S0-BMY-972

S. Pub. 105–20

1997–1998

OFFICIAL

Congressional Directory

105th CONGRESS

Convened January 7, 1997

Joint Committee on Printing
United States Congress

United States Government Printing Office
Washington, DC

Printed on recycled paper

NOTES

Closing date for compilation of the *Congressional Directory* was June 4, 1997.

[Republicans in roman, Democrats in *italic*, Independents in **bold**.]

The following changes have occurred in the membership of the 105th Congress since the election of November 5, 1996:

Name	Resigned or [Died]	Successor	Elected	Sworn in
REPRESENTATIVES				
Jo Ann Emerson, 8th MO [1]	....	....	....	
Frank Tejeda, 28th TX	[Jan. 30, 1997] ..	*Ciro D. Rodriguez*	Apr. 12, 1997 ..	Apr. 17, 1997
Bill Richardson, 3d NM [2]	Feb. 13, 1997	Bill Redmond	May 13, 1997 ..	May 20, 1997

[1] Changed party affiliation from Independent to Republican January 8, 1997. [2] Resigned to take office as United States Representative to the United Nations.

The following changes occurred in the membership of the 104th Congress after the election of November 8, 1994:

Name	Resigned or [Died]	Successor	Elected or [Appointed]	Sworn in
SENATORS				
Ben Nighthorse Campbell, CO [1].	....	....	....	
Bob Packwood, OR	Oct. 1, 1995	*Ron Wyden*	Jan. 30, 1996 ...	Feb. 6, 1996
Robert Dole, KS	June 11, 1996 ...	Sheila Frahm	[June 11, 1996]	June 11, 1996
Do	......do	Sam Brownback	Nov. 5, 1996	Nov. 27, 1996
REPRESENTATIVES				
Nathan Deal, 9th GA [2]	....	....	....	
Greg Laughlin, 14th TX [3] ...	....	....	....	
Billy Tauzin, 3d LA [4]	....	....	....	
Mel Reynolds, 2d IL	Oct. 1, 1995	*Jesse L. Jackson, Jr.*	Dec. 12, 1995 ..	Dec. 14, 1995
Norman Y. Mineta, 15th CA	Oct. 10, 1995	Tom Campbell	Dec. 12, 1995 ..	Dec. 15, 1995
Mike Parker, 4th MS [5]	....	....	....	
Jimmy Hayes, 7th LA [6]	....	....	....	
Walter R. Tucker III, 37th CA.	Dec. 15, 1995 ...	*Juanita Millender-McDonald.*	Mar. 26, 1996 ..	Apr. 16, 1996
Ron Wyden, 3d OR [7]	Feb. 5, 1996	*Earl Blumenauer*	May 21, 1996 ..	May 30, 1996
Kweisi Mfume, 7th MD	Feb. 18, 1996	*Elijah E. Cummings* ..	Apr. 16, 1996 ..	Apr. 25, 1996
Bill Emerson, 8th MO	[June 22, 1996]	Jo Ann Emerson [8]	Nov. 5, 1996	
Charles Wilson, 2d TX	Oct. 9, 1996	....	....	
Sam Brownback, 2d KS [9]	Nov. 27, 1996 ...	Jim Ryun [10]	Nov. 5, 1996	
Ray Thornton, 2d AR	Jan. 1, 1997	....	....	

[1] Changed party affiliation from Democrat to Republican March 3, 1995. [2] Changed party affiliation from Democrat to Republican April 10, 1995. [3] Changed party affiliation from Democrat to Republican June 26, 1995. [4] Changed party affiliation from Democrat to Republican August 6, 1995. [5] Changed party affiliation from Democrat to Republican November 10, 1995. [6] Changed party affiliation from Democrat to Republican December 1, 1995. [7] Resigned to take office as Senator. [8] Elected as a Republican in special election to fill unexpired term (election held simultaneously with general election in which she was elected as an Independent to the 105th Congress); since the House of Representatives had adjourned *sine die,* no swearing-in took place. [9] Resigned to take office as Senator. [10] Elected in general election to the 105th Congress; however, Kansas law states: "In the event that any vacancy occurs...on or after the date of any general election of state officers and before the term of office in which the vacancy has occurred expires, votes cast for the office of congressman in the district in which such vacancy occurs shall be deemed to have been cast to fill such vacancy for the unexpired term, as well as for election for the next regular term." Since the House of Representatives had adjourned *sine die,* no swearing-in took place.

FOREWORD

The Congressional Directory is one of the oldest working handbooks in the United States government. While there have been directories of one form or another since the first Congress of the United States in 1789, the Congressional Directory for the first session of the 30th Congress (1847) is considered by scholars and historians to be the first official edition because it is the first to be ordered and paid for by the Congress. With the addition of biographical sketches of legislators in 1867, the Congressional Directory attained its modern format.

The Congressional Directory is published by the United States Senate in partnership with the Government Printing Office, at the direction of the Joint Committee on Printing under the authority of Title 44, Section 721 of the U.S. Code.

Senate
John W. Warner, VA, *Chairman.*
Thad Cochran, MS
Mitch McConnell, KY
Wendell H. Ford, KY
Daniel K. Inouye, HI

House
Bill Thomas, CA, *Vice Chairman.*
Robert W. Ney, OH
Kay Granger, TX
Steny H. Hoyer, MD
Sam Gejdenson, CT

For sale by the U.S. Government Printing Office, Superintendent of Documents,
Mail Stop: SSOP, Washington, DC 20402.

Available via the World Wide Web: http://www.access.gpo.gov

Paper Cover ISBN 0–16–055119–6
Casebound ISBN 0–16–055120–X

ACKNOWLEDGMENT

The Joint Committee on Printing acknowledges with gratitude the commitment and dedication of the employees of the Government Printing Office who compiled and published this directory. Led by Ms. Kathryn McConnell, Project Manager, a team of eight writer-editors and keyboard specialists undertook this mammoth initiative, completing it in just five months. The members of the team included Senior Writer-Editor Lorena Beauchesne, Writer-Editors Joyce Carlton and Selene Dalecky, and Keyboard Specialists Audrey Brown, C.C. Price, Sherian K. Roberts and Dana Zimmerman who suffered a stroke during the project, but through her determination and dedication, recovered and returned to complete her work. Volunteering his time to assist with project research was Peter Byrd, an employee of the Capitol Guide Service.

Along with these individuals, other employees of the Government Printing Office, including Janice Sterling, who designed the cover, and Jerry Fairbanks, Jack Fulmer, Mike Glaser, Bob Keller, Ben Lopez, Rick McElroy, Stephen Naumann and Dave Turney, who maintained graphic systems development, contributed to this publication. Bernie Horn served as the Congressional Printing Management Liaison.

John Warner

John W. Warner
Chairman
Joint Committee on Printing

CONTENTS

Name Index on p. 1087

105th Congress*

THE VICE PRESIDENT

AL GORE, Democrat, of Carthage, TN; born March 31, 1948; graduated, Harvard University, 1969, with honors; attended Vanderbilt School of Religion, 1971–72; Vanderbilt Law School, 1974–76; engaged in homebuilding business; former investigative reporter and editorial writer; served in the U.S. Army, 1969–71; Vietnam veteran; member: Jaycees, American Legion, VFW, Farm Bureau; married the former Tipper Aitcheson, 1970; four children: Karenna, Kristin, Sarah, and Albert III; elected to the 95th Congress, November 2, 1976; reelected to three succeeding Congresses; elected to the U.S. Senate, November 6, 1984, for the term expiring January 3, 1991; reelected November 6, 1990; elected Vice President, November 3, 1992; resigned Senate seat on January 1, 1993; took oath of office January 20, 1993; reelected November 1996.

The Ceremonial Office of the Vice President is S–212 in the Capitol.
The Vice President has offices in the Dirksen Senate Office Building, the Old Executive Office Building (OEOB) and the White House (West Wing).

Chief of Staff.—Ronald Klain, OEOB, Room 276, 456–6605.
Deputy Chief of Staff.—David Strauss, OEOB, Room 280, 456–7021.
Counsel.—Kumiki Gibson, OEOB, Room 268, 456–7022
Deputy Counsel and Director of Legislative Affairs.—Charles Burson, S–212, 224–8391.
National Security Advisor.—Leon S. Fuerth, OEOB, Room 290, 395–4213.
Chief Domestic Policy Advisor.—Donald Gips, OEOB, Room 286, 456–6222.
Senior Policy Advisor.—Elaine C. Kamarck, OEOB, Room 271, 456–2816.
Director of Communications.—Lorraine Voles, OEOB, Room 272, 456–7035.
Director of Scheduling.—Kim Tilley, OEOB, Room 283, 395–4245.
Director of Advance.—Dennis Alpert, OEOB, Room 281, 456–7935.
Special Assistant to the Vice President and Chief of Staff to Mrs. Gore.—Susan Liss, OEOB, Room 200, 456–6640.
Executive Assistant.—Heather Marabeti, West Wing, 456–2326.

*Biographies are based on information furnished or authorized by the respective Senators and Representatives.

SENATORS - 105TH CONGRESS

Republicans in roman (55). Democrats in *italic (45).*

Abraham, Spencer, MI
Akaka, Daniel K., HI
Allard, Wayne, CO
Ashcroft, John, MO
Baucus, Max, MT
Bennett, Robert F., UT
Biden, Joseph R., Jr., DE
Bingaman, Jeff, NM
Bond, Christopher S., MO
Boxer, Barbara, CA
Breaux, John B., LA
Brownback, Samuel Dale, KS
Bryan, Richard H., NV
Bumpers, Dale, AR
Burns, Conrad R., MT
Byrd, Robert C., WV
Campbell, Ben Nighthorse, CO
Chafee, John H., RI
Cleland, Max, GA
Coats, Dan, IN
Cochran, Thad, MS
Collins, Susan M., ME
Conrad, Kent, ND
Coverdell, Paul, GA
Craig, Larry E., ID
D'Amato, Alfonse M., NY
Daschle, Thomas A., SD
DeWine, Mike, OH
Dodd, Christopher J., CT
Domenici, Pete V., NM
Dorgan, Byron L., ND
Durbin, Richard J., IL
Enzi, Michael B., WY
Faircloth, Lauch, NC
Feingold, Russell D., WI
Feinstein, Dianne, CA
Ford, Wendell H., KY
Frist, Bill, TN
Glenn, John, OH
Gorton, Slade, WA
Graham, Bob, FL
Gramm, Phil, TX
Grams, Rod, MN
Grassley, Charles E., IA
Gregg, Judd, NH
Hagel, Chuck, NE
Harkin, Tom, IA
Hatch, Orrin G., UT
Helms, Jesse, NC
Hollings, Ernest F., SC
Hutchinson, Tim, AR
Hutchison, Kay Bailey, TX
Inhofe, James M., OK
Inouye, Daniel K., HI
Jeffords, James M., VT
Johnson, Tim, SD
Kempthorne, Dirk, ID
Kennedy, Edward M., MA
Kerrey, J. Robert, NE
Kerry, John F., MA
Kohl, Herb, WI
Kyl, Jon, AZ
Landrieu, Mary, LA
Lautenberg, Frank R, NJ
Leahy, Patrick J., VT
Levin, Carl, MI
Lieberman, Joseph I., CT
Lott, Trent, MS
Lugar, Richard G., IN
Mack, Connie, FL
McCain, John, AZ
McConnell, Mitch, KY
Mikulski, Barbara A., MD
Moseley-Braun, Carol, IL
Moynihan, Daniel P., NY
Murkowski, Frank H., AK
Murray, Patty, WA
Nickles, Don, OK
Reed, Jack, RI
Reid, Harry, NV
Robb, Charles S., VA
Roberts, Pat, KS
Rockefeller, John D., IV, WV
Roth, William V., Jr., DE
Santorum, Rick, PA
Sarbanes, Paul S., MD
Sessions, Jeff, AL
Shelby, Richard C., AL
Smith, Bob, NH
Smith, Gordon, OR
Snowe, Olympia J., ME
Specter, Arlen, PA
Stevens, Ted, AK
Thomas, Craig, WY
Thompson, Fred, TN
Thurmond, Strom, SC
Torricelli, Robert G., NJ
Warner, John W., VA
Wellstone, Paul David, MN
Wyden, Ron, OR

REPRESENTATIVES - 105TH CONGRESS

Republicans in roman (228). Democrats in *italic* (206). Independent in **bold** (1). Total 435.

Abercrombie, Neil, HI (1st)
Ackerman, Gary L., NY (5th)
Aderholt, Robert, AL (4th)
Allen, Thomas H., ME (1st)
Andrews, Robert E., NJ (1st)
Archer, Bill, TX (7th)
Armey, Dick, TX (26th)
Bachus, Spencer, AL (6th)
Baesler, Scotty, KY (6th)
Baker, Richard H., LA (6th)
Baldacci, John Elias, ME (2nd)
Ballenger, Cass, NC (10th)
Barcia, James A., MI (5th)
Barr, Bob, GA (7th)
Barrett, Bill, NE (3rd)
Barrett, Thomas M., WI (5th)
Bartlett, Roscoe G., MD (6th)
Barton, Joe, TX (6th)
Bass, Charles, NH (2nd)
Bateman, Herbert H., VA (1st)
Becerra, Xavier, CA (30th)
Bentsen, Kenneth F., Jr., TX (25th)
Bereuter, Doug, NE (1st)
Berman, Howard L., CA (26th)
Berry, Marion, AR (1st)
Bilbray, Brian P., CA (49th)
Bilirakis, Michael, FL (9th)
Bishop, Sanford, GA (2nd)
Blagojevich, Rod, IL (5th)
Bliley, Thomas J., Jr., VA (7th)
Blumenauer, Earl, OR (3rd)
Blunt, Roy, MO (7th)
Boehlert, Sherwood L., NY (23rd)
Boehner, John A., OH (8th)
Bonilla, Henry, TX (23rd)
Bonior, David E., MI (10th)
Bono, Sonny, CA (44th)
Borski, Robert A., PA (3rd)
Boswell, Leonard L., IA (3rd)
Boucher, Rick, VA (9th)
Boyd, Allen, FL (2nd)
Brady, Kevin, TX (8th)
Brown, Corrine, FL (3rd)
Brown, George E., Jr., CA (42nd)
Brown, Sherrod, OH (13th)
Bryant, Ed, TN (7th)
Bunning, Jim, KY (4th)
Burr, Richard M., NC (5th)
Burton, Dan, IN (6th)
Buyer, Steve, IN (5th)
Callahan, Sonny, AL (1st)
Calvert, Ken, CA (43rd)
Camp, Dave, MI (4th)
Campbell, Tom, CA (15th)
Canady, Charles T., FL (12th)
Cannon, Christopher B., UT (3rd)
Capps, Walter Holden, CA (22nd)
Cardin, Benjamin L., MD (3rd)
Carson, Julia M., IN (10th)
Castle, Michael N., DE (At Large)
Chabot, Steve, OH (1st)
Chambliss, Saxby, GA (8th)
Chenoweth, Helen, ID (1st)
Christensen, Jon, NE (2nd)
Clay, William (Bill), MO (1st)
Clayton, Eva, NC (1st)
Clement, Bob, TN (5th)
Clyburn, James E., SC (6th)
Coble, Howard, NC (6th)
Coburn, Thomas A., OK (2nd)
Collins, Mac, GA (3rd)
Combest, Larry, TX (19th)
Condit, Gary A., CA (18th)
Conyers, John, Jr., MI (14th)
Cook, Merrill, UT (2nd)
Cooksey, John, LA (5th)
Costello, Jerry F., IL (12th)
Cox, Christopher, CA (47th)
Coyne, William J., PA (14th)
Cramer, Bud, AL (5th)
Crane, Philip M., IL (8th)
Crapo, Michael D., ID (2nd)
Cubin, Barbara, WY (At Large)
Cummings, Elijah E., MD (7th)
Cunningham, Randy (Duke), CA (51st)
Danner, Pat, MO (6th)
Davis, Danny K., IL (7th)
Davis, Jim, FL (11th)
Davis, Thomas M., III, VA (11th)
Deal, Nathan, GA (9th)
DeFazio, Peter A., OR (4th)
DeGette, Diana, CO (1st)
Delahunt, William D., MA (10th)
DeLauro, Rosa L., CT (3rd)
DeLay, Tom, TX (22nd)
Dellums, Ronald V., CA (9th)
Deutsch, Peter, FL (20th)
Diaz-Balart, Lincoln, FL (21st)
Dickey, Jay, AR (4th)
Dicks, Norman D., WA (6th)
Dingell, John D., MI (16th)
Dixon, Julian C., CA (32nd)
Doggett, Lloyd, TX (10th)
Dooley, Calvin M., CA (20th)
Doolittle, John T., CA (4th)
Doyle, Michael F., PA (18th)
Dreier, David, CA (28th)
Duncan, John J., Jr., TN (2nd)

Dunn, Jennifer, WA (8th)
Edwards, Chet, TX (11th)
Ehlers, Vernon, MI (3rd)
Ehrlich, Robert, Jr., MD (2nd)
Emerson, Jo Ann, MO (8th)
Engel, Eliot L., NY (17th)
English, Phil, PA (21st)
Ensign, John, NV (1st)
Eshoo, Anna G., CA (14th)
Etheridge, Bob, NC (2nd)
Evans, Lane, IL (17th)
Everett, Terry, AL (2nd)
Ewing, Thomas W., IL (15th)
Farr, Sam, CA (17th)
Fattah, Chaka, PA (2nd)
Fawell, Harris W., IL (13th)
Fazio, Vic, CA (3rd)
Filner, Bob, CA (50th)
Flake, Floyd H., NY (6th)
Foglietta, Thomas M., PA (1st)
Foley, Mark, FL (16th)
Forbes, Michael, NY (1st)
Ford, Harold E., Jr., TN (9th)
Fowler, Tillie K., FL (4th)
Fox, Jon, PA (13th)
Frank, Barney, MA (4th)
Franks, Bob, NJ (7th)
Frelinghuysen, Rodney P., NJ (11th)
Frost, Martin, TX (24th)
Furse, Elizabeth, OR (1st)
Gallegly, Elton, CA (23rd)
Ganske, Greg, IA (4th)
Gejdenson, Sam, CT (2nd)
Gekas, George W., PA (17th)
Gephardt, Richard A., MO (3rd)
Gibbons, Jim, NV (2nd)
Gilchrest, Wayne T., MD (1st)
Gillmor, Paul E., OH (5th)
Gilman, Benjamin A., NY (20th)
Gingrich, Newt, GA (6th)
Gonzalez, Henry B., TX (20th)
Goode, Virgil H., Jr., VA (5th)
Goodlatte, Robert W. (Bob), VA (6th)
Goodling, William F., PA (19th)
Gordon, Bart, TN (6th)
Goss, Porter J., FL (14th)
Graham, Lindsey, SC (3rd)
Granger, Kay, TX (12th)
Green, Gene, TX (29th)
Greenwood, James C., PA (8th)
Gutierrez, Luis V., IL (4th)
Gutknecht, Gil, MN (1st)
Hall, Ralph M., TX (4th)
Hall, Tony P., OH (3rd)
Hamilton, Lee H., IN (9th)
Hansen, James V., UT (1st)
Harman, Jane, CA (36th)
Hastert, J. Dennis, IL (14th)
Hastings, Alcee L., FL (23d)
Hastings, Doc, WA (4th)
Hayworth, J. D., AZ (6th)
Hefley, Joel, CO (5th)
Hefner, W.G. (Bill), NC (8th)
Herger, Wally, CA (2nd)
Hill, Rick, MT (At Large)
Hilleary, Van, TN (4th)
Hilliard, Earl F., AL (7th)
Hinchey, Maurice D., NY (26th)
Hinojosa, Rubén, TX (15th)
Hobson, David L., OH (7th)
Hoekstra, Peter, MI (2nd)
Holden, Tim, PA (6th)
Hooley, Darlene, OR (5th)
Horn, Steve, CA (38th)
Hostettler, John, IN (8th)
Houghton, Amo, NY (31st)
Hoyer, Steny H., MD (5th)
Hulshof, Kenny, MO (9th)
Hunter, Duncan, CA (52nd)
Hutchinson, Asa, AR (3rd)
Hyde, Henry J., IL (6th)
Inglis, Bob, SC (4th)
Istook, Ernest J., Jr., OK (5th)
Jackson, Jesse L., Jr., IL (2nd)
Jefferson, William J., LA (2nd)
Jenkins, William L. (Bill), TN (1st)
John, Chris, LA (7th)
Johnson, Eddie Bernice, TX (30th)
Johnson, Jay W., WI (8th)
Johnson, Nancy L., CT (6th)
Johnson, Sam, TX (3rd)
Jones, Walter B., NC (3rd)
Kanjorski, Paul E., PA (11th)
Kaptur, Marcy, OH (9th)
Kasich, John R., OH (12th)
Kelly, Sue, NY (19th)
Kennedy, Joseph P., II, MA (8th)
Kennedy, Patrick J., RI (1st)
Kennelly, Barbara B., CT (1st)
Kildee, Dale E., MI (9th)
Kilpatrick, Carolyn C., MI (15th)
Kim, Jay, CA (41st)
Kind, Ron, WI (3rd)
King, Peter T., NY (3rd)
Kingston, Jack, GA (1st)
Kleczka, Gerald D., WI (4th)
Klink, Ron, PA (4th)
Klug, Scott L., WI (2nd)
Knollenberg, Joe, MI (11th)
Kolbe, Jim, AZ (5th)
Kucinich, Dennis, OH (10th)
LaFalce, John J., NY (29th)
LaHood, Ray, IL (18th)
Lampson, Nick, TX (9th)
Lantos, Tom, CA (12th)
Largent, Steve, OK (1st)
Latham, Tom, IA (5th)
LaTourette, Steven, OH (19th)
Lazio, Rick A., NY (2nd)
Leach, James A., IA (1st)
Lee, Sheila Jackson, TX (18th)
Levin, Sander M., MI (12th)
Lewis, Jerry, CA (40th)
Lewis, John, GA (5th)
Lewis, Ron, KY (2nd)
Linder, John, GA (11th)
Lipinski, William O., IL (3rd)
Livingston, Bob, LA (1st)
LoBiondo, Frank, NJ (2nd)
Lofgren, Zoe, CA (16th)
Lowey, Nita M., NY (18th)
Lucas, Frank, OK (6th)

Luther, Bill, MN (6th)
Maloney, Carolyn B., NY (14th)
Maloney, Jim, CT (5th)
Manton, Thomas J., NY (7th)
Manzullo, Donald, IL (16th)
Markey, Edward J., MA (7th)
Martinez, Matthew G., CA (31st)
Mascara, Frank, PA (20th)
Matsui, Robert T., CA (5th)
McCarthy, Carolyn, NY (4th)
McCarthy, Karen, MO (5th)
McCollum, Bill, FL (8th)
McCrery, Jim, LA (4th)
McDade, Joseph M., PA (10th)
McDermott, Jim, WA (7th)
McGovern, Jim, MA (3rd)
McHale, Paul, PA (15th)
McHugh, John M., NY (24th)
McInnis, Scott, CO (3rd)
McIntosh, David M., IN (2nd)
McIntyre, Mike, NC (7th)
McKeon, Howard P. (Buck), CA (25th)
McKinney, Cynthia, GA (4th)
McNulty, Michael R., NY (21st)
Meehan, Martin T., MA (5th)
Meek, Carrie, FL (17th)
Menendez, Robert, NJ (13th)
Metcalf, Jack, WA (2nd)
Mica, John L., FL (7th)
Millender-McDonald, Juanita, CA (37th)
Miller, Dan, FL (13th)
Miller, George, CA (7th)
Minge, David, MN (2nd)
Mink, Patsy T., HI (2nd)
Moakley, John Joseph, MA (9th)
Molinari, Susan, NY (13th)
Mollohan, Alan B., WV (1st)
Moran, James P., VA (8th)
Moran, Jerry, KS (1st)
Morella, Constance A., MD (8th)
Murtha, John P., PA (12th)
Myrick, Sue, NC (9th)
Nadler, Jerrold, NY (8th)
Neal, Richard E., MA (2nd)
Nethercutt, George, WA (5th)
Neumann, Mark, WI (1st)
Ney, Robert W., OH (18th)
Northup, Anne Meagher, KY (3rd)
Norwood, Charlie, GA (10th)
Nussle, Jim, IA (2nd)
Oberstar, James L., MN (8th)
Obey, David R., WI (7th)
Olver, John W., MA (1st)
Ortiz, Solomon P., TX (27th)
Owens, Major R., NY (11th)
Oxley, Michael G., OH (4th)
Packard, Ron, CA (48th)
Pallone, Frank, Jr., NJ (6th)
Pappas, Mike, NJ (12th)
Parker, Mike, MS (4th)
Pascrell, William J., Jr., NJ (8th)
Pastor, Ed, AZ (2nd)
Paul, Ron, TX (14th)
Paxon, Bill, NY (27th)
Payne, Donald M., NJ (10th)
Pease, Edward A., IN (7th)
Pelosi, Nancy, CA (8th)
Peterson, Collin C., MN (7th)
Peterson, John E., PA (5th)
Petri, Thomas E., WI (6th)
Pickering, Charles W. (Chip) Jr., MS (3rd)
Pickett, Owen B., VA (2nd)
Pitts, Joseph R., PA (16th)
Pombo, Richard W., CA (11th)
Pomeroy, Earl, ND (At Large)
Porter, John Edward, IL (10th)
Portman, Rob, OH (2nd)
Poshard, Glenn, IL (19th)
Price, David E., NC (4th)
Pryce, Deborah, OH (15th)
Quinn, Jack, NY (30th)
Radanovich, George, CA (19th)
Rahall, Nick J., II, WV (3rd)
Ramstad, Jim, MN (3rd)
Rangel, Charles B., NY (15th)
Redmond, Bill, NM (3rd)
Regula, Ralph, OH (16th)
Reyes, Silvestre, TX (16th)
Riggs, Frank, CA (1st)
Riley, Bob, AL (3rd)
Rivers, Lynn Nancy, MI (13th)
Rodriguez, Ciro, TX (28th)
Roemer, Timothy J., IN (3rd)
Rogan, James E., CA (27th)
Rogers, Harold, KY (5th)
Rohrabacher, Dana, CA (45th)
Ros-Lehtinen, Ileana, FL (18th)
Rothman, Steven R., NJ (9th)
Roukema, Marge, NJ (5th)
Roybal-Allard, Lucille, CA (33rd)
Royce, Ed, CA (39th)
Rush, Bobby L., IL (1st)
Ryun, Jim, KS (2nd)
Sabo, Martin Olav, MN (5th)
Salmon, Matt, AZ (1st)
Sanchez, Loretta, CA (46th)
Sanders, Bernard, VT (At Large)
Sandlin, Max, TX (1st)
Sanford, Mark, SC (1st)
Sawyer, Tom, OH (14th)
Saxton, Jim, NJ (3rd)
Scarborough, Joe, FL (1st)
Schaefer, Dan, CO (6th)
Schaffer, Bob, CO (4th)
Schiff, Steven H., NM (1st)
Schumer, Charles E., NY (9th)
Scott, Robert C. (Bobby), VA (3rd)
Sensenbrenner, F. James, Jr., WI (9th)
Serrano, José E., NY (16th)
Sessions, Pete, TX (5th)
Shadegg, John, AZ (4th)
Shaw, E. Clay, Jr., FL (22nd)
Shays, Christopher, CT (4th)
Sherman, Brad, CA (24th)
Shimkus, John M., IL (20th)
Shuster, Bud, PA (9th)
Sisisky, Norman, VA (4th)
Skaggs, David E., CO (2nd)
Skeen, Joe, NM (2nd)
Skelton, Ike, MO (4th)
Slaughter, Louise M., NY (28th)
Smith, Adam, WA (9th)

Smith, Christopher H., NJ (4th)
Smith, Lamar S., TX (21st)
Smith, Linda, WA (3rd)
Smith, Nick, MI (7th)
Smith, Robert F. (Bob), OR (2nd)
Snowbarger, Vince, KS (3rd)
Snyder, Vic, AR (2nd)
Solomon, Gerald B. H., NY (22nd)
Souder, Mark, IN (4th)
Spence, Floyd, SC (2nd)
Spratt, John M., Jr., SC (5th)
Stabenow, Debbie, MI (8th)
Stark, Fortney Pete, CA (13th)
Stearns, Cliff, FL (6th)
Stenholm, Charles W., TX (17th)
Stokes, Louis, OH (11th)
Strickland, Ted, OH (6th)
Stump, Bob, AZ (3rd)
Stupak, Bart, MI (1st)
Sununu, John E., NH (1st)
Talent, James M., MO (2nd)
Tanner, John S., TN (8th)
Tauscher, Ellen, CA (10th)
Tauzin, W. J. (Billy), LA (3rd)
Taylor, Charles H., NC (11th)
Taylor, Gene, MS (5th)
Thomas, Bill, CA (21st)
Thompson, Bennie G., MS (2nd)
Thornberry, William (Mac), TX (13th)
Thune, John, SD (At Large)
Thurman, Karen L., FL (5th)
Tiahrt, Todd, KS (4th)
Tierney, John, MA (6th)
Torres, Esteban Edward, CA (34th)
Towns, Edolphus, NY (10th)
Traficant, James A., Jr., OH (17th)
Turner, Jim, TX (2nd)
Upton, Fred, MI (6th)
Velázquez, Nydia M., NY (12th)
Vento, Bruce F., MN (4th)
Visclosky, Peter J., IN (1st)
Walsh, James T., NY (25th)
Wamp, Zach, TN (3rd)
Waters, Maxine, CA (35th)
Watkins, Wes, OK (3rd)
Watt, Melvin, NC (12th)
Watts, J.C., OK (4th)
Waxman, Henry A., CA (29th)
Weldon, Curt, PA (7th)
Weldon, Dave, FL (15th)
Weller, Jerry, IL (11th)
Wexler, Robert, FL (19th)
Weygand, Robert A., RI (2nd)
White, Rick, WA (1st)
Whitfield, Edward, KY (1st)
Wicker, Roger, MS (1st)
Wise, Robert E., Jr., WV (2nd)
Wolf, Frank R., VA (10th)
Woolsey, Lynn, CA (6th)
Wynn, Albert R., MD (4th)
Yates, Sidney R., IL (9th)
Young, C. W. Bill, FL (10th)
Young, Don, AK (At Large)
DELEGATES
Christian-Green, Donna, VI
Faleomavaega, Eni F. H., AS
Norton, Eleanor Holmes, DC
Underwood, Robert A., GU
RESIDENT COMISSIONER
Romero-Barceló, Carlos, PR

STATE DELEGATIONS - 105TH CONGRESS

Number before names designates Congressional district. Republicans in roman. Democrats in *italic.* Independent in **bold.**

ALABAMA

SENATORS
Richard C. Shelby
Jeff Sessions

REPRESENTATIVES
[Republicans 5, Democrats 2]
1. Sonny Callahan
2. Terry Everett
3. Bob Riley
4. Robert Aderholt
5. *Bud Cramer*
6. Spencer Bachus
7. *Earl F. Hilliard*

ALASKA

SENATORS
Ted Stevens
Frank H. Murkowski

REPRESENTATIVE
[Republican 1]

At Large - Don Young

ARIZONA

SENATORS
John McCain
Jon Kyl

REPRESENTATIVES
[Republicans 5, Democrat 1]
1. Matt Salmon
2. *Ed Pastor*
3. Bob Stump
4. John Shadegg
5. Jim Kolbe
6. J.D. Hayworth

ARKANSAS

SENATORS
Dale Bumpers
Tim Hutchinson

REPRESENTATIVES
[Republicans 2, Democrats 2]
1. *Marion Berry*
2. *Vic Snyder*
3. Asa Hutchinson
4. Jay Dickey

CALIFORNIA

SENATORS
Dianne Feinstein
Barbara Boxer

REPRESENTATIVES
[Republicans 23, Democrats 29]
1. Frank Riggs
2. Wally Herger
3. *Vic Fazio*
4. John T. Doolittle
5. *Robert T. Matsui*
6. *Lynn Woolsey*
7. *George Miller*
8. *Nancy Pelosi*
9. *Ronald V. Dellums*
10. *Ellen Tauscher*
11. Richard W. Pombo
12. *Tom Lantos*
13. *Fortney Pete Stark*
14. *Anna G. Eshoo*
15. Tom Campbell
16. *Zoe Lofgren*
17. *Sam Farr*

18. *Gary A. Condit*
19. George Radanovich
20. *Calvin M. Dooley*
21. Bill Thomas
22. *Walter Holden Capps*
23. Elton Gallegly
24. *Brad Sherman*
25. Howard P. (Buck) McKeon
26. *Howard L. Berman*
27. James E. Rogan
28. David Dreier
29. *Henry A. Waxman*
30. *Xavier Becerra*
31. *Matthew G. Martinez*
32. *Julian C. Dixon*
33. *Lucille Roybal-Allard*
34. *Esteban Edward Torres*
35. *Maxine Waters*
36. *Jane Harman*
37. *Juanita Millender-McDonald*
38. Steve Horn
39. Ed Royce
40. Jerry Lewis
41. Jay Kim
42. *George E. Brown, Jr.*
43. Ken Calvert
44. Sonny Bono
45. Dana Rohrabacher
46. *Loretta Sanchez*
47. Christopher Cox
48. Ron Packard
49. Brian Bilbray
50. *Bob Filner*
51. Randy (Duke) Cunningham
52. Duncan Hunter

COLORADO

SENATORS
Ben Nighthorse Campbell
Wayne Allard

REPRESENTATIVES
[Republicans 4, Democrats 2]
1. *Diana L. DeGette*
2. *David E. Skaggs*
3. Scott McInnis
4. Bob Schaffer
5. Joel Hefley
6. Dan Schaefer

CONNECTICUT

SENATORS
Christopher J. Dodd
Joseph I. Lieberman

REPRESENTATIVES
[Republicans 2, Democrats 4]
1. *Barbara B. Kennelly*
2. *Sam Gejdenson*
3. *Rosa L. DeLauro*
4. Christopher Shays
5. *Jim Maloney*
6. Nancy L. Johnson

DELAWARE

SENATORS
William V. Roth, Jr.
Joseph R. Biden, Jr.

REPRESENTATIVE
[Republican 1]
At Large - Michael N. Castle

FLORIDA

SENATORS
Bob Graham
Connie Mack

REPRESENTATIVES
[Republicans 15, Democrats 8]
1. Joe Scarborough
2. *Allen Boyd*
3. *Corrine Brown*
4. Tillie Fowler
5. *Karen L. Thurman*
6. Cliff Stearns
7. John L. Mica
8. Bill McCollum
9. Michael Bilirakis
10. C.W. Bill Young
11. *Jim Davis*
12. Charles T. Canady
13. Dan Miller
14. Porter J. Goss
15. Dave Weldon
16. Mark Foley
17. *Carrie Meek*
18. Ileana Ros-Lehtinen
19. *Robert Wexler*
20. *Peter Deutsch*
21. Lincoln Diaz-Balart
22. E. Clay Shaw, Jr.
23. *Alcee L. Hastings*

GEORGIA

SENATORS
Paul Coverdell
Max Cleland

REPRESENTATIVES
[Republicans 8, Democrats 3]
1. Jack Kingston
2. *Sanford Bishop*
3. Mac Collins
4. *Cynthia McKinney*
5. *John Lewis*
6. Newt Gingrich
7. Bob Barr
8. Saxby Chambliss
9. Nathan Deal
10. Charlie Norwood
11. John Linder

HAWAII

SENATORS
Daniel K. Inouye
Daniel K. Akaka

REPRESENTATIVES
[Democrats 2]
1. *Neil Abercrombie*
2. *Patsy T. Mink*

IDAHO

SENATORS
Larry Craig
Dirk Kempthorne

REPRESENTATIVES
[Republicans 2]
1. Helen Chenoweth
2. Michael D. Crapo

ILLINOIS

SENATORS
Carol Moseley-Braun
Richard J. Durbin

REPRESENTATIVES
[Republicans 10, Democrats 10]
1. *Bobby L. Rush*
2. *Jesse L. Jackson, Jr.*
3. *William O. Lipinski*
4. *Luis V. Gutierrez*
5. *Rod Blagojevich*
6. Henry J. Hyde
7. *Danny K. Davis*
8. Philip M. Crane
9. *Sidney R. Yates*
10. John Edward Porter
11. Jerry Weller
12. *Jerry F. Costello*
13. Harris W. Fawell
14. J. Dennis Hastert
15. Thomas W. Ewing
16. Donald Manzullo
17. *Lane Evans*
18. Ray LaHood
19. *Glenn Poshard*
20. John M. Shimkus

INDIANA

SENATORS
Richard G. Lugar
Dan Coats

REPRESENTATIVES
[Republicans 6, Democrats 4]
1. *Peter J. Visclosky*
2. David M. McIntosh
3. *Timothy J. Roemer*
4. Mark Souder
5. Steve Buyer
6. Dan Burton
7. Edward A. Pease
8. John Hostettler
9. *Lee H. Hamilton*
10. *Julia M. Carson*

IOWA

SENATORS
Charles E. Grassley
Tom Harkin

REPRESENTATIVES
[Republicans 4, Democrats 1]
1. James A. Leach

2. Jim Nussle
3. *Leonard L. Boswell*
4. Greg Ganske
5. Tom Latham

KANSAS

SENATORS
Samuel Dale Brownback
Pat Roberts

REPRESENTATIVES
[Republicans 4]
1. Jerry Moran
2. Jim Ryun
3. Vince Snowbarger
4. Todd Tiahrt

KENTUCKY

SENATORS
Wendell H. Ford
Mitch McConnell

REPRESENTATIVES
[Republicans 5, Democrats 1]
1. Edward Whitfield
2. Ron Lewis
3. Ann Meagher Northup
4. Jim Bunning
5. Harold Rogers
6. *Scotty Baesler*

LOUISIANA

SENATORS
John B. Breaux
Mary Landrieu

REPRESENTATIVES
[Republicans 5, Democrats 2]
1. Bob Livingston
2. *William J. Jefferson*
3. W.J. (Billy) Tauzin
4. Jim McCrery
5. John Cooksey
6. Richard H. Baker
7. *Chris John*

MAINE

SENATORS
Olympia J. Snowe
Susan Collins

REPRESENTATIVES
[Democrats 2]
1. *Thomas H. Allen*
2. *John Elias Baldacci*

MARYLAND

SENATORS
Paul S. Sarbanes
Barbara A. Mikulski

REPRESENTATIVES
[Republicans 4, Democrats 4]
1. Wayne T. Gilchrest
2. Robert Ehrlich, Jr.
3. *Benjamin L. Cardin*
4. *Albert R. Wynn*
5. *Steny H. Hoyer*
6. Roscoe G. Bartlett
7. *Elijah E. Cummings*
8. Constance A. Morella

MASSACHUSETTS

SENATORS
Edward M. Kennedy
John F. Kerry

REPRESENTATIVES
[Democrats 10]
1. *John W. Olver*
2. *Richard E. Neal*
3. *Jim McGovern*
4. *Barney Frank*
5. *Martin T. Meehan*
6. *John Tierney*
7. *Edward J. Markey*
8. *Joseph P. Kennedy II*
9. *John Joseph Moakley*
10. *William D. Delahunt*

MICHIGAN

SENATORS
Carl Levin
Spencer Abraham

REPRESENTATIVES
[Republicans 6, Democrats 10]
1. *Bart Stupak*
2. Peter Hoekstra
3. Vernon Ehlers
4. Dave Camp
5. *James A. Barcia*
6. Fred Upton
7. Nick Smith
8. *Debbie Stabenow*
9. *Dale E. Kildee*
10. *David E. Bonior*
11. Joe Knollenberg
12. *Sander M. Levin*
13. *Lynn Nancy Rivers*
14. *John Conyers, Jr.*
15. *Carolyn C. Kilpatrick*
16. *John D. Dingell*

MINNESOTA

SENATORS
Paul David Wellstone
Rod Grams

REPRESENTATIVES
[Republicans 2, Democrats 6]
1. Gil Gutknecht
2. *David Minge*
3. Jim Ramstad
4. *Bruce F. Vento*
5. *Martin Olav Sabo*
6. *Bill Luther*
7. *Collin C. Peterson*
8. *James Oberstar*

MISSISSIPPI

SENATORS
Thad Cochran
Trent Lott

REPRESENTATIVES
[Republicans 3, Democrats 2]
1. Roger Wicker
2. *Bennie G. Thompson*
3. Charles W. (Chip) Pickering, Jr.
4. Mike Parker
5. *Gene Taylor*

MISSOURI

SENATORS
Christopher S. Bond
John Ashcroft

REPRESENTATIVES
[Republicans 4, Democrats 5]
1. *William (Bill) Clay*
2. James M. Talent
3. *Richard A. Gephardt*
4. *Ike Skelton*
5. *Karen McCarthy*
6. *Pat Danner*
7. Roy D. Blunt
8. Jo Ann Emerson
9. Kenny Hulshof

MONTANA

SENATORS
Max Baucus
Conrad Burns

REPRESENTATIVE
[Republican 1]
At Large - Rick Hill

NEBRASKA

SENATORS
J. Robert Kerrey
Chuck Hagel

REPRESENTATIVES
[Republicans 3]
1. Doug Bereuter
2. Jon Christensen
3. Bill Barrett

NEVADA

SENATORS
Harry Reid
Richard H. Bryan

REPRESENTATIVES
[Republicans 2]
1. John Ensign
2. Jim Gibbons

NEW HAMPSHIRE

SENATORS
Robert C. Smith
Judd Gregg

REPRESENTATIVES
[Republicans 2]
1. John E. Sununu
2. Charles Bass

NEW JERSEY

SENATORS
Frank R. Lautenberg
Robert G. Torricelli

REPRESENTATIVES
[Republicans 7, Democrats 6]
1. *Robert E. Andrews*
2. Frank LoBiondo
3. Jim Saxton
4. Christopher H. Smith
5. Marge Roukema
6. *Frank Pallone, Jr.*
7. Bob Franks
8. *William J. Pascrell, Jr.*
9. *Steven R. Rothman*
10. *Donald M. Payne*
11. Rodney Frelinghuysen
12. Mike Pappas
13. *Robert Menendez*

NEW MEXICO

SENATORS
Pete V. Domenici
Jeff Bingaman

REPRESENTATIVES
[Republicans 3]
1. Steven H. Schiff
2. Joe Skeen
3. Bill Redmond

NEW YORK

SENATORS
Daniel P. Moynihan
Alfonse M. D'Amato

REPRESENTATIVES
[Republicans 13, Democrats 18]
1. Michael Forbes
2. Rick A. Lazio
3. Peter T. King
4. *Carolyn McCarthy*
5. *Gary L. Ackerman*
6. *Floyd H. Flake*
7. *Thomas J. Manton*
8. *Jerrold Nadler*
9. *Charles E. Schumer*
10. *Edolphus Towns*
11. *Major R. Owens*
12. *Nydia M. Velázquez*
13. Susan Molinari
14. *Carolyn B. Maloney*
15. *Charles B. Rangel*
16. *José E. Serrano*
17. *Eliot L. Engel*
18. *Nita M. Lowey*
19. Sue Kelly
20. Benjamin A. Gilman
21. *Michael R. McNulty*
22. Gerald B.H. Solomon
23. Sherwood L. Boehlert
24. John M. McHugh
25. James T. Walsh
26. *Maurice D. Hinchey*
27. Bill Paxon
28. *Louise M. Slaughter*
29. *John J. LaFalce*
30. Jack Quinn
31. Amo Houghton

NORTH CAROLINA

SENATORS
Jesse Helms
Lauch Faircloth

REPRESENTATIVES
[Republicans 6, Democrats 6]
1. *Eva Clayton*
2. *Bob Etheridge*
3. Walter B. Jones
4. *David Price*
5. Richard M. Burr
6. Howard Coble
7. *Mike McIntyre*
8. *W.G. (Bill) Hefner*
9. Sue Myrick
10. Cass Ballenger
11. Charles H. Taylor
12. *Melvin Watt*

NORTH DAKOTA

SENATORS
Kent Conrad
Byron L. Dorgan

REPRESENTATIVE
[Democrat 1]

At Large - *Earl Pomeroy*

OHIO

SENATORS
John Glenn
Mike DeWine

REPRESENTATIVES
[Republicans 11, Democrats 8]
1. Steve Chabot
2. Rob Portman
3. *Tony P. Hall*
4. Michael G. Oxley
5. Paul E. Gillmor
6. *Ted Strickland*
7. David L. Hobson
8. John A. Boehner
9. *Marcy Kaptur*
10. *Dennis Kucinich*
11. *Louis Stokes*
12. John R. Kasich
13. *Sherrod Brown*
14. *Tom Sawyer*
15. Deborah Pryce
16. Ralph Regula
17. *James A. Traficant, Jr.*
18. Robert A. Ney
19. Steven LaTourette

OKLAHOMA

SENATORS
Don Nickles
James M. Inhofe

REPRESENTATIVES
[Republicans 6]
1. Steve Largent
2. Thomas A. Coburn
3. Wes Watkins
4. J.C. Watts
5. Ernest J. Istook, Jr.
6. Frank Lucas

OREGON

SENATORS
Ron Wyden
Gordon Smith

REPRESENTATIVES
[Republican 1, Democrats 4]
1. *Elizabeth Furse*
2. Robert F. (Bob) Smith
3. *Earl Blumenauer*
4. *Peter A. DeFazio*
5. *Darlene Hooley*

PENNSYLVANIA

SENATORS
Arlen Specter
Rick Santorum

REPRESENTATIVES
[Republicans 10, Democrats 11]
1. *Thomas M. Foglietta*
2. *Chaka Fattah*
3. *Robert A. Borski*
4. *Ron Klink*

5. John E. Peterson
6. *Tim Holden*
7. Curt Weldon
8. James C. Greenwood
9. Bud Shuster
10. Joseph M. McDade
11. *Paul E. Kanjorski*
12. *John P. Murtha*
13. Jon Fox
14. *William J. Coyne*
15. *Paul McHale*
16. Joseph R. Pitts
17. George W. Gekas
18. *Michael F. Doyle*
19. William F. Goodling
20. *Frank Mascara*
21. Philip English

RHODE ISLAND

SENATORS
John H. Chafee
Jack Reed

REPRESENTATIVES
[Democrats 2]
1. *Patrick J. Kennedy*
2. *Robert A. Weygand*

SOUTH CAROLINA

SENATORS
Strom Thurmond
Ernest F. Hollings

REPRESENTATIVES
[Republicans 4, Democrats 2]
1. Mark Sanford
2. Floyd Spence
3. Lindsey Graham
4. Bob Inglis
5. *John M. Spratt, Jr.*
6. *James E. Clyburn*

SOUTH DAKOTA

SENATORS
Thomas A. Daschle
Tim Johnson

REPRESENTATIVE
[Republican 1]

At Large - John Thune

TENNESSEE

SENATORS
Bill Frist
Fred Thompson

REPRESENTATIVES
[Republicans 5, Democrats 4]
1. William L. (Bill) Jenkins
2. John J. Duncan, Jr.
3. Zach Wamp
4. Van Hilleary
5. *Bob Clement*
6. *Bart Gordon*
7. Ed Bryant
8. *John S. Tanner*
9. *Harold E. Ford, Jr.*

TEXAS

SENATORS
Phil Gramm
Kay Bailey Hutchison

REPRESENTATIVES
[Republicans 13, Democrats 17]
1. *Max Sandlin*
2. *Jim Turner*
3. Sam Johnson
4. *Ralph M. Hall*
5. Pete Sessions
6. Joe Barton
7. Bill Archer
8. Kevin Brady
9. *Nick Lampson*
10. *Lloyd Doggett*
11. *Chet Edwards*
12. Kay Granger
13. William (Mac) Thornberry
14. Ron Paul
15. *Rubén Hinojosa*
16. *Silvestre Reyes*
17. *Charles W. Stenholm*
18. *Sheila Jackson Lee*
19. Larry Combest
20. *Henry B. Gonzalez*
21. Lamar S. Smith
22. Tom DeLay

23. Henry Bonilla
24. *Martin Frost*
25. *Kenneth F. Bentsen, Jr.*
26. Dick Armey
27. *Solomon P. Ortiz*
28. *Ciro Rodriguez*
29. *Gene Green*
30. *Eddie Bernice Johnson*

UTAH

SENATORS
Orrin Hatch
Robert F. Bennett

REPRESENTATIVES
[Republicans 3]
1. James V. Hansen
2. Merrill Cook
3. Christopher B. Cannon

VERMONT

SENATORS
Patrick J. Leahy
James M. Jeffords

REPRESENTATIVE
[Independent 1]

At Large - **Bernard Sanders**

VIRGINIA

SENATORS
John W. Warner
Charles S. Robb

REPRESENTATIVES
[Republicans 5, Democrats 6]
1. Herbert H. Bateman
2. *Owen B. Pickett*
3. *Robert C. (Bobby) Scott*
4. *Norman Sisisky*
5. *Virgil H. Goode, Jr.*
6. Robert W. (Bob) Goodlatte
7. Thomas J. Bliley, Jr.
8. *James P. Moran*
9. *Rick Boucher*
10. Frank R. Wolf
11. Thomas M. Davis III

WASHINGTON

SENATORS
Slade Gorton
Patty Murray

REPRESENTATIVES
[Republicans 6, Democrats 3]
1. Rick White
2. Jack Metcalf
3. Linda Smith
4. Doc Hastings
5. George Nethercutt
6. *Norman D. Dicks*
7. *Jim McDermott*
8. Jennifer Dunn
9. *Adam Smith*

WEST VIRGINIA

SENATORS
Robert C. Byrd
John D. Rockefeller IV

REPRESENTATIVES
[Democrats 3]
1. *Alan B. Mollohan*
2. *Robert E. Wise, Jr.*
3. *Nick J. Rahall II*

WISCONSIN

SENATORS
Herb Kohl
Russell D. Feingold

REPRESENTATIVES
[Republicans 4, Democrats 5]
1. Mark Neumann
2. Scott L. Klug
3. *Ron Kind*

4. *Gerald D. Kleczka*
5. *Thomas M. Barrett*
6. Thomas E. Petri
7. *David R. Obey*
8. *Jay W. Johnson*
9. F. James Sensenbrenner, Jr.

WYOMING

SENATORS
Craig Thomas
Michael B. Enzi

REPRESENTATIVE
[Republican 1]

At Large - Barbara Cubin

AMERICAN SAMOA

DELEGATE
[Democrat 1]

Eni F.H. Faleomavaega

DISTRICT OF COLUMBIA

DELEGATE
[Democrat 1]

Eleanor Holmes Norton

GUAM

DELEGATE
[Democrat 1]

Robert A. Underwood

PUERTO RICO

RESIDENT COMMISSIONER
[Democrat 1]

Carlos Romero-Barceló

VIRGIN ISLANDS

DELEGATE
[Democrat 1]

Donna Christian-Green

ALABAMA

(Population 1995, 4,253,000)

SENATORS

RICHARD C. SHELBY, Republican, of Tuscaloosa, AL; born in Birmingham, AL on May 6, 1934; attended the public schools; A.B., University of Alabama, 1957; LL.B., University of Alabama School of Law, 1963; attorney; admitted to the Alabama bar in 1961 and commenced practice in Tuscaloosa; member, Alabama State Senate, 1970–78; law clerk, Supreme Court of Alabama, 1961–62; city prosecutor, Tuscaloosa, 1963–71; U.S. Commissioner, Northern District of Alabama, 1966–70; special assistant attorney general, State of Alabama, 1968–70; chairman, legislative council of Alabama Legislature, 1977–78; former president, Tuscaloosa County Mental Health Association; member of Alabama Code Revision Committee, 1971–75; member: Phi Alpha Delta legal fraternity, Tuscaloosa County; Alabama and American bar associations; First Presbyterian Church of Tuscaloosa; Exchange Club; American Judicature Society; Alabama Law Institute; married the former Annette Nevin in 1960; two children: Richard C., Jr. and Claude Nevin; committees: Appropriations; Banking, Housing, and Urban Affairs; Special Committee on Aging; chair, Select Committee on Intelligence; elected to the 96th Congress, November 7, 1978, and reelected to the three succeeding Congresses; elected to the U.S. Senate on November 4, 1986; reelected on November 3, 1992.

Office Listings

http://www.senate.gov/senator/shelby.html senator@shelby.senate.gov

110 Hart Senate Office Building, Washington, DC 20510–0103 224–5744
Administrative Assistant.—Tom Young. FAX: 224–3416
Personal Secretary/Appointments.—Anne Caldwell.
Press Secretary.—Laura Cox.
P.O. Box 2570, Tuscaloosa, AL 35403 .... (205) 759–5047
Federal Building, Room 321, 1800 5th Avenue North, Birmingham, AL 35203 ...... (205) 731–1384
308 U.S. Court House, 113 St. Joseph Street, Mobile, AL 36602 .... (205) 694–4164
B28–A U.S. Courthouse, 15 Lee Street, Montgomery, AL 36104 .... (205) 223–7303
Huntsville International Airport, 1000 Glenn Hearn Boulevard, Box 20127, Huntsville, AL 35824 .... (205) 772–0460

* * *

JEFFERSON BEAUREGARD SESSIONS III, Republican, of Mobile, AL; born in Hybard, AL on December 24, 1946; graduated Wilcox County High School, Camden, AL; B.A., Huntingdon College, Montgomery, AL, 1969; J.D., University of Alabama, Tuscaloosa, 1973; U.S. Army Reserves, captain, 1973–86; attorney; admitted to the Alabama bar in 1973 and commenced practice for Guin, Bouldin and Porch in Russellville, 1973–75; Assistant U.S. Attorney, South District of Alabama, 1975–77; attorney for Stockman & Bedsole, 1977–81; U.S. Attorney, South District of Alabama, 1981–93; attorney for Stockman, Bedsole and Sessions, 1993–94; Attorney General, State of Alabama, 1994–96; member: Huntingdon College Board of Trustees; delegate, General Conference, United Methodist Church; Montgomery Lions Club; Mobile United Methodist Inner City Mission; American Bar Association; Ashland Place United Methodist Church; married the former Mary Blackshear, 1969; three children: Ruth, Mary and Samuel; committees: Environment and Public Works; Judiciary; Select Committee on Ethics; Joint Economic; elected to the U.S. Senate, November 5, 1996.

Office Listings

http://www.senate.gov/senator/sessions.html senator@sessions.senate.gov

495 Russell Senate Office Building, Washington, DC 20510–0104 224–4124
Chief of Staff.—Armand DeKeyser. FAX: 224–3149
Scheduler.—Kate Hollis.
Executive Assistant.—Peggi Jeffreys.
Press Secretary.—John Cox.
General Counsel.—Kristi Lee.
341 Federal Building, 1800 Fifth Avenue, North Birmingham, AL 35203 .... (202) 690–3167
Staff.—Keith Ensey, Virginia Amason. FAX: 731–0221
Federal Courthouse, 113 St. Joseph Street, Room 437, Mobile, AL 36604 .... (334) 690–3167
Staff.—Stormie Jansen. FAX: 690–3174
Federal Courthouse, Room B27, 15 Lee Street, Montgomery, AL 36104 .... (334) 265–9507
State Director.—Chuck Spurlock. FAX: 834–2823
Suite 200, AmSouth, 200 Clinton Avenue, N.W., Huntsville, AL 35801 .... (205) 533–0979
Staff.—Angela Colvert, Jana Dollar. FAX: 533–0745

REPRESENTATIVES

FIRST DISTRICT

SONNY CALLAHAN, Republican, of Mobile, AL; born in Mobile, September 11, 1932; graduated McGill Institute (high school), Mobile, 1950; University of Alabama, Mobile (night school), 1959–60; served in U.S. Navy, seaman, 1952–54; businessman, The Finch Companies, 1964–84; membership, Mobile Area Chamber of Commerce; Alabama House of Representatives, 1970–78; Alabama State Senate, 1978–82; married to the former Karen Reed; six children: Scott, Patrick, Shawn, Chris, Kelly and Cameron (deceased); elected to the 99th Congress on November 6, 1984; reelected to each succeeding Congress; serves on the Committee on Appropriations; chairman, Foreign Operations Subcommittee.

Office Listings

http://www.house.gov/callahan callahan@hr.house.gov

2418 Rayburn House Office Building, Washington, DC 20515–0101 225–4931
Chief of Staff/Press Secretary.—Jo Bonner. FAX: 225–0562
Legislative Director.—Nancy Tippins.
Personal Secretary.—Helen Vulevich.
Suite 126, 2970 Cottage Hill Road, Mobile, AL 36606 .... (334) 690–2811
District Representative.—Taylor Ellis. FAX: 473–4750

Counties: Baldwin, Clarke, Escambia, Mobile, Monroe, and Washington. Population (1990), 577,226.

ZIP Codes: 36425–27, 36431, 36439, 36441, 36444–45, 36449, 36451, 36456–58, 36460–61, 36470–71, 36475, 36480–81, 36482 (part), 36483, 36501–02, 36504–05, 36507, 36509–13, 36515, 36518, 36521–23, 36525–30, 36532–33, 36535–36, 36538–45, 36547–51, 36553, 36555–56, 36558–62, 36564, 36567–69, 36571–72, 36574–76, 36578–87, 36590, 36601–19, 36633, 36640–41, 36652, 36660, 36663, 36670–71, 36685, 36688–89, 36691, 36693, 36695, 36784 (part)

* * *

SECOND DISTRICT

TERRY EVERETT, Republican, of Enterprise, AL; born February 15, 1937, in Dothan, AL; attended Enterprise State Junior College; newspaper publisher; president: Premium Home Builders, Everett Land Development Company, Union Springs Newspapers, Inc.; owner and operator, Hickory Ridge Farms; chairman, board of directors, Dothan Federal Savings Bank; Alabama Press Association; chairman of the board, Union Springs Newspapers, Inc.; married to Barbara Pitts Everett; committees; Agriculture, National Security, and Veterans' Affairs; elected on November 3, 1992 to the 103rd Congress; reelected to each succeeding Congress.

Office Listings

everett@hr.house.gov

208 Cannon House Office Building, Washington, DC 20515–0102 225–2901
Administrative Assistant.—H. Clay Swanzy. FAX: 225–8913
Legislative Director.—Wade H. Heck.
Press Secretary.—Mike Lewis.
Personal Secretary.—Joanna Varoutsos.
3500 Eastern Boulevard, No. 250, Montgomery, AL 36116 .... (205) 277–9113
Federal Building, 100 West Troy Street, Dothan, AL 36303 .... (205) 794–9680
City Hall Building, Main Street, Opp, AL 36467 .... (205) 493–9253

Counties: Autauga, Barbour, Bullock, Butler, Coffee, Conecuh, Covington, Crenshaw, Dale, Elmore, Geneva, Henry, Houston, Montgomery, and Pike. Population (1990), 577,227.

ZIP Codes: 36001, 36003–06, 36007–10, 36012, 36013–18, 36020, 36022, 36024–27, 36028–30, 36033–38, 36041–42, 36046 (part), 36048–49, 36051–54, 36057, 36061–62, 36064, 36067, 36069 (part), 36071–72, 36078, 36080–81, 36089, 36092, 36104 (part), 36105 (part), 36106 (part), 36107 (part), 36108 (part), 36109, 36110 (part), 36111–12, 36113 (part), 36114–16, 36117 (part), 36120–21, 36123–25, 36301–04, 36310–14, 36315–23, 36330–31, 36340, 36343–46, 36348, 36349–53, 36360–63, 36370–71, 36073–74, 36076, 36079, 36373–76, 36401, 36420, 36429, 36432, 36442, 36453–56, 36467, 36468–69, 36473–78, 36483, 36749

THIRD DISTRICT

ROBERT RILEY, Republican, of Ashland, AL; born on October 3, 1944 in Talladega, AL; graduated from Clay County High School, MO, 1962; B.A. in business administration, University of Alabama, 1965; businessman: owner of Midway Ford, Chrysler, Plymouth, Dodge and Jeep Eagle, and of Midway Transit Trucking Company; involved in commercial and residential real estate; cattleman; Ashland City Council, 1972–76; member: First Baptist Church of Ashland, Ashland Jaycees, Alabama Cattlemen's Association, APEA; Shriner; Mason; married Patsy Adams Riley, 1964; four children: Rob, Jenice, Minda and Krisalyn; committees: National Security, Banking and Financial Services; subcommittees: Military Readiness, Military Research and Development, Depot Caucus, Capital Markets and Securities, Oversight and Investigations; elected to the 105th Congress.

Office Listings

510 Cannon House Office Building, Washington, DC 20515–0103 225–3261
Chief of Staff.—Earl Whipple. FAX: 225–6827
Legislative Director/Military Affairs Director.—Dan Gans.
Legislative Assistant.—John Heroux.
Legislative Assistant/Systems Manager.—Julia Rotch.
Press Secretary.—Mike Scanlon.
Scheduler/Office Manager.—Debbie McBride.
104 Federal Building, Anniston, AL 36202 .... (205) 236–5655
FAX: 237–9203
107 Federal Building, Opelika, AL 36801 .... (334) 745–6221
FAX: 742–0109

Counties: Bibb, Calhoun, Chambers, Chilton, Clay, Cleburne, Coosa, Lee, Macon, Randolph, Russell, St. Clair, Talladega and Tallapoosa. CITIES AND TOWNSHIPS: Moody, Alexander City, Alpine, Bon Air, Brent, Brierfield, Centerville, Childersburg, Clanton, Cropwell, Goodwater, Green Pond, Hissop, Hollins, Jemison, Kellyton, Leeds, Lincoln, Margaret, Odenville, Pell City, Ragland, Riverside, Rockford, Springville, Sycamore, Sylacauga, Talladega, Thorsby, Wattsville, Weogufka, West Blockton, Woodstock, Ashville, Steele, Armstrong, Autaugaville, Billingsley, Booth, Central, Deatsville, East Tallassee, Equality, Fort Davis, Hardaway, Shorter, Tallassee, Tuskegee, Tuskegee Institute, Verbena, Anniston, Oxford, Blue Mountain, Alexandria, Ashland, Bynum, Choccolocco, Cragford, Daviston, DeArmanville, Delta, Eastaboga, Edwardsville, Fruithurst, Graham, Heflin, Jacksonville, Lineville, Millerville, Munford, Muscadine, Newell, Ohatchee, Piedmont, Ranburne, Roanoke, Wadley, Weaver, Wedowee, Wellington, Woodland, Jones, Maplesville, Stanton, Randolph, Lawley, Opelika, Auburn, Auburn University, Camp Hill, Cottonton, Cusseta, Dadeville, Valley, Five Points, Fort Mitchell, Hatchechubbee, Holy Trinity, Hurtsboro, Jackson's Gap, Lafayette, Lanett, Langdale, Loachapoka, Notasulga, Phenix City, Pittsview, River View, Salem, Seale, Shawmut, Smiths, Standing Rock, Waverly, Fairfax, Fort McClellan, Hobson City, Rock Mills. Population (1990), 577,227.

ZIP Codes: 35004, 35010, 35014, 35032, 35034–35, 35040, 35042, 35044–45, 35052, 35054, 35072, 35074, 35081–82, 35084–85, 35089, 35094 (part), 35096, 35112, 35115 (part), 35120–21, 35125, 35131, 35133, 35135–36, 35146 (part), 35149–50, 35160, 35171, 35173 (part), 35182–84, 35188, 35228, 35905, 35953, 35972, 35987, 36002–03, 36006, 36008, 36013 (part), 36014, 36021–23, 36026, 36027 (part), 36031, 36039, 36045, 36075, 36078, 36080, 36083, 36087–88, 36091, 36201–06, 36250–51, 36253–58, 36260–74, 36276–80, 36749, 36750, 36769, 36790, 36792–93, 36801–03, 36830–31, 36849, 36850–56, 36858–89, 36860–64, 36865–69, 36871–72, 36874–76, 36877–79

* * *

FOURTH DISTRICT

ROBERT ADERHOLT, Republican, of Haleyville, AL; born in Haleyville, July 22, 1965; graduate, Birmingham Southern University; J.D., Cumberland School of Law, Samford University; attorney; assistant legal advisor to Governor Fob James, 1995–96; Haleyville municipal judge, 1992–96; George Bush delegate, Republican National Convention, 1992; Republican nominee for the 17th District, Alabama House of Representatives, 1990; married to the former Caroline McDonald; committee: Appropriations; elected to the 105th Congress.

Office Listings

1007 Longworth House Office Building, Washington, DC 20515 225–4876
Chief of Staff.—Brian Rell. FAX: 225–5587
Legislative Director.—Mark Busching.
Legislative Assistant.—Mark Zelden.
Scheduler.—Alison Klukas.
1710 Alabama Avenue, Room 247, Jasper, AL 35501 .... (205) 221–2310
District Coordinator.—Melissa Waldron. FAX: 221–9035
District Field Coordinator.—Bill Harris.

Counties: Blount, Cherokee, Cullman, DeKalb, Etowah, Fayette, Franklin, Lamar, part of Lawrence, Marion, Marshall, Pickens (part), Walker, and Winston. Population (1990), 577,227.

ZIP Codes: 35006 (part), 35013, 35016, 35019, 35031, 35033, 35038, 35049, 35053, 35055–56, 35062 (part), 35063 (part), 35070, 35077, 35079, 35083, 35087, 35097–98, 35121, 35126 (part), 35130, 35133, 35139, 35148, 35172, 35175, 35179, 35180 (part), 35403 (part), 35442, 35447, 35461, 35466, 35481, 35501–02, 35540–46, 35548–55, 35559–60, 35563–65, 35570–82, 35584–87, 35592–94, 35619 (part), 35621–22, 35643 (part), 35650–51, 35653, 35672 (part), 35747, 35755, 35760, 35768, 35776, 35901–06, 35950, 35952, 35954, 35957, 35959–64, 35966–67, 35971–76, 35978, 35980–81, 35983–84, 35986, 35988–90, 35999, 36275

* * *

FIFTH DISTRICT

BUD CRAMER, Democrat, of Huntsville, AL; born in Huntsville, August 22, 1947; graduated, Huntsville High School, 1965; B.A., University of Alabama, Tuscaloosa, 1969, ROTC; J.D., University of Alabama School of Law, Tuscaloosa, 1972; U.S. Army, 1972; captain, U.S. Army Reserves, 1976–78; attorney; instructor, University of Alabama School of Law, Tuscaloosa; director of clinical studies program, 1972–73; assistant district attorney, Madison County, AL, 1973–75; private law practice, Huntsville, AL, 1975–80; district attorney, Madison County, 1981–90; member: Alabama District Attorneys Association; National District Attorneys Association; founder, National Children's Advocacy Center, Huntsville; National Center for Missing and Exploited Children; American Bar Association, 1975–present; State of Alabama Bar Association, 1972–present; American Bar Association's National Legal Resource Center for Child Advocacy and Protection; awards and honors: received certificate of appreciation, presented by President Ronald Reagan, for outstanding dedication and commitment in promoting safety and well-being of children from the President's Child Safety Partnership, 1987; 1986 recipient of the Vincent De Francis Award, presented by the American Humane Association; selected as National Public Citizen of the Year, 1984; Alabama District Attorneys Investigators Association, "District Attorney of the Year, 1986"; Methodist; widower; one daughter: Hollan C. Gaines; elected to the 102nd Congress, November 6, 1990; reelected to each succeeding Congress; member: Committee on Transportation and Infrastructure, Committee on Science.

Office Listings

http://www.house.gov/cramer budmail@hr.house.gov

2416 Rayburn House Office Building, Washington, DC 20515–0105 225–4801
Administrative Assistant.—John Hay.
Executive Assistant.—Samantha Smith.
Legislative Assistants: Shar Hendrick, Amy Strain.
403 Franklin Street, Huntsville, AL 35801 .... (205) 551–0190
District Coordinator.—Joe Vallely.
Morgan County Courthouse, Box 668, Decatur, AL 35602 .... (205) 355–9400
737 East Avalon Avenue, Muscle Shoals, AL 35661 .... (205) 381–3450

Counties: Colbert, Jackson, Lauderdale, Lawrence, Limestone, Madison, and Morgan. Population (1990), 577,227.

ZIP Codes: 35087, 35601–03, 35610–11, 35615–18, 35619 (part), 35620–22, 35630–31, 35633, 35640, 35643 (part), 35645–49, 35652–53, 35660–62, 35670–71, 35672 (part), 35673–74, 35677, 35739–42, 35744–46, 35748–52, 35754–55, 35758–68, 35771–76, 35801–08, 35810–12, 35814–16, 35824, 35958, 35966, 35971, 35978–79

* * *

SIXTH DISTRICT

SPENCER BACHUS, Republican, of Vestavia Hills, AL; born in Birmingham, AL, December 28, 1947; B.A., Auburn University, 1969; J.D., University of Alabama, 1972; law firm, Bachus, Dempsey, Carson, and Steed, senior partner; member: Huntor Street Baptist Church; Alabama State Representative, Senator; school board, Republican Party Chair; five children: Warren, Stuart, Elliott, Candace, and Lisa; elected to the 103rd Congress, November 3, 1992; reelected to each succeeding Congress.

Office Listings

http://www.house.gov/sbachus bachus@hr.house.gov

442 Cannon House Office Building, Washington, DC 20515–0106 225–4921
Administrative Assistant.—Jennifer Oldham Hatcher.
Executive Assistant.—Gerry Cashin.
Press Secretary.—Jeff Emerson.
Suite 107, 1900 International Park Drive, Birmingham, AL 35243 .... (205) 969–2296
P.O. Drawer 569, 3500 McFarland Boulevard, Northport, AL 35476 .... (205) 333–9894

Counties: Bibb, Jefferson, Shelby, and Tuscaloosa. CITIES AND TOWNSHIPS: Adamsville, Alabaster, Argo, Brookside, Brookwood, Calera, Cardiff, Columbiana, County Line, Fultondale, Gardendale, Graysville, Harpersville, Helena, Homewood, Hoover, Hueytown, Irondale, Kimberly, Leeds, Maytown, Montevallo, Morris, Mountain Brook, Mulga, North Johns, Northport, Pelham, Pleasant Grove, Sumiton, Sylvan Springs, Trafford, Trussville, Vestavia Hills, Vincent, Warrior, West Blocton, West Jefferson, Wilsonville, Wilton, and portions of Bessemer, Birmingham, Tarrant, Tuscaloosa, and West Blocton. Population (1990), 577,226.

ZIP Codes: 35005, 35006 (part), 35007, 35015, 35023 (part), 35035–36, 35040–41, 35043, 35048, 35051, 35060, 35061 (part), 35062 (part), 35063 (part), 35068, 35071, 35073, 35078, 35080, 35091, 35094 (part), 35111 (part), 35114, 35115 (part), 35116–19, 35123–24, 35126 (part), 35127, 35137, 35142–44, 35146 (part), 35147, 35172, 35173 (part), 35176, 35178, 35180 (part), 35181, 35185–87, 35205 (part), 35206 (part), 35207 (part), 35209–10, 35211 (part), 35212 (part), 35213, 35214 (part), 35215 (part), 35216, 35217 (part), 35219–20, 35222 (part), 35223, 35224 (part), 35226, 35231, 35233 (part), 35235–36, 35238, 35242–44, 35253, 35255–56, 35294, 35298, 35401 (part), 35404 (part), 35405 (part), 35406 (part), 35444, 35446, 35452, 35457–58, 35463, 35468, 35476 (part), 35478, 35480 (part)

* * *

SEVENTH DISTRICT

EARL F. HILLIARD, Democrat, of Birmingham, AL; born in Birmingham on April 9, 1942, son of the late William Nelson and Iola Hilliard; attended public schools of Birmingham; B.A., Morehouse College, Atlanta, GA, 1964; J.D., Howard University, Washington, DC, 1967; M.B.A., Atlanta University School of Business, Atlanta, GA, 1970; married Mary Franklin of Atlanta, GA; two children: Alesia and Earl, Jr.; attorney, admitted to the Alabama bar, 1968; commenced practice in Birmingham; member of Mt. Moriah Baptist Church, Pratt City; member: National Bar Association and State of Alabama Bar Association; member of the Tuskegee University Trustee Board, 1986–92; member of the Miles College Law School Trustee Board, 1982–92; elected: Alabama House of Representatives, 1974 and 1978; elected: First Chairman of Alabama Black Legislative Caucus, 1975; elected: Alabama State Senate, 1980–83, 1986 and 1990; chairman, Senate Commerce, Transportation and Utility Committee, 1990–92; chairman, Jefferson County Senate Delegation, 1986–92; chairman, Senate Judiciary Committee, 1982–86; elected November 3, 1992 to the 103rd Congress; reelected to each succeeding Congress.

Office Listings

1007 Longworth House Office Building, Washington, DC 20515–0107	225–2665
Chief of Staff.—Elvira Willoughby.	FAX: 226–0772
Administrative Assistant.—Tunstall Wilson.	
Scheduler.—Tara Sallee.	
Press Secretary.—Kenneth Mullinax.	
Federal Building, Room 204, Tuscaloosa, AL 35401	(205) 752–3578
District Office Manager.—Kay Presley.	FAX: 349–2450
Vance Federal Building, 1800 Fifth Avenue North, Birmingham, AL 35203	(205) 328–2841
	FAX: 251–6817
Federal Building, Room 109, Selma, AL 36701	(205) 872–2684
District Office Manager.—Betty Calloway.	FAX: 875–8270
Federal Building, 15 Lee Street, Room 301, Montgomery, AL 36104	(205) 875–8270
District Office Manager.—Robert Lane.	FAX: 263–4338

Counties: BIBB COUNTY; city of Eoline. CHOCTAW COUNTY; cities and townships of Bolinger, Butler, Choctaw, Cromwell, Gilbertown, Halsell, Jachin, Lavaca, Lisman, Melvin, Needham, Pennington, Pushmataha, Riderwood, Silas, Cullomburg, Toxey, and Yantley. DALLAS COUNTY; cities and townships of Browns, Marion Junction, Minter, Orrville, Plantersville, Safford, Sardis, and Selma. GREENE COUNTY; cities and townships of Boligee, Clinton, Eutaw, Knoxville, Mantua, and West Greene. HALE COUNTY; cities and townships of Akron, Gallion, Greensboro, Moundville, Newbern, Sawyerville, and Stewart. JEFFERSON COUNTY; cities and townships of Bessemer, Birmingham, Dolomite, Fairfield, McCalla, and Tarrant. LOWNDES COUNTY; cities and townships of Benton, Burkeville, Farmersville, Fort Deposit, Hayneville, Letohatchee, and Lowndesboro. MARENGO COUNTY; cities and townships of Dayton, Demopolis, Dixons Mills, Faunsdale, Jefferson, Linden, Magnolia, Myrtlewood, Nanafalia, Putnam, Shortleaf, Sweet Water, and Thomaston. MONTGOMERY COUNTY; cities and townships of Boylston, Montgomery, Ramer, and West Side. PERRY COUNTY; cities and townships of Marion, Sprott, Suttle, and Uniontown. PICKENS COUNTY; cities and townships of Aliceville, Carrollton, Ethelsville, Gordo, McShan, and Reform. SUMTER COUNTY; cities and townships of Bellamy, Coatopa, Cuba, Emelle, Epes, Gainesville, Geiger, Livingston, Panola, Sumterville, Ward, Whitfield, and York. TUSCALOOSA COUNTY; cities and townships of Coaling, Cottondale, Duncanville, Tuscaloosa, and Vance. WILCOX COUNTY; cities and townships of Alberta, Annemanie, Arlington, Boykin, Camden, Catherine, Coy, Furman, Lamison, Lower Peachtree, McWilliams, Millers Ferry, Oak Hill, Pineapple, Pine Hill, Prairie, and Snow Hill. Population (1990), 577,227.

ZIP Codes: 35020–21, 35023 (part), 35034, 35042, 35061 (part), 35064, 35111 (part), 35201–04, 35205 (part), 35206 (part), 35207 (part), 35208, 35211 (part), 35212 (part), 35214 (part), 35215 (part), 35217 (part), 35218, 35221, 35222 (part), 35224 (part), 35228, 35232, 35233 (part), 35234, 35237, 35259, 35263, 35283, 35291–92, 35401 (part), 35402, 35403 (part), 35404 (part), 35405 (part), 35406 (part), 35440–43, 35449, 35453, 35456, 35459–64, 35469–71, 35474, 35476 (part), 35477, 35480 (part), 35485–87, 35490–91, 36032, 36040, 36043, 36046 (part), 36047, 36069 (part), 36101–03, 36104 (part), 36105 (part), 36106 (part), 36107 (part), 36108 (part), 36110 (part), 36113 (part), 36117 (part), 36435–36, 36446, 36482 (part), 36524, 36570, 36701–03, 36720, 36722–23, 36726–28, 36732, 36736, 36738, 36740, 36742, 36744, 36748–49, 36751 (part), 36752–54, 36756, 36758–59, 36761–65, 36767–69, 36773, 36775–76, 36779, 36782–83, 36784 (part), 36785–86, 36901, 36903–04, 36906–08, 36910–13, 36916, 36919, 36921–22, 36925

ALASKA

(Population 1995, 604,000)

SENATORS

TED STEVENS, Republican, of Girdwood, AK; born in Indianapolis, IN, November 18, 1923; graduated UCLA, 1947; Harvard Law School, 1950; served as first lieutenant (pilot), 1943–46; 14th Air Force in China, 1944–45; practiced law in Washington, DC, and Fairbanks, AK, 1950–53; U.S. attorney, Fairbanks, 1953–56; legislative counsel, U.S. Department of the Interior, 1956–57; assistant to the Secretary of the Interior (Fred Seaton), 1958–59; appointed solicitor of the Department of the Interior by President Eisenhower, 1960; opened law office, Anchorage, AK, 1961; Alaska House of Representatives, 1964–68; has served in U.S. Senate since December 24, 1968; assistant Republican leader, 1977–85; committees: chair, Appropriations; Commerce, Science and Transportation; Governmental Affairs; Rules and Administration; Joint Committee on the Library; married Catherine Chandler of Anchorage; one daughter; five children with first wife, Ann Cherrington (deceased, 1978); member: American, Federal, California, Alaska, and District of Columbia bar associations; member: Rotary, American Legion, Veterans of Foreign Wars, Igloo No. 4 Pioneers of Alaska.

Office Listings

http://www.senate.gov/~stevens senator__stevens@stevens.senate.gov

522 Hart Senate Office Building, Washington, DC 20510–0201 224–3004
Chief of Staff.—Lisa Sutherland.
Legislative Director.—Earl Comstock.
Administrative Director.—Carol M. White.
Scheduling Director.—DeLynn Henry.
Press Secretary.—Mitch Rose.
222 West Seventh Avenue, No. 2, Anchorage, AK 99513 .... (907) 271–5915
Federal Building, Room 206, Box 4, 101 12th Avenue, Fairbanks, AK 99701 .... (907) 456–0261
Federal Building, Room 965, Box 020149, Juneau, AK 99802 .... (907) 586–7400
120 Trading Bay Road, Suite 350, Kenai, AK 99611 .... (907) 283–5808
109 Main Street, Ketchikan, AK 99901 .... (907) 225–6880

* * *

FRANK H. MURKOWSKI, Republican, of Fairbanks, AK; born in Seattle, WA, March 28, 1933; graduated, Ketchikan High School, 1951; attended University of Santa Clara, 1951–53; B.A., economics, Seattle University, 1955; U.S. Coast Guard, active duty, 1955–56; banker; Alaska Commissioner of Economic Development, 1966–70; president, Alaska Bankers Association, 1972; president, Alaska Chamber of Commerce, 1977; president, Alaska National Bank, Fairbanks, 1971–80; member: Elks, Lions, Pioneers of Alaska, Young Presidents Organization, NRA; married the former Nancy Rena Gore, 1954; six children: Carol, Lisa, Michael, Eileen, Mary, and Brian; committees: chair, Energy and Natural Resources; Finance; Veterans' Affairs; Select Committee on Ethics; elected to the U.S. Senate, November 4, 1980, for the six-year term beginning January 5, 1981; elected to second term November 4, 1986; reelected November 3, 1992.

Office Listings

http://www.senate.gov/~murkowski email@murkowski.senate.gov

322 Hart Senate Office Building, Washington, DC 20510–0202 224–6665
Administrative Assistant.—Andrew Lundquist.
Communications Director.—Chuck Kleeschulte.
Legislative Director.—Alexander Polinsky.
Executive Assistant/Scheduler.—Janet Klinger.
U.S. Federal Building, 222 West Seventh Avenue, Box 1, Anchorage, AK 99513–7570 .... (907) 271–3735
U.S. Federal Building, 101 12th Avenue, Box 7, Fairbanks, AK 99701 .... (907) 456–0233
U.S. Federal Building, P.O. Box 1647, Juneau, AK 99802 .... (907) 586–7400
120 Trading Bay Road, Box 260, Kenai AK, 99611 .... (907) 283–5808
109 Main Street, Ketchikan, AK 99901 .... (907) 225–6880
851 East Westpoint Drive, Wasilla, AK 99654 .... (907) 376–7665

REPRESENTATIVE

AT LARGE

DONALD E. YOUNG, Republican, of Fort Yukon, AK; born in Meridian, CA, on June 9, 1933; A.A., Yuba Junior College; B.A., Chico State College, Chico, CA; Honorary Doctorate of Laws, University of Alaska, Fairbanks; State House of Representatives, 1966–70; U.S. Army, 41st Tank Battalion, 1955–57; elected member of the State Senate, 1970–73; served on the Fort Yukon City Council for six years, serving four years as mayor; educator for nine years; river boat captain; member: National Education Association, Elks, Lions, Jaycees; married Lula Fredson of Fort Yukon; two children: Joni and Dawn; elected to the 93rd Congress in a special election, March 6, 1973, to fill the vacancy created by the death of Congressman Nick Begich; reelected to each succeeding Congress; chairman, Resources Committee; member: Transportation and Infrastructure Committee.

Office Listings

http://www.house.gov/donyoung donyoung@mail.house.gov

2331 Rayburn House Office Building, Washington, DC 20515–0201 225–5765
Administrative Assistant.—Lloyd Jones. FAX: 225–0425
Press Secretary.—Jennifer Wise.
Staff Director.—Pamela Kish.
Executive Secretary.—Jessica Scallon.
222 West Seventh Avenue, No. 3, Room 200, Anchorage, AK 99513 .... (907) 271–5978
101 12th Avenue, Box 10, Fairbanks, AK 99701 .... (907) 456–0210
401 Federal Building, Box 1247, Juneau, AK 99802 .... (907) 586–7400
109 Main Street, Ketchikan, AK 99902 .... (907) 225–6880
Suite 260, 120 Trading Bay Road, Kenai, AK 99611 .... (907) 283–5808

Population (1990), 550,043.

ZIP Codes: 99501–24, 99540, 99549–59, 99561, 99563–69, 99571–81, 99583, 99585–90, 99599, 99602–15, 99619–22, 99624–28, 99630–36, 99639, 99641, 99643–45, 99647–52, 99654–55, 99657–59, 99661–65, 99667–72, 99674, 99676–79, 99681–84, 99686–89, 99691, 99693–94, 99701–12, 99714, 99716, 99720–27, 99729–30, 99732–34, 99736–53, 99755–73, 99775, 99777–78, 99780–86, 99788–89, 99791, 99801–03, 99811, 99820–21, 99824–27, 99829–30, 99832–33, 99835–36, 99840–41, 99901, 99918–19, 99921–23, 99925–29

ARIZONA

(Population 1995, 4,218,000)

SENATORS

JOHN McCAIN, Republican, of Phoenix, AZ; born in Panama Canal Zone on August 29, 1936; graduated Episcopal High School, Alexandria, VA, 1954; graduated, U.S. Naval Academy, Annapolis, MD, 1958; National War College, Washington, DC, 1973; retired captain (pilot), U.S. Navy, 1958–81; military awards: Silver Star, Bronze Star, Legion of Merit, Purple Heart, and Distinguished Flying Cross; chair, International Republican Institute; married to the former Cindy Hensley; seven children: Doug, Andy, Sidney, Meghan, Jack, Jim, and Bridget; chairman: Senate Commerce, Science and Transportation Committee; member: Armed Services and Indian Affairs committees; elected on November 1, 1982 to the U.S. House of Representatives; reelected to the 99th Congress in 1984; elected to the U.S. Senate on November 4, 1986; reelected in 1992.

Office Listings

http://www.senate.gov/~mccain senator_mccain@mccain.senate.gov

241 Russell Senate Office Building, Washington, DC 20510–0303 224–2235
Chief of Staff.—Mark Salter. TDD: 224–7132
Legislative Director.—Ann Sauer.
Press Secretary.—Nancy Ives.
Personal Secretary.—Ellen Cahill.
Office Manager.—Debbie Paul.
2400 East Arizona Biltmore Circle, Suite 1150, Building No. 1, Phoenix, AZ 85016 .... (602) 952–2410
TDD: 952–0170
1839 South Alma School Road, Suite 375, Mesa, AZ 85210 .... (602) 491–4300
450 West Paseo Redondo, Suite 200, Tucson, AZ 85701 .... (602) 670–6334

* * *

JON KYL, Republican, of Phoenix, AZ; born in Oakland, NE on April 25, 1942; graduated Bloomfield High School, Bloomfield, IA, 1960; B.A., University of Arizona, Tucson, 1964 (Phi Beta Kappa, Phi Kappa Phi); LL.B., University of Arizona, 1966; editor-in-chief, *Arizona Law Review*; attorney, admitted to the Arizona State bar, 1966; former partner in Phoenix law firm of Jennings, Strouss and Salmon, 1966–86; chairman, Phoenix Chamber of Commerce (1984–85); married to the former Caryll Louise Collins; two children: Kristine and Jon; elected to the 100th Congress on November 4, 1986; reelected to each succeeding Congress; member: Judiciary, Energy and Natural Resources, and Intelligence committees.

Office Listings

http://www.senate.gov/~kyl info@kyl.senate.gov

724 Hart Senate Office Building, Washington, DC 20515 224–4521
Chief of Staff.—Ted Maness.
Senior Policy Advisor.—Jeanine Esperne.
Senior Policy Advisor.—Tim Glazewski.
Press Secretary.—Vince Sollitto.
Suite 120, 2200 East Camelback Road, Phoenix, AZ 85016 .... (602) 840–1891
Suite 220, 7315 North Oracle, Tucson, AZ 85704 .... (520) 575–8633

REPRESENTATIVES

FIRST DISTRICT

MATT SALMON, Republican, of Mesa, AZ; born in Salt Lake City, UT, January 21, 1958; graduated, Mesa High School, 1976; B.A., Arizona State University, Temple, 1981; M.P.A., Brigham Young University, Provo, UT, 1986; telecommunications executive; community affairs manager, U.S. West Communications, Phoenix, AZ; Arizona State Senate, 1991–95: assistant majority leader, 1993–95; chairman, Rules Committee, 1993–95; Appropriations and Finance committees and Appropriations Subcommittee on Education; member: East Valley Child Crisis

Center; Council on Families, Youth and Children; Mesa United Way; Arizona Science and Technology Museum; committees: International Relations, Science; subcommittees: International Operations and Human Rights; Asia and the Pacific; Energy and Environment; Space and Aeronautics; married to the former Nancy Huish; four children: Lara, Jacob, Katie, and Matthew, Jr.; elected to the 104th Congress in November 1994; reelected to the 105th Congress.

Office Listings

http://www.house.gov/salmon msalmon@hr.house.gov

115 Cannon House Office Building, Washington, DC 20515–0301 225–2635
Chief of Staff.—Robert Glazier. FAX: 225–3405
Office Manager/Scheduler.—Julia Koppius.
Press Secretary.—Sara Kane.
Legislative Director.—Mike Paranzino.
401 West Baseline Road, Suite 209, Tempe, AZ 85283 .... (602) 831–2900
District Director.—Terree Wasley. FAX: 831–2700

County: Maricopa County; Ahwatukee, Gilbert. Cities and townships: Chandler, Mesa, Phoenix, Scottsdale, Tempe. Population (1990), 610,872.

ZIP Codes: 85003–4, 85006, 85008, 85012–14, 85016, 85018, 85040, 85044–45, 85048, 85201–03, 85205, 85210, 85213, 85215, 85224–26, 85233, 85248–49, 85251, 85257, 85281–84

* * *

SECOND DISTRICT

ED PASTOR, Democrat, of Phoenix, AZ; born in Claypool, AZ, on June 28, 1943; attended public schools in Miami, AZ; graduate of Arizona State University; B.A., chemistry, 1966; J.D., Arizona University, 1974; member, Governor Raul Castro's staff; taught chemistry, North High School; former deputy director of Guadalupe Organization, Inc.; elected supervisor, board of supervisors, Maricopa County; served three terms in Congress; served, board of directors for the National Association of Counties; vice chairman, Employment Steering Committee; president, Arizona County Supervisors Association; member, executive committee of the Arizona Association of Counties; resigned, May, 1991; elected by special election September 24, 1991 to fill the vacancy caused by the resignation of Morris K. Udall; elected November 3, 1992 to the 103rd Congress; appointed to Democratic Steering and Policy Committee; member: Appropriations Committee, Subcommittee on Energy and Water Development, Subcommittee on Rural Development, Agriculture and Related Agencies; elected to the 104th Congress, November 1994; appointed to the House Committee on Agriculture; member: Subcommittee on General Commodities, Subcommittee on Risk Management and Specialty Crops; House Committee on Oversight, Joint Committee on the Library of Congress; chairman, Hispanic Caucus; married to Verma Pastor; two daughters: Yvonne and Laura; board of directors, Neighborhood Housing Services of America, National Association of Latino Elected Officials; served as director at large, ASU Alumni Association; founding board member, ASU Los Diablos Alumni Association; served on board of directors for National Council of La Raza, Arizona Joint Partnership Training Council, National Conference of Christians and Jews, Friendly House, Chicanos Por La Causa, Phoenix Economic Growth Corporation, Sun Angel Foundation; vice president, Valley of the Sun United Way; advisory member, Boys Club of Metropolitan Phoenix.

Office Listings

http://www.house.gov/pastor ed.pastor@mail.house.gov

223 Cannon House Office Building, Washington, DC 20515–0302 225–4065
Administrative Assistant.—Gene Fisher.
802 North Third Avenue, Phoenix, AZ 85003 .... (602) 256–0551
District Director.—Ron Piceno.
2432 East Broadway Boulevard, Tucson, AZ 85719 .... (602) 624–9986
Southern Arizona District Director.—Linda Leatherman.
Suite 117, 281 West 24th Street, Yuma, AZ 85364 .... (602) 726–3324
District Representative.—Charlene Fernandez.

Counties: Maricopa (part), Pima (part), Pinal (part), Santa Cruz, and Yuma. Population (1990), 610,871.

ZIP Codes: 85001–02, 85003 (part), 85004 (part), 85005, 85006 (part), 85007 (part), 85008 (part), 85009 (part), 85013 (part), 85017 (part), 85019 (part), 85025, 85030–31, 85033 (part), 85034 (part), 85035 (part), 85040 (part), 85041, 85043 (part), 85044 (part), 85063, 85073–74, 85222 (part), 85223, 85230, 85283 (part), 85301 (part), 85311, 85318, 85321–22, 85323 (part), 85326 (part), 85333, 85336–37, 85338 (part), 85339 (part), 85341, 85347, 85349–50, 85352, 85353 (part), 85356, 85364–66, 85611, 85614 (part), 85624, 85628, 85634, 85637 (part), 85639–40, 85645 (part), 85646, 85648, 85701–02, 85705 (part), 85706 (part), 85711 (part), 85713 (part), 85714, 85716 (part), 85717, 85719 (part), 85722, 85733, 85735–36, 85745 (part), 85746 (part)

THIRD DISTRICT

BOB STUMP, Republican, of Tolleson, AZ; born in Phoenix, AZ, April 4, 1927; graduated, Tolleson High School, 1947; B.S., Arizona State University, 1951; cotton farmer; served in the U.S. Navy, 1943–46; Arizona House of Representatives, four terms, 1959–67; Arizona State Senate, five terms, 1967–76, president of Arizona Senate, 1975–76; member: VFW; Veterans of Underage Military Service; Barry M. Goldwater Scholarship and Excellence in Education Foundation; three children: Karen, Bob, and Bruce; elected to the 95th Congress, November 2, 1976; reelected to each succeeding Congress; member: vice-chairman, Committee on National Security; chairman, Committee on Veterans' Affairs; Republican Steering Committee.

Office Listings

211 Cannon House Office Building, Washington, DC 20515–0303 225–4576
Administrative Assistant.—Lisa Jackson. FAX: 225–6328
Appointment Secretary.—Dolores Dunn.
230 North First Avenue, Room 2001, Phoenix, AZ 85025 .... (602) 379–6923
District Assistant.—Bruce Bartholomew. FAX: 271–0611
District Assistant.—Arlene Y. Lassila.

Counties: Coconino (part), La Paz, Maricopa (part), Mohave, Navajo (part), and Yavapai. Population (1990), 610,871.

ZIP Codes: 85023 (part), 85024 (part), 85027 (part), 85033 (part), 85035 (part), 85037, 85039, 85043 (part), 85301 (part), 85302 (part), 85303, 85304 (part), 85305, 85306 (part), 85307–08, 85310, 85312, 85320, 85323 (part), 85324–25, 85326 (part), 85328, 85332, 85334–35, 85338 (part), 85340, 85342–46, 85348, 85351, 85353 (part), 85354–55, 85357–63, 85371–75, 85380–82, 85390, 86001 (part), 86002–03, 86004 (part), 86015–16, 86018, 86020–23, 86030, 86034, 86036, 86039, 86042–44, 86046, 86301–04, 86312–13, 86320–27, 86329–35, 86336 (part), 86337–38, 86340–43, 86401–03, 86405, 86411–12, 86427, 86430–38, 86440–45

* * *

FOURTH DISTRICT

JOHN B. SHADEGG, Republican, of Phoenix, AZ; born in Phoenix on October 22, 1949; graduated Camelback High School; B.A., University of Arizona, Tucson, 1972; J.D., University of Arizona, 1975; Air National Guard, 1969–75; admitted to the Arizona bar, 1976; law offices of John Shadegg; special counsel, Arizona House Republican Caucus, 1991–92; special assistant attorney general, 1983–90; advisor, U.S. Sentencing Commission; founding director/executive committee member, Goldwater Institute for Public Policy; member/former president, Crime Victim Foundation; chairman, Arizona Juvenile Justice Advisory Council; advisory board, Salvation Army; vestry, Christ Church of the Ascension Episcopal, 1989–91; member, Law Society, ASU College of Law; chairman, Arizona Republican Caucus, 1985–87; chairman, Proposition 108—Two-Thirds Tax Limitation Initiative, 1992; member, Fiscal Accountability and Reform Efforts (FARE) Committee, 1991–92; counsel, Arizonans for Wildlife Conservation (No on Proposition 200), 1992; Victims Bill of Rights Task Force, 1989–90; married to Shirley Shadegg; two children: Courtney and Stephen; member: Budget, Resources, and Government Reform and Oversight committees; elected to the 104th Congress; reelected to the 105th Congress.

Office Listings

http://www.house.gov/shadegg jshadegg@hr.house.gov

503 Cannon House Office Building, Washington, DC 20515 225–3361
Chief of Staff.—Chris Mulholland. FAX: 225–3462
Legislative Assistants: Myron Ebell, Jason Whiting, Robert Franciosi.
Legislative Correspondent.—Eric Schlecht.
Staff Assistant.—Brent Bice.
301 East Bethany Home Road, Suite 178, Phoenix, AZ 85014 .... (602) 263–5300
District Director.—Jennifer Macdonald.
Office Manager/Scheduler.—Pat Corbin.

County: MARICOPA COUNTY; cities of Glendale (part), Paradise Valley, Phoenix (part), Scottsdale (part). Population (1990), 610,871.

ZIP Codes: 85003 (part), 85007 (part), 85009 (part), 85012 (part), 85013, 85014 (part), 85015, 85016 (part), 85017 (part), 85018 (part), 85019 (part), 85020–22, 85023 (part), 85024 (part), 85027 (part), 85028–29, 85032, 85051, 85250 (part), 85251 (part), 85253, 85254 (part), 85258 (part), 85260 (part), 85301 (part), 85302 (part), 85304 (part), 85306 (part)

FIFTH DISTRICT

JIM KOLBE, Republican, of Tucson, AZ; born in Evanston, IL, June 28, 1942; graduated, U.S. Capitol Page School, Washington, DC, 1960; B.A., political science, Northwestern University, Evanston, IL, 1965; M.B.A., Stanford University, CA, 1967; study abroad program, International School of America, 1962–63; served in Vietnam, U.S. Navy, lieutenant, 1967–69; lieutenant commander, U.S. Naval Reserves (inactive); vice president, Wood Canyon Corporation, Sonoita, AZ; consultant, real estate development and political affairs; Arizona State Senator, 1977–82; served on Appropriations, Education, and Agriculture committees, chairman of Judiciary Committee; special assistant to Governor Ogilvie of Illinois, 1972–73; board of directors, Arizona Foundation for Children; board of directors, Tucson Community Bank; presidential appointment, Commission on Presidential Scholars; director of operations, Vietnam Orphans Airlift, San Francisco, 1975; committees: Appropriations, Budget; elected to the 99th Congress on November 6, 1984; reelected to each succeeding Congress.

Office Listings

http://www.house.gov.kolbe

205 Cannon House Office Building, Washington, DC 20515–0305 225–2542
Chief of Staff.—Laurie Fenton.
Office Manager/Scheduler.—Natalie Zoll.
Suite 112, 1661 North Swan, Tucson, AZ 85712 .... (602) 881–3588
District Director.—Patricia Klein.
Suite B–160, 77 Calle Portal, Sierra Vista, AZ 85635 .... (602) 459–3115

Counties: Cochise, Graham (part), Pima (part), and Pinal (part). Population (1990), 610,871.

ZIP Codes: 85222 (part), 85231 (part), 85245, 85531, 85535–36, 85543, 85546, 85548, 85551–52, 85602–10, 85613, 85614 (part), 85615–17, 85619–23, 85625–27, 85629 (part), 85630, 85631 (part), 85632–33, 85635–38, 85641, 85643–44, 85645 (part), 85652–55, 85670–71, 85703–04, 85705 (part), 85706 (part), 85708 (part), 85710 (part), 85711 (part), 85712, 85713 (part), 85714 (part), 85715, 85716 (part), 85718, 85719 (part), 85725–26, 85730–32, 85734, 85737–38, 85740–43, 85745 (part), 85746 (part), 85747–49, 85751

* * *

SIXTH DISTRICT

JOHN D. HAYWORTH, JR., Republican, of Scottsdale, AZ; born in High Point, NC, on July 12, 1958; graduated, High Point Central High School, 1976; B.A., speech communications and political science, *cum laude*, North Carolina State University, Raleigh, 1980; broadcaster, public relations consultant, insurance agent; member: Rotary Club of Phoenix (Paul Harris Fellow), Boy Scouts of America (Eagle Scout); married Mary Denise Yancey Hayworth, 1989; three children: Nicole, Hannah, and John Micah; elected to the 104th Congress; reelected to the 105th Congress.

Office Listings

http://www.house.gov/hayworth hayworth@hr.house.gov

1023 Longworth House Office Building, Washington, DC 20515 225–2190
Administrative Assistant.—Steve Bloch. FAX:225–3263
Legislative Director.—Glenn Buberl.
Executive Assistant.—Tricia Evans.
Legislative Assistant.—Katharine Mottley.
1300 South Milton, Suite 207, Flagstaff, AZ 86001 .... (520) 556–8760
Office Manager.—Patty Brookins.
1017 South Gilbert, Suite 203, Mesa, AZ 85204 .... (602) 926–4151
Office Manager.—Jan Lemon.

Counties: Apache, Cocconino (part), Gila, Graham (part), Greenlee, Maricopa (part), Navajo (part), and Pinal (part). CITIES AND TOWNSHIPS: Alpine, Apache Junction, Bapchule, Blue, Bylas, Carefree, Cashion, Casa Grande, Cave Creek, Chandler, Chandler Heights, Chinle, Cibeque, Clay Springs, Claypool, Clifton, Concho, Coolidge, Dennehotso, Duncan, Eagar, Eloy, Flagstaff, Florence, Fountain Hills, Fort Apache, Fort Defiance, Forest Lakes, Ganado, Gilbert, Globe, Gold Canyon, Greer, Happy Jack, Hayden, Heber, Higley, Holbrook, Houck, Indian Wells, Joseph City, Kaibito, Kayenta, Kearny, Lake Montezuma, Lakeside, Laveen, Leupp, Lukachukai, Lupton, Mammoth, Many Farms, Maricopa, McNary, Mesa, Miami, Morenci, Mormon Lake, Munds Park, Nazlini, Nutrioso, Overgaard, Paradise Valley, Payson, Peridot, Petrified Forest NP, Phoenix, Picacho, Pine, Pinedale, Pinetop, Pinon, Queen Creek, Queen Valley, Red Valley, Rio Verde, Rock Point, Roosevelt, Round Rock, Sacaton, Saint Johns, Saint Michaels, San Carlos, Sanders, San Manuel, Sawmill, Scottsdale, Sedona, Shonto, Show Low, Snowflake, Springerville, Stanfield, Strawberry, Sun Lakes, Sun Valley, Superior, Taylor, Teec Nos Pos, Tolleson, Tonto Basin, Tortilla Flat, Tsaile, Tuba City, Valley Farms, Vernon, White Mountain Lake, Whiteriver, Window Rock, Winkelman, Winslow, Woodruff, Young. Population (1990), 610,872.

ZIP Codes: 85024, 85027–28, 85032, 85040, 85044, 85048, 85054, 85076, 85201–08, 85210, 85213–17, 85219–22, 85224–28, 85231–37, 85239, 85241–42, 85247–51, 85253, 85254–60, 85262–64, 85268–69, 85272–73, 85278, 85287, 85290–92, 85296, 85329, 85331, 85339, 85353, 85359–40, 85377, 85501–02, 85528, 85530, 85532–34, 85541–542, 85544–45, 85547, 85550, 85553–54, 85618, 85631, 85901, 85911–12, 85920, 85922–23, 85925–38, 85940–42, 86001–02, 86004, 86011, 86017, 86024–25, 86028–29, 86031–33, 86035, 86038, 86045, 86047, 86053–54, 86336, 86341–42, 86503–08, 86510–15, 86535, 86538–40, 86544–45, 86547, 86549, 86556.

ARKANSAS

(Population 1995, 2,484,000)

SENATORS

DALE BUMPERS, Democrat, of Charleston, AR; born in Charleston, August 12, 1925; graduated, University of Arkansas; J.D., Northwestern University, 1951; admitted to Arkansas bar, 1952; served in U.S. Marine Corps, 1943–46, staff sergeant; past president, Charleston Chamber of Commerce; past president: Charleston School Board, Franklin County Board of Education; past chairman: United Fund, Boy Scout Fund, and Cancer Fund; Governor of Arkansas, 1970–74; married the former Betty Flanagan, 1949; three children: Brent, Bill, and Brooke; committees: Appropriations; Energy and Natural Resources; Small Business; elected to the U.S. Senate, November 5, 1974; reelected November 4, 1980, November 4, 1986, and November 3, 1992.

Office Listings

http://www.senate.gov/~bumpers senator@bumpers.senate.gov

229 Dirksen Senate Office Building, Washington, DC 20510–0401 224–4843
Administrative Assistant.—Mary E. Davis.
Executive Secretary.—Jo Nobles.
Press Secretary.—David Eskola.
Legislative Director.—Rich Glick.
Scheduler.—Henry Woods.
3108 Federal Building, Little Rock, AR 72201 .... (501) 324–6286

* * *

TIM HUTCHINSON, Republican, of Bentonville, AR; born in Bentonville, August 11, 1949; graduated from Springdale High School, Springdale, AR, 1967; B.A., Bob Jones University, Greenville, SC, 1972; M.A., University of Arkansas, Fayetteville, 1990; college instructor, John Brown University; co-owner, KBCV radio station, 1982–89; Arkansas State Legislature, 1985–92; member: Kiwanis, Chamber of Commerce, Our Farm Board, Northwest Community College Foundation, Emmanuel Baptist Church; married the former Donna Jean King, 1970; three children; Timothy and Jeremy (twins), Joshua; committees: Environment and Public Works, Labor and Human Resources, Veterans' Affairs; elected to November 3, 1992 to the 103rd Congress; elected in November 1996 to the U.S. Senate.

Office Listings

http://www.senate.gov/~hutchinson senator.hutchinson@hutchinson.senate.gov

245 Dirksen Senate Office Building, Washington, DC 20510 224–2353
Chief of Staff.—Todd Deatherage. FAX: 228–3973
Deputy Chief of Staff.—Lisa Smittcamp.
Legislative Director.—Jo Ann Webb.
2527 Federal Building, Little Rock, AR 72201 .... (501) 324–6336
FAX: 324–5320

REPRESENTATIVES

FIRST DISTRICT

MARION BERRY, Democrat, of Gillett, AR; born in Bayou Meto Community, August 27, 1942; graduated, DeWitt High School; B.S., pharmacy, University of Arkansas, 1965; partner and general manager, family farm; appointed Special Assistant to the President for Agricultural Trade and Food Assistance, 1993; member, Arkansas Soil and Water Conservation Commission, 1986–94, serving as chairman in 1992; Gillett city councilman, 1976–80; married the former Carolyn Lowe in 1962; two children: Ann Coggin and Mitchell; cochairman, Democratic Blue Dog Coalition's Medicaid Task Force; committee: Agriculture; elected to the 105th Congress.

Office Listings

1407 Longworth House Office Building, Washington, DC 20515 225–4076
Chief of Staff.—Bruce Harris. FAX: 225–5602
Scheduler.—Sara Bland.
Legislative Director.—Courtenay McKinnon.
615 South Main, Suite 211, Jonesboro, AR 72401 .... (501) 972–4600

FAX: 972–4605

Counties: Arkansas, Clay, Cleburne, Craighead, Crittenden, Cross, Fulton, Greene, Independence, Izard, Jackson, Lawrence, Lee, Lonoke, Mississippi, Monroe, Phillips, Poinsett, Prairie, Randolph, St. Francis, Searcy, Sharp, Stone, and Woodruff. Population (1990), 588,588.

ZIP Codes: 72003–07, 72014, 72017, 72020–21, 72023–24, 72026, 72029, 72031, 72036–38, 72040–44, 72046, 72048, 72051, 72055, 72059–60, 72064, 72066–67, 72069, 72072–75, 72083, 72086, 72101, 72108, 72112, 72121 (part), 72123, 72130–31, 72134, 72137, 72140, 72153, 72160, 72165–66, 72169–70, 72176, 72179, 72301, 72303, 72310–13, 72315–17, 72319–22, 72324–33, 72335, 72338–42, 72346–48, 72350–55, 72358–60, 72364–70, 72372–74, 72376–77, 72381, 72383–84, 72386–87, 72389–92, 72394–97, 72401–03, 72410–17, 72419, 72421–22, 72424–38, 72440–45, 72447, 72449–51, 72453–62, 72464–67, 72469–76, 72478–79, 72482, 72501, 72503, 72512–13, 72515–17, 72519–34, 72536, 72538–40, 72542–43, 72546, 72550, 72553–57, 72560–62, 72564–69, 72571–73, 72575–79, 72581, 72583–85, 72587, 72610, 72617, 72633, 72636, 72639, 72645, 72650, 72663, 72669, 72675, 72679–80, 72686

* * *

SECOND DISTRICT

VIC SNYDER, Democrat, of Little Rock, AR; born in Medford, OR, September 27, 1947; graduated from Medford High School, 1965; corporal, U.S. Marine Corps, 1967–69, including one year in Vietnam with Headquarters Company, First Marine Division; B.A., chemistry, 1975, Willamette University, Salem, OR; M.D., 1979, University of Oregon Health Sciences Center, Portland; family practice residency, 1979–82, University of Arkansas for Medical Sciences; family practice physician in central Arkansas, 1982–96; medical missions to Cambodian refugee camps in Thailand, El Salvadoran refugee camps in Honduras, a West African mission hospital in Sierra Leone, and an Ethiopian refugee camp in Sudan; J.D., 1988, University of Arkansas at Little Rock School of Law; Arkansas State Senator, 1991–96; board member, Historic Preservation Alliance of Arkansas and Arkansas Historical Society; member: Arkansas Academy of Family Practice, American Academy of Family Practice, Arkansas Medical Society, Arkansas Bar Association, Arkansas Wildlife Federation, Ducks Unlimited, Arkansas Nature Conservancy; committees: Veterans' Affairs, National Security; subcommittees: Military Installations and Facilities, Military Procurement; elected November 1996 to the 105th Congress.

Office Listings

http://www.house.gov/snyder/index.html snyder.congress@mail.house.gov

1319 Longworth House Office Building, Washington, DC 20515 225–2506
Staff Director.—Ed Fry. FAX: 225–5903
Press Aide.—Rusty Logan.
1527 Federal Building, 700 West Capitol Avenue, Little Rock, AR 72201 .... (501) 324–5941
District Director.—John Yates. FAX: 324–6029
Deputy District Director.—Shawn Mittledorf.

Counties: Conway, Faulkner, Perry, Pulaski, Saline, Van Buren, White, and Yell. Population (1990), 587,412.

ZIP Codes: 71909–10, 72001–02, 72010–13, 72015–16, 72018, 72020, 72022, 72025, 72027–28, 72030–33, 72039, 72045, 72047, 72052–53, 72058, 72060–61, 72063, 72065, 72067, 72068, 72070, 72076, 72080–82, 72085, 72088–89, 72099, 72102–03, 72106–07, 72110–11, 72113–22, 72124–27, 72131, 72135–37, 72139, 72141–43, 72145, 72149, 72153, 72156–57, 72164, 72167, 72173, 72178, 72180–81, 72183, 72190, 72201–07, 72209–12, 72214–17, 72219, 72221, 72225, 72227, 72231, 72295, 72629, 72645, 72824, 72827–29, 72833–34, 72838, 72841–42, 72853, 72857, 72860

* * *

THIRD DISTRICT

ASA HUTCHINSON, Republican, of Bentonville, AR; born in Bentonville, December 3, 1950; B.S., accounting, Bob Jones University, 1972; J.D., University of Arkansas Law School, 1974; admitted to the Arkansas bar in 1975 and began practice in Bentonville; Bentonville City Attorney, 1976; United States Attorney, 1982–85; chairman, Arkansas State Republican Committee, 1990–95; married the former Susan Burrell in 1973; four children: Asa III, Sara, John Paul, and Seth; elected to the 105th Congress.

Office Listings

http://www.house.gov/hutchinson asa.hutchinson@mail.house.gov

1535 Longworth House Office Building, Washington, DC 20515–0403 225–4301
Chief of Staff.—David Olive. FAX: 225–5713
Executive Assistant/Scheduler.—Diana Ludlow.
Legislative Director.—Stacy Shrader.
30 South Sixth Street, Room 248, Fort Smith, AR 72901 .... (501) 782–7787

Federal Building, Harrison, AR 72601 .... (501) 741–6900
Federal Building, Fayetteville, AR 72701 .... (501) 422–5258

Counties: Baxter, Benton, Boone, Carroll, Crawford, Franklin, Johnson, Logan, Madison, Marion, Newton, Polk, Pope, Scott, Sebastian, and Washington. Population (1990), 589,523.

ZIP Codes: 71740, 71932, 71937, 71944–46, 71953, 71972–73, 72063, 72080, 72519, 72531, 72537–38, 72544, 72601–02, 72611, 72613, 72615–19, 72623–24, 72626, 72628, 72630, 72632–35, 72638, 72640–42, 72644–45, 72648, 72651, 72653, 72655, 72658, 72660–62, 72666, 72668, 72670, 72672, 72675, 72677, 72679, 72682–83, 72685–87, 72701–03, 72711–12, 72714, 72717–19, 72721–22, 72727–30, 72732–42, 72744–45, 72747, 72749, 72751–53, 72756–57, 72760–62, 72764–66, 72768–70, 72773–76, 72801, 72820–21, 72823, 72826–27, 72830, 72832–35, 72837–43, 72845–47, 72851–52, 72854–56, 72858, 72863, 72865, 72901–04, 72906, 72913–14, 72916–17, 72921, 72923–24, 72926–28, 72930, 72932–38, 72940–41, 72943–52, 72955–56, 72958–59

* * *

FOURTH DISTRICT

JAY DICKEY, Republican, of Pine Bluff, AR; born in Pine Bluff on December 14, 1939; graduated, Pine Bluff High School; University of Arkansas, Fayetteville, AR (B.A., 1961, J.D., 1963); two Taco Bell Restaurants; former state chairman, Christian Legal Society; past president, Pine Bluff Jaycees; recipient, Jaycees Distinguished Service Award; former board member, Bank of Bearden, Guaranty Savings and Loan Association, Pine Bluff Chamber of Commerce; member: Ducks Unlimited, life member of National Rifle Asociation, Pillars Club of the United Way, Century Club of the Boy Scouts; four children: John, Laura, Ted, and Rachel; elected on November 3, 1992 to the 103rd Congress; reelected to each succeeding Congress.

Office Listings
http://www.house.gov/dickey

2453 Rayburn House Office Building, Washington, DC 20515–0404 225–3772
Director/Press Secretary.—Anthony Hulen.
Legislative Director.—Jennifer Hartman.
Executive Assistant/Scheduler.—Jennifer Weams.
Room 2521, 100 East Eighth Avenue, Pine Bluff, AR 71601 .... (501) 536–3376
District Director.—Allen Maxwell.
Suite 201, 100 Reserve, Hot Springs, AR 71901 .... (501) 623–5800

Counties: Ashley, Bradley, Calhoun, Chicot, Clark, Cleveland, Columbia, Dallas, Desha, Drew, Garland, Grant, Hempstead, Hot Spring, Howard, Jefferson, Lafayette, Lincoln, Little River, Miller, Montgomery, Nevada, Ouachita, Pike, Sevier, and Union. Population (1990), 585,202.

ZIP Codes: 71601–03, 71611, 71613, 71630–31, 71635, 71638–40, 71642–44, 71646–47, 71649, 71651–56, 71658–63, 71665–67, 71670–71, 71674–78, 71701, 71720–22, 71724–26, 71728, 71730–31, 71740, 71742–45, 71747–53, 71758–59, 71762–66, 71768, 71770, 71772, 71801, 71820, 71822–23, 71825–28, 71831–42, 71845–47, 71851–53, 71855, 71857–62, 71864–66, 71901–02, 71909, 71913–14, 71921–23, 71929, 71933, 71935, 71940–43, 71949–52, 71956–62, 71964–65, 71968–71, 71998–99, 72004, 72046, 72057, 72072–73, 72079, 72084, 72087, 72104–05, 72128–29, 72132–33, 72150, 72152, 72168, 72175, 72182, 72379, 75502

CALIFORNIA

(Population 1995, 31,589,000)

SENATORS

DIANNE FEINSTEIN, Democrat, of San Francisco, CA; born June 22, 1933 in San Francisco; B.A., Stanford University, 1955; elected to San Francisco Board of Supervisors, 1970–78; president of Board of Supervisors: 1970–71, 1974–75, 1978; mayor of San Francisco, 1978–88; candidate for governor of California, 1990. Recipient: Distinguished Woman Award, *San Francisco Examiner;* Achievement Award, Business and Professional Women's Club, 1970; Golden Gate University, California, LL.D. (hon.), 1979; SCOPUS Award for Outstanding Public Service, American Friends of the Hebrew University of Jerusalem; University of Santa Clara, D.P.S. (hon.); University of Manila, D.P.A. (hon.), 1981; Antioch University, LL.D. (hon.), 1983; Los Angeles Anti-Defamation League of B'nai B'rith's Distinguished Service Award, 1984; French Legion d'Honneur from President Mitterand, 1984; Mills College, LL.D. (hon.), 1985; U.S. Army's Commander's Award for Public Service, 1986; Brotherhood/Sisterhood Award, National Conference of Christians and Jews, 1986; Paulist Fathers Award, 1987; Episcopal Church Award for Service, 1987; U.S. Navy Distinguished Civilian Award, 1987; Silver Spur Award for Outstanding Public Service, San Francisco Planning and Urban Renewal Association, 1987; ''All Pro Management Team Award'' for No. 1 Mayor, *City and State* Magazine, 1987; Community Service Award Honoree for Public Service, 1987; American Jewish Congress, 1987; President's Award, St. Ignatius High School, San Francisco, 1988; Coro Investment in Leadership Award, 1988; President's Medal, University of California at San Francisco, 1988; University of San Francisco, D.H.L. (hon.), 1988. Member: Coro Foundation, Fellowship, 1955–56; California Women's Board of Terms and Parole, 1960–66, executive committee; U.S. Conference of Mayors, 1983–88; Mayor's Commission on Crime, San Francisco; Bank of California, director, 1988–89; San Francisco Education Fund's Permanent Fund, 1988–89; Japan Society of Northern California, 1988–89; Inter-American Dialogue, 1988-present; Trilateral Commission, 1988; Biderberg Foreign Policy Conference, Baden, Germany, 1991; married to Dr. Bertram Feinstein (dec.); married January 20, 1980 to Richard C. Blum; one child; three stepchildren; Jewish; committees: Foreign Relations, Judiciary, Rules and Administration, Joint Committee on the Library; elected to the U.S. Senate by special election, November 3, 1992, to fill the vacancy caused by the resignation of Senator Pete Wilson, for the term ending January 3, 1995; reelected to six-year term, November 8, 1994.

Office Listings

http://www.senate.gov/~feinstein senator@feinstein.senate.gov

331 Hart Senate Office Building, Washington, DC 620510–0504 224–3841
Chief of Staff.—Michael McGill.
Legislative Director.—Susy Elfving.
Communications Director.—Susan Kennedy.
Suite 1030, 750 B Street, San Diego, CA 92101 .... (619) 231–9712
Suite 2446, Federal Office Building, 1130 O Street, Fresno, CA 93721 .... (209) 485–7430
Suite 3670, 525 Market Street, San Francisco, CA 94105 .... (415) 536–6868
Suite 915, 11111 San Monica Boulevard, Los Angles, CA 90025 .... (310) 914–7300

* * *

BARBARA BOXER, Democrat, of Greenbrae, CA; born in Brooklyn, NY, November 11, 1940; B.A., economics, Brooklyn College, 1962; stockbroker and economic researcher with securities firms on Wall Street, 1962–65; journalist and associate editor, *Pacific Sun* newspaper, 1972–74; congressional aide, Fifth Congressional District, California, 1974–76; elected Marin County Board of Supervisors, 1976–82; first woman president, Marin County Board of Supervisors; member: United States Holocaust Memorial Council; married Stewart Boxer, 1962; two adult children: Doug and Nicole; elected November 2, 1982 to 98th Congress; reelected to the 99th–102nd Congresses; Government Operations Committee, Armed Services Committee, Select Committee on Children, Youth, and Families, Budget Committee, 1985–90, Merchant Marine and Fisheries Committee, House Whip at Large; committees: Appropriations, Environment and Public Works, Banking, Housing and Urban Affairs, Budget; subcommittees: VA, HUD, and Independent Agencies; Interior; Legislative Branch; District of Columbia (ranking); Transportation and Infrastructure; Superfund, Waste Control and Risk Assessment; Clean Air, Private Property and Nuclear Safety; Financial Services and Technology (ranking); International Finance; Financial Institutions; elected to the U.S. Senate on November 3, 1992 for the six-year term beginning January 3, 1993.

Office Listings

http://www.senate.gov/~boxer senator@boxer.senate.gov

112 Hart Senate Office Building, Washington, DC 20510–0501 224–3553
Administrative Assistant.—Karen Olick.
Policy Director/Counsel.—Drew Littman.
Legislative Director.—Liz Tankersley.
Suite 240, 1700 Montgomery Street, San Francisco, CA 94111 .... (415) 403–0100
Chief of Staff.—Sam Chapman.
Suite 545, 2250 East Imperial Highway, El Segundo, CA 90245 .... (310) 414–5700
Suite 6544, 650 Capitol Mall, Sacramento, CA 95814 .... (916) 448–2787
Suite 210, 210 North E Street, San Bernadino, CA 92401 .... (909) 888–8525
Suite 990, 525 B Street, San Diego, CA 92101 .... (619) 239–3884
Suite 130, 2300 Tulare Street, Fresno, CA 93721 .... (209) 497–5109

REPRESENTATIVES

FIRST DISTRICT

FRANK DUNCAN RIGGS, Republican, of Windsor, CA; graduated, San Rafael High School, San Rafael, CA; St. Mary's Golden Gate University, San Francisco, CA, 1980: B.A. in administration of justice, *summa cum laude*; served in the U.S. Army, military police investigator, 1972–75; real estate developer and vice president of an educational software company; former police officer and deputy sheriff; member, Windsor School Board, two-term board president; member: California State Job Training Coordinating Council, Governor's Committee for Employment of Disabled Persons; married Cathy Anne Riggs, 1980; three children: Matt, Ryan, and Sarah; elected to the 104th Congress; reelected to the 105th Congress.

Office Listings

1714 Longworth House Office Building, Washington, DC 20515 225–3311
Chief of Staff/Press Secretary.—Beau Phillips.
Legislative Director.—Mark J. Davis.
Scheduler.—Kara Noe.
Staff Assistant.—Robert W. Collins.
1700 Second Street, Suite 378, Napa, CA 94559 .... (707) 254–7308
District Director.—Darrell Shull. (800) 723–0201
Office Manager.—Kay Rendelman.
710 East Street, Suite 100, Eureka, CA 95501 .... (707) 441–8701
Office Director.—Vee Sorenson. (800) 481–9724
188 Mason Mall, No. 8, Crescent City, CA 95531 .... (707) 464–1656
Field Representative.—Bob Berkowitz.

Counties: DEL NORTE COUNTY; cities and townships of Crescent City, Fortdeck, Gasquet, Klamath, Prison, Smith River. HUMBOLDT COUNTY; cities and townships of Alderpoint, Areata, Bayside, Blocksburg, Blue Lake, Burcka, Carlotta, Eureka, Ferndale, Fortuna, Garberville, Hoopa, Hydseville, Kneeland, Korbel, Loleta, McKinlayville, Myers Flat, Orick, Petrolia, Redcrest, Redway, Rio Del, Scotia, Trinidad, Whitehorn, Willow Creek. LAKE COUNTY; cities and townships of Clearlake, Clearlake Oaks, Clearlake Park, Cobb, Glenhaven, Kelseyville, Lakeport, Lower Lake, Lucerne, Middletown, Nice, Upper Lake. MENDOCINO COUNTY; cities and townships of Albion, Boonville, Calpella, Compiche, Covelo, Elk, Finley, Fort Bragg, Gualala, Hopland, Laytonville, Little River, Manchester, Mendocino, Philo, Piercy, Point Arena, Potter Valley, Redwood Valley, Talmage, Ukiah, Willits, Yorkville. NAPA COUNTY; cities and townships of American Canyon, Angwin, Aetna Springs, Calistoga, Deer Park, Oakville, Pope Valley, Rutherford, and St. Helena. SOLONA COUNTY (part); cities and townships of Cordelia, Fairfield, Suisun, Travis AFB, Vacaville. SONOMA COUNTY (part); cities and townships of Alexander Valley, Cloverdale, Geyserville, Healdsburg, Mark West, Santa Rosa (part), and Windsor. Population (1990), 524,264.

ZIP Codes: 94508, 94515, 94533, 94535, 94562, 94567, 94573–74, 94585, 94590 (part), 95404, 95406, 95409 (part), 95410–11, 15414–15, 95418, 95420, 95422–28, 95432, 95435, 95437, 95440–41, 95443, 95445, 95448, 95449, 95451, 95453–54, 95456–61, 95464, 95466–70, 95481–82, 95485, 95489–90, 95492–94, 95501, 95521, 95524–25, 95528, 95531–32, 95536, 95540, 95543, 95546–51, 95554–55, 95558, 95560, 95562, 95565, 95567, 95569–70, 95573, 95687, 95688, 95696

* * *

SECOND DISTRICT

WALLY HERGER, Republican, of Marysville, CA; born in Sutter County, CA, May 20, 1945; graduated East Nicolaus High School; attended California State University, Sacramento, CA; cattle rancher; small businessman; member, East Nicolaus High School Board of Trustees, 1977–80; California State Assemblyman, 1980–86; member: National Federation of Independent Business, Sutter County Taxpayers Association, Yuba-Sutter Farm Bureau, California Cattlemen's Association, California Chamber of Commerce, Big Brothers/Big Sisters Board of Directors, South Yuba Rotary Club; married to the former Pamela Sargent; eight children; committees: Budget, Ways and Means; elected to the 100th Congress, November 4, 1986; reelected to each succeeding Congress.

Office Listings

2433 Rayburn House Office Building, Washington, DC 20515–0502 225–3076
Administrative Assistant.—John P. Magill.
Legislative Director.—Rich Nolan.
Press Secretary.—Steve Thompson.
Executive Assistant/Scheduler.—Pamela Mattox.
Suite 104, 55 Independence Circle, Chico, CA 95926 .... (916) 893–8363
District Director.—Fran Peace.
410 Hemsted Drive, Suite 104, Redding, CA 96002 .... (916) 223–5898

Counties: BUTTE COUNTY; cities of Bangor, Berry Creek, Biggs, Butte Meadows, Chico, Clipper Mills, Cohasset, Durham, Feather Falls, Forbestown, Forest Ranch, Magalia, Nelson, Oroville, Palermo, Paradise, Pulga, Richardson Springs, Richvale, and Stirling City. LASSEN COUNTY; cities of Bieber, Doyle, Herlong, Janesville, Madeline, Nubieber, Ravendale, Standish, Susanville, Termo, Wendel, and Westwood. MODOC COUNTY; cities of Adin, Alturas, Canby, Cedarville, Eagleville, Fort Bidwell, Lake City, Likely, Litchfield, and Lookout. NEVADA COUNTY; cities of Floriston, Grass Valley, Nevada City, North San Juan, Penn Valley, Rough and Ready, and Truckee. PLUMAS COUNTY; cities of Beckwourth, Belden, Blairsden, Canyon Dam, Chester, Chilcoot, Clio, Crescent Mills, Cromberg, Graegle, Greenville, Keddie, Meadow Valley, Portola, Quincy, Spring Garden, Storrie, Taylorsville, Twain, and Vinton. SHASTA COUNTY; cities of Anderson, Bella Vista, Big Bend, Burney, Cassel, Castella, Central Valley, Cottonwood, Fall River Mills, French Gulch, Glenburn, Hat Creek, Igo, Lakehead, Manzanita Lake, McArthur, Millville, Montgomery Creek, Oak Run, O'Brien, Old Station, Ono, Palo Cedro, Platina, Project City, Redding, Round Mountain, Shingletown, Summit City, Whiskeytown, and Whitmore. SIERRA COUNTY; cities of Alleghany, Calpine, Downieville, Goodyear Bar, Loyalton, Sattley, Sierra City, and Sierraville. SISKIYOU COUNTY; cities of Callahan, Cecilville, Dorris, Dunsmuir, Edgewood, Enterprise, Etna, Forks of Salmon, Fort Jones, Gazelle, Greenview, Grenada, Happy Camp, Hilt, Hornbrook, Horse Creek, Kamath River, Macdoel, McCloud, Montague, Mount Hebron, Mount Shasta, Pondosa, Sawyers Bar, Scott Bar, Seiad Valley, Shasta, Somes Bar, Tulelake, Weed, and Yreka. TRINITY COUNTY; cities of Bir Bar, Burnt Ranch, Denny, Douglas City, Forest Glen, Hayfork, Helena, Hyampom, Island Mountain, Junction City, Lewiston, Mad River, Ruth, Salyer, Trinity Center, Weaverville, and Zenia. YUBA COUNTY; cities of Beale A.F.B., Browns Valley, Brownsville, Camptonville, Challenge, Dobbins, Marysville, Olivehurst, Oregon House, Rackerby, Smartville, Strawberry Valley, and Wheatland. Population (1990), 573,322.

ZIP Codes: 95478, 95495, 95526–27, 95535, 95552, 95563, 95568, 95595, 95602, 95692, 95712, 95724, 95728, 95901, 95903, 95910, 95914–16, 95917 (part), 95918–19, 95921–25, 95926 (part), 95927–30, 95934–36, 95938, 95940–42, 95944–47, 95948 (part), 95949, 95952, 95954 (part), 95956, 95958–62, 95965–69, 95971–78, 95980–81, 95983–84, 95986, 96001–03, 96006–11, 96013–17, 96019–20, 96022–25, 96027–28, 96030–36, 96037–43, 96044–52, 96054, 96056–60, 96062, 96064–66, 96067–73, 96076–77, 96079, 96084–89, 96091, 96093–97, 96099, 96101, 96103–06, 96108–19, 96121–96126, 96128–30, 96132, 96134–37, 96160–62

* * *

THIRD DISTRICT

VIC FAZIO, Democrat, of West Sacramento, CA; born in Winchester, MA, October 11, 1942; B.A., Union College, Schenectady, NY, 1965; graduate work in public administration, California State University, Sacramento; Coro Foundation Fellow; congressional and legislative consultant, 1966–75; member, California State Assembly, 1975–78; former director, assembly majority staff; former assistant to the speaker of the Assembly; former member: Sacramento County Charter Commission, Sacramento County Planning Commission, and National Conference of State Legislatures; former vice president, Planning and Conservation League; co-founder, *California Journal* magazine; member: UNICO, Air Force Association, Navy League, Democratic State Central Committee; married to the former Judy Kern; four children: Dana, Anne (d. 1995), Kevin, and Kristie; committees: Appropriations; Subcommittee on Legislative Branch and Subcommittee on Agriculture; ranking member, Energy and Water Development; Democratic Steering Committee; chairman, Democratic Caucus; elected to the 96th Congress, November 7, 1978; reelected to each succeeding Congress.

Office Listings

http://www.house.gov/fazio/welcome.html

2113 Rayburn House Office Building, Washington, DC 20515–0503 225–5716
Chief of Staff.—Monica Maples.
Legislative Director.—Janice Morris.
Executive Assistant.—Lisa Davison.
722B Main Street, Woodland, CA 95695–3407 .... (916) 666–5521
District Director.—Val Dolcini.
332 Pine Street, No. F, Red Bluff, CA 96080–3312 .... (916) 529–5629

Counties: Colusa, Glenn, Sutter, Tehama, Yolo, the eastern portion of Solano County, the northern portion of Sacramento County, the southern portion of Butte County. CITIES AND TOWNSHIPS: Antelope Arbuckle, Artois, Birds Landing,

Broderick, Brooks, Butte, Capay, Carmichael (part), Citrus Heights (part), Clarksburg, College, Colusa, Corning, Cottonwood, Dairyville, Davis, Dixon, Dunnigan, East Nicolaus, El Macero, Elk Creek, Elmira, Elverta, Esparto, Fair Oaks, Flournoy, Gerber, Glenn, Gridley, Grimes, Guinda, Hamilton, Knights Landing, Live Oak, Lodoga, Los Molinos, Madison, Manton, Maxwell, McClellan AFB, Meridian, Mill Creek, Mineral, Nicolaus, North Highlands, Orland, Paskenta, Paynes Creek, Pleasant Grove, Princeton, Proberta, Red Bluff, Rio Linda, Rio Oso, Rio Vista, Robbins, Rumsey, Sacramento, Sites, Stonyford, Sutter, Sycamore, Tehama, Trowbridge, Tudor, Vacaville, Vina, West Sacramento, Williams, Willows, Winters, Woodland, Yolo, Yuba, and Zamora. Population (1990), 571,374.

ZIP Codes: 94512, 94571 (part), 94585 (part), 95605–07, 95608 (part), 95609, 95610 (part), 95612, 95616–18, 95620 (part), 95621 (part), 95622, 95625–27, 95628 (part), 95637, 95645, 95653, 95659–60, 95668, 95671, 95673 (part), 95674, 95676, 95679, 95687 (part), 95688 (part), 95691, 95694–95, 95697–98, 95776, 95798–99, 95821 (part), 95834 (part), 95835–36, 95837 (part), 95838 (part), 95841, 95842 (part), 95843, 95860, 95864 (part), 95912–13, 95917 (part), 95920, 95926 (part), 95931–32, 95937, 95939, 95943, 95948 (part), 95950–51, 95953, 95955, 95957, 95963, 95970, 95979, 95982, 95987–88, 95991–93, 96021–22, 96029, 96035, 96055, 96059, 96061, 96063, 96074–75, 96078, 96080, 96090, 96092

* * *

FOURTH DISTRICT

JOHN T. DOOLITTLE, Republican, of Rocklin, CA; born in Glendale, CA, October 30, 1950; graduated Cupertino High School, Cupertino, CA, 1968; University of California at Santa Cruz, 1972; University of the Pacific, McGeorge School of Law, 1978; lawyer; member: California bar; elected to the California State Senate, 1980; reelected 1984 and 1988; served as chairman of the Senate Republican Caucus, May 1987–April 1990; married the former Julia Harlow, 1979; two children: John, Jr. and Courtney Doolittle; elected to the 102nd Congress, November 6, 1990; elected in 1992 to newly drawn fourth congressional district.

Office Listings

http://www.house.gov/doolittle

1526 Longworth House Office Building, Washington, DC 20515–0504 225–2511
Executive Assistant.—Annemarie Metzger. FAX: 225–5444
District Coordinator.—Richard Robinson.
Legislative Director.—Kevin Ring.
2130 Professional Drive, Suite 190, Roseville, CA 95661 .... (916) 786–5560
Administrative Assistant.—David Lopez. FAX: 786–6364

Counties: Alpine, Amador, Calaveras, El Dorado, Mono, Placer, Sacramento (part), and Tuolumne. CITIES OF: Angels, Arnold, Auburn, Cameron Park, Carmichael (part), Citrus Heights (part), Columbia, Diamond Springs, East Sonora, El Dorado Hills, Fair Oaks, Folsom, Groveland-Big Oak Flat, Ione, Jackson, Jamestown, Kings Beach, Lincoln, Loomis, Mammoth Lakes, Meadow Vista, Mono Vista, Murphys, North Auburn, Orangevale, Phoenix Lake-Cedar Ridge, Placerville, Pollock Pines, Rockin, Roseville, San Andreas, Shingle Springs, Sonora, Soulsbyville, South Lake Tahoe, Sunnyside-Tahoe City, Sutter Creek, Tuolumne City, and Twain Harte. Population (1990), 571,033.

ZIP Codes: 93512, 93517, 93529, 93541, 93546, 95221–25, 95228–29, 95232–33, 95245–52, 95254–55, 95257, 95305, 95309–10, 95321–22, 95327, 95329, 95335, 95346–47, 95364, 95370, 95372–73, 95375, 95379, 95383, 95601–04, 95610 (part), 95611, 95613–14, 95619, 95621 (part), 95623, 95628 (part), 95629–31, 95633–36, 95640, 95642–43, 95646, 95648, 95650–51, 95654, 95656, 95658, 95661–67, 95669, 95672, 95675, 95677–78, 95681–82, 95684–85, 95689, 95699, 95701, 95703, 95709, 95713–15, 95717, 95720–22, 95726, 95735–36, 95746–47, 95762–63, 95765, 95842 (part), 95954 (part), 96107, 96120, 96133, 96140, 96142–43, 96145–46, 96148, 96150–58

* * *

FIFTH DISTRICT

ROBERT T. MATSUI, Democrat, of Sacramento, CA, born in Sacramento, September 17, 1941; graduated, C.K. McClatchy High School, 1959; A.B., University of California, Berkeley, 1963; J.D., Hastings College of Law, University of California, 1966; admitted to the California bar in 1967 and commenced practice in Sacramento; Sacramento City Council, District 8, 1971–75; reelected, 1975–78; chairman, budget-finance committee, 1976–78; vice mayor, 1977; chairman, law and legislative committee, 1978; chairman, U.S. Congressman John E. Moss reelection campaign committee; member, California Democratic Central Committee, 1973–78; president, Active 20–30 Club, 1972; vice president, Sacramento Safety Council; board member, United Crusade and Sacramento Rotary Club; officer and director, Sacramento Metropolitan Chamber of Commerce; Jaycee Young Man of the Year, 1973; married the former Doris K. Okada, 1966; one child, Brian Robert; member, Ways and Means Committee; elected to the 96th Congress, November 7, 1978; reelected to each succeeding Congress.

Office Listings

http://www.house.gov/matsui

2308 Rayburn House Office Building, Washington, DC 20515–0505 225–7163

Administrative Assistant.—Tom Keaney. FAX: 225–0566
Executive Assistant.—Shirley Queja.
8058 Federal Building, 650 Capitol Mall, Sacramento, CA 95814 .... (916) 551–2846
District Director.—Collette Johnson-Schulke.

County: SACRAMENTO COUNTY; City of Sacramento (part): Population (1990), 573,684.

ZIP Codes: 94207, 94274, 94299, 95608 (part), 95624 (part), 95673 (part), 95758 (part), 95812–20, 95821 (part), 95822–25, 95826 (part), 95827 (part), 95828, 95829 (part), 95831, 95832 (part), 95833, 95834 (part), 95837 (part), 95838 (part), 95851–53, 95864 (part), 95865–66

* * *

SIXTH DISTRICT

LYNN WOOLSEY, Democrat, of Petaluma, CA; born in Seattle, WA, on November 3, 1937; graduated from Lincoln High School, Seattle; B.S., University of San Francisco, 1981; president and founder, Woolsey Personnel Service, 1980–92; human resources manager, Harris Digital Telephone Systems, 1969–80; elected member, Petaluma City Council, 1984–92; vice mayor, 1989 and 1992; member: Sonoma County National Women's Political Caucus, chair; Sonoma County Commission on the Status of Women, chair; Business and Professional Women; National Organization for Women; Sierra Club; Sonoma County Hazardous Materials Management Commission, chair; Association of Bay Area Governments, Regional Hazardous Materials Representative; CAL Energy Commission, advisory committee; four children: Joseph Critchett, Michael Woolsey, Ed Critchett, Amy Critchett; elected on November 3, 1992 to the 103rd Congress; reelected to each succeeding Congress.

Office Listings

http://www.house.gov/woolsey

439 Cannon House Office Building, Washington, DC 20515–0506 225–5161
Administrative Assistant.—Mark Isaac.
Press Secretary.—Tom Roth.
1101 College Avenue, Suite 200, Santa Rosa, CA 95404 .... (707) 542–7182
District Director.—Danielle Tinman.

Counties: Marin County and Sonoma County; including cities of Santa Rosa, Sebastapol, Cotati, Petaluma, and Sonoma to Golden Gate Bridge. Population (1990), 571,227.

ZIP Codes: 94901, 94903–04, 94912–15, 94920, 94922–25, 94927–31, 94933, 94937–42, 94945–57, 94960, 94963–66, 94970–73, 94975–79, 95401, 95403 (part), 95404 (part), 95405, 95407, 95409 (part), 95412, 95416, 95419, 95421, 95430–31, 95433, 95436 (part), 95439, 95442, 95444, 95446, 95448 (part), 95450, 95452, 95462, 95465, 95471–73, 95476, 95480, 95486–87, 95492 (part), 95497

* * *

SEVENTH DISTRICT

GEORGE MILLER, Democrat, of Martinez, CA; born in Richmond, CA, May 17, 1945; attended Martinez public schools; Diablo Valley College; graduated, 1968, San Francisco State College; J.D., 1972, University of California at Davis School of Law; member: California State bar, Davis Law School Alumni Association; served five years as legislative aide to Senate majority leader, California State Legislature; past chairman and member of Contra Costa County Democratic Central Committee; past president of Martinez Democratic Club; married to the former Cynthia Caccavo; two children: George and Stephen; committees: Education and the Workforce and Resources, ranking member; elected to the 94th Congress, November 5, 1974; reelected to each succeeding Congress.

Office Listings

http://www.house.gov/georgemiller gmiller@hr.house.gov

2205 Rayburn House Office Building, Washington, DC 20515–0507 225–2095
Administrative Assistant.—Daniel Weiss.
Personal Secretary.—Sylvia Arthur.
Room 14, 367 Civic Drive, Pleasant Hill, CA 94523 .... (510) 602–1880
District Administrator.—David A. Tucker.
Room 281, 3220 Blume Drive, Richmond, CA 94806 .... (510) 262–6500

Counties: Contra Costa (part), Solaro (part). CITIES AND TOWNSHIPS: Benicia, Concord, Cordelia Village (part), Crockett, El Cerrito, El Sobrante, Hercules, Kensington, Martinez, Pinole, Pittsburg, Port Costa, Richmond, Rodeo, San Pablo, Suisun City (part), and Vallejo. Population (1990), 526,191.

ZIP Codes: 94510, 94518 (part), 94519, 94520 (part), 94521 (part), 94522, 94523 (part), 94524–25, 94527, 94530, 94547 (part), 94549 (part), 94553 (part), 94564 (part), 94565 (part), 94569, 94572 (part), 94585 (part), 94589 (part), 94590 (part), 94591–92, 94596 (part), 94598 (part), 94801–02, 94803 (part), 94804–08, 94820

* * *

EIGHTH DISTRICT

NANCY PELOSI, Democrat, of San Francisco, CA; born in Baltimore, MD, March 26, 1940; daughter of the late Representative Thomas D'Alesandro, Jr., of MD; graduated, Institute of Notre Dame High School, 1958; B.A., Trinity College, Washington, DC (major, political science; minor, history), 1962; northern chair, California Democratic Party, 1977–81; state chair, California Democratic Party, 1981–83; chair, 1984 Democratic National Convention Host Committee; finance chair, Democratic Senatorial Campaign Committee, 1985–86; member: Democratic National Committee; California Democratic Party Executive Committee; San Francisco Library Commission; Board of Trustees, LSB Leakey Foundation; married Paul F. Pelosi, 1963; five children: Nancy Corinne, Christine, Jacqueline, Paul, Jr., and Alexandra; elected by special election, June 2, 1987, to the 100th Congress to fill the vacancy caused by the death of Sala Burton; reelected to each succeeding Congress.

Office Listings

http://www.house.gov/pelosi sf.nancy@mail.house.gov

2457 Rayburn House Office Building, Washington, DC 20515–0508 225–4965
Administrative Assistant.—Judith K. Lemons. FAX: 225–8259
Legislative Director.—Carolyn Bartholomew.
Room 145378, 450 Golden Gate Avenue, San Francisco, CA 94102 .... (415) 556–4862
District Director.—Fred Ross.

County and City of San Francisco: That part not contained in the 12th District. Population (1990), 573,247.

ZIP Codes: 94014 (part), 94102–11, 94112 (part), 94114 (part), 94115, 94117 (part), 94118–21, 94123–26, 94128–30, 94131 (part), 94132 (part), 94133–35, 94139–42, 94144–47, 94152, 94159, 94164, 94188

* * *

NINTH DISTRICT

RONALD V. DELLUMS, Democrat, of Oakland, CA; born in Oakland, November 24, 1935; educated at McClymonds High School and Oakland Technical High School; Oakland City College, A.A., 1958; San Francisco State College, B.A., 1960; University of California, M.S.W., 1962; honorary doctor of law, Wilberforce University, 1975; served in U.S. Marine Corps, two years active duty, honorable discharge; member, Berkeley City Council, 1967–71; psychiatric social worker, Department of Mental Hygiene, 1962–64; program director, Bayview Community Center, 1964–65; associate director, then director, Hunters Point Youth Opportunity Center, 1965–66; planning consultant, Bay Area Social Planning Council, 1966–67; director, Concentrated Employment Program, San Francisco Economic Opportunity Council, 1967–68; senior consultant, Social Dynamics, Inc. (specializing in manpower programs), 1968–70; part-time lecturer, San Francisco State College, University of California, and Berkeley Graduate School of Social Welfare; married Leola (Roscoe) Higgs; three children; elected to the 92nd Congress November 3, 1970; reelected to each succeeding Congress.

Office Listings

http://www.house.gov/dellums

2108 Rayburn House Office Building, Washington, DC 20515–0509 225–2661
Administrative Assistant.—Carlottia A.W. Scott. FAX: 225–9817
Legislative Director.—Charles Stephenson.
1301 Clay Street, Suite 1000–N, Oakland, CA 94612 .... (415) 763–0370
General Counsel.—H. Lee Halterman.
District Director.—Sandre Swanson.

Counties: ALAMEDA COUNTY; cities of Alameda, Albany, Berkeley, Emeryville, Kensington, and Piedmont. OAKLAND COUNTY; (part). Population (1990), 573,458.

ZIP Codes: 94501 (part), 94601–02, 94603 (part), 94604, 94605 (part), 94606–10, 94611 (part), 94612–13, 94618–20, 94621 (part), 94623–24, 94661–62, 94701–10, 94720

TENTH DISTRICT

ELLEN TAUSCHER, Democrat, of Pleasanton, CA; born in East Newark, NJ, November 15, 1951; graduated, Harrison High School, Harrison, NJ, 1969; B.S., early childhood education, Seton Hall University; founder and CEO, The Registry Companies, first national child care provider pre-employment screening service, 1992-present; one of the first women to hold a seat on the New York Stock Exchange (1977-79); Wall Street trader and investment banker, 1979-88; author of *The Child Care Source Book*; created Tauscher Foundation, which has provided $150,000 to California and Texas elementary schools for purchase of computer equipment; member: NARAL, CARAL, Planned Parenthood, Seton Hall University Board of Regents; endorsed by Emily's List; cochair, Dianne Feinstein's 1992 and 1994 senatorial campaigns; married William Y. Tauscher in 1989; one child, Katherine; elected to the 105th Congress.

Office Listings

http://www.house.gov/tauscher ellen.tauscher@mail.house.gov

1440 Longworth House Office Building, Washington, DC 20515 225–1880
Chief of Staff.—Katie Merrill. FAX: 225–5914
Legislative Director.—Peter Muller.
Press Secretary.—Dave Lemmon.
Scheduler.—Laura Faer.
1801 North California Boulevard, Suite 103, Walnut Creek, CA 94596 .... (510) 932–8899
District Director.—Michelle Henry. FAX: 932–8519
Congressional Aides: David Bowlby, Sandra Jones, Kathleen Kilcline, Jennifer Renk.
100 Civic Plaza, Suite 242, Dublin, CA 94549 .... (510) 829–0813
Congressional Aide.—Marco Milanese.
420 West Third Street, Antioch, CA 94509. .... (510) 757–7187
Congressional Aide.—Phillip Arndt.

Counties: Contra Costa (part), Alameda (part). CITIES AND TOWNSHIPS: Alamo, Antioch, Blackhawk, Bethel Island, Brentwood, Byron, Castro Valley (part), Clayton, Concord (part), Danville, Diablo, Discovery Bay, Dublin, Hayward (part), Lafayette, Livermore, Moraga, Oakley, Orinda, Pleasanton, Pleasant Hill, San Ramon, San Leandro (part), San Lorenzo (part), Sunol, and Walnut Creek. Population (1990), 572,008.

ZIP Codes: 94506–07, 94509, 94511, 94513–14, 94516–17, 94518 (part), 94521 (part), 94523, 94525–26, 94528, 94546 (part), 94548, 94549 (part), 94550–51, 94552 (part), 94556, 94561, 94563, 94566, 94568, 94575, 94578 (part), 94580 (part), 94583, 94586, 94588, 94595, 94596, 94598, 95209

* * *

ELEVENTH DISTRICT

RICHARD W. POMBO, Republican, of Tracy, CA; born in Tracy, January 8, 1961; attended California State University at Pomona; rancher; Tracy city councilman, 1990–91; cofounder, San Joaquin County Citizens Land Alliance; member, Tracy Rotary Club; married to Annette Pombo since 1983; three children: Richard Jr., Rena and Rachel; committees: Agriculture, Natural Resources; subcommittee assignments include areas covering specialty crops, domestic and international agricultural marketing, livestock, farm credit, water policy, mining; elected November 3, 1992 to the 103rd Congress; reelected to the each succeeding Congress.

Office Listings

http://www.house.gov/pombo/pombo.htm pombo@house.gov

1519 Longworth House Office Building, Washington, DC 20515–0511 225–1947
Press Secretary.—Mike Hardiman. FAX: 226–0861
Legislative Director.—Christopher D'Arcy.
Scheduler/Office Manager.—Eileen O'Brien Werner.
2321 West March Lane, Suite 205, Stockton, CA 95207 .... (209) 951–3091
Chief of Staff/District Director.—Steve Ding.

Counties: Sacramento (part), San Joaquin. CITIES AND TOWNSHIPS: Stockton, Rancho Cordova, Galt Lodi, Manteca, and Tracy. Population (1990), 571,772.

ZIP Codes: 94571 (part), 95201–10, 95212–13, 95215, 95219–20, 95227, 95231, 95234, 95236–37, 95240–42, 95253, 95258, 95267, 95269, 95304, 95320, 95330, 95336 (part), 95361 (part), 95366 (part), 95376 (part), 95378, 95385, 95608 (part), 95615, 95624 (part), 95632, 95638–39, 95641, 95655, 95670, 95680, 95683, 95686, 95690, 95693, 95741–42, 95758 (part), 95759, 95826 (part), 95827 (part), 95829 (part), 95830, 95832 (part)

TWELFTH DISTRICT

TOM LANTOS, Democrat, of San Mateo, CA; born in Budapest, February 1, 1928; during World War II active in anti-Nazi underground; came to the United States in 1947 on academic scholarship; B.A., University of Washington, 1949; M.A., University of Washington, 1950; Ph.D., University of California, 1953, Phi Beta Kappa; professor of economics; consultant, TV news analyst and commentator; member, Millbrae Board of Education, 1950–66; administrative assistant, economic and foreign policy adviser, U.S. Senate; married to Annette Tillemann; two married daughters: Annette Tillemann-Dick and Katrina Lantos-Swett; 16 grandchildren; elected to the 97th Congress, November 4, 1980; reelected to each succeeding Congress; member, Committee on International Relations; ranking member, Subcommittee on International Operations and Human Rights; Government Reform and Oversight; cochairman of the permanent U.S. Congressional Delegation to the European Parliament of the European Union; cochairman, Congressional Human Rights Caucus; member, U.S. Holocaust Council.

Office Listings

http://www.house.gov/lantos talk2tom@hr.house.gov

2217 Rayburn House Office Building, Washington, DC 20515–0512 225–3531
Administrative Assistant.—Robert R. King.
Office Manager.—Brigid H. Davis.
Suite 820, 400 El Camino Real, San Mateo, CA 94402 .... (415) 342–0300
District Representative.—Evelyn Szelenyi.
Office Manager.—Dorothy Powell.

Counties: SAN MATEO COUNTY; cities of Brisbane, Burlingame, Colma, Daly City, Foster City, Hillsborough, Millbrae, Montara, Moss Beach, Pacifica, Redwood Shores, San Bruno, San Mateo, and South San Francisco. SAN FRANCISCO COUNTY; city of San Francisco. Population (1990), 571,535.

ZIP Codes: 94002 (part), 94005, 94010 (part), 94011, 94014 (part), 94015–17, 94030, 94037–38, 94044, 94065 (part), 94066, 94080, 94112 (part), 94114 (part), 94116, 94117 (part), 94122, 94127, 94131 (part), 94132 (part), 94401–04

* * *

THIRTEENTH DISTRICT

FORTNEY PETE STARK, Democrat, of Hayward, CA; born in Milwaukee, WI, November 11, 1931; graduated from Wauwatosa, WI, High School, 1949; Massachusetts Institute of Technology, B.S., 1953; University of California, Berkeley, M.B.A., 1960; East Bay Skills Center, Oakland, G.E.D. (honorary), 1972; served in U.S. Air Force, 1955–57, first lieutenant; banker, founder, and president, Security National Bank, Walnut Creek, CA, 1963–72; trustee, California Democratic Council; chairman, board of trustees, Starr King School of Ministry, Berkeley; trustee, Graduate Theological Union, Berkeley; sponsor, Northern California American Civil Liberties Union; board member: Housing Development Corporation and Council for Civic Unity; director, Common Cause, 1971–72; five children: Jeffrey Peter, Beatrice Stark Winslow, Thekla Stark Wainwright, Sarah Stark Ramirez, and Fortney Stark III; married to Deborah Roderick; committee: Ways and Means (senior member); elected to the 93rd Congress, November 7, 1972; reelected to each succeeding Congress.

Office Listings

petemail@hr.house.gov

239 Cannon House Office Building, Washington, DC 20515–0513 225–5065
Administrative Assistant.—William K. Vaughan. FAX: 226–3805
Personal Assistant.—Ella M. Mumphard.
Suite 500, 22320 Foothill Boulevard, Hayward, CA 94541 .... (510) 247–1388
District Administrator.—Annie Zatlin.

County: ALAMEDA COUNTY; communities of Castro Valley (part), Hayward, San Leandro, San Lorenzo, cities of Oakland (part), Union City, Fremont, Newark, Milpitas, San Jose (part), and Sunnyvale (part). Population (1990), 572,441.

ZIP Codes: 94089 (part), 94536–45, 94546 (part), 94552 (part), 94555, 94557, 94560, 94577, 94578 (part), 94579–80, 94587, 94603 (part), 94605 (part), 94614, 94621 (part), 95002, 95035 (part), 95131 (part), 95132 (part), 95134 (part), 95143

FOURTEENTH DISTRICT

ANNA G. ESHOO, Democrat, of Atherton, CA; born December 13, 1942; attended Canada College; San Mateo supervisor, 1983–92; served on House Committees on Science, Space, and Technology, and Merchant Marine and Fisheries; currently serves on House Committee on Commerce, including its subcommittees on Telecommunications, Trade and Consumer Protection, and Health and Environment; has served as a Democratic regional whip since 1993; selected to co-chair the House Medical Technology Caucus, 1994; elected on November 3, 1992 to the 103rd Congress; reelected to each succeeding Congress.

Office Listings

http://www-eshoo.house.gov annagram@house.gov

308 Cannon House Office Building, Washington, DC 20515–0514 225–8104
Chief of Staff.—John Flaherty. FAX: 225–8890
Executive Assistant.—Karen Chapman.
Legislative Director.—Jill Ehrlich.
698 Emerson Street, Palo Alto, CA 94301 .... (415) 323–2984
District Director.—Bruce Ives.
Scheduler.—Margaret Abe.

Counties: San Mateo, Santa Clara. CITIES AND TOWNSHIPS: Belmont, San Carlos, Redwood City, Woodside, Menlo Park, Atherton, Portola Valley, Half Moon Bay, La Honda, East Palo Alto, Palo Alto, Stanford, Mountain View, Los Altos, Los Altos Hills, Sunnyvale, and Cupertino. Population (1990), 571,131.

ZIP Codes: 94002 (part), 94010 (part), 94018, 94019 (part), 94020–28, 94039–43, 94060–64, 94065 (part), 94070 (part), 94074, 94086 (part), 94087–88, 94089 (part), 94301–06, 94309, 95014 (part), 95015–16, 95030 (part), 95051 (part), 95070 (part), 95129 (part)

* * *

FIFTEENTH DISTRICT

TOM CAMPBELL, Republican, of Campbell, CA; born August 14, 1952, in Chicago, IL; B.A., M.A. (awarded simultaneously), economics, University of Chicago, 1973; J.D., *magna cum laude,* Harvard Law School, 1976, and editor of *Harvard Law Review*; Ph.D., economics, University of Chicago, 1980 (Lilly Fellowship); admitted to the Illinois and District of Columbia bars in 1976; law professor, Stanford University (tenured, 1987); represented California's 12th District in U.S. House of Representatives, 1989–92, and has represented 15th District since December 1995; member, California Senate, 1993–95; director, Bureau of Competition, Federal Trade Commission, 1981–83; White House Fellow, 1980–81; member, White House Task Force on Women, 1981; term member, Council on Foreign Relations, 1981–86; United States Supreme Court Clerk, Justice Byron White, 1977–78; attorney, Winston and Shawn, Chicago, 1978–80; member: San Francisco Council on Foreign Relations, 1983–88, Chicago Council on Foreign Relations, 1978–80; council member, American Bar Association, 1983–88; married to Susanne Martin Campbell since 1978; member, International Relations and Banking and Financial Services committees; rated single most fiscally responsible member of Congress by the National Taxpayers Union, 1992.

Office Listings

http://www.house.gov/campbell campbell@hr.house.gov

2221 Rayburn House Office Building, Washington, DC 20515 225–2631
Chief of Staff.—Karin M. Pipkin. FAX: 225–6788
Legislative Director.—Charlie DeWitt.
Scheduler.—Annabelle Romero.
910 Campis Way, Suite 1C, Campbell, CA 95008 .... (408) 371–7337
FAX: 371–7925

Counties: Santa Clara, Santa Cruz. CITIES AND TOWNSHIPS: Ben Lomond, Boulder Creek, Brookdale, Burbank, Cambrian Park, Campbell, Cupertino (part), Davenport, Felton, Holy City, Lexington Hills, Los Gatos, Monte Sereno, Mt. Hermon, Redwood Estates, San Jose (part), Santa Clara (part), Santa Cruz (part), Saratoga (part), Scotts Valley, Soquel, Sunnyvale (part), and Watsonville (part). Population (1990), 572,485.

ZIP Codes: 94086 (part), 94089 (part), 95005–09, 95011, 95014 (part), 95017–18, 95026, 95030 (part), 95031–32, 95041, 95044, 95050 (part), 95051 (part), 95052–56, 95060 (part), 95061, 95065 (part), 95066–67, 95070 (part), 95071, 95073 (part), 95110 (part), 95117–20, 95123 (part), 95124, 95125 (part), 95126 (part), 95128 (part), 95129 (part), 95130, 95136 (part), 95138 (part), 95139, 95141 (part), 95153–55, 95157–60, 95170, 95171, 95173

SIXTEENTH DISTRICT

ZOE LOFGREN, Democrat, of San Jose, CA; born in San Mateo, CA, December 21, 1947; graduated Gunn High School, 1966; B.A., Stanford University, Stanford, CA, 1970; J.D., Santa Clara Law School, Santa Clara, CA, 1975; admitted to the California bar, 1975; District of Columbia bar, 1981; Supreme Court, 1986; member: board of trustees, San Jose Evergreen Community College District, 1979–81; board of supervisors, Santa Clara County, CA, 1981–94; member: Committee on Science; Judiciary Committee; Subcommittee on Crime; married John Marshall Collins, 1978; two children: Sheila and Johnny; elected to the 104th Congress; reelected to the 105th Congress.

Office Listings

http://www.house.gov/lofgren zoegram@hr.house.gov

118 Cannon House Office Building, Washington, DC 20515–0516 225–3072
Chief of Staff.—Mavis E. Toscano. FAX: 225–5336
Executive Assistant.—Doris M. Barnes.
Legislative Assistant.—Jason M. Mahler.
Press Secretary.—Genet Garamendi.
635 North First Street, San Jose, CA 95112 .... (408) 271–8700
Staff Assistant.—Dolores A. Jufiar.

County: SANTA CLARA COUNTY; most of the City of San Jose, the southernmost portion of the City of Milpitas, Gilroy, Morgan Hill, San Martin and unincorporated portions of southern Santa Clara County. Population (1990), 571,551.

ZIP Codes: 95013, 95020 (part), 95021, 95023 (part), 95035 (part), 95036–38, 95042, 95046, 95050 (part), 95103, 95106, 95108–09, 95110 (part), 95111–13, 95115–16, 95121–22, 95123 (part), 95125 (part), 95126 (part), 95127, 95128 (part), 95131, 95132 (part), 95133, 95134 (part), 95135, 95136 (part), 95138 (part), 95140, 95141 (part), 95148, 95150–52, 95156, 95161, 95172–73

* * *

SEVENTEENTH DISTRICT

SAM FARR, Democrat, of Carmel, CA; born July 4, 1941; attended Carmel public schools; B.S., biology, Willamette University, Salem, OR; studied at the Monterey Institute of International Studies; served in the Peace Corps for two years in Colombia, South America; worked as a consultant and employee of the California Assembly; elected to the California Assembly, 1980–93; member: Committees on Education, Insurance, and Natural Resources; married to Shary Baldwin; one daughter, Jessica; elected by special election on June 8, 1993, to fill the vacancy caused by the resignation of Leon Panetta; reelected to each succeeding Congress.

Office Listings

http://www.house.gov/farr samfarr@mail.house.gov

1117 Longworth House Office Building, Washington, DC 20515–0517 225–2861
Administrative Assistant.—Rochelle Dornatt.
Legislative Director.—Debbie Merrill.
Press Secretary.—Mike Diamond.
380 Alvarado Street, Monterey, CA 93940 .... (408) 649–3555
District Representative.—Donna Blitzer.
701 Ocean Avenue, Santa Cruz, CA 95060 .... (408) 429–1976
100 West Alisal, Salinas, CA 93901 .... (408) 424–2229

Counties: Monterey, San Benito, Santa Cruz (southern half). Population (1990), 570,981.

ZIP Codes: 93426 (part), 93450, 93451 (part), 93901–02, 93905–08, 93912, 93915, 93920–28, 93930, 93932–33, 93940–44, 93950, 93953–55, 93960, 93962, 95001, 95003–04, 95010, 95012, 95019, 95020 (part), 95023 (part), 95024, 95039, 95043, 95045, 95060 (part), 95062–64, 95065 (part), 95073 (part), 95075, 95076 (part), 95077

EIGHTEENTH DISTRICT

GARY A. CONDIT, Democrat, of Ceres, CA; born in Tulsa OK, April 20, 1948; attended Modesto Junior College and Cal State University, Stanislaus; B.A., political science, 1972; Ceres City Council, 1972–76; mayor, Ceres, 1974–76; Stanislaus County Board of Supervisors, 1976–82, chairman, 1980; California State Assembly, 1982–89; former Assembly Assistant Majority Leader; former chairman and vice-chairman, Assembly Governmental Organization Committee and chairman of the Subcommittee on Sports and Entertainment; past chair, Assembly Rural Caucus; Legislator of the Year for California Narcotic Officers Association, 1986; Legislator of the Year for California Rifle and Pistol Association, 1986, 1988; married to Carolyn P. Condit; two children: Chad and Cadee; committees: Agriculture, Elections Reapportionment and Constitutional Amendments, Environmental Safety and Toxic Materials, International Trade and Intergovernmental Relations, Human Services, Governmental Organization, Revenue and Taxation, Ways and Means, Ways and Means Subcommittee on Education, Joint Committee on States Economy, Joint Committee on Fair Allocation and Classification, Special Committee on Community Colleges, and Select Committee on California Youth; member: House Agriculture Committee and subcommittees on Risk Management and Specialty Crops and Livestock, Dairy and Poultry; Government Reform and Oversight; subcommittees on National Economic Growth, Natural Resources, and Regulatory Affairs and National Security, International Affairs, and Criminal Justice; elected to the 101st Congress by special election on September 12, 1989 to fill the vacancy caused by the resignation of Tony Coelho; reelected to each succeeding Congress.

Office Listings

http://www.house.gov/gcondit gary.condit@mail.house.gov

2444 Rayburn House Office Building, Washington, DC 20515–0518 225–6131
Legislative Assistants.—Steve Jones, Ken Tyndal, Joel Perez, Robert Guenther. FAX: 225–0819
920 16th Street, Suite C, Modesto, CA 95354 .... (209) 527–1914
Chief of Staff.—Mike Lynch.
415 West 18th Street, Merced, CA 95340 .... (209) 383–4455

Counties: Merced, Stanislaus. FRESNO COUNTY; city of Firebaugh. MADERA COUNTY; city of Madera. SAN JOAQUIN COUNTY; city of Ripon. Population (1990), 571,393.

ZIP Codes: 92634, 93242, 93610 (part), 93616 (part), 93620, 93622 (part), 93635, 93637, 95301, 95303 (part), 95312–13, 95317, 95321 (part), 95322, 95329, 95333–34, 95337, 95339–42, 95344–48, 95350–58, 95360, 95361 (part), 95363, 95365–69, 95374, 95376, 95380–82, 95385–88, 95389 (part)

* * *

NINETEENTH DISTRICT

GEORGE RADANOVICH, Republican, of Mariposa, CA; born June 20, 1955; graduated, Mariposa County High School; B.A., California State Polytechnic University, 1978; assistant manager, Yosemite Bank, 1980–83; opened Mariposa County's first winery, 1986; charter member and president of the Mariposa Wine Grape Growers Association; founder, Mariposa Creek Parkway, 1985; treasurer, Mariposa Historical Society, 1982–83; member: Wine Institute, California Farm Bureau, California Association of Wine Grape Growers; Chambers of Commerce; California Ag Leadership, class XXI; chairman: Mariposa County Board of Supervisors, Mariposa County Planning Commission; executive director of the California State Mining and Mineral Museum Association; committees: Budget and Resources; subcommittees: Water and Power Resources; National Parks and Public Lands; Endangered Species Task Force; elected to the 104th Congress; reelected to the 105th Congress.

Office Listings

http://www.house.gov/radanovich george@hr.house.gov

213 Cannon House Office Building, Washington, DC 20515 225–4540
Chief of Staff.—John McCamman.
Executive Assistant.—Lisa Ford.
Legislative Director.—Tom Pyle.
Press Secretary/Counsel.—Will Dwyer.
2377 West Shaw, Suite 105, Fresno, CA 93711 .... (209) 248–0800
District Director.—Steve Samuelian. FAX: (209) 248–0169

Counties: FRESNO COUNTY; cities and townships of Auberry, Big Creek, Clovis (part), Del Rey (part), Dinuba (part), Dunlap, Fowler (part), Fresno, Friant, Hume, Huntington Lake, Kerman, Kings Canyon, Lakeshore, Miramonte, Orange

Cove (part), Piedra, Pinedale, Prather, Reedley (part), Sanger (part), Shaver Lake, Squaw Valley, Tollhouse, and Wishon. MADERA COUNTY; cities and townships of Ahwahnee, Bass Lake, Chowchilla (part), Coarsegold, Madera (part), Mono Hot Springs, North Fork, Oakhurst, O'Neals, and Raymond. MARIPOSA COUNTY; cities and townships of Fish Camp, Cathey's Valley (part), Coulterville (part), El Portal, Mariposa, Midpines, and Yosemite National Park. TULARE COUNTY; cities and townships of Badger, Dinuba (part), Exeter (part), Ivanhoe, Kaweah, Lemoncove, Lindsay (part), Orosi (part), Sequoia National Park, Three Rivers, Visalia (part), and Woodlake. Population (1990), 573,043.

ZIP Codes: 93221 (part), 93235, 93237, 93244, 93247 (part), 93262, 93271, 93277 (part), 93286, 93291 (part), 93292 (part), 93601–05, 93610 (part), 93611–14, 93616 (part), 93618 (part), 93621, 93623, 93625 (part), 93626, 93629, 93630 (part), 93633–34, 93637 (part), 93638–39, 93641, 93643–45, 93646 (part), 93647 (part), 93649–51, 93653, 93654 (part), 93657 (part), 93664, 93667, 93669, 93675, 93701 (part), 93702 (part), 93703–05, 93706 (part), 93710–11, 93720, 93722 (part), 93725 (part), 93726–29, 93744, 93747, 93755, 93790–94, 95306, 95311, 95318, 95338, 95345, 95389

* * *

TWENTIETH DISTRICT

CALVIN M. DOOLEY, Democrat, of Visalia, CA; born in Hanford, CA, January 11, 1954; M.S., management, Sloan Fellow, Stanford University, 1986–87; B.S., agricultural economics, University of California at Davis; administrative assistant to State Senator Rose Ann Vuich; past vice president, Tulare County Farm Bureau; member, House Agricultural Committee; ranking member, Subcommittee on Forestry, Resource Conservation and Research; member, Subcommittee on Livestock, Dairy and Poultry; member, Resources Committee and subcommittees on Energy and Mineral Resources and Water and Power; founder and cochair, New Democratic Coalition; cochair, Western Water Caucus; cochair, Congressional Biotechnology Caucus; Education and Industry Liaison, Oil and Gas Forum; cochair, Democratic Caucus Health Care Task Force; member, Rural Health Care Coalition; past cochair, Western Water Caucus; married to the former Linda Phillips; two children: Brooke and Emily; elected to the 102nd Congress on November 6, 1990; reelected to each succeeding Congress.

Office Listings

1227 Longworth House Office Building, Washington, DC 20515–0520 225–3341
Administrative Assistant.—Lisa Quigley.
Legislative Director.—Emily Beizer.
Press Secretary.—Jim Proulx.
224 West Lacey Boulevard, Hanford, CA 93230 .... (209) 585–8171
(800) 464–4294

Counties: Kings County. FRESNO COUNTY; western portion not in the Nineteenth District including western part of Fresno. KERN COUNTY; western portion not in the Twenty-First District including western part of Bakersfield. TULARE COUNTY; western portion not in Nineteenth or Twenty First District including western part of Visalia and Tulare. Population (1990), 573,282.

ZIP Codes: 93201–02, 93203 (part), 93204, 93206, 93210, 93212, 93215–17, 93219–20, 93227, 93230, 93232, 93234, 93239, 93241–42, 93245, 93249–50, 93256, 93257 (part), 93261, 93263 (part), 93266, 93270 (part), 93272, 93274 (part), 93275, 93277 (part), 93280, 93282, 93291 (part), 93305 (part), 93306 (part), 93307 (part), 93308 (part), 93309 (part), 93311 (part), 93312 (part), 93313 (part), 93382–83, 93606–09, 93615, 93616 (part), 93618 (part), 93622 (part), 93624, 93625 (part), 93627, 93630 (part), 93631, 93640, 93646 (part), 93647 (part), 93648, 93652, 93654 (part), 93656, 93657 (part), 93660, 93662, 93666, 93668, 93670, 93673, 93701 (part), 93702 (part), 93706 (part), 93707–09, 93712, 93714–18, 93721, 93722 (part), 93725 (part), 93745, 93771–79

* * *

TWENTY-FIRST DISTRICT

BILL THOMAS, Republican, of Bakersfield, CA; born in Wallace, ID, December 6, 1941; graduated, Garden Grove High School, 1959; A.A., Santa Ana Community College, 1961; B.A., San Francisco State University, 1963; M.A., San Francisco State University, 1965; professor, Bakersfield Community College, 1965–74; served in California State Assembly, 1974–78; member: Agriculture, Revenue and Taxation, and Rules committees; selected by the American Council of Young Political Leaders as a delegate to the Soviet Union, 1977; member: Ways and Means Committee; member, Subcommittee on Trade; chairman, Subcommittee on Health; chairman, House Oversight Committee; married to the former Sharon Lynn Hamilton, 1968; two children: Christopher and Amelia; elected to the 96th Congress, November 7, 1978; reelected to each succeeding Congress.

Office Listings

http://www.house.gov/billthomas

2208 Rayburn House Office Building, Washington, DC 20515–0521 225–2915

Administrative Assistant.—Cathy Abernathy.
Legislative Director.—Robert S. Winters.
Scheduler.—Julie Hasler.
Suite 220, 4100 Truxtun Avenue, Bakersfield, CA 93309 .... (805) 327–3611
319 West Murray Street, Visalia, CA 93291 .... (209) 627–6549

Counties: KERN COUNTY; cities and townships of Arvin, Bakersfield, Bodfish, Boron, Buttonwillow, Caliente, California City, Cantil, China Lake, Edison, Edwards, Fellows, Frazier Park, Glennville, Havilah, Inyokern, Keene, Kernville, Lake Isabella, Lebec, Maricopa, McKittrick, Mojave, Monolith, North Edwards, Onyx, Randsberg, Ridgecrest, Rosamond, Taft, Tehachapi, Tupman, Weldon, Willow Springs, Wofford Heights, and Woody. TULARE COUNTY; cities and townships of California Hot Springs, Camp Nelson, Ducor, Farmersville, Lindsay, Porterville, Posey, Springville, Strathmore, Terra Bella, Tulare, and Visalia. Population (1990), 571,300.

ZIP Codes: 93203 (part), 93205–08, 93218, 93220, 93222–26, 93238, 93240, 93247 (part), 93251–52, 93255, 93257 (part), 93258, 93260, 93265, 93267–68, 93270 (part), 93274 (part), 93275–76, 93277 (part), 93278–79, 93283, 93285, 93287, 93291 (part), 93301–04, 93305 (part), 93306 (part), 93307 (part), 93308 (part), 93309 (part), 93310, 93311 (part), 93312 (part), 93313 (part), 93380–89, 93501–02, 93504–05, 93516, 93518–19, 93523–24, 93527, 93531, 93554, 93555 (part), 93556, 93560–61, 93596

* * *

TWENTY-SECOND DISTRICT

WALTER H. CAPPS, Democrat, of Santa Barbara, CA; born on May 5, 1934, in Omaha, NE; graduated, Benson High School, Omaha, 1952; B.A., Portland State University, 1958; M.S.T., Yale Divinity School, 1961; M.A., 1963, and Ph.D., 1965, Yale University; professor and chair, Religious Studies Department, University of California Santa Barbara (UCSB), 1964–96; developed first college class dealing with Vietnam War; past director, Center for the Study of Democratic Institutions, UCSB; leading scholar, author of 14 books, and nationally recognized leader on issues of American democracy, veterans' affairs, and peace and conflict studies; cofounder of a veterans' center for the central coast region; recipient of Corita Kent Peace Award; nominated for Albert Schweitzer Humanitarian Award; former California State Chair, National Endowment for the Humanities; member, Federation of State Humanities Councils; served on board of advisors of the Smithsonian Institution's Center for the Study of the Vietnam Generation and as advisor to the Vietnam Veterans Outreach Program; member: Grace Lutheran Church, American Academy of Religion, Center for Common Good; married to Lois G. Capps since 1960; three children: Lisa, Todd, and Laura; committees: Science, International Relations; elected to the 105th Congress.

Office Listings

walter.capps@mail.house.gov

1118 Longworth House Office Building, Washington, DC 20515 225–3601
Chief of Staff.—Jeremy Rabinovitz. FAX: 225–5632
Legislative Director.—Lisa Moreno.
Senior Legislative Assistant.—Randolph Harrison.
Press Secretary.—Lisa Finkel.
Scheduler.—Thu Pham.
1411 Marsh Street, Suite 205, San Luis Obispo, CA 93401 .... (805) 546–8348
District Representatives.—Ann McMahon, Betsy Umhofer. FAX: 546–8368
1428 Chapala Street, Santa Barbara, CA 93101 .... (805) 730–1710
District Director.—Liz Giffin. FAX: 730–9153
Senior District Representative.—Sharon Siegel.

Counties: SAN LUIS OBISPO COUNTY; cities and townships of Arroyo Grande, Atascadero, Avila Beach, Bradley, Cambria, Cayucos, Cholame, Creston, California Valley, Grover Beach, Halcyon, Harmony, Los Osos, Morro Bay, Nipomo, Oceano, Paso Robles, Pismo Beach, San Luis Obispo, San Miguel, San Simeon, Santa Margarita, Shandon, Pozo, and Templeton. SANTA BARBARA COUNTY; cities and townships of Buellton, Casmalia, Cuyama, Ellwood, Gaviota, Goleta, Guadalupe, Isla Vista, Lompoc, Los Olivos, Los Alamos, Montecito, Santa Barbara, Santa Maria, Santa Ynez, Solvang, Summerland, Vandenberg Air Force Base, Orcutt, and Ballard. Population (1990), 572,891.

ZIP Codes: 93101, 93013 (part), 93014, 93067, 93101–03, 93105–11, 93116–18, 93120–21, 93130, 93140, 93150, 93160, 93190, 93214, 93254, 93401–03, 93405–10, 93412, 93420–24, 93426 (part), 93427–38, 93440–49, 93451 (part), 93452–57, 93460–61, 93463–65, 93479

* * *

TWENTY-THIRD DISTRICT

ELTON GALLEGLY, Republican, of Simi Valley, CA; born in Huntington Park, CA, March 7, 1944; graduated Huntington Park High School, 1962; attended Los Angeles State College;

businessman; member, Simi Valley City Council, 1979; mayor, city of Simi Valley, 1980–86; Congressional Human Rights Caucus; chairman: Subcommittee on the Western Hemisphere; member: Courts and Intellectual Property, Immigration and Claims, National Parks and Public Land subcommittees; Congressional Fire Services Caucus; chairman, Task Force on Urban Search and Rescue; former vice-chairman and chairman, Ventura County Association of Governments; former member, board of directors, Moorpark College Foundation; delegate to 1988 Republican National Convention; married the former Janice L. Shrader, 1974; four children: Shawn G., Shawn P., Kevin, and Shannon; elected to the 100th Congress, November 4, 1986; reelected to each succeeding Congress.

Office Listings

2427 Rayburn House Office Building, Washington, DC 20515–0523 225–5811
Administrative Assistant.—Dennis Parobek.
Legislative Director.—Vince Morelli.
Press Secretary.—Nora Bomar.
Office Manager.—Carolyn Hall.
300 Esplanade Drive, Suite 1800, Oxnard, CA 93030–1262 .... (805) 485–2300
District Director.—Paula Sheil. (800) 423–0023

Counties: VENTURA COUNTY; cities and townships of Bell Canyon, Camarillo, Fillmore, Meiners Oaks, Moorpark, Oak View, Ojai, Oxnard, Piru, Point Mugu, Port Hueneme, Santa Paula, Santa Susana, Saticoy, Simi Valley, Somis, Thousand Oaks, and Ventura. SANTA BARBARA COUNTY; city of Carpinteria. Population (1990), 571,483.

ZIP Codes: 90265 (part), 91304 (part), 91307 (part), 91311 (part), 91361 (part), 91362 (part), 93001–07, 93010–12, 93013 (part), 93015–16, 93020, 93021, 93023–24, 93030–35, 93040–44, 93060–63, 93065–66, 93093, 93222 (part), 93225 (part), 93252 (part)

* * *

TWENTY-FOURTH DISTRICT

BRAD J. SHERMAN, Democrat, of Sherman Oaks, CA; born in Los Angeles, October 24, 1954; B.A., *summa cum laude,* UCLA, 1974; J.D., *magna cum laude,* Harvard Law School, 1979; admitted to the California bar in 1979 and began practice in Los Angeles; attorney, CPA, certified tax law specialist; elected to the California State Board of Equalization, 1990, serving as chairman, 1991–95; elected to the 105th Congress.

Office Listings

1524 Longworth House Office Building, Washington, DC 20515 225–5911
Chief of Staff.—Michael Day. FAX: 225–5879
Scheduler.—Dan Lichtenberg.
Legislative Assistants.—Don MacDonald; Tracy Shapiro.
21031 Ventura Boulevard, Suite 1010, Woodland Hills, CA 91364 .... (818) 999–1990
FAX: 999–2287
2100 East Thousand Oaks Boulevard, No. C, Thousand Oaks, CA 91362 .... (805) 449–2372
Senior Field Representative.—John Anderson. FAX: 449–2375
Field Representatives.—Ken Goldman, Evita Mendiola, Sean Stalbaum.

County: LOS ANGELES COUNTY; cities of Agoura, Calabasas, Canoga Park, Encino, Hidden Hills, Malibu, Reseda, Tarzana, Topanga, West Hills, Westlake Village, Woodland Hills, and parts of Chatsworth, Northridge, Sherman Oaks, and Van Nuys. VENTURA COUNTY; cities of Oak Park, Newbury Park, Thousand Oaks, Westlake, and parts of Bell Canyon. Population (1990), 572,563.

ZIP Codes: 90264, 90265, 90290, 91301–03, 91304 (part), 91305, 91306 (part), 91307 (part), 91308–09, 91311 (part), 91316, 91320, 91324 (part), 91325 (part), 91335, 91337, 91356–59, 91360 (part), 91361 (part), 91362 (part), 91364–65, 91367, 91372, 91376, 91385, 91401 (part), 91403 (part), 91404, 91406 (part), 91408, 91411 (part), 91416, 91423 (part), 91436, 91604 (part), 91607 (part)

* * *

TWENTY-FIFTH DISTRICT

HOWARD P. (BUCK) McKEON, Republican, of Santa Clarita, CA; born in Los Angeles, CA, September 9, 1938; graduated, Verdugo Hills High School, Tujunga, CA; B.S., Brigham Young University; owner, Howard and Phil's Western Wear; mayor and city councilman, Santa Clarita, 1987–92; member: board of directors, Canyon Country Chamber of Commerce; California Republican State Central Committee; advisory council, Boy Scouts of America; president and trustee, William S. Hart School District, 1979–87; chairman and director, Henry Mayo Newhall Memorial Hospital, 1983–87; chairman and founding director, Valencia National Bank, 1987–92; honorary chairman, Red Cross Community Support Campaign, 1992; honorary chairman, Leukemia Society Celebrity Program, 1990 and 1994; president, Republican Freshman Class of the 103rd Congress; married to the former Patricia Kunz, 1962; six children: Tamara, Howard D., John Matthew, Kimberly, David Owen, and Tricia; elected on November 3, 1992 to the 103rd Congress; reelected to each succeeding Congress.

Office Listings

http://www.house.gov/mckeon tellbuck@hr.house.gov

307 Cannon House Office Building, Washington, DC 20515–0525 225–1956
Chief of Staff.—Bob Cochran. FAX: 226–0683
Executive Assistant/Appointments.—Marcy Benson.
Press Secretary/District Director.—Armando Azarloza.
23929 West Valencia Boulevard, Suite 410, Santa Clarita, CA 91355 .... (805) 254–2111
1008 West Avenue, M–4, Suite D, Palmdale, CA 93551 .... (805) 948–7833

County: Los Angeles County (part); cities and townships of Acton, Canyon Country, Canyon Country/Acqua Dulce, Castaic, Castaic/Saugus/Val Verde, Chatsworth, Granada Hills, Lake Hughes/Elizabeth, Lake Los Angeles. Lancaster, Lancaster/Quartz Hills, Little Rock, Llano, Neenach, Newhall, North Hills/Sepulveda, Northridge, Palmdale, Palmdale/Leona Valley, Pearblossom, Santa Clarita, Stevenson Ranch, Valencia, Valyermo, West Hills. Population (1990), 573,105.

ZIP Codes: 91304 (part), 91306 (part), 91310, 91311 (part), 91313, 91321 (part), 91324 (part), 91325 (part), 91326–28, 91342 (part), 91343 (part), 91344 (part), 91345 (part), 91350 (part), 91351, 91354–55, 91380–81, 91384, 91386, 91393–94, 93243, 93510, 93532, 93534–36, 93539, 93543–44, 93550–53, 93584, 93586, 93590–91

* * *

TWENTY-SIXTH DISTRICT

HOWARD L. BERMAN, Democrat, of Mission Hills, CA (representing the San Fernando Valley and parts of Los Angeles); born April 15, 1941 in Los Angeles; B.A., international relations, UCLA, 1962; LL.B., UCLA School of Law, 1965; California Assembly Fellowship Program, 1965–70; Vista volunteer, 1966–67; admitted to the California bar, 1966; practiced law until election to California Assembly in 1972; named assembly majority leader in first term; served as chair of the Assembly Democratic Caucus and policy research management committee; member: regional board of the Anti-Defamation League; past president, California Federation of Young Democrats; Distinguished Alumnus of UCLA, 1977; married to the former Janis Schwartz; two children: Brinley and Lindsey; elected to the 98th Congress on November 2, 1982 and reelected to each succeeding Congress; member, Judiciary and International Relations committees; ranking member, Subcommittee on Asia and the Pacific.

Office Listings

2231 Rayburn House Office Building, Washington, DC 20515–0526 225–4695
Administrative Assistant.—Gene Smith.
Legislative Director.—Bari Schwartz.
Personal Secretary.—Nancy Milburn.
10200 Sepulveda Boulevard, Suite 300, Mission Hills, CA 91345 .... (818) 891–0543
Administrative Assistant.—Tom Waldman.

County: Los Angeles County; portions of the city of Los Angeles, including all or part of the communities of Arleta, Lakeview Terrace, Mission Hills, North Hollywood, North Hills, Pacoima, Panorama City, Sun Valley, Sylmar, Valley Village, and Van Nuys; and the city of San Fernando. Population (1990), 571,523.

ZIP Codes: 91040 (part), 91331, 91340, 91342 (part), 91343 (part), 91344 (part), 91345 (part), 91352 (part), 91395, 91401 (part), 91402, 91405, 91406 (part), 91411 (part), 91504 (part), 91505 (part), 91601 (part), 91602 (part), 91605 (part), 91606, 91607 (part)

* * *

TWENTY-SEVENTH DISTRICT

JAMES E. ROGAN, Republican, of Glendale, CA; born in San Francisco, August 21, 1957; B.A., University of California, Berkeley, 1979; J.D., UCLA Law School, 1983; admitted to the California bar in 1984 and began practice in Los Angeles; attorney; member, California State Assembly, 1994–96, serving as Assembly Majority Leader in 1996; Glendale Municipal Court

Judge, 1990–94; Los Angeles County Deputy District Attorney, 1985–90; married to Christine Rogan since 1988; two children, Dana and Claire; elected to the 105th Congress.

Office Listings

502 Cannon House Office Building, Washington, DC 20515	225–4176
Chief of Staff.—Greg Mitchell.	FAX: 225–5828
Legislative Director/Press Secretary.—David J. Joergenson.	
Legislative Assistants: Myron M. Jacobson, Wendi F. Lynagh.	
Systems Administrator.—Ann C. Mooney.	
199 South Los Robles Avenue, Suite 560, Pasadena, CA 91101	(818) 577–3969
District Director.—Denise R. Milinkovich.	FAX: (818) 577–5581
Deputy District Director.—Robert Wyatt.	
Staff Assistants: Elizabeth L. Bloom, Linda Bonar.	
Field Representatives: Brian Saenger, Sabrina C. Schick.	

County: LOS ANGELES.

ZIP Codes: 91001, 91011, 91020, 91030, 91040, 91042, 91101–08, 91201–08, 91501–06.

* * *

TWENTY-EIGHTH DISTRICT

DAVID DREIER, Republican, of San Dimas, CA; born in Kansas City, MO, July 5, 1952; Claremont McKenna College, B.A. (cum laude), political science, 1975; Claremont Graduate School, M.A., American Government, 1976; Winston S. Churchill Fellow; Phi Sigma Alpha; director, corporate relations, Claremont McKenna College, 1975–78; member: board of governors, James Madison Society; Republican State Central Committee of California; Los Angeles Town Hall; named Outstanding Young Man of America and Outstanding Young Californian, 1976 and 1978; director, marketing and government affairs, Industrial Hydrocarbons, 1979–80; vice president, Dreier Development, 1985–present; author of congressional reform package incorporated into the House Rules; elected to the 97th Congress, November 4, 1980; reelected to each succeeding Congress.

Office Listings

http://www.house.gov/dreier

411 Cannon House Office Building, Washington, DC 20515–0528	225–2305
Administrative Assistant.—Bradley W. Smith.	FAX: 225–7018
Legislative Director.—Vince Randazzo.	
Scheduler/Projects.—Janice McKinney.	
112 North Second Avenue, Covina, CA 91723	(818) 339–9078
Field Representative.—Mark Harmsen.	(909) 592–2857

County: LOS ANGELES COUNTY; cities of Arcadia, Azusa, Bradbury, Claremont, Covina, Duarte, Glendora, Industry, LaPuente, La Verne, Angeles Forest, Monrovia, Pasadena, Pomona, Rowland Heights, San Dimas, San Gabriel, Sierra Madre, Temple City, Valinda, Walnut, West Covina. Population (1990), 572,927.

ZIP Codes: 91006 (part), 91007, 91009, 91010 (part), 91016 (part), 91024–25, 91066, 91077, 91107 (part), 91116, 91702 (part), 91711, 91722 (part), 91723–24, 91731 (part), 91740 (part), 91744 (part), 91748 (part), 91750, 91767 (part), 91768 (part), 91773, 91775 (part), 91776 (part), 91780, 91788, 91789 (part), 91790 (part), 91791, 91792 (part), 91793

* * *

TWENTY-NINTH DISTRICT

HENRY A. WAXMAN, Democrat, of Los Angeles, CA; born in Los Angeles, September 12, 1939; B.A., political science, UCLA, 1961; J.D., School of Law; admitted to the California State bar, 1965; served three terms as California State Assemblyman; former chairman, California Assembly Health Committee, Select Committee on Medical Malpractice, and Committee on Elections and Reapportionment; president, California Federation of Young Democrats, 1965–67; member: Guardians of the Jewish Home for the Aged, American Jewish Congress, Sierra Club; member: Commerce and Government Reform and Oversight committees; married the former Janet Kessler, 1971; two children: Carol Lynn and Michael David; elected to the 94th Congress, November 5, 1974; reelected to each succeeding Congress.

Office Listings

http://www.house.gov/waxman

2408 Rayburn House Office Building, Washington, DC 20515–0529 225–3976
Administrative Assistant.—Philip M. Schiliro. FAX: 225–4099
Legislative Assistant.—Patricia Delgado.
Personal Secretary/Office Manager.—Norah Lucey Mail.
Suite 600, 8436 West Third Street, Los Angeles, CA 90048 .... (213) 651–1040
Administrative Assistant.—Howard Elinson.
Coordinator.—Keiko Shimabukuro.

County: Los Angeles County; cities of Beverly Hills, Pacific Palisades, Santa Monica, West Hollywood, Los Angeles (part), North Hollywood (part), and Sherman Oaks (part). Population (1990), 571,566.

ZIP Codes: 90004 (part), 90005 (part), 90010 (part), 90020 (part), 90024–25, 90026 (part), 90027 (part), 90028 (part), 90029 (part), 90035 (part), 90036 (part), 90038 (part), 90039 (part), 90046, 90048 (part), 90049 (part), 90064 (part), 90067, 90068 (part), 90069, 90072–73, 90077–78, 90093, 90209–13, 90265 (part), 90272, 90290 (part), 90401–04, 90405 (part), 90406–11, 91010 (part), 91403 (part), 91413, 91423 (part), 91601 (part), 91602 (part), 91604 (part), 91607 (part), 91608, 91610, 91614

* * *

THIRTIETH DISTRICT

XAVIER BECERRA, Democrat, of Los Angeles, CA; born in Sacramento, CA, on January 26, 1958; graduated McClatchy High School, Sacramento, 1976; B.A., Stanford University, 1980; J.D., Stanford Law School, 1984; admitted to California bar, 1985; attended Universidad de Salamanca, 1978–79; staff attorney, "Reggie Fellow", Legal Assistance Corporation of Central Massachusetts, 1984–85; administrative assistant for State Senator Art Torres, California State Legislature, 1986; Deputy Attorney General, Office of the Attorney General, State of California, 1987–90; Assemblyman, California State Legislature, 1990–92; member: Mexican American State Legislators Policy Institute; Mexican American Bar Association; chairperson: Hispanic Employee Advisory Committee to the State Attorney General, 1989; honorary member: Association of California State Attorneys and Administrative Law Judges; former member: steering committee, Greater Eastside Voter Registration Project; Construction and General Laborers Union, Local 185 (Sacramento); married to Dr. Carolina Reyes; elected on November 3, 1992 to the 103rd Congress; reelected to each succeeding Congress.

Office Listings

1119 Longworth House Office Building, Washington, DC 20515–0530 225–6235
Administrative Assistant.—Krista Atteberry. FAX: 225–2202
Press Secretary.—Estela B. Mendoza.
District Administrator.—Henry Lozano.
Suite 200, 2435 Colorado Boulevard, Los Angeles, CA 90041 .... (213) 550–8962
FAX: 550–1440

County: Los Angeles County (part); city of Los Angeles (part). Population (1990), 572,538.

ZIP Codes: 90004 (part), 90005 (part), 90006 (part), 90010 (part), 90012 (part), 90019 (part), 90020 (part), 90023 (part), 90026 (part), 90027 (part), 90028 (part), 90029 (part), 90031, 90032 (part), 90033 (part), 90038 (part), 90039 (part), 90041 (part), 90042, 90050, 90057 (part), 90063 (part), 90065 (part), 90070

* * *

THIRTY-FIRST DISTRICT

MATTHEW G. MARTINEZ, Jr., Democrat, of Monterey Park, CA; born in Walsenburg, CO, February 14, 1929; Roosevelt High School, Los Angeles, 1949; received certificate of competence, Los Angeles Trade Technical School, 1959; served in U.S. Marine Corps, private first class, 1947–50; small businessman and building contractor; appointed: Monterey Park Planning Commission, 1971–74; elected mayor, Monterey Park, 1974–75; city councilman, Monterey Park, 1974–80; California State Legislature, 1980–82; member: Communications Workers of America, VFW, American Legion, Latin Business Association, Monterey Park Chamber of Commerce, Navy League; board, San Gabriel Valley YMCA; past president, Rotary Club; five children: Matthew, Diane, Susan, Michael, and Carol Ann; elected to the 97th Congress by special election, July 13, 1982, to fill the vacancy created by the resignation of George Danielson; reelected to each succeeding Congress.

Office Listings

2234 Rayburn House Office Building, Washington, DC 20515–0531 225–5464
Administrative Assistant/Chief of Staff.—Maxine A. Grant. FAX: 225–5467
320 South Garfield Avenue, Suite 214, Alhambra, CA 91801 .... (818) 458–4524

County: LOS ANGELES COUNTY; cities of Alhambra, Azusa, Baldwin Park, El Monte, South El Monte, Irwindale, Monterey Park, Rosemead, San Gabriel, South San Gabriel, and portions of East Los Angeles, East San Gabriel, Citrus CDP, Glendora, Industry City, Los Angeles, Temple City, Vincent CDP, and West Covina. Population (1990), 572,643.

ZIP Codes: 90022 (part), 90032 (part), 90063 (part), 91006 (part), 91010 (part), 91016 (part), 91030 (part), 91702 (part), 91706 (part), 91722 (part), 91731 (part), 91732–34, 91740 (part), 91754, 91770 (part), 91775 (part), 91776 (part), 91778, 91790 (part), 91801 (part), 91802–03

* * *

THIRTY-SECOND DISTRICT

JULIAN C. DIXON, Democrat, of Los Angeles, CA; born in Washington, DC, August 8, 1934; graduated, Dorsey High School, Los Angeles, CA, 1953; B.S., Los Angeles State College, 1962; LL.B., Southwestern University, Los Angeles, 1967; served in U.S. Army, sergeant, 1957–60; member of California State Assembly, 1972–78; chairman, Democratic Caucus; member: Assembly Committee on Criminal Justice, Ways and Means, Select Committee on Corrections, Joint Committee on the Revision of the Penal Code; vice chairman, Assembly Select Committee on Health Sciences Education; secretary, Law Enforcement and Criminal Justice Task Force; member: National Conference of State Legislatures Executive Committee; Committee on Appropriations; member, Appropriations Subcommittee on Commerce, Justice, State, and Judiciary; Appropriations Subcommittee on National Security; member: Subcommittee on the District of Columbia; member: Permanent Select Committee on Intelligence; chairman, Congressional Black Caucus, 98th Congress; married to Bettye Lee Dixon; one child: Cary Cordon; elected to the 96th Congress, November 7, 1978; reelected to each succeeding Congress.

Office Listings

2252 Rayburn House Office Building, Washington, DC 20515–0532 225–7084
Administrative Assistant.—Andrea (Tracy) Holmes. FAX: 225–4091
Appointment Secretary.—Deanne R. Samuels.
Legislative Director.—Paul Cunningham.
Wateridge, Suite 208, 5100 West Goldleaf Circle, Los Angeles, CA 90056 .... (213) 678–5424
Administrative Assistant.—Patricia Miller. FAX: 678–6026

County: LOS ANGELES COUNTY; cities of Culver City, Los Angeles City (part), communities of Crenshaw, West Adams, Mid City, Leimert Park, Exposition Park, South Central (part), Baldwin Hills, Mar Vista, Beverlywood, Palms, Rancho Park (part), Cheviot Hills, and unincorporated communities of Windsor HIlls, View Park and Ladera Heights. Population (1990), 572,595.

ZIP Codes: 90005 (part), 90006 (part), 90007 (part), 90008, 90010 (part), 90016, 90018, 90019 (part), 90034, 90035 (part), 90036 (part), 90037 (part), 90043, 90044 (part), 90045 (part), 90047 (part), 90048 (part), 90056, 90062, 90064 (part), 90066 (part), 90075–76, 90082, 90089, 90230 (part), 90231–33, 90291 (part), 90292 (part), 90302 (part), 90405 (part)

* * *

THIRTY-THIRD DISTRICT

LUCILLE ROYBAL-ALLARD, Democrat, of Los Angeles, CA; born on June 12, 1941, in Los Angeles, CA; B.A., California State University, Los Angeles, 1965; elected to the California State Assembly, 1987–92; awards: 1992 Environmental Achievement Award, California Sierra Club; 1992 Feminist of the Year Award, National Organization for Women; 1991 Star Legislator Award, Los Angeles Women's Legislative Coalition; 1990 and 1991, Highest Legislative Rating, California League of Conservation Voters; 1990 Legislator of the Year, University of California Student Association; Humanitarian Award, Los Angeles Commission on Assaults Against Woman; Public Service Award, Asian Business Association; Public Service Award (three-time winner), East Los Angeles Jaycees; Outstanding Achievement Award, National Association of Hispanic CPAs; Hispanic Woman of the '80s Award, Mexican American Women's National Association; President's Award, Latin American Professional Women's Association; Award for Work on Domestic Violence, Los Angeles County Board of Supervisors; The President's Public Service Award, County of Los Angeles; married in 1981 to Edward T. Allard III; four children, Lisa Marie, Ricardo, Angela, and Guy Mark; chair, California Democratic Congressional Delegation; committees: Budget, Banking and Financial Services; subcommittees:

Financial Institutions and Consumer Credit, and Capital Markets, Securities and Government-Sponsored Enterprises; elected on November 3, 1993 to the 103rd Congress; reelected to each succeeding Congress.

Office Listings

2435 Rayburn House Office Building, Washington, DC 20515–0533 225–1766
Chief of Staff.—Henry J. Contreras.
Legislative Director.—Peter Wong.
Communications Director.—Sherry Greenberg.
Legislative Aides: Ellen Riddleberger, Kathleen Sengstock, Adriana Martinez.
Office Manager/Scheduler.—Valerie McMullin.
Staff Assistant.—Jonathan Long.

County: LOS ANGELES COUNTY; cities of Bell, Bell Gardens, Boyle Heights, Commerce, Cudahy, Downtown Los Angeles, East Los Angeles, Florence, Huntington Park, Maywood, Paramount, Pico Union, South Gate, Vernon, Walnut Park, and Westlake. Population (1990), 572,595.

ZIP Codes: 90001 (part), 90005 (part), 90006 (part), 90007 (part), 90011 (part), 90012 (part), 90013–15, 90017, 90020 (part), 90021, 90022 (part), 90023 (part), 90026 (part), 90030, 90033 (part), 90040 (part), 90051, 90053–55, 90057 (part), 90058 (part), 90060, 90063 (part), 90071, 90079, 90086–87, 90091, 90201, 90255 (part), 90262 (part), 90270, 90280 (part), 90301 (part)

* * *

THIRTY-FOURTH DISTRICT

ESTEBAN EDWARD TORRES, Democrat, of La Puente, CA; born in Miami, AZ, January 27, 1930; moved to East Los Angeles in 1936; graduated from James A. Garfield High School in 1949; studied under GI Bill, Los Angeles Art Center, 1953; East Los Angeles College, 1959; California State University at Los Angeles, 1963; postgraduate studies, University of Maryland, 1965, economics; American University, 1966, international relations; Honorary Doctorate Degree, National University, San Diego, 1987; married the former Arcy Sanchez of Los Angeles, January 22, 1955; five children: Carmen (Ms. Raul Garcia), Rena, Camille, Selina, and Steve; enlisted in U.S. Army, 1949; honorably discharged as a Korean conflict veteran in 1953 (stationed in Germany) with the rank of sergeant first class; employed by the Chrysler Corporation, Los Angeles, 1954; elected chief shop steward, 1958, United Auto Workers UAW Local 230; appointed UAW organizer, western region 6; appointed international representative, UAW, Washington, DC, office, 1963; director, UAW Inter-American Bureau for Caribbean and Latin American Affairs, 1964–68; returned to Los Angeles, cofounded The East Los Angeles Community Union (TELACU); served as chief executive officer, TELACU, 1968–74; member, Los Angeles County Commission on Economic Development, 1970–72; commissioner, Mexican American Education Commission, 1970–72; president, Congress Mexican American Unity, 1969–70; president, Plaza de la Raza Cultural Center, 1973; vice president, National Congress for Community Economic Development, 1974; board of visitors, School of Architecture, UCLA, 1973–74; resigned TELACU; candidate for U.S. Congress, 30th Congressional District, 1974, San Gabriel Valley, CA; consultant, Committee to Incorporate East Los Angeles; member, Citizens National Committee on Broadcasting, 1975; appointed by UAW President Leonard Woodcock as assistant director of UAW International Affairs Department, Washington, DC; delegate and consultant to international trade union conferences, Latin America and Western Europe; delegate to IMF Central Committee meetings, Geneva, Switzerland; consultant, U.S. Congress Office of Technology Assessment, 1976; presidential appointment and U.S. Senate confirmation as U.S. Permanent Representative to United Nations Educational, Scientific, and Cultural Organization (UNESCO), with rank of Ambassador, Paris, France, 1977; chairman, Geneva Group, 1978; delegate and vice president to UNESCO General Conference, Paris, 1978; elected to UNESCO Executive Board, 1978; appointed special assistant to President Jimmy Carter; director, White House Office of Hispanic Affairs, 1979; affiliations include: trustee, American College in Paris; trustee, Florida International University School of Business and Organizational Sciences; U.S. Commission for UNESCO; U.S. Committee for UNICEF; Pan-American Development Foundation; Veterans of Foreign Wars, VFW Post 6315, Pico Rivera, CA; elected to the 98th Congress, November 2, 1982; reelected to each succeeding Congress; chairman, Congressional Hispanic Caucus, 1987; appointed official observer, Geneva Arms Reduction Talks, 1986–90; Democratic deputy whip; member, Committee on Appropriations; Subcommittee on Foreign Operations, Export Financing and Related Programs.

Office Listings

http://www.house.gov/torres arcoiris@hr.house.gov

2368 Rayburn House Office Building, Washington, DC 20515–0534 225–5256

Chief of Staff.—Albert S. Jacquez. FAX: 225–9711
Legislative Director/Systems Manager.—Phil Alperson.
Press Secretary.—Roderic Olvera Young.
Executive Assistant.—Lisa Esquivel.
8819 Whittier Boulevard, Suite 101, Pico Rivera, CA 90660 .... (310) 695–0702
Chief of Staff.—James Casso. FAX: 692–2216

County: LOS ANGELES COUNTY; cities of Bassett, Industry, East Los Angeles, Hacienda Heights, Los Nietos, La Puente, Montebello, Norwalk, Pico Rivera, Santa Fe Springs, Valinda, and Whittier. Population (1990), 573,047.

ZIP Codes: 90022 (part), 90040 (part), 90063 (part), 90601, 90602 (part), 90604 (part), 90605 (part), 90606–08, 90610, 90638 (part), 90640, 90650 (part), 90651–52, 90659, 90660 (part), 90661, 90665, 90670 (part), 90701 (part), 91706 (part), 91715–16, 91744 (part), 91745 (part), 91746–47, 91748 (part), 91749, 91770 (part), 91790 (part), 91792 (part)

* * *

THIRTY-FIFTH DISTRICT

MAXINE WATERS, Democrat, of Los Angeles, CA; born in St. Louis, MO, August 15, 1938; B.A., California State University; honorary degrees, Spelman College, Atlanta, GA, North Carolina A&T State University, Howard University, Central State University, Bishop College, Morgan State University; elected to California State Assembly, 1976; reelected every two years thereafter; member: Assembly Democratic Caucus, Board of TransAfrica Foundation, National Women's Political Caucus; chairperson, Ways and Means Subcommittee on State Administration; chair, Joint Committee on Public Pension Fund Investments; married to Sidney Williams, U.S. Ambassador to the Commonwealth of the Bahamas; two children: Karen and Edward; founding member, National Commission for Economic Conversion and Disarmament; member of the board, Center for National Policy; Clara Elizabeth Jackson Carter Foundation (Spelman College); Minority AIDS Project; committees: Banking and Financial Services, Veterans' Affairs; elected to the 102nd Congress on November 6, 1990; reelected to each succeeding Congress.

Office Listings

2344 Rayburn House Office Building, Washington, DC 20515–0535 225–2201
Chief of Staff.—Leah Allen.
Legislative Director.—Bill Zavarello.
Press Secretary.—Vernon Richardson.
Personal Secretary.—Betty Edwards.
10124 South Broadway, Los Angeles, CA 90003 .... (213) 757–8900
District Director.—Mike Murase, Esq.

County: LOS ANGELES COUNTY; census tracts: 2244–46, 2264, 2265, 2267, 2281–89, 2291–94, 2311, 2317–19, 2321–23, 2325–28, 2371–79. 2381–86, 2391–99, 2401–09, 2411, 2412, 2421–29, 2431, 5325, 5326.01, 5326.02, 5327–30, 5331–30, 5331.01, 5331.02, 5332, 5335, 5345, 5347–50, 5351.01, 5351.02, 5352, 5353, 5355, 5356.01, 5356.02, 5357, 5358.01, 5358.02, 5359–62, 5505–08, 6001, 6002.01, 6002.02, 6003.01, 6003.02, and 6004; partial census tracts: 2312 (blocks 104, 107, 204, and 212), 2316 (block groups 1, 2, and 3, and blocks 501, 502, and 503), 2266 (blocks 207 and 213), 5324 (portions not contained in the Thirtieth District), 5354 (all except portions in the city of Lynwood), and 5514 (portions not contained in the Thirty-Second District). Population (1990), 570,882.

ZIP Codes: 90001 (part), 90002 (part), 90003 (part), 90007 (part), 90011 (part), 90037 (part), 90044 (part), 90045 (part), 90047 (part), 90058 (part), 90061 (part), 90247 (part), 90248 (part), 90249 (part), 90250 (part), 90251, 90255 (part), 90260 (part), 90262 (part), 90301 (part), 90302 (part), 90303–10, 90312

* * *

THIRTY-SIXTH DISTRICT

JANE HARMAN, Democrat, of Rolling Hills, CA; born in New York, NY; graduated, University High School, Los Angeles, 1962; B.A., Smith College, Northampton, MA, 1966; J.D., Harvard University Law School, Cambridge, MA, 1969; attorney, admitted to the District of Columbia bar, 1969; counsel for Jones, Day, Reavis and Pogue; director, secretary, and outside general counsel for Harman International Industries; special counsel, Department of Defense, 1979; member, L.A. County High Technology Committee; founding member, South Bay Alliance for Choice; board member and former vice chair, Center for National Policy; board member, International Human Rights Law Group; member, Visiting Committee, John F. Kennedy School of Government, Harvard University; married to Sidney Harman, 1980; four children: Brian Lakes Frank, Hilary Lakes Frank, Daniel Geier Harman, and Justine Leigh Harman; elected on November 3, 1992 to the 103rd Congress; reelected to each succeeding Congress.

Office Listings

http://www.house.gov/harman jharman@hr.house.gov

325 Cannon House Office Building, Washington, DC 20515–0536 225–8220
Chief of Staff.—Mark Kadesh. FAX: 226–0684
Legislative Director.—David Flanders.
Office Manager/Scheduler/Executive Assistant.—Laura Flores.
1217 El Prado Avenue, Torrance, CA 90501 .... (310) 783–8220
FAX: 787–8425
583¾ Venice Boulevard, Suite E, Venice, CA 90291 .... (301) 581–9011
FAX: 581–9237

County: LOS ANGELES COUNTY (part); cities of Avalon, El Segundo, Hawthorne (part), Hermosa Beach, Lawndale, Lomita, Los Angeles (part), Manhattan Beach, Marina del Rey, Palos Verdes Estates, Rancho Palos Verdes, Redondo Beach, Rolling Hills, Rolling Hills Estates, Torrance, and West Carson. Population (1990), 573,663.

ZIP Codes: 90009, 90045 (part), 90066 (part), 90080, 90083, 90230 (part), 90245, 90247 (part), 90248 (part), 90249 (part), 90250 (part), 90254, 90260 (part), 90266, 90274, 90277–78, 90291 (part), 90292 (part), 90293–96, 90405 (part), 90501 (part), 90502 (part), 90503–05, 90507–10, 90704, 90710 (part), 90717 (part), 90731 (part), 90732, 90734, 90744 (part), 90803 (part)

* * *

THIRTY-SEVENTH DISTRICT

JUANITA MILLENDER-McDONALD, Democrat, of Carson, CA; born in Birmingham, AL, September 7, 1938; graduated from University of Redlands, CA; graduate work at California State University–Long Beach and University of Southern California; teacher, director of gender equity programs; coordinator of Career Education, Los Angeles Unified School District; member, California State Assembly, 1992–96, serving as California's representative, Education Commission of the States (executive committee), and vice chair, Commerce Committee, National Conference of State Legislatures; first woman chair, Assembly Revenue and Taxation Committee, 1995–96; first woman chair, Assembly Insurance Committee, 1994; first woman vice chair, Assembly Governmental Organization Committee, 1993; mayor pro tempore, Carson City Council, 1991–92; member, Carson City Council, 1990; life member, NAACP; member, Alpha Kappa Alpha Sorority; board of directors, Southern California SCLC; board of trustees, Second Baptist Church; serves on the National Commission on Teaching and America's Future; married since 1955 to James McDonald, Jr.; five children: Valerie, Angela, Sherryll, and Keith; elected to the 105th Congress.

Office Listings

millendermcdonald@hr.house.gov

419 Cannon House Office Building, Washington, DC 20515–0537 225–7924
Chief of Staff.—Andrea Martin. FAX: 225–7926
Legislative Director.—Marcers Mason.
Scheduler.—Alex Hanson.
Press Secretary.—Alex Hanson.
One Civic Plaza, Suite 650, Carson, CA 90745 .... (310) 549–0537
FAX: 549–3810

County: LOS ANGELES COUNTY; cities of Carson, Compton, Gardena, Long Beach (part), Lynwood. Population (1990), 572,049.

ZIP Codes: 90002, 90003, 90044, 90054, 90061, 90062, 90220–90224, 90247, 90248, 90262, 90280, 90706, 90710, 90717, 90723, 90744–90747, 90805–90807, 90810, 90813

* * *

THIRTY-EIGHTH DISTRICT

STEPHEN HORN, Republican, of Long Beach, CA; born in Gilroy, CA, May 31, 1931; graduated, San Benito County High School, Hollister, CA, 1949; A.B., with Great Distinction, political science, Stanford University, CA, 1953; M.P.A., Harvard University, 1955; Ph.D., political science, Stanford University, 1958; Strategic Intelligence Reserve, SP–7, U.S. Army, 1954–62; congressional fellow, American Political Science Association, 1958–59; administrative assistant to Secretary of Labor James P. Mitchell, 1959–60; legislative assistant to U.S. Senator Thomas H. Kuchel (R–CA), 1960–66; senior fellow in governmental studies, Brookings Institution, 1966–69; dean of graduate studies and research, American University, 1969–70; president, California State University, Long Beach, 1970–88; trustee professor of political science, California State University, Long Beach, 1988–93; vice chairman/member, U.S. Commission on Civil Rights, 1969–82; member, National Institute of Corrections, 1970–88, chairman, 1985–87; author, *The Cabinet and Congress*, 1960; *Unused Power: The Work of the Senate Committee on Appropriations*, 1970; co-author, *Congressional Ethics: The View from the House*, 1975; lecturer on human rights, education, and American government in 15 countries for USIA, 1975–79; fellow, National Academy of Public Administration, 1986–; chairman, American Association of State Colleges and Universities, 1985–86; named "one of the 100 most effective university presidents in the United States," 1986; married to the former Nini Moore; two children: Marcia and Stephen; elected on November 8, 1994 to the 104th Congress; reelected to the 105th Congress.

Office Listings

http://www.house.gov/horn

438 Cannon House Office Building, Washington, DC 20515–0538 225–6676
Administrative Assistant.—David Bartel. FAX: 226–1012
Legislative Director.—Douglas Johnson.
Press Secretary.—Matthew Phillips.
District Administrator.—Connie Sziebl.
4010 Watson Plaza Drive, Suite 160, Lakewood, CA 90712 .... (562) 425–1336
FAX: 425–4591

County: LOS ANGELES COUNTY; cities of Bellflower, Downey, Lakewood, Long Beach, Los Angeles, (San Pedro), Paramount, and Signal Hill. Population (1990), 572,657.

ZIP Codes: 90239–42, 90280 (part), 90660 (part), 90706–07, 90711–12, 90713 (part), 90714, 90723 (part), 90731 (part), 90733, 90802, 90803 (part), 90804, 90805 (part), 90806 (part), 90807 (part), 90808 (part), 90809, 90810 (part), 90813 (part), 90814, 90815 (part), 90822, 90831–32, 90840, 90842, 90844–48, 90853

* * *

THIRTY-NINTH DISTRICT

ED ROYCE, Republican, of Fullerton, CA; born on October 12, 1951 in Los Angeles, CA; B.A., California State University, Fullerton, 1977; small business owner; controller; corporate tax manager; California State Senate, 1982–92; member: Fullerton Chamber of Commerce; board member, Literacy Volunteers of America; California Interscholastic Athletic Foundation board of advisers; married Marie Therese Porter, 1985; elected on November 3, 1992 to the 103rd Congress; reelected to each succeeding Congress.

Office Listings

http://www.house.gov/royce

1133 Longworth House Office Building, Washington, DC 20515–0539 225–4111
Chief of Staff.—Joan Bates Korich. FAX: 226–0335
Legislative Director.—Thor Ronay.
Press Secretary.—John Doherty.
305 North Harbor Boulevard, Suite 300, Fullerton, CA 92632 .... (714) 992–8081
Administrative Assistant.—Marcia Gilchrist.

Counties: ORANGE COUNTY; the north and west part including the cities of Anaheim (part), Brea, Fullerton, La Habra, Placentia, Yorba Linda, Buena Park, Cypress, La Palma, Stanton, Los Alamitos, Seal Beach. LOS ANGELES COUNTY; cities of Artesia, Cerritos, Hawaiian Gardens, La Habra Heights, La Mirada, Lakewood, and Whittier. Population (1990), 573,574.

ZIP Codes: 90602 (part), 90603, 90604 (part), 90605 (part), 90609, 90620 (part), 90621–24, 90630 (part), 90631 (part), 90632–33, 90637, 90638 (part), 90639, 90650 (part), 90670 (part), 90680 (part), 90701 (part), 90702–03, 90713 (part), 90715–16, 90720 (part), 90721, 90740 (part), 90808 (part), 90815 (part), 92601, 92621 (part), 92631, 92632 (part), 92633–35, 92670 (part), 92686 (part), 92801 (part), 92805 (part), 92806 (part)

* * *

FORTIETH DISTRICT

JERRY LEWIS, Republican, of Redlands, CA; born in Seattle, WA, October 21, 1934; graduated, San Bernardino High School, 1952; B.A., UCLA, 1956; graduate intern in public affairs, Coro Foundation; life underwriter; former member, San Bernardino School Board; served in California State Assembly, 1968–78; insurance executive, 1959–78; married to Arlene Willis; seven children; elected to the 96th Congress, November 7, 1978; reelected to each succeeding Congress.

Office Listings
http://www.house.gov/jerrylewis

2112 Rayburn House Office Building, Washington, DC 20515–0540 225–5861
Administrative Assistant.—Arlene Willis. FAX: 225–6498
Associate Staff/Appropriations Committee.—Letitia White.
Deputy Chief of Staff/Press Secretary.—Dave LesStrang.
1150 Brookside Avenue, No. J5, Redlands, CA 92373 .... (909) 862–6030
District Representative.—Corrine Spears.

Counties: Inyo, San Bernardino. CITIES AND TOWNSHIPS: Adelanto, Amboy, Angelus Oaks, Apple Valley, Argus, Arrowbear Lake, Baker, Barstow, Big Bear City, Big Bear Lake, Big Pine, Bishop, Blue Jay, Bryn Mawr, Big River, Cadiz, Cedar Glen, Cedar Pines Park, Cima, Colton, Crestline, Crest Park, Daggett, Death Valley, Earp, East Highlands, Highland, Essex, Etiwanda, Fawnskin, Forest Falls, Ft. Irwin, George AFB, Green Valley Lake, Guasti, Havasu Lake, Helendale, Hesperia, Hinckley, Independence, Joshua Tree, Kelso, Lake Arrowhead, Landers, Loma Linda, Lone Pine, Lucerne Valley, Ludlow, Mentone, Morongo Valley, Mountain Pass, Mt. Baldy, Needles, Newberry Springs, Nipton, Olancha, Oro Grande, Parker Dam, Phelan, Pinon Hills, Pioneertown, Redlands, Rimforest, Running Springs, San Bernardino, Shoshone, Skyforest, Sugarloaf, Trona, 29 Palms, Twin Peaks, Victorville, Vidal, Westend, Wrightwood, Yermo, Yucaipa, Yucca Valley. Population (1990), 573,625.

ZIP Codes: 91739, 91743, 91759, 92242, 92252, 92256, 92267–68, 92277–78, 92280, 92284–85, 92301, 92304–05, 92307, 92309–12, 92314–15, 92317–19, 92321–28, 92332–33, 92338, 92339, 92341–42, 92345–47, 92351–52, 92354, 92356, 92359, 92363–66, 92368, 92371–75, 92378, 92382, 92384, 92386, 92389, 92391–92, 92394, 92397–99, 92404, 92407–10, 93513–15, 93526, 93545, 93549, 93562, 93564

* * *

FORTY-FIRST DISTRICT

JAY KIM, Republican, of Diamond Bar, CA; born on March 27, 1939 in Seoul, Korea; B.A., civil engineering, University of Southern California, 1967; M.A., civil engineering, University of Southern California; M.P.A., California State University, 1979; served, Republic of Korean Army, 1959–61; civil engineer, founder of JAYKIM Engineers, a transportation design firm; member, city council, Diamond Bar, CA, 1990–91; mayor, Diamond Bar, 1991–92; member, American Society of Civil Engineers, American Public Works Association; married June Kim, 1961; three children: Richard, Kathy, and Eugene; committees: Transportation and International Relations; elected on November 3, 1992 to the 103rd Congress.

Office Listings
http://www.house.gov/kim

435 Cannon House Office Building, Washington, DC 20515–0540 225–3201
Chief of Staff.—Matt Reynolds. FAX: 226–1485
District Director.—Peter Stevens.
1131 West Sixth Street, Suite 160A, Ontario, CA 91762 .... (909) 988–1055
18200 Yorba Linda Boulevard, Suite 203A, Yorba Linda, CA 92686 .... (714) 572–8574

Counties: Los Angeles (part), Orange (part), and San Bernardino (part). CITIES AND TOWNSHIPS: Anaheim (part), Brea (part), Chino, Diamond Bar, La Habra Heights (part), Montclair, Ontario (part), Placentia (part), Pomona (part), Rowland Heights (part), Upland, Yorba Linda (part) and Walnut (part). Population (1990), 572,663.

ZIP Codes: 90631 (part), 91708–10, 91721 (part), 91748 (part), 91761 (part), 91762 (part), 91763, 91764 (part), 91765–66, 91767 (part), 91768 (part), 91784, 91786 (part), 91789 (part), 92807 (part), 92808 (part), 92821–22, 92870, 92886–87

* * *

FORTY-SECOND DISTRICT

GEORGE E. BROWN, JR., Democrat, of San Bernardino, CA; born in Holtville, CA, March 6, 1920; graduated from University of California at Los Angeles with B.A. in industrial physics; employed by city of Los Angeles for 12 years in personnel, engineering, and management positions; management consultant; second lieutenant, infantry, World War II; mayor and city councilman, Monterey Park, 1954–58; State assemblyman, 1958–62; married Marta Marcias Brown, 1988; two children, David and Dale; elected to the 88th Congress, November 6, 1962; reelected to the 89th, 90th, and 91st Congresses; unsuccessfully sought election to U.S. Senate in 1970; member: Agriculture Committee; ranking minority, Committee on Science; member, Technology Assessment Board; elected to the 93rd Congress, November 7, 1972; reelected to each succeeding Congress.

Office Listings

http://www.house.gov/georgebrown talk2geb@hr.house.gov

2300 Rayburn House Office Building, Washington, DC 20515–0542 225–6161
Administrative Assistant.—Bill Grady. FAX: 225–8671
Legislative Director.—Corinne Colgan.
Executive Assistant.—Ruth Hogue.
657 La Cadena Drive, Colton, CA 92324 .... (909) 825–2472
District Administrator.—Wilmer D. Carter.

County: SAN BERNARDINO COUNTY (part); Census tracts: 10–12, 14–16, 18, 23–26, 28–70, 74.01, 75–77; partial census tracts: 3, 4, 6.01, 17, and 21, all have portions in the city of Ontario; 13, 20, portions in the city of Fontana; 22, portions in the cities of Fontana and Ontario; 27, portions in the city of Rialto, except for the noncontiguous portion; 71, all except portions south of Fern Street and its southwesterly extension to an intersection within the city limits of Grand Terrace and portions in the city of Grand Terrace; 72, all except portions in the city of Loma Linda and blocks 324 and 326 and the portion of block 401 in the city of Redlands; 73, portions in the cities of Colton and San Bernardino; 74.02, all except the unincorporated portions of block groups 1–3; 79, 101, and 102.02, and Rancho Cucomongo. Population (1990), 571,844.

ZIP Codes: 91701 (part), 91729, 91730 (part), 91737, 91739, 91743, 91758, 91761 (part), 91762 (part), 91764 (part), 91786 (part), 92313, 92324 (part), 92334–35, 92336 (part), 92346 (part), 92377, 92401–02, 92404 (part), 92405–06, 92407 (part), 92408 (part), 92410 (part), 92411, 92414, 92416, 92418, 92507 (part)

* * *

FORTY-THIRD DISTRICT

KEN CALVERT, Republican, of Corona, CA; born June 8, 1953 in Corona; Chaffey College (CA), A.A., 1973; San Diego State University, B.A. in economics, 1975; congressional aide to Rep. Victor V. Veysey, CA; general manager, Jolly Fox Restaurant, Corona, 1975–79; Marcus W. Meairs Co., Corona, 1979–81; president and general manager, Ken Calvert Real Properties, 1981–92; County Youth Chairman, Rep. Veysey's District, 1970, then 43rd District, 1972; Corona/Norco Youth Chairman for Nixon, 1968 and 1972; Reagan-Bush campaign worker, 1980; cochair, Wilson for Senate Campaign, 1982; Riverside Republican Party, chairman, 1984–88; cochairman, George Deukmejian election, 1978, 1982 and 1986; cochairman, George Bush election, 1988; cochairman, Pete Wilson Senate elections, 1982 and 1988; cochairman, Pete Wilson for Governor election, 1990; member: Riverside County Republican Winners Circle, charter member; Corona/Norco Republican Assembly, former vice president; Lincoln Club of Riverside County, chairman and charter member, 1986–90; Corona Rotary Club, president, 1991; Corona Elks; Navy League of Corona/Norco; Corona Chamber of Commerce, past president, 1990; Norco Chamber of Commerce; County of Riverside Asset Leasing, chairman; Corona/Norco Board of Realtors; Monday Morning Group; Corona Group, past chairman; Economic Development Partnership, executive board; Corona Community Hospital Corporate 200 Club; Silver Eagles (March AFB Support Group), charter member; Corona Airport Advisory Commission; committees: Science, Agriculture, and Resources; elected November 3, 1992 to the 103rd Congress.

Office Listings

1034 Longworth House Office Building, Washington, DC 20515–0543 225–1986
Administrative Assistant.—Ed Slevin. FAX: 225–2004
Legislative Director.—David Ramey.
Press Secretary.—David Ramey.
District Manager.—Sue Miller.
3400 Central Avenue, Suite 200, Riverside, CA 92506 .... (909) 784–4300

County: RIVERSIDE COUNTY; cities and townships of Canyon Lake, Corona, El Cerrito, Glen Avon, Highgrove, Home Gardens, Lake Elsinore, Lakeland Village, March AFB, Mira Loma, Moreno Valley, Murrieta, Murrieta Hot Springs, Norco, Pedley, Perris, Quail Valley, Riverside, Rubidoux, Sedco Hills, Sunnyslope, Temecula, Wildomar, and Woodcrest. Population (1990), 571,231

ZIP Codes: 91718–19, 91720 (part), 91752, 91760, 92501–06, 92507 (part), 92508–09, 92513–19, 92530–32, 92543 (part), 92545 (part), 92553 (part), 92557 (part), 92562 (part), 92563 (part), 92564, 92570 (part), 92571 (part), 92572, 92584 (part), 92586 (part), 92587 (part), 92590 (part), 92591 (part), 92592 (part), 92595, 92596 (part)

* * *

FORTY-FOURTH DISTRICT

SONNY BONO, Republican, of Palm Springs, CA; born in Detroit, MI, February 16, 1935; graduated, Inglewood High School, Inglewood, CA, 1952; restaurateur, entertainer, songwriter, and producer; elected mayor of Palm Springs, 1988–92, by the largest margin in the city's history; balanced the city budget and eliminated a $2.5 million deficit without imposing new taxes; oversaw the creation of a master plan for urban renewal and secured federal assistance for expansion of Palm Springs Regional Airport; married Mary Whitaker Bono, 1986; four children: Christy, Chastity, Chesare, and Chianna; elected to the 104th Congress; reelected to the 105th Congress.

Office Listings

http://www.house.gov/bono

512 Cannon House Office Building, Washington, DC 20515 225–5330
Administrative Director.—Brian Nestande. FAX: 225–2961
Legislative Director.—Curt Hollmann.
Executive Director.—Beverly Swain.
Press Secretary.—Frank Cullen, Jr.
1555 South Palm Canyon Drive, Suite G101, Palm Springs, CA 92264 .... (619) 320–1076
District Director.—Joy Schlendorf.
23119–A Cottonwood Avenue, Suite 208, Moreno Valley, CA 92553 .... (909) 653–4466
Director of Constituent Liaison.—Linda Valter.
Constituent Liaison.—Tom Dryden.

County: RIVERSIDE COUNTY; that part not contained in the forty-third District, cities and townships of Aguanga, Anza, Banning, Bermuda Dunes, Beaumont, Blythe, Cabazon, Calimesa, Cathedral City, Cherry Valley, Coachella, Desert Center, Desert Hot Springs, Gilman Hot Springs, Hemet, Homeland, Idyllwild, Indian Wells, Indio, La Quinta, Mecca, part of Menifee, most of Moreno Valley, Mountain Center, part of Murrieta, North Palm Springs, North Shore, Nuevo, Oasis, Palm Desert, Palm Springs, Perris, Pinyon Pines, Rancho Mirage, Romoland, Salton City, San Jacinto, part of Sun City, part of Temecula, Thermal, Thousand Palms, Whitewater and Winchester. Population (1990), 571,583.

ZIP Codes: 92060, 92201–02, 92210, 92220, 92223, 92225–26, 92230, 92234–36, 92239–40, 92253–55, 92258, 92260–64, 92270, 92272, 92274 (part), 92276, 92282, 92320, 92324 (part), 92373 (part), 92375, 92399 (part), 92536 (part), 92539, 92543 (part), 92544, 92545 (part), 92548–49, 92552, 92553 (part), 92554–56, 92557 (part), 92561, 92563 (part), 92567, 92570 (part), 92571 (part), 92581–83, 92584 (part), 92585, 92586 (part), 92587 (part), 92591 (part), 92592 (part), 92593, 92596 (part)

* * *

FORTY-FIFTH DISTRICT

DANA ROHRABACHER, Republican, of Huntington Beach, CA; born in Coronado, CA, on June 21, 1947; graduated Palos Verdes High School, CA, 1965; attended Los Angeles Harbor College, Wilmington, CA, 1965–67; B.A., Long Beach State College, CA, 1969; M.A., University of Southern California, Los Angeles, 1975; writer/journalist; speechwriter and special assistant to the President, The White House, Washington, D.C., 1981–88; assistant press secretary, Reagan/Bush Committee, 1980; reporter, City News Service/Radio News West, and editorial writer, *Orange County Register*, 1972–80; elected on November 8, 1988, to the 101st Congress; reelected to each succeeding Congress.

Office Listings

http://www.house.gov/rohrabacher

2338 Rayburn House Office Building, Washington, DC 20515–0545 225–2415
Legislative Director.—Richard T. (Rick) Dykema. FAX: 225–0145
Communications Director.—Dale Neugebauer.
16162 Beach Boulevard, Suite 304, Huntington Beach, CA 92647–3813 .... (714) 847–2433
District Director.—Kathleen M. Hollingsworth. FAX: 847–5153

County: ORANGE COUNTY; communities of Stanton, Midway City, Westminster, Huntington Beach, Newport Beach (part), Costa Mesa, Cypress (part), Garden Grove (part), Fountain Valley, Buena Park (part), Anaheim (part), Surfside, Seal Beach and Sunset Beach. Population (1990), 570,874.

ZIP Codes: 90620 (part), 90630 (part), 90680 (part), 90720 (part), 90740 (part), 90742–43, 92605, 92615, 92626 (part), 92627 (part), 92628, 92641 (part), 92644 (part), 92645–49, 92655, 92659, 92660 (part), 92661–62, 92663 (part), 92683 (part), 92684, 92704 (part), 92707 (part), 92708 (part), 92728, 92801 (part), 92804 (part)

* * *

FORTY-SIXTH DISTRICT

LORETTA SANCHEZ, Democrat, of Anaheim, CA; born in Lynwood, CA, January 7, 1960; graduate of Chapman University; graduate studies at American University; specializes in assisting public agencies with finance matters; member, congressional Women's and Hispanic caucuses; married to Steven Phbrixey; committees: Education and the Workforce, National Security; elected to the 105th Congress.

Office Listings

1529 Longworth House Office Building, Washington, DC 20515–0546 225–2965
Chief of Staff.—Steve Jost. FAX: 225–5859
Legislative Director.—Mauro Morales.
Legislative Assistant.—Laura Rodriguez.
Legislative Correspondents.—Katie Efstratis, Aylin Kuyumcu.
Office Manager/Scheduler.—Cynthia Contreras.
12397 Lewis Street, Suite 101, Garden Grove, CA 92840 .... (714) 621–0102
District Director.—Nancy Ramirez. FAX: 621–0410
Field Representatives.—Armando Ramirez, Xuan Vu.
Press Secretary.—Josie Cabiglio.

County: ORANGE COUNTY; cities of Anaheim (west and north-south Anaheim Stadium-Disneyland corridor), Buena Park, Costa Mesa, Fountain Valley, Garden Grove, Irvine, Orange, Santa Ana, Stanton, Tustin, and Westminster (north of San Diego Freeway). Population (1990), 571,380.

ZIP Codes: 92626 (part), 92632 (part), 92640, 92641 (part), 92642–43, 92644 (part), 92668 (part), 92680 (part), 92683 (part), 92701 (part), 92702–03, 92704 (part), 92705 (part), 92706 (part), 92707 (part), 92708 (part), 92710–12, 92714 (part), 92716–17, 92799, 92801 (part), 92802–03, 92804 (part), 92805 (part), 92806 (part), 92812, 92814–15, 92817, 92840

* * *

FORTY-SEVENTH DISTRICT

CHRISTOPHER COX, Republican, of Newport Beach, CA; born in St. Paul, Ramsey County, MN, October 16, 1952; graduated, St. Thomas Academy, St. Paul, 1970; B.A., University of Southern California, Los Angeles, 1973; J.D., Harvard Law School, Cambridge, MA, 1977; M.B.A., Harvard Business School, Boston, MA, 1977; attorney; admitted to the California bar in 1978 and commenced practice in Los Angeles; law clerk, U.S. Court of Appeals, San Francisco, CA, and Honolulu, HI, 1977–78; associate, Latham and Watkins, Newport Beach, CA, 1978–84; cofounder, Context Corporation, St. Paul, MN, 1984–86; partner, Latham and Watkins, Newport Beach, CA, 1984–86; senior associate counsel to the President, The White House, 1986–88; member: Republican Associates, California Republican Assembly, Rotary Club of Orange County; married to Rebecca Gernhardt Cox; two children: Charles and Kathryn; elected November 8, 1988, to the 101st Congress; reelected to each succeeding Congress.

Office Listings

http://www.house.gov/chriscox ccox@hr.house.gov

2402 Rayburn House Office Building, Washington, DC 20515–0547 225–5611
Chief of Staff.—Jan Fujiwara. FAX: 225–9177
Scheduler/Secretary.—Linda Hansen.
Suite 430, 4000 MacArthur Boulevard, Newport Beach, CA 92660 .... (714) 756–2244
District Representative.—Greg Haskin.
Scheduler/Secretary.—Susi Kulda.

County: ORANGE COUNTY; that part not contained in the Thirty-eighth, Thirty-ninth, Forty-second, and Forty-third Districts, includes Aliso Viejo (part), Anaheim (part), Corona del Mar, Foothill Ranch, Irvine, Laguna Beach, Laguna Hills, Lake Forest, Mission Viejo (part), Newport Beach (part), Orange, Silverado, Trabuco Canyon, Santa Ana (part), Tustin, and Villa Park. Population (1990), 571,380.

ZIP Codes: 92602–04, 92606, 92612, 92618, 92620, 92625, 92630, 92650–54, 92656–57, 92660, 92691, 92705, 92776, 92778–82, 92805–08, 92856–57, 92859, 92861, 92863–65, 92867–69

* * *

FORTY-EIGHTH DISTRICT

RON PACKARD, Republican, of Oceanside, CA; born in Meridian, ID, January 19, 1931; graduated, Meridian High School, 1948; attended Brigham Young University, Provo, UT, 1948–50; Portland State University, Portland, 1952–53; D.M.D., University of Oregon Dental School, Portland, OR, 1957; lieutenant, U.S. Navy Dental Corps, 1957–59; dentist; Carlsbad School District Board, 1960–72; director, Carlsbad Chamber of Commerce, 1972–76; member: Carlsbad Planning Commission, 1974–76; Carlsbad City Council, 1976–78; Carlsbad chairman of the Boy Scouts of America, 1977–79; mayor of Carlsbad, 1978–82; member: North County Armed Services YMCA; North County Transit District; San Diego Association for Government; Coastal Policy Committee and Transportation Policy Committee; California League of Cities; president, San Diego Division of the League of California Cities; Mormon Church; married to the former Jean Sorenson; seven children: Chris, Debbie, Jeff, Vicki, Scott, Lisa, and Theresa; elected on November 2, 1982, to the 98th Congress; reelected to each succeeding Congress; member: House Appropriations Committee.

Office Listings

http://www.house.gov/packard rep.packard@hr.house.gov

2162 Rayburn House Office Building, Washington, DC 20515–0548 225–3906
Administrative Assistant.—David Coggin. FAX: 225–0134
Legislative Director.—Ray Mock.
Executive Assistant/Scheduler.—Mary Kouvelis.
221 East Vista Way, Suite 205, Vista, CA 92084 .... (619) 631–1364
629 Camino del los Mares, Suite 204, San Clemente, CA 92673 .... (714) 496–2343
District Director.—Michael Eggers.

Counties: Portions of San Diego, Riverside and Orange.

ZIP Codes: 92003, 92008 (part), 92026 (part), 92028, 92036 (part), 92049, 92054, 92056 (part), 92057–59, 92061, 92065 (part), 92066, 92068, 92069 (part), 92070, 92082 (part), 92083 (part), 92084 (part), 92085–86, 92088, 92536 (part), 92562 (part), 92589, 92590 (part), 92591 (part), 92592 (part), 92607, 92624, 92629, 92630 (part), 92653 (part), 92656 (part), 92672–75, 92677 (part), 92678, 92679 (part), 92688, 92690, 92691 (part), 92692–93

* * *

FORTY-NINTH DISTRICT

BRIAN BILBRAY, Republican, of Imperial Beach, CA; born in Coronado, CA, January 28, 1951; graduated Mar Vista High School; attended South Western College; tax consultant; city council, Imperial Beach, CA, 1976–78; mayor, Imperial Beach, 1978–85; San Diego County Board of Supervisors, 1985–95; member, Fleet Reserve Association; married Karen Bilbray, 1984; five children: Scott Palmer, Kristen Palmer, Shannan Palmer, Bryan Patrick Bilbray, and Briana Bilbray; elected to the 104th Congress; reelected to the 105th Congress.

Office Listings

http://www.house.gov/bilbray bilbray@hr.house.gov

1530 Longworth House Office Building, Washington DC 20515–0549 225–2040
Chief of Staff.—John Woodard.
Legislative Director.—Dave Schroeder.
Press Secretary.—Ion Valaskakis.
Office Manager/Scheduler.—Suzanne Michel.
1011 Camino Del Rio South, Suite 330, San Diego, CA 92108 .... (619) 291–1430
District Director.—Steve Danon.

County: SAN DIEGO (part), Imperial Beach, Coronado. Population (1990), 573,362.

ZIP Codes: 91932 (part), 91933, 91942 (part), 92014, 92037, 92038–39, 92101, 92102 (part), 92103, 92104 (part), 92105 (part), 92106–12, 92113 (part), 92115 (part), 92116–18, 92119 (part), 92120 (part), 92121 (part), 92122 (part), 92123, 92124 (part), 92133, 92135, 92137–38, 92140, 92160, 92163–64, 92166–69, 92171, 92175–78, 92186, 92188–90, 92192–95, 92197

* * *

FIFTIETH DISTRICT

BOB FILNER, Democrat, of San Diego, CA; born on September 4, 1942, in Pittsburgh, PA; B.A., Cornell University, Ithaca, NY, 1963; M.A., University of Delaware, 1969; Ph.D., Cornell University, 1973; professor, San Diego State University, 1970–92; San Diego Board of Education, 1979–83 (president, 1982); San Diego City Council, 1987–92 (deputy mayor, 1990); member: Sierra Club, NAACP, Navy League, Gray Panthers, Economic Conversion Council, Common Cause, ACLU, ADL, NWPC, MAPA; married in 1985 to Jane Merrill Filner; two children: Erin and Adam; elected on November 3, 1992 to the 103rd Congress; reelected to each succeeding Congress.

Office Listings

330 Cannon House Office Building, Washington, DC 20515–0550 225–8045
Chief of Staff.—Francisco Estrada. FAX: 225–9073
Executive Secretary.—Kara Hughes.
Legislative Director.—Francisco Estrada.
District Administrator.—Lisa Hirsch Medina.
333 F Street, Suite A, Chula Vista, CA 91910 .... (619) 422–5963

County: SAN DIEGO COUNTY (part); cities of Bonita, Chula Vista, Lemon Grove (part), National City, San Diego (part) and Spring Valley (part). Population (1990), 573,463.

ZIP Codes: 91902, 91908–15, 91932 (part), 91941 (part), 91945 (part), 91947–48, 91950–51, 91977 (part), 92102 (part), 92104 (part), 92105 (part), 92113 (part), 92114 (part), 92115 (part), 92136, 92139, 92143, 92149, 92153–54, 92162, 92165, 92170, 92173–74

* * *

FIFTY-FIRST DISTRICT

RANDY (DUKE) CUNNINGHAM, Republican, of Del Mar, CA; born in Los Angeles, CA, December 8, 1941; graduated, Shelbina High School, Shelbina, MO; University of Missouri, B.S. in education, 1964, and M.S. in education, 1965; M.B.A., National University, San Diego, CA; dean, School of Aviation and Flight Training, and businessman; coached swim teams at Hinsdale and at the University of Missouri, training 36 All Americans, two Olympic gold and silver medalists; member: Naval Aviation Hall of Fame, 1986–present; Golden Eagles, 1985–present; Miramar Aviation Hall of Fame, 1974–present; American Fighter Aces Association, 1972–present; author of ''Fox Two,'' on his experiences as a naval aviator, and produced ''Top Gun—The Story Behind the Story'' video about his career as a fighter pilot instructor at Miramar NAS; joined the Navy at the age of 25 and became one of the most highly decorated fighter pilots in the Vietnam War; retired in 1987 with the rank of commander; married the former Nancy Jones; three children: Randall Todd, April, and Carrie; member: National Security and Economic and Educational Opportunities committees; elected to the 102nd Congress, November 6, 1990; reelected to each succeeding Congress.

Office Listings

http://www.house.gov/cunningham

227 Cannon House Office Building, Washington, DC 20515–0551 225–5452
Chief of Staff.—Frank C. Collins III. FAX: 225–2558
Legislative Director.—W. Lindsay Lloyd III.
Executive Assistant.—Sharon Dorazio.
Press Secretary.—Patrick McSwain.
613 West Valley Parkway, Suite 320, Escondido, CA 92025 .... (619) 737–8438
District Director.—Kathy Stafford-Taulbee.

County: SAN DIEGO COUNTY; city of San Diego, in part or in whole the communities of San Carlos, Sorrento Valley, Tierrasanta, Mira Mesa, Rancho Bernardo, Peñasquitos, Carmel Valley and Scripps Ranch. Also in part or in whole the cities of Cardiff-by-the-Sea, Carlsbad, Del Mar, Encinitas, Escondido, Oceanside, Poway, Solana Beach, San Marcos, Valley Center, Vista Raindora and Rancho Santa Fe. Population (1990), 572,982.

ZIP Codes: 92007, 92008 (part), 92009, 92014 (part), 92018, 92023–25, 92026 (part), 92027, 92029–30, 92033, 92040 (part), 92056 (part), 92064 (part), 92065 (part), 92067, 92069 (part), 92071 (part), 92074–75, 92079, 92082 (part), 92083 (part), 92084 (part), 92119 (part), 92120 (part), 92121 (part), 92122 (part), 92124 (part), 92126–31, 92142, 92145, 92159, 92172, 92191, 92196, 92198

* * *

FIFTY-SECOND DISTRICT

DUNCAN HUNTER, Republican, of Alpine, CA; born in Riverside, CA, May 31, 1948; graduated, Rubidoux High School, 1966; J.D., Western State University, 1976; first lieutenant, U.S. Army Airborne, 1969–71; trial lawyer; admitted to the California bar, 1976; commenced practice in San Diego; member: Baptist Church, Navy League; married the former Lynne Layh, 1973; two sons: Duncan Duane and Robert Samuel; elected to the 97th Congress, November 4, 1980; reelected to each succeeding Congress.

Office Listings

2265 Rayburn House Office Building, Washington, DC 20515–0552 225–5672
Administrative Assistant.—Victoria Middleton. FAX: 225–0235
Office Manager/Appointment Secretary.—Melinda Patterson.
Press Secretary.—Harald Stavenas.
366 South Pierce Street, El Cajon, CA 92020 .... (619) 579–3001
Suite G, 1101 Airport Road, Imperial, CA 92251 .... (619) 353–5420
Suite C, 1410 Main Street, Ramona, CA 92065 .... (619) 788–3630

Counties: Imperial County, San Diego County. CITIES AND TOWNSHIPS: Alpine, Bard, Barona I.R., Borrego Springs, Boulder Park, Boulevard, Brawley, Calexico, Calipatria, Campo, Descanso, Dulzura, El Centro NAF, El Cajon, El Centro, Guatay, Indian Res., Jacumba, Jamul, Julian, Lakeside, La Mesa, Lemon Grove, Mount Laguna, Pine Valley, Potrero, Poway, Ramona, San Diego, Santee, Seeley, Spring Valley, Tecate, Glamis, Heber, Holtville, Imperial, Mecca, Niland, Ocotillo, Palo Verde, Plaster City, Thermal, Westmoreland, and Winterhaven. Population (1990), 573,203.

ZIP Codes: 91901, 91903, 91905–06, 91916–17, 91931, 91934–35, 91941 (part), 91942 (part), 91943–44, 91945 (part), 91946, 91948, 91962–63, 91976, 91977 (part), 91978–80, 91987, 91990–91, 92004, 92019–22, 92036 (part), 92040 (part), 92064 (part), 92065 (part), 92071 (part), 92072, 92090, 92114 (part), 92115 (part), 92119 (part), 92120 (part), 92222, 92227, 92231–33, 92243–44, 92249–51, 92254, 92257, 92259, 92266, 92269, 92273, 92274 (part), 92275, 92281, 92283

COLORADO

(Population 1995, 3,747,000)

SENATORS

BEN NIGHTHORSE CAMPBELL, Republican, of Ignacio, CO; born in Auburn, CA, April 13, 1933; attended Placer High School, Auburn, CA, 1951; quit high school to join Air Force (where he got his GED); attended graduation exercises and received a diploma in 1991; B.A., San Jose State, 1957; attended Meiji University in Toyko, Japan, as special research student, 1960–64; served in U.S. Air Force in Korea, airman second class, 1951–53; jewelry designer who has won more than 200 first-place and best-of-show awards; rancher who raised, trained, and showed horses; All-American in judo, captain of the U.S. Olympic Judo Team in 1964, gold medal in the Pan-American Games of 1963; elected to Colorado State Legislature in 1982, serving 1983–86 on the Agriculture and Natural Affairs and Business and Labor committees; appointed advisor to the Colorado Commission on International Trade and Colorado Commission on the Arts and Humanities; voted by colleagues one of "Ten Best Legislators" in the Denver Post-News Center 4 survey, 1984; "1984 Outstanding Legislator" award from Colorado Bankers Association; inducted into the Council of 44 Chiefs, Northern Cheyenne Indian Tribe; member of Durango Chamber of Commerce, American Quarter Horse Association, American Paint Horse Association, American Brangus Association, American Indian Education Association, Colorado Pilots Association, Aircraft Owners and Pilot Association; senior technical advisor, U.S. Judo Association; married Linda Price, July 23, 1966; two children: Colin and Shanan; elected to the 100th Congress, November 4, 1986; reelected to the 101st and 102nd Congresses; appointed to Committees on Agriculture, Interior and Insular Affairs, and Small Business; elected to the U.S. Senate on November 3, 1992 for the six-year term beginning January 3, 1993; committees: Energy and Natural Resources; Veterans' Affairs; Indian Affairs, chair; Appropriations; chair, Subcommittee on Treasury, Postal Service, and General Government; vice chair, Subcommittee on National Parks, Historic Preservation, and Recreation.

Office Listings

http://www.senate.gov/senator/campbell.html

380 Russell Senate Office Building, Washington, DC 20510–0605 224–5852
Chief of Staff.—Ginnie Kontnik.
Legislative Director.—Warren Schaeffer.
Executive Assistant.—Jeani Frickey.
Press Secretary.—Alton Dillard.
1129 Pennsylvania Street, Denver, CO 80203 .... (303) 866–1900
743 Horizon Court, Suite 366, Grand Junction, CO 81506 .... (970) 241–6631
835 Second Avenue, Suite 228, Durango, CO 81301 .... (970) 247–1609
720 North Main Street, Suite 410, Pueblo, CO 81003 .... (719) 542–6987
19 Old Town Square, Suite 238, Ft. Collins, CO 80524 .... (970) 224–1909
105 East Vermijo, Suite 600, Colorado Springs, CO 80903 .... (719) 636–9092

WAYNE ALLARD, Republican, of Loveland, CO; born in Fort Collins, CO, December 2, 1943; graduated, Fort Collins High School, 1963; preveterinary studies, Colorado State University, 1964; Doctor of Veterinary Medicine, Colorado State University, 1968; received veterinarian license in Colorado; Chief Health Officer, Loveland, CO, 1970–78; Larimer County Board of Health, 1978–82; Colorado State Senate, 1982–90; chair, Health and Human Services Committee and majority caucus; member: American Veterinary Medical Association, National Federation of Independent Business, Chamber of Commerce, Loveland Rotary, American Animal Hospital Association, American Board of Veterinary Practitioners, Companion Animal; married to the former Joan Elizabeth Malcolm; two children: Christi and Cheryl; committees: Banking, Housing, and Urban Affairs; Environment and Public Works; Intelligence; elected to the 102nd Congress, November 6, 1990; reelected to each succeeding Congress; elected to the U.S. Senate on November 6, 1996.

Office Listings

http://www.senate.gov/senator/allard.html

513 Hart Senate Office Building, Washington, DC 20510–0604 224–5941
Chief of Staff.—Roy Palmer. FAX: 224–6471
Administrative Assistant.—Mike Bennett.
Scheduler.—Wendy Evans.
Suite 215, 7340 East Caley, Englewood, CO 80111 .... (303) 220–7414
Suite 3Q, 3400 16th Street, Greeley, CO 80631 .... (970) 351–7582
Suite 106, 228 North Cascade Avenue, Colorado Springs, CO 80903 .... (719) 634–6071

411 Thatcher Building, Fifth and Main Streets, Pueblo, CO 81003 .... (719) 545–9751
215 Federal Building, 400 Rood Avenue, Grand Junction, CO 81501 .... (970) 245–9553

* * *

REPRESENTATIVES

FIRST DISTRICT

DIANA L. DEGETTE, Democrat, of Denver, CO; born on July 29, 1957, in Tachikowa, Japan; B.A., political science, *magna cum laude*, The Colorado College, 1979; J.D., New York University School of Law, 1982 (Root Tilden Scholar); attorney with McDermott, Hansen, and Reilly; Colorado Deputy State Public Defender, Appellate Division, 1982-84; Colorado House of Representatives, 1992-96; board of directors, Planned Parenthood, Rocky Mountain Chapter; member and formerly on board of governors, Colorado Bar Association; member, Colorado Women's Bar Association; past memberships: board of trustees, The Colorado College; Denver Women's Commission; board of directors, Colorado Trial Lawyers Association; former editor, *Trial Talk* magazine; listed in 1994-96 edition of *Who's Who in America*; elected to the 105th Congress.

Office Listings

1404 Longworth House Office Building, Washington, DC 20515–0601 225–4431
Administrative Assistant.—Lisa B. Cohen. FAX: 225–5842
Appointment Secretary.—Bertha Ramlow.
Press Secretary.—Chris Robichoux.
1400 Glenarm Place, Suite 202, Denver, CO 80203 .... (303) 844–4988
District Administrator.—Edgar Neel.

Counties: Adams (part), Arapahoe (part), Denver, Jefferson (part). Population (1990), 549,068.

ZIP Codes: 80010 (part), 80011 (part), 80014 (part), 80022 (part), 80024, 80037, 80040–42, 80045, 80110 (part), 80111 (part), 80112 (part), 80123 (part), 80201–11, 80212 (part), 80214 (part), 80216–20, 80221 (part), 80222–25, 80226 (part), 80227 (part), 80229 (part), 80230, 80231 (part), 80232 (part), 80235 (part), 80236 (part), 80237–39, 80243–44, 80248–52, 80254–56, 80259, 80261–66, 80270–71, 80273–75, 80279–81, 80290–95

* * *

SECOND DISTRICT

DAVID E. SKAGGS, Democrat, of Boulder, CO; born in Cincinnati, OH, on February 22, 1943; B.A., Wesleyan University, Middletown, CT, 1964; LL.B., Yale Law School, New Haven, CT, 1967; served in U.S. Marine Corps, captain, 1968–71; U.S. Marine Corps Reserves, 1971–77, promoted to major, 1975; attorney; admitted to the New York State bar, 1968, and the Colorado State bar, 1971, and commenced practice in Boulder; administrative assistant to former Congressman Timothy Wirth, 1975–77; elected to the Colorado House of Representatives, 1980–86; House Minority Leader, 1982–85; married the former Laura Locher, 1987; one son, Matthew; two stepchildren: Clare and Will; elected to the 100th Congress on November 4, 1986; reelected to each succeeding Congress.

Office Listings

http://www.house.gov/skaggs skaggs@hr.house.gov

1124 Longworth House Office Building, Washington, DC 20515–0602 225–2161
Chief of Staff.—Stephen Saunders.
Executive Assistant.—Kelly Nelson.
Press Secretary.—Brooke Anderson.
Suite 130, 9101 Harlan Street, Westminster, CO 80030 .... (303) 650–7886
District Director.—Susan Damour.

Counties: Adams (part), Boulder, Clear Creek, Gilpin, Jefferson (part). Population (1990), 549,072.

ZIP Codes: 80001, 80002 (part), 80003–06, 80020 (part), 80021, 80025–28, 80030, 80033 (part), 80034, 80038, 80212 (part), 80214 (part), 80215 (part), 80221 (part), 80229 (part), 80233 (part), 80234 (part), 80241 (part), 80301–04, 80306–10, 80314, 80321–23, 80328–29, 80401 (part), 80403 (part), 80422, 80427, 80436, 80438, 80439 (part), 80444, 80452, 80455, 80466, 80471, 80474, 80476, 80481, 80501 (part), 80502–03, 80504 (part), 80510, 80516, 80533, 80540 (part), 80544, 80601 (part), 80614

THIRD DISTRICT

SCOTT McINNIS, Republican, of Glenwood Springs, CO; born and raised in Glenwood Springs; graduated from Glenwood Springs High School; attended Mesa College in Grand Junction; received B.A. in business administration from Fort Lewis College in Durango; earned law degree from St. Mary's University in San Antonio; worked as police officer in Glenwood Springs, 1976; director of the Valley View Hospital; director of personnel at Holy Cross Electric Association; served in the Colorado legislature; chaired the Committee on Agriculture, Livestock, and Natural Resources; served on the Judiciary, Local Government and Appropriations Committee for 10 years; House majority leader, 1990–92; the only elected official ever to receive the Florence Sabin Award for contributions to rural health care and received several awards from the United Veterans Commission of Colorado; member, Colorado Tourism Board; Colorado Ski Country's Legislator of the Year and Legislative Achievement of the Decade; received the Lee Atwater Leadership Award for outstanding contributions and extraordinary achievements in public service; twice received the National Federation of Independent Business and Guardian of Small Business Award; married to the former Lori Smith; three children: Daxon, Tessa, and Andrea; elected November 3, 1992 to the 103rd Congress; reelected to each succeeding Congress; serves on the Committee on Rules.

Office Listings

215 Cannon House Office Building, Washington, DC 20515–0603 225–4761
FAX: 226–0622
Chief of Staff.—Stephannie Finley.
Legislative Director.—David Bernhardt.
Press Secretary.—Will Bos.
District Administrator.—Roger Gomez.

327 North Seventh Street, Grand Junction, CO 81501 .... (303) 245–7107
FAX: 245–2194

134 West B Street, Pueblo, CO 81003 .... (719) 543–8200
FAX: 543–8204

Old Main Post Office-Professional Building, 1060 Main Avenue, Suite 101, Durango, CO 81301 .... (303) 259–2754
FAX: 259–2762

Hotel Colorado, 526 Pine Street, Suite 111, Glenwood Springs, CO 81601 .... (303) 928–0637
FAX: 928–0630

Counties: Alamosa, Archuleta, Chaffee, Conejos, Costilla, Custer, Delta, Dolores, Douglas (part), Eagle, Fremont (part), Garfield, Grand, Gunnison, Hinsdale, Huerfano, Jackson, Jefferson (part), Lake, La Plata, Mesa, Mineral, Moffat, Montezuma, Montrose, Ouray, Park, Pitkin, Pueblo, Rio Blanco, Rio Grande, Routt, Saguache, San Juan, San Miguel, and Summit. Population (1990), 549,062.

ZIP Codes: 80104 (part), 80118 (part), 80127 (part), 80131, 80135 (part), 80420–21, 80423–24, 80426, 80428–30, 80432, 80433 (part), 80434–35, 80440–43, 80446–49, 80451, 80456, 80459, 80461, 80463, 80467–69, 80470 (part), 80473, 80475, 80477–80, 80482–83, 80487–88, 80498, 80816, 80820, 80827, 81001–08, 81019, 81022–23, 81025, 81040, 81055, 81066, 81069, 81089, 81101, 81120–38, 81140–41, 81143–44, 81146–49, 81151–55, 81157, 81201 (part), 81210–11, 81212 (part), 81215, 81220, 81224–25, 81228, 81230, 81232, 81233 (part), 81235–37, 81239, 81241–43, 81247–49, 81251–52, 81253 (part), 81301–02, 81320–21, 81323–35, 81401–02, 81410–11, 81413–16, 81418–20, 81422–35, 81501–06, 81520–27, 81601–02, 81610–12, 81615, 81620–21, 81623–26, 81628, 81630–33, 81635–43, 81645–50, 81652–58

* * *

FOURTH DISTRICT

BOB SCHAFFER, Republican, of Fort Collins, CO; born in Cincinnati, OH, July 24, 1962; B.S., political science, University of Dayton, 1984; legislative assistant; Colorado State Senator, 1987–96; former press secretary for Republican Senators, Colorado General Assembly; named National Legislator of the Year, 1995, by National Republican Legislators Association, Business Legislator of the Year by Colorado Association of Commerce and Industry, Guardian of Small Business by the National Federation of Independent Business, and Taxpayer Champion by the Colorado Union of Taxpayers; married to Maureen Schaffer; four children: Jennifer, Emily, Justin and Sarah; committees: Education and the Workforce, Agriculture, Resources; elected to the 105th Congress.

Office Listings

212 Cannon House Office Building, Washington, DC 20515 225–4676
Chief of Staff.—Susan Wadhams. FAX: 225–5870
Legislative Assistants.—Cory Flohr, Rob Nanfelt, Marcus Dunn.
Legislative Correspondent.—Scott Slusher.
Scheduler.—Brandi Graham.
Rocky Mountain Bank Building, 315 West Oak Street, Suite 307, Fort Collins, CO 80521 .... (970) 493–9132
District Director.—Tom Lynch. FAX: 493–9144
Field Representative.—Sean Murphy.
Press Secretary.—Nancy Hunter.
705 S. Division Avenue, Sterling, CO 80571 .... (970) 522–1788
District Aide.—Marge Klein. FAX: 522–1789
Madison and Main Building, 801 Eighth Street, Suite 220E, Greeley, CO 80631 ... (970) 353–3507
FAX: 353–3509

Counties: Adams (part), Arapahoe (part), Baca, Bent, Cheyenne, Crowley, Elbert, Kiowa, Kit Carson, Larimer, Las Animas, Lincoln, Logan, Morgan, Otero, Phillips, Prowers, Sedgwick, Washington, Weld, and Yuma. Population (1990), 549,070.

ZIP Codes: 69128, 69140, 69168, 80011 (part), 80013 (part), 80015 (part), 80016 (part), 80018 (part), 80022 (part), 80101–03, 80105, 80106 (part), 80107, 80117, 80134 (part), 80136–37, 80229 (part), 80234 (part), 80241 (part), 80511–15, 80517, 80520–26, 80530, 80532, 80534–43, 80545–50, 80601 (part), 80610–12, 80615, 80620–24, 80631–34, 80640, 80642–46, 80648–54, 80701, 80720–23, 80726–29, 80731–37, 80740–47, 80749–51, 80754–55, 80757–59, 80801–02, 80804–07, 80810, 80812, 80815, 80818, 80821–25, 80828, 80830, 80834–36, 80861–62, 81020–21, 81024, 81027–30, 81032–34, 81036, 81038–39, 81041–47, 81049–50, 81052, 81054, 81057–59, 81062–64, 81067, 81070–71, 81073–74, 81076–77, 81081–82, 81084, 81087, 81090–92

* * *

FIFTH DISTRICT

JOEL HEFLEY, Republican, of Colorado Springs, CO; born in Ardmore, OK, on April 18, 1935; graduated, Classen High School, Oklahoma City, OK, 1953; B.A., Oklahoma Baptist University, Shawnee, 1957; M.A., Oklahoma State University, Stillwater, 1962; Gates Fellow, Harvard University, Cambridge, MA, 1984; management consultant; executive director, Community Planning and Research Council, 1966–86; Colorado State House of Representatives, 1977–78; Colorado State Senate, 1979–86; member: committees on National Security, Resources, Small Business; assistant minority whip, 1989–94; married the former Lynn Christian, 1961; three children: Janna, Lori, and Juli; elected to the 100th Congress on November 4, 1986; reelected to each succeeding Congress.

Office Listings

2351 Rayburn House Office Building, Washington, DC 20515–0605 225–4422
Scheduler.—Anna Osborne. FAX: 225–1942
104 South Cascade Avenue, Suite 105, Colorado Springs, CO 80903 .... (719) 520–0055
District Director.—Connie Scott Solomon.
Creekside II, 6053 South Quebec Street, Suite 103, Englewood, CO 80111 .... (303) 843–0401
Office Manager.—Angela D'Aurio.

Counties: Arapahoe, Douglas, El Paso, Fremont (part), and Teller. Population (1990), 549,066.

ZIP Codes: 80015 (part), 80016 (part), 80104 (part), 80106 (part), 80111 (part), 80112 (part), 80116, 80118 (part), 80120 (part), 80121 (part), 80122 (part), 80124–26, 80132–33, 80134 (part), 80135 (part), 80161, 80808–09, 80813–14, 80816–17, 80819, 80827, 80829, 80831–33, 80840–41, 80860, 80863–64, 80866, 80901, 80903–11, 80913–22, 80925–26, 80928–37, 80949, 80960, 80962, 81201 (part), 81212 (part), 81221–23, 81226, 81233 (part), 81240, 81244, 81253 (part)

* * *

SIXTH DISTRICT

DAN SCHAEFER, Republican, of Lakewood, CO; born on January 25, 1936, in Guttenberg, IA; B.A., Niagara University, Niagara, NY, 1961; public relations consultant, 1967–83; Colorado General Assembly, 1977–78; Colorado State Senate, 1979–83; member: West Chamber of Commerce, South Metro Chamber of Commerce, Golden Chamber of Commerce, Englewood Chamber of Commerce, Evergreen Chamber of Commerce, Conifer Chamber of Commerce, Century Club, Chatfield YMCA, Chatfield Jaycees; Honorary Doctor of Laws (1986), Niagara University, Niagara, NY; married the former Mary Lenney, 1959; four children: Danny, Darren, Joel, and Jennifer; elected by special election on March 29, 1983, to fill the vacancy caused by the death of Congressman-elect John L. Swigert; reelected to each succeeding Congress.

Office Listings

http://www.house.gov/schaefer schaefer@hr.house.gov

2160 Rayburn House Office Building, Washington, DC 20515–0606 225–7882
Chief of Staff.—Holly Propst.
Senior Legislative Assistant.—Patrick O'Keefe.
Press Secretary.—Dana Perino.
Suite 101, 3615 South Huron Street, Englewood, CO 80110 .... (303) 762–8890
District Director.—Andree Krause.

Counties: Arapahoe (part) and Jefferson (part). Population (1990), 549,056.

ZIP Codes: 80010 (part), 80011 (part), 80012 (part), 80013 (part), 80014 (part), 80015 (part), 80017, 80044, 80110 (part), 80111 (part), 80120 (part), 80121, 80122 (part), 80123 (part), 80127 (part), 80150–51, 80154–55, 80160 (part), 80162, 80214 (part), 80215 (part), 80226, 80227 (part), 80228, 80231 (part), 80232 (part), 80235, 80236 (part), 80401 (part), 80402, 80403 (part), 80419, 80433 (part), 80439 (part), 80453–54, 80457, 80465, 80470 (part)

CONNECTICUT

(Population 1995, 3,275,000)

SENATORS

CHRISTOPHER J. DODD, Democrat, of East Haddam, CT; born in Willimantic, CT, May 27, 1944, son of Thomas J. and Grace Murphy Dodd; graduated, Georgetown Preparatory School, 1962; B.A., English Literature, Providence College, 1966; J.D., University of Louisville School of Law, 1972; admitted to Connecticut bar, 1973; served in U.S. Army Reserves, 1969–75; Peace Corps volunteer, Dominican Republic, 1966–68; elected to the 94th Congress, November 5, 1974; reelected to the 95th and 96th Congresses; first elected to the U.S. Senate, November 4, 1980; reelected for six-year terms November 4, 1986, and November 3, 1992; founded the Senate Children's Caucus; served on the Rules Committee, Judiciary Committee, and Science and Technology Committee; appointed to the Select Committee on the Outer Continental Shelf and the Select Committee on Assassinations; committees: Foreign Relations; Banking, Housing and Urban Affairs; Labor and Human Resources; Rules and Administration; ranking member: Subcommittee on Western Hemisphere, Peace Corps, Narcotics and Terrorism; Subcommittee on Financial Services and Technology; Subcommittee on Securities; Subcommittee on Children and Families.

Office Listings

http://www.senate.gov/~dodd sen_dodd@dodd.senate.gov

444 Russell Senate Office Building, Washington, DC 20510–0702 224–2823
Legislative Director.—Shawn Maher.
Putnam Park, 100 Great Meadow Road, Wethersfield, CT 06109 .... (203) 240–3470
State Director.—Ed Mann.

* * *

JOSEPH I. LIEBERMAN, Democrat, of New Haven, CT; born in Stamford, CT, February 24, 1942; attended Stamford public schools; B.A., Yale University, 1964; law degree, Yale Law School, 1967; Connecticut State Senate, 1970–80; majority leader, 1974–80; honorary degrees: Yeshiva University, University of Hartford; Connecticut's 21st attorney general, 1983; reelected in 1986; author of "The Power-Broker" (Houghton Mifflin Company, 1966), a biography of late Democratic Party chairman John M. Bailey; "The Scorpion and the Tarantula" (Houghton Mifflin Company, 1970), a study of early efforts to control nuclear proliferation; "The Legacy" (Spoonwood Press, 1981), a history of Connecticut politics from 1930–80; and "Child Support in America" (Yale University Press, 1986); married to Hadassah Lieberman; children: Matthew, Rebecca, Ethan, and Hana; committees: Armed Services, Environment and Public Works, Governmental Affairs, Small Business; member, Gulf Pollution Task Force; vice chairman, Democratic Leadership Council; elected on November 8, 1988, to the U.S. Senate for the six-year term beginning on January 3, 1989.

Office Listings

http://www.senate.gov/~lieberman senator_lieberman@lieberman.senate.gov

706 Hart Senate Office Building, Washington, DC 20510–0703 224–4041
Administrative Assistant.—William Andresen. FAX: 224–9750
Executive Assistant.—Carleen Morris.
Legislative Director.—William B. Bonvillian.
One State Street, 14th Floor, Hartford, CT 06103 .... (860) 549–8463
State Director.—Sherry Brown.

REPRESENTATIVES

FIRST DISTRICT

BARBARA B. KENNELLY, Democrat, of Hartford, CT; born in Hartford, July 10, 1936; graduated, Mount St. Joseph Academy, West Hartford; B.A., economics, Trinity College, Washington, DC; certificate of completion, Harvard-Radcliffe Program in Business Administration, Harvard Business School, Cambridge, MA; M.A., government, Trinity College, Hartford; honorary doctorates: Sacred Heart University, Bridgeport, CT, 1981; Mount Holyoke College, South Hadley, MA, 1984; University of Hartford, West Hartford, CT, 1985; St. Mary's College, Notre Dame, IN, 1986; Simmons College, Boston, MA; Teikyo Post University, Waterbury, CT: Secretary of the State of Connecticut, 1979–82; Hartford Court of Common Council, 1975–79; vice chairman, House Democratic Caucus; member, House Ways and Means Committee; subcommittee: Social Security; four children; elected to the 97th Congress, January 12, 1982; reelected to each succeeding Congress.

Office Listings

http://www.house.gov/kennelly kennelly@mail.house.gov

201 Cannon House Office Building, Washington, DC 20515–0701 225–2265
Administrative Assistant.—Ross Brown. FAX: 225–1031
Executive Assistant.—Emma Lee Harrell.
One Corporate Center, Hartford, CT 06103 .... (860) 278–8888
District Director.—Robert Croce.

Counties: Hartford (part), Middlesex (part), and Tolland (part). Population (1990), 548,016.

ZIP Codes: 06001 (part), 06002, 06016, 06023, 06025, 06026 (part), 06028, 06033, 06037, 06040, 06043 (part), 06045, 06049, 06064, 06066 (part), 06067, 06073–74, 06088, 06095, 06102–06, 06107 (part), 06108–12, 06114–15, 06117–20, 06123, 06126–29, 06131–34, 06137–38, 06140–47, 06231 (part), 06232, 06248 (part), 06414, 06415 (part), 06416, 06424 (part), 06447, 06456, 06480

* * *

SECOND DISTRICT

SAM GEJDENSON, Democrat, of Bozrah, CT; born in Eschwege, Germany, in an American displaced persons camp, May 20, 1948; graduated, Norwich Free Academy, Norwich, CT, 1966; A.S., Mitchell Junior College, New London, CT, 1968; B.A., University of Connecticut, Storrs, 1970; farmer; broker, FAI Trading Company; chairman, Bozrah Town Committee, 1973; member: Connecticut House of Representatives, 1974–78; Big Brothers/Big Sisters of Southeastern Connecticut and Bozrah Grange; past member, Norwich Quinebaug Cancer Society; married to Betsy Henley-Cohn; two children: Mia and Ari; elected to the 97th Congress, November 4, 1980; reelected to each succeeding Congress.

Office Listings

http://www.house.gov/gejdenson bozrah@hr.house.gov

1401 Longworth House Office Building, Washington, DC 20515–0702 225–2076
Administrative Assistant.—Rich Davis. FAX: 225–4977
Acting Press Secretary.—Rich Davis.
Scheduler.—Jonathan Lenzner.
P.O. Box 2000, Norwich, CT 06360 .... (203) 886–0139
District Director.—Naomi Otterness.
94 Court Street, Middletown, CT 06457 .... (203) 346–1123

Counties: Middlesex (part), New London, Tolland (part), and Windham. Population (1990), 548,041.

ZIP Codes: 06029, 06043 (part), 06066 (part), 06071 (part), 06075, 06076–77, 06084, 06226, 06230, 06231 (part), 06233–35, 06237–39, 06241–47, 06248 (part), 06249–51, 06254–56, 06258–60, 06262–68, 06277–82, 06320, 06330–37, 06339–40, 06349–51, 06353–55, 06357, 06359–60, 06365, 06370–80, 06382–85, 06387–89, 06409, 06412, 06415 (part), 06417 (part), 06419 (part), 06420, 06423, 06424 (part), 06426, 06438–39, 06441–42, 06457, 06469, 06475, 06498

* * *

THIRD DISTRICT

ROSA L. DELAURO, Democrat, of New Haven, CT; born in New Haven, March 2, 1943; graduated, Laurelton Hall High School; attended London School of Economics, Queen Mary College, London, 1962–63; B.A., *cum laude*, history and political science, Marymount College, NY, 1964; M.A., international politics, Columbia University, NY, 1966; executive assistant to Mayor Frank Logue, city of New Haven, 1976–77; executive assistant/development administrator, city of New Haven, 1977–78; chief of staff, Senator Christopher Dodd, 1980–87; executive director, Countdown '87, 1987–88; executive director, Emily's List, 1989–90; married to Stanley Greenberg; three children: Anna, Kathryn, and Jonathan; elected to the 102nd Congress, November 6, 1990; reelected to each succeeding Congress.

Office Listings

436 Cannon House Office Building, Washington, DC 20515–0703 225–3661
Administrative Assistant.—Maura Keefe.
Legislative Director.—Catoyina McDonald.
Press Secretary.—Stacy Beck.
59 Elm Street, New Haven, CT 06510 .... (203) 562–3718
District Director.—Steve Hudak.

Counties: Fairfield (part), Middlesex (part), and New Haven (part). CITIES AND TOWNSHIPS: North Branford, Clinton, Durham, East Haven, Guilford, Hamden, Killingworth, Madison, Middlefield, Milford, New Haven, North Branford, Northford, North Haven, Orange, Rockfall, Stratford, Wallingford, West Haven, and Woodbridge. Population (1990), 547,765.

ZIP Codes: 06405, 06410 (part), 06413, 06417 (part), 06419 (part), 06422, 06437, 06443, 06455, 06460, 06471–73, 06477, 06481, 06492, 06497 (part), 06501–31

* * *

FOURTH DISTRICT

CHRISTOPHER SHAYS, Republican, of Stamford, CT; born in Stamford on October 18, 1945; graduated, Darien High School, Darien, CT, 1964; B.A., Principia College, Elsah, IL, 1968; M.B.A., New York University Graduate School of Business, 1974; M.P.A., New York University Graduate School of Public Administration, 1978; member, Peace Corps, Fiji Islands, 1968–70; business consultant; college instructor, realtor; executive aide, Trumbull First Selectman, 1971–72; Connecticut House of Representatives, 1974–87; married Betsi Shays, 1968; one daughter, Jeramy; elected by special election, August 18, 1987, to the 100th Congress to fill the vacancy caused by the death of Stewart B. McKinney; reelected to each succeeding Congress.

Office Listings

http://www.house.gov/shays cshays@hr.house.gov

1502 Longworth House Office Building, Washington, DC 20515–0704 225–5541
Chief of Staff.—Betsy Wright-Hawkings. FAX: 225–9629
Executive Assistant.—Diana White.
Second Floor, 888 Washington Boulevard, Stamford, CT 06901–2927 .... (203) 357–8277
10 Middle Street, Bridgeport, CT 06604–4223 .... (203) 579–5870
Norwalk, CT .... (203) 866–6469

County: FAIRFIELD COUNTY (part); cities of Bridgeport, Darien, Greenwich, New Canaan, Monroe, Norwalk, Stamford, Trumbull and Westport. Population (1990), 547,765.

ZIP Codes: 06430, 06432, 06436, 06468, 06490, 06601–02, 06604–08, 06610, 06611, 06807, 06820, 06829–31, 06836, 06840, 06850–56, 06870, 06878, 06880, 06881, 06901–07, 06911–12

* * *

FIFTH DISTRICT

JAMES H. MALONEY, Democrat, of Danbury, CT; born in Quincy, MA, September 17, 1948; graduated, St. Sebastian High School, Needham, MA; B.A., *cum laude*, Harvard University, 1972; J.D., Boston University School of Law, 1980; attorney; admitted to the Connecticut bar, 1980; VISTA volunteer; State Senator, representing Bethel, Danbury, New Fairfield, 1986–95; married the former Mary Draper, 1980; three children: Adele, Ellen, and Anna; committees: National Security, Banking and Financial Services; subcommittees: Military Personnel, Military Procurement, Housing and Community Opportunity; elected to the 105th Congress on November 5, 1996.

Office Listings

1213 Longworth House Office Building, Washington, DC 20515–0705 225–3822
Chief of Staff.—Tricia Haisten.
Legislative Director.—Jeffrey Cooper.
Executive Assistant.—Mattie Barrow.
Press Secretary.—Nichole Glushakow.
Suite 210, 135 Grant Street, Waterbury, CT 06702–1911 .... (203) 573–1418
Deputy Chief of Staff/Counsel.—Phil Lewis.

Counties: Fairfield (part) amd New Haven (part). CITIES AND TOWNSHIPS: Ansonia, Beacon Falls, Botsford, Bethany, Bethel, Brookfield, Cheshire, Danouny, Derby, Easton, Georgetown, Huntington, Meriden, Monroe, Middlebury, Newtown, Naugatuck, New Fairfield, Oxford, Prospect, Redding, Ridgefield, Sandy Hook, Seymour, Shelton, Southbury, Union City, Woodbridge, Waterbury, Weston, West Redding, Wilton, and Wolcott. Population (1990), 547,764.

ZIP Codes: 06401, 06403–04, 06410 (part), 06418, 06430 (part), 06440, 06450, 06454, 06468 (part), 06470 (part), 06478, 06482–83, 06484 (part), 06488 (part), 06489 (part), 06497 (part), 06524 (part), 06525 (part), 06611 (part), 06612, 06702, 06704–06, 06708, 06710, 06712, 06716, 06720–26, 06762 (part), 06770, 06784 (part), 06801, 06804, 06810–13, 06875–77, 06880 (part), 06883, 06896, 06897 (part)

* * *

SIXTH DISTRICT

NANCY L. JOHNSON, Republican, of New Britain, CT; born in Chicago, IL, on January 5, 1935, daughter of Gertrude (Smith) and Noble W. Lee (deceased); attended University of Chicago Laboratory School, 1951; University of Chicago, 1953; B.A., Radcliffe College, *cum laude,* Cambridge, MA, 1957; attended University of London (English Speaking Union Scholarship), 1958; Connecticut State Senate, 1977–82; member, board of directors, United Way of New Britain; president, Sheldon Community Guidance Clinic; Unitarian Universalists Society of New Britain; founding president, Friends of New Britain Public Library; member: board of directors, New Britain Bank and Trust; New Britain Museum of American Art; adjunct professor (political science), Central Connecticut State College; married Dr. Theodore Herbert Johnson, 1958; three children: Lindsey, Althea, and Caroline; elected on November 2, 1982, to the 98th Congress; reelected to each succeeding Congress.

Office Listings

343 Cannon House Office Building, Washington, DC 20515–0706 225–4476
Chief of Staff.—Dave Karvelas. FAX: 225–4488
Press Secretary.—Andrea Hofelich.
Executive Assistant.—Margo Nousen.
Suite 200, 480 Myrtle Street, New Britain, CT 06053 .... (203) 223–8412
District Director.—Marianne Calnen.

Counties: Fairfield (part), Hartford (part), Litchfield, New Haven (part), and Tolland (part). Population (1990), 547,765.

ZIP Codes: 06001, 06010–11, 06013, 06018–22, 06024, 06026 (part), 06027, 06031–32, 06034–35, 06039, 06050–53, 06057–63, 06065, 06068–70, 06071 (part), 06072, 06078–79, 06081–83, 06085, 06089–94, 06096, 06098, 06444, 06467, 06479, 06487, 06488 (part), 06489 (part), 06750–59, 06762 (part), 06763, 06776–79, 06781–83, 06784 (part), 06785–87, 06790–91, 06793–96, 06798

DELAWARE

(Population 1995, 717,000)

SENATORS

WILLIAM V. ROTH, JR., Republican, of Wilmington, DE; born in Great Falls, MT, July 22, 1921; B.A., University of Oregon; M.B.A., Harvard Business School; LL.B., Harvard Law School; enlisted as private in U.S. Army, 1943; served in Pacific; Bronze Star, discharged in 1946 as captain; married to Jane K. Richards; two children: William V. Roth III and Katharine Kellond Roth; Episcopalian; member, Delaware and California bars, admitted to practice before U.S. Supreme Court; chairman of Delaware Republican State Committee, 1961–64; Republican National Committee, 1961–64; committees: chair, Finance; Governmental Affairs; Joint Economic; Joint Committee on Taxation; elected U.S. Representative at Large from Delaware to the 90th Congress, November 8, 1966; reelected to the 91st Congress; elected to the U.S. Senate, November 3, 1970, for the term ending January 3, 1977; reelected November 2, 1976; reelected to each succeeding Congress.

Office Listings

http://www.senate.gov/~roth

104 Hart Senate Office Building, Washington, DC 20510–0801 224–2441
Administrative Assistant.—John M. Duncan.
Scheduling Secretary.—Susie Cohen.
Press Secretary.—Brian Tassinari.
3021 Federal Building, 844 King Street, Wilmington, DE 19801 .... (302) 573–6291
2215 Federal Building, 300 South New Street, Dover, DE 19904 .... (302) 674–3308
12 The Circle, Georgetown, DE 19947 .... (302) 856–7690

* * *

JOSEPH R. BIDEN, JR., Democrat, of Wilmington, DE; born in Scranton, PA, November 20, 1942; educated at St. Helena's School, Wilmington, DE; Archmere Academy, Claymont, DE; A.B., history and political science, University of Delaware; J.D., Syracuse University College of Law; married to Jill Tracy Biden; three children: Joseph R. Biden III, Robert Hunter Biden, and Ashley Blazer Biden; admitted to the bar, December 1968, Wilmington, DE; engaged in private practice until 1972; served on New Castle County Council, 1970–72; elected to the U.S. Senate, November 1972, for the term ending January 3, 1979; reelected November 1978, November 1984, and November 1990; committees: Foreign Relations (ranking); Judiciary.

Office Listings

http://www.senate.gov/~biden senator@biden_senate.gov

221 Russell Senate Office Building, Washington, DC 20510–0802 224–5042
Chief of Staff.—Bernard Toon. FAX: 224–0139
Legislative Director.—Jane Woodfin.
Communications Director.—Larry Spinelli.
J.C. Boggs Federal Building, 844 King Street, Wilmington, DE 19801 .... (302) 573–6345
J. Allen Frear Building, 300 South New Street, Dover, DE 19901 .... (302) 678–9483
Georgetown Professional Center, Suite 108, 600 South DuPont Highway, Georgetown, DE 19947 .... (302) 856–9275

REPRESENTATIVE

AT LARGE

MICHAEL N. CASTLE, Republican, of Wilmington, DE; born on July 2, 1939 in Wilmington; graduate of Tower Hill School, 1957; B.S., economics, Hamilton College, Clinton, NY, 1961; J.D., Georgetown University Law School, 1964; attorney; admitted to the District of Columbia and Delaware bars, 1964; commenced practice in Wilmington; Delaware House of Representatives, 1966–67; Delaware Senate, 1968–76; Lieutenant Governor of Delaware, 1981–85; Governor, 1985–92; awarded honorary degrees: Wesley College, 1986; Widener College, 1986; Delaware State University, 1986; Hamilton College, 1991; Jefferson Medical College, Philadelphia, PA, 1992; active in the National Governors Association, serving three years as chairman of the Human Resources Committee; co-vice chairman for NGA's Task Force on Health Care with President Clinton; past president of the Council of State Governments; past chairman of the Southern Governors Association; chaired the Republican Governors Association, 1988; American Diabetes Association's C. Everett Koop Award for Health Promotion and Awareness, 1992; member: Delaware Bar Association, American Bar Association; former member: National Governors Association, Republican Governors Association, National Assessment Governing Board, Council of State Governors, Southern Governors Association; honorary board of directors, Delaware Greenways; committees: Banking and Financial Services, Economic and Educational Opportunities; Permanent Select Committee on Intelligence; subcommittees: chair, Domestic and International Monetary Policy; vice chair, Children, Youth and Families; cofounder, House Republican Education Caucus; cochairman, Congressional Task Force to the National Campaign to Reduce Teen Pregnancy; House Social Security Task Force; House Tobacco Task Force; selected as one of seven regional whips for the 110-member freshman class; married Jane DiSabatino, 1992; elected to the 103rd Congress on November 3, 1992; reelected to each succeeding Congress.

Office Listings

http://www.house.gov/castle delaware@hr.house.gov

1207 Longworth House Office Building, Washington, DC 20515–0801 225–4165
Administrative Assistant.—Paul Leonard. FAX: 225–2291
Communications Director.—Kristin Nolt.
Legislative Director.—Booth Jameson.
3 Christina Centre, 201 North Walnut Street, Wilmington, DE 19801 .... (302) 428–1902
Office Director.—Jeff Dayton. FAX: 428–1950
J. Allen Frear Federal Building, 300 South New Street, Dover, DE 19901 .... (302) 736–1666
FAX: 736–6580

Counities: Kent, New Castle, and Sussex. CITIES AND TOWNSHIPS: Brookside, Camden, Claymont, Delaware City, Dover, Edgemoor, Elsmere, Georgetown, Harrington, Highland, Acres, Kent Acres, Laurel, Lewes, Middletown, Milford, Millsboro, New Castle, Newark, Pike Creek, Rising Sun-Lebanon, Rodney Village, Seaford, Smyrna, Stanton, Talleyville, Wilmington, Wilmington Minor, and Woodside East. Population (1990), 666,696.

ZIP Codes: 19701–03, 19706–11, 19713–15, 19720, 19730, 19732–34, 19736, 19801–10, 19850, 19899, 19901, 19903, 19930–31, 19933–34, 19936, 19938–47, 19950–56, 19958, 19960–64, 19966–71, 19973, 19975, 19977, 19979–80

FLORIDA

(Population 1995, 14,166,000)

SENATORS

BOB GRAHAM, Democrat, of Miami Lakes, FL; born in Coral Gables, FL, on November 9, 1936; graduated, Miami High School, 1955; B.S., University of Florida, Gainesville, 1959; LL.B., Harvard Law School, Cambridge, MA, 1962; lawyer; admitted to the Florida bar, 1962; builder and cattleman; elected to the Florida State House of Representatives, 1966; Florida State Senate, 1970–78; Governor of Florida, 1978–86; married the former Adele Khoury in 1959; four children: Gwendolyn Patricia, Glynn Adele, Arva Suzanne, and Kendall Elizabeth; committees: Energy and Natural Resources; Environment and Public Works; Finance; Veterans' Affairs; Select Committee on Intelligence; elected to the U.S. Senate on November 4, 1986.

Office Listings

http://www.senate.gov/~graham bob_graham@graham.senate.gov

524 Hart Senate Office Building, Washington, DC 20510–0903 224–3041
Administrative Assistant.—Ken Klein. TDD: 224–5621
Legislative Director.—Russell Sullivan.
Press Secretary.—Kimberly James.
P.O. Box 3050, Tallahassee, FL 32315 .... (904) 422–6100
State Director.—Mary Chiles.
Suite 3270, 101 East Kennedy Boulevard, Tampa, FL 33602 .... (813) 228–2476
Suite 1715, 44 West Flagler Street, Miami, FL 33130 .... (305) 536–7293

* * *

CONNIE MACK, Republican, of Cape Coral, FL; born in Philadelphia, PA, on October 29, 1940; graduated, Fort Myers High School, 1959; B.A., marketing, University of Florida, Gainesville, 1966; banker, 1966–82; member: Fort Myers Chamber of Commerce; Kiwanis Club; board of directors, Palmer Drug Abuse Center; Fort Myers Rotary; appointed to Federal Reserve Board (Miami Branch); married the former Priscilla Hobbs in 1960; two children: Debbie and Connie IV; elected on November 2, 1982 to the 98th Congress; reelected to each succeeding Congress; committees: Finance; Banking, Housing, and Urban Affairs; Joint Economic; elected on November 8, 1988 to the U.S. Senate for the term beginning January 3, 1989.

Office Listings

http://www.senate.gov/~mack connie@mack.senate.gov

517 Hart Senate Office Building, Washington, DC 20510–0904 224–5274
Chief of Staff.—Mitch Bainwol. FAX: 224–8022
Administrative Assistant.—John Reich.
Legislative Director.—Greg Waddell.
Suite 704, 777 Brickell, Miami, FL 33131 .... (305) 530–7100
Suite 602, 600 North Westshore Boulevard, Tampa, FL 33609 .... (813) 225–7683
Suite 27, 1342 Colonial Boulevard, Fort Myers, FL 33907 .... (941) 275–6252

REPRESENTATIVES

FIRST DISTRICT

JOE SCARBOROUGH, Republican, of Pensacola, FL; born in Atlanta, GA, April 9, 1963; graduated, Catholic High School, Pensacola; B.A. in history, University of Alabama, 1985; law degree, University of Florida, 1990; admitted to the Florida bar, 1991; served on the executive board of the Escambia-Santa Rosa Bar Association; board of directors for the Navy League of the Pensacola area; Emerald Coast Pediatric Primary Care; member: Gulf Coast Economics Club, Chamber of Commerce, Inns of Court, Challenger Committee, Rotary Club, Young Lawyers Association, and Fellowship of Christian Athletes; attends First Baptist Church of Pensacola, where he often teaches Sunday School; married to the former Melanie Hinton; two children: Joey and Andrew; serves on the House National Security and Government Operations committees; elected to the 104th Congress; reelected to the 105th Congress.

Office Listings
http://www.house.gov/scarborough

1523 Longworth House Office Building, Washington, DC 20515 225–4136
Chief of Staff/Press Secretary.—Rachel Cacioppo. FAX: 225–3414
Military Affairs, Foreign Affairs.—Bart Roper.
Legislative Director.—James Geoffrey.
Office Manager.—Susan Waren.

Counties: Bay, Escambia, Holmes, Okaloosa, Santa Rosa, and Walton. CITIES AND TOWNSHIPS: Bonifay, Carryville, Crestview, DeFuniak Springs, Destin, Fountain, Freeport, Ft. Walton Beach, Gulf Breeze, Laurel Hill, Lynn Haven, Noma, Panama City, Paxton, Pensacola, Sunnyside, Westville, Youngstown. Population (1990), 577,226.

ZIP Codes: 32401, 32405, 32407, 32408, 32409, 32413, 32425, 32427, 32428, 32433, 32437, 32439, 32440, 32455, 32459, 32462, 32464, 32466, 32501, 32503, 32504, 32505, 32506, 32507, 32508, 32514, 32526, 32531, 32533, 32534, 32535, 32536, 32541, 32542, 32547, 32548, 32561, 32564, 32565, 32566, 32567, 32568, 32569, 32570, 32571, 32578, 32579, 32580, 32583

* * *

SECOND DISTRICT

ALLEN BOYD, Jr., Democrat, of Monticello, FL; born in Valdosta, GA, June 6, 1945; graduated, Jefferson County High School, Monticello, 1963; B.S., Florida State University, 1969; partner and general manager, F.A. Boyd and Sons, Inc., family farm corporation; first lieutenant, U.S. Army 101st Airborne Division, Vietnam, 1969–71, receiving the CIB and other decorations; Florida House of Representatives, 1989–96; elected majority whip; chaired Governmental Operations Committee (1992–94) and House Democratic Conservative Caucus (Blue Dogs); member: Peanut Producers Association; Farm Bureau; Cattlemen's Association; local historical association, Chamber of Commerce, and Kiwanis; board member, National Cotton Council; member, First United Methodist Church; married the former Stephannie Ann Roush, 1970; four children: Fred Allen Boyd III (d), Suzanne, John, and David; elected to the 105th Congress.

Office Listings

1237 Longworth House Office Building, Washington, DC 20515 225–5235
Chief of Staff.—Bob Doyle. FAX: 225–5615
Legislative Director.—Eve Young.
Legislative Assistant/Systems Manager.—Chris Schloesser.
Legislative Assistants.—Diane Pratt, Jason Quaranto.
Executive Assistant/Scheduler.—Jenny Ornes.
301 South Monroe Street, No. 108, Tallahassee, FL 32301 .... (904) 561–3979
FAX: 681–2902
30 W. Government Street, Panama City, FL 32401 .... (904) 785–0812
District Director.—Bill Bassett. FAX: 763–3764

Counties: Calhoun, Columbia (part), Dixie, Franklin, Gadsden, Gilchrist, Gulf, Hamilton, Jackson, Jefferson, Lafayette, Leon, Liberty, Madison, Suwannee, Taylor, Wakulla, and Washington. CITIES AND TOWNSHIPS: Alford, Altha, Apalachicola, Bascom, Blountstown, Bonifay, Branford, Bristol, Campbellton, Carrabelle, Caryville, Chattahoochee, Chipley, Clarksville, Cottondale, Crawfordville, Cypress, Day, Eastpoint, Ebro, Fountain, Graceville, Grand Ridge, Greensboro, Greenville, Greenwood, Gretna, Havana, Hosford, Jasper, Jennings, Kinard, Lake City, Lamont, Lanark Village, Lee, Live Oak, Lloyd, Lynn Haven, MacClenny, Madison, Malone, Marianna, Mayo, McAlpin, Mexico Beach, Miccosukee, Midway, Monticello, Mount Pleasant, O'Brien, Olustee, Panacea, Panama City, Pinetta, Port St. Joe, Quincy, Saint Marks, Salem, Sanderson, Shady Grove, Sneads, Sopchoppy, Steinhatchee, Sumatra, Sunnyside, Tallahassee, Telogia, Trenton, Vernon, Wacissa, Wausau, Wellborn, Wewahitchka, White Springs, Woodville, and Youngstown. Population (1990), 562,519.

ZIP Codes: 32008, 32013, 32038, 32052–55, 32059–60, 32062, 32066, 32071, 32087, 32094, 32096, 32301, 32303–04, 32306, 32308, 32310–12, 32320–22, 32324, 32327–28, 32331, 32333–34, 32336, 32340, 32344, 32346–47, 32350–51, 32356, 32358–59, 32401, 32403–05, 32409, 32413, 32420–21, 32423–28, 32430–31, 32437–38, 32440, 32442–46, 32449, 32455–56, 32460, 32462, 32464–66, 32578, 32165, 32619, 32621, 32626, 32643, 32648, 32669, 32680, 32693

* * *

THIRD DISTRICT

CORRINE BROWN, Democrat, of Jacksonville, FL; born in Jacksonville on November 11, 1946; B.S., Florida A&M University, 1969; master's degree, Florida A&M University, 1971; education specialist degree, University of Florida; honorary doctor of law, Edward Waters College; faculty member: Florida Community College in Jacksonville, University of Florida, and

Edward Waters College; served in the Florida House of Representatives for 10 years; first woman elected chairperson of the Duval County Legislative Delegation; served as a consultant to the Governor's Committee on Aging; committees: Transportation and Infrastructure, Veterans' Affairs; subcommittees: Surface Transportation, Aviation, and Hospitals and Health Care; member: Congressional Black Caucus, Women's Caucus, Progressive Caucus; one child, Shantrel; elected on November 3, 1992 to the 103rd Congress; reelected to each succeeding Congress.

Office Listings

1610 Longworth House Office Building, Washington, DC 20515–0903 225–0123
Administrative Assistant.—E. Ronnie Simmons. FAX: 225–2256
Appointment Secretary.—Darla E. Smallwood.
Executive Assistant.—Carolyn Wilson Newton.
Legislative Director.—Joyce Rodgers.
314 Palmetto Street, Jacksonville, FL 32202 .... (904) 354–1652

Counties: Clay (part), Duval (part), Flagler (part), Lake (part), Orange (part), Putnam (part), St. Johns (part), Seminole (part), and Volusia (part). CITIES AND TOWNSHIPS: Altamonte Springs (part), Apopka (part), Bunnell (part), Crescent City, Daytona Beach (part), Debary, DeLand (part), DeLeon Springs, East Palatka, Green Cove Springs (part), High Springs (part), Holden Heights (part), Jacksonville (part), Lake City (part), Lockhart (part), Macclenny (part), Maitland (part), Mount Dora (part), Oak Ridge (part), Ocala (part), Orange Park (part), Orlando (part), Orlovista (part), Palatka (part), Pierson (part), Pine Hills (part), Sanford (part), South Apopka (part), St Augustine (part), Tangelo Park, Watertown (part), Wekiva Springs (part), West De Land (part), Williston (part), Winter Garden (part), and Winter Park (part). Population (1990), 562,519.

ZIP Codes: 00222, 00229, 32033, 32043, 32073, 32084, 32086, 32092, 32095, 32102, 32110, 32112, 32114, 32117, 32124, 32130, 32131, 32134, 32137, 32139, 32140, 32145, 32148, 32177, 32180, 32181, 32187, 32189, 32190, 32202, 32204, 32205, 32206, 32207, 32208, 32209, 32210, 32211, 32212, 32215, 32216, 32218, 32219, 32220, 32221, 32223, 32225, 32244, 32246, 32254, 32257, 32258, 32259, 32656, 32701, 32702, 32703, 32707, 32712, 32713, 32714, 32720, 32724, 32725, 32726, 32746, 32750, 32751, 32757, 32763, 32767, 32771, 32773, 32776, 32779, 32784, 32789, 32798, 32801, 32804, 32805, 32808, 32809, 32810, 32811, 32818, 32819, 32835, 32836, 32839, 34761, 34787

* * *

FOURTH DISTRICT

TILLIE FOWLER, Republican, of Jacksonville, FL; born on December 23, 1942 in Milledgeville, Georgia; B.A. and J.D., Emory University, Atlanta, GA, 1964, 1967; attorney, admitted to Georgia bar, 1967; legislative assistant, Congressman Robert G. Stevens, Jr., 1967–70; general counsel, deputy counsel, associate director of legislative affairs, White House Office of Consumer Affairs, 1970–71; member, Jacksonville City Council, 1985–92; president, Jacksonville City Council, 1989–90; member: Emory University Alumni Board of Governors; Civil Justice Reform Act Advisory Group for the United States District Court, Middle District of Florida; American Red Cross, Northeast Florida Chapter; honorary member, St. Vincent's Health Care System Advisory Board; married L. Buck Fowler, 1968; two children: Tillie and Elizabeth; elected on November 3, 1992 to the 103rd Congress; reelected to each succeeding Congress.

Office Listings
http://www.house.gov/fowler

413 Cannon House Office Building, Washington, DC 20515–0904 225–2501
Administrative Assistant.—David Gilliland. FAX: 225–9318
Legislative Director.—William Klein.
Scheduler/Executive Assistant.—Lynn Miller.
4452 Hendricks Avenue, Jacksonville, FL 32207 .... (904) 739–6600
140 South Atlantic Avenue, Ormond Beach, FL 32176 .... (904) 672–0754

Counties: DUVAL COUNTY (part); cities and townships of Bryceville and Jacksonville. FLAGLER COUNTY (part); cities and townships of Bunnell, Flagler Beach, Hastings, and Palm Coast. NASSAU COUNTY; cities and townships of Callahan, Fernandina Beach, Hilliard, and Yulee. ST. JOHNS COUNTY (part); cities and townships of Ponte Verda Beach, and Saint Augustine. VOLUSIA COUNTY (part); cities and townships of Daytona Beach, Ormond Beach, Pierson, and Seville. Population (1990), 562,518.

ZIP Codes: 32009, 32011, 32033, 32034, 32046, 32063, 32082, 32084, 32086, 32092, 32095, 32097, 32110, 32114, 32117, 32118, 32124, 32130, 32136, 32137, 32145, 32164, 32174, 32176, 32180, 32204, 32205, 32207, 32208, 32210, 32211, 32216, 32217, 32218, 32219, 32229, 32221, 32223–27, 32233–34, 32244, 32246, 32250, 32254, 32256, 32257, 32258, 32259, 32266, 32277

FIFTH DISTRICT

KAREN L. THURMAN, Democrat, of Dunnellon, FL; born in Rapid City, SD, on January 12, 1951; graduated, Satellite High School, Satellite Beach, FL, 1969; Santa Fe Community College 1969–71; B.A., University of Florida, Gainesville, 1973; attended University of Florida Graduate School, 1973; mathematics teacher, Dunnellon Middle School; Florida State Senate, 1982–92; Dunnellon City Council, 1975–82; elected mayor, city of Dunnellon, 1979–81; member: State Sentencing Guidelines Commission; Future Farmers of America, board of directors; State Public Service Commission; Withlacoochee Regional Water Supply Authority; Regional Energy Action Committee; Coastal Impact Study; chairman, Job Training Partnership Act Coordinating Council; Comprehensive Plan; National Conference of State Legislatures; Southern Regional Education Board; married John Patrick Thurman, 1973; two children: McLin and Liberty Lee; elected on November 3, 1992 to the 103rd Congress; reelected to each succeeding Congress.

Office Listings

http://www.house.gov/thurman

130 Cannon House Office Building, Washington, DC 20515–0905 225–1002
Administrative Assistant.—Nora Matus.
Scheduler.—Joan Rodriguez Hall.
Legislative Director.—Robert Dobek.
District Administrator.—Anne Morgan.
2224 Highway 44 West, Inverness, FL 34453 .... (904) 344–3044
5700 SW 34th Street, Suite 425, Gainesville, FL 32608 .... (904) 336–6614
5623 U.S. 19 South, Suite 206, New Port Richey, FL 34652 .... (813) 849–4496

Counties: Alachua (part), Citrus, Dixie, Gilchrist, Hernando, Levy (part), Marion (part), Pasco (part), and Sumter. CITIES AND TOWNSHIPS: Alachua (part), Bayonet Point (part), Beacon Square, Beverly Hills, Brookridge, Brooksville, Bushnell, Chiefland, Citrus Springs, Cross City, Crystal River, Dunnellon, Elfers (part), Floral City, Gainesville (part), Hernando, Hernando Beach, High Point, High Springs (part), Holiday, Homosassa, Homosassa Springs, Hudson (part), Inverness, Jasmine Estates, Lake Panasoffkee, New Port Richey, New Port Richey East, Newberry, Ocala (part), Port Richey, Ridge Manor, South Brooksville, Spring Hill, Sugarmill Woods, Timber Pines, Wildwood, and Williston (part). Population (1990), 562,518.

ZIP Codes: 32008, 32038, 32044, 32054, 32055, 32061, 32094, 32113, 32134, 32148, 32601, 32603, 32605, 32606, 32607, 32608, 32609, 32611, 32615, 32618, 32621, 32622, 32625, 32626, 32631, 32640, 32643, 32666, 32667, 32668, 32669, 32680, 32686, 32693, 32694, 32696, 33513, 33525, 33538, 33597, 34428, 34429, 34431, 34432, 34433, 34434, 34436, 34442, 34446, 34448, 34449, 34450, 34452, 34453, 34461, 34465, 34473, 34481, 34482, 34498, 34601, 34602, 34606, 34607, 34608, 34609, 34610, 34613, 34614, 34652, 34653, 34654, 34655, 34667, 34668, 34689, 34690, 34691

* * *

SIXTH DISTRICT

CLIFF B. STEARNS, Republican, of Ocala, FL; born in Washington, DC, April 16, 1941; graduated, Woodrow Wilson High, Washington, DC, 1959; B.S., electrical engineering, George Washington University, Washington, DC, 1963; Air Force ROTC Distinguished Military Graduate; graduate work, University of California, Los Angeles, 1965; served, U.S. Air Force (captain), 1963–67; businessman; past president: Silver Springs Kiwanis; member: Marion County/Ocala Energy Task Force, Tourist Development Council, Ocala Board of Realtors, American Hotel/Motel Association in Florida, American Hotel/Motel Association of the United States, Grace Presbyterian Church; board of directors, Boys Club of Ocala; trustee: Munroe Regional Hospital; married to the former Joan Moore; three children: Douglas, Bundy, and Scott; elected November 8, 1988, to the 101st Congress; reelected to each succeeding Congress.

Office Listings

http://www.house.gov/stearns cstearns@hr.house.gov

2352 Rayburn House Office Building, Washington, DC 20515–0906 225–5744
Administrative Assistant.—Jack Seum. FAX: 225–3973
Legislative Director.—Veronica Crowe.
Executive Assistant.—Marcia Summers.
115 Southeast 25th Avenue, Ocala, FL 34471 .... (904) 351–8777
District Manager.—Sharon Brooks. FAX: 351–8011
Leesburg Office Park Ltd., 734 North Third Street, Suite 517CD, Leesburg, FL 34748 .... (904) 326–8285
FAX: 326–9430
1726 Kinglsey Avenue, Suite 8, Orange Park, FL 32073 .... (904) 269–3203
FAX: 269–3343

Counties: Baker, Bradford, Clay (part), Duval (part), Lake (part), Marion (part), Putnam (part), Sumter, and Union. CITIES AND TOWNSHIPS: Ocala, Leesburg, Orange Park, and Jacksonville (part). Population (1990), 562,518.

ZIP Codes: 00222, 00229, 32038, 32040, 32043, 32044, 32054, 32058, 32061, 32063, 32065, 32068, 32073, 32083, 32087, 32091, 32112, 32113, 32134, 32139, 32140, 32148, 32159, 32177, 32179, 32195, 32210, 32220, 32221, 32222, 32234, 32244, 32609, 32615, 32617, 32622, 32631, 32640, 32656, 32666, 32667, 32668, 32686, 32694, 32696, 32702, 32726, 32735, 32757, 32776, 32778, 32784, 33513, 33514, 33525, 33538, 33597, 33809, 33837, 33868, 34420, 34432

* * *

SEVENTH DISTRICT

JOHN L. MICA, Republican, of Winter Park, FL; born in Binghamton, NY, on January 27, 1943; graduated, Miami-Edison High School, Miami, FL; B.A., University of Florida, 1967; president, MK Development; managing general partner, Cellular Communications; former government affairs consultant, Mica, Dudinsky and Associates; executive director, Local Government Study Commissions, Palm Beach County, 1970–72; executive director, Orange County Local Government Study Commission, 1972–74; Florida State House of Representatives, 1976–80; administrative assistant, U.S. Senator Paula Hawkins, 1980–85; Florida State Good Government Award, 1973; one of five Florida Jaycees Outstanding Young Men of America, 1978; member: Kiwanis, Crime Line Board, Tiger Bay Club, Beth Johnson Mental Health Board, PTA Board, Chamber of Commerce, Florida Blue Key; brother of former Congressman Daniel A. Mica; married the former Patricia Szymanek, 1972; two children: D'Anne Leigh and John Clark; elected on November 3, 1992 to the 103rd Congress; reelected to each succeeding Congress.

Office Listings

http://www.house.gov/mica/mica.htm john.mica@mail.house.gov

106 Cannon House Office Building, Washington, DC 20515–0907 225–4035
Administrative Assistant.—Russell L. Roberts. FAX: 226–0821
Legislative Director/Press Secretary.—Sharon Pinkerton.
1211 Semoran Boulevard, Suite 117, Casselberry, FL 32707 .... (407) 657–8080
840 Deltona Boulevard, Deltona, FL 32725 .... (407) 860–1499
1396 Dunlawton Avenue, Port Orange, FL 32127 .... (904) 756–9798

Counties: ORANGE COUNTY; city of Apopka (part). SEMINOLE COUNTY; cities and townships of Altamonte Springs, Casselberry, Chuluota, Fern Park, Forest City, Geneva, Heathrow, Lake Mary, Longwood, Oviedo, Sanford (part), Tuscawilla, and Winter Springs. VOLUSIA COUNTY; cities and townships of Daytona Beach (part), Daytona Beach Shores, Deland (part), Deltona, Edgewater, Lake Helen, New Smyrna Beach, Oak Hill, Orange City, Ponce Inlet, Port Orange, and South Daytona. Population, (1990), 562,518.

ZIP Codes: 32114 (part), 32115–16, 32118 (part), 32119–23, 32124 (part), 32127, 32129, 32130 (part), 32132, 32141, 32168–70, 32701 (part), 32703 (part), 32706, 32707 (part), 32708, 32712 (part), 32713 (part), 32714 (part), 32715–16, 32718–19, 32720 (part), 32724 (part), 32725, 32728, 32730, 32732, 32738, 32744, 32746 (part), 32747, 32750 (part), 32751 (part), 32752, 32754 (part), 32759, 32763 (part), 32764–66, 32771 (part), 32772, 32773 (part), 32774, 32779 (part), 32791, 32792 (part), 32795, 32808 (part), 32810 (part), 32818 (part), 32860

* * *

EIGHTH DISTRICT

BILL MCCOLLUM, Republican, of Longwood, FL; born in Brooksville, FL, July 12, 1944; graduated, Hernando High School, 1962; B.A., 1965, and J.D., 1968, University of Florida, Gainesville; U.S. Navy, 1969–72 (active duty), Reserves, commander; lawyer; admitted to the Florida bar in 1968 and commenced practice in Orlando, 1973; former partner, Pitts, Eubanks and Ross; member: American, Florida, and Orange County bar associations; Florida Blue Key, Phi Delta Phi, and Omicron Delta Kappa; Kiwanis; Sertoma Club of Apopka; American Legion; Who's Who in America; Reserve Officers Association; Naval Reserve Officers Association; Military Order of World Wars; former chairman, Seminole County Republican Executive Committee; married the former Ingrid Seebohm, 1971; three sons: Douglas, Justin, and Andrew; elected to the 97th Congress, November 4, 1980; reelected to each succeeding Congress; member: Judiciary Committee; chairman, Crime Subcommittee; vice chairman, Banking and Financial Services Committee; Financial Institutions and Consumer Credit Subcommittee; House Select Committee on Intelligence.

Office Listings

http://www.house.gov/mccollum

2266 Rayburn House Office Building, Washington, DC 20515–0908 225–2176
FAX: 225–0999

Chief of Staff.—Doyle Bartlett.
Legislative Assistant.—Karl Kaufmann.
Office Manager.—Lisa Weigle.
605 East Robinson Street, No. 650, Orlando, FL 32801 .... (407) 872–1962
District Representative.—John Ariale.

Counties: Orange (part) and Osceola (part). CITIES AND TOWNSHIPS: Apopka, Belle Isle, Bithlo, Christmas, Edgewood, Oakland, Ocoee, Orlando, Maitland, Winter Park, Windermere, Winter Garden, Zellwood, Lake Buena Vista, Taft, Tangerine, Kissimmee, and Buena Ventura Lake. Population (1990), 711,689.

ZIP Codes: 32703 (part), 32709, 32712 (part), 32733, 32745, 32751 (part), 32757 (part), 32789 (part), 32790, 32792 (part), 32793, 32798, 32801 (part), 32802–03, 32804 (part), 32805 (part), 32806–07, 32808 (part), 32809, 32810 (part), 32811 (part), 32812, 32814, 32817, 32818 (part), 32819 (part), 32820–33, 32835 (part), 32836–37, 32839 (part), 32853–54, 32856–57, 32859, 32862, 32867, 32872, 33848, 34734, 34740, 34741 (part), 34742–43, 34744 (part), 34745, 34760, 34761 (part), 34771 (part), 34777, 34786, 34787 (part)

* * *

NINTH DISTRICT

MICHAEL BILIRAKIS, Republican, of Palm Harbor, FL; born July 16, 1930, in Tarpon Springs, FL; raised in western Pennsylvania; B.S. in engineering, University of Pittsburgh, 1955–59; accounting, George Washington University, Washington, DC, 1959–60; J.D., University of Florida, Gainesville, 1961–63; U.S. Air Force, 1951–55; attorney and small businessman, petroleum engineer, aerospace contract administrator, geophysical engineer (offshore oil exploration), steelworker, and judge of various courts for eight years; honors in college include Phi Alpha Delta Annual Award for Outstanding Law Graduate and president of the student body of School of Engineering and Mines; honors after college, civil activities, and organizations include Citizen of the Year Award for Greater Tarpon Springs, 1972–73; founder and charter president of Tarpon Springs Volunteer Ambulance Service; past president and four-year director of Greater Tarpon Springs Chamber of Commerce; past president, Rotary Club of Tarpon Springs; board of governors, Pinellas Suncoast Chamber of Commerce; board of development, Anclote Manor Psychiatric Hospital, AHEPA; elected commander, Post 173 American Legion, Holiday, FL (1977–79, two terms); 33rd degree Mason and Shriner; member: West Pasco Bar Association, American Judicature Society, Florida and American bar associations, University of Florida Law Center Association and Gator Booster, American Legion, and Veterans of Foreign Wars; holds college level doctorate teaching certificate; member: Juvenile Diabetes Association, Elks, Eastern Star and White Shrine of Jerusalem, Royaler of Jesters of Egypt Temple Shrine District, Air Force Association; former member: Clearwater Bar Association, National Contract Management Association, American Society of Mining, Metallurgical and Petroleum Engineers, and Creative Education Foundation; married the former Evelyn Miaoulis, 1959; two children: Manuel and Gus; elected to the 98th Congress, November 2, 1982; reelected to each succeeding Congress.

Office Listings
http://www.house.gov/bilirakis

2240 Rayburn House Office Building, Washington, DC 20515–0909 225–5755
Administrative Assistant.—Patricia Faber. FAX: 225–4085
Legislative/Media Counsel.—Todd Tuten.
Scheduler.—Douglas Menorca.
Suite 1600, 1100 Cleveland Street, Clearwater, FL 34615 .... (813) 441–3721
Director of District Operations.—Sonja Stefanadis.
4111 Land O'Lakes Boulevard, Suite 306, Land O'Lakes, FL 34639 .... (813) 996–7441

Counties: Hillsborough (part), Pasco (part), and Pinellas (part). CITIES AND TOWNSHIPS: Aripeka, Bearss, Brandon, Brooksville, Carrollwood Village, Clearwater, Countryside, Crystal Springs, Dade City, Dale Mabry, Dunedin, Eastlake Woodlands, Elfers, Feather Sound, Holiday, Howard Franklin, Hudson, Hunters Green, Land O'Lakes, Lutz, New Port Richey, Odessa, Oldsmar, Ozona, Palm Harbor, Plant City, Quail Hollow, Safety Harbor, San Antonio, Seffner, Seven Springs Veterans Village, Smitter, St. Leo, St. Pete, Tarpon Springs, Thonotosassa, Valrico, Wesley Chapel, and Zephyrhills. Population (1990), 562,518.

ZIP Codes: 33510 (part), 33524, 33525 (part), 33526–27, 33537, 33539, 33540 (part), 33541, 33543–44, 33549 (part), 33556, 33564, 33565 (part), 33574, 33576 (part), 33584 (part), 33592, 33594 (part), 33613 (part), 33617, 33618 (part), 33624–26, 33637 (part), 33647, 33682, 33684–86, 33688, 33694, 33716 (part), 34608 (part), 34610 (part), 34615, 34616 (part), 34617–19, 34620 (part), 34621, 34622 (part), 34623, 34624 (part), 34625, 34629, 34630 (part), 34639, 34652 (part), 34653 (part), 34654 (part), 34655–56, 34660, 34667 (part), 34669 (part), 34673–74, 34677, 34679, 34681–85, 34688–89, 3 4690 (part), 34695, 34697–98

TENTH DISTRICT

C.W. BILL YOUNG, Republican, of Indian Rocks Beach, FL; born in Harmarville, PA, December 16, 1930; elected Florida's only Republican State Senator in 1960; reelected 1964, 1966, 1967 (special election), and 1968, serving as minority leader from 1963 to 1970; national committeeman, Florida Young Republicans, 1957–59; state chairman, Florida Young Republicans, 1959–61; member, Florida Constitution Revision Commission, 1965–67; he and his wife, Beverly, have three sons; elected to the 92nd Congress, November 3, 1970; reelected to each succeeding Congress; member: Committee on Appropriations, Republican Executive Committee on Committees, Select Intelligence Committee; chairman, Appropriations Subcommittee on National Security.

Office Listings

2407 Rayburn House Office Building, Washington, DC 20515–0910 225–5961
Executive Assistant.—Douglas M. Gregory. FAX: 225–9764
Legislative Director.—Harry Glenn.
Suite 627, 144 First Avenue South, St. Petersburg, FL 33701 .... (813) 893–3191
Administrative Assistant.—George N. Cretekos.
Suite 606, 801 West Bay Drive, Largo, FL 33640 .... (813) 581–0980

County: PINELLAS COUNTY (part). Population (1990), 562,518.

ZIP Codes: 33504, 33701, 33702 (part), 33703–15, 33716 (part), 33731, 33733–34, 33736–43, 33784, 34616 (part), 34620 (part), 34622 (part), 34624 (part), 34630 (part), 34635, 34640–44, 34646–49, 34664–66

* * *

ELEVENTH DISTRICT

JIM DAVIS, Democrat, of Tampa, FL; born October 11, 1957, in Tampa; B.A., Washington and Lee University, 1979; J.D., University of Florida Law School, 1982; admitted to the Florida bar in 1982 and began practice with Carlton Fields law firm in Tampa; partner, Bush, Ross, Gardner, Warren and Rudy law firm, 1988–96; member, Florida House of Representatives, 1988–96, serving as majority leader from 1994 to 1996; member of the Tampa, Brandon and Riverview chambers of commerce and Old Seminole Heights Preservation Committee; married to Peggy Bessent Davis since 1986; two sons, Peter and William; selected Democratic freshman class president for the 105th Congress.

Office Listings

http://www.house.gov/jimdavis

327 Cannon House Office Building, Washington, DC 20515 225–3376
Chief of Staff.—Suzanne F. Farmer. FAX: 225–5652
Scheduler/Executive Assistant.—Joan R. Hall.
Legislative Director.—Tricia Barrentine.
Press Secretary.—Brian K. Edwards.
3315 Henderson Boulevard, No. 100, Tampa, FL 33609 .... (813) 354–9217
District Director.—T. Clay Phillips. FAX: 354–9514

County: HILLSBOROUGH COUNTY (part); cities of Apollo Beach (part), Bloomingdale (part), Brandon (part), Carrollwood, Del Rio, East Lake-Orient Park, Egypt Lake, Gibsonton, Lake Magdalene (part), Mango (part), Palm River-Clair Mel, Riverview, Tampa, Temple Terrace, Town 'N' Country. Population (1990), 562,519.

ZIP Codes: 33509, 33510 (part), 33511 (part), 33534, 33549 (part), 33550, 33569 (part), 33572 (part), 33584 (part), 33587, 33594 (part), 33601–12, 33613 (part), 33614–17, 33618 (part), 33619, 33621–23, 33629–31, 33634–35, 33637 (part), 33672–75, 33677, 33679–82, 33684–88, 33690, 33695, 33697

* * *

TWELFTH DISTRICT

CHARLES T. CANADY, Republican, of Lakeland, FL; born June 22, 1954 in Lakeland; Lakeland Senior High School; B.A., Haverford College (PA), 1976; J.D., Yale Law School, 1979; attorney, Lakeland, 1979–92; member, Florida House of Representatives, 1984–90; recipient: President's Award, Florida Public Library Association, 1988; Crime Fighters Award, Florida Department of Law Enforcement, 1989; board member: Volunteers in Service to the Elderly, Carenet, HUG (home for unwed mothers), Community Council on Substance Abuse, United Cerebral Palsy; member, Boy Scout Advisory Council; married the former Jennifer Houghton, 1996; elected November 3, 1992 to the 103rd Congress; reelected to each succeeding Congress.

Office Listings

1222 Longworth House Office Building, Washington, DC 20515–0912 225–1252
Administrative Assistant.—Tracey St. Pierre. FAX: 225–2279
Scheduler.—Athena Buonome.
District Administrator.—Sue Loftin.
Federal Building, 124 South Tennessee Avenue, Lakeland, FL 33801 .... (813) 688–2651
FAX: 683–4453

Counties: DeSoto, Hardee, Highlands (part), Hillsborough (part), Pasco (part), and Polk (part). CITIES AND TOWNSHIPS: Arcadia, Auburndale, Avon Park (part), Bartow, Bowling Green, Brandon (part), Combee Settlement, Dade City, Dade City North, Dover, Dundee, Eagle Lake, Fort Meade, Frostproof, Haines City (part), Highland City, Kathleen, Lacoochee, Lake Alfred, Lake Wales, Lakeland, Mulberry, Plant City (part), Southeast Arcadia, Wauchula, Winter Haven and Zephyrhills (part). Population (1990), 562,519.

ZIP Codes: 33503, 33509, 33511 (part), 33524, 33525 (part), 33526–27, 33530, 33537, 33539, 33540 (part), 33547 (part), 33564, 33565 (part), 33566–67, 33569 (part), 33574, 33593, 33594 (part), 33801–09, 33811, 33813, 33820, 33823 (part), 33825 (part), 33827, 33830 (part), 33834–35, 33838–41, 33843–47, 33849–56, 33860, 33863, 33856, 33867, 33868 (part), 33870 (part), 33871, 33873, 33877, 33880–85, 33890, 33982, 33966–68

* * *

THIRTEENTH DISTRICT

DAN MILLER, Republican, of Bradenton, FL; born in Highland Park, MI, on May 30, 1942; graduated Manatee High School, Bradenton, 1960; B.S., B.A., University of Florida, Gainesville, 1964; M.B.A., Emory University, Atlanta, GA, 1965; Ph.D., Louisiana State University, Baton Rouge, 1970; former partner, Miller Enterprises; married the former Glenda Darsey, 1968; two children: Daniel Darsey and Kathryn C.; elected on November 3, 1992 to the 103rd Congress; reelected to each succeeding Congress.

Office Listings

http://www.house.gov/danmiller

102 Cannon House Office Building, Washington, DC 20515–0913 225–5015
Administrative Assistant.—Matt Kibbe. FAX: 226–0828
Legislative Director.—Marty Reiser.
District Administrator.—Ralph DeVitto.
1751 Mound, Suite A–2, Sarasota, FL 34236 .... (813) 951–6643
2424 Manatee Avenue, Suite 104, Bradenton, FL 34205 .... (813) 747–9081

Counties: Charlotte (part), Hillsborough (part), Manatee, and Sarasota. CITIES AND TOWNSHIPS: Anna Maria, Apollo Beach (part), Bayshore Gardens, Bee Ridge, Bradenton, Bradenton Beach, Cortez, Desoto Lakes, Ellenton, Englewood (part), Fruitville, Gulf Gate Estates, Holmes Beach, Kensington Park, Lake Sarasota, Lauerl, Longboat Key, Memphis, Nokomis, North Port, North Sarasota, Osprey, Palmetto, Plantation, Port Charlotte (part), Ridge Wood Heights, Ruskin, Samoset, Sarasota, Sarasota Springs, Siesta Key, South Bradenton, South Gate Ridge, South Sarasota, South Venice, Southgate, Sun City Center, The Meadows, Vamo, Venice, Venice Gardens, Warm Mineral Springs, West Bradenton, West Samoset, Whitfield and Mimauma. Population (1990), 562,518.

ZIP Codes: 33547 (part), 33569 (part), 33570–71, 33572 (part), 33573, 33586, 33598, 33948 (part), 33952 (part), 33953 (part), 33954 (part), 33980 (part), 34201–03, 34205–10, 34215–22, 34223 (part), 34224 (part), 34228–43, 34250–51, 34264, 34270, 34272, 34274–78, 34280–82, 34284–85, 34287, 34292–93, 34295

* * *

FOURTEENTH DISTRICT

PORTER J. GOSS, Republican, of Sanibel, FL; born in Waterbury, CT, November 26, 1938; B.A., Yale University, New Haven, CT, 1960; served, U.S. Army, second lieutenant, 1960–62; clandestine services officer, CIA, 1962–72; newspaper publisher, small business owner; councilman/mayor, city of Sanibel, 1974–82; chairman, Lee County Commission, 1985–86; commissioner, Lee County, District 1, 1983–88; director, National Audubon Society; chairman, State Advisory Committee on Coastal Management; vice chairman, West Coast Inland Navigational District; past chairman, Metropolitan Planning Organization; port commissioner, Southwest Florida Regional Airport; member: Southwest Florida Mental Health District Board, Canterbury School, Lee County Mental Health Center, Sanibel-Captiva Conservation Foundation, Westminster Presbyterian Church; married to the former Mariel Robinson; four children: Leslie, Chauncey, Mason, and Gerrit; elected November 8, 1988, to the 101st Congress; reelected to each succeeding Congress.

Office Listings

http://www.house.gov/goss

108 Cannon House Office Building, Washington, DC 20515–0914 225–2536
FAX: 225–6820

Chief of Staff.—Sheryl Wooley.
Administrative Assistant/Counsel to Rules Subcommittee on Legislative and Budget Process.—Wendy Selig.
Legislative Director.—Merrell Moorhead.
Office Manager/Scheduler.—Maggie Knutson.
Press Secretary.—Natasha DeWees.
Senior Legislative Assistant.—Kirsten Madison.
Suite 303, Barnett Center, 2000 Main Street, Fort Myers, FL 33901 .... (813) 332–4677
FAX: 332–1743
Suite 212, Building F, 3301 Tamiam: Trail East, Naples, FL 33962 .... (813) 774–8060
FAX: 774–7262
75 Taylor Street, Punta Gorda, FL 33950 .... (813) 639–0051

Counties: Charlotte (part), Collier, and Lee. Population (1990), 562,518.

ZIP Codes: 33901–43, 33945–57, 33959, 33961–64, 33969–72, 39975, 33980 (part), 33981–83, 33990–91, 33993–94 33999, 34133–35, 34137–43, 34145–46, 34223 (part), 34224 (part)

* * *

FIFTEENTH DISTRICT

DAVE WELDON, Republican, of Palm Bay, FL; born in Long Island, NY, August 31, 1953; graduated Farmingdale High School, Farmingdale, NY, 1971; B.S., biochemistry, State University of New York, Stony Brook, 1978; M.D., State University of New York, Buffalo, 1981; U.S. Army Major, 1981–87; physician, internal medicine; member: American College of Physicians, Florida Medical Association, Brevard County Medical Society, Retired Officers Association, Good Samaritan Club, Brevard Veterans Council, Vietnam Veterans of Brevard, American Legion; founder, Space Coast Family Forum; married Nancy Weldon, 1979; one child, Katherine; elected to the 104th Congress; reelected to the 105th Congress.

Office Listings

http://www.house.gov/weldon fla15@hr.house.gov

216 Cannon House Office Building, Washington, DC 20515–0915 225–3671
Administrative Assistant.—Dana Gartzke. FAX: 225–3516
Office Manager.—Barbara Reynolds.
Legislative Director.—Stuart Burns.
Press Secretary.—April Lassiter.
2725 Saint John Street, Building C, Melbourne, FL 32940 .... (407) 632–1776
FAX: 639–8595

Counties: Brevard, Indian River, Osceola (part), and Polk (part). Population (1990), 562,519.

ZIP Codes: 32754 (part), 32775, 32780–83, 32796, 32815, 32901–10, 32920, 32922–27, 32931–32, 32934–37, 32940–41, 32948–68, 32970–71, 32976, 32978, 33402 (part), 33420 (part), 33823 (part), 33830 (part), 33837, 33844 (part), 33845, 33850 (part), 33851, 33853 (part), 33858, 33868 (part), 33877, 34739, 34741 (part), 34744 (part), 34746–47, 34758–59, 34769–70, 34771 (part), 34772–73, 34972 (part)

* * *

SIXTEENTH DISTRICT

MARK A. FOLEY, Republican, of West Palm Beach, FL; born in Newton, MA, September 8, 1954; graduated Lake Worth High School, Lake Worth, FL; attended Palm Beach Community College, Lake Worth; president, Foley Smith and Associates, Inc., real estate company; Florida House of Representatives, 1990–92; Florida Senate (Agriculture Committee chairman), 1992–94; Lake Worth city commissioner, 1977; Lake Worth vice mayor, 1983–84; elected to the 104th Congress.

Office Listings
mfoley@hr.house.gov

506 Cannon House Office Building, Washington, DC 20515 225–5792
Chief of Staff/Press Secretary.—Kirk Fordham. FAX: 225–3132
Executive Assistant/Scheduler.—Michele Famiglietti.
Legislative Director.—Sean Dougherty.
4440 PGA Boulevard, Suite 406, Palm Beach Gardens, FL 33410 .... (407) 627–6192
District Manager.—Ed Chase. FAX: 626–4749
250 Northwest Country Club Drive, Port St. Lucie, FL 34986 .... (407) 878–3181
District Manager.—Anne Decker. FAX: 871–0651

Counties: Glades, Hendry, Highlands, Martin, Okeechobee, Palm Beach, and St. Lucie. Population (1990), 562,519.

ZIP Codes: 33401 (part), 33403 (part), 33404 (part), 33406 (part), 33407 (part), 33409 (part), 33410 (part), 33411 (part), 33412, 33413 (part), 33414 (part), 33415 (part), 33417–18, 33430 (part), 33437 (part), 33440 (part), 33455, 33458, 33461 (part), 33463 (part), 33467 (part), 33468–69, 33470 (part), 33471, 33475, 33477–78, 33498 (part), 33825 (part), 33852, 33857, 33870 (part), 33871–72, 33920 (part), 33930, 33935, 33944, 33960, 34945 (part), 34946 (part), 34947 (part), 34949, 34950 (part), 34951 (part), 34952–53, 34957–58, 34972 (part), 34973, 34974 (part), 34981 (part), 34982–85, 34986 (part), 34987 (part), 34990, 34992, 34994–97

* * *

SEVENTEENTH DISTRICT

CARRIE P. MEEK, Democrat, of Miami, FL; born in Tallahassee, FL, on April 29, 1926; attended Florida A&M Laboratory School, Tallahassee; graduated, Florida A&M High School, Tallahassee, 1943; B.S., Florida A&M University, Tallahassee, 1946; M.S., University of Michigan, Ann Arbor, 1948; Florida Atlantic University, Boca Raton; instructor, Florida A&M University, Tallahassee; instructor, Bethune Cookman-College, Daytona Beach, FL; professor, Miami-Dade Community College; planner, Dade County Model City Program; Florida House of Representatives, 1979–82; Florida Senate, 1982–92; special assistant to the vice president, Miami-Dade Community College; recipient, 1995 Governor LeRoy Collins Lifetime Achievement Award and 1997 Spirit of Dr. Martin Luther King Jr. Award; three children: Lucia Davis Raiford, Sheila Davis Kinui, and Kendrick Meek; elected on November 3, 1992 to the 103rd Congress; reelected to each succeeding Congress.

Office Listings
http://www.house.gov/meek

401 Cannon House Office Building, Washington, DC 20515–0917 225–4506
Chief of Staff.—Peggy Demon. FAX: 226–0777
Deputy Chief of Staff.—John Schelble.
Press Secretary/Legislative Assistant.—Tola Thompson.
District Office Manager.—Cynthia Allen.
25 West Flagler Street, Suite 1015, Miami, FL 33130 .... (305) 381–9541

County: DADE COUNTY (part); cities and townships of Allapattah, Andover, Belle Meade, Biscayne Gardens, Biscayne Park (part), Brownsville (part), Bunche Park, Carol City (part), Coconut Grove (part), Coral Gables (part), Crestview, Cutler Ridge (part), El Portal, Florida City (part), Gladeview, Glenvar Heights, Golden Glades, Goulds (part), Hialeah (part), Homestead (part), Homestead AFB, Howard, Kendall (part), Lake Lucerne, Leisure City (part), Lemon City, Liberty City, Little Haiti, Little River, Miami (part), Miami Shores (part), Morningside, Naranja, Norland (part), North Miami (part), North Miami Beach (part), Norwood, Ojus (part), Opa-locka, Opa-locka North, Overtown, Palmetto Estates, Perrine (part), Pinewood, Princeton (part), Richmond Heights (part), Rolling Oaks, Scott Lake, South Miami (part), South Miami Heights (part), Washington Park, West Little River, Westview and Wynwood. Population (1990), 570,981.

ZIP Codes: 33012 (part), 33013 (part), 33014 (part), 33030 (part), 33032 (part), 33033 (part), 33034 (part), 33039, 33054, 33055 (part), 33056, 33090, 33101, 33125 (part), 33127, 33128 (part), 33129 (part), 33130 (part), 33132 (part), 33133 (part), 33136 (part), 33137 (part), 33138 (part), 33142 (part), 33143 (part), 33145 (part), 33146 (part), 33147 (part), 33150 (part), 33151, 33153, 33155 (part), 33156 (part), 33157 (part), 33160 (part), 33161 (part), 33162 (part), 33164, 33167–68, 33169 (part), 33170 (part), 33176 (part), 33177 (part), 33179 (part), 33180 (part), 33181 (part), 33186 (part), 33188, 33189 (part), 33190 (part), 33238, 33242, 33261

* * *

EIGHTEENTH DISTRICT

ILEANA ROS-LEHTINEN, Republican, of Miami, FL; born July 15, 1952 in Havana, Cuba; B.A., English, Florida International University; M.S., educational leadership, Florida International University; doctoral candidate in education, University of Miami; certified Florida school teacher; founder and former owner, Eastern Academy; elected to Florida House of Representatives, 1982; elected to Florida State Senate, 1986; former president, Bilingual Private School Association; regular contributor to leading Spanish-language newspaper; during House tenure, married then-State Representative Dexter Lehtinen; two children: Amanda Michelle and Patricia Marie; elected on August 29, 1989 to the 101st Congress; reelected to each succeeding Congress; member, International Relations and Government Reform and Oversight committees.

Office Listings

127 Cannon House Office Building, Washington, DC 20515–0918 225–3931
Chief of Staff.—Arthur Estopinan. FAX: 225–5620
Legislative Director.—Jay O'Callaghan.
Press Secretary.—Juan Cortinas.
Appointment Secretary.—William S. Burlew.
Suite 240, 5757 Blue Lagoon Drive, Miami, FL 33126 .... (305) 262–1800

County: DADE COUNTY (part); cities and townships of Coral Gables, Florida City, Homestead, Key Biscayne, Miami, Miami Beach, South Miami, and West Miami. Population (1990), 562,519.

ZIP Codes: 33030 (part), 33031 (part), 33032 (part), 33033 (part), 33034 (part), 33035 (part), 33092, 33109, 33111, 33114, 33116, 33119, 33122 (part), 33124, 33125 (part), 33126 (part), 33128 (part), 33129 (part), 33130 (part), 33131, 33132 (part), 33133 (part), 33134–35, 33136 (part), 33139 (part), 33142 (part), 33143 (part), 33144 (part), 33145 (part), 33146 (part), 33149, 33155 (part), 33156 (part), 33157 (part), 33158 (part), 33165 (part), 33170 (part), 33173 (part), 33174 (part), 33175 (part), 33176 (part), 33177 (part), 33186 (part), 33189 (part), 33190 (part), 33197, 33233, 33243, 33245, 33255, 33257, 33283, 33296, 33299

* * *

NINETEENTH DISTRICT

ROBERT WEXLER, Democrat, of Boca Raton, FL; born on January 2, 1961 in Queens, NY; graduate of Hollywood Hills High School; University of Florida, 1982; George Washington University Law School, 1985; admitted to the Florida bar in 1985; former attorney; Florida State Senator, 1990-96; member: Palm Beach Planning and Zoning Commission, 1989-90, Palm Beach County Democratic Executive Committee, 1989-92, Palm Beach County Affordable Housing Committee, 1990-91, Florida Bar Association, South Palm Beach County Jewish Federation, Palm Beach County Anti-Defamation League; married to the former Laurie Cohen; three children: Rachel, Zachary, and Hannah; committees: Judiciary, International Relations; subcommittees: Crime, Immigration and Claims, International Operations and Human Rights, Asia and the Pacific; elected to the 105th Congress on November 5, 1996.

Office Listings

1609 Longworth House Office Building, Washington, DC 20515–0919 225–3001
Chief of Staff.—Suzanne Stoll. FAX: 225–5974
Legislative Director.—Susan Silver.
Executive Assistant.—Lisa White.
Press Secretary.—Betsy Rothstein.
2500 North Military Trail, Suite 100, Boca Raton, FL 33434 .... (561) 988–6302
District Director.—Eric Johnson.

Counties: Broward and Palm Beach. CITIES AND TOWNSHIPS: Boca Raton, Boynton Beach, Deerfield Beach, Delray Beach, Fort Lauderdale, Tamarac, and West Palm Beach.

ZIP Codes: 33063–69, 33071, 33073, 33075–77, 33093, 33097, 33309, 33319–21, 33349, 33351, 33424–26, 33428, 33431–37, 33442–46, 33460, 33462–65, 33467, 33481–82, 33484, 33486–87, 33496–99

* * *

TWENTIETH DISTRICT

PETER DEUTSCH, Democrat, of Lauderhill, FL; born in New York, NY on April 1, 1957; graduated, Horace Mann School, New York City, 1975; B.A., Swarthmore College, 1979; J.D., Yale Law School, New Haven, CT, 1982; attorney; admitted to Florida bar, 1983; elected to the Florida State House, 1982; member, Jewish Foundation Board of Directors; married the former Lori Ann Coffino, 1989; two children: Johnathan Michael and Danielle Brooke; elected on November 3, 1992 to the 103rd Congress; reelected to each succeeding Congress.

Office Listings
pdeutsch@hr.house.gov

425 Cannon House Office Building, Washington, DC 20515–0920 225–7931
Administrative Assistant.—Jim Smith. FAX: 225–8456
Legislative Director.—Elizabeth Mullin.
Scheduler/Legislative Aide.—Jacqueline Martins.
District Administrator.—Henry Ellenbogen.
10100 Pines Boulevard, Pembroke Pines, FL 33025 .... (305) 437–3936
FAX: 437–4776

Counties: Broward (part), Dade (part), and Monroe. Population (1990), 562,518.

ZIP Codes: 33001, 33021 (part), 33023 (part), 33024, 33025 (part), 33026–29, 33030 (part), 33031 (part), 33032 (part), 33033 (part), 33034 (part), 33035 (part), 33036–37, 33040–45, 33050–52, 33070, 33081–82, 33084, 33156 (part), 33157 (part), 33158 (part), 33170 (part), 33177 (part), 33187 (part), 33189 (part), 33190 (part), 33196 (part), 33256, 33301 (part), 33312 (part), 33313 (part), 33314, 33315 (part), 33317 (part), 33318, 33319 (part), 33322–26, 33328–32, 33338, 33351 (part), 33388

* * *

TWENTY-FIRST DISTRICT

LINCOLN DIAZ-BALART, Republican, of Miami, FL; born in Havana, Cuba on August 13, 1954; graduated, American School of Madrid, Spain, 1972; B.A., New College of the University of South Florida, Sarasota, 1976; J.D., Case Western Reserve University Law School, 1979; attorney; admitted to the Florida bar, 1979; partner, Fowler, White, Burnett, Hurley, Banick and Strickroot, P.A., Miami; Florida State House, 1986–89; Florida State Senate, 1989–92; founding member, Miami-Westchester Lions Club; member, Organization for Retarded Citizens; member: Foreign Affairs Committee (currently on leave), Rules Committee; vice chairman, Committee on Rules of the House; House Oversight Committee; 1992–94: national vice chairman, National Republican Congressional Committee; chairman, Republican Research Committee Task Force on Latin American and Carribean Affairs; member: Congressional Hispanic Caucus, executive committee; Congresional Human Rights Caucus; married the former Cristina Fernandez, 1976; two children: Lincoln Gabriel and Daniel; elected on November 3, 1992 to the 103rd Congress; reelected to each succeding Congress.

Office Listings
http://www.house.gov/diaz-balart

431 Cannon House Office Building, Washington, DC 20515–0921 225–4211
Chief of Staff/Administrative Assistant.—Stephen D. Vermillion III.
Legislative Director.—Elizabeth Humphrey.
Press Secretary.—Yanik Maria Fenton.
8525 NW 53 Terrace, Suite 102, Miami, FL 33166 .... (305) 470–8555
District Director.—Ana M. Carbonell.

County: DADE COUNTY (part); cities of Carol City (part), Country Club, Doral, Hammocks, Hialeah (part), Hialeah Gardens, Kendale Lakes, Kendall (part), Kendall Lakes West, Lindgren Acres, Miami Lakes, Miami Springs, Palm Springs North, Sunset (part), Sweetwater, Tamiami and Virginia Gardens. Population (1990), 562,519.

ZIP Codes: 33010–11, 33012 (part), 33013 (part), 33014 (part), 33015–17, 33055 (part), 33102, 33122 (part), 33126 (part), 33142 (part), 33144 (part), 33147 (part), 33152, 33159, 33165 (part), 33166, 33172, 33173 (part), 33174 (part), 33175 (part), 33176 (part), 33177 (part), 33178, 33182–85, 33186 (part), 33187 (part), 33193, 33196 (part), 33247, 33265–66

* * *

TWENTY-SECOND DISTRICT

E. CLAY SHAW, JR., Republican, of Fort Lauderdale, FL; born in Miami, FL, April 19, 1939; graduated, Miami Edison Senior High School, 1957; B.A., Stetson University, Deland, FL, 1961; M.B.A., University of Alabama, 1963; J.D., Stetson University College of Law, 1966; former certified public accountant; lawyer; admitted to the Florida State bar in 1966 and commenced practice in Fort Lauderdale; admitted to practice before the federal court in the Southern District of Florida and the U.S. Supreme Court; assistant city attorney, Fort Lauderdale, 1968; chief city prosecutor, 1968–69; assistant municipal judge, 1969–71; city commissioner, 1971–72; vice mayor, 1973–75; mayor, 1975–80; member: executive committee, U.S. Conference of Mayors; executive committee, Republican National Committee; president, National

Conference of Republican Mayors; U.S. special ambassador, Papua, New Guinea (President Ford); director, Fort Lauderdale Chamber of Commerce; vice chairman, Sun Belt Mayor's Task Force; Broward County Charter Commission; national vice chairman, Mayors for Reagan, 1980; member, St. Anthony's Church; married the former Emilie Costar, 1960; four children: Mimi Shaw Carter, Jennifer Shaw Wilder, E. Clay Shaw III, and John Charles Shaw; elected to the 97th Congress, November 4, 1980; reelected to each succeeding Congress.

Office Listings

2267 Rayburn House Office Building, Washington, DC 20515–0922 225–3026
Chief of Staff and Tax Counsel.—Scott Spear. FAX: 225–8398
Press Secretary.—Scott Brenner.
1512 East Broward Boulevard, Fort Lauderdale, FL 33301 .... (305) 522–1800
District Director.—Dorothy Stuart.
222 Lakeview Avenue, No. 162, West Palm Beach, FL 33401 .... (407) 832–3007

Counties: Aventura, Bal Harbour, Bay Harbor Islands, Biscayne Park, Boca Raton, Boynton Beach, Bring Breezes, Cloud Lake, Dania, Deerfield Beach, Delray Beach, Fort Lauderdale, Glen Ridge, Golden Beach, Gulf Stream, Hallandale, Highland Beach, Hillsboro Beach, Hollywood, Hypoluxo, Indian Creek, Juno Beach, Lake Park, Lake Worth, Lantana, Lauderdale by the Sea, Lazy Lake, Lighthouse Point, Manalapan, Miami, Miami Beach, Miami Shores, North Bay Village, North Miami, North Miami Beach, North Palm Beach, Oakland Park, Ocean Ridge, Palm Beach, Palm Beach Gardens, Palm Beach Shores, Pembroke Park, Pompano Beach, Rivera Beach, Sea Ranch Lakes, South Palm Beach, Surfside, West Palm Beach, and Wilton Manors.

ZIP Codes: 33004 (part), 33009 (part), 33019, 33020 (part), 33023 (part), 33060 (part), 33062, 33064 (part), 33132 (part), 33138 (part), 33139 (part), 33140, 33141, 33154, 33160, 33161 (part), 33162 (part), 33169 (part), 33179 (part), 33180, 33181 (part), 33301 (part), 33304 (part), 33305, 33306, 33308, 33309 (part), 33311 (part), 33316 (part), 33334 (part), 33401 (part), 33403 (part), 33404 (part), 33405, 33406 (part), 33408, 33410 (part), 33431 (part), 33432 (part), 33435 (part), 33441 (part), 33460 (part), 33480, 33483 (part), 33487 (part)

* * *

TWENTY-THIRD DISTRICT

ALCEE L. HASTINGS, Democrat, of Miramar, FL; born in Altamonte, FL, on September 5, 1936; graduated, Crooms Academy, Sanford, FL, 1954; B.A., Fisk University, Nashville, TN, 1958; Howard University, Washington, D.C.; J.D., Florida A&M University, Tallahassee, 1963; attorney; admitted to the Florida bar, 1963; circuit judge, U.S. District Court Judge for the Southern District of Florida; U.S. Federal Judge; member: African Methodist Episcopal Church, NAACP, Miami-Dade Chamber of Commerce, Family Christian Association, ACLU, Southern Poverty Law Center, National Organization for Women, Planned Parenthood, Women and Children First, Inc., Sierra Club, Cousteau Society, Broward County Democratic Executive Committee, Dade County Democratic Executive Committee, Lauderhill Democratic Club, Hollywood Hills Democratic Club, Pembroke Pines Democratic Club, Urban League, National Bar Association, Florida Chapter of the National Bar Association, T.J. Reddick Bar Association, National Conference of Black Lawyers, Simon Wiesenthal Center, The Furtivist Society; Progressive Black Police Officers Club, International Black Firefighters Association; three children: Alcee Lamar II, Chelsea, and Leigh; elected on November 3, 1992 to the 103rd Congress; reelected to each succeeding Congress.

Office Listings

http://www.house.gov/alceehastings hastings@hr.house.gov

1039 Longworth House Office Building, Washington, DC 20515–0923 225–1313
Legislative Director.—Ann Jacobs.
District Administrator.—Arthur W. Kennedy.
2701 West Oakland Park Boulevard, Suite 200, Oakland Park, FL 33311 .... (305) 733–2800
5725 Corporate Way, Suite 208, West Palm Beach, FL 33407 .... (407) 684–0565

Counties: Broward (part), Dade (part), Hendry (part), Martin (part), Okeechobee (part), Palm Beach (part), and St. Lucie (part). Population (1990), 562,519.

ZIP Codes: 33004 (part), 33008, 33009 (part), 33020 (part), 33021 (part), 33023 (part), 33025 (part), 33060 (part), 33064 (part), 33068 (part), 33069 (part), 33073 (part), 33074, 33083, 33169 (part), 33179 (part), 33269, 33301 (part), 33304 (part), 33305 (part), 33309 (part), 33311 (part), 33312 (part), 33313 (part), 33315 (part), 33316 (part), 33317 (part), 33319 (part), 33334 (part), 33340, 33345, 33401 (part), 33402 (part), 33403 (part), 33404 (part), 33406 (part), 33407 (part), 33408 (part), 33409 (part), 33411 (part), 33413 (part), 33414 (part), 33415 (part), 33416, 33419, 33430 (part), 33431 (part), 33432 (part), 33435 (part), 33438–39, 33440 (part), 33441 (part), 33442 (part), 33444 (part), 33445 (part), 33447, 33459, 33460 (part), 33461 (part), 33462 (part), 33470 (part), 33476, 33483 (part), 33486 (part), 33487 (part), 33491, 33493, 34945 (part), 34946 (part), 34947 (part), 34948, 34950 (part), 34951 (part), 34954, 34956, 34972 (part), 34974 (part), 34979, 34981 (part), 34986 (part), 34987 (part), 34988

GEORGIA

(Population 1995, 7,201,000)

SENATORS

PAUL D. COVERDELL, Republican, of Atlanta, GA; born January 20, 1939 in Des Moines, IA; graduated, Lee's Summit High School, Lee's Summit, MO, 1957; B.S., journalism, University of Missouri, 1961; served as an officer, U.S. Army in Okinawa, Taiwan and Korea, 1962–64; founder and chairman of the board, Coverdell and Company, Inc.; Georgia State Senate, 1970–89; chairman, Georiga Republican Party, 1985–87; director, U.S. Peace Corps, 1989–91; Good Government Award, Atlanta Jaycees, 1976; Ten Leading State Legislators, *Atlanta Journal/Constitution,* 1980; NRLA Legislator of the Year, 1982; Liberty Bell Award, Atlanta Bar Association, 1982; Honorable William E. Brock Award, 1984; Hermione Weil Alexander Fund Award of Appreciation, 1984, for the battle against drunk driving; Atlanta Fulton County League of Women Voters, second Sidney Marcus Public Service Award, 1985; Leadership Atlanta, Leadership Georgia; 1989 Distinguished Service Award, Georgia Republican Party; Georgia Institute of Technology Distinguished Service Award, 1989; Distinguished Service Award from the Georgia Association for Retarded Citizens, 1984; married to Nancy Nally Coverdell; Republican Conference Secretary; committees: Agriculture, Nutrition and Forestry; Appropriations; Energy and Natural Resources; Veterans' Affairs; Special Committee on Aging; elected to the U.S. Senate in a special runoff election, November 24, 1992, for the six-year term beginning January 3, 1993.

Office Listings

http://www.senate.gov/~coverdell senator@coverdell.senate.gov

200 Russell Senate Office Building, Washington, DC 20510–1004 224–3643
Administrative Director.—Molly Dye.
Legislative Director.—Alex Albert.
Director of Constituent Services.—Shirley Puchalski.
Suite 300, 100 Coloney Square, 1175 Peachtree Street, Atlanta, GA 30361 .... (404) 347–2202
Suite 1208, 699 Broad Street, Augusta, GA 30901 .... (706) 722–0032
10 Eleventh Street, Columbus, GA 31901 .... (706) 322–7920
503 South Thornton Avenue, Dalton, GA 30720 .... (706) 226–1925
Suite 1502, Two East Bryan Street, Savannah, GA 31401 .... (912) 238–3244
22 North Main Street, Moultrie, GA 31768 .... (912) 985–8113
582 Walnut Street, Macon, GA 31297 .... (912) 742–0205

JOSEPH MAXWELL CLELAND, Democrat, of Lithonia, GA; born in Atlanta, GA, August 24, 1942; graduated, Lithonia High School, 1960; B.A., Stetson University, Deland, FL, 1964 (honorary doctorate); M.A., honorary doctorate, Emory University, 1968; captain, U.S. Army, 1965–68; Bronze Star for Meritorious Service, Silver Star for Gallantry in Action; Georgia State Senate, 1971–75; Secretary of State, Georgia, 1983–96; consultant, Committee on Veterans' Affairs, U.S. Senate, 1975; staff member, Committee on Veterans' Affairs, U.S. Senate, 1975–77; administrator of U.S. Veterans' Administration, 1977–81; committees: Armed Services; Governmental Affairs; Small Business; elected to the 105th Congress.

Office Listings

http://www.senate.gov/~cleland senator__max__cleland@cleland.senate.gov

463 Dirksen Senate Office Building, Washington, DC 20510–1001 224–3521
Administrative Assistant.—Wayne Howell. FAX: 224–0072
Legislative Director.—Bill Johnstone.
Press Secretary.—Jennifer Wardrep.
Scheduler.—Erica Brooks.
Executive Assistant.—Carole Dabbs.
75 Spring Street, S.W., Suite 1700, Atlanta, GA 30303 .... (404) 331–4811
State Director.—Bill Chapman. FAX: 331–5439
Deputy State Directors.—Curtis Atkinson, Elsie Hand.

REPRESENTATIVES

FIRST DISTRICT

JACK KINGSTON, Republican, of Savannah, GA; born on April, 24, 1955 in Bryan, TX; Michigan State University, 1973–74; University of Georgia, 1974–78; insurance salesman; vice president, Palmer and Cay/Carswell; Georgia State Legislature, 1984–92; member: Savannah Health Mission, Isle of Hope Community Association, Christ Church; married Elizabeth Morris Kingston, 1979; four children: Betsy, John, Ann, and Jim; committees: Agriculture, Ways and Means; elected on November 3, 1992 to the 103rd Congress; reelected to each succeeding Congress.

Office Listings

http://www.house.gov/kingston

1507 Longworth House Office Building, Washington, DC 20515–1001 225–5831
Staff Director.—Karleen Mahn. FAX: 226–2269
Legislative Director.—Diana Burns.
Legislative Assistant.—Karen Roberson.
Press Secretary.—Robyn Ridgley.
6605 Abercorn Street, Suite 102, Savannah, GA 31405 .... (912) 352–0101
Statesboro Federal Building No. 220, Statesboro, GA 30458 .... (912) 489–8797
208 Tebeau Street, Waycross, GA 31501 .... (912) 287–1180
Federal Building, Room 304, Brunswick, GA 31520 .... (912) 265–9010

Counties: Appling, Bacon, Brantley, Bryan, Bulloch, Camden, Candler, Charlton, Chatham (part), Effingham (part), Emanuel, Evans, Glynn, Liberty, Long, McIntosh, Montgomery, Pierce, Tattnall, Toombs, Ware, and Wayne. Population (1990), 589,546.

ZIP Codes: 30308–9, 30415, 30417, 30420–21, 30427, 30436, 30438–39, 30442, 30446, 30450, 30452–3, 30455, 30458, 30467, 30474, 30822, 31301–05, 31312–14, 31316, 31319–24, 31326–29, 31331, 31404 (part), 31405 (part), 31406 (part), 31407, 31408 (part), 31409, 31410 (part), 31411, 31419, 31503, 31516, 31518, 31520, 35122 31525, 31527, 31537, 31542–43, 31545, 31548, 31551, 31553, 31555, 31557–8 31560, 31565–66, 31568–69

* * *

SECOND DISTRICT

SANFORD BISHOP, Democrat, of Columbus, GA; born on February 4, 1947 in Mobile, AL; attended Mobile County public schools; B.A., Morehouse College, 1968; J.D., Emory College, 1971; attorney; admitted to the Georgia and Alabama bars; Georgia House of Representatives, 1977–91; Georgia Senate, 1991–93; former member: executive board, Chattahoochee Council; Boy Scouts of America; YMCA; Sigma Pi Phi fraternity; Kappa Alpha Psi fraternity; 32nd degree Mason, Shriner; member: Fourth Street Baptist Church, Columbus, GA; committees: Agriculture, Veterans' Affairs; elected to the 103rd Congress; reelected to each succeeding Congress.

Office Listings

1632 Longworth House Office Building, Washington, DC 20515–1002 225–3631
Administrative Assistant.—Nadine Chatman. FAX: 225–1117
Legislative Director.—Cheryll Johnson.
Communications Director.—Selby McCach.
District Director.—Hobby Stripling.
Room 201, 225 Pine Avenue, Albany, GA 31701 .... (912) 439–8067
The Rankin, 17 Tenth Street, Columbus, GA 31901 .... (706) 323–6894
101 South Main, City Hall, Dawson, GA 31742 .... (912) 995–3991
Southern Trust Building, 682 Cherry Street, Suite 1113, Macon, GA 31201 .... (912) 741–2221
Room 211, 401 North Patterson, Valdosta, GA 31601 .... (912) 247–9705

Counties: Baker, Bibb (part), Brooks, Calhoun, Chattahoochee, Clay, Colquitt (part), Crawford (part), Crisp (part), Decatur, Dooly (part), Dougherty (part), Early, Grady, Houston (part), Lee (part), Lowndes (part), Macon, Marion, Meriwether (part), Miller, Mitchell, Muscogee (part), Peach (part), Quitman, Randolph, Schley, Seminole, Stewart, Sumter, Talbot, Taylor, Terrell, Thomas, and Webster. Population (1990), 591,699.

ZIP Codes: 30021 (part), 30066 (part), 30218, 30222, 30251, 30293, 30354 (part), 30572, 30646 (part), 30669, 31006–07, 31008 (part), 31013, 31015 (part), 31025, 31028 (part), 31030 (part), 31036 (part), 31039, 31041, 31051, 31057–58, 31063, 31066 (part), 31068, 31069 (part), 31070, 31076, 31078, 31081, 31088 (part), 31091–92, 31093 (part), 31098 (part), 31201 (part), 31204 (part), 31206 (part), 31210 (part), 31211 (part), 31601 (part), 31602 (part), 31625–26, 31629, 31638, 31643, 31701 (part), 31702–03, 31705 (part), 31706, 31707 (part), 31709, 31711, 31713, 31715–17, 31720, 31723–26, 31728–30, 31732, 31734–43, 31745–46, 31751–54, 31756, 31759, 31761–62, 31763 (part), 31764–

67, 31768 (part), 31770, 31773, 31777–80, 31784–87, 31792, 31797, 31799, 31801 (part), 31803, 31805–06, 31810, 31812, 31814–15, 31816 (part), 31821, 31824–25, 31827, 31832, 31836, 31901 (part), 31902–03, 31904 (part), 31905, 31906 (part), 31907 (part), 31908

* * *

THIRD DISTRICT

MAC COLLINS, Republican, of Hampton, GA; born in Jackson, October 14, 1944; graduated, Jackson High School, 1962; owner, Collins Trucking Company, Inc.; Georgia State Senate, 1989–92; chairman, Butts County Commission, 1977–80; chairman, Butts County Republican Party, 1981–82; director, Georgia Forestry Association; 32nd degree Mason; member: American Legislative Exchange Council and National Conference of State Legislatures; married the former Julie Watkins, 1964; four children: Crystal, Mike, Andy, and April; committee: Ways and Means; deputy whip; elected on November 3, 1992 to the 103rd Congress; reelected to each succeeding Congress.

Office Listings

http://www.house.gov/maccollins rep3mac@hr.house.gov

1131 Longworth House Office Building, Washington, DC 20515–1003 225–5901
Administrative Assistant.—Betty Monro. FAX: 225–2515
Legislative Director.—Bo Bryant.
Executive Assistant.—Anne Derouen Jasien.
173 North Main Street, Jonesboro, GA 30336 .... (770) 603–3395
District Administrator.—Ronnie Chance.
2121 Wynnton Road, Columbus, GA 31906 .... (706) 327–7229

Counties: Clayton (part), Coweta, Fayette, Harris, Henry (part), Lamar, Meriwether (part), Monroe, Muscogee, Pike, and Spalding. Population (1990), 591,328.

ZIP Codes: 30027 (part), 30049 (part), 30050 (part), 30051, 30205–06, 30212, 30213 (part), 30214, 30220, 30223–24, 30228 (part), 30229, 30233 (part), 30234 (part), 30236–37, 30244 (part), 30248 (part), 30249 (part), 30250, 30253 (part), 30257, 30258, 30259–60, 30263–66, 30268 (part), 30269, 30273, 30274 (part), 30275–77, 30281 (part), 30284–87, 30289–90, 30292, 30295, 30296 (part), 30337 (part), 30349 (part), 30354 (part), 31004, 31016, 31029, 31030, 31031 (part), 31038 (part), 31046, 31052 (part), 31066 (part), 31086, 31097, 31210 (part), 31211 (part), 31801 (part), 31804, 31807–08, 31811, 31816 (part), 31820, 31822 (part), 31823, 31826, 31829–31, 31833 (part), 31901, 31904 (part), 31906, 31907, 31909, 30002 (part), 30021 (part), 30030 (part), 30031, 30032 (part), 30033 (part), 30035 (part), 30036–37, 30049 (part), 30058 (part), 30061, 30065, 30071 (part), 30072, 30074, 30079 (part), 30083 (part), 30084 (part), 30085–86, 30087 (part), 30088 (part), 30091, 30093, 30136 (part), 30174 (part), 30207 (part), 30208 (part), 30209, 30221 (part), 30226, 30243 (part), 30244 (part), 30245 (part), 30246–47, 30249 (part), 30253 (part), 30278, 30281 (part), 30305 (part), 30306 (part), 30307 (part), 30309 (part), 30317 (part), 30319 (part), 30322, 30324 (part), 30326 (part), 30329, 30340, 30341 (part), 30345, 30347, 30359, 30360 (part), 30362, 30366, 30376, 31119

* * *

FOURTH DISTRICT

CYNTHIA McKINNEY, Democrat, of Decatur, GA; born in Atlanta, GA, on March 17, 1955; graduated St. Joseph High School, Atlanta; A.B., University of Southern California, 1978; attended Fletcher School of Law and Diplomacy; currently enrolled in Ph.D. program; Georgia State House of Representatives, 1988–92; member, NAACP; one child, Coy Grandison, Jr.; elected on November 3, 1992 to the 103rd Congress; reelected to each succeeding Congress.

Office Listings

http://www.house.gov/mckinney cymck@hr.house.gov

124 Cannon House Office Building, Washington, DC 20515–1011 225–1605
Legislative Director.—David Taylor.
Press Secretary/Legislative Assistant.—Omar Jabard.
246 Sycamore Street, Suite 110, Decatur, GA 30030 .... (404) 377–6900
District Director.—Gary Cox.

Counties: DeKalb, Gwinnett (part). CITIES: Avodale Estates, Chamblee, Conyers, Decatur, Doraville, Druid Hills, Duluth (part), Lawrenceville (part), Liburn, Loganville (part), Mountain Park, Norcross, North Decatur, North Druid Hills, Scottdale, Snellville, Stone Mountain and Tucker. Population (1990), 588,293.

ZIP Codes: 30002 (part), 30021 (part), 30030 (part), 30031, 30032 (part), 30033 (part), 30034, 30035, (part), 30036–37, 30049 (part), 30058 (part), 30072, 30079 (part), 30083, 30084 (part), 30086, 30087 (part), 30091, 30093, 30136 (part), 30174 (part), 30207 (part), 30208 (part), 30209, 30221 (part), 30226, 30243 (part), 30244 (part), 30245 (part), 30246–47, 30249 (part), 30253 (part), 30278, 30281 (part).

FIFTH DISTRICT

JOHN LEWIS, Democrat, of Atlanta, GA; born in Pike County, AL on February 21, 1940; graduated Pike County Training School, Brundidge, AL, 1957; B.A., American Baptist Theological Seminary, Nashville, TN, 1961; B.A., Fisk University, Nashville, TN, 1963; civil rights leader; Atlanta City Council, 1982–86; member: Martin Luther King Center for Social Change, African American Institute, Robert F. Kennedy Memorial; married the former Lillian Miles in 1968; one child, John Miles Lewis; elected to the 100th Congress on November 4, 1986; member: Committee on Ways and Means; Subcommittee on Health; appointed chief deputy Democratic whip in the 102nd Congress; reelected to each succeeding Congress.

Office Listings

229 Cannon House Office Building, Washington, DC 20515–1005 225–3801
Administrative Assistant.—Robert Bossin. FAX: 225–0351
Suite 1920, 100 Peachtree Street SW, Atlanta, GA 30303 .... (404) 659–0116
Director of Constituent Services.—Love Williams.

Counties: Clayton (part), Cobb (part), DeKalb (part), and Fulton (part). Population (1990), 586,485.

ZIP Codes: 30001 (part), 30030 (part), 30032 (part), 30050 (part), 30059 (part), 30213 (part), 30268 (part), 30272, 30274 (part), 30291, 30296 (part), 30301–04, 30305 (part), 30306 (part), 30307 (part), 30308, 30309 (part), 30310–14, 30315 (part), 30316 (part), 30317 (part), 30318 (part), 30319 (part), 30320–21, 30324 (part), 30325, 30326 (part), 30327–28, 30330–34, 30336, 30337 (part), 30338 (part), 30339 (part), 30342–44, 30348, 30349 (part), 30350 (part), 30353, 30354 (part), 30355, 30357–58, 30361, 30364, 30367, 30370–71, 30374, 30377–79, 31131

* * *

SIXTH DISTRICT

NEWT GINGRICH, Republican, of Marietta, GA; born in Harrisburg, PA, June 17, 1943; graduated, Baker High School, Columbus, GA, 1961; B.A., Emory University, Atlanta, GA, 1965; M.A., Tulane University, New Orleans, LA, 1968, and Ph.D., European History, 1971; teacher, West Georgia College, Carrollton, 1970–78; member: Kiwanis, Georgia Conservancy, American Association for the Advancement of Science, World Futurist Society; cofounder and member, Conservative Opportunity Society; general chairman, GOPAC; married to the former Marianne Ginter; two children: Kathy and Jackie Sue; elected to the 96th Congress, November 7, 1978; reelected to each succeeding Congress; elected House Republican Whip, March 1989; elected Speaker of the House, January 1995.

Office Listings

http://www.house.gov/gingrich georgia@hr.house.gov

2428 Rayburn House Office Building, Washington, DC 20515–1006 225–4501
Administrative Assistant.—Greg Wright. FAX: 225–4656
Legislative Director.—Krister Holladay.
Press Secretary.—Christina Martin.
Executive Assistant.—Rachael Robinson.
3823 Roswell Road, Suite 200, Marietta, GA 30062 .... (404) 565–6398
Chief of Staff.—Nancy Desmond. FAX: 565–6824

Counties: Cherokee (part), Cobb (part), DeKalb (part), Fulton (part), and Gwinnett (part). CITIES AND TOWNSHIPS: Doraville, Dunwoody, Marietta, Norcross, Roswell, South Springs, and Smyrna. Population (1990), 587,118.

ZIP Codes: 30001 (part), 30007, 30059–60 (part), 30061–63, 30064 (part), 30065–68, 30073 (part), 30075–77, 30080–81, 30082 (part), 30092 (part), 30101–02 (part), 30114–15 (part), 30120 (part), 30132 (part), 30136, 30137 (part), 30142 (part), 30144, 30152 (part), 30155 (part), 30188–89 (part), 30195, 30201–02 (part), 30243 (part), 30245 (part), 30327–28 (part), 30339, 30342 (part), 30350, 30174 (part), 30356, 30360 (part), 30518 (part)

* * *

SEVENTH DISTRICT

BOB BARR, Republican, of Smyrna, GA; born in Iowa City, IA, November 5, 1948; graduated, Community High School, Tehran, Iran, 1966; B.A., University of Southern California, 1970; M.A., international affairs, George Washington University, 1972; J.D., Georgetown University, 1977; member of the Georgia and Florida bars; former president, Southeastern Legal Foundation, 1990–91; private practice, 1978–86 and 1991–94; prior services: appointed the U.S.

Attorney for the Northern District of Georgia, 1986–90; Central Intelligence Agency, 1971–78; member: Kiwanis, National Rifle Association, National Federation of Independent Business, and Chamber of Commerce; attends First United Methodist Church, Marietta, GA; married the former Jerilyn Dobbin, 1986; four children and four grandchildren; committees: Judiciary, Banking and Financial Services, Veterans' Affairs; subcommittees: General Oversight and Investigations; Education, Training, and Employment; Housing; elected to the 104th Congress; reelected to the 105th Congress.

Office Listings

http://www.house.gov/barr bbarr@hr.house.gov

1607 Longworth House Office Building, Washington, DC 20515 225–2931
Chief of Staff.—Dan Levinson. FAX: 225–2944
Administrative Assistant.—Jeff Beedlove.
Legislative Director/Press Secretary.—Carter Cornick.
999 Whitlock Avenue, Marietta, GA 30064 .... (404) 429–1776

Counties: Bartow, Carroll, Chattooga, Cobb (part), Douglas, Floyd, Haralson, Heard, Paulding, Polk, and Troup. Population (1990), 588,071.

ZIP Codes: 30001 (part), 30020, 30057, 30059 (part), 30060 (part), 30062 (part), 30064 (part), 30073 (part), 30080 (part), 30082 (part), 30101 (part), 30102–05, 30108–10, 30113, 30116–18, 30120–21, 30123–25, 30129, 30132 (part), 30133–35, 30137–41, 30145, 30147, 30150, 30153, 30161–65, 30170–73, 30176, 30178–80, 30182, 30184–85, 30187, 30217, 30219, 30230, 30240–41, 30253 (part), 30261, 30730–31, 30747, 30753, 31139, 31833 (part)

* * *

EIGHTH DISTRICT

SAXBY CHAMBLISS, Republican, of Moultrie, GA; born in Warrenton, NC on November 10, 1943; graduated, C.E. Byrd High School, Shreveport, LA, 1962; B.A., University of Georgia, 1966; J.D., University of Tennessee College of Law, 1968; served on the state bar of Georgia's Disciplinary Review Panel, 1969; member: Moultrie-Colquitt County Economic Development Authority, Colquitt County Economic Development Corporation; married the former Julianne Frohbert, 1966; two children: Lia Chambliss Baker and C. Saxby "Bo," Jr.; Agriculture and National Security committees; elected to the 104th Congress; reelected to the 105th Congress.

Office Listings

http://www.house.gov/chambliss saxby@hr.house.gov

1708 Longworth House Office Building, Washington, DC 20515 225–6531
Chief of Staff.—Rob Leebern. FAX: 225–3013
Executive Assistant.—Teresa Ervin.
Legislative Director.—Chris Cox.
Press Secretary.—Mary Brown Brewer.
3312 Northside Drive, Building D, Suite 232, Macon, GA 31210 .... (912) 475–0665
1707 First Avenue, SE, Suite B, Moultrie, GA 31768 .... (912) 891–3474
District Director.—Bill Stembridge.

Counties: Atkinson, Ben Hill, Berrien, Bibb (part), Bleckley, Clinch, Coffee, Colquitt (part), Cook, Crisp (part), Dodge, Dooly (part), Dougherty (part), Echols, Houston (part), Irwin, Jeff Davis, Johnson, Jones (part), Lanier, Laurens, Lee (part), Lowndes (part), Pulaski, Telfair, Tift, Treutlen, Turner, Twiggs (part), Wheeler, Wilcox, and Worth. Population (1990), 591,615.

ZIP Codes: 30204, 30257, 30286, 30410–12, 30428, 30457, 30470, 3073, 31001, 31004–5, 31008 31011–14, 31020 (part), 31023, 31028–30 31036 (part), 31037, 31044 (part), 31047, 31050, 31052 (part), 31055, 31060, 31066 (part), 31069 (part), 31071, 31072–73, 31077,–79, 31083–84, 31088 (part), 31091–93, 31095, 31097–98 31201 (part), 31202–03, 31204 (part), 31205, 31206 (part), 31207–09, 31210 (part), 31211 (part), 31212–13, 31294, 31297–98, 31501–3, 31510, 31512–13, 31519, 31532–33, 31537, 31539, 31544, 31549–50, 31554, 31563–64 31567, 31622–24, 31630–31, 31634–35, 31639, 31642, 31645–46, 31648

* * *

NINTH DISTRICT

NATHAN DEAL, Republican, of Lula, GA; born in Millen, GA on August 25, 1942; graduated, Washington County High School, Sandersville, 1960; B.A., Mercer University, Macon, GA, 1964; J.D., Mercer University, Walter F. George School of Law, Macon, GA, 1966; admitted to the Georgia bar, 1966; captain, U.S. Army, 1966–68; Georgia State Senate, 1981–92; president pro tempore, 1991–92; married the former Emilie Sandra Dunagan, 1966; four children: Jason, Mary Emily, Carrie, and Katie; elected on November 3, 1992 to the 103rd Congress; reelected to each succeeding Congress.

Office Listings

1406 Longworth House Office Building, Washington, DC 20515–1009 225–5211
Chief of Staff.—Mark Maddox.
Press Secretaries.—Mark Maddox, Lance Compton.
109 North Main Street, Lafayette, GA 30728 .... (706) 638–7042
P.O. Box 1015, Gainesville, GA 30503 .... (770) 535–2592
Suite 108, 415 East Walnut Avenue, Dalton, GA 30721 .... (706) 226–5320

Counties: Catoosa, Cherokee (part), Dade, Dawson, Fannin, Forsyth, Gilmer, Gordon, Habersham, Hall, Lumpkin, Murray, Pickens, Rabun, Stephens, Towns, Union, Walker, White, and Whitfield. CITIES AND TOWNSHIPS: Adairsville, Alpharetta (part), Alto, Baldwin, Ball Ground, Blairsville, Blue Ridge, Calhoun, Canton, Chatsworth, Cherry Log, Chestnut Mountain, Chickamauga, Cisco, Clarkesville, Clayton, Clermont, Cleveland, Cohutta, Crandall, Cumming, Dahlonega, Dalton, Dawsonville, Demorest, Dillard, East Ellijay, Eastanollee, Ellijay, Epworth, Eton, Fairmount, Flintsone, Flowery Branch, Fort Oglethorpe, Gainesville, Gillsville, Habersham, Helen, Hiawassee, Holly Springs, Jasper, LaFayette, Lakemont, Lebanon, Lookout Mountain, Lula, Marble Hill, Martin, McCaysville, Mineral Bluff, Morgantown, Mount Airy, Mountain City, Murrayville, Nelson, Oakman, Oakwood, Plainville, Rabun Gap, Ranger, Resaca, Ringgold, Rising Fawn, Rock Spring, Rocky Face, Rossville, Sautee, Suches, Sugar Valley, Talking Rock, Tallulah Falls, Tate, Tennga, Tiger, Toccoa, Toccoa Falls, Trenton, Tunnel Hill, Waleska, Wildwood, Wiley, Woodstock, and Young Harris. Population (1990), 586,222.

ZIP Codes: 30103, 30107, 30114 (part), 30130–31, 30136 (part), 30139, 30142–43, 30146, 30148, 30151, 30174 (part), 30175, 30177, 30183 (part), 30188 (part), 30201 (part), 30202 (part), 30501–04, 30506–07, 30510 (part), 30511–13, 30518 (part), 30522–23, 30525, 30527–28, 30531, 30533–35, 30537–46, 30548 (part), 30552, 30554–55, 30557, 30559–60, 30562–64, 30566–68, 30571–73, 30575–77, 30580–82, 30598, 30641, 30665, 30701, 30703, 30705, 30707–08, 30710–11, 30720–22, 30724–26, 30728, 30731–36, 30738–42, 30746, 30750–53, 30755–57

* * *

TENTH DISTRICT

CHARLES W. NORWOOD, JR., Republican, of Evans, GA; born in Valdosta, GA, on July 27, 1941; graduated, Baylor Military High School, Chattanooga, TN, 1959; B.S., Georgia Southern University, Statesboro, 1964; D.D.S., Georgetown University Dental School, Washington, DC, 1967; served as captain, U.S. Army, 1967–69, including tour of duty in Vietnam with the 173rd Airborne Brigade; awarded the Combat Medic Badge and two Bronze Stars; dentistry practice, Augusta, GA, 1969; elected president of the Georgia Dental Association, 1983; member: Commerce Committee and Economic and Educational Opportunities Committee; subcommittees: Energy and Power, Health and Environment, Workforce Protections; member, Trinity-on-the-Hill United Methodist Church, Augusta, GA; started several small businesses over the years, including Northwood Tree Nursery in Evans, GA, and Park Avenue Fabrics in Augusta, GA; married Gloria Norwood, 1962; two children: Charles and Carlton; two grandchildren; elected on November 8, 1994 to the 104th Congress; reelected to each succeeding Congress.

Office Listings
ga10@hr.house.gov

1707 Longworth House Office Building, Washington, DC 20515–1010 225–4101
Chief of Staff.—John Walker.
Legislative Director.—Jim Hagan.
Senior Legislative Assistant.—Dan LaPre.
Legislative Assistant.—Gabe Sterling.
Communications Director.—John Stone.
1056 Claussen Road, Suite 226, Augusta, GA 30907 .... (706) 733–7066
District Director.—Michael Shaffer.
Constituent Services Director.—CSM James K. Hussey (Ret).
Office Manager/Constituent Services.—Nellie Torres.
Constituent Services.—Dana Pavey.
3720 Atlanta Highway, Suite 1, Athens, GA 30606 .... (706) 208–8919
3914 Mullikin Road, Evans, GA 30809 .... (706) 651–1420

Counties: Baldwin, Burke, Butts, Columbia, Elbert, Emanuel, Glascock, Green, Hancock, Jasper, Jefferson, Johnson, Jones, Laurens, Lincoln, McDuffie, Oglethorpe, Putnam, Richmond (part), Taliaferro, Warren, Washington, Wilkes (part), and Wilkinson. Population (1990), 591,644.

ZIP Codes: 30216, 30233–34, 30255, 30401, 30413, 30425, 30434, 30441, 30447, 30448, 30454, 30456, 30463, 30466, 30471, 30477, 30619, 30624, 30630–31, 30634–5, 30642, 30648, 30660, 30664–5, 30667–9, 30671, 30673, 30678, 30802–3, 30805, 30808–21, 30823–24, 30828, 30830, 30833, 30901, 30903–19, 31002–3, 31018–19, 31021–22, 31024, 31031–35, 31038, 31040, 31042, 31045, 31049, 31054, 31061, 31064–65, 31067, 31075, 31082, 31085, 31087, 31089, 31090, 31094, 31096

ELEVENTH DISTRICT

JOHN LINDER, Republican, of Atlanta, GA; born on September 9, 1942 in Deer River, MN; graduate, Deer River High School, 1957; B.S., 1963, and D.D.S., 1967, University of Minnesota; captain, U.S. Air Force, 1967–69; former dentist; president, Linder Financial Corporation; Georgia State Representative, 1975–80, 1983–90; member: Georgia GOP, Rotary Club, American Legion; married Lynne Peterson Linder, 1963; two children: Matt and Kristine; elected on November 3, 1992 to the 103rd Congress; reelected to each succeding Congress.

Office Listings

http://www.house.gov/linder jlinder@hr.house.gov

1005 Longworth House Office Building, Washington, DC 20515–1004 225–4272
Administrative Assistant.—Henry Plaster. FAX: 225–4696
Legislative Director.—Rob Woodall.
Scheduler.—Elizabeth Reid.
220 College Avenue, Suite 520, Athens, GA 30601 .... (706) 355–9909
3675 Crestwood Boulevard, Suite 530, Duluth, GA 30136 .... (770) 931–9550

Counties: Banks, Barrow, Clarke, Franklin, Gwinnett, Hart, Jackson, Madison, Morgan, Newton, Oconee, Rockdale, Walton
CITIES: Athens, Duluth

ZIP Codes: 30049 (part), 30058 (part), 30071 (part), 30084 (part), 30087 (part), 30091–2, 30093 (part), 30136 (part), 30155, 33174 (part), 30203, 30207–11, 30219, 30221, 30226, 30235, 30243 (part), 30244 (part), 30245 (part), 30246 (part), 30247 (part), 30249, 30253 (part), 30255, 30262 (part), 30270, 30278 (part), 30279, 30281 (part), 30510 (part), 30511 (part), 30516, 30517 (part), 30518 (part), 30519–21, 30529, 30538 (part), 30547, 30548 (part), 30549, 30553, 30554 (part), 30558, 30565, 30567, 30575 (part), 30601–9, 30612–13, 30620–23, 30625 (part), 30627 (part), 30628 (part), 30629, 30633, 30638–29, 30664, 30641, 30643, 30645–47, 30650 (part), 30655–56, 30662–3 (part), 30666, 30677 (part), 30680, 30683 (part)

HAWAII

(Population 1995, 1,187,000)

SENATORS

DANIEL K. INOUYE, Democrat, of Honolulu, HI; born in Honolulu, September 7, 1924; A.B., government and economics, University of Hawaii, 1950; J.D., George Washington University Law School, 1952; majority leader, Territorial House of Representatives, 1954–58; Territorial Senate, 1958–59; enlisted as private, 442nd Infantry Regimental Combat Team, 1943; battlefield commission, second lieutenant, 1944; served in France and Italy; retired captain, U.S. Army; Methodist; married the former Margaret Shinobu Awamura of Honolulu; one son, Daniel Ken Inouye, Jr.; committees: Appropriations; Commerce, Science and Transportation; Rules and Administration; Indian Affairs; Joint Committee on Printing; elected July 28, 1959, to the 86th Congress; reelected to the 87th Congress; elected to the U.S. Senate, November 6, 1962, for the term ending January 3, 1969; reelected for each succeeding term.

Office Listings

http://www.senate.gov/~inouye senator@inouye.senate.gov

722 Hart Senate Office Building, Washington, DC 20510–1102 224–3934
Administrative Assistant.—Patrick H. DeLeon. TDD: 224–1233
Office Manager.—Beverly MacDonald.
Personal Secretary.—Sally Watanabe.
Legislative Director.—Margaret Cummisky.
Suite 7325, 300 Ala Moana Boulevard, Honolulu, HI 96850 .... (808) 541–2542
Hilo Auxiliary Office, 101 Aupuni Street, No. 205, Hilo, HI 96720 .... (808) 935–0844

* * *

DANIEL K. AKAKA, Democrat, of Honolulu, HI; born in Honolulu, September 11, 1924; graduated, Kamehameha High School, 1942; University of Hawaii, 1948–66, bachelor of education, professional certificate, master of education; served in the U.S. Army, 1945–47; teacher, 1953–60; vice principal, 1960; principal, 1963–71; program specialist, 1968–71; director, 1971–74; director and special assistant in human resources, 1975–76; member, Kawaiahao Church; board of directors, Hanahauoli School; Act 4 Educational Advisory Commission; Library Advisory Council; Na Hookama O Pauahi Scholarship Committee, Kamehameha Schools; commissioner, Manpower and Full Employment Commission; minister of music, Kawaiahao Church; married to the former Mary Mildred Chong; five children: Millannie, Daniel, Jr., Gerard, Alan, and Nicholas; committees: Energy and Natural Resources, Governmental Affairs, Veterans' Affairs, Indian Affairs; elected to the 95th Congress, November 2, 1976; reelected to succeeding Congresses; elected November 6, 1990 to the U.S. Senate to complete the unexpired term of the late Senator Spark Matsunaga; reelected to the 104th and 105th Congresses.

Office Listings

http://www.senate.gov/senator/akaka.html

720 Hart Senate Office Building, Washington, DC 20510–1103 224–6361
Administrative Assistant.—James Sakai. FAX: 224–2126
Legislative Director.—Patrick O. McGarey.
Office Manager/Personal Secretary.—Patricia L. Hill.
Room 3104, Prince Kuhio Building, P.O. Box 50144, Honolulu, HI 96850 .... (808) 522–8970
District Coordinator.—Michael T. Kitamura. FAX: 545–4683

REPRESENTATIVES

FIRST DISTRICT

NEIL ABERCROMBIE, Democrat, of Honolulu, HI; born in Buffalo, NY, June 26, 1938; graduated from Williamsville High School, Williamsville, NY; B.A., Union College, 1959; Ph.D., University of Hawaii, 1974; candidate for election to the U.S. Senate, 1970; Hawaii House of Representatives, 1974–78; Hawaii State Senate, 1978–86; elected to the U.S. House of Representatives on September 20, 1986, to fill the vacancy caused by the resignation of Cecil

Heftel; Honolulu City Council, 1988–90; married to Nancie Caraway; elected to the 102nd Congress, November 6, 1990; reelected to each succeeding Congress.

Office Listings

http://www.house.gov/abercrombie

1233 Longworth House Office Building, Washington, DC 20515–1101	225–2726
Chief of Staff.—Alan Yamamoto.	
Legislative Director.—Alan Yamamoto.	
Communications Director.—Mike Slackman.	
Room 4104, 300 Ala Moana Boulevard, Honolulu, HI 96850	(808) 541–2570
District Director.—Steve Beaudry.	

County: HONOLULU COUNTY (part); cities and townships of Aiea Pearl City, Ewa Beach, Honolulu, Mililani (part), and Waipahu (part). Population (1990), 554,119.

ZIP Codes: 96701, 96706, 96782, 96789, 96801–28, 96830, 96835–39, 96850, 96898

* * *

SECOND DISTRICT

PATSY MINK, Democrat, of Honolulu, HI; born on December 6, 1927, in the village of Paia on Maui, HI; graduated from Maui High School, 1944; attended Wilson College, Chambersburg, PA; University of Nebraska; B.A., University of Hawaii, 1948; J.D., University of Chicago Law School, 1951; attorney, practicing in Hawaii; lecturer, University of Hawaii, 1952–56 and 1959–62; Hawaii House of Representatives, 1956–58; Hawaii Senate, 1958–59, 1962–64; elected to the U.S. House of Representatives, 89th–94th Congresses, 1965–77; unsuccessful candidate to the U.S. Senate in 1976; Assistant Secretary of State, 1977–78; president, Americans for Democratic Action, 1978–82; Honolulu city council, 1983–87; married to John Francis Mink; one child, Gwendolyn; elected to the 101st Congress by special election on September 22, 1990 to fill the vacancy caused by the resignation of Daniel Akaka; reelected to each succeeding Congress.

Office Listings

2135 Rayburn House Office Building, Washington, DC 20515–1102	225–4906
Legislative Director.—Laura Efurd.	FAX: 225–4987
Office Manager.—Helen Lewis.	
Room 5104, Prince Kuhio Federal Building, PO Box 50124, Honolulu, HI 96850	(800) 541–1986
Administrative Assistant.—Colleen Saiki.	FAX: 538–0233

Counties: Hawaii, Honolulu (part), Kalawao, Kauai, and Maui. Population (1990), 554,110.

ZIP Codes: 96703–05, 96707–08, 96710, 96712–22, 96725–34, 96738–86, 96788, 96790–93, 96795–97, 96862

IDAHO

(Population 1995, 1,163,000)

SENATORS

LARRY E. CRAIG, Republican, of Payette, ID; born July 20, 1945 in Council, ID; attended Midvale public schools; graduated, University of Idaho; student body president, University of Idaho, 1968–69; graduate work in economics and the politics of developing nations, George Washington University, 1970; Idaho State president and national vice president, Future Farmers of America, 1966–67; Idaho State Senate (three terms); chairman, Senate Commerce and Labor Committee; member: National Foundation for Defense Analysis; Idaho State Republican Executive Committee, 1976–78; president, Young Republican League of Idaho, 1976–77; chairman, Republican Central Committee, Washington County, 1971–72; board of directors, National Rifle Association; policy chairman, Republican Study Committee, 1990; farmer-rancher, Midvale area, for 10 years; married to the former Suzanne Thompson; three children: Mike, Shae, and Jay; chairman, Senate Republican Policy Committee; Senate cochairman, Congressional Coalition on Adoption; cofounder and cochair, Senate Private Property Rights Caucus; cochairman, Congressional Leaders United for a Balanced Budget (CLUBB); committees: Appropriations; Energy and Natural Resources; Agriculture, Nutrition and Forestry; Veterans' Affairs; Special Committee on Aging; subcommittees: chairman, Forests and Public Land Management; Energy Research and Development; Water and Power; Forestry, Conservation, and Rural Revitalization; Research, Nutrition and General Legislation; Energy and Water Development Appropriations; Labor, HHS and Education Appropriations; Legislative Branch Appropriations; Military Construction Appropriations; VA, HUD and Independent Agencies Appropriations; elected to the 97th Congress, November 4, 1980; reelected to each succeeding Congress; elected to the U.S. Senate, November 6, 1990; reelected November, 1996.

Office Listings

http://www.senate.gov/~craig   larry__craig@craig.senate.gov

313 Hart Senate Office Building, Washington, DC 20510–1203 224–2752
Chief of Staff.—Michael O. Ware. FAX: 224–2573
Executive Assistant.—Heather Neal.
Legislative Director/Counsel.—Brooke M. Roberts.
Press Secretary.—Michael Frandsen.

Room 149, 304 North Eighth Street, Boise, ID 83702 .... (208) 342–7985
FAX: 343–2458

103 North Fourth Street, Coeur d'Alene, ID 83814 .... (208) 667–6130
FAX: 765–1743

846 Main Street, Lewiston, ID 83501 .... (208) 743–0792
FAX: 746–7275

250 South Fourth Street, Pocatello, ID 83201 .... (208) 236–6817
FAX: 236–6820

1292 Addison Avenue East, Twin Falls, ID 83301 .... (208) 734–6780
FAX: 734–3905

Suite 240, 2539 Channing Way, Idaho Falls, ID 83404 .... (208) 523–5541
FAX: 552–0135

* * *

DIRK KEMPTHORNE, Republican, of Boise, ID; born October 29, 1951 in San Diego, CA; B.A., University of Idaho, 1975; mayor, city of Boise; 1986–93, U.S. Conference of Mayors Advisory Board, 1991–93; chairman, U.S. Conference of Mayors; first vice president, Association of Idaho Cities, 1991–93; Idaho public affairs manager, FMC Corporation, 1983–86; executive vice president, Idaho Home Builders Association, 1978–81; executive assistant to the director, Idaho Department of Lands, 1976–78; student body president, University of Idaho, 1974–75; board of directors, Parents and Youth Against Drug and Alcohol Abuse (PAYADA); honorary chairman, Working Partners, Ltd.; married to the former Patricia Merrill of Boise; two children: Heather and Jeff; committees: Armed Services, Environment and Public Works, Small Business; elected to the U.S. Senate, November 3, 1992, for the six-year term beginning January 5, 1993.

Office Listings

http://www.senate.gov/~kempthorne   dirk__kempthorne@kempthorne.senate.gov

304 Russell Senate Office Building, Washington, DC 20510–1202 224–6142

Legislative Director.—W.H. (Buzz) Fawcett. FAX: 224–5893
Special Assistant and Scheduler.—Tyler Dougherty. TDD: 224–8523
Press Secretary.—Mark Snider.
Office Manager.—Stephanie Schisler.
304 North Eighth, Room 338, Boise, ID 83701 .... (208) 334–1776
Chief of Staff.—Phil Reberger.
118 North Second Street, Coeur d'Alene, ID 83814 .... (208) 664–5490
2539 Channing Way, Room 240, Idaho Falls, ID 83404 .... (208) 522–9779
401 Second Street North, Room 106, Twin Falls, ID 83301 .... (208) 734–2515
250 South Fourth, Room 207, Pocatello, ID 83201 .... (208) 236–6775
618 D Street, Room E, Lewiston, ID 83501 .... (208) 743–1492
704 Blaine Street, Room 1, Caldwell, ID 83605 .... (208) 455–0360
220 East Fifth Street, Room 105, Moscow, ID 83843 .... (208) 883–9783

REPRESENTATIVES

FIRST DISTRICT

HELEN P. CHENOWETH, Republican, of Boise, ID; born in Topeka, KS, January 27, 1938; graduated, Grants Pass High School, Grants Pass, OR; attended Whitworth College, Spokane, WA; self-employed medical and legal management consultant; guest instructor, University of Idaho School of Law; recruited physicians to towns and clinics in Northwest from medical schools nationwide; state executive director of Idaho Republican Party, 1975–77; chief of staff to then-Congressman Steve Symms; co-owner, Consulting Associates, Inc.; nationally recognized spokeswoman for private property rights; committees: Resources, Agriculture, Veterans' Affairs; subcommittees: Energy and Mineral Resources; National Parks and Public Lands; Resource Conservation, Research, and Forestry; married to Nicholas Signor Chenoweth; two children: Michael and Margaret; elected to the 104th Congress; reelected to the 105th Congress.

Office Listings

http://www.house.gov/chenoweth ask.helen/@mail.house.gov

1727 Longworth House Office Building, Washington, DC 20515–1201 225–6611
Chief of Staff.—Keith Rupp. FAX: 226–3029
Legislative Director.—Gregory Peek.
Executive Assistant/Scheduler.—Liz Denny.
Office Manager/System Administrator.—Dean Lester.
304 North Eighth Street, Room 454, Boise, ID 83702 .... (208) 336–9831
District Director.—Jim Gambrell.
Caseworkers: Tereasa Sinigiani, Rhonda Tilden.
Press Secretary.—Khris Bershers.
Legislative Assistant.—Judy Boyle.
621 Main, Suite G, Lewiston, ID 83501 .... (208) 746–4613
District Representative.—Scott Carlton.
118 North Second Street, Suite 2, Coeur d'Alene, ID 83814 .... (208) 667–0127
District Representative.—Heather Sawyer.

Counties: Ada (part), Adams, Benewah, Boise, Bonner, Boundary, Canyon, Clearwater, Gem, Idaho, Kootenai, Latah, Lewis, Nez Perce, Owyhee, Payette, Shoshone, Valley, and Washington. Population (1990), 503,357.

ZIP Codes: 83501, 83520–26, 83530, 83533–49, 83551–55, 83602, 83604–05, 83610–12, 83615–17, 83619–20, 83622, 83624, 83626, 83628–32, 83634–39, 83641–46, 83650–52, 83654–61, 83666, 83669–72, 83676–77, 83701–09, 83720–32, 83801–14, 83821, 83823–27, 83830, 83832–37, 83839–43, 83845–55, 83857–58, 83860–62, 83864–67, 83869–74, 83876

* * *

SECOND DISTRICT

MICHAEL D. CRAPO, Republican, of Idaho Falls, ID; born in Idaho Falls on May 20, 1951; graduated, Idaho Falls High School, Idaho Falls, 1969; B.A., Brigham Young University, Provo, UT, 1973; J.D., Harvard University Law School, Cambridge, MA, 1977; attorney; admitted to the California bar, 1977; admitted to the Idaho bar, 1979; law clerk, Hon. James M. Carter, Judge of the U.S. Court of Appeals for the Ninth Circuit, San Diego, CA, 1977–78; associate attorney, Gibson, Dunn, and Crutcher, San Diego, 1978–79; attorney, Holden, Kidwell, Hahn and Crapo, 1979–92; partner, 1983–92; Idaho State Senate, 1984–92, assistant majority leader, 1987–89, president pro tempore, 1989–92; member: American Bar Association, Boy Scouts of America, Idaho Falls Rotary Club, 1984–88; committees: Commerce, Resources; house majority leadership, strategic planning leader; deputy whip; Republican Policy Committee; married the former Susan Diane Hasleton, 1974; five children: Michelle, Brian, Stephanie, Lara, and Paul; elected on November 3, 1992 to the 103rd Congress; reelected to each succeeding Congress.

Office Listings

http://www.house.gov/crapo askmike@mail.house.gov

437 Cannon House Office Building, Washington, DC 20515–1202	225–5531
Administrative Assistant.—Jane Gorsuch.	FAX: 225–8216
Executive Assistant.—Dorothy Boger.	
Legislative Director.—Will Hollier.	
Communications Director.—Susan Wheeler.	
Suite 325, 304 North Eighth Street, Boise, ID 83702	(208) 334–1953
Chief of Staff.—John Hoehne.	
628 Blue Lakes Boulevard North, Twin Falls, ID 83301	(208) 734–7219
2539 Channing, Suite 260, Idaho Falls, ID 83404	(208) 523–6701
Room 220, Federal Building, 250 South Fourth, Pocatello, ID 83201	(208) 236–6734

Counties: Ada (part), Bannock, Bear Lake, Bingham, Blaine, Bonneville, Butte, Camas, Caribou, Cassia, Clark, Custer, Elmore, Franklin, Fremont, Gooding, Jefferson, Jerome, Lemhi, Lincoln, Madison, Minidoka, Oneida, Power, Teton, and Twin Falls. Population (1990), 503,392.

ZIP Codes: 83201–06, 83209–15, 83217–18, 83220–21, 83223, 83226–30, 83232–39, 83241, 83243–46, 83250–56, 83260–63, 83271–72, 83274, 83276–78, 83280–81, 83283, 83285–87, 83301–03, 83311–14, 83316, 83318, 83320–28, 83330, 83332–38, 83340–44, 83346–50, 83352–55, 83401–06, 83420–25, 83427–29, 83431, 83433–38, 83440, 83442–46, 83448–52, 83454–55, 83462–69, 83601, 83623–24, 83627, 83633, 83647–48, 83701, 83702 (part), 83703 (part), 83705 (part), 83706 (part), 83707, 83712, 83720–27, 83729–30, 83733, 83735, 83756–57

ILLINOIS

(Population, 1995 11,830,000)

SENATORS

CAROL MOSELEY-BRAUN, Democrat, of Chicago, IL; born August 16, 1947 in Chicago; J.D., University of Chicago Law School, 1972; prosecutor in the U.S. Attorney's Office for three years; Illinois House of Representatives, 1978–87; first woman and first African-American to serve as assistant majority leader of the Illinois House; elected as Cook County Recorder of Deeds, 1987–92: first woman and first African-American to hold executive office in Cook County; one child; elected to the U.S. Senate, November 3, 1992, for the six-year term beginning January 3, 1993; committees: Banking, Housing and Urban Affairs; Finance; Special Committee on Aging.

Office Listings

http://www.senate.gov/~moseley-braun senator@moseley-braun.senate.gov

320 Hart Senate Office Building, Washington, DC 20510–1303 224–2854
Chief of Staff.—Bill Matea.
Press Secretary.—Michael Briggs.
Administrative Director.—Paula Effertz.
Suite 3900, Kluczynski Federal Building, 230 South Dearborn Street, Chicago, IL 60604–1690 .... (312) 353–5420
State Director.—Jill Zwick.
Henson Robinson House, 520 South Eighth Street, Springfield, IL 62703–1607 ..... (217) 492–4126
6 Executive Drive, Suite 6, Fairview Heights, IL 62208 .... (618) 632–7242

* * *

RICHARD J. DURBIN, Democrat, of Springfield, IL; born in East St. Louis, IL, November 21, 1944, son of William and Ann Durbin; graduated, Assumption High School, East St. Louis; B.S., foreign service and economics, Georgetown University, Washington, DC, 1966; J.D., Georgetown University Law Center, 1969; attorney, admitted to the Illinois bar in 1969 and began practice in Springfield; legal counsel to Lieutenant Governor Paul Simon, 1969–72; legal counsel to Illinois Senate Judiciary Committee, 1972–82; parliamentarian, Illinois Senate, 1969–82; president, New Members Democratic Caucus, 98th Congress; associate professor of medical humanities, Southern Illinois University School of Medicine, Springfield; married the former Loretta Schaefer, 1967; three children: Christine, Paul, and Jennifer; committees: Budget, Governmental Affairs, Judiciary; subcommittees: Administrative Oversight and the Courts; Immigration; Technology, Terrorism and Government Information; elected to the 98th Congress, November 2, 1982; reelected to each succeeding Congress; elected to the U.S. Senate, November 1996.

Office Listings

http://www.senate.gov/senator/durbin.html dick@durbin.senate.gov

364 Russell Senate Office Building, Washington, DC 20510–1304 224–2152
Chief of Staff.—Ed Greelegs. TTY: 224–8180
Legislative Director.—Tom Faletti.
Executive Assistant.—Kathy Anderson.
Press Secretary.—Melissa Merz.
230 South Dearborn, Kluczynski Building 38th Floor, Chicago, IL 60604 .... (312) 353–4952
Chief of Staff.—Mike Daly.
525 South Eighth Street, Springfield, IL 62703 .... (217) 492–4062
Director.—Bill Houlihan.
Mercantile Bank Building of Southern Illinois, 123 South 10th Street, Suite 414, Mt. Vernon, IL 62864 .... (618) 244–7441

REPRESENTATIVES

FIRST DISTRICT

BOBBY RUSH, Democrat, of Chicago, IL; born on November 23, 1946 in Georgia; served in U.S. Army, 1963–68; B.A., with honors, Roosevelt University, Chicago; M.A., University of Illinois, Chicago; Democratic Ward Committeeman, second ward, Chicago, 1984, 1988; Democratic State Central Committeeman, First Congressional District, 1990; deputy chairman, Illinois Democratic Party, 1990; Department of Commerce and Community Affairs Illinois Enterprise Zone Award; Operation PUSH Outstanding Young Man award; Henry Booth House Outstanding Community Service Award; South End Jaycees Outstanding Business and Professional Achievement award; Chicago Black United Communities Distinguished Political Leadership Award; cofounder, Illinois Black Panther Party; married to Carolyn Rush; five children; elected on November 3, 1992 to the 103rd Congress; reelected to each succeeding Congress.

Office Listings

http://www.house.gov/rush brush@hr.house.gov

131 Cannon House Office Building, Washington, DC 20515–1301 225–4372
Administrative Assistant.—Maurice Daniel. FAX: 226–0333
Legislative Director.—Robert Walsh, Esq.
655 East 79th Street, Chicago, IL 60619 .... (312) 224–6500
District Administrator.—Stanley Watkins. FAX: 224–9624

County: COOK COUNTY (part); cities and townships of Alsip (part), Blue Island, Evergreen Park, Merrionette Park, and Oak Lawn. Population (1990), 571,530.

ZIP Codes: 60406 (part), 60453 (part), 60609 (part), 60615 (part), 60616 (part), 60617 (part), 60619, 60620 (part), 60621 (part), 60628 (part), 60629 (part), 60632 (part), 60636 (part), 60637 (part), 60642, 60643 (part), 60649 (part), 60652 (part), 60653 (part), 60655, 60658 (part)

* * *

SECOND DISTRICT

JESSE L. JACKSON, JR., Democrat, of Chicago, IL; born in Greenville, SC, March 11, 1965; B.S., business management, *magna cum laude,* North Carolina A&T State University, 1987; M.A., Chicago Theological Seminary, 1989; J.D., University of Illinois College of Law, 1993; member, Congressional Black Caucus, Congressional Progressive Caucus; elected secretary of the Democratic National Committee's Black Caucus; national field director, National Rainbow Coalition, 1993–95; member, Rainbow/Push Action Network; married to the former Sandra Lee Stevens; committees: Banking and Financial Services, Small Business; elected to the 105th Congress.

Office Listings

312 Cannon House Office Building, Washington, DC 20515–1302 225–0773
Chief of Staff.—Licia Green. FAX: 225–0899
Legislative Director.—Hilary Weinstein.
Legislative Assistants: Tariq Ahmed, Rodney Emery, George Seymore.
Press Secretary.—Frank Watkins.
17926 South Halsted, Homewood, IL 60430 .... (708) 798–6000
FAX: 798–6160

County: COOK COUNTY (part); cities and townships of Blue Island, Burnham, Calumet City, Calumet Park, Chicago (part), Chicago Heights, Country Club Hills Crestwood, Dixmoor, Dolton, East Hazel Crest, Flossmoor, Ford Heights, Glenwood, Harvey, Hazel Crest, Homewood, Markham, Matteson, Midlothian, Oak Forest, Olympia Fields, Park Forest, Phoenix, Posen, Riverdale, Robbins, South Holland, and Tinley Park. Population (1990), 571,530.

ZIP Codes: 60406 (part), 60409 (part), 60411 (part), 60419, 60422, 60423 (part), 60425 (part), 60426 (part), 60429, 60430 (part), 60443 (part), 60445 (part), 60452 (part), 60461, 60466 (part), 60469, 60472, 60473 (part), 60477 (part), 60478 (part), 60617 (part), 60620 (part), 60621 (part), 60627, 60628 (part), 60633 (part), 60636 (part), 60643 (part), 60649 (part)

* * *

THIRD DISTRICT

WILLIAM O. LIPINSKI, Democrat, of Chicago, IL; born in Chicago on December 22, 1937; graduated, St. Patrick High School, Chicago, 1956; attended Loras College, Dubuque, IA, 1956–57; served in U.S. Army Reserves, 1961–67; alderman, Chicago City Council, 1975–83; chairman, City Council Education Committee; delegate, Democratic National Convention, 1976, 1984, and 1988; past president, Kiwanis Club; member: Polish National Alliance, Chicago Historical Society; 23rd Ward Democratic Committeeman, 1974–present; married the former Rose

Marie Lapinski, 1962; two children: Laura and Dan; award: Man of the Year, Area 4, Chicago Park District, January 1983; committees: Democratic Steering, Transportation and Infrastructure; subcommittees: Aviation (ranking member), Railroads; elected on November 2, 1982, to the 98th Congress; reelected to each succeeding Congress.

Office Listings

1501 Longworth House Office Building, Washington, DC 20515–1303 225–5701
Legislative Director.—Jeffrey Goodell.
Executive Assistant.—Beverly Griffin.
5832 South Archer Avenue, Chicago, IL 60638 .... (312) 886–0481
Administrative Assistant.—George Edwards.
12717 South Ridgeland Avenue, Palos Heights, IL 60463 .... (708) 371–7460

County: COOK COUNTY (part); cities and townships of Alsip, Argo, Bedford Park, Berwyn, Bridgeview, Burr Ridge, Chicago, Chicago Ridge, Cicero, Countryside, Crestwood Midlothian, Forest Park, Hickory Hills, Hinsdale, Hometown, Hodgkins, Indian Head Park, Justice Burbank, LaGrange, Lyons, McCook, North Riverside, Oak Forest, Oak Lawn, Oak Park, Orland Park, Palos Heights, Palos Hills, Palos Park, Proviso, Riverside, Stickney, Summit Brookfield, Tinley Park, Western Springs, Willow Springs, and Worth. Population (1990), 571,531

ZIP Codes: 60130 (part), 60304 (part), 60402, 60415, 60426 (part), 60445 (part), 60452 (part), 60453 (part), 60454–56, 60457 (part), 60458–59, 60462 (part), 60463, 60464 (part), 60465 (part), 60477 (part), 60478 (part), 60480 (part), 60482, 60499, 60501, 60513 (part), 60521 (part), 60525 (part), 60534 (part), 60546 (part), 60558 (part), 60629 (part), 60632 (part), 60638, 60644 (part), 60650 (part), 60652 (part), 60658 (part), 60804 (part)

* * *

FOURTH DISTRICT

LUIS V. GUTIERREZ, Democrat, of Chicago, IL; born on December 10, 1953, in Chicago; B.A., Northeastern Illinois University, 1974; alderman; social worker, State of Illinois; teacher; married in 1977 to Soraida Arocho Gutierrez; two children: Omaira and Jessica; elected on November 3, 1992 to the 103rd Congress; reelected to each succeeding Congress.

Office Listings

luisg@hr.house.gov

2438 Rayburn House Office Building, Washington, DC 20515–1304 225–8203
Chief of Staff.—Doug Scofield.
Legislative Director.—Jennice Fuentes.
Scheduler/Office Manager.—Lisa Esquivel.
Press Secretary.—Billy Weinberg.
3181 North Elston Avenue, Chicago, IL 60618 .... (773) 509–0999
2132 West 21st Street, Chicago, IL 60608 .... (773) 579–0902

County: COOK COUNTY (part); cities of Berkeley (part), Brookfield (part), Chicago (part), Ciero (part), Elmwood Park (part), Forest Park (part), Hillside (part), Maywood (part), Melrose Park (part), Northlake (part), Oak Park (part), Stickney (part), Stone Park (part), and Westchester (part). Population (1990), 571,530.

ZIP Codes: 60130 (part), 60141, 60153 (part), 60154 (part), 60160 (part), 60162 (part), 60163 (part), 60164 (part), 60165 (part), 60304 (part), 60513 (part), 60608 (part), 60609 (part), 60612 (part), 60614 (part), 60616 (part), 60618 (part), 60622 (part), 60623 (part), 60625 (part), 60629 (part), 60632 (part), 60635 (part), 60636 (part), 60639 (part), 60641 (part), 60644 (part), 60647 (part), 60650 (part), 60651 (part), 60657 (part)

* * *

FIFTH DISTRICT

ROD R. BLAGOJEVICH, Democrat, of Chicago, IL; born in Chicago, December 10, 1956; B.A., Northwestern University, 1979; J.D., Pepperdine University Law School; admitted to the Illinois bar in 1984 and began community law practice in Chicago; Assistant Cook County State's Attorney, 1986–88; Illinois House of Representatives, 1972–96; married Patricia Blagojevich in 1990; one child, Amy; elected to the 105th Congress.

Office Listings

501 Cannon House Office Building, Washington, DC 20515 225–4061

Chief of Staff.—John Wyma. FAX: 225–5603
Legislative Director.—Chris Davis.
Press Secretary.—Matt Devine.
Executive Assistant.—Tabitha O'Man.
4064 North Lincoln Avenue, Chicago, IL 60618 .... (773) 868–3240
District Administrator.—Deborah Pascal. FAX: 868–0036

County: COOK COUNTY (part); cities and townships of Chicago, Franklin Park, River Grove, Harwood Heights, Norridge, Schiller Park (part), Elmwood Park (part), Melrose Park (part), Maywood, and Northlake. Population (1990), 571,530.

ZIP Codes: 60131 (part), 60153 (part), 60160 (part), 60161, 60164 (part), 60165 (part), 60171, 60176 (part), 60197–98, 60610 (part), 60611 (part), 60613 (part), 60614 (part), 60618 (part), 60622 (part), 60625 (part), 60630 (part), 60631 (part), 60634, 60635 (part), 60639 (part), 60640 (part), 60641 (part), 60646 (part), 60647 (part), 60656 (part), 60657 (part), 60659 (part)

* * *

SIXTH DISTRICT

HENRY J. HYDE, Republican, of Wood Dale, IL; born in Chicago, April 18, 1924; graduated St. George High School, Evanston, IL, 1942; B.S.S., Georgetown University, 1947; J.D., Loyola University School of Law, Chicago, 1949; ensign, U.S. Navy, 1944–46; commander, U.S. Naval Reserves (retired); admitted to the Illinois bar, January 9, 1950; State Representative in Illinois General Assembly, 1967–74; majority leader, Illinois House of Representatives, 1971–72; married the late Jeanne Simpson, 1947; four children: Henry, Jr., Robert, Anthony, Laura; elected to the 94th Congress, November 5, 1974; reelected to each succeeding Congress.

Office Listings

http://www.house.gov/hyde

2110 Rayburn House Office Building, Washington, DC 20515–1306 225–4561
Administrative Assistant.—Judy Wolverton.
Press Secretary.—Sam Stratman.
Suite 200, 50 East Oak Street, Addison, IL 60101 .... (708) 832–5950
Executive Assistants: Patrick Durante, Alice Horstman.

Counties: Cook County (part) and DuPage (part). CITIES: Addison, Bensenville, Bloomingdale, Carol Stream, Des Plaines, Elk Grive Village, Elmhurst, Glen Ellyn, Glendale Heights, La Grange Park, Lombard, Park Ridge, Roselle, Schiller Park, Villa Park, Westchester, Wheaton. TOWNSHIPS: Addison, Bloomingdale, Elk Grove, Leyden Proviso, Maine, Milton and York. Population (1990), 571,530.

ZIP Codes: 60005 (part), 60007 (part), 60008 (part), 60009, 60016 (part), 60017–19, 60025 (part), 60056 (part), 60068, 60101, 60103 (part), 60106, 60108, 60126, 60131 (part), 60137 (part), 60138–39, 60143, 60148 (part), 60154 (part), 60157 (part), 60162 (part), 60172 (part), 60173 (part), 60176 (part), 60181 (part), 60187 (part), 60188 (part), 60191, 60513 (part), 60515 (part), 60521 (part), 60525 (part), 60558 (part), 60559 (part), 60631 (part), 60666, 60714 (part)

* * *

SEVENTH DISTRICT

DANNY K. DAVIS, Democrat, of Chicago, IL; born in Parkdale, AR, September 6, 1941; B.A., Arkansas A.M. & N. College, 1961; M.A., Chicago State University; Ph.D., Union Institute, Cincinnati, OH; educator and health planner-administrator; board of directors, National Housing Partnership; Cook County Board of Commissioners, 1990–96; former alderman of the Chicago City Council's 29th ward, receiving the Independent Voters of Illinois "Best Alderman Award" for 1980–81, 1981–82, and 1989–90; cochair, Clinton-Gore-Braun '92; founder and past president, Westside Association for Community Action; past president, National Association of Community Health Centers; 1987 recipient of Leon M. Despres Award; married to Vera G. Davis; two sons, Jonathan and Stacey; committees: Small Business, Government Reform and Oversight; subcommittees: Postal Service; Government Management, Information and Technology; Empowerment; Tax Finance and Exports; elected on March 19, 1996, to the 105th Congress.

Office Listings

1208 Longworth House Office Building, Washington, DC 20515–1307 225–5006
Chief of Staff.—Roxanne Smith. FAX: 225–5641
Legislative Director.—Ira Cohen.
333 West Arthington Street, Suite 130, Chicago, IL 60024. .... (773) 533–7520

County: COOK COUNTY (part); cities and townships of Bellwood, Berkley, Broadview, Chicago, Forest Park, Hillside, Maywood, Oak Park, River Forest, Westchester and Elmwood Park. Population (1990), 571,530.

ZIP Codes: 60104, 60130 (part), 60153 (part), 60154 (part), 60160 (part), 60162 (part), 60163 (part), 60301–03, 60304 (part), 60305, 60425 (part), 60546 (part), 60601–07, 60608 (part), 60609 (part), 60610 (part), 60611 (part), 60612 (part), 60614 (part), 60615 (part), 60616 (part), 60621 (part), 60622 (part), 60623 (part), 60624, 60635 (part), 60637 (part), 60639 (part), 60644 (part), 60650 (part), 60651 (part), 60653 (part), 60654, 60661, 60664, 60680–81, 60690

* * *

EIGHTH DISTRICT

PHILIP M. CRANE, Republican, of Wauconda, IL; born in Chicago, November 3, 1930; educated at DePauw University, Hillsdale College, University of Michigan, and University of Vienna, and received M.A. and Ph.D. degrees from Indiana University; honorary doctor of laws, Grove City College, Grove City, PA, 1973; honorary doctor of political science, Francisco Marroquin University, Guatemala, 1979; U.S. Army, active duty, 1954–56; two years, advertising manager, Hopkins Syndicate, Inc.; taught at Indiana University for three years before moving to Bradley University, Peoria, IL, in 1963, where he taught United States and Latin American history until 1967; director of schools, Westminster Academy, Northbrook, IL, 1967–68; in 1962, employed by the Republican Party as a public relations expert; in 1964, served as director of research for the Illinois Goldwater Organization; at the request of Richard Nixon, served as one of his advisors and researchers on political and national issues, 1964–68; in 1976 served as chairman of Illinois Citizens for Reagan Committee; trustee of Hillsdale College; chairman, American Conservative Union, 1977–79; director of the Intercollegiate Studies Institute; serves with more than 60 U.S. Senators and Representatives on the National Advisory Board of Young Americans for Freedom; chairman of Republican Study Committee, 1983; appointed by President Reagan to the Commission on the Bicentennial of the United States Constitution; married Arlene Catherine Johnson of Chicago; eight children: Catherine Anne, Susanna Marie, Jennifer Elizabeth, Rebekah Caroline, George Washington V, Rachel Ellen, Sarah Emma, and Carrie Esther; elected to the 91st Congress by special election, November 25, 1969, to fill the vacancy caused by the resignation of Donald Rumsfeld; reelected to each succeeding Congress; member, Committee on Ways and Means.

Office Listings

233 Cannon House Office Building, Washington, DC 20515–1308 225–3711
Chief of Staff.—Kirt Johnson.
Scheduler.—Sandra Wiseman.
Press Secretary.—Steven Behn.
1450 South New Wilke Road, Arlington Heights, IL 60005 .... (847) 394–0790
District Representative.—Jack McKenney.
300 North Milwaukee Avenue, Suite C, Lake Villa, IL 60046 .... (847) 265–9000

Counties: COOK COUNTY; cities of Barrington, Hanover, Palatine, Schaumburg, part of Elk Grove and part of Wheeling. LAKE COUNTY; cities of Antioch, Avon, Cuba, Ela, Fremont, Grant, Lake Villa, Newport, Warren and Wauconda. Population (1990), 571,530.

ZIP Codes: 60002, 60004 (part), 60005 (part), 60006, 60007 (part), 60008 (part), 60010 (part), 60011, 60013 (part), 60020, 60030 (part), 60031, 60041, 60042 (part), 60046–47, 60048 (part), 60050 (part), 60056 (part), 60060 (part), 60067, 60073–75, 60078, 60081 (part), 60083, 60084 (part), 60085 (part), 60087 (part), 60092, 60094–95, 60099 (part), 60103 (part), 60107, 60120 (part), 60159, 60168, 60172 (part), 60173 (part), 60192–96

* * *

NINTH DISTRICT

SIDNEY R. YATES, Democrat, of Chicago, IL; born in Chicago, August 27, 1909; graduated, Lakeview High School in Chicago; Bachelor of Philosophy, University of Chicago, 1931; J.D., University of Chicago, 1933; served in the U.S. Navy for 26 months; released from active duty with rank of lieutenant; attorney at law since 1933; assistant attorney for Illinois State bank receiver, 1935–37; assistant attorney general attached to Illinois Commerce Commission as traction attorney, 1937–40; editor of "Bulletin of Decalogue Society of Lawyers," 1947; married Adeline J. Holleb of Chicago in 1935; one son, Stephen R. Yates; member: American Bar Association, American Veterans' Committee, Chicago Bar Association, Illinois State Bar Association, Chicago Council on Foreign Relations, City Club of Chicago, Decalogue Society of Lawyers; Kennedy Center trustee; regent emeritus, Smithsonian Institution; U.S. Holocaust Memorial Council; elected to the 81st Congress on November 2, 1948; reelected to the 82nd, 83rd,

84th, 85th, 86th, and 87th Congresses; U.S. representative to Trusteeship Council of the United Nations with rank of Ambassador, 1963–64; committee: Appropriations; subcommittees: Foreign Operations, Export Financing and Related Programs; Interior (ranking minority); elected to the 89th Congress, November 3, 1964; reelected to each succeeding Congress.

Office Listings

2109 Rayburn House Office Building, Washington, DC 20515–1309 225–2111
Chief of Staff/Administrative Assistant.—Mary Anderson Bain. FAX: 225–3493
Room 3920, 230 South Dearborn Street, Chicago, IL 60604 .... (312) 353–4596
Room 2700, 2100 Ridge Avenue, Evanston, IL 60201 .... (708) 328–2610

County: COOK COUNTY (part). Cities: Chicago (part), Evanston, Glenview, Golf, Lincolnwood, Morton Grove, Niles, Skoki. Population (1990), 571,530.

ZIP Codes: 60025, 60029, 60053, 60076–77, 60201–03, 60208, 60613 (part), 60626, 60630 (part), 60631 (part), 60640 (part), 60645, 60646 (part), 60656 (part), 60657 (part), 60659 (part), 60660, 60670, 60714 (part)

* * *

TENTH DISTRICT

JOHN EDWARD PORTER, Republican, of Wilmette, IL; born in Evanston, IL, June 1, 1935; graduated from Evanston Township High School, 1953; attended Massachusetts Institute of Technology, Cambridge, MA, 1953–54; B.S.B.A., Northwestern University School of Business, Evanston, IL, 1957; J.D. with distinction, University of Michigan Law School, Ann Arbor, 1961 (*Michigan Law Review*); served in U.S. Army Signal Corps (Reserves), 1958–64; engaged in the practice of law in Evanston, IL; admitted to practice before the Supreme Court of the United States, U.S. Court of Claims, and the Illinois State bar; honor law graduate attorney, U.S. Department of Justice, Washington, DC, 1961–63; member, Illinois State Legislature, 1973–79; member or officer of many civic and philanthropic organizations; member since 1981 of the Appropriations Committee; subcommittees: ranking member, Labor, Health and Human Services, and Education; Foreign Operations, Export Financing, and Related Programs; founder and cochairman, Congressional Human Rights Caucus; married the former Kathryn Suzanne Cameron, 1974; five children: John, David, Donna, Robyn, and Ann; elected to the 96th Congress by special election, January 22, 1980; reelected to each succeeding Congress.

Office Listings

http://www.house.gov/porter

2373 Rayburn House Office Building, Washington, DC 20515–1310 225–4835
Administrative Assistant.—Robert Bradner. FAX: 225–0157
Legislative Director.—Julie Deboldt.
Scheduler.—Lynn Guhse.
Suite 102, 200 Wilmot Road, Deerfield, IL 60015 .... (708) 940–0202
Executive Assistant.—Ginny Hotaling.
Press Secretary.—David Kohn.
601–A County Building, 18 North County Street, Waukegan, IL 60085 .... (708) 662–0101
1650 Arlington Heights Road, Arlington Heights, IL 60004 .... (708) 392–0303

Counties: Cook (part) and Lake (part). Population (1990), 571,530.

ZIP Codes: 60004 (part), 60005 (part), 60015, 60016 (part), 60022, 60025 (part), 60026, 60029, 60030 (part), 60035, 60037, 60040, 60043–45, 60048 (part), 60056 (part), 60060 (part), 60061–62, 60064–65, 60069–70, 60079, 60082, 60085 (part), 60087 (part), 60088–91, 60093, 60096, 60099 (part)

* * *

ELEVENTH DISTRICT

JERRY WELLER, Republican, of Morris, IL; born in Streator, IL, July 7, 1957; graduated, Dwight High School, 1975; B.A., agriculture, University of Illinois, 1979; aide to Congressman Tom Corcoran, 1980–81; aide to John R. Block (U.S. Secretary of Agriculture), 1981–85; former State Representative, 1988–94; National Republican Legislative Association Legislator of the Year; listed in the 1990 *Almanac of Illinois Politico*; member: Ways and Means Committee; Subcommittee on Oversight and Social Security; assistant majority whip, House Republican Steering Committee; elected to the 104th Congress; reelected to the 105th Congress.

Office Listings
http://www.house.gov/weller

130 Cannon House Office Building, Washington, DC 20515 225–3635
Administrative Assistant.—Jim Hayes. FAX: 225–3521
Executive Assistant.—Alan Tennille.
Legislative Director.—Bill Himpler.
Senior Legislative Assistant.—Gina Elmore.
Joliet Congressional District Office, 51 West Jackson Street, Suite 100, Joliet, IL 60432 .... (815) 740–2028
Press Secretary.—Kimberly Clarke.
Ottawa Congressional District Office, 628–30, Columbus Street, Suite 205, Ottawa, IL 61350 .... (815) 433–0085
District Manager.—Reed Wilson.

Counties: Cook (part), Grundy, Kankakee (part), La Salle (part), and Will (part). Population (1990), 571,528.

ZIP Codes: 60401, 60407–08, 60409 (part), 60410, 60411 (part), 60416–17, 60421, 60423 (part), 60424, 60425 (part), 60432–34, 60435 (part), 60436 (part), 60437–38, 60442, 60444, 60447 (part), 60448–49, 60450 (part), 60451, 60466 (part), 60468, 60470–71, 60473 (part), 60474–76, 60479, 60481, 60531, 60537, 60551, 60557, 60901 (part), 60913–15, 60931, 60935, 60940–41, 60944, 60950, 60954, 60964 (part), 61316, 61332, 61334 (part), 61341, 61342 (part), 61348, 61350, 61354 (part), 61358 (part), 61360, 61364 (part), 61370 (part), 61371–73, 61377 (part)

* * *

TWELFTH DISTRICT

JERRY F. COSTELLO, Democrat, of Belleville, IL; born in East St. Louis, on September 25, 1949; graduated, Assumption High, East St. Louis, 1968; A.A., Belleville Area College, IL, 1970; B.A., Maryville College of the Sacred Heart, St. Louis, MO, 1973; law enforcement official, 1970–80; elected chairman of the county board, St. Clair County, 1980–88; member: East-West Gateway Coordinating Council, Metro Counties of Illinois, Southwestern Illinois Leadership Council, Southwestern Illinois Small Business Finance Alliance, Light Rail Transit Committee; chairman, St. Clair Heart Fund drive and United Way drive, 1985; cochairman of the St. Clair, County March of Dimes, 1988; married the former Georgia Jean Cockrum, 1968; three children: Jerry II, Gina Keen, and John; committees: Transportation and Infrastructure, Budget; elected by special election to the 100th Congress on August 9, 1988, to fill the vacancy caused by the death of Charles Melvin Price; reelected to each succeeding Congress.

Office Listings
http://www.house.gov/costello jfcil12@hr.house.gov

2454 Rayburn House Office Building, Washington, DC 20515–1312 225–5661
Administrative Assistant.—Brian Lott. FAX: 225–0285
1363 Niedringhaus Avenue, Granite City, IL 62040 .... (618) 451–7065
Suite 210, 8787 State Street, East Saint Louis, IL 62203 .... (618) 397–8833
327 West Main Street, Belleville, IL 62220 .... (618) 233–8026

Counties: Alexander, Jackson, Madison (part), Monroe, Perry, Randolph, St. Clair, Union, and Williamson (part). Population (1990), 571,530.

ZIP Codes: 62002 (part), 62010 (part), 62018 (part), 62024 (part), 62040 (part), 62048, 62059–60, 62071, 62084, 62087, 62090, 62095, 62201–08, 62214, 62217, 62220–23, 62225, 62232–33, 62234 (part), 62236–44, 62246, 62248, 62254–61, 62264–65, 62269, 62272, 62274, 62277–80, 62282, 62285–86, 62288–90, 62292, 62295, 62297–98, 62832, 62888, 62901–03, 62905–07, 62913–16, 62918, 62920–22, 62924, 62926–27, 62929, 62932–33, 62940, 62942, 62949–50, 62952, 62957–58, 62961–62, 62966, 62969, 62971, 62975, 62988, 62990, 62993–94, 62997–98

* * *

THIRTEENTH DISTRICT

HARRIS W. FAWELL, Republican, of Naperville, IL; born in West Chicago, March 25, 1929; graduated from West Chicago Community High School; undergraduate, North Central College, Naperville, IL, 1947–49; LL.D., Chicago-Kent College of Law, Chicago, 1949–52; engaged in private practice of law, Fawell, James and Brooks, Naperville, 1954–84; member, Du Page County, IL, and American bar associations; U.S. District Court Trial Bar; Illinois and American trial lawyers associations; American Judicature Society; highest legal ability rating ''A'' of Martindale-Hubbell law directory; general counsel, Illinois Association of Park Districts, 1977–84; member, Illinois State Senate, 1963–77; former chairman, Education and Public

Welfare-Health committees, Illinois Senate; former member, Illinois Commission on Children, 1967–77; former chairman, School Law Section Council, Illinois State Bar Association; active in many civic associations; elected Fellow of the Chicago-Kent College of Law Honor Council "for contribution to the College of Law and high standards of legal profession," 1981; former assistant State's attorney, DuPage County, IL; Illinois congressional representative to the Full Committee of the National Republican Congressional Committee; Speaker's Group on Health Care Reform; married to the former Ruth Johnson; three children: Richard, Jane, and John; member, Wesley Methodist Church, Naperville, IL; committees: Economic and Educational Opportunities, Science; subcommittees: Employer-Employee Relations, Energy and Environment, Republican Policy, Workforce Protections; elected to the 99th Congress on November 6, 1984; reelected to each succeeding Congress.

Office Listings

2159 Rayburn House Office Building, Washington, DC 20515–1313 225–3515
Chief of Staff.—Alan Mertz. FAX: 225–9420
Executive Assistant.—Sue Geibel.
Suite 100, 115 West 55th Street, Clarendon Hills, IL 60514 .... (708) 655–2052
District Director.—Barbara Graham.

Counties: Cook (part), DuPage (part), and Will (part). Population (1990), 571,531.

ZIP Codes: 60137 (part), 60148 (part), 60181 (part), 60187 (part), 60431 (part), 60432 (part), 60435 (part), 60436 (part), 60439–40, 60441 (part), 60457 (part), 60462 (part), 60464 (part), 60465 (part), 60477 (part), 60480 (part), 60504 (part), 60514, 60515 (part), 60516–17, 60519, 60521 (part), 60522, 60532, 60535, 60540, 60544 (part), 60566, 60559 (part), 60561, 60563–67

* * *

FOURTEENTH DISTRICT

J. DENNIS HASTERT, Republican, of Yorkville, IL; born in Aurora, IL, on January 2, 1942; graduated, Oswego High School, 1960; B.A., Wheaton College, IL, 1964; M.S., Northern Illinois University, DeKalb, 1967; teacher/coach, Yorkville High School; partner, family restaurant business; member, Illinois General Assembly House of Representatives, 1980–86; Republican spokesman for the Appropriations II Committee; chairman, Joint Committee on Public Utility Regulation; member, Legislative Audit Commission; named one of Illinois' 20 top legislators in 1985 by *Chicago Sun-Times*; member, Yorkville Lions Club; board of directors, Aurora Family Support Center; married the former Jean Kahl in 1973; two children: Joshua and Ethan; elected to the 100th Congress on November 4, 1986; reelected to each succeeding Congress.

Office Listings

2241 Rayburn House Office Building, Washington, DC 20515–1314 225–2976
Chief of Staff.—Scott Palmer. FAX: 225–0697
Scheduler.—Amy Jensen.
Legislative Director.—S. Tandi Thomas.
27 North River Street, Batavia, IL 60510 .... (630) 406–1114
Office Manager.—Lisa Post.

Counties: DeKalb, DuPage (part), Kane, Kendall, La Salle (part), Lee. CITIES AND TOWNSHIPS Amboy, Ashton, Aurora, Barrington Hills (part), Bartlett (part), Batavia, Big Rock, Bristol, Burlington, Carol Stream (part), Carpentersville, Clare, Compton, Cornell, Cortland, DeKalb, Dixon, Dundee, East and West, Earlville, Elburn, Elgin, Esmond, Forreston, Franklin Grove, Geneva, Genoa, Gilberts, Hampshire, Harmon, Hinckley, Kaneville, Kingston, Kirkland, Lee, Leland, Malta, Maple Park, Mendota, Millbrook, Millington, Minooka (part), Montgomery, Mooseheart, Nelson, Newark, North Aurora, Oswego, Paw Paw, Plano, Plato Center, St. Charles, Sandwich, Shabbona, Sleepy Hollow, Somonauk, South Elgin, Steward, Sublette, Sugar Grove, Sycamore, Virgil, Warrenville (part), Wasco, Waterman, Wayne, West Brooklyn, West Chicago, Wheaton (part), Winfield, Yorkville. Population (1990), 571,530.

ZIP Codes: 60010 (part), 60103 (part), 60109, 60110–12, 60115, 60118–21, 60123, 60129, 60134–36, 60140, 60144–46, 60150–51, 60170, 60174–75, 60177–78, 60182–85, 60187 (part), 60188 (part), 60190, 60447, 60504–07, 60510–12, 60518, 60520, 60530–31, 60536–39, 60542–43, 60545, 60548, 60550, 60552–56, 60560, 61006, 61021, 61030–31, 61042, 61058, 61310, 61318–19, 61342, 61353, 61367, 61378

* * *

FIFTEENTH DISTRICT

THOMAS W. EWING, Republican, of Pontiac, IL; born September 19, 1935, in Atlanta, IL; B.S., Milikin University, 1957; awarded Juris Doctorate degree, John Marshall Law School,

1968; Illinois House of Representatives, 17 years; assistant Republican minority leader, 1982–90; minority leader, 1990; delegate, Republican National Convention, 1980, 1984, and 1988; secretary, Illinois Delegation; delegation floor whip, 1984; named "National Legislator of the Year" by National Republican Legislators Association, 1988; farm owner and businessman; married to Connie Ewing; six children; committees: Agriculture, Transportation and Infrastructure; subcommittees: chairman, Risk Management and Specialty Crops; Aviation; Water Resources and Environment; Department Operations; Nutrition and Foreign Agriculture; elected by special election on July 2, 1991 to fill the vacancy caused by the resignation of Edward Madigan; reelected to each succeeding Congress.

Office Listings

http://www.house.gov/ewing

2417 Rayburn House Office Building, Washington, DC 20515–1315 225–2371
Chief of Staff.—Terry Greene.
Legislative Director.—Eric Nicoll.
Executive Assistant.—Karen Kaumeier.
210 West Water Street, Pontiac, IL 61764 .... (815) 844–7660
2401 East Washington Street, Bloomington, IL 61704 .... (309) 662–9371
Room 307, 102 East Main Street, Urbana, IL 61801 .... (217) 328–0165
Suite A, 120 North Vermilion, Danville, IL 61832 .... (217) 431–8230

Counties: Champaign, De Witt, Douglas, Edgar, Ford, Iroquois, Kankakee (part), Livingston, McLean (part), Piatt, and Vermilion. CITIES AND TOWNSHIPS: Pontiac, Bloomington-Normal, Champaign-Urbana, Danville, and Kankakee. Population (1990), 571,532.

ZIP Codes: 60420, 60460, 60901 (part), 60911–12, 60917–22, 60924, 60926–34, 60936, 60938–39, 60941–42, 60945–46, 60948–49, 60951–53, 60955–57, 60959–63, 60964 (part), 60966–70, 60973–74, 61311, 61313, 61319, 61321 (part), 61333, 61364 (part), 61701–02, 61704, 61720, 61722, 61724, 61726–28, 61730–31, 61735–37, 61739–41, 61743, 61744 (part), 61745 (part), 61748 (part), 61749–50, 61752–53, 61758, 61761 (part), 61764, 61769–70, 61773, 61775–78, 61801, 61810–18, 61820–21, 61824–26, 61830–34, 61839–59, 61862–66 61870–78, 61880, 61882–84, 61910, 61911 (part), 61913, 61917, 61919, 61924, 61929–30, 61932–33, 61936, 61940–42, 61944, 61949, 61953, 61955–56, 62423, 62474, 62512, 62552 (part)

* * *

SIXTEENTH DISTRICT

DONALD MANZULLO, Republican, of Egan, IL; born on March 24, 1944 in Rockford, IL; B.A., American University, Washington, DC, 1987; J.D., Marquette University Law School, Milwaukee, WI, 1970; president, Ogle County Bar Association, 1971, 1973; advisor, Oregon Ambulance Corporation; founder, Oregon Youth, Inc.; admitted to Illinois bar, 1970; member: State of Illinois and City of Oregon chambers of commerce, Friends of Severson Dells, Natural Land Institute, Ogle County Historic Society, Northern Illinois Alliance for the Arts, Aircraft Owners and Pilots Association, Ogle County Pilots Association, Kiwanis International, Illinios Farm Bureau, Ogle County Farm Bureau, National Federation of Independent Business, Citizens Against Government Waste; married Freda Teslik Manzullo, 1982; three children: Niel, Noel, and Katherine; elected on November 3, 1992 to the 103rd Congress; reelected to each succeeding Congress.

Office Listings

409 Cannon House Office Building, Washington, DC 20515–1316 225–5676
Chief of Staff.—Doug Thomas.
415 South Mulford Road, Rockford, IL 61108 .... (815) 394–1231
Press Secretary.—Christopher Hamrick.
District Director.—Pamela Bunting.
181 Virginia Avenue, Crystal Lake, IL 60014 .... (815) 356–9800
Caseworker.—Nada Johnson.

Counties: Boone, Jo Daviess, McHenry, Ogle (part), Stephenson, and Winnebago. Population (1990), 571,530.

ZIP Codes: 60012, 60013 (part), 60014, 60021, 60033–34, 60039, 60042 (part), 60050 (part), 60051, 60071–72, 60080, 60081 (part), 60084 (part), 60097–98, 60102, 60113, 60129 (part), 60142, 60152, 60180, 61001, 61006 (part), 61007 (part), 61008, 61010–13, 61015–16, 61018–20, 61024–25, 61027–28, 61030 (part), 61031 (part), 61032, 61036, 61038–39, 61041, 61043–45, 61047–50, 61052, 61053 (part), 61054 (part), 61059, 61060, 61061 (part), 61062–63, 61065, 61067, 61068 (part), 61070, 61072–73, 61075–77, 61078 (part), 61079–80, 61084–85, 61087–89, 61101–12, 61114–15, 61125–26, 61130–32

* * *

SEVENTEENTH DISTRICT

LANE EVANS, Democrat, of Rock Island, IL; born in Rock Island on August 4, 1951; graduated, Alleman High School, Rock Island, 1969; B.A., Augustana College, Rock Island, 1974; J.D., Georgetown University Law Center, Washington, DC, 1978; admitted to Illinois bar in 1978 and commenced practice in Rock Island; served in U.S. Marine Corps, 1969–71; attorney for the Western Illinois Legal Foundation, 1978–79; national staff of Kennedy for President campaign, 1980; entered private practice as a partner in Community Legal Clinic, 1982; legal representative for ACLU, APRI, and LULAC, 1979; awards: Vietnam Veterans of America "National Legislator of the Year" (1985), President's Award for Outstanding Achievement, 1990; elected on November 2, 1982 to the 98th Congress; reelected to each succeeding Congress.

Office Listings

2335 Rayburn House Office Building, Washington, DC 20515–1317 225–5905
Administrative Assistant.—Dennis King. FAX: 225–5396
Office Manager.—Eda Robinson.
Press Secretary.—Steve Vetzner.
Room 5, 1535 47th Avenue, Moline, IL 61265 .... (309) 793–5760
District Representative.—Phil Hare.
1640 North Henderson, Galesburg, IL 61401 .... (309) 342–4411

Counties: Adams (part), Bureau, Carroll, Fulton, Hancock, Henderson, Henry, Knox, McDonough, Mercer, Ogle (part), Rock Island, Warren, and Whiteside. Population (1990), 571,530.

ZIP Codes: 61007 (part), 61014, 61017, 61021 (part), 61030 (part), 61037, 61046, 61051, 61053, 61054 (part), 61061 (part), 61064 (part), 61071, 61074, 61078 (part), 61081, 61091, 61201, 61204, 61230–44, 61250–52, 61254, 61256–65, 61270, 61272–79, 61281–85, 61301 (part), 61312, 61314–15, 61317, 61320, 61322–23, 61328–30, 61337–38, 61342 (part), 61344–46, 61349, 61354 (part), 61356, 61359, 61361–62, 61368, 61374, 61376, 61379, 61401–02, 61410–20, 61422–23, 61425, 61427–28, 61430–43, 61447–50, 61452–55, 61458–60, 61462, 61465–78, 61480, 61482, 61484–86, 61488–90, 61501, 61519–20, 61524, 61529, 61531, 61542–44, 61553, 61563, 61572, 62301 (part), 62311, 62313, 62316, 62318, 62320–21, 62325–27, 62329–30, 62334, 62336, 62338–39, 62341, 62346, 62348–49, 62351, 62354, 62358–59, 62367, 62373–74, 62376, 62379–80, 62422, 62624, 62644

* * *

EIGHTEENTH DISTRICT

RAY LAHOOD, Republican, of Peoria, IL; born December 6, 1945, in Peoria; graduate of Spalding High School; Canton Junior College, Canton, IL; B.S., education and sociology, Bradley University, Peoria, IL, 1971; previous memberships: Academy of Our Lady/Spalding Board of Education (president), Notre Dame High School Board (president), Peoria Area Retarded Citizens Board of Directors, Bradley University National Alumni Board (president) and Peoria Area Chamber of Commerce Board; junior high school teacher, director of Rock Island County Youth Services Bureau, chief planner for Bi-State Metropolitan Planning Commission, administrative assistant to Congressman Tom Railsback and chief of staff for Congressman Bob Michel; member, Illinois House of Representatives, 1982; Peoria Economic Development Council Board of Directors, Heartland Water Resources Council, Children's Hospital of Illinois Advisory Board, Peoria Rotary Club, Junior League Community Advisory Committee, United Way Pillars Society and Holy Family Church; married Kathy Dunk LaHood, 1967; four children: Darin, Amy, Sam, and Sara; committees: Agriculture, Transportation and Infrastructure, Veterans' Affairs; subcommittee: Benefits; elected November 8, 1994 to the 104th Congress; reelected to the 105th Congress.

Office Listings

http://www.house.gov/lahood

329 Cannon House Office Building, Washington, DC 20515–1318 225–6201
Administrative Assistant.—Diane Liesman. FAX: 225–9249
Legislative Director.—Chris Guidry.
Legislative Assistant/Counsel.—David Kunz.
Scheduler/Office Manager.—Joan Mitchell.
100 Monroe Street NE, Room 100, Peoria, IL 61602 .... (309) 671–7027
District Administrative Assistant.—Mary Alice Erickson. FAX: 671–7309
Office Manager.—Sheri Lemaster.
236 West State Street, Jacksonville, IL 62650 .... (217) 245–1431

Office Manager.—Sally Dahman. FAX: 243–6852
Staff Assistant.—Diane Hequet.
3050 Montvale Drive, Suite D, Springfield, IL 62704 .... (217) 793–0808
Office Manager.—Donna Rapps Miller. FAX: 793–9724
Staff Assistant.—Judy Hinds.

Counties: Cass, Logan, Macon (part), Marshall, Mason, McLean (part), Menard, Morgan, Peoria, Putnam, Sangamon (part), Stark, Tazewell, and Woodford. CITIES: Atlanta, Auburn, Bartonville, Beardstown, Chatham (part), Chillicothe, Creve Coeur, Decatur (part), Delavan, East Peoria, El Paso, Elmwood, Eureka, Havana, Henry, Heyworth, Jacksonville, Lacon, Leland Grove (part), Lincoln, Manilo, Marquette Heights, Mason City, Metamora, Minonk, Morton, Mount Pulaski, Normal (part), North Pekin, Pekin, Peoria, Peoria Heights, Petersburg, Riverton, Roanoke, Rochester, Rome, Sherman, South Jacksonville, Springfield (part), Tremont, Verden (part), Virginia, Washington and West Peoria. Population (1990), 571,580.

ZIP Codes: 61326–27, 61335–36, 61340, 61363, 61369, 61375, 61377, 61421, 61424, 61426, 61449–51, 61474–80, 61482–86, 61488–91, 61501, 61516–18, 61523, 61525–26, 61528–37, 61539–41, 61544–48, 61550, 61552, 61554–55, 61558–62, 61564–65, 61567–72, 61567–72, 61600–07, 61611–15, 61626, 61628–30, 61632–41, 61643–44, 61650–56, 61720–25, 61728–29, 61731–45, 61747, 61751–56, 61759–60, 61771–72, 61774, 62512, 62515, 62518–20, 62526, 62534–36, 62538–39, 62541, 62543, 62545, 62548, 62551, 62557–58, 62561, 62563, 62571,62573, 62601, 62611–13, 62616–18, 62622, 62625–29, 62631, 62633–34, 62636, 62638, 63640, 62642–44, 62649–51, 62655–56, 62659–62, 62664–68, 62670–71, 62673–75, 62677, 62681–82, 62688–89, 62691–95, 61702, 62704, 62707, 62761, 62765, 62786

* * *

NINETEENTH DISTRICT

GLENN POSHARD, Democrat, of Marion, IL; born in Herald, White County, IL, October 30, 1945; graduated, Carmi Township High School, Carmi, IL, 1962; Southern Illinois University, Carbondale, B.S., 1970, M.S., 1974, Ph.D., 1984; served in U.S. Army, specialist 5, 1962–65; farmer, teacher, school administrator; Illinois State Senate, 1984–88; member: Lions Club, VFW, American Legion, Chamber of Commerce, AMVETS; married to the former Jo Roetzel; two children: Dennis and Kris; committees: Transportation and Infrastructure, Small Business; elected November 8, 1988 to the 101st Congress; reelected to each succeeding Congress.

Office Listings

2334 Rayburn House Office Building, Washington, DC 20515–1319 225–5201
Chief of Staff.—David Stricklin. FAX: 225–1541
New Route 13 West, Marion, IL 62959 .... (618) 993–8532
District Office Manager.—Judy Hampton..

Counties: Christian (part), Clark, Clay, Coles, Crawford, Cumberland, Edwards, Effingham, Franklin, Gallatin, Hamilton, Hardin, Jasper, Johnson, Lawrence, Macon (part), Massac, Moultrie, Pope, Pulaski, Richland, Saline, Shelby, Wabash, Wayne, White, and Williamson (part). Population (1990), 571,530.

ZIP Codes: 61756, 61911 (part), 61912–14, 61920, 61925, 61928, 61931, 61937–38, 61943, 61951, 61957, 62080, 62083 (part), 62401, 62410–11, 62413–15, 62417, 62419–22, 62424–28, 62431–34, 62436, 62438–52, 62454, 62458–69, 62473–81, 62501, 62510, 62513–14, 62521–23, 62525, 62526 (part), 62532, 62534, 62537, 62544, 62547, 62549–50, 62552 (part), 62553–55, 62557, 62565, 62567, 62568 (part), 62571, 62574, 62805–06, 62809–12, 62814–15, 62817–25, 62827–30, 62833–46, 62849–52, 62854–56, 62858–63, 62865, 62867–69, 62871, 62874, 62878–79, 62884, 62886–87, 62890–91, 62895–97, 62899, 62908, 62910, 62912, 62917, 62919, 62921–23, 62926, 62928, 62930–35, 62938–39, 62941, 62943–44, 62946–48, 62951, 62953–56, 62959–60, 62963–65, 62967, 62970, 62972–74, 62976–77, 62979, 62982–85, 62987, 62991–92, 62995–96, 62999

* * *

TWENTIETH DISTRICT

JOHN M. SHIMKUS, Republican, of Collinsville, IL; born on February 21, 1958, in Collinsville; graduated from Collinsville High School; B.S., West Point Military Academy, West Point, NY, 1980; teaching certificate, Christ College, Irvine, CA, 1990; graduate school, Southern Illinois University, Edwardsville; U.S. Army Reserves, 1980–85; government and history teacher, Collinsville High School; Collinsville township trustee, 1989; Madison county treasurer, 1990–96; married the former Karen Muth, 1987; two children, David and Joshua; elected to the 105th Congress.

Office Listings

http://www.house.gov/shimkus

512 Cannon House Office Building, Washington, DC 20515 225–5271
Chief of Staff.—Craig Roberts. FAX: 225–5880
Legislative Director.—Stan Blankenburg.
301 North Sixth Street, Suite 100, Springfield, IL 62701 .... (217) 492–5090
District Director.—Brad Carlson. FAX: 492–5096

Counties: Adams (part), Bond, Brown, Calhoun, Christian (part), Clinton, Fayette, Greene, Jefferson, Jersey, Macoupin, Madison (part), Marion, Montgomery, Pike, Sangamon (part), Schuyler, Scott, and Washington. Population (1990), 571,480.

ZIP Codes: 61452, 62001, 62002 (part), 62006, 62009, 62010 (part), 62011–17, 62018 (part), 62019, 62021–23, 62024 (part), 62025–28, 62030–34, 62035 (part), 62036–37, 62040 (part), 62044–47, 62049–54, 62056, 62058, 62061–63, 62065, 62067, 62069–70, 62074–82, 62083 (part), 62085–86, 62088–89, 62091–94, 62097, 62214–16, 62218–19, 62230–31, 62234 (part), 62245–47, 62249–50, 62252–53, 62262–63, 62265–66, 62268, 62271, 62273, 62275, 62281, 62283–84, 62293 (part), 62294 (part), 62301 (part), 62305–06, 62312, 62314, 62319, 62323–24, 62332, 62340, 62343–47, 62352–53, 62355–57, 62360–63, 62365–66, 62370, 62372, 62375, 62378, 62418, 62458, 62471, 62511, 62517, 62530–31, 62533, 62536, 62538, 62540, 62546, 62556, 62558, 62560, 62568 (part), 62570, 62572, 62610, 62621, 62624, 62626, 62629 (part), 62630, 62639–40, 62649, 62663, 62667, 62672, 62674, 62676, 62681, 62683, 62685–86, 62690, 62694, 62701, 62702 (part), 62703, 62704 (part), 62705, 62707 (part), 62708, 62718, 62791, 62801, 62803, 62807–08, 62810, 62814, 62816, 62830–31, 62838, 62846, 62848–49, 62853–54, 62857, 62864, 62866, 62870, 62872, 62875–77, 62880–83, 62885, 62889, 62892–94, 62898

INDIANA

(Population 1995, 5,803,000)

SENATORS

RICHARD G. LUGAR, Republican, of Indianapolis, IN; born in Indianapolis, April 4, 1932; graduated, Shortridge High School, 1950; B.A., Denison University, Granville, OH; Rhodes Scholar, B.A., M.A., Pembroke College, Oxford, England, 1956; served in the U.S. Navy, 1957–60; businessman; treasurer, Lugar Stock Farms, Inc., a livestock and grain operation; vice president and treasurer, 1960–67, Thomas L. Green and Co., manufacturers of food production machinery; member, Indianapolis Board of School Commissioners, 1964–67; mayor of Indianapolis, 1968–75; member, advisory board, U.S. Conference of Mayors, 1969–75; National League of Cities, advisory council, 1972–75, president, 1971; Advisory Commission on Intergovernmental Relations, 1969–75, vice chairman, 1971–75; board of trustees, Denison University and the University at Indianapolis; advisory board, Indiana University-Purdue University at Indianapolis; visiting professor of political science, director of public affairs, Indiana Central University; 31 honorary doctorates; recipient of Fiorello LaGuardia Award, 1975; GOP National Convention Keynote Speaker, 1972; SFRC chairman, 1985–86; NRSC chairman, 1983–84; member, St. Luke's Methodist Church; married the former Charlene Smeltzer, 1956; four children; chairman, Agriculture, Nutrition, and Forestry Committee; member: Select Committee on Intelligence, Arms Control Observer Group, Senate Foreign Relations Committee; elected to the U.S. Senate, November 2, 1976, for the six-year term beginning January 4, 1977; reelected on November 2, 1982, November 8, 1988, and November 8, 1994.

Office Listings

http://www.senate.gov/senator/lugar.html senator_lugar@lugar.senate.gov

306 Hart Senate Office Building, Washington, DC 20510–1401 224–4814
Administrative Assistant.—Martin W. Morris.
Legislative Director.—Dan Diller.
Press Secretary.—Mark Schoeff.
Scheduler.—Randy Pritchard.
10 West Market Street, Room 1180, Indianapolis, IN 46204 .... (317) 226–5555
Federal Building, Room 122, 101 NW Martin Luther King Boulevard, Evansville, IN 47708 .... (812) 465–6313
Federal Building, Room 3158, 1300 South Harrison Street, Fort Wayne, IN 46802–3487 .... (219) 422–1505
5530 Sohl Avenue, Room 103, Hammond, IN 46320 .... (219) 937–5380
Federal Center, Room 103, 1201 East 10th Street, Jeffersonville, IN 47132 .... (812) 288–3377

* * *

DAN COATS, Republican, of Fort Wayne, IN; born in Jackson, MI, May 16, 1943; graduated, Jackson High School, 1961; B.A., Wheaton College, Wheaton, IL, 1965; J.D., Indiana University School of Law, *cum laude,* 1971; associate editor of the *Indiana Law Review*; staff sergeant, U.S. Army, 1966–68; attorney, admitted to the Indiana State bar in 1972 and commenced practice in Fort Wayne; Mutual Security Life Insurance Company, Fort Wayne, assistant vice president and counsel for mortgage loan and real estate investments; district director, U.S. Representative Dan Quayle, 1976–80; board member: board of visitors, Wheaton College; Big Brothers/Big Sisters of America; International Republican Institute; Military Academy Board of Advisors, West Point; Center for Effective Compassion; numerous honorary board memberships; member: McLean Presbyterian Church; Quest Club, Fort Wayne, Indiana; Emil Verbin Society; honors: Indiana University School of Law, Distinguished Alumni Award, 1995; L. Mendel Rivers Award, 1993; numerous National Federation of Independent Business, Guardian of Small Business awards; Region 5 Head Start Man of the Year, 1991; numerous Watchdog of the Treasury awards; 1986 Leadership Award, Coalition for Peace Through Strength; Spirit of Enterprise award; Sagamore of the Wabash, 1985; 1988 Congressional Baseball Game, MVP; honorary degrees: Huntington College, Doctor of Public Service, 1995; Wheaton College, Doctor of Laws, 1992; Olivet College, Doctor of Laws, 1987; married Marcia Ann Crawford, 1965; three children: Laura (Mrs. Mark Russo), Lisa (Mrs. Edward Wolf), and Andrew; two grandchildren: Christopher and Michael Russo; elected to the 97th Congress, November 4, 1980, representing Indiana's 4th District; reelected to each succeeding Congress; Republican leader, House Select Committee on Children, Youth, and Families; member of House Energy and Commerce Committee; appointed by Indiana Governor Robert Orr, December, 1988, to the U.S. Senate seat vacated by Vice President-elect Dan Quayle; sworn in as U.S. Senator, January 3,

1989; elected November 6, 1990 to complete the term ending January 3, 1993; reelected for the six-year term ending January 2, 1999; member, Senate Committee on Armed Services; chairman, Subcommittee on AirLand Forces; member, Senate Committee on Labor and Human Resources; chairman, Subcommittee on Children and Families; member, Senate Select Committee on Intelligence; Midwest regional whip.

Office Listings

http://www.senate.gov/~coats

404 Russell Office Building, Washington, DC 20510–1403 224–5623
Chief of Staff.—Sharon Soderstrom.
Press Secretary.—Tim Goeglein.
Legislative Director.—Brent Orrell.
Scheduler.—Karen Parker.
1180 Market Tower, 10 West Market Street, Indianapolis, IN 46204 .... (317) 226–5555
State Director.—William Dull.
Federal Building, Room 3158, 1300 South Harrison Street, Fort Wayne, IN 46802 (219) 422–1505
Building 66, Room 103, 1201 East 10th Street, Jeffersonville, IN 47132 .... (812) 288–3377
101 NW Seventh Street, Evansville, IN 47708 .... (812) 465–6313
8585 Broadway, Suite 490, Merrillville, IN 46410 .... (219) 736–9084

REPRESENTATIVES

FIRST DISTRICT

PETER J. VISCLOSKY, Democrat, of Merrillville, IN; born in Gary, IN, on August 13, 1949; graduated, Andrean High School, Merrillville, 1967; B.S., accounting, Indiana University Northwest, Gary, 1970; J.D., University of Notre Dame Law School, Notre Dame, IN, 1973; LL.M., international and comparative law, Georgetown University Law Center, Washington, DC, 1982; attorney, 1974–76; admitted to the Indiana State bar, 1974, the District of Columbia Bar, 1978, and the U.S. Supreme Court Bar, 1980; associate staff, U.S. House of Representatives, Committee on Appropriations, 1977–80, Committee on the Budget, 1980–82; practicing attorney, Merrillville law firm, 1983–84; married to Anne Marie O'Keefe; two children: John Daniel and Timothy Patrick; elected to the 99th Congress on November 6, 1984; reelected to each succeeding Congress.

Office Listings

http://www.house.gov/visclosky

2464 Rayburn House Office Building, Washington, DC 20515–1401 225–2461
Administrative Assistant.—Charles Brimmer. FAX: 225–2493
Legislative Director.—Cameron Griffith.
Executive Assistant/Scheduler.—Lisa Zawadzki.
Press Assistant.—Dwayne Lawler.
215 West 35th Avenue, Gary, IN 46408 .... (219) 884–1177
District Director.—David Rozmanich.
166 Lincolnway, Valparaiso, IN 46383 .... (219) 464–0315
6070 Central Avenue, Portage, IN 46368 .... (219) 763–2904

Counties: Lake (part) and Porter (part). Population (1990), 554,416.

ZIP Codes: 46302, 46303 (part), 46304, 46307 (part), 46311 (part), 46312, 46319–25, 46327, 46341 (part), 46342, 46347 (part), 46348 (part), 46355, 46360 (part), 46368, 46373 (part), 46375 (part), 46383–84, 46391 (part), 46393–94, 46401–05, 46406 (part), 46407–11

* * *

SECOND DISTRICT

DAVID M. McINTOSH, Republican, of Muncie, IN; born on June 8, 1958 in Oakland, CA; graduate of East Noble High School; Yale University, 1980; law degree, University of Chicago, 1983; member of the Indiana State bar and the U.S. Supreme Court bar; special assistant to President Reagan for domestic affairs, special assistant to Attorney General Meese in the Reagan Administration, liaison to President's Commission on Privatization and specialized in constitutional legal policy at the Justice Department, special assistant to Vice President Quayle, executive director of the President's Council on Competitiveness, deputy legal counsel to Vice President Quayle; former fellow, Hudson Institute Competitiveness Center; senior fellow, Citizens for a Sound Economy; founded the Federalist Society for Law and Public Policy (currently national cochairman); committees: Government Reform and Oversight, Economic and Educational Opportunities; chairman, National Economic Growth, Natural Resources and Regulatory Affairs Subcommittee; married to Ruthie McIntosh; elected to the 104th Congress; reelected to the 105th Congress.

Office Listings

1208 Longworth House Office Building, Washington, DC 20515 225–3021
Chief of Staff.—Devin Anderson. FAX: 225–3382
Communications Director.—Chris Jones.
Legislative Director.—Mark Epley.
Scheduler/Executive Assistant.—Betsy Thraves.
2900 West Jackson Street, Suite 101, Muncie, IN 47304 .... (317) 747–5566
FAX: 747–5586
The Paramount Centre, 1134 Meridian, Anderson, IN 46016 .... (317) 640–2919
2581 Seventh Street, Columbus, IN 47201.

Counties: Bartholomew (part), Decatur, Delaware, Henry (part), Jay (part), Madison, Randolph, Rush, Shelby, and Wayne. Population (1990), 554,416.

ZIP Codes: 46011–18, 46176, 47201–03, 47240, 47283, 47362, 47302–08, 47371, 47374–75, 47394

* * *

THIRD DISTRICT

TIM ROEMER, Democrat, of South Bend, IN; born in South Bend, October 30, 1956; graduated, Penn High School, Mishawaka, IN, 1975; B.A., political science, University of California, San Diego, 1979; M.A. (1981) and Ph.D. (1985), international relations, University of Notre Dame, South Bend, IN; staff assistant, Congressman John Brademas, U.S. Congress; defense, trade, and foreign policy adviser to Senator Dennis DeConcini; adjunct professor, The American University; married the former Sally Johnston, 1989; two children: Patrick and Matthew; elected to the 102nd Congress; reelected to each succeeding Congress.

Office Listings

http://www.house.gov/roemer troemer@hr.house.gov

407 Cannon House Office Building, Washington, DC 20515–1403 225–3915
Administrative Assistant.—Mark Brown. FAX: 225–6798
Legislative Director.—Carole Stringer.
Press Secretary.—Desiree Green.
217 North Main Street, South Bend, IN 46601 .... (219) 288–3301
District Director.—Julie Vuckovich.

Counties: Elkhart, Kosciusko (part), La Porte, St. Joseph, and Starke (part). Population (1990), 554,416.

ZIP Codes: 46301, 46340, 46341 (part), 46345–46, 46348 (part), 46350, 46360 (part), 46365, 46371, 46382, 46390, 46391 (part), 46502, 46506 (part), 46507, 46514–17, 46526, 46530, 46531 (part), 46532, 46536, 46538, 46540, 46542–46, 46550, 46552–54, 46556, 46561, 46567 (part), 46573, 46574 (part), 46580 (part), 46581, 46590, 46595, 46601, 46604, 46612–17, 46619–20, 46624, 46626, 46628–29, 46634–35, 46637, 46660, 46680, 46732 (part)

* * *

FOURTH DISTRICT

MARK E. SOUDER, Republican, of Fort Wayne, IN; born in Grabill, IN, July 18, 1950; graduated from Leo High School, 1968; B.S., Indiana University, Fort Wayne, 1972; M.B.A., University of Notre Dame Graduate School of Business, 1974; partner, Historic Souder's of Grabill; majority owner of Souder's General Store; vice president, Our Country Home, fixture manufacturing business; attends Emmanuel Community Church; served as economic development liaison for then-Representative Dan Coats (IN–4th District); appointed Republican staff director of the House Select Committee on Children, Youth and Families, 1984; legislative director and deputy chief of staff for Congressman Coats; member: Grabill Chamber of Commerce, former head of Congressional Action Committee of Ft. Wayne Chamber of Commerce; committees: Economic and Educational Opportunities, Government Reform and Oversight, Small Business; married the former Diane Zimmer, 1974; three children: Brooke, Nathan, and Zachary; elected to the 104th Congress; reelected to the 105th Congress.

Office Listings

http://www.house.gov/souder souder@hr.house.gov

508 Cannon House Office Building, Washington, DC 20515 225–4436
Administrative Assistant.—Ziad Ojakli. FAX: 225–3479
Legislative Director/Counsel.—Chris Donesa.
Press Secretary.—Angela Flood.
Scheduler.—Dawn Gerson.
1300 South Harrison, Room 3105, Fort Wayne, IN 46802 .... (219) 424–3041
District Director.—Mark Wickershan.

Counties: Adams, Allen, DeKalb, Huntington, Jay, Lagrange, Noble, Steuben, Wells, and Whitley. Population (1990), 554,416.

ZIP Codes: 46700–46799, 46800–46899

* * *

FIFTH DISTRICT

STEVE BUYER, Republican, of Monticello, IN; born in Rensselaer, IN, November 26, 1958; graduated from North White High School in 1976; B.S., business administration, The Citadel, 1980; J.D., Valparaiso University School of Law, 1984; admitted to the Virginia and Indiana bars; U.S. Army Judge Advocate General Corps, 1984–87, assigned Deputy to the Attorney General of Indiana, 1987–88; family law practice, 1988–92; U.S. Army Reserves, 1980–present; major; legal counsel for the 22nd Theatre Army in Operations Desert Shield and Desert Storm; married to the former Joni Lynn Geyer; two children: Colleen and Ryan; elected to the 103rd Congress, November 3, 1992; reelected to each succeeding Congress; member, Veterans' Affairs, National Security, and Judiciary committees.

Office Listings

http://www.house.gov/buyer

326 Cannon House Office Building, Washington, DC 20515 225–5037
Administrative Assistant.—Kelly Craven.
Scheduler/Office Manager.—Eveie Green.
Legislative Director.—Myrna Dugan.
Press Secretary.—Pat Hinton.
120 East Mulberry Street, Room 106, Kokomo, IN 46901 .... (317) 454–7551
District Director.—Linda Worsham.
204A North Main Street, Monticello, IN 47960 .... (219) 583–9819

Counties: Benton, Blackford, Carroll, Cass, Fulton, Grant, Howard, Jasper, Kosciusko (part), Lake (part), Marshall, Miami, Newton, Porter (part), Pulaski, Starke (part), Vermillion (part), Wabash, Warren, and White. Population (1990), 554,415.

ZIP Codes: 46065 (part), 46068 (part), 46076 (part), 46303 (part), 46307 (part), 46310, 46311 (part), 46341 (part), 46347 (part), 46349, 46356, 46366, 46372, 46373 (part), 46374, 46375 (part), 46377, 46379–81, 46392, 46406 (part), 46410 (part), 46501, 46504, 46506, 46508, 46510–11, 46513, 46524, 46534, 46537, 46539, 46555, 46562 (part), 46563, 46566, 46567 (part), 46570, 46572, 46574 (part), 46580 (part), 46732 (part), 46901–04, 46910–17, 46919–23, 46925–26, 46928–33, 46935–43, 46945–47, 46950–53, 46957–62, 46965, 46967–68, 46970–71, 46974–75, 46977–80, 46982–92, 46994–96, 46998, 47336, 47348, 47359, 47842 (part), 47847, 47854, 47875, 47917, 47918 (part), 47921–23, 47925–26, 47928–29, 47942–44, 47946, 47948, 47950–51, 47957, 47959–60, 47963–64, 47966, 47970 (part), 47971, 47973–78, 47980, 47982, 47984, 47986, 47991, 47993, 47995, 47997

* * *

SIXTH DISTRICT

DAN BURTON, Republican, of Indianapolis, IN; born in Indianapolis, June 21, 1938; graduated, Shortridge High School, 1956; Indiana University, 1956–57, Cincinnati Bible Seminary, 1958–60; served in the U.S. Army, 1957–58; U.S. Army Reserves, 1958–64; businessman, insurance and real estate firm owner since 1968; served, Indiana House of Representatives, 1967–68 and 1977–80; Indiana State Senate, 1969–70 and 1981–82; president: Volunteers of America, Indiana Christian Benevolent Association, Committee for Constitutional Government, and Family Support Center; member, Jaycees; 33rd degree Mason, Scottish rite division; married the former Barbara Jean Logan, 1959; three children: Kelly, Danielle Lee, and Danny Lee II; elected on November 2, 1982, to the 98th Congress; reelected to each succeeding Congress.

Office Listings

http://www.house.gov/burton

2411 Rayburn House Office Building, Washington, DC 20515–1406 225–2276

Administrative Assistant.—Kevin Binger. FAX: 225–0016
Executive Assistant.—Leah Tolson.
Office Manager.—Jill Schroeder.
Press Secretary.—Kevin Long.
8900 Keystone at the Crossing, Suite 1050, Indianapolis, IN 46240 .... (317) 848–0201
435 East Main Street, Suite J–3, Greenwood, IN 46142 .... (317) 882–3640
District Director.—Jim Atterholt.

Counties: Boone (part), Clinton, Hamilton, Hancock, Henry (part), Johnson (part), Marion (part), and Tipton. Population (1990), 554,416.

ZIP Codes: 46030–35, 46038–41, 46045, 46047, 46049–50, 46055, 46057–58, 46060, 46065, 46067–68, 46069 (part), 46072, 46074, 46076, 46077 (part), 46106, 46107 (part), 46113 (part), 46117, 46129, 46131 (part), 46140, 46142–43, 46148 (part), 46151 (part), 46154, 46158 (part), 46160 (part), 46162 (part), 46163 (part), 46164 (part), 46181, 46184, 46186–87, 46203 (part), 46214 (part), 46217 (part), 46219 (part), 46220 (part), 46222 (part), 46224 (part), 46227 (part), 46229 (part), 46230, 46231 (part), 46234 (part), 46236 (part), 46237 (part), 46239 (part), 46240, 46241 (part), 46247, 46250, 46256 (part), 46259 (part), 46260 (part), 46268 (part), 46278 (part), 46280, 46290, 46936, 46979 (part), 47201 (part), 47384 (part)

* * *

SEVENTH DISTRICT

EDWARD A. PEASE, Republican, of Terre Haute, IN; born in Terre Haute, May 22, 1951; B.A. with Distinction, 1973, and J.D., *cum laude,* 1977, Indiana University; postgraduate study in English, Indiana State University, 1978–84; admitted to the Indiana bar in 1977 and began practice in Brazil, IN; vice president for university advancement, Indiana State University; city attorney, Brazil, 1980; department attorney, Clay County Department of Public Welfare, 1978–79; partner, Thomas, Thomas and Pease, Attorneys at Law, 1977–84; Indiana Senate, 1980–92; member, former chapter adviser, and former national president, Pi Kappa Alpha Fraternity; member, Phi Beta Kappa and Phi Eta Sigma scholastic fraternities; member of the advisory council and chairman of the National Order of the Arrow Committee, National Council of Boy Scouts of America; member: executive committee, Wabash Valley Council, Boy Scouts of America; board of directors, National Interfraternity Conference; lay leader, First United Methodist Church of Brazil; elected to the 105th Congress.

Office Listings

226 Cannon House Office Building, Washington, DC 20515–1407 225–5805
Administrative Assistant.—Bill Maxam.
Legislative Director.—Kate Wallem.
Legislative Assistant.—Amy Bulander.
Scheduler.—Terra Awalt.
107 Federal Building, Terre Haute, IN 47808 .... (812) 238–1619
District Director.—Brian Kerns.
107 Halleck Building, Lafayette, IN 47901 .... (317) 423–1661

Counties: Boone (part), Clay, Fountain, Hendricks, Monroe (part), Montgomery, Morgan (part), Owen, Parke, Putnam, Tippecanoe, Vermillion (part), and Vigo. Population (1990), 554,416.

ZIP Codes: 46052, 46058, 46069 (part), 46071, 46075, 46077 (part), 46102–03, 46105, 46111–12, 46113 (part), 46118, 46120–21, 46122, 46125, 46128, 46135, 46147, 46149, 46151 (part), 46157, 46158 (part), 46165–68, 46170–72, 46175, 46180, 46231 (part), 46234 (part), 46278 (part), 47403 (part), 47404 (part), 47407, 47408 (part), 47427, 47429, 47431, 47433, 47438, 47455–56, 47459, 47460 (part), 47464, 47471, 47802–05, 47807–09, 47811, 47830–34, 47836–37, 47840–41, 47842 (part), 47845–46, 47850–51, 47853, 47856–60, 47862–63, 47866, 47868–72, 47874, 47876–78, 47880–81, 47884–85, 47901–07, 47916, 47918, 47920, 47924, 47930–33, 47940–41, 47949, 47952, 47954–55, 47958, 47962, 47965, 47967–69, 47981, 47983, 47985, 47987–90, 47992, 47994

* * *

EIGHTH DISTRICT

JOHN NATHAN HOSTETTLER, Republican, of Blairsville, IN; born in Evansville, IN, June 19, 1961; graduated from North Posey High School, Poseyville, IN, 1979; B.S.M.E., Rose-Hulman Polytechnic University, 1983; performance engineer, Southern Indiana Gas and Electric; Baptist; married the former Elizabeth Hamman, 1983; four children: Matthew, Amanda, Jaclyn and Jared; elected to the 104th Congress; reelected to the 105th Congress; committees: National Security, Agriculture; subcommittees: Military Installations; Research and Development; Department Operations, Nutrition and Foreign Agriculture; Resources Conservation; Research and Forestry.

Office Listings

http://www.house.gov/hostettler johnhost@hr.house.gov

1404 Longworth House Office Building, Washington, DC 20515 225–4636
Legislative Director.—David Parry. FAX: 225–4688
Communications Director.—Melissa Merz.
One City Centre, Suite 208, 120 North Seventh Street, Bloomington, IN 47404 ..... (812) 334–1111
Administrative Assistant.—Melinda Plaisier.
Federal Building, Room 124, 101 NW Martin Luther King, Jr. Boulevard, Evansville, IN 47708 .... (812) 465–6484
Area Director.—Carolyn Johnson-Millender. (800) 392–6269

Counties: Daviess, Gibson, Greene, Knox, Lawrence, Martin, Monroe (part), Orange, Pike, Posey, Sullivan, Vanderburgh, and Warrick. CITIES AND TOWNSHIPS: Bedford, Bicknell, Bloomfield, Bloomington (part), Boonville, Chandler, Evansville, Fort Branch, French Lick, Highland (Vanderburgh Co.), Jasonville, Linton, Loogootee, Melody Hill, Mitchell, Mount Vernon, Newburgh, Oakland City, Orleans, Paoli, Petersburg, Princeton, Sullivan, Vincennes, and Washington. Population (1990), 554,416.

ZIP Codes: 47108 (part), 47118 (part), 47125 (part), 47138 (part), 47140 (part), 47401–02, 47403 (part), 47404 (part), 47405–08, 47420–21, 47424 (part), 47426, 47430, 47431 (part), 47432 (part), 47433 (part), 47434, 47436–39, 47441, 47443, 47445, 47446 (part), 47449, 47451–54, 47457–58, 47459 (part), 47460 (part), 47462, 47465, 47467, 47468 (part), 47469–71, 47501, 47512, 47516, 47519, 47522, 47524, 47528–30, 47535, 47553 (part), 47557 (part), 47558 (part), 47561 (part), 47562 (part), 47564 (part), 47567 (part), 47568 (part), 47573, 47578 (part), 47580 (part), 47581 (part), 47584–85, 47590–91, 47596–98, 47601, 47610, 47612–14, 47615 (part), 47616, 47618–20, 47629–31, 47633, 47634 (part), 47635 (part), 47637–40, 47647–49, 47654, 47660, 47665–66, 47670–71, 47683, 47700–06, 47708, 47710–16, 47719–22, 47724, 47727–28, 47730–37, 47739–41, 47744, 47747, 47750, 47838 (part), 47848–49, 47449, 47850 (part), 47852, 47855, 47861, 47864–65, 47872 (part), 47874 (part), 47879, 47882 (part)

* * *

NINTH DISTRICT

LEE H. HAMILTON, Democrat, of Nashville, IN; born in Daytona Beach, FL, April 20, 1931; graduated, Central High School, 1948, Evansville, IN; B.A., DePauw University; attended Goethe University, Frankfurt, Germany, 1952–53; J.D., Indiana University School of Law, 1956; lawyer; married to the former Nancy Ann Nelson; three children: Tracy Lynn Souza, Deborah Lee Hamilton, and Douglas Nelson Hamilton; elected to the 89th Congress, November 3, 1964; reelected to each succeeding Congress.

Office Listings

http://www.house.gov/hamilton

2314 Rayburn House Office Building, Washington, DC 20515–1409 225–5315
Chief of Staff.—Jonathan Friedman.
Executive Assistant.—Nora Coulter.
Press Secretary.—Holly Baker.
Room 107, 1201 East 10th Street, Jeffersonville, IN 47130 .... (812) 288–3999
Toll Free in Indiana. .... (800) 892–3232
Administrative Assistant.—Wayne Vance.

Counties: Bartholomew (part), Brown, Clark, Crawford, Dearborn, Dubois, Fayette, Floyd, Franklin, Harrison, Jackson, Jefferson, Jennings, Ohio, Perry, Ripley, Scott, Spencer, Switzerland, Union, and Washington. Population (1990), 554,416.

ZIP Codes: 46127 (part), 46133 (part), 46160 (part), 46164 (part), 46173 (part), 46181 (part), 47001, 47006, 47010–12, 47016–25, 47030–43, 47060, 47102, 47104, 47106–08, 47110–12, 47114–20, 47122–26, 47129–31, 47135–43, 47145–47, 47150–51, 47160–67, 47170, 47172, 47174–75, 47177, 47199, 47201 (part), 47203 (part), 47220, 47223–24, 47227–32, 47235–36, 47240 (part), 47243, 47245, 47249–50, 47260, 47262, 47264 (part), 47265, 47270, 47273–74, 47281–82, 47283 (part), 47322, 47325, 47327, 47331, 47352 (part), 47353, 47387 (part), 47401 (part), 47435, 47448, 47452, 47468 (part), 47513–15, 47520–21, 47523 (part), 47525, 47527, 47531–32, 47536–37, 47541–42, 47545–47, 47550–52, 47555–56, 47574–77, 47579–80, 47586, 47588, 47590, 47601, 47611, 47615, 47617, 47634

* * *

TENTH DISTRICT

JULIA CARSON, Democrat, of Indianapolis; born in Louisville, KY, July 8, 1938; graduated, Crispus Attucks High School, Indianapolis, 1955; attended: Martin University, Indianapolis; Indiana University-Purdue University at Indianapolis; manager, businesswoman; Indiana House of Representatives, 1972–76; Indiana Senate, 1976–90; as Indianapolis center township trustee, 1990–96, targeted fraud and waste to eliminate the city's $20-million debt; twice named Woman of the Year by the *Indianapolis Star*; two children; committees: Banking and Financial Services, Veterans' Affairs; subcommittees: Housing, Health; elected on November 5, 1996, to the 105th Congress.

Office Listings

1541 Longworth House Office Building, Washington, DC 20515–1410 225–4011
Office Manager.—Winnie Donaldson. FAX: 225–5633
Legislative Director.—David Wildes.
Press Secretary/Legislative Assistant.—Stephen Thibodeau.
Staff Assistant.—Erin Kraabel.
46 East Ohio Street, 441A Federal Building, Indianapolis, IN 46204–1910 .... (317) 226–7331
District Director.—Fran Quigley. FAX: 226–7330

County: MARION COUNTY; city of Indianapolis (part), township of Center, parts of the townships of Decatur, Lawrence, Perry, Pike, Warren, Washington, and Wayne, included are the cities of Beech Grove and Lawrence (part). Population (1990), 554,416.

ZIP Codes: 46107 (part), 46201–02, 46203 (part), 46204–05 46208, 46214 (part), 46216, 46217 (part), 46218, 46219 (part), 46220 (part), 46221, 46222 (part), 46224 (part), 46225, 46226 (part), 46227 (part), 46229 (part), 46231 (part), 46234 (part), 46236 (part), 46237 (part), 46239 (part), 46241 (part), 46254, 46256 (part), 46260 (part), 46268 (part), 46278 (part)

IOWA

(Population 1995, 2,842,000)

SENATORS

CHARLES E. GRASSLEY, Republican, of Cedar Falls, IA; born in New Hartford, IA, September 17, 1933; graduated, New Hartford Community High School, 1951; B.A., University of Northern Iowa, 1955; M.A., University of Northern Iowa, 1956; doctoral studies, University of Iowa, 1957–58; farmer; member, Iowa State Legislature, 1959–74; Farm Bureau, State and County Historical Society, Masons, Baptist Church, and International Association of Machinists, 1962–71; married the former Barbara Ann Speicher, 1954; five children: Lee, Wendy, Robin Lynn, Michele Marie, and Jay Charles; committees: Agriculture, Nutrition, and Forestry; Budget; Finance; Judiciary; chair, Special Committee on Aging; Joint Committee on Taxation; elected to the 94th Congress, November 5, 1974; reelected to the 95th and 96th Congresses; elected to the U.S. Senate, November 4, 1980, for the six-year term beginning January 3, 1981; reelected for each succeeding term.

Office Listings

http://www.senate.gov/~grassley chuck_grassley@grassley.senate.gov

135 Hart Senate Office Building, Washington, DC 20510–1501	224–3744
Chief of Staff.—Ken Cunningham.	FAX: 224–6020
Press Secretary.—Jill Kozeny.	
Legislative Director.—Ken Cunningham.	
721 Federal Building, 210 Walnut Street, Des Moines, IA 50309–2140	(515) 284–4890
State Administrator.—Henry C. Wulff.	
206 Federal Building, 101 First Street SE, Cedar Rapids, IA 52401–1227	(319) 363–6832
103 Federal Courthouse Building, 320 Sixth Street, Sioux City, IA 51101–1244	(712) 233–1860
210 Waterloo Building, 531 Commercial Street, Waterloo, IA 50701–5497	(319) 232–6657
116 Federal Building, 131 East Fourth Street, Davenport, IA 52801–1513	(319) 322–4331
307 Federal Building, 8 South Sixth Street, Council Bluffs, IA 51501	(712) 322–7103

* * *

TOM HARKIN, Democrat, of Cumming, IA; born in Cumming, November 19, 1939; graduated from Dowling Catholic High School, Des Moines; B.S., Iowa State University, Ames, 1962; LL.B., Catholic University of America, Washington, DC, 1972; U.S. Navy, 1962–67; LCDR, U.S. Naval Reserves; admitted to the bar, 1972, Des Moines; married the former Ruth Raduenz, 1968; two daughters: Amy and Jenny; committees: Agriculture, Nutrition, and Forestry; Appropriations; Labor and Human Resources; Small Business; elected to the 94th Congress, November 5, 1974; reelected to four succeeding Congresses; elected November 6, 1984 to the U.S. Senate; reelected November 6, 1990 for the term expiring January 3, 1997.

Office Listings

http://www.senate.gov/~harkin tom_harkin@harkin.senate.gov

531 Hart Senate Office Building, Washington, DC 20510–1502	224–3254
Administrative Assistant.—Dan Smith.	TDD: 224–4633
Legislative Director.—Peter Reinecke.	
Press Secretary.—Jodie Silverman.	
Federal Building, Room 733, 210 Walnut Street, Des Moines, IA 50309	(515) 284–4574
150 First Avenue NE, Suite 370, Cedar Rapids, IA 52401	(319) 365–4504
Federal Building, Room 314–B, 131 East Fourth Street, Davenport, IA 52801	(319) 322–1338
Federal Building, Room 110, 320 Sixth Street, Sioux City, IA 51101	(712) 252–1550
Federal Building, Room 315, 350 West Sixth Street, Dubuque, IA 52001	(319) 582–2130

REPRESENTATIVES

FIRST DISTRICT

JAMES A. LEACH, Republican, of Davenport, IA; born in Davenport, October 15, 1942; graduated, Davenport High School, 1960; B.A., Princeton University, 1964; M.A., School of Advanced International Studies of Johns Hopkins University, 1966; further graduate studies at the London School of Economics, 1966–68; staff member of U.S. Congressman Donald Rumsfeld, 1965–66; foreign service officer assigned to the Department of State, 1968–69; administrative assistant to the director of the Office of Economic Opportunity, 1969–70; foreign service officer assigned to the Arms Control and Disarmament Agency, 1970–73; member: U.S. delegation to the Geneva Disarmament Conference, 1971–72; U.S. delegation to the United Nations General Assembly, 1972; U.S. delegation to the United Nations Conference on Natural Resources, 1975; U.S. Advisory Commission on International Educational and Cultural Affairs, 1975–76; Federal Home Loan Bank Board of Des Moines, 1975–76; president, Flamegas Companies, Inc., family business, 1973–76; member: Bettendorf Chamber of Commerce; National Federation of Independent Business; Davenport Elks, Moose, Rotary; Episcopal Church; married to the former Elisabeth Foxley; two children, Gallagher and Jenny; elected to the 95th Congress, November 2, 1976; reelected to each succeeding Congress; chairman, Banking and Financial Services Committee; member: International Relations Committee, Arms Control and Foreign Policy Caucus, Rural Caucus, Arts Caucus, Northeast-Midwest Coalition, House Wednesday Group, Congressional Human Rights Caucus, Environmental and Energy Study Conference, Congressional Caucus for Women's Issues.

Office Listings

http://www.house.gov/leach

2186 Rayburn House Office Building, Washington, DC 20515–1501 225–6576
Administrative Assistant.—Bill Tate. FAX: 226–1278
209 West Fourth Street, Davenport, IA 52801 .... (319) 326–1841
District Director.—Tom Cope.
102 South Clinton, Suite 505, Iowa City, IA 52240 .... (319) 351–0789
District Staff Assistant.—Ginny Burrus.
308 10th Street SE, Cedar Rapids, IA 52403 .... (319) 363–4773
District Staff Assistant.—Brian Fagan.

Counties: Cedar, Clinton, Johnson, Jones, Linn, Louisa, Muscatine, and Scott. Population (1990), 555,229.

ZIP Codes: 52037, 52070, 52202, 52205, 52207, 52212–14, 52216, 52218–19, 52226–28, 52230, 52233, 52235, 52240–42, 52244–46, 52252–55, 52302, 52305–06, 52310, 52312, 52314, 52317, 52319–24, 52328, 52331, 52333, 52336–38, 52340–41, 52343–44, 52350, 52352, 52358, 52362, 52401–10, 52499, 52640, 52646, 52653, 52701, 52720–22, 52726–33, 52736–39, 52742, 52745–61, 52765–69, 52771–74, 52776–78, 52801–09

* * *

SECOND DISTRICT

JIM NUSSLE, Republican, of Manchester, IA; born in Des Moines, IA, June 27, 1960; graduated, Carl Sandburg High School, 1978; attended Ronshoved Hojskole, Denmark, 1978–79; Luther College, Decorah, IA, 1983; Drake University Law School, Des Moines, IA, 1985; admitted to the bar, January 1986; Delaware County Attorney, 1986–90; two children: Sarah and Mark; committees: Ways and Means, Budget; subcommittee: Trade; elected to the 102nd Congress; reelected to each succeeding Congress.

Office Listings

nussleia@hr.house.gov

303 Cannon House Office Building, Washington, DC 20515–1502 225–2911
Chief of Staff.—Rich Meade. FAX: 225–9129
3641 Kimball Avenue, Suite LL2, Waterloo, IA 50702 .... (319) 235–1109
2255 John F. Kennedy Road, Asbury Square, Space 20, Unit 4, Dubuque, IA 52002 .... (319) 557–7740
23 Third Street NW, Suite 103, Mason City, IA 50401 .... (515) 423–0303
712 West Main Street, Manchester, IA 52057 .... (319) 927–5141
District Administrator.—Cheryl Madlom.

Counties: Allamakee, Benton, Black Hawk, Bremer, Buchanan, Butler, Cerro Gordo, Chickasaw, Clayton, Delaware, Dubuque, Fayette, Floyd, Grundy, Howard, Iowa, Jackson, Mitchell, Tama, Winneshiek, and Worth. CITIES AND TOWNSHIPS: Asbury, Belle Plaine, Bellevue, Cascade (part), Cedar Falls, Charles City, Clear Lake, Cresco, Decorah, Denver, Dubuque, Dyersville, Elkader, Evansdale, Grundy Center, Guttenberg, Hudson, Independence, Jesup, La Porte City, Manchester, Maquoketa, Marengo, Mason City, Monona, New Hampton, Nora Springs, Northwood, Oelwein, Osage, Parkersburg, Reinbeck, Sumner, Tama, Toledo, Traer, Vinton, Waterloo, Waukon, Waverly, West Union and Williamsburg. Population (1990), 555,494.

ZIP Codes: 50173, 50401, 50426, 50428, 50433–35, 50440, 50444, 50446, 50448, 50454–61, 50464, 50466–69, 50471–72, 50475–77, 50479, 50481–82, 50601–09, 50611–13, 50616, 50619–32, 50634–36, 50638, 50641–45, 50647–55, 50657–62, 50664–71, 50673–77, 50680–82, 50701–04, 50706–07, 51246, 52001–04, 52030–33, 52035–36, 52038–50, 52052–57, 52060, 52064–66, 52068–79, 52101, 52130–36, 52140–44, 52146–47, 52149–51, 52154–66, 52168–72, 52175, 52203,

52206–10, 52215, 52217, 52220, 52223–25, 52228–29, 52236–37, 52249, 52251, 52257, 52301, 52307–09, 52313, 52315–16, 52318, 52325–26, 52329–30, 52332, 52334, 52339, 52342, 52345–49, 52351, 52354, 52361

* * *

THIRD DISTRICT

LEONARD L. BOSWELL, Democrat, of Davis City, IA; born in Harrison County, MO, on January 10, 1934; graduated from Lamoni High School, 1952; B.A., Graceland College, Lamoni, IA, 1969; lieutenant colonel, U.S. Army, 1956–76; awards: two Distinguished Flying Crosses, two Bronze Stars, Soldier's Medal; Iowa State Senate, 1984–96; Iowa State Senate President, 1992–96; lay minister, RLDS Church; member: American Legion, Disabled American Veterans of Foreign Wars, Iowa Farm Bureau, Iowa Cattlemen's Association, Graceland College Board of Trustees; Farmer's Co-op Grain and Seed Board of Directors, 1979–93 (president for 13 years); married Darlene ''Dody'' Votava Boswell, 1955; three children: Cindy, Diana and Joe; committees: Agriculture, Transportation and Infrastructure; subcommittees: Risk Management and Specialty Crops; Livestock, Dairy and Poultry; elected to the 105th Congress.

Office Listings

rep.boswell.ia03@mail.house.gov

1029 Longworth House Office Building, Washington, DC 20515–1503 225–3806
Chief of Staff.—John Norris. FAX: 225–5608
Legislative Director.—E.H. ''Ned'' Michalek.
Scheduler/Office Manager.—Sandy Carter.
Systems Administrator/Legislative Assistant.—Cornelia V. Murphy.
Legislative Assistants.—Alex Fischer; Eric Witte.
Press Secretary.—Jeani Murray.
Staff Assistant.—Lynh Nguyen.

709 Furnas Street, Suite 1, Osceola, IA 50213 .... (515) 342–4801
District Director.—Cindy Cox. FAX: 342–4354

Counties: Adams, Appanoose, Clarke, Davis, Decatur, Des Moines, Henry, Jasper, Jefferson, Keokuk, Lee, Lucas, Mahaska, Marion, Marshall, Monroe, Page, Poweshiek, Ringgold, Story Taylor, Union, Van Buren, Wapello, Warren, Washington, and Wayne. Population (1990), 555,299.

ZIP Codes: 50001, 50005, 50008, 50010–13, 50027–28, 50030, 50044, 50046–47, 50049, 50051–52, 50054–57, 50060–62, 50065, 50067–68, 50074, 50078, 50103–06, 50108, 50112, 50116, 50118–20, 50123–25, 50127, 50133–45, 50147–51, 50153–54, 50157–58, 50160–63, 50165–66, 50168, 50170–72, 50174, 50201, 50207–08, 50210–11, 50213–14, 50219, 50221–22, 50225, 50228–29, 50232, 50234, 50236, 50238–42, 50244, 50247–48, 50251–56, 50258, 50262, 50264, 50268, 50272, 50275, 50278, 50609, 50621, 50637, 50801, 50830–31, 50833, 50835–36, 50839–42, 50844–45, 50848, 50850–52, 50854, 50857, 50859–63, 51601, 51630–32, 51636–38, 51646–47, 51651, 51656, 52201, 52211, 52222, 52231–32, 52247–48, 52250, 52327, 52335, 52353, 52355–56, 52359, 52404, 52501, 52530–31, 52533–38, 52540, 52542–44, 52548–56, 52560–63, 52565–77, 52580–81, 52583–86, 52588, 52590–91, 52593–95, 52601, 52619–21, 52623–27, 52630–32, 52635, 52637–39, 52641, 52644–45, 52647–52, 52654–60

* * *

FOURTH DISTRICT

GREG GANSKE, Republican, of Des Moines, IA; born March 31, 1949, in New Hampton, IA; graduated, University of Iowa School of Medicine; general surgery training at Oregon Health Science Center; reconstructive surgery training under Nobel Laureate Joe Murray at Harvard; plastic and reconstructive surgeon, practiced in Des Moines; lieutenant colonel in the U.S. Army Reserves; active manager of 160 acres of farmland; married Corrine Mikkelsen; three children: Ingrid, Bridget, and Karl; elected to the 104th Congress; reelected to the 105th Congress.

Office Listings

http://www.house.gov/ganske rep.ganske@mail.house.gov

1108 Longworth House Office Building, Washington, DC 20515–1504 225–4426
Chief of Staff.—John Barnes.
Appointment Secretary/Office Manager.—Amy Bonham.

Federal Building, 210 Walnut Street, Suite 717, Des Moines, IA 50309 .... (515) 284–4634
District Director.—Luke Roth.

40 Pearl Street, Council Bluffs, IA 51503 .... (515) 323–5976
Field Representative.—Ben Post.

Counties: ADAIR COUNTY; cities and townships of Adair, Bridgewater, Fontanelle, Greenfield, and Orient. AUDUBON COUNTY; cities and townships of Audubon, Brayton, Exira, Gray, and Kimballton. CASS COUNTY; cities and townships of Anita,

Atlantic, Cumberland, Griswold, Lewis, Marne, Massena, and Wiota. DALLAS COUNTY; cities and townships of Adel, Bouton, Dallas Center, DeSoto, Dexter, Granger, Linden, Minburn, Perry, Redfield, Van Meter, Waukee, and Woodward. FREMONT COUNTY; cities and townships of Farragut, Hamburg, Imogene, Randolph, Riverton, Sidney, Tabor, and Thurman. GUTHRIE COUNTY; cities and townships of Bagley, Bayard, Casey, Guthrie Center, Jamaica, Menlo, Panora, Stuart, and Yale. HARRISON COUNTY; cities and townships of Dunlap, Little Sioux, Logan, Magnolia, Mo. Valley, Modale, Mondamin, Persia, Pisgah, and Woodbine. MADISON COUNTY; cities and townships of Bevington, Earlham, East Peru, Macksburg, Patterson, St. Charles, Truro, and Winterset. MILLS COUNTY; cities and townships of Emerson, Glenwood, Hastings, Henderson, Malvern, Pacific Junction, and Silver City. MONTGOMERY COUNTY; cities and townships of Elliot, Grant, Red Oak, Stanton, and Villisca. POLK COUNTY; cities and townships of Alleman, Altoona, Ankeny, Bondurant, Clive, Des Moines, Elkhart, Grimes, Johnston, Mitchellville, Pleasant Hill, Polk City, Runnells, Sheldahl, Urbandale, West Des Moines, and Windsor Heights. POTTAWATTAMIE COUNTY; cities and townships of Avoca, Carson, Council Bluffs, Crescent, Hancock, Macedonia, McClelland, Minden, Neola, Oakland, Treynor, and Underwood, Walnut. SHELBY COUNTY; cities and townships of Defiance, Earling, Elkhorn, Harlan, Irwin, Kirkman, Panama, Portsmouth, Shelby, Tennant, and Westphalia. Population (1990), 555,276.

ZIP Codes: 50002–03, 50007, 50009, 50020–22, 50025–26, 50029, 50032–33, 50035, 50038–39, 50042, 50048, 50061, 50063, 50066, 50069–70, 50072–73, 50076, 50109–11, 50115, 50117, 50128, 50131, 50146, 50149, 50155, 50164, 50167, 50169, 50216, 50218, 50220, 50222, 50226, 50228, 50233, 50237, 50240, 50243, 50250, 50257, 50261, 50263, 50265–66, 50273–74, 50276–77, 50301–06, 50309–17, 50320–22, 50325, 50333, 50393–94, 50837, 50843, 50846–47, 50849, 50853, 50858, 50864, 51446–47, 51454, 51501–03, 51510, 51521, 51525–37, 51540–46, 51548–57, 51559–66, 51570–71, 51573–79, 51639–40, 51645, 51648–50, 51652–54

* * *

FIFTH DISTRICT

TOM LATHAM, Republican, of Alexander, IA; born July 14, 1948 in Hampton, IA; attended Alexander Community School; graduated Cal (Latimer) Community College, 1966; attended Wartburg College, 1966–67; Iowa State University, 1976–70; agriculture business major; marketing representative, independent insurance agent, bank teller and bookkeeper; member and past president, Nazareth Lutheran Church; past chairman, Franklin County Extension Council; secretary, Republican Party of Iowa; 5th District representative, Republican State Central Committee; cochairman, Franklin County Republican Central Committee; Iowa delegation whip; member: 1992 Republican National Convention, Iowa Farm Bureau Federation, Iowa Soybean Association, American Seed Trade Association, Iowa Corn Growers Association, Iowa Seed Association, Agribusiness Association of Iowa, I.S.U. Extension Citizens Advisory Council; married Mary Katherine (Kathy) Latham, 1975; three children: Justin, Jennifer, and Jill; elected to the 104th Congress; reelected to the 105th Congress.

Office Listings

http://www.house.gov/latham latham@hr.house.gov

516 Cannon House Office Building, Washington, DC 20515–1505 225–5476
Chief of Staff.—Vicky Vermaat. FAX: 225–3301
Operations and Communications Director.—James D. Carstensen.
Legislative Director.—Scott McCoy.
Staff Assistant.—Elizabeth Gordon.
123 Albany Avenue, SE, Suite 1, Orange City, IA 51041 .... (712) 737–8708
Chief of Staff.—Vicky Vermont. FAX: 737–3456
526 Pierce Street, Sioux City, IA 51101 .... (712) 277–2114
Special Assistant.—Shane Keith. FAX: 277–0932
20 West Sixth Street, Spencer, IA 51301 .... (712) 262–6480
Staff Assistant.—Lois Clark. FAX: 262–6673
1411 First Avenue South, Suite A, Fort Dodge, IA 50501 .... (515) 573–2738
Staff Assistant.—Andrew Warren. FAX: 576–7141

Counties: Boone, Buena Vista, Calhoun, Carroll, Cherokee, Clay, Crawford, Dickinson, Emmet, Fort Dodge, Franklin, Greene, Hamilton, Hancock, Hardin, Humboldt, Ida, Kossuth, Lyon, Monona, O'Brien, Osceola, Palo Alto, Plymouth, Pocahontas, Sac, Sioux, Sioux City, Webster, Winnebago, Woodbury, and Wright. Population (1990), 555,457.

ZIP Codes: 50006, 50010, 50031, 50034, 50036, 50039–41, 50043, 50050, 50058–59, 50064, 50071, 50075, 50101–02, 50107, 50122, 50126, 50129–30, 50132, 50152, 50156, 50206, 50212, 50217, 50223, 50227, 50230–31, 50235, 50244, 50246, 50249, 50258–59, 50269, 50271, 50420–21, 50423–24, 50427, 50430–32, 50436, 50438–39, 50441, 50446–47, 50449–53, 50465, 50470, 50473, 50475, 50478, 50480, 50483–84, 50501, 50510–11, 50514–25, 50527–33, 50535–36, 50538–46, 50548, 50551–54, 50556–63, 50565–71, 50573–83, 50585–88, 50590–95, 50597–99, 50601, 50627, 50633, 50640, 50672, 50680, 51001–12, 51014–20, 51022–31, 51033–41, 51044–63, 51101–11, 51201, 51230–32, 51234–35, 51237–50, 51301, 51330–31, 51333–34, 51338, 51340–47, 51349–51, 51354–55, 51357–58, 51360, 51363–66, 51401, 51430–33, 51436, 51439–45, 51448–55, 51458–63, 51465–67, 51520, 51523, 51527–28, 51558, 51572

KANSAS

(Population 1995, 2,565,000)

SENATORS

SAM BROWNBACK, Republican, of Topeka, KS; born in Garrett, KS, September 12, 1956; graduated, Prairie View High School, 1974; B.S. with honors, Kansas State University, Manhattan, KS, 1978; J.D., University of Kansas, Lawrence, 1982; Kansas bar; attorney, broadcaster, teacher; U.S. House of Representatives, 1994–96; State Secretary of Agriculture, 1986–93; White House Fellow, Office of the U.S. Trade Representative, 1990–91; member: Topeka Fellowship Council, Kansas Bar Association, Kansas State University and Kansas University alumni associations; married the former Mary Stauffer, 1982; three children: Abby, Andy, and Liz; committees: Governmental Affairs; Commerce, Science, and Transportation; Foreign Relations; Joint Economic; subcommittees: chair, Oversight of Government Management, Restructuring, and the District of Columbia; Aviation; Communications; Consumer Affairs, Foreign Commerce, and Tourism; Manufacturing and Competitiveness; Near Eastern and South Asian Affairs; elected to the U.S. Senate in November 1996, to fill the remainder of the vacancy caused by the resignation of former Senator Bob Dole.

Office Listings

http://www.senate.gov/~brownback/ sam__brownback@brownback.senate.gov

303 Hart Senate Office Building, Washington, DC 20510 224–6521
Chief of Staff.—Tim McGivern. FAX: 228–1265
Scheduler.—Emily Wellman.
Legislative Director.—Paul Ryan.
Communications Director.—Bob Murray.
612 South Kansas, Topeka, KS 66603 .... (913) 233–2503
FAX: 233–2616
1001–C North Broadway, Pittsburg, KS 66762 .... (316) 231–6040
FAX: 231–6347
225 Nort Market, Suite 120, Wichita, KS 67202 .... (316) 264–8066
FAX: 264–9078
11111 West 95th, Suite 245, Overland Park, KS 66214 .... (913) 492–6378
FAX: 492–7253

* * *

PAT ROBERTS, Republican, of Dodge City, KS; born in Topeka, KS, April 20, 1936; graduated, Holton High School, Holton, KS, 1954; B.S., journalism, Kansas State University, Manhattan, KS, 1958; captain, U.S. Marine Corps, 1958–62; editor and reporter, Arizona newspapers, 1962–67; aide to Representative Keith Sebelius, 1969–80; aide to Senator Frank Carlson, 1967–68; U.S. House of Representatives, 1980–96; founding member: bipartisan Caucus on Unfunded Mandates, House Rural Health Care Coalition; shepherded the 1996 Freedom to Farm Act through the House and Senate; awards: honorary American Farmer, Future Farmers of America; 1993 Wheat Man of the Year, Kansas Association of Wheat Growers; Golden Carrot Award, Public Voice; Golden Bulldog Award, Watchdogs of the Treasury; numerous Guardian of Small Business awards, National Federation of Independent Business; 1995 Dwight D. Eisenhower Medal, Eisenhower Exchange Fellowship; married the former Franki Fann, 1969; three children: David, Ashleigh, and Anne-Wesley; committees: Agriculture, Nutrition, and Forestry; Armed Services; Senate Select Committee on Ethics; Select Committee on Intelligence; subcommittees: Production and Price Competitiveness, Readiness; elected to the U.S. Senate in November 1996.

Office Listings

http://www.senate.gov/senator/roberts.html

302 Hart Senate Office Building, Washington, DC 20510 224–4774
Administrative Assistant.—Leroy Towns. FAX: 224–3514
Press Secretary.—Jackie Cottrell.
Scheduler.—Maggie Ward.
100 Military Plaza, P.O. Box 550, Dodge City, KS 67801 .... (316) 227–2244
District Director.—Phyllis Ross. FAX: 227–2264
155 North Market Street, Suite 120, Wichita, KS 67202 .... (316) 263–0416
District Director.—Karin Wisdom. FAX: 263–0273
State Agricultural Representative.—Mel Thompson.
Frank Carlson Federal Building, 444 SE Quincy, Room 392, Topeka, KS 66683 .... (913) 295–2745
State Casework Director.—Betty Duwe. FAX: 235–3665
District Director.—Gilda Lintz.
4200 Somerset, Suite 152, Prairie Village, KS 66208 .... (913) 648–3103

State Director.—Mike Harper. FAX: 648–3106
District Director.—Ramona Corbin.

REPRESENTATIVES

FIRST DISTRICT

JERRY MORAN, Republican, of Hays, KS; born in Great Bend, KS, May 29, 1954; B.S., economics, 1976, and J.D., 1981, University of Kansas; M.B.A. candidate, Fort Hays State University; partner, Jeter and Moran, Attorneys at Law, Hays, KS; former bank officer and university instructor; represented 37th District in Kansas Senate, 1989–97, serving as vice president in 1993–95 and majority leader in 1995–97; Special Assistant Attorney General, State of Kansas, 1982–85; Deputy Attorney, Rooks County, 1987–95; governor, board of governors, University of Kansas School of Law, 1990 (vice president, 1993–94; president, 1994–95); member: board of directors, Kansas Chamber of Commerce and Industry, 1996–97; Hays Chamber of Commerce; Northwest Kansas and Ellis County bar associations; Phi Alpha Delta legal fraternity; Rotary Club; Lions International; board of trustees, Fort Hays State University Endowment Association; married to Robba Moran; two children, Kelsey and Alex; committees: Agriculture, International Relations, Veterans' Affairs; elected to the 105th Congress.

Office Listings

http://www.house.gov/moranks01

1217 Longworth House Office Building, Washington, DC 20515–1601 225–2715
Chief of Staff.—Tom Hemmer. FAX: 225–5124
Legislative Director.—Kari Austin.
Press Secretary.—Doug McGinn.
Office Manager—Becky Kuhn.
Room 203, Davis Hall, Ft. Hays State University, Hays KS 67601 .... (913) 628–6401
District Representative.—Karla Werth. FAX: 628–3791
335 North Washington Street, Suite 180, Hutchinson, KS 67504 .... (316) 665–6138
District Representative.—Patty Kerr. FAX: 665–6360

Counties: Barber, Barton, Chase, Cheyenne, Clark, Clay, Cloud, Comanche, Decatur, Dickinson, Edwards, Ellis, Ellsworth, Finney, Ford, Gove, Graham, Grant, Gray, Greeley, Hamilton, Haskell, Hodgeman, Jewell, Kearny, Kiowa, Lane, Lincoln, Logan, Lyon, McPherson, Marion (part), Marshall, Meade, Mitchell, Morris, Morton, Ness, Norton, Osborne, Ottawa, Pawnee, Phillips, Pratt, Rawlins, Reno, Republic, Rice, Rooks, Rush, Russell, Saline, Scott, Seward, Sheridan, Sherman, Smith, Stafford, Stanton, Stevens, Thomas, Trego, Wabaunsee, Wallace, Washington, and Wichita. Population (1990), 619,370.

ZIP Codes: 66401, 66403, 66406–07, 66411–12, 66423, 66427, 66431, 66433, 66438, 66501, 66507–08, 66518, 66526, 66541, 66544, 66548, 66610, 66801, 66830, 66833–35, 66838, 66840 (part), 66843, 66845–46, 66849–851, 66854, 66858–62, 66864–65, 66866 (part), 66868–69, 66872–73, 66901, 66930–33, 66935–46, 66948–49, 66951–53, 66955–56, 66958–64, 66966–68, 66970, 67015, 67021, 67028–29, 67035, 67053–54, 67057, 67059, 67063, 67065–66, 67070–71, 67073, 67104, 67107–09, 67112, 67117, 67124, 67127, 67134, 67138, 67143, 67155, 67401–02, 67410, 67414, 67416–18, 67420, 67422–23, 67425, 67427–32, 67436–39, 67441–52, 67454–60, 67463–70, 67472–76, 67478–85, 67487–88, 67490–92, 67501–02, 67504–05, 67510–26, 67529–30, 67543–48, 67550, 67552–54, 67556–57, 67559–70, 67572–79, 67581–85, 67601, 67621–23, 67625–32, 67634–54, 67656–61, 67663–65, 67667, 67669–76, 67701, 67730–41, 67743–45, 67747–49, 67751–53, 67755–59, 67761–62, 67764, 67801, 67831, 67834–44, 67846, 67849–51, 67853–65, 67867–71, 67874, 67876–80, 67882, 67901, 67905, 67950–54

* * *

SECOND DISTRICT

JIM RYUN, Republican, of Topeka, KS; born on April 29, 1947, in Wichita, KS; graduated, Wichita East High school, 1965; B.S., photojournalism, University of Kansas; product development consultant, president of Jim Ryun Sports, Inc., professional photographer, and author of two books; represented the U.S. in three consecutive Olympics (1964, 1968, 1972): silver medal in the 1500-meter race, 1968, and World Record Holder in the 880-yard, one-mile, and 1500-meter races; awards: Sports Illustrated Sportsman of the Year, 1966; AAU Sullivan Award; Jaycees of America Top Ten Young Men of the United States, 1968; married Anne Snider Ryun, 1969; four children: Heather, Ned, Drew, and Catharine; elected to the 105th Congress.

Office Listings

511 Cannon House Office Building, Washington, DC 20515 225–6601
Chief of Staff.—Daniel Schneider. FAX: 225–7986
Press Secretary.—Jeanie Mamo.
Legislative Director.—Paul Webster.
820 SE Quincy Street, Suite 100, Topeka, KS 66612 .... (913) 232–4500
Chief of Staff.—Michelle Butler Latham. FAX: 232–4512
The Stilwell Hotel, 701 North Broadway, Suite A, Pittsburg, KS 66762 .... (316) 232–6100
Regional Representative.—Jim Allen. FAX: 232–6105

Counties: Allen, Anderson, Atchison, Bourbon, Brown, Cherokee, Coffey, Crawford, Doniphan, Douglas (part), Franklin, Geary, Jackson, Jefferson, Labete, Leavenworth, Linn, Nemaha, Neosho, Osage, Pottawatomie, Riley, Shawnee, Wilson, and Woodson. Population (1990), 619,391.

ZIP Codes: 66002, 66006 (part), 66007–08, 66010, 66014–17, 66020, 66023–24, 66025 (part), 66027, 66032–33, 66035, 66039–43, 66044 (part), 66048, 66050, 66052, 66054, 66056, 66058, 66060, 66066–67, 66070, 66072–73, 66075–80, 66086–88, 66090–91, 66092 (part), 66093–95, 66097, 66401–04, 66406–09, 66413–20, 66422, 66424–26, 66428–29, 66431–32, 66434–36, 66439–42, 66449–51, 66502, 66509–10, 66512, 66514–17, 66520–24, 66527–28, 66531–40, 66542–43, 66546–52, 66554, 66601, 66603–12, 66614–19, 66647, 66667, 66675, 66683, 66701, 66710–14, 66716–17, 66720, 66724–25, 66727–28, 66732–36, 66738–43, 66746, 66748–49, 66751, 66753–62, 66767, 66769–73, 66775–83, 66834, 66839, 66849, 66852, 66854, 66856–57, 66870–72, 67330, 67332, 67336–37, 67341–42, 67351, 67354, 67356–57, 67487

* * *

THIRD DISTRICT

VINCENT K. SNOWBARGER, Republican, of Olathe, KS; born in Kankakee, IL, September 9, 1950; graduated from Shawnee Mission South High School, Overland Park, KS, 1967; B.A., history, Southern Nazarene University, Bethany, OK, 1971; M.A., political science, University of Illinois, 1974; J.D., University of Kansas, 1977; attorney, admitted to Kansas bar in 1977; Assistant Public Defender, 32nd judicial circuit, 1983–86; Olathe City Planning Commission, 1982–84; Kansas House of Representatives, 1985–97; majority leader, 1993–97; member: Rotary International, Olathe Area Chamber of Commerce, Mid-America Nazarene College Foundation, National Federation of Independent Business; married Carolyn McMahon Snowbarger, 1972; two children: Jeffrey and Matthew; committees: vice chair, Government Reform and Oversight; Banking and Financial Services; Small Business; subcommittees: Capital Markets, Securities, and Government-Sponsored Enterprises; Human Resources and Intergovernmental Relations; National Economic Growth, Natural Resources and Regulatory Affairs; Tax, Finance, and Exports; assistant majority whip; elected to the 105th Congress.

Office Listings

http://www.house.gov/snowbarger rep.snowbarger@mail.house.gov

509 Cannon House Office Building, Washington, DC 20515 225–2865
Chief of Staff/Press Secretary.—Kevin Yowell. FAX: 225–5897
Legislative Director.—Jonathan Fellows.
Legislative Assistants: John Kerr, Amy Smith, Patrick Wilson.
Scheduler/Office Manager.—Bonnie Matles.
Constituent Relations Director.—Jennifer Eisenbrandt.
182 Federal Building, 500 State Avenue, Kansas City, KS 66101 .... (913) 621–0832
8826 Santa Fe Drive, Suite 350, Overland Park, KS 66212 .... (913) 383–2013
647 Massachusetts, Suite 207, Lawrence, KS 66044 .... (913) 342–9313
FAX: 294–4122

Counties: Douglas (part), Johnson, Miami, Wyandotte

ZIP Codes: 66006 (part), 66012, 66013, 66018, 66019, 66021, 66025 (part), 66026, 66030, 66031, 66036, 66044 (part), 66046, 66047, 66049, 66051, 66053, 66061–64, 66071, 66083, 66085, 66092 (part), 66101–06, 66109–13, 66115, 66117–19, 66160, 66201–27, 66282, 66285

FOURTH DISTRICT

TODD TIAHRT, Republican, of Goddard, KS; born in Vermillion, SD, June 15, 1951; attended South Dakota School of Mines and Technology; B.A., Evangel College, Springfield, MO, 1975; M.B.A., Southwest Missouri State, 1989; proposal manager, The Boeing Company; married the former Vicki Holland, 1976; three children: Jessica, John, and Luke; member, Appropriations Committee; elected to the 104th Congress; reelected to the 105th Congress.

Office Listings

http://www.house.gov/tiahrt tiahrt@hr.house.gov

428 Cannon House Office Building, Washington, DC 20515 225–6216
Administrative Assistant.—Matt Schlapp. FAX: 225–3489
Legislative Director.—Jeff Kahrs.
Scheduler.—Sarah Sunday.
155 North Market Street, Suite 400, Wichita, KS 67202 .... (316) 262–8992
District Director.—Pam Porvaznik. FAX: 262–5309
Communications Director.—Dave Hanna.
325 North Penn, Suite 9, Independence, KS 67301 .... (316) 331–8056
Southeast Kansas Coordinator.—Monica Green. FAX: 331–8074

Counties: Butler, Chautauqua, Cowley, Elk, Grenwood, Harper, Harvey, Kingman, Montgomery, Sedgwick, and Sumner. Population (1990), 619,374.

ZIP Codes: 66507, 66842, 66853, 66855, 66860, 66863, 66866, 66870, 66952, 67001–05, 67008–10, 67012–13, 67016–20, 67022–27, 67030–32, 67035–39, 67041–42, 67045, 67047, 67049–52, 67056, 67058, 67060, 67062, 67067–68, 67072, 67074, 67101, 67103, 67105–06, 67108, 67110–12, 67117–20, 67122–23, 67131–33, 67135, 67137, 67140, 67142, 67144, 67146–47, 67149, 67150–52, 67154, 67156, 67159, 67202–21, 67223, 67227–28, 67230–33, 67235, 67239, 67301, 67333–35, 67337, 67340, 67343–47, 67349, 67351–52, 67355, 67360–61, 67363–64

KENTUCKY

(Population 1995, 3,860,000)

SENATORS

WENDELL H. FORD, Democrat, of Owensboro, KY; born in Daviess County, KY, September 8, 1924; University of Kentucky; served in the U.S. Army, 1944–46, Kentucky National Guard, 1949–62; former partner, E.M. Ford and Company Insurance; former chief assistant to the Governor of Kentucky; State Senator, 1965–67; Lieutenant Governor, 1967–71; Governor, 1971–74; president of the Kentucky and national Jaycees; Junior Chamber of Commerce; chairman, National Democratic Governors Caucus, 1973–74; member, Democratic National Committee, 1976; member of Carter-Mondale Steering Committee and chairman of National Democratic Campaign Committee, 1976; chairman, Democratic Senatorial Campaign Committee; recipient of awards from the March of Dimes, Veterans of Foreign Wars, U.S. National Guard Association, American Legion, Boy Scouts of America, National Cancer Society, Kentucky Educational Television, Kentucky Housing Corporation, National Association of Regional Councils, Kentucky Council of Area Development Districts; son of the late Mr. and Mrs. E.M. Ford; holds honorary degrees from Universities of Kentucky, Morehead, Eastern Kentucky, Murray State, Kentucky Wesleyan, Spalding University, Union College, and Brescia College; married the former Jean Neel, 1943; two children: Shirley (Mrs. William Dexter) and Steven; five grandchildren; assistant majority leader, 1991; committees: Commerce, Science and Transportation; Energy and Natural Resources; Rules and Administration; Joint Committee on Printing; elected to the U.S. Senate, November 5, 1974, for the term ending January 3, 1981; reelected to each succeeding term; elected Democratic Whip on November 13, 1990; reelected November 10, 1992, December 2, 1994, and December 3, 1996.

Office Listings

http://www.senate.gov/~ford wendell_ford@ford.senate.gov

173A Russell Senate Office Building, Washington, DC 20510–1701 224–4343
Legislative Director.—Charles Smith.
Office Manager.—Robert Paxton.
Communications Director.—Meg Conlon.
Administrative Assistant.—Rob Mangas.
Executive Secretary.—Missy Smith.
Press Secretary.—Mark L. Day.
Room 1072, 600 Martin Luther King Jr. Place, Louisville, KY 40202 .... (502) 582–6251
Room 204, 343 Waller Avenue, Lexington, KY 40504 .... (606) 233–2484
305 Federal Building, Owensboro, KY 42301 .... (502) 685–5158
19 U.S. Post Office and Courthouse, Covington, KY 41011 .... (606) 491–7929

* * *

MITCH McCONNELL, Republican, of Louisville, KY; born in Colbert County, AL, February 20, 1942; graduated Manual High School, Louisville, 1960, president of the student body; B.A. with honors, University of Louisville, 1964, president of the student council, president of the student body of the College of Arts and Sciences; J.D., University of Kentucky Law School, 1967, president of student bar association, outstanding oral advocate; attorney, admitted to the Kentucky bar, 1967; chief legislative assistant to U.S. Senator Marlow Cook, 1968–70; Deputy Assistant U.S. Attorney General, 1974–75; elected judge/executive of Jefferson County, KY, 1977, reelected 1981; president, Kentucky Association of County Judge/Executives, 1982; named Outstanding Young Man in Jefferson County, 1974; named Outstanding Young Man in Kentucky, 1977; named Conservationist of the Year by the League of Kentucky Sportsmen, 1983; founder and chairman, Kentucky Task Force on Exploited and Missing Children, 1982; cochairman, National Child Tragedies Coalition, 1981; advisory board member, National Institute of Justice, 1982–84; appointed chairman of the Council of Elected Officials by Republican National Committee Chairman Haley Barbour; member, Crescent Hill Baptist Church, Louisville, KY; three children: Elly, Claire, and Porter; married Elaine Chao, president of the United Way of America, February 6, 1993; committees: Agriculture, Nutrition, and Forestry; Appropriations; Labor and Human Resources; Rules and Administration; Joint Committee on Printing; elected to the U.S. Senate, November 6, 1984, for the term expiring January 3, 1991; reelected November 6, 1990, for the term expiring January 3, 1997.

Office Listings

http://www.senate.gov/~mcconnell senator@mcconnell.senate.gov

120 Russell Senate Office Building, Washington, DC 20510–1702 224–2541

Administrative Assistant.—Steven J. Law. FAX: 224–2499
Personal Secretary/Scheduler.—Susan Oursler.
Communications Director.—Mildred Cooper.
Gene Snyder Courthouse, 601 West Broadway, Suite 630, Louisville, KY 40202 ... (502) 582–6304
State Director.—Larry Cox.
1885 Dixie Highway, Suite 345, Fort Wright, KY 41011 .... (606) 578–0188
Suite N, 1501 South Main Street, London, KY 40740 .... (606) 864–2026
Irving Cobb Building, 602 Broadway Street, Paducah, KY 42001 .... (502) 442–4554
155 East Main, Room 210, Lexington, KY 40507 .... (606) 252–1781
Federal Building, Room 102, 241 Main Street, Bowling Green, KY 42101 .... (502) 781–1673

REPRESENTATIVES

FIRST DISTRICT

EDWARD WHITFIELD, Republican, of Hopkinsville, KY; born in Hopkinsville, May 25, 1943; graduated, Madisonville High School, Madisonville, KY; B.S., University of Kentucky, Lexington, 1965; J.D., University of Kentucky, 1969; attended American University's Wesley Theological Seminary, Washington, DC; first lieutenant, U.S. Army Reserves, 1967–73; attorney, private practice, 1970–79; vice president, CSX Corporation, 1979–90; admitted to bar: Kentucky, 1970, and Florida, 1993; began practice in 1970 in Hopkinsville, KY; member, Kentucky House, 1973, one term; married to Constance Harriman Whitfield; one child, Kate; elected to the 104th Congress; reelected to the 105th Congress.

Office Listings

edky01@hr.house.gov

1541 Longworth House Office Building, Washington, DC 20515 225–3115
Administrative Director.—Rob Freeman.
Legislative Director.—Karen Long.
Press Secretary.—Ashley Hopkins.
Policy Director.—Larry Van Hoose.
First Floor, 317 West Ninth Street, Hopkinsville, KY 42240 .... (502) 885–8079
Field Representative.—Michael Pape. FAX: 885–8598
P.O. Box 717, Monroe County Courthouse, Thompkinsville, KY 42167 .... (502) 487–9509
Field Representative.—Sandy Simpson. FAX: 487–0019
Room 307, Municipal Building, 222 First Street, Henderson, KY 42420 .... (502) 826–4180
Field Representative.—Neil Johnson. FAX: 826–6783
Room 104, 100 Fountain Avenue, Paducah, KY 42001 .... (502) 442–6901
Field Representative.—Amy Bowland. FAX: 442–6805

Counties: Adair, Allen, Ballard, Butler, Caldwell, Calloway, Carlisle, Christian, Clinton, Crittenden, Cumberland, Fulton, Graves, Henderson, Hickman, Hopkins, Livingston, Logan, Lyon, McCracken, McLean, Marshall, Monroe, Muhlenberg, Ohio, Russell, Simpson, Todd, Trigg, Union, and Webster. Population (1990), 614,226.

ZIP Codes: 42001–03, 42020–29, 42031–33, 42035–41, 42044–51, 42053–56, 42058–61, 42063–64, 42066, 42069–71, 42076, 42078–79, 42081–88, 42120, 42122, 42129 (part), 42133–35, 42140, 42153, 42155, 42157, 42164, 42167, 42170, 42201–02, 42204, 42206, 42209, 42211, 42215–17, 42219–21, 42223, 42232, 42234, 42236, 42240–41, 42251–52, 42254, 42256, 42261–62, 42265–68, 42273–76, 42280, 42283, 42286–88, 42320–28, 42330, 42332–33, 42337–39, 42343–45, 42347, 42349–50, 42352, 42354, 42357–58, 42361, 42365–67, 42369–72, 42374, 42376, 42378, 42403–04, 42406, 42408–11, 42413, 42420, 42431, 42436–37, 42440–42, 42444–45, 42450–53, 42455–64, 42565, 42601–02, 42629, 42642, 42711, 42714–15, 42717, 42723 (part), 42728 (part), 42730, 42731 (part), 42735, 42741, 42742 (part), 42752–53, 42759, 42761, 42768

* * *

SECOND DISTRICT

RON LEWIS, Republican, of Cecilia, KY; born in South Shore, KY, September 14, 1946; graduated, McKell High School, 1964; B.A., University of Kentucky, 1969; M.A., higher education, Morehead State University, 1981; U.S. Navy Officer Candidate School, 1972; laborer, Morehead State, Armco Steel Corporation; Kentucky Highway Department, Eastern State Hospital; sales for Ashland Oil; teacher, Watterson College, 1980; minister, White Mills Baptist Church; named to the National Security Committee (Military Procurement and Military Personnel subcommittees) and Agriculture Committee (Risk Management and Specialty Crops and Resource Conservation, Research, and Forestry subcommittees); member, Elizabethtown Chamber of Commerce; past president, Hardin and Larue County jail ministry; member, Serverus Valley Ministerial Association; honored for his voting record by U.S. Term Limits, League of Private Property Rights, Council for Citizens Against Government Waste, National Federation of Independent Business; named a ''Guardian of Seniors' Rights'' by Tax Fairness for Seniors; cosponsored term limits legislation, welfare reform; voted to pass the Congressional Accountability Act; chairman, Congressional Family Caucus; member, GOP Task Force on Regulatory Reform; married the former Kayi Gambill, 1966; two children: Ronald Brent and Allison Faye; elected to the 104th Congress; reelected to the 105th Congress.

Office Listings

412 Cannon House Office Building, Washington, DC 20515–1702 226–3501
Chief of Staff.—Greg Van Tatenhove.
Legislative Director.—Helen McCarthy.
Press Secretary.—John McGary.
Scheduler.—Jane Riddleberger.
312 North Mulberry Street, Elizabethtown, KY 42701 .... (502) 765–4360
District Administrator.—Sam Willett.
Federal Building, Room B–18, 241 East Main Street, Bowling Green, KY 42101 .. (502) 842–9896
Federal Building, Room B–17, 423 Frederica Street, Owensboro, KY 42303 .... (502) 688–8858

Counties: Barren, Breckinridge, Bullitt, Casey, Daviess, Edmonson, Grayson, Green, Hancock, Hardin, Hart, Jefferson (part), Larue, Lincoln (part), Marion, Meade, Metcalfe, Nelson, Spencer, Taylor, Warren, and Washington. Population (1990), 614,833.

ZIP Codes: 40004, 40008–09, 40012–13, 40020, 40023, 40028, 40033, 40037, 40040, 40046–49, 40051–52, 40060, 40062–63, 40069, 40071, 40076, 40078, 40104, 40106–11, 40114–15, 40117, 40118 (part), 40119, 40121, 40140, 40142–46, 40150, 40152–53, 40155, 40157, 40159–62, 40164–65, 40170–71, 40175–78, 40214 (part), 40219 (part), 40223 (part), 40228 (part), 40229, 40243 (part), 40245 (part), 40253, 40269, 40272 (part), 40291 (part), 40299 (part), 40328, 40330, 40437 (part), 40442, 40448, 40484 (part), 40489 (part), 42101–04, 42122–24, 42127–28, 42129 (part), 42130–31, 42141–42, 42151–52, 42154, 42156, 42159–60, 42163, 42166, 42169–71, 42207, 42210, 42214, 42235, 42250, 42257, 42259, 42270, 42274–75, 42284–85, 42301–03, 42334, 42348, 42351, 42355–56, 42361, 42366, 42368, 42375–76, 42378, 42516, 42528, 42539, 42541, 42566, 42567 (part), 42701–02, 42712–13, 42716, 42718–19, 42721–22, 42723 (part), 42724, 42726, 42728 (part), 42729, 42731 (part), 42732–33, 42736, 42740, 42742 (part), 42743, 42746, 42748–49, 42754–55, 42757–58, 42762, 42764–65, 42776, 42782–84, 42787–88

* * *

THIRD DISTRICT

ANNE MEAGHER NORTHUP, Republican, of Louisville, KY; born on January 22, 1948 in Louisville; graduated from Sacred Heart Academy, Louisville, 1966; graduated from St. Mary's College, South Bend, IN, 1970; Kentucky State Legislature, 1987–96; board member: Greater Louisville Public Radio, Inc., Community Advisory Board for the Junior League of Louisville, Hospice of Louisville, Kentucky Cancer Consortium, Partnership for Kentucky School Reform; member, Institute for Republican Women; married Robert Wood Northup, 1969; six children: David, Katie, Joshua, Kevin, Erin, Mark; elected to the 105th Congress.

Office Listings

1004 Longworth House Office Building, Washington, DC 20515 225–5401
Chief of Staff.—Terry Carmack. FAX: 225–5776
Legislative Director.—Kristi Craig.
Press Secretary.—Patrick Neely.
600 Martin Luther King, Jr. Place, Suite 216, Louisville, KY 40202 .... (502) 582–5129
FAX: 582–5897

County: JEFFERSON COUNTY. POPULATION (1990), 613,603.

ZIP Codes: 40059 (part), 40118 (part), 40201–22, 40223 (part), 40228 (part), 40241–42, 40243 (part), 40258, 40272 (part), 40291 (part), 40299 (part)

* * *

FOURTH DISTRICT

JIM BUNNING, Republican, of Southgate, KY; born in Southgate, October 23, 1931; graduated, St. Xavier High School, Cincinnati, OH, 1949; B.S., Xavier University, Cincinnati, OH, 1953; professional baseball player; investment broker and agent; president, Jim Bunning Agency, Inc.; member of Kentucky State Senate (minority floor leader), 1979–83; member: Ft. Thomas City Council, 1977–79; appointed member, Ohio, Kentucky, and Indiana Regional

Council of Governments, Cincinnati, OH; National Committeeman, Republican National Committee, 1983–92; appointed member, President's National Advisory Board on International Education Programs, 1984–88; member: board of directors of Kentucky Special Olympics, Ft. Thomas (KY) Lions Club, Brighton Street Center Community Action Group; married the former Mary Catherine Theis, 1952; nine children: Barbara, Jim and Joan, Cathy, Bill and Bridgett, Mark, David and Amy; elected to the 100th Congress, November 4, 1986; reelected to each succeeding Congress.

Office Listings

rep.jim.banning@mail.house.gov

2437 Rayburn House Office Building, Washington, DC 20515–1704 225–3465
Administrative Assistant.—David A. York.
Legislative Director.—Jon Deuser.
Office Manager/Executive Secretary.—Joan L. Manning.
Suite 160, 1717 Dixie Highway, Fort Wright, KY 41011 .... (606) 342–2602
District Administrator.—Debbie McKinney.
Suite 236, The Federal Building, 1405 Greenup Avenue, Ashland, KY 41101 .... (606) 325–9898

Counties: Boone, Boyd, Bracken, Campbell, Carroll, Carter, Elliott, Fleming, Gallatin, Grant, Greenup, Henry, Kenton, Lewis, Mason, Oldham, Owen, Pendleton, Robertson, Rowan, Shelby, and Trimble. Population (1990), 614,245.

ZIP Codes: 40003, 40006–07, 40010–11, 40014, 40019, 40022, 40026, 40031, 40036, 40045, 40050, 40055–58, 40059 (part), 40065–68, 40070, 40075–77, 40245 (part), 40313, 40317, 40319, 40327, 40351, 40355, 40359, 40363, 40379 (part), 40389, 41001–02, 41004–12, 41014–18, 41022, 41030, 41033–35, 41037, 41039–46, 41048–49, 41051–53, 41055–56, 41059, 41061–64, 41071–76, 41080, 41083, 41085–86, 41091–98, 41101–02, 41105, 41121, 41127–29, 41131–32, 41135, 41137, 41139, 41141–44, 41146, 41149, 41156, 41163–64, 41166, 41168–71, 41173–75, 41177, 41179, 41181, 41183, 41189, 41631, 42133

* * *

FIFTH DISTRICT

HAROLD ROGERS, Republican, of Somerset, KY; born in Barrier, KY, December 31, 1937; graduated, Wayne County High School, 1955; attended Western Kentucky University, 1956–57; A.B., University of Kentucky, 1962; LL.B., University of Kentucky Law School, 1964; lawyer, admitted to the Kentucky State bar, 1964; commenced practice in Somerset; member, North Carolina and Kentucky National Guard, 1957–64; associate, Smith and Blackburn, 1964–67; private practice, 1967–69; Commonwealth Attorney, Pulaski and Rockcastle Counties, KY, 1969–80; delegate, Republican National Convention, 1972, 1976, 1980, 1984, and 1988; Republican nominee for lieutenant governor, KY, 1979; past president, Kentucky Commonwealth Attorneys Association; member and past president, Somerset-Pulaski County Chamber of Commerce and Pulaski County Industrial Foundation; founder, Southern Kentucky Economic Development Council, 1986; member, Chowder and Marching Society, 1981–present; member, Energy and Commerce Committee, 1981–82; member, House Appropriations Committee, 1983–present; married the former Shirley McDowell, 1957; three children: Anthony, Allison, and John Marshall; elected to the 97th Congress, November 4, 1980; reelected to each succeeding Congress.

Office Listings

2468 Rayburn House Office Building, Washington, DC 20515–1705 225–4601
Administrative Assistant.—Kevin Fromer. FAX: 225–0940
Office Manager.—Julia Casey.
Press Secretary.—Susan Zimmerman.
203 East Mount Vernon Street, Somerset, KY 42501 .... (606) 679–8346
District Administrator.—Robert L. Mitchell.
601 Main Street, Hazard, KY 41701 .... (606) 439–0794
806 Hambley Boulevard, Pikeville, KY 41501 .... (606) 432–4388

Counties: Bell, Breathitt, Clay, Floyd, Harlan, Jackson, Johnson, Knott, Knox, Laurel, Lawrence (part), Lee, Leslie, Letcher, Magoffin, Martin, McCreary, Menifee, Morgan, Owsley, Perry, Pike, Pulaski, Rockcastle, Wayne, Whitley, and Wolfe. Population (1990), 614,119.

ZIP Codes: 40316, 40322, 40336, 40341, 40345–46, 40365, 40387, 40402–03, 40409, 40417, 40419 (part), 40420, 40434, 40445, 40447, 40456, 40460, 40481, 40486, 40488, 40492, 40701–02, 40729–30, 40734, 40737, 40740–43, 40745, 40754–55, 40759, 40763, 40769, 40771, 40801, 40803, 40806–08, 40810, 40813, 40815–16, 40818–20, 40823, 40825–31, 40840, 40843–47, 40849, 40854–56, 40858, 40861–63, 40865, 40867–68, 40870, 40873–74, 40902–03, 40906, 40913–15, 40921, 40923, 40927, 40930, 40932, 40935, 40939–41, 40943–44, 40946, 40949, 40953, 40955, 40958, 40962, 40964–65, 40972, 40977, 40979, 40982–83, 40988, 40995, 40997, 40999, 41124, 41159 (part), 41201, 41203–04, 41214–16, 41219, 41222, 41224, 41226, 41228, 41230–32, 41234, 41237–38, 41240, 41250, 41254–58, 41260,

41262–69, 41271, 41274, 41301, 41306, 41310–11, 41314–15, 41317, 41321, 41327–28, 41331–33, 41338–40, 41342–44, 41346, 41348, 41351, 41357–58, 41360, 41363–70, 41377, 41385–86, 41390, 41396–97, 41406–09, 41412–13, 41419, 41421–22, 41425–26, 41441, 41443, 41451, 41457, 41464–66, 41472, 41474, 41477, 41501–03, 41512–14, 41517–20, 41522, 41524, 41527–29, 41531, 41534–40, 41542–49, 41551, 41553–55, 41557–72, 41574, 41601–07, 41612, 41614–16, 41619, 41621–22, 41626–27, 41629–33, 41635–37, 41639–40, 41642–43, 41645, 41647, 41649–51, 41653, 41655, 41659–60, 41663, 41666–69, 41701–02, 41712–14, 41719–23, 41725, 41727–33, 41735–36, 41739–40, 41743, 41745–46, 41749, 41751, 41754, 41756, 41759–60, 41762–66, 41771–78, 41801, 41804–05, 41810–12, 41815, 41817, 41819, 41821–26, 41828–29, 41831–40, 41843–45, 41847–49, 41855, 41858–59, 41861–62, 42501–02, 42518–19, 42532–33, 42536, 42544, 42553, 42558, 42564, 42567 (part), 42603, 42607, 42611, 42613, 42631, 42633–35, 42638, 42640, 42643, 42647, 42649, 42653, 42655

* * *

SIXTH DISTRICT

SCOTTY BAESLER, Democrat, of Lexington, KY; born in Athens, KY on July 9, 1941; B.S., University of Kentucky, Lexington, 1963; captain, University of Kentucky Basketball Team, 1963; J.D., University of Kentucky College of Law, 1966; served as staff sergeant in the U.S. Army Reserves, 1966–72; attorney; elected vice-mayor, Lexington, 1974–77, district judge, Fayette County, 1978–81, and mayor, Lexington, 1982–92; member: National League of Cities, U.S. Conference of Mayors, Kentucky League of Cities; awards: Preservation Award (Historic Commission), 1984, Greek Hellenic Award, National Conference of Christians and Jews Brotherhood Award, Carl D. Perkins Memorial Award, 1986, William Booth D.C.L. Award (Salvation Army), 1986, Distinguished Member, Kentucky Academy of Science, 1988, Henry T. Duncan Memorial Award (Fayette County Bar Association), 1988, Governor's Arts Award, 1989, Better Life Award, Kentucky Association of Health Care Facilities, 1989, Citizen Planner of the Year, 1990; married to Alice Dudley Woods Baesler, 1963; two children: Scott and Ashley; two grandchildren: Fritts, and Adeline; elected on November 3, 1992 to the 103rd Congress; reelected to each succeeding Congress.

Office Listings

http://www.house.gov/baesler baesler@hr.house.gov

2463 Rayburn House Office Building, Washington, DC 20515–1706 225–4706
Chief of Staff.—Chuck Atkins.
Legislative Director.—Cheryl Brownell.
Scheduler/Office Manager.—Sharyn Alexander.
Suite 318, 401 West Main Street, Lexington, KY 40507 .... (606) 253–1124
District Office Manager.—Bob Wiseman.
Room 104, Franklin County Courthouse, Frankfort, KY 40601 .... (502) 875–1512
Caseworker.—Phyllis Highley.

Counties: Anderson, Bath, Bourbon, Boyle, Clark, Estill, Fayette, Franklin, Garrard, Harrison, Jessamine, Lincoln (part), Madison, Mercer, Montgomery, Nicholas (part), Powell, Scott, and Woodford. Population (1990), 614,270.

ZIP Codes: 40306, 40310, 40311 (part), 40312, 40324, 40330, 40334, 40336–37, 40339–40, 40342, 40346–48, 40350, 40353, 40356–58, 40360–62, 40366, 40370–72, 40374, 40376, 40379 (part), 40380, 40383, 40385, 40390–92, 40403, 40410, 40415, 40419 (part), 40422–23, 40426, 40437 (part), 40440, 40444, 40452, 40461, 40464, 40468, 40471–72, 40475–76, 40484 (part), 40489 (part), 40501–05, 40507–17, 40522–24, 40533, 40544, 40555, 40574–96, 40601–04, 41003, 41031, 42567 (part)

LOUISIANA

(Population 1995, 4,342,000)

SENATORS

JOHN BREAUX, Democrat, of Crowley, LA; born in Crowley on March 1, 1944; graduated, St. Michael's High School, Crowley, 1961; B.A., University of Southwestern Louisiana, Lafayette, 1965; J.D., Louisiana State University, Baton Rouge, 1967; law partner, Brown, McKernan, Ingram and Breaux, 1967–68; legislative assistant to Congressman Edwin W. Edwards, 1968–69; district assistant to Congressman Edwards, 1969–72; member: Louisiana Bar Association and Acadia Parish Bar Association; board of directors, International Rice Festival Association; member: Crowley Jaycees; Crowley Chamber of Commerce; Pi Lambda Beta, prelaw fraternity; Phi Alpha Delta, law fraternity; Lambda Chi Alpha, social fraternity; Student Bar Association, L.S.U.; U.S.L. tennis team; Moot Court finalist, L.S.U., 1966; winner, American Legion Award; married the former Lois Gail Daigle in 1964; four children: John I. Jr., William Lloyd, Elizabeth Andre, and Julia; elected to the 92nd Congress by special election, September 30, 1972; reelected to the seven succeeding Congresses; chairman, Subcommittee on the Conservation of Wildlife and Fisheries and the Environment, 1979–86; elected to U.S. Senate November 4, 1986; chairman, Democratic Senatorial Campaign Committee, 1989–90; member, chairman, Democratic Leadership Council (1991–93), elected Democratic chief deputy whip, 104th Congress; reelected to second Senate term November 3, 1992; committees: Commerce, Science, and Transportation; Finance; ranking Democrat, Special Committee on Aging.

Office Listings

http://www.senate.gov/~breaux senator@breaux.senate.gov

516 Hart Senate Office Building, Washington, DC 20510 224–4623
Chief of Staff.—Tommy Hudson.
Legislative Director.—Darla Romfo.
Executive Assistant.—Susie Owens.
Press Secretary.—Bette Phelan.
Federal Building, Room 103, 705 Jefferson Street, Lafayette, LA 70501 .... (318) 262–6871
One American Place, Suite 2030, Baton Rouge, LA 70825 .... (504) 382–2050
Room 102–A, 211 North Third Street, Monroe, LA 71201 .... (318) 325–3320
Hale Boggs Federal Building, Suite 1005, 501 Magazine Street, New Orleans, LA 70130 .... (504) 589–2531

* * *

MARY L. LANDRIEU, Democrat, of Baton Rouge, LA; born in Alexandria, VA, November 23, 1955; B.A., Louisiana State University, 1977; real estate broker, specializing in townhouse development; represented New Orleans District House 90 in Louisiana Legislature, 1979–87; State Treasurer, 1987–95; vice chair, Louisiana Council on Child Abuse; member, Business and Professional Women; majority council member, Emily's List; past national president, Women's Legislative Network; past vice president, Women Executives in State Government; delegate to every Democratic national convention since 1979; married to E. Frank Snellings; one child, Connor; committees: Energy and Natural Resources; Agriculture, Nutrition, and Forestry; Small Business; elected to the 105th Congress.

Office Listings

http://www.senate.gov/senator/landrieu.html senator@landr.senate.gov

702 Hart Senate Office Building, Washington, DC 20510–1802 224–5824
Administrative Assistant.—Norma Jane Sabiston. FAX: 224–9735
Legislative Director.—Ben Cannon.
Executive Director.—Gina Warner.
Press Secretary.—Rich Masters.
Hale Boggs Federal Building, Room 1010, 501 Magazine Street, New Orleans, LA 70130 .... (504) 589–2427
U.S. Courthouse, 300 Fannin Street, Suite 2240, Shreveport, LA 71101–3086 .... (318) 676–3085
U.S. Postal Building, 707 Florida Street, Baton Rouge, LA 70801 .... (504) 389–0395

REPRESENTATIVES

FIRST DISTRICT

BOB LIVINGSTON, Republican, of Metairie, LA; born in Colorado Springs, CO, April 30, 1943; graduated, St. Martin's High School, New Orleans, 1960; B.A., economics, Tulane University, 1967; J.D., Tulane University Law School, 1968; admitted to the Louisiana bar, 1968; commenced practice in New Orleans; trial attorney in the law firm of Livingston and Powers; served in the U.S. Navy, 1961–63; graduate, Loyola Institute of Politics, 1973; Assistant U.S. Attorney, deputy chief, Criminal Division, 1970–73; received special achievement award as "Outstanding Assistant U.S. Attorney" in 1973; chief special prosecutor and chief, Armed Robbery Division, Orleans Parish district attorney's office, 1974–75; chief prosecutor, organized crime unit, Louisiana attorney general's office, 1975–76; member: various business, civic, veterans, and bar associations; married the former Bonnie Robichaux, 1965; four children: Robert L. III, Richard Godwin, David Barkley, and SuShan Alida; elected to the 95th Congress, August 27, 1977, in a special election to fill the vacancy caused by the resignation of Richard A. Tonry; reelected to each succeeding Congress; chairman, Appropriations Committee.

Office Listings

2406 Rayburn House Office Building, Washington, DC 20515–1801 225–3015
Administrative Assistant.—J. Allen Martin. FAX: 225–0739
Legislative Assistant.—Paul Cambon.
Executive Secretary.—Jane Graham.
111 Veterans Boulevard, Metairie, LA 70005 .... (504) 589–2753
District Representative.—Rick Legendre.
2055 Second Street, Slidell, LA 70458 .... (504) 643–7733
3101 East Causeway Approach, Mandeville, LA 70448 .... (504) 626–3144
428 East Boston Street, Covington, LA 70433 .... (504) 892–7304
300 East Thomas Street, Hammond, LA 70401 .... (504) 542–9617

Counties: Jefferson Parish (part), Orleans Parish (part), St. Tammany Parish, Tangipahoa Parish, Washington Parish. Population (1990), 602,859.

ZIP Codes: 70001–06, 70009–11, 70033, 70053, 70055, 70056 (part), 70058 (part), 70059, 70062 (part), 70063–64 (part), 70065 (part), 70072 (part), 70115 (part), 70118 (part), 70119 (part), 70121, 70122 (part), 70123–24, 70401, 70403, 70420–22, 70426–27, 70429, 70431, 70433–34, 70436–38, 70442, 70443–46, 70448, 70450–52, 70454–61, 70463–67, 70469–70

* * *

SECOND DISTRICT

WILLIAM J. JEFFERSON, Democrat, of New Orleans, LA; born in Lake Providence, LA, March 14, 1947; graduated, G.W. Griffin High School, Lake Providence, LA, 1965; B.A., political science and English, Southern University and A&M College, Baton Rouge, LA, 1969; J.D., Harvard Law School, Cambridge, MA, 1972; admitted to the bar, New Orleans, LA, 1972; attorney, Jefferson, Bryan, Jupiter, Lewis and Blanson, New Orleans; first lieutenant, U.S. Army, J.A.G. Corps, 1975; member, board of trustees, Greater St. Stephen's Baptist Church; Urban League of Greater New Orleans; Southern University Foundation Board; Louisiana State Senate, March, 1980–January 2, 1991; married the former Andrea Green in 1970; five children: Jamila, Jalila, Jelani, Nailah, and Akilah; elected to the 102nd Congress; reelected to each succeeding Congress.

Office Listings

240 Cannon House Office Building, Washington, DC 20515–1802 225–6636
Administrative Assistant.—Lionel Collins.
Executive Secretary/Scheduler.—Kristin Spoerl.
Communications Director.—Jean LaPlace.
1012 Boggs Federal Building, 501 Magazine Street, New Orleans, LA 70130 .... (504) 589–2274
District Office Manager.—Stephanie Edwards.

County: New Orleans Parish (part). Population (1990), 602,689.

ZIP Codes: 70001 (part), 70003 (part), 70053–54, 70056 (part), 70058 (part), 70062 (part), 70063, 70065 (part), 70067 (part), 70072 (part), 70073, 70094 (part), 70096, 70112–14, 70115 (part), 70116–17, 70118 (part), 70119 (part), 70121 (part), 70122 (part), 70123 (part), 70125–31, 70139, 70141, 70150–4, 70156–58, 70160–61, 70163, 70165, 70170, 70172, 70174–79, 70182, 70185–87, 70189–90

THIRD DISTRICT

W.J. (BILLY) TAUZIN, Republican, of Thibodaux, LA; born in Chackbay, LA, June 14, 1943; graduated, Thibodaux High School, 1961; B.A., history, prelaw, Nicholls State University, 1964; honor student, Hall of Fame graduate, student body president, 1962–64; J.D., Louisiana State University, 1967, while serving four years in Louisiana State Senate, legislative aide; lawyer; admitted to the Louisiana bar in 1968; commenced practice in Houma, LA.; law partner, Marcel, Marcel, Fanguy and Tauzin, 1968–72; private practice, 1972; partner, Sonnier and Tauzin, 1976; married Cecile Bergeron Tauzin; five children by previous marriage: Kristie René, W.J. (Billy) III, John Ashton, Thomas Nicholas, and Michael James; served in Louisana State Legislature, 1971–80; elected to the 96th Congress, May 22, 1980, in a special election to fill the vacancy caused by the resignation of David C. Treen; reelected to each succeeding Congress; Freshman Representative, Democratic Steering and Policy Committee; member, Commerce and Natural Resources Committees; cochairman, Congressional Coalition for America; chairman, Telecommunications, Trade, and Consumer Protection Subcommittee of Commerce.

Office Listings

2183 Rayburn House Office Building, Washington, DC 20515–1803 .... (202) 225–4031
Administrative Assistant.—Emily Young Shaw.
Federal Building, Suite 107, Houma, LA 70360 .... (504) 876–3033
District Representative.—Jeri Theriot.
210 East Main Street, New Iberia, LA 70560 .... (318) 367–8231
District Representative.—Jan Viator.
Ascension Parish Courthouse East, 828 South Irma Boulevard, Gonzales, LA 70737 .... (504) 621–8490
District Representative.—Ina Smiley.
8201 West Judge Perez Drive, Chalmette, LA 70043 .... (504) 271–1707
District Coordinator.—Peggy Bourgeous.

Counties: PARISHES. Assumption, Iberia, Lafourche, Plaquemines, St. Bernard, St. Charles, St. Mary, and Terrebonne. JEFFERSON PARISH: That part not contained in the First District and the Second District. Ascension, St. James, St. John the Baptist, Iberville (Precinct 4 only). ST. MARTIN PARISH: District 1 (precincts 2 and 5). Population (1990), 602,950.

ZIP Codes: 70030–32, 70036–41, 70043–44, 70046–47, 70049–52, 70056 (part), 70057, 70058 (part), 70066, 70067 (part), 70068–71, 70075–76, 70078–80, 70082–87, 70090–92, 70301–02, 70339–46, 70352–61, 70363–64, 70372–75, 70377, 70380–81, 70390–95, 70397, 70421, 70513–14, 70518 (part), 70522–23, 70538, 70540, 70544, 70552, 70560, 70562, 70569, 70582 (part), 70707, 70716, 70718, 70723, 70725, 70728, 70734 (part), 70737 (part), 70738, 70743, 70763, 70769 (part), 70774, 70778, 70788 (part)

* * *

FOURTH DISTRICT

JIM McCRERY, Republican, of Shreveport, LA; born in Shreveport, September 18, 1949; graduated Leesville High, Los Angeles, 1967; B.A., Louisiana Tech University, Ruston, 1971; J.D., Louisiana State University, Baton Rouge, 1975; attorney; admitted to the Louisiana bar in 1975 and commenced practice in Leesville, LA; Jackson, Smith, and Ford (Leesville), 1975–78; assistant city attorney, Shreveport, 1979–80; district manager, U.S. Representative Buddy Roemer, 1981–82; legislative director, U.S. Representative Buddy Roemer, 1982–84; board of directors, Louisiana Association of Business and Industry, 1986–87; chairman, Regulatory Affairs Committee, Louisiana Forestry Association, 1987; regional manager for Government Affairs, Georgia-Pacific Corporation, 1984–88; elected by special election to the 100th Congress, April 16, 1988, to fill the vacancy caused by the resignation of Charles E. (Buddy) Roemer; reelected to each succeeding Congress.

Office Listings

http://www.house.gov/mccrery mccrery@hr.house.gov

2104 Rayburn House Office Building, Washington, DC 20515–1804 225–2777
Chief of Staff.—Richard Hunt. FAX: 225–8039
6425 Youree Drive, Suite 350, Shreveport, LA 71105 .... (318) 798–2254
Western District Manager.—Allyn Murphy.
Southgate Plaza Shopping Center, 1606 South Fifth Street, Leesville, LA 71446 .... (318) 238–0778
District Manger.—Linda Wright.

Counties: PARISHES. Allen, Beauregard, Bienville, Bossier, Caddo, Claiborne, Desoto, Natchitoches, Red River, Sabine, Vernon, and Webster. Population (1990), 602,816.

ZIP Codes: 70634, 70637–39, 70642, 70644, 70651–54, 70656, 70657, 70659, 70660, 70662, 71001–04, 71006–09, 71014, 71018, 71019, 71021, 71023–25, 71027–30, 71032–34, 71036–40, 71043–52, 71055, 71058, 71060, 71061, 71063–

73, 71075, 71078–80, 71101, 71104–13, 71115, 71118, 71134, 71135, 71138, 71152, 71164, 71166, 71171, 71172, 71403, 71411, 71414, 71416, 71419, 71426, 71429, 71434, 71437–39, 71443, 71444, 71446, 71447, 71449, 71450, 71452, 71455–62, 71468, 71469, 71474–76, 71486, 71496, 71497

* * *

FIFTH DISTRICT

JOHN COOKSEY, Republican, of Monroe, LA born in Alexandria, LA, August 20, 1941; graduated, LaSalle High School, Olla, LA; graduated, Louisiana State University, Baton Rouge, Louisiana State University Medical School, New Orleans; Air Force, 1967–69, served in northern Thailand during Vietnam War; Air National Guard, 1970–71; physician-ophthalmologist; professional: Ochsner Medical Foundation in New Orleans; private medical practice in Monroe, LA; made five medical mission trips to Maua Methodist Hospital in Maua, Kenya, where he performed eye surgery; in 1986; raised enough money through private donations to build a modern eye clinic at the Maua Hospital to be used by local and visiting ophthalmologists; received Downtown Rotary Club Paul Harris Fellow Award in 1989 for his humanitarian work in Africa; member: Louisiana State Medical Society, Louisiana Association of Business and Industry, Monroe Chamber of Commerce, National Federation of Independent Business, St. Paul United Methodist Church (laity leader); president, Ouachita Parish Medical Society; president, Ophthalmology Association; boards: Board of Trustees of the Billy Pomeroy Caney Conference Center (chairman), Louisiana Association of Business and Industry, Public Affairs Research; married former Ann Grabill, 1967; three children: Karen, Carol Ann, and Catherine; committees: Agriculture, Transportation and Infrastructure; subcommittees: Veterans' Affairs; Aviation; Resource Conservation, Research, and Forestry; General Farm Commodities; Hospitals and Health Care; Public Building and Economic Development (vice chair); elected to the 105th Congress.

Office Listings

http://www.house.gov/cooksey

319 Cannon House Office Building, Washington, DC 20515–1805 225–8490
FAX: 225–5639
Administrative Assistant.—Lee Fletcher.
Legislative Director.—Jim Phalen.
Office Manager.—Sally Buikema.
Press Secretary.—Camp Kaufman.

1101 Hudson Lane, Suite B, Monroe, LA 71201 .... (318) 330–9998
FAX: 330–9950
District Director.—Dr. Dwight Vines.

2019 MacArthur Drive, Suite B, Building 10, Alexandria, LA 71301 .... (318) 448–1777
FAX: 473–8163
Co-District Managers.—Bob Stewart, Susan DeKeyzer.

Counties: PARISHES. Avoyelles, Caldwell, Catahoula, Concordia, Evangeline (part), East Carroll, Franklin, Grant, Jackson, LaSalle, Lincoln, Madison, Morehouse, Rapides, Richland, Tensas, Union, West Carroll, Win.

ZIP Codes: 70031–32, 70036–43, 70094, 70118, 70301, 70340–44, 70380, 70420–22, 70426–27, 70431, 70510, 70512–25, 70582, 70586, 70630–31, 70675, 70710–21, 70738, 70764, 70806, 70994, 71001–09, 71014–17, 71110–12, 71216, 71218–20, 71222–28, 71301, 71316, 71318, 71320–25, 71401–07, 71409–12, 71414–15, 71433

* * *

SIXTH DISTRICT

RICHARD H. BAKER, Republican, of Baton Rouge, LA; born in New Orleans, LA on May 22, 1948; graduated, University High School; Louisiana State University, Baton Rouge; real estate broker; Louisiana House of Representatives, 1972–86; chairman, Committee on Transportation, Highways, and Public Works, 1980–86; member: Southern Legislative Conference, ALEC, Central Area Homebuilders, East Baton Rouge Airport Commission, Baton Rouge Lodge No. 372 Central Region Planning Commission; married the former Kay Carpenter in 1969; two children: Brandon and Julie; committees: Transportation and Infrastructure, Banking and Financial Services; subcommittees: chairman, Capital Markets, Securities, and Government-Sponsored Enterprises; Housing and Community Opportunity; Water Resources and Environment; elected to the 100th Congress on November 4, 1986; reelected to each succeeding Congress.

Office Listings

434 Cannon House Office Building, Washington, DC 20515–1806 225–3901
Staff Director/Press Secretary.—Paul Sawyer. FAX: 225–7313
Executive Assistant/Scheduler.—Lynn Kirk.
5555 Hilton Avenue, Suite 100, Baton Rouge, LA 70808 .... (504) 929–7711
Chief of Staff.—Christina Kyle Casteel. FAX: 929–7688

Counties: Ascension, East Baton Rouge, East Feliciana, Iberville, Livingston, Pointe Coupee, St. Helena, West Baton Rouge, West Feliciana. CITIES: Addis, Albany, Angola, Baker, Batchelor, Baton Rouge, Bayou Goula, Blanks, Brittany, Brusly, Bueche, Carville, Clinton, Denham Springs, Duplessis, Erwinville, Ethel, Fordoche, French Settlement, Geismar, Glynn, Gonzales, Greenburg, Greenwell Springs, Grosse Tete, Hardwood, Holden, Innis, Jackson, Jarreau, Labarre, Lakeland, Lettsworth, Livingston, Livonia, Lottie, Maringouin, Maurepas, Morganza, New Roads, Norwood, Oscar, Pine Grove, Plaquemine, Port Allen, Prairieville, Pride, Rosedale, Rougon, Slaughter, Sorrento, Springfield, St. Amant, St. Francisville, St. Gabriel, Sunshine, Torbert, Tunica, Ventress, Wakefield, Walker, Watson, Weyanoke, White Castle, Wilson, Zachary.

ZIP Codes: 70704, 70707, 70710–12, 70714–22, 70726–30, 70732–33, 70734, 70736–37, 70739–40, 70742, 70744, 70747–49, 70751–57, 70759–62, 70764–65, 70767, 70779–70, 70772–78, 70780–89, 70791, 70801–96

* * *

SEVENTH DISTRICT

CHRIS JOHN, Democrat, of Crowley, LA; born in Crowley, January 5, 1960; graduated, Notre Dame High School, Acadia Parish, 1978; B.A., business administration, Louisiana State University, 1982; vice president in charge of office operations, John N. John Truckline, Inc.; aide to father, Louisiana State Representative John N. John, Jr., 1974–82; elected chairman of Acadiana Delegation while serving in Louisiana House of Representatives, 1988–96; charter member, Crowley Chamber of Commerce; member: Crowley Kiwanis Club, Acadia Chapter of Ducks Unlimited, Knights of Columbus; past vice president, Acadiana Sportsmen's League; former Crowley city councilman; married to Payton Smith; elected to the 105th Congress.

Office Listings

http://www.house.gov/john

1504 Longworth House Office Building, Washington, DC 20515 225–2031
Chief of Staff.—Lynn Hershey. FAX: 225–5724
556 Jefferson Street, Suite 100, Lafayette, LA 70501 .... (318) 235–6322
District Director.—Louis Perret. FAX: 235–6072
Executive Assistant.—Karl DeRouen.
1101 Lakeshore Drive, Suite 306, Lake Charles, LA 70601 .... (318) 433–1747
Executive Assistant.—Lynn Jones. FAX: 433–0974

Counties: PARISHES. Acadia, Allen, Calcasieu, Cameron, Evangeline, Jefferson Davis, Lafayette, St. Landry, Vermilion, Vernon, St. Martin (part). That part not contained in the Third District. Population (1990), 602,921.

ZIP Codes: 70501–03, 70505–96, 59708–12, 70515–16, 70518, 70520, 70524–29, 70531–35, 70537, 70541–43, 70546, 70548–52, 70554–56, 70558–59, 70570–71, 70575–81, 70575–75–81, 70583–86, 70589, 70591–92, 70601–02, 70605–07, 70609, 70611–12, 70615–16, 70629–33, 70638, 70640, 70643, 70645–48, 70650, 70655, 70658, 70661, 70663–64, 70668–69, 7750, 71345, 71353, 71358, parts of 70506, 70528, 70586

MAINE

(Population, 1995 1,241,000)

SENATORS

OLYMPIA J. SNOWE, Republican, of Auburn, ME; born in Augusta, ME, February 21, 1947; graduated from Edward Little High School, Auburn, ME, 1965; B.A., University of Maine, Orono, 1969; member, Holy Trinity Greek Orthodox Church of Lewiston-Auburn; active member of civic and community organizations; elected to the Maine House of Representatives, 1973, to the seat vacated by the death of her first husband, the late Peter Snowe; reelected for a full two-year term in 1974; elected to the Maine Senate, 1976; chaired the Joint Standing Committee on Health and Institutional Services; elected to the 96th Congress, November 7, 1978—the youngest Republican woman, and first Greek-American woman, elected; reelected to the 97th through 103rd Congresses; past member: House Budget Committee; House Foreign Affairs Committee; leading member of the former House Select Committee on Aging, ranking Republican on its Subcommittee on Human Services; Senate committees: Armed Services; Budget; Commerce, Science and Transportation; Small Business; subcommittees: Acquisition and Technology; Personnel; Seapower; Aviation; Manufacturing and Innovation; chair, Oceans and Fisheries; Surface Transportation and Merchant Marine; married to former Maine Governor John R. McKernan, Jr.; elected to the U.S. Senate, November 8, 1994, for the six-year term beginning January 3, 1995.

Office Listings

http://www.senate.gov/~snowe olympia@snowe.senate.gov

250 Russell Senate Office Building, Washington, DC 20510	224–5344
Chief of Staff.—Kevin L. Raye.	
Executive Assistant.—Rochelle B. Meyer.	
Communications Director.—W. Davis Lackey, Jr.	
Legislative Director.—Jane Q. Calderwood.	
2 Great Falls Plaza, Suite 7B, Auburn, ME 04210	(207) 786–2451
68 Sewall Street, Suite 101C, Augusta, ME 04330	(207) 622–8292
One Cumberland Place, Suite 306, Bangor, ME 04401	(207) 945–0432
231 Main Street, P.O. Box 215, Biddeford, ME 04005	(207) 282–4144
3 Canal Plaza, Suite 601, P.O. Box 188, Portland, ME 04112	(207) 874–0883
169 Academy Street, Suite 3, Presque Isle, ME 04769	(207) 764–5124

* * *

SUSAN COLLINS, Republican, of Bangor, ME; born on December 7, 1952, in Caribou, ME; graduated, Caribou High School, 1971; B.A., *magna cum laude,* Phi Beta Kappa, St. Lawrence University, Canton, NY; Outstanding Alumni Award, St. Lawrence University, 1992; staff director, Senate Subcommittee on the Oversight of Government Management, 1981–87; for 12 years, principal advisor on business issues to former Senator William S. Cohen; Commissioner of Professional and Financial Regulation for Maine Governor John R. McKernan, Jr., 1987; New England administrator, Small Business Administration, 1992–93; appointed Deputy Treasurer of Massachusetts, 1993; executive director, Husson College Center for Family Business, 1994–96; committees: Labor and Human Resources, Governmental Affairs, Special Committee on Aging; subcommittee: chair, Permanent Subcommittee on Investigations; elected on November 5, 1996, to the U.S. Senate.

Office Listings

http://www.senate.gov/senator/collins.html

172 Russell Senate Office Building, Washington, DC 20510–1904	224–2523
Chief of Staff.—Steven Abbott.	FAX: 224–2693
Communications Director.—Mark Woodward.	
Legislative Director.—Don Green.	
P.O. Box 655, 202 Harlow Street, Room 204, Bangor, ME 04401	(207) 945–0417
State Representative.—Judy Cuddy.	FAX: 990–4604
168 Capitol Street, Augusta, ME 04330	(207) 622–8414
State Representative.—Valerie Emerson.	FAX: 622–5884
109 Alfred Street, Biddeford, ME 04005	(207) 283–1101
State Representative.—Cliff Garvey.	FAX: 283–4054
11 Lisbon Street, Lewiston, ME 04240	(207) 784–6969
State Representative.—Dan Demeritt.	FAX: 782–6475
25 Sweden Street, Suite A, Caribou, ME 04736	(207) 493–5873

State Representative.—Philip Bosse.
10 Moulton Street, Portland, ME 04101 .... (207) 780–3575
FAX: 828–0380

REPRESENTATIVES

FIRST DISTRICT

THOMAS H. ALLEN, Democrat, of Portland, ME; born in Portland, April 16, 1945; graduated, Deering High School, Portland; Bowdoin College, Phi Beta Kappa; Oxford University, Rhodes scholar; Harvard University, J.D.; Bowdin College Board of Trustees; board of directors of Shalom House and the United Way of Greater Portland; president, Portland Stage Company; Executive and Legislative Policy committees; Maine Municipal Association; chair, Governor's Task Force on Foster Care; Portland city council and mayor; married to Diana Allen; two children: Gwen and Kate; committees: National Security, Government Reform and Oversight; elected to the 105th Congress.

Office Listings

rep.tomallen@mail.house.gov

1630 Longworth House Office Building, Washington, DC 20515 225–6166
Chief of Staff.—Jacqueline Potter. FAX: 225–5590
Executive Assistant/Scheduler.—Jean Waskow.
Legislative Director.—Stella Livanios.
Legislative Assistants: Todd Stein, Jon Chase, Andrew Hysell.
Legislative Correspondents: Beth Beausang, Alexis Gilman.
234 Oxford Street, Portland, ME 04101 .... (207) 774–5019
District Director.—Bill Johnson. FAX 871–0720
Communications Director.—Mark Sullivan.
Office Manager/Scheduler.—Rosemary Ginn.
Case Workers: Ann Goodridge, John McLaughlin, Mark Ouellette.

Counties: Cumberland, Kennebec, Knox, Lincoln, Sagadahoc, and York. Population (1990), 591,442.

ZIP Codes: 03901–11, 04001–11, 04013–17, 04019–22, 04024, 04027–30, 04032, 04037–43, 04046–51, 04053–58, 04060–64, 04066–88, 04090–96, 04101–10, 04112, 04116, 04210–12, 04216–17, 04219–21, 04223–28, 04230–31, 04233–41, 04243, 04250–61, 04263, 04265–68, 04270–71, 04273–76, 04278–92, 04294, 04330, 04332–33, 04338, 04341–55, 04357–64, 04401–02, 04406, 04408, 04410–19, 04421–24, 04426–31, 04433–35, 04438, 04441–44, 04446, 04448–51, 04453–65 04467–69, 04471–76, 04478–79, 04481–82, 04485, 04487–93, 04495–97, 04516, 04526, 04530, 04535–39, 04541–44, 04547–49, 04551–56, 04558, 04562–65, 04567–68, 04570–76, 04578–79, 04605–09, 04611–15, 04617–19, 04622–25, 04627–31, 04634–35, 04637–38, 04640, 04643–46, 04648–50, 04652–62, 04664–69, 04671–81, 04683–86, 04690–94, 04730, 04732–47, 04749–51, 04756–70, 04772–77, 04779–88, 04841, 04843, 04846–65, 04901, 04903, 04908, 04910–12, 04915, 04917–18, 04920–30, 04932–33, 04935–45, 04947, 04949–58, 04961–67, 04969–76, 04978–79, 04981–89, 04992

* * *

SECOND DISTRICT

JOHN E. BALDACCI, Democrat, of Bangor, ME; born in Bangor, January 30, 1955; graduated Bangor High School, 1973; B.A., history, University of Maine, Orono, 1986; restaurant operator, Momma Baldacci's Restaurant, Bangor, ME; Bangor City Council, 1978–81; Maine State Senator 1982–94; married Karen Weston Baldacci, 1982; one child, Jack; committees: Agriculture, Small Business; regional whip; elected November 8, 1994, to the 104th Congress; reelected to the 105th Congress.

Office Listings

http://www.house.gov/baldacci baldacci@hr.house.gov

1740 Longworth House Office Building, Washington, DC 20515–1902 225–6306
Administrative Assistant.—Larry Benoit.
Press Secretary.—Doug Dunbar.
Office Manager.—Kristi Garland.
P.O. Box 858, 202 Harlow Street, Bangor, ME 04401 .... (207) 942–6935
157 Main Street, Lewiston, ME 04240 .... (207) 782–3704
445 Main Street, Presque Isle, ME 04769 .... (207) 764–1036

Counties: Androscoggin, Aroostook, Franklin, Hancock, Kennebec (part), Oxford, Penobscot, Piscataquis, Somerset, Waldo (part), and Washington. Population (1990), 591,442.

ZIP Codes: 04010, 04016, 04022, 04037, 04041, 04051, 04058, 04064, 04068, 04080–81, 04088, 04210–12, 04216–17, 04219–21, 04223–28, 04230–31, 04234, 04236–41, 04243, 04250–59, 04261–63, 04266–68, 04270–71, 04273–76, 04278–86, 04287 (part), 04288–92, 04294, 04401–02, 04406, 04408, 04410–19, 04421–24, 04426–31, 04433–35, 04438, 04441–44, 04446, 04448–51, 04453, 04455–64, 04467–68, 04471–76, 04478–79, 04485, 04487–93, 04495–97, 04605–09, 04611–19, 04622–31, 04634–35, 04637–38, 04640, 04642–44, 04646, 04648–50, 04652–62, 04664–69, 04671–81, 04683–85, 04690–94, 04730, 04732–40, 04742–47, 04749–51, 04756–69, 04772–77, 04779–87, 04910–12, 04915, 04920–21, 04923–30, 04932–33, 04936, 04938–39, 04942–45, 04947, 04950–51, 04953–58, 04961, 04963–67, 04969–72, 04974–76, 04978–79, 04981–86, 04992

MARYLAND

(Population 1995, 5,042,000)

SENATORS

PAUL S. SARBANES, Democrat, of Baltimore, MD; born in Salisbury, MD, February 3, 1933, son of Spyros and Matina Sarbanes; graduated, Wicomico Senior High School, 1950; A.B., Princeton University, 1954, *magna cum laude* and Phi Beta Kappa; Rhodes scholar, Balliol College, Oxford, England, 1954–57, first-class B.A. honours in School of Philosophy, Politics and Economics; LL.B., *cum laude*, Harvard Law School, 1960; admitted to practice by Maryland Court of Appeals, 1960; law clerk to Judge Morris A. Soper, U.S. Court of Appeals for the Fourth Circuit, 1960–61; associate in Baltimore law firms Piper and Marbury, 1961–62, and Venable, Baetjer and Howard, 1965–70; administrative assistant to Walter W. Heller, chairman of the Council of Economic Advisers, 1962–63; executive director, Charter Revision Commission of Baltimore City, 1963–64; elected to the Maryland House of Delegates in November 1966, serving from 1967–71; member, Greek Orthodox Cathedral of the Annunciation, Baltimore, MD; married Christine Dunbar of Brighton, England; three children: John Peter, Michael Anthony, and Janet Matina; committees: Banking, Housing, and Urban Affairs; Budget; Foreign Relations; Joint Economic; elected to 92nd Congress on November 3, 1970; reelected to 93rd and 94th Congresses; elected to the U.S. Senate, November 2, 1976, for the six-year term beginning January 3, 1977; reelected November 2, 1982, November 8, 1988 and November 8, 1994.

Office Listings

http://www.senate.gov/~sarbanes senator@sarbanes.senate.gov

309 Hart Senate Office Building, Washington, DC 20510 224–4524
Chief of Staff.—Peter Marudas. FAX: 224–1651
Deputy Chief of Staff.—Julie Kehrli. TDD: 224–3452
Legislative Director.—Julie Kehrli.
Appointment Secretary.—Elise Gillette.
Press Secretary.—Jesse Jacobs.
1518 Tower I, Suite 1010, 100 South Charles Street, Baltimore, MD 21201 .... (410) 962–4436
1110 Bonifant Street, Suite 450, Silver Spring, MD 20910 .... (301) 589–0797
141 Baltimore Street, Cumberland, MD 21502 .... (301) 724–0695
111 Baptist Street, Suite 115, Salisbury, MD 21801 .... (410) 860–2131
Box 331, 15499 Potomac River Drive, Cobb Island, MD 20625 .... (301) 259–2404

* * *

BARBARA A. MIKULSKI, Democrat, of Baltimore, MD; born in Baltimore on July 20, 1936; B.A., Mount St. Agnes College, 1958; M.S.W., University of Maryland School of Social Work, 1965; former social worker for Catholic Charities and city of Baltimore; served as adjunct professor, Department of Sociology, Loyola College; elected to Baltimore City Council, 1971; Democratic nominee for U.S. Senate in 1974, winning 43 percent of vote; elected to U.S. Congress in 1976; first woman appointed to Energy and Commerce Committee; served on Merchant Marine and Fisheries Committee; elected to U.S. Senate in November 1986 with 61 percent of the vote; reelected in November 1992 with 71 percent of the vote; became first woman representing the Democratic Party to be elected to a Senate seat not previously held by her husband and the first Democratic woman ever to serve in both houses of Congress; committees: Appropriations (ranking member of VA, HUD and Independent Agencies Subcommittee), Labor and Human Resources (ranking member of Aging Subcommittee); secretary of Democratic Conference for 105th Congress, first woman to be elected to a leadership post.

Office Listings

http://www.senate.gov/~mikulski senator@mikulski.senate.gov

709 Hart Senate Office Building, Washington, DC 20510–2003 224–4654
Chief of Staff.—Shaila Aery. TDD: 224–5223
Legislative Director.—Roberta Haeberle.
World Trade Center, Suite 253, Baltimore, MD 21202 .... (410) 962–4510
State Director.—Mike Morrill.
Suite 202, 60 West Street, Annapolis, MD 21401 .... (410) 263–1805
Suite 208, 9658 Baltimore Boulevard, College Park, MD 20740 .... (410) 345–5517
94 West Washington Street, Hagerstown, MD 21740 .... (410) 797–2826
Suite 1, Building B, 1201 Pemberton, Salisbury, MD 21801

REPRESENTATIVES

FIRST DISTRICT

WAYNE T. GILCHREST, Republican, of Kennedyville, MD; born on April 15, 1946, in Rahway, NJ; graduated from Rahway High School, 1964; attended Wesley College, Dover, DE; B.A. in history, Delaware State College, Dover, 1973; graduate studies, Loyola University, Baltimore, MD, 1984–present; served in the U.S. Marine Corps, 1964–68; awarded the Purple Heart, Bronze Star, Navy Commendation Medal, Navy Unit Citation, and others; government and history teacher, Kent County High School, 1973–present; member: Kent County Teachers Association, American Legion, Veterans of Foreign Wars, Order of the Purple Heart, Kennedyville Methodist Church; married to the former Barbara Rawley; three children: Kevin, Joel, and Katie; elected to the 102nd Congress; reelected to each succeeding Congress.

Office Listings

332 Cannon House Office Building, Washington, DC 20515–2001 225–5311
Administrative Assistant.—Tony Caligiuri. FAX: 225–0254
Office Manager/Scheduler.—Cyndy Dingus.
Legislative Director.—Dan Walsh.
521 Washington Avenue, Chestertown, MD 21620 .... (410) 778–9407
One Plaza East, Salisbury, MD 21801 .... (410) 749–3184
Arundel Center North, 101 Crain Highway, NW, Suite 509, Glen Burnie, MD 21061 .... (410) 760–3372
District Director.—Emmett Duke.

Counties: Anne Arundel (part), Caroline, Cecil, Dorchester, Kent, Queen Anne's, Somerset, Talbot, Wicomico, Worcester, and Baltimore city (part). Population (1990), 597,684.

ZIP Codes: 20755 (part), 21012 (part), 21032 (part), 21037 (part), 21054 (part), 21060, 21061 (part), 21076 (part), 21108 (part), 21113 (part), 21114 (part), 21122 (part), 21144 (part), 21146 (part), 21225 (part), 21226, 21240, 21401 (part), 21402–04, 21601, 21607, 21609–13, 21617, 21619–20, 21622–29, 21631–32, 21634–73, 21675–79, 21801–03, 21810–11, 21813–14, 21816–17, 21821–22, 21824, 21826, 21829–30, 21835–38, 21840–42, 21849–53, 21856–58, 21861–75, 21901–04, 21911–22, 21930

* * *

SECOND DISTRICT

ROBERT L. EHRLICH, Jr., Republican, of Timonium, MD; born in Arbutus, MD on November 25, 1957; A.B., Princeton University, 1979 (academic-athletic scholarship recipient); J.D., Wake Forest University, 1982 (scholarship recipient); admitted to Maryland bar, 1983; Associate, Ober, Kaler, Grimes, and Shriver, 1982–92; Of Counsel, Ober, Kaler, Grimes, and Shriver, 1992–94; associate, Ober, Kaler, Grimes, and Shriver, 1982–92; elected to Maryland House of Delegates, November 9, 1986; reelected on November 6, 1990; married to the former Kendel Sibiski; member: Banking and Financial Services and Government Reform and Oversight Committees; elected to the 104th Congress on November 9, 1994; reelected to the 105th Congress.

Office Listings

http://www.house.gov/lattanze.loyola.edu:80/research/ehrlich/index.html ehrlich@house.gov

315 Cannon House Office Building, Washington, DC 20515–2002 225–3061
Chief of Staff.—Steve L. Kreceski. FAX: 225–3094
1407 York Road, Suite 304, Lutherville, MD 21093 .... (410) 337–7222
Chief Administrator.—Karl Aumann.
45 North Main Street, Bel Air, MD 21014 .... (410) 838–2517
Government Building, 7701 Wise Avenue, 2nd Floor, Dundalk, MD 21222
511–B Eastern Avenue, Essex, MD 21221
Pasadena.—TBA

Counties: Anne Arundel (part), Baltimore (part), and Harford. Population (1990), 597,683.

ZIP Codes: 21001, 21005, 21009–10, 21012 (part), 21013–15, 21017–18, 21021, 21023–24, 21027–28, 21030–31, 21034, 21040, 21047, 21050–53, 21056–57, 21074 (part), 21078, 21082, 21084–85, 21087, 21092, 21093 (part), 21101, 21105, 21107 (part), 21108 (part), 21111, 21117 (part), 21120, 21122 (part), 21128 (part), 21130–32, 21136 (part), 21139, 21146 (part), 21152–54, 21155 (part), 21156, 21160–62, 21204 (part), 21206 (part), 21212 (part), 21219–21, 21222 (part), 21224 (part), 21234 (part), 21236 (part), 21237 (part), 21239 (part), 21284–86

THIRD DISTRICT

BENJAMIN L. CARDIN, Democrat, of Baltimore, MD; born in Baltimore, October 5, 1943; attended Baltimore public schools; graduated Baltimore City College, 1961; B.A., University of Pittsburgh, PA, 1964, *cum laude*; J.D., University of Maryland, Baltimore, 1967, (first in class); attorney; admitted to Maryland bar November 1967 and began practice in Baltimore; member of the Maryland House of Delegates, 1967–86; Speaker of House of Delegates, 1979–86; chairman, Ways and Means Committee, 1974–79; vice chairman, Ways and Means Committee, 1971–73; member, Presidential Advisory Committee on Federalism; chairman, State Federal Assembly, National Council of State Legislators, 1980–81; member, National Council of State Legislators, executive committee; member, Council of State Governments, executive committee, 1979–86; cochairman, Legislative Policy Committee, Maryland General Assembly, 1979–86; trustee, Baltimore Museum of Art; member, Baltimore Jewish Community Relations Council; trustee, Baltimore Council on Foreign Affairs; member, Associated Jewish Charities Welfare Fund; member, board of visitors of the University of Maryland School of Law; trustee, St. Mary's College; chairman, Maryland Legal Services Corporation; MACO Legislator of the Year Award, 1984; commissioner, Commission on Security and Cooperation in Europe; married the former Myrna Edelman, 1964; two children, Michael and Deborah; committees: Ways and Means; Standards and Official Conduct; elected to the 100th Congress, November 4, 1986; reelected to each succeeding Congress.

Office Listings

http://www.house.gov/cardin cardin@hr.house.gov

104 Cannon House Office Building, Washington, DC 20515–2003 225–4016
Administrative Assistant.—David Koshgarian.
Office Manager.—Amy Daiger.
Suite 201, 540 East Belvedere Avenue, Baltimore, MD 21212 .... (410) 433–8886
District Office Director.—Bailey Fine.
Press Secretary.—Suan Sullam.

Counties: Anne Arundel (part), Baltimore (part), Howard (part), and Baltimore city (part). Population (1990), 597,680.

ZIP Codes: 20755 (part), 20794 (part), 21042 (part), 21043 (part), 21044 (part), 21045 (part), 21046, 21055, 21061 (part), 21076 (part), 21090, 21093 (part), 21113 (part), 21117 (part), 21128 (part), 21133 (part), 21136 (part), 21144 (part), 21150, 21201 (part), 21202 (part), 21204 (part), 21205 (part), 21206 (part), 21207 (part), 21208 (part), 21209 (part), 21210 (part), 21211 (part), 21212 (part), 21213 (part), 21214 (part), 21215 (part), 21218 (part), 21222 (part), 21223 (part), 21224 (part), 21225 (part), 21227 (part), 21228 (part), 21229 (part), 21230, 21231 (part), 21234 (part), 21236 (part), 21237 (part), 21239 (part), 21244 (part), 21281

* * *

FOURTH DISTRICT

ALBERT R. WYNN, Democrat, of Largo, MD; born in Philadelphia, PA, on September 10, 1951; graduated DuVal High School, Lanham, 1969; B.S., University of Pittsburgh, PA, 1973; attended Howard University Graduate School of Political Science, 1974; J.D., Georgetown University Law School, Washington, DC, 1977; attorney; admitted to the Maryland bar, 1979; Maryland House of Delegates, 1983–86; Maryland State Senate, 1987–92; executive director, Prince George's County Consumer Protection Commission, 1979–82; member: Kappa Alpha Psi Fraternity; J. Franklyn Bourne Bar Association; board of directors, Consumer Credit Counseling Service; Prince George's County Economic Development Corporation; Ploughman and Fisherman; delegate to the Democratic National Convention, 1984 and 1988; elected on November 3, 1992 to the 103rd Congress; reelected to each succeeding Congress.

Office Listings

http://www.house.gov/wynn albert.wynn@mail.house.gov

418 Cannon House Office Building, Washington, DC 20515–2004 225–8699
Administrative Assistant.—James C. Ballentine.
Legislative Director.—Claudia Arko.
Press Secretary.—Elena Temple.
Suite 316, 9200 Basil Court, Landover, MD 20785 .... (301) 350–5055
Suite 201, 8601 Georgia Avenue, Silver Spring, MD 20910 .... (301) 588–7328
Suite 208, 6009 Oxon Hill Road, Oxon Hill, MD 20745 .... (301) 839–5570

Counties: Montgomery (part) and Prince George's (part). CITIES AND TOWNSHIPS: Adelphi, Bladensburg, Bowie, Brentwood, Burtonsville, Camp Springs, Capital Heights, Clinton, District Heights, Forestville, Fort Washington, Glenarden, Glenn Dale, Hyattsville, Landover, Lanham, Marlow Heights, Mitchellville, Mount Rainier, Oxon Hill, Riverdale, Seabrook, Seat Pleasant, Silver Spring, Suitland, Takoma Park, Temple Hills, and Upper Marlboro. Population (1990), 597,690.

ZIP Codes: 20706 (part), 20710 (part), 20712, 20720 (part), 20721 (part), 20722 (part), 20731, 20735 (part), 20737 (part), 20743–47, 20748 (part), 20749–50, 20752–53, 20757, 20769 (part), 20772 (part), 20781 (part), 20782 (part), 20783 (part), 20784 (part), 20785, 20789, 20791, 20866 (part), 20901 (part), 20903 (part), 20904 (part), 20905 (part), 20906 (part), 20907–08, 20910 (part), 20911–14, 20916, 20918

* * *

FIFTH DISTRICT

STENY H. HOYER, Democrat, of Mechanicsville, MD; born in New York, NY, June 14, 1939; graduated Suitland High School; B.S., University of Maryland, 1963; J.D., Georgetown University Law Center, 1966; Honorary Doctor of Public Service, University of Maryland, 1988; admitted to the Maryland Bar Association, 1966; practicing attorney, 1966–90; Maryland State Senate, 1967–79; vice chairman, Prince George's County Senate delegation, 1967–69; chairman, Prince George's County Senate delegation, 1969–75; president, Maryland Senate, 1975–79; member, State Board for Higher Education, 1978–81; ranking member, Subcommittee on Treasury Postal/General Government; wife, Judith Pickett, deceased, February 6, 1997; three children: Susan, Stefany, and Anne; elected to the 97th Congress, May 19, 1981, by special election; reelected to each succeeding Congress; member: Appropriations Committee, House Oversight Committee, Joint Committee on Printing, Democratic Steering Committee, Commission on Security and Cooperation in Europe (Helsinki Commission).

Office Listings

1705 Longworth House Office Building, Washington, DC 20515–2005 225–4131
Administrative Assistant.—Betsy Bossart.
Legislative Director.—Melissa Schulman.
U.S. Federal Courthouse, Suite 310, 6500 Cherrywood Lane, Greenbelt, MD 20770 .... (301) 474–0119
Suite 101, 21A Industrial Park Drive, Waldorf, MD 20602 .... (301) 705–9633

Counties: Anne Arundel (part), Calvert, Charles, Prince George's (part), and St. Mary's. Population (1990), 597,681.

ZIP Codes: 20601–04, 20606–13, 20615–26, 20628–30, 20632, 20634, 20636–37, 20639–40, 20643, 20645–46, 20650, 20653, 20656–62, 20664, 20667, 20670, 20674–78, 20680, 20684–90, 20692–93, 20695, 20703–05, 20706 (part), 20707 (part), 20708–09, 20710 (part), 20711, 20714–19, 20720 (part), 20721 (part), 20722 (part), 20724–26, 20732–33, 20735 (part), 20736, 20737 (part), 20738, 20740–41, 20748 (part), 20751, 20754, 20755 (part), 20758, 20764–65, 20768, 20769 (part), 20770–71, 20772 (part), 20773, 20775–76, 20778–79, 20781 (part), 20782 (part), 20783 (part), 20784 (part), 20787–88, 20794 (part), 20903 (part), 21032 (part), 21035, 21037 (part), 21054 (part), 21106, 21113 (part), 21114 (part), 21140, 21401 (part)

* * *

SIXTH DISTRICT

ROSCOE G. BARTLETT, Republican, of Frederick, MD; born June 3, 1926 in Moreland, KY; House service, January 3, 1993 to present; rank, 77th (1 of 108); University of Maryland, Ph.D.; retired professor; engineer; married to Ellen Bartlett; 10 children; elected on November 3, 1992 to the 103rd Congress; reelected to each succeeding Congress.

Office Listings

322 Cannon House Office Building, Washington, DC 20515–2006 225–2721
Chief of Staff.—Jim Backlin.
Legislative Director.—Scott Plecs.
Office Manager/Scheduler/Deputy Press Secretary.—Sallie Taylor.
100 West Franklin Street, Hagerstown, MD 21740 .... (301) 797–6043
5831 Buckeystown Pike, Suite E, Frederick, MD 21704 .... (301) 694–3030
15 Main Street, Suite 110, Westminster, MD 21157 .... (410) 857–1115
50 Broadway, Frostburg, MD 21532 .... (301) 689–0034

Counties: Allegany, Carroll, Frederick, Garrett, Howard (part), and Washington. CITIES AND TOWNSHIPS: Ballenger Creek, Boonsboro, Braddock Heights, Bridgeport, Brunswick, Clover Hill, Columbia (part), Cresaptown-Bel Air, Cumberland, Discovery-Spring Garden, Eldersburg, Ellicott City (part), Emmitsburg, Frederick, Frostburg, Green Valley, Hagerstown, Halfway, Hampstead, Hancock, Jessup (part), La Vale, Linganore-Bartonsville, Long Meadow, Manchester, Middletown, Mount Aetna, Mount Airy, Mountain Lake Park, North Laurel (part), Oakland (Carroll Co.), Oakland (Garrett Co.), Savage-Guilford (part), Sykesville, Taneytown, Thurmont, Walkersville, Westernport, Westminster, Westminster South and Williamsport. Population (1990), 597,688.

ZIP Codes: 20701, 20723, 20759, 20763, 20777 (part), 20794 (part), 20833 (part), 20838 (part), 20839, 20841, 20842 (part), 20850 (part), 20854 (part), 20855 (part), 20871 (part), 20872 (part), 20874 (part), 21029, 21036, 21041, 21042 (part), 21043 (part), 21044 (part), 21045 (part), 21048, 21074 (part), 21079 (part), 21080, 21088, 21102, 21104 (part), 21107 (part), 21136 (part), 21155 (part), 21157–58, 21163 (part), 21183 (part), 21227 (part), 21501–05, 21520–24, 21528–32, 21536, 21538–43, 21545, 21550, 21555–57, 21560–62, 21623, 21629, 21701–05, 21710–11, 21713–14, 21716–23, 21725, 21727, 21733–34, 21737–38, 21740–42, 21750, 21754–59, 21762, 21764, 21766–70, 21771 (part), 21773–80, 21782–84, 21787–88, 21790–95, 21797–98, 26726 (part)

* * *

SEVENTH DISTRICT

ELIJAH EUGENE CUMMINGS, Democrat, of Baltimore, MD; born in Baltimore, on January 18, 1951; graduated, Baltimore City College High School, 1969; B.S., political science, Phi Beta Kappa, Howard University, Washington, DC, 1973; J.D., University of Maryland Law School, 1976; attorney; admitted to the Maryland bar in 1976; delegate, Maryland State Legislature, 1982–96; chairman, Maryland Legislative Black Caucus, 1984; speaker pro tempore, Maryland General Assembly, 1995–96; vice chairman, Constitutional and Administrative Law Committee; vice chairman, Economic Matters Committee; president, sophomore class, student government treasurer and student government president at Howard University; member: Governor's Commission on Black Males, New Psalmist Baptist Church in Baltimore, MD; founded the Maryland Bootcamp Aftercare Program in July 1991 to address the self-sufficiency of young male and female ex-offenders; active in civic affairs and recipient of numerous community awards; one child: Jennifer; committees: House Democratic Policy, National Security, International Affairs, Criminal Justice; subcommittees: Surface Transportation, Civil Service; elected to the 104th Congress by special election, April 1996; reelected to the 105th Congress.

Office Listings

http://www.house.gov/cummings

1632 Longworth House Office Building, Washington, DC 20515	225–4741
Chief of Staff.—Deidra Bishop.	FAX: 225–3178
Communications Director.—Anthony McCarthy.	
3000 Druid Park Drive, Baltimore, MD 21515	(410) 367–1900
	FAX: 367–5331
7900 Liberty Road, Baltimore, MD 21207	(410) 496–2010
	FAX: 496–2015
754 Frederick Road, Baltimore, MD 21228	(410) 719–8777
	FAX: 455–0110

County: Baltimore County (part) and Baltimore city (part). Population (1980), 527,485.

ZIP Codes: 21043 (part), 21104 (part), 21117 (part), 21133 (part), 21136 (part), 21163 (part), 21201 (part), 21202 (part), 21203, 21205 (part), 21206 (part), 21207, 21208 (part), 21209 (part), 21210 (part), 21211 (part), 21212 (part), 21213 (part), 21214 (part), 21215–18, 21223 (part), 21224 (part), 21227 (part), 21228–29, 21231 (part), 21235, 21239 (part), 21241, 21244, 21270, 21297–98

* * *

EIGHTH DISTRICT

CONSTANCE A. MORELLA, Republican, of Bethesda, MD; born in Somerville, MA, February 12, 1931; graduated, Somerville High School, 1948; A.B., Boston University, 1954; M.A., The American University, Washington, DC, 1967; professor, Montgomery College, 1970–86; honorary doctoral degrees from American University, Norwich University, Dickinson College, Mount Vernon College, and University of Maryland University College; member, policy committee of 1995 White House Conference on Aging; cochair, Congressional Coalition on Population and Development; cochair, Congressional Caucus on Women's Issues; cochair, Older Americans Caucus; delegate, Maryland General Assembly, 1979–86; trustee, Capitol College, Laurel, MD; former chair, Arms Control and Foreign Policy Caucus; charter member of Global Legislators for a Balanced Environment (GLOBE); married Anthony C. Morella, 1954; three children: Paul, Mark, and Laura; guardian of six children (of late sister): Christine, Catherine, Louise, Paul, Rachel, and Ursula; member: Government Reform and Oversight Committee; chair, Technology Subcommittee of Committee on Science; elected to the 100th Congress, November 4, 1986; reelected to each succeeding Congress.

Office Listings

rep.morella@mail.house.gov

106 Cannon House Office Building, Washington, DC 20515–2008	225–5341

FAX: 225–1389

Administrative Assistant.—William C. Miller.
Chief of Staff.—David A. Nathan.
Executive Assistant.—Patricia Donnelly.
Legislative Director.—Cindy Hall.

51 Monroe Street, No. 507, Rockville, MD 20850 .... (301) 424–3501
FAX: 424–5992

District Director.—Minnie Anderson.

County: MONTGOMERY COUNTY (part); cities and townships of Ashton, Barnesville, Beallsville, Bethesda, Boyds, Brinklow, Brookeville, Burtonsville, Cabin John, Chevy Chase, Clarksburg, Damascus, Derwood, Dickerson, Gaithersburg, Garrett Park, Germantown, Glen Echo, Highland, Kensington, Mount Airy (part), Olney, Poolesville, Potomac, Rockville, Sandy Spring, Silver Spring (part), Spencerville, and Wheaton (part). Population (1990), 597,682.

ZIP Codes: 20707 (part), 20777 (part), 20812, 20813–18, 20824–25, 20827, 20830, 20832, 20833 (part), 20837–39, 20841, 20842 (part), 20847–55, 20858–62, 20866 (part), 20868, 20871 (part), 20872, 20874–80, 20882, 20884–86, 20891, 20895–96, 20898, 20901 (part), 20902, 20904 (part), 20905 (part), 20906 (part), 20910 (part), 20915, 21771 (part)

MASSACHUSETTS

(Population 1995, 6,074,000)

SENATORS

EDWARD M. KENNEDY, Democrat, of Barnstable, MA; born in Boston, MA, February 22, 1932, son of Joseph P. and Rose F. Kennedy; graduated, Milton Academy, 1950; A.B., Harvard College, 1956; International Law School, The Hague, the Netherlands, 1958; LL.B., University of Virginia Law School, 1959; enlisted in the U.S. Army as a private and served in France and Germany, 1951–53; elected to the Senate, November 6, 1962, to fill the unexpired term of his brother John F. Kennedy; reelected November 3, 1964, November 3, 1970, November 2, 1976, November 2, 1982, November 8, 1988, and November 8, 1994; member: Labor and Human Resources, Judiciary, Armed Services, and Joint Economic committees; married to Victoria Reggie Kennedy; children: Kara, Edward M., Jr., Patrick J., Curran, and Caroline.

Office Listings

http://www.senate.gov/~kennedy senator@kennedy.senate.gov

315 Russell Senate Office Building, Washington, DC 20510–2101 224–4543
Administrative Assistant.—Gerard Kavanaugh. FAX: 224–2417
Legislative Director.—Carey Parker. TDD: 224–1819
John F. Kennedy Federal Building, 2400–A, Boston, MA 02203 .... (617) 565–3170
Administrative Assistant.—Barbara Souliotis. TDD: 565–4045

* * *

JOHN F. KERRY, Democrat, of Boston, MA; born in Denver, CO, December 11, 1943; graduated, St. Paul's School, Concord, NH, 1962; B.A., Yale University, New Haven, CT, 1966; J.D., Boston College Law School, Boston, MA, 1976; served, U.S. Navy, discharged with rank of lieutenant; decorations: Silver Star, Bronze Star with Combat "V", three Purple Hearts, various theatre campaign decorations; attorney, admitted to Massachusetts bar, 1976; appointed first assistant district attorney, Middlesex County, 1977; elected lieutenant governor, Massachusetts, 1982; married to Teresa Heinz; elected to the U.S. Senate, November 6, 1984 for the six-year term beginning January 3, 1985; reelected November 1990 and November 1996; appointed to Democratic Leadership for 104th and 105th Congresses; chairman, Steering Committee; committees: Banking, Housing, and Urban Affairs; Commerce, Science, and Transportation; Intelligence; Foreign Relations.

Office Listings

http://www.senate.gov/~kerry/index2.htm john__kerry@kerry.senate.gov

421 Russell Senate Office Building, Washington, DC 20510–2102 224–2742
Administrative Assistant.—David J. Leiter. FAX: 224–8525
Legislative Director.—Scott Bunton.
Personal Secretary.—Patricia Ferrone.
One Bowdoin Square, 10th Floor, Boston, MA 02114 .... (617) 565–8519
Suite 311, 222 Milliken Place, Fall River, MA 02722 .... (508) 677–0522

REPRESENTATIVES

FIRST DISTRICT

JOHN W. OLVER, Democrat, of Amherst, MA; born on September 3, 1936 in Honesdale, PA; B.S., Rensselaer Polytechnic Institute, 1955; M.A., Tufts University, 1956; taught for two years at Franklin Technical Institute, Boston, MA; Ph.D., Massachusetts Institute of Technology, 1961; chemistry professor, University of Massachusetts-Amherst; Massachusetts House, 1968–72; Massachusetts Senate, 1972–91; became first Democrat since the Spanish-American War to represent the First Congressional District, 1991; elected by special election on June 4, 1991 to fill the vacancy caused by the death of Silvio Conte; member: Budget Committee, Science Committee, Basic Research Subcommittee, Energy and Environment Subcommittee; married to Rose Olver; one daughter, Martha; elected on November 3, 1992 to the 103rd Congress; reelected to each succeeding Congress.

Office Listings

http://www.house.gov/olver olver@hr.house.gov

1027 Longworth House Office Building, Washington, DC 20515 225–5335
Chief of Staff/Legislative Director.—Hunter Ridgway.
Press Secretary.—Leslie Lillard.
Legislative Correspondent.—Eleanor Thompson.
Scheduler.—Patrick Riccards.
Administrative Assistant.—Jonathan D. Klein. FAX: 226–1224
881 Main Street, Room 223, Fitchburg, MA 01420 .... (508) 343–0777
187 High Street, Holyoke, MA 01040 .... (413) 532–7010
78 Center Street, Pittsfield, MA 01201 .... (413) 442–0946

Counties: Berkshire, Franklin, Hampden (part), Hampshire (part), Middlesex (part), and Worcester (part). Population (1990), 601,643.

ZIP Codes: 01002, 01004–05, 01007–08, 01011–12, 01026–27, 01029, 01031–34, 01037–41, 01050, 01054, 01059, 01066, 01068, 01070–74, 01075 (part), 01077, 01082 (part), 01084–86, 01088–90, 01093–94, 01096–98, 01201–03, 01220, 01222–23, 01225–27, 01229–30, 01235–38, 01240, 01242–45, 01247, 01252–60, 01262, 01264, 01266–67, 01270, 01301–02, 01330–31, 01337–44, 01346–47, 01349–51, 01354–55, 01360, 01364, 01366–68, 01370, 01373, 01375–76, 01378–80, 01420, 01430–31, 01436, 01438, 01440–41, 01452–53, 01462 (part), 01466, 01468–69, 01473–75, 01477, 01531, 01535, 01585

* * *

SECOND DISTRICT

RICHARD E. NEAL, Democrat, of Springfield, MA; born in Springfield, February 14, 1949; graduated, Springfield Technical High School, 1968; B.A., American International College, Springfield, 1972; M.A., University of Hartford Barney School of Business and Public Administration, CT, 1976; instructor and lecturer; assistant to mayor of Springfield, 1973–78; Springfield City Council, 1978–84; mayor, city of Springfield, 1984–88; member: Massachusetts Mayors Association; Adult Education Council; American International College Alumni Association; Boys Club Alumni Association; Emily Bill Athletic Association; Cancer Crusade; John Boyle O'Reilly Club; United States Conference of Mayors; Valley Press Club; Solid Waste Advisory Committee for the State of Massachusetts; Committee on Leadership and Government; Mass Jobs Council; trustee: Springfield Libraries and Museums Association, Springfield Red Cross, Springfield YMCA; married to the former Maureen Conway; four children: Rory Christopher, Brendan Conway, Maura Katherine, and Sean Richard; elected on November 8, 1988, to the 101st Congress; reelected to each succeeding Congress.

Office Listings

http://www.house.gov/neal

2236 Rayburn House Office Building, Washington, DC 20515–2102 225–5601
Administrative Assistant.—Ann Brozek. FAX: 225–8112
Executive Assistant.—JoAnn Healy.
Press Secretary.—Bill Tranghese.
Federal Building, Room 309, 1550 Main Street, Springfield, MA 01103–1422 .... (413) 785–0325
District Manager.—James Leydon.
4 Congress Street, Milford, MA 01757 .... (508) 634–8198
Office Manager.—Virginia Purcell.

Counties: Hampden (part), Hampshire (part), Norfolk (part), and Worcester (part). Population (1990), 601,642.

ZIP Codes: 01001, 01009–10, 01013–14, 01020–22, 01028, 01030, 01035–36, 01053, 01056–57, 01060–61, 01063, 01069, 01075 (part), 01079–81, 01082 (part), 01083, 01092, 01095, 01101–09, 01115–16, 01118–19, 01128–29, 01138–39, 01151, 01501 (part), 01504, 01506–09, 01515–16, 01518, 01521, 01524, 01526–27, 01529, 01537–38, 01540, 01542, 01550, 01562, 01566, 01569–71, 01586, 01588 (part), 01590, 01611, 01747, 01756, 01757 (part), 02019 (part), 02038 (part)

* * *

THIRD DISTRICT

JIM McGOVERN, Democrat, of Worcester, MA; born in Worcester, November 20, 1959; B.A., M.P.A., American University; legislative director and senior aide to Congressman Joe Moakley (D–South Boston); led the 1989 investigation into the murders of six Jesuit priests and two lay women in El Salvador; managed George McGovern's (D–SD) 1984 presidential campaign in Massachusetts and delivered his nomination speech at the Democratic National

Convention; board of directors, Jesuit International Volunteers; former volunteer, Mt. Carmel House, an emergency shelter for battered and abused women; married to Lisa Murray McGovern; committee: Transportation and Infrastructure; subcommittees: Surface Transportation; Water and the Environment; elected to the 105th Congress.

Office Listings

james.mcgovern@mail.house.gov

512 Cannon House Office Building, Washington, DC 20515–2103 225–6101
Chief of Staff.—Bernie Robinson. FAX: 225–5759
Senior Legislative Assistant: Foreign Affairs, Education.—Cindy Buhl.
Press Secretary.—John Del Cecato.
Special Assistant/Office Manager.—Christine Leonard.
34 Mechanic Street, First Floor, Worcester, MA 01608 .... (508) 831–7356
District Director.—Gladys Rodriguez-Parker. FAX: 754–0982
District Representatives.—Joseph Bisceglia, Vicki Zwerdling.
1 Park Street, Attleboro, MA 02703. .... (508) 431–8025.
District Representative.—Shirley Cohelo. FAX: 431–8017
218 South Main Street, Room 204, Fall River, MA 02721 .... (508) 677–0140
District Representative.—Patrick Norton. FAX: 677–0992

Counties: Bristol (part), Middlesex (part), Norfolk (part), and Worcester (part). CITIES AND TOWNSHIPS: Attleborough, North Attleborough, Auburn (part), Berlin, Boylston, West Boylston, Clinton, Dartmouth, Fall River, Foxborough, Franklin, Grafton, Holden, Holliston, Hopkinton, Lancaster, Mansfield, Medway, Northborough, Northbridge, Paxton, Plainville, Princeton, Rutland, Seekonk, Shrewsbury, Somerset, Sterling, Swansea, Upton, Westborough, Westport, Worcester, and Wrentham. Population (1990), 601,642.

ZIP Codes: 01501 (part), 01503, 01505, 01510, 01517, 01519–20, 01522–23, 01532, 01534, 01536, 01539, 01541, 01543, 01545, 01560–61, 01564, 01568, 01580–83, 01587, 01588 (part), 01601–10, 01612–15, 01655, 01721 (part), 01746, 01748, 01752 (part), 01757 (part), 01784, 02019 (part), 02031, 02035 (part), 02038 (part), 02048 (part), 02053, 02070, 02093, 02703 (part), 02714, 02721 (part), 02722, 02723 (part), 02724–26, 02740 (part), 02747 (part), 02748 (part), 02760–63, 02766 (part), 02771, 02777, 02790 (part), 02791

* * *

FOURTH DISTRICT

BARNEY FRANK, Democrat, of Newton, MA; born in Bayonne, NJ, March 31, 1940; graduated, Bayonne High School, 1957; B.A., Harvard College, 1962; graduate student in political science, Harvard University, 1962–67; teaching fellow in government, Harvard College, 1963–66; J.D., Harvard University, 1977; admitted to the Massachusetts bar, 1979; executive assistant to Mayor Kevin White of Boston, 1968–71; administrative assistant to U.S. Congressman Michael F. Harrington, 1971–72; member, Massachusetts Legislature, 1973–80; elected to the 97th Congress, November 4, 1980; reelected to each succeeding Congress.

Office Listings

http://www.house.gov/frank

2210 Rayburn House Office Building, Washington, DC 20515–2104 225–5931
Administrative Assistant.—Peter Kovar. FAX: 225–0182
Executive Assistant.—Maria Giesta.
29 Crafts Street, Newton, MA 02158 .... (617) 332–3920
District Director.—Dorothy Reichard.
222 Milliken Place, Third Floor, Fall River, MA 02721 .... (508) 674–3551
89 Main Street, Bridgewater, MA 02324 .... (508) 697–9403
558 Pleasant Street, Room 309, New Bedford, MA 02740 .... (508) 999–6462

Counties: Bristol (part), Middlesex (part), Norfolk (part), and Plymouth (part). CITIES AND TOWNSHIPS: Acushnet, Berkley, Bridgewater, Brookline, Carver, Dighton, Dover, East Bridgewater, Easton (part), Fairhaven, Fall River (part), Foxboro (part), Freetown, Halifax, Hanson, Lakeville, Mansfield (part), Marion, Mattapoisett, Middleborough, Millis, New Bedford, Newton, Norfolk, Norton, Pembroke, Plympton, Raynham, Rehoboth, Rochester, Rockland (part), Sharon, Sherborn, Wareham, Wellesley, and West Bridgewater. Population (1990), 601,642.

ZIP Codes: 01770, 02030, 02035 (part), 02048 (part), 02054, 02056, 02067, 02146–47, 02158–62, 02164–68, 02181, 02195, 02324, 02327, 02330, 02333, 02337–38, 02341, 02346–47, 02350, 02356 (part), 02358–59, 02366–67, 02370 (part), 02375 (part), 02379, 02532 (part), 02538, 02571, 02576, 02702, 02712, 02715, 02717, 02719–20, 02721 (part), 02723 (part), 02738–46, 02764, 02766 (part), 02767–70, 02779–80, 02790 (part)

FIFTH DISTRICT

MARTIN T. MEEHAN, Democrat, of Lowell, MA; born in Lowell, December 30, 1956; graduated from Lowell High School, 1974; B.A., University of Lowell, 1978; M.P.A., Suffolk University, Boston, MA, 1981; J.D., Suffolk University Law School, 1986; attorney; admitted to the Massachusetts bar, 1986; First Assistant District Attorney for Middlesex County; Deputy Secretary of State; married Ellen Murphy, July 1996; elected on November 3, 1992 to the 103rd Congress; reelected to each succeeding Congress.

Office Listings

http://www.house.gov/meehan mtmeehan@hr.house.gov

318 Cannon House Office Building, Washington, DC 20515–2105 225–3411
FAX: 226–0771
Administrative Assistant.—Steve Joncas.
Press Secretary.—Will Keyser.
11 Kearney Square, Lowell, MA 01852 .... (508) 459–0101
Bay State Building, Suite 806, 11 Lawrence Street, Lawrence, MA 01840 .... (508) 681–6200
Walker Building, Room 102, 255 Main Street, Mastborough, MA 01752 .... (508) 460–9292

Counties: Essex (part), Middlesex (part), and Worcester (part). Population (1990), 601,643.

ZIP Codes: 01432–33, 01450–51, 01460, 01462 (part), 01463–64, 01467, 01471–72, 01525, 01718–20, 01721 (part), 01730 (part), 01740–41, 01742 (part), 01745, 01749, 01752 (part), 01754, 01772, 01773 (part), 01775–76, 01778 (part), 01810, 01821–22, 01824, 01826–27, 01840–43, 01844 (part), 01850–54, 01862–63, 01865–66, 01876, 01879, 01886, 02193 (part)

* * *

SIXTH DISTRICT

JOHN F. TIERNEY, Democrat, of Salem, MA; born on September 18, 1951 in Salem; graduated, Salem High School; B.A., political science, Salem State College, 1973; J.D., Suffolk University, 1976; attorney, admitted to the Massachusetts bar in 1976; sole practitioner, 1976–80; partner, Tierney, Kalis and Lucas, 1981–96; member: Salem Chamber of Commerce, 1976–96 (president, 1995); trustee, Salem State College, 1992–97; married Patrice M. Tierney, 1997; elected to the 105th Congress.

Office Listings

120 Cannon House Office Building, Washington, DC 20515–2106 225–8029
FAX: 225–5915
Executive Assistant.—Mary Flanagan.
Chief of Staff/Press Secretary.—David Williams.
Legislative Specialist.—Harry Hoglander.
Legislative Assistant.—Laura Geer.
Legislative Correspondent.—Allen Segal.
17 Peabody Square, Peabody, MA 01960 .... (508) 531–1669
FAX: 531–1996
District Director.—Gary Barrett.
Room 410, Lynn City Hall, Lynn, MA 01902 .... (617) 595–7375
FAX: 595–7492
160 Main Street, Haverhill, MA 01830 .... (508) 469–1942
FAX: 469–9021

Counties: Essex, Middlesex. CITIES AND TOWNSHIPS: Amesbury, Bedford, Beverly, Boxford, Burlington, Danvers, Essex, Georgetown, Gloucester, Groveland, Hamilton, Haverhill, Ipswich, Lynn, Lynnfield, Manchester by the Sea, Marblehead, Merrimac, Middletown, Nahant, Newbury, Newburyport, North Andover, North Reading, Peabody, Reading (part), Rockport, Rowley, Salem, Salisbury, Saugus, Swampscott, Topsfield, Wenham, West Newbury, and Wilmington

Zip Codes: 01803, 01830, 01833, 01838, 01845, 01860, 01864, 01867, 01887, 01901, 01906–8, 01913, 01915, 01921, 01923, 01929–30, 01938, 01940, 01944–45, 01949–50, 01960, 01966, 01969–70, 01983–85

* * *

SEVENTH DISTRICT

EDWARD J. MARKEY, Democrat, of Malden, MA; born in Malden, July 11, 1946; graduated, Malden Catholic High School, 1964; B.A., Boston College, 1968; J.D., Boston College Law School, 1972; lawyer; served in the U.S. Army Reserves, 1968–73; member, Massachusetts House of Representatives, 1973–76; elected to the 94th Congress, November 2, 1976, to fill the vacancy caused by the death of Representative Torbert H. Macdonald, and at the same time elected to the 95th Congress; reelected to each succeeding Congress.

Office Listings
http://www.house.gov/markey

2133 Rayburn House Office Building, Washington, DC 20515–2107 225–2836
Administrative Assistant.—David Moulton.
Executive Assistant.—Nancy Morrissey.
Legislative Director.—Jeff Duncan.
5 High Street, Suite 101, Medford, MA 02155 .... (617) 396–2900
188 Concord Street, Suite 102, Framingham, MA 01701 .... (508) 875–2900

Counties: Middlesex (part) and Suffolk (part). Population (1990), 601,642.

ZIP Codes: 01701, 01721 (part), 01742 (part), 01760, 01773, 01778 (part), 01801, 01867 (part), 01880, 01888, 01890, 02140 (part), 02144 (part), 02145 (part), 02148–49, 02151–52, 02154–55, 02172 (part), 02173–76, 02180, 02181 (part), 02193 (part), 02254

* * *

EIGHTH DISTRICT

JOSEPH P. KENNEDY II, Democrat, of Boston, MA; born in Brighton, MA, September 24, 1952; son of Senator Robert F. Kennedy of New York; nephew of President John F. Kennedy; nephew of Senator Edward M. Kennedy of Massachusetts; B.A., University of Massachusetts, Amherst, 1976; community services administrator, 1977–79; founder and president, Citizens Energy Group, 1979–86, Citizens Conservation Corps, 1981; chairman, Canadian Robert F. Kennedy Memorial; married Beth Kelly; two children: Joseph P. III and Matthew; elected to the 100th Congress on November 4, 1986; reelected to each succeeding Congress.

Office Listings
http://www.house.gov/josephkennedy

2242 Rayburn House Office Building, Washington, DC 20515–2110 225–5111
Administrative Assistant.—Matt O'Neil. FAX: 225–9322
Scheduler/Personal Secretary.—Beth Kennedy.
Press Secretary.—Amy Simmons.
Professional Staff.—Jonathan Miller.
The Schrafft Center, Suite 605, 525 Main Street, Charlestown, MA 02129 .... (617) 242–0200
801 Tremont Street, Roxbury, MA 02118 .... (617) 445–1281

Counties: Middlesex (part) and Suffolk (part). CITIES AND TOWNSHIPS: Belmont, Boston, Cambridge, Chelsea, Roxbury, Somerville, and Watertown. Population (1990), 601,643.

ZIP Codes: 02108 (part), 02112, 02114 (part), 02115, 02116 (part), 02117, 02118 (part), 02119 (part), 02120, 02121 (part), 02122 (part), 02123, 02124 (part), 02125 (part), 02126 (part), 02128–29, 02130 (part), 02131 (part), 02133–35, 02136 (part), 02138–39, 02140 (part), 02141–43, 02144 (part), 02145 (part), 02146 (part), 02149 (part), 02150 (part), 02151 (part), 02155 (part), 02163, 02172 (part), 02178–79, 02199, 02208–09, 02215 (part), 02238, 02258, 02272

* * *

NINTH DISTRICT

JOHN JOSEPH MOAKLEY, Democrat, of South Boston, MA; born April 27, 1927; graduated from Suffolk University Law School, 1956 with doctor of jurisprudence; served in the U.S. Navy, 1943–46; member: Massachusetts and District of Columbia bars; began the practice of law in Boston, 1957; elected to the Massachusetts House of Representatives, 1952, and served as Democratic majority whip, 1957; elected to the Massachusetts State Senate, 1964; member, Boston City Council, 1971; honorary doctorate, public administration, from Suffolk University, 1977; honorary doctorate of laws, New England School of Law; honorary doctorate, political science, Northeastern University; married Evelyn Duffy of Cambridge, MA, 1957; elected to the 93rd Congress, November 7, 1972; reelected to each succeeding Congress; ranking Democrat minority, Rules Committee.

Office Listings

http://www.house.gov/moakley jmoakley@hr.house.gov

235 Cannon House Office Building, Washington, DC 20515–2109 225–8273
Chief of Staff.—Kevin Ryan. FAX: 225–3984
Legislative Director.—Ellen Harrington.
Press Secretary.—Karin Walser.
Office Manager.—Steve LaRose.
World Trade Center, Suite 220, Boston, MA 02110 .... (617) 565–2920
District Director.—Fred Clark.
Crocker Building, 4 Court Street, Taunton, MA 02780 .... (617) 824–6676

Counties: Bristol (part), Norfolk (part), Plymouth (part), and Suffolk (part). Population (1990), 601,643.

ZIP Codes: 02021, 02026, 02030 (part), 02032, 02052, 02062, 02071–72, 02081 (part), 02090, 02101, 02107, 02108 (part), 02109–11, 02113, 02114 (part), 02116 (part), 02118 (part), 02119 (part), 02121 (part), 02122 (part), 02124 (part), 02125 (part), 02126 (part), 02127, 02130 (part), 02131 (part), 02132, 02136 (part), 02137, 02153, 02156, 02177, 02184, 02186 (part), 02187, 02190 (part), 02192, 02194, 02203, 02205, 02210, 02212, 02222, 02269, 02334, 02356 (part), 02357, 02368 (part), 02375 (part), 02401 (part), 02402 (part), 02403–05, 02718, 02767 (part), 02780 (part)

* * *

TENTH DISTRICT

WILLIAM D. DELAHUNT, Democrat, of Quincy, MA; born in Boston, July 18, 1941; B.A., political science, Middlebury College, VT; M.A., J.D., Boston College Law School, 1967; U.S. Coast Guard Reserves, 1963–71; admitted to the Massachusetts bar in 1967 and began practice in Boston; assistant majority leader, Massachusetts House of Representatives, 1973–75; Norfolk County District Attorney, 1975–96; president, Massachusetts District Attorneys Association, 1985; invitee, Council of Young American Political Leaders fact-finding mission to Poland, 1979; named citizen of the Year by South Shore Coalition for Human Rights, 1983; delegate, Human Rights Project on justice system fact-finding mission to Cuba, 1988; invitee, Anti-Defamation League of B'nai B'rith fact-finding mission to Israel, 1990; chairman, development committee, South Shore Association for Retarded Citizens; Democratic State Committeeman, Norfolk District; president, Police Athletic League; advisory board member, Jane Doe Safety Fund; honoree of Boston Area Rape Crisis Center for contribution to preventing sexual assault, 1993; New England Region honoree, Anti-Defamation League, 1994; Massachusetts Bar Association Public Service Award, 1994; member, board of directors, RYKA Rose Foundation; two daughters, Kirsten and Kara; elected to the 105th Congress.

Office Listings

1517 Longworth House Office Building, Washington, DC 20515 225–3111
Chief of Staff.—Steve Schwadron. FAX: 225–5658
146 Main Street, Hyannis, MA 02601 .... (508) 771–0666
Regional Representative.—Mark Forest.
15 Cottage Avenue, Fourth Floor, Quincy, MA 02169 .... (617) 770–3700
Regional Representative.—Paul O'Sullivan.
166 Main Street, Brockton, MA 02401 .... (508) 584–6666
225 Water Street, Plymouth, MA 02360 .... (508) 747–5500

Counties: Barnstable, Dukes, Nantucket, Norfolk (part), and Plymouth (part). Population (1990), 601,642.

ZIP Codes: 02018, 02020, 02025, 02040–41, 02043, 02045, 02047, 02050–51, 02055, 02059–61, 02065–66, 02169–71, 02186 (part), 02188–89, 02190 (part), 02191, 02322, 02331–32, 02338 (part), 02339, 02343, 02345, 02351, 02360–62, 02364, 02368 (part), 02370 (part), 02371, 02381–82, 02401 (part), 02402 (part), 02403, 02532 (part), 02534–37, 02539–43, 02551, 02552–54, 02556–57, 02559, 02560–65, 02568, 02573–75, 02584, 02601, 02630–39, 02640–55, 02657, 02659–64, 02666–73, 02675, 02703 (part), 02713

MICHIGAN

(Population 1995, 9,549,000)

SENATORS

CARL M. LEVIN, Democrat, of Detroit, MI; born in Detroit, June 28, 1934; graduated, Central High School, Detroit, 1952; Swarthmore College, Swarthmore, PA, 1956; Harvard Law School, Boston, MA, 1959; lawyer; Grossman, Hyman and Grossman, Detroit, 1959–64; assistant attorney general and general counsel for Michigan Civil Rights Commission, 1964–67; chief appellate defender for city of Detroit, 1968–69; counsel, Schlussel, Lifton, Simon, Rands and Kaufman, 1971–73; counsel, Jaffe, Snider, Raitt, Garratt and Heuer, 1978–79; admitted to the Michigan bar in 1959; member, City Council of Detroit, 1969–77; president, City Council of Detroit, 1974–77; member: Congregation T'Chiyah; American, Michigan and Detroit bar associations; former instructor at Wayne State University and the University of Detroit; married the former Barbara Halpern, 1961; three daughters: Kate, Laura, and Erica; elected to the U.S. Senate, November 7, 1978, for the six-year term beginning January 3, 1979; reelected November 6, 1984, November 6, 1990, and November 5, 1996.

Office Listings

http://www.senate.gov/~levin senator@levin.senate.gov

459 Russell Senate Office Building, Washington, DC 20510–2202 224–6221
Administrative Assistant.—Gordon Kerr.
Legislative Director.—Rich Arenberg.
Executive Secretary.—Helen Galen.
Press Secretary.—Kathleen McShea.
McNamara Building, Room 1860, 477 Michigan Avenue, Detroit, MI 48226 .... (313) 226–6020
Federal Building, Room 720, 110 Michigan Street, NW, Grand Rapids, MI 49503 (616) 456–2531
1810 Michigan National Tower, 124 West Allegan Street Lansing, MI 48933 .... (517) 377–1508
Suite 303, 623 Ludington Street, Escanaba, MI 49829 .... (906) 789–0052
301 East Genesee, Saginaw, MI 48607 .... (517) 754–2494
Federal Building, Room 102, 145 Water Street, Alpena, MI 49707 .... (517) 354–5520
30500 VanDyke, Suite 206, Warren, MI 48093 .... (810) 573–9145
15100 Northline Road, Room 107, Southgate, MI 48195 .... (313) 285–8596
207 Grandview Parkway, Suite 104, Traverse City, MI 49684 .... (616) 947–9569

* * *

SPENCER ABRAHAM, Republican, of Auburn Hills, MI; born in East Lansing, MI, June 12, 1952; graduated, East Lansing High School; graduated, Michigan State University, 1974; J.D., Harvard Law School, Cambridge, MA, 1978; admitted to District of Columbia and State of Michigan bars; chairman, Michigan GOP, 1983–89; cochairman, NRCC, 1990–92; office counsel, Miller Canfield, Paddock, and Stone, 1992–94; deputy chief of staff to Vice President Quayle, 1990; founder and board member, Federalist Society; founder and president, *Harvard Journal of Law and Public Policy*; married to Jane Hershey Abraham; three children: Betsy, Julie, and Spencer; committees: Budget; Commerce, Science, and Transportation; Judiciary; elected to the 104th Congress.

Office Listings

http://www.senate.gov/~abraham michigan@abraham.senate.gov

329 Dirksen Senate Office Building, Washington, DC 20510–2203 224–4822
Chief of Staff.—Jim Pitts. FAX: 224–8834
Legislative Director.—Cesar Conda.
Press Secretary.—Joe McMonigle.
Office Manager.—Katja Bullock.
3738 28th Street SE, Grand Rapids, MI 49512 .... (616)975–1112
FAX: 975–1119
200 North Capitol Avenue, Lansing, MI 48933 .... (517) 484–1984
FAX: 484–3099
202 West Washington Street, Marquette, MI 49855 .... (906) 226–9466
FAX: 226–9464
301 East Genesee Street, Saginaw, MI 48607 .... (517) 752–4400
FAX: 752–4492
26222 Telegraph Road, Southfield, MI 48034 .... (810) 350–0510
State Director.—Laurie Bink. FAX: 350–0420

REPRESENTATIVES

FIRST DISTRICT

BART T. STUPAK, Democrat, of Menominee, MI; born in Milwaukee, WI, on February 29, 1952; graduated, Gladstone High School, Gladstone, MI, 1970; B.S., Saginaw Valley State College, 1977; J.D., Thomas Cooley Law School, 1981; attorney; admitted to the Michigan bar, 1981; Michigan State House of Representatives, 1989–90; member: Elks Club; State Employees Retirement Association; Sons of the American Legion; Wildlife Unlimited; National Rifle Association; Knights of Columbus; national committeeman, Boy Scouts of America; married to the former Laurie Ann Olsen; two children: Ken and Bart, Jr.; elected on November 3, 1992 to the 103rd Congress; reelected to each succeeding Congress.

Office Listings

http://www.house.gov/stupak stupak@hr.house.gov

1410 Longworth House Office Building, Washington, DC 20515–2201	225–4735 FAX: 225–4744
Chief of Staff.—Jim Hart.	
Legislative Director.—Dave Buchanan.	
Press Secretary.—Bob Meissner.	
District Administrator.—Scott Schloegel.	
1120 East Front Street, Suite D, Traverse City, MI 49686	(616) 929–4711
902 Ludington Street, Escanaba, MI 49829	(906) 786–4504
1229 West Washington, Marquette, MI 49855	(906) 228–3700
111 East Chisholm, Alpena, MI 49707	(517) 356–0690
2 South Street, Suite 3, Crystal Falls, MI 49920	(906) 875–3751
616 Sheldon Avenue, Room 213, Houghton, MI 49931	(906) 482–1371

Counties: Alger, Alpena, Antrim, Baraga, Benzie, Charlevoix, Cheboygan, Chippewa, Crawford (part), Delta, Dickinson, Emmet, Gogebic, Grand Traverse, Houghton, Iron, Kalkaska, Keweenaw, Leelanau, Luce, Mackinac, Marquette, Menominee, Montmorency, Ontonagon, Otsego, Presque Isle, and Schoolcraft. Population (1990), 580,956.

ZIP Codes: 48619, 49610–13, 49615–17, 49620–22, 49627–30, 49633, 49635–37, 49640, 49643, 49646–50, 49653–54, 49659, 49664, 49666, 49670, 49673–74, 49676, 49680, 49682, 49683 (part), 49684–85, 49690, 49701, 49705–07, 49709–13, 49715–30, 49733, 49735–37, 49738 (part), 49740, 49743–49, 49751–53, 49755, 49756 (part), 49757, 49759–62, 49764–66, 49768–70, 49774–77, 49779–83, 49788–93, 49795–97, 49799, 49801–02, 49805–08, 49812–22, 49825–27, 49829, 49831, 49833–41, 49843, 49845, 49847–49, 49852–55, 49858, 49861–64, 49866, 49868–74, 49876–81, 49883–87, 49890–96, 49901–03, 49905, 49908, 49910–13, 49915–22, 49924–25, 49927, 49929–31, 49934–35, 49938, 49942–43, 49945–48, 49950, 49952–53, 49955, 49958–65, 49967–71

* * *

SECOND DISTRICT

PETER HOEKSTRA, Republican, of Holland, MI; born in Groningen, the Netherlands, on October 30, 1953; graduated, Holland Christian High School; B.A., Hope College, Holland, 1975; M.B.A., University of Michigan, 1977; vice president for product management, Herman Miller, Inc.; married to the former Diane Johnson; three children: Erin, Allison, and Bryan; elected on November 3, 1992 to the 103rd Congress; reelected to each succeeding Congress.

Office Listings

http://www.house.gov/hoekstra tellhoek@hr.house.gov

1122 Longworth House Office Building, Washington, DC 20515–2202	225–4401 FAX: 226–0779
Administrative Assistant.—Amy Plaster.	
Scheduler/Executive Assistant.—Cindy Harrington.	
District Director of Policy.—Bill Huizenga.	
Press Secretary.—Jon Brandt.	
Legislative Counsel.—Chris LaGrand.	
Suite 320, 31 East Eighth Street, Holland, MI 49423	(616) 395–0030
900 Third Street, Suite 203, Muskegon, MI 40440	(616) 722–8386
210½ North Mitchell Street, Cadillac, MI 49601	(616) 775–0050

Counties: Allegan (part), Barry (part), Lake, Manistee, Mason, Muskegon, Newaygo, Oceana, Ottawa, and Wexford. Population (1990), 580,956.

ZIP Codes: 48462 (part), 49010 (part), 49035, 49046 (part), 49058 (part), 49060 (part), 49070, 49078 (part), 49080 (part), 49303–04, 49307, 49309, 49311–14, 49315 (part), 49318, 49323 (part), 49327–28, 49330, 49333 (part), 49335, 49337–38, 49344, 49348 (part), 49349, 49401–06, 49408–12, 49415–31, 49434–37, 49440–46, 49448–49, 49451–61, 49463–64, 49504, 49601, 49613–14, 49618–20, 49623, 49625–26, 49634, 49638, 49642, 49644–45, 49649, 49656–57, 49660, 49663 (part), 49668, 49675, 49683 (part), 49689

THIRD DISTRICT

VERNON J. EHLERS, Republican, of Grand Rapids, MI; born Feburary 6, 1934 in Pipestone, MN; educated at home by his parents; attended Calvin College, Ph.D. in nuclear physics from University of California at Berkeley; tenure of service in teaching, scientific research, and community service; NATO post-doctoral research fellow; research physicist at Lawrence Berkeley Laboratory and lecturer in physics at the University of California; named an Outstanding Educator of the Year, 1970–73; co-authored two books on the environment: *Earthkeeping in the '90s: Stewardship of Creation* and *Earthkeeping: Christian Stewardship of Natural Resources;* co-authored two books on world hunger; elected to the Kent County Commission, 1975; elected to the State House of Representatives, 1983; appointed to INTERSET, a science advisory committee; chairman, National Conference of State Legislatures Environment Committee; science advisor to then-Congressman Gerald Ford; president of his class during the 104th Congress, midwest regional vice president during the 103rd Congress; serves as a member of the House Republican Transition Team; assigned to lead efforts in revamping the U.S. House of Representatives computer system; full-time career in public office, 1983; member and former elder of Eastern Avenue Christian Reformed Church, Grand Rapids; married to the former Johanna Meulink; four children: Heidi, Brian, Marla, and Todd; vice chairman: Science Committee, House Oversight Committee; member: Transportation and Infrastructure Committee, Federal EPA Clean Air Act Advisory Committee; chaired Senate Natural Resources and Environmental Affairs Committee, Senate Committee on Public and Mental Health, Senate Appropriations subcommittees on Higher Education and Public Health; elected to the 103rd Congress, December, 1993 in a special election; reelected to each succeeding Congress.

Office Listings

http://www.house.gov/ehlers@hr.house.gov congehlr@hr.house.gov

1717 Longworth House Office Building, Washington, DC 20515–2203 225–3831
Administrative Assistant.—Bill McBride.
Office Manager.—Loraine Kehl.
166 Federal Building, Grand Rapids, MI 49503 .... (616) 451–8383
District Administrator.—Beth Bandstra.

Counties: Allegan, Barry (part), Ionia, and Kent, Montcalm, Ottowa. CITIES AND TOWNSHIPS: Ada, Allengan, Allendale, Alto, Bailey (part), Belding, Belmont, Byron Center, Caledonia, Cannonsburg, Casnovia, Cedar Springs, Comstock Park, Clarksville, Conklin, Delton (part), Dorr, Fenwick (part), Freeport, Gowen, Grandville, Grand Rapids, Grant, Greenville (part), Hastings, Hubbardston (part), Ionia, Kent City, Kentwood, Lake Odessa, Lowell, Lyons, Marne, Middleville, Muir, Nashville, Orleans, Palo, Pewamo, Portland, Rockford, Sand Lake, Saranac, Smyrna, Sparta, Sunfield, Wayland, Woodland, and Wyoming. Population (1990), 580,956.

ZIP Codes: 48809, 48815, 48834, 48838, 48845–46, 48849 (part), 48851, 48860, 48865, 48870, 48873, 48875–76, 48881, 48887, 48890, 48897, 49010, 49046 (part), 49058 (part), 49073 (part), 49301–03, 49306, 49315–19, 49321, 49323 (part), 49325–27, 49330–31, 49333 (part), 49341, 49343, 49345, 49348, 49351, 49355–57, 49401, 49403, 49418, 49435, 49468, 49501, 49503–10, 49512, 49514–16, 49518, 49523, 49530, 49544, 49546, 49548, 49550, 49555, 49560, 49588, 49851, 49880

* * *

FOURTH DISTRICT

DAVE CAMP, Republican, of Midland, MI; born in Midland, July 9, 1953; graduated, H.H. Dow High School, Midland, 1971; B.A., Albion College, Albion, MI, 1975, *magna cum laude*; J.D., University of California San Diego, 1978; attorney, member of State Bar of Michigan, State Bar of California, District of Columbia bar, U.S. Supreme Court; U.S. District Court, Eastern District of Michigan and Southern District of California; Midland County Bar Association; law practice, Midland, 1979–91; Special Assistant Attorney General, 1980–84; administrative assistant to Congressman Bill Schuette, Michigan's 10th Congressional District, 1985–87; State Representative, Michigan's 102nd district, 1989–91; former president of Young Business People's Group; former member, Michigan's 10th Congressional District Republican Executive Committee; member, Midland County Republican Executive Committee; appointed to House Committee on Agriculture, Committee on Small Business; member, Committee on Ways and Means; assistant majority whip; National Republican Congressional Committee, Executive Committee; Rural Health Care Coalition; married September 10, 1994 to Nancy Keil; elected to 102nd Congress, November 6, 1990; reelected to each succeeding Congress.

Office Listings

http://www.house.gov/camp davecamp@hr.house.gov

137 Cannon House Office Building, Washington, DC 20515–2204 225–3561
FAX: 225–9679
Chief of Staff.—John Guzik.
Communications Director.—Jennifer Murray.
Legislative Director/Administrative Assistant.—Behrends Foster.
Scheduler.—Tamara Syrek.
135 Ashman Street, Midland, MI, 48640 .... (517) 631–2552
308 West Main Street, Owosso, MI 48867 .... (517) 723–6759
3508 West Houghton Lake Drive, Houghton Lake, MI 48629 .... (517) 366–4922

Counties: CLARE COUNTY; cities of Clare, Farwell, Harrison, Lake, and Lake George. CLINTON COUNTY; cities of Bath, DeWitt, Eagle, Elsie, Eureka, Fowler, Maple Rapids, Ovid, St. Johns, and Westphalia. CRAWFORD COUNTY; city of Grayling. GLADWIN COUNTY; cities of Beaverton, Bentley, Gladwin, and Rhodes. GRATIOT COUNTY; cities of Alma, Ashley, Bannister, Breckenridge, Elm Hall, Elwell, Ithaca, Middleton, North Star, Perrinton, Pompeii, Riverdale, Sumner, St. Louis, and Wheeler. ISABELLA COUNTY; cities of Blanchard, Mt. Pleasant, Rosebush, Shepherd, Weidman, and Winn. MECOSTA COUNTY; cities of Big Rapids, Mecosta, Morley, Paris, Remus, Rodney, and Stanwood. MIDLAND COUNTY; cities of Coleman, Edenville, Laporte, Midland, North Bradley, Poseyville, and Sanford. MISSAUKEE COUNTY; cities of Falmouth, Lake City, McBain, Merritt, and Moorestown. MONTCALM COUNTY; cities of Alger, Amble, Butternut, Carson City, Cedar Lake, Coral, Crystal, Edmore, Entrican, Fenwick, Gowen, Greenville, Howard City, Lakeview, Langston, Maple Hill, McBride, Pierson, Sand Lake, Sheridan, Sidney, Six Lakes, Stanton, Trufant, Vestaburg, and Vickeryville. OGEMAW COUNTY; cities of Lupton, Oakley, Prescott, Rose City, Skidway Lake, South Branch, and West Branch. OSCEOLA COUNTY; cities of Evart, Hersey, LeRoy, Reed City, Sears, and Tustin. OSCODA COUNTY; cities of Comins, Fairview, Lovells, Luzerne, Mio, and Red Oak. ROSCOMMON COUNTY; cities of Higgins Lake, Houghton Lake, Houghton Lake Heights, Prudenville, Roscommon, and St. Helen. SAGINAW COUNTY; cities of Bridgeport, Burt, Chesaning, Fosters, Freeland, Hemlock, Merrill, Oakley, Shields, and University Center. SHIAWASSEE COUNTY; cities of Bancroft, Chapin, Corunna, Henderson, Laingsburg, Morrice, New Lothrup, Owosso, Perry, and Shaftsburg. Population (1990), 580,956.

ZIP Codes: 48414 (part), 48415 (part), 48417 (part), 48433 (part), 48449 (part), 48457 (part), 48460 (part), 48601 (part), 48603 (part), 48604 (part), 48608–10, 48612, 48614–22, 48623 (part), 48624–30, 48632–33, 48635–37, 48640–42, 48647, 48649, 48651–57, 48661–62, 48722 (part), 48724, 48728, 48743, 48756, 48761, 48801, 48804, 48806–08, 48811–12, 48817 (part), 48818, 48820, 48822, 48829–35, 48837–38, 48840–41, 48845, 48847–48, 48850, 48852–53, 48856, 48857 (part), 48858, 48862, 48866, 48867 (part), 48871, 48872 (part), 48873–75, 48877–80, 48882–86, 48888–89, 48891, 48893–94, 48896, 48906, 49305, 49307, 49310, 49320, 49322, 49326, 49329, 49332, 49336, 49338–40, 49342–43, 49346–47, 49631–32, 49639, 49651, 49655, 49657, 49663 (part), 49665, 49667, 49677, 49679, 49688, 49738 (part), 49756 (part)

* * *

FIFTH DISTRICT

JAMES A. BARCIA, Democrat, of Bay City, MI; born in Bay City, February 25, 1952; B.A., Saginaw Valley State University, 1974; serves on the Public Works and Transportation Committee and the Science, Space and Technology Committee; State Representative, 1976–82; State Senator, 1983–92; as a State Senator, served as assistant democratic whip, vice-chairperson of Natural Resources and Environmental Affairs Committee and Technology and Energy Committee, and member of the Agriculture and Forestry Committee; cofounder, Coalition of Michigan Sportsmen; member, Bay Area Chamber of Commerce; life member, Veterans of Foreign Wars National Home; member, National Rifle Association; member, Fraternal Order of Eagles, Gladwin County Aerie No. 3292; honorary lay member, The Michigan Association of Osteopathic Physicians and Surgeons; Michigan Jaycees Top Five IMPACT award; Bay City Jaycees Distinguished Service Award; Safari Club International's ''Legislator of the Year''; AMVETS award; married to Vicki Bartlett Barcia; elected on November 3, 1992 to the 103rd Congress; reelected to each succeeding Congress.

Office Listings

http://www.house.gov/barcia jbarcia@hr.house.gov

2419 Rayburn House Office Building, Washington, DC 20515–2205 225–8171
FAX: 225–2168
Chief of Staff.—Jim Lewis.
Legislative Assistants: Kristen Valade, Heather MacMillan, Rob Ryan.
Executive Assistant.—Carisa Henze.
Press Secretary.—Laura Yntema.
301 East Genesee, Suite 502, Saginaw, MI 48607 .... (517) 754–6075
503 North Euclid, Bay City, MI 48706 .... (517) 667–0003
5409 Pierson Road, Flushing, MI 48433 .... (810) 732–7501

Counties: Alcona, Arenac, Bay, Genesee (part), Huron, Iosco, Lapeer (part), Saginaw (part), Sanilac, and Tuscola. Population (1990), 580,956.

ZIP Codes: 48032, 48097 (part), 48401, 48410, 48412 (part), 48413, 48415 (part), 48416 (part), 48417 (part), 48419–22, 48423 (part), 48426–27, 48430 (part), 48432, 48433 (part), 48434–35, 48437, 48441, 48444 (part), 48445, 48446 (part), 48450, 48453–54, 48456, 48457 (part), 48458, 48460 (part), 48461, 48463–72, 48475, 48504 (part), 48505 (part), 48506 (part), 48531, 48601 (part), 48602, 48603 (part), 48604 (part), 48605–07, 48610–11, 48613, 48623 (part), 48631, 48634, 48642, 48650, 48652, 48658–59, 48701, 48703, 48705–08, 48720–21, 48722 (part), 48723, 48725–50, 48754–55, 48757–70

* * *

SIXTH DISTRICT

FRED UPTON, Republican, of St. Joseph, MI; born in St. Joseph on April 23, 1953; graduated, Shattuck School, Fairbault, MN, 1971; B.A., journalism, University of Michigan, Ann Arbor, 1975; field manager, Dave Stockman Campaign, 1976; staff member, Congressman Dave Stockman, 1976–80; legislative assistant, Office of Management and Budget, 1981–83; deputy director of Legislative Affairs, 1983–84; director of Legislative Affairs, 1984–85; member: First Congregational Church, Emil Verbin Society; married to the former Amey Rulon-Miller; elected to the 100th Congress on November 4, 1986; reelected to each succeeding Congress.

Office Listings

talk2fsu@hr.house.gov

2333 Rayburn House Office Building, Washington, DC 20515–2206 225–3761
Administrative Assistant.—Joan Hillebrands. FAX: 225–4986
Executive Assistant.—Liz Pavlich.
800 Centre, Suite 106, 800 Ship Street, St. Joseph, MI 49085 .... (616) 982–1986
Mall Plaza, Suite 180, 157 South Kalamazoo Mall, MI 49007 .... (616) 385–0039

Counties: Allegan (part), Berrien, Cass, Kalamazoo, St. Joseph, and Van Buren. CITIES AND TOWNSHIPS: Allegan, Augusta, Bangor, Baroda, Benton Harbor, Berrien Springs, Berrien Center, Bloomingdale, Breedsville, Bridgman, Buchanan, Burr Oak, Cassopolis, Centreville, Climax, Coloma, Colon, Comstock, Constantine, Covert, Decatur, Delton, Dowagiac, Eau Claire, Edwardsburg, Fulton, Galesburg, Galien, Gobles, Grand Junction, Hagar Shores, Harbert, Hartford, Hickory Corners, Jones, Kalamazoo, Kendall, Lacota, Lakeside, Lawrence, Lawton, Leonidas, Marcellus, Mattawan, Mendon, Nazareth, New Troy, New Buffalo, Niles, Nottawa, Oshtemo, Otsego, Paw Paw, Plainwell, Portage, Pullman, Richland, Riverside, Sawyer, Schoolcraft, Scotts, Sodus, South Haven, St. Joseph, Stevensville, Sturgis, Three Oaks, Three Rivers, Union Pier, Union, Vandalia, Vicksburg, Watervliet, and White Pigeon. Population (1990), 580,956.

ZIP Codes: 49001–09, 49010 (part), 49012–13, 49019, 49022–23, 49026–27, 49030 (part), 49031–32, 49034 (part), 49038–39, 49040 (part), 49041–43, 49045, 49046 (part), 49047, 49052 (part), 49053, 49055–57, 49060 (part), 49061–67, 49071–72, 49074–75, 49077, 49078 (part), 49079, 49080 (part), 49081, 49083–85, 49087–88, 49090–91, 49093, 49095, 49097–99, 49101–03, 49106–07, 49111–13, 49115–17, 49119–20, 49125–30, 49450

* * *

SEVENTH DISTRICT

NICK SMITH, Republican, of Addison, MI; born in Addison on November 5, 1934; attended Addison Community Schools; B.A., Michigan State University, East Lansing, MI, 1957; M.S., University of Delaware, 1959; served as captain, military intelligence, U.S. Air Force, 1959–61; elected to Addison Township as trustee, supervisor, and county board member; member: Addison Community Hospital Board; State chairman, Agriculture Stabilization and Conservation Service; director, Michigan Farm Bureau; National Director of Energy for the U.S. Department of Agriculture; Michigan House of Representatives, 1978–82; Michigan State Senate, 1982–92; member: National Delegation on U.S.-Soviet Cooperation and Trade; awards: Kellogg Foundation Fellow, Outstanding Young Men of America; married the former Bonnalyn Atwood, 1960; four children: Julianna Smith Bellinger, Bradley LeGrand, Elizabeth Smith Burnette, and Stacia Kathleen; elected on November 3, 1992 to the 103rd Congress; reelected to each succeeding Congress.

Office Listings

http://www.house.gov/nicksmith repsmith@hr.house.gov

306 Cannon House Office Building, Washington, DC 20515–2207 225–6276
Administrative Assistant.—Kurt Schmautz.
Legislative Director.—Alec Rogers.
Executive Assistant/Scheduler.—Mary Christ.
121 South Cochran Avenue, Charlotte, MI 48813 .... (517) 543–0055
209 East Washington, Suite 217E, Jackson, MI 49201 .... (517) 783–4486
118 West Church Street, Adrian, MI 49221 .... (517) 265–5012
81 South 20th Street, Battle Creek, MI 49015 .... (616) 965–9066

Counties: Barry (part), Branch, Calhoun, Eaton, Hillsdale, Jackson, Lenawee, and Washtenaw (part). Population (1990), 580,957.

ZIP Codes: 48115, 48118 (part), 48158 (part), 48176 (part), 48813, 48821, 48827, 48837, 48849 (part), 48861, 48876, 48890, 48906–08, 48911, 48917, 49011, 49015–18, 49020–21, 49028–29, 49030 (part), 49033, 49034 (part), 49036, 49038, 49040 (part), 49046 (part), 49050–51, 49052 (part), 49058 (part), 49068, 49073 (part), 49076, 49082, 49089, 49092, 49094, 49096, 49201–04, 49220–21, 49224, 49227–28, 49229 (part), 49230, 49232–42, 49245–50, 49252–59, 49261–69, 49271–72, 49274–84, 49285 (part), 49286–89

* * *

EIGHTH DISTRICT

DEBBIE STABENOW, Democrat, of Lansing, MI; born in Gladwin, MI on April 29, 1950; graduated, Clare High School; B.A., Michigan State University, East Lansing, MI, 1972; M.S.W., Michigan State University, East Lansing, 1975; Michigan House of Representatives, 1979–90; Michigan State Senate, 1991–94; Ingham County Commissioner, 1975–78, chair for two years; two children: Todd and Michelle; committees: Agriculture, Science; elected to the 105th Congress, November 6, 1996.

Office Listings

1516 Longworth House Office Building, Washington, DC 20515–2208 .... 225–4872 FAX: 225–5820
Administrative Assistant.—Maggie Springer.
Executive Assistant/Scheduler.—John Kerekes.
Legislative Assistants: Elizabeth Rutledge, David Dumke, Bridget Gonzales.
3401 East Saginaw No. 214, Lansing, MI 48912 .... (517) 336–7777 FAX: 336–7236
District Director.—Teresa Plachetka.
2900 East Grand River, Howell, MI 48843 .... (517) 545–2195 FAX: 545–2430
2503 South Linden, Flint, MI 48503 .... (810) 230–8275 FAX: 230–8521

Counties: Genesee (part), Ingham, Livingston, Oakland (part), Shiawasse (part), and Washtenaw (part). Population (1990), 580,956.

ZIP Codes: 48103 (part), 48105 (part), 48106, 48108 (part), 48113, 48116, 48118 (part), 48130 (part), 48137, 48139, 48143, 48158 (part), 48169, 48176 (part), 48178 (part), 48189, 48197 (part), 48350 (part), 48353 (part), 48357 (part), 48380 (part), 48414 (part), 48418, 48429–30, 48433 (part), 48436, 48439 (part), 48442 (part), 48449 (part), 48451, 48473, 48476, 48503 (part), 48504 (part), 48507 (part), 48532 (part), 48805, 48816, 48817 (part), 48819, 48823–26, 48827 (part), 48836, 48840 (part), 48842–44, 48854, 48857 (part), 48863–64, 48867 (part), 48872 (part), 48892, 48895, 48901, 48906 (part), 48909–10, 48911 (part), 49912, 48915, 48917 (part), 48933, 49251, 49264 (part), 49285 (part)

* * *

NINTH DISTRICT

DALE E. KILDEE, Democrat, of Flint, MI; born in Flint, September 16, 1929; graduated, St. Mary High School, 1947; B.A., Sacred Heart Seminary, Detroit, 1952; M.A., University of Michigan, Ann Arbor, 1961; graduate studies in history and political science, University of Peshawar, Pakistan, under Rotary Foundation Fellowship; teacher, University of Detroit High School, 1954–56; Flint Central High School, 1956–64; served as State Representative, 1965–74; State Senator, 1975–77; member: Optimists, Urban League, Knights of Columbus, Phi Delta Kappa national honorary fraternity, American Federation of Teachers; life member, National Association for the Advancement of Colored People; married to the former Gayle Heyn, 1965; three children: David, Laura, and Paul; elected to the 95th Congress, November 2, 1976; re-elected to each succeeding Congress.

Office Listings

dkildee@hr.house.gov

2187 Rayburn House Office Building, Washington, DC 20515–2209 .... 225–3611 FAX: 225–6393
Administrative Assistant.—Christopher J. Mansour.
Legislative Director.—Larry Rosenthal.
Business Manager/Personal Secretary.—Dorothy Makris.
316 West Water Street, Flint, MI 48503 .... (810) 239–1437 FAX: 239–1439
1829 North Perry Street, Pontiac, MI 48340 .... (810) 373–9337 FAX: 373–6955
District Director.—Tiffany Anderson-Flynn.

Counties: GENESEE COUNTY (part); cities and townships of Atlas, Burton, Davison, Flint (part), Goodrich, Grand Blanc, Grand Blanc Township (part), and Holly (Groveland Township only). LAPEER COUNTY (part); cities and townships of Almont, Attica, Dryden, Hadley, Imlay City, Lapeer, and Metamora. OAKLAND COUNTY; cities and townships of Auburn Hills, Clarkston, Davisburg, Drayton Plains (part), Lake Orion, Lakeville, Leonard, Oakland, Ortonville (Brandon Township), Oxford, Pontiac, Rochester, Rochester Hills, Waterford. Population (1990), 580,956.

ZIP Codes: 48003, 48306 (part), 48307–09, 48321, 48326, 48327–30, 48340, 48341, 48342–43, 48346–48, 48350, 48359–63, 48366–67, 48370–71, 48411, 48412 (part), 48423 (part), 48428, 48438, 48439 (part), 48440, 48442 (part), 48444 (part), 48446 (part), 48455, 48462 (part), 48501–02, 48503, 48504 (part), 48505–06, 48507 (part), 48509, 48519, 48529, 48532 (part)

* * *

TENTH DISTRICT

DAVID E. BONIOR, Democrat, of Mount Clemens, MI; born in Detroit, MI, June 6, 1945; graduated, Notre Dame High School, 1963; B.A., University of Iowa, 1967; M.A., history, Chapman College (CA), 1972; served in the U.S. Air Force, 1968–72; member, Michigan House of Representatives, 1973–77; author, "The Vietnam Veteran: A History of Neglect"; married to Judy Bonior; three children: Julie, Andy, and Stephen; elected to the 95th Congress, November 2, 1976; reelected to each succeeding Congress.

Office Listings

2207 Rayburn House Office Building, Washington, DC 20515–2210 225–2106
Suite 305, 59 North Walnut Street, Mount Clemens, MI 48043–5659 .... (810) 469–3232
Admistrative Assistants: Edward Bruley, Christine Koch.
101 Federal Building, 526 Water Street, Port Huron, MI 48060 .... (810) 987–8889

Counties: Macomb (part) and St. Clair. Population (1990), 580,956.

ZIP Codes: 48001–02, 48004–06, 48014, 48021 (part), 48022–23, 48026–28, 48032, 48035–36, 48038–51, 48054, 48059–65, 48066 (part), 48074, 48079–82, 48094, 48096, 48097 (part), 48236 (part), 48306 (part), 48314 (part), 48315 (part), 48316 (part), 48317 (part), 48318, 48416 (part), 48444 (part)

* * *

ELEVENTH DISTRICT

JOE KNOLLENBERG, Republican, of Bloomfield Hills, MI; born in Mattoon, IL, November 28, 1933; graduated Eastern Illinois University, B.S.; operated family insurance agency; Troy Chamber of Commerce, past vice chairman; Birmingham Cable TV Community Advisory Board, past member; St. Bede's Parish Council, past president and board member; Evergreen School PTA, past president; Bloomfield Glens Homeowners Association, past president; Cranbrook Homeowners Association, past president; Southfield Ad Hoc Park and Recreational Development Committee, past coordinator; Southfield Mayor's Wage and Salary Committee, past member; married to the former Sandra Moco; two sons, Martin and Stephen; member of the Committee on Banking, Finance, and Urban Affairs; Committee on Small Business; elected to the Freshman Class Leadership, liaison to the National Republican Congressional Committee; 104th committees: Appropriations, Economic and Educational Opportunities; elected on November 3, 1992, to the 103rd Congress; reelected to each succeeding Congress.

Office Listings

http://www.house.gov/knollenberg

1511 Longworth House Office Building, Washington, DC 20515–2211 225–5802
Chief of Staff.—Craig Piercy. FAX: 226–2356
Legislative Director.—Devon Zeppelin.
Press Secretary.—Frank Maisano.
30833 Northwestern Highway, Suite 214, Farmington Hills, MI 48334 .... (313) 851–1366
15439 Middlebelt, Livonia, MI 48154 .... (313) 425–7557

Counties: Oakland (part) and Wayne (part). CITIES AND TOWNSHIPS: Beverly Hills, Birmingham, Birmingham Farms, Bloomfield Hills, Bloomfield Township, Commerce Township, Farmington, Farmington Hills, Franklin, Highland, Keego Harbo, Lathrup Village, Livonia (part), Lyon Township, Milford, New Hudson, Northville (part), Novi, Orchard Lake Village, Redford, South Lyon, Southfield (part), Sylvan Lake, Union Lake, Walled Lake, West Bloomfield Township, White Lake, Wixom and Wolverine Lake. Population (1990), 580,956.

ZIP Codes: 48009 (part), 48012, 48025, 48034, 48037, 48075 (part), 48076, 48086, 48150 (part), 48151–53, 48154 (part), 48165, 48167 (part), 48178 (part), 48239 (part), 48240 (part), 48301–04, 48320, 48322–23, 48324 (part), 48325, 48331–36, 48356, 48357 (part), 48374–77, 48380 (part), 48381–82, 48383 (part), 48386 (part), 48390, 48393

TWELFTH DISTRICT

SANDER M. LEVIN, Democrat, of Royal Oak, MI; born in Detroit, MI on September 6, 1931; graduated, Central High School, Detroit, 1949; B.A., University of Chicago, 1952; M.A., Columbia University, New York, NY, 1954; LL.B., Harvard University, Cambridge, MA, 1957; attorney, admitted to the Michigan bar in 1958 and commenced practice in Detroit, MI; member: Oakland Board of Supervisors, 1961–64; Michigan Senate, 1965–70; Democratic floor leader in State Senate; served on the Advisory Committee on the Education of Handicapped Children in the Department of Health, Education, and Welfare, 1965–68; chairman, Michigan Democratic Party, 1968–69; Democratic candidate for governor, 1970 and 1974; fellow, Kennedy School of Government, Institute of Politics, Harvard University, 1975; assistant administrator, Agency for International Development, 1977–81; married the former Victoria Schlafer, 1957; four children: Jennifer, Andrew, Madeleine, and Matthew; elected on November 2, 1982 to the 98th Congress; reelected to each succeeding Congress.

Office Listings

slevin@hr.house.gov

2209 Rayburn Office House Building, Washington, DC 20515 225–4961
Administrative Assistant.—Hilarie Chambers.
Scheduler.—Carol Ditta Ertel.
Suite 130, 2107 East 14 Mile Road, Sterling Heights, MI 48310 .... (810) 268–4444
District Administrator.—Diana McBroom.

Counties: Macomb County (part) and Oakland County (part). CITIES: Berkley, Center Line, Clawson, East Pointe (part), Ferndale, Hazel Park, Huntington Woods, Madison Heights, Oak Park, Pleasant Ridge, Royal Oak, Royal Oak Township, Southfield, Sterling Heights, Troy, Utica, Warren. Population (1990), 580,956.

ZIP Codes: 48007, 48015, 48017, 48020–21, 48030, 48067–73, 48075, 48083–84, 48089–93, 48098–99, 48220, 48237, 48310–18

* * *

THIRTEENTH DISTRICT

LYNN NANCY RIVERS, Democrat, of Ann Arbor, MI; born in Au Gres, MI, December 19, 1956; graduate, Au Gres-Sims High School, 1975; B.A., University of Michigan, 1987; J.D., Wayne State University, 1992; Ann Arbor Board of Education (trustee), 1984–92; member, Michigan House of Representatives; State Representative, 1993–94; married Joseph A. Rivers, 1975; two children: Bridgitte and Jeanne; elected to the 104th Congress on November 6, 1994; reelected to the 105th Congress.

Office Listings

http://www.house.gov/rivers/welcome.html lrivers@hr.house.gov

1724 Longworth House Office Building, Washington, DC 20515 225–6261
Administrative Assistant.—Gayle Boesky. FAX: 225–3404
Executive Assistant.—Donna Childers.
Legislative Director.—Gayle Boesky.
Deputy Administrative Assistant.—Shelley Simpson.
Federal Building, Wayne, MI 48184 .... (313) 722–1411
106 East Washington, Ann Arbor, MI 48104 .... (313) 741–4210

Counties: Washtenaw (part) and Wayne (part). CITIES AND TOWNSHIPS: Ann Arbor, Ann Arbor Township, Augusta Township, Belleville, Canton Township, Dearborn Heights, Garden City, Huron Township, Inkster, Livonia, Northville, Northville Township, Pittsfield Township, Plymouth, Plymouth Township, Romulus, Salem Township, Scio Township, Sumpter Township, Superior Township, Van Buren Township, Wayne, Westland, Ypsilanti, and Ypsilanti Township. Population (1990), 580,967.

ZIP Codes: 48103 (part), 48104, 48105 (part), 48107, 48108 (part), 48109, 48111–12, 48125 (part), 48134 (part), 48135–36, 48141, 48150 (part), 48154 (part), 48164 (part), 48167 (part), 48170, 48174 (part), 48175, 48178 (part), 48184–85, 48187–88, 48190, 48191 (part), 48197 (part), 48198, 48242

FOURTEENTH DISTRICT

JOHN CONYERS, JR., Democrat, of Detroit, MI; born May 16, 1929, in Detroit, son of John and Lucille Conyers; graduated from Wayne State University (B.A., 1957); graduated from Wayne State Law School (LL.B., June 1958); served as officer in the U.S. Army Corps of Engineers, one year in Korea; awarded combat and merit citations; married to Monica Esters-Conyers; engaged in many civil rights and labor activities; legislative assistant to Congressman John D. Dingell, December 1958 to May 1961; appointed Referee for the Workmen's Compensation Department, State of Michigan, by Governor John B. Swainson in October 1961; former vice chairman of Americans for Democratic Action; vice chairman of National Advisory Council of ACLU; member: Kappa Alpha PSI, Wolverine Bar, NAACP, Tuskebee Airmen, Inc.; ranking minority member, Judiciary Committee; member: Subcommittee of Courts and Intellectual Property, Subcommittee on the Constitution; dean, Congressional Black Caucus; elected to 89th Congress, November 3, 1964; reelected to each succeeding Congress.

Office Listings

http://www.house.gov/conyers jconyers@hr.house.gov

2426 Rayburn House Office Building, Washington, DC 20515–2214	225–5126
Office Manager.—Carla Brooks.	FAX: 225–0072
Federal Building, Room 669, 231 West Lafayette, Detroit, MI 48226	(313) 961–5670
	FAX: 226–2085

County: WAYNE COUNTY (part). CITY AND TOWNSHIPS of Detroit (part), Dearborn Heights, Grosse Pointe Shores, Gross Pointe Woods, Highland Park. Population (1990), 580,956.

ZIP Codes: 48203, 48205 (part), 48212 (part), 48217 (part), 48219, 48221, 48223, 48224 (part), 48225, 48227 (part), 48228 (part), 48234 (part), 48235, 48236 (part), 48238 (part), 48239 (part)

* * *

FIFTEENTH DISTRICT

CAROLYN C. KILPATRICK, Democrat, of Detroit, MI; born in Detroit, June 25, 1945; attended Ferris State University; graduate, Western Michigan University, 1972; M.S., education administration, University of Michigan, 1977; teacher; served in Michigan House of Representatives, 1979-96; member, Detroit Substance Abuse Advisory Council; former chair, Michigan Legislative Black Caucus; participated in first-of-its-kind African Trade Mission; delegate, U.N. International Women's Conference; led Michigan Department of Agriculture delegation to International Agriculture Show, Nairobi, Kenya; awards: Anthony Wayne Award for leadership, Wayne State University; Burton-Abercrombie Award, 15th Democratic Congressional District; Distinguished Legislator Award, University of Michigan; named Woman of the Year by Gentlemen of Wall Street, Inc.; listed in *Who's Who in Black America* and *Who's Who in American Politics*; two children, Kwame and Ayanna; committees: Banking and Financial Services; Government Reform and Oversight; elected to the 105th Congress.

Office Listings

503 Cannon House Office Building, Washington, DC 20515	225–2261
Administrative Assistant.—Beverlyn Hilton.	FAX: 225–5730
Executive Assistant.—Gerri Houston.	
Legislative Director.—James Williams.	
Legislative Assistant/Press Secretary.—Kimberly Roudolph.	
Systems Director/Legislative Assistant.—Derrick Miller.	
1274 Library Street, Suite 1B, Detroit, MI 48226	(313) 965–9004
District Director.—Cecilia Walker.	FAX: 965–9006

County: WAYNE COUNTY (part). Population (1990), 580,956.

ZIP Codes: 48201–02, 48204, 48206–18, 48224, 48226, 48229–33, 48236, 48243–44, 48227–28, 48235, 48238

SIXTEENTH DISTRICT

JOHN D. DINGELL, Democrat, of Dearborn, MI; born in Colorado Springs, CO, July 8, 1926; B.S., Georgetown University, 1949; J.D., Georgetown University Law School, 1952; World War II veteran; assistant Wayne County prosecutor, 1953–55; married to the former Deborah Insley; member: Migratory Bird Conservation Commission; elected to the 84th Congress in a special election to fill the vacant seat of his late father, the Honorable John D. Dingell, December 13, 1955; reelected to the 85th and all succeeding Congresses; ranking member, Commerce Committee.

Office Listings

2328 Rayburn House Office Building, Washington, DC 20515–2216 225–4071
Chief of Staff.—Marda J. Robillard.
Legislative Director.—R. Daniel Beattie.
Office Manager.—Nancy Garrett.
5465 Schaefer Road, Dearborn, MI 48126–3277 .... (313) 846–1276
23 East Front Street, Suite 103, Monroe, MI 48161 .... (313) 243–1849

Counties: WAYNE COUNTY(part); cities and townships of Allen Park, Brownstown Township, Dearborn, Dearborn Heights (part), Flat Rock, Gibraltar, Grosse Ile Township, Lincoln Park, Melvindale, Riverview, Rockwood, Southgate, Taylor, Trenton, Woodhaven, and Wyandotte. MONROE COUNTY; cities and townships of Azalia, Carleton, Dundee, Erie, Ida, Lambertville, LaSalle, Luna Pier, Maybee, Milan (part), Monroe, Newport, Ottawa Lake, Petersburg, Samaria, S. Rockwood, and Temperance. Population (1990), 580,956.

ZIP Codes: 48101, 48110, 48117, 48120–22, 48124–26, 48127 (part), 48128, 48131, 48133–34 (part), 48138, 48140, 48144–46, 48157, 48159, 48160 (part), 48161, 48166, 48173, 48177, 48179–80, 48182–83, 48192, 48195, 49267, 49270

MINNESOTA

(Population 1995, 4,610,000)

SENATORS

PAUL D. WELLSTONE, Democrat, of Northfield, MN; born in Washington, DC, July 21, 1944; attended Wakefield and Yorktown High Schools, Arlington, VA; B.A., political science, University of North Carolina, Chapel Hill, 1965; Ph.D., political science, University of North Carolina, Chapel Hill, 1969; professor of political science, Carleton College, Northfield, MN, 1969–90; director of the Minnesota Community Energy Program; member, Democratic Farmer Labor Party and numerous peace and justice organizations; publisher of two books: "How the Rural Poor Got Power" and "Powerline"; published several articles; married to the former Sheila Ison; three children: David, Marcia, and Mark; committees: Labor and Human Resources, Small Business, Indian Affairs, Veterans' Affairs, Foreign Relations; Labor subcommittees on Aging, Children and Families, and Education; elected to the U.S. Senate, November 6, 1990, for the six-year term beginning on January 3, 1991.

Office Listings

http://www.senate.gov/~wellstone senator@wellstone.senate.gov

136 Hart Senate Office Building, Washington, DC 20510–2303 224–5641
Administrative Assistant.—Kari J. Moe. FAX: 224–8438
Office Manager.—Kevin Lane.
Legislative Director.—Mike Epstein.
Court International Building, 2550 University Avenue West, St. Paul, MN 55114–1025 .... (612) 645–0323
State Director.—Jeff Blodgett.
105 Second Avenue South, Virginia, MN 55792 .... (218) 741–1074
417 Litchfield Avenue SW, Willmar, MN 56201 .... (612) 231–6041

* * *

ROD GRAMS, Republican, of Ramsey, MN; born on February 4, 1948 in Princeton, MN; graduated, St. Francis High School in Anoka; attended Anoka-Ramsey Junior College and Brown Institute in Minneapolis, and Carroll College in Helena, MT; producer and anchorman (1982–91): KMSP–TV (Minneapolis/St. Paul, MN), KFBB–TV (Great Falls, MT), WSAU–TV (Wausau, WI), and WIFR–TV (Rockford, IL); homebuilder; land developer, president and CEO, Sun Ridge Builders, Inc., 1985; U.S. House of Representatives, 1992–94; four children: Michelle, Tammy, Rhiannon, and Morgan; committees: Banking, Housing, and Urban Affairs; Energy and Natural Resources, Foreign Relations, Budget, and Joint Economic; serves on the Senate task forces on Term Limits, Unfunded Mandates, and Balanced Budget Amendment; appointed to the Working Group on Entitlements; Republican whip for the 103rd Congress; elected on November 3, 1992 to the 103rd Congress elected to the U.S. Senate on November 8, 1994.

Office Listings

http://www.senate.gov/~grams mail_grams@grams.senate.gov

257 Dirksen Senate Office Building, Washington, DC 20510–2304 224–3244
Chief of Staff.—Chris Erikstrup. FAX: 228–0956
Press Secretary.—Peter Hong.
Legislative Director.—Pat Eveland.
Executive Assistant.—Cindy Waters.
Office Manager.—Elizabeth Heir.
2013 Second Avenue North, Anoka, MN 55303 .... (612) 427–5921
State Director.—Merna Pease. FAX: 427–8872

REPRESENTATIVES

FIRST DISTRICT

GILBERT W. GUTKNECHT, Republican, of Rochester, MN; born in Cedar Falls, IA, March 20, 1951; graduated, Cedar Falls High School; B.A., University of Northern Iowa; real estate broker and auctioneer; member: Knights of Columbus, Chamber of Commerce; served as State

Representative, 1982–94, floor leader, House Republican Caucus; married Mary Catherine Gutknecht, 1972; three children: Margie, Paul, and Emily; elected to the 104th Congress; reelected to the 105th Congress.

Office Listings

http://www.house.gov/gutknecht gil@hr.house.gov

425 Cannon House Office Building, Washington, DC 20515 225–2472
Chief of Staff/Press Director.—Matt Miller.
Legislative Director.—John Rothrock.
Executive Assistant.—Lidia Hupp.
Legislative Assistants: Brian Harte, Jon Peterson, Adam Stenberg.

Counties: BLUE EARTH COUNTY; cities of Amboy, Eagle Lake, Garden City, Good Thunder, Lake Crystal, Madison Lake, Mankato, Mapleton, North Mankato, Pemberton, St. Clair, Vernon Center. DAKOTA COUNTY; cities of Farmington, Hampton, Randolph. DODGE COUNTY; cities of Claremont, Dodge Center, Hayfield, Kasson, Mantorville, West Concord. EXOTA COUNTY; City of Viola. FARIBAULT COUNTY; cities of Blue Earth, Bricelyn, Delavan, Easton, Elmore, Frost, Huntley, Kiester, Minnesota Lake, Walters, Wells, Winnebago. FILLMORE COUNTY; cities of Canton, Chatfield, Fountain, Harmony, Lanesboro, Mabel, Ostrander, Peterson, Preston, Rushford, Spring Valley, Whalan, Wykoff. FREEBORN COUNTY; cities of Albert Lea, Alden, Clarks Grove, Conger, Emmons, Freeborn, Geneva, Glenville, Hartland, Hayward, Hollandale, London, Myrtle, Oakland, Twin Lakes. GOODHUE COUNTY; cities of Cannon Falls, Dennison, Goodhue, Kenyon, Pine Island, Red Wing, Wanamingo, Welch, Zumbrota. HOUSTON COUNTY; cities of Brownsville, Caledonia, Eitzen, Hokah, Houston, La Crescent, Spring Grove. LE SUEUR COUNTY; cities of Cleveland, Elysian, Kasota, Kilkenny, Le Center, Le Sueur, Montgomery, New Prague, Waterville. LONSDALE COUNTY; City of Veseli. MOWER COUNTY; cities of Adams, Austin, Brownsdale, Dexter, Elkton, Grand Meadow, Lansing, LeRoy, Lyle, Racine, Rose Creek, Sargeant, Taopi, Waltham. OLMSTED COUNTY; cities of Byron, Dover, Eyota, Oronoco, Rochester, Stewartville. RICE COUNTY; cities of Dundas, Lonsdale, Morristown, Nerstrand, Northfield, Warsaw, Webster. SCOTT COUNTY; cities of Elko, Jordan, New Market. STEELE COUNTY; cities of Blooming Prairie, Ellendale, Hope, Medford, Meriden, Owatonna. WABASHA COUNTY; cities of Elgin, Hammond, Kellogg, Lake City, Mazeppa, Millville, Plainview, Reads Landing, Theilman, Wabasha, Zumbro Falls. WASECA COUNTY; cities of Janesville, New Richland, Otisco, Waldorf, Waseca. WINONA COUNTY; cities of Altura, Dakota, Goodview, Homer, Lewiston, Minnesota City, Rollingstone, St. Charles, Stockton, Utica, Winona. Population (1990), 546,887.

ZIP Codes: 55009, 55018–21, 55024 (part), 55026–27, 55031 (part), 55033 (part), 55041, 55044 (part), 55046, 55047 (part), 55049–50, 55052–54, 55057, 55060, 55065–66, 55087–88, 55089 (part), 55352, 55901–06, 55909–10, 55912, 55917–27, 55929, 55931–36, 55938–47, 55949–57, 55959–65, 55967–79, 55981–83, 55985–88, 55990–92, 56001–03, 56007, 56009–10, 56011 (part), 56013–14, 56016–17, 56020, 56023–29, 56031–37, 56042–43, 56045–48, 56050–52, 56055, 56057–58, 56061, 56063–65, 56067–70, 56071 (part), 56072, 56076–78, 56080, 56082, 56089–93, 56096–98, 56219, 56257

* * *

SECOND DISTRICT

DAVID MINGE, Democrat, of Montevideo, MN; born in Clarkfield, MN, March 19, 1942; B.A. in history, St. Olaf College, Northfield, MN, 1964; J.D., University of Chicago, 1967; professor, University of Wyoming Law School, 1970–77; attorney, 1977–92; Montevideo School Board member; married to Karen Aaker Minge; two children: Erik and Olaf; elected on November 3, 1992 to the 103rd Congress; reelected to each succeeding Congress.

Office Listings

http://www.house.gov/minge dminge@hr.house.gov

1415 Longworth House Office Building, Washington, DC 20515–2302 225–2331
Chief of Staff.—Ross Peterson.
Executive Assistant/Scheduler.—Alana Christensen.
Communications Director.—Amy Gromer.
District Director.—Herb Halvorson.
542 First Street South, Montevideo, MN 56205 .... (320) 269–9311
205 East Fourth Street, Chaska, MN 55318 .... (612) 448–6567
P.O. Box 367, 938 Fourth Avenue, Windom, MN 56101 .... (507) 831–0015

Counties: Big Stone, Brown, Carver, Chippewa, Cottonwood, Jackson, Kandiyohi, Lac qui Parle, Lincoln, Lyon, McLeod, Martin, Meeker, Murray, Nicollet, Nobles, Pipestone, Redwood, Renville, Rock, Scott (part), Sibley, Stearns (part), Swift, Watonwan, Wright, and Yellow Medicine. Population (1990), 546,887.

ZIP Codes: 55301–02, 55307, 55312–15, 55317–18, 55320 (part), 55321–22, 55324–25, 55328–29, 55330 (part), 55331 (part), 55332–36, 55338–39, 55342, 55349–50, 55352–55, 55358, 55359 (part), 55360, 55362–63, 55366–68, 55370, 55372 (part), 55374 (part), 55376 (part), 55379–81, 55382 (part), 55383, 55385–90, 55394–97, 55399, 55442 (part), 55473, 55583, 56011 (part), 56019, 56021–22, 56030–31, 56039, 56041, 56044, 56053–54, 56056, 56058, 56060, 56062, 56071 (part), 56073–75, 56081–85, 56087–88, 56101, 56110–23, 56125–29, 56131–34, 56136–45, 56147, 56149–53, 56155–62, 56164–76, 56178–81, 56183, 56185–87, 56201, 56207–12, 56214–16, 56218, 56220, 56222–33, 56237–41, 56243, 56245–47, 56249–58, 56260, 56262–66, 56270–73, 56276–89, 56291–95, 56297, 56312, 56362

THIRD DISTRICT

JIM RAMSTAD, Republican, of Minnetonka, MN; born in Jamestown, ND, May 6, 1946; University of Minnesota, B.A., Phi Beta Kappa, 1968; George Washington University, J.D. with honors, 1973; first lieutenant, U.S. Army Reserves, 1968–74; elected to the Minnesota Senate, 1980; reelected 1982, 1986; assistant minority leader; attorney; adjunct professor; board member: United Handicapped Federation, Children's Heart Fund, Lake Country Food Bank, Hazelden Foundation National Advisory Council, and Violence Against Women Coalition; member: Ways and Means Committee; elected to the 102nd Congress, November 6, 1990; reelected to each succeeding Congress.

Office Listings

mn03@hr.house.gov

103 Cannon House Office Building, Washington, DC 20515–2303 225–2871
Administrative Assistant.—Dean Peterson.
Legislative Director.—Karin Hope.
Executive Assistant/Scheduler.—Margaret Johnson.
Room 152, 8120 Penn Avenue South, Bloomington, MN 55431 .... (612) 881–4600
District Director.—Shari Nichols.

Counties: Dakota (part), Hennepin (part), Scott (part). CITIES AND TOWNSHIPS: Bloomington, Brooklyn Center, Brooklyn Park, Burnsville, Champlin, Corcoran, Dayton, Deephaven, Eden Prarie, Edina, Excelsior, Greenwood, Hanover, Haasan, Hopkins, Independence, Long Lake, Loretto, Maple Grove, Maple Plain, Medicine Lake, Medina, Minnetonka Beach, Minnetonka, Minnetrista, Mound, Orono, Osseo, Plymouth, Rockford, Rogers, Saint Bonifacius, Savage, Shorewood, Spring Park, Tonka Bay, Wayzata, and Woodland. Population (1990), 546,888.

ZIP Codes: 55044 (part), 55305–06, 55311, 55316, 55323, 55327–28, 55331, 55337, 55340–41, 55343, 55344–47, 55356–57, 55359, 55361, 55364, 55369, 55373–75, 55378, 55384, 55387, 55391, 55420, 55423, 55424 (part), 55425, 55428–31, 55435 (part), 55436 (part), 55437–38, 55439 (part), 55441–47

* * *

FOURTH DISTRICT

BRUCE F. VENTO, Democrat-Farmer-Labor, of St. Paul, MN; born in St. Paul, October 7, 1940; graduated, Johnson High School, St. Paul, 1958; A.A., University of Minnesota, 1961; B.S., with honors, Wisconsin State University, 1965; graduate work, University of Minnesota; teacher; served in Minnesota House of Representatives, 1971–76, assistant majority leader and committee chairman; chairman of the Ramsey County Delegation; vice-chairman of the Judiciary Committee; chairman of the General Legislation and Veterans Affairs Committee; member of Democratic-Farmer-Labor (DFL) Party; awards/recognition from: National Council of Senior Citizens, National Audubon Society, National Taxpayers Union, Izaak Walton League, National Parks and Conservation Association, National Parks and Recreation Association, Sierra Club, Minnesota Federation for the Blind, St. Paul Chamber of Commerce, American Legion, National Alliance to End Homelessness, YMCA-Youth in Government; activities include Minnesota Education Council, Commission on Minnesota's Future, Merrick Day Activity Center Board of Retarded, Target Area "C" Advisory Council poverty program, Phalen Area Community Council, YMCA; member, Presentation Church; three sons: Michael, Peter, and John; committees: Banking and Financial Services, Resources; ranking member, Subcommittee on Financial Institutions and Consumer Credit; subcommittees: Housing and Community Development; National Parks, Forests and Lands; Water and Power Resources; elected to the 95th Congress, November 2, 1976; reelected to each succeeding Congress.

Office Listings

http://www.house.gov/vento vento@hr.house.gov

2304 Rayburn House Office Building, Washington, DC 20515–2304 225–6631
Administrative Assistant.—Lawrence Romans. FAX: 225–1968
Appointment Secretary.—Mary Ann Daly.
Room 727, 175 East Fifth Street, St. Paul, MN 55101 .... (612) 224–4503
District Director.—Molly Grove.
Appointment Secretary.—Linda Wason.

Counties: Dakota and Ramsey. Population (1990), 546,887.

ZIP Codes: 55075, 55101, 55112–14, 55116–18, 55120, 55126–27, 55418

FIFTH DISTRICT

MARTIN OLAV SABO, Democrat-Farmer-Labor, of Minneapolis, MN; born in Crosby, ND, February 28, 1938; graduated Alkabo High School, ND, 1955; B.A., Augsburg College, Minneapolis, MN, 1959; graduate studies, University of Minnesota, 1960; served in the Minnesota House of Representatives, 1961–78; served as house Democrat-Farmer-Labor minority leader, 1969–73; Speaker of the House, 1973–78; presidential appointee to the National Advisory Commission on Intergovernmental Relations; president, National Conference of State Legislatures; president, National Legislative Conference; chairman, Intergovernmental Relations Committee of the National Conference of State Legislatures; Nuclear Test Ban Leadership Award, 1992; Arms Control Leadership Award, 1988; Endowment for Leadership in Community and Public Service, established in his name, 1994; Distinguished Service Award from the Committee on Education Funding, 1994; inducted into the Scandinavian American Hall of Fame, October 12, 1994; honorary lifetime member, Hospital and Nursing Home Employees Union, Local No. 113, SEIU AFL–CIO; Minneapolis Jaycees Man of the Year Award, 1973–74; Augsburg College Distinguished Alumnus Citation; Lloyd M. Short Merit Award of the Minnesota Chapter of the American Society for Public Administration; ranking member, Budget Committee; Appropriations Committee; member, Democratic Steering Committee; subcommittees: National Security and Transportation; married the former Sylvia Lee, 1963; two children: Karin and Julie; elected to the 96th Congress, November 7, 1978; reelected to each succeeding Congress.

Office Listings

http://www.house.gov/sabo martin.sabo@mail.house.gov

2336 Rayburn House Office Building, Washington, DC 20515–2305 225–4755
Administrative Assistant.—Michael Erlandson.
Chief of Staff.—Michael Erlandson.
Press Secretary.—Marc Kimball.
Scheduler.—Bonnie Gottwald.
462 Federal Courts Building, 110 South Fourth Street, Minneapolis, MN 55401 .... (612) 348–1649

County: HENNEPIN COUNTY (part); cities of Crystal, Edina (part), Ft. Snelling, Minneapolis, New Hope, Richfield, Robbinsdale, Population (1990), 546,887.

ZIP Codes: 55401–19, 55422–24, 55426–30, 55435–36, 55450 (part), 55454–55, 55487

* * *

SIXTH DISTRICT

WILLIAM P. (BILL) LUTHER, Democrat, of Stillwater, MN; born in Fergus Falls, MN, on June 27, 1945; graduated, Fergus Falls High School, 1963; B.S., University of Minnesota, 1967; J.D., University of Minnesota, 1970; admitted to the State bar in 1970; member: Minnesota State House, 1975–76; Minnesota State Senate, 1977–94; Senate assistant majority leader, 1983–94; member, St. Alphonsus Catholic Church; married to Darlene Luther; two children: Alexander and Alicia; committees: Small Business, Science; elected to the 104th and 105th Congresses.

Office Listings

http://www.house.gov/luther/welcome.html tell.bill@mail.house.gov

1419 Longworth House Office Building, Washington, DC 20515–2306 225–2271
Chief of Staff.—Theodore M. Thompson. FAX: 225–3368
Legislative Director.—John Edgell.
Office Manager.—Christopher Hoven.
Legislative Assistants: Nick Gerten, Sean McDonough.
Suite 150, 1811 Weir Drive, Woodbury, MN 55125 .... (612) 730–4949

Counties: ANOKA COUNTY; Cities and townships of Andover, Anoka, Bethel, Blaine, Burns, Cedar, Centerville, Circle Pines, Columbia Heights, Coon Rapids, East Bethel, Fridley, Ham Lake, Hilltop, Lexington, Lino Lakes, Oak Grove, Ramsey, St. Francis, Spring Lake Park; DAKOTA COUNTY; Apple Valley, Coates, Eagan, Farmington, Hastings, Inver Grove Heights, Lakeville, Marshan, Nininger, Ravenna, Rosemount, Vermillion; WASHINGTON COUNTY; Afton, Bayport, Birchwood, Cottage Grove, Dellwood, Forest Lake, Forest Lake, Hugo, Lake Elmo, Lakeland, Lakeland Shores, Landfall, Mahtomedi, Marine, Newport, New Scandia, Oakdale, Oak Park Heights, Pine Springs, St. Mary's Pt, St. Paul Park, Stillwater, West Lakeland, White Bear Lake, Willemie, and Woodbury.

ZIP Codes: 55001, 55003, 55005, 55011–12, 55014, 55016, 55024–25, 55031, 55033, 55038, 55040, 55042–44, 55047, 55055, 55068, 55070–71, 55073, 55075–77, 55079, 55082–83, 55085, 55089–90, 55092, 55109–10, 55115, 55119, 55121–26, 55128, 55303–04, 55306, 55330, 55337, 55372, 55421, 55430, 55432, 55433–34, 55444, 55448–49

SEVENTH DISTRICT

COLLIN C. PETERSON, Democrat, of Detroit Lakes, MN; born in Fargo, ND, June 29, 1944; graduated from Glyndon (MN) High School, 1962; B.A., Moorhead State University, 1966: (business administration and accounting); U.S. Army National Guard, 1963–69; CPA, owner and partner; Minnesota State Senator, 1976–86; member: AOPA, Safari Club, Ducks Unlimited, American Legion, Sea Plane Pilots Association, Pheasants Forever, Benevolent Protective Order of Elks, Cormorant Lakes Sportsmen Club; three children: Sean, Jason, and Elliott; elected to the 102nd Congress, November 6, 1990; reelected to each succeeding Congress.

Office Listings

http://www.house.gov/collinpeterson tocollin.peterson@mail.house.gov

1314 Longworth House Office Building, Washington, DC 20515–2307 225–2165
Assistants: Victoria Hight, Rob Larew, Heather Westlund, Diane Gerten, Nick Gerten, Hannah Richert, Dana Hagerty.
Lake Avenue Plaza Building, Suite 107, 714 Lake Avenue, Detroit Lakes, MN 56501 .... (218) 847–5056
110 Second Street South, Suite 112, Waite Park, MN 56387 .... (612) 259–0559
Minnesota Wheat Growers Building, 2603 Wheat Drive, Red Lake, MN 56750 ..... (218) 253–4356

Counties: Becker, Beltrami, Benton, Clay, Clearwater, Douglas, Grant, Hubbard, Kittson, Lake of the Woods, Mahnomen, Marshall, Morrison, Norman, Otter Tail, Pennington, Polk, Pope, Red Lake, Richland, Roseau, Stearns, Stevens, Todd, Traverse, Wadena, and Wilkin. Population (1990), 546,888.

ZIP Codes: 56301–56701

* * *

EIGHTH DISTRICT

JAMES L. OBERSTAR, Democrat, of Chisholm, MN; born in Chisholm, September 10, 1934; graduated, Chisholm High School, 1952; B.A., *summa cum laude*, French and political science, College of St. Thomas, St. Paul, MN, 1956; M.A., European area studies, College of Europe, Bruges, Belgium, 1957; Laval University, Canada; Georgetown University, former teacher of English, French, and Creole; served as administrative assistant to the late Congressman John A. Blatnik, 1963–74; administrator of the House Public Works Committee, 1971–74; cochair: Congressional Travel and Tourism Caucus, Democratic Study Group, Great Lakes Task Force; National Water Alliance, Northeast Midwest Congressional Coalition, Steel Caucus, Conference of Great Lakes Congressmen (chairman); married Jean Kurth, 1993; six children: Thomas Edward, Katherine Noelle, Anne-Therese, Monica Rose, Charlie, and Lindy; committee: Transportation and Infrastructure, ranking Democrat; elected to the 94th Congress, November 5, 1974; reelected to each succeeding Congress.

Office Listings

http://www.house.gov/oberstar oberstar@hr.house.gov

2366 Rayburn House Office Building, Washington, DC 20515–2308 225–6211
Deputy Administrative Assistant.—William Richard.
Office Manager.—Jill Beatty.
Legislative Director.—Chip Gardiner.
Communications Director.—Mary Kerr.
231 Federal Building, Duluth, MN 55802 .... (218) 727–7474
District Manager.—Jackie Morris.
Chisholm City Hall, 316 West Lake Street, Chisholm, MN 55719 .... (218) 254–5761
District Representative.—Jacquelyn Hirvela.
Brainerd City Hall, 501 Laurel Street, Brainerd, MN 56401 .... (218) 828–4400
District Representative.—Ken Hasskamp.
Elk River City Hall, 13065 Orono Parkway, Elk River, MN 55330 .... (612) 241–0188
District Representative.—Ken Hasskamp.

Counties: Aitkin, Benton (part), Carlton, Cass, Chisago, Cook, Crow Wing, Isanti, Itasca, Kanabec, Koochiching, Lake, Mille Lacs, Morrison (part), Pine, St. Louis, and Sherburne (part) Cities of Brainerd, Chisholm, Cloquet, Duluth, Elk River, Grand Rapids, Hibbing, International Falls, and Little Falls. Population (1990), 546,887.

ZIP Codes: 55002, 55004, 55006–08, 55012–13, 55017, 55025 (part), 55029–30, 55032, 55036–37, 55040, 55045, 55051, 55056, 55063, 55067, 55069, 55070, 55072, 55073 (part), 55074, 55079–80, 55084, 55092, 55172, 55308–09, 55319, 55330 (part), 55371, 55377, 55398, 55601–07, 55609, 55612–16, 55701–13, 55716–27, 55729 55731–36, 55738, 55741–42, 55744–55746 55748–58, 55760–69, 55771–73, 55775, 55777–99, 55801–08, 55810–12, 55815–16, 55974, 56304 (part), 56313, 56317, 56329–30, 56333, 56338, 56342, 56344, 56350, 56353, 56357–59, 56363–64, 56367 (part), 56377 (part), 56379 (part), 56386, 56401, 56425, 56430–31, 56433, 56435, 56441–42, 56444, 56447–50, 56452, 56455–56, 56459, 56461, 56463, 56465–66, 56468–69, 56472–74, 56477, 56479, 56481, 56484–85, 56623, 56626–33, 56636–37, 56639, 56641, 56649, 56653–55, 56657–62, 56668–69, 56672, 56679–81, 56688

MISSISSIPPI

(Population 1995, 2,697,000)

SENATORS

THAD COCHRAN, Republican, of Jackson, MS; born in Pontotoc, MS, December 7, 1937; graduated, Byram High School, 1955; B.A., University of Mississippi, 1959; J.D., University of Mississippi Law School, 1965; received a Rotary Foundation Fellowship and studied international law and jurisprudence at Trinity College, University of Dublin, Ireland, 1963–64; served in U.S. Navy, 1959–61; admitted to Mississippi bar in 1965; board of directors, Jackson Rotary Club, 1970–71; Outstanding Young Man of the Year Award, Junior Chamber of Commerce in Mississippi, 1971; president, young lawyers section of Mississippi State bar, 1972–73; cochairman of the Sunbelt Caucus, 1994; married the former Rose Clayton of New Albany, MS, 1964; two children: Clayton and Katherine; elected to the 93rd Congress, November 7, 1972; reelected to 94th and 95th Congresses; elected to the U.S. Senate, November 7, 1978, for the six-year term beginning January 3, 1979; subsequently appointed by the governor, December 27, 1978, to fill the vacancy caused by the resignation of Senator James O. Eastland; reelected November 6, 1984; reelected November 6, 1990 without opposition; reelected November 5, 1996; chair: subcommittees on Agriculture, Rural Development and Related Agencies, and Production and Price Competitiveness; committees: Appropriations, Governmental Affairs, Agriculture, Nutrition and Forestry and Rules Administration, Joint Committee on the Library, Joint Committee on Printing; elected chairman of the Senate Republican Conference in 1990; reelected chairman, 1992 and 1994.

Office Listings

http://www.senate.gov/~cochran senator@cochran.senate.gov

326 Russell Senate Office Building, Washington, DC 20510–2402 224–5054
Chief of Staff.—Mark Eikeenum.
Legislative Director.—James Lofton.
Administrative Assistant.—Haley Fisackerly.
Legislative Director.—M.D.B. Carlisle.
Suite 614, 188 East Capitol Street, Jackson, MS 39201 .... (601) 965–4459
Administrative Assistant.—Wiley Carter.
P.O. Box 1434, Oxford, MS 38655 .... (601) 236–1018

* * *

TRENT LOTT, Republican, of Pascagoula, MS; born October 9, 1941, in Grenada, MS, son of Chester P. and Iona (Watson) Lott; University of Mississippi, B.P.A., 1963, J.D., 1967; served as field representative for the University of Mississippi, 1963–65; acting law alumni secretary of the Ole Miss Alumni Association, 1966–67; practiced law in Pascagoula in 1967 with Bryan and Gordon law firm; administrative assistant to Congressman William M. Colmer, 1968–72; member: Sigma Nu social fraternity, Phi Alpha Delta legal fraternity, Jackson County Bar Association, American Bar Association, the Masons, First Baptist Church of Pascagoula; married Patricia E. Thompson of Pascagoula, 1964; two children: Chester T., Jr. and Tyler Elizabeth; elected to the 93rd Congress, November 7, 1972; reelected to each succeeding Congress; member, Judiciary Committee, Merchant Marine and Fisheries, 93rd Congress; Committee on Rules and Post Office and Civil Service Committee, 94th and 95th Congresses; chairman, House Republican Research Committee, 96th Congress; House Republican Whip, Committee on Rules, 97th–100th Congresses; member, Committee on Small Business, 101st Congress; member, Committee on Budget, 102nd Congress; chairman, Republican Committee on Committees, 102nd Congress; member, Committee on Energy and Natural Resources, Joint Committee on the Reorganization of Congress, Secretary of Republican Conference, 103rd Congress; member, Committee on Ethics, 101st and 102nd Congresses; member, Committee on Armed Services, Committee on Commerce, Science and Transportation, 101st–103rd Congresses; elected on November 8, 1988 to the U.S. Senate for the term beginning January 3, 1989; elected to the 104th Congress; elected Senate majority whip; committees: Commerce, Science, and Transportation; Finance; Rules and Administration; subcommittees; Aviation; Communications; International Trade; Long-Term Growth, Debt and Deficit Reduction.

Office Listings

http://www.senate.gov/~lott senatorlott@lott.senate.gov

487 Russell Senate Office Building, Washington, DC 20510–2403 224–6253

Chief of Staff.—John Lundy. FAX: 224–2262
Scheduler.—Hardy Lott.
Press Secretary.—Elizabeth Mavar.
Legislative Director.—Carl Biersack.
245 East Capitol Street, Jackson, MS 39201 .... (601) 965–4644
3100 South Pascagoula Street, Pascagoula, MS 39567 .... (601) 762–5400
One Government Plaza, Gulfport, MS 39502 .... (601) 864–1988
101 South Lafayette, Starkville, MS 39759 .... (601) 323–1414
911 Jackson Avenue, Oxford, MS 38655 .... (601) 234–3774
20 East Washington Street, Greenwood, MS 38930 .... (601) 453–5681

REPRESENTATIVES

FIRST DISTRICT

ROGER F. WICKER, Republican, of Tupelo, MS; born in Pontotoc, MS, July 5, 1951; graduated Pontotoc High School; B.A. and J.D., University of Mississippi, 1973; Ole Mississippi Law School, 1975; attorney-at-law; member: Lions Club, Promise Keepers; president, Associated Student Body, 1972–73; Ole Miss Hall of Fame; Sigma Nu Fraternity; Omicron Delta Kappa; Phi Delta Phi; *Mississippi Law Journal*, 1973–75; Air Force ROTC; U.S. Air Force, 1976–80; lieutenant colonel, U.S. Air Force Reserves, 1980–present; Lee County Public Defender, 1984–87; Tupelo City Judge pro tempore, 1986–87; private law practice, 1982–94; served as president of Tupelo Community Theatre; president, Lee County Young Lawyers; North Mississippi Medical Center Development Council; member: Community Development Foundation Education Roundtable, CDF Skills and Technology Task Force; deacon, Sunday School teacher, adult choir of First Baptist Church, Tupelo, MS; married to Gayle Long Wicker; three children: Margaret, Caroline, and McDaniel; member: Mississippi State Senate, 1988–94; chairman: Electric Committee (1992), Public Health and Welfare Committee (1993); previous committees: Education, Judiciary, Finance, Elections, and Constitution; Senate Rules Committee (1993); U.S. House Rules Committee staff for Representative Trent Lott, 1980–82; Appropriations Committee; president, Republican freshman class, 1995; elected to the 104th Congress, November 6, 1994; reelected to the 105th Congress.

Office Listings

http://www.house.gov/wicker rwicker@hr.house.gov

206 Cannon House Office Building, Washington, DC 20515–2401 225–4306
Administrative Assistant/Press Secretary.—Kyle Steward.
Chief of Staff.—John Keast.
Legislative Director.—Chris Pedigo.
500 West Main Street, Suite 210, P.O. Box 1482, Tupelo, MS 38802 .... (601) 844–5437
8625 Highway 51 North, Southhaven, MS 38671 .... (601) 342–3942

Counties: Alcorn, Benton, Calhoun, Chickasaw, Choctaw, DeSoto, Grenada (part), Itawamba, Lafayette, Lee, Marshall, Monroe, Montgomery (part), Oktibbeha (part), Panola (part), Pontotoc, Prentiss, Tallahatchie (part), Tate, Tippah, Tishomingo, Union, Webster, and Yalobusha. Population (1990), 514,548.

ZIP Codes: 38601–03, 38606 (part), 38610–11, 38618–20, 38625, 38627, 38629, 38632–35, 38637–38, 38641–42, 38647–52, 38654–55, 38658–59, 38661, 38663, 38665, 38668, 38671, 38673–74, 38677, 38679–80, 38683, 38685, 38801–03, 38820–21, 38824–29, 38833–34, 38838–39, 38841, 38843–44, 38846–52, 38855–60, 38862–66, 38868–71, 38873–74, 38876–80, 38913–16, 38920, 38921 (part), 38922, 38925 (part), 38927, 38929 (part), 38948–49, 38951, 38953, 38955, 38961–62, 38965, 38967 (part), 39730, 39735, 39737, 39740, 39744–46, 39747 (part), 39750–52, 39756, 39767, 39769, 39771–72, 39776

* * *

SECOND DISTRICT

BENNIE THOMPSON, Democrat, of Bolton, MS; born in Bolton, January 28, 1948; graduated, Hinds County Agriculture High School; B.A., Tougaloo College, 1968; M.S., Jackson State University, 1972; teacher; Bolton Board of Aldermen, 1969–73; mayor of Bolton, 1973–79; Hinds County Board of Supervisors, 1980–93; married to the former London Johnson, Ph.D.; one daughter, BendaLonne; committee assignments: Agriculture, Merchant Marine and Fisheries, Small Business; member: Congressional Black Caucus, Sunbelt Caucus, Rural Caucus, Progressive Caucus; Housing Assistance Council; NAACP 100 Black Men of Jackson, MS; Southern Regional Council; Kappa Alpha Psi Fraternity; elected in a special election to the 103rd Congress; reelected to each succeeding Congress.

Office Listings

http://www.house.gov/thompson ms2nd@hr.house.gov

1408 Longworth House Office Building, Washington, DC 20515–2402 225–5876
Executive Assistant.—Marsha G. McCraven. FAX: 225–5898
Legislative Director/Press Secretary.—Edward Jackson.
Office Manager.—Minnie Langham.
107 West Madison Street, P.O. Box 610, Bolton, MS 39041–0610 .... (601) 866–9003
District Director.—Charles Horhn.
Quitman County Court House, 230 Chestnut Street, Marks, MS 38646 .... (601) 326–3090
Mound Bayou City Hall, Room 134, 106 West Green Street, Mound Bayou, MS 38762 .... (601) 741–9003
221 West Market Street, Suite 5, Greenwood, MS 38930 .... (601) 455–9003
901 Courthouse Lane, Greenville, MS 38701 .... (601) 335–9003

Counties: Attala (part), Bolivar, Carroll, Claiborne, Coahoma, Grenada (part), Hinds (part), Holmes, Humphreys, Issaquena, Jefferson, Leake (part), Leflore, Madison (part), Montgomery (part), Panola (part), Quitman, Sharkey, Sunflower, Tallahatchie (part), Tunica, Warren, Washington, and Yazoo. Population (1990), 514,845.

ZIP Codes: 38606 (part), 38609, 38614, 38617, 38619, 38620–23, 38626, 38628, 38630–31, 38639, 38643–46, 38657–58, 38662, 38664–66, 38669–70, 38676, 38701–04, 38720–23, 38725–26, 38729–33, 38736–40, 38744–46, 38748–49, 38751, 38753–56, 38758–65, 38767–69, 38771–74, 38776, 38778–82, 38901, 38912, 38917, 38921 (part), 38923–24, 38925 (part), 38926–28, 38929 (part), 38930, 38940–47, 38950, 38952, 38954, 38957–61, 38963–64, 38966, 38967 (part), 39038–40, 39041 (part), 39045, 39046 (part), 39049, 39051 (part), 39054–55, 39056 (part), 39060–61, 39063–64, 39066 (part), 38967, 39069–72, 39079, 39081, 39086, 39088, 39090 (part), 39094–97, 39207–09, 39110 (part), 39113, 39115, 39130, 39144, 39146, 39150, 39154 (part), 39156, 39158–60, 39162–63, 39166, 39169–73, 39175 (part), 39176–77, 39179–82, 39189, 39192, 39194, 39206 (part), 39209 (part), 39213 (part), 39216 (part), 39352, 39653, 39661, 39668, 39747 (part), 39862

* * *

THIRD DISTRICT

CHARLES W. (CHIP) PICKERING, Jr., Republican, of Laurel, MS; born on August 10, 1963; B.A., business administration, University of Mississippi, 1986; M.B.A., Baylor University; farmer; legislative aide to Senate Majority Leader Trent Lott, 1992–96; Bush administration appointee, U.S. Department of Agriculture, 1989–91; Southern Baptist missionary to Budapest, Hungary, 1986–87; married to the former Leisha Jane Prather; four children: Will, Ross, Jackson, and Asher; committees: Transportation and Infrastructure, Agriculture, Science; assistant whip at large, Policy Committee; elected to the 105th Congress.

Office Listings

http://www.house.gov/pickering c.pickering@mail.house.gov

427 Cannon House Office Building, Washington, DC 20515–2403 225–5031
Chief of Staff.—Susan Connell. FAX: 225–5797
Press Secretary.—Quinton Dickerson.
Legislative Director.—John Rothrock.
Scheduler.—Christi Bradley.
110–D Airport Road, Pearl, MS, 39208 .... (601) 932–2410
District Director.—James B. Huff. FAX: 965–4598
2100 Ninth Street, Suite 302, Meridian, MS 39301 .... (601) 693–6681
Staff Assistants: Lynne Compton, Carol Mabry. FAX: 693–1801
2080 Airport Road, Suite D, Columbus, MS 39702 .... (601) 327–2766
District Representative.—Henry Moseley. FAX: 328–4570
Special Assistant.—Clara Peterson.

Counties and Townships: Aponaug, Attala (part), Berea, Carmack, Clarke, Clay, East, Ethel, Jasper, Jones (part), Kemper, Lauderdale, Leake (part), Liberty Chapel, Lowndes, Madison (part), McCool, Neshoba, Newton, Northwest, Noxubee, Oktibbeha (part), Providence, Rankin, Scott, South Central, Smith, Thompson, Wayne (part), Williamsville, Winston and Zama. Jones County: Carthage, Ebenezer, Erata, Freeny, Glade, Good Hope, Lena, Madden, Myrick School, Northeast High, Northwest High, Rustin, Salem, Shady Grove, Sharon, Singleton, South Carthage, and Walnut Grove. Madison County: Madisonville, Madison, Lorman/Cavelier, Ridgeland, and Trace Habor. Oktibbeha County: Adaton, Bell Schoolhouse, Bradley, Central Starkville, Craig Springs, East Starkville, Gillespie Street, Hickory Grove, Northeast Starkville, North Longview, North Starkville, Osborn, Oktoc, Self Creek, Sessums, South Longview, South Starkville, and West Starkville. Wayne County: Big Rock, Chaparral, Coit, Diamond, Eucutta, Yellow Creek, Hiwannee, and Matherville. Population (1990), 515,314.

ZIP Codes: 39042–44, 39046 (part), 39047, 39051 (part), 39057, 39067, 39073–74, 39076, 39080, 39087, 39090 (part), 39092, 39094, 39098, 39107–09, 39110 (part), 39114, 39116–17, 39119, 39145, 39148, 39151–53, 39157 (part), 39158, 39161, 39167–68, 39189, 39193, 39208, 39211 (part), 39213 (part), 39218, 39283, 39288, 39298, 39301–05, 39307, 39320, 39323, 39325–28, 39330, 39332, 39335–39, 39341–42, 39345–48, 39350, 39352–56, 39358–61, 39363–67, 39422, 39439, 39440 (part), 39441–42, 39460, 39477, 39480–81, 39701–05, 39736, 39739, 39741, 39743, 39753–55, 39759 (part), 39762, 39766, 39773

FOURTH DISTRICT

MIKE PARKER, Republican, of Brookhaven, MS; born in Laurel, MS, on October 31, 1949, son of Rev. and Mrs. Milton Paul Parker; graduated, Franklin High School, Meadville, MS, 1967; B.A., William Carey College, Hattiesburg, MS, 1970; small businessman; member, Faith Presbyterian Church; married to the former Rosemary Prather; three children: Michael Adrian, Marisa, and Thomas Welch; committees: Appropriations, Budget; subcommittees: Energy and Water Development, Military Construction; elected on November 8, 1988, to the 101st Congress; reelected to each succeeding Congress.

Office Listings

http://www.house.gov/parker

2445 Rayburn House Office Building, Washington, DC 20515–2404 225–5865
FAX: 225–5886
Chief of Staff.—Arthur Rhodes.
Executive Assistant/Scheduler.—Pat Stewart-Holland.
245 East Capitol Street, Jackson, MS 39201 .... (601) 352–1355
FAX: 352–9044
Executive Administrator.—Ed Cole.

Counties: Adams, Amite, Copiah, Covington, Franklin, Hinds (part), Jefferson Davis, Jones (part), Lawrence, Lincoln, Marion, Pike, Simpson, Walthall, and Wilkinson. Population (1990), 513,853.

ZIP Codes: 39041 (part), 39044, 39049, 39056 (part), 39059, 39062, 39066 (part), 39077–78, 39082–83, 39086, 39111–12, 39114, 39119–22, 39140, 39144, 39149, 39154 (part), 39157 (part), 39165, 39168, 39170, 39174, 39175 (part), 39190–91, 39201–05, 39206 (part), 39207, 39209 (part), 39211 (part), 39212, 39213 (part), 39215, 39216 (part), 39225, 39236, 39269, 39282, 39284, 39286, 39289, 39296, 39401 (part), 39421, 39427–29, 39436–37, 39440 (part), 39459, 39464, 39470, 39474, 39478–80, 39482–84, 39601, 39629–33, 39635, 39638, 39641, 39643, 39645, 39647–48, 39652–54, 39656–57, 39661–69, 39759 (part)

* * *

FIFTH DISTRICT

GENE TAYLOR, Democrat, of Bay St. Louis, MS; born in New Orleans, LA on September 17, 1953; graduated from De LaSalle High School, New Orleans, LA, 1971; B.A., Tulane University, New Orleans, LA, 1974; graduate studies in business and economics, August 1978–April 1980; U.S. Coast Guard Reserves, 1971–84, first class petty officer, search and rescue boat skipper; sales representative, Stone Container Corporation, 1977–89; city councilman, Bay St. Louis, 1981–83; State Senator, 1983–89; member: American Legion, Rotarian, Boys and Girls Club of the Gulf Coast; committees: National Security, Transportation and Infrastructure; married the former Margaret Gordon, 1978; three children: Sarah, Emily, Gary; elected to the 101st Congress by special election on October 17, 1989, to fill the vacancy caused by the death of Larkin Smith; reelected to each succeeding Congress.

Office Listings

2447 Rayburn House Office Building, Washington, DC 20515–2405 225–5772
FAX: 225–7074
Administrative Assistant.—Wayne Weidie.
Legislative Director.—Stephen Peranich.
Executive Secretary/Scheduler.—Molly Burns.
2424 Fourteenth Street, Gulfport, MS 39501 .... (601) 864–7670
FAX: 864–3099
District Manager.—Beau Gex.
215 Federal Building, 701 Main Street, Hattiesburg, MS 39401 .... (601) 582–3246
FAX: 582–3452
706 Watts Avenue, Pascagoula, MS 39567 .... (601) 762–1770
FAX: 762–7957

Counties: Forrest, George, Greene, Hancock, Harrison, Jackson, Lamar, Pearl River, Perry, Stone, and Wayne (part). CITIES AND TOWNSHIPS: Biloxi, Gulfport, Hattiesburg, Pascagoula. Population (1990), 514,656.

ZIP Codes: 38827, 39322, 39324, 39362, 39367, 39401, 39402–03, 39406–07, 39423, 39425–26, 39451–52, 39455–57, 39461–66, 39470, 39475–76, 39482, 39501–03, 39505–07, 39520–22, 39525, 39529–35, 39552–53, 39555–56, 39558, 39560–65, 39567–69, 39571–74, 39576–77, 39581

MISSOURI

(Population 1995, 5,324,000)

SENATORS

CHRISTOPHER S. (KIT) BOND, Republican, of Mexico, MO; born March 6, 1939, in St. Louis; B.A., *cum laude*, Woodrow Wilson School of Public and International Affairs of Princeton University, 1960; J.D., valedictorian, University of Virginia, 1963; held a clerkship with the U.S. Court of Appeals for the Fifth Circuit until 1964; practiced law in Washington, DC, and returned to Missouri, 1967; assistant attorney general of Missouri, 1969; state auditor, 1970; governor of Missouri, 1973–77, 1981–85; one child, Samuel Reid Bond; U.S. Senator, elected November 4, 1986; reelected on November 3, 1992; committees: chairman, Small Business; Appropriations; Budget; Environment and Public Works.

Office Listings

http://www.senate.gov/~bond/comm.html kit__bond@bond.senate.gov

274 Russell Senate Office Building, Washington, DC 20510–2503 224–5721
Administrative Assistant.—David Israelite. FAX: 224–8149
Legal Counsel.—Brent Franzel.
Chief of Staff.—Julie Dammann.
Scheduling Secretary.—Kelli Jones.
Rivergate Business Center, 600 Broadway, Suite 400, Kansas City, MO 64105 ...... (816) 471–7141
308 East High, Suite 202, Jefferson City, MO 65101 .... (314) 634–2488
8000 Maryland, Suite 440, St. Louis, MO 63105 .... (314) 727–7773
Room 705, 1736 Sunshine, Springfield, MO 65804 .... (417) 881–7068
Federal Building, Room 214, 339 Broadway, Cape Girardeau, MO 63701 .... (314) 334–7044

* * *

JOHN DAVID ASHCROFT, Republican, of Willard, MO; born in Chicago, IL, May 9, 1942; graduated, Hillcrest High School, Springfield, MO; A.B. *cum laude*, Yale University, 1964; J.D., University of Chicago School of Law, 1967; admitted to the Springfield bar, 1967; Governor of Missouri, 1985–93; Attorney General of Missouri, 1976–85; State Auditor of Missouri, 1973–75; married Janet Elise Ashcroft, 1967; three children: Martha, John Robert, and Andrew; committees: Commerce, Science and Transportation; Judiciary; Foreign Relations; elected to the U.S. Senate in November 1994.

Office Listings

http://www.senate.gov/~ashcroft/ john__ashcroft@ashcroft.senate.gov

316 Hart Senate Office Building, Washington, DC 20510–2502 224–6154
Chief of Staff.—David Ayres.
Executive Assistant.—Janet Potter.
Communications Director.—Steve Hilton.
Appointments.—Andy Beach.
Suite 202, 308 East High, Jefferson City, MO 65101 .... (573) 635–7292
Rivergate Business Center, 600 Broadway, Suite 400, Kansas City, MO 64105 ...... (816) 471–7141
8000 Maryland Avenue, Suite 440, St. Louis, MO 63105 .... (314) 725–4484
Plaza Towers, Suite 705, 1736 East Sunshine, Springfield, MO 65804 .... (417) 881–7068
Room 214, 339 Broadway, Cape Girardeau, MO 63701 .... (573) 334–7044

REPRESENTATIVES

FIRST DISTRICT

WILLIAM (BILL) CLAY, Democrat, of St. Louis, MO; born in St. Louis, April 30, 1931; B.S., St. Louis University, 1953, history and political science; real estate broker; manager, life insurance company, 1959–61; alderman, 26th ward, St. Louis, 1959–64; wrote and sponsored Fair Employment Law, 1963; developed agenda and workshops and attended Summer White House Conference, 1966, as delegate from Missouri; married Carol A. Johnson; three children: Vicki, William, Jr., and Michelle; member, House Committee on Education and the Workforce; elected to the 91st Congress, November 5, 1968; reelected to each succeeding Congress.

Office Listings
http://www.house.gov/clay

2306 Rayburn House Office Building, Washington, DC 20515–2501 .... 225–2406 FAX: 225–1725
Administrative Assistant.—Harriet Pritchett Grigsby.
Legislative Director.—Michele Bogdanovich.
5261 Delmar Boulevard, St. Louis, MO 63108 .... (314) 367–1970
District Assistant.—Pearlie Evans.
12755 New Halls Ferry Road, Florissant, MO 63033 .... (314) 839–9148 FAX: 839–9318
District Coordinator.—Virginia Cook.

Counties: St. Louis County (part) and St. Louis City (part). Population (1990), 568,285.

ZIP Codes: 63031 (part), 63033 (part), 63034, 63042 (part), 63074 (part), 63101, 63102 (part), 63103, 63104 (part), 63105–08, 63110 (part), 63112–13, 63114 (part), 63115, 63117 (part), 63118 (part), 63119 (part), 63120–21, 63122 (part), 63124 (part), 63130, 63132 (part), 63133, 63134 (part), 63135–38, 63140 (part), 63143 (part), 63144–45, 63147, 63155–56, 63166, 63169, 63177–79, 63182, 63188, 63197

* * *

SECOND DISTRICT

JAMES M. TALENT, Republican, of Chesterfield, MO; born in St. Louis, MO, on October 18, 1956; graduated from Kirkwood High School, 1973; B.A., Washington University, St. Louis, 1978; J.D., University of Chicago Law School, 1981; attorney; admitted to the Missouri bar, 1981; clerk for Judge Richard Posner, U.S. Court of Appeals, 7th Circuit; associate of Moller, Talent, Kuelthau, and Welch; counsel of Lashly and Baer; Missouri State House of Representatives, 1985–92, elected minority leader, 1989–92; member: West County Chamber of Commerce; Chesterfield Chamber of Commerce; Twin Oaks Presbyterian Church; related to Congressman Richard A. Gephardt; married the former Brenda Lyons, 1984; three children: Michael, Kathleen, and Christine; elected on November 3, 1992 to the 103rd Congress; reelected to each succeeding Congress.

Office Listings
http://www.house.gov/talent talentmo@house.gov

1022 Longworth House Office Building, Washington, DC 20515–2502 .... 225–2563 FAX: 225–2563
Administrative Assistant.—Mark Strand.
Office Manager.—Michelle Blotevogel.
Legislative Director.—Michael McLaughlin.
820 South Maine Street, Suite 206, Saint Charles, MO 63301 .... (314) 949–6826
District Director.—Barbara Cooper.
555 N. New Ballas Road, Suite 315, St. Louis, MO 63141 .... (314) 872–9561

Counties: St. Charles (part) and St. Louis (part). Population (1990), 568,306.

ZIP Codes: 63005 (part), 63006, 63011, 63017, 63021–22, 63025 (part), 63026 (part), 63031 (part), 63032, 63033 (part), 63038, 63040, 63042 (part), 63043–45, 63069 (part), 63074 (part), 63088, 63114 (part), 63117 (part), 63119 (part), 63122 (part), 63124 (part), 63127 (part), 63128 (part), 63131, 63132 (part), 63134 (part), 63140 (part), 63141, 63146, 63301–02, 63303 (part), 63304 (part), 63338, 63366 (part), 63373, 63376 (part), 63386

* * *

THIRD DISTRICT

RICHARD A. GEPHARDT, Democrat, of St. Louis, MO; born in St. Louis, January 31, 1941; graduated, Southwest High School, 1958; B.S., Northwestern University, 1962; J.D., University of Michigan Law School, 1965; admitted to the Missouri bar in 1965; commenced practice in St. Louis; attorney, partner, Thompson and Mitchell law firm, 1965–77; served in Missouri Air National Guard, 1965–71; chairman, Young Lawyer's Section, the Bar Association of Metropolitan St. Louis, 1971–73; Democratic Committeeman, 1968–71; alderman of 14th ward, city of St. Louis, 1971–77; member: Third Baptist Church (St. Louis), Kiwanis, Boy Scouts of America, Children's United Research Effort, Missouri Bar Association, and the Bar Association of Metropolitan St. Louis; married the former Jane Ann Byrnes, 1966; three children: Matthew, Christine, and Katherine; member, Democratic Caucus; past chairman, Democratic Leadership Council; Democratic leader; first Democratic presidential candidate to announce in the 1988 national election; elected to the 95th Congress, November 2, 1976; reelected to each succeeding Congress.

Office Listings

http://www.house.gov.gephardt gephardt@hr.house.gov

1226 Longworth House Office Building, Washington, DC 20515–2503 225–2671
Administrative Assistant.—Rod Sippel.
Legislative Director.—James Hawley.
11140 South Towne Square, Room 201, St. Louis, MO 63123 .... (314) 894–3400
District Director.—Mary Renick.

Counties: Jefferson, Sainte, Genevieve, St. Louis (part), and St. Louis City (part). Population (1990), 568,326.

ZIP Codes: 63010, 63012, 63016, 63019–20, 63023, 63025 (part), 63026 (part), 63028, 63030, 63041, 63047–53, 63065–66, 63069 (part), 63070, 63087, 63102 (part), 63104 (part), 63109, 63110 (part), 63111, 63116, 63117 (part), 63118 (part), 63119 (part), 63122 (part), 63123, 63125–26, 63127 (part), 63128 (part), 63129, 63139, 63143 (part), 63151, 63157–58, 63163, 63627, 63640, 63661, 63670, 63673

* * *

FOURTH DISTRICT

IKE SKELTON, Democrat, of Lexington, MO; born in Lexington, December 20, 1931; graduated, Lexington High School, 1949; attended Wentworth Military Academy, Lexington; graduated, University of Missouri: A.B., 1953, LL.B., 1956; attended University of Edinburgh (Scotland), 1953; lawyer; admitted to the Missouri bar in 1956 and commenced practice in Lexington; elected, State Senate, 1970; reelected, 1974; prosecuting attorney, Lafayette County, 1957–60; special assistant attorney general, 1961–63; member: Phi Beta Kappa honor society, Missouri Bar Association, Lions, Elks, Masons, Boy Scouts, First Christian Church; married the former Susan B. Anding, 1961; three children: Ike, James, and Page; elected to the 95th Congress, November 2, 1976; reelected to each succeeding Congress.

Office Listings

2227 Rayburn House Office Building, Washington, DC 20515–2504 225–2876
Administrative Assistant.—Jack Pollard.
Appointments.—Melanie Moosally.
Legislative Director.—Lara Battles.
514–B North West 7 Highway, Blue Springs, MO 64014 .... (816) 228–4242
District Representative.—Robert Hagedorn.
319 South Lamine, Sedalia, MO 65301 .... (816) 826–2675
1401 Southwest Boulevard, Jefferson City, MO 65109 .... (573) 635–3499
219 North Adams, Lebanon, MO 65536 .... (417) 532–7964

Counties: Bates, Benton, Camden, Cass, Cole, Dallas, Henry, Hickory, Jackson (part), Johnson, Laclede, Lafayette, Maries, Miller, Moniteau, Morgan, Osage, Pettis, Pulaski, St. Clair, Saline, Vernon, and Webster. Population (1990), 569,146.

ZIP Codes: 63548, 64001, 64011–12, 64014 (part), 64015 (part), 64017, 64019–22, 64029 (part), 64034 (part), 64037, 64040, 64061, 64063 (part), 64067, 64070–71, 64074, 64075 (part), 64076, 64078, 64080, 64082 (part), 64083, 64090, 64093, 64096–97, 64147 (part), 64701, 64720, 64722–26, 64728, 64730, 64733–35, 64738–43, 64744 (part), 64745–47, 64750–52, 64760–61, 64763, 64765, 64767, 64770–72, 64776, 64778–81, 64783, 64784 (part), 64788, 64790, 65001, 65011, 65013–14, 65016–18, 65020, 65023–26, 65032, 65034–35, 65037–38, 65040, 65042, 65046–55, 65058, 65061–62, 65064–65, 65072, 65074–76, 65078–79, 65081–85, 65101–02, 65109–10, 65287, 65301–02, 65305, 65320–21, 65323–27, 65329–30, 65332–40, 65344–45, 65347–51, 65354–55, 65360, 65443, 65452, 65457, 65459, 65461–63, 65470, 65473, 65486, 65534, 65536, 65550, 65552, 65556, 65567, 65572, 65580, 65582–83, 65590–91, 65622, 65632, 65634, 65636, 65644, 65648, 65650, 65652, 65662, 65668, 65674, 65685, 65706, 65713, 65722, 65724, 65727, 65732, 65735, 65742, 65746, 65757, 65764, 65767, 65774, 65779, 65783, 65786–87

* * *

FIFTH DISTRICT

KAREN MCCARTHY, Democrat, of Kansas City, MO; born in Haverhill, MA, March 18, 1947; graduated, Shawnee Mission East High School, Shawnee Mission, KS, 1965; University of Kansas, Lawrence, 1969; B.S. (English) and M.A. (English), University of Missouri, Kansas City, 1976; M.B.A., University of Kansas, 1986; educator; Stern Brothers and Company Investment Bankers; Midwest Research Institute; Marion Merrell Dow; Missouri State Representative; president, National Conference of State Legislatures; president, Leadership America Alumni Board; Harvard Fellow, Institute of Politics, Kennedy School of Government; Japan Fellow, U.S.-Japan Leadership Program; National Democratic Institute for International Affairs instructor; American Council of Young Political Leaders; member, University of Kansas School of Business Board of Advisors; member: Missouri House of Representatives, 1977–95; chair, Ways and Means Committee, 1983–95; elected to the 104th Congress; reelected to the 105th Congress.

Office Listings

1232 Longworth House Office Building, Washington, DC 20515 225–4535
Administrative Assistant/Press Secretary.—Howard Bauleke. FAX: 225–4403
Executive Assistant.—Becky Banta-Kunn.
Legislative Director.—Christopher Yatooma.
Room 935, 811 Grand, Kansas City, MO 64106–1997 .... (816) 842–4545
District Director.—Gerard Grimaldi.
Room 217, 301 West Lexington, Independence, MO 64050–3724 .... (816) 833–4545

County: JACKSON COUNTY (part); cities and townships of Grandview, Greenwood, Independence, Lee's Summit, Raytown, and Sugar Creek. Population (1990), 569,130.

ZIP Codes: 64015 (part), 64016 (part), 64030, 64034 (part), 64050, 64052–55, 64056 (part), 64057 (part), 64058 (part), 64063 (part), 64064 (part), 64065, 64081, 64082 (part), 64100–02, 64105–06, 64108–14, 64120, 64123–34, 64136–39, 64145–46, 64147 (part), 64148–49, 64196, 64198–99

* * *

SIXTH DISTRICT

PAT DANNER, Democrat, of Kansas City North, MO; born January 13, 1934, in Louisville, KY; public schools in Bevier, MO; graduated *cum laude* from Northeast Missouri State University, B.A., political science; small business owner; appointed to subcabinet position, Carter administration, 1977–81; first and only woman to serve as chair of a regional planning commission; elected to the Missouri Senate, 1982, 1986, and 1990; committees: Transportation and Infrastructure; chair, Education; vice chair, Aging, Families, and Mental Health; Gubernatorial Missouri Scholars Academy Commission; married to C. Markt Meyer; four children: Stephen, Stephanie, Shane, and Shavonne; elected November 3, 1992 to the 103rd Congress; reelected to each succeeding Congress.

Office Listings

1323 Longworth House Office Building, Washington, DC 20515–2506 .... (202) 225–7041
Chief of Staff.—Cathie H. McCarley.
Administrative Assistant.—Doug Gray. FAX: 225–8221
Legislative Director.—Chris Bohannon.
5754 North Broadway, Building 3, Suite 2, Kansas City, MO 64118 .... (816) 455–2256
District Administrator.—Lou Carson. FAX: 255–4153
U.S. Post Office, 201 South Eighth Street, St. Joseph, MO 64501 .... (816) 233–9818
District Administrator.—Rosie Haertling. FAX: 233–9848

Counties: Andrew, Atchison, Buchanan, Caldwell, Carroll, Chariton, Clay, Clinton, Cooper, Daviess, DeKalb, Gentry, Grundy, Harrison, Holt, Howard, Jackson (part), Linn, Livingston, Mercer, Nodaway, Platte, Putnam, Ray, Schuyler, Sullivan, and Worth. Population (1990), 569,131.

ZIP Codes: 63535–36, 63541, 63544–46, 63548, 63551, 63556–61, 63565–67, 64013, 64014 (part), 64015 (part), 64016 (part), 64017–18, 64024, 64028, 64029 (part), 64035–36, 64048, 64056 (part), 64057 (part), 64060, 64062, 64066, 64068, 64072–73, 64075 (part), 64077, 64079, 64084–85, 64088 (part), 64089, 64092, 64098, 64116–19, 64150–58, 64161, 64163–68, 64192, 64195, 64401–02, 64420–24, 64426–49, 64451–59, 64461, 64463, 64465–71, 64473–87, 64489–94, 64496–99, 64501–08, 64601, 64620–25, 64628, 64630–33, 64635–61, 64664–65, 64667–68, 64670–74, 64676–77, 64679, 64681–83, 64686–89, 65025, 65046, 65068, 65230, 65233, 65236–37, 65244, 65246, 65248, 65250, 65254, 65256–57, 65261, 65274, 65276, 65279, 65281, 65286–87, 65322, 65347–48, 65354

* * *

SEVENTH DISTRICT

ROY D. BLUNT, Republican, of Bolivar, MO; born in Niangua, MO, January 10, 1950; president, Southwest Baptist University; author; two-term Missouri Secretary of State; past chair: Missouri Housing Development Commission, Governor's Council on Literacy; past cochair, Missouri Opportunity 2000 Commission; past member, Project Democracy Commission for Voter Participation in the United States; past board member, American Council of Young Political Leaders; served as first chairman of the Missouri Prison Fellowship; named one of the Ten Outstanding Young Americans, 1986; married to Roseann Blunt; three children: Matt, Amy, and Andy; committees: Transportation and Infrastructure, Agriculture, International Relations; subcommittees: vice chair, Aviation; Livestock, Dairy, and Poultry; Economic Policy and Trade; elected to the 105th Congress.

Office Listings

508 Cannon House Office Building, Washington, DC 20515–2507 225–6536
Chief of Staff.—Gregg Hartley. FAX: 225–5604
Appointment Secretary.—Kathy Palmateer.
Press Secretary.—Dan Wadlington.
2740-B East Sunshine, Springfield, MO 65802 .... (417) 889–1800
302 Joplin Street, Suite 302, Joplin, MO 64801 .... (417) 781–1041

Counties: Barry, Barton, Cedar, Christian, Dade, Douglas, Greene, Jasper, Lawrence, McDonald, Newton, Ozark, Polk, Stone, and Taney. Population (1990), 568,017.

ZIP Codes: 64728, 64744 (part), 64748, 64755–56, 64759, 64803, 64830–36, 64840–44, 64847–50, 64854–59, 64861–70, 64873–74, 65436, 65463, 65470, 65536, 65543, 65572, 65590, 65632, 65636, 65644, 65654, 65660, 65662, 65667, 65670, 65672, 65674, 65604–05, 65607–14, 65616–20, 65622–27, 65629–31, 65633, 65635, 65637–38, 65640–41, 65646–50, 65652–53, 65655–59, 65661, 65663–64, 65666, 65669, 65672, 65674–76, 65679–82, 65685–86, 65701–02, 65704–08, 65707–08, 65710–15, 65717–18, 65720–23, 65725–34, 65737–42, 65744–45, 65747, 65751–62, 65764–73, 65775, 65781, 65784–85, 65790, 65793, 65801–10

* * *

EIGHTH DISTRICT

JO ANN EMERSON, Republican, of Cape Girardeau, MO; born in Washington, DC, September 16, 1950; B.A., political science, Ohio Wesleyan University, Delaware, OH, 1972; Senior Vice President of Public Affairs, American Insurance Association; director, State Relations and Grassroots Programs, National Restaurant Association; deputy communications director, National Republican Congressional Committee; member: PEO Women's Service Group, Cape Girardeau, MO; Copper Dome Society, Southeast Missouri State University; advisory committee, Children's Inn, National Institutes of Health; advisory board, Arneson Institute for Practical Politics and Public Affairs, Ohio Weslyan University; four children: Elizabeth, Abigail, Victoria, and Katharine; committees: Agriculture, Small Business, Transportation and Infrastructure; elected to the 105th Congress.

Office Listings

http://www.house.gov/emerson joann.emerson@mail.house.gov

132 Cannon House Office Building, Washington, DC 20515–2508 225–4404
Office Manager/Scheduler.—Kacky Garner.
Communications Director/Legislative Assistant.—Pete Jeffries.
Legislative Director/Executive Director.—David LaValle.
Legislative Assistants.—Kelly Glenn, Seaver Sowers.
Legislative Assistant/Systems Administrator.—Julie Pickett.
Staff Assistant.—Margaret Goodin.
339 Broadway, Cape Girardeau, MO 63701 .... (573) 335–0101
Chief of Staff.—Lloyd Smith.
612 North Pine Street, Rolla, MO 65401 .... (573) 364–2455
22 East Columbia, Farmington, MO 63640 .... (573) 756–9755

Counties: Bollinger, Butler, Cape Girardeau, Carter, Crawford, Dent, Dunklin, Howell, Iron, Madison, Mississippi, New Madrid, Oregon, Pemiscot, Perry, Phelps, Reynolds, Ripley, St. Francois, Scott, Shannon, Stoddard, Texas, Washington, Wayne, and Wright. Population (1990), 568,385.

ZIP Codes: 63036, 63071, 63601, 63620–26, 63628–33, 63636–41, 63645–46, 63648, 63650–51, 63653–56, 63660, 63662–65, 63674–75, 63701, 63730, 63732–33, 63735–36, 63738–40, 63742–45, 63747–36, 63738–40, 63742–45, 63747–48, 63750–55, 63758, 63760, 63762–72, 63774–75, 63779–87, 63801, 63820–30, 63833–34, 63837–41, 63845–53, 63855, 63857, 63860, 63862–63, 63866–71, 63873–82, 63901, 63931–37, 63939–45, 63947, 63950–55, 63856, 63960–67, 65014, 65401, 65433, 65436, 65438–41, 65444, 65446, 65449, 65451, 65453, 65456, 65461–62, 65464, 65466, 65468, 65470, 65479, 65483–84, 65501, 65529, 65532, 65535, 65540–42, 65545, 65548, 65550, 65552, 65555, 65557, 65559–60, 65564–66, 65570–71, 65573, 65586, 65588–89, 65606, 65609, 65626, 65637, 65660, 65662, 65667, 65688–90, 65692, 65702, 65704, 65711, 65717, 65775, 65777–78, 65788–91, 6579

* * *

NINTH DISTRICT

KENNY HULSHOF, Republican, of Columbia, MO; born on May 22, 1958 in Sikestown, MO; graduated from Thomas W. Kelly High School, Benton, MO; agriculture economics degree, University of Missouri School of Agriculture, 1980; J.D., University of Mississippi Law School, 1983; attorney, admitted to Missouri and Mississippi bars in 1983; Assistant Public Defender, 32nd judicial circuit, 1983–86; Assistant Prosecuting Attorney, Cape Girardeau, MO, 1986–89; Assistant Attorney General, State of Missouri, 1989–96; member: Newman Center Catholic Church, Boone County Farm Bureau, Farm House Foundation, Ducks Unlimited; committee: Ways and Means; married Renee Howell Hulshof, 1994; elected to the 105th Congress.

Office Listings

http://www.house.gov/hulshof

1728 Longworth House Office Building, Washington, DC 20515 225–2956
FAX: 225–5712
Administrative Assistant.—Matt Miller.
Executive Assistant/Scheduler.—Sara Kennedy.
Legislative Director.—Manning Feraci.

33 Broadway, Suite 280, Columbia, MO 65203 .... (573) 449–5111
FAX: 229–5312

Counties: Adair, Audrain, Boone, Callaway, Clark, Franklin, Gasconade, Knox, Lewis, Lincoln, Macon, Marion, Monroe, Montgomery, Pike, Ralls, Randolph, St. Charles (part), Scotland, Shelby, and Warren. Population (1990), 568,347.

ZIP Codes: 63001, 63005 (part), 63013–15, 63023, 63037, 63039, 63055–56, 63060–61, 63068, 63069 (part), 63072, 63073, 63077, 63079–80, 63084, 63089–91, 63303 (part), 63304 (part), 63330, 63332–34, 63336, 63339, 63341–53, 63357, 63359, 63361–65, 63366 (part), 63367, 63369–70, 63371, 63376 (part), 63377, 63379, 63381–85, 63387–90, 63401, 63430–43, 63445–48, 63450–54, 63456–74, 63501, 63530–40, 63541, 63543–44, 63546–47, 63549, 63552, 63555, 63558–59, 63563, 63567, 63755, 64012, 64075, 65010, 65014, 65022, 65036, 65039, 65041, 65043, 65056, 65059, 65061–63, 65066–67, 65069, 65077, 65080, 65201–03, 65205, 65231–32, 65239–40, 65243–44, 65245, 65247, 65251, 65255–60, 65262–65, 65270, 65275, 65278–80, 65282–85, 65338, 65347, 65707, 65778

MONTANA

(Population 1995, 870,000)

SENATORS

MAX BAUCUS, Democrat, of Helena, MT; born in Helena, December 11, 1941; graduated, Helena High School, 1959; B.A. in economics, Stanford University, 1964; LL.B., Stanford University Law School, 1967; attorney, Civil Aeronautics Board, 1967–71; attorney, George and Baucus law firm, Missoula, MT; married to the former Wanda Minge; one child, Zeno; member, Montana and District of Columbia bar associations; served in Montana House of Representatives, 1973–74; elected to the 94th Congress, November 5, 1974; reelected to the 95th Congress; elected to the U.S. Senate, November 7, 1978 for the six-year term beginning January 3, 1979; subsequently appointed December 15, 1978, to fill the vacancy caused by the resignation of Senator Paul Hatfield; reelected November 6, 1984 and to each succeeding term; member: Finance Committee; Agriculture, Nutrition and Forestry Committee; Select Committee on Intelligence; Joint Committee on Taxation; ranking minority member, Environment and Public Works Committee.

Office Listings

http://www.senate.gov/~baucus max@baucus.senate.gov

511 Hart Senate Office Building, Washington, DC 20510–2602 224–2651
Chief of Staff.—David Castagnette.
Legislative Director.—Brian Cavey.
Press Secretary.—Tim Warner.
207 North Broadway, Billings, MT 59101 .... (406) 657–6790
State Director.—Sharon Peterson. (800) 332–6106
P.O. Box 1689, Bozeman, MT 59771 .... (406) 586–6104
Silver Bow Center, 125 West Granite, Butte, MT 59701 .... (406) 782–8700
118 Fifth Street South, Great Falls, MT 59401 .... (406) 761–1574
23 South Last Chance Gulch, Helena, MT 59601 .... (406) 449–5480
Chief of Staff.—Doug Mitchell.
Scheduler.—Holly Luck.
220 First Avenue East, Kalispell, MT 59901 .... (406) 756–1150
Room 102, 211 North Higgins, Missoula, MT 59802 .... (406) 329–3123

* * *

CONRAD BURNS, Republican, of Billings, MT; born in Gallatin, MO, on January 25, 1935; graduated, Gallatin High School, 1952; attended University of Missouri, Columbia, 1953–54; served, U.S. Marine Corps, corporal, 1955–57; farm broadcaster and auctioneer; county commissioner, Yellowstone County, 1986; member: Rotary, American Legion, National Association of Farm Broadcasters, American Association of Farm Broadcasters, Atonement Lutheran Church; married to the former Phyllis Kuhlmann; two children: Keely and Garrett; committees: Appropriations; Commerce, Science, and Transportation; Energy and Natural Resources; Small Business; Special Committee on Aging; elected to the U.S. Senate on November 8, 1988, for the six-year term beginning January 3, 1989; reelected November 8, 1994, for the six-year term beginning January 4, 1995.

Office Listings

http://www.senate.gov/~burns conrad_burns@burns.senate.gov

183 Dirksen Senate Office Building, Washington, DC 20510–2603 224–2644
Administrative Assistant.—Leo Giacometto.
Senior Legislative Director.—Mark Baker.
Executive Assistant/Scheduler.—Jennifer Parson.
Office Manager.—Margo Rushing.
208 North Montana Avenue, Suite 202–A, Helena, MT 59601 .... (406) 449–5401
2708 First Avenue North, Billings, MT 59101 .... (406) 252–0550
321 First Avenue North, Great Falls, MT 59401 .... (406) 452–9585
415 North Higgins, Missoula, MT 59802 .... (406) 329–3528
324 West Towne, Glendive, MT 59330 .... (406) 365–2391
211 Haggerty Lane, Bozeman, MT 59715 .... (406) 586–4450
125 West Granite, Suite 211, Butte, MT 59701 .... (406) 723–3277
575 Sunset Boulevard, Suite 101, Kalispell, MT 59901 .... (406) 257–3360

REPRESENTATIVE

AT LARGE

RICK HILL, Republican, of Helena, MT; born on December 30, 1946; B.S., economics and political science, St. Cloud State University; businessman; served as Republican precinct committeeman and state committeeman from Lewis and Clark County; served on board of directors, Montana Science and Technology Alliance; chair, State Worker's Compensation Board, 1993–96; past chairman, Helena Chamber of Commerce and State Republican Party Government Affairs Committee; past president, Professional Insurance Agents and Green Meadow Country Club; member: Montana Ambassadors, Montana Contractors Association, National Surety Bond Association, National Rifle Association, National Ski Patrol, *Who's Who in American Finance and Industry*; married to Betti Hill; three grown sons; committees: Banking and Financial Services, Resources, Small Business, Republican Policy; elected to the 105th Congress.

Office Listings

rickhill@mail.house.gov

1037 Longworth House Office Building, Washington, DC 20515 225–3211
FAX: 225–5687
Chief of Staff.—Mike Pieper.
Legislative Director.—Richard Jones.
Legislative Assistant/Systems Administrator.—Warren Tryon.
Legislative Assistant.—Rob Hobart.
Scheduler.—Anne-Marie Wade.

33 South Last Chance Gulch, Aspen Court Building 2C, Helena, MT 59601 .... (406) 443–7878
FAX: 449–3637
State Director.—Peggy Trenk.
Western Field Representative.—Roger Halver.

27 North 27th Street, Billings, MT 59101 .... (406) 256–1019
FAX: 256–3185
Eastern Field Representative.—Larry Herzog.

Counties: Beaverhead, Big Horn, Blaine, Broadwater, Carbon, Carter, Cascade, Chouteau, Custer, Daniels, Dawson, Deer Lodge, Fallon, Fergus, Flathead, Gallatin, Garfield, Glacier, Golden Valley, Granite, Hill, Jefferson, Judith Basin, Lake, Lewis and Clark, Liberty, Lincoln, Madison, McCone, Meagher, Mineral, Missoula, Mussellshell Park, Petroleum, Phillips, Pondera, Powder River, Powell, Prairie, Ravalli, Richland, Roosevelt, Rosebud, Sanders, Sheridan, Silver Bow, Stillwater, Sweet Grass, Teton, Toole, Treasure, Valley, Wheatland, Wibaux, Yellowstone, and Yellowstone National Park. Population (1990), 799,065.

ZIP Codes: 59001–03, 59006–08, 59010–20, 59022, 59024–39, 59041, 59043–44, 59046–47, 59050–55, 59057–59, 59061–72, 59074–79, 59081–83, 59085–89, 59101–08, 59111–12, 59114–17, 59201, 59211–15, 59217–19, 59221–26, 59230–31, 59240–45, 59247–48, 59250, 59252–63, 59270, 59273–76, 59301, 59311–19, 59322–24, 59326–27, 59330, 59332–33, 59336–39, 59341–45, 59347–49, 59351, 59353–54, 59401, 59403–06, 59410–12, 59414, 59416–22, 59424–25, 59427, 59430, 59432–36, 59440–48, 59450–54, 59456–57, 59460–69, 59471–474, 59477, 59479–80, 59482–87, 59489, 59501, 59520–32, 59535, 59537–38, 59540, 59542, 59544–47, 59601, 59604, 59624, 59626, 59631–36, 59638–45, 59647–48, 59701–03, 59710–11, 59713–17, 59720–22, 59724–25, 59727–33, 59735–36, 59739–41, 59743, 59745–52, 59754–56, 59758–62, 59771–72, 59801–03, 59806–07, 59820–21, 59823–37, 59840–48, 59851–56, 59858–60, 59863–68, 59870–75, 59901, 59903–04, 59910–23, 59925–37

NEBRASKA

(Population 1995, 1,637,000)

SENATORS

J. ROBERT KERREY, Democrat, of Omaha, NE; born in Lincoln, NE, August 27, 1943; graduated, Northeast High School, Lincoln, 1961; B.S. degree in pharmacy, University of Nebraska, Lincoln, 1966; served, U.S. Navy, lieutenant (jg), 1966–69; restaurateur; Governor of Nebraska, 1983–87; member: VFW, American Legion, Disabled American Veterans, Vietnam Veterans of America, Chamber of Commerce, Medal of Honor Society; two children: Benjamin and Lindsey; committees: Agriculture, Nutrition and Forestry; Finance; vice chairman, Select Committee on Intelligence; elected to the U.S. Senate on November 8, 1988 for the six-year term beginning January 3, 1989; reelected November 8, 1994 for the six-year term beginning January 4, 1995.

Office Listings

http://www.senate.gov/~kerrey/pages/index3.html bob@kerrey.senate.gov

141 Hart Senate Office Building, Washington, DC 20510–2704 224–6551
Interim Chief of Staff.—Sheila Nix.
Administrative Director.—Mary Conklin.
Communications Director.—Greg Weiner.
Schedulers: Mary Sherman (DC); Cindy Dwyer (State and National).
7602 Pacific Street Omaha, NE 68114 .... (402) 391–3411
Federal Building, 100 Centennial Mall North, Lincoln, NE 68508 .... (402) 437–5109
2106 First Avenue, Scottsbluff, NE 69361 .... (308) 632–3595

* * *

CHUCK HAGEL, Republican, of Omaha, NE; born in North Platte, NE, October 4, 1946; graduated, St. Bonaventure High School, Columbus, NE, 1964; Brown Institute for Radio and Television, Minneapolis, MN; University of Nebraska, Omaha; served with U.S. Army in Vietnam, 1968, receiving two Purple Hearts, other decorations; president, McCarthy and Company, Omaha, NE; president and CEO, Private Sector Council (PSC), Washington, DC; deputy director and CEO, Economic Summit of Industrialized Nations (G–7 Summit), 1990; president and CEO, World USO; cofounder, director, and executive vice president, VANGUARD Cellular Systems, Inc.; cofounder and chairman of VANGUARD subsidiary, Communications Corporation International, Ltd.; president, Collins, Hagel and Clarke, Inc.; former deputy administrator, Veterans' Administration; former administrative assistant to Congressman John Y. McCollister; former newscaster and talk show host, Omaha radio stations KBON and KLNG; member: American Legion; Veterans of Foreign Wars; Disabled American Veterans; Military Order of the Purple Heart; Business-Government Relations Council, Washington, DC; Council for Excellence in Government; University of Nebraska Chancellors Club; board of directors, Omaha Chamber of Commerce; board of trustees: Bellevue University, Hastings College, Heartland Chapter of the American Red Cross; chairman: Building Campaign, Great Plains Chapter of Paralyzed Veterans of America; 10th Anniversary Vietnam Veterans' Memorial; board of directors and national advisory committee, Friends of the Vietnam Veterans' Memorial; board of directors, Arlington National Cemetery Historical Society; chairman of the board, No Greater Love, Inc.; awards: first-ever World USO Leadership Award; International Men of Achievement; Outstanding Young Men of America; Distinguished Alumni Award, University of Nebraska, Omaha, 1988; Freedom Foundation (Omaha Chapter) 1993 Recognition Award; married the former Lillian Ziller, 1985; two children, Allyn and Ziller; committees: Banking, Housing and Urban Affairs; Foreign Relations; Special Committee on Aging; subcommittees: Financial Services and Technology; Housing Opportunity and Community Development; International Finance; East Asian and Pacific Affairs; European Affairs; chair, International Economic Policy, Export, and Trade Promotion; deputy Republican whip; elected to the U.S. Senate on November 5, 1996.

Office Listings

http://www.senate.gov/senator/hagel.html chuck_hagel@hagel.senate.gov

346 Russell Senate Office Building, Washington, DC 20510 224–4224

Administrative Assistant.—Sheila Ross. FAX: 224–5213
Office Manager.—Gladys Gordon.
Press Secretary.—Deb Fiddelke.
Scheduler.—Brenda Hart.
Legislative Counsel.—Derek Schmidt.

11301 Davenport Street, Suite 2, Omaha, NE 68154 .... (402) 758–8981 FAX: 758–9165
State Director.—Tom Janssen.

294 Federal Building, 100 Centennial Mall North, Lincoln, NE 68508 .... (402) 476–1400 FAX: 476–0605
Constituent Services Director.—Dorothy Anderson.

4009 Sixth Avenue, Suite 9, Kearney, NE 68847.
Constituent Services Representative.—Julie Brooker.

300 East Third Street, North Platte, NE 69101 .... (308) 534–2006 FAX: 534–1150
Constituent Services Representative.—Carol Gale.

1010 Avenue T, Scottsbluff, NE 69361 .... (308) 632–6032 FAX: 632–6295
Constituent Services Representative.—Lee Ann McLaughlin.
Field Representative.—Mary B. Crawford.

REPRESENTATIVES

FIRST DISTRICT

DOUG BEREUTER, Republican, of Lincoln, NE; born in York, NE, October 6, 1939, son of Rupert and Evelyn Bereuter; graduated, Utica High School, Utica, NE, 1957; B.A., University of Nebraska, Lincoln, 1961; Sigma Alpha Epsilon; M.C.P., Harvard University, 1966; M.P.A., Harvard University, 1973; counterintelligence officer, First Infantry Division, U.S. Army, 1963–65; urban development consultant in states surrounding Nebraska; associate professor at University of Nebraska and Kansas State University; visiting lecturer, Harvard University; State Senator, Nebraska Unicameral Legislature, 1974–78; vice chairman, Appropriations Committee and Committee on Administrative Rules and Regulations, 1977–78; chaired the Urban Development Committee of the National Conference of State Legislatures, 1977–78; member, Select Committee on Post-Secondary Education Coordination, 1977–78; Legislative Conservationist of the Year Award by the Nebraska and National Wildlife Federation in 1980; division director, Nebraska Department of Economic Development, 1967–68; director, State Office of Planning and Programming, 1968–70; appointee, Federal-State Relations Coordinator for Nebraska State Government, 1967–70; member: State Crime Commission 1969–71; Phi Beta Kappa; Sigma Xi; board of trustees, Nebraska Wesleyan University; member: State Department Commission on Security and Economic Assistance, 1983–84, National Commission on Agricultural Trade and Export Policy 1985–86; congressional delegate to the United Nations, 1987; member: Committee on International Relations, vice chairman; Committee on Banking and Financial Services; House Delegation to the North Atlantic Assembly, chairman; House Interparliamentary Delegation to the European Parliament; married Louise Meyer Bereuter, 1962; two children: Eric and Kirk; elected to the 96th Congress and each succeeding Congress.

Office Listings

2348 Rayburn House Office Building, Washington, DC 20515–2701 225–4806
Administrative Assistant.—Susan Olson.
Office Manager.—Robin Evans.
Appointment/Personal Secretary.—Marcia Smith.

1045 K Street, Lincoln, NE 68508 .... (402) 438–1598
District Office Manager.—Jim Barr.

502 North Broad Street, Fremont, NE 68025 .... (402) 727–0888

Counties: Burt, Butler, Cass (part), Cedar, Colfax, Cuming, Dakota, Dixon, Dodge, Gage, Johnson, Lancaster, Madison, Nemaha, Otoe, Pawnee, Richardson, Saline, Saunders, Seward, Stanton, Thurston, Washington, Wayne, and York. Population (1990), 526,297.

ZIP Codes: 68001–04, 68008, 68014–20, 68023, 68025, 68029–31, 68033, 68036–42, 68044–45, 68047, 68050, 68055, 68057–58, 68061–63, 68065–68, 68070–73, 68301, 68304–05, 68307, 68309–10, 68313–14, 68316–21, 68323–24, 68328–33, 68336–37, 68339, 68341, 68343–49, 68355, 68357–60, 68364, 68366–68, 68371–72, 68374, 68376, 68378–82, 68401–05, 68407, 68409–10, 68413–15, 68417–23, 68428, 68430–34, 68437–39, 68441–43, 68445–48, 68450, 68453–58, 68460–67, 68500–510, 68512, 68514, 68516–17, 68520–24, 68526–29, 68531–32, 68542, 68621, 68624, 68626, 68629, 68632–33, 68635, 68641, 68643, 68648–50, 68657–59, 68661, 68664, 68667, 68669, 68701, 68710, 68715–17, 68723, 68727–28, 68731–33, 68738–41, 68743, 68745, 68748–49, 68751–52, 68757–58, 68762, 68768, 68770–71, 68774, 68776, 68779, 68781, 68784–85, 68787–88, 68790–92

* * *

SECOND DISTRICT

JON CHRISTENSEN, Republican, of Omaha, NE; born in St. Paul, NE, February 20, 1963; graduated, St. Paul High School, St. Paul; graduated, Midland Lutheran College, 1985; J.D.,

South Texas College of Law, Houston, 1989; elected freshman class president; member of the student senate; cofounded Midland's Fellowship of Christian Athletes; served as president of Law Week; clerk, Vision and Elkins law firm, interned at Windle Turley, P.C. law firm and the banking divisions of Chamberlin Hrdlicka, Dallas; admitted to the Nebraska State bar, 1992; vice president, COMReP, Inc.; marketing director, Connecticut Mutual Insurance Co.; insurance executive; formed Aquila Group, Inc.; member: Nebraska Farm Bureau; Nebraska Cattlemen's Association, National Federation of Independent Business; Northwest Rotary Club; American, Nebraska, and Omaha bar associations; ABA's Real Estate; Probate and Trust Division, National and Omaha Associations of Life Underwriters; cochairman, American Diabetes Association's Celebrity Breakfast; married Meredith Stewart Maxfield, 1987; committee: Ways and Means; subcommittees: Health and Social Security.

Office Listings

talk2jon@house.gov

1020 Longworth House Office Building, Washington, DC 20515 225–4155
Administrative Assistant.—Steven Thomlison. FAX: 225–3032
Legislative Director.—Mark Fahleson.
Legislative Aides: Patricia Fava, Pam Davidson, Paul Gresens.
Press Secretary.—Chris Hull.
8712 West Dodge Road, Room 350, Omaha, NE 68114 .... (402) 397–9944
District Director.—Bill Protexter. FAX: 397–8787
Deputy District Director.—Krista Neumann.
Constituent Liaisons: Terry Van Keuren, Dwain Marlowe, Karie Keown.

Counties: Douglas and Sarpy; cities of Bellevue, Bennington, Boys Town, Elkhorn, Gretna, La Vista, Omaha, Offutt AFB, Papillion, Plattsmouth, Ralston, Springfield, Valley, Waterloo. Population (1990), 526,567.

ZIP Codes: 68005, 68007, 68010, 68022, 68028, 68046, 68048 (part), 68059, 68064, 68069, 68102, 68104–08, 68111–18, 68122–24, 68127–28, 68130–38, 68142, 68144, 68147, 68152, 68154, 68157, 68164

* * *

THIRD DISTRICT

WILLIAM E. (BILL) BARRETT, Republican, of Lexington, NE; born in Lexington on February 9, 1929; graduate of Lexington High School; B.A., Hastings College, Hastings, NE, 1951; classes at Universities of Connecticut, Nebraska, and Colorado; served in the U.S. Navy, 1951–52; career in real estate and insurance since 1956; president, Barrett-Housel and Associates, Inc., 1970–90; appointed to Nebraska Unicameral Legislature in 1979; elected to Nebraska Legislature in 1980, 1984, 1988; elected Speaker of the Nebraska Legislature, 1987–90; named Legislator of the Year by the National Republican Legislators Association, 1990; named one of the five most influential State legislators by the *Lincoln Star*, 1988; member: Lexington School Board, 1962–68; Lexington Planning Commission; Lexington Airport Authority; Greater Lexington Development Corporation; organizational memberships: Nebraska Association of Insurance Agents; National Association of Insurance Agents; past president, Dawson County Board of Realtors; past treasurer, Nebraska Realtors Association; Realtors National Marketing Institute; American Institute of Real Estate Appraisers; National Association of Realtors; National Association of Realtors' honorary fraternity, Omega Tau Rho; certified instructor, Nebraska Real Estate Commission; member: Nebraska Jaycees (past president); Lexington Rotary Club (past president); American Legion; elder, Presbyterian Church; trustee, Hastings College; married Elsie Carlson Barrett, 1952; four children: William, David, Elizabeth, and Jane; committees: Agriculture, Education and Labor; elected to the 102nd Congress, November 6, 1990; reelected to each succeeding Congress.

Office Listings

http://www.house.gov/billbarrett

1213 Longworth House Office Building, Washington, DC 20515–2703 225–6435
Administrative Assistant.—Jeralyn P. Finke.
Press Secretary.—Julie Ryan.
Scheduler/Office Manager.—Anna Castner.
312 West Third Street, Grand Island, NE 68801 .... (308) 381–5555
1811 Avenue A, Scottsbluff, NE 69361 .... (308) 632–3333

Counties: Adams; Antelope; Arthur; Banner; Blaine; Boone; Box Butte; Boyd; Brown; Buffalo; Chase; Cherry; Cheyenne; Clay; Custer; Dawes; Dawson; Deuel; Dundy; Fillmore; Franklin; Frontier; Furnas; Garden; Garfield; Gosper; Grant; Greeley; Hall; Hamilton; Harlan; Hayes; Hitchcock; Holt; Hooker; Howard; Jefferson; Kearney; Keith; Keya Paha; Kimball; Knox; Lincoln; Logan; Loup; McPherson; Merrick; Morrill; Nance; Nuckolls; Perkins; Phelps; Pierce; Platte;

Polk; Red Willow; Rock; Scotts Bluff; Sheridan; Sherman; Sioux; Thayer; Thomas; Valley; Webster; Wheeler. Population (1990), 525,521.

ZIP Codes: 68303, 68315–16, 68322, 68325–27, 68335, 68338, 68340–42, 68350–52, 68354, 68361–62, 68365, 68367, 68370–71, 68375, 68377, 68401, 68406, 68416, 68424, 68429, 68436, 68440, 68444, 68452–53, 68464, 68601–02, 68620, 68622–23, 68625, 68627–28, 68630–31, 68634, 68636–38, 68640, 68642–44, 68647, 68651–55, 68660, 68662–63, 68665–66, 68711, 68713–14, 68718–20, 68722, 68724–26, 68729–30, 68734–35, 68737–38, 68742, 68746–47, 68752–53, 68755–56, 68758–61, 68763–67, 68769, 68771–73, 68777–78, 68780–81, 68783, 68786, 68789, 68801–03, 68810, 68812–29, 68831–38, 68840–44, 68846–48, 68850, 68852–56, 68858–66, 68868–76, 68878–83, 68901–02, 68920, 68922–30, 68932–52, 68954–61, 68963–64, 68966–67, 68969–82, 69001, 69020–46, 69101, 69103, 69120–23, 69125, 69127–35, 69138, 69140–57, 69161–63, 69165–71, 69201, 69210–12, 69214, 69216–21, 69301, 69331, 69333–37, 69339–41, 69343, 69345–58, 69360–61, 69363, 69365–67

NEVADA

(Population 1995, 1,530,000)

SENATORS

HARRY REID, Democrat, of Searchlight NV; born in Searchlight on December 2, 1939; graduated, Basic High School, Henderson, NV, 1957; associate degree in science, Southern Utah State College, 1959; B.S., Utah State University, Phi Kappa Phi, 1961; J.D., George Washington School of Law, Washington, DC, 1964; admitted to the Nevada State bar in 1963, a year before graduating from law school; while attending law school, worked as a U.S. Capitol police officer; city attorney, Henderson, 1964–66; member and chairman, South Nevada Memorial Hospital Board of Trustees, 1967–69; elected: Nevada State Assembly, 1969–70; Lieutenant Governor, State of Nevada, 1970–74; served, executive committee, National Conference of Lieutenant Governors; chairman, Nevada Gaming Commission, 1977–81; member: Nevada State, Clark County and American bar associations; married the former Landra Gould in 1959; five children: Lana, Rory, Leif, Josh, and Key; elected to the 98th Congress on November 2, 1982 and reelected to the 99th Congress; elected to the U.S. Senate on November 4, 1986; reelected November 3, 1992; committees: Appropriations; Environment and Public Works; vice chairman, Select Committee on Ethics; Special Committee on Aging; Indian Affairs; subcommittees: ranking member, Energy and Water Development; Drinking Water, Fisheries and Wildlife.

Office Listings

http://www.senate.gov/~reid senator_reid@reid.senate.gov

528 Hart Senate Office Building, Washington, DC 20510–2803 224–3542
Personal Secretary.—Janice Shelton. FAX: 224–7327
Administrative Assistant.—Reynaldo L. Martinez.
Legislative Director.—Larry Werner.
Press Secretary.—Susan McCue.
Room 302, 600 East Williams, Carson City, NV 89701 .... (702) 882–7343
300 Las Vegas Boulevard South, Suite 1610, Las Vegas, NV 89101 .... (702) 474–0041
400 S. Virginia Street, No. 902, Reno, NV 89501 .... (702) 686–5750

* * *

RICHARD H. BRYAN, Democrat, of Las Vegas, NV; born on July 16, 1937 in Washington, DC; graduated, Las Vegas High School, Las Vegas, 1955; B.A., University of Nevada, Reno, 1959; LL.B., University of California Hastings College of Law, 1963; second lieutenant, U.S. Army, 1959–60; served in U.S. Army Reserves; attorney, began practice in Nevada, 1963; appointed public defender, 1966–68; Nevada State Assembly, 1968–72; Nevada State Senate, 1972–78; Nevada Attorney General, 1979–83; Governor of Nevada, 1983–89; married the former Bonnie Fairchild, 1962; three children: Richard, Jr., Leslie, and Blair; member: Committees on Banking, Housing and Urban Affairs; Commerce, Science and Transportation; Finance; Select Committee on Intelligence; Democratic Senatorial Campaign Committee; Democratic Steering Committee; subcommittees: ranking member, Financial Institutions and Regulatory Relief; Housing Opportunity and Community Development; Securities; Consumer Affairs, Foreign Commerce and Tourism; Science, Technology and Space; elected to the U.S. Senate on November 8, 1988 for the six-year term commencing January 3, 1989; reelected November 8, 1994.

Office Listings

http://www.senate.gov/~bryan senator@bryan.senate.gov

364 Russell Senate Office Building, Washington, DC 20510–2804 224–6244
Administrative Assistant.—Jean Neal. FAX: 224–1867
Legislative Counsel.—Opal Winebrenner.
Legislative Director.—Andrew Vermilye.
Suite 304, 600 East Williams Street, Carson City, NV 89701 .... (702) 885–9111
Suite 1110, 300 Las Vegas Boulevard, Las Vegas, NV 89101 .... (702) 388–6605

REPRESENTATIVES

FIRST DISTRICT

JOHN ENSIGN, Republican, of Las Vegas, NV; born in Roseville, CA, March 25, 1958; graduated E.W. Clark High School, Las Vegas, 1976; B.S., University of Las Vegas,

1976–79; Oregon State University, 1981; Colorado State University, 1985; veterinarian; general manager of a casino; member: Las Vegas Southwest Rotary, Las Vegas Chamber of Commerce, Sigma Chi fraternity, Prison Fellowship, Meadows Christian Fellowship; married Darlene Ensign, 1987; two children, Trevor and Siena; committees: Ways and Means, Resources; subcommittee: Human Resources; elected to the 104th Congress; reelected to the 105th Congress.

Office Listings

http://www.house.gov/ensign ensign@hr.house.gov

414 Cannon House Office Building, Washington, DC 20515 225–5965
FAX: 225–3119
Chief of Staff.—Mark Emerson.
Legislative Director.—J. Scott Bensing.
Press Secretary.—Katie Baur.
Scheduler.—Ziba Ayeen.
1000 East Sahara Avenue, Suite D, Las Vegas, NV 89104 .... (702) 731–1801
FAX: 731–1863
District Director.—Sonia Joya.

County: CLARK COUNTY (part); cities of Henderson, Las Vegas, and North Las Vegas. Population (1990), 600,957.

ZIP Codes: 89014–16, 89030–31, 89101–04, 89106–10, 89112, 89114–28, 89130, 89132, 89160, 89170, 89180, 89185, 89191, 89193

* * *

SECOND DISTRICT

JAMES A. GIBBONS, Republican, of Reno, NV; born in Sparks, NV, December 16, 1944; B.S., geology, and M.S., mining geology, University of Nevada at Reno; J.D., Southwestern University; admitted to the Nevada bar in 1982 and began practice in Reno; colonel, U.S. Air Force, 1967–71; vice commander of the Nevada Air Guard since 1975; pilot, Delta Airlines; mining geologist; mining and water rights attorney; Nevada State Assemblyman, 1989–93; member: advisory board, Committee to Aid Abused Women; Nevada Landman's Association; American Association of Petroleum Landsmen; Nevada Bar Association; National Conference Board; University of Nevada Alumni Association; Reno Board of Realtors; board of directors, Nevada Council on Economic Education; Nevada Development Authority; married Theresa D. Snelling in 1986; three children: Christopher, Jennifer, and Jimmy; committees: Resources and National Security; elected to the 105th Congress.

Office Listings

1116 Longworth House Office Building, Washington, DC 20515 225–6155
FAX: 225–5679
Chief of Staff/Press Secretary.—Michael L. Dayton.
Legislative Director.—Stephen S. Swan.
Senior Legislative Assistant.—Jack Victory.
Legislative Assistants: John Fileppo, Peggy Gordon, Dawn Suitor.
Office Manager/Scheduler.—Ashley E. McKinney.
400 South Virginia Street, Suite 502, Reno, NV 89501 .... (702) 686–5760
FAX: 686–5711
District Office Manager.—Deanna Lazovich.
Constituent Service Representatives: Toni Angelini, Daniel Grimmer, Patricia Phillips.
850 South Durango Drive, Suite 107, Las Vegas, NV 89128 .... (702) 255–1651
FAX: 255–1927
Regional Field Representative.—Jeanne Rice.
Western Folklife Center, 501 Railroad Street, Suite 202, Elko, NV 89801 .... (702) 777–7920
FAX: 777–7922
Regional Representative.—Claude Ackerman.

Counties: All of the state of Nevada except for parts of Clark County. Population (1990), 600,876.

ZIP Codes: 89001, 89003–10, 89013, 89015 (part), 89017–25, 89028–29, 89030 (part), 89031 (part), 89036, 89039–43, 89045–47, 89049, 89103 (part), 89107 (part), 89108 (part), 89111, 89113, 89115 (part), 89117 (part), 89118 (part), 89122 (part), 89124 (part), 89128 (part), 89129, 89130 (part), 89131, 89133–34, 89301, 89310–11, 89314–19, 89402–15, 89418–34, 89436, 89438–40, 89442, 89444–45, 89447–51, 89501–07, 89509–13, 89515, 89520, 89523, 89550, 89557, 89564, 89570, 89701–06, 89721, 89801–03, 89820–26, 89828, 89830–35, 89883

NEW HAMPSHIRE

(Population 1995, 1,148,000)

SENATORS

ROBERT C. SMITH, Republican, of Tuftonboro, NH; born in Trenton, NJ, March 30, 1941; B.S., government and history, Lafayette College, Easton, PA, 1965; served, U.S. Navy, 1965–67; one year of duty in Vietnam, five years in U.S. Naval Reserves; teacher, realtor; married to the former Mary Jo Hutchinson; three children: Jennifer, Robert, Jr., and Jason; elected to the U.S. House, 1985–90; served on Armed Services Committee, Science and Technology Committee, Veterans' Affairs Committee, Small Business Committee, and Select Committee on Children, Youth and Families; elected to the U.S. Senate, November 6, 1990; reelected November 5, 1996; committees: Armed Services; Environment and Public Works; chairman, Select Committee on Ethics; Senate Steering Committee.

Office Listings

http://www.senate.gov/~smith opinion@smith.senate.gov

307 Dirksen Senate Office Building, Washington, DC 20510–2903 224–2841
Administrative Assistant.—Patrick J. Pettey.
Legislative Director/General Counsel.—Rick Valentine.
Press Secretary.—Lisa B. Harrison.
Office Manager.—Nancy B. Post.
Suite 100, 1750 Elm Street, Manchester, NH 03104 .... (603) 634–5000
State Director.—Mark Aldrich.
One Harbour Place, Portsmouth, NH 03801 .... (603) 433–1667
1st Floor, 3 Glen Avenue, Berlin, NH 03570 .... (603) 752–2600

* * *

JUDD GREGG, Republican, of Greenfield, NH; born in Nashua, NH, February 14, 1947; graduated Phillips Exeter Academy, 1965; A.B., Columbia University, New York City, 1969; J.D., 1972, and LL.M., 1975, Boston University; attorney, admitted to the New Hampshire bar, 1972; commenced practice in Nashua; practiced law, 1975–80; member, Governor's Executive Council, 1978–80; president, Crotched Mountain Rehabilitation Foundation; married to the former Kathleen MacLellan, 1973; three children: Molly, Sarah, and Joshua; committees: Appropriations, Budget, Labor and Human Resources; elected to the 97th Congress, November 4, 1980 and reelected to the 98th–100th Congresses; elected Governor of New Hampshire, 1988–92; elected to the U.S. Senate, November 3, 1992, for the six-year term beginning January 3, 1993.

Office Listings

http://www.senate.gov/~gregg mailbox@gregg.senate.gov

393 Russell Senate Office Building, Washington, DC 20510–2902 224–3324
Administrative Assistant.—Stanley Sokul.
Office Manager.—Suzanne Hoffman.
Legislative Director.—Alyssa Shooshan.
State Director.—Joel Maiola.
125 North Main Street, Concord, NH 03301 .... (603) 225–7115
28 Webster Street, Manchester, NH 03104 .... (603) 622–7979
99 Pease Boulevard, Portsmouth, NH 03801 .... (603) 431–2171
3 Glen Avenue, Berlin, NH 03570 .... (603) 752–2604

REPRESENTATIVES

FIRST DISTRICT

JOHN E. SUNUNU, Republican, of Bedford, NH; born on September 10, 1964 in Boston, MA; graduated from Salem High School, Salem, MA, 1982; B.S. in mechanical engineering, Massachusetts Institute of Technology, 1986; M.S., mechanical engineering, Massachusetts Institute of Technology, 1987; M.B.A., Harvard University Business School, Boston, MA, 1991; Chief Financial Officer and Director of Operations, Teletrol Systems, Inc.; married Catherine Holloran Sununu, 1988; two children: John Hayes and Grace; committees: Budget, Governmental Reform and Oversight, Small Business; subcommittees: Natural Resources Working Group; vice chair, Regulatory Affairs; Government Management, Information and Technology; elected to the 105th Congress.

Office Listings

rep.sununu@mail.house.gov

1229 Longworth House Office Building, Washington, DC 20515–2901 225–5456
Chief of Staff.—Paul Collins. FAX: 225–5822
Legislative Director.—Jay Contis.
Scheduler.—Sheri Keniston.
1750 Elm Street, Suite 101, Manchester, NH 03104 .... (603) 641–9536
FAX: 641–9561

Counties: Belknap, Carroll, Hillsborough, Rockingham, Strafford. CITIES: Manchester, Laconia, Portsmouth, Rochester, Dover. Population (1990), 554,360.

ZIP Codes: 03032, 03034, 03036–38, 03040–42, 03044–45, 03053–54, 03077, 03101–02, 03103 (part), 03104–05, 03106 (part), 03108–10, 03218, 03220, 03225–27, 03234, 03237, 03246–47, 03253–54, 03256, 03259, 03261, 03263, 03276 (part), 03289–91, 03801–02, 03804, 03809–10, 03811 (part), 03812–20, 03824–27, 03830, 03832–33, 03835–42, 03844–60, 03862, 03864–65, 03867–75, 03878, 03882–87, 03890, 03894, 03896, 03897

* * *

SECOND DISTRICT

CHARLES FOSTER BASS, Republican, of Petersborough, NH; born on January 8, 1952, in Boston, MA; graduated, Holderness School, Plymouth, NH, 1970; B.A., Dartmouth College, NH, 1974; vice president, High Standard Inc., Dublin, NH; chairman, Columbia Architectural Products, Beltsville, MD; New Hampshire State Representative, 1982–88; vice chairman, Judiciary Committee; New Hampshire State Senate 1988–92; chairman, Public Affairs and Ethics committees; cochairman, Economic Development Committee; member: Monadnock Rotary Club (president, 1992–93); Anoskeag Veterans; Altermont Lodge, FA&M; trusteeships: New Hampshire Higher Education Assistance Foundation, Monadnock Conservancy, New Hampshire Humanities Council; committees: Budget, Government Reform and Oversight; subcommittees: vice chairman, Civil Service; Government Management, Information and Technology; married Lisa Levesque Bass, 1989; two children: Lucy and Jonathan; elected to the 104th Congress; reelected to the 105th Congress.

Office Listings

http://www.house.gov/bass cbass@hr.house.gov

1728 Longworth House Office Building, Washington, DC 20515–2902 225–5206
Chief of Staff.—Suzanne Hellmann.
Legislative Director.—Darwin Cusack.
District Director.—Paul Collins.
Press Secretary.—Brian Sansoni.
142 North Main Street, Concord, NH 03301 .... (603) 226–0249
170 Main Street, Nashua, NH 03062 .... (603) 889–8772

Counties: Belknap (part), Cheshire, Coos, Grafton, Hillsborough (part), Merrimack (part), Rockingham (part), Sullivan. Population (1990), 554,892.

ZIP Codes: 03031, 03033, 03043, 03047–49, 03051, 03055, 03057, 03060–63, 03070–71, 03073, 03076, 03079, 03082, 03084, 03086–87, 03103 (part), 03106 (part), 03215–17, 03221–24, 03229–33, 03235, 03238, 03240–45, 03251–52, 03255, 03257, 03260, 03262, 03264–66, 03268–69, 03272–75, 03276 (part), 03278–82, 03284–85, 03287, 03293, 03301–04, 03431, 03440–52, 03455–58, 03461–62, 03464–70, 03561, 03570, 03574–76, 03579–85, 03588–90, 03592, 03595, 03597–98, 03601–09, 03740–41, 03743, 03745–46, 03748–55, 03765–66, 03768–74, 03777, 03779–82, 03784–85, 03811 (part), 03263 (part)

NEW JERSEY

(Population 1995 7,945,000)

SENATORS

FRANK R. LAUTENBERG, Democrat, of Cliffside Park, NJ, born in Paterson, NJ; on January 23, 1924; Nutley High School, Nutley, NJ, 1941; B.S., economics, Columbia University School of Business, New York, NY, 1949; U.S. Army Signal Corps, 1942–46; data processing firm founder and CEO, 1952–82; commissioner of the Port Authority of New York and New Jersey, 1978–82; commissioner, New Jersey Economic Development Authority; member: U.S. Holocaust Memorial Council; Advisory Council of the Graduate School of Business, Columbia University; Helsinki Commission; four children: Ellen, Nan, Lisa and Joshua; committees: Environment and Public Works, Budget, Appropriations, Select Committee on Intelligence; subcommittees: ranking member, Superfund, Waste Control and Risk Assessment; Drinking Water, Fisheries and Wildlife; Transportation; Commerce, Justice, State and the Judiciary; Defense; VA, HUD and Independent Agencies; Foreign Operations; elected to the U.S. Senate November 2, 1982, for the six-year term beginning January 3, 1983; appointed by the Governor on December 27, 1982, to complete the unexpired term of Nicholas F. Brady; reelected 1988 and 1994.

Office Listings

http://www.senate.gov/~lautenberg frank__lautenberg@lautenberg.senate.gov

506 Hart Senate Office Building, Washington, DC 20510–3002 224–4744
Administrative Assistant.—Eve Lubalin. FAX: 224–9707
Legislative Director.—Bruce King.
Scheduler.—Derick Mams.
State Director.—Christy Davis.
One Newark Center, Fourth Floor, Newark, NJ 07102 .... (201) 645–3030
Barrington Commons, Suites 18–19, 208 White Horse Pike, Barrington, NJ 08007 (609) 757–5353

* * *

ROBERT G. TORRICELLI, Democrat, of Englewood, NJ; born in Franklin Lakes, NJ, August 25, 1951; graduated, Storm King High School, Cornwall on Hudson, NY, 1970; B.A., 1974, Rutgers College; J.D., 1977, Rutgers School of Law; M.P.A., Harvard University, 1980; admitted to the New Jersey bar, 1978; began practice in Washington, DC, 1981; deputy legislative counsel, Governor Brendan T. Byrne, 1975–77; counsel to Vice President Walter F. Mondale, 1978–81; member, New Jersey and American bar associations; board of governors, Rutgers University, 1977–83; elected to 98th Congress, House of Representatives, on November 2, 1982, and reelected for six successive terms; elected to the U.S. Senate in November, 1996; member, Council on Foreign Relations; committees: Governmental Affairs, Judiciary, Rules and Administration; subcommittees: Antitrust, Business Rights and Competition; Constitution Federalism and Property Rights.

Office Listings

http://www.senate.gov/senator/torricelli.html senator__torricelli@torricelli.senate.gov

113 Dirksen Senate Office Building, Washington, DC 20510 224–3224
Legislative Director.—Eric Shuffler. FAX: 224–8567
Administrative Assistant.—Jamie P. Fox.
One Riverfront Plaza, Third Floor, Newark, NJ 07102 .... (201) 624–5555
State Director.—Deborah Lux. FAX: 639–2878

* * *

REPRESENTATIVES

FIRST DISTRICT

ROBERT E. ANDREWS, Democrat, of Haddon Heights, NJ; born in Camden, NJ, August 4, 1957; graduated, Triton High School, Runnemede, NJ, 1975; B.S., political science, Bucknell University, Phi Beta Kappa, Lewisburg, PA, 1979; J.D., Cornell Law School, Ithaca, NY, 1982;

Camden County Freeholder, 1986–90; Camden County Freeholder Director, 1988–90; elected by special election on November 6, 1990 to fill the vacancy caused by the resignation of James Florio; elected at the same time to the 102nd Congress; reelected to each succeeding Congress.

Office Listings

randrews@hr.house.gov

2439 Rayburn House Office Building, Washington, DC 20515–3001 225–6501
Administrative Assistant.—David Socolow.
506A White Horse Pike, Haddon Heights, NJ 08035 .... (609) 546–5100
Chief of Staff.—David Applebaum.

Counties: BURLINGTON COUNTY; cities and townships of Maple Shade, Palmyra, Riverton. CAMDEN COUNTY: cities and townships of Audubon, Audubon Park, Barrington, Bellmawr, Berlin, Berlin Township, Brooklawn, Camden, Chesilhurst, Clementon, Collingswood, Gibbsboro, Gloucester City, Gloucester Township, Haddon Heights, Haddon Township (part), Hi-Nella, Laurel Springs, Lawnside, Lindenwold, Magnolia, Mt. Ephraim, Oaklyn, Pennsauken, Pine Hill, Pine Valley, Runnemede, Somerdale, Stratford, Tavistock, Voorhees, Winslow, Woodlynne. GLOUCESTER COUNTY: cities and townships of Deptford, E. Greenwich, Greenwich, Logan Township, Mantua (part), Monroe, National Park, Paulsboro, Washington Township, and Wenonah. Population (1990), 594,630.

ZIP Codes: 08002 (part), 08003 (part), 08004 (part), 08007, 08009 (part), 08012, 08014, 08020–21, 08026–27, 08029–32, 08033 (part), 08035, 08037 (part), 08039, 08043 (part), 08045, 08049, 08051 (part), 08052 (part), 08056 (part), 08059, 08061, 08063, 08065 (part), 08066, 08077 (part), 08078, 08080 (part), 08081, 08083–84, 08085 (part), 08086, 08089 (part), 08090–91, 08093, 08094 (part), 08096 (part), 08097, 08099, 08101–07, 08108 (part), 08109 (part), 08110

* * *

SECOND DISTRICT

FRANK A. LOBIONDO, Republican, of Vineland, NJ; born in Bridgeton, NJ, May 12, 1946; graduated, Georgetown Preparatory School, Rockville, MD, 1964; St. Joseph's University, Philadelphia, PA, 1968; operations manager, LoBiondo Brothers Motor Express; New Jersey State Assemblyman, 1988–94; chairman, General Assembly Economic and Community Development, Agriculture and Tourism Committee, 1988–94; member: Cumberland County Board of Freeholders, 1985–88; board of directors, Literacy Volunteers of America, Cape May County Chapter; Vineland Rotary, 1987–95 (honorary as of January 1, 1995); board of directors, Young Men's Christian Association; honorary chairman, Cumberland County Hospice annual fundraising drive, 1992; chairman, American Heart Association, Cumberland County Chapter, 1989–90; founder, Cumberland County Environmental Health Task Force; president, Cumberland County Guidance Center, 1982–84; director, Young Men's Christian Association, 1978–84; member, Cape May County Chamber of Commerce (honorary as of January 1, 1995); married to Jan Dwyer LoBiondo; two children: Adina and Amy; elected to the 104th Congress; reelected to the 105th Congress.

Office Listings

http://www.house.gov/lobiondo lobiondo@hr.house.gov

222 Cannon House Office Building, Washington, DC 20515–3002 225–6572
Administrative Assistant.—Mary Annie Harper. FAX: 225–3318
Executive Assistant.—Carolyn Maloney.
5914 Main Street, Mays Landing, NJ 08330 .... (609) 625–5008
Staff Assistant.—Crystal Neill.

Counties: ATLANTIC COUNTY. Cities and townships: Absecon, Atlantic City, Brigantine, Buena, Cardiff, Collings Lake, Cologne, Corbin City, Dorothy, Egg Harbor, Estell Manor, Galloway, Hammonton, Landisville, Leeds Point, Linwood, Longport, Margate, Mays Landing, Milmay, Minotola, Mizpah, Newtonville, Northfield, Oceanville, Pleasantville, Pomona, Port Republic, Richland, Somers Point, Ventnor. BURLINGTON COUNTY (part). Cities and townships: Chatsworth, New Gretna. CAPE MAY COUNTY. Cities and townships: Avalon, Bargaintown, Beesley's, Belleplain, Burleigh, Cape May, Cap May C.H., Cape May Point, Cold Springs, Del Haven, Dennisville, Dias Creek, Eldora, Erma, Fishing Creek, Goshen, Green Creek, Greenfield, Marmora, Ocean City, Ocean View, Rio Grande, Sea Isle, South Dennis, South Seaville, Stone Harbor, Strathmere, Tuckahoe, Villas, Whitesboro, Wildwood, Woodbine. CUMBERLAND COUNTY. Cities and townships: Bridgeton, Cedarville, Centerton, Deerfield, Delmont, Dividing Creek, Dorchester, Elwood, Fairton, Fortescue, Greenwich, Heislerville, Hopewell, Leesburg, Mauricetown, Millville, Newport, Port Elizabeth, Port Norris, Rosenhayn, Shiloh, Vineland. GLOUCESTER COUNTY (part). Cities and townships: Clayton, Ewan, Franklinville, Glassboro, Harrisonville, Malaga, Mantua, Mickleton, Mullica Hill, Newfield, Pitman, Richwood, Sewell, Swedesboro, Williamstown, Woodbury. SALEM COUNTY. Cities and townships: Alloway, Carney's Point, Daretown, Deepwater, Elmer, Elsinboro, Hancocks Bridge, Monroeville, Norma, Pedricktown, Penns Grove, Pennsville, Quinton, Salem, and Woodstown. Population (1990), 594,630.

ZIP Codes: 08001, 08023, 08025, 08028, 08037–39, 08051 (part), 08062, 08067, 08069–72, 08074, 08079, 08080, 08085, 08094–96, 08098, 08201–04, 08210, 08212–15, 08217, 08219–21, 08223, 08225–26, 08230–32, 08240–48, 08250–52, 08260, 08270, 08302, 08310–24, 08326–30, 08332, 08340–50, 08352–53, 08360, 08400–04, 08406

THIRD DISTRICT

JIM SAXTON, Republican, of Mt. Holly, NJ; born in Nicholson, PA, January 22, 1943; graduated, Lackawanna Trail High School, Factoryville, PA, 1961; B.A., education, East Stroudsburg State College, PA, 1965; graduate courses in elementary education, Temple University, Philadelphia, PA, 1968; public school teacher, 1965–68; realtor, owner of Jim Saxton Realty Company, 1968–85; New Jersey General Assembly, 1976–82; State Senate, 1982–84; chairman, State Republican Platform Committee, 1983; former member: Chamber of Commerce, Association of the U.S. Air Force, Leadership Foundation of New Jersey, Boy Scouts of America, Rotary International; former chairman: American Cancer Committee; two children: Jennifer and Martin; elected to the 98th Congress by special election on November 6, 1984; reelected to each succeeding Congress.

Office Listings

339 Cannon House Office Building, Washington, DC 20515–3003 225–4765
Administrative Assistant.—Tom Houston. FAX: 225–0778
Press Secretary.—Gary Gallant.
Executive Assistant.—Courtney Johnson.
Legislative Correspondent.—Scott Rudder.
100 High Street, Mount Holly, NJ 08060 .... (609) 261–5800
District Representative/Business Manager.—Sandra Condit.
1 Maine Avenue, Cherry Hill, NJ 08002 .... (609) 428–0520
7 Hadley Avenue, Toms River, NJ 08753 .... (908) 914–2020

Counties: BURLINGTON COUNTY; that part not contained in the Third and Fourth Districts. CAMDEN COUNTY; municipalities of Cherry Hill, Haddonfield, Merchantville, and Waterford. OCEAN COUNTY; that part not contained in the Third and Fourth Districts. Population (1990), 594,630.

ZIP Codes: 08002, 08054, 08055, 08731, 08754

* * *

FOURTH DISTRICT

CHRISTOPHER H. SMITH, Republican, of Robbinsville, NJ; born in Rahway, NJ, March 4, 1953; B.A., Trenton State College, 1975; attended Worcester College, England, 1974; businessman; executive director, New Jersey Right to Life Committee, Inc., 1976–78; married to the former Marie Hahn, 1976; four children: Melissa Elyse, Christopher, and Michael; Catholic; member: Committee on International Relations; vice chairman, Committee on Veterans' Affairs; cochairman, Commission on Security and Cooperation in Europe, 1995; cochairman, Congressional Pro-Life Caucus; subcommittees: chairman, International Operations and Human Rights; Western Hemisphere; Hospitals and Health Care; elected to the 97th Congress, November 4, 1980; reelected to each succeeding Congress.

Office Listings

2370 Rayburn House Office Building, Washington, DC 20515–3004 225–3765
Chief of Staff.—Mary Noonan. FAX: 225–7768
Press Secretary.—Ken Wolfe.
Office Manager.—Patricia Coll.
1540 Kuser Road, Suite A9, Hamilton, NJ 08619 .... (609) 585–7878
Regional Director.—Joyce Golden.
38–A Whiting Shopping Center, Whiting, NJ 08759 .... (908) 350–2300
Regional Director.—Loretta Charbonneau.

Counties: BURLINGTON COUNTY; municipalities of Bordentown City, Bordentown Township, Burlington City, Burlington Township, Chesterfield, Eastampton, Fieldsboro, Florence, Mansfield, North Hanover, Springfield, Westampton, and Wrightstown (part). MERCER COUNTY; municipalities of East Windsor, Hamilton, Highstown, Trenton, and Washington Township. MONMOUTH COUNTY; municipalities of Allentown, Brielle, Farmingdale, Howell, Manasquan, Millstone Township, Roosevelt, Spring Lake Hts. (part), Upper Freehold, Wall. OCEAN COUNTY; municipality of Bay Head, Brick, Dover Township (part), Jackson, Lakehurst, Lakewood, Manchester, Mantoloking, Plumstead, Pt. Pleasant, and Pt. Pleasant Beach. Population (1990), 594,630.

ZIP Codes: 07719 (part), 07726 (part), 07727, 07728 (part), 07731, 07753 (part), 07762 (part), 08010 (part), 08016, 08022, 08041, 08046 (part), 08060 (part), 08068 (part), 08501, 08505, 08510, 08512 (part), 08514–15, 08518, 08520 (part), 08526–27, 08533, 08535, 08554–55, 08561, 08562 (part), 08601–11, 08618 (part), 08619 (part), 08620, 08629, 08638 (part), 08640 (part), 08641 (part), 08645–47, 08648 (part), 08650, 08666, 08677, 08690 (part), 08691 (part), 08695, 08701, 08720, 08723–24, 08730, 08733, 08736 (part), 08738–39, 08742, 08750 (part), 08755 (part), 08757 (part), 08759 (part)

FIFTH DISTRICT

MARGE ROUKEMA, Republican, of Ridgewood, NJ; born on September 19, 1929; graduated, Montclair State College in New Jersey with B.A., political science and English; pursued interests in government by studying urban and regional planning at Rutgers University; married to Dr. Richard W. Roukema; three children: Greg, Todd (deceased), and Meg; teacher, history, and English, Livingston and Ridgewood, NJ; Trustee and Vice President, Ridgewood Board of Education, 1970–73; chairman, Ridgewood Better Government Committee; member: Mayor's Advisory Charter Study Commission; New Jersey Business and Professional Women; College Club of Ridgewood; Distributive Education Clubs of American Congressional Advisory Board; active member, board of directors of public service organizations including: Ridgewood Family Counseling Service; Leukemia Society of Northern New Jersey; Ridgewood Senior Citizens Housing Corporation (cofounder); Spring House, residential center for the treatment of alcoholism; Spectrum for Living; awards: National PTA Children's Advocacy Award; Concord Coalition's House Honor Roll; U.S. Chamber of Commerce Spirit of Enterprise Award; committee member: Banking and Financial Services; Education and the Workforce; elected to the 97th Congress, November 4, 1980; reelected to each succeeding Congress.

Office Listings

2469 Rayburn House Office Building, Washington, DC 20515–3005 225–4465
Administrative Assistant.—Steve Wilson. FAX: 225–9048
Press Secretary.—Craig Shearman.
Scheduler.—Artemis Rentzis.
1200 E. Ridgewood Avenue, Ridgewood, NJ 07450 .... (201) 447–3900
District Administrator.—David Zuidema. FAX: 447–3749
1500 Route 517, Allamuchy, NJ 07820 .... (908) 850–4747
FAX: 850–3406

Counties: BERGEN COUNTY; cities and townships of Allendale, Alpine, Bergenfield, Closter, Cresskill, Demarest, Dumont, Emerson, Fair Lawn, Franklin Lakes, Glen Rock, Harrington Park, Haworth, Hillsdale, Hohokus, Mahwah, Midland Park, Montvale, Northvale, Norwood, Oakland, Old Tappan, Oradell, Paramus, Park Ridge, Ramsey, Ridgewood, River Vale, Rochelle Park, Rockleigh, Saddle River, Tenafly, Upper Saddle River, Waldwick, Washington, Westwood, Woodcliff Lake, and Wyckoff. PASSAIC COUNTY; cities and townships of Haskell, Hawthorne, Hewitt, Newfoundland, North Haledon, Oak Ridge, Wanaque, and West Milford. SUSSEX COUNTY; cities and townships of Andover Borough, Andover Township, Agusta, Branchville, Frankford, Franklin, Fredon, Glenwood, Green, Hamburg, Hampton, Hardyston, Highland Lakes, Lafayette, Layton, McAfee, Montague, Newtown, Sandyston, Stillwater (Middleville), Stockholm, Sussex, Swartswood, Tranquility, Vernon, Walpack Center, and Wantage. WARREN COUNTY; cities and townships of Allamuchy, Alpha, Belvidere, Blairstown, Buttzville, Columbia, Franklin, Frelinghuysen, Greenwich, Hackettstown, Hardwick, Harmony, Hope, Independence, Knowlton, Landing, Liberty, Lopatcong, Mansfield, Oxford, Pahaquarry, Phillipsburg, Pohatcong, Washington Borough, Washington Township, White. Population (1990), 594,630.

ZIP Codes: 07401, 07410 (part), 07416–23, 07424 (part), 07428, 07430, 07432, 07435–36, 07438 (part), 07446, 07450–51, 07452 (part), 07456 (part), 07458, 07460 (part), 07461–63, 07465 (part), 07480–81, 07495, 07506, 07507, 07508 (part), 07620–21, 07624, 07626–28, 07630, 07640–42, 07645, 07647–48, 07649 (part), 07652–53, 07656, 07662 (part), 07670 (part), 07675, 07820, 07821 (part), 07822–23, 07825–27, 07829–33, 07837–40, 07844, 07846, 07848, 07850, 07851 (part), 07855, 07860 (part), 07863, 07865, 07874 (part), 07875, 07877, 07879–82, 08802, 08804, 08808, 08827, 08865, 08886

* * *

SIXTH DISTRICT

FRANK PALLONE, JR., Democrat, of Long Branch, NJ; born in Long Branch, October 30, 1951; B.A., Middlebury College, Middlebury, VT, 1973; M.A., Fletcher School of Law and Diplomacy, 1974; J.D., Rutgers University School of Law, 1978; member of the bar: Florida, New York, Pennsylvania, and New Jersey; attorney, Marine Advisory Service; assistant professor, Cook College, Rutgers University Sea Grant Extension Program; counsel, Monmouth County, NJ, Protective Services for the Elderly; instructor, Monmouth College; Long Branch City Council, 1982–88; New Jersey State Senate, 1983–88; married the former Sarah Hospodor, 1992; elected to the 100th Congress by special election on November 8, 1988 to fill the vacancy caused by the death of the Hon. James J. Howard; reelected to each succeeding Congress.

Office Listings

420 Cannon House Office Building, Washington, DC 20515–3006 225–4671
Administrative Assistant.—Tim Yahl. FAX: 225–9665
Legislative Director.—Rick Kessler.
Press Secretary.—Ted Loud.
District Director.—Mike Beson.
504 Broadway, Long Branch, NJ 07740 .... (908) 571–1140
FAX: 870–3890

67/69 Church Street, Kilmer Square, New Brunswick, NJ	(908) 249–8892
	FAX: 249–1335
Room 33, I.E.I. Airport Plaza, Highway 36, Hazlet, NJ	(908) 264–9104
	FAX: 739–4668

Counties: MONMOUTH COUNTY; cities and townships of Aberdeen, Allenhurst, Asbury Park, Atlantic Highlands, Avon-by-the-Sea, Belford, Belmar, Bradley Beach, Deal, Hazlet, Highlands, Keansburg, Keyport, Leonardo, Loch Arbour, Long Branch, Matawan, Middletown, Monmouth Beach, Navesink, Neptune, Neptune City, Ocean Grove, Red Bank, Sea Birght, Sea Girt, South Belmar, Spring Lake, Spring Lake Heights, Union Beach. MIDDLESEX COUNTY; cities and townships of Dunellen, Edison, Highland Park, Metuchen, Milltown, New Brunswick, North Brunswick, Old Bridge, Parlin, Piscataway, Sayerville, South Amboy, South River, Spotswood.

ZIP Codes: 07080 (part), 07701 (part), 07711 (part), 07712 (part), 07716–18, 07719 (part), 07720–21, 07722 (part), 07723 (part), 07730 (part), 07732, 07734 (part), 07735, 07737, 07740 (part), 07747 (part), 07748 (part), 07750, 07752, 07753 (part), 07754, 07756, 07758, 07760 (part), 07762 (part), 08736 (part), 08750 (part), 08812 (part), 08816 (part), 08817–18, 08820 (part), 08824 (part), 08831 (part), 08837 (part), 08840 (part), 08846 (part), 08850 (part), 08854 (part), 08855, 08857, 08859, 08871–72, 08873 (part), 08878–79, 08882, 08884 (part), 08899, 08901, 08902 (part), 08903–04, 08906, 08988–89

* * *

SEVENTH DISTRICT

BOB FRANKS, Republican, of New Providence, NJ; born on September 21, 1951 in Hackensack, NJ; B.A., DePauw University, Indiana, 1973; J.D., Southern Methodist University, Dallas, TX, 1976; elected to New Jersey General Assembly, 1979–92; assembly majority conference leader, 1986–89; assembly policy chairman, 1992; member: Long-Term Planning Committee, Overlook Hospital Association, 1982–present, Children's Specialized Board of Managers, 1982–present; committees: Budget, Transportation and Infrastructure; elected on November 3, 1992 to the 103rd Congress; reelected to each succeeding Congress.

Office Listings

http://www.house.gov/bobfranks franksnj@hr.house.gov

225 Cannon House Office Building, Washington, DC 20515–3007	225–5361
Chief of Staff.—Bill Ulrey.	FAX: 225–9460
Scheduler/Office Manager.—Karen Cologne.	
Legislative Director.—Michael Harrington.	
Deputy Chief of Staff/Press Secretary.—Janet Thompson.	
2333 Morris Avenue, Suite B–8, Union, NJ 07083	(908) 686–5576
	FAX: 688–7390
Suite 4, 73 Main Street, Woodbridge, NJ 07095	(908) 602–0075

Counties: ESSEX COUNTY; municipalities Maplewood (part) and Millburn (part). MIDDLESEX COUNTY; municipalities of Edison (part), Middlesex, South Plainfield, and Woodbridge (part). SOMERSET COUNTY; municipalities of Bound Brook, Bridgewater (part), Franklin, Hillsborough, Green Brook, Manville, Millstone, North Plainfield, South Bound Brook, Warren, and Watchung. UNION COUNTY. Municipalities of Berkeley Heights, Clark, Cranford, Fanwood, Garwood, Kenilworth, Linden (part), Mountainside, New Providence, Plainfield, Roselle Park, Scotch Plains, Springfield, Summit, Union (part), Westfield, and Winfield. Population (1990), 594,629.

ZIP Codes: 07001, 07008 (part), 07016, 07023, 07027, 07033, 07036 (part), 07040 (part), 07041, 07059 (part), 07060–63, 07064 (part), 07066 (part), 07067, 07076, 07078 (part), 07080 (part), 07081, 07083 (part), 07088 (part), 07090–92, 07095, 07203 (part), 07204, 07208 (part), 07901–02, 07920 (part), 07922, 07974, 08502 (part), 08528, 08540 (part), 08805, 08807 (part), 08812 (part), 08820 (part), 08821, 08823, 08830, 08832, 08835–36, 08837 (part), 08840 (part), 08846 (part), 08853, 08854 (part), 08861 (part), 08863, 08873 (part), 08875, 08876 (part), 08880, 08890

* * *

EIGHTH DISTRICT

WILLIAM J. PASCRELL, JR., Democrat, of Paterson, NJ; born in Paterson, January 27, 1937; B.A., journalism, and M.A., philosophy, Fordham University; veteran, U.S. Army and Army Reserves; educator; New Jersey General Assembly, 1988–96: elected Minority Leader Pro Tempore; mayor of Paterson, 1990–96; named Mayor of the Year by bipartisan NJ Conference of Mayors, 1996; started Paterson's first Economic Development Corporation; married to the former Elsie Marie Botto; three children: William III, Glenn, and David; committees: Transportation and Infrastructure, Small Business; subcommittees: Surface Transportation, Water Resources and Environment; elected to the 105th Congress.

Office Listings

1722 Longworth House Office Building, Washington, DC 20515 .... 225–5751 FAX: 225-5782
Chief of Staff.—Thomas J. Edwards.
Office Manager.—Margaret J. VanTassell.
Press Contact.—David Filippelli.
Legislative Director.—Ross Galin.
200 Federal Plaza, Suite 500, Paterson, NJ 07505 .... (201) 523–5152 FAX: 523–0637
District Director.—Bill Maer.

Counties: ESSEX COUNTY: cities of Belleville, Bloomfield, Cedar Grove. Glen Ridge, Maplewood, Montclair, Nutley, South Orange, Verona, West Orange. PASSAIC COUNTY: Cities of Clifton, Haledon, Little Falls, North Haledon, Passaic, Paterson, Pompton Lakes, Prospect Park, Totowa, Wayne, and West Paterson.

ZIP Codes: 07011–15, 07055, 07024, 07442, 07470, 07501–5, 07508–10, 07512–14, 07524

* * *

NINTH DISTRICT

STEVE ROTHMAN, Democrat, of Fair Lawn, NJ; born in Englewood, NJ, October 14, 1952; graduate, Tenafly High School, 1970; B.A., Syracuse University, Syracuse, NY, 1974; LL.B., Washington University School of Law, St. Louis, MO, 1977; attorney; as two-term mayor of Englewood, NJ, spearheaded business growth and installed a fiscally conservative management team, transforming Englewood's bond rating from one of the worst to the best in Bergen County; judge, Bergen County Surrogate Court, 1993–96; founding member, New Democratic Coalition; principal cosponsor, Higher Education Accumulation Program (HEAP) Act; two children; committees: Judiciary, International Relations; subcommittees: Crime; International Economic Policy and Trade; elected to the 105th Congress.

Office Listings

http://www.house.gov/rothman steven.rothman@mail.house.gov

1607 Longworth House Office Building, Washington, DC 20515 .... 225–5061 FAX: 225–5851
Chief of Staff.—Chuck Young.
Executive Assistant/Scheduler.—Mary Flanagan.
Communications Director.—Phil Goldberg.
Legislative Director.—Jim Wall.
Legislative Assistants.—Raffi Hamparian, Heather Pearlman.
25 Main Street, Court Plaza, Hackensack, NJ 07601–7089 .... (201) 646–0808 FAX: 646–1944
District Director.—Adam Zellner.
130 Central Avenue, Jersey City, NJ 07306–2118 .... (201) 798–1366 FAX: 798–1725
Office Director.—Mike Gallo.

Counties: BERGEN COUNTY. Cities and towns of Bogota, Carlstadt, Cliffside Park, East Rutherford, Edgewater, Elmwood Park, Englewood, Englewood Cliffs, Fair Lawn (part), Fairview, Fort Lee, Garfield, Hackensack, Hasbrouck Heights, Leonia, Little Ferry, Lodi, Lyndhurst, Maywood, Moonachie, New Milford, North Arlington, Palisades Park, Ridgefield, Ridgefield Park, River Edge, Rutherford, Saddle Brook, South Hackensack, Teaneck, Teterboro, Wallington, and Wood Ridge. HUDSON COUNTY. Cities and towns of Kearny (ward 1: districts 1, 2, and 6; ward 3; and ward 4: districts 5–7), Secaucus, North Bergen, and Jersey City. Population (1990), 594,630.

ZIP Codes: 07010, 07014 (part), 07020, 07022, 07024, 07026, 07029 (part), 07031, 07032 (part), 07047 (part), 07057, 07070–75, 07087 (part), 07094, 07096, 07306 (part), 07307–08, 07310 (part), 07407, 07410 (part), 07452 (part), 07601–08, 07631–32, 07643–44, 07646, 07649 (part), 07650, 07657, 07660–61, 07662 (part), 07666, 07670 (part)

* * *

TENTH DISTRICT

DONALD M. PAYNE, Democrat, of Newark, NJ; born in Newark, July 16, 1934; graduated, Barringer High School, Newark, 1952; B.A., Seton Hall University, South Orange, NJ, 1957; businessman; elected to the Essex County Board of Chosen Freeholders, 1972–78; elected to the Newark Municipal Council, 1982–88; president, YMCA of the USA, 1970–73; member: NAACP, Council on Foreign Relations, Bethlehem Baptist Church; former chairman, Congressional Black Caucus; serves on the advisory council of the U.S. Committee for UNICEF; Advisory Commission on Intergovernmental Relations; board of directors: Congressional Black Caucus Foundation, Congressional Award Foundation, National Endowment for Democracy; widower; three children: elected on November 8, 1988 to the 101st Congress; reelected to each succeeding Congress.

Office Listings

2244 Rayburn House Office Building, Washington, DC 20515–3010 225–3436
Administrative Assistant.—Maxine James. FAX: 225–4160
Legislative Director/Press Secretary.—Kerry McKenney.
50 Walnut Street, Room 1016, Newark, NJ 07102 .... (201) 645–3213
District Director.—Richard T. Thigpen. FAX: 645–5902
333 North Broad Street, Elizabeth, NJ 07202 .... (908) 629–0222
FAX: 629–0221

Counties: ESSEX COUNTY. municipalities of East Orange, Irvington, Maplewood (districts 5, 9, 12, 21), Montclair (ward 3 (districts 1–8), ward 4 (districts 2–7)), Newark (wards South, East (districts 22, 25, 29, 30, 32–34), West (districts 3, 6, 7, 9, 10, 11, 13, 15–43, 45), Central (districts 1–13, 15–24, 28, 29, 32, 34–42)), Orange, South Orange (districts 2, 12), West Orange (ward 2 (districts 3, 4), ward 3, ward 5 (districts 1, 2, 4, 5)). HUDSON COUNTY; municipalities of Bayonne (ward 3 (districts 13–15, 18, 19)), Jersey City (ward A (districts 1–8, 10, 14–17, 19–32), ward B (districts 11–15), ward E (district 27), ward F (districts 2, 3, 14, 16–21, 23–26)). UNION COUNTY; municipalities of Elizabeth (ward 1 (district 6), ward 2 (districts 2–6, 8, 10), ward 3, ward 4 (districts 1–3, 5–12), ward 5 (districts 1–2, 4–11), ward 6 (districts 6, 8, 10, 12)), Hillside, Linden (ward 1 (districts 1–3), wards 2–6, ward 8 (districts 1, 3), ward 9 (district 5), ward 10 (districts 2–4)), Rahway, Roselle, Union (districts 7, 8, 38). Population (1990), 594,630.

ZIP Codes: 07002 (part), 07017–19, 07028 (part), 07036 (part), 07040 (part), 07042 (part), 07044 (part), 07050–51, 07052 (part), 07065, 07066 (part), 07079 (part), 07083 (part), 07088 (part), 07101, 07102 (part), 07103, 07105 (part), 07106, 07107 (part), 07108, 07111–12, 07114 (part), 07201 (part), 07202 (part), 07203 (part), 07205, 07206 (part), 07207, 07208 (part), 07304 (part), 07305 (part)

* * *

ELEVENTH DISTRICT

RODNEY P. FRELINGHUYSEN, Republican, of Morristown, NJ; born in New York, NY, April 29, 1946; graduated Hobart College, NY, 1969; attended graduate school in Connecticut; named Legislator of the Year by the Veterans of Foreign Wars, the New Jersey Association of Mental Health Agencies, and the New Jersey Association of Retarded Citizens; honored by numerous organizations; served in the New Jersey General Assembly, 1983–94; chairman, Assembly Appropriations Committee, 1988–89 and 1992–94; member: Morris County Board of Chosen Freeholders, 1974–83 (director, 1980); served on: Welfare and Mental Health boards; Human Services and Private Industry councils; served, U.S. Army, 93rd Engineer Battalion; honorably discharged, 1971; member: American Legion and Veterans of Foreign Wars; Morris County state and federal aid coordinator and administrative assistant, 1972; married to Virginia Frelinghuysen; two children: Louisine and Sarah; committee: Appropriations; subcommittees: VA, HUD and Independent Agencies; Energy and Water Development; District of Columbia.

Office Listings

http://www.house.gov/frelinghuysen njeleven@hr.house.gov

514 Cannon House Office Building, Washington, DC 20515–3011 225–5034
Chief of Staff.—Donna Mullins.
Press Secretary.—Trent Duffy.
Senior Legislative Aide.—Ed Krenik.
Constitutent Service Director.—Laura Scobey.
One Morris Street, Morristown, NJ 07960 .... (201) 984–0711
District Manager.—Betty Denecke.

Counties: ESSEX COUNTY. CITIES AND TOWNSHIPS: Caldwell, Essex Fells, Fairfield Township, Livingston, Millburn (part), North Caldwell, Roseland, West Caldwell. MORRIS COUNTY. Cities and townships: Bernardsville, Municipalities of Boonton Town, Boonton Township, Brookside, Budd Lake, Butler, Califon, Cedar Knolls, Chatham Borough, Chaptham Township, Chester Borough, Chester Township, Convent Station, Denville, Dover Town, East Hanover, Flanders, Florham Park, Gillette, Green Pond, Green Village, Hanover, Harding, Hibernia, Ironia, Jefferson, Kenvill, Kinnelon, Lake Hiawatha, Lake Hopatcong, Landing, Ledgewood, Lincoln Park, Long Valley, Madison, Mendham Borough, Mendham Township, Millington, Mine Hill, Montville, Morris Plains, Morris Township, Morristown, Mount Arlington, Mountain Lakes, Mount Olive, Mount Tabor, Netcong, Newfoundland, New Vernon, Oak Ridge, Parsippany-Troy Hills, Passaic Township, Pequannock, Picatinny, Pine Brook, Randolph, Riverdale, Rockaway Borough, Rockaway Township, Roxbury, Schooley's Mountain, Stanhope, Stirling, Succasunna, Towaco, Victory Gardens, Washington Township, Wharton, and Whippany. PASSAIC COUNTY. Bloomingdale. SOMERSET COUNTY. Cities and townships: Bernards Township, Bridgewater (part), Raritan Borough, and Somerville. SUSSEX COUNTY. Cities and townships: Byram, Hopatcong, Ogdensburg, Sparta, and Stanhope. Population (1990), 594,630.

ZIP Codes: 07004–07, 07009 (part), 07021, 07034–35, 07039, 07045–46, 07052 (part), 07054, 07058, 07059 (part), 07068, 07078 (part), 07082, 07403, 07405, 07438 (part), 07439–40, 07444, 07456 (part), 07457, 07460 (part), 07801–02, 07821 (part), 07826–28, 07834, 07836, 07840, 07842–43, 07845, 07847, 07849–50, 07851 (part), 07852–53, 07856–57, 07860 (part), 07866, 07869–71, 07874 (part), 07876, 07878, 07885, 07920 (part), 07924 (part), 07926–28, 07930, 07932–33, 07935–36, 07938–40, 07945–46, 07950, 07960–63, 07970, 07976, 07980–81, 08807 (part), 08869, 08876 (part)

TWELFTH DISTRICT

MICHAEL (MIKE) PAPPAS, Republican, of Rocky Hill, NJ; born in New Brunswick, NJ, December 29, 1960; graduated, Alma Preparatory School, Zarephath, NJ; attended Seton Hall University, South Orange, NJ; insurance executive and partner, Pappas Insurance Agency; chairman, Human Services and Education Steering Committee, National Association of Counties; member, National Policy Forum, Republican National Committee; president, New Jersey Association of Counties, 1994; past chairman, New Jersey Judicial Unification Transition Committee; Somerset County Freeholder, 1984–96, serving as director, deputy director, and board of social services chairman; Franklin township councilman, 1982–87; mayor of Franklin, 1983–84; spearheaded Somerset County Youth Council; board of trustees, Somerset Medical Center; past member: Somerset County 4–H Association, Franklin Township Lions Club, Order of AHEPA, Central Jersey Club of the Deaf; Franklin Township Lions Club Citizen of the Year award, 1988; Somerville Area Jaycees Distinguished Service Award, 1992; one child; assistant majority whip; committees: National Security, Government Reform and Oversight, Small Business; elected to the 105th Congress.

Office Listings

http://www.house.gov/pappas

1710 Longworth House Office Building, Washington, DC 20515 225–5801
FAX: 225–6025
Administrative Assistant.—Jeffrey Krilla.
Legislative Director.—Paul Pisano.
Legislative Assistants: Bill Burlew, Jack Grimes.
Press Secretary.—Sean Spicer.
Scheduler.—Elan Liang.

8 Main Street, Flemington, NJ 08822 .... (908) 284–1138
FAX: 284–2577
(800) 955–2587
District Director.—Diane Naar.

30 South Street, Freehold, NJ 07728 .... (908) 462–8499
FAX: 462–8467
(800) 965–2597
Senior Staff Assistant.—Phyllis Deroian.

Counties: HUNTERDON COUNTY; cities and towns of Alexandria, Bethlehem, Bloomsbury, Califon, Clinton Town, Clinton Township, Delaware, East Amwell, Flemington, Franklin, Frenchtown, Glen Gardner, Hampton, High Bridge, Holland, Kingwood, Lambertville, Lebanon Borough, Lebanon Township, Milford, Raritan, Readington, Stockton, Tewksbury, Union, West Amwell. MERCER COUNTY part; cities and townships of Ewing, Hopewell Borough, Hopewell Township, Lawrence, Pennington, Princeton Borough, Princeton Township, West Windsor. MIDDLESEX COUNTY (part); cities and townships of Cranbury, East Brunswick, Helmetta, Jamesburg, Monroe, Plainsboro, South Brunswick. MONMOUTH COUNTY (part); cities and townships of Colts Neck, Eatontown, Englishtown, Fair Haven, Freehold Borough, Freehold Township, Holmdel, Interlaken, Little Silver, Manalapan, Marlboro, Middletown (part), Ocean, Oceanport, Rumson, Shrewsbury Borough, Shrewsbury Township, Tinton Falls, West Long Branch. SOMERSET COUNTY (part); cities and townships of Bedminster, Bernardsville, Branchburg, Far Hills, Montgomery, Peapack-Gladstone, and Rocky Hill. Population (1990), 594,630.

ZIP Codes: 07701 (part), 07702–04, 07709, 07711 (part), 07712 (part), 07713, 07722 (part), 07723 (part), 07724, 07726 (part), 07728 (part), 07733, 07734 (part), 07738–39, 07746, 07748 (part), 07751, 07753 (part), 07754, 07755, 07757, 07760 (part), 07763–65, 07777, 07830, 07921, 07924, 07931, 07934, 07977–79, 08502 (part), 08504, 08512, 08525, 08530, 08534, 08536, 08540 (part), 08541–44, 08550–51, 08553, 08556–60, 08570, 08618 (part), 08625, 08628, 08638 (part), 08648 (part), 08691 (part), 08801–04, 08809–10, 08816, 08822, 08824–29, 08831, 08833–34, 08848, 08850 (part), 08852, 08858, 08867–68, 08870, 08876 (part), 08884 (part), 08885, 08887–89

* * *

THIRTEENTH DISTRICT

ROBERT MENENDEZ, Democrat, of Union City, NJ; born in New York City, NY, on January 1, 1954; graduated, Union Hill High School, 1972; B.A., St. Peter's College, Jersey City, NJ, 1976; J.D., Rutgers Law School, Newark, NJ, 1979; attorney; admitted to the New Jersey bar, 1980; elected to the Union City Board of Education, 1974–78; mayor of Union City, 1986–92; New Jersey Assembly, 1987–91; New Jersey State Senate, 1991–92; chairman, New Jersey Hispanic Leadership Program; member: New Jersey Hispanic Elected Officials Organization; New Jersey Mayors Coalition; president and cofounder, Alliance Civic Association; married the former Jane Jacobsen, 1976; two children: Alicia and Robert; elected on November 3, 1992 to the 103rd Congress; reelected to each succeeding Congress.

Office Listings

http://www.house.gov/menendez

1730 Longworth House Office Building, Washington, DC 20515–3013 225–7919
FAX: 226–0792
Administrative Assistant.—Michael Hutton.
Legislative Assistant.—Pedro Pablo Permuy.

911 Bergen Avenue, Jersey City, NJ 07306 .... (201) 222–2828
FAX: 222–0188

654 Avenue C, Bayonne, NJ 07002 .... (201) 823–2900
275 Hobart Street, Perth Amboy, NJ 08861 .... (908) 324–6212

Counties: Essex (part), Hudson (part), Middlesex (part), and Union (part). Cities and townships: Bayonne (part), Carteret, East Newark, Elizabeth (part), Guttenberg, Harrison Township, Hoboken, Jersey City (part), Kearny (part), Linden (part), Newark, North Bergen (part), Port Reading, Perth Amboy, Sewaren, Union City, Weehawken, West New York, Woodbridge (part). Population (1990), 594,630.

ZIP Codes: 07002, 07008, 07029–30, 07032, 07036, 07047, 07064, 07077, 07087, 07093, 07095, 07097, 07099, 07102, 07104–05, 07107, 07114, 07201–02, 07208, 07300, 07302–06, 07308–11, 07399, 08861–62

NEW MEXICO

(Population 1995, 1,685,000)

SENATORS

PETE V. DOMENICI, Republican, of Albuquerque, NM; born in Albuquerque, May 7, 1932; graduate of St. Mary's High School, 1954; University of New Mexico, B.S., 1966; Denver University, LL.D., 1958; admitted to New Mexico bar, 1958; elected to Albuquerque City Commission, 1966; chairman (ex officio mayor), 1967; married Nancy Burk, 1958; eight children: Lisa, Peter, Nella, Clare, David, Nanette, Helen, and Paula; committees: chairman, Budget; Appropriations; Energy and Natural Resources; Governmental Affairs; Indian Affairs; elected to the U.S. Senate, November 7, 1972, for the term ending January 3, 1979; reelected 1978, 1984, 1990 and 1996.

Office Listings

http://www.senate.gov/~domenici senator__domenici@domenici.senate.gov

328 Hart Senate Office Building, Washington, DC 20510–3101 224–6621
FAX: 224–7371
Administrative Assistant.—Charles Gentry.
Executive Assistant.—Larry W. Dye.
Legislative Director.—Kay Davies.
Press Secretary.—Chris Gallegos
Personal Secretary.—Angela Raish.
Federal Building, Suite 120, 625 Silver Avenue SW, Albuquerque, NM 87102 ...... (505) 766–3481
Federal Building, 1065 South Main Street, Building D–13, Suite I, Las Cruces, NM 88005 .... (505) 526–5475
Room 302, 120 South Federal Place, Santa Fe, NM 87501 .... (505) 988–6511
Federal Building, 140 Roswell, NM 88201 .... (505) 623–6170

* * *

JEFF BINGAMAN, Democrat, of Santa Fe, NM; born in El Paso, TX, October 3, 1943; raised in Silver City, NM; graduate of Western High (now Silver High), 1961; B.A., government, Harvard University, 1965; J.D., Stanford Law School, 1968; served in the U.S. Army Reserves, 1968–74; served as Assistant New Mexico Attorney General, 1969, as counsel to the State constitutional convention; private practice, 1970–78; served as New Mexico Attorney General, 1979–82; committees: Armed Services, Energy and Natural Resources, Labor and Human Resources, Joint Economic; elected to the U.S. Senate November 2, 1982, for the six-year term beginning January 3, 1983; reelected 1988 and 1994; member of the Methodist Church; married to the former Anne Kovacovich; one son, John.

Office Listings

http://www.senate.gov/~bingaman senator__bingaman@bingaman.senate.gov

703 Hart Senate Office Building, Washington, DC 20510–3102 224–5521
TDD: 224–1792
Administrative Assistant.—Patrick Von Bargen.
Legislative Director.—Trudy Vincent.
Press Secretary.—Kristen Ludecke.
Personal Assistant.—Virginia White.
Loretto Town Centre, Suite 148, 505 South Main, Las Cruces, NM 88001 .... (505) 523–6561
625 Silver Avenue SW, Suite 130, Albuquerque, NM 87102 .... (505) 766–3636
105 West Third Street, Suite 409, Roswell, NM 88201 .... (505) 622–7113
119 East Marcy, Suite 101, Santa Fe, NM 87501 .... (505) 988–6647

REPRESENTATIVES

FIRST DISTRICT

STEVEN SCHIFF, Republican, Albuquerque, NM; born in Chicago, IL on March 18, 1947; B.A., University of Illinois, Chicago, political science, 1968; J.D., University of New Mexico Law School, 1972; colonel, U.S. Air Force Reserves; assistant district attorney of Bernalillo County, NM, 1972–77; trial attorney, 1977–79; assistant city attorney and counsel for Albuquerque Police Department, 1979–81; district attorney, Bernalillo County, 1980–88; member:

Civitan International, New Mexico and National District Attorneys associations, Albuquerque Lodge of B'nai B'rith, Albuquerque Humane Association; married to the former Marcia Lewis; two children: Jaimi and Daniel; vice chairman, Government Reform and Oversight Committee; member: Science, Judiciary, and Standards of Official Conduct committees; elected to the 101st Congress on November 8, 1988; reelected to each succeeding Congress.

Office Listings

2404 Rayburn House Office Building, Washington, DC 20515–3101 225–6316
Executive Assistant.—Maureen Harrison. FAX: 225–4975
Legislative Director.—Troy Benavidez.
Press Secretary.—J. Barry Bitzer.
Suite 140, 625 Silver Avenue SW, Albuquerque, NM 87102 .... (505) 766–2538
Chief of Staff.—Mary Martinek.

Counties: Bernalillo (part), Sandoval (part), Santa Fe (part), Torrance, Valencia (part). Population (1990), 505,491.

ZIP Codes: 87002 (part), 87008–09, 87016, 87031 (part), 87032, 87035–36, 87043, 87047, 87057, 87059, 87061, 87063, 87068 (part), 87070, 87102–04, 87105 (part), 87106–13, 87114 (part), 87116, 87118–23, 87124 (part), 87125, 87153–54, 87176, 87184, 87190–92, 87194–99, 88319, 88321

* * *

SECOND DISTRICT

JOE R. SKEEN, Republican, of Picacho, NM; born in Roswell, NM, June 30, 1927; B.S., engineering, Texas A&M University, 1950; served in the U.S. Navy, 1945–46; U.S. Air Force Reserves, 1949–52; soil and water engineer, Zuni and Ramah Navajo Indians, 1951, returning to the family sheep ranching operation in Lincoln County, NM, which was purchased from his grandmother; operated a flying service, Ruidoso, NM; member, New Mexico State Senate, 1960–70, serving as minority leader for six years; served three years as State Republican chairman; Republican nominee for lieutenant governor, 1970, and GOP nominee for governor, 1974 and 1978; elected to Congress from New Mexico's Second District as a write-in candidate, 1980, after the incumbent died in office and the Republican Party was denied a place on the ballot by the courts; member: New Mexico Woolgrowers Association; New Mexico Cattle Growers Association; New Mexico Farm and Livestock Bureau; Conquistadore Council, Boy Scouts of America; Elks; Eagles; married to the former Mary Helen Jones, two children: Lisa and Mike; Catholic; elected to the 97th Congress, November 4, 1980; reelected to each succeeding Congress.

Office Listings

2367 Rayburn House Office Building, Washington, DC 20515–3102 225–2365
Administrative Assistant.—Suzanne Eisold. FAX: 225–9599
Executive Assistant/Office Manager.—Lin Rhode.
Press Secretary.—Sherry Kiesling.
Federal Building, Room 257, Roswell, NM 88201 .... (505) 622–0055
1065–B, South Main, Suite A, Las Cruces, NM 88005 .... (505) 527–1771

Counties: Bernalillo (part), Catron, Chaves, Cibola (part), DeBaca, Dona Ana, Eddy; Grant, Guadalupe, Hidalgo, Lea, Lincoln, Luna, Otero, Sierra, Socorro, and Valencia (part). Population (1990), 504,659.

ZIP Codes: 87002 (part), 87006–07, 87011, 87014, 87020 (part), 87022–23, 87026, 87028, 87031 (part), 87034, 87038, 87040, 87042, 87049–51, 87055, 87062, 87068, 87105, 87185, 87711, 87724, 87801, 87815, 87820–21, 87823–25, 87827–32, 87901, 87930–33, 87935–37, 87939–43, 88001–06, 88008–09, 88011–12, 88020–34, 88036, 88038–49, 88052–56, 88058, 88061–63, 88065, 88072, 88114, 88119, 88134, 88136, 88201–02, 88210–11, 88213 88220–21, 88230–32, 88240–41, 88250, 88252–56, 88260, 88262–68, 88301, 88310–12, 88314, 88316–18, 88323–25, 88330, 88336–54, 88417, 88431–32, 88435

* * *

THIRD DISTRICT

BILL REDMOND, Republican, of Santa Fe, NM; B.A., Ministry and Administration, Lincoln Christian College, IL, 1979; Masters-Philosophy Science, Counseling, History, and Administration, Lincoln Christian Seminary, 1988; attended Murray State University; U.S. Army Reserve, Army Chaplain Candidate Program; special education instructor, 1980–83; author; free- lance writer; teacher at University of New Mexico; member, New Mexico Republican State Central

Committee; delegate: New Mexican Republican Pre-Primary Convention, Quadrennial Presidential Convention in New Mexico; Republican Distribution Coordinator for Los Alamos County; active in Boy Scouts of America; Big Brother; Foster Parent; minister of Sante Fe Christian Church; managed Santa Fe Youth and Family Roller Rink; adult basic education instructor for University of New Mexico at the Los Alamos Detention Center and UNLMA Campus; married 22 years to Shirley Raye Redmond; two children: Bethany Joy, Jordan Andrew; committees: (call office); elected to 105th Congress by special election to replace Bill Richardson, who became Ambassador to United Nations.

Office Listings

2268 Rayburn House Office Building, Washington, DC, 20515–3103 225–6190
Chief of Staff.—Cathy Jewell. FAX: 226–1331
Legislative Director.—Jennifer Hamann.
Press Secretary.—Jennifer Bennett.
1494 South St. Francis Drive, Santa Fe, NM 87505 .... (505) 988–7230
District Director.—Michael (Mike) Burita.

Counties: Bernalillo (part), Cibola (part), Colfax, Curry, Harding, Los Alamos, McKinley, Mora, Quay, Rio Arriba, Roosevelt, Sandoval (part), San Juan, San Miguel, Santa Fe (part), Taos, and Union. Population (1990), 504,919.

ZIP Codes: 87001, 87004–05, 87010, 87012–13, 87015, 87017–18, 87020 (part), 87021, 87024–25, 87027, 87029, 87037, 87041, 87044–46, 87048, 87052–53, 87056, 87064, 87072, 87083, 87114 (part), 87124 (part), 87174, 87301, 87305, 87310–13, 87315–17, 87319–28, 87347, 87357, 87364–65, 87375, 87401–02, 87410, 87412–13, 87415–21, 87455, 87461, 87499, 87501–02, 87504–06, 87510–16, 87518–25, 87527–33, 87535, 87537, 87539–40, 87544, 87547–53, 87556–58, 87560, 87562–67, 87569, 87571, 87573–75, 87577–83, 87701, 87710, 87712–15, 87718, 87722–23, 87725, 87728–36, 87740, 87742–43, 87745–47, 87749–50, 87752–53, 88101–03, 88111–13, 88115–16, 88118, 88120–26, 88130, 88132–33, 88135, 88401, 88410–12, 88414–16, 88418–19, 88421–24, 88426–27, 88429–30, 88434, 88436–37, 88439

NEW YORK

(Population 1995, 18,136,000)

SENATORS

DANIEL PATRICK MOYNIHAN, Democrat, of Oneonta, NY; born in Tulsa, OK, March 16, 1927; attended City College of New York; served in the U.S. Navy, 1944–47, gunnery officer, U.S.S. *Quirinus;* Tufts College, B.N.S., 1946, B.A., *cum laude*, 1948; Fletcher School of Law and Diplomacy, M.A., 1949, Ph.D., 1961, LL.D., 1968; Fulbright Fellow, London School of Economics and Political Science, 1950–51; assistant to Governor Averell Harriman of New York, 1955–58; delegate to the Democratic national conventions, 1960, 1976; served as a cabinet or subcabinet officer to Presidents Kennedy, Johnson, Nixon, and Ford: Ambassador to India, 1973–75; U.S. Permanent Representative to the United Nations, 1975–76; member, National Commission to Reform Social Security; member, National Economic Commission; member, President's Science Advisory Committee; director, American Association for the Advancement of Science; member, American Academy of Arts and Sciences, American Philosophical Society, National Academy of Public Administration; teacher of government at Russell Sage College, Cornell University School of Industrial Relations, Syracuse University, Harvard University; 60 honorary degrees from colleges and universities; Meritorious Service Award, U.S. Department of Labor, 1965; Arthur S. Flemming Award as ''an architect of the Nation's program to eradicate poverty,'' 1965; International League for Human Rights, 1975 award; Syracuse University Centennial Medal; recipient: 1986 Encyclopedia Britannica Award; Seal Medallion of the Central Intelligence Agency; married to the former Elizabeth Brennan; three children: Timothy Patrick, Maura Russell, and John McCloskey; committees: Environment and Public Works; Finance; Rules and Administration; Joint Committee on the Library; Joint Committee on Taxation; elected to the U.S. Senate, November 2, 1976, for the six-year term beginning January 3, 1977; reelected for each succeeding term.

Office Listings

http://www.senate.gov/~moynihan senator@dpm.senate.gov

464 Russell Senate Office Building, Washington, DC 20510–3201 224–4451
Chief of Staff.—Tony Bullock. TDD: 224–6821
Press Secretary.—Dan Maffei.
Legislative Director.—Gray Maxwell.
Suite 6200, 405 Lexington Avenue, New York, NY 10174 .... (212) 661–5150
28 Church Street, Buffalo, NY 14202 .... (716) 846–4097
214 Main Street, Oneonta, NY 13820 .... (607) 433–2310

* * *

ALFONSE M. D'AMATO, Republican, of Island Park, NY; born in Brooklyn, NY, August 1, 1937; graduated, Chaminade High School, Mineola, NY, 1955; B.S., Syracuse University, College of Business Administration, Syracuse, NY, 1959; J.D., Syracuse Law School, 1961; Honorary Doctor of Laws, New York Law School, 1982; attorney; admitted to the New York State bar in 1962; Nassau County Public Administrator, 1965–68; town of Hempstead, NY, receiver of taxes, 1969; Hempstead Town Supervisor, 1971–77; presiding supervisor, Town of Hempstead, and vice chairman, Nassau County Board of Supervisors, 1977–80; honors: National Council of Young Israel, Humanitarian Award; New York State Order, Sons of Italy, ''Man of the Year''; member: Knights of Columbus; Island Park Volunteer Fire Department, Lions Club, Sons of Italy, and Sacred Heart R.C. Church; four children: Lisa, Lorraine, Daniel, and Christopher; elected to the U.S. Senate, November 4, 1980; reelected November 3, 1992, for the six-year term beginning January 3, 1993; committees: chairman, Banking, Housing and Urban Affairs; Finance; subcommittees: Taxation and IRS Oversight; Health Care; International Trade; cochairman, Helsinki Commission.

Office Listings

http://www.senate.gov/damato senator_al@damato.senate.gov

520 Hart Senate Office Building, Washington, DC 20510–3202 224–6542
Administrative Assistant.—Michael Kinsella. FAX: 224–5871
Personnel Director.—Claudia Breggia.
Scheduler.—Lecia Corbisiero.
Seven Penn Plaza, Suite 600, Seventh Avenue, New York, NY 10001 .... (212) 947–7390
Leo O'Brien Office Building, Room 420, Albany, NY 12207 .... (518) 472–4343

Federal Building, Room 620, 111 West Huron Street, Buffalo, NY 14202 .... (716) 846–4111
304 Federal Building, 100 State Street, Rochester, NY 14614 .... (716) 263–5866
1259 Federal Office Building, P.O. Box 7216, Syracuse, NY 13261–7216 .... (315) 423–5471

REPRESENTATIVES

FIRST DISTRICT

MICHAEL PATRICK FORBES, Republican, of Quogue, NY; born in Riverhead, NY, on July 16, 1952; graduated Westhampton Beach High, Westhampton, NY, 1971; State University of New York at Albany, 1983, B.A.; regional director, Small Business Administration; principal liaison for Chamber of Commerce of the United States; Knights of Columbus; Southampton Elks; Irish-American Society of the Hamptons; owned a public relations and marketing business, 1980s; member: Appropriations Committee; elected to the 104th Congress, November 8, 1994; reelected to the 105th Congress.

Office Listings

http:/www.house.gov/forbes mpforbes@hr.house.gov

502 Cannon House Office Building, Washington, DC 20515–3201 225–3826
FAX: 225–3143
Administrative Assistant/Chief of Staff.—Anne Stanley.
Scheduler/Office Manager.—Kate Fernstrom.
Press Secretary.—Tom Springer.
1500 William Floyd Parkway, Shirley, NY 11967 .... (516) 345–9000
Office Manager.—Diana Weir.

County: SUFFOLK COUNTY (part); cities and townships of Brookhaven, East Hampton, Riverhead, Shelter Island, Smithtown, Southampton, and Southold. Population (1990), 580,338.

ZIP Codes: 11772, 11777, 11787

* * *

SECOND DISTRICT

RICK A. LAZIO, Republican, of Brightwaters, NY; born on March 13, 1958 in Amityville, NY; A.B., Vassar College, Poughkeepsie, NY, 1980; J.D., American University, Washington College of Law; partner, Glass, Lazio, and Glass, Attorneys at Law; admitted to New York bar in 1984; Suffolk County Legislature, 1989–92; married in 1990 to Patricia Ann Moriarty Lazio; two daughters, Molly Ann and Kelsey; elected on November 3, 1992 to the 103rd Congress; reelected to each succeeding Congress.

Office Listings

http://www.house.gov/lazio lazio@hr.house.gov

314 Cannon House Office Building, Washington, DC 20515–3202 225–3335
FAX: 225–4669
Chief of Staff.—David Horne.
Office Manager/Scheduler.—Tara Shelley.
126 West Main Street, Babylon, NY 11702 .... (516) 893–9010

County: SUFFOLK COUNTY (part); cities of Amityville, Babylon, Bay Shore, Bayport, Baywood, Bohemia, Brentwood, Brightwaters, Central Islip, Commack (part), Copiague, Deer Park, Dix Hills (part), East Farmingdale, East Islip, Elwood (part), Greenlawn (part), Hauppauge (part), Holbrook (part), Holtsville (part), Huntington (part), Huntington Station (part), Islandia, Islip, Islip Terrace, Lindenhurst, Melville (part), North Amityville, North Babylon, North Bay Shore, North Great River, North Lindenhurst, Oakdale, Ronkonkoma, Sayville, South Huntington (part), West Babylon, West Bay Shore, West Islip, West Sayville, Wheatley Heights and Wyandanch. Population (1990), 580,337.

ZIP Codes: 11701–07, 11715 (part), 11716–18, 11722, 11725 (part), 11726, 11729–30, 11731 (part), 11735 (part), 11739, 11740 (part), 11741 (part), 11742 (part), 11743 (part), 11746 (part), 11747 (part), 11751–52, 11757, 11769–70, 11779 (part), 11782, 11788 (part), 11795–96, 11798

* * *

THIRD DISTRICT

PETER T. KING, Republican, of Seaford, NY; born on April 5, 1944 in Manhattan, NY; B.A., St. Francis College, NY, 1965; J.D., University of Notre Dame Law School, IN, 1968;

served, U.S. Army Reserve National Guard, specialist 5, 1968–73, admitted to New York bar, 1968; attorney; Deputy Nassau County Attorney, 1972–74, executive assistant to the Nassau County Executive, 1974–76; general counsel, Nassau Off-Track Betting Corporation, 1977; Hempstead Town Councilman, 1978–81; Nassau County Comptroller, 1981–92; member: Ancient Order of Hiberians, Long Island Committee for Soviet Jewry, Sons of Italy, Knights of Columbus, 69th Infantry Veterans Corps, American Legion; married in 1967 to Rosemary Wiedl King; two children: Sean and Erin; elected on November 3, 1992 to the 103rd Congress; reelected to each succeeding Congress.

Office Listings

http://www.house.gov/king peter.king@mail.house.gov

403 Cannon House Office Building, Washington, DC 20515–3203 .... (202) 225–7896
Administrative Assistant.—Jonathan Hymes. FAX: 226–2279
Executive Assistant/Personal Secretary.—Carolyn Radcliff.
Press Assistant.—Daniel Michaelis.
1003 Park Boulevard, Massapequa Park, NY 11762 .... (516) 541–4225
District Administrator.—Randolph Yunker. FAX: 541–6602

County: NASSAU COUNTY (part); cities and townships of Albertson (part), Baldwin (part), Bellmore, Bethpage, Brookville, Cove Neck, East Norwich (part), East Rockaway, Farmingdale, Flower Hill (part), Freeport (part), Glen Cove (part), Glen Head, Glenwood Landing, Greenvale (part), Hicksville, Island Park, Jericho, Levittown (part), Lido Beach, Locust Valley, Long Beach, Lynbrook (part), Manhasset (part), Massapequa, Massapequa Park, Matinecock, Merrick, Mill Neck, Muttontown, North Bellmore (part), North Massapequa, North Merrick (part), North Wantagh, Oceanside, Old Bethpage, Old Brookville, Old Westbury, Oyster Bay, Oyster Bay Cove, Plainedge, Plainview (part), Plandome, Point Lookout, Port Washington (part), Roslyn (part), Sea Cliff, Seaford, Searingtown (part), Syosset (part), Upper Brookville, Wantagh, Westbury (part), Woodbury (part). Population (1990), 580,337.

ZIP Codes: 11030 (part), 11050 (part), 11507 (part), 11510 (part), 11518, 11520 (part), 11542 (part), 11545, 11547, 11548 (part), 11558, 11560–61, 11563 (part), 11566 (part), 11568–69, 11572, 11576 (part), 11578–79, 11590 (part), 11710 (part), 11714, 11732 (part), 11735, 11753, 11756 (part), 11762, 11765, 11771, 11783, 11791 (part), 11793, 11797 (part), 11801, 11803 (part), 11804

* * *

FOURTH DISTRICT

CAROLYN McCARTHY, Democrat, of Mineola, NY; born in Brooklyn, NY, January 5, 1944; graduated, Mineola High School, 1962; graduated, nursing school, 1964; licensed practical nurse in ICU Section, Glen Cove Hospital; married Dennis McCarthy, 1967; widowed on December 7, 1993, when her husband was killed and her only son, Kevin, severely wounded in the Long Island Railroad Massacre; turned personal nightmare into a crusade against violence—speaking out with other families of the Long Island tragedy, not just to the victims of the shooting but to crime victims across the country; honorary member of the board, Americans Against Gun Violence; member: board of directors for "Guns for Goods"; board of directors, New Yorkers Against Gun Violence; board of directors, New York City "Stop the Violence" campaign; elected to the 105th Congress.

Office Listings

1725 Longworth House Office Building, Washington, DC 20515 225–5516
Chief of Staff.—Beneva Schullte. FAX: 225–5758
Executive Assistant.—Sean McDonough.
Legislative Assistants: Andrew Goldberg, Gerry O'Sullivan.
Legislative Correspondent.—Stacey Minograd.
Staff Assistant/Tour Coordinator.—Christina Pagett.
One Fulton Avenue, Hempstead, NY .... (516) 489–7066
FAX: 489–7283

Countries: NASSAU (part). Cities and townships of Atlantic Beach, Baldwin, Carle Place, Cedarhurst, East Meadow, East Williston, Elmont, Floral Park, Franklin Square, Freeport, Garden City, Hempstead, Hewlett, Inwood, Lakeview, Lawrence, Levittown, Lynbrook, Malverne, Mineola, New Hyde Park, North Bellmore, Rockville Centre, Roosevelt, Salisbury, Stewart Manor, Uniondale, Valley Stream, Wantagh, West Hempstead, Williston Park, and Woodmere.

ZIP Codes: 11001, 11003, 11010, 11040 (part), 11501, 11509, 11510, 11514, 11516, 11520, 11530, 11550, 11552–54, 11557, 11559, 11563, 11565, 11570, 11575, 11580–81, 11590, 11596, 11598, 11696, 11710, 11756, 11793

FIFTH DISTRICT

GARY L. ACKERMAN, Democrat, of Queens, NY; born in Brooklyn, NY, on November 19, 1942; graduate, Queens College, Flushing, NY; attended St. John's University, Jamaica, NY; public school teacher; newspaper editor; businessman; New York State Senate, 1979–83; married to the former Rita Tewel; three children: Lauren, Corey, and Ari; elected by special election on March 1, 1983, to the 98th Congress, to fill the vacancy caused by the death of Benjamin Rosenthal; reelected to each succeeding Congress.

Office Listings

http://www.house.gov/ackerman

2243 Rayburn House Office Building, Washington, DC 20515–3205 225–2601
Administrative Assistant.—Jedd Moskowitz.
Executive Assistant.—Seth Applebaum.
218–14 Northern Boulevard, Bayside, NY 11361 .... (718) 423–2154
District Office Administrator.—Arthur Flug.
229 Main Street, Huntington, NY 11743 .... (516) 423–2154
Assistant District Administrator.—Anne McShane.

Counties: Nassau (part), Queens (part), Suffolk (part). CITIES AND TOWNSHIPS: Asharoken, Auburndale, Bay Terrace, Bayside, Bayville, Bell Park Gardens, Bell Park Manor, Centerport, Centre Island, Clearview, Cold Spring Harbor, Commack, Deepdale, Douglaston, Douglaston Manor, East Commack, East Hills, East Northport, Eatons Neck, Electchester, Elwood, Flushing, Fort Salonga, Fresh Meadows, Glen Oaks, Glen Cove, Great Neck, Great Neck Estates, Great Neck Gardens, Great Neck Plaza, Greenlawn, Greenvale, Halesite, Herricks, Hillcrest, Hollis Court Gardens, Hollis Hills, Huntington, Huntington Bay, Huntington Manor, Huntington Station, Kensington, Kew Gardens Hills, Kings Point, Lake Success, Lattingtown, Laurel Hollow, Little Neck, Lloyd Harbor, Lloyd Neck, Lower Melville, Manor Haven, Melville, Middleville, North Shore Towers, Northport, Oakland Gardens, Plainview, Pomonok, Port Washington, Port Washington North, Queensboro Hill, Roslyn, Roslyn Estates, Roslyn Harbor, Roslyn Heights, Russell Gardens, Saddle Rock, Saddle Rock Estates, Sands Point, Searington, Smithtown, Thomaston, University Gardens, Vernon Valley, West Hills, West Neck, Windsor Park, Woodbury. Population (1990), 580,337.

ZIP Codes: 11004 (part), 11005, 11020–25, 11027, 11030 (part), 11040 (part), 11042 (part), 11050 (part), 11051, 11054, 11351–52, 11354 (part), 11355 (part), 11357 (part), 11358–59, 11360 (part), 11361–64, 11365 (part), 11366 (part), 11367 (part), 11386, 11426 (part), 11427 (part), 11507 (part), 11542 (part), 11548 (part), 11560 (part), 11576 (part), 11577 (part), 11579 (part), 11709, 11721, 11724, 11725 (part), 11731 (part), 11740 (part), 11743 (part), 11746 (part), 11747 (part), 11754 (part), 11768, 11771 (part), 11787 (part), 11788 (part), 11791 (part), 11797 (part), 11803 (part)

* * *

SIXTH DISTRICT

FLOYD H. FLAKE, Democrat, of Rosedale, Queens, NY; born in Los Angeles, CA on January 30, 1945; graduated G.W. Carver High School, Houston, TX, 1962; B.A., Wilberforce University, Wilberforce, OH, 1967; B.A., Payne Theological Seminary, Wilberforce, OH, 1970; attended Northeastern University, Boston, MA, 1974–76; St. John's University, Jamaica, NY, 1980–84, Doctorate of Ministry (candidate, 1995); pastor of Allen A.M.E. Church, Jamaica, NY, 1976–present; founder: Allen Housing Development Fund Corporation, Allen Christian School and Multi-Purpose Center, Allen Home Care Agency, Allen Housing Corporation, Allen Neighborhood Preservation and Development Corporation; member, NAACP; married the former Margaret Elaine McCollins, 1975; four children: Aliya, Nailah, Rasheed, and Hasan; elected to the 100th Congress on November 4, 1986; reelected to each succeeding Congress.

Office Listings

1035 Longworth House Office Building, Washington, DC 20515–3206 225–3461
Executive Staff Director.—Edwin Reed. FAX: 226–4169
Legislative Director.—Sean Peterson.
Communications Director/Deputy Staff Director.—Marshall Mitchell.
Office Manager.—Pat Fisher.
196–06 Linden Boulevard, St. Albans, NY 11412 .... (718) 949–5600
20–08 Seagirt Boulevard, Far Rockaway, NY 11691 .... (718) 327–9791

County: QUEENS COUNTY (part). Cities and townships of Arverne, Cambria Heights, Edgemere, Far Rockaway, Floral Park, Glen Oaks, Hammels, Hollis, Jamaica, Kew Gardens, Laurelton, New Hyde Park, Ozone Park, Queens Village, Richmond Hill, Rosedale, St. Albans, South Ozone Park, Springfield Gardens, and Woodhaven. Population (1990), 580,337.

ZIP Codes: 11001 (part), 11004 (part), 11040 (part), 11411–13, 11415 (part), 11416 (part), 11417–20, 11421 (part), 11422, 11423 (part), 11426 (part), 11427 (part), 11428–30, 11432 (part), 11433–34, 11435 (part), 11436, 11690, 11691 (part), 11692 (part), 11693

SEVENTH DISTRICT

THOMAS J. MANTON, Democrat, of Sunnyside, Queens, NY; born of Irish immigrant parents in Manhattan, New York City, on November 3, 1932; graduated, St. John's Preparatory School, Brooklyn, NY, 1950; St. John's University, 1958, B.B.A.; St. John's Law School (nights), 1962, LL.B.; served in U.S. Marine Corps, 1951–53; member, New York City Police Department, 1955–60; marketing representative, IBM Corporation, 1960–64; admitted to New York State bar, 1963; private practice of law, 1964–84; member: New York City Council, 1970–84, Queens County Bar Association; Catholic War Veterans, Post 870; past president, St. Patrick's Society of Queens; elected chairman, executive committee, Queens County Democratic Organization, 1986; married to the former Diane Schley; four children: Catherine, Thomas, John, and Jeanne; elected to the 99th Congress, November 6, 1984; reelected to each succeeding Congress.

Office Listings

tmanton@hr.house.gov

2235 Rayburn House Office Building, Washington, DC 20510–3207 225–3965
Administrative Assistant.—Steven Vest.
Legislative Director/Counsel.—Elaine Simek.
Office Manager.—John Olmsted.
Legislative Assistant.—Jim Mathews.
46–12 Queens Boulevard, Sunnyside, NY 11104 .... (718) 706–1400
District Chief of Staff.—Fran Kraft.
2114 Williamsbridge Road, Bronx, NY 10461 .... (718) 931–1400

Counties: Bronx (part), Queens (part). Population (1990), 580,337.

ZIP Codes: 10461, 10462, 10465 (part), 10467 (part), 10469 (part), 11101 (part), 11102 (part), 11103 (part), 11104, 11106, 11354 (part), 11356, 11357 (part), 11368 (part), 11369 (part), 11370 (part), 11371, 11372 (part), 11373 (part), 11377 (part), 11378 (part), 11379 (part), 11380, 11385 (part)

* * *

EIGHTH DISTRICT

JERROLD L. NADLER, Democrat, of New York, NY; born in Brooklyn, NY, on June 13, 1947; graduated from Stuyvesant High School, 1965; B.A., Columbia University, 1970; J.D., Fordham University, 1978; New York State Assembly, 1977–92; member: American Jewish Congress, ACLU, National Abortion Rights Action League, AIPAC, National Organization for Women, United States Holocaust Memorial Council; married, 1976; one child; elected to the 102nd Congress on November 3, 1992 to fill the vacancy caused by the death of Congressman Ted Weiss; at the same time elected to the 103rd Congress; reelected to each succeeding Congreess.

Office Listings

http://www.house.gov/nadler nadler@hr.house.gov

2448 Rayburn House Office Building, Washington, DC 20515–3208 225–5635
Chief of Staff.—Amy Green. FAX: 225–6923
Legislative Director.—David Lachmann.
Suite 910, 11 Beach Street, New York, NY 10013 .... (212) 334–3270
Chief of Staff.—Neil Goldstein. FAX: 334–5259
District Administrator.—Linda Rosenthal.
52 Neptune Avenue, Brooklyn, NY 11224 .... (718) 373–3198
Brooklyn Director.—Bradley Korn. FAX: 996–0039

Counties: Kings (part), New York (part). Population (1990), 580,337.

ZIP Codes: 10001 (part), 10003 (part), 10004–08, 10010 (part), 10011 (part), 10012 (part), 10013 (part), 10014, 10016 (part), 10018 (part), 10019 (part), 10023 (part), 10024 (part), 10025 (part), 10036 (part), 10038 (part), 10041, 10048, 10101, 10103 (part), 10104–05, 10106 (part), 10107 (part), 10108, 10113, 10118 (part), 10119–23, 10129, 10249, 10268, 10270–72, 10274, 10276, 10278–81, 11204 (part), 11214 (part), 11215 (part), 11218 (part), 11219 (part), 11220 (part), 11223 (part), 11224 (part), 11230 (part), 11231 (part), 11232 (part), 11235 (part)

NINTH DISTRICT

CHARLES E. SCHUMER, Democrat, of Brooklyn and Queens, NY; born in Brooklyn, November 23, 1950; graduated valedictorian, Madison High School; Harvard University, *magna cum laude*, 1971; J.D. with honors, Harvard Law School, 1974; admitted to the New York State bar in 1975; elected to the New York State Assembly, 1974; served on Judiciary, Health, Education, and Cities committees; chairman, subcommittee on City Management and Governance, 1977; chairman, Committee on Oversight and Investigation, 1979; reelected to each succeeding legislative session until December 1980; married Iris Weinshall, 1980; two children: Jessica Emily and Alison Emma; committees: Banking and Financial Services; Judiciary; Housing and Community Opportunity; Financial Institutions and Consumer Credit; Immigration and Claims; ranking member, Crime; elected to the 97th Congress, November 4, 1980 reelected to each succeeding Congress.

Office Listings

2211 Rayburn House Office Building, Washington, DC 20515–3209 225–6616
Administrative Assistant.—Ben Chevat.
Director of Commnunications.—Josh Isay.
Executive Assistant.—Clare Coleman.
118–21 Queens Boulevard, Forest Hills, NY 11375 .... (718) 268–8200
90–16 Rockaway Beach Boulevard, Rockaway, NY 11693 .... (718) 945–9200
1628 Kings Highway, Brooklyn, NY 11229 .... (718) 627–9700
District Administrator.—Florence Stachel.

Counties: KINGS COUNTY (part); cities and townships of Bergen Beach, Brighton Beach, Canasie, Flatbush, Flatlands, Gerritsen Beach, Georgetowne, Kensington, Manhattan Beach, Marine Park, Midwood, Mill Basin, Park Slope, Parkville, Sheepshead Bay, Windsor Terrace. QUEENS COUNTY (part); cities and townships of Belle Harbor, Breezy Point, Briarwood, Broad Channel, Far Rockaway, Forest Hills, Glendale, Hamilton Beach, Howard Beach, Kew Gardens, Lindenwood, Middle Village, Neponsit, Ozone Park, Rego Park, Richmond Hill, Ridgewood, Rockway Point, Roxbury, West Lawrence, and Woodhaven. Population (1990), 580,338.

ZIP Codes: 11204 (part), 11210 (part), 11215 (part), 11218 (part), 11223 (part), 11224 (part), 11226, 11229, 11230 (part), 11234 (part), 11235 (part), 11236 (part), 11239, 11374 (part), 11375 (part), 11379 (part), 11385 (part), 11414, 11415 (part), 11416 (part), 11417 (part), 11418 (part), 11421 (part), 11435 (part), 11691 (part), 11692 (part), 11693 (part), 11694–95, 11697

* * *

TENTH DISTRICT

EDOLPHUS TOWNS, Democrat, of Brooklyn, NY; born in Chadbourn, NC, on July 21, 1934; graduated, West Side High School, Chadbourn, 1952; B.S., North Carolina A&T State University, Greensboro, 1956; master's degree in social work, Adelphi University, Garden City, NY, 1973; U.S. Army, 1956–58; teacher, Medgar Evers College, Brooklyn, NY, and for the New York City public school system; deputy hospital administrator, 1965–71; deputy president, Borough of Brooklyn, 1976–82; member: Kiwanis, Boy Scouts Advisory Council, Salvation Army, Phi Beta Sigma Fraternity; married the former Gwendolyn Forbes in 1960; two children: Darryl and Deidra; elected on November 2, 1982, to the 98th Congress; reelected to each succeeding Congress.

Office Listings

2232 Rayburn House Office Building, Washington, DC 20515–3210 225–5936
Administrative Assistant.—Brenda Pillors. FAX: 225–1018
Scheduler.—Gerri Taylor.
Second Floor, 545 Broadway, Brooklyn, NY 11206 .... (718) 387–8696
Special Assistant.—Jennifer Joseph. FAX: 387–8045
16 Court Street, Suite 1505, Brookyln, NY 11241 .... (718) 855–8018
District Director.—Karen Johnson.

County: KINGS COUNTY (part). Population (1990), 580,335.

ZIP Codes: 11201 (part), 11203 (part), 11205 (part), 11206 (part), 11207 (part), 11208 (part), 11210 (part), 11211 (part), 11212 (part), 11213 (part), 11215 (part), 11216 (part), 11217 (part), 11218 (part), 11219 (part), 11221 (part), 11231 (part), 11233 (part), 11234 (part), 11236 (part), 11238 (part), 11239–42, 11241

ELEVENTH DISTRICT

MAJOR R. OWENS, Democrat, of Brooklyn, NY; born in Memphis, TN, June 28, 1936; attended Hamilton High School, Memphis, TN; B.A., with high honors Morehouse College, 1956; M.S., Atlanta University, 1957; chairman, Brooklyn Congress of Racial Equality; vice president, Metropolitan Council of Housing, 1964; community coordinator, Brooklyn Public Library, 1965; executive director, Brownsville Community Council, 1966; commissioner, New York City Community Development Agency, 1968–73; director, community media library program at Columbia University, 1974; New York State Senate, 1974–82; chairman, Senate Democratic Operations Committee; Brooklyn borough president declared September 10, 1971, "Major R. Owens Day"; served on International Commission on Ways of Implementing Social Policy to Ensure Maximum Public Participation and Social Justice for Minorities at The Hague, the Netherlands, 1972; published author and lecturer on library science; featured speaker, White House Conference on Libraries, 1979; recognized authority in community development; married to Maria A. Owens of New York City; the children of their blended family are Christopher, Geoffrey, Millard, Carlos, and Cecelia; appointed chairman of the House Subcommittee on Select Education and Civil Rights, 1987; chairman of the Congressional Black Caucus Budget Task Force; appointed chairman of the Congressional Black Caucus Education Braintrust from the 98th Congress to the present; appointed chairman of the Congressional Black Caucus Task Force on Haiti from the 103rd Congress to the present; senior member, Government Reform and Oversight and Economic and Educational Opportunities committees; elected to the 98th Congress, November 2, 1982; reelected to each succeeding Congress.

Office Listings

2305 Rayburn House Office Building, Washington, DC 20515 225–6231
Administrative Assistant.—Jacqueline Ellis. FAX: 226–0112
Legislative Director.—Paul Seltman.
Acting Press Secretary.—Jacqueline Ellis.
Scheduler.—Debbie Aledo-Simpson.
289 Utica Avenue, Brooklyn, NY 11213 .... (718) 773–3100
District Office Director.—Daniel Simonette. FAX: 735–7143
1310 Cortelyou Road, Brooklyn, NY 11226 .... (718) 940–3213

County: KINGS COUNTY (part). Population (1990), 580,337.

ZIP Codes: 11201 (part), 11203 (part), 11205 (part), 11210 (part), 11212 (part), 11213 (part), 11215 (part), 11216 (part), 11217 (part), 11218 (part), 11225–26, 11230 (part), 11233 (part), 11234 (part), 11236 (part), 11238 (part), 11243

* * *

TWELFTH DISTRICT

NYDIA M. VELAZQUEZ, Democrat, of New York City; born in Yabucoa, Puerto Rico, March 28, 1953; University of Puerto Rico, B.A. in political science, 1974; New York University, M.A. in political science, 1976; faculty member, University of Puerto Rico, 1976–81; adjunct professor, Hunter College of the City University of New York, 1981–83; special assistant to Congressman Ed Towns, 1983; member, City Council of New York City, 1984–86; national director of Migration Division Office, Department of Labor and Human Resources of Puerto Rico, 1986–89; director, Department of Puerto Rican Community Affairs in the United States, 1989–92; elected on November 3, 1992 to the 103rd Congress.

Office Listings

http://www.house.gov/velazquez

1221 Longworth House Office Building, Washington, DC 20515 225–2361
Chief of Staff.—Rick Jauert. FAX: 226–0327
815 Broadway, Brooklyn, NY 11206 .... (718) 599–3658
District Administrator.—George Siberon. FAX: 599–4537
50–07 108th Street, Queens, NY .... (718) 699–2602
173 Avenue B, New York, NY 10009 .... (212) 673–3997

Counties: Kings (part), New York (part), Queens (part). Population (1990), 580,340.

ZIP Codes: 10002 (part), 10003 (part), 10009 (part), 10012 (part), 10013 (part), 10038 (part), 10110 (part), 10112 (part), 10114 (part), 11201 (part), 11205 (part), 11206 (part), 11207 (part), 11208 (part), 11211 (part), 11215 (part), 11217 (part), 11219 (part), 11220 (part), 11221 (part), 11222 (part), 11231 (part), 11232 (part), 11237, 11368 (part), 11369 (part), 11370 (part), 11372 (part), 11373 (part), 11377 (part), 11378 (part), 11385 (part)

THIRTEENTH DISTRICT

SUSAN MOLINARI, Republican, of Staten Island and Brooklyn, NY; born in Staten Island, NY, March 27, 1958; graduated from St. Joseph Hill Academy, Staten Island, 1976; B.A., *cum laude*, State University of New York, Albany, 1980; M.A., with honors, State University of New York, Albany, 1981; member, New York City Council, 1985–90; minority leader, New York City Council; daughter of Representative Guy V. Molinari; elected to the 101st Congress by special election on March 20, 1990 to fill the vacancy caused by the resignation of Guy Molinari; reelected to each succeeding Congress; married Representative Bill Paxon, Republican, of New York, July 3, 1994.

Office Listings

http://www.house.gov/molinari molinari@hr.house.gov

2411 Rayburn House Office Building, Washington, DC 20515–3213 225–3371
Administrative Assistant.—Peter Rintye. FAX: 226–1272
Office Manager.—Sally Collins.
Press Secretary.—James Mazarella.
14 New Dorp Lane, Staten Island, NY 10306 .... (718) 987–8400
District Manager.—Barbara Palumbo.
9818 Fourth Avenue, Brooklyn, NY 11209 .... (718) 630–5277
Constituent Representative.—Eileen Long.

County: KINGS COUNTY (part); RICHMOND COUNTY. Population (1990), 580,337.

ZIP Codes: 10301–14, 11204 (part), 11209, 11214 (part), 11219 (part), 11220 (part), 11223 (part), 11228

* * *

FOURTEENTH DISTRICT

CAROLYN B. MALONEY, Democrat, of New York City, NY; born on February 19, 1948 in Greensboro, NC; B.A., Greensboro College, Greensboro, NC, 1968; various positions, New York City Board of Education, 1970–77; legislative aide, New York State Assembly, senior program analyst, 1977–79; executive director of advisory council, 1979–82; director of special projects, New York State Senate Office of the Minority Leader; New York City council member, 1982–93; chairperson, New York City Council Committee on Contracts; member: Council Committee on Aging, National Organization of Women, Common Cause, Sierra Club, Americans for Democratic Action, New York City Council Committee on Housing and Buildings, Citizens Union, Grand Central Business Improvement District, Harlem Urban Development Corporation (1982–91), Commission on Early Childhood Development Programs, Council of Senior Citizen Centers of New York City, 1982–87; married Clifton H. W. Maloney, 1976; two children: Virginia Marshall Maloney and Christina Paul Maloney; elected on November 3, 1992 to the 103rd Congress; reelected to each succeeding Congress.

Office Listings

http://www.house.gov/maloney

1330 Longworth House Office Building, Washington, DC 20515 .... (202) 225–7944
Administrative Assistant.—Ben Chevat. FAX: 225–4709
Legislative Director.—Jim Datri.
110 East 59th Street, 2nd Floor, New York, NY 10022 .... (202) 832–6531
28–11 Astoria Boulevard, Long Island City, NY 11102 .... (718) 932–1804
619 Lorimer Street, Brooklyn, NY 11211 .... (718) 349–1260

Counties: Kings (part); New York (part); Queens (part). Cities and townships: Astoria, Brooklyn (part), Greenpoint, Manhattan (part), Queens (part), Roosevelt Island. Population (1990), 580,337.

ZIP Codes: 10001 (part), 10002 (part), 10003 (part), 10009 (part), 10010 (part), 10011 (part), 10016 (part), 10017, 10018 (part), 10019 (part), 10020–22, 10023 (part), 10024 (part), 10025 (part), 10026 (part), 10028, 10029 (part), 10036 (part), 10044, 10055, 10103 (part), 10106 (part), 10107 (part), 10110 (part), 10111–12, 10118 (part), 10126, 10128, 10131, 10150–57, 10158 (part), 10159–61, 10162–63, 10165–78, 10185, 11102 (part), 11103 (part), 11105 (part), 11206 (part), 11211 (part), 11222 (part), 11370 (part)

FIFTEENTH DISTRICT

CHARLES B. RANGEL, Democrat-Liberal, of New York, NY; born in Harlem, NY, June 11, 1930; attended DeWitt Clinton High School; served in U.S. Army, 1948–52; awarded the Purple Heart, Bronze Star for Valor, U.S. and Korean presidential citations and three battle stars while serving in combat with the Second Infantry Division in Korea; honorably discharged with rank of staff sergeant; after military duty, completed high school, 1953; graduated from New York University School of Commerce, student under the G.I. bill, 1957 dean's list; graduated from St. John's University School of Law, dean's list student under a full three-year scholarship, 1960; lawyer; admitted to practice in the courts of the State of New York, U.S. Federal Court, Southern District of New York, and U.S. Customs Court; appointed assistant U.S. attorney, Southern District of New York, 1961; legal counsel, New York City Housing and Redevelopment Board, Neighborhood Conservation Bureau; general counsel, National Advisory Commission on Selective Service, 1966; served two terms in the New York State Assembly, 1966–70; active in 369th Veterans Association, Community Education Program, and Martin Luther King, Jr. Democratic Club; married Alma Carter; two children: Steven and Alicia; elected to the 92nd Congress, November 3, 1970; reelected to each succeeding Congress.

Office Listings

rangel@hr.house.gov

2354 Rayburn House Office Building, Washington, DC 20510–3215 225–4365
Executive Assistant.—Patricia O. Bradley. FAX: 225–0816
163 West 125th Street, New York, NY 10027 .... (212) 663–3900
District Administrator.—Vivian E. Jones.
2110 First Avenue, New York, NY 10029 .... (212) 348–9630

Counties: Bronx (part), New York (part), and Queens (part). Population (1990), 580,337.

ZIP Codes: 10024 (part), 10025 (part), 10026 (part), 10027, 10029 (part), 10030–35, 10037, 10039–40, 10115–16, 10463 (part), 11105 (part)

* * *

SIXTEENTH DISTRICT

JOSÉ E. SERRANO, Democrat, of Bronx, NY; born in Mayagüez, PR, October 24, 1943; Dodge Vocational High School, Bronx, NY; attended Lehman College, City University of New York, NY; served with the U.S. Army Medical Corps, 1964–66; employed by the Manufacturers Hanover Bank, 1961–69; Community School District 7, 1969–74; New York State Assemblyman, 1974–90; chairman, Consumer Affairs Committee, 1979–83; chairman, Education Committee, 1983–90; married in 1979 to the former Mary Staucet; five children: Lisa Trapenese, Jose Marco, Benjamin, Jonathan Brucker, and Justine Brucker; elected to the 101st Congress by special election March 28, 1990 to fill the vacancy caused by the resignation of Robert Garcia; reelected to each succeeding Congress.

Office Listings

http://www.house.gov/serrano jserrano@hr.house.gov

2342 Rayburn House Office Building, Washington, DC 20515–3216 225–4361
Special Counsel/Chief of Staff.—Ellyn Toscano.
Executive Assistant.—Pichy Marty.
Legislative Director.—Lucy Hand.
Scheduler.—Clara Wagner.
890 Grand Concourse, Bronx, NY 10451–2828 .... (212) 538–5400
District Director.—Cheryl Simmons-Oliver.

County: BRONX COUNTY (part). Cities and townships: Bronx. Population (1990), 580,338.

ZIP Codes: 10451 (part), 10452 (part), 10453 (part), 10454–56, 10457 (part), 10458 (part), 10459, 10460 (part), 10461 (part), 10462 (part), 10465 (part), 10467 (part), 10468 (part), 10472–74

* * *

SEVENTEENTH DISTRICT

ELIOT L. ENGEL, Democrat, of Bronx, NY; born in Bronx, NY, on February 18, 1947; B.A., Hunter-Lehman College, 1969; M.A., City University of New York, 1973; New York

Law School, 1987; married Patricia Ennis Engel, 1980; three children: Julia, Jonathan, and Philip; teacher and counselor in the New York City public school system, 1969–77; elected to the New York legislature, 1977–88; chaired the Assembly Committee on Alcoholism and Substance Abuse and subcommittee on Mitchell-Lama Housing (twelve years prior to his election to Congress); committee: Commerce; subcommittees: Telecommunications, Trade and Consumer Protection; Finance and Hazardous Materials; Oversight and Investigations; member: Congressional Human Rights Caucus, Democratic Study Group on Health, and Long Island Sound Caucus; cochairman, Albanian Issues Caucus; board member, Congressional Ad Hoc Committee on Irish Affairs; elected on November 8, 1988 to the 101st Congress; reelected to each succeeding Congress.

Office Listings

http://www.house.gov/engel engeline@hr.house.gov

2303 Longworth House Office Building, Washington, DC 20515–3217 225–2464
Administrative Assistant.—John F. Calvelli.
Office Manager.—Pamela K. Segal.
3655 Johnson Avenue, Bronx, NY 10463 .... (718) 796–9700
Chief of Staff.—Arnold I. Linhardt.
Director of Communications.—Joseph O'Brien.

Counties: Bronx (part), Westchester (part). CITIES AND TOWNSHIPS: Parts of Bronx, Yonkers, Mount Vernon, New Rochelle and Pelham. Population (1990), 580,337.

ZIP Codes: 10451 (part), 10452 (part), 10453 (part), 10457 (part), 10458 (part), 10463 (part), 10466, 10467 (part), 10468 (part), 10469 (part), 10470–71, 10475 (part), 10550 (part), 10551, 10552 (part), 10553 (part), 10701 (part), 10702, 10703 (part), 10704 (part), 10705 (part), 10710 (part), 10801 (part), 10802, 10803 (part), 10804 (part), 10805 (part)

* * *

EIGHTEENTH DISTRICT

NITA M. LOWEY, Democrat, of Harrison, NY; born in New York, NY, July 5, 1937; graduated, Bronx High School of Science, 1955; B.S., Mount Holyoke College, 1959; assistant to Secretary of State for Economic Development and Neighborhood Preservation, and deputy director, Division of Economic Opportunity, 1975–85; Assistant Secretary of State, 1985–87; member: boards of directors, Close-Up Foundation, Effective Parenting Information for Children; Windward School, Downstate (New York Region); Westchester Jewish Conference; Westchester Opportunity Program, National Committee of the Police Corps; Women's Network of the YWCA; Legal Awareness for Women, National Women's Political Caucus of Westchester; American Jewish Committee of Westchester; married Stephen Lowey, 1961; three children: Dana, Jacqueline, and Douglas; elected on November 8, 1988 to the 101st Congress; reelected to each succeeding Congress.

Office Listings

http://www.house.gov/lowey nitamail@hr.house.gov

2421 Rayburn House Office Building, Washington, DC 20515–3218 225–6506
Administrative Assistant.—Howard Wolfson. FAX: 225–0546
Executive Assistant.—Randy Stokes.
Suite 310, 222 Mamaroneck Avenue, White Plains, NY 10605 .... (914) 428–1707
District Administrator.—Patricia Keegan.

Counties: Bronx (part), Queens (part), Westchester (part). Cities and townships; Harrison, Larchmont, Mamaroneck, Mount Vernon, Port Chester, Rye Brook, Purchase, Rye, Scarsdale, White Plains, Yonkers, Tuckahoe, Creshwood, Bronxville, Eastchester, New Rochelle, Pelham, City Island, Country Club, Edgewater, Locust Point, Spencer Estates, Throggs Neck, Flushing, Holliswood, Jamaica Estates, Kew Garden Hills, Lefrak City, Queens Valley, West Cunningham Park, Fresh Meadows, and Rego Park. Population (1990), 580,337.

ZIP Codes: 10464, 10465 (part), 10469 (part), 10475 (part), 10528, 10530 (part), 10538, 10543, 10550 (part), 10552 (part), 10553 (part), 10573, 10577, 10580, 10583 (part), 10601 (part), 10602, 10604 (part), 10605 (part), 10606 (part), 10607 (part), 10701 (part), 10703 (part), 10704 (part), 10705 (part), 10706 (part), 10707 (part), 10708–09, 10710 (part), 10801 (part), 10803 (part), 10804 (part), 10805 (part), 11354 (part), 11355 (part), 11357 (part), 11360 (part), 11365 (part), 11366 (part), 11367 (part), 11368 (part), 11373 (part), 11374 (part), 11375 (part), 11379 (part), 11423 (part), 11427 (part), 11431, 11432 (part), 11435 (part), 11439

NINETEENTH DISTRICT

SUE W. KELLY, Republican, of Katonah, NY; born in Lima, OH, September 26, 1936; graduated, Lima Central High School; B.A., Denison University, Granville, OH, 1958; M.A., Sarah Lawrence College, Bronxville, NY, 1985; educator, small business owner, patient advocate, rape crisis counselor, community leader; member: League of Women Voters, American Association of University Women, PTA, Bedford Recreation Committee; member, Bedford Presbyterian Church; married Edward W. Kelly, 1960; four children: Eric, Sean, Charity, and Tim; committees: Transportation and Infrastructure, Small Business, and Banking and Financial Services; elected to the 104th Congress; reelected to the 105th Congress.

Office Listings

http://www.house.gov/suekelly dearsue@hr.house.gov

1222 Longworth House Office Building, Washington, DC 20515 225–5441
Chief of Staff.—Dennis Lambert.
Legislative Director.—Steve Hall.
Press Secretary.—Dan Boston.
21 Old Main Street, Room 205, Fishkill, NY 12524 .... (914) 897–5200
District Director.—Chris Fish.
105 South Bedford Road, Room 312–A, Mt. Kisco, NY 10549 .... (914) 241–6340

Counties: DUTCHESS COUNTY (part); cities and townships of Amenia, Beekman, Castle Point, Chelsea, City of Poughkeepsie, Dover, Dover Plains, East Fishkill, Fishkill (not including City of Beacon), Glenham, Holmes, Hopewell Junction, Hughsonville, LaGrange (part), Millbrook, New Hamburg, Pawling, Poughquag, Stormville, Unionvale, Verbank, Wappinger, Wappingers Falls, Washington, Wassiac, Wingdale. Post Offices: Billings (part of Town of Union Vale, E. Fiskkill), Clinton Corners (part of Town of Washington), LaGrangeville (part of Town of Unionvale), Pleasant Valley (part of LaGrange, Union Vale), Salt Point (part of Town of Washington). ORANGE COUNTY (part); cities and townships of Campbell Hall, Cornwall, Cornwall-on-Hudson, Ft. Montgomery, Hamptonburgh, Highlands, Highland Falls, Mountainville, New Windsor, Rock Tavern, Vails Gate, West Point. Post Offices: Bear Mountain (part of Town of Highlands), Central Valley (part of Town of Highlands), Montgomery (part of Town of Hamptonburgh), Newburgh (part of Town of New Windsor), Salisbury Mills (part of Town of Cornwall), Washingtonville (part of New Windsor, Hamptonburgh). PUTNAM COUNTY; cities and townships of Baldwin Place, Brewster, Carmel, Cold Spring, Garrison, Kent, Lake Peekskill, Mahopac, Mahopac Falls, Patterson, Philipstown, Putnam Valley, Southeast. WESTCHESTER COUNTY; cities and townships of Amawalk, Armonk, Baldwin Place, Bedford, Bedford Hills, Briarcliff Manor/Scarborough, Buchanan, Chappaqua, city of Peekskill, city of White Plains (North Part), Cortlandt, Crompound, Cross River, Croton Falls, Croton-on-Hudson, Golden's Bridge, Granite Springs, Hawthorne, Jefferson Valley, Katonah, Lewisboro, Lincolndale, Maryknoll, Millwood, Mohegan Lake, Montrose, Mount Kisco, Mount Kisco, Mount Pleasant, New Castle, North Castle, North Salem, North Tarrytown, Ossining, Peekskill, Pleasantville, Pound Ridge, Purdys, Shenorock, Shrub Oak, Somers, South Salem, Thornwood, Valhalla, Verplanck, Waccabuc, Yorktown, and Yorktown Heights. Population (1990), 580,337.

ZIP Codes: 10501, 10504–07, 10509–12, 10514, 10516–21, 10524, 10526–27, 10532, 10535–37, 10540–42, 10545–49, 10560, 10562, 10566, 10570, 10576 10578–79, 10587–90, 10591 (part), 10594, 10595 (part), 10596–98, 10602, 10603 (part), 10911, 10916–17, 10922, 10928, 10953, 10992, 10996, 12501, 12510–12, 12514, 12518, 12520, 12522, 12524, 12527, 12531, 12533, 12537, 12540 12545, 12549, 12550 (part), 12553, 12560, 12563–64, 12569–70, 12575 (part), 12577 (part), 12578, 12582, 12584–85, 12590 (part), 12592, 12594, 12601 (part), 12602, 12603 (part)

* * *

TWENTIETH DISTRICT

BENJAMIN A. GILMAN, Republican, of Middletown, NY; born in Poughkeepsie, NY, December 6, 1922; graduated from Middletown High School, 1941; B.S., Wharton School of Business and Finance, University of Pennsylvania, 1946; LL.B., New York Law School, 1950; veteran of World War II, 20th Air Force, 19th Bomb Group; awarded Distinguished Flying Cross and Air Medal for 35 missions over Japan; appointed assistant attorney general, New York State Department of Law, 1953; formed the law firm of Gilman and Gilman, 1955, in Middletown, NY; attorney for New York State's Temporary Commission on the Courts; served for three terms in the New York State Assembly from the 95th District, 1967–72; member: Southeastern Water Commission; Middletown, Orange County, New York State and American bar associations; the Association of the Bar of the City of New York; New York and American Trial Lawyers Associations; member of Orange County Republican Committee, American Legion, V.F.W., Masonic War Veterans Beth El Post No. 29, JWV (national legislative chairman), BPOE No. 1097, Hoffman Lodge of F&AM, AAONMS of Cyprus Temple (Albany), International Narcotic Enforcement Officers Association, Zeta Beta Tau fraternity, Otisville Grange, Hudson-Delaware Boy Scout Council, Lamont-Doherty Geological Observatory Advisory Council, advisory committee of NYS Division of Youth's Start Center; past president of Capitol Hill Shrine Club, former board chairman of Middletown Little League, vice president of Orange County Mental Health Association and Orange County Heart Association; lieutenant colonel, Civil Air Patrol, congressional branch; member: Le Societe des 40 Hommes et 8 Chevaux; colonel, New York Guard; three children: Jonathan, Harrison, Susan; chairman, International Relations Committee, 1995; member, Government Reform and Oversight Committee; former member of Foreign Affairs Committee, Post Office, Energy Security Working Group, Select Committee on Narcotics Abuse and Control, Select Committee on Hunger; congressional delegate to United Nations General Assembly, 11th Special Session (1981); member: U.S.-Ukraine Famine Commission; U.S.-Mexican Interparliamentary Conference; cochairman, U.S.-European Interparliamentary Conference; congressional advisor to Law of the Sea Conference; United States Military Academy Board of Visitors, 1973–83; Presidential Commission on World Hunger; Task Force on the Handicapped; cochairman, ad hoc committee on Irish Affairs; vice chairman, House Task Force on POWs and MIAs; Foundation for Better Health; Good Samaritan Hospital, Suffern, NY; board of directors, World Hunger Year; elected to the 93rd Congress, November 7, 1972; reelected to each succeeding Congress.

Office Listings

http://www.house.gov/gilman robert.becker@mail.house.gov

2449 Rayburn House Office Building, Washington, DC 20515–3220 225–3776
Administrative Assistant.—Nancy L. Colandrea. FAX: 225–2541
Legislative Director.—Todd Burger.
Press Assistant.—Andrew Zarutskie.
P.O. Box 358, 407 East Main Street, Middletown, NY 10940–0358 .... (914) 343–6666
District Office Manager.—Amalia Aumick.
377 Route 59, Monsey, NY 10954–3498 .... (914) 357–9000
32 Main Street, Hastings-on-Hudson, NY 10706–1602 .... (914) 478–5550

Counties: Orange (part), Rockland, Sullivan (part), Westchester (part). CITIES AND TOWNSHIPS of Bethel, Blooming Grove, Chester (Orange Co.), Clarks, Crawford, Deer Park, Goshen, Greenburgh, Greenville (Orange Co.), Haverstraw, Highland, Mamakating, Middletown, Minisink, Monroe, Montgomery, Mount Hope, Orange (Rockland Co.), Port Jervis, Ramapo, Stony Point, Thompson (part), Tuxedo, Wallkill, Warwick, Wawayanda, Woodbury and Yonkers (part). Population (1990), 580,338.

ZIP Codes: 10502–03, 10520 (part), 10522–23, 10530 (part), 10532 (part), 10533 (part), 10552 (part), 10560 (part), 10566 (part), 10570 (part), 10581, 10583 (part), 10591 (part), 10594 (part), 10595 (part), 10601 (part), 10603 (part), 10606 (part), 10607, 10629, 10701 (part), 10705 (part), 10706 (part), 10710 (part), 10801 (part), 10901, 10910–15, 10916 (part), 10917–21, 10923, 10924 (part), 10925–27, 10928 (part), 10930–33, 10940 (part), 10941, 10943, 10950–52, 10954, 10956, 10958–60, 10962–65, 10968–70, 10973–77, 10979–90, 10992 (part), 10993–95, 10996 (part), 10998 (part), 12518 (part), 12520 (part), 12543 (part), 12546 (part), 12549 (part), 12550 (part), 12553 (part), 12566 (part), 12575 (part), 12577 (part), 12583 (part), 12586 (part), 12701 (part), 12719 (part), 12720, 12721 (part), 12722, 12723 (part), 12725 (part), 12726 (part), 12727, 12729, 12732, 12734 (part), 12736 (part), 12737 (part), 12739 (part), 12743, 12745 (part), 12746, 12748 (part), 12749, 12750 (part), 12752 (part), 12760 (part), 12764 (part), 12766 (part), 12768 (part), 12769, 12770 (part), 12771, 12775 (part), 12777 (part), 12778, 12780–82, 12783 (part), 12785, 12786 (part), 12788 (part), 12790 (part), 12792

* * *

TWENTY-FIRST DISTRICT

MICHAEL R. MCNULTY, Democrat, of Green Island, NY; born in Troy, Rensselaer County, NY, September 16, 1947; graduated St. Joseph's Institute, Barrytown, NY, 1965; attended Loyola University, Rome Center, Rome, Italy, 1967–68; B.A., Holy Cross College, Worcester, MA, 1969; attended Hill School of Insurance, New York City, 1970; insurance broker; town supervisor, Green Island, NY, 1969–77; mayor, village of Green Island, 1977–83; New York State Assembly, 1983–88; member: Albany County Democratic Executive Committee, Green Island Democratic Committee, New York State Democratic Committee; board of directors, Capital Region Technology Development Council; delegate, Democratic National Convention, 1972; married the former Nancy Ann Lazzaro, 1971; four children: Michele, Angela, Nancy, and Maria; elected on November 8, 1988 to the 101st Congress; reelected to each succeeding Congress.

Office Listings

http://www.house.gov/mcnulty mmcnulty@hr.house.gov

2442 Rayburn House Office Building, Washington, DC 20515–3221 225–5076
Chief of Staff.—Lana R. Helfrich. FAX: 225–5077
Press Secretary.—Charles Segal.
Legislative Director.—Jim Glenn.
Leo W. O'Brien Federal Building, Albany, NY 12207 .... (518) 465–0700
U.S. Office, Schenectady, NY 12305 .... (518) 374–4547
33 Second Street, Troy, NY 12180 .... (518) 271–0822
9 Market Street, Amsterdam, NY 12010 .... (518) 843–3400

Counties: Albany, Montgomery (part), Rensselaer (part), Saratoga (part), and Schenectady. Population (1990), 580,337.

ZIP Codes: 12007–09, 12010 (part), 12019 (part), 12023, 12027 (part), 12041, 12045–47, 12053–56, 12059, 12061 (part), 12066–67, 12068 (part), 12069, 12070 (part), 12072, 12077, 12083–85, 12086 (part), 12087, 12107, 12110, 12120,

12122 (part), 12128, 12137, 12141, 12143–44, 12147, 12148 (part), 12150, 12157 (part), 12158–59, 12161, 12163, 12166, 12177, 12180 (part), 12182 (part), 12183, 12186, 12188 (part), 12189, 12193, 12198 (part), 12200–12, 12220, 12224–25, 12260, 12300–09, 12325, 12345, 12469 (part), 12508 (part), 12550 (part), 13317 (part)

* * *

TWENTY-SECOND DISTRICT

GERALD B.H. SOLOMON, Republican, of Glens Falls, NY; born in Okeechobee, FL, August 14, 1930; graduated from Bethlehem Central High School, Delmar, NY; attended Siena College, Albany, NY, and St. Lawrence University, Canton, NY; served in the U.S. Marine Corps, 1951–59; founding partner of insurance and investment firm; member, New York State Assembly, 1973–78; Queensbury town supervisor and Warren County legislator, 1968–72; member: president, Chamber of Commerce, First Presbyterian Church, Masons, Kiwanis, Grange, Farm Bureau, Jaycees, Queensbury Fire Department, Elks Lodge, Boy Scouts, Oriental Shrine, Amvets, Marine Corps League, American Legion, Disabled American Veterans; married the former Freda Parker of Monongahela, PA, 1955; five children: Susan, Daniel, Robert, Linda, and Jeffrey; elected to the 96th Congress, November 7, 1978; reelected to each succeeding Congress.

Office Listings

http://www.house.gov/solomon

2206 Rayburn House Office Building, Washington, DC 20515–3222 225–5614
Administrative Assistant.—Geoffrey Gleason. FAX: 225–6234
Personal Secretary.—Dorothy Cook.
Press Secretary.—Dan Amon.
Gaslight Square, Saratoga Springs, NY 12801 .... (518) 587–9800
21 Bay Street, Glens Falls, NY 12801 .... (518) 792–3031
337 Fairview Avenue, Hudson, NY 12534 .... (518) 828–0181

Counties: Columbia, Dutchess (part), Essex (part), Greene, Rensselaer (part), Saratoga (part), Schoharie (part), Warren, Washington. Population (1990), 582,340.

ZIP Codes: 12015, 12017–18, 12019 (part), 12020, 12022–24, 12026, 12027 (part), 12028–29, 12033, 12037, 12040, 12042, 12050–52, 12057–58, 12060, 12061 (part), 12062–63, 12065–66, 12071, 12074–76, 12082–83, 12087, 12089–90, 12092, 12094, 12106, 12114–15, 12118, 12120–21, 12122 (part), 12123–25, 12130–36, 12138, 12140, 12148 (part), 12151, 12153–54, 12156, 12157 (part), 12162, 12165, 12167 (part), 12168–74, 12176, 12180 (part), 12181, 12182 (part), 12184–85, 12192, 12195–96, 12198 (part), 12405, 12407, 12413–15, 12418, 12422–24, 12427, 12430–31, 12436–37, 12439, 12442, 12444, 12450–52, 12454, 12460, 12463, 12468, 12470, 12473, 12482, 12485, 12492, 12496, 12501–4, 12506–07, 12513–14, 12516–17, 12521, 12523, 12526, 12529–30, 12534, 12538, 12540 (part), 12541, 12544–47, 12565, 12567, 12569–72, 12574, 12578, 12580–81, 12583, 12585, 12590 (part), 12593, 12601 (part), 12603 (part), 12801, 12803–04, 12808–11, 12814–17, 12819–24, 12826–28, 12831–39, 12841, 12843–46, 12848–50, 12852–56, 12860–63, 12865–66, 12870–74, 12878, 12883–87, 12893, 12913 (part), 12928, 12932, 12942, 12946, 12956, 12960, 12974, 12987, 12997–98

* * *

TWENTY-THIRD DISTRICT

SHERWOOD L. BOEHLERT, Republican, of New Hartford, NY; born in Utica, September 28, 1936; graduated from Whitesboro Central High School; Utica College, A.B., 1961; served in the U.S. Army, 1956–58; Wyandotte Chemicals Corporation, 1961–64; 1964–72, chief of staff for Congressman Alexander Pirnie; 1973–79, chief of staff for Congressman Donald J. Mitchell; past president, Administrative Assistants Association, U.S. House of Representatives; elected 1979, Oneida County Executive; member: board of directors, Utica College Foundation; St. John the Evangelist Church, New Hartford; Distinguished Service Award, New York Air Force Association; Honorary Doctoral Degree, Utica College of Syracuse University; Federal 100: Readers' Choice Award, *Federal Computer Week* magazine; Environmental Leadership Award, League of Conservation Voters of America; married to the former Marianne Willey; four children; member: Committee on Science, Committee on Transportation and Infrastructure; chairman, Water Resources and Environment Subcommittee; elected on November 2, 1982 to the 98th Congress; reelected to each succeeding Congress.

Office Listings

http://www.house.gov/boehlert boehlert@hr.house.gov

2246 Rayburn House Office Building, Washington, DC 20515–3223 225–3665
Chief of Staff.—Dean D'Amore.
Executive Assistent.—Julie Phillips.
Alexander Pirnie Federal Office Building, Room 200, 10 Broad Street, Utica, NY 13501 .... (315) 793–8146
District Director.—Jeanne Donalty.

Counties: Broome (part), Chenango, Delaware (part), Herkimer (part), Madison, Montgomery (part), Oneida, Otsego, and Schoharie (part). Population (1990), 580,337.

ZIP Codes: 12031, 12036, 12043, 12064, 12071, 12093, 12113, 12116, 12149, 12155, 12160, 12167 (part), 12175, 12187, 12194, 12197, 12421, 12434, 12438, 12455, 12459, 12474, 12724, 12776, 13030 (part), 13032, 13035 (part), 13037 (part), 13040, 13042 (part), 13043, 13052 (part), 13054, 13061, 13072, 13082, 13085, 13122 (part), 13123–24, 13133–34, 13136, 13155, 13157, 13162–63, 13301, 13303–04, 13308–10, 13313–15, 13316 (part), 13317 (part), 13318–23, 13326, 13328, 13329 (part), 13332–38, 13339 (part), 13340–42, 13346, 13348–50, 13352, 13354–55, 13357, 13361–65, 13401–03, 13406–11, 13413, 13415, 13417–18, 13421, 13424–25, 13428–29, 13431–32, 13434–35, 13438–40, 13442, 13450, 13452, 13455–57, 13459–61, 13464–66, 13468–69, 13471, 13475–80, 13482, 13483 (part), 13484–92, 13494–95, 13501–05, 13730, 13731 (part), 13733, 13739–40, 13744–47, 13750–53, 13755, 13757–58, 13775–78, 13780, 13782, 13786–88, 13796, 13801, 13804, 13806–10, 13813 (part), 13814–15, 13820, 13825, 13830, 13832–34, 13837–39, 13841 (part), 13842–44, 13846–49, 13856, 13859–61, 13862 (part), 13901 (part)

* * *

TWENTY-FOURTH DISTRICT

JOHN M. MCHUGH, Republican, of Pierrepont Manor, NY; born in Watertown, NY, on September 29, 1948; graduated from Watertown High School, 1966; B.A., Utica College of Syracuse University; M.A., Nelson A. Rockefeller Graduate School of Public Affairs; assistant to the city manager, Watertown; liaison with local governments for New York State Senator H. Douglas Barclay; elected to the New York State Senate, 1984–92; member: American Society of Young Political Leaders; Jefferson County Farm Bureau; BPOE of Watertown; National Conference of State Legislatures; Council of State Governments' Eastern Regional Conference Committee on Fiscal Affairs; U.S. Trade Representative's Intergovernmental Policy Advisory Committee on Trade; committees: National Security, Government Reform and Oversight, International Relations; subcommitees: chairman, Panel on Morale, Welfare, and Recreation; Military Installations and Facilities; Research and Development; chairman, Postal Service; National Security, International Affairs and Criminal Justice; Asia and the Pacific; Africa; cochairman, Army Caucus; cochairman, Congressional Study Group on Canada; U.S. Military Academy Board of Vistors; National Postal Museum Advisory Commission; Congressional Rural Caucus; Great Lakes Task Force; Older Americans Caucus; Sportsmen's Caucus; Northeast Agriculture Caucus; Task Force on Agriculture; Fire Services Caucus; Rural Health Care Coalition; Forestry 2000 Task Force; National Security Caucus; Northern Border Caucus; Regulatory Reform Caucus; elected on November 3, 1992 to the 103rd Congress; reelected to each succeeding Congress.

Office Listings

416 Cannon House Office Building, Washington, DC 20515–3224 225–4611
Chief of Staff.—Cary R. Brick.
Administrative Secretary.—Donna M. Bell.

Counties: Clinton, Essex (part), Franklin, Fulton, Hamilton, Herkimer (part), Jefferson, Lewis, Oswego, St. Lawrence. CITIES AND TOWNSHIPS: Adams, Adams Center, Akwesasne, Albion, Alexandria Bay, Altmar, Altona, Amboy, Amsterdam (part), Antwerp, Arietta, Ausable Chasm, AuSable Forks, Balmat, Bangor, Barnes Corners, Batchellerville, Beaver Falls, Beaver River, Beekmantown, Belfort, Belleville, Bellmont, Benedict, Benson, Bernhards Bay, Big Moose, Black Brook, Black River, Bleecker, Blue Mountain Lake, Bluff Point, Bombay, Boonville (part), Bouquet, Boysen Bay, Boylston, Brainardsville, Brandon, Brandeth Park, Brantingham, Brasher Falls, Brasier Corners, Brier Hill, Brighton, Broadalbin, Brownville, Brushton, Burke, Cadyville, Calcium, Canada Lake, Canton, Cape Vincent, Caroga Lake, Carthage, Castorland, Cedar River, Central Square, Champion, Champlain, Chase Mills, Chasm Falls, Chateaugay, Chaumont, Chazy, Chesterfield, Childwold, Chippewa Bay, Churubusco, Clare, Clayburg, Clayton, Cleveland, Cliffhaven, Clifton, Clinton, Clintonville, Cold Brook, Colton, Constable, Constableville, Constantia, Coopersville, Copenhagen, Cork Center, Cranberry Lake, Crary Mills, Crater Club, Croghan, Crystaldale, Dannemora, Dart's Lake, Deerland, Deer River, Deferiet, Degrasse, DeKalb, DeKalb Junction, Denmark, Depauville, DePeyster, Dexter, Diana, Dickinson, Dickinson Center, Dolgeville, Duane, Eagle Bay, Eagle's Nest, Edwards, Ellenburg, Ellenburg Center, Ellenburg Corners, Ellenburg Depot, Ellisburg, Elmdale, Emeryville, Ephratah, Essex, Evans Mills, Felts Mills, Fine, Fineview, Fishers Landing, Flackville, Fonda (part) (R.R. No. 1), Fort Covington, Fort Drum, Fort Jackson, Fort Johnson (part), Fort Plain (part), Fowler, Franklin, Frontenanc, Fullerville, Fulton, Gabriels, Glen Park, Glenfield, Gloversville, Gouverneur, Granby, Great Bend, Green Lake, Greig, Grenell, Grindstone Island, Hagaman (part), Hailesboro, Hammond, Hannawa Falls, Hannibal, Harkness, Harrietstown, Harrisburg, Harrisville, Hastings, Helena, Henderson, Henderson Harbor, Hermon, Herrings, Heuvelton, Higgins Bay, High Market, Hoffmeister, Hogansburg, Hope, Hopkinton, Hounsfield, Indian Lake, Ingraham, Inlet, Irona, Jay, Jericho, Joe Indian Pond, Johnstown, Keeseville, Kirschnerville, Knapps, Lacona, LaFargeville, Lake Clear, Lake Ozonia, Lake Pleasant, Lawrence, Lawrenceville, Le Ray, Lewis, Leyden, Limekiln, Limerick, Lisbon, Lobdell, Long

Lake, Loon Lake, Lorraine, Louisville, Lowville, Lycoming, Lyme, Lyon Mountain, Lyonsdale, Lyons Falls, Macomb, Madrid, Mallory, Malone, Mannsville, Maple View, Martinsburg, Martville (part), Massawepie, Massena, Mayfield, Meco, Merrill, Mexico, Minetto, Moffittsville, Moira, Montague, Mooers, Mooers Forks, Morehouse, Morley, Morrisonville, Morristown, Moss Lake, Mountain Lake, Mountain View, Murray Island, Natural Bridge, Naumburg, New Bremen, New Haven, Newkirks, Newton Falls, Nicholville, Norfolk, North Bangor, Northampton, North Bush, North Lawrence, North Stockholm, Northville, Norway, Norwood, Ogdensburg, Ohio, Old Forge, Onchiota, Oppenheim, Orleans, Orwell, Osceola, Oswegatchie, Oswego, Otter Lake, Owls Head, Oxbow, Oxbow Lake, Palermo, Pamelia, Parish, Parishville, Paul Smiths, Peasleeville, Peck's Park, Pennellville, Perth, Perrys Mills, Peru, Petries Corners, Philadelphia, Phoenix, Piercefield, Pierrepont, Pierrepont Manor, Pinckney, Pine Lake, Piseco, Pitcairn, Plattsburgh, Plattsburgh AFB, Plessis, Point-Au-Roche, Point Vivian, Port Douglas, Port Kent, Port Leyden, Potsdam, Pulaski, Purdy's Mills, Pyrites, Rainbow Lake, Raquette Lake, Ray Brook (part), Raymondville, Reber, Redfield, Redford, Redwood, Rensselaer Falls, Richland, Richville, Riverview, Rodman, Rooseveltown, Rosiere, Rossie, Round Island, Rouses Point, Russell, Russia, Rutland, Sabael, Sabattis, Sackets Harbor, St. Johnsville, St. Regis Falls, St. Regis Indian Reservation, Salisbury Center, Salmon River, Sammonsville, Sand Ridge, Sandy Creek, Sanfordville, Santa Clara, Saranac, Saranac Inn, Saranac Lake (part), Schroeppel, Schuyler Falls, Scriba, Sciota, Silver Lake, Smithville, Somerville, South Colton, South Rutland, Speculator, Spy Lake, Standish, Star Lake, Sterling, Stockholm, Stratford, Sunmount, Swastika, Thendara, Theresa, Thousand Island Pk., Three Mile Bay, Trout River, Tupper Lake, Turin, Union Falls, Unionville, Upper Jay, Upper St. Regis, Valcour, Vermontville, Volney, Waddington, Wadhams, Wanakena, Watertown, Waverly, Watson, Webb, Wellesley Island, Wells, West Bangor, West Chazy, West Leyden, West Monroe, Westport, West Stockholm, Westville, Whallonsburg, Wheelerville, Whippleville, Williamstown, Willsboro, Wilna, Winthrop, Woodville, and Worth. Population (1990), 580,338.

ZIP Codes: 11220 (part), 11231 (part), 11234 (part), 12010 (part), 12025, 12032, 12068 (part), 12070 (part), 12078, 12086 (part), 12095, 12108, 12117, 12134, 12139, 12164, 12190, 12812, 12842, 12847, 12864, 12901, 12910–12, 12913 (part), 12914–24, 12926–27, 12929–30, 12933–37, 12939–41, 12944–45, 12949–50, 12952–53, 12955, 12957–59, 12962, 12965–70, 12972–73, 12975–81, 12983 (part), 12985–86, 12989–90, 12992–96, 13028, 13036, 13042 (part), 13044, 13069 (part), 13074, 13076, 13083, 13093, 13103, 13107, 13111 (part), 13114–15, 13121, 13126, 13131–32, 13135, 13142, 13144–45, 13156 (part), 13167, 13302, 13305, 13309, 13312, 13316 (part), 13324–25, 13327, 13329 (part), 13331, 13339 (part), 13343, 13345, 13353, 13360, 13367–68, 13404, 13416, 13420, 13426, 13433, 13436–37, 13452, 13454, 13470–73, 13483 (part), 13489, 13493, 13601, 13603, 13605–08, 13610–28, 13630–43, 13645–52, 13654–62, 13664–85, 13687–88, 13690–97, 13699

* * *

TWENTY-FIFTH DISTRICT

JAMES T. WALSH, Republican, of Syracuse, NY; born in Syracuse, June 19, 1947, son of U.S. Representative William F. Walsh; B.A., St. Bonaventure University, Olean, NY, 1970; marketing executive; president, Syracuse Common Council; member: Syracuse Board of Estimates; board of trustees of Erie Canal Museum, advisory council of the Catholic Schools Drug-Free Schools and Communities Consortium, Valley Men's Club, South Side Businessmen's Club, Nine Mile Republican Club, Onondaga Anglers Association, Oneida Lake Association, Otisco Lake Association; married the former Diane Elizabeth Ryan, 1974; three children: James (Jed), Benjamin, and Maureen; elected on November 8, 1988 to the 101st Congress; reelected to each succeeding Congress.

Office Listings

http://www.house.gov/walsh rep.james.walsh@mail.house.gov

2351 Rayburn House Office Building, Washington, DC 20515–3225	225–3701
Administrative Assistant.—Art Jutton.	FAX: 225–4042
Scheduler.—Michelle Crowley.	
Legislative Assistant.—John Simmons.	
P.O. Box 7306, Syracuse, NY 13261	(315) 423–5657
District Representative.—John McGuire.	FAX: 423–5669
1 Lincoln Street, Auburn, NY 13021	(315) 255–0649
45 Church Street, Cortland, NY, 13045	(315) 758–3918

Counties: BROOME COUNTY; cities and townships of Bible School Park, Johnson City, Killawog, Lisle, Maine, Whitney Point; CAYUGA COUNTY; cities and townships of Auburn, Cato, Fair Haven, Martville, Meridian, Montezuma, Port Byron, Sterling, Weedsport; CORTLAND COUNTY; cities and townships of Blodgett Mills, Cincinnatus, Cortland, Cuyler, East Freetown, East Homer, Harford, Homer, Little York, Marathon, McGraw, Preble, Truxton, Willet; TIOGA COUNTY: cities and townships of Berkshire, Newark Valley, Richford; ONONDAGA COUNTY: cities and townships of Apulia Station, Baldwinsvile, Brewerton, Camillus, Cicero, Clay, Delphi Falls, DeWitt, East Syracuse, Elbridge & Hart Lot, Fabius, Fayetteville, Jamesville, Jordan, Kirkville, Lafayette, Liverpool, Lysander, Manlius, Marcellus, Marietta, Mattydale, Memphis, Minoa, Mottville, Nedrow, North Syracuse, Onondaga, Oran, Plainville, Pompey, Salina, Skaneateles, Skaneateles Falls, Solvay, Tully, Warners. Population (1990), 580,337.

ZIP Codes: 13020, 13021 (part), 13022 (part), 13027, 13029, 13031, 13033, 13039–41, 13045, 13050–51, 13055–57, 13060, 13063–64, 13066, 13077–78, 13080, 13082, 13084, 13087–90, 13094, 13101, 13104, 13108, 13110–13, 13116–17, 13119–20, 13125, 13137–38, 13140–41, 13152–53, 13156, 13158–59, 13164, 13166, 13201–07, 13208–12, 13214–15, 13217, 13220–21, 13250, 13261, 13736–38, 13784, 13790, 13794, 13797, 13802–03, 13811, 13835, 13862–63

TWENTY-SIXTH DISTRICT

MAURICE D. HINCHEY, Democrat, of Saugerties, NY; born in New York, NY, on October 27, 1938; graduated, Saugerties High School, 1956; B.S., State College, New Paltz, NY, 1968; M.A., State College, New Paltz, 1969; seaman first class, U.S. Navy, 1956–59; teacher, public administrator; elected to the New York State Assembly, 1975–92; member: New York Council of State Governments, National Conference of State Legislatures; married to Ilene Marder Hinchey; three children (including two sons by previous marriage): Maurice Scott, Josef, and Michelle Rebecca; elected on November 3, 1992 to the 103rd Congress; reelected to each succeeding Congress.

Office Listings

http://www.house.gov/hinchey hinchey@hr.house.gov

1313 Longworth House Office Building, Washington, DC 20515–3226 225–6335
Administrative Assistant.—Eleanor Nash-Brown.
Legislative Director.—Christopher Arthur.
Press Secretary.—Erik Smith.
291 Wall Street, Kingston, NY 12401 .... (914) 331–4466
Federal Building, Binghamton, NY 13901 .... (607) 773–2768
114 Prospect Street, Ithaca, NY 14850 .... (607) 273–1388

Counties: BROOME COUNTY; towns of Binghamton, Chenango (part), Conklin, Dickinson, Kirkwood, Sanford, Union, and Vestal; city of Binghamton. DELAWARE COUNTY; towns of Deposit, Hancock, and Tompkins. DUTCHESS COUNTY; city of Beacon. ORANGE COUNTY; town and city of Newburgh. SULLIVAN COUNTY; towns of Callicoon, Delaware, Fallsburg, Fremont, Liberty, Neversink, Rockland, and Thompson (part). TIOGA COUNTY; towns of Barton, Candor, Nichols, Owego, Spencer, and Tioga. TOMPKINS COUNTY; towns of Caroline, Danby, Dryden, Enfield, and Ithaca; city of Ithaca. ULSTER COUNTY; towns of Denning, Esopus, Gardiner, Hardenburgh, Hurley, Kingston, Lloyd, Marbletown, Marlborough, New Paltz, Olive, Plattekill, Rochester, Rosendale, Saugerties, Shandaken, Shawangunk, Ulster, Wawarsing, and Woodstock; city of Kingston. Population (1990), 580,338.

ZIP Codes: 12401, 12404, 12406, 12409–12, 12416–17, 12419–20, 12426, 12428–29, 12432–33, 12435, 12440–41, 12443, 12446, 12447–49, 12453, 12456–58, 12461–62, 12464–66, 12471–72, 12475, 12477, 12480–81, 12483–84, 12486–87, 12489–91, 12493–95, 12498, 12505, 12508, 12515, 12525, 12528, 12542, 12547–48, 12550, 12561, 12566, 12568, 12586, 12588–89, 12701, 12723–25, 12728, 12733–34, 12736, 12738, 12740–42, 12745, 12747–48, 12753–54, 12758–61, 12763, 12765–68, 12775–76, 12779, 12782–84, 12787–89, 12791, 13053, 13062, 13068, 13732, 13734, 13736–37, 13742, 13743–45, 13748–49, 13754, 13756, 13760, 13774, 13783, 13790, 13795, 13811–12, 13826–27, 13839–40 13845, 13847, 13850, 13856, 13862, 13864–65, 13901–05 14817, 14850, 14851, 14853, 14859, 14881, 14883, 14892, 14896

* * *

TWENTY-SEVENTH DISTRICT

BILL PAXON, Republican, of Williamsville, NY; born in Buffalo, NY, April 29, 1954; graduated, St. Joseph's Collegiate Institute, Buffalo, NY, 1968; B.A., Canisius College, Buffalo, NY, 1977; Erie County legislator, 1978–82; New York State Assembly, 1982–88; member, Commerce Committee; Telecommunications and Finance Subcommittee; chairman of the National Republican Congressional Committee; married to Congresswoman Susan Molinari (R-Staten Island); elected on November 8, 1988 to the 101st Congress; reelected to each succeeding Congress.

Office Listings

bpaxon@hr.house.gov

2436 Rayburn House Office Building, Washington, DC 20515–3227 225–5265
Chief of Staff.—Michael Hook. FAX: 225–5910
Appointments Secretary.—Marilyn Abel.
Administrative Assistant.—David Marventano.
Press Secretary.—Eric Cote.
5500 Main Street, Williamsville, NY 14221 .... (716) 634–2324
10 East Main Street, Victor, NY 14564 .... (716) 742–1600
268 West Genesee Street, Auburn, NY 13021 (by appointment) .... (800) 453–8330
216 East Main Street, Batavia, NY 14020 (by appointment) .... (800) 453–8330
131 Main Street, Geneseo, NY 14454 (by appointment) .... (800) 453–8330
10 Leach Road, Lyons, NY 14489 (by appointment) .... (800) 453–8330
117 Fall Street, Seneca Falls, NY 13148 (by appointment) .... (800) 453–8330
36 North Main Street, Warsaw, NY 14569 (by appointment) .... (800) 453–8330
611 West Washington Street, Geneva, NY 14456 (by appointment) .... (800) 453–8330

Counties: Cayuga (part), Erie (part), Genesee, Livingston, Monroe (part), Ontario, Seneca (part), Wayne, and Wyoming. Population (1990), 580,337.

ZIP Codes: 13021 (part), 13034, 13065, 13143, 13146, 13148 (part), 13154, 13156 (part), 13165 (part), 14001 (part), 14003, 14004 (part), 14005, 14009, 14011, 14013, 14020–21, 14024, 14030 (part), 14031, 14032 (part), 14036–40, 14042, 14051, 14052 (part), 14054, 14056, 14058, 14059 (part), 14066, 14068, 14082–83, 14086 (part), 14102, 14113, 14125, 14130, 14139 (part), 14143, 14145, 14167, 14169, 14215 (part), 14221 (part), 14225 (part), 14226 (part), 14228 (part), 14231, 14413–14, 14416 (part), 14422–25, 14427, 14428 (part), 14432–33, 14435, 14437, 14443–44, 14449, 14450 (part), 14453–54, 14456 (part), 14461–63, 14466, 14469, 14471–72, 14474–75, 14480–82, 14485–89, 14502 (part), 14504–06, 14510–13, 14514 (part), 14516–20, 14522, 14525, 14530, 14532–33, 14534 (part), 14536–39, 14541 (part), 14542, 14543 (part), 14544–51, 14554–58, 14560–61, 14563, 14564 (part), 14568–69, 14572, 14580 (part), 14584–85, 14586 (part), 14589–92, 14623 (part), 14624 (part), 14822, 14836, 14846

* * *

TWENTY-EIGHTH DISTRICT

LOUISE McINTOSH SLAUGHTER, Democrat, of Fairport, NY; born in Harlan County, KY, August 14, 1929; graduated from University of Kentucky with a B.S. in bacteriology; master's degree in public health; elected to Monroe County legislature, two terms, 1976–79; elected to New York State Assembly, two terms, 1982–86; Woman of the Year, 1987, Rochester Women's Political Caucus; married to Robert Slaughter; three daughters; two grandchildren; elected to 100th Congress on November 4, 1986; reelected to each succeeding Congress; majority whip at large; member: Committee on Government Reform and Oversight; Committee on the Budget.

Office Listings

http://www.house.gov/slaughter louiseny@hr.house.gov

2347 Rayburn House Office Building, Washington, DC 20515–3228 225–3615
Chief of Staff.—Thomas Bantle.
Legislative Director.—Anne Grady.
Press Secretary.—Kelly Sullivan.
3120 Federal Building, Rochester, NY 14614 .... (716) 232–4850
District Director.—Michael Keane.

County: MONROE COUNTY (part). Cities and townships: Brighton, E. Rochester, Greece, Henetta, Irondequoit, Penfield, Perinton, Pittsford, Rochester, Webster. Population (1990), 580,337.

ZIP Codes: 14445 (part), 14450 (part), 14467, 14468 (part), 14502 (part), 14515 (part), 14526 (part), 14534 (part), 14543 (part), 14564 (part), 14580 (part), 14586 (part), 14601–05, 14606, 14607–12, 14613, 14614–23, 14625–26, 14627 (part), 14650, 14660, 14692

* * *

TWENTY-NINTH DISTRICT

JOHN J. LAFALCE, Democrat, of Tonawanda, NY; born in Buffalo, October 6, 1939; graduated from Canisius High School; Canisius College, B.S. 1961; Villanova Law School, J.D. 1964; captain, U.S. Army, 1965–67; law clerk, Office of General Counsel, Department of the Navy, 1963; former lecturer on law, George Washington University, 1965–66; practiced law in Buffalo; member, New York State Senate, 1971–72; member, New York State Assembly, 1973–74; elected to the 94th Congress, November 5, 1974; reelected to each succeeding Congress; ranking minority member, Committee on Small Business; member, Committee on Banking and Financial Services; married Patricia Fisher, 1979.

Office Listings

2310 Rayburn House Office Building, Washington, DC 20515–3229 225–3231
Administrative Assistant.—Ronald J. Maselka.
Communications Director.—Gary A. Luczak.
Main U.S. Post Office, 615 Main Street, Niagara Falls, NY 14302 .... (716) 284–9976
Federal Building, 111 West Huron Street, Buffalo, NY 14202 .... (716) 846–4056
409 South Union Street, Spencerport, NY 14559 .... (716) 352–4777

Counties: Niagara, Orleans. ERIE COUNTY; cities and townships of Buffalo (part), Grand Island, Tonawanda. MONROE COUNTY; cities and townships of Clarkson, Gates, Hamlin, Ogden, Parma, Rochester (part) and Sweden. Population (1990), 580,336.

ZIP Codes: 14001, 14008, 14012, 14028, 14067, 14072, 14092, 14094, 14098, 14102, 14105, 14107–09, 14120, 14126, 14131–32, 14144, 14150, 14172, 14174, 14201 (part), 14202 (part), 14203 (part), 14204 (part), 14205 (part), 14207, 14209, 14213, 14214 (part), 14215 (part), 14217, 14222 (part), 14223, 14301–06, 14410 (part), 14411, 14420, 14428 (part), 14429, 14430 (part), 14442, 14452, 14464, 14468, 14470, 14473, 14476–77, 14479, 14508, 14514 (part), 14559, 14571, 14606 (part), 14624 (part)

THIRTIETH DISTRICT

JACK QUINN, Republican, of Hamburg, NY; born on April 13, 1951 in Buffalo, NY; B.A., Siena College, Loudonville, NY, 1973; M.A., State University of New York, Buffalo, 1978; teacher; councilman, Hamburg, 1982–84; town supervisor, Hamburg, 1985–92; founder, DARE, 1984; married the former Mary Beth McAndrews, 1974; two children: Jack III and Kara Elizabeth; elected on November 3, 1992 to the 103rd Congress; reelected to each succeeding Congress.

Office Listings

331 Cannon House Office Building, Washington, DC 20515–3230 .... 225–3306 FAX: 226–0347
Legislative Director.—Beth Meyers.
Legislative Assistants: Cassandra McClam, Michael Pietkiewicz, Aura Kenny, Dan Skopee.
Legislative Correspondent.—Erin Pierce.
Brisbane Building, 403 Main Street, Suite 240, Buffalo, NY 14203–2199 .... (716) 845–5257 FAX: 847–0323
Administrative Assistant.—Mary Lou Palmer.

County: ERIE COUNTY (part); cities and townships of Boston, Brant, Buffalo (part), Cheektowaga, Colden, Concord, Collins, East Aurora, Eden, Elma, Evans, Hamburg, Holland, Lackawanna, Lancaster, North Boston, North Collins, Orchard Park, Sardinia, and Seneca. Population (1990), 580,337.

ZIP Codes: 14006, 14010, 14025–27, 14030 (part), 14033–34, 14043, 14047, 14052, 14057, 14059, 14061, 14069, 14070, 14075, 14080, 14085, 14086, 14091, 14110–12, 14127, 14134, 14139–41, 14170, 14201–06, 14208–16, 14218–21, 14223–27, 14263

* * *

THIRTY-FIRST DISTRICT

AMO HOUGHTON, Republican, of Corning, NY; born in Corning on August 7, 1926; grandson of former Congressman Alanson B. Houghton of New York; graduated, St. Paul's School, Concord, NH; B.A., Harvard University, Cambridge, MA, 1950; M.A., Harvard Business School, 1952; honorary doctoral degrees: Alfred University, NY, 1963; Albion College, MI, 1964; Centre College, Danville, KY, 1966; Clarkson College of Technology, Potsdam, NY, 1968; Elmira College, NY, 1982; Hartwick College, Oneonta, NY, 1983; Houghton College, NY, 1983; St. Bonaventure University, NY, 1987; Hobart and William Smith College, 1991; served in the U.S. Marine Corps, 1945–46; executive officer, Corning Glass Works, Corning, NY, 1951–86; member: Grace Commission, Business Council of New York State, Business Advisory Commission for Governor of New York, Labor-Industry Coalition for International Trade, Corning Chamber of Commerce, Corning Rotary Club, Corning Elk's Club; trustee, Brookings Institution; International Relations Committee, Ways and Means Committee; Subcommittee on Africa; married to Priscilla Dewey Houghton; elected to the 100th Congress on November 4, 1986; reelected to each succeeding Congress.

Office Listings

http://www.house.gov/houghton houghton@hr.house.gov

1110 Longworth House Office Building, Washington, DC 20515–3231 .... 225–3161 FAX: 225–5574
Staff Director.—Brian Fitzpatrick.
Office Manager.—Vickie M. Austin.
Legislative Director.—Marijo Gorney.
32 Denison Parkway West, Corning, NY 14830 .... (607) 937–3333
Federal Building, Room 122, Jamestown, NY 14702–0908 .... (716) 484–0252
Westgate Plaza, West State Street, Olean, NY 14760 .... (716) 372–2127
268 Genesee Street, Auburn, NY 13021 .... (315) 255–3045

Counties: Allegany; Cattaraugus; Cayuga (part); Chautauqua; Chemung; Schuyler; Seneca (part); Steuben; Tompkins (part); Yates. Population (1990), 580,337.

ZIP Codes: 13021 (part), 13026, 13045 (part), 13068 (part), 13071, 13073, 13081, 13092, 13102, 13118, 13139, 13147, 13148 (part), 13152 (part), 13160, 13165 (part), 14029, 14041–42, 14048, 14060, 14062–63, 14065, 14070 (part), 14081 (part), 14101, 14129, 14133, 14135–36, 14138, 14141 (part), 14166, 14168, 14171, 14173, 14415, 14418, 14441, 14456 (part), 14478, 14507, 14521, 14527, 14529, 14541 (part), 14572, 14588, 14701–02, 14706–12, 14714–24, 14726–33, 14735–45, 14747–60, 14766–67, 14769–70, 14772, 14774–75, 14777–79, 14781–88, 14801–10, 14812–16, 14818–27, 14830, 14837–45, 14847, 14850 (part), 14854–58, 14859 (part), 14860–61, 14863–65, 14867–74, 14876–80, 14882, 14883 (part), 14884–85, 14886 (part), 14887–89, 14891, 14892 (part), 14893–95, 14897–98, 14901–05

NORTH CAROLINA

(Population 1995, 7,195,000)

SENATORS

JESSE HELMS, Republican, of Raleigh, NC; born in Monroe, NC, October 18, 1921; attended Wingate College and Wake Forest College; U.S. Navy, 1942–45; former city editor, *Raleigh Times*; administrative assistant to U.S. Senator Willis Smith, 1951–53, and to U.S. Senator Alton Lennon, 1953; executive director, North Carolina Bankers Association, 1953–60; executive vice president, WRAL–TV and Tobacco Radio Network, 1960–72; member, Raleigh City Council, chairman of Law and Finance Committee, 1957–61; deacon and Sunday School teacher, Hayes Barton Baptist Church, Raleigh; recipient of two Freedom Foundation awards for radio-television editorials; recipient of annual citizenship awards from North Carolina American Legion, North Carolina Veterans of Foreign Wars, and Raleigh Exchange Club; recipient of Outstanding Service Award of the Council Against Communist Aggression, the Richard Henry Lee Award, and the Order of Lafayette Freedom Award; former trustee, Meredith College, John F. Kennedy College, Delaware Law School, Campbell University, and Wingate College; president, Raleigh Rotary Club, 1969–70; 33rd degree Mason: Grand Orator, Grand Lodge of Masons of North Carolina, 1964–65, 1982, 1991; member, board of directors, North Carolina Cerebral Palsy Hospital; member, board of directors of Camp Willow Run, a youth camp for Christ at Littleton, NC; married Dorothy Jane Coble of Raleigh, October 31, 1942; three children: Jane (Mrs. Charles R. Knox), Nancy (Mrs. John C. Stuart), and Charles; seven grandchildren; committees: Agriculture, Nutrition, and Forestry; chairman, Foreign Relations; Rules and Administration; elected to the U.S. Senate, November 7, 1972, for the term ending January 3, 1979; reelected in 1978, 1984, 1990 and 1996.

Office Listings

htttp://www.senate.gov/~helms jesse__helms@helms.senate.gov

403 Dirksen Senate Office Building, Washington, DC 20510–3301 224–6342
Administrative Assistant.—James W.C. Broughton.
Personal Secretary.—Patricia H. Devine.
Century Post Office Building, P.O. Box 2888, Fayetteville Street Mall, Raleigh, NC 27602 .... (919) 856–4630
Staff Director.—Frances P. Jones.
Post Office Building, P.O. Box 2944, Hickory, NC 28603 .... (704) 322–5170
Staff Director.—Josephine R. Murray.

* * *

LAUCH FAIRCLOTH, Republican, of Clinton, NC; born January 14, 1928 on a farm in Sampson County, NC; farmer, businessman; North Carolina State Highway Commission, chairman; North Carolina Secretary of Commerce, six years; one child; elected to the U.S. Senate, November 3, 1992, for the six-year term beginning January 3, 1993; committees: Banking, Housing, and Urban Affairs; Appropriations; Small Business.

Office Listings

http://www.senate.gov/~faircloth senator@faircloth.senate.gov

317 Hart Senate Office Building, Washington, DC 20510–3305 224–3154
Chief of Staff.—Jonathan R. Hill.
Legislative Director.—James Hyland.
Scheduler.—Fraley Connell.
310 New Bern Avenue, Suite 120, Raleigh, NC 27601 .... (919) 856–4791
401 West Trade Street, Suite 219, Charlotte, NC 28202 .... (704) 375–1993
37 Battery Park, Suite 16, Asheville, NC 28801 .... (704) 254–3099
251 Main Street, Suite 422, Winston Salem, NC 27101 .... (910) 631–5313
901 Highway 321, Suite 134, Hickory, NC 28601 .... (704) 345–6260

REPRESENTATIVES

FIRST DISTRICT

EVA CLAYTON, Democrat, of Littleton, NC; born on September 16, 1934 in Savannah, GA; B.S., biology, Johnson C. Smith University, Charlotte, NC, 1955; M.S., biology and general science, North Carolina Central University, Durham, 1965; executive director, Soul City Foundation; director, North Carolina Health Manpower Development Programs, University of North Carolina at Chapel Hill; founder, Technical Resources Ltd., 1981; elected Warren County commissioner, 1982–90; member: Association of County Officials; Housing Assistance Council; former member, North Carolina Housing Finance Agency, Fair Housing Commission, and Judicial Compensation Commission; member: Committee on Agriculture and Committee on Small Business (ranking miniority); Subcommittee on Procurement, Exports and Business Opportunities; married to Theaoseus T. Clayton, Sr.; four children: Joanne, Theaoseus, Jr., Martin, and Reuben; elected to the 102nd Congress by special election on November 3, 1992 to fill the vacancy caused by the death of Walter B. Jones, Sr.; reelected to each succeeding Congress.

Office Listings

eclayton@hr.house.gov

222 Cannon House Office Building, Washington, DC 20515–3301 225–3101
Administrative Assistant.—Johnny Barnes.
Executive Assistant.—Jean Chippel.
Legislative Director.—Johnny Barnes.
Press Secretary/Legislative Assistant.—Veda Lamar.
400 West Fifth Street, Greenville, NC 27838 .... (919) 758–8800
134 North Main Street, Warrenton, NC 27589 .... (919) 257–4800

Counties: Beaufort (part), Bertie, Bladen (part), Chowan, Columbus (part), Craven (part), Cumberland (part), Duplin (part), Edgecombe (part), Gates, Greene, Halifax (part), Hertford, Jones (part), Lenoir (part), Martin (part), Nash (part), New Hanover (part), Northampton, Pasquotank (part), Pender (part), Perquimans, Pitt (part), Vance (part), Warren, Washington, Wayne (part), Wilson (part). Population (1990), 552,394.

ZIP Codes: 27536 (part), 27551, 27553, 27556, 27563, 27570, 27584, 27589, 27594, 27801 (part), 27802, 27803 (part), 27804 (part), 27805–06, 27811–14, 27817–18, 27820–21, 27822 (part), 27823, 27827–29, 27831–32, 27834 (part), 27835, 27837 (part), 27838–45, 27847–49, 27850 (part), 27853–55, 27857, 27858 (part), 27859, 27860 (part), 27861–62, 27863 (part), 27866–67, 27869, 27870 (part), 27871–74, 27876–77, 27881, 27883 (part), 27884, 27886 (part), 27887–88, 27889 (part), 27890–91, 27892 (part), 27893 (part), 27894–95, 27897, 27909 (part), 27910, 27919, 27922, 27924, 27926, 27928, 27930, 27932, 27935, 27937–38, 27942, 27944, 27946, 27957, 27962, 27967, 27969–70, 27979–80, 27983, 27985–86, 28105 (part), 28301 (part), 28302, 28303 (part), 28304 (part), 28305 (part), 28306 (part), 28311 (part), 28337 (part), 28349, 28390 (part), 28398–99, 28401 (part), 28402, 28403 (part), 28405 (part), 28421, 28423–24, 28429 (part), 28431 (part), 28433–34, 28435 (part), 28436, 28448, 28453 (part), 28454 (part), 28456 (part), 28472 (part), 28501 (part), 28502–03, 28513 (part), 28523, 28526, 28530, 28532 (part), 28538, 28551, 28554, 28560 (part), 28562 (part), 28573, 28580, 28585 (part), 28715 (part)

* * *

SECOND DISTRICT

BOB ETHERIDGE, Democrat, of Lillington, NC; born in Sampson County, NC, August 7, 1941; B.S., business administration, 1965, Campbell University, NC; graduate studies in economics, North Carolina State University, 1967; U.S. Army, 1965–67; businessman, bank director, licensed realtor; North Carolina General Assembly, 1978–88; North Carolina Superintendent of Public Instruction, 1988–96; Harnett County commissioner, 1972–76, serving as chairman of the board in 1974–76; past member: National Council of Chief State School Officers; Governor's Executive Cabinet; advisory board, Mathematics/Science Education Network; Board of the NC Council on Economic Education; board of trustees, NC Symphony; board of trustees, UNC Center of Public Television; Harnett County Mental Health Board; NC Law and Order Commission; member and past president, Occoneechee Boy Scout Council; received Lillington Jaycees Distinguished Service Award and Lillington Community Service Award; elder, Presbyterian Church; married the former Faye Cameron in 1965; three children: Brian, Catherine, and David; committees: Agriculture, Science; elected to the 105th Congress.

Office Listings

1641 Longworth House Office Building, Washington, DC 20515 225–4531
Administrative Assistant.—Julie Dwyer. FAX: 225–5662
Legislative Director.—Pat Devlin.
Press Secretary.—Robert Gibbs.
Executive Assistant.—Kim Williams.
3310 Croasdaile Drive, Suite 301, Durham, NC 27705 .... (919) 383–7548
607 First Street, Lillington, NC 27564 .... (910) 814–0335

Counties: Durham (part), Edgecombe (part), Franklin, Granville (part), Halifax (part), Harnett, Johnston, Lee, Moore (part), Nash (part), Vance (part), Wake (part), and Wilson (part). Population (1990), 552,378.

ZIP Codes: 27281 (part), 27330–31, 27376, 27501, 27504–06, 27508–09, 27514 (part), 27520 (part), 27521–22, 27524–25, 27526 (part), 27529 (part), 27536 (part), 27542–43, 27544 (part), 27546, 27549, 27552, 27555, 27557, 27560 (part), 27564, 27565 (part), 27568–69, 27576–77, 27581 (part), 27587 (part), 27589 (part), 27591 (part), 27592 (part), 27593, 27596 (part), 27597 (part), 27603 (part), 27701 (part), 27702, 27703 (part), 27704 (part), 27705 (part), 27706 (part), 27707 (part), 27708, 27712 (part), 27713 (part), 27715, 27801 (part), 27803 (part), 27804 (part), 27807, 27809, 27816, 27819, 27822 (part), 27850 (part), 27851–52, 27856, 27864, 27868, 27870 (part), 27878, 27880, 27882, 27886 (part), 27893 (part), 28315 (part), 28323, 28326, 28327 (part), 28334 (part), 28335, 28339, 28350, 28355, 28356 (part), 28368, 28373–74, 28387 (part), 28388, 28390 (part), 28394

* * *

THIRD DISTRICT

WALTER BEAMAN JONES, Republican, of Farmville, NC; born in Farmville, February 10, 1943; graduated Hargrave Military Academy, Chatham, VA, 1961; B.A., Atlantic Christian College, Wilson, NC, 1966; served in North Carolina National Guard; self-employed, sales; member: North Carolina General Assembly House of Representatives, 1983–92; married to Joe Anne Whitehurst Jones; one child, Ashley Elizabeth Jones Scarborough; elected to the 104th Congress; reelected to the 105th Congress.

Office Listings

427 Cannon House Office Building, Washington, DC 20515–3303 225–3415
Administrative Assistant.—Glen Downs. FAX: 225–3286
Executive Assistant.—Gloria Curry.
District Office, 102 C Eastbrook Drive, Greenville, NC 27858 .... (919) 931–1003
District Office Manager.—Millicent A. Lilley.

Counties: Beaufort (part), Camden, Carteret, Craven (part), Currituck, Dare, Duplin (part), Hyde, Jones (part), Lenoir (part), Martin (part), Onslow (part), Pamlico, Pasquotank (part), Pender (part), Pitt (part), Sampson, Tyrrell and Wayne (part); CITIES: Atlantic Beach, Ayden (part), Beaufort, Belhaven, Burgaw, Clinton, Elizabeth City (part), Emerald Isle, Fremont, Goldsboro, Greenville (part), Havelock, Jacksonville (part), Kill Devil Hills, Kinston (part), Kitty Hawk, Morehead City, Mount Olive, Nags Head, New Bern (part), Newport, River Bend, Trent Woods, Wallace (part), Washington (part) and Winterville. Population (1990), 552,387.

ZIP Codes: 27530–32, 27633–34, 27806 (part), 27808, 27810 (part), 27824 (part) 27825, 27826 (part), 27828 (part), 27829 (part), 27830, 27834 (part), 27835, 27836, 27858 (part), 27860 (part), 27863 (part), 27865 (part), 27875, 27879, 27883 (part), 27885 (part), 27889 (part), 27892 (part), 27909 (part), 27915–17, 27920 27921 (part), 27923, 27925 (part), 27927, 27929, 27936, 27937 (part), 27939, 27941, 27943, 27944 (part), 27946 (part) 27947–50, 27953–54, 27956, 27958 (part), 27959–60. 27964–66, 27968, 27970 (part), 27972, 27973 (part) 27974, 27976, 27978, 27981–82, 28318 (part), 28325, 28328, 28333, 28341 (part), 28364 (part), 28365, 28366 (part), 28382, 28385, 28393 (part), 28420 (part), 28421 (part), 28425 (part), 28435 (part), 28441 (part), 28443 (part), 28444 (part), 28445 (part), 28446, 28447 (part), 28453 (part), 28454 (part), 28457 (part), 28458 (part), 28463, 28464, 28466 (part), 28471 (part), 28478 (part), 28501 (part), 28502–03, 28508–12, 28513 (part), 28515–16, 28518–20, 28521 (part), 28522, 28523 (part), 28524–25, 28527–29, 28530 (part), 28531 (part), 28532 (part), 28533, 28537, 28539 (part), 28540 (part), 28541, 28544 (part), 28546 (part), 28551 (part), 28552–53, 28555–57, 28560 (part), 28562 (part), 28570–72, 28573 (part), 28574 (part) 28575, 28577, 27578 (part), 28579, 28581, 28582 (part), 28583, 28584 (part), 28585 (part), 28586 (part), 28587, 28589, 28590 (part), 28594

* * *

FOURTH DISTRICT

DAVID PRICE, Democrat, of Chapel Hill, NC; born in Erwin, TN, August 17, 1940; B.A., Morehead Scholar, University of North Carolina; Bachelor of Divinity, 1964, and Ph.D., political science, 1969, Yale University; professor of political science and public policy, Duke University; author of four books on Congress and the American political system; served North Carolina's Fourth District in the U.S. House of Representatives, 1987–94; in the 102nd Congress, wrote and pushed to passage the Scientific and Advanced Technology Bill and sponsored the Home Ownership Assistance Act; past chairman and executive director, North Carolina Democratic Party; Hubert Humphrey Public Service Award, American Political Science Association, 1990; member, North Carolina's Transit 2001 Commission; past chairman of the board and Sunday School teacher, Binkley Memorial Baptist Church; married to Lisa Price; two children, Karen and Michael; committee: Appropriations; subcommittees: VA, HUD, and Independent Agencies; Treasury, Postal Service, and General Government; elected to the 105th Congress.

Office Listings

david.price@mail.house.gov
2162 Rayburn House Office Building, Washington, DC 20515 225–1784
Administrative Assistant.—William Moore. FAX: 225–2014
Senior Legislative Assistants: Jean-Louise Beard, Mark Harkins.
Legislative Assistants: Chuck Cushman, Darek Newby, Kimberly Manno.
Congressional Liaison.—Don Owens.
225 Hillsborough Street, Suite 490, Raleigh, NC 27603. .... (919) 832–2456
FAX: 832–2559

1777 Fordham Boulevard, Suite 202, Chapel Hill, NC 27514 .... (919) 967–7924 FAX: 967–8324

Counties: Chatham, Orange (part), Wake (part). Cities and townships of Angier, Apex, Bear Creek, Bennett, Bonlee, Bynum, Carrboro, Cary, Cedar Grove, Efland, Chapel Hill, Clayton, Creedmoor, Eagle Rock, Fuquay-Varina, Garner Goldston, Gulf, Hillsborough, Mebane, Pittsboro, Sanford, Siler City, Snow Camp, Holly Springs, Hurdle Mills, Knightdale, Middlesex, Moncure, Morrisville, New Hill, Rolesville, Timberlake, Wake Forest, Wendell, Willow Spring, Zebulon, and Raleigh. Population (1990), 552,387.

ZIP Codes: 27207, 27208 (part), 27213, 27228, 27231, 27243, 27252, 27256, 27278 (part), 27302 (part), 27312, 27330, 27344, 27349 (part), 27501 (part), 27502, 27510–13, 27514 (part), 27515–16, 27519, 27520 (part), 27526, 27529, 27540, 27541 (part), 27545, 27559, 27560, 27562, 27571, 27587, 27588, 27591, 27592, 27599, 27601–15, 27619–20, 27622–29, 27636, 27650, 27658, 27695, 27705 (part), 27707 (part)

* * *

FIFTH DISTRICT

RICHARD BURR, Republican, of Winston-Salem, NC; born in Charlottesville, VA on November 30, 1955; graduated Reynolds High School, Winston-Salem, NC, 1974; B.A., communications, Wake Forest University, Winston-Salem, NC, 1978; sales manager, Carswell Distributing; membership: Reynolds Rotary Club; cochairman, North Carolina Taxpayers United, National Policy Forum Council on Economic Growth and Workplace Opportunity; member: Commerce Committee; married to Brooke Fauth Burr, 1984; two children: Tyler and William; elected to the 104th Congress; reelected to the 105th Congress.

Office Listings

http://www.house.gov/burr mail2nc5@hr.house.gov

1431 Longworth House Office Building, Washington, DC 20515 .... 225–2071 FAX: 225–2995
- Administrative Assistant.—Jim Dornan.
- Legislative Director.—Doug Bassett.
- Legislative Assistants: Hope Lanier, Ann Thomas Griffin, Chuck Greene, Patrick Sullivan.
- Press Secretary.—Alicia Peterson.

2000 West First Street, Piedmont Plaza Two, Room 508, Winston-Salem, NC 27104 .... (910) 631–5125
- District Staff Director.—Dean Myers.

Counties: ALLEGHANY COUNTY; cities of Ennice, Glade Valley, Laurel Springs, Piney Creek, Roaring Gap, Sparta, and Whitehead. ASHE COUNTY; cities of Creston, Crumpler, Fleetwood, Glendale Springs, Grassy Creek, Jefferson, Lansing, Todd, Warrensville, and West Jefferson. BURKE COUNTY (part); cities of Drexel, Glen Alpine, and Morganton. CALDWELL COUNTY (part); city of Lenoir. CASWELL COUNTY; cities of Blanch, Leasburg, Milton, Pelham, Prospect Hill, Providence, Semora, and Yanceyville. DURHAM COUNTY (part); city of Rougemont. FORSYTH COUNTY (part); cities of Belews Creek, Bethania, Kernersville, Rural Hall, Tobaccoville, Walkertown, and Winston-Salem. GRANVILLE COUNTY (part); cities of Bullock, Oxford, and Stovall. GUILFORD COUNTY (part); Browns Summit, McLeansville, Mebane, Stokesdale, and Summerfield. PERSON COUNTY; cities of Roxboro and Timberlake. ROCKINGHAM COUNTY; cities of Eden, Madison, Mayodan, Stoneville, Reidsville, Ruffin, and Wentworth. STOKES COUNTY; cities of Danbury, Germanton, King, Lawsonville, Pine Hall, Pinnacle, Sandy Ridge, and Walnut Cove. SURRY COUNTY; cities of Ararat, Dobson, Elkin, Low Gap, Mount Airy, Pilot Mountain, Siloam, State Road, Toast, and Westfield. WARREN COUNTY; city of Vaughan. WATAUGA COUNTY; cities of Banner Elk, Blowing Rock, Boone, Deep Gap, Sugar Grove, Vilas, and Zionville. WILKES COUNTY (part); cities of Boomer, North Wilkesboro, Thurmond, and Wilkesboro. Population (1990), 552,386.

ZIP Codes: 27007, 27009–10, 27016–17, 27019, 27021–22, 27024–25, 27027, 27030–31, 27041–43, 27045 (part), 27046–49, 27050 (part), 27051–53, 27101 (part), 27103 (part), 27104 (part), 27105 (part), 27106 (part), 27107 (part), 27109, 27113–16, 27127 (part), 27212, 27214 (part), 27284 (part), 27285, 27288–89, 27291, 27301 (part), 27302 (part), 27305, 27311, 27314–15, 27320, 27326, 27343, 27357 (part), 27358, 27375, 27379, 27507, 27565, 27572 (part), 27573, 27582–83, 27586, 28604, 28605 (part), 28606–07, 28615, 28617–19, 28621 (part), 28623, 28626–29, 28631, 28640, 28643–44, 28645 (part), 28654 (part), 28655, 28659 (part), 28663, 28668, 28675–76, 28679–80, 28683–84, 28691–95, 28697 (part), 28698

* * *

SIXTH DISTRICT

HOWARD COBLE, Republican, of Greensboro, NC; born in Greensboro, March 18, 1931; attended Appalachian State University, Boone, NC, 1949–50; A.B., history, Guilford College, Greensboro, NC, 1958; J.D., University of North Carolina School of Law, Chapel Hill, 1962; enlisted in U.S. Coast Guard as a seaman recruit, 1952; active duty, 1952–56 and 1977–78; reserve duty, 1960–82; presently holds rank of captain; last reserve duty assignment, commanding officer, U.S. Coast Guard Reserve Unit, Wilmington, NC; attorney; admitted to North Carolina bar, 1966; field claim representative and superintendent, auto insurance, 1961–67; elected to North Carolina House of Representatives, 1969; assistant U.S. attorney, Middle District of

North Carolina, 1969–73; commissioner (secretary), North Carolina Department of Revenue, 1973–77; North Carolina House of Representatives, 1979–83; practiced law with law firm of Turner, Enochs and Sparrow, Greensboro, NC, 1979–84; member: Alamance Presbyterian Church, American Legion, Veterans of Foreign Wars of the United States, Lions Club, Greensboro Bar Association, North Carolina Bar Association, North Carolina State Bar; North Carolina State cochairman, American Legislative Exchange Council, 1983–84; elected to the 99th Congress on November 6, 1984; reelected to each succeeding Congress.

Office Listings

coblenc6@hr.house.gov

2239 Rayburn House Office Building, Washington, DC 20515–3306 225–3065
Administrative Assistant/Press Secretary.—Ed McDonald.
Executive Assistant.—Carolyn Seale.
Suite 247, 324 West Market Street, Greensboro, NC 27401–2544 .... (910) 333–5005
Office Manager.—Chris Beaman.
Suite 200B, 155 Northpoint Avenue, High Point, NC 27262–7723 .... (910) 886–5106
P.O. Box 814, Graham, NC 27253–0814 .... (910) 229–0159
P.O. Box 1813, Lexington, NC 27293–1813 .... (910) 248–8230
Suite 101, 241 Sunset Avenue, Asheboro, NC 27203–5658 .... (910) 626–3060

Counties: Alamance (part), Davidson (part), Davie (part), Guilford (part), Randolph, Rowan (part). Population (1990), 552,385.

ZIP Codes: 27014, 27028 (part), 27107 (part), 27117, 27127 (part), 27201, 27203–04, 27208 (part), 27214 (part), 27215–16, 27217 (part), 27230, 27233, 27235, 27239, 27244 (part), 27248, 27249 (part), 27253 (part), 27258 (part), 27260 (part), 27261, 27262 (part), 27263–64, 27265 (part), 27282 (part), 27283, 27284 (part), 27292 (part), 27298–99, 27301 (part), 27302 (part), 27310, 27313, 27316–17, 27325 (part), 27340, 27341 (part), 27342, 27344 (part), 27349 (part), 27350–51, 27355, 27357 (part), 27358–59, 27360 (part), 27361, 27370–71, 27373, 27377 (part), 27401 (part), 27403 (part), 27404, 27405 (part), 27406 (part), 27407 (part), 27408 (part), 27409–10, 27413, 27416, 27419, 27425, 27427, 27429, 27435, 28023 (part), 28071 (part), 28137 (part), 28138 (part), 28144 (part), 28146 (part)

* * *

SEVENTH DISTRICT

MIKE McINTYRE, Democrat, of Lumberton, NC; born in Robeson County, August 6, 1956; B.A., Phi Beta Kappa Morehead Scholar, 1978, and J.D., 1981, University of North Carolina; upon graduation, received the Algernon Sydney Sullivan Award for ''unselfish interest in the welfare of his fellow man''; attorney; past president, Lumberton Economic Advancement for Dowtown; formerly on board of directors of Lumberton Rotary Club, Chamber of Commerce and a local group home for the mentally handicapped; active in Boy Scouts of America and Lumberton PTA; married to the former Dee Strickland; two children; committees.

Office Listings

http://www.house.gov.mcintyre congmcintyre@mail.house.gov

1605 Longworth House Office Building, Washington, DC 20515–3307 225–2731
Chief of Staff/Press Secretary.—Dean Mitchell. FAX: 225–5773
Chief of Constituent Services.—Vivian Lipford.
Deputy Legislative Director.—Bill Bondshu.
Systems Manager/Legislative Assistant.—Jamie Norment.
Legislative Assistant.—Felicia Cummings.
Room 218, Federal Building, 301 Green Street, Fayetteville, NC 28401 .... (910) 323–0260
District Director.—Judith Kirchman. FAX: 323–0069
Room 208, Post Office Building, 152 Front Street North, Wilmington, NC 28401 (910) 815–4959
Constituent Services Assistant.—Pam Campbell-Dereef. FAX: 815–4543
701 Elm Street, Lumberton, NC 28358 .... (910) 671–6223
District Executive Assistant.—Marie Thompson. FAX: 739–5085

Counties: Bladen (part), Brunswick, Columbus (part), Cumberland (part), New Hanover (part), Onslow (part), Pender (part), and Robeson (part). Population (1990), 552,386.

ZIP Codes: 28301 (part), 28303 (part), 28304 (part), 28305 (part), 28306 (part), 28307 (part), 28311 (part), 28314 (part), 28319–20, 28324, 28332, 28337 (part), 28340, 28342, 28344 (part), 28348, 28356 (part), 28358–59, 28362, 28369, 28372, 28375, 28383, 28390 (part), 28391, 28392, 28395, 28401 (part), 28403 (part), 28405 (part), 28406–07, 28409, 28412, 28420, 28422, 28428, 28429 (part), 28430, 28431 (part), 28432, 28438–39, 28442, 28443 (part), 28445, 28449–52, 28455, 28456 (part), 28459–63, 28465, 28467–70, 28472 (part), 28479–80, 28539, 28540 (part), 28542–43, 28544 (part), 28546 (part)

EIGHTH DISTRICT

W.G. (BILL) HEFNER, Democrat, of Concord, NC; born in Elora, TN, April 11, 1930; former entertainer and broadcast executive; married Nancy Hill, 1952; two children: Stacye and Shelly; committee: Appropriations; subcommittees: ranking member, Military Construction; National Security; appointed deputy whip for the 100th through 103rd Congress; appointed to leadership advisory group for 104th Congress; elected to the 94th Congress, November 5, 1974; reelected to each succeeding Congress.

Office Listings

2470 Rayburn House Office Building, Washington, DC 20515–3308 225–3715
Administrative Assistant.—Bill McEwen. FAX: 225–4036
Legislative Director.—Irene Schecter.
Executive Assistant.—Ellen Young.
P.O. Box 385, 101 South Union Street, Concord, NC 28026 .... (704) 786–1612
P.O. Box 4220, 507 West Innes Street, Salisbury, NC 28144 .... (704) 636–0635
P.O. Box 1503, 230 East Franklin Street, Rockingham, NC 28379 .... (910) 997–2070
P.O. Box 372, Carthage, NC 28327 .... (910) 949–2912
District Administrator.—J. Elvin Jackson.

Counties: Anson, Cabarrus, Cumberland (part), Hoke, Iredell (part), Mecklenburg (part), Montgomery, Moore (part), Richmond, Robeson (part), Rowan (part), Scotland, Stanly, Union. Population (1990), 552,387.

ZIP Codes: 27008, 27013 (part), 27209, 27229, 27242, 27247, 27251, 27259, 27281 (part), 27306, 27325 (part), 27341 (part), 27356, 27371, 28001–02, 28007, 28009, 28023 (part), 28025–27, 28031, 28036 (part), 28041, 28071 (part), 28072, 28075, 28078 (part), 28079, 28081–83, 28088, 28091, 28097, 28102–03, 28105 (part), 28107–12, 28115 (part), 28119, 28124–25, 28127–29, 28133, 28135, 28137 (part), 28138 (part), 28144 (part), 28145, 28146 (part), 28163, 28170, 28173–74, 28213 (part), 28215 (part), 28262 (part), 28303 (part), 28304 (part), 28306 (part), 28307 (part), 28309, 28314 (part), 28315 (part), 28327 (part), 28330–31, 28338, 28343, 28345, 28347, 28351–53, 28357, 28361, 28363–64, 28367, 28371, 28376–79, 28384, 28386, 28387 (part), 28390 (part), 28396

* * *

NINTH DISTRICT

SUE MYRICK, Republican, of Charlotte, NC; born in Tiffin, OH, August 1, 1941; graduated Port Clinton High School, Port Clinton, OH; attended Heidelberg College; former president and CEO, Myrick Advertising and Myrick Enterprises; mayor of Charlotte, NC, 1987–91; Charlotte City Council, 1983–85; active with the National League of Cities and the U.S. Conference of Mayors; served on former President Bush's Affordable Housing Commission; member: Charlotte Chamber of Commerce, Muscular Dystrophy Association, March of Dimes, Elks Auxiliary, PTA, Cub Scout den mother, United Methodist Church; founder, Charitable Outreach Society; married Ed Myrick, 1977; five children; elected to the 104th Congress; reelected to the 105th Congress.

Office Listings

http://www.house.gov/myrick myrick@hr.house.gov

509 Cannon House Office Building, Washington, DC 20515 225–1976
Administrative Assistant.—J.T. Taylor. FAX: 225–3389
Executive Assistant.—Susan Ludwick.
1901 Roxborough Road, Suite 211, Charlotte, NC 28211 .... (704) 367–0852
224 South New Hope Road, Suite H, Gastonia, NC .... (704) 861–1976

Counties: Cleveland (part); Gaston (part); Mecklenburg (part). Population (1990), 552,387.

ZIP Codes: 28006 (part), 28012 (part), 28016–17, 28020, 28021 (part), 28032, 28034, 28036 (part), 28042, 28052 (part), 28053, 28054 (part), 28056, 28073, 28077, 28078 (part), 28086 (part), 28090 (part), 28098 (part), 28101, 28105 (part), 28106, 28114 (part), 28115 (part), 28120, 28126, 28130, 28134 (part), 28150 (part), 28152 (part), 28164 (part), 28169, 28202 (part), 28203 (part), 28204 (part), 28205 (part), 28207 (part), 28208 (part), 28209 (part), 28210 (part), 28211 (part), 28212, 28213 (part), 28214 (part), 28215 (part), 28216 (part), 28217 (part), 28218, 28220–22, 28224–27, 28229–37, 28247, 28256, 28262 (part), 28269 (part), 28270, 28273 (part), 28277–78, 28283, 28297, 28299, 28532 (part)

TENTH DISTRICT

CASS BALLENGER, Republican, of Hickory, NC; born in Hickory, December 6, 1926; graduated, Episcopal High School, Alexandria, VA, 1944; attended University of North Carolina, Chapel Hill, 1944–45; B.A., Amherst College, Amherst, MA, 1948; served in U.S. Naval Air Corps, aviation cadet, 1944–45; founder and president, Plastic Packaging, Inc.; North Carolina House of Representatives, 1974–76; North Carolina Senate, 1976–86; member: Catawba County Board of Commissioners, 1966–74 (chairman, 1970–74); Advisory Budget Commission, White House Advisory Committee, Community Ridge Day Care Center, Hickory Rotary Club, Hickory United Fund, Lenoir-Rhyne College Board of Development, Salvation Army Board of Directors, Florence Crittenton Home Board of Directors, Greater Hickory Chamber of Commerce (director); sustaining member, North Carolina School of the Arts; patron: North Carolina Symphony, North Carolina Arts Society; married the former Donna Davis, 1952; three children: Lucinda Ballenger-Brinkley, Melissa Ballenger Jordan, and Dorothy Davis Ballenger Weaver; two grandsons: Matthew Jordan and William Eriksen Jordan; deputy whip, 104th Congress; member, International Relations and Economic and Educational Opportunities committees; elected to the 99th Congress, November 4, 1986, to complete the unexpired term of James Broyhill; reelected to each succeeding Congress.

Office Listings

cass@mailhr.house.gov

2238 Rayburn House Office Building, Washington, DC 20515–3310 225–2576
Administrative Assistant.—Patrick M. Murphy. FAX: 225–0316
Legislative Director.—Leslie Gallagher.
Executive Assistant.—Mary McLartey.
P.O. Box 1830, Hickory, NC 28603 .... (704) 327–6100
District Director.—Tommy Luckadoo.
P.O. Box 1881, Clemmons, NC 27012 .... (919) 766–9455
District Representative.—Marsha Sucharski.

Counties: Alexander, Avery, Buncombe (part), Burke (part), Caldwell (part), Catawba, Davie (part), Forsyth (part), Henderson (part), Iredell (part), Lincoln, McDowell (part), Mitchell, Polk (part), Rutherford (part), Wilkes (part), and Yadkin. Population (1990), 552,386.

ZIP Codes: 27006, 27011–12, 27018, 27020, 27023, 27028 (part), 27040, 27045 (part), 27050 (part), 27055, 27103 (part), 27104 (part), 27105 (part), 27106 (part), 27127 (part), 28006 (part), 28010, 28018, 28021 (part), 28033, 28037, 28080, 28092–93, 28115 (part), 28123, 28139 (part), 28164 (part), 28166 (part), 28167 (part), 28168, 28601–04, 28605 (part), 28609–14, 28616, 28621 (part), 28622, 28624, 28630, 28634–38, 28641–42, 28645 (part), 28646–53, 28654 (part), 28657–58, 28659 (part), 28660–62, 28664–67, 28669–71, 28673, 28677 (part), 28678, 28681–83, 28685, 28688–90, 28696, 28697 (part), 28699, 28704 (part), 28705, 28711 (part), 28720, 28730, 28732, 28742 (part), 28746, 28752 (part), 28756 (part), 28760, 28765, 28777, 28792 (part), 28803 (part), 28804 (part)

* * *

ELEVENTH DISTRICT

CHARLES H. TAYLOR, Republican, of Brevard, NC; born in Brevard on January 23, 1941; graduated from Brevard High School; B.A., Wake Forest University, 1963; J.D., Wake Forest University, 1966; tree farmer; member: North Carolina Board of Transportation, North Carolina Energy Policy Council; vice chairman, Western North Carolina Environmental Council; chairman, North Carolina Parks and Recreation Council; member, North Carolina State House, 1967–73; minority leader, 1969–73; North Carolina State Senator and minority leader, 1973–75; married to the former Elizabeth Owen; three children: Owen, Bryan, and Charles Robert; member, Board of Visitors to the Military Academy; committees: Appropriations; vice chairman, Subcommittee on Commerce, State, Justice and the Judiciary; Subcommittee on Interior; chairman, Subcommittee on the District of Columbia; elected to the 102nd Congress on November 6, 1990; reelected to each succeeding Congress.

Office Listings

chtaylor@hr.house.gov

231 Cannon House Office Building, Washington, DC 20515–3311 225–6401
Administrative Assistant.—Roger France. FAX: 225–0519
Suite 330, 22 South Park Square, Asheville, NC 28801 .... (704) 251–1988
106 North Main Street, Rutherfordton, NC 28139 .... (704) 286–8750
211 Seventh Avenue West, Hendersonville, NC 28791 .... (704) 697–8539
Cherokee County Courthouse, Murphy, NC 28906 .... (704) 837–3249
200 South Lafayette Street, Shelby, NC 28150 .... (704) 484–6971

Counties: Buncombe (part), Cherokee, Clay, Cleveland (part), Graham, Haywood, Henderson (part), Jackson, McDowell (part), Macon, Madison, Polk (part), Rutherford (part), Swain, Transylvania, Yancey. Population (1990), 552,387.

ZIP Codes: 28019, 28024, 28038, 28040 (part), 28043, 28074, 28076, 28086 (part), 28089, 28090 (part), 28114 (part), 28136, 28139 (part), 28150 (part), 28151, 28152 (part), 28160, 28167 (part), 28701–03, 28704 (part), 28707–10, 28711 (part), 28712–14, 28715 (part), 28716–19, 28721–29, 28731, 28733–41, 28742 (part), 28743, 28745, 28747–51, 28752 (part), 28753–55, 28756 (part), 28757–58, 28761–63, 28766, 28768, 28770–76, 28778–84, 28786–90, 28792 (part), 28793, 28801 (part), 28802, 28803 (part), 28804 (part), 28805–06, 28813–16, 28901–06, 28909

* * *

TWELFTH DISTRICT

MELVIN WATT, Democrat, of Charlotte, NC; born in Charlotte on August 26, 1945; graduated, York Road High School, Charlotte, 1963; B.S., business adminisration, University of North Carolina, Chapel Hill, 1967; J.D., Yale University Law School, New Haven, CT, 1970; attorney; admitted to the District of Columbia bar, 1970, admitted to the North Carolina bar, 1971; began practice with Chambers, Stein, Ferguson and Becton, 1971–92; North Carolina State Senate, 1985–86; life member: NAACP; member: Mount Olive Presbyterian Church; Mecklenburg County Bar Association, past president; Johnston C. Smith University Board of Visitors; Central Piedmont Community College Foundation; North Carolina Association of Black Lawyers; North Carolina Association of Trial Lawyers; Legal Aid of Southern Piedmont; NationsBank Community Development Corporation; Charlotte Chamber of Commerce; Sports Action Council; Auditorium-Coliseum-Civic Center Authority; United Way; Mint Museum; Inroads, Inc.; Family Housing Services; Public Education Forum; Dilworth Community Development Association; Cities in Schools; West Charlotte Business Incubator; Housing Authority Scholarship Board; Morehead Scholarship Selection Committee, Forsyth Region; married the former Eulada Paysour, 1968; two children: Brian and Jason; elected on November 3, 1992 to the 103rd Congress; reelected to each succeeding Congress.

Office Listings

http://www.house.gov/watt melmail@hr.house.gov

1230 Longworth House Office Building, Washington, DC 20515–3312	225–1510
Administrative Assistant.—Joan Kennedy.	FAX: 225–1512
214 North Church Street, Suite 130, Charlotte, NC 28202	(704) 344–9950
	FAX: 344–9971
315 East Chapel Hill, Suite 202, Durham, NC 27701	(919) 688–3004
	FAX: 688–0940
301 South Green Street, Suite 210, Greensboro, NC 27401	(910) 379–9403
District Director.—Don Baker.	FAX: 379–9429

Counties: ALAMANCE COUNTY; cities and townships of Altamahau, Burlington, Elon College, Graham, Haw River, and Mebane. DAVIDSON COUNTY; cities of Lexington, Rougemont, and Welcome. DURHAM COUNTY; cities of Bahama and Durham. FORSYTH COUNTY; cities of Kernersville and Winston-Salem. GASTON COUNTY; cities of Gastonia and Lowell. GUILFORD COUNTY; cities and townships of Gibsonville, Greensboro, High Point, Jamestown, McLeansville, and Whitsett. IREDELL COUNTY; cities and townships of Mooresville, Troutman, and Statesville. MECKLENBURG COUNTY; cities and townships of Charlotte, Davidson, Huntersville, and Pineville. ORANGE COUNTY; city of Hillsborough. ROWAN COUNTY; cities and townships of Cleveland, East Spencer, Salisbury, Spencer, Thomasville, and Woodleaf. Population (1990), 552,387.

ZIP Codes: 27013 (part), 27054, 27101 (part), 27102, 27105 (part), 27107 (part), 27108, 27120, 27127 (part), 27202, 27217 (part), 27244 (part), 27249 (part), 27253 (part), 27258 (part), 27260 (part), 27262 (part), 27265 (part), 27278 (part), 27282 (part), 27284 (part), 27292 (part), 27293, 27301 (part), 27302 (part), 27360 (part), 27374, 27377 (part), 27401 (part), 27402, 27403 (part), 27405 (part), 27406 (part), 27407 (part), 27408 (part), 27415, 27417, 27420, 27438, 27455, 27503, 27541, 27572 (part), 27701 (part), 27703 (part), 27704 (part), 27705 (part), 27706 (part), 27707 (part), 27709, 27712 (part), 27713 (part), 27717, 27722, 28012 (part), 28036 (part), 28039, 28052 (part), 28054 (part), 28078 (part), 28098 (part), 28115 (part), 28134 (part), 28144 (part), 28146 (part), 28159, 28166 (part), 28202 (part), 28203 (part), 28204 (part), 28205 (part), 28206, 28207 (part), 28208 (part), 28209 (part), 28210 (part), 28211 (part), 28213 (part), 28214 (part), 28215 (part), 28216 (part), 28217 (part), 28219, 28241, 28244, 28246, 28262 (part), 28266, 28269 (part), 28273 (part), 28280–81, 28284, 28677 (part)

NORTH DAKOTA

(Population 1995, 641,000)

SENATORS

KENT CONRAD, Democrat, of Bismarck, ND; born in Bismarck on March 12, 1948; graduated Wheelus High School, Tripoli, Libya, 1966; attended University of Missouri, Columbia, 1967; B.A., Stanford University, CA, 1971; M.B.A., George Washington University, Washington, DC, 1975; assistant to tax commissioner, Bismarck, 1974–80; director, management planning and personnel, North Dakota Tax Department, March–December 1980; tax commissioner, State of North Dakota, 1981–86; married Lucy Calautti, February 1987; one child by former marriage: Jessamyn Abigail; elected to the U.S. Senate on November 4, 1986; committees: Agriculture, Nutrition and Forestry; Budget; Finance; Indian Affairs; Select Committee on Ethics; was not a candidate for a second term to Senate seat he had won in 1986; subsequently elected by special election on December 4, 1992 to fill the vacancy caused by the death of Senator Quentin Burdick, whose term will expire January 3, 1995; took the oath of office on December 14, 1992 and continued his Senate service without interruption; reelected November 8, 1994.

Office Listings

http://www.senate.gov/~conrad senator@conrad.senate.gov

530 Hart Senate Office Building, Washington, DC 20510–3403 224–2043
Chief of Staff.—Kent Hall. FAX: 224–7776
Legislative Directors.—Bob Foust, Tom Mahr, Mary Naylor.
Federal Building, Room 228, Third and Rosser, Bismarck, ND 58501 .... (701) 258–4648
State Director.—Lynn Clancy.
Federal Building, Suite 104, 102 North Fourth Street, Grand Forks, ND 58203 ...... (701) 775–9601
Federal Building, Room 306, 657 Second Avenue North, Fargo, ND 58102 .... (701) 232–8030
TDD: 232–2139
Suite 105, 100 First Street SW, Minot, ND 58701 .... (701) 852–0703

* * *

BYRON L. DORGAN, Democrat, of Bismarck, ND; born in Dickinson, ND, May 14, 1942; graduated, Regent High School, 1961; B.S., University of North Dakota, 1965; M.B.A., University of Denver, 1966; North Dakota State Tax Commissioner, 1969–80, the only elected state tax commissioner in the nation; received 80 percent of the vote in 1976 tax commissioner reelection bid; chairman, Multi-State Tax Commission, 1972–74; executive committee member, National Association of Tax Administrators, 1972–75; selected by the *Washington Monthly* as one of the outstanding state officials in the United States, 1975; chosen by one of North Dakota's leading newspapers as the individual with the greatest influence on State government, 1977; elected to Congress, 1980; elected president of Democratic freshman class during first term; reelected, 1982, with 72 percent of the vote; reelected to Congress in 1984 with 78.5 percent of the vote, setting three election records in North Dakota—largest vote ever received by a statewide candidate, largest vote by a U.S. House candidate, and largest majority by a U.S. House candidate; his 242,000 votes in 1984 were the most received anywhere in the nation by an opposed House candidate; served on three congressional committees during first term in Congress: Agriculture, Small Business, and Veterans' Affairs; named to the Ways and Means Committee, January 1983; called the real successor to Bill Langer and the State's most exciting office holder in generations, by the 1983 *Book of America*; 1990 *New York Times* editorial said, ''Mr. Dorgan sets an example for political statesmanship''; named to Select Committee on Hunger in 1985; chairman, International Task Force on Select Committee on Hunger; reelected in 1986; reelected in 1988 with 71 percent of the votes, reelected again in 1990; elected to the U.S. Senate on November 3, 1992; first sworn in on December 15, 1992 to fill remainder of term in North Dakota's open Senate seat, then sworn in January 5, 1993 for six-year term; committees: Commerce, Science and Transportation; Appropriations; Energy and Natural Resources; Indian Affairs; Democratic Policy Committee; assistant Democratic floor leader, 104th Congress; married to Kim Dorgan; four children: Scott, Shelly (deceased), Brendon, and Haley.

Office Listings

http://www.senate.gov/~dorgan senator@dorgan.senate.gov

713 Hart Senate Office Building, Washington, DC 20510–3405 224–2551

FAX: 224–1193

Administrative Assistant.—Lucy Calautti.
Communications Director.—Barry E. Piatt.
Office Manager.—Marlene Eide.
State Coordinator.—Bob Valeu.

Third Floor, Federal Building, Bismarck, ND 58501 .... (701) 250–4618
FAX: 250–4484

110 Roberts Street, Fargo, ND 58102 .... (701) 239–5389
FAX: 239–5512

102 North Fourth Street, Room 108, Grand Forks, ND 58201 .... (701) 746–9126
FAX: 746–9122

100 First Street SW, Suite 105, Minot, ND 58701 .... (701) 852–0703
FAX: 838–8196

REPRESENTATIVE

AT LARGE

EARL RALPH POMEROY, Democrat-NPL, of Valley City, ND; born on September 2, 1952 in Valley City; B.A. and J.D., University of North Dakota, Grand Forks, 1974, 1979; graduate research in legal history at the University of Durham, England, 1975–76; attorney; admitted to North Dakota bar, 1979; North Dakota House of Representatives, 1980–84; insurance commissioner of North Dakota, 1985–92; president, National Association of Insurance Commissioners, 1990; married Laurie Kirby, 1986; two children: Kathryn and Scott; member: Budget and Agriculture committees; elected on November 3, 1992 to the 103rd Congress; reelected to each succeeding Congress.

Office Listings

epomeroy@hr.house.gov

1533 Longworth House Office Building, Washington, DC 20515 225–2611
FAX: 226–0893

Administrative Assistant.—Karen Frederickson.
Legislative Director.—Bart Chilton.
Press Secretary.—Donald Marshall.

Room 376, Federal Building, 220 East Rosser Avenue, Bismarck, ND 58501 .... (701) 224–0355

Room 266, Federal Building, 657 Second Avenue North, Fargo, ND 58012 .... (701) 235–9760

State Director.—Gail Skaley.

Population (1990), 638,800.

ZIP Codes: 56548 (part), 56744 (part), 57255 (part), 57260 (part), 57270 (part), 57430 (part), 57632 (part), 57634 (part), 57638 (part), 57648 (part), 57660 (part), 58001–18, 58020–21, 58023–24, 58027, 58029, 58030 (part), 58031, 58032 (part), 58033, 58035–40, 58041 (part), 58042–43, 58045–49, 58051–52, 58053 (part), 58054, 58056–65, 58067–69, 58071–72, 58075, 58077–79, 58081, 58102–03, 58105, 58107–09, 58201–02, 58205–06, 58210, 58212–16, 58218–20, 58222–24, 58225 (part), 58227–31, 58233, 58235–41, 58243–46, 58248–51, 58253–62, 58264–67, 58269–70, 58271 (part), 58272–79, 58281–82, 58301, 58310–11, 58313, 58315–25, 58327–33, 58335, 58337–39, 58341–46, 58348, 58351–53, 58355–57, 58359–63, 58365–74, 58377, 58379–82, 58384–86, 58401–02, 58411–12, 58413 (part), 58415–18, 58420–33, 58436 (part), 58438, 58439 (part), 58440–45, 58447–48, 58450–52, 58454–56, 58458, 58460–61, 58463–67, 58469, 58471–84, 58486–90, 58492, 58494–97, 58501–02, 58504–05, 58520–21, 58523–24, 58528–33, 58535, 58537–38, 58540–42, 58544–45, 58547, 58549, 58551–55, 58558–66, 58568–73, 58575–77, 58579–81, 58601–02, 58620–22, 58623 (part), 58625–27, 58630–32, 58634, 58636, 58637 (part), 58638–47, 58649–57, 58701–02, 58704, 58710–16, 58718, 58720–23, 58725, 58727–28, 58730–41, 58744, 58746–50, 58752, 58755–63, 58765, 58768–73, 58775–76, 58778–79, 58781–85, 58787–90, 58792–95, 58801–02, 58830–33, 58835, 58838, 58843–45, 58847, 58849–50, 58852–56, 59221 (part), 59270 (part), 59275 (part)

OHIO

(Population 1995, 11,151,000)

SENATORS

JOHN GLENN, Democrat, of Columbus, OH; born in Cambridge, OH, July 18, 1921; graduated New Concord (OH) High School, 1939; B.S., Muskingum College; U.S. Marine Corps, colonel (retired), 1942–65; combat World War II and Korean war (awards and decorations); NASA astronaut, 1959–65, first American to orbit the Earth, ***Friendship 7, 1962***; member, board of trustees, Muskingum College; business, vice president, Royal Crown, 1966–68; president, Royal Crown International, 1967–69; board of directors, Questor Corporation 1970–74; member of numerous U.S. and international aviation, aeronautic, and scientific organizations; Presbyterian (elder); married the former Anna Margaret Castor, 1942; two children: David and Lyn; committees: Armed Services, Governmental Affairs, Special Committee on Aging, Select Committee on Intelligence; elected to the U.S. Senate, November 5, 1974; reelected November 4, 1980, November 4, 1986, and November 3, 1992, for term the ending January 3, 1999.

Office Listings

http://www.senate.gov/~glenn senator.glenn@glenn.senate.gov

503 Hart Senate Office Building, Washington, DC 20510–3501 224–3353
Administrative Assistant.—Mary Jane Veno.
Executive Assistant.—Nicole Dauray.
Legislative Director.—Ron Grimes.
Room 600, 200 North High Street, Columbus, OH 43215 .... (614) 469–6697
Anthony J. Celebrezze Building, 1240 East Ninth Street, Room 2957, Cleveland, OH 44199 .... (216) 522–7095
Federal Building, Suite 10407, 550 Main Street, Cincinnati, OH 45202 .... (513) 684–3265
234 North Summit Street, Room 726, Toledo, OH 43604 .... (419) 259–7592

* * *

MIKE DeWINE, Republican, of Columbus, OH; born in Springfield, OH, January 5, 1947; Yellow Springs High School; B.S., Miami University, Oxford, OH, 1969; graudated, J.D., Ohio Northern University, 1972; attorney, admitted to the Ohio State bar, 1972; Greene County assistant and prosecuting attorney, 1976–80; Ohio State Senator, 1980–82; U.S. Representative, 1983–91; Lieutenant Governor of Ohio, 1991–95; married the former Frances Stizvewing, 1967; eight children: Patrick, Jill, Becky, John, Brian, Alice, Mark, and Anna; committees: Judiciary; Labor and Human Resources; Select Committee on Intelligence; elected to the U.S. Senate in November 1994 for the six-year term beginning January 3, 1995.

Office Listings

http://www.senate.gov/~dewine senator_dewine@dewine.senate.gov

140 Russell Senate Office Building, Washington, DC 20510 224–2315
Chief of Staff.—Laurel Pressler. FAX: 224–6519
Communications Director.—Charles Boesel.
Legislative Director.—Robert Hoffman.
Press Secretary.—Mary Brown Brewer.
Office Manager.—Cole Thomas.
105 East Street, Room 1515, Cincinnati, OH 45202 .... (513) 763–8260
District Representative.—Jana Morford. FAX: 763–8268
600 Superior Avenue East, Room 2450, Cleveland, OH 44114 .... (216) 522–7272
FAX: 522–2239
37 West Broad Street, Room 970, Columbus, OH 43215 .... (614) 469–6774
FAX: 469–7419
Dime Bank Building, 200 Putnam Street, Suite 522, Marietta, OH 45750 .... (614) 373–2317
FAX: 373–8689
234 North Summit Street, Room 716, Toledo, OH 43604 .... (419) 259–7535
FAX: 259–7575
265 South Allison Avenue, Room 105, Xenia, OH 45385 .... (937) 376–3080
State Director.—Barbara Briggs. FAX: 376–3387

REPRESENTATIVES

FIRST DISTRICT

STEVE CHABOT, Republican, of Cincinnati, OH; born in Cincinnati, OH, January 22, 1953; attended LaSalle High School, Cincinnati; B.A., College of William and Mary, Williamsburg, VA, 1975; J.D., Salmon P. Chase College of Law, 1978; former school teacher; private practice lawyer, 1978–94; Hamilton County commissioner, 1990–94; member, Cincinnati City Council, 1985–90; chairman, County Council's Urban Development and Law and Public Safety committees; married Donna Chabot, 1973; two children: Randy and Erica; committees: Judiciary, International Relations, Small Business; subcommittees: Commercial and Administrative Law, Crime, International Economic Policy and Trade, Africa and Empowerment; elected to the 104th Congress; reelected to the 105th Congress.

Office Listings

129 Cannon House Office Building, Washington, DC 20515 225–2216
Chief of Staff.—Fred Nelson. FAX: 225–3012
Legislative Director.—Kevin Fitzpatrick.
Office Director.—Cynthia Kielb.
105 West Fourth Street, Suite 1115, Cincinnati, OH 45202 .... (513) 684–2723
District Director.—Shannon Jones. FAX: 421–8722

County: Hamilton County (part); cities of Bridgetown North, Cheviot, Cincinnati (part), Cleves, Covedale, Deer Park (part), Dent, Elmwood Place, Finneytown, Forest Park, Glendale (part), Golf Manor, Greenhills, Groesbeck, Lincoln Heights, Lockland, Mack North, Mack South, Monfort Heights East, Monfort Heights South, Mount Healthy, Mount Healthy Heights, North College Hill, Northbrook, Northgate, Pleasant Run (part), Pleasant Run Farm (part), Silverton, St. Bernard, White Oak, White Oak East, White Oak West and Woodlawn. Population (1990), 570,900.

ZIP Codes: 45001–02, 45033, 45051–52, 45200 (part), 45201, 45202, 45203 (part), 45204–05, 45206 (part), 45207 (part), 45208 (part), 45210, 45211, 45212 (part), 45213 (part), 45214 (part), 45215 (part), 45216, 45217 (part), 45218, 45219 (part), 45220 (part), 45221–24, 45225 (part), 45227 (part), 45229 (part), 45231–33, 45236 (part), 45237–38, 45239, 45240 (part), 45243 (part), 45246–48, 45250, 45251–52, 45254, 45258, 45262

* * *

SECOND DISTRICT

ROB PORTMAN, Republican, of Cincinnati, OH; born in Cincinnati, December 19, 1955; graduated Cincinnati Country Day School; B.A., Dartmouth College, 1979; J.D., University of Michigan Law School, 1984; admitted to the Ohio and Washington, DC bars, 1984; attorney, private practice, (six years); associate counsel to former President Bush, 1989; deputy assistant to the president and director, White House Office of Legislative Affairs, 1989–91; married June Dudley Portman, 1986; three children; committee: Ways and Means; subcommittees: Oversight and Social Security; cochair National Commission on Restructuring the Internal Revenue Service; elected by special election on May 4, 1993 to fill the vacancy caused by the resignation of William Gradison; reelected to the each succeeding Congress.

Office Listings

http://www.house.gov/portman portmail@hr.house.gov

238 Cannon House Office Building, Washington, DC 20515–3502 225–3164
Chief of Staff.—John M. Bridgeland.
Legislative Director.—Barbara Pate.
Communications Director.—Brian Besanceney.
8044 Montgomery Road, Suite 540, Cincinnati, OH 45236 .... (513) 791–0381
District Manager.—Gloria Griffiths.

Counties: Adams; Brown; Clermont; Hamilton (part); Warren (part). Population (1990), 570,902.

ZIP Codes: 45101 (part), 45102–03, 45106, 45107 (part), 45111–13, 45115, 45118 (part), 45119–21, 45122 (part), 45130–31, 45133 (part), 45140 (part), 45142 (part), 45144 (part), 45145, 45147, 45148 (part), 45150, 45153, 45154 (part), 45156–57, 45160, 45162 (part), 45166–68, 45171 (part), 45174, 45176, 45200 (part), 45201, 45203 (part), 45206–07, 45208 (part), 45209–10, 45212–13, 45214 (part), 45215 (part), 45217 (part), 45219 (part), 45220 (part), 45225 (part), 45226–28, 45229 (part), 45230, 45236, 45239, 45240 (part), 45242–45, 45249 (part), 45255, 45697 (part)

THIRD DISTRICT

TONY P. HALL, Democrat, of Dayton; born in Dayton, OH, January 16, 1942; graduated from Fairmont High School, Kettering, OH, 1960; A.B., Denison University, Granville, OH, 1964; Honory Doctor of Laws degrees from Asbury College and Eastern College; named Little All-American in football; most valuable player, Ohio Conference; Peace Corps volunteer, 1966–67; realtor; member, Ohio General Assembly—State Representative, 1969–72, State Senator, 1973–78; member: Montgomery County Democratic Party; board of managers, Air Force Museum Foundation; board of trustees, Holiday Aid; board of advisors, Aviation Trail, Inc.; advisory committee, Emergency Resource Bank of the Dayton Area Chapter of the American Red Cross; awards: United States Committee for UNICEF 1995 Children's Legislative Advocate Award; U.S. AID Presidential End Hunger Award; Distinguished Service Against Hunger Award from Bread of the World; Tree of Life Award from the Jewish National Fund; Golden Apple Award from the National Association of Nutrition and Aging Services Programs; NCAA Silver Anniversary Award; Freedom Award from the Asian Pacific American Chamber of Commerce; 1992 Silver World Food Day medal from the Food and Agriculture Organization of the United Nations; married the former Janet Dick, 1972; one child: Jyl; elected to the 96th Congress, November 7, 1978; reelected to each succeeding Congress.

Office Listings

1432 Longworth House Office Building, Washington, DC 20515–3503 225–6465
Chief of Staff.—Rick Carne.
Rules Committee Associate Staff/Press Secretary.—Michael Gessel.
Legislative Director.—David Goldberg.
Personal Secretary/Office Manager.—Bonnie Ruestow.
501 Federal Building, 200 West Second Street, Dayton, OH 45402 .... (513) 225–2843
District Director.—Bryan J. Bucklew.

County: MONTGOMERY COUNTY. All of Montgomery County with the exception of the western portion of German Township. Population (1990), 570,901.

ZIP Codes: 45309, 45315, 45322, 45325, 45327 (part), 45342–43, 45345, 45354, 45370 (part), 45377, 45401–10, 45414–20, 45422–24, 45426–29, 45430 (part), 45431 (part), 45432 (part), 45433 (part), 45439, 45440 (part), 45449, 45458 (part), 45459 (part), 45469, 45479

* * *

FOURTH DISTRICT

MICHAEL G. OXLEY, Republican, of Findlay, OH; born in Findlay, February 11, 1944, son of George Garver and Marilyn Maxine; graduated, Findlay Senior High School, 1962; B.A., government, Miami University, Oxford, OH, 1966; J.D., Ohio State University College of Law, Columbus, 1969; admitted to Ohio bar, 1969; FBI special agent, Washington, DC, Boston, and New York City, 1969–72; attorney, Oxley, Malone, Fitzgerald, Hollister, 1972–81; elected to Ohio House of Representatives, 1972, from 82nd District, which includes all or parts of four northwestern Ohio counties; reelected, 1974, 1976, 1978, and 1980; member: financial institutions committee and State government committee; ranking minority member, judiciary and criminal justice committee; member: Trinity Lutheran Church, Findlay, OH; American, Ohio, and Findlay Bar Associations; Sigma Chi Fraternity; Omicron Delta Kappa Men's Honorary Fraternity; the Society of Former Special Agents of the FBI; Rotary International; Ohio Association of Township Trustees and Clerks; Ohio Farm Bureau; Findlay Area Chamber of Commerce; married to the former Patricia Pluguez of Philadelphia, 1971; one son, Chadd; member: Commerce Committee; Subcommittees on Telecommunications and Finance (vice chairman); Commerce, Trade and Hazardous Materials (chairman); elected to the 97th Congress, June 25, 1981, in a special election to fill the vacancy caused by the death of Tennyson Guyer; reelected to each succeeding Congress.

Office Listings

http://www.house.gov/oxley oxley@hr.house.gov

2233 Rayburn House Office Building, Washington, DC 20515-3504 225–2676
Administrative Assistant.—Jim Conzelman.
Legislative Assistant.—Bob Foster.
Press Secretary.—Peggy Peterson.
Office Manager/Personal Secretary.—Debi Deimling.
3121 West Elm Plaza, Lima, OH 45805–2516 .... (419) 999–6455
100 East Main Cross Street, Findlay, OH 45840–3311 .... (419) 423–3210
Room 314, 24 West Third Street, Mansfield, OH 44902–1299 .... (419) 522–5757

Counties: Allen, Auglaize (part), Crawford, Hancock, Hardin, Knox (part), Logan (part), Marion, Morrow, Richland, and Wyandot. Population (1990), 570,901.

ZIP Codes: 43005–06, 43011 (part), 43014, 43019 (part), 43022, 43028, 43037, 43048 (part), 43050, 43302 (part), 43310 (part), 43316 (part), 43323, 43326, 43330, 43331 (part), 43337 (part), 43340 (part), 43343 (part), 43345 (part), 43346, 43347 (part), 43351–59, 43822 (part), 43843 (part), 44628 (part), 44802 (part), 44809, 44813 (part), 44818 (part), 44820, 44822–23, 44825, 44827, 44830 (part), 44833 (part), 44843, 44844 (part), 44849, 44853, 44856, 44860, 44862, 44875, 44878, 44881–82, 44887, 44900 (part), 44901, 44902 (part), 44903 (part), 44904, 44906–07, 45302, 45306, 45317 (part), 45318 (part), 45333–34, 45336, 45340, 45353, 45356 (part), 45360, 45363, 45365 (part), 45373 (part), 45380 (part), 45383 (part), 45801–02, 45804–10, 45812, 45814, 45816, 45817 (part), 45819–20, 45830 (part), 45833 (part), 45835–36, 45839–41, 45843 (part), 45845, 45846 (part), 45850, 45854, 45856 (part), 45858 (part), 45859, 45865, 45867, 45868 (part), 45869 (part), 45870–71, 45872 (part), 45877 (part), 45881, 45884, 45885 (part), 45887 (part), 45888–90, 45894 (part), 45895 (part), 45896–97

* * *

FIFTH DISTRICT

PAUL E. GILLMOR, Republican, of Old Fort, OH; born in Tiffin, OH, February 1, 1939; graduated, Old Fort High School, Old Fort, OH, 1957; B.A., Ohio Wesleyan University, Delaware, 1961; J.D., University of Michigan Law School, Ann Arbor, 1964; served in the U.S. Air Force, captain, 1965–66; attorney; admitted to the Ohio bar, 1965; commenced practice in Tiffin, OH; Ohio State Senate, 1967–88; minority leader and president, Ohio State Senate; married the former Karen Lako, 1983; five children: Linda, Julie, Paul Michael, Adam, and Connor; member: Commerce Committee; elected to the 101st Congress on November 8, 1988; reelected to each succeeding Congress.

Office Listings

http://www.house.gov/gillmor

1203 Longworth House Office Building, Washington, DC 20515–3505 225–6405
Administrative Assistant.—Mark Wellman.
Executive Assistant.—Karen Parker.
120 Jefferson Street, Second Floor, Port Clinton, OH 43452 .... (419) 734–1999
1655 North Clinton Street, C–2, Defiance, OH 43512 .... (419) 782–1996
148 East South Boundary Street, Perrysburg, OH 43551 .... (419) 872–2500
County Administration Building, Norwalk, OH 44857 .... (419) 668–0206

Counties: Defiance, Erie, Henry, Huron, Lorain (part), Mercer (part), Ottawa (part), Paulding, Putnam, Sandusky, Seneca, Van Wert, Williams, Wood (part). Population (1990), 570,901.

ZIP Codes: 43316 (part), 43402, 43406–08, 43410, 43412 (part), 43413–14, 43416, 43420, 43430–33, 43435–43, 43445 (part), 43446, 43447 (part), 43448–52, 43456–58, 43462–64, 43465 (part), 43466–69, 43501–02, 43505–06, 43510–12, 43516–21, 43522 (part), 43523–27, 43529–32, 43534–36, 43541, 43543, 43545, 43548–51, 43553–57, 43565, 43567 (part), 43569–70, 44089 (part), 44801, 44802 (part), 44803–04, 44807, 44811 (part), 44814–15, 44817, 44818 (part), 44824, 44828–29, 44830 (part), 44836–37, 44839, 44841, 44844 (part), 44845–46, 44847 (part), 44850, 44854–55, 44861, 44867, 44870, 44883, 44890 (part), 45813, 45815, 45817 (part), 45821, 45827, 45830 (part), 45831, 45832 (part), 45833 (part), 45837, 45844 (part), 45848–49, 45851, 45853, 45855, 45856 (part), 45858 (part), 45861, 45864, 45868 (part), 45872 (part), 45873, 45875–76, 45877 (part), 45879–80, 45886 (part), 45893

* * *

SIXTH DISTRICT

TED STRICKLAND, Democrat, of Lucasville, OH: born in Lucasville, August 4, 1941; B.A., history, Asbury College, 1963; M. Div., Asbury College, 1967; M.A., 1967; M.A., Ph.D. (1980), counseling psychology, University of Kentucky; psychologist and educator: director of a Methodist children's home, professor at Shawnee State University, and consulting psychologist at Southern Ohio Correctional Facility; married to Francis Smith Strickland; elected to the 103rd and 105th Congresses; committee memberships during 103rd Congress: Education and Labor, Small Business.

Office Listings

336 Cannon House Office Building, Washington, DC 20515–3506 225–5705
Chief of Staff.—Mark Lotwis. FAX: 225–5907
Legislative Director.—Sara Franko.
Press Secretary.—Jess Goode.
Legislative Aid (for Education).—Greg Hargett.
1236 Gallia Street, Portsmouth, OH 45662 .... (614) 353–5171
254 Front Street, Marietta, OH 45750 .... (614) 376–0868

Counties: Athens, Clinton, Gallia, Highland, Hocking, Jackson, Lawrence, Meigs, Pike, Ross (part), Scioto, Vinton, Warren (part), and Washington. Population (1990), 570,901.

ZIP Codes: 43101, 43106 (part), 43111, 43115, 43127, 43135 (part), 43137 (part), 43138, 43142, 43144, 43145 (part), 43149, 43152, 43154 (part), 43158, 43160 (part), 43164 (part), 43766 (part), 45005, 45032, 45034, 45036 (part), 45039–41, 45054, 45065–66, 45068 (part), 45101 (part), 45105, 45107 (part), 45110, 45114, 45118 (part), 45122 (part), 45123, 45132, 45133 (part), 45135, 45138, 45140 (part), 45142 (part), 45144 (part), 45146, 45148 (part), 45152, 45154 (part), 45155, 45158–59, 45162 (part), 45164–65, 45169 (part), 45171 (part), 45172, 45177, 45327 (part), 45342 (part), 45458, 45459 (part), 45601, 45611–12, 45613 (part), 45616–18, 45620–22, 45624, 45626, 45628, 45629 (part), 45630, 45633–34, 45636, 45638 (part), 45640, 45642, 45644 (part), 45646–48, 45650–54, 45656 (part), 45657, 45660–62, 45670–73, 45677, 45679, 45681–84, 45685 (part), 45687, 45690, 45692–93, 45694 (part), 45697 (part), 45698, 45701 (part), 45710 (part), 45716–17, 45732 (part), 45741 (part), 45761 (part), 45764 (part), 45766 (part)

* * *

SEVENTH DISTRICT

DAVID L. HOBSON, Republican, of Springfield, OH; born in Cincinnati, OH, October 17, 1936; graduated from Withrow High School, Cincinnati, 1954; B.A., Ohio Wesleyan University, Delaware, OH, 1958; J.D., Ohio State College of Law, Columbus, 1963; admitted to the Kentucky bar, 1965; airman, Ohio Air National Guard, 1958–63; businessman; member: VFW Post No. 1031, Springfield Rotary, Shrine Club No. 5121, Moose No. 536, Elks No. 51; member: board of Ohio Wesleyan University; appointed to Ohio State Senate, 1982; Ohio State Senator, 1984–90; majority whip, 1986–88; president pro tempore, 1988–90; married the former Carolyn Alexander, 1958; three children: Susan Marie, Lynn Martha, Douglas Lee; elected to the 102nd Congress on November 6, 1990; reelected to each succeeding Congress; member: Appropriations and Budget committees.

Office Listings

http://www.house.gov/hobson

1514 Longworth House Office Building, Washington, DC 20515–3507 225–4324
Chief of Staff.—Mary Beth Carozza.
Press Secretary.—Scott Milburn.
Legislative Director.—Kenny Kraft.
Washington Scheduler.—Ginny Gano.
Room 220, Post Office Building, 150 North Limestone Street, Springfield, OH 45501–1121 .... (513) 325–0474
212 South Broad Street, Lancaster, OH 43130–4389 .... (614) 654–5149

Counties: Champaign, Clark, Fairfield, Fayette, Greene, Logan (part), Pickaway (part), Ross (part), Union. Population (1990), 570,902.

ZIP Codes: 43002 (part), 43007, 43009–10, 43015, 43017 (part), 43029 (part), 43036, 43040 (part), 43044 (part), 43045, 43046 (part), 43047, 43060 (part), 43061 (part) 43062 (part), 43064 (part), 43066 (part), 40367 (part), 40368 (part), 43070 (part), 43072 (part), 43076 (part), 43077 (part), 43078 (part), 43083 (part), 43084 (part), 43102 (part), 43103 (part), 43105 (part), 43106 (part), 43107 (part), 43109 (part), 43110 (part), 43112 (part), 43113 (part), 43115 (part), 43116 (part), , 43123 (part), 43125 (part), 43128 (part), 43130, 43135 (part), 43136 (part), 43137 (part), 43138 (part), 43140 (part), 43142 (part), 43143 (part), 43145 (part), 43146 (part), 43147 (part), 43150 (part), 43153 (part), 43154 (part), 43155 (part), 43156, 43157 (part), 43160 (part), 43163 (part), 43164 (part), 43311 (part), 43318 (part), 43319 (part), 43336, 43342 (part), 43343 (part), (43344 (part), 43345 (part), 43357 (part), 43358 (part), 43360 (part), 43725 (part), 45301 (part), 45305 (part), 45307 (part), 45314 (part), 45316 (part), 45319 (part), 45323 (part), 45324 (part), 45335 (part), 45341 (part), 45344 (part), 45349 (part), 45368 (part), 45369 (part), 45370 (part), 45372 (part), 45384 (part), 45385 (part), 45387 (part), 45389 (part), 45424 (part), 45430 (part), 45431 (part), 45432 (part), 45433 (part), 45434 (part), 45440 (part), 45458 (part), 45459 (part), 45501–06, 45601 (part), 45628 (part), 45644 (part).

* * *

EIGHTH DISTRICT

JOHN A. BOEHNER, Republican, of West Chester, OH; born in Reading, OH, November 17, 1949; graduated, Moeller High School, Cincinnati, OH, 1968; B.S., Xavier University, 1977; president, Nucite Sales, Inc.; Ohio House of Representatives, 1984–90; ranking Republican member, Commerce and Labor Committee; Energy and Environment Committee; Judiciary and Criminal Justice; elected, Union Township Trustees, 1981; elected, president, Union Township Board of Trustees, 1984; member: St. John Catholic Church, Ohio Farm Bureau; Lakota Hills Homeowners Association; Knights of Columbus, Pope John XXIII; Union Chamber of Commerce, American Heart Association Board, Butler County Mental Health Association cochair, YMCA Capital Campaign; Union Elementary School PTA; Middletown Chamber of Commerce; American Legion Post 218 of Middletown Butler County Trustees and Clerks Association; married the former Deborah Gunlack, 1973; two children: Lindsay, Tricia; elected to the 102nd Congress and each succeeding Congress.

Office Listings

http://www.house.gov/boehner

1011 Longworth House Office Building, Washington, DC 20515–3508 225–6205
Deputy Chief of Staff.—Brian Gaston. FAX: 225–0704
Press Secretary.—Dave Schnittger.
8200 Beckett Park Drive, Suite 202, Hamilton, OH 45011 .... (513) 870–0151
12 South Plum Street, Troy, Ohio 45373 .... (513) 339–1524

Counties: Auglaize (part), Butler, Darke, Mercer (part), Miami, Montgomery (part), Preble, and Shelby. Population (1990), 570,901.

ZIP Codes: 43072 (part), 45003 (part), 45004, 45011–15, 45030 (part), 45036 (part), 45042, 45044, 45050, 45053 (part), 45055–56, 45061–64, 45067, 45069–70, 45240 (part), 45303, 45304 (part), 45308, 45309 (part), 45310–12, 45317 (part), 45318 (part), 45320–21, 45322 (part), 45326, 45327 (part), 45328–32, 45337–39, 45344 (part), 45345–48, 45350–52, 45356 (part), 45358–59, 45361–62, 45371 (part), 45373 (part), 45378, 45380 (part), 45381 (part), 45382, 45383 (part), 45388, 45390, 45416, 45417 (part), 45426, 45822, 45826, 45828, 45832 (part), 45838, 45844 (part), 45846 (part), 45860, 45862–63, 45866, 45869 (part), 45874, 45882–83, 45885 (part), 45886 (part), 45887 (part), 45891, 45894 (part), 45898–99, 47390 (part)

* * *

NINTH DISTRICT

MARCY KAPTUR, Democrat, of Toledo, OH; born in Toledo on June 17, 1946; Roman Catholic; graduated, St. Ursula Academy, Toledo, 1964; B.A., University of Wisconsin, Madison, 1968; Master of Urban Planning, University of Michigan, Ann Arbor, 1974; attended University of Manchester, England, 1974; urban planner; assistant director for urban affairs, domestic policy staff, White House, 1977–79; member: American Planning Association and American Institute of Certified Planners board of directors, National Center for Urban Ethnic Affairs advisory committee, Gund Foundation, board of directors, University of Michigan Urban Planning Alumni Association; NAACP Urban League; Polish Museum; Polish American Historical Association; Lucas County Democratic Party Executive Committee; Democratic Women's Campaign Association; Lucas County Democratic Business and Professional Women's Club; Fulton County Democratic Women's Club; Little Flower Parish Church; member: Appropriations Committee; cochair: Congressional Competitiveness Caucus; House Auto Parts Task Force; Northeast-Midwest Congressional Coalition; Fair Trade Caucus; elected on November 2, 1982 to the 98th Congress; reelected to each succeeding Congress.

Office Listings

http://www.house.gov/kaptur

2311 Rayburn House Office Building, Washington, DC 20515–3509 225–4146
Chief of Staff.—Fariborz S. Fatemi.
Press Secretary.—Steve Fought.
Legislative Director.—Roberta Jeanquart.
Appointment Secretary.—Norma Olsen.
Federal Building, Room 719, 234 Summit Street, Toledo, OH 43604 .... (419) 259–7500

Counties: Fulton; Lucas; Ottawa; Wood. Cities and townships: Archbold, Berkey, Bowling Green, Bono, Curtice, Clay Center, Delta, Dunbridge, Elmore, Fayette, Genoa, Grand Rapids, Graytown, Harbor View, Holland, Lemoyne, Luckey, Lyons, Maumee, Martin, Metamora, Millbury, Monclova, Neapolis, Northwood, Oak Harbor, Oregon, Pemberville, Perrysburg, Pettisville, Portage, Rossford, Rocky Ridge, Stony Ridge, Swanton, Sylvania, Toledo, Walbridge, Waterville, Wauseon, Whitehouse, Williston, and Woodville. Population (1990), 570,901.

ZIP Codes: 43402 (part), 43408, 43412, 43416 (part), 43430, 43432, 43434, 43441, 43443 (part), 43445, 43447, 43449 (part), 43450 (part), 43451 (part), 43458, 43460 (part), 43463, 43465, 43468, 43469 (part), 43502, 43504, 43515, 43521, 43522 (part), 43528, 43533, 43537, 43540, 43542, 43547, 43551 (part), 43552–53, 43558, 43560, 43566–67, 43571, 43602–20, 43623–24, 43635, 43682, 43697, 43699

* * *

TENTH DISTRICT

DENNIS KUCINICH, Democrat, of Cleveland, OH; born in Cleveland, October 8, 1946; B.A., M.A., speech and communications, Case Western Reserve University, 1973; editor, professor; Ohio Senate, 1994–96; named outstanding Ohio Senator by National Association of Social Workers for his work on health and social welfare issues; mayor of Cleveland, 1977–79; clerk of the municipal court, 1975–77; Cleveland city councilman, 1969–75; one child, Jackie; committees: Education and the Workforce, Government Reform and Oversight; subcommittees: Early Childhood, Youth and Families; Human Resources and Intergovernmental Relations; National Economic Growth; elected to the 105th Congress.

Office Listings

1730 Longworth House Office Building, Washington, DC 20515 225–5871
Chief of Staff.—John Edgell. FAX: 225–5745
Scheduler/Office Manager.—Michael Yarborough.
14400 Detroit Avenue, Lakewood, OH 44107 .... (216) 228–8850
FAX: 228–6465

County CUYAHOGA COUNTY(part); cities and townships of Bay Village, Berea, Brooklyn, Brooklyn Heights, Cleveland, Cuyahaga Heights, Fairview Park, Lakewood, Newberg Heights, North Olmsted, Olmsted Falls, Olmsted Township, Parma, Rocky River, Seven Hills, Strongsville, Westlake. Population (1990), 570,903.

ZIP Codes: 44017, 44070, 44102, 44105, 44107, 44109, 44111, 44113–16, 44125–26, 44129–31, 44134–36, 44138, 44140, 44144–45

* * *

ELEVENTH DISTRICT

LOUIS STOKES, Democrat, of Shaker Heights, OH; born in Cleveland, OH, February 23, 1925, son of Charles and Louise Stokes, both deceased; educated at Cleveland College of Western Reserve University, 1946–48; Cleveland Marshall Law School, 1948–53, Juris Doctor degree; veteran of U.S. Army, 1943–46, honorably discharged; practicing attorney in Cleveland, OH, since 1954; numerous civic awards including Cleveland Branch, NAACP, and the U.S. Commission on Civil Rights; past chairman, Ohio State Bar Association Criminal Justice Committee; past chairman, Congressional Black Caucus; past president: Congressional Black Caucus Foundation; board of trustees, the Martin Luther King, Jr. Center for Social Change: executive committee, Cuyahoga County Democratic Party; lectured and wrote articles for universities and bar associations; member of numerous civic and legal organizations; Methodist, St. Paul A.M.E. Zion Church; married Jeanette (Jay) Francis; four children: Shelley, Angela, Louis C., and Lorene; brother of the late Carl B. Stokes, former mayor of Cleveland, OH, and Ambassador to the Republic of Seychelles; elected to the 91st Congress, November 5, 1968; reelected to each succeeding Congress; member: Committee on Appropriations; subcommittees: Labor, Health and Human Services, and Education, and District of Columbia; ranking minority member, VA, HUD and Independent Agencies; former chairman, House Permanent Select Committee on Intelligence; Committee on Standards of Official Conduct (Ethics Committee); House Select Committee on Assassinations.

Office Listings

2365 Rayburn House Office Building, Washington, DC 20515–3511 225–7032
Administrative Assistant.—Fredette West. FAX: 225–1339
Personal Secretary.—Sallie Bell.
3645 Warrensville Center Road, Suite 204, Shaker Heights, OH 44122 .... (216) 522–4900
District Manager.—Jewell Gilbert.

County: CUYAHOGA COUNTY (part). CITIES: Beachwood (part), Bedford Heights, Brooklyn (part), Cleveland (part), Cleveland Heights, East Cleveland, Euclid, Garfield Heights (part), Linndale, Maple Heights (part), Oakwood (part), Orange, Richmond Heights (part), Shaker Heights, South Euclid, University Heights, Warrensville Heights, and Woodmere. Population (1990), 570,901.

ZIP Codes: 44022 (part), 44100 (part), 44103–04, 44105 (part), 44106, 44107 (part), 44108, 44109 (part), 44110, 44111 (part), 44112, 44113 (part), 44114 (part), 44115, 44117, 44118–20, 44121 (part), 44122 (part), 44123 (part), 44124 (part), 44125 (part), 44127 (part), 44128, 44132, 44135 (part), 44137, 44143 (part), 44146, 44199

* * *

TWELFTH DISTRICT

JOHN R. KASICH, Republican, of Westerville, OH; born in McKees Rocks, PA, May 13, 1952; graduated, Sto-Rox High School, McKees Rocks, 1970; B.A., political science, Ohio State University, Columbus, 1974; administrative assistant to State Senator Donald Lukens, 1975–77; Ohio State Legislature, 1979–82; chairman, Health and Human Services Committee; member: board of trustees, Concord Counseling Service, Westerville, OH; awards: Outstanding Young Men in America Award, 1976; Watchdog of the Treasury Award, 1979; Watchdog of the Treasury's "Golden Bulldog Award," 1983–92; Northland Community Council President's Award, 1981–82; American Security Council's Leadership Award, Guardian of Small Business Award, 1983–92; Spirit of Enterprise Award, 1988–93; Taxpayer's Friend Award, 1989–91; Ohio Health Care Association's "Buckeye Award"; National American Wholesale Grocers Association, "Thomas Jefferson Award," 1992; "Champion of the Merit Shop," 1985–92, Associated Builders and Contractors; National Association of Wholesaler-Distributors; "Congressional Leadership Award," 1994; NAWGA, "Thomas Jefferson Award for Distinguished Service," 1994; elected to the 98th Congress and each succeeding Congress; member, House National Security Committee; chairman, House Budget Committee.

Office Listings

http://www.house.gov/kasich

1131 Longworth House Office Building, Washington, DC 20515–3512	225–5355
Chief of Staff/Legislative Director.—Don Thibaut.	
Executive Assistant.—Mimi McCarthy.	
Press Secretary.—Bruce A. Cuthbertson.	
Suite 500, 200 North High Street, Columbus, OH 43215	(614) 469–7318
Office Manager.—Sally A. Testa.	

Counties: Delaware, Franklin (part), Licking (part). Population (1990), 570,902.

ZIP Codes: 43001, 43003 (part), 43004, 43011 (part), 43013, 43015, 43017–18, 43021, 43023, 43031–33, 43035, 43054, 43055 (part), 43061–62, 43065–66, 43071, 43073–74, 43080–81, 43201 (part), 43205 (part), 43206 (part), 43207 (part), 43209, 43211 (part), 43213, 43224 (part), 43227 (part), 43232 (part), 43235 (part)

* * *

THIRTEENTH DISTRICT

SHERROD BROWN, Democrat, of Lorain, OH; born on November 9, 1952 in Mansfield, OH; B.A., Yale University, 1974; M.A., education and public administration, Ohio State University, 1979; Ohio House of Representatives, 1975–83; Ohio Secretary of State, 1983–91; Eagle Scout, Boy Scouts of America; two children: Emily and Elizabeth; elected to the 103rd Congress; reelected to each succeeding Congress.

Office Listings

sherrod@hr.house.gov http://www.house.gov/sherrodbrown

1407 Longworth House Office Building, Washington, DC 20515–3513	225–3401
Chief of Staff/Legislative Director.—Rhod Shaw.	FAX: 225–2266
Press Secretary.—Steve Fought.	
5201 Abbe Road, Elyria, OH 44035	(216) 934–5100
Medina County Administration Building, 144 North Broadway, Medina, OH 44256	(216) 722–9262
15561 West High Street, Middlefield, OH 44062	(216) 632–3913

Counties: Cuyahoga (part), Geauga (part), Lorain (part), Medina, Portage (part), Summit (part), Trumbull (part). Population (1990), 570,894.

ZIP Codes: 44001, 44011–12, 44024, 44026, 44028 (part), 44033–36, 44039, 44044, 44046, 44052–56, 44062, 44065, 44067, 44072, 44074, 44087, 44089 (part), 44212, 44215, 44233–35, 44251, 44253–54, 44256, 44258, 44271–75, 44280, 44281, 44288 (part), 44321 (part), 44638 (part), 44691 (part),

* * *

FOURTEENTH DISTRICT

THOMAS C. SAWYER, Democrat, of Akron, OH; born in Akron on August 15, 1945; graduated Buchtel High School, Akron, 1963; B.A., University of Akron, 1968; M.A., University of Akron, 1970; former public school teacher; adminstrator, State school for delinquent boys; legislative agent, Public Utilities Commission; Ohio House of Representatives (chairman, Education Committee and member, Ohio Board of Regents), 1977–83; mayor of Akron, 1984–86; married the former Joyce Handler, 1968; one child, Amanda; elected to the 100th Congress on November 4, 1986; reelected to each succeeding Congress.

Office Listings

1414 Longworth House Office Building, Washington, DC 20515–3514 225–5231
Administrative Assistant.—Mary Anne Walsh. FAX: 225–5278
Executive Assistant/Office Manager.—Dianne Tomasek.
411 Wolf Ledges Parkway, Suite 105, Akron, OH 44311–1105 .... (216) 375–5710
District Administrator.—Judi Shapiro. TDD: 375–5443

Counties: Portage (part), Stark (part), Summit (part). Population (1990), 570,900.

ZIP Codes: 44141 (part), 44203 (part), 44210, 44216 (part), 44221–24, 44230 (part), 44236 (part), 44240, 44250, 44260 (part), 44262, 44264, 44266, 44278, 44281 (part), 44286, 44301–14, 44319, 44320–21, 44325, 44328, 44333–34, 44372, 44614 (part), 44685 (part), 44720 (part)

* * *

FIFTEENTH DISTRICT

DEBORAH PRYCE, Republican, of Columbus, OH; born on July 29, 1951 in Warren, OH; B.A., *cum laude,* Ohio State University, Columbus, 1973; J.D., Capital University Law School, Columbus, OH, 1976; attorney; admitted to the Ohio bar in 1976; administrative law judge, Ohio Department of Insurance, 1976–78; first assistant city prosecutor, senior assistant city attorney, and assistant city attorney, Columbus City Attorney's Office, 1978–85; judge, Franklin County Municipal Court, presiding judge for two terms; Ohio Supreme Court Victims of Crime Award, 1986–92; attorney, Hamilton, Kramer, Myers & Cheek, 1992; YWCA Woman of the Year Award, 1995; member, Ohio Supreme Court Committee on Dispute Resolution; chairperson, Municipal Court Subcommittee; member: Jail Capacity Management Board, Domestic Violence Task Force, Corrections Planning Board, Alliance for Cooperative Justice Policy Board, Columbus Inns of Court and Action for Children, Franklin County Alcohol, Drug Addiction and Mental Health Services (ADAMH) Advisory Committee; American Council of Young Political Leaders, delegate to Australia, 1986; session member, former deacon and stewardship chair, Indianola Presbyterian Church; married Randy Walker, 1980; two children: Kelly and Caroline; 103rd Congress freshman class interim; 103rd Congress freshman class policy director; 104th Congress transition team; Rules Committee, Legislative Process Subcommittee; former member, Banking and Financial Services, Government Operations committee; assistant majority whip, NRCC Executive Committee; elected to the 103rd Congress; reelected to each succeeding Congress.

Office Listings

http://www.house.gov/pryce/welcome.html pryce15@hr.house.gov

221 Cannon House Office Building, Washington, DC 20515–3515 225–2015
Administrative Assistant.—Tom Wolfe. FAX: 226–0986
Legislative Director.—Tim Day.
Executive Assistant.—Holly Bauterbaugh.
Room 400, 200 North High Street, Columbus, OH 43215 .... (614) 469–5614
District Representative.—Marcee McCreary.

Counties: Franklin (part), Madison, Pickaway (part). Population (1990), 570,902.

ZIP Codes: 43002, 43017 (part), 43026, 43064 (part), 43065 (part), 43085 (part), 43110, 43119, 43123, 43125–26, 43137, 43140, 43146 (part), 43162, 43201–02, 43204, 43205 (part), 43206 (part), 43207, 43210, 43212, 43214, 43215 (part), 43216 (part), 43220–23, 43227 (part), 43228, 43232 (part), 43235.

* * *

SIXTEENTH DISTRICT

RALPH REGULA, Republican, of Navarre, OH; born in Beach City, OH, December 3, 1924; B.A., Mount Union College, Alliance, OH, 1948; LL.B., William McKinley School of Law, Canton, OH, 1952; U.S. Navy, 1944–46; attorney at law; admitted to Ohio bar and began practice in Navarre, OH, 1952; Ohio House of Representatives, 1965–66, and Ohio Senate, 1967–72; member: Ohio State Board of Education, 1960–64; Saint Timothy Episcopal Church, Massillon, OH; board of trustees, Mount Union College; honorary member, board of advisors, Walsh College; Kiwanis; Grange; trustee, Stark County Historical Society; married Mary Ann Rogusky, 1950; three children: Martha, David, and Richard; committee: Appropriations; elected to the 93rd Congress, November 7, 1972; reelected to each succeeding Congress.

Office Listings

http://www.house.gov/regula

2309 Rayburn House Office Building, Washington, DC 20515–3516 225–3876
FAX: 225–3059

Executive Secretary.—Sylvia Snyder.

Appropriations.—Barbara Wainman; Connie Veillette.

Legal Counsel.—Karen Buttaro.

Staff Director/Press Secretary.—Connie Veillette.

4150 Belden Village Street NW, Suite 408, Canton, OH 44718 .... (330) 489–4414

District Director.—Darryl Revoldt.

Counties: Ashland, Holmes, Knox (part), Stark (part), Wayne. Population (1990), 570,902.

ZIP Codes: 43006, 43014, 43022, 43028, 43050, 44214 (part), 44216 (part), 44217 (part), 44230 (part), 44270, 44276, 44287, 44601, 44606, 44608, 44610, 44611, 44613, 44614, 44617–18, 44626, 44627–8, 44630, 44632, 44633, 44636, 44637, 44638, 44640–41, 44643–46, 44648, 44650, 44652, 44654, 44657, 44659, 44660–62, 44666–67, 44669–70, 44676–77, 44687–90, 44691 (part), 44701–11, 44714, 44718, 44720, 44721, 44730, 44735, 44805, 44838, 44840, 44842, 44859, 44864, 44866, 44874, 44880

* * *

SEVENTEENTH DISTRICT

JAMES A. TRAFICANT, JR., Democrat, of Poland, OH; born in Youngstown, OH, May 8, 1941, son of James A., Sr., and Agnes Traficant; graduated, Cardinal Mooney High School, Youngstown, 1959; B.S., education, University of Pittsburgh, 1963; M.S., administration, 1973, and M.S., counseling, Youngstown State University, 1976; sheriff, Mahoning County, Youngstown, 1981–85; executive director, Mahoning County Drug Program, Inc., 1970–81; consumer finance director, Youngstown Community Action Program; instructed classes on drugs and alcohol, Youngstown State University and Kent State University; national lecturer, drug and alcohol abuse and juvenile problems; drug and alcohol abuse instructor, Ohio Peace Officer Training Institute and Ohio State Highway Patrol; State manager, Girard Life Insurance; committee: Transportation and Infrastructure; ranking member, Coast Guard and Maritime Transporation Subcommittee; married to the former Patricia Choppa; two children: Robin and Elizabeth; elected to the 99th Congress on November 6, 1984; reelected to each succeeding Congress.

Office Listings

telljim@hr.house.gov

2446 Rayburn House Office Building, Washington, DC 20515–3517 225–5261
FAX: 225–3719

Chief of Staff.—Paul Marcone.

Legislative Assistants: Dan Blair, Kim Harris, Charles McCrudden, James Welfley.

Office Manager.—Brian Clark.

125 Market Street, Youngstown, OH 44503 .... (216) 788–2414

Suite 503, 5555 Youngstown-Warren Road, Niles, OH 44406 .... (216) 652–5649

East Liverpool Office, 109 West Third Street, East Liverpool, OH 43920 .... (216) 385–5921

Counties: Columbiana, Mahoning, Trumbull (part). Population (1990), 570,900.

ZIP Codes: 44401, 44403–06, 44408 (part), 44410 (part), 44412 (part), 44416, 44417 (part), 44418, 44420, 44422, 44424–25, 44427 (part), 44429 (part), 44431 (part), 44436–38, 44440, 44442, 44443 (part), 44444 (part), 44446, 44449 (part), 44451–53, 44454 (part), 44460 (part), 44471, 44473, 44481 (part), 44483 (part), 44484–85, 44490 (part), 44491 (part), 44500–07, 44509–12, 44514–15, 44601 (part), 44609 (part), 44619, 44625 (part), 44634 (part), 44657 (part), 44665, 44672

* * *

EIGHTEENTH DISTRICT

ROBERT WILLIAM NEY, Republican, of Columbus, OH; born in Wheeling, WV, July 5, 1954; graduated, St. John's High School, Bellaire, OH; B.S., Ohio State University, Columbus; chairman, Finance Insurance and Banking (13 years); member: Elks, Lions, Kiwanis, and NRA; two children: Robert William II and Kayla Marie; committees: Banking and Financial Services; Government Reform and Oversight; Transportation and Infrastructure; deputy whip; elected to the 104th Congress; relected to the 105th Congress.

Office Listings

http://www.house.gov/ney/welcome.html bobney@hr.house.gov

1024 Longworth House Office Building, Washington, DC 20515–1004 225–6265

Chief of Staff.—David DiStefano. FAX: 225–3394
Legislative Director.—David Heil.
Press Secretary.—Neil Volz.
Legislative Assistants: Daun Forester, Jeff Janas, Maria Robinson.
3201 Belmont Street, Room 604, Bellaire, OH 43906 .... (614) 676–1960
District Director.—Michael Carey. FAX: 676–1983
152 Second Street, NE, Hilton-Fairfield Building 200, New Philadelphia, OH 44663 .... (330) 364–6380
District Field Representative.—Lesley Applegarth FAX: 364–7675
Masonic Temple Building, 38 North Fourth Street, Room 502, Zanesville, OH 43701 .... (614) 452–7023
District Field Representative.—Joe Rose. FAX: 452–7191
401 Market Street, Room 719, Steubenville, OH 43952 .... (614) 283–3716
District Field Representative.—Dennis Watson. FAX: 283–1915

Counties: Belmont, Carroll, Columbiana (part), Coshocton, Guernsey, Harrison, Jefferson, Licking (part), Monroe, Morgan, Muskingum, Noble, Perry, and Tuscarawas. Population (1990), 570,900.

ZIP Codes: 43710–11, 43713, 43716–19, 43722–23, 43724 (part), 43725 (part), 43729, 43732 (part), 43733, 43736, 43747, 43749–50, 43752, 43754–55, 43757, 43759, 43768, 43772–73, 43778–80, 43784, 43786, 43788–89, 43793, 43803, 43804 (part), 43805, 43811, 43812 (part), 43821 (part), 43822 (part), 43824, 43828, 43832, 43836–37, 43840, 43842 (part), 43843 (part), 43844–45, 43901–03, 43905–10, 43912–17, 43920, 43925–28, 43930–35, 43937–48, 43950–53, 43960–64, 43966–68, 43970–74, 43976–77, 43979, 43981, 43983–86, 43988–89, 44408 (part), 44413, 44415, 44423, 44427 (part), 44431 (part), 44432, 44441, 44443 (part), 44445, 44454 (part), 44455, 44460 (part), 44490 (part), 44492–93, 44607, 44608 (part), 44609 (part), 44612 (part), 44615 (part), 44620–22, 44624 (part), 44625 (part), 44626 (part), 44629, 44631, 44637 (part), 44639, 44643 (part), 44651, 44653, 44654 (part), 44656, 44657 (part), 44663, 44671, 44675, 44678–79, 44680 (part), 44681 (part), 44682–83, 44686, 44688 (part), 44693, 44695, 44697, 44699, 45715 (part), 45727, 45730, 45734, 45744 (part), 45745–46, 45767, 45768 (part), 45774, 45789

* * *

NINETEENTH DISTRICT

STEVEN C. LATOURETTE, Republican, of Madison Village, OH; born on July 22, 1954; graduated, Cleveland Heights High School, 1972; B.A., University of Michigan, 1976; J.D., Cleveland State University, 1979; assistant public defender, Lake County, OH, Public Defender's Office, 1980–83; associated with Painesville firm of Cannon, Stern, Aveni and Krivok, 1983–86; Baker, Hackenberg and Collins, 1986–88; prosecuting attorney, Lake County, OH, 1988–94; served on the Lake County Budget Commission; executive board of the Lake County Narcotics Agency; chairman, County Task Force on Domestic Violence; trustee, Cleveland Policy Historical Society; director, Regional Forensic Laboratory; member: Lake County Association of Police Chiefs, Ohio Prosecuting Attorneys Association, and National District Attorneys Association; appointed to serve as a fellow of the American College of Prosecuting Attorneys; married Susan LaTourette; four children: Sarah, Sam, Clare, and Amy; committees: Banking and Financial Services, Transportation and Infrastructure, Government Reform and Oversight; subcommittees: Public Buildings and Economic Development; Surface Transportation; Water Resources and Environment, National Security, International Affairs and Criminal Justice; Domestic and International Monetary Policy; elected to the 104th Congress; reelected to the 105th Congress.

Office Listings

1239 Longworth House Office Building, Washington, DC 20515–3519 225–5731
Chief of Staff.—Brian Durdle. FAX: 225–9114
Legislative Director.—Michael Riith.
Office Administrator/District Scheduler.—Kathy Dalton.
1 Victoria Place, Room 320, Painesville, OH 44077 .... (216) 352–3939
FAX: 352–3622

Counties: Ashtabula, Cuyahoga (part), Lake. CITIES AND TOWNSHIPS: Andover, Ashtabula, Austinburg, Beachwood, Bedford, Bentleyville, Berea, Brecksville, Broadview Heights, Brook Park, Chagrin Falls, Concord, Conneaut, Dorset, Eastlake, Fairport, Fairport Harbor, Garfield Heights, Gates Mills, Geneva, Geneva on the Lake, Grand River, Highland Heights, Hunting Valley, Independence, Jefferson, Kingsville, Kirtland, Kirtland Hills, Lakeline, Lyndhurst, Madison, Maple Heights, Mayfield, Mayfield Heights, Mayfield Village, Mentor, Mentor on the Lake, Midpark, Middleburg Heights, Moreland Hills, North Kingsville, North Perry, North Royalton, Oakwood Village, Orwell, Painesville, Parma Heights, Pepper Pike, Perry, Pierpont, Richmond Heights, Roaming Shores, Rock Creek, Rome, Solon, Strongsville, Timberlake, Unionville, Waite Hill, Walton Hills, Wickliffe, Williamsfield, Willoughby, Willoughby Hills, Willowick, Windsor. Population (1990), 570,901.

ZIP Codes: 44003–04, 44010, 44017 (part), 44022–23, 44030, 44032, 44040–41, 44045, 44047–48, 44057, 44060–61, 44068, 44076–77, 44081–82, 44084–85, 44088, 44092–95, 44099, 44122 (part), 44124, 44130–31, 44133, 44136, 44139, 44141–43, 44146

OKLAHOMA

(Population 1995, 3,278,000)

SENATORS

DON NICKLES, Republican, of Ponca City, OK; born in Ponca City, December 6, 1948; graduated, Ponca City High School, 1967; B.S., business administration, Oklahoma State University, 1971; served in National Guard, 1970–76; vice president and general manager, Nickles Machine Corporation; served in Oklahoma State Senate, 1979–80; cofounder and member, Oklahoma Coalition for Peace Through Strength; served on the boards of: Ponca City United Way, St. Mary's Catholic Church Parish Council, Chamber of Commerce, Kay County Council for Retarded Children; chairman of the National Republican Senatorial Committee, 1988–90; chairman, Republican Policy Committee, 1991–95; assistant majority leader, 1996; member: Rotary Club, Fellowship of Christian Athletes; married to the former Linda Lou Morrison; four children: Don, Jenny, Kim, and Robyn; committees: Budget; Energy and Natural Resources; Finance; Governmental Affairs; Rules and Administration; elected to the U.S. Senate, November 4, 1980, for the six-year term beginning January 3, 1981; reelected November 4, 1986; reelected November 3, 1992 for the six-year term beginning January 3, 1993.

Office Listings

http://www.senate.gov/~nickles senator@nickles.senate.gov

133 Hart Senate Office Building, Washington, DC 20510–3602 224–5754
Administrative Assistant.—Bret Bernhardt. FAX: 224–6008
Communications Director.—Brook Simmons.
Press Secretary.—Gayle Osterberg.
Legislative Director.—Diane Mocry.
Scheduler.—Darci Davis.
1820 Liberty Tower, Oklahoma City, OK 73102 .... (405) 231–4941
National Bank Building, Suite 206, 601 D Avenue, Lawton, OK 73501 .... (405) 357–9878
3310 Mid-Continent Tower, 409 South Boston, Tulsa, OK 74103–4007 .... (918) 581–7651
1916 Lake Road, Ponca City, OK 74604 .... (405) 767–1270

* * *

JAMES M. INHOFE, Republican, of Tulsa, OK; born in Des Moines, IA on November 17, 1934; graduated Central High School, Tulsa, OK, 1953; B.A., University of Tulsa, OK, 1959; served in the U.S. Army, private first class, 1957–58; businessman; active pilot; president, Quaker Life Insurance Company; Oklahoma House of Representatives, 1967–69; Oklahoma State Senate, 1969–77; mayor of Tulsa, 1978–84; member, First Presbyterian Church of Tulsa; married to the former Kay Kirkpatrick; four children: Jim, Perry, Molly, and Katy; five grandchildren; committees: Armed Services, Environment and Public Works, Indian Affairs, Select Committee on Intelligence; elected to the 100th Congress on November 4, 1986; reelected to each succeeding Congress; elected to the unexpired term of Senator David Boren upon his resignation from the U.S. Senate on November 16, 1994.

Office Listings

http://www.senate.gov/~inhofe

453 Russell Senate Office Building, Washington, DC 20510 224–4721
Press Secretary.—Gary Hoitsma.
Administrative Assistant.—Herb Johnson.
Legislative Director.—Ruth Van Mark.
Scheduler.—Phillis Kreis.
Suite 530, 1924 South Utica, Tulsa, OK 74104 .... (918) 748–5111
Suite 2701, 204 North Robinson, Oklahoma City, OK 73102 .... (405) 231–4381
Suite 104, 302 North Independence, Enid, OK 73701 .... (405) 234–5104
Suite 106, 215 East Choctaw, McAlester, OK 74501 .... (918) 426–0933

REPRESENTATIVES

FIRST DISTRICT

STEVE LARGENT, Republican, of Tulsa, OK; born in Tulsa, September 28, 1954; graduated from Putnam City High School; B.S., University of Tulsa, 1976; professional athlete: National

Football League; pass receiver, Seattle Seahawks; inducted into the Pro Football Hall of Fame, 1995; proprietor, advertising and marketing consulting firm; serves on advisory board, Tulsa Area Salvation Army; board of trustees, University of Tulsa; remains active with the Fellowship of Christian Athletes and Focus on the Family; attends Fellowship Bible Church, Tulsa; married Terry Largent; four children: Casie, Kyle, Kelly, and Kramer; committees: Budget, Science, Commerce; subcommittees: Energy and Environment, Space and Aeronautics; elected to the 104th Congress; reelected to the 105th Congress.

Office Listings

http://www.house.gov/largent

410 Cannon House Office Building, Washington, DC 20510 225–2211
Administrative Assistant.—Terry Allen. FAX: 225–9817
Legislative Director.—Marie Wheat.
Press Secretary.—Nick Thimmesch.
Legislative Assistants: Bob Bolster, Paul Webster.
2424 East 21st Street, Suite 510, Tulsa, OK 74114 .... (918) 749–0014

Counties: Tulsa, Wagoner (part). Population (1990), 524,264.

ZIP Codes: 74008 (part), 74011, 74012 (part), 74013, 74014–15 (part), 74015 (part), 74021 (part), 74033 (part), 74036 (part), 74037, 74043, 74047 (part), 74050, 74055 (part), 74063 (part), 74066 (part), 74070 (part), 74073 (part), 74101–05, 74106 (part), 74107, 74108 (part), 74110, 74112, 74114, 74115, 74116 (part), 74117, 74119–21, 74126 (part), 74127 (part), 74128–30, 74132 (part), 74133–37, 74145–50, 74152–53, 74152, 74155–59, 74169–72, 74182, 74184, 74189, 74192–94, 74337 (part), 74352 (part), 74403 (part), 74429, 74434 (part), 74436 (part), 74446, 74457–58, 74467, 74477

* * *

SECOND DISTRICT

THOMAS ALLEN COBURN, Republican, of Muskogee, OK; born in Casper, WY, March 14, 1948; graduated, Central High School, Muskogee, OK, 1966; B.S., Oklahoma State University, 1970; Oklahoma University Medical School, 1983; manufacturing manager, Coburn Ophthalmic Division, Coburn Optical Industries, 1970–78; family physician, 1983–present; member: American Medical Association, Oklahoma State Medical Association, East Central County Medical Society, American Academy of Family Practice; member, First Baptist Church, ordained deacon; teacher, adult classes, First Baptist Church; promise keepers, Medical Mission Trip to Iraq and Haiti; married Carolyn Denton Coburn, 1968; three children: Callie Coburn Bonds, Katie, and Sarah.

Office Listings

511 Cannon House Office Building, Washington, DC 20515 225–2701
Administrative Director.—John Stirrup. FAX: 225–3038
Senior Legislative Assistants: Cheryl Crate, Doug Farry.
Scheduler.—Heather Barnthouse.
215 State Street, Suite 815, Muskogee, OK 74401 .... (918) 687–2533
Chief of Staff.—Karl Ahlgren. FAX: 682–8503
Press Secretary.—Fount Holland.
Scheduler.—Gwen Coburn.
120 South Missouri Street, Room 105, Claremore, OK 74017 .... (918) 341–9336
Field Representative.—Jo Rainbolt. FAX: 341–9437

Counties: Adair, Cherokee, Craig, Creek, Delaware, Haskell, Mayes, McIntosh, Muskogee, Nowata, Okfuskee, Okmulgee, Osage, Ottawa, Pawnee, Rogers, Sequoyah, and Wagoner. Population (1990), 524,264.

ZIP Codes: 74001–02, 74010, 74014–18, 74021, 74027–28, 74030–31, 74035–36, 74039, 74041–42, 74044, 74046–48, 74052–56, 74060, 74063, 74066–68, 74070–72, 74080, 74083–84, 74106, 74108, 74116, 74126–27, 74131–32, 74149, 74301, 74330–33, 74335, 74337–40, 74342–44, 74346–47, 74349–50, 74352–55, 74358–70, 74401–03, 74421–23, 74426–29, 74431–32, 74434–38, 74440–41, 74444–47, 74450–52, 74454–72, 74477, 74552, 74637, 74829, 74833, 74835, 74845, 74859, 74860, 74862, 74880, 74882, 74931, 74936, 74941, 74943–46, 74948, 74954–55, 74960, 74962, 74964–65

* * *

THIRD DISTRICT

WES WATKINS, Republican, of Stillwater, OK; born in DeQueen, AR, December 15, 1938; B.S., M.S., Oklahoma State University; president, World Export Services, Inc., an oil, real estate, and telecommunications investment company; served 14 years in U.S. House of Representatives; founding member, Congressional Trade Caucus; past president, House Rural Caucus and U.S. Congress Prayer Breakfast Group; served two years in Oklahoma Senate; married to Lou Watkins; three children; committee: Ways and Means; elected to the 105th Congress.

Office Listings

2312 Rayburn Building, Washington, DC 20515 225–4565
Chief of Staff/Press Secretary.—Leslie Belcher. FAX: 225–5966
Executive Assistant/Office Manager.—Judy Shaffer.
Legislative Assistant/System Manager.—Jeff Hampton.
Legislative Assistants: Scott Raab, Jeff Stromberg.
118 Carl Albert Federal Building, McAlester, OK 74501 .... (918) 423–5951
Caseworker/Office Manager.—Sue Bollinger. FAX: 423–1457
Community and Constituent Services.—Betty Ford.
1511 Cimarron Plaza, Stillwater, OK 74075 .... (405) 743–1400
Caseworker.—Nancy Rogers. FAX: 743–0680
Staff Assistant.—Jamee Majid.
P.O. Box 1600, Ada, OK 74820 .... (405) 436–1980
Caseworker/Office Manager.—Sissy Kiser. FAX: 332–7421
Community and Constituent Services.—Dustin Rowe.

Counties: Atoka, Bryan, Carter, Choctaw, Coal, Hughes, Johnston, Latimer, Le Flore, Lincoln, Love, McCurtain, Marshall, Murray, Pawnee (part), Payne, Pittsburg, Pontotoc, Pottawatomie, Pushmataha, and Seminole. Population (1990), 524,264.

ZIP Codes: 73027 (part), 73030, 73032, 73045 (part), 73046 (part), 73054 (part), 73063 (part), 73073 (part), 73081 (part), 73086–88, 73098 (part), 73401–03, 73430, 73432, 73435–37, 73438 (part), 73439–41, 73443, 73446–50, 73452–53, 73455, 73456 (part), 73458–61, 73463, 74020, 74023 (part), 74026, 74030 (part), 74032 (part), 74038, 74045, 74058–59, 74062, 74074 (part), 74075–76, 74079 (part), 74085 (part), 74425, 74430, 74432 (part), 74442, 74501–02, 74521–23, 74525–26, 74528–31, 74533–36, 74538, 74540, 74542–43, 74545–49, 74553–60, 74561 (part), 74562–63, 74565, 74567, 74569–72, 74574, 74576–78, 74650, 74701–02, 74720–24, 74726–31, 74733–38, 74740–41, 74743, 74745, 74747–48, 74750, 74752–56, 74759–61, 74763–64, 74766, 74801–02, 74818, 74820–21, 74824–27, 74829 (part), 74830, 74831 (part), 74832, 74833 (part), 74834, 74835 (part), 74836–38, 74839 (part), 74840, 74842–44, 74848–50, 74851 (part), 74852, 74854–56, 74857 (part), 74859 (part), 74863–64, 74865 (part), 74866–69, 74871, 74872 (part), 74873, 74875, 74878, 74881 (part), 74883 (part), 74884, 74901–02, 74930, 74932, 74935, 74937, 74939–40, 74941 (part), 74942, 74947, 74949, 74951, 74953, 74956–57, 74959, 74963, 74966

* * *

FOURTH DISTRICT

JULIUS C. WATTS, Jr., Republican, of Norman, OK; born in Eufaula, OK, November 18, 1957; graduated Eufaula High School, 1976; B.A., journalism, University of Oklahoma; esquire management, esquire property; quarterback, CFL, 1981–86; ordained minister, 1993; youth minister, 1987–95; Oklahoma Corporation Commission, 1991–95; commission chairman, 1992–95; served on the National Drinking Water Advisory Council, Electricity Committee of the National Association of Regulatory Utility Commissioners; member, Fellowship of Christian Athletes, Oklahoma Special Olympics; national speaking tour, Anti-Drug Campaign; honorary chairman, Susan Komen Breast Cancer Foundation; married Frankie Jean Watts in 1977; five children: LaKesha, Jerrell, Jennifer, Julia, and Troy.

Office Listings

1210 Longworth House Office Building, Washington, DC 20515–3604 225–6165
Legislative Director.—Douglas J. Lamude. FAX: 225–3512
Press Secretary.—Pam Pryor.
Suite 120, 2420 Springer Drive, Norman, OK 73069 .... (405) 329–6500
Chief of Staff.—Mike Hunter.
Suite 205, 601 D Avenue, Lawton, OK 73501 .... (405) 357–2131
District Representative.—Suzanne Hogan.

Counties: Cleveland, Comanche, Cotton, Garvin, Grady, Jackson, Jefferson, McClain, Oklahoma (part), Stephens, and Tillman. Population (1990), 524,265.

ZIP Codes: 73443, 73446–50, 73453, 73455, 73458–59, 73461, 73463, 74832, 74834, 74836–37, 74839, 74842–44, 74848–49, 74852, 74854–55, 74860, 74865–69, 74871–73, 74875, 74880, 74929

FIFTH DISTRICT

ERNEST J. ISTOOK, JR., Republican, of Oklahoma City, OK; born in Fort Worth, TX, on February 11, 1950; graduated, Castleberry High School, Ft. Worth, 1967; B.A., Baylor University, 1971; J.D., Oklahoma City University, 1976; attorney; admitted to the Oklahoma bar, 1977; reporter, WKY, KOMA, 1972–77; city councilman, Warr Acres, 1982–86; library board chairman, Oklahoma City, 1985–86; director, Warr Acres Chamber of Commerce, 1986–92; Oklahoma State House of Representatives, 1986–92; married the former Judy Bills, 1973; five children: Butch, Chad, Amy, Diana, and Emily; elected on November 3, 1992 to the 103rd Congress; reelected to each succeding Congress.

Office Listings

http://www.house.gov/istook/welcome.htm

119 Cannon House Office Building, Washington, DC 20515–3605 225–2132
Administrative Assistant/Legislative Director.—Steve Jones. FAX: 226–1463
Office Manager/Scheduler.—Kim Rubin.
Press Secretary.—Kristy Khachigian.
Suite 505, 5400 North Grand Boulevard, Oklahoma City, OK 73112 .... (405) 942–3636
Fifth and Grand, Ponca City, OK 74601 .... (405) 762–6778
Suite 205, First Court Place, Bartlesville, OK 74003 .... (918) 336–5546

Counties: Canadian (part); Kay; Logan; Noble; Oklahoma (part); Osage (part); Washington. CITIES AND TOWNSHIPS: Bartlesville, Bethany, Edmond, Cashion, Choctaw, Collinsville, Crescent, Glencoe, Edmond, El Reno, Guthrie, Harrah, Jones, Luther, Marshall, Meridian, Mustang, Norman, Orlando, Stillwater, Perry, Piedmont, Talala, Yale, Yukon, Oklahoma City, Ponca City, Billings, Blackwell, Cordell, Fairfax, Kaw City, Nardin, Newkirk, Raiston, Red Rock, Shidler, Tonkawa, Enid, Newalla, Wellston. Population (1990), 524,264.

ZIP Codes: 73007–08, 73013, 73020 (part), 73027, 73028, 73034 (part), 73044, 73045 (part), 73049 (part), 73050, 73054, 73056, 73058, 73061, 73063, 73064 (part), 73073 (part), 73077, 73078 (part), 73083, 73084 (part), 73085, 73099 (part), 73103, 73106–08, 73109 (part), 73111, 73112, 73114, 73116 (part), 73118, 73119 (part), 73120, 73121, 73122 (part), 73123, 73127–28, 73131, 73132, 73134, 73137, 73142, 73146–48, 73151, 73156–57, 73162, 73177–79, 73184, 73757, 74003–06, 74009, 74022, 74029, 74051, 74056, 74061, 74070, 74601–04, 74630–33, 74641, 74644, 74646–47, 74651–53, 74857 (part)

* * *

SIXTH DISTRICT

FRANK DEAN LUCAS, Republican, of Cheyenne, OK; born in Cheyenne, January 6, 1960; attended Oklahoma State University, Stillwater, 1982; rancher and farmer; served in Oklahoma State House of Representatives, 1989–94; secretary, House Republican Caucus, 1991–94; member: Oklahoma Farm Bureau, Oklahoma Cattlemen's Association, and Oklahoma Shorthorn Association; married to Lynda Bradshaw Lucas; three children: Jessica, Ashlea, and Grant; elected to the 103rd Congress; reelected to each succeeding Congress.

Office Listings

http://www.house.gov/lucas

107 Cannon House Office Building, Washington, DC 20515–3606 225–5565
Press Secretary.—Randy Swanson.
Legislative Assistants: Maura McGilvray, Owen Pinkerton. FAX: 225–8698
Legislative Counsel.—Natalie Rule.
Legislative Assistant/Systems Administrator.—Amy Blair.
109 Old Post Office Building, 215 Dean A. McGee Avenue, Oklahoma City, OK 73102 .... (405) 576–5511
Chief of Staff.—Allen B. Wright.
Federal Building, P.O. Box 3612, Enid, OK 73701 .... (405) 233–9224
Field Representative.—Curt Roggow.
2728 Williams Avenue, Suite F, Woodward, OK 73801 .... (405) 256–5752
Field Representative.—Tammie R. Smith.

Counties: Alfalfa, Beacer, Beckham, Blaine, Caddo, Canadian (part), Cimarron, Custer, Dewey, Ellis, Garfield, Grant, Greer, Harmon, Harper, Kingfisher, Kiowa, Major, Oklahoma (part), Roger Mills, Texas, Washita, Woods, and Woodward. Population (1990), 524,264.

ZIP Codes: 73001, 73005, 73006 (part), 73009, 73014–15, 73016 (part), 73017 (part), 73021–22, 73024, 73028 (part), 73029, 73033, 73036, 73038, 73040–43, 73047–48, 73053, 73056 (part), 73059 (part), 73062, 73064, 73073 (part), 73078 (part), 73079 (part), 73085, 73090, 73092 (part), 73094, 73096, 73099, 73101–02, 73103 (part), 73104–06, 73109 (part), 73111 (part), 73115, 73117 (part), 73119 (part), 73121, 73124–26, 73129 (part), 73132 (part), 73133, 73135–36, 73139 (part), 73143–44, 73146, 73149 (part), 73152, 73154–55, 73159, 73160 (part), 73169, 73176, 73179 (part), 73190, 73541 (part), 73544, 73547, 73550, 73552 (part), 73554 (part), 73559 (part), 73564, 73566 (part), 73571,

73601, 73620, 73622, 73624–28, 73632, 73638–39, 73641–42, 73644–48, 73650–51, 73654–56, 73658–64, 73666–69, 73673, 73701–03, 73706, 73716–20, 73722–31, 73733–39, 73741–44, 73746–47, 73749–50, 73753–56, 73757 (part), 73758–64, 73766, 73768, 73770–73, 73801–03, 73832, 73834–35, 73838, 73840–44, 73847–49, 73851–53, 73855, 73857–60, 73901, 73931–33, 73935, 73937–39, 73942, 73944–46, 73947 (part), 73948–51, 74630 (part), 74636, 74640, 74643, 74646 (part)

OREGON

(Population 1995, 3,141,000)

SENATORS

RON WYDEN, Democrat, of Portland, OR; born in Wichita, KS, on May 3, 1949; graduated from Palo Alto High School, 1967; B.A. in political science, with distinction, Stanford University, 1971; J.D., University of Oregon Law School, 1974; attorney; member, American Bar Association; former director, Oregon Legal Services for the Elderly; former public member, Oregon State Board of Examiners of Nursing Home Administrators; cofounder and codirector, Oregon Gray Panthers, 1974–80; married the former Laurie Oseran, 1978; two children: Adam David and Lilly Anne; elected to the 97th Congress, November 4, 1980; reelected to each succeeding Congress; elected to the U.S. Senate on January 30, 1996 to fill the unexpired term of Senator Bob Packwood; committees: Budget; Commerce, Science and Transportation, Energy and Natural Resources; Environment and Public Works; Special Committee on Aging.

Office Listings

http://www.senate.gov/~wyden senator@wyden.senate.gov

717 Hart Senate Office Building, Washington, DC 20510 224–5244
Chief of Staff.—Josh Kardon.
Legislative Director.—Carole Grunberg.
Communications Director.—David Seldin.
Scheduler.—Bruck Ehrle.
500 NE Multnomah Street, Suite 320, Portland, OR 97232 .... (503) 326–7525
151 West Seventh Avenue, Suite 435, Eugene, OR 97401 .... (541) 431–0229
The Federal Courthouse, 310 West Sixth Street, Room 118, Medford, OR 97501 .. (541) 858–5122
The Jamison Building, 131 NW Hawthorne Avenue, Suite 107, Bend, OR 97701 .. (541) 330–9142
Sac Annex Building, 105 Fir Street, Suite 210, LaGrande, OR 97850 .... (541) 962–7691
777 13th Street, SE, Suite 110, Salem, OR 97310 .... (503) 589–4555

* * *

GORDON HAROLD SMITH, Republican, of Pendleton, OR; born May 25, 1952, in Pendleton, B.A., 1976, Brigham Young University; LL.B, 1979, Southwestern University; served as law clerk to Justice H. Vernon Payne of the New Mexico Supreme Court and practiced law in Arizona; elected to State of Oregon Senate, 1993; elected Oregon Senate President, 1994; president/owner of Smith Frozen Foods, Inc. since 1981; committees: Budget, Energy and Natural Resources, Foreign Relations; elected to the U.S. Senate in November 1996; married Sharon Lankford Smith in 1975; three children: Brittany, Garrett, Morgan.

Office Listings

http://www.senate.gov/~gsmith oregon@gsmith.senate.gov

B–40 Dirksen Senate Office Building, Suite 2, Washington, DC20510–1001 224–3753
Chief of Staff.—Kurt Pfotenhauer.
Legislative Director.—Penny Schiller.
Office Manager.—Lynn Hemmerich.
Press Secretary.—John Easton.
1220 SW Third, Suite 618, Wyatt Federal Building, Portland, OR 97204 .... (503) 326–3386
FAX: 326–2900

REPRESENTATIVES

FIRST DISTRICT

ELIZABETH FURSE, Democrat, of Hillsboro, OR; born on October, 13, 1936 in Nairobi, Kenya; B.A., Evergreen State College, WA, 1974; attended, Northwestern School of Law, Portland, OR, 1978–79; community activist; co-owner, Helvetia Vineyards, Hillsboro, OR; cofounder and director, Oregon Peace Institute, 1985–91; community organizer, Citizens Train, 1988; founder, Black Sash (a South African women's anti-apartheid group); Oregon Legal Services, 1980–86; member: Rotary International, Downtown Portland, District 510; Oregonians Against Gun Violence; Durfee Award, an international award for the effective use of the legislative process to benefit a community, 1986; lobbied Congress to pass legislation restoring legal status to three Oregon tribes, 1980–86; well known for her work on behalf of low-income women, farm workers and Native Americans; American Leadership Forum Fellow, 1991; married in 1980 to John Platt; two children: Amanda and John; committee: Commerce; subcommittees: Energy and Power; Health and Environment; Telecommunications and Finance; Commerce, Trade and Hazardous Materials; cochair, cofounder of the Congressional Diabetes Caucus; founder of Congressional Sustainable Development Caucus; member, Congressional Education Caucus, Internet Caucus; Law Enforcement Caucus; Older Americans Caucus; elected on November 3, 1992 to the 103rd Congress; reelected to each succeeding Congress.

Office Listings

http://www.house.gov/furse/welcome.html rep.elizabeth.furse@hr.house.gov

316 Cannon House Office Building, Washington, DC 20515–3701 225–0855
Legislative Director.—Christopher Porter.
Executive Assistant.—Lesley Bennett.
Press Secretary.—Sarah Anderson.
Administrative Assistant.—Jennie Kugel. FAX: 225–9497
860 Montgomery Park, 2701 NW Vaughn Street, Portland, OR 97210 .... (503) 326–2901

Counties: Clackamas (part), Clatsop, Columbia, Multnomah (part), Washington, and Yamhill. Population (1990), 524,264.

ZIP Codes: 97005–07, 97016, 97018, 97034 (part), 97035 (part), 97048, 97051, 97053–54, 97056, 97062 (part), 97064, 97075–77, 97101–03, 97106–19, 97121–25, 97127–28, 97130–31, 97132 (part), 97133–36, 97138, 97140 (part), 97141, 97143–49, 97200–01, 97203 (part), 97204–05, 97207–10, 97219 (part), 97221, 97223–25, 97228–29, 97231, 97240, 97258, 97304 (part), 97338 (part), 97341, 97343–44, 97361 (part), 97364–69, 97371 (part), 97372, 97376, 97378, 97380, 97388, 97390 (part), 97391, 97394, 97498 (part)

* * *

SECOND DISTRICT

ROBERT F. (BOB) SMITH, Republican, of Medford, OR; born June 16, 1931 in Portland, OR; B.A., business administration and economics, Willamette University, 1953; rancher and businessman; House majority leader and speaker pro tempore of Oregon Legislature, 1964–66; Speaker of the House, 1968–72; State Senator, 1972–82, and Senate Republican Leader, 1978–82; served six terms in the U.S. House of Representatives (1983–95); board of trustees, Willamette University; married Kaye Tomlinson in 1966; three children: Christopher, Matthew and Tiffany; chairman, Agriculture Committee; elected to the 105th Congress.

Office Listings

1126 Longworth House Office Building, Washington, DC 20515 225–6730
Administrative Assistant.—Brian MacDonald. FAX: 225–5774
Office Manager.—Sara Coon.
Press Secretary.—Ron Reese.
Legislative Director.—Doug Badger.
843 East Main, Suite 400, Medford, OR 97504 .... (541) 776–4646
District Director.—John Snider. FAX: 779–0204

Counties: Baker, Crook, Deschutes, Gilliam, Grant, Harney, Hood River, Jackson, Jefferson, Josephine (part), Klamath, Lake, Malheur, Morrow, Sherman, Umatilla, Union, Wallowa, Wasco, and Wheeler. Population (1990), 568,464.

ZIP Codes: 97001, 97014 (part), 97021, 97029, 97031, 97033, 97037, 97039–41, 97044, 97050, 97057–58, 97063, 97065, 97425, 97501–04, 97520, 97522–24, 97525 (part), 97526 (part), 97527, 97530–31, 97532 (part), 97533–34, 97535 (part), 97536–40, 97541 (part), 97543–44, 97601–04, 97620–27, 97630, 97632–41, 97701–02, 97707–08, 97710–12, 97720–22, 97730–41, 97750–54, 97756, 97758–61, 97801, 97810, 97812–14, 97817–21, 97823–28, 97830–31, 97833–46, 97848, 97850, 97856–57, 97859, 97861–62, 97864–65, 97867–70, 97872–77, 97880, 97882–86, 97901–09, 97910 (part), 97911, 97913–14, 97917–20

* * *

THIRD DISTRICT

EARL BLUMENAUER, Democrat, of Portland, OR; born on August 16, 1948 in Portland; graduated from Centennial High School; Lewis and Clark College, J.D., Northwestern School of Law; assistant to the president, Portland State University; served in Oregon State Legislature 1973–78; chaired revenue and school finance committee; Multnomah County Commissioner, 1978–85; Portland City Commissioner 1986–96; served on Governor's Commission on Higher Education, National League of Cities Transportation Committee, National Civic League board of directors, Oregon Environmental Council, Oregon Public Broadcasting; elected to the U.S. House of Representatives on May 21, 1996 to fill the vacancy created by Representative Ron Wyden's election to the Senate, two children: Jon and Anne.

Office Listings

1113 Longworth House Office Building, Washington, DC 20515 225–4811
Administrative Assistant.—Bob Crane. FAX: 225–8941
Legislative Director.—Stephanie Vance.
Press Secretary.—Pat Forguy.
Scheduler.—Stephanie Henley.
516 SE Morrison Street, Suite 250, Portland, OR 97214 .... (503) 231–2300

Counties: Multnomah, Clakamus.

ZIP Codes: 97009 (part), 97010, 97011, 97015, 97019, 97024, 97028, 97030, 97049, 97055, 97060, 97067, 97080, 97202, 97203, 97206, 97210 (part), 97211–18, 97219 (part), 97220, 97222, 97227, 97229 (part), 97230, 97231–33, 97236, 97242, 97266, 97267 (part)

* * *

FOURTH DISTRICT

PETER A. DeFAZIO, Democrat, of Springfield, OR; born in Needham, MA, May 27, 1947; B.A., Tufts University, 1969; M.S., University of Oregon, 1977; aide to Representative Jim Weaver, 1977–82; Lane County commissioner, 1983–86; committees: Resources, Transportation and Infrastructure; elected to the 100th Congress, November 4, 1986; reelected to each succeeding Congress.

Office Listings
http://www.house.gov/defazio/index.htm

2134 Rayburn House Office Building, Washington, DC 20515–3704 225–6416
Administrative Assistant.—Penny Dodge.
Legislative Director.—Jeff Stier.
151 West Seventh Avenue, Eugene, OR 97401 .... (503) 465–6732
District Coordinator.—Betsy Boyd. (800) 944–9603
P.O. Box 1557, Coos Bay, OR 97420 .... (503) 269–2609
P.O. Box 2460, Roseberg, OR 97470 .... (503) 440–3523

Counties: Benton (part), Coos, Curry, Douglas, Josephine (part), Lane, Linn. Population (1990), 568,465.

ZIP Codes: 97321, 97324, 97326–27, 97329, 97330 (part), 97333, 97335–36, 97339, 97345–46 (part), 97348, 97350 (part), 97355, 97358 (part), 97360, 97370, 97374 (part), 97377 (part), 97386, 97389, 97390 (part), 97401–08, 97409–17, 97419–20, 97423–24, 97426–32, 97434–44, 97446–70, 97472–73, 97476–82, 97484, 97486–97, 97499, 97526 (part), 97532

* * *

FIFTH DISTRICT

DARLENE HOOLEY, Democrat, of West Linn, OR; born on April 4, 1939; B.S., education, Oregon State University; teacher and girls' sports coach; past member: Oregon House of Representatives, West Linn City Council, Clackamas County Board of Commissioners; married to John Hooley; two children, Chad and Erin; committees: Banking and Financial Services, Science; elected to the 105th Congress.

Office Listings

1419 Longworth House Office Building, Washington, DC 20515 225-5711
Chief of Staff.—Joan Mooney. FAX: 225–5699
Executive Assistant/Scheduler.—Margaret Ellis.
Press Secretary.—David Danzig.
Legislative Director.—Lori Denham.
315 Mission Street, Suite 101, Salem, OR 97302 .... (503) 588–9100
District Director.—Beth Bernard.

Counties: Benton (part); Clackamas (part); Lincoln; Marion; Polk; Tillamook; cities of Salem, Corvallis, and Tillamook. Population (1990), 568,466.

ZIP Codes: 97002, 97004, 97009 (part), 97013, 97015, 97017, 97020, 97022–23, 97026 (part), 97027 (part), 97032, 97034 (part), 97035–36, 97038, 97042, 97045, 97055, 97062 (part), 97068 (part), 97070–71, 97107–08, 97112, 97118, 97122, 97130–31, 97134–37, 97141, 97143, 97147, 97149, 97222, 97267 (part), 97268 (part), 97301–03, 97304 (part), 97305–06, 97308–09, 97321 (part), 97325 (part), 97326, 97330–31, 97333, 97338 (part), 97341–47, 97350 (part), 97351 (part), 97352, 97357, 97359–60, 97361 (part), 97362, 97364–73, 97375–76, 97378, 97380–81, 97383–85, 97390–94, 97498

PENNSYLVANIA

(Population 1995, 12,072,000)

SENATORS

ARLEN SPECTER, Republican, of Philadelphia, PA; born in Wichita, KS, February 12, 1930; graduated, Russell High School, Russell, KS, 1947; University of Pennsylvania, 1951, B.A., international relations, Phi Beta Kappa; Yale Law School, LL.B., 1956; board of editors, *Law Journal*; served in U.S. Air Force, 1951–53, attaining rank of first lieutenant; member, law firm of Dechert, Price and Rhoads before and after serving two terms as district attorney of Philadelphia, 1966–74; married the former Joan Levy, who was elected to the city council of Philadelphia in 1979; two sons: Shanin and Stephen; served as assistant counsel to the Warren Commission, 1964; served on Pennsylvania's State Planning Board, The White House Conference on Youth, The National Commission on Criminal Justice, and the Peace Corps National Advisory Council; elected to the U.S. Senate, November 4, 1980, for the six-year term beginning January 5, 1981; committees: Veterans' Affairs, chair; Appropriations; chair, Judiciary; Governmental Affairs; subcommittees: Agriculture; Rural Development, and Related Agencies; Defense; Foreign Operations; chair, Labor, Health and Human Services; ranking member, Transportation; Antitrust, Business Rights, and Competition; Immigration; Technology, Terrorism, and Government Information.

Office Listings

http://www.senate.gov/~specter senator__specter@specter.senate.gov

530 Hart Senate Office Building, Washington, DC 20510–3802 224–4254
Administrative Assistant.—Craig Snyder. FAX: 228–1229
Legislative Director.—Dan Renberg.
Office Manager.—Jill Schugardt.
Press Secretary.—Jon Ullyot.
Suite 9400, 600 Arch Street, Philadelphia, PA 19106 .... (215) 597–7200
Federal Building, Suite 2017, Liberty Avenue/Grant Street, Pittsburgh, PA 15222 .. (412) 644–3400
Federal Building, Room 107, Sixth and State Streets, Erie, PA 16501 .... (814) 453–3010
Federal Building, Room 1159, 228 Walnut Street, Harrisburg, PA 17101 .... (717) 782–3951
Post Office Building, Room 201, 5th and Hamilton Streets, Allentown, PA 18101 (610) 434–1444
310 Spruce Street, No. 201, Scranton, PA 18503 .... (717) 346–2006
South Main Towers, Room 306, 116 South Main Street, Wilkes Barre, PA 18701 (717) 826–6265

* * *

RICHARD JOHN SANTORUM, Republican, of Mount Lebanon, PA; born in Winchester, VA, May 10, 1958; graduated Carmel High School, 1976; B.A., Pennsylvania State University, 1980; M.B.A., University of Pittsburgh, 1981; J.D., Dickinson School of Law, 1986; admitted to the Pennsylvania bar; member: Rotary, Bethel Park USC; Italian Sons and Daughters Association; Knights of Columbus; Big Brothers and Sisters of Greater Pittsburgh Advisory Board; Tyrolean Society, Western Pennsylvania; Sons of Italy; administrative assistant to State Senator J. Doyle Corman (R.-Centre), 1981–86: director of the Senate Local Government Committee, 1981–84; director of the Senate Transportation Committee, 1984–86; associate attorney, Kirkpatrick and Lockhart, Pittsburgh, PA, 1986–90; married Karen Garver Santorum, 1990; three children: Elizabeth Anne, Richard John, Jr., and Dainel James; committees: Agriculture, Nutrition and Forestry; Armed Services; Rules and Administration; Special Committee on Aging; subcommittess: chairman, Forestry, Conservation and Rural Revitalization; chairman, Acquisition and Technology; elected to the 102nd Congress; reelected to each succeeding Congress; elected as U.S. Senator in 104th Congress on November 8, 1994.

Office Listings

http://www.senate.gov/~santorum senator@santorum.senate.gov

120 Russell Senate Office Building, Washington, DC 20510 224–6324
Chief of Staff.—Mark Rodgers. FAX:228-0604
Executive Assistant.—Ramona Ely.
Legislative Director.—Michael Hershey.
Office Manager.—David Hall.
1705 West 26th Street, Erie, PA 16508 .... (814) 454–7114
FAX: 459–2096
221 Strawberry Square, Harrisburg, PA 17101 .... (717) 231–7540
FAX: 231–7542
3804 Federal Building, 504 West Hamilton Street, Allentown, PA 18015 .... (610) 770–0142
FAX: 770–0911
Regency Square, Suite 202, Route 220 North, Altoona, PA 16001 .... (814) 946–7023

	FAX: 946–7025
Widener Building, One South Penn Square, Suite 960, Philadelphia, PA 19107	(215) 864–6900
	FAX: 597–4771
Landmarks Building, One Station Square, Suite 250, Pittsburgh, PA 15219	(412) 562–0533
	FAX: 562–4313
527 Linden Street, Scranton, PA 18503	(717) 344–8799
	FAX: 344–8906

REPRESENTATIVES

FIRST DISTRICT

THOMAS M. FOGLIETTA, Democrat, of Philadelphia, PA; born in Philadelphia, December 3, 1928; graduated, South Catholic High School, 1945; B.A., St. Joseph's College, 1949; J.D., Temple University School of Law, 1952; lawyer; member: Supreme Court of the United States, Supreme Court of Pennsylvania, Courts of Common Pleas of Philadelphia County; Municipal Court of Philadelphia; youngest city councilman in Philadelphia's history, 1955; minority leader of Philadelphia's City Council; regional director, U.S. Department of Labor, 1976; elected to the 97th Congress, November 4, 1980; reelected to each succeeding Congress.

Office Listings

http://www.house.gov/foglietta/yopage.htm mailtoma@hr.house.gov

242 Cannon House Office Building, Washington, DC 20515–3801	225–4731
Administrative Assistant/Counsel.—Anthony Green.	FAX: 225–0088
Executive Assistant.—Kathleen Carmody.	
Legislative Director.—Barbara Zylinski.	
William J. Green Building, Room 10402, 600 Arch Street, Philadelphia, PA 19106	(215) 925–6840
1806 South Broad Street, Philadelphia, PA 19148	(215) 463–8702
1510 West Cecil B. Moore Avenue, Suite 304, Philadelphia, PA 19121	(215) 236–5430
The Colony Building, 511–13 Welsh Street, Chester, PA 19013	(610) 874–7094

Counties: Delaware (part); Philadelphia (part). Cities and townships: Chester City (part), Eddystone Borough, Colwyn Borough, Tinicum Township, Darby Township (part), Folcroft Borough, Darby Township (part), Glenolden Borough, Darby Township (part). Population (1990), 565,842.

ZIP Codes: 19013 (part), 19015 (part), 19023 (part), 19029, 19032, 19036 (part), 19074 (part), 19079 (part), 19102 (part), 19106 (part), 19107 (part), 19108, 19112–13, 19120 (part), 19121 (part), 19222 (part), 19123 (part), 19124 (part), 19125 (part), 19126 (part), 19129 (part), 19130 (part), 19132 (part), 19133 (part), 19134 (part), 19138 (part), 19140 (part), 19141, 19142 (part), 19143 (part), 19144 (part), 19145 (part), 19146 (part), 19147 (part), 19148, 19150 (part), 19153, 19160

* * *

SECOND DISTRICT

CHAKA FATTAH, Democrat, of Philadelphia, PA; born in Philadelphia; attended Overbrook High School, Community College of Philadelphia, University of Pennsylvania's Wharton School; M.A., University of Pennsylvania's Fels School of State and Local Government, 1986; Harvard University's John F. Kennedy School of Government; recognized for outstanding leadership in *Time* magazine, and in *Ebony* magazine as one of 50 Future Leaders; recipient, Pennsylvania Public Interest Coalition's State Legislator of the Year Award; Pennsylvania State Senate, 1988–94; State House of Representatives, 1982–88; created the Jobs Project; in Pennsylvania House of Representatives, sponsored 1987 Employment Opportunities Act; supported Ben Franklin Technology Center, a conduit for securing government contracts for African-American and women-owned businesses; founded Graduate Opportunities Conference; chairman of the executive committee of the Pennsylvania Higher Education Assistance Agency; convened and led a task force, Child Development Initiative; supported measures to reform the Philadelphia Housing Authority; formed the Drug-Free Program; founded American Cities Conference and Foundation; trustee, Lincoln University and Community College of Philadelphia; member, Mt. Carmel Baptist Church; married to the former Patricia Renfroe, Esq.; three children; committees: Government Reform and Oversight, Education and the Workforce; subcommittees: Human Resources and Intergovernmental Relations, District of Columbia.

Office Listings
http://www.house.gov/fattah

1205 Longworth House Office Building, Washington, DC 20515–3802 225–4001
Administrative Assistant/Legislative Director.—Claudia Pharis.
Press Secretary.—Lydia Sermons.
4104 Walnut Street, Philadelphia, PA 19104 .... (215) 387–6404

Counties: Delaware (part), Philadelphia (part). Population (1990), 565,650.

ZIP Codes: 19101 (part), 19102 (part), 19103 (part), 19104 (part), 19119 (part), 19121, 19126 (part), 19129, 19130 (part), 19131–32, 19138–39, 19140 (part), 19141 (part), 19143 (part), 19144, 19146 (part), 19150, 19151 (part)

* * *

THIRD DISTRICT

ROBERT A. BORSKI, Democrat, of Philadelphia, PA; born in Philadelphia on October 20, 1948; graduated, Frankford High School, Philadelphia, 1966; B.A., University of Baltimore, Baltimore, MD, 1971; former stockbroker; member, Philadelphia Stock Exchange; elected to the Pennsylvania House of Representatives, 1976, 1978, and 1980; five children: Jill, Darci, Jen, Robert, and Maggie; elected on November 2, 1982 to the 98th Congress; reelected to each succeeding Congress.

Office Listings
rborski@hr.house.gov

2182 Rayburn House Office Building, Washington, DC 20515–3803 225–8251
Administrative Assistant.—Alan Slomowitz. FAX: 225–4628
Scheduler.—Danielle Pettine.
7141 Frankford Avenue, Philadephia, PA 19135 .... (215) 335–3355
District Director.—John F. Dempsey.
2630 Memphis Street, Philadelphia, PA 19125 .... (215) 426–4616

Counties: Philadelphia (part). Population (1990), 565,860.

ZIP Codes: 19106 (part), 19107 (part), 19111, 19114–16, 19120 (part), 19122 (part), 19123 (part), 19124, 19125 (part), 19133 (part), 19134 (part), 19135–37, 19140 (part), 19147 (part), 19149, 19152, 19154

* * *

FOURTH DISTRICT

RON KLINK, Democrat, of Jeannette, PA; born September 23, 1951, in Canton, OH; graduated Meyersdale High School, 1969; reporter and anchorman, KDKA–TV, Pittsburgh, PA; awards: Associated Press, Golden Quill; member: Youngwood (PA) Volunteer Fire Department; board member, Forbes Road Vocational Technical School, Monroeville, PA; partner, Dagwood's Restaurant; married the former Linda Hogan, August 27, 1977; two children, Matthew and Juliana; elected on November 3, 1992 to the 103rd Congress; reelected to each succeeding Congress.

Office Listings

125 Cannon House Office Building, Washington, DC 20515–3804 225–2565
Administrative Assistant.—Mary Kiernan. FAX: 226–2274
Legislative Director.—Peter Madaus.
North Huntingdon Township, 11279 Center Highway, North Huntingdon, PA 15642 .... (800) 453–5078 FAX:(412) 864–8681
Suite 305, Beaver Trust Building, 250 Insurance Street, Beaver, PA 15009–2761 .. (412) 728–3005
Cranberry Township Municipal Building, 2525 Rochester Road, Suite 207, Cranberry Township, PA 16066–6422 .... (412) 772–6080
The Castleton, 134 North Mercer Street, New Castle, PA 16101–3715 .... (412) 654–9036
2692 Leechburg Road, Lower Burrell, PA 15068–0343 .... (412) 335–4518

Counties: Allegheny (part), Beaver, Butler (part), Lawrence, Westmoreland (part). CITIES AND TOWNSHIPS: Adams, Aliquippa, Allegheny, Ambridge, Arnold Baden, Beaver, Beaver Falls, Bessemer, Big Beaver, Brackenridge, Bradford Woods,

Bridgewater, Brighton, Buffalo, Center, Cheswick, Chippewa, Clinton, Conway, Cranberry, Darlington, Daugherty, Delmont, East Deer, East Rochester, East Vandergrift, Eastvale, Economy, Ellport, Ellwood City, Enon Valley Export, Fallstown, Fawn, Frankfort Spring, Franklin, Frazer, Freedom, Georgetown Glasgow, Greene, Hanover, Harmony, Harrison, Hickory, Homewood, Hookstown, Hopewell, Hyde Park, Independence, Industry, Irwin, Jackson, Jeannette, Koppel, Little Beaver, Lower Burrell, Mahoning, Manor, Marion, Mars, Marshall Middlesex, Midland, Monaca, Murrysville, Neshannock, New Beaver, New Brighton, New Castle, New Galilee, New Kensington, New Sewickley, New Wilmington, North Beaver, North Huntingdon, North Irwin, North Sewickley, Ohioville, Patterson, Patterson Heights, Penn, Perry, Pine, Plain Grove, Plum, Potter, Pulaski, Raccoon, Richland, Rochester, S.N.P.J., Salem, Saxonburg, Scott, Seven Fields, Shenango, Shippingport, Slippery Rock, South Beaver, South Heights, South New Castle, Taylor, Tarentum, Trafford, Union, Upper Burrell, Valencia, Vandergrift, Vanport Volant, Wampum, Washington, Wayne, West Deer, West Mayfield, White, Wilmington, Zelienople. Population (1990), 570,901.

ZIP Codes: 15001, 15003, 15005, 15009–10, 15014–15, 15024, 15026–27, 15030, 15042–44, 15050, 15052, 15059, 15061, 15065–66, 15068, 15074, 15076–77, 15081, 15084–86, 15090, 15239, 15340, 15343, 15601, 15613, 15623, 15626, 15629, 15636, 15641–42, 15644, 15656, 15665, 15668, 15675, 15690, 16001, 16037, 16046, 16055–56, 16059, 16063, 16101–02, 16105, 16112, 16115, 16117, 16120, 16123, 16132, 16136, 16141–43, 16156–57, 16160, 16650

* * *

FIFTH DISTRICT

JOHN PETERSON, Republican, of Pleasantville, PA; born in Titusville, PA, December 25, 1938; attended Pennsylvania State University; served in U.S. Army, 1958–64; past owner of supermarket; served in Pennsylvania House of Representatives, 1977–84, and in Pennsylvania Senate, 1985–96; Pleasantville borough councilman, 1968–77; past president: Pleasantville Lions Club, Titusville Chamber of Commerce, Pleasantville PTA, and Pleasantville Borough Council; formerly served on: board of directors of Titusville Hospital and University of Pittsburgh's Titusville and Bradford campuses, advisory board of Pennsylvania State University School of Forest Resources, and advisory committee of the University of Pittsburgh Graduate School of Public Health; married Saundra J. Watson in 1966; one son, Richard; member, Resources and Educational Opportunities committees; elected to the 105th Congress.

Office Listings

1020 Longworth House Office Building, Washington, DC 20515 225–5121
FAX: 225–5796
Chief of Staff.—Bob Ferguson.
Legislative Director.—Bob Moran.
Senior Legislative Assistant.—Jill Hershey.
Press Secretary.—Andrea Andrews.

115 West Spring Street, Titusville, PA 16801 .... (814) 827–3985
FAX: 827–7307

1524 West College Avenue, State College, PA 16801 .... (814) 238–1776
FAX: 238–1918

224 Liberty Street, Suite 3, Warren, PA 16364 .... (814) 726–3910
FAX: 726–0269

Counties: Armstrong (part), Cameron, Centre (part), Clarion (part), Clearfield (part), Clinton, Crawford (part), Elk, Forest, Jefferson, Lycoming (part), McKean, Potter, Tioga, Union, Venango, Warren. Population (1990), 570,901.

ZIP Codes: 15711, 15715, 15730, 15733, 15740, 15744, 15763 (part), 15764, 15767, 15770, 15776, 15778, 15780–81, 15784, 15801, 15821–25, 15827–29, 15831–32, 15834, 15840–41, 15843, 15845–47, 15851, 15853, 15857, 15860–61, 15863–65, 15868, 15870, 16028, 16035–36, 16038 (part), 16049, 16054, 16058, 16213–14, 16216, 16217 (part), 16220–25, 16230–35, 16239–40, 16242 (part), 16248, 16253–55, 16257–61, 16301, 16312–14, 16317, 16319, 16321–23, 16326–29, 16331–34, 16335 (part), 16340–47, 16350–54, 16360–62, 16364–65, 16370–75, 16402, 16404–05, 16407 (part), 16416, 16420, 16434, 16436, 16438 (part), 16701, 16720, 16724–35, 16738, 16740, 16743–46, 16748–51, 16801–05, 16820, 16822–23, 16826–28, 16832, 16835, 16840–41, 16844, 16848, 16851–54, 16856, 16864, 16865 (part), 16868, 16871–72, 16875, 16877, 16882, 16901, 16911–12, 16915, 16917–18, 16920–23, 16927–30, 16932–33, 16935–43, 16946–48, 16950, 17720–24, 17726, 17727, 17729, 17734, 17738–39, 17740, 17744, 17745, 17747–48, 17750–51, 17759–60,17767, 17769, 17773 17776, 17778–79, 17810, 17829, 17835, 17837, 17844–45, 17847, 17855–56, 17880, 17883, 17885–87, 17889

* * *

SIXTH DISTRICT

TIM HOLDEN, Democrat, of St. Clair, PA; born in Pottsville, PA, on March 5, 1957; attended St. Clair High School, St. Clair; Fork Union Military Academy; University of Richmond, Richmond, VA; B.A., Bloomsburg State College, 1980; sheriff of Schuylkill County, PA, 1985–93; licensed insurance broker and real estate agent, John J. Holden Insurance Agency and Holden Realty Company, St. Clair; member: Pennsylvania Sheriffs Association, Fraternal Order of Police, St. Clair Fish and Game Association, Benevolent and Protective Order of the Elks Lodge 1533; member, Rural Health Care Coalition; elected to the 103rd Congress; reelected to each succeeding Congress.

Office Listings

1421 Longworth House Office Building, Washington, DC 20515–3806	225–5546
Administrative Assistant.—Tom Gajewski.	FAX: 226–0996
Legislative Director.—Bruce Andrews.	
Communications Director.—Trish Reilly.	
Projects Director.—Bill Hanley.	
Berks County Services Center, 633 Court Street, Reading, PA 19601	(610) 371–9931
	FAX: 371–9939
Room 303, Meridian Bank Building, 101 North Centre Street, Pottsville, PA 17901	(717) 622–4212
	FAX: 628–2561
Market Square, Northumberland County Court House, Sunbury, PA 17801	(717) 988–1902

Counties: Berks, Schuylkill, Montgomery (Pottstown area), Northumberland (parts). CITIES AND TOWNSHIPS: Alburtis, Andreas, Ashland, Auburn, Bally, Barnesville, Barto, Beaver Meadows, Bechtelsville, Bernville, Bethel, Birdsboro, Blue Ball, Blandon, Bowers, Bowmansville, Boyertown, Branch Dale, Brockton, Breinigsville, Centerport, Coaldale, Cressona, Cumbola, Dalmatia, Danville, Deer Lake, Dewart, Donaldson, Dornsife, Douglassville, Earlville, East Earl, East Greenville, Elverson, Fleetwood, Frackville, Friedensburg, Geigertown, Gilberton, Girardville, Goodville, Gordon, Hamburg, Hazelton, Hegins, Helfenstein, Hereford, Herdon, Joliett, Junedale, Kaska, Kelayres, Kempton, Kenhorst, Klingerstown, Locustdale, Lost Creek, Lyon Station, Mahanoy City, Mahanoy Plane, Mar Lin, Mary D, Maxatawny, McAdoo, McEwensville, Mertztown, Middleport, Milton, Minersville, Mohrsville, Monocacy Station, Morea, Morgantown, Mount Aetna, Mount Penn, Muir, Muncy, Narvon, Nesquehoning, New Berlinville, New Holland, New Philadelphia, New Ringgold, Northumberland, Nuremberg, Oley, Oneida, Orwigsburg, Palo Alto, Palm, Paxinos, Pennside, Pine Forge, Pine Grove, Pitman, Port Carbon, Port Clinton, Pottstown, Pottsville, Quakake, Ravine, Reading, Reamstown, Red Hill, Rehrersburg, Reinholds, Ringtown, Riverside, Robesonia, Sacramento, Saint Clair, Seltzer, Shamokin, Shartlesville, Shenandoah, Sheppton, Shillington, Shoemakersville, Shuylkill Haven, Sinking Spring, Snydertown, Spring Glen, Stevens, Stony Run, Strausstown, Summit Hill, Summit Station, Sunbury, Tamaqua, Temple, Terre Hill, Topton, Turbotville, Tower City, Tremont, Tuscarora, Valley View, Virginville, Watsontown, Weatherly, Wernersville, West Lawn, West Reading, Womelsdorf, Wyomissing, Zion Grove, Zionsville; POST OFFICES: Dalmatia, Danville, Dornsife, Herndon, Leck Kill, McEwensville, Milton, Montandon, Northumberland, Pitman, Pottstown, Riverside, Sunbury, Syndertown, Turbotville, Watsontown. Population (1990), 570,901.

ZIP Codes: 17017, 17026, 17089, 17449, 17507, 17519, 17528, 17555, 17557, 17567, 17569, 17578, 17581, 17756, 17801, 17860, 17868, 17872, 17877, 17901, 17921–23, 17925, 17929–31, 17933–36, 17938–39, 17941–46, 17948–49, 17951–55, 17957, 17959–61, 17963–66, 17967–68, 17970, 17972, 17974, 17976, 17978–83, 17985, 18011, 18031, 18041, 10856, 18070, 18076, 18092, 18201, 18211, 18214, 18216, 18218, 18220, 18230–32, 18237, 18240, 18240–42, 18245, 18248, 18250, 18252, 18255, 19464, 19503–04, 19505–08, 19510–12, 19516–18, 19520, 19522,–23, 19526, 19529–30, 19533–36, 19538–43, 19545, 19547–51, 19554–55, 19557, 19559–60, 15962, 19564–65, 19567, 19601–07, 19609–12, 19640

* * *

SEVENTH DISTRICT

CURT WELDON, Republican, of Aston, PA; born in Marcus Hook, PA, on July 22, 1947; B.A., West Chester State College, PA, 1969; graduate work, Cabrini College, Wayne, PA; Temple and St. Joseph's Universities, Philadelphia, PA; administrator and teacher; mayor of Marcus Hook Borough, 1977–82; member, Delaware County Council, 1981–86; chairman, Delaware Valley Regional Planning Commission; member: Lower Delco Lions Club, United Way of Southeastern Pennsylvania, American Red Cross in Media, Marcus Hook Fire Company, Viscose Fire Company, Sacred Heart Medical Center, Neumann College, Delaware County Industrial Development Authority, Delaware County Community Action Agency, Delaware County Hero Scholarship Fund, Boy Scout Troop No. 418, Darby-Colwyn-William Penn School District Education Association; awards: 1984 Man of the Year from Delaware County Irish-American Association; 1984 Man of the Year from the Chester Business and Professional Association; married the former Mary Gallagher in 1972; five children: Karen, Kristen, Kimberly, Curt, and Andrew; elected to the 100th Congress on November 4, 1986; reelected to each succeeding Congress.

Office Listings

http://www.house.gov/weldon curtpa7@hr.house.gov

2452 Rayburn House Office Building, Washington, DC 20515–3807	225–2011
Administrative Assistant.—Doug Ritter.	FAX: 225–8137
Executive Assistant.—Sarah Young.	
Legislative Director.—Nancy Lifset.	
1554 Garrett Road, Upper Darby, PA 19082	(610) 259–0700
District Representative.—Patrick Patterson.	FAX: (215) 596–4665
30 South Valley Road, Suite 212, Paoli, PA 19301	(610) 640–9064

Counties: Chester (part), Delaware (part), Montgomery (part). Population (1990), 565,746.

ZIP Codes: 19003 (part), 19008, 19010 (part), 19013 (part), 19014 (part), 19015, 19017–18, 19022–23, 19026, 19028, 19033, 19037, 19039, 19041, 19043, 19050 (part), 19052, 19061, 19063–65, 19070, 19073, 19074, 19076, 19078–

79, 19081–83, 19085 (part), 19086, 19094, 19301, 19312, 19317, 19319, 19331, 19333, 19342, 19355, 19373, 19395, 19405–06, 19425, 19421, 19432, 19442, 19460, 19468, 19475, 19481 (part),

* * *

EIGHTH DISTRICT

JAMES C. GREENWOOD, Republican, of Erwinna, PA; born on May 4, 1951, in Philadelphia, PA; graduated, Council Rock High School; B.A., Dickinson College, Carlisle, PA, 1973; legislative assistant, Pennsylvania State Representative John S. Renninger, 1972–76; head house parent, The Woods Schools, 1974–76; campaign coordinator, Renninger for Congress Committee, 1976; caseworker, Bucks County Children and Youth Social Service Agency, 1977–80; Pennsylvania State Representative, 1980–86; Pennsylvania State Senator, 1986–93; chairman: Joint State Government Commission Task Force on Services to Children and Youth, Pennsylvania Legislative Children's Caucus; member, Joint State Government Commission Task Force on Commonwealth Efficiency Study; vice chairman, Assembly on the Legislature of the National Conference of State Legislatures; board of directors: Pennsylvania Trauma Systems Foundation, Pennsylvania Energy Development Authority, Pennsylvania Higher Education Assistance Agency; member: Governor's Commission for Children and Families, Children's Trust Fund Board, Joint Legislative Air and Water Pollution Control and Conservation Committee; Committee on the Environment of the Eastern Regional Conference of the Council of State Governments, Permanency Planning Task Force; board of directors: Bucks County Council on Alcoholism, Parents Anonymous, Today Inc., The Woods Schools; Public Citizen of the Year, 1990; Pennsylvania Chapter of the National Federation of Independent Business, Guardian of Small Business Award, 1989 and 1991; Pennsylvania Association of Retarded Citizens, Outstanding Legislator, 1989; Progressive Education for Rubella Children Award, 1987; Pennsylvania Association of Rehabilitation Facilities, Distinguished Service Award, 1987; National Head Injury Foundation, Award of Appreciation, 1986; Humane Society of the United States Award, 1983; committees: Commerce, Education and the Work Force; married to the former Christina Paugh; four children: Robert, Andrew, Laura, Kathryn; elected on November 3, 1992 to the 103rd Congress; reelected to each succeeding Congress.

Office Listings

http://www.house.gov/greenwood

2436 Rayburn House Office Building, Washington, DC 20515–3808 225–4276
Administrative Assistant.—Jordan P. Krauss. FAX: 225–9511
Scheduler.—Mary Corcoran.
Legislative Director.—Judy Borger.
69 East Oakland Avenue, Doylestown, PA 18901 .... (215) 348–7511
District Director.—Pete Johnson.
One Oxford Valley, Suite 800, Langhorne, PA 19047 .... (215) 752–7711

Counties: Bucks, Montgomery (part). Population (1990), 565,787.

ZIP Codes: 18036 (part), 18039, 18041 (part), 18054 (part), 18055 (part), 18073 (part), 18077, 18081, 18901, 18910–13, 18914, 18915 (part), 18916–17, 18920–23, 18925–31 18932 (part), 18933–35, 18936 (part), 18938, 18940, 18942–44, 18946–47, 18949–50, 18951 (part), 18953–56, 18960, 18962–63, 18964 (part), 18966, 18968, 18969 (part), 18970, 18972, 18974, 18976–77, 18980–81, 19002 (part), 19006 (part), 19007, 19020–21, 19030, 19040 (part), 19044 (part), 19047, 19053–59, 19067, 19090 (part), 19440 (part), 19446 (part), 19454 (part)

* * *

NINTH DISTRICT

BUD SHUSTER, Republican, of Everett, PA; born in Glassport, PA, January 23, 1932; B.S., University of Pittsburgh; M.B.A., Duquesne University; Ph.D., American University; served in the U.S. Army (infantry and counterintelligence); former vice president of RCA's computer division and founder and chairman of a computer software company (NYSE); member: Phi Beta Kappa, Sigma Chi (Significant Sig Award), ODK, Chowder and Marching Society; married Patricia Rommel; five children: Peg, Bill, Deb, Bob, and Gia; elected to the 93rd Congress, November 7, 1972; elected president of the 46-member GOP freshman class; reelected to each succeeding Congress, winning both Republican and Democratic nominations (1976, 1980, 1986, 1988, 1990, 1992, 1994); delegate, Republican National Convention (1976, 1980, 1984, 1988, 1992 and 1996); elected chairman of the Republican Policy Committee for the 96th Congress; appointed member of House Budget Committee; elected as ranking member of Full Public Works and Transportation Committee; chairman of Transportation and Infrastructure Committee; serves on Select Intelligence Committee; elected chairman of the National Transportation Policy

Study Commission; authored award winning book, "*Believing In America*" (William Morrow), 1983; paperback edition (Berkeley), 1984; member, The Authors Guild.

Office Listings

2188 Rayburn House Office Building, Washington, DC 20515–3809 225–2431
Chief of Staff.—Tim Hugo.
Office Manager.—Tracy G. Mosebey.
Legislative Director.—John P. McAllister.
Press Secretary.—Jeff Nelligan.
RD 2, Box 711, Altoona, PA 16601 .... (814) 946–1653
179 East Queen Street, Chambersburg, PA 17201 .... (717) 264–8308
1214 Oldtown Road, No. 4, Clearfield, PA 16830 .... (814) 765–9106

Counties: Bedford, Blair, Centre (part), Clearfield (part), Franklin, Fulton, Huntingdon, Juniata, Mifflin, Perry (part), Snyder. Population (1990), 565,803.

ZIP Codes: 15521–22, 15533, 15534 (part), 15535–37, 15539, 15540 (part), 15545 (part), 15550, 15554, 15559 (part), 15714 (part), 15721, 15722 (part), 15724 (part), 15738, 15742 (part), 15753, 15757 (part), 15767 (part), 15801 (part), 15848, 15866, 15868 (part), 15926 (part), 15946 (part), 16601–03, 16611, 16613 (part), 16614–17, 16619–23, 16625, 16627, 16631, 16633–40, 16641 (part), 16644–48, 16650–52, 16655–57, 16659–65, 16666 (part), 16667, 16668 (part), 16669–74, 16675 (part), 16678–85, 16686 (part), 16689, 16691–95, 16821, 16830 (part), 16833–34, 16838–40, 16847, 16849, 16858 (part), 16860 (part), 16861, 16863 (part), 16865 (part), 16866 (part), 16870 (part), 16876, 16877 (part), 16878 (part), 16879, 17002, 17004, 17007, 17009, 17013 (part), 17014, 17021, 17029, 17035 (part), 17044, 17045 (part), 17049, 17051–52, 17053 (part), 17054, 17056, 17058–60, 17062 (part), 17063, 17066, 17075–76, 17082, 17084, 17086, 17094, 17099, 17201, 17210–15, 17217–25, 17228–29, 17231–33, 17235–40, 17241 (part), 17243–44, 17246–47, 17249–57, 17260–68, 17270–72, 17324 (part)

* * *

TENTH DISTRICT

JOSEPH M. McDADE, Republican, of Clarks Summit, PA; born in Scranton, PA, September 29, 1931, son of John B. and Genevieve McDade; attended St. Paul's School and Scranton Preparatory School; graduated with honors from the University of Notre Dame, 1953, B.A., political science; graduated from University of Pennsylvania, 1956, LL.B.; honorary LL.D., St. Thomas Aquinas College; honorary doctor of laws, University of Scranton; Marywood College Presidential Medal; L.H.D., Misreicordia College, 1981; H.H.D., Kings College, 1981; LL.D., Mansfield State College, 1982; clerkship in office of Chief Federal Judge John W. Murphy, Middle District of Pennsylvania; engaged in general practice of law; served as Scranton city solicitor, 1962; married to the former Sarah Scripture, Rome, NY; one child: Jared; four children by previous marriage: Joseph, Aileen, Deborah, and Mark; member: James Wilson Law Club, Knights of Columbus, Elks Club, Scranton Chamber of Commerce; American, Pennsylvania, and Lackawanna County bar associations; elected to the 88th Congress, November 6, 1962; reelected to each succeeding Congress.

Office Listings

2107 Rayburn House Office Building, Washington, DC 20515–3810 225–3731
Administrative Assistant.—John Enright. FAX: 225–9594
Appointment Secretary.—Linda Hewitt.
Legislative Director.—John Enright.
514 Scranton Life Building, Scranton, PA 18503 .... (717) 346–3834
Field Representative.—Michael Russen.
Herman Schneebeli Federal Building, 240 West Third Street, Suite 230, Williamsport, PA 17701 .... (717) 327–8161
Staff Assistant.—Ruth Calistri.

Counties: Bradford, Lackawanna, Pike, Sullivan, Susquehanna, Wayne, and Wyoming. LYCOMING COUNTY; city of Williamport and townships of Armstrong, Brady, Cascade, Clinton, Eldred, Fairfield, Franklin, Gamble, Hepburn, Jackson, Jordan, Lewis, Loyalsock, Lycoming, McIntyre, McNett; Mill Creek, Moreland, Muncy, Muncy Creek, Old Lycoming, Penn, Plunketts Creek, Shrewsbury, Upper Fairfield, Wolf, and Woodward, and the boroughs of Duboistown, Hughesville, Montgomery, Montoursville, Muncy, Picture Rocks, and South Williamsport. MONROE COUNTY; townships of Barrett, Coolbaugh, Jackson, Middle Smithfield, Paradise, Pocono, Price and Smithfield and the boroughs of Delaware Water Gap, East Stroudsburg (part districts 2 and 3) and Mt. Pocono. Population (1990), 565,681.

ZIP Codes: 16910, 16914, 16925–26, 16945, 16947, 17701, 17703, 17724, 17728, 17731, 17735, 17737, 17742–44, 17752, 17754, 17756, 17758–59, 17762–63, 17765, 17768, 17770–71, 17774, 18301, 18320, 18323–28, 18332, 18335–37, 18340–42, 18344, 18349–50, 18355–57, 18360, 18370–72, 18403, 18405, 18407, 18410–11, 18413–17, 18419–21, 18424–28, 18430–31, 18433–41, 18443–47, 18449, 18451–66, 18469–73, 18501–10, 18512, 18517–19, 18612, 18614–16, 18618–19, 18623, 18625–26, 18628–30, 18632, 18636, 18641, 18653, 18657, 18801, 18810, 18812–18, 18820–34, 18837, 18839–40, 18842–48, 18850–51, 18853–54

ELEVENTH DISTRICT

PAUL E. KANJORSKI, Democrat, of Nanticoke, PA; born in Nanticoke, April 2, 1937; U.S. Capitol Page School, Washington, DC, 1954; attended, Wyoming Seminary, Kingston, PA, Temple University, Philadelphia, PA, Dickinson School of Law, Carlisle, PA; served in U.S. Army, private, 1960–61; attorney, admitted to Pennsylvania State bar, 1966; began practice in Wilkes Barre, PA, November 7, 1966; member: House Banking and Financial Services Committee; Government Reform and Oversight Committee; ranking member: Capital Markets, Securities, and Government-Sponsored Enterprises Subcommittee; married to the former Nancy Marie Hickerson; one daughter, Nancy; elected to the 99th Congress on November 6, 1984; reelected to each succeeding Congress.

Office Listings

paul.kanjorski@hr.house.gov

2353 Rayburn House Office Building, Washington, DC 20515–3811 225–6511
Chief of Staff.—Karen Feather.
Legislative Director.—Mike Radway.
Executive Assistant.—Donna Giobbi.
Press Secretary.—Christopher McCannell.
10 East South Street, Wilkes Barre, PA 18701 .... (717) 825–2200

Counties: Carbon, Columbia, Luzerne, Monroe (part), Montour, Northumberland (part). Population (1990), 565,913.

ZIP Codes: 17756 (part), 17772 (part), 17774 (part), 17777 (part), 17814–15, 17820, 17821 (part), 17824 (part), 17826, 17828, 17832, 17834, 17839–40, 17846 (part), 17847 (part); 17851, 17858–59, 17860, 17866–67, 17872 (part), 17878, 17881, 17884, 17888, 17920, 17921 (part), 17927, 18012, 18030, 18058 (part), 18071, 18201 (part), 18210, 18211 (part), 18212, 18216, 18219, 18221–25, 18229–30, 18234, 18235 (part), 18237 (part), 18239, 18241 (part), 18243–44, 18246–47, 18249, 18250–51, 18254, 18255 (part), 18256, 18301 (part), 18322–23, 18330–31, 18333–34, 18346–48, 18350, 18352–54, 18360 (part), 18424 (part), 18466 (part), 18601–03, 18610–11, 18612 (part), 18614 (part), 18615 (part), 18617, 18618 (part), 18621–22, 18624, 18627, 18631, 18634–35, 18636 (part), 18637, 18640 (part), 18641 (part), 18642–44, 18651, 18654–56, 18660–61, 18700–10, 18773

* * *

TWELFTH DISTRICT

JOHN P. MURTHA, Democrat, of Johnstown, PA; graduated, Ramsey High School, Mount Pleasant, PA; Kiskiminetas Spring School; B.A. in economics, University of Pittsburgh; graduate study at Indiana University of Pennsylvania; married Joyce Bell; three children: Donna Sue and twin sons, John and Patrick; served in Marine Corps as an enlisted Marine commissioned as an officer; discharged as a first lieutenant; maintained active reserve officer status; volunteered for one year of active duty in Vietnam as a major; served with 1st Marines, a Marine infantry regiment, 1966–67, south of Danang; awarded Bronze Star Medal with combat "V", two Purple Heart medals, Vietnamese Cross of Gallantry, and service medals; retired colonel, U.S. Marine Corps Reserves; elected to Pennsylvania House of Representatives in 1969, served continuously until elected to U.S. House of Representatives; recipient of Pennsylvania Distinguished Service Medal and Pennsylvania Meritorious Service Medal (the commonwealth's two highest honors); created the John P. Murtha Award for student assistance at the University of Pittsburgh at Johnstown; received Honorary Doctor of Humanities, Mount Aloysius Junior College; elected to the 93rd Congress, February 5, 1974; reelected to each succeeding Congress; member, Appropriations Committee.

Office Listings

http://www.house.gov/murtha murtha@hr.house.gov

2423 Rayburn House Office Building, Washington, DC 20515–3812 225–2065
Executive Assistant.—William N. Allen.
Administrator.—Winifred Frederick.
Scheduling Coordinator.—Colette Marchesini.
P.O. Box 780, Johnstown, PA 15907 .... (814) 535–2642
District Administrative Assistant.—John Hugya.

Counties: ARMSTRONG COUNTY (part); cities and townships of Adrian, Apollo, Cadogan, Cowansville, Dayton, Distant, Edmon, Elderton, Ford City, Ford Cliff, Freeport, Kittanning, Leechburg, Manorville, McGrann, North Apollo, NuMine, Oak Ridge, Parker, Rural Valley, Sagamore, Schenley, Seminole, Shelocta, Spring Church, Templeton, Worthington, Yatesboro. CAMBRIA COUNTY; cities and townships of Ashville, Barnesboro, Beaverdale, Belsano, Blandburg, Carrolltown, Cassandra, Chest Springs, Coalport, Colver, Coupon, Cresson, Dunlo, Dysart, Ebensburg, Elmora, Elton, Emeigh Fallentimber, Flinton, Gallitzin, Glasgow, Hastings, Johnstown, Lilly, Loretto, Marsteller, Mineral Point, Nanty Glo, Nicktown, Parkhill, Patton, Portage, Revloc, Saint Benedict, Saint Boniface, Saint Michael, Salix, Sidman, South Fork, Spangler, Summerhill, Twin Rocks, Wilmore. CLARION COUNTY (part); cities and townships of East Brady, Mayport, New Bethlehem. FAYETTE COUNTY (part); cities and townships of Chalkhill, Chestnut Ridge, Connellsville, Dickerson

Run, Dunbar, Fairchance, Farmington, Gibbon Glade, Hopwood, Leisenring, Lemont Furnace, Markleysburg, Mill Run, Mount Braddock, Ohiopyle, Oliver, Smithfield, Uniontown, Vanderbilt, West Leisenring. INDIANA COUNTY; cities and townships of Alverda, Arcadia, Armagh, Aultman, Beyer, Black Lick, Blairsville, Brush Valley, Chambersville, Cherry Tree, Clarksburg, Clune, Clymer, Commodore, Coral, Creekside, Dilltown, Dixonville, Ernest, Gipsy, Glen Campbell, Heilwood, Hillsdale, Home, Homer City, Indiana, Josephine, Juneau, Kent, Lucernemines, Marchand, Marion Center, McIntyre, Mentlce, New Florence, North Point, Penn Run, Plumville, Robinson, Rochester Mills, Rossiter, Saltsburg, Seward, Smicksburg, Starford, Strongstown, Vintondale, West Lebanon. SOMERSET COUNTY; cities and townships of Acosta, Addison, Berlin, Boswell, Boynton, Cairnbrook, Central City, Confluence, Davidsville, Fairhope, Fort Hill, Friedens, Garrett, Glencoe, Gray, Hidden Valley, Hollsopple, Hooversville, Jenners, Jennerstown, Jerome, Kantner, Listie, Markleton, Meyersdale, New Baltimore, Quecreek, Rockwood, Salisbury, Seanor, Shanksville, Sipesville, Somerset, Springs, Stoystown, Tire Hill, Ursina, Wellersburg, West Salisbury, Windber. WESTMORELAND COUNTY (part); cities and townships of Acme, Alverton, Avonmore, Bolivar, Bradenville, Calumet, Champion, Derry, Donegal, Greensburg, Hostetter, Jones Mills, Latrobe, Laughlintown, Ligonier, Loyalhanna, Luxor, Mammoth, Mount Pleasant New Alexandria, New Derry, Norvelt, Pleasant Unity, Rector, Ruffs Dale, Salina, Scottdale, Slickville, Southwest, Stahlstown, Tarrs, Torrance, United, Vandergrift, Whitney, Youngstown. Population (1990), 565,794.

ZIP Codes: 15401 (part), 15411, 15421, 15422 (part), 15424, 15425 (part), 15430–31, 15436–37, 15440, 15445, 15455–56, 15459, 15464–65, 15470, 15472, 15478, 15485, 15501–02, 15520, 15530–32, 15538, 15540–43, 15544, 15546–49, 15551–53, 15555, 15557–58, 15560–65, 15601 (part), 15610, 15612, 15613 (part), 15618, 15620–22, 15627–28, 15629 (part), 15630, 15638, 15646, 15650, 15655–56, 15658, 15661–62, 15664, 15666, 15670–71, 15673–74, 15676–77, 15679–82, 15683 (part), 15684–89, 15690 (part), 15693, 15696, 15701, 15710, 15712–14, 15716–17, 15720, 15722–25, 15727–29, 15731–32, 15734, 15736–39, 15741–42, 15745–48, 15750–52, 15754, 15756, 15757 (part), 15758–63, 15765, 15771–75, 15777, 15779, 15783, 15901–02, 15904–07, 15909, 15920–31, 15934–38, 15940, 15942–46, 15948–49, 15951–63, 16028 (part), 16049, 16201, 16210–12, 16218, 16222, 16226, 16228, 16229 (part), 16236, 16238, 16240, 16242 (part), 16244–46, 16249–50, 16253, 16256, 16259, 16262–63, 16613, 16619, 16624, 16627 (part), 16629–30, 16636, 16639–41, 16644, 16646, 16668, 16675

* * *

THIRTEENTH DISTRICT

JON D. FOX, Republican, of Elkins Park, PA; born in Abington, PA, April 22, 1947; graduated Cheltenham High School, Wyncote, PA, 1965; B.A., Pennsylvania State University, 1969; J.D., Delaware Law Schoool (now Widener University School of Law); admitted to the Pennsylvania State bar; awarded the Lindsay Law Prize for excellence in legal research; U.S. General Services Administration, Washington, DC; guest lecturer for the Presidential Classroom for Young Americans; served in the U.S. Air Force Reserves as a technical sargeant, 1969–75; Montgomery City commissioner, 1991–94; vice chairman, Board of Commissioners; assistant district attorney in Montgomery County, 1976–80; Abington Township commissioner, 1980–84; represented 153rd Legislative District in Pennsylvania House of Representatives, 1984–90; member: House Appropriations and Education committees; House Select committees on Services for the Handicapped and Long-Term Care; Republican chairman, House Special Education Subcommittee; chairman, Mental Health Task Force of the Children's Legislative Caucus; founder/chairman, Legislative Coalition Against Drug and Alcohol Abuse; member: Legislative Coalition for Libraries, Pennsylvania Firefighters Legislative Caucus; served on the boards of Montgomery County Legal Aid, Eastern Montgomery County Red Cross, Jewish Community Relations Council (neighborhood division), Aldersgate Youth Service Bureau, Montgomery County Spinal Cord Association, American Cancer Society, Manor Junior College, Willow Grove Senior Citizens Center, the Citizen's Committee for Environmental Control, F&AM Friendship Lodge No. 400 (Jenkintown), Friends of the Abington Free Library, Glenside Kiwanis, Optimist Club of Lower Montgomery County, North Penn Elks, North Penn Veterans of Foreign Wars, Lansdale American Legion, Abington Senior Citizens Support Council, and Advisory Council to the Montgomery County Office on Aging and Adult Services; co-founded, Montgomery County AIDS Task Force, 1987, which resulted in the creation of the Montgomery County Department of Health, 1989; married to the former Judithanne Wilbert, 1992; committiees: Banking and Financial Services, Transportation and Infrastructure; elected to the 104th Congress; reelected to the 105th Congress.

Office Listings

jonfox@hr.house.gov

435 Cannon House Office Building, Washington, DC 20515–3813 225–6111
FAX: 225–3155
Chief of Staff.—Jan W. Friis, Jr.
Legislative Director.—Kristen McSwain.
Communications Director.—Tony Swanick.
Scheduler.—Jennifer Unterberger.

Logan Square Shopping Center, 1768 Markley Street, Norristown, PA 19401 .... (610) 272–8400
FAX: 272–8532
District Administrator.—Eric Willcox.
Office Manager.—Marie Cavanaugh.
Caseworkers: Linda Gerhard, Amy Griffith, Coley Adams.

Easton and Edge Hill Roads, Abington, PA 19001–4305 .... (215) 885–3500
FAX: 885–6828
Office Manager.—Janice Harvey.
Caseworkers: Julie Nahill, Judy Mazzola.
Staff Assistants: Ralph Goldstein, Walter Waeltz.

Narberth Borough Hall, 100 Conway Avenue, Narberth, PA 19072–2202 .... (610) 667–6020

County: MONTGOMERY COUNTY; cities and townships of Abington, Ambler, Ardmore, Audubon, Bala Cynwyd, Blue Bell, Bryn Athyn, Bryn Mawr, Cheltenham, Collegeville, Conshohocken, East Norriton, Eagleville, Elkins Park, Elroyboro, Erdenheim, Flourtown, Fort Washingotn, Franconia, Gladwyn, Glenside, Gwynedd, Gwynedd Valley, Harleysville, Hatboro, Hatfield Haverford, Huntingdon Valley, Jenkintown, Kulpsville, Lafayette Hills, Lansdale, Limerick, Lower Frederick, Lower Gwynedd, Lower Merion, Lower Moreland, Lower Pottsgrove, Lower Providence, Lower Salford, Malborough, Maple Glen, Meadowbrook, Melrose Park, Merion, Miguion, Montgomery, Narberth, Norristown, North Wales, Oaks, Penlyn, Plymouth, Perkiomen, Plymouth Meeting, Pottstown, Oreland, Radnor, Rockledge, Rosemont, Roslyn, Rydal, Salford, Schwenksville, Skippack, Souderton, Springfield, Springhouse, Swarthmore, Telford, Towamencin, Trappe, Villanova, Upper Dublin, Upper Gwynedd, Upper Merion (part), Upper Moreland, Upper Providence, Upper Salford, West Conshohocken, West Norriton, West Point, WhiteMarsh, Whitpain, Willow Grove, Worcester, Wyncote, Wyndmoor. Population (1990), 565,793.

ZIP Codes: 18915, 18918, 18924, 18932, 18936, 18957–58, 18964, 18969, 18971, 18979, 19001 (part), 19002 (part), 19003, 19004 (part), 19006, 19009, 19010 (part), 19012, 19025 (part), 19027 (part), 19031 (part), 19034–35, 19038 (part), 19040–41, 19046 (part), 19066 (part), 19072 (part), 19075, 19083, 19085 (part), 19087, 19090, 19095–96, 19401 (part), 19403 (part), 19407–09, 19422 (part), 19423, 19426, 19428 (part), 19430, 19436–38, 19440, 19443–44, 19446, 19450–54, 19456, 19460, 19462, 19464, 19468, 19473, 19477, 19481, 19486, 19490 (part)

* * *

FOURTEENTH DISTRICT

WILLIAM J. COYNE, Democrat, of Pittsburgh; born in Pittsburgh, PA August 24, 1936; graduated, Central Catholic High School, Pittsburgh, 1954; graduated, Robert Morris College, Pittsburgh, 1965, B.S. accounting; served in U.S. Army, 1955–57, Korea; member: Pennsylvania State Legislature, 1970–72; Pittsburgh City Council, 1974–80, Pittsburgh Housing Authority, and Governor's Justice Commission; chairman, public works committee; board member, Opportunities Industrialization Center; elected to the 97th Congress, November 4, 1980; reelected to each succeeding Congress; member, Ways and Means Committee; subcommittees: Oversight, Human Resources; Congressional Steel and Human Rights Caucuses; Steering Committee for the Northeast-Midwest Congressional Coalition.

Office Listings

2455 Rayburn House Office Building, Washington, DC 20515–3814 225–2301
Administrative Assistant.—Coleman J. Conroy. FAX: 225–1844
2009 Federal Building, 1000 Liberty Avenue, Pittsburgh, PA 15222 .... (412) 644–2870
District Administrator.—James P. Rooney.

County: ALLEGHENY COUNTY; cities of Aleppo, Avalon, Bell Acres, Bellevue, Ben Avon, Ben Avon Heights, Crafton, Edgewood, Emsworth, Franklin Park, Greentree, Homestead, Ingram, Leetsdale, McKees Rocks, Mount Oliver, Pittsburgh, Rosslyn Farms, Sewickley Heights, Sewickley Hills, Thornburg, West View; townships of Collier, Hampton, Kennedy, Kilbuck, Leet, McCandless, Neville, Ohio, Pennsbury Village, Robinson, Ross, Stowe. Population (1990), 565,787.

ZIP Codes: 15003 (part), 15017 (part), 15044 (part) 15056, 15090 (part), 15091, 15101 (part), 15106 (part), 15108 (part), 15136 (part), 15201, 15203–04, 15205 (part), 15206–09, 15210 (part), 15211–15, 15216 (part), 15217, 15218 (part), 15219, 15220 (part), 15221 (part), 15222, 15224–25, 15226 (part), 15230, 15232–33, 15240, 15242 (part), 15245, 15290, 15299

* * *

FIFTEENTH DISTRICT

PAUL MCHALE, Democrat, of Bethlehem, PA; born on July 26, 1950, in Bethlehem; B.A., Phi Beta Kappa, Lehigh University, PA, 1972; J.D., Georgetown University Law School, Washington, DC, 1977; attorney; admitted to the Pennsylvania bar, 1977; served in U.S. Marine Corps, 1972–74; served in U.S. Marine Corps Reserves; served on active duty in Persian Gulf, August-October, 1990; volunteered for Desert Storm duty, January-April, 1991; awarded Navy Commendation Medal; currently serves in 157th IMA Detachment; attorney in private practice, 1977–82 and 1991–93; Pennsylvania House of Representatives, 1982–91; married to Kathy McHale, who was elected to his vacant seat in the Pennsylvania House of Representatives; three children: Matthew, Mary, and Luke; committee memberships: Committee on National Security and Committee on Science; cofounder, House National Guard and Reserve Components Caucus; elected on November 3, 1992 to the 103rd Congress; reelected to each succeeding Congress.

Office Listings

http://www.house.gov/mchale mchale@hr.house.gov

217 Cannon House Office Building, Washington, DC 20515–3815 225–6411
Chief of Staff.—Christine Messina-Boyer. FAX: 225–5320
Executive Assistant.—Sally Derr.
Legislative Director.—Melissa Kolossar.
26 East Third Street, Bethlehem, PA 18015–1392 .... (215) 866–0916
District Administrator.—Tom Mohr. FAX: 867–8210
Hamilton Financial Center, One Center Square, Allentown, PA 18101–2192 .... (215) 439–8861
FAX: 439–0598
168 Main Street, Pennsburg, PA 18073–1398 .... (215) 541–0614
FAX: 541–0617

Counties: LEHIGH COUNTY; cities of Alburtis, Allentown, Breinigsville, Catasauqua, Center Valley, Coopersburg, Coplay, East Texas, Emmaus, Fogelsville, Germansville, Laury's Station, Lehigh Valley, Macungie, New Tripoli, Old Zionsville, Orefield, Schnecksville, Slatedale, Slatington, Trexlertown, Whitehall, Zionsville. MONTGOMERY COUNTY; cities of East Greenville, Gilbertsville, Palm, Pennsburg, Red Hill. NORTHAMPTON COUNTY; cities of Bangor, Bath, Bethlehem, Cherryville, Danielsville, Easton, Freemansburg, Hellertown, Martins Creek, Mount Bethel, Nazareth, Northampton, Pen Argyl, Portland, Roseto, Stockertown, Tatamy, Treichlers, Walnutport, and Wind Gap. Population (1990), 565,810.

ZIP Codes: 18002, 18011, 18013–18, 18031–32, 18034–38, 18041–44, 18046, 18049, 18051–53, 18055, 18059, 18062–64, 18066–70, 18072–73, 18076, 18078–80, 18083, 18085–88, 18091–92, 18101–06, 18343, 18351, 19525

* * *

SIXTEENTH DISTRICT

JOSEPH R. PITTS, Republican, of Kenneth Square, PA; born in Lexington, KY, October 10, 1939; B.A., philosophy and religion, Asbury College, KY; served in U.S. Air Force, 1963–69, rising from second lieutenant to captain; nursery business owner and operator; math and science teacher, Great Valley High School, Malvern, PA, 1969–72; teacher, Mortonsville Elementary School, Versailles, KY; member: Pennsylvania House of Representatives, 1972–96, serving as chairman of Appropriations Committee, 1989–96, and of Labor Relations Committee, 1981–88; married the former Virginia M. Pratt in 1961; three children: Karen, Carol, and Daniel; elected to the 105th Congress.

Office Listings

504 Cannon House Office Building, Washington, DC 20515–3816 225–2411
Chief of Staff.—Bill Wichterman. FAX: 225–2013
Legislative Director.—Patrick Sullivan.
Press Secretary.—Tonya Neff.
P.O. Box 837, Unionville Road, Unionville, PA 19375 .... (610) 429–4581
FAX: 444–5750

Counties: LANCASTER (part); cities and townships of Adamstown, Bart, Bausman, Bird-in-Hand, Blue Ball, Bowmansville, Brownstown, Christiana, Conestoga, Denver, Drumore, East Earl, East Petersburg, Martindale, Gap, Goodville, Gordonville, Holtwood, Intercourse, Kinzers, Kirkwood, Lampeter, Lancaster, Leola, Lititz, Rothsville, Millersville, Narvon, New Holland, New Province, Paradise, Peach Bottom, Pequea, Quarryville, Reamstown, Refton, Rohrerstown, Reinholds, Ronks, Smoketown, Stevens, Strasburg, Talmage, Terre Hill, West Willow, Willow Street, Witmer. CHESTER (part); cities and townships of Atglen, Avondale, Brandamore, Chadds Ford, Chatham, Chester Springs, Cheyney, Coatesville, Cochranville, Downingtown, Elverson, Exton, Glen Mills, Glenmoore, Honey Brook, Kelton, Kemblesville, Kennett Square, Landenberg, Lewisville, Lincoln University, Lionville, Lyndell, Mendenhall, Modena, New London, Nottingham, Oxford, Parker Ford, Parkesburg, Phoenixville, Pottstown, Pocopson, Pomeroy, Sadsburyville, Saint Peters, Soudersburg, Spring City, Steelville, Suplee, Thorndale, Toughkenamon, Unionville, Uwchland, Wagontown, West Chester, Westtown. Population (1990), 565,804.

ZIP Codes: 17503–09, 17516 (part), 17517–20, 17522, 17527–29, 17532, 17534–37, 17538, 17540, 17543, 17545 (part), 17551 (part), 17555, 17557, 17560, 17562–69, 17572, 17576–85, 17601 (part), 17602, 17603 (part), 17604–08, 19310–11, 19316, 19317 (part), 19318–20, 19330, 19335, 19341, 19342 (part), 19343–44, 19346–48, 19350–54, 19355 (part), 19357–58, 19360, 19362–63, 19365–67, 19369–72, 19374–76, 19380–83, 19390, 19395, 19425, 19457, 19460 (part), 19464 (part), 19470, 19475 (part), 19480, 19501, 19520

SEVENTEENTH DISTRICT

GEORGE GEKAS, Republican, of Harrisburg, PA; born in Harrisburg on April 14, 1930; graduated, William Penn High School, 1948; B.A., Dickinson College, Carlisle, PA, 1952; LL.B. and J.D., Dickinson School of Law, Carlisle, 1958; served as corporal in U.S. Army, 1953–55; attorney, admitted to the Pennsylvania bar in 1959, and commenced practice in Harrisburg; served as assistant district attorney, Dauphin County, PA, 1960–66; Pennsylvania House of Representatives, 1966–74; Pennsylvania Senate, 1976–82; member: American Judicature Society; Harrisburg Historical Society; board of trustees, Orthodox Church of Greater Harrisburg; Police Athletic League; March of Dimes Campaign; Cancer Crusade; United Church of Harrisburg; married the former Evangeline Charas in 1971; elected on November 2, 1982 to the 98th Congress; reelected to each succeeding Congress.

Office Listings

http://www.house.gov/gekas

2410 Rayburn House Office Building, Washington, DC 20515–3817 225–4315
FAX: 225–8440
Administrative Assistant.—Allan Cagnoli.
Executive Assistant.—Seth Johnson.
Press Secretary.—Jim Campi.
Second Floor, 3605 Vartan Way, Harrisburg, PA 17110 .... (717) 541–5507
222 South Market Street, Suite 102–A, Elizabethtown, PA 17022 .... (800) 210–0206
FAX: 367–6602
108–B Municipal Building, 400 South Eighth Street, Lebanon, PA 17042–6794 ..... (717) 273–1451
FAX: 273–1673

Counties: Cumberland (part), Dauphin, Lancaster (part), Lebanon, and Perry (part). Population (1990), 565,742.

ZIP Codes: 16930 (part), 16938 (part), 17005–06, 17017–18, 17020, 17022 (part), 17023–24, 17028 (part), 17030–32, 17033 (part), 17034, 17035 (part), 17036–37, 17040, 17045 (part), 17047–48, 17053 (part), 17057, 17061, 17062 (part), 17068–69, 17071, 17074, 17078 (part), 17080, 17090, 17097–98, 17100–05, 17108–13, 17502 (part), 17701, 17703, 17720, 17722–23, 17724 (part), 17727–28, 17730, 17737 (part), 17739, 17740 (part), 17742, 17744, 17749, 17752, 17754, 17756, 17758 (part), 17759, 17761–63, 17765 (part), 17769, 17771, 17772 (part), 17774 (part), 17776–77, 17801, 17810, 17812–13, 17821 (part), 17823, 17824 (part), 17827, 17829–31, 17833, 17835–37, 17841–45, 17846 (part), 17847, 17850, 17853, 17855–57, 17860–62, 17864–65, 17867–68, 17870, 17872 (part), 17876–77, 17880–83, 17885–89, 17941 (part), 17978 (part), 17980 (part)

* * *

EIGHTEENTH DISTRICT

MICHAEL F. DOYLE, Democrat, of Swissvale, PA; born in Swissvale, PA, August 5, 1953; graduated, Swissvale Area High School, 1971; B.S., Pennsylvania State University, 1975; co-owner, Eastgate Insurance Agency, Inc., 1983; elected and served as finance and recreation chairman, Swissvale, Borough Council, 1977–81; member: Leadership Pittsburgh Alumni Association, Lions Club, Ancient Order of the Hibernians, Italian Sons and Daughters of America, and Penn State Alumni Association; member: Democratic Caucus, Democratic Study Group, Pennsylvania Democratic Delegation, Congressional Steel Caucus, Travel and Tourism CMO, AdHoc Committee on Irish Affairs, and National Italian-American Foundation; married Susan Beth Doyle, 1975; four children: Michael, David, Kevin, and Alexandra; committees: Science, Veterans' Affairs; subcommittees: Basic Research, Energy and Environment, Hospitals and Health Care; elected November 8, 1994 to the 104th Congress; reelected to the 105th Congress.

Office Listings

http://www.house.gov/doyle rep.doyle@mail.house.gov

1218 Longworth House Office Building, Washington, DC 20515 225–2135
Administrative Assistant/Legislative Director.—David Lucas.
Office Manager/Scheduler.—Chris Swartz.
11 Duff Road, Penn Hills, PA 15235 .... (412) 241–6055
District Coordinator/Administrative Assistant.—Dan Rihn.
541 Fifth Avenue, McKeesport, PA 15132 .... (412) 664–4049

County: ALLEGHENY (part). CITIES AND TOWNSHIPS: Aspinwall, Baldwin Borough, Baldwin Township, Blawnox, Braddock, Braddock Hills, Brentwood, Carnegie, Castle Shannon, Chalfant, Churchill, Clairton, Dormont, Dravosburg, Duquesne, E. McKeesport, E. Pittsburgh, Elizabeth Borough, Elizabeth Township, Etna, Forest Hills, Forward Township, Fox Chapel, Glassport, Harmar, Heidelberg, Indiana, Jefferson, Liberty, Lincoln, McKeesport, Millvale, Monroeville, Mt. Lebanon, Munhall, North Braddock, North Versailles, Oakmont, O'Hara Township, Penn Hills, Pitcairn, Pleasant Hills, Port Vue, Rankin, Reserve, Swissvale, Shaler Township, Scott, Sharpsburg, South Park, South Versailles, Springdale Borough, Springdale Township, Trafford, Turtle Creek, Verona, Versailles, Wall, West Elizabeth, West Homestead, West Mifflin, Whitaker, Whitehall, White Oak, Wilkins, Wilkinsburg, and Wilmerding. Population (1990), 565,781.

ZIP Codes: 15017–18, 15020, 15024–25, 15028, 15034–35, 15037–38, 15045, 15047, 15049, 15051, 15063, 15075, 15085, 15088, 15101, 15104, 15106, 15110, 15112, 15116, 15120, 15122, 15129–33, 15135, 15137, 15139–40, 15144–48, 15207, 15209–10, 15212, 15214–16, 15218, 15220–21, 15223, 15226–28, 15234–36, 15238, 15243, 15332

* * *

NINETEENTH DISTRICT

WILLIAM F. GOODLING, Republican, of Jacobus, PA; born December 5, 1927 in Loganville, PA; graduated from William Penn Senior High School, York, PA; B.S., University of Maryland; M.Ed, Western Maryland College; doctoral studies, Pennsylvania State University; various teaching positions including principal, West York Area High School; supervisor of student teachers for Pennsylvania State University; superintendent, Spring Grove Area schools; president, Dallastown area School Board; served in U.S. Army, 1946–48; member: Lions, various health associations, and Loganville United Methodist Church; married to the former Hilda Wright; two children: Todd and Jennifer; chair, Committee on Economic and Educational Opportunities; member: Committee on International Relations; elected to the 94th Congress, November 5, 1974; reelected to each succeeding Congress.

Office Listings

2263 Rayburn House Office Building, Washington, DC 20515–3819 225–5836
Executive Assistant/Communications Director.—Tim Stadnaus.
Executive Assistant/Legislative Director.—Kimberly Strycharz.
Federal Building, 200 South George Street, York, PA 17405 .... (717) 843–8887
2020 Yale Avenue, Camp Hill, PA 17011 .... (717) 763–1988
District Coordinator.—Nancy Newcomer.
Room 301, 140 Baltimore Street, Gettysburg, PA 17325 .... (717) 334–3430
212 North Hanover Street, Carlisle, PA 17013 .... (717) 243–5432

Counties: ADAMS COUNTY; cities of Abbottstown, Arendtsville, Aspers, Bendersville, Biglerville, East Berlin, Fairfield, Gardners, Gettysburg, Littlestown, McKnightstown, McSherrystown, New Oxford, Orrtanna. CUMBERLAND COUNTY: cities of Boiling Springs, Carlisle, Camp Hill, Enola, Grantham, Lemoyne, Mechanicsburg, Mt. Holly Springs, Newburg, New Cumberland, Newville, Shippensburg, Shiremanstown, Summerdale, Walnut Bottom, West Fairview, Wormleysburg; townships of Cooke, Dickinson, Hampden (Part, Precincts 01 North and 01 South), Hopewell, Lower Allen, Lower Frankford, Lower Mifflin, Middlesex, Monroe, North Middleton, North Newton, Penn, Shippensburg, South Middleton, South Newton, Southamption, Upper Allen, Upper Frankford, Upper Mifflin and West Pennsboro and the Boroughs of Camp Hill, Carlisle, Lemoyne, Mt. Holly Springs, New Cumberland, Newburg, Newville, Shippensburg (Cumberland County Portion), West Fairview and Wormleysburg. YORK COUNTY; cities and townships of Airville, Brodbecks, Brogue, Dallastown, Delta, Dillsburg, Dover, Emigsville, East Prospect, Etters, Felton, Fawn Grove, Glen Rock, Hanover, Hellam, Jacobus, Lewisberry, Loganville, Manchester, Mount Wolf, New Freedom, New Park, Red Lion, Spring Grove, Shrewsbury, Stewartstown, Seven Valleys, Thomasville, Wellsville, Windsor, Wrightsville, York, York Haven, York New Salem, Yoe, York Springs. Population (1990), 565,831.

ZIP Codes: 17007–17407

* * *

TWENTIETH DISTRICT

FRANK R. MASCARA, Democrat, of Charleroi, PA; born January 19, 1930; graduated from Belle Vernon High School, Belle Vernon, PA; B.S., California University of Pennsylvania, California, PA; served in the U.S. Army, 1946–47; educator, businessman and public accountant; Washington County controller, 1974–80; chairman, Washington County commissioners, 1980–94; member, California University of Pennsylvania; Board of Trustees; Port of Pittsburgh commissioner; Middle Monongahela Valley Industrial Development Authority; National Society of Public Accountants, 1954; married Dolores Mascara, 1954; four children: Frank, Karen, Mark, and Jon; committees: Transportation and Infrastructure, Veterans' Affairs; elected on November 8, 1994 to the 104th Congress; relected to the 105th Congress.

Office Listings

1531 Longworth House Office Building, Washington, DC 20515–3820 225–4665
Administrative Assistant.—Bill Sember. FAX: 225–3377
Press Secretary.—Bonnie Lowrey.
Secretary.—Becky Banta-Kuhn.
93 High Street, Waynesburg, PA 15370 .... (412) 852–2182
96 North Main Street, Washington, PA 15301 .... (412) 228–4326
47 East Penn Street, Uniontown, PA 15402 .... (412) 437–5078

Counties: Greene, Washington. ALLEGHENY COUNTY (part); cities and townships of Crescent, Findlay, Moon, North Fayette, South Fayette and Upper St. Clair, Boroughs of Bethel Park, Bridgeville, Coraopolis, Edgeworth, Glenfield, Haysville,

McDonald (Allegheny County Portion), Oakdale, Osborne and Sewickley. FAYETTE COUNTY (part); city of Uniontown, townships of Brownsville, Bullskin, Franklin, German, Jefferson, Lower Tyrone, Luzerne, Menallen, Nicholson, Perry, Redstone, Saltlick, South Union, Springhill, Upper Tyrone and Washington and the Boroughs of Belle Venon, Brownsville, Dawson, Everson, Fayette City, Masontown, Newell, Perryopolis, Point Marion. WESTMORELAND COUNTY (part); cities of Greensburg, Monessen, townships of Hempfield, Rostraver, Sewickley, South Huntingdon, Boroughs of Adamsburg, Arona, Hunker, Madison, New Stanton, North Belle Vernon, Smithton, South Greensburg, Southwest Greensburg, Sutersville, West Newton, and Youngwood. Population (1990), 565,815.

ZIP Codes: 15001 (part), 15003 (part), 15004, 15012 (part), 15017 (part), 15019, 15021–22, 15026 (part), 15028–29, 15031, 15033, 15036, 15038, 15042 (part), 15043 (part), 15050 (part), 15052 (part), 15053–56, 15057 (part), 15059 (part), 15060–61, 15063 (part), 15064, 15066 (part), 15067, 15071 (part), 15074 (part), 15078, 15081, 15106 (part), 15108, 15126 (part), 15142, 15301, 15310–17, 15320–25, 15327, 15329–31, 15332 (part), 15333–34, 15336–42, 15344–54, 15356–68, 15370, 15376 (part), 15377 (part), 15378–80, 15401, 15410, 15412–13, 15415–17, 15419–23, 15424 (part), 15425, 15427–40, 15442–51, 15454–56, 15458–70, 15472–78, 15479 (part), 15480, 15482–84, 15485 (part), 15486, 15488–90, 15492, 15557 (part), 15610 (part), 15622 (part), 15631, 15666 (part), 15683 (part), 26525 (part)

* * *

TWENTY-FIRST DISTRICT

PHIL S. ENGLISH, Republican, of Erie, PA; born in Erie, June 20, 1956; B.A., University of Pennsylvania, political science; chief of staff, State Senator Melissa Hart; executive director, State Senate Finance Committee; married Christiane Weschler-English, 1992; elected to the 104th Congress; reelected to the 105th Congress.

Office Listings

http://www.house.gov/english

1721 Longworth House Office Building, Washington, DC 20515–3821 225–5406
Administrative Assistant.—Bob HolsteFAX: 225–5406
Office Manager.—Nancy Billet.
Press Secretary.—Doug Graham.
Legislative Director.—Karin Johns.
Modern Toal Square, 310 French Street, Suite 107, Erie, PA 16507 .... (814) 456–2038
312 Chestnut Street, Meadville, PA 16335 .... (814) 724–8414
City Annex Building, 900 North Hermitage Road, Suite 6, Hermitage, PA 16148 .. (412) 342–6132
The Butler Mall, 310 New Castle Road, Suite 140, Butler PA 16001 .... (412) 285–7005

Counties: Butler (part), Crawford (part), Erie, and Mercer. Population (1990), 565,802.

ZIP Codes: 16001, 16051 (part), 16057 (part), 16105 (part), 16110–11, 16113–14, 16121, 16123 (part), 16124–25, 16127 (part), 16130–31, 16133–34, 16137, 16142 (part), 16143 (part), 16145–46, 16148, 16150–51, 16153–54, 16156 (part), 16159 (part), 16161, 16311 (part), 16314 (part), 16316, 16317 (part), 16327–28, 16335, 16342 (part), 16354 (part), 16360, 16362 (part), 16401, 16403–04, 16405 (part), 16406, 16407 (part), 16410–13, 16415, 16416 (part), 16417, 16421–24, 16426–28, 16430, 16432–33, 16434 (part), 16435, 16438, 16440–43, 16500–12, 16514–15

RHODE ISLAND

(Population 1995, 990,000)

SENATORS

JOHN H. CHAFEE, Republican, of Warwick, RI; born in Providence, RI, October 22, 1922; graduated, Deerfield Academy, 1940; entered Yale University, 1940 and left in February 1942 to enlist in U.S. Marine Corps; served in original landing on Guadalcanal, August 1942; commissioned second lieutenant, participated in fighting in Okinawa; B.A., Yale University, 1947; LL.B., Harvard Law School, 1950; admitted to bar in Rhode Island, 1950; recalled to active duty in Marines in Korean conflict, 1951; served in Korea as rifle company commander; discharged with rank of captain, 1952; total active duty time in Marine Corps, 5½ years; practiced law in Providence, 1952–63; member, Rhode Island House of Representatives, 1957–63; minority leader, 1959–63; Governor of Rhode Island, 1963–69; chairman, Republican Governors Association, 1968; Secretary of the Navy, January 1969 to May 1972; Chubb fellow, Yale University, 1966; board of visitors, John F. Kennedy School of Government, Harvard University, 1969–72; Yale University, board of trustees, 1972–78; honorary degrees: Brown University, Providence College, University of Rhode Island, Rhode Island College, Roger Williams College, Salve Regina College, Suffolk University, Jacksonville University, Bryant College; Legislator of the Year Award; National League of Women Voters, 1992; Environmental Law Institute Award, 1991; 1992 Audubon Medal; 1992 Excellence in Health Care Award; married the former Virginia Coates; five children: Zechariah, Lincoln, John, Jr., Georgia, and Quentin; elected to the U.S. Senate, November 2, 1976, for the six-year term beginning January 3, 1977, first Republican Senator elected from Rhode Island in 46 years; reelected November 2, 1982; reelected November 8, 1988; reelected November 8, 1994; Senate committees: chairman, Environment and Public Works; Finance; Select Committee on Intelligence; Joint Committee on Taxation.

Office Listings

http.//www.senate.gov/senator/chafee.html senator__chafee@chafee.senate.gov

505 Dirksen Senate Office Building, Washington, DC 20510–3902 224–2921
Chief of Staff.—David A. Griswold.
Personal/Appointment Secretary.—Kathy Bell.
Press Secretary.—Nicholas Graham.
10 Dorrance Street, Suite 221, Providence, RI 02903 .... (401) 528–5294
Director.—Keith Lang.

* * *

JACK REED, Democrat, of Cranston, RI; born in Providence, RI, November 12, 1949; graduated, La Salle Academy, Providence, RI, 1967; B.S., U.S. Military Academy, West Point, NY, 1971; M.P.P., Kennedy School of Government, Harvard University, 1973; J.D., Harvard Law School, 1982; served in the U.S. Army, 1967–79; associate professor, Department of Social Sciences, U.S. Military Academy, West Point, NY, 1978–79; 2nd BN (Abn) 504th Infantry, 82nd Airborne Division, Fort Bragg, NC; platoon leader, company commander, battalion staff officer, 1973–77; military awards: Army commendation medal with Oak Leaf Cluster, ranger, senior parachutist, jumpmaster, expert infantryman's badge; lawyer; admitted to the Washington, DC bar, 1983; elected to the Rhode Island State Senate, 1985–90; committees: Banking, Housing, and Urban Affairs; Labor and Human Resources; Special Committee on Aging; elected to the 102nd Congress on November 6, 1990; served three terms in the U.S. House of Representatives; elected to the U.S. Senate, November 5, 1996 for the six-year term beginning January 7, 1997.

Office Listings

http://www.senate.gov/senator/reed.html

320 Hart Senate Office Building, Washington, DC 20510–3903 .... (202) 224–4642
Administrative Assistant.—J.B. Poersch.
Office Manager.—Suzanne Hassett.
Legislative Director.—Neil Campbell.
Press Secretary.—Betsy Mullins.
201 Hillside Road, Suite 200, Cranston, RI 02920 .... (401) 943–3100
Chief of Staff.—Raymond Simone.
Office Manager.—Lynne Lombardi.
Federal Courthouse, 1 Exchange Terrace, Room 418, Providence, RI 02903–1757 (401) 528–5200
Deputy Chief of Staff.—Todd Andrews.

REPRESENTATIVES

FIRST DISTRICT

PATRICK JOSEPH KENNEDY, Democrat, of Providence, RI; born on July 14, 1967, in Brighton, MA; graduated, Phillips Academy, Andover, MA; B.A., Providence College, Providence, RI, 1991; Rhode Island State Legislature, 1988–94; member: Rhode Island Special Olympics (board of directors), Rhode Island March of Dimes, Rhode Island Lung Association, Rhode Island Mental Health Association, Rhode Island Chapter of National Committee for the Prevention of Child Abuse; elected to the 104th and 105th Congresses.

Office Listings

http://www.house.gov/patrickkennedy

1505 Longworth House Office Building, Washington, DC 20515	225–4911 FAX: 225–3290
Administrative Assistant.—Tony Marcella.	
Staff Director.—William Burke.	
Legislative Director.—Deanna Kirtman.	
286 Main Street, Suite 600, Pawtucket, RI 02860	(401) 729–5600 FAX: 729–5608
District Director.—Mike Mello.	
Press Secretary.—Larry Berman.	
Newport Post Office 3 20, Thames Street, Newport, RI 02840	(401) 841–0440 FAX: 841–0441
Woonsocket Post Office, 127 Social Street, Woonsocket, RI 02895	(401) 762–2288

Counties: Bristol, Newport, Providence. CITIES AND TOWNSHIPS: Barrington, Bristol, Burrillville, Central Falls, Cumberland, East Providence, Jamestown, Lincoln, Little Compton, Middleton, Newport, North Providence, North Smithfield, Providence, Pawtucket, Portsmouth, Smithfield, Tiverton, Warren, Woonsocket. Population (1990), 501,677.

ZIP Codes: 01871, 02801–02, 02806, 02809, 02824, 02826, 02828 (part), 02830, 02835, 02837–40, 02842, 02860–61, 02863–65, 02871–72, 02876, 02878, 02885, 02895–96, 02903 (part), 02906, 02908 (part), 02911–12, 02914–17, 02940

* * *

SECOND DISTRICT

BOB WEYGAND, Democrat, of North Kingstown, RI; born on May 10, 1948; B.F.A., 1971, and B.S., civil and environmental engineering, 1976, University of Rhode Island; landscape architect; former Lieutenant Governor of Rhode Island; served in Rhode Island House of Representatives, 1985–93, providing leadership on environmental protection issues and housing and land use policy reform; chaired state delegation, White House Conference on Aging, 1995; named Legislator of the Year by the Rhode Island League of Cities and Towns, 1988; Leadership Award, American Planning Association, 1992; former board member, Save the Bay; past president and director, Rhode Island Parks Association; past chairman: Rhode Island Small Business Advocacy Council, Rhode Island Long Term Care Coordinating Council, Rhode Island Land Use Commission, Rhode Island Scenic Highway Board; member: United Way of Rhode Island, Meeting Street Center, Big Brothers of Rhode Island; married to the former Frances A. Scullian; three children: Jennifer, Allison, and Robert, Jr.; elected to the 105th Congress.

Office Listings

507 Cannon House Office Building, Washington, DC 20515	225–2735 FAX: 225–5976
Chief of Staff.—James M. Russo.	
Executive Assistant.—Rhiannon E. Burruss.	
Press Secretary.—Jennifer Bramley.	
Legislative Director.—Kevin M. Wilson.	
Suite 205, The Summit West, 300 Centerville Road, Warwick, RI 02886	(401) 732–9400
District Director.—Leigh Ann Woisard.	

Counties: Kent, Providence (part), Washington. CITIES AND TOWNSHIPS: Ashaway, Bradford, Cranston, Johnston, Kingston, Narragansett Pier, Providence (part), Wakefield-Peacedale, Warwick, West Warwick and Westerly. Population (1990), 501,787.

ZIP Codes: 02804, 02807–08, 02812–16, 02818, 02821–27, 02828 (part), 02829–32, 02836, 02839, 02852, 02854, 02857–59, 02873–75, 02877, 02879–83, 02886–89, 02891–94, 02898, 02903 (part), 02905, 02907, 02908 (part), 02909–10, 02919–20

SOUTH CAROLINA

(Population 1995, 3,673,000)

SENATORS

STROM THURMOND, Republican, of Aiken, SC; attorney and educator; committees: chairman, Senate Armed Services Committee; ranking member, Judiciary; senior member, Veterans' Affairs. Family: born December 5, 1902, in Edgefield, SC; son of John William and Eleanor Gertrude (Strom) Thurmond; married Jean Crouch, 1947 (deceased January 6, 1960); married Nancy Moore, 1968; four children: Nancy Moore (deceased April 14, 1993), James Strom II, Juliana Gertrude, and Paul Reynolds. *Education:* 1923 graduate of Clemson University; studied law at night under his father, admitted to South Carolina bar, 1930, and admitted to practice in all federal courts, including the U.S. Supreme Court. *Professional career:* teacher and athletic coach (1923–29), county superintendent of education (1929–33), city attorney and county attorney (1930–38), State Senator (1933–38), circuit judge (1938–46), Governor of South Carolina (1947–51), serving as chairman of Southern Governors Conference (1950); practiced law in Edgefield, SC (1930–38) and in Aiken, SC (1951–55); adjunct professor of political science at Clemson University and distinguished lecturer at the Strom Thurmond Institute; member, President's Commission on Organized Crime and Commission on the Bicentennial of the Constitution. *Military service:* Reserve officer for 36 years; while serving as judge, volunteered for active duty in World War II the day war was declared against Germany; served with Headquarters First Army (1942–46), American, European, and Pacific theaters; participated in Normandy invasion with 82nd Airborne Division and landed on D-day; awarded 5 battle stars and 18 decorations, medals, and awards, including the Legion of Merit with Oak Leaf Cluster, Bronze Star Medal with "V", Purple Heart, Belgian Order of the Crown, and French Croix de Guerre; major general, U.S. Army Reserves. *Honors and awards:* past national president of Reserve Officers Association (ROA) of the United States (1954–55); Clemson University Alumni Association Distinguished Service Award (1961), Clemson Medallion (1981) and Clemson University Athletic Hall of Fame (1983); Disabled American Veterans Outstanding and Unselfish Service Awards (1964 and 1981); Military Order of World Wars Distinguished Service Award (1964); Order of AHEPA Dedicated Public Service Award (1968); WIS Radio-TV (Columbia, SC) "South Carolinian of the Year" (1968); 33rd degree Mason (1969); first president of ROA to receive "Minuteman of the Year Award" (1971); Noncommissioned Officers Association L. Mendel Rivers Award for Legislative Action (1971); Congressional Medal of Honor Society National Patriots Award (1974); The Retired Officers Association Distinguished Service Award (1974); Association of U.S. Army Distinguished Service Citation (1974); American Legion Distinguished Public Service Award (1975); Medal of the Knesset, Israel (1982); Distinguished Service Medal (1984); Military Order of the Purple Heart Congressional Award (1976); AMVETS Silver Helmet Congressional Award (1977); Veterans of Foreign Wars Dwight D. Eisenhower Service Award (1977) and Congressional Award (1985); Touchdown Club of Washington, DC, "Mr. Sam" Award for contributions to sports (1978); South Carolina Trial Lawyers Association Service Award (1980); Navy League of U.S. Meritorious Service Citation (1980); American Judges Association Distinguished Service Citation (1981); South Carolina Hall of Fame (1982); Audie Murphy Patriotism Award (1982); National Guard Association of United States, Harry S. Truman Distinguished Service Award (1982); New York Board of Trade "Textile Man of the Year" (1984); Napoleon Hill Gold Medal Humanitarian Achievement Award (1985); Order of the Palmetto Award; Presidential Citizens Medal by President Ronald Reagan, 1989; Noncommissioned Officers Association Lifetime Legislative Achievement Award, 1990; Adjutants General Association of the United States, George Washington Freedom Award, 1991; U.S. Marshals Service America's Star Award, 1991; ROA; Presidential Medal of Freedom by President George Bush, 1992; over 20 honorary degrees; numerous Watchdog of the Treasury awards and Guardian of Small Business awards. International awards: Order of Distinguished Diplomatic Service Merit Medal, South Korea (1974); Order of Kim Khanh Award, Republic of Vietnam (1975); Grand Cross in the Order of Orange-Nassau, the Netherlands (1982); numerous other distinctions; U.S. Army Ranger Hall of Fame Medal (1994); Senior Army Reserve Commanders Association Hall of Fame Medal (1995). Named in his honor: Thurmond Hall at Winthrop College, SC (1939); Strom Thurmond High School, Edgefield County, SC (1961); Strom Thurmond Student Center, Charleston Southern University at Charleston, SC (1972); Strom Thurmond Federal Building, Columbia, SC (1975); The Strom Thurmond Institute of Government and Public Affairs at The Strom Thurmond Center for Excellence in Government and Public Service at Clemson University, Clemson, SC (1981); Strom Thurmond Chairs and Scholarships (1981), and Strom Thurmond Auditorium (1982) at University of South Carolina School of Law, Columbia, SC; life-sized statue erected on Edgefield town square by people of Edgefield County, SC (1984), and on streets in several South Carolina cities; Strom Thurmond Lake, Dam and Highway, Clarks Hill, SC, 1987; Strom Thurmond Mall, Columbia, SC, 1988; has endowed 52 scholarships at 45 colleges and universities, and established the Strom

Thurmond Foundation, which assists in educating 80 to 100 needy, worthy students annually; Strom Thurmond Soldier Service Center, Fort Jackson, Columbia, SC, 1991; Strom Thurmond Room, U.S. Capitol, 1991; Strom Thurmond Highway (Interstate 20 from the Georgia Line to Florence, SC), 1992; Strom Thurmond Biomedical Research Center, Medical University of South Carolina, Charleston, SC (1993); Strom Thurmond National Guard Armory, Edgefield, SC (1994). *Memberships and affiliations:* Baptist; Shriner; South Carolina and American bar associations; numerous defense, veterans, civic, fraternal, and farm organizations. *Political activities:* States Rights Democratic candidate for president of the United States (1948), carrying four states and receiving 39 electoral votes; delegate to six Democratic national conventions (chairman of South Carolina delegation and national committeeman, 1948); switched from Democratic to Republican Party (September 16, 1964); delegate to five Republican national conventions (chairman of South Carolina delegation, 1984); elected to the U.S. Senate, November 2, 1954, as a write-in candidate (first person in U.S. history elected to a major office in this manner) for term ending January 3, 1961; resigned as U.S. Senator April 4, 1956, to place the office in a primary, pursuant to a promise made to the people during the 1954 campaign; renominated and reelected to the Senate in 1956, resuming duties on November 7, 1956; reelected for each succeeding term; served as president pro tempore of the U.S. Senate, 1981–87, and currently since 1995.

Office Listings

http://www.senate.gov/~thumond senator@thurmond.senate.gov

217 Russell Senate Office Building, Washington, DC 20510–4001 224–5972
Chief of Staff.—R.J. (Duke) Short.
Executive Assistant.—Holly Richardson.
Press Secretary.—Chris Kelley Cimko.
Thurmond Federal Building, 18365 Assembly Street, Columbia, SC 29201 .... (803) 765–5494
State Director.—Warren Abernathy.
Federal Building, 211 York Street NE, Aiken, SC 29801 .... (803) 649–2591
Federal Building, 334 Meeting Street, Charleston, SC 29501 .... (803) 727–4596
McMillan Federal Building, 401 West Evans Street, Florence, SC 29501 .... (803) 662–8873

* * *

ERNEST F. HOLLINGS, Democrat, of Charleston, SC; born in Charleston, January 1, 1922; son of Wilhelmine Meyer and Adolph G. Hollings; graduated, The Citadel, B.A., 1942; University of South Carolina, LL.B., 1947; LL.D. The Citadel, June 1959; lawyer; member of Charleston County, South Carolina, and American bar associations; admitted to practice before South Carolina Supreme Court, U.S. District Court, U.S. Circuit Court of Appeals, U.S. Tax Court, U.S. Customs Court, and U.S. Supreme Court; member, St. John's Lutheran Church; member, Court of Adjudication, Lutheran Church in America; Armed Forces, 1942–45, served overseas from Africa to Austria, 33 months; 353rd Antiaircraft Artillery; 3rd, 36th, and 45th Divisions, captain; member, highest honor society at The Citadel—The Round Table; president of the alumni (the Association of Citadel Men), 1954; at the University of South Carolina Law School—member, Honor Society, Wig and Robe, *South Carolina Law Review*, and president of Law Federation; honorary doctor of letters degree, Benedict College, Columbia, SC, 1971; Charleston Junior Chamber of Commerce Distinguished Service Award as Young Man of the Year, 1953; U.S. Junior Chamber of Commerce, one of ten Outstanding Young Men of the United States, 1954; South Carolina Veteran of the Year, 1957; member, Hibernian Society, Arion Society, Sertoma Club; Charleston Rifle Club; Mason, LeCandeur No. 36, AFM; Shriner, Omar Temple; BPOE Lodge No. 242; American Legion, Post No. 10; Charleston Chamber of Commerce; Veterans of Foreign Wars; Captain John L. Weeks Post No. 3142; elected to South Carolina General Assembly from Charleston County, 1948, 1950, and 1952; chairman, Charleston County legislative delegation; speaker pro tempore, South Carolina House of Representatives; elected twice by unanimous vote, 1951, 1953; elected lieutenant governor, November 2, 1954; elected governor, November 4, 1958; served as Governor, 1959–63; appointed to Hoover Commission May 15, 1955; appointed by President Eisenhower to Advisory Commission on Intergovernmental Relations, December 1959; reappointed by President Kennedy, February 1962; chairman, Regional Advisory Council on Nuclear Energy; instituted technical training program in South Carolina, Nuclear Space Commission, and Commission on Higher Education; married to the former Rita Louise Liddy of Charleston, SC; four children: Michael Milhous, Helen Hayne, Patricia Salley, and Ernest Frederick Hollings III; author of "The Case Against Hunger—A Demand for a National Policy," 1970; elected to the U.S. Senate, November 8, 1966, to complete the unexpired term of the late Senator Olin D. Johnston; elected to full six-year term November 5, 1968; reelected 1974, 1980, 1986 and 1992; ranking member: Senate Commerce, Science and Transportation Committee; other committee assignments: Appropriations, Budget.

Office Listings

http://www.senate.gov/~hollings senator@hollings.senate.gov

125 Russell Senate Office Building, Washington, DC 20510–4002 224–6121
Administrative Assistant.—David Rudd.
Executive Assistant.—Karen Kollmansperger.
Home Secretary.—Sam B. King, III.
Appointments Secretary.—Robin McCain.
Press Secretary.—Maury Lane.
Room 1551, 1835 Assembly Street, Columbia, SC 29201 .... (803) 765–5731
Custom House, Suite 112, 200 East Bay Street, Charleston, SC 29401 .... (803) 727–4525
103 Federal Building, Spartanburg, SC 29301 .... (864) 585–3702
126 Federal Building, Greenville, SC 29603 .... (864) 233–5366

REPRESENTATIVES

FIRST DISTRICT

MARSHALL (MARK) CLEMENT SANFORD, Jr., Republican, of Charleston, SC; born May 28, 1960, in Ft. Lauderdale, FL; attended high school in Beaufort, SC; B.A., Furman University, 1983; M.B.A., University of Virginia's Darden School of Business, 1988; owner, real estate investment firm; member: Preservation Society of Charleston, National Trust; attends St. Stephen's Episcopal Church; married Jennifer Sullivan Sanford, 1989; three children: Marshall, Landon and Bolton; elected on November 8, 1994 to the 104th Congress; reelected to the 105th Congress; Joint Economic Committee, Government Reform and Oversight Committee, International Relations Committee.

Office Listings

http://www.house.gov/sanford sanford@hr.house.gov

1223 Longworth House Office Building, Washington, DC 20515–4001 225–3176
Administrative Assistant.—Greg Engeman.
Legislative Director.—David John.
Office Manager.—Mary Green.
Suite 640, Federal Building, 334 Meeting Street, Charleston, SC 29403 .... (803) 727–4175
206 Laurel Street, Conway, SC 29526 .... (803) 248–2660
829 East Front Street, Georgetown, SC 29440 .... (803) 527–6868
Staff Assistant.—Elma Harrelson.

Counties: Berkeley (part), Charleston (part), Dorchester (part), Georgetown, Horry. Population (1990), 581,125.

ZIP Codes: 29018 (part), 29081 (part), 29082 (part), 29401–12, 29414–15, 29417–18, 29426–27, 29429, 29432 (part), 29433, 29435, 29437–39, 29445–49, 29451–52, 29455–56, 29458, 29460, 29463–64, 29470–71, 29472 (part), 29474–75, 29477, 29481 (part), 29482, 29483 (part), 29484, 29487–88, 29493–94, 29902–05, 29910–11, 29913–16, 29918, 29920–24, 29927–29, 29931–36, 29939–41, 29943–45

* * *

SECOND DISTRICT

FLOYD SPENCE, Republican, of Lexington, SC; born in Columbia, SC, April 9, 1928; on July 3, 1988, married the former Deborah Ellen Williams of Lexington, SC; father of four sons with the late Lula Hancock Drake Spence: David, Zach, Benjamin and Caldwell; Lexington High School, SC, student body president; attended University of South Carolina on an athletic scholarship; B.A. in English, 1952, president South Carolina Association of Student Governments, junior class president, battalion subcommander of USN–ROTC, captain of track team, member of Kappa Alpha Order social fraternity, honor council honor board, student council, football team, basketball team, YMCA; named to Omicron Delta Kappa honorary leadership fraternity, Kappa Sigma Kappa honorary service fraternity, dean's list, *Who's Who Among Students in American Colleges and Universities,* selected Outstanding Senior and recipient of Algernon-Sydney Sullivan Award as outstanding male student at University of South Carolina in 1952, Fellowship of Christian Athletes; author and lecturer on communism and national defense, coauthor, *Can You Afford This House?, The Case Against the Reckless Congress, Who's Who in the South and Southwest, Who's Who in American Politics,* and *Outstanding Personalities of the South;* attended college on football scholarship; University of South Carolina Law School, J.D., 1956; editor of *South Carolina Law Quarterly*; chief justice of Phi Alpha Delta legal fraternity and vice president of the Law Federation; enlisted as a recruit in Naval Reserves when in high school, commissioned upon graduation from college, served aboard U.S.S. *Carter Hall* (LSD–3) and U.S.S. *LSM–397* in European, Arctic, Atlantic and Caribbean theaters of operations, retired as captain; present rank, captain, U.S. Naval Reserves; former group commander, all Naval Reserve units, Columbia, SC, area; South Carolina House of Representatives, 1956–62; elected to South Carolina Senate in 1966, reelected in 1968; minority leader of South Carolina Senate, 1966–70; chairman of Joint Senate-House Internal Security Committee in South Carolina, 1967–70; lawyer; former partner in law firm of Callison and Spence, West Columbia, SC; former Sunday School teacher and council member, St. Peter's Lutheran Church; first president of Lexington County Historical Society; former county chairman and member of board of directors of Mid-Carolina Mental Health Association; Sons of Confederate Veterans, commander of Wade Hampton Camp; advisory board of Civil Air Patrol; former circuit vice president and counselor-at-large, University of South Carolina Alumni Association; executive board member of the Indian Waters Council of the Boy Scouts of America; Silver Beaver Award; member of Farm Bureau, Chamber of Commerce, American Legion, Veterans of Foreign Wars, Lexington Voiture, Reserve Officers Association, Naval Reserve Association, U.S. Supreme Court Bar, Lexington County, South Carolina, and American bar associations, American Judicature Society, American Trial Lawyers Association, South Carolina Historical Society, South Caroliniana Society, Columbia Carillon, Archeological Society of South Carolina, University of South Carolina Association of Lettermen; graduate of Defense Strategy Seminar at National War College, graduate of National Security Seminar of Industrial College of the Armed Forces; chairman, Committee on National Security; member, Committee on Veterans' Affairs; elected to the 92nd Congress in November 1970; reelected to each succeeding Congress.

Office Listings

2405 Rayburn House Office Building, Washington, DC 20515–4002 225–2452
Chief of Staff.—Craig H. Metz. FAX: 225–2455
Executive Assistant.—Caroline S. Bryson.
Legislative Director.—Miriam E. A. Wolff.
220 Stoneridge Drive, Suite 202, Columbia, SC 29210 .... (803) 254–5120
1681 Chestnut Street NE, P.O. Box 1609, Orangeburg, SC 29116–1609 .... (803) 536–4641
66 East Railroad Avenue, P.O. Box 550, Estill, SC 29918 .... (803) 625–3177
807 Port Republic Street, Suite 2, P.O. Box 1538, Beaufort, SC 29901 .... (803) 521–2530
1 Town Center Court, Hilton Head Island, SC 29928 .... (803) 842–7212

Counties: Aiken (part), Allendale, Barnwell, Beaufort (part), Calhoun (part), Colleton (part), Hampton, Jasper, Lexington, Orangeburg (part), Richland (part). CITIES AND TOWNSHIPS: Aiken (part), Allendale, Ballentine, Barnwell, Batesburg, Beaufort, Blackville, Bluffton, Blythewood, Brunson, Cayce, Chapin, Columbia (part), Cooaawhatchie, Cope, Cordova, Crocketville, Daufuskie Island, Early Branch, Elko, Estill, Fairfax, Furman, Garnett, Gaston, Gifford, Gilbert, Hampton, Hardeeville, Hilda, Hilton Head Island, Irmo, Islandston, Kline, Leesville, Lexington, Livingston, Lodge, Luray, Martin, Miley, Montmorenci, Neeses, North, Norway, Orangeburg, Pelion, Pineland, Port Royal, Ridgeland, Ruffin, Scotia, Springfield, St. Helena Island, St. Matthews (part), State Park, Swansea, Sycamore, Tillman, Ulmer, Varnville, Walterboro (part), West Columbia, White Rock, Williams, Williston, Windsor, Yemassee. Population (1990), 581,111.

ZIP Codes: 29002, 29006, 29016, 29033, 29036, 29038, 29039, 29053, 29054, 29054, 29063, 29070, 29071, 29072, 29073, 29076, 29082, 29107, 29112, 29113, 29115 (part), 29116 (part), 29123, 29135 (part), 29146, 29147, 29160, 29169, 29170 (part), 29171–72, 29177, 29201 (part), 29202 (part), 29203 (part), 29204 (part), 29205 (part), 29206 (part), 29207 (part), 29208 (part), 29209 (part), 29210–12, 29214 (part), 29215 (part), 29216 (part), 29217 (part), 29218 (part), 29221 (part), 29223 (part), 29224 (part), 29228 (part), 29230 (part), 29240 (part), 29250 (part), 29260 (part), 29290 (part), 29292 (part), 29475, 29488 (part), 29493, 29801 (part), 29802 (part), 29083 (part), 29804 (part), 29810, 29812–14, 29817, 29826–27, 29836, 29839, 29846, 29849, 29853, 29856, 29901–05, 29910–13, 29915–16, 29918, 29920–29, 29932–36, 29938–40, 29943–45, 29948

* * *

THIRD DISTRICT

LINDSEY GRAHAM, Republican, of Seneca; born in Seneca, July 9, 1955; graduated, Daniel High School, Central, SC; B.A., University of South Carolina, 1977; M.A. in public administration, 1978; awarded J.D., 1981; joined the U.S. Air Force, 1982; served in the Base Legal and as area defense counsel; assigned to Rhein Main Air Force Base, Germany, 1984; chief prosecutor for U.S. Air Forces; Meritorius Service Medal for Active Duty Tour in Europe; presently, major in the South Carolina Air National Guard serving as base staff judge advocate at McEntyre Air National Guard Base, Eastover, SC; established private law practice, 1988; former member, South Carolina House of Representatives; Home Health Care Legislator of the year, 1992; assistant county attorney for Oconee County, 1988–92; city attorney for Central, SC, 1990–94; member: Seneca Sertoma, Walhalla Rotary, Anderson Chamber of Commerce, American Legion Post 120, Retired Officers Association; served as fundraising chairman, Oconee County Chapter of the American Cancer Society; board member, Rosa Clark Free Medical Clinic in Seneca, SC; appointed to Judicial Arbitration Commission by the Chief Justice of the Supreme Court; attends Corinth Baptist Church; committees: Education and the Workforce, National Security, International Relations; subcommittees: Workforce Protection, Postsecondary Education, Training and Lifelong Learning, Military Procurement, Military Personnel, International Economic Policy and Trade, International Operations and Human Rights; elected to the 104th Congress on November 8, 1994; reelected to the 105th Congress.

Office Listings

http://www.house.gov/graham

1429 Longworth House Office Building, Washington, DC 20515	225–5301
Chief of Staff.—Richard Perry.	FAX: 225–3216
Press Secretary.—Lisa Brennen.	
101 Federal Building, P.O. Box 4126, Anderson, SC 29622	(864) 224–7401
District Director.—Jane Goolsby.	
129 Federal Building, 120 Main Street, Greenwood, SC 29646	(864) 223–8251
5 Federal Building, 211 York Street NE, Aiken, SC 29801	(803) 649–5571

Counties: ABBEVILLE COUNTY; cities and townships of Abbeville, Calhoun Falls, Donalds, Due West, Lowndesville. AIKEN COUNTY; cities and townships of Aiken, Bath, Belvedere, Clearwater, Graniteville, Gloverville, Jackson, Langley, Monetta, New Ellenton, North Augusta, Ridge Spring, Vaucluse, Ward, Warrenville. ANDERSON COUNTY; Anderson, Belton, Honea Path, Iva, LaFrance, Pelzer, Pendleton, Sandy Springs, Starr, Townville, Williamston, Piedmont. EDGEFIELD COUNTY; cities and townships of Edgefield, Johnston, Modoc, Trenton. GREENWOOD COUNTY; cities and townships of Bradley, Callison, Greenwood, Hodges, Ninety Six, Shoals Junction, Troy, Ware Shoals. LAURENS COUNTY; cities and townships of Clinton, Cross Hill, Gray Court, Joanna, Laurens, Mountville, Waterloo, Fountain Inn, Enoree. MCCORMICK COUNTY; cities and townships of Clarks Hill, McCormick, Modoc, Mt. Carmel, Parksville, Plum Branch, Willington. OCONEE COUNTY; cities and townships of Fair Play, Long Creek, Madison, Mountain Rest, Newry, Richland, Salem, Seneca, Tamassee, Walhalla, Westminister, West Union. PICKENS COUNTY; cities and townships of Cateechee, Central Dacusville, Easley, Easley P.O., Liberty, Norris, Pickens, Six Mile, Sunset, Clemson, Clemson University. SALUDA COUNTY; cities and townships of Monetta, Ridge Spring, Saluda, Ward. Population (1990), 581,104.

ZIP Codes: 29006 (part), 29037 (part), 29059 (part), 29070 (part), 29105, 29124, 29127 (part), 29129, 29137 (part), 29138, 29146 (part), 29164, 29166, 29620–25, 29627 (part), 29628, 29630–33, 29635 (part), 29638–41, 29643, 29646–49, 29648, 29653, 29654 (part), 29655–59, 29661 (part), 29664–67, 29669 (part), 29671, 29673 (part), 29675–79, 29682, 29684–86, 29689, 29691, 29692 (part), 29693–94, 29696–97, 29801, 29809–10, 29812–14, 29816–17, 29819, 29821–22, 29824, 29826–29, 29831–32, 29834–36, 29838–41, 29844–51, 29853, 29856, and 29650, 29802

* * *

FOURTH DISTRICT

BOB INGLIS, Republican, of Greenville, SC; born in Savannah, GA, on October 11, 1959 (hometown, Bluffton, SC); graduated, May River Academy, Bluffton, SC, 1977; A.B., Duke University, Durham, NC, 1981; J.D., University of Virginia Law School, Charlottesville, VA, 1984; attorney; admitted to the South Carolina bar, 1984; formerly shareholder, Leatherwood, Walker, Todd and Mann, P.C.; Fourth District Chairman, South Carolinians to Limit Congressional Terms; Leadership Greenville; United Way Loaned Executive; Second Presbyterian Church; married the former Mary Anne Williams, 1982; four children, Robert Durden, Jr., Mary Ashton, Anne McCullough, and Mabel Andrews; elected on November 3, 1992 to the 103rd Congress; reelected to each succeeding Congress.

Office Listings

binglis@hr.house.gov

1237 Longworth House Office Building, Washington, DC 20515–4004	225–6030
Chief of Staff/Legislative Director.—Jeff Fedorchak.	FAX: 226–1177
Executive Administrator.—Cherié Sveiven.	
Press Secretary.—Jill Gerber.	
201 Magnolia Street, Suite 108, Spartanburg, SC 29301	(864) 582–6422
	FAX: 573–9478
300 East Washington Street, Suite 101, Greenville, SC 29601	(864) 232–1141
	FAX: 233–2160
405 West Main Street, McDade and Fant Building, Union, SC 29379	(864) 427–2205
	FAX: 429–8879

Counties: Greenville, Laurens (part), Spartanburg, Union. Population (1990), 581,113.

ZIP Codes: 29031, 29178, 29301–7, 29316, 29318, 29320–23, 29329–31, 29333–36, 29338, 29340–42, 29346, 29348–49, 29353, 29356, 29364–65, 29368–69, 29372, 29379, 29385, 29388, 29601–16, 29635, 29650–51, 29654, 29661–62, 29669, 29673, 29680–81, 29683, 29687–88, 29690

FIFTH DISTRICT

JOHN M. SPRATT, Jr., Democrat, of York, SC; born in Charlotte, NC, November 1, 1942; graduated, York High School, 1960; A.B., Davidson College, 1964; president of student body and Phi Beta Kappa, Davidson College; M.A., economics, Oxford University, Corpus Christi College (Marshall Scholar), 1966; LL.B., Yale Law School, 1969; admitted to the South Carolina Bar in 1969; active duty, U.S. Army, 1969–71, discharged as captain; served as member of Operations Analysis Group, Office of the Assistant Secretary of Defense (Comptroller), received Meritorious Service Medal; private practice of law 1971–82, Spratt, McKeown and Spratt in York, SC; York County attorney, 1973–82; president, Bank of Fort Mill, 1973–82; president, Spratt Insurance Agency, Inc.; president, York Chamber of Commerce; chairman, Winthrop College Board of Visitors; chairman, Divine Saviour Hospital Board; board of visitors, Davidson and Coker Colleges; president, Western York County United Fund; board of directors, Piedmont Legal Services; House of Delegates, South Carolina bar; elder, First Presbyterian Church, York; member, National Security Committee, Subcommittee on Procurement; Budget Committee, ranking mamber; married Jane Stacy Spratt, 1968; three daughters: Susan, Sarah and Catherine; elected to the 98th Congress, November 2, 1982; reelected to each succeeding Congress.

Office Listings

http://www.house.gov/spratt jspratt@hr.house.gov

1536 Longworth House Office Building, Washington, DC 20515–4005 225–5501
Administrative Assistant.—Ellen Buchanan. FAX: 225–0464
Press Secretary.—Chuck Fant.
P.O. Box 350, Rock Hill, SC 29731 .... (803) 327–1114
District Administrator.—Robert Hopkins.
39 East Calhoun Street, Sumter, SC 29150 .... (803) 773–3362
P.O. Box 25, Darlington, SC 29532–0025 .... (803) 393–3998

Counties: Cherokee, Chester, Chesterfield, Darlington (part), Dillon, Fairfield, Kershaw, Lancaster, Lee (part), Marlboro, Newberry, Sumter (part), and York. Population (1990), 581,131.

ZIP Codes: 29001 (part), 29009–10, 29014–15, 29016 (part), 29017, 29020, 29031 (part), 29032, 29036 (part), 29037 (part), 29040, 29045 (part), 29046, 29051 (part), 29055, 29058, 29062, 29065, 29067 (part), 29074, 29075 (part), 29078 (part), 29080, 29101 (part), 29102 (part), 29104, 29106, 29108, 29114 (part), 29122, 29125 (part), 29126, 29127 (part), 29128, 29130 (part), 29131 (part), 29132, 29134, 29145, 29150–52, 29154, 29162 (part), 29168, 29175–76, 29178 (part), 29180 (part), 29183, 29323 (part), 29325, 29330 (part), 29332, 29340, 29342, 29351, 29355, 29360, 29370, 29372 (part), 29384, 29388 (part), 29520, 29550 (part), 29584, 29593 (part), 29644 (part), 29645, 29654 (part), 29692 (part), 29702–06, 29709–10, 29712, 29714–15, 29717–20, 29724, 29726–31, 29733, 29741–45

* * *

SIXTH DISTRICT

JAMES E. CLYBURN, Democrat, of Columbia, SC; born in Sumter, SC, on July 21, 1940; graduated, Mather Academy, Camden, SC, 1957; B.S., South Carolina State University, Orangeburg, 1962; attended University of South Carolina Law School, Columbia, 1972–74; South Carolina State Human Affairs Commissioner; Assistant to the Governor for Human Resource Development; executive director, South Carolina Commission for Farm Workers, Inc.; director, Neighborhood Youth Corps and New Careers; counselor, South Carolina Employment Security Commission; member: NAACP, lifetime member; Southern Regional Council; Omega Psi Phi Fraternity, Inc.; Arabian Temple, No. 139; Nemiah Lodge No. 51 F&AM; married to the former Emily England; three children: Mignon, Jennifer and Angela; elected on November 3, 1992 to the 103rd Congress; reelected to each succeeding Congress.

Office Listings

http://www.house.gov/clyburn jclyburn@hr.house.gov

319 Cannon House Office Building, Washington, DC 20515–4006 225–3315
Administrative Assistant/Legislative Director.—Yelberton Watkins. FAX: 225–2313
Press Secretary.—Dorothy Givens.
Office Manager.—Lisa Toporek.
Appointments.—Pamela McDonald.
1703 Gervais Street, Columbia, SC 29201 .... (803) 799–1100
FAX: 799–9060
181 East Evans Street, Suite 314, Post Office Box 6286, Florence, SC 29502 .... (803) 662–1212
FAX: 662–8474
North Charleston City Hall, 4900 LaCrosse Road, North Charleston, SC 29418 ..... (803) 747–9660
FAX: 744–2715

Counties: Bamberg County; cities and townships of Bamberg, Denmark, Erhardt, Olar. Berkeley County; cities and townships of Bethera, Cross, Huger, Jamestown, Pineville, Russellville, Saint Stephen, Wando. Calhoun County;

city of Cameron (part). CHARLESTON COUNTY; cities and townships of Adams Run, Charleston (part), Edisto Island, Hollywood, Johns Island (part), Ravenel (part), Wadmalaw Island (part). CLARENDON; cities and townships of Alcolu, Davis Station, Gable, Manning, New Zion, Rimini, Summerton, Turbeville. COLLECTON COUNTY; cities and townships of Cottageville, Green Pond, Jacksonboro, Lodge (part), Round O, Saint George, Smoaks, Walterboro (part), Williams. COLUMBIA COUNTY; city of Columbia (part). DARLINGTON COUNTY; cities and townships of Darlington (part), Lamar (part). DORCHESTER COUNTY; cities and townships of Dorchester, Harleyville, Reevesville. FLORENCE COUNTY; cities and townships of Coward, Effingham, Florence, Johnsonville, Lake City, Olanta, Pamplico, Scranton, Timmonsville. MARION COUNTY; cities and townships of Centenary, Gresham, Marion, Mullins, Nichols, Rains, Sellers. LEE COUNTY; cities and townships of Bishopville (part), Elliott, Lynchburg. ORANGEBURG COUNTY; cities and townships of Bowman, Branchville (part), Cope (part), Elloree, Eutawville, Holly Hill, Orangeburg (part), Rowesville, Santee, Vance. RICHLAND COUNTY; cities and townships of Blythewood, Eastover, Gadsden, Hopkins (part). SUMTER COUNTY; cities and townships of Mayesville, Pinewood, Rembert, Sumter (part), Wedgefield. WILLIAMSBURG COUNTY; cities and townships of Cades, Greeleyville, Hemingway, Kingstree, Lane, Nesmith, Salters, Trio. Population (1990), 581,133.

ZIP Codes: 29001, 29003, 29010 (part), 29016 (part), 29018, 29030 (part), 29038 (part), 29041–42, 29044, 29046–48, 29051–52, 29056, 29059, 29061 (part), 29069 (part), 29080–81, 29082 (part), 29102, 29104, 29111, 29114–15, 29116 (part), 29125, 29128, 29131, 29133, 29142, 29148, 29150 (part), 29151, 29153–54, 29161–63, 29168, 29201–05, 29206 (part), 29209, 29211, 29223, 29240, 29401 (part), 29403, 29405, 29407, 29411–12, 29415, 29426, 29430, 29432 (part), 29435–38, 29446, 29448–50, 29452–53, 29455 (part), 29468 29470 (part), 29471, 29474, 29476–77, 29479, 29481, 29487 (part), 29488 (part), 29492–93, 29501–06, 29518–19, 29530, 29532 (part), 29541, 29546, 29554–56, 29560, 29564, 29571, 29574, 29580–81, 29583, 29589–92, 29595, 29843

SOUTH DAKOTA

(Population 1995, 729,000)

SENATORS

THOMAS A. DASCHLE, Democrat, of Aberdeen, SD; born in Aberdeen on December 9, 1947; attended private and public schools; B.A., South Dakota State University, 1969; served in U.S. Air Force Strategic Air Command, first lieutenant, 1969–72; representative for financial investment firm; legislative assistant to former South Dakota Senator James Abourezk; member, American Legion, Catholic Church, South Dakota Jaycees; awards: only the third South Dakotan in 43 years to receive the Ten Outstanding Young Men from the U.S. Jaycees (1981), National Commander's Award by the Disabled American Veterans (1980), Person of the Year by the National Association of Concerned Veterans, Eminent Service Award by East River (South Dakota) Electric Power Cooperative, Friend of Education by the South Dakota Education Association; VFW Congressional Award, Veterans of Foreign Wars, 1997; founder, American Grown Foundation (1987); board member, Rural Voice; Committee on Agriculture, Nutrition, and Forestry; subcommittees: Production and Price Competitiveness; Forestry, Conservation, and Rural Revitalization; chairman, Democratic Policy Committee; married the former Linda Hall in 1984; three children: Kelly, Nathan, and Lindsay; elected to the 96th Congress, November 7, 1978; and reelected to the three succeeding Congresses; elected Rocky Mountain region whip (1979); served as whip-at-large (1982–86), elected to the House Steering and Policy Committee (1983); elected to the U.S. Senate on November 4, 1986; elected Senate Democratic Leader in December 1994 for the 104th Congress.

Office Listings

509 Hart Senate Office Building, Washington, DC 20510–4103 224–2321
Administrative Assistant.—Peter M. Rouse.
Scheduler.—Nancy Erickson.
Press Secretary.—Ranit Schmelzer.
810 South Minnesota Avenue, Sioux Falls, SD 57104 .... (605) 334–9596
20 Sixth Avenue, SW, Suite B, Aberdeen, SD 57401 .... (605) 225–8823
816 Sixth Street, Rapid City, SD 57701 .... (605) 348–7551

* * *

TIM JOHNSON, Democrat, of Vermillion, SD, born in Canton, SD, December 28, 1946; B.A., University of South Dakota, 1969; Phi Beta Kappa; M.A., political science, University of South Dakota, 1970; post-graduate study in political science, Michigan State University, 1970–71; J.D., University of South Dakota, 1975; married Barbara Brooks, 1969; three children: Brooks, Brendan and Kelsey Marie; Lutheran; budget advisor to the Michigan State Senate Appropriations Committee, 1971–72; admitted to the South Dakota bar in 1975 and began private law practice in Vermillion; served as Clay County Deputy State's Attorney, 1985; elected to the South Dakota House of Representatives, 1978; reelected, 1980; elected to the South Dakota State Senate, 1982; reelected, 1984; served on the Joint Appropriations Committee and the Senate Judiciary Committee; named Outstanding Citizen of Vermillion (1983); received South Dakota Education Association's "Friend of Education" Award (1983); Billy Sutton Award for Legislative Achievement (1984); elected to the U.S. House of Representatives, 1986; reelected to each succeeding Congress; delegate, Democratic National Convention, 1988–92; elected to the U.S. Senate, 1996; committees: Agriculture, Nutrition and Forestry; Banking, Housing and Urban Affairs; Budget; Energy and Natural Resources.

Office Listings

502 Hart Senate Office Building, Washington, DC 20510 224–5842
Chief of Staff.—Drey Samuelson.
Administrative Assistant.—Greg Billings.
Legislative Director.—Dwight Fettig.
Communications Director.—Kris Bess.
Scheduler.—Cindy Reesman.
515 South Dakota Avenue, Sioux Falls, SD 57104 .... (605) 332–8896
State Director.—Sharon Bertram.
405 East Omaha Street, Rapid City, SD 57701 .... (605) 341–3990
Deputy Chief of Staff.—Steve Jarding.
20 Sixth Avenue SW, Suite C, Aberdeen, SD 57401 .... (605) 226–3440

REPRESENTATIVE

AT LARGE

JOHN R. THUNE, Republican, of Pierre, SD; born in Pierre, January 7, 1961; graduated, Jones County High School, 1979; B.S., business administration, Biola University, CA; M.B.A., University of South Dakota, 1984; executive director, South Dakota Municipal League; board of directors, National League of Cities; executive director, South Dakota Republican Party, 1989–91; appointed State Railroad Director, 1991; former congressional legislative assistant and deputy staff director; married Kimberly Joy Weems in 1984; two children: Brittany and Larissa; elected to the 105th Congress.

Office Listings

506 Cannon House Office Building, Washington, DC 20515–4101	225–2801
Chief of Staff.—Herb Jones.	FAX: 225–5823
Legislative Director.—Jafar Karim.	
Press Secretary.—Christine Iverson.	
2310 West 41st Street, Sioux Falls, SD 57105	(605) 331–1010
	FAX: 331–0651
621 6th Street, Suite 100A, Rapid City, SD 57701	(605) 342–5135
	FAX: 342–5291

Population (1990), 699,999.

ZIP Codes: 51001 (part), 51023 (part), 56138 (part), 56164 (part), 56219 (part), 57001–04, 57005 (part), 57006–07, 57010, 57012–25, 57026 (part), 57027–29, 57030 (part), 57031–33, 57034 (part), 57035–48, 57049 (part), 57050–59, 57060 (part), 57061–67, 57068 (part), 57069–77, 57078 (part), 57100–07, 57115–16, 57118, 57201–02, 57210, 57212–27, 57229–39, 57241–52, 57255 (part), 57256–59, 57260 (part), 57261–66, 57268–69, 57270 (part), 57271–74, 57276, 57278–79, 57301, 57310–17, 57319, 57321–25, 57328–32, 57334–42, 57344–46, 57348–50, 57353–59, 57361–71, 57373–76, 57379–86, 57401–02, 57420–29, 57430 (part), 57432–42, 57445–46, 57448–52, 57454–57, 57460–63, 57465–77, 57479, 57481, 57483, 57501, 57520–23, 57526–29, 57531–34, 57536–38, 57540–45, 57547–48, 57551–53, 57555, 57557, 57559–60, 57562–64, 57566–72, 57574, 57576–81, 57584–85, 57601, 57620–23, 57625–26, 57628–31, 57632 (part), 57633, 57634 (part), 57636, 57638 (part), 57639–47, 57648 (part), 57649–54, 57656–58, 57660 (part), 57661, 57701–02, 57706, 57708–09, 57714–20, 57722, 57724 (part), 57725, 57729–30, 57732, 57735–38, 57741–42, 57744–45, 57747–48, 57750–52, 57754–67, 57769–70, 57772–80, 57782–85, 57787–88, 57790–95, 58030 (part), 58032 (part), 58041 (part), 58053 (part), 58413 (part), 58436 (part), 58439 (part), 58623 (part), 58637 (part), 68719 (part), 69201 (part), 69211 (part), 69212 (part), 69216 (part), 69218 (part), 69337 (part), 69343 (part)

TENNESSEE

(Population 1995, 5,256,000)

SENATORS

WILLIAM H. FRIST, Republican, of Nashville, TN; born on February 22, 1952 in Nashville; graduated, Montgomery Bell Academy, Nashville, 1970; A.B., Princeton University, Woodrow Wilson School of Public and International Affairs, 1974; M.D., Harvard Medical School, 1978, with honors; residency in general surgery (1978–84) and thoracic surgery (1983–84), Massachusetts General Hospital; cardiovascular and transplant fellowship, Stanford University Medical Center, 1985–86; heart and lung transplant surgeon; founding director, Vanderbilt Transplant Center; teaching faculty, Vanderbilt University Medical Center, 1986–93; staff surgeon, Nashville Veterans' Administration Hospital; board certified in both general surgery and cardiothoracic surgery; Medical Center Ethics Committee, 1991–93; chairman, Tennessee Medicaid Task Force, 1992–93; recipient: Distinguished Service Award, Tennessee Medical Association; president, Middle Tennessee Heart Association; member: Smithsonian Institution's Board of Regents, Princeton University Board of Trustees, American College of Surgeons, Society of Thoracic Surgeons, Southern Thoracic Surgical Association, American College of Chest Physicians; American Medical Association, Tennessee Medical Association, American Society of Transplant Surgeons, Association of Academic Surgery, International Society for Heart and Lung Transplantation, Tennessee Transplant Society, Alpha Omega Alpha, Rotary Club, United Way de Tocqueville Society; board member: YMCA Foundation of Metropolitan Nashville, Sergeant York Historical Association; commercial pilot; author of 100 scientific articles, chapters and abstracts (subjects: fibroblast growth factor, thoracic surgery, artificial heart, transplantation, immunosuppression); author of *Transplant* (Atlantic Monthly Press, 1989); co-editor, *Grand Rounds in Transplantation* (Chapman and Hall, 1995); married Karyn McLaughlin Frist, 1981; three children: Harrison, Jonathan, and Bryan; elected to the 104th Congress, November 8, 1994; committees: Commerce, Science and Transportation; Budget; Labor and Human Resources; Small Business; Foreign Relations; chairman: Subcommittee on Public Health and Safety and Subcommittee on Science, Technology and Space.

Office Listings

http://www.senate.gov/~frist senator__frist@frist.senate.gov

565 Dirksen Senate Office Building, Washington, DC 20510–4205 224–3344
Chief of Staff.—Lee Rawls.
Legislative Director.—Bill Testerman.
Press Secretary.—Keith Still.
Executive Assistant/ Scheduler.—Romona Lessen.
28 White Bridge Road, Suite 211, Nashville, TN 37205 .... (615) 352–9411
State Director.—Emily Reynolds.
5100 Poplar Avenue, Suite 605, Memphis, TN 38137 .... (901) 683–1910
6000 Building, Suite 2303, 5704 Marlin Road, Chattanooga, TN 37411 .... (423) 894–2203
South Royal Depot Building, 584 South Royal Street, Jackson, TN 38301 .... (901) 425–9655
10368 Wallace Alley Street, Suite 7, Kingsport, TN 37663 .... (423) 323–1252
Twelve Oaks Executive Park, Building One, Suite 170, 5401 Kingston Pike, Knoxville, TN 37919 .... (423) 602–7977

* * *

FRED THOMPSON, Republican, of Nashville, TN; born on August 19, 1942 in Sheffield, AL; graduated Lawrence County High School, Lawrenceburg, TN, 1960; B.S., Memphis State University, Memphis, TN, 1964; J.D., Vanderbilt University, Nashville, TN, 1967; attorney; Assistant U.S. Attorney, 1969–72; admitted to the Tennessee bar, 1967; member: Nashville, Tennessee and American bar associations; minority counsel, Senate Select Committee on Presidential Campaign Activities (Watergate Committee), 1973–74; special counsel to Governor Lamar Alexander (Tennessee) during the first three months of his administration in 1980; special counsel, Senate Foreign Relations Committee (Haig Confirmation), 1980–81; special counsel, Senate Intelligence Committee, 1982; member, Appellate Court Nominating Commission for the State of Tennessee, 1985–87; appeared in 18 major motion pictures; three children: Fred D., Jr., Elizabeth Thompson Hollins and Daniel L.; committees: chairman, Governmental Affairs; Judiciary; elected to the 104th Congress; reelected to the 105th Congress.

Office Listings

http://www.senate.gov/~thompson senator_thompson@thompson.senate.gov

523 Dirksen Senate Office Building, Washington, DC 20510 224–4944
Chief of Staff.—Tom Daffron. FAX: 228–3679
Press Secretary.—Alex Pratt.
Legislative Director.—Hannah Sistare.
3322 West End Avenue, Suite 120, Nashville, TN 37203 .... (615) 736–5129
Federal Building, Suite 403, Memphis, TN 38103 .... (901) 544–4224
Post Office Building, 501 Main Street, Suite 315, Knoxville, TN 37902 .... (615) 545–4253
Federal Building, 109 South Highland Street, Suite B–9, Jackson, TN 38301 .... (901) 423–9344
6100 Building, Suite 4404, Chattanooga, TN 37411 .... (615) 756–1328
Tri-City Regional Airport, Suite 103, Blountville, TN 37617 .... (615) 323–6217

* * *

REPRESENTATIVES

FIRST DISTRICT

WILLIAM LEWIS JENKINS, Republican, of Rogersville, TN; born on November 29, 1936 in Detroit, MI; graduated from Rogersville High School, 1954; B.B.A from Tennessee Tech, Cookville, 1957; served in the U.S. Army Military Police, second lieutenant, 1959–60; J.D., University of Tennessee College of Law, Knoxville, TN, 1961; admitted to the Rogersville bar, 1962; attorney; farmer; commissioner of conservation; circuit judge; energy advisor to Governor Lamar Alexander; TVA board member; Tennessee State Senate, 1962–70; Speaker of the House, 1968–70; delegate to the Republican National Convention, 1988; member: American Legion, Masonic Lodge, Tennessee Bar Association, Tennessee Farm Bureau; married Mary Kathryn Jenkins, 1959; four children: Rebecca, Georgeanne Price, William, Jr., Douglas; elected to the 105th Congress.

Office Listings

1708 Longworth House Office Building, Washington, DC 20515–4201 225–6356
Chief of Staff.—Jeff Anderson. FAX: 225–5714
Executive Assistant/Office Manager.—Beth Point.
Legislative Director.—Brenda Otterson.
320 West Center Street, Kingsport, TN 37662 .... (423) 247–8161
FAX: 247–1834

Counties: Carter, Cocke, Greene, Hancock, Hawkins, Jefferson, Johnson, Knox, Sevier, Sullivan, Unicoi, Washington. Population (1990), 541,875.

ZIP Codes: 37601–05, 37614–18, 37620–21, 37625, 37640–45, 37650, 37656–60, 37662–65, 37669, 37680–84, 37686–88, 37690–92, 37694, 37699, 37711, 37713, 37722, 37725, 37727, 37731, 37738, 37743–44, 37753, 37760, 37764–65, 37806, 37809–11, 37818, 37820–21, 37843, 37857, 37862–65, 37868–69, 37871, 37873, 37876–77, 37883, 37890–91

* * *

SECOND DISTRICT

JOHN J. DUNCAN, Jr., Republican, of Knoxville, TN; born in Lebanon, TN, July 21, 1947; University of Tennessee, B.S. degree in journalism, 1969; National Law Center, George Washington University, J.D. degree, 1973; served in both the Army National Guard and the U.S. Army Reserves, retiring with the rank of captain; private law practice in Knoxville, 1973–81; appointed State Trial Judge by Governor Lamar Alexander in 1981 and elected to a full eight-year term in 1982 without opposition, receiving the highest number of votes of any candidate on the ballot that year; member: American Legion 40 and 8, Elks, Sertoma Club, Masons, Scottish Rite and Shrine; present or past board member: Red Cross, Girl's Club, YWCA, Sunshine Center for the Mentally Retarded, Beck Black Heritage Center, Knoxville Union Rescue Mission, Senior Citizens Home Aid Service; active elder at Eastminster Presbyterian Church; married to the former Lynn Hawkins; four children: Tara, Whitney, John J. III, and Zane; committees: Transportation and Infrastructure, Resources; elected to both the 100th Congress (special election) and the 101st Congress in separate elections held on November 8, 1988; reelected to each succeeding Congress.

Office Listings

http://www.house.gov/duncan jjduncan@hr.house.gov

2400 Rayburn House Office Building, Washington, DC 20515–4202 225–5435
Administrative Assistant.—Judy Whitbred. FAX: 225–6440
800 Market Street, Suite 110, Knoxville, TN 37902 .... (423) 523–3772
Suite 419, 200 East Broadway, Maryville, TN 37801 .... (423) 984–5464
Courthouse, Athens, TN 37303 .... (423) 745–4671

Counties: Blount, Bradley (part), Knox (part), Loudon, McMinn, Monroe. CITIES AND TOWNSHIPS: Alcoa, Athens, Cleveland (part), Eagleton Village, Englewood, Etowah, Farragut, Halls (Knox Co.), Knoxville, Lenoir City, Loudon, Madisonville, Maryville, Powell, Seymour (part), South Cleveland (part), Sweetwater. Population (1990), 541,864.

ZIP Codes: 37303–04, 37309, 37310 (part), 37311 (part), 37312 (part), 37314, 37322 (part), 37325–26, 37329, 37331, 37354, 37358 (part), 37370–71, 37385, 37701, 37705 (part), 37709 (part), 37721 (part), 37737, 37742, 37754 (part), 37764 (part), 37771 (part), 37774 (part), 37777, 37779 (part), 37801–04, 37806 (part), 37807 (part), 37826 (part), 37830 (part), 37846 (part), 37849 (part), 37853, 37865 (part), 37871 (part), 37874 (part), 37878, 37880 (part), 37882, 37885–86, 37900–02, 37909, 37912, 37914–17, 37918 (part), 37919 (part), 37920 (part), 37921–23, 37924 (part), 37927–30, 37931 (part), 37932 (part), 37933, 37938 (part), 37939–40, 37950, 37995–98

* * *

THIRD DISTRICT

ZACHARY P. (ZACH) WAMP, Republican, of Chattanooga, TN; born on October 28, 1957 in Fort Benning, GA; graduated, McCallie School, Chattanooga, 1976; attended University of North Carolina at Chapel Hill and University of Tennessee; member, Red Bank Baptist Church; commercial and industrial real estate broker; named Chattanooga Business Leader of the Year; chairman, Hamilton County Republican Party; regional director, Tennessee Republican Party; received Tennessee Jaycees' Outstanding Young Tennessean Award in 1996, U.S. Chamber of Commerce Spirit of Enterprise Award, Citizens Against Government Waste "A" Rating, National Taxpayers Union Friend of the Taxpayers Award; recognized by the Citizens Taxpayers Association of Hamilton County, the National Federation of Independent Business and the Concord Coalition for casting tough votes to reduce spending; married Kimberly Watts Wamp, 1985; two children: Weston and Coty; elected to the 104th Congress; reelected to the 105th Congress.

Office Listings

http://www.house.gov/wamp

423 Cannon House Office Building, Washington, DC 20515–4203 225–3271
Chief of Staff.—Helen Hardin. FAX: 225–3494
Legislative Director.—Bob Castro.
Press Secretary.—Dick Kopper.
Scheduler.—Lisa Reynolds.
6100 Building, Eastgate Center, 5721 Marlin Road, Suite 3400, Chattanooga, TN 37411 .... (423) 894–7400
District Director.—Robin Derryberry. FAX: 894–8621
District Scheduler.—Paula Albornoz.
Office Manager.—Beverly Mauldin.
Federal Building, Suite 100, 200 Administration Road, Oak Ridge, TN 37830 .... (423) 483–3336
District Director.—Ann Cook. FAX: 576–3221
Field Representative.—Jack Copeland.

Counties: Anderson, Bledsoe, Bradley (part), Grundy, Hamilton, Marion, Meigs, Morgan, Polk, Roane, Sequatchie, Van Buren. CITIES AND TOWNSHIPS: Chattanooga, Cleveland, Oak Ridge, Pikeville, Dunlap, Jasper, South Pittsburg, Tracy City, Decatur, Wartburg, Benton, Kingston, Harriman, Spencer. Population (1990), 541,866.

ZIP Codes: 37110, 37301–02, 37305, 37307–08, 37310 (part), 37311 (part), 37312 (part), 37313, 37315–17, 37320, 37322–23, 37326–27, 37333, 37336, 37338–41, 37343, 37347, 37350–51, 37353, 37356–57, 37361–67, 37369, 37373–74, 37377, 37379–80, 37387, 37391, 37396–97, 37401–12, 37415–16, 37419, 37421–22, 37450, 37705, 37710, 37716–17, 37719, 37726, 37748, 37754 (part), 37763, 37769–70, 37828–31, 37840, 37845, 37849 (part), 37852, 37854, 37872, 37880, 37887, 37919 (part), 37931 (part), 38581, 38585

* * *

FOURTH DISTRICT

VAN HILLEARY, Republican, of Spring City, TN; born on June 20, 1959, in Dayton, TN; graduated, Rhea County High School, Dayton, TN; B.S., University of Tennessee, Knoxville, 1981; Cumberland School of Law, Samford University, 1990; member: Presbyterian Church,

American Legion, Veterans of Foreign Wars, Kiwanis International; major, USAF Reserves, 1982–present; served two volunteer tours in Persian Gulf during Operation Desert Shield and Desert Storm; flew 24 missions on a C–130 aircraft while in the Persian Gulf; U.S. Air Medals, the Aerial Achievement Medal, the National Service Medal, Kuwait Liberation Medal, Southwest Asia Campaign Medal and the Outstanding Unit Ribbon; director, Planning and Business Development at SSM Industries, Inc., Spring City, TN; admitted to the Tennessee bar, 1991; elected November 8, 1994 to the 104th Congress; reelected to the 105th Congress.

Office Listings

http://www.house.gov/hilleary hilleary@hr.house.gov

114 Cannon House Office Building, Washington, DC 20515–4204 225–6831
Acting Chief of Staff.—Elaine Robinson. FAX: 225–4520
Legislative Director.—Roger Morse.
Press Secretary.—Ed Frank.
1502 North Main Street, Crossville, TN 38555 .... (615) 484–1114
400 West Main Street, Suite 304, Morristown, TN 37814 .... (423) 587–0396
300 South Jackson Street, Tullahoma, TN 37388 .... (615) 393–4764

Counties: Bedford, Campbell, Claiborne, Coffee, Cumberland, Fentress, Franklin, Giles, Grainger, Hamblen, Hardin, Knox (part), Lawrence, Lincoln, Moore, Pickett, Rhea, Scott, Union, Warren, Wayne, White. Population (1990), 541,868.

ZIP Codes: 37018, 37020 (part), 37026 (part), 37034 (part), 37037 (part), 37047 (part), 37060 (part), 37091 (part), 37110 (part), 37144 (part), 37153 (part), 37160, 37166 (part), 37180 (part), 37183, 37190 (part), 37306, 37318, 37321, 37324, 37327–28, 37330, 37332, 37334–35, 37337–38, 37342, 37345, 37348, 37352, 37355, 37357, 37359–60, 37365 (part), 37367, 37372, 37375–76, 37378, 37379 (part), 37381–82, 37388–89, 37394–95, 37397 (part), 37398, 37705 (part), 37707–08, 37709 (part), 37711 (part), 37714, 37715 (part), 37719, 37721 (part), 37723–24, 37726, 37729–30, 37731 (part), 37732–33, 37748 (part), 37752, 37754 (part), 37755–57, 37762, 37765–66, 37769 (part), 37770, 37773, 37778, 37779 (part), 37806 (part), 37807 (part), 37811 (part), 37813 (part), 37814 (part), 37815–16, 37819, 37825, 37829, 37840 (part), 37841–42, 37843 (part), 37845, 37847–48, 37851–52, 37854 (part), 37860–61, 37866–67, 37869 (part), 37870, 37872, 37877 (part), 37879, 37881 (part), 37887–88, 37890 (part), 37891 (part), 37892, 38449 (part), 38451 (part), 38453, 38455–57, 38459–60, 38463 (part), 38464 (part), 38468–69, 38472 (part), 38473, 38474 (part), 38477–78, 38481, 38483 (part), 38486 (part), 38488, 38504 (part), 38549 (part), 38550, 38553 (part), 38555, 38556 (part), 38559, 38565, 38570 (part), 38574 (part), 38577 (part), 38578–79, 38581 (part), 38583 (part), 38585, 38587, 38589

* * *

FIFTH DISTRICT

BOB CLEMENT, Democrat, of Nashville, TN; born in Nashville, September 23, 1943; graduated, Hillsboro High School, Nashville, 1962; B.S., University of Tennessee, Knoxville, 1967; M.B.A., Memphis State University, TN, 1968; served in U.S. Army, lieutenant, 1969–71; served in Tennessee Army National Guard, lieutenant colonel, 1971–present; member, Tennessee Public Service Commission, 1973–79; TVA Board Member, 1979–81; partner, Charter Equities, 1981–83; president, Cumberland University, Lebanon, TN, 1983–87; Tennessee chairman, American Heart Association, 1989; member: American Legion, Girl Scouts of America, Jaycees, Lions Club, Rotary Club, United Way; committees: Transportation and Infrastructure, International Relations; married the former Mary Carson, 1976; four children: Greg, Jeff, Elizabeth and Rachel; elected to the 100th Congress by special election, January 19, 1988, to fill the vacancy caused by the resignation of Bill Boner; reelected to each succeeding Congress.

Office Listings

http://www.house.gov/clement bob.clement@mail.house.gov

2229 Rayburn House Office Building, Washington, DC 20515–4205 225–4311
Chief of Staff.—Alex Haught.
Executive Assistant.—Carolyn Waugh.
Legislative Director.—Todd Bouldin.
Press Secretary.—Catheryne Pully.
552 U.S. Courthouse, Nashville, TN 37203 .... (615) 736–5295
Administrative Assistant.—Bart Herbison.
Suite 103, 2701 Jefferson Street, Nashville, TN 37208 .... (615) 320–1363
Suite 201, 101 5th Avenue West, Springfield, TN 37172 .... (615) 384–6600

Counties: Davidson (part), Robertson (part); cities of Belle Meade, Forest Hills, Goodlettsville (Davidson County portion), Greenbrier, Lakewood, Millersville (part), Nashville-Davidson (part), Oak Hill, Springfield (part) and White House (part). Population (1990), 541,909.

ZIP Codes: 37010, 37013, 37015 (part), 37027 (part), 37032 (part), 37035 (part), 37048 (part), 37049 (part), 37072 (part), 37073, 37076 (part), 37080 (part), 37082 (part), 37086 (part), 37115–16, 37122 (part), 37135 (part), 37138 (part), 37141, 37143, 37146 (part), 37148 (part), 37152, 37154, 37171–72, 37188 (part), 37189, 37191 (part), 37201–04, 37205 (part), 37206–22, 37228–29, 37232, 37235, 37250

SIXTH DISTRICT

BART GORDON, Democrat, of Murfreesboro, TN; born January 24, 1949, Murfreesboro; graduated, Central High School, Murfreesboro, 1967; B.S. *cum laude*, Middle Tennessee State University, Murfreesboro, 1971; J.D., University of Tennessee College of Law, Knoxville, 1973; admitted to the Tennessee State bar, 1974; opened private law practice in Murfreesboro, 1974; elected to the Tennessee Democratic Party's executive committee, 1974; appointed executive director of the Tennessee Democratic Party, 1979; elected the first full-time chairman of the Tennessee Democratic Party, 1981; resigned chairmanship, 1983, to successfully seek congressional seat; member, St. Mark's Methodist Church, Murfreesboro; past chairman: Rutherford County United Givers Fund and Rutherford County Cancer Crusade; board member: Rutherford County Chamber of Commerce, MTSU Foundation; elected to the 99th Congress on November 6, 1984; reelected to each succeeding Congress; member: Commerce Committee and Science Committee.

Office Listings

http://www.house.gov/gordon bart@hr.house.gov

2201 Rayburn House Office Building, Washington, DC 20515–4206 225–4231
FAX: 225–6887
Administrative Assistant.—Eric Altshule.
Executive Assistant/Scheduler.—Ellen Helm.
P.O. Box 1986, 106 South Maple Street, Murfreesboro, TN 37133 .... (615) 896–1986
District Administrative Assistant.—Kent Syler.
P.O. Box 1140, 17 South Jefferson, Cookeville, TN 38501 .... (615) 528–5907

Counties: Cannon, Clay, Davidson (part), DeKalb, Jackson, Macon, Marshall, Overton, Putnam, Rutherford, Smith, Sumner, Trousdale, Williamson, Wilson. CITIES AND TOWNSHIPS: Murfreesboro, Hendersonville, Gallatin, Mt. Juliet, Lebanon, Brentwood, Franklin, Lewisburg, Cookeville, Livingston, and Lafayette. Population (1990), 541,977.

ZIP Codes: 37012, 37014, 37016, 37019, 37022, 37024, 37026 (part), 37027 (part), 37030–31, 37034 (part), 37037, 37046, 37047 (part), 37048 (part), 37049 (part), 37057, 37059–60, 37062–66, 37068, 37071, 37072 (part), 37074–75, 37076 (part), 37077, 37083, 37085–88, 37091 (part), 37095, 37110 (part), 37118–19, 37122, 38129–30, 37132–33, 37135 (part), 37136, 37138 (part), 37144 (part), 37145, 37148 (part), 37149–51, 37153, 37166–67, 37179, 37184, 37186, 37188 (part), 37190 (part), 37211 (part), 37220 (part), 37221 (part), 38472 (part), 38501–03, 38505, 38541–45, 38547–48, 38551–52, 38554, 38560, 38562–64, 38567–69, 38570 (part), 38573, 38574 (part), 38575, 38580, 38582, 38588

* * *

SEVENTH DISTRICT

EDWARD BRYANT, Republican, of Henderson, TN; born in Jackson, TN, on September 7, 1948; graduated, Jackson High School; B.A., 1970, and J.D., 1972, University of Mississippi; vice president, Sigma Nu; member: military honorary society, leadership society; Army officer, ROTC in the Military Intelligence Branch, 1970; captain, Judge Advocate General Corps; teacher, U.S. Military Academy in West Point, NY, 1977–78; president, Madison County Bar Association, boards of Rotary, Little League, Fellowship of Christian Athletes; member, Tennessee Farm Bureau; U.S. Attorney for the Western District of Tennessee; led an office of 29 attorneys who prosecuted Tennessee's largest mass murder case; ranked among the top nationally in the prosecution of violent criminals; one of the first to establish a task force to investigate abuse and fraud in the health care system; member, Agriculture and Judiciary committees; married Cyndi Lemons Bryant, 1971; three children: Drew, Josh and Matt; elected to the 104th Congress; reelected to the 105th Congress.

Office Listings

http://www.house.gov/bryant

408 Cannon House Office Building, Washington, DC 20515–4207 225–2811
FAX: 225–2989
Chief of Staff.—P.K. Rehbein.
Legislative Director.—Mark Johnson.
Press Secretary.—Justin Hunter.
Executive Assistant.—Polly Payne.
5909 Shelby Oaks Drive, Suite 213, Memphis, TN 38134 .... (901) 382–5811
District Field Representative.—Ken Scroggs.
330 North Second Street, Clarksville, TN 37040–3210 .... (615) 503–0391
District Staff Assistant.—Woody Parker.
810½ South Garden Street, Columbia, TN 38401 .... (615) 381–8100
District Staff Assistant.—Becky Moon.

Counties: Cheatham, Chester, Decatur, Dickson, Fayette, Hardeman, Henderson, Hickman, Lewis, McNairy, Maury, Montgomery, Perry, Robertson (part), Shelby (part). Population (1990), 541,937.

ZIP Codes: 37015 (part), 37025 (part), 37029, 37032 (part), 37033 (part), 37035 (part), 37036, 37040–41, 37042 (part), 37043–44, 37050 (part), 37051–52, 37054–55, 37061, 37062 (part), 37078, 37079 (part), 37080 (part), 37082 (part),

37096–98, 37101, 37134, 37137, 37140, 37142, 37146 (part), 37147, 37165, 37175 (part), 37178 (part), 37181, 37185, 37187, 37191 (part), 38002, 38008, 38010, 38014, 38017 (part), 38018, 38028–29, 38036, 38039, 38042–46, 38048, 38049 (part), 38052, 38057, 38060–61, 38066–68, 38074, 38075 (part), 38076, 38115, 38116 (part), 38118 (part), 38125, 38128 (part), 38130, 38134, 38138, 38163, 38168, 38175, 38181, 38183–84, 38187, 38237–38, 38305 (part), 38310–11, 38313 (part), 38315, 38321 (part), 38326–29, 38332, 38334, 38339–40, 38341 (part), 38345, 38347, 38351–52, 38356 (part), 38357, 38359, 38361, 38363, 38365, 38366 (part), 38367–68, 38370–72, 38374–77, 38379–81, 38387 (part), 38388, 38390 (part), 38392 (part), 38393, 38425, 38450, 38452, 38454 (part), 38458, 38461 (part), 38463 (part), 38464 (part), 38471, 38475, 38476 (part), 38485 (part), 38486 (part), 38487 (part), 42223 (part)

* * *

EIGHTH DISTRICT

JOHN S. TANNER, Democrat, of Union City, TN; born at Dyersburg Army Air Base in Halls, TN, on September 22, 1944; attended elementary and high school in Union City; B.S., University of Tennessee at Knoxville, 1966; J.D., University of Tennessee at Knoxville, 1968; served, U.S. Navy, lieutenant, 1968–72; Tennessee Army National Guard, colonel, 1974–present; attorney; admitted to the Tennessee bar in 1968 and commenced practice in Union City; member, Elam, Glasgow, Tanner and Acree law firm until 1988; businessman; elected to Tennessee House of Representatives, 1976–88; chairman, House Committee on Commerce, 1987–89; member: Obion County Chamber of Commerce, Obion County Cancer Society, Union City Rotary Club, Obion County Bar Association, American Legion, Masons, First Christian Church (Disciples of Christ) of Union City; married to the former Betty Ann Portis; two children: Elizabeth Tanner Atkins and John Portis; elected on November 8, 1988 to the 101st Congress; reelected to each succeeding Congress; member: National Security and Science committees.

Office Listings

http://www.house.gov/tanner/index.htm   john.tanner@mail.house.gov

1127 Longworth House Office Building, Washington, DC 20515–4208 225–4714
Administrative Assistant.—Vickie Walling. FAX: 225–1765
Legislative Director.—F. Douglas Thompson.
Personal Secretary.—Kathy Becker.
203 West Church Street, Union City, TN 38261 .... (901) 885–7070
District Director.—Joe Hill.
Federal Building, Room B–7, Jackson, TN 38301 .... (901) 423–4848
2836 Coleman Road, Memphis, TN 38128 .... (901) 382–3220

Counties: Benton, Carroll, Crockett, Dyer, Gibson, Haywood, Henry, Houston, Humphreys, Lake, Lauderdale, Madison, Obion, Shelby (part), Stewart, Tipton, and Weakley. Population (1990), 541,907.

ZIP Codes: 37023, 37028, 37050 (part), 37058, 37079 (part), 37175 (part), 37178 (part), 37191 (part), 38001, 38004, 38006–07, 38011–12, 38015, 38017 (part), 38019, 38021, 38023–25, 38030, 38033–34, 38037, 38040–41, 38047, 38049 (part), 38050, 38053–54, 38056, 38058–59, 38063, 38069–71, 38075 (part), 38077, 38079 (part), 38080, 38104 (part), 38107 (part), 38108, 38119 (part), 38127, 38128 (part), 38133 (part), 38134 (part), 38135 (part), 38201, 38220–27, 38229–33, 38235–36, 38240–42, 38251, 38253–56, 38258–61, 38271, 38301–03, 38305 (part), 38308, 38313 (part), 38314, 38316–18, 38320, 38321 (part), 38324, 38330–31, 38333, 38336–38, 38341 (part), 38342–44, 38346, 38348, 38355, 38356 (part), 38358, 38369, 38378, 38382, 38389, 338391, 38392 (part)

* * *

NINTH DISTRICT

HAROLD E. FORD, JR., Democrat, of Memphis, TN; born in Memphis, May 11, 1970; son of the Honorable Harold E. Ford (D, TN–09, 1974–96) and Dorothy Bowles Ford; B.A. in American History, University of Pennsylvania, 1992; cofounded monthly newspaper, "The Vision" while at the University of Pennsylvania; J.D., University of Michigan School of Law, 1996; special assistant, Department of Commerce Economic Development Administration; Special Assistant, Justice/Civil Rights Cluster, President Clinton's 1992 transition team; aide to U.S. Senator James Sasser, Senate Budget Committee; coordinator of 1992 and 1994 reelection campaigns of U.S. Representative Harold E. Ford; member: Mt. Moriah-East Baptist Church; committee: Education and the Workforce; subcommittees: Postsecondary Education, Training, and Lifelong Learning; Oversight and Investigations; elected to the 105th Congress.

Office Listings

http://www.house.gov/ford

1523 Longworth House Office Building, Washington, DC 20515–4209 225–3265
Chief of Staff.—Mark Yates. FAX: 225–5663
Legislative Director.—David Sutphen.
Communications Director.—Mark Schuermann.

Federal Office Building, Suite 369, 167 North Main Street, Memphis, TN 38103 .. (901) 544–4131
FAX: 544–4329

County: SHELBY COUNTY; city of Memphis. Population (1990), 541,981.

ZIP Codes: 38100–01, 38103, 38104 (part), 38105–06, 38107 (part), 38109, 38111–15, 38116 (part), 38117, 38119 (part), 38120 (part), 38122, 38124, 38126, 38127, 38128 (part), 38131–32, 38141 (part), 38152, 38173–74, 38182, 38186

TEXAS

(Population 1995, 18,724,000)

SENATORS

PHIL GRAMM, Republican, of College Station, TX; born in Fort Benning, GA, July 8, 1942, son of Sergeant and Mrs. Kenneth M. Gramm; B.B.A. and Ph.D., economics, University of Georgia, Athens, 1961–67; professor of economics, Texas A&M University, College Station, 1967–78; author of several books including: "The Evolution of Modern Demand Theory" and "The Economics of Mineral Extraction"; Episcopalian; married Dr. Wendy Lee Gramm, of Waialua, HI, 1970; two sons: Marshall and Jeff; coauthor of the Gramm-Latta I Budget, the Gramm-Latta II Omnibus Reconciliation Act and the Gramm-Rudman-Hollings balanced budget bill; committees: Agriculture, Nutrition and Forestry; Banking, Housing and Urban Affairs; Budget; Finance; elected to the U.S. House of Representatives as a Democrat in 1978, 1980 and 1982; resigned from the House on January 5, 1983 upon being denied a seat on the House Budget Committee; reelected as a Republican in a special election on February 12, 1983; elected to the U.S. Senate on November 6, 1984; reelected in 1990 and 1996; elected chairman, U.S. Senate Steering Committee, 1997–98; elected chairman, National Republican Senatorial Committee for the 1991–92 term and reelected for the 1993–94 term.

Office Listings

http://www.senate.gov/senator/gramm.html

370 Russell Senate Office Building, Washington, DC 20510–4302 224–2934
Chief of Staff.—Ruth Cymber.
Legislative Director.—Richard Ribbentrop.
Press Secretary.—Lawrence A. Neal.
State Director.—Ed Hodges.
Suite 1500, 2323 Bryan, Dallas, TX 75201 .... (214) 767–3000
222 East Van Buren, Harlingen, TX 78550 .... (210) 423–6118
712 Main Street, Houston, TX 77002 .... (713) 229–2766
404 East Ramsey Road, San Antonio, TX 78216 .... (210) 366–9494
1205 Texas, Lubbock, TX 79401 .... (806) 472–7533
310 North Mesa, El Paso, TX 79901 .... (915) 534–6896
100 East Ferguson, Tyler, TX 75702 .... (903) 593–0902

* * *

KAY BAILEY HUTCHISON, Republican, of Dallas, TX; raised in La Marque, TX; graduate of the University of Texas at Austin and University of Texas School of Law; Texas House of Representatives, 1972–76; appointed vice chair of the National Transportation Safety Board, 1976; senior vice president and general counsel, RepublicBank Corporation, and later co-founded Fidelity National Bank of Dallas; owned McCraw Candies, Inc.; political and legal correspondent for KPRC–TV, Houston; Episcopalian, married to Ray Hutchison; member: development boards of SMU and Texas A&M schools of business; trustee of The University of Texas Law School Foundation; elected Texas State Treasurer, 1990; committees: Appropriations; Commerce, Science and Transportation; Rules and Administration; elected to the U.S. Senate by special election on June 5, 1993 to fill the vacancy caused by the resignation of Lloyd Bentsen.

Office Listings

http://www.senate.gov/~hutchison senator@hutchison.senate.gov

283 Russell Senate Office Building, Washington, DC 20510–4303 224–5922
Chief of Staff.—Tom Houston. FAX: 224–0776
Deputy Chief of Staff.—Lindsey Parham.
Legislative Counsel.—Shelby Weiss.
Legislative Director.—Larry DiRita.
961 Federal Building, 300 East 8th Street, Austin, TX 78701 .... (512) 482–5834
10440 North Central Expressway, Suite 1160, LB 606, Dallas, Texas 75231 .... (214) 361–3500
1919 Smith Street, Suite 800, Houston, TX 77024 .... (714) 653–3456
500 Chestnut Street, Suite 1570, Abilene, Texas 79602 .... (915) 676–2839
8023 Vantage Drive, Suite 460, San Antonio, Texas 78230 .... (210) 340–2885

REPRESENTATIVES

FIRST DISTRICT

MAX SANDLIN, Democrat, of Marshall, TX; born on September 29, 1952 in Texarkana, AR; graduated, Atlanta High School, TX; B.A., Baylor University, Waco, TX, 1975; J.D., Baylor University School of Law, 1978; admitted to the bar, Marshall, TX, 1978; board certified in family law; county judge, Harrison County, 1986–89; county court of law judge, Harrison County, 1989–96; partner, Sandlin & Buckner, 1982–96; vice president, Howell and Sandlin, Inc., 1989–96; president, East Texas Fuels, Inc., 1992–96; coach, Marshall Youth Baseball, Softball and Basketball Association; member: Texas Ranger Association Foundation, Marshall Chamber of Commerce, East Texas Housing and Finance Corporation (board of directors and treasurer), Oil, Gas and Mineral Law section of the State Bar of Texas; awards: National Mock Trial Championship Team, Outstanding Young Alumni, Baylor University; Texas Department of Human Services award for services to abused children; married Leslie Howell Sandlin, 1982; four children: Hillary, Max III, Emily, Christian; elected to the 105th Congress.

Office Listings

http://www.house.gov/sandlin

214 Cannon House Office Building, Washington, DC 20515–4301 225–3035
Chief of Staff.—Paul F. Rogers.
Legislative Director.—Lynn Marquis.
Communications Director/Press Secretary.—Andrew C. Dodson.
Office Manager/Scheduler.—Angela Jones.
1300 East Pinecrest Drive, Suite 30, Marshall, TX 75670 .... (903) 938–8386
FAX: 935–5772
P.O. Box 248, New Boston, TX 75570 .... (903) 628–5594
FAX: 628–3155
P.O. Box 538, Sulphur Springs, TX 75482–0538 .... (903) 885–8682
FAX: 885–2976

Counties: Bowie, Camp, Cass, Delta, Franklin, Gregg, Harrison, Hopkins, Hunt, Lamar, Marion, Morris, Nacogdoches, Panola, Red River, Rusk, Smith, Titus, Upshur, Wood. Population (1990), 566,217.

ZIP Codes: 75135, 75401, 75403, 75411–12, 75415–17, 75420, 75421–23, 75426, 75428, 75431–37, 75441, 75448, 75451, 75453, 75455, 75457–58, 75460, 75468–71, 75473–74, 75477, 75478, 75480–82, 75486, 75494, 75496, 75497, 75501–05, 75550–51, 75555–70, 75571–74, 75601–08, 75630–31, 75633, 75635, 75637–39,75640–44, 75647, 75650–53, 75656–58, 75659–63, 75666–71, 75680–89, 75691–93, 75694, 75757, 75760, 75765, 75773, 75783, 75785, 75788–89, 75937, 75943, 75944, 75946, 75958, 75961–63, 75978

* * *

SECOND DISTRICT

JIM TURNER, Democrat, of Crockett, TX; born on February 6, 1946; B.A., M.A., business administration, and LL.B., University of Texas; captain, U.S. Army; represented Fifth District in Texas Senate; Texas House of Representatives, 1981–84; Special Counsel for Legislative Affairs and Executive Assistant to the Governor, 1984–85; chairman, Texas Commission on Children and Youth, 1993; member, Select Committee on Public Education and Texas Punishment Standards Commission, 1993; sponsored legislation to establish, and served as member of the State Ethics Commission; former mayor of Crockett; past president, Crockett Chamber of Commerce; deacon and Sunday School teacher, First Baptist Church; named Legislator of the Year by the Texas Association for the Education of Young Children and Outstanding State Senator by the Texas Youth Commission; married to Ginny Turner; two children, John and Susan; committees: National Security; Government Reform and Oversight; subcommittees: Military Procurement; Military Research and Development; National Security, International Affairs and Criminal Justice; National Economic Growth, Natural Resources and Regulatory Affairs; elected to the 105th Congress.

Office Listings

TX02@mail.house.gov

1508 Longworth House Office Building, Washington, DC 20515–430 225–2401
Chief of Staff.—Steve Patterson. FAX: 225–5955
Legislative Director.—Elizabeth Hurley.
Executive Assistant/General Counsel.—Laurie Knight.
Press Secretary.—Kevin McHargue.
701 North First Street, Room 201, Lufkin, TX 75901–3008 .... (409) 637–1770

District Caseworkers.—Norma Butler, Lorri Donnahoe. FAX: 632–8588
P.O. Box 780, 605 North Goliad, Suite 102, Crockett, TX 75835 .... (409) 544–8414
Field Representative.—Patricia Lucas. FAX: 544–3102
420 West Green Avenue, Orange, TX 77630 .... (409) 883–4990
Field Representative.—Ann Gray. FAX: 883–5149

Counties: Angelina, Cherokee, Grimes, Hardin, Houston, Liberty, Montgomery (part), Nacogdoches (part), Newton, Orange, Polk, Sabine, San Augustine, San Jacinto, Shelby, Trinity, Tyler, Walker. Population (1990), 566,217.

ZIP Codes: 75757, 75763 (part), 75764, 75766, 75780, 75784–85, 75789, 75830, 75834–35, 75841, 75843–45, 75847, 75849, 75851, 75856, 75858, 75862, 75865, 75873, 75901–03, 75915, 75925–39, 75941–42, 75947–49, 75951, 75954, 75959–61, 75963, 75966, 75968–80, 77301, 77326–28, 77331–32, 7734–35, 77340–42, 77350–51, 77357–60, 77363–65, 77367–72, 77374, 77376, 77378, 77519, 77533, 77535, 77538, 77561, 77564, 77575, 77582, 77585, 77611–12, 77614–16, 77618, 77624–26, 77630–32, 77639, 77656, 77659, 7760, 77662–64, 77670, 77711, 77830–31, 77851, 77861, 77868, 77873, 77875–77

* * *.

THIRD DISTRICT

SAM JOHNSON, Republican, of Dallas, TX; born San Antonio, TX, October 11, 1930; B.S., business administration, Southern Methodist University, Dallas, TX, 1951; M.A., international affairs, George Washington University, Washington, DC, 1974; served in Air Force, 29 years: Korea and Vietnam (POW in Vietnam, six years, ten months); director, Air Force Fighter Weapons School; flew with Air Force Thunderbirds Precision Flying Demonstration Team; graduate of Armed Services Staff College and National War College; military awards: two Silver Stars, two Legions of Merit, Distinguished Flying Cross, one Bronze Star with Valor, two Purple Hearts, four Air Medals, and three Outstanding Unit awards; ended career with rank of colonel and Air Division commander; retired, 1979; opened homebuilding company, 1979; served seven years in Texas House of Representatives; Smithsonian Board of Regents; U.S./Russian Joint Commission on POW/MIA; member: Executive Board of Dedman College, Southern Methodist University; Associated Texans Against Crime; Texas State Society; married the former Shirley L. Melton, 1950; three children, Dr. James Robert Johnson, Shirley Virginia (Gini) Mulligan, Beverly Briney; elected to Texas State House of Representatives, 1984; elected to U.S. House of Representatives by special election on May 18, 1991 to fill the vacancy caused by the resignation of Steve Bartlett; elected on November 3, 1992 to the 103rd Congress; reelected to each succeeding Congress.

Office Listings

http://www.house.gov/samjohnson sam.tx03@mail.house.gov

1030 Longworth House Office Building, Washington, DC 20515–4303 225–4201
Administrative Assistant.—Mark Franz.
Legislative Director.—Michael Hansen.
Press Secretary.—Mindy Tucker.
District Director.—Mary Lynn Murrell.
Suite 610, 9400 North Central Expressway, Dallas, TX 75231 .... (214) 739–0182
Suite 204, 1912 Avenue K, Plano, TX 75074 .... (214) 423–2017

Counties: Dallas, Garland, Mesquite, Richardson, Sachse, Wylie. Population (1990), 566,217.

ZIP Codes: 75002, 75023, 75025, 75034, 75041 (part), 75042 (part), 75043, 75044, 75048, 75069, 75074–75, 75080–82, 75088, 75093–94, 75098, 75149–50, 75181–82, 75216, 75240, 75243, 75244 (part), 75252 (part), 75253 (part), 75275, 75283–84, 75355, 75359, 75367, 75372, 75378, 75382, 75391

* * *

FOURTH DISTRICT

RALPH M. HALL, Democrat, of Rockwall, TX; born in Fate, TX, May 3, 1923; graduated, Rockwall High School, 1941; attended Texas Christian University, University of Texas, and received LL.B., Southern Methodist University, 1951; lieutenant (senior grade), U.S. Navy, carrier pilot, 1942–45; lawyer; admitted to the Texas bar in 1951 and commenced practice in Rockwall; former president and chief executive officer, Texas Aluminum Corporation; past general counsel, Texas Extrusion Company, Inc.; past organizer, chairman, board of directors, now chairman of board, Lakeside National Bank of Rockwall (now Lakeside Bancshares, Inc.); past chairman, board of directors, Lakeside News, Inc.; past vice chairman, board of directors, Bank of Crowley; president, North and East Trading Company; vice president, Crowley Holding Co.; county judge, Rockwall County, 1950–62; member, Texas State Senate, 1962–72; member: First Methodist Church; American Legion Post 117; VFW Post 6796, Rockwall Rotary Club, and Rotary Clubs International; committees: Commerce, Science; subcommitties: Energy and Power, Health and the Environment, Telecommunications and Finance, Space; married the former Mary Ellen Murphy, 1944; three sons: Hampton, Brett and Blakeley; elected to the 97th Congress, November 4, 1980; reelected to each succeeding Congress.

Office Listings

rmhall@hr.house.gov

2236 Rayburn House Office Building, Washington, DC 20515–4304 225–6673
Administrative Assistant.—James D. Cole. FAX: 225–3332
Legislative Assistant.—Grace Warren.
104 North San Jacinto Street, Rockwall, TX 75087–2508 .... (214) 771–9118
District Assistant.—E.K. Slaughter. FAX: 722–0907
119 Federal Building, Sherman, TX 75090–5917 .... (903) 892–1112
District Assistant.—Judy Rowton. FAX: 868–0264
211 Federal Building, Tyler, TX 75072–7222 .... (903) 597–3729
District Assistant.—Martha Glover. FAX: 597–0726

Counties: COLLIN COUNTY (part); cities and townships of Anna, Blue Ridge, Celina, Copeville, Farmersville, Howe, Josephine, Lavon, McKinney (part), Melissa, Nevada, Princeton, Westminister, Weston, Wylie. COOKE COUNTY (part); cities and townships of Callisburg, Era, Gainesville, Lake Kiowa, Lindsay, Muenster, Myra, Valley View. DALLAS COUNTY (part); cities and townships of Rowlett (part), Sachse (part), Sunnyvale (part). DENTON COUNTY (part); cities and townships of Aubrey, Denton (part), Krum, Little Elm, Pilot Point, Sanger. FANNIN COUNTY; cities and townships of Bailey, Bonham, Dodd City, Ector, Gober, Honey Grove, Ivanhoe, Ladonia, Leonard, Ravenna, Savoy, Telephone, Trenton, Windom. GRAYSON COUNTY; cities and townships of Bells, Collinsville, Denison, Dorchester, Gordonville, Gunter, Pottsboro, Sadler, Sherman, Southmayd, Tioga, Tom Bean, Van Alstyne, Whitesboro, Whitewright. GREGG COUNTY (part); cities and townships of Easton Gladewater, Judson, Kilgore, Longview (part), White Oak. HUNT COUNTY (part); cities and townships of Caddo Mills, Celeste, Greenville (part), Quinlan. KAUFMAN COUNTY (part); cities and townships of Crandall, Elmo, Forney, Kaufman, Kemp, Mabank, Terrell. RAINS COUNTY ; cities and townships of East Tawakoni, Emory, Point. ROCKWALL COUNTY; cities and townships of Fate, Heath, Rockwall, Royse City. SMITH COUNTY (part); cities and townships of Bullard, Flint, Lindale, Troup, Tyler (part), Whitehouse, Winona. VAN ZANDT COUNTY; cities and townships of Ben Wheeler, Canton, Edgewood, Fruitvale, Grand Saline, Van, Wills Point. Population, 566,217.

ZIP Codes: 75009, 75020–21, 75030, 75048, 75058, 75069 (part), 75070 (part), 75076, 75087, 75088 (part), 75090–91, 75097, 75098 (part), 75103, 75114 (part), 75117–18, 75121, 75126–27, 75132, 75135 (part), 75140, 75142, 75143 (part), 75147 (part), 75159 (part), 75160, 75169, 75182 (part), 75189, 75200 (part), 75401 (part), 75403, 75404 (part), 75407, 75409, 75413–14, 75418, 75423–24, 75438, 75439, 75440, 75442–43, 75446–47, 75449, 75452, 75453 (part), 75454, 75458, 75459, 75472, 75474–76, 75479, 75488–91, 75492 (part), 75494 (part), 75495, 75601 (part), 75602 (part), 75603 (part), 75604 (part), 75605 (part), 75606–08 (part), 75610–11, 75613, 75641, 75647 (part), 75660, 75662 (part), 75663 (part), 75693, 75701 (part), 75702 (part), 75703, 75704 (part), 75705 75708 (part), 75710, 75711 (part), 75712, 75713, 75750, 75754, 75757 (part), 75758 (part), 75762, 75771, 75789 (part), 75790–92, 76201, 76202, 76203, 76204, 76233 (part), 76240, 76241, 76245, 76249, 76250, 76252, 76258, 76264, 76266, 76268, 76271, 76272, 76273

* * *

FIFTH DISTRICT

PETE SESSIONS, Republican, of Dallas, TX; born on March 22, 1955; graduate, Southwestern University, 1978; worked for Southwestern Bell and Bell Communications Research (formerly Bell Labs), 1978–94, rising to the position of district manager; past vice president for public policy, National Center for Policy Analysis, 1994–95; board member, East Dallas YMCA; past chairman, East Dallas Chamber of Commerce; past district chairman, White Rock Council of the Boy Scouts of America; member, East Dallas Rotary Club; married to Nita Sessions; two children, Bill and Alex; committees: Government Reform and Oversight, Banking and Financial Services, Science; subcommittees: vice chair, Government Management, Information and Technology; Civil Service; Postal Service; Capital Markets, Securities and Government-Sponsored Enterprises; Housing and Community Opportunity; Basic Research; elected on November 5, 1996, to the 105th Congress.

Office Listings

http://www.house.gov/sessions petes@mail.house.gov

1318 Longworth House Office Building, Washington, DC 20515 225–2231
Chief of Staff.—Scott Styles. FAX: 225–5878
Press Secretary.—Pam Arruda.
Legislative Director.—Robert Shea.
Legislative Assistants.—Charles Bouer, Guy Harrison, Eric Rizzo.
10677 East NW Highway, No. 410, Dallas, TX 75238 .... (214) 349–9996
District Director.—Chris Homan. FAX: 349–0738
104 East Corsicana Street, Athens, TX 75751 .... (903) 675–8288
Regional Director.—Charlie Hawn. FAX: 675–8351

Counties: Anderson, Brazos (part), Dallas (part), Freestone, Henderson, Kaufman (part), Leon, Limestone, Madison, Robertson, Smith (part). CITIES AND TOWNSHIPS: Athens, Bremond, Brownsboro, Bryan, Buffalo, Calvert, Cayuga, Centerville, Chandler, Concord, Coolidge, Crandall, Cuney, Dallas, Donie, Elkhart, Eustace, Fairfield, Ferris, Flynn, Franklin, Frankston, Groesbeck, Gun Barrel City, Hearne, Jewett, Kaufman, Kemp, Kirvin, Kose, Larue, Leona, Mabank, Garland, Lancaster, Hutchins, Seagoville, Mesquite, Madisonville, Malakoff, Marquez, Mart, Mexia, Midway, Montalba, Mount Calm, Munford, Murchison, New Baden, Normangee, North Zulch, Oakwood, Palestine, Poyner, Prairie Hill, Rosser, Scurry, Streetman, Teague, Tehuacana, Tennessee Colony, Thornton, Tinidad, Tyler, Wheelock, Wortham. Population (1990), 566,217.

ZIP Codes: 75040 (part), 75041 (part), 75042 (part), 75043 (part), 75046 (part), 75114, 75124–25, 75134 (part), 75141, 75142 (part), 75143 (part), 75147 (part), 75148, 75149 (part), 75150 (part), 75157–58, 75159 (part), 75163, 75180 (part), 75181 (part), 75185 (part), 75187 (part), 75201 (part), 75204 (part), 75205 (part), 75206 (part), 75207 (part), 75209 (part), 75214 (part), 75217 (part), 75218 (part), 75219 (part), 75221, 75223 (part), 75226 (part), 75227 (part), 75228 (part), 75235 (part), 75238 (part), 75239 (part), 75241 (part), 75246 (part), 75253 (part), 75371, 75701 (part), 75702 (part), 75704 (part), 75708 (part), 75709, 75712 (part), 75751, 75756, 75758–59, 75763, 75770, 75782, 75801–02, 75831–33, 75838–40, 75846, 75848, 75850, 75852–53, 75855, 75859–61, 75865, 76629, 76635, 76642, 76653, 76664, 76667, 76673, 76678, 76686–87, 76693, 77801 (part), 77802 (part), 77803 (part), 77806, 77822, 77837, 77850, 77855–56, 77859, 77864, 77870–72

* * *

SIXTH DISTRICT

JOE BARTON, Republican, of Ennis, TX; born in Waco, TX, September 15, 1949; graduated Waco High School, 1968; B.S., industrial engineering, Texas A&M University, College Station, 1972; M.S., industrial administration, Purdue University, West Lafayette, IN, 1973; plant manager, assistant to the vice president, Ennis Business Forms, Inc., 1973–81; awarded White House Fellowship, 1981–82; served as aide to James B. Edwards, secretary, Department of Energy; member, Natural Gas Decontrol Task Force in the Office of Planning, Policy and Analysis; worked with the Department of Energy task force in support of the President's Private Sector Survey on Cost Control; natural gas decontrol and project cost control consultant, Atlantic Richfield Company; cofounder, Houston County Volunteer Ambulance Service, 1976; vice president, Houston County Industrial Development Authority, 1980; chairman, Crockett Parks and Recreation Board, 1979–80; vice president, Houston County Chamber of Commerce, 1977–80; member, Dallas Energy Forum; married to Janet Sue Winslow Barton; three children: Brad, Alison and Kristin; Methodist; elected to the 99th Congress on November 6, 1984; reelected to each succeeding Congress.

Office Listings

http://www.house.gov/barton rep.barton@mail.house.gov

2264 Rayburn House Office Building, Washington, DC 20515–4306 225–2002
Administrative Assistant.—Cathy Gillespie. FAX: 225–3052
Communications Director.—Craig Murphy.
Legislative Director.—Beth Hall.
Scheduler.—Pam Lewis.
Suite 101, 303 West Knox, Ennis, TX 75119–3942 .... (817) 543–1000
4521 South Hulen Street, Suite 210, Fort Worth, TX 76109 .... FAX: 225–3052
805 F Washington Street, Arlington, TX 76011 .... (817) 543–1000

Counties: Dallas (part), Ellis (part), Johnson (part), Parker (part), Tarrant (part). CITIES AND TOWNSHIPS: Aledo, Anneta, Anneta North, Anneta South, Azle (part), Bedford, Benbrook (part), Briar Oaks, Burleson (part), Colleyville, Coppell (part), Crowley (part), Dallas (part), Dalworthington Gardens (part), Ennis (part), Euless, Flower Mound (part), Fort Worth (part), Grand Prairie (part), Grapevine, Haltom City (part), Haslet (part), Hudson Oaks, Hurst, Irving (part), Joshua (part), Keene (part), Keller, Mansfield (part), Midlothian (part), Newark (part), North Richland Mills, Oak Leaf, Ovilla, Pantego (part), Pecan Hill (part), Red Oak (part), Richland Hills (part), Southlake (part), Watauga, Waxahachie (part), Weatherford (part), Westlake (part), Willow Park. Population (1990), 566,217.

ZIP Codes: 75019 (part), 75050 (part), 75052 (part), 75063 (part), 75119 (part), 75154 (part), 75165 (part), 76008, 76013 (part), 76015 (part), 76016, 76017 (part), 76018 (part), 76020 (part), 76021, 76022 (part), 76028 (part), 76034 (part), 76036 (part), 76039 (part), 76040 (part), 76051 (part), 76052 (part), 76053 (part), 76054 (part), 76058, 76059 (part), 76063 (part), 76065 (part), 76086 (part), 76092, 76095, 76103 (part), 76109 (part), 76110 (part), 76112 (part), 76116 (part), 76117 (part), 76118 (part), 76123 (part), 76126 (part), 76132 (part), 76133 (part), 76148, 76179 (part), 76248 (part), 76262

* * *

SEVENTH DISTRICT

BILL ARCHER, Republican, of Houston, TX; born in Houston, March 22, 1928; graduated from St. Thomas High School, salutatorian, 1945; attended Rice University, 1945–46; University of Texas, B.B.A., LL.B. (with honors), 1946–51; served in the U.S. Air Force, 1951–53; captain, USAF Reserves; councilman and mayor pro tempore, city of Hunters Creek Village,

1955–62; elected to Texas House of Representatives, 1966; reelected, 1968; attorney and businessman; president, Uncle Johnny Mills, Inc., 1953–61; member of Saint Anne's Catholic Church; member, Sigma Alpha Epsilon fraternity; chosen Houston Sigma Alpha Epsilon Man of the Year; St. Thomas High School Alumnus Award; Houston B'nai B'rith Man of the Year Award; member, Phi Delta Phi legal fraternity; life member, Houston Livestock Show and Rodeo; Guardian of Small Business award, National Federation of Independent Business Watchdog of the Treasury Award; National Alliance of Senior Citizens Golden Age Hall of Fame award; president, Texas State Society of Washington, DC, 1974–75; Spring Branch-Memorial Chamber of Commerce Most Representative Citizen award; Brotherhood Award, National Conference of Christians and Jews; University of Texas 1981 Distinguished Alumnus Award; five children, two step children, and seven grandchildren; married to the former Sharon Sawyer; elected to the 92nd Congress, November 3, 1970; reelected to each succeeding Congress; chairman, Committee on Ways and Means; Joint Committee on Taxation; official Congressional Trade Adviser; member, White House Commission on Regulatory Reform, 1975–76; chairman, Republican Study Committee Task Force on Regulatory Reform, 1975–76; member, National Commission on Social Security Reform, 1982–83; member, Republican Leadership's Task Force on Health, 1992–93; chairman, Leader's Economic Task Force, 1993; awards: Free Congress Foundation's Sound Dollar, 1994; Golden Bulldog Award, Watchdog of the Treasury; The Jefferson Award, Citizens for a Sound Economy, 1994; The National Association of Private Enterprise Entrepreneurs Perfect Partner Award, 1993; American Society of Association Executives, Beacon Award, 1992; American Business Council of the Gulf Countries, Open Door to the Middle East Award, 1993.

Office Listings

http://www.house.gov/archer

1236 Longworth House Office Building, Washington, DC 20515–4307 225–2571
FAX: 225–4381

Administrative Assistant.—Don Carlson.

Legislative Director.—Noelle Montano Hawley.

Appointment Secretary.—Linda Figura.

Press Secretary.—James Wilcox.

10000 Memorial Drive, No. 620, Houston, TX 77024–3490 .... (713) 682–8828
FAX: 680–8070

County: HARRIS COUNTY; cities of Barker, Cypress, Houston (part), Katy (part), Tomball (part), and Waller (part). Population (1990), 566,217.

ZIP Codes: 77005 (part), 77019 (part) 77024, 77027, 77040 (part), 77041 (part), 77042 (part), 77043, 77046, 77055, 77056–57, 77057, 77063 (part), 77064 (part), 77065, 77070 (part), 77072 (part), 77077, 77079, 77080 (part), 77081 (part), 77082 (part), 77083 (part), 77084 (part), 77086 (part), 77094–95, 77098 (part), 77099 (part), 77218–19 (part), 77224, 77227, 77240–42, 77243 (part), 77244, 77256–57, 77269, 77277 (part), 77279, 77280 (part), 77282, 77411 (part), 77413, 77429, 77433, 77446, 77447 (part), 77449 77450 (part), 77484 (part), 77491–92, 77493 (part), 77494 (part)

* * *

EIGHTH DISTRICT

KEVIN BRADY, Republican, of The Woodlands, TX; born in Vermillion, SD, November 4, 1955; B.S., business, University of South Dakota; served in Texas House of Representatives, 1991–96—the first Republican to capture the 15th District seat since the 1800s; awards: Achievement Award, Texas Conservative Coalition; Outstanding Young Texan (one of five), Texas Jaycees; Ten Best Legislators for Families and Children, State Bar of Texas; Legislative Standout, Dallas Morning News; Scholars Achievement Award for Excellence in Public Service, North Harris Montgomery Community College District; Victims Rights Equalizer Award, Texans for Equal Justice Center; Support for Family Issues Award, Texas Extension Homemakers Association; chair, Council of Chambers of Greater Houston; president, East Texas Chamber Executive Association; president, South Montgomery County Woodlands Chamber of Commerce, 1985-present; director, Texas Chamber of Commerce Executives; Rotarian; attends Saints Simon and Jude Catholic Church; married to Cathy Brady; elected to the 105th Congress.

Office Listings

1531 Longworth House Office Building, Washington, DC 20515–4308 225–4901

Chief of Staff.—Doug Centilli.

Press Secretary.—Bill Greene.

Legislative Director.—Barry Brown.

616 FM 1960 West, Suite 325, Houston, TX 77090 .... (281) 895–8892

District Director.—Jamey Webster.

111 East University Drive, Suite 216, College Station, TX 77840 .... (409) 846–6068
Staff Assistant.—Scott Pool.

COUNTIES: Austin (part), Brazos (part), Harris, (part), Montgomery (part), Washington. CITIES AND TOWNSHIPS: Bellville, Brenham, Bryan (part), College Station, Conroe (part), Houston(part), Humble (part), Kingwood, Oak Ridge North, Panorama Village, Pinehurst, Sealy (part), Shenandoah, Spring, The Woodlands, Tomball, and Woodbranch. Population (1990), 566,217.

ZIP Codes: 77064 (part), 77066 (part), 77068 (part), 77069 (part), 77070 (part), 77073 (part), 77090 (part), 77268, 77301 (part), 77302, 77303 (part), 77304, 77325, 77327 (part), 77333, 77336, 77338 (part), 77339, 77345, 77346 (part), 77347, 77355–57, 77362, 77365, 77372–73, 77375, 77377, 77378 (part), 77379–89, 77391, 77396 (part), 77418, 77426, 77429 (part), 77447 (part), 77452, 77474 (part), 77484 (part), 77532 (part), 77801 (part), 77802, 77803 (part), 77805–06, 77807 (part), 77833–35, 77840–45, 77862, 77866, 77880–81, 78931, 78944, 78950 (part)

* * *

NINTH DISTRICT

NICHOLAS V. LAMPSON, Democrat, of Beaumont, TX; born in Beaumont, February 14, 1945; graduated, South Park High School, Beaumont, TX, 1964; B.S., biology, Lamar University, Beaumont, 1968; M.Ed., Lamar University, 1971; teacher; elected Jefferson County Tax Assessor-Collector; member: Young Men's Business Lease, Clean Air and Water, Sierra International, Knights of Columbus; married to the former Susan Floyd; two children: Hilary, Stephanie; committees: Science, Resources; elected to the 105th Congress.

Office Listings

417 Cannon House Office Building, Washington, DC 20515–4309 225–6565
Administrative Assistant.—Randy White. FAX: 225–5547
Legislative Director.—Jacquelyn Davis.
Appointment Secretary/Office Manager.—Julie Byrom.
Suite B–104, 300 Willow Street, Beaumont, TX 77701 .... (409) 838–0061
FAX: 832–0738
Suite 216, 601 Rosenbert, Galveston, TX 77550 .... (409) 762–5877
FAX: 763–4133

Counties: Chambers, Galveston, Harris (part), Jefferson. CITIES: Baytown, Beaumont, Galveston, Port Arthur, Texas City. Population (1990), 566,217.

ZIP Codes: 77044 (part), 77049 (part), 77058 (part), 77062 (part), 77346 (part), 77396 (part), 77510, 77511 (part), 77514, 77517–18, 77520 (part), 77521 (part), 77532 (part), 77539, 77546 (part), 77550–55, 77560, 77562 (part), 77563, 77565, 77568, 77573–74, 77579–80, 77590–92, 77597, 77598 (part), 77613, 77617, 77619, 77622–23, 77627, 77629, 77640–43, 77650–51, 77655, 77661, 77665, 77701–10, 77713, 77720, 77726

* * *

TENTH DISTRICT

LLOYD DOGGETT, Democrat, of Austin, TX; born October 6, 1946 in Austin; graduated, Austin High School; B.B.A., University of Texas, Austin, 1967; J.D., University of Texas, 1970; president, University of Texas Student Body; associate editor, *Texas Law Review*; Outstanding Young Lawyer, Austin Association of Young Lawyers; president, Texas Consumer Association; member, First United Methodist Church; admitted to the Texas State bar, 1971; Texas State Senate, 1973–85, elected at age 26; Senate author of 124 state laws and Senate sponsor of 63 House bills enacted into law; elected president pro tempore of Texas Senate; served as acting governor; named Outstanding Young Texan by Texas Jaycees; Arthur B. DeWitty Award for outstanding achievement in human rights, Austin NAACP; honored for work by Austin Rape Crisis Center, Planned Parenthood of Austin; Austin Chapter, American Institute of Architects; Austin Council on Alcoholism; Disabled American Veterans; justice on Texas Supreme Court, 1989–94; chairman, Supreme Court Task Force on Judicial Ethics, 1992–94; judge (Mexican-American Bar of Texas), 1993; adjunct professor, University of Texas School of Law, 1989–94; James Madison Award, Texas Freedom of Information Foundation, 1990; First Amendment Award, National Society of Professional Journalists, 1990; member: Science Committee and Subcommittee on Basic Research, Budget Committee, Democratic Caucus Task Force on Crime, Democratic Caucus Parliamentary Group; married Libby Belk Doggett, 1969; two children: Lisa and Cathy; elected to the 104th Congress; reelected to the 105th Congress.

Office Listings

http://www.house.gov/doggett doggett@hr.house.gov

126 Cannon House Office Building, Washington, DC 20515–4310 225–4865
Chief of Staff.—Leo Coco.
Staff Assistant.—Matt Miller.
Press Secretary.—Evelyn Knolle.
763 Federal Building, Austin, TX 78701 .... (512) 916–5921
District Director.—Path Everitt.

County: TRAVIS COUNTY (part); cities and townships of Anderson Mill (part), Austin (part), Jollyville (part), Lakeway (part), Lost Creek, Onion Creek, Pflugerville, Tanglewood Forest, Wells Branch, West Lake Hills and Windemere. Population (1990), 566,217.

ZIP Codes: 73301, 73344, 78600, 78602, 78605 (part), 78606, 78610–12, 78616–17, 78619–20, 78621 (part), 78622, 78635, 78636 (part), 78640, 78641 (part), 78644, 78648 (part), 78650–53, 78654 (part), 78655 (part), 78656, 78659 (part), 78660–63, 78665, 78666 (part), 78667, 78669, 78676, 78700–05, 78710–13, 78716–39, 78741–69, 78771–74, 78776, 78778–89, 78941 (part), 78942 (part), 78953, 78957 (part), 78959 (part)

* * *

ELEVENTH DISTRICT

CHET EDWARDS, Democrat, of Waco, TX; born in Corpus Christi, TX, November 24, 1951; graduated Memorial High School, Houston, TX, 1970; B.A., Texas A&M University, College Station, 1974; M.B.A., Harvard Business School, Boston, MA, 1981; served as legislative assistant to Texas Congressman Olin "Tiger" Teague, 1974–77; marketing representative, Trammell Crow Company, 1981–85; president, Edwards Communications, Inc.; member, Texas State Senate, 1983–90; member of the Waco Chamber of Commerce; married to the former Lea Ann Wood; one son: John; elected to the 102nd Congress, November 6, 1990; reelected to each succeeding Congress.

Office Listings

328 Cannon House Office Building, Washington, DC 20515–4311 225–6105
FAX: 225–0350
Administrative Assistant.—Jay Neel.
Legislative Director.—Ned Michalek.
Press Secretary.—Vance Gore.
710 Clifton-Robinson Tower, 700 S. University Parks Drive, Waco, TX 76706–1093 .... (817) 752–9600
FAX: 752–7769
District Director.—Jim Haddox.

Counties: Bell, Bosque, Coryell, Falls, Hamilton, Hill, Lampasas, McCulloch (part), McLennan, Milam, Mills, San Saba. CITIES: Killeen, Temple, Waco. Population (1990), 566,217.

ZIP Codes: 76043 (part), 76432 (part), 76433 (part), 76436 (part), 76442 (part), 76443 (part), 76457 (part), 76471 (part), 76501–04, 76511–13, 76517–20, 76522–26, 76527 (part), 76528, 76530–31, 76533–34, 76537–44, 76550, 76552, 76554–59, 76561, 76564–66, 76567 (part), 76569–71, 76573, 76576, 76577 (part), 76579–80, 76621 (part), 76624 (part), 76630, 76632–34, 76637–38, 76640, 76643, 76649 (part), 76652, 76653 (part), 76654–57, 76661, 76664 (part), 76665, 76671, 76673 (part), 76675, 76677, 76680, 76682, 76684–85, 76687 (part), 76689, 76690 (part), 76691 (part), 76700–08, 76710–12, 76714, 76716, 76801, 76803–04, 76823 (part), 76824, 76827, 76832, 76844, 76853, 76857, 76864, 76870, 76871 (part), 76872 (part), 76877, 76880, 76890 (part), 77857, 77859 (part), 78605 (part), 78608, 78613, 78639 (part), 78641 (part), 78642, 78645, 78673–74, 78947 (part)

* * *

TWELFTH DISTRICT

KAY GRANGER, Republican, of Fort Worth, TX; born in Greenville, TX, January 18, 1943; B.S., *magna cum laude*, 1965, and Honorary Doctorate of Humane Letters, 1992, Texas Wesleyan University; owner, Kay Granger Insurance Agency, Inc.; former public school teacher; elected mayor of Fort Worth, 1991, serving three terms; during her tenure, Fort Worth received All-America City Award from the National Civic League; former Fort Worth councilwoman; past chair, Fort Worth Zoning Commission; past board member: Dallas-Fort Worth International Airport, North Texas Commission, Fort Worth Convention and Visitors Bureau, U.S. Conference of Mayors Advisory Board; Business and Professional Women's Woman of the Year, 1989; three grown children: Jady, Brandon and Chelsea; first woman Republican to represent Texas in the U.S. House; committees: Budget, Transportation and Infrastructure, Government Reform and Oversight; Speaker's Advisory Group on Corrections; assistant Republican whip; elected to the 105th Congress.

Office Listings
http://www.house.gov/granger

515 Cannon House Office Builiding, Washington, DC 20515 225–5071
Chief of Staff.—Ken Mehlman. FAX: 225–5683
Legislative Director.—Bruce Butler.
Communications Director.—Ron Bonjean.
Scheduler.—Nancy Scott.
1600 West Seventh Street, Suite 740, Fort Worth, TX 76102 .... (817) 338–0909
District Director.—Paula Good. (817) 335–5852

Counties: Johnson (part), Parker (part), Tarrant (part). Population (1990), 254,109.

ZIP Codes: 76009, 76020, 76022, 76031, 76036, 76044, 76050, 76052–53, 76058, 76063, 76094, 76066, 76487, 76082, 76086, 76087, 76490, 76102–04, 76106–11, 76114–18, 76122, 76125–27, 76129, 76131–35, 76140, 76148, 76179, 76180

* * *

THIRTEENTH DISTRICT

WILLIAM M. (MAC) THORNBERRY, Republican, of Amarillo, TX; born in Clarendon, TX, July 15, 1958; graduated, Clarendon High School; B.A., Texas Tech University; University of Texas, law degree; rancher, attorney; admitted to the Texas bar, 1983; member: Texas and Southwestern Cattle Raisers, Children's Rehabilitation Center; married Sarah Adams, 1986; two children: Will and Mary Kemp; elected to the 104th Congress; reelected to the 105th Congress.

Office Listings

1535 Longworth House Office Building, Washington, DC 20515–4313 225–3706
Administrative Assistant/Press Secretary.—Tommy Thompson. FAX: 225–3486
Office Manager.—Diane Lasyone.
724 South Polk, Suite 400, Amarillo, TX 79101 .... (806) 371–8844
District Office Manager.—Melodi Moore-Byrd.
811 Sixth Street, Suite 130, Wichita Falls, TX 76301 .... (817) 767–0541
District Office Manager.—Drucie Scaling.

Counties: ARCHER COUNTY; cities of Archer City, Holliday, Megarel, Scotland, and Windhorst. ARMSTRONG COUNTY; cities of Claude and Wayside. BAYLOR COUNTY; cities of Red Springs and Seymour. BRISCOE COUNTY; cities of Quitaque and Silverton. CARSON COUNTY; cities of Carson, Nazareth, Panhandle, Skellytown, and White Deer. CASTRO COUNTY; cities of Dimmitt and Hereford. CHILDRESS COUNTY; cities of Carey, Childress, Kirkland, and Tell. CLAY COUNTY; cities of Bellevue, Bluegrove, Byers, Henrietta, and Petrolia. COLLINGSWORTH COUNTY; cities of Dodson, Quail, Samnorwood, and Wellington. COTTLE COUNTY; cities of Cee Vee, Chalk, and Paducah. CROSBY COUNTY; Cone, Crosbyton, Lorenzo, and Ralls. DENTON COUNTY; cities of Denton and Krum. DICKENS COUNTY; cities of Afton, Dickens, Mcadoo, and Spur. DONLEY COUNTY; Clarendon, Hedley, and Lelia Lake. FLOYD COUNTY; cities of Aiken, Dougherty, Floydada, Lakeview, Lockney, and South Plains. FOARD COUNTY; city of Crowell. GARZA COUNTY; cities of Justiceburg and Post. GRAY COUNTY; cities of Lefors, McLean, and Pampa. HALE COUNTY; cities of Abernathy, Cotton Center, Edmonson, Happy, Plainview, Petersburg, and Quail. HALL COUNTY; cities of Estelline, Memphis, and Turkey. HARDEMAN COUNTY; cities of Chillicothe and Quanah. HEMPHILL COUNTY; city of Canadian. HUTCHINSON COUNTY; cities of Borger, Fritch, Sanford, and Stinnett. KING COUNTY; cities of Dumont and Guthrie. KNOX COUNTY; cities of Benjamin, Goree, Knox City, Munday, Truscott, and Vera. LAMB COUNTY; Amherst, Earth, Fieldton, Lamb, Littlefield, Olton, Spade, Springlake, and Sudan. LIPSCOMB COUNTY; cities of Booker, Darrouzett, Follett, Higgins, and Lipscomb. LUBBOCK COUNTY; cities of Lubbock and Slaton. LYNN COUNTY; cities of New Home, O'Donnell, Tahoka, and Wilson. MONTAGUE COUNTY; cities of Bowie, Forestburg, Montague, Nocona, Ringgold, and Saint Jo. MOTLEY COUNTY; cities of Flomot, Matador, Northfield, and Roaring Springs. POTTER COUNTY; cities of Amarillo, and Bushland. WHEELER COUNTY; cities of Allison, Briscoe, Mobeetie, Shamrock, Twitty, and Wheeler. ROBERTS COUNTY; city of Miami. SWISHER COUNTY; cities of Happy, Kress, and Tulia. WICHITA COUNTY; Burkburnett, Electra, Iowa Park, Kamay, Sunset, and Wichita Falls. WILBARGER COUNTY; city of Vernon. Population (1990), 566,217.

ZIP Codes: 76201, 76228 , 76230, 76239, 76249, 76251, 76255, 76261, 76265, 76270, 76301–11, 76351–52, 76354, 76357, 76360, 76363–67, 76369–71, 76377–80, 76383–84, 76389, 79003, 79005, 79007–08, 79011–12, 79014, 79019, 79021, 79024, 79027, 79031–32, 79034, 79036, 79039, 79041–43, 79046, 79051–52, 79054, 79056–57, 79059, 79061, 76063–66, 79068, 79072–73, 79077–80, 79082–83, 79085, 79088, 79090, 79094–97, 79101–11, 79114, 79117–22, 79124, 79159–60, 79201, 79220–27, 79229–41, 79243–46, 79248, 79250–52, 79255–61, 79311–12, 79321–22, 79326, 79330, 79339, 79343, 79351, 79356–57, 79364, 79369–71, 79373, 79381, 79383, 79401, 79403–04, 79415, 79505, 79529

* * *

FOURTEENTH DISTRICT

RON E. PAUL, Republican, of Surfside Beach, TX; born in Pittsburgh, PA, August 20, 1935; B.A., Gettysburg College, 1957; M.D., Duke College of Medicine, North Carolina, 1961; captain, U.S. Air Force, 1963–68; obstetrician and gynecologist; represented Texas' 22nd District in the U.S. House of Representatives, 1976–84; married the former Carol Wells in 1957; five children: Ronnie, Lori, Pyeatt, Rand, Robert and Joy LeBlanc; elected to the 105th Congress.

Office Listings

http://www.house.gov/paul rep.paul@mail.house.gov

203 Cannon House Office Building, Washington, DC 20515–4314 225–2831
Chief of Staff.—Tom Lizardo. FAX: 226–4871
Legislative Director.—Joseph Becker.
Press Secretary.—Michael Sullivan.

MLK Federal Building, 312 South Main, Victoria, TX 77901 .... (512) 576–1231
FAX: 576–0381

Counties: Aransas, Austin (part), Bastrop, Blanco, Brazoria (part), Burleson, Caldwell, Calhoun, Colorado, Fayette, Gonzales, Hays, Jackson, Lavaca, Lee, Matagorda, Refugio, Travis (part), Victoria, Waller (part), Wharton, Williamson (part). Population (1990), 566,217.

ZIP Codes: 76527 (part), 76567 (part), 76574, 76577 (part), 76578, 77412, 77414–15, 77418–19, 77420 (part), 77422 (part), 77423 (part), 77426, 77428, 77431–32, 77434, 77435 (part), 77436–37, 77440, 77442–43, 77445–46, 77447 (part), 77448, 77452–58, 77460, 77462–63, 77465–68, 77470, 77473–75, 77480, 77482–83, 77484 (part), 77485 (part), 77486 (part), 77488, 77833, 77835–36, 77838–39, 77852–53, 77863, 77878–80, 77901–05, 77950–52, 77954, 77957, 77960–64, 77967–79, 77982–91, 77993–95, 78071 (part), 78102–04, 78107, 78108 (part), 78115, 78119 (part), 78122–25, 78130 (part), 78140 (part), 78141–42, 78145–46, 78154–56, 78159, 78162, 78164, 78336 (part), 78340, 78358, 78368 (part), 78377, 78382, 78387 (part), 78389, 78391, 78393, 78603–04, 78614–15, 78621 (part), 78626–29, 78632, 78634, 78638, 78648 (part), 78655 (part), 78658, 78659 (part), 78664, 78666 (part), 78670, 78677, 78680–81, 78931–35, 78938, 78940, 78941 (part), 78942 (part), 78943–46, 78947 (part), 78948–52, 78954, 78956, 78957 (part), 78959 (part), 78960–64

* * *

FIFTEENTH DISTRICT

RUBÉN HINOJOSA, Democrat, of Mercedes, TX; born in Mercedes, August 20, 1940; B.B.A., 1962, and M.B.A., 1980, University of Texas; president and chief financial officer, H&H Foods, Inc.; board of directors, National Livestock and Meat Board and Texas Beef Industry Council, 1989–93; past president and past chairman of the board of directors, Southwestern Meat Packers Association; chairman and member of board of trustees, South Texas Community College, 1993–96; past public member, Texas State Bar Board of Directors; former adjunct professor, Pan American University School of Business; elected member, Texas State Board of Education, 1975–84; past director, Rio Grande Valley Chamber of Commerce, Knapp Memorial Hospital Board of Trustees, and Our Lady of Mercy Church Board of Catholic Advisors; past member, board of trustees, Mercedes Independent School District; former U.S. Jaycee Ambassador to Colombia and Ecuador; married to Martha L. Hinojosa; five children: Ruben, Jr., Laura, Iliana, Kaitlin and Karen; elected to the 105th Congress.

Office Listings

rep.hinojosa@mail.house.gov

1032 Longworth House Office Building, Washington, DC 20515–4315 225–2531
Chief of Staff.—Rita Jaramillo. FAX: 225–5688
Legislative Director.—Anton Papich.
Senior Legislative Assistant/Grants Coordinator.—Mari Ann Hollis.
Legislative Assistants: Diego De La Garza, Sarah Shipman, Rolando Valdez.
Special Assistant/Office Manager/Scheduler.—Laura Flores.

311 North 15th Street, McAllen, TX 78501 .... (210) 682–5545
Acting District Director.—Esther Garcia. FAX: 682–0141

Counties: Bee, Brooks, DeWitt, Goliad, Hidalgo, Jim Wells (part), Karnes, Klegerg (part), Live Oak, San Patricio, and Willacy (part). Population (1990), 566,217.

ZIP Codes: 78001, 78002 (part), 78005, 78007–08, 78011–12, 78014, 78017, 78019–22, 78026, 78050, 78052–53, 78057 (part), 78060–62, 78064–65, 78067, 78071 (part), 78072, 78073 (part), 78075–76, 78101 (part), 78111, 78113–14, 78116–18, 78119 (part), 78121, 78140 (part), 78143–44, 78147, 78151, 78153, 78160–61, 78332–33, 78336 (part), 78341–42, 78349–50, 78352–53, 78355, 78357, 78359–62, 78368 (part), 78370, 78372, 78374 (part), 78375–76, 78383–84, 78387 (part), 78390, 78410 (part), 78501–04, 78516, 78536–40, 78543, 78545, 78547–49, 78557–58, 78560, 78562–65, 78569 (part), 78570, 78572, 78576–77, 78579, 78582, 78584–85, 78588–89, 78591, 78595–96

SIXTEENTH DISTRICT

SYLVESTRE REYES, Democrat, of El Paso, TX; born in Canutillo, TX, on November 10, 1944; graduated, Canutillo High School, 1964; associate degree, El Paso Community College, 1976; attended University of Texas, Austin, 1964–65, and El Paso, 1965–66; served in U.S. Army, 1966–68, Vietnam combat veteran; U.S. Border Patrol, chief patrol agent, 26½ years, retired December 1, 1995; member: Canutillo School Board, 1968–69, 21st Century Democrats, El Paso County Democrats, and Unite El Paso; married the former Carolina Gaytan, 1968; three children: Monica, Rebecca and Silvestre Reyes, Jr.; elected on November 5, 1996 to the 105th Congress.

Office Listings

514 Cannon House Office Building, Washington, DC 20515–4316 225–4831
Chief of Staff.—Enrique Gallegas. FAX: 225–2016
Press Secretary.—Dora Tovar.
Office Manager/Personal Secretary.—Alison Houle.
Suite 400, 310 North Mesa, El Paso, TX 79901 .... (915) 534–4400
District Director.—Irma Sanchez.

County: El Paso: CITIES AND TOWNSHIPS of Anthony, Canutillo, Clint, El Paso, Fabens, San Elizario, Socorro, Tornillo. Population (1990), 566,217.

ZIP Codes: 79835, 79838, 79901–08, 79912, 79915–16, 79918, 79922, 79924–25, 79927, 79930, 79932, 79934–36

* * *

SEVENTEENTH DISTRICT

CHARLES W. STENHOLM, Democrat, of Avoca, TX; born in Stamford, TX, October 26, 1938; graduated, Stamford High School, 1957; graduated, Tarleton State Junior College, 1959; B.S., Texas Tech University, 1961; M.S., Texas Tech University, 1962; honorary doctor of laws, McMurry University; honorary doctor of laws, Abilene Christian University; farmer; past president, Rolling Plains Cotton Growers and Texas Electric Cooperatives; former member, Texas State ASC Committee; former State Democratic executive committeeman, 30th senatorial district; member, Stamford Exchange Club and Lions Club; past president: Stamford Chamber of Commerce, United Way and Little League; member, Bethel Lutheran Church; married to the former Cynthia (Cindy) Ann Watson; three children: Chris, Cary and Courtney Ann; elected to the 96th Congress, November 7, 1978; reelected to each succeeding Congress.

Office Listings

http://www.house.gov/stenholm texas17@hr.house.gov

1211 Longworth House Office Building, Washington, DC 20515–4317 225–6605
Administrative Assistant.—Lois Auer. FAX: 225–2234
Legislative Director.—Becca Tice.
Press Assistant.—John Haugen.
P.O. Box 1237, Stamford, TX 79553 .... (915) 773–3623
P.O. Box 1101, Abilene, TX 79604 .... (915) 673–7221
33 East Twohig Avenue, No. 318, San Angelo, Texas 76903 .... (915) 655–7994

Counties: Borden, Brown, Callahan, Coke, Coleman, Comanche, Concho, Dawson, Eastland, Erath, Fisher, Haskell, Hood, Howard, Jack, Jones, Kent, Martin, Mitchell, Nolan, Palo Pinto, Runnels; Scurry, Shackelford, Somervell, Stephens, Stonewall, Taylor, Throckmorton, Tom Green (part), Wise, Young. Population (1990), 566,217.

ZIP Codes: 76023, 76026, 76035, 76043, 76045, 76048–49, 76067–68, 76070–71, 76073, 76077–78, 76225, 76234, 76246, 76260, 76267, 76350, 76359, 76372, 76374, 76388, 76401–2, 76424, 76426–27, 76429–33, 76435, 76437–38, 76442–50, 76452–56, 76458–66, 76468–72, 76474–76, 76481, 76483, 76484, 76486, 76491, 76801, 76804, 76821, 76823, 76827–28, 76834, 76837, 76845, 76851, 76855, 76857–58, 76861–62, 76865–66, 76873, 76875, 76878, 76882, 76884, 76886, 76888, 76889, 76890, 76901 (part), 76902, 76903 (part), 76904 (part), 76905 (part), 76933, 76937, 76945, 76949, 76953, 79331, 79377, 79501–04, 79506, 79508, 79510–12, 79515–21, 79525–28, 79530, 79532–50, 79553, 79556, 79560–63, 79565–67, 79600–09, 79697–99, 79713, 79720–21, 79733, 79738, 79748, 79749, 79782–83

EIGHTEENTH DISTRICT

SHEILA JACKSON LEE, Democrat, of Houston, TX; born in Queens, NY, on January 12, 1950; graduated, Jamaica High School; B.A., Yale University, New Haven, CT, 1972; J.D., University of Virginia Law School, 1975; practicing attorney for 12 years; AKA Sorority, Houston Area Urban League, American Bar Association; staff counsel, U.S. House Select Committee on Assassinations, 1977–78; admitted to the Texas bar, 1975; city council (at large), Houston, 1990–94; Houston Municipal Judge, 1987–90; married Dr. Elwyn Cornelius Lee, 1973; two children: Erica Shelwyn and Jason Cornelius Bennett; elected to the 104th Congress; reelected to the 105th Congress.

Office Listings

http://www.house.gov/jacksonlee tx18@lee.house.gov

410 Cannon House Office Building, Washington, DC 20515–4318 225–3816
Administrative Assistant.—Kathi Wilkes.
Legislative Director.—Leon Buck.
Communications Director.—John Brennan.
Scheduler.—Mary Sykes.
1919 Smith Street, Suite 1180, Mickey Leland Building, Houston, TX 77002 .... (713) 655–0050
District Director.—Tom Combs.
420 West 19th Street, Houston, TX 77008 .... (713) 861–4070

County: Harris County (part). CITIES: Houston. Population (1990), 566,217.

ZIP Codes: 77001–10, 77012–14, 77016–22, 77024–26, 77028–30, 77032–33, 77037–40, 77043–44, 77047–52, 77054–56, 77060–61, 77064, 77066–67, 77073, 77075–76, 77078, 77080–81, 77086–88, 77091–93, 77097–98, 77201–03, 77205–06, 77208, 77210, 77212, 77216, 77219, 77221, 77226, 77228, 77230, 77238, 77240–41, 77250–53, 77255, 77265, 77267, 77277, 77288, 77291–92, 77297–99, 77338, 77396

* * *

NINETEENTH DISTRICT

LARRY COMBEST, Republican, of Lubbock, TX; born in Memphis, TX, March 20, 1945; graduated from Panhandle High School, 1963; B.B.A., West Texas State University, Canyon, TX, 1969; farmer, Agriculture Stabilization and Conservation Service of U.S. Department of Agriculture, 1971; legislative assistant to U.S. Senator John Tower of Texas, 1971–78; State treasurer for Senator Tower's reelection, 1978; owner, Combest Distributing Company, 1978–84; teacher, 1970; member: St. John's Methodist Church; Lubbock Historical Society; "Who's Who in American Politics," 1971; "Personalities of the South," 1972; married to the former Sharon McCurry; two children: Tonya and Haydn; elected to the 99th Congress on November 6, 1984; reelected to each succeeding Congress.

Office Listings

http://www.house.gov/combest

1511 Longworth House Office Building, Washington, DC 20515–4319 225–4005
Administrative Assistant.—Robert Lehman.
Office Manager.—Lynn E. Cowart.
Federal Building, Room 611, 1205 Texas Avenue, Lubbock, TX 79401 .... (806) 763–1611
District Representative.—Jimmy D. Clark.
No. 205, 3800 East 42nd Street, Odessa, TX 79762 .... (915) 550–0743
Office Manager.—Jenny Welsh.
No. 205, 5809 South Western, Amarillo, TX 79110 .... (806) 353–3945
Office Manager.—Danelle Barber.

Counties: Andrews, Bailey, Cochran, Dallam, Deaf Smith, Ector (part), Gaines, Hansford, Hartley, Hockley, Lubbock (part), Midland (part), Moore, Ochiltree, Oldham, Parmer, Randall, Sherman, Terry, Yoakum. Population (1990), 566,217.

ZIP Codes: 79001, 79009–10, 79013, 79015–16, 79018, 79022, 79025, 79029, 79033, 79035, 79040, 79044–45, 79051, 79053, 79058, 79062, 79070, 79081, 79084, 79086–87, 79091–93, 79098, 79103, 79106 (part), 79109 (part), 19110, 79114, 79118–20, 79121 (part), 79159–60, 79189, 79311, 79313–14, 79316, 79320, 79323,–25, 79329, 79336, 79338, 79342, 79344–47, 79350, 79353, 79355, 79358–60, 79363, 79364 (part), 79366 (part), 79367, 79372, 79376, 79378–80, 79382, 79401, 79403 (part), 79404 (part), 79405–07, 79410–11, 79412 (part), 79413, 79414, 79415 (part), 79416 (part), 79423–24, 79452–53, 79464, 79489–91, 79493, 79499, 79701 (part), 79703, (part), 79705 (part), 79707–09, 79714, 79741, 79758–59, 79761 (part), 79762 (part), 79763 (part) 79764–65, 79767–68, 79776

TWENTIETH DISTRICT

HENRY B. GONZALEZ, Democrat, of San Antonio, TX; born in San Antonio, May 3, 1916; son of Leonides (deceased) and Genevieve Gonzalez (deceased), descendants of the original colonists of the State of Durango in northern Mexico, who fled their country as the result of the revolution and moved to San Antonio in 1911; attended San Antonio College, University of Texas, and St. Mary's University School of Law (J.D. and LL.B.), which conferred on him an honorary doctor of laws degree in 1965; honorary doctor of humanities degree, Our Lady of the Lake College, 1973; honorary doctor of laws degree, University of the District of Columbia, 1984; first elected to public office in 1953; served three years on the San Antonio City Council, and as mayor pro tempore for part of the second term; served as chief probation officer of Bexar County Juvenile Court; worked for bilingual publications, San Antonio Housing Authority, taught math and citizenship classes in veterans training program; elected to the State Senate of Texas in 1956, reelected in 1960; married Bertha Cuellar, 1940; eight children: Henry, Rose Mary (Mrs. Ramos), Charles, Bertha (Mrs. Terry Denzer), Stephen, Genevieve, Francis and Anna Maria (Mrs. Mark Ihle); 21 grandchildren; elected to the 87th Congress on November 4, 1961, to fill the unexpired term of Paul J. Kilday; reelected to each succeeding Congress; ranking member, Banking and Financial Services Committee; previously served as chairman, Subcommittee on Housing and Community Opportunity and on the ad hoc Subcommittee on Robinson-Patman Act, antitrust legislation, and related matters; member, Select Committee on the Missing in Action in Southeast Asia; House Select Committee on Assassinations, vice chairman, 94th Congress; served seven times as a House delegate to the U.S.-Mexico Interparliamentary Conference; member, National Commission on Consumer Finance (terminated December 1972).

Office Listings

2413 Rayburn House Office Building, Washington, DC 20515–4320 225–3236
Legislative Director.—Tod Wells.
Executive Assistant.—Christine Ochoa.
Federal Building, B–124, 727 East Durango Boulevard, San Antonio, TX 78206 ... (210) 472–6195
(210) 472–6199

County: BEXAR COUNTY (part); cities of Alamo Heights (part), Atascosa (part), Balcones Heights, Castle Hills (part), Lackland AFB, Leon Valley (part), Macdona Somerset (part), San Antonio (part), and Terrell Hills (part), Von Ormy (part). Population (1990), 566,217.

ZIP Codes: 78002 (part), 78052 (part), 78054, 78069 (part), 78073 (part), 78201, 78202 (part), 78203 (part), 78204 (part), 78205 (part), 78206–07, 78208 (part), 78209 (part), 78210 (part), 78212 (part), 78213 (part), 78215 (part), 78216 (part), 78217 (part), 78218 (part), 78219 (part), 78225 (part), 78226–29, 78230 (part), 78233 (part), 78234, 78236–37, 78238 (part), 78240 (part), 78242, 78245 (part), 78250 (part), 78251 (part), 78252, 78268, 78279, 78291

* * *

TWENTY-FIRST DISTRICT

LAMAR SMITH, Republican, of San Antonio, TX; born in San Antonio on November 19, 1947; graduated from Texas Military Institute, San Antonio, 1965; B.A., Yale University, New Haven, CT, 1969; management intern, Small Business Administration, Washington, DC, 1969–70; business and financial writer, *The Christian Science Monitor*, Boston, MA, 1970–72; J.D., Southern Methodist University School of Law, Dallas, TX, 1975; admitted to the State bar of Texas, 1975, and commenced practice in San Antonio with the firm of Maebius and Duncan, Inc.; elected chairman of the Republican Party of Bexar County, TX, 1978 and 1980; elected District 57–F State Representative, 1981; elected Precinct 3 Commissioner of Bexar County, 1982 and 1984; partner, Lamar Seeligson Ranch, Jim Wells County, TX; married to Beth Schaefer; two children: Nell Seeligson and Tobin Wells; elected to the 100th Congress on November 4, 1986; reelected to each succeeding Congress; committees: Judiciary, Budget; House GOP Economic Task Force.

Office Listings

http://www.house.gov/lamarsmith lamars@hr.house.gov

2443 Rayburn House Office Building, Washington, DC 20515–4321 225–4236
Chief of Staff.—John Lampmann. FAX: 225–8628
Office Manager/Scheduler.—Elissa Pruett.
First Federal Building, Suite 640, 1100 North East Loop 410, San Antonio, TX 78209 .... (210) 821–5024
District Director.—O'Lene Stone.
Suite 318, 221 East Main, Round Rock, TX 78664 .... (512) 218–4208

Suite 104, 201 West Wall Street, Midland, TX 79701 .... (915) 687–5232
Suite 302, 33 East Twohig Street, San Angelo, TX 76903 .... (915) 653–3971
1006 Junction Highway, Kerrville, TX 78028 .... (512) 895–1414

Counties: Bandera, Bexar (part), Burnet, Comal, Gillespie, Glasscock, Guadalupe, Irion, Kendall, Kerr, Kimble, Llano, Mason, McCullough, (part), Menard, Midland (part), Real, Schleicher, Sterling, Tom Green (part), Williamson. Population (1990), 566,217.

ZIP Codes: 76527, 76537, 76820, 76825, 76831, 76841–42, 76848–49, 76854, 76856, 76859, 76869, 76874, 76885, 76901–06, 76930, 76934–36, 76939, 76941, 76951, 76955, 76957–58, 78003–4, 78006, 78010, 78013, 78023–25, 78027–29, 78055, 78058, 78063, 78074, 78108, 78115, 78123, 78130–33, 78148, 78154–56, 78163, 78209, 78212–13, 78216–18, 78230–32, 78239, 78247, 78258–59, 78261, 78265–66, 78270, 78278, 78283, 78292–99, 78605, 78607–09, 78611, 78613, 78618, 78623–24, 78626–28, 78631, 78634, 78638–39, 78641–43, 78654, 78664, 78669–75, 78680–81, 78717, 78727–29, 78750, 78759, 78828, 78833 78873, 78879, 78883, 78885, 79701–05, 79707, 78710–11, 79739

* * *

TWENTY-SECOND DISTRICT

TOM DELAY, Republican, of Sugar Land, TX; born in Laredo, TX, April 8, 1947; graduated Calallan High School, Corpus Christi, 1965; attended Baylor University, Waco, TX, 1967; B.S., University of Houston, TX, 1970; businessman; Texas House of Representatives, 1979–84; member: Oyster Creek Rotary, Fort Bend 100 Club; Chamber of Commerce; board member, Youth Opportunities Unlimited; married to the former Christine Furrh; one child: Danielle; elected by colleagues to No. 3 leadership post as majority whip for 104th Congress; elected to the 99th Congress on November 6, 1984; reelected to each succeeding Congress.

Office Listings

http://tomdelay.house.gov thewhip@mail.house.gov

341 Cannon House Office Building, Washington, DC 20515–4322 225–5951
Administrative Assistant.—Ed Buckham.
Appointment Secretary.—Pam Mattox.
Press Secretary.—Tony Rudy.
Legislative Assistants/Committee on Appropriations: Lori Eisner, Monica Kladakis.
Suite 285, 12603 Southwest Freeway, Stafford, TX 77477 .... (281) 240–3700

Counties: BRAZORIA COUNTY; city and townships of Alvin, Angleton, Danbury, Lake Jackson, Liverpool, Manvel, Rosharon, Pearland. FORT BEND COUNTY; city and townships of Beasley, Fulshear, Guy, Katy, Kindleton, Missouri C, Needville, Orchard, Richmond, Rosenberg, Simonton, Stafford, Sugar Land, Thompson, Fresno, Houston. HARRIS COUNTY; cities and townships of Friendswood, Houston, LaPorte, Seabrook. Population (1990), 566,217.

ZIP Codes: 77005, 77012, 77025, 77035–36, 77041–42, 77045–46, 77055, 77058–59, 77062–63, 77072, 77074–75, 77077, 77081–84, 77089, 77096, 77098–99, 77417, 77440–41, 77444, 77450, 77457, 77459, 77461, 77464, 77469, 77471, 77476–79, 77481, 77489, 77511–12, 77515, 77534, 77545–46, 77566, 77571, 77577–78, 77581, 77583–84, 77586

* * *

TWENTY-THIRD DISTRICT

HENRY BONILLA, Republican, of San Antonio, TX; born in San Antonio on January 2, 1954; graduated South San Antonio High School, 1972; B.J., University of Texas, Austin, 1976; Executive Producer for Public Affairs, KENS-TV, San Antonio; Executive News Producer, KENS-TV, San Antonio; National Federation of Independent Business Guardian of Small Business Award, 1994; League of Private Property Owners Champion of Private Property Rights Award, 1994; Watchdogs of the Treasury Golden Bulldog Award, 1994; U.S Hispanic Chamber of Commerce President's Award, 1994; American Heart Association of Texas Legislator of the Year, 1994; Vocational Home Economics Teachers Association of Texas Golden Flame Award, 1994; Hispanic Heritage Conference Eagle Award, 1993; University of Texas Ex-Students Association Outstanding Young Texas Ex Award, 1993; San Antonio Hispanic Chamber of Commerce Corporate Community Service Award, 1990; San Antonio Hispanic Chamber of Commerce Leadership Award, 1989; married the former Deborah JoAnn Knapp, 1981; two children: Alicia Knapp and Austin Elliott, 1988; elected on November 3, 1992 to the 103rd Congress; reelected to each succeeding Congress; committee: Appropriations.

Office Listings

1427 Longworth House Office Building, Washington, DC 20515–4323 225–4511
Administrative Assistant.—Steve Ruhlen. FAX: 225–2237
11120 Wurzbach, Suite 300, San Antonio, TX 78230 .... (210) 697–9055
District Director.—Phil Ricks.
1300 Matamoros Street, Room 113B, Laredo, TX 78040 .... (210) 726–4682
Federal Courthouse Building, Room 101, 111 East Broadway, Del Rio, TX 78840 (210) 774–6547
4400 North Big Spring, No. 211, Midland, TX 79705 .... (915) 686–8833

Counties: BEXAR COUNTY (part); cities and townships of San Antonio, Helotes, Fair Oaks Ranch. BREWSTER COUNTY; cities and townships of Alpine, Marathon, Big Bend National Park, Terlingua, Lajitas. CRANE COUNTY; city of Crane. CROCKETT COUNTY; city of Ozona. CULBERSON COUNTY; cities and townships of Van Horn, Kent, Lobo, Pine Springs. DIMMIT COUNTY; cities and townships of Carrizo Springs, Big Wells, Brundage, Asherton, Catarina. ECTOR COUNTY (part); city of Odessa. EDWARDS COUNTY; cities and townships of Rock Springs, Barksdale. EL PASO COUNTY (part); cities and townships of El Paso, Horizon City, Fort Bliss. HUDSPETH COUNTY; cities and townships of Dell City, Allamoore, Sierra Blanca, McNary Fort Hancock, Salt Flat. JEFF DAVIS COUNTY; cities and townships of Fort Davis, Valentine. KINNEY; cities and townships of Brackettville, Fort Clark Springs, Spofford. LOVING COUNTY; city of Mentone. MAVERICK COUNTY; cities and townships of Eagle Pass, Normandy, Quemado, El Indio. MEDINA COUNTY; cities and townships of Hondo, Castroville, La Coste, Devine, D'Hanis, Natalia, Yancey, Riomedina, Mico. MIDLAND COUNTY (part); city of Midland. PECOS COUNTY; cities and townships of Fort Stockton, Iraan, Sheffield, Bakersfield, Coyanosa, Girvin, Imperial. PRESIDIO COUNTY; cities and townships of Presidio, Marfa, Shafter, Redford. REAGAN COUNTY; cities and townships of Big Lake, Best. REEVES COUNTY; cities and townships of Pecos, Toyah, Saragosa, Balmorhea, Orla, Toyahvale. SUTTON COUNTY; city of Sonora. TERRELL COUNTY cities and townships of Dryden, Sanderson. UPTON; cities and townships of McCamey, Rankin, Midkiff. UVALDE COUNTY; cities and townships of Uvalde, Sabinal, Knippa, Concan, Utopia. VAL VERDE COUNTY; cities and townships of Del Rio, Comstock, Langtry, Juno, Loma Alta. WARD.; cities and townships of Monahans, Barstow, Wickett, Grandfalls, Pyote, Royalty. WEBB COUNTY; cities and townships Laredo, Bruni, Mirando City, Oilton. WINKLER COUNTY; cities Kermit, Wink. ZAVALA COUNTY; cities and townships of Crystal City, La Pryor, Batesville. Population (1990), 566,217.

ZIP Codes: 78002 (part), 78009, 78016, 78023 (part), 78039–44, 78054, 78057 (part), 78059 (part), 78066, 78069, 78073 (part), 78101 (part), 78108 (part), 78109, 78112, 78148, 78150, 78152, 78203 (part), 78210 (part), 78211 (part), 78214 (part), 78217 (part), 78218 (part), 78219, 78220 (part), 78221 (part), 78222, 78224 (part), 78227 (part), 78229 (part), 78232 (part), 78233 (part), 78235, 78236 (part), 78237 (part), 78238–39, 78240 (part), 78242, 78244–45, 78247 (part), 78250 (part), 78251–53, 78263–64, 78268, 78344, 78369, 78371, 78801–02, 78827, 78829–30, 78832, 78834, 78836–42, 78850, 78852–53, 78860–61, 78870–72, 78877, 78881, 78884, 78886

* * *

TWENTY-FOURTH DISTRICT

MARTIN FROST, Democrat, of Dallas, TX; born in Glendale, CA, January 1, 1942; graduated R.L. Paschal High School, Fort Worth, TX, 1960; B.A. and B.J., University of Missouri, Columbia, MO, 1964; J.D., Georgetown Law Center, Washington, DC, 1970; served in U.S. Army Reserves, 1966–72; lawyer; law clerk for Federal Judge Sarah T. Hughes; legal commentator for channel 13; vice president and board member, Dallas Democratic Forum, 1976–77; admitted to the Texas bar in 1970 and commenced practice in Dallas; active leader in civic, community, and political affairs; board member, Oak Cliff Chamber of Commerce, American Cancer Society, and Oak Cliff Conservation League; member: Oak Cliff Lions Club, American Jewish Committee, Temple Emanu-El in Dallas, Dallas and Texas bar associations; staff writer for the *Congressional Quarterly Weekly,* 1965–67; married the former Valerie Hall of Fort Worth, TX, 1976; three daughters: Alanna, Mariel and Camille; elected to the 96th Congress, November 7, 1978; reelected to each succeeding Congress; member, Rules Committee; chairman, Democratic Congressional Campaign Committee.

Office Listings

http://www.house.gov/frost frost@hr.house.gov

2459 Rayburn House Office Building, Washington, DC 20515–4324 225–3605
Administrative Assistant.—Ronnie Carleton. FAX: 225–4951
Press Secretary.—Askia Suruma.
Executive Assistant.—Vera Lou Durigon.
Legislative Director.—Susan McAvoy.
3020 South East Loop 820, Fort Worth, TX 76140 .... (817) 293–9231
District Director.—Cinda Crawford.
506 NCNB Oak Cliff Tower, 400 South Zang Boulevard, Dallas, TX 75208 .... (214) 948–3401
100 North Main Street, Room 534, Corsicana, TX 76010 .... (903) 874–0760

Counties: Dallas (part), Ellis (part), Navarro, Tarrant (part). CITIES AND TOWNSHIPS: Fort Worth, Dallas, Arlington, Duncanville, Grand Prairie, DeSoto, Cedar Hill, Mansfield, Kennedale, Waxahachi, Ennis, Corsicana, Red Oak, Cockrell Hill, Glenn Heights, Lancaster, Wilmer, Maypearl, Milford, Avalon, Italy, Forreston, Ferris, Nash, Boyce, Palmer, Rockett, Bardwell, Rice, Chatfield, Kerens, Forest, Dawson, Richland, Purdon, Barry, Blooming Grove, Powell, Emhouse, Roane. Population (1990), 566,217.

ZIP Codes: 75050, 75051–52, 75101–02, 75104, 75105, 75110, 75115–16, 75119–20, 75125, 75134, 75137–38, 75141, 75144, 75146, 75151–53, 75154–55, 75165, 75167, 75168 (part), 75172, 75203 75208, 75211, 75222, 75224, 75233,

75235–36, 75241, 75249, 75260, 75262–63, 75264 (part), 75265, 75266–67 (part), 75277 (part), 75283–86 (part), 75301 (part), 75303 (part), 75310 (part), 75312 (part), 75320 (part), 75323 (part), 75326 (part), 75350 (part), 75353 (part), 75363–64 (part), 75373 (part), 75387–88 (part), 75391–98 (part), 75859, 76004–07, 76010–15, 76017–18, 76041, 76050, 76060, 76063–65, 76084, 76103–05, 76112, 76115, 76119, 76134, 76140, 76623, 76626, 76639, 76641, 76648, 76651, 76670, 76679, 76681

* * *

TWENTY-FIFTH DISTRICT

KENNETH F. BENTSEN, Jr., Democrat, of Houston, TX; born in Houston, June 3, 1959; graduated, Deerfield Academy, 1977; B.A., University of St. Thomas, Houston, 1982; M.P.A., American University, Washington, DC, 1985; attends First Presbyterian Church; legislative assistant to Ronald D. Coleman, 1983–87; served as associate staff to the U.S. House Committee on Appropriations; investment banker, 1987–94; chair, Harris County Democratic Party, 1990–1993; serves on Banking and Financial Services and Small Business Committees; married the former Tamra Kiehn, 1990; two children: Louise and Meredith; elected to the 104th Congress; reelected to the 105th Congress.

Office Listings

http://www.house.gov/bentsen bentsen@hr.house.gov

128 Cannon House Office Building, Washington, DC 20515–4325 225–7508
Chief of Staff.—Vince Willmore. FAX: 225–2947
Press Secretary.—Jerremy Warren.
Executive Assistant.—Brenda O'Lenick.
Legislative Director.—Bradley Edgell.
Federal Building, Suite 12102, 515 Rusk Street, Houston, TX 77002 .... (713) 229–2244
Suite 810, 1001 East Southmore, Pasadena, TX 77504 .... (713) 473–4334

Counties: Harris, Cities and townships: Barrett Station, Baytown, Bellaire, Channel View, Deer Park, Highlands, Houston, LaPorte, Morgans Point, Pasadena Southside Place, West University Place. Population (1990), 566,217.

ZIP Codes: 77005, 77015, 77025, 77030, 77031, 77034–36, 77042, 77045, 77230–31, 77047–49, 77053–54, 77059, 77061, 77063, 77071–72, 77074, 77081, 77085, 77087, 77089, 77096, 77099, 77225, 77234–35, 77245, 77254, 77265, 77277, 77289, 77401–02, 77489, 77502–08, 77520–21, 77530, 77532, 77536, 77562, 77571–72

* * *

TWENTY-SIXTH DISTRICT

DICK ARMEY, Republican, of Irving, TX; born in Cando, ND, on July 7, 1940; graduated Cando High School, 1958; B.A., Jamestown College, Jamestown, ND, 1963; M.A., University of North Dakota, Grand Forks, 1964; Ph.D., University of Oklahoma, Norman, 1969; faculty, economics, University of Montana, 1964–65; assistant professor, West Texas State University, 1967–68; assistant professor, Austin College, 1968–72; associate professor, North Texas State University, 1972–77; chairman, Department of Economics, North Texas State University, 1977–83; economic consultant and adviser; Distinguished Fellow of the Fisher Institute, Dallas, TX; Omicron Delta Epsilon, economics honor society; Southwestern Social Sciences Association; Missouri Valley Economics Association; former deacon, Presbyterian Church; married to the former Susan Byrd; five children: Kathryn, David, Chip, Scott and Scott; elected to the 99th Congress on November 6, 1984; reelected to each succeeding Congress.

Office Listings

http://www.house.gov/armey

301 Cannon House Office Building, Washington, DC 20515–4326 225–7772
Administrative Assistant.—Paul Morrell.
Legislative Director.—Gayland Barksdale.
Press Secretary.—Michele Davis.
9901 Valley Ranch Parkway E, No. 3050, Irving, TX 75063 .... (972) 556–2500
District Director.—Jean Campbell.

Counties: Collin (part), Dallas (part), Denton (part), Tarrant (part). Cities and townships: Addison (part), Argyle, Carrollton, Coppell (part), Corinth, Dallas (part), Denton (part), Double Oak, Farmers Branch (part), Flower Mound, Frisco (part), Grand Prairie (part), Grapevine (part), Hickory Creeks, Highland Village, Irving (part), Lake Dallas, Lewisville (part), McKinney (part), Plano (part), Richardson (part), Roanoke, Southlake (part). Population (1990), 566,217.

ZIP Codes: 75001, 75006–08, 75010–11, 75015–16, 75019, 75023–25, 75028–29, 75034, 75038–39, 75050, 75053, 75056–57, 75060–63, 75065, 75067–70, 75075, 75078, 75080–81, 75083–85, 75093, 75220, 75229, 75234, 75240, 75243, 75244, 75248, 75251, 75252, 75253, 75287, 75379, 75380, 75381, 76051, 76201

TWENTY-SEVENTH DISTRICT

SOLOMON P. ORTIZ, Democrat, of Corpus Christi, TX; born in Robstown, TX, on June 3, 1938; attended Robstown High School; attended Del Mar College, Corpus Christi; officers certificate, Institute of Applied Science, Chicago, IL, 1962; officers certificate, National Sheriffs Training Institute, Los Angeles, CA, 1977; served in U.S. Army, Sp4c. 1960–62; insurance agent; Nueces County constable, 1965–68; Nueces County commissioner, 1969–76; Nueces County sheriff, 1977–82; member: Congressional Hispanic Caucus (chairman, 102nd Congress); Congressional Hispanic Caucus Institute (chairman of the board, 102nd Congress); Army Caucus; Depot Caucus; Sheriffs' Association of Texas, National Sheriffs' Association, Corpus Christi Rotary Club, American Red Cross, United Way; honors: *Who's Who among Hispanic Americans;* Man of the Year, International Order of Foresters (1981); Conservation Legislator of the Year for the Sportsman Clubs of Texas (1986), Boss of the Year by the American Businesswomen Association (1980); National Government Hispanic Business Advocate, U.S. Hispanic Chamber of Commerce (1992); Leadership Award, Latin American Management Association (1991); National Security Leadership Award, American Security Council (1992); Tree of Life Award, Jewish National Fund (1987); two children: Yvette and Solomon, Jr.; elected on November 2, 1982 to the 98th Congress; reelected to each succeeding Congress.

Office Listings

2136 Rayburn House Office Building, Washington, DC 20515–4327 225–7742
Administrative Assistant.—Florencio H. Rendon. FAX: 226–1134
Executive Assistant/Scheduling.—Joe Galindo.
Deputy Chief of Staff.—Vickie Plunkett.
Press Secretary.—Cathy Travis.
Suite 510, 3649 Leopard, Corpus Christi, TX 78408 .... (512) 883–5868
Suite 200, 3505 Boca Chica Boulevard, Brownsville, TX 78521 .... (210) 541–1242

Counties: Cameron; Kenedy; Kleberg (part); Nueces; Willacy (part). Population (1990), 566,217.

ZIP Codes: 78330, 78338–39, 78343, 78347, 78351, 78363, 78373, 78379–80, 78385, 78400–09, 78410 (part), 78411–19, 78469–71, 78473–78, 78520–23, 78526, 78535, 78550–52, 78559, 78561, 78566–68, 78569 (part), 78575, 78578, 78580, 78583, 78586, 78590, 78592–94, 78597–98

* * *

TWENTY-EIGHTH DISTRICT

CIRO RODRIGUEZ, Democrat, of San Antonio, TX born in Piedras Negras, Mexico; attended San Antonio College; B.A in Political Science, St. Mary's University; M.A., Our Lady of the Lake University; former Texas State House of Representatives, 1987–97; dean, House Bexar County Legislative Delegation; taught undergraduate and graduate courses at Worden School of Social Work; member: Harlendale Independent School District School Board; Local and Consent Calendar Committee, chairman; Public Health Committee; Higher Education Committee; Legislative Study Group, vice chairman; caseworker, The Department of Mental Health and Mental Retardation; faculty associate, Our Lady of the Lake University in San Antonio; consultant, Intercultural Development Research Association; married to Carolina Pena; one daughter: Xochil Daria; committees: National Security; Veterans Affairs; subcommittees: Benefits, Readiness; elected to 105th Congress in special election, sworn in on April 17, 1997.

Office Listings

323 Cannon House Office Bulding, Washington, DC 20515–4328 225–1640
Chief of Staff.—Jeff Mendelsohn. FAX: 225-1641
Legislative Director.—Mark Gillman.
Legislative Aide.—Asim Ghafoor.
Legislative Assistant.—Farah L. Press.
Executive Assistant.—Stephen T. Hofmann.
Suite 115, 1313 South East Military Drive, San Antonio, TX 78214–2851 .... (210) 924–7383
District Director.—Norma Reyes.
Suite 5, 202 East St. Joseph Street, San Diego, Texas 78384 .... (512) 279–3907

Counties: Atascosa, Bexar, Comal, Duval, Frio, Guadalupe, Jim Hogg, Jim Wells, La Salle, McMullen, Starr, Wilson, Zapata.

ZIP Codes: 78001, 78005, 78007–8, 78011–12, 78014, 78017, 78019, 78021, 78026, 78050, 78052 (part) 78053, 78057, 78061–62, 78064–65, 78067, 78072, 78073 (part), 78076, 78101, 78108 (part), 78109, 78112, 78114, 78121, 78124,

78130 (part), 78132 (part), 78143, 78147, 78148 (part), 78152, 78154 (part), 78155 (part), 78160–61, 78202 (part), 78203 (part), 78204 (part), 78205 (part), 78210 (part), 78211 (part), 78214, 78218 (part), 78219 (part), 78220–24, 78225 (part), 78233 (part), 78235, 78239 (part), 78244, 78263–64, 78280, 78322 (part), 78333, 78341–42, 78344 (part), 78349, 78357, 78360–61, 78372, 78375–76, 78384, 78536, 78545, 78547–48, 78564, 78582, 78584–85, 78588, 78591

* * *

TWENTY-NINTH DISTRICT

GENE GREEN, Democrat, of Houston, TX; born on October 17, 1947 in Houston; B.A., University of Houston, 1971; admitted Texas bar, 1977; business manager, attorney; Texas State Representative, 1973–85; Texas State Senator, 1985–92; member: Houston Bar Association, Texas Bar Association, American Bar Association, Communications Workers of America, Aldine Optimist Club, Gulf Coast Conservation Association, Texas Historical Society, Lindale Lions Club, Congressional Hispanic Caucus, Congressional Steel Caucus, Urban Caucus, and Sportsmen's Caucus; married on January 23, 1970 to Helen Albers; two children: Angela and Christopher; elected on November 3, 1992 to the 103rd Congress; reelected to each succeeding Congress.

Office Listings

http://www.house.gov/green ggreen@hr.house.gov

1024 Longworth House Office Building, Washington, DC 20515–4329 225–1688
FAX: 225–9903

Administrative Assistant.—Moses C. Mercado.
Executive Assistant/Scheduling.—DeAnna Rodriguez.
Grants Coordinator.—Catherine Herrington.
Staff Assistant.—Rochelle Tafolla.
Legislative Assistant.—Ron Lord.
Legislative Assistant.—Mike Hollon.
Press Secretary.—Elizabeth Miller.

5502 Lawndale, Houston, TX 77023 .... (713) 923–9961
FAX: 923–4758

420 West 19th Street Houston, TX 77008 .... (713) 880–4364
FAX: 880–5916

County: HARRIS COUNTY (part); cities and townships of Houston, Humble (part), Pasadena (part), Channelview, Galena Park, Jacinto City, La Porte (part), South Houston. Population (1990), 566,217.

ZIP Codes: 77009, 77011–17, 77020, 77022–23, 77026, 77028, 77032, 77034, 77037–39, 77044, 77049–50, 77060, 77066–67, 77073, 77076, 77078, 77087, 77090, 77093, 77396, 77502–04, 77506, 77508, 77530, 77547, 77587

* * *

THIRTIETH DISTRICT

EDDIE BERNICE JOHNSON, Democrat, of Dallas, TX; born on December, 3, 1935 in Waco, TX; nursing diploma, St. Mary's at Notre Dame, 1955; B.S., nursing, Texas Christian, 1967; M.P.A, Southern Methodist, 1976; proprietor, Eddie Bernice Johnson and Associates consulting and airport concession management; Texas House of Representatives, 1972–77; Carter administration appointee, 1977–81; Texas State Senate, 1986–92; member, St. John Baptist Church, Dallas; member, American Nurses Association; member, Links, Inc., Dallas Chapter; member, Dallas Black Chamber of Commerce; life member, NAACP; member, Charter 100 of Dallas; member, Girlfriends, Inc.; honorary member, Delta Kappa Gama Society International Women Educators Organization, Epsilon Chapter; life member, YWCA; executive committee member, United Way of Metropolitan Dallas; member, Women's Council of Dallas; member and past president, National Council of Negro Women; member, Democratic Women of Dallas County; member, Dallas Urban League; member, Dallas County Democratic Progressive Voters League; member, past national vice president and past national secretary, National Order of Women Legislators; member, National Black Nurses Association; member, Goals for Dallas; Emma V. Kelly Achievement Award, Grant Temple Daughters of IBPOE of W, 1973; first woman to chair a major House committee in the Texas Legislature; Libertarian of the Year, ACLU, 1978; Women Helping Women Award, Soroptimist International of Dallas and Southwest Region, 1979; Outstanding Citizenship Award, National Conference of Christians and Jews, 1985; NAACP Juanita Craft Award in Politics, NAACP, Dallas Chapter, 1989; Legislative Action Award, Texas Association of Community Action Agencies, 1989; ''She Knows Where She is Going,'' Girls Inc., 1990; Distinguished Public Service Award, Prairie View

A&M University, 1990; Eartha M.M. White Award, outstanding achievement as a businesswoman, National Business League, 1990; Outstanding Service Award, KKDA Radio, 1991; National Association of Negro Business and Professional Women and Clubs Achievement in Government, 1991; Outstanding Service Award, Sigma Pi Phi Fraternity, 1991; Certificate of Commendation, City of Dallas, 1991; Outstanding Service Award, the Child Care Group, 1991; Legislator of the Year award, Dallas Alliance for the Mentally Ill, 1991; member, Alpha Kappa Alpha Sorority, Inc., Dallas Chapter; 1993 Meritorious Award, the National Black Nurses Foundation, Inc.; 1993 Award for Achievement in Equal Employment Opportunity, U.S. Department of Energy; 1994 Leadership Commendation, Campaign To Keep America Warm; one child, Dawrence Kirk; elected on November 3, 1992 to the 103rd Congress; reelected to each succeeding Congress.

Office Listings

http://www.house.gov/ebjohnson

1123 Longworth House Office Building, Washington, DC 20515–4330 225–8885
Legislative Director.—Horace Jennings. FAX: 226–1477
Communications Director.—Mike Greene.

2515 McKinney Avenue, Suite 1565, Dallas, TX 75201 .... (214) 922–8885
District Director.—Shallie Bey.
Scheduler.—Ronnie Veals. FAX: 922–7028

Counties: Dallas. CITIES AND TOWNSHIPS: Dallas, De Soto, Farmer's Branch, Irving, Lancaster. Population (1990), 566,217.

ZIP Codes: 75015–17, 75019, 75038–39, 75050–51, 75053, 75060–63, 75074–75, 75083, 75085, 75094, 75115, 75134, 75141, 75146, 75149, 75201–04, 75206–12, 75214–17, 75220–21, 75223–24, 75226–29, 75232–33, 75235–37, 75241–42, 75244, 75246–47, 75250–51, 75258, 75261, 75270, 75315, 75339, 75342, 75354–56, 75371, 75374, 75376, 75380, 75389

UTAH

(Population 1995, 1,951,000)

SENATORS

ORRIN G. HATCH, Republican, of Salt Lake City, UT; born in Pittsburgh, PA, March 22, 1934; B.S., Brigham Young University, Provo, UT, 1959; LL.B., University of Pittsburgh, 1962; practiced law in Salt Lake City, UT and Pittsburgh, PA; senior partner, Hatch and Plumb law firm, Salt Lake City; worked his way through high school, college, and law school at the metal lathing building trade; member, AFL–CIO; holds ''av'' rating in Martindale-Hubbell Law Directory; member, Salt Lake County Bar Association, Utah Bar Association, American Bar Association, Pennsylvania Bar Association, Allegheny County Bar Association, numerous other professional and fraternal organizations; member, Church of Jesus Christ of Latter-day Saints; honorary doctorate, University of Maryland; honorary doctor of laws: Pepperdine University and Southern Utah State University; honorary national ski patroller; Help Eliminate Litter and Pollution (HELP) Association; author of numerous national publications; married to Elaine Hansen of Newton, UT; six children: Brent, Marcia, Scott, Kimberly, Alysa and Jess; elected to the U.S. Senate, November 2, 1976, for the six-year term beginning January 3, 1977; reelected on November 2, 1982; reelected to six-year term November 8, 1988; reelected to six-year term November 8, 1994; author: ''The Equal Rights Amendment Extension: A Critical Analysis'' in the *Harvard Journal of Law and Public Policy*, and ''Should the Capital Vote in Congress? A Critical Analysis of the D.C. Representation Amendment'' in the *Fordham Urban Law Journal*; ''Alternative Dispute Resoultion in the Federal Government: A View from Congress,'' *Touro Law Review*, vol. 4, No. 1, fall 1987; ''The First Amendment and Our National Heritage,'' *Oklahoma City University Law Review*, vol. 12, No. 3, fall 1987; ''Avoidance of Constitutional Conflicts,'' *University of Pittsburgh Law Review*, vol. 48, No. 4, summer 1987; ''The Role of Congress in Sentencing: The United States Sentencing Commission, Mandatory Minimum Sentences, and the Search for a Certain and Effective Sentencing System,'' by Senator Orrin Hatch, *Wake Forest Law Review*, vol. 28, No. 2, summer 1993; committees: chairman, Judiciary; Finance; Indian Affairs; Select Committee on Intelligence.

Office Listings

http://www.senate.gov/~hatch senator_hatch@hatch.senate.gov

135 Russell Senate Office Building, Washington, DC 20510–4402 224–5251
Administrative Assistant.—Robert Dibblee.
Press Secretary.—J. Paul Smith.
8402 Federal Building, Salt Lake City, UT 84138 .... (801) 524–4380
State Director.—Melanie Bowen.
1410 Federal Building, Ogden, UT 84401 .... (801) 625–5672
109 Federal Building, Provo, UT 84601 .... (801) 375–7881
197 East Tabernacle, Room 2, St. George, UT 84770 .... (801) 634–1795

* * *

ROBERT F. BENNETT, Republican, of Salt Lake City, UT; born September 18, 1933 in Salt Lake City; B.S., University of Utah, 1957; chief executive officer of Franklin Quest, Salt Lake City; chief congressional liaison; U.S. Department of Transportation chairman of Utah Education Strategic Planning Commission; awards: ''Entrepreneur of the Year,'' *Inc.* magazine, 1989, Light of Learning Award, 1989; author, *Gaining Control*; married to Joyce McKay; children: James, Julie, Robert, Wendy, Heather, and Heidi; committees: Appropriations; Banking, Housing, and Urban Affairs; Small Business; Joint Economic; elected to the U.S. Senate, November 3, 1992, for the six-year term beginning January 3, 1993.

Office Listings

http://www.senate.gov/~bennett senator@bennett.senate.gov

431 Dirksen Senate Office Building, Washington, DC 20510–4403 224–5444
Administrative Assistant.—James Barker.
Legislative Director.—Chip Yost.
Office Manager.—Sandy Knickman.
4225 Wallace F. Bennett Federal Building, Salt Lake City, UT 84138 .... (801) 524–5933
State Director.—Dixie Minson.
1410 Federal Building, 324 25th Street, Ogden, UT 84401 .... (801) 625–5675
51 South University Avenue, Provo, UT 84601–4424 .... (801) 379–2525

Federal Building, 196 E. Tabernacle Street, St. George, UT 84770–3474 .... (801) 628–5514
82 North 100 East, Cedar City, UT 84720 .... (801) 865–1335

REPRESENTATIVES

FIRST DISTRICT

JAMES V. HANSEN, Republican, of Farmington, UT; born in Salt Lake City, UT, August 14, 1932; B.S., University of Utah, 1961; U.S. Navy, 1951–55; president, James V. Hansen Insurance Agency; president, Woodland Springs Development Company; member, Utah House of Representatives, 1973–80—last term, Speaker of the House; recipient, Legislator of the Year Award, 1980; member, Rotary Club; recipient, Citizen of the Year Award; member, Church of Jesus Christ of Latter-day Saints (Mormon); married the former Ann Burgoyne, 1958; five children: Susan, Joseph James, David Burgoyne, Paul William and Jennifer; committees: National Security, Resources, Intelligence; subcommittees: chairman, National Parks, Forests, and Lands, Water and Power, Research and Development; Military Reconstruction; elected to the 97th Congress, November 4, 1980; reelected to each succeeding Congress.

Office Listings
http://www.house.gov/hansen

2466 Rayburn House Office Building, Washington, DC 20515–4401 225–0453
Administrative Assistant.—Nancee W. Blockinger. FAX: 225–5857
1017 Federal Building, 324 25th Street, Ogden, UT 84401 .... (801) 393–8362
State District Director.—Steve Peterson.
435 East Tabernacle, Suite 301, St. George, UT 84770 .... (801) 628–1071
Field Office Representative.—Rick Arial.

Counties: Beaver, Box Elder, Cache, Davis, Iron, Juab, Millard, Rich, Salt Lake (part), Tooele, Washington, and Weber. Population (1990), 574,286.

ZIP Codes: 83254 (part), 84010, 84014–16, 84018, 84022, 84025, 84028–29, 84037–39, 84041, 84050, 84054, 84056, 84064, 84067, 84069, 84071, 84074, 84077, 84080, 84083, 84086–87, 84301–02, 84304–21, 84325–26, 84328–40, 84400–05, 84409, 84624, 84628, 84630–31, 84635–36, 84638–40, 84644–45, 84648–49, 84656, 84710, 84712–20, 84722–23, 84725–26, 84728–29, 84731–38, 84740–43, 84745–47, 84749–53, 84755–65, 84767, 84770, 84772–76, 84779–80

* * *

SECOND DISTRICT

MERRILL COOK, Republican, of Salt Lake City, UT; born in Philadelphia, PA, May 6, 1946; graduated, East High School, Salt Lake City; B.A., University of Utah, 1969; M.B.A., Harvard University, 1971; business management consultant, Arthur D. Little, Inc., Cambridge, MA, 1971–74; founder and president, Cook Slurry Company, Salt Lake City; KALL talk show host, Merrill Cook Show, 1995; Reagan delegate to Republican National Convention, 1976; member, Central Committee of the Utah Republican Party, 1980s; married the former Camille Sanders, 1969; five children: Brian, Alison, Barbara, David, and Michelle; committees: Banking and Financial Services, Transportation and Infrastructure, Science; subcommittees: Capital Markets, Securities, and Government-Sponsored Enterprises; Housing and Community Opportunity; Aviation; Space and Aeronautics; Surface Transportation; Technology; elected to the 105th Congress on November 5, 1996.

Office Listings
merrill.cook@mail.house.gov

1431 Longworth House Office Building, Washington, DC 20515–4402 225–3011
Chief of Staff.—David Irvine. FAX: 225–5638
Legislative Director.—Janet Jenson.
Press Secretary.—Marnie Funk.
Scheduler.—Marcy Benson.
Federal Building, 125 South State Street, Suite 2311, Salt Lake, UT 84138 ...... (801) 524–4394
District Director.—Rob Jeppson. FAX: 524–5994

COUNTIES: Salt Lake. CITIES: Alta, Bluffdale, Draper, Midvale, Murray, Riverton, Salt Lake City, Sandy, South Salt Lake City, South Jordan, Taylorsville, West Jordan. Population (1990), 574,241.

ZIP Codes: 84020 (part), 84044 (part), 84047, 84049, 84070, 84091–92, 84100–06, 84107 (part), 84108–17, 84119 (part), 84120 (part), 84121–27, 84130–45, 84147–48, 84150–52, 84180, 84184, 84189, 84199

THIRD DISTRICT

CHRISTOPHER B. CANNON, Republican, of Mapleton, UT; born in Salt Lake City, UT, October 20, 1950; B.S., university studies, Brigham Young University, 1974; graduate work at Harvard School of Business, 1974–75; J.D., Brigham Young University, 1977–80; admitted to the Utah bar in 1980 and began practice in Provo, UT; attorney, Robinson, Seiler and Glazier; former associate solicitor and deputy associate solicitor, Department of the Interior; cofounder, Geneva Steel, Provo; founder, Cannon Industries, Salt Lake City; president and, subsequently, chairman, of Cannon Industries, Salt Lake City; member, Utah Republican Party Elephant Club and Finance Committee; Utah chairman, Lamar Alexander for President; Utah finance chairman, Bush-Quayle '92; married the former Claudia Ann Fox in 1978; seven children: Rachel, Jane, Laura, Emily, Elizabeth, Jonathan, Matthew; elected to the 105th Congress.

Office Listings

cannon.ut03@mail.house.gov

118 Cannon House Office Building, Washington, DC 20515–4403 .... 225–7751 FAX: 225–5629

Administrative Assistant.—Chuck Warren.
Office Administrator/Scheduler.—Meredith Rasmussen.
Legislative Correspondent.—Chris McKay.
Legislative Director.—Steve Taggart.
Press Secretary.—Peter Valcasce.
Legislative Assistants: Claude Hrvatin, Nathan Glazier.
Staff Assistant.—Gregory Roney.

Room 317, 51 South University Drive, Provo, UT 84601 .... (801) 397–2500

Counties: Carbon, Daggett, Duchesne, Emery, Garfield, Grand, Kane, Morgan, Piute, Salt Lake (part), San Juan, Sanpete, Sevier, Summit, Uintah, Utah, Wasatch, and Wayne. Population (1990), 574,323.

ZIP Codes: 84001–04, 84007–08, 84013, 84017–18, 84021–24, 84025–27, 84030–33, 84035–36, 84039, 84042–44, 84046, 84049–53, 84055, 84057–63, 84066, 84068, 84072–73, 84076, 84078–79, 84082, 84085, 84098, 84104, 84115 (part), 84116 (part), 84118 (part), 84119 (part), 84120 (part), 84123 (part) 84501, 84510–13, 84515–16, 84518, 84520–23, 84525–37, 84539–40, 84601–04, 84606, 84620–23, 84626–27, 84629–30, 84632–34, 84642–43, 84646–47, 84651–55, 84657, 84660, 84662–65, 84667, 84701, 84710–12, 84715–18, 84723–24, 84726, 84729–30, 84732, 84734–36, 84739–41, 84743–44, 84747, 84749–50, 84554–55, 84758–59, 84762, 84766–67, 84773, 84775–76

VERMONT

(Population 1995, 585,000)

SENATORS

PATRICK J. LEAHY, Democrat, of Burlington, VT; born in Montpelier, VT, March 31, 1940, son of Howard and Alba Leahy; graduate of St. Michael's High School, Montpelier, 1957; B.A., St. Michael's College, 1961; J.D., Georgetown University, 1964; lawyer, admitted to the Vermont bar, 1964; admitted to the District of Columbia bar, 1979; admitted to practice before the U.S. Supreme Court, 1968; the Second Circuit Court of Appeals in New York, 1966, the Federal District Court of Vermont, 1965, and the Vermont Supreme Court, 1964; State's attorney, Chittenden County, 1966–74; vice president, National District Attorneys Association, 1971–74; married the former Marcelle Pomerleau, 1962; three children: Kevin, Alicia and Mark; ranking minority member, Agriculture, Nutrition and Forestry Committee; Appropriations Committee: Subcommittee on Foreign Operations (ranking minority member), Subcommittee on VA, HUD and Independent Agencies (senior Democrat), Subcommitteee on Interior; Judiciary Committee: Subcommittee on Antitrust, Business Rights and Competition (ranking minority member), Subcommittee on Technology, Terrorism and Government Information (senior Democrat); first Democrat and youngest person in Vermont to be elected to the U.S. Senate; elected to the Senate on November 5, 1974; reelected November 6, 1986 and November 3, 1993.

Office Listings

http://www.senate.gov/~leahy senator_leahy@leahy.senate.gov

433 Russell Senate Office Building, Washington, DC 20510–4502 224–4242
Chief of Staff.—Luke Albee.
Deputy Chief of Staff.—Clara Kircher.
Legislative Director.—John P. Dowd.
Press Secretary.—David Carle.
Federal Building, Room 338, Montpelier, VT 05602 .... (802) 229–0569
Legislative Assistant.—Robert G. Paquin.
199 Main Street, Courthouse Plaza, Burlington, VT 05401 .... (802) 863–2525
Director.—Chuck Ross.

* * *

JAMES M. JEFFORDS, Republican, of Shrewsbury, VT; born in Rutland, VT, May 11, 1934; attended public schools in Rutland; received B.S.I.A. degree from Yale, New Haven, CT, 1956; graduate work, Harvard, Cambridge, MA, 1962, LL.B.; served in the U.S. Navy as lieutenant (jg.); captain, U.S. Naval Reserves (retired June 1990); admitted to the Vermont bar, 1962, and began practice in Rutland; State Senator, 1967–68; attorney general, State of Vermont, 1969–73; committees: chairman: Labor and Human Resources; Finance; Veterans' Affairs; Special Committee on Aging; cochairman: Northeast-Midwest Coalition; married to Elizabeth Daley; two children: Leonard and Laura; elected to the 94th Congress, November 5, 1974; reelected to each succeeding Congress; elected to the U.S. Senate, November 8, 1988, for the six-year term beginning January 3, 1989; reelected to the 104th Congress.

Office Listings

http://www.senate.gov/~jeffords vermont@jeffords.senate.gov

728 Hart Senate Office Building, Washington, DC 20510–4503 224–5141
Administrative Assistant.—Susan Boardman Russ.
Legislative Director.—Ken Connolly.
Office Manager.—Jim Eismeier.
Scheduler.—Pamela Ploof.
58 State Street, Montpelier, VT 05602 .... (802) 223–5273
Lindholm Building, 2nd Floor, 2 South Main Street, Rutland, VT 05701 .... (802) 773–3875
Suite 100, 95 St. Paul Street, Burlington, VT 05401 .... (802) 658–6001

REPRESENTATIVE

AT LARGE

BERNARD SANDERS, Independent, of Burlington, VT; born in Brooklyn, NY, September 8, 1941; graduated from Madison High School, Brooklyn, B.S., political science, University of

Chicago, 1964; carpenter, writer, college professor; mayor of Burlington, VT, 1981–89; married to the former Jane O'Meara, 1988; four children: Levi, Heather, Carina and David; elected to the 102nd Congress on November 6, 1990; reelected to each succeding Congress.

Office Listings

http://www.house.gov/bernie bernie@hr.house.gov

213 Cannon House Office Building, Washington, DC 20515–4501 225–4115
Administrative Assistant.—Ruthan Wirman. FAX: 225–6790
Legislative Director/Senior Policy Advisor.—Bill Goold.
Press Secretary.—Tina Wisell.
1 Church Street, Burlington, VT 05401 .... (802) 862–0697

Population (1990), 562,677.

ZIP Codes: 05001, 05030–56, 05058–62, 05065, 05067–77, 05079, 05081, 05083–86, 05088, 05089, 05091, 05101, 05141–44, 05146, 05148–56, 05158–59, 05161, 05201, 05250–55, 05257, 05260–62, 05301, 05302, 05303, 05304, 05340–46, 05350–63, 05401–05, 05406, 05407, 05440–48, 05449, 05450–66, 05468–74, 05476–78, 05481–83, 05485–92, 05494–95, 05601, 05602, 05640–41, 05647–58, 05660–70, 05672–82, 05701, 05702, 05730–53, 05757–70, 05772–78, 05819–30, 05832–33, 05836–43, 05845–51, 05853, 05855, 05857–63, 05866–68, 05871–75, 05901–07

VIRGINIA

(Population 1995, 6,618,000)

SENATORS

JOHN W. WARNER, Republican, of Alexandria, VA; born February 18, 1927; grandson of John W. and Mary Tinsley Warner of Amherst County, VA, son of the late Dr. John W. Warner and Martha Budd Warner; left high school in 1944 to serve in the U.S. Navy, released from active duty, third class electronics technician, July 1946; graduated Washington and Lee University (engineering), 1949; entered University of Virginia Law School, 1949; U.S. Marine Corps, served in Korea as first lieutenant, communications officer, 1st Marine Air Wing, September 1950–May 1952; received LL.B. from University of Virginia, 1953; former owner and operator of Atoka, a cattle and crops farm, 1961–94; law clerk to E. Barrett Prettyman, late chief judge for the U.S. Court of Appeals for D.C. Circuit, 1953–54; private law practice, 1954–56; assistant U.S. attorney, 1956–60; private law practice, 1960–69; trustee, Protestant Episcopal Cathedral, Mount St. Albans, 1967–72; member, board of trustees, Washington and Lee University, 1968–79; presidential appointments: Under Secretary, U.S. Navy, February 1969–April 1972; Secretary, U.S. Navy, May 1972–April 1974; Department of Defense delegate to Law of Sea Conferences, 1969–72, head of U.S. delegation for Incidents at Sea Conference, treaty signed in Moscow, May 1972; administrator, American Revolution Bicentennial Administration, April 1974–October 1976; committees: Armed Services; Environment and Public Works; chairman, Rules and Administration; Labor and Human Resources; Small Business; Special Committee on Aging; Joint Commmittee on the Library; Joint Committee on Printing; chairman, Airland Forces Subcommittee; Transportation and Infrastructure Subcommittee; member: National Security Working Group, Commission on Roles and Capabilities of U.S. Intelligence; U.S. delegate to the 12th special session of the U.N. General Assembly devoted to disarmament, 1982; appointed in 1985 as Senate observer to Geneva arms control talks with the Soviet Union; elected to the U.S. Senate, November 7, 1978, took oath of office in Richmond, VA, January 2, 1979; reelected on November 6, 1984, November 6, 1990, and November 4, 1996.

Office Listings

senator@warner.senate.gov

225 Russell Senate Office Building, Washington, DC 20510–4601 224–2023
Administrative Assistant.—Susan Magill.
Executive Assistant/Secretary.—Eileen Mandel.
Press Secretary.—Eric Ruff.
235 Federal Building, 180 West Main Street, Abingdon, VA 24210 .... (540) 628–8158
600 East Main Street, Richmond, VA 23219 .... (804) 771–2579
4900 World Trade Center, Norfolk, VA 23510 .... (540) 441–3079
1003 First Union Bank Building, 213 South Jefferson Street, Roanoke, VA 24011 (540) 857–2676

* * *

CHARLES S. ROBB, Democrat, of McLean, VA; born on June 26, 1939 in Phoenix, AZ; graduated from Mount Vernon High School, Fairfax, VA, 1957; B.B.A., University of Wisconsin, Madison, 1961; J.D., University of Virginia, 1973; served in U.S. Marine Corps, 1961–70; law clerk, U.S. Court of Appeals, 1973–74; associate, law firm of Williams, Connelly and Califano, 1974–77; partner, Hunton and Williams, 1986–88; elected Lieutenant Governor of Virginia, 1978–82; elected Governor of Virginia, 1982–86; member: American Bar Association, Virginia Bar Association, Virginia State bar, Council on Foreign Relations, Coalition for a Democratic Majority, Trilateral Commission, National Leadership Commission on Health Care, 1986–89; chairman, Democratic Leadership Council, 1986–88; National Commission on the Public Service, 1987–89; chairman, Jobs for America's Graduates, Inc., 1987–90; Center for Strategic and International Studies; Center for Democratic Institutions; Center for Democracy; assistant Senate Democratic whip for the South; cochairman, Business Roundtable; member: Committee on Foreign Relations, Armed Services Committee, Joint Economic Committee, Democratic Senate Campaign Committee, Select Committee on Intelligence; Deficit Reduction Caucus; ranking member, Senate Subcommittee on East Asian and Pacific Affairs; vice chairman of the Democratic Policy Committee, Congressional Competitiveness Committee, Congressional Arts Caucus; chairman, Democratic Senatorial Campaign Committee, 1991–92; married the former Lynda Bird Johnson, 1967; three children: Lucinda, Catherine and Jennifer; elected to the U.S. Senate on November 8, 1988 for the six-year term beginning January 3, 1989; re-elected November 8, 1994 for the six-year term beginning January 4, 1995.

Office Listings

http://www.senate.gov/~robb senator@robb.senate.gov

154 Russell Senate Office Building, Washington, DC 20510–4603 224–4024
FAX: 224–8689
Chief of Staff.—Thomas J. Lehner.
Legislative Director.—Ridge Schuyler.
Press Secretary.—Karen Gravois.
1001 East Broad Street, Richmond, VA 23219 .... (804) 771–2221
FAX: 771–8313
State Director.—Rob Jones.

REPRESENTATIVES

FIRST DISTRICT

HERBERT H. BATEMAN, Republican, of Newport News, VA; born in Elizabeth City, NC, August 7, 1928; College of William and Mary, Williamsburg, VA, B.A., 1949; Georgetown University Law Center, J.D., 1956; attorney; married the former Laura Yacobi, 1954; two children: Herbert H., Jr. and Laura Margaret; teacher at Hampton High School, 1949–51; enlisted in U.S. Air Force, 1951, discharged first lieutenant, 1953; law clerk for Judge Walter M. Bastian, U.S. Court of Appeals, District of Columbia Circuit, 1956–57; elected and reelected to the Virginia State Senate in 1967, 1971, 1975 and 1979; committee assignments: finance, courts of justice, transportation, and rehabilitation and social service; former member and chairman, agriculture, conservation and natural resources; member: Joint Legislative Audit and Review Commission; Coal and Energy Study Commission, 1979–82; chairman: Consumer Credit Study Committee, 1970–74; Study of Virginia Milk Commission, 1972–74; public positions: board of commissioners, Peninsula Ports Authority of Virginia, 1968–73; chairman, Peninsula Arena-Auditorium Authority; civic activities: board of directors, Peninsula Economic Development Council; general legal counsel, U.S. Jaycees, 1964–65; president, Virginia Jaycees, 1962–63; board of directors, Newport News Chapter, American Red Cross; president and campaign chairman, Peninsula United Fund; Braxton-Perkins Post, American Legion; professional and fraternal affiliations: Omicron Delta Kappa, Phi Delta Phi, Pi Kappa Alpha, and American Judicature Society; committees: National Security, Transportation and Infrastructure; subcommittees: chair, Subcommittee on Military Readiness, Merchant Marine Panel; cochair, Congressional Aviation and Space Caucus; Military Research and Development; Morale, Welfare and Recreation Panel; Surface Transportation; Water Resources and Environment; elected to the 98th Congress, November 2, 1982; reelected to each succeeding Congress.

Office Listings

http://www.house.gov/bateman

2350 Rayburn House Office Building, Washington, DC 20515–4601 225–4261
Administrative Assistant.—Daniel Scandling.
Executive Assistant.—Margaret C. Haar.
Legislative Director.—Peter Kirkham.
Suite 803, 739 Thimble Shoals Boulevard, Newport News, VA 23606 .... (757) 873–1132
District Director.—Dolores Benton.
4712 Southpoint Parkway, Fredericksburg, VA 22407 .... (540) 898–2975
Box 447, Accomack, VA 23301 .... (757) 787–7836

Counties: Accomack, Caroline, Gloucester, Hanover (part), James City (part), King George, Lancaster, Mathews, Middlesex, Northampton, Northumberland, Spotsylvania (part), Stafford, Westmoreland, York. CITIES AND TOWNSHIPS: Accomac, Achilles, Alfonso, Ark, Assawoman, Ashland, Atlantic, Bavon, Beaverdam, Beaverlett, Bellamy, Belle Haven, Bena, Birdsnest, Blakes, Bloxom, Bohannon, Bowling Green, Brooke, Burgess, Callao, Cape Charles, Capeville, Cheriton, Chincoteague, Craddockville, Coles Point, Colonial Beach, Corbin, Cardinal, Christchurch, Church View, Cobbs Creek, Dahlgren, Davis Wharf, Deltaville, Diggs, Dogue, Doswell, Dutton, Eastville, Exmore, Edwardsville, Foster, Franktown, Fredericksburg, Garrisonville, Gloucester, Gloucester Point, Greenbackville, Greenbush, Grimstead, Gwynn, Hacksneck, Hague, Hallwood, Hampton, Hanover, Harborton, Hardyville, Hartfield, Hartwood, Haynes, Heathsville, Horntown, Hudgins, Hyacinth, Irvington, Jamaica, James Store, Jamestown, Jamesville, Jenkins Bridge, Jersey, Kilmarnock, King George, Kinsale, Keller, Lackey, Ladysmith, Lancaster, Laneview, Lanexa, Lee Mont, Lewisetta, Lightfoot, Lively, Locust Hill, Locustville, Lottsburg, Machipongo, Mappsville, Marionville, Maryus, Mathews, Mechanicsville, Mears, Melfa, Merry Point, Miles, Milford Mobjack, Modest Town, Mollusk, Montross, Moon, Morattico, Mount Holly, Nassawadox, Naxera, Nelsonia, New Church, New Point, Newport News, Ninde, Norge, North, Nuttsville, Oak Hall, Oldhams, Onancock, Onemo, Onley, Ophelia, Ordinary, Oyster, Painter, Parksley, Partlow, Port Haywood, Port Royal, Pungoteague, Quinby, Rappahannock Academy, Redart, Reedville, Regina, Rescue, Rollins Fork, Ruby, Ruther Glen, Saluda, Sanford, Saxis, Schley, Seaford, Sealston, Seaview, Severn, Shiloh, Sparta, Spotsylvania, Stafford, Studley, Susan, Tangier, Tasley, Temperanceville, Toano, Topping, Townsend, Urbanna, Wachapreague, Wake, Wardtown, Ware Neck, Warner, Warter View, Wattsville, Weems, Weirwood, Westmoreland, White Marsh, White Stone, Wicomico, Wicomico Church, Williamsburg, Willis Wharf, Withams, Woodford, Woods Cross Roads, Yorktown, Zacata, and Zanoni. Population (1990), 562,758.

ZIP Codes: 22401, 22405–08, 22427, 22432, 22435, 22443, 22448, 22456, 22460, 22469, 22471, 22473, 22480, 22482, 22485, 22488, 22503, 22507, 22511, 22514, 22520, 22530, 22535, 22538, 22539, 22546, 22553–55, 22570, 22572, 22578–80, 23005, 23015, 23043, 23047, 23060–62, 23069, 23070–72, 23089–90, 23111, 23124, 23127, 23149, 23162,

23168, 23185–88, 23192, 23301–03, 23306–08, 23310, 23313, 23316, 23336–37, 23341, 23345, 23347, 23350, 23354, 23356–59, 23389, 23395–96, 23398–99, 23401, 23404–05, 23407–10, 23412–23, 23426–27, 23440–43, 23480, 23483, 23486, 23488, 23601–03, 23605–06, 23651, 23661–66, 23669, 23690, 23692–23693, 23696

* * *

SECOND DISTRICT

OWEN B. PICKETT, Democrat, of Virginia Beach, VA; born in Richmond, VA, on August 31, 1930; graduated, Henry Clay High School, Ashland, VA, 1947; B.S., Virginia Polytechnic Institute and State University, Blacksburg, VA, 1952; LL.B., University of Richmond Law School, VA, 1955; attorney (former senior partner in Pickett, Lyle, Siegel, Drescher and Croshaw, Virginia Beach, VA); admitted to the Virginia State bar in 1955 and commenced practice in Richmond; certified public accountant; served in the Virginia House of Delegates, 1972–86; committee assignments: Finance; Appropriations; National Security; Resources, Privileges and Elections; Health, Welfare and Institutions; Chesapeake and Its Tributaries; chairman, Appropriations Subcommittee on Retirement; chairman, Appropriations Subcommittee on Public Education; chairman, Health, Welfare and Institutions Subcommittee on Health Standards; chairman, Privileges and Elections Subcommittee on Election Laws; chairman, Virginia Democratic State Central Committee, 1980–82; chairman, Second Congressional District Democratic Committee, 1978–82; chairman, Democratic City Committee of Virginia Beach, 1967–72; executive committee, Southern Growth Policies Board; member: Virginia Bar Association, District of Columbia Bar Association, American Bar Association, Virginia Beach Bar Association (former president), Norfolk-Portsmouth Bar Association, Health Lawyers General Counsel Association, Virginia Trial Lawyers Association, Fourth Circuit Judicial Conference, Hampton Roads Maritime Association, American Institute of Certified Public Accountants, Oceana Lions Club, Princess Anne Ruritan Club (former president), Princess Anne Rotary Club (honorary member), Meals on Wheels Advisory Board; Mason, Scottish rite, Shriner; Jesters; married the former Sybil Catherine Kelly in 1952; three daughters: Laura, Karen, and Mary; elected to the 100th Congress on November 4, 1986; reelected to each succeeding Congress.

Office Listings

opickett@hr.house.gov

2430 Rayburn House Office Building, Washington, DC 20515–4602 225–4215
Staff Director.—Jeanne Evans.
Legislative Director.—Albert A. Oetken.
Director of Systems/Finance and Scheduler.—Donna T. Wooten.
Communications Director.—Morris Rowe.
112 East Little Creek Road, Suite 216, Norfolk, VA 23505 .... (804) 583–5892
2710 Virginia Beach Boulevard, Virginia Beach, VA 23452 .... (804) 486–3710

Counties: Norfolk (part), Virginia Beach (part). Population (1990), 562,276

ZIP Codes: 23450, 23451 (part), 23452, 23454–55, 23456 (part), 23457–59, 23462, 23464 (part), 23466–67, 23503, 23504 (part), 23505 (part), 23507 (part), 23508 (part), 23509 (part), 23510 (part), 23511, 23513 (part), 23517 (part), 23518, 23521

* * *

THIRD DISTRICT

ROBERT C. (BOBBY) SCOTT, Democrat, of Newport News, VA; born in Washington, DC, on April 30, 1947; graduated from Groton High School; B.A., Harvard University; J.D., Boston College Law School; served in the Massachusetts National Guard; attorney; admitted to the Virginia bar; Virginia House of Representatives, 1978–83; Virginia State Senate, 1983–92; member: Sigma Pi Phi Fraternity, Peninsula Chamber of Commerce, NAACP, Alpha Phi Alpha Fraternity, March of Dimes Board of Directors; Peninsula Legal Aid Center Board of Directors; elected on November 3, 1992 to the 103rd Congress; reelected to each succeeding Congress.

Office Listings

2464 Rayburn House Office Building, Washington, DC 20515–4603 225–8351
Chief of Staff.—Joni L. Ivey.
Senior Counsel.—B. Norris Vassar.
Legislative Assistants: Denise Forte, Theresa Thompson, Brian Woolfolk.
Communicatons Director.—Laurence Dillard.
2600 Washington Avenue, Suite 1010, Newport News, VA 23607 .... (804) 380–1000
FAX: 928–6694

501 North Second Street, Richmond, VA 23219–1321 .... (804) 644–4845
FAX: 644–5106

Counties: Charles City, Essex, Henrico (part), King and Queen, King William, New Kent, Prince George (part), and Surry. CITIES: Hampton (part), Hopewell (part), Newport News (part), Norfolk (part), Petersburg (part), Portsmouth (part), Richmond (part), and Suffolk (part). Population (1990), 562,431.

ZIP Codes: 22070 (part), 22436–39, 22454, 22460, 22472, 22476, 22504, 22509, 22548, 22559–60, 22570, 22572, 23009, 23011, 23023, 23029–30, 23060 (part), 23069, 23075 (part), 23085–86, 23089 (part), 23091, 23106, 23108, 23110, 23111 (part), 23115, 23124, 23126, 23140–41, 23147–48, 23150 (part), 23156, 23161, 23177, 23181, 23185 (part), 23201–19, 23220 (part), 23221 (part), 23222 (part), 23223 (part), 23224 (part), 23225 (part), 23227 (part), 23228 (part), 23231 (part), 23234 (part), 23240–41, 23260–61, 23435 (part), 23501, 23502 (part), 23504 (part), 23505 (part), 23506, 23507 (part), 23508 (part), 23509 (part), 23510 (part), 23513 (part), 23514, 23517 (part), 23518 (part), 23523, 23601 (part), 23602 (part), 23603 (part), 23604, 23605 (part), 23607 (part), 23608, 23612, 23661 (part), 23663 (part), 23664 (part), 23666 (part), 23669 (part), 23670, 23701 (part), 23702 (part), 23703 (part), 23704 (part), 23707 (part), 23803 (part), 23805 (part), 23839, 23846, 23860 (part), 23875 (part), 23881 (part), 23883, 23899

* * *

FOURTH DISTRICT

NORMAN SISISKY, Democrat, of Cavalier Farms, Petersburg, VA; born June 9, 1927, in Richmond; educated at John Marshall High School, Richmond; Virginia Commonwealth University, B.S. in business administration, 1949; married the former Rhoda Brown, 1949; four sons: Mark, Terry, Richard and Stuart; seven grandchildren; served in the U.S. Navy, 1945–46; Virginia House of Delegates, 1974–82; committee assignments: Appropriations; Health, Welfare and Institutions; Labor and Commerce; Finance; Chesapeake and Its Tributaries; former owner and former president, Pepsi-Cola Bottling Company of Petersburg, Inc.; former chairman of the board, National Soft Drink Association; past president, Appomattox Industrial Development Corporation; former member, Virginia State University Board of Visitors; former trustee, Virginia State University Foundation; former commissioner, Petersburg Hospital Authority; former director, Southside Virginia Emergency Crew and Community Resource Development Board; former member, Quad Cities Beautification Committee; recipient of Outstanding Service to Children in Virginia Award, 1978; honorary doctor of laws, Virginia State University; honorary doctor of humane letters, Virginia Commonwealth University; elected to the 98th Congress, November 2, 1982; reelected to each succeeding Congress.

Office Listings

2371 Rayburn House Office Building, Washington, DC 20515–4604 225–6365
FAX: 226–1170
Administrative Assistant.—Jan Faircloth.
Press Secretaries: Kelley Ross, Perry Floyd.
Executive Assistant/Scheduler.—Michelle Tolbert.
309 County Street, Portsmouth, VA 23704 .... (757) 393–2068
43 Rives Road, Petersburg, VA 23805 .... (757) 732–2544
Emporia Executive Center, 425 H South Main Street, Emporia, VA 23847 .... (757) 634–5575

Counties: Amelia, Brunswick, Chesterfield (part), Dinwiddie, Goochland, Greensville, Isle of Wight, Louisa, Nottoway, Powhatan, Prince George (part), Southampton, Sussex; cities and townships of Chesapeake, Colonial Heights, Emporia, Franklin, Hopewell (part), Petersburg (part), Portsmouth (part), Suffolk (part), Virginia Beach (part). Population (1990), 562,466.

ZIP Codes: 22942 (part), 22947, 23002, 23024 (part), 23038 (part), 23039, 23054, 23063, 23065, 23067, 23083, 23084 (part), 23093, 23101–03, 23105, 23113 (part), 23117, 23120 (part), 23129, 23139, 23146 (part), 23153, 23160, 23170, 23233 (part), 23304, 23314–15, 23320–23, 23324 (part), 23325 (part), 23326–28, 23397, 23424, 23430, 23432–34, 23435 (part), 23436–39, 23456 (part), 23464 (part), 23481, 23487, 23523 (part), 23700, 23701 (part), 23702 (part), 23704 (part), 23705, 23707 (part), 23801, 23803 (part), 23804, 23805 (part), 23821–22, 23824 (part), 23827–30, 23831 (part), 23832 (part), 23833, 23834 (part), 23837, 23840–45, 23847, 23850–51, 23856–57, 23859, 23860 (part), 23866–68, 23870, 23872–74, 23875 (part), 23876, 23878–79, 23881 (part), 23882, 23884–85, 23887–90, 23893–94, 23897–98, 23920 (part), 23922, 23930, 23938, 23955, 23966

* * *

FIFTH DISTRICT

VIRGIL H. GOODE, Jr., Democrat, of Rocky Mount, VA; born in Richmond, VA, October 17, 1946; B.A., University of Virginia, 1969; J.D., University of Virginia Law School, 1973; served in Virginia Army National Guard; admitted to the Virginia bar in 1973; attorney; member, Virginia State Senate, 1973–97; former member: Ruritan Chamber of Commerce, Jaycees; married Lucy Dodson Goode in 1991; one daughter, Catherine; elected to the 105th Congress.

Office Listings

1520 Longworth House Office Building, Washington, DC 20515–4605 225–4711
Chief of Staff.—Jim Severt. FAX: 225–5681
Legislative Assistant/Office Manager.—Lesley Robertson.
Legislative Assistant.—Tom Hance.
Virgil Goode Building, 70 East Court Street, Suite 215, Rocky Mount, VA 24151 (540) 484–1254
FAX: 484–1459

Counties: ALBEMARLE COUNTY; cities and townships of Charlotteville, Batesville, Covesville, Esmont, Greenwood, Hatton, Ivy, Keene, Keswick, North Garden, Scottsville. APPOMATTOX COUNTY; cities and townships of Appomattox, Evergreen, Pamplin, Spout Spring. BEDFORD COUNTY; cities and townships of Bedford, Big Island, Goodview, Coleman Falls, Forest, Goode, Huddleston, Lowry, Thaxton. BUCKINGHAM COUNTY; cities and townships of Andersonville, Arvonia, Buckingham, Dillwyn, Buckingham, New Canton. CAMPBELL COUNTY; cities and townships of Altavista, Brookneal, Concord, Evington, Gladys, Long Island, Lynch Station, Naruna, Rustburg. CHARLOTTE COUNTY; cities and townships of Barnesville, Charlotte Court House, Cullen, Drakes Branch, Keysville, Phenix, Randolph, Red House, Red Oak, Saxe, Wylliesburg. CUMBERLAND COUNTY; cities and townships of Carterville, Cumberland. DANVILLE COUNTY; city of Danville. FLUVANNA COUNTY; cities and townships of Bremo Bluff, Bybee, Carysbrook, Columbia, Fort Union, Kents Store, Palmyra, Troy. FRANKLIN COUNTY; cities and townships of Boones Mill, Callaway, Ferrum, Glade Hill, Henry, Redwood, Penhook, Rocky Mount, Union Hall, Waidsboro, Wirtz. HALIFAX COUNTY; cities and townships of Alton, Clover, Cluster Springs, Crystal Hall, Denniston, Halifax, Ingram, Lennig, Mayo, Nathalie, Republican Grove, Scottsburg, Turbeville, Vernon Hill, Virgilina. HENRY COUNTY; cities and townships of Axton, Bassett, Collinsville, Fieldale, Ridgeway, Spencer, Stanleytown. LUNENBURG COUNTY; cities and townships of Tamworth, Dundas, Fort Mitchell, Kenbridge, Lunenburg, Rehoboth, Victoria. MARTINSVILLE COUNTY; city of Martinsville. MECKLENBURG COUNTY; cities and townships of Baskerville, Blackridge, Boydton, Bracey, Chase City, Clarksville, Forksville, LaCross, Palmer Springs, Skipwith, South Hill, Union Level Buffalo Junction, Nelson. NELSON COUNTY; cities and townships of Afton, Arrington, Faber, Lovingston, Massies Mill, Nellysford, Montebello, Gladstone, Norwood, Piney River, Roseland, Schuyler, Shipman, Tye River, Tyro, Wingina. PATRICK COUNTY; cities and townships of Ararat, Claudville, Critz, Meadows of Dan, Patrick Springs, Stuart, Vesta, Woolwine. PITTSYLVANIA COUNTY; cities and townships of Blairs, Callands, Cascade, Chatham, Pittsville, Sandy Level, Dry Fork, Gretna, Hurt, Java, Keeling, Ringgold, Sutherlin. PRINCE EDWARD COUNTY; cities and townships of Green Bay, Farmville, Darlington, Heights, Green Bay, Hampden-Sydney, Meherrin, Prospect, Rice, South Boston. Population (1990), 562,268.

ZIP Codes: 22920 (part), 22922 (part), 22938 (part), 22942 (part), 22949, 22951 (part), 22952 (part), 22954, 22958, 22963–64, 22967 (part), 22969 (part), 22971, 22974 (part), 22976, 23004, 23022, 23027, 23038 (part), 23040, 23055, 23083 (part), 23084, 23123, 23822, 23901, 23911, 23915, 23916 (part), 23917, 23919 (part), 23920 (part), 23921, 23923–24, 23927, 23934–44, 23947, 23950, 23952, 23954, 23957–60, 23962–64, 23966–68, 23970, 23973–74, 23976, 24053–55, 24059 (part), 24065, 24067, 24069, 24076–78, 24079 (part), 24082, 24088–89, 24092, 24095, 24101 (part), 24102, 24104, 24105 (part), 24112–15, 24120 (part), 24121–22, 24133, 24137, 24139, 24146, 24148, 24151, 24161, 24165, 24168, 24171, 24174, 24176 (part), 24177–78, 24179 (part), 24184–85, 24312 (part), 24317, 24325, 24328, 24333 (part), 24343, 24348 (part), 24351–52, 24380 (part), 24381, 24464, 24501 (part), 24502 (part), 24503 (part), 24517, 24520, 24521 (part), 24522–23, 24526–31, 24534–36, 24538–41, 24549–51, 24553 (part), 24554, 24556–58, 24563–66, 24568–71, 24576–77, 24580–81, 24585–86, 24588–89, 24590 (part), 24592–94, 24596–99

* * *

SIXTH DISTRICT

ROBERT W. (BOB) GOODLATTE, Republican, of Roanoke, VA; born on September 22, 1952 in Holyoke, MA; B.A., Bates College, Lewiston, ME, 1974; J.D., Washington and Lee University, 1977; Massachusetts bar, 1977, Virginia bar, 1978; began practice in Roanoke, VA, 1979; district director for Congressman M. Caldwell Butler, 1977–79; attorney, sole practitioner, 1979–81; partner, 1981–92; chairman, sixth district, VA, Republican Committee, 1983–88; member, Civitan Club of Roanoke (president, 1989–90); former member, Building Better Boards Advisory Council; member: Parent Teachers Association, Fishburn Park Elementary School; assistant majority whip; member: House Republican Policy Committee; committees: Judiciary, Agriculture; subcommittees: chairman, Department Operations, Nutrition and Foreign Agriculture; Courts and Intellectual Property; Livestock, Dairy and Poultry; The Constitution; married in 1974 to Maryellen Flaherty; two children: Jennifer and Robert; elected on November 3, 1992 to the 103rd Congress; reelected to each succeeding Congress.

Office Listings

http://www.house.gov/goodlatte talk2bob@hr.house.gov

123 Cannon House Office Building, Washington, DC 20515–4606 225–5431
Administrative Assistant.—Tim Phillips. FAX: 225–9681
Legislative Counsel.—David Lehman.
Legislative Assistant.—Kevin Kramp.
10 Franklin Road, SE, 540 Crestar Plaza, Roanoke, VA 24011 .... (703) 857–2672
District Director.—Pete Larkin. FAX: 857–2675
919 Main Street, Suite 300, Lynchburg, VA 24504 .... (804) 845–8306
FAX: 845–8245
114 North Central Avenue, Staunton, VA 24401 .... (703) 885–3861
FAX: 885–3930
2 South Main Street, First Floor, Suite A, Harrisonburg, VA 22801 .... (703) 432–2391
FAX: 432–6593

Counties: Alleghany, Amherst, Augusta, Bath, Bedford (part), Botetourt, Highland, Roanoke (part), Rockbridge, and Rockingham (part). CITIES: Buena Vista, Clifton Forge, Covington, Harrisonburg, Lexington, Lynchburg, Roanoke, Salem, Staunton, and Waynesboro. Population (1990), 562,572

ZIP Codes: 22801, 22811–12, 22815, 22820–21, 22827 (part), 22830–34, 22840–41, 22843, 22846, 22848, 22849 (part), 22850 (part), 22853 (part), 22920 (part), 22922 (part), 22939, 22951 (part), 22952 (part), 22967 (part), 22980, 24001–20, 24022–38, 24051 (part), 24059 (part), 24064, 24066, 24070 (part), 24077, 24079 (part), 24083, 24085, 24090, 24101 (part), 24130, 24153, 24175, 24176 (part), 24179 (part), 24401, 24411–13, 24415–16, 24420–22, 24426 (part), 24430–33, 24435, 24437–42, 24444–45, 24448–50, 24457–60, 24463, 24465, 24467–69, 24471–77, 24479, 24482–87, 24501 (part), 24502 (part), 24503 (part), 24504–06, 24521 (part), 24533, 24553 (part), 24555, 24572, 24574, 24578–79, 24595, 26807 (part)

* * *

SEVENTH DISTRICT

TOM J. BLILEY, JR., Republican, of Richmond, VA; born in Chesterfield County, January 28, 1932; graduated, Benedictine High School, 1948; B.A., history, Georgetown University, 1952; served three years in the U.S. Navy, leaving active duty with the rank of lieutenant; elected to Richmond City Council, 1968; appointed vice mayor, 1968; reelected to council and appointed mayor, 1970–77; former board member, National League of Cities; past president, Virginia Municipal League; former board member, Metropolitan Richmond Chamber of Commerce; board member, Central Richmond Association; Virginia Home for Boys, board of governors; former board member, Crippled Children's Hospital; former member, board of visitors, Virginia Commonwealth University; former board member, Southern Bank and Trust Company; married the former Mary Virginia Kelley, 1957; two children: Mary Vaughan and T.J. (Jerry) III; elected to the 97th Congress, November 4, 1980; reelected to each succeeding Congress.

Office Listings

http://www.house.gov/bliley

2409 Rayburn House Office Building, Washington, DC 20515–4607 225–2815
Chief of Staff.—Linda Pedigo.
Legislative Director.—Brent Del Monte.
Suite 101, 4914 Fitzhugh Avenue, Richmond, VA 23230 .... (804) 771–2809
District Office Representative.—Kathy Costigan.
Suite 207, Culpeper Office Park, 763 Madison Road, Culpeper, VA 22701 .... (540) 825–8960
District Office Representative.—Anita Essalih.

Counties: Albemarle (part), Chesterfield (part), Culpeper, Greene, Hanover (part), Henrico (part), Madison, Orange, Spotsylvania (part). CITY: Richmond (part). Population (1990), 652,643.

ZIP Codes: 22407 (part), 22433, 22508, 22534, 22542, 22553 (part), 22565, 22567–68, 22701, 22709, 22711, 22713–15, 22718–19, 22721–27, 22729–33, 22735–38, 22740 (part), 22741, 22743, 22748, 22901 (part), 22903 (part), 22923, 22929, 22931–32, 22935–37, 22940, 22942 (part), 22943, 22945–48, 22953, 22957, 22959–60, 22965, 22968, 22972–73, 22987, 22989, 23005 (part), 23015, 23060 (part), 23075 (part), 23111 (part), 23112, 23113 (part), 23120 (part), 23146 (part), 23150 (part), 23192, 23220 (part), 23221 (part), 23222 (part), 23223 (part), 23224 (part), 23225 (part), 23226, 23227 (part), 23228 (part), 23229–30, 29231 (part), 23233 (part), 23234 (part), 23235–37, 23250, 23255, 23288, 23294, 23831 (part), 23832 (part), 23834 (part)

* * *

EIGHTH DISTRICT

JAMES P. MORAN, Democrat, of Alexandria, VA; born May 16, 1945, in Buffalo, NY; College of Holy Cross, B.A.; Bernard Baruch Graduate School of Finance—City University of New York; University of Pittsburgh Graduate School of Public and International Affairs, M.P.A.; University of Southern California Graduate School, Urban Policy and Management; formerly an investment broker with A.G. Edwards and Sons, Inc.; staff member on Senate Appropriations Committee; budgetary and fiscal policy specialist for Library of Congress; comptroller for the U.S. Department of Health, Education and Welfare; auditor, accountant, and senior budget analyst for U.S. Department of Health, Education and Welfare; served on city council of Alexandria, 1979–82; vice mayor of Alexandria from 1982–84, mayor from 1985–90; elected to the 102nd Congress, November 6, 1990; reelected to each succeeding Congress; married to the former Mary Howard; five children: James, Michael, Patrick, Mary and Dorothy.

Office Listings

http://www.house.gov/moran jim.moran@hr.house.gov

1214 Longworth House Office Building, Washington, DC 20515–4608 225–4376
FAX: 225–0017

Chief of Staff.—Paul Reagan.
Legislative Director.—Michael Brown.
Scheduling Secretary.—Mary Miller.
5115 Franconia Road, Suite B, Alexandria, VA 22302 .... (703) 971–4700
District Manager.—Susie Warner.

Counties: Arlington, Fairfax (part). CITIES: Alexandria, Falls Church. Population (1990), 562,484.

ZIP Codes: 22003 (part), 22015, 22021 (part), 22031 (part), 22039, 22040, 22041 (part), 22042 (part), 22043 (part), 22044 (part), 22046 (part), 22060, 22067, 22079, 22101 (part), 22102 (part), 22106, 22121–22, 22150, 22151 (part), 22152 (part), 22153, 22156, 22158–59, 22161, 22201–07, 22209–11, 22213, 22215–19, 22222, 22226–7, 22229, 22234, 22302–10, 22311 (part), 22312 (part), 22313–14, 22333–34, 22336

* * *

NINTH DISTRICT

RICK BOUCHER, Democrat, of Abingdon, VA; born in Washington County, VA, August 1, 1946; graduated from Abingdon High School in 1964; B.A. degree from Roanoke College in 1968; J.D. degree from the University of Virginia School of Law in 1971; associate, Milbank, Tweed, Hadley and McCloy, New York, NY; partner, Boucher and Boucher, Abingdon, VA; elected to the Virginia State Senate in 1975 and reelected in 1979; former chairman of the Oil and Gas Subcommittee of the Virginia Coal and Energy Commission; former member: Virginia State Crime Commission, Virginia Commission on Interstate Cooperation, Law and Justice Committee of the National Conference of State Legislatures; member: board of directors of the First Virginia Bank, Damascus; Abingdon United Methodist Church; Kappa Alpha order; Phi Alpha Delta legal fraternity; American Bar Association, Virginia Bar Association, Association of the Bar of the City of New York; recipient of the Abingdon Jaycees Outstanding Young Businessman Award, 1975; member: Committee on Commerce, assistant whip; Committee on the Judiciary; elected to the 98th Congress on November 2, 1982; reelected to each succeeding Congress.

Office Listings

http://www.house.gov/boucher ninthnet@hr.house.gov

2245 Rayburn House Office Building, Washington, DC 20515–4609 225–3861
Chief of Staff.—Andy Wright. FAX: 225–0442
Deputy Chief of Staff/Comunications Director.—Joe Shoemaker.
188 East Main Street, Abingdon, VA 24210 .... (703) 628–1145
District Administrator.—Donna M. Stanley.
311 Shawnee Avenue East, Big Stone Gap, VA 24219 .... (703) 523–5450
P.O. Box 1268, 112 North Washington Avenue, Pulaski, VA 24301 .... (703) 980–4310

Counties: Bland, Buchanan, Carroll, Craig, Dickenson, Floyd, Giles, Grayson, Lee, Montgomery, Pulaski, Roanoke (part), Russell, Scott, Smyth, Tazewell, Washington, Wise, Wythe. CITIES: Bristol, Galax, Norton, and Radford. Population (1990), 562,380.

ZIP Codes: 24051 (part), 24058, 24059 (part), 24060, 24068, 24070 (part), 24072–73, 24079 (part), 24084, 24086–87, 24091, 24093–94, 24105 (part), 24108, 24111, 24120 (part), 24124, 24126–29, 24131–32, 24134, 24136, 24138, 24141–43, 24147, 24149–50, 24162, 24167, 24201, 24210, 24215–21, 24224–26, 24228, 24230, 24236–37, 24239, 24243–46, 24248–51, 24256, 24258, 24260, 24263, 24265–66, 24269–73, 24277, 24279–83, 24285, 24289, 24292–93, 24301, 24311, 24312 (part), 24313–16, 24318–19, 24321–24, 24326–27, 24329–30, 24333 (part), 24340, 24347, 24348 (part), 24350, 24354, 24360–61, 24363, 24366, 24368, 24370, 24373–75, 24377–79, 24380 (part), 24382, 24601–09, 24611–14, 24616, 24618–20, 24622, 24624, 24627–28, 24630–31, 24633–35, 24637, 24639–41, 24646–47, 24649, 24651, 24655–59

* * *

TENTH DISTRICT

FRANK R. WOLF, Republican, of Vienna, VA; born in Philadelphia, PA, January 30, 1939; B.A., Pennsylvania State University, 1961; LL.B., Georgetown University Law School, 1965; served in the U.S. Army Signal Corps (Reserves); lawyer, admitted to the Virginia State bar; legislative assistant for former U.S. Congressman Edward G. Biester, Jr., 1968–71; assistant to Secretary of the Interior Rogers C.B. Morton, 1971–74; Deputy Assistant Secretary for Congressional and Legislative Affairs, Department of the Interior, 1974–75; member, Vienna Presbyterian Church; married to the former Carolyn Stover; five children: Frank, Jr., Virginia, Anne, Brenda, and Rebecca; elected to the 97th Congress, November 4, 1980; reelected to each succeeding Congress.

Office Listings
http://www.house.gov/wolf

241 Cannon House Office Building, Washington, DC 20515–4610 225–5136
FAX: 225–0437
Legislative Director.—Janet Shaffron.
Appropriations Associate Staff.—Lori-Beth Feld Hua.
Press Secretary.—David Whitestone.
13873 Park Center Road, Suite 130, Herndon, VA 20171 .... (703) 709–5800
110 North Cameron Street, Winchester, VA 22601 .... (540) 667–0900

Counties: Clarke, Fairfax (part), Fauquier, Frederick, Loudoun, Page, Prince William (part), Rappahannock, Rockingham (part), Shenandoah, Warren. CITIES: Manassas, Manassas Park, and Winchester. Population (1990), 562,664.

ZIP Codes: 20101–02, 20106–10, 20111 (part), 20112 (part), 20113, 20115–22, 20124 (part), 20128–32, 20134–44, 20146–48, 20151–53, 20155–56, 20158, 20160, 20164–69, 20170 (part), 20171–72, 20175–78, 20180–82, 20184–88, 20191, 22028 (part), 22030 (part), 22033, 22039 (part), 22066, 22102 (part), 22124, 22181 (part), 22182 (part), 22192 (part), 22601–64, 22712, 22716, 22720, 22728, 22734 (part), 22739, 22740 (part), 22742, 22746 (part), 22747–48

* * *

ELEVENTH DISTRICT

THOMAS M. DAVIS, Republican, of Falls Church, VA; born in Minot, ND, on January 5, 1949; graduated, U.S. Capitol Page School; graduated, Amherst College with honors in political science; law degree, University of Virginia; attended officer candidate school; served in the U.S. Army Reserves; member: Fairfax County Board of Supervisors, 1980–94, chairman, 1992–94; vice president and general counsel of PRC, Inc., Mclean, VA; past president, Washington Metropolitan Council of Governments; founding member and past president, Bailey's Crossroads Rotary Club; committees: Transportation and Infrastructure; Science; Government Reform and Oversight; chairman, District of Columbia Subcommittee; married the former Petty Rantz, 1973; three children: Carlton, Pamela and Shelley; elected to the 104th Congress; reelected to the 105th Congress.

Office Listings
http://www.house.gov/tomdavis tomdavis@hr.house.gov

224 Cannon House Office Building, Washington, DC 20515–4611 225–1492
FAX: 225–3071
Chief of Staff.—John Hishta.
Legislative Director.—Chip Highsmith.
Press Secretary.—John Hishta.
Executive Assistant.—Hana Brilliant.
7018 Evergreen Court, Annandale, VA 22003 .... (703) 916–9610
FAX: 916–9617
District Director.—Linda O'Meara.
Herndon Town Hall, 730 Elden Street, Second Floor, Herndon, VA 22070 .... (703) 437–1726
FAX: 437–3004
Constituent Service Director.—Ann Wharam.
Dominion Center, 13554 Minnieville Road, Woodbridge, VA 22192 .... (703) 590–4599
FAX: 590–4740
Constituent Service Director.—George Massey.

Counties: Fairfax (part), Prince William (part). CITIES: Reston, Herndon, Vienna, city of Fairfax, Annandale, Burke, Fairfax Station, Occoquan, Woodbridge, Lake Ridge, Dale City, Dumfries, Quantico. Population (1990), 562,497.

ZIP Codes: 22003, 22009, 22015 (part), 22020 (part), 22024 (part), 22026 (part), 22027, 22030 (part), 22031–32, 22035, 22038, 22039 (part), 22041 (part), 22042 (part), 22043 (part), 22044 (part), 22046 (part), 22070 (part), 22071 (part), 22079 (part), 22090–91, 22094, 22102 (part), 22111 (part), 22116, 22124 (part), 22125, 22134, 22151 (part), 22152 (part), 22172, 22180, 22181 (part), 22182 (part), 22183, 22191, 22192 (part), 22193 (part), 22194, 22302 (part), 22311 (part), 22312 (part)

WASHINGTON

(Population 1995, 5,431,000)

SENATORS

SLADE GORTON, Republican, of Seattle, WA; born January 8, 1928, in Chicago, IL; graduated from high school in Evanston, IL, 1945; enlisted in U.S. Army, 1945–46; A.B., international relations, Dartmouth, 1950; LL.B., with honors, Columbia University Law School, New York, NY, 1953; admitted to bar, Washington State, 1953; service in U.S. Air Force, 1953–56, retired colonel, USAF Reserves; elected to Washington State House of Representatives, 46th District, Seattle, 1958; reelected 1960, 1962, 1964, 1966, (majority leader) 1967–68; elected Washington State Attorney General, 1968; reelected 1972, 1976; member, National Association of Attorneys General, 1969–80, president 1976–77; Wyman Award winner, 1980; member: President's Consumer Advisory Council, 1975–77; Washington State Law and Justice Commission, 1969–80, chairman 1969–70; State Criminal Justice Training Commission, 1969–80, chairman 1969–76; married Sally Clark of Selah, WA, 1958; three children: Tod, Sarah Jane, and Rebecca Lynn; committees: Appropriations; Budget; Commerce, Science, and Transportation; Energy and Natural Resources; Indian Affairs; elected to the U.S. Senate, November 4, 1980, for the six-year term beginning January 3, 1981; unsuccessful candidate for reelection, November 4, 1986; elected to the U.S. Senate on November 8, 1988 for the six-year term beginning January 3, 1989.

Office Listings

http://www.senate.gov/~gorton

730 Hart Senate Office Building, Washington, DC 20510–4701 224–3441
Chief of Staff.—Tony Williams. FAX: 224–9393
Administrative Assistant/Legislative Director.—Sam Spina.
Press Secretary.—Melissa Dollaghan.
10900 N.E. Fourth Street, Room 2110, Bellevue, WA 98004 .... (206) 451–0103
State Director.—Veda Jellen. FAX: 451–0234
697 U.S. Courthouse, West 920 Riverside, Spokane, WA 99201 .... (509) 353–2507
FAX: 353–2547
Federal Office Building, 500 West 12th Street, Vancouver, WA 98660 .... (360) 696–7838
FAX: 696–7844
420 The Tower, 402 East Yakima Avenue, Yakima, WA 98901 .... (509) 248–8084
FAX: 248–8167
1530 Grandridge Boulevard, Suite 212, Kennewick, WA 99336 .... (509) 783–0640
FAX: 735–7559

* * *

PATTY MURRAY, Democrat, of Seattle, WA; born October 11, 1950 in Seattle; B.A., Washington State University, 1972; teacher, lobbyist; school board member, 1985–89; Washington State Senate, 1988–92; Shoreline Community Cooperative School, parent volunteer, 1977–84; Shoreline Community College, parent education instructor for Crystal Springs, 1984–87; citizen lobbyist for environmental and educational issues, 1983–88; elected: board of directors, Shoreline School District, 1985–89, two-term president and legislative representative; Washington State Senate, first district, 1988–92; Washington State Legislator of the Year, 1990; Democratic whip, 1990–92; member: Education, Ways and Means, Commerce and Labor committees; Domestic Timber Processing Select Committee; Open Government Select Committee; chairperson, School Transportation Safety Task Force; married Rob Murray, 1972; two children: Randy and Sara; committees: Appropriations, Budget, Labor and Human Resources, Veterans' Affairs, Ethics; elected to the U.S. Senate, November 3, 1992, for the six-year term beginning January 3, 1993.

Office Listings

http://www.senate.gov/~murray senate_murray@murray.senate.gov

111 Russell Senate Office Building, Washington, DC 20510–4704 224–2621
Chief of Staff.—Patricia Akiyama. FAX: 224–0238
Legislative Director.—Ric Ilgenfritz. TDD: 224–4430
Press Secretary.—Rex Carney.
2988 Jackson Federal Building, 915 Second Avenue, Seattle, WA 98174 .... (206) 553–5545
State Director.—Dan Evans.
140 Federal Building, 500 West 12th, Vancouver, WA 98660 .... (206) 696–7797

West 601 First Avenue, Spokane, WA 99201 .... (509) 624–9515
2930 Wetmore Avenue, Suite 903, Everett, WA 98201 .... (206) 259–6515
FAX: 259–7152
402 E. Yakima Avenue, Suite 390, Yakima, WA 98901 .... (509) 453–7462
FAX: 453–7731

REPRESENTATIVES

FIRST DISTRICT

RICK WHITE, Republican, of Bainbridge Island, WA; born in Bloomington, IN, on November 6, 1953; B.A., Dartmouth College, Hanover, NH, 1975; attended Pantheon-Sorbonne in Paris; J.D., Georgetown University, Washington, DC, 1980; partner, Perkins Coie law firm; private sector jobs ranging from dock foreman to assembly line worker to grill cook; founder and director, Books for Kids, (a literacy program); services: YMCA's Indian Guides program, Law Explorers advisor for Boy Scouts; elder, Rolling Bay Presbyterian Church; member of Leadership Tomorrow; leader, Republican Party Farm Team (encouraging young professionals to get involved in the party); served on Queen Anne Community Council, 1986–88; delegate to various districts; committee: Commerce; subcommittees: Telecommunications and Finance; Commerce; Trade, and Hazardous Materials; married Vikki Kennedy, 1982; four children: Kathleen, Emily, Charlotte and Richard; elected to the 104th Congress; reelected to the 105th Congress.

Office Listings

http://www.house.gov/white

116 Cannon House Office Building, Washington, DC 20515 225–6311
Administrative Assistant.—Michael Gallagher.
Legislative Director.—Leslie Dunlap.
Scheduler/Office Manager.—Amonica Richardson.
Press Secretary.—Connie Correll.
21905 64th Avenue West, Suite 101, Mountlake Terrace, WA 98043 .... (206) 640–0233
Chief of Staff.—Randy Pepple.
District Director.—Roberta Clark.
1050 NE Hostmark Street, Poulsbo, WA 98370 .... (800) 422–5521

Counties: King (part), Kitsap (part), Snohomish (part). CITIES AND TOWNSHIPS: Bainbridge Island, Bellevue, Bothell, Bremerton, Edmonds, Everett, Hansville, Indianola, Keyport, Kingston, Kirkland, Lynnwood, Mountlake Terrace, Port Gamble, Poulsbo, Redmond, Seabeck, Seattle, Silverdale, Suquamish, Woodinville, Medina. Population (1990), 540,745.

ZIP Codes: 98004 (part), 98005 (part), 98007 (part), 98008 (part), 98009, 98011, 98012 (part), 98020, 98021 (part), 98026, 98033–34, 98036, 98037 (part), 98039, 98041, 98043, 98046, 98052 (part), 98061, 98072 (part), 98073, 98083, 98103 (part), 98110, 98117 (part), 98133 (part), 98155 (part), 98177, 98204 (part), 98208 (part), 98272 (part), 98275 (part), 98290 (part), 98310 (part), 98312 (part), 98314–15, 98340, 98342, 98345–46, 98364, 98370, 98380 (part), 98383, 98392–93

* * *

SECOND DISTRICT

JACK METCALF, Republican, of Langley, WA; born in Marysville, WA, November 30, 1927; B.A., Pacific Lutheran University, 1951; University of Washington, 1966; owner of the Log Castle Bed and Breakfast, Langley; teacher, Everett High School; U.S. Army, 1946–47; member: U.S. Fish and Wildlife Service patrol boat skipper with U.S. Marshal Authority, 1947–48; United We Stand America, Concord Coalition, South Whidby Washington Historical Society, South Whidby Washington Kiwanis, Wildcat Steelhead Club, Back Country Horsemen—Skagit County Chapter; Washington State House, 1960–64; Washington State Senate, 1966–74, 1980–92; Washington State Senate assistant Republican whip; chairman, Senate Environmental and Natural Resources Committee, 1988–92; married Norma Metcalf, 1948; four children: Marta, Gayle, Ann and Lea; elected to the 104th Congress; reelected to the 105th Congress.

Office Listings

1510 Longworth House Office Building, Washington, DC 20515–4702 225–2605
Chief of Staff.—Lew Moore. FAX: 225–4420
Deputy Chief of Staff.—Chris Strow.
Legislative Director.—Eric Strom.
Legislative Assistants: Vergil Cabasco, Jeff Mackey, Brad Marshall.
Press Secretary.—Kevin McDermott.
2930 Wetmore Avenue, Suite 901, Everett, WA 98201 .... (206) 252–3188

District Director.—Roy Atwood. (800) 562–1385
Office Manager.—Norma Smith.
322 North Commercial Street, Suite 203, Bellingham, WA 98225 .... (360) 733–4500
Office Manager.—Fairalee Markusen.

Counties: Island, San Juan, Skagit, Snohomish (part), and Wetcom. CITIES AND TOWNSHIPS: Bellingham, Everett, Mt. Vernon. Population (1990), 540,739.

ZIP Codes: 98101, 98116 (part), 98200 (part), 98201, 98203 (part), 98204–07, 98208 (part), 98220–23, 98225–27, 98230, 98232–33, 98235–41, 98243–53, 98255–64, 98266–68, 98270, 98272–73, 98276–81, 98283–84, 98286–87, 98290 (part), 98292–95, 98297, 98305, 98320, 98324–26, 98331, 98334, 98339, 98343, 98350, 98357–58, 98362, 98365, 98368, 98376, 98381–82, 98520 (part), 98524, 98526, 98535–36, 98541 (part), 98546, 98548, 98550 (part), 98552, 98557, 98560, 98562–63, 98566, 98569, 98571, 98575, 98583–84, 98587–88, 98592

* * *

THIRD DISTRICT

LINDA A. SMITH, Republican, of Vancouver, WA; born July 16, 1950 in LaJunta, CO; graduated, Fort Vancouver High School, Vancouver, 1968; attends Glad Tidings Church, Vancouver; manager of seven tax preparation offices for nine years; committees: Resources, Endangered Species Act Task Force, Small Business; subcommittees: National Parks and Public Lands; Fisheries, Wildlife and Oceans; Procurement, Exports and Business Opportunities; chairperson, Subcommittee on Taxation and Finance; Washington State Representative, 1983–86; Washington State Senate, 1987–94; chairperson, Children and Family Services Committee; vice chairperson, Republican Caucus; author: Washington State Initiative 134—The Fair Campaign Practices Act—and Washington State Initiative 601; married Vernon Thomas Smith, 1968; two children: Sheri and Robert; elected to the 104th Congress; reelected to the 105th Congress.

Office Listings

http://www.house.gov/lindasmith asklinda@hr.house.gov

1217 Longworth House Office Building, Washington, DC 20515–4703 226–3536
Chief of Staff.—Patrick Fiske. FAX: 225–3478
Legislative Director.—Ted Case.
Executive Assistant.—Shirley Smits.
719 Sleater-Kinney Road, Suite 214, Lacey, WA 98503 .... (360) 923–9393
FAX: 923–9429
1220 Main Street, Suite 310, Vancouver, WA 98660 .... (360) 695–6292
FAX: 695–6197

Counties: CLARK COUNTY; cities and townships of Amboy, Ariel, Battle Ground, Brush Prairie, Camas, Heisson, La Center, Ridgefield, Vancouver, Washougal, Woodland, Yacolt. COWLITZ COUNTY; cities and townships of Carrolls, Castle Rock, Cougar, Kalama, Kelso, Longview, Ryderwood, Silverlake, Toutle. GRAYS HARBOR COUNTY (part); cities and townships of Cosmopolis, Elma, Grayland, McCleary, Malone, Oakville, Satsop, Westport. KLICKITAT COUNTY (part); cities and townships of Appleton, Bingen, Dallesport, Husum, Klickitat, Lyle, Trout Lake, Wahkiacus, White Salmon, Wishram. LEWIS COUNTY; cities and townships of Adna, Centralia, Chehalis, Cinebar, Curtis, Doty, Ethel, Galvin, Glenoma, Mineral, Morton, Mossyrock, Napavine, Onalaska, Packwood, Pe Ell, Randle, Salkum, Silver Creek, Toledo, Vader, Winlock. PACIFIC COUNTY; cities and townships of Bay Center, Chinook, Ilwaco, Lebam, Long Beach, Menlo, Nahcotta, Naselle, Ocean Park, Oysterville, Raymond, Seaview, South Bend, Tokeland. PIERCE COUNTY; township of Elbe. SKAMANIA COUNTY; cities and townships of Carson, North Bonneville, Stevenson, Underwood. THURSTON COUNTY (part); cities and townships of Littlerock, Olympia, and Rochester. WAHKIAKUM COUNTY; cities and townships of Cathlamet, Grays River, Rosburg, Skamokawa. Population (1990), 540,745.

ZIP Codes: 98330, 98336, 98355–56, 98361, 98377, 98501–03, 98506, 98522, 98527, 98531–33, 98537–39, 98541–42, 98544, 98547, 98554, 98556–57, 98559, 98561, 98564–65, 98568, 98570, 98572, 98577, 98579 98581–83, 98585–86, 98590–91, 98593, 98595–96, 98601–07, 98609–12, 98614, 98616–17, 98621–26, 98628–29, 98631–32, 98635, 98637–45, 98647–51, 98660–66, 98668, 98670–75, 98682, 98684–86

* * *

FOURTH DISTRICT

DOC HASTINGS, Republican, of Pasco, WA; born in Spokane, WA, on February 7, 1941; graduated, Pasco High School, 1959; attended Columbia Basin College and Central Washington State University, Ellensborg, WA; U.S. Army Reserves, 1963–69; president, Columbia Basin Paper and Supply; board of directors, Yakima Federal Savings and Loan; member: Washington State House of Representatives, 1979–87; Republican Caucus chairman, assistant majority leader, National Platform Committee, 1984; president: Pasco Chamber of Commerce, Pasco Downtown Development Association; Pasco Jaycees (chamber president); committees: National Security, Resources; chairman, Franklin County Republican Central Committee, 1974–78; delegate,

Republican National Convention, 1976–84; married Claire Hastings, 1967; three children: Kirsten, Petrina and Colin; elected to the 104th Congress; reelected to the 105th Congress.

Office Listings

1229 Longworth House Office Building, Washington, DC 20515 225–5816
Administrative Assistant.—Ed Cassidy. FAX: 225–3251
Scheduler/Office Manager.—Linda Bradley.
Press Secretary.—Sheila Riggs.
320 North Johnson, Suite 500, Kennewick, WA 99336 .... (509) 783–0310
FAX: 735–9573
302 East Chestnut, Yakima, WA 98901 .... (509) 452–3243
FAX: 452–3438
25 North Wenatchee Avenue, Suite 202, Wenatchee, WA 98801 .... (509) 662–4294
FAX: 662–4295

Counties: ADAMS COUNTY; city of Othello. BENTON COUNTY; cities and townships of Benton City, Kennewick, Paterson, Plymouth, Prosser, Richland, West Richland. CHELAN COUNTY; cities and townships of Ardenvoir, Cashmere, Chelan, Chelan Falls, Dryden, Entiat, Leavenworth, Malaga, Manson, Monitor, Peshastin, Stehekin, Wenatchee. DOUGLAS COUNTY; cities and townships of Bridgeport, Leahy, Mansfield, Orondo, Palisades, Rock Island, Waterville, Wenatchee. FRANKLIN COUNTY; cities and townships of Connell, Eltopia, Kahlotus, Mesa, Pasco, Windust. GRANT COUNTY; cities and townships of Beverly, Coulee City, Electric City, Ephrata, George, Grand Coulee, Hartline, Marlin, Mattawa, Moses Lake, Quincy, Royal City, Soap Lake, Stratford, Warden, Wilson Creek. KITTITAS COUNTY; cities and townships of Cle Elum, Easton, Ellensburg, Hyak, Kittitas, Ronald, Roslyn, South Cle Elum, Thorp, Vantage. KLICKITAT COUNTY; cities and townships of Alderdale, Appleton, Bickleton, Bingen, Centerville, Dallesport, Glenwood, Goldendale, Husum, Klickitat, Lyle, Roosevelt, Trout Lake, White Salmon, Wishram. OKANOGAN COUNTY; cities and townships of Brewster, Carlton, Conconully, Coulee Dam, Elmer City, Loomis, Malott, Methow, Nespelem, Okanogan, Omak, Oroville, Pateros, Riverside, Tonasket, Twisp, Wauconda, Winthrop. YAKIMA COUNTY; cities and townships of Brownstown, Buena, Cowiche, Grandview, Granger, Harrah, Mabton, Moxee, Naches, Outlook, Parker, Selah, Sunnyside, Tieton, Toppenish, Wapato, White Swan, Yakima, Zillah. Population (1990), 540,744.

ZIP Codes: 98068, 98605, 98613, 98619, 98620, 98801–02, 98807, 98811–17, 98819, 98821–24, 98826–34, 98836–37, 98840–41, 98843–53, 98855–60, 98862, 98901–04, 98907–09, 98920–23, 98925–26, 98930, 98932–44, 98946–48, 98950–53, 99115–16, 99123–24, 99133, 99135, 99155, 99301–02, 99320–22, 99326, 99330, 99335–37, 99343, 99344 (part), 99345–46, 99350, 99352, 99356–57

* * *

FIFTH DISTRICT

GEORGE R. NETHERCUTT, JR., Republican, of Spokane, WA; born in Spokane, October 7, 1944; graduated from North Central High School; B.A., Washington State University, 1967; J.D., Gonzaga University School of Law, 1971; served as law clerk to Federal Judge Ralph Plummer, U.S. District Court, Anchorage, AK; served as staff counsel and chief of staff to U.S. Senator Ted Stevens (R–Alaska), 1972–77; private law practice: served as town attorney for eastern Washington communities of Reardan, Creston and Almira; cofounder, Vanessa Behan Crisis Nursery; past president, Spokane County Juvenile Diabetes Foundation; past chairman, Spokane County Republican Party; member: Spokane Central Lions, Sigma Nu Fraternity, Spokane Masonic Lodge No. 34, Scottish rite, El Katif Shrine, Masonic Temple Foundation Trustees, Spokane School Levy Advisory Foundation; committee: Appropriations; Agriculture, National Security and Interior subcommittees; married to the former Mary Beth Socha of Summerville, SC; two children: Meredith and Elliott; elected to the 104th Congress, November 8, 1994; reelected to the 105th Congress.

Office Listings

http://www.house.gov/nethercutt grnwa05@hr.house.gov

1527 Longworth House Office Building, Washington, DC 20515 225–2006
Chief of Staff.—Edward Feddeman.
Legislative Director.—Amy Flachbart.
Press Secretary.—Ken Lisaius.
West 920 Riverside Suite 594, Spokane, WA 99201 .... (509) 353–2374
District Director.—Mike Gruber.
District Scheduler.—Dennis Mitchell.

Counties: Adams (part), Asotin, Columbia, Ferry, Garfield, Lincoln; Pend Oreille, Spokane, Stevens, Walla Walla, Whitman. Population (1990), 540,744.

ZIP Codes: 99001, 99003–06, 99008–09, 99011–14, 99016–23, 99025–27, 99029–34, 99036–37, 99039–40, 99101–02, 99103 (part), 99104–05, 99107, 99109–11, 99113–14, 99117–19, 99121–22, 99124–26, 99128 (part), 99129–31, 99133 (part), 99134, 99136–41, 99143–44, 99146–54, 99156 (part), 99157–61, 99163, 99165–67, 99169–71, 99173–74, 99176, 99179–81, 99185, 99201–16, 99218–20, 99223, 99228, 99323–24, 99327–29, 99332–33, 99341, 99344 (part), 99347–48, 99359–63, 99371, 99401–03

SIXTH DISTRICT

NORMAN D. DICKS, Democrat, of Bremerton, WA; born in Bremerton, December 16, 1940; graduated, West Bremerton High School, 1959; B.A., political science, University of Washington, 1963; J.D., University of Washington School of Law, 1968; admitted to Washington bar, 1968; joined the staff of Senator Warren G. Magnuson in 1968 as legislative assistant and appropriations assistant, named administrative assistant in 1973 and held that post until he resigned to campaign for Congress in February 1976; in Congress received a first-term appointment to the House Appropriations Committee; currently serves on subcommittees on National Security and Natural Resources; appointed to Permanent House Select Committee on Intelligence, 1991; ranking Democrat, Intelligence Committee; member, Democratic Caucus; member of Washington, DC and Washington State bars; serves on the Board of Visitors of the U.S. Air Force Academy and is a member of the Puget Sound Naval Bases Association and the Navy League of the United States; married the former Suzanne Callison, 1967; two sons: David and Ryan; elected to the 95th Congress; reelected to each succeeding Congress.

Office Listings

2467 Rayburn House Office Building, Washington, DC 20515–4706 225–5916
Legislative Director.—Pete Modaff.
Press Secretary.—George Behan.
Suite 2244, 1717 Pacific Avenue, Tacoma, WA 98402 .... (206) 593–6536
District Representative.—Mike Weinman.
Suite 301, 500 Pacific Avenue, Bremerton, WA 98310 .... (360) 479–4011
Deputy District Directors: Amy Morrison, Cheri Williams.

Counties: CLALLAM COUNTY: cities and townships of Forks, Port Angeles, La Push, Sequim, Sekiu, Neah Bay. GRAYS HARBOR COUNTY: cities and townships of Aberdeen, Hoquiam, Montesano, Ocean City, Ocean Shores, Moclips. JEFFERSON COUNTY: cities and townships of Port Townsend, Quilcene. KITSAP COUNTY: cities and townships of Bremerton (part), Port Orchard, Gorst. MASON COUNTY: cities and townships of Shelton, Belfair, Allyn, Union. PIERCE COUNTY: cities and townships of Tacoma (part), Gig Harbor, Lakebay, Lakewood. Population (1990), 540,742.

ZIP Codes: 98303, 98305, 98310 (part), 98312 (part), 98320, 98322, 98324–26, 98329, 98331–35, 98337, 98339, 98343, 98349, 98350–51, 98353, 98357–59, 98362, 98365–66, 98368, 98376, 98378, 98380 (part), 98381–82, 98384, 98386, 98388, 98394–95, 98401, 98402 (part), 98403, 98404 (part), 98405–07, 98408 (part), 98409 (part) 98411–12, 98415, 98421 (part), 98442, 98444 (part), 98464–67, 98492, 98494, 98497, 98498 (part), 98499 (part), 98520, 98524, 98526, 98528, 98535–36, 98537 (part) 98546, 98548, 98550, 98552, 98555, 98560, 98562–63, 98566, 98569, 98571, 98575, 98584, 98587–88, 98592

* * *

SEVENTH DISTRICT

JIM MCDERMOTT, Democrat, of Seattle, WA; born in Chicago, IL, on December 28, 1936; B.S., Wheaton College, Wheaton, IL, 1958; M.D., University of Illinois Medical School, Chicago, 1963; residency in adult psychiatry, University of Illinois Hospitals, 1964–66; residency in child psychiatry, University of Washington Hospitals, Seattle, 1966–68; served, U.S. Navy Medical Corps, lieutenant commander, 1968–70; psychiatrist; Washington State House of Representatives, 1971–72; Washington State Senate, 1975–87; Democratic nominee for governor, 1980; regional medical officer, Sub-Saharan Africa, U.S. Foreign Service, 1987–88; practicing psychiatrist and assistant clinical professor of psychiatry, University of Washington, Seattle, 1970–83; member: Washington State Medical Association; King County Medical Society; American Psychiatric Association; St. Mark's Episcopal Church, Seattle; two grown children: Katherine and James; elected on November 8, 1988, to the 101st Congress; reelected to each succeeding Congress; member: Committee on Ways and Means; ranking member, Committee on Standards of Official Conduct.

Office Listings

2349 Rayburn House Office Building, Washington, DC 20515–4707 225–3106
Administrative Assistant.—Charles M. Williams.
Executive Assistant.—Wilda E. Chisolm.
Suite 1212, 1809 Seventh Avenue, Seattle, WA 98101–1313 .... (206) 553–7170
District Administrator.—Nancy F. James.

County: KING COUNTY (part); CITIES AND TOWNSHIPS: Vashon, Burton, Dockton, Seattle (part). Population (1990), 542,000.

ZIP Codes: 98013, 98028, 98055 (part), 98070, 98101–2, 98103 (part), 98104–05, 98106 (part), 98107, 98108 (part), 98109, 98111–12, 98114–16, 98117 (part), 98118 (part), 98119, 98121–22, 98124–25, 98126 (part), 98129, 98133 (part), 98134, 98136, 98144–45, 98146 (part), 98150–51, 98154, 98155 (part), 98161, 98164, 98168 (part), 98174, 98178 (part), 98181, 98184–85, 98191, 98195, 98199

* * *

EIGHTH DISTRICT

JENNIFER DUNN, Republican, of Bellevue, WA; born July 29, 1941 in Seattle, WA; B.A., Stanford University, 1963; chairman, Washington State Republican Party, 1981–92; member, Republican National Committee: vice chairman, Western Region; U.S. delegate to the 30th United Nations Commission on the Status of Women, 1984, 1990; member, Preparatory Commission for the 1985 World Conference on the Status of Women; presidential appointee: President's Advisory Council on Voluntary Services, President's Advisory Council on Historic Preservation, Executive Committee of the Small Business Administration Advisory Council; received Shavano Summit Award for Excellence in National Leadership, Hillsdale College, 1984; member: Seattle Junior League, Board of Epiphany School, Advisory Board for KUOW–FM (National Public Radio), Metropolitan Opera National Council, Henry M. Jackson Foundation, International Women's Forum, and International Republican Institute; committees: Ways and Means, House Oversight; serves as House Republican Conference Secretary; two children: Bryant and Reagan; elected to the 103rd Congress; reelected to each succeeding Congress.

Office Listings

http://www.house.gov/dunn dunnwa08@hr.house.gov

432 Cannon House Office Building, Washington, DC 20515–4708 225–7761
Chief of Staff.—Phil Bond. FAX: 225–8673
Office Manager/Scheduler.—Linda Suter.
Legislative Director.—Tim Hugo.
Suite 201, 50 116th Avenue SE, Bellevue, WA 98004 .... (206) 450–0161
District Contact.—Jane Muffitt.

Counties: KING COUNTY; cities and townships of Auburn, Baring, Beaux Arts Village, Bellevue, Black Diamond, Carnation, Duvall, Enumclaw, Fall City, Issaquah, Kent, Mercer Island, Maple Valley, New Castle, North Bend, Preston, Redmond (part), Renton (part), Skykomish, Snoqualmie, Summit, Woodinville. PIERCE COUNTY; cities and townships of Ashford, Bonney Lake, Buckley, Carbonado, Eatonville, Elbe, Graham, Orting, Puyallup (part), Roy, South Prairie, Spanaway, Sumner, Wilkeson. Population (1990), 540,742.

ZIP Codes: 98001 (part), 98002 (part), 98004 (part), 98005 (part), 98006, 98007 (part), 98008 (part), 98009–10, 98014–15, 98019 (part), 98021–22, 98024–25, 98027, 98031 (part), 98032 (part), 98035, 98038, 98040, 98042, 98045, 98050–51, 98052 (part), 98053, 98055 (part), 98056 (part), 98057, 98058 (part), 98059, 98064–65, 98068, 98072 (part), 98224, 98288, 98304, 98321, 98323, 98328 (part), 98330 (part), 98338 (part), 98344, 98348 (part), 98360 (part), 98372 (part), 98373–74, 98385, 98387 (part), 98390 (part), 98396, 98446 (part), 98580 (part)

* * *

NINTH DISTRICT

ADAM SMITH, Democrat, of Tacoma, WA; born on June 15, 1965, in Washington, DC; graduated from Tyee High School, 1983; graduated from Fordham University, NY, 1987; law degree, University of Washington, 1990; admitted to the Washington bar in 1991; prosecutor for the city of Seattle; Washington State Senate, 1990–96; member, Kent Drinking Driver Task Force; board member, Judson Park Retirement Home; committees: Resources, National Security; married Sara Smith, 1993; elected to the 105th Congress.

Office Listings

1505 Longworth House Office Building, Washington, DC 20515 225–8901
Office Director.—Linda Danforth. FAX: 225–5893
Legislative Director.—Lesley Turner.
Communications Director.—Alixandria Weise.
3600 Port of Tacoma Road E, Suite 308, Tacoma, WA 98424 .... (206) 926–6683
District Director.—Amy Ruble. FAX: 926–1321

Counties: King (part), Pierce (part), Thurston (part). Population (1990), 540,744.

ZIP Codes: 98001, 98002 (part), 98003, 98023, 98032, 98055 (part), 98058, 98059, 98065, 98146, 98148, 98166, 98168, 98178, 98188, 98198, 98371–73, 98404, 98444–47, 98498, 98499, 98501, 98503, 98512, 98513, 98516, 98530–31, 98576, 98580 (part), 98589, 98597

WEST VIRGINIA

(Population 1995, 1,828,000)

SENATORS

ROBERT C. BYRD, Democrat, of Sophia, WV; born November 20, 1917; Baptist; married Erma Ora James; two daughters: Mrs. Mohammad (Mona Byrd) Fatemi and Mrs. Jon (Marjorie Byrd) Moore; six grandchildren: Erik, Darius and Fredrik Fatemi, and Michael (deceased), Mona and Mary Anne Moore; committees: Appropriations, Armed Services, Rules and Administration, sworn in to the U.S. Senate on January 3, 1959; reelected for each succeeding term.

Office Listings

senator__byrd@byrd.senate.gov

311 Hart Senate Office Building, Washington, DC 20510–4801 224–3954
Chief of Staff.—Barbara Videnieks.
Administrative Assistant.—Lisa Tuite.
Press Secretary.—Ann Adler.
Suite 1019, 500 Quarrier Street, Charleston, WV 25301 .... (304) 342–5855
State Liaison.—Anne Barth.

* * *

JOHN D. ROCKEFELLER IV, Democrat, of Charleston, WV; born in New York City, NY, June 18, 1937; graduated, Phillips Exeter Academy, Exeter, NH, 1954; A.B., Harvard University, Cambridge, MA, 1961; honorary degrees: J.D., West Virginia University, Marshall University, Davis and Elkins College, Dickinson College, University of Alabama, University of Cincinnati; doctor of humanities, West Virginia Institute of Technology; doctor of public service, Salem College; Vista volunteer, Emmons, WV, 1964; West Virginia House of Delegates, 1966–68; elected Secretary of State of West Virginia, 1968; president, West Virginia Wesleyan College, 1973–76; Governor of West Virginia, 1976–84; married to the former Sharon Percy; four children: John, Valerie, Charles and Justin; committees: Commerce, Science and Transportation; Finance; Veterans' Affairs; elected to the U.S. Senate, November 6, 1984.

Office Listings

http://www.senate.gov/~rockefeller senator@rockefeller.senate.gov

531 Hart Senate Office Building, Washington, DC 20510–4802 224–6472
Administrative Assistant.—R. Lane Bailey. FAX: 224–7665
Legislative Director.—Tamera M. Stanton.
405 Capitol Street, Suite 608, Charleston, WV 25301 .... (304) 347–5372
207 Prince Street, Beckley, WV 25801 .... (304) 253–9704
118 Adams Street, Suite 301, Fairmont, WV 26554 .... (304) 367–0122

REPRESENTATIVES

FIRST DISTRICT

ALAN B. MOLLOHAN, Democrat, of Fairmont, WV; born in Fairmont on May 14, 1943, son of former Congressman Robert H. Mollohan and Helen Holt Mollohan; graduated, Greenbrier Military School, Lewisburg, WV, 1962; A.B., College of William and Mary, Williamsburg, VA, 1966; J.D., West Virginia University College of Law, Morgantown, 1970; captain, U.S. Army Reserves, 1970–83; admitted to the West Virginia bar in 1970 and commenced practice in Fairmont; admitted to the District of Columbia bar in 1975; member, First Baptist Church, Fairmont; married the former Barbara Whiting, 1976; five children: Alan, Robert, Andrew, Karl and Mary Kathryn; elected on November 2, 1982, to the 98th Congress; reelected to each succeeding Congress.

Office Listings

2346 Rayburn House Office Building, Washington, DC 20515–4801 225–4172

Chief of Staff.—Elizabeth Whyte.
Personal Secretary.—Ann Marie Packo.
Press Secretary.—Ron Hudok.
209 P.O. Box 1400, Post Office Building, Clarksburg, WV 26302–1400 .... (304) 623–4422
Room 13, 389 Spruce Street, Morgantown, WV 26505–5563 .... (304) 292–3019
4311 P.O. Box 145, Federal Building, Parkersburg, WV 26101–0145 .... (304) 428–0493
315 Federal Building, Wheeling, WV 26003–2900 .... (304) 232–5390

Counties: Barbour, Brooke, Doddridge, Grant, Hancock, Harrison, Marion, Marshall, Mineral, Monongalia, Ohio, Pleasants, Preston, Ritchie, Taylor, Tucker, Tyler, Wetzel, Wood. CITIES AND TOWNSHIPS: Albright, Alma, Alvy, Anmoore, Arthur, Arthurdate, Auburn, Aurora, Barrackville, Baxter, Bayard, Beech Bottom, Belington, Belleville, Belleville, Bellview, Belmont, Bens Run, Benwood, Berea, Bethany, Big Run, Blacksville, Blandville, Booth, Brandonville, Bretz, Bridgeport, Bristol, Brownton, Bruceton Mills, Burlington, Burnt House, Burton, Cabins, Cairo, Cameron, Carolina, Cassville, Center Point, Central Station, Century, Chester, Clarksburg, Coburn, Colfax, Colliers, Core, Corinth, Cove, Cuzzart, Dallas, Davis, Davisville, Dawmont, Dellslow, Dorcas, Eglon, Elk Garden, Ellenboro, Elm Grove, Enterprise, Eureka, Everettville, Fairmont, Fairview, Farmington, Flemington, Follansbee, Folsom, Fort Ashby, Fort Neal, Four states, Friendly, Galloway, Glen Dale, Glen Easton, Goffs, Gormania, Grafton, Grant Town, Granville, Greenwood, Gypsy, Hambleton, Harrisville, Hastings, Haywood, Hazelton, Hebron, Hendricks, Hepzibah, Highland, Hundred, Idamay, Independence, Industrial, Jacksonburg, Jere, Jordan, Junior, Keyser, Kingmont, Kingwood, Knob Fork, Lahmansville, Lima, Littleton, Lost Creek, Lumberport, MacFarlan, Mahone, Maidsville, Mannington, Masontown, Maysville, McMechen, McWhorter, Meadowbrook, Medley, Metz, Middlebourne, Mineralwells, Moatsville, Monongah, Montana Mines, Morgantown, Moundsville, Mount Clare, Mount Storm, Mountain, New Creek, New Cumberland, New England, New Manchester, New Martinsville, New Milton, Newburg, Newell, North Parkersburg, Nutter Fort, Osage, Owings, Paden City, Parkersburg, Parsons, Pennsboro, Pentress, Petersburg, Petroleum, Philippi, Piedmont, Pine Grove, Porters Falls, Proctor, Pullman, Pursglove, Rachel, Reader, Red Creek, Reedsville, Reynoldsville, Riegeley, Rivesville, Rocket Center, Rockport, Rosemont, Rowlesburg, Saint George, Saint Marys, Salem, Shinnston, Shirley, Short Creek, Simpson, Sistersville, Smithburg, Smithfield, Smithville, Spelter, Stonewood, Terra Alta, Thomas, Thornton, Toll Gate, Triadelphia, Tunnelton, Valley Grove, Vienna, Volga, Wadestown, Walker, Wallace, Wana, Warwood, Washington, Watson, Waverly Weirton, Wellsburg, Wendel, West Liberty, West Milford, West Union, Westover, Wheeling Wick, Wilbur, Wiley Ford, Wileyville, Williamstown, Wilson, Wilsonburg, Windsor Heights, Wolf Summit, Worthington, Wyatt. Population (1990), 598,056.

ZIP Codes: 15376 (part), 15377 (part), 26003, 26030–41, 26047, 26050, 26055–56, 26058–60, 26062, 26070, 26074–75, 26101–05, 26130 (part), 26133 (part), 26134–35, 26142, 26143 (part), 26144, 26146, 26148–50, 26155, 26159, 26161–62, 26167, 26169–70, 26175, 26178, 26180–81, 26184–87, 26190, 26301–02, 26320, 26322–23, 26325, 26327–28, 26330 (part), 26332, 26336–37, 26339, 26344, 26346, 26347 (part), 26348, 26354, 26360–62, 26366–67, 26369, 26375, 26377, 26378 (part), 26383, 26385–86, 26401–02, 26404, 26407–08, 26411, 26415, 26419, 26421–22, 26424, 26426, 26431, 26434–38, 26440 (part), 26442, 26448, 26451, 26456, 26459, 26461–63, 26554–55, 26559–63, 26566, 26568, 26570–72, 26574–76, 26578, 26581, 26582 (part), 26585–88, 26589 (part), 26591

* * *

SECOND DISTRICT

ROBERT E. WISE, JR., Democrat, of Clendenin, WV; born in Washington, DC, on January 6, 1948; graduated, George Washington High School, 1966; A.B., Duke University, Durham, NC, 1970; B.A., Tulane University College of Law, New Orleans, LA, 1975; attorney, admitted to West Virginia State bar in 1976 and commenced practice in Charleston; legislative counsel, Judiciary Committee of the West Virginia House of Delegates, 1977–78; director, West Virginians for Fair and Equitable Assessment of Taxes, Inc., 1977–80; West Virginia Senate, 1980–82; member: American Bar Association, West Virginia State bar; committees: Transportation and Infrastructure; Government Reform and Oversight; married Sandra Casber White, 1984; two children: Robert and Alexandra; elected on November 2, 1982 to the 98th Congress; reelected to each succeeding Congress.

Office Listings

http://www.house.gov/wise bobwise@hr.house.gov

2434 Rayburn House Office Building, Washington, DC 20515–4802 225–2711
Administrative Assistant.—Lowell Johnson.
Legislative Director.—Jane Mellow.
Press Secretary.—Rod Blackstone.
4710 Chimney Drive, Charleston, WV 25302 .... (304) 342–7170
222 West John Street, Martinsburg, WV 25401 .... (304) 264–8810

Counties: Berkeley, Braxton, Calhoun, Clay, Gilmer, Hampshire, Hardy, Jackson, Jefferson, Kanawha, Lewis, Mason, Morgan, Nicholas, Pendleton, Putnam, Randolph, Roane, Upshur, and Wirt. Population (1990), 597,921.

ZIP Codes: 25003, 25005, 25008 (part), 25009–13, 25015, 25018–19, 25021, 25024–26, 25028, 25030, 25033, 25034 (part), 25035, 25037, 25039, 25043, 25045–46, 25047 (part), 25049–54, 25059 (part), 25061, 25063–64, 25067, 25070–71, 25075, 25079–84, 25086, 25088, 25093, 25095, 25102–03, 25105–14, 25122–26, 25130, 25132–34, 25136 (part), 25141–43, 25147–50, 25154, 25156, 25158, 25159 (part), 25160, 25162–66, 25168–69, 25172, 25177, 25181–82, 25187, 25193, 25201–06, 25208–10, 25211 (part), 25212–14, 25231, 25234, 25235 (part), 25237, 25239–40, 25241 (part), 25242–53, 25255–62, 25264–68, 25270–72, 25274–76, 25279–81, 25283, 25285–87, 25300–04, 25306, 25309, 25311–15, 25320–39, 25357, 25360, 25362, 25501–03, 25506, 25508 (part), 25510 (part), 25513, 25515, 25520 (part), 25521, 25523, 25524 (part), 25526, 25529, 25536, 25540, 25541 (part), 25544, 25546, 25550, 25557, 25560, 25563–65, 25567–69, 25570 (part), 25571 (part), 25572–73, 26130 (part), 26133 (part), 26136–39, 26141, 26143 (part), 26145, 26147,

26151–53, 26158, 26160, 26164, 26173, 26179, 26202, 26205, 26207, 26261, 26321, 26335, 26338, 26342–43, 26350–51, 26372, 26376, 26378 (part), 26384, 26409, 26412, 26423, 26430, 26439, 26443, 26445–47, 26452, 26504, 26601, 26610–12, 26616–21, 26623–27, 26629, 26631, 26633–34, 26636, 26638–41, 26651, 26656 (part), 26660, 26662, 26667, 26671, 26675–76, 26678–79, 26681 (part), 26683–84, 26688, 26690–91

* * *

THIRD DISTRICT

NICK RAHALL II, Democrat, of Beckley, WV; born in Beckley, May 20, 1949; graduated, Woodrow Wilson High School, Beckley, 1967; A.B., Duke University, Durham, NC, 1971; graduate work, George Washington University, Washington, DC; colonel in U.S. Air Force Civil Air Patrol; president of the West Virginia Society of Washington, DC; business executive; sales representative, WWNR radio station; president, Mountaineer Tour and Travel Agency, 1974; president, West Virginia Broadcasting; named: Coal Man of the Year, *Coal Industry News*, 1979; ''Young Democrat of the Year'', Young Democrats, 1980; 1984 West Virginia American Legion Distinguished Service Award recipient; delegate, Democratic national conventions, 1972, 1976, 1980, 1984; member, Democratic Congressional Campaign Committee; member: Rotary, Elks, Moose, Eagles, NAACP, National Rifle Association, AF & AM, RAM, Mount Hope Commandery, Shrine Club, Benie Kedeem Temple in Charleston, Beckley Presbyterian Church; chairman and founder, Congressional Coal Group; member: Democratic Leadership Council, Congressional Black Caucus, Democratic Study Group, Energy and Environment Study Conference, Congressional Arts Caucus, Congressional Travel and Tourism Caucus, Congressional Textile Caucus, Congressional Truck Caucus, Congressional Steel Caucus, Automobile Task Force, Congressional Rural Caucus; serves on Resources and Transportation and Infrastructure committees; ranking minority member, Surface Transportation Subcommittee; three children: Rebecca Ashley, Nick Joe III, and Suzanne Nicole; elected to the 95th Congress, November 2, 1976; reelected to each succeeding Congress.

Office Listings

nrahall@hr.house.gov

2269 Rayburn House Office Building, Washington, DC 20515–4803	225–3452
Administrative Assistant.—Kent Keyser.	FAX: 225–9061
Legislative Assistants: Birdie Kyle, Jim Boia, Craig Clapper.	
Press Secretary.—Kent Keyser.	
815 Fifth Avenue, Huntington, WV 25701	(304) 522–6425
110½ Main Street, Beckley, WV 25801	(304) 252–5000
RK Building, Logan, WV 25601	(304) 752–4934
1005 Federal Building, Bluefield, WV 24701	(304) 325–6222
101 North Court Street, Lewisburg, WV 24901	(304) 647–3228

Counties: Boone, Cabell, Fayette, Greenbrier, Lincoln, Logan, McDowell, Mercer, Mingo, Monroe, Pocahontas, Raleigh, Summers, Wayne, Webster, and Wyoming. Population (1990), 597,500.

ZIP Codes: 24701, 24710, 24712, 24714–17, 24719, 24724, 24726–27, 24729, 24731–33, 24735–40, 24747, 24751, 24801, 24807–11, 24813, 24815–32, 24834–36, 24839, 24841–62, 24866–74, 24877–84, 24886–92, 24894–99, 25004, 25007, 25008 (part), 25022, 25044, 25047 (part), 25048, 25060, 25062, 25076, 25121, 25135, 25140, 25159 (part), 25174, 25180, 25183, 25188–89, 25211 (part), 25235 (part), 25241 (part), 25504–05, 25507, 25508 (part), 25510 (part), 25511–12, 25514, 25517, 25519, 25520 (part), 25524 (part), 25530, 25534–35, 25537, 25541 (part), 25545, 25547, 25555, 25559, 25562, 25570 (part), 25571 (part), 25601, 25606–08, 25611–12, 25614, 25617–21, 25623–25, 25628–39, 25642–54, 25661 (part), 25663, 25665–67, 25669–72, 25674, 25676–78, 25682, 25684–88, 25690–94, 25696–97, 25699, 25701–29, 25770–79, 25801–02, 25810–11, 25813, 25816–18, 25820, 25823, 25825 (part), 25826–28, 25832, 25836, 25839, 25841, 25843–45, 25847–49, 25851, 25853, 25856–57, 25860, 25865, 25870–71, 25873, 25875–78, 25880 (part), 25882, 25902, 25905–09, 25911, 25913, 25915–16, 25918–22, 25926–28, 25932–34, 25939, 25943, 25951 (part), 25969 (part), 25971, 25979 (part), 25989 (part), 26681 (part)

WISCONSIN

(Population 1995, 5,123,000)

SENATORS

HERB KOHL, Democrat, of Milwaukee, WI; born in Milwaukee on February 7, 1935; graduated, Washington High School, Milwaukee, 1952; B.A., University of Wisconsin, Madison, 1956; M.B.A., Harvard Graduate School of Business Administration, Cambridge, MA, 1958; LL.D., Cardinal Stritch College, Milwaukee, WI, 1986 (honorary); served, U.S. Army Reserves, 1958–64; businessman; president, Herbert Kohl Investments; owner, Milwaukee Bucks NBA basketball team; past chairman, Milwaukee's United Way Campaign; State chairman, Democratic Party of Wisconsin, 1975–77; honors and awards: Pen and Mike Club Wisconsin Sports Personality of the Year, 1985; Wisconsin Broadcasters Association Joe Killeen Memorial Sportsman of the Year, 1985; Greater Milwaukee Convention and Visitors Bureau Lamplighter Award, 1986; Wisconsin Parkinsons Association Humanitarian of the Year, 1986; Kiwanis Milwaukee Award, 1987; committees: Appropriations, Judiciary, Special Committee on Aging; elected to the U.S. Senate, November 8, 1988, for the six-year term beginning January 3, 1989.

Office Listings

http://www.senate.gov/~kohl senator_kohl@kohl.senate.gov

330 Hart Senate Office Building, Washington, DC 20510–4903 224–5653
Legislative Director.—Kate Sparks.
Chief of Staff.—Paul Bock.
Communications Director.—Brad Fitch.
Executive Secretary.—Arlene Branca.
205 East Wisconsin Avenue, Milwaukee, WI 53202 .... (414) 297–4451
Suite 312, 14 West Muffin Street, Madison, WI 53703 .... (608) 264–5338
Suite 206, Graham Avenue, Eau Claire, WI 54701 .... (715) 832–8424
Suite 235, 4321 West College Avenue, Appleton, WI 54914 .... (414) 738–1640

* * *

RUSSELL FEINGOLD, Democrat, of Middleton, WI; born March 2, 1953 in Janesville, WI; graduated from Craig High School, Janesville, WI in 1971; B.A., University of Wisconsin-Madison, 1975; Rhodes scholar, Oxford University, 1977; J.D., Harvard Law School, 1979; practicing attorney with Foley and Lardner and with LaFollette and Sinykin, both in Madison, WI, 1979–85; Wisconsin State Senate, January 1983 to January 1993; married to Mary Feingold; four children: daughters Jessica and Ellen, stepsons Sam Speerschneider and Ted Speerschneider; elected to the U.S. Senate, November 3, 1992, for the six-year term beginning January 3, 1993.

Office Listings

http://www.senate.gov/~feingold russell_feingold@feingold.senate.gov

502 Hart Senate Office Building, Washington, DC 20510–4904 224–5323
Administrative Assistant.—Mary Murphy.
Legislative Director.—Susanne Martinez.
Press Secretary.—Mary Bottari.
517 East Wisconsin Avenue, Milwaukee, WI 53202 .... (414) 276–7282
8383 Greenway Boulevard, Middleton, WI 53562 .... (608) 828–1200
State Coordinator.—Janet Piraino.
Staff Director.—Ruth LaRocque.
317 First Street, Room 107, Wausau, WI 54401 .... (715) 848–5660
425 State Street, Room 232, LaCrosse, WI 54603 .... (608) 782–5585
1640 Main Street, Green Bay, WI 54302 .... (414) 465–7508

REPRESENTATIVES

FIRST DISTRICT

MARK W. NEUMANN, Republican, of Janesville, WI; born on February 27, 1954; attended East Troy High School, 1972; B.S., University of Wisconsin, Whitewater, 1975; M.S., University of Wisconsin, River Falls, 1977; homebuilder; member of St. Matthew's Evangelical Lutheran Church of Janesville; past president of the Milton Chamber of Commerce; member: Optimist Club, Forward Janesville, South Central Wisconsin Builders Association, National Federation of Independent Business, Janesville Board of Realtors, director of the Boys and Girls Club of Janesville, Board of Regents of Wisconsin Lutheran College; recipient of the Entrepreneur of the Year Award from the University of Wisconsin-Whitewater Entrepreneurship Program; committees: Appropriations, Budget; subcommittees: VA, HUD and Independent Agencies; District of Columbia; married, Sue Anne (Link) Neumann, 1973; three children: Andrew, Tricia and Matthew; elected to the 104th Congress; reelected to the 105th Congress.

Office Listings

http://www.house.gov/neumann mneumann@hr.house.gov

415 Cannon House Office Building, Washington, DC 20515 225–3031
Chief of Staff.—Chuck Pike.
One Parker Place, Room 495, Janesville, WI 53545 .... (608) 752–4050
City Hall, 100 State Street, Beloit, WI 53511 .... (608) 363–0751
City Hall, 9 South Broad Street, Elkhorn, WI 53121 .... (414) 723–7122
6530 Sheridan Road, Room 5, Kenosha, WI 53143 .... (414) 654–1901
Racine County Courthouse, 730 Wisconsin Avenue, Racine, WI 53403 .... (414) 637–0510

Counties: Green (part), Jefferson (part), Kenosha, Racine, Rock, Walworth, Waukesha (part). Population (1990), 543,530.

ZIP Codes: 53101–02, 53104–05, 53108–09, 53114–15, 53119 (part), 53120–21, 53125–26, 53128, 53130 (part), 53138–42, 53147–48, 53149 (part), 53152, 53157–59, 53167–68, 53170–71, 53176–77, 53179, 53181–82, 53184–85, 53186 (part), 53190 (part), 53191–92, 53194–95, 53400, 53402–06, 53501–02, 53505, 53508 (part), 53511, 53520, 53521 (part), 53522 (part), 53525, 53528 (part), 53534 (part), 53536–37, 53542, 53545–46, 53550, 53563 (part), 53566 (part), 53570 (part), 53574 (part), 53576, 53585 (part)

* * *

SECOND DISTRICT

SCOTT KLUG, Republican, of Madison, WI; born on January 16, 1953 in Milwaukee, WI; graduated from Marquette University High School, 1971; B.A., history, Lawrence University, Appleton, WI, 1975; M.A., journalism, Northwestern University, 1972; M.B.A., University of Wisconsin, Madison, 1990; news reporter and news anchor for WKOW–TV; investigative reporter for WJLA–TV; vice president, business development, Blunt, Ellis, and Loem; married to the former Theresa Mary Summers; three children: Keefe, Brett and Collin; elected to the 102nd Congress on November 6, 1990; reelected to each succeeding Congress.

Office Listings

http://www.house.gov/klug badger02@hr.house.gov

1224 Longworth House Office Building, Washington, DC 20515–4902 225–2906
Chief of Staff.—Kris Beininger-Andrews.
Legislative Director.—Pat Browne.
Press Secretary.—Pamela Arruda-Lambo.
Office Manager/Scheduler.—Laura Imhoff.
Room 600, 16 North Carroll Street, Madison, WI 53703 .... (608) 257–9200
District Director.—Judy Lowell.

Counties: Columbia, Dane, Dodge (part), Green (part), Iowa, Jefferson (part), Lafayette, Richland, and Sauk. Population (1990), 543,532.

ZIP Codes: 53016, 53032, 53034, 53035 (part), 53039, 53059 (part), 53078 (part), 53094 (part), 53503–04, 53506–07, 53508 (part), 53510, 53515–17, 53521 (part), 53522 (part), 53523 (part), 53526–27, 53528 (part), 53529–33, 53534 (part), 53535, 53540–41, 53543 (part), 53544, 53553, 53554 (part), 53555–58, 53559 (part), 53560–62, 53565, 53566 (part), 53569 (part), 53570 (part), 53571–72, 53573 (part), 53574 (part), 53575, 53577–80, 53581 (part), 53582–84, 53585 (part), 53586–88, 53589 (part), 53590, 53593, 53594 (part), 53597–99, 53700–01, 53703–08, 53711, 53713–19, 53803, 53807 (part), 53811 (part), 53817, 53818 (part), 53901, 53910 (part), 53911–13, 53916, 53923 (part), 53924 (part), 53925, 53926 (part), 53928, 53932–33, 53935, 53936 (part), 53937, 53940–44, 53948 (part), 53951, 53954 (part), 53955, 53956 (part), 53959–62, 53963 (part), 53965 (part), 53968 (part), 53969, 54634 (part), 61001 (part), 61060 (part), 61075 (part), 61087 (part), 61089 (part)

* * *

THIRD DISTRICT

RON KIND, Democrat, of La Crosse, WI; born in La Crosse, March 16, 1963; B.A., Harvard University, 1985; M.A., London School of Economics, 1986; J.D., University of Minnesota Law

School, 1990; admitted to the Wisconsin bar, 1990; state prosecutor, La Crosse County District Attorney's Office; board of directors, La Crosse Boys and Girls Club, Coulee Council on Alcohol and Drug Abuse, Wisconsin Harvard Club; member: Wisconsin Bar Association, La Crosse County Bar Association; married Tawni Zappa in 1994; one son, Jonathan; member: Committee on Resources and Committee on Education and the Workforce; elected to the 105th Congress.

Office Listings

1713 Longworth House Office Building, Washington, DC 20515–4903 225–5506
Chief of Staff.—Alan MacLeod. FAX: 225–5739
Press Secretary.—Kevin Kennedy.
Legislative Director.—Sylvia Gaudette.
Executive Assistant.—Kathryn Baer.
205 5th Avenue South, Suite 227, La Crosse, WI 54601 .... (608) 782–2558
District Director.—Loren Kannenberg.
131 S. Barstow Street, Suite 301, Eau Claire, WI 54701 .... (715) 831–9214

Counties: Barron, Buffalo, Chippewa (part), Clark (part), Crawford, Dunn, Eau Claire (part), Grant, Jackson, La Crosse, Monroe (part), Pepin, Pierce, Polk (part), St. Croix, Trempealeau, and Vernon. Population (1990), 543,533.

ZIP Codes: 53518, 53543 (part), 53554 (part), 53569 (part), 53573 (part), 53581 (part), 53589 (part), 53801–02, 53804–06, 53807 (part), 53808–10, 53811 (part), 53812–13, 53816, 53818 (part), 53820–21, 53824–27, 53924 (part), 53929 (part), 53968 (part), 54001–05, 54007–17, 54020–28, 54082, 54420 (part), 54436, 54446, 54456, 54465 (part), 54466 (part), 54601–03, 54610–12, 54614–17, 54619 (part), 54621–26, 54627 (part), 54628, 54629 (part), 54630–32, 54634 (part), 54635–36, 54638 (part), 54639–40, 54642 (part), 54644–45, 54650–52, 54653 (part), 54654–55, 54656 (part), 54657–59, 54661, 54664–65, 54667, 54669, 54701–03, 54720–23, 54725, 54726 (part), 54727 (part), 54728 (part), 54730 (part), 54733–38, 54739 (part), 54740–44, 54746–47, 54749–51, 54754–56, 54757 (part), 54758–65, 54767, 54768 (part), 54769–70, 54771 (part), 54772–73, 54805, 54810, 54812, 54813 (part), 54818, 54822, 54824, 54826, 54829 (part), 54841, 54857, 54866, 54868, 54889

* * *

FOURTH DISTRICT

GERALD D. KLECZKA, Democrat, of Milwaukee, WI; born in Milwaukee, November 26, 1943; graduated Don Bosco High School, Milwaukee, 1961; attended University of Wisconsin, Milwaukee; served in the Wisconsin Air National Guard, 1963–69; served in Wisconsin Assembly, 1969–74; Wisconsin Senate, 1975–84; member: LaFarge Lifelong Learning Institute, Thomas More Foundation, Polish National Alliance-Milwaukee Society, Polish American Congress, South Side Democratic Party Unit, State and Milwaukee County Democratic Party; married the former Bonnie L. Scott, 1978; elected to the 98th Congress by special election, April 3, 1984, reelected to each succeeding Congress.

Office Listings

jerry4wi@hr.house.gov

2301 Rayburn House Office Building, Washington, DC 20515–4904 225–4572
Administrative Assistant.—Jennifer McKenzie.
Press Secretary.—Barbara Warner.
5032 West Forest Home Avenue, Milwaukee, WI 53219 .... (414) 297–1140
Chief of Staff.—Kathryn Hein.
414 West Moreland Boulevard, Suite 105, Waukesha, WI 53186 .... (414) 549–6360

Counties: Milwaukee (part), Waukesha (part). CITIES AND TOWNSHIPS: Milwaukee (part), Waukesha (part), Pewaukee (part), Big Bend, Cudahy, Greendale, Hales Corners, Franklin, New Berlin, Mukwonago, Vernon, Muskego, Oak Creek, South Milwaukee, West Allis, West Milwaukee, St. Francis, and Greenfield. Population (1990), 543,527.

ZIP Codes: 53072 (part), 53103, 53110, 53129, 53130 (part), 53132, 53146, 53149 (part), 53150–51, 53154, 53172, 53186 (part), 53187–88, 53193, 53202 (part), 53204, 53207, 53214 (part), 53215, 53219–21, 53227–28, 53233

* * *

FIFTH DISTRICT

THOMAS M. BARRETT, Democrat, of Milwaukee, WI; born December 8, 1953 in Milwaukee; B.A., University of Wisconsin, Madison, 1976; J.D. with honors, University of Wisconsin, Madison Law School, 1980; attorney; Wisconsin State Assembly, 1984–89; Wisconsin State Senate, 1989–92; member, Wisconsin State bar; married Kristine Mansfield Barrett, 1991; two children: Thomas John and Anne Elizabeth; elected on November 3, 1992 to the 103rd Congress; reelected to each succeeding Congress.

Office Listings

http://www.house.gov/barrett telltom@hr.house.gov

1224 Longworth House Office Building, Washington, DC 20515–4905 225–3571
Administrative Assistant/Press Secretary.—Janet Piraino. FAX: 225–1396
Associate Administrator.—Jan Miller.
Legislative Director.—Sharon Robinson.
Suite 618, 135 West Wells Street, Milwaukee, WI 53203 .... (414) 297–1331
District Director.—Anne DeLeo.

Counties: Milwaukee County (part): CITIES AND TOWNSHIPS: Bayside, Brown Deer, Fox Point, Glendale, River Hills, Shorewood, Wauwatosa and Whitefish Bay. Population (1990), 543,530.

ZIP Codes: 53201, 53202 (part), 53203, 53205–06, 53208–10, 53211 (part), 53212–13, 53216, 53217 (part), 53218, 53222–26, 53233

* * *

SIXTH DISTRICT

THOMAS E. PETRI, Republican, of Fond du Lac, WI; born in Marinette, WI, May 28, 1940; graduated, Lowell P. Goodrich High School, 1958; B.A., Harvard University, Cambridge, MA, 1962; J.D., Harvard Law School, 1965; admitted to the Wisconsin state and Fond du Lac county bar associations, 1965; commenced practice in Fond du Lac in 1970; lawyer; law clerk to Federal Judge James Doyle, 1965; Peace Corps volunteer, 1966–67; White House aide, 1969; elected to the Wisconsin State Senate in 1972; reelected in 1976 and served until April 1979; married; one daughter; elected to the 96th Congress by special election, April 3, 1979, to fill the vacancy caused by the death of William A. Steiger; reelected to each succeeding Congress.

Office Listings

http://www.house.gov/petri tompetri@hr.house.gov

2262 Rayburn House Office Building, Washington, DC 20515–4906 225–2476
Administrative Assistant/Legislative Director.—Joseph Flader.
Communications Director.—Niel Wright.
Office Manager.—Linda Towse.
845 South Main Street, No. 160, Fond du Lac, WI 54935 .... (414) 922–1180
District Director.—Sue Kerkman.
115 Washington Avenue, Oshkosh, WI 54901 .... (414) 231–6333

Counties: Adams; Brown (part); Calumet (part); Fond du Lac (part); Green Lake; Juneau; Manitowoc (part); Marquette; Monroe (part); Outagamie (part); Sheboygan (part); Waupaca; Waushara; Winnebago. CITIES AND TOWNSHIPS: Adams, Adrian, Algoma, Alto, Angelo (part), Armenia, Ashford (part), Auburn, Aurora, Bear Creek, Berlin, Big Falls, Big Flats, Black Wolf, Bloomfield, Brandon, Brillion, Brooklyn, Brothertown, Buchanan, Buffalo, Byron, Byron, Caledonia, Calumet, Camp Douglas, Campbellspot, Cascade, Cato, Centeville, Charleston, Chilton, Chitton, Clayton, Clearfield, Cleveland, Clifton, Clintonville, Colburn, Coloma, Combined Locks, Cooperstown (part), Crystal Lake, Cutler, Dakota, Dayton, Deerfield, Dell Prairie, Douglas, DuPont, Easton, Eaton, Eden, Eldorado, Elkhart Lake, Elroy, Embarras, Empire, Endeavor, Fairwater, Farmington, Finley, Fond du Lac, Forest, Fountain, Francis Creek, Franklin, Fremont, Friendship, Germantown, Gibson Kossuth, Glenbeulah, Glendale, Grant, Green Lake, Greenbush, Greenfield, Hancock, Harris, Harrison, Helvetia, Hilbert, Holland, Hustler, Iola, Jackson, Jefferson (part), Kellnersville, Kendall, Kiel, Kildare, Kimberly, Kingston, Lafayette (part), LaGrange, Lamartine, Larabee, Lebanon, Lemonwier, Leola, Leon, Liberty, Lima, Lincoln, Lind, Linding, Lisbon, Little Chute, Little Wolf, Lohrville, Lyndon, Lyndon Station, Mackford, Manchester, Manitowoc, Maple Grove, Maribel, Marion, Markesan, Marquette, Marshfield, Matteson, Mauston, Mecan, Meeme, Menasha, Menasha, Metomer, Mishicot, Mitchel, Monroe, Montello, Moundville, Mount Morris, Mukwa, Munawa, Munitowoc, Necedah, Neerah, Nekimi, Nepeuskon, Neshkoro, New Chester, New Haven, New Holstein, New Lisbon, New London, New Lyme (part), Newton, North Fon du Lac, Norwalk, Oakdale, Oakfield, Oakfield, Oasis, Ogdensburg, Omro, Orange, Osceola, Oshkosh, Oxford, Packwaukee, Plainfield, Plymouth, Potter, Poygan, Poysippi, Preston, Princeton, Quincy, Rantoul, Redgranite, Reedsville, Rhine, Richfield, Richford, Ridgeville, Ripon, Rockland, Rome, Rose, Rosendale, Royalton, Rushford, Russell, Saxeville, Scandinavia, Schleswig, Scott, Seneca, Sheboygan Falls, Sheldon, Sherwood, Shields, Springfield, Springvale, Springville, Springwater, St. Cloud, St. Lawrence, St. Marie, St. Nazianz, Stockbridge, Strongs Prairie, Summit, Taycheedah, Tomah, Tomah Seven Mile Creek, Two Creeks, Two Rivers, Union, Union Center, Utica, Valders, Vinland, Waldo, Warren, Waupaca, Waupun, Wautoma, Wellington, Wells (part), Westfield, Weyauwega, Whitelaw, Wild Rose, Wilton, Winchester, Winnecome, Wolf River, Wonewoc, Woodville, Wrightstown (part), Wyeville, Wyoming. Population (1990), 543,652.

ZIP Codes: 53006 (part), 53009, 53010 (part), 53011 (part), 53014–15, 53019–20, 53023, 53026, 53031, 53040 (part), 53042, 53044, 53048 (part), 53049, 53057, 53061–63, 53065, 53070 (part), 53073 (part), 53079, 53081 (part), 53083 (part), 53085, 53088, 53093 (part), 53910 (part), 53919–21, 53923 (part), 53926 (part), 53927, 53929 (part), 53930–31, 53934, 53936 (part), 53939, 53945–47, 53948 (part), 53949–50, 53952–53, 53954 (part), 53956 (part), 53963 (part), 53964, 53965 (part), 54110 (part), 54123, 54126 (part), 54129, 54130 (part), 54160, 54169, 54170 (part), 54206 (part), 54207, 54208 (part), 54214, 54215 (part), 54220, 54227–28, 54230, 54232, 54240–41, 54245, 54247, 54413, 54457 (part), 54466 (part), 54486 (part), 54613, 54618, 54619 (part), 54620, 54627 (part), 54629 (part), 54637, 54638 (part), 54641, 54642 (part), 54643, 54646, 54648–49, 54653 (part), 54656 (part), 54660, 54662, 54666, 54670–71, 54901–04, 54909 (part), 54911 (part), 54915, 54921 (part), 54922 (part), 54923, 54926–27, 54929–30, 54932–36, 54940 (part), 54941, 54943, 54945–47, 54949, 54950 (part), 54952, 54956 (part), 54957, 54960, 54961 (part), 54962–65, 54966 (part), 54967–68, 54970–71, 54974–77, 54979–80, 54981 (part), 54982–86, 54990

SEVENTH DISTRICT

DAVID R. OBEY, Democrat, of Wausau, WI; born in Okmulgee, OK, October 3, 1938; graduated Wausau High School, 1956; M.A. in political science, University of Wisconsin, 1960 (graduate work in Russian government and foreign policy); elected to the Wisconsin Legislature from Marathon County's 2nd District at the age of 24; reelected three times; assistant Democratic floor leader; married Joan Lepinski of Wausau, WI, 1962; two sons: Craig David and Douglas David; elected to the 91st Congress by special election, April 1, 1969, to fill the vacancy created by resignation of Melvin R. Laird; reelected to each succeeding Congress; ranking member, House Committee on Appropriations; Subcommittee on Labor, Health and Human Services, and Education, ranking member; ex officio member of all subcommittees; and former chairman, Joint Economic Committee.

Office Listings

2462 Rayburn House Office Building, Washington, DC 20515–4907 225–3365
Staff Director.—Joseph R. Crapa.
Executive Assistant/Personal Secretary.—Carly M. Burns.
Press Secretary.—Kori Hardin.
Federal Building, 317 First Street, Wausau, WI 54403 .... (715) 842–5606
District Representative.—Jerry Madison.

Counties: Ashland; Bayfield; Burnett; Chippewa (part); Clark (part); Douglas; Eau Claire (part); Iron; Lincoln; Marathon; Oneida (part); Polk (part); Portage; Price; Rusk; Sawyer; Taylor; Washburn; Wood. Population (1990), 543,529.

ZIP Codes: 54006, 54024 (part), 54401–02, 54405–07, 54408 (part), 54409 (part), 54410–12, 54413 (part), 54414 (part), 54415, 54417, 54419, 54421–23, 54425–26, 54427 (part), 54429, 54432–34, 54435 (part), 54443, 54447–49, 54451–55, 54457 (part), 54458–60, 54463 (part), 54466 (part), 54467, 54469–71, 54473–76, 54479–81, 54484, 54487–90, 54494, 54498, 54499 (part), 54501 (part), 54513–15, 54517, 54524–30, 54532, 54534, 54536–37, 54546 (part), 54547–50, 54552, 54555–56, 54559, 54563–65, 54702 (part), 54703 (part), 54724, 54726 (part), 54727 (part), 54729, 54731–32, 54739 (part), 54745, 54748, 54757 (part), 54766, 54768 (part), 54771 (part), 54801, 54806, 54813 (part), 54814, 54815, 54816–17, 54819–21, 54824 (part), 54825, 54827–28, 54829 (part), 54830, 54832, 54833, 54834–40, 54842–51, 54852, 54853–56, 54858–59, 54861–62, 54864–65, 54867, 54870–76, 54880, 54888, 54890–91, 54893–96, 54909 (part), 54921 (part)

* * *

EIGHTH DISTRICT

JAY JOHNSON, Democrat, of Green Bay, WI; born in Bessemer, MI, September 30, 1943; associate B.A., political science, Gogebic Community College, Ironwood, MI, 1963; B.A., speech, Northern Michigan University, Marquette, 1965; M.A., radio and television, Michigan State University, Lansing, 1970; private first class, information specialist, U.S. Army, 1966–68, broadcaster and journalist, 1964–96: television anchor/reporter, WFRV–TV (Channel 5), 1981–87, WLUK–TV (Channel 11) since 1987; past president, Family Violence Center, Green Bay; vice president for communications, United Way of Brown County; board of directors, Wisconsin United Way; advisory board, Libertas; state board, Easter Seals of Wisconsin; married the former JoLee Works, 1982; two stepchildren: Joanna Carlson, Chris Carlson; committees: Transportation and Infrastructure, Agriculture; subcommittees: Water Resources and the Environment; Coast Guard and Maritime Transportation; Livestock, Dairy, and Poultry; General Farm Commodities; elected to the 105th Congress on November 5, 1996.

Office Listings

http://www.house.gov/jayjohnson jay.johnson@mail.house.gov

1313 Longworth House Office Building, Washington, DC 20515 225–5665
Chief of Staff.—Karisa Johnson. FAX: 225–5729
Legislative Director.—George F. Shevlin IV.
Press Secretary.—Todd Sandman.
211 North Broadway Street, Suite 103, Green Bay, WI 54303 .... (414) 430–1776
300 North Woods Edge Drive, Suite 101, Appleton, WI 54914 .... (414) 731–7586
District Director.—Paul Willems.

Counties: Brown (part); Calumet (part); Door; Florence; Forest; Kewaunee; Langlade; Manitowoc (part); Marinette; Menominee; Oconto; Oneida (part); Outagamie (part); Shawano; Vilas. Population (1990), 543,404.

ZIP Codes: 49935 (part), 49936, 54101–04, 54106–08, 54110 (part), 54111–15, 54119–21, 54124–25, 54126 (part), 54127–28, 54130 (part), 54131, 54135–41, 54143, 54149–54, 54155 (part), 54156–57, 54159, 54161–62, 54164–66, 54170 (part), 54171–77, 54180, 54182, 54201–02, 54204–05, 54206 (part), 54208 (part), 54209–13, 54215 (part), 54216–17, 54226, 54229, 54231, 54234–35, 54246, 54300–08, 54324, 54408 (part), 54409 (part), 54414 (part), 54416, 54418,

54424, 54427 (part), 54428, 54430, 54435 (part), 54444–45, 54450, 54462, 54463 (part), 54464, 54465 (part), 54485, 54486 (part), 54491, 54499 (part), 54501 (part), 54511–12, 54516, 54519–21, 54531, 54538 (part), 54539–42, 54545, 54546 (part), 54554, 54557, 54558 (part), 54560–62, 54566–67, 54568 (part), 54911 (part), 54912–14, 54922 (part), 54928, 54931, 54940 (part), 54942, 54944, 54948, 54950 (part), 54951, 54956 (part), 54961 (part), 54969, 54978

* * *

NINTH DISTRICT

F. JAMES SENSENBRENNER, Jr., Republican, of Menomonee Falls, WI; born in Chicago, IL, June 14, 1943; graduated from Milwaukee Country Day School, 1961; A.B., Stanford University, 1965; J.D., University of Wisconsin Law School, 1968; admitted to the Wisconsin bar, 1968; commenced practice in Cedarburg, WI; admitted to practice before the U.S. Supreme Court in 1972; attorney; elected to the Wisconsin Assembly in 1968, reelected in 1970, 1972 and 1974; elected to Wisconsin Senate in a special election in 1975 and reelected in 1976, serving as assistant minority leader; staff member of former U.S. Congressman J. Arthur Younger of California in 1965; member: Waukesha County Republican Party, Wisconsin Bar Association, Riveredge Nature Center, Friends of Museum, and American Philatelic Society; married the former Cheryl Warren, 1977; two sons: Frank James III and Robert Alan; elected to the 96th Congress, November 7, 1978; reelected to each succeeding Congress.

Office Listings

http://www.house.gov/sensenbrenner sensen09@hr.house.gov

2332 Rayburn House Office Building, Washington, DC 20515–4909 225–5101
Administrative Assistant.—Todd R. Schultz.
Legislative Director.—Robert Cook.
Office Manager.—Arlene I. Davis.
Press Secretary.—Kathy Benz.
Room 154, 120 Bishops Way, Brookfield, WI 53005 .... (414) 784–1111
Home Secretary.—Tom Schreibel.

Counties: Dodge (part), Fond du Lac (part), Jefferson (part), Ozaukee, Sheboygan (part), Washington, Waukesha (part). Population (1990), 543,532.

ZIP Codes: 53002–09, 53010 (part), 53012–13, 53016–18, 53021–22, 53024, 53027, 53029, 53032–39, 53040 (part), 53044 (part), 53045–48, 53050–52, 53056, 53058–60, 53064, 53066, 53069, 53070 (part), 53072 (part), 53074–78, 53080–82, 53083 (part), 53085 (part), 53086, 53089, 53091–92, 53094–95, 53099, 53118, 53119 (part), 53122, 53127, 53137, 53153, 53156 (part), 53178, 53183, 53186 (part), 53188 (part), 53217 (part), 53224 (part), 53523 (part), 53538 (part), 53549, 53551, 53557, 53579, 53594 (part), 53916, 53922, 53963 (part)

WYOMING

(Population 1995, 480,000)

SENATORS

CRAIG THOMAS, Republican, of Casper, WY; born February 17, 1933 in Cody, WY; graduated from Cody High School; B.S., University of Wyoming, 1955; served in the U.S. Marine Corps, captain, 1955–59; small businessman; vice president, Wyoming Farm Bureau, 1960–66; American Farm Bureau, 1966–75; general manager, Wyoming Rural Electric Association, 1975–89; member: Wyoming House of Representatives, 1984–89; committees: Energy and Natural Resources, Environment and Public Works, Foreign Relations, Indian Affairs; subcommittees: chairman, Parks, Historic Preservation and Recreation; Transportation and Infrastructure; European Affairs; Forests and Public Land Management; Drinking Water, Fisheries and Wildlife; chairman, East Asian and Pacific Affairs; Near Eastern and South Asian Affairs; International Economic Policy, Export and Trade Promotion; married to Susan Thomas; four children: Peter, Paul, Lexi and Patrick; elected to the U.S. House of Representatives by special election, April 25, 1989 to fill the vacancy caused by the resignation of Dick Cheney; reelected to each succeeding Congress; elected to the U.S. Senate in November 1994 for the term beginning January 3, 1995.

Office Listings

http://www.senate.gov/~thomas craig@thomas.senate.gov

109 Hart Senate Office Building, Washington, DC 20510 224–6441
Chief of Staff.—Elizabeth Brimmer. FAX: 224–1724
Legislative Director.—Dan Naatz.
Press Secretary.—Dan Kunsman.
Administrative Director.—Stacy Robert.
2201 Federal Building, Casper, WY 82601 .... (307) 261–6413
State Director.—Bobbi Brown. FAX: 265–6706
2120 Capitol Avenue, Suite 2009, Cheyenne, WY 82009 .... (307) 772–2451
Field Representative.—Ruthann Norris. FAX: 638–3512
2632 Foothills Boulevard, Suite 101, Rock Springs, WY 82901 .... (307) 362–5012
Field Representative.—Pati Smith. FAX: 362–5129
325 West Main, Suite F, Riverton, WY 82501 .... (307) 856–6642
Field Representative.—Pam Buline. FAX: 856–5901
40 South Main Street, Suite 206, Sheridan, WY 82801 .... (307) 672–6456
Field Representative.—Jackie Van Mark. FAX: 672–8227

* * *

MICHAEL B. ENZI, Republican, of Gillette, WY; born in Bremerton, WA, February 1, 1944; B.S., accounting, George Washington University, 1966; M.B.A., Denver University, 1968; served in Wyoming National Guard, 1967–73; accounting manager and computer programmer, Dunbar Well Service, 1985–97; director, Black Hills Corporation, a New York stock exchange company, 1992–96; member, founding board of directors, First Wyoming Bank of Gillette, 1978–88; owner, with wife, of NZ Shoes; served in Wyoming House of Representatives, 1987–91, and in Wyoming State Senate, 1991–96; mayor of Gillette, 1975–82; commissioner, Western Interstate Commission for Higher Education, 1995–96; served on the Education Commission of the States, 1989–93; president, Wyoming Association of Municipalities, 1980–82; president, Wyoming Jaycees, 1973–74; member, Lions Club; elder, Presbyterian Church; Eagle Scout; married Diana Buckley in 1969; three children: Amy, Brad and Emily; committees: Banking, Housing and Urban Affairs; Labor and Human Resources; Small Business; Special Committee on Aging; elected to the U.S. Senate in November, 1996 for the six-year term beginning January 7, 1997.

Office Listings

http://www.senate.gov/~enzi senator@enzi.senate.gov

116 Hart Senate Office Building, Washington, DC 20510 224–3424
Chief of Staff.—George "Flip" McConnaughey.
Legislative Director.—Katherine Brunett-McGuire.
Press Secretary.—Coy Knobel.
Office Manager.—Evora Williams.
Federal Building, Suite 2007, Cheyenne, WY 82001 .... (307) 772–2477
FAX: 772–2480

510 South Gillette Avenue, Gillette, WY 82716	(307) 682–6268 FAX: 682–6501
Federal Center, Suite 3201, 100 East B Street, Casper, WY 82601	(307) 261–6572 FAX: 261–6574
1285 Sheridan Avenue, Suite 210, Cody, WY 82414	(307) 527–9444 FAX: 527–9476
545 West Broadway, Jackson, WY 83001	(307) 739–9507 FAX: 739–9520
P.O. Box 12470, Jackson, WY 83002	

REPRESENTATIVE

AT LARGE

BARBARA CUBIN, Republican, of Casper, WY; born November 30, 1946, in Cody, WY; graduated, Natrona County High School; B.S., Creighton University, 1969; manager, substitute teacher, social worker, chemist; member of Saint Stephen's Episcopal Church; founding member of the Casper Suicide Prevention League, Casper Service League; president, Southridge Elementary School Parent/Teacher Organization; Mercer House, president and executive member; Casper Self Help Center, board member; Seton House, board member; Central Wyoming Rescue Mission, volunteer cook and server, Wyoming State Choir and Casper Civic Chorale, Cub Scout leader, Sunday School teacher at Saint Stephen's Episcopal Church; past memberships: executive committee of the Energy Council; chairman, Center for Legislators Energy and Environment Research (CLEER); National Council of State Legislatures; vice chairman, Energy Committee; 1994 Edison Electric Institutes' Wyoming Legislator of the Year and Toll Fellowship from the Council of State Governments, 1990; Wyoming House of Representatives committees, 1987–92: Minerals, Business and Economic Development, Revenue, Transportation; chairperson, Joint Interim Economic Development Subcommittee; Wyoming Senate committees, 1993–94: Travel, Recreation, Wildlife, Cultural Resources, Revenue; Republican activities: chair, Wyoming Senate Conference, 1992–94; precinct committeewoman, 1988–94; legislative liaison and member, Natrona County Republican Women; 1992 Wyoming State Convention Parliamentarian; delegate, Wyoming State Convention, 1990, 1992 and 1994; State Legislative Candidate Recruitment Committee for the Wyoming Republican Party in 1988, 1990 and 1992; married to Frederick W. (Fritz) Cubin; two children: William (Bill) and Frederick III (Eric); elected to the 104th Congress; reelected to the 105th Congress; committees: Resources, Science; subcommittees: chair, Energy and Mineral Resources; ex officio chair, National Parks and Public Lands; Commerce subcommittees on Finance and Hazardous Materials, and Health and Environment.

Office Listings

1114 Longworth House Office Building, Washington, DC 20515	225–2311
Chief of Staff.—Patty McDonald.	FAX: 225–3057
Legislative Director.—Marian Marshal.	
Senior Legislative Assistants: Dave DuBose, Steve Rice.	
Press Secretary.—Tom Wiblemo.	
100 East B Street, Suite 4003, Casper, WY 82601	(307) 261–6595
District Representatives: Jackie King, Vivian Stokes.	FAX: 261–6597
2015 Federal Building, Cheyenne, WY 82001	(307) 772–2595
District Representative.—Elaine McCauley.	FAX: 772–2597
2515 Foothill Boulevard, Suite 204, Rock Springs, WY 82901	(307) 362–4095
District Representative.—Katia Legerski.	FAX: 362–4097
State Director.—Martha Phillips.	

Population (1990), 455,975

ZIP Codes: 59030 (part), 59311 (part), 69352 (part), 69358 (part), 82001, 82003, 82007, 82009, 82050–55, 82057, 82059–63, 82070–71, 82080–84, 82190, 82201, 82210, 82212–15, 82217–25, 82227–29, 82240, 82242–44, 82301, 82310, 82321–25, 82327, 82329, 82331–32, 82334–36, 82401, 82410–12, 82414, 82420–23, 82425–28, 82430, 82431 (part), 82432–35, 82440–43, 82450, 82501, 82510, 82512–16, 82520, 82523–24, 82601–02, 82604, 82609, 82615, 82620, 82630–31, 82633, 82635–40, 82642–44, 82648–49, 82701, 82710–16, 82720–21, 82723–25, 82727, 82729–32, 82801, 82831, 82832 (part), 82833–40, 82842, 82844–45, 82901–02, 82922–23, 82925–26, 82929–30, 82932–39, 82941–45, 83001, 83011–14, 83025, 83101, 83110–16, 83118–24, 83126–28

AMERICAN SAMOA

(Population 1995, 60,000)

DELEGATE

ENI F.H. FALEOMAVAEGA, Democrat, of Vailoatai Pago Pago, AS; graduate of Kahuku High School, Hawaii, 1962; B.A., Brigham Young University, 1966; J.D., University of Houston Law School, 1972; LL.M., University of California, Berkeley, 1973; enlisted in U.S. Army, 1966–69, Vietnam veteran; captain, USAR, Judge Advocate General Corps, 1982–92; adminstrative assistant to American Samoa's Delegate to Washington, 1973–75; staff counsel, Committee on Interior and Insular Affairs, 1975–81; deputy attorney general, American Samoa, 1981–84; elected Lieutenant Governor, American Samoa, 1984–89; member: Committee on Foreign Affairs, Committee on Resources, Congressional Human Rights Caucus, Congressional Travel and Tourism Caucus, Democratic Study Group, Congressional Arts Caucus, Congressional Hispanic Caucus; admitted to U.S. Supreme Court and American Samoa bars; member: National Conference of lieutenant governors, National Association of Secretaries of State, Veterans of Foreign Wars, Navy League of the United States, National American Indian Prayer Breakfast Group, Pago Pago Lions Club; married to Hinanui Bambridge Cave of Tahiti; five children; elected as the American Samoan Delegate to the 101st Congress, November 8, 1988; reelected to each succeeding Congress.

Office Listings

http://www.house.gov/faleomavaega

2422 Rayburn House Office Building, Washington, DC 20515–5201 225–8577
Executive Assistant/Office Manager.—Nancy Leong. FAX: 225–8757
Legislative Director.—Martin Yerick.
Administrative Assistant/Public Affairs Coordinator.—Ali'imau Scanlan.
P.O. Drawer X, Pago Pago, AS 96799 .... (684) 633–1372
FAX: 633–2680

ZIP Codes: 96799

* * *

DISTRICT OF COLUMBIA

DELEGATE

ELEANOR HOLMES NORTON, Democrat, of Washington, DC; born in Washington, DC, June 13, 1937; graduated from Dunbar High School, 1955; B.A., Antioch College, 1960; M.A., Yale Graduate School, 1963; J.D., Yale Law School, 1964; honorary degrees: Tougalvo University, 1992; University of Southern Connecticut, 1992; Fisk University, 1991; University of Hartford, 1990; Ohio Wesleyan University, 1990; Wake Forest University, 1990; Colgate University, 1989; Drury College, 1989; Florida International University, 1989; St. Lawrence University, 1989; University of Wisconsin, 1989; Rutgers University, 1988; St. Joseph's College, 1988; University of Lowell, 1988; Sojourner-Douglas College, 1987; Salem State College, 1987; Haverford College, 1986; Lesley College, 1986; New Haven University, 1986; University of San Diego, 1986; Bowdoin College, 1985; Antioch College, 1985; Tufts University, 1984; University of Massachusetts, 1983; Smith College, 1983; Medical College of Pennsylvania, 1983; Spelman College, 1982; Syracuse University, 1981; Yeshiva University, 1981; Lawrence University, 1981; Emanuel College, 1981; Wayne State University, 1980; Gallaudet College, 1980; Denison University, 1980; New York University, 1978; Howard University, 1978; Brown University, 1978; Wilberforce University, 1978; Georgetown University, 1977; City College of New York, 1975; Marymount College, 1974; Princeton University, 1973; Bard College, 1971; Cedar Crest College, 1969; chair, Equal Employment Opportunity Commission, 1977–81; professor of law, Georgetown University, 1982–90; chair, New York Commission on Human Rights, 1970–76; executive assistant to the mayor of New York City (concurrent appointment); law clerk, Judge A. Leon Higginbotham, Federal District Court, 3rd Circuit; attorney, admitted to practice by examination in the District of Columbia and Pennsylvania and in the U.S. Supreme Court; One Hundred Most Important Women (*Ladies Home Journal*, 1988); One Hundred Most Powerful Women in Washington (The *Washingtonian* magazine, September 1989); Ralph E. Shikes Bicentennial Fellow, Harvard Law School, 1987; Visiting Phi Beta Kappa Scholar, 1985; Visiting Fellow, Harvard University, John F. Kennedy School of Government, spring 1984; Distinguished Public Service Award, Center for National Policy, 1985; Chancellor's Distinguished Lecturer, University of California Law School (Boalt Hall) at Berkeley, 1981; Yale Law School Association Citation of Merit Medal to the Outstanding Alumnus of the Law School, 1980; Harper Fellow, Yale Law School, 1976, (for "a person . . . who has made a distinguished contribution to the public life of the nation . . ."); Rockefeller Foundation, trustee, 1982–90; Community Foundation of Greater Washington, board; Yale Corporation, 1982–88; Council on Foreign Relations; Overseas Development Council; U.S. Committee to Monitor the Helsinki accords; Carter Center, Atlanta, Georgia; boards of Martin Luther King, Jr. Center for Social Change and Environmental Law Institute; Workplace Health Fund; ranking minority member, Subcommittee on the District of Columbia, Government Reform and Oversight Committee; member, Water Resources and Environment Subcommittee, Public Buildings and Economic Development Subcommittee, Transportation and Infrastructure Committee; vice chair, Congressional Caucus for Women's Issues; divorced; two children: John and Katherine; elected to the 102nd Congress on November 6, 1990; reelected November 2, 1992 and November 8, 1994.

Office Listings

http://www.house.gov/norton

1424 Longworth House Office Building, Washington, DC 20515–5100 225–8050
Administrative Assistant/Press Secretary.—Donna Brazile. FAX: 225–3002
Legislative Director.—Brian Seward.
Executive Assistant.—Larry Hoster.

Population (1980): 606,000 (plus).

ZIP Codes: 20000–13, 20015–20, 20024, 20026, 20029–30, 20032–33, 20035–40, 20041 (part), 20042, 20044–53, 20055–60, 20062–71, 20073–76, 20080–82, 20084, 20088, 20090, 20097–98, 20201–31, 20233–35, 20239–42, 20244–45, 20250–51, 20260–61, 20265–66, 20268, 20305–07, 20310, 20314–15, 20317–19, 20324, 20330, 20332–38, 20350, 20360–63, 20370–76, 20380, 20388–89, 20391, 20401–16, 20418–25, 20427–31, 20433, 20435–36, 20439–42, 20444, 20451, 20453, 20456, 20460, 20463, 20468–70, 20472, 20500–07, 20510, 20515, 20520–21, 20523–27, 20530–44, 20546–55, 20557–60, 20565–66, 20570–73, 20575–81, 20585–86, 20590–91, 20593–95, 20597, 20599

* * *

GUAM

(Population 1996 est., 157,000)

DELEGATE

ROBERT A. UNDERWOOD, Democrat, of Yoña, GU; born in Tamuning, July 13, 1948; graduated from John F. Kennedy High School, 1965; B.A. (1969) and M.A. (1971), history, California State University; Ed.D., University of Southern California, 1987; administrator and curriculum writer in Guam public schools, 1972–76; retired as a full professor of education, University of Guam, 1992; director, bilingual education service center for Micronesia, dean of the College of Education and academic vice president; chair, Chamorro Language Commission, 1977–89; member: Guam Review Board for Historical Preservation; board member: Guam Council on the Humanities; married the former Lorraine Aguilar; five children: Sophia, Roberto, Ricardo, Ramon, and Raphael; elected to the U.S. House of Representatives on November 7, 1992; reelected to each succeeding Congress; committees: Resources, National Security.

Office Listings

http://www.house.gov/underwood guamtodc@hr.house.gov

424 Cannon House Office Building, Washington, DC 20515–5301 225–1188
Chief of Staff.—Terri Schroeder. FAX: 226–0341
Legislative Director.—John Whitt.
Office Manager.—Myat M. Khaing.
Press Secretary.—Keith Parsky.
Personal Secretary/Scheduler.—Angie Borja.
120 Father Duenas Avenue, Suite 107, Agana, GU 96910 .... (671) 477–4272
FAX: 477–2587

ZIP Codes: 96910–12, 96921, 96931–32

PUERTO RICO

(Population 1996 est., 3,819,000)

RESIDENT COMMISSIONER

CARLOS ROMERO-BARCELÓ, New Progressive Party, of San Juan, born on September 4, 1932 in Santurce; B.A., Yale University, 1953; LL.B., J.D., University of Puerto Rico, 1956; attorney; president, Citizens for State 51, 1965–67; mayor of San Juan, 1969–77; member, board of directors, U.S. Conference of Mayors and National League of Cities, 1976; president, National League of Cities, 1976; president, New Progressive Party, 1974–85 and 1989–92; elected Governor of Puerto Rico, 1977–85; chairman, Southern Governors Association, 1980–81; Senate of Puerto Rico, 1986–89; honorary degree, LL.D., University of Bridgeport, 1977; awards: Lifetime Achievement Award, *Hispanic Magazine*, 1993; U.S. Attorney General's Medal for Eminent Public Service, U.S. Department of Justice, 1981; Special Gold Medal Award, Achievements in Bilingual Education, Spanish Institute, New York, 1979; James J. and Jane Hoey Award for Interracial Justice, Catholic Interracial Council, New York, 1977; Outstanding Young Man of the Year, Jaycees, 1968; author, "Statehood Is for the Poor," New Progressive Party, 1978; author, article, "U.S.A.: The Case for Statehood," *Foreign Affairs*, 1980; married Kathleen R. Donnelly, 1966; four children: Carlos, Andrés, Juan Carlos, and Melinda; elected as a Democrat/New Progessive Party candidate on November 3, 1992 to the 103rd Congress; reelected to each succeeding Congress.

Office Listings

http://www.house.gov/romero-barcelo

428 Cannon House Office Building, Washington, DC 20515–5401	225–2615
Administrative Assistant.—Pedro Rivera-Casiano.	FAX: 225–2154
Legislative Director.—Marcia Schmitz.	225–5039
Legislative Assistant.—Luis Bacó.	225–5029
Office Manager.—Alba Bernart.	
P.O. Box 4751, Old San Juan, PR 00902	(809) 723–6333
P.O. Box 946, Ponce, PR 00731	(809) 841–3300

ZIP Codes: 00601–07, 00616–17, 00623–24, 00627, 00636–38, 00641, 00646–47, 00650–53, 00656, 00659–60, 00662–64, 00669–94, 00698, 00703–05, 00715, 00718–23, 00725–26, 00729–41, 00744–45, 00751, 00754, 00757, 00765–67, 00769, 00771–73, 00775–78, 00780–86, 00791–92, 00794–95, 00901–02, 00906–31, 00934–36, 00940, 00949–54, 00956–63, 00965–71, 00976–78

* * *

VIRGIN ISLANDS

(Population 1996 est., 97,000)

DELEGATE

DONNA CHRISTIAN–GREEN, Democrat, of St. Croix, VI; B.S., St. Mary's College, Notre Dame, IN, 1966; M.D., George Washington University School of Medicine, 1970; physician, family medicine; Acting Commissioner of Health, 1994–95; medical director, St. Croix Hospital, 1987–88; founding member and vice president, Virgin Islands Medical Institute; trustee, National Medical Association; past secretary and two-time past president, Virgin Islands Medical Society; founding member and trustee, Caribbean Youth Organization; member: Democratic National Committee, Virgin Islands Democratic Territorial Committee (past vice chair), Substance Abuse Coalition, St. Dunstan's Episcopal School Board of Directors, Caribbean Studies Association, Women's Coalition of St. Croix, St. Croix Environmental Association; past chair, Christian Education Committee, Friedensthal Moravian Church; past member: Virgin Islands Board of Education, Democratic Platform Committee; delegate to the 1984, 1988 and 1992 Democratic national conventions; cohost, Straight Up TV interview program, 1993; two daughters, Rabiah Layla and Karida Yasmeen; member, Congressional Black Caucus and Congressional Women's Caucus; committee: Resources; subcommittees: Energy and Mineral Resources, National Parks and Public Lands; elected to the 105th Congress.

Office Listings

1711 Longworth House Office Building, Washington, DC 20515–5501	225–1790
Administrative Assistant.—Lorraine Hill.	FAX: 225–5517
Legislative Director.—Brian Modeste.	
Press Secretary.—James O'Bryan, Jr.	
Executive Assistant/Appointments Secretary.—Monique Clendinen.	
Building 2, Bay 3, Vitraco Mall, St. Thomas, VI 00802	(809) 774–4408
Office Manager.—Steven Steele.	FAX: 778–8033
Space No. 3MM, Sunny Isle Shopping Center, St. Croix, VI 00820	(809) 778–5900
Staff Assistant.—Shelley Thomas.	FAX: 778–5111

Cities and townships: Charlotte Amalie, St. Thomas, Cruz Bay, St. John, Cristiansted, St. Croix, Frederiksted, St. Croix.

Zip Codes: 00801–04, 00820–24, 00830–31, 00840–41, 00850–51

ASSIGNMENTS OF SENATORS TO COMMITTEES

[Republicans in roman (55); Democrats in *italic* (45); total, 100]

Senator	Committees (Standing, Joint, Special, Select) and Subcommittees
Abraham	Budget. Commerce, Science and Transportation — Communications; Consumer Affairs, Foreign Commerce and Tourism; Science, Technology and Space; Surface Transportation and Merchant Marine; Manufacturing and Competitiveness. Judiciary — Constitution, Federalism and Property Rights; Immigration.
Akaka	Energy and Natural Resources —National Parks, Historic Preservation and Recreation; Water and Power. Govrnmental Affairs — International Security, Proliferation and Federal Services. Veterans' Affairs. Indian Affairs.
Allard	Banking, Housing and Urban Affairs — Financial Institutions and Regulatory Relief; Housing Opportunity and Community Development; Securities. Environment and Public Works — Clean Air, Wetlands, Private Property and Nuclear Safety; Superfund, Waste Control and Risk Assessment. Select Committee on Intelligence.
Ashcroft	Commerce, Science and Transportation — Aviation; Communications; Consumer Affairs, Foreign Commerce and Tourism; Manufacturing and Competitiveness; Surface Transportation and Merchant Marine. Foreign Relations — African Affairs; European Affairs; Near Eastern and South Asian Affairs. Judiciary — Constitution, Federalism and Property Rights; Youth Violence.
Baucus	Agriculture, Nutrition and Forestry — Marketing, Inspection and Product Promotion; Forestry, Conservation and Rural Revitalization. Environment and Public Works — Transportation and Infrastructure. Finance — Health Care; International Trade; Taxation and IRS Oversight. Select Committee on Intelligence. Joint Committee on Taxation.
Bennett	Appropriations — Energy and Water Development; Foreign Operations; Interior; Legislative Branch; Transportation. Banking, Housing and Urban Affairs — Financial Services and Technology; International Finance; Securities. Small Business. Joint Economic Committee.
Biden	Foreign Relations — European Affairs; International Economic Policy, Export and Trade Promotion. Judicary — Youth Violence; Technology, Terrorism and Government Information.
Bingaman	Armed Services — Acquisition and Technology; Airland Forces; Strategic Forces.

Senator	Committees (Standing, Joint, Special, Select) and Subcommittees
	Energy and Natural Resources — Energy Research and Development, Production and Regulation; National Parks, Historic Preservation and Recreation. Labor and Human Resources — Children and Families; Public Health and Safety. Joint Economic Committee.
Bond	Appropriations — Agriculture, Rural Development and Related Agencies; Defense; Labor, Health and Human Services, and Education; Transportation; VA, HUD and Independent Agencies. Budget. Environment and Public Works — Drinking Water, Fisheries and Wildlife; Transportation and Infrastructure. Small Business, *chairman*.
Boxer	Appropriations — District of Columbia; Interior; Legislative Branch; VA, HUD and Independent Agencies. Banking, Housing and Urban Affairs — Financial Institutions and Consumer Credit; International Finance; Financial Services and Technology. Budget. Environment and Public Works — Clean Air, Wetlands, Private Property and Nuclear Safety; Superfund, Waste Control and Risk Assessment; Transportation and Infrastructure.
Breaux	Commerce, Science and Transportation — Aviation; Communications; Oceans and Fisheries; Surface Transportation and Merchant Marine; Consumer Affairs, Foreign Commerce and Tourism. Finance — International Trade; Social Security and Family Policy; Taxation and IRS Oversight. Special Committee on Aging.
Brownback	Commerce, Science and Transportation — Aviation; Communications; Consumer Affairs, Foreign Commerce and Tourism; Manufacturing and Competitivness. Foreign Relations — International Operations; Near Eastern and South Asian Affairs; Western Hemisphere, Peace Corps, Narcotics and Terrorism. Governmental Affairs — Oversight of Government Management, Restructuring and the District of Columbia; Investigations. Joint Economic Committee.
Bryan	Banking, Housing and Urban Affairs — Financial Institutions and Regulatory Relief; Housing Opportunity and Community Development; Securities. Commerce, Science, and Transportation — Aviation; Consumer Affairs, Foreign Commerce and Tourism; Manufacturing and Competitiveness; Science, Technology and Space; Surface Transportation and Merchant Marine. Finance — Health Care; Long-Term Growth, Debt and Deficit Reduction; Taxation and IRS Oversight. Select Committee on Intelligence.
Bumpers	Appropriations — Agriculture, Rural Development and Related Agencies; Commerce, Justice, State and Judiciary; Defense; Interior, Labor, Health and Human Services, and Education. Energy and Natural Resources. Small Business.
Burns	Appropriations — Agriculture, Rural Development and Related Agencies; Energy and Water Development; Interior; Military Construction; VA, HUD and Independent Agencies. Commerce, Science and Transportation — Aviation; Communications; Consumer Affairs, Foreign Commerce and Tourism; Science, Technology and Space; Surface Transportation and Merchant Marine. Energy and Natural Resources — Forest and Public Land Management; National Parks, Historic Preservation and Recreation.

Senator	Committees (Standing, Joint, Special, Select) and Subcommittees
	Small Business. Special Committee on Aging.
Byrd	Appropriations — Defense; Energy and Water Development; Interior; Transportation; Agriculture, Rural Development and Related Agencies. Armed Services — Airland Forces; Strategic Forces; Seapower. Rules and Administration.
Campbell	Appropriations — Commerce, Justice, State and Judiciary; Foreign Operations; Interior; Treasury, Postal Service and General Government; VA, HUD and Independent Agencies. Energy and Natural Resources — Energy Research and Development Production and Regulation; National Parks, Historic Presrvation and Recreation; Water and Power. Veterans' Affairs. Indian Affairs, *chairman*.
Chafee	Environment and Public Works, *chairman*. Finance — Health Care; Social Security and Family Policy; International Trade. Select Committee on Intelligence. Joint Committee on Taxation.
Cleland	Armed Services — Airland Forces; Personnel; Readiness. Governmental Affairs — International Security; Proliferation and Federal Services; Oversight of Government Management, Restructuring and the District of Columbia; Investigations. Small Business.
Coats	Armed Services — Airland Forces; Personnel; Readiness. Labor and Human Resources — Children and Families; Public Health and Safety. Select Committee on Intelligence.
Cochran	Agriculture, Nutrition and Forestry — Marketing, Inspection and Product Promotion; Production and Price Competitiveness. Appropriations — Agriculture, Rural Development and Related Agencies; Defense; Energy and Water Development; Interior; Labor, Health and Human Services, and Education. Governmental Affairs — Investigations; International Security, Proliferation and Federal Services. Rules and Administration. Joint Committee on the Library. Joint Committee on Printing.
Collins	Governmental Affairs — International Security, Proliferation and Federal Services; Investigations. Labor and Human Resources — Children and Families; Public Health and Safety. Special Committee on Aging.
Conrad	Agriculture, Nutrition and Forestry — Forestry, Conservation and Rural Revitalization; Research, Nutrition and General Legislation. Budget. Finance — International Trade; Taxation and IRS Oversight; Health Care. Indian Affairs. Select Committee on Ethics.
Coverdell	Agriculture, Nutrition and Forestry — Forestry, Conservation and Rural Revitalization; Marketing, Inspection and Product Promotion. Foreign Affairs — East Asian and Pacific Affairs; International Economic Policy, Export and Trade Promotion; Western Hemisphere, Peace Corps, Narcotics and Terrorism. Small Business.
Craig	Agriculture, Nutrition and Forestry — Forestry, Conservation, and Rural Revitalization; Research, Nutrition and General Legislation.

Senator	Committees (Standing, Joint, Special, Select) and Subcommittees
	Appropriations — Energy and Water Development; Labor, Health and Human Services, and Education; Legislative Branch; Military Construction; VA, HUD and Independent Agencies. Energy and Natural Resources — Energy Research and Development; Forests and Public Land Management; Water and Power. Veterans' Affairs. Special Committee on Aging.
D'Amato	Banking, Housing and Urban Affairs, *chaiman.* Finance — International Trade; Taxation and IRS Oversight; Health Care.
Daschle	Agriculture, Nutrition and Forestry — Production and Price Competitiveness; Forestry, Conservation and Rural Revitalization.
DeWine	Judiciary — Antitrust, Business Rights and Competition; Youth Violence. Labor and Human Resources — Employment and Training; Public Health and Safety. Select Committee on Intelligence.
Dodd	Banking, Housing and Urban Affairs — Housing Opportunity and Community Development; Securities; Financial Institutions and Regulatory Relief. Foreign Relations — International Operations; European Affairs; Western Hemisphere, Peace Corps, Narcotics and Terrorism. Labor and Human Resources — Children and Families; Employment and Training. Rules and Administration.
Domenici	Appropriations — Commerce, Justice, State and Judiciary; Defense; Energy and Water Development; Interior; Transportation. Budget, *chairman.* Energy and Natural Resources — Energy Research and Development, Production and Regulation; Forests and Public Land Management. Governmental Affairs — International Security, Proliferation and Federal Services; Investigations. Indian Affairs.
Dorgan	Appropriations — Defense; Energy and Water Development; Interior; Legislative Branch. Commerce, Science and Transportation — Aviation; Science, Technology and Space; Surface Transportation and Merchant Marine; Communications; Manufacturing and Competitiveness. Energy and Natural Resources — Forests and Public Land Management; Water and Power. Indian Affairs.
Durbin	Budget. Governmental Affairs — International Security, Proliferation and Federal Services; Investigations. Judiciary — Administrative Oversight and the Courts; Immigration; Technology, Terrorism and Government Information.
Enzi	Banking, Housing and Urban Affairs — Financial Institutions and Regulatory Relief; Financial Services and Technology; Housing Opportunity and Community Development. Labor and Human Resources — Employment and Training; Public Health and Safety. Small Business. Special Committee on Aging.
Faircloth	Appropriations — Labor, Health and Human Services, and Education; Military Construction; Transportation; Treasury and General Government; District of Columbia. Banking, Housing and Urban Affairs — Financial Institutions and Regulatory Relief; Housing Opportunity and Community Development; Securities.

Senator	Committees (Standing, Joint, Special, Select) and Subcommittees
	Small Business.
Feingold	Budget. Foreign Relations — African Affairs; East Asian and Pacific Affairs. Judiciary — Administrative Oversight and the Courts; Constitution, Federalism and Property Rights. Special Committee on Aging.
Feinstein	Foreign Relations — East Asian and Pacific Affairs; Near Eastern and South Asian Affairs; International Operations. Judiciary — Immigration; Terrorism, Technology and Government Information; Youth Violence. Rules and Administration. Joint Committee on the Library.
Ford	Commerce, Science and Transportation — Aviation; Communications; Consumer Affairs, Foreign Commerce and Tourism. Energy and Natural Resources — Energy Research and Development, Production and Regulation; Water and Power. Rules and Administration. Joint Committee on Printing.
Frist	Budget. Commerce, Science and Transportation — Aviation; Communications; Manufacturing and Competitiveness; Surface Transportation and Merchant Marine; Science, Technology and Space. Labor and Human Resources — Children and Families; Public Health and Safety. Foreign Relations — African Affairs; East Asian and Pacific Affairs; International Economic Policy, Export and Trade Promotion. Small Business.
Glenn	Armed Services — Airland Forces; Readiness; Strategic Forces. Governmental Affairs — Investigations. Special Committee on Aging. Select Committee on Intelligence.
Gorton	Appropriations — Agriculture, Rural Development and Related Agencies; Energy and Water Development; Interior; Labor, Health and Human Services, and Education; Transportation. Budget. Commerce, Science and Tranportation — Aviation; Communications; Consumer Affairs, Foreign Commerce and Tourism; Oceans and Fisheries. Energy and Natural Resources — Energy Research and Development, Production and Regulation; Water and Power. Indian Affairs.
Graham	Energy and Natural Resources — Energy Research and Development, Production and Regulation; Forests and Public Land Management; National Parks, Historic Preservation and Recreation. Environment and Public Works — Clean Air, Wetlands, Private Property and Nuclear Safety; Transportation and Infrastructure; Superfund, Waste Control and Risk Assessment. Finance — International Trade; Long-Term Growth, Debt and Deficit Reduction; Health Care. Veterans' Affairs. Select Committee on Intelligence.
Gramm	Agriculture, Nutrition and Forestry — Production and Price Competitions; Research, Nutrition and General Legislation. Finance — Health Care; International Trade; Social Security and Family Policy.

Senator	Committees (Standing, Joint, Special, Select) and Subcommittees
	Banking, Housing and Urban Affairs — Financial Institutions and Regulatory Relief; Securities; International Finance. Budget.
Grams	Banking, Housing and Urban Affairs — Financial Institutions and Regulatory Relief; Financial Services and Technology; International Finance. Budget. Energy and Natural Resources — Energy Research and Development, Production and Regulation; National Parks, Historic Preservation and Recreation. Foreign Relations — African Affairs; Near Eastern and South Asian Affairs; International Operations. Joint Economic Committee.
Grassley	Agriculture, Nutrition and Forestry — Forestry, Conservation and Rural Revitalization; Production and Price Competitiveness. Budget. Finance — International Trade; Health Care; Taxation and IRS Oversight. Judiciary — Administrative Oversight and the Courts; Immigration; Youth Violence. Special Committtee on Aging, *chairman*. Joint Committee on Taxation.
Gregg	Appropriations — Commerce, Justice, State and Judiciary; Defense; Foreign Operations; Labor, Health and Human Services, and Education; Interior. Budget. Labor and Human Resources — Aging; Children and Families.
Hagel	Banking, Housing and Urban Affairs — Financial Services and Technology; Housing Opportunity and Community Development; International Finance. Foreign Relations — East Asian and Pacific Affairs; European Affairs; International Economic Policy, Export and Trade Promotion. Special Committee on Aging.
Harkin	Agriculture, Nutrition and Forestry. Appropriations — Agriculture, Rural Development and Related Agencies; Defense; Foreign Operations; Labor, Health and Human Services, and Education; VA, HUD and Independent Agencies. Labor and Human Resources — Public Health and Safety; Employment and Training. Small Business.
Hatch	Finance — Health Care; International Trade; Taxation and IRS Oversight. Judiciary, *chairman* — Antitrust, Business Rights, and Competition; Constitution, Federalism and Property Rights; Technology, Terrorism and Government Information. Indian Affairs. Select Committee on Intelligence.
Helms	Agriculture, Nutrition, and Forestry — Marketing, Inspection and Product Promotion; Production and Price Competitiveness. Foreign Relations, *chairman* — International Operations; Western Hemisphere, Peace Corps, Narcotics and Terrorism; Near Eastern and South Asian Affairs. Rules and Administration.
Hollings	Appropriations — Commerce, Justice, State and Judiciary; Defense; Energy and Water Development; Interior; Labor, Health and Human Services, and Education. Budget. Commerce, Science and Transportation — Communications; Aviation; Manufacturing and Competitiveness.

Senator	Committees (Standing, Joint, Special, Select) and Subcommittees
Hutchinson	Environment and Public Works — Clean Air, Wetlands, Private Property and Nuclear Safety; Drinking Water, Fisheries and Wildlife. Labor and Human Resources — Aging; Children and Families. Veterans Affairs.
Hutchison	Appropriations — Commerce, Justice, State and Judiciary; Defense; District of Columbia; Labor, Health and Human Services, and Education; Military Construction. Commerce, Science and Transportation —Aviation; Science, Technology and Space; Communications; Surface Transportation and Merchant Marine; Oceans and Fisheries. Rules and Administration.
Inhofe	Armed Services — Airland Forces; Readiness; Strategic Forces. Environment and Public Works — Clean Air, Wetlands, Private Property and Nuclear Safety; Superfund, Waste Control and Risk Assessment; Transportation and Infrastructure. Indian Affairs. Select Committee on Intelligence.
Inouye	Appropriations — Commerce, Justice, State and Judiciary; Defense; Foreign Operations; Labor, Health and Human Services, and Education; Military Construction. Commerce, Science and Transportation — Aviation; Communications; Oceans and Fisheries; Surface Transportation and Merchant Marine. Rules and Administration. Indian Affairs. Joint Committee on Printing.
Jeffords	Labor and Human Resources, *chairman* — Employment and Training; Public Health and Safety. Finance — Health Care; Social Security and Family Policy; Taxation and IRS Oversight. Veterans' Affairs. Special Committee on Aging.
Johnson	Agriculture, Nutrition and Forestry — Production and Price Competitiveness; Research, Nutrition and General Legislation. Banking, Housing and Urban Affairs — Financial Institutions and Regulatory Relief; Financial Services and Technology; Securities. Budget. Energy and Natural Resources — Energy Research and Development, Production and Regulation; Forests and Public Land Management.
Kempthorne	Armed Services — Airland Forces; Strategic Forces; Personnel. Environment and Public Works — Drinking Water, Fisheries and Wildlife; Transportation and Infrastructure. Small Business.
Kennedy	Armed Services — Acquisition and Technology; Personnel; Seapower Judiciary — Constitution, Federalism and Property Rights; Immigration. Labor and Human Resources — Employment and Training; Public Health and Safety. Joint Economic Committee.
Kerrey	Agriculture, Nutrition and Forestry — Marketing, Inspection, and Production Promotion; Production and Price Competitiveness. Finance — Health Care; International Trade; Taxation and IRS Oversight. Select Committee on Intelligence.
Kerry	Banking, Housing and Urban Affairs — Financial Services and Technology; Housing Opportunity and Community Development; Securities.

Senator	Committees (Standing, Joint, Special, Select) and Subcommittees
	Commerce, Science and Transportation — Communications; Oceans and Fisheries; Science, Technology and Space. Foreign Relations — East Asian and Pacific Affairs; International Operations; Western Hemisphere, Peace Corps, Narcotics and Terrorism. Small Business. Select Committee on Intelligence.
Kohl	Appropriations — Agriculture, Rural Development and Related Agencies; Energy and Water Development; Labor, Health and Human Services, and Education; Transportation; Treasury and General Government. Judiciary — Administrative Oversight and the Courts; Youth Violence; Antitrust, Business Rights and Competition. Special Committee on Aging.
Kyl	Energy and Natural Resources — Forests and Public Land Management; Water and Power. Judiciary — Administrative Oversight and the Courts; Immigration; Technology, Terrorism and Government Information. Select Committee on Intelligence.
Landrieu	Agriculture, Nutrition and Forestry — Marketing, Inspection and Product Promotion; Production and Price Competitiveness. Energy and Natural Resources — Energy Research and Development, Production and Regulation; Forests and Public Land Management; National Parks, Historic Preservation and Recreation. Small Business.
Lautenberg	Appropriations — Commerce, Justice, State and Judiciary; Defense; Foreign Operations; Transportation; VA, HUD and Independent Agencies. Budget. Environment and Public Works — Drinking Water, Fisheries and Wildlife; Superfund, Waste Control and Risk Assessment. Select Committee on Intelligence.
Leahy	Agriculture, Nutrition, and Forestry — Research, Nutrition and General Legislation; Forestry, Conservation and Rural Revitalization. Appropriations — Agriculture, Rural Development and Related Agencies; Defense; Foreign Operations; Interior; VA, HUD and Independent Agencies. Judiciary — Antitrust, Business Rights and Competition.
Levin	Armed Services — Acquisition and Technology; Airland Forces; Strategic Forces. Governmental Affairs — International Security, Proliferation and Federal Services; Investigations. Small Business. Select Committee on Intelligence.
Lieberman	Armed Services — Airland Forces; Acquisition and Technology. Environment and Public Works — Clean Air, Wetlands, Private Property and Nuclear Safety; Drinking Water, Fisheries and Wildlife. Governmental Affairs — Oversight of Government Management, Restructuring and the District of Columbia; Investigations. Small Business.
Lott	Commerce, Science and Transportation — Aviation; Communications. Finance — International Trade; Long-Term Growth, Debt and Deficit Reduction; Taxation and IRS Oversight. Rules and Administration.
Lugar	Agriculture, Nutrition, and Forestry, *chairman*. Foreign Relations — East Asian and Pacific Affairs; European Affairs; Western Hemisphere, Narcotics and Terrorism. Select Committee on Intelligence.

Senator	Committees (Standing, Joint, Special, Select) and Subcommittees
Mack	Banking, Housing, and Urban Affairs — Financial Institutions and Regulatory Relief; Housing Opportunity and Community Development; Financial Services and Technology. Finance — International Trade; Long-Term Growth, Debt and Deficit Reduction; Taxation and IRS Oversight. Joint Economic Committee.
McCain	Armed Services — Personnel; Readiness; Seapower. Commerce, Science and Transportation, *chairman*. Indian Affairs.
McConnell	Agriculture, Nutrition and Forestry — Marketing, Inspection, and Product Promotion; Research, Nutrition and General Legislation. Appropriations — Agriculture, Rural Development and Related Agencies; Commerce, Justice, State and Judiciary; Defense; Energy and Water Development; Foreign Operations. Labor and Human Resources — Children and Families; Employment and Training. Rules and Administration. Joint Committee on Printing.
Mikulski	Appropriations — Commerce, Justice, State and Judiciary; Foreign Operations; Transportation; Treasury and General Government; VA, HUD and Independent Agencies. Labor and Human Resources — Aging; Public Health and Safety.
Moseley-Braun	Banking, Housing, and Urban Affairs — Financial Institutions and Regulatory Relief; Housing Opportunity and Community Development; International Finance. Finance — International Trade; Social Security and Family Policy; Health Care. Special Committee on Aging.
Moynihan	Environment and Public Works — Superfund, Waste Control, and Risk Assessment; Transportation and Infrastructure. Finance — International Trade; Social Security and Family Policy; Taxation and IRS Oversight. Rules and Administration. Joint Committee on the Library. Joint Committtee on Taxation.
Murkowski	Energy and Natural Resources, *chairman*. Finance — International Trade; Long-Term Growth, Debt and Deficit Reduction; Taxation and IRS Oversight. Veteran's Affairs. Indian Affairs.
Murray	Appropriations — Energy and Water Development; Foreign Operations; Military Construction; Transportation; Labor, Health and Human Services, and Education. Budget. Labor and Human Resources — Aging; Children and Families. Veterans' Affairs. Select Committee on Ethics.
Nickles	Budget. Energy and Natural Resources — Energy Research and Development, Production and Regulation; National Parks, Historic Preservation and Recreation. Finance — Social Security and Family Policy; Taxation and IRS Oversight; Health Care. Governmental Affairs — International Security, Proliferation and Federal Services; Investigations. Rules and Administration.
Reed	Banking, Housing and Urban Affairs — Financial Institutions and Regulatory Relief; Housing Opportunity and Community Development; International Finance. Labor and Human Resources — Children and Families; Public Health and Safety.

Senator	Committees (Standing, Joint, Special, Select) and Subcommittees
	Special Committee on Aging.
Reid	Appropriations — Energy and Water Development; Interior; Labor, Health and Human Services, and Education; Military Construction; Transportation. Environment and Public Works — Drinking Water, Fisheries and Wildlife; Transportation and Infrastructure. Special Committee on Aging. Select Committee on Ethics. Indian Affairs.
Robb	Armed Services — Personnel; Readiness; Seapower. Foreign Relations — East Asian and Pacific Affairs; Near Eastern and South Asian Affairs; Western Hemisphere, Peace Corps, Narcotics and Terrorism. Select Committee on Intelligence. Joint Economic Committee.
Roberts	Agriculture, Nutrition and Forestry — Forestry, Conservation and Rural Revitalization; Production and Price Competitiveness. Armed Services — Acquisition and Technology; Airland Forces; Readiness. Select Committee on Ethics. Select Committee on Intelligence.
Rockefeller	Commerce, Science and Transportation — Aviation; Communications; Manufacturing and Competitiveness; Science, Technology and Space. Finance — International Trade; Health Care; Social Security and Family Policy. Veterans' Affairs.
Roth	Finance, *chairman* — International Trade; Health Care; Taxation and IRS Oversight. Governmental Affairs — Investigations; Oversight of Government Management, Restructuring and the District of Columbia. Joint Economic Committee. Joint Committee on Taxation.
Santorum	Agriculture, Nutrition and Forestry — Forestry, Conservation and Rural Revitalization; Research, Nutrition and General Legislation. Armed Services — Airland Forces; Personnel; Seapower; Acquisition and Technology. Rules and Administration. Special Committee on Aging.
Sarbanes	Banking, Housing and Urban Affairs. Budget. Foreign Relations — African Affairs; European Affairs; International Economic Policy, Export and Trade Promotion; Near Eastern and South Asian Affairs. Joint Economic Committee.
Sessions	Environment and Public Works — Clean Air, Wetlands, Private Property and Nuclear Safety: Superfund, Waste Control and Risk Assessment. Judiciary — Administrative Oversight and the Courts; Youth Violence. Select Committee on Ethics. Joint Economic Committee.
Shelby	Appropriations — Defense; Foreign Operations; Transportation; Treasury and General Government; VA, HUD and Independent Agencies. Banking, Housing and Urban Affairs — Financial Institutions and Regulatory Relief; Housing Opportunity and Community Development; Securities. Special Committee on Aging. Select Committee on Intelligence.

Senator	Committees (Standing, Joint, Special, Select) and Subcommittees
Smith, B.	Armed Services — Acquisition and Technology; Seapower, Strategic Forces. Environment and Public Works — Superfund, Waste Control and Risk Assessment; Transportation and Infrastructure. Select Committee on Ethics, *chairman.*
Smith, G.	Budget. Energy and Natural Resources — Energy Research and Development, Production and Regulation; Forests and Public Land Management; Water and Power. Foreign Relations — European Affairs; International Operations; Near Eastern and South Asian Affairs.
Snowe	Armed Services — Acquisition and Technology; Personnel; Seapower. Budget. Commerce, Science and Transportation — Aviation; Manufacturing and Competitiveness; Oceans and Fisheries; Surface Transportation and Merchant Marine. Small Business.
Specter	Appropriations — Agriculture, Rural Development and Related Agencies; Defense; Foreign Operations; Labor, Health and Human Services, and Education; Transportation. Governmental Affairs — International Security, Proliferation and Federal Services; Oversight of Government Management, Restructuring and the District of Columbia; Investigations. Judiciary — Antitrust, Business Right and Competition; Immigration; Technology, Terrorism, and Government Information. Veterans' Affairs, *chairman.*
Stevens	Appropriations, *chairman.* — Commerce, Justice, State and Judiciary; Defense; Foreign Operations; Interior; Legislative Branch; VA, HUD and Independent Agencies. Commerce, Science and Transportation — Aviation; Communications; Oceans and Fisheries; Science, Technology and Space; Surface Transportation and Merchant Marine. Governmental Affairs — International Security, Proliferation and Federal Services; Investigations. Rules and Administration. Joint Committee on the Library.
Thomas	Energy and Natural Resources — Forests and Public Land Management, National Parks, Historic Preservation and Recreation. Environment and Public Works — Drinking Water, Fisheries and Wildlife; Transportation and Infrastructure. Foreign Relations — East Asian and Pacific Affairs; International Economic Policy, Export and Trade Promotion; European Affairs. Indian Affairs.
Thompson	Governmental Affairs, *chairman.* Judiciary — Constitution, Federalism and Property Rights; Technology, Terrorism and Government Information; Youth Violence.
Thurmond	Armed Services, *chairman.* Judiciary — Administrative Oversight and the Courts; Antitrust, Business Rights and Competition; Constitution, Federalism and Property Rights. Veterans' Affairs.
Torricelli	Governmental Affairs — International Security, Proliferation and Federal Services; Investigations. Judiciary — Antitrust, Business Rights and Competition; Constitution, Federation and Property Rights; Youth Violence. Rules and Administration.

Senator	Committees (Standing, Joint, Special, Select) and Subcommittees
Warner	Armed Services — Airland Forces; Seapower; Strategic Forces. Environment and Public Works — Drinking Water, Fisheries and Wildlife; Superfund, Waste Control and Risk Assessment; Transportation and Infrastructure. Labor and Human Resources — Aging; Employment and Training. Rules and Administration, *chairman.* Small Business. Special Committee on Aging. Joint Committee on the Library. Joint Committee on Printing, *chairman.*
Wellstone	Labor and Human Resources — Children and Families; Employment and Training. Small Business. Foreign Relations — European Affairs; International Economic Policy, Export and Trade Promotion; Near Eastern and South Asian Affairs. Veterans' Affairs. Indian Affairs.
Wyden	Budget. Commerce, Science and Transportation — Aviation; Communications; Surface Transportation and Merchant Marine. Environment and Public Works — Drinking Water, Fisheries and Wildlife. Energy and Natural Resources — Energy Research and Development, Production and Regulation; Forests and Public Land Management; Water and Power. Special Committee on Aging.

ASSIGNMENTS OF REPRESENTATIVES TO COMMITTEES

[Republicans in roman (228); Democrats in *italic* (206); Independent in **bold** (1); total, 435]

Representative	Committees (Standing, Joint, Special, Select) — Subcommittees
Abercrombie	National Security — Military Installations and Facilities; Military Research and Development. Resources — Fisheries Conservation, Wildlife and Oceans.
Ackerman	Banking and Financial Services — Financial Institutions and Consumer Credit; Capital Markets, Securities and Government Sponsored Enterprises. International Relations — International Operations and Human Rights; The Western Hemisphere.
Aderholt	Appropriations — District of Columbia; Transportation; Treasury, Postal Service and General Government.
Allen	National Security — Military Procurement; Military Research and Development. Government Reform and Oversight — District of Columbia; Human Resources.
Andrews	Education and the Workforce — Workforce Protections; Postsecondary Education, Training and Life-Long Learning. International Relations — Asia and the Pacific; The Western Hemisphere.
Archer	Ways and Means. Joint Committee on Taxation.
Armey	Office of the Majority Leader.
Bachus	Banking and Financial Services — General Oversight and Investigations; Capital Markets, Securities and Government Sponsored Enterprises. Veterans' Affairs — Health. Transportation and Infrastructure — Railroads; Surface Transportation.
Baesler	Agriculture — Risk Management and Specialty Crops; Forestry, Resource Conservation and Research. Budget.
Baker	Banking and Financial Services — Housing and Community Opportunity; Capital Markets, Securities and Government Sponsored Enterprises. Transportation and Infrastructure — Water Resources and Environment; Surface Transportation.
Baldacci	Agriculture — Forestry, Resource Conservation and Research; Risk Management and Specialty Crops. Small Business — Tax, Finance and Exports.
Ballenger	Education and the Workforce — Workforce Protections; Employer-Employee Relations. International Relations — The Western Hemisphere; International Operations and Human Rights.
Barcia	Transportation and Infrastructure — Water Resources and Environment; Surface Transportation. Science — Basic Research; Technology.
Barr	Banking and Financial Services — Domestic and International Monetary Policy; Financial Institutions and Consumer Credit. Judiciary — Crime; The Constitution.

Representative	Committees (Standing, Joint, Special, Select) — Subcommittees
	Government Reform and Oversight — National Economic Growth, Natural Resources and Regulatory Affairs; National Security, International Affairs and Criminal Justice.
Barrett, B. of Nebraska	Agriculture — General Farm Commodities; Forestry, Resource Conservation, and Research. Education and the Workforce — Workforce Protections; Postsecondary Education, Training and Life-Long Learning.
Barrett, T. of Wisconsin	Banking and Financial Services — Financial Institutions and Consumer Credit; Capital Markets, Securities and Government Sponsored Enterprises. Government Reform and Oversight — Human Resources; National Security, International Affairs and Criminal Justice.
Bartlett	National Security — Military Personnel; Military Research and Development. Science — Space and Aeronautics; Technology. Small Business — Government Programs and Oversight.
Barton	Science — Basic Research; Space and Aeronautics. Commerce — Oversight and Investigations; Health and Environment; Telecommunications, Trade and Consumer Protection.
Bass	Budget — Transportation and Infrastructure; Aviation; Surface Transportation. Permanent Select Committee on Intelligence — Human Intelligence, Analysis and Counterintelligence.
Bateman	National Security — Military Readiness; Military Research and Development. Transportation and Infrastructure — Surface Transportation; Water Resources and Environment.
Becerra	Ways and Means — Health; Social Security.
Bentsen	Banking and Financial Services — Financial Institutions and Consumer Credit; Domestic and International Monetary Policy. Budget.
Bereuter	Banking and Financial Services — Financial Institutions and Consumer Credit; Housing and Community Opportunity. International Relations — Asia and the Pacific; International Economic Policy and Trade.
Berman	Judiciary — Courts and Intellectual Property; Immigration and Claims. International Relations — Asia and the Pacific. Standards of Official Conduct.
Berry	Agriculture — Forestry, Resource Conservation and Research; Department Operations, Nutrition and Foreign Agriculture. Small Business.
Bilbray	Commerce — Finance and Hazardous Materials; Health and Environment; Oversight and Investigations.
Bilirakis	Commerce — Health and Environment; Energy and Power. Veterans' Affairs — Health.
Bishop	Agriculture — Risk Management and Specialty Crops; Department Operations, Nutrition and Foreign Agriculture. Permanent Select Committee on Intelligence — Human Intelligence, Analysis and Counterintelligence.
Blagojevich	Government Reform and Oversight — Government Management, Information and Technology; National Security, International Affairs and Criminal Justice. National Security — Military Procurement; Military Research and Development.
Bliley	Commerce.

Representative	Committees (Standing, Joint, Special, Select) — Subcommittees
Blumenauer	Transportation and Infrastructure — Railroads; Water Resources and Environment.
Blunt	Agriculture — Livestock, Dairy and Poultry. International Relations — The Western Hemisphere; International Economic Policy and Trade. Transportation and Infrastructure — Aviation.
Boehlert	Transportation and Infrastructure — Water Resources and Environment; Railroads. Science — Basic Research. Permanent Select Committee on Intelligence — Technical and Tactical Intelligence.
Boehner	Agriculture — General Farm Commodities; Livestock, Dairy and Poultry. House Oversight.
Bonilla	Appropriations — Agriculture, Rural Development, Food and Drug Administration and Related Agencies; Labor, Health and Human Services and Education; National Security.
Bonior	Office of the Democratic Whip.
Bono	Judiciary — Courts and Intellectual Property; Immigration and Claims. National Security — Military Personnel; Military Procurement.
Borski	Transportation and Infrastructure — Water Resources and Environment; Railroads.
Boswell	Transportation and Infrastructure — Aviation; Water Resources and Environment. Agriculture — Risk Management and Specialty Crops; Livestock, Dairy and Poultry.
Boucher	Commerce — Telecommunications, Trade and Consumer Protection; Energy and Power. Judiciary — Courts and Intellectual Property.
Boyd	National Security — Military Installations and Facilities; Military Procurement. Small Business — Government Programs and Oversight; Regulatory Reform and Paperwork Reduction.
Brady	Resources — Energy and Mineral Resources. Science — Space and Aeronautics; Technology. International Relations — International Economic Policy and Trade; The Western Hemisphere.
Brown, C. of Florida	Transportation and Infrastructure — Surface Transportation; Aviation. Veterans' Affairs — Health.
Brown, G. of California	Agriculture — Department Operations, Nutrition and Foreign Agriculture; Forestry, Resource Conservation and Research. Science.
Brown, S. of Ohio	Commerce — Health and Environment; Energy and Power. International Relations — Asia and the Pacific.
Bryant	Agriculture — Risk Management and Specialty Crops. Judiciary — Immigration and Claims; The Constitution; Commercial and Administrative Law.
Bunning	Budget. Ways and Means — Social Security.
Burr	Commerce — Energy and Power; Health and Environment; Oversight and Investigations.
Burton	International Relations — The Western Hemisphere; International Operations and Human Rights. Government Reform and Oversight.

Representative	Committees (Standing, Joint, Special, Select) — Subcommittees
Buyer	National Security — Military Personnel; Military Installations and Facilities. Judiciary — Crime. Veterans' Affairs — Oversight and Investigations.
Callahan	Appropriations — Foreign Operations, Export Financing and Related Programs; Transportation; Energy and Water Development.
Calvert	Science — Space and Aeronautics; Energy and Environment. Resources — Energy and Mineral Resources; Water and Power.
Camp	Ways and Means — Trade; Human Resources.
Campbell	Banking and Financial Services — Financial Institutions and Consumer Credit; Capital Markets, Securities and Government Sponsored Enterprises. International Relations — Africa; International Economic Policy and Trade.
Canady	Agriculture — Department Operations, Nutrition and Foreign Agriculture. Judiciary — The Constitution; Courts and Intellectual Property.
Cannon	Judiciary — Courts and Intellectual Property; Immigration and Claims. Resources — Water and Power; Energy and Mineral Resources. Committee on Science — Space and Aeronautics; Technology.
Capps	International Relations — Asia and the Pacific; The Western Hemisphere. Science — Basic Research; Space and Aeronautics.
Cardin	Ways and Means — Health. Budget.
Carson	Banking and Financial Services — Housing and Community Opportunity. Veterans' Affairs — Health.
Castle	Banking and Financial Services — Domestic and International Monetary Policy; Housing and Community Opportunity. Education and the Workforce — Early Childhood, Youth and Families; Postsecondary Education, Training and Life-Long Learning. Permanent Select Committee on Intelligence — Human Intelligence, Analysis and Counterintelligence.
Chabot	Judiciary — Commercial and Administrative Law; Crime. International Relations — International Economic Policy and Trade; Africa. Small Business — Empowerment.
Chambliss	Agriculture — General Farm Commodities; Risk Management and Specialty Crops; Forestry, Resource Conservation and Research. National Security — Military Readiness; Military Research and Development.
Chenoweth	Agriculture — Forestry, Resource Conservation and Research. Resources — National Parks and Public Lands; Water and Power; Forests and Forest Health. Veterans' Affairs — Health.
Christensen	Ways and Means — Health; Social Security.
Christian-Green	Resources — National Parks and Public Lands; Energy and Mineral Resources.
Clay	Education and the Workforce.
Clayton	Agriculture — Forestry, Resource Conservation, and Research; Department Operations, Nutrition and Foreign Agriculture. Budget.

Representative	Committees (Standing, Joint, Special, Select) — Subcommittees
Clement	Transportation and Infrastructure — Railroads; Coast Guard and Maritime Transportation. International Relations — International Economic Policy and Trade.
Clyburn	Transportation and Infrastructure — Surface Transportation; Aviation. Veterans' Affairs — Oversight and Investigations.
Coble	Judiciary — Courts and Intellectual Property; Crime. Transportation and Infrastructure — Coast Guard and Maritime Transportation; Surface Transportation.
Coburn	Commerce — Energy and Power; Health and Environment; Oversight and Investigations. Science — Energy and Environment.
Collins	Ways and Means — Human Resources; Social Security.
Combest	Agriculture — General Farm Commodities; Risk Management and Specialty Crops; Forestry, Resource Conservation and Research. Small Business — Regulatory Reform and Paperwork Reduction.
Condit	Agriculture — Risk Management and Specialty Crops; Livestock, Dairy and Poultry. Government Reform and Oversight — National Economic Growth, Natural Resources and Regulatory Affairs; National Security, International Affairs and Criminal Justice.
Conyers	Judiciary — Courts and Intellectual Property; The Constitution.
Cook	Banking and Financial Services — Capital Markets, Securities and Government Sponsored Enterprises; Housing and Community Opportunity. Science — Space and Aeronautics; Technology. Transportation and Infrastructure — Aviation; Surface Transportation.
Cooksey	Agriculture — Forestry, Resource Conservation and Research; General Farm Commodities. Transportation and Infrastructure — Aviation; Public Buildings and Economic Development. Veterans' Affairs — Health.
Costello	Transportation and Infrastructure — Aviation; Surface Transportation. Budget.
Cox	Commerce — Oversight and Investigations; Telecommunications, Trade and Consumer Protection. Government Reform and Oversight — Civil Service.
Coyne	Ways and Means — Human Resources; Oversight.
Cramer	Transportation and Infrastructure — Surface Transportation; Aviation. Science — Space and Aeronautics.
Crane	Ways and Means — Trade; Health. Joint Committee on Taxation.
Crapo	Commerce — Finance and Hazardous Materials; Energy and Power; Oversight and Investigations. Resources — Fisheries Conservation, Wildlife and Oceans; Water and Power.
Cubin	Resources — Energy and Mineral Resources. Commerce — Finance and Hazardous Materials; Health and Environment.
Cummings	Government Reform and Oversight — Civil Service; National Security, International Affairs and Criminal Justice. Transportation and Infrastructure — Aviation; Surface Transportation.

Representative	Committees (Standing, Joint, Special, Select) — Subcommittees
Cunningham	Appropriations — District of Columbia; Legislative; National Security.
Danner	Transportation and Infrastructure — Aviation; Surface Transportation. International Relations — International Economic Policy and Trade.
Davis, D. of Illinois	Government Reform and Oversight — Postal Service; Government Management, Information and Technology. Small Business — Empowerment; Tax, Finance and Exports.
Davis, J. of Florida	Budget. International Relations.
Davis, T. of Virginia	Government Reform and Oversight — District of Columbia; Government Management, Information and Technology. Science — Space and Aeronautics; Technology. Transportation and Infrastructure — Aviation; Public Buildings and Economic Development.
Deal	Commerce — Telecommunications, Trade and Consumer Protection; Finance and Hazardous Materials; Health and Environment. Education and the Workforce — Postsecondary Education, Training and Life-Long Learning.
DeFazio	Transportation and Infrastructure — Aviation; Surface Transportation. Resources — Water and Power.
DeGette	Commerce — Finance and Hazardous Materials; Health and Environment.
Delahunt	Judiciary — Courts and Intellectual Property; Commercial and Administrative Law. Resources — National Parks and Public Lands.
DeLauro	Offices of the Chief Deputy Democratic Whips. Appropriations — Agriculture, Rural Development, Food and Drug Administration and Related Agencies; Labor, Health and Human Services and Education.
DeLay	Appropriations — Transportation; VA, HUD and Independent Agencies. Office of the Majority Whip.
Dellums	National Security — Military Procurement.
Deutsch	Commerce — Health and Environment; Energy and Power; Oversight and Investigations.
Diaz-Balart	Rules — Rules and Organization of the House.
Dickey	Appropriations — Agriculture, Rural Development, Food and Drug Administration and Related Agencies; Labor, Health and Human Services and Education; Energy and Water Development.
Dicks	Appropriations — Interior; National Security; Military Construction. Permanent Select Committee on Intelligence — Technical and Tactical Intelligence.
Dingell	Commerce.
Dixon	Appropriations — Commerce, Justice, State and Judiciary; District of Columbia; National Security. Permanent Select Committee on Intelligence — Human Intelligence, Analysis and Counterintelligence.
Doggett	Budget. Resources.
Dooley	Agriculture — Livestock, Dairy and Poultry; Forestry, Resource Conservation and Research. Resources — Energy and Mineral Resources; Water and Power.

Representative	Committees (Standing, Joint, Special, Select) — Subcommittees
Doolittle	Agriculture — Forestry, Resource Conservation and Research; Risk Management and Specialty Crops. Resources — Water and Power; Forests and Forest Health. Joint Economic Committee.
Doyle	Veterans' Affairs — Health. Science — Energy and Environment; Technology.
Dreier	Rules — Rules and Organization of the House.
Duncan	Resources — National Parks and Public Lands; Energy and Mineral Resources. Transportation and Infrastructure — Aviation; Public Buildings and Economic Development.
Dunn	Ways and Means — Trade; Oversight.
Edwards	Offices of the Chief Deputy Democratic Whips. Appropriations — Energy and Water Development; Military Construction.
Ehlers	Science — Energy and Environment; Technology. Transportation and Infrastructure — Aviation; Water Resources and Environment. House Oversight. Joint Committee on the Library.
Ehrlich	Banking and Financial Services — Financial Institutions and Consumer Credit; Housing and Community Opportunity. Budget.
Emerson	Agriculture — Forestry, Resource Conservation and Research; General Farm Commodities. Transportation and Infrastructure — Surface Transportation; Water Resources and Environment. Small Business — Regulatory Reform and Paperwork Reduction; Empowerment.
Engel	Commerce — Telecommunications, Trade and Consumer Protection; Finance and Hazardous Materials; Oversight and Investigations.
English	Ways and Means — Human Resources; Oversight. Small Business — Empowerment; Tax, Finance and Exports. Science — Energy and Environment.
Ensign	Ways and Means — Human Resources; Health. Resources — National Parks and Public Lands; Water and Power.
Eshoo	Commerce — Health and Environment; Telecommunications, Trade and Consumer Protection.
Etheridge	Agriculture — Risk Management and Specialty Crops; General Farm Commodities. Science — Basic Research.
Evans	National Security — Military Procurement; Military Readiness. Veterans' Affairs.
Everett	Agriculture — Risk Management and Specialty Crops; Forestry, Resource Conservation and Research. Veterans' Affairs — Oversight and Investigations. National Security — Military Procurement; Military Installations and Facilities.
Ewing	Agriculture — Risk Management and Specialty Crops; Department Operations, Nutrition and Foreign Agriculture. Transportation and Infrastructure — Aviation; Surface Transportation. Science — Basic Research; Technology. Joint Economic Committee.
Faleomavaega	International Relations — International Operations and Human Rights; Asia and the Pacific. Resources — National Parks and Public Lands.

Representative	Committees (Standing, Joint, Special, Select) — Subcommittees
Farr	Agriculture — Forestry, Resource Conservation and Research; Livestock, Dairy and Poultry. Resources — Fisheries Conservation, Wildlife and Oceans; Water and Power.
Fattah	Government Reform and Oversight — Postal Service; National Economic Growth, Natural Resources and Regulatory Affairs. Education and the Workforce — Employer-Employee Relations; Early Childhood, Youth and Families.
Fawell	Science — Energy and Environment. Education and the Workforce — Employer-Employee Relations; Workforce Protections; Oversight and Investigations.
Fazio	Appropriations — Energy and Water Development; Agriculture, Rural Development, Food and Drug Administration and Related Agencies; Legislative.
Filner	Transportation and Infrastructure — Surface Transportation; Railroads. Veterans' Affairs — Benefits.
Flake	Banking and Financial Services — Domestic and International Monetary Policy; Capital Markets, Securities and Government Sponsored Enterprises. Small Business — Empowerment.
Foglietta	Appropriations — Transportation; Foreign Operations, Export Financing and Related Programs.
Foley	Agriculture — Risk Management and Specialty Crops; Department Operations, Nutrition and Foreign Agriculture. Science — Energy and Environment; Space and Aeronautics. Banking and Financial Services.
Forbes	Appropriations — Commerce, Justice, State and Judiciary; Foreign Operations, Export Financing and Related Programs; Treasury, Postal Service and General Government.
Ford	Education and the Workforce — Oversight and Investigations; Postsecondary Education, Training and Life-Long Learning. Government Reform and Oversight.
Fowler	National Security — Military Installations and Facilities; Military Readiness. Transportation and Infrastructure — Surface Transportation; Railroads.
Fox	Banking and Financial Services — Domestic and International Monetary Policy; Housing and Community Opportunity. International Relations — Asia and the Pacific. Transportation and Infrastructure — Aviation; Railroads.
Frank	Banking and Financial Services — Domestic and International Monetary Policy; Housing and Community Opportunity. Judiciary — Courts and Intellectual Property.
Franks	Budget. Transportation and Infrastructure — Surface Transportation; Railroads; Water Resources and Environment.
Frelinghuysen	Appropriations — Energy and Water Development; VA, HUD and Independent Agencies; Foreign Operations, Export Financing and Related Programs.
Frost	Rules — Legislative and Budget Process.
Furse	Commerce — Finance and Hazardous Materials; Health and Environment; Energy and Power.
Gallegly	Resources — National Parks and Public Lands. Judiciary — Courts and Intellectual Property; Immigration and Claims. International Relations — The Western Hemisphere.

Representative	Committees (Standing, Joint, Special, Select) — Subcommittees
Ganske	Commerce — Finance and Hazardous Materials; Health and Environment; Oversight and Investigations.
Gejdenson	House Oversight. International Relations — International Economic Policy and Trade. Joint Committee on the Library. Joint Committee on Printing.
Gekas	Judiciary — Commercial and Administrative Law; Crime.
Gephardt	Office of the Democratic Leader.
Gibbons	National Security — Military Readiness; Military Research and Development. Resources — National Parks and Public Lands; Energy and Mineral Resources. Permanent Select Committee on Intelligence — Technical and Tactical Intelligence.
Gilchrest	Transportation and Infrastructure — Water Resources and Environment; Coast Guard and Maritime Transportation. Resources — Fisheries Conservation, Wildlife and Oceans; National Parks and Public Lands.
Gillmor	Commerce — Finance and Hazardous Materials; Telecommunications, Trade and Consumer Protection.
Gilman	International Relations. Government Reform and Oversight — Postal Service; Human Resources.
Gingrich	Office of the Speaker.
Gonzalez	Banking and Financial Services.
Goode	Agriculture — Forestry, Resource Conservation and Research; Risk Management and Specialty Crops. Small Business — Regulatory Reform and Paperwork Reduction.
Goodlatte	Agriculture — Livestock, Dairy and Poultry; Department Operations, Nutrition and Foreign Agriculture. Judiciary — Courts and Intellectual Property; The Constitution.
Goodling	Education and the Workforce — Postsecondary Education, Training and Life-Long Learning; Early Childhood, Youth and Families; Employer-Employee Relations. International Relations — International Operations and Human Rights.
Gordon	Commerce — Energy and Power; Telecommunications, Trade and Consumer Protection. Science — Space and Aeronautics; Technology.
Goss	Rules — Legislative and Budget Process. Permanent Select Committee on Intelligence.
Graham	Education and the Workforce — Workforce Protections; Postsecondary Education, Training and Life-Long Learning. International Relations — International Operations and Human Rights; International Economic Policy and Trade. National Security — Military Personnel; Military Procurement.
Granger	Budget. Transportation and Infrastructure — Aviation; Surface Transportation; Railroads. House Oversight. Joint Committee on Printing.
Green	Commerce — Telecommunications, Trade and Consumer Protection; Health and Environment.
Greenwood	Commerce — Finance and Hazardous Materials; Health and Environment; Oversight and Investigations. Education and the Workforce; Early Childhood, Youth and Families; Postsecondary Education, Training and Life-Long Learning.

Representative	Committees (Standing, Joint, Special, Select) — Subcommittees
Gutierrez	Banking and Financial Services — Housing and Community Opportunity; Capital Markets, Securities and Government Sponsored Enterprises. Veterans' Affairs — Health.
Gutknecht	Science — Basic Research; Technology. Budget.
Hall, R. of Texas	Science — Space and Aeronautics; Energy and Environment. Commerce — Energy and Power; Health and Environment; Finance and Hazardous Materials.
Hall, T. of Ohio	Rules — Rules and Organization of the House.
Hamilton	International Relations. Joint Economic Committee.
Hansen	National Security — Military Procurement; Military Readiness. Resources — National Parks and Public Lands; Forests and Forest Health. Standards of Official Conduct.
Harman	National Security — Military Research and Development; Military Personnel. Permanent Select Committee on Intelligence — Technical and Tactical Intelligence.
Hastert	Office of the Chief Deputy Majority Whip. Commerce — Energy and Power; Health and Environment; Telecommunications, Trade and Consumer Protection. Government Reform and Oversight — National Economic Growth, Natural Resources and Regulatory Affairs; National Security, International Affairs and Criminal Justice.
Hastings, A. of Florida	International Relations — Africa; Asia and the Pacific. Science — Space and Aeronautics.
Hastings, D. of Washington	Rules — Legislative and Budget Process.
Hayworth	Ways and Means — Human Resources; Social Security. Veterans' Affairs — Benefits.
Hefley	National Security — Military Installations and Facilities; Military Research and Development. Small Business. Resources — National Parks and Public Lands.
Hefner	Appropriations — Military Construction; National Security.
Herger	Budget. Ways and Means — Trade.
Hill	Banking and Financial Services — Capital Markets, Securities and Government Sponsored Enterprises; Housing and Community Opportunity. Resources — National Parks and Public Lands; Forests and Forest Health. Small Business — Government Programs and Oversight.
Hilleary	National Security — Military Installations and Facilities; Military Research and Development. Budget. Education and the Workforce — Oversight and Investigations; Early Childhood, Youth and Families.
Hilliard	Agriculture — Livestock, Dairy and Poultry; Forestry, Resource Conservation and Research. International Relations — International Operations and Human Rights; International Economic Policy and Trade.
Hinchey	Banking and Financial Services — Housing and Community Opportunity; Domestic and International Monetary Policy. Resources — National Parks and Public Lands; Forests and Forest Health.

Representative	Committees (Standing, Joint, Special, Select) — Subcommittees
	Joint Economic Committee.
Hinojosa	Education and the Workforce — Employer-Employee Relations; Postsecondary Education, Training and Life-Long Learning. Small Business.
Hobson	Appropriations — National Security; VA, HUD and Independent Agencies; Military Construction. Budget.
Hoekstra	Education and the Workforce — Oversight and Investigations; Workforce Protections. Budget.
Holden	Agriculture — Livestock, Dairy and Poultry; Forestry, Resource Conservation and Research. Transportation and Infrastructure.
Hooley	Banking and Financial Services — Housing and Community Opportunity; General Oversight and Investigations. Science — Energy and Environment.
Horn	Government Reform and Oversight — Government Management, Information and Technology; District of Columbia. Transportation and Infrastructure — Water Resources and Environment; Surface Transportation.
Hostettler	Agriculture — Forestry, Resource Conservation and Research; Livestock, Dairy and Poultry. National Security — Military Installations and Facilities; Military Research and Development.
Houghton	Ways and Means — Trade; Health. International Relations — Africa.
Hoyer	Appropriations — Labor, Health and Human Services and Education; Treasury, Postal Service and General Government; Military Construction. Joint Committee on Printing. House Oversight.
Hulshof	Ways and Means — Social Security; Oversight.
Hunter	National Security — Military Procurement; Military Readiness.
Hutchinson	Judiciary — Crime; The Constitution. Transportation and Infrastructure — Aviation; Surface Transportation. Veterans' Affairs — Health.
Hyde	Judiciary — The Constitution. International Relations — International Operations and Human Rights.
Inglis	Budget. Judiciary — Commercial and Administrative Law; The Constitution.
Istook	Appropriations — Labor, Health and Human Services and Education; Treasury, Postal Service and General Government; National Security.
Jackson	Banking and Financial Services — Housing and Community Opportunity; Domestic and International Monetary Policy. Small Business — Government Programs and Oversight; Empowerment.
Jefferson	Ways and Means — Trade; Human Resources.
Jenkins	Agriculture — Forestry, Resource Conservation and Research; Livestock, Dairy and Poultry. Judiciary — Immigration and Claims; The Constitution.
John	Agriculture — Forestry, Resource Conservation and Research; General Farm Commodities. Resources — Energy and Mineral Resources.

Representative	Committees (Standing, Joint, Special, Select) — Subcommittees
Johnson, E., of Texas	Transportation and Infrastructure — Surface Transportation; Aviation. Science — Technology; Energy and Environment.
Johnson, J. of Wisconsin	Transportation and Infrastructure — Coast Guard and Maritime Transportation; Water Resources and Environment. Agriculture — Livestock, Dairy and Poultry; General Farm Commodities.
Johnson, N. of Connecticut	Ways and Means — Oversight; Health.
Johnson, S., of Texas	Education and the Workforce — Early Childhood, Youth and Families. Ways and Means — Health; Social Security.
Jones	Resources — Fisheries Conservation, Wildlife and Oceans; National Parks and Public Lands. National Security — Military Research and Development; Military Readiness. Banking and Financial Services.
Kanjorski	Banking and Financial Services — Capital Markets, Securities and Government Sponsored Enterprises; Domestic and International Monetary Policy. Government Reform and Oversight — Government Management, Information and Technology; National Economic Growth, Natural Resources and Regulatory Affairs.
Kaptur	Appropriations — Agriculture, Rural Development, Food and Drug Administration and Related Agencies; VA, HUD and Independent Agencies; Legislative.
Kasich	National Security — Military Readiness; Military Research and Development. Budget.
Kelly	Banking and Financial Services — Financial Institutions and Consumer Credit; Housing and Community Opportunity. Transportation and Infrastructure — Surface Transportation; Water Resources and Environment. Small Business — Regulatory Reform and Paperwork Reduction.
Kennedy, J. of Massachusetts	Banking and Financial Services — Domestic and International Monetary Policy; Housing and Community Opportunity. Veterans' Affairs — Health.
Kennedy, P. of Rhode Island	National Security — Military Research and Development; Military Personnel. Resources — National Parks and Public Lands; Fisheries Conservation, Wildlife and Oceans.
Kennelly	Ways and Means — Social Security.
Kildee	Education and the Workforce — Early Childhood, Youth and Families; Postsecondary Education, Training and Life-Long Learning. Resources — National Parks and Public Lands; Forests and Forest Health.
Kilpatrick	Banking and Financial Services — Financial Institutions and Consumer Credit; General Oversight and Investigations. House Oversight. Joint Committee on the Library.
Kim	Transportation and Infrastructure — Public Buildings and Economic Development; Water Resources and Environment. International Relations — Asia and the Pacific; The Western Hemisphere.
Kind	Education and the Workforce — Oversight and Investigations; Postsecondary Education, Training and Life-Long Learning. Resources — National Parks and Public Lands; Water and Power.

Representative	Committees (Standing, Joint, Special, Select) — Subcommittees
King	Banking and Financial Services — Financial Institutions and Consumer Credit; General Oversight and Investigations; Capital Markets, Securities and Government Sponsored Enterprises. International Relations — International Operations and Human Rights; Asia and the Pacific.
Kingston	Appropriations — Agriculture, Rural Development, Food and Drug Administration and Related Agencies; Foreign Operations, Export Financing and Related Programs; Military Construction.
Kleczka	Ways and Means — Health; Oversight.
Klink	Commerce — Oversight and Investigations; Telecommunications, Trade and Consumer Protection.
Klug	Commerce — Health and Environment; Telecommunications, Trade and Consumer Protection; Finance and Hazardous Materials.
Knollenberg	Appropriations — Energy and Water Development; Foreign Operations, Export Financing and Related Programs; VA, HUD and Independent Agencies. Education and the Workforce — Employer-Employee Relations.
Kolbe	Appropriations — Commerce, Justice, State and Judiciary; Interior; Treasury, Postal Service and General Government.
Kucinich	Government Reform and Oversight — National Economic Growth, Natural Resources and Regulatory Affairs; Human Resources. Education and the Workforce.
LaFalce	Banking and Financial Services — Financial Institutions and Consumer Credit; Housing and Community Opportunity. Small Business.
LaHood	Agriculture — Department Operations, Nutrition and Foreign Agriculture; Forestry, Resource Conservation and Research. Transportation and Infrastructure — Aviation; Surface Transportation. Veterans' Affairs — Benefits.
Lampson	Science — Space and Aeronautics. Transportation and Infrastructure.
Lantos	Government Reform and Oversight — National Security, International Affairs and Criminal Justice; Human Resources. International Relations — International Operations and Human Rights; International Economic Policy and Trade.
Largent	Commerce — Telecommunications, Trade and Consumer Protection; Finance and Hazardous Materials; Energy and Power.
Latham	Appropriations — Agriculture, Rural Development, Food and Drug Administration and Related Agencies; Commerce, Justice, State and Judiciary; Legislative.
LaTourette	Transportation and Infrastructure — Public Buildings and Economic Development; Surface Transportation; Water Resources and Environment. Government Reform and Oversight — Postal Service; National Economic Growth, Natural Resources and Regulatory Affairs; National Security, International Affairs and Criminal Justice. Banking and Financial Services — Domestic and International Monetary Policy; General Oversight and Investigations.
Lazio	Banking and Financial Services — Housing and Community Opportunity; Capital Markets, Securities and Government Sponsored Enterprises. Commerce — Finance and Hazardous Materials; Health and Environment.
Leach	Banking and Financial Services. International Relations — Asia and the Pacific.
Lee	Judiciary — Crime; Commercial and Administrative Law. Science — Basic Research; Space and Aeronautics.

Representative	Committees (Standing, Joint, Special, Select) — Subcommittees
Levin	Ways and Means — Human Resources; Social Security.
Lewis, J. of California	Appropriations — VA, HUD and Independent Agencies; National Security. Permanent Select Committee on Intelligence — Technical and Tactical Intelligence.
Lewis, J. of Georgia	Offices of the Chief Deputy Democratic Whips. Ways and Means — Health.
Lewis, R. of Kentucky	Agriculture — Risk Management and Specialty Crops; Forestry, Resource Conservation and Research; Livestock, Dairy and Poultry. National Security — Military Personnel; Military Procurement.
Linder	Rules — Legislative and Budget Process.
Lipinski	Transportation and Infrastructure — Aviation; Railroads.
Livingston	Appropriations.
LoBiondo	Small Business — Regulatory Reform and Paperwork Reduction; Empowerment. Transportation and Infrastructure — Coast Guard and Maritime Transportation; Water Resources and Environment.
Lofgren	Judiciary — Courts and Intellectual Property; Immigration and Claims. Science — Energy and Environment; Space and Aeronautics.
Lowey	Appropriations — Labor, Health and Human Services and Education; Foreign Operations, Export Financing and Related Programs.
Lucas	Agriculture — Livestock, Dairy, and Poultry; Forestry, Resource Conservation and Research; General Farm Commodities. Banking and Financial Services — Domestic and International Monetary Policy; Capital Markets, Securities and Government Sponsored Enterprises.
Luther	Science — Basic Research; Space and Aeronautics. International Relations.
Maloney, C. of New York	Banking and Financial Services — Financial Institutions and Consumer Credit; Domestic and International Monetary Policy. Government Reform and Oversight — Government Management, Information and Technology; National Security, International Affairs and Criminal Justice. Joint Economic Committee.
Maloney, J. of Connecticut	Banking and Financial Services — Housing and Community Opportunity. National Security — Military Personnel; Military Procurement.
Manton	Commerce — Finance and Hazardous Materials; Telecommunications, Trade and Consumer Protection.
Manzullo	Small Business — Government Programs and Oversight; Tax, Finance and Exports. International Relations — International Economic Policy and Trade; Asia and the Pacific. Banking and Financial Services.
Markey	Commerce — Finance and Hazardous Materials; Energy and Power; Telecommunications, Trade and Consumer Protection. Resources — National Parks and Public Lands.
Martinez	Education and the Workforce — Workforce Protections; Early Childhood, Youth and Families. International Relations — The Western Hemisphere; Asia and the Pacific.
Mascara	Veterans' Affairs — Benefits. Transportation and Infrastructure — Surface Transportation; Water Resources and Environment.

Representative	Committees (Standing, Joint, Special, Select) — Subcommittees
Matsui	Ways and Means — Trade; Human Resources.
McCarthy, C. of New York	Education and the Workforce — Employer-Employee Relations; Postsecondary Education, Training and Life-Long Learning. Small Business — Government Programs and Oversight; Tax, Finance and Exports.
McCarthy, K. of Missouri	Commerce — Telecommunications, Trade and Consumer Protection; Energy and Power.
McCollum	Banking and Financial Services — Financial Institutions and Consumer Credit. Judiciary — Crime Courts and Intellectual Property. Permanent Select Committee on Intelligence — Human Intelligence, Analysis and Counterintelligence.
McCrery	Ways and Means — Human Resources; Health. Joint Economic Committee.
McDade	Appropriations — Interior; National Security Energy and Water Development.
McDermott	Budget. Ways and Means — Trade.
McGovern	Transportation and Infrastructure — Surface Transportation; Water Resources and Environment.
McHale	National Security — Military Readiness; Military Research and Development. Science — Energy and Environment; Technology.
McHugh	National Security — Military Installations and Facilities; Military Research and Development. Government Reform and Oversight — Postal Service; National Security, International Affairs and Criminal Justice. International Relations — Asia and the Pacific; Africa.
McInnis	Rules — Rules and Organization of the House.
McIntosh	Education and the Workforce — Early Childhood, Youth and Families; Postsecondary Education, Training and Life-Long Learning. Government Reform and Oversight — National Economic Growth, Natural Resources and Regulatory Affairs; Human Resources. Small Business — Regulatory Reform and Paperwork Reduction.
McIntyre	Agriculture — Risk Management and Specialty Crops; General Farm Commodities. National Security — Military Procurement.
McKeon	Education and the Workforce — Postsecondary Education, Training and Life-Long Learning; Oversight and Investigations. National Security — Military Procurement, Military Readiness.
McKinney	Banking and Financial Services — Financial Institutions and Consumer Credit; General Oversight and Investigations. International Relations — International Operations and Human Rights; The Western Hemisphere.
McNulty	Ways and Means — Oversight; Trade.
Meehan	National Security — Military Research and Development; Military Readiness. Judiciary — Crime. Commercial and Administrative Law.
Meek	Appropriations — Treasury, Postal Service and General Government; VA, HUD and Independent Agencies.
Menendez	Offices of the Chief Deputy Democratic Whips. International Relations — The Western Hemisphere; Africa. Transportation and Infrastructure — Water Resources and Environment; Surface Transportation.

Representative	Committees (Standing, Joint, Special, Select) — Subcommittees
Metcalf	Banking and Financial Services — Financial Institutions and Consumer Credit; Domestic and International Monetary Policy; Housing and Community Opportunity. Transportation and Infrastructure — Aviation; Surface Transportation.
Mica	Transportation and Infrastructure — Railroads; Surface Transportation. Government Reform and Oversight — Civil Service; National Security, International Affairs and Criminal Justice. House Oversight.
Millender-McDonald	Small Business — Regulatory Reform and Paperwork Reduction; Tax, Finance and Exports. Transportation and Infrastructure — Surface Transportation; Aviation.
Miller, D. of Florida	Appropriations — Labor, Health and Human Services and Education; Interior. Budget.
Miller, G. of California	Education and the Workforce — Early Childhood, Youth and Families; Workforce Protections. Resources — Water and Power.
Minge	Agriculture — General Farm Commodities; Forestry, Resource Conservation and Research. Budget.
Mink	Budget. Education and the Workforce — Early Childhood, Youth and Families; Oversight and Investigations.
Moakley	Rules — Legislative and Budget Process.
Molinari	Transportation and Infrastructure — Railroads; Aviation; Water Resources and Environment. Budget.
Mollohan	Appropriations — Commerce, Justice, State and Judiciary; VA, HUD and Independent Agencies. Budget.
Moran, J. of Virginia	Appropriations — District of Columbia; Interior.
Moran, J. of Kansas	Agriculture — Forestry, Resource Conservation and Research; Risk Management and Specialty Crops; General Farm Commodities. International Relations — International Economic Policy and Trade. Veterans' Affairs — Health.
Morella	Science — Technology; Basic Research. Government Reform and Oversight — Civil Service; District of Columbia.
Murtha	Appropriations — National Security; Interior.
Myrick	Rules — Rules and Organization of the House.
Nadler	Transportation and Infrastructure — Railroads; Surface Transportation. Judiciary — Commercial and Administrative Law; The Constitution.
Neal	Ways and Means — Trade; Social Security.
Nethercutt	Appropriations — Agriculture, Rural Development, Food and Drug Administration and Related Agencies; Interior; National Security. Science — Space and Aeronautics.
Neumann	Appropriations — District of Columbia; VA, HUD and Independent Agencies. Budget.

Representative	Committees (Standing, Joint, Special, Select) — Subcommittees
Ney	Banking and Financial Services — Domestic and International Monetary Policy; Housing and Community Opportunity; General Oversight and Investigations. House Oversight. Joint Committee on the Library. Joint Committee on Printing. Transportation and Infrastructure — Surface Transportation; Water Resources and Environment.
Northup	Appropriations — District of Columbia; Labor, Health and Human Services and Education; Treasury, Postal Service and General Government.
Norton	Transportation and Infrastructure — Public Buildings and Economic Development; Surface Transportation. Government Reform and Oversight — District of Columbia; Civil Service.
Norwood	Commerce — Energy and Power; Health and Environment. Education and the Workforce — Oversight and Investigations.
Nussle	Ways and Means — Trade. Budget.
Oberstar	Transportation and Infrastructure.
Obey	Appropriations — Labor, Health and Human Services and Education.
Olver	Appropriations — Military Construction; Transportation.
Ortiz	National Security — Military Installations and Facilities; Military Readiness. Resources — Fisheries Conservation, Wildlife and Oceans; Energy and Mineral Resources.
Owens	Government Reform and Oversight — Postal Service; Government Management, Information and Technology. Education and the Workforce — Workforce Protections; Early Childhood, Youth and Families.
Oxley	Commerce — Finance and Hazardous Materials; Telecommunications, Trade and Consumer Protection.
Packard	Appropriations — Foreign Operations, Export Financing and Related Programs; Transportation; Military Construction.
Pallone	Resources — National Parks and Public Lands; Fisheries Conservation, Wildlife and Oceans. Commerce — Finance and Hazardous Materials; Health and Environment; Energy and Power.
Pappas	Government Reform and Oversight — Civil Service; Human Resources. National Security — Military Procurement; Military Research and Development. Small Business; Tax, Finance and Exports.
Parker	Appropriations — Energy and Water Development; Military Construction. Budget.
Pascrell	Transportation and Infrastructure — Surface Transportation; Water Resources and Environment. Small Business — Empowerment.
Pastor	Appropriations — Energy and Water Development; Transportation.
Paul	Banking and Financial Services — Financial Institutions and Consumer Credit; Domestic and International Monetary Policy. Education and the Workforce — Workforce Protections; Early Childhood, Youth and Families.
Paxon	Commerce — Finance and Hazardous Materials; Energy and Power.

Representative	Committees (Standing, Joint, Special, Select) — Subcommittees
Payne	Education and the Workforce — Employer-Employee Relations; Early Childhood, Youth and Families. International Relations — International Operations and Human Rights; Africa.
Pease	Judiciary — Courts and Intellectual Property; Immigration and Claims. Transportation and Infrastructure — Aviation; Surface Transportation.
Pelosi	Appropriations — Foreign Operations, Export Financing and Related Programs; Labor, Health and Human Services and Education. Permanent Select Committee on Intelligence — Human Intelligence, Analysis and Counterintelligence.
Peterson, C. of Minnesota	Agriculture — Livestock, Dairy and Poultry; Forestry, Resource Conservation and Research. Veterans' Affairs — Health.
Peterson, J. of Pennsylvania	Education and the Workforce — Early Childhood, Youth and Families; Postsecondary Education, Training and Life-Long Learning. Resources — Fisheries Conservation, Wildlife and Oceans; Forests and Forest Health.
Petri	Transportation and Infrastructure — Surface Transportation; Water Resources and Environment. Education and the Workforce — Employer-Employee Relations; Postsecondary Education, Training and Life-Long Learning.
Pickering	Agriculture — Forestry, Resource Conservation and Research; Livestock, Dairy and Poultry. Transportation and Infrastructure — Aviation; Surface Transportation. Science — Basic Research; Space and Aeronautics.
Pickett	National Security — Military Personnel; Military Readiness; Military Research and Development. Resources — Water and Power.
Pitts	Budget. Transportation and Infrastructure — Aviation; Railroads; Surface Transportation.
Pombo	Agriculture — Forestry, Resource Conservation and Research; Livestock, Dairy and Poultry; Risk Management and Specialty Crops. Resources — National Parks and Public Lands; Water and Power.
Pomeroy	Agriculture — Forestry, Resource Conservation and Research; Risk Management and Specialty Crops. Budget.
Porter	Appropriations — Labor, Health and Human Services and Education; Foreign Operations, Export Financing and Related Programs; Military Construction.
Portman	Ways and Means — Oversight; Social Security. Government Reform and Oversight.
Poshard	Small Business — Government Programs and Oversight. Transportation and Infrastructure — Water Resources and Environment; Aviation.
Price	Appropriations — Treasury, Postal Service and General Government; VA, HUD and Independent Agencies.
Pryce	Rules — Legislative and Budget Process.
Quinn	Transportation and Infrastructure — Water Resources and Environment; Railroads; Surface Transportation. Veterans' Affairs — Benefits.

Representative	Committees (Standing, Joint, Special, Select) — Subcommittees
Radanovich	Budget. Resources — National Parks and Public Lands; Water and Power; Forests and Forest Health.
Rahall	Transportation and Infrastructure — Surface Transportation; Aviation; Water Resources and Environment. Resources — National Parks and Public Lands; Energy and Mineral Resources.
Ramstad	Ways and Means — Trade; Oversight.
Rangel	Ways and Means — Trade. Joint Committee on Taxation.
Redmond	Assignments not available at press time.
Regula	Appropriations — Interior; Commerce, Justice, State and Judiciary; Transportation.
Reyes	National Security — Military Installations and Facilities; Military Research and Development. Veterans' Affairs — Benefits.
Riggs	Education and the Workforce — Early Childhood, Youth and Families; Postsecondary Education, Training and Life-Long Learning. Transportation and Infrastructure — Water Resources and Environment; Surface Transportation.
Riley	Banking and Financial Services — Capital Markets, Securities and Government Sponsored Enterprises; General Oversight and Investigations. National Security — Military Readiness; Military Research and Development.
Rivers	Science — Basic Research; Technology. Budget.
Rodriguez	National Security. Veterans' Affairs.
Roemer	Science — Energy and Environment. Education and the Workforce — Postsecondary Education, Training and Life-Long Learning; Early Childhood, Youth and Families.
Rogan	Commerce — Telecommunications, Trade and Consumer Protection; Energy and Power.
Rogers	Appropriations — Commerce, Justice, State and Judiciary; Energy and Water Development; Transportation.
Rohrabacher	Science — Space and Aeronautics; Energy and Environment. International Relations — International Economic Policy and Trade; Asia and the Pacific.
Romero-Barceló	Education and the Workforce — Postsecondary Education, Training and Life-Long Learning. Resources — National Parks and Public Lands; Energy and Mineral Resources.
Ros-Lehtinen	Government Reform and Oversight — National Security, International Affairs and Criminal Justice; District of Columbia. International Relations — The Western Hemisphere; International Operations and Human Rights; International Economic Policy and Trade.
Rothman	International Relations — International Economic Policy and Trade. Judiciary — Crime.
Roukema	Banking and Financial Services — Financial Institutions and Consumer Credit; Housing and Community Opportunity. Education and the Workforce — Employer-Employee Relations; Postsecondary Education, Training and Life-Long Learning.

Representative	Committees (Standing, Joint, Special, Select) — Subcommittees
Roybal-Allard	Banking and Financial Services — Financial Institutions and Consumer Credit; Capital Markets, Securities and Government Sponsored Enterprises. Budget.
Royce	Banking and Financial Services — Domestic and International Monetary Policy; Financial Institutions and Consumer Credit. International Relations — Asia and the Pacific; Africa.
Rush	Commerce — Energy and Power; Telecommunications, Trade and Consumer Protection.
Ryun	Banking and Financial Services — Financial Institutions and Consumer Credit. National Security — Military Personnel; Military Procurement. Small Business — Regulatory Reform and Paperwork Reduction.
Sabo	Appropriations — National Security; Transportation; District of Columbia.
Salmon	International Relations — International Operations and Human Rights; Asia and the Pacific. Science — Energy and Environment; Space and Aeronautics.
Sanchez	Education and the Workforce — Oversight and Investigations; Postsecondary Education, Training and Life-Long Learning. National Security — Military Research and Development.
Sanders	Banking and Financial Services — Domestic and International Monetary Policy; Housing and Community Opportunity. Government Reform and Oversight — Human Resources; National Economic Growth, Natural Resources and Regulatory Affairs.
Sandlin	Transportation and Infrastructure — Railroads; Surface Transportation.
Sanford	International Relations — Africa; The Western Hemisphere. Government Reform and Oversight — Postal Service; Government Management, Information and Technology. Joint Economic Committee.
Sawyer	Commerce — Telecommunications, Trade and Consumer Protection; Finance and Hazardous Materials; Oversight and Investigations.
Saxton	National Security — Military Procurement; Military Installations and Facilities. Joint Economic Committee. Resources — Fisheries Conservation, Wildlife and Oceans.
Scarborough	Government Reform and Oversight — Government Management, Information and Technology; National Economic Growth, Natural Resources and Regulatory Affairs. National Security — Military Research and Development; Military Installations and Facilities. Education and the Workforce — Oversight and Investigations.
Schaefer	Commerce — Energy and Power; Telecommunications, Trade and Consumer Protection. Veterans' Affairs — Benefits.
Schaffer	Agriculture — Forestry, Resource Conservation and Research. Education and the Workforce — Workforce Protections; Postsecondary Education, Training and Life-Long Learning. Resources — Forests and Forest Health.
Schiff	Government Reform and Oversight — Human Resources; National Security, International Affairs and Criminal Justice. Science — Energy and Environment; Basic Research. Judiciary — Crime; Commercial and Administrative Law.

Representative	Committees (Standing, Joint, Special, Select) — Subcommittees
Schumer	Banking and Financial Services — Financial Institutions and Consumer Credit; Capital Markets, Securities and Government Sponsored Enterprises. Judiciary — Immigration and Claims; Crime.
Scott	Education and the Workforce — Early Childhood, Youth and Families. Judiciary — The Constitution.
Sensenbrenner	Judiciary — Courts and Intellectual Property. Science.
Serrano	Appropriations — Legislative; Agriculture, Rural Development, Food and Drug Administration and Related Agencies.
Sessions	Banking and Financial Services — Capital Markets, Securities and Government Sponsored Enterprises; Housing and Community Opportunity. Government Reform and Oversight — Civil Service; Postal Service; Government Management, Information and Technology. Science — Basic Research.
Shadegg	Budget. Resources — National Parks and Public Lands; Water and Power. Government Reform and Oversight — National Economic Growth, Natural Resources and Regulatory Affairs; National Security, International Affairs and Criminal Justice.
Shaw	Ways and Means — Human Resources; Trade.
Shays	Government Reform and Oversight — Human Resources; National Security, International Affairs and Criminal Justice. Budget.
Sherman	Budget. International Relations — The Western Hemisphere; International Economic Policy and Trade.
Shimkus	Commerce — Telecommunications, Trade and Consumer Protection; Energy and Power.
Shuster	Transportation and Infrastructure. Permanent Select Committee on Intelligence — Human Intelligence, Analysis and Counterintelligence.
Sisisky	National Security — Military Readiness; Military Installations and Facilities. Small Business — Regulatory Reform and Paperwork Reduction.
Skaggs	Appropriations — Commerce, Justice, State and Judiciary; Interior. Permanent Select Committee on Intelligence — Human Intelligence, Analysis and Counterintelligence; Technical and Tactical Intelligence.
Skeen	Appropriations — Agriculture, Rural Development, Food and Drug Administration and Related Agencies; Interior; National Security.
Skelton	National Security — Military Personnel; Military Procurement. Permanent Select Committee on Intelligence — Technical and Tactical Intelligence.
Slaughter	Rules — Rules and Organization of the House.
Smith, A. of Washington	National Security — Military Installations and Facilities; Military Procurement. Resources — Water and Power.
Smith of New Jersey	International Relations — International Operations and Human Rights; The Western Hemisphere. Veterans' Affairs — Health.
Smith of Texas	Budget. Judiciary — Immigration and Claims; Commercial and Administrative Law.

Representative	Committees (Standing, Joint, Special, Select) — Subcommittees
Smith, L. of Washington	Resources — National Parks and Public Lands; Water and Power. Small Business — Government Programs and Oversight; Tax, Finance and Exports.
Smith of Michigan	Agriculture — Livestock, Dairy and Poultry; Forestry, Resource Conservation and Research; Department Operations, Nutrition and Foreign Agriculture; Risk Management and Specialty Crops. Budget.
Smith of Oregon	Agriculture. Resources — National Parks and Public Lands; Water and Power.
Snowbarger	Banking and Financial Services — Capital Markets, Securities and Government Sponsored Enterprises. Government Reform and Oversight — National Economic Growth, Natural Resources and Regulatory Affairs; Human Resources. Small Business — Tax, Finance and Exports.
Snyder	National Security — Military Installations and Facilities; Military Procurement. Veterans' Affairs — Oversight and Investigations.
Solomon	Rules — Rules and Organization of the House; Legislative and Budget Process.
Souder	Education and the Workforce — Early Childhood, Youth and Families; Postsecondary Education, Training and Life-Long Learning. Small Business — Empowerment. Government Reform and Oversight — National Security, International Affairs and Criminal Justice; Human Resources.
Spence	National Security — Military Procurement. Veterans' Affairs — Oversight and Investigations.
Spratt	National Security — Military Procurement. Budget.
Stabenow	Agriculture — Forestry, Resource Conservation and Research; General Farm Commodities. Science — Technology.
Stark	Ways and Means — Health; Human Resources. Joint Committee on Taxation. Joint Economic Committee.
Stearns	Commerce — Energy and Power; Telecommunications, Trade and Consumer Protection. Veterans' Affairs — Health.
Stenholm	Agriculture.
Stokes	Appropriations — Labor, Health and Human Services and Education; VA, HUD and Independent Agencies.
Strickland	Commerce — Finance and Hazardous Materials; Health and Environment.
Stump	National Security — Military Installations and Facilities; Military Procurement. Veterans' Affairs — Oversight and Investigations.
Stupak	Commerce — Health and Environment; Finance and Hazardous Materials; Oversight and Investigations.
Sununu	Budget. Government Reform and Oversight — Government Management, Information and Technology; National Economic Growth, Natural Resources and Regulatory Affairs. Small Business — Government Programs and Oversight.
Talent	National Security — Military Procurement; Military Personnel. Education and the Workforce — Employer-Employee Relations. Small Business.

Representative	Committees (Standing, Joint, Special, Select) — Subcommittees
Tanner	Ways and Means — Social Security; Oversight.
Tauscher	Transportation and Infrastructure — Surface Transportation; Water Resources and Environment. Science.
Tauzin	Commerce — Telecommunications, Trade and Consumer Protection; Finance and Hazardous Materials. Resources — Fisheries Conservation, Wildlife and Oceans; Energy and Mineral Resources.
Taylor, C. of North Carolina	Appropriations — Commerce, Justice, State and Judiciary; Interior; District of Columbia.
Taylor, G. of Mississippi	National Security — Military Personnel; Military Readiness. Transportation and Infrastructure — Water Resources and Environment; Surface Transportation.
Thomas	House Oversight. Ways and Means — Health; Trade. Joint Committee on Taxation. Joint Committee on the Library. Joint Committee on Printing.
Thompson	Agriculture — General Farm Commodities; Department Operations, Nutrition and Foreign Agriculture. Budget.
Thornberry	Resources — Energy and Mineral Resources; Water and Power. National Security — Military Personnel; Military Procurement. Joint Economic Committee.
Thune	Agriculture — Department Operations, Nutrition and Foreign Agriculture; General Farm Commodities. Transportation and Infrastructure — Surface Transportation; Water Resources and Environment.
Thurman	Ways and Means — Oversight.
Tiahrt	Appropriations — District of Columbia; Military Construction; Transportation.
Tierney	Education and the Workforce — Employer-Employee Relations; Postsecondary Education, Training and Life-Long Learning. Government Reform and Oversight — National Economic Growth, Natural Resources and Regulatory Affairs.
Torres	Appropriations — Foreign Operations, Export Financing and Related Programs; Transportation. Banking and Financial Services.
Towns	Government Reform and Oversight — Human Resources. Commerce — Health and Environment; Energy and Power; Finance and Hazardous Materials.
Traficant	Transportation and Infrastructure — Public Buildings and Economic Development; Aviation. Science — Space and Aeronautics.
Turner	National Security — Military Procurement; Military Research and Development. Government Reform and Oversight — National Economic Growth, Natural Resources and Regulatory Affairs; National Security, International Affairs and Criminal Justice.
Underwood	National Security — Military Installations and Facilities; Military Personnel; Military Readiness. Resources — National Parks and Public Lands.
Upton	Commerce — Energy and Power; Health and Environment; Telecommunications, Trade and Consumer Protection. Education and the Workforce — Early Childhood, Youth and Families; Postsecondary Education, Training and Life-Long Learning.

Representative	Committees (Standing, Joint, Special, Select) — Subcommittees
Velázquez	Banking and Financial Services — Housing and Community Opportunity; Domestic and International Monetary Policy. Small Business — Empowerment.
Vento	Banking and Financial Services — Financial Institutions and Consumer Credit; Capital Markets, Securities and Government Sponsored Enterprises. Resources — National Parks and Public Lands; Forests and Forest Health.
Visclosky	Appropriations — Energy and Water Development; National Security.
Walsh	Appropriations — Agriculture, Rural Development, Food and Drug Administration and Related Agencies; VA, HUD and Independent Agencies; Legislative.
Wamp	Appropriations — Interior; Legislative; Military Construction.
Waters	Banking and Financial Services — Capital Markets, Securities and Government Sponsored Enterprises; General Oversight and Investigations. Judiciary — The Constitution.
Watkins	Ways and Means — Human Resources; Oversight.
Watt	Banking and Financial Services — Financial Institutions and Consumer Credit; Capital Markets, Securities and Government Sponsored Enterprises. Judiciary — The Constitution; Immigration and Claims.
Watts	National Security — Military Personnel; Military Procurement. Transportation and Infrastructure — Aviation; Surface Transportation.
Waxman	Government Reform and Oversight. Commerce — Health and Environment; Oversight and Investigations.
Weldon, C. of Pennsylvania	National Security — Military Readiness; Military Research and Development. Science — Energy and Environment; Technology.
Weldon, D. of Florida	Science — Space and Aeronautics. Banking and Financial Services — Financial Institutions and Consumer Credit; Domestic and International Monetary Policy.
Weller	Ways and Means — Social Security; Oversight.
Wexler	International Relations — Asia and the Pacific; International Operations and Human Rights. Judiciary — Crime; Immigration and Claims.
Weygand	Budget. Small Business — Government Programs and Oversight; Tax, Finance and Exports.
White	Commerce — Finance and Hazardous Materials; Telecommunications, Trade and Consumer Protection; Energy and Power.
Whitfield	Commerce — Health and Environment; Energy and Power.
Wicker	Appropriations — Labor, Health and Human Services and Education; Military Construction; VA, HUD and Independent Agencies.
Wise	Transportation and Infrastructure — Railroads; Water Resources and Environment. Government Reform and Oversight — National Security, International Affairs and Criminal Justice.
Wolf	Appropriations — Transportation; Foreign Operations, Export Financing and Related Programs; Treasury, Postal Service and General Government.

Representative	Committees (Standing, Joint, Special, Select) — Subcommittees
Woolsey	Budget. Education and the Workforce — Workforce Protections; Postsecondary Education, Training and Life-Long Learning.
Wynn	Commerce — Telecommunications, Trade and Consumer Protection; Energy and Power.
Yates	Appropriations — Foreign Operations, Export Financing and Related Programs; Interior.
Young of Florida	Appropriations — National Security; Labor, Health and Human Services and Education; Legislative. Permanent Select Committee on Intelligence — Technical and Tactical Intelligence.
Young of Alaska	Resources. Transportation and Infrastructure — Coast Guard and Maritime Transportation; Water Resources and Environment.

STANDING COMMITTEES OF THE SENATE

[Republicans in roman, Democrats in *italic*]

[Room numbers beginning with SD are in the Dirksen Building, SH in the Hart Building, and SR in the Russell Building; Capitol numbers begin with S]

Agriculture, Nutrition and Forestry

328A Russell Senate Office Building 20510–6000

phone 224–2035, Agriculture Hotline 224–2587

http://www.senate.gov/committee/agriculture.html

meets first and third Wednesdays of each month

Richard G. Lugar, of Indiana, *Chairman*

Jesse Helms, of North Carolina.
Thad Cochran, of Mississippi.
Mitch McConnell, of Kentucky.
Paul Coverdell, of Georgia.
Rick Santorum, of Pennsylvania.
Pat Roberts, of Kansas.
Chuck Grassley, of Iowa.
Phil Gramm, of Texas.
Larry E. Craig, of Idaho.

Tom Harkin, of Iowa.
Patrick J. Leahy, of Vermont.
Kent Conrad, of North Dakota.
Thomas A. Daschle, of South Dakota.
Max Baucus, of Montana.
J. Robert Kerrey, of Nebraska.
Mary L. Landrieu, of Louisiana.
Tim Johnson, of South Dakota.

SUBCOMMITTEES

Forestry, Conservation and Rural Revitalization

Mr. Santorum, *Chairman*

Mr. Grassley
Mr. Coverdell
Mr. Roberts
Mr. Craig

Mr. Conrad
Mr. Leahy
Mr. Daschle
Mr. Baucus

Marketing Inspection and Product Promotion

Mr. Coverdell, *Chairman*

Mr. Helms
Mr. Cochran
Mr. McConnell

Mr. Baucus
Mr. Kerrey
Ms. Landrieu

Production and Price Competitiveness

Mr. Cochran, *Chairman*

Mr. Roberts
Mr. Helms
Mr. Grassley
Mr. Gramm

Mr. Kerrey
Mr. Daschle
Mr. Johnson
Ms. Landrieu

Research, Nutrition and General Legislation

Mr. McConnell, *Chairman*

Mr. Gramm
Mr. Craig
Mr. Santorum

Mr. Leahy
Mr. Conrad
Mr. Johnson

STAFF

Committee on Agriculture, Nutrition and Forestry (SR–328A), 224–2035

Agriculture Hotline 224–2587.

Majority Staff Director.—Chuck Conner.
Chief Clerk.—Robert E. Sturm.
Senior Professional Staff.—Randy Green.
Chief Counsel.—Dave Johnson.
Counsel.—Michael Knipe.
Financial Clerk.—Debbie Schwertner.
Hearing Clerk.—Daniel Spellacy.
Chief Economist.—Andrew Morton.
Press Secretary.—Andy Fisher.
Staff Assistant.—Kathryn Boots.
Credit Counsel.—Marcia Asquith.
Commodity Programs.—Darrell Choat.
Research.—Karl Glasener.
Nutrition.—Beth Johnson.
Food Safety.—Terri Nintemann.
Marketing Program.—Terri Snow.
Conservation.—David Stawick.
GPO Printer.—Barbara Ward.
Minority Staff Director.—Dan Smith.
Chief Counsel.—Mark Halverson.
Deputy Chief Counsel.—Andy Fish.
Staff Assistant.—Donna Claycomb.
Economist.—Stephanie Mercier.
Trade.—Kate Howard.
Research.—Phil Schwab.

Appropriations

S–128 The Capitol 20510–6025, phone 224–3471

http://www.senate.gov/committee/appropriations.html

meets upon call of the chairman

Ted Stevens, of Alaska, *Chairman.*

Thad Cochran, of Mississippi.
Arlen Specter, of Pennsylvania.
Pete V. Domenici, of New Mexico.
Christopher S. Bond, of Missouri.
Slade Gorton, of Washington.
Mitch McConnell, of Kentucky.
Conrad Burns, of Montana.
Richard C. Shelby, of Alabama.
Judd Gregg, of New Hampshire.
Robert F. Bennett, of Utah.
Ben Nighthorse Campbell, of Colorado.
Larry Craig, of Idaho.
Lauch Faircloth, of North Carolina.
Kay Bailey Hutchison, of Texas.

Robert C. Byrd, of West Virginia.
Daniel K. Inouye, of Hawaii.
Ernest F. Hollings, of South Carolina.
Patrick J. Leahy, of Vermont.
Dale Bumpers, of Arkansas.
Frank R. Lautenberg, of New Jersey.
Tom Harkin, of Iowa.
Barbara A. Mikulski, of Maryland.
Harry Reid, of Nevada.
Herb Kohl, of Wisconsin.
Patty Murray, of Washington.
Byron Dorgan, of North Dakota.
Barbara Boxer, of California.

SUBCOMMITTEES

[The chairman and the ranking minority member are ex officio members of all subcommittees of which they are not regular members.]

Agriculture, Rural Development and Related Agencies

Mr. Cochran, *Chairman*

Mr. Specter	*Mr. Bumpers*
Mr. Bond	*Mr. Harkin*
Mr. Gorton	*Mr. Kohl*
Mr. McConnell	*Mr. Byrd*
Mr. Burns	*Mr. Leahy*

Commerce, Justice, State and Judiciary

Mr. Gregg, *Chairman*

Mr. Stevens	*Mr. Hollings*
Mr. Domenici	*Mr. Inouye*
Mr. McConnell	*Mr. Bumpers*
Mrs. Hutchison	*Mr. Lautenberg*
Mr. Campbell	*Ms. Mikulski*

Defense

Mr. Stevens, *Chairman*

Mr. Cochran	*Mr. Inouye*
Mr. Specter	*Mr. Hollings*
Mr. Domenici	*Mr. Byrd*
Mr. Bond	*Mr. Leahy*
Mr. McConnell	*Mr. Bumpers*
Mr. Shelby	*Mr. Lautenberg*
Mr. Gregg	*Mr. Harkin*
Mrs. Hutchison	*Mr. Dorgan*

District of Columbia

Mr. Faircloth, *Chairman*

Mrs. Hutchison	*Mrs. Boxer*

Energy and Water Development

Mr. Domenici, *Chairman*

Mr. Cochran	*Mr. Reid*
Mr. Gorton	*Mr. Byrd*
Mr. McConnell	*Mr. Hollings*
Mr. Bennett	*Mrs. Murray*
Mr. Burns	*Mr. Kohl*
Mr. Craig	*Mr. Dorgan*

Foreign Operations

Mr. McConnell, *Chairman*

Mr. Specter	*Mr. Leahy*
Mr. Gregg	*Mr. Inouye*
Mr. Shelby	*Mr. Lautenberg*
Mr. Bennett	*Mr. Harkin*
Mr. Campbell	*Ms. Mikulski*
Mr. Stevens	*Mrs. Murray*

Interior

Mr. Gorton, *Chairman*

Mr. Stevens	*Mr. Byrd*
Mr. Cochran	*Mr. Leahy*
Mr. Domenici	*Mr. Bumpers*
Mr. Burns	*Mr. Hollings*
Mr. Bennett	*Mr. Reid*
Mr. Gregg	*Mr. Dorgan*
Mr. Campbell	*Mrs. Boxer*

Labor, Health and Human Services, and Education

Mr. Specter, *Chairman*

Mr. Cochran	*Mr. Harkin*
Mr. Gorton	*Mr. Hollings*
Mr. Bond	*Mr. Inouye*
Mr. Gregg	*Mr. Bumpers*
Mr. Faircloth	*Mr. Reid*
Mr. Craig	*Mr. Kohl*
Mrs. Hutchison	*Mrs. Murray*

Legislative Branch

Mr. Bennett, *Chairman*

Mr. Stevens	*Mr. Dorgan*
Mr. Craig	*Mrs. Boxer*

Military Construction

Mr. Burns, *Chairman*

Mrs. Hutchison	*Mrs. Murray*
Mr. Faircloth	*Mr. Reid*
Mr. Craig	*Mr. Inouye*

Transportation

Mr. Shelby, *Chairman*

Mr. Domenici	*Mr. Lautenberg*
Mr. Specter	*Mr. Byrd*
Mr. Bond	*Ms. Mikulski*
Mr. Gorton	*Mr. Reid*
Mr. Bennett	*Mr. Kohl*
Mr. Faircloth	*Mrs. Murray*

Treasury and General Government

Mr. Campbell, *Chairman*

Mr. Shelby	*Mr. Kohl*
Mr. Faircloth	*Ms. Mikulski*

VA, HUD and Independent Agencies

Mr. Bond, *Chairman*

Mr. Burns	*Ms. Mikulski*
Mr. Stevens	*Mr. Leahy*
Mr. Shelby	*Mr. Lautenberg*
Mr. Campbell	*Mr. Harkin*
Mr. Craig	*Mrs. Boxer*

STAFF

Committee on Appropriations (S–128), 224–3471.
Staff Director.—Steven J. Cortese, 4–4566.
Deputy Staff Director.—Lisa Sutherland, 4–5164.

Assistant Staff Director.—Christine Ciccone (S–125), 4–8921.
Chief Clerk.—Dona Pate (S–128), 4–2316.
Senior Counsel.—Al McDermott (S–125), 4–5647.
Communications Director.—John Raffetto (S–128), 4–0992.
Professional Staff: John J. Conway (SD–114), 4–7222; Robert W. Putnam (SD–114), 4–7221; Mary Beth Nethercutt (S–128), 4–1526.
Security Manager.—Justin Weddle (SD–119), 4–7205.
Staff Assistants: Jane Kenny (S–128), 4–2667; Doug Shaftel (S–128), 4–1453.
Minority Staff Director.—James H. English (S–205), 4–7200.
Deputy Staff Director.—Terry Sauvain (SD–144), 4–0338.
Professional Staff: Mary Dewald (S–205), 4–7292; C. Richard D'Amato (SH–123), 4–3088.
Editorial and Printing (SD–126): Richard L. Larson, 4–7265; Robert M. Swartz, 4–7217; Bernard F. Babik, 4–7267; Carole C. Lane, 4–7266.
Clerical Assistants (SD–118): Norman L. Edwards, 4–7264; Joseph C. Chase, 4–0331.

Subcommittee on Agriculture, Rural Development and Related Agencies (SD–136), 4–7219
Clerk.—Rebecca Davies.
Professional Staff Member.—Martha Poindexter, 4–2836.
Staff Assistant.—Jimmie Reynolds, 4–5270.
Minority Clerk.—Galen Fountain (SH–123), 4–7202.
Staff Assistant.—Carole Geagley, 4–7240.

Subcommittee on Commerce, Justice, State and Judiciary (S–146A), 4–7243
Clerk.—Jim Morhard.
Professional Staff Members: Kevin Linskey, 4–0856; Paddy Link (S–146A), 4–0918.
Staff Assistant.—Dana Quam, 4–7464.
Minority Clerk.—Scott Gudes (SH–123), 4–7298.
Staff Assistant.—Emelie East, 4–7209.

Subcommittee on Defense (SD–122), 4–7239
Clerk.—Steven J. Cortese.
Professional Staff: Sid Ashworth, 4–3378; Susan Hogan, 4–7296; Jay Kimmitt, 4–7206; Gary Reese, 4–7207; Mary C. Marshall, 4–6817; John J. Young, 4–7232.
Staff Assistant.—Mazie R. Mattson, 4–7204.
Minority Clerk.—Charles J. Houy (SD–117), 4–7293.
Professional Staff Member.—C. Richard D'Amato (SD–160), 4–3088.
Staff Assistant.—Emelie East, 4–7209.

Subcommittee on District of Columbia (SD–142), 4–2731
Clerk.—Mary Beth Nethercutt.
Minority Clerk.—Terry Sauvain (SD–144), 4–0338.
Staff Assistant.—Liz Blevins (SD–156), 4–4403.

Subcommittee on Energy and Water Development (SD–131), 4–7261
Clerk.—Alex W. Flint.
Professional Staff Member.—W. David Gwaltney, 4–0332.
Staff Assistant.—Lashawnda Leftwich, 4–7234
Minority Clerk.—Greg Daines (SD–156), 4–0335.
Staff Assistant.—Liz Blevins (SD–156), 4–4403.

Subcommittee on Foreign Operations, Export Financing and Related Programs (S–125), 4–7274
Clerk.—Robin Cleveland (SD–142), 4–5095.
Professional Staff Member.—Will Smith (SD–142), 4–2104.
Minority Clerk.—Tim Rieser (SH–123), 4–7284.
Professional Staff Member.—Emelie East, 4–7209.

Subcommittee on Interior and Related Agencies (SD–127), 4–7262
Clerk.—Bruce Evans (SD–131), 4–7257.
Professional Staff: Ginny James (SD–131), 4–7350; Anne McInerney (SD–131), 4–2168.
Minority Clerk.—Sue E. Masica (SH–123), 4–5271.
Staff Assistant.—Carole Geagley (SH–123), 4–7240.

Subcommittee on Labor, Health and Human Services, and Education (SD–184), 4–7643
Clerk.—Craig A. Higgins (SD–184), 4–7643.
Professional Staff Members: Bettilou Taylor, 4–7216; Dale Cabaniss, 4–1396.
Staff Assistant.—Lula Edwards, 4–7236.
Minority Clerk.—Marsha Simon (SH–123), 4–7288.
Staff Assistant.—Carole Geagley (SH–123), 4–7240.

Subcommittee on Legislative Branch, 4–9420
Clerk.—Christine Ciccone (S–125) 4–8921.
Minority Clerk.—James H. English (S–205), 4–7200.

Subcommittee on Military Construction (SD–140), 4–7271
Clerk.—Sid Ashworth, 4–3378.

Committee on Appropriations (S–128), 224–3471—CONTINUED

Minority Clerk.—C. Richard D'Amato (SD–123), 4–3088.
Staff Assistant.—Emelie East, 4–7209.

Subcommittee on Transportation and Related Agencies (SD–133), 4–0330

Clerk.—Wally Burnett, 4–2175.
Professional Staff Members: Anne Miano, 4–7213; Joyce C. Rose, 4–7281.
Minority Clerk.—Peter Rogoff (SH–123), 4–7245.
Staff Assistant.—Carole Geagley (SH–123), 4–7240.

Subcommittee on Treasury and General Government (S–128), 4–7337

Clerk.—Pat Raymond (SD–190), 4–1394.
Professional Staff Member.—Tammy Perrin (SD–190), 4–9145.
Staff Assistant.—Lula Edwards (SD–190), 4–7236.
Minority Clerk.—Barbara A. Retzlaff (SD–196), 4–6280.
Staff Assistant.—Liz Blevins (SD–156), 4–4403.

Subcommittee on VA, HUD and Independent Agencies (SD–131), 4–7253

Clerk.—John Kamarck.
Professional Staff Member.—Carolyn E. Apostolou, 4–7238.
Staff Assistant.—Lashawnda Leftwich, 4–7234.
Minority Clerk.—Sally Chadbourne (SD–134), 4–7231.
Staff Assistant.—Liz Blevins (SD–156), 4–4403.

Armed Services

228 Russell Senate Office Building 20510–6050

phone 224–3871, http://www.senate.gov/committee/armed_services.html

meets every Tuesday and Thursday

Strom Thurmond, of South Carolina, *Chairman.*

John Warner, of Virginia.
John McCain, of Arizona.
Dan Coats, of Indiana.
Bob Smith, of New Hampshire.
Dirk Kempthorne, of Idaho.
James M. Inhofe, of Oklahoma.
Rick Santorum, of Pennsylvania.
Olympia J. Snowe, of Maine.
Pat Roberts, of Kansas.

Carl Levin, of Michigan.
Edward M. Kennedy, of Massachusetts.
Jeff Bingaman, of New Mexico.
John Glenn, of Ohio.
Robert C. Byrd, of West Virginia.
Charles S. Robb, of Virginia.
Joseph I. Lieberman, of Connecticut.
Max Cleland, of Georgia.

SUBCOMMITTEES

[The chairman and the ranking minority member are ex officio members of all subcommittees.]

Acquisition and Technology

Mr. Santorum, *Chairman*

Mr. Smith
Ms. Snowe
Mr. Roberts

Mr. Lieberman
Mr. Kennedy
Mr. Bingaman

Airland Forces

Mr. Coats, *Chairman*

Mr. Warner
Mr. Kempthorne
Mr. Inhofe
Mr. Santorum
Mr. Roberts

Mr. Glenn
Mr. Bingaman
Mr. Byrd
Mr. Lieberman
Mr. Cleland

Personnel

Mr. Kempthorne, *Chairman*

Mr. McCain	*Mr. Cleland*
Mr. Coats	*Mr. Kennedy*
Ms. Snowe	*Mr. Robb*

Readiness

Mr. Inhofe, *Chairman*

Mr. McCain	*Mr. Robb*
Mr. Coats	*Mr. Glenn*
Mr. Roberts	*Mr. Cleland*

Seapower

Mr. Warner, *Chairman*

Mr. McCain	*Mr. Kennedy*
Mr. Smith	*Mr. Byrd*
Mr. Santorum	*Mr. Robb*
Ms. Snowe	*Mr. Lieberman*

Strategic Forces

Mr. Smith, *Chairman*

Mr. Warner	*Mr. Bingaman*
Mr. Kempthorne	*Mr. Glenn*
Mr. Inhofe	*Mr. Byrd*

STAFF

Committee on Armed Services (SR–228), 224–3871.
Staff Director.—Les Brownlee.
Deputy Staff Director.—George W. Lauffer.
Chief Clerk.—Melinda M. Koutsoumpas.
Deputy Chief Clerk.—Marie Fabrizio Dickinson.
General Counsel.—Scott W. Stucky.
Assistant Counsel.—Ann M. Mittermeyer.
Communications Director.—Christine Kelley Cimko.
Security Manager.—Cindy Pearson.
Systems Administrator.—Roslyne D. Turner.
Printing and Documents Clerk.—Larry J. Hoag.
Receptionist.—Christopher J. MacNaughton.
Research Assistant.—Pamela L. Farrell.
Staff Assistants: Patricia L. Banks, Shawn H. Edwards, Cristina W. Fiori, J. Reaves McLeod, Sarah J. Ritch, Moultrie D. Roberts, Jennifer L. Wallace.
Minority Staff Director.—David S. Lyles.
Special Assistant.—Christine E. Cowart.
Minority Counsels: Peter K. Levine, Richard D. DeBobes, Madelyn R. Creedon.
Staff Assistants: Jan Gordon, Jennifer A. Lambert.
Subcommittee on Acquisition and Technology
Professional Staff Member.—Jonathan L. Etherton.
Minority Staff Member.—Peter K. Levine.
Subcommittee on Airland Forces
Professional Staff Member.—John R. Barnes.
Minority Staff Members: Creighton Greene, Daniel J. Cox, Jr.
Subcommittee on Personnel
Professional Staff Member.—Charles S. Abell.
Minority Staff Member.—Patrick T. Henry.
Subcommittee on Readiness
Professional Staff Member.—Cord A. Sterling.
Minority Staff Member.—Michael J. McCord.
Subcommittee on Seapower
Professional Staff Member.—Steven C. Saulnier.
Minority Staff Member.—Creighton Greene.

Committee on Armed Services (SR–228), 224–3871—CONTINUED

Subcommittee on Strategic Forces

Professional Staff Member.—Eric H. Thoemmes.

Minority Staff Member.—Madelyn R. Creedon.

Majority Professional Staff Members for:

Arms Control/Counterproliferation.—Lucia Monica Chavez.

Aviation Systems.—Stephen L. Madey, Jr.

Budget Tracking.—Lawrence J. Lanzillotta.

Civilian Nominations.—Scott W. Stucky.

Energy Issues.—Paul M. Longsworth.

Environmental Issues.—Ann M. Mittermeyer.

Intelligence Issues.—Eric H. Thoemmes.

International Security Policy.—Bert K. Mizusawa.

Military Construction/Base Closure.—George W. Lauffer.

Military Nominations.—Charles S. Abell.

Regional Security.—John H. Miller.

Minority Professional Staff Members for:

Acquisition Policy.—Peter K. Levine.

Arms Control/Proliferation Issues.—Richard W. Fieldhouse.

Aviation Systems.—Creighton Greene.

Budget Tracking.—Michael J. McCord.

Civilian Nominations.—Peter K. Levine.

Defense Security Assistance.—Richard D. DeBobes.

Energy Issues.—Madelyn R. Creedon.

Environmental Issues.—Peter K. Levine.

Foreign Policy/Peacekeeping/UN/Multilateral Issues/Treaties.—Richard D. DeBobes.

Intelligence Issues.—Andrew W. Johnson.

Military Nominations.—Patrick T. Henry.

Military Construction/Base Closure.—Michael J. McCord.

Military Strategy.—Richard D. DeBobes.

Banking, Housing and Urban Affairs

534 Dirksen Senate Office Building 20510–6075
phone 224–7391, http://www.senate.gov/committee/banking.html

meets last Tuesday of each month

Alfonse M. D'Amato, of New York, *Chairman.*

Phil Gramm, of Texas.
Richard C. Shelby, of Alabama.
Connie Mack, of Florida.
Lauch Faircloth, of North Carolina.
Robert F. Bennett, of Utah.
Rod Grams, of Minnesota.
Wayne Allard, of Colorado.
Michael B. Enzi, of Wyoming.
Chuck Hagel, of Nebraska.

Paul S. Sarbanes, of Maryland.
Christopher J. Dodd, of Connecticut.
John F. Kerry, of Massachusetts.
Richard H. Bryan, of Nevada.
Barbara Boxer, of California.
Carol Moseley-Braun, of Illinois.
Tim Johnson, of South Dakota.
Jack Reed, of Rhode Island.

SUBCOMMITTEES

[The chairman and ranking minority member are ex officio, nonvoting members of all subcommittees.]

Financial Institutions and Regulatory Relief

Mr. Faircloth, *Chairman*

Mr. Allard
Mr. Enzi
Mr. Shelby
Mr. Mack
Mr. Grams
Mr. Gramm

Mr. Bryan
Mr. Johnson
Mrs. Boxer
Ms. Moseley-Braun
Mr. Reed

Financial Services and Technology

Mr. Bennett, *Chairman*

Mr. Hagel	*Mrs. Boxer*
Mr. Mack	*Mr. Kerry*
Mr. Grams	*Mr. Dodd*
Mr. Enzi	*Mr. Johnson*

Housing Opportunity and Community Development

Mr. Mack, *Chairman*

Mr. Faircloth	*Mr. Kerry*
Mr. Enzi	*Mr. Reed*
Mr. Shelby	*Mr. Dodd*
Mr. Allard	*Mr. Bryan*
Mr. Hagel	*Ms. Moseley-Braun*

International Finance

Mr. Grams, *Chairman*

Mr. Hagel	*Ms. Moseley-Braun*
Mr. Gramm	*Mrs. Boxer*
Mr. Bennett	*Mr. Reed*

Securities

Mr. Gramm, *Chairman*

Mr. Shelby	*Mr. Dodd*
Mr. Allard	*Mr. Johnson*
Mr. Bennett	*Mr. Kerry*
Mr. Faircloth	*Mr. Bryan*

STAFF

Committee on Banking, Housing and Urban Affairs (SD–534), 224–7391.
Staff Director.—Howard A. Menell.
Chief Counsel.—Phil Bechtel.
Counsels: Holidae Hayes, Joe Mondello, Doug Nappi, Laura Unger.
Chief Clerk.—Joe Kolinski.
Press Secretary.—E. Richard Mills.
Professional Staff: Melody Fennel, David Hardiman, Helena Grannis, Madelyn Simmons, Al Wooten.
Financial Economists: Peggy Kuhn, Lendell Porterfield.
Legislative Assistant.—David Hardiman.
Staff Assistants: Sloan Deerin, Peter Barrett.
Executive Assistants: Mark Hoffman, Doris Mahoney.
Editor.—George Whittle.
Editorial Assistants: Donna Krause, Irene Whitson.
Democratic Staff:
Staff Director/Chief Counsel.—Steve Harris.
Senior Counsel.—Marty Gruenberg.
Chief International Counsel.—Patrick Mulloy.
Counsels: Sarah Bloom Raskin, Andrew Lowenthal.
Staff Assistants: Yael Belkind, Amy Randel, Carolyn Smith.
Majority Staff Director, Securities Subcommittee.—Wayne Abernathy.
Majority Staff Director, Financial Institutions and Regulatory Relief Subcommittee.—[Vacant].
Majority Staff Director, International Finance Subcommittee.—Dave Berson.
Majority Staff Director, Housing Opportunity and Community Development Subcommittee.—Chris Lord.
Majority Deputy Staff Director, Housing Opportunity and Community Development Subcommittee.—Kari Davidson.
Majority Staff Director, Financial Services and Technology Subcommittee.—Robert Cresanti.

Budget

621 Dirksen Senate Office Building 20510–6100

phone 224–0642, http://www.senate.gov/committee/budget.html

meets first Thursday of each month

Pete V. Domenici, of New Mexico, *Chairman.*

Charles E. Grassley, of Iowa.
Don Nickles, of Oklahoma.
Phil Gramm, of Texas.
Christopher S. Bond, of Missouri.
Slade Gorton, of Washington.
Judd Gregg, of New Hampshire.
Olympia J. Snowe, of Maine.
Spencer Abraham, of Michigan.
Bill Frist, of Tennessee.
Rod Grams, of Minnesota.
Gordon H. Smith, of Oregon.

Frank R. Lautenberg, of New Jersey.
Ernest F. Hollings, of South Carolina.
Kent Conrad, of North Dakota.
Paul S. Sarbanes, of Maryland.
Barbara Boxer, of California.
Patty Murray, of Washington.
Ron Wyden, of Oregon.
Russell D. Feingold, of Wisconsin.
Tim Johnson, of South Dakota.
Richard Durbin, of Illinois.

(No Subcommittees)

STAFF

Committee on Budget (SD–621), 224–0642.
Majority Staff Director.—G. William Hoagland, 4–0769.
Assistant Staff Director/Director of—
Appropriations Activities.—Carole McGuire, 4–0537.
Budget Process and Energy.—Austin Smythe, 4–0539.
Director of Budget Review.—Anne Miller, 4–5398.
Senior Policy Analyst.—Jim Capretta, 4–0834.
Senior Analyst for—
Agriculture and Natural Resources and Community Development.—Ricardo Rel, 4–6588.
Budget Review.—Cheri Reidy, 4–0557.
Education, Social Service and Justice.—Lisa Cieplak, 4–0564.
Government Finance and Management.—Jim Hearn, 4–2370.
Transportation and Science.—Brian Riley, 4–3023.
Income Security and Veterans.—Michael Ruffner, 4–0797.
Communications Director.—Bob Stevenson, 4–5289.
Communications Assistant.—Amy Call, 4–6815.
Chief Economist.—Amy Smith, 4–0566.
Chief Counsel.—Beth Smerko Felder, 4–0531.
Legislative Counsel.—Kay Davies, 4–0543.
Legal Assistant.—Karen Ricoy, 4–1602.
Budget Analyst.—Scott Burnison, 4–0838.
Analyst for Defense.—Winslow Wheeler, 4–0529.
Analyst for International Affairs.—Alice Grant, 4–0833.
Administrative Director.—Kathleen Dorn, 4–6988.
Staff Assistants: Mieko Nakabayashi, 4–0536; Andrea Shank, 4–2574.
Fellow.—Marc Sumerlin, 4–0857.
Minority Staff Director.—Bruce King, 4–9712.
Staff Assistant.—Nell Mays, 4–0533.
Director for Planning.—Sander Lurie, 4–6822.
Director of Budget Review and Analysis/Senior Analyst for Medicare.—Sue Nelson, 4–0560.
Senior Analyst for—
Agriculture, Commerce and Community, and Regional Development.—Phil Karsting, 4–0544.
Education and Health/Appropriations Coordinator.—Amy Peck Abraham, 4–0559.
Energy, Environment, and Science and Technology.—Matt Greenwald, 4–0538.
Analyst for—
General Government and Veterans.—John Cahill, 4–0835.
Defense, International Affairs and Justice.—Jon Rosenwasser, 4–0865.
Transportation.—Mitch Warren, 4–0535.

Chief Economist.—Jim Klumpner, 4–7925.
General Counsel.—Jodi Grant, 4–1458.
Tax Counsel.—Martin Morris, 4–0837.
Budget Analyst.—Barry Strumpf, 4–0550.
Non-Designated:
Chief Clerk.—Lynne Seymour, 4–0191.
Computer Systems Administrator.—Diane Bath, 4–6576.
Publicants Department.—Alex Green, 4–0855.
Staff Assistants: Victor Block, 4–9547; Deena McMullen, 4–0565; George Woodall, 4–0796.

Commerce, Science and Transportation

508 Dirksen Senate Office Building 20510–6125

phone 224–5115, http://www.senate.gov/committee/commerce.html

meets first and third Tuesdays of each month

John McCain, of Arizona, *Chairman*

Ted Stevens, of Alaska.
Conrad Burns, of Montana.
Slade Gorton, of Washington.
Trent Lott, of Mississippi.
Kay Bailey Hutchison, of Texas.
Olympia J. Snowe, of Maine.
John Ashcroft, of Missouri.
Bill Frist, of Tennessee.
Spencer Abraham, of Michigan.
Sam Brownback, of Kansas.

Ernest F. Hollings, of South Carolina.
Daniel K. Inouye, of Hawaii.
Wendell H. Ford, of Kentucky.
John D. Rockefeller, IV, of West Virginia.
John F. Kerry, of Massachusetts.
John B. Breaux, of Louisiana.
Richard H. Bryan, of Nevada.
Byron L. Dorgan, of North Dakota.
Ron Wyden, of Oregon.

SUBCOMMITTEES

Aviation

Mr. Gorton, *Chairman*

Mr. Stevens
Mr. Burns
Mr. Lott
Mrs. Hutchison
Mr. Ashcroft
Mr. Frist
Ms. Snowe
Mr. Brownback

Mr. Ford
Mr. Hollings
Mr. Inouye
Mr. Bryan
Mr. Rockefeller
Mr. Breaux
Mr. Dorgan
Mr. Wyden

Communications

Mr. Burns, *Chairman*

Mr. Stevens
Mr. Gorton
Mr. Lott
Mr. Ashcroft
Mrs. Hutchison
Mr. Abraham
Mr. Frist
Mr. Brownback

Mr. Hollings
Mr. Inouye
Mr. Ford
Mr. Kerry
Mr. Breaux
Mr. Rockefeller
Mr. Dorgan
Mr. Wyden

Consumer Affairs, Foreign Commerce and Tourism

Mr. Ashcroft, *Chairman*

Mr. Gorton
Mr. Abraham
Mr. Burns
Mr. Brownback

Mr. Breaux
Mr. Ford
Mr. Bryan

Manufacturing and Competitiveness

Mr. Abraham, *Chairman*

Ms. Snowe
Mr. Aschcroft
Mr. Frist
Mr. Brownback

Mr. Bryan
Mr. Hollings
Mr. Dorgan
Mr. Rockefeller

Oceans and Fisheries

Ms. Snowe, *Chairman*

Mr. Stevens
Mr. Gorton
Mrs. Hutchison

Mr. Kerry
Mr. Inouye
Mr. Breaux

Science, Technology and Space

Mr. Frist, *Chairman*

Mr. Burns
Mrs. Hutchison
Mr. Stevens
Mr. Abraham

Mr. Rockefeller
Mr. Kerry
Mr. Bryan
Mr. Dorgan

Surface Transportation and Merchant Marine

Mrs. Hutchison, *Chairwoman*

Mr. Stevens
Mr. Burns
Ms. Snowe
Mr. Frist
Mr. Abraham
Mr. Ashcroft

Mr. Inouye
Mr. Breaux
Mr. Dorgan
Mr. Bryan
Mr. Wyden

STAFF

Committee on Commerce, Science and Transportation (SD–508), 224–5115.
Staff Director.—John Raidt.
Policy Director.—Mark Buse.
General Counsel.—Kevin Sabo.
Press Secretary.—Pia Pialorsi.
Democratic Chief Counsel and Staff Director.—Ivan Schlager.
Democratic General Counsel.—James S.W. Drewry.
Staff:
Jennifer Aitken
Denise Anderson
Lloyd G. Ator
Ann D. Begeman
Lauren (Pete) Belvin
Carl W. Bentzel
Moses Boyd
Lance D. Bultena
Charlotte Casey
Penni Compton
Penny Dalton
Floyd Deschamps*
Gregg Elias
Leslie M. Ellis
Paul Feeney
Robert L. Foster
Matthew T. Frekko
Yvonne T. Gowdy
Clyde J. Hart
Stephen Hartell
Lila H. Helms
Ann Hodges
Michael E. Inners
Vanessa E. Jones
Kevin M. Joseph
Summer L. Keel
Rebecca A. Kojm
Kevin Krufky
Susan MacDonald
Thomas Melius
Denis P. O'Donovan
Rosalind M. Parker
Pia Pialorsi
Gretchen Stevenson Post
Virginia Pounds
Elizabeth Prostic
Michael W. Reynolds
James D. Reilly*
Andrew Rivas
James A. Sartucci*
Ivan Schlager
Brett Scott
Arlene M. Sidell
Theresa (Dianne) Smith*
Scott B. Verstandig
Joani Wales
Samuel E. Whitehorn
Patrick H. Windham
Kate T. Wing
Jessica Yoo

*Associated with Committee.

Energy and Natural Resources

304 Dirksen Senate Office Building 20510–6510

phone 224–4971, fax 224–6163, http://www.senate.gov/committee/energy.html

meets third Wednesday of each month

Frank H. Murkowski, of Alaska, *Chairman.*

Pete V. Domenici, of New Mexico.
Don Nickles, of Oklahoma.
Larry E. Craig, of Idaho.
Ben Nighthorse Campbell, of Colorado.
Craig Thomas, of Wyoming.
Jon Kyl, of Arizona.
Rod Grams, of Minnesota.
Gordon H. Smith, of Oregon.
Slade Gorton, of Washington.
Conrad Burns, of Montana.

Dale Bumpers, of Arkansas.
Wendell H. Ford, of Kentucky.
Jeff Bingaman, of New Mexico.
Daniel K. Akaka, of Hawaii.
Byron L. Dorgan, of North Dakota.
Bob Graham, of Florida.
Ron Wyden, of Oregon.
Tim Johnson, of South Dakota.
Mary L. Landrieu, of Louisiana.

SUBCOMMITTEES

[The chairman and the ranking minority member are ex officio members of all subcommittees.]

Energy Research, Development, Production and Regulation

Mr. Nickles, *Chairman*

Mr. Domenici, *Vice Chairman*

Mr. Craig
Mr. Grams
Mr. Gorton
Mr. Campbell
Mr. Smith

Mr. Ford
Mr. Bingaman
Mr. Graham
Mr. Wyden
Mr. Johnson
Ms. Landrieu

Forests and Public Land Management

Mr. Craig, *Chairman*

Mr. Burns, *Vice Chairman*

Mr. Domenici
Mr. Thomas
Mr. Kyl
Mr. Smith

Mr. Dorgan
Mr. Graham
Mr. Wyden
Mr. Johnson
Ms. Landrieu

National Parks, Historic Preservation and Recreation

Mr. Thomas, *Chairman*

Mr. Campbell, *Vice Chairman*

Mr. Grams
Mr. Nickles
Mr. Burns

Mr. Bingaman
Mr. Akaka
Mr. Graham
Ms. Landrieu

Water and Power

Mr. Kyl, *Chairman*

Mr. Smith, *Vice Chairman*

Mr. Gorton
Mr. Campbell
Mr. Craig

Mr. Akaka
Mr. Ford
Mr. Dorgan
Mr. Wyden

STAFF

Committee on Energy and Natural Resources (SD–304), 224–4971, fax 224–6163.
Staff Director.—Gregg Renkes, 4–1004.
Calendar Clerk.—Mia Miranda (SD–317), 4–7147.
Chief Clerk.—Carol Craft (SD–358), 4–7153.
Chief Counsel.—Gary Ellsworth (SD–358), 4–7141.
Computer Systems Administrator.—Chris Kimball (SD–317), 4–7163.
Counsels: Karen Hunsicker (SH–312), 4–3543; Maureen Koetz (SH–312), 4–7932; Mike Poling (SH–212), 4–8276; Kelly Johnson, (SH–212), 4–3329.
Director of Communications.—David Fish (SD–364), 4–5861.
Communications Assistant.—Derek Jumper (SD–364), 4–2039.
Executive Assistant to Chief Counsel.—Camille H. Flint (SD–358), 4–5070.
Executive Assistant to Staff Director.—Gerry Gentry (SD–358), 4–5305.
Financial Clerk.—Nancy Hall (SD–317), 4–3606.
Printer.—Jack Sprinkle (SD–304), 4–7302.
Printer/Editor.—Richard Smit (SD–304), 4–3118.
Professional Staff Members: David Garman (SD–308), 4–7933; Jim O'Toole (SD–362), 4–5161; Mark Rey (SD–306), 4–2878; Howard Useem (SD–308), 4–6567; Michael Menge (SD–306), 4–9607; Brian Malnak (SH–212), 4–8119.
Receptionist.—Amy Sparck (SD–304), 4–2694.
Senior Counsel.—Jim Beirne (SH–312), 4–2564.
Staff Assistants: Judy Brown (SD–308) 4–7556; Julia Gustafson (SD–362), 4–1219; Jo Meuse (SH–212), 4–4756; Betty Nevitt (SH–312), 4–0765; Shawn Taylor (SD–308), 4–7875.
Minority Staff Director.—Tom Williams (SD–312), 4–7145.
Counsels: Kira Finkler, 4–8164; Mary Katherine Ishee, 4–7865.
Senior Counsel.—David Brooks, 4–9863.
Minority Clerk/Office Manager.—Vicki Thorne, 4–3607.
Receptionist.—Elizabeth MacDonald, 4–6836.
Chief Counsel.—Sam Fowler, 4–7571.
Staff Assistants: Diane Balamoti, 4–7934; Teri Breland, 4–5915.

Environment and Public Works

410 Dirksen Senate Office Building 20510–6175
phone 224–6176, http://www.senate.gov/committee/environment.html

meets first and third Thursdays of each month

John H. Chafee, of Rhode Island, *Chairman.*

John W. Warner, of Virginia.
Bob Smith, of New Hampshire.
Dirk Kempthorne, of Idaho.
James M. Inhofe, of Oklahoma.
Craig Thomas, of Wyoming.
Christopher S. Bond, of Missouri.
Tim Hutchinson, of Arkansas.
Wayne Allard, of Colorado.
Jeff Sessions, of Alabama.

Max Baucus, of Montana.
Daniel Patrick Moynihan, of New York.
Frank R. Lautenberg, of New Jersey.
Harry Reid, of Nevada.
Bob Graham, of Florida.
Joseph I. Lieberman, of Connecticut.
Barbara Boxer, of California.
Ron Wyden, of Oregon.

SUBCOMMITTEES

[John H. Chafee, as chairman of the committee, serves as an ex officio member of each subcommittee.]

Clean Air, Wetlands, Private Property and Nuclear Safety

Mr. Inhofe, *Chairman*

Mr. Hutchinson
Mr. Allard
Mr. Sessions

Mr. Graham
Mr. Lieberman
Mrs. Boxer

Drinking Water, Fisheries and Wildlife

Mr. Kempthorne, *Chairman*

Mr. Thomas	*Mr. Reid*
Mr. Bond	*Mr. Lautenberg*
Mr. Warner	*Mr. Lieberman*
Mr. Hutchinson	*Mr. Wyden*

Superfund, Waste Control and Risk Assessment

Mr. Smith, *Chairman*

Mr. Warner	*Mr. Lautenberg*
Mr. Inhofe	*Mr. Moynihan*
Mr. Allard	*Mrs. Boxer*
Mr. Sessions	*Mr. Graham*

Transportation and Infrastructure

Mr. Warner, *Chairman*

Mr. Smith	*Mr. Baucus*
Mr. Kempthorne	*Mr. Moynihan*
Mr. Bond	*Mr. Reid*
Mr. Inhofe	*Mr. Graham*
Mr. Thomas	*Mrs. Boxer*

STAFF

Committee on Environment and Public Works (SD–410), phone 224–6176

Recording for Committee Agenda, 224–1179.

Majority FAX (SD–410), 224–5167; (SH–415), 224–2322.

Staff Director/Chief Counsel.—Steven J. Shimberg, 4–7854.

Deputy Staff Director.—Jimmie Powell, 4–2376.

Office Manager.—Marie Balderson, 4–4764.

Counsels: Thomas Gibson (SH–415), 4–5761; Linda Jordan, 4–3255; Ann Klee (SH–505), 4–0554; Jeff Merrifield (SH–415), 4–2699; Stephen Odell (SD–410), 4–7940; Jason Patlis (SH–415), 4–9134; Andrew Wheeler (SH–505), 4–0146.

Professional Staff: Daniel Corbett, 4–7863; Stephanie Daigle, 4–5642; Dan Delich (SH–415), 4–5762; Ann Loomis (SH–415), 4–3211; Catherine Taylor (SH–415), 4–1615.

Editorial Director.—Duane Nystrom (SH–407), 4–7841.

Staff Assistant/Legislative Correspondent.—Eric King, 4–2829.

Staff Assistants: Elaine Herrick, 4–7189; Abigail Kinnison, 4–3107; Irene Sarate, 4–7855.

System Administrator.—Carolyn Streeter (SH–415), 4–5763.

Financial Clerk.—Stephanie Brewster (SH–505), 4–7844.

Receptionist.—Camille Sanders, 4–2991.

Minority FAX (SD–456), 4–1273; (SH–508), 8–0574.

Minority Staff Director.—J. Thomas Sliter (SD–456), 4–8832.

General Counsel.—Michael W. Evans, 4–8832.

Office Manager.—Karen Piccione, 4–3974.

Counsels: David W. Hoskins, (SH–508), 4–0748; Barbara Roberts (SD–456), 4–2969.

Professional Staff: Jo-Ellen Darcy (SH–508), 4–3247; Cliff L. Rothenstein (SH–508), 4–9097; Kathryn Ruffalo, 4–3333.

System Administrator.—Janet Burrell, 4–3598.

Staff Assistant.—Michael Hill, 4–3975.

Finance

219 Dirksen Senate Office Building 20510–6200

phone 224–4515, fax 224–5920, http://www.senate.gov/committee/finance.html

meets second and fourth Tuesdays of each month

William V. Roth, Jr., of Delaware, *Chairman.*

John H. Chafee, of Rhode Island.
Charles E. Grassley, of Iowa.
Orrin G. Hatch, of Utah.
Alfonse M. D'Amato, of New York.
Frank H. Murkowski, of Alaska.
Don Nickles, of Oklahoma.
Phil Gramm, of Texas.
Trent Lott, of Mississippi.
James M. Jeffords, of Vermont.
Connie Mack, of Florida.

Daniel Patrick Moynihan, of New York.
Max Baucus, of Montana.
John D. Rockefeller, IV, of West Virginia.
John Breaux, of Louisiana.
Kent Conrad, of North Dakota.
Bob Graham, of Florida.
Carol Moseley-Braun, of Illinois.
Richard H. Bryan, of Nevada.
J. Robert Kerrey, of Nebraska.

SUBCOMMITTEES

[The chairman and the ranking minority member are ex officio members of all subcommittees]

Health Care

Mr. Gramm, *Chairman*

Mr. Roth
Mr. Chafee
Mr. Grassley
Mr. Hatch
Mr. D'Amato
Mr. Nickles
Mr. Jeffords

Mr. Rockefeller
Mr. Baucus
Mr. Conrad
Mr. Graham
Ms. Moseley-Braun
Mr. Bryan
Mr. Kerrey

International Trade

Mr. Grassley, *Chairman*

Mr. Roth
Mr. Chafee
Mr. Hatch
Mr. D'Amato
Mr. Murkowski
Mr. Gramm
Mr. Lott
Mr. Mack

Mr. Moynihan
Mr. Baucus
Mr. Rockefeller
Mr. Breaux
Mr. Conrad
Mr. Graham
Ms. Moseley-Braun
Mr. Kerrey

Long-Term Growth, Debt and Deficit Reduction

Mr. Mack, *Chairman*

Mr. Murkowski
Mr. Lott

Mr. Graham
Mr. Bryan

Social Security and Family Policy

Mr. Chafee, *Chairman*

Mr. Nickles
Mr. Gramm
Mr. Jeffords

Mr. Breaux
Mr. Moynihan
Mr. Rockefeller
Ms. Moseley-Braun

Taxation and IRS Oversight

Mr. Nickles, *Chairman*

Mr. Roth	*Mr. Baucus*
Mr. Grassley	*Mr. Moynihan*
Mr. Hatch	*Mr. Breaux*
Mr. D'Amato	*Mr. Conrad*
Mr. Murkowski	*Mr. Bryan*
Mr. Lott	*Mr. Kerrey*
Mr. Jeffords	
Mr. Mack	

STAFF

Committee on Finance (SD–219), 224–4515, fax 224–5920.
Staff Director/Chief Counsel.—Lindy L. Paull.
Economist/Chief Budget Analyst.—Joan Woodward.
Health/Social Security Analyst.—Alexander Vachon.
Chief Clerk.—Jane Butterfield.
Chief Editor.—Bruce Anderson.
Chief Health Analyst.—Julia James.
Chief Investigator.—Eric Thorson.
Chief Tax Counsel.—Mark Prater.
Tax Counsels: Rosemary Becchi, Douglas Fisher, Brigitta Gulya, Samuel Olchyk, Lori Peterson, Tom Roesser.
Trade Counsel.—Jeremy Preiss.
Correspondence Manager.—Sallie Cribbs.
Health Analyst.—Dennis Smith.
Hearing Clerks: Mark Blair, Darcell M. Savage.
International Trade Counsel.—Erik Autor.
Press Secretary.—Virginia Koops.
Deputy Press Secretary.—Christina Pearson.
General Counsel.—Frank Polk.
Receptionists: Churchill Hooff, Connie Foster.
Staff Assistants: Myrtle Agent, Donna Ridenour (Health).
System Administrator.—Janet Blum.
Legislative Fellow.—Robert Baker.
Minority Staff Director/Chief Counsel.—Mark A. Patterson (SH–203), 4–5315.
Minority Chief Economist.—David Podoff.
Minority Chief International Trade Counsel.—Deborah Adele Lamb.
Minority Chief Tax Counsels: Nick Giordano, Jonathan Talisman.
Minority Office Manager.—Jon Resnick.
Minority Professional Staff Members (Medicaid): Laird Burnett, Kristen Testa.
Minority Receptionist.—LaShawn Lewis.
Minority Research Assistant.—Rakesh Singh.
Minority Professional Staff (Welfare).—Douglas Steiger.
Minority Senior Health Counselor (NY Issues).—Faye Drummond.
Minority Tax Counsels: Patricia McClanahan, Maury I. Passman.
Minority Trade Counsel.—Linda Menghetti.

Foreign Relations

450 Dirksen Senate Office Building 20510–6225
phone 224–4651, http://www.senate.gov/committee/foreign.html

Jesse Helms, of North Carolina, *Chairman.*

Richard G. Lugar, of Indiana.
Paul Coverdell, of Georgia.
Chuck Hagel, of Nebraska.
Gordon H. Smith, of Oregon.
Craig Thomas, of Wyoming.
Rod Grams, of Minnesota.
John Ashcroft, of Missouri.
Bill Frist, of Tennessee.
Sam Brownback, of Kansas.

Joseph R. Biden, Jr., of Delaware.
Paul S. Sarbanes, of Maryland.
Christopher J. Dodd, of Connecticut.
John F. Kerry, of Massachusetts.
Charles S. Robb, of Virginia.
Russell D. Feingold, of Wisconsin.
Dianne Feinstein, of California.
Paul D. Wellstone, of Minnesota.

SUBCOMMITTEES

[The chairman and ranking minority member of the full committee are ex officio members of each subcommittee on which they do not serve as members.]

African Affairs

Mr. Ashcroft, *Chairman*

Mr. Grams
Mr. Frist

Mr. Feingold
Mr. Sarbanes

East Asian and Pacific Affairs

Mr. Thomas, *Chairman*

Mr. Frist
Mr. Lugar
Mr. Coverdell
Mr. Hagel

Mr. Kerry
Mr. Robb
Mr. Feingold
Mrs. Feinstein

European Affairs

Mr. Smith, *Chairman*

Mr. Lugar
Mr. Ashcroft
Mr. Hagel
Mr. Thomas

Mr. Biden
Mr. Wellstone
Mr. Sarbanes
Mr. Dodd

International Economic Policy, Export and Trade Promotion

Mr. Hagel, *Chairman*

Mr. Thomas
Mr. Frist
Mr. Coverdell

Mr. Sarbanes
Mr. Biden
Mr. Wellstone

International Operations

Mr. Grams, *Chairman*

Mr. Helms
Mr. Brownback
Mr. Smith

Mrs. Feinstein
Mr. Dodd
Mr. Kerry

Near Eastern and South Asian Affairs

Mr. Brownback, *Chairman*

Mr. Smith
Mr. Grams
Mr. Helms
Mr. Ashcroft

Mr. Robb
Mrs. Feinstein
Mr. Wellstone
Mr. Sarbanes

Western Hemisphere, Peace Corps, Narcotics and Terrorism

Mr. Coverdell, *Chairman*

Mr. Helms
Mr. Lugar
Mr. Brownback

Mr. Dodd
Mr. Kerry
Mr. Robb

STAFF

Committee on Foreign Relations (SD–450), 224–4651.
Staff Director.—James W. Nance.
Chief Counsel.—Thomas C. Kleine.
Minority Staff Director.—Edwin K. Hall.
Minority Counsel.—Brian McKeon.
Chief Clerk.—Barbara F. Allem.

Professional Staff:
Stephen E. Biegun
Marshall Billingslea
Ellen Bork
Edward P. Levine
Elisabeth J. DeMoss
Daniel W. Fisk
G. Garrett Grigsby
Michael H. Haltzel
Gina Marie Hathaway
Sandra S. Mason
Christopher M. Moore
Patricia A. McNerney
Janice M. O'Connell
Diana L. Ohlbaum
Danielle M. Pletka
Nancy H. Stetson
Puneet Talwar
Marc A. Thiessen
Christopher J. Walker
Elizabeth Y. Wilson

Support Staff:
Beatriz G. Alonso
Andrew Anderson
Jacqueline Aronson
Sue Campbell
Sherry Grandjean
Debbie Johnson
Cheryl Kimball
Caroline Mullen
Ed Mullen
Colleen Noonan
Susan Oursler
Dawn Ratliff
Julie Raulston
Kathryn M. Taylor
Natasha Watson
Joanna Woodard

Governmental Affairs

340 Dirksen Senate Office Building 20510–6250
phone 224–4751, http://www.senate.gov/committee/governmental_affairs.html
Hearing Room—342 Dirksen Senate Office Building, phone 224–4941

meets first Thursday of each month

Fred Thompson, of Tennessee, *Chairman.*

William V. Roth, Jr., of Delaware.
Ted Stevens, of Alaska.
Susan Collins, of Maine.
Sam Brownback, of Kansas.
Pete V. Domenici, of New Mexico.
Thad Cochran, of Mississippi.
Don Nickles, of Oklahoma.
Arlen Specter, of Pennsylvania.

John Glenn, of Ohio.
Carl Levin, of Michigan.
Joseph I. Lieberman, of Connecticut.
Daniel K. Akaka, of Hawaii.
Richard J. Durbin, of Illinois.
Robert G. Torricelli, of New Jersey.
Max Cleland, of Georgia.

SUBCOMMITTEES

[The chairman and the ranking minority member are ex officio members of all subcommittees.]

International Security, Proliferation and Federal Services

Mr. Cochran, *Chairman*

Mr. Stevens
Ms. Collins
Mr. Domenici
Mr. Nickles
Mr. Specter

Mr. Levin
Mr. Akaka
Mr. Durbin
Mr. Torricelli
Mr. Cleland

Oversight of Government Management, Restructing and the District of Columbia

Mr. Brownback, *Chairman*

Mr. Roth	*Mr. Lieberman*
Mr. Specter	*Mr. Cleland*

Permanent Subcommittee on Investigations

Ms. Collins, *Chairwoman*

Mr. Roth	*Mr. Glenn*
Mr. Stevens	*Mr. Levin*
Mr. Brownback	*Mr. Lieberman*
Mr. Domenici	*Mr. Akaka*
Mr. Cochran	*Mr. Durbin*
Mr. Nickels	*Mr. Torricelli*
Mr. Specter	*Mr. Cleland*

STAFF

Committee on Governmental Affairs (SD–340), 224–4751.
Staff Director/Counsel.—Hannah S. Sistare.
Chief Counsel.—Frederick Ansell.
Senior Counsel.—Richard Hertling.
Communications Director.—Paul Clark.
Systems Administrator.—Christopher Lamond.
Minority Staff Director.—Leonard Weiss (SD–326), 4–2627.
Chief Clerk.—Michal Sue Prosser.
Counsels: Ellen B. Brown, Paul Noe.
Professional Staff: Susanne Marshall, Kristine Simmons, Curtis Silvers, William Greenwalt.
Legislative Correspondent.—Mark Lenker.
Staff Assistant/Librarian.—Carrie Outhier.
Staff Assistants: John Knepper, Michael Wussow.
Minority Counsels: Brian Dettelbach, David Plocher.
Minority Professional Staff: Randy Rydell, Christopher Kline, Jane McFarland, Sebastian O'Kelly.
Minority Staff Assistant.—Michael Slater.
Subcommittee on Special Investigations (SR–100), 4–2000
Chief Counsel.—Michael J. Madigan.
Senior Counsel.—J. Mark Tipps.
Minority Chief Counsel.—Alan Baron (SR–193), 4–2627.
Subcommittee on Oversight of Government Management, Restructing and the District of Columbia (SH–432), 4–3682
Staff Director.—Ronald Utt.
Minority Staff Director.—[Vacant] (SH–613A), 4–5538.
Minority Legislative Assistant/Counsel.—Laurie Rubenstein.
Chief Clerk.—Esmeralda Amos.
Permanent Subcommittee on Investigations (SR–100), 4–3721
Staff Director.—Timothy Shea.
Minority Staff Director.—[Vacant] (SH–601), 4–9157.
Minority Counsel.—John Sopko.
Chief Clerk.—[Vacant].
Subcommittee on International Security, Proliferation and Federal Services (SH–446), 4–2254
Staff Director.—Mitchel Kugler.
Minority Staff Director.—Linda Gustitus (SH–446), 4–4551.
Chief Clerk.—Julie Sander.

Judiciary

224 Dirksen Senate Office Building 20510–6275

phone 224–5225, fax 224–9102, http://www.senate.gov/committee/judiciary.html

Orrin G. Hatch, of Utah, *Chairman.*

Strom Thurmond, of South Carolina.	*Patrick J. Leahy,* of Vermont.
Charles E. Grassley, of Iowa.	*Edward M. Kennedy,* of Massachusetts.
Arlen Specter, of Pennsylvania.	*Joseph R. Biden, Jr.,* of Delaware.
Fred Thompson, of Tennessee.	*Herbert H. Kohl,* of Wisconsin.
Jon Kyl, of Arizona.	*Dianne Feinstein,* of California.
Mike DeWine, of Ohio.	*Russell D. Feingold,* of Wisconsin.
John Ashcroft, of Missouri.	*Richard J. Durbin,* of Illinois.
Spencer Abraham, of Michigan.	*Robert G. Torricelli,* of New Jersey.
Jeff Sessions, of Alabama.	

SUBCOMMITTEES

Administrative Oversight and the Courts

Mr. Grassley, *Chairman*

Mr. Thurmond	*Mr. Durbin*
Mr. Sessions	*Mr. Feingold*
Mr. Kyl	*Mr. Kohl*

Antitrust, Business Rights and Competition

Mr. DeWine, *Chairman*

Mr. Hatch	*Mr. Kohl*
Mr. Thumond	*Mr. Torricelli*
Mr. Specter	*Mr. Leahy*

Constitution, Federalism and Property Rights

Mr. Ashcroft, *Chairman*

Mr. Hatch	*Mr. Feingold*
Mr. Abraham	*Mr. Kennedy*
Mr. Thurmond	*Mr. Torricelli*
Mr. Thompson	

Immigration

Mr. Abraham, *Chairman*

Mr. Grassley	*Mr. Kennedy*
Mr. Kyl	*Mrs. Feinstein*
Mr. Specter	*Mr. Durbin*

Technology, Terrorism and Government Information

Mr. Kyl, *Chairman*

Mr. Hatch	*Mrs. Feinstein*
Mr. Specter	*Mr. Biden*
Mr. Thompson	*Mr. Durbin*

Youth Violence

Mr. Sessions, *Chairman*

Mr. Thompson	*Mr. Biden*
Mr. DeWine	*Mr. Torricelli*
Mr. Ashcroft	*Mr. Kohl*
Mr. Grassley	*Mrs. Feinstein*

STAFF

Committee on Judiciary (SD–224), 224–5225.
Chief Counsel/Staff Director.—Manus Cooney.
Deputy Chief Counsel.—Sharon Post.
Deputy Staff Director/Chief Clerk.—Anna Cabral.
Chief Intellectual Property Counsel.—Edward J. Damach.
Counsels: Shawn Bentley, Larry Block, Michael Hirshland, Brian Jones, Paul Larkin, Pat Murphy, Steven Schlesinger.
Professional Staff Members: Rob Foreman, Patricia Knight.
Chief Investigator.—Michael Hubbard.
Deputy Investigator.—Cristina Rios.
Investigator.—Melissa Riley.
GPO Printers: Walter Jung, Elaine T. Cummings, Heinz Mohle.
Documents Clerk.—Phil Shipman.
Press Secretary.—Jeanne Lopatto.
Assistant Press Secretary.—Lindsay Welch.
Research Director/Library Administrator.—Grant Madsen.
Deputy Chief Clerk.—Lara Maxfield.
Systems Administrator.—Cesar Yabor.
Executive Assistant.—Gus Mutscher.
Mail Clerk/Legislative Correspondent.—Allison Vinson.
Staff Assistants: Jasen Adams, Troy Dow, Paul Joklik, Michael Kennedy, Ann Murphy, Steve Tepp.
Nominations Clerk.—B.J. Runyon.
Fellow.—Bruce Artim.
Receptionist.—Pat McDaniel.
Legislative Correspondent.—Caroline Marriott.
Minority Chief Counsel.—Bruce Cohen (SD–148), 4–7703.
Senior Counsel.—Beryl Howell.
Counsels: Trish Aspland, John McGrail, Ed Pagano, Marla Grossman.
Professional Staff.—Laura Weintraub.
Investigator.—Mary DeOreo.
Deputy to the Chief Counsel.—Ed Barron.
Staff Assistants: Mike Carrasco, Andrea Dew, Kevin Flynn, John Lamy.

Subcommittee on Administrative Oversight and the Courts (SH–308), 224–6736
Chief Counsel.—Kolan Davis.
Counsels: John McMickle, Jennifer Shaw.
Chief Clerk.—Laura Dove.
Minority Chief Counsel.—Victoria Bassetti (SD–153), 4–4022.
Chief Clerk/Counsel.—Katie Segal.

Subcommittee on Antitrust, Business Rights and Competition (SD–161), 224–9424
Chief Counsel.—Louis Dupart.
General Counsel.—Helen Rhee.
Senior Counsel.—Joseph Desanctis.
Minority Chief Counsel/Staff Director.—Jon Leibowitz (SH–815), 4–3406.
Staff Assistant.—Alicia Jennings.

Subcommittee on the Constitution, Federalism and Property Rights (SD–524), 4–8081
Counsel.—Rudy Rhodes.
Minority Counsel.—Michael O'Leary, (SH–807), 4–5573.

Subcommittee on Immigration (SD–323), 4–6098
Chief Counsel.—Lee Leberman Otis.
Counsel: Elizabeth Kessler, Ray Kethledge.
Office Manager.—Trudy Settles.
Minority Staff Director.—Michael Myers, (SD–522), 4–7878.
Counsel.—Patty First.
General Counsel.—Melody Barnes.
Pearson Fellow.—Joe Pomper.
Special Counsel.—Tom Perez.
Staff Assistant/Legislative Correspondent.—Michael Mershon.

Subcommittee on Technology, Terrorism and Government Information (SH–325), 4–6791
Chief Counsel.—Stephen Higgins.
Counsel.—Janice Roberts-Kephart.
Legislative Assistant.—Elizabeth Maier.
Minority Chief Counsel/Staff Director.—[Vacant], (SH–807), 224–4933.
Counsels: Jamie Grodsky, Neil Quinter.
Deputy Counsel.—David Hantman.

Subcommittee on Youth Violence (SD–163), 4–7572
Chief Counsel.—Kristi Lee.
Counsel.—Rhet DeHart.
Minority Chief Counsel.—[Vacant], (SH–305), 4–0558.
Staff Director.—Chris Putala.
Counsel.—David Schanzer.

Labor and Human Resources

428 Dirksen Senate Office Building 20510–6300
phone 224–5375, http://www.senate.gov/committee/labor.html

meets second and fourth Wednesdays of each month

James M. Jeffords, of Vermont, *Chairman.*

Dan Coats, of Indiana.
Judd Gregg, of New Hampshire.
Bill Frist, of Tennessee.
Mike DeWine, of Ohio.
Michael B. Enzi, of Wyoming.
Tim Hutchinson, of Arkansas.
Susan M. Collins, of Maine.
John W. Warner, of Virginia.
Mitch McConnell, of Kentucky.

Edward M. Kennedy, of Massachusetts.
Christopher J. Dodd, of Connecticut.
Tom Harkin, of Iowa.
Barbara A. Mikulski, of Maryland.
Jeff Bingaman, of New Mexico.
Paul D. Wellstone, of Minnesota.
Patty Murray, of Washington.
Jack Reed, of Rhode Island.

SUBCOMMITTEES

[The chairman and the ranking minority member are ex officio voting members of all subcommittees.]

Aging

Mr. Gregg, *Chairman*

Mr. Hutchinson
Mr. Warner

Ms. Mikulski
Mrs. Murray

Children and Families

Mr. Coats, *Chairman*

Mr. Gregg
Dr. Frist
Mr. Hutchinson
Ms. Collins
Mr. McConnell

Mr. Dodd
Mr. Bingaman
Mr. Wellstone
Mrs. Murray
Mr. Reed

Employment and Training

Mr. DeWine, *Chairman*

Mr. Jeffords
Mr. Enzi
Mr. Warner
Mr. McConnell

Mr. Wellstone
Mr. Kennedy
Mr. Dodd
Mr. Harkin

Public Health and Safety

Dr. Frist, *Chairman*

Mr. Jeffords
Mr. Coats
Mr. DeWine
Mr. Enzi
Ms. Collins

Mr. Kennedy
Mr. Harkin
Ms. Mikulski
Mr. Bingaman
Mr. Reed

STAFF

Committee on Labor and Human Resources (SD–428), 224–5375, fax 228–5044, TDD 224–1975.

Staff Director.—Mark Powden (SH–835), 4–6770.
Deputy Staff Director.—Susan K. Hattan, 4–6770.
Director, Education Policy.—Pamela Devitt, 4–6770.
Professional Staff Members: Sherry Kaiman, Jennifer Smulson, Patricia Morrissey, Scott Giles, Rayne Pollack, 4–6770.
Educational Policy Research Assistant.—Heidi Mohlman, 4–6770.
Pension Policy Advisor.—Diann Howland, 4–6770.
Labor Counsel.—Leslie Silverman, 4–6770.
Director, Health Policy.—Paul Harrington, 4–3191.
Health Policy Advisors: James W. Hawkins, III, Sharon Winn, 4–3191.
Director, Children's Policy.—Kimberly Barnes-O'Connor, 4–6770.
Children's Policy Research Assistant.—Brian Jones, 4–6770.
Communications Director.—Joseph Karpinski, 4–6770.
Editor.—Uwe Timpke (SH–132), 4–7657.
Computer Systems Administrator.—Sharon Bauman, 4–7657.
Receptionists: Deborah Collier, Carolyn Dupree, 4–3191.
Staff Assistants: Declan Cashman (SH–835), 4–3191; Erin Guild (SH–835), 4–6770; Roger Elliott (SD–428), 4–5375.
Administrative Assistant.—Nadine Arrington (SD–428), 4–3656.
Minority Staff Director/Chief Counsel.—Nick Littlefield (SD–644), 4–5465.
Chief Economist.—Gerard Kavanaugh, 4–4879.
Counsel.—Jeffrey Teitz (SH–527), 4–7675.
Chief Labor Counsel.—Susan Greene (SH–440), 4–5441.
Chief Education Counsel.—Marianna Pierce (SH–639), 4–5501.
Education Advisor.—Danica Petroshius (SH–639), 4–5501.
Professional Staff Members: Robert Silverstein, Sabrina Corlette, (SH–113), 4–6265.
Staff Assistants: Jonathan Halpern (SH–527), 4–6572; Jeffrey Huang (SD–644), 4–9789; Stephanie Williams (SH–440), 4–5363; Sarah Reinstein (SH–639), 4–5510; Adabelle Schmitt (SH–527), 4–6065; Colleen Richards, 4–7751.

Subcommittee on Children and Families (SH–625), 4–5800

Staff Director/Chief Counsel.—Stephanie Monroe Johnson.
Counsels: Vincent Ventemiglia, Townsend Lange.
Professional Staff Member.—William Stancyzkiewicz.
Staff Assistant.—Mary Smith.
Minority Professional Staff Members: Suzanne Day, Jane Loewenson, (SH–404), 4–5630.
Counsel.—Brooke Byers-Goldman.

Subcommittee on Aging (SH–615), 4–0136

Staff Director.—Kimberly Spaulding.
Counsel.—Anthi Jones.
Professional Staff Member.—Heather Koop.
Minority Staff Director.—Lynne Lawrence (SH–113), 4–1493.
Legislative Aide.—Kerry O'Toole.

Subcommittee on Public Health and Safety (SD–422), 4–7139

Staff Director.—Susan Ramthun.
Health Legislative Assistant.—Jennifer Van Horn.
Professional Staff Members: Kathryn Braden, David Larson.
Minority Staff Director.—David Nexon (SH–725), 4–7675.

Subcommittee on Employment and Training (SH–608), 4–2962

Staff Director.—Dwayne Sattler.
Chief Counsel.—Saira Sultan.
Professional Staff Members: Aaron L. Grau, Kari K. Kern.
Minority Staff Director.—Brian Ahlberg (SH–717), 4–5641.

Rules and Administration

[Legislative Reorganization Act of 1946]

305 Russell Senate Office Building 20510–6325

phone 224–6352, http://www.senate.gov/committee/rules.html

meets second and fourth Wednesdays of each month

John W. Warner, of Virginia, *Chairman*

Jesse Helms, of North Carolina.
Ted Stevens, of Alaska.
Mitch McConnell, of Kentucky.
Thad Cochran, of Mississippi.
Rick Santorum, of Pennsylvania.
Don Nickles, of Oklahoma.
Trent Lott, of Mississppi.
Kay Bailey Hutchison, of Texas.

Wendell H. Ford, of Kentucky.
Robert C. Byrd, of West Virginia.
Daniel K. Inouye, of Hawaii.
Daniel Patrick Moynihan, of New York.
Christopher J. Dodd, of Connecticut.
Dianne Feinstein, of California.
Robert G. Torricelli, of New Jersey.

(No Subcommittees)

STAFF

Staff Director.—Grayson F. Winterling, 4–8824.
Chief Counsel.—Bruce K. Kasold, 4–3448.
Deputy Staff Director.—Edward Edens, 4–6678.
Democratic Staff Director/Chief Counsel.—Kennie L. Gill (SR–479), 4–6351.
Administrative Assistant.—Carole J. Blessington (SR–479), 4–0278.
Counsel.—Stewart Verdery (SR–305) 4–2204.
Democratic Elections Counsel.—Douglas M. Chapin, Jr. (SR–479), 4–5648.
Senior Professional Staff Member.—John N. McConnell (SR–305), 4–2233.
Professional Staff Members: Mary Louise Faunce (SR–305), 4–7717; Sherry Little (SR–305), 4–0192; Brian Raines (SR–305), 4–6913.
Democratic Professional Staff Member.—Jonthan B. Clay (SR–479), 4–0279.
Director, Administration and Policy.—Christopher D. Shunk (SH–144), 4–9528.
Senior Auditor.—Kimberly J. Austin (SH–144) 4–5549.
Auditor.—Janet Bowers. (SH–144), 4–6282.
Manager, Publications.—Lana R. Slack (SR–B04), 4–0296.
Office Manager.—Lory G. Breneman (SR–305), 4–0281.
Staff Assistants: Patrick Henry (SR–305), 4–8925; Jessica Menold, 4–3870.
Democratic Staff Assistant.—Jennifer S. Bryant, 4–2475.

Small Business

[Created pursuant to S. Res. 58, 81st Congress]

428A Russell Senate Office Building 20510–6350

phone 224–5175, fax 224–4885, http://www.senate.gov/committee/small_business.html

meets first Wednesday of each month

Christopher S. Bond, of Missouri, *Chairman*

Conrad Burns, of Montana.
Paul Coverdell, of Georgia.
Dirk Kempthorne, of Idaho.
Robert F. Bennett, of Utah.
John W. Warner, of Virginia.
William Frist, of Tennessee.
Olympia J. Snowe, of Maine.
Lauch Faircloth, of North Carolina.
Michael Enzi, of Wyoming.

John F. Kerry, of Massachusetts.
Dale Bumpers, of Arkansas.
Carl Levin, of Michigan.
Tom Harkin, of Iowa.
Joseph I. Lieberman, of Connecticut.
Paul D. Wellstone, of Minnesota.
Max Cleland, of Georgia.
Mary Landrieu, of Louisiana.

(No Subcommittees)

STAFF

Staff Director/Chief Counsel.—Louis Taylor.
Deputy Chief Counsel.—Paul Cooksey.
Communications Director.—Ken Bricker.
Senior Advisor on Regulatory Affairs.—Suey Howe.
Professional Staff.—Susan McMillan.
Employment and Benefits Counsel.—Stephen Sola.
Tax and Finance Counsel.—Mark Warren.
Counsel.—Jack Bartling.
Chief Clerk.—Bettie Mohart.
Executive Assistant.—Lori Rosso.
Legislative Clerk.—Karen Ponzurick.
Administrative Clerk.—Teresa Hoggard.
Staff Assistants: Dreama Towe, Dines Warren.
Minority Staff: Patricia R. Forbes, 4–8496.
Legislative Aides: David DiMartino, Jim Jones, Gregg Rothschild.

Veterans' Affairs

412 Russell Senate Office Building 20510–6375
phone 224–9126, http://www.senate.gov/committee/veterans.html

meets first Wednesday of each month

Arlen Specter, of Pennsylvania, *Chairman.*

Frank H. Murkowski, of Alaska.
Strom Thurmond, of South Carolina.
James M. Jeffords, of Vermont.
Ben Nighthorse Campbell, of Colorado.
Larry E. Craig, of Idaho.
Tim Hutchinson, of Arkansas.

John D. Rockefeller, IV, of West Virginia.
Bob Graham, of Florida.
Daniel K. Akaka, of Hawaii.
Paul D. Wellstone, of Minnesota.
Patty Murray, of Washington.

(No Subcommittees)

STAFF

Majority Staff Director.—Charles C. Battaglia.
General Counsel.—William F. Tuerk.
Special Counsel.—Michael J. Rotko.
Professional Staff: David J. Balland, Charles C. Yoder.
Chief Clerk.—Dennis G. Doherty.
Executive Assistant.—Linda H. Reamy.
Legislative Correspondents: William S. Foster, Thomas R. Dower.
Receptionist.—Rosalie L. Ducosin.
Minority Staff (SH–202), 224–2074.
Minority Staff Director/Chief Counsel.—James R. Gottlieb.
Minority General Counsel.—William E. Brew.
Minority Chief Clerk.—Elinor P. Tucker.
Minority Special Projects Director.—Charlotte R. Moreland.
Minority Staff Assistant.—Joanne Gavalec.

SELECT AND SPECIAL COMMITTEES OF THE SENATE

Committee on Indian Affairs

[Created pursuant to S. Res. 4, 95th Congress; amended by S. Res. 71, 103d Congress]

838 Hart Senate Office Building 20510–2251

phone 224–2251, fax 224–5929

http:/www.senate.gov/~scia

meets first Wednesday of each month

Ben Nighthorse Campbell, of Colorado, *Chairman.*

Daniel K. Inouye, of Hawaii, *Vice Chairman.*

Frank H. Murkowski, of Alaska.
John McCain, of Arizona.
Slade Gorton, of Washington.
Pete V. Domenici, of New Mexico.
Craig Thomas, of Wyoming.
Orrin G. Hatch, of Utah.
James M. Inhofe, of Oklahoma.

Kent Conrad, of North Dakota.
Harry Reid, of Nevada.
Daniel K. Akaka, of Hawaii.
Paul D. Wellstone, of Minnesota.
Byron L. Dorgan, of North Dakota.

Majority Staff Director.—Gary Bohnee.
Minority Staff Director/Chief Counsel.—Patricia M. Zell.
Majority General Counsel.—Paul Moorehead.
Minority Counsels: Noelle Kahanu, Loretta Tuell, Raho Ortiz
Minority Professional Staff Member.—Michael D. Jackson.
Chief Clerk.—Eleanor McComber.
Assistant to the Staff Director.—Steve Clark.
Legislative Assistant to the Minority.—Hawley Manwarring.
Systems Administrator.—Greg Farrer.
Receptionist.—Amy Sagalkin.
Printer/Editor.—John Mogavero.

Select Committee on Ethics

[Created pursuant to S. Res. 4, 95th Congress]

220 Hart Senate Office Building 20510–6425, phone 224–2981, fax 224–7416

http://www.senate.gov/committee/ethics.html

Bob Smith, of New Hampshire, *Chairman.*

Harry Reid, of Nevada, *Vice Chairman.*

Pat Roberts, of Kansas.
Jeff Sessions, of Alabama.

Patty Murray, of Washington.
Kent Conrad, of North Dakota.

Staff Director/Chief Counsel.—Victor Baird.
Counsels: Elizabeth A. Ryan, Adam Bramwell.
Chief Clerk.—Annette M. Gillis.
Professional Staff.—Marie Mullis.
Special Assistant for Financial Disclosure.—John Lewter.
Staff Assistant for Financial Disclosure.—Victoria H. Le Grand.
Systems Administrator.—Danny Remmington.
Staff Assistants: Dawne Vermon, Lauren Partner.

Select Committee on Intelligence

[Created pursuant to S. Res. 400, 94th Congress]

211 Hart Senate Office Building 20510–6475, phone 224–1700

http://www.senate.gov/committee/intelligence.html

Richard C. Shelby, of Alabama, *Chairman.*

J. Robert Kerrey, of Nebraska, *Vice Chairman.*

John H. Chafee, of Rhode Island.
Richard G. Lugar, of Indiana.
Mike DeWine, of Ohio.
Jon Kyl, of Arizona.
James M. Inhofe, of Oklahoma.
Orrin G. Hatch, of Utah.
Pat Roberts, of Kansas.
Wayne Allard, of Colorado.
Dan Coats, of Indiana.

John Glenn, of Ohio.
Richard H. Bryan, of Nevada.
Bob Graham, of Florida.
John F. Kerry, of Massachusetts.
Max Baucus, of Montana.
Charles S. Robb, of Virginia.
Frank R. Lautenberg, of New Jersey.
Carl Levin, of Michigan.

Ex Officio

Trent Lott, of Mississippi.

Thomas A. Daschle, of South Dakota.

Staff Director.—Taylor W. Lawrence.
Minority Staff Director.—Christopher C. Straub.
Chief Clerk.—Kathleen P. McGhee.

Special Committee on Aging

Reauthorized pursuant to S. Res. 4, 95th Congress

G–31 Dirksen Senate Office Building 20510–6400, phone 224–5364, fax 224–8660

http://www.senate.gov/committee/aging.html

Charles E. Grassley, of Iowa, *Chairman.*

James M. Jeffords, of Vermont.
Larry E. Craig, of Idaho.
Conrad Burns, of Montana.
Richard C. Shelby, of Alabama.
Rick Santorum, of Pennsylvania.
John W. Warner, of Virginia.
Chuck Hagel, of Nebraska.
Susan Collins, of Maine.
Mike Enzi, of Wyoming.

John B. Breaux, of Louisiana.
John Glenn, of Ohio.
Harry Reid, of Nevada.
Herb Kohl, of Wisconsin.
Russell D. Feingold, of Wisconsin.
Carol Moseley-Braun, of Illinois.
Ron Wyden, of Oregon.
Jack Reed, of Rhode Island.

Staff Director.—Ted Totman.
Chief Clerk.—Patricia Hameister.
Counsel.—Liz Liess.
Press Secretary.—Monte Shaw.
Professional Staff: Hope Hegstrom, Rebecca Jones, Tom Walsh.
Chief Investigator.—Emilia DiSanto.
Hearing Clerk.—Angela Hill.
Staff Assistants: Gina Falconio, Meredith Levenson, Wendy Moltrup, La Vita Westbrook.
GPO Printer.—Joyce Ward.
Minority Staff (SH–628), 224–1467, fax 224–9926.
Staff Director.—Bruce Lesley.
Professional Staff: Kenneth Cohen, Allison Denny.
Staff Assistant.—Julianna Arnold.

National Republican Senatorial Committee

425 Second Street NE, 20002, phone 675–6000

Mitch McConnell, of Kentucky, *Chairman.*

National Republican Senatorial Committee: 675–6000, fax 675–6058.

Executive Director.—Steven J. Law.
Treasurer.—Stan Huckaby.
Director of:
Finance.—Albert Mitchler.
Corporate Affairs.—Ed Rahal.
Communications.—Mike Russell.
Research.—Don Todd.
Administration.—Stephen Ratchford.
National Field Director.—Dave Hansen.
Legal Counsel.—Craig Engle.

Sally Abraham
Eric Anderson
Yvonne Barazi
Lance Baird
Tim Barnes
Robert Bennett
Kristen Branch
Tom Bucci
Patrick Callahan
Keith Carter
Scott Carter
Doug Congdon
Christina Culver
Tom Donovan
Mike Dorrler
Margee Dotter
Stephen Edelen
Anne Ekern
Craig Engle
Semmes Evans
Sarah Fehrer
Mark Fennel
Amy Ford Bradley
Francese Franch
Chip Gately
Katherine Gibbs
Christopher Greer
Robert Griffin
Joseph Grogan
Dave Hansen
Katie Harrison
Jean Hinz
Carey Hollensteiner
Anastasia Hontzas
Stan Huckaby
J.C. Ignaszewski
Myra Johnston
Mike Kroeger
Brian Larkin
Steven Law
Scott Lewis
Matt Lowe
David Lugar
Chris Maiorana
Jan McBride
Albert Mitchler
Geoffrey Mullins
Monica Noe
Ed Payne
Courtney Phillips
Heather Pinsker
Smila Rabicoff
Ed Rahal
Stephen Raines
Stephen Ratchford
Amy Rempfer
Jeff Richards
Doug Robinson
Jim Ross
Stuart Roy
Mike Russell
Eric Schoell
Glenn Spencer
Susan Spoto
Grant Swindells
Don Todd
Mary Ellen Tomlin
Laura Van Hove
Katherine Waldrop
Beth Walker
Jeff Webb
Joliett Wiggins
Sean Yeakel

Republican Policy Committee

347 Russell Senate Office Building, phone 224–2946, fax 224–1235

http:/www.senate.gov/~rpc/

Larry E. Craig, of Idaho, *Chairman.*

The Policy Committee consists of 22 members of which the Senate Republican Leadership and chairmen of Senate committees are ex officio members.

STAFF

Staff Director.—Jade West.
Deputy Staff Director for Policy.—Candida Perotti Wolff.
Deputy Staff Director and Counsel.—Lincoln Oliphant.
Administrative Director.—Wes Harris.
Analysts:
Yvonne Bartoli (Defense/National Security Issues).
Jack Clark (Labor Issues; Legislative Coordinator).
Jim Jatras (Foreign Affairs and Social Issues).
Judy Myers (Agriculture and Commerce Issues).

Mark Whitenton (Energy and Environmental Issues).
J.T. Young (Chief Economist and Health Policy Issues).

Professional Staff:
Staff Assistant.—Paul Coyer.
Research Director/Station Operator.—Ken Foss.
Communications Director.—Gerry Fritz.
System Administrator/Technology Coordinator.—Marlo Meuli.
Editor.—Judy Gorman Prinkey.
Editor, RVA's/Station Operator.—Tom Pulju.
Station Operator/Special Projects.—Jennifer Spann.
Government Printing Office Liaison.—George Stephens.

Senate Republican Conference

405 Hart Senate Office Building, phone 224–2764

Chairman.—Connie Mack, of Florida.
Secretary.—Paul Coverdell, of Georgia.
Committee Chairmen:
Policy.—Larry Craig, of Idaho.
Campaign.—Mitch McConnell, of Kentucky.
Committees.—Slade Gorton, of Washington.

STAFF

Conference of the Majority (SH–405), 224–2764.
Chief of Staff.—Mitch Bainwol.
Deputy of the Chief of Staff.—Missy Cortese.
Deputy Staff Director.—Vertell F. Simmons.
Staff Assistant.—Candice Woodruff.
Counsel to the Chairman.—Kimberly Cobb.
Communications Advisor.—Laura Dove, Missy Cortese.
Director of Radio Services.—Dave Hodgdon.
Multimedia Designer.—Akram S. Khan.
Broadcast and Communications Advisor.—Michael Klein.
Senior Graphic Designer.—Chris Angrisani.
Senior Photographer.—Jurandir Menezes.
Deputy Staff Director for Communications Services.—Kris Seeger.
Television Technical Director.—Henry Peterson.
Art Director.—Karen Portik.
Director of Television Services.—Anne Rackley.
Television Photographer.—Bryan Rager.
Deputy Director for Communications Strategy.—Mark Mills.
Systems Engineer/Multimedia Producer.—William Taylor.
Producer, Radio Department.—Diedre Woodbyme.

Secretary of the Conference Staff (SD–513), 224–1326.
Chief of Staff.—Kyle McSlarrow.
Director of Communications.—Jonathan Baron.
Deputy Press Secretary.—Amy McKinley.
Assistant to Chief of Staff.—Sarah Heckel.

Senate Democratic Leadership Committees

Suites S–118, S–318, and ST–50 The Capitol, phones 224–5551, 4–2939 and 4–5554

Suites SH–419, SH–512, SH–619 and SH–712, Hart Senate Office Building,

phones 4–3232, 4–1414, 4–1430 and 4–9048

Tom Daschle, of South Dakota, *Chairman.*

STAFF

Staff Director.—Joel Johnson (SH–419), 4–3232.
Deputy Staff Director.—Debra Silimeo (SH–712).
Special Assistant.—Kim Kolvisto (SH–419).
Senior Speech Writer/Researcher.—David Corbin (SH–712).
Chief Floor Assistant to the Democratic Leader.—Lula Davis (S–118), 4–5551.
Floor Staff's Office: Gary Myrick, Paul Brown (S–118), 4–5551.
Executive Assistant to the Democratic Leader.—Alice Aughtry (S–118), 4–5551.
Press Secretary to the Democratic Leader.—Ranit Schmelzer (S–318), 4–2939.
Press Secretary's Office: Mary Rowley (Deputy), Mary Helen Fuller, Staci Schiller (S–318), 4–2939.
Chief Clerk.—Marian Bertram (SH–419), 4–5554.
Systems Administrator.—Jeff Hecker (SH–419), 4–5554.

Democratic Policy Committee

Tom Daschle, of South Dakota, *Chairman.*

Harry M. Reid, of Nevada, *Co-Chairman.*

Regional Chairs:
Patty Murray, of Washington.
J. Robert Kerrey, of Nebraska.
Jack Reed, of Rhode Island.
Max Cleland, of Georgia.

Members:
John Glenn, of Ohio.
Ernest F. Hollings, of South Carolina.
Dale Bumpers, of Arkansas.
Paul S. Sarbanes, of Maryland.
Daniel Patrick Moynihan, of New York.
John D. Rockefeller, IV, of West Virginia.
Charles S. Robb, of Virginia.
Daniel Akaka, of Hawaii.
Byron L. Dorgan, of North Dakota.
Carol Moseley-Braun, of Illinois.
Russell D. Feingold, of Wisconsin.
Joseph I. Lieberman, of Connecticut.
Paul Wellstone, of Minnesota.
Dianne Feinstein, of California.
Ron Wyden, of Oregon.
Robert Torricelli, of New Jersey.

Ex Officio:
Wendell H. Ford, of Kentucky.
Barbara Mikulski, of Maryland.

STAFF

Democratic Policy Committee (S–118), 224–5551.
Staff Director.—Lenna Aoki (SH–619), 4–3232.
Domestic Policy Staff: Lauren Griffin, Ted Zegers, Rob Sweeney, Scott McCullers (SH–619), 4–3232.
Foreign and Defense Policy.—Heidi Bonner (SH–419), 4–3232.
Staff Assistant/Research.—Masha Pastuhov-Pastein (SH–712), 4–9048.
Staff Assistant.—Octavia Shaw (SH–419), 4–3232.
Voting Records: Marian Bertram, Doug Connolly, Mike Mozden, Jennifer Lloyd, Clare Amoruso (ST–50), 4–5554.
Publications: Marguerite Beck-Rex (Editor), Kobye Noel (Deputy), Katharine Moore, Adrian Dorris (SH–512), 4–1414.
Television Services (Channel 6).— Marc Cahill (SH–619), 4–7358.

Democratic Steering and Coordination Committee

Room 712 Hart Senate Office Building, phone 224–9048, FAX 224–5976

John F. Kerry, of Massachusetts, *Chairman.*

Members:
Daniel K. Inouye, of Hawaii.
Robert C. Byrd, of West Virginia.
Edward M. Kennedy, of Massachusetts.
Joseph R. Biden, Jr., of Delaware.
Wendell H. Ford, of Kentucky.
Patrick J. Leahy, of Vermont.
Christopher J. Dodd, of Connecticut.
Tom Harkin, of Iowa.
Max Baucus, of Montana.
Bob Graham, of Florida.
Kent Conrad, of North Dakota.
Carl Levin, of Michigan.
Richard H. Bryan, of Nevada.
Herbert H. Kohl, of Wisconsin.
Barbara Boxer, of California.
John B. Breaux, of Louisiana.
Tom Daschle, of South Dakota.
Frank Lautenberg, of New Jersey.
Jeff Bingaman, of New Mexico.

STAFF

Associate Director.—Rusty Grieff (SH–712), 4–9048.
Outreach Advisor/Intergovernmental Liaison.—Paul Thornell (SH–712), 4–0224.

Democratic Technology and Communications Committee

619 Hart Senate Office Building, phone 224–1430

John D. Rockefeller, IV, of West Virginia, *Chairman.*

Members:
John Glenn, of Ohio.
Ernest Hollings, of South Carolina.
Patty Murray, of Washington.
Charles S. Robb, of Virginia.
Jeff Bingaman, of New Mexico.
Christopher J. Dodd, of Connecticut.
Frank Lautenberg, of New Jersey.
Kent Conrad, of North Dakota.

Ex Officio:
Tom Daschle, of South Dakota.
Wendell H. Ford, of Kentucky.
Barbara Mikulski, of Maryland.
John B. Breaux, of Louisiana.

STAFF

Staff Director.—Laura Quinn.
Associate Director.—Kim Gerson.
Administrator.—Mary Helen Fuller.
Associate Radio Producer/Technician.—Joel Bilheimer.
Press Assistant.—Jim Papa.
Broadcast Services: Clare Flood, Kevin Kelleher, Brian Jones.

Democratic Conference

709 Hart Senate Office Building, phone 224–4654, fax 228–4513

Secretary.—Barbara A. Mikulski, of Maryland.
Liaison to Leadership.—Roberta Haeberle.

Democratic Senatorial Campaign Committee

430 South Capitol Street SE 20003, phone 224–2447 fax 485–3120

J. Robert Kerrey, of Nebraska, *Chairman.*

Robert G. Torricelli, of New Jersey, *Vice Chairman.*

Program Chairs:
Majority Trust:
John D. Rockefeller, IV, of West Virginia
Max Baucus, of Montana
Tom Harkin, of Iowa

Select and Special Senate Committees Roundtable:
Richard H. Bryan, of Nevada
Jack Reed, of Rhode Island

Labor Council:
Edward M. Kennedy, of Massachusetts
Paul Wellstone, of Minnesota
Leadership Circle:
Charles S. Robb, of Virginia
Kent Conrad, of North Dakota
Women's Council:
Dianne Feinstein, of California
Mary Landrieu, of Louisiana
Political Whips:
Joseph I. Lieberman, of Connecticut
Richard J. Durbin, of Illinois

STAFF

Executive Director.—Paul Johnson.
Deputy Executive Director.—Rita Lewis.
Political.—Steven C. Hildebrand.
Director, Research.—Peter Lindstrom.
Deputy Director, Research.—Patty Gaul.
Labor Liaison.—Dick Murphy.
Finance Director.—Tracey Buckman.
Deputy Finance Director.—Lisa Cowell.
Majority Trust.—Stephanie Cooper.
Leadership Circle.—Sheila Dwyer.
DSCC Roundtable.—Amy Edwards.
Fundraising Assistants: Tim Tozer, Rebecca Mandell, Abigail Phillips, Keeley Cain.
Director of Computer Operations.—Jeff Ferguson.
Deputy Director of Computer Operations.—Tim Nelson.
Systems Analyst.—John Donahue.
Director of Direct Mail.—Debra Davey.
Comptroller.—Darlene Setter.
Deputy Comptroller.—Katherine Buchanan.
Operations.—Mable Squire, Darlene Setter, Katie Buchaman.
General Counsel.—Robert Bauer, Judy Corley.
Auditor.—Amy Gilbert.

OFFICERS AND OFFICIALS OF THE SENATE

Capitol Telephone Directory, 224–3121

Senate room prefixes:

Capitol-S, Russell Senate Office Building-SR

Dirksen Senate Office Building-SD, Hart Senate Office Building-SH

PRESIDENT OF THE SENATE

Vice President of the United States and President of the Senate.—Al Gore.

The Ceremonial Office of the Vice President is S–212 in the Capitol. The Vice President has offices in the Dirksen Office Building, Old Executive Office Building (OEOB) and the White House (West Wing).

Executive Assistant to the Vice President.—Heather Marabeti, 456–2326.
Chief of Staff and Counselor to the Vice President.—Ronald Klain, OEOB Room 276, 456–6605.
Director of Communications.—Lorraine Voles, OEOB Room 272, 456–7035.
National Security Advisor.—Leon S. Fuerth, OEOB Room 290, 395–4213.
Counsel.—Charles Burson, OEOB Room 268, 456–7022.
Special Assistant to the Vice President and Chief of Staff to Mrs. Gore.—Susan Liss, OEOB Room 200, 456–6640.
Policy Advisors:
Donald Gips, OEOB Room 288, 456–6222.
Elaine C. Kamarck, OEOB Room 273, 456–2816.
Director of Scheduling.—Kim Tilley, OEOB Room 283, 395–4245.
Director of Advance.—Dennis W. Alpert, OEOB Room 281, 456–7935.
Director of Correspondence.—Bill Mason, OEOB Room 202, 224–2424.

PRESIDENT PRO TEMPORE

S–237 The Capitol, phone 224–5972

President Pro Tempore of the Senate.—Strom Thurmond.

MAJORITY LEADER

S–230 The Capitol, phone 224–3135, fax 224–4639

Majority Leader.—Trent Lott.
Chief of Staff.—Dave Hoppe.
Deputy Chief of Staff.—Alison Carroll.
Administrative Assistant.—Susan W. Wells.
Counsels to the Republican Leader: Steve Seale, Bill Gribbin, Rolf Lundberg, Robert Wilkie.
Assistants to the Republican Leader: Keith Hennessey, Randy Scheunemann, Eric Womble.
Press Secretary.—Susan Irby.
Deputy Press Secretary.—Kirsten Shaw.
Scheduler.—Hardy Lott.
Assistant to the Scheduler.—Marcy Thoms.
Staff Assistants: Lee Clearwater, Dan Dukes, Celeste Embrey, Ginger Gregory, Christine McCarlie, Julie Morrison, Sally Walburn.

ASSISTANT MAJORITY LEADER

S–208 The Capitol, phone 224–2708, fax 224–3913

Assistant Majority Leader.—Don Nickles.
Chief of Staff.—Doug Badger.
Deputy Chief of Staff.—Eric Ueland.
Director of Research and Administration.—Debbie Price.
Counsel.—Barbara Olson.
Chief Economist.—Hazen Marshall.
Policy Advisor.—Stacey Hughes.
Policy Assistant.—Scott Whitaker.
Floor Assistant.—Matt Kirk.
Staff Assistant.—Lori Goins.

DEMOCRATIC LEADER

S–221 The Capitol, phone 224–5556, fax 224–6603

Democratic Floor Leader.—Tom Daschle.
Chief of Staff.—Peter Rouse.
Deputy Chief of Staff.—Laura Petrou.
Legislative Director.—Laura Petrou.
Chief Counsel.—Larry Stein.
Counsel.—Glenn Ivey.
Scheduler.—Nancy Erickson.
Assistant Scheduler.—Stephanie Peterson.
Special Assistants: Ashley Magargee, Pat Sarcone.
Staff Assistants: Sue Christensen, Matt Lyons.
Press Secretary.—Ranit Schmelzer, 224–2939.
Assistant Press Secretary.—Molly Rowley, 224–2939.
Office Manager.—Kelly Cordes, 224–2321.

DEMOCRATIC WHIP

S–148 The Capitol, phone 224–2158

Democratic Whip.—Wendell H. Ford.
Executive Assistant.—Missy Smith.
Staff Assistant.—Joe Hart.
Receptionists/Secretaries.—Terri Ayres, Helen Walker.
Press.—Mark L. Day.
Counsel.—Rob Mangas.

OFFICE OF THE SECRETARY

S–208 The Capitol, phone 224–2115

GARY L. SISCO, Secretary of the Senate, elected and sworn in on October 1, 1996; born and raised in Bolivar, TN; B.S., University of Mississippi, 1967; M.S., George Washington University, 1970; served in the U.S. Army, 1968–70; rejoined IBM's Memphis Data Processing Division, 1970; executive assistant for Senator Howard H. Baker, Jr.; appointed manager for Lamar Alexander's campaign for governor of Tennessee, 1974; served as administrative assistant to U.S. Congressman Robin Beard, 1975–77; real estate investment business in Nashville, TN, 1977–96; Secretary Sisco is married and has three children.

Secretary of the Senate.—Gary Sisco, 224–3622.
Administrative Assistant.—Jon Lynn Kerchner, 224–3627.
Assistant Secretary of the Senate.—Sharon Zelaska (S–312), 224–2114.
Accounts Manager.—Marilyn Sayler, 224–7099.
General Counsel.—Keith Simmons, 224–8789.
Seminar Program Coordinator.—Jill Armstrong (SH–231B), 224–5347.
Director for Information Systems.—Cheri Allen, 224–2020.
Bill Clerk.—Kathleen Alvarez (ST–45), 224–2120.
Assistant Bill Clerk.—Mary Ann Clarkson, 224–2118.
Director, Captioning Services.—Peter Jepsen (ST–54), 224–4321.
Conservation and Preservation, Bookbinder.—Carl Fritter, 224–4550.
Curator.—Diane Skvarla (S–411), 224–2955.
Editor, Daily Digest.—Thomas G. Pellikaan (ST–56), 224–2658.
Assistant Editor.—Linda E. Sebold.
Director, Printing and Document Services.—Barry Wolk (SH–B04), 224–0205.
Assistant Superintendent.—Douglas Bowers.
Enrolling Clerk.—Thomas J. Lundregan (S–139), 224–8427.
Assistant Enrolling Clerk.—Charlene McDevitt.
Executive Clerk.—David G. Marcos (S–138), 224–4341.
Assistant Executive Clerk.—Michelle Haynes.
Financial Clerk.—Stuart F. Balderson (SH–127), 224–3205.
Assistant Financial Clerk.—Timothy S. Wineman, 224–3208.
Historian.—Richard A. Baker (SH–201), 224–6900.
Associate Historian.—Donald A. Ritchie, 224–6816.
Director, Interparliamentary Services.—Sally Walsh (SH–808), 224–3047.
Journal Clerk.—William D. Lackey (S–135), 224–4650.
Assistant Journal Clerk.—Mark Lacovara, 224–3629.
Keeper of Stationery.—Stephen G. Bale (SD–B43), 224–0581.
Assistant Keeper of Stationery.—Michael McGhee, 224–4771.
Legislative Clerk.—Scott Bates (S–134), 224–3630.
Assistant Legislative Clerk.—David J. Tinsley, 224–4350.
Librarian.—Gregory Harness (acting), (S–332), 224–3313.
Special Assistant, Office Services.—Daniel W. Pelham (SH–B04), 224–1483.
Assistant Special Assistant.—Rogers Ferguson (SB–36), 224–1483.
Chief Reporter, Official Reporters of Debates.—Ronald Kavulick (ST–41), 224–3152.
Coordinator of the Record.—Scott Sanborn.
Morning Business Editor.—Ken Dean (ST–41), 224–3960.
Parliamentarian.—Robert B. Dove (S–133), 224–6128.
Senior Assistant Parliamentarian.—Alan Frumin.
First Assistant Parliamentarian.—Kevin Kayes.
Superintendent, Public Records.—Pamela B. Gavin (SH–232), 224–0322.
Assistant Superintendent.—Elizabeth Williams, 224–0329.
Lobby Registrar.—Mark Ward, 224–0758.
Campaign Finance.—Raymond Davis, 224–0761.
Ethics and Disclosure.—Susan Morgan, 224–0763.
Senate Chief Counsel for Employment.—Jean Manning (SH–143), 224–5424.
Director, Senate Gift Shop.—Ernie LePire (SR–180), 224–7308.
Principal, Senate Page School.—Kathryn S. Weeden, 224–3926.
Director, Senate Security.—Michael P. DiSilvestro (S–406), 224–5632.
Deputy Director.—Jeriel S. Garland.

OFFICE OF THE CHAPLAIN

204A Hart Senate Office Building, phone 224–2510, fax 224–9686

LLOYD JOHN OGILVIE, Chaplain of the U.S. Senate; born in Kenosha, WI, September 2, 1930; educated in the public schools of Kenosha; B.A., Lake Forest College; M.Th., Garrett Theological Seminary; D.D., Whitworth College; H.L.D., University of Redlands; D.H., Moravian College and Seminary; LL.D., Eastern College; New College, University of Edinburgh, Edinburgh, Scotland; student pastor, Gurnee Community Church, Gurnee, IL; pastor: Winnetka Presbyterian Church, Winnetka, IL (1956–62); First Presbyterian Church, Bethlehem, PA (1962–72); First Presbyterian Church, Hollywood, CA (1972–95); Chaplain of the U.S. Senate (1995); media communicator, author, and frequent speaker throughout the nation; awards: Distinguished Service Citation, Lake Forest College; Preacher of the Year Award and Angel Award (Religion in Media); Silver Angel Award, 1982, 1986; Gold Medallion Book Award, 1985; William Booth Award, 1992; married to Mary Jane Jenkins-Ogilvie; three children: Heather, Scott, and Andrew.

Chaplain of the Senate.—Lloyd John Ogilvie, M.Th., D.D., H.L.D., D.H., and LL.D.
Executive Assistant.—Kathy Rusty.

OFFICE OF THE SERGEANT AT ARMS

S–321 The Capitol, phone 224–2341, fax 224–7690

GREGORY S. CASEY, Sergeant at Arms, U.S. Senate; elected on September 6, 1996. Born on January 27, 1953 in Boise, Idaho; graduated from the University of Idaho with a major in political science and history, 1976, and did graduate work in legislative affairs through the Library of Congress; 1977–78, executive vice president of the Homebuilders Association of South West Idaho; 1979–80, vice president and general manager of Pioneer Title Company of Ada and Canyon counties; 1981–86, staff assistant, legislative director, administrative assistant and chief of staff to Congressman Larry Craig; 1986–90, president and chief executive officer, Idaho Association of Commerce and Industry; 1990–96, chief of staff, Senator Larry Craig.

Sergeant at Arms.—Gregory S. Casey.
Deputy Sergeant at Arms.—Loretta Fuller-Symms.
Administrative Assistant.—Larry Harris.
Executive Assistants: Jeri Thomson, Marie Angus, Laura Parker, Becky Daugherty.
Director of—
Facilities.—Karen Ellis (ST–53, Capitol), 224–1692.
Financial Management.—Chris Dey (Postal Square), 224–6292.
Human Resources.—Doug Fertig (SH–143), 224–2889.
Customer Support.—Liz McAlhany (Postal Square), 224–1113.
Computer Center.—Tracy Williams (Postal Square), 224–1113.
Service Department.—Russell Jackson (SD–G84), 224–2705.
Telecommunications.—Duane Ravenberg (SD–180), 224–4300.
Photographic Studio.—Steve Benza (Postal Square), 224–6000.
Recording Studio.—David Bass (ST–71, Capitol), 224–4977.
Postmaster.—Harry Green (SD–B23), 224–5353.
State Office Liaison.—Jeanne Tessieri (Postal Square), 224–5409.
Manager of—
Health Promotion Seminars.—Sara Oursler (SD–G14), 224–7952.
Placement Office.—Yvonne Costello (SH–142), 224–9167.
Chief of—
U.S. Capitol Police.—Gary Abrecht (119 D Street NE), 224–9806.
Capitol Guide Service.—Ted Daniel (Capitol Rotunda), 224–5750.

OFFICE OF THE MAJORITY SECRETARY

S–337 The Capitol, phone 224–3835, fax 224–3267

Secretary for the Majority.—Elizabeth Greene, S–226, 224–6191.
Assistant Secretary for the Majority.—David Schiappa.

S–226 Republican Cloakroom, phone 224–6191

Cloakroom Assistants: John (Brad) Holsclaw, Laura Martin, Hilary Newlin, Mike Smythers.

S–123 Republican Legislative Scheduling, phone 224–5456

Floor Assistant.—Greer Amburn.

OFFICE OF THE MINORITY SECRETARY

S–309 The Capitol, phone 224–3735, fax 224–0211

Secretary for the Minority.—Martin P. Paone.
Assistant Secretary for the Minority.—Lula Davis.
Administrative Assistant to the Secretary.—Sue Ann Spatz.
Staff Assistant.—Maura Farley.
Cloakroom Assistants: Leonard Oursler, Paul Cloutier, Christina Krasow, Brian Griffin.

OFFICE OF THE LEGISLATIVE COUNSEL

668 Dirksen Senate Office Building, phone 224–6461, fax 224–0567

Legislative Counsel.—Francis L. Burk, Jr.

Senior Counsels: James W. Fransen, Arthur Rynearson, William F. Jensen III, Gary L. Endicott, Gregory A. Scott.

Assistant Counsels: Anthony C. Coe, Mark J. Mathiesen, Polly W. Craighill, William R. Baird, Mark S. Sigurski, Timothy D. Trushel, Cornelia A. Burr, J. Elizabeth Aldridge, Charles E. Armstrong, Laura M. Ayoud, Janine L. Johnson, Robin B. Bates, Mary K. MacMillan, Ruth A. Ernst, Thomas E. Cole, John A. Goetcheus.

Staff Attorney.—Janell K. Bentz.

Office Manager.—Suzanne D. Pearson.

Assistant Office Manager.—Joanne T. Cole.

Senior Staff Assistant.—Donna M. Erwin.

Staff Assistants: Susan G. Baird, Donna L. Pasqualino, Rhonda H. Dickens, Kimberly Bourne.

Receptionist.—Angela Brodigan.

OFFICE OF SENATE LEGAL COUNSEL

642 Hart Senate Office Building, phone 224–4435, fax 224–3391

Senate Legal Counsel.—Thomas B. Griffith.

Deputy Senate Legal Counsel.—Morgan J. Frankel.

Assistant Senate Legal Counsels: Steven F. Huefner, Monica P. Dolin.

Administrative Assistant.—Kathleen M. Parker.

Systems Administrator.—Barbara L. Thoreson.

Legal Assistant.—Sara Fox Jones.

STANDING COMMITTEES OF THE HOUSE

Republicans in roman; Democrats in *italic*; Independent in **bold.**

[Room numbers beginning with H are in the Capitol, with CHOB in the Cannon House Office Building, with LHOB in the Longworth House Office Building, with RHOB in the Rayburn House Office Building, with H1 in O'Neill House Office Building, and with H2 in the Ford House Office Building]

Agriculture

1301 Longworth House Office Building, phone 225–2171, fax 225–0917

http://www.house.gov/agriculture

meets first Tuesday of each month

Robert F. (Bob) Smith, of Oregon, *Chairman.*

Larry Combest, of Texas, *Vice Chairman.*

Bill Barrett, of Nebraska.
John A. Boehner, of Ohio.
Thomas W. Ewing, of Illinois.
John T. Doolittle, of California.
Bob Goodlatte, of Virginia.
Richard W. Pombo, of California.
Charles T. Canady, of Florida.
Nick Smith, of Michigan.
Terry Everett, of Alabama.
Frank D. Lucas, of Oklahoma.
Ron Lewis, of Kentucky.
Helen Chenoweth, of Idaho.
John N. Hostettler, of Indiana.
Ed Bryant, of Tennessee.
Mark Foley, of Florida.
Saxby Chambliss, of Georgia.
Ray LaHood, of Illinois.
Jo Ann Emerson, of Missouri.
Jerry Moran, of Kansas.
Roy Blunt, of Missouri.
Charles W. (Chip) Pickering, of Mississippi.
Bob Schaffer, of Colorado.
John R. Thune, of South Dakota.
William L. Jenkins, of Tennessee.
John Cooksey, of Louisiana.

Charles W. Stenholm, of Texas.
George E. Brown, Jr., of California.
Gary A. Condit, of California.
Collin C. Peterson, of Minnesota.
Calvin M. Dooley, of California.
Eva M. Clayton, of North Carolina.
David Minge, of Minnesota.
Earl F. Hilliard, of Alabama.
Earl Pomeroy, of North Dakota.
Tim Holden, of Pennsylvania.
Scotty Baesler, of Kentucky.
Sanford D. Bishop, Jr., of Georgia.
Bennie G. Thompson, of Mississippi.
Sam Farr, of California.
John Elias Baldacci, of Maine.
Marion Berry, of Arkansas.
Virgil H. Goode, Jr., of Virginia.
Mike McIntyre, of North Carolina.
Debbie Stabenow, of Michigan.
Bob Etheridge, of North Carolina.
Christopher John, of Louisiana.
Jay W. Johnson, of Wisconsin.
Leonard L. Boswell, of Iowa.

SUBCOMMITTEES

[The chairman and ranking minority member are ex officio members of all subcommittees.]

Department Operations, Nutrition and Foreign Agriculture

Mr. Goodlatte, *Chairman*

Mr. Ewing, *Vice Chairman*

Mr. Canady
Mr. Smith
Mr. Foley
Mr. LaHood
Mr. Thune

Ms. Clayton
Mr. Thompson
Mr. Berry
Mr. Brown
Mr. Bishop

Forestry, Resource Conservation and Research

Mr. Combest, *Chairman*

Mr. Barrett, *Vice Chairman*

Mr. Doolittle
Mr. Pombo
Mr. Smith
Mr. Everett
Mr. Lucas
Mr. Lewis
Ms. Chenoweth
Mr. Hostettler
Mr. Chambliss
Mr. LaHood
Ms. Emerson
Mr. Moran
Mr. Pickering
Mr. Schaffer
Mr. Jenkins
Mr. Cooksey

Mr. Dooley
Mr. Brown
Mr. Farr
Ms. Stabenow
Mr. John
Mr. Peterson
Ms. Clayton
Mr. Minge
Mr. Hilliard
Mr. Pomeroy
Mr. Holden
Mr. Baesler
Mr. Baldacci
Mr. Berry
Mr. Goode

General Farm Commodities

Mr. Barrett, *Chairman*

Mr. Combest, *Vice Chairman*

Mr. Boehner
Mr. Lucas
Mr. Chambliss
Ms. Emerson
Mr. Moran
Mr. Thune
Mr. Cooksey

Mr. Minge
Mr. Thompson
Mr. McIntyre
Ms. Stabenow
Mr. Etheridge
Mr. John
Mr. Johnson

Livestock, Dairy and Poultry

Mr. Pombo, *Chairman*

Mr. Boehner, *Vice Chairman*

Mr. Goodlatte
Mr. Smith
Mr. Lucas
Mr. Lewis
Mr. Hostettler
Mr. Blunt
Mr. Pickering
Mr. Jenkins

Mr. Peterson
Mr. Hilliard
Mr. Holden
Mr. Johnson
Mr. Condit
Mr. Dooley
Mr. Farr
Mr. Boswell

Risk Management and Specialty Crops

Mr. Ewing, *Chairman*

Mr. Combest, *Vice Chairman*

Mr. Doolittle
Mr. Pombo
Mr. Smith
Mr. Everett
Mr. Lewis
Mr. Bryant
Mr. Foley
Mr. Chambliss
Mr. Moran

Mr. Condit
Mr. Baesler
Mr. Bishop
Mr. Pomeroy
Mr. Baldacci
Mr. Goode
Mr. McIntyre
Mr. Etheridge
Mr. Boswell

STAFF

Committee on Agriculture (1301 LHOB), 225–2171, fax 225–0917.
Majority Staff Director.—Paul Unger (1301 LHOB), 5–2171.
Chief Counsel.—John E. Hogan (1304 LHOB), 5–5944.
Associate Counsels: Gerald Jackson, 5–5944; Lance Kotschwar (1304 LHOB), 5–5944.
Policy Director.—William E. O'Conner (1301 LHOB), 5–2171.
Legislative Director.—Pete Thomson (1301 LHOB), 5–2171.
Committee Administrator.—Diane Keyser (1301 LHOB), 5–2171.
Office Manager.—Sharon Rusnak (1305 LHOB), 5–0317.
Communications Director.—David Redmond (1303 LHOB), 5–4050.
Deputy Communications Director.—David Spooner (1303 LHOB), 5–3329.
Printing Editor.—James Cahill (1301 LHOB), 5–2183.
Hearing Clerk.—Wanda Worsham (1336 LHOB), 5–2342.
Assistant to Majority Staff Director.—Jason Vaillancourt (1301 LHOB), 5–0020.
Assistant Hearing Clerk/Scheduler.—Callista Bisek (1301 LHOB), 5–0029.
Information Systems.—J. Merrick Munday (1126 LHOB), 6–8472.
Senior Professional Staff Members: Dave Ebersole (1336 LHOB), 5–2342; Lynn Gallagher (1301 LHOB), 5–0029.
Professional Staff Members: Bryce R. Quick, 5–0029; John Goldberg (1432–P LHOB), 5–4980; Sharla Moffett (1336 LHOB), 5–4946; David Tenny (1336 LHOB), 5–0316.
Legislative Staff Assistant.—Debbie Smith (1304 LHOB), 5–5944.
Legislative Assistants: Brian Hard (1430 LHOB), 5–4916; Christopher Matthews.
Staff Assistants: Ryan Weston (1741–P), 5–4593; Mason Wiggins (1301–A LHOB), 5–4927; Monique Brown, (1336 LHOB), 5–2342; Lara Zinda (1301–A), 5–2171; James Burns.
Director, Subcommittee on:
Forestry, Resource and Conservation.—Russell Laird (1336 LHOB), 5–1130.
Risk Management and Specialty Crops.—Stacy Carey (1741–P LHOB), 5–2171.
Department Operations, Nutrition and Foreign Agriculture.—Kevin Kramp (1430 LHOB), 5–0171.
General Farm Commodities.—Mike Neruda (1430 LHOB), 5–0184.
Livestock, Dairy and Poultry.—Christopher D'Arcy (1432–P LHOB), 5–1564.
Congressional Fellow.—Joy Mulinex (1304 LHOB), 5–4544.
Minority Staff Director.—Stephen Haterius (1305 LHOB), 5–0014.
Minority Counsel.—Vernie Hubert (1305 LHOB), 5–0420.
Deputy Minority Counsel.—Julie Paradis (1305 LHOB), 5–9381.
Minority Associate Counsel.—Andy Baker (1002 LHOB), 5–3069.
Minority Economist.—Chip Conley (1041 LHOB), 5–2349.
Minority Press Coordinator.—John Haugen (1305 LHOB), 5–6872.
Minority Consultants: Curt Mann (1002 LHOB), 5–1867; John Riley (1305 LHOB), 5–7987; Beau Greenwood (1002–A LHOB), 5–8903; Danelle Farmer (1002–A LHOB), 5–4453; Russell Middleton (1002–B), 5–1496.
Staff Assistant.—Sharon Rusnak (1305 LHOB), 5–6878.
Congressional Fellow.—Mac Warren (1002–B LHOB), 5–0720.

Appropriations

H–218 The Capitol, phone 225–2771

http://www.house.gov/appropriations

meets first Wednesday of each month and on call of the Chairman

Bob Livingston, of Louisiana, *Chairman.*

Joseph M. McDade, of Pennsylvania.
C.W. Bill Young, of Florida.
Ralph Regula, of Ohio.
Jerry Lewis, of California.
John Edward Porter, of Illinois.
Harold Rogers, of Kentucky.
Joe Skeen, of New Mexico.
Frank R. Wolf, of Virginia.
Tom DeLay, of Texas.
Jim Kolbe, of Arizona.
Ron Packard, of California.
Sonny Callahan, of Alabama.
James T. Walsh, of New York.
Charles H. Taylor, of North Carolina.
David L. Hobson, of Ohio.
Ernest J. Istook, Jr., of Oklahoma.
Henry Bonilla, of Texas.
Joe Knollenberg, of Michigan.
Dan Miller, of Florida.
Jay Dickey, of Arkansas.
Jack Kingston, of Georgia.
Mike Parker, of Mississippi.
Rodney P. Frelinghuysen, of New Jersey.
Roger F. Wicker, of Mississippi.
Michael P. Forbes, of New York.
George R. Nethercutt, Jr., of Washington.
Mark W. Neumann, of Wisconsin.
Randy (Duke) Cunningham, of California.
Todd Tiahrt, of Kansas.
Zach Wamp, of Tennessee.
Tom Latham, of Iowa.
Anne M. Northup, of Kentucky.
Robert B. Aderholt, of Alabama.

David R. Obey, of Wisconsin.
Sidney R. Yates, of Illinois.
Louis Stokes, of Ohio.
John P. Murtha, of Pennsylvania.
Norman D. Dicks, of Washington.
Martin Olav Sabo, of Minnesota.
Julian C. Dixon, of California.
Vic Fazio, of California.
W.G. (Bill) Hefner, of North Carolina.
Steny H. Hoyer, of Maryland.
Alan B. Mollohan, of West Virginia.
Marcy Kaptur, of Ohio.
David E. Skaggs, of Colorado.
Nancy Pelosi, of California.
Peter J. Visclosky, of Indiana.
Thomas M. Foglietta, of Pennsylvania.
Esteban Edward Torres, of California.
Nita M. Lowey, of New York.
José E. Serrano, of New York.
Rosa L. DeLauro, of Connecticut.
James P. Moran, of Virginia.
John W. Olver, of Massachusetts.
Ed Pastor, of Arizona.
Carrie P. Meek, of Florida.
David E. Price, of North Carolina.
Chet Edwards, of Texas.

SUBCOMMITTEES

[Under committee rules, Mr. Livingston as chairman of the full committee, and Mr. Obey, as the ranking minority member of the full committee, are authorized to sit as members of all subcommittees.]

Agriculture, Rural Development, Food and Drug Administration, and Related Agencies

Mr. Skeen, *Chairman*

Mr. Walsh
Mr. Dickey
Mr. Kingston
Mr. Nethercutt
Mr. Bonilla
Mr. Latham

Ms. Kaptur
Mr. Fazio
Mr. Serrano
Ms. DeLauro

Commerce, Justice, State and Judiciary

Mr. Rogers, *Chairman*

Mr. Kolbe
Mr. Taylor
Mr. Regula
Mr. Forbes
Mr. Latham

Mr. Mollohan
Mr. Skaggs
Mr. Dixon

District of Columbia

Mr. Taylor, *Chairman*

Mr. Neumann	*Mr. Moran*
Mr. Cunningham	*Mr. Sabo*
Mr. Tiahrt	*Mr. Dixon*
Ms. Northup	
Mr. Aderholt	

Energy and Water Development

Mr. McDade, *Chairman*

Mr. Rogers	*Mr. Fazio*
Mr. Knollenberg	*Mr. Visclosky*
Mr. Frelinghuysen	*Mr. Edwards*
Mr. Parker	*Mr. Pastor*
Mr. Callahan	
Mr. Dickey	

Foreign Operations, Export Financing and Related Programs

Mr. Callahan, *Chairman*

Mr. Porter	*Ms. Pelosi*
Mr. Wolf	*Mr. Yates*
Mr. Packard	*Ms. Lowey*
Mr. Knollenberg	*Mr. Foglietta*
Mr. Forbes	*Mr. Torres*
Mr. Kingston	
Mr. Frelinghuysen	

Interior

Mr. Regula, *Chairman*

Mr. McDade	*Mr. Yates*
Mr. Kolbe	*Mr. Murtha*
Mr. Skeen	*Mr. Dicks*
Mr. Taylor	*Mr. Skaggs*
Mr. Nethercutt	*Mr. Moran*
Mr. Miller	
Mr. Wamp	

Labor, Health and Human Services, and Education

Mr. Porter, *Chairman*

Mr. Young	*Mr. Obey*
Mr. Bonilla	*Mr. Stokes*
Mr. Istook	*Mr. Hoyer*
Mr. Miller	*Ms. Pelosi*
Mr. Dickey	*Ms. Lowey*
Mr. Wicker	*Ms. DeLauro*
Ms. Northup	

Legislative

Mr. Walsh, *Chairman*

Mr. Young	*Mr. Serrano*
Mr. Cunningham	*Mr. Fazio*
Mr. Wamp	*Ms. Kaptur*
Mr. Latham	

Military Construction

Mr. Packard, *Chairman*

Mr. Porter
Mr. Hobson
Mr. Wicker
Mr. Kingston
Mr. Parker
Mr. Tiahrt
Mr. Wamp

Mr. Hefner
Mr. Olver
Mr. Edwards
Mr. Dicks
Mr. Hoyer

National Security

Mr. Young, *Chairman*

Mr. McDade
Mr. Lewis
Mr. Skeen
Mr. Hobson
Mr. Bonilla
Mr. Nethercutt
Mr. Istook
Mr. Cunningham

Mr. Murtha
Mr. Dicks
Mr. Hefner
Mr. Sabo
Mr. Dixon
Mr. Visclosky

Transportation

Mr. Wolf, *Chairman*

Mr. DeLay
Mr. Regula
Mr. Rogers
Mr. Packard
Mr. Callahan
Mr. Tiahrt
Mr. Aderholt

Mr. Sabo
Mr. Foglietta
Mr. Torres
Mr. Olver
Mr. Pastor

Treasury, Postal Service and General Government

Mr. Kolbe, *Chairman*

Mr. Wolf
Mr. Istook
Mr. Forbes
Ms. Northup
Mr. Aderholt

Mr. Hoyer
Ms. Meek
Mr. Price

VA, HUD and Independent Agencies

Mr. Lewis, *Chairman*

Mr. DeLay
Mr. Walsh
Mr. Hobson
Mr. Knollenberg
Mr. Frelinghuysen
Mr. Neumann
Mr. Wicker

Mr. Stokes
Mr. Mollohan
Ms. Kaptur
Ms. Meek
Mr. Price

STAFF

Committee on Appropriations (H–218, The Capitol), 225–2771.
Clerk and Staff Director.—James W. Dyer.
Staff Assistants: Dennis M. Kedzior, John R. Mikel, Charles Parkinson, Stan Skocki, Mark C. Corallo.
Communications Director.—Elizabeth Morra.
Administrative Assistant.—Gerard J. Chouinard.
Administrative Aides: Diann Kane, Tracey LaTurner.
Office Assistant.—Theodore Powell.
Editor.—Larry Boarman (B–301A RHOB), 5–2851.
Administrative Aide.—Cathy Edwards.
Computer Operations (B–305 RHOB), 5–2718: Dale Oak, Michael S. Weinberger, Kenneth M. Marx, Timothy J. Buck, Carrie Campbell.
Minority Staff Director.—Scott Lilly (1016 LHOB), 5–3481.
Staff Assistants: David Reich, William H. Stone.
Administrative Aides: Nancy Madden, Robert Bonner.

Surveys and Investigations Staff (H2–283 FHOB), 5–3881:
Chief.—R.W. Vandergrift, Jr.
Deputy Director.—Robert Reitwiesner.
Assistant Director.—Robert Pearre.
Investigators: Michael O. Glynn, Noble L. Holmes, Dennis K. Lutz, Douglas D. Nosik, L. Michael Welsh, Herman C. Young.
Administrative Officer.—Ann M. Stull.
Secretaries: Victoria V. Decatur-Brodeur, Regina L. Martinez, Johannah P. O'Keefe, Tracey E. Russell, Joyce C. Stoyer, Dorothy M. Williams.

Subcommittee on Agriculture, Rural Development, Food and Drug Administration, and Related Agencies (2362 RHOB), 5–2638
Staff Assistants: Timothy K. Sanders, Carol A. Murphy, John Ziolkowski.
Administrative Aide.—Joanne Orndorff.
Minority Staff Assistant.—Del Davis (1016 LHOB), 5–3481.

Subcommittee on Commerce, Justice, State, Judiciary, and Related Agencies (H–309), 5–3351
Staff Assistants: James M. Kulikowski, Therese McAuliffe, Jennifer Miller.
Minority Staff Assistant.—Patricia Schlueter (1016 LHOB), 5–3481.

Subcommittee on the District of Columbia (H–147), 5–5338
Staff Assistant.—Americo S. Miconi.
Minority Staff Assistant.—Cheryl Smith (1016 LHOB), 5–3481.

Subcommittee on Energy and Water Development (2362 RHOB), 5–3421
Staff Assistants: James D. Ogsbury, Jeanne L. Wilson, Robert A. Schmidt, Donald McKinnon.
Administrative Aide.—Sandra T. Farrow.
Minority Staff Assistant.—Mark W. Murray (1016 LHOB), 5–3481.

Subcommittee on Foreign Operations, Export Financing and Related Programs (H–150), 5–2041
Staff Assistants: Charles O. Flickner, Jr., William B. Inglee, John G. Shank.
Administrative Aide.—Lorinda Maes.
Minority Staff Assistant.—Mark W. Murray (1016 LHOB), 5–3481.

Subcommittee on Interior and Related Agencies (B–308 RHOB), 5–3081
Staff Assistants: Deborah A. Weatherly, Loretta C. Beaumont, Joel Kaplan, Christoper Topik.
Administrative Aide.—Angie Perry.
Minority Staff Assistant.—Del Davis (1016 LHOB), 5–3481.

Subcommittee on Departments of Labor, Health and Human Services, Education, and Related Agencies (2358 RHOB), 5–3508
Staff Assistants: S. Anthony McCann, Robert L. Knisely, Susan E. Quantius, Michael Myers.
Administrative Aide.—Francine Mack.
Minority Staff Assistant.—Mark Mioduski, Cheryl Smith (1016 LHOB), 5–3481.

Subcommittee on Legislative (H–147), 5–5338
Staff Assistant.—Edward E. Lombard.
Minority Staff Assistant.—Gregory R. Dahlberg (1016 LHOB), 5–3481.

Subcommittee on Military Construction (B–300 RHOB), 5–3047
Staff Assistants: Elizabeth C. Dawson, Henry E. Moore.
Administrative Aide.—Mary Arnold.
Minority Staff Assistant.—Mark W. Murray (1016 LHOB), 5–3481.

Subcommittee on National Security (H–149), 5–2847

Staff Assistants:

Kevin M. Roper
Douglas Gregory
Tina Jonas
Alicia Jones
Paul Juola
David F. Kilian
Steven Nixon
Juliet Pacquing
John G. Plashal
Patricia Ryan
Gregory J. Walters

Administrative Aides: Stacy Trimble, Jennifer Mummert.

Minority Staff Assistant.—Gregory Dahlberg (1016 LHOB), 5–3481.

Subcommittee on Department of Transportation and Related Agencies (2358 RHOB), 5–2141

Staff Assistants: John T. Blazey, Richard Efford, Stephanie Gupta.

Administrative Aide.—Linda J. Muir.

Minority Staff Assistant.—Cheryl Smith (1016 LHOB), 5–3481.

Subcommittee on Treasury, Postal Service and General Government (B–307 RHOB), 5–5834

Staff Assistants: Michelle Mrdeza, Elizabeth Phillips, Jeffrey Ashford.

Administrative Aide.—Melanie Marshall.

Minority Staff Assistant.—Patricia Schlueter (1016 LHOB), 5–3481.

Subcommittee on VA, HUD and Independent Agencies (H–143), 5–3241

Staff Assistants: Frank M. Cushing, Paul E. Thomson, Timothy Peterson, Valerie Baldwin.

Minority Staff Assistant.—Del Davis (1016 LHOB), 5–3481.

Banking and Financial Services

2129 Rayburn House Office Building, phone 225–7502

http://www.house.gov/banking

meets first Tuesday of each month

James A. Leach, of Iowa, *Chairman*

Bill McCollum, of Florida.
Marge Roukema, of New Jersey.
Doug Bereuter, of Nebraska.
Richard H. Baker, of Louisiana.
Rick Lazio, of New York.
Spencer Bachus III, of Alabama.
Michael Castle, of Delaware.
Peter King, of New York.
Tom Campbell, of California.
Edward Royce, of California.
Frank D. Lucas, of Oklahoma.
Jack Metcalf, of Washington.
Robert Ney, of Ohio.
Robert L. Ehrlich, Jr., of Maryland.
Bob Barr, of Georgia.
Jon Fox, of Pennsylvania.
Sue W. Kelly, of New York.
Ron Paul, of Texas.
Dave Weldon, of Florida.
Jim Ryun, of Kansas.
Merrill Cook, of Utah.
Vince Snowbarger, of Kansas.
Bob Riley, of Alabama.
Rick Hill, of Montana.
Pete Sessions, of Texas.
Steven LaTourette, of Ohio.
Donald A. Manzullo, of Illinois.
Mark Foley, of Florida.
Walder B. Jones, of North Carolina.

Henry B. Gonzalez, of Texas.
John J. LaFalce, of New York.
Bruce F. Vento, of Minnesota.
Charles E. Schumer, of New York.
Barney Frank, of Massachusetts.
Paul E. Kanjorski, of Pennsylvania.
Joseph P. Kennedy II, of Massachusetts.
Floyd H. Flake, of New York.
Maxine Waters, of California.
Carolyn B. Maloney, of New York.
Luis V. Gutierrez, of Illinois.
Lucille Roybal-Allard, of California.
Thomas M. Barrett, of Wisconsin.
Nydia M. Velázquez, of New York.
Melvin Watt, of North Carolina.
Maurice Hinchey, of New York.
Gary Ackerman, of New York.
Ken Bentsen, of Texas.
Jesse Jackson, Jr., of Illinois.
Cynthia McKinney, of Georgia.
Carolyn C. Kilpatrick, of Michigan.
Jim Maloney, of Connecticut.
Darlene Hooley, of Oregon.
Julia Carson, of Indiana.
Esteban Edward Torres, of California.

Bernard Sanders, of Vermont.

SUBCOMMITTEES

Capital Markets, Securities and Government Sponsored Enterprises

Mr. Baker, *Chairman*

Mr. Lucas, *Vice Chairman*

Mr. Cook
Mr. Snowbarger
Mr. Riley
Mr. Hill
Mr. Sessions
Mr. Lazio
Mr. Bachus
Mr. King
Mr. Campbell
1 vacancy

Mr. Kanjorski
Mr. Schumer
Mr. Flake
Ms. Waters
Mr. Gutierrez
Mr. Vento
Ms. Roybal-Allard
Mr. Barrett
Mr. Watt
Mr. Ackerman

Domestic and International Monetary Policy

Mr. Castle, *Chairman*

Mr. Fox, *Vice Chairman*

Mr. LaTourette
Mr. Royce
Mr. Lucas
Mr. Metcalf
Mr. Ney
Mr. Barr
Mr. Paul
Mr. Weldon
2 vacancies

Mr. Flake
Mr. Frank
Mr. Kennedy
Mr. Kanjorski
Ms. Velázquez
Ms. Maloney
Mr. Hinchey
Mr. Bentsen
Mr. Jackson

Mr. Sanders

Financial Institutions and Consumer Credit

Ms. Roukema, *Chairwoman*

Mr. McCollum, *Vice Chariman*

Mr. Bereuter
Mr. King
Mr. Campbell
Mr. Royce
Mr. Metcalf
Mr. Ehrlich
Mr. Barr
Ms. Kelly
Mr. Paul
Mr. Weldon
Mr. Ryun
1 vacancy

Mr. Vento
Mr. LaFalce
Mr. Schumer
Ms. Maloney
Mr. Barrett
Mr. Watt
Ms. Roybal-Allard
Mr. Ackerman
Mr. Bentsen
Ms. McKinney
Ms. Kilpatrick

General Oversight and Investigations

Mr. Bachus, *Chairman*

Mr. Riley, *Vice Chairman*

Mr. LaTourette
Mr. King
Mr. Ney
1 vacancy

Ms. Waters
Ms. McKinney
Ms. Kilpatrick
Ms. Hooley

Housing and Community Opportunity

Mr. Lazio, *Chairman*

Mr. Ney, *Vice Chairman*

Ms. Roukema
Mr. Bereuter
Mr. Baker
Mr. Castle
Mr. Ehrlich
Mr. Fox
Ms. Kelly
Mr. Cook
Mr. Hill
Mr. Sessions
Mr. Metcalf

Mr. Kennedy
Mr. Gutierrez
Ms. Velázquez
Mr. Frank
Mr. Hinchey
Mr. Jackson
Mr. LaFalce
Mr. Maloney
Ms. Hooley
Ms. Carson

Mr. Sanders

STAFF

Committee on Banking and Financial Services (2129 RHOB), 225–7502.
Staff Director.—Anthony Cole.
General Counsel.—Gary Parker, 6–3241.
Minority Staff Director.—Kelsay Meek, 5–7057.

Budget

309 Cannon House Office Building 20515–6065, phone 226–7270, fax 226–7174
http://www.house.gov/budget
meets first Wednesday of each month

John R. Kasich, of Ohio, *Chairman.*

David L. Hobson, of Ohio.
Christopher Shays, of Connecticut.
Wally Herger, of California.
Jim Bunning, of Kentucky.
Lamar S. Smith, of Texas.
Dan Miller, of Florida.
Bob Franks, of New Jersey.
Nick Smith, of Michigan.
Bob Inglis, of South Carolina.
Susan Molinari, of New York.
Jim Nussle, of Iowa.
Peter Hoekstra, of Michigan.
John B. Shadegg, of Arizona.
George P. Radanovich, of California.
Charles F. Bass, of New Hampshire.
Mark W. Neumann, of Wisconsin.
Mike Parker, of Mississippi.
Bob Ehrlich, of Maryland.
Gil Gutknecht, of Minnesota.
Van Hilleary, of Tennessee.
Kay Granger, of Texas.
John E. Sununu, of New Hampshire.
Joseph Pitts, of Pennsylvania.

John M. Spratt, of South Carolina.
Jim McDermott, of Washington.
Alan B. Mollohan, of West Virginia.
Jerry F. Costello, of Illinois.
Patsy T. Mink, of Hawaii.
Earl Pomeroy, of North Dakota.
Lynn Woolsey, of California.
Lucille Roybal-Allard, of California.
Lynn N. Rivers, of Michigan.
Lloyd Doggett, of Texas.
Bennie G. Thompson, of Mississippi.
Benjamin L. Cardin, of Maryland.
David Minge, of Minnesota.
Scotty Baesler, of Kentucky.
Ken Bentsen, of Texas.
Jim Davis, of Florida.
Brad Sherman, of California.
Robert A. Weygand, of Rhode Island.
Eva M. Clayton, of North Carolina.

(No Subcommittees)

Committee on Budget (309 CHOB), 226–7270.
Chief of Staff.—Richard E. May.
Assistant to Chief of Staff.—Tracie Sandlin.
Deputy Staff Director.—Art Sauer.
Chief Counsel.—Jim Bates.
Assistant Counsel.—Carl Christie.

Receptionist.—Cindi Cooper.
Administrative Officer.—Brynne K. Crowe.
Printer/Systems Manger.—Dick Magee.
Economist.—Tom Loo.
Analysts: Lilnda Barnett, Jim Cantwell, Bret Coulson, Gary Guthrie, Greg Hampton, Shirley Lee, Mike Lofgren, Roger Mahan, Kathy Ormiston, Paul Restuccia, Dede Spitznagel, Rob Warner.
Director of—
Budget Policy.—Pat Knudsen.
Communications.—Adrien MacGillivrary.
Budget Priorities.—Wayne Struble.
Minority Staff Director/Chief Counsel.—Tom Kahn.
Executive Assistant to Staff Director.—Linda Bywaters.
Office Manager.—Beth Vilsack.
Budget Analysts: Shelley Amdur, Craig Bomberger, Hugh Brady, Mike Jones, Susan Warner, Andrea Weathers.
Chief Economist.—Al Davis.
Director of Policy.—Richard Kogan.
Counsel.—Paul Seltman.

Commerce

2125 Rayburn House Office Building, phone 225–2927

http://www.house.gov/commerce

meets fourth Tuesday of each month

Thomas J. Bliley, Jr., of Virginia, *Chairman.*

Paul E. Gillmor, of Ohio, *Vice Chairman.*

W.J. (Billy) Tauzin, of Louisiana.
Michael G. Oxley, of Ohio.
Michael Bilirakis, of Florida.
Dan Schaefer, of Colorado.
Joe Barton, of Texas.
J. Dennis Hastert, of Illinois.
Fred Upton, of Michigan.
Cliff Stearns, of Florida.
Bill Paxon, of New York.
Scott L. Klug, of Wisconsin.
James C. Greenwood, of Pennsylvania.
Michael D. Crapo, of Idaho.
Christopher Cox, of California.
Nathan Deal, of Georgia.
Steve Largent, of Oklahoma.
Richard Burr, of North Carolina.
Brian P. Bilbray, of California.
Ed Whitfield, of Kentucky.
Greg Ganske, of Iowa.
Charles W. Norwood, Jr., of Georgia.
Rick White, of Washington.
Tom A. Coburn, of Oklahoma.
Rick Lazio, of New York.
Barbara Cubin, of Wyoming.
James E. Rogan, of California.
John Shimkus, of Illinois.

John D. Dingell, of Michigan.
Henry A. Waxman, of California.
Edward J. Markey, of Massachusetts.
Ralph M. Hall, of Texas.
Rick Boucher, of Virginia.
Thomas J. Manton, of New York.
Edolphus Towns, of New York.
Frank Pallone, Jr., of New Jersey.[1]
Sherrod Brown, of Ohio.
Bart Gordon, of Tennessee.
Elizabeth Furse, of Oregon.
Peter Deutsch, of Florida.
Bobby L. Rush, of Illinois.
Anna G. Eshoo, of California.
Ron Klink, of Pennsylvania.
Bart Stupak, of Michigan.
Eliot L. Engel, of New York.
Thomas C. Sawyer, of Ohio.
Albert R. Wynn, of Maryland.
Gene Green, of Texas.
Karen McCarthy, of Missouri.
Ted Strickland, of Ohio.
Diana DeGette, of Colorado.

Representative Bill Richardson (D–NM) resigned as a Member of the House of Representatives on February 13, 1997; he was subsequently sworn in as the Ambassador to the United Nations on that same date.

[1] Representative Frank Pallone, Jr. (D–NJ) was elected to the Committee on Commerce for the 105th Congress on February 13, 1997, pursuant to H. Res. 58, which passed the House on February 13, 1997. Previously, Mr. Pallone had been on sabbatical leave from the Committee since the beginning of the 105th Congress.

SUBCOMMITTEES

[The chairman and ranking minority member are ex officio members, with vote, of all subcommittees.]

Energy and Power

Mr. Schaefer, *Chairman*

Mr. Crapo, *Vice Chairman*

Mr. Bilirakis	*Mr. Hall*
Mr. Hastert	*Ms. Furse*
Mr. Upton	*Mr. Rush*
Mr. Stearns	*Ms. McCarthy*
Mr. Paxon	*Mr. Wynn*
Mr. Largent	*Mr. Markey*
Mr. Burr	*Mr. Boucher*
Mr. Whitfield	*Mr. Towns*
Mr. Norwood	*Mr. Pallone*
Mr. White	*Mr. Brown*
Mr. Coburn	*Mr. Gordon*
Mr. Rogan	*Mr. Deutsch*
Mr. Shimkus	*1 vacancy*

Finance and Hazardous Materials

Mr. Oxley, *Chairman*

Mr. Tauzin, *Vice Chairman*

Mr. Paxon	*Mr. Manton*
Mr. Gillmor	*Mr. Stupak*
Mr. Klug	*Mr. Engel*
Mr. Greenwood	*Mr. Sawyer*
Mr. Crapo	*Mr. Strickland*
Mr. Deal	*Ms. DeGette*
Mr. Largent	*Mr. Markey*
Mr. Bilbray	*Mr. Hall*
Mr. Ganske	*Mr. Towns*
Mr. White	*Mr. Pallone*
Mr. Lazio	*Ms. Furse*
Ms. Cubin	

Health and Environment

Mr. Bilirakis, *Chairman*

Mr. Hastert, *Vice Chairman*

Mr. Barton	*Mr. Brown*
Mr. Upton	*Mr. Waxman*
Mr. Klug	*Mr. Towns*
Mr. Greenwood	*Mr. Pallone*
Mr. Deal	*Mr. Deutsch*
Mr. Burr	*Mr. Stupak*
Mr. Bilbray	*Mr. Green*
Mr. Whitfield	*Mr. Strickland*
Mr. Ganske	*Ms. DeGette*
Mr. Norwood	*Mr. Hall*
Mr. Coburn	*Ms. Furse*
Mr. Lazio	*Ms. Eshoo*
Ms. Cubin	

Oversight and Investigations

Mr. Barton, *Chairman*

Mr. Cox, *Vice Chairman*

Mr. Greenwood	*Mr. Klink*
Mr. Crapo	*Mr. Waxman*
Mr. Burr	*Mr. Deutsch*
Mr. Bilbray	*Mr. Stupak*
Mr. Ganske	*Mr. Engel*
Mr. Coburn	*Mr. Sawyer*

Telecommunications, Trade and Consumer Protection

Mr. Tauzin, *Chairman*

Mr. Oxley, *Vice Chairman*

Mr. Schaefer
Mr. Barton
Mr. Hastert
Mr. Upton
Mr. Stearns
Mr. Gillmor
Mr. Klug
Mr. Cox
Mr. Deal
Mr. Largent
Mr. White
Mr. Rogan
Mr. Shimkus

Mr. Markey
Mr. Boucher
Mr. Gordon
Ms. Eshoo
Mr. Engel
Mr. Wynn
Mr. Manton
Mr. Rush
Mr. Klink
Mr. Sawyer
Mr. Green
Ms. McCarthy

STAFF

Committee on Commerce (2125 RHOB), 225–2927.
Chief of Staff.—James E. Derderian.
Director of Communications.—Joseph Collins.
Deputy Communications Director.—Christina Gungoll.
Deputy Press Secretary.—Rodney Hoppe.
General Counsel.—Charles Ingebretson.
Counsels: Douglas Bennett, David Cavicke, Howard Cohen, John Cohrssen, L. Rodger Currie, Frederick Eames, Robert Gordon, Curry Ann Hagerty, Edward Hearst, Steven Irizarry, Joseph Kelliher, Nandan Kenkeremath, John Lepore, Justin Weaver Lilley, Robert Meyers, John Stroman Morabito, Mark Paoletta, Patricia Paoletta, Linda Dallas Rich, Stephen Sayle, Alan Slobodin, Joseph Stanko, Jr., Catherine VanWay, William Walters, John Marc Wheat.
Investigative Counsel.—Matthew Denton Saylor.
Junior Counsel.—Fernanda Dau Fisher.
Chief Legislative Clerk.—Darlene McMullen.
Legislative Clerks: Michael Flood, Jr., Anthony Habib, James Alan Hill, C. Barbara Loza, Melissa Clark Niceswanger, Clifford Riccio, Jr., Donn Salvosa, Carter Smith, Michael Twinchek.
Legislative Analyst.—Michael O'Rielly.
Administrative Coordinator.—Marie Elena Burns.
Professional Investigative Staff Member.—William Duncan Wood.
Professional Staff Members: Eric Berger, B. Paige Estep, Hugh Halpern, Kerry Locke, Troy Timmons, Kristina White.
Comptroller.—Anthony Sullivan.
Chief Economist.—Harold Furchtgott-Roth.
Staff Assistants: Matthew Bosher, John Crawford, Nora Demirjian, Brian Elms, Peter Sheffield, Robert Simison, Christopher Wright.
Personnel Specialist.—Gabriele Glynn.
Systems Administrator.—John Clocker.
Printer.—Joseph P. Patterson, Jr.
Minority Staff Director/Chief Counsel.—Reid P.F. Stuntz.
Deputy Staff Director.—Dennis Fitzgibbons.
Counsels: Alison Berkes, Richard Frandsen, Andrew Levin, Sue Sheridan, William Tyndall, Consuela Washington.
Professional Staff Members: Kathleen Holcombe, Mansel Bruce Gwinn, Bridgette Taylor.
Senior Secretary.—Donna Sheets.
Senior Secretary/Assistant LAN Administator.—Carla Van't Hoff Hultberg.
Investigator.—Christopher Knauer.
Chief Clerk.—Sharon E. Davis.
Finance Assistant.—Raymond Kent.

Education and the Workforce

2181 Rayburn House Office Building, phone 225–4527 fax 225–9571
http://www.house.gov/eeo

meets second and fourth Tuesdays of each month

William F. Goodling, of Pennsylvania, *Chairman.*

Thomas E. Petri, of Wisconsin, *Vice Chairman.*

Marge Roukema, of New Jersey.
Harris W. Fawell, of Illinois.
Cass Ballenger, of North Carolina.
Bill Barrett, of Nebraska.
Peter Hoekstra, of Michigan.
Howard P. (Buck) McKeon, of California.
Michael N. Castle, of Delaware.
Sam Johnson, of Texas.
James M. Talent, of Missouri.
James C. Greenwood, of Pennsylvania.
Joe Knollenberg, of Michigan.
Frank Riggs, of California.
Lindsey O. Graham, of South Carolina.
Mark E. Souder, of Indiana.
David M. McIntosh, of Indiana.
Charles W. Norwood, Jr., of Georgia.
Ron Paul, of Texas.
Bob Schaffer, of Colorado.
John Peterson, of Pennsylvania.
Fred Upton, of Michigan.
Nathan Deal, of Georgia.
Van Hilleary, of Tennessee.
Joe Scarborough, of Florida.

William (Bill) Clay, of Missouri.
George Miller, of California.
Dale E. Kildee, of Michigan.
Matthew G. Martinez, of California.
Major R. Owens, of New York.
Donald M. Payne, of New Jersey.
Patsy T. Mink, of Hawaii.
Robert E. Andrews, of New Jersey.
Tim Roemer, of Indiana.
Robert C. Scott, of Virginia.
Lynn C. Woolsey, of California.
Carlos A. Romero-Barceló, of Puerto Rico.
Chaka Fattah, of Pennsylvania.
Rubén Hinojosa, of Texas.
Carolyn McCarthy, of New York.
John Tierney, of Massachusetts.
Ron Kind, of Wisconsin.
Loretta Sanchez, of California.
Harold Ford, Jr., of Tennessee.
Dennis J. Kucinich, of Ohio.

SUBCOMMITTEES

Early Childhood, Youth and Families

Mr. Riggs, *Chairman*

Mr. Castle, *Vice Chairman*

Mr. Johnson
Mr. Souder
Mr. Paul
Mr. Goodling
Mr. Greenwood
Mr. McIntosh
Mr. Peterson
Mr. Upton
Mr. Hilleary

Mr. Martinez
Mr. Miller
Mr. Scott
Mr. Fattah
Mr. Kildee
Mr. Owens
Mr. Payne
Mr. Mink
Mr. Roemer

Employer-Employee Relations

Mr. Fawell, *Chairman*

Mr. Knollenberg, *Vice Chairman*

Mr. Talent
Mr. Petri
Ms. Roukema
Mr. Ballenger
Mr. Goodling

Mr. Payne
Mr. Fattah
Mr. Hinojosa
Ms. McCarthy
Mr. Tierney

Oversight and Investigations

Mr. Hoekstra, *Chairman*

Mr. Norwood, *Vice Chairman*

Mr. Hilleary
Mr. Scarborough
Mr. McKeon
Mr. Fawell

Ms. Mink
Mr. Kind
Ms. Sanchez
Mr. Ford

Postsecondary Education, Training and Life-Long Learning

Mr. McKeon, *Chairman*

Mr. Graham, *Vice Chairman*

Mr. Goodling	*Mr. Kildee*
Mr. Petri	*Mr. Andrews*
Ms. Roukema	*Mr. Roemer*
Mr. Barrett	*Ms. Woolsey*
Mr. Greenwood	*Mr. Romero-Barceló*
Mr. McIntosh	*Mr. Hinojosa*
Mr. Schaffer	*Ms. McCarthy*
Mr. Peterson	*Mr. Tierney*
Mr. Castle	*Mr. Kind*
Mr. Riggs	*Ms. Sanchez*
Mr. Souder	*Mr. Ford*
Mr. Upton	*1 vacancy*
Mr. Deal	

Workforce Protections

Mr. Ballenger, *Chairman*

Mr. Fawell, *Vice Chairman*

Mr. Barrett	*Mr. Owens*
Mr. Hoekstra	*Mr. Miller*
Mr. Graham	*Mr. Martinez*
Mr. Paul	*Mr. Andrews*
Mr. Schaffer	*Ms. Woolsey*

STAFF

Committee on Education and the Workforce (2181 RHOB), 225–4527.

Staff Director.—Jay Eagen.
Parliamentary Counsel.—Jo-Marie St. Martin.
Parliamentary Assistant.—Linda Stevens.
Workplace Policy Counsel.—Kathy (Marshall) Gillespie.
Workplace Policy Coordinator.—Randy Johnson.
Communications Director.—Cheri Jacobus.
Senior Education Policy Advisor.—Sally G. Lovejoy.
Education Policy Coordinator.—Vic Klatt.
Office Managers: Pat Koch, Linda Castleman (H2–230 FHOB), 5–6558.
Office Manager/Intern Coordinator.—Deborah L. Samantar (B–346A RHOB), 5–7101.
Budget Analyst.—Susan Firth (B–346A RHOB), 5–7101.
Clerk.—Silvia R. Riley.
Deputy Clerk.—Dianna J. Ruskowsky.
Documents Clerk.—Rob Borden (B–346A RHOB), 5–7101.
Calendar Clerk/Advance.—Cindy Von Gogh.
Media Assistant.—Kevin MacMillan.
Actuary/Professional Staff Member.—Russell J. Mueller (B–346A RHOB), 5–7101.
Legislative Associate.—Leigh Studthaws (B–346A RHOB), 5–7101.
Legislative Assistants: Mary Ann Fitzgerald, Denzel McGuire (H2–230 FHOB), 5–6558.
Professional Staff: Mark Brennee (B–346A RHOB), 5–7101; Mary (Gardner) Clagett (H2–230 FHOB), 5–6558; George Conant (H2–230 FHOB), 5–6558; Emilia DiSanto (B–346A RHOB), 5–7101; David Frank (B–346A RHOB), 5–7101; Ed Gilroy (B–346A RHOB), 5–7101; Marc Lampkin (2178 RHOB), 6–6910; Derrick Max (B–346A RHOB), 5–7101; Hans Meeder (H2–230 FHOB), 5–6558; Erika Otto (H2–230 FHOB), 5–6558; D'Arcy Philps (H2–230 FHOB), 5–6558; Ashley Rehr (B–346A RHOB), 5–7101; Molly Salmi (B–346A RHOB), 5–7101; Lynn Selmser (H2–230A FHOB), 5–6558; Sally Stroup (H2–230 FHOB), 5–6558; Kent Talbert (H2–230 FHOB), 5–6558; Gary L. Visscher (B–346A RHOB), 5–7101.
Staff Assistants: Linda Castleman; Amanda Day (B–346A RHOB), 5–7101; Mark Eckard (H2–230 FHOB), 5–6558; Leigh Lanning (B–346A RHOB), 5–7101; Amy (Swisher) Lozupone; Kevin MacMillan; Deanna Waldron (2178 RHOB), 5–6910; Karen (Coleman) Wayson.
Receptionist/Staff Assistant.—Trent Barton.
Computer Systems Manager/Staff Assistant.—Nikki Carter (2257–A RHOB), 5–1743.

Committee on Education and the Workforce (2181 RHOB), 225–4527—CONTINUED

Minority Staff (2101 Rayburn) 225–3725, fax 226–4864

Staff Director.—Gail Weiss.
General Counsel.—Broderick Johnson.
Deputy Counsel/Press.—Mark Zuckerman.
Executive Assistant.—Elisabeth Lotkin.
Administrative Assistant/Secretary.—Anita Johnson.
Receptionist.—Shannon McNulty.
Staff Aide.—Miriam Hess.

Minority Staff (1040 Longworth) 226–1881, fax 226–1882

Senior Legislative Associate/Education.—Marshall Grigsby, 225–7116.
Legislative Associates/Education: Patricia Crawford, 6–1881; David Evans, 6–2068; Cheryl Johnson, 5–7118; Alex Nock, 6–2068.
Education Coordinator.—June Harris, 6–2068.
Staff Assistant.—Margo Huber.—6–2068.

Minority Staff (112 CHOB) 226–1881

Senior Legislative Associate/Labor.—Peter Rutledge, 225–7117.
Legislative Associate/Labor: Maria Cuprill.
Counsel/Coordinator.—Brian Kennedy, 6–1881.
Staff Assistant.—Jennifer Cordero.
Education Coordinator.—June Harris.
Legislative Associates/Education: Rick Jerue, Sara Platt Davis.
Staff Assistant/Education.—[Vacant].
Labor Counsel/Coordinator.—Brian V. Kennedy.
Legislative Associate/Labor.—Maria Cuprill.
Staff Assistant/Labor.—Anne Gillespie.

Government Reform and Oversight

2157 Rayburn House Office Building, phone 225–5074, fax 225–3974, TTY 225–6852

http://www.house.gov/reform

meets second Tuesday of each month

Dan Burton, of Indiana, *Chairman.*

Benjamin A. Gilman, of New York.
J. Dennis Hastert, of Illinois.
Constance A. Morella, of Maryland.
Christopher Shays, of Connecticut.
Steven H. Schiff, of New Mexico.
Christopher Cox, of California.
Ileana Ros-Lehtinen, of Florida.
John McHugh, of New York.
Stephen Horn, of California.
John L. Mica, of Florida.
Thomas M. Davis, III, of Virginia.
David M. McIntosh, of Indiana.
Mark E. Souder, of Indiana.
Joe Scarborough, of Florida.
John Shadegg, of Arizona.
Steven C. LaTourette, of Ohio.
Marshall (Mark) Sanford, of South Carolina.
John E. Sununu, of New Hampshire.
Pete Sessions, of Texas.
Mike Pappas, of New Jersey.
Vince Snowbarger, of Kansas.
Bob Barr, of Georgia.
Rob Portman, of Ohio.

Henry A. Waxman, of California.
Tom Lantos, of California.
Bob Wise, of West Virginia.
Major R. Owens, of New York.
Edolphus Towns, of New York.
Paul E. Kanjorski, of Pennsylvania.
Gary A. Condit, of California.
Carolyn B. Maloney, of New York.
Thomas M. Barrett, of Wisconsin.
Eleanor Holmes Norton, of the District of Columbia.
Chaka Fattah, of Pennsylvania.
Elijah E. Cummings, of Maryland.
Dennis Kucinich, of Ohio.
Rod R. Blagojevich, of Illinois.
Danny K. Davis, of Illinois.
John F. Tierney, of Massachusetts.
Jim Turner, of Texas.
Thomas H. Allen, of Maine.
Harold E. Ford, Jr., of Tennessee.

Bernard Sanders

SUBCOMMITTEES

[The chairman and ranking minority member are ex officio members of all subcommittees]

Civil Service

Mr. Mica, *Chairman*

Mr. Pappas, *Vice Chairman*

Ms. Morella	*Mr. Cummings*
Mr. Cox	*Ms. Norton*
Mr. Sessions	*1 vacancy*

District of Columbia

Mr. T. Davis, *Chairman*

Ms. Morella, *Vice-Chairwoman*

Ms. Ros-Lehtinen	*Ms. Norton*
Mr. Horn	*Mr. Allen*

Government Management, Information and Technology

Mr. Horn, *Chairman*

Mr. Sessions, *Vice Chairman*

Mr. T. Davis	*Ms. Maloney*
Mr. Scarborough	*Mr. Kanjorski*
Mr. Sanford	*Mr. Owens*
Mr. Sununu	*Mr. Blagojevich*
1 vacancy	*Mr. D. Davis*

Human Resources

Mr. Shays, *Chairman*

Mr. Snowbarger, *Vice Chairman*

Mr. Gilman	*Mr. Towns*
Mr. McIntosh	*Mr. Kucinich*
Mr. Souder	*Mr. Allen*
Mr. Pappas	*Mr. Lantos*
Mr. Schiff	**Mr. Sanders**
	Mr. Barrett

National Economic Growth, Natural Resources and Regulatory Affairs

Mr. McIntosh, *Chairman*

Mr. Sununu, *Vice Chairman*

Mr. Hastert	**Mr. Sanders**
Mr. Scarborough	*Mr. Tierney*
Mr. Shadegg	*Mr. Turner*
Mr. LaTourette	*Mr. Kanjorski*
Mr. Snowbarger	*Mr. Condit*
Mr. Barr	*Mr. Kucinich*
1 vacancy	*Mr. Fattah*

National Security, International Affairs and Criminal Justice

Mr. Hastert, *Chairman*

Mr. Souder, *Vice Chairman*

Mr. Shays
Mr. Schiff
Ms. Ros-Lehtinen
Mr. McHugh
Mr. Mica
Mr. Shadegg
Mr. LaTourette
Mr. Barr

Mr. Barrett
Mr. Lantos
Mr. Wise
Mr. Condit
Mr. Blagojevich
Ms. Maloney
Mr. Cummings
Mr. Turner

Postal Service

Mr. McHugh, *Chairman*

Mr. Sanford, *Vice Chairman*

Mr. Gilman
Mr. LaTourette
Mr. Sessions

Mr. Fattah
Mr. Owens
Mr. D. Davis

STAFF

Committee on Government Reform and Oversight (2157 RHOB), 225–5074.
Majority Staff Director.—Kevin Binger.
Deputy Staff Director.—Daniel R. Moll.
Chief Counsel.—John Patrick Rowley III.
Counsel.—Jonathan Yates.
Financial and Human Resources Manager.—Grace Washbourne.
Systems Administrator.—Corinne Zaccagnini.
Office Manager.—Robin Butler.
Chief Clerk.—Judith McCoy.
Assistant Chief Clerk/Calendar Clerk.—Teresa Austin.
Director of Communications.—[Vacant].
Press Assistant.—Michael Donohue.
Oversight Coordinator.—David N. Bossie.
Chief Investigative Counsel.—Barbara Comstock.
Senior Investigative Counsels: J. Timothy Griffin, James Rodio.
Investigators: Joseph W. Harrison, Kristi Remington, Laurie Taylor, Kevin Long.
Investigative Clerk.—James J. Schumann.
Director of Procurement Policy.—William Scott O'Neill.
Professional Staff Members: Jane Cobb, Brian Caudill, Jeff Schaffner, Michael Delph.
Staff Assistants: Paul LeBeau, David Jones, Karl Lady, John Mastranadi, Amy Davenport.

Subcommittee on Civil Service (B371–C), 5–6427, fax 5–2392
Staff Director.—George Nesterczuk.
Counsel.—Gary M. Ewing.
Professional Staff Members: Edward J. Lynch, Susan Mosychuk.
Clerk.—Caroline Fiel.

Subcommittee on the District of Columbia (B349–A), 5–6751, fax 5–4960
Staff Director.—Ronald Hamm.
Counsel.—Howard Denis.
Professional Staff Members: Roland Gunn, Bob Dix.
Press Secretary/Professional Staff Member.—Anne M. Mack.
Clerk.—Ellen C. Brown.

Subcommittee on Government Management, Information and Technology (B–373 RHOB), 5–5147, fax 5–2373
Staff Director/Counsel.—Russell George.
Professional Staff Members: Anna D. Gowans Miller, Mark Uncapher, Mark Brasher.
Staff Assistant.—Andrea Miller.

Subcommittee on Human Resources and Intergovernmental Relations (B–372 RHOB), 5–2548, fax 5–2382
Staff Director/Counsel.—Lawrence J. Halloran.
Associate Counsel.—Doris F. Jacobs.
Professional Staff Members: Christopher Allred, Robert A. Newman, Anne Marie Finley, Marcia Sayer.
Clerk.—R. Jared Carpenter.

Subcommittee on National Economic Growth, Natural Resources and Regulatory Affairs (B–377 RHOB), 5–4407, fax 5–2441
Staff Director.—Mildred Webber.
Chief Counsel.—Todd Gaziano.
Counsel.—Larisa Dobriansky.
Professional Staff Members: Chip Griffin, Karen Barnes.
Clerk.—Cynthia Stamm.

Subcommittee on National Security, International Affairs and Criminal Justice (B–373 RHOB), 5–2577, fax 5–2373
Staff Director/Chief Counsel.—Robert Charles.
Special Counsel.—Michele Lang.
Defense Counsel.—Jim Wilon.
Professional Staff Member.—Andrew Richardson.
Special Assistant.—Sean C. Littlefield.
Senior Policy Coordinator.—Tom Brierton.
Clerk.—Ianthe Saylor.

Subcommittee on the Postal Service (B349–C), 5–3741, fax 5–2544
Staff Director.—Dan Blair.
Professional Staff Member/Chief Investigator.—Robert Taub.
Senior Professional Staff Member.—Steve Williams.
Counsel.—Heea Vazirani-fales.
Office/System Administrator and Legislative Assistant.—Jane Hatcherson.
Clerk.—Jennifer Tracy.

House Oversight

1309 Longworth House Office Building, phone 225–8281

http://www.house.gov/cho

William M. Thomas, of California, *Chairman.*

Robert W. Ney, of Ohio.
John A. Boehner, of Ohio.
Vernon J. Ehlers, of Michigan.
Kay Granger, of Texas.
John L. Mice, of Florida.

Sam Gejdenson, of Connecticut.
Steny H. Hoyer, of Maryland.
Carolyn C. Kilpatrick, of Michigan.

(No Subcommittees)

STAFF

Committee on House Oversight (1309 LHOB), 225–8281
Staff Director.—Stacy Carlson.
Staff Director, Franking Commission.—Jack Dail (140 LHOB), 5–9337.
Office Manager.—Janet Giuliani.
Counsels: Roman Buhler, Dan Crowley.
Assistant Counsels: Mark Blencowe, Catherine Fanucchi.
Professional Assistants: Becca Aslin, George Hadijski.
Professional Staff Members: Karen Buhler (Franking Commission), (140 LHOB), 5–9337; Valerie Kazanjian, Reynold Schweickhardt, Otto Wolff, Chris Wright, Mary Sue Englund.
Staff Assistants: Julie Benevedes, Laura Buhl, Kerrie Freeborn, Wayne Parris, Carla Tully.
Minority Staff Director.—Tom Jurkovich (1339 LHOB), 5–2061.
Minority Counsel.—Charlie Howell, 5–2061.
Professional Staff Members: Don DeArmon, Connie Goode, Stacy Hefner, Ellen McCarthy, Herb Stone, 5–2061.

International Relations

2170 Rayburn House Office Building, phone 225–5021
http://www.house.gov/internation__relations
meets first Tuesday of each month
Benjamin A. Gilman, of New York, *Chairman*

William F. Goodling, of Pennsylvania.
James A. Leach, of Iowa.
Henry J. Hyde, of Illinois.
Doug Bereuter, of Nebraska.
Christopher H. Smith, of New Jersey.
Dan Burton, of Indiana.
Elton Gallegly, of California.
Ileana Ros-Lehtinen, of Florida.
Cass Ballenger, of North Carolina.
Dana Rohrabacher, of California.
Donald A. Manzullo, of Illinois.
Edward A. Royce, of California.
Peter T. King, of New York.
Jay Kim, of California.
Steve Chabot, of Ohio.
Mark Sanford, of South Carolina.
Matt Salmon, of Arizona.
Amo Houghton, of New York.
Tom Campbell, of California.
Jon Fox, of Pennsylvania.
John McHugh, of New York.
Lindsey Graham, of South Carolina.
Roy Blunt, of Missouri.
Jerry Moran, of Kansas.
Kevin Brady, of Texas.

Lee H. Hamilton, of Indiana.
Sam Gejdenson, of Connecticut.
Tom Lantos, of California.
Howard L. Berman, of California.
Gary L. Ackerman, of New York.
Eni F.H. Faleomavaega, of American Samoa.
Matthew G. Martinez, of California.
Donald M. Payne, of New Jersey.
Robert E. Andrews, of New Jersey.
Robert Menendez, of New Jersey.
Sherrod Brown, of Ohio.
Cynthia McKinney, of Georgia.
Alcee L. Hastings, of Florida.
Pat Danner, of Missouri.
Earl Hilliard, of Alabama.
Walter Capps, of California.
Brad Sherman, of California.
Robert Wexler, of Florida.
Steve Rothman, of New Jersey.
Bob Clement, of Tennessee.
Bill Luther, of Minnesota.
Jim Davis, of Florida.

SUBCOMMITTEES

Africa

Mr. Royce, *Chairman*

Mr. Houghton
Mr. Chabot
Mr. Sanford
Mr. Campbell
Mr. McHugh

Mr. Menendez
Mr. Payne
Mr. Hastings
vacancy

Asia and the Pacific

Mr. Bereuter, *Chairman*

Mr. Leach
Mr. Rohrabacher
Mr. King
Mr. Kim
Mr. Salmon
Mr. Fox
Mr. McHugh
Mr. Manzullo
Mr. Royce

Mr. Berman
Mr. Faleomavaega
Mr. Andrews
Mr. Brown
Mr. Martinez
Mr. Hastings
Mr. Capps
Mr. Wexler

International Operations and Human Rights

Mr. Smith, *Chairman*

Mr. Goodling
Mr. Hyde
Mr. Burton
Mr. Ballenger
Mr. King
Mr. Salmon
Mr. Graham
Ms. Ros-Lehtinen

Mr. Lantos
Ms. McKinney
Mr. Ackerman
Mr. Faleomavaega
Mr. Payne
Mr. Hilliard
Mr. Wexler

Western Hemisphere

Mr. Gallegly, *Chairman*

Mr. Ballenger	*Mr. Ackerman*
Mr. Sanford	*Mr. Martinez*
Mr. Smith	*Mr. Andrews*
Mr. Burton	*Mr. Menendez*
Ms. Ros-Lehtinen	*Ms. McKinney*
Mr. Kim	*Mr. Capps*
Mr. Blunt	*Mr. Sherman*
Mr. Brady	

International Economic Policy and Trade

Ms. Ros-Lehtinen, *Chairwoman*

Mr. Manzullo	*Mr. Gejdenson*
Mr. Chabot	*Ms. Danner*
Mr. Campbell	*Mr. Hilliard*
Mr. Graham	*Mr. Sherman*
Mr. Blunt	*Mr. Rothman*
Mr. Moran	*Mr. Clement*
Mr. Brady	*Mr. Lantos*
Mr. Bereuter	1 vacancy
Mr. Rohrabacher	

STAFF

Committee on International Relations (2170 RHOB), 225–5021.

Chief of Staff.—Richard J. Garon.
Chief Counsel.—Stephen G. Rademaker.
Investigative Counsel.—John Mackey.
Senior Professional Staff Members: Frank Record, J. Walker Roberts.
Senior Professional Staff Member/Counsel.—Hillel Weinberg.
Counsel.—Mark Kirk.
Administrative Director.—Nancy Bloomer.
Communications Director.—Gerald Lipson.
Professional Staff Members: Paul Berkowitz, Deborah Bodlander, Peter Brookes, Ronald Crump, Mark Gage, Kristen Gilley, John Herzberg, David Jung, Lester Munson, Roger Noriega.
Legislative Information Coordinator.—Laura L. Rush.
Budget/Fiscal Affairs Officer.—Shelly Livingston.
Protocol Officer.—Linda Solomon.
Classified Materials/Travel.—Curtis Banks.
Information Systems Manager.—Cheryl Earnshaw.
Senior Staff Associate.—Jo Weber.
Staff Associates: Christopher Baugh, Parker H. Brent, Caroline Cooper, Allison Kieman, Kimberly Roberts, Beverly Vitarelli.
Special Assistant.—Richard Stafford.

Democratic Office.—(B–360 RHOB), 5–6735.
Chief of Staff.—Michael H. Van Dusen.
Coordinator, Regional Issues.—Christopher Kojm.
Counsel.—Mara Rudman.
Public Affairs.—Christopher Madison.
Professional Staff Members: Elana Broitman, F. Marian Chambers, Robert Hathaway, Cliff Kupchan, Denis McDonough, Kenneth V. Nelson, Martin C. Sletzinger, David A. Weiner.
Administrative Director.—William M. Cox.
Clerk.—Carol G. Doherty.

Subcommittee on International Economic Policy and Trade (702 OHOB), 5–3345.
Staff Director.—Maurice Tamargo.
Professional Staff Member.—Yleem Poblete.
Staff Associate.—[Vacant.]
Democratic Professional Staff Member.—Amos Hochstein.

Subcommittee on Asia and the Pacific (B–359 RHOB), 6–7825.
Staff Director.—Michael P. Ennis.
Professional Staff Member.—Dan Martz.
Staff Associate.—Jon Peterson.

Committee on International Relations (2170 RHOB), 225–5021—CONTINUED

Democratic Professional Staff Member.—Richard Kessler.

Subcommittee on International Operations and Human Rights (B–358 RHOB), 5–5748.

Staff Director/Chief Counsel.—Grover Joseph Rees.

Professional Staff Member.—Douglas Anderson.

Staff Associate.—Elise Kenderian.

Democratic Professional Staff Member.—Robert King.

Subcommittee on the Western Hemisphere (2401–A RHOB), 6–7820.

Staff Director.—Vince Morelli.

Professional Staff Member.—[Vacant].

Staff Associate.—Anita Winsor Edwards.

Democratic Professional Staff Member.—David Adams.

Subcommittee on Africa (705 OHOB–1), 6–7812.

Staff Director.—Tom Sheehy.

Professional Staff Member.—Gregory B. Simpkins.

Staff Associate.—Shannon Gawronski.

Democratic Professional Staff Member.—Jodi Christiansen.

Judiciary

2138 Rayburn House Office Building, phone 225–3951

http://www.house.gov/judiciary

meets every Tuesday

Henry J. Hyde, of Illinois, *Chairman.*

F. James Sensenbrenner, Jr., of Wisconsin.
Bill McCollum, of Florida.
George W. Gekas, of Pennsylvania.
Howard Coble, of North Carolina.
Lamar S. Smith, of Texas.
Steven Schiff, of New Mexico.
Elton Gallegly, of California.
Charles T. Canady, of Florida.
Bob Inglis, of South Carolina.
Bob Goodlatte, of Virginia.
Stephen E. Buyer, of Indiana.
Sonny Bono, of California.
Ed Bryant, of Tennessee.
Steve Chabot, of Ohio.
Bob Barr, of Georgia.
William L. Jenkins, of Tennessee.
Asa Hutchinson, of Arkansas.
Edward A. Pease, of Indiana.
Christopher Cannon, of Utah.

John Conyers, Jr., of Michigan.
Barney Frank, of Massachusetts.
Charles E. Schumer, of New York.
Howard L. Berman, of California.
Rick Boucher, of Virginia.
Jerrold Nadler, of New York.
Robert C. Scott, of Virginia.
Melvin Watt, of North Carolina.
Zoe Lofgren, of California.
Shelia Jackson Lee, of Texas.
Maxine Waters, of California.
Martin T. Meehan, of Massachusetts.
William Delahunt, of Massachusetts.
Robert Wexler, of Florida.
Steven R. Rothman, of New Jersey.

SUBCOMMITTEES

Commercial and Administrative Law

Mr. Gekas, *Chairman*

Mr. Schiff
Mr. Smith
Mr. Inglis
Mr. Bryant
Mr. Chabot

Mr. Nadler
Ms. Lee
Mr. Meehan
Mr. Delahunt

The Constitution

Mr. Canady, *Chairman*

Mr. Hyde
Mr. Inglis
Mr. Bryant
Mr. Jenkins
Mr. Goodlatte
Mr. Barr
Mr. Hutchinson

Mr. Scott
Ms. Waters
Mr. Conyers
Mr. Nadler
Mr. Watt

Courts and Intellectual Property

Mr. Coble, *Chairman*

Mr. Sensenbrenner
Mr. Gallegly
Mr. Goodlatte
Mr. Bono
Mr. Cannon
Mr. McCollum
Mr. Canady

Mr. Frank
Mr. Conyers
Mr. Berman
Mr. Boucher
Ms. Lofgren
Mr. Delahunt

Crime

Mr. McCollum, *Chairman*

Mr. Schiff	*Mr. Schumer*
Mr. Buyer	*Ms. Lee*
Mr. Chabot	*Mr. Meehan*
Mr. Barr	*Mr. Wexler*
Mr. Hutchinson	*Mr. Rothman*
Mr. Gekas	
Mr. Coble	

Immigration and Claims

Mr. Smith, *Chairman*

Mr. Gallegly	*Mr. Watt*
Mr. Bono	*Mr. Schumer*
Mr. Jenkins	*Mr. Berman*
Mr. Pease	*Ms. Lofgen*
Mr. Cannon	*Mr. Wexler*
Mr. Bryant	

STAFF

Committee on the Judiciary (2138 RHOB), 225–3951.
Chief of Staff/General Counsel.—Thomas E. Mooney.
Staff Director/Counsel.—Joseph V. Wolfe.
Deputy General Counsel.—Jon Dudas.
Deputy Staff Director/Counsel.—Diana L. Schacht.
Counsel/Parliamentarian.—Daniel M. Freeman.
Counsels: Joseph Gibson, Peter Levinson (B–353 RHOB), 5–2825, Rick Filkins.
Executive Assistant to General Counsel.—Sheila F. Klein.
Assistant to General Counsel.—Michelle H. Pelletier.
Office Manager.—Annelie E. Weber.
Press Secretary.—Samuel F. Stratman (2110 RHOB), 5–4561.
Financial Clerk.—James B. Farr.
Legislative Correspondent.—Arthur R. Yoon.
Computer Systems Coordinator.—Sharon L. Hammersla.
Calendar Clerk.—Lynn Alcock (B–336 RHOB), 5–5026.
Publications Clerk.—Joseph McDonald (B–29 CHOB), 5–0408.
Receptionist.—Ann Jemison.
Assistant Clerk.—Kenneth Prater.
Subcommittee on Commercial and Administrative Law (B–353 RHOB), 5–2825
Chief Counsel.—Raymond V. Smietanka.
Counsel.—Charles E. Kern II.
Clerk/Research Assistant.—Susana Gutierrez.
Staff Assistant.—Audray Clement.
Subcommittee on the Constitution (806 OHOB), 6–7680
Chief Counsel.—Kathryn Hazeem Lehman.
Assistant Counsels: Keri D. Harrison, John H. Ladd, Robert Corry.
Staff Assistant.—Brett Shogren.
Subcommittee on Courts and Intellectual Property (B–351–A RHOB), ext. 5–5741.
Chief Counsel.—Mitch Glazier.
Counsels: Blaine Merritt, Vince Garlock.
Staff Assistants: Veronica Eligan, Eunice Goldring.
Subcommittee on Crime (207 CHOB), 5–3926
Chief Counsels: Paul J. McNulty.
Counsels: Glenn R. Schmitt, Daniel J. Bryant, Nicole R. Nason.
Research Assistant.—Aerin D. Bryant.
Staff Assistant.—Kara R. Norris.
Subcommittee on Immigration, and Claims (B–370B RHOB), 5–5727
Chief Counsel.—Cordia A. Strom.
Counsels: Edward R. Grant, George Fishman.
Clerk.—Cynthia Blackston.
Staff Assistant.—Judy Knott.

National Security

2120 Rayburn House Office Building, phone 225–4151, fax 225–9077

http://www.house.gov/nsc

meets every Tuesday

Floyd D. Spence, of South Carolina, *Chairman.*

Bob Stump, of Arizona.
Duncan Hunter, of California.
John R. Kasich, of Ohio.
Herbert H. Bateman, of Virginia.
James V. Hansen, of Utah.
Curt Weldon, of Pennsylvania.
Joel Hefley, of Colorado.
Jim Saxton, of New Jersey.
Stephen E. Buyer, of Indiana.
Tillie K. Fowler, of Florida.
John H. McHugh, of New York.
James M. Talent, of Missouri.
Terry Everett, of Alabama.
Roscoe G. Bartlett, of Maryland.
Howard P. (Buck) McKeon, of California.
Ron Lewis, of Kentucky.
J.C. Watts, Jr., of Oklahoma.
William M. (Mac) Thornberry, of Texas.
John N. Hostettler, of Indiana.
Saxby Chambliss, of Georgia.
Van Hilleary, of Tennessee.
Joe Scarborough, of Florida.
Walter B. Jones, of North Carolina.
Lindsey Graham, of South Carolina.
Sonny Bono, of California.
Jim Ryun, of Kansas.
Michael Pappas, of New Jersey.
Riley, of Alabama.
Jim Gibbons, of Nevada.

Ronald V. Dellums, of California.
Ike Skelton, of Missouri.
Norman Sisisky, of Virginia.
John M. Spratt, Jr., of South Carolina.
Solomon P. Ortiz, of Texas.
Owen B. Pickett, of Virginia.
Lane Evans, of Illinois.
Gene Taylor, of Mississippi.
Neil Abercrombie, of Hawaii.
Martin T. Meehan, of Massachusetts.
Robert A. Underwood, of Guam.
Jane Harman, of California.
Paul McHale, of Pennsylvania.
Patrick J. Kennedy, of Rhode Island.
Rod R. Blagojevich, of Illinois.
Silvestre Reyes, of Texas.
Tom Allen, of Maine.
Vic Snyder, of Arkansas.
Jim Turner, of Texas.
F. Allen Boyd, Jr., of Florida.
Adam Smith, of Washington.
Loretta Sanchez, of California.
James H. Maloney, of Connecticut.
Mike McIntrye, of North Carolina.
Ciro D. Rodriguez, of Texas.

SUBCOMMITTEES

Military Installations and Facilities

Mr. Hefley, *Chairman*

Mr. McHugh
Mr. Hostettler
Mr. Hilleary
Mr. Scarborough
Mr. Stump
Mr. Saxton
Mr. Buyer
Ms. Fowler
Mr. Everett

Mr. Ortiz
Mr. Sisisky
Mr. Abercrombie
Mr. Underwood
Mr. Reyes
Mr. Snyder
Mr. Boyd
Mr. Smith

Military Personnel

Mr. Buyer, *Chairman*

Mr. Talent
Mr. Bartlett
Mr. Lewis
Mr. Watts
Mr. Thornberry
Mr. Graham
Mr. Bono
Mr. Ryun

Mr. Taylor
Mr. Skelton
Mr. Pickett
Mr. Underwood
Ms. Harman
Mr. Kennedy
Mr. Maloney

Military Procurement

Mr. Hunter, *Chairman*

Mr. Spence
Mr. Stump
Mr. Hansen
Mr. Saxton
Mr. Talent
Mr. Everett
Mr. McKeon
Mr. Lewis
Mr. Watts
Mr. Thornberry
Mr. Graham
Mr. Bono
Mr. Ryun
Mr. Pappas

Mr. Skelton
Mr. Dellums
Mr. Spratt
Mr. Evans
Mr. Blagojevich
Mr. Allen
Mr. Snyder
Mr. Turner
Mr. Boyd
Mr. Smith
Mr. Maloney
Mr. McIntyre

Military Readiness

Mr. Bateman, *Chairman*

Mr. Kasich
Ms. Fowler
Mr. Chambliss
Mr. Jones
Mr. Riley
Mr. Gibbons
Mr. Hunter
Mr. Hansen
Mr. Weldon
Mr. McKeon

Mr. Sisisky
Mr. Ortiz
Mr. Pickett
Mr. Evans
Mr. Taylor
Mr. Meehan
Mr. Underwood
Mr. McHale
1 vacancy

Military Research and Development

Mr. Weldon, *Chairman*

Mr. Bartlett
Mr. Kasich
Mr. Bateman
Mr. Hefley
Mr. McHugh
Mr. Hostettler
Mr. Chambliss
Mr. Hilleary
Mr. Scarborough
Mr. Jones
Mr. Pappas
Mr. Riley
Mr. Gibbons

Mr. Pickett
Mr. Abercrombie
Mr. Meehan
Mr. Harman
Mr. McHale
Mr. Kennedy
Mr. Blagojevich
Mr. Reyes
Mr. Allen
Mr. Turner
Ms. Sanchez

Special Oversight Panel on Morale, Welfare and Recreation

Mr. McHugh, *Chairman*

Mr. Stump
Mr. Bateman
Mr. Bartlett
Mr. Watts
Mr. Chambliss
Mr. Scarborough
Mr. Jones

Mr. Meehan
Mr. Sisisky
Mr. Ortiz
Mr. Pickett
Mr. Underwood
1 vacancy

Special Oversight Panel on the Merchant Marine

Mr. Bateman, *Chairman*

Mr. Hunter
Mr. Weldon
Mr. Saxton
Ms. Fowler
Mr. Scarborough
2 vacancies

Mr. Abercombie
Mr. Taylor
Ms. Harman
Mr. Kennedy
Mr. Allen
Mr. Smith

STAFF

Committee on National Security (2120 RHOB), 225–4151.
Staff Director.—Andrew Ellis.
Deputy Staff Director.—Robert S. Rangel.
General Counsel.—Henry J. Schweiter.
Executive Assistant to the Staff Director.—Laura R. Hass.
Press Secretary.—Maureen P. Cragin.
Press Assistant.—B. Ryan Vaart.
Counsels: Lee Halterman, Hugh N. Johnston, Jr..
Professional Staff Members: Rita D. Argenta, Brenda J. Wright, Kathleen A. Lipovac, Steven A. Thompson, Michael R. Higgins, George O. Withers, Jeffrey M. Schwartz, Philip W. Grone, Andrea K. Aquino, Roger M. Smith, Peter J. Berry, Mieke Y. Eoyang, Subrata Ghoshroy, Robert W. Lautrup, Joseph F. Boessen, Christian P. Zur, John F. Sullivan, Lara L. Roholt.
Staff Assistants: Frank A. Barnes, Peggy Cosseboom, Ernest B. Warrington, Jr., Diane W. Bowman, Tracy W. Finck, Sheila A. McDowell, Karen V. Steube, Rebecca J. Anfinson, William M. Marsh, Heather L. Hescheles, R. Christian Barger, Laura M. Billings, Bridget M. Keator, Nancy M. Warner, Aaron M. McKay.

Resources

1324 Longworth House Office Building, phone 225–2761

http://www.house.gov/resources

meets first Wednesday of each month

Don Young, of Alaska, *Chairman.*

W.J. (Billy) Tauzin, of Louisiana.
James V. Hansen, of Utah.
Jim Saxton, of New Jersey.
Elton Gallegly, of California.
John J. Duncan, Jr., of Tennessee.
Joel Hefley, of Colorado.
John T. Doolittle, of California.
Wayne T. Gilchrest, of Maryland.
Ken Calvert, of California.
Richard W. Pombo, of California.
Barbara Cubin, of Wyoming.
Helen Chenoweth, of Idaho.
Linda Smith, of Washington.
George P. Radanovich, of California.
Walter B. Jones, of North Carolina.
William M. (Mac) Thornberry, of Texas.
John B. Shadegg, of Arizona.
John Ensign, of Nevada.
Robert F. Smith, of Oregon.
Chris Cannon, of Utah.
Kevin Brady, of Texas.
John Peterson, of Pennsylvania.
Rick Hill, of Montana.
Bob Schaffer, of Colorado.
Jim Gibbons, of Nevada.
Michael D. Crapo, of Idaho.

George Miller, of California.
Edward J. Markey, of Massachusetts.
Nick J. Rahall II, of West Virginia.
Bruce F. Vento, of Minnesota.
Dale E. Kildee, of Michigan.
Peter DeFazio, of Oregon.
Eni F.H. Faleomavaega, of American Samoa.
Neil Abercrombie, of Hawaii.
Solomon P. Ortiz, of Texas.
Owen Pickett, of Virginia.
Frank Pallone, Jr., of New Jersey.
Calvin M. Dooley, of California.
Carlos A. Romero-Barceló, of Puerto Rico.
Maurice D. Hinchey, of New York.
Robert A. Underwood, of Guam.
Sam Farr, of California.
Patrick J. Kennedy, of Rhode Island.
Adam Smith, of Washington.
William D. Delahunt, of Massachusetts.
Chris John, of Louisiana.
Donna Christian-Green, of Virgin Islands.
Ron Kind, of Wisconsin.
Lloyd Doggett, of Texas.

SUBCOMMITTEES

[The chairman and ranking minority member are non-voting ex officio members of all subcommittees on which they do not hold a regular assignment.]

Energy and Mineral Resources

Ms. Cubin, *Chairwoman*

Mr. Tauzin
Mr. Duncan
Mr. Calvert
Mr. Thornberry
Mr. Cannon
Mr. Brady
Mr. Gibbons

Mr. Romero-Barceló
Mr. Rahall
Mr. Ortiz
Mr. Dooley
Mr. John
Ms. Christian-Green
1 vacancy

Fisheries Conservation, Wildlife and Oceans

Mr. Saxton, *Chairman*

Mr. Tauzin
Mr. Gilchrest
Mr. Jones
Mr. Peterson
Mr. Crapo

Mr. Abercrombie
Mr. Ortiz
Mr. Pallone
Mr. Farr
Mr. Kennedy

National Parks and Public Lands

Mr. Hansen, *Chairman*

Mr. Gallegly
Mr. Duncan
Mr. Hefley
Mr. Gilchrest
Mr. Pombo
Ms. Chenoweth
Ms. Smith
Mr. Radanovich
Mr. Jones
Mr. Shadegg
Mr. Ensign
Mr. R. Smith
Mr. Hill
Mr. Gibbons

Mr. Faleomavaega
Mr. Markey
Mr. Rahall
Mr. Vento
Mr. Kildee
Mr. Pallone
Mr. Romero-Barceló
Mr. Hinchey
Mr. Underwood
Mr. Kennedy
Mr. Delahunt
Ms. Christian-Green
Mr. Kind

Forests and Forest Health

Ms. Chenoweth, *Chairwoman*

Mr. Hansen
Mr. Doolittle
Mr. Randovich
Mr. Peterson
Mr. Hill
Mr. Schaffer

Mr. Hinchey
Mr. Vento
Mr. Kildee
3 vacancies

Water and Power

Mr. Doolittle, *Chairman*

Mr. Calvert
Mr. Pombo
Ms. Chenoweth
Ms. Smith
Mr. Radanovich
Mr. Thornberry
Mr. Shadegg
Mr. Ensign
Mr. R. Smith
Mr. Cannon
Mr. Crapo

Mr. DeFazio
Mr. Miller
Mr. Pickett
Mr. Dooley
Mr. Farr
Mr. A. Smith
Mr. Kind
3 vacancies

STAFF

Committee on Natural Resources (1324 LHOB), 225–2761.
Chief of Staff.—Lloyd Jones.
Executive Assistant to the Chief of Staff.—Linda Livingston.
Chief Counsel.—Elizabeth Megginson.
Deputy Chief Counsel.—Lisa Pittman.
Special Assistant to the Chief Counsel.—Marcia Stewart.
Counsel/Legislative Staff.—Duane Gibson.
Counsel.—Tim Glidden, 5–6869.
Communications Director.—Steve Hansen, 5–7749.
Chief Clerk/Administrator.—Christine Kennedy, 5–5150.
Deputy Chief Clerk.—Deborah Callis, 5–7736.
Full Committee Clerk.—Cherié Sexton, 6–3926.
Chief Financial Officer.—Margherita Woods, 5–2925.
Legislative Calendar Clerk.—Ann Vogt.
Investigative/Legislative Staff: Chris Fluhr, 5–2761; Christopher Kearney, 6–7384; Kurt Christensen, 6–7388; John Rishel, 6–0242.
Legislative Staff Members: Cynthia Ahwinona, 6–0382; T.E. Manase Mansur, 6–7400.
Systems Administrator.—Jose Guillen, 5–1975.
Printing Clerk.—Marion Tucker, 6–3529.
Receptionist.—Karen Needy.
Staff Assistant.—James Davin, 5–8182.
Minority Staff (1329 LHOB), 225–6065
Staff Director.—John Lawrence.
Chief Counsel.—Jeff Petrich.
Administrative Assistant.—Ann Owens.
Legislative Research Assistant.—Carrie Yourd Moore.
Staff Assistant.—Josef Novonty.
Legislative Staff (509 OHOB), 226–2311: Rick Healy, Deborah Lanzone, Marie Howard Fabrizio, Steve Lanich.
Counsels: Liz Birnbaum, Christopher Stearns.
Administrative Staff.—Joycelyn Johnson.
Legislative Staff (522 OHOB): Jean Flemma, Chris Mann, Karen Steuer.
Sea Grant Fellow.—Dan Terrell.
Subcommittee on National Parks and Public Lands (812 OHOB), 226–7736
Staff Director.—Allen Freemyer.
Legislative Staff.—Steve Hodapp.
Clerks: Nancy Laheeb, Mary Anne Harper.
Subcommittee on Fisheries Conservation, Wildlife and Oceans (805 OHOB), 226–0200
Staff Director.—Harry Burroughs.
Legislative Staff: Dave Whaley, John Rayfield, Bonnie Bruce, Sharon McKenna.
Clerks: Michelle Sparck, Kathleen Miller.
Subcommittee on Energy and Mineral Resources (1626 LHOB), 225–9297
Staff Director.—Bill Condit.
Legislative Staff.—Sharla Bickley.
Clerk.—Dawn Criste.
Subcommittee on Water and Power (818 OHOB), 225–8331
Staff Director.—Robert Faber.
Legislative Staff.—Valerie West.
Clerk.—Lara Chamberlain.
Subcommittee on Forests and Forest Health (1337 LHOB), 225–0691
Staff Director.—Bill Simmons.
Legislative Staff.—Anne Heissenbuttel.
Clerk.—Kathy Crook.

Rules

H–312 The Capitol, phone 225–9191

http://www.house.gov/rules

meets every Tuesday

Gerald B.H. Solomon, of New York, *Chairman.*

David Dreier, of California.
Porter Goss, of Florida.
John Linder, of Georgia.
Deborah Pryce, of Ohio.
Lincoln Diaz-Balart, of Florida.
Scott McInnis, of Colorado.
Doc Hastings, of Washington.
Sue Myrick, of North Carolina.

John Joseph Moakley, of Massachusetts.
Martin Frost, of Texas.
Tony P. Hall, of Ohio.
Louise Slaughter, of New York.

SUBCOMMITTEES

Legislative and Budget Process

Mr. Goss, *Chairman*

Mr. Linder
Ms. Pryce
Mr. Hastings
Mr. Solomon

Mr. Frost
Mr. Moakley

Rules and Organization of the House

Mr. Dreier, *Chairman*

Mr. Diaz-Balart
Mr. McInnis
Ms. Myrick
Mr. Solomon

Mr. Hall
Ms. Slaughter

STAFF

Chief Counsel.—William D. Crosby, Jr..
Staff Director.—Dan Keniry.
Office Manager.—Peter Hamm.
Clerk.—Bryan Roth.
Press Secretary.—Dan Amon (HB–26), 5–7985.
Legislative Manager.—Celeste West.
Legislative Assistants: Jim Doran, 5–7985; Erin Fleming, Eric Pelletier, Veronica Rolocut, Gena Woolner.
Minority Staff Director.—George C. Crawford (H–152).
Deputy Staff Director.—David Pomerantz.
Assistant to Ranking Member.—Deborah Spriggs.
Professional Staff: John Daniel, Sophie Hayford, Jeff Lockwood, Kevin Ryan, Leanita Shelby (234 CHOB), 5–9486.
Associate Staff: David Bernhardt, 5–4761; Brian Bieron, 5–2305; Ed Cassidy, 5–5816; William Evans, 5–4272; Michael Gessel, 5–6465; Geoff Gleason, 5–5614; Elizabeth Humphrey, 5–4211; Lisa Konwinski, 5–3615; Ken Moffitt, 5–1976; Darren Wilcox, 5–2536; Chris Pearce, 5–2015; Kristi Walseth, 5–3605.

Subcommittee on Rules and Organization of the House, (421 CHOB), 225–8925
Counsel.—Vincent Randazzo.
Minority Staff Director.—Michael Gessel.

Subcommittee on Legislative and Budget Process, (421 CHOB), 225–1547
Counsel.—Merrel Moorehead.
Minority Staff Director.—Kristi Walseth.

Science

2320 Rayburn House Office Building, phone 225–6371, fax 225–0891

http://www.house.gov/science/welcome.html

meets second and fourth Wednesdays of each month

F. James Sensenbrenner, Jr., of Wisconsin, *Chairman.*

Sherwood L. Boehlert, of New York.
Harris W. Fawell, of Illinois.
Constance A. Morella, of Maryland.
Curt Weldon, of Pennsylvania.
Dana Rohrabacher, of California.
Steven Schiff, of New Mexico.
Joe Barton, of Texas.
Ken Calvert, of California.
Roscoe G. Bartlett, of Maryland.
Vernon J. Ehlers, of Michigan.
Dave Weldon, of Florida.
Matt Salmon, of Arizona.
Thomas M. Davis, of Virginia.
Gil Gutknecht, of Minnesota.
Mark Foley, of Florida.
Thomas W. Ewing, of Illinois.
Charles W. (Chip) Pickering, of Mississippi.
Chris Cannon, of Utah.
Kevin Brady, of Texas.
Merrill Cook, of Utah.
Phil English, of Pennsylvania.
George R. Nethercutt, Jr., of Washington.
Tom A. Coburn, of Oklahoma.
Pete Sessions, of Texas.

George E. Brown, Jr., of California.
Ralph M. Hall, of Texas.
Bart Gordon, of Tennessee.
James A. Traficant, Jr., of Ohio.
Tim Roemer, of Indiana.
Robert E. (Bud) Cramer, Jr., of Alabama.
James A. Barcia, of Michigan.
Paul McHale, of Pennsylvania.
Eddie Bernice Johnson, of Texas.
Alcee L. Hastings, of Florida.
Lynn N. Rivers, of Michigan.
Zoe Lofgren, of California.
Michael F. Doyle, of Pennsylvania.
Sheila Jackson Lee, of Texas.
Bill Luther, of Minnesota.
Walter H. Capps, of California.
Debbie Stabenow, of Michigan.
Bob Etheridge, of North Carolina.
Nick Lampson, of Texas.
Darlene Hooley, of Oregon.
Ellen O. Tauscher, of California.

SUBCOMMITTEES

[The chairman and ranking minority member are ex officio members, with vote, of all subcommittees.]

Basic Research

Mr. Schiff, *Chairman*

Mr. Boehlert
Ms. Morella
Mr. Barton
Mr. Gutknecht
Mr. Ewing
Mr. Pickering
Mr. Sessions

Mr. Barcia
Mr. Etheridge
Ms. Rivers
Ms. Lee
Mr. Luther
Mr. Capps

Energy and Environment

Mr. Calvert, *Chairman*

Mr. Fawell
Mr. C. Weldon
Mr. Rohrabacher
Mr. Schiff
Mr. Ehlers
Mr. Salmon
Mr. Foley
Mr. English
Mr. Coburn

Mr. Roemer
Mr. McHale
Mr. Doyle
Ms. Hooley
Mr. Hall
Ms. Johnson
Ms. Lofgren
1 vacancy

Space and Aeronautics

Mr. Rohrabacher, *Chairman*

Mr. Barton
Mr. Calvert
Mr. Bartlett
Mr. D. Weldon
Mr. Salmon
Mr. Davis
Mr. Foley
Mr. Pickering
Mr. Cannon
Mr. Brady
Mr. Cook
Mr. Nethercutt

Mr. Cramer
Mr. Hall
Mr. Traficant
Mr. Hastings
Ms. Lee
Mr. Luther
Ms. Lofgren
Mr. Capps
Mr. Lampson
Mr. Gordon

Technology

Ms. Morella, *Chairwoman*

Mr. C. Weldon
Mr. Bartlett
Mr. Ehlers
Mr. Davis
Mr. Gutknecht
Mr. Ewing
Mr. Cannon
Mr. Brady
Mr. Cook

Mr. Gordon
Ms. Johnson
Ms. Rivers
Ms. Stabenow
Mr. Barcia
Mr. McHale
Mr. Doyle
1 vacancy

STAFF

Committee on Science (2320 RHOB), 225–6371, fax 225–0113.
Chief of Staff.—Todd R. Schultz, 5–8772.
Deputy Chief of Staff.—Phil Kiko, 5–4275.
Chief Counsel.—Barry Beringer, 5–8500.
Budget Analyst.—Kathee McCright, 5–9662.
Director of Communications.—Katy McGregor, 5–4275.
Deputy Director of Communications.—Adrienne Woodward, 5–4275.
Project Director.—Bob Cook, 5–1546.
Counsel.—Beth Sokul, 5–9662.
Associate Counsel.—Scott Geesey, 5–0125.
Chief Clerk/Administrator.—Tish Schwartz, 5–5975.
Special Assistant to the Chief of Staff.—Anne Dressendorfer, 5–7574.
Legislative Clerk.—Vivian Tessieri, 5–8121.
Finance Clerk.—Diane Hill, 5–6371.
Systems Manager.—Tom Vanek, 5–4414.
Senior Legislative Assistant.—Karen Pearce, 5–5967.
Senior Staff Assistant.—Cheryl Faunce, 5–1445.
Staff Assistants: Carolyn Ryan, 5–7593; Angie Harris, 5–6371.
GPO Printer.—Terri Allison, 5–8123.
Democratic Staff Director.—Robert E. Palmer, 5–6375.
Democratic Counsel.—Michael Rodemeyer, 5–6375.
Democratic Legislative Director.—William A. Stiles, 5–8483.
Democratic Professional Staff Members: Jean Fruci, 5–8115; Richard M. Obermann, 5–4482; James Paul, 6–3639; Daniel Pearson, 5–4494; Michael D. Quear, 5–6917; Elizabeth Robinson, 5–8896; William S. Smith, 5–4439; James H. Turner, 5–8128; James Wilson, 5–2634.
Democratic Senior Staff Assistant.—Mary A. Sanchez, 5–6375.
Democratic Staff Assistants: Terese B. McDonald, 5–6375; Martha L. Ralston, 5–8844.

Subcommittee on Basic Research (B374 RHOB), fax 5–7815
Staff Director.—Tom Weimer, 5–9662.
Professional Staff Member.—Kristine Dietz, 5–7206.
Oversight Coordinator.—Christopher Roosa, 5–5848.
Legislative Assistant.—Kirstin Travers, 5–7255.
Staff Assistant.—Jennifer Disharoon.

Subcommittee on Energy and Environment (B374 RHOB), fax 6–6983
Staff Director.—Harlan Watson, 5–9662.

Professional Staff Members: Larry Hart, 5–7281; Steve Eule, 5–7504.
Legislative Assistant.—Kirstin Travers, 5–7255.
Staff Assistant.—Liz Hickam, 5–9662.
Subcommittee on Space and Aeronautics (2321 RHOB), fax 5–6415
Staff Director.—Shana Dale, 5–7858.
Professional Staff Members: Jim Muncy, 5–7858; Eric Sterner, 5–7802; Bill Buckeyq, 5–4320.
Legislative Assistant.—JuliAnna Potter, 5–2070.
Staff Assistant.—Rich Stombres, 5–7858.
Subcommittee on Technology (2319 RHOB), fax 5–4438
Staff Director.—Richard Russell, 5–8844.
Professional Staff Members: Ben Wu, 5–0278; Jeff Grove, 5–7950.
Counsel.—Donna Farmer, 5–7518.
Staff Assistant.—Kathi Kromer, 5–7538.

Small Business

2361 Rayburn House Office Building, phone 225–5821, fax 225–3587

http://www.house.gov/ssmbiz

meets second Thursday of each month

Jim Talent, of Missouri, *Chairman.*

Larry Combest, of Texas.
Joel Hefley, of Colorado.
Donald A. Manzullo, of Illinois.
Roscoe G. Bartlett, of Maryland.
Linda Smith, of Washington.
Frank LoBiondo, of New Jersey.
Sue W. Kelly, of New York.
Mark E. Souder, of Indiana.
Steve Chabot, of Ohio.
Jim Ryun, of Kansas.
Vince Snowbarger, of Kansas.
Michael Pappas, of New Jersey.
Phil English, of Pennsylvania.
David McIntosh, of Indiana.
Jo Ann Emerson, of Missouri.
Rick Hill, of Montana.
John Sununu, of New Hampshire.
1 vacancy

John LaFalce, of New York.
Norman Sisisky, of Virginia.
Floyd H. Flake, of New York.
Glenn Poshard, of Illinois.
Nydia M. Velázquez, of New York.
John Baldacci, of Maine.
Jesse Jackson, Jr., of Illinois.
Juanita Millender-McDonald, of California.
Robert Weygand, of Rhode Island.
Danny Davis, of Illinois.
Allen Boyd, Jr., of Florida.
Carolyn McCarthy, of New York.
Bill Pascrell, Jr., of New Jersey.
Virgil Goode, Jr., of Virginia.
2 vacancies

SUBCOMMITTEES

Empowerment

Mr. Souder, *Chairman*

Mr. LoBiondo
Mr. Chabot
Mr. English
Ms. Emerson
vacancy

Ms. Velázquez
Mr. Flake
Mr. Davis
Mr. Pascrell
Mr. Jackson

Government Programs and Oversight

Mr. Bartlett, *Chairman*

Mr. Manzullo
Ms. Smith
Mr. Hill
Mr. Sununu
1 vacancy

Mr. Poshard
Mr. Jackson
Mr. Weygand
Mr. Boyd
Ms. McCarthy

Regulatory Reform and Paperwork Reduction

Ms. Kelly, *Chairwoman*

Mr. Combest
Mr. LoBiondo
Mr. Ryun
Mr. McIntosh
Ms. Emerson

Mr. Sisisky
Mr. Goode
Mrs. Millender-McDonald
Mr. Boyd
1 vacancy

Tax, Finance and Exports

Mr. Manzullo, *Chairman*

Ms. Smith, *Vice Chairwoman*

Mr. Snowbarger
Mr. Pappas
Mr. English
1 vacancy

Mr. Baldacci
Mrs. Millender-McDonald
Mr. Weygand
Mr. Davis
Ms. McCarthy

STAFF

Committee on Small Business (2361 RHOB), 225–5821, fax 225–3587.
Staff Director.—Mary C. McKenzie.
Chief Counsel.—Harry Katrichis.
Counsels: James C. Hale, Ligia Salcedo-McWilliams, Charles E. Rowe III, Jennifer S. Woodbury.
Chief Clerk.—Rebecca Ward.
Professional Staff: Katherine Kless, Nancy M. Piper, Jeff Polich, Jeff Tucker.
Press Secretary.—Kristin Young.
Research Assistant.—Karen Richardson.
Legislative Assistant.—Emily Murphy.
Systems Administrator.—Susan Ely.
Staff Assistant—Peter Brechtel, 6–2630.
Minority Staff Director.—Jeanne M. Roslanowick (B–343C RHOB), 225–4038, fax 225–7209.
Chief Counsel.—Thomas G. Powers.
Professional Staff: Patricia R. Hennessey, 6–3420; Patricia A. Lord, 5–4038; Dean Sagar, 6–3420; Pamela Reid, 6–3420.
Chief Economist.—Marilyn Seiber.
Subcommittee on Empowerment (B–363 RHOB), 226–2630, fax 225–8950
Staff Director.—Alvin Felzenberg.
Subcommittee on Government Programs and Oversight (B–363 RHOB), 225–8944, fax 225–8950
Staff Director.—Nelson Crowther.
Subcommittee on Regulatory Reform and Paperwork Reduction (B–363 RHOB), 225–9368, fax 225–8950
Staff Director.—Laurence McCredy.
Subcommittee on Tax, Finance and Exports (B–363 RHOB), 225–7797, fax 225–8950
Staff Director.—Philip Eskeland.

Standards of Official Conduct

HT–2 The Capitol, phone 225–7103, fax 225–7392

James, V. Hansen, of Utah, *Chairman.*

6 vacancies

Howard L. Berman, of California.
6 vacancies

(No Subcommittees)

STAFF

Staff Director/Chief Counsel.—Theordor J. Van Der Meid.
Counsels: Virginia Johnson, David Laufman, John Vargo, Charles Willoughby.
Staff Assistants: Margarita Mestre, Chris Weinstein, Joanne White.

Transportation and Infrastructure

2165 Rayburn House Office Building, phone 225–9446, fax 225–6782

http://www.house.gov/transportation

meets first Wednesday of each month

Bud Shuster, of Pennsylvania, *Chairman.*

Don Young, of Alaska.
Thomas E. Petri, of Wisconsin.
Sherwood L. Boehlert, of New York.
Herbert H. Bateman, of Virginia.
Howard Coble, of North Carolina.
John J. Duncan, Jr., of Tennessee.
Susan Molinari, of New York.
Thomas W. Ewing, of Illinois.
Wayne T. Gilchrest, of Maryland.
Jay Kim, of California.
Stephen Horn, of California.
Bob Franks, of New Jersey.
John L. Mica, of Florida.
Jack Quinn, of New York.
Tillie K. Fowler, of Florida.
Vernon J. Ehlers, of Michigan.
Spencer Bachus, of Alabama.
Steven C. LaTourette, of Ohio.
Sue W. Kelly, of New York.
Ray LaHood, of Illinois.
Richard H. Baker, of Louisiana.
Frank Riggs, of California.
Charles F. Bass, of New Hampshire.
Robert W. Ney, of Ohio.
Jack Metcalf, of Washington.
Jo Ann Emerson, of Missouri.
Edward A. Pease, of Indiana.
Roy Blunt, of Missouri.
Joseph R. Pitts, of Pennsylvania.
Asa Hutchinson, of Arkansas.
Merrill Cook, of Utah.
John Cooksey, of Louisiana.
John R. Thune, of South Dakota.
Charles W. (Chip) Pickering, Jr., of Mississippi.
Kay Granger, of Texas.
Jon D. Fox, of Pennsylvania.
Thomas M. Davis, of Virginia.
Frank A. LoBiondo, of New Jersey.
J.C. Watts, Jr., of Oklahoma.

James L. Oberstar, of Minnesota.
Nick J. Rahall II, of West Virginia.
Robert A. Borski, of Pennsylvania.
William O. Lipinski, of Illinois.
Robert E. Wise, Jr., of West Virginia.
James A. Traficant, Jr., of Ohio.
Peter A. DeFazio, of Oregon.
Bob Clement, of Tennessee.
Jerry F. Costello, of Illinois.
Glenn Poshard, of Illinois.
Robert E. (Bud) Cramer, Jr., of Alabama.
Eleanor Holmes Norton, of the District of Columbia.
Jerrold Nadler, of New York.
Pat Danner, of Missouri.
Robert Menendez, of New Jersey.
James E. Clyburn, of South Carolina.
Corrine Brown, of Florida.
James A. Barcia, of Michigan.
Bob Filner, of California.
Eddie Bernice Johnson, of Texas.
Frank Mascara, of Pennsylvania.
Gene Taylor, of Mississippi.
Juanita Millender-McDonald, of California.
Elijah E. Cummings, of Maryland.
Earl Blumenauer, of Oregon.
Max Sandlin, of Texas.
Ellen O. Tauscher, of California.
Bill Pascrell, Jr., of New Jersey.
Jay W. Johnson, of Wisconsin.
Leonard L. Boswell, of Iowa.
James P. McGovern, of Massachusetts.
Tim Holden, of Pennsylvania.
Nick Lampson, of Texas.

SUBCOMMITTEES

[The chairman and ranking minority member of the committee are ex officio members of all subcommittees.]

Aviation

Mr. Duncan, *Chairman*

Mr. Blunt
Ms. Molinari
Mr. Ewing
Mr. Ehlers
Mr. LaHood
Mr. Bass
Mr. Metcalf
Mr. Pease
Mr. Pitts
Ms. Hutchinson
Mr. Cook
Mr. Cooksey
Mr. Pickering
Ms. Granger
Mr. Fox
Mr. Davis
Mr. Watts

Mr. Lipinski
Mr. Boswell
Mr. Poshard
Mr. Rahall
Mr. Traficant
Mr. DeFazio
Mr. Costello
Mr. Cramer
Ms. Danner
Mr. Clyburn
Ms. Brown
Ms. Johnson
Ms. Millender-McDonald
Mr. Cummings

Coast Guard and Maritime Transportation

Mr. Gilchrest, *Chairman*

Mr. LoBiondo
Mr. Young
Mr. Coble

Mr. Clement
Mr. Johnson
1 vacancy

Public Buildings and Economic Development

Mr. Kim, *Chairman*

Mr. Cooksey
Mr. Duncan
Mr. LaTourette
Mr. Davis

Mr. Traficant
Ms. Norton
2 vacancies

Railroads

Ms. Molinari, *Chairwoman*

Ms. Granger
Mr. Boehlert
Mr. Franks
Mr. Mica
Mr. Quinn
Ms. Fowler
Mr. Bachus
Mr. Pitts
Mr. Fox

Mr. Wise
Mr. Blumenauer
Mr. Borski
Mr. Lipinski
Mr. Clement
Mr. Nadler
Mr. Filner
Mr. Sandlin

Surface Transportation

Mr. Petri, *Chairman*

Mr. Pickering
Mr. Bateman
Mr. Coble
Mr. Ewing
Mr. Horn
Mr. Franks
Mr. Mica
Mr. Quinn
Ms. Fowler
Mr. Bachus
Mr. LaTourette
Ms. Kelly
Mr. LaHood
Mr. Baker
Mr. Riggs
Mr. Bass
Mr. Ney
Mr. Metcalf
Ms. Emerson
Mr. Pease
Mr. Pitts
Mr. Hutchinson
Mr. Cook
Mr. Thune
Ms. Granger
Mr. Watts

Mr. Rahall
Mr. DeFazio
Mr. Cramer
Ms. Danner
Mr. Clyburn
Ms. Brown
Mr. Barcia
Mr. Filner
Ms. Johnson
Ms. Millender-McDonald
Mr. Costello
Ms. Norton
Mr. Nadler
Mr. Menendez
Mr. Taylor
Mr. Cummings
Mr. Sandlin
Ms. Tauscher
Mr. Pascrell
Mr. McGovern

Water Resources and Environment

Mr. Boehlert, *Chairman*

Mr. Thune
Mr. Young
Mr. Petri
Mr. Bateman
Ms. Molinari
Mr. Gilchrest
Mr. Kim
Mr. Horn
Mr. Franks
Mr. Quinn
Mr. Ehlers
Mr. LaTourette
Ms. Kelly
Mr. Baker
Mr. Riggs
Mr. Ney
Ms. Emerson
Mr. LoBiondo

Mr. Borski
Mr. Johnson
Mr. Wise
Mr. Poshard
Mr. Menendez
Mr. Barcia
Mr. Mascara
Mr. Taylor
Mr. Blumenauer
Ms. Tauscher
Mr. Pascrell
Mr. Boswell
Mr. McGovern
Mr. Rahall
1 vacancy

STAFF

Committee on Transportation and Infrastructure (2165 RHOB), 225–9446, fax 225–6782.

Chief of Staff.—Jack L. Schenendorf.

Deputy Chief of Staff.—Michael Strachn.

Counsel.—Charles Ziegler.

Administrator.—Carol Wood.

Director of Communications.—Jeff Nelligan.

Deputy Administrator/Financial Officer.—Mary Moll.

Professional Staff Member for Budget and Economic Development.—William J. Hughes (2251 RHOB), 6–5434.

Professional Staff Member for Outreach.—Patricia Law.

Special Assistant to the Chairman.—Darrell Wilson.

Special Assistant to the Chief of Staff.—Kathy Guilfoy.

Director of Committee Facilities/Travel.—Jimmy Miller.
Computer Systems Manager.—Keven Sard.
Executive Staff Assistant.—Cheryl McCullough.
Counsel for Investigations.—Paul Rosenzweig (587 FHOB), 5–5504.
Staff Assistant for Investigations.—Michael Robinson (587 FHOB), 5–5504.
Editor/Legislative Calendar Clerk.—Joan H. Botuck, 5–9960.
Associate Editor/Legislative Calendar Clerk.—Gilda Shirley, 5–9960.
GPO Print Specialist.—Edna Lanier, 5–9960.
Staff Assistants: Jeffrey Fedorko, Mary Beth Will, Denise Beshaw, Kevin Blose, Justin Harclerode, Todd Krueckeberg, Leneal Scott.
Minority Staff Director.—David Heymsfeld (2163 RHOB), 5–4472.
Chief Counsel.—Sante J. Esposito.
Administrator.—Joy B. Bryson.
Director of Communications.—Eric K. Federing.
Executive Staff Assistant.—Sheila R. Lockwood.
Staff Assistant.—Dara Schlieker.

Subcommittee on Aviation (2251 RHOB), 6–3220 fax 5–4629
Majority Counsel.—David Schaffer.
Professional Staff Members: Donna McLean, Jim Coon.
Staff Assistant.—Dianne Rogers.
Minority Senior Professional Staff Member.—David Traynham.
Counsel.—Mary Walsh, 5–9161.
Assistant Counsel.—Michelle Mihin.

Subcommittee on Coast Guard and Maritime Transportation (589 FHOB), 6–3552
Majority Counsel.—Rebecca Dye.
Professional Staff Member.—Lee Edward.
Staff Assistant.—Marsha Canter.
Minority Senior Professional Staff Member.—John Cullather (585 FHOB), 6–3587.
Staff Assistant.—Rose M. Hamlin.

Subcommittee on Public Buildings and Economic Development (586 FHOB), 5–3014, fax 226–1898
Senior Professional Staff Member.—Richard C. Barnett.
Counsel.—Suzanne Te Beau.
Executive Staff Assistant.—Barbara Bannister.
Minority Senior Professional Staff Member.—Susan Brita, (585 F40B), 5–9961.
Counsel.—Ward McCarragher.
Staff Assistant.—Rose Hamlin.

Subcommittee on Railroads (B–376 RHOB), 6–0727
Counsel.—Glenn Scammel.
Professional Staff Member.—Alice Tornquist.
Staff Assistant.—Jennifer Southwick.
Minority Senior Professional Staff Member.—John V. Wells (2251 RHOB), 5–9161.
Counsel.—Trinita Brown.
Staff Assistant.—Michelle Mihin.

Subcommittee on Surface Transportation (B–370A RHOB), 225–6715, fax 225–4623
General Counsel.—Roger Nober.
Counsel.—Susan Lent.
Professional Staff Members: Debra A. Gebhardt, Christopher Bertram, Adam Tsao.
Staff Assistant.—Linda D. Scott.
Minority Senior Professional Staff Member.—Kenneth House (B–375 RHOB), 5–9989, fax 225–4627.
Transportation Economist.—Rosalyn Millman.
Counsel.—Ward McCarragher.
Staff Assistant.—Steve DuBois.

Subcommittee on Water Resources and Environment (B–376 RHOB), 225–4360, fax 226–5435
Senior Counsel.—Benjamin H. Grumbles.
Counsel.—Susan Bodine.
Senior Professional Staff Member.—Marcus Peacock.
Assistant Counsels.—Lee D. Forsgren.
Professional Staff Member.—Jeffrey T. More.
Staff Assistants: Donna Campbell, Hannah Howe.
Minority Counsel.—Kenneth J. Kopocis (B–375 RHOB), 5–0060, fax 225–4627.
Assistant Counsel.—Barbara Rogers.
Chief Economist.—Arthur Chan.
Staff Assistant.—Pamela Stevens Keller.

Veterans' Affairs

355 Cannon House Office Building, phone 225–3527, fax 225–5486
http://www.house.gov/va
meets first Tuesday of each month

Bob Stump, of Arizona, *Chairman.*

Christopher H. Smith, of New Jersey.
Michael Bilirakis, of Florida.
Floyd Spence, of South Carolina.
Terry Everett, of Alabama.
Stephen E. Buyer, of Indiana.
Jack Quinn, of New York.
Spencer Bachus, of Alabama.
Cliff Stearns, of Florida.
Dan Schaefer, of Colorado.
Jerry Moran, of Kansas.
John Cooksey, of Louisiana.
Asa Hutchinson, of Arkansas.
J.D. Hayworth, of Arizona.
Helen Chenoweth, of Idaho.
Ray LaHood, of Illinois.

Lane Evans, of Illinois.
Joseph P. Kennedy II, of Massachusetts.
Bob Filner, of California.
Luis V. Gutierrez, of Illinois.
James E. Clyburn, of South Carolina.
Corrine Brown, of Florida.
Michael F. Doyle, of Pennsylvania.
Frank Mascara, of Pennsylvania.
Collin Peterson, of Minnesota.
Julia Carson, of Indiana.
Silvestre Reyes, of Texas.
Vic Snyder, of Arizona.
1 vacancy

SUBCOMMITTEES

[The chairman and ranking minority member are ex officio members of all subcommittees.]

Benefits

Mr. Quinn, *Chairman*

Mr. Schaefer
Mr. Hayworth
Mr. LaHood
1 vacancy

Mr. Filner
Mr. Mascara
Mr. Reyes
1 vacancy

Health

Mr. Stearns, *Chairman*

Mr. Smith
Mr. Bilirakis
Mr. Bachus
Mr. Moran
Mr. Cooksey
Mr. Hutchinson
Ms. Chenoweth

Mr. Gutierrez
Mr. Kennedy
Ms. Brown
Mr. Doyle
Mr. Peterson
Ms. Carson

Oversight and Investigations

Mr. Everett, *Chairman*

Mr. Stump
Mr. Spence
Mr. Buyer

Mr. Clyburn
Mr. Snyder
1 vacancy

STAFF

Committee on Veterans' Affairs (335 CHOB), 225–3527, fax 225–5486.
Staff Director/Chief Counsel.—Carl Commenator.
Deputy Chief Counsel.—Patrick Ryan (335 CHOB), 5–3541.
Assistant General Counsel.—Sloan Rappoport (337 CHOB), 5–9164.
Legislative Coordinator.—Jeanne M. McNally, 5–9112.
Professional Staff Members: Daniel Devine (337 CHOB), 5–3527; Arthur Wu, 6–3670.
Democratic Professional Staff Member.—Thomas O'Donnell (2335 RHOB), 5–5905.
Staff Assistants: Sally Elliott (335 CHOB), 5–3527; Allison Clarke (338 CHOB), 5–9154; Ira Greenspan (337 CHOB), 5–9165; Mary E. Petrella (213 CHOB), 5–4576; Pat Tippett (335 CHOB), 5–3527.
Administrative and Financial Clerk.—Mary McDermott, 5–8557.
Printing Clerk.—Jeremiah Tan (400 CHOB), 5–3535.
Democratic Staff Director.—Michael Durishin (333 CHOB), 5–9756.
Subcommittee on Health
Staff Director.—Ralph Ibson (338 CHOB), 5–9154.
Professional Staff Member.—John Roerty (338 CHOB), 5–9154.
Subcommittee on Benefits
Staff Director.—Michael Brinck (337 CHOB), 5–9164.
Professional Staff Member.—Paige McManus (337 CHOB), 5–9164.
Democratic Professional Staff Member.—Jill Cochran (333 CHOB), 5–9756.
Democratic Executive Assistant.—Elizabeth Kilker (333 CHOB), 5–9756.
Subcommittee on Oversight and Investigations
General Counsel/Staff Director.—Kingston Smith (335 CHOB), 5–3527.
Democratic Administrative Assistant/Executive Assistant.—Deborah Smith (333 CHOB), 5–9756.

Ways and Means

1102 Longworth House Office Building, phone 225–3625

http://www.house.gov/ways__means

meets second Wednesday of each month

Bill Archer, of Texas, *Chairman.*

Philip M. Crane, of Illinois.
Bill Thomas, of California.
E. Clay Shaw, Jr., of Florida.
Nancy L. Johnson, of Connecticut.
Jim Bunning, of Kentucky.
Amo Houghton, of New York.
Wally Herger, of California.
Jim McCrery, of Louisiana.
Dave Camp, of Michigan.
Jim Ramstad, of Minnesota.
Jim Nussle, of Iowa.
Sam Johnson, of Texas.
Jennifer Dunn, of Washington.
Mac Collins, of Georgia.
Rob Portman, of Ohio.
Phil English, of Pennsylvania.
John E. Ensign, of Nevada.
Jon Christensen, of Nebraska.
Wes Watkins, of Oklahoma.
J.D. Hayworth, of Arizona.
Jerry Weller, of Illinois.
Kenny Hulshof, of Missouri.

Charles B. Rangel, of New York.
Fortney Pete Stark, of California.
Robert T. Matsui, of California.
Barbara B. Kennelly, of Connecticut.
William J. Coyne, of Pennsylvania.
Sander M. Levin, of Michigan.
Benjamin L. Cardin, of Maryland.
Jim McDermott, of Washington.
Gerald D. Kleczka, of Wisconsin.
John Lewis, of Georgia.
Richard E. Neal, of Massachusetts.
Michael R. McNulty, of New York.
William J. Jefferson, of Louisiana.
John S. Tanner, of Tennessee.
Xavier Becerra, of California.
Karen L. Thurman, of Florida.

SUBCOMMITTEES

Health

Mr. Thomas, *Chairman*

Ms. Johnson	*Mr. Stark*
Mr. McCrery	*Mr. Cardin*
Mr. Ensign	*Mr. Kleczka*
Mr. Christensen	*Mr. Lewis*
Mr. Crane	*Mr. Becerra*
Mr. Houghton	
Mr. Johnson	

Human Resources

Mr. Shaw, *Chairman*

Mr. Camp	*Mr. Levin*
Mr. McCrery	*Mr. Stark*
Mr. Collins	*Mr. Matsui*
Mr. English	*Mr. Coyne*
Mr. Ensign	*Mr. McDermott*
Mr. Hayworth	
Mr. Watkins	

Oversight

Ms. Johnson, *Chairwoman*

Mr. Portman	*Mr. Coyne*
Mr. Ramstad	*Mr. Kleczka*
Ms. Dunn	*Mr. McNulty*
Mr. English	*Mr. Tanner*
Mr. Watkins	*Ms. Thurman*
Mr. Weller	
Mr. Hulshof	

Social Security

Mr. Bunning, *Chairman*

Mr. Johnson	*Ms. Kennelly*
Mr. Collins	*Mr. Neal*
Mr. Portman	*Mr. Levin*
Mr. Christensen	*Mr. Tanner*
Mr. Hayworth	*Mr. Becerna*
Mr. Weller	
Mr. Hulshof	

Trade

Mr. Crane, *Chairman*

Mr. Thomas	*Mr. Matsui*
Mr. Shaw	*Mr. Rangel*
Mr. Houghton	*Mr. Neal*
Mr. Camp	*Mr. McDermott*
Mr. Ramstad	*Mr. McNulty*
Ms. Dunn	*Mr. Jefferson*
Mr. Herger	
Mr. Nussle	

STAFF

Committee on Ways and Means (1102 LHOB), 225–3625.

Chief of Staff.—A.L. Singleton.

Chief Tax Counsel.—James D. Clark (1135 LHOB), 5–5522.

Communications Director.—Ari Fleischer (1101 LHOB), 5–8933.

Professional Assistants: Paul Auster (1135 LHOB), 5–5522; Meredith Broadbent (1104 LHOB), 5–6649; Scott Brenner (1101 LHOB), 5–8933; Steve Whitaker (1104 LHOB), 5–6649; Amy York (B–316 RHOB), 5–9263; Cassle Bevan (B–317), 5–1025; Dean Rosen (1136 LHOB), 5–3943; Ann-Maire Lynch; Allison Giles; Timothy L. Hanford (1135 LHOB), 5–5522; John L. Harrington (1135 LHOB), 5–5522; Margaret Hostetler (1136 LHOB), 5–3943; Ann LaBelle (1136 LHOB), 5–7601;

Committee on Ways and Means (1102 LHOB), 225–3625—CONTINUED

William McKenney (1135 LHOB), 5–7601; Norah H. Moseley (1135 LHOB), 5–5522; Christopher A. Smith (1102 LHOB), 5–3625; Michael A. Superata (1136 LHOB), 5–7601; Matthew Weidinger (B–317 RHOB), 5–1025.

Staff Assistants: Barbara Adgate (1135 LHOB), 5–5522; Traci Altman (1102 LHOB), 5–3625; Scott Auster (1102 LHOB); Darren Bearson (1135 LHOB); William T. Crippen (1102 LHOB), 5–3625; Crissie Curtis (1136 LHOB); Peter Davila (B–316 RHOB); Melissa Douglas (1136 LHOB); Reginald Greene (1201B LHOB), 5–3625; Tom Hardy (1104 LHOB); Karen Humbel (1102 LHOB), 5–3625; Katherine Keith (B–316 RHOB), 5–9263; Diane Kirkland (1102 LHOB), 5–3625; David Laughter (1102 LHOB), 5–3625; Jennifer Moyer (1104 LHOB); Margaret Pratt (B–317 RHOB), 5–1025; Nancy Runge (1136 LHOB), 5–3943; David Savercool (1102 LHOB), 5–3625; Bradley Schreiber (1102 LHOB), 5–3625; Scot Smith (B–317 RHOB), 5–1025; Carren Turko (1139C LHOB), 5–3625; Walter Wukasch (1102 LHOB), 5–3625.

Minority Chief Counsel.—Janice Mays (1106 LHOB), 5–4021.

Minority Professional Assistants: John Buckley (1106 LHOB); Deborah G. Colton (1128 LHOB); Ellen Dadisman (1139A LHOB); Kathleen O'Connell (1106 LHOB); Franklin C. Phifer, Jr. (1240 LHOB); Beth Kuntz Vance (1139B LHOB); Mary Jane Wignot (1139B LHOB); Bruce Wilson (1139B LHOB); Sandy Casber Wise (1106 LHOB); Mildeen Worrell (1106 LHOB); Maureen Pritchard; William Vaughn (1139–A LHOB).

Minority Staff Assistants: Harriett Lawler, Chela Sullivan, Judy Talbert.

Subcommittee on Trade (1104 LHOB), 5–6649

Staff Director.—Thelma J. Askey.

Staff Assistants: Tom Hardy, Jennifer Moyer.

Trade Counsel.—Angela Ellard.

Professional Assistants: Meredith Broadbent, Steve Whitaker.

Subcommittee on Oversight (1136 LHOB), 5–7601

Staff Director.—Donna Steele Flynn.

Staff Assistant.—Crissie Curtis.

Professional Assistants: William McKenney, Michael A. Superata, Ann LaBelle.

Subcommittee on Human Resources (B–317 RHOB), 5–1025

Staff Director.—Ron Haskins.

Staff Assistants: Margaret Pratt, Scot Smith.

Professional Assistants: Matt Weidinger, Cassie Bevan.

Subcommittee on Health (1136 LHOB), 5–3943

Staff Director.—Charles N. Kahn III.

Staff Assistants: Nancy Runge, Melissa Douglas.

Professional Assistants: Dean Rosen, Allison Giles, Ann-Marie Lynch.

Subcommittee on Social Security (B–316 RHOB), 5–9263

Staff Director.—Kim Hildred.

Staff Assistants: Katherine Keith, Peter Davila.

Professional Assistant.—Amy York.

Tax Staff (1135 LHOB), 5–5522.

Staff Director.—James D. Clark.

Staff Assistants: Barbara Adgate, Darren Bearson.

Professional Assistants: Paul Auster, Timothy L. Hanford, John L. Harrington, Norah H. Moseley.

SELECT AND SPECIAL COMMITTEES OF THE HOUSE

Permanent Select Committee on Intelligence

H–405 The Capitol, phone 225–4121

[Created pursuant to H. Res. 658, 95th Congress]

Porter J. Goss, of Florida, *Chairman.*

C.W. Bill Young, of Florida.
Jerry Lewis, of California.
Bud Shuster, of Pennsylvania.
Bill McCollum, of Florida.
Michael N. Castle, of Delaware.
Sherwood L. Boehlert, of New York.
Charles F. Bass, of New Hampshire.
Jim Gibbons, of Nevada.

Norman D. Dicks, of Washington.
Julian C. Dixon, of California.
David E. Skaggs, of Colorado.
Nancy Pelosi, of California.
Jane Harman, of California.
Ike Skelton, of Missouri.
Sanford D. Bishop, of Georgia.

SUBCOMMITTEES

Human Intelligence, Analysis and Counterintelligence

Mr. McCollum, *Chairman*

Mr. Shuster
Mr. Castle
Mr. Bass

Mr. Skaggs
Mr. Dixon
Ms. Pelosi
Mr. Bishop

Technical and Tactical Intelligence

Mr. Lewis, *Chairman*

Mr. Young
Mr. Boehlert
Mr. Gibbons

Mr. Dicks
Mr. Skaggs
Ms. Harman
Mr. Skelton

STAFF

Chief Counsel.—Patrick B. Murray.
Deputy Chief Counsel.—Christopher Barton.
Democratic Counsel.—Michael W. Sheehy, 5–7690.
Chief Clerk.—Lydia M. Olson.
Staff Director.—John I. Millis.
Staff Assistants: Christopher Baugh, Anne Fogarty, Delores Jackson, Ilene Romack, 5–7690; Kelli Short.
Chief of Registry/Security.—Mary Jane Maguire.
Deputy Chief of Registry/Security.—William McFarland.
Professional Staff: Catherine D. Eberwein, Mary Engebreth,L. Christine Healey, 5–7690; Calvin Humphrey, 5–7690; Kenneth M. Kodama, 5–7690; T. Kirk McConnell, 5–7690; Michael C. Meermans, Thomas Newcomb, Susan M. Ouellette, Diane S. Roark, Timothy R. Sample, Wendy Selig.
Speaker's Designee.—Gardner Peckham.
Minority Leader's Designee.—Brett O'Brien, 5–7690.

National Republican Congressional Committee

320 First Street SE 20003, phone 479–7000

John Linder, of Georgia, *Chairman.*

Executive Committee
Chairman.—Ed Royce, of California.
Vice Chairman.—Deb Pryce, of Ohio.
Vice Chairman.—Jim McCrery, of Louisiana.
Vice Chairman.—Michael Crapo, of Idaho.

Members

Bob Barr, of Georgia
Charlie Bass, of New Hampshire.
Sherwood Boehlert, of New York.
Dave Camp, of Michigan.
Chris Cannon, of Utah.
Jon Christensen, of Nebraska.
Thomas Coburn, of Oklahoma.
Tom Davis, of Virginia.
John Doolittle, of California.
Jo Ann Emerson, of Missouri.
John Ensign, of Nevada.
Tom Ewing, of Illinois.
Mark Foley, of Florida.
Bob Franks, of New Jersey.
Gil Gutknecht, of Minnesota.
Doc Hastings, of Washington.
Dave Hobson, of Ohio.
Ray LaHood, of Illinois.
Rick Lazio, of New York.
Jerry Moran, of Kansas.
Sue Myrick, of North Carolina.
Anne Northup, of Kentucky.
Chip Pickering, of Mississippi.
John Thune, of South Dakota.
Jerry Weller, of Illinois.
Roger Wicker, of Mississippi.

STAFF

Executive Director.—Sam Dawson, 479–7020.
Deputy Executive Director.—Mark Anderson, 479–7020.
Political Director.—Ed Brookover, 479–7050.
Communications Director.—Rich Galen, 479–7070.
Research Director.—Bill Clark, 479–7060.
Finance Director.—Grace Cummings, 479–7030.
Administration Director.—Donna Singleton, 479–7025.
Counsel.—Bruce Mehlman, 479–7020.

Republican Policy Committee

2471 Rayburn House Office Building, phone, 225–6168
meets every Wednesday

Christopher Cox, of California, *Chairman.*

Republican Leadership
Speaker.—Newt Gingrich, of Georgia.
Majority Leader.—Dick Armey, of Texas.
Majority Whip.—Tom DeLay, of Texas.
Conference Chairman.—John Boehner, of Ohio.
Conference Vice Chairman.—Susan Molinari, of New York.
Conference Secretary.—Jennifer Dunn, of Washington.
NRCC Chairman.—John Linder, of Georgia.
104th Class Representative.—David McIntosh, of Indiana.
104th Class Representative.—Sue Myrick, of North Carolina.
105th Class Representative.—John Thune, of South Dakota.

Committee Chairmen:
Rules Committee.—Gerald Solomon, of New York.
Ways and Means Committee.—Bill Archer, of Texas.
Appropriations Committee.—Bob Livingston, of Louisiana.
Budget Committee.—John R. Kasich, of Ohio.
Commerce Committee.—Tom Bliley, of Virginia.

Regional and Small States Representatives:
Richard Pombo, of California.
Bob Barr, of Georgia.
Nick Smith, of Michigan.
Todd Tiahrt, of Kansas.
Rob Portman, of Ohio.
Ben Gilman, of New York.
Floyd Spence, of South Carolina.
Tom Coburn, of Louisiana.
Jack Metcalf, of Washington.
Doug Bereuter, of Nebraska.

Four Class Representatives:
Sophomore Class.—Jim Greenwood, of Pennsylvania.
Sophomore Class.—Ed Royce, of California.
Freshman Class.—Dave Weldon, of Florida.
Freshman Class.—John Shadegg, of Arizona.

Members-at-Large:
Wayne Allard, of Colorado.
Helen Chenoweth, of Idaho.
Bill Goodling, of Pennsylvania.
Mel Hancock, of Missouri.
Bob Inglis, of South Carolina.
Steve Largent, of Oklahoma.
Ron Lewis, of Kentucky.
Jim Saxton, of New Jersey.
Cliff Stearns, of Florida.
Jerry Weller, of Illinois.

STAFF

Republican Policy Committee (2471 RHOB), 225–6168.
Executive Director.—Benedict S. Cohen.
Director, Communications/Senior Policy Analyst.—Antony Korenstein.
Policy Analyst/Committee Coordinator.—Steven J. Ricks.

House Republican Conference

1010 Longworth House Office Building, phone 225–5107

John A. Boehner, of Ohio, *Chairman.*

Susan Molinari, of New York, *Vice Chairman.*

Jennifer Dunn, of Washington, *Secretary.*

STAFF

Executive Director.—Barry Jackson.
Director of:
Policy.—Brian Gaston.
Outreach.—Joyce Hamilton.
Members Services.—Dwayne Kratt.
Communications.—Paula Nowakowski.
Information Services.—Andy Weixler.
Press Secretary.—Terry Holt.
Press Assistant.—Chad Kolton.
Staff Assistant.—Jonathan Day.
Conference Coordinator.—Brenda Benjamin.
Policy and Planning Coordinator.—Christy Carson.
Policy Analyst.—Cindy Herrle.
Communications Assistant.—Amy Ricketts.
General Counsel.—Marc Lampkin.
Grassroots Coordinator.—Jeff Dobrozsi.

House Republican Steering Committee

H–233 The Capitol, phone, 225–0600

Newt Gingrich, *Chairman.*

Susan Molinari, of New York.
Jennifer Dunn, of Washington.
Dick Armey, of Texas.
Tom DeLay, of Texas.
John Boehner, of Ohio.
Christopher Cox, of California.
John Linder, of Georgia.
Bill Paxon, of New York.
Bob Livingston, of Louisiana.
John Kasich, of Ohio.
Gerald (Jerry) Solomon, of New York.
Bill Archer, of Texas.
David Dreier, of California.
Bill Young, of Florida.
Denny Hastert, of Illinois.
Tom Latham, of Iowa.
Bud Shuster, of Pennsylvania.
John McHugh, of New York.
Cass Ballenger, of North Carolina.
Joe Barton, of Texas.
Bob Stump, of Arizona.
Don Young, of Arkansas.
Saxby Chambliss, of Georgia.
Lindsey Graham, of South Carolina.
Roy Blunt, of Missouri.

Staff Contact: Martha Morrison.

Democratic Congressional Campaign Committee

430 South Capitol Street SE 20003, phone 863–1500

Chairman.—Martin Frost, Representative from Texas.
Vice Chairman.—Nancy Pelosi, Representative from California.

Ex Officio Members:
Richard A. Gephardt, of Missouri.
David Bonior, of Michigan.
Vic Fazio, of California.
Barbara B. Kennelly, of Connecticut.
Rosa L. DeLauro, of Connecticut.
Chet Edwards, of Texas.
John Lewis, of Georgia.

Co-chairs, Full Committee:
Bill Brewster, of Oklahoma.
Robert (Bud) Cramer Jr., of Alabama.
Peter Deutsch, of Florida.
Barney Frank, of Massachusetts.
William (Jeff) Jefferson, of Louisiana.
Joseph P. Kennedy, II, of Massachusetts.
Carolyn B. Maloney, of New York.
Patricia Schroeder, of Colorado.
Charles W. Stenholm, of Texas.
Pat Williams, of Alabama.

Oversight Subcommittee, At-Large Members:
Sherrod Brown, of Ohio.
James E. Clyburn, of South Carolina.
Norman D. Dicks, of Washington.
Anna G. Eshoo, of California.
Patsy Mink, of Hawaii.
Pete Peterson, of Florida.
Earl Pomeroy, of North Dakota.

Leader's Appointees:
Neil Abercrombie, of Hawaii.
Jerry F. Costello, of Illinois.
Chaka Fattah, of Pennsylvania.
Bart Gordon, of Tennessee.
James A. Hayes, of Louisiana.
Patrick J. Kennedy, of Rhode Island.
Nita M. Lowey, of New York.
Karen McCarthy, of Missouri.
James P. Moran, of Virginia.
Donald M. Payne, of New Jersey.
Tim Roemer, of Indiana.

Vice Chairs, Speaker's Club:
Norman Y. Mineta, of California.
John (Jack) Murtha, of Pennsylvania.

Co-chairs, Chairmen's Council:
John D. Dingell, of Michigan.
David R. Obey, of Wisconsin.

Co-chair, Democratic House and Senate Council:
Robert T. Matsui, of California.

State Representatives:
Tom Bevill, of Alabama.
Blanche Lambert Lincoln, of Arizona.
Calvin M. Dooley, of California.
David E. Skaggs, of Colorado.
Samuel Gejdenson, of Connecticut.
Sam Gibbons, of Florida.
Cynthia A. McKinney, of Georgia.
Patsy Mink, of Hawaii.
Richard J. Durbin, of Illinois.
Lee H. Hamilton, of Indiana.
Scotty Baesler, of Kentucky.
William (Jeff) Jefferson, of Louisiana.
Steny Hoyer, of Maryland.
Richard E. Neal, of Massachusetts.
John D. Dingell, of Michigan.
James L. Oberstar, of Minnesota.
Bennie G. Thompson, of Mississippi.
Harold L. Volkmer, of Missouri.
Robert G. Torricelli, of New Jersey.
Gary L. Ackerman, of New York.
Charlie Rose, of North Carolina.
Thomas C. Sawyer, of Ohio.
Ron Wyden, of Oregon.
John (Jack) Murtha, of Pennsylvania.
Jack Reed, of Rhode Island.
James E. Clyburn, of South Carolina.
Harold E. Ford, of Tennessee.
Greg Laughlin, of Texas.
Norman D. Dicks, of Washington.
Gerald D. Kleczka, of Wisconsin.

STAFF

Democratic Congressional Campaign Committee, 430 South Capitol Street SE, 20003, 863–1500, fax 485–3512.
Executive Director.—Matt Angle, 485–3424.
Deputy to the Executive Director.—Kelly Powis, 485–3405.
Special Assistant to the Chairman.—Rob Griner, 485–3441.
Legal Counsels: Robert F. Bauer, Perkins Coie, 628–6600.

Communications Division
Communications Director.—Dan Sallick, 485–3432.
Press Spokesperson.—Stephanie Cohen, 485–3517.
Communications: Jodi Sakol, 485–3414; Dave Dougherty, 485–3502; Sid Voorakkara, 485–3502.
Communications Assistant.—Lisa Sohen, 485–3509.

Computer Resources Division
Technical Analyst.—Troy Barker, 485–3409.

Administration Division
Chief Financial Officer.—Janica Kyriacopoulos, 485–3455.
Controller.—Jackie Forte-Mackay, 485–3411.
Office Administrator.—Jacqui Vaughn, 485–3413.
Accounts Manager.—Jimmia Hammond, 485–3408.
Administration.—Cindy McGill, 485–3457; Glynis Mason, 485–3402.
Projects Assistant.—Milly Velez, 485–3502 (TTD 855–1000).
Receptionist.—Claudette Street, 863–1500.

Direct Mail
Director, Direct Mail.—Liz Fisher, 485–3421.
Director, Mail Coordinator.—Heather Nalitt, 485–3447.

Finance Division
Director of—
Chairman's Council.—Karla Kirk, 485–3430.
Member Fundraising.—Dotti Mavromatis, 485–3420.Susan Maiers, 485–3406.
House and Senate Council.—Rod Kassir, 485–3508.
Washington Fundraising.—Erin Graefe, 485–3519.
Member Fundraising Assistant: Rebecca Ruppert, 485–3447;
Speakers' Trust, National Finance.—Jonathan Mantz, 485–3422.
Speakers' Trust, Regional Directors: Colleen Browne, 485–3415; Ty Harrell, 485–3453; Marc Abrams, 485–3418; Kate Walton, 485–3458; Lane Luskey, 485–3505.
Finance Assistant.—Alan Moore, 485–3403.
Finance Research Coordinator.—Patrick Manning, 485–3439.
Finance Researchers: Bill Chapman, 485–3428; Shawn Sachs, 485–3501.
Consultant, Democratice House and Senate Counse.—Susanne Hassler, 863–1500 ext. 468.

Political Division
Political Director.—Rob Engel, 485–3448.
Political.—Stacey Silvia, 485–3433; Randy Dukes, 485–3515.
Director of—
National Field.—Paul Frick, 485–3442.
Southern Field.—Mike Henry, 485–3425.
Western Field.—Marty Stone, 863–1500.

Financial Services Director.—Darrel Thompson, 485–3419.
Financial Services.—Camisha Abels, 485–3443; Ed Welch, 863–1500.
Consultant.—Mark Gersh, NCEC, 639–8300.

Strategic Planning and Research Division
Stategic Planning and Research Director.—Peter Cari, 485–3507.
Research Deputy Director.—David Hawkins, 485–3521.
Policy and Issues Director.—John Williams, 485–3501.
Research: Nicole Anzia, 485–3435; Chris Orlando, 485–3438; Frank Rizzo.
Research Assistant.—Kristin Lentz, 863–1500.

Harriman Communications Center
Director.—Dennis Hayden, 485–3412.
Deputy Director.—Amy Gleklen, 485–3503.
Receptionist.—Kenya Dickerson, 485–3400.
Communications: Todd Glass, 485–3440; Greg Speed, 863–1500.
Technicians: Alyson Curcio, Dennis Ballard, Carol Rachou, Kevin Greenberg, Jeff Herberger, 485–3400.

Democratic Policy Committee

Room H–301 The Capitol, phone 225–6760

Chairman.—Richard A. Gephardt, Representative from Missouri.
Co-Chair.—*Eva M. Clayton,* Representative from North Carolina.
Co-Chairmen:
George Miller, Representative from California.
John M. Spratt, Representative from South Carolina.
Richard J. Durbin, Representative from Illinois.
Kweisi Mfume, Representative from Maryland.
David R. Obey, Representative from Wisconsin.

STAFF

Democratic Policy Committee (H–301, The Capitol).
Executive Director.—Craig Hanna.
Counsel.—Faith Rivers.
Special Assistant for Communication.—Melissa Narins.
Communication Analysts: Martha Coven, Paul Frick.
Advisors for—
Domestic Policy.—Andie King.
Foreign Policy.—Brett O'Brien.
Policy.—Jim Hawley.

Democratic Caucus Staff

1420 Longworth House Office Building, phone 226–3210

Vic Fazio, of California, *Chairman.*

Barbara B. Kennelly, of Connecticut, *Vice Chairman.*

STAFF

Chief of Staff.—Monica Maples.
Policy Director.—Julie Tippens.
Executive Assistant.—Andy Klineman.
Assistants to the Vice Chairman: Tara Lichtenfels, Michael Prucker.
Program Coordinator.—Sean Marcus.
Staff Assistant.—Brendan Kelsay.
Research Assistants: Jessica Gibson, Carrie Nixon.

OFFICERS AND OFFICIALS OF THE HOUSE

OFFICE OF THE SPEAKER

The Capitol, Room H–232, phone 225–0600

The Speaker.—Newt Gingrich.
Chief of Staff.—Arne Christenson, H–228.
Assistant to the Chief of Staff.—Christy Suprenant.
Director of Administration/General Counsel.—Steve Greiner.
Deputy Director of Administration.—Anne Beighey.
Office Manager.—Kathleen Taylor.
Director of Speaker Operations.—Rachel Robinson.
Scheduler.—Ann Mercorella.
Director of Planning.—David Winston.
Information Resources Manager.—D.J. Smith.
Assistants to the Speaker.—Jack Howard.
Staff Assistants.—Veloris Jean Edwards, Shirley Fitzgerald, Steve Hanser, Heather Hopkins, Lena Moore.
Assistants to the Speaker for Policy: Ed Kutler, Gardner Peckham, Karen Feaga.
Senior Policy Assistant.—Sue Yang.
Policy Assistants.—Chris Scheve, Brett Palmer.

SPEAKER'S PRESS OFFICE

The Capitol, Room H–236, phone 225–2800

Communications Director.—Tom Blank.
Press Secretary.—Christina Martin.
Deputy Press Secretary.—Andrew Weinstein.
Assistant Press Secretary.—Sandra Hernandez.
Deputy Communications Coordinator.—Kara Kindermann.
Special Assistant to the Speaker.—Robert George.
Staff Assistant: Kevin Schweers.

SPEAKER'S FLOOR OFFICE

The Capitol, Room H–209, phone 225–2204

Senior Floor Assistant.—Len Swinehart.
Floor Assistants: Ron Lasch, Jay Pierson, Martha Morrison, Mark Peterson.

SPEAKER'S CONGRESSIONAL OFFICE

2428 Rayburn House Office Building, phone 225–4501

Chief of Staff.—Nancy Desmond.
Legislative Director.—Krister Holladay.
Legislative Assistants: Rob Hood, Missy Jenkins, Lavin Gartland.

OFFICE OF THE MAJORITY LEADER

The Capitol, Room H–329, phone 225–4000

Majority Leader.—Dick Armey.
Chief of Staff.—Kerry Knott.
Deputy Chief of Staff.—Brian Gunderson.
Assistant to Chief of Staff.—Dina Habib.

Scheduler.—Leah Levy.
General Counsel/Director of Policy.—Peter Davidson.
Director of Special Projects.—Jim Wilkinson.
Press Secretary.—Michele Davis, 225–6007.
Press.—Patrick Shortridge.
Communications Assistant.—Brenna Hapes.
Policy Coordinator/Floor Assistant.—David Hobbs.
Floor Assistant.—Siobhan McGill.
Legislative Assistant.—Kimberly Franbach.
Assistants to Majority Leader: April McKinney, Kristin Lewandowski, Tyler Storey.
Policy Analysts: Horace Cooper, Dean Clancy, John Sampson.
Committee Liaison.—Ginni Thomas.
Deputy Committee Liaison.—Sigal Mandelker.
Director of Information Systems.—D.J. Smith.
Staff Assistants: Amanda Scoggins, Carla Bauer.

OFFICE OF THE MAJORITY WHIP

The Capitol, Room H–107, phone 225–0197

Majority Whip.—Tom DeLay.
Administrative Aide.—Jim Morrell.
Chief of Staff.—Ed Buckham.
Chief Floor Assistant.—Scott Hatch.
Communications Director.—John P. Feehery.
Deputy Chief of Staff.—Scott B. Palmer.
Director of Scheduling.—Pam Mattox.
Office Manager.—Deana Funderburk.
Policy Assistant.—Tim Berry.
Policy Director.—Ralph P. Hellmann.
Press Secretary.—Tony Rudy.
Research Director.—Steven Robinson.
Special Assistant to the Majority Whip.—Susan Hirschmann.
Special Assistant to the Chief of Staff.—Shannon Graves.
Special Assistant to the Chief Deputy Whip.—Samuel G. Lancaster.

OFFICE OF THE CHIEF DEPUTY MAJORITY WHIP

The Capitol, Room H–105, phone 225–0197

Chief Deputy Majority Whip.—J. Dennis Hastert.
Assistant to Chief Deputy Whip.—Samuel G. Lancaster.
Chief of Staff.—Scott B. Palmer.
Special Assistant.—Laurel Snapper.

OFFICE OF THE DEMOCRATIC LEADER

The Capitol, Room H–204, phone 225–0100

Democratic Leader.—Richard A. Gephardt.
Chief of Staff.—Steven Elmendorf.
Special Assistant.—Charles Jefferson.
Senior Advisor.—George Kundanis.
Communications Director.—Laura Nichols.
Office Manager.—Karen Brooke.
Staff Assistants: Josh Ackil, Mike Messmer, Shanti Ochs.
Assistant to the Chief of Staff.—Steve Cooper.
Research Director.—Bill Frymoyer.
Administrative Assistant.—Sharon Daniels.
Deputy Chief of Staff.—David Plouffe.
Executive Floor Assistant.—Marti Thomas.
Floor Assistant.—Daniel Turton.
General Counsel.—Michael Wessel.

OFFICE OF THE DEMOCRATIC WHIP

The Capitol, Room H–307, phone 225–3130

Democratic Whip.—David E. Bonior.
Administrative Assistant.—Sarah Dufendach.
Executive Floor Assistant.—Kathleen Gille.
Floor Assistant.—Jerry Hartz.
Deputy Floor Assistant.—Matthew Gelman.
Legislative Director.—Miles Lackey.
Press Secretary.—Gretchen Kline.
Speech Writer.—Paul Orzvlak.
Research Director.—Miles Lackey.
Staff Assistants: Anne Maginnis, Fred Miller.
Scheduler.—Paula Short.

OFFICES OF THE CHIEF DEPUTY DEMOCRATIC WHIPS

Deputy Democratic Whips:
Rose L. DeLauro, 436 CHOB, 5–3661.
Chet Edwards, 2459 RHOB, 5–6105.
John Lewis, 229 CHOB, 5–7780.
Robert Menendez, 405 CHOB, 225–7919.

HOUSE OFFICES AND STAFF

OFFICE OF THE CLERK

The Capitol, Room H–154, phone 225–7000

ROBIN H. CARLE, Clerk of the House of Representatives; born in Albuquerque, NM, June 1, 1955; B.A., English; Macalester College, St. Paul, MN, 1977; Republican National Committee: western field representative, 1977–80; director of political education, deputy political director, 1983–85; chief of staff, 1985–88; director of campaign operations, 1993–94; executive director, Nevada republican Central Committee, 1981–83; executive secretary to U.S. Department of Health and Human Services, 1989–92; chief of staff, U.S. Department of Health and Human Services, 1992–93; elected January 4, 1995, as Clerk of the House for the 104th Congress.

Clerk.—Robin H. Carle.
Assistant Clerk.—Ray Strong.
Assistant Clerk/Personnel.—Julie Perrier.
General Counsel (Acting).—Geraldine Gennet.
Chief of—
Legislative Computer Systems.—Dick Langley, (2401 RHOB), 225–1182.
Official Reporters.—Ray A. Boyum, (1718 LHOB), 225–2627.
Legislative Operations.—Gigi Kelaher, (HT–13 The Capitol), 225–7925.
Legislative Information.—Deborah Jo Turner; (H2–696), 225–1772.
Legislative Resource Center.—John Kornacki, (B–106 CHOB), 226–5200.
Coordinator, Page Program.—Karen Quinn (H–154), 225–7000.
Majority Chief of Pages.—Peggy Sampson, 225–7350.
Minority Chief of Pages.—Wren Ivester, 225–7330.
Service Groups—
Majority Cloakroom Manager.—Time Harroun, 225–7350.
Minority Cloakroom Manager.—Barry Sullivan, 225–7330.
Congresswoman's Suite.—225–4196.
Members and Family Room.—225–6369.
Prayer Room.—225–8070.

CHIEF ADMINISTRATIVE OFFICER

The Capitol, Room H–112, phone 225–6900

[Authorized by House Resolution 423, 102nd Congress, enacted April 9, 1992]

JEFF TRANDAHL, B.A. in government/politics/English from University of Maryland; various professional experiences including office of U.S. Senator James Abdnor (South Dakota) from 1982 to 1987; office of Congresswoman Virginia Smith (Nebraska) and House Committee on Appropriations from 1987 to 1990; office of Congressman Pat Roberts (Kansas) from 1990 to 1995; office of the Clerk of the House from 1995 to 1996; Chief Administrative Officer (acting) from 1996 to present; involved in various professional and social organizations.

Chief Administrative Officer.—Jeff Trandahl (acting).
Executive Assistant.—Rachel Kahler, H–112, 225–6900.
Administrative Assistant.—Jo Jorgenson, H–112, 225–6900.
Counsel to Chief Administrative Officer.—Michael J. Dorsey, H1–612, 225–4899.
Associate Administrator for—
Finance.—[Vacant], 263 CHOB, 225–6514.
Human Resources.—Kay E. Ford, 263 CHOB, 225–6514.
Procurement and Purchasing.—William Norton (acting), H1–719, 225–2921.
House Information Resources.—Ken Miller, H2–631, 225–9276.
Media/Support Services.—Helene Flanagan, B–217 LHOB, 225–3321.
Director, Internal Control and Continuous Improvement.—[Vacant], H1–611, 226–1854.
Deputy Director, Internal Control and Continuous Improvement.—William L. Sturdevant, H1–611, 225–7352.

CHAPLAIN

The Capitol, Room HB–25, phone 225–2509

JAMES DAVID FORD, D.D., Chaplain of the House of Representatives, first elected Chaplain by the 96th Congress, reelected by succeeding Congresses; graduated from Gustavus Adolphus College, St. Peter, MN; M. Div. from Augustana Seminary, Rock Island, IL; Doctor of Divinity from Wagner College, New York City; served as pastor of Lutheran Church, Ivanhoe, MN, and Cadet Chaplain of U.S. Military Academy, West Point, NY, for 18 years.

Chaplain of the House.—Rev. James David Ford, D.D.

HOUSE INFORMATION RESOURCES

Ford House Office Building, H2–631, 20515, phone 225–7017, fax 226–3482

OFFICE OF THE ATTENDING PHYSICIAN

The Capitol, Room H–166, phone 225–5421

(If no answer, call Capitol Operator 224–2145)

Attending Physician.—Dr. John F. Eisold: after office hours, (301) 279–0963.
Administrative Assistant.—Robert J. Burg: after office hours, (703) 719–7783.

OFFICE OF INSPECTOR GENERAL

Ford House Office Building, H2–485, phone 226–1250

Inspector General.—John W. Lainhart IV.
Deputy Inspector General.—Robert B. Frey III.
Administrative Assistant.—Mary M. Chaney.
Secretary.—Pamela Leigh.
Director, Performance and Financial Audits.—G. Kenneth Eichelman.
Auditors-in-Charge: Opal Marie Hughes, Anne M. Murphy.
Auditors: Shari L. Palumbo, Laurence B. Hawkins.
Director, Information Systems Audits.—David I. Berran.
Auditors-in-Charge: Edward D. Slevin, Robert J. Batta.
Auditors: Stephen D. Lockhart, Donna K. Hughes.
Director, Computer Assisted Audit Techniques.—Teresa J. Mosby.
Specialist.—Michael E. Benner.
Director, Contract Audit Services.—Craig W. Silverthorne.
Assistant Director, Contract Audit Services.—Susan L. Sharp.
Director, Investigations.—Thomas C. Buchanan.

OFFICE OF THE LAW REVISION COUNSEL

Ford House Office Building, H2–304 20515–6711, phone 226–2411, fax 225–0010

Law Revision Counsel.—John R. Miller (acting).
Senior Counsels: Jerald J. Director, Kenneth I. Paretzky.
Assistant Counsels: Jane W. Lawrence, Peter G. LeFevre, Ralph V. Seep, Richard B. Simpson, Alan G. Skutt, Robert M. Sukol, Deborah Z. Yee.
Staff Assistants: Debra L. Johnson, Jean Orlando, William M. Short, Dulcie M. Violette.
Computer Systems Manager.—Hal Norman.
Printing Editors.—Wayne W. Grigsby, Robert A. Prather.
Senior Programmer Analyst.—Eric Loach.

OFFICE OF THE LEGISLATIVE COUNSEL

136 Cannon House Office Building, phone 225–6060

Legislative Counsel.—David E. Meade.
Deputy Legislative Counsel.—Pope Barrow.
Assistant Counsels: Wade Ballou, Douglass Bellis, Timothy Brown, Paul C. Callen, Sherry Chriss, Steven Cope, Robert Cover, Camille Davidson, Susan Fleishman, Ira Forstater, Rosemary Gallagher, Pete Goodloe, Stanley Grimm, Edward Grossman, James Grossman, Curt C. Haensel, Jean Harmann, Yvonne Haywood, Lawrence Johnston, Jacqueline A. Jones, Gregory M. Kostka, Edward Leong, David Mendelsohn, Pierre Poisson, Rebecca Rosenberg, Lisa M. Satterfield, Hank Savage, Willoughby G. Sheane, Jr., Sandra Strokoff, Mark A. Synnes, Hunter C. Torny, Robert Weinhagen, James Wert, Noah L. Wofsy.
Office Administrator.—Lynne Richardson.
Assistant Office Administrator.—Renate Stehr.
Staff Assistants: Debra Birch, Patricia Floyd, Michael J. Gallagher, Nancy M. Cassavechia, Bruce A. Robertson, M. Elaine Sagman, Catherine Searcy, Craig A. Sterkx.
Information Systems Analyst.—James Goepel.
Publications Coordinator.—Frederick Dichter.

OFFICE OF THE PARLIAMENTARIAN

The Capitol, Room H–209, phone 225–7373

Parliamentarian.—Charles W. Johnson III.
Deputy Parliamentarians: Thomas G. Duncan, John V. Sullivan.
Assistant Parliamentarians: Muftiah M. McCartin, Thomas J. Wickham.
Clerk.—Gay S. Topper.
Assistant Clerk.—Brian C. Cooper.

OFFICE OF THE SERGEANT AT ARMS

The Capitol, Room H–124, phone 225–2456

WILSON LIVINGOOD, Sergeant at Arms of the U.S. House of Representatives; born on October 1, 1936 in Philadelphia, PA; B.S., police administration, Michigan State University; career record: special agent, U.S. Secret Service's Dallas Field Office, 1961–69; assistant to the special agent in charge of the Presidential Protective Division, 1969; special agent in charge of the Office of Protective Forces, 1970; inspector, Office of Inspection, 1978–82; special agent in charge, Houston Field Office, 1982–86; deputy assistant director, Office of Training, 1986–89; executive assistant to the Director of Secret Service, 1989–95; elected 36th Sergeant at Arms of the U.S. House of Representatives, January 4, 1995, for the 104th Congress; reelected for the 105th Congress.

Sergeant at Arms.—Bill Livingood.
Deputy Sergeant at Arms.—Jim Varey.
Executive Assistant.—Kerri Hanley.
Directors—
Police Services.—Tom Keating.
Special Events.—Don Kellaher.
Identification Services.—Melissa Franger.
Staff Assistants: Pat Schaap, Karen Forriest, Doris Boyd.

Chamber Security.—Bill Sims.
  Assistant Supervisor.—Richard Wilson.
House Garages and Parking Security.—Pat Lanigan.
Assistants to Sergeant at Arms: Ed Nichols, Jim Kaelin, Kevin Brennan, Pamela Kidd, Pam Ahearn.
Manager, Appointments/Public Information Center.—Susan Lowe.
Staff Assistant.—Theodore Lancaster.

JOINT COMMITTEES

Joint Economic Committee

G01 Dirksen Senate Office Building 20510–6432

phone 224–5171

[Created pursuant to sec. 5(a) of Public Law 304, 79th Congress]

Jim Saxton, Representative from New Jersey, *Chairman.*
Connie Mack, Senator from Florida, *Vice Chairman.*

HOUSE

Donald A. Manzullo, of Illinois.
Marshall (Mark) Sanford, of South Carolina.
William M. (Mac) Thornberry, of Texas.
John T. Doolittle, of California.
Jim McCrery, of Louisiana.

Fortney Pete Stark, of California.
Lee H. Hamilton, of Indiana.
Maurice D. Hinchey, of New York.
Carolyn B. Maloney, of New York.

SENATE

William V. Roth, Jr., of Delaware.
Robert F. Bennett, of Utah.
Rod Grams, of Minnesota.
Sam Brownback, of Kansas.
Jeff Sessions, of Alabama.

Jeff Bingaman, of New Mexico.
Paul S. Sarbanes, of Maryland.
Edward M. Kennedy, of Maine.
Charles S. Robb, of Virginia.

STAFF

Joint Economic Committee (SD–G01), 4–5171.
Executive Director.—Chris Frenze 224–5171.
Chief Counsel to the Vice Chairman.—Shelley Hymes (SH–805), 224–7683.
Counselor to the Vice Chairman.—Jeff Styles (SH–802A), 224–7056.
Policy Analyst to the Vice Chairman.—Alan Petigny (SH–802), 224–7578.
Senior Economist to the Vice Chairman.—Bob Stein (SH–805), 224–0377.
Staff Assistant to the Vice Chairman.—Dennis McKeon (SH–805), 224–0374.
Systems Specialist to the Vice Chairman.—Akram Khan (SH–802), 224–3183.
Chief Economist and Tax Advisor to the Vice Chairman.—Paul Merski (SH–805), 224–2989.
Senior Economists: Reed Garfiled 225–2223; Hayden Bryan (H1–102), 226–3228.
Macro Economist.—Chief Bob Keleher (H1–102), 224–3227.
Economist.—Dan Miller 225–0371.
Finance Director.—Colleen Healy (SD–G01), 224–5171.
Press Secretary.—Mary Hewitt (SD–G09), 224–0379.
Professional Staff Members: Andrew Quinlan (SD–G05), 224–0373; Roni Singleton (SD–G07); 224–0381.
Systems Administrator.—Jack Hubbert (SD–G03), 224–0365.
Research Analyst.—Shahira ElBogdady 225–0370.
Staff Assistants: Brenda Janowiak, 224–7943; Victoria Norcross (SD–G01), 224–7171; Amy Pardo 226–3234.
Administrative Assistant.—Juanita Morgan (SD–G01), 224–0368.

Joint Committee on the Library

William M. Thomas, Representative from California, *Chairman.*
Ted Stevens, Senator from Alaska, *Vice Chairman.*

HOUSE

Robert W. Ney, of Ohio.
Veron J. Ehlers, of Michigan.
Carolyn C. Kilpatrick, of Michigan.
Sam Gejdenson, of Connecticut.

SENATE

John W. Warner, of Virginia.
Thad Cochran, of Mississippi.
Daniel Patrick Moynihan, of New York.
Dianne Feinstein, of California.

Joint Committee on Printing

818 Hart Senate Office Building 20510, phone 224–5241, fax 224–1176

[Created by act of August 3, 1846 (9 Stat. 114); U.S. Code 44, section 101]

John W. Warner, Senator from Virginia, *Chairman.*
William M. Thomas, Representative from California, *Vice Chairman.*

SENATE

Thad Cochran, of Mississippi.
Mitch McConnell, of Kentucky.
Wendell H. Ford, of Kentucky.
Daniel K. Inouye, of Hawaii.

HOUSE

Robert W. Ney, of Ohio.
Kay Granger, of Texas.
Steny H. Hoyer, of Maryland.
Sam Gejdenson, of Connecticut.

STAFF

Staff Director.—Eric C. Peterson.
Deputy Staff Director.—Linda C. Kemp.
Deputy Staff Director for the Senate.—George Cartagena.
Staff Director for the Minority.—Robert T. Mansker.
Deputy Staff Director for the Minority.—John Chambers.
Chief Clerk.—Virginia C. Sandahl.
Professional Staff: Jim Bradley, Mary Beth Lawler, Craven Rand.

Joint Committee on Taxation

[Created by Public Law 20, 69th Congress]

1015 Longworth House Office Building 20515–6453, phone 225–3621

Bill Archer, Representative from Texas, *Chairman.*
William V. Roth, Jr., Senator from Delaware, *Vice Chairman.*

HOUSE

Philip M. Crane, of Illinois.
William M. Thomas, of California.
Charles B. Rangel, of New York.
Fortney Pete Stark, of California.

SENATE

John H. Chafee, of Rhode Island.
Charles E. Grassley, of Iowa.
Daniel Patrick Moynihan, of New York.
Max Baucus, of Montana.

STAFF

Joint Committee on Taxation (1015 LHOB), 225–3621.
Chief of Staff.—Kenneth J. Kies.
Deputy Chief of Staff/Law.—Mary M. Schmitt (H1–A104 OHOB), 6–3270.
Deputy Chief of Staff/Revenue Analysis.—Bernard A. Schmitt (H1–A621 OHOB), 6–7575.
Associate Deputy Chiefs: Joseph M. Mikrut (1618 LHOB), 5–7377; Carolyn E. Smith (SD–204), 4–5561; Thomas F. Koerner (H1–A618 OHOB), 6–7575.
Administrative Assistant.—Michael E. Boren (1015 LHOB), 5–3621.
Chief Clerk.—John H. Bloyer (1620 LHOB), 5–2647.
Special Assistant.—Leon W. Klud (1618 LHOB), 5–7377.
Senior Legislation Counsels: Laurie A. Matthews (1622 LHOB), 5–3780; H. Benjamin Hartley (1616 LHOB), 5–7377; Harold E. Hirsch (SH–836), Melvin C. Thomas (1618 LHOB), 5–7377;
Legislation Counsels: Steven D. Arkin (H1–A104 OHOB), 6–3270; Kent L. Killelea (1622 LHOB), 5–7377; Alysa M. McDaniel (H1–A104 OHOB), 6–3270; Joseph W. Nega (1618 LHOB), 5–7377; Judy K. Owens (1616–LHOB), 5–7377; Barry L. Wold (SD–204), 4–5561. Maxine B. Terry (H1–A104), 6–3270.
Business Tax Counsel.—Barbara M. Angus (HD–204), 4–5561.
Senior Economists: Thomas A. Barthold (1616 LHOB), 5–7377; Patrick A. Driessen (H1–A620 OHOB), 6–7575; William T. Sutton (H1–A622 OHOB), 6–7575.
Economists: Christopher Giosa, (H1–A619), 6–7575; Robert P. Harvey (H1–A618), 6–7575; Ronald A. Jeremias (H1–A622 OHOB), 6–7575; Gary Koeing (H1–A622 OHOB), *6–7575; Pamela H. Moomau (H1–A620 OHOB), 6–7575; Barbara J. Robles* (H1–A618 OHOB), 6–7575; Maxine B. Terry (H1–A104), 6–3270; Michael A. Udell (H1–A622 OHOB), 6–7575; Judy Xanthopoulos (H1–A619 OHOB), 6–7575.
Statistical Analyst.—Melani M. Houser (H1–615 OHOB), 6–7575.
Director of Tax Resources.—Tracy Nadel (H1–A614 OHOB), 5–7575.
Tax Resources Specialist.—Melissa O'Brien (H1–A614 OHOB), 6–7575.
Senior Refund Counsel.—Norman J. Brand (3565 IRS), 2–3580.
Refund Counsels: Robert C. Gotwald (3565 IRS), 622–3580; Carl E. Bates.
Secretaries: Carolyn D. Abraham (SD–204), 4–5561; Jean B. Best (H1–A615 OHOB), 6–7575; Debbie D. Davis (H1–A615 OHOB), 6–7575; Teresa S. Grimes (1015 LHOB), 5–3621; M.L. Sharon Jedlicka (SD–204), 4–5561; R. Julie Mitchell (3565 IRS), 622–3580; Jo Piraneo (H1–A107 OHOB), 6–3270; Lucia J. Rogers (H1–A615 OHOB), 6–7575; Diane M. Sordi (1620 LHOB), 5–7377; Christine J. Simmons (1620 LHOB), 5–7377; Pam Williams (1015 LHOB) 5–3621; Joanne Yanusz (1620 LHOB), 5–7377.
Computer Specialists: William J. Dahl; Diana L. Nelson, (H1–A104 OHOB), 6–3270.
Senior Staff Assistant: Debra L. McMullen (1620 LHOB), 5–2647.
Staff Assistants: Neval E. McMullen (1620 LHOB), 5–2647; Richard L. Scott (1620 LHOB), 5–2647; Thomas A. St. Clair (1620 LHOB), 5–2647.

CONGRESSIONAL ADVISORY BOARDS, COMMISSIONS, GROUPS

BOARD OF VISITORS TO THE AIR FORCE ACADEMY

Title 10, U.S.C., Section 9355(a)

BOARD OF VISITORS TO THE MILITARY ACADEMY

Title 10, U.S.C., Section 4355(a)

BOARD OF VISITORS TO THE NAVAL ACADEMY

Title 10, U.S.C., Section 6968(a)

Memberships Not Available At Press Time

BROADCASTING BOARD OF GOVERNORS

Created by Public Law 103–236

330 Independence Avenue SW, Suite 3360, 20547, phone 401–3736, fax 401–6605

Chairman.—David Burke.

GOVERNORS

Tom Korologos
Edward Kaufman
Bette Bao Lord
Carl Spielvogel
Cheryl Halpern
Marc Nathanson
Alberto Mora
AJospeh Duffey
(ex officio member)

STAFF

Chief of Staff.—Kathleen Harrington.
Director of Evaluations/Analysis.—Brian Conniff.
Legal Counsel.—John Lindburg.
Program Review Officer.—Bruce Sherman.
Congressional Liaison.—Jon Beard.
Budget Analyst.—Michael Ringler.
Executive Assistant.—Brenda Thomas.
Staff Assistant.—Carolyn Ford.

CANADA–UNITED STATES INTERPARLIAMENTARY GROUP

Created by Public Law 86–42, 22 U.S.C., 1928a–1928d, 276d–276g

The Capitol, Room S–208, 224–3047

Senate Delegation:
Chairman.—Frank H. Murkowski, Senator from Alaska.
Vice Chairman.—[Vacant.]
Member.—[Vacant.]

COMMISSION ON CONGRESSIONAL MAILING STANDARDS

Created by Public Law 93–191

140 Cannon House Office Building, phone 225–9337

Chairman.—William M. Thomas, Representative from California.
John Boehner, Representative from Ohio.
Robert W. Ney, Representative from Ohio.
Steny Hoyer, Representative from Maryland.
William Clay, Representative from Missouri.
Martin Frost, Representative from Texas.

STAFF

Majority Staff Director.—Jack Dail 140, 225–9337.
Staff Assistants: Karen S. Buehler, Kerrie Freeborn.
Minority Staff Assistants: Constance Goode Bell, Ellen McCarthy 1339, 225–2061.

COMMISSION ON SECURITY AND COOPERATION IN EUROPE

234 Ford House Office Building, phone 225–1901

Alfonse D'Amato, of New York, *Chairman.*

Christopher H. Smith, of New Jersey, *Co-Chairman.*

Ben Nighthorse Campbell, of Colorado.
Dirk Kempthorne, of Idaho.
Spencer Abraham, of Michigan
Frank R. Lautenberg, of New Jersey.
Harry Reid, of Nevada.
Bob Graham, of Florida.
Russell D. Feingold, of Wisconsin.
John Edward Porter, of Illinois.
Frank R. Wolf, of Virginia.
Matt Salmon, of Arizona.
Jon Christensen, of Nebraska.
Steny H. Hoyer, of Maryland.
Edward J. Markey, of Massachusetts.
Benjamin L. Cardin, of Maryland.

EXECUTIVE BRANCH COMMISSIONERS

Department of State.—John Shattuck.
Department of Defense.—[Vacant].
Department of Commerce.—[Vacant].

COMMISSION STAFF

Chief of Staff.—Michael R. Hathaway.
Deputy Chief of Staff.—Dorothy Taft.
Office Administrator.—Maria Coll.
Communications Director.—Chadwick Gore.
Staff Assistant/Systems Administrator.—Peter Santighian.
Counselors: Erika B. Schlager, Marlene Kaufmann.
Senior Advisor.—Richard P. Livingston.
Staff Advisors: Orest Deychakiwsky, John Finerty, Robert Hand, Janice Helwig, Ronald McNamara, Michael Ochs.
Printing Clerk.—Sandy List.
Fellow.—Karen Lord.

COMMISSION ON THE WEST CENTRAL FRONT OF THE UNITED STATES CAPITOL

Created by Public Law 95–94 (91 Stat. 653, 681–682)

Membership Not Available At Press Time

CONGRESSIONAL AWARD FOUNDATION

Created by Public Law 96–114; amended by Public Law 102–457

379 Ford House Office Building 20515, phone (202) 226–0130, fax (202) 226–0131

Chairman.—Thomas D. Campbell, Thomas D. Campbell and Associates Inc., (703) 683–0773.

Vice Chairmen:

Ray N. Ivey, Consolidated Natural Gas Company, (412) 227–1185.
Charles F. Smithers, Jr., Paine Webber Incorporated, (202) 370–8710.
Secretary.—Edwin S. Jayne, AFSCME, (202) 429–1000.
Treasurer.—Janice Griffin, The Prudential Insurance Company of America, (202) 293–1141.
National Director.—Kendall S. Hartman, The Congressional Award Foundation, (202) 226–0130.

Members:

Frank H. Arlinghaus, Jr., Physician, Red Bank, NJ, (908) 747–1180.
Max Baucus, Senator from Montana, (202) 224–2651.
Thomas Hale Boggs, Jr., Esquire, Patton, Boggs and Blow, (212) 457–6040.
Thomas M. Bresnahan III, The Chevron Companies, (202) 408–5800.
Mark A. Carano, Food Marking Institute, (202) 452–8444.
Maxine C. Champion, Nestle USA, Inc., (202) 296–4100.
Elaine L. Chao, The Heritage Foundation, (202) 546–4400.
Larry E. Craig, Senator from Idaho, (202) 224–2752.
Roderick A. DeArment, Covington and Burling, (202) 662–5900.
Jerry A. Edgerton, MCI Telecommunications Inc., (703) 902–6111.
Ralph B. Everett, Paul, Hastings, Janofsky and Walker, (202) 508–9500.
John M. Falk, Esquire, Falk Law Firm, (202) 872–8123.
Glen D. Gaddy, Law Engineering, (703) 968–4718.
Robert B. Harding, Groom and Nordberg, (202) 857–0620.
Candice Shy Hooper, Hooper, Hooper, Owen and Gould, (202) 638–7780.
David W. Hunt, Esquire, Legal Counsel, Washington, DC, (202) 944–4639.
W. Russell King, Freeport-McMoRan, Inc., (202) 737–1400.
General Richard L. Lawson, USAF (Ret.), National Mining Association, (202) 463–2625.
George R. Layne, Fairfax Station, VA, (703) 250–8471.
Michael L. Lunceford, Mary Kay Foundation, (214) 905–5730.
Mary E. McAuliffe, Union Pacific Corporation, (202) 662–0110.
Judith A. McHale, Discovery Communications, Inc., (301) 986–1999.
Eugene Moos, Department of Agriculture, (202) 720–3111.
Sir James Murray K.C.M.G., New York, NY, (718) 852–3320.
Alexander V. Netchvolodoff, Cox Enterprises, (202) 296–4933.
Walker F. Nolan, Edison Electric Institute, (202) 508–5400.
Donald Payne, Representative from New Jersey, (202) 225–3436.
Nancy Gibson Prowitt, Alcalde and Fay, (703) 841–0626
Galen J. Reser, PepsiCo, Inc., (914) 253–2862.
Michael A. Reza, Funders Mortgage Corporation, (818) 915–8351.
Oliver G. Richard III, Columbia Gas System, Inc., (302) 429–5211.
Charles E. Sandler, American Petroleum Institute, (202) 682–8400.
William F. Sittmann, American Gaming Association, (202) 637–6500.
Richard L. Thompson, Bristol-Myers Squibb Company, (202) 783–0900.
Rex B. Wackerle, Bank of America, (202) 383–3430.

CONGRESSIONAL CLUB

2001 New Hampshire Avenue, NW 20008, phone 332–1155, fax 797–0698

President.—Mrs. David Hobson.
Vice Presidents:
(1st) Mrs. John Breaux.
(2d) Mrs. Bill Archer.
(3d) Mrs. John Tanner.
(4th) Mrs. David McIntosh.
(5th) Mrs. Mac Collins.
Treasurer.—Mrs. David Minge.
Recording Secretary.—Mrs. Calvin Dooley.
Corresponding Secretary.—Mrs. Jon Kyl.

FRANKLIN DELANO ROOSEVELT MEMORIAL COMMISSION

Created by Public Law 94–371

632 Dirksen Senate Office Building, phone 228–2491, fax 228–1010

Co-Chairs:
Mark O. Hatfield, Senator from Oregon.
Daniel K. Inouye, Senator from Hawaii.

Commissioners Appointed by the President:
Jack W. Theimer, of San Francisco, CA.
Barbara Handman, of New York, NY.
Lester S. Hyman, Esq., of Washington, DC.
David B. Roosevelt, of Westport, CT.

Appointed by the Senate:
Alfonse M. D'Amato, of New York.
Mark O. Hatfield, of Oregon.
Daniel K. Inouye, of Hawaii.
Carl M. Levin, of Michigan.

Appointed by the House:
Maurice D. Hinchey, of New York.
Jerry Lewis, of California.
Phil English, of Pennsylvania.
1 Vacancy

STAFF

Executive Director.—Dorann H. Gunderson.
Office Manager.—Colleen J. Carolan.

House Delegation:
Chairman.—[Vacant.]
Vice Chairman.—[Vacant.]
Members:
[Vacant.]
[Vacant.]
[Vacant.]
[Vacant.]
[Vacant.]
[Vacant.]
Staff:
Director, Office of Interparliamentary Services.—Sally Walsh.

HOUSE OFFICE BUILDING COMMISSION

Title 40, U.S.C. 175–176

The Capitol, Room H–326, phone 225–0600

Chairman.—Newt Gingrich, Speaker of the House of Representatives.
Dick Armey, House Majority Leader.
Richard A. Gephardt, House Minority Leader.

HOUSE OF REPRESENTATIVES PAGE BOARD

Established by House Resolution 611, 97th Congress

The Capitol, Room H–154, phone 225–7000

Chairwoman.—Tille K. Fowler, Representative from Florida.

Members:
Jim Kolbe, Representative from Arizona.
Dale Kildee, Representative from Michigan.
Robin Carle, Clerk of the House.
Wilson Livingood, Sergeant at Arms of the House.

Staff Contact:
Karen Quinn, Office of the Clerk, Page Program Administator.

INTERPARLIAMENTARY UNION

Created by 49 Stat. 425, 22 U.S.C., 276a

The Capitol, Room S–208, phone 224–3047

OFFICERS OF THE UNITED STATES GROUP FOR THE 105TH CONGRESS

President.—[Vacant.]
Vice President.—[Vacant.]
[Vacant.]
[Vacant.]
Secretary.—[Vacant.]
Treasurer.—[Vacant.]
At Large Members of Executive Committee:
[Vacant.]
[Vacant.]
[Vacant.]
Honorary Members: Edward J. Derwinski, Robert T. Stafford.
Executive Secretary.—Gary Sisco, Secretary of the Senate.
Administrative Secretary.—Robin H. Carle, Clerk of the House of Representatives.

JAPAN–UNITED STATES FRIENDSHIP COMMISSION

Created by Public Law 94–118

1120 Vermont Avenue NW, Suite 925, 20005, phone 275–7712, fax 275–7413

Chairman.—Dr. Richard Wood, Dean, Yale Divinity School.
Vice Chairman.—Glen S. Fukushima, AT&T Japan, Ltd.
Executive Director.—Dr. Eric J. Gangloff.
Assistant Executive Director.—Margaret P. Mihori.
CULCON Program Officer.—Pamela L. Fields.

Members:
Hon. David Longanecker, Assistant Secretary for Higher Education Programs, U.S. Department of Education.
[Vacant], Assistant Secretary of State for East Asian and Pacific Affairs, U.S. Department of State.
Hon. Jane Alexander, Chairman, National Endowment for the Arts.
[Vacant], Chairman, National Endowment for the Humanities.
Hon. Joseph D. Duffey, Director, United States Information Agency.
David I. Hitchcock, Bethesda MD.
Hon. Frank H. Murkowski, U.S. Senate.
George H. Takei, Los Angeles CA.
Hon. Thomas Petri, U.S. House of Representatives.
Hon. John D. Rockefeller IV, U.S. Senate.
Dr. Carol Gluck, Dept. of History, Columbia University.
Jeffrey M. Lepon, Partner, Lepon, McCarthy, White and Holzworth.
Burnill F. Clark, President, KCTS/TV, Seattle.
Thomas E. McLain, Partner, Perkins Cole.
Ira Wolf, Director, Japan Relations and Vice President Eastman Kodak, Tokyo.
Hon. Robert Wise, U.S House of Representatives.

MEXICO–UNITED STATES INTERPARLIAMENTARY GROUP

Created by Public Law 82–420, 22 U.S.C. 276h–276k

The Capitol, Room S–208, phone 224–3047

Senate Delegation:
Chairman.—Kay Bailey Hutchison, of Texas.
Vice Chairman.—*Christopher J. Dodd,* of Connecticut.

House Delegation:
Chairman.—Jim Kolbe, of Arizona.

STAFF

Director, Office of Interparliamentary Services.—Sally Walsh.

MIGRATORY BIRD CONSERVATION COMMISSION

Created by act of February 18, 1929, 16 U.S.C. 715a

Department of the Interior Building 20240, phone (703) 358–1716, fax (703) 358–2223

Chairman.—Bruce Babbitt, Secretary of the Interior.
John Breaux, Senator from Louisiana.
Thad Cochran, Senator from Mississippi.
John D. Dingell, Representative from Michigan.
Curt Weldon, Representative from Pennsylvania.
Dan Glickman, Secretary of Agriculture.
Carol M. Browner, Administrator of Environmental Protection Agency.
Secretary.—Jeffery M. Donahoe.

NORTH ATLANTIC ASSEMBLY

Created by Public Law 84–689, 22 U.S.C., 1928z

Headquarters: Place du Petit Sablon 3, B–1000 Brussels, Belgium

President.—William V. Roth, Jr.
Vice Presidents:
Rep. Jerry Solomon, United States.
M. Claude-Gerard Marcus, France.
M. Rafael Estrella, Spain.
M. Pedro Holstein-Campillo, Portugal.

Treasurer.—Sir Geoffrey Johnson Smith, United Kingdom.
Chairman, U.S. Senate Delegation.—Senator William V. Roth, Jr.
Vice Chairman, U.S. Senate Delegation.—[Vacant].
House of Representatives
Chairman.—Douglas Bereuter.

STAFF

Secretary, Senate Delegation.—Ian Brzezinski, Office of Senator Roth, 104 Senate Hart Office Building 20510, 224–2441.
Secretary, House Delegation.—John Herzberg, Committee on Foreign Affairs, 2170 Rayburn House Office Building, 20515 225–8095.
Director of Interparliamentary Services.—Sally Walsh, Office of the Secretary of the Senate, SH–231B, U.S. Senate 20510, 224–3047.

PERMANENT COMMITTEE FOR THE OLIVER WENDELL HOLMES DEVISE FUND

Created by act of Congress approved Aug. 5, 1955 (Public Law 246, 84th Congress), to administer Oliver Wendell Holmes Devise Fund, established by same act

Library of Congress 20540, phone 707–5383

Chairman Ex Officio.—James H. Billington.
Administrative Officer for the Devise.—James H. Hutson, 707–5383.

SENATE ARMS CONTROL OBSERVER GROUP

637 Hart Senate Office Building 20510, phone 224–2163

Reauthorized by House Resolution 105, 101st Congress

Senate Majority Leader.—Trent Lott, Senator from Mississippi.
Senate Minority Leader.—Thomas Daschle, Senator from South Dakota.
Administrative Co-Chairman.—Ted Stevens, Senator from Alaska.
Administrative Co-Chairman.—Robert C. Byrd, Jr., Senator from West Virginia.
Senate President Pro Tempore.—Strom Thurmond, Senator from South Carolina.
Co-Chairman.—Richard Lugar, Senator from Indiana.
Co-Chairman.—Jesse Helms, Senator from North Carolina.
Co-Chairman.—Carl Levin, Senator from Michigan.
Members:
John Chafee, Senator from Rhode Island.
Thad Cochran, Senator from Mississippi.
Jon Kyl, Senator from Arizona.
Don Nickles, Senator from Oklahoma.
Bob Smith, Senator from New Hampshire.
Olympia Snowe, Senator from Maine.
John Warner, Senator from Virginia.
Dale Bumpers, Senator from Arkansas.
Joseph R. Biden, Jr., Senator from Delaware.
John Glenn, Senator from Ohio.
Edward Kennedy, Senator from Massachusetts.
J. Robert Kerrey, Senator from Nebraska.
John Kerry, Senator from Massachusetts.
Daniel Patrick Moynihan, Senator from New York.
Paul Sarbanes, Senator from Maryland.
1 Vacancy.
Staff: John Roots, Dick D'Amato.

SENATE OFFICE BUILDING COMMISSION

Created by the act of April 28, 1904 (33 Stat. 481), as amended by the act of July 11, 1947 (61 Stat. 307), the act of August 1, 1953 (67 Stat. 328), and the act of August 3, 1956 (70 Stat. 966)

Members:
Ted Stevens, Senator from Alaska.
Jesse Helms, Senator from North Carolina.
Thad Cochran, Senator from Mississippi.
[Vacant.]
[Vacant.]
J. Bennett Johnston, Jr., Senator from Louisiana.
Daniel Patrick Moynihan, Senator from New York.
[Vacant.]
[Vacant.]

U.S. ASSOCIATION OF FORMER MEMBERS OF CONGRESS

330 A Street NE 20002, phone (202) 543–8676, fax 543–7145

President.—Louis Frey, of Florida.
Vice President.—Matthew F. McHugh, of New York.
Treasurer.—John N. Erlenborn, of Illinois.
Secretary.—H. Martin Lancaster, of North Carolina.
Immediate Past President.—Lindy Boggs, of Louisiana.
Honorary Co-chairmen: Gerald R. Ford, of Michigan; Walter F. Mondale, of Minnesota.
Executive Director.—Linda A. Reed.
Counselors: J. Glenn Beall, Jr., of Maryland; Elford A. Cederberg, of Michigan; Edward J. Derwinski, of Illinois; John S. Monagan, of Connecticut; Frank E. Moss, of Utah; James M. Quigley, of Pennsylvania; Thomas F. Railsback, of Illinois; Carlton R. Sickles, of Maryland.

U.S. CAPITOL HISTORICAL SOCIETY

Congressional Charter, October 20, 1978, Public Law 95–493, 95th Congress, 92 Stat. 1643

200 Maryland Avenue NE 20002, phone 543–8919, fax 544–8244

Chairman of the Board.—Robert L. Breeden.
President.—Clarence J. Brown, of Ohio.
Treasurer.—L. Neale Cosby.
General Secretary.—Suzanne C. Dicks.
Vice Presidents.—Michael F. Dineen, Bryce Larry Harlow, Gary G. Hymel, Carmella La Spada, James D. (Mike) McKevitt.

Executive Committee:
Robert L. Breeden
Clarence J. Brown
L. Neale Cosby
Michael Dineen
Amory Houghton
Gary G. Hymel
James D. (Mike) McKevitt
Lee J. Stillwell
Rudy A. Vignone

STAFF

Chief Historian.—Donald R. Kennon.
Associate Historian.—Rebecca Rogers.

U.S. CAPITOL PRESERVATION COMMISSION

Created pursuant to Public Law 100–696

Co-Chairmen:
Strom Thurmond, Senate President Pro Tempore.
Newt Gingrich, Speaker of the House.
House Members:
Richard K. Armey, Majority Leader.
Richard A. Gephardt, Minority Leader.
[Vacant], House Co-Chair Appointment.
William M. Thomas, Chairman, House Oversight Committee.
Sam Gejdenson, Ranking Member, House Oversight Committee.
William M. Thomas, Chairman, Joint Committee on the Library Designee.
[Vacant], Speaker's Appointment.
[Vacant], Minority Leader Appointment.
Senate Members:
Trent Lott, Majority Leader.
Thomas A. Daschle, Minority Leader.
[Vacant], Co-Chair Appointment.
John Warner, Chairman, Rules Committee.
Wendell H. Ford, Ranking Member, Rules Committee.
Ted Stevens, Chairman, Joint Committee on the Library.
[Vacant], President Pro Tempore Appointment.
[Vacant], Minority Leader Appointment.
Architect of the Capitol.—Alan M. Hantman.
Advisory Board Members:
Lindy Boggs, Co-Chairperson.
Preston Robert Tisch, Co-Chairman.
Dwayne O. Andreas.
Robert M. Bass.
Richard H. Jenrette.
William Murray.
Walter J. Stewart.
Franklin A. Thomas.
William L. Weiss.
Diane Wolf.

U.S. HOUSE OF REPRESENTATIVES FINE ARTS BOARD

Created by Public Law 101–696

1309 Longworth House Office Building, phone 225–8281

Chairman.—William M. Thomas, of California.

Members:
Robert W. Ney, of Ohio.
Veron J. Ehlers, of Michigan.
Carolyn Kilpatrick, of Michigan.
Sam Gejdenson, of Connecticut.

Staff Contact:
Stacy Carlson, Staff Director, Committee on House Oversight, 225–8281.

U.S. SENATE COMMISSION ON ART

Created by Public Law 100–696

The Capitol, Room S–411, phone 224–2955

Chairman.—Trent Lott, of Mississippi.
Vice Chairman.—*Thomas A. Daschle,* of South Dakota.

Members:
Strom Thurmond, of South Carolina.
Wendell H. Ford, of Kentucky.
John W. Warner, of Virginia.

STAFF

Executive Secretary.—Gary Sisco.
Curator.—Diane K. Skvarla.
Administrator.—Scott M. Strong.
Collections Manager.—John B. Odell.
Registrar.—Melinda K. Smith.
Museum Specialist.—Richard L. Doerner.

OTHER CONGRESSIONAL OFFICIALS AND SERVICES

ARCHITECT OF THE CAPITOL

ARCHITECT'S OFFICE

SB–15 The Capitol, phone 228–1793, fax 228–1893, http://www.aoc.gov

Architect of the Capitol.—Alan M. Hantman.
Assistant Architect of the Capitol.—[Vacant].
Administrative Assistant.—Ben C. Wimberly, 228–1819.
Budget Officer.—Stuart Pregnall, 228–1225.
Director of Engineering.—Dan E. Hanlon, 228–4832.
Executive Officer.—Herbert M. Franklin, 228–1205.
General Counsel.—Charles K. Tyler, 225–1210.
Superintendent (Capitol).—Roberto J. Miranda, 228–8800.
Landscape Architect.—Matthew Evans, 224–6645.
Air Conditioning Engineer.—[Vacant], 226–3180.
Chief Engineer (Power Plant).—Lenard Gibson (acting), 225–4380.
Electrical Engineer.—Vinod K. Wadhwa, 226–3470.
Electronic Engineer.—Ronald Schenk (acting), 224–9827.
Curator.—Barbara Wolanin, HT–3, 228–2700.

SENATE OFFICE BUILDINGS

G45 Dirksen Senate Office Building, phone 224–3141, fax 224–0652

Superintendent.—Lawrence Stoffel.
Deputy Superintendent.—Jerry Shaw.
Assistant Superintendents: Chester Kirk, Stephen Ayers.

HOUSE OFFICE BUILDINGS

B–341 Rayburn House Office Building, phone 225–3003

Superintendent.—Robert Miley.
Deputy Superintendent.—Robert Gleich.
Assistant Superintendents.—Margaret Donnelly, Bill Wood.

CAPITOL TELEPHONE EXCHANGE

180 Dirksen Senate Office Building, phone 224–2145

Supervisors: Joan Sartori, Martha Brick, Barbara Broce.

CHILD CARE CENTERS

HOUSE OF REPRESENTATIVES CHILD CARE CENTER

501 First Street SE 20003, phone 225–9684, fax 225–6908

Director.—Natalie Gitelman.

SENATE EMPLOYEES' CHILD CARE CENTER

190 D Street NE 20510, phone 224–1461, fax 228–3686

Director.—Shirley V. Letourneau.

COMBINED AIRLINES TICKET OFFICES (CATO)
1925 North Lynn Street Suite 801, Arlington VA 22209
phone (703) 522–8664, fax (703) 522–0616

General Manager.—Charles A. Dinardo.
Assistant General Manager.—Susan B. Willis.

B–222 Longworth House Office Building, phone (703) 522–2286

Supervisor.—Michelle Gelzer.

B06 Russell Senate Office Building, phone (703) 522–2286

Supervisor.—Sonja Noll.

CONGRESSIONAL DAILY DIGEST

HOUSE SECTION
HT–13 The Capitol, phone 225–7925

Editors: Maura Patricia Kelly, Elsa B. Thompson.

SENATE SECTION
ST–56 The Capitol, phone 224–2658, fax 224–1220

Editor.—Thomas G. Pellikaan.
Assistant Editor.—Linda E. Sebold.

CONGRESSIONAL RECORD INDEX OFFICE
U.S. Government Printing Office, Room C–738
North Capitol and H Streets NW 20401, phone 512–0275

Director.—Michael J. McCabe (acting), 512–0072.
Deputy Director.—Marcia Oleszewski, 512–0280.
Historian of Bills.—Barbre A. Brunson, 512–0274.
Editors: Grafton J. Daniels, Philip C. Hart, Michael M. Sardone.
Indexers: Dorothy G. Bryant, Ytta B. Carr, Tucker Greer, Karl M. Operle, Jason Parsons, Patricia J. Slater, Jodi L. Solomon.

CAPITOL GUIDE SERVICE AND CONGRESSIONAL SPECIAL SERVICES OFFICE
Crypt of the Capitol 20510
Message Line 225–6827, Special Services 224–4048, TTY 224–4048

Director.—Ted Daniel, ST13, 225–6832.

LIAISON OFFICES

AIR FORCE
B–322 Rayburn House Office Building, phone 225–6656, fax 475–0680

Chief.—Col. Marty Dupont.
Deputy Chief.—LtCol. Kim Dougherty.
Action Officers: LtCol. Manny Fernandez, Maj. Steve Wallender.
Legislative Liaison Specialist.—Donna Warren.
Legislative Liaison Assistant.—Melissa Hammonds.

182 Russell Senate Office Building, phone 224–2481, fax 685–2575

Chief.—Col. Jeff McChesney.

Liaison Officer.—LtCol. Briggs Shade.
Legislative Liaison Specialist.—Cheryl S. Cromwell.

ARMY

B–325 Rayburn House Office Building, phone 225–3853, fax 475–1561

Chief.—Col. Dan Fleming.
Liaison Officers: LtCol. Noreen Hoethaus, LtCol. Daphne Sahlin, LtCol. Earl Smith.
Administrative Assistant.—Sgt. Carol Reid.
Chief Congressional Caseworker.—Ethel McCann.
Congressional Caseworkers: Cindy Swift-Dojcak, Prevolia Harper.

R–183 Russell Senate Office Building, phone 224–2881, fax 685–2570

Chief.—Col. Randall Bookout.
Deputy Chief.—LtCol. Mike DeYoung.
Liaison Officer.—Maj. Wanda Good.
Chief, Casework Liaison.—Margaret T. Tyler.
Casework Liaison Officers: Cathy Abell, Brigitte H. Hanes, Sgt. Tanti Rowland.

COAST GUARD

B–320 Rayburn House Office Building, phone 225–4775, fax 426–6081

Liaison Officer.—Cdr. John Gentile.
Assistant Liaison Officers: Lt. Carla J. Grantham, Lt. L. Brad Mynatt.

183 Russell Senate Office Building, phone 224–2913, fax 755–1695

Liaison Officer.—J. Miko.
Liaison Assistant.—Liz Moses.

NAVY/MARINE CORPS

B–324 Rayburn House Office Building, phone 225–7124

Director.—Capt. Dale Snodgrass, USN.
Deputy Director.—Cdr. Fritz Roegge, USN.
USN Liaison Officers: LtCdr. Travis Hayes, USN, (contracts); Lt. Tracy Barkhimer, USN; Lt. Tony Horton, USN; Lt. Paul Tierney, USN; Lt. Steve West, USN.
Yeoman.—YN1 (SW/PJ) Dwight R. Scott, USN.
Director USMC.—Lt. Col. John Kelley, USMC.
USMC Liaison Officer.—Maj. Norm Cooling, USMC.
Administrative Clerks: GySgt. Harry Jenkins, USMC; Sgt. Blanca Burnley, USMC.

182 Russell Senate Office Building, phone 224–4681

Principal Deputy.—Capt. Barry M. Costello.
Assistant Deputies: Cdr. Sean Fogarty, USN; Col. Terrence Paul, USMC.
USN Liaison Officers: Lt. Gary Mayes, USN; Lt. Peter Olson, USN.
Assistant Liaison Officers: SSgt. Terry Petrovich, USMC; Sgt. Rodolfo Altamirano, USMC; YNZ (SS) Matthew Hawes, USN.

GENERAL ACCOUNTING OFFICE

Room 7125, 441 G Street 20548, phone 512–4400

Director.—Helen H. Hsing.
Legislative Advisers: Richard P. Roscoe, 512–3505; Richard M. Stana, 512–4301; Doris E.L. Cannon, 512–5407.
Associate Legislative Adviser.—Michael C. Zola, 512–8330.

OFFICE OF PERSONNEL MANAGEMENT

B–332 Rayburn House Office Building, phone 225–4955 or 632–6296

Chief.—Charlene E. Luskey.
Civil Service Representative.—Elnora E. Lewis.
Administrative Assistant.—Joseph A. Gill.

VETERANS' AFFAIRS

B–328 Rayburn House Office Building, phone 225–2280, fax 453–5225

Director.—Philip R. Mayo.
Assistant Director.—Linda Jurvelin.
Liaison Assistant.—Terry Cerda.
Representatives: Paul Downs, Pamela Mugg.

321 Hart Senate Office Building, phone 224–5351, fax 453–5218

Director.—Philip R. Mayo.
Assistant Director.—Linda Jurvelin.
Liaison Assistant.—Joan C. Lee.
Representative.—Patricia J. Covington.
Secretary.—Reo R. Johnson.

OFFICE OF THE ATTENDING PHYSICIAN

H–166 The Capitol, phone 225–5421

(If no answer call Capitol Operator 224–2145)

Attending Physician.—Dr. John F. Eisold (after office house (301) 279–0963).
Administrative Assistant.—Robert J. Burg (after office hours (703) 719–7783).

PAGE SCHOOLS

SENATE

Daniel Webster Senate Page Residence 20510, fax 224–1838

Principal.—Kathryn S. Weeden, 224–1838.
English.—Lynne Sacks, 8–1024.
Mathematics.—Stephen Perencevich, 8–1018.
Science.—Duncan Forbes, 8–1025.
Social Studies.—Michael Bowers, 8–1012.
Administrative Assistant.—Janice M. Yocco, 4–3927.

HOUSE OF REPRESENTATIVES

LJ–A5 Library of Congress 20540–9996, phone 225–9000, fax 225–9001

Principal.—Robert F. Knautz.
Administrative Assistant.—Sue Ellen Stickley.
English.—Randall R. Mawer.
Guidance.—Donna D. Wilson.
Languages.—Linda Glenn Miranda.
Mathematics.—Barbara R. Bowen.
Science.—Robert S. Nelson.
Social Studies.—Ronald L. Weitzel.
Technology.—Doborah A. Lindsay.

RAILROAD TICKET OFFICE

S–101 The Capitol, phone 224–5948, fax 228–0431

Manager (Amtrak).—Robert E. Scolaro.

U.S. CAPITOL POLICE

119 D Street NE 20510

Office of the Chief 224–9806, Communications 224–5151, Emergency 224–0911

U.S. CAPITOL POLICE BOARD

Sergeant at Arms, U.S. Senate.—Gregory S. Casey.
Sergeant at Arms, U.S. House of Representatives.—Wilson Livingood.
Architect of the Capitol.—Alan M. Hantman.

OFFICE OF THE CHIEF

Chief of Police.—Gary L. Abrecht.
Administrative Assistant.—Lt. Timothy J. Connors.
Assistant Chief of Police.—Robert R. Howe.
Administrative Assistant.—Sgt. Jane E. Frederick.
General Counsel.—John T. Caulfield.
Deputy Counsel.—Ken O. Benjamin.
Internal Affairs Division Commander.—Vicki L. Frye.
Assistant Commander.—Lt. John J. Delucca.
Office of Financial Management.—James B. Holmberg.
Public Information Officer.—Sgt. Daniel R. Nichols.

ADMINISTRATIVE SERVICES BUREAU

Bureau Commander.—Deputy Chief Fentress A. Hickman.
Executive Officer.—Inspector Stephen W. Ring.
Human Resources Management Director.—Daniel J. Strodel.
Training Division.—Capt. Mack A. Kennedy.
Property Management Division.—Lt. James W. Proctor, Jr.
Planning and Development Division.—Lt. Michael A. Borowski.
Information Management Division.—Douglas W. Pippin.
Recruiting and Investigations Section.—Lt. Stephen Istvan.
Personnel Management and Development Section.—Gail McNamara.
Personnel/Payroll Systems.—Jan E. Jones.
Federal Law Enforcement Training Center.—Lt. Stanley J. Grochowski.
Entry Level Training Section.—Lt. Thomas P. Reynolds.
In-Service Training Section.—Lt. Alan D. Morris.
Physical Specialties Section.—Lt. Lawrence K. Morgan.

PROTECTIVE SERVICES BUREAU

Bureau Commander.—Deputy Chief Steven D. Bahrns.
Protective Intelligence Division.—Capt. David F. Callaway.
Criminal Investigations Division.—Capt. Price S. Goldston.
Technical Security Division.—Capt. Gilman Udell.
Assistant Technical Security Division.—Lt. Michael Conway.
Dignitary Protection Division Commander.—Capt. Michael C. Preloh.
Assistant Dignitary Protection Division Commander.—Lt. James M. Belka.

UNIFORM SERVICES BUREAU

Bureau Commander.—Deputy Chief James P. Rohan.
Executive Assistant.—Lt. Robert L. Dicks.

Capitol Division Commander.—Inspector Christopher M. McGaffin.
Capt. Caroline Fields
Capt. Gregory D. Parman
Lt. Robert V. Howse
Lt. Thomas L. Smith, Sr.
Lt. William H. Emory
Lt. Harry I. Wall

First Responder Unit: Lt. Lawrence F. Loughery, Lt. Billy R. Frye.
Gallery Security Section.—Lt. George B. Hawco.

Senate Division Commander.—Inspector Michael J. Boyle.
Capt. Alan J. Yaworske
Lt. Debora J. Brooke
Lt. Ruth B. Micer
Lt. Thomas H. Noord
Lt. Robert S. Rosencrans

House Division Commander.—Inspector Marsha E. Krug.

Capt. Larry D. Thompson
Lt. Michael G. Komara
Lt. David E. Pasierb
Lt. Cornelius W. Heine, Jr.
Lt. William G. Kaval, Jr.

Patrol Division Commander.—Inspector Jospeh S. Parisi, Jr.

Capt. Joseph M. Alukonis
Lt. Thomas G. O'Brien
Lt. Shirley J. Johnson
Lt. John T. Mattingly

Canine Section.—Lt. Charles L. Shelton.
Containment and Emergency Response Team.—Lt. Patrick J. Kerrigan.

Operations Division Commander.—Inspector Joseph R. Luteran.
Watch Commanders: Insp. Michael A. Jarboe, Insp. Mark G. Herbst, Capt. Frank M. Ziemba, Jr., Capt. Edward L. Bailor, Capt. Mark A. Sullivan.
Communications Section: Capt. William E. Uber, Lt. Edward F. Lopez, Lt. Donald R. Dixon.
Services Section.—Capt. Edward L. Bailor.
Special Events Unit.—Lt. Wesley D. Mahr.

WESTERN UNION TELEGRAPH CO.

242–A Cannon House Office Building, phone 225–4553/4554, fax 225–5499

Manager.—Gladys R. Crockett.

105th Congress
Nine-Digit Postal ZIP Codes

Senate Post Office (20510): The four-digit numbers in these tables were assigned by the Senate Committee on Rules and Administration. Mail to all Senate offices is delivered by the main Post Office in the Dirksen Senate Office Building.

Senate Committees

Committee on Agriculture, Nutrition, and Forestry	–6000
Committee on Appropriations	–6025
Committee on Armed Services	–6050
Committee on Banking, Housing, and Urban Affairs.	–6075
Committee on the Budget	–6100
Committee on Commerce, Science, and Transportation.	–6125
Committee on Energy and Natural Resources	–6150
Committee on Environment and Public Works	–6175
Committee on Finance	–6200
Committee on Foreign Relations	–6225
Committee on Governmental Affairs	–6250
Committee on Indian Affairs	–6450
Committee on the Judiciary	–6275
Committee on Labor and Human Resources	–6300
Committee on Rules and Administration	–6325
Committee on Small Business	–6350
Committee on Veterans' Affairs	–6375
Committee on Aging (Special)	–6400
Committee on Ethics (Select)	–6425
Committee on Intelligence (Select)	–6475
Committee to Investigate White Water Development Corporation and Related Matters (Special).	6485

Joint Committee Offices, Senate Side

Joint Economic Committee	–6602
Joint Committee on the Library	–6625
Joint Committee on Printing	–6650
Joint Committee on Taxation	–6675

Senate Leadership Offices

President Pro Tempore	–7000
Chaplain	–7002
Majority Leader	–7010
Assistant Majority Leader	–7012
Secretary for the Majority	–7014
Minority Leader	–7020
Assistant Minority Leader	–7022
Secretary for the Minority	–7024
Democratic Policy Committee	–7050
Republican Conference	–7060
Secretary to the Republican Conference	–7062
Republican Policy Committee	–7064
Republican Steering Committee	–7066
Arms Control Observer Group	–7070

Senate Officers

Secretary of the Senate	–7100
Curator of Art and Antiquities	–7102
Disbursing Office	–7104
Document Room	–7106
Historian	–7108
Interparliamentary Services	–7110
Senate Library	–7112
Office of Senate Security	–7114
Office of Public Records	–7116
Office of Official Recorders of Debates	7117
Stationery Room	–7118
Office of Printing Services	7120
U.S. Capitol Preservation Commission	–7122
Office of Conservation and Preservation	–7124
Senate Gift Shop	–7128
Legal Counsel, Employment Management Relations.	–7130
Senate Sergeant at Arms	–7200
General Counsel	–7201
Computer Center	–7202
Facilities	–7204
Finance Division	–7205
Barber Shop	–7206
Beauty Shop	–7208
Capitol Guides	–7209
Parking	–7210
Human Resources	–7212
Health Promotion/Employee Assistance Program	–7213
Placement/Seminars	–7214
Photographic Studio	–7216
Capitol Police	–7218
Senate Post Office	–7220
Senate Recording Studio	–7222
Senate Service Department	–7224
Telecommunications	–7226
Congressional Special Services Office	–7228
Customer Relations	7230

Other Offices on the Senate Side

Senate Legal Counsel	–7250
Senate Legislative Counsel	–7275
Architect of the Capitol	–8000
Superintendent of Senate Buildings	–8002
Office of Technology Assessment	–8025
Amtrak Ticket Office	–9010
Airlines Ticket Office (CATO)	–9014
Senate Child Care Center	–9022
Senate Credit Union	–9026
Periodical Press Gallery	–7234
Press Gallery	–7238
Press Photo Gallery	–7242
Radio and TV Gallery	–7246
Webseter Hall	7248
Restaurant	–8050
Office of Compliance	–9061
Social Security Liaison	9064
Veterans Liaison	9054
Western Union	–9058
Office of Senate Fair Employment Practices	–9060
Caucus on International Narcoties Control	9070
Army Liaison	9082
Air Force Liaison	9083
Coast Guard Liaison	9084
Navy Liaison	9085
Marine Liaison	9086

House Post Office (20515): The four-digit numbers in these tables were assigned by the Postmaster of the House of Representatives. Mail to all House offices is delivered by the main Post Office in the Longworth House Office Building.

House Committees, Leadership and Officers

U.S. House of Representatives	–0001
Cannon House Office Building	–0002
Rayburn House Office Building	–0003
Longworth House Office Building	–0004
O'Neill House Office Building	–0005
Ford House Office Building	–0006
The Capitol	–0007
Committee on Agriculture	–6001
Committee on Appropriations	–6015
Committee on Banking and Financial Services	–6050
Committee on the Budget	–6065
Committee on Commerce	–6115
Committee on Economic and Educational Opportunities.	–6100
Committee on Government Reform and Oversight	–6143
Committee on House Oversight	–6157
Committee on International Relations	–6128
Committee on National Security	6035
Committee on Resources	–6201
Committee on Rules	–6269
Committee on Science	–6301
Committee on Small Business	–6315
Committee on Standards of Official Conduct	–6328
Committee on Transportation and Infrastructure	–6256
Committee on Veterans' Affairs	–6335
Committee on Ways and Means	–6348
Select Committee on Intelligence	–6415

Joint Committee Offices, House side

Joint Economic Committee	–6432
Joint Committee on the Library	–6439
Joint Committee on Printing	–6445
Joint Committee on Taxation	–6453

House Leadership Offices

Office of the Speaker	–6501
Office of the Majority Leader	–6502
Office of the Majority Whip	–6503
Office of the Deputy Majority Whip	–6504
Democratic Caucus	–6524
Democratic Congressional Campaign Committee	–6525
Democratic Personnel Committee	–6526
Democratic Steering and Policy Committee	–6527
Democratic Cloakroom	–6528
Office of the Minority Leader	–6537
Office of the Minority Whip	–6538
House Republican Conference	–6544
House Republican Research Committee	–6545
Legislative Digest (Republican Conference)	–6546
Republican Congressional Committee, National	–6547
Republican Policy Committee	–6549
Republican Cloakroom	–6650

House Officers

Office of the Clerk	–6601
Legislative Operations	–6602
Reporters of Debates	–6603
Reporters to Committees	–6615
Legislative Information	–6605
House Library	–6606
Office of Printing Services	–6611
Records and Registration	–6612
Office of Telecommunications	–6617
Office of Fair Employment Practices	–6616
House Recording Studio	–6613
Legislative Computer Systems	–6618
Office of Employee Assistance	–6619
House Document Room	–6622
Office of Photography	–6623
Periodical Press Gallery	–6624
Press Gallery	–6625
Publication Distribution	–6626
Radio-TV Correspondents Gallery	–6627
Democratic Pages	–6530
Republican Pages	–6552
Office of the Sergeant at Arms	–6634
Office of the Chaplain	–6655
Office of Finance	–6604
Office Systems Management	–6607
Office Furnishings	–6554
Office Supply Service	–6608
Postal Operations	–9998
House Placement Office	–6609

House Commissions and Offices

Commission on Security and Cooperation in Europe.	–6460
Commission on Congressional Mailing Standards	–6461
Office of the Law Revision Counsel	–6711
Office of the Legislative Counsel	–6721
Office of the Parliamentarian	–6731
General Counsel	–6532
House Historian	–6701
Architect of the Capitol	–6906
Attending Physician	–6907
Congressional Budget Office	–6925
Daily Digest	–6930
Executive Communications	–6938
Federal Election Commission (Clerk)	–6939

Liaison Offices

Air Force	–6854
Army	–6855
Coast Guard	–6856
Navy	–6857
Office of Personnel Management	–6858
Veterans' Administration	–6859

TERMS OF SERVICE

EXPIRATION OF THE TERMS OF SENATORS

CLASS III.—SENATORS WHOSE TERMS OF SERVICE EXPIRE IN 1999

[34 Senators in this group: Republicans, 16; Democrats, 18]

Name	Party	Residence
Bennett, Robert F.	R.	Salt Lake City, UT.
Bond, Christopher S.	R.	Mexico, MO.
Boxer, Barbara	D.	Greenbrae, CA.
Breaux, John B.	D.	Crowley, LA.
Brownback, Samuel Dale [1]	R.	Topeka, KS.
Bumpers, Dale	D.	Charleston, AR.
Campbell, Ben Nighthorse [2]	R.	Ignacio, CO.
Coats, Dan	R.	Fort Wayne, IN.
Coverdell, Paul [3]	R.	Atlanta, GA.
D'Amato, Alfonse	R.	Island Park, NY.
Daschle, Thomas A.	D.	Aberdeen, SD.
Dodd, Christopher J.	D.	Norwich, CT.
Dorgan, Byron L. [4]	D.	Bismarck, ND.
Faircloth, Lauch	R.	Clinton, NC.
Feingold, Russell D.	D.	Middleton, WI.
Ford, Wendell H.	D.	Owensboro, KY.
Glenn, John	D.	Columbus, OH.
Graham, Bob	D.	Miami Lakes, FL.
Grassley, Charles E.	R.	New Hartford, IA.
Gregg, Judd	R.	Greenfield, NH.
Hollings, Ernest F.	D.	Charleston, SC.
Inouye, Daniel K.	D.	Honolulu, HI.
Kempthorne, Dirk	R.	Boise, ID.
Leahy, Patrick J.	D.	Burlington, VT.
McCain, John	R.	Phoenix, AZ.
Mikulski, Barbara A.	D.	Baltimore, MD.
Moseley-Braun, Carol	D.	Chicago, IL.
Murkowski, Frank H.	R.	Fairbanks, AK.
Murray, Patty	D.	Seattle, WA.
Nickles, Don	R.	Ponca City, OK.
Reid, Harry	D.	Las Vegas, NV.
Shelby, Richard C.	R.	Tuscaloosa, AL.
Specter, Arlen	R.	Philadelphia, PA.
Wyden, Ron [5]	D.	Portland, OR.

[1] Senator Brownback was elected on November 5, 1996 to fill the remainder of the term of Senator Bob Dole. He took the oath of office on November 27, 1996. This seat was filled by Senator Sheila Frahm, who had been appointed, ad interim, on June 11, 1996 by the Governor.

[2] Senator Campbell changed parties March 3, 1995.

[3] Senator Coverdell was elected in a runoff election on Nov. 24, 1992, for the 6-year term beginning on Jan. 3, 1993.

[4] Senator Dorgan was elected to a 6-year term on Nov. 3, 1992, and subsequently was appointed by the Governor Dec. 14, 1992 to fill the vacancy caused by the resignation of Senator Kent Conrad.

[5] Senator Wyden was elected on January 30, 1996 to fill the vacancy caused by the resignation of Senator Bob Packwood.

CLASS I.—SENATORS WHOSE TERMS OF SERVICE EXPIRE IN 2001

[33 Senators in this group: Republicans, 19; Democrats, 14]

Name	Party	Residence
Abraham, Spencer	R.	Auburn Hills, MI.
Akaka, Daniel K.[1]	D.	Honolulu, HI.
Ashcroft, John	R.	Ballwin, MO.
Bingaman, Jeff	D.	Santa Fe, NM.
Bryan, Richard H.	D.	Las Vegas, NV.
Burns, Conrad R.	R.	Billings, MT.
Byrd, Robert C.	D.	Sophia, WV.
Chafee, John H.	R.	Warwick, RI.
Conrad, Kent[2]	D.	Bismarck, ND.
DeWine, Mike	R.	Cedarville, OH.
Feinstein, Dianne[3]	D.	San Francisco, CA.
Frist, William H.	R.	Nashville, TN.
Gorton, Slade	R.	Seattle, WA.
Grams, Rod	R.	Ramsey, MN.
Hatch, Orrin G.	R.	Salt Lake City, UT.
Hutchison, Kay Bailey[4]	R.	Dallas, TX.
Jeffords, James M.	R.	Shrewsbury, VT.
Kennedy, Edward M.	D.	Boston, MA.
Kerrey, J. Robert	D.	Omaha, NE.
Kohl, Herb	D.	Milwaukee, WI.
Kyl, Jon	R.	Phoenix, AZ.
Lautenberg, Frank R.	D.	Cliffside Park, NJ.
Lieberman, Joseph I.	D.	New Haven, CT.
Lott, Trent	R.	Pascagoula, MS.
Lugar, Richard G.	R.	Indianapolis, IN.
Mack, Connie	R.	Cape Coral, FL.
Moynihan, Daniel Patrick	D.	Oneonta, NY.
Robb, Charles S.	D.	McLean, VA.
Roth, William V., Jr	R.	Wilmington, DE.
Santorum, Rick	R.	Pittsburgh, PA.
Sarbanes, Paul S.	D.	Baltimore, MD.
Snowe, Olympia J.	R.	Auburn, ME.
Thomas, Craig	R.	Casper, WY.

[1] Senator Akaka was appointed Apr. 28, 1990 by the Governor to fill the vacancy caused by the death of Senator Spark M. Matsunaga, and took the oath of office on May 16, 1990. He was elected in a special election, on Nov. 6, 1990, for the remainder of the unexpired term.

[2] Senator Conrad resigned his term from Class III after winning a special election on Dec. 4, 1992 to fill the vacancy caused by the death of Senator Quentin Burdick. Senator Conrad's seniority in the Senate continues without a break in service. He took the oath of office on Dec. 15, 1992.

[3] Senator Feinstein won the special election held on Nov. 3, 1992 to fill the vacancy caused by the resignation of Senator Pete Wilson. She took the oath of office on Nov. 10, 1992. This seat was filled pending the election by gubernatorial appointee, Senator John Seymour.

[4] Senator Hutchison won the special election held on June 5, 1993 to fill remainder of the term of Senator Lloyd Bentsen. She took the oath of office on June 14, 1993. She won the seat from Senator Bob Krueger, who had been appointed, ad interim, on Jan. 21, 1993 by the Governor.

CLASS II.—SENATORS WHOSE TERMS OF SERVICE EXPIRE IN 2003

[33 Senators in this group: Republicans, 20; Democrats, 13]

Name	Party	Residence
Allard, Wayne	R.	Loveland, CO.
Baucus, Max	D.	Missoula, MT.
Biden, Joseph R., Jr	D.	Hockessin, DE.
Cleland, Max	D	Lithonia, GA.
Cochran, Thad	R.	Jackson, MS.
Collins, Susan M.	R.	Bangor, ME.
Craig, Larry E.	R.	Boise, ID.

CLASS II.—SENATORS WHOSE TERMS OF SERVICE EXPIRE IN 2003—CONTINUED

[33 Senators in this group: Republicans, 20; Democrats, 13]

Name	Party	Residence
Domenici, Pete V.	R.	Albuquerque, NM.
Durbin, Richard J.	D.	Springfield, IL.
Enzi, Michael B.	R.	Gillette, WY.
Gramm, Phil	R.	College Station, TX.
Hagel, Chuck	R.	Omaha, NE.
Harkin, Tom	D.	Cumming, IA.
Helms, Jesse	R.	Raleigh, NC.
Hutchinson, Tim	R.	Bentonville, AR.
Inhofe, James M.	R.	Tulsa, OK.
Kerry, John F.	D.	Boston, MA.
Johnson, Tim	D.	Vermillion, SD.
Landrieu, Mary	D.	Baton Rouge, LA.
Levin, Carl	D.	Detroit, MI.
McConnell, Mitch	R.	Louisville, KY.
Reed, Jack	D.	Cranston, RI.
Roberts, Pat	R.	Dodge City, KS.
Rockefeller, John D., IV	D.	Charleston, WV.
Sessions, Jeff	R.	Mobile, AL.
Smith, Bob	R.	Tuftonboro, NH.
Smith, Gordon	R.	Pendleton, OR.
Stevens, Ted	R.	Anchorage, AK.
Thompson, Fred	R.	Nashville, TN.
Thurmond, Strom	R.	Aiken, SC.
Torricelli, Robert G.	D.	Engelwood, NJ.
Warner, John W.	R.	Middleburg, VA.
Wellstone, Paul David	D.	Northfield, MN.

CONTINUOUS SERVICE OF SENATORS

[Republicans in roman (55); Democrats in *italic* (45); total, 100]

Rank	Name	State	Beginning of present service
1	Thurmond, Strom [1]	South Carolina	Nov. 7, 1956. ‡
2	*Byrd, Robert C.*†	West Virginia	Jan. 3, 1959.
3	*Kennedy, Edward M.*[2]	Massachusetts	Nov. 7, 1962. ‡
4	*Inouye, Daniel K.*†	Hawaii	Jan. 3, 1963.
5	*Hollings, Ernest F.*[3]	South Carolina	Nov. 9, 1966. ‡
6	Stevens, Ted [4]	Alaska	Dec. 24, 1968.
7	Roth, William V., Jr.† [5]	Delaware	Jan. 1, 1971.
8	*Biden, Joseph R., Jr.*	Delaware	Jan. 3, 1973.
8	Domenici, Pete V.	New Mexico	Jan. 3, 1973.
8	Helms, Jesse	North Carolina	Jan. 3, 1973.
9	*Glenn, John*[6]	Ohio	Dec. 24, 1974.
10	*Ford, Wendell H.*[7]	Kentucky	Dec. 28, 1974.
11	*Bumpers, Dale*	Arkansas	Jan. 3, 1975.
11	*Leahy, Patrick J.*	Vermont	Jan. 3, 1975.
12	Chafee, John H.	Rhode Island	Dec. 29, 1976.
13	Hatch, Orrin G.†	Utah	Dec. 30, 1976.
13	Lugar, Richard G.	Indiana	Dec. 30, 1976.
14	*Moynihan, Daniel P.*	New York	Jan. 3, 1977.
14	*Sarbanes, Paul S.*†	Maryland	Jan. 3, 1977.
15	*Baucus, Max* † [8]	Montana	Dec. 15, 1978.
16	Cochran, Thad † [9]	Mississippi	Dec. 27, 1978.
17	Warner, John W.[10]	Virginia	Jan. 2, 1979.
18	*Levin, Carl*	Michigan	Jan. 3, 1979.
19	D'Amato, Alfonse M.	New York	Jan. 3, 1981.
19	*Dodd, Christopher J.*†	Connecticut	Jan. 3, 1981.
19	Grassley, Charles E.†	Iowa	Jan. 3, 1981.
19	Murkowski, Frank H.	Alaska	Jan. 3, 1981.
19	Nickles, Don	Oklahoma	Jan. 3, 1981.
19	Specter, Arlen	Pennsylvania	Jan. 3, 1981.
20	*Lautenberg, Frank R.*[11]	New Jersey	Dec. 27, 1982.
21	*Bingaman, Jeff*	New Mexico	Jan. 3, 1983.
22	*Kerry, John F.*[12]	Massachusetts	Jan. 2, 1985.
22	Gramm, Phil †	Texas	Jan. 2, 1985.
23	*Harkin, Tom* †	Iowa	Jan. 3, 1985.
23	McConnell, Mitch	Kentucky	Jan. 3, 1985.
24	*Rockefeller, John D., IV*[13]	West Virginia	Jan. 15, 1985.
25	Bond, Christopher S.	Missouri	Jan. 6, 1987.
25	*Breaux, John B.*†	Louisiana	Jan. 6, 1987.
25	*Conrad, Kent*	North Dakota	Jan. 6, 1987.
25	*Daschle, Thomas A.*†	South Dakota	Jan. 6, 1987.
25	*Graham, Bob*	Florida	Jan. 6, 1987.
25	McCain, John †	Arizona	Jan. 6, 1987.
25	*Mikulski, Barbara A.*†	Maryland	Jan. 6, 1987.
25	*Reid, Harry* †	Nevada	Jan. 6, 1987.
25	Shelby, Richard C.†	Alabama	Jan. 6, 1987.
26	*Bryan, Richard H.*	Nevada	Jan. 3, 1989.
26	Burns, Conrad	Montana	Jan. 3, 1989.
26	Coats, Dan † [14]	Indiana	Jan. 3, 1989.
26	Gorton, Slade [15]	Washington	Jan. 3, 1989.
26	Jeffords, James M.	Vermont	Jan. 3, 1989.
26	*Kerrey, J. Robert*	Nebraska	Jan. 3, 1989.
26	*Kohl, Herb*	Wisconsin	Jan. 3, 1989.
26	*Lieberman, Joseph I.*	Connecticut	Jan. 3, 1989.
26	Lott, Trent †	Mississippi	Jan. 3, 1989.

CONTINUOUS SERVICE OF SENATORS—CONTINUED

[Republicans in roman (55); Democrats in *italic* (45); total, 100]

Rank	Name	State	Beginning of present service
26	Mack, Connie †	Florida	Jan. 3, 1989.
26	*Robb, Charles S.*	Virginia	Jan. 3, 1989.
27	*Akaka, Daniel K.*† [16]	Hawaii	Apr. 28, 1990.
28	Smith, Robert C.† [17]	New Hampshire	Dec. 7, 1990.
29	Craig, Larry E.†	Idaho	Jan. 3, 1991.
29	*Wellstone, Paul D.*	Minnesota	Jan. 3, 1991.
30	*Feinstein, Dianne* [18]	California	Nov. 10, 1992.‡
31	*Dorgan, Byron* † [19]	North Dakota	Dec. 14, 1992.
32	Bennett, Robert F.	Utah	Jan. 3, 1993.
32	*Boxer, Barbara*†	California	Jan. 3, 1993.
32	Campbell, Ben Nighthorse † [20]	Colorado	Jan. 3, 1993.
32	Coverdell, Paul [21]	Georgia	Jan. 3, 1993.
32	Faircloth, Lauch	North Carolina	Jan. 3, 1993.
32	*Feingold, Russell*	Wisconsin	Jan. 3, 1993.
32	Gregg, Judd†	New Hampshire	Jan. 3, 1993.
32	Kempthorne, Dirk	Idaho	Jan. 3, 1993.
32	*Moseley-Braun, Carol*	Illinois	Jan. 3, 1993.
32	*Murray, Patty*	Washington	Jan. 3, 1993.
33	Hutchison, Kay Bailey [22]	Texas	June 5, 1993.
34	Inhofe, James M. † [23]	Oklahoma	Nov. 16, 1994.
35	Thompson, Fred [24]	Tennessee	Dec. 9, 1994.
36	Abraham, Spencer	Michigan	Jan. 3, 1995.
36	Ashcroft, John	Missouri	Jan. 3, 1995.
36	DeWine, Mike †	Ohio	Jan. 3, 1995.
36	Frist, Bill	Tennessee	Jan. 3, 1995.
36	Grams, Rod †	Minnesota	Jan. 3, 1995.
36	Kyl, Jon †	Arizona	Jan. 3, 1995.
36	Santorum, Rick †	Pennsylvania	Jan. 3, 1995.
36	Snowe, Olympia J. †	Maine	Jan. 3, 1995.
36	Thomas, Craig †	Wyoming	Jan. 3, 1995.
37	*Wyden, Ron* † [25]	Oregon	Feb. 6, 1996.
38	Brownback, Samuel D.† [26]	Kansas	Nov. 26, 1996.
39	Hagel, Chuck	Nebraska	Jan. 3, 1997.
40	Allard, Wayne†	Colorado	Jan. 6, 1997.
40	*Cleland, Max*	Georgia	Jan. 6, 1997.
40	Collins, Susan	Maine	Jan. 6, 1997.
40	*Durbin, Richard J.*†	Illinois	Jan. 6, 1997.
40	Enzi, Michael B.	Wyoming	Jan. 6, 1997.
40	Hutchinson, Tim†	Arkansas	Jan. 6, 1997.
40	*Johnson, Tim*†	South Dakota	Jan. 6, 1997.
40	*Landrieu, Mary*	Louisiana	Jan. 6, 1997.
40	*Reed, Jack*†	Rhode Island	Jan. 6, 1997.
40	Roberts, Pat†	Kansas	Jan. 6, 1997.
40	Sessions, Jeff	Alabama	Jan. 6, 1997.
40	Smith, Gordon	Oregon	Jan. 6, 1997.
40	*Torricelli, Robert G.*†	New Jersey	Jan. 6, 1997.

† Served in the House of Representatives previous to service in the Senate.

‡ Senators elected to complete unexpired terms begin their terms on the day following the election.

1 Senator Thurmond also served in the Senate by appointment from Dec. 24, 1954, to Jan. 3, 1955; was elected Nov. 2, 1954, as a write-in candidate for the term ending Jan. 3, 1961, and served from Jan. 3, 1955, until his resignation Apr. 4, 1956; reelected Nov. 6, 1956, to fill the vacancy caused by his own resignation; switched from the Democratic to Republican party Sep. 16, 1964.

2 Senator Kennedy was elected Nov. 6, 1962, to complete the unexpired term caused by the resignation of Senator John F. Kennedy.

3 Senator Hollings was elected Nov. 8, 1966, to complete the unexpired term caused by the death of Senator Olin D. Johnston.

[4] Senator Stevens was appointed Dec. 23, 1968 by the Governor to fill the vacancy caused by the death of Senator Edward L. Bartlett.

[5] Senator Roth was appointed Jan. 1, 1971 by the Governor to fill the vacancy caused by the resignation of Senator John J. Williams.

[6] Senator Glenn was elected Nov. 5, 1974, for the 6-year term commencing Jan. 3, 1975; subsequently appointed Dec. 24, 1974, to fill the vacancy caused by the resignation of Senator Howard M. Metzenbaum.

[7] Senator Ford was elected Nov. 5, 1974, for the 6-year term commencing Jan. 3, 1975; subsequently appointed Dec. 28, 1974, to fill the vacancy caused by the resignation of Senator Marlow W. Cook.

[8] Senator Baucus was elected Nov. 7, 1978, for the 6-year term commencing Jan. 3, 1979; subsequently appointed Dec. 15, 1978, to fill the vacancy caused by the resignation of Senator Paul Hatfield.

[9] Senator Cochran was elected Nov. 6, 1978, for the 6-year term commencing Jan. 3, 1979; subsequently appointed Dec. 27, 1978, to fill the vacancy caused by the resignation of Senator James Eastland.

[10] Senator Warner was elected Nov. 6, 1978, for the 6-year term commencing Jan. 3, 1979; subsequently appointed Jan. 2, 1979, to fill the vacancy caused by the resignation of Senator William Scott.

[11] Senator Lautenberg was elected Nov. 2, 1982, for the 6-year term commencing Jan. 3, 1983; subsequently appointed Dec. 27, 1982, to fill the vacancy caused by the resignation of Senator Nicholas F. Brady.

[12] Senator Kerry was elected Nov. 6, 1984, for the 6-year term commencing Jan. 3, 1985; subsequently appointed Jan. 2, 1985, to fill the vacancy caused by the resignation of Senator Paul E. Tsongas.

[13] Senator Rockefeller was elected Nov. 6, 1984, for the 6-year term commencing Jan. 3, 1985; did not take his seat until Jan. 15, 1985.

[14] Senator Coats was appointed Jan. 3, 1989 by the Governor. Senator Coats won a special election in November 1990 for the remainder of Senator Dan Quayle's unexpired term.

[15] Senator Gorton also served a six-year term from Jan. 3, 1981–Jan. 3, 1987.

[16] Senator Akaka was appointed Apr. 28, 1990 by the Governor to fill the vacancy caused by the death of Senator Spark M. Matsunaga. Subsequently elected on Nov. 6, 1990 to complete the unexpired term.

[17] Senator Smith was elected Nov. 6, 1990, for the 6-year term commencing Jan. 3, 1991; subsequently appointed Dec. 7, 1990, to fill the vacancy caused by the resignation of Senator Gordon J. Humphrey.

[18] Senator Feinstein was elected on Nov. 3, 1992 to fill the vacancy caused by the resignation of Senator Pete Wilson. She replaced appointed Senator John Seymour when she took the oath of office on Nov. 10, 1992.

[19] Senator Dorgan was elected to a 6-year term on Nov. 3, 1992 and subsequently was appointed by the Governor on Dec. 14, 1992 to complete the unexpired term of Senator Kent Conrad.

[20] Senator Campbell changed parties, March 3, 1995.

[21] Senator Coverdell was elected in a runoff election on Nov. 24, 1992.

[22] Senator Hutchison won a special election on June 5, 1993 to fill the vacancy caused by the resignation of Senator Lloyd Bentsen. She won the seat from Senator Bob Krueger, who had been appointed on Jan. 21, 1993 by the Governor.

[23] Senator Inhofe was elected to fill an unexpired term until January 3, 1997.

[24] Senator Thompson was elected to fill an unexpired term until January 3, 1997.

[25] Senator Wyden was elected on January 30, 1996 to fill the vacancy caused by the resignation of Senator Bob Packwood.

[26] Senator Brownback was elected on November 5, 1996 to fill the vacancy caused by the resignation of Senator Bob Dole. He replaced appointed Senator Sheila Frahm when he took the oath of office on November 27, 1996.

CONGRESSES IN WHICH REPRESENTATIVES HAVE SERVED, WITH BEGINNING OF PRESENT SERVICE

[* Elected to fill a vacancy; Republicans in roman (228); Democrats in *italic* (206); Independent in **bold** (1); total, 435]

Name	State	District	Congresses (inclusive)	Beginning of present service
24 terms, not consecutive				
Yates, Sidney R	IL	9	81st to 87th, 89th to 105th.	Jan. 3, 1965.
22 terms, consecutive				
Dingell, John D	MI	16	*84th to 105th	Dec. 13, 1955.
19 terms, consecutive				
Gonzalez, Henry B	TX	20	*87th to 105th	Nov. 4, 1961.
18 terms, consecutive				
McDade, Joseph M	PA	10	88th to 105th	Jan. 3, 1963.
17 terms, consecutive				
Conyers, John, Jr	MI	14	89th to 105th	Jan. 3, 1965.
Hamilton, Lee H	IN	9	89th to 105th	Jan. 3, 1965.
17 terms, not consecutive				
Brown, George E., Jr	CA	42	88th to 91st, 93d to 105th.	Jan. 3, 1973.
15 terms, consecutive				
Clay, William (Bill)	MO	1	91st to 105th	Jan. 3, 1969.
Crane, Philip M	IL	8	*91st to 105th	Nov. 25, 1969.
Obey, David R	WI	7	*91st to 105th	Apr. 1, 1969.
Stokes, Louis	OH	11	91st to 105th	Jan. 3, 1969.
14 terms, consecutive				
Archer, Bill	TX	7	92d to 105th	Jan. 3, 1971.
Dellums, Ronald V	CA	9	92d to 105th	Jan. 3, 1971.
Rangel, Charles B	NY	15	92d to 105th	Jan. 3, 1971.
Spence, Floyd	SC	2	92d to 105th	Jan. 3, 1971.
Young, C.W. Bill	FL	10	92d to 105th	Jan. 3, 1971.
13 terms, consecutive				
Gilman, Benjamin A	NY	20	93d to 105th	Jan. 3, 1973.
Moakley, John Joseph	MA	9	93d to 105th	Jan. 3, 1973.
Murtha, John P	PA	12	*93d to 105th	Feb. 5, 1974.
Regula, Ralph	OH	16	93d to 105th	Jan. 3, 1973.
Shuster, Bud	PA	9	93d to 105th	Jan. 3, 1973.
Stark, Fortney Pete	CA	13	93d to 105th	Jan. 3, 1973.
Young, Don	AK	At L.	*93d to 105th	Mar. 6, 1973.
12 terms, consecutive				
Goodling, William	PA	19	94th to 105th	Jan. 3, 1975.
Hefner, W.G. (Bill)	NC	8	94th to 105th	Jan. 3, 1975.
Hyde, Henry J	IL	6	94th to 105th	Jan. 3, 1975.
LaFalce, John J	NY	29	94th to 105th	Jan. 3, 1975.
Markey, Edward J	MA	7	*94th to 105th	Nov. 2, 1976.
Miller, George	CA	7	94th to 105th	Jan. 3, 1975.
Oberstar, James L	MN	8	94th to 105th	Jan. 3, 1975.
Waxman, Henry A	CA	29	94th to 105th	Jan. 3, 1975.

CONGRESSES IN WHICH REPRESENTATIVES HAVE SERVED, WITH BEGINNING OF PRESENT SERVICE—CONTINUED

[* Elected to fill a vacancy; Republicans in roman (228); Democrats in *italic* (206); Independent in **bold** (1); total, 435]

Name	State	District	Congresses (inclusive)	Beginning of present service
11 terms, consecutive				
Bonior, David E	MI	10	95th to 105th	Jan. 3, 1977.
Dicks, Norman D	WA	6	95th to 105th	Jan. 3, 1977.
Gephardt, Richard A	MO	3	95th to 105th	Jan. 3, 1977.
Kildee, Dale E	MI	9	95th to 105th	Jan. 3, 1977.
Leach, James A	IA	1	95th to 105th	Jan. 3, 1977.
Livingston, Bob	LA	1	*95th to 105th	Aug. 27, 1977.
Rahall, Nick J, II	WV	3	95th to 105th	Jan. 3, 1977.
Skelton, Ike	MO	4	95th to 105th	Jan. 3, 1977.
Stump, Bob	AZ	3	95th to 105th	Jan. 3, 1977.
Vento, Bruce F	MN	4	95th to 105th	Jan. 3, 1977.
11 terms, not consecutive				
Mink, Patsy	HI	2	89th to 94th, *101st to 105th.	Sept. 22, 1990.
10 terms, consecutive				
Bereuter, Doug	NE	1	96th to 105th	Jan. 3, 1979.
Dixon, Julian C	CA	32	96th to 105th	Jan. 3, 1979.
Fazio, Vic	CA	3	96th to 105th	Jan. 3, 1979.
Frost, Martin	TX	24	96th to 105th	Jan. 3, 1979.
Gingrich, Newt	GA	6	96th to 105th	Jan. 3, 1979.
Hall, Tony P	OH	3	96th to 105th	Jan. 3, 1979.
Lewis, Jerry	CA	40	96th to 105th	Jan. 3, 1979.
Matsui, Robert T	CA	5	96th to 105th	Jan. 3, 1979.
Petri, Thomas E	WI	6	*96th to 105th	Apr. 3, 1979.
Porter, John Edward	IL	10	*96th to 105th	Jan. 22, 1980.
Sabo, Martin Olav	MN	5	96th to 105th	Jan. 3, 1979.
Sensenbrenner, F. James, Jr.	WI	9	96th to 105th	Jan. 3, 1979.
Solomon, Gerald B.H	NY	22	96th to 105th	Jan. 3, 1979.
Stenholm, Charles W	TX	17	96th to 105th	Jan. 3, 1979.
Tauzin, W.J. (Billy)	LA	3	*96th to 105th	May 17, 1980.
Thomas, Bill	CA	21	96th to 105th	Jan. 3, 1979.
9 terms, consecutive				
Bliley, Thomas J., Jr.	VA	7	97th to 105th	Jan. 3, 1981.
Coyne, William J	PA	14	97th to 105th	Jan. 3, 1981.
Dreier, David	CA	28	97th to 105th	Jan. 3, 1981.
Foglietta, Thomas M	PA	1	97th to 105th	Jan. 3, 1981.
Frank, Barney	MA	4	97th to 105th	Jan. 3, 1981.
Gejdenson, Sam	CT	2	97th to 105th	Jan. 3, 1981.
Hall, Ralph M	TX	4	97th to 105th	Jan. 3, 1981.
Hansen, James V	UT	1	97th to 105th	Jan. 3, 1981.
Hoyer, Steny H	MD	5	*97th to 105th	May 19, 1981.
Hunter, Duncan	CA	52	97th to 105th	Jan. 3, 1981.
Kennelly, Barbara B	CT	1	*97th to 105th	Jan. 12, 1982.
Lantos, Tom	CA	12	97th to 105th	Jan. 3, 1981.
Martinez, Matthew G	CA	31	*97th to 105th	July 13, 1982.
McCollum, Bill	FL	8	97th to 105th	Jan. 3, 1981.
Oxley, Michael G	OH	4	*97th to 105th	June 25, 1981.
Rogers, Harold	KY	5	97th to 105th	Jan. 3, 1981.
Roukema, Marge	NJ	5	97th to 105th	Jan. 3, 1981.

CONGRESSES IN WHICH REPRESENTATIVES HAVE SERVED, WITH BEGINNING OF PRESENT SERVICE—CONTINUED

[* Elected to fill a vacancy; Republicans in roman (228); Democrats in *italic* (206); Independent in **bold** (1); total, 435]

Name	State	District	Congresses (inclusive)	Beginning of present service
Schumer, Charles E	NY	9	97th to 105th	Jan. 3, 1981.
Shaw, E. Clay, Jr	FL	22	97th to 105th	Jan. 3, 1981.
Skeen, Joe	NM	2	97th to 105th	Jan. 3, 1981.
Smith, Christopher H	NJ	4	97th to 105th	Jan. 3, 1981.
Wolf, Frank R	VA	10	97th to 105th	Jan. 3, 1981.
8 terms, consecutive				
Ackerman, Gary L	NY	5	*98th to 105th	Mar. 1, 1983.
Bateman, Herbert H	VA	1	98th to 105th	Jan. 3, 1983.
Berman, Howard L	CA	26	98th to 105th	Jan. 3, 1983.
Bilirakis, Michael	FL	9	98th to 105th	Jan. 3, 1983.
Boehlert, Sherwood L	NY	23	98th to 105th	Jan. 3, 1983.
Borski, Robert A	PA	3	98th to 105th	Jan. 3, 1983.
Boucher, Rick	VA	9	98th to 105th	Jan. 3, 1983.
Burton, Dan	IN	6	98th to 105th	Jan. 3, 1983.
Evans, Lane	IL	17	98th to 105th	Jan. 3, 1983.
Gekas, George W	PA	17	98th to 105th	Jan. 3, 1983.
Johnson, Nancy L	CT	6	98th to 105th	Jan. 3, 1983.
Kaptur, Marcy	OH	9	98th to 105th	Jan. 3, 1983.
Kasich, John R	OH	12	98th to 105th	Jan. 3, 1983.
Kleczka, Gerald D	WI	4	*98th to 105th	Apr. 3, 1984.
Levin, Sander M	MI	12	98th to 105th	Jan. 3, 1983.
Lipinski, William O	IL	3	98th to 105th	Jan. 3, 1983.
Mollohan, Alan B	WV	1	98th to 105th	Jan. 3, 1983.
Ortiz, Solomon P	TX	27	98th to 105th	Jan. 3, 1983.
Owens, Major R	NY	11	98th to 105th	Jan. 3, 1983.
Packard, Ron	CA	48	98th to 105th	Jan. 3, 1983.
Saxton, Jim	NJ	3	*98th to 105th	Nov. 6, 1984.
Schaefer, Dan	CO	6	*98th to 105th	Mar. 29, 1983.
Sisisky, Norman	VA	4	98th to 105th	Jan. 3, 1983.
Spratt, John M., Jr	SC	5	98th to 105th	Jan. 3, 1983.
Torres, Esteban Edward ...	CA	34	98th to 105th	Jan. 3, 1983.
Towns, Edolphus	NY	10	98th to 105th	Jan. 3, 1983.
Wise, Robert E., Jr	WV	2	98th to 105th	Jan. 3, 1983.
8 terms, not consecutive				
Watkins, Wes	OK	3	95th to 101th, 105th.	Jan. 3, 1997.
7 terms, consecutive				
Armey, Dick	TX	26	99th to 105th	Jan. 3, 1985.
Ballenger, Cass	NC	10	*99th to 105th	Nov. 4, 1986.
Barton, Joe	TX	6	99th to 105th	Jan. 3, 1985.
Callahan, Sonny	AL	1	99th to 105th	Jan. 3, 1985.
Coble, Howard	NC	6	99th to 105th	Jan. 3, 1985.
Combest, Larry	TX	19	99th to 105th	Jan. 3, 1985.
DeLay, Tom	TX	22	99th to 105th	Jan. 3, 1985.
Fawell, Harris W	IL	13	99th to 105th	Jan. 3, 1985.
Gordon, Bart	TN	6	99th to 105th	Jan. 3, 1985.
Kanjorski, Paul E	PA	11	99th to 105th	Jan. 3, 1985.
Kolbe, Jim	AZ	5	99th to 105th	Jan. 3, 1985.
Manton, Thomas J	NY	7	99th to 105th	Jan. 3, 1985.
Traficant, James A., Jr	OH	17	99th to 105th	Jan. 3, 1985.

CONGRESSES IN WHICH REPRESENTATIVES HAVE SERVED, WITH BEGINNING OF PRESENT SERVICE—CONTINUED

[* Elected to fill a vacancy; Republicans in roman (228); Democrats in *italic* (206); Independent in **bold** (1); total, 435]

Name	State	District	Congresses (inclusive)	Beginning of present service
Visclosky, Peter J	IN	1	99th to 105th	Jan. 3, 1985.
7 terms, not consecutive				
Smith, Robert F (Bob)	OR	2	98th to 103d, 105th	Jan. 3, 1997.
6 terms, consecutive				
Baker, Richard H	LA	6	100th to 105th	Jan. 3, 1987.
Bunning, Jim	KY	4	100th to 105th	Jan. 3, 1987.
Cardin, Benjamin L	MD	3	100th to 105th	Jan. 3, 1987.
Clement, Bob	TN	5	*100th to 105th	Jan. 25, 1988.
Costello, Jerry F	IL	12	*100th to 105th	Aug. 11, 1988.
DeFazio, Peter A	OR	4	100th to 105th	Jan. 3, 1987.
Duncan, John J., Jr	TN	2	*100th to 105th	Nov. 9, 1988.
Flake, Floyd H	NY	6	100th to 105th	Jan. 3, 1987.
Gallegly, Elton	CA	23	100th to 105th	Jan. 3, 1987.
Hastert, J. Dennis	IL	14	100th to 105th	Jan. 3, 1987.
Hefley, Joel	CO	5	100th to 105th	Jan. 3, 1987.
Herger, Wally	CA	2	100th to 105th	Jan. 3, 1987.
Houghton, Amo	NY	31	100th to 105th	Jan. 3, 1987.
Kennedy, Joseph P., II	MA	8	100th to 105th	Jan. 3, 1987.
Lewis, John	GA	5	100th to 105th	Jan. 3, 1987.
McCrery, Jim	LA	5	*100th to 105th	Apr. 26, 1988.
Morella, Constance A	MD	8	100th to 105th	Jan. 3, 1987.
Pallone, Frank, Jr	NJ	6	*100th to 105th	Nov. 9, 1988.
Pelosi, Nancy	CA	8	*100th to 105th	June 9, 1987.
Pickett, Owen B	VA	2	100th to 105th	Jan. 3, 1987.
Sawyer, Tom	OH	14	100th to 105th	Jan. 3, 1987.
Shays, Christopher	CT	4	*100th to 105th	Sep. 9, 1987.
Skaggs, David E	CO	2	100th to 105th	Jan. 3, 1987.
Slaughter, Louise M	NY	28	100th to 105th	Jan. 3, 1987.
Smith, Lamar S	TX	21	100th to 105th	Jan. 3, 1987.
Upton, Frederick S	MI	6	100th to 105th	Jan. 3, 1987.
Weldon, Curt	PA	7	100th to 105th	Jan. 3, 1987.
5 terms, consecutive				
Andrews, Robert E	NJ	1	*101st to 105th	Nov. 7, 1990.
Condit, Gary A	CA	18	*101st to 105th	Sept. 12, 1989.
Cox, Christopher	CA	47	101st to 105th	Jan. 3, 1989.
Engel, Eliot L	NY	17	101st to 105th	Jan. 3, 1989.
Gillmor, Paul E	OH	5	101st to 105th	Jan. 3, 1989.
Goss, Porter J	FL	14	101st to 105th	Jan. 3, 1989.
Lowey, Nita M	NY	18	101st to 105th	Jan. 3, 1989.
McDermott, Jim	WA	7	101st to 105th	Jan. 3, 1989.
McNulty, Michael R	NY	21	101st to 105th	Jan. 3, 1989.
Molinari, Susan	NY	13	*101st to 105th	Mar. 20, 1990.
Neal, Richard E	MA	2	101st to 105th	Jan. 3, 1989.
Parker, Mike	MS	4	101st to 105th	Jan. 3, 1989.
Paxon, Bill	NY	27	101st to 105th	Jan. 3, 1989.
Payne, Donald M	NJ	10	101st to 105th	Jan. 3, 1989.
Poshard, Glenn	IL	19	101st to 105th	Jan. 3, 1989.
Rohrabacher, Dana	CA	45	101st to 105th	Jan. 3, 1989.
Ros-Lehtinen, Ileana	FL	18	*101st to 105th	Aug. 29, 1989.
Schiff, Steven H	NM	1	101st to 105th	Jan. 3, 1989.

CONGRESSES IN WHICH REPRESENTATIVES HAVE SERVED, WITH BEGINNING OF PRESENT SERVICE—CONTINUED

[* Elected to fill a vacancy; Republicans in roman (228); Democrats in *italic* (206); Independent in **bold** (1); total, 435]

Name	State	District	Congresses (inclusive)	Beginning of present service
Serrano, José, E	NY	16	*101st to 105th	Mar. 20, 1990.
Stearns, Cliff	FL	6	101st to 105th	Jan. 3, 1989.
Tanner, John S	TN	8	101st to 105th	Jan. 3, 1989.
Taylor, Gene	MS	5	*101st to 105th	Oct. 18, 1989.
Walsh, James T	NY	25	101st to 105th	Jan. 3, 1989.
5 terms, not consecutive				
Abercrombie, Neil	HI	1	*99th, 102d to 105th.	Jan. 3, 1991.
Paul, Ron	TX	14	94th, 96th to 98th, 105th.	Jan. 3, 1997.
Price, David	NC	4	100th to 103d, 105th.	Jan 3. 1997.
4 terms, consecutive				
Barrett, Bill	NE	3	102d to 105th	Jan. 3, 1991.
Boehner, John A	OH	8	102d to 105th	Jan. 3, 1991.
Camp, Dave	MI	4	102d to 105th	Jan. 3, 1991.
Clayton, Eva	NC	1	*102d to 105th	Nov. 4, 1992.
Cramer, Bud	AL	5	102d to 105th	Jan. 3, 1991.
Cunningham, Randy (Duke).	CA	51	102d to 105th	Jan. 3, 1991.
DeLauro, Rosa L	CT	3	102d to 105th	Jan. 3, 1991.
Dooley, Calvin M	CA	20	102d to 105th	Jan. 3, 1991.
Doolittle, John T	CA	4	102d to 105th	Jan. 3, 1991.
Edwards, Chet	TX	11	102d to 105th	Jan. 3, 1991.
Ewing, Thomas W	IL	15	*102d to 105th	July 2, 1991.
Gilchrest, Wayne T	MD	1	102d to 105th	Jan. 3, 1991.
Hobson, David L	OH	7	102d to 105th	Jan. 3, 1991.
Jefferson, William J	LA	2	102d to 105th	Jan. 3, 1991.
Johnson, Sam	TX	3	*102d to 105th	May 18, 1991.
Klug, Scott L	WI	2	102d to 105th	Jan. 3, 1991.
Moran, James P	VA	8	102d to 105th	Jan. 3, 1991.
Nadler, Jerrold	NY	8	*102d to 105th	Nov. 4, 1992.
Nussle, Jim	IA	2	102d to 105th	Jan. 3, 1991.
Olver, John W	MA	1	*102d to 105th	June 4, 1991.
Pastor, Ed	AZ	2	*102d to 105th	Sep. 24, 1991.
Peterson, Collin C	MN	7	102d to 105th	Jan. 3, 1991.
Ramstad, Jim	MN	3	102d to 105th	Jan. 3, 1991.
Roemer, Timothy J	IN	3	102d to 105th	Jan. 3, 1991.
Sanders, Bernard	VT	At L.	102d to 105th	Jan. 3, 1991.
Taylor, Charles H	NC	11	102d to 105th	Jan. 3, 1991.
Waters, Maxine	CA	35	102d to 105th	Jan. 3, 1991.
3 terms, consecutive				
Bachus, Spencer	AL	6	103d to 105th	Jan. 3, 1993.
Baesler, Scotty	KY	6	103d to 105th	Jan. 3, 1993.
Barcia, James A	MI	5	103d to 105th	Jan. 3, 1993.
Barrett, Thomas M	WI	5	103d to 105th	Jan. 3, 1993.
Bartlett, Roscoe G	MD	6	103d to 105th	Jan. 3, 1993.
Becerra, Xavier	CA	30	103d to 105th	Jan. 3, 1993.
Bishop, Sanford	GA	2	103d to 105th	Jan. 3, 1993.
Bonilla, Henry	TX	23	103d to 105th	Jan. 3, 1993.

CONGRESSES IN WHICH REPRESENTATIVES HAVE SERVED, WITH BEGINNING OF PRESENT SERVICE—CONTINUED

[* Elected to fill a vacancy; Republicans in roman (228); Democrats in *italic* (206); Independent in **bold** (1); total, 435]

Name	State	District	Congresses (inclusive)	Beginning of present service
Brown, Corrine	FL	3	103d to 105th	Jan. 3, 1993.
Brown, Sherrod	OH	13	103d to 105th	Jan. 3, 1993.
Buyer, Steve	IN	5	103d to 105th	Jan. 3, 1993.
Calvert, Ken	CA	43	103d to 105th	Jan. 3, 1993.
Canady, Charles T	FL	12	103d to 105th	Jan. 3, 1993.
Castle, Michael N	DE	At L.	103d to 105th	Jan. 3, 1993.
Clyburn, James E	SC	6	103d to 105th	Jan. 3, 1993.
Collins, Mac	GA	3	103d to 105th	Jan. 3, 1993.
Crapo, Michael D	ID	2	103d to 105th	Jan. 3, 1993.
Danner, Pat	MO	6	103d to 105th	Jan. 3, 1993.
Deal, Nathan	GA	9	103d to 105th	Jan. 3, 1993.
Deutsch, Peter	FL	20	103d to 105th	Jan. 3, 1993.
Diaz-Balart, Lincoln	FL	21	103d to 105th	Jan. 3, 1993.
Dickey, Jay	AR	4	103d to 105th	Jan. 3, 1993.
Dunn, Jennifer	WA	8	103d to 105th	Jan. 3, 1993.
Ehlers, Vernon	MI	3	103d to 105th	Jan. 25, 1994.
Eshoo, Anna G	CA	14	103d to 105th	Jan. 3, 1993.
Everett, Terry	AL	2	103d to 105th	Jan. 3, 1993.
Farr, Sam	CA	17	*103d to 105th	June 16, 1993.
Filner, Bob	CA	50	103d to 105th	Jan. 3, 1993.
Fowler, Tillie	FL	4	103d to 105th	Jan. 3, 1993.
Franks, Bob	NJ	7	103d to 105th	Jan. 3, 1993.
Furse, Elizabeth	OR	1	103d to 105th	Jan. 3, 1993.
Goodlatte, Robert W. (Bob).	VA	6	103d to 105th	Jan. 3, 1993.
Green, Gene	TX	29	103d to 105th	Jan. 3, 1993.
Greenwood, James C	PA	8	103d to 105th	Jan. 3, 1993.
Gutierrez, Luis V	IL	4	103d to 105th	Jan. 3, 1993.
Harman, Jane	CA	36	103d to 105th	Jan. 3, 1993.
Hastings, Alcee L	FL	23	103d to 105th	Jan. 3, 1993.
Hilliard, Earl F	AL	7	103d to 105th	Jan. 3, 1993.
Hinchey, Maurice D	NY	26	103d to 105th	Jan. 3, 1993.
Hoekstra, Peter	MI	2	103d to 105th	Jan. 3, 1993.
Holden, Tim	PA	6	103d to 105th	Jan. 3, 1993.
Horn, Steve	CA	38	103d to 105th	Jan. 3, 1993.
Inglis, Bob	SC	4	103d to 105th	Jan. 3, 1993.
Istook, Ernest J., Jr	OK	5	103d to 105th	Jan. 3, 1993.
Johnson, Eddie Bernice	TX	30	103d to 105th	Jan. 3, 1993.
Kim, Jay	CA	41	103d to 105th	Jan. 3, 1993.
King, Peter T	NY	3	103d to 105th	Jan. 3, 1993.
Kingston, Jack	GA	1	103d to 105th	Jan. 3, 1993.
Klink, Ron	PA	4	103d to 105th	Jan. 3, 1993.
Knollenberg, Joseph	MI	11	103d to 105th	Jan. 3, 1993.
Largent, Steve	OK	1	103d to 105th	Nov. 29, 1994.
Lazio, Rick A	NY	2	103d to 105th	Jan. 3, 1993.
Lewis, Ron	KY	2	*103d to 105th	May 17, 1994.
Linder, John	GA	4	103d to 105th	Jan. 3, 1993.
Lucas, Frank	OK	6	103d to 105th	Jan. 3, 1993.
Maloney, Carolyn B	NY	14	103d to 105th	May 17, 1994.
Manzullo, Donald	IL	16	103d to 105th	Jan. 3, 1993.
McHale, Paul	PA	15	103d to 105th	Jan. 3, 1993.
McHugh, John M	NY	24	103d to 105th	Jan. 3, 1993.
McInnis, Scott	CO	3	103d to 105th	Jan. 3, 1993.

CONGRESSES IN WHICH REPRESENTATIVES HAVE SERVED, WITH BEGINNING OF PRESENT SERVICE—CONTINUED

[* Elected to fill a vacancy; Republicans in roman (228); Democrats in *italic* (206); Independent in **bold** (1); total, 435]

Name	State	District	Congresses (inclusive)	Beginning of present service
McKeon, Howard P. (Buck).	CA	25	103d to 105th	Jan. 3, 1993.
McKinney, Cynthia	GA	11	103d to 105th	Jan. 3, 1993.
Meehan, Martin T	MA	5	103d to 105th	Jan. 3, 1993.
Meek, Carrie	FL	17	103d to 105th	Jan. 3, 1993.
Menendez, Robert	NJ	13	103d to 105th	Jan. 3, 1993.
Mica, John L	FL	7	103d to 105th	Jan. 3, 1993.
Miller, Dan	FL	13	103d to 105th	Jan. 3, 1993.
Minge, David	MN	2	103d to 105th	Jan. 3, 1993.
Pombo, Richard W	CA	11	103d to 105th	Jan. 3, 1993.
Pomeroy, Earl	ND	At L.	103d to 105th	Jan. 3, 1993.
Portman, Rob	OH	2	*103d to 105th	May 4, 1993.
Pryce, Deborah	OH	15	103d to 105th	Jan. 3, 1993.
Quinn, Jack	NY	30	103d to 105th	Jan. 3, 1993.
Roybal-Allard, Lucille	CA	33	103d to 105th	Jan. 3, 1993.
Royce, Ed	CA	39	103d to 105th	Jan. 3, 1993.
Rush, Bobby L	IL	1	103d to 105th	Jan. 3, 1993.
Scott, Robert C. (Bobby)	VA	3	103d to 105th	Jan. 3, 1993.
Smith, Nick	MI	7	103d to 105th	Jan. 3, 1993.
Stupak, Bart	MI	1	103d to 105th	Jan. 3, 1993.
Talent, James M	MO	2	103d to 105th	Jan. 3, 1993.
Thompson, Bennie	MS	2	*103d to 105th	Apr. 13, 1993.
Thurman, Karen L	FL	5	103d to 105th	Jan. 3, 1993.
Velázquez, Nydia M	NY	12	103d to 105th	Jan. 3, 1993.
Watt, Melvin	NC	12	103d to 105th	Jan. 3, 1993.
Woolsey, Lynn	CA	6	103d to 105th	Jan. 3, 1993.
Wynn, Albert R	MD	4	103d to 105th	Jan. 3, 1993.
3 terms, not consecutive				
Riggs, Frank	CA	1	102nd, 104th to 105th.	Jan. 3, 1995.
2 terms, consecutive				
Baldacci, John Elias	ME	2	104th and 105th	Jan. 3, 1995.
Barr, Bob	GA	7	104th and 105th	Jan. 3, 1995.
Bass, Charles	NH	2	104th and 105th	Jan. 3, 1995.
Bentsen, Kenneth E., Jr	TX	25	104th and 105th	Jan. 3, 1995.
Bilbray, Brian	CA	49	104th and 105th	Jan. 3, 1995.
Blumenauer, Earl	OR	3	*104th and 105th	May 30, 1996.
Bono, Sonny	CA	44	104th and 105th	Jan. 3, 1995.
Bryant, Ed	TN	7	104th and 105th	Jan. 3, 1995.
Burr, Richard M	NC	5	104th and 105th	Jan. 3, 1995.
Campbell, Tom	CA	15	*104th and 105th	Dec. 15, 1995.
Chabot, Steve	OH	1	104th and 105th	Jan. 3, 1995.
Chambliss, Saxby	GA	8	104th and 105th	Jan. 3, 1995.
Chenoweth, Helen	ID	1	104th and 105th	Jan. 3, 1995.
Christensen, Jon	NE	2	104th and 105th	Jan. 3, 1995.
Coburn, Thomas A	OK	2	104th and 105th	Jan. 3, 1995.
Cubin, Barbara	WY	At L.	104th and 105th	Jan. 3, 1995.
Cummings, Elijah	MD	7	*104th and 105th	Apr. 25, 1996.
Davis, Thomas, III	VA	11	104th and 105th	Jan. 3, 1995.
Doggett, Lloyd	TX	10	104th and 105th	Jan. 3, 1995.
Doyle, Michael F	PA	18	104th and 105th	Jan. 3, 1995.

CONGRESSES IN WHICH REPRESENTATIVES HAVE SERVED, WITH BEGINNING OF PRESENT SERVICE—CONTINUED

[* Elected to fill a vacancy; Republicans in roman (228); Democrats in *italic* (206); Independent in **bold** (1); total, 435]

Name	State	District	Congresses (inclusive)	Beginning of present service
Ehrlich, Robert, Jr	MD	2	104th and 105th	Jan. 3, 1995.
Emerson, Jo Ann	MO	8	*104th and 105th	Nov. 5, 1996.
English, Philip	PA	21	104th and 105th	Jan. 3, 1995.
Ensign, John	NV	1	104th and 105th	Jan. 3, 1995.
Fattah, Chaka	PA	2	104th and 105th	Jan. 3, 1995.
Foley, Mark	FL	16	104th and 105th	Jan. 3, 1995.
Forbes, Michael	NY	1	104th and 105th	Jan. 3, 1995.
Fox, Jon	PA	13	104th and 105th	Jan. 3, 1995.
Frelinghuysen, Rodney	NJ	11	104th and 105th	Jan. 3, 1995.
Ganske, Greg	IA	4	104th and 105th	Jan. 3, 1995.
Graham, Lindsey	SC	3	104th and 105th	Jan. 3, 1995.
Gutknecht, Gilbert W	MN	1	104th and 105th	Jan. 3, 1995.
Hastings, (Doc)	WA	4	104th and 105th	Jan. 3, 1995.
Hayworth, J.D	AZ	6	104th and 105th	Jan. 3, 1995.
Hilleary, Van	TN	4	104th and 105th	Jan. 3, 1995.
Hostettler, John	IN	8	104th and 105th	Jan. 3, 1995.
Jackson, Jesse, Jr.	IL	2	*104th and 105th	Dec. 14, 1995.
Jones, Walter B.	NC	3	104th and 105th	Jan. 3, 1995.
Kelly, Sue	NY	19	104th and 105th	Jan. 3, 1995.
Kennedy, Patrick J	RI	1	104th and 105th	Jan. 3, 1995.
LaHood, Ray	IL	18	104th and 105th	Jan. 3, 1995.
Latham, Tom	IA	5	104th and 105th	Jan. 3, 1995.
LaTourette, Steven	OH	19	104th and 105th	Jan. 3, 1995.
Lee, Sheila Jackson	TX	18	104th and 105th	Jan. 3, 1995.
LoBiondo, Frank	NJ	2	104th and 105th	Jan. 3, 1995.
Lofgren, Zoe	CA	16	104th and 105th	Jan. 3, 1995.
Luther, William	MN	6	104th and 105th	Jan. 3, 1995.
Mascara, Frank	PA	20	104th and 105th	Jan. 3, 1995.
McCarthy, Karen	MO	5	104th and 105th	Jan. 3, 1995.
McIntosh, David M	IN	2	104th and 105th	Jan. 3, 1995.
Metcalf, Jack	WA	2	104th and 105th	Jan. 3, 1995.
Millender-McDonald, Juanita.	CA	37	*104th and 105th	Apr. 16, 1996.
Myrick, Sue	NC	9	104th and 105th	Jan. 3, 1995.
Nethercutt, George	WA	5	104th and 105th	Jan. 3, 1995.
Neumann, Mark	WI	1	104th and 105th	Jan. 3, 1995.
Ney, Robert A	OH	18	104th and 105th	Jan. 3, 1995.
Norwood, Charlie	GA	10	104th and 105th	Jan. 3, 1995.
Portman, Rob	OH	2	104th and 105th	Jan. 3, 1995.
Radanovich, George	CA	19	104th and 105th	Jan. 3, 1995.
Rivers, Lynn Nancy	MI	13	104th and 105th	Jan. 3, 1995.
Salmon, Matt	AZ	1	104th and 105th	Jan. 3, 1995.
Sanford, Mark	SC	1	104th and 105th	Jan. 3, 1995.
Scarborough, Joe	FL	1	104th and 105th	Jan. 3, 1995.
Shadegg, John	AZ	4	104th and 105th	Jan. 3, 1995.
Smith, Linda	WA	3	104th and 105th	Jan. 3, 1995.
Souder, Mark	IN	4	104th and 105th	Jan. 3, 1995.
Tate, Randy	WA	9	104th and 105th	Jan. 3, 1995.
Thornberry, William	TX	13	104th and 105th	Jan. 3, 1995.
Tiahrt, Todd	KS	4	104th and 105th	Jan. 3, 1995.
Wamp, Zachary Paul	TN	3	104th and 105th	Jan. 3, 1995.
Watts, J.C	OK	4	104th and 105th	Jan. 9, 1995.
Weldon, Dave	FL	15	104th and 105th	Jan. 3, 1995.

CONGRESSES IN WHICH REPRESENTATIVES HAVE SERVED, WITH BEGINNING OF PRESENT SERVICE—CONTINUED

[* Elected to fill a vacancy; Republicans in roman (228); Democrats in *italic* (206); Independent in **bold** (1); total, 435]

Name	State	District	Congresses (inclusive)	Beginning of present service
Weller, Jerry	IL	11	104th and 105th	Jan. 3, 1995.
White, Rick	WA	1	104th and 105th	Jan. 3, 1995.
Whitfield, Edward	KY	1	104th and 105th	Jan. 3, 1995.
Wicker, Roger	MS	1	104th and 105th	Jan. 3, 1995.
2 terms, not consecutive				
Strickland, Ted	OH	6	103d and 105th	Jan. 3, 1997.
1 term				
Aderholt, Robert	AL	4	105th	Jan. 3, 1997.
Allen, Thomas H.	ME	1	105th	Jan. 3, 1997.
Berry, Marion	AR	1	105th	Jan. 3, 1997.
Blagójevich, Rod	IL	5	105th	Jan. 3, 1997.
Blunt, Roy	MO	7	105th	Jan. 3, 1997.
Boswell, Leonard L.	IA	3	105th	Jan. 3, 1997.
Boyd, Allen	FL	2	105th	Jan. 3, 1997.
Brady, Kevin	TX	8	105th	Jan. 3, 1997.
Cannon, Christopher B.	UT	3	105th	Jan. 3, 1997.
Capps, Walter H.	CA	22	105th	Jan. 3, 1997.
Carson, Julia M.	IN	10	105th	Jan. 3, 1997.
Cook, Merrill	UT	2	105th	Jan. 3, 1997.
Cooksey, John	LA	5	105th	Jan. 3, 1997.
Davis, Danny K.	IL	7	105th	Jan. 3, 1997.
Davis, Jim	FL	11	105th	Jan. 3, 1997.
DeGette, Diana	CO	1	105th	Jan. 3, 1997.
Delahunt, William D.	MA	10	105th	Jan. 3, 1997.
Etheridge, Bob	NC	2	105th	Jan. 3, 1997.
Ford, Harold E., Jr.	TN	9	105th	Jan. 3, 1997.
Gibbons, Jim	NE	2	105th	Jan. 3, 1997.
Goode, Vigil H., Jr.	VA	5	105th	Jan. 3, 1997.
Granger, Kay	TX	12	105th	Jan. 3, 1997.
Hill, Rick	MT	At L.	105th	Jan. 3, 1997.
Hinojosa, Rubén	TX	15	105th	Jan. 3, 1997.
Hooley, Darlene	OR	5	105th	Jan. 3, 1997.
Hulfshof, Kenny	MO	9	105th	Jan. 3, 1997.
Hutchinson, Asa	AR	3	105th	Jan. 3, 1997.
Jenkins, William L. (Bill)	TN	1	105th	Jan. 3, 1997.
John, Chris	LA	7	105th	Jan. 3, 1997.
Johnson, Jay W.	WI	8	105th	Jan. 3, 1997.
Kilpatrick, Carolyn C.	MI	15	105th	Jan. 3, 1997.
Kind, Ron	WI	3	105th	Jan. 3, 1997.
Kucinich, Dennis	OH	10	105th	Jan. 3, 1997.
Lampson, Nick	TX	9	105th	Jan. 3, 1997.
Maloney, Jim	CT	5	105th	Jan. 3, 1997.
McCarthy, Carolyn	NY	4	105th	Jan. 3, 1997.
McGovern, Jim	MA	9	105th	Jan. 3, 1997.
McIntyre, Mike	NC	7	105th	Jan. 3, 1997.
Moran, Jerry	KS	1	105th	Jan. 3, 1997.
Northup, Anne Meagher	KY	3	105th	Jan. 3, 1997.
Pappas, Mike	NJ	12	105th	Jan. 3, 1997.
Pascrell, William J., Jr.	NJ	8	105th	Jan. 3, 1997.
Pease, Edward A.	IN	7	105th	Jan. 3, 1997.
Peterson, John E.	PA	5	105th	Jan. 3, 1997.

CONGRESSES IN WHICH REPRESENTATIVES HAVE SERVED, WITH BEGINNING OF PRESENT SERVICE—CONTINUED

[* Elected to fill a vacancy; Republicans in roman (228); Democrats in *italic* (206); Independent in **bold** (1); total, 435]

Name	State	District	Congresses (inclusive)	Beginning of present service
Pickering, Charles W. (Chip), Jr..	MS	3	105th	Jan. 3, 1997.
Pitts, Joseph R.	PA	16	105th	Jan. 3, 1997.
Redmond, Bill	NM	3	*105th	May 20, 1997.
Reyes, Silvestre	TX	16	105th	Jan. 3, 1997.
Riley, Bob	AL	3	105th	Jan. 3, 1997.
Rodriguez, Ciro	TX	28	*105th	Apr. 16, 1997.
Rogan, James E.	CA	27	105th	Jan. 3, 1997.
Rothman, Steven R.	NJ	9	105th	Jan. 3, 1997.
Ryun, Jim	KS	2	*105th	Jan. 3, 1997.
Sanchez, Loretta	CA	46	105th	Jan. 3, 1997.
Sandlin, Max	TX	1	105th	Jan. 3, 1997.
Schaffer, Bob	CO	4	105th	Jan. 3, 1997.
Sessions, Pete	TX	12	105th	Jan. 3, 1997.
Sherman, Brad	CA	24	105th	Jan. 3, 1997.
Shimkus, John M.	IL	20	105th	Jan. 3, 1997.
Smith, Adam	WA	9	105th	Jan. 3, 1997.
Snowbarger, Vince	KS	3	105th	Jan. 3, 1997.
Snyder, Vic	AR	2	105th	Jan. 3, 1997.
Stabenow, Debbie	MI	8	105th	Jan. 3, 1997.
Sununu, John E.	NH	1	105th	Jan. 3, 1997.
Tauscher, Ellen	CA	10	105th	Jan. 3, 1997.
Thune, John	SD	At L.	105th	Jan. 3, 1997.
Tierney, John	MA	6	105th	Jan. 3, 1997.
Turner, Jim	TX	2	105th	Jan. 3, 1997.
Wexler, Robert	FL	19	105th	Jan. 3, 1997.
Weygand, Robert A	RI	2	105th	Jan. 3, 1997.
RESIDENT COMMISSIONER				
Romero-Barceló, Carlos [1]	PR	....	103d to 105th	Jan. 3, 1993.
DELEGATES				
Christian-Green, Donna	VI	....	105th	Jan. 3, 1997.
Faleomavaega, Eni F.H	AS	....	101st to 105th	Jan. 3, 1989.
Norton, Eleanor Holmes	DC	....	102d to 105th	Jan. 3, 1991.
Underwood, Robert A	GU	....	103d to 105th	Jan. 3, 1993.

[1] New Progressive Party.

NOTE: Members elected by special election are considered to begin service on the date of the election, except for those elected after a sine die adjournment. If elected after the Congress has adjourned for the session, Members are considered to begin their service on the day after the election.

STATISTICAL INFORMATION *

VOTES CAST FOR SENATORS IN 1992, 1994, AND 1996

[The figures show the vote for the Democratic and Republican nominees, except as otherwise indicated. Compiled from official statistics obtained by the Clerk of the House. Figures in the last column, for the 1996 election, may include totals for more candidates than the ones shown.]

State	Vote						Total vote cast in 1996
	1992		1994		1996		
	Democrat	Republican	Republican	Democrat	Republican	Democrat	
Alabama	1,022,698	522,015	...	...	786,436	681,651	1,499,393
Alaska	92,065	127,163	...	...	177,893	23,977	231,916
Arizona	436,321	771,395	600,999	442,510	...	...	...
Arkansas	553,635	366,373	...	...	445,942	400,241	846,183
California	5,173,467	4,644,182	3,817,025	3,979,152	...	...	...
	[1] 5,853,651	4,093,501	...	...	...	...	...
Colorado	803,725	662,893	...	...	750,315	667,600	1,459,601
Connecticut	577,662	572,036	334,833	443,793	...	...	...
Delaware	...	...	111,074	84,540	105,088	165,465	275,591
Florida	3,245,565	1,716,505	2,894,726	1,210,412	...	...	...
Georgia	1,108,416	1,073,282	...	...	1,073,969	1,103,993	2,259,224
	[2] 618,877	635,114	...	...	...	...	...
Hawaii	208,266	97,928	86,320	256,189	...	...	...
Idaho	208,036	270,468	...	...	283,532	198,422	497,233
Illinois	2,631,229	2,126,833	...	...	1,728,824	2,384,028	4,250,722
Indiana	900,148	1,267,972	1,039,625	470,799	...	...	...
Iowa	351,561	899,761	...	...	571,807	634,166	1,224,054
Kansas	349,525	706,246	...	...	652,677	362,380	1,052,300
	...	...	...	...	574,021	461,344	[3] 1,064,716
Kentucky	836,888	476,604	...	...	724,794	560,012	1,307,046
Louisiana	([a])	...	...	...	847,157	852,945	1,700,102
Maine	...	...	308,244	186,042	298,422	266,226	606,777
Maryland	1,307,610	533,688	559,908	809,125	...	...	...
Massachusetts	...	...	894,000	1,265,997	1,143,120	1,334,135	2,555,942
Michigan	...	...	1,578,770	1,300,960	1,500,106	2,195,738	3,762,575
Minnesota	...	...	869,653	781,860	901,194	1,098,430	2,182,905
Mississippi	...	...	418,333	189,752	240,647	624,154	878,662
Missouri	1,057,967	1,221,901	1,060,149	633,697	...	...	...
Montana	...	...	218,542	131,845	182,111	201,935	407,490
Nebraska	...	...	260,668	317,297	379,933	281,904	661,837
Nevada	253,150	199,413	156,020	193,804	...	...	...
New Hampshire	234,982	249,591	...	...	242,257	227,355	491,873
New Jersey	...	...	966,244	1,033,487	1,227,351	1,519,154	2,883,466
New Mexico	...	...	213,025	249,989	357,171	164,356	551,821
New York	2,943,001	2,652,822	1,711,760	2,528,387	...	...	...
North Carolina	1,194,015	1,297,892	...	...	1,345,833	1,173,875	2,556,456
North Dakota	179,347	118,162	99,390	137,157	...	...	...
	[4] 103,246	55,194	...	...	...	...	...
Ohio	2,444,419	2,028,300	1,836,556	1,348,213	...	...	...
Oklahoma	494,350	757,876	542,390	392,488	670,610	474,162	1,183,150
Oregon	639,851	717,455	...	...	624,370	677,336	1,360,230
Pennsylvania	2,224,966	2,358,125	1,735,691	1,648,481	...	...	...
Rhode Island	...	...	222,856	122,532	127,368	230,676	364,371
South Carolina	591,030	554,175	...	...	619,859	510,951	1,161,231
South Dakota	217,095	108,733	...	...	157,954	166,533	324,487
Tennessee	...	...	[5] 885,998	565,930	1,091,554	654,937	1,778,664
			[6] 834,226	623,164	...	...	...
Texas	...	...	2,604,218	1,639,615	3,027,680	2,428,776	5,527,441
Utah	301,228	420,069	357,297	146,938	...	...	...
Vermont	154,762	123,854	106,505	85,868	...	...	...
Virginia	...	...	882,213	938,376	1,235,744	1,115,982	2,354,715
Washington	1,197,973	1,020,829	947,821	752,352	...	...	...
West Virginia	...	...	130,441	290,495	139,088	456,526	595,614
Wisconsin	1,290,662	1,129,599	636,989	912,662	...	...	...
Wyoming	...	...	118,754	79,287	114,116	89,103	211,077

* Statistical material edited by Peter A. Byrd.

[a] Under Louisiana State law, a candidate receiving at least 51 percent of the vote cast in the primary election is elected to the congressional seat.

[1] A special election was held on Nov. 3, 1992 for the unexpired term of Senator Alan Cranston.

[2] A runoff election was held on Nov. 24, 1992. The November 3d election did not produce a winner with a clear majority.

[3] Sam Brownback was elected by Special Election on Nov. 5, 1996 to fill the unexpired term of Senator Bob Dole.

[4] A special election was held on Dec. 4, 1992 to fill the vacancy caused by the death of Senator Quentin Burdick.

[5] Fred Thompson was elected by special election on Nov. 8, 1994 to fill the unexpired term of Senator Al Gore.

[6] William Frist was elected for full term on Nov. 8, 1994.

VOTES CAST FOR REPRESENTATIVES, RESIDENT COMMISSIONER, AND DELEGATES IN 1992, 1994, AND 1996

[The figures, compiled from official statistics obtained by the Clerk of the House, show the votes for the Democratic and Republican nominees, except as otherwise indicated. Figures in the last column, for the 1996 election, may include totals for more candidates than the ones shown. Population changes reflected in the 1990 census caused the reapportionment of congressional districts; those changes are reflected in the 1992 election results.]

State and district	Vote cast in 1992		State and district	Vote cast in 1994		State and district	Vote cast in 1996		Total vote cast in 1996
	Democrat	Republican		Republican	Democrat		Republican	Democrat	
AL:			AL:			AL:			
1st	78,742	128,874	1st	103,432	50,227	1st	132,206	69,470	205,417
2d	109,335	112,906	2d	124,465	44,694	2d	132,563	74,317	209,793
3d	119,175	73,800	3d	53,757	93,924	3d	98,353	92,325	195,047
4th	157,907	66,934	4th	....	119,436	4th	102,741	99,250	205,917
5th	160,060	77,951	5th	86,923	88,693	5th	86,727	114,442	205,547
6th	126,062	146,599	6th	155,047	41,030	6th	180,781	69,592	254,859
7th	144,320	36,086	7th	34,814	116,150	7th	52,142	136,651	192,113
AK:			AK:			AK:			
At large	102,378	111,849	At large	118,537	68,172	At large	138,834	85,114	233,700
AZ:			AZ:			AZ:			
1st	130,715	113,613	1st	101,350	70,627	1st	135,634	89,738	225,372
2d	90,693	41,257	2d	32,797	62,589	2d	38,786	81,982	126,101
3d	88,830	158,906	3d	145,396	61,939	3d	175,231	88,214	263,445
4th	70,572	156,330	4th	116,714	69,760	4th	150,486	74,857	225,343
5th	77,256	172,867	5th	149,514	63,436	5th	179,349	67,597	260,898
6th	124,251	97,074	6th	107,060	81,321	6th	121,431	118,957	255,287
AR:			AR:			AR:			
1st	149,558	64,618	1st	83,147	95,290	1st	88,436	105,280	199,450
2d	154,946	53,978	2d	72,473	97,580	2d	104,548	114,841	219,389
3d	117,775	125,295	3d	129,800	61,883	3d	137,093	102,994	246,132
4th	102,918	113,009	4th	87,469	81,370	4th	125,956	72,391	198,347
CA:			CA:			CA:			
1st	119,676	113,266	1st	106,870	93,717	1st	110,243	96,522	222,119
2d	71,780	167,247	2d	137,864	55,959	2d	144,913	80,401	238,326
3d	122,149	96,092	3d	89,964	97,093	3d	91,134	118,663	221,737
4th	129,489	141,155	4th	144,936	82,505	4th	164,048	97,948	271,315
5th	158,250	58,698	5th	52,905	125,042	5th	52,940	142,618	202,460
6th	190,322	98,171	6th	88,940	137,642	6th	86,278	156,958	253,836
7th	153,320	54,822	7th	45,698	116,105	7th	42,542	137,089	190,917
8th	191,906	25,693	8th	30,528	137,642	8th	25,739	175,216	207,738
9th	164,265	53,707	9th	40,448	129,233	9th	37,126	154,806	200,968
10th	134,635	145,702	10th	138,916	90,523	10th	133,633	137,726	283,183
11th	90,539	94,453	11th	99,302	55,794	11th	107,477	65,536	181,096
12th	157,205	53,278	12th	57,228	118,408	12th	49,276	149,049	207,908
13th	123,795	64,953	13th	45,555	97,344	13th	53,385	114,408	175,539
14th	146,873	101,202	14th	78,475	120,713	14th	71,571	148,773	229,633
15th	168,617	82,875	15th	80,266	119,921	15th	132,737	79,048	226,868
16th	96,661	49,843	16th	40,409	74,935	16th	43,197	94,020	143,207
17th	151,565	49,947	17th	74,380	87,222	17th	73,856	115,116	195,545
18th	139,704	....	18th	44,046	91,106	18th	52,695	108,827	165,586
19th	101,619	100,590	19th	104,435	72,912	19th	137,402	58,452	206,379
20th	72,679	39,388	20th	43,836	57,394	20th	45,276	65,381	115,705
21st	68,058	127,758	21st	116,874	47,517	21st	125,916	50,694	191,152
22d	87,328	131,242	22d	102,987	101,424	22d	107,987	118,299	244,186
23d	88,225	115,504	23d	114,043	47,345	23d	118,880	70,035	199,507
24th	141,742	99,835	24th	91,806	95,342	24th	93,629	106,193	214,848
25th	72,233	113,611	25th	110,301	53,445	25th	122,428	65,089	196,203
26th	73,807	36,453	26th	28,423	55,145	26th	29,332	67,525	102,515
27th	83,805	105,521	27th	88,341	70,267	27th	95,310	82,014	189,930
28th	76,525	122,353	28th	110,179	50,022	28th	113,389	69,037	186,885
29th	160,312	67,141	29th	53,801	129,413	29th	52,857	145,278	214,817
30th	48,800	20,034	30th	18,741	43,943	30th	15,078	58,283	80,590
31st	68,324	40,873	31st	34,926	50,541	31st	28,705	69,285	102,690
32d	150,644	....	32d	22,190	98,017	32d	18,768	124,712	151,427
33d	32,010	15,428	33d	....	33,814	33d	8,147	47,478	57,828
34th	91,738	50,907	34th	40,068	72,439	34th	36,852	94,730	138,440
35th	102,941	17,417	35th	18,390	65,688	35th	13,116	92,762	108,488
36th	125,751	109,684	36th	93,127	93,939	36th	98,538	117,752	224,459
37th	97,159	....	37th	....	64,166	37th	15,399	87,247	102,646
38th	82,108	92,038	38th	85,225	53,681	38th	88,136	71,627	167,645
39th	81,728	122,472	39th	113,641	49,696	39th	120,761	61,392	192,290
40th	63,881	129,563	40th	115,728	48,003	40th	98,821	44,102	152,261
41st	58,777	101,753	41st	82,100	50,043	41st	83,934	47,346	143,445
42d	79,780	69,251	42d	56,259	58,888	42d	51,170	52,166	103,336
43d	88,468	88,987	43d	84,500	59,342	43d	97,247	67,422	177,640
44th	81,693	110,333	44th	95,521	65,370	44th	110,643	73,844	191,518
45th	88,508	123,731	45th	124,875	55,849	45th	125,326	68,312	205,522
46th	45,435	55,659	46th	50,616	33,004	46th	46,980	47,964	102,784
47th	76,924	165,004	47th	154,071	53,669	47th	160,078	70,362	243,777
48th	67,415	140,935	48th	143,570	43,523	48th	145,814	59,558	221,391
49th	127,280	106,170	49th	90,283	85,597	49th	108,806	86,657	206,768
50th	77,293	39,531	50th	36,955	59,214	50th	38,351	73,200	118,340

VOTES CAST FOR REPRESENTATIVES, RESIDENT COMMISSIONER, AND DELEGATES IN 1992, 1994, AND 1996—CONTINUED

[The figures, compiled from official statistics obtained by the Clerk of the House, show the votes for the Democratic and Republican nominees, except as otherwise indicated. Figures in the last column, for the 1996 election, may include totals for more candidates than the ones shown. Population changes reflected in the 1990 census caused the reapportionment of congressional districts; those changes are reflected in the 1992 election results.]

State and district	Vote cast in 1992		State and district	Vote cast in 1994		State and district	Vote cast in 1996		Total vote cast in 1996
	Democrat	Republican		Republican	Democrat		Republican	Democrat	
51st	85,148	141,890	51st	138,547	57,374	51st	149,032	66,250	229,024
52d	88,076	112,995	52d	109,201	53,024	52d	116,746	53,104	178,321
CO:			CO:			CO:			
1st	156,629	70,902	1st	61,978	93,123	1st	79,540	112,631	197,839
2d	164,790	88,470	2d	80,723	105,938	2d	97,865	145,894	255,784
3d	114,480	143,293	3d	145,365	63,427	3d	183,523	82,953	266,476
4th	101,957	139,884	4th	136,251	52,202	4th	137,012	92,837	244,067
5th	62,550	173,096	5th	138,674	....	5th	188,805	73,660	262,465
6th	91,073	142,021	6th	124,079	49,701	6th	146,018	88,600	234,618
CT:			CT:			CT:			
1st	112,838	75,113	1st	46,865	88,946	1st	53,666	145,169	215,136
2d	83,197	119,416	2d	79,167	79,188	2d	100,332	106,544	223,249
3d	112,022	84,952	3d	53,110	111,261	3d	59,335	137,108	211,352
4th	58,666	147,816	4th	109,436	34,962	4th	121,949	75,902	201,712
5th	74,791	104,891	5th	93,471	57,579	5th	98,782	105,359	215,130
6th	60,373	166,967	6th	123,101	44,159	6th	113,020	104,225	227,756
DE:			DE:			DE:			
At large	117,426	153,037	At large	137,945	51,793	At large	185,577	73,258	266,831
FL:			FL:			FL:			
1st	118,941	100,349	1st	112,901	70,389	1st	175,946	66,495	242,545
2d	167,215	60,425	2d	74,011	117,404	2d	94,122	138,151	232,400
3d	91,915	63,114	3d	46,895	63,845	3d	62,196	98,085	160,281
4th	103,531	135,883	4th	([1])	....	4th	([1])	....	....
5th	129,698	114,356	5th	94,093	125,780	5th	100,051	161,050	261,101
6th	76,419	144,195	6th	148,698	....	6th	161,527	78,908	240,442
7th	96,945	125,823	7th	131,711	47,747	7th	143,667	87,832	231,557
8th	65,145	141,977	8th	131,376	....	8th	136,515	65,794	202,326
9th	110,135	158,028	9th	177,253	....	9th	161,708	73,809	235,517
10th	114,809	149,606	10th	([1])	....	10th	114,443	57,375	171,820
11th	100,984	77,640	11th	72,119	76,814	11th	78,881	108,522	187,403
12th	92,346	100,484	12th	106,123	57,203	12th	122,584	76,513	199,097
13th	115,767	158,881	13th	([1])	....	13th	173,671	96,098	269,904
14th	....	220,351	14th	([1])	....	14th	176,992	63,842	240,834
15th	132,412	128,873	15th	117,027	100,513	15th	139,014	115,981	270,350
16th	101,237	157,322	16th	122,734	88,646	16th	175,714	98,827	294,541
17th	102,784	....	17th	....	75,741	17th	14,525	114,638	129,165
18th	52,142	104,755	18th	([1])	....	18th	123,659	....	123,665
19th	177,423	103,867	19th	75,779	147,591	19th	99,101	188,766	287,867
20th	130,959	91,589	20th	72,516	114,615	20th	85,777	159,256	245,033
21st	....	([1])	21st	90,948	....	21st	125,469	....	125,473
22d	91,625	128,400	22d	119,690	69,215	22d	137,098	84,517	221,618
23d	84,249	44,807	23d	....	([1])	23d	36,907	102,161	139,089
GA:			GA:			GA:			
1st	75,808	103,932	1st	88,788	27,197	1st	108,616	50,622	159,238
2d	95,789	54,593	2d	33,429	65,383	2d	75,282	88,256	163,538
3d	94,271	114,107	3d	94,717	49,828	3d	120,251	76,538	196,789
4th	123,819	126,495	4th	90,063	65,566	4th	92,985	127,157	220,142
5th	147,445	56,960	5th	37,999	85,094	5th	....	136,555	136,555
6th	116,196	158,761	6th	119,432	66,700	6th	174,155	127,135	301,290
7th	111,374	82,915	7th	71,265	65,978	7th	112,009	81,765	193,774
8th	108,472	86,220	8th	89,591	53,408	8th	93,619	84,506	178,125
9th	113,024	77,919	9th	57,568	79,145	9th	132,532	69,662	202,194
10th	108,426	93,059	10th	96,099	51,192	10th	96,723	88,054	184,777
11th	120,168	44,221	11th	37,533	71,560	11th	145,821	80,940	226,761
HI:			HI:			HI:			
1st	129,332	41,575	1st	76,623	94,754	1st	80,053	86,732	172,206
2d	131,454	40,070	2d	42,891	124,431	2d	55,729	109,178	180,963
ID:			ID:			ID:			
1st	140,985	90,983	1st	111,728	89,826	1st	132,344	125,899	264,778
2d	81,450	139,783	2d	143,593	47,936	2d	157,646	67,625	229,248
IL:			IL:			IL:			
1st	209,258	43,453	1st	36,038	112,474	1st	25,659	174,005	203,113
2d	182,614	31,957	2d	....	93,998	2d	....	172,648	183,543
3d	162,165	93,128	3d	78,163	92,353	3d	67,214	137,153	209,916
4th	90,452	26,154	4th	15,384	46,695	4th	....	85,278	91,135
5th	132,889	90,738	5th	75,328	63,065	5th	65,768	117,544	183,326
6th	86,891	165,009	6th	115,664	37,163	6th	132,401	68,807	205,954
7th	182,811	35,346	7th	24,011	93,457	7th	27,241	149,568	181,095
8th	96,419	132,887	8th	88,225	47,654	8th	127,763	74,068	205,305
9th	162,942	64,760	9th	48,419	94,404	9th	71,763	124,319	196,082
10th	85,400	155,230	10th	114,884	38,191	10th	145,626	65,144	210,773
11th	135,387	107,860	11th	97,241	63,150	11th	109,896	102,388	212,284
12th	168,762	68,115	12th	52,419	101,391	12th	55,890	150,005	209,519

VOTES CAST FOR REPRESENTATIVES, RESIDENT COMMISSIONER, AND DELEGATES IN 1992, 1994, AND 1996—CONTINUED

[The figures, compiled from official statistics obtained by the Clerk of the House, show the votes for the Democratic and Republican nominees, except as otherwise indicated. Figures in the last column, for the 1996 election, may include totals for more candidates than the ones shown. Population changes reflected in the 1990 census caused the reapportionment of congressional districts; those changes are reflected in the 1992 election results.]

State and district	Vote cast in 1992		State and district	Vote cast in 1994		State and district	Vote cast in 1996		Total vote cast in 1996
	Demo- crat	Repub- lican		Repub- lican	Demo- crat		Repub- lican	Demo- crat	
13th	82,985	179,257	13th	124,312	45,709	13th	141,651	94,693	236,344
14th	75,294	155,271	14th	110,204	33,891	14th	134,432	74,332	208,764
15th	97,190	142,167	15th	108,857	50,874	15th	121,019	90,065	211,084
16th	113,555	142,388	16th	117,238	48,736	16th	137,523	90,575	228,100
17th	156,233	103,719	17th	79,471	95,312	17th	109,240	120,008	231,173
18th	114,413	156,533	18th	119,838	78,332	18th	143,110	98,413	241,523
19th	187,156	83,526	19th	81,995	115,045	19th	75,751	158,668	237,955
20th	154,869	119,219	20th	88,964	108,034	20th	120,926	119,688	240,618
IN:			IN:			IN:			
1st	147,054	64,770	1st	52,920	68,612	1st	56,418	133,553	193,113
2d	130,881	90,593	2d	93,592	78,241	2d	123,113	85,105	212,883
3d	121,269	89,834	3d	58,878	72,497	3d	80,699	114,288	197,312
4th	134,907	82,468	4th	88,584	71,235	4th	121,344	81,740	207,880
5th	107,973	112,492	5th	111,031	45,224	5th	125,191	63,578	211,111
6th	71,952	186,499	6th	136,876	40,815	6th	193,193	59,661	257,857
7th	88,005	129,189	7th	104,359	55,941	7th	130,010	72,705	209,840
8th	125,244	108,054	8th	93,529	84,857	8th	109,860	106,201	219,864
9th	160,980	70,057	9th	84,315	91,459	9th	96,442	128,123	226,844
10th	69,362	35,049	10th	117,604	64,378	10th	72,796	85,965	162,373
IA:			IA:			IA:			
1st	81,600	178,042	1st	110,448	69,461	1st	129,242	111,595	244,596
2d	131,570	134,536	2d	111,076	86,087	2d	127,827	109,731	239,299
3d	121,063	125,931	3d	111,862	79,310	3d	111,895	115,914	234,875
4th	158,610	94,045	4th	111,935	98,824	4th	133,419	119,790	256,509
5th	....	196,942	5th	114,796	73,627	5th	147,576	75,785	225,479
KS:			KS:			KS:			
1st	83,620	194,912	1st	169,531	49,477	1st	191,899	63,948	261,145
2d	151,019	109,801	2d	135,725	71,025	2d	131,592	114,644	252,078
3d	110,071	169,929	3d	102,218	78,401	3d	139,169	126,848	279,264
4th	143,671	117,070	4th	111,653	99,366	4th	128,486	119,544	256,391
KY:			KY:			KY:			
1st	128,524	83,088	1st	64,849	62,387	1st	111,473	96,684	208,157
2d	126,894	79,684	2d	90,535	60,867	2d	125,433	90,483	215,916
3d	148,066	132,689	3d	67,238	67,663	3d	126,625	125,326	251,951
4th	86,890	139,634	4th	96,695	33,717	4th	149,135	68,939	218,074
5th	95,760	115,255	5th	82,291	21,318	5th	117,842	....	117,853
6th	135,613	87,816	6th	49,032	70,085	6th	100,231	125,999	226,230
LA:			LA:			LA:			
1st	....	([3])	1st	([2])	....	1st	([2])	....	....
2d	([3])	....	2d	....	([2])	2d	....	([3])	....
3d	([3])	....	3d	....	([2])	3d	([2])	....	....
4th	194,831	....	4th	....	([2])	4th	([3])	....	....
5th	90,079	153,501	5th	([2])	....	5th	135,990	97,363	233,353
6th	....	245,178	6th	([2])	....	6th	([3])	....	....
7th	([2])	....	7th	....	([2])	7th	....	241,800	241,800
ME:			ME:			ME:			
1st	232,696	125,236	1st	136,316	126,373	1st	140,354	173,745	314,164
2d	130,824	153,022	2d	97,754	109,615	2d	70,856	206,439	285,636
MD:			MD:			MD:			
1st	112,771	120,084	1st	120,975	57,712	1st	131,033	81,825	212,876
2d	88,658	165,443	2d	125,162	74,275	2d	143,075	88,344	231,419
3d	163,354	58,869	3d	47,966	117,269	3d	63,229	130,204	193,433
4th	136,902	45,166	4th	30,999	93,148	4th	24,700	142,094	166,794
5th	118,312	97,982	5th	69,211	98,821	5th	91,806	121,288	213,094
6th	106,224	125,564	6th	122,809	63,411	6th	132,853	100,910	233,788
7th	152,689	26,304	7th	22,007	97,016	7th	22,929	115,764	138,695
8th	77,042	203,377	8th	143,449	60,660	8th	152,538	96,229	249,146
MA:			MA:			MA:			
1st	135,049	113,828	1st	....	150,047	1st	115,801	129,232	245,111
2d	131,215	76,795	2d	72,732	117,178	2d	49,885	162,995	227,411
3d	115,587	131,473	3d	115,810	93,689	3d	115,694	135,044	255,097
4th	182,633	70,665	4th	....	168,942	4th	72,701	183,844	256,637
5th	133,844	96,206	5th	60,734	140,725	5th	....	183,429	185,137
6th	130,248	159,165	6th	120,952	113,481	6th	132,642	133,002	276,379
7th	174,837	78,262	7th	80,674	146,246	7th	76,407	177,053	253,570
8th	149,903	....	8th	....	113,224	8th	27,303	147,126	174,620
9th	175,550	54,291	9th	63,369	146,287	9th	66,079	172,009	238,152
10th	189,342	75,887	10th	78,487	172,753	10th	123,520	160,745	295,923
MI:			MI:			MI:			
1st	144,857	117,056	1st	89,660	121,433	1st	69,957	181,486	256,791
2d	86,265	155,577	2d	146,164	46,097	2d	165,608	83,603	253,699
3d	95,927	162,451	3d	136,711	43,580	3d	169,466	72,791	247,043
4th	87,573	157,337	4th	145,176	50,544	4th	159,561	79,691	243,645

VOTES CAST FOR REPRESENTATIVES, RESIDENT COMMISSIONER, AND DELEGATES IN 1992, 1994, AND 1996—CONTINUED

[The figures, compiled from official statistics obtained by the Clerk of the House, show the votes for the Democratic and Republican nominees, except as otherwise indicated. Figures in the last column, for the 1996 election, may include totals for more candidates than the ones shown. Population changes reflected in the 1990 census caused the reapportionment of congressional districts; those changes are reflected in the 1992 election results.]

State and district	Vote cast in 1992		State and district	Vote cast in 1994		State and district	Vote cast in 1996		Total vote cast in 1996
	Demo-crat	Repub-lican		Repub-lican	Demo-crat		Repub-lican	Demo-crat	
5th	147,618	93,098	5th	61,342	126,456	5th	65,542	162,675	232,451
6th	89,020	144,083	6th	121,923	42,348	6th	146,170	66,243	215,834
7th	....	133,972	7th	115,621	57,326	7th	120,227	93,725	218,544
8th	135,517	131,906	8th	109,663	95,383	8th	115,836	141,086	262,421
9th	133,956	111,798	9th	89,148	97,096	9th	89,733	136,856	231,200
10th	138,193	114,918	10th	73,862	121,876	10th	106,444	132,829	244,281
11th	117,725	168,940	11th	154,696	69,168	11th	169,165	99,303	276,618
12th	137,514	119,357	12th	92,762	103,508	12th	94,235	133,436	232,475
13th	127,642	105,169	13th	77,908	89,573	13th	89,907	123,133	217,658
14th	165,496	32,036	14th	26,215	128,463	14th	22,152	157,722	183,695
15th	148,908	31,849	15th	20,074	119,442	15th	16,009	143,683	162,600
16th	156,964	75,694	16th	71,159	105,849	16th	78,723	136,854	220,612
MN:			MN:			MN:			
1st	206,369	72,367	1st	117,613	95,328	1st	137,486	123,147	261,062
2d	132,156	131,587	2d	98,881	114,289	2d	107,807	144,083	262,353
3d	104,606	200,240	3d	173,223	62,211	3d	205,816	87,350	293,583
4th	159,796	101,744	4th	88,344	115,638	4th	94,110	145,831	255,759
5th	174,139	77,093	5th	73,258	121,515	5th	70,109	158,261	246,041
6th	100,016	133,564	6th	113,190	113,740	6th	129,988	164,921	295,481
7th	133,886	130,396	7th	102,623	108,023	7th	80,132	170,936	251,599
8th	167,104	83,823	8th	79,818	153,161	8th	69,460	185,333	275,338
MS:			MS:			MS:			
1st	121,664	82,952	1st	80,553	47,192	1st	123,724	55,998	182,966
2d	133,361	41,248	2d	49,270	68,014	2d	65,263	102,503	171,933
3d	162,864	37,710	3d	39,826	83,163	3d	115,443	68,658	188,144
4th	130,927	43,705	4th	38,200	82,939	4th	112,444	66,836	183,663
5th	120,766	67,619	5th	48,575	73,179	5th	71,114	103,415	177,445
MO:			MO:			MO:			
1st	158,693	74,482	1st	50,303	97,061	1st	51,857	131,659	187,653
2d	148,729	157,594	2d	154,882	70,480	2d	165,999	100,372	270,726
3d	174,000	90,006	3d	80,997	117,601	3d	90,202	137,300	232,755
4th	176,977	74,475	4th	65,616	137,876	4th	81,650	153,566	240,789
5th	151,014	93,562	5th	77,120	100,391	5th	61,803	144,223	213,971
6th	148,887	119,637	6th	71,709	140,108	6th	72,064	169,006	246,282
7th	99,762	160,303	7th	112,228	77,836	7th	162,558	79,306	250,584
8th	86,730	147,398	8th	129,320	48,987	8th	23,477	83,084	[4] 222,854
9th	124,694	118,811	9th	92,301	103,443	9th	123,580	117,685	250,230
MT:			MT:			MT:			
At large	203,711	189,570	At large	148,715	171,372	At large	211,975	174,516	404,426
NE:			NE:			NE:			
1st	96,309	142,713	1st	117,967	70,369	1st	157,108	67,152	224,260
2d	119,512	113,828	2d	92,516	90,750	2d	125,201	88,447	219,938
3d	67,457	170,857	3d	159,919	41,943	3d	167,758	48,833	216,591
NV:			NV:			NV:			
1st	128,278	84,217	1st	73,769	72,333	1st	86,472	75,081	172,593
2d	157,328	91,126	2d	83,121	74,243	2d	162,310	97,742	277,192
NH:			NH:			NH:			
1st	108,578	135,936	1st	97,017	42,481	1st	123,939	115,462	247,577
2d	74,866	67,225	2d	157,328	91,126	2d	122,957	105,824	243,260
NJ:			NJ:			NJ:			
1st	153,525	65,123	1st	41,505	108,155	1st	44,287	160,413	210,734
2d	132,465	98,315	2d	102,566	56,151	2d	133,131	83,890	220,718
3d	94,012	151,368	3d	115,750	54,441	3d	157,503	81,590	245,278
4th	84,514	149,095	4th	109,818	49,537	4th	146,404	77,565	230,114
5th	67,579	196,198	5th	139,964	41,275	5th	181,323	62,956	254,333
6th	118,266	100,949	6th	55,287	88,922	6th	73,402	124,635	203,478
7th	105,761	132,174	7th	98,814	64,231	7th	128,821	97,285	232,571
8th	96,742	84,674	8th	70,494	68,661	8th	92,609	98,861	193,091
9th	139,188	88,179	9th	57,651	99,984	9th	89,005	117,646	210,930
10th	117,287	30,160	10th	21,524	74,622	10th	22,086	127,126	151,060
11th	68,871	188,165	11th	127,868	50,211	11th	169,091	78,742	255,158
12th	83,035	174,216	12th	125,939	55,977	12th	135,811	125,594	269,221
13th	93,670	44,529	13th	24,071	67,688	13th	25,427	115,459	146,473
NM:			NM:			NM:			
1st	76,600	128,426	1st	119,996	42,316	1st	109,290	71,635	193,078
2d	73,157	94,838	2d	89,966	45,316	2d	95,091	74,915	170,006
3d	122,850	54,569	3d	53,515	99,900	3d	56,580	124,594	[a] 185,271
NY:			NY:			NY:			
1st	111,908	87,248	1st	72,045	78,692	1st	90,001	93,816	235,506
2d	91,320	94,208	2d	86,857	40,358	2d	97,105	53,055	203,172
3d	116,915	108,574	3d	98,628	77,774	3d	111,310	93,145	259,409
4th	97,007	98,723	4th	87,815	65,286	4th	78,004	119,946	236,238
5th	105,953	82,883	5th	63,665	89,581	5th	59,394	116,005	224,495

VOTES CAST FOR REPRESENTATIVES, RESIDENT COMMISSIONER, AND DELEGATES IN 1992, 1994, AND 1996—CONTINUED

[The figures, compiled from official statistics obtained by the Clerk of the House, show the votes for the Democratic and Republican nominees, except as otherwise indicated. Figures in the last column, for the 1996 election, may include totals for more candidates than the ones shown. Population changes reflected in the 1990 census caused the reapportionment of congressional districts; those changes are reflected in the 1992 election results.]

State and district	Vote cast in 1992	
	Democrat	Republican
6th	96,972	18,725
7th	72,280	46,218
8th	132,172	25,548
9th	111,424	....
10th	93,801	....
11th	76,724	....
12th	55,926	12,288
13th	68,738	92,144
14th	97,059	92,034
15th	101,229	....
16th	80,927	6,741
17th	94,758	16,511
18th	115,841	74,076
19th	92,854	119,047
20th	66,826	150,301
21st	149,319	83,845
22d	86,896	136,909
23d	61,835	139,774
24th	47,675	113,408
25th	101,422	119,282
26th	112,763	98,389
27th	89,906	126,997
28th	140,908	93,806
29th	120,758	85,294
30th	102,519	114,921
31st	52,010	133,758
NC:		
1st	116,078	54,457
2d	113,693	93,893
3d	101,739	80,759
4th	171,299	89,345
5th	117,835	102,086
6th	67,200	162,822
7th	92,414	66,536
8th	113,162	71,842
9th	74,583	153,650
10th	79,206	149,033
11th	108,003	130,158
12th	127,262	49,402
ND:		
At large	169,273	117,442
OH:		
1st	120,190	....
2d	75,924	177,720
3d	146,072	98,733
4th	92,608	147,346
5th	....	187,860
6th	122,720	119,252
7th	66,237	164,195
8th	62,033	176,362
9th	178,879	53,011
10th	103,788	136,433
11th	154,718	43,866
12th	68,761	170,297
13th	134,486	88,889
14th	165,335	78,659
15th	94,907	110,390
16th	90,224	158,489
17th	216,503	40,743
18th	166,189	77,229
19th	138,465	124,606
OK:		
1st	106,619	119,211
2d	118,542	87,657
3d	155,934	51,725
4th	140,841	58,235
5th	107,579	123,237
6th	134,734	64,068
OR:		
1st	152,917	140,986
2d	90,036	184,163
3d	208,028	50,235
4th	199,372	79,733

State and district	Vote cast in 1994	
	Republican	Democrat
6th	13,956	68,596
7th	....	58,935
8th	21,132	103,268
9th	30,371	90,783
10th	7,995	74,264
11th	6,311	59,850
12th	....	37,322
13th	83,509	32,060
14th	50,290	96,795
15th	....	74,566
16th	....	57,157
17th	16,896	70,486
18th	55,636	91,663
19th	100,173	70,696
20th	120,334	52,345
21st	68,745	131,916
22d	129,579	57,064
23d	124,486	40,786
24th	108,278	34,032
25th	96,363	81,710
26th	82,917	90,852
27th	122,592	52,160
28th	61,321	110,987
29th	69,290	97,619
30th	106,551	58,577
31st	106,898	....
NC:		
1st	42,602	66,827
2d	79,207	62,122
3d	72,464	65,013
4th	77,773	76,558
5th	84,741	63,194
6th	98,355	....
7th	58,849	62,670
8th	57,140	62,845
9th	82,374	44,379
10th	107,829	42,939
11th	115,826	76,862
12th	29,933	57,655
ND:		
At large	105,988	123,134
OH:		
1st	92,997	72,822
2d	150,128	43,730
3d	72,314	105,342
4th	139,841	....
5th	135,879	49,335
6th	91,263	87,861
7th	140,124	....
8th	148,338	....
9th	38,665	118,120
10th	95,226	70,918
11th	33,705	114,220
12th	114,608	57,294
13th	86,422	93,147
14th	89,106	96,274
15th	112,912	46,480
16th	137,322	45,781
17th	43,490	149,004
18th	103,115	87,926
19th	99,997	89,701
OK:		
1st	107,085	63,753
2d	82,479	75,943
3d	41,147	115,731
4th	80,251	67,237
5th	136,877	....
6th	106,961	45,399
OR:		
1st	120,846	121,147
2d	134,255	90,822
3d	43,211	161,624
4th	78,947	158,981

State and district	Vote cast in 1996		Total vote cast in 1996
	Republican	Democrat	
6th	13,986	102,799	153,238
7th	24,826	78,848	151,185
8th	25,005	123,809	197,860
9th	27,829	102,556	178,160
10th	6,827	97,125	153,666
11th	5,369	87,559	133,934
12th	7,824	58,947	100,185
13th	74,836	51,448	183,921
14th	42,641	122,504	211,303
15th	5,951	108,680	155,236
16th	2,878	86,971	130,722
17th	11,488	97,891	153,797
18th	51,656	118,194	213,574
19th	98,705	83,975	243,986
20th	122,479	77,756	245,812
21st	62,630	136,964	267,608
22d	119,467	94,192	265,794
23d	118,653	50,436	226,149
24th	108,777	43,692	209,946
25th	106,327	103,199	242,136
26th	78,946	117,097	238,437
27th	117,818	91,679	260,311
28th	85,038	133,084	250,094
29th	66,438	126,210	238,399
30th	97,320	97,686	241,405
31st	119,395	49,502	225,718
NC:			
1st	54,666	108,759	165,028
2d	98,951	113,820	216,629
3d	118,159	68,887	188,579
4th	126,466	157,194	288,984
5th	130,177	74,320	209,698
6th	167,828	58,022	228,543
7th	75,811	87,487	165,440
8th	81,676	103,129	186,908
9th	147,755	83,078	234,710
10th	158,585	65,103	226,597
11th	132,860	91,257	228,025
12th	46,581	124,675	174,399
ND:			
At large	113,684	144,833	263,010
OH:			
1st	118,324	94,719	218,424
2d	186,853	58,715	259,473
3d	75,732	144,583	227,203
4th	147,608	69,096	227,761
5th	145,892	81,170	238,523
6th	111,907	118,003	229,926
7th	158,087	61,419	233,001
8th	165,815	61,515	235,943
9th	46,040	170,617	221,334
10th	104,546	110,723	225,696
11th	28,821	153,546	189,039
12th	151,667	78,762	237,434
13th	87,108	148,690	244,505
14th	95,307	124,136	228,435
15th	156,776	64,665	221,441
16th	159,314	64,902	231,827
17th	....	218,283	239,968
18th	117,365	108,332	233,843
19th	135,012	101,152	246,819
OK:			
1st	143,415	57,996	210,407
2d	112,273	90,120	202,393
3d	98,526	86,647	191,508
4th	106,923	73,950	185,373
5th	148,362	57,594	212,791
6th	113,499	64,173	177,672
OR:			
1st	126,146	144,588	278,604
2d	164,062	97,195	266,056
3d	65,259	165,922	247,909
4th	76,649	177,270	269,856

VOTES CAST FOR REPRESENTATIVES, RESIDENT COMMISSIONER, AND DELEGATES IN 1992, 1994, AND 1996—CONTINUED

[The figures, compiled from official statistics obtained by the Clerk of the House, show the votes for the Democratic and Republican nominees, except as otherwise indicated. Figures in the last column, for the 1996 election, may include totals for more candidates than the ones shown. Population changes reflected in the 1990 census caused the reapportionment of congressional districts; those changes are reflected in the 1992 election results.]

State and district	Vote cast in 1992		State and district	Vote cast in 1994		State and district	Vote cast in 1996		Total vote cast in 1996
	Demo-crat	Repub-lican		Repub-lican	Demo-crat		Repub-lican	Demo-crat	
5th	174,443	97,984	5th	121,369	114,015	5th	125,409	139,521	272,636
PA:			PA:			PA:			
1st	150,172	35,419	1st	22,595	99,669	1st	20,734	145,210	165,945
2d	164,355	47,906	2d	19,824	120,553	2d	23,047	168,887	191,937
3d	130,828	86,787	3d	55,209	92,702	3d	54,681	121,120	175,801
4th	186,684	48,484	4th	66,509	119,115	4th	79,448	142,621	222,167
5th	....	188,911	5th	145,335	....	5th	116,303	76,627	193,003
6th	108,312	99,694	6th	68,610	90,023	6th	80,061	115,193	196,729
7th	91,623	180,648	7th	137,480	59,845	7th	165,087	79,875	246,666
8th	114,095	129,593	8th	110,499	44,559	8th	133,749	79,856	226,322
9th	....	182,406	9th	146,688	....	9th	142,105	50,650	192,822
10th	....	189,414	10th	106,992	50,635	10th	124,670	75,536	208,540
11th	138,875	68,112	11th	51,295	101,966	11th	60,339	128,258	188,609
12th	166,916	....	12th	53,147	117,825	12th	58,643	136,815	195,481
13th	127,685	126,312	13th	96,254	88,073	13th	120,304	120.220	245,979
14th	165,633	61,311	14th	53,221	105,310	14th	78,921	122,922	202,578
15th	111,419	99,520	15th	71,602	72,073	15th	82,803	109,812	200,363
16th	74,741	137,823	16th	109,759	47,680	16th	124,511	78,598	209,602
17th	65,881	150,158	17th	133,788	....	17th	150,678	57,911	208,616
18th	96,655	154,024	18th	83,881	101,784	18th	86,829	120,410	214,990
19th	74,798	98,599	19th	124,496	....	19th	130,716	74,944	208,963
20th	114,898	111,591	20th	84,156	95,251	20th	97,004	113,394	210,402
21st	70,802	150,729	21st	89,439	84,796	21st	106,875	104,004	210,888
RI:			RI:			RI:			
1st	48,092	135,982	1st	76,069	89,832	1st	49,199	121,781	175,425
2d	144,450	49,998	2d	56,348	119,659	2d	58,458	118,827	184,318
SC:			SC:			SC:			
1st	59,908	121,938	1st	97,803	47,769	1st	138,467	....	143,572
2d	....	148,667	2d	133,307	....	2d	158,229	....	175,942
3d	119,119	75,660	3d	90,123	59,932	3d	114,273	73,417	189,525
4th	94,182	99,879	4th	109,626	39,396	4th	138,165	54,126	194,792
5th	112,031	70,866	5th	70,967	77,311	5th	81,455	97,335	179,949
6th	120,647	64,149	6th	50,259	88,635	6th	51,974	120,132	173,054
SD:			SD:			SD:			
At large ...	230,070	89,375	At large ..	112,054	183,036	At large ..	186,393	119,547	323,203
TN:			TN:			TN:			
1st	47,809	114,797	1st	102,947	34,691	1st	117,676	58,657	181,708
2d	52,887	148,377	2d	128,937	....	2d	150,953	61,020	213,574
3d	105,693	102,763	3d	84,583	73,839	3d	113,408	85,714	201,444
4th	98,984	50,340	4th	81,539	60,489	4th	103,091	73,331	178,063
5th	125,233	49,417	5th	61,692	95,953	5th	46,201	140,264	193,783
6th	120,177	86,289	6th	88,759	90,933	6th	94,599	123,846	227,571
7th	72,062	125,101	7th	102,587	65,851	7th	126,737	64,512	193,742
8th	136,852	....	8th	55,573	97,951	8th	55,024	123,681	183,898
9th	123,276	60,606	9th	69,226	94,805	9th	70,951	116,345	190,414
TX:			TX:			TX:			
1st	152,209	....	1st	63,911	86,480	1st	93,105	102,697	199,170
2d	118,625	92,176	2d	66,071	87,709	2d	89,838	102,908	196,971
3d	....	201,569	3d	157,011	....	3d	142,325	47,654	195,026
4th	128,008	83,875	4th	67,267	99,303	4th	71,065	132,126	207,177
5th	98,567	62,419	5th	58,521	61,877	5th	80,196	70,922	151,119
6th	73,933	189,140	6th	152,038	44,286	6th	160,800	26,713	208,516
7th	....	169,407	7th	116,873	....	7th	152,024	28,187	186,831
8th	53,473	179,349	8th	148,473	....	8th	51,370	....	[5] 51,370
9th	118,690	96,270	9th	81,353	71,643	9th	52,870	59,225	[6] 112,095
10th	177,233	68,646	10th	80,382	113,738	10th	97,204	132,066	234,991
11th	119,999	58,033	11th	52,876	76,667	11th	74,549	99,990	175,935
12th	125,492	74,432	12th	43,959	96,372	12th	98,349	69,859	170,204
13th	117,892	77,514	13th	79,466	63,923	13th	116,098	56,066	173,627
14th	135,930	54,412	14th	68,793	86,175	14th	99,961	93,200	195,699
15th	86,351	56,549	15th	41,119	61,527	15th	50,914	86,347	138,594
16th	66,731	61,870	16th	37,409	49,815	16th	35,271	90,260	127,784
17th	136,213	69,958	17th	72,108	83,497	17th	91,429	99,678	192,994
18th	111,422	56,080	18th	28,153	84,790	18th	27,165	110,523	137,688
19th	47,325	162,057	19th	120,641	....	19th	156,910	38,316	195,226
20th	103,755	....	20th	36,035	60,114	20th	47,616	88,190	138,409
21st	62,827	190,979	21st	165,595	....	21st	205,830	60,338	269,307
22d	67,812	150,221	22d	120,302	38,826	22d	126,056	59,030	185,086
23d	63,797	98,259	23d	73,815	44,101	23d	101,332	59,596	163,839
24th	104,174	70,042	24th	58,062	65,019	24th	54,551	82,503	139,637
25th	98,975	73,192	25th	53,321	61,959	25th	21,892	29,396	[6] 51,288
26th	55,237	150,209	26th	135,398	39,763	26th	163,708	58,623	222,342
27th	87,022	66,853	27th	44,693	65,325	27th	50,964	97,350	150,600

VOTES CAST FOR REPRESENTATIVES, RESIDENT COMMISSIONER, AND DELEGATES IN 1992, 1994, AND 1996—CONTINUED

[The figures, compiled from official statistics obtained by the Clerk of the House, show the votes for the Democratic and Republican nominees, except as otherwise indicated. Figures in the last column, for the 1996 election, may include totals for more candidates than the ones shown. Population changes reflected in the 1990 census caused the reapportionment of congressional districts; those changes are reflected in the 1992 election results.]

State and district	Vote cast in 1992		State and district	Vote cast in 1994		State and district	Vote cast in 1996		Total vote cast in 1996
	Demo-crat	Repub-lican		Repub-lican	Demo-crat		Repub-lican	Demo-crat	
28th	122,457	....	28th	28,777	73,986	28th	34,191	110,148	146,135
29th	64,064	34,609	29th	15,952	44,102	29th	28,381	61,751	91,472
30th	107,831	37,853	30th	25,848	73,166	30th	28,425	79,397	113,072
UT:			UT:			UT:			
1st	68,712	160,037	1st	104,954	57,664	1st	150,126	65,866	219,779
2d	127,738	118,307	2d	85,507	66,911	2d	129,963	100,283	236,321
3d	135,029	84,019	3d	61,839	91,505	3d	106,220	98,178	207,715
VT:			VT:			VT:			
At large	22,279	86,901	At large	98,523	At large	....	83,021	23,830	(7) 254,706
VA:			VA:			VA:			
1st	89,814	133,537	1st	142,930	45,173	1st	165,574	....	167,235
2d	99,253	77,797	2d	56,375	81,372	2d	57,586	106,215	163,996
3d	132,432	35,780	3d	28,080	108,532	3d	25,781	118,603	144,418
4th	147,649	68,286	4th	71,678	115,055	4th	43,516	160,100	203,666
5th	133,031	60,030	5th	83,555	95,308	5th	70,869	120,323	197,923
6th	84,618	127,309	6th	126,455	....	6th	133,576	61,485	199,361
7th	....	211,618	7th	176,941	....	7th	189,644	51,206	252,505
8th	138,542	102,717	8th	79,568	120,281	8th	64,562	152,334	229,421
9th	133,284	77,985	9th	72,133	102,876	9th	58,055	122,908	189,077
10th	75,775	144,471	10th	153,311	....	10th	169,266	59,145	235,013
11th	114,172	103,119	11th	98,216	84,104	11th	138,758	74,701	216,482
WA:			WA:			WA:			
1st	148,844	113,897	1st	100,554	94,110	1st	141,948	122,187	264,135
2d	133,207	107,365	2d	107,430	89,096	2d	124,655	122,728	256,944
3d	138,043	108,583	3d	100,188	85,826	3d	123,117	122,230	245,347
4th	106,556	103,028	4th	92,828	81,198	4th	108,647	96,502	205,149
5th	135,965	110,443	5th	110,057	106,074	5th	131,618	105,166	236,784
6th	152,933	66,664	6th	75,322	105,480	6th	71,337	155,467	235,910
7th	222,604	54,149	7th	49,091	148,353	7th	49,341	209,753	259,094
8th	87,611	155,874	8th	140,409	44,165	8th	170,691	90,340	261,031
9th	110,902	91,910	9th	77,833	72,451	9th	99,199	105,236	209,867
WV:			WV:			WV:			
1st	172,924	....	1st	43,590	103,177	1st	....	171,334	171,334
2d	143,988	59,102	2d	51,691	90,757	2d	63,933	141,551	205,484
3d	122,279	64,012	3d	42,382	74,967	3d	....	145,550	145,550
WI:			WI:			WI:			
1st	147,495	104,352	1st	83,937	82,817	1st	118,408	114,148	232,801
2d	108,291	183,366	2d	133,734	55,406	2d	154,557	110,467	269,374
3d	108,664	146,903	3d	89,338	65,758	3d	112,146	121,967	234,650
4th	173,482	84,872	4th	78,225	93,789	4th	98,438	134,470	233,284
5th	162,344	71,085	5th	51,145	87,806	5th	47,384	141,179	192,569
6th	128,232	143,875	6th	119,384	....	6th	169,213	55,377	231,719
7th	166,200	91,772	7th	81,706	97,184	7th	103,365	137,428	240,898
8th	81,792	191,704	8th	114,319	65,065	8th	119,398	129,551	249,157
9th	77,362	192,898	9th	141,617	....	9th	197,910	67,740	265,875
WY:			WY:			WY:			
At large	77,418	113,882	At large	104,426	81,022	At large	116,004	85,724	209,983

VOTES CAST FOR REPRESENTATIVES, RESIDENT COMMISSIONER, AND DELEGATES IN 1992, 1994, AND 1996—CONTINUED

Commonwealth of Puerto Rico	Vote						Total vote cast in **1996**
	1992		**1994**		**1996**		
	Popular Democrat	New Progressive	Popular Democrat	New Progressive	New Progressive	Popular Democrat	
Resident Commissioner (4-year term)	891,176	904,067	....	....	973,654	904,048	1,946,529

District of Columbia	Vote						Total vote cast in **1996**
	1992		**1994**		**1996**		
	Democrat	Republican	Democrat	Republican	Republican	Democrat	
Delegate At large	166,808	20,108	154,988	13,828	11,306	134,996	149,998

Guam	Vote						Total vote cast in **1996**
	1992		**1994**		**1996**		
	Democrat	Republican	Democrat	Republican	Republican	Democrat	
Delegate At large	18,462	14,921	....	36,379	....	34,395	34,395

Virgin Islands	Vote						Total vote cast in **1996**
	1992		**1994**		**1996**		
	Democrat	Republican	Democrat	Independent	Republican	Democrat	
Delegate At large	14,084	8,913	13,817	16,561	3,973	4,162	(8) 15,351

American Samoa	Vote						Total vote cast in **1996**
	1992		**1994**		**1996**		
	Democrat	Republican	Democrat	Republican	Republican	Democrat	
Delegate At large	7,955	2,263	6,517	2,116	....	6,321	(9) 11,192

1 Under Florida State law, the names of those with no opposition are not printed on the ballot.
2 Under Louisiana State law, the names of those with no opposition are not printed on the ballot.
3 Under Louisiana State law, a candidate receiving at least 51 percent of the vote cast in the primary election is elected to the congressional seat.
4 The Independent candidate was elected with 112,472 votes, and was also elected on a separate ballot as a Republican by a special election to fill the vacancy in the seat for the remainder of the 104th Congress. The member changed party affiliation to Republican after the organization of the 105th Congress.
5 A runoff election was held on December 10, 1996. Both candidates in the runoff election were Republicans; the winner received 30,366 votes.
6 A runoff election was held on December 10, 1996.
7 The independent candidate was elected with 140,678 votes.
8 A runoff election was held on November 19, 1996 between the Democratic and Independent candidates. The Democratic candidate was elected with 12,869 votes.
9 A runoff election was held on November 19, 1996.

SESSIONS OF CONGRESS

[Closing date for this table was April 8, 1997. See additional notes at end of the table.]

MEETING DATE AND PLACES OF CONGRESS: The Constitution (Article I, section 4) originally provided that ''The Congress shall assemble at least once in every Year, and such Meeting shall be on the first Monday in December, unless they shall by law appoint a different day.'' Pursuant to a resolution of the Congress of the Confederation in 1788, the first session of the First Congress under the Constitution convened March 4, 1789. Up to and including May 20, 1820, 18 acts were passed providing for the meeting of Congress on other days in the year. The Congress met regularly on the first Monday in December until 1934, when the 20th amendment to the Constitution became effective, changing the meeting of Congress to January 3. Please see note 3, at the end of this table, concerning extraordinary sessions of the Congress, as well as the next table about special sessions of the Senate. The first and second sessions of the First Congress were held in New York City; subsequently, including the first session of the Sixth Congress, Philadelphia was the meeting place; since then Congress has convened in Washington.

Congress	Session	Date of beginning	Date of adjournment	Length in days	Recesses: Senate	Recesses: House	President pro tempore of the Senate [1]	Speaker of the House of Representatives
1st	1	Mar. 4, 1789	Sept. 29, 1789	210			John Langdon,[2] of New Hampshire	Frederick A.C. Muhlenberg, of Pennsylvania.
	2	Jan. 4, 1790	Aug. 12, 1790	221			......do..	
	3	Dec. 6, 1790	Mar. 3, 1791	88			......do..	
2d *	1	Oct. 24, 1791	May 8, 1792	197			Richard Henry Lee, of Virginia	Jonathan Trumbull, of Connecticut.
	2	Nov. 5, 1792	Mar. 2, 1793	119			John Langdon, of New Hampshire.	
3d *	1	Dec. 2, 1793	June 9, 1794	190			......do Ralph Izard, of South Carolina	Frederick A.C. Muhlenberg, of Pennsylvania.
	2	Nov. 3, 1794	Mar. 3, 1795	121			Henry Tazewell, of Virginia.	
4th *	1	Dec. 7, 1795	June 1, 1796	177			......do Samuel Livermore, of New Hampshire	Jonathan Dayton, of New Jersey.
	2	Dec. 5, 1796	Mar. 3, 1797	89			William Bingham, of Pennsylvania.	
5th *	1	May 15, 1797[3]	July 10, 1797	57			William Bradford, of Rhode Island	Do.
	2	Nov. 13, 1797	July 16, 1798	246			Jacob Read, of South Carolina Theodore Sedgwick, of Massachusetts	George Dent, of Maryland.[4]
	3	Dec. 3, 1798	Mar. 3, 1799	91			John Laurence, of New York. James Ross, of Pennsylvania.	
6th	1	Dec. 2, 1799	May 14, 1800	164			Samuel Livermore, of New Hampshire Uriah Tracy, of Connecticut	Theodore Sedgwick, of Massachusetts.
	2	Nov. 17, 1800	Mar. 3, 1801	107	Dec. 23–Dec. 30, 1800	Dec. 23–Dec. 30, 1800	John E. Howard, of Maryland. James Hillhouse, of Connecticut.	
7th *	1	Dec. 7, 1801	May 3, 1802	148			Abraham Baldwin, of Georgia	Nathaniel Macon, of North Carolina.
	2	Dec. 6, 1802	Mar. 3, 1803	88			Stephen R. Bradley, of Vermont.	
8th	1	Oct. 17, 1803[3]	Mar. 27, 1804	163			John Brown, of Kentucky Jesse Franklin, of North Carolina	Do.
	2	Nov. 5, 1804	Mar. 3, 1805	119			Joseph Anderson, of Tennessee.	
9th	1	Dec. 2, 1805	Apr. 21, 1806	141			Samuel Smith, of Maryland	Do.
	2	Dec. 1, 1806	Mar. 3, 1807	93			......do.	
10th	1	Oct. 26, 1807[3]	Apr. 25, 1808	182			......do	Joseph B. Varnum, of Massachusetts.
	2	Nov. 7, 1808	Mar. 3, 1809	117			Stephen R. Bradley, of Vermont. John Milledge, of Georgia.	
11th *	1	May 22, 1809	June 28, 1809	38			Andrew Gregg, of Pennsylvania	Do.
	2	Nov. 27, 1809	May 1, 1810	156			John Gaillard, of South Carolina.	
	3	Dec. 3, 1810	Mar. 3, 1811	91			John Pope, of Kentucky.	
12th	1	Nov. 4, 1811[3]	July 6, 1812	245			William H. Crawford, of Georgia	Henry Clay, of Kentucky.
	2	Nov. 2, 1812	Mar. 3, 1813	122			......do.	
13th	1	May 24, 1813	Aug. 2, 1813	71			......do	Do.

SESSIONS OF CONGRESS—CONTINUED

[Closing date for this table was April 8, 1997. See additional notes at end of the table.]

MEETING DATE AND PLACES OF CONGRESS: The Constitution (Article I, section 4) originally provided that "The Congress shall assemble at least once in every Year, and such Meeting shall be on the first Monday in December, unless they shall by law appoint a different day." Pursuant to a resolution of the Congress of the Confederation in 1788, the first session of the First Congress under the Constitution convened March 4, 1789. Up to and including May 20, 1820, 18 acts were passed providing for the meeting of Congress on other days in the year. The Congress met regularly on the first Monday in December until 1934, when the 20th amendment to the Constitution became effective, changing the meeting of Congress to January 3. Please see note 3, at the end of this table, concerning extraordinary sessions of the Congress, as well as the next table about special sessions of the Senate. The first and second sessions of the First Congress were held in New York City; subsequently, including the first session of the Sixth Congress, Philadelphia was the meeting place; since then Congress has convened in Washington.

Congress	Session	Date of beginning	Date of adjournment	Length in days	Recesses		President pro tempore of the Senate[1]	Speaker of the House of Representatives
					Senate	House		
	2	Dec. 6, 1813	Apr. 18, 1814	134			Joseph B. Varnum, of Massachusetts.	
	3	Sept. 19, 1814[3]	Mar. 3, 1815	166			John Gaillard, of South Carolina	Langdon Cheves,[5] of South Carolina.
14th	1	Dec. 4, 1815	Apr. 30, 1816	148			do	Henry Clay, of Kentucky.
	2	Dec. 2, 1816	Mar. 3, 1817	92			do.	
15th *	1	Dec. 1, 1817	Apr. 20, 1818	141	Dec. 24–Dec. 29, 1817	Dec. 24–Dec. 29, 1817	do	Do.
	2	Nov. 16, 1818	Mar. 3, 1819	108			James Barbour, of Virginia.	
16th	1	Dec. 6, 1819	May 15, 1820	162			John Gaillard, of South Carolina	Do.
	2	Nov. 13, 1820	Mar. 3, 1821	111			do	John W. Taylor,[6] of New York.
17th	1	Dec. 3, 1821	May 8, 1822	157			do	Philip P. Barbour, of Virginia.
	2	Dec. 2, 1822	Mar. 3, 1823	92			do.	
18th	1	Dec. 1, 1823	May 27, 1824	178			do	Henry Clay, of Kentucky.
	2	Dec. 6, 1824	Mar. 3, 1825	88			do.	
19th *	1	Dec. 5, 1825	May 22, 1826	169			Nathaniel Macon, of North Carolina	John W. Taylor, of New York.
	2	Dec. 4, 1826	Mar. 3, 1827	90			do.	
20th	1	Dec. 3, 1827	May 26, 1828	175			Samuel Smith, of Maryland	Andrew Stevenson, of Virginia.
	2	Dec. 1, 1828	Mar. 3, 1829	93	Dec. 24–Dec. 29, 1828	Dec. 24–Dec. 29, 1828	do.	
21st *	1	Dec. 7, 1829	May 31, 1830	176			do	Do.
	2	Dec. 6, 1830	Mar. 3, 1831	88			Littleton Waller Tazewell, of Virginia.	
22d	1	Dec. 5, 1831	July 16, 1832	225			do	Do.
	2	Dec. 3, 1832	Mar. 2, 1833	91			Hugh Lawson White, of Tennessee.	
23d	1	Dec. 2, 1833	June 30, 1834	211			George Poindexter, of Mississippi	Do.
	2	Dec. 1, 1834	Mar. 3, 1835	93			John Tyler, of Virginia	John Bell,[7] of Tennessee.
24th	1	Dec. 7, 1835	July 4, 1836	211			William R. King, of Alabama	James K. Polk, of Tennessee.
	2	Dec. 5, 1836	Mar. 3, 1837	89			do.	
25th *	1	Sept. 4, 1837[3]	Oct. 16, 1837	43			do	Do.
	2	Dec. 4, 1837	July 9, 1838	218			do.	
	3	Dec. 3, 1838	Mar. 3, 1839	91			do.	
26th	1	Dec. 2, 1839	July 21, 1840	233			do	Robert M.T. Hunter, of Virginia.
	2	Dec. 7, 1840	Mar. 3, 1841	87			do.	
27th *	1	May 31, 1841[3]	Sept. 13, 1841	106			Samuel L. Southard, of New Jersey	John White, of Kentucky.
	2	Dec. 6, 1841	Aug. 31, 1842	269			Willie P. Mangum, of North Carolina.	
	3	Dec. 5, 1842	Mar. 3, 1843	89			do.	
28th	1	Dec. 4, 1843	June 17, 1844	196			do	John W. Jones, of Virginia.
	2	Dec. 2, 1844	Mar. 3, 1845	92			do.	
29th *	1	Dec. 1, 1845	Aug. 10, 1846	253			David R. Atchison, of Missouri	John W. Davis, of Indiana.
	2	Dec. 7, 1846	Mar. 3, 1847	87			do.	
30th	1	Dec. 6, 1847	Aug. 14, 1848	254			do	Robert C. Winthrop, of Massachusetts.

	2	Dec. 4, 1848	Mar. 3, 1849	90			......do.	
31st *	1	Dec. 3, 1849	Sept. 30, 1850	302			William R. King, of Alabama	Howell Cobb, of Georgia.
	2	Dec. 2, 1850	Mar. 3, 1851	92			......do.	
32d *	1	Dec. 1, 1851	Aug. 31, 1852	275			......do	Linn Boyd, of Kentucky.
	2	Dec. 6, 1852	Mar. 3, 1853	88			David R. Atchison, of Missouri.	
33d *	1	Dec. 5, 1853	Aug. 7, 1854	246			......do	Do.
	2	Dec. 4, 1854	Mar. 3, 1855	90			Jesse D. Bright, of Indiana. Lewis Cass, of Michigan.	
34th	1	Dec. 3, 1855	Aug. 18, 1856	260			Jesse D. Bright, of Indiana	Nathaniel P. Banks, of Massachusetts.
	2	Aug. 21, 1856[3]	Aug. 30, 1856	10			......do.	
	3	Dec. 1, 1856	Mar. 3, 1857	93			James M. Mason, of Virginia. Thomas J. Rusk, of Texas.	
35th *	1	Dec. 7, 1857	June 14, 1858	189	Dec. 23, 1857–Jan. 4, 1858	Dec. 23, 1857–Jan. 4, 1858	Benjamin Fitzpatrick, of Alabama	James L. Orr, of South Carolina.
	2	Dec. 6, 1858	Mar. 3, 1859	88	Dec. 23, 1858–Jan. 4, 1859	Dec. 23, 1858–Jan. 4, 1859	......do.	
36th *	1	Dec. 5, 1859	June 25, 1860	202			Benjamin Fitzpatrick, of Alabama	William Pennington, of New Jersey.
	2	Dec. 3, 1860	Mar. 3, 1861	93			Jesse D. Bright, of Indiana. Solomon Foot, of Vermont.	William Pennington, of New Jersey.
37th *	1	July 4, 1861[3]	Aug. 6, 1861	34			......do	Galusha A. Grow, of Pennsylvania.
	2	Dec. 2, 1861	July 17, 1862	228			......do.	
	3	Dec. 1, 1862	Mar. 3, 1863	93	Dec. 23, 1862–Jan. 5, 1863	Dec. 23, 1862–Jan. 5, 1863	......do.	
38th *	1	Dec. 7, 1863	July 4, 1864	209	Dec. 23, 1863–Jan. 5, 1864	Dec. 23, 1863–Jan. 5, 1864	......do	Schuyler Colfax, of Indiana.
	2	Dec. 5, 1864	Mar. 3, 1865	89	Dec. 22, 1864–Jan. 5, 1865	Dec. 22, 1864–Jan. 5, 1865	Daniel Clark, of New Hampshire. ......do.	
39th *	1	Dec. 4, 1865	July 28, 1866	237	Dec. 6–Dec. 11, 1865 Dec. 21, 1865–Jan. 5, 1866	Dec. 6–Dec. 11, 1865 Dec. 21, 1865–Jan. 5, 1866	Lafayette S. Foster, of Connecticut Benjamin F. Wade, of Ohio.	Do.
	2	Dec. 3, 1866	Mar. 3, 1867	91	Dec. 20, 1866–Jan. 3, 1867	Dec. 20, 1866–Jan. 3, 1867	......do.	
40th *	1	Mar. 4, 1867	Dec. 1, 1867	273	Mar. 30–July 3, 1867 July 20–Nov. 21, 1867	Mar. 30–July 3, 1867 July 20–Nov. 21, 1867	......do	Do.
	2	Dec. 2, 1867	Nov. 10, 1868	345	Dec. 20, 1867–Jan. 6, 1868 July 27–Sept. 21, 1868 Sept. 21–Oct. 16, 1868 Oct. 16–Nov. 10, 1868	Dec. 20, 1867–Jan. 6, 1868 July 27–Sept. 21, 1868 Sept. 21–Oct. 16, 1868 Oct. 16–Nov. 10, 1868		
	3	Dec. 7, 1868	Mar. 3, 1869	87	Dec. 21, 1868–Jan. 5, 1869	Dec. 21, 1868–Jan. 5, 1869	......do	Theodore M. Pomeroy,[8] of New York.
41st *	1	Mar. 4, 1869	Apr. 10, 1869	38			Henry B. Anthony, of Rhode Island	James G. Blaine, of Maine.
	2	Dec. 6, 1869	July 15, 1870	222	Dec. 22, 1869–Jan. 10, 1870	Dec. 22, 1869–Jan. 10, 1870	......do.	
	3	Dec. 5, 1870	Mar. 3, 1871	89	Dec. 23, 1870–Jan. 4, 1871	Dec. 22, 1870–Jan. 4, 1871	......do.	
42d *	1	Mar. 4, 1871	Apr. 20, 1871	48			......do	Do.
	2	Dec. 4, 1871	June 10, 1872	190	Dec. 21, 1871–Jan. 8, 1872	Dec. 21, 1871–Jan. 8, 1872	......do.	
	3	Dec. 2, 1872	Mar. 3, 1873	92	Dec. 20, 1872–Jan. 6, 1873	Dec. 20, 1872–Jan. 6, 1873	......do.	
43d *	1	Dec. 1, 1873	June 23, 1874	204	Dec. 19, 1873–Jan. 5, 1874	Dec. 19, 1873–Jan. 5, 1874	Matthew H. Carpenter, of Wisconsin	Do.
	2	Dec. 7, 1874	Mar. 3, 1875	87	Dec. 23, 1874–Jan. 5, 1875	Dec. 23, 1874–Jan. 5, 1875	......do	
44th *	1	Dec. 6, 1875	Aug. 15, 1876	254	Dec. 20, 1875–Jan. 5, 1876	Dec. 21, 1875–Jan. 5, 1876	Henry B. Anthony, of Rhode Island. Thomas W. Ferry, of Michigan	Michael C. Kerr,[9] of Indiana. Samuel S. Cox,[10] of New York, pro tempore. Milton Sayler,[11] of Ohio, pro tempore.
	2	Dec. 4, 1876	Mar. 3, 1877	90			......do	Samuel J. Randall, of Pennsylvania.
45th *	1	Oct. 15, 1877[3]	Dec. 3, 1877	50			......do	Do.
	2	Dec. 3, 1877	June 20, 1878	200	Dec. 15, 1877–Jan. 10, 1878	Dec. 15, 1877–Jan. 10, 1878	......do.	
	3	Dec. 2, 1878	Mar. 3, 1879	92	Dec. 20, 1878–Jan. 7, 1879	Dec. 20, 1878–Jan. 7, 1879	......do.	

SESSIONS OF CONGRESS—CONTINUED

[Closing date for this table was April 8, 1997. See additional notes at end of the table.]

MEETING DATE AND PLACES OF CONGRESS: The Constitution (Article I, section 4) originally provided that "The Congress shall assemble at least once in every Year, and such Meeting shall be on the first Monday in December, unless they shall by law appoint a different day." Pursuant to a resolution of the Congress of the Confederation in 1788, the first session of the First Congress under the Constitution convened March 4, 1789. Up to and including May 20, 1820, 18 acts were passed providing for the meeting of Congress on other days in the year. The Congress met regularly on the first Monday in December until 1934, when the 20th amendment to the Constitution became effective, changing the meeting of Congress to January 3. Please see note 3, at the end of this table, concerning extraordinary sessions of the Congress, as well as the next table about special sessions of the Senate. The first and second sessions of the First Congress were held in New York City; subsequently, including the first session of the Sixth Congress, Philadelphia was the meeting place; since then Congress has convened in Washington.

Congress	Session	Date of beginning	Date of adjournment	Length in days	Recesses		President pro tempore of the Senate [1]	Speaker of the House of Representatives
					Senate	House		
46th	1	Mar. 18, 1879 [3]	July 1, 1879	106			Allen G. Thurman, of Ohio	Samuel J. Randall, of Pennsylvania.
	2	Dec. 1, 1879	June 16, 1880	199	Dec. 19, 1879–Jan. 6, 1880	Dec. 19, 1879–Jan. 6, 1880	do.	
	3	Dec. 6, 1880	Mar. 3, 1881	88	Dec. 23, 1880–Jan. 5, 1881	Dec. 23, 1880–Jan. 5, 1881	do.	
47th *	1	Dec. 5, 1881	Aug. 8, 1882	247	Dec. 22, 1881–Jan. 5, 1882	Dec. 22, 1881–Jan. 5, 1882	Thomas F. Bayard, of Delaware David Davis, of Illinois.	J. Warren Keifer, of Ohio.
	2	Dec. 4, 1882	Mar. 3, 1883	90			George F. Edmunds, of Vermont.	
48th	1	Dec. 3, 1883	July 7, 1884	218	Dec. 24, 1883–Jan. 7, 1884	Dec. 24, 1883–Jan. 7, 1884	do	John G. Carlisle, of Kentucky.
	2	Dec. 1, 1884	Mar. 3, 1885	93	Dec. 24, 1884–Jan. 5, 1885	Dec. 24, 1884–Jan. 5, 1885	do.	
49th *	1	Dec. 7, 1885	Aug. 5, 1886	242	Dec. 21, 1885–Jan. 5, 1886	Dec. 21, 1885–Jan. 5, 1886	John Sherman, of Ohio	Do.
	2	Dec. 6, 1886	Mar. 3, 1887	88	Dec. 22, 1886–Jan. 4, 1887	Dec. 22, 1886–Jan. 4, 1887	John J. Ingalls, of Kansas.	
50th	1	Dec. 5, 1887	Oct. 20, 1888	321	Dec. 22, 1887–Jan. 4, 1888	Dec. 22, 1887–Jan. 4, 1888	do	Do.
	2	Dec. 3, 1888	Mar. 3, 1889	91	Dec. 21, 1888–Jan. 2, 1889	Dec. 21, 1888–Jan. 2, 1889	do.	
51st *	1	Dec. 2, 1889	Oct. 1, 1890	304	Dec. 21, 1889–Jan. 6, 1890	Dec. 21, 1889–Jan. 6, 1890	do	Thomas B. Reed, of Maine.
	2	Dec. 1, 1890	Mar. 3, 1891	93			Charles F. Manderson, of Nebraska.	
52d	1	Dec. 7, 1891	Aug. 5, 1892	251			do	Charles F. Crisp, of Georgia.
	2	Dec. 5, 1892	Mar. 3, 1893	89	Dec. 22, 1892–Jan. 4, 1893	Dec. 22, 1892–Jan. 4, 1893	Isham G. Harris, of Tennessee.	
53d *	1	Aug. 7, 1893 [3]	Nov. 3, 1893	89			do	Do.
	2	Dec. 4, 1893	Aug. 28, 1894	268		Dec. 21, 1893–Jan. 3, 1894	do.	
	3	Dec. 3, 1894	Mar. 3, 1895	97		Dec. 23, 1894–Jan. 3, 1895	Matt W. Ransom, of North Carolina. Isham G. Harris, of Tennessee.	
54th	1	Dec. 2, 1895	June 11, 1896	193			William P. Frye, of Maine	Thomas B. Reed, of Maine.
	2	Dec. 7, 1896	Mar. 3, 1897	87	Dec. 22, 1896–Jan. 5, 1897	Dec. 22, 1896–Jan. 5, 1897	do.	
55th *	1	Mar. 15, 1897 [3]	July 24, 1897	131			do	Do.
	2	Dec. 6, 1897	July 8, 1898	215	Dec. 18, 1897–Jan. 5, 1898	Dec. 18, 1897–Jan. 5, 1898	do.	
	3	Dec. 5, 1898	Mar. 3, 1899	89	Dec. 21, 1898–Jan. 4, 1899	Dec. 21, 1898–Jan. 4, 1899	do.	
56th	1	Dec. 4, 1899	June 7, 1900	186	Dec. 20, 1899–Jan. 3, 1900	Dec. 20, 1899–Jan. 3, 1900	do	David B. Henderson, of Iowa.
	2	Dec. 3, 1900	Mar. 3, 1901	91	Dec. 20, 1900–Jan. 3, 1901	Dec. 21, 1900–Jan. 3, 1901	do.	
57th *	1	Dec. 2, 1901	July 1, 1902	212	Dec. 19, 1901–Jan. 6, 1902	Dec. 19, 1901–Jan. 6, 1902	do	Do.
	2	Dec. 1, 1902	Mar. 3, 1903	93	Dec. 20, 1902–Jan. 5, 1903	Dec. 20, 1902–Jan. 5, 1903	do.	
58th *	1	Nov. 9, 1903 [3]	Dec. 7, 1903	29			do	Joseph G. Cannon, of Illinois.
	2	Dec. 7, 1903	Apr. 28, 1904	144	Dec. 19, 1903–Jan. 4, 1904	Dec. 19, 1903–Jan. 4, 1904	do.	
	3	Dec. 5, 1904	Mar. 3, 1905	89	Dec. 21, 1904–Jan. 4, 1905	Dec. 21, 1904–Jan. 4, 1905	do.	
59th *	1	Dec. 4, 1905	June 30, 1906	209	Dec. 21, 1905–Jan. 4, 1906	Dec. 21, 1905–Jan. 4, 1906	do	Do.
	2	Dec. 3, 1906	Mar. 3, 1907	91	Dec. 20, 1906–Jan. 3, 1907	Dec. 20, 1906–Jan. 3, 1907	do.	
60th	1	Dec. 2, 1907	May 30, 1908	181	Dec. 21, 1907–Jan. 6, 1908	Dec. 21, 1907–Jan. 6, 1908	do	Do.
	2	Dec. 7, 1908	Mar. 3, 1909	87	Dec. 19, 1908–Jan. 4, 1909	Dec. 19, 1908–Jan. 4, 1909	do.	
61st *	1	Mar. 15, 1909 [3]	Aug. 5, 1909	144			do	Do.

	2	Dec. 6, 1909	June 25, 1910	202	Dec. 21, 1909–Jan. 4, 1910	Dec. 21, 1909–Jan. 4, 1910	......do.	
	3	Dec. 5, 1910	Mar. 3, 1911	89	Dec. 21, 1910–Jan. 5, 1911	Dec. 21, 1910–Jan. 5, 1911	......do.	
62d	1	Apr. 4, 1911[3]	Aug. 22, 1911	141			......do.[12]	Champ Clark, of Missouri.
	2	Dec. 4, 1911	Aug. 26, 1912	267	Dec. 21, 1911–Jan. 3, 1912	Dec. 21, 1911–Jan. 3, 1912	Augustus O. Bacon, of Georgia[13] Frank B. Brandegee, of Connecticut[14] Charles Curtis, of Kansas[15] Jacob H. Gallinger, of New Hampshire[16] Henry Cabot Lodge, of Massachusetts.[17]	
	3	Dec. 2, 1912	Mar. 3, 1913	92	Dec. 19, 1912–Jan. 2, 1913	Dec. 19, 1912–Jan. 2, 1913	Augustus O. Bacon, of Georgia[18] Jacob H. Gallinger, of New Hampshire.[19]	
63d *	1	Apr. 7, 1913[3]	Dec. 1, 1913	239			James P. Clarke, of Arkansas	Do.
	2	Dec. 1, 1913	Oct. 24, 1914	328	Dec. 23, 1913–Jan. 12, 1914	Dec. 23, 1913–Jan. 12, 1914	......do.	
	3	Dec. 7, 1914	Mar. 3, 1915	87	Dec. 23–Dec. 28, 1914	Dec. 23–Dec. 28, 1914	......do.	
64th	1	Dec. 6, 1915	Sept. 8, 1916	278	Dec. 17, 1915–Jan. 4, 1916	Dec. 17, 1915–Jan. 4, 1916	......do.[20]	Do.
	2	Dec. 4, 1916	Mar. 3, 1917	90	Dec. 22, 1916–Jan. 2, 1917	Dec. 22, 1916–Jan. 2, 1917	Willard Saulsbury, of Delaware.	Champ Clark, of Missouri.
65th *	1	Apr. 2, 1917[3]	Oct. 6, 1917	188			......do	Do.
	2	Dec. 3, 1917	Nov. 21, 1918	354	Dec. 18, 1917–Jan. 3, 1918	Dec. 18, 1917–Jan. 3, 1918	......do.	
	3	Dec. 2, 1918	Mar. 3, 1919	92			......do.	
66th	1	May 19, 1919[3]	Nov. 19, 1919	185	July 1–July 8, 1919	July 1–July 8, 1919	Albert B. Cummins, of Iowa	Frederick H. Gillett, of Massachusetts.
	2	Dec. 1, 1919	June 5, 1920	188	Dec. 20, 1919–Jan. 5, 1920	Dec. 20, 1919–Jan. 5, 1920	......do.	
	3	Dec. 6, 1920	Mar. 3, 1921	88			......do.	
67th *	1	Apr. 11, 1921[3]	Nov. 23, 1921	227			......do	Do.
	2	Dec. 5, 1921	Sept. 22, 1922	292	Dec. 22, 1921–Jan. 3, 1922	Dec. 22, 1921–Jan. 3, 1922	......do.	
	3	Nov. 20, 1922[3]	Dec. 4, 1922	15			......do.	
	4	Dec. 4, 1922	Mar. 3, 1923	90			......do.	
68th	1	Dec. 3, 1923	June 7, 1924	188	Dec. 20, 1923–Jan. 3, 1924	Dec. 20, 1923–Jan. 3, 1924	......do	Do.
	2	Dec. 1, 1924	Mar. 3, 1925	93	Dec. 20–Dec. 29, 1924	Dec. 20–Dec. 29, 1924	......do.	
69th *	1	Dec. 7, 1925	July 3, 1926	209	Dec. 22, 1925–Jan. 4, 1926	Dec. 22, 1925–Jan. 4, 1926	George H. Moses, of New Hampshire	Nicholas Longworth, of Ohio.
	2	Dec. 6, 1926	Mar. 4, 1927	88	Dec. 22, 1926–Jan. 3, 1927	Dec. 22, 1926–Jan. 3, 1927	......do.	
70th	1	Dec. 5, 1927	May 29, 1928	177	Dec. 21, 1927–Jan. 4, 1928	Dec. 21, 1927–Jan. 4, 1928	......do	Do.
	2	Dec. 3, 1928	Mar. 3, 1929	91	Dec. 22, 1928–Jan. 3, 1929	Dec. 22, 1928–Jan. 3, 1929	......do.	
71st *	1	Apr. 15, 1929[3]	Nov. 22, 1929	222	June 19–Aug. 19, 1929	June 19–Sept. 23, 1929	......do	Do.
	2	Dec. 2, 1929	July 3, 1930	214	Dec. 21, 1929–Jan. 6, 1930	Dec. 21, 1929–Jan. 6, 1930	......do.	
	3	Dec. 1, 1930	Mar. 3, 1931	93	Dec. 20, 1930–Jan. 5, 1931	Dec. 20, 1930–Jan. 5, 1931	......do.	
72d	1	Dec. 7, 1931	July 16, 1932	223	Dec. 22, 1931–Jan. 4, 1932	Dec. 22, 1931–Jan. 4, 1932	......do	John N. Garner, of Texas.
	2	Dec. 5, 1932	Mar. 3, 1933	89			......do.	
73d *	1	Mar. 9, 1933[3]	June 15, 1933	99			Key Pittman, of Nevada	Henry T. Rainey,[21] of Illinois.
	2	Jan. 3, 1934	June 18, 1934	167			......do.	
74th	1	Jan. 3, 1935	Aug. 26, 1935	236			......do	Joseph W. Byrns,[22] of Tennessee.
	2	Jan. 3, 1936	June 20, 1936	170	June 8–June 15, 1936	June 8–June 15, 1936	......do	William B. Bankhead,[23] of Alabama.
75th	1	Jan. 5, 1937	Aug. 21, 1937	229			......do	Do.
	2	Nov. 15, 1937[3]	Dec. 21, 1937	37			......do.	
	3	Jan. 3, 1938	June 16, 1938	165			......do.	
76th	1	Jan. 3, 1939	Aug. 5, 1939	215			......do	Do.[24]
	2	Sept. 21, 1939[3]	Nov. 3, 1939	44			......do.	
	3	Jan. 3, 1940	Jan. 3, 1941	366	July 11–July 22, 1940	July 11–July 22, 1940	......do.[25]	Sam Rayburn,[26] of Texas.
77th	1	Jan. 3, 1941	Jan. 2, 1942	365			William H. King,[27] of Utah Pat Harrison,[28] of Mississippi; Carter Glass,[29] of Virginia.	Do.
	2	Jan. 5, 1942	Dec. 16, 1942	346			Carter Glass, of Virginia.	
78th	1	Jan. 6, 1943	Dec. 21, 1943	350	July 8–Sept. 14, 1943	July 8–Sept. 14, 1943	......do	Do.

SESSIONS OF CONGRESS—CONTINUED

[Closing date for this table was April 8, 1997. See additional notes at end of the table.]

MEETING DATE AND PLACES OF CONGRESS: The Constitution (Article I, section 4) originally provided that "The Congress shall assemble at least once in every Year, and such Meeting shall be on the first Monday in December, unless they shall by law appoint a different day." Pursuant to a resolution of the Congress of the Confederation in 1788, the first session of the First Congress under the Constitution convened March 4, 1789. Up to and including May 20, 1820, 18 acts were passed providing for the meeting of Congress on other days in the year. The Congress met regularly on the first Monday in December until 1934, when the 20th amendment to the Constitution became effective, changing the meeting of Congress to January 3. Please see note 3, at the end of this table, concerning extraordinary sessions of the Congress, as well as the next table about special sessions of the Senate. The first and second sessions of the First Congress were held in New York City; subsequently, including the first session of the Sixth Congress, Philadelphia was the meeting place; since then Congress has convened in Washington.

Congress	Session	Date of beginning	Date of adjournment	Length in days	Recesses		President pro tempore of the Senate [1]	Speaker of the House of Representatives
					Senate	House		
	2	Jan. 10, 1944	Dec. 19, 1944	345	Apr. 1–Apr. 12, 1944 June 23–Aug. 1, 1944 Sept. 21–Nov. 14, 1944	Apr. 1–Apr. 12, 1944 June 23–Aug. 1, 1944 Sept. 21–Nov. 14, 1944	Carter Glass, of Virginia..	
79th	1	Jan. 3, 1945	Dec. 21, 1945	353	Aug. 1–Sept. 5, 1945	July 21–Sept. 5, 1945	Kenneth McKellar, of Tennessee	Sam Rayburn, of Texas.
	2	Jan. 14, 1946	Aug. 2, 1946	201		Apr. 18–Apr. 30, 1946	......do.	
80th	1	Jan. 3, 1947	Dec. 19, 1947	351	July 27–Nov. 17, 1947 [30]	July 27–Nov. 17, 1947 [30]	Authur H. Vandenberg, of Michigan	Joseph W. Martin, Jr., of Massachusetts.
	2	Jan. 6, 1948	Dec. 31, 1948	361	June 20–July 26, 1948 [30] Aug. 7–Dec. 31, 1948	June 20–July 26, 1948 [30] Aug. 7–Dec. 31, 1948	......do.	
81st	1	Jan. 3, 1949	Oct. 19, 1949	290			Kenneth McKellar, of Tennessee	Sam Rayburn, of Texas.
	2	Jan. 3, 1950	Jan. 2, 1951	365	Sept. 23–Nov. 27–1950	Apr. 6–Apr. 18, 1950 Sept. 23–Nov. 27, 1950	......do.	
82d	1	Jan. 3, 1951	Oct. 20, 1951	291		Mar. 22–Apr. 2, 1951 Aug. 23–Sept. 12, 1951	......do	Do.
	2	Jan. 8, 1952	July 7, 1952	182		Apr. 10–Apr. 22, 1952	......do.	
83d	1	Jan. 3, 1953	Aug. 3, 1953	213		Apr. 2–Apr. 13, 1953	Styles Bridges, of New Hampshire	Joseph W. Martin, Jr., of Massachusetts.
	2	Jan. 6, 1954	Dec. 2, 1954	331	Aug. 20–Nov. 8, 1954 Nov. 18–Nov. 29, 1954	Apr. 15–Apr. 22, 1954 Adjourned sine die Aug. 20, 1954	......do.	
84th	1	Jan. 5, 1955	Aug. 2, 1955	210	Apr. 4–Apr. 13, 1955	Apr. 4–Apr. 13, 1955	Walter F. George, of Georgia	Sam Rayburn, of Texas.
	2	Jan. 3, 1956	July 27, 1956	207	Mar. 29–Apr. 9, 1956	Mar. 29–Apr. 9, 1956	......do.	
85th	1	Jan. 3, 1957	Aug. 30, 1957	239	Apr. 18–Apr. 29, 1957	Apr. 18–Apr. 29, 1957	Carl Hayden, of Arizona	Do.
	2	Jan. 7, 1958	Aug. 24, 1958	230	Apr. 3–Apr. 14, 1958	Apr. 3–Apr. 14, 1958	......do.	
86th	1	Jan. 7, 1959	Sept. 15, 1959	252	Mar. 26–Apr. 7, 1959	Mar. 26–Apr. 7, 1959	......do	Do.
	2	Jan. 6, 1960	Sept. 1, 1960	240	Apr. 14–Apr. 18, 1960 May 27–May 31, 1960 July 3–Aug. 8, 1960	Apr. 14–Apr. 18, 1960 May 27–May 31, 1960 July 3–Aug. 15, 1960	......do.	
87th	1	Jan. 3, 1961	Sept. 27, 1961	268		Mar. 30–Apr. 10, 1961	......do	Do. [31]
	2	Jan. 10, 1962	Oct. 13, 1962	277		Apr. 19–Apr. 30, 1962	......do	John W. McCormack, [32] of Massachusetts.
88th	1	Jan. 9, 1963	Dec. 30, 1963	356		Apr. 11–Apr. 22, 1963	......do	Do.
	2	Jan. 7, 1964	Oct. 3, 1964	270	July 10–July 20, 1964 Aug. 21–Aug. 31, 1964	Mar. 26–Apr. 6, 1964 July 2–July 20, 1964 Aug. 21–Aug. 31, 1964	......do.	
89th	1	Jan. 4, 1965	Oct. 23, 1965	293			......do	Do.

	2	Jan. 10, 1966	Oct. 22, 1966 ...	286	Apr. 7–Apr. 13, 1966 .... June 30–July 11, 1966	Apr. 7–Apr. 18, 1966 .... June 30–July 11, 1966	......do.	
90th	1	Jan. 10, 1967	Dec. 15, 1967 ..	340	Mar. 23–Apr. 3, 1967 .... June 29–July 10, 1967 Aug. 31–Sept. 11, 1967 Nov. 22–Nov. 27, 1967	Mar. 23–Apr. 3, 1967 .... June 29–July 10, 1967 Aug. 31–Sept. 11, 1967 Nov. 22–Nov. 27, 1967	......do	Do.
	2	Jan. 15, 1968	Oct. 14, 1968 ...	274	Apr. 11–Apr. 17, 1968 .... May 29–June 3, 1968 June 3–July 8, 1968 Aug. 2–Sept. 4, 1968	Apr. 11–Apr. 22, 1968 .... May 29–June 3, 1968 June 3–July 8, 1968 Aug. 2–Sept. 4, 1968	......do.	
91st	1	Jan. 3, 1969	Dec. 23, 1969 ..	355	Feb. 7–Feb. 17, 1969 .... Apr. 3–Apr. 14, 1969 July 2–July 7, 1969 Aug. 13–Sept. 3, 1969 Nov. 26–Dec. 1, 1969	Feb. 7–Feb. 17, 1969 .... Apr. 3–Apr. 14, 1969 May 28–June 2, 1969 July 2–July 7, 1969 Aug. 13–Sept. 3, 1969 Nov. 6–Nov. 12, 1969 Nov. 26–Dec. 1, 1969	Richard B. Russell, of Georgia	John W. McCormack, of Massachusetts.
	2	Jan. 19, 1970	Jan. 2, 1971	349	Feb. 10–Feb. 16, 1970 .... Mar. 26–Mar. 31, 1970 Sept. 2–Sept. 8, 1970 Oct. 14–Nov. 16, 1970 Nov. 25–Nov. 30, 1970 Dec. 22–Dec. 28, 1970	Feb. 10–Feb. 16, 1970 .... Mar. 26–Mar. 31, 1970 May 27–June 1, 1970 July 1–July 6, 1970 Aug. 14–Sept. 9, 1970 Oct. 14–Nov. 16, 1970 Nov. 25–Nov. 30, 1970 Dec. 22–Dec. 29, 1970	......do.	
92d	1	Jan. 21, 1971	Dec. 17, 1971 ..	331	Feb. 11–Feb. 17, 1971 .... Apr. 7–Apr. 14, 1971 May 26–June 1, 1971 June 30–July 6, 1971 Aug. 6–Sept. 8, 1971 Oct. 21–Oct. 26, 1971 Nov. 24–Nov. 29, 1971	Feb. 10–Feb. 17, 1971 .... Apr. 7–Apr. 19, 1971 May 27–June 1, 1971 July 1–July 6, 1971 Aug. 6–Sept. 8, 1971 Oct. 7–Oct. 12, 1971 Oct. 21–Oct. 26, 1971 Nov. 19–Nov. 29, 1971	......do. [33] .... Allen J. Ellender, [34] of Louisiana.	Carl B. Albert, of Oklahoma.
	2	Jan. 18, 1972	Oct. 18, 1972 ...	275	Feb. 9–Feb. 14, 1972 .... Mar. 30–Apr. 4, 1972 May 25–May 30, 1972 June 30–July 17, 1972 Aug. 18–Sept. 5, 1972	Feb. 9–Feb. 16, 1972 .... Mar. 29–Apr. 10, 1972 May 24–May 30, 1972 June 30–July 17, 1972 Aug. 18–Sept. 5, 1972	......do. [35] James O. Eastland, [36] of Mississippi.	
93d	1	Jan. 3, 1973	Dec. 22, 1973 ..	354	Feb. 8–Feb. 15, 1973 .... Apr. 18–Apr. 30, 1973 May 23–May 29, 1973 June 30–July 9, 1973 Aug. 3–Sept. 5, 1973 Oct. 18–Oct. 23, 1973 Nov. 21–Nov. 26, 1973	Feb. 8–Feb. 19, 1973 .... Apr. 19–Apr. 30, 1973 May 24–May 29, 1973 June 30–July 10, 1973 Aug. 3–Sept. 5, 1973 Oct. 4–Oct. 9, 1973 Oct. 18–Oct. 23, 1973 Nov. 15–Nov. 26, 1973	......do	Do.

SESSIONS OF CONGRESS—CONTINUED

[Closing date for this table was April 8, 1997. See additional notes at end of the table.]

MEETING DATE AND PLACES OF CONGRESS: The Constitution (Article I, section 4) originally provided that "The Congress shall assemble at least once in every Year, and such Meeting shall be on the first Monday in December, unless they shall by law appoint a different day." Pursuant to a resolution of the Congress of the Confederation in 1788, the first session of the First Congress under the Constitution convened March 4, 1789. Up to and including May 20, 1820, 18 acts were passed providing for the meeting of Congress on other days in the year. The Congress met regularly on the first Monday in December until 1934, when the 20th amendment to the Constitution became effective, changing the meeting of Congress to January 3. Please see note 3, at the end of this table, concerning extraordinary sessions of the Congress, as well as the next table about special sessions of the Senate. The first and second sessions of the First Congress were held in New York City; subsequently, including the first session of the Sixth Congress, Philadelphia was the meeting place; since then Congress has convened in Washington.

Congress	Session	Date of beginning	Date of adjournment	Length in days	Recesses		President pro tempore of the Senate [1]	Speaker of the House of Representatives
					Senate	House		
	2	Jan. 21, 1974	Dec. 20, 1974	334	Feb. 8–Feb. 18, 1974 Mar. 13–Mar. 19, 1974 Apr. 11–Apr. 22, 1974 May 23–May 28, 1974 Aug. 22–Sept. 4, 1974 Oct. 17–Nov. 18, 1974 Nov. 26–Dec. 2, 1974	Feb. 7–Feb. 13, 1974 Apr. 11–Apr. 22, 1974 May 23–May 28, 1974 Aug. 22–Sept. 11, 1974 Oct. 17–Nov. 18, 1974 Nov. 26–Dec. 3, 1974	James O. Eastland, of Mississippi..	
94th	1	Jan. 14, 1975	Dec. 19, 1975	340	Mar. 26–Apr. 7, 1975 May 22–June 2, 1975 June 27–July 7, 1975 Aug. 1–Sept. 3, 1975 Oct. 9–Oct. 20, 1975 Oct. 23–Oct. 28, 1975 Nov. 20–Dec. 1, 1975	Mar. 26–Apr. 7, 1975 May 22–June 2, 1975 June 26–July 8, 1975 Aug. 1–Sept. 3, 1975 Oct. 9–Oct. 20, 1975 Oct. 23–Oct. 28, 1975 Nov. 20–Dec. 1, 1975	......do	Carl B. Albert, of Oklahoma.
	2	Jan. 19, 1976	Oct. 1, 1976	257	Feb. 6–Feb. 16, 1976 Apr. 14–Apr. 26, 1976 May 28–June 2, 1976 July 2–July 19, 1976 Aug. 10–Aug. 23, 1976 Sept. 1–Sept. 7, 1976	Feb. 11–Feb. 16, 1976 Apr. 14–Apr. 26, 1976 May 27–June 1, 1976 July 2–July 19, 1976 Aug. 10–Aug. 23, 1976 Sept. 2–Sept. 8, 1976	......do.	
95th	1	Jan. 4, 1977	Dec. 15, 1977	346	Feb. 11–Feb. 21, 1977 Apr. 7–Apr. 18, 1977 May 27–June 6, 1977 July 1–July 11, 1977 Aug. 6–Sept. 7, 1977	Feb. 9–Feb. 16, 1977 Apr. 6–Apr. 18, 1977 May 26–June 1, 1977 June 30–July 11, 1977 Aug. 5–Sept. 7, 1977 Oct. 6–Oct. 11, 1977	......do	Thomas P. O'Neill, Jr., of Massachusetts.
	2	Jan. 19, 1978	Oct. 15, 1978	270	Feb. 10–Feb. 20, 1978 Mar. 23–Apr. 3, 1978 May 26–June 5, 1978 June 29–July 10, 1978 Aug. 25–Sept. 6, 1978	Feb. 9–Feb. 14, 1978 Mar. 22–Apr. 3, 1978 May 25–May 31, 1978 June 29–July 10, 1978 Aug. 17–Sept. 6, 1978	......do.	

96th	1	Jan. 15, 1979	Jan. 3, 1980	354	Feb. 9–Feb. 19, 1979 .... Apr. 10–Apr. 23, 1979 May 24–June 4, 1979 June 27–July 9, 1979 Aug. 3–Sept. 5, 1979 Nov. 20–Nov. 26, 1979 Adjourned sine die, Dec. 20, 1979	Feb. 8–Feb. 13, 1979 .... Apr. 10–Apr. 23, 1979 May 24–May 30, 1979 June 29–July 9, 1979 Aug. 2–Sept. 5, 1979 Nov. 20–Nov. 26, 1979 Adjourned sine die, Jan. 3, 1980	Warren G. Magnuson, of Washington ..	Do.
	2	Jan. 3, 1980	Dec. 16, 1980 ..	349	Apr. 3–Apr. 15, 1980 .... May 22–May 28, 1980 July 2–July 21, 1980 Aug. 6–Aug. 18, 1980 Aug. 27–Sept. 3, 1980 Oct. 1–Nov. 12, 1980 Nov. 25–Dec. 1, 1980	Feb. 13–Feb. 19, 1980 .... Apr. 2–Apr. 15, 1980 May 22–May 28, 1980 July 2–July 21, 1980 Aug. 1–Aug. 18, 1980 Aug. 28–Sept. 3, 1980 Oct. 2–Nov. 12, 1980 Nov. 21–Dec. 1, 1980	......do Milton Young, of North Dakota.[37]	
97th	1	Jan. 5, 1981	Dec. 16, 1981 ..	347	Feb. 6–Feb. 16, 1981 .... Apr. 10–Apr. 27, 1981 June 25–July 8, 1981 Aug. 3–Sept. 9, 1981 Oct. 7–Oct. 14, 1981 Nov. 24–Nov. 30, 1981	Feb. 6–Feb. 17, 1981 .... Apr. 10–Apr. 27, 1981 June 26–July 8, 1981 Aug. 4–Sept. 9, 1981 Oct. 7–Oct. 13, 1981 Nov. 23–Nov. 30, 1981	Strom Thurmond, of South Carolina	Do.
	2	Jan. 25, 1982	Dec. 23, 1982 ..	333	Feb. 11–Feb. 22, 1982 .... Apr. 1–Apr. 13, 1982 May 27–June 8, 1982 July 1–July 12, 1982 Aug. 20–Sept. 8, 1982 Oct. 1–Nov. 29, 1982	Feb. 10–Feb. 22, 1982 .... Apr. 6–Apr. 20, 1982 May 27–June 2, 1982 July 1–July 12, 1982 Aug. 20–Sept. 8, 1982 Oct. 1–Nov. 29, 1982	Strom Thurmond, of South Carolina.	Thomas P. O'Neill, Jr., of Massachusetts.
98th	1	Jan. 3, 1983	Nov. 18, 1983 ..	320	Jan. 3–Jan. 25, 1983 .... Feb. 3–Feb. 14, 1983 Mar. 24–Apr. 5, 1983 May 26–June 6, 1983 June 29–July 11, 1983 Aug. 4–Sept. 12, 1983 Oct. 7–Oct. 17, 1983	Jan. 6–Jan. 25, 1983 .... Feb. 17–Feb. 22, 1983 Mar. 24–Apr. 5, 1983 May 26–June 1, 1983 June 30–July 11, 1983 Aug. 4–Sept. 12, 1983 Oct. 6–Oct. 17, 1983	......do	Do.
	2	Jan. 23, 1984	Oct. 12, 1984 ...	264	Feb. 9–Feb. 20, 1984 .... Apr. 12–Apr. 24, 1984 May 24–May 31, 1984 June 29–July 23, 1984 Aug. 10–Sept. 5, 1984	Feb. 9–Feb. 21, 1984 .... Apr. 12–Apr. 24, 1984 May 24–May 30, 1984 June 29–July 23, 1984 Aug. 10–Sept. 5, 1984	......do.	
99th	1	Jan. 3, 1985	Dec. 20, 1985 ..	352	Jan. 7–Jan. 21, 1985 .... Feb. 7–Feb. 18, 1985 Apr. 4–Apr. 15, 1985 May 9–May 14, 1985 May 24–June 3, 1985 June 27–July 8, 1985 Aug. 1–Sept. 9, 1985 Nov. 23–Dec. 2, 1985	Jan. 3–Jan. 21, 1985 .... Feb. 7–Feb. 19, 1985 Mar. 7–Mar. 19, 1985 Apr. 4–Apr. 15, 1985 May 23–June 3, 1985 June 27–July 8, 1985 Aug. 1–Sept. 4, 1985 Nov. 21–Dec. 2, 1985	......do	Do.
	2	Jan. 21, 1986	Oct. 18, 1986 ...	278	Feb. 7–Feb. 17, 1986 .... Mar. 27–Apr. 8, 1986 May 21–June 2, 1986 June 26–July 7, 1986 Aug. 15–Sept. 8, 1986	Feb. 6–Feb. 18, 1986 .... Mar. 25–Apr. 8, 1986 May 22–June 3, 1986 June 26–July 14, 1986 Aug. 16–Sept. 8, 1986	......do.	

SESSIONS OF CONGRESS—CONTINUED

[Closing date for this table was April 8, 1997. See additional notes at end of the table.]

MEETING DATE AND PLACES OF CONGRESS: The Constitution (Article I, section 4) originally provided that "The Congress shall assemble at least once in every Year, and such Meeting shall be on the first Monday in December, unless they shall by law appoint a different day." Pursuant to a resolution of the Congress of the Confederation in 1788, the first session of the First Congress under the Constitution convened March 4, 1789. Up to and including May 20, 1820, 18 acts were passed providing for the meeting of Congress on other days in the year. The Congress met regularly on the first Monday in December until 1934, when the 20th amendment to the Constitution became effective, changing the meeting of Congress to January 3. Please see note 3, at the end of this table, concerning extraordinary sessions of the Congress, as well as the next table about special sessions of the Senate. The first and second sessions of the First Congress were held in New York City; subsequently, including the first session of the Sixth Congress, Philadelphia was the meeting place; since then Congress has convened in Washington.

Con-gress	Ses-sion	Date of beginning	Date of adjourn-ment	Length in days	Recesses		President pro tempore of the Senate [1]	Speaker of the House of Representatives
					Senate	House		
100th ..	1	Jan. 6, 1987	Dec. 22, 1987 ..	351	Jan. 6–Jan. 12, 1987 .... Feb. 5–Feb. 16, 1987 Apr. 10–Apr. 21, 1987 May 21–May 27, 1987 July 1–July 7, 1987 Aug. 7–Sept. 9, 1987 Nov. 20–Nov. 30, 1987	Jan. 8–Jan. 20, 1987 .... Feb. 11–Feb. 18, 1987 Apr. 9–Apr. 21, 1987 May 21–May 27, 1987 July 1–July 7, 1987 July 15–July 20, 1987 Aug. 7–Sept. 9, 1987 Nov. 10–Nov. 16, 1987 Nov. 20–Nov. 30, 1987	John C. Stennis, of Mississippi	James C. Wright, Jr., of Texas.
	2	Jan. 25, 1988	Oct. 22, 1988 ...	272	Feb. 4–Feb. 15, 1988 .... Mar. 4– Mar. 14, 1988 Mar. 31–Apr. 11, 1988 Apr. 29–May 9, 1988 May 27–June 6, 1988 June 29–July 6, 1988 July 14–July 25, 1988 Aug. 11–Sept. 7, 1988	Feb. 9–Feb. 16, 1988 .... Mar. 31–Apr. 11, 1988 May 26–June 1, 1988 June 30–July 7, 1988 July 14–July 26, 1988 Aug. 11–Sept. 7,1988	......do.	
101st ..	1	Jan. 3, 1989	Nov. 22, 1989 ..	324	Jan. 4–Jan. 20, 1989 .... Jan. 20–Jan. 25, 1989 Feb. 9–Feb. 21, 1989 Mar. 17–Apr. 4, 1989 Apr. 19–May 1, 1989 May 18–May 31, 1989 June 23–July 11, 1989 Aug. 4–Sept. 6, 1989	Jan. 4–Jan. 19, 1989 .... Feb. 9–Feb. 21, 1989 Mar. 23–Apr. 3, 1989 Apr. 18–Apr. 25, 1989 May 25–May 31, 1989 June 29–July 10, 1989 Aug. 5–Sept. 6, 1989	Robert C. Byrd, of West Virginia	Do. Thomas S. Foley, [38] of Washington.
	2	Jan. 23, 1990	Oct. 28, 1990 ...	260	Feb. 8–Feb. 20, 1990 .... Mar. 9–Mar. 20, 1990 Apr. 5–Apr. 18, 1990 May 24–June 5, 1990 June 28–July 10, 1990 Aug. 4–Sept. 10, 1990	Feb. 7–Feb. 20, 1990 .... Apr. 4–Apr. 18, 1990 May 25–June 5, 1990 June 28–July 10, 1990 Aug. 4–Sept. 5, 1990	......do.	

102d ...	1	Jan. 3, 1991	Jan. 3, 1992	366	Feb. 7–Feb. 19, 1991 Mar. 22–Apr. 9, 1991 Apr. 25–May 6, 1991 May 24–June 3, 1991 June 28–July 8, 1991 Aug. 2–Sept. 10, 1991 Nov. 27, 1991–Jan. 3, 1992	Feb. 6–Feb. 19, 1991 Mar. 22–Apr. 9, 1991 May 23–May 29, 1991 June 27–July 9, 1991 Aug. 2–Sept. 11, 1991 Nov. 27, 1991–Jan. 3, 1992	......do	Do.
	2	Jan. 3, 1992	Oct. 9, 1992	281	Jan. 3–Jan. 21, 1992 Feb. 7–Feb. 18, 1992 Apr. 10–Apr. 28, 1992 May 21–June 1, 1992 July 2–July 20, 1992 Aug. 12–Sept. 8, 1992	Jan. 3–Jan. 22, 1992 Apr. 10–Apr. 28, 1992 May 21–May 26, 1992 July 2–July 7, 1992 July 9–July 21, 1992 Aug. 12–Sept. 9, 1992	......do.	
103d ...	1	Jan. 5, 1993	Nov. 26, 1993	326	Jan. 7–Jan. 20, 1993 Feb. 4–Feb. 16, 1993 Apr. 7–Apr. 19, 1993 May 28–June 7, 1993 July 1–July 13, 1993 Aug. 7–Sept. 7, 1993 Oct. 7–Oct. 13, 1993 Nov. 11–Nov. 16, 1993	Jan. 6–Jan. 20, 1993 Jan. 27–Feb. 2, 1993 Feb. 4–Feb. 16, 1993 Apr. 7–Apr. 19, 1993 May 27–June 8, 1993 July 1–July 13, 1993 Aug. 6–Sept. 8, 1993 Sept. 15–Sept. 21, 1993 Oct. 7–Oct. 12, 1993 Nov. 10–Nov. 15, 1993	Robert C. Byrd, of West Virginia	Thomas S. Foley, of Washington.
	2	Jan. 25, 1994	Dec. 1, 1994	311	Feb. 11–Feb. 22, 1994 Mar. 26–Apr. 11, 1994 May 25–June 7, 1994 July 1–July 11, 1994 Aug. 25–Sept. 12, 1994 Oct. 8–Nov. 30, 1994	Jan. 26–Feb. 1, 1994 Feb. 11–Feb. 22, 1994 Mar. 24–Apr. 12, 1994 May 26–June 8, 1994 June 30–July 12, 1994 Aug. 26–Sept. 12, 1994 Oct. 8–Nov. 29, 1994	......do.	
104th ..	1	Jan. 4, 1995	Jan. 3, 1996	365	Feb. 16–Feb. 22, 1995 Apr. 7–Apr. 24, 1995 May 26–June 5, 1995 June 30–July 10, 1995 Aug. 11–Sept. 5, 1995 Sept. 29–Oct. 10, 1995 Nov. 20–Nov. 27, 1995	Feb. 16–Feb. 21, 1995 Mar. 16–Mar. 21, 1995 Apr. 7–May 1, 1995 May 3–May 9, 1995 May 25–June 6, 1995 June 30–July 10, 1995 Aug. 4–Sept. 6, 1995 Sept. 29–Oct. 6, 1995 Nov. 20–Nov. 28, 1995	Strom Thurmond, of South Carolina	Newt Gingrich, of Georgia.
	2	Jan. 3, 1996	Oct. 4, 1996	276	Jan. 10–Jan. 22, 1996 Mar. 29–Apr. 15, 1996 May 24–June 3, 1996 June 28–July 8, 1996 Aug. 2–Sept. 3, 1996	Jan. 9–Jan. 22, 1996 Mar. 29–Apr. 15, 1996 May 23–May 29, 1996 June 28–July 8, 1996 Aug. 2–Sept. 4, 1996	......do.	
105th ..	1	Jan. 7, 1997	....	....	Jan. 9–Jan. 21, 1997 Feb. 13–Feb. 24, 1997 Mar. 21–Apr. 7, 1997	Jan. 9–Jan. 20, 1997 Jan. 21–Feb. 4, 1997 Feb. 13–Feb. 25, 1997 Mar. 21–Apr. 8, 1997	......do	Do.

* Indicates that a special session of the Senate was convened during a Congress. Please see the following table, SPECIAL SESSIONS OF THE SENATE, for more information.

[1] For many years the appointment or election of a President pro tempore was held by the Senate to be for the occasion only, so that more than one appear in several sessions and in others none was chosen. Since Mar. 12, 1890, they have served until "the Senate otherwise ordered." Since 1949, the position has gone to the most senior member of the majority (see note 37 for a minority party exception).

[2] Elected to count the vote for President and Vice President, which was done Apr. 6, 1789, a quorum of the Senate then appearing for the first time. John Adams, Vice President, appeared Apr. 21, 1789, and took his seat as President of the Senate.

[3] Article II, section 3 of the Constitution provides that the President "may, on extraordinary occasions, convene both Houses, or either of them." This procedure occurs only if the Congress is convened by presidential proclamation. Extraordinary sessions have been called by the Chief Executive to urge the Congress to focus on important national issues. These are separate sessions of Congress, unless otherwise noted.

[4] Elected Speaker pro tempore for Apr. 20, 1798, and again for May 28, 1798.

[5] Elected Speaker Jan. 19, 1814, to succeed Henry Clay, of Kentucky, who resigned Jan. 19, 1814.

[6] Elected Speaker Nov. 15, 1820, to succeed Henry Clay, of Kentucky, who resigned Oct. 28, 1820.

[7] Elected Speaker June 2, 1834, to succeed Andrew Stevenson, of Virginia, who resigned.

[8] Elected Speaker Mar. 3, 1869, and served 1 day.

[9] Died Aug. 19, 1876.

[10] Appointed Speaker pro tempore Feb. 17, May 12, June 19.

[11] Appointed Speaker pro tempore June 4.

[12] Resigned as President pro tempore Apr. 27, 1911.

[13] Elected to serve Jan. 11–17, Mar. 11–12, Apr. 8, May 10, May 30 to June 1 and 3, June 13 to July 5, Aug. 1–10, and Aug. 27 to Dec. 15, 1912.

[14] Elected to serve May 25, 1912.

[15] Elected to serve Dec. 4–12, 1911.

[16] Elected to serve Feb. 12–14, Apr. 26–27, May 7, July 6–31, Aug. 12–26, 1912.

[17] Elected to serve Mar. 25–26, 1912.

[18] Elected to serve Aug. 27 to Dec. 15, 1912, Jan. 5–18, and Feb. 2–15, 1913.

[19] Elected to serve Dec. 16, 1912, to Jan. 4, 1913, Jan. 19 to Feb. 1, and Feb. 16 to Mar. 3, 1913.

[20] Died Oct. 1, 1916.

[21] Died Aug. 19, 1934.

[22] Died June 4, 1936.

[23] Elected June 4, 1936.

[24] Died Sept. 15, 1940.

[25] Died Nov. 10, 1940.

[26] Elected Sept. 16, 1940.

[27] Elected Nov. 19, 1940.

[28] Elected Jan. 6, 1941; died June 22, 1941.

[29] Elected July 10, 1941.

[30] Extraordinary session of the Congress called by President Harry Truman. The extraordinary session was convened after a recess period, and it did not begin a new session.

[31] Died November 16, 1961.

[32] Elected Jan. 10, 1962.

[33] Died Jan. 21, 1971.

[34] Elected Jan. 22, 1971.

[35] Died July 27, 1972.

[36] Elected July 28, 1972.

[37] Milton Young, of North Dakota, was elected President pro tempore for one day, Dec. 5, 1980, which was at the end of his 36-year career in the Senate. He was Republican, which was the minority party at that time.

[38] Elected Speaker June 6, 1989, to succeed James C. Wright, Jr., of Texas, who resigned.

SPECIAL SESSIONS OF THE SENATE

From 1789 to 1933 presidential and congressional terms began on March 4, although the Congress generally did not meet until the first Monday in December. When a new President was to take office, his predecessor would call the Senate into special session to confirm the nominations for the Cabinet and other significant posts. Special sessions also were convened to consider the ratification of treaties. Incumbent presidents also called special sessions from time to time to allow Senators to consider vacancies and other executive business. Special sessions are called by presidential proclamation.

[Except as noted below, all special sessions were convened to consider executive nominations.]

Congress	Year	Date of beginning	Date of adjournment
2d	1791	Friday, March 4	Friday, March 4.
3d	1793	Monday, March 4	Monday, March 4.
4th	1795	Monday, June 8 [1]	Friday, June 26.
5th	1797	Saturday, March 4	Saturday, March 4.
	1798	Tuesday, July 17	Thursday, July 19.
7th	1801	Wednesday, March 4	Thursday, March 5.
11th	1809	Saturday, March 4	Tuesday, March 7.
15th	1817	Monday, March 4	Wednesday, March 6.
19th	1825	Friday, March 4	Wednesday, March 9.
21st	1829	Wednesday, March 4	Tuesday, March 17.
25th	1837	Saturday, March 4	Friday, March 10.
27th	1841	Thursday, March 4	Monday, March 15.
29th	1845	Tuesday, March 4	Thursday, March 20.
31st	1849	Monday, March 5	Friday, March 23.
32d	1851	Tuesday, March 4	Thursday, March 13.
33d	1853	Friday, March 4	Monday, April 11.
35th	1857	Wednesday, March 4	Saturday, March 14.
	1858	Tuesday, June 15	Wednesday, June 16.
36th	1859	Friday, March 4	Thursday, March 10.
	1860	Tuesday, June 26 [2]	Thursday, June 28.
37th	1861	Monday, March 4	Thursday, March 28.
38th	1863	Wednesday, March 4	Saturday, March 14.
39th	1865	Saturday, March 4	Saturday, March 11.
40th	1867	Monday, April 1	Saturday, April 20.
41st	1869	Monday, April 12	Thursday, April 22.
42d	1871	Wednesday, May 10 [3]	Saturday, May 27.
43d	1873	Tuesday, March 4	Wednesday, March 26.
44th	1875	Friday, March 5	Wednesday, March 24.
45th	1877	Monday, March 5	Saturday, March 17.
47th	1881	Friday, March 4	Friday, May 20.
	1881	Monday, October 10	Saturday, October 29.
49th	1885	Wednesday, March 4	Thursday, April 2.
51st	1889	Monday, March 4	Tuesday, April 2.
53d	1893	Saturday, March 4	Friday, April 15.
55th	1897	Thursday, March 4	Wednesday, March 10.
57th	1901	Monday, March 4	Saturday, March 9.
58th	1903	Thursday, March 5	Thursday, March 19.
59th	1905	Saturday, March 4	Saturday, March 18.
61st	1909	Thursday, March 4	Saturday, March 6.
63d	1913	Tuesday, March 4	Monday, March 17.
65th	1917	Monday, March 5	Friday, March 16.
67th	1921	Friday, March 4	Tuesday, March 15.
69th	1925	Wednesday, March 4	Wednesday, March 18.
71st	1929	Monday, March 4	Tuesday, March 5.
	1930	Monday, July 7 [4]	Monday, July 21.
73d	1933	Saturday, March 4	Monday, March 6.

[1] To consider the Jay Treaty. [2] To consider treaties. [3] To consider the Washington Treaty. [4] To consider the Naval Arms Treaty.

JOINT SESSIONS, JOINT MEETINGS, AND INAUGURATIONS

1st–105th CONGRESSES, 1789–1997 [1]

The parliamentary difference between a joint session and a joint meeting has evolved over time. In recent years the distinctions have become clearer: a joint session is more formal, and occurs upon the adoption of a concurrent resolution; a joint meeting occurs when each body adopts a unanimous consent agreement to recess to meet with the other legislative body.

The Speaker of the House of Representatives usually presides over joint sessions and joint meetings; however, the President of the Senate does preside over counts of the electoral votes, as required by the Constitution.

In the earliest years of the Republic, 1789 and 1790, when the national legislature met in New York City, joint gatherings were held in the Senate Chamber in Federal Hall. In Philadelphia, when the legislature met in Congress Hall, such meetings were held in the Senate Chamber, 1790–1793, and in the Hall of the House of Representatives, 1794–1799. Once the Congress moved to the Capitol in Washington in 1800, the Senate Chamber again was used for joint gatherings through 1805. Since 1809, with few exceptions, joint sessions and joint meetings have occurred in the Hall of the House.

Presidential messages on the state of the Union were once known as ''Annual Messages,'' but since the 80th Congress have been called ''State of the Union Addresses.'' After President Adams' Annual Message on November 22, 1800, these addresses were read by clerks to the individual bodies until President Wilson resumed the practice of delivering them to joint sessions on December 2, 1913.

In some instances more than one joint gathering has occurred on the same day. For example, on January 6, 1941, Congress met in joint session to count electoral votes for President and Vice President, and then met again in joint session to receive President Roosevelt's Annual Message.

Congress has hosted inaugurations since the first occasion in 1789. They always have been formal joint gatherings, and sometimes they also were joint sessions. Inaugurations were joint sessions when both houses of Congress were in session, and they processed to the ceremony as part of the business of the day. In many cases, however, one or both houses were not in session or were in recess at the time of the ceremony. In the table below, inaugurations that were not joint sessions are listed in the second column. Those that were joint sessions are so identified and described in the third column.

JOINT SESSIONS, JOINT MEETINGS, AND INAUGURATIONS

1st–105th CONGRESSES, 1789–1997

[See notes at end of table]

Congress & Date	Type	Occasion, topic, or location	Name and position of dignitary (where applicable)
		NEW YORK CITY	
1st CONGRESS			
Apr. 6, 1789	Joint session	Counting electoral votes	N.A.
Apr. 30, 1789	......do	Inauguration and church service [2]	President George Washington; Right Reverend Samuel Provoost, Senate-appointed Chaplain.
Jan. 8, 1790	......do	Annual Message	President George Washington.
		PHILADELPHIA	
Dec. 8, 1790	......do	......do	Do.
2d CONGRESS			
Oct. 25, 1791	......do	......do	Do.
Nov. 6, 1792	......do	......do	Do.
Feb. 13, 1793	......do	Counting electoral votes	N.A.
3d CONGRESS			
Mar. 4, 1793	Inauguration	Senate Chamber	President George Washington.
Dec. 3, 1793	Joint session	Annual Message	Do.
Nov. 19, 1794	......do	......do	Do.
4th CONGRESS			
Dec. 8, 1795	......do	......do	Do.

JOINT SESSIONS, JOINT MEETINGS, AND INAUGURATIONS—CONTINUED

1st–105th CONGRESSES, 1789–1997

[See notes at end of table]

Congress & Date	Type	Occasion, topic, or location	Name and position of dignitary (where applicable)
Dec. 7, 1796	Joint session	Annual Message	President George Washington.
Feb. 8, 1797	......do	Counting electoral votes	N.A.
5th CONGRESS			
Mar. 4, 1797	Inauguration	Hall of the House	President John Adams.
May 16, 1797	Joint session	Relations with France	Do.
Nov. 23, 1797	......do	Annual Message	Do.
Dec. 8, 1798	......do	......do	Do.
6th CONGRESS			
Dec. 3, 1799	......do	......do	Do.
Dec. 26, 1799	......do	Funeral procession and oration in memory of George Washington [3].	Representative Henry Lee.
		WASHINGTON	
Nov. 22, 1800	......do	Annual Message	President John Adams.
Feb. 11, 1801	......do	Counting electoral votes [4]	N.A.
7th CONGRESS			
Mar. 4, 1801	Inauguration	Senate Chamber	President Thomas Jefferson.
8th CONGRESS			
Feb. 13, 1805	Joint session	Counting electoral votes	N.A.
9th CONGRESS			
Mar. 5, 1805	Inauguration	Senate Chamber	President Thomas Jefferson.
10th CONGRESS			
Feb. 8, 1809	Joint session	Counting electoral votes	N.A.
11th CONGRESS			
Mar. 4, 1809	Inauguration	Hall of the House	President James Madison.
12th CONGRESS			
Feb. 10, 1813	Joint session	Counting electoral votes	N.A.
13th CONGRESS			
Mar. 4, 1813	Inauguration	Hall of the House	President James Madison.
14th CONGRESS			
Feb. 12, 1817	Joint session	Counting electoral votes [5]	N.A.
15th CONGRESS			
Mar. 4, 1817	Inauguration	In front of Brick Capitol	President James Monroe.
16th CONGRESS			
Feb. 14, 1821	Joint session	Counting electoral votes [6]	N.A.
17th CONGRESS			
Mar. 5, 1821	Inauguration	Hall of the House	President James Monroe.
18th CONGRESS			
Dec. 10, 1824	House address[7]	Address	Speaker Henry Clay; General Gilbert du Motier, Marquis de Lafayette.
Feb. 9, 1825	Joint session	Counting electoral votes [8]	N.A.
19th CONGRESS			
Mar. 4, 1825	Inauguration	Hall of the House	President John Quincy Adams.
20th CONGRESS			
Feb. 11, 1829	Joint session	Counting electoral votes	N.A.
21st CONGRESS			
Mar. 4, 1829	Inauguration	East Portico [9]	President Andrew Jackson.
22d CONGRESS			
Feb. 13, 1833	Joint session	Counting electoral votes	N.A.
23d CONGRESS			
Mar. 4, 1833	Inauguration	Hall of the House [10]	President Andrew Jackson.
Dec. 31, 1834	Joint session	Lafayette eulogy	Representative and former President John Quincy Adams; ceremony attended by President Andrew Jackson.
24th CONGRESS			
Feb. 8, 1837	......do	Counting electoral votes	N.A.
25th CONGRESS			
Mar. 4, 1837	Inauguration	East Portico	President Martin Van Buren.

JOINT SESSIONS, JOINT MEETINGS, AND INAUGURATIONS—CONTINUED

1st–105th CONGRESSES, 1789–1997

[See notes at end of table]

Congress & Date	Type	Occasion, topic, or location	Name and position of dignitary (where applicable)
26th CONGRESS			
Feb. 10, 1841	Joint session	Counting electoral votes	N.A.
27th CONGRESS			
Mar. 4, 1841	Inauguration	East Portico	President William Henry Harrison.
28th CONGRESS			
Feb. 12, 1845	Joint session	Counting electoral votes	N.A.
29th CONGRESS			
Mar. 4, 1845	Inauguration	East Portico	President James Knox Polk.
30th CONGRESS			
Feb. 14, 1849	Joint session	Counting electoral votes	N.A.
31st CONGRESS			
Mar. 5, 1849	Inauguration	East Portico	President Zachary Taylor.
July 10, 1850	Joint session	Oath of office to President Millard Fillmore [11].	N.A.
32d CONGRESS			
Feb. 9, 1853	......do	Counting electoral votes	N.A.
33d CONGRESS			
Mar. 4, 1853	Inauguration	East Portico	President Franklin Pierce.
34th CONGRESS			
Feb. 11, 1857	Joint session	Counting electoral votes	N.A.
35th CONGRESS			
Mar. 4, 1857	Inauguration	East Portico	President James Buchanan.
36th CONGRESS			
Feb. 13, 1861	Joint session	Counting electoral votes	N.A.
37th CONGRESS			
Mar. 4, 1861	Inauguration	East Portico	President Abraham Lincoln.
Feb. 22, 1862	Joint session	Reading of Washington's farewell address.	John W. Forney, Secretary of the Senate.
38th CONGRESS			
Feb. 8, 1865	......do	Counting electoral votes	N.A.
39th CONGRESS			
Mar. 4, 1865	Inauguration	East Portico	President Abraham Lincoln.
Feb. 12, 1866	Joint session	Memorial to Abraham Lincoln	George Bancroft, historian; ceremony attended by President Andrew Johnson.
40th CONGRESS			
Feb. 10, 1869	......do	Counting electoral votes	N.A.
41st CONGRESS			
Mar. 4, 1869	Inauguration	East Portico	President Ulysses S. Grant.
42d CONGRESS			
Feb. 12, 1873	Joint session	Counting electoral votes [12]	N.A.
43d CONGRESS			
Mar. 4, 1873	Inauguration	East Portico	President Ulysses S. Grant.
Dec. 18, 1874	Joint meeting	Reception of King Kalakaua of Hawaii	Speaker James G. Blaine; David Kalakaua, King of the Hawaiian Islands.[13]
44th CONGRESS			
Feb. 1, 1877 Feb. 10, 1877 Feb. 12, 1877 Feb. 19, 1877 Feb. 20, 1877 Feb. 21, 1877 Feb. 24, 1877 Feb. 26, 1877 Feb. 28, 1877 Mar. 1, 1877 Mar. 2, 1877	Joint session	Counting electoral votes [14]	N.A.
45th CONGRESS			
Mar. 5, 1877	Inauguration	East Portico	President Rutherford B. Hayes.

JOINT SESSIONS, JOINT MEETINGS, AND INAUGURATIONS—CONTINUED

1st–105th CONGRESSES, 1789–1997

[See notes at end of table]

Congress & Date	Type	Occasion, topic, or location	Name and position of dignitary (where applicable)
46th CONGRESS			
Feb. 9, 1881	Joint session	Counting electoral votes	N.A.
47th CONGRESS			
Mar. 4, 1881	Inauguration	East Portico	President James A. Garfield.
Feb. 27, 1882	Joint session	Memorial to James A. Garfield	James G. Blaine, former Speaker, Senator, and Secretary of State; ceremony attended by President Chester A. Arthur.
48th CONGRESS			
Feb. 11, 1885	......do	Counting electoral votes	N.A.
Feb. 21, 1885	......do	Completion of Washington Monument	Representative John D. Long; Representative-elect John W. Daniel [15]; ceremony attended by President Chester A. Arthur.
49th CONGRESS			
Mar. 4, 1885	Inauguration	East Portico	President Grover Cleveland.
50th CONGRESS			
Feb. 13, 1889	Joint session	Counting electoral votes	N.A.
51st CONGRESS			
Mar. 4, 1889	Inauguration	East Portico	President Benjamin Harrison.
Dec. 11, 1889	Joint session	Centennial of George Washington's first inauguration.	Melville W. Fuller, Chief Justice of the United States; ceremony attended by President Benjamin Harrison.
52d CONGRESS			
Feb. 8, 1893	......do	Counting electoral votes	N.A.
53d CONGRESS			
Mar. 4, 1893	Inauguration	East Portico	President Grover Cleveland.
54th CONGRESS			
Feb. 10, 1897	Joint session	Counting electoral votes	N.A.
55th CONGRESS			
Mar. 4, 1897	Inauguration	In front of original Senate Wing of Capitol.	President William McKinley.
56th CONGRESS			
Dec. 12, 1900	Joint meeting	Centennial of the Capital City	Representatives James D. Richardson and Sereno E. Payne, and Senator George F. Hoar; ceremony attended by President William McKinley.
Feb. 13, 1901	Joint session	Counting electoral votes	N.A.
57th CONGRESS			
Mar. 4, 1901	Inauguration	East Portico	President William McKinley.
Feb. 27, 1902	Joint session	Memorial to William McKinley	John Hay, Secretary of State; ceremony attended by President Theodore Roosevelt and Prince Henry of Prussia.
58th CONGRESS			
Feb. 8, 1905	......do	Counting electoral votes	N.A.
59th CONGRESS			
Mar. 4, 1905	Inauguration	East Portico	President Theodore Roosevelt.
60th CONGRESS			
Feb. 10, 1909	Joint session	Counting electoral votes	N.A.
61st CONGRESS			
Mar. 4, 1909	Inauguration	Senate Chamber [16]	President William Howard Taft.
62d CONGRESS			
Feb. 12, 1913	Joint session	Counting electoral votes	N.A.
Feb. 15, 1913	......do	Memorial for Vice President James S. Sherman [17].	Senators Elihu Root, Thomas S. Martin, Jacob H. Gallinger, John R. Thornton, Henry Cabot Lodge, John W. Kern, Robert M. LaFollette, John Sharp Williams, Charles Curtis, Albert B. Cummins, George T. Oliver, James A. O'Gorman; Speaker Champ Clark; President William Howard Taft.
63d CONGRESS			
Mar. 4, 1913	Inauguration	East Portico	President Woodrow Wilson.

JOINT SESSIONS, JOINT MEETINGS, AND INAUGURATIONS—CONTINUED

1st–105th CONGRESSES, 1789–1997

[See notes at end of table]

Congress & Date	Type	Occasion, topic, or location	Name and position of dignitary (where applicable)
Apr. 8, 1913	Joint session	Tariff message	President Woodrow Wilson.
June 23, 1913	......do	Currency and bank reform message	Do.
Aug. 27, 1913	......do	Mexican affairs message	Do.
Dec. 2, 1913	......do	Annual Message	Do.
Jan. 20, 1914	......do	Trusts message	Do.
Mar. 5, 1914	......do	Panama Canal tolls	Do.
Apr. 20, 1914	......do	Mexico message	Do.
Sept. 4, 1914	......do	War tax message	Do.
Dec. 8, 1914	......do	Annual Message	Do.
64th CONGRESS			
Dec. 7, 1915	......do	......do	Do.
Aug. 29, 1916	......do	Railroad message (labor-management dispute).	Do.
Dec. 5, 1916	......do	Annual Message	Do.
Feb. 3, 1917	......do	Severing diplomatic relations with Germany.	Do.
Feb. 14, 1917	......do	Counting electoral votes	N.A.
Feb. 26, 1917	......do	Arming of merchant ships	President Woodrow Wilson.
65th CONGRESS			
Mar. 5, 1917	Inauguration	East Portico	Do.
Apr. 2, 1917	Joint session	War with Germany	Do.
Dec. 4, 1917	......do	Annual Message/War with Austria-Hungary.	Do.
Jan. 4, 1918	......do	Federal operation of transportation systems.	Do.
Jan. 8, 1918	......do	Program for world's peace	Do.
Feb. 11, 1918	......do	Peace message	Do.
May 27, 1918	......do	War finance message	Do.
Nov. 11, 1918	......do	Terms of armistice signed by Germany	Do.
Dec. 2, 1918	......do	Annual Message	Do.
Feb. 9, 1919	......do	Memorial to Theodore Roosevelt	Senator Henry Cabot Lodge, Sr.; ceremony attended by former President William Howard Taft.
66th CONGRESS			
Aug. 8, 1919	......do	Cost of living message	President Woodrow Wilson.
Sept. 18, 1919	......do	Address	President pro tempore Albert B. Cummins; Speaker Frederick H. Gillett; Representative and former Speaker Champ Clark; General John J. Pershing.
Feb. 9, 1921	......do	Counting electoral votes	N.A.
67th CONGRESS			
Mar. 4, 1921	Inauguration	East Portico	President Warren G. Harding.
Apr. 12, 1921	Joint session	Federal problem message	Do.
Dec. 6, 1921	......do	Annual Message	Do.
Feb. 28, 1922	......do	Maintenance of the merchant marine	Do.
Aug. 18, 1922	......do	Coal and railroad message	Do.
Nov. 21, 1922	......do	Promotion of the American merchant marine.	Do.
Dec. 8, 1922	......do	Annual Message [18]	Do.
Feb. 7, 1923	......do	British debt due to the United States	Do.
68th CONGRESS			
Dec. 6, 1923	......do	Annual Message	President Calvin Coolidge.
Feb. 27, 1924	......do	Memorial to Warren G. Harding	Charles Evans Hughes, Secretary of State; ceremony attended by President Calvin Coolidge.
Dec. 15, 1924	......do	Memorial to Woodrow Wilson	Dr. Edwin Anderson Alderman, President of the University of Virginia; ceremony attended by President Calvin Coolidge.
Feb. 11, 1925	......do	Counting electoral votes	N.A.
69th CONGRESS			
Mar. 4, 1925	Inauguration	East Portico	President Calvin Coolidge.
Feb. 22, 1927	Joint session	George Washington birthday message	Do.
70th CONGRESS			
Feb. 13, 1929	......do	Counting electoral votes	N.A.
71st CONGRESS			
Mar. 4, 1929	Inauguration	East Portico	President Herbert Hoover.
72d CONGRESS			
Feb. 22, 1932	Joint session	Bicentennial of George Washington's birth.	Do.

JOINT SESSIONS, JOINT MEETINGS, AND INAUGURATIONS—CONTINUED

1st–105th CONGRESSES, 1789–1997

[See notes at end of table]

Congress & Date	Type	Occasion, topic, or location	Name and position of dignitary (where applicable)
Feb. 6, 1933	Joint meeting	Memorial to Calvin Coolidge	Arthur Prentice Rugg, Chief Justice of the Supreme Judicial Court of Massachusetts; ceremony attended by President Herbert Hoover.
Feb. 8, 1933	Joint session	Counting electoral votes	N.A.
73d CONGRESS			
Mar. 4, 1933	Inauguration	East Portico	President Franklin Delano Roosevelt.
Jan. 3, 1934	Joint session	Annual Message	Do.
May 20, 1934	......do	100th anniversary, death of Lafayette	André de Laboulaye, Ambassador of France; President Franklin Delano Roosevelt; ceremony attended by Count de Chambrun, great-grandson of Lafayette.
74th CONGRESS			
Jan. 4, 1935	......do	Annual Message	President Franklin Delano Roosevelt.
May 22, 1935	......do	Veto message	Do.
Jan. 3, 1936	......do	Annual Message	Do.
75th CONGRESS			
Jan. 6, 1937	......do	Counting electoral votes	N.A.
Do	......do	Annual Message	President Franklin Delano Roosevelt.
Jan. 20, 1937	Inauguration	East Portico	President Franklin Delano Roosevelt; Vice President John Nance Garner.[19]
Jan. 3, 1938	Joint session	Annual Message	President Franklin Delano Roosevelt.
76th CONGRESS			
Jan. 4, 1939	......do	......do	Do.
Mar. 4, 1939	......do	Sesquicentennial of the 1st Congress	Do.
June 9, 1939	Joint meeting	Reception[20]	George VI and Elizabeth, King and Queen of the United Kingdom.
Sept. 21, 1939	Joint session	Neutrality address	President Franklin Delano Roosevelt.
Jan. 3, 1940	......do	Annual Message	Do.
May 16, 1940	......do	National defense message	Do.
77th CONGRESS			
Jan. 6, 1941	......do	Counting electoral votes	N.A.
Do	......do	Annual Message	President Franklin Delano Roosevelt.
Jan. 20, 1941	......do	Inauguration, East Portico	President Franklin Delano Roosevelt; Vice President Henry A. Wallace.
Dec. 8, 1941	......do	War with Japan	President Franklin Delano Roosevelt.
Dec. 26, 1941	Joint meeting	Address[21]	Winston Churchill, Prime Minister of the United Kingdom.
Jan. 6, 1942	Joint session	Annual Message	President Franklin Delano Roosevelt.
78th CONGRESS			
Jan. 7, 1943	......do	......do	Do.
May 19, 1943	Joint meeting	Address	Winston Churchill, Prime Minister of the United Kingdom.
Nov. 18, 1943	......do	Moscow Conference	Cordell Hull, Secretary of State.
79th CONGRESS			
Jan. 6, 1945	Joint session	Counting electoral votes	N.A.
Do	......do	Annual Message	President Roosevelt was not present. His message was read before the Joint Session of Congress.
Jan. 20, 1945	Inauguration	South Portico, The White House[22]	President Franklin Delano Roosevelt; Vice President Harry S. Truman.
Mar. 1, 1945	Joint session	Yalta Conference	President Franklin Delano Roosevelt.
Apr. 16, 1945	......do	Prosecution of the War	President Harry S. Truman.
May 21, 1945	......do	Bestowal of Congressional Medal of Honor on Tech. Sgt. Jake William Lindsey.	General George C. Marshall, Chief of Staff, U.S. Army; President Harry S. Truman.
June 18, 1945	Joint meeting	Address	General Dwight D. Eisenhower, Supreme Commander, Allied Expeditionary Force.
Oct. 5, 1945	......do	......do	Admiral Chester W. Nimitz, Commander-in-Chief, Pacific Fleet.
Oct. 23, 1945	Joint session	Universal military training message	President Harry S. Truman.
Nov. 13, 1945	Joint meeting	Address	Clement R. Attlee, Prime Minister of the United Kingdom.
May 25, 1946	Joint session	Railroad strike message	President Harry S. Truman.
July 1, 1946	......do	Memorial to Franklin Delano Roosevelt	John Winant, U.S. Representative on the Economic and Social Council of the United Nations; ceremony attended by President Harry S. Truman and Mrs. Franklin Delano Roosevelt.

JOINT SESSIONS, JOINT MEETINGS, AND INAUGURATIONS—CONTINUED

1st–105th CONGRESSES, 1789–1997

[See notes at end of table]

Congress & Date	Type	Occasion, topic, or location	Name and position of dignitary (where applicable)
80th CONGRESS			
Jan. 6, 1947	Joint session	State of the Union Address [23]	President Harry S. Truman.
Mar. 12, 1947	......do	Greek-Turkish aid policy	Do.
May 1, 1947	Joint meeting	Address	Miguel Aleman, President of Mexico.
Nov. 17, 1947	Joint session	Aid to Europe message	President Harry S. Truman.
Jan. 7, 1948	......do	State of the Union Address	Do.
Mar. 17, 1948	......do	National security and conditions in Europe.	Do.
Apr. 19, 1948	......do	50th anniversary, liberation of Cuba	President Harry S. Truman; Guillermo Belt, Ambassador of Cuba.
July 27, 1948	......do	Inflation, housing, and civil rights	President Harry S. Truman.
81st CONGRESS			
Jan. 5, 1949	......do	State of the Union Address	Do.
Jan. 6, 1949	......do	Counting electoral votes	N.A.
Jan. 20, 1949	......do	Inauguration, East Portico	President Harry S. Truman; Vice President Alben W. Barkley.
May 19, 1949	Joint meeting	Address	Eurico Gaspar Dutra, President of Brazil.
Jan. 4, 1950	Joint session	State of the Union Address	President Harry S. Truman.
May 31, 1950	Joint meeting	Address	Dean Acheson, Secretary of State.
82d CONGRESS			
Jan. 8, 1951	Joint session	State of the Union Address	President Harry S. Truman.
Feb. 1, 1951	Joint meeting [24]	North Atlantic Treaty Organization	General Dwight D. Eisenhower.
Apr. 2, 1951	......do	Address	Vincent Auriol, President of France.
Apr. 19, 1951	......do	Return from Pacific Command	General Douglas MacArthur.
June 21, 1951	......do	Address	Galo Plaza, President of Ecuador.
Sept. 24, 1951	......do	......do	Alcide de Gasperi, Prime Minister of Italy.
Jan. 9, 1952	Joint session	State of the Union Address	President Harry S. Truman.
Jan. 17, 1952	Joint meeting	Address	Winston Churchill, Prime Minister of the United Kingdom.
Apr. 3, 1952	......do	......do	Juliana, Queen of the Netherlands.
May 22, 1952	......do	Korea	General Matthew B. Ridgway.
June 10, 1952	Joint session	Steel industry dispute	President Harry S. Truman.
83d CONGRESS			
Jan. 6, 1953	......do	Counting electoral votes	N.A.
Jan. 20, 1953	......do	Inauguration, East Portico	President Dwight D. Eisenhower; Vice President Richard M. Nixon.
Feb. 2, 1953	......do	State of the Union Address	President Dwight D. Eisenhower.
Jan. 7, 1954	......do	......do	Do.
Jan. 29, 1954	Joint meeting	Address	Celal Bayar, President of Turkey.
May 4, 1954	......do	......do	Vincent Massey, Governor General of Canada.
May 28, 1954	......do	......do	Haile Selassie I, Emperor of Ethiopia.
July 28, 1954	......do	......do	Syngman Rhee, President of South Korea.
84th CONGRESS			
Jan. 6, 1955	Joint session	State of the Union Address	President Dwight D. Eisenhower.
Jan. 27, 1955	Joint meeting	Address	Paul E. Magliore, President of Haiti.
Feb. 29, 1956	......do	......do	Giovanni Gronchi, President of Italy.
May 17, 1956	......do	......do	Dr. Sukarno, President of Indonesia.
85th CONGRESS			
Jan. 5, 1957	Joint session	Middle East message	President Dwight D. Eisenhower.
Jan. 7, 1957	......do	Counting electoral votes	N.A.
Jan. 10, 1957	......do	State of the Union Address	President Dwight D. Eisenhower.
Jan. 21, 1957	......do	Inauguration, East Portico	President Dwight D. Eisenhower; Vice President Richard M. Nixon.
May 9, 1957	Joint meeting	Address	Ngo Dinh Diem, President of Vietnam.
Jan. 9, 1958	Joint session	State of the Union Address	President Dwight D. Eisenhower.
June 5, 1958	Joint meeting	Address	Theodor Heuss, President of West Germany.
June 18, 1958	......do	......do	Carlos F. Garcia, President of the Philippines.
86th CONGRESS			
Jan. 9, 1959	Joint session	State of the Union Address	President Dwight D. Eisenhower.
Jan. 21, 1959	Joint meeting	Address	Arturo Frondizi, President of Argentina.
Feb. 12, 1959	Joint session	Sesquicentennial of Abraham Lincoln's birth.	Fredric March, actor; Carl Sandburg, poet.
Mar. 11, 1959	Joint meeting	Address	Jose Maria Lemus, President of El Salvador.
Mar. 18, 1959	......do	......do	Sean T. O'Kelly, President of Ireland.
May 12, 1959	......do	......do	Baudouin, King of the Belgians.
Jan. 7, 1960	Joint session	State of the Union Address	President Dwight D. Eisenhower.
Apr. 6, 1960	Joint meeting	Address	Alberto Lleras-Camargo, President of Colombia.

JOINT SESSIONS, JOINT MEETINGS, AND INAUGURATIONS—CONTINUED

1st–105th CONGRESSES, 1789–1997

[See notes at end of table]

Congress & Date	Type	Occasion, topic, or location	Name and position of dignitary (where applicable)
Apr. 25, 1960	Joint meeting	Address	Charles de Gaulle, President of France.
Apr. 28, 1960	......do	......do	Mahendra, King of Nepal.
June 29, 1960	......do	......do	Bhumibol Adulyadej, King of Thailand.
87th CONGRESS			
Jan. 6, 1961	Joint session	Counting electoral votes	N.A.
Jan. 20, 1961	......do	Inauguration, East Portico	President John F. Kennedy; Vice President Lyndon B. Johnson.
Jan. 30, 1961	......do	State of the Union Address	President John F. Kennedy.
May 4, 1961	Joint meeting	Address	Habib Bourguiba, President of Tunisia.
May 25, 1961	Joint session	Urgent national needs: foreign aid, defense, civil defense, and outer space.	President John F. Kennedy.
July 12, 1961	Joint meeting	Address	Mohammad Ayub Khan, President of Pakistan.
Sept. 21, 1961	......do	......do	Manuel Prado, President of Peru.
Jan. 11, 1962	Joint session	State of the Union Address	President John F. Kennedy.
Feb. 26, 1962	Joint meeting	Friendship 7: 1st United States orbital space flight.	Lt. Col. John H. Glenn, Jr., USMC; Friendship 7 astronaut.
Apr. 4, 1962	......do	Address	João Goulart, President of Brazil.
Apr. 12, 1962	......do	......do	Mohammad Reza Shah Pahlavi, Shahanshah of Iran.
88th CONGRESS			
Jan. 14, 1963	Joint session	State of the Union Address	President John F. Kennedy.
May 21, 1963	Joint meeting	Flight of Faith 7 Spacecraft	Maj. Gordon L. Cooper, Jr., USAF, Faith 7 astronaut.
Nov. 27, 1963	Joint session	Assumption of office	President Lyndon B. Johnson.
Jan. 8, 1964	......do	State of the Union Address	Do.
Jan. 15, 1964	Joint meeting	Address	Antonio Segni, President of Italy.
May 28, 1964	......do	......do	Eamon de Valera, President of Ireland.
89th CONGRESS			
Jan. 4, 1965	Joint session	State of the Union Address	President Lyndon B. Johnson.
Jan. 6, 1965	......do	Counting electoral votes	N.A.
Jan. 20, 1965	......do [25]	Inauguration, East Portico	President Lyndon B. Johnson; Vice President Hubert H. Humphrey.
Mar. 15, 1965	......do	Voting rights	President Lyndon B. Johnson.
Sept. 14, 1965	Joint meeting	Flight of Gemini 5 Spacecraft	Lt. Col. Gordon L. Cooper, Jr., USAF; and Charles Conrad, Jr., USN; Gemini 5 astronauts.
Jan. 12, 1966	Joint session	State of the Union Address	President Lyndon B. Johnson.
Sept. 15, 1966	Joint meeting	Address	Ferdinand E. Marcos, President of the Philippines.
90th CONGRESS			
Jan. 10, 1967	Joint session	State of the Union Address	President Lyndon B. Johnson.
Apr. 28, 1967	Joint meeting	Vietnam policy	General William C. Westmoreland.
Oct. 27, 1967	......do	Address	Gustavo Diaz Ordaz, President of Mexico.
Jan. 17, 1968	Joint session	State of the Union Address	President Lyndon B. Johnson.
91st CONGRESS			
Jan. 6, 1969	......do	Counting electoral votes [26]	N.A.
Jan. 9, 1969	Joint meeting	Apollo 8: 1st flight around the moon	Col. Frank Borman, USAF; Capt. James A. Lowell, Jr., USN; Lt. Col. William A. Anders, USAF; Apollo 8 astronauts.
Jan. 14, 1969	Joint session	State of the Union Address	President Lyndon B. Johnson.
Jan. 20, 1969	......do [25]	Inauguration, East Portico	President Richard M. Nixon; Vice President Spiro T. Agnew.
Sept. 16, 1969	Joint meeting	Apollo 11: 1st lunar landing	Neil A. Armstrong; Col. Edwin E. Aldrin, Jr., USAF; and Lt. Col. Michael Collins, USAF; Apollo 11 astronauts.
Jan. 22, 1970	Joint session	State of the Union Address	President Richard M. Nixon.
Feb. 25, 1970	Joint meeting	Address	Georges Pompidou, President of France.
June 3, 1970	......do	......do	Dr. Rafael Caldera, President of Venezuela.
Sept. 22, 1970	......do	Report on prisoners of war	Col. Frank Borman, Representative to the President on Prisoners of War.
92d CONGRESS			
Jan. 22, 1971	Joint session	State of the Union Address	President Richard M. Nixon.
Sept. 9, 1971	......do	Economic policy	Do.
Do	Joint meeting	Apollo 15: lunar mission	Col. David R. Scott, USAF; Col. James B. Irwin, USAF; and Lt. Col. Alfred M. Worden, USAF; Apollo 15 astronauts.
Jan. 20, 1972	Joint session	State of the Union Address	President Richard M. Nixon.
June 1, 1972	......do	European trip report	Do.
June 15, 1972	Joint meeting	Address	Luis Echeverria Alvarez, President of Mexico.

JOINT SESSIONS, JOINT MEETINGS, AND INAUGURATIONS—CONTINUED

1st–105th CONGRESSES, 1789–1997

[See notes at end of table]

Congress & Date	Type	Occasion, topic, or location	Name and position of dignitary (where applicable)
93d CONGRESS			
Jan. 6, 1973	Joint session	Counting electoral votes	N.A.
Jan. 20, 1973	Inauguration	East Portico	President Richard M. Nixon; Vice President Spiro T. Agnew.
Dec. 6, 1973	Joint meeting	Oath of office to Vice President Gerald R. Ford.	Vice President Gerald R. Ford; ceremony attended by President Richard M. Nixon.
Jan. 30 1974	Joint session	State of the Union Address	President Richard M. Nixon.
Aug. 12, 1974	......do	Assumption of office	President Gerald R. Ford.
Oct. 8, 1974	......do	Economy	Do.
94th CONGRESS			
Jan. 15, 1975	......do	State of the Union Address	President Gerald R. Ford.
Apr. 10, 1975	......do	State of the World message	Do.
June 17, 1975	Joint meeting	Address	Walter Scheel, President of West Germany.
Nov. 5, 1975	......do	......do	Anwar El Sadat, President of Egypt.
Jan. 19, 1976	Joint session	State of the Union Address	President Gerald R. Ford.
Jan. 28, 1976	Joint meeting	Address	Yitzhak Rabin, Prime Minister of Israel.
Mar. 17, 1976	......do	......do	Liam Cosgrave, Prime Minister of Ireland.
May 18, 1976	......do	......do	Valery Giscard d'Estaing, President of France.
June 2, 1976	......do	......do	Juan Carlos I, King of Spain.
Sept. 23, 1976	......do	......do	Dr. William R. Tolbert, Jr., President of Liberia.
95th CONGRESS			
Jan. 6, 1977	Joint session	Counting electoral votes	N.A.
Jan. 12, 1977	......do	State of the Union Address	President Gerald R. Ford.
Jan. 20, 1977	Inauguration	East Portico	President Jimmy Carter; Vice President Walter F. Mondale.
Feb. 22, 1977	Joint meeting	Address	Pierre Elliot Trudeau, Prime Minister of Canada.
Apr. 20, 1977	Joint session	Energy	President Jimmy Carter.
Jan. 19, 1978	......do	State of the Union Address	Do.
Sept. 18, 1978	......do	Middle East Peace agreements	Do.; joint session attended by Anwar El Sadat, President of Egypt, and by Menachem Begin, Prime Minister of Israel.
96th CONGRESS			
Jan. 23, 1979	......do	State of the Union Address	Do.
June 18, 1979	......do	Salt II agreements	Do.
Jan. 23, 1980	......do	State of the Union Address	Do.
97th CONGRESS			
Jan. 6, 1981	......do	Counting electoral votes	N.A.
Jan. 20, 1981	......do[25]	Inauguration, West Front	President Ronald Reagan; Vice President George Bush.
Feb. 18, 1981	......do	Economic recovery	President Ronald Reagan.
Apr. 28, 1981	......do	Economic recovery—inflation	Do.
Jan. 26, 1982	......do	State of the Union Address	Do.
Jan. 28, 1982	Joint meeting	Centennial of birth of Franklin Delano Roosevelt.	Dr. Arthur Schlesinger, historian; Senator Jennings Randolph; Representative Claude Pepper; Averell Harriman, former Governor of New York[27]; former Representative James Roosevelt, son of President Roosevelt.
Apr. 21, 1982	......do	Address	Beatrix, Queen of the Netherlands.
98th CONGRESS			
Jan. 25, 1983	Joint session	State of the Union Address	President Ronald Reagan.
Apr. 27, 1983	......do	Central America	Do.
Oct. 5, 1983	Joint meeting	Address	Karl Carstens, President of West Germany.
Jan. 25, 1984	Joint session	State of the Union Address	President Ronald Reagan.
Mar. 15, 1984	Joint meeting	Address	Dr. Garett FitzGerald, Prime Minister of Ireland.
Mar. 22, 1984	......do	......do	François Mitterand, President of France.
May 8, 1984	......do	Centennial of birth of Harry S. Truman	Representatives Ike Skelton and Alan Wheat; former Senator Stuart Symington; Margaret Truman Daniel, daughter of President Truman; and Senator Mark Hatfield.
May 16, 1984	......do	Address	Miguel de la Madrid, President of Mexico.
99th CONGRESS			
Jan. 7, 1985	Joint session	Counting electoral votes	N.A.

JOINT SESSIONS, JOINT MEETINGS, AND INAUGURATIONS—CONTINUED

1st–105th CONGRESSES, 1789–1997

[See notes at end of table]

Congress & Date	Type	Occasion, topic, or location	Name and position of dignitary (where applicable)
Jan. 21, 1985	Inauguration	Rotunda[28]	President Ronald Reagan; Vice President George Bush.
Feb. 6, 1985	Joint session	State of the Union Address	President Ronald Reagan.
Feb. 20, 1985	Joint meeting	Address	Margaret Thatcher, Prime Minister of the United Kingdom.
Mar. 6, 1985	......do	......do	Bettino Craxi, President of the Council of Ministers of Italy.
Mar. 20, 1985	......do	......do	Raul Alfonsin, President of Argentina.
June 13, 1985	......do	......do	Rajiv Gandhi, Prime Minister of India.
Oct. 9, 1985	......do	......do	Lee Kuan Yew, Prime Minister of Singapore.
Nov. 21, 1985	Joint session	Geneva Summit	President Ronald Reagan.
Feb. 4, 1986	......do	State of the Union Address	Do.
Sept. 11, 1986	Joint meeting	Address	Jose Sarney, President of Brazil.
Sept. 18, 1986	......do	......do	Corazon C. Aquino, President of the Philippines.
100th CONGRESS			
Jan. 27, 1987	Joint session	State of the Union Address	President Ronald Reagan.
Nov. 10, 1987	Joint meeting	Address	Chaim Herzog, President of Israel.
Jan. 25, 1988	Joint session	State of the Union Address	President Ronald Reagan.
Apr. 27, 1988	Joint meeting	Address	Brian Mulroney, Prime Minister of Canada.
June 23, 1988	......do	......do	Robert Hawke, Prime Minister of Australia.
101st CONGRESS			
Jan. 4, 1989	Joint session	Counting electoral votes	N.A.
Jan. 20, 1989	Inauguration	West Front	President George Bush; Vice President Dan Quayle.
Feb. 9, 1989	Joint session	Building a Better America	President George Bush.
Mar. 2, 1989	Joint meeting	Bicentennial of the 1st Congress	President Pro Tempore Robert C. Byrd; Speaker James C. Wright, Jr.; Representatives Lindy Boggs, Thomas S. Foley, and Robert H. Michel; Senators George Mitchell and Robert Dole; Howard Nemerov, Poet Laureate of the United States; David McCullough, historian; Anthony M. Frank, Postmaster General; former Senator Nicholas Brady, Secretary of the Treasury.
June 7, 1989	......do	Address	Benazir Bhutto, Prime Minister of Pakistan.
Oct. 4, 1989	......do	......do	Carlos Salinas de Gortari, President of Mexico.
Oct. 18, 1989	......do	......do	Roh Tae Woo, President of South Korea.
Nov. 15, 1989	......do	Address	Lech Walesa, chairman of Solidarnośc labor union, Poland.
Jan. 31, 1990	Joint session	State of the Union Address	President George Bush.
Feb. 21, 1990	Joint meeting	Address	Vaclav Hável, President of Czechoslovakia.
Mar. 7, 1990	......do	......do	Giulio Andreotti,President of the Council of Ministers of Italy.
Mar. 27, 1990	......do	Centennial of birth of Dwight D. Eisenhower.	Senator Robert Dole; Walter Cronkite, television journalist; Winston S. Churchill, member of British Parliament and grandson of Prime Minister Churchill; Clark M. Clifford, former Secretary of Defense; James D. Robinson III, chairman of Eisenhower Centennial Foundation; Arnold Palmer, professional golfer; John S.D. Eisenhower, former Ambassador to Belgium and son of President Eisenhower; Representatives Beverly Byron, William F. Goodling, and Pat Roberts.
June 26, 1990	......do	Address	Nelson Mandela, Deputy President of the African National Congress, South Africa.
Sept. 11, 1990	Joint session	Invasion of Kuwait by Iraq	President George Bush.
102d CONGRESS			
Jan. 29, 1991	......do	State of the Union Address	Do.
Mar. 6, 1991	......do	Conclusion of Persian Gulf War	Do.
Apr. 16, 1991	Joint meeting	Address	Violeta B. de Chamorro, President of Nicaragua.

JOINT SESSIONS, JOINT MEETINGS, AND INAUGURATIONS—CONTINUED

1st–105th CONGRESSES, 1789–1997

[See notes at end of table]

Congress & Date	Type	Occasion, topic, or location	Name and position of dignitary (where applicable)
May 16, 1991	Joint meeting	Address	Elizabeth II, Queen of the United Kingdom; joint meeting also attended by Prince Philip.
Nov. 14, 1991	......do	......do	Carlos Saul Menem, President of Argentina.
Jan. 28, 1992	Joint session	State of the Union Address	President George Bush.
Apr. 30, 1992	Joint meeting	Address	Richard von Weizsäcker, President of Germany.
June 17, 1992	......do	......do	Boris Yeltsin, President of Russia.
103d CONGRESS			
Jan. 6, 1993	Joint session	Counting electoral votes	N.A.
Jan. 20, 1993	Inauguration	West Front	President William J. Clinton; Vice President Albert Gore.
Feb. 17, 1993	Joint session	Economic Address[29]	President William J. Clinton.
Sept. 22, 1993	......do	Health care reform	Do.
Jan. 25, 1994	......do	State of the Union Address	Do.
May 18, 1994	Joint meeting	Address	Narasimha Rao, Prime Minister of India.
July 26, 1994	......do	Addresses	Hussein I, King of Jordan; Yitzhak Rabin, Prime Minister of Israel.
Oct. 6, 1994	......do	Address	Nelson Mandela, President of South Africa.
105th CONGRESS			
Jan. 24, 1995	Joint session	State of the Union Address	President William J. Clinton.
July 26, 1995	Joint meeting	Address	Kim Yong-sam, President of South Korea[30].
Oct. 11, 1995	......do	Close of the Commemoration of the 50th Anniversary of World War II.	Speaker Newt Gingrich; Vice President Albert Gore; President Pro Tempore Strom Thurmond; Representatives Henry J. Hyde and G. V. "Sonny" Montgomery; Senators Daniel K. Inouye and Robert Dole; former Representative Robert H. Michel; General Louis H. Wilson (ret.), former Commandant of the Marine Corps.
Dec. 12, 1995	......do	Address	Shimon Peres, Prime Minister of Israel.
Jan. 30, 1996	Joint session	State of the Union Address	President William J. Clinton.
Feb. 1, 1996	Joint meeting	Address	Jacques Chirac, President of France.
July 10, 1996	......do	......do	Benyamin Netanyahu, Prime Minister of Israel.
Sept. 11, 1996	......do	......do	John Bruton, Prime Minister of Ireland.
105th CONGRESS			
Jan. 9, 1997	Joint session	Counting electoral votes	N.A.
Jan. 20, 1997	Inauguration	West Front	President William J. Clinton, Vice President Albert Gore.
Feb. 4, 1997	Joint session	State of the Union Address[31]	President William J. Clinton.
Feb. 27, 1997	Joint meeting	Address	Edurado Frei, President of Chile.

[1] Closing date for this table was May 12, 1997.

[2] The oath of office was administered to George Washington outside on the gallery in front of the Senate Chamber, after which the Congress and the President returned to the chamber to hear the inaugural address. They then proceeded to St. Paul's Chapel for the "divine service" performed by the Chaplain of the Congress. Adjournment of the ceremony did not occur until the Congress returned to Federal Hall.

[3] Funeral oration was delivered at the German Lutheran Church in Philadelphia.

[4] Because of a tie in the electoral vote between Thomas Jefferson and Aaron Burr, the House of Representatives had to decide the election. Thirty-six ballots were required to break the deadlock, with Jefferson's election as President and Burr's as Vice President on February 17. The Twelfth Amendment was added to the Constitution to prevent the 1800 problem from recurring.

[5] During most of the period while the Capitol was being reconstructed following the fire of 1814, the Congress met in the "Brick Capitol," constructed on the site of the present Supreme Court building. This joint session took place in the Representatives' chamber on the 2d floor of the building.

[6] The joint session to count electoral votes was dissolved because the House and Senate disagreed on Missouri's status regarding statehood. The joint session was reconvened the same day and Missouri's votes were counted.

[7] While this occasion has historically been referred to as the first joint meeting of Congress, the Journals of the House and of the Senate indicate that Lafayette actually addressed the House of Representatives, with some of the Senators present as guests of the House. Similar occasions, when members of the one body were invited as guests of the other, include the Senate address by Queen Wilhelmina of the Netherlands on Aug. 6, 1942, and the House address by General H. Norman Schwarzkopf on May 8, 1991.

[8] Although Andrew Jackson won the popular vote by a substantial amount and had the highest number of electoral votes from among the several candidates, he did not receive the required majority of the electoral votes. The responsibility for choosing the new President therefore devolved upon the House of Representatives. As soon as the Senators left the chamber, the balloting proceeded, and John Quincy Adams was elected on the first ballot.

[9] The ceremony was moved outside to accommodate the extraordinarily large crowd of people who had come to Washington to see the inauguration.

[10] The ceremony was moved inside because of cold weather.

[11] Following the death of President Zachary Taylor, Vice President Millard Fillmore took the presidential oath of office in a special joint session in the Hall of the House.

JOINT SESSIONS, JOINT MEETINGS, AND INAUGURATIONS—CONTINUED

1st–105th CONGRESSES, 1789–1997

[12] The joint session to count electoral votes was dissolved three times so that the House and Senate could resolve several electoral disputes.

[13] Because of a severe cold and hoarseness, the King could not deliver his speech, which was read by former Representative Elisha Hunt Allen, then serving as Chancellor and Chief Justice of the Hawaiian Islands.

[14] The contested election between Rutherford B. Hayes and Samuel J. Tilden created a constitutional crisis. Tilden won the popular vote by a close margin, but disputes concerning the electoral vote returns from four states deadlocked the proceedings of the joint session. Anticipating this development, the Congress had created a special commission of five Senators, five Representatives, and five Supreme Court Justices to resolve such disputes. The Commission met in the Supreme Court Chamber (the present Old Senate Chamber) as each problem arose. In each case, the Commission accepted the Hayes' electors, securing his election by one electoral vote. The joint session was convened on 15 occasions, with the last on March 2, just three days before the inauguration.

[15] The speech was written by former Speaker and Senator Robert C. Winthrop, who could not attend the ceremony because of ill health.

[16] Because of a blizzard, the ceremony was moved inside, where it was held as part of the Senate's special session. President William Howard Taft took the oath of office and gave his inaugural address after Vice President James S. Sherman's inaugural address and the swearing-in of the new senators.

[17] Held in the Senate Chamber.

[18] This was the first Annual Message broadcast live on radio.

[19] This was the first inauguration held pursuant to the Twentieth Amendment, which changed the date from March 4 to January 20. The Vice Presidential oath, which previously had been given earlier on the same day in the Senate Chamber, was added to the inaugural ceremony as well, but the Vice Presidential inaugural address was discontinued.

[20] A joint reception for the King and Queen of the United Kingdom was held in the Rotunda, authorized by Senate Concurrent Resolution 17, 76th Congress. Although the concurrent resolution was structured to establish a joint meeting, the Senate, in fact, adjourned rather than recessed as called for by the resolution.

[21] Delivered in the Senate Chamber.

[22] The oaths of office were taken in simple ceremonies at the White House because the expense and festivity of a Capitol ceremony were thought inappropriate because of the war. The Joint Committee on Arrangements of the Congress was in charge, however, and both the Senate and the House of Representatives were present.

[23] This was the first time the term "State of the Union Address" was used for the President's Annual Message. Also, it was the first time the address was shown live on television.

[24] An informal meeting in the Coolidge Auditorium of the Library of Congress.

[25] According to the Congressional Record, the Senate adjourned prior to the inaugural ceremonies, even though the previously adopted resolution had stated the adjournment would come immediately following the inauguration. The Senate Journal records the adjournment as called for in the resolution, hence this listing as a joint session.

[26] The joint session to count electoral votes was dissolved so that the House and Senate could resolve the dispute regarding a ballot from North Carolina. The joint session was reconvened the same day and the North Carolina vote was counted.

[27] Because the Governor had laryngitis, his speech was read by his wife, Pamela.

[28] The ceremony was moved inside because of extremely cold weather.

[29] This speech was mislabeled in many sources as a State of the Union Address.

[30] President Kim Yong-sam was in Washington for the dedication of the Korean Veterans' Memorial, held the day after this joint meeting.

[31] This was the first State of the Union Address carried live on the Internet.

REPRESENTATIVES UNDER EACH APPORTIONMENT

State	Constitutional apportionment	First Census, 1790	Second Census, 1800	Third Census, 1810	Fourth Census, 1820	Fifth Census, 1830	Sixth Census, 1840	Seventh Census, 1850	Eighth Census, 1860	Ninth Census, 1870	Tenth Census, 1880	Eleventh Census, 1890	Twelfth Census, 1900	Thirteenth Census, 1910 [1]	Fifteenth Census, 1930	Sixteenth Census, 1940	Seventeenth Census, 1950	Eighteenth Census, 1960	Nineteenth Census, 1970	Twentieth Census, 1980	Twenty-First Census, 1990
Alabama	......	......	......	[2]1	3	5	7	7	6	8	8	9	9	10	9	9	9	8	7	7	7
Alaska	......	......	......	......	......	......	......	......	......	......	......	......	......	......	......	......	[2]1	1	1	1	1
Arizona	......	......	......	......	......	......	......	......	......	......	......	......	......	[2]1	1	2	2	3	4	5	6
Arkansas	......	......	......	......	......	[2]1	1	2	3	4	5	6	7	7	7	7	6	4	4	4	4
California	......	......	......	......	......	......	[2]2	2	3	4	6	7	8	11	20	23	30	38	43	45	52
Colorado	......	......	......	......	......	......	......	......	......	[2]1	1	2	3	4	4	4	4	4	5	6	6
Connecticut	5	7	7	7	6	6	4	4	4	4	4	4	5	5	6	6	6	6	6	6	6
Delaware	1	1	1	2	1	1	1	1	1	1	1	1	1	1	1	1	1	1	1	1	1
Florida	......	......	......	......	......	......	[2]1	1	1	2	2	2	3	4	5	6	8	12	15	19	23
Georgia	3	2	4	6	7	9	8	8	7	9	10	11	11	12	10	10	10	10	10	10	11
Hawaii	......	......	......	......	......	......	......	......	......	......	......	......	......	......	......	......	[2]1	2	2	2	2
Idaho	......	......	......	......	......	......	......	......	......	......	[2]1	1	1	2	2	2	2	2	2	2	2
Illinois	......	......	......	[2]1	1	3	7	9	14	19	20	22	25	27	27	26	25	24	24	22	20
Indiana	......	......	......	[2]1	3	7	10	11	11	13	13	13	13	13	12	11	11	11	11	10	10
Iowa	......	......	......	......	......	......	[2]2	2	6	9	11	11	11	11	9	8	8	7	6	6	5
Kansas	......	......	......	......	......	......	......	......	1	3	7	8	8	8	7	6	6	5	5	5	4
Kentucky	......	2	6	10	12	13	10	10	9	10	11	11	11	11	9	9	8	7	7	7	6
Louisiana	......	......	......	[2]1	3	3	4	4	5	6	6	6	7	8	8	8	8	8	8	8	7
Maine	......	......	......	[3]7	7	8	7	6	5	5	4	4	4	4	3	3	3	2	2	2	2
Maryland	6	8	9	9	9	8	6	6	5	6	6	6	6	6	6	6	7	8	8	8	8
Massachusetts	8	14	17	[3]13	13	12	10	11	10	11	12	13	14	16	15	14	14	12	12	11	10
Michigan	......	......	......	......	......	[2]1	3	4	6	9	11	12	12	13	17	17	18	19	19	18	16
Minnesota	......	......	......	......	......	......	......	[2]2	2	3	5	7	9	10	9	9	9	8	8	8	8
Mississippi	......	......	......	[2]1	1	2	4	5	5	6	7	7	8	8	7	7	6	5	5	5	5
Missouri	......	......	......	......	1	2	5	7	9	13	14	15	16	16	13	13	11	10	10	9	9
Montana	......	......	......	......	......	......	......	......	......	......	[2]1	1	1	2	2	2	2	2	2	2	1
Nebraska	......	......	......	......	......	......	......	......	[2]1	1	3	6	6	6	5	4	4	3	3	3	3
Nevada	......	......	......	......	......	......	......	......	[2]1	1	1	1	1	1	1	1	1	1	1	2	2
New Hampshire	3	4	5	6	6	5	4	3	3	3	2	2	2	2	2	2	2	2	2	2	2
New Jersey	4	5	6	6	6	6	5	5	5	7	7	8	10	12	14	14	14	15	15	14	13
New Mexico	......	......	......	......	......	......	......	......	......	......	......	......	......	[2]1	1	2	2	2	2	3	3
New York	6	10	17	27	34	40	34	33	31	33	34	34	37	43	45	45	43	41	39	34	31
North Carolina	5	10	12	13	13	13	9	8	7	8	9	9	10	10	11	12	12	11	11	11	12
North Dakota	......	......	......	......	......	......	......	......	......	......	[2]1	1	2	3	2	2	2	2	1	1	1
Ohio	......	......	[2]1	6	14	19	21	21	19	20	21	21	21	22	24	23	23	24	23	21	19
Oklahoma	......	......	......	......	......	......	......	......	......	......	......	......	[2]5	8	9	8	6	6	6	6	6
Oregon	......	......	......	......	......	......	......	[2]1	1	1	1	2	2	3	3	4	4	4	4	5	5
Pennsylvania	8	13	18	23	26	28	24	25	24	27	28	30	32	36	34	33	30	27	25	23	21
Rhode Island	1	2	2	2	2	2	2	2	2	2	2	2	2	3	2	2	2	2	2	2	2
South Carolina	5	6	8	9	9	9	7	6	4	5	7	7	7	7	6	6	6	6	6	6	6
South Dakota	......	......	......	......	......	......	......	......	......	......	[2]2	2	2	3	2	2	2	2	2	1	1
Tennessee	......	[2]1	3	6	9	13	11	10	8	10	10	10	10	10	9	10	9	9	8	9	9
Texas	......	......	......	......	......	......	[2]2	2	4	6	11	13	16	18	21	21	22	23	24	27	30
Utah	......	......	......	......	......	......	......	......	......	......	......	[2]1	1	2	2	2	2	2	2	3	3
Vermont	......	2	4	6	5	5	4	3	3	3	2	2	2	2	1	1	1	1	1	1	1
Virginia	10	19	22	23	22	21	15	13	11	9	10	10	10	10	9	9	10	10	10	10	11
Washington	......	......	......	......	......	......	......	......	......	......	[2]1	2	3	5	6	6	7	7	7	8	9
West Virginia	......	......	......	......	......	......	......	......	......	3	4	4	5	6	6	6	6	5	4	4	3
Wisconsin	......	......	......	......	......	......	[2]2	3	6	8	9	10	11	11	10	10	10	10	9	9	9
Wyoming	......	......	......	......	......	......	......	......	......	......	[2]1	1	1	1	1	1	1	1	1	1	1
Total	65	106	142	186	213	242	232	237	243	293	332	357	391	435	435	435	437	435	435	435	435

[1] No apportionment was made in 1920.

[2] The following representation was added after the several census apportionments indicated when new States were admitted and is included in the above table:

First. Tennessee, 1.
Second. Ohio, 1.
Third. Alabama, 1; Illinois, 1; Indiana, 1; Louisiana, 1; Mississippi, 1.
Fifth. Arkansas, 1; Michigan, 1.
Sixth. California, 2; Florida, 1; Iowa, 2; Texas, 2; Wisconsin, 2.
Seventh. Minnesota, 2; Oregon, 1.
Eighth. Nebraska, 1; Nevada, 1.
Ninth. Colorado, 1.
Tenth. Idaho, 1; Montana, 1; North Dakota, 1; South Dakota, 2; Washington, 1; Wyoming, 1.
Eleventh. Utah, 1.
Twelfth. Oklahoma, 5.
Thirteenth. Arizona, 1; New Mexico, 1.
Seventeenth. Alaska, 1; Hawaii, 1.

[3] Twenty Representatives were assigned to Massachusetts, but 7 of them were credited to Maine when that area became a State.

COURT OF IMPEACHMENT

The Senate has sat as a Court of Impeachment in the cases of the following accused officials, with the result stated, for the periods named:

WILLIAM BLOUNT, a Senator of the United States from Tennessee; charges dismissed for want of jurisdiction: Monday, December 17, 1798, to Monday, January 14, 1799.

JOHN PICKERING, judge of the United States district court for the district of New Hampshire; removed from office; Thursday, March 3, 1803, to Monday, March 12, 1804.

SAMUEL CHASE, Associate Justice of the Supreme Court of the United States; acquitted; Friday, November 30, 1804, to Friday, March 1, 1805.

JAMES H. PECK, judge of the United States district court for the district of Missouri; acquitted; Monday, April 26, 1830, to Monday, January 31, 1831.

WEST H. HUMPHREYS, judge of the United States district court for the middle, eastern, and western districts of Tennessee; removed from office; Wednesday, May 7, 1862, to Thursday, June 26, 1862.

ANDREW JOHNSON, President of the United States; acquitted; Tuesday, February 25, 1868, to Tuesday, May 26, 1868.

WILLIAM W. BELKNAP, Secretary of War; acquitted; Friday, March 3, 1876, to Tuesday, August 1, 1876.

CHARLES SWAYNE, judge of the United States district court for the northern district of Florida; acquitted; Wednesday, December 14, 1904, to Monday, February 27, 1905.

ROBERT W. ARCHBALD, associate judge, United States Commerce Court; removed from office; Saturday, July 13, 1912, to Monday, January 13, 1913.

GEORGE W. ENGLISH, judge of the United States district court for the eastern district of Illinois; resigned office November 4, 1926; Court of Impeachment adjourned to December 13, 1926, when, on request of House managers, impeachment proceedings were dismissed.

HAROLD LOUDERBACK, judge of the United States district court for the northern district of California; acquitted; Monday, May 15, 1933, to Wednesday, May 24, 1933.

HALSTED L. RITTER, judge of the United States district court for the southern district of Florida; removed from office; Monday, April 6, 1936, to Friday, April 17, 1936.

HARRY E. CLAIBORNE, judge of the United States district court of Nevada; removed from office; Tuesday, October 7, 1986, to Thursday, October 9, 1986.

ALCEE L. HASTINGS, judge of the United States district court for the southern district of Florida; removed from office; Wednesday, October 18, 1989, to Friday, October 20, 1989.

WALTER L. NIXON, judge of the U.S. district court for the southern district of Mississippi; removed from office; Wednesday, November 1, 1989, to Friday, November 3, 1989.

DELEGATES, REPRESENTATIVES, AND SENATORS SERVING IN THE 1st–105th CONGRESSES [1]

As of May 20, 1997, 11,538 individuals have served: 9,697 in the House of Representatives, 1,221 in the Senate, and 620 in both Houses. Total serving in the House of Representatives (including individuals serving in both bodies) is 10,316. Total for Senate (including individuals serving in both bodies) is 1,841.[2]

State	Date Became Territory	Date Entered Union	Delegates	Representatives Only	Senators Only	Both Houses	Total, Not Including Delegates
Alabama	Mar. 3, 1817	Dec. 14, 1819 (22d)	1	163	24	15	202
Alaska	Aug. 24, 1912	Jan. 3, 1959 (49th)	9	4	5	0	9
Arizona	Feb. 24, 1863	Feb. 14, 1912 (48th)	11	22	7	3	32
Arkansas	Mar. 2, 1819	June 15, 1836 (25th)	3	81	22	9	112
California		Sept. 9, 1850 (31st)		306	32	11	348
Colorado	Feb. 28, 1861	Aug. 1, 1876 (38th)	3	48	23	9	80
Connecticut		Jan. 9, 1788 (5th)		186	28	25	239
Delaware		Dec. 7, 1787 (1st)		48	35	13	96
Florida	Mar. 30, 1822	Mar. 3, 1845 (27th)	5	92	25	5	122
Georgia		Jan. 2, 1788 (4th)		243	37	20	300
Hawaii	June 14, 1900	Aug. 21, 1959 (50th)	10	5	2	3	10
Idaho	Mar. 3, 1863	July 3, 1890 (43d)	9	23	19	5	47
Illinois	Feb. 3, 1809	Dec. 3, 1818 (21st)	3	423	27	22	472
Indiana	May 7, 1800	Dec. 11, 1816 (19th)	3	290	26	17	333
Iowa	June 12, 1838	Dec. 28, 1846 (29th)	2	167	22	11	200
Kansas	May 30, 1854	Jan. 29, 1861 (34th)	2	103	22	9	134
Kentucky		June 1, 1792 (15th)		306	36	28	370
Louisiana	Mar. 24, 1804	Apr. 30, 1812 (18th)	2	140	34	13	187
Maine		Mar. 15, 1820 (23d)		140	18	18	176
Maryland		Apr. 28, 1788 (7th)		250	28	27	305
Massachusetts		Feb. 6, 1788 (6th)		381	20	28	429
Michigan	Jan. 11, 1805	Jan. 26, 1837 (26th)	7	243	24	13	281
Minnesota	Mar. 3, 1849	May 11, 1858 (32d)	3	116	23	11	150
Mississippi	Apr. 17, 1798	Dec. 10, 1817 (20th)	5	108	27	16	151
Missouri	June 4, 1812	Aug. 10, 1821 (24th)	3	287	33	8	328
Montana	May 26, 1864	Nov. 8, 1889 (41st)	5	25	13	6	44
Nebraska	May 30, 1854	Mar. 1, 1867 (37th)	6	83	27	7	117
Nevada	Mar. 2, 1861	Oct. 31, 1864 (36th)	2	25	19	4	48
New Hampshire		June 21, 1788 (9th)		117	35	25	177
New Jersey		Dec. 18, 1787 (3d)		293	47	14	354
New Mexico	Sept. 9, 1850	Jan. 6, 1912 (47th)	13	20	12	3	35
New York		July 26, 1788 (11th)		1,388	35	22	1,445
North Carolina		Nov. 21, 1789 (12th)		300	33	17	350
North Dakota [3]	Mar. 2, 1861	Nov. 2, 1889 (39th)	11	21	15	6	42
Ohio [4]		Mar. 1, 1803 (17th)	2	613	35	18	666
Oklahoma	May 2, 1890	Nov. 16, 1907 (46th)	4	69	11	5	85
Oregon	Aug. 14, 1848	Feb. 14, 1859 (33d)	2	54	31	5	90
Pennsylvania		Dec. 12, 1787 (2d)		983	32	21	1,035
Rhode Island		May 29, 1790 (13th)		60	36	10	106
South Carolina		May 23, 1788 (8th)		194	39	14	247
South Dakota [3]	Mar. 2, 1861	Nov. 2, 1889 (40th)	11	24	16	9	49
Tennessee		June 1, 1796 (16th)	2	240	38	18	296
Texas		Dec. 29, 1845 (28th)		222	20	10	252
Utah	Sept. 9, 1850	Jan. 4, 1896 (45th)	7	31	12	3	46
Vermont		Mar. 4, 1791 (14th)		80	24	15	119
Virginia		June 25, 1788 (10th)		375	24	26	425
Washington	Mar. 2, 1853	Nov. 11, 1889 (42d)	10	64	13	9	86
West Virginia		June 20, 1863 (35th)		90	22	8	120
Wisconsin	Apr. 20, 1836	May 29, 1848 (30th)	6	166	19	7	192
Wyoming	July 25, 1868	July 10, 1890 (44th)	4	14	17	3	34

[1] March 4, 1789 until May 20, 1997.

[2] Some of the larger states split into smaller states as the country grew westward (e.g., part of Virginia became West Virginia); hence, some individuals represented more than one state in the Congress.

[3] North and South Dakota were formed from a single territory on the same date, and they shared the same delegates before statehood.

[4] The Territory Northwest of the River Ohio was established as a district for purposes of temporary government by the Act of July 13, 1787. Virginia ceded the land beyond the Ohio River, and delegates representing the district first came to the 6th Congress, March 4, 1799.

NOTE: Information was supplied by the Congressional Research Service.

POLITICAL DIVISIONS OF THE U.S. SENATE AND HOUSE OF REPRESENTATIVES FROM 1855 (34th CONGRESS) TO 1997 (105th CONGRESS)

[All Figures Reflect Immediate Result of Elections. Figures supplied by the Clerk of the House]

Congress	Years	SENATE					HOUSE				
		No. of Senators	Democrats	Republicans	Other parties	Vacancies	No. of Representatives	Democrats	Republicans	Other parties	Vacancies
34th	1855–1857	62	42	15	5	....	234	83	108	43	....
35th	1857–1859	64	39	20	5	....	237	131	92	14	....
36th	1859–1861	66	38	26	2	....	237	101	113	23	....
37th	1861–1863	50	11	31	7	1	178	42	106	28	2
38th	1863–1865	51	12	39	....	....	183	80	103	....	....
39th	1865–1867	52	10	42	....	....	191	46	145	....	....
40th	1867–1869	53	11	42	....	....	193	49	143	....	1
41st	1869–1871	74	11	61	....	2	243	73	170	....	....
42d	1871–1873	74	17	57	....	....	243	104	139	....	....
43d	1873–1875	74	19	54	....	1	293	88	203	....	2
44th	1875–1877	76	29	46	....	1	293	181	107	3	2
45th	1877–1879	76	36	39	1	....	293	156	137	....	....
46th	1879–1881	76	43	33	....	....	293	150	128	14	1
47th	1881–1883	76	37	37	2	....	293	130	152	11	....
48th	1883–1885	76	36	40	....	....	325	200	119	6	....
49th	1885–1887	76	34	41	....	1	325	182	140	2	1
50th	1887–1889	76	37	39	....	....	325	170	151	4	....
51st	1889–1891	84	37	47	....	....	330	156	173	1	....
52d	1891–1893	88	39	47	2	....	333	231	88	14	....
53d	1893–1895	88	44	38	3	3	356	220	126	10	....
54th	1895–1897	88	39	44	5	....	357	104	246	7	....
55th	1897–1899	90	34	46	10	....	357	134	206	16	1
56th	1899–1901	90	26	53	11	....	357	163	185	9	....
57th	1901–1903	90	29	56	3	2	357	153	198	5	1
58th	1903–1905	90	32	58	....	....	386	178	207	....	1
59th	1905–1907	90	32	58	....	....	386	136	250	....	....
60th	1907–1909	92	29	61	....	2	386	164	222	....	....
61st	1909–1911	92	32	59	....	1	391	172	219	....	....
62d	1911–1913	92	42	49	....	1	391	228	162	1	....
63d	1913–1915	96	51	44	1	....	435	290	127	18	....
64th	1915–1917	96	56	39	1	....	435	231	193	8	3
65th	1917–1919	96	53	42	1	....	435	[1] 210	216	9	....
66th	1919–1921	96	47	48	1	....	435	191	237	7	....
67th	1921–1923	96	37	59	....	....	435	132	300	1	2
68th	1923–1925	96	43	51	2	....	435	207	225	3	....
69th	1925–1927	96	40	54	1	1	435	183	247	5	....
70th	1927–1929	96	47	48	1	....	435	195	237	3	....
71st	1929–1931	96	39	56	1	....	435	163	267	1	4
72d	1931–1933	96	47	48	1	....	435	[2] 216	218	1	....
73d	1933–1935	96	59	36	1	....	435	313	117	5	....
74th	1935–1937	96	69	25	2	....	435	322	103	10	....
75th	1937–1939	96	75	17	4	....	435	333	89	13	....
76th	1939–1941	96	69	23	4	....	435	262	169	4	....
77th	1941–1943	96	66	28	2	....	435	267	162	6	....
78th	1943–1945	96	57	38	1	....	435	222	209	4	....
79th	1945–1947	96	57	38	1	....	435	243	190	2	....
80th	1947–1949	96	45	51	....	....	435	188	246	1	....
81st	1949–1951	96	54	42	....	....	435	263	171	1	....
82d	1951–1953	96	48	47	1	....	435	234	199	2	....
83d	1953–1955	96	46	48	2	....	435	213	221	1	....
84th	1955–1957	96	48	47	1	....	435	232	203	....	....
85th	1957–1959	96	49	47	....	....	435	234	201	....	....
86th	1959–1961	98	64	34	....	....	[3] 436	283	153	....	....
87th	1961–1963	100	64	36	....	....	[4] 437	262	175	....	....
88th	1963–1965	100	67	33	....	....	435	258	176	....	1
89th	1965–1967	100	68	32	....	....	435	295	140	....	....
90th	1967–1969	100	64	36	....	....	435	248	187	....	....
91st	1969–1971	100	58	42	....	....	435	243	192	....	....
92d	1971–1973	100	54	44	2	....	435	255	180	....	....
93d	1973–1975	100	56	42	2	....	435	242	192	1	....
94th	1975–1977	100	60	37	2	....	435	291	144	1	....
95th	1977–1979	100	61	38	1	....	435	292	143	....	....
96th	1979–1981	100	58	41	1	....	435	277	158	....	....
97th	1981–1983	100	46	53	1	....	435	242	192	1	....
98th	1983–1985	100	46	54	....	....	435	269	166	....	....
99th	1985–1987	100	47	53	....	....	435	253	182	....	....
100th	1987–1989	100	55	45	....	....	435	258	177	....	....
101st	1989–1991	100	55	45	....	....	435	260	175	....	....
102d	1991–1993	100	56	44	....	....	435	267	167	1	....
103d	1993–1995	100	57	43	....	....	435	258	176	1	....
104th	1995–1997	100	48	52	....	....	435	204	230	1	....
105th	1997–1999	100	45	55	....	....	435	207	226	2	....

[1] Democrats organized House with help of other parties.
[2] Democrats organized House due to Republican deaths.
[3] Proclamation declaring Alaska a State issued January 3, 1959.
[4] Proclamation declaring Hawaii a State issued August 21, 1959.

GOVERNORS OF THE STATES AND TERRITORIES

State or territory	Capital	Governor	Party	Term of service	Expiration of term	Salary
				Years		
STATE						
Alabama	Montgomery	Fob James, Jr	R	[c] 4	Jan. 1999	[1] $87,643
Alaska	Juneau	Tony Knowles	D	[c] 4	Dec. 1998	[2] 81,648
Arizona	Phoenix	Fife Symington	R	[c] 4	Mar. 1999	[3] 75,000
Arkansas	Little Rock	Mike Huckabee	R	[e] 4	Dec. 1998	[1] 60,000
California	Sacramento	Pete Wilson	R	[c] 4	Jan. 1999	[3] 120,000
Colorado	Denver	Roy Romer	D	[c] 4	Jan. 1999	[1] 70,000
Connecticut	Hartford	John G. Rowland	R	[b] 4	Jan. 1999	[1] 78,000
Delaware	Dover	Thomas R. Carper	D	[c] 4	Jan. 2001	[2] 95,000
Florida	Tallahassee	Lawton Chiles	D	[c] 4	Jan. 1999	[1] 104,817
Georgia	Atlanta	Zell Miller	D	[c] 4	Jan. 1999	[1] 92,088
Hawaii	Honolulu	Benjamin J. Cayetano	D	[c] 4	Dec. 1998	[1] 94,780
Idaho	Boise	Phil Batt	R	[b] 4	Jan. 1999	[1] 85,000
Illinois	Springfield	Jim Edgar	R	[b] 4	Jan. 1999	[2] 103,097
Indiana	Indianapolis	Evan Bayh	D	[f] 4	Jan. 2001	[2] 77,200
Iowa	Des Moines	Terry E. Branstad	R	[b] 4	Jan. 1999	[1] 98,200
Kansas	Topeka	Bill Graves	R	[c] 4	Jan. 1999	[1] 80,340
Kentucky	Frankfort	Breretan C. Jones	D	[c] 4	Dec. 1999	[1] 81,647
Louisiana	Baton Rouge	Edwin W. Edwards	D	[c] 4	Jan. 2000	[1] 73,440
Maine	Augusta	John R. McKernan, Jr	R	[c] 4	Jan. 1999	[1] 70,000
Maryland	Annapolis	Parris N. Glendening	D	[c] 4	Jan. 1999	[1] 120,000
Massachusetts	Boston	William F. Weld	R	[b] 4	Jan. 2001	[3] 100,000
Michigan	Lansing	John Engler	R	[b] 4	Jan. 1999	[1] 121,166
Minnesota	St. Paul	Arne H. Carlson	R	[b] 4	Jan. 1998	[1] 114,506
Mississippi	Jackson	Kirk Fordice	R	[c] 4	Jan. 2000	[1] 83,160
Missouri	Jefferson City	Mel Carnahan	D	[c] 4	Jan. 2001	[1] 88,500
Montana	Helena	Marc Racicot	R	[c] 4	Jan. 2001	[1] 59,310
Nebraska	Lincoln	E. Benjamin Nelson	D	[c] 4	Jan. 1999	[1] 65,000
Nevada	Carson City	Robert J. Miller	D	[c] 4	Nov. 1998	[1] 90,000
New Hampshire	Concord	Stephen Merrill	R	[b] 2	Jan. 2001	[1] 86,235
New Jersey	Trenton	Christine Todd Whitman	R	[c] 4	Jan. 1998	[1] 85,000
New Mexico	Santa Fe	Gary E. Johnson	R	[c] 4	Jan. 2000	[1] 95,000
New York	Albany	George E. Pataki	R	[b] 4	Jan. 1999	[1] 130,000
North Carolina	Raleigh	James B. Hunt, Jr	D	[c] 4	Jan. 2001	[1] 98,600
North Dakota	Bismarck	Edward T. Schafer	R	[b] 4	Jan. 2001	71,042
Ohio	Columbus	George V. Voinovich	R	[c] 4	Jan. 1999	[1] 115,762
Oklahoma	Oklahoma City	Frank Keating	R	[c] 4	Jan. 1999	[1] 70,000
Oregon	Salem	Dr. John A. Kitzhaber	D	[f] 4	Jan. 1999	[3] 80,000
Pennsylvania	Harrisburg	Tom Ridge	R	[c] 4	Jan. 1999	[1] 105,000
Rhode Island	Providence	Lincoln C. Almond	R	[c] 4	Jan. 1999	[2] 69,900
South Carolina	Columbia	David M. Beasley	R	[c] 4	Jan. 1999	[1] 103,998
South Dakota	Pierre	William J. Janklow	R	[c] 4	Jan. 1999	[1] 79,875
Tennessee	Nashville	Ned Ray McWherter	D	[c] 4	Jan. 1999	[1] 85,000
Texas	Austin	George W. Bush	R	[c] 4	Jan. 1999	[1] 99,120
Utah	Salt Lake City	Michael O. Leavitt	R	[b] 4	Jan. 2001	[1] 83,200
Vermont	Montpelier	Howard Dean	D	[b] 2	Jan. 1999	[3] 80,730
Virginia	Richmond	George Allen	R	[a] 4	Jan. 1998	[2] 110,000
Washington	Olympia	Gary Locke	D	[d] 4	Jan. 2001	[1] 121,000
West Virginia	Charleston	Gaston Caperton	D	[c] 4	Jan. 2001	[2] 90,000
Wisconsin	Madison	Tommy G. Thompson	R	[b] 4	Jan. 1999	[1] 101,861
Wyoming	Cheyenne	Jim Geringer	R	[c] 4	Jan. 1999	[2] 92,000
COMMONWEALTH OF PUERTO RICO						
Puerto Rico	San Juan	Pedro Rosselló	[4] N.P./D.	[b] 4	Jan. 2001	[1] 70,000
TERRITORIES						
Guam	Agana	Carl T.C. Gutierrez	D	[c] 4	Jan. 1999	[1] 90,000
Virgin Islands	Charlotte Amalie	Roy L. Schneider, M.D.	D	[c] 4	Jan. 2001	[1] 100,000
American Samoa	Pago Pago	Peter Tali Coleman	R	[a] 4	Jan. 2001	[1] 50,000
Northern Mariana Islands.	Saipan, Marianas	Lorenzo Iglesias DeLeon Guerrero.	R	[c] 4	....	[1] 50,000
Trust Territory of the Pacific Islands.	Palau Island	Leslie Turner [5]	D	....	....	....

[a] Cannot succeed himself. [b] No limit. [c] Can serve 2 consecutive terms. [d] Can serve 3 consecutive terms. [e] Can serve 4 consecutive terms. [f] Can serve no more than 8 years in a 12-year period.

[1] Use of executive mansion and fund for maintenance and expenses. [2] Executive mansion furnished. [3] No executive mansion; nominal appropriation for expenses. [4] New Progressive Party/Democrat. [5] By Secretarial Order 3119, July 10, 1987, the position of High Commissioner of the Trust Territories was abolished and the duties were transferred to the Assistant Secretary of the Interior for Territorial and International Affairs. The only remaining part of the original Trust Territory is the island of Palau.

PRESIDENTS AND VICE PRESIDENTS AND THE CONGRESSES COINCIDENT WITH THEIR TERMS [1]

President	Vice President	Service	Congresses
George Washington	John Adams	Apr. 30, 1789–Mar. 3, 1797	1, 2, 3, 4.
John Adams	Thomas Jefferson	Mar. 4, 1797–Mar. 3, 1801	5, 6.
Thomas Jefferson	Aaron Burr	Mar. 4, 1801–Mar. 3, 1805	7, 8.
Do	George Clinton	Mar. 4, 1805–Mar. 3, 1809	9, 10.
James Madison	......do. [2]	Mar. 4, 1809–Mar. 3, 1813	11, 12.
Do	Elbridge Gerry [3]	Mar. 4, 1813–Mar. 3, 1817	13, 14.
James Monroe	Daniel D. Tompkins	Mar. 4, 1817–Mar. 3, 1825	15, 16, 17, 18.
John Quincy Adams	John C. Calhoun	Mar. 4, 1825–Mar. 3, 1829	19, 20.
Andrew Jackson	......do. [4]	Mar. 4, 1829–Mar. 3, 1833	21, 22.
Do	Martin Van Buren	Mar. 4, 1833–Mar. 3, 1837	23, 24.
Martin Van Buren	Richard M. Johnson	Mar. 4, 1837–Mar. 3, 1841	25, 26.
William Henry Harrison [5]	John Tyler	Mar. 4, 1841–Apr. 4, 1841	27.
John Tyler		Apr. 6, 1841–Mar. 3, 1845	27, 28.
James K. Polk	George M. Dallas	Mar. 4, 1845–Mar. 3, 1849	29, 30.
Zachary Taylor [5]	Millard Fillmore	Mar. 5, 1849–July 9, 1850	31.
Millard Fillmore		July 10, 1850–Mar. 3, 1853	31, 32.
Franklin Pierce	William R. King [6]	Mar. 4, 1853–Mar. 3, 1857	33, 34.
James Buchanan	John C. Breckinridge	Mar. 4, 1857–Mar. 3, 1861	35, 36.
Abraham Lincoln	Hannibal Hamlin	Mar. 4, 1861–Mar. 3, 1865	37, 38.
Do. [5]	Andrew Johnson	Mar. 4, 1865–Apr. 15, 1865	39.
Andrew Johnson		Apr. 15, 1865–Mar. 3, 1869	39, 40.
Ulysses S. Grant	Schuyler Colfax	Mar. 4, 1869–Mar. 3, 1873	41, 42.
Do	Henry Wilson [7]	Mar. 4, 1873–Mar. 3, 1877	43, 44.
Rutherford B. Hayes	William A. Wheeler	Mar. 4, 1877–Mar. 3, 1881	45, 46.
James A. Garfield [5]	Chester A. Arthur	Mar. 4, 1881–Sept. 19, 1881	47.
Chester A. Arthur		Sept. 20, 1881–Mar. 3, 1885	47, 48.
Grover Cleveland	Thomas A. Hendricks [8]	Mar. 4, 1885–Mar. 3, 1889	49, 50.
Benjamin Harrison	Levi P. Morton	Mar. 4, 1889–Mar. 3, 1893	51, 52.
Grover Cleveland	Adlai E. Stevenson	Mar. 4, 1893–Mar. 3, 1897	53, 54.
William McKinley	Garret A. Hobart [9]	Mar. 4, 1897–Mar. 3, 1901	55, 56.
Do. [5]	Theodore Roosevelt	Mar. 4, 1901–Sept. 14, 1901	57.
Theodore Roosevelt		Sept. 14, 1901–Mar. 3, 1905	57, 58.
Do	Charles W. Fairbanks	Mar. 4, 1905–Mar. 3, 1909	59, 60.
William H. Taft	James S. Sherman [10]	Mar. 4, 1909–Mar. 3, 1913	61, 62.
Woodrow Wilson	Thomas R. Marshall	Mar. 4, 1913–Mar. 3, 1921	63, 64, 65, 66.
Warren G. Harding [5]	Calvin Coolidge	Mar. 4, 1921–Aug. 2, 1923	67.
Calvin Coolidge		Aug. 3, 1923–Mar. 3, 1925	68.
Do	Charles G. Dawes	Mar. 4, 1925–Mar. 3, 1929	69, 70.
Herbert C. Hoover	Charles Curtis	Mar. 4, 1929–Mar. 3, 1933	71, 72.
Franklin D. Roosevelt	John N. Garner	Mar. 4, 1933–Jan. 20, 1941	73, 74, 75, 76, 77.
Do	Henry A. Wallace	Jan. 20, 1941–Jan. 20, 1945	77, 78, 79.
Do. [5]	Harry S. Truman	Jan. 20, 1945–Apr. 12, 1945	79.
Harry S. Truman		Apr. 12, 1945–Jan. 20, 1949	79, 80, 81.
Do	Alben W. Barkley	Jan. 20, 1949–Jan. 20, 1953	81, 82, 83.
Dwight D. Eisenhower	Richard M. Nixon	Jan. 20, 1953–Jan. 20, 1961	83, 84, 85, 86, 87.
John F. Kennedy [5]	Lyndon B. Johnson	Jan. 20, 1961–Nov. 22, 1963	87, 88, 89.
Lyndon B. Johnson		Nov. 22, 1963–Jan. 20, 1965	88, 89.
Do	Hubert H. Humphrey	Jan. 20, 1965–Jan. 20, 1969	89, 90, 91.
Richard M. Nixon	Spiro T. Agnew [11]	Jan. 20, 1969–Dec. 6, 1973	91, 92, 93.
Do. [13]	Gerald R. Ford [12]	Dec. 6, 1973–Aug. 9, 1974	93.
Gerald R. Ford		Aug. 9, 1974–Dec. 19, 1974	93.
Do	Nelson A. Rockefeller [14]	Dec. 19, 1974–Jan. 20, 1977	93, 94, 95.
James Earl (Jimmy) Carter	Walter F. Mondale	Jan. 20, 1977–Jan. 20, 1981	95, 96, 97.
Ronald Reagan	George Bush	Jan. 20, 1981–Jan. 20, 1989	97, 98, 99, 100, 101.
George Bush	Dan Quayle	Jan. 20, 1989–Jan. 20, 1993	101, 102, 103.
William J. Clinton	Albert Gore	Jan. 20, 1993–	103, 104, 105.

[1] From 1789 until 1933, the terms of the President and Vice President and the term of the Congress coincided, beginning on March 4 and ending on March 3. This changed when the 20th amendment to the Constitution was adopted in 1933. Beginning in 1934 the convening date for Congress became January 3, and beginning in 1937 the starting date for the Presidential term became January 20. Because of this change, the number of Congresses overlapping with a Presidential term increased from two to three, although the third only overlaps by a few weeks.

[2] Died Apr. 20, 1812.

[3] Died Nov. 23, 1814.

[4] Resigned Dec. 28, 1832, to become United States Senator.

[5] Died in office.

[6] Died Apr. 18, 1853.

[7] Died Nov. 22, 1875.

[8] Died Nov. 25, 1885.

[9] Died Nov. 21, 1899.

[10] Died Oct. 30, 1912.

[11] Resigned Oct. 10, 1973.

[12] First Vice President nominated by the President and confirmed by the Congress pursuant to the 25th amendment to the Constitution; took the oath of office on Dec. 6, 1973.

[13] Resigned from office.

[14] Nominated to be Vice President by President Gerald R. Ford on Aug. 20, 1974; confirmed by the Senate on Dec. 10, 1974; confirmed by the House and took the oath of office on Dec. 19, 1974.

CAPITOL BUILDINGS AND GROUNDS

UNITED STATES CAPITOL

Overview of the Building and Its Function

The United States Capitol is among the most architecturally impressive and symbolically important buildings in the world. It has housed the meeting chambers of the Senate and the House of Representatives for almost two centuries. Begun in 1793, the Capitol has been built, burnt, rebuilt, extended, and restored; today, it stands as a monument not only to its builders but also to the American people and their government.

As the focal point of the government's Legislative Branch, the Capitol is the centerpiece of the Capitol Complex, which includes the six principal Congressional office buildings and three Library of Congress buildings constructed on Capitol Hill in the 19th and 20th centuries.

In addition to its active use by Congress, the Capitol is a museum of American art and history. Each year, it is visited by an estimated seven to ten million people from around the world.

A fine example of 19th-century neoclassical architecture, the Capitol combines function with aesthetics. Its designs derived from ancient Greece and Rome evoke the ideals that guided the Nation's founders as they framed their new republic. As the building was expanded from its original design, harmony with the existing portions was carefully maintained.

Today, the Capitol covers a ground area of 175,170 square feet, or about 4 acres, and has a floor area of approximately 16½ acres. Its length, from north to south, is 751 feet 4 inches; its greatest width, including approaches, is 350 feet. Its height above the base line on the east front to the top of the Statue of Freedom is 287 feet 5½ inches; from the basement floor to the top of the dome is an ascent of 365 steps. The building contains approximately 540 rooms and has 658 windows (108 in the dome alone) and approximately 850 doorways.

The building is divided into five levels. The first, or ground, floor is occupied chiefly by committee rooms and the spaces allocated to various congressional officers. The areas accessible to visitors on this level include the Hall of Columns, the Brumidi Corridor, the restored Old Supreme Court Chamber, and the Crypt beneath the rotunda, where historical exhibits are presented.

The second floor holds the Chambers of the House of Representatives (in the south wing) and the Senate (in the north wing) as well as the offices of the congressional leadership. This floor also contains three major public areas. In the center under the dome is the rotunda, a circular ceremonial space that also serves as a gallery of paintings and sculpture depicting significant people and events in the Nation's history. The rotunda is 96 feet in diameter and rises 180 feet 3 inches to the canopy. The semicircular chamber south of the rotunda served as the Hall of the House until 1857; now designated National Statuary Hall, it houses part of the Capitol's collection of statues donated by the States in commemoration of notable citizens. The Old Senate Chamber northeast of the rotunda, which was used by the Senate until 1859, has been returned to its mid-19th-century appearance.

The third floor allows access to the galleries from which visitors to the Capitol may watch the proceedings of the House and the Senate when Congress is in session. The rest of this floor is occupied by offices, committee rooms, and press galleries.

The fourth floor and the basement/terrace level of the Capitol are occupied by offices, machinery rooms, workshops, and other support areas.

Location of the Capitol

The Capitol is located at the eastern end of the Mall on a plateau 88 feet above the level of the Potomac River, commanding a westward view across the Capitol Reflecting Pool to the Washington Monument 1.4 miles away and the Lincoln Memorial 2.2 miles away. The geographic location of the head of the Statue of Freedom that surmounts the Capitol dome is described by the National Geodetic Survey as latitude 38°53′23.31098″ north and longitude 77°00′32.62262″ west.

Before 1791, the Federal Government had no permanent site. The early Congresses met in eight different cities: Philadelphia, Baltimore, Lancaster, York, Princeton, Annapolis, Trenton, and New York City. The subject of a permanent capital for the government of the United

States was first raised by Congress in 1783; it was ultimately addressed in Article I, Section 8 of the Constitution (1787), which gave the Congress legislative authority over "such District (not exceeding ten Miles square) as may, by Cession of Particular States, and the Acceptance of Congress, become the Seat of the Government of the United States. . . ."

In 1788, the state of Maryland ceded to Congress "any district in this State, not exceeding ten miles square," and in 1789 the State of Virginia ceded an equivalent amount of land. In accordance with the "Residence Act" passed by Congress in 1790, President Washington in 1791 selected the area that is now the District of Columbia from the land ceded by Maryland (private landowners whose property fell within this area were compensated by a payment of £25 per acre); that ceded by Virginia was not used for the capital and was returned to Virginia in 1846. Also under the provisions of that Act, he selected three Commissioners to survey the site and oversee the design and construction of the capital city and its government buildings. The Commissioners, in turn, selected the French engineer Pierre Charles L'Enfant to plan the new city of Washington. L'Enfant's plan, which was influenced by the gardens at Versailles, arranged the city's streets and avenues in a grid overlaid with baroque diagonals; the result is a functional and aesthetic whole in which government buildings are balanced against public lawns, gardens, squares, and paths. The Capitol itself was located at the elevated east end of the Mall, on the brow of what was then called Jenkins' Hill. The site was, in L'Enfant's words, "a pedestal waiting for a monument."

Selection of a Plan

L'Enfant was expected to design the Capitol and to supervise its construction. However, he refused to produce any drawings for the building, claiming that he carried the design "in his head"; this fact and his refusal to consider himself subject to the Commissioners' authority led to his dismissal in 1792. In March of that year the Commissioners announced a competition, suggested by Secretary of State Thomas Jefferson, that would award $500 and a city lot to whoever produced "the most approved plan" for the Capitol by mid-July. None of the 17 plans submitted, however, was wholly satisfactory. In October, a letter arrived from Dr. William Thornton, a Scottish-trained physician living in Tortola, British West Indies, requesting an opportunity to present a plan even though the competition had closed. The Commissioners granted this request.

Thornton's plan depicted a building composed of three sections. The central section, which was topped by a low dome, was to be flanked on the north and south by two rectangular wings (one for the Senate and one for the House of Representatives). President Washington commended the plan for its "grandeur, simplicity and convenience," and on April 5, 1793, it was accepted by the Commissioners; Washington gave his formal approval on July 25.

Brief Construction History

1793–1829

The cornerstone was laid by President Washington in the building's southeast corner on September 18, 1793, with Masonic ceremonies. Work progressed under the direction of three architects in succession. Stephen H. Hallet (an entrant in the earlier competition) and George Hadfield were eventually dismissed by the Commissioners because of inappropriate design changes that they tried to impose; James Hoban, the architect of the White House, saw the first phase of the project through to completion.

Construction was a laborious and time-consuming process: the sandstone used for the building had to be ferried on boats from the quarries at Aquia, Virginia; workers had to be induced to leave their homes to come to the relative wilderness of Capitol Hill; and funding was inadequate. By August 1796 the Commissioners were forced to focus the entire work effort on the building's north wing so that it at least could be ready for government occupancy as scheduled. Even so, some third-floor rooms were still unfinished when the Congress, the Supreme Court, the Library of Congress, and the courts of the District of Columbia occupied the Capitol in late 1800.

In 1803, Congress allocated funds to resume construction. A year earlier, the office of the Commissioners had been abolished and replaced by a Superintendent of the City of Washington. To oversee the renewed construction effort, Benjamin Henry Latrobe was appointed architect. The first professional architect and engineer to work in America, Latrobe modified Thornton's plan for the south wing to include space for offices and committee rooms; he also introduced alterations to simplify the construction work. Latrobe began work by removing a squat, oval, temporary building known as "the Oven," which had been erected in 1801 as a meeting place for the House of Representatives. By 1807 construction on the south wing was sufficiently advanced that the House was able to occupy its new legislative chamber, and the wing was completed in 1811.

In 1808, as work on the south wing progressed, Latrobe began the rebuilding of the north wing, which had fallen into disrepair. Rather than simply repair the wing, he redesigned the interior of the building to increase its usefulness and durability; among his changes was the addition of a chamber for the Supreme Court. By 1811, he had completed the eastern half of this wing, but funding was being increasingly diverted to preparations for a second war with Great Britain. By 1813, Latrobe had no further work in Washington and so he departed, leaving the north and south wings of the Capitol connected only by a temporary wooden passageway.

The War of 1812 left the Capitol, in Latrobe's later words, ''a most magnificent ruin'': on August 24, 1814, British troops set fire to the building, and only a sudden rainstorm prevented its complete destruction. Immediately after the fire, Congress met for one session in Blodget's Hotel, which was at Seventh and E Streets, NW. From 1815 to 1819, Congress occupied a building erected for it on First Street, NE, on part of the site now occupied by the Supreme Court Building. This building later came to be known as the Old Brick Capitol.

Latrobe returned to Washington in 1815, when he was rehired to restore the Capitol. In addition to making repairs, he took advantage of this opportunity to make further changes in the building's interior design (for example, an enlargement of the Senate Chamber) and introduce new materials (for example, marble discovered along the upper Potomac). However, he came under increasing pressure because of construction delays (most of which were beyond his control) and cost overruns; finally, he resigned his post in November 1817.

On January 8, 1818, Charles Bulfinch, a prominent Boston architect, was appointed Latrobe's successor. Continuing the restoration of the north and south wings, he was able to make the chambers for the Supreme Court, the House, and the Senate ready for use by 1819. Bulfinch also redesigned and supervised the construction of the Capitol's central section. The copper-covered wooden dome that topped this section was made higher than Bulfinch considered appropriate to the building's size (at the direction of President James Monroe and Secretary of State John Quincy Adams). After completing the last part of the building in 1826, Bulfinch spent the next few years on the Capitol's decoration and landscaping. In 1829, his work was done and his position with the government was terminated. In the 20 years following Bulfinch's tenure, the Capitol was entrusted to the care of the Commissioner of Public Buildings.

1830–1868

The Capitol was by this point already an impressive structure. At ground level, its length was 351 feet 7½ inches and its width was 282 feet 10½ inches. Up to the year 1827—records from later years being incomplete—the project cost was $2,432,851.34. Improvements to the building continued in the years to come (running water in 1832, gas lighting in the 1840s), but by 1850 its size could no longer accommodate the increasing numbers of senators and representatives from newly admitted States. The Senate therefore voted to hold another competition, offering a prize of $500 for the best plan to extend the Capitol. Several suitable plans were submitted, some proposing an eastward extension of the building and others proposing the addition of large north and south wings. However, Congress was unable to decide between these two approaches, and the prize money was divided among five architects. Thus, the tasks of selecting a plan and appointing an architect fell to President Millard Fillmore.

Fillmore's choice was Thomas U. Walter, a Philadelphia architect who had entered the competition. On July 4, 1851, in a ceremony whose principal oration was delivered by Secretary of State Daniel Webster, the President laid the cornerstone for the northeast corner of the House wing in accordance with Walter's plans. Over the next 14 years, Walter supervised the construction of the extensions, ensuring their compatibility with the architectural style of the existing building. However, because the Aquia Creek sandstone used earlier had already deteriorated noticeably, he chose to use marble for the exterior. For the veneer, Walter selected marble quarried at Lee, MA, and for the columns he used marble from Cockeysville, MD.

Walter faced several significant challenges during the course of construction. Chief among these was the steady imposition by the government of additional tasks without additional pay. Aside from his work on the Capitol extensions and dome, Walter designed the wings of the Patent Office building, extensions to the Treasury and Post Office buildings, and the Marine barracks in Pensacola and Brooklyn. When the Library of Congress in the Capitol's west central section was gutted by a fire in 1851, Walter was commissioned to restore it. He also encountered obstacles in his work on the Capitol extensions. His location of the legislative chambers was changed in 1853 at the direction of President Franklin Pierce, based on the suggestions of the newly appointed supervising engineer, Captain Montgomery C. Meigs. In general, however, the project progressed rapidly: the House of Representatives was able to meet in its new chamber on December 16, 1857, and the Senate first met in its present chamber on January 4, 1859. The old House chamber was later designated National Statuary Hall. In 1861 most construction was suspended because of the Civil War, and the Capitol was used briefly as a military barracks, hospital, and bakery. In 1862 work on the entire building was resumed.

As the new wings were constructed, more than doubling the length of the Capitol, it became apparent that the dome erected by Bulfinch no longer suited the building's proportions. In 1855 Congress voted for its replacement based on Walter's design for a new, fireproof cast-iron dome. The old dome was removed in 1856, and 5,000,000 pounds of new masonry was placed on the existing rotunda walls. Iron used in the dome construction had an aggregate weight of 8,909,200 pounds and was lifted into place by steam-powered derricks.

In 1859, Thomas Crawford's plaster model for the Statue of Freedom, designed for the top of the dome, arrived from the sculptor's studio in Rome. With a height of 19 feet 6 inches, the statue was almost 3 feet taller than specified, and Walter was compelled to make revisions to his design for the dome. When cast in bronze by Clark Mills at his foundry on the outskirts of Washington, it weighed 14,985 pounds. The statue was lifted into place atop the dome in 1863, its final section being installed on December 2 to the accompaniment of gun salutes from the forts around the city.

The work on the dome and the extensions was completed under the direction of Edward Clark, who had served as Walter's assistant and was appointed Architect of the Capitol in 1865 after Walter's resignation. In 1866, the Italian-born artist Constantino Brumidi finished the canopy fresco, a monumental painting entitled *The Apotheosis of George Washington.* The Capitol extensions were completed in 1868.

1869–1902

Clark continued to hold the post of Architect of the Capitol until his death in 1902. During his tenure, the Capitol underwent considerable modernization. Steam heat was gradually installed in the Old Capitol. In 1874 the first elevator was installed, and in the 1880s electric lighting began to replace gas lights.

Between 1884 and 1891, the marble terraces on the north, west, and south sides of the Capitol were constructed. As part of the grounds plan devised by landscape architect Frederick Law Olmsted, these terraces not only added over 100 rooms to the Capitol but also provided a broader, more substantial visual base for the building.

On November 6, 1898, a gas explosion and fire in the original north wing dramatically illustrated the need for fireproofing. The roofs over the Statuary Hall wing and the original north wing were reconstructed and fireproofed, the work being completed in 1902 by Clark's successor, Elliott Woods. In 1901 the space in the west central front vacated by the Library of Congress was converted to committee rooms.

1903–1970

During the remainder of Woods' service, which ended with his death in 1923, no major structural work was required on the Capitol. The activities performed in the building were limited chiefly to cleaning and refurbishing the interior. David Lynn, the Architect of the Capitol from 1923 until his retirement in 1954, continued these tasks. Between July 1949 and January 1951, the corroded roofs and skylights of both wings and the connecting corridors were replaced with new roofs of concrete and steel, covered with copper. The cast-iron and glass ceilings of the House and Senate chambers were replaced with ceilings of stainless steel and plaster, with a laylight of carved glass and bronze in the middle of each. The House and Senate chambers were completely remodeled, improvements such as modern air conditioning and lighting were added, and acoustical problems were solved. During this renovation program, the House and Senate vacated their chambers on several occasions so that the work could progress.

The next significant modification made to the Capitol was the east front extension. This project was carried out under the supervision of Architect of the Capitol J. George Stewart, who served from 1954 until his death in 1970. Begun in 1958, it involved the construction of a new east front 32 feet 6 inches east of the old front, faithfully reproducing the sandstone structure in marble. The old sandstone walls were not destroyed; rather, they were left in place to become a part of the interior wall and are now buttressed by the addition. The marble columns of the connecting corridors were also moved and reused. Other elements of this project included repairing the dome, constructing a subway terminal under the Senate steps, reconstructing those steps, cleaning both wings, birdproofing the building, providing furniture and furnishings for the 90 new rooms created by the extension, and improving the lighting throughout the building. The project was completed in 1962. Subsequent work in the 1960s was concentrated chiefly on the construction of the Rayburn House Office Building and on the maintenance and repair of the Capitol.

1971–Present

During the nearly 25-year tenure (1971–1995) of the ninth Architect of the Capitol, George M. White, FAIA, the building was both modernized and restored. Electronic voting equipment was installed in the House chamber in 1973; facilities were added to allow television coverage of the House and Senate debates in 1979 and 1986, respectively; and improved climate control, electronic surveillance systems, and new computer and communications facilities have been added to bring the Capitol up-to-date. The Old Senate Chamber, National Statuary Hall, and the Old Supreme Court Chamber, on the other hand, were restored to their mid-19th-century appearance by 1976 for the Nation's Bicentennial celebration.

In 1983, work began on the strengthening, renovation, and preservation of the west front of the Capitol. Structural problems had developed over the years because of defects in the original foundations, deterioration of the sandstone facing material, alterations to the basic building fabric (a fourth-floor addition and channeling of the walls to install interior utilities), and damage from the fires of 1814 and 1851 and the 1898 gas explosion

To strengthen the structure, over one thousand stainless steel tie rods were set into the building's masonry. More than 30 layers of paint were removed, and damaged stonework was repaired or replicated. Ultimately, 40 percent of the sandstone blocks were replaced with limestone. The walls were treated with a special consolidant and then painted to match the marble wings. The entire project was completed in 1987, well ahead of schedule and under budget.

A related project, completed in January 1993, effected the repair of the Olmsted terraces, which had been subject to damage from settling, and converted the terrace courtyards into several thousand square feet of meeting space.

As the Capitol enters its third century, restoration and modernization work continues. Major projects include conservation of the Rotunda canopy and frieze and the Statue of Freedom, creation of murals in three first-floor House corridors, replacement of worn Minton tiles in the Senate corridors, and repair and restoration of the House monumental stairs. Permanent television broadcasting facilities have been installed in the Senate Chamber, and the subway system linking the Capitol with the Dirksen and Hart Senate Office Buildings has been replaced with a new system.

The tenth Architect of the Capitol, Alan M. Hantman, AIA, was appointed in January 1997. A program of barrier removal begun in the 1970's continues in compliance with the Americans with Disabilities Act. Planning and design work for a Capitol Visitor Center is under way; the Center, subject to authorization and funding, will be located under the East Front Plaza and will contain exhibits, orientation displays, theaters, and other facilities to make the visitor's experience in the Capitol more informative and meaningful.

HOUSE OFFICE BUILDINGS

Cannon House Office Building

An increased membership of the Senate and House resulted in a demand for additional rooms for the accommodations of the Senators and Representatives. On March 3, 1903, the Congress authorized the erection of a fireproofed office building for the use of the House Members. It was designed by the firm of Carrere & Hastings of New York City in the Beaux Arts style. The first brick was laid July 5, 1905, in square No. 690, and formal exercises were held at the laying of the cornerstone on April 14, 1906, in which President Theodore Roosevelt participated. The building was completed and occupied January 10, 1908. A subsequent change in the basis of congressional representation made necessary the building of an additional story in 1913–14. The total cost of the building, including site, furnishings, equipment, and the subway connecting the House Office Building with the U.S. Capitol, amounted to $4,860,155. This office building contains about 500 rooms, and was considered at the time of its completion fully equipped for all the needs of a modern building for office purposes.

Pursuant to authority in the Second Supplemental Appropriations Act, 1955, and subsequent action of the House Office Building Commission, remodeling of the Cannon Building began in 1966. The estimated cost of this work, $5,200,000, was included in total appropriation of $135,134,000 for the additional House Office Building project. Pursuant to the provisions of Public Law 87–453, approved May 21, 1962, the building was named in honor of the late Honorable Joseph G. Cannon of Illinois, who was serving as Speaker at the time the building was constructed.

Longworth House Office Building

Under legislation contained in the authorization act of January 10, 1929, and in the urgent deficiency bill of March 4, 1929, provisions were made for an additional House Office

Building, to be located on the west side of New Jersey Avenue (opposite the first House Office Building). The building was designed by the Allied Architects of Washington in the Neoclassical Revival style.

The cornerstone was laid June 24, 1932, and the building was completed and ready for beneficial occupancy April 20, 1933. It contains 251 two-room suites and 16 committee rooms. Each suite and committee room is provided with a storeroom. Eight floors are occupied by Members. The basement and subbasement contain shops and mechanics needed for the proper maintenance of the building. The cost of this building, including site, furnishings, and equipment, was $7,805,705. Pursuant to the provisions of Public Law 87–453, approved May 21, 1962, the building was named in honor of the late Honorable Nicholas Longworth of Ohio, who was serving as Speaker when the second House Office Building was constructed.

Rayburn House Office Building and Other Related Changes and Improvements

Under legislation contained in the Second Supplemental Appropriations Act, 1955, provision was made for construction of an additional fireproofed office building, and other appurtenant and necessary facilities for the use of the House of Representatives; for acquisition of real property located south of Independence Avenue in the vicinity of the Capitol Grounds for purposes of construction of such building and facilities and as additions to the Capitol Grounds; for changes to the present House Office Buildings; and for changes or additions to the subway systems.

All work was carried forward by the Architect of the Capitol under the direction of the House Office Building Commission at an authorized limit of cost to be fixed by such Commission. Appropriations totaling $135,279,000 were provided to carry forward this project.

Under this program, property consisting of eight city squares was acquired. Contracts were let for necessary architectural and engineering services for reconstruction of a section of Tiber Creek sewer running through the site for excavations and foundations, structural steel, superstructure, furniture and furnishings for the new building; for a cafeteria in the courtyard of the existing Longworth House Office Building; for remodeling of the Cannon House Office Building; for improved lighting and other improvements in the Longworth House Office Building; and for an underground garage in the courtyard of the Cannon House Office Building and two underground garages in squares 637 and 691 south of the Rayburn and Longworth buildings.

The Rayburn Building is connected to the Capitol by a subway from the center of the Independence Avenue upper garage level to the southwest corner of the Capitol. Designs for the building were prepared by the firm of Harbeson, Hough, Livingston & Larson of Philadelphia, Associate Architects. The building contains 169 congressional suites; full-committee hearing rooms for 9 standing committees, 16 subcommittee hearing rooms, committee staff rooms and other committee facilities; a large cafeteria and other restaurant facilities; an underground garage accommodating 1,600 automobiles; and a variety of liaison offices, press and television facilities, maintenance and equipment shops or rooms, and storage areas. This building has nine stories and a penthouse for machinery.

The cornerstone was laid May 24, 1962, by the Honorable John W. McCormack, Speaker of the House of Representatives. President John F. Kennedy participated in the cornerstone laying and delivered the address.

A portion of the basement floor was occupied beginning March 12, 1964, by House of Representatives personnel moved from the George Washington Inn property. Full occupancy of the Rayburn Building, under the room-filing regulations, was begun February 23, 1965, and completed April 2, 1965. Pursuant to the provisions of Public Law 87–453, approved May 21, 1962, the building was named in honor of the late Honorable Sam Rayburn of Texas, who was serving as Speaker at the time the third House Office Building was constructed.

Two buildings have been purchased and adapted for office use by the House of Representatives. The eight-story Congressional Hotel across from the Cannon on C Street SE was acquired in 1957 and subsequently altered for office use and a dormitory for the Pages. It has 124,000 square feet. It was known as House Office Building Annex No. 1, until it was named the "Thomas P. O'Neill, Jr. House of Representatives Office Building" in honor of the former Speaker of the House, pursuant to House Resolution 402, approved September 10, 1990. House Office Building Annex No. 2, named the "Gerald R. Ford House of Representatives Office Building" by the same resolution, was acquired in 1975 from the General Services Administration. The structure, located at Second and D Streets SW, was built in 1939 for the Federal Bureau of Investigation as a fingerprint file archives. This building has approximately 432,000 square feet of space.

SENATE OFFICE BUILDINGS

Richard Brevard Russell Senate Office Building

The demand for an office building for the Representatives was greater because of their larger membership, and the Senate had been supplied with additional office space by the purchase of the Maltby Building, then located on the northwest corner of B Street and New Jersey Avenue NW. This building provided only a temporary need, and when it was condemned as an unsafe structure, the requirement arose for the Senators to have safer and more commodious office space. Under authorization of the Act of April 28, 1904, square 686 on the northeast corner of Delaware Avenue and B Street NE was purchased as a site for the Senate Office Building. The plans for the House Office Building were adapted for the Senate Office Building by the firm of Carrere & Hastings, with the exception that the side of the building fronting on First Street NE was temporarily omitted. The cornerstone was laid without special exercises on July 31, 1906, and the building was occupied March 5, 1909. In 1931, the completion of the fourth side of the building was commenced. In 1933 it was completed, together with alterations to the C Street facade, and the construction of terraces, balustrades, and approaches. The cost of the completed building, including the site, furnishings, equipment and the subway connecting the Senate Office Building with the United States Capitol, was $8,390,892.

The building was named the ''Richard Brevard Russell Senate Office Building'' by Senate Resolution 296, 92nd Congress, agreed to October 11, 1972, as amended by Senate Resolution 295, 96th Congress, agreed to December 3, 1979.

Everett McKinley Dirksen Senate Office Building

Under legislation contained in the Second Deficiency Appropriations Act, 1948, Public Law 80–785, provision was made for an additional office building for the United States Senate with limits of cost of $1,100,000 for acquisition of the site and $20,600,000 for constructing and equipping the building.

The authorized limit of cost for construction and equipment of the building was increased to $23,446,000 by the Legislative Branch Appropriations Act, 1958, Public Law 85–85, and to $24,196,000 by the Second Supplemental Appropriations Act, 1959, Public Law 86–30. All work was carried forward by the Architect of the Capitol under the direction of the Senate Office Building Commission. The New York firm of Eggers & Higgins served as the consulting architects.

The site was acquired and cleared in 1948–49 at a total cost of $1,011,492.

A contract for excavation, concrete footings and mats for the new building was awarded in January 1955, in the amount of $747,200. Groundbreaking ceremonies were held January 26, 1955.

A contract for the superstructure of the new building was awarded September 9, 1955, in the amount of $17,200,000. The cornerstone was laid July 13, 1956.

As a part of this project, a new underground subway system was installed from the Capitol to both the Old and New Senate Office Buildings.

An appropriation of $1,000,000 for furniture and furnishings for the new building was provided in the Supplemental Appropriations Act, 1958, Public Law 85–170. An additional appropriation of $283,550 was provided in the Second Supplemental Appropriations Act, 1959, Public Law 86–30. The building was accepted for beneficial occupancy October 15, 1958.

The building was named the ''Everett McKinley Dirksen Senate Office Building'' by Senate Resolution 296, 92nd Congress, agreed to October 11, 1972 and Senate Resolution 295, 96th Congress, agreed to December 3, 1979.

Philip A. Hart Senate Office Building

Construction as an extension to the Dirksen Senate Office Building was authorized by the Supplemental Appropriations Act, 1973, Public Law 92–607, approved October 31, 1972; legislation enacted in subsequent years (ending with Public Law 96–69, approved September 16, 1979) increased the scope of the project and established a total cost ceiling of $137,700,400. The firm of John Carl Warnecke & Associates served as Associate Architect for the project.

Senate Resolution 525, passed August 30, 1976, amended by Senate Resolution 295, 96th Congress, agreed to December 3, 1979, provided that upon completion of the extension it would be named the ''Philip A. Hart Senate Office Building'' to honor the Senator from Michigan.

The contract for clearing of the site, piping for utilities, excavation, and construction of foundation was awarded in December 1975. Groundbreaking took place January 5, 1976. The contract for furnishing and delivery of the exterior stone was awarded in February

1977, and the contract for the superstructure, which included wall and roof systems and the erection of all exterior stonework, was awarded in October 1977. The contract for the first portion of the interior and related work was awarded in December 1978. A contract for interior finishing was awarded in July 1980. The first suite was occupied on November 22, 1982. Alexander Calder's mobile/stabile *Mountains and Clouds* was installed in the building's atrium in November 1986.

CAPITOL POWER PLANT

During the development of the plans for the Cannon and Russell Buildings, the question of heat, light, and power was considered. The Senate and House wings of the Capitol were heated by separate heating plants. The Library of Congress also had in use a heating plant for that building. Finally it was determined that the need for heating and lighting, with power for elevators, could be adequately met by the construction of a central power plant to furnish all heat and power, as well as light, for the Capitol group of buildings.

Having determined the need for a central power plant, a site was selected in Garfield Park, bounded by New Jersey Avenue, South Capitol Street, Virginia Avenue, and E Street SE. Since this park was a Government reservation, an appropriation of money was not required to secure title. The determining factors leading to the selection of this site were its nearness to the tracks of what is now the Penn Central Railroad and its convenient distance to the river and to the buildings to be served by the plant.

The dimensions of the Capitol Power Plant, which was constructed under authorization of the act of April 28, 1904, and completed and placed in operation in 1910, were 244 feet 8 inches by 117 feet. There are two radial brick chimneys 174 feet in height (reduced from 212 feet to 174 feet in 1951–52) and 11 feet in diameter at the top.

The buildings originally served by the Capitol Power Plant were connected to it by a reinforced-concrete steam tunnel 7 feet high by 4½ feet wide, with walls approximately 12 inches thick. This tunnel originated at the Capitol Power Plant and terminated at the Senate Office Building, with connecting tunnels for the Cannon House Office Building, the Capitol, and the Library of Congress. Subsequently it was extended to the Government Printing Office and the Washington City Post Office, with steam lines extended to serve the Longworth House Office Building, the Supreme Court Building, the John Adams Building of the Library of Congress, and the Botanic Garden.

In September 1951, when the demand for electrical energy was reaching the maximum capacity of the Capitol Power Plant, arrangements were made to purchase electrical service from the local public utility company and to discontinue electrical generation. The heating and cooling functions of the Capitol Power Plant were expanded in 1935, 1939, 1958, 1973, and 1980.

U.S. CAPITOL GROUNDS

A DESCRIPTION OF THE GROUNDS

Originally a wooded wilderness, the U.S. Capitol Grounds today provide a parklike setting for the Nation's Capitol, offering a picturesque counterpoint to the building's formal architecture. The grounds immediately surrounding the Capitol are bordered by a stone wall and cover an area of 58.8 acres. Their boundaries are Independence Avenue on the south, Constitution Avenue on the north, First Street NE/SE on the east, and First Street NW/SW on the west. Over 100 varieties of trees and bushes are planted around the Capitol, and thousands of flowers are used in seasonal displays. In contrast to the building's straight, neoclassical lines, most of the walkways in the grounds are curved. Benches along the paths offer pleasant spots for visitors to appreciate the building, its landscape, and the surrounding areas, most notably the Mall to the west.

The grounds were designed by Frederick Law Olmsted (1822–1903), who planned the expansion and landscaping of the area that was performed from 1874 to 1892. Olmsted, who also designed New York's Central Park, is considered the greatest American landscape architect of his day. He was a pioneer in the development of public parks in America, and many of his designs were influenced by his studies of European parks, gardens, and estates. In describing his plan for the Capitol grounds, Olmsted noted that "The ground is in design part of the Capitol, but in all respects subsidiary to the central structure." Therefore, he was careful not to group trees or other landscape features in any way that would distract the viewer from the Capitol. The use of sculpture and other ornamentation has also been kept to a minimum.

Many of the trees on the Capitol grounds have historic or memorial associations. Among the oldest is the "Cameron Elm" near the House entrance. This tree was named in honor of the Pennsylvania Senator who ensured its preservation during Olmsted's landscaping project.

Other trees commemorate members of Congress and other notable citizens, national organizations, and special events. In addition, over 30 States have made symbolic gifts of their state trees to the Capitol grounds. Many of the trees on the grounds bear plaques that identify their species and their historic significance. The eastern part of the grounds contains the greatest number of historic and commemorative trees.

At the East Capitol Street entrance to the Capitol Plaza are two large rectangular stone fountains. The bottom levels now contain plantings, but at times in the past they have been used to catch the spillover from the fountains. At other times, both levels have held plantings. Six massive red granite lamp piers topped with light fixtures in wrought-iron cages, and 16 smaller bronze light fixtures, line the paved plaza. Seats are placed at intervals along the sidewalks. Three sets of benches are enclosed with wrought-iron railings and grilles; the roofed bench was originally a shelter for streetcar passengers.

The northern part of the grounds offers a shaded walk among trees, flowers, and shrubbery. A small, hexagonal brick structure named the Summer House may be found in the northwest corner of the grounds. This structure contains shaded benches, a central ornamental fountain, and three public drinking fountains. In a small grotto on the eastern side of the Summer House, a stream of water flows and splashes over rocks to create a pleasing sound and cool the summer breezes.

The two round stone towers in the western portion of the grounds contain air shafts for the Capitol ventilation system. The southern tower provides air for the House Chamber area; the northern tower supplies the Senate.

A BRIEF HISTORY OF THE GROUNDS BEFORE OLMSTED

The land on which the Capitol stands was first occupied by the Manahoacs and the Monacans, who were subtribes of the Algonquin Indians. Early settlers reported that these tribes occasionally held councils not far from the foot of the hill. This land eventually became a part of Cerne Abbey Manor, and at the time of its acquisition by the Federal Government it was owned by Daniel Carroll of Duddington.

The "Residence Act" of 1790 provided that the Federal Government should be established in a permanent location by the year 1800. In early March 1791 the Commissioners of the City of Washington, who had been appointed by President George Washington, selected the French engineer Pierre Charles L'Enfant to plan the new federal city. L'Enfant decided to locate the Capitol at the elevated east end of the Mall (on what was then called Jenkins' Hill); he described the site as "a pedestal waiting for a monument."

At this time the site of the Capitol was a relative wilderness partly overgrown with scrub oak. Oliver Wolcott, a signer of the Declaration of Independence, described the soil as an "*exceedingly stiff* clay, becoming dust in dry and mortar in rainy weather." A muddy creek with swampy borders flowed at the base of the hill, and an alder swamp bordered by tall woods occupied the place where the Botanic Garden now stands. The city's inhabitants, like L'Enfant and Washington, expected that the capital would grow to the east, leaving the Capitol and the White House essentially on its outskirts. For some years the land around the Capitol was regarded as a common, crossed by roads in several directions and intended to be left as an open area.

In 1825, a plan was devised for imposing order on the Capitol grounds, and it was carried out for almost 15 years. The plan divided the area into flat, rectangular grassy areas bordered by trees, flower beds, and gravel walks. The growth of the trees, however, soon deprived the other plantings of nourishment, and the design became increasingly difficult to maintain in light of sporadic and small appropriations. John Foy, who had charge of the grounds during most of this period, was "superseded for political reasons," and the area was then maintained with little care or forethought. Many rapidly growing but short-lived trees were introduced and soon depleted the soil; a lack of proper pruning and thinning left the majority of the area's vegetation ill-grown, feeble, or dead. Virtually all was removed by the early 1870's, either to make way for building operations during Thomas U. Walter's enlargement of the Capitol or as required by changes in grading to accommodate the new work on the building or the alterations to surrounding streets.

THE OLMSTED PLAN

The mid-19th-century extension of the Capitol, in which the House and Senate wings and the new dome were added, required also that the Capitol grounds be enlarged, and in 1874 Frederick Law Olmsted was commissioned to plan and oversee the project. As noted above, Olmsted was determined that the grounds should complement the building. In addition, he addressed an architectural problem that had persisted for some years: from the west—the direction in which the city was clearly growing—the earthen terraces at the building's base made it seem inadequately supported at the top of the hill. The solution, Olmsted believed, was to construct marble terraces on the north, west, and south sides of the building, thereby causing it to ''gain greatly in the supreme qualities of stability, endurance, and repose.'' He submitted his design for these features in 1875, and after extensive study it was approved.

Work on the grounds began in 1874, concentrating first on the east side and then progressing to the west, north, and south sides in 1875. First, the ground was reduced in elevation. Almost 300,000 cubic yards of earth and other material were eventually removed, and over 200 trees were transplanted. New sewer, gas, and water systems were installed. The soil was then enriched with fertilizers to provide a suitable growth medium for new plantings. Paths and roadways were graded and their foundations were laid.

By 1876, gas and water service was completed for the entire grounds, and electrical lamp-lighting apparatuses had been installed. Stables and workshops had been removed from the northwest and southwest corners. A streetcar system north and south of the west grounds had been relocated farther from the Capitol, and ornamental shelters were in place at the north and south car-track termini. The granite and bronze lamp piers and ornamental bronze lamps for the east plaza area were completed.

Work accelerated in 1877. By this time, according to Olmsted's report, ''altogether 7,837 plants and trees [had] been set out.'' However, not all had survived: hundreds were stolen or destroyed by vandals, and, as Olmsted explained, ''a large number of cattle [had] been caught trespassing.'' Other work met with less difficulty. Foot-walks were laid with artificial stone, a mixture of cement and sand, and approaches were paved with concrete. An ornamental iron trellis had been installed on the northern east-side walk, and another was under way on the southern walk. An underground air duct for ventilating the Hall of the House was laid to a temporary opening in the west side of the hill.

The 1878 appointment of watchmen to patrol the grounds was quite effective in preventing further vandalism, allowing the lawns to be completed and much shrubbery to be added. Also in that year, the roads throughout the grounds were paved.

Most of the work required on the east side of the grounds was completed by 1879, and effort thus shifted largely to the west side. The Pennsylvania Avenue approach was virtually finished, and work on the Maryland Avenue approach had begun. The stone walls on the west side of the grounds were almost finished, and the red granite lamp piers were placed at the eastward entrance from Pennsylvania Avenue.

In the years 1880–82, many features of the grounds were completed. These included the walls and coping around the entire perimeter, the approaches and entrances, the tower for the House air shaft, and the Summer House. Work on the terraces began in 1882, and most work from this point until 1892 was concentrated on these structures.

In 1885, Olmsted retired from superintendency of the terrace project; he continued to direct the work on the grounds until 1889. Landscaping work was performed to adapt the surrounding areas to the new construction, grading the ground and planting shrubs at the bases of the walls, as the progress of the masonry work allowed. Some trees and other types of vegetation were removed, either because they had decayed or as part of a careful thinning-out process.

In 1886, Olmsted recommended that the Senate side of the Capitol be supplied with fresh air through a duct and tower similar to those on the House side. This project was completed in 1889–90. In 1888, the wrought-iron lamp frames and railings were placed at the Maryland Avenue entrance, making it the last to be completed. In 1892, the streetcar track that had extended into grounds from Independence Avenue was removed.

THE GROUNDS AFTER OLMSTED

In the last years of the 19th century, work on the grounds consisted chiefly of maintenance and repairs as needed. Trees, lawns, and plantings were tended, pruned, and thinned to allow their best growth. This work was quite successful: by 1894, the grounds were so deeply shaded by trees and shrubs that Architect of the Capitol Edward Clark recommended an all-night patrol by watchmen to ensure public safety. A hurricane in September 1896 damaged or destroyed a number of trees, requiring extensive removals in the following year. Also in 1897, electric lighting replaced gas lighting in the grounds.

Between 1910 and 1935, 61.4 acres north of Constitution Avenue were added to the grounds. Approximately 100 acres was added in subsequent years, bringing the total area to 274 acres. In 1981, the Architect of the Capitol developed the Master Plan for future development of the U.S. Capitol grounds and related areas.

Since 1983, increased security measures have been put into effect, including the installation of barriers at vehicular entrances. However, the area still functions in many ways as a public park, and visitors are welcome to use the walks to tour the grounds. Demonstrations and ceremonies are often held on the grounds. During the summer, many high-school bands perform in front of the Capitol, and a series of evening concerts by the bands of the Armed Forces is offered free of charge on the east front plaza. On various holidays, concerts by the National Symphony Orchestra are held on the west front lawn.

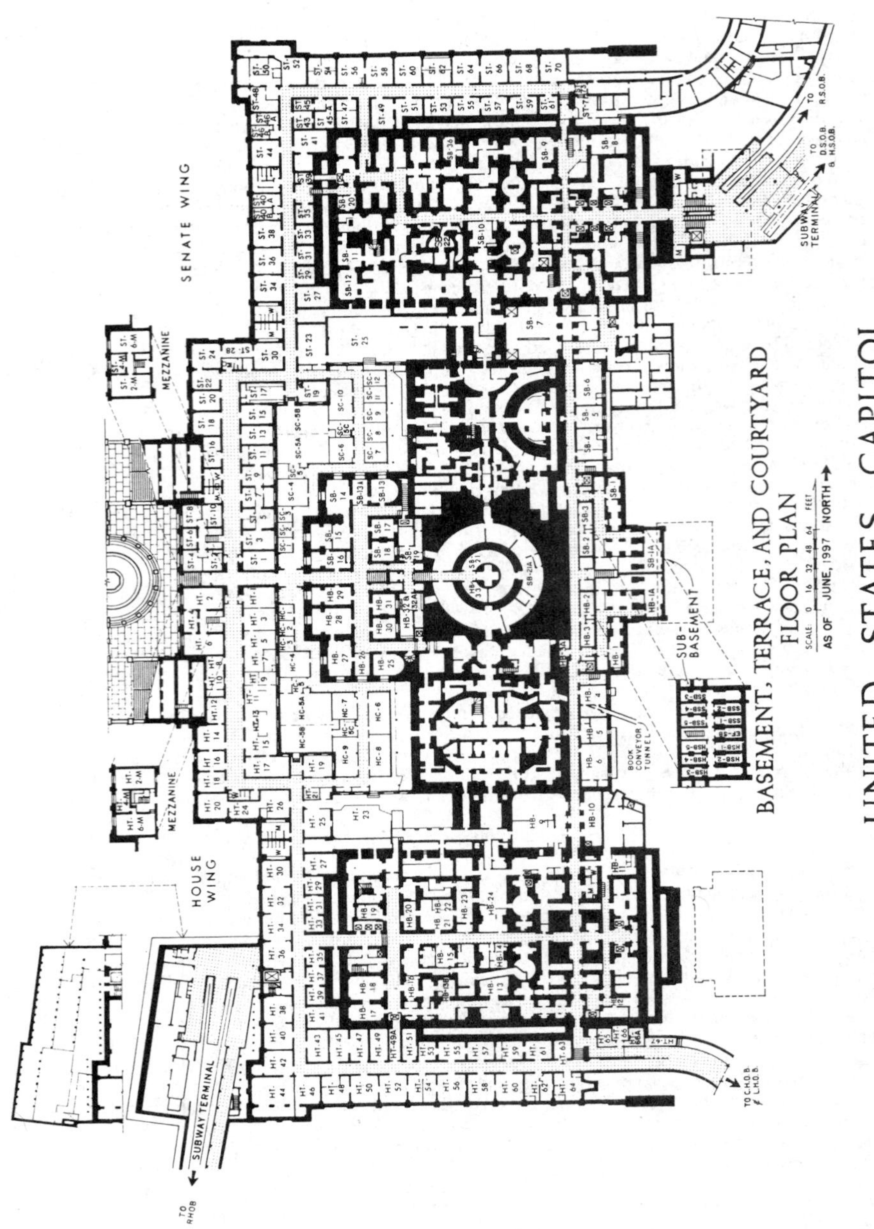
SENATE WING
HOUSE WING
MEZZANINE
SUBWAY TERMINAL
SUB-BASEMENT
BOOK CONVEYOR TUNNEL
TO RHOB
TO C.H.O.B. & L.H.O.B.
TO D.S.O.B. & H.S.O.B.
TO R.S.O.B.
BASEMENT, TERRACE, AND COURTYARD
FLOOR PLAN
SCALE: 0 16 32 48 64 FEET
AS OF JUNE, 1997 NORTH
UNITED STATES CAPITOL

ROOMS IN BASEMENT, TERRACE, AND COURTYARDS OF THE CAPITOL

HOUSE SIDE

BASEMENT

HB–1, 6. House Sergeant at Arms.
HB–1A. Clerk of the House.
HB–4. Library of Congress–Capitol Station.
HB–9, 10. House Restaurant. Coffee shop.
HB–13. Speaker of the House.
HB–13B. Democratic Leader.
HB–15. Architect of the Capitol. House engineers.
HB–16, 17, 18. Committee on Appropriations.
HB–19. Architect of the Capitol. Elevator operators.
HB–20, 21, 22, 23, 24. House Restaurant. Kitchen.
HB–25. House Chaplain.
HB–28, 29, 31, 32, 32A, 33. Architect of the Capitol.
HB–26, 27. Committee on Rules.

TERRACE

HT–2, 2M, 4, 4M, 6, 6M. Committee on Standards of Official Conduct.
HT–3, 5, 7. Architect of the Capitol. Curator.
HT–8, 10. Clerk of the House. Pages.
HT–9, 11, 13, 15, 17. Clerk of the House. Legislative Operations.
HT–12, 14, 16, 18. Architect of Capitol. Flag office.
HT–20, 23, 24, 25, 26, 49, 49A, 62. Architect of the Capitol. Mechanical rooms.
HT–30, 32, 34, 36. Architect of the Capitol. Sheetmetal shop.
HT–33. Architect of the Capitol. Carpenter's key shop.
HT–35, 37, 39. Architect of the Capitol. Elevator shop.
HT–38, 40, 41. Architect of the Capitol. Electrical shop.
HT–42, 44, 62. Architect of the Capitol.
HT–43. Architect of the Capitol. Paint shop.
HT–45, 47. Architect of the Capitol. Laborers' shop.
HT–46. Architect of the Capitol. Plumbers' shop.
HT–50, 52. Clerk of the House. Document Room.
HT–53, 55, 57. House television control.
HT–56, 65, 66, 66A, 67. Committee on Appropriations.
HT–58, 59, 60, 61. Clerk of the House. Official Reporters of Debates.

COURTYARD

HC–4, 5A, 5B, 6, 7, 8, 9. Conference / Hearing rooms.
HC–5. Foyer.
HC–5C. Kitchen.

SENATE SIDE

BASEMENT

SB–1. Senate Restaurant. Banquet Department.
SB–7. Senate Restaurant. Kitchen.
SB–8. Senate Sergeant at Arms. Recording studio.
SB–9. Senate Sergeant at Arms.
SB–10. Senate Restaurant. Carry-Out.
SB–11, 12. Architect of the Capitol. Senate engineers.
SB–13, 13A, 14, 15, 16, 17, 18, 19, 21, 21A. Architect of the Capitol.
SB–20. Secretary of the Senate.
SB–22. Architect of the Capitol. Masonry shop.
SB–23. Senate Sergeant at Arms. Custodial service.
SB–36. Secretary of the Senate. Newspaper room.

TERRACE

ST–1, 3, 5, 7, 9, 11, 17, 18. Capitol Police.
ST–13, 15. Capitol Guide Service.
ST–16. Architect of the Capitol. Insulation shop.
ST–19, 23, 24, 25, 27, 28, 30, 49, 52, 59, 61, 68. Architect of the Capitol. Mechanical rooms.
ST–20, 53, 60, 62. Senate Sergeant at Arms. Custodial service.
ST–34, 36, 38. Senate Sergeant at Arms. Senate television control.
ST–41, 44. Secretary of the Senate. Official Reporters of Debates.
ST–45, 45A. Assistant Majority Leader.
ST–47, 48, 70. Senate Sergeant at Arms.
ST–50. Democratic Policy Committee.
ST–51, 52, 64, 66. Architect of the Capitol. Paint shop.
ST–54. Secretary of the Senate. Captioning services.
ST–55. Democratic Leader.
ST–56, 58. Secretary of the Senate. Daily Digest.
ST–57. Republican Policy Committee.
ST–71, 73. Senate Sergeant at Arms. Recording studio (old Senate subway tunnel).

COURTYARD

SC–4, 5A, 5B, 6, 10. Conference / Hearing rooms.
SC–5. Foyer.
SC–5C. Kitchen.
SC–7, 8. Democratic Leader.
SC–11, 12. Republican Leader.

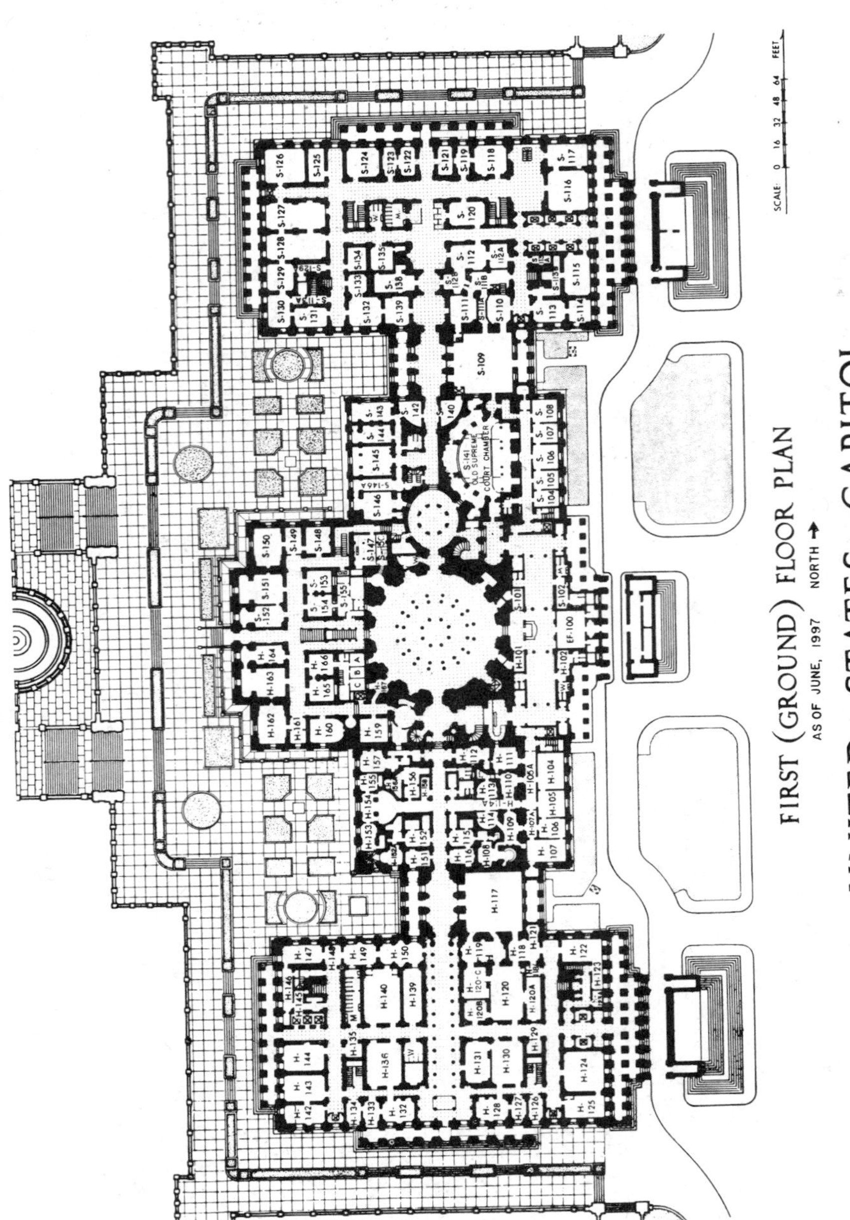
FIRST (GROUND) FLOOR PLAN
AS OF JUNE, 1997 NORTH →
UNITED STATES CAPITOL
SCALE: 0 16 32 48 64 FEET
S-141 OLD SUPREME COURT CHAMBER

ROOMS ON FIRST (GROUND) FLOOR OF THE CAPITOL

HOUSE SIDE

Hall of Columns.
Hall of Capitols.
Great Experiment Hall.
Westward Expansion Hall.

H–101. House Post Office.
H–104, 105. Chief Deputy Majority Whip.
H–105A, 106, 107, 107A, 108, 109, 110, 113, 114, 114A, 115, 116. Majority Whip.
H–111, 112. Chief Administrative Officer.
H–117. House Restaurant [Ernest Petinaud Room].
H–118, 118A, 120A, 120B, 121. House Restaurant.
H–119, 120C. House Restaurant. Kitchen.
H–120 House Restaurant [Charles E. Bennett Room].
H–122, 123. Private dining room (Speaker).
H–123A. House Restaurant. Catering Office.
H–124, 125. Sergeant at Arms.
H–126. Parliamentarian.
H–127, 128. Speaker of the House.
H–129. Wright Patman Congressional Federal Credit Union.
H–130, 131. Members' private dining rooms.
H–132, 151. Democratic Leader.
H–133, 134. Republican Conference.
H–135. Subcommittee on Defense (Appropriations).
H–136, 137. Committee on Ways and Means.
H–139. Committee on International Relations.
H–140. Committee on Appropriations [George Mahon Room].
H–142, 143. Subcommittee on HUD–Independent Agencies (Appropriations).
H–144, 145, 146, 148. Committee on Appropriations.
H–147. Subcommittee on Legislative-D.C. (Appropriations).
H–149. Subcommittee on National Security (Appropriations).
H–150. Subcommittee on Foreign Operations (Appropriations).
H–152, 152A. Committee on Rules.
H–153, 154, 155, 156, 156A, 158. Clerk of the House.
H–159, 160, 161, 162, 165, 166, 166A, 166B, 166C, 167. Attending Physician.
H–163, 164. Committee on House Oversight.

SENATE SIDE

Brumidi Corridors.

S–101. Railroad Ticket Office.
S–102. Capitol Guide Service.
S–109, 110, 112, 112A, 112B, 114, 115. Senate Restaurant.
S–111, 111A, 111B, 113B. Senate Restaurant. Kitchen.
S–113. Senate Restaurant [Styles Bridges Room].
S–113A. Senate Restaurant. Catering Office.
S–116, 117. Committee on Foreign Relations.
S–118, 119, 121. Democratic Policy Committee.
S–120. Reception Room (Restaurant) [Hugh Scott Room].
S–122, 123. Secretary of the Senate. Bill Clerk and Morning Business Clerk.
S–125, 126, 127, 128, 129, 129A, 130, 130A, 131. Committee on Appropriations.
S–132, 133. Secretary of the Senate. Parliamentarian.
S–134. Secretary of the Senate. Legislative Clerk.
S–135. Secretary of the Senate. Journal Clerk.
S–138. Secretary of the Senate. Executive Clerk and Office Services [Arthur H. Vandenberg Room].
S–139. Secretary of the Senate. Engrossing and Enrolling Clerks.
S–141. Old Supreme Court Chamber.
S–145. Senate Wives' Reception Room.
S–146. Committee on Appropriations.
S–146A. Subcommittee on Commerce, Justice, State, and the Judiciary (Appropriations).
S–147. Architect of the Capitol.
S–148, 149, 150. Democratic Whip.
S–151. Committee on Rules.
S–153, 154. Attending Physician. First Aid.
S–155. Attending Physician.
S–156. Capitol Guide Service. Congressional Special Services Office.

CRYPT

EF–100. Reception Room (center, East Front).

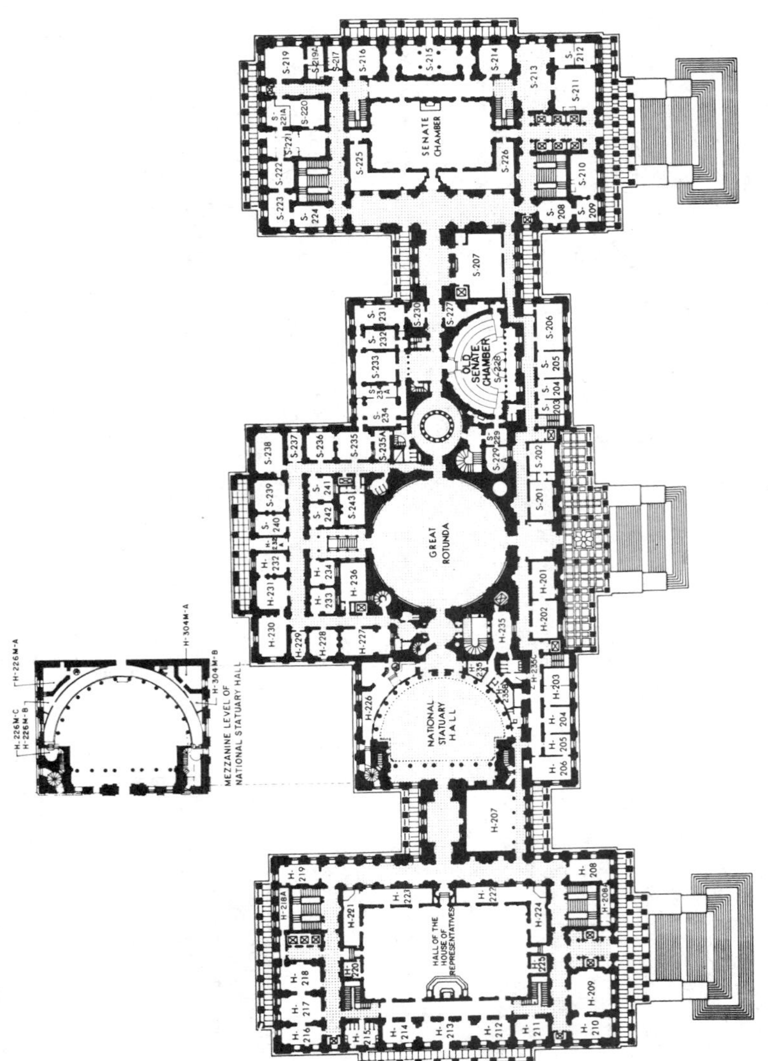

SECOND (PRINCIPAL) FLOOR PLAN

scale: 0 16 32 48 64 feet

AS OF JUNE, 1997 NORTH →

UNITED STATES CAPITOL

ROOMS ON SECOND (PRINCIPAL) FLOOR OF THE CAPITOL

HOUSE SIDE

National Statuary Hall.
Hall of the House of Representatives.

H–201, 202, 203, 204, 205, 206. Democratic Leader.
H–207. House Reception Room [Sam Rayburn Room].
H–208, 208A. Committee on Ways and Means.
H–209, 210. Speaker's Rooms.
H–211. Parliamentarian.
H–212, 213, 214. Representatives' retiring rooms.
H–216, 217, 218, 218A. Committee on Appropriations.
H–219. Majority Leader.
H–220. Speaker's floor office.
H–221, 223. Republican cloakroom.
H–222, 224. Democratic cloakroom.
H–225. Democratic Leader's floor office.
H–226, 226M–A, 226M–B, 226M–C. Majority Leader.
H–227, 228, 229, 230, 231, 232, 232A, 233, 236. Speaker of the House.
H–234. Prayer Room.
H–235, 235A, 235B, 235C. Congressional Women's Reading Room [Lindy Claiborne Boggs Room].
H–304M-A, 304M-B (mezzanine). Periodical Press Gallery.

SENATE SIDE

Senate Chamber.
Balcony [Robert J. Dole Balcony].

S–207. Senators' Conference Room [Mike Mansfield Room].
S–208, 209. Assistant Majority Leader.
S–210. Assistant Majority Leader. [John F. Kennedy Room].
S–211. Secretary of the Senate [Lyndon B. Johnson Room].
S–212. Vice President.
S–213. Senate Reception Room.
S–214. Ceremonial Office of the Vice President.
S–215. Senators' retiring room [Marble Room].
S–216. President's Room.
S–219, 219A, 220. Secretary of the Senate.
S–221, 221A, 222, 223, 224. Democratic Leader [Robert C. Byrd Rooms].
S–225. Democratic cloakroom.
S–226. Republican cloakroom.
S–227, 231, 232, 233, 234, 234A, 235, 235A, 236. Republican Leader.
S–228. Old Senate Chamber.
S–229, 229A, 229M. Republican Legislative Scheduling Office.
S–230. Republican Leader [Howard H. Baker, Jr., Room].
S–237. President Pro Tempore.
S–238. [Strom Thurmond Room].

ROTUNDA

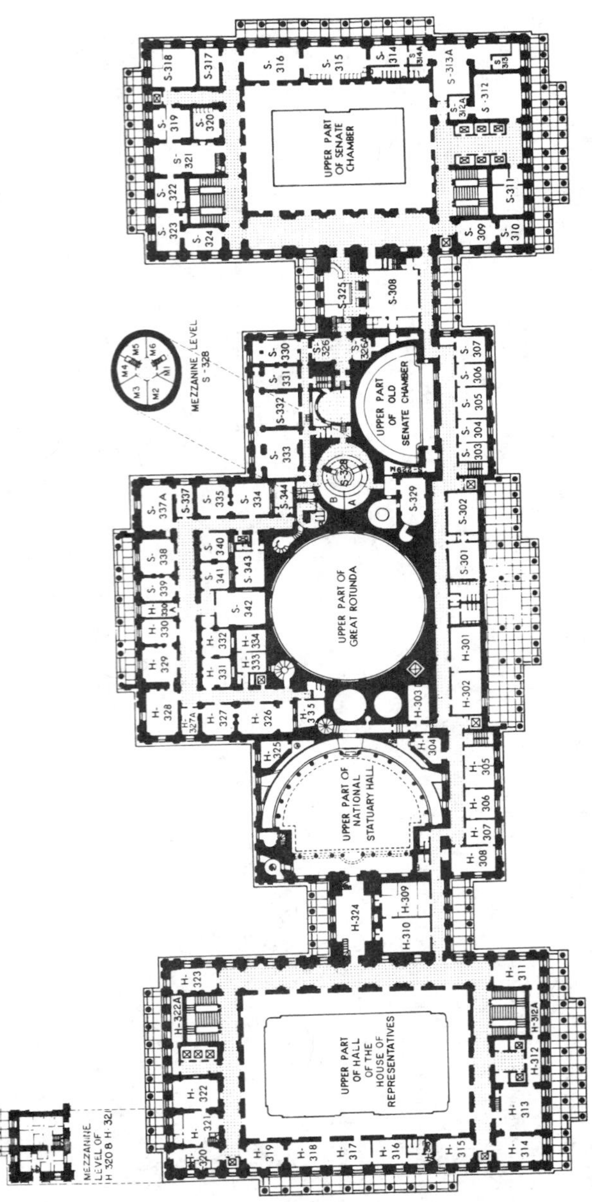

THIRD (GALLERY) FLOOR PLAN

scale: 0 16 32 48 64 feet

AS OF JUNE, 1997 NORTH →

UNITED STATES CAPITOL

ROOMS ON THIRD (GALLERY) FLOOR OF THE CAPITOL

HOUSE SIDE

H–301, 302, 303. Democratic Policy Committee.
H–304, 304M-A, 304M-B. Periodical Press Gallery.
H–305, 306, 307, 308. Democratic Whip.
H–309, 310. Subcommittee on Commerce, Justice, State, and the Judiciary (Appropriations).
H–311, 312, 312A, 313, 314. Committee on Rules.
H–315, 315A, 316, 317, 318, 319. Press Gallery.
H–320, 320M, 321, 321M, 322, 322A. Radio and Television Correspondents' Gallery.
H–323. Committee on Appropriations.
H–324, 324M. Members' Families Room. [Thomas P. O'Neill, Jr. Room].
H–325, 327A, 328, 329, 330, 330A, 331, 332, 335. Majority Leader.
H–326, 327, 333, 334, 335. Speaker of the House.

SENATE SIDE

S–308. Radio and Television Studio.
S–309, 310. Democratic Secretary.
S–311. Senate Wives' Lounge.
S–312, 312A. Assistant Secretary of the Senate.
S–313, 313A, 314, 314A, 315, 316. Press Gallery.
S–317. Press Photographers' Gallery.
S–318. Democratic Policy Committee.
S–319, 321, 322, 323, 324. Sergeant at Arms.
S–320. Periodical Press Gallery.
S–325. Radio and Television Correspondents' Gallery.
S–326. Hallway.
S–331, 332, 333. Secretary of the Senate. Senate Library.
S–337, 337A. Secretary for the Majority.

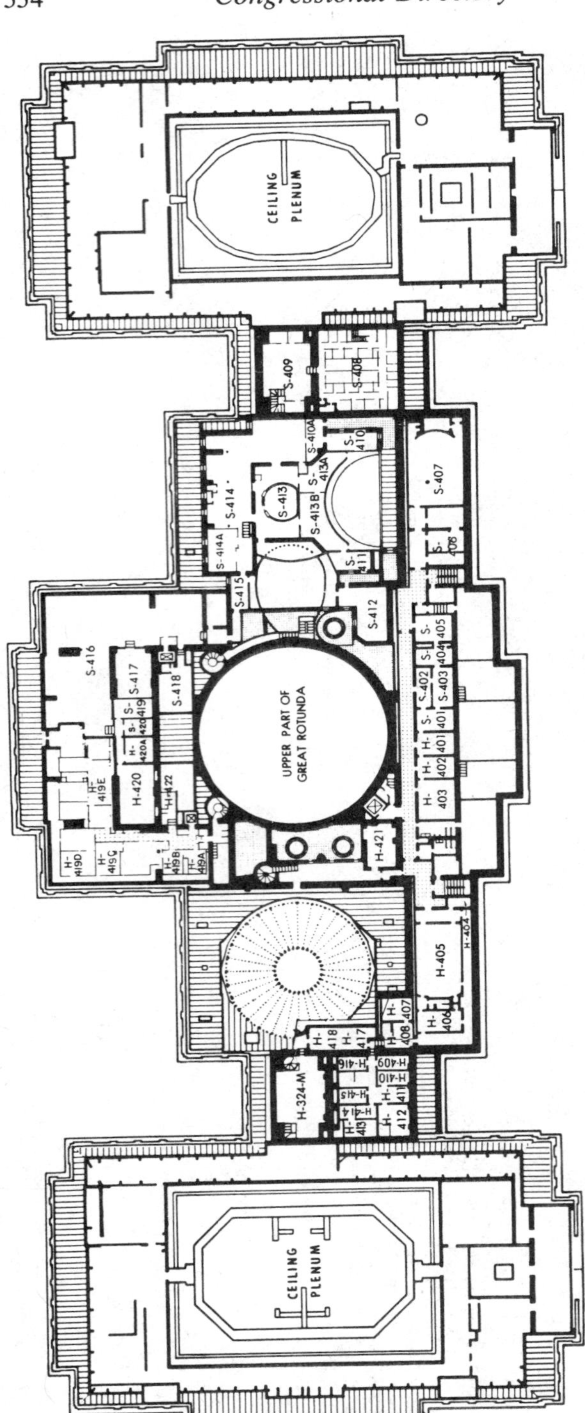

FOURTH (ATTIC) FLOOR PLAN

scale: 0 16 32 48 64 feet

AS OF JUNE, 1997 NORTH →

UNITED STATES CAPITOL

ROOMS ON FOURTH (ATTIC) FLOOR OF THE CAPITOL

HOUSE SIDE

H–324M (mezzanine). Members' Families Room.
H–405. Permanent Select Committee on Intelligence.
H–419A, 419B, 419C, 419D, 419E. Speaker of the House.
H–420, H–420A, 421. Architect of the Capitol.

SENATE SIDE

S–406. Secretary of the Senate. Senate Security.
S–408, 409. Radio and Television Correspondents' Gallery.
S–410. Secretary of the Senate. Conservation and Preservation.
S–411, 413A, 413B. Secretary of the Senate. Curator of Art.
S–412, 417. Architect of the Capitol. Mechanical rooms.
S–413, 414, 415, 416, 418. Secretary of the Senate. Senate Library.
S–414A, 419, 420. Secretary of the Senate.

Note: To reach H–405 and S–406—Use express elevator on the first floor at southeast wall of the Crypt, and take to fourth floor of Capitol.

Maps edited by Jay Bon and Peter Byrd.

SEATING ARRANGEMENT IN THE SENATE CHAMBER

As of Feb. 24, 1997

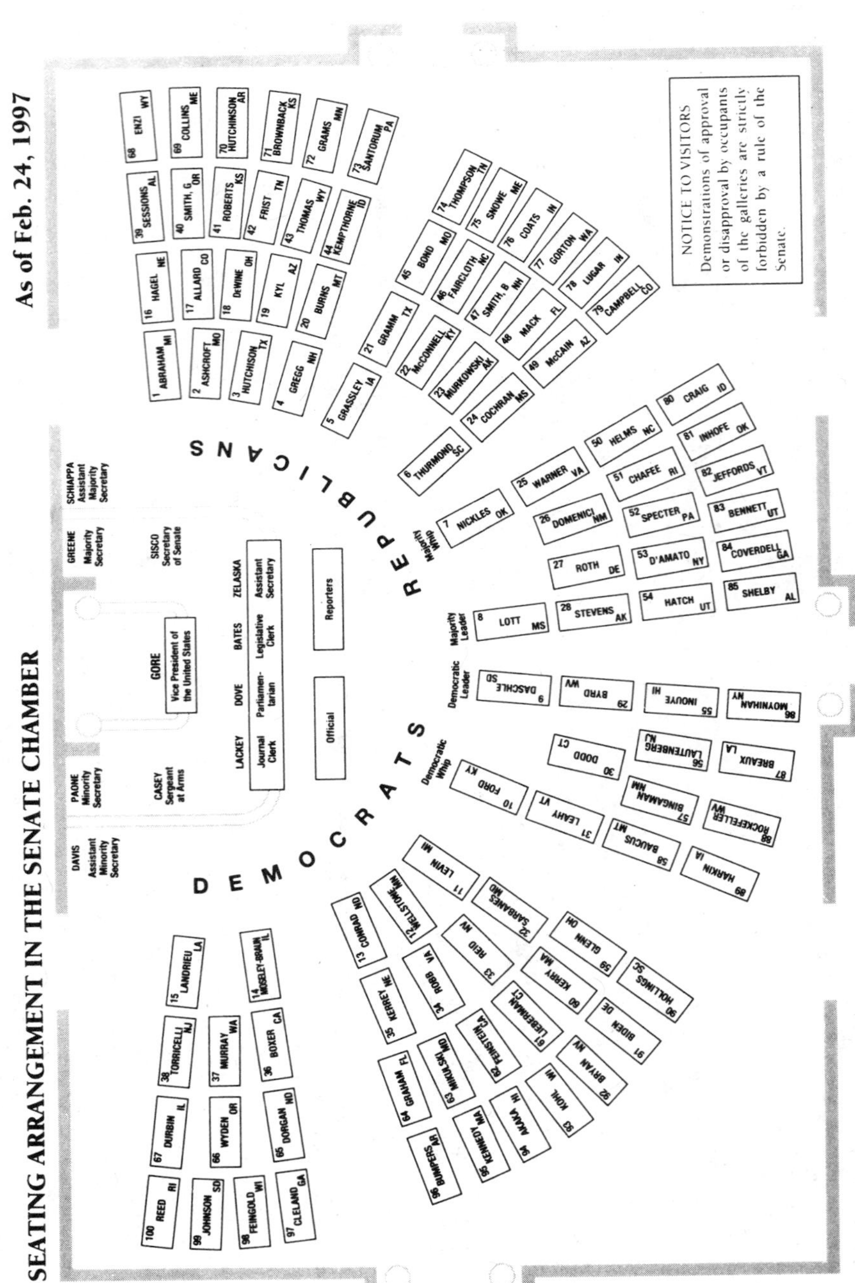

DIRECTORY OF THE SENATE — 105th Congress

AL GORE, Vice President of the United States and President of the Senate
STROM THURMOND, President pro tempore
TRENT LOTT, Majority Leader
TOM DASCHLE, Democratic Leader
DON NICKLES, Assistant Majority Leader (Whip)
WENDELL H. FORD, Democratic Whip

Gary Sisco, Secretary of the Senate
Greg Casey, Sergeant-at-Arms
Elizabeth B. Greene, Secretary for the Majority
Martin P. Paone, Secretary for the Minority
Robert B. Dove, Parliamentarian
Dr. Lloyd J. Ogilvie, Chaplain

REPUBLICANS IN ROMAN (55); DEMOCRATS IN *ITALIC* (45); TOTAL 100

Abraham, Spencer, MI, 1
Akaka, Daniel K., HI, 94
Allard, Wayne, CO, 17
Ashcroft, John, MO, 2
Baucus, Max, MT, 58
Bennett, Robert F., UT, 83
Biden, Joseph R., Jr., DE, 91
Bingaman, Jeff, NM, 57
Bond, Christopher S., MO, 45
Boxer, Barbara, CA, 36
Breaux, John B., LA, 87
Brownback, Samuel Dale, KS, 71
Bryan, Richard H., NV, 92
Bumpers, Dale, AR, 96
Burns, Conrad R., MT, 20
Byrd, Robert C., WV, 29
Campbell, Ben Nighthorse, CO, 79
Chafee, John H., RI, 51
Cleland, Max, GA, 97
Coats, Dan, IN, 76
Cochran, Thad, MS, 24
Collins, Susan M., ME, 69
Conrad, Kent, ND, 13
Coverdell, Paul, GA, 84
Craig, Larry E., ID, 80
D'Amato, Alfonse M., NY, 53
Daschle, Thomas A., SD, 9
DeWine, Mike, OH, 18
Dodd, Christopher J., CT, 30
Domenici, Pete V., NM, 26
Dorgan, Byron L., ND, 65
Durbin, Richard J., IL, 67
Enzi, Michael B., WY, 68
Faircloth, Lauch, NC, 46
Feingold, Russell D., WI, 98
Feinstein, Dianne, CA, 62
Ford, Wendell H., KY, 10
Frist, Bill, TN, 42
Glenn, John, OH, 59
Gorton, Slade, WA, 77
Graham, Bob, FL, 64
Gramm, Phil, TX, 21
Grams, Rod, MN, 72
Grassley, Charles E., IA, 5
Gregg, Judd, NH, 4
Hagel, Chuck, NE, 16
Harkin, Tom, IA, 89
Hatch, Orrin G., UT, 54
Helms, Jesse, NC, 50
Hollings, Ernest F., SC, 90
Hutchinson, Tim, AR, 70
Hutchison, Kay Bailey, TX, 3
Inhofe, James M., OK, 81
Inouye, Daniel K., HI, 55
Jeffords, James M., VT, 82
Johnson, Tim, SD, 99
Kempthorne, Dirk, ID, 44
Kennedy, Edward M., MA, 95
Kerrey, J. Robert, NE, 35
Kerry, John F., MA, 60
Kohl, Herb, WI, 93
Kyl, Jon, AZ, 19
Landrieu, Mary, LA, 15
Lautenberg, Frank R, NJ, 56
Leahy, Patrick J., VT, 31
Levin, Carl, MI, 11
Lieberman, Joseph I., CT, 61
Lott, Trent, MS, 8
Lugar, Richard G., IN, 78
Mack, Connie, FL, 48
McCain, John, AZ, 49
McConnell, Mitch, KY, 22
Mikulski, Barbara A., MD, 63
Moseley-Braun, Carol, IL, 14
Moynihan, Daniel P., NY, 86
Murkowski, Frank H., AK, 23
Murray, Patty, WA, 37
Nickles, Don, OK, 7
Reed, Jack, RI, 100
Reid, Harry, NV, 33
Robb, Charles S., VA, 34
Roberts, Pat, KS, 41
Rockefeller, John D., IV, WV, 88
Roth, William V., Jr., DE, 27
Santorum, Rick, PA, 73
Sarbanes, Paul S., MD, 32
Sessions, Jeff, AL, 39
Shelby, Richard C., AL, 85
Smith, Bob, NH, 47
Smith, Gordon, OR, 40
Snowe, Olympia J., ME, 75
Specter, Arlen, PA, 52
Stevens, Ted, AK, 28
Thomas, Craig, WY, 43
Thompson, Fred, TN, 74
Thurmond, Strom, SC, 6
Torricelli, Robert G., NJ, 38
Warner, John W., VA, 25
Wellstone, Paul David, MN, 12
Wyden, Ron, OR, 66

Hall of the House of Representatives

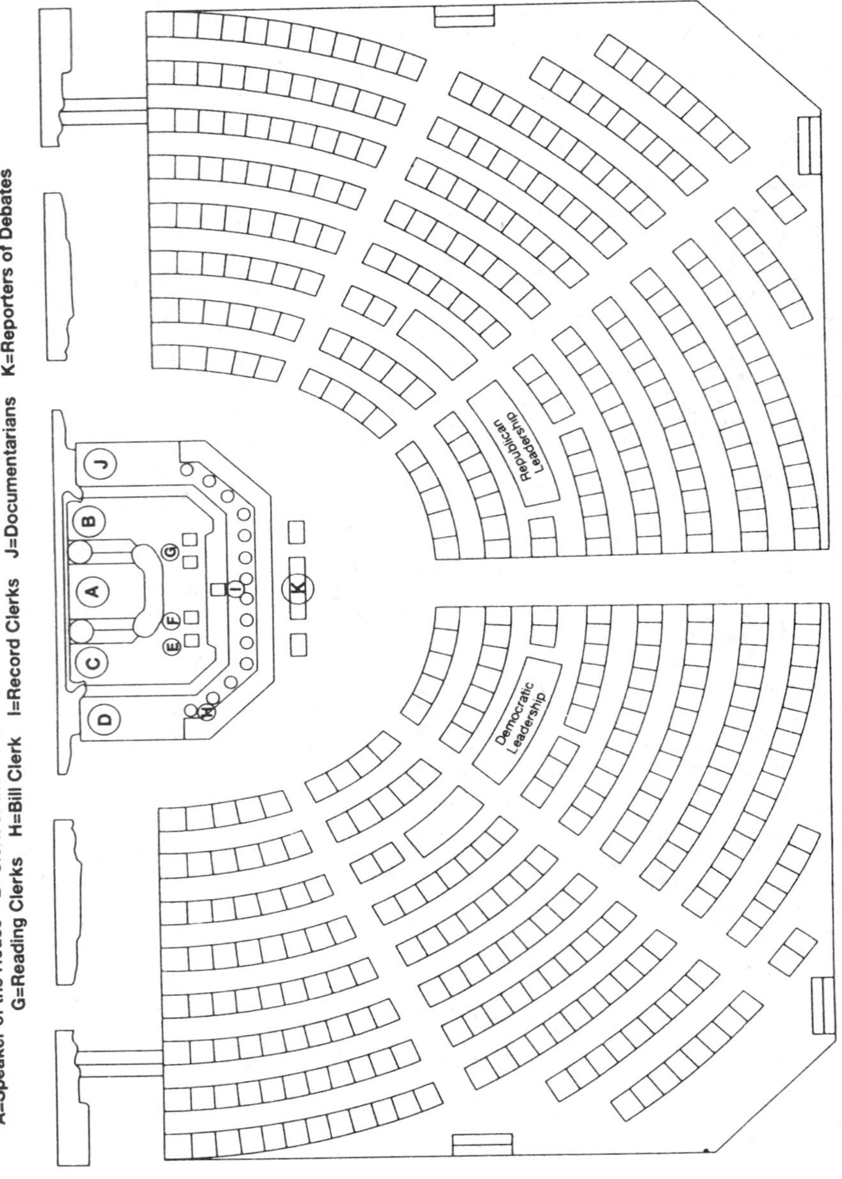

LEGISLATIVE BRANCH AGENCIES

CONGRESSIONAL BUDGET OFFICE

(Created by Public Law 93–344)

H2–410 Ford House Office Building, Second and D Streets SW 20515, phone 226–2621

Director.—June E. O'Neill, 6–2700.
Deputy Director.—James L. Blum, 6–2702.
General Counsel.—Gail Del Balzo, 5–1971.
Director, Office of Intergovernmental Relations.—Stanley L. Greigg, 6–2600.
Assistant Director for—
Macroeconomic Analysis.—Robert A. Dennis, 6–2784.
Budget Analysis.—Paul N. Van de Water, 6–2800.
National Security.—Cindy Williams, 6–2900.
Tax Analysis.—Rosemary D. Marcuss, 6–2687.
Health and Human Resources.—Joseph A. Antos, 6–2668.
Natural Resources and Commerce.—Jan Paul Acton, 6–2940.
Special Studies.—Arlene Holen, 6–2606.

GENERAL ACCOUNTING OFFICE

441 G Street 20458

Comptroller General of the United States.—James F. Hinchman (acting), 512–5600, fax 512–6722.
Deputy Comptroller General of the United States.—[Vacant].
Assistant Comptroller General for—
Planning and Reporting.—J. Dexter Peach, 512–5900, fax 512–5725.
Operations.—Joan M. Dodaro, 512–5800, fax 512–3322.
Assistant Comptroller General.—Richard Fogel, 512–8442, fax 512–5507.

OFFICES

General Counsel.—Robert Murphy, 512–5400, fax 512–7703.
Assistant Comptroller General for Policy.—Brian Crowley, 512–6100, fax 512–4844.
Assistant Comptroller General for Information Management and Communications.—John Harman, 512–6623, fax 512–6742.
Director, Office of—
Affirmative Action/Civil Rights.—Nilda Aponte, 512–6388, fax 512–4818.
Chief Accountant.—Philip T. Calder, 512–7353, fax 512–4844.
Chief Economist.—James L. Bothwell, 512–6209, fax 512–5366.
Congressional Relations.—Helen H. Hsing, 512–4400, fax 512–7919.
Counseling and Career Development.—Howard N. Johnson, 512–8343, fax 512–4276.
Inspector General.—Frances Garcia, 512–5748, fax 512–2539.
International Audit Organization Liaison.—Linda L. Weeks (acting), 512–4707, fax 512–4021.
Personnel.—Patrica M. Rodgers, 512–4500, fax 512–8869.
Public Affairs.—Cleve E. Corlett, 512–4800, fax 512–7726.
Program Planning.—Paul Jones, 512–6190, fax 512–9068.
Recruitment.—Stephen J. Kenealy (acting), 512–4900, fax 512–2539.
Special Investigations.—Donald J. Wheeler (acting), 512–7455, fax 371–2442.
Training Institute.—Anne Klein, 512–8674, fax 512–8947.
Executive Director for Federal Accounting Standards Advisory Board.—Wendy M. Comes, 512–7357, fax 512–7366.
Executive Director for Joint Financial Management Improvement Program.—Doris Chew (acting), 512–9201, fax 512–9593.
Chief for Personnel Appeals Board.—Leroy D. Clark, 512–6137, fax 512–7522.

DIVISIONS

Assistant Comptroller General, Division of—

Accounting and Information Management.—Gene L. Dodaro, 512–2600, fax 512–9193.

Directors: Peter V. Aliferis, 512–9459; Jack L. Brock, 512–6406; Linda M. Calbom, 512–9508; David L. Clark, 512–9489; Robert F. Dacey, 512–3317; Robert W. Gramling, 512–9406; Gregory M. Holloway, 512–3406; Lisa G. Jacobson, 512–9095; Frank W. Reilly, 512–6252; Paul L. Posner, 512–9573; Rona Stillman, 512–6412; Jeffrey C. Steinhoff, 512–9450; Joel C. Willemssen, 512–6408.

General Government.—Johnny C. Finch, 512–2700, fax 512–3938.

Directors: Tim Bowling, 512–7802; Nancy Kingsbury, 512–7824; Norman J. Rabkin, 512–3610; L. Nye Stevens, 512–8676; Jean G. Stromberg, 512–8678; Linda Willis, 512–8633.

Health, Education and Human Services.—Richard L. Hembra, 512–6806, fax 512–5806.

Directors: David P. Baine, 512–6807; Stephen P. Backhus, 512–7111; Carlotta Joyner, 512–7014; Gregory J. McDonald, 512–6805; Jane Ross, 512–7215; William Scanlon, 512–7114; Bernice Steinhardt, 512–7119.

National Security and International Affairs.—Henry L. Hinton, Jr., 512–4300, fax 512–7686.

Directors: Kwai-Cheung Chan, 512–3092; Clarence C. Crawford, 512–4126; Richard A. Davis, 512–3504; Joseph F. Delfico, 512–6153; Mark E. Gebicke, 512–5140; Donna M. Heivilin, 512–6152; Benjamin Nelson, 512–4128; Louis J. Rodrigues, 512–4841; David R. Warren, 512–8412.

Resources, Community and Economic Development.—Keith O. Fultz, 512–3200, fax 512–8774.

Directors: John H. Anderson, Jr., 512–2834; Judy England-Joseph, 512–7631; Michael Cryszkowiec, 512–3200; Peter F. Guerrero, 512–6111; Robert A. Robinson, 512–5138; Victor S. Rezendes, 512–3841; Jim Wells, 512–3200.

FIELD OFFICES

Managers:

Atlanta.—Ralph V. Carlone, 2635 Century Parkway, Suite 700, Atlanta GA 30345, (404) 679–1900, fax (404) 679–1819.

Boston.—Michelle L. Roman (acting), Room 575, 10 Causeway Street, Boston MA 02222, (617) 565–7500, fax (617) 565–5909.

Chicago.—Leslie G. Aronovitz, Suite 700, 200 W. Adams Street, Chicago IL 60606–5219, (312) 220–7600, fax (312) 220–7726.

Dallas.—Robert A. Peterson, Suite 2200, 1999 Bryan Street, Dallas TX 75201–6848, (214) 777–5600, fax (214) 777–5758.

Denver.—Thomas J. Brew, Suite 800, 1244 Speer Boulevard, Denver CO 80204–3581, (303) 572–7306, fax (303) 572–7433.

Kansas City.—James R. Watts, Suite 600, Broadmoor Place, 5799 Broadmoor, Mission KS 66202–2408, (913) 384–7440, fax (913) 384–7517.

Los Angeles.—Martin M. Ferber, Los Angeles World Trade Center, 350 South Figueroa Street, Suite 1010, Los Angeles CA 90071, (213) 830–1000, fax (213) 830–1180.

Norfolk.—Neal P. Curtin, Suite 300, 5029 Corporate Woods Drive, Virginia Beach VA 23462, (757) 552–8100, fax (757) 552–8197.

San Francisco.—Thomas J. Schulz, Suite 1200, 301 Howard Street, San Francisco CA 94105–2252, (415) 904–2000, fax (415) 904–2111.

Seattle.—James K. Meissner, 701 Fifth Avenue, Suite 2700, Seattle WA 98104, (206) 287–4800, fax (206) 287–4872.

GOVERNMENT PRINTING OFFICE

732 North Capitol Street NW 20401
phone 512–0000, http://www.access.gpo.gov

Public Printer.—Michael F. DiMario, 512–2034, fax 512–1347.

Deputy Public Printer.—[Vacant], 512–2036.

Director for—

Equal Employment Opportunity.—J. Emory Crandall (acting), 512–2014.

Labor and Employee Relations.—Neal Fine, 512–0198.

Materials Management Service.—Thomas M. Hughes, 512–0935.

Manager for—

Printing Procurement Department.—Meredith L. Arneson, 512–0327.

Superintendent for—
Contract Management.—Lewis W. Gardner, Jr., 512–0485.
Term Contracts.—Raymond Sullivan, 512–0320.
Purchase Division.—M. Clive Walker, 512–0528.
Eastern Regional Operations.—Douglas R. MacBride, 512–0412, fax 512–0381.
Western Regional Operations.—Jerome Durrington, 512–0412, fax 512–0381.
Director for—
Engineering Service.—Joseph A. Palank, 512–1031.
Information Resources Management.—Patricia R. Gardner, 512–1594.
Occupational Health and Environmental Services.—William T. Harris, 512–1210.
Administrative Support.—Raymond J. Garvey, 512–1084.
Comptroller.—Robert B. Holstein, 512–2073.
Planning.—Thomas J. Muldoon, 512–0851.
Personnel.—Edward A. Blatt, 512–1111.
Superintendents:
Congressional Printing Management.—Charles C. Cook, Sr., 512–0224, fax 512–1101.
Departmental Account Representative.—Robert G. Cox, 512–0238, fax 512–1260.
Typography and Design.—John W. Sapp, 512–0212.
Quality Control and Technical Department.—[Vacant], 512–0766.
Director, Institute for Federal Printing and Publishing.—Lois Schutte, 512–1283.
General Counsel.—Anthony J. Zagami, 512–0033.
Deputy General Counsel.—Drew Spalding, 512–0033.
Director, Congressional, Legislative and Public Affairs.—[Vacant], 512–1991, fax 512–1293.
Administrative Law Judge.—Stuart M. Foss, 512–0008.
Inspector General.—Thomas J. Muldoon (acting), 512–0039.
Director, Office of Budget.—William M. Guy, 512–0832.
Director, Policy Coordination Staff.—Vincent F. Arendes, 512–0263.
Manager, Production Department.—Donald L. Ladd, 512–0707.
Superintendents:
Binding.—John W. Crawford, 512–0593.
Electronic Photocomposition.—Robert E. Schwenk, 512–0625.
Press.—Willis M. Streets, 512–0673.
Production Planning.—Philip J. Markett, Jr., 512–0233.
Manager for—
Electronic Systems Development.—[Vacant], 512–0682.
Graphic Systems Development.—Russell A. Duncan, Jr., 512–0731.
Superintendent of Documents.—Wayne P. Kelley, Jr., 512–0571, fax 512–1434.
Director for—
Documents Sales.—James D. Young, 512–2332.
Office of Electronic Information Dissemination.—[Vacant], 512–1622.
Library Programs.—James D. Young (acting), 512–1114.

REGIONAL PRINTING PROCUREMENT OFFICES

Region 1: *Manager.*—Roger S. White, 28 Court Square, Boston MA 02108–2504, (617) 720–3680, fax (617) 720–0281.
Region 2 (I):
Manager.—James T. Reingruber, Southampton Office Park, Suite A–190, 928 Jaymore Road, Southampton PA 18966–3820, (215) 364–6465, fax (215) 364–6479.
Assistant Manager.—[Vacant], GPO Satellite Printing Procurement Office, Moorhead Federal Office Building, Room 501, 1000 Liberty Avenue, Pittsburgh PA 15222–4000, (412) 644–2858, fax (412) 355–3694.
Region 2 (II):
Manager.—Francis P. Dillon, 201 Varick Street, Room 709, New York NY 10014–4879, (212) 620–3321, fax (212) 620–3378.
Region 3 (I):
Manager.—Chris J. Brown, Government Printing Office, Rapid Response Center (Procurement), Building 136, Washington Navy Yard, First and N Streets SE 20403, (202) 755–2110, fax (202) 755–0287.
Region 3 (II):
Manager.—Robert M. Blake, 11836 Canon Boulevard, Suite 400, Newport News VA 23606–2555, (757) 873–2800, fax (757) 873–2805.
Region 4:
Manager.—Douglas M. Faour, 1888 Emery Street, Suite 110, Two Park Place, Atlanta GA 30318–2542, (404) 605–9160, fax (404) 605–9185.

Assistant Manager.—James A. Wainscott, GPO Satellite Printing Procurement Office, L. Mendel Rivers Federal Building, Room 122, 334 Meeting Street, Charleston SC 29403–6417, (803) 723–9379, fax (803) 723–0534.

Region 5 (I):

Manager.—Thomas E. Nepi, 200 North LaSalle Street, Suite 810, Chicago IL 60601–1055, (312) 353–3916, fax (312) 886–3163.

Region 5 (II):

Manager.—Aurelio E. Morales, 1335 Dublin Road, Suite 112–B, Columbus OH 43215–7034, (614) 488–4616, fax (614) 488–4577.

Region 6: *Manager.*—Lorraine B. Horton, Old Post Office Building, Room 328, 815 Olive Street, St. Louis MO 63101–1597, (314) 241–0349, fax (314) 241–4154.

Region 7:

Manager.—Richard W. Wildbrett, U.S. Courthouse and Federal Office Building, Room 3D4, 1100 Commerce Street, Dallas TX 75242–0395, (214) 767–0451, fax (214) 767–4101.

Assistant Manager.—Lowell W. Borton, GPO Satellite Printing Procurement Office, Building 1552, Door No. 2, Kelley Air Force Base TX 78241–5000, (210) 924–4245, fax (210) 924–4848.

Assistant Manager.—Gerard J. Finnegan, GPO Satellite Printing Procurement Office, U.S. Customs Building, Room 310, 423 Canal Street, New Orleans LA 70130–2352, (504) 589–2538, fax (504) 589–2542.

Assistant Manager.—Timothy J. Ashcraft, GPO Satellite Printing Procurement Office, 3420 D Avenue, Suite 100, Tinker Air Force Base OK 73145–9188, (405) 231–4146, fax (405) 231–4125.

Region 8: *Manager.*—Judy Ruehle, Denver Federal Center, Building 53, Room D–1010, Denver CO 80225–0347, (303) 236–5292, fax (303) 236–5304.

Region 9 (I):

Manager.—James A. Davidson, 3950 Paramount Boulevard, Room 220, Lakewood CA 90712–4144, (310) 982–1130, fax (310) 982–1147.

Assistant Manager.—Eileen P. Hall-Splendorio, GPO Satellite Printing Procurement Office, Valley Center Office Building, 2221 Camino Del Rio South, San Diego CA 92108–3609, (619) 497–6050, fax (619) 497–6054.

Region 9 (II):

Manager.—John J. O'Connor, 536 Stone Road, Suite One, Benicia CA 94510–1170, (707) 748–1970, fax (707) 748–1980.

Region 10: *Manager.*—Michael J. Atkins, Federal Center South, 4735 East Marginal Way South, Seattle WA 98134–2397, (206) 764–3726, fax (206) 764–3301.

REGIONAL PRINTING PLANT

Denver: *Manager.*—Judy Ruehle, Denver Federal Center, Building 53, Room D–1010, Denver CO 80225–0347, (303) 236–5292, fax (303) 236–5304.

BOOKSTORES

Washington, DC area:

U.S. Government Printing Office, (Main Bookstore), 710 North Capitol Street NW Washington DC 20401, (202) 512–0132.

1510 H Street NW (McPherson), Washington DC 20005, (202) 653–5075.

8660 Cherry Lane, Laurel MD 20707, Warehouse Sales Outlet, (301) 953–7974, (301) 792–0262.

Alabama: O'Neill Building, 2021 Third Avenue North, Birmingham AL 35203, (205) 731–1056.

California:

ARCO Plaza, C–Level, 505 South Flower Street, Los Angeles CA 90071, (213) 239–9844.

Room 141–S, Marathon Plaza, 303 Second Street, San Francisco CA 94107, (415) 512–2770.

Colorado:

Room 117, Byron G. Rogers Federal Building and U.S. Courthouse, 1961 Stout Street, Denver CO 80294, (303) 844–3964.

Norwest Banks Building, 201 West Eighth Street, Pueblo CO 81003, (719) 544–3142.

Public Documents Distribution Center, PO Box 4007, Pueblo CO 81003, (719) 948–2240.

Florida: Room 100, Federal Building, 100 West Bay Street, Jacksonville FL 32202, (904) 353–0569.

Georgia: 120 First Union Plaza, 999 Peachtree Street NE, Atlanta GA 30309, (404) 347–1900.
Illinois: One Congress Center, Room 124, 401 South State Street, Chicago IL 60605, (312) 353–5133.
Massachusetts: Thomas P. O'Neill Building, 10 Causeway Street, Room 169, Boston MA 02222, (617) 720–4180.
Michigan: Suite 160, Patrick V. McNamera Federal Building, 477 Michigan Avenue, Detroit MI 48226, (313) 226–7816.
Missouri: 120 Bannister Mall, 5600 East Bannister Road, Kansas City MO 64137, (816) 767–8225.
New York: Room 110, Jacob K. Javits Federal Building, 26 Federal Plaza, New York NY 10278, (212) 264–3825.
Ohio:
Room 1653, Anthony J. Celebrezze Federal Building, 1240 East Ninth Street, Cleveland OH 44199, (216) 522–4922.
Room 207, Federal Building, 200 North High Street, Columbus OH 43215, (614) 469–6956.
Oregon: 1305 SW First Avenue, Portland OR 97201–5801, (503) 221–6217.
Pennsylvania:
Robert Morris Building, 100 North 17th Street, Philadelphia PA 19103, (215) 636–1900.
Room 118, William S. Moorehead Federal Building, 1000 Liberty Avenue, Pittsburgh PA 15222, (412) 644–2721.
Texas:
Room 1C50, Earle Cabell Federal Building and U.S. Courthouse, 1100 Commerce Street, Dallas TX 75242, (214) 767–0076.
Texas Crude Building, 801 Travis Street, Suite 120, Houston TX 77002, (713) 228–1187.
Washington: Room 194, Henry M. Jackson Federal Building, 915 Second Avenue, Seattle WA 98174, (206) 553–4270.
Wisconsin: Suite 150, Reuss Federal Plaza, 310 West Wisconsin Avenue, Milwaukee WI 53203, (414) 297–1304.

Orders to:

Superintendent of Documents,
PO Box 371954, Pittsburgh PA 15250–7954
phone (202) 512–1800, fax (202) 512–2250
http://www.access.gpo.gov/su_docs

LIBRARY OF CONGRESS

10 First Street SE 20540, phone 707–5000, fax 707–5844

OFFICE OF THE LIBRARIAN, LM 608

Librarian of Congress.—James H. Billington, 707–5205.
Confidential Assistant to the Librarian.—Janet Chase.
Deputy Librarian.—Donald L. Scott, 707–5215.
Chief of Staff.—Jo Ann C. Jenkins, 707–0351.
Senior Advisor for Diversity.—Jo Ann C. Jenkins.
Director of Security.—Kenneth E. Lopez, 707–8708.

CONGRESSIONAL RELATIONS OFFICE, LM 611

Legislative Liaison Officer.—[Vacant], 707–6577.
Director, Congressional Relations Office.—Geraldine Otramba, 707–6577.

DEVELOPMENT OFFICE, LM 605

Director.—Norma K. Baker, 707–5753.

OFFICE OF SPECIAL EVENTS AND PUBLIC PROGRAMS, LM 605

Special Events Officers: Nancy R. Mitchell, 707–9543; Kim H. Moden, 707–1523.

NATIONAL DIGITAL LIBRARY PROGRAM, LM 637

Director.—Laura E. Campbell, 707–3300.

DIGITAL CONVERSION (AMERICAN MEMORY), LA G04

Operations Manager.—Nancy Eichacker, 707–1335.

Technical Coordinator.—Carl Fleischhauer, 707–8330.

USER SERVICES, LM 629

Project Manager.—Martha Dexter, 707–0805.
Electronic Programs Manager.—Robert G. Zich, 707–8330.

DIGITAL LIBRARY VISITORS CENTER, LM Atrium

Coordinator.—Judith R. Farley, 707–8475.

OFFICE OF COMMUNICATIONS, LM 611

Director/Senior Editor.—Peter Braestrup, 707–1535.
LOC Associates/Civilization, 707–2905.
The Gazette, 707–0970.
Editor.—Gail Fineberg, 707–9194.

PUBLIC AFFAIRS OFFICE, LM 105

Public Affairs Officer.—Jill D. Brett, 707–2905.
Editor, Calendar of Events.—Helen Dalrymple, 707–1940.
Editor, Library of Congress Information Bulletin.—Guy V. Lamolinara, 7–9217.
Media Director.—Craig L. D'Ooge, 707–9189.

OFFICE OF ASSOCIATE LIBRARIAN FOR HUMAN RESOURCES SERVICES, LM 643

Associate Librarian.—Lloyd A. Pauls, 707–5659.

AFFIRMATIVE ACTION AND SPECIAL PROGRAMS OFFICE, LM 623

Chief.—[Vacant], 707–4565.

TARGETED RECRUITMENT DIVISION, LM 107

Chief.—[Vacant], 707–2541.

TESTING AND VALIDATION DIVISION, LM 107

Chief.—Tommy Shaw, 707–7192.

DISPUTE RESOLUTION CENTER, LM 624

Director.—André Carl Whisenton, 707–6024.

EQUAL EMPLOYMENT OPPORTUNITY COMPLAINTS OFFICE, LM 626

Director.—André Carl Whisenton, 707–6024.

OFFICE OF THE DIRECTOR OF PERSONNEL, LM 648

Director.—Ben Benitez, 707–6080.

CLASSIFICATION AND POSITION MANAGEMENT OFFICE, LM 643

Chief.—Donald R. Ware, 707–7195.

EMPLOYEE RELATIONS OFFICE, LM 636

Chief.—Elizabeth L. Carl (acting), 707–6402.

EMPLOYEE ASSISTANCE GROUP, LM 636

American Sign Language Interpreting Services Program.—707–6361, TTY 707–6362.

EMPLOYMENT OFFICE, LM 647

Chief.—[Vacant], 707–2939.

STAFFING AND RECRUITMENT GROUP, LM 647

Group Leader.—[Vacant], 707–2034.

TECHNICAL SERVICES GROUP, LM 648

Group Leader.—Herbert L. Junious, 707–2939.

LABOR MANAGEMENT RELATIONS OFFICE, LM 653

Chief.—Harry Yee, 707–1414.

OFFICE OF COUNSEL FOR PERSONNEL, LM 653

Counsel.—Peter J. Watters, 707–6197.

PAY AND PERSONNEL INFORMATION OFFICE, LM 107

Chief.—Nora J. Bardak, 707–0289.

TRAINING AND DEVELOPMENT OFFICE, LM 644

Chief.—James W. Browning, 707–6432.

OFFICE OF THE DIRECTOR FOR FINANCIAL SERVICES, LM 613

Director.—John D. Webster, 707–5189.

ACCOUNTING DIVISION, LM 617

Chief.—John A. Husovsky, 707–5225.

BUDGET OFFICE, LM 613

Budget Officer.—[Vacant], 707–5186.

DISBURSING OFFICE, LM 613

Disbursing Officer.—Reginald F. Massie, 707–5202.

FINANCIAL SYSTEMS OFFICE, LM 613

Financial Systems Officer.—Jamie L. McCullough, 707–4160.

OFFICE OF THE DIRECTOR OF INFORMATION TECHNOLOGY SERVICES, LM G51

Director.—Herbert S. Becker, 707–6207.

DATA ADMINISTRATION STAFF, LM G51

Administrator.—Mary Kay D. Ganning, 707–9709.

RESOURCES MANAGEMENT STAFF, LM G51

Manager.—Judith L. Stork (acting), 707–9739.

TECHNOLOGY ASSESSMENT STAFF, LM G51

Manager.—James S. Graber, 707–9628.

COMPUTER OPERATIONS GROUP, LM G51

Group Leader.—Henry C. Johnson, 707–9588.

PRODUCTION SYSTEMS GROUP 1, LM G51

Group Leader.—Richard W. Genter, 707–9577.

PRODUCTION SYSTEMS GROUP 2, LM G51

Group Leader.—Mercedes Ondich, 707–9669.

SYSTEMS DEVELOPMENT GROUP 1, LM G51

Group Leader.—Ivey S. Andrews, 707–9689.

SYSTEMS DEVELOPMENT GROUP 2, LM G51

Group Leader.—Maryle G. Ashley, 707–9641.

SYSTEMS DEVELOPMENT GROUP 3, LM G51

Group Leader.—Ivey S. Andrews (acting), 707–9557.

SYSTEMS DEVELOPMENT GROUP 4, LM G51

Group Leader.—Larry T. Fizgerald, 707–3995.

SYSTEMS ENGINEERING GROUP, LM G51

Group Leader.—Judith L. Stork, 707–9739.

USER SUPPORT GROUP, LM G51

Group Leader.—Michael F. Handy, 707–8338.

OFFICE OF THE DIRECTOR FOR INTEGRATED SUPPORT SERVICES, LM 327

Director.—Linda J. Washington, 707–1393.

CONTRACTS AND LOGISTICS SERVICES, LCA

Chief.—Charles S. Fulmore, 707–8616.

FACILITY SERVICES, LM 327

Facility Services Officer.—Gary L. Capriotti, 707–7512.

HEALTH SERVICES, LM G40

Health Services Officer.—Sandra Charles, 707–8035.

OFFICE SYSTEMS SERVICES, LM G23

Chief.—Elizabeth M. Zaic, 707–5590.

PROTECTIVE SERVICES, LM G03

Protective Services Officer.—[Vacant], 707–6367.

SAFETY SERVICES, LM B28

Safety Services Officer.—Carter L. Silcox (acting), 707–6204.

OFFICE OF THE GENERAL COUNSEL, LM 601

General Counsel.—[Vacant], 707–6316.

OFFICE OF THE INSPECTOR GENERAL, LM 630

Inspector General.—John W. Rensbarger, 707–6314.

PERSONNEL SECURITY OFFICE, LM B15

Personnel Security Officer.—Cynthia Wilkins, 707–5618.

OFFICE OF THE LIBRARIAN EMERITUS, LM 225K

The Librarian of Congress Emeritus.—Daniel J. Boorstin, 707–1500.

CONGRESSIONAL RESEARCH SERVICE

OFFICE OF THE DIRECTOR OF THE CONGRESSIONAL RESEARCH SERVICE, LM205

Director.—Daniel P. Mulhollan, 707–5775.

OFFICE OF THE ASSOCIATE DIRECTOR FOR FINANCE AND ADMINISTRATION, LM208

Associate Director.—Susan C. Finsen, 707–8851.

OFFICE OF THE ASSOCIATE DIRECTOR FOR RESEARCH, LM 208

Associate Director.—Kent M. Ronhovde, 707–6464.

OFFICE OF THE ASSOCIATE DIRECTOR FOR POLICY COMPLIANCE, LM 205

Associate Director.—Hugh L. Elsbree, Jr., 707–8924.

AMERICAN LAW DIVISION, LM 227

Chief.—Richard C. Ehlke, 707–6006.

CONGRESSIONAL REFERENCE DIVISION, LM 215

Chief.—[Vacant], 707–8900.

ECONOMICS DIVISION, LM 325

Chief.—Donald W. Kiefer, 707–7800.

EDUCATION AND PUBLIC WELFARE DIVISION, LM 320

Chief.—Royal Shipp, 707–6228.

ENVIRONMENT AND NATURAL RESOURCES POLICY DIVISION, LM 423

Chief.—John L. Moore, 707–7232.

FOREIGN AFFAIRS AND NATIONAL DEFENSE DIVISION, LM 315

Chief.—Charlotte P. Preece, 707–7654.

GOVERNMENT DIVISION, LM 303

Chief.—Michael L. Koempel, 707–0165.

LIBRARY SERVICES DIVISION, LM 221

Chief.—Stephanie V. Williams, 707–5804.

SCIENCE POLICY RESEARCH DIVISION, LM 413

Chief.—Eric A. Fischer, 707–7071.

COPYRIGHT OFFICE

OFFICE OF THE REGISTER OF COPYRIGHTS AND ASSOCIATE LIBRARIAN FOR COPYRIGHT SERVICES, LM 403

Register of Copyrights and Associate Librarian for Copyright Services.—Marybeth Peters, 707–8350.

OFFICE OF THE ASSOCIATE REGISTER FOR POLICY AND INTERNATIONAL AFFAIRS, LM 403

Associate Register for Policy and International Affairs.—Shira Perlmutter, 707–8350.

OFFICE OF THE ASSOCIATE REGISTER FOR NATIONAL COPYRIGHT PROGRAMS, LM 403

Associate Register for National Copyright Programs.—Mary Berghaus Levering, 707–8350.

COPYRIGHT ACQUISITIONS DIVISION, LM 438C

Chief.—Laila Mulgaokar, 707–7125.

OFFICE OF THE COPYRIGHT GENERAL COUNSEL, LM 407

General Counsel.—[Vacant], 707–8380.

OFFICE OF THE ASSOCIATE REGISTER OF COPYRIGHTS FOR OPERATIONS, LM 403

Associate Register of Copyrights for Operations.—Michael Pew, 707–8370.

CATALOGUING DIVISION, LM 513

Chief.—William Collins, 707–8040.

EXAMINING DIVISION, LM 445

Chief.—Nanette Petruzzelli, 707–8200.

INFORMATION AND REFERENCE DIVISION, LM 453

Chief.—Joan A. Doherty, 707–6800.

LICENSING DIVISION, LM 454

Chief.—Walter D. Sampson, 707–8130.

RECEIVING AND PROCESSING DIVISION, LM 435

Chief.—Susie J. Barfield, 707–7700.

LAW LIBRARY

OFFICE OF THE LAW LIBRARIAN, LM 240

Law Librarian.—Rubens Medina, 707–5065.

DIRECTORATE OF LAW LIBRARY SERVICES, LM 240

Director.—Margaret E. Whitlock, 707–5376.

COLLECTION SERVICES OFFICE, LM 233

Chief.—Rose Marie Clemandot, 707–5067.

PUBLIC SERVICES, LM 201

Chief.—Robert N. Gee, 707–5080.

DIRECTORATE OF LEGAL RESEARCH, LM 240

Director.—Daniel H. Zafren, 707–4351.

EASTERN LAW DIVISION, LM 235

Chief.—Tao-tai Hsia, 707–5085.

WESTERN LAW DIVISION, LM 235

Chief.—Robert L. Nay, 707–5077.

LIBRARY SERVICES

OFFICE OF THE ASSOCIATE LIBRARIAN FOR LIBRARY SERVICES, LM 642

Associate Librarian.—Winston Tabb, 707–6240.

OFFICE OF THE DIRECTOR FOR ACQUISITIONS AND SUPPORT SERVICES, LM 642

Director.—[Vacant], 707–5137.

ACQUISITIONS BIBLIOGRAPHIC SUPPORT PROJECT, LM 534

Chief.—[Vacant], 707–4508.

AUTOMATION PLANNING AND LIAISON OFFICE, LM 532

Chief.—Susan M. Hayduchok, 707–0125.

EXCHANGE AND GIFT DIVISION, LM 632

Chief.—Donald P. Panzera, 707–5243.

NETWORK DEVELOPMENT AND MARC STANDARDS OFFICE, LM 639

Chief.—Sally H. McCallum, 707–6237.

ORDER DIVISION, LM G35

Chief.—Michael W. Albin, 707–5361.

OVERSEAS OPERATIONS DIVISION, LM 637

Chief.—Judy C. McDermott, 707–5273.

SERIAL RECORD DIVISION, LM 515

Chief.—Kimberly W. Dobbs, 707–5302.

TECHNICAL PROCESSING AND AUTOMATION INSTRUCTION OFFICE, LM 530

Chief.—Judith P. Cannan, 707–2031.

OFFICE OF THE DIRECTOR FOR AREA STUDIES COLLECTIONS, LM 633

Director.—Carolyn T. Brown (acting), 707–1902.

AFRICAN AND MIDDLE EASTERN DIVISION, LA 130A

Chief.—Beverly Ann Gray, 707–7937.

ASIAN DIVISION, LA 130

Chief.—Mya Helen Poe, 707–5919.

EUROPEAN DIVISION, LJ 100

Chief.—John Van Oudenaren, 707–4543.

EUROPEAN READING ROOM SECTION, LJ 100

Head, European Reference.—[Vacant], 707–8498.

FEDERAL RESEARCH DIVISION, LA 5284

Chief.—Louis R. Mortimer, 707–3900.

HISPANIC DIVISION, LJ 205

Chief.—Georgette M. Dorn, 707–5400.

OFFICE OF SCHOLARLY PROGRAMS, LM 225M

Director.—Prosser Gifford, 707–1517.

POETRY AND LITERATURE CENTER, LJ A10

Poet Laureate Consultant in Poetry.—[Vacant], 707–5394.

OFFICE OF THE DIRECTOR FOR CATALOGUING, LM 642

Director.—Beacher J.E. Wiggins (acting), 707–5333.

ARTS AND SCIENCES CATALOGUING DIVISION, LM 501

Chief.—Beacher J.E. Wiggins, 707–5342.

CATALOGUING IN PUBLICATION DIVISION, LM 542

Chief.—John P. Celli, 707–9797.

CATALOGUING POLICY AND SUPPORT OFFICE, LA 311

Chief.—Barbara B. Tillett, 707–4380.

DECIMAL CLASSIFICATION DIVISION, LM 556

Chief.—David A. Smith, 707–2264.

HISTORY AND LITERATURE CATALOGUING DIVISION, LM 541

Chief.—Jeffrey Heynen, 707–5194.

REGIONAL AND COOPERATIVE CATALOGUING DIVISION, LM 535

Chief.—John D. Byrum, Jr., 707–5196.

SOCIAL SCIENCES CATALOGUING DIVISION, LM 527

Chief.—Regene C. Ross, 707–5281.

SPECIAL MATERIALS CATALOGUING DIVISION, LM 547

Chief.—Susan H. Vita, 707–7211.

OFFICE OF THE DIRECTOR FOR NATIONAL SERVICES, LM 642

Director.—Winston Tabb (acting), 707–6240.

CATALOGUING DISTRIBUTION SERVICE, LA 230

Chief.—[Vacant], 707–6120.

CENTER FOR THE BOOK, LM 650

Director.—John Y Cole, Jr., 707–5221.

FEDERAL LIBRARY AND INFORMATION CENTER COMMITTEE, MSA

Executive Director.—Susan M. Tarr, 707–4801.

INTERPRETIVE PROGRAMS OFFICE, LA G25

Interpretive Programs Officer.—Irene U. Chambers, 707–5223.

OFFICE OF THE DIRECTOR FOR NATIONAL LIBRARY SERVICE FOR THE BLIND AND PHYSICALLY HANDICAPPED, TSA

Director.—Frank Kurt Cylke, 707–5104.

PUBLISHING OFFICE, LM 602

Director.—W. Ralph Eubanks, 707–5093.
Retail Marketing Officer.—Anna S. Lee, 707–7715.

VISITOR SERVICES OFFICE, LJ G05

Visitor Services Officer.—Teresa V. Sierra, 707–5277.

OFFICE OF DIRECTOR FOR PRESERVATION, LM G21

Director.—Diane Nester Kresh, 707–5213.

BINDING AND COLLECTIONS CARE DIVISION, LM G20

Chief.—Debra McKern, 707–5625.

CONSERVATION DIVISION, LM G38

Conservation Officer.—[Vacant], 707–5634.

PHOTODUPLICATION SERVICE, LA 123

Chief.—R. Kevin Flood (acting), 707–5650.

PRESERVATION REFORMATTING DIVISION, LM G05

Chief.—Irene Schubert (acting), 707–5918.

PRESERVATION RESEARCH AND TESTING DIVISION, LM G38

Chief.—Chandru J. Shahani, 707–5607.

OFFICE OF THE DIRECTOR FOR PUBLIC SERVICE COLLECTIONS, LM 642

Director.—Diane Nester Kresh (acting), 707–5330.

AMERICAN FOLKLIFE CENTER, LJ G08

Director.—Alan Jabbour, 707–6590.

CHILDREN'S LITERATURE CENTER, LJ 100

Chief.—Sybille A. Jagusch, 707–5535.

COLLECTIONS MANAGEMENT DIVISION, LJ G56

Chief.—Steven J. Herman, 707–7400.

GEOGRAPHY AND MAP DIVISION, LM B02

Chief.—Ralph E. Ehrenberg, 707–8530.

HUMANITIES AND SOCIAL SCIENCES DIVISION, LJ 109

Chief.—Stephen E. James, 707–5530.

LOAN DIVISION, LJ G09

Chief.—L. Christopher Wright, 707–5345.

MANUSCRIPT DIVISION, LM 102

Chief.—James H. Hutson, 707–5383.

MOTION PICTURE, BROADCASTING AND RECORDED SOUND DIVISION, LM 338

Chief.—David J. Francis, 707–5840.

MUSIC DIVISION, LM 113

Chief.—Jon W. Newsom (acting), 707–5503.

NATIONAL REFERENCE SERVICE

Chief.—Barbara R. Morland, 707–5522.

PRINTS AND PHOTOGRAPHS DIVISION, LM 339

Chief.—Nancy A. Davenport (acting), 707–5836.

REFERENCE SECTION, LM 339

Head.—Mary M. Ison, 707–8867.

RARE BOOK AND SPECIAL COLLECTIONS DIVISION, LJ Dk B

Chief.—Nancy A. Davenport (acting), 707–5434.

SCIENCE AND TECHNOLOGY DIVISION, LA 5204

Chief.—William J. Sittig, 707–5664.

SERIAL AND GOVERNMENT PUBLICATIONS DIVISION, LM 133

Chief.—Karen Renninger, 707–5647.

UNITED STATES BOTANIC GARDEN

245 First Street SW 20024

Public Information Recording 225–7099, fax 225–1561

Director.—Alan M. Hantman (acting), Architect of the Capitol, 8–1793.
Executive Director.—Jeffrey P. Cooper-Smith, 5–6670.
Supervisory Secretary.—Elizabeth A. Spar, 5–5002.
Botanist.—Sarah McNaull, 6–8333.
Conservatory Manager.—Rob Pennington, 5–6646 or 5–6647.
Maintenance Foreman.—Kenneth L. Murphy, 563–3228.
Production Facility Manager.—Carla Pastore, 563–1222.

THE CABINET

Vice President of the United States	AL GORE.
Secretary of State	MADELEINE ALBRIGHT.
Secretary of the Treasury	ROBERT E. RUBIN.
Secretary of Defense	WILLIAM S. COHEN.
Attorney General	JANET RENO.
Secretary of the Interior	BRUCE BABBITT.
Secretary of Agriculture	DANIEL R. GLICKMAN.
Secretary of Commerce	WILLIAM M. DALEY.
Secretary of Labor	ALEXIS M. HERMAN.
Secretary of Health and Human Services	DONNA E. SHALALA.
Secretary of Housing and Urban Development	ANDREW CUOMO.
Secretary of Transportation	RODNEY SLATER.
Secretary of Energy	FEDERICO PEÑA.
Secretary of Education	RICHARD W. RILEY.
Secretary of Veterans' Affairs	JESSE BROWN.
Director, Office of Management and Budget	FRANKLIN RAINES.
Chair, Council of Economic Advisers	JANET YELLEN.
U.S. Ambassador to the United Nations	WILLIAM RICHARDSON.
U.S. Trade Representative	CHARLENE BARSHEFSKY.
Administrator, Environmental Protection Agency	CAROL M. BROWNER.
Director, Office of National Drug Control Policy	BARRY R. MCCAFFREY.
Administrator, Small Business Administration	AIDA ALVAREZ.
Chief of Staff	ERSKINE BOWLES.
Council to the President	THOMAS F. (MACK) MCLARTY.
Director, Central Intelligence Agency	GEORGE J. TENET (designate).
Director, Federal Emergency Management Agency	JAMES LEE WITT.

EXECUTIVE

THE PRESIDENT

WILLIAM JEFFERSON CLINTON, Democrat, of Arkansas; born in Hope, AR, August 19, 1946; attended public schools in Hope and Hot Springs, AR; B.S., Georgetown University, 1968; Rhodes Scholar, Oxford University, England, 1968–70; J.D., Yale Law School, 1973; professor, University of Arkansas, 1973–76; attorney general, State of Arkansas, 1977–79; counsel, Wright, Lindsey, and Jennings, Little Rock, 1981–83; elected Governor of Arkansas, 1979–81 and 1983–92; chair: National Governor's Association; the Education Commission of the States; the Lower Mississippi Delta Development Commission; the Southern Growth Policies Board; Democratic Governor's Association; Democratic Leadership Council; married to Hillary Rodham Clinton; one daughter, Chelsea; elected the 42nd President of the United States, November 3, 1992; inaugurated January 20, 1993; reelected November 1996.

EXECUTIVE OFFICE OF THE PRESIDENT

THE WHITE HOUSE OFFICE

1600 Pennsylvania Avenue 20500

Old Executive Office Building (OEOB), 17th Street and Pennsylvania Avenue 20500

phone 456–1414, http://www.whitehouse.gov

The President of the United States.—William J. Clinton.
Deputy Assistant to the President and Director of Oval Office Operations.—Nancy Hernreich.
Special Assistant to the President and Records Manager.—Janis F. Kearney.
Special Assistant for Personal Correspondence.—Maureen F. Lewis.
Special Assistant to the President.—Carolyn Huber.
Counselor to the President and Special Envoy to the Americas.—Thomas F. (Mack) McLarty.

CABINET AFFAIRS

phone 456–2572

Assistant to the President and Cabinet Secretary.—Kathryn O. Higgins.
Deputy Assistant to the President and Deputy Secretary to the Cabinet.—Stephen B. Silverman.
Special Assistant to the President for Cabinet Affairs.—Anne E. McGuire.
Special Assistant to the Cabinet Secretary and Director of Surrogate Scheduling.—David J. Beaubaire.
Special Assistant to the Cabinet Secretary.—Rhonda H. Jackson.

CHIEF OF STAFF

phone 456–6797

Chief of Staff to the President.—Erskine B. Bowles.
Assistants to the President and Deputy Chiefs of Staff: Sylvia M. Mathews, John D. Podesta.
Senior Advisors to the Chief of Staff: John Angell, Beverly L. Barnes, Thomas J. Vellenga.
Special Assistant to the Chief of Staff.—Jason S. Goldberg.
Deputy Chief of Staff for Policy and Planning.—Rahm I. Emanuel.
Counselor to the President.—Douglas B. Sonik.

STRATEGIC PLANNING AND COMMUNICATIONS

phone 456–2640, speechwriting phone 456–2777

Assistant to the President and Coordinator of Strategic Planning/Communications.—Donald A. Baer.

Assistant to the President and Deputy Director of Communications.—Ann F. Lewis.

Assistant to the President and White House Press Secretary.—Michael McCurry, 456–2673.

Assistant to the Press Secretary.—Julie E. Mason, 456–2673.

Special Assistant to the President and Deputy Press Secretary.—Barry J. Toiv.

Deputy Assistant to the President and Deputy Press Secretary for Operations.—Mary E. Glynn, 456–2580.

Deputy Press Secretary.—Joseph P. Lockhart.

Assistant Press Secretaries: Kathleen M. McKiernan, April K. Mellody, 456–2580.

Deputy Assistant to the President and Director of Speechwriting.—Michael Waldman, Room 196, 456–2777.

Special Assistant to the President and Director of Research.—Ann Walker, Room 197, 456–7845.

CORRESPONDENCE

phone 456–7610

Special Assistant to the President and Director of Correspondence and Presidential Messages.—Jim Dorskind, OEOB, Room 94, 456–5460.

Deputy Director.—Daniel W. Buckhardt, OEOB, Room 90, 456–7610.

Special Assistant for Personal Correspondence.—Mildred C. Alston, 456–2957.

Director for—

Presidential Messages.—Carmen Fowler, OEOB, Room 91, 456–5505.

Presidential Letters and Messages.— Reuben L. Musgrave, Jr., OEOB, Room 94, 456–5518.

Presidential Inquiries.—Jamie Shell Williams, OEOB, Room 39, 456–2724.

Agency Liaison.—Dorethea S. Smith, OEOB, Room 6, 456–5480.

First Lady's Correspondence.—Alice Pushkar, OEOB, Room 18, 456–2941.

GENERAL COUNSEL

phone 456–2632

Counsel to the President.—Charles F. Ruff.

Executive Assistant to the Counsel to the President.—Ora Theard.

Assistant to the President and Deputy Counsel to the President.—Bruce Lindsey, 456–2668.

Deputy Assistant to the President and Deputy Counsel to the President.—Cheryl D. Mills, 456–6611.

Executive Assistant to the Deputy Counsel.—Odetta S. Walker, 456–6611.

Special Counsel to the President.—Lanny J. Davis, 456–7900.

Assistant Counsel to the President.—Robert W. Schroeder, OEOB, Room 128, 456–7903.

Special Assosciate Counsel to the President.—John Yarowsky, OEOB, Room 130, 456–7903.

Associate Counsels to the President: Dawn M. Chirwa, OEOB, Room 130, 456–7903; William P. Marshall, OEOB, Room 128, 456–6219; Miriam R. Nemetz, OEOB, Room 482, 456–5092; Michelle M. Peterson, OEOB, Room 128, 456–7900; Karen A. Popp, OEOB, Room 128, 456–7594; Kathleen M. Whalen, OEOB, Room 136, 456–6229; Wendy S. White, OEOB, Room 136, 456–7361.

DOMESTIC POLICY COUNCIL

phone 456–2216

Assistant to the President for Domestic Policy.—Bruce N. Reed.

Executive Assistant.—Cathy R. Mays, 456–6515.

Deputy Assistants to the President for Domestic Policy: Christopher C. Jennings, OEOB, 456–5560; Elena Kagan, OEOB, 456–5584.

Senior Advisor to the President.—Ira Magaziner, OEOB, Room 216, 456–6406.

FIRST LADY'S OFFICE

phone 456–6266

The First Lady.—Hillary Rodham Clinton.
Assistant to the President and Chief of Staff to the First Lady.—Margaret A. Williams.
Assistant to the Chief of Staff to the First Lady.—Peggy A. Lewis, OEOB, Room 100.
Deputy Assistant to the President and—
Deputy Chief of Staff to the First Lady.—Melanne Verveer, OEOB, Room 100.
Press Secretary to the First Lady.—G. N. Lattimore, OEOB, Room 104, 456–2960.
Special Assistant to the President and Social Secretary.—Judith A. Stock, 456–7136.

INTERGOVERNMENTAL AFFAIRS

phone 456–2896

Assistant to the President and Director for Intergovernmental Affairs.—Marcia L. Hale.
Deputy Assistants to the President and Deputy Directors of Intergovernmental Affairs: John B. Emerson, OEOB, Room 148; John P. Hart, OEOB, Room 106; Kevin O'Keefe, OEOB, Room 106.

LEGISLATIVE AFFAIRS

phone 456–2230

Senior Advisor to the President and Director for Legislative Affairs.—John Hilley.
Deputy Assistant to the President and Deputy Director for Legislative Affairs.—Susan Brophy.
Special Assistant to the Director.—Elisa Millsap.
Special Assistant to the Deputy Director.—Tripp Donnelly.
Special Assistant to the President for Legislative Affairs.—Donald F. Goldberg, 456–2230.
Deputy Assistant to the President for Legislative Affairs.—Alphonso Maldon, 456–6620.
Deputy Assistant to the President for Legislative Affairs, (Senate).—[Vacant], 456–6493.
Special Assistants (Senate): Paul R. Carey, Barbara Chow, Tracey Thornton.
Deputy Assistant to the President for Legislative Affairs, (House).—Janet Murguia, 456–6620.
Special Assistants (House): Ananias Blocker III, Peter G. Jacoby, Daniel Tate, 456–6620.
Special Assistant to the Director and Director of Congressional Correspondence and Messages.—Christopher F. Walker, 456–7500.

MANAGEMENT AND ADMINISTRATION

phone 456–2861

Assistant to the President for Management and Administration.—Jodie Torkelson.
Director of the White House Conference Center.—Patti C. Cogdell, 456–7507
White House Personnel Liaison.—Kelli R. McClure.
Executive Assistant.—Theresa Wildman.

NATIONAL ECONOMIC COUNCIL

Old Executive Office Building 20500, phone 456–6630

Assistant to the President for Economic Policy and Director of the National Economic Council.—Gene B. Sperling.
Deputy Assistant to the President for Economic Policy and Chief of Staff.—Kathleen M. Wallman, 456–5803.
Assistant to the President for International Economic Affairs.—Daniel K. Tarallo.
Special Assistants to the President for Economic Policy: Elwood (Elgie) Holstein, OEOB, Room 221, 456–2800; Dorothy Robyn, OEOB, Room 226, 456–2801; Jake Siewart, OEOB, Room 234½, 456–2800.
Directors to the National Economic Council: Lael Brainard, OEOB, Room 330, 395–5104; Thomas Kalil, OEOB, Room 230, 456–2802; Jonathan A. Kaplan, OEOB, Room 233, 456–6630; Mark J. Mazur, OEOB, Room 318, 395–5147.
Director to the National Economic Council/National Security Council for International Economic Policy.—Malcolm R. Lee, OEOB, Room 389, 456–9291.

OFFICE OF THE VICE PRESIDENT

phone 456–2326

The Vice President.—Al Gore.

Executive Assistant to the Vice President.—Heather Marabeti, 456–2326.

Chief of Staff and Counselor to the Vice President.—Ronald Klain, OEOB, Room 276, 456–6605.

Director of Communications.—Lorraine Voles, OEOB, Room 272, 456–7035.

National Security Advisor.—Leon S. Fuerth, OEOB, Room 298, 395–4213.

Counsel.—Charles Burson, OEOB, Room 266, 456–7020.

Special Assistant to the Vice President and Chief of Staff to Mrs. Gore.—Susan Liss, OEOB, Room 200, 456–6640.

Policy Advisors:

Donald Gips, OEOB, Room 288, 456–6222.

Elaine C. Kamarck, OEOB, Room 273, 456–2816.

Director of Scheduling.—Kim Tilley, OEOB, Room 287, 395–4245.

Director of Advance.—Dennis W. Alpert, OEOB, Room 279, 456–7935.

Director of Correspondence.—Bill Mason, Room 202, 224–2424.

POLITICAL AFFAIRS

phone 456–6257

Assistant to the President and Director of Political Affairs.—Craig T. Smith.

Deputy Assistants to the President and Deputy Directors for Political Affairs: Minyon Moore, 456–6625; Karen Skelton, 456–6625.

Special Assistant to the Director.—Gordon Li.

Special Assistant to the President for Political Affairs.—Linda L. Moore.

Chief of Staff for Political Affairs.—Cynthia Jasso Rotunno.

PRESIDENTIAL PERSONNEL

phone 456–6676

Assistant to the President and Director of Presidential Personnel.—Bob J. Nash.

Deputy Assistant to the President and Deputy Director.—Patsy L. Thomasson.

Special Assistants to the President and Associate Directors: Peggy A. Clark, OEOB, Room 141, 456–7831; Elizabeth A. Montoya, Room OEOB, 151, 456–6676.

Deputy Associate Directors: Walker Bass, Elizabeth A. Martinez, Andrea Esquer.

OFFICE OF PUBLIC LIAISON

phone 456–2930

Special Assistant to the President and Director for Public Liaison.—

Executive Assistant to the Director.—Ruby G. Moy.

Deputy Assistant to the President and Deputy Director for Public Liaison.—Doris Matsui.

Special Assistant to the President and Staff Director.—Lee Satterfield.

Special Assistant to the President and Senior Advisor for Public Liaison.—Richard Socarides.

Counsel to the President.—Maria Echareste.

Special Assistants to the President for Public Liaison: Cheryl Carter, Robert B. Johnson, Suzanna Valdez.

Associate Directors: Marilyn DiGiacobbe, Jay Footlik, Flo McAfee, Dan Wexler, William H. White, Jr., Barbara Woolley.

Special Assistants: Ann Eder, Craig Gardenswartz, Christa Robinson, Brian G. Scott, Marjorie Tarmey.

SCHEDULING AND ADVANCE

phone 456–7560

Deputy Assistant to the President and Director of Advance.—Dan K. Rosenthal.

Deputy Assistants to the President and Directors of Scheduling: Anne W. Hawley, Stephanie S. Street.

Deputy Assistant to the President and Deputy Director of Press Advance.—Catherine A. Cornelius, OEOB, Room 185.5.

Special Assistant to the President and Director of Scheduling for the First Lady.—Patricia S. Doyle, OEOB, Room 185.5.

Special Assistant to the President and Director of Advance for the First Lady.—Kelly Craighead, OEOB, Room 188.

Special Assistants to the President and Deputy Directors of Scheduling for the President: Nicole L. Elkon, OEOB, Room 184, 456–6481; Lucie F. Naphin, OEOB, Room 184, 456–5328; Patrick M. Steel, OEOB, Room 184, 456–2920.

Special Assistant to the President and Trip Director.—Andrew Friendly, OEOB, Room 185.5, 456–7560.

STAFF SECRETARY

phone 456–2702

Assistant to the President and Staff Secretary.—Todd Stern.

Deputy Assistant to the President and Deputy Staff Secretary.—Phillip Caplan.

Special Assistant to the President and Deputy Staff Secretary.—Helen P. Howell.

Special Assistant to the Staff Secretary and Presidential Aide.—Stephen D. Goodin, 456–1831.

Administrative Assistant to the Staff Secretary.—Frances R. (Fran) Wessel.

Administrative Assistants: Barbara Barclay, Carolyn E. Cleveland.

VISITOR'S OFFICE

phone 456–2322

Director.—Melinda N. Bates.

Deputy Director and Director of Special Events.—Robyn G. Dickey, 456–7136.

Associate Director.—Marc Hoberman.

Assistant Director.—Holly H. Holt.

WHITE HOUSE MILITARY OFFICE

Deputy Assistant to the President and Director.—Alan P. Sullivan, 456–2150.

Chief of Staff.—Col. James A. Hawkins, U.S. Air Force.

Air Force Aide to the President.—Lt. Col. Robert Patterson, 757–1253.

Army Aide to the President.—Maj. Dana J. H. Pittard, 757–1253.

Coast Guard Aide to the President.—[Vacant], 395–1747.

Marine Corps Aide to the President.—Maj. Charles H. Raderstorf, 757–1253.

Naval Aide to the President.—Cdr. John M. Richardson, 757–1253.

Commander, White House Communications Agency.—[Vacant], 757–5530.

Commanding Officer, Camp David.—Cdr. Robert Ramsay, 456–2810.

Commanding Officer, HMX–1.—Col. Frederick Geier, 757–1415.

Presidential Pilot.—LtCol. Mark. S. Donnelly, (301) 981–2817.

Chief, White House Transportation Agency.—Leroy Borden, White House Garage, 456–2660.

White House Medical Unit.—Capt. Connie Mariano, U.S. Navy, 757–2481.

COUNCIL OF ECONOMIC ADVISERS

Chair.—Janet L. Yellen, OEOB, Room 314, 395–5042.

Chief of Staff.—Michele M. Jolin, OEOB, Room 320, 395–5084.

Member.—Alicia H. Munnell, OEOB, Room 314, 395–5036.

Member.—Jeffrey A. Frankel, OEOB, Room 315, 395–5046.

COUNCIL ON ENVIRONMENTAL QUALITY

phone 456–6224, http://www.whitehouse.gov/CEQ

Chair.—Kathleen McGinty, OEOB, Room 360.

Chief of Staff.—Shelley Fidler.

Deputy Chief of Staff.—Wesley Warren.

General Counsel.—Dinah Bear.

Associate General Counsel.—Elisabeth Blaug.

Associate Director for—

Toxics and Environmental Protection.—Bradley M. Campbell.

NEPA.—Ray Clark.

Congressional Relations.—Michelle Denton.

Natural Resources.—Thomas C. Jensen.

Communications.—Brian J. Johnson.

Special Assistant to the Chair.—Robert Kapla.

Associate Director for—

Transportation and Land Management.—Linda Lance.
Sustainable Development.—Keith E. Laughlin.
Associate Director.—Nilda Mesa.
Administrative Officer.—Carolyn Mosley.
Associate Director for Global Environment.—David B. Sandalow.
Special Assistant for Outreach and Planning.—Michael Terrell.
Associate Director of Public Liaison.—Beth Viola.

CENTRAL INTELLIGENCE AGENCY

Washington DC 20505, phone (703) 482–1100

Director.—George J. Tenet (designate).
Deputy Director, Administration.—Richard D. Calder.
Director of Congressional Affairs.—John Moseman, (703) 482–6121.
Congressional Inquiries.—(703) 482–6136.

FOREIGN INTELLIGENCE ADVISORY BOARD

phone 456–2352

Chairman.—Warren B. Rudman (acting).
Vice Chairman.—Warren B. Rudman.

MEMBERS

Gen. Lew Allen, Jr., USAF
Zoe Baird
Ann Z. Caracristi
Sidney D. Drell
Thomas F. Eagleton
Anthony S. Harrington
Robert J. Hermann
Harold W. Pote
Lois D. Rice
Maurice Sonnenberg

Executive Director.—Randy W. Deitering (acting), OEOB, Room 340, 395–5075.
Assistant Director.—Linda England, OEOB, Room 340, 456–2915.

NATIONAL SECURITY COUNCIL

Old Executive Office Building 20503, phone 456–9491

MEMBERS

The President.—William J. Clinton.
The Vice President.—Al Gore.
The Secretary of State.—Madeleine K. Albright.
The Secretary of Defense.—William Cohen.

STATUTORY ADVISERS

Director of Central Intelligence.—George Tenet (designate).
Chairman, Joint Chiefs of Staff.—Gen. John M. Shalikashvili.
Assistant to the President for National Security Affairs.—Samuel (Sandy) R. Berger (acting).
Deputy Assistant to the President for National Security Affairs.—James B. Steinberg.
Executive Assistants to the Assistant and Deputy Assistant to the President for National Security Affairs.—Peter E. Bass, Diana Helwig.
Special Assistant to the Deputy for National Security.—Kristen K. Cicio.

OFFICE OF ADMINISTRATION

Special Assistant to the President for Management and Administration and Director of the Office of Administration.—Patsy L. Thomasson, OEOB, Room 145, 456–2861.
Special Assistant to the Director.—Kristin L. White, OEOB, Room 145, 456–2015.
Deputy Director.—John W. Cressman, OEOB, Room 480, 395–6963.
Assistant to the Deputy Director for Administrative Operations.—Ada L. Posey, NEOB, Room 5001, 395–7100.
Director, Information Systems and Technology Division.—James L. MacDonald, Jr., NEOB, Room 4208, 395–6403.

OFFICE OF MANAGEMENT AND BUDGET

Old Executive Office Building (OEOB), 20503, phone 395–4840

Director.—Franklin D. Raines, Room 252, 395–4742.
Special Assistant to the Director.—Rebecca Culberson, Room 251, 456–7255.
Deputy Director.—Jack Lew, Room 260, 395–6190.
Deputy Director for Management.—John A. Koskinen, Room 260, 395–6190.
Assistant to the Director for Management Issues.—Edward DeSeve, Room 252, 395–4742.
Associate Director for Administration.—[Vacant], Room 254, 395–3060.
Assistant Director for Budget Review.—Barry B. Anderson, Room 258, 395–4630.
Deputy Assistant Director for—
Budget Analysis and Systems.—Philip R. Dame, NEOB, Room 6001, 395–7503.
Budget Review and Concepts.—Richard P. Emery, Jr., NEOB, Room 6204, 395–4632.
Associate Director for—
Communications.—Larry Haas, Room 253, 395–7254.
Economic Policy.—Joseph J. Minarik, Room 244, 395–5873.
General Government and Finance.—Michael Deich, Room 246, 395–3120.
Health/Personnel.—Nancy-Ann Min, Room 262, 395–5178.
Human Resources.—Kenneth S. Apfel, Room 260, 395–4844.
Legislative Affairs.—Charles Kieffer, Room 243, 395–4790.
National Security and International Affairs.—Gordon Adams, Room 238, 395–4657.
Natural Resources, Energy and Science.—T.J. Glauthier, Room 246, 395–4561.
Deputy Associate Director for—
Housing, Treasury, and Finance.—Alan B. Rhinesmith, NEOB, Room 9201, 395–4516.
Transportation, Commerce and Justice.—Kenneth L. Schwartz, NEOB, Room 9202, 395–4892.
Health.—Barry Clendenin, NEOB, Room 7025, 395–4922.
VA/Personnel.—Bruce Long, NEOB, Room 7007, 395–7388.
Human Resources.—Barry White, NEOB, Room 8201, 395–6150.
International Affairs.—Philip A. DuSault, NEOB, Room 10002, 395–4770.
National Security.—Phebe N. Vickers, NEOB, Room 10001, 395–4572.
Energy and Science.—Kathleen Peroff, NEOB, Room 8002, 395–3404.
Natural Resources.—Ronald M. Cogswell, NEOB, Room 8001, 395–4586.
General Counsel.—Robert G. Damus, Room 262, 395–5044.
Assistant Director for Legislative Reference.—Jim Murr, Room 7202, 395–4864.
Controller.—Edward DeSeve, OEOB, Room 350, 395–3585.
Administrator, Office of—
Federal Procurement Policy.—Steven Kelman, Room 352, 395–5802.
Information and Regulatory Affairs.—Sally Katzen, Room 350, 395–4852.

OFFICE OF NATIONAL DRUG CONTROL POLICY

Executive Office of the President 20502, phone 395–6700

Director.—Barry R. McCaffrey, Room 800.
Deputy Director.—Hoover Adger, M.D., M.P.H., Room 856.
Chief of Staff.—Janet Crist, 750 17th Street, Room 804, 395–6732.
Director of—
Demand Reduction.—Dan Schecter (acting), Room 710, 395–6733.
Supply Reduction.—Bob Brown (acting), Room 713, 395–6604.
Associate Director, Bureau of State and Local Affairs.—John Navarette (acting), Room 731, 395–6632.
Director of—
Administration.—Tilman Dean, Room 701, 395–6732.
Programs, Budget and Evaluation.—John T. Carnevale, Room 518, 395–6725.
Counter-Drug Technology Assessment Center.—Albert E. Brandenstein, Room 310, 395–6758.
Public Affairs.—Don Maple (acting), Room 843, 395–6618.

OFFICE OF SCIENCE AND TECHNOLOGY POLICY

Executive Office Building 20500, phone 456–7116

Assistant to the President for Science and Technology and Director.—John H. Gibbons, OEOB, Room 424, 456–7116, fax 456–6021.

Associate Director for—

Environment.—Rosina Bierbaum (acting), OEOB, Room 443, 456–6077, fax 456–6025.

National Security and International Affairs.—Kerri-Ann Jones, OEOB, Room 494, 456–2894, fax 456–6028.

Science.—Clifford Gabriel, (acting), OEOB, Room 432.5, 456–6127, fax 456–6027.

Technology.—Henry Kelly (acting), OEOB, Room 423, 456–6033, fax 456–6023.

Deputy Director for—

Management and General Counsel.—Jonathan Foster, OEOB, Room 428.5, 456–2735, fax 456–6049.

Policy.—Timothy Newell, OEOB, Room 428, 456–6011, fax 456–6019.

Assistant Director for—

Budget and Administration.—Barbara Ferguson, OEOB, Room 431, 456–6001, fax 456–6022.

International.—Deanna Behring, OEOB, Room 494, 456–6058, fax 456–6028.

Life Sciences.—Rachel Levinson, OEOB, Room 438, 456–6137, fax 456–6027.

National Security.—Bruce MacDonald, OEOB, Room 492, 456–6068, fax 456–6028.

Physical Sciences and Engineering.—Beverly Hartline, OEOB, Room 432, 456–6128, fax 456–6027.

Social and Behavioral Sciences.—Daryl Chubin, OEOB, Room 438, 456–6129, fax 456–6027.

Space and Aeronautics.—Jefferson Hofgard, OEOB, Room 423, 456–6043, fax 456–6023.

Executive Secretary for—

National Science and Technology Council (NSTC).—Angela Phillips Diaz, OEOB, Room 435, 456–6100, fax 456–6026.

President's Committee of Advisors for Science and Technology (PCAST).—Angela Phillips Diaz, OEOB, Room 435, 456–6100, fax 456–6026.

Special Assistant and Scheduler.—Susanne Bachtel, OEOB, Room 424, 456–7116, fax 456–6021.

OFFICE OF U.S. TRADE REPRESENTATIVE

Winder Building, 600 17th Street 20506, phone 395–5797

Ambassador, U.S. Trade Representative.—Charlene Barshefsky, Room 209A, 395–3204.

Chief of Staff.—Nancy Lea Mond.

Ambassador, Deputy U.S. Trade Representative.—Jeffrey M. Lang.

Ambassador, Senior Counsel and Negotiator.—Ira Shapiro.

Senior Counsel and Negotiator.—Peter Scher.

Ambassador and Chief Textile Negotiator.—Rita Hayes.

Deputy Chief Textile Negotiator.—Caroyl L. Miller, Room 309, 395–3026.

Counselor to the U.S. Trade Representative.—Ellen Frost, Room 216, 395–5636.

General Counsel.—Sue Esserman.

Deputy General Counsel.—Irving Williamson.

Director of Scheduling.—Colleen McCarthy.

Assistant U.S. Trade Representative for—

Administration.—John Hopkins, Room 125, 395–5797.

Agriculture.—Jim Murphy.

Asia and the Pacific.—Donald Phillips.

Congressional Affairs.—Liz Arky.

Economic Affairs.—David A. Walters, Room 516, 395–3583.

Policy Coordination.—Frederick Montgomery, Room 501A, 395–3475.

Environment and Natural Resources.—Jennifer Haverkemp, Room 415, 395–7320.

Europe and the Mediterranean.—Chris Marcich, Room 323, 395–4620.

WTO and Multilateral Affairs.—Dorothy Dwoskin, Room 509, 395–6843.

Trade and Development.—Jon Rosenbaum, Room 515, 395–6971.

Industry.—Donald Phillips, Room 420, 395–5656.

Intergovernmental Affairs and Public Liaison.—Phyllis Jones.

China.—Robert B. Cassidy.

Public Affairs.—Jay Ziegler.

Services, Investment and Intellectual Property.—Wendy Cutler.

Monitoring and Enforcement.—A. Jane Bradley.

U.S.-Pacific Trade and Investment Commission.—Nancy J. Adams.

Associate Trade Representative for Western Hemisphere.—Peter F. Allgeier, Room 523, 395–6135.

Deputy Chief of Geneva Mission.—Andrew Stoler.

PRESIDENT'S COMMISSION ON WHITE HOUSE FELLOWSHIPS

712 Jackson Place NW, 20503 395–4522

Chairman.—Marjorie Benton.
Director.—Jacqueline Blumenthal.
Associate Director.—Gail Britton.
Education Director.—Joseph Walsh.
Administrative Officer.—Victoria Smith.
Executive Assistant.—Deborah Moody.

PRESIDENT'S COMMITTEE ON MENTAL RETARDATION

200 Independence Avenue SW, HHH Building, Room 352–G, 619–0634

Chairperson.—Valerie J. Bradley, President, Human Services Research Institute, 2335 Massachusetts Avenue, Cambridge MA 02140, (617) 876–0426, fax (617) 492–7401.

COMMITTEE MEMBERS

Lorenzo H. Aguilar-Melancon, El Paso TX, (915) 577–0990, fax (915) 577–9099.
Jane L. Browning, Severna Park MD.
Robert D. Dinerstein, J.D., Associate Dean for Academic Affairs, Washington College of Law at American University, Washington DC, (202) 274–4141, fax (202) 274–4015.
Steven M. Eidelman, Executive Director, Joseph P. Kennedy Jr., Foundation, Washington DC, (202) 393–1250, fax (202) 824–0351.
Ann M. Forts, Center Harbor NH.
Gisselle Acevedo Franco, J.D., Director, Communications and Public Relations Medpartners, Long Beach CA, (310) 497–4989, fax (310) 497–4985.
Joyce A. Keller, Waterford MI, (810) 352–5272, fax (810) 352–5279.
John F. Kennedy, J.D., President, Reaching Up, Inc., New York NY, (212) 754–6750, (212) 754–0203.
K. Charlie Lakin, Ph.D., Director of the Rehabilitation Research and Training Center on Community Living Integration, University of Minnesota, Minneapolis MN, (612) 624–5005, fax (612) 625–6619.
Ruth Luckasson, J.D., Regents Professor and Professor of Special Education, College of Education, University of New Mexico, Albuquerque NM, (505) 277–7231, (505) 277–8360.
T.J. Monroe, Cincinnati OH.
Michael L. Remus, Director of Special Education, Kansas State Board of Education, Topeka KS, (913) 291–3097, fax (913) 296–1413.
Tom E.C. Smith, Ed.D., Associate Professor, Department of Teacher Education, University of Arkansas at Little Rock, Little Rock AR, (501) 569–3016, fax (501) 569–8694.
Deborah M. Spitalnik, Ph.D., Executive Director, University Affiliated Programs of New Jersey (UAPNJ), Brookwood II, Piscataway NJ, (908) 235–4447, fax (908) 235–5059.
Cathy Ficker Terrill, Vice-President of Quality and Strategic Planning, Ray Graham Association, Elmhurst IL, (630) 530–4554, fax (630) 832–7337.
Jacqueline B. Victorian, MSW, Executive Director, Independent Living, Inc., Baton Rouge LA, (504) 924–7998, (504) 924–7715.
Barbara Yoshioka Wheeler, Ph.D., Associate Professor of Clinical Pediatrics, University Affiliated Program, Mailstop #53, Children's Hospital of Los Angeles, Los Angeles, CA, (213) 669–2300, fax 213–953–0439.
Sheryl White-Scott, M.D., Director, Adult Health Services, Westchester Institute for Human Development, Valhalla, NY, (914) 285–8714, fax (914) 285–1973.
Virginia J. Williams, MA, Norfolk, VA.

EX OFFICIO MEMBERS

The Honorable Donna E. Shalala, Secretary, U.S. Department of Health and Human Services (DHHS), Washington DC, (202) 690–7000.
The Honorable Janet Reno, Attorney General, U.S. Department of Justice (DoJ), Washington DC, (202) 514–2001.
Secretary of Labor, U.S. Department of Labor (DoL), Washington DC, (202) 219–8271.
Secretary of Housing and Urban Development, U.S. Department of Housing and Urban Development (HUD), Washington DC, (202) 708–0417.
Harris Wofford, Chief Executive Officer, Corporation for National and Community Service, Washington DC, (202) 606–5000.
The Honorable Richard W. Riley, Secretary of Education, U.S. Department of Education (DoE), Washington DC, (202) 401–3000.
Gilbert Casellas, Chair, Equal Employment Opportunity Commission (EEOC), Washington DC, (202) 663–4900, fax (202) 663–7022.
Marca Bristo, Chair, National Council on Disability (NCD), Washington DC, (202) 272–2004, fax (202) 272–2022.
Commissioner of Social Security, Social Security Administration (SSA), Baltimore MD, (202) 358–6000, (202) 358–6077 or 6078.
Executive Director.—Gary Blumenthal, (202) 619–0634.
Deputy Executive Director.—John L. Pride, (202) 619–0634.

WHITE HOUSE OFFICE FOR WOMEN'S INITIATIVES AND OUTREACH

phone (202) 456–7300, fax (202) 456–7311

Director.—Betsy Myers.
Deputy Director.—Lisa Ross.

DEPARTMENT OF AGRICULTURE

Jamie L. Whitten Building, Independence Avenue and 14th Street SW 20250
phone (202) 720–3631, hhtp://www.usda.gov

DAN GLICKMAN, of Kansas, born in Wichita, November 24, 1944; graduated Southeast High School, 1962; B.A., University of Michigan, 1966; J.D., George Washington University, 1969; admitted to the bar in Kansas in 1969 and in Michigan in 1970, commenced practice in Washington, DC; attorney and businessman; trial attorney for U.S Securities and Exchange Commission, 1969–70; partner in the law firm of Sargent, Klenda and Glickman, 1973–76; served on Wichita School Board, 1973–76; president of Wichita School Board, 1975–76; member: American Bar Association, National Conference of Christians and Jews, Arthritis Foundation, Big Brothers; married to the former Rhoda Yura, 1966; two children: Jonathan and Amy; represented the 4th Congressional District of Kansas in the U.S. House of Representatives, 1977–95; committees: House Permanent Select Committee on Intelligence, chairman during the 103rd Congress; subcommittees: chairman, General Commodities, Department Operations and Nutrition; Crime and Criminal Justice, Economic and Commercial Law; Administrative Law and Government Relations; Science, Space and Technology, Environment and Aviation; nominated Secretary of Agriculture on December 28, 1994; confirmed on March 30, 1995.

Secretary of Agriculture.—Dan Glickman, Room 200–A, (202) 720–3631.
Chief of Staff.—Greg Frazier.
Deputy Chiefs of Staff: Patrick Steele; Reba Evans.
Counsel.—Janet Potts, Room 214–A.
Special Assistant to the President/Personnel.—Carl Whillock, Room 216–A, 720–2406.
Special Assistant, International.—Paul Drazek, Room 220–A, 720–2046.
Special Assistants:—Anne Kennedy, Room 200–A, 720–3631; Eric Olsen, Room 210–A, 720–3631.
Executive Secretariat.—Lynne Finnerty, Room 116–A, 720–7100.
Deputy Secretary.—Richard Rominger, Room 202B–A, 720–6158.
Executive Assistant.—Charlie Rawls, Room 202B–A, 720–6158.
Chief Financial Officer (acting).—Irwin T. David, Room 143–W, 720–5539.
General Counsel.—James Gilliland, Room 107–W, 720–3351.
Inspector General.—Roger Viadero, Room 117–W, 720–8001.
Chief Economist.— Keith Collins, Room 227–E, 720–4164.
Chief Information Officer.—Ann F. Thompson Reed, Room 416–W, 720–3152.
Director of Communications.—Tom Amontree, Room 402–A, 720–4623.
Under Secretary for Natural Resources and Environment.—James Lyons, Room 217–E, 720–7173.
Chief of Forest Service.—Mike Dombeck, Auditors Building, 205–1661.
Natural Resources Conservation Service.—Paul W. Johnson, Room 5105–S, BG, 720–4525.
Farm and Foreign Agricultural Services.—Dallas Smith, Acting, Room 205–E, 720–3111.
Administrator for Consolidated Farm Services Agency.—Randy Weber (acting), Room 3086–S, BG, 720–3467.
Administrator for Foreign Agricultural Service.—Gus Schumacher, Room 5071–S, BG, 720–3935.
Economic and Community Development.—Jill Long-Thompson, Room 205–W, 720–4581.
Administrator for Rural Utilities Service.—Wally Beyer, Room 4051–S, BG, 720–9540.
Rural Housing and Community Development Service.—Jan Shadburn (acting), 690–1533.
Rural Business and Cooperative Development Service.—Dayton Watkins, Room 5045–S, BG, 690–4730.
Food, Nutrition and Consumer Services.—Mary Ann Keeffe (acting), Room 240–E, 720–7711.
Administrator for Food and Consumer Service.—Bill Ludwig, Room 803, PC, 305–2062.
Food Safety.—Thomas Billy (acting), Room 331–E, 720–7025.
Administrator for Food Safety and Inspection Service.—Thomas Billy, Room 331–E, 720–7025.
Research, Education and Economics.—Floyd Horn (acting), Room 217–W, 720–8885.
Administrator for Agricultural Research Service.—Floyd Horn, Room 302–A, 720–3656.

Cooperative State Research, Education, and Extension Service.—Bob Robinson.
Economic Research Service.—Susan Offutt, Room 1226–NYA, 219–030.
National Agricultural Statistics Service.—Donald Bay (acting), Room 4147–S, BG, 720–2707.
Assistant Secretary for Congressional Relations.—J. David Carlin, Room 213–A, 720–7095.
Director, Office of Congressional Relations.—Vince Ancell, Room 213–A, 720–7095.
Director, Intergovernmental Affairs.—Veronica DelaGarza, Room 219–A, 720–6643.
Marketing and Regulatory Service.—Michael V. Dunn, Room 228–W, 720–4256.
Administrator for Agricultural Marketing Service.—Lon Hatamiya, Rm 3071–S, BG, 720–5115.
Animal and Plant Health Inspection Service.—Terry Medley, Room 313, 720–3861.
Grain Inspection, Packers and Stockyards Administrator.—James R. Baker, Room 1094–S, BG, 720–0219.
Administrator.—Pearlie Reed, Room 240–W, 720–3291.
Operations.—Ira L. Hobbs, Room 1575–S, BG, 720–3937.
Personnel.—Roger L. Bensey, Room 316–W, 720–3585.
Office of Administrative Law Judges.—Victor Palmer, Chief Judge, Room 1055–S, BG, 720–6645.
Board of Contract Appeals.—Judge Edward Houry, Chairman, Room 2912–S, 720–6110.
Office of the Judicial Officer.—Donald A. Campbell, Room 510–A, 720–4764.

GENERAL COUNSEL

Jamie L. Whitten Building, Room 106–W, phone 720–3351

General Counsel.—James Gilliland.
Deputy General Counsel.—Bonnie L. Luken.
Associate General Counsel for:
Rural Development.—Arnold Grundeman, 720–6187.
Natural Resources.—James Perry, 720–9311.
Assistant General Counsel for:
Community Development.—[Vacant].
Electric and Telephone.—Michael W. Kelly, 720–2764.
Natural Resources.—Michael Gippert, 720–7121.
International Affairs: Commodity Programs and Food Assistant Programs.—Thomas V. Conway,729–6883.
Assistant General Counsel, Division of:
Food and Nutrition.—Ronald Hill, 720–6181.
International Affairs and Commodity Programs.—Ralph Linden, 720–9246.
Legislation, Litigation, Research and Operations.—James Michael Kelly, 501–7515.
Legislative Affairs.—David Grahn, 720–5354.
Litigation.—[Vacant].
General Law.—Kenneth E. Cohen, 720–5565.
Regulatory and Marketing.—John Golden, 720–3155.
Marketing.—Kenneth Vail, 720–5293.
Resource Management Specialist.—Deborah L. Vita, 720–4861.

INSPECTOR GENERAL

Inspector General.—Roger C. Viadero, Room 117–W.
Deputy Inspector General.—Joyce Fleischmann, Room 117–W, 720–7431.
Executive Assistant to the Inspector General.—Sharon Friend, Room 113–W, 720–4979.
Assistant Inspector General for Audit.—James R. Ebbitt, Room 403–E, 720–3306.
Policy Development and Resources Management.—Paula F. Hayes, Room 5–E, 720–6979.

ASSISTANT SECRETARY FOR ADMINISTRATION

Jamie L. Whitten Building, Room 240–W, phone 720–3291

Assistant Secretary for Administration.—Pearlie Reed (acting).
Deputy Assistant Secretary for Administration.—Christine Pytel, (acting), Room 240–W, 720–3590.
Special Assistant.—Tia Young, Room 240–W, 720–3291.

BOARD OF CONTRACT APPEALS

South Agriculture Building, Room 2912, phone 720–6110

Chairman and Administrative Judge.—Edward Houry.
Vice Chair and Administrative Judge.—Marilynn M. Eaton, 690–0710.
Administrative Judges: Sean Doherty, 720–7242; Howard A. Pollack, 720–2583; Robert M. M. Seto, 720–2066.
Chief Counsel.—Merrie C. Shager, 720–6229.
Recorder.—Elaine M. Hillard, 720–7023.
Deputy Recorder.—Delores Sanders, 720–9023.

OFFICE OF ADMINISTRATIVE LAW JUDGES

South Agriculture Building, Room 1055–S, phone 720–6645

Chief Administrative Law Judge.—Victor W. Palmer.
Secretary to the Chief Administrative Law Judge.—Roxanne Lane.
Administrative Law Judges: Dorothea A. Baker, Room 1045–S, 720–8305; Edwin S. Bernstein, Room 1049–S, 720–8161; James W. Hunt, Room, 1049–S, 720–6383.
Hearing Clerk.—Joyce A. Dawson, Room 1081–S, 720–4443.

OFFICE OF THE JUDICIAL OFFICER

Jamie L. Whitten Building, Room 510–A, phone 720–4764

Judicial Officer.—William G. Jensen.
Assistant.—Michael J. Stewart, Room 508–A, 720–9268.

OFFICE OF SMALL AND DISADVANTAGED BUSINESS UTILIZATION

South Agriculture Building, Room 1323–S, phone 720–7117

Director.—Sharon Harris.

OFFICE OF OPERATIONS

South Agriculture Building, Room 1575–S, phone 720–3937

Director.—Ira L. Hobbs.
Deputy Director.—Reba Pittman Evans, 720–1762.
Associate Director for Operations.—Priscilla B. Carey, 720–3937.
Associate Deputy Director, Civil Rights Enforcement and Adjudicating Program.—Robert Franco, Room 1575, 720–5681.
Medical Officer.—Oleh Jacykewycw, Room 1039 720–3893.
National Information Technology Center (NITC).
Director.—[Vacant], PO Box 205, 8930 Ward Parkway, Kansas City MO 64141, (816) 926–6501.
Supervisory Computer Specialist.—E. Sue Rachlin, 3825 East Mulberry Street, Fort Collins CO 80524, (303) 498–1510.

POLICY ANALYSIS AND COORDINATION CENTER

INFORMATION RESOURCES MANAGEMENT

Jamie L. Whitten Building, Room 414–W, phone 720–8833

Chief Information Officer.—Anne F. Thomson Reed (acting).
Associate Deputy Chief Information Officer.—Hollace Twining.
Senior Policy Advisor for Field Service Center Oversight.—William E. Gardner, 720–3482.

HUMAN RESOURCES MANAGEMENT

Jamie L. Whitten Building, Room 316–W, phone 720–3585

Director.—Roger L. Bensey.Deputy Director.—Robert W. Whiting, 720–3586.
Division Directors:
Compensation and Employment Division.—Charles S. Warrick, Room 309–S, 720–6104.

Employee Relations and Development.—[Vacant].
Safety and Health Management.—James Stevens, Room 3304–S, 720–8248.
Automated Personnel Systems.—Joan B. Golden, Room 342–W, 720–2973.
Human Resources Services.—Denise Leger-Lee, Room 31–W, 720–7797.

CIVIL RIGHTS

Jamie L. Whitten Building Room 326–W, phone 720–5212

Director.—Lloyd Wright.
Deputy Directors: Jeremy Wu, Room 326–W, 720–5212; Susan Reilly, Room 326–W, 720–5212.

PROCUREMENT AND PROPERTY MANAGEMENT

South Agriculture Building, Room 110–W, phone 720–6841

Director.—Warren R. Ashworth.
Division Directors:
Procurement Policy.—David Shea, Room 1550, 720–6206.
Property Management.—Denise Patterson, Room 1524, 720–7283.
Disaster Management and Coordination Staff.—Leonard Mandrgoc, Room 302–S, 720–5711.

MODERNIZATION OF ADMINISTRATIVE PROCESSES

Jamie L. Whitten Building, Room 110–W, 720–6841

Director.—David Skeen.

OFFICE OF THE CHIEF FINANCIAL OFFICER

Jamie L. Whitten Building, Room 143–W, phone 720–0727

Chief Financial Officer.—[Vacant].
Deputy Chief Financial Officer.—Irwin T. David, Room 143–W, 720–0727.
Associate Chief Financial Officer.—Allan S. Johnson, Room 4094–S, 720–8345.
Division Chiefs:
Fiscal Policy.—Richard Guyer, Room 3023–S, 690–0291.
Planning and Accountability.—Patricia Wensel, Room 3027, 720–1175.
Financial Systems Reporting and Analysis.—David Suing, Room 3033–S, 720–1174.
Working Capital Fund Budget and Fiscal Services Division.—[Vacant], Room 4094–S, 720–1547.
Executive Services Staff.—Gary Barber, Room 4088–S, 720–1221.
Director, National Finance Center.—John Hall, PO Box 60000, New Orleans LA 70160, (504) 255–5200, fax (504) 255–5548.

OFFICE OF THE CHIEF ECONOMIST

Jamie L. Whitten Building, Room 227–E, phone 720–4164

Chief Economist.—Keith Collins.
Deputy Chief Economist.—James Glauber, 720–6185.
Chairperson.—Gerald A. Bange, Room 5143–S, 720–6030.
Chief Meteorologist.—Albert Peterlin, Room 5143–S, 720–8651.
World Agricultural Outlook Board, Supervisory Meteorologist.—Raymond P. Motha, Room 5133–S, 720–9807.
National Weather Service, Supervisory Meteorologist.—Douglas LeComte, Room 5844–S.

OFFICE OF RISK ASSESSMENT AND COST BENEFIT ANALYSIS

South Agriculture Building, Room 5248–S, phone 720–8022

Director.—Alwynelle (Nell) Ahl.
Deputy Director.—Ronald Meekhof.

OFFICE OF BUDGET AND PROGRAM ANALYSIS

Jamie L. Whitten Building, Room 101–A, phone 720–3323

Director.—Stephen B. Dewhurst.
Associate Director.—Lawrence Wachs, 720–5303.
Deputy Director, Budget, Legislative and Regulatory Systems.—Dennis Kaplan, Room 125–E, 720–6667.
Deputy Director Program Analysis.—Scott Steele, Room 126–W, 720–3396.

OFFICE OF THE EXECUTIVE SECRETARIAT

Jamie L. Whitten Building, Room 116–A, phone 720–7100

Director.—Lynne Finnerty.
System Administrator.—Al Henderson.

NATIONAL APPEALS BOARD

3101 Park Center Drive, Room 1113, Alexandria VA 22302

Director.—Norman G. Cooper, (703) 305–2708
Deputy Director for Hearings and Administration.—Robert J. Day, Jr., (703) 305–1151

OFFICE OF COMMUNICATIONS

Jamie L. Whitten Building, Room 404–A, phone 720–4623

Director.—Thomas S. Amontree.
Deputy Director.—Sedelta Verble.
Press Secretary.—[Vacant].
Special Assistant to the Secretary.—Samuel E. Thornton.
Director, National Service.—Joel S. Berg.
Division Directors:
Video Teleconferencing and Radio.—Larry A. Quinn, Room 1618–S, 720–6072.
Design Graphics and Exhibits.—Eva Cuevas, Room 518–A, 720–2267.
Photography and Photo Library.—William C. Tarpenning, Room 4404–S, 720–6633.
Printing Officer.—Alvin Senter, Room 501–A, 720–7175.

UNDER SECRETARY FOR NATURAL RESOURCES AND ENVIRONMENT

Jamie L. Whitten Building, Room 21709–E, phone 720–7173

Under Secretary.—Jim Lyons.
Deputy Under Secretary of:
Forestry.—Adela Backiel.
Conservation.—Tom Hebert.

FOREST SERVICE

Fourth Floor, Auditors Building, 201 14th Street SW 20250, phone 205–1661

Chief.—Michael P. Dombeck.
Associate Chief.—David G. Unger.
Director, Office of Public Affairs.—Christopher Holmes (acting), 205–1760.

ADMINISTRATION

Deputy Chief.—Kathleen Connelly, Second Floor, Auditors Building, 205–1709.
Associate Deputy Chief.—Clyde Thompson, 205–1709; Christine Pytel, 205–1784.
Staff Directors:
Information Systems and Technology.—John B. Arthur, 235–8607.
Fiscal and Accounting Services.—James R. Turner, (703) 235–8130.
Human Resources Programs.—Irving Thomas, (703) 235–8834.
Personnel Management.—Dale Nelson, (703) 235–8102, ext. 3005.
Property and Procurement.—Allen W. Smith, (703) 235–8007.

Civil Rights.—Luther Burse, (703) 235–2931.

NATIONAL FOREST SYSTEM

Third Floor, Auditors Building

Deputy Chief.—[Vacant].
Associate Deputy Chief.—Janice H. McDougle, 205–1465.
Associate Deputy Chief.—Bertha C. Gillam (acting), 205–1523.
Staff Directors:
Ecosystem Management Coordination.—Chris Risbrudt, 205–0895.
Engineering.—Gerald T. Coghlan (acting), 205–1400.
Lands.—Eleanor S. Towns, 205–1248.
Minerals and Geology.—Larry O. Gadt, 205–1224.
Recreation.—Lyle Laverty, 205–1643.
Timber Management.—David L. Hessel, 205–1185.
Watershed and Air Management.—Arthur Bryant, 205–1473.
Wildlife Management.—Robert D. Nelson, 205–1205.

PROGRAMS AND LEGISLATION

Auditors Building, Fifth Floor, phone 205–1663

Chief.—Ronald E. Stewart.

RESEARCH

Auditors Building, First Floor, phone 205–1665

Deputy Chief.—Jerry A. Sesco.
Associate Deputy Chiefs: Thomas E. Hamilton, 205–1507; Eldon W. Ross, 205–1702.
Staff Assistant.—Rita Stevens, 205–1076.
Staff Directors:
Forest Environment Research.—Richard V. Smythe, 205–1524.
Forest Fire and Atmospheric Sciences Research.—William T. Sommers, 205–1561.
Forest Insect and Disease Research.—James L. Stewart, 205–1532.
Forest Inventory and Economics.—H. Fred Kaiser, Jr., 205–1747.
Forest Products and Harvesting Research.—[Vacant], 205–1565.
Forest Management Research.—Stanley L. Krugman, 205–1547.

STATE AND PRIVATE FORESTRY

Auditors Building, Second Floor, phone 205–1331

Deputy Chief.—Joan M. Comanor.
Associate Deputy Chief.—William L. McCleese, 205–1331.
Staff Assistants: Richard Wright; Robert Tippeconnic; Pamela Godsay, 205–0832.
Staff Directors:
Cooperative Forestry.—Steve McDonald (acting), 205–1389.
Fire and Aviation Management.—Mary Jo Lavin, 205–1494.
Fire and Atmospheric Science.—William T. Sommers, 205–1561.
Forest Pest Management.—Ann M. Bartuska, 205–1665.

INTERNATIONAL FORESTRY

Deputy Chief.—David A. Harcharik, 205–1575.
Associate Deputy Chief.—David A. Harcharik, 205–1575.
Staff Directors:
International Forestry Operations.—Michael Martin (acting), (703) 235–9461.
International Forestry Policy and Planning.—Bertha Gillam (acting), 205–1571.

NATURAL RESOURCES CONSERVATION SERVICE

Chief.—Paul W. Johnson, 720–4525.
Associate Chief.—Pearlie Reed, 720–4525.
Director, Legislative Affairs.—Danny D. Sells, 720–2771.

Director, Office of Public Affairs.—David C. White, 720–3210.
Strategic Natural Resource Issues:
Special Assistants to the Chiefs: Gary A. Margheim, Ann E. Carey, 690–2500; Max Schnepf, 720–2889; Craig Cox, 720–8644.
Program Manager.—Jim Cubie, 690–2632.
Senior Partnership Policy and Program Coordinator.—Judy Doerner, 547–6223.
Deputy Chief for Management.—Thomas A. Weber, 720–6297.
National IRM Leader.—William E. Gardner, 720–7847.
Information Resources Management Division.—Thomas Christensen (acting), 720–0646.
Directors of—
Information Technology Center, Ft. Collins CO—Bernard A. Shafer, (970) 282–1974.
Management Services Division.—Edward M. Biggers, Jr., 720–4811.
Financial Management Division.—J. Keith Laird, 720–5904.
NHQ Administrative Support Division.—Gerlene Inman, 720–4102.
Human Resources Management Division.—Karen W. Amorose, 720–2227.
Quality Management and Program Evaluation Division.—Katherine Gugulis, 720–8388.
Correspondence Management.—Stephanie Edelen, 690–0023.
EEO Manager.—Jo Williams, 720–8118.
Astro Team Leader.—Patricia Cecil, 720–5904.
Director, National Employee Development Center, FT. Worth, TX.—Charles Adams, 817–334–5401, ext. 3225.
National Business Management Center.—Roy R. Twidt, 817–334–5424, ext. 3765.
Deputy Chief for Natural Resources Conservation Programs.—Lawrence A. Clark, 720–4527.
Director, Civil Rights Division.—Arun C. Basu, 720–5373.
Director of 1890/HACU Initiatives.—Maxine Barron, 720–1829.
Special Assistant for Management Issues.—James E. Tatum, 690–2877.
Special Assistant for RC&D.—Barbara T. Osgood, 720–2241.
Director:
Community Assistance and Resource Development Division.—Humberto Hernandez, 720–2847.
Watersheds and Wetlands Division.—Warren M. Lee, 720–3527.
Conservation and Ecosystem Assistance Division.—Lloyd E. Wright, 720–1845.
Budget Planning and Analysis Division.—Robert Reaves, 720–4533.
International Conservation Division.—Hari Eswaran, 720–2218.
Deputy Chief for Soil Science and Resource Assessment.—Gary A. Margheim, 720–4630.
Director:
Soils Division.—Horace Smith, 720–1819.
Resource Economics and Social Sciences Division.—Jerome Hammond, 720–2307.
Biological Conservation Sciences Division.—Gary Nordstrom, 720–2587.
Conservation Engineering Division.—Richard Van Klaveren, 720–2520.
Natural Resources Inventory Division.—Peter F. Smith, 720–5420.

FARM SERVICE AGENCY

Administrator.—Bruce Weber, (acting), Room 3086–S, 720–3467.
Associate Administrator.—Bruce Weber.
Advisory and Corporate Operations Staff.—William Waggener (acting), Room 0323–S, 690–3682.
Executive Secretariat.—Sandra Smith, Room 0071–S, 720–9564.
Civil Rights and Small Business Utilization Staff.—Willie D. Cook, Room 5400 (L–ST), 418–9076.
Legislative Liaison Staff.—Ronald Schrader, Room 3613–S, 720–3865.
Public Affairs Staff.—Marlyn Aycock (acting), Room 3624–S, 720–5237.
Economic and Policy Analysis Staff.—Larry A. Walker, Room 3741–S, 720–3451.
Deputy Administrator for Farm Programs.—Richard Newman, Room 3612–S, 720–3175.
Assistant Deputy Administrator for Farm Programs.—Parks Shackelford, Room 3612–S, 720–8513.
Compliance and Production Adjustment Division.—Audrey D. Sharp, Room 3630–S, 720–7641.
Price Support Division.—Grady Bilberry, Room 4095–S, 720–7901.
Conservation and Environmental Programs Division.—George Denley, Room 4714–S, 720–6221.
Tobacco and Peanuts Division.—Charles Hatcher, Room 5750–S, 720–7413.
Emergency and Noninsured Assistance Program Division.—Leona Dittus, Room 6099–S, 720–3168.

Deputy Administrator for Loan Programs.—Carolyn Cooksie, Room 3605–S, 720–4671.
Assistant Deputy Administrator.—Almeda Cole (acting), Room 3605–S, 720–7597.
Program Development and Economic Enhancement Division.—Bobby Reynolds, Room 4919–S, 720–3647.
Loan Making Division.—James Radintz, Room 5438–S, 720–1632.
Loan Servicing and Property Management Division.—Veldon Hall, Room 5449–S, 720–4572.
Deputy Administrator for Program Delivery and Field Operations.—John Stencel, Room 3096–S, 690–2807.
Assistant Deputy Administrator.—Elnora Dooms, Room 3096–S, 690–2806.
Operations Analysis Staff.—Thomas McCann, Room 2720–S, 690–2532.
Area Offices:
Northeast Area.—Tim Carter, Room 3718–S, 720–4746.
Southeast Area.—William Wheeler, Room 3717–S, 720–3593.
Southwest Area.—Trudy Kareus, Room 3720–S, 720–7889.
Northwest Area.—Alan Durick (acting), Room 3718–S, 720–6941.
Midwest Area.—Robert Soukup, Room 3709–S, 720–6803.
Deputy Administrator for Commodity Operations.—[Vacant], Room 3080–S, 720–3217.
Assistant Deputy Administrator.—Vicki Hicks, Room 3080–S, 720–7565.
Procurement and Donations Division.—Skip Brown (acting), Room 5755–S, 720–5074.
Warehouse and Inventory Division.—Steve Gill (acting), Room 5962–S, 720–2121.
Kansas City Commodity Office.—Alan King, (816) 926–6301.
Deputy Administrator for Management.—George Aldaya, Room 3095–S, 720–3438.
Assistant Deputy Administrator.—Earl Hadlock, Room 3095–S, 720–3833.
Management Services Division.—John Williams, Room 6603–S, 720–3138.
Human Resources Division.—Francis X. Riley, Jr., Room 5200 (L–ST), 418–8950.
Budget Division.—David Hall, Room 4720–S, 720–3674.
Information Technology Services Division.—Barry Ohler, Room 5768–S, 720–5320.
Financial Management Division.—James Little, Room 1206 POC, 305–1386.
Kansas City Management Office.—Jim Ray (acting), (816) 823–1260.

RISK MANAGEMENT AGENCY

Administrators.—Kenneth Ackerman, Room 3609–S, 720–2803.
Associate Administrators:
Suzette Dittrich, Room 3609–S, 720–2533; Tekle Mulugeta, Room 6090–S, 720–5533.
Deputy Administrator for:
Insurance Services.—Robert Prchal, Room 6709–S, 690–4494.
Compliance.—Garland Westmoreland, Room 6092–S, 720–5828.
Research and Development.—Timothy Witt, Kansas City, (816) 926–7394.

FOREIGN AGRICULTURAL SERVICE

South Agriculture Building, phone 720–3935

ADMINISTRATOR

Administrator.—August Schumacher, Jr., Room 5071–S, 720–3935.
General Sales Manager.—Christopher E. Goldthwait, Room 5071–S, 720–5173.
Associate Administrator.—Timothy J. Galvin, Room 5081–S, 720–5691.
Assistant to the Administrator.—Kevin Smith, Room 5061–S, 690–3062.
Deputy Administrator for—
Export Credits.—Mary Chambliss, Room 4077–S, 720–6301.
Commodity and Marketing Programs.—James V. Parker, Room 5089A–S, 720–4761.
International Trade Policy.—Patricia Sheikh (acting), Room 5075–S, 720–6887.
Foreign Agricultural Affairs.—Daniel Conable, Room 5702–S, 720–6138.
International Cooperation and Development.—Lynnett Wagner, Room 3008–S, 690–0776.
Director of—
Civil Rights Staff.—Mae C. Massey, Room 5083–S, 720–7233.
Legislative Affairs Staff.—Robert Cummings (acting), Room 5065–S, 720–6829.
Information Division.—Maureen Quinn, Room 5074–S, 720–7115.
Compliance Review Staff.—Robert Riston, Room 4957–S, 720–6713.
Budget Staff.—Hal Wynn.

FOREIGN AGRICULTURAL AFFAIRS

Deputy Administrator.—Daniel B. Conable, Room 5702–S, 720–6138.
Assistant Deputy Administrator.—Theodore Horoschak, Room 5702–S, 720–3253.
Executive Assistant to Deputy Administrator.—Thomas A. Hamby, 5082–S, 690–4053.
Assistant to Deputy Administrator.—Ronald P. Verdonk, 5702–S, 720–6878.
Area Officers:
Europe Team.—Philip A. Letarte, Room 5098–S, 720–6727.
Africa and Middle East.—Larry Pasnasuk, Room 5094–S, 720–7053.
Western Hemisphere.—William Westman, Room 5094–S, 720–3221.
North Asia and Oceania.—Wayne Molstad, Room 5095–S, 720–3080.
Southeast Asia, Russia and Poland.—Weyland Beeghly, Room 5095–S, 720–2690.
Representation, Foreign Visitors and Protocol Staff Chief.—Allen Alexander, Room 5088–S, 720–6725.
Field Communications Officer.—Kent Sisson, 6072–S, 205–2930.

INTERNATIONAL TRADE POLICY

Deputy Administrator.—Patricia Sheikh (acting), Room 5075–S, 720–6887.
Assistant Deputy Administrator.—[Vacant], Room 5055–S, 720–4055.
Assistant to the Deputy Administrator.—Randy Zeitner, Room 5501–S, 720–1061.
Director, Office of Food Safety and Technical Services.—Lloyd Harbert, Room 5547–S, 720–1301.
Marketing Specialist.—Leroy Barrett, Room 5543–S, 720–7054.
Director, Multilateral Trade Policy Affairs Division.—Geoffrey Wiggin, Room 5530–S, 720–1312.
MTN Analysis Team.—Alan Hrapsky, Room 5532–S, 720–6278.
Trade Barriers Analysis Team.—Robert Spitzer, Room 5540–S, 720–6064.
Director, Inter-America and Western Europe Division.—Craig Thorn, Room 5506–S, 720–1340.
Western Europe Team.—Carol Chesley, Room 5522–S, 720–1322.
Inter-America Team.—Carol Goodloe, Room 5510–S, 720–1335.
Director, Asia, Africa and Eastern Europe Division.—Patricia Sheikh, Room 5509–S, 720–1289.
Deputy Director.—Robert Curtis, Room 5509–S, 720–1289.
Chief of—
International Economic and Financial Analysis Branch.—David Pendlum, Room 3055–S, 720–1293.
Trade and Marketing Analysis Branch.—Michael J. Dwyer, Room 3059–S, 720–3124.
Export Sales Reporting Branch.—Thomas B. McDonald, Room 5959–S, 720–3273.
Director, Import Polices and Programs Division.—Carol M. Harvey, Room 5533–S, 720–2916.
Import Quota Team.—Stephen Hammond, Room 5535–S, 720–5676.
Import Policies Team.—Diana C. Wanamaker, Room 5527–S, 720–1330.

EXPORT CREDITS

Deputy Administrator.—Mary Chambliss (acting), Room 4077–S, 720–6301.
Assistant Deputy Administrator.—Glenn D. Whiteman, Room 4077–S, 720–4274.
Director, Emerging Markets Office.—James O'Meara, Room 6506–S, 720–0368.
Director, Program Development Division.—Kerry Reynolds, Room 4506–S, 720–4221.
Manager for—
Asia, Africa and the Middle East.—Lynne Reich, Room 4514–S, 720–4216.
Latin America and the Caribbean.—Dorothy Whitehead, Room 4516–S, 720–0625.
Eastern Europe and the FSU.—James Higgiston, Room 4524–S, 720–5319.
Director, CCC Operations Division.—Lawrence McElvain, Room 4521–S, 720–6211.
Deputy Director.—Robert Simpson, Room 4519–S, 720–6211.
Director of—
PL 480 Operations Division.—Constance Delaplane, Room 4549–S, 720–3664.
Director, CCC Program Support Division.—Ira Branson, Room 4077–S, 720–3573.

COMMODITY AND MARKETING PROGRAMS

Deputy Administrator.—James V. Parker, Room 5089A–S, 720–4761.
Assistant Deputy Administrator.—Frank Tarrant, Room 5089A–S, 720–1595.
Assistant Deputy Administrator.—Elizabeth Callanan, Room 5089A–S, 720–7791.

Assistant to the Deputy Administrator.—Beverly J. Simmons, Room 5087–S, 720–9059.
Director, Marketing Operations Staff.—Denise Fetters (acting), Room 4932–S, 720–4327.
Deputy Director.—Denise Fetters, Room 4932–S, 720–5521.
Director of—
Planning and Evaluation Staff.—John Nuttall, Room 5550–S, 690–1198.
Tobacco, Cotton and Seeds Division.—Lana Bennett (acting), Room 5946–S, 720–9516.
Deputy Director for—
Marketing.—Lynn Abbott, Room 5646–S, 720–9518.
Analysis.—Lana Bennett, Room 5646–S, 720–9487.
Director, Horticultural and Tropical Products Division.—Frank J. Piason, Room 5647–S, 720–6590.
Deputy Director for—
Marketing.—Robert Tisch, Room 5944–S, 720–7931.
Analysis.—Howard Wetzel, Room 5647–S, 720–3423.
Director, Forest Products Division.—J. Lawrence Blum, Room 4647–S, 720–0638.
Deputy Director for—
Marketing.—Thomas Westcott, Room 4647–S, 720–0638.
Analysis.—David Young, Room 4651–S, 720–1296.
Director, Oilseeds and Products Division.—Lana Bennett, Room 5646–S, 720–9516.
Deputy Director for—
Marketing.—Lynn Abbott, Room 5640–S, 720–8809.
Analysis.—Lana Bennett, Room 5646-S, 720–0472.
Director, Grain and Feed Division.—Robert Riemenschneider, Room 5603–S, 720–6219.
Deputy Director for—
Marketing.—Francine Radler, Room 5603–S, 720–4168.
Analysis.—H. Lee Schatz, Room 5617–S, 720–4935.
Director, Dairy, Livestock and Poultry Divison.—John Reddington, Room 5935–S, 720–8031.
Deputy Director for—
Marketing.—Robert Wicks, Room 5935–S, 720–1353.
Analysis.—Max Bowser, Room 5934–S, 720–1350.
Director of—
AgExport Services Division.—Charles Alexander, Room 4939–S, 720–6343.
Production Estimates and Crop Assessment Division.—Edwin I. Cissel, Room 6053–S, 720–0888.

INTERNATIONAL COOPERATION AND DEVELOPMENT

Room 3002 South Agriculture Building, phone 690–0776

Deputy Administrator.—Lynnett Wagner, Room 3008–S, 690–0776.
Assistant Deputy Administrator.—John Miranda (acting), Room 3010–S, 690–0775.
Directors for—
International Organizations Division.—Richard Kelm, Room 3123–S, 690–1801.
Food Industries Division.—Frank Fender, Room 3245–S, 690–3737.
Leader:
Cochran Fellowship Program.—Gary Laidig, Room 3844–S, 690–1734.
Trade and Investment Program.—Richard Rortvedt, Room 3250–S, 690–3985.
Professional Development Program.—Margaret Hively, Room 3247–S, 690–1141.
Director, Research and Scientific Exchange Division.—Whetten Reed, Room 3222–S, 690–4872.
Deputy Director.—Linda Lynch, Room 3202–S, 690–4872.
Leader:
Scientific Exchange Program.—Whetten Reed, Room 3222–S, 690–4872.
Binational Research Program.—Whetten Reed.
Foreign Currency Research Program.—Whetten Reed.
Reimbursable Research Program.—Richard Affleck, Room 3202–S, 720–2589.
Director of—
Far Eastern Regional Research Office New Delhi, India.—James Thomas, 9–011–91–11–600–651.
Development Resources Division.—Arlene Mitchell, Room 3219–S, 690–1924.
Deputy Director.—[Vacant], Room 3219–S, 690–1924.
Chief of—
Africa, Asia, and Europe Branch.—Robert Wilson, Room 3225–S, 690–1945.
Natural Resources and the Environment Branch.—[Vacant], Room 3211–S, 690–1918.
Inter-American and International Programs Branch.—Andres Delgado, Room 3239–S, 690–2946.

UNDER SECRETARY FOR RURAL DEVELOPMENT
Jamie L. Whitten Building, phone 720–4581

Under Secretary.—Jill Long Thompson.
Deputy Under Secretary, Operations and Management.—Inga Smulkstys.
Deputy Under Secretary, Policy and Planning.—Art Campbell, 720–8653.

RURAL HOUSING SERVICE

South Agriculture Building, Room 5014, phone 690–1533

Administrator.—Jan Shadburn (acting).
Associate Administrator.—Eileen Fitgerald (acting), 720–5614.
Confidential Assistant.—Bill Simpson, Room 5033, 720–5593.
Deputy Administrator, Single Family Housing.—Ronnie Tharrington, Room 5013–S, 720–5177.
Single Family Housing Processsing Division.—William Toney, Room 5334, 720–1474.
Single Family Housing Servicing and Property Management Division.—Thomas Hannah, Room 5309–S, 720–1452.
Deputy Administrator, Multi-Family Housing.—Charles Werwein, Room 5013–S, 720–3773.
Multi-Family Housing Processing Division.—Obediah Baker, Room 5337–S, 720–1604.
Deputy Administrator, Community Programs.—John Bowles, Room 6304, 720–1490.

MANAGEMENT

Deputy Administrator, Operations and Management.—Leonard Hardy, Room 5007–S, 720–7015.
Controller.—Victoria Bateman, Room 6871–S, 720–9593.
Civil Rights Staff.—Cheryl Prejean Greaux, Room 6333–S.
Office of Communications.—Clark Ray, Room 5039–S, 720–6903.
Director, Budget Division.—Al Darke, Room 6900–S, 720–9593.
Financial Management Division.—Sherie Hinton Henry, Room 6869, 690–0300.
Chief, Information Officer.—Joseph Perez, Room 6425, 690–0326.
Director:
IRM Customer Services Division.—Sheri McFarlane, Room 6430–S, 720–6700.
Management Services Division.—Vic Agresti, (703) 235–5500.
Information Technology Division.—Jim Campbell, 1520 Market Street, St. Louis MO 63103, (314) 539–2835.
Systems Services Division.—[Vacant], St. Louis MO, (314) 539–6490.
Assistant Controller.—Terry Young, St. Louis MO, (314) 539–2425.
Assistant Administrator for Human Resources.—Timothy Ryan, 501 School Street, Third Floor, 245–5561.
Assistant Administrator for Procurement and Administrative Services.—Chris Gomez, Room 5038, 720–9746.
Director, Division of:
Support Services.—Michael Clark, Room 0166, 720–9716.
Procurement Management.—Elaine Larison, Room 6445–S, 690–9820.
Property and Supply Management.—Herman White, 1520 Market Street, St. Louis MO 63103, (314) 539–2411.

RURAL BUSINESS-COOPERATIVE DEVELOPMENT SERVICE

Administrator.—Dayton Watkins, Room 5045–S, 690–4730.
Associate Administrator.—Wilbur T. Peer, Room 5045–S, 720–6165.
Deputy Administrator for Business Programs.—Willliam F. Hagy, III, 5050–S, 720–7287.
Director:
Processing Division.—Dwight Carmon, 6321–S, 690–4100.
Servicing Division.—Carolyn Parker, Room 6333, 690–4103.
Specialty Leaders.—Joseph R. Binder, Room 5402, 720–1400.
Deputy Administrator for Cooperative Services Programs.—Randall Torgerson, Room 4014–S.
Assistant Deputy Administrator.—James E. Haskell, Room 4014–S, 720–8460.
Director, Division of:
Cooperative Marketing.—Thomas Stafford, Room 4204–S, 690–0368.
Cooperative Management.—John R. Dunn, Room 4206–S, 690–1374.
Cooperative Development.—John Wells, Room 4218–S, 720–3350.

Deputy Administrator, Community Development.—Victor Vazquez, Reporters Building, Room 704, 690–0289.

Associate Deputy Administrator.—J. Norman Reid, Reporters Building, Room 701, 260–6332.

Director, Empowerment Program Division.—Dr. Richard Wetherill, Reporters Building, Room 701, 619–7983.

Director, Community Resource Development Division.—John Dean, Reporters Building, Room 701, 619–0358.

Deputy Administrator for Policy and Planning.—[Vacant], Room 5024–S, 690–0569.

Confidential Assistant to the Deputy Under Secretary for Policy and Planning.—Alicia Peterson, Room 5024, 690–0569.

Chief Budget Officer.—James R. Newby, Room 206–W, 720–4581.

Director:

Rural Initiatives and Partnerships.—Wayne Fawbush, Room 5027–S, 205–2860.

National Partnership Office.—James Scanlon, Room 4227–S, 690–2394.

Research, Analysis, and Information.—Ted Butler, Room 5308–S, 690–3859.

ALTERNATIVE AGRICULTURE RESEARCH AND COMMERCIALIZATION CORPORATION

Director.—W. Bruce Crain, Room 0156–S, 690–1633.

Deputy Director.—Dr. Robert E. Armstrong, Room 0156–S, 690–1641.

RURAL UTILITIES SERVICE

Administrator.—Wally Beyer, Room 4051–S, 720–9540.

Deputy Administrator, Program Operations.—Adam M. Golodner, Room 4051–S, 720–9542.

Deputy Administrator, Water and Wastewater.—John P. Romano (designee), Room 4048–S, 720–0962.

Confidential Assistant to the Administrator.—Carolyn Phillips, Room 4051–S, 720–9540.

Borrower and Program Support:

Director, Administrative Liaison Staff.—Richard E. Lynch, Room 4064–S, 720–1382.

Program Advisor, Program/Financial Services Staff.—Larry A. Belluzzo, Room 4031–S, 720–1265.

Director, Program Accounting Services Division.—Roberta D. Purcell, Room 2221–S, 720–9450.

Electric Program:

Assistant Administrator.—Blaine D. Stockton, Jr., Room 4037–S, 720–9545.

Deputy Assistant Administrator.—Alexander M. Cockey, Jr., Room 4037–S, 720–9545.

Director, Division of:

Northern Region.—Thomas W. Nusbaum, Room 0243–S, 720–1420.

Southern Region.—James A. Ruspi, Room 0221–S, 720–0848.

Power Supply.—Thomas L. Eddy, Room 0270–S, 720–6436.

Electric Staff.—George J. Bagnall, Room 1246–S, 720–1900.

Telecommunications Program:

Assistant Administrator.—Robert Peters, Room 4056–S, 720–9554.

Deputy Assistant Administrator.—Barbara L. Eddy, Room 4056–S, 720–9554.

Directors:

Northeast Area.—Gerald Nugent, Jr., Room 2859–S, 720–8268.

Southeast Area.—Craig R. Wulf, Room 2870–S, 720–0715.

Northwest Area—Jerry H. Brent, Room 2813–S, 720–0733.

Southwest Area—Ken B. Chandler, Room 2808–S, 720–0800.

Advanced Telecommunications Services Division.—Barbara L. Eddy (acting), Room 4056–S, 720–9554.

Telecommunications Standards Division.—Orren E. Cameron, Room 2835–S, 720–8663.

Assistant Administrator, Water and Wastewater Program.—Richard H. Mansfield, Room 4048–S, 690–2670.

Director, Water Programs Division.—[Vacant], Room 4048–S, 690–2670.

Director, Engineering and Environmental Staff.—Gary J. Morgan, Room 4040–S, 720–8328.

UNDER SECRETARY FOR FOOD, NUTRITION AND CONSUMER SERVICES
Jamie L Whitten Building, Room 240–E, phone 720–7711, fax 690–3100

Under Secretary.—Mary Ann Keeffe (acting).
Deputy Under Secretary.—Mary Ann Keeffe, Room 240–E.

FOOD AND CONSUMER SERVICE

3101 Park Center Drive Alexandria VA 22302, phone (703) 305–2061

Administrator.—Bill Ludwig, Room 803.
Associate Administrators.—George A. Braley, (703) 305–2060; Amanda Dew Manning, (703) 305–1609.
Director, Office of Analysis and Evaluation.—Michael E. Fishman (acting), Room 208, (703) 305–2017.

GOVERNMENTAL AFFAIRS AND PUBLIC INFORMATION

Deputy Administrator.—Darlene Barnes (acting), Room 806, (703)305–2039.
Director of:
Public Information.—Darlene Barnes, Room 806, (703) 305–2039.
Governmental Affairs.—Frank Ippolito, Room 805, (703) 305–2010.

MANAGEMENT

Deputy Administrator.—Joseph Leo, Room 808, (703) 305–2030.
Associate Deputy Administrator.—Janice Lilja, Room 808, (703) 305–2032.
Divisional Directors:
Administrative Services.—Paul Braun, Room 909, (703) 305–2232.
Civil Rights.—Gloria McColl (acting), Room 802, (703) 305–2195.
Information Technology.—Claude Correll, Room 322, (703) 305–2754.
Human Resources.—Floyd Wheeler, Room 614, (703) 305–2326.

FINANCIAL MANAGEMENT

Deputy Administrator/Comptroller.—Gary Maupin, Room 409, (703) 305–2046.
Divisional Directors:
Accounting.—James Belcher, Room 415, (703) 305–2850.
Budget.—Arthur French (acting), Room 423, (703) 305–2189.
Grants Management.—Lou Pastura, Room 412, (703) 305–2048.
Program Information.—Richard Platt (acting), Room 405, (703) 305–2159.

FOOD STAMP PROGRAM

Deputy Administrator.—Yvette Jackson, Room 710, (703) 305–2026.
Associate Deputy Administrator.—Bonny O'Neil, Room 710, (703) 305–2022.
Divisional Directors:
Benefit Redemption.—Tim O'Connor, Room 706, (703) 305–2756.
Program Accountability.—Abigail Nichols, Room 907, (703) 305–2414.
Program Development.—Art Foley, Room 720, (703) 305–2490.
EBT Coordinator.—Jeff Cohen, Room 716, (703) 305–2517.

SPECIAL NUTRITION PROGRAMS

Deputy Administrator.—Ronald Vogel (acting), Room 510, (703) 305–2052.
Associate Deputy Administrator.—Ronald Vogel, Room 510, (703) 305–2054.
Divisional Directors:
Child Nutrition.—Robert Eadie (acting), Room 1006, (703) 305–2590.
Food Distribution.—Les Johnson, Room 502, (703) 305–2680.
Nutrition and Technical Services.—Carole Davis (acting), Room 607, (703) 305–2585.
Supplemental Food Programs.—Stanley Garnett, Room 517, (703) 305–2746.

OFFICE OF CONSUMER AFFAIRS

Director.—Graydon Forrer (acting), Room 813B, phone (703) 305–2281.

CENTER FOR NUTRITION POLICY AND PROMOTION

1120 20th Street NW, Suite 200 N, phone 418–2312, fax 208–2322

Executive Director.—Eileen Kennedy.
Director for:
Nutrition Promotion Staff.—William Layden, 208–2331.
Nutrition Policy Staff.—Carol Kramer LeBlanc, 418–0243.

FOOD SAFETY AND INSPECTION SERVICE

Jamie L. Whitten Building, Room 331–E, phone 720–7025, fax 690–4437

Administrator.—Thomas J. Billy.
Deputy Administrator for:
Office of Management.—Alberta Frost, Room 347–E, 720–4425.
Office of Field Operations.—Craig Reed, Room 344–E, 720–5190.
Office of Policy, Program Development and Evaluation.—Margaret O'K. Glavin, Room 350–E, 720–2709.
Office of Public Health and Science.—Kaye Wachsmuth (acting), Room 341–E, 720–2644.
Director:
Civil Rights Staff.—Cynthia Mercado, Room 1144–S, 205–0743.
Food Safety Executive and Management Coordination Staff.—Judith Riggins (acting), Room 327–E, 720–8911.
Legislative Liaison Staff.—Linda Swacina, Room 1165–S, 720–3897.
Food Safety Education and Communications Staff.—Susan Conley, Room 1175–S, 720–7943.

UNDER SECRETARY FOR RESEARCH, EDUCATION AND ECONOMICS

Jamie L. Whitten Building, Room 217–W, 720–8885

Under Secretary.—Catherine Woteki (acting), Room 217–W, 720–8885.
Deputy Under Secretary.—Floyd Horn (acting), Room 217–W, 720–8885.

AGRICULTURAL RESEARCH SERVICE

Administration Building, Room 303–A, phone 720–3656, fax 720–5427

Administrator.—Floyd Horn (acting) Room 302–A, 720–3656.
Associate Administrator.—Robert J. Reginato, Room 302–A, 720–3658.
Assistant Administrator for—
Technology Transfer.—Richard M. Parry, Jr., Room 358–A, 720–3973.
Deputy Assistant Administrator.—Michael D. Ruff, Room 414, Building 005, BARC–West, Beltsville MD, (301) 504–5734.
International Research.—A.R. Bennett (acting), Room 102, Building 005, BARC–West, Beltsville MD, (301) 504–5605.
Director, Budget and Program Management Staff.—Joseph S. Garbarino, Room 358–A, 720–4421.
Director, Information Staff.—Robert W. Norton, Room 450, 6303 Ivy Lane, Greenbelt MD 20770, 344–2340.
Legislative Advisor.—Marshall Tarkington, Room 353–A, 720–7141.

ADMINISTRATIVE AND FINANCIAL MANAGEMENT

South: Jamie L. Whitten Federal Building, Room 324A

Deputy Administrator.—Jane L. Giles, Room 324A, 690–2575.
Special Assistant to the Deputy Administrator.—S.R. Leaman, Room 314A, 690–2585.
Associate Deputy Administrator, Administrative Management.—W.G. Horner, Room 814, 6305 Ivy Lane Lane, Greenbelt MD 20770, (301) 344–3646.
Associate Deputy Administrator, Financial Management.—Gene Spory, Room 820, 6305 Ivy Lane Lane, Greenbelt MD 20770, (301) 344–8106.
Director, Human Resources.—James Bradley, Room 809, 6303 Ivy Lane, Greenbelt MD 20770, (301) 344–1518.

NATIONAL PROGRAM STAFF

Beltsville Agricultural Research Center, Building 005, Room 125, Beltsville MD 20705

phone (301) 504–5084, fax (301) 504–6191

Deputy Administrator.—Edward B. Knipling, Room 125, Building 005, (301) 504–5084.
Program Planning Advisor.—David Rust, Room 112, Building 005, (301) 504–6233.
Associate Deputy Administrator.—
Natural Resources and Sustainable Agricultural Systems.—[Vacant], Room 134, Building 005, (301) 504–7987.
Animal Production, Product Value and Safety.—[Vacant], Room 138, (301) 504–6252.
Crop Production, Product Value and Safety.—Judy St. John, Room 133, Building 005, (301) 504–6252.
Research Program Safety Officer.—Michael Kiley, Room 208, Building 005, (301) 504–5737.
National Program Leader:
Soil Erosion.—Richard Amerman, Room 233, Building 005, Room 233, (301) 504–6441.
Water Quality/Water Management.—Dale Bucks, Room 233B, (301) 504–7034.
Oilseeds and Bioscience.—Dwayne Buxton, Room 212, (301) 504–5541.
Biological Control.—Raymond I. Carruthers, Room 220, (301) 504–5930.

NATIONAL AGRICULTURAL LIBRARY

Route 1, Beltsville, MD 20705, phone (301) 504–5248, fax (301) 504–7042

Director.—Pamela O.J. Andre, Room 200–A, (301) 504–5248.
Deputy Director.—Keith Russell, Room 200, (301) 504–6780.
Associate Director for:
Automation.—Gary McCone, Room 204, (301) 504–5018, fax (301) 504–5472.
Technical Services.—Sally Sinn, Room 203, (301) 504–7294, fax (301) 504–5472.
Public Services.—Maria Pisa, Room 203, (301) 504–5834, fax (301) 504–5472.

AREA OFFICES

Director, Beltsville Area.—Kenneth D. Murrell, Room 223, Building 003, BARC–West, Beltville MD 29705, (301) 504–6078.
Associate Area Director.—Phyllis E. Johnson, Room 223, Building 003, BARC–West, Beltsville MD 29705, (301) 504–5193.
Director, North Atlantic Area.—Herbert L. Rothbart, 600 East Mermaid Line, Wyndmoor PA 19038, (215) 233–6593.
Associate Area Director.—Frank Greene, (215) 233–6668.
Director, South Atlantic Area.—Roger Breeze, PO Box 5677, College Station Road, Athens GA 30613 (706) 546–3311.
Associate Area Director.—Richard S. Soper, (706) 546–3328.
Director, Mid South Area.—Thomas J. Army, PO Box 225, Stoneville MS 38776, (601) 686–5265.
Director, Midwest Area.—Richard L. Dunkle, Room 2004, 1815 North University Street, Peoria IL 61604–0000, (700) 360–4602.
Associate Area Director.—Eldean D. Gerloff, Room 2002, 1815 North University Street, Peoria IL 61604, (700) 360–4251.
Director, Pacific West Area.—[Vacant], room 2030, 800 Buchanan Street, Albany CA 94710, (510) 559–6060.
Director, Northern Plains Area.—Wilbert H. Blackburn, Room S–150, 1201 Oakridge Drive, Fort Collins CO 80525–5562, (970) 229–5557.
Associate Area Director.—James R. Welsh, (970) 229–5595.
Director, Southern Plains Area.—Charles A. Onstad, Suite 230, 7607 Eastmark Drive, College Station TX 77840, (409) 260–9346.

REGIONAL RESEARCH CENTERS

Director, Eastern Regional Research Center.—John P. Cherry, 600 East Mermaid Lane, Wyndmoor PA 19038, (215) 233–6595.
Director, Western Regional Research Center.—Antoinette A. Betschart, 800 Buchanan Street, Albany CA 94710–0000, (510) 559–6060.
Director, Southern Regional Research Center.—John Patrick Jordan, 1100 Robert E. Lee Boulevard, New Orleans LA 70179–0000, (504) 286–4212.

Director, National Center for Agricultural Utilization Research.—Peter B. Johnsen, Rom 2038, 1815 North University Street, Peoria IL 61604–0000, (309) 681–6541.

NUTRITIONAL RESEARCH CENTERS

Director, Beltsville Human Nutrition Research Center.—Joseph T. Spence, Room 223, Building 308, BARC-East, Beltsville MD 20705, (301) 504–8157.

Director, Children's Human Nutrition Research Center.—Dennis M. Bier, Baylor College of Medicine, 1100 Bates Street, Houston TX 77030, (713) 798–7022.

Director, Grand Forks Human Nutrition Research Center.—Forrest Nielson, PO Box 7166, University Station, Grand Forks ND 58202, (701) 795–8456.

Director, Human Nutrition Research Center on Aging.—Dr. Irwin Rosenberg, 711 Washington Street, Boston MA 02111, (617) 556–3331.

Director, Western Human Nutrition Research Center.—Dr. Janet King, Building 1110, PO Box 29997, The Presidio of San Francisco CA 94129, (415) 556–9697.

COOPERATIVE STATE RESEARCH, EDUCATION AND EXTENSION SERVICE

Jamie L. Whitten Building, Room 305–A, phone 720–4423, fax 447–8987

Aerospace Building, 901 D Street 20250–2200

Administrator.—B.H. Robinson, Room 304–A, 720–4423.
Associate Administrator.—Colien Hefferan, 720–7441.
Deputy Administrator for:
Plant and Animal Production, Protection, and Processing.—Edward M. Wilson, Aerospace Building, Room 862–K, 401–4329, fax 401–4888.
Natural Resources and Environment.—Ralph Otto, Room 812, Aerospace Building, 401–4555, fax 401–1706.
Rural, Economic and Social Development.—Robert Koppman, Room 3409, South Building, 720–7506; fax 690–3162.
Families, 4H and Nutrition.—Alma Hobbs, Room 3441, South Building, 720–5853, fax 690–2469.
Partnerships.—George Cooper, Room 3851, South Building, 720–5623, fax 720–4924.
Competitive Research Grants and Awards Management.—Sally Rockey, Room 328, Aerospace Building, 401–1761, fax 401–1782.
Science and Education Resources Development.—K. Jane Coulter, Room 338–A, Whitten Building, 720–3877, fax 720–3945.
Communications, Technology, and Distance Education.—Barbara White, Room 3328, South Building, 720–6133, fax 690–0289.

ECONOMIC RESEARCH SERVICE

1301 New York Avenue 20005–4788, phone 219–0300, fax 219–0146

Administrator.—Susan E. Offutt, Room 1226.
Associate Administrator.—T. Kelley White, Room 1226, 219–0302.
Division Directors:
Commercial Agriculture.—Katherine Smith, Room 732, 219–0700, fax 219–0759.
Food and Consumer Economics.—Betsey Kuhn, Room 1128, 219–0880, fax 219–0869.
Information Services.—Bruce Greenshields, Room 228, 219–0310, fax 219–8924.
Natural Resources and Environment.—Margot Anderson, Room 524, 219–0455, fax 219–0029.
Rural Economy.—Richard Long (acting), Room 314, 219–0530, fax 219–0202.
Office of Energy and New Uses.—Roger Conway, Room 1232, 219–1941, fax 501–6338.

NATIONAL AGRICULTURAL STATISTICS SERVICE

South Agriculture Building, Room 4117—S, phone 720–2707, fax 720–9013

Administrator.—Donald M. Bay.
Executive Assistant to the Administrator.—Janice A. Goodwin, 720–5141.
Associate Administrator.—Richard D. Allen, Room 4117–S, 720–4333, fax 720–9013.
Deputy Administrator for—
Field Operations.—Fred S. Barrett, Room 4133–S, 720–3638, fax 720–0507.
Divisional Directors:

Estimates.—Frederic A. Vogel, Room 5801–S, 720–3896, fax 690–1311.
Research.—Ronald Bosecker, Room 305, 3251 Old Lee Highway, Fairfax VA 22030, (703) 235–5211, fax (703) 235–3386.
Survey Management.—Carol House, Room 4801–S, 720–4557, fax 720–8738.
Systems and Information.—Phillip L. Zellers, Room 5847–S, 720–2984, fax 720–9909.

ASSISTANT SECRETARY FOR MARKETING AND REGULATORY PROGRAMS

Jamie A. Whitten Building, Room 228–W, phone 720–4256, fax 720–5775

Assistant Secretary.—Michael V. Dunn.
Deputy Assistant Secretary.—Shirley R. Watkins, 720–7813.
Special Assistant to the Assistant Secretary.—Chris Sarcone, 720–5759.
Confidential Assistant to the Secretary.—Jennifer Yezak, 720–4031.

AGRICULTURAL MARKETING SERVICE

South Agriculture Building, Room 3071–S, phone 720–5115, fax 720–8477

Administrator.—Lon Hatamiya, 720–5115.
Director for:
Compliance.—David N. Lewis, Room 3529–S, 720–6766, fax 205–5772.
Legislative and Regulatory Review.—Sandra K. Hogan, Room 3510–S, 720–3203, fax 720–7135.
Information Staff.—Connie X. Crunkleton, Room 3510–S, 720–8998, fax 720–7135.
Assistant Administrator, Executive Resources.—Gary E. Scavongelli, Room 3074–S, 720–4658, fax 690–0476.
Deputy Assistant Administrator, Financial Management.—Joseph A. Roeder, Room 3969–S, 720–7511, fax 720–8882.
Deputy Administrator for Management Services.—Richard E. Walters, Room 3528–S, 720–7047, fax 720–7692.
Civil Rights Staff Officer.—Connie T. Bails, Room 3068–S, 720–0583, fax 720–5059.

MARKETING PROGRAMS

Deputy Administrator for Marketing Programs.—Kenneth C. Clayton, Room 3069–S, 720–4276, fax 720–8477.
Assistant Deputy Administrator.—Barbara A. Claffey, Room 3063–S, 690–4024, fax 720–8477.
Divisional Directors:
Cotton.—Mary E. Atienza, Room 2641–S, 720–3193, fax 690–1718.
Dairy.—Richard M. McKee, Room 2968–S, 720–4392, fax 690–0552.
Fruit and Vegetable.—Robert C. Keeney, Room 2077–S, 720–4722, fax 720–0565.
Livestock and Seed.—Barry L. Carpenter, Room 2092–S, 720–5705, fax 720–3499.
Poultry.—D. Michael Holbrook, Room 3932–S, 720–4476, fax 690–3165.
Science and Technology.—William J. Franks, Room 3507–S, 720–5231, fax 720–6496.
Tobacco.—John P. Duncan III, Room 502 Annex, 205–0567, fax 205–4099.
Transportation and Marketing.—Eileen S. Stommes, Room 4006–S, 690–1300, fax 690–0338.

ANIMAL AND PLANT HEALTH INSPECTION SERVICE

Jamie L. Whitten Building, Room 312–E, phone 720–3668, fax 720–3054

Administrator.—Terry L. Medley.
Associate Administrator.—Donald W. Luchsinger (acting), 720–3861.
Chief of Staff.—Richard T. Certo, Room 308–E, 720–2463.
Science Advisor.—Sally L. McCommon, Room 316–E, 720–8014.
Civil Rights Enforcement and Compliance.—Clarence M. Lemon, 4700 River Road, Unit 92, Riverdale MD 20737, (301) 734–6312.
Information Technology.—Michael C. Gregoire, Unit 92, Riverdale, (301) 734–3762.

LEGISLATIVE AND PUBLIC AFFAIRS

South Building, Room 1147, phone 720–2511, fax 720–3982

Director.—Patrick T. Collins (acting), Room 1147–S, 720–2511.

Deputy Director.—Paula Henstridge, 720–3981.
Assistant Directors:
Public Affairs.—Richard McNanny, Unit 51, Riverdale, (301) 734–7799.
Executive Correspondence.—Lynn Quarles, Unit 49, Riverdale, (301) 734–7776.
FOIA.—Michael Marquis, Unit 50, Riverdale, (301) 734–8296.

POLICY AND PROGRAM DEVELOPMENT

4700 River Road, Unit 118, Riverdale MD 20737
phone (301) 734–3771, fax (301) 734–5899

Director.—William S. Wallace (acting).
Unit Chiefs:
Planning, Evaluation and Monitoring.—Kenneth E. Waters, Unit 120, Riverdale, (301) 734–8889.
Policy Analysis and Development.—Janet W. Beirs, Unit 119, Riverdale, (301) 734–6698.
Regulatory Analysis and Development.—Richard F. Kelly, Riverdale, (301) 734–5956.
Environmental Analysis and Documentation.—(rotating) Unit 117, Riverdale, (301) 734–4391.
Risk Analysis.—(rotating), Unit 117, (301) 734–4391.

ORGANIZATION AND PROFESSIONAL DEVELOPMENT

4700 River Road, Riverdale MD 20737, phone (301) 734–5100, fax (301) 734–4966

Director.—Sharon A. Coursey, Unit 23, Riverdale.
Service Delivery Units/Deputy Directors:
PPQ.—Bill Wade, 7340 Exective Way, Suite A, Frederick MD 21701, (301) 663–0342, fax (301) 663–3240.
VS/AC.—Asia Elsbree, (301) 734–8111.
IS, ADC.—Richard Fraser, Kathy Trickey, (301) 734–5747.
MRP/Support.—Tim Blackburn, (301) 734–5738.
AMS.—Jan Williams, 1741 South Building, 690–3018, fax 720–6308.
Conflict Prevention.—Sheila Clemons, (301) 734–5100.
Organizational Development.—Jane Berkow, (301) 734–5735.

ANIMAL DAMAGE CONTROL

South Building, Room 1624–S, 720–2054, fax 690–0053.

Deputy Administrator.—Bob R. Acord.
Associate Deputy Administrator.—William H. Clay, 720–2054.
Assistant to the Deputy Administrator.—Susan Bright (acting), 720–2054.
Director for—
Operational Support Staff.—[Vacant], 4700 River Road, Riverdale MD 20737, (301) 734–8281, fax (301) 734–5157.
Resource Management Staff.—Joanne Garrett, Riverdale, (301) 734–7941, fax (301) 734–5157.

INTERNATIONAL SERVICES

Jamie L. Whitten Building, Room 324–E, phone 720–7593, fax 690–1484

Deputy Administrator.—Carl W. Castleton (acting).
Associate Deputy Administrator.—Dan J. Sheesley (acting), 720–7021.
Divisional Directors:
Operational Support.—Mary S. Neal, 4700 River Road, Unit 67, Riverdale, MD 20737, (301) 734–8892.
Resource Management Support.—Freida Skaggs (acting), Unit 65, Riverdale, (301) 734–5214.
Trade Support Team.—John Greifer (acting), South Building, Room 1128, 720–7677.

MANAGEMENT AND BUDGET

Jamie L. Whitten Building, Room 308–E, phone 720–5123, fax 690–0686

Deputy Administrator.—Phyllis B. York.

Associate Deputy Administrator.—[Vacant].
Divisional Directors:
Investigative and Enforcement Services.—Ron D. Stanley, Unit 85, 4700 River Road, Riverdale MD 20737, (301) 734–6491.
Management Services.—Joanne L. Munno, Unit 81, Riverdale, 20737–1234, (301) 734–6502.
Budget and Accounting.—Kevin Shea, Unit 57, Riverdale, 20737–1232, (301) 734–8014.
MRP Human Resources.—Larry T. Thackston, Room 1709–S, 720–6377.
Resources Management Systems and Evaluation Staff.—Frank C. Vollmerhausen, Unit 52, Riverdale 20737–1232, (301) 734–8864.

PLANT PROTECTION AND QUARANTINE

Jamie L. Whitten Building, Room 302–E, phone 720–5601, fax 690–0472

Deputy Administrator.—Alfred S. Elder (acting).
Associate Deputy Administrator.—Charles Schwalbe, 720–4441.
Assistant to the Deputy Administrator.—Paul Eggert, (301) 734–7764.
Veterinary Medical Officer.—Ronald B. Caffey, (301) 734–7633.
Director of—
Biotechnology and Scientific Services.—John H. Payne, 4700 River Road, Unit 98, Riverdale MD 20737, (303) 734–7602, fax (301) 734–8724.
Center for Plant Health Science and Technology.—Matt Royer, Unit 133, Riverdale, (301) 734–6600, fax (301) 734–8192.
Phytosanitary Issues Management.—Robert G. Spaide, Unit 131, Riverdale, (301) 734–8261, fax (301) 734–7639.
Operational Support.—Sidney E. Cousins, Unit 131, Riverdale, (301) 734–8261, fax (301) 734–7639.
Technical Information Systems.—Tracy Bowman, (301) 734–5518.
Biological Assessment and Taxonomic Support.—Rebecca Bech, (301) 734–5215.
Boll Weevil.—Gary Cunningham, (301) 734–8676.
Biocontrol.—Dale Meyerdirk, (301) 734–5667.
Resource Management Support.—Mona Grupp, Unit 130, Riverdale, (301) 734–7764, fax (301) 734–8434.

ANIMAL CARE

4700 River Road, Riverdale MD 20737, phone (301) 734–4980, fax (301) 734–4328

Director.—W. Ron DeHaven (acting).

VETERINARY SERVICES

Jamie L. Whitten Building, Room 320–E, phone 720–5193, fax 690–4171

Deputy Administrator.—Joan M. Arnoldi.
Associate Deputy Administrator.—[Vacant].
Special Assistant to the Deputy Administrator.—Richard L. Rissler, (301) 734–8093.
Assistant Director, Operational Support.—John L. Williams, Unit 33, Riverdale, (301) 734–8093, fax (301) 734–8818.
Chief Staff Veterinarian for:
Brucellosis Eradication.—Granville H. Frye, (301) 734–8711.
National Animal Health Programs.—[Vacant], (301) 734–5909.
Emergency Programs.—Joseph F. Annelli, (301) 734–8073.
National Center for Import and Export.—Gary S. Colgrove, Unit 38, Riverdale, (301) 734–8364, fax (301) 734–3222.
Center for Veterinary Biologics.—David A. Espeseth, Unit 148, Riverdale, (301) 734–8245, fax (301) 734–8910.
Resource Management Staff.—Louise R. Lothery, Unit 44, Riverdale, (301) 734–7517, fax (301) 734–7393.

GRAIN INSPECTION, PACKERS AND STOCKYARDS ADMINISTRATION

South Agriculture Building, Room 1094, phone 720–0219, fax 205–9237

Administrator.—James R. Baker.
Deputy Administrator for Grain Inspection.—David R. Shipman, Room 1092, 720–9170.

Deputy Administrator for Packers and Stockyards.—Harold Davis (acting), Room 3039, 720–7051.

Confidential Assistant to the Administrator.—F. Martin Rookard, Room 1097, 720–0217.

Assistant to the Administrator for EEO/CR.—Eugene Bass, Room 1634, 720–0216.

Public Affairs.—Dana Stewart, Room 1093, 720–5091.

Executive Resources Staff.—Robert E. Soderstrom, Room 0634, 720–0231, fax 720–4628.

Chief, International Monitoring Staff.—John Pitchford, Room 1627, 720–0231, fax 720–0226.

Division Director:

Compliance.—Neil E. Porter, Room 1647, 720–8262, fax 690–2755.

Field Management.—David Orr (acting), Room 1641, 720–0228, fax 720–1015.

Technical Services.—Steven N. Tanner, 10383 North Executive Hills Boulevard, Kansas City MO 64153–1394, (816) 891–0401, (816) 891–0478.

DEPARTMENT OF COMMERCE

Herbert C. Hoover Building

14th Street between Pennsylvania and Constitution Avenues 20230

phone 482–2000, http://www.doc.gov

WILLIAM M. DALEY, Secretary of Commerce; born August 9, 1948 in Chicago IL; B.S., Loyola University, 1970; J.D., John Marshall Law School, 1975; admitted to Illinois bar, 1975; served in Army National Guard/Air National Guard, 1970–76; Partner in law firm of Daley and George, 1975–85; partner (1985–89) and Of Counsel (1989–90) in law firm of Mayer, Brown and Platt; Vice Chairman (1989–90) and President and Chief Operating Officer (1990–93) of Amalgamated Bank of Chicago; Special Counsel to the President for the North American Free Trade Agreement, 1993; partner in law firm of Mayer, Brown and Platt, 1993–97; married to Loretta Aukstik, 1970; three children: William R., Lauren, and Maura; nominated on December 13, 1996, by President Clinton; confirmed by the U.S. Senate on January 30, 1997, to be Secretary of Commerce; sworn in on February 10, 1997.

OFFICE OF THE SECRETARY

Secretary of Commerce.—William M. Daley.
  Deputy Secretary.—[Vacant], Room 5838, 482–4625.
  Counselor to the Secretary.—[Vacant], Room 5865, 482–5485.
  Chief of Staff.—Paul Donovan, Room 5858, 482–4246.
    Director, Office of:
      Executive Secretariat.—Bettie Baca, Room 5516, 482–3934.
      Scheduling.—Dalia E. Elalfi Traynham, Room 5583, 482–5880.
      Public Affairs.—Mary Hanley, Room 5415, 482–8290.
      Business Liaison.—Cheryl Bruner, Room 5062, 482–1360.
      White House Liaison.—Parnice Green, Room 5717, 482–1684.
      Consumer Affairs.—Lajuan Johnson, Room 5718, 482–5001.

OFFICE OF THE DEPUTY SECRETARY

Deputy Secretary.—[Vacant], Room 5838, 482–4625.
Associate Deputy Secretary.—Kent Hughes, Room 5027, 482–6315.

GENERAL COUNSEL

General Counsel.—[Vacant], Room 5870, 482–4772.
Deputy General Counsel.—Paul Joffe, Room 5870, 482–4772.

ASSISTANT SECRETARY FOR LEGISLATIVE AND INTERGOVERNMENTAL AFFAIRS

Assistant Secretary.—Jane Bobbitt, Room 5421, 482–3663.
Deputy Assistant Secretary.—Ellen Bloom, Room 5421, 482–3663.

ASSISTANT SECRETARY FOR ADMINISTRATION

Herbert C. Hoover Building, Room 5830, 482–4951

Chief Financial Officer and Assistant Secretary for Administration.—Raymond G. Kammer, Jr. (acting).

Deputy Assistant Secretary.—[Vacant].
Director for:
Human Resources Management.—Elizabeth W. Stroud, Room 5001, 482–4807.
Deputy Director.—[Vacant], Room 5001, 482–4807.
Director, Office of:
Personnel Operations.—H. James Reese, Room 5005, 482–3827.
Programs and Policies.—Pamela E. Rankin, Room 5102, 482–3982.
Automated Systems and Pay Policy.—Diane Atchinson, Room 5118, 482–4425.
Budget, Management and Information, and Deputy Chief Information Officer.—Alan P. Balutis, Room 5820, 482–3490.
Director, Office of:
Budget.—Mark E. Brown, Room 5818, 482–4648.
Management and Organization.—Stephen C. Browning, Room 5327, 482–3707.
Information Planning and Review.—Lisa Westerbach, Room 6625, 482–0335.
Information Policy and Technology.—James E. McNamee, Room 6899, 482–3201.
Computer Services.—Patrick F. Smith, Room 1030 SILLS, (703) 487–4724.
Decision Analysis Center.—Charles Treat, Room 5026, 482–1314.
Executive Budgeting and Assistance Management.—Sonya G. Stewart, Room 6026, 482–4299.
Office of Executive Assistance Management.—John J. Phelan, III, Room 6020, 482–4115.
Office of Executive Budgeting.—Thomas D. Jones, Room 6839, 482–4458.
Financial Management and Deputy Chief Financial Officer.—John D. Newell, Room 6827, 482–1207.
Deputy Director for Financial Management.—Douglas K. Day, Room 6827, 482–0590.
Director, Office of:
Financial Management Systems.—Joseph Sclafani, Room 10 IC, (301) 258–4505.
Financial Policy and Assistance.—Theodore A. Johnson, Room 6819, 482–0754.
Acquisition Management.—Kenneth Buck (acting), Room 6424, 482–0191.
Director:
Acquisition Services.—Howard Price, Room 6516, 482–1966.
Acquisition Policy and Programs.—Michael Sade, Room 6424, 482–4248.
Systems Analysis and Organizational Performance.—Stephen C. Willett, Room 6424, 482–4248.
Security and Administrative Services.—Hugh L. Brennan, Room 6316, 482–1200.
Director, Office of:
Administrative Operations.—Robert A. Galpin, Room 2852, 482–3721.
Security.—Steven E. Garmon, Room 1069, 482–4371.
Safety and Building Management.—Robert Heinemann, Room 6316, 482–4935.
Real Estate Policy and Major Programs.—James M. Andrews, Room 1040, 482–3580.
Civil Rights.—Courtland Cox, Room 6010, 482–3940.
Chief:
Programs Planning and Systems Division.—David R. Lewis, Room 6010, 482–5691.
Compliance Division.—Kimberly Walton, Room 6010, 482–4993.
Systems and Telecommunications Management.—Ronald P. Hack, Room 6082, 482–0120.
Director, Office of:
Telecommunications Management.—Thomas Zetty, Room 6608, 482–3501.
Information Systems.—[Vacant], Room 6066, 482–2855.
Technical Support.—George Imber, Room 6616, 482–0873.

INSPECTOR GENERAL

Herbert C. Hoover Building, Room 7898–C, 482–4661

Inspector General.—Frank DeGeorge.
Deputy Inspector General.—[Vacant], 482–3516.
Executive Assistant.—Mary L. Casey, 482–1318.
Congressional Liaison Officer.—Jessica Rickenbach, 482–3052.
Counsel to the Inspector General.—Elizabeth T. Barlow, Room 7892, 482–5992.
Assistant Inspector General for Inspections and Program Evaluations.—Johnnie E. Frazier, Room 7886–B, 482–2754.
Deputy Assistant Inspector General for Inspections and Program Evaluations.—Jill A. Gross, Room 7886–B, 482–2754.
Audits.—George E. Ross, Room 7721, 482–1934.

Deputy Assistant Inspector General for:
Audits.—William E. Todd, Room 7721, 482–1934.
Environmental and Technology.—Ronald D. Lieberman, SSMC3, Suite 4404, (301) 713–2070.
Regional Audits.—Larry B. Gross, Room 7721, 482–0745.
Systems Evaluation.—Judith J. Gordon, Room 7876, 482–0185.
Deputy Assistant Inspector General for Systems Evaluation.—Allen R. Crawley, Room 7876,482–0185.
Investigations.—Damon L. Barbat, Room 7087, 482–0934.
Deputy Assistant Inspector General for Investigations.—Kathy A. Friebel, Room 7087, 482–0934.
Compliance and Administration.—[Vacant], Room 7099–A, 482–4266.
Human Resources Management Officer.—James D. Back, Room 7713, 482–4948.
Budget Officer.—Ann Carman, Room 7099–A, 482–1025.
Press Inquiries and FOIA Requests.—Office of Counsel, Room 7892, 482–5992.

UNDER SECRETARY FOR ECONOMICS AND STATISTICS ADMINISTRATION

Herbert C. Hoover Building, Room 4848, phone 482–3727, fax 482–0432

Under Secretary.—Everett M. Ehrlich.
Deputy Under Secretary.—Paul A. London, Room 4850, 482–3523.
Associate Under Secretary.—John Gray, Room 4843, 482–2760.
Executive Director.—James K. White, Room 4840, 482–2405.
Chief Economist.—James L. Price, Room 4868–A, 482–4885.
Director, Office of:
Administration.—B. Jerome Jackson, Room 4093, 482–3884.
Stat-USA.—Kenneth W. Rogers, Room 4878, 482–1405.
Economic Conditions.—Carl E. Cox, Room 4861, 482–4871.
Policy Development.—Jeffrey L. Mayer, Room 4858, 482–1727.
International Macroeconomic Analysis.—Sumiye O. Okubo, Room 4868, 482–1675.

BUREAU OF ECONOMIC ANALYSIS

1441 L Street NW 20230, phone 606–9600, fax 606–5311

Director.—J. Steven Landefeld, Room 6006.
Deputy Director.—Betty Barker, Room 6005, 606–9602.
Administrative Officer.—Sheila A. Robinson, Room 3013, 606–5556, fax 606–5323.
Associate Director for:
National Income Expenditures and Wealth.—[Vacant], Room 5006, 606–9715.
Regional Economics.—Hugh W. Knox, Room 6064, 606–9605.
International Economics.—Gerald A. Pollack, Room 6004, 606–9604.
Chief Economist.—Jack E. Triplett, Room 6060, 606–9603.
Chief Statistician.—Robert P. Parker, Room 6065, 606–9607.
Division Chiefs:
Balance of Payments.—Christopher L. Bach, Room 8024, 606–9545, fax 606–5314.
Computer Systems and Services.—Alan C. Lorish, Room 3051, 606–9909, fax 606–5315.
Current Business Analysis.—Douglas R. Fox, Room 6040, 606–9683, fax 606–5313.
Government.—Karl Galbraith, Room 5071, 606–9778, fax 606–5349.
Interindustry Economics.—Ann M. Lawson, Room 8066, 606–9462, fax 606–5316.
International Investment.—Gerald A. Pollack (acting), Room 6004, 606–9604, fax 606–5311.
National Income and Wealth.—Leon W. Taub, Room 5006, 606–9722, fax 606–5320.
Regional Economic Analysis.—John R. Kort, Room 4048, 606–9221, fax 606–5321.
Regional Economic Measurement.—Robert Brown, Room 4005, 606–9246, fax 606–5322.
Public Information Office.—Staff, Room 6027, 606–9900, fax 606–5310.
News Media Contact.—Larry Moran, Room 6043, 606–9691, fax 606–5310.

BUREAU OF THE CENSUS

(Use Washington DC 20233 for mailings to all locations.)

Federal Office Building Number 3, Suitland MD 20746 (FOB–3)

Federal Office Building Number 4, Suitland MD 20746 (FOB–4)

Iverson Mall, Marlow Heights MD 20748 (IM)

Washington Plaza Number 1, Upper Marlboro MD 20772 (WP–1)

Washington Plaza Number 2, Upper Marlboro MD 20772 (WP–2)

Director.—Martha Farnsworth Riche, FOB–3, Room 2049, (301) 457–2135, fax (301) 457–3761.

Deputy Director.—[Vacant], FOB–3, Room 2049, (301) 457–2138, fax (301) 457–3761.

Principal Associate Director and Chief Financial Officer.—[Vacant], FOB–3, Room 2037, (301) 457–2469, fax (301) 457–1902.

Principal Associate Director for Programs.—Paula J. Schneider, FOB–3, Room 2037, (301) 457–2092, fax (301) 457–1902.

Associate Director for:

Administration/Controller.—Nancy A. Potok, FOB–3, Room 2025, (301) 457–2473, fax (301) 457–1902.

Information Technology.—[Vacant], FOB–3, Room 2065, (301) 457–2168, fax (301) 457–1609.

Field Operations.—Marvin D. Raines, FOB–3, Room 2027, (301) 457–2072, fax (301) 457–1902.

Communications.—Philip L. Sparks, FOB–3, Room 2069, (301) 457–2158, fax (301) 457–2063.

Economic Programs.—Frederick T. Knickerbocker, FOB–3, Room 2061, (301) 457–2112, fax (301) 457–3761.

Decennial Census.—Robert W. Marx, FOB–3, Room 2031, (301) 457–2131, fax (301) 457–1902.

Demographic Programs.—Nancy M. Gordon, FOB–3, Room 2061, (301) 457–2126, fax (301) 457–3761.

Methodology and Standards.—Cynthia Z. F. Clark, FOB–3, Room 2031, (301) 457–2160, fax (301) 457–1902.

Assistant Director for Economic Programs.—Thomas L. Mesenbourg, FOB–3, Room 3045, (301) 457–2932.

Divisions and Offices:

Acquisition and Security Division.—Mark M. Taylor, FOB–3, Room 1533, (301) 457–1827.

Administrative and Customer Services Division.—Walter C. Odom, Jr., FOB–3, Room 2150, (301) 457–2228.

Agriculture and Financial Statistics Division.—Ewen M. Wilson, IM, Room 437, (301) 457–8555.

Budget Division.—Daniel F. Owens, FOB–3, Room 3430, (301) 457–3909.

Census 2000 Publicity Office.—Kenneth C. Meyer, FOB–3, Room 3049, (301) 457–2964.

Chief Economist.—John C. Haltiwanger, WP2, Room 221, (301) 457–1848.

Computer Assisted Survey Research Office.—Robert N. Tinari, SH, (301) 457–1381.

Computer Services Division.—Debra D. Williams, FOB–3, Room 1025, (301) 457–1734.

Customer Liaison Office.—John Ambler (acting), FOB–3, Room 3525, (301) 457–2479.

Data Preparation Division.—Judith N. Petty, Jeffersonville, IN, (812) 288–3344.

Decennial Management Division.—John Thompson, FOB–3, Room 3586, (301) 457–3946.

Decennial Policy and Design Office.—Patricia Berman (acting), FOB–3, Room 3574, (301) 457–3960.

Decennial Statistical Studies Division.—Ruth Ann Killion, FOB–3 Room 3785, (301) 457–4242.

Decennial Systems and Contracts Management Office.—Michael J. Longini, FOB–3, Room 3045, (301) 457–2933.

Demographic Statistical Methods Division.—P. Jay Waite, FOB–3, Room 3785, (301) 457–4242.

Demographic Surveys Division.—Chester E. Bowie, FOB–3, Room 3324, (301) 457–3773.

Economic Planning and Coordination Division.—John P. Govoni, FOB–3, Room 2584, (301) 457–2558.

Economic Statistical Methods and Programming Division.—Charles P. Pautler, Jr., FOB–4, Room 3015, (301) 457–1312.
Equal Employment Opportunity Office.—Carol Shaw, FOB–3, Room 3071, (301) 457–2853.
Field Division.—[Vacant], FOB–3, Room 1703, (301) 457–2031.
Finance Division.—Mary Kohlmeier, WP1, Room 412, (301) 457–1272.
Financial and Administrative Systems Division.—[Vacant], FOB–3, Room 3102, (301) 457–3115.
Foreign Trade Division.—C. Harvey Monk, Jr., FOB–3, Room 2104, (301) 457–2255.
Geography Division.—Joel L. Morrison, WP1, Room 651, (301) 457–1132.
Governments Division.—Gordon W. Green, WP2, Room 407, (301) 457–1489.
Housing and Household Economic Statistics Division.—Daniel H. Weinberg, IM, Room 307, (301) 763–8550.
Human Resources Division.—Marilia A. Matos, FOB–3, Room 3260, (301) 457–3721.
Information Systems Support and Review Office.—James E. Steed, FOB–3, Room 1071, (301) 457–1881.
Manufacturing and Construction Division.—David W. Cartwright, FOB–4, Room 2102–A, (301) 457–4593.
Marketing Services Office.—W. Donald Wynegar, FOB–3, Room 3023, (301) 457–2155.
Policy Office.—M. Catherine Miller, FOB–3, Room 2430, (301) 457–2520.
Population Division.—John F. Long (acting), FOB–3, Room 2011, (301) 457–2071.
Public Information Office.—Laverne V. Collins, FOB–3, Room 2705, (301) 457–2804.
Services Division.—Carole A. Ambler, FOB–3, Room 2633, (301) 457–2668.
Statistical Research Division.—Tommy Wright, FOB–4, Room 3202, (301) 457–1030.
Systems Support Division.—Richard W. Swartz, FOB–3, Room 1342, (301) 457–2117.
Technologies Management Office.—John W. Marshall, FOB–3, Room 1649, (301) 457–1943.
Telecommunications Office.—Larry J. Patin, FOB–3, Room 1101, (301) 457–1793.

BUREAU OF EXPORT ADMINISTRATION

Herbert C. Hoover Building, Room 3898, phone 482–1455, fax 482–2387

Under Secretary.—William A. Reinsch.
Deputy Under Secretary.—[Vacant], Room 3892, 482–1427.
Director, Office of Administration.—Robert Kugelman, Room 3889, 482–1900.
Assistant Secretary for Export Administration.—Sue E. Eckert, Room 3886–C, 482–5491.
Deputy Assistant Secretary for Export Administration.—Iain Baird, Room 3886–C, 482–5711.
Director, Office of Strategic Industries and Economic Security.—[Vacant], Room 3878, 482–4506.
Divisional Directors:
Defense Trade.—William J. Denk, Room 3878, 482–3695.
Strategic Analysis.—Brad I. Botwin, Room 3878, 482–4060.
Economic Analysis.—Karen Swasey, Room 3878, 482–5953.
Director, Office of Exporter Services.—Eileen Albanese, Room 1091, 482–4532.
Divisional Directors:
Exporter Counseling.—Laverne Smith, Room 1099–D, 482–4811.
Regulatory Policy.—Larry Christiansen, 482–0074.
Compliance and Special Licenses.—Deborah Kappler, 482–0062.
Export Seminar.—Rodney Menas, 482–6031.
Operations.—Cheryl Suggs, 482–3298.
Director, Office of Chemical and Biological Control and Treaty Compliance.—Steven C. Goldman, Room 2093, 482–3825.
Divisional Directors:
Treaty Compliance.—Charles Guernieri, 482–4044.
Chemical and Biological Controls.—James Seeveratnam, 482–3343.
Director, Office of Strategic Trade and Foreign Policy Controls.—James A. Lewis, Room 2628, 482–0092.
Divisional Directors:
Strategic Trade.—[Vacant], 482–5400.
Foreign Policy Controls.—Joan Roberts, 482–4252.
Director, Office of Nuclear and Missile Technology Controls.—[Vacant], Room 2631, 482–4188.

Divisional Directors:
Nuclear Technology Controls.—Joseph Chuchla, 482–4188.
Missile Technology Controls.—Raymond Jones, 482–4188.
Assistant Secretary for Export Enforcement.—[Vacant], Room 3727, 482–1561.
Deputy Assistant Secretary for Export Enforcement.—Frank Deliberti, 482–3618.
Director, Office of:
Antiboycott Compliance.—William V. Skidmore, Room 6098, 482–5914.
Export Enforcement.—Mark Menefee, Room 4616, 482–2252.
Enforcement Support.—Tom Andrunkonis, Room 4065, 482–4255.
Domestic Field Offices:
Boston.—Joseph Leone, New Boston Federal Building, Room 350, 10 Causeway Street, Boston MA 02222, (617) 565–6030, fax (617)565–6039.
Chicago.—Reid Pederson, 2400 East Devon, Suite 300, Des Plaines, IL 60018, (312) 353–6640, fax (312) 353–8008.
Dallas.—Leonard Patak, 525 Griffin Street, Room 622, Dallas, TX 75202, (214) 767–9294, fax (214) 767–9299.
Los Angeles.—Robert Schoonmaker, 2601 Main Street, Suite 310, Irvine, CA 92714–6299, (714) 251–9001, fax (714) 251–9103.
Florida.—Lyndon Berezowsky, 200 East Las Olas Boulevard, Suite 1260, Fort Lauderdale, FL 33301, (954) 356–7540, fax (954) 356–7549.
New York.—Josephine Fontana-Moran, Two Teleport Drive, Suite 201, Staten Island, NY 10311–1001, (718) 370–0070, fax (718) 370–0826.
Northern California.—Randall Sike, 96 North Third Street, Suite 250, San Jose, CA 95112–5572, (408) 291–4204, fax (408) 291–4320.
Mid-Atlantic.—Richard Sherwood, 8001 Forbes Place, Room 201, Springfield, VA 22151–0838, (703) 487–4950, fax (703) 487–4955.

ECONOMIC DEVELOPMENT ADMINISTRATION

Herbert C. Hoover Building, Room 7800, fax 482–0995

Assistant Secretary.—Phillip A. Singerman, 482–5081.
Deputy Assistant Secretary.—Wilbur F. Hawkins, 482–4067.
Office of:
Chief Counsel.—Edward Levin, Room 7001, 482–4687, fax 482–5671.
Program Operations.—Chester J. Straub, Room 7824, 482–3081, fax 501–8007.
Communications and Congressional Liaison.—Ella M. Rusinko, Room 7810, 482–5314, fax 273–4873.
Program Research and Evaluation.—Awilda R. Marquez, Room 7001–A, 482–4687, fax 482–5671.

INTERNATIONAL TRADE ADMINISTRATION

Under Secretary.—Stuart E. Eizenstat, Room 3850, 482–2867, fax 482–4821.
Deputy Under Secretary.—Timothy J. Hauser, Room 3842, 482–3917, fax 482–2925.
Counselor.—Jan H. Kalicki, Room 3427, 482–3500, fax 482–6330.
Trade Promotion Coordinating Committee Secretariat.—Jeri Jensen-Moran, Room 3051, 482–5455, fax 482–4821.
Office of:
Legislative and Intergovernmental Affairs.—Jerry L. Bonham, Room 3424, 482–3105, fax 482–0900.
Public Affairs.—James P. Desler, Room 3414, 482–3809, fax 482–5819.
Chief Counsel for International Commerce.—Eleanor Roberts Lewis, Room 5624, 482–0937, fax 482–4076.
Chief Counsel for Import Administration.—Stephen J. Powell, Room 3622, 482–0915, fax 482–4912.

ADMINISTRATION

Director of Administration.—Alan Neuschatz, Room 3827, 482–5855, fax 482–6825.
Director, Office of:
Financial Management.—Mitchell Luxenberg, Room 4012, 482–3788, fax 482–4066.
Information Resources Management.—Bernard McMahon, Room 4800, 482–3801, fax 482–4066.

Organization and Management Support.—Mary Ann McFate, Room 4001, 482–5436, fax 482–4066.

Human Resources Management.—James T. King, Jr., Room 4808, 482–3505, fax 482–4066.

U.S. AND FOREIGN COMMERCIAL SERVICE

Assistant Secretary and Director General.—Lauri J. Fitz–Pegado, Room 3802, 482–5777, fax 482–5013.

Deputy Assistant Secretary.—[Vacant], Room 3802, 482–0725, fax 482–5013.

Office of Information Systems.—[Vacant], Room 1848, 482–5291, fax 482–0251.

Human Resources Development Staff.—Scott Bozek, Room 3813, 482–2392, fax 482–1629.

Office of Planning.—[Vacant], Room 3809, 482–4996, fax 482–2391.

Deputy Assistant Secretary for:

International Operations.—Deplores R. Harrod, Room 3130, 482–6228, fax 482–3159.

Office of Foreign Service Personnel.—Nancy Kripner (acting), Room 3226, 482–2368, fax 482–1629.

Director for:

Europe.—George Knowles, Room 3130, 482–1599, fax 481–3159.

Western Hemisphere.—Richard Lenehan, Room 3130, 482–2736, fax 481–3159.

East Asia and Pacific.—Alice Davenport, Room 1229, 482–2422, fax 481–5179.

Africa, Near East and South Asia.—Jenelle Matheson (acting), Room 1223, 482–4836, fax 481–5179.

Multilateral Development Bank Operations.—Janet Thomas (acting), Room 1107, 482–3399, fax 481–0927.

Export Promotion Services.—Mary Fran Kirchner, Room 32810, 482–6220, fax 482–2526.

Director, Office of:

Trade Events Management.—[Vacant], Room 2107 482–4705, fax 482–5398.

Public/Private Initiatives.—[Vacant], Room 2116 482–4231, fax 482–0115.

Export Information and Research Services.—[Vacant], Room 2202 482–4909, fax 482–0973.

Domestic Operations.—Daniel J. McLaughlin, Room 3810, 482–4767, fax 482–0687.

Office of Operations.—[Vacant], Room 3811, 482–2975, fax 482–0687.

Regional Directors:

Eastern Region.—Thomas Cox, (410) 962–4539.

Mid–Eastern Region.—Gordon B. Thomas, (513) 684–2944.

Mid–Western Region.—Sandra Gerley, (314) 425–3300.

Western.—Keith Bovetti, (415) 705–2310.

ASSISTANT SECRETARY FOR IMPORT ADMINISTRATION

Assistant Secretary.—Robert S. LaRussa (acting), Room 3099–B, 482–1780, fax 482–0947.

Director for Policy and Analysis.—Richard Moreland, Room 3093, 482–1768, fax 482–0947.

Director for:

Office of Policy.—David Mueller, Room 3713, 482–4412, fax 2308.

Office of Accounting.—Christian Marsh, Room 3087–B, 482–2210, fax 482–4795.

Foreign Trade Zones.—John DaPonte, Room 3716, 482–2862, fax 482–0002.

Statutory Import Programs Staff.—Frank Creel, Room 4211, 482–1660, fax 482–0949.

Deputy Assistant Secretary for Antidumping Countervailing Duty Enforcement I.—Barbara Stafford, Room 3099, 482–5497, fax 482–1059.

Director, Office of:

Antidumping Countervailing Duty Enforcement I.—Susan Kuhbach, Room 3707, 482–0112, fax 482–5439.

Antidumping Countervailing Duty Enforcement II.—Gary Taverman, Room 3709, 482–0161, fax 482–4776.

Antidumping Countervailing Duty Enforcement III.—Laurie Parkhill, Room 4203, 482–4733, fax 482–1390.

Antidumping Countervailing Duty Enforcement II.—Jeffrey Bialos, Room 3099–B, 482–1780, fax 482–0947.

Antidumping Countervailing Duty Enforcement IV.—Holly Kuga, Room 3064, 482–4737, fax 482–5105.

Antidumping Countervailing Duty Enforcement V.—David Binder, Room 3086, 482–1779, fax 482–4776.

Antidumping Countervailing Duty Enforcement VI.—Barbara Tillman, Room 4012, 482–2786, fax 482–4001.

Antidumping Countervailing Duty Enforcement III.—Joseph Spetrini, Room 3069–A, 482–2104, fax 273–0957.
Antidumping Countervailing Duty Enforcement VII.—Roland MacDonald, Room 7866, 482–3793, fax 482–1388.
Antidumping Countervailing Duty Enforcement VIII.—Richard Weible, Room 7856, 482–1103, fax 482–1388.
Antidumping Countervailing Duty Enforcement IX.—Edward Yang, Room 7860, 482–0460, fax 482–1388.

ASSISTANT SECRETARY FOR MARKET ACCESS AND COMPLIANCE

Assistant Secretary.—William W. Ginsberg (acting), Room 3868–A, 482–3022, fax 482–5444.
Deputy Assistant Secretary.—[Vacant], Room 3868–A, 482–4769, fax 482–5444.
Deputy Assistant Secretary for:
Agreements Compliance.—Douglas C. Olin, Room 3413, 482–5767, fax 482–6097.
Director, Office of:
Multilateral Affairs.—Nancy Morgan, (acting), Room 3513, 482–0603, fax 482–5939.
Policy Coordination.—Peter Hale, Room 3312, 482–5341, fax 482–5545.
NAFTA Secretariat.—James Holbien, Room 2061, 482–5438, fax 482–0148.
Trade Compliance Center.—[Vacant], Room 3415, 482–1191, fax 482–6097.
Western Hemisphere.—Regina Vargo, Room 3826, 482–5324, fax 482–4736.
Latin American and the Caribbean.—Walter Bastian, Room 3025, 482–2436, fax 482–4726.
NAFTA.—[Vacant], Room 3022, 482–0305, fax 482–5865.
Inter-American Affairs.—Stephan Jacobs, Room 3025, 482–2314, fax 482–4726
Europe.—Franklin J. Vargo, Room 3863, 482–5638, fax 482–4098.
European Union and Regional Affairs.—Charles Ludolph, Room 3036, 482–5276, fax 482–2155.
Eastern Europe, Russia and Independent States.—Susanne Lotarski, Room 3319, 482–1104, fax 482–4505.
Africa and the Near East.—Judith Barnett (acting), Room 33819, 482–4925, fax 482–6083.
Africa.—Sally K. Miller, Room 2037, 482–4227, fax 482–5198.
The Near East.—Thomas Parker, Room 2029B, 482–1860, fax 482–0878.
Asia and the Pacific.—Nancy Linn Patton, Room 3203, 482–5251, fax 482–4760.
China Economic Area.—Donald Forest, Room 2317, 482–5527, fax 482–1576.
Korea and Southeast Asia.—Susan Blackman, Room 3203, 482–1695, fax 482–4760.
South Asia and Oceania.—Richard Harding, Room 2308, 482–2955, fax 482–5330.
Japan.—Marjory Searing, Room 2820, 482–4527, fax 482–0469.
Japan Trade Policy.—Philip Agress, Room 2820, 482–1820, fax 482–0469.
Japan Commercial Programs.—Robert Francis, Room 2328, 482–2425, fax 482–0469.

ASSISTANT SECRETARY FOR TRADE DEVELOPMENT

Assistant Secretary.—Raymond E. Vickery, Jr., Room 3832, 482–1461, fax 482–5697.
Deputy Assistant Secretary.—David Marchick, Room 3832, 482–1112, fax 482–5697.
Director, Office of:
Export Promotion Coordination.—Gary Enright, Room 2003, 482–4501, fax 481–1999.
Trade Information Center.—Wendy H. Smith, Room 7424, 482–0543, fax 482–4473.
Trade and Economic Analysis.—Jonathan C. Menes, Room 2825, 482–5145, fax 482–4614.
Advocacy Center.—T.S. Chung, Room 3814A, 481–3896, fax 482–3508.
Planning Coordination and Resource Management.—Robert Pearson, Room 3223, 482–4921, fax 482–4462.
Basic Industries.—Michael J. Copps, Room 4043, 482–0614, fax 482–5666.
Automotive Affairs.—Henry Misisco, Room 4036, 482–0554, fax 482–0784.
Materials, Metals, and Chemicals.—Robert Riley, Room 4039, 482–0575, fax 482–1436.
Energy, Infrastructure and Machinery.—Andrew Vitali, Room 4056, 482–0169, fax 482–5361.
Technology and Aerospace Industries.—Ellis R. Mottur, Room 2800A, 482–1872, fax 482–0856.
Aerospace.—Sally H. Bath, Room 2128, 482–1229, fax 482–0856.
Computer and Business Equipment.—John McPhee, Room 2806, 482–0572, fax 482–0952.
Microelectronics, Medical Equipment and Instrumentation.—Jeffrey Gren, Room 1015, 482–2587, fax 482–0975.

Telecommunications.—Robin Layton, Room 4324, 482–4466, fax 482–5834.
Service Industries and Finance.—Graham Whatley (acting), Room 1128, 482–5261, fax 482–4775.
Export Trading Company Affairs.—W. Dawn Busby, Room 1800, 48–5131, fax 482–1790.
Finance.—[Vacant], Room 1104, 482–3277, fax 482–5702.
Service Industries.—Josephine Ludolph, Room 1124, 482–3575, fax 482–2669.
Textiles, Apparel and Consumer Goods Industries.—Troy H. Cribb, Room 3001A, 482–3737, fax 482–2331.
Textiles and Apparel.—D. Michael Hutchinson, Room 3100, 482–5078, fax 482–2331.
Consumer Goods.—J. Hayden Boyd, Room 3013, 482–0337, fax 482–3981.
Environmental Technologies Exports.—Anne L. Alonzo, Room 1101, 482–5225, fax 482–5665.
Tourism Industries.—Leslie R. Doggett, Room 1860, 482–0140, fax 482–4279.

MINORITY BUSINESS DEVELOPMENT AGENCY

Director.—Joan Parrott–Fonseca, Room 5053, 482–5061, fax 501–4698.
Deputy Director.—Paul R. Webber, IV (acting), Room 5053, 482–2654.
Assistant Director for:
Operations.—Paul R. Webber, IV, Room 5087, 482–3237.
External Affairs.—Barbara J. Maddox, Room 5063, 482–3007.

NATIONAL OCEANIC AND ATMOSPHERIC ADMINISTRATION

Under Secretary for Oceans and Atmosphere.—Donald J. Baker, Room 5128, 482–3436, fax 482–8203.
Assistant Secretary.—Terri Garcia (acting), Room 5804, 482–3567.
Deputy Under Secretary.—Diana H. Josephson, Room 5810, 482–5135.
Chief Scientist.—Al Beeton, Room 5128, 482–2977.
Deputy Assistant Secretary.—Will E. Martin, Room 5805, 482–6076.
Assistant Administrator for:
Fisheries.—Rolland A. Schmitten, (301) 713–2239, fax (301) 713–2258.
Oceanic and Atmospheric Research.—Ned A. Ostenso, (301) 713–2458, fax (301) 713–5167.
Ocean Services and Coastal Zone Management.—William S. Wilson, (301) 606–4140.
Weather Services.—Elbert W. Friday, Jr., (301) 713–0689.
Satellite and Information Services.—Robert S. Winokur, (301) 457–5115.
General Counsel.—Monica Medina, 482–4080.
Chief Financial Officer and Chief Administrative Officer.—Joseph Kammerer, Room 6811, 482–2291.
Director, Office of Public and Constituents Affairs.—Lori A. Arguelles, Room 6203, 482–4190.
NOAA Corps Operations.—Rear Admiral Sigmund R. Peterson, Room 505, 11400 Rockville Pike, Rockville, MD, (301) 412–0110, fax (301) 413–0410.
Sustainable Development and Intergovernmental Affairs.—John K. Bullard, 482–3384.

PATENT AND TRADEMARK OFFICE

2021 Jefferson Davis Highway, Arlington, VA 22202
phone (703) 305–8600, fax (703) 305–8664

Assistant Secretary of Commerce and Commissioner of Patents and Trademarks.—Bruce A. Lehman, Suite 906, Crystal Park 2, 2121 Crystal Drive, Arlington, VA, (703) 305–8600.
Executive Assistant to the Assistant Secretary and Commissioner.—Paul Salmon, Crystal Park 2, Suite 906, 2121 Crystal Drive, Arlington, VA (703) 305–8600.
Acting Deputy Assistant Secretary of Commerce and Acting Deputy Commissioner of Patents and Trademarks.—Lawrence J. Goffney, Jr., Crystal Park 2, Suite 910, 212 Crystal Drive, Arlington, VA (703) 305–8700.
Chief Administrative Patent Judge of the Board of Patents Appeals and Interferences.—Bruce H. Stoner, Jr., Room 10C01, Crystal Gateway 2, (703) 308–9797.

Vice Chief Administrative Patent Judge.—Richard Schafer, Room 10C01, Crystal Gateway 2, (703) 308–9797.

Vice Chief Administrative Patent Judge.—Gary V. Harkcom, Room 10C01, Crystal Gateway 2, (703) 308–9797.

Administrative Patent Judges:

Neal E. Abrams, Lee Barrett, Ian Calvert, James T. Carmichael, Marc L. Caroff, Irwin C. Cohen, Murriel Crawford, Mary F. Downey, Joan Ellis, Michael R. Fleming, Charles F. Frankfort, Bradley R. Garris, Teddy Gron, Kenneth W. Hairston, Adriene L. Hanlon, Edward C. Kimlin, Errol A. Krass, Jameson Lee, William E. Lyddane, John C. Martin, Harrison McCandlish, Anthony R. McFarlane, Fred E. McKelvey, John McQuade, James M. Meister, Edward J. Meros, Andrew H. Metz, Jeffrey Nase, Terry J. Owens, Chung Pak, William F. Pate, III, Jerry Smith, John D. Smith, Ronald H. Smith, William F. Smith, Michael Sofocleous, Lawrence J. Staab, Joan Thierstein, James D. Thomas, Richard Torczon, Stanley M. Urynowicz, Thomas A. Waltz, Charles Warren, Cameron Weiffenbach, Elizabeth C. Weimar, Sherman Winters, Crystal Gateway 2, Room 10C01, (703) 308–9797.

Deputy Associate Commissioner for Administration and Quality Services.—Theresa A. Brelsford, Suite 819,Crystal Park 1, 2011 Crystal Drive, Arlington VA, (703) 305–9100, fax (703) 305–9265.

Assistant Commissioner for Patents.—[Vacant], Suite 910 Crystal Park 2, 2121 Crystal Drive, Arlington VA, (703) 305–8800, fax (703) 305–8825.

Deputy Assistant Commissioner for:

Patents.—Edward R. Kazenske, Suite 910, Crystal Park 2, 2121 Crystal Drive, Arlington VA, (703) 305–8800, fax (703) 305–8825.

Patent Policy and Projects.—Stephen G. Kunin, Suite 910, Crystal Park 2, 2121 Crystal Drive, Arlington VA, (703) 305–8850, fax (703) 305–8825.

Administrator for Search and Information Resources Administration.—Fred Schmidt, Suite 700, Crystal Park 3, 2231 Crystal Drive, Arlington VA (703) 308–6900.

Patent Group Directors:

1110.—John E. Kittle, Room 8D19 (703) 308–1495, fax 305–3600.

1200.—Richard V. Fisher, Room 3D09, (703) 308–0193, fax 308–4556.

1300.—John Terapane, Room 5D19, (703) 308–1193, fax 305–3601.

1500.—Theodore Morris, Room 7D09, (703) 308–2359, fax 305–3596.

1800.—John J. Doll, Room 12A05, (703) 308–1123, fax 305–7230.

2100.—Stewart J. Levy, Room 11D37, (703) 308–0658, fax 305–3431.

2200.—Robert E. Garrett, Room 4B03, (703) 306–4174, fax 306–4195.

2300.—Joseph Rolla, Room 4A23, (703) 305–9700, fax 308–5355.

2400.—Gerald Goldberg, Room 6A27, (703) 308–5543, fax 308–6743.

2500.—Janice A. Howell, Room 3A2, (703) 308–0530, fax 305–3594.

2600.—Nicholas Godici, Room 8A23, (703) 305–4800, fax 305–9508.

3100.—Margaret Focarine (acting) Room 8D19, (703) 308–1134, fax 305–7687.

3200.—Ethel Rollins-Cross, Room 10A12, (703) 308–1078, fax 305–3579.

3300.—John L. Love, Room 6D37, (703) 308–0873, fax 305–3590.

3400.—Donald G. Kelly, Room 3D19, (703) 308–0975, fax 305–3463.

3500.—Al Lawrence Smith, Room 3D19, (703) 308–1200, fax 305–3597.

Assistant Commissioner for Trademarks.—Philip G. Hampton, II, Suite 10B10, South Tower, 2900 Crystal Drive, Arlington VA, (703) 308–8900, fax 308–7220.

Deputy Assistant Commissioner for Trademarks.—Robert M. Anderson, Suite 10B10, South Tower, 2900 Crystal Drive, Arlington VA &03) 308–8900, fax 308–7220.

Chief Administrative Trademark Judge for the Trademark Trial and Appeal Board.—J. David Sams, Suite 9A03, South Tower, 2900 Crystal Drive, Arlington VA (03) 308–9300 ext. 200.

Administrative Trademark Judges.—Carlisle Walters, Room 9D09, 308–9300 ext. 154; Ellen Seeherman, Room 9A09, ext. 206; Robert F. Cissel, Room 9A21, ext. 201; Paula T. Hairston, Room 9A05, ext. 222; G. Douglas Hohein, Room 9D01, ext. 203; Janet E. Rice, Room 9A07, ext. 205; Rany L. Simms, Room 9A25, ext. 207; Elmer W. Hanak III, Room 9A17, ext. 202; T. Jeffrey Quinn, Room 9A13, ext. 204.

Solicitor.—Nancy J. Linck, Suite 918, Crystal Park 2, 2121 Crystal Drive, Arlington VA, (703) 305–9035, fax 305–9373.

Deputy Solicitor.—Albin F. Drost, Suite 918, Crystal Park 2, 2121 Crystal Drive, Arlington VA (703) 305–9035, fax 305–9373.

Associate and Assistant Solicitors:

Kevin G. Baer, David Ball, Karen A. Buchanan, Thaddeus J. Burns, Scott A. Chambers, Maryann Capria, Kenneth R. Corsello, Linda M. Isacson, Craig R. Kaufman, Kevin T. Kramer, Joseph G. Piccolo, Nancy C. Slutter, John Whealan, Suite 918, Crystal Park 2, 2121 Crystal Drive, Arlington VA (703) 305–9035, fax 305–9373.

Associate Commissioner and Chief Information Officer.—Bradford R. Huther, Suite 904, Crystal Park 2, 2121 Crystal Drive, Arlington VA (703) 305–9200.

Chief Information Officer.—Dennis Shaw, Suite 1004, Crystal Park 2, 2121 Crystal Drive, (703) 305–9400.

Administrator of the Office of Legislative and International Affairs.—Robert Stoll, Suite 902, Crystal Park 2, 2121 Crystal Drive, Arlington VA (703) 305–9300, fax 305–8885.

Attorneys:

Lynne G. Beresford, Lois Boland, Peter Fowler, H. Dieter Hoinkes, Michael Keplinger, Keith Kupferschmid, Linda Louris, Howard Richman, Lee Schroeder, G. Lee Skillington, Timothy Trainer, Jo Ellen Urban, Richard Wilder, Alice Zalik, Suite 902, 2121 Crystal Drive, Crystal Park 2, Arlington VA (703) 305–9300, fax 305–8885.

Director of Congressional Affairs.—Matthew Pappas, Suite 902, 2121 Crystal Drive, Crystal Park 2, Arlington VA, (703) 305–9300, fax 305–8885.

Congressional Liaison.—Janie F. Cooksey, Suite 902, 2121 Crystal Drive, Crystal Park 2, Arlington VA, (703) 305–9300, fax, 305–8885.

Director, Office of Public Affairs.—Richard Maulsby, Suite 100, Crystal Park 2, 2121 Crystal Drive, Arlington VA, (703) 305–8341.

TECHNOLOGY ADMINISTRATION

Under Secretary.—Mary L. Good, Room 4824, 482–1575.

Deputy Under Secretary.—Gary Bachula, Room 4822, 482–1091.

Director, Congressional Affairs.—Judy Jablow, Room 4822, 482–2123.

Staff Director.—Joyce S. Hasty, Room 4823, 482–5804.

Director, Public Affairs, PNGV.—Virginia Miller, Room 7060, 482–6030.

Chief Counsel.—Mark Mohannon, Room 4835, 482–1984.

OFFICE FOR TECHNOLOGY POLICY

Assistant Secretary.—Graham Mitchell, Room 4814–C, 482–1581, fax 482–4817.

Deputy Assistant Secretary.—Kelly Carnes, Room 4814–C, 482–1403.

Director, Office of:

Strategic Planning, Public Affairs.—Cheryl Mendonsa, Room 4814–C, 482–3037.

International Policy.—Phyllis Genther–Yoshida (acting), Room 4817, 482–5150.

Manufacturing Competitiveness.—Cary Gravett, Room 4841, 482–5524.

Technology Competitiveness.—Jon Paugh, Room 4418, 482–6101.

NATIONAL INSTITUTE OF STANDARDS AND TECHNOLOGY

Director.—Raymond Kammer, Administration, Room A1134, (301) 975–2300.

Deputy Director.—Robert E. Hebner (acting), Administration, Room A1134, (301) 975–2300.

Deputy Chief Counsel.—Michael R. Rubin, Administration, Room A813, (301) 975–2308.

Director for Congressional and Legislative Affairs.—Esther C. Cassidy, Administration, Room A1111, (301) 975–3080.

Director, Office of:

National Quality Program.—Harry S. Hertz, Administration, Room A537, (301) 975–2360.

Program Office.— Elaine Bunten–Mines, Administration, Room A1000, (301) 975–2667.

Human Resources Management.—Ellen Dowd, Administration, Room A123, (301) 975–3000.

Civil Rights.—Alvin Lewis, Building 820, Room 665, (301) 975–2037.

International and Academic Affairs.—B. Stephen Carpenter, Administration, Room A505, (301) 975–3069.

NIST/Boulder Laboratories.—David W. Norcross, Building One, Boulder, CO, (303) 497–3237.

Chief Financial Officer.—Hratch Semerjian (acting), Administration, Room A1134, (301) 975–2300, fax (301) 948–5603.

Director, Advanced Technology Program.—Lura Powell, Administration, Room A603, (301) 975–5187.

Deputy Director, Advanced Technology Program.—Brian Belanger, Administration, Room A603, (301) 975–5187, fax (301) 869–1150.

Director, Manufacturing Extension Partnership.—Kevin Carr, Building 301, Room C121, (301) 975–5454.

Deputy Director, Manufacturing Extension Partnership.—Roger Kilmer, Building 301, Room C121, (301) 975–5454, fax (301) 963–6556.

Director of Technology Services.—Peter Heydemann, Building 820, Room 306, (301) 975–4500.

Deputy Director of Technology Services.—David Edgerly, Building 820, Room 306, (301) 975–4500, fax (301) 975–2183.

Director of Administration.—Jorge Urrutia, Administration, Room A1105, (301) 975–2390.

Deputy Director of Administration.—Karl Bell, Administration, Room A1105, (301) 975–2390, fax (301) 926–7203.

Chief, Public and Business Affairs.—Matthew Heyman, Administration, Room A903, (301) 975–2758, fax (301) 926–1630.

Director, Electronics and Electrical Engineering Laboratory.—Judson French, Metrology, Room B358, (301) 975–2220.

Deputy Director, Electronics and Electrical Engineering Laboratory.—Alan Cookson (acting), Metrology, Room B358, (301) 975–2220, fax (301) 975–4091.

Director, Manufacturing Engineering Laboratory.—Richard Jackson, Metrology, Room B322, (301) 975–3400.

Deputy Director, Manufacturing Engineering Laboratory.—Howard Bloom, Metrology, Room B322, (301) 975–3400, fax (301) 948–5668.

Director, Chemical Science and Technology Laboratory.— Hratch Semerjian, Chemistry, Room A317, (301) 975–3143.

Deputy Director, Chemical Science and Technology Laboratory.—William Koch, Chemistry, Room A317, (301) 975–3143, fax (301) 975–3845.

Director, Physics Laboratory.—Katharine Gebbie, Physics, Room B160, (301) 975–4200.

Deputy Director, Physics Laboratory.—William Ott, Physics, Room B160, (301) 975–4200, fax (301) 975–3038.

Director, Materials Science and Engineering Laboratory.—[Vacant].

Deputy Director, Materials Science and Engineering Laboratory.—Dale Hall (acting), Room B309, (301) 975–5658, fax (301) 926–8349.

Director, Building and Fire Research Laboratory.—Richard Wright, III, Building 226, Room B216, (301) 975–5900.

Deputy Director, Building and Fire Research Laboratory.—Jack E. Snell, Building 226, Room B216, (301) 975–5900, fax (301) 975–4032.

Director, Information Technology Laboratory.—Shukri Wakid, Technology, Room A231, (301) 975–2900.

Deputy Director, Information Technology Laboratory Deputy Director.—[Vacant], fax (301) 840–1357.

NATIONAL TELECOMMUNICATIONS AND INFORMATION ADMINISTRATION

Herbert C. Hoover Building, Room 4898, fax 482–1635

Assistant Secretary for Communications and Information.—Larry Irving, 482–1840.

Deputy Assistant Secretary.—Shirl G. Kinney, 482–1830.

Director, Congressional Affairs.—Kristan Van Hook, 482–1551.

Chief Counsel.—Barbara Wellbery, Room 4713, 482–1816, fax 482–3244.

Director, Public Affairs.—Paige Darden (acting), Room 4897, 482–7002, fax 482–1635.

Associate Administrator:

Office of Telecommunications and Information Applications.—Bernadette McGuire–Rivera, Room 4096, 482–5802, fax 501–8009.

International Affairs.—Jack Gleason (acting), Room 4701, 482–1866, fax 482–1865.

Policy Analysis and Development.—Kathryn Brown, Room 4725, 482–1880, fax 482–6173.

Spectrum Management.—Richard D. Parlow, Room 4099, 482–1850, fax 482–4396.

Office of Policy Coordination Management.—[Vacant], Room 4892, 482–1835, fax 482–0979.

Director, Institute for Telecommunications Sciences.—William F. Utlaut, Boulder CO, (303) 497–3500, fax 303 497–5993.

NATIONAL TECHNICAL INFORMATION SERVICE

FORBES Building, 5285 Port Royal Road, Room 200, Springfield VA 22161

(703) 482–4093

Director.—Donald R. Johnson, (703) 487–4636.
Deputy Director.—Donald Corrigan.

PRESIDENT'S EXPORT COUNCIL

Authorized by Executive Orders 12131, 12534, 12551 12610, 12692, 12774, 12869, and 12974 (May 1979 through September 1995).

Room 2015–B, Department of Commerce 20230, (202) 482–1124.

Chairman.—C. Michael Armstrong, Chairman of the Board and Chief Executive Officer, GM Hughes Electronics Corporation.

Vice Chairman.—Elizabeth J. Coleman, Chairman of the Board, Maidenform, Inc.

Private Sector Members:

J. Joe Adorjan, President, and Chief Operating Officer, Borg-Warner Security Corporation.
John J. Barry, International President, International Brotherhood of Electrical Workers.
Carol Bartz, Chairman and Chief Executive Officer, Autodesk, Inc.
George F. Becker, International President, United Steelworkers of America.
Frank Biondi, President and Chief Executive Officer, MCA, Inc.
Edgar Bronfman, Jr., President and Chief Executive Officer, Joseph E. Seagram and Sons, Inc.
Dean L. Buntrock, Chairman and Chief Executive Officer, WMX Technologies, Inc.
John F. Carlson, Retired, Chairman and Chief Executive Officer, CRAY Research, Inc.
Susan Corrales-Diaz, President and Chief Executive Officer, Systems Integrated.
Lawrence Ellison, Chairman, President, and Chief Executive Officer, Oracle Corporation.
Ellen R. Gordon, President, Tootsie Roll Industries, Inc.
Joseph T. Gorman, Chairman and Chief Executive Officer, TRW, Inc.
Steven Green, Chairman and Chief Executive Officer, The CEENIS Property Fund.
Ray R. Irani, Chairman, President, and Chief Executive Officer, Occidental Petroleum Corporation.
Michael H. Jordan, Chairman and Chief Executive Officer, Westinghouse Electric Corporation.
Thomas G. Labrecque, Chairman and Chief Executive Officer, Chase Manhattan Corporation.
Les McCraw, Chairman and Chief Executive Officer, Fluor Corporation.
John F. McDonnell, Chairman, McDonnell, Douglas Corporation.
John J. Moores, Chairman, JMI, Inc.
Richard Notebart, Chairman and Chief Executive Officer, Ameritech.
Dennis J. Picard, Chairman and Chief Executive Officer, Raytheon Company.
Safi Qureshey, Chairman and Chief Executive Officer, AST Research.
Frank Savage, Chairman, Alliance Capital Management International.
Kathryn C. Turner, Chairman and Chief Executive Officer, Standards Technology, Inc.
Thomas N. Urban, President, Pioneer Hi-Bred International, Inc.
C.J. Wang, Ph.D., Chairman, International Corporation of America.

Congressional Members: Eva Clayton, Representative from North Carolina. Richard Gephardt, Representative from Missouri. Ernest F. Hollings, Senator from South Carolina. James M. Jeffords, Senator from Vermont. Nancy L. Johnson, Representative from Connecticut. Nancy L. Kassebaum, Senator from Kansas. Daniel P. Moynihan, Senator from New York. Charles B. Rangel, Representative from New York. Bill Richardson, Representative from New Mexico. Paul S. Sarbanes, Senator from Maryland.

Executive Branch Members:

William H. Daley, Secretary of Commerce.
Martin Kamack, President and Chairman of Export-Import Bank of the United States.
Madleine Albright, Secretary of State.
Charlene Barshefsky, United States Trade Representative. Designate.
Philip Lader, Administrator, U.S. Small Business Administration.
Alexis Herman, Secretary of Labor.
Dan Glickman, Secretary of Agriculture.
Robert Rubin, Secretary of the Treasury.

Staff:

Executive Director.—Stuart E. Eizenstat, Under Secretary of Commerce for International Trade.

Staff Director/Executive Secretary.—Sylvia Lino Prosak.

DEPARTMENT OF DEFENSE

The Pentagon 20301–1155, phone (703) 545–6700

fax (703) 695–3362/693–2161, www.dtic.dla.mil/defenselink

WILLIAM S. COHEN, Secretary of Defense; nominated by President William Clinton; confirmed by the U.S. Senate and took the oath of office on January 24, 1997; born August 28, 1940; B.A. in Latin from Bowdoin College; LL.B. cum laude from Boston University Law School; served three terms in the House of Representatives from Maine's Second Congressional District (1973–79) and three terms in the U.S. Senate for the State of Maine (1979–97).

JOHN WHITE, Deputy Secretary of Defense, nominated by President William Clinton; confirmed by the U.S. Senate and sworn in on June 22, 1995; M.A. and Ph.D. in economics from the Maxwell Graduate School at Syracuse University, and a B.S. in industrial and labor relations from Cornell University; most recently served as the chairman of the Commission on Roles and Missions for the Armed Forces; served as director of the Center for Business and Government at the Kennedy School of Government at Harvard University; general manager of the Integration and Systems Products Division and vice president of the Eastman Kodak Company (1988–92); CEO and chairman of the board of Interactive Systems Corporation (1981–88); deputy director of the Office of Management and Budget (1978–81); Assistant Secretary of Defense for Manpower, Reserve Affairs and Logistics (1977–78); senior vice president, Rand Corporation (1968–77).

OFFICE OF THE SECRETARY

Pentagon, Room 3E880, 20301–1000, phone (703) 695–5261, fax (703) 697–9080

Secretary of Defense.—William S. Cohen.

OFFICE OF THE DEPUTY SECRETARY

Pentagon, Room 3E944, 20301–1000, phone (703) 695–6352

Deputy Secretary of Defense.—John White.

EXECUTIVE SECRETARIAT

Pentagon, Room 3E880, 20301–1000, phone (703) 695–0825, fax (703) 697–9080

Executive Secretary.—Col. James N. Mattis, USMC.

UNDER SECRETARY OF DEFENSE FOR ACQUISITION AND TECHNOLOGY

Pentagon, Room 3E933, 20301, phone (703) 695–2381

Under Secretary.—Paul G. Kaminski.
  Principal Deputy Under Secretary.—Noel Longuemare.
  Director, Defense Research and Engineering.—Anita K. Jones.
    Assistant to the Secretary of Defense for Nuclear and Chemical and Biological Defense Programs.—Harold R. Smith, Jr.
  Deputy Under Secretary for—
    Acquisition Reform.—*[Vacant].*
    Advanced Technology.—John M. Bachkosky.
    Environmental Security.—Sherri W. Goodman.
    Logistics.—John F. Phillips.
    Space.—Robert V. Davis.
    International & Commercial Programs.—Paul J. Hopper.
    Industrial Affairs & Installations.—John B. Goodman.
  Director, Small and Disadvantaged Business Utilization.—Robert L. Neal, Jr.

UNDER SECRETARY OF DEFENSE FOR POLICY
Pentagon, Room 4E808, 20301–2000, phone (703) 697–7200

Under Secretary.—Walter Slocombe.
Principal Deputy Under Secretary.—Jan M. Lodal.
Assistant Secretary of Defense for—
International Security Affairs.—Franklin D. Kramer.
International Security Policy.—Franklin C. Miller (acting).
Strategy and Requirements.—Edward L. Warner III.
Special Operations and Low-Intensity Conflict.—H. Allen Holmes.
Director, Net Assessment.—Andrew W. Marshall.
Defense Advisor, US Mission NATO.—[Vacant].
Deputy to the USD(P) for Policy Suport.—Linton Wells II.

COMPTROLLER
Pentagon, Room 3E822, 20301–1100, phone (703) 695–3237

Under Secretary/Chief Financial Officer.—John J. Hamre.
Principal Deputy Under Secretary.—Alice C. Maroni.
Director, Program Analysis and Evaluation.—William J. Lynn III.

PERSONNEL AND READINESS
Pentagon, Room 3E764, 20301–4000, phone (703) 695–5254.

Under Secretary.—Edwin Dorn.
Principal Deputy Under Secretary.—Fred Pang.
Assistant Secretary for—
Force Management Policy.—Fred Pang.
Health Affairs.—[Vacant].
Reserve Affairs.—Deborah R. Lee.
Deputy Under Secretary for—
Readiness.—L. Finch.
Program Integration.—Jeanne Fites.

GENERAL COUNSEL
Pentagon, Room 3E980, 20301–1600, phone (703) 695–3341, fax (703) 614–9789

General Counsel.—Judith A. Miller.
Principal Deputy General Counsel.—F. Whitten Peters (703) 697–7248.

OPERATIONAL TEST AND EVALUATION
Pentagon, Room 3E318, 20301–1700, phone (703) 697–3654, fax (703) 693–5248

Director.—Philip E. Coyle III.

INSPECTOR GENERAL
400 Army Navy Drive, Room 1000, Arlington VA 22202–2884
phone (703) 695–4249, fax (703) 693–4749, hotline (703) 693–5080

Inspector General.—Eleanor Hill.

ASSISTANT SECRETARY FOR COMMAND, CONTROL, COMMUNICATIONS AND INTELLIGENCE (C^3I)
Pentagon, Room 3E172, 20301–3040, phone (703) 695–0348

Assistant Secretary.—Emmett Paige, Jr.

ASSISTANT SECRETARY FOR LEGISLATIVE AFFAIRS
Pentagon, Room 3E966, 20301–1300, phone (703) 697–6210, fax (703) 697–8299

Assistant Secretary.—Sandra K. Stuart.

ASSISTANT TO THE SECRETARY OF DEFENSE FOR INTELLIGENCE OVERSIGHT

Crown Ridge Building, 4035 Ridge Top Road, Suite 210, Fairfax VA 22030 phone (703) 275–6575

Assistant to the Secretary.—Walter Jajko.

ASSISTANT SECRETARY FOR PUBLIC AFFAIRS

Pentagon, Room 2E800, 20301–1400, phone (703) 697–9312, fax (703) 695–1149 public inquiries (703) 697–5737

Assistant Secretary.—Kenneth H. Bacon.

ADMINISTRATION AND MANAGEMENT

Pentagon, Room 3D972, 20301–1950, phone (703) 695–4436

Director.—David O. Cooke.

DEPARTMENT OF DEFENSE FIELD ACTIVITIES

AMERICAN FORCES INFORMATION SERVICE

601 North Fairfax Street Room 300, EFC Plaza, Alexandria VA 22314–2007 phone (703) 428–1200

Director.—Jordan E. Rizer.
Deputy Director.—Capt. W.R. Harlow, USN, Room 300, (703) 428–1202.
General Counsel.—M. Filice, Room 300, (703) 428–1204.
Director for Armed Forces Radio and Television Services.—Melvin W. Russell, Room 360, (703) 428–0616.

CIVILIAN HEALTH AND MEDICAL PROGRAM OF THE UNIFORMED SERVICES

Director.—Capt. John E. Montgomery, MSC, USN, phone (303) 361–1313.

DEPARTMENT OF DEFENSE EDUCATION ACTIVITY

4040 North Fairfax Drive, Arlington VA 22303–1635 school information (703) 696–4236

Director.—Dr. Lillian Gonzalez.
Deputy Director.—Bartley A. Lagomarsino, (703) 696–4545.
General Counsel.—Robert Terzian, (703) 696–4387.

DEPARTMENT OF DEFENSE HUMAN RESOURCES FIELD ACTIVITY

1400 Key Boulevard, Suite B200, Arlington VA 22209–5144, phone (703) 696–2788

Director.—Edwin Dorn
Deputy Director.—Jeanne Fites.

DEFENSE MEDICAL PROGRAMS ACTIVITY

Skyline 6, 5109 Leesburg Pike, Suite 502, Falls Church VA 22041–3201 phone (703) 697–2113

Director.—Edward D. Martin, MD.

DEFENSE PRISONER OF WAR/MISSING PERSONNEL OFFICE

1745 Jefferson Davis Highway, Suite 800, Arlington VA 22201

Director.—James S. Wold, USAF (Retired).
Deputy Director.—Alan Liotta.

DEFENSE TECHNOLOGY SECURITY ADMINISTRATION

400 Army Navy Drive, Suite 300, Arlington VA 22202, phone (703) 604–5215

Director.—David S. Tarbell.
Deputy Director.—Peter M. Sullivan.
Assistant Director.—George Menas, (703) 604–5912.
Director for—
Policy.—Frank Bray, (703) 604–8032.
License Directorate.—James P. Woody, (703) 604–4859.
Resource Management.—Howard P. Ady III, (703) 604–4836.
Technology Security Operations.—F. Michael Maloof, (703) 604–5926.
Technology Directorate.—Clarence M. Griffin, (703) 604–5217.

ECONOMIC ADJUSTMENT

400 Army Navy Drive, Suite 200, Arlington VA 22202–2884, phone (703) 604–6020

Director.—Paul J. Dempsey.
Deputy Director.—Helene M. O'Connor (acting).
Western Region Manager.—Richard R. Kinnier, (206) 524–1845.

WASHINGTON HEADQUARTERS SERVICES

Pentagon, Room 3D972, 20301, phone (703) 695–4436

Director.—David O. Cooke.
Director for—
Budget and Finance.—Joe Friedl, Jr., Room 3B287, (703) 697–6760.
Correspondence and Directives.—Larry Curry, Room 3B946, (703) 687–8261.
Federal Voting Assistance Office.—Phyllis J. Taylor, Room 1B457, (703) 695–0663.
Information Operations and Reports.—Robert Drake, Room 1204, Crystal Gateway No. 3, 1215 Jefferson Davis Highway, Arlington VA 22202, (703) 604–4569.
Personnel and Security.—Al Papenfus, Room 3B347, (703) 697–1703.
Real Estate and Facilities.—L. Walter Freeman, Room 3C345, (703) 697–7241.
General Counsel.—Thomas R. Brooks, Room 1E197, (703) 693–7374.

JOINT CHIEFS OF STAFF

OFFICE OF THE CHAIRMAN

Pentagon, Room 2E872, 20318–0001, phone (703) 697–9121

Chairman.—Gen. John M. Shalikashvili, USA.
Vice Chairman.—Gen. Joseph W. Ralston, USAF, Room 2E860, (703) 614–8948, (703) 614–2500.
Assistant to Chairman, Joint Chiefs of Staff.—LtGen. Richard B. Myers, USAF, Room 2E868, (703) 695–4605.

JOINT STAFF

Director.—Vice Adm. Dennis Blair, USN, Room 2E936, (703) 614–5221.
Vice Director.—Maj. Gen. Stephen T. Rippe, USA, Room 2E936, (703) 614–5223.
Director for—
Manpower and Personnel, J–1.—Brig. Gen. Patrick O. Adams, USAF, Room 1E948, (703) 697–6098.

Intelligence, J–2.—Maj. Gen. James C. King, USA, Room 1E884, (703) 697–9773.
Operations, J–3.—Lt. Gen. Peter Pace, USMC, Room 2D874, (703) 697–3702.
Logistics, J–4.—Lt. Gen. John J. Cusick, USA, Room 2E828, (703) 697–7000.
Strategic Plans and Policy, J–5.—Vice Adm. John S. Redd, USN, Room 2E996, (703) 695–5618.
Command, Control, Communications and Computer Systems, J–6.—Lt. Gen. Douglas D. Buchholz, USA, Room 2D860, (703) 695–6478.
Operational Plans and Interoperability, J–7.—Maj. Gen. David A. Sawyer, USAF, Room 2B865A, (703) 697–9031.
Force Structure, Resource, and Assessment, J–8.—Lt. Gen. David J. McCloud, USAF, Room 1E962, (703) 697–8853.

DEFENSE AGENCIES

BALLISTIC MISSILE DEFENSE ORGANIZATION

Pentagon, Room 1E1081, 20301–7100, phone (703) 695–8040

Director.—Lt. Gen. L. Lyles, USAF, (703) 693–3025.
Deputy Director.—Rear Adm. R. West, USN, (703) 695–7060.

DEFENSE ADVANCED RESEARCH PROJECTS AGENCY

3701 North Fairfax Drive, Arlington VA 22203–1714, phone (703) 696–2444

Director.—Larry Lynn (acting).
Deputy Director.—Dr. H. Lee Buchanan III, (703) 696–2402.

DEFENSE COMMISSARY AGENCY

Fort Lee VA 23801–6300, phone (804) 734–8721

Director.—Maj. Gen. Richard E. Beale, Jr., USA, (Retired).
Chief Executive Officer.—Charles M. Wiker.

LIAISON OFFICE

Pentagon, Room 5E487, 20330–5130, phone (703) 614–9225

Director.—Daniel W. Sclater.

DEFENSE CONTRACT AUDIT AGENCY

8725 John J. Kingman Road, Suite 2135, Fort Belvoir VA 22060–6219
phone (703) 767–3200

Director.—William H. Reed.
Deputy Director.—Michael J. Thibault, (703) 767–3272.

DEFENSE FINANCE AND ACCOUNTING SERVICE

Crystal Mall Building No. 3, 1931 Jefferson Davis Highway, Arlington VA 22240–5191
phone (703) 607–2616

Director.—Richard F. Keevey, Room 425.
Principal Deputy Director.—Gary W. Amlin, Room 425, (703) 607–1467.

DEFENSE INFORMATION SYSTEMS AGENCY

701 South Court House Road, Arlington VA 22204–2199, phone (703) 607–6020

Director.—Lt. Gen. Albert J. Edmonds, USAF, Room 4222, (703) 607–6001.

Deputy Director.—Maj. Gen. D.J. Kelley, USA, Room 4222, (703) 607–6010.

DEFENSE INTELLIGENCE AGENCY

Pentagon, Room 3E258, 20340–1001, phone (703) 695–0071

Director.—Lt. Gen. Patrick M. Hughes, USA.
Deputy Director.—Jeremy C. Clark, Room 3E258, (703) 697–5128.

DEFENSE INVESTIGATIVE SERVICE

1340 Braddock Place, Alexandria VA 22314–1651, phone (703) 325–5324

Director.—Margaret R. Munson.

DEFENSE LEGAL SERVICES AGENCY

Pentagon, Room 3E980, 20301–1600, phone (703) 695–3341

Director/General Counsel.—Judith A. Miller.
Principal Deputy Director.—F. Whitten Peters, (703) 697–7248.

DEFENSE LOGISTICS AGENCY

8725 John J. Kingman Road, Suite 0119, Ft. Belvoir VA 22060–6221 phone (703) 767–4012

Director.—Lt. Gen. George T. Babbitt, USAF, (703) 767–5200.
Principal Deputy Director.—Maj. Gen. Ray E. McCoy, USA, (703) 767–5222.

DEFENSE SECURITY ASSISTANCE AGENCY

1111 Jefferson Davis Highway, Suite 303, Arlington VA 22202, phone (703) 604–6604

Director.—Lt. Gen. Thomas G. Rhame, USA.
Deputy Director.—H. Diehl McKalip, (703) 604–6606.

DEFENSE SPECIAL WEAPONS AGENCY

6801 Telegraph Road, Alexandria VA 22310, phone (703) 325–7004

Director.—Maj. Gen. G.L. Curtin, USAF, Room 200.
Deputy Director.—Dr. G.W. Ullrich 2024, (703) 325–7300.

NATIONAL IMAGERY AND MAPPING AGENCY

8613 Lee Highway, Fairfax VA 22031–2137, phone (703) 275–5900

Director.—Rear Adm. J.J. Dantone, Jr., USN (acting).
Deputy Director of—
Operations.—Leo Hazlewood.
Systems and Technology.—William Mularie.
Corporate Affairs.—W. Douglas Smith.

NATIONAL SECURITY AGENCY/CENTRAL SECURITY SERVICE

Ft. George G. Meade, MD 20755, phone (301) 688–6311

Director.—Lt. Gen. Kenneth A. Minihan, USAF.
Deputy Director.—William P. Crowell.

ON–SITE INSPECTION AGENCY

Fairchild Building, 300 West Service Road, Dulles Airport, Chantilly VA 22021
mailing address: Washington DC 20041–0498, phone (703) 742–4480

Director.—Brig. Gen. Thomas E. Kuenning, USAF, (703) 810–4449.
Principal Deputy Director.—Joerg H. Menzil, (703) 810–4446.

JOINT SERVICE SCHOOLS

DEFENSE ACQUISITION UNIVERSITY

President.—Thomas H. Crean, (703) 845–6733.

JOINT MILITARY INTELLIGENCE COLLEGE

President.—A. Denis Clift, (202) 231–3344.

DEFENSE SYSTEMS MANAGEMENT COLLEGE

Commandant.—Brig. Gen. R. Black, USA, (703) 805–3360.

NATIONAL DEFENSE UNIVERSITY
Fort McNair, Fourth and P Streets SW, 20319–6000, phone (202) 685–3912

President.—Lt. Gen. Ervin J. Rokke, USAF, Room 228, (202) 685–3922.
Vice President.—Ambassador William G. Walker, (202) 685–3923.

INFORMATION RESOURCES MANAGEMENT COLLEGE

Dean of the College.—J.F. Smith, Jr., (202) 685–3884.

ARMED FORCES STAFF COLLEGE

Commandant.—Brig. Gen. William R. Looney III, USAF, Room A201.

INDUSTRIAL COLLEGE OF THE ARMED FORCES

Commandant.—Maj. Gen. John S. Cowings, USA, Room 200, (202) 685–4337.

NATIONAL WAR COLLEGE

Commandant.—Rear Adm. Michael A. McDevitt, USN, Room 113, (202) 685–4312.

UNIFORMED SERVICES UNIVERSITY OF THE HEALTH SCIENCES
4301 Jones Bridge Road, Bethesda MD 20814, phone (301) 295–3030

President.—James A. Zimble, M.D., Room A1005, (301) 295–3013.

DEPARTMENT OF THE AIR FORCE

Pentagon, 1670 Air Force, 20330–1670, phone (703) 697–7376, fax 693–7553

SECRETARY OF THE AIR FORCE

Secretary of the Air Force.—Dr. Sheila E. Widnall, Room 4E871, (703) 697–7376.
Confidential Assistant.—Norma J. Pearce.
Staff Assistant.—TSgt. Dean M. Huber.
Military Assistant.—[Vacant], (703) 697–8141.
Secretary to the Military Assistant.—Karen Tibus.
Deputy Military Assistant.—Maj. Walter D. Givhan, (703) 697–7376.
Military Aide.—Maj. Stephen J. Gensheimer, (703) 697–8141.
Protocol.—Capt. Alan T. Lake.

Executive Administrative Assistant.—SSgt. Shari L. Miller, (703) 697–3288.
Executive Assistant.—SM Sgt. Roddy L. Stanback.
Deputy Executive Assistant.—SSgt. Thomas A. Stuhl, Jr.
NCOIC Administrative Support.—SSgt. Daniel J. McKinley.

SECRETARY'S STAFF GROUP

Chief.—Col. Stephen P. Randolph, Room 4D865, (703) 695–1323.
Deputy Chief.—LtCol. David Williamson, (703) 695–8704.
Policy and Issues Analysts: Maj. Linda C. Jackson, (703) 695–8710; LtCol. Susan K. Mashiko, (703) 695–8713; Maj. Paul H. Dijulio, (703) 695–8724; Maj. Randy O'Connor, (703) 695–1326.
Speech Writer.—Maj. Edith A. Disler, (703) 695–8726.
Public Affairs Advisor.—Maj. Alvina K. Mitchell, (703) 695–8723.
Special Actions Officer.—Patricia Ryder, (703) 695–1325.
Superintendent.—MSgt. Joseph P. Wahl, (703) 695–1324.

UNDER SECRETARY OF THE AIR FORCE

Pentagon, 1670 Air Force, Room 4E886 20330–1670

Under Secretary.—Rudy F. de Leon, (703) 697–1361.
Confidential Assistant.—Margaret Souleyret.
Consultant.—James F. Boatright, (703) 697–1362.
Military Assistant.—LtCol. Timothy Milbrath, (703) 697–1361.
Executive Officer.—LtCol. Sharon Dunbar.
Executive NCOs.—SSgt. Kimala Riche, SSgt. Brian McHugh, (703) 697–6572.

DEPUTY UNDER SECRETARY FOR INTERNATIONAL AFFAIRS

Pentagon, 1080 Air Force, Room 4E334 20330–1080

Deputy Under Secretary.—Robert D. Bauerlein, (703) 614–8475.
Principal Assistant Deputy.—MG Clinton V. Horn, (703) 695–7261.
Assistant Deputy Under Secretary.—BG William E. Stevens.
Military Assistant.—Col. Marc J. Neifert.
Executive Officer.—LtCol. Joseph A. Spann.

DIRECTOR FOR SMALL AND DISADVANTAGED BUSINESS UTILIZATION

Pentagon, 1060 Air Force, Room 5E271 20330–1060

Director.—Anthony J. DeLuca, (703) 697–1950.

ASSISTANT SECRETARY FOR MANPOWER, RESERVE AFFAIRS, INSTALLATIONS AND ENVIRONMENT

Pentagon, 1660 Air Force 20330–1660

Air Force Review Boards Agency, 1535 Command Drive, EE Wing Andrews Air Force Base, MD 20762–7002 (AAFB)

Air Force Personnel Council, 1535 Command Drive, EE Wing Andrews Air Force Base, MD 20762–7002 (AAFB)

Civilian Appellate Review Agency, 1535 Command Drive, EE Wing Andrews Air Force Base, MD 20762–7002 (AAFB)

Air Force Base Conversion Agency, Metro Center Building 1700 North Moore Street, Arlington VA 22209–2808 (ROSSLYN)

Assistant Secretary.—Rodney A. Coleman, Pentagon, Room 4E1020, (703) 697–2302.
Military Assistant.—Col. Charles E. Stallworth II, (703) 697–2303.

PRINCIPAL DEPUTY ASSISTANT SECRETARY FOR MANPOWER, RESERVE AFFAIRS, INSTALLATIONS AND ENVIRONMENT

Principal Deputy Assistant Secretary.—Phillip P. Upschulte, Room 4E1020, (703) 697–6300.
Military Assistant.—LtCol. Carolyn A. Gavares, (703) 697–1258.
Executive Officer.—Capt. Shelia O. Uphoff, Room 4E985, (703) 697–4356.

DEPUTY ASSISTANT SECRETARY FOR FORCE MANAGEMENT AND PERSONNEL

Deputy Assistant Secretary.—Ruby B. DeMesme, Room 5E977, (703) 614–4751.
Military Assistant for—
Force Support.—LtCol. James R. Holaday.
Military Personnel.—Maj. Joseph W. Mazzola.
Assistant Deputy for—
Civilian Personnel.—Charlene M. Bradley.
Health Affairs.—Carol J. Thompson.

DEPUTY ASSISTANT SECRETARY FOR RESERVE AFFAIRS

Deputy Assistant Secretary.—Bryan E. Sharratt, Room 5C938, (703) 697–6375.
Assistant for—
Air Force Reserve Affairs Matters.—Col. Philip P. Steptoe, (703) 697–6429.
Counterdrug Policy and Civil Air Patrol Matters.—LtCol. David K. Pitman.
Total Force Policy Matters.—LtCol. Robert G. Sidelko.
Executive Administrative Assistant.—CM Sgt. William E. Brake.
Assistant for ANG Matters.—Col. Ronald C. Manning.
Military Executive for Air Reserve Forces Policy Division.—Maj. Joel R. Maynard.

DEPUTY ASSISTANT SECRETARY FOR INSTALLATIONS

Deputy Assistant Secretary.—Jimmy G. Dishner, Room 4C940, (703) 695–3592.
Military Assistant.—Jon A. Roop, (703) 697–6456.
Director for Installations Management.—Lawrence Leehy, (703) 697–7244.
Military Assistant for Reserve Affairs.—LtCol. Karen D. Kohlhaas, (703) 697–4391.
Director for Facility Management Programs.—Col. William Drake, (703) 697–7003.
Assistant for—
Base Closure and Realignment.—LtCol. Marcia Malcomb, (703) 697–7070.
Installation Management.—James A. Anderson.
Office Assistant.—Nancy Garrow, (703) 697–7244.

AIR FORCE REAL ESTATE AGENCY

Director.—William E. Edwards, Bolling Air Force Base, Building 5683, (202) 767–4275.
Realty Specialists:
Catherine M. Dee (202) 767–4383; Barbara J. Jenkins (202) 767–4184; Robert F. Menke (202) 767–4031; Virginia C. Owensby (202) 767–4186; Jon E. Peterson, (202) 767–4189; Charles G. Skidmore (202) 767–4033; Julia A. Talbott (202) 767–4193; Carol M. Xander (202) 767–4034.

DEPUTY ASSISTANT SECRETARY FOR ENVIRONMENT, SAFETY AND OCCUPATIONAL HEALTH

Deputy Assistant Secretary.—Thomas W.L. McCall, Jr., Pentagon, Room 5C866, (703) 697–9297.
MA to the Deputy Assistant Secretary.—BG Lawrence F. Sheehan, Jr.
Deputy for—
Public Health/Chief of Staff.—Col. Craig Postlewaite, (703) 697–1016.
Technology and International Activities.—Col. Rick Drawbaugh, (703) 697–0997.
Resource Management.—Terry Yonkers, (703) 697–0989.
Cleanup and Operations.—LtCol. Mark Hamilton, (703) 693–7548.
Readiness/Guard and Reserve Affairs.—LtCol. Ed Stern, (703) 614–8458.

Assistant Deputy for—
Pollution Prevention.—LtCol. John Garland, (703) 697–1016.
Assistant Deputy for Conservation.—Maj. Mohsen Parhizkar, (703) 695–5978.
Community-Based Program Integration.—Marilyn Null, (703) 693–7705.
Assistant Deputy for Environmental Planning.—Jean Reynolds, (703) 697–0800.
Bioenvironmental Engineering Fellow.—Capt. Roger Nelson, (703) 697–9298.

AIR FORCE REVIEW BOARDS AGENCY

Director.—Joe G. Lineberger, AAFB Building 1535, (301) 981–3137.
Assistant Director.—Col. David L. Oles, (301) 981–5739.
Assistant Secretary for Inquiries.—Perryn B. Ashmore, (301) 981–3119.

AIR FORCE BOARD FOR CORRECTION OF MILITARY RECORDS

Executive Director.—Burton M. Mack, AAFB Building 1535, (301) 981–3502.
Chief Examiners.—John J. D'Orazio, Raymond H. Weller, Frederik Weller.
Administrative Supervisor.—SM Sgt. Susan Ayala, (301) 981–6025.
Inquiries.—[Vacant], (301) 981–3502.

AIR FORCE BASE CONVERSION AGENCY

Director.—[Vacant], Rosslyn Metro Center Building, Suite 2300, (703) 696–5501.
Deputy Director.—Albert Lowas, (703) 696–5502.
Special Assistant for—
Real Property.—Gil Sailer, (703) 696–5566.
Real Estate.—Michael Ruzila, (703) 696–5567.
Personal Property.—Helen Commodore, (703) 696–5574.
External Affairs.—Joyce Frank, (703) 696–5533.
Chief of—
Executive Services.—Joyce Truett, (703) 696–5505.
Administration.—Bev Robertson, (703) 696–5507.
Data Systems.—Tom King, (703) 696–5515.
Legal Counsel.—Doug Baur, (703) 696–5522.
Resource Management.—Cortina Cooley, (703) 696–5566.
Environmental.—John Smith, (703) 696–5522.

AIR FORCE PERSONNEL COUNCIL

Director.—Col. David L. Olsen, AAFB Building 1535, (301) 981–5739.
Deputy Director/Senior Personnel Advisor.—Col. Cheryl M. Harris, (301) 981–3138.
Senior Medical Advisor.—Col. Henry F. Davis, (301) 981–5353.
Senior Legal Advisor.—Col. Lloyd F. LeRoy, (301) 981–5739.
Chief, Air Force Discharge Review Board.—Col. Marion J. Martin, (301) 981–3516.
Air National Guard Advisor.—Col. Marion J. Martin.
Decoration Air Force Reserve Advisor.—Col. James W. Shumand III, (301) 981–5342.
Executive Secretary/Attorney/Advisor on Clemency and Parole.—James D. Johnston, (301) 981–5329.
Chief, DOD Civilian/Military Service Review Board.—James D. Johnston, (301) 981–3504.

AIR FORCE CIVILIAN APPELLATE REVIEW OFFICE

Director.—Sophie A. Clark, AAFB Building 1535, (301) 981–7071.
Acting Chief, Appellate Liaison Unit.—[Vacant], (301) 981–8152.

DEPUTY ASSISTANT SECRETARY FOR EQUAL OPPORTUNITY

Deputy.—Dennis M. Collins, Pentagon, Room 4C942, (703) 697–6586.
Military Assistant.—Alan R. Van Epps.

ASSISTANT SECRETARY FOR FINANCIAL MANAGEMENT AND COMPTROLLER OF THE AIR FORCE

Pentagon, 1130 Air Force, 20330–1130
(CGN) Air Force Cost Analysis Agency, Crystal Gateway North
1111 Jefferson Davis Highway, Suite 403, Arlington VA 22202–1430

Assistant Secretary.—Robert F. Hale, Room 4E984, (703) 693–6457.
Military Assistant.—LtCol. Richard B. Weathers, (703) 697–1974.

PRINCIPAL DEPUTY ASSISTANT SECRETARY FOR FINANCIAL MANAGEMENT

Principal Deputy Assistant Secretary.—John W. Beach, Pentagon, Room 4E984, (703) 697–4464.
Executive.—LtCol. Robert J. Modrovsky, (703) 697–5065.

EXECUTIVE SERVICES

Superintendent.—SM Sgt. Preston Dunn, Room 4D181, (703) 695–9134.
Chief, Information Management.—SSgt. LaDonne White, (703) 695–2524.

DEPUTY ASSISTANT SECRETARY FOR BUDGET

Deputy Assistant Secretary.—MG George T. Stringer, Room 4D131, (703) 695–1875.
Executive Officer.—LtCol. Keith Bell.
Deputy.—Robert D. Stuart, (703) 695–1877.
Executive Assistant.—MSgt. Brenda Bowie.

DIRECTORATE OF BUDGET AND APPROPRIATIONS LIAISON

Director.—Col. Philip E. Ruter, Room 5D911, (703) 614–8110.
Division Chief for—
Appropriations Liaison.—LtCol. Garry G. Savner.
Budget Liaison.—Nancy W. Drury.

DIRECTORATE OF BUDGET MANAGEMENT AND EXECUTION

Director.—Robert W. Zook, Room 4D120, (703) 697–1220.
Executive Officer.—Maj. Barbara Gilchrist.
Assistant for—
Future Budget System.—Dennis T. Bryson, SSC/SBFB, 201 E. Moore Drive, Gunter AFS, AL 36114–3005, (205) 596–2708.
Information Control.—Edward Parker, Pentagon, Room 5D110, (703) 614–4411.
Budget Execution and Control.—George J. Gallagaher, (703) 695–4938.
Policy and Procedures.—Marti A. Maust, Room 4D150, (703) 697–8250.
Special Programs.—Olga Crerar, Room 5C132, (703) 614–1283.
Revolving Funds.—Pat Zarodkiewicz, Room 4D164, (703) 614–3803.

DIRECTORATE OF BUDGET INVESTMENT

Director.—Cathlynn B. Sparks, Room 4D132, (703) 695–9737.
Deputy Director.—Michael J. Novel.
Executive Officer.—Capt. Johnny Wilson.
Assistant for—
Aircraft Procurement and Technology Programs.—Col. Galen Bessert, Room 5C129, (703) 614–5701.
Military Construction and Family Housing.—Tracy Meyer, Room 5D110, (703) 697–1724.
Program Control and Integration.—Michael J. Novel, Room 5C116, (703) 614–4994.
Security Assistance.—Dana Gilmour, Room 4D223, (703) 695–3980.

DIRECTORATE OF BUDGET OPERATIONS

Director.—BG Everett G. Odgers, Room 4D120, (703) 697–0627.

Executive Officer.—Maj. James Sisson.
Assistant for—
Integration Management.—LtCol. Dave Goossens, Room 5D110, (703) 614–4096.
Mission Operations.—Col. John Thompson, (703) 614–3801.
Personnel and Training.—LtCol. Al Detrick, (703) 697–5596.

DIRECTORATE OF BUDGET PROGRAMS

Director.—Col. Gordon Kage, Room 5D110, (703) 614–3642.
Deputy Director.—LtCol. Carl Schweinfurth.

DEPUTY ASSISTANT SECRETARY FOR COST AND ECONOMICS

Deputy Assistant Secretary.—Leroy T. Baseman, Room 4D159, (703) 697–5311.
Executive Assistant.—TSgt. Wayne Ferguson, (703) 697–5313.
Associate Deputy Assistant Secretary.—John C. Graser, (703) 697–5312.
Commander, Air Force Cost Analysis Agency.—Col.(S) Eddie Weeks, CGN Suite 403, Arlington VA 22202–1430, (703) 604–0388.
Deputy to Commander.—Joseph Wagner.
Technical Director for Cost and Economics.—John T. Dorsett, (703) 604–0387.
Director for—
Cost Analysis.—Col.(S) Eddie Weeks, Pentagon, Room 4D178, (703) 697–0734.
Economics and Business Management.—Walter J. Hosey, Room 4D167, (703) 697–1152.

DEPUTY ASSISTANT SECRETARY FOR MANAGEMENT SYSTEMS

Deputy Assistant Secretary.—A. Ernest Fitzgerald, Room 5C886, (703) 697–7832.

DEPUTY ASSISTANT SECRETARY FOR FINANCIAL OPERATIONS

Deputy Assistant Secretary.—John J. Nethery, Room 5E989, (703) 697–2905.
Director for—
Comptroller Support.—Col. Richard Schuetz, Room 4E137, (703) 695–0550.
Financial Systems and Reporting.—Tony Coluuci, Room 4E139, (703) 697–6465.
Audit Liaison and Follow-up.—Vaughn E. Schlunz, Room 4C228, (703) 697–2905.
Internal Management Controls.—Arnold B. Brodsky, Room 4D164, (703) 693–7066.
Special Assistant.—Joseph A. Roj, Room 4C138, (703) 614–4180.

ASSISTANT SECRETARY FOR ACQUISITION
Pentagon, 1060 Air Force 20330–1060
1919 South Eads Street, Suite 100, Arlington VA 22022–3053

Assistant Secretary.—Arthur L. Money, Pentagon, Room 4E964, (703) 697–6361.
Military Assistant.—John R. Ward, (703) 695–7311.
Executive.—Alan T. Evans.

PRINCIPAL DEPUTY ASSISTANT SECRETARY FOR ACQUISITION

Principal Deputy Assistant Secretary.—LtG. George K. Muellner, Room 4E964, (703) 697–6363.
Executive.—LtCol. Steven W. Brown, (703) 695–7311.
Chief, Executive Services Division.—CM Sgt. Linda D. Brown, Room 4E969, (703) 697–8331.

PRINCIPAL DEPUTY ASSISTANT SECRETARY FOR ACQUISITION AND MANAGEMENT

Principal Deputy Assistant Secretary.—Darlene A. Druyun, Room 4E969, (703) 614–8000.

Military Assistant.—LtCol. Jeffrey C. Dodson, (703) 614–8001.

MISSION AREA DIRECTORATE FOR INFORMATION DOMINANCE

Mission Area Director.—BG David A. Nagy, Room 4E128, (703) 697–3624.
Deputy.—Col. Bruce R. Queen.
Executive Officer.—Maj. Jerry M. Jankowiak.

DEPUTY ASSISTANT SECRETARY FOR CONTRACTING

Deputy Assistant Secretary.—BG Timothy P. Malishenko, Room 4C261, (703) 695–6332.
Associate Deputy Assistant Secretary.—W. Lee Evey, Room 4C261, (703) 695–7810.
Assistant Deputy.—Col. Curtis N. Newill, (703) 697–7807.
Operational Contracting Division.—Col. Bradley Orton, Room 4C276, (703) 695–1913.
Systems and Logistics Contracting Division.—Col. Stephen Busch, Room 4C323, (703) 697–7714.
Contract Policy Division.—Col. Terry Raney, Room 4C314, (703) 697–9441.
Contracting Systems Division.—Col. Richard Heffner, Room 4C251, (703) 695–4982.
Contract Support Division.—Col. Thomas Brown, Room 4B262, (703) 695–2128.

DEPUTY ASSISTANT SECRETARY FOR MANAGEMENT POLICY AND PROGRAM INTEGRATION

Deputy Assistant Secretary.—Blaise J. Durante, Room 4C331, (703) 697–2227.
Associate Deputy Assistant Secretary.—Col. Barry G. Morgan, (703) 697–6915.
Chief of—
Acquisition Management Operations (Military Assistant).—Maj. Thomas J. Barth, Room 4C331, (703) 697–6513.
Acquisition Career Management and Resources Division.—Joseph G. Diamond, Room 4D347, (703) 695–8352.
Acquisition Management Policy Division.—Col. Chris Waln, Room 4C344, (703) 697–6513.
Program Integration Division.—Col. Terry L. Blaven, Room 4C347, (703) 614–5672.

MISSION AREA DIRECTORATE FOR GLOBAL REACH

Mission Area Director.—BG Tome H. Walters, Jr., Room 4E342, (703) 695–3020.
Deputy Director.—Col. Peter J. Bein, (703) 697–7304.
Division Chief for—
Mobility.—Col. Mark Volcheff, Room 5D167, (703) 695–7992.
Special Missions and Training.—Col. Donn Kegel, (703) 697–9234.
Program, Budget and Congressional.—LtCol. William C. Maisch, Room 5E325, (703) 697–0523.

DIRECTORATE FOR SPECIAL PROGRAMS

Director.—Col. Neil G. Kacena, Room 5D230, (703) 695–1256.
Deputy Director.—Col. Oscar W. Johnston, (703) 695–1256.
Chief of—
Special Program Operations.—LtCol. Randall Soileau, (703) 697–6174.
Special Studies Division.—LtCol. Robert Gierard, (703) 695–6681.
Advanced Technology Division.—Col.(S) Robert J. Schraeder, (703) 697–5353.
Advanced Electronic Programs Division.—Col. James W. Smail, (703) 697–6994.

MISSION AREA DIRECTORATE FOR GLOBAL POWER

Mission Area Director.—BG Bruce A. Carlson, Room 4E312, (703) 695–2147.
Chief, Program Integration Division and Management Support Office.—Barbara A. Westgate, Room 4E312, (703) 697–7505.
Division Chief for—
Air Superiority.—Col. Melvin L. Greene, Room 5E381, (703) 614–3555.

Theater Air Defense.—Col. Bill Pearson, Room 4D337, (703) 695–0328.
Power Projection.—Col. Robert L. Ostrander, Room 5E279, (703) 697–7715.
Command Systems.—Col. Kevin J. O'Connor, Room 5E373, (703) 697–0660.

MISSION AREA DIRECTORATE FOR SPACE AND NUCLEAR DETERRENCE

Director.—BG James R. Beale, Room 4D330, (703) 695–1904.
Deputy Director.—Col. Richard W. Skinner.
Division Chief for—
Space C4I.—[Vacant], Room 4D269, (703) 695–9644.
Space Lauch.—Col.(S) Marlon Yankee, Room 4D269, (703) 695–9640.
Satellite.—Col.(S) Michael Mantz, Room 5C269, (703) 614–8445.
IBM Modernization.—Col.(S) James Warner, Room 5D543, (703) 697–8123.
Mission Support, Congressional and Budget.—Lt. Col. Robert Fisher, Room 4D284, (703) 695–5311.

DEPUTY ASSISTANT SECRETARY FOR SCIENCE, TECHNOLOGY AND ENGINEERING

Deputy Assistant Secretary.—Dr. Helmut Hellwig, Building 1919, Room S–100, (703) 602–9301.
Associate Deputy Assistant Secretaries:
Col.(S) Jack L. Blackhurst, (703) 602–9200.
Col. George Williams, Pentagon, Room 4C283, (703) 697–1417.

AIR FORCE PROGRAM EXECUTIVE OFFICERS

Executive Officer for Airlift and Trainers.—BG Richard V. Reynolds, Pentagon, Room 5A266, (703) 693–7289.
Program Director, C–17.—BG Charles L. Johnson II, 2590 Loop Road West, Wright-Patterson AFB, OH 45433–7142, (937) 255–1545.
Executive Officer for—
Battle Management Programs.—John M. Gilligan, Pentagon, Room 4D317, (703) 693–8071.
Fighter and Bomber Programs.—MG Robert F. Raggio, Room 5D270, (703) 697–9400.
Program Director for—
B–2.—Col. Jay Jabour, 2275 D Street, Suite 4, Wright-Patterson AFB, OH 45433–7221, (513) 255–9484.
F–16.—Col. Larry H. Cooper, 1981 Third Street, Suite 105, Wright-Patterson AFB, OH 45433–7205, (513) 255–6151.
F–22.—BG Michael C. Mushala, 2130 Fifth Street, Building 50, Wright-Patterson AFB, OH 45433–7003, (937) 255–4167.
Space Programs.—Brent R. Collins, Pentagon, Room 4D279, (703) 693–8076.
Program Director for—
MILSATCOM.—Col. Joseph B. Sovey, 2420 Vela Way, Suite 1467–A8, Los Angeles AFB, CA 90245–4659, (310) 336–4877.
Space-Based Infrared Systems (SBIRS).—BG (Sel) Craig P. Weston, 185 Discoverer Boulevard, Suite 2512, Los Angeles AFB, CA 90245–4695, (310) 363–1807.
EELV.—Col. Richard W. McKinney, 2420 Vela Way, Suite 1467, Los Angeles AFB, CA 90245–4659, (310) 363–4614.
Launch Systems.—Col. Jeffery J. Norton, 160 Skynet Street, Suite 1215, Los Angles AFB, CA 90245–4683, (310) 363–3915.
ICBM.—Col. Terrence G. Crossey, 6014 Dogwood Avenue, Hill AFB, UT 84056–5816, (801) 777–8644.
Executive Officer for—
Command, Control and Communications Systems.—BG Berwyn A. Reiter, Pentagon, Room 4D287, (703) 693–8065.
Weapons.—Harry E. Shulte, Room 4C328, (703) 695–8343.
Joint Logistics Systems.—Oscar A. Goldfarb, Room 5D544, (703) 695–9049.

JOINT STRIKE FIGHTER TECHNOLOGY PROGRAM

Director.—Rear Adm. Craig E. Steidle, 1745 Jefferson Davis Highway, Arlington VA 22202–3251, (703) 602–7640.

Deputy Director.—BG Leslie F. Kenne.

JOINT LOGISTICS SYSTEMS CENTER

Commander.—BG David A. Herrelko, 1864 Fourth Street, Suite 1, Wright-Patterson AFB, OH 45433–7131, (937) 255–0401.

ASSISTANT SECRETARY FOR SPACE

Pentagon, 1640 Air Force 20330–1640

Assistant Secretary.—[Vacant], Room 4E998, (703) 693–5996.
Military AssistanT.—[Vacant].

PRINCIPAL DEPUTY ASSISTANT SECRETARY FOR SPACE

Principal Deputy Assistant Secretary.—[Vacant], Room 4C958, (703) 697–8531.
Executive Officer.—Capt. Ed Wilson.

DEPUTY ASSISTANT SECRETARY FOR SPACE PLANS AND POLICY

Deputy Assistant Secretary.—Richard M. McCormick, Room 4E998, (703) 693–5799.
Director, Space Policy Planning and Strategy.—Col. Robert Cox, Room 4D939, (703) 697–0301.
Chief of—
Space Programming.—Maj. Ed Phillips, (703) 695–2317.
Space Policy.—LtCol. Vic Villhard.
Space Plans.—Maj. Marty Whelan.
Interdepartmental Space Affairs.—LtCol. Steve Opel.

SPECIAL PROJECTS

Director.—BG Robert E. Larned, Room 4C1052, (703) 697–8675.
Executive Officer.—Capt. Elaine Eldridge.

OFFICE OF SPACE SYSTEMS

Director.—BG Howard J. Mitchell, Room 4C1052, (703) 614–2212.
Executive Officer.—Capt. Bryan Cannon.

GENERAL COUNSEL

Pentagon, 1740 Air Force 20330–1740

General Counsel.—Sheila C. Cheston, Room 4E856, (703) 697–0941.
Principal Deputy.—Matthew D. Slater, (703) 697–4406.
Special Counsel/Military Assistant.—LtCol. Johnny H. Edwards, (703) 697–8418.
Deputy General Counsel for—
Installations and Environment.—Fred W. Kuhn, Room 4C921, (703) 695–4691.
Civilian Personnel and Fiscal Law.—Walter A. Willson, Room 4C916, (703) 695–4975.
International Affairs.—Michael W. Zehner, Room 4C941, (703) 697–5196.
Contractor Responsibility.—Steven A. Shaw, Room 4C941, (703) 693–9818.
Acquisition.—John P. Janecek, Room 4D980, (703) 697–3900.
Military Affairs.—Florence W. Madden, Room 4C948, (703) 695–5663.

INSPECTOR GENERAL

Pentagon, 1140 Air Force 20330–1140

Inspector General.—LtG. Richard T. Swope, Room 4E1076, (703) 697–6733.
Deputy Inspector General.—MG William B. Davitte, (703) 697–4351.

Executive Officer.—LtCol. Robert A. Ciola, (703) 697–4787.
Advisor for—
Reserve Matters.—Col. Kirk Bentson, Room 4E1082, (703) 697–0066.
Air National Guard Matters.—Col. David Kirtley.

OFFICE OF THE INSPECTOR GENERAL

Director of—
Inquiries Directorate.—Col. Robert Rhodes, Room 4E1082, (703) 695–3653.
Inspection Directorate.—Col. David Sconnenberg, Room 4E1078, (703) 697–7050.
Special Investigations.—Col. Charles Azykas, Room 4E1081, (703) 697–0411.
Senior Officials Inquiries.—Col. Jon Bear, (703) 693–5032.

ADMINISTRATIVE ASSISTANT TO THE SECRETARY

Pentagon, 1720 Air Force 20330–1720

170 Luke Avenue, Suite 300, Bolling AFB 20332–5113 (BAFB)

Administrative Assistant.—William A. Davidson, Pentagon, Room 4D881, (703) 695–9492.
Director for Operations Support.—Col. David J. Semon, (703) 695–9607.
Military Assistant.—LtCol. Edward Patrick.
Executive Assistant.—Capt. Sandra Sullivan.

CIVILIAN PERSONNEL DIVISION

Chief.—Peggy S. Park, Room 4C882, (703) 697–1162.

AIR FORCE EXECUTIVE DINING ROOM

Facility Manager.—Alfonso C. Sisneros, Room 4D852A, (703) 697–1112.

DIRECTORATE FOR PLANS, PROGRAMS AND BUDGET

Director.—Col. David Ferguson, Room 5E122, (703) 697–9057.

MILITARY PERSONNEL DIVISION

Chief.—LtCol. Judy Best, Room 4C882, (703) 614–9363.

DIRECTORATE FOR SECURITY AND INVESTIGATIVE PROGRAMS

Director.—Gene Boesch, Room 5D972, (703) 693–2013.

AUDITOR GENERAL

1120 Air Force Pentagon, 20330–1120

4170 Hebble Creek Road, Suite 1, Wright-Patterson AFB OH 45433–5644 (WPAFB)

5023 Fourth Street, March AFB CA 95218–1852 (MAFB)

Auditor General.—Jackie R. Crawford, Room 4E168, (703) 614–5626.

AIR FORCE AUDIT AGENCY

Assistant Auditor General for—
Operations.—Thomas F. Bachman, Arlington Plaza, Room 506, (703) 696–8026.
Resource Management.—James R. Lonon, Rosslyn Metro Center Building, Room 402, (703) 696–5975.
Acquisition and Logistics Audits.—Kenneth E. Gregory, WPAFB, (513) 257–6355.
Financial and Support Audits.—James R. Speer, MAFB, (909) 655–7011.
Field Activities.—Karla W. Corcoran, Arlington Plaza, Room 502, (703) 696–8031.

DIRECTORATE OF LEGISLATIVE LIAISON

1160 Air Force Pentagon, 20330–1160
Rayburn House Office Building, 20515–6854 (RHOB)
Russell Senate Office Building, 20510 (RSOB)

Director.—MG Lansford E. Trapp, Jr., Pentagon, Room 4D927, (703) 697–8153.
Deputy Director.—BG(s) Randy C. Gelwix.
Executive.—Capt. Michael LoGrande, (703) 697–5321.
Assistant Executive.—MSgt. Jacques Marshall, (703) 697–4142.
Chief of—
House Liaison Office.—Col. Marty Dupont, B322 RHOB, (202) 685–4531.
Senate Liaison Office.—LtCol. Richard Pgatt, SR182 RSOB, (202) 685–2573.
Weapons Systems Liaison Division.—Col. Steve Gress, Pentagon, Room 5D928, (703) 697–6711.
Programs and Legislation Division.—Col. Stephen D. Bull III, Room 5D927, (703) 697–5322.
Issues Team.—Lt. Col. Steve Farrow, Room 4D961, (703) 695–0137.
Air Operations Office.—Col. Paul Rouse, Room 5D912, (703) 697–1500.
Legislative Research Office.—Fred Bumgarner, Room 5D934, (703) 695–2552.
Executive Director for Operations.—Col. John K. Wilson III, Room 4D927, (703) 697–4142.

CONGRESSIONAL INQUIRY DIVISION

Chief.—Col. Nicki Watts, Room 5D883, (703) 697–3783.
Chief of—
Inquiry Branch.—LtCol. Beth Unklesbay, Room 5D878, (703) 695–7204.
White House Liaison.—Maj. Mark Wasserman, Room 5D883, (703) 697–3731.
Information Management Branch.—MSgt. Willette Jodee, Room 5D875, (703) 697–3020.

DIRECTORATE OF PUBLIC AFFAIRS

Pentagon, 1690 Air Force 20330–1690

Director.—BG Ronald T. Sconyers, Room 4D922, (703) 697–6061.
Deputy Director.—Col. Hal Smarkola.
Executive Officer.—LtCol.(S) Andrew Walker.

PUBLIC AFFAIRS STAFF GROUP

Chief.—Col. Alan DeFend, Room 5C935, (703) 697–2842.
Public Affairs Advisors for—
SECAF.—LtCol.(S) Alvina Mitchell, (703) 695–1323.
CSAF.—LtCol. Mike Wiley.
CMSAF.—CM Sgt.(S) Mike Brown.

COMMUNITY RELATIONS DIVISION

Chief of—
Community Relations.—Walt Werner, Room 5C945, (703) 693–2775.
Bands and Music.—Maj. Frank Hudson, Room 4A120, (703) 695–0019.
Civil Affairs.—Maj. Ron Lovas, Room 5C945, (703) 697–1128.
Environmental.—Gerda Parr, Room 4A120, (703) 614–1325.
Public Affairs Resource Library.—SSgt. Donna Burgess, (703) 697–4100.

MEDIA RELATIONS DIVISION

Chief of—
Media Relations.—LtCol. Virginia Pribyla, Room 5C879, (703) 695–0640.
Operations.—Maj. Ed Worley.
Support.—LtCol.(S) Laura Feldman.
Media Training.—Maj. Felicia Tavares, Room 5C885, (703) 695–7793.

RESOURCES DIVISION

Chief, Strategic Plans.—Col. Terry Tyrell, Room 4A120, (703) 697–5838.
Reserve Advisor.—Col. Tony Epifano, (703) 697–6725.
Chief, Resource.—Joyce Richardson (acting), (703) 697–6702.
Wartime and Quality.—Maj. Ken McClellan, (703) 697–5226.
Chief, Technology Team.—Capt. Terry Bowman, (703) 695–8561.
Acting Chief, Human Resource Development.—Capt. Todd Viciam, (703) 697–6703.

SECURITY REVIEW

Chief.—June Forte, Room 5D227, (703) 697–3222.

INTERNAL INFORMATION

Chief.—LtCol. Sanford McClaurin, Room 4A120, (703) 695–7793.

NATIONAL AFFAIRS

Chief.—LtCol. Napolean Byars, Room 5C687, (703) 695–9664.

CHIEF OF STAFF

Pentagon, 1670 Air Force 20330–1670

Chief of Staff.—Gen. Ronald R. Fogleman, Room 4E924, (703) 697–9225.
Executive Officer.—Col. Trudy Clark.
Director, Operations Group.—Col. Doug Fraser, Room 4E941, (703) 697–5540.
Vice Chief of Staff.—Gen. Thomas S. Moorman, Jr., Room 4E936, (703) 695–7911.
Chief Master Sergeant of the Air Force.—CM Sgt. Eric Benken, Room 4B948, (703) 695–0498.
Special Assistant for National Defense Review.—MG Charles D. Link, Room 4D956, (703) 693–3473.

CHIEF OF SAFETY

9700 G Avenue SE, Suite 240, Kirtland AFB NM 87117–5670

Chief of Safety/Director, Air Force Safety Center.—BG Orin L. Godsey, (505) 846–2372.

SAFETY ISSUES DIVISION (PENTAGON LIAISON)

Pentagon, 1400 Air Force 20330–1400

Director.—Col. Kerry May, Room 5E161, (703) 695–7280.

DIRECTOR OF SECURITY FORCES

Pentagon, 1340 Air Force 20330–1340

Director of Security Forces/Commander, USAF Force Protection Agency.—BG Richard A. Coleman, Jr., Room BC917, (703) 693–9002.

SCIENTIFIC ADVISORY BOARD

Pentagon, 1180 Air Force 20330–1180.

Chairman.—Dr. Gene H. McCall, Room 5D982, (703) 697–4811.

DIRECTORATE OF SERVICES

Pentagon, 1770 Air Force 20330–1770

Crystal Gateway North, Arlington VA 22202–4306 (CGN)

Director.—BG Patrick O. Adams, 413 CGN, (703) 604–0010.

DEPUTY CHIEF OF STAFF FOR PLANS AND PROGRAMS

Pentagon, 1070 Air Force 20330–1070

Deputy Chief of Staff.—LtG. Lawrence P. Farrell, Jr., Room 4E315, (703) 697–2405.
Director for Manpower, Organization and Quality.—BG Larry W. Northington, Room 5C465, (703) 695–7686.
Deputy Director for Manpower, Organization and Quality.—Col. Robert E. Corsi.
Director of Programs.—MG John W. Handy, Room 4E339, (703) 697–2405.
Deputy Director.—BG Joseph H. Wehrle, Jr.
Director for Strategic Planning.—MG David W. McIlvoy, Room 5E171, (703) 697–3117.
Deputy Director.—Clark Murdock, (703) 695–2161.

DIRECTORATE OF TEST AND EVALUATION

Pentagon, 1650 Air Force 20330–1650

Director.—LtG.(R) Howard W. Leaf, Room 4E995, (703) 697–4774.

AIR FORCE HISTORIAN

Bolling AFB, 170 Luke Avenue, Suite 400, 20332–5113

Air Force Historian.—Dr. Richard P. Hallion, (202) 767–5764.
Executive Officer.—Maj. Chip Hunt.

AIR FORCE SCIENTIST

Pentagon, 1060 Air Force 20330–1060

Chief Scientist.—Dr. Edward A. Feigenbaum, Pentagon, Room 4E320, (703) 697–7842.

AIR FORCE RESERVE

Pentagon, 1150 Air Force 20330–1150

Chief, Air Force Reserve/Commander, Air Force Reserve Center.—MG Robert A. McIntosh, Room 5C916, (703) 695–9225.
Deputy.—BG John A Bradley, (703) 694–7307.

NATIONAL GUARD BUREAU

Pentagon, 2500 Army 20310–2500

Chief.—LtG. Edward D. Baca, Room 2E394, (703) 695–6987.
Air National Guard:
Director.—MG Donald W. Shepperd, Room 2E378, (703) 693–4750.
Deputy Director.—BG Paul A. Weaver, Jr.

SURGEON GENERAL

Bolling AFB, 170 Luke Avenue, Building 5681, Suite 400, 20332–5113

Surgeon General.—Charles H. Roadman II, (202) 767–4343.
Deputy Surgeon General/Chief, Medical Services Corps.—MG Michael K. Wyrick, (202) 767–5050.
Executive Officer.—Maj. Mark A. Presson, (202) 767–4343.
Director of—
Medical Service Corps.—Col. Neil G. Patterson, (202) 767–4351.
Biomedical Sciences.—Col. Jerry W. Ross, (202) 767–1177.
Assistant Surgeon General, Dental Services/Cdr., 89th Medical Group, AMC.—BG Theodore C. Almquist, (202) 767–5070.
Director for—
Medical Inquiries and Information.—Col. Diana L. Kupchella, (202) 767–5046.
Medical Readiness Doctrine/Planning and Nursing Services.—BG Linda J. Stierle, (202) 767–5054.
Health Care Studies and Evaluations.—Col. Arthur Aenchbacher, (202) 767–0090.

CHIEF OF THE CHAPLAIN SERVICE
Bolling AFB, 112 Luke Avenue 20332–9050

Chief.—Chaplain (MG) Arthur S. Thomas, Room 316, (202) 767–4577.
Deputy.—Chaplain (BG) William J. Dendinger, Room 313, (202) 767–4599.

JUDGE ADVOCATE GENERAL
Pentagon, 1420 Air Force 20330–1420
1501 Wilson Boulevard, Suite 810, Rosslyn VA 22209–2403 (ROSSLYN)
172 Luke Avenue, Suite 336, Bolling AFB 20332 (BAFB)

Judge Advocate General.—MG Ryan G. Hawley, Pentagon, Room 4E112, (703) 614–5732.
Deputy Judge Advocate General.—MG Andrew M. Egeland, Jr.
Director for—
Civil Law and Litigation.—Col. Paul L. Black, ROSSLYN, (703) 696–9040.
USAF Judiciary.—Col. Richard F. Rothenburg, BAFB, (202) 767–1535.

LEGAL SERVICES

Commander, Air Force Legal Services Agency.—Col. Richard F. Rothenburg, BAFB, (202) 404–8758.

DEPUTY CHIEF OF STAFF FOR PERSONNEL
Pentagon, 1040 Air Force 20330–1040

Deputy Chief of Staff.—LtG. Michael D. McGinty, Room 4E194, (703) 697–6088.
Assistant Deputy.—Roger M. Blanchard.
Director for—
Civilian Personnel Policy and Personnel Plans.—Sandra Grese, Room 4E228, (703) 695–2141.
Military Personnel Policy.—BG John F. Regni, Room 4E178, (703) 697–5221.
Personnel Programs, Education and Training.—BG Michael S. Kudlacz, Room 4E144, (703) 697–1228.

DEPUTY CHIEF OF STAFF FOR AIR AND SPACE OPERATIONS
Pentagon, 1630 Air Force 20330–1630

Deputy Chief of Staff.—LtG. John P. Jumper, Room 4E1032, (703) 697–9991.
Assistant Deputy.—MG Donald L. Peterson, (703) 697–9881.
Mobilization Assistant.—MG Louis A. Crigler, Room 4E1041, (703) 695–5069.
Director for—
Intelligence, Surveillance and Reconnaissance.—MG John P. Casciano, Room 4A932, (703) 695–5613.
Command and Control.—MG(Sel) Charles R. Henderson, Room 4C1059, (703) 695–1833.
Operational Requirements.—MG Gregory S. Martin, Room 4E1021, (703) 695–3018.
Operations and Training.—MG(s) Terryl J. Schwalier, Room 4E1046, (703) 695–9067.
Joint Matters.—MG(Sel) Charles J. Wax, Room 4E1047, (703) 693–9244.
Nuclear and Counterproliferation.—MG Thomas H. Neary, Room 4E1048, (703) 695–5833.
Weather.—BG Fred P. Lewis, Room 4A1084, (703) 614–7258.
Deputy Director for—
Command and Control.—BG James E. Sandstrom, Room 4C1059, (703) 695–1833.
Intelligence, Surveillance and Reconnaissance.—BG Arthur D. Sikes, Room 4A932, (703) 697–2548.

DEPUTY CHIEF OF STAFF FOR INSTALLATIONS AND LOGISTICS
Pentagon, 1030 Air Force 20330–1030
Crystal Gateway North, Arlington VA 22202–4306 (CGN)

Deputy Chief of Staff.—MG William P. Hallin, Pentagon, Room 4E260, (703) 695–3153.

Assistant Deputy.—R.L. Orr (SES), (703) 695–6236.
Director of—
Supply.—BG Leon A. Wilson, Jr., (703) 697–2822.
Transportation.—BG(Sel) Mary L. Saunders, Room 4B285, (703) 697–4206.
Maintenance.—BG Michael E. Zettler, Room 4E278, (703) 695–2775.
The Civil Engineer.—MG Eugene A. Lupia, Room 5D422, (703) 697–9221.
Director of Services.—Arthur J. Myers, 413 CGN, (703) 604–0010.

DEPUTY CHIEF OF STAFF FOR COMMUNICATIONS AND INFORMATION
Pentagon, 1250 Air Force 20330–1250

Deputy Chief of Staff.—LtG. William J. Donahue, Room 5B477, (703) 695–6324.
Assistant Deputy.—MG George P. Lampe, Room 5B485, (703) 695–4440.
Director of—
Mission Systems.—[Vacant], Room 5B525, (703) 697–0478.
Architectures and Technology.—William C. James, Room 5B478, (703) 695–2906.
Plans, Policy and Resources.—Col. Michael A. Cuoio, Room 5B486, (703) 697–3943.

DEPARTMENT OF THE ARMY

The Pentagon, 20310, phone (703) 695–2442

OFFICE OF THE SECRETARY
Pentagon, Room 3E700, 20310–0101, phone (703) 695–3211, fax (703) 697–8036

Secretary of the Army.—Togo D. West, Jr.
Senior Military Assistant.—Col. T. Michael Crews, (703) 695–1717.
Military Assistants to the Secretary: LtCol. Mary Brown; LtCol. Monique Hale, (703) 695–1717.

OFFICE OF THE UNDER SECRETARY
Pentagon, Room 3E733, 20310–0102, phone (703) 695–4311, fax (703) 695–1525

Under Secretary.—Joseph R. Reeder.
Executive to the Under Secretary.—Col. Thomas G. Bowden, (703) 697–9806.
Military Assistants to the Under Secretary: LtCol. Alexander D. Perwich, (703) 695–4491; Maj. Thomas F. Lynch, (703) 697–7834.

ASSISTANT SECRETARY FOR CIVIL WORKS
Pentagon, Room 2E570, 20310–0108, phone (703) 697–8986, fax (703) 697–3366

Assistant Secretary.—H. Martin Lancaster.
Principal Deputy Assistant Secretary.—John F. Zirschky, (703) 697–4671.
Executive Officer.—Col. Robert J. Sperberg, Room 2E569, (703) 697–9809.
Military Assistant.—LtCol. Robert Crear, (703) 695–0482.
Administrative Officer.—Ruth K. Huff, (703) 693–3656.
Deputy, Assistant Secretary for—
Policy and Legislation.—Michael L. Davis, Room 2E569, (703) 697–1370.
Management and Budget.—Steven Dola, Room 7126, 20 Massachusetts Avenue, 20314–1000, (703) 761–0128.

ASSISTANT SECRETARY FOR FINANCIAL MANAGEMENT AND COMPTROLLER
Pentagon, Room 3E606, 20310–0109, phone (703) 697–8121, fax (703) 693–5389

Assistant Secretary.—Helen T. McCoy.
Principal Deputy Assistant Secretary.—Neil R. Ginnetti, (703) 695–2254.
Executive Officer.—Col. Hugh B. Tant III, (703) 695–2216.

Deputy Assistant Secretary for—
Financial Operations.—Ernest J. Gregory, Room 3E575, (703) 697–3857.
Resource Analysis and Business Practices.—Robert Raynsford (acting), Room 3A712 (703) 697–7629.
Army Budget.—MG Roger G. Thompson, Jr., Room 3A662, (703) 697–3937.
Director for U.S. Cost and Economic Analysis Center.—Robert W. Young, Room 436, 5611 Columbia Pike, Falls Church VA 22041–5050, (703) 681–3217.

ASSISTANT SECRETARY FOR INSTALLATIONS, LOGISTICS AND ENVIRONMENT

Pentagon, Room 2E614, 20310–0110, phone (703) 695–6527, fax (703) 614–5975

Assistant Secretary.—Robert M. Walker.
Principal Deputy Assistant Secretary.—Alma Boyd Moore, (703) 695–9508.
Executive Officer.—Col. David R. Powers, (703) 695–6527.
Deputy Assistant Secretary for—
Installations and Housing.—Paul W. Johnson, Room 3E581, (703) 697–8161.
Logistics.—Eric A. Orsini, Room 3E620, (703) 697–9030.
Environment, Safety and Occupational Health.—Raymond J. Fatz, Room 2E577, (703) 695–7824.

ASSISTANT SECRETARY FOR MANPOWER AND RESERVE AFFAIRS

Pentagon, Room 2E594, 20310–0111, phone (703) 697–9253, fax (703) 614–5975

Assistant Secretary.—Sara E. Lister.
Principal Deputy Assistant Secretary.—Archie D. Barrett, (703) 695–1164.
Executive Officer.—Col. William A. Brown III, (703) 697–9253.
Deputy Assistant Secretary for—
Force Management, Manpower and Resources.—Jayson L. Spiegel, Room 2E580, (703) 695–9652.
DA Review Boards and Equal Employment Opportunity Compliance and Complaints Review.—Thomas R. Cuthbert, Crystal Mall Building 4, Room 200, 1941 Jefferson Davis Highway, Arlington VA 20360, (703) 607–1597.
Reserve Affairs Mobilization Readiness and Training.—Todd A. Weiler, Room 23580, (703) 695–3721.
Military Personnel Management and Equal Opportunity Policy.—John P. McLaurin III, Room 2E580, (703) 697–2631.
Civilian Personnel Policy.—Carol A. Smith, Room 2C681, (703) 695–4237.

ASSISTANT SECRETARY FOR RESEARCH, DEVELOPMENT AND ACQUISITION

Pentagon, Room 2E672, 20310–0103, phone (703) 695–6153, fax (703) 697–4003

Assistant Secretary.—Gilbert F. Decker.
Executive Officer.—Col. Dean Ertwine, (703) 695–5749.
Military Deputy.—LtG. Ronald V. Hite, (703) 697–0356.
Deputy Assistant Secretary for—
Research and Technology.—A. Fenner Milton, Room 3E374, (703) 697–1646.
Procurement.—Kenneth J. Oscar, Room 2E661, (703) 695–2488.
Plans, Programs and Policy.—Keith Charles, Room 3E432, (703) 697–0387.

GENERAL COUNSEL

Pentagon, Room 2E722, 20310–0104, phone (703) 697–9235, fax (703) 697–6553

General Counsel.—William T. Coleman III.
Principal Deputy General Counsel.—Lawrence M. Baskir, (703) 697–4807.
Executive Officer.—Col. John Greenbaugh, (703) 697–9235 .
Deputy General Counsel for—
Acquisition.—Frank J. Sando (acting), Room 2E725, (703) 697–5120.
Civil Works and Environment.—Earl H. Stockdale, Jr., Room 2D717, (703) 693–3024.
Ethics and Fiscal.—Matt Reres, Room 2E725, (703) 695–4296.
Operations and Personnel.—T.W. Taylor, 2E725, (703) 695–0562.

ADMINISTRATIVE ASSISTANT

Pentagon, Room 3E733, 20310–0105, phone (703) 695–2442, fax (703) 697–6194

Administrative Assistant.—Joel B. Hudson.
Deputy Administrative Assistant.—Sandra R. Riley, (703) 695–5879.
Director of Policy and Plans.—Fritz W. Kirklighter (acting), Room 3D746, (703) 697–6900.
Executive Director for Headquarters Services (Washington).—Sandra R. Riley.
Director of—
Equal Employment Opportunity.—Debra A. Muse, Room 5A532, (703) 697–4313.
Information Management Support Center.—Michael Selves, Room 1E600, (703) 693–5425.
Defense Supply Service (Washington).—Col. Kimberly Smith, Room 1E230, (703) 693–5425.
Defense Telecommunications Service (Washington).—Michael A. Newton, 1700 North Moore Street, Suite 1475, Arlington VA 22209–1903, (703) 696–8636.
Personnel and Employment Services (Washington).—Peter B. Horn, Room 1E530, (703) 697–2691.
Safety, Security and Support Services (Washington).—Fritz W. Kirklighter (acting), Room 3E746, (703) 697–6900.
Space and Building Management Service (Washington).—R. Wes Blaine, Room 1A123, (703) 695–7555.
Single Agency Manager.—Fred Budd, Room 1D1000, (703) 697–4264.

DIRECTOR FOR INFORMATION SYSTEMS FOR COMMAND, CONTROL, COMMUNICATIONS AND COMPUTERS

Pentagon, Room 3E458, 20310–0107, phone (703) 697–7494, fax (703) 695–3091

Director.—LtG. Otto J. Guenther.
Vice Director.—David Borland, (703) 695–6604.
Executive Officer.—Col. James D. Bryan, (703) 695–5503.
Director of—
Army Information.—Miriam F. Browning, Room 3C570, (703) 697–5693.
Programs and Architecture.—Col. Lamar Murphy (acting), Room 3C560, (703) 614–0508.
Architecture.—Col. Jeremiah F. Garretson, Room 1C670, (703) 614–0517.

INSPECTOR GENERAL

Pentagon, Room 1E736, 20310–1700, phone (703) 695–1500, fax (703) 697–4705

Inspector General.—LtG. Jared L. Bates.
Deputy Inspector General.—MG Larry R. Jordan, (703) 695–1501.
Executive Officer.—Col. Richard E. Evans, Room 1E736, (703) 695–1502.

AUDITOR GENERAL

3101 Park Center Drive, Alexandria VA 22303
phone (703) 681–9809, fax (703) 681–9860

Auditor General.—Francis E. Reardon.
Deputy Auditor General for—
Financial Audits.—Thomas Druzgal, (703) 681–9839.
Logistical Audits.—C.A. Arigo, (703) 681–9690.
Policy and Operations Management.—Stephen E. Keefer, (703) 681–9820.
Acquisition and Force Management Audits.—Thomas W. Brown, (703) 681–9574.

DEPUTY UNDER SECRETARY OF THE ARMY (INTERNATIONAL AFFAIRS)

Pentagon, Room 3E412, 20310–0102, phone (703) 697–5075, fax (703) 697–3145

Deputy Under Secretary.—LtG. (Retired) Claude M. Kicklighter.
Chief of Staff.—Col. Kevin T. Hanretta, (703) 697–4664.

Military Deputy.—MG Joseph G. Garrett III, Room 3E516, (703) 697–3111.

DEPUTY UNDER SECRETARY OF THE ARMY (OPERATIONS RESEARCH)

Pentagon, Room 2E660, 20310–0102, phone (703) 695–0083, fax (703) 693–3897

Deputy Under Secretary.—Walter W. Hollis.
Executive Officer.—LtCol. John A. Marriott, (703) 697–0366.

LEGISLATIVE LIAISON

Pentagon, Room 2C631, 20310–1600, phone (703) 697–6767, fax (703) 697–3847

Chief.—MG Morris J. Boyd.
Deputy Chief.—Sheila McCready, (703) 695–6368.
Assistant Deputy.—Col. William D. McGill II, (703) 695–6368.
Special Assistant for Legislative Affairs for Intelligence.—Robert J. Winchester, (703) 695–3918.
Executive Officer.—Col. Wilson A. Shatzer, (703) 695–3524.
Chief of—
Congressional Inquiry.—Col. Louis Duet, Room 2D631, (703) 697–8381.
House Liaison.—Col. Dan Fleming, Room B325, Rayburn House Office Building, Washington DC, (202) 225–3853.
Senate Liaison.—Col. Randy Bookout, Room SR 183, Senate Russell Office Building, Washington DC, (202) 224–2881.
Investigation and Legislative.—Col. Gil Fegley, Room 2C634, (703) 697–2106.
Programs.—Col. Louis Kronenberger, Room 2C638, (703) 697–9915.

PUBLIC AFFAIRS

Pentagon, Room 2E636, 20310–1500, phone (703) 695–5135, fax (703) 693–8362

Chief.—BG John G. Meyer, Jr.
Deputy Chief.—Col. Robert E. Gaylord, (703) 697–4482.
Executive Officer.—Col. Carl J. Kropf, (703) 697–4200.
Chief of—
Public Communication.—Col. John A. Smith, Room 2E637, (703) 695–4462.
Plans, Operations and Policy.—Col. Eugenia Thornton, Room 2E631, (703) 695–2992.
Command Information.—William Drobnick, Room 2E625, (703) 697–4640.

ARMED RESERVE FORCES POLICY COMMITTEE

Pentagon, Room 2B684, 20310–0112, phone (703) 697–0226, fax (703) 697–4369

Chairman.—MG John T. Crowe.
Deputy Chairman.—MG James S. Rueger, (703) 695–3391.

SMALL AND DISADVANTAGED BUSINESS UTILIZATION

Pentagon, Room 2A712, 20310–0106, phone (703) 695–9800, fax (703) 693–3898

Director.—Tracey L. Pinson.
Deputy Director.—Sarah A. Cross, (703) 697–2868.
Senior Military Advisor.—Col. John E. Schweppe, (703) 697–8113.

ARMY STAFF AND SELECTED AGENCIES

Pentagon, 20310–0200, phone (703) 697–7994.

Chief of Staff.—Gen. Dennis J. Reimer, Room 3E668, (703) 695–2077.
Vice Chief of Staff.—Gen. Ronald H. Griffith, Room 3E666, (703) 695–4371.
Assistant Vice Chief of Staff.—LtG. Jay M. Garner, Room 3E658, (703) 697–8232 .
Director of Army Staff.—LtG. John A. Dubia, Room 3D665, (703) 695–3542.

Director, Office of—

Management.—Col. Daniel J. Sullivan, Room 3D658, (703) 695–0294.

Program Analysis and Evaluation.—MG David K. Heebner, Room 3C718, (703) 695–4617.

INTELLIGENCE

Pentagon, Room 2E646, 20310–1000, phone (703) 695–3033, fax (703) 697–8849

Deputy Chief of Staff.—MG Claudia J. Kennedy (acting).

Assistant Deputy Chiefs: Mark W. Ewing, (703) 697–4644; BG Michael E. Dunlavely, Room 2E482, (703) 695–3053.

Director, Office of—

Foreign Intelligence.—Col. William H. Speer, Room 2B515, (703) 614–0572.

Foreign Liaison.—Col. John A. Almborg, Room 2E484, (703) 697–0562.

Intelligence Information Management.—Col. Gary A. Millan, Room 2C472, (703) 695–3369.

Intelligence Policy.—Col. John C. Hammond, Room 2E473, (703) 695–6295.

Intelligence Plans, Program and Budget.—Col. Richard F. Riccardelli, Room 2E477, (703) 695–5001.

Reserve Affairs.—Col. Walter J. Stewart, Room 2B478, (703) 693–6396.

LOGISTICS

Pentagon, Room 3E560, 20310–0500, phone (703) 695–4102, fax (703) 614–6702

Deputy Chief of Staff.—LtG. John G. Coburn.

Assistant Deputy Chief of Staff.—MG Charles C. Cannon, Jr., (703) 697–5301.

Director, Office of—

Resource Management.—Stephen R. Burdt, Room 1E560, (703) 614–4391.

Plans and Operations.—BG Hawthorne L. Proctor, Room 2C567, (703) 695–3282.

Transportation, Energy, and Troop Support.—BG Boyd E. King, Room 1E580, (703) 695–0955.

Supply and Maintenance.—MG Charles Mahan, Room 2E554, (703) 697–8401.

OPERATIONS AND PLANS

Pentagon, Room 3E634, 20310–0400, phone (703) 695–2904, fax (703) 697–5572

Deputy Chief of Staff.—LtG. Eric K. Shinseki.

Assistant Deputy Chief of Staff.—MG John R. Riggs, (703) 697–5180.

Assistant Deputy Chief of Staff for—

Mobilization and Reserve Affairs.—MG Paul G. Rehkamp, Room 3B518, (703) 695–3447.

Joint Affairs.—BG Howard Von Kaenel, Room 3E530, (703) 695–5032.

Force Development.—MG Ronald E. Adams, Room 3A522, (703) 697–5116.

Director, Office of—

Strategy, Plans and Policy.—BG Howard Von Kaenel, Room 3E530, (703) 695–5032.

Training.—BG James Dubik, Room 1E542, (703) 614–8198.

Requirements.—BG John P, Rose, Room 3A522, (703) 695–0527.

Force Programs.—BG Kevin P. Byrnes, Room 3A522, (703) 695–6772.

Operations Readiness and Mobilization.—MG David L. Grange, Room BF751B, (703) 695–0526.

PERSONNEL

Pentagon, Room 2E736, 20310–0300, phone (703) 695–6003, fax (703) 695–3195

Deputy Chief of Staff.—LtG. Frederick E. Vollrath.

Assistant Deputy Chief of Staff.—MG Larry R. Ellis, (703) 695–2250.

Assistant Deputy Chief of Staff for Manpower and Reserve Affairs.—MG Kent H. Hillhouse, 2D738, (703) 614–3367.

Director, Office of—

Military Personnel Management.—MG Thomas Sikora, Room 2B736, (703) 695–2497.

Plans, Resources and Operations.—Col. Mark R. Lewis, Room 2C725, (703) 695–4729.
Manprint.—Jack H. Hiller, Room 2C739, (703) 697–7384.
Human Resources.—Col. Vickie Longenecker, Room 2B662, (703) 697–3018.

ASSISTANT CHIEF OF STAFF INSTALLATION MANAGEMENT

Pentagon, Room 1E668, 20310–0600, phone (703) 693–3233, fax (703) 693–3507

Assistant Chief of Staff.—MG R. W. House.
Deputy Assistant.—Janet C. Menig.

CORPS OF ENGINEERS

Pulaski Buliding, Room 8228, 20 Massachusetts Avenue, 20314
phone (202) 761–0001, fax (202) 761–0359

Chief.—LtG. Joe Ballard.
Deputy Chief.—MG Albert J. Genetti, Jr., (202) 761–0002.

SURGEON GENERAL

Skyline Place 5, Room 672, 5109 Leesburg Pike, Falls Church VA 22041–3258
phone (703) 681–3000, fax (703) 681–0243

Surgeon General.—LtG. Ronald R. Blanck.
Deputy Surgeon General.—MG John J. Cuddy, (703) 681–3002.

NATIONAL GUARD BUREAU

Pentagon, Room 2E394, 20310–2500, phone (703) 695–6987, fax (703) 693–3422

Chief.—LtG. Edward D. Baca.
Vice Chief.—MG Russell C. Davis, (703) 695–3544.
Director, Army National Guard.—MG William A. Javas, Jr., Room 2E408, (703) 697–5559.

ARMY RESERVE

Pentagon, Room 3E390, 20310–2400, phone (703) 697–1784, fax (703) 695–4380

Chief.—MG Max Baratz.
Deputy Chief.—BG James R. Helmly, (703) 697–1260.
Deputy Chief (IMA).—Col. Robert M. Diamond, (703) 695–4733.

JUDGE ADVOCATE

Pentagon, Room 2E444, 20310–2200, phone (703) 697–5152, fax (703) 695–8370.

Judge Advocate General.—MG Michael J. Nardotti, Jr.
Assistant Judge Advocate General.—MG Kenneth D. Gray, (703) 697–6309.
Assistant Deputy Chief for—
Civil Law and Litigation.—BG Walter B. Huffman, Room 2E432, (703) 695–5947.
Military Law and Operations.—BG John D. Altenberg, Jr., Room 2E432, (703) 697–4769.

CHIEF OF CHAPLAINS

Pentagon, Room 1E416, 20310–2700, phone (703) 695–1135, fax (703) 695–9824

Chief.—MG Donald W. Shea.
Deputy Chief.—BG Gaylord T. Gunhus, (703) 695–1135.

ARMY CENTER OF MILITARY HISTORY

Franklin Court Building, 1099 14th Street NW, Room 208, 20005–3402

phone (202) 761–5400, fax (202) 761–5390

Chief.—BG John W. Mountcastle.
Deputy Chief.—Col. Stephen E. Wilson, Room 206, (202) 761–5401.
Chief Historian.—Jeffrey J. Clarke, Room 210, (202) 761–5402.

MAJOR ARMY COMMANDS

U.S. Army Materiel Command.—Gen. Johnnie E. Wilson, 5001 Eisenhower Avenue, Room 1OE08, Alexandria VA 22333–0001, (703) 617–9625.
U.S. Army Corps of Engineers.—LtG. Joe N. Ballard, 20 Massachuetts Avenue NW, Room 8228, Washington DC 20314, (202) 761–0001.
U.S. Army Criminal Investigation Command.—BG Daniel A. Doherty, Building 1465, Room 303, Fort Belvoir VA 22060–5506, (703) 806–0400.
U.S. Army Forces Command.—Gen. David A. Bramlett, Fort McPherson GA 30330–6000, (404) 669–5054.
U.S. Army Intelligence and Security Command.—BG John D. Thomas, Jr., Nolan Building, Room 2F01B, Fort Belvoir VA 22060–5246, (703) 706–1603.
U.S. Army Medical Command.—LtG. Ronald R. Blanck, Fort Sam Houston TX 78234, (703) 681–3000.
U.S. Army Military District of Washington.—MG Robert T. Foley, 1900 Half Street NW, Washington DC 20319–5000, (202) 685–2807.
U.S. Army Military Traffic Management Command.—MG Mario F. Montero, Jr., 5611 Columbia Pike, Room 701, Falls Church VA 22041–5050, (703) 681–6724.
U.S. Army Special Operations Command.—LtG. Peter J. Schoomaker, Fort Bragg NC 28307–5200, (910) 432–3000.
U.S. Army Training and Doctrine Command.—Gen. William W. Hartzog, Fort Monroe VA 23651–5000, (757) 727–3514.
U.S. Army South.—MG Lawson W. Magruder III, APO AA 34004–5000.
Eighth U.S. Army.—LtG. Richard F. Timmons, APO AP 96205.
U.S. Army Pacific.—LtG. William M. Steele, Fort Shafter Hawaii 96858–5100, (808) 438–2206.
U.S. Army Europe and 7th Army.—Gen. William W. Crouch, APO AE 09014.

DEPARTMENT OF THE NAVY

Pentagon 20350–1000, phone (703) 695–3131

OFFICE OF THE SECRETARY

Pentagon, Room 4E686, phone (703) 695–3131

Secretary of the Navy.—Hon. John H. Dalton.
Executive Assistant and Naval Aide.—Capt. L.W. Crenshaw, (703) 695–4603.
Military Assistant and Marine Corps Aide.—Col. J.R. Battaglini, USMC, (703) 695–5133.
Administrative Aide.—Cdr. K.S. Lipold, Room 4E687, (703) 695–5410.
Naval Aide.—[Vacant]. (703) 695–5050.
Special Assistant for—
Legal and Legislative Affairs.—Cdr. J. Daniel McCarthy, Room 4E725, (703) 697–6935.
Public Affairs.—Capt. C.D. Connor, Room 4E748, (703) 697–7491.
Administrative Officer.—Zoe Walker, Room 4E687, (703) 697–3334.

OFFICE OF THE UNDER SECRETARY

Pentagon, Room 4E714, phone (703) 695–3141

Under Secretary of the Navy.—Hon. Richard Danzig.
Executive Assistant and Naval Aide.—Capt. Kevin Cosgriff, (703) 695–2140.
Special Assistant and Marine Corps Aide.—Col. J. Paxton, USMC, (703) 695–2002.
Assistant for Administration.—Roy L. Carter.

Auditor General.—Richard Shaffer, Nassif Building, Room 501–B, (703) 756–2117.

PROGRAM APPRAISAL

Pentagon, Room 4D730, phone (703) 697–9396, fax (703) 694–3477

Director.—Vice Adm. C.C. Lautenbacher, Jr.
Deputy Director.—[Vacant].
Executive Assistant.—Cdr. Steven L. Briganti.

GENERAL COUNSEL

Pentagon, Room 4E724; CP–5 and 6, Crystal Plaza Building, No. 5, 6
2211 Jefferson Davis Highway, Arlington VA 20360
phone (703) 614–1994

General Counsel.—Hon. Steven H. Honigman.
Principal Deputy Counsel.—Leigh A. Bradley, (703) 614–5066.
Deputy General Counsel.—Eugene P. Angrist.
Associate General Counsel for Management.—Fred A. Phelps, Room 480, (CP–5), (703) 602–2743.
Associate General Counsel for Litigation.—Arthur H. Hildebrandt, Room 1000, (CP–6), (703) 602–3176.
Assistant General Counsel for—
Research, Development and Acquisition.—Barry J. Plunkett, Room 4C748, (703) 614–6985.
Manpower and Reserve Affairs.—[Vacant] Room 4E725, (703) 614–5066.
Installations and Environment.—John C. Turnquist, Room 4D434, (703) 614–1101.
Financial Management/Counsel for the Comptroller.—Margaret A. Olsen, Room 4C719, (703) 614–5588
Ethics.—Kenneth J. Wernick, Room 480, (CP–5), (703) 602–2727.

INSPECTOR GENERAL

901 M Street SE, Room 100, Washington DC 20374–5006, phone 433–2000

Inspector General.—Vice Adm. James Fitzgerald.
Deputy Naval Inspector General.—Jill Vines Loftus.

LEGISLATIVE AFFAIRS

Pentagon, Room 5C760, phone (703) 697–7146, fax (703) 694–7089

Chief.—Rear Adm. Norbert R. Ryan, Jr.
Deputy Chief.—LtCdr. Michael Hewitt.
Executive Assistant.—LtCdr. Michael Hewitt.
Director for—
Administration and Support.—Ms. Pris Matthews, (703) 695–4816.
Congressional Correspondence Control.—Veronica Leonard, (703) 695–6357.
Legislation.—Capt. Richard F. Walsh, (703) 695–5276.
Navy Programs.—Capt. Patrick W. Dunne, (703) 693–2919.
Public Affairs and Contract Notifications.—LtCdr. Scott D. Harris, Room 5C768, (703) 695–0395.
Principal Deputy for—
House Liaison.—Capt. Del O. Snodgrass, (202) 225–7808.
Senate Liaison.—Capt. Barry M. Costello, (202) 685–6006.

OFFICE OF INFORMATION

Pentagon, Room 2E340, phone (703) 697–7391

Chief.—Rear Adm. Kendell Pease.
Deputy Chief.—Capt. James P. Mitchell, (703) 697–6724.
Executive Assistant.—LtCdr. Frank Thorp.
Assistant Chief for—
Administration and Resource Management.—William Mason.

Naval Media Center.—LtCdr. Susan M. Haeg.
Media Operations.—Cdr. Steven Pietropaoli.
Plans, Policy, and Community Programs.—[Vacant].

JUDGE ADVOCATE GENERAL

Pentagon, Room 4E474 Pentagon

200 Stovall Street, Hoffman Building 2 (HB–2), Alexandria VA 22332-2400

phone (703) 614–7420, fax (703) 325–9152

Judge Advocate General.—Rear Adm. Harold E. Grant.
Executive Assistant.—Capt. Donald J. Guter.
Deputy Judge Advocate General.—Rear Adm. Carlson M. Legrand, (HB–2), (703) 325–9820, fax (703) 325–7227.
Executive Assistant to the Deputy Judge Advocate General.—LtCdr. Mark D. Lawton, (703) 325–9820, fax (703) 325–7227.
Assistant Judge Advocate General for Civil Law.—Capt. Richard B. Schiff, (HB–2), (703) 325–9850.
Deputy Assistant Judge Advocate General for—
Administrative Law.—Capt. James F. Duffy, (703) 604–8200.
Admiralty.—Capt. Rand R. Pixa, (703) 325–9744.
Civil Affairs.—Cdr. Timothy M. McGuan, (703) 325–9752.
Claims, Investigations and Tort Litigation.—Capt. Ginger C. Paad, (703) 325–9880, fax (703) 325–2159.
General Litigation.—Capt. John K. Henebery, (703) 325–9870.
International and Operational Law.—Capt. Charles A. Allen, (703) 697–9161.
Legal Assistance.—Cdr. David B. Clement, (703) 325–7928.
Special Programs.—Cdr. Timothy J. Nagle, (703) 325–9536.
Assistant Judge Advocate General for Military Justice.—Col. David C. Hauge, USMC, Building 111, 1st Floor, Washington Navy Yard, 20374–1111, (202) 433–6030, fax (202) 433–6489.
Deputy Assistant Judge Advocate General for Criminal Law.—Capt. Richard M. Mollison, (202) 433–5895.
Assistant Judge Advocate General for Operations and Management.—Capt. Thomas A. Morrison, (HR–2), (703) 325–9820.
Deputy Assistant Judge Advocate General for—
Management and Plans.—Capt. Kenneth R. Bryant, (703) 325–8312.
Military Personnel.—Capt. Richard A. Stevens, (703) 325–9830, fax (703) 325–7429.
Reserve and Retired Personnel Programs.—Cdr. Jeanne McGann, (703) 325–9736, fax (703) 325–9152.
Special Assistants to the Judge Advocate General—
Command Master Chief.—LNCM Michael S. Reed, (703) 325–9830.
Comptroller.—Dennis J. Oppman, (703) 325–0786.
Inspector General.—Capt. Steven D. Peterson, (703) 325–9850, fax (703) 325–7227.
Public Affairs Officer.—Carolyn Alison, (703) 325–9820.

ASSISTANT SECRETARY FOR MANPOWER AND RESERVE AFFAIRS

Pentagon, Room 4E788, phone (703) 697–2179

Assistant Secretary.—Dr. Bernard Rostker.
Executive Assistant.—Capt. Stewart Barnett.
Military Assistant and Marine Corps Aide.—Col. Mary Lowery, (703) 697–0975.
Deputy Assistant Secretary for—
Civilian Personnel Policy and Equal Employment Opportunity.—Betty S. Welch.
Director of Congressional and Employee Inquiries.—Norm Chamberland, (703) 696–0389, fax (703) 696–0508.
Force Support and Families.—William W. Tate.
Manpower.—Karen S. Heath.
Personnel Policy.—Charles Tompkins.
Reserve Affairs.—Wade Sanders.
Principal Deputy Assistant Secretary.—Karen Heath.

NAVAL COUNCIL OF PERSONNEL BOARDS

Ballston Center Tower 2, Room 907

801 North Randolph Street, Arlington VA 22203–1989

phone (703) 696–4355, fax 696–4556

Director.—Capt. J.L. Johnson.
Deputy Director.—[Vacant].
Executive Assistant.—J.W. Kinder.
Counsel.—Cdr. R. Fiske.
Special Correspondence Officer.—Janice B. Overman.
Executive Secretary for—
Disability Evaluation System.—[Vacant].
Naval Clemency and Parole Board.—LtCol. G. Lyon.
Naval Discharge Review Board.—[Vacant].

BOARD FOR CORRECTION OF NAVAL RECORDS

Arlington Annex Room 2432, Arlington VA 20370

phone (703) 614–1316, fax (703) 694–9857

Executive Director.—W. Dean Pfieffer.
Deputy Executive Director.—Robert D. Zsalman.
Administrative Officer.—Ev Sellers.

BOARD FOR DECORATIONS AND MEDALS

Building 36 Washington Navy Yard, Washington DC 20374

Senior Member.—Vice Adm. James Fitzgerald.
Decorations/Medals Specialist and Recorder.—Barbara Wilson.

ASSISTANT SECRETARY FOR RESEARCH, DEVELOPMENT AND ACQUISITION

Pentagon, Room 4E732, phone (703) 695–6315

Assistant Secretary.—John W. Douglas.
Executive Assistant and Naval Aide.—Capt. Joseph Carnevale.
Special Assistant and Marine Corps Aide.—Col. David L. Saddler.
Principal Deputy Assistant Secretary.—Rear Adm. M.P. Sullivan, Room 4E731, (703) 697–4928.
Deputy Assistant Secretary for—
Air Programs.—William A. Stussie.
PPR.—William J. Schaefer, Jr.
C4I.—Dr. Marvin Langston.
Expeditionary Forces.—BG Michael A. Hough.
Ships.—Michael C. Hammes.
MUW Programs.—[Vacant].

NAVAL RESEARCH

Ballston Tower 1, Room 907, 800 North Quincy Street, Arlington VA 22217

phone (703) 696–4258

Chief.—Rear Adm. Paul G. Goffney II.
Deputy Chief of Naval Research/Technical Director.—Fred E. Saalfeld, (703) 696–4517.
Assistant Chief.—Capt. Richard J. Scott, Jr., (703) 696–4261.

ASSISTANT SECRETARY FOR FINANCIAL MANAGEMENT AND COMPTROLLER

Pentagon, Room 4E768, phone (703) 697–2325

Assistant Secretary and Comptroller.—Hon. Deborah P. Christie.
Executive Assistant and Naval Aide.—Capt. Mark E. Easton.
Special Assistant and Marine Corps Aide.—Maj. Beverly J. Runelfson.

Principal Deputy Assistant Secretary.—Gladys J. Commons, (703) 695–3377.
Director, Office of Budget and Reports.—Rear Adm. James F. Amerault.
Director, Office of Financial Operations.—A. Anthony Tisone.
Counsel.—Margaret A. Olsen, Room 4C717, (703) 697–5588.

ASSISTANT SECRETARY FOR INSTALLATIONS AND ENVIRONMENT
Pentagon, Room 4E780, phone (703) 693–4529

Assistant Secretary.—Robert B. Pirie, Jr.
Principal Deputy.—[Vacant].
Executive Assistant and Naval Aide.—Capt. Andrew D. Brunhart.
Special Assistant and Marine Corps Aide.—LtCol. Larry A. Johnson.
Deputy Assistant Secretary—
Shore Resources.—Richard O. Thomas, (703) 693–0657.
Conversion and Redevelopment.—William J. Cassidy, Jr., (703) 693–4527.
Environment and Safety.—Elsie Munsell, (703) 614–1303.
Installations and Facilities.—Duncan Holaday, (703) 695–3491.
Director, Operational Safety and Survivability.—Richard F. Healing, Crystal Plaza Building No. 5, Room 162, (703) 602–2882.

CHIEF OF NAVAL OPERATIONS
Pentagon, Room 4E660, phone (703) 695–0532, fax (703) 693–9408

Chief.—ADM J.L. Johnson.
Vice Chief.—ADM H.W. Gehman, Jr.
Assistant Vice Chief.—[Vacant].
Director, Naval Nuclear Propulsion Program.—ADM F.L. Bowman.
Special Assistant for—
Public Affairs Support.—Rear Adm. Kendell Pease, (703) 697–7391.
Safety Matters.—Rear Adm. F.M. Dirren.
Inspection Support.—Vice Adm. J.R. Fitzgerald.
Legal Services.—Rear Adm. Harold Grant, (703) 614–4720.
Legislative Support.—Rear Adm. N.R. Ryan.
Naval Investigative Matters and Security.—[Vacant].
Material Inspections and Surveys.—Rear Adm. H.F. Herrera.
Deputy Chief of Naval Operations for—
Logistics.—Vice Adm. W.J. Hancock.
Manpower and Personnel.—Vice Adm. D.T. Oliver.
Plans, Policy, and Operations.—Vice Adm. J.O. Ellis, Jr.
Resources, Warfare Requirements, and Assessments.—Vice Adm. D.L. Tilling.
Director, Office of—
Naval Intelligence.—Rear Adm. Michael Cramer, (703) 695–0124.
Naval Medicine/Surgeon General.—Vice Adm. Harold M. Koenig, MC, (202) 653–1144.
Naval Reserve.—Rear Adm. Thomas Hall, (703) 695–5353.
Naval Training.—Vice Adm. Timothy Wright, (904) 452–4810.
Space and Electronic Warfare.—Vice Adm. Walter Davis, (703) 695–3239.
Test and Evaluation and Technology Requirements.—Rear Adm. Thomas Ryan, (703) 697–5533.
Chief of Chaplains.—Rear Adm. Donald Muchow, (703) 614–4043.
Oceanographer.—Rear Adm. P.E. Tobin.

BUREAU OF MEDICINE AND SURGERY
Potomac Annex 23d and E Streets, Washington DC 20372
phone (202) 653–1144, fax 653–0101

Chief.—Vice Adm. Harold M. Koenig, MC.

NAVAL AIR SYSTEMS COMMAND
2531 Jefferson Plaza Building Nos. 1 and 2 Room 1200, Arlington VA 20361–0001
phone (703) 604–2822

Commander.—Vice Adm. John A. Lockard.

NAVAL SEA SYSTEMS COMMAND

2531 Jefferson Davis Highway, Room 12E10 Building 3, Arlington VA 22242–5160
phone (703) 602–3381

Commander.—Vice Adm. George R. Sterner.

NAVAL SUPPLY SYSTEMS COMMAND

Mechanicsburg PA, phone (717) 790–6206

Commander.—Rear Adm. R.M. Mitchell, Jr., SC.

NAVAL HOSPITAL

Commanding Officer.—Rear Adm. Richard I. Ridenour (Medical Command), 8901 Wisconsin Avenue, Bethesda MD 20614, (301) 295–2206.

NATIONAL NAVAL MEDICAL CENTER

Commander.—Rear Adm. Richard I. Ridenour (Medical Command), Bethesda MD 20889–5600, (301) 295–5800, fax (301) 295–6521.

NAVAL COMPUTER AND TELECOMMUNICATIONS COMMAND

4401 Massachusetts Avenue, Washington DC 20394
phone (202) 764–0356, fax 764–0357

Commander.—Capt. M.P. Finn.

NAVAL FACILITIES ENGINEERING COMMAND

Hoffman Building No. 2 (HB–2), 200 Stovall Street, Alexandria VA 22332–2300
phone (703) 325–0400, fax (703) 325–0024

Commander.—Rear Adm. D.J. Nash, CEC.

OFFICE OF NAVAL INTELLIGENCE

4251 Suitland Road, Washington DC 20395–5720
phone (301) 669–3011, fax (301) 669–3099

Director.—Rear Adm. Michael W. Cramer.

NAVAL CRIMINAL INVESTIGATIVE SERVICE COMMAND

901 M Street SE, Washington DC 20388, phone (202) 433–8800, fax 433–9619

Director.—Roy D. Nedrow.

NAVAL SECURITY GROUP COMMAND

Naval Security Station, 3801 Nebraska Avenue, Washington DC 20393
phone (202) 764–0786, fax 764–0329

Commander.—Rear Adm. Thomas F. Stevens.

MILITARY SEALIFT COMMAND

Building No. 210, Washington Navy Yard, 9th and M Streets SE
Washington DC 20398–5540
phone (202) 685–5001, fax 685–5020

Commander.—Vice Adm. Philip M. Quast.

NAVAL LEGAL SERVICE COMMAND
Hoffman Building No. 2 (HB–2), 200 Stovall Street, Alexandria VA 22332
phone (703) 325–9820, fax (703) 325–7227

Commander.—Rear Adm. C.M. LeGrand.

NAVAL SPACE COMMAND
Building 180, Dahlgren VA 22448, phone (703) 663–6100

Commander.—Rear Adm. Katharine Laughton.

SPACE AND NAVAL WARFARE SYSTEMS COMMAND
2451 Crystal Drive, No. 5 Crystal Park, Arlington VA 22202
phone (703) 602–3006, fax (703) 602–1659

Commander.—Rear Adm. George F.A. Wagner.

NAVAL DISTRICT OF WASHINGTON
901 M Street SE, Washington DC 20374–5001, phone 433–2777, fax 433–2207

Commandant.—Rear Adm. Robert L. Ellis, Jr.
Chief of Staff.—Capt. Jeff Sweet.
Public Affairs Officer.—Lt. Dave Waterman.

U.S. NAVAL ACADEMY
Annapolis MD 21402–5000, phone (410) 293–1000

Superintendent.—ADM Charles R. Larson, 293–1500.
Commandant of Midshipmen.—Capt. William Thomas R. Bogle, 293–7005.

U.S. MARINE CORPS HEADQUARTERS
Pentagon, Room 4E714, Washington DC, phone (703) 614–1235

Commandant.—Gen. C.C. Krulak.
Aide-de-Camp.—LtCol. J.R. Allen.
Sergeant Major of the Marine Corps.—Sgt. Maj. L.G. Lee.
Assistant Commandant.—Gen. R.I. Neal.
Legislative Assistant.—BG R.L. West.
Military Assistant.—Col. John Holly.
Counsel for the Commandant.—Peter M. Murphy, (703) 614–2150.
Inspector General of the Marine Corps.—MG Peter D. Williams (703) 614–1533.
Fiscal Director of the Marine Corps.—H. Lee Dixson, (703) 614–2590.
Chaplain.—Capt. G.W. Pucciarelli, USN.
Dental Officer.—Capt. L. Herrman, USN.
Judge Advocate.—BG T.G. Hess.
Medical Officer.—Capt. A. Diaz, USN.
Deputy Chief of Staff for—
Aviation.—LtG. T.R. Dake.
Installations and Logistics.—MG J.D. Stewart.
Manpower and Reserve Affairs.—LtG. C.A. Mutter.
Plans, Policies, and Operations.—LtG. M.R. Steele.
Programs and Resources.—LtG. Jeffrey W. Oster, (703) 614–3435.
Assistant Chief of Staff, Command, Control, Communications, Computer, and Intelligence.—MG D.A. Richwine.
Director of—
Intelligence.—Col. Bruce A. Harder.
Marine Corps History and Museums.—[Vacant].

MARINE BARRACKS
Eighth and I Streets SE, Washington DC 20390, phone 433–4094

Commanding Officer.—Col. David G. Dotterrer.

TRAINING AND EDUCATION DIVISION

Quantico VA 22134, phone (703) 640–3730, fax (703) 640–3724

Director.—BG B.B. Knutson, Jr.

DEPARTMENT OF EDUCATION

600 Independence Avenue SW 20202
phone 401–3000, fax 401–0596, http://www.ed.gov

RICHARD W. RILEY, born in Greenville County, SC, January 2, 1933; B.A., cum laude, Furman University, 1954; served for two years as an officer in the U.S. Navy; received law degree, University of South Carolina School of Law, 1959; legal counsel, Judiciary Committee of the U.S. Senate; joined his family's law firm in Greenville and Simpsonville, 1960; South Carolina State representative, 1963–67; State Senator, 1967–77; elected Governor, 1978; awards: South Carolina Education Association's Friend of Education Award; the 1983 Government Responsibility Award from the Martin Luther King, Jr. Center; 1981 Connie Award for special conservation achievement by the National Wildlife Federation; member: National Assessment Governing Board; Carnegie Foundation Task Force on Meeting the Needs of Young Children; Duke Endowment; Institute Fellow at the John F. Kennedy School of Government at Harvard University; senior partner with the South Carolina law firm of Nelson, Mullins, Riley and Scarborough; married to the former Ann Osteen Yarborough; four children; nominated by President Clinton to be Secretary of Education on January 20, 1993; confirmed by the U.S. Senate, January 21, 1993, and sworn in January 22, 1993.

OFFICE OF THE SECRETARY

Room 6161, phone 401–3000, fax 401–0596

Secretary of Education.—Richard W. Riley.
Chief of Staff.—Frank S. Holleman, Room 6153, 401–1110.
Deputy Chief of Staff.—Leslie Thornton, Room 6142, 401–1110.
Director, Office of Public Affairs.—David Frank, Room 6113, 401–3026, fax 401–3130 or 401–0954.

OFFICE OF THE DEPUTY SECRETARY

Room 6236, phone 401–1000, fax 401–3093

Deputy Secretary.—Marshall Smith (acting).
Chief of Staff.—Michele Cavataio.
Director of—
Corporate Liaison Staff.—Margarita Colmenares, 401–9500.
Office of Educational Technology.—Linda Roberts, 401–1444.
Office of Small and Disadvantaged Business Utilization.—Viola J. Sanchez, 7th and D Streets SW, Room 3120, 20202, 708–9820, fax 401–6477.

OFFICE FOR CIVIL RIGHTS

330 C Street SW, Room 5000, 20202, phone 401–5557, fax 205–9862 or 205–9889

Assistant Secretary.—Norma V. Cantú.
Deputy Assistant Secretary.—Raymond C. Pierce, Room 5114A, 205–9556.
Special Assistant/Legal.—Arthur Coleman, Room 5012D, 205–5557.
Executive Assistant.—Arthur Coleman (acting), Room 5012D, 205–5557.
Director of—
Enforcement, East.—Susan Bowers, Room 5112A, 205–8217.
Enforcement, West.—Cathy Lewis (acting), Room 5112B, 205–8217.
Resource Management Group.—Paul Fairley, Room 5117, 205–5415.
Program Legal Group.—Eileen Hanrahan (acting), Room 5044, 205–8635.

National Coordinator for Desegregation.—Archie Meyer, 19th Floor, 61 Forsyth Street, Atlanta, GA 30303, 404–562–6352.

OFFICE OF THE UNDER SECRETARY

Room 6236, phone 401–1000, fax 260–7113 or 401–4353

Under Secretary.—Marshall Smith (acting).

Director of—

Management Operations Staff.—Douglas F. Flamm, Room 5154, 205–0685, fax 401–7638.

Planning and Evaluation Service.—Alan L. Ginsburg, Room 4162, 401–3132, fax 401–3036.

Budget Service.—Thomas P. Skelly, Room 5264, 401–1700, fax 401–6139.

OFFICE OF INSPECTOR GENERAL

330 C Street SW, Room 4006, 20202, phone 205–5439, fax 205–8238

Inspector General.—Thomas R. Bloom.

Deputy Inspector General.—John P. Higgins, Jr.

Counsel to the Inspector General.—Ellen Bass, Room 4044, 205–8041.

Assistant Inspector General for—

Investigation Services.—Dianne Van Riper, Room 4106, 205–8762.

Audit Services.—Steven McNamara, Room 4200, 205–8200.

Executive Officer, Planning, Analysis, and Management Services.—Robert K. Nagle, Room 4022, 205–5400.

OFFICE OF THE GENERAL COUNSEL

Room 5400, phone 401–6000, fax 401–5391

General Counsel.—Judith Winston.

Special Counsel/Executive Assistant.—Robert Wexler.

Senior Counsel.—Theodore Sky.

Deputy General Counsel of—

Program Service.—Steven Y. Winnick.

Postsecondary and Departmental Service.—Felix Baxter.

Regulations and Legislation Service.—Jamienne S. Studley.

OFFICE OF SPECIAL EDUCATION AND REHABILITATIVE SERVICES

330 C Street SW, Room 3006, 20202, phone 205–5465, fax 205–9252

Assistant Secretary.—Judith Heumann.

Special Assistant.—Prudence Lezy (acting).

Deputy Assistant Secretary.—Howard Moses.

Executive Administrator.—Andrew J. Pepin, Room 3110, 205–9439.

Director of—

Office of Special Education Programs.—Thomas Hehir, Room 3086, 205–5507, fax 260–0416.

National Institute on Disability and Rehabilitation Research.—Katherine D. Seelman, Room 3060, 205–8134, fax 205–8997.

Commissioner of Rehabilitation Services Administration.—Fredric K. Schroeder, Room 3026, 205–5482, fax 205–9874.

Associate Commissioner of—

Program Operations.—Mark Shoob, (acting), Room 3036, 205–9406, fax 205–9874.

Developmental Programs.—Tom Finch (acting), Room 3038, 205–8292, fax 260–9424.

OFFICE OF THE CHIEF INFORMATION OFFICER

7th and D Streets SW, Room 5102, 20202, phone 708–8391

Chief Information Officer.—Gloria Parker (acting).

OFFICE OF LEGISLATION AND CONGRESSIONAL AFFAIRS

Room 6337, phone 401–0020, fax 401–1438

Assistant Secretary.—Kay L. Casstevens.
Administrative Specialist.—Elnora Walker.
Deputy Assistant Secretary.—Scott Fleming, 401–1028.
Director of—
Legislation Staff.—Charlotte Frass, 401–1028.
Congressional Affairs Staff.—Scott Fleming, 401–1028.

OFFICE OF INTERGOVERNMENTAL AND INTERAGENCY AFFAIRS

Room 6442, phone 401–0404, fax 401–8607

Assistant Secretary.—Gilberto Mario Moreno.
Chief of Staff.—Edward Augustus, 401–3407.
Team Director of—
Interagency, International, and National Services.—Henry Smith, fax 401–2508.
Community Services.—John McGrath, Room 3163, 401–1309, fax 205–0676.
Intergovernmental and Constituent Services.—Michelle L. Doyle.
Regional Services.—Wilson Goode, fax 401–8552.

OFFICE OF THE CHIEF FINANCIAL OFFICER

Room 4366, phone 401–0085, fax 401–0006

Chief Financial Officer.—Mitchell L. Laine (acting).
Deputy Chief Financial Officer.—Mitchell L. Laine, Room 4300, 401–0207.
Executive Assistant.—William Burrow, 401–0250.
Special Assistant/Operations.—Marilyn McCarroll, Room 4316, 401–0322, fax 401–2455.
Director of—
Contracts and Purchasing Operations.—Glenn Perry, Room 3600, 7th and D Streets SW 20202, 708–9781, fax 205–0323.
Financial Improvement, Receivables and Post Audit Operations.—Hazel Fiers, Room 3131, 401–1194, fax 401–1198.
Grants Policy and Oversight Staff.—Mary P. Liggett, 7th and D Streets SW, Room 3652, 20202, 708–8263, fax 205–0667.
Financial Payments and Cash Management Operations.—Charlie Coleman, Room 3211, 401–1776, fax 205–0765.
Financial Reporting and Systems Operations.—Gloria Jarmon, Room 3116, 401–0561, fax 401–8341.

OFFICE OF MANAGEMENT

Room 2164, phone 401–0470, fax 401–0485

Director.—Gary Rasmussen.
Deputy Director.—Mary Ellen Dix.
Chief of Staff.—Jim Borches.
Group Director of—
Equal Employment Opportunity Group.—Mary Ellen Dix (acting), Room 2468, 401–3560, fax 205–5760.
Family Policy Compliance Group.—LeRoy Rooker, Room 1366, 260–3887, fax 260–9001.
Human Resources Group.—Veronica D. Trietsch, Room 1168, 401–0553, fax 401–0520.

Management Systems Improvement Group.—Joseph Colantuoni, 401–8534.
Office of Hearings and Appeals.—Frank J. Furey, Room 2100, 490 L'Enfant Plaza, SW 20202, 619–9700, fax 619–9726.
Labor Relations Group.—James Keenan, Room 1467, 401–3927.
Real Property Group.—David Hakola, Room 2339, 401–0506, fax 401–0828.
Quality Workplace Group.—Tony Conques, Room 2400, 401–0900, fax 732–1534 or 401–1033.
Information Resources Group.—Gloria Parker, Room 4682, 7th and D Streets SW, 20202, 401–3200, fax 708–9886.
Health and Environmental Safety Group—Diane Schmitz, Room A404, 401–0156.
Training and Development Group.—Ingrid Kolb, Room 1100, 401–1973, fax 401–0434.

OFFICE OF POSTSECONDARY EDUCATION

7th and D Streets SW, Room 4082, 20202, phone 708–5547, fax 708–9814

Assistant Secretary.—David A. Longanecker.
Chief of Staff.—Diane E. Rogers.
Deputy Assistant Secretary for—
Policy, Planning and Innovation.—Maureen McLaughlin, Room 4060, 205–2987, fax 401–5749.
Higher Education Programs.—Claudio R. Prieto, 600A, 1250 Maryland Avenue SW 20202, 708–8596, fax 708–9046.
Student Financial Assistant Programs.—Elizabeth M. Hicks, Room 4004, 260–6536.
Service Director of—
Policy, Training, and Analysis Service.—Nina Winkler, Room 3060, 708–5217, fax 205–0786.
Accounting and Financial Management Service.—Linda Paulsen, Room 4624, 206–6824.
Program Systems Service.—Gerard A. Russomano, Room 4640, 708–7701.
Institutional Participation and Oversight Service.—Marianne Phelps, Room 3905, 708–6040.
Debt Collection Service.—Thomas Pestka, Room 5114, 708–4764, fax 708–8875.

OFFICE OF EDUCATIONAL RESEARCH AND IMPROVEMENT

555 New Jersey Avenue NW, Room 600, 20208, phone 219–1385, fax 219–1466

Assistant Secretary.—[Vacant].
Senior Program Advisor.—Alicia Coro, 219–2000.
Chief of Staff.—Sandra Garcia, Room 602E, 219–1385.
Deputy Assistant Secretary for—
Policy and Planning.—Charles E. Hansen, Room 600G, 219–2050.
Operations.—Charles E. Hansen (acting), Room 600G, 219–2050.
Commissioner of National Center for Education Statistics.—Pascal D. Forgione, Jr., Room 400F, 219–1828, fax 219–1736.
Director of—
National Institute on Student Achievement, Curriculum and Assessment.—Joseph Conaty, Room 510H, 219–2079, fax 219–2135.
National Institute on the Education of At-Risk Students.—Edward Fuentes, Room 610E, 219–1895, fax 219–2035.
National Institute on Early Childhood Development and Education.—Naomi Karp, Room 522, 219–1935, fax 273–4678
National Institute on Educational Governance, Finance, Policymaking, and Management.—Deborah Iman, Room 608B, 219–2032, fax 219–1528.
National Institute on Postsecondary Education, Libraries, and Lifelong Learning.—Carole B. LaCampagne, Room 627H, 219–2064, fax 501–3005.
Office of Reform Assistance and Dissemination.—Ronald Cartwright (acting), Room 500E, 219–2164, fax 219–2106.

National Library of Education.—Blane K. Dessy, Room 202A, 219–2226, fax 219–1970.
Media and Information Services.—Cynthia H. Dorfman, Room 306C, 219–1892, fax 219–1321.
Library Programs.—Robert Klassen, Room 300Q, 219–1300, fax 219–1725.

OFFICE OF ELEMENTARY AND SECONDARY EDUCATION

1250 Maryland Avenue SW, Room 4000, 20202, phone 401–0113, 205–0303

Assistant Secretary.—Gerald N. Tirozzi.
Deputy Assistant Secretary.—James Kohlmoos (acting).
Deputy Assistant Secretary.—Phyllis Barajas (acting).
Chief of Staff.—Sarah Lisenby.
Director of—
Impact Aid Programs.—Catherine Schagh, Room 4200, 260–3858, fax 205–0088.
School Improvement Programs.—Arthur Cole, Room 4500, 260–3693, fax 205–0302.
Compensatory Education Programs.—Mary Jean LeTendre, Room 4400, 260–0826, fax 260–7764.
Goals 2000 Program.—Thomas Fagan, Room 4000, 401–0039.
Office of Migrant Education.—Bayla F. White, Room 4100, 260–1164, fax 205–0089.
Safe and Drug Free Schools Program.—William Modzeleski, Room 604, 260–3954, fax 260–7767.
Office of Indian Education.—Saundra Spaulding (acting), Room 4300, 260–3774, fax 260–7779.

OFFICE OF BILINGUAL EDUCATION AND MINORITY LANGUAGE AFFAIRS

330 C Street SW, Room 5082, 20202, phone 205–5463, fax 205–8737 or 205–8680

Director.—Delia Pompa.
Deputy Director.—Dang Pham.
Management Resources and Policy Officer.—Ileana A. Fresen, Room 5090.
Coordinator of—
East Region Cluster.—Luis Catarineau, Room 5615, 205–9907.
Midwest Region Cluster.—John Ovard, Room 5624, 205–5576.
West Region Cluster.—Mary Mahony, Room 5609, 205–9803.

OFFICE OF VOCATIONAL AND ADULT EDUCATION

330 C Street SW, Room 4090, 20202, phone 205–5451, fax 205–8748

Assistant Secretary.—Patricia W. McNeil.
Deputy Assistant Secretary.—[Vacant].
Director of—
Adult Education and Literacy Division.—Ronald S. Pugsley, Room 4428, 205–8270, fax 205–8973.
Vocational-Tech Education Division.—Winifred I. Warnat, Room 4315, 205–9441, fax 205–5522.
National Programs Division.—Dennis Berry, Room 4512, 205–9650, fax 205–8793.

DEPARTMENT OF ENERGY

James Forrestal Building, 1000 Independence Avenue SW 20585

phone (202) 586–5000, http://www.doe.gov

FEDERICO F. PEÑA, Secretary of Energy; born in Laredo, TX, March 15, 1947; B.A., University of Texas at Austin, 1968; J.D., 1971; president and chief executive officer, Peña Investment Advisors, Inc., 1991–93; of counsel, Brownstein, Hyatt, Farber and Strickland, PC, 1992–93; city mayor, city and county of Denver, 1983–91; served in Colorado House of Representatives, 1978–82; House minority leader, 1981, specialized in school finance reform; attorney; private practice and civil rights litigation, 1972–82; past member, U.S. Alternative Fuels Council; past member, Metropolitan Transportation Development Commission; member, New World Airport Commission; president, Colorado Advisory Council on Mexico; board member, Piton Foundation; married to the former Ellen Hart; two children: Nelia Joan and Cristina Lucila. The 12th Secretary of Transportation, 1993–97; confirmed by the U.S. Senate and sworn in as the 8th Secretary of Energy on March 12, 1997.

OFFICE OF THE SECRETARY

Secretary of Energy.—Federico F. Peña, 586–6210.
Deputy Secretary.—Charles B. Curtis, 586–5500.
Associate Deputy Secretary for Field Management.—Franklin G. Peters (acting), 586–2850.
Associate Deputy Secretary for Energy Programs.—C. Kyle Simpson, 586–5000.
Associate Deputy Secretary for National Security Programs.—Madelyn R. Creedon, 586–5000.
Under Secretary.—Thomas P. Grumbly, 586–6479.
Inspector General.—John C. Layton, 586–4393.
General Counsel.—Eric J. Fygi (acting), 586–5284.
Secretary of Energy Advisory Board.—David W. Cheney (acting), 586–4383.
Assistant Secretary for—
Congressional, Public and Intergovernmental Affairs.—Robert M. Alcock (acting), 586–5450.
Energy Efficiency and Renewable Energy.—Christine A. Ervin, 586–9220.
Defense Programs.—Victor H. Reis, 586–2177.
Human Resources and Administration.—Archer L. Durham, 586–8010.
Policy and International Affairs.—Marc Chupka (acting), 586–5800.
Environmental Management.—Alvin L. Alm, 586–7710.
Environment, Safety and Health.—Dr. Tara J. O'Toole, 586–6151.
Fossil Energy.—Patricia Fry Godley, 586–6660.
Administrator for Energy Information Administration.—Jay E. Hakes, 586–4361.
Director, Office of—
Chief Financial Officer.—Elizabeth E. Smedley (acting), 586–4171.
Civilian Radioactive Waste Management.—Lake H. Barrett (acting), 586–6842.
Economic Impact and Diversity.—Corilis S. Moody, 586–8383.
Energy Research.—Dr. Martha Krebs, 586–5430.
Fissile Materials Disposition.—Howard R. Canter (acting), 586–2695.
Hearings and Appeals.—George B. Breznay, 426–1566.
Nonproliferation and National Security.—Kenneth E. Baker (acting), 586–0645.
Nuclear Energy, Science and Technology.—Terry Lash, 586–6450.
Quality Management.—Archer L. Durham (acting), 586–5363.
Worker and Community Transition.—Robert W. DeGrasse, Jr., 586–7550.

MAJOR FIELD ORGANIZATIONS

OPERATIONS OFFICES

Managers:
Albuquerque.—Bruce Twining, (505) 845–6049.
Chicago.—Cherri Langenfeld, (708) 972–2110.
Idaho.—John M. Wilcynski, (208) 526–5665.
Nevada.—Terry A. Vaeth (acting), (702) 295–3211.
Oakland.—James M. Turner, (510) 637–1800.
Oak Ridge.—James C. Hall, (615) 576–4444.
Richland.—John D. Wagoner, (509) 376–7395.
Savannah River.—Mario P. Fiori, (803) 725–2277.

FIELD OFFICES

Managers:
Golden.—Frank M. Stewart, Jr., (303) 275–4778.
Ohio.—Jon P. Hamric, (513) 865–3977.
Rocky Flats.—Jesse M. Roberson, (303) 966–2025.

POWER MARKETING ADMINISTRATIONS

Administrator, Power Administration—
Alaska.—Rodney L. Adelman, (202) 586–2008.
Bonneville.—Randall W. Hardy, (503) 230–5101.
Southeastern Area.—Charles A. Borchardt, (706) 213–3800.
Southwestern Area.—Michael A. Diehl, (918) 595–6601.
Western Area.—John M. Shafer, (303) 275–1513.

FEDERAL ENERGY TECHNOLOGY CENTER

Director.—Rita A. Bajura, (304) 285–4931.

NAVAL REACTORS OFFICES

Managers:
Pittsburgh.—Henry A. Cardinali, (412) 476–7200.
Schenectady.—Philip E. Salm, (518) 395–4690.

NAVAL PETROLEUM RESERVES

Directors:
California.—O. Jay Williams, (805) 763–6011.
Colorado, Utah, Wyoming (Oil Shale Reserves).—Clarke D. Turner, (307) 261–5161.

FEDERAL ENERGY REGULATORY COMMISSION

Washington DC 20426

Chair.—Elizabeth Anne Moler, 208–0000.
Commissioners:
William L. Massey, 208–0366.
Donald F. Santa, Jr., 208–0377.
James J. Hoecker, 208–0383.
Vicky A. Bailey, 208–0388.
Executive Director and Chief Financial Officer.—Christie McGue, 208–0300.
Director, Office of External Affairs.—Rebecca F. Schaffer, 208–0004.

DEPARTMENT OF HEALTH AND HUMAN SERVICES

200 Independence Avenue SW 20201, http://www.os.dhhs.gov

DONNA E. SHALALA, of Wisconsin, Secretary of Health and Human Services, nominated by President Clinton, January 20, 1993; confirmed by the Senate, January 21, 1993; sworn in on January 22, 1993; bornin Cleveland, OH, on February 14, 1941; B.A., Western College for Women, 1962; PhD, Maxwell School of Citizenship and Public Affairs, Syracuse University, 1970; volunteered for the U.S. Peace Corps, and spent two years teaching in Iran 1962–64; served as assistant to the director of the Metropolitan Studies Program, lecturer in social science and assistant to the dean at the Maxwell School of Citizenship and Public Affairs at Syracuse 1966–70; taught political science at Bernard Baruch College 1970–72; taught politics and education at Teachers College, Columbia University 1972–79; Spencer Academy of Education, 1972–73; John Simon Guggenheim Fellow, 1975–76; visiting professor, Yale Law School, 1976; Leadership Fellow with the Japan Society 1987; director and treasurer of the Municipal Assistance Corporation, 1975–77; served in the Carter Administration as Assistant Secretary for Policy Development and Research, Department of Housing and Urban Development 1977–80; member: Board of the Children's Defense Fund 1980–92, Chair, 1992; member: Committee for Economic Development; director and trustee Spelman College; the Brookings Institute; the Carnegie Foundation; Spencer Foundation; Institute for International Economics; Council of Foreign Relations; National Collegiate Athlete Association Foundation; New York Urban Coalition and the National Women's Law Center; member: National Science Board of Commission on the Future of the National Science Foundation; Advisory Committee to the Director of the National Institutes of Health, NIH Office of Minority Program's Fact Finding Team; Carnegie Commission of Science, Technology and Government; Higher Education Colloguium on Science Facilities; Knight Commission on Intercollegiate Athletes; and the Steering Committee of the Bishop Desmond Tutu Southern African Refugee Scholarship Fund; received honorary degrees from 17 colleges and universities; lectured and written extensively on matters dealing with education, urban fiscal, political, tax, social science and government financing issues.

OFFICE OF THE SECRETARY

Secretary of Health and Human Services.—Donna E. Shalala, PhD, 690–7000.
Confidential Assistant to the Secretary.—Jolinda Gaither.
Executive Staff Analyst to the Secretary.—Virginia Boldon.
Counselor to the Secretary.—[Vacant].
Chief of Staff.—William Corr, 690–7431.

OFFICE OF THE DEPUTY SECRETARY

Deputy Secretary.—Kevin Thurm, 690–7431.
Special Assistant to the Deputy Secretary.—Lisa Gilmore, 690–6133.
Staff Assistant to the Deputy Secretary.—Vivian Grishkot, 690–7431.
Counselor to the Deputy Secretary.—[Vacant].
Director of Intergovernmental Affairs.—John Monahan, 690–6060.
Chair, Departmental Appeals Board.—Norval D. Settle, 690–7707.

ASSISTANT SECRETARY FOR LEGISLATION

Assistant Secretary-Designate.—Richard J. Tarplin, 690–7627, fax 690–7380.
Principal Deputy Assistant Secretary.—Richard J. Tarplin, 690–7627.
Deputy Assistant Secretary for—
Congressional Liaison.—Irene B. Bueno, 690–6786.
Health.—Karen L. Pollitz, 690–7450.
Human Services.—Mary M. Bourdette, 690–6311.

ASSISTANT SECRETARY FOR MANAGEMENT AND BUDGET

Assistant Secretary.—John J. Callahan, 690–6396, fax 690–5405.
Principal Deputy Assistant Secretary.—Elizabeth M. James, 690–6061.
Deputy Assistant Secretary, Policy Initiatives.—Lavarne Burton, 690–8218.
Deputy Assistant Secretary for—
Grants and Acquisition Management.—Terrence J. Tychan, 690–6901.
Small and Disadvantaged Business Utilization.—Verl Zanders, 690–7300.
Budget.—Dennis P. Williams, 690–7393.
Finance.—George H. Strader, 690–7084.
Human Resources.—Evelyn White, 690–6191.
Information Resources Management.—Neil J. Stillman, 690–6162.
Director, Office of—
Facilities Services.—Peggy Dodd, 619–1755.
OS Equal Employment Opportunity.—Barbara B. Aulenbach, 619–1564.

ASSISTANT SECRETARY FOR PLANNING AND EVALUATION

Assistant Secretary.—[Vacant].
Principal Deputy Assistant Secretary.—David F. Garrison, 690–7858.
Executive Assistant.—Jeffrey Merkowitz, fax 690–6518.
Deputy Assistant Secretary—
Health Policy.—Gary Claxton, 690–6870.
Human Services Policy.—Ann Rosewater, 690–7409.
Program Systems.—Susanne Stoiber, 690–8774.
Science Policy.—William Raub, 690–5874.

ASSISTANT SECRETARY FOR PUBLIC AFFAIRS

Assistant Secretary.—Melissa Skolfield, 690–7850.
Deputy Assistant Secretary for—
Policy and Communication.—Laurie Boeder, 690–6853.
Media.—Victor Zonana, 690–6343; fax 690–6247.
Director, Division of—
Freedom of Information/Privacy.—Ross Cirrincione, 690–7453.
News.—P. Campbell Gardett, 690–6343.

OFFICE FOR CIVIL RIGHTS

Director.—Dennis Hayashi, 619–0403.
Deputy Director.—Omar V. Guerrero, 619–0403.
Confidential Assistant to the Director.—[Vacant].
Executive Assistant to the Director.—[Vacant].
Associate Deputy Director for—
Management Planning and Evaluation.—Omar V. Guerrero, (acting), 619–0403.
Program Operations.—Ronald G. Copeland, 619–0553, fax 619–3437.

OFFICE OF CONSUMER AFFAIRS

808 17th Street NW, Suite 800, 20006

Director.—Leslie L. Byrne, 565–0040.
Deputy Director.—[Vacant].
Director, Office of—
Business, Consumer and International Liaison.—Patricia A. Faley, 634–4329, fax 634–4135.
Planning, Budget, and Evaluation.—E. Waverly Land, 634–4177.
Policy and Education Development.—Howard Seltzer, 634–4319.
Public and Legislative Affairs.—[Vacant].

OFFICE OF PUBLIC HEALTH AND SCIENCE

Assistant Secretary for Health.—[Vacant].
Principal Deputy Assistant Secretary.—Jo Ivey Boufford, MD, 690–7694.
Deputy Assistant Secretary for Health.—Ciro Sumaya, MD, 690–7694.
Executive Officer.—Harold P. Thompson, 205–0677.
Surgeon General.—Audrey F. Manley, MD, MPH, (acting), 690–7694.
Deputy Assistant Secretary, Office of—
Disease Prevention and Health Promotion.—Claude E. Fox, MD, 205–8611.
Minority Health.—Clay E. Simpson, (301) 443–5084.
Population Affairs.—Thomas Kring, (acting), (301) 594–4000.
Women's Health.—Susan J. Blumenthal, MD, 690–7650.
Director, Office of—
Emergency Preparedness.—Robert Knouss, MD, (301) 443–1167.
HIV/AIDS Policy.—Eric Goosby, MD, 690–5560.
International Health and Refugee Health.—Linda A. Vogel, (301) 443–1774.
Research Integrity.—Christopher Pascal, (acting), (301) 443–3400.
President's Council on Physical Fitness and Sports.—Sandra P. Perlmutter, 272–3426.

OFFICE OF THE GENERAL COUNSEL

fax [Immediate Office] 690–7998, fax [Admin. Office] 690–5452

General Counsel.—Harriet S. Rabb, 690–7741.
Deputy General Counsel.—Beverly Dennis, III, 690–7721.
Legal Counsel.—[Vacant].
Program Review.—Anna L. Durand, 690–6318.
Regulation.—Renee Landers, 690–6318.
Executive Officer.—Donald E. Watts, 690–7705.
Associate General Counsel for.—
Business and Administrative Law Division.—Leslie Clune, 619–0150.
Children, Family and Aging Division.—Robert Keith, (acting), 690–8005.
Civil Rights Division.—George Lyon, 619–0900.
Ethics Division/Special Counsel for Ethics.—Jack Kress, 690–7258.
Food and Drug Division.—Margaret Porter, (301) 827–1137.
Health Care Financing Division.—Robert Jaye, (acting), 619–0300.
Legislation Division.—Sondra S. Wallace, 690–7760.
Public Health Division.—Richard Riseberg, (301) 443–2644.

OFFICE OF THE INSPECTOR GENERAL

330 Independence Avenue SW, 20201

Inspector General.—June Gibbs Brown, 619–3148.
Executive Assistant to the Inspector General.—Marcia J. Van Note, 619–7675.
Special Assistant to the Inspector General.—Jenny Banner-Wheeler, 619–3081.
Principal Deputy Inspector General.—Michael F. Mangano, 619–3146.
Chief Counsel to the Inspector General.—D. McCarty Thornton, 619–0335.
Deputy Inspector General for—
Audit Services.—Thomas D. Roslewicz, 619–3155.
Enforcement and Compliance.—Eileen T. Boyd, 690–0070.
Evaluation and Inspections.—George F. Grob, 619–0480.
Investigations.—John E. Hartwig, 619–3208.
Management and Policy.—Dennis J. Duquette, 619–3185.

ADMINISTRATION ON AGING

330 Independence Avenue SW, 20201

Assistant Secretary for Aging.—[Vacant], 401–4541.
Deputy Assistant Secretary.—Vicki Shepard, 401–4541.
Deputy to the Deputy Assistant Secretary, Governmental Affairs and Elder Rights.—William F. Benson, 401–4541.
Special Assistant for Legislation, Public Affairs and White House Liaison.—Moya Benoit Thompson, 401–4541.

ADMINISTRATION FOR CHILDREN AND FAMILIES

370 L'Enfant Promenade SW, 20447

Assistant Secretary.—[Vacant], 401–9200.
Principal Deputy Assistant Secretary.—Olivia A. Golden, 401–2337.
Deputy Assistant Secretary for—
Policy and External Affairs.—[Vacant], 401–9200.
Program Operations.—Laurence Love, 401–9200.
Director, Regional Operations Staff.—Diann Dawson, 401–4802.
Commissioner—
Children, Youth, and Families.—James Harrell, (acting), 205–8347.
Associate Commissioner—
Child Care Bureau.—Joan Lombardi, 401–6947.
Children's Bureau.—Carol W. Williams, 205–8618.
Developmental Disabilities.—Bob Williams, 690–6590.
Family and Youth Services Bureau.—Terry Lewis, 205–8086.
Head Start Bureau.—Helen Taylor, 205–8572.
Native Americans.—Gary N. Kimble, 690–7776.
Director, Office of—
Child Support Enforcement.—[Vacant], 402–9200.
Community Services.—Donald Sykes, 401–9333.
Family Assistance.—Lavinia Limon, 401–9275.
Program Support.—Norman Thompson, 401–9238.
Refugee Resettlement.—Lavinia Limon, 401–9246.

AGENCY FOR HEALTH CARE POLICY AND RESEARCH

2101 East Jefferson Street, Rockville MD 20852

Administrator.—John M. Eisenberg, (301) 594–6662.
Deputy Administrator.—Lisa Simpson, (301) 594–6662.
Director, Office of—
Policy Analysis.—Larry T. Patton, (301) 594–1321.
Forum for Quality and Effectiveness in Health Care.—Douglas B. Kamerow, (301) 594–4015.
Management.—Williard B. Evans, Jr., (301) 594–1433.
Planning and Evaluation.—Phyllis M. Zucker, (301) 594–1455.
Scientific Affairs.—Linda Demlo, (301) 594–1398.
Director, Center for—
Cost and Financing Studies.—Ross H. Arnett, III, (301) 594–1400.
Organization and Delivery Studies.—Irene Fraser, (301) 594–1410.
Health Care Technology.—Douglas B. Kamerow, (301) 594–4015.
Health Information Dissemination.—Christine G. Williams, (301) 594–1360.
Information Technology.—J. Michael Fitzmaurice, (301) 594–1483.
Outcomes and Effectiveness Research.—Carolyn M. Clancy, (301) 594–1357.
Primary Care Research.—Carolyn M. Clancy, (acting), (301) 594–1357.
Quality Measurement and Improvement.—Sandra Robinson, (acting), (301) 594–1352.

AGENCY FOR TOXIC SUBSTANCES AND DISEASE REGISTRY

1600 Clifton Road NE, Atlanta GA 30333

Administrator.—David Satcher, (404) 639–7000.
Deputy Administrator.—Claire V. Broome, (404) 639–7000.
Assistant Administrator.—Barry L. Johnson, (404) 639–7000.
Deputy Assistant Administrator.—William D. Adams, (404) 639–7000.

CENTERS FOR DISEASE CONTROL AND PREVENTION

1600 Clifton Road NE, Atlanta GA 30333

Director.—David Satcher, (404) 639–3291.
Deputy Director.—Claire V. Broome, (404) 639–3294
Associate Director for—
Communications.—Vicki Freimuth, (404) 639–7290.
International Health.—Melinda Moore, (acting), (770) 488–1085.
Management and Operations.—Arthur C. Jackson, (404) 639–3256.
Minority Health.—Robert G. Robinson, (acting), (404) 639–3703.
Policy, Planning and Evaluation.—Jeffrey R. Harris, (acting), (404) 639–7060.
Science.—Dixie E. Snider, (404) 639–3701.
Washington.—Donald E. Shriber, (202) 690–8598.
Director, Office of—
Equal Employment Opportunity.—Sue J. Porter, (404) 639–0336.
Health Communication.—Vicki Freimuth, (404) 639–7290.
Health and Safety.—Jonathan Y. Richmond, (404) 639–2453.
Program Planning and Evaluation.—Jeffrey R. Harris, (acting), (404) 639–7060.
Program Support.—Arthur C. Jackson, (404) 639–3256.
Public Affairs.—Vicki Freimuth, (404) 639–7290.
Women's Health.—Wanda Jones, (404) 639–7230.
Director, Program Office—
Epidemiology.—Stephen B. Thacker, (404) 639–3661.
National Immunization.—Walter A. Orenstein, (404) 639–8200.
National Vaccine.—Vicki Freimuth, (404) 639–7290.
Public Health Practice.—Edward L. Baker, (404) 639–1900.
Director, National Center for—
Chronic Disease Prevention and Health Promotion.—James S. Marks, (404) 488–5401.
Environmental Health.—Richard J. Jackson, (404) 488–7000.
Health Statistics.—Edward J. Sondik, (301) 436–7016.
HIV, STD, and TB Prevention.—Helene Gayle, (404) 639–8000.
Infectious Disease.—James M. Hughes, (404) 639–3401.
Injury Prevention and Control.—Mark L. Rosenberg, (404) 488–4696.
Director, National Institute—
Occupational Safety and Health.—Linda Rosenstock, (404) 639–3771.

FOOD AND DRUG ADMINISTRATION

5600 Fishers Lane, Rockville MD 20857

Commissioner.—[Vacant].
Lead Deputy Commissioner for Operations.—Michael A. Friedman MD, (301) 827–3310.
Deputy Commissioner/Senior Advisor.—Mary Pendergast, (301) 827–3330.
Chief Counsel.—Margaret Jane Porter, (301) 827–1137.
Senior Advisor for Science.—Elkan Blout, PhD, (301) 827–3340.
Deputy Commissioner for—
External Affairs.—Sharon Smith Holston, (301) 827–3450.
Management and Systems.—Robert J. Byrd, (301) 827–3443.
Policy.—William B. Schultz, (301) 827–3370.
Associate Commissioner for—
Consumer Affairs.—Charles A. Gaylord, (acting), (301) 827–5006.
Health Affairs.—Stuart L. Nightingale, MD, (301) 443–6143.
Legislative Affairs.—Diane Thompson, (301) 827–0087.
Planning and Evaluation.—Paul L. Coppinger, (301) 827–5292.
Public Affairs.—James O'Hara, (301) 443–1130.
Regulatory Affairs.—Ronald G. Chesemore, (301) 827–3101.
Science.—Bernard A. Schwetz, DVM, PhD, (Arkansas), (501) 543–7517.
Director, Center for—
Biologics Evaluation and Research.—Katherine C. Zoon, PhD, (301) 827–0548.
Devices and Radiological Health.—D. Bruce Burlington, MD, (301) 443–4690.
Drug Evaluation and Research.—Janet Woodcock, MD, (301) 594–5400.
Food Safety and Applied Nutrition.—Fred R. Shank, PhD, (202) 205–4850.
Toxicological Research.—Bernard Schwetz, DVM, PhD, (501) 543–7517.
Veterinary Medicine.—Stephen Sundlof, DVM, PhD, (301) 594–1740.

HEALTH CARE FINANCING ADMINISTRATION

200 Independence Avenue SW, 20201

Administrator.—Bruce C. Vladeck, 690–6726.
Deputy Administrator.—Sally Richardson, (acting), 690–5727.
Executive Associate Administrator.—[Vacant].
Associate Administrator for—
External Affairs.—Pamela Gentry, 690–8390.
Operations and Resource Management.—Steven Pelovitz, (410) 786–3160.
Policy.—Kathleen Buto, 690–7063.
Director of—
Hearings.—Anthony Tirone, (acting), (410) 786–6763.
Legislative and Intergovernmental Affairs.—Deborah Chang, (202) 690–5894.
Managed Care.—Dennis Siebert, (202) 690–5727.
Medicaid Bureau.—Judy Moore, (acting), (410) 786–3230.
Office of the Actuary.—Richard Foster, (410) 786–6374.
Policy Development.—Barbara Wynn, (410) 786–5674.
Director, Bureau of—
Data Management and Strategy.—Regina McPhillips, (410) 786–1800.
Health Standards and Quality.—Peter Bouxsein, (410) 786–4287.
Program Operations.—Gary Kavanaugh, (acting), (410) 786–5876.
Director, Office of—
Attorney Advisor.—Jacqueline Vaughn, (acting), (410) 786–3176.
Beneficiary Relations.—Frank Sokolik, (410) 786–3206.
Financial and Human Resources.—Michelle Snyder, (410) 786–1051.
Freedom of Information and Privacy Office.—Glenn Kendall, (410) 786–5352.
Media Relations.—[Vacant].
Professional Relations.—Rondalyn Haughton, (202) 690–7874.

HEALTH RESOURCES AND SERVICES ADMINISTRATION

5600 Fishers Lane, Rockville MD 20857

Administrator.—Claude E. Fox, MD, MPH, (acting), (301) 443–2216.
Deputy Administrator.—Thomas Morford, (301) 443–2194.
Chief Medical Officer.—William A. Robinson, MD, MPH, (301) 443–0458.
Associate Administrator for—
AIDS.—Joseph O'Neill, MD, MPH, (301) 443–4588.
Communications.—Charlotte Mehuron, (301) 443–3376.
Equal Opportunity and Civil Rights.—J. Calvin Adams, (301) 443–5636.
Minority Health.—Ileana Herrell, PhD, (301) 443–2964.
Operations and Management.—James Corrigan, (acting), (301) 443–2053.
Planning, Evaluation, and Legislation.—Ronald H. Carlson, (301) 443–2460.
Director, Bureau of—
Health Professions.—Neil Sampson, (acting), (301) 443–5795.
Health Resources Development.—Joseph F. O'Neill, MD, MS, MPH, (acting), (301) 443–1993.
Maternal and Child Health.—Audrey H. Nora, MD, (301) 443–2170.
Primary Health Care.—Marilyn H. Gaston, MD, (301) 594–4110.

INDIAN HEALTH SERVICE

5600 Fishers Lane, Rockville MD 20857

Director.—Michael H. Trujillo, MD, ASG, (301) 443–1083.
Deputy Director.—Michel Lincoln.
Chief Medical Officer.—Kermit C. Smith, DO, (acting).
Director of—
Congressional and Legislative Affairs.—Michael Mahsetky, (301) 443–1083.
Equal Employment Opportunity/Civil Rights Staff.—Cecelia Heftel, (301) 443–2700.
Field Operations.—Duane L. Jeanotte (acting).
Headquarters Operations.—Luana L. Reyes.
Urban Indian Health Program Staff.—Arvada J. Nelson, (acting), (302) 443–4680.

Director, Office of—
Management Support.—Robert G. McSwain, (301) 443–6290.
Public Affairs.—Tony Kendrick, (301) 443–3593.
Public Health.—Robert H. Harry, DDS, (acting), (301) 443–3024.
Tribal Programs.—Douglas P. Black, (301) 443–1104.
Tribal Self-Governance.—Paula Williams, (301) 443–7821.

NATIONAL INSTITUTES OF HEALTH

9000 Rockville Pike, Bethesda MD 20892

Director.—Harold E. Varmus, (301) 496–2433.
Deputy Director.—Ruth L. Kirschstein, MD, (301) 496–2433.
Deputy Director, Office of—
Extramural Research.—Wendy Baldwin, PhD, (301) 496–1096.
Intramural Research.—Michael M. Gottesman, MD, (301) 496–1921.
Management.—Anthony L. Itteilag, (301) 496–3271.
Assistant Director, Office of—
Program Coordination.—Vida Beaven, PhD, (301) 496–3553.
Associate Director for—
Administration.—Leamon M. Lee, PhD, (301) 496–4466.
AIDS Research.—William E. Paul, MD, (301) 496–0357.
Behavioral and Social Science Research.—Norman B. Anderson, PhD, (301) 402–1146.
Clinical Research.—John I. Gallin, MD, (301) 496–4114.
Communications.—R. Anne Thomas, (301) 496–4461.
Disease Prevention.—William R. Harlan, MD, (301) 496–1508.
Legislative Policy and Analysis.—Diane S. Wax, (301) 496–3471.
Research on Minority Health.—John Ruffin, PhD, (301) 402–1366.
Research on Women's Health.—Vivian W. Pinn, MD, (301) 402–1770.
Research Services.—Stephen A. Ficca, (301) 496–2215.
Science Policy.—Lana R. Skirboll, PhD, (301) 496–3152.
Director, Office of—
Community Liaison.—Janyce Hedetniemi, (301) 496–3931.
Equal Opportunity.—Naomi Churchill, Esq., (301) 496–6301.
Financial Management.—Francine Little, (301) 496–4477.
Human Resource Management.—Stephen C. Benowitz, (301) 496–3592.
Director—
Warren G. Magnuson Clinical Center.—John I. Gallin, MD, (301) 496–4114.
Fogarty International Center.—Philip E. Schambra, PhD, (301) 496–1415.
National Center for Research Resources.—Judith L. Vaitukaitis, MD, (301) 496–5793.
National Library of Medicine.—Donald A.B. Lindberg, MD, (301) 496–6221.
Division of Computer Research and Technology.—William L. Risso, (acting), (301) 496–5703.
Division of Research Grants.—Elvera Ehrenfeld, PhD, (301) 435–1114.
Director, National Institute—
Aging.—Richard J. Hodes, MD, (301) 496–9265.
Alcohol Abuse and Alcoholism.—Enoch Gordis, MD, (301) 443–3885.
Allergy and Infectious Diseases.—Anthony Fauci, MD, (203) 496–2263.
Arthritis, Musculoskeletal and Skin Diseases.—Stephen I. Katz, MD, PhD, (301) 496–4353.
Cancer.—Richard Klausner, MD, (301) 496–5615.
Child Health and Human Development.—Duane F. Alexander, MD, (301) 496–3454.
Deafness and Other Communication Disorders.—James B. Snow, Jr, MD, (301) 402–0900.
Dental Research.—Harold C. Slavkin, DDS, (301) 496–3571.
Diabetes, Digestive and Kidney Diseases.—Phillip Gorden, MD, (301) 496–5877.
Drug Abuse.—Alan I. Leshner, PhD, (301) 443–6480.
Environmental Health Sciences.—Kenneth Olden, PhD, (919) 541–3201.
Eye.—Carl Kupfer, MD, (301) 496–2234.
General Medical Sciences.—Marvin Cassman, PhD, (301) 594–2172.
Heart, Lung and Blood.—Claude J.M. Lenfant, MD, (301) 496–5166.
Human Genome Research.—Francis S. Collins, MD, PhD, (301) 496–0844.
Mental Health.—Stephen E. Hyman, MD, (301) 443–3673.
Neurological Disorders and Stroke.—Zach W. Hall, PhD, (301) 496–9746.
Nursing Research.—Patricia A. Grady, RN, PhD, (301) 496–8230.

PROGRAM SUPPORT CENTER

5600 Fishers Lane, Rockville MD 20857

Director.—Lynnda M. Regan, (301) 443–3921.
Chief Financial Officer.—John C. West, (301) 443–1478.
Director of—
Human Resources.—Thomas M. King, (301) 443–1200.
Information Technology.—Lawrence S. Cohan, (301) 443–2374.
Operations.—Richard W. Harris, (301) 443–2516.

SUBSTANCE ABUSE AND MENTAL HEALTH SERVICES ADMINISTRATION

5600 Fishers Lane Rockville, MD 20857

Administrator.—Nelba R. Chavez, PhD, (301) 443–4795.
Deputy Administrator.—Paul Schwab, (301) 443–4795.
Director, Equal Employment Opportunity.—Pedro J. Morales, (301) 443–4447.
Associate Administrator—
AIDS.—Adolfo Mata, (acting), (301) 443–8461.
Alcohol Prevention and Treatment Policy.—Bettina M. Scott, PhD (acting), (301) 443–7905.
Communications.—Mark Weber, (301) 443–8956.
Managed Care.—Eric Goplerud, PhD, (301) 443–2817.
Minority Concerns.—DeLoris James-Hunter, PhD, (301) 443–0365.
Policy and Program Coordination.—Mary C. Knipmeyer, PhD, (301) 443–4111.
Women's Programs.—Ulonda Shamwell, (acting), (301) 443–5184.
Director of—
Applied Studies.—Donald Goldstone, MD, (301) 443–1038.
Extramural Activities Review.—Jane E. Taylor, PhD, (301) 443–4266.
Program Services.—Richard T. Kopanda, Executive Officer, (301) 443–3875.
Director, Center for—
Mental Health Services.—Bernard S. Arons, MD, (301) 443–0001.
Substance Abuse Prevention.—Stephania O'Neill, (acting), (301) 443–0365.
Substance Abuse Treatment.—David J. Mactas, (301) 443–5700.

THE PRESIDENT'S COUNCIL ON PHYSICAL FITNESS AND SPORTS

701 Pennsylvania Avenue NW, Suite 250, 20004–2608, phone 272–3421, fax 504–2064
http://www.whitehouse.gov/wh/pcpfs/html/

Co-Chairs:—Florence Griffith Joyner, Tom McMillen.
Council Members:
Elizabeth Arendt
Ralph Boston
Timothy Finchem
Zina Garrison-Jackson
Jimmie Heuga
Jim Kelly
Deborah Slaner Larkin
Al Mead, III
Kevin Saunders
Jeff Blatnick
Don Casey
Rockne Freitas
Veronica Goldberg
Calvin Hill
Judith Kieffer
Ira Leesfield
Jack Mills
Amber Travsky
Executive Director.—Sandra Perlmutter.

DEPARTMENT OF HOUSING AND URBAN DEVELOPMENT

HUD Building, 451 Seventh Street SW 20410, phone (202) 708–6417, http://www.hud.gov

ANDREW CUOMO, Secretary of Housing and Urban Development; born in Queens, NY on December 6, 1957; B.A., Fordham University, 1979; law degree, Albany Law School, 1982; campaign manager for Governor Mario M. Cuomo, 1982; served as special assistant to the governor; served as an assistant district attorney in Manhattan; partner, law firm of Blutrich, Falcone and Miller; founded HELP, the nation's largest private provider of transitional housing for the homeless, 1986; founded the Genesis Project, which develops innovative approaches to urban revitalization, community development and tenant management; named commission chairman for the New York City Commission on the Homeless by Mayor David Dinkins, 1991; served as Assistant Secretary for Community Planning and Development at the Department of Housing and Urban Development; married to Kerry Kennedy Cuomo; two children, twins Cara and Mariah; nominated by President Clinton to be Secretary of Housing and Urban Development on December 20, 1996; confirmed by the U.S. Senate and sworn in on January 29, 1997.

OFFICE OF THE SECRETARY

Secretary of Housing and Urban Development.—Andrew Cuomo, Room 10000, 708–0417.
Chief of Staff.—Michael A. Stegman (acting), Room 10000, 708–2713.
Senior Advisor to the Secretary.—Roberta Achtenberg, Room 10226, 708–3636.
Director, Special Advisor to the Secretary for EEO/Labor Management.—Mari Barr (acting), Room 10126, 708–3633.
Director, Special Actions Office.—Art Agnos, Room 10234, 708–1547.

OFFICE OF THE DEPUTY SECRETARY

Deputy Secretary.—Dwight P. Robinson, Room 10100, 708–0123.
Assistant to the Deputy Secretary for Management Planning and Operations.—Albert M. Miller (acting), Room 10100, 708–0759.

ASSISTANT TO THE DEPUTY SECRETARY FOR FIELD MANAGEMENT

Assistant to the Deputy Secretary for Field Management.—John E. Wilson, Room 7106, 708–2426.

ASSISTANT TO THE SECRETARY FOR LABOR RELATIONS

Assistant to the Secretary for Labor Relations.—[Vacant], Room 7118, 708–0370.

SMALL AND DISADVANTAGED BUSINESS UTILIZATION

Director.—Casimir Bonkowski, Room 3130, 708–1428.

OFFICE OF FAIR HOUSING AND EQUAL OPPORTUNITY

Assistant Secretary.—[Vacant], Room 5100, 708–4252.
Director of Beaumont Fair Housing Office.—Joseph James, (409) 838–7500.
Deputy Assistant Secretary for Enforcement and Investigations.—Susan Forward, Room 5106, 708–4211, ext. 108.

Director, Office of—
Program Compliance/Disability Rights.—[Vacant], Room 5242, 708–2618, ext. 345.
Fair Housing Initiatives and Voluntary Programs.—Maxine Cunningham, Room 5234, 708–0800, ext. 308.
Investigations.—Sara K. Pratt, Room 5204, 708–0836, ext. 221.
Deputy Assistant Secretary for Operations and Management.—Sandra D. Chavis, Room 5100, 708–3855.
Director, Office of Management and Field Coordination.—Theodore R. Daniels, Room 5124, 708–4150, ext. 147.
Director, Office of Policy and Regulatory Initiatives.—Peter Kaplan, Room 5135, 708–2906.

OFFICE OF ADMINISTRATION

Assistant Secretary.—Marilynn A. Davis, Room 10110, 708–0940.
Director, Office of Executive Scheduling.—Andrew Rivera, Room 10158, 708–1238.
Special Assistant, Office of HUD CARES.—Patricia A. Newton, Room 10158, 619–8127.
Director, Executive Secretariat.—Ann Aldrich, Room 10139, 708–3054.
Deputy Assistant Secretary, Office of Management and Planning.—[Vacant], 708–0306.
Director of—
Information Technology.—Steven M. Yohai, Room 4160, 708–0306.
Budget.—[Vacant], Room 3270, 708–3296.
Procurement and Contracts.—Craig E. Durkin, Room 5272, 708–1290.
Human Resources.—Joanne W. Simms, Room 2162, 708–2000.
Administrative and Management Services.—Marie P. Kissick, Room 5168, 708–3123.
Special Actions.—Art Agnos, Room 10234, 708–1547.
Management and Planning.—Joseph Webb (acting), 708–1027.

OFFICE OF DEPARTMENTAL OPERATIONS AND COORDINATION

Director.—Frank L. Davis, Room 9241, 708–2806.

OFFICE OF GENERAL COUNSEL

General Counsel.—George L. Weidenfeller (acting), Room 10214, 708–2244.
Office of the Deputy General Counsel for:
Civil Rights and Litigation.—[Vacant], Room 10216, 708–1240.
Programs and Regulations.—Paul M. Ceja (acting), Room 10214, 708–0636.
Operations.—George L. Weidenfeller, Room 10240, 708–2864.
Associate General Counsel, Office of—
Assisted Housing and Community Development.—Robert S. Kenison, Room 8162, 708–0212.
Program Enforcement.—John W. Herold, Room 10182, 708–2568.
Finance and Regulatory Enforcement.—John P. Kennedy, Room 9256, 708–2203.
Human Resources.—Sam E. Hutchinson, Room 10242, 708–0888.
Insured Housing.—John J. Daly, Room 9236, 708–1274.
Legislation and Regulations.—George L. Weidenfeller (acting), Room 10240, 708–2864.
Litigation and Fair Housing Enforcement.—Carole W. Wilson, Room 10258, 708–0300.

OFFICE OF COMMUNITY PLANNING AND DEVELOPMENT

Assistant Secretary.—[Vacant], Room 7100, 708–2690.
General Deputy Assistant Secretary.—Howard B. Glaser, Room 7100, 708–2960.
Deputy Assistant Secretary for Economic Development.—Jacquie M. Lawing, Room 7100, 708–0270.
Director, Office of Economic Development.—Roy O. Priest, Room 7136, 708–2290.
Deputy Assistant Secretary for Grant Programs.—Kenneth C. Williams, Room 7214, 708–6367.
Director, Office of—
Block Grant Assistance.—Dick Kennedy, Room 7286, 708–3587.
Affordable Housing-Programs.—Gordon McKay, Room 7164, 708–2685.
Deputy Assistant Secretary for Operations.—[Vacant], Room 7214, 401–8932.
Director, Office of Technical Assistance and Management.—Donna Abbenante, Room 7228, 708–3532.

Deputy Assistant Secretary for Planning and Community Viability.—[Vacant], Room 7204, 708–2484.

Director, Office of Community Viability.—Richard H. Broun, Room 7240, 708–2894 ext. 4439.

Deputy Assistant Secretary for Empowerment Zones.—[Vacant], Room 7134, 708–8851.

OFFICE OF THE CHIEF FINANCIAL OFFICER

Chief Financial Officer.—John A. Knubel (designate), Room 10164, 708–1946 ext. 3899.

Director, Office of Chief Financial Officer for Accounting.—William H. Eargle, Jr., Room 2206, 708–3310 ext. 3840.

Deputy Chief Financial Officer for Finance.—William Dobrzkowski, Room 10166, 708–0650.

Director, Office of—

Financial Planning and Asset and Management.—Wallace H. Garner, Room 10170, 708–0654.

Financial Systems Integration.—David J. Epstein, Room 10174, 708–0646.

Internal Control and Audit Resolution.—Owen M. Jones, Room 10176, 708–0638.

OFFICE OF INSPECTOR GENERAL

Inspector General.—Susan Gaffney, Room 8256, 708–0430.

Deputy Inspector General.—John J. Connors, Room 8256, 708–0430.

Assistant Inspector General, Office of Audit.—Kathryn Kuhl-Inclan, Room 8286, 708–0364.

Counsel to the Inspector General, Office of Legal Counsel.—Judith Hetherton, Room 8260, 708–1613.

Assistant Inspector General, Office of—

Management and Policy.—Robert H. Martin, Room 8254, 708–0006.

Investigation.—Patrick J. Neri, Room 8274, 708–0390.

OFFICE OF HOUSING

Assistant Secretary for Housing—Federal Housing Commissioner.—Nicolas P. Retsinas, Room 9100, 708–3600.

General Deputy Assistant Secretary.—Stephanie A. Smith, Room 9100, 708–3600.

Associate General Deputy Assistant Secretary.—James E. Schoenberger, Room 9106, 708–1490.

Comptroller, Office of Housing–FHA.—Kathryn M. Rock, Room 5132, 401–8800.

Deputy Comptroller, Housing–FHA.—C. Duncan Macrae, Room 5130, 755–7503.

Director, Office of—

Accounting and Analysis.—John Chin, Room 5136, 401–0450.

Financial Services.—Christopher Peterson, Room 2108, 708–0614.

Deputy Assistant Secretary for Multifamily Housing Programs.—John H. Greer, Room 6106, 708–2495.

Director, Office of—

Asset Management and Disposition.—Linda D. Cheatham, Room 6134, 708–3000.

Multifamily Housing Development.—Albert B. Sullivan, Room 6160, 708–3730.

Deputy Assistant Secretary for Operations.—Sarah Rosen, Room 9138, 708–1104.

Director, Office of—

Management.—Cheryl Wright-Mayes (acting), Room 9114, 708–1014.

Housing Budget and Field Resource.—Linda S. Reid, Room 9206, 401–8975.

Deputy Assistant Secretary for Single Family Housing.—Emelda P. Johnson, Room 9282, 708–3175.

Director, Office of—

Insured Single Family Housing.—[Vacant], Room 9162, 708–3046.

Lender Activities and Land Sales Registration.—Morris E. Carter, Room 9156, 708–1515.

ASSISTANT SECRETARY FOR CONGRESSIONAL AND INTERGOVERNMENTAL RELATIONS

Assistant Secretary.—Hal C. DeCell III, Room 10120, 708–0380.
Deputy Assistant Secretary, Office of—
Congressional Relations.—John C. Biechman.
Intergovernmental Relations.—Choco G. Meza.
Legislation.—[Vacant].
Plans and Policy.—Preston V. Lee.

OFFICE OF LEAD HAZARD CONTROL

Director.—David E. Jacobs, Room 3202, 755–1785.

OFFICE OF FEDERAL HOUSING ENTERPRISE OVERSIGHT

Director.—[Vacant], Fourth Floor, 414–3800.

OFFICE OF PUBLIC AND INDIAN HOUSING

Assistant Secretary.—Kevin Marchman (acting), Room 4100, 708–0950.
General Deputy Assistant Secretary.—Michael B. Janis, Room 4100, 755–0702.
Director, Office of—
Management and Planning.—Nancy E. Gelb (acting), Room 4244, 708–0920.
Troubled Agency Recovery.—[Vacant], Room 4122, 708–0099.
Comptroller, Public and Indian Housing.—Barbara L. Burkhalter, Room 4122, 708–0099.
Deputy Assistant Secretary, Native American Programs.—Dominic A. Nessi, (303) 675–1600.
Deputy Assistant Secretary, Policy, Program and Legislative Initiatives.—[Vacant], Room 4100, 708–3343.

OFFICE OF POLICY DEVELOPMENT AND RESEARCH

Assistant Secretary.—Michael A. Stegman, Room 8100, 708–1600.
General Deputy Assistant Secretary.—Lawrence L. Thompson, Room 8100, 708–1600, ext. 248.
Financial Institutions Regulation Staff.—Harold L. Bunce, Room 8204, 708–3080, ext. 304.
Deputy Assistant Secretary for—
Economic Affairs.—Frederick J. Eggers, Room 8204, 708–3080, ext. 302.
Policy Development.—Paul A. Leonard, Room 8108, 708–3896, ext. 240.
Research, Evaluation and Monitoring.—Margery A. Turner, Room 8146, 708–4230, ext. 117.

GOVERNMENT NATIONAL MORTGAGE ASSOCIATION

President.—Kevin G. Chavers, Room 6100, 708–0926.
Executive Vice President.—George S. Anderson, Room 6100, 708–0926.
Vice President, Office of—
Customer Service.—[Vacant], Room 6214, 708–4141.
Finance.—Michael J. Najjum (acting), Room 6218, 401–2064.
Multifamily Programs.—S. Daniel Raley, Room 6230, 708–2043.
Program Administration.—Thomas R. Weakland, Room 6204, 708–2884.
Policy, Planning and Risk Management.—J. Nicholas Shelly (acting), Room 6226, phone 708–2772.

OFFICE OF DEPARTMENTAL EQUAL EMPLOYMENT OPPORTUNITY

Director.—Mari Barr (acting), Room 10126, 708–3633.
Director, Office of Affirmative Action and Equal Employment Opportunity.—William O. Anderson (acting), Room 4300, 755–0341 ext. 127.

ASSISTANT SECRETARY FOR PUBLIC AFFAIRS

Assistant Secretary.—Jonathan J. Cowan (acting), Room 10132, 708–0980.
Director, Office of—
Press Relations.—William A. Connelly, Room 10138, 708–0685 ext. 115.
Policy Support.—Charles S. Cogan, Room 10130, 708–0120, ext. 120.

FIELD OFFICES

Boston MA.—Mary Lou K. Crane, New England Secretary's Representative, Thomas P. O'Neill, Jr. Federal Building, Room 375, 10 Causeway Street, Boston MA 02222–1092, (617) 565–5234.

Bangor ME.—[Vacant], State Coordinator, First Floor, 99 Franklin Street, Bangor ME 04401–4925, (207) 945–0467.

Burlington VT.—William Peters (acting), State Coordinator, PO Box 879, U.S. Federal Building, Room 244, 11 Elmwood Avenue, Burlington VT 05402–0879, (802) 951–6290.

Hartford CT.—[Vacant], State Coordinator, 330 Main Street, First Floor, Hartford CT 06106–1860, (860) 240–4522.

Manchester NH.—David B. Harrity, State Coordinator, Norris Cotton Federal Building, 275 Chestnut Street, Manchester NH 03101–2487, (603) 666–7681.

Providence RI.—Nancy D. Smith, State Coordinator, Sixth Floor, 10 Weybosset Street, Providence RI 02903–2808, (401) 528–5351.

New York NY Regional.—Maxine Griffith, New York/New Jersey Secretary's Representative, 26 Federal Plaza, New York NY 10278–0068, (212) 264–6500.

Albany NY.—John Petricco, Area Coordinator, 52 Corporate Circle, Albany NY 12203–5121, (518) 464–4200.

Buffalo NY.—Kenneth J. LoBene, Area Coordinator, 465 Main Street, Lafayette Court, Buffalo NY 14203–1780, (716) 846–5755.

Camden NJ.—Elmer L. Roy, Area Coordinator, Hudson Building, 800 Hudson Square, Second Floor, Camden NJ 08102–1156, (609) 757–5081.

Newark NJ.—Diane J. Johnson, State Coordinator, One Newark Center, 13th Floor, Newark NJ 07102–5260, (201) 622–7900.

Philadelphia PA Regional.—Karen A. Miller, Mid-Atlantic Secretary's Representative, Wanamaker Building, 100 Penn Square East, Philadelphia PA 19107–3380, (215) 656–0500.

Baltimore MD.—Harold D. Young (acting), State Coordinator, City Crescent Building, 10 South Howard Street, Fifth Floor, Baltimore MD 21201–2505, (410) 962–2520.

Charleston WV.—Frederick S. Roncaglione (acting), State Coordinator, Suite 708, 405 Capitol Street, Charleston WV 25301–1795, (304) 347–7000.

Pittsburgh PA.—Richard M. Nemoytin, Area Coordinator, U.S. Post Office and Courthouse Building, 339 Sixth Avenue, Pittsburgh PA 15222–2515, (412) 644–6428.

Richmond VA.—Maryann Wilson, State Coordinator, 3600 West Broad Street, 3600 Centre, Richmond VA 23230–4920, (804) 278–4507.

Washington DC.—Jessica A. Franklin, DC Coordinator, 820 First Street NE, Washington DC 20002–4205, (202) 275–9206.

Wilmington DE.—[Vacant], State Coordinator, Suite 850, 824 Market Street, Wilmington DE 19801–3016, (302) 573–6300.

Atlanta GA.—Davey L. Gibson, Southeast/Caribbean Secretary's Representative, 75 Spring Street SW, Atlanta GA 30303–3388, (404) 331–5136.

Birmingham AL.—Heager L. Hill, State Coordinator, Beacon Ridge Tower, 600 Beacon Parkway West, Room 300, Birmingham AL 35209–3144, (205) 290–7617.

Coral Gables FL.—Jose Cintron, State Coordinator, Gables 1 Tower, 1320 South Dixie Highway, Coral Gables, FL 33146–2911, (305) 662–4500.

Columbia SC.—Choice Edwards, State Coordinator, Strom Thurmond Federal Building, 1835 Assembly Street, Columbia SC 29201–2480, (803) 765–5592.

Greensboro NC.—James E. Blackmon, State Coordinator, Koger Building, 2306 West Meadowview Road, Greensboro NC 27407–3707, (910) 547–4000.

Jackson MS.—Patricia A. Hoban-Moore, State Coordinator, Doctor A.H. McCoy Federal Building, Room 910, 100 West Capitol Street, Jackson MS 39269–1016, (601) 965–4738.

Jacksonville FL.—James P. Walker, Jr., Area Coordinator, Southern Bell Tower, 301 West Bay Street, Suite 2200, Jacksonville FL 32202–5121, (904) 232–2626.

Louisville KY.—Robert D. Kuhale, State Coordinator, PO Box 1044, 601 West Broadway, Louisville KY 40201–1044, (502) 585–5251.

Knoxville TN.—Mark J. Brezina (acting), Area Coordinator, Third Floor, John J. Duncan Federal Building, 710 Locust Street, Knoxville TN 37902–2526, (423) 545–4384.

Memphis TN.—Ginger Van Ness (acting), Area Coordinator, One Memphis Place, Suite 1200, 200 Jefferson Avenue, Memphis TN 38103–2335 (901) 544–3367.
Nashville TN.—Ginger Van Ness, State Coordinator, Suite 200, 251 Cumberland Bend Drive, Nashville TN 37228–1803, (615) 736–5213.
Orlando FL.—George A. Milburn (acting), Area Coordinator, Langley Building, Suite 270, 3751 Maguire Boulevard, Orlando FL 32803–3032, (407) 648–6441.
Caribbean.—Michael A. Colon, Coordinator, New San Juan Building, 159 Carlos E. Chardon Avenue, San Juan PR 00918–1804, (809) 766–6121.
Chicago IL Regional.—Edwin W. Eisendrath, Midwest Secretary's Representative, Ralph H. Metcalfe Federal Building, 77 West Jackson Boulevard, Chicago IL 60604–3507, (312) 353–5680.
Cincinnati OH.—William J. Harris, Area Coordinator, 525 Vine Street, Cincinnati OH 45202–3188, (513) 684–3451.
Cleveland OH.—Douglas W. Shelby, Area Coordinator, Renaissance Building, 1350 Euclid Avenue, Suite 500, Cleveland OH 44115–1815, (216) 522–4065.
Columbus OH.—Deborah Williams, State Coordinator, 200 North High Street, Columbus OH 43215–2499, (614) 469–5737.
Detroit MI.—Regina P. Freeman Solomon, State Coordinator, Patrick V. McNamara Federal Building, 477 Michigan Avenue, Detroit MI 48226–2592, (313) 266–7900.
Grand Rapids MI.—[Vacant], Area Coordinator, Trade Center Building, Third Floor, 50 Louis Street NW, Grand Rapids MI 49503–2648, (616) 456–2100.
Indianapolis IN.—William P. Shaw, State Coordinator, 151 North Delaware Street, Indianapolis IN 46204–2526, (317) 226–6303.
Milwaukee WI.—Delbert F. Reynolds, State Coordinator, Henry S. Reuss Federal Plaza, Suite 1380, 310 West Wisconsin Avenue, Milwaukee WI 53203–2289, (414) 297–3214.
Flint MI.—[Vacant], Area Coordinator, The Federal Building, 605 North Saginaw Street, Suite 200, Flint MI 48502–2043, (810) 766–5108.
Minneapolis MN.—Thomas T. Feeney, State Coordinator, 220 Second Street South, Minneapolis MN 55401–2195, (612) 370–3000.
Springfield IL.—[Vacant], Area Coordinator, 509 West Capitol Street, Suite 206, Springfield IL 62704–1906, (217) 492–4085.
Fort Worth TX Regional.—Stephen R. Weatherford, Southwest Secretary's Representative, PO Box 2905, 1600 Throckmorton, Fort Worth TX 76113–2905, (817) 885–5401.
Albuquerque NM.—Michael R. Griego, State Coordinator, 625 Truman Street NE, Albuquerque NM 87110–6472, (505) 262–6463.
Dallas TX.—C. Donald Babers, Area Coordinator, Room 860, 525 Griffin Street, Dallas TX 75202–5007, (214) 767–8359.
Houston TX.—George H. Rodriguez, Area Coordinator, Norfolk Tower, Suite 200, 2211 Norfolk, Houston TX 77098–4096, (713) 834–3274.
Little Rock AR.—Bobbie Joe McCoy, TCBY Tower, 425 W. Capitol Avenue, Suite 900, Little Rock AR 72201–3488, (501) 324–5931.
Lubbock TX.—Miguel C. Rincon Jr., (acting), Area Coordinator, George H. Mahon Federal Building and United States Courthouse, 1205 Texas Avenue, Lubbock TX 79401–4093, (806) 472–7275.
New Orleans LA.—Jason Gamlin, State Coordinator, Hale Boggs Federal Building, 501 Magazine Street, New Orleans LA 70130–3099, (504) 589–7200.
Oklahoma City OK.—Margaret R. Milner, State Coordinator, 500 W. Main Street, Suite 400, Oklahoma City OK 73102–2233, (405) 553–7401.
San Antonio TX.—A. Cynthia Leon, Area Coordinator, Washington Square Building, 800 Dolorosa, San Antonio TX 78207–4563, (210) 229–6800.
Shreveport LA.—Martha N. Sakre, 401 Edwards Street, Suite 1510, Shreveport LA 71101–3107, (318) 676–3385.
Tulsa OK.—James S. Colgan, Area Coordinator, 50 East 15th Street, Tulsa OK 74119–4030, (918) 581–7434.
Kansas City KS Regional.—Elmer Binford (acting), Great Plains Secretary's Representative, Gateway Tower II, 400 State Avenue, Kansas City KS 66101–2406, (913) 551–5462.
Des Moines IA.—William H. McNarney, State Coordinator, Room 239, 210 Walnut Street, Des Moines IA 50309–2155, (515) 284–4512.
Omaha NE.—Ernest T. Gratz, State Coordinator, 10909 Mill Valley Road, Omaha NE 68154–3955, (402) 492–3100.
St. Louis MO.—Kenneth G. Lange, Area Coordinator, 1222 Spruce Street, Third Floor, St. Louis MO 63103–2836, (314) 539–6583.
Denver CO Regional.—Anthony J. Hernandez, Rocky Mountains Secretary's Representative, First Interstate Tower North, 633 17th Street, Denver CO 80202–3607, (303) 672–5440.
Casper WY.—William L. Garrett, State Coordinator, Federal Office Building, Room 4229, 100 East B Street, Casper WY 82602–1918, (307) 261–5252.

Fargo ND.—Keith Elliott, State Coordinator, Federal Building, 657 Second Avenue, Room 366, Fargo ND 58108–2483, (701) 239–5136.

Helena MT.—Richard C. Brinck, State Coordinator, Federal Office Building, Drawer 10095, 301 S. Park, Helena MT 59626–0095, (406) 441–1298.

Salt Lake City UT.—John Milchick, Jr., State Coordinator, 257 Tower Building, Suite 550, 257 East, 200 South, Salt Lake City UT 84111–2048, (801) 524–5241.

Sioux Falls SD.—Dwight A. Peterson, State Coordinator, 2500 W. 49th Street, Suite I–201, Sioux Falls SD 57105–6558, (605) 330–4223.

San Francisco CA Regional.—Arthur C. Agnos, Pacific/Hawaii Secretary's Representative, Phillip Burton Federal Building and U.S. Courthouse, 450 Golden Gate Avenue, PO Box 36003, San Francisco CA 94102–3448, (415) 436–6532.

Fresno CA.—Yvielle Edwards-Lee, Area Coordinator, 1630 East Shaw Avenue, Suite 138, Fresno CA, 93710–8193, (209) 487–5033.

Honolulu HI.—Gordan Y. Furutani, State Coordinator, Seven Waterfront Plaza, 500 Ala Moana Boulevard, Suite 500, Honolulu HI 96813–4918, (808) 522–8175.

Los Angeles CA.—Jacqueline J. Slayton, Area Coordinator, AT&T Center, 611 West Sixth Street, Suite 800, Los Angeles CA 90017–3127, (213) 894–7122.

Phoenix AZ.—Tery Goddard, State Coordinator, Two Arizona Center, 400 North Fifth Street, Suite 1600, Phoenix AZ 85004–2361, (602) 379–4434.

Reno NV.—[Vacant], Area Coordinator, 1575 Delucchi Lane, Suite 114, Reno NV 89502–6581, (702) 784–5356.

Sacramento CA.—Rafael Metzger, Area Coordinator, 777 12th Street, Suite 200, Sacramento CA 95814–1997, (916) 498–5220.

San Diego CA.—Charles J. Wilson, Area Coordinator, Mission City Corporate Center, 2365 Northside Drive, Suite 300, San Diego CA 92108–2712, (619) 557–5310.

Santa Ana CA.—Dave Westerfield (acting), Area Coordinator, 3 Hutton Centre Drive, Suite 500, Santa Ana CA 92707–5764, (714) 957–1702.

Las Vegas NV.—Paul A. Pradia, State Coordiantor, Altrim Building, Suite 700, 333 North Rancho Drive, Los Vegas NV 89106–3714, (702) 388–6500.

Tucson AZ.—Sharon Atwell (acting), Area Coordinator, Security Pacific Bank Plaza, 33 North Stone Avenue, Suite 700, Tucson AZ 85701–1467, (602) 670–6237.

Seattle WA Regional.—Robert N. Santos, Northwest/Alaska Secretary's Representative, Seattle Federal Office Building, 909 First Avenue, Suite 200, Seattle WA 98104–1000, (206) 220–5101.

Anchorage AK.—Arlene L. Patton, State Coordinator, University Plaza Building, 949 East 36th Avenue, Suite 401, Anchorage AK 99508–4399, (907) 271–4170.

Boise ID.—Gary L. Gillespie, State Coordinator, Plaza IV, Suite 220, 800 Park Boulevard, Boise ID 83712–7743, (208) 334–1990.

Portland OR.—Mark E. Pavolka, State Coordinator, 400 Southwest Sixth Avenue, Suite 700, Portland OR 97204–1632, (503) 326–2561.

Spokane WA.—Robert J. Seamons (acting), Area Coordinator, Farm Credit Bank Building, Eighth Floor East, West 601 First Avenue, Spokane WA 99204–0317, (509) 353–2510.

DEPARTMENT OF THE INTERIOR

Interior Building, 1849 C Street 20240, phone (202) 208–3100, http://www.doi.gov

BRUCE BABBITT, Secretary of the Interior, sworn in on January 22, 1993, as the 47th Secretary; born June 27, 1938; B.A., Notre Dame, student body president; M.S., University of Newcastle in England, Marshall Scholar; J.D., Harvard; Attorney General of Arizona, 1975–78; Governor of Arizona, 1978–87; chairman, Democratic Governors Association, 1985; candidate for Democratic nomination for President, 1988; married to the former Hattie Coons; two children: Christopher and T.J.

OFFICE OF THE SECRETARY

Interior Building, Room 6156, phone 208–7351, fax 208–5048

Secretary of the Interior.—Bruce Babbitt.
Special Assistant to the Secretary.—Maura K. McManimon.
Chief of Staff.—Ann H. Shields.

OFFICE OF THE DEPUTY SECRETARY

Interior Building, Room 5100, phone 208–7351

Deputy Secretary.—John R. Garamendi.
Office of the Special Trustee for American Indians.—Paul M. Homan.

EXECUTIVE SECRETARIAT

Interior Building, Room 6217, phone 208–3181

Assistant to the Secretary and Director.—Juliette A. Falkner, Room 6215, 208–3181.

CONGRESSIONAL AND LEGISLATIVE AFFAIRS

Interior Building, Room 6256, phone 208–7693

Assistant to the Secretary and Director.—Melanie L. Beller, 208–7683.
Deputy Director.—Geoff Webb.
Deputy Director for Legislative and Intergovernmental Affairs.—Danny Consenstein.
Legislative Counsel.—Jane Lyder, Room 6245, 208–6797.

OFFICE OF COMMUNICATIONS

Interior Building, Room 7214, phone 208–6416

Director.—Michael Gauldin.
Deputy Director.—Lisa Guide, Room 7217.
Press Secretary.—Mary Helen Thompson, Room 7219.
Information Officers: Steve Brooks, Stephanie Hanna, John E. Wright, 208–3171.

OFFICE OF THE SOLICITOR

Interior Building, Room 6352, phone 208–4423

Solicitor.—John D. Leshy.
Deputy Solicitor.—Edward B. Cohen, Room 6353, 208–4813.
Associate Solicitor for—
Administration.—Robert S. More, Room 7460, 208–6115.
Conservation and Wildlife.—Robert L. Baum, Room 6560, 208–4344.

General Law.—Timothy S. Elliott (acting), Room 6514, 208–4722.
Indian Affairs.—David C. Etheridge (acting), Room 6454, 208–4361.
Land and Water Resources.—Paul B. Smyth (acting), Room 6411, 208–4506.
Mineral Resources.—Peter J. Schaumberg (acting), Room 6311, 208–4036.

OFFICE OF THE INSPECTOR GENERAL

Interior Building, Room 5341, phone 208–5745, fax 208–4998

Inspector General.—Wilma A. Lewis, Room 5359.
Chief of Staff and General Counsel.—Richard Reback, Room 5359, 208–4618.
Assistant Inspector General for—
Management and Policy.—Sharon D. Eller, Room 5355, 208–4618.
Audits.—Robert Williams, Room 5356, 208–4252.
Investigations.—John R. Sinclair, Room 5352, 208–6752.

ASSISTANT SECRETARY FOR POLICY, MANAGEMENT AND BUDGET

Interior Building, Room 6130, phone 208–4203

Assistant Secretary.—Bonnie R. Cohen.
Staff Assistant.—Justin Johnston, 208–4203.
Director Office of Hearings and Appeals.—Barry Hill, 4015 Wilson Boulevard, Arlington VA 22203, (703) 235–3810.
Deputy Assistant Secretary for Human Resources.—[Vacant], 208–4727.
Director, Office for Equal Opportunity.—Melodee Stith, Room 1324, 208–5693.
Director, Office of—
National Service and Educational Partnerships.—Dolores Chacon, 208–6403.
Personnel Policy.—Dolores Chacon (acting), Room 5201, 208–6761.
Chief, Ethics Staff.—Gabriele J. Paone, Room 5140, 208–7960.
Deputy Assistant Secretary for Policy and International Affairs.—Brooks B. Yeager, 208–5978.
Director, Office of—
Environmental Policy and Compliance.—Willie Taylor, Room 2024, 208–3891.
Insular Affairs.—Allen Stayman, Room 4311, 208–4736.
Managing Risk and Public Safety.—L. Michael Kaas, Room 7358, 208–3760.
Policy Analysis.—William Bettenberg (acting), Room 4411, 208–3805.
Deputy Assistant Secretary for Budget and Finance.—Robert J. Lamb, 208–7966.
Director, Office of—
Acquisition and Property Management.—Paul A. Dennett, Room 5512, 208–3668.
Budget.—Mary Ann Lawler, Room 4100, 208–5308.
Financial Management.—Schuyler Lesher, Room 7258, 208–4701.
Information Resources Management.—Donald Lasher, Room 5312, 208–6194.
Director of Planning and Performance Management.—Jody Kusek, Room 5124, 208–1818.
Chief Executive Officer, Interior Service Center.—Claudia P. Schechter, Room 5115, 208–6254.
Chief Operating Officer, ISC.—[Vacant].
Director, Office of Aircraft Services.—Elmer Hurd, Boise Idaho, (208) 387–5750.

ASSISTANT SECRETARY FOR FISH AND WILDLIFE AND PARKS

Interior Building, Room 3156, phone 208–4416

Assistant Secretary.—[Vacant].
Deputy Assistant Secretary.—Donald J. Barry, 208–7400.
Assistant to the Assistant Secretary.—Joseph E. Doddridge, Room 3142, 208–3928.
Counselor to the Assistant Secretary for Fish and Wildlife and Parks.—William L. Leary, Room 3153, 208–5347.

U.S. FISH AND WILDLIFE SERVICE

1849 C Street NW, Washington DC 20240, phone 208–4416, fax 208–4473

Director.—John G. Rogers (acting), 208–4545.
Deputy Director.—Jay L. Gerst (acting), 208–4717.
Chief, Office for Human Resources.—Nathaniel Brown, 208–3195.

Assistant Director for—

External Affairs.—Daniel M. Ashe, 208–4500.

Chief, Office of—

Congressional and Legislative Services.—Lori C. Williams, 208–5403.

Public Affairs.—Phil Million, 208–4131.

Federal Aid.—Robert E. Lange, Jr., (703) 358–2156.

International Affairs.—Marshall P. Jones, 208–6393.

Ecological Services.—Jamie R. Clark, 208–4646.

Fisheries.—Gary B. Edwards, 208–6394.

Policy, Budget and Administration.—Paul W. Henne (acting), 208–4888.

Refuges and Wildlife.—Robert G. Streeter, 208–5333.

Regional Directors:

Region 1.—Michael J. Spear, Eastside Federal Complex, 911 Northeast 11th Avenue, Portland OR 97232–4181, (503) 231–6118, fax (503) 872–2716.

Region 2.—Nancy M. Kaufman, PO Box 1306, Room 1306, 500 Gold Avenue SW, Albuquerque NM 87103, (505) 248–6282, fax (505) 248–6845.

Region 3.—William F. Hartwig, Federal Building, Fort Snelling, Twin Cities MN 55111, (612) 725–3563, fax (612) 725–3501.

Region 4.—Noreen K. Clough, 1875 Century Boulevard, Atlanta GA 30345, (404) 679–4000, fax (404) 679–4006.

Region 5.—Ronald E. Lambertson, 300 Westgate Center Drive, Hadley MA 01035–9589, (413) 253–8300, fax (413) 253–8308.

Region 6.—Ralph O. Morgenweck, PO Box 25486, Denver Federal Center, Denver CO 80225, (303) 236–7920, fax (303) 236–8295.

Region 7.—David B. Allen, 1011 East Tudor Road, Anchorage AK 99503, (907) 786–3542, fax (907) 786–3306.

NATIONAL PARK SERVICE

Interior Building, Room 3104, phone 208–4621, fax 208–7520

Director.—Roger Kennedy.

Deputy Director.—Denis Galvin (acting), 208–3818.

Chief of Staff.—Renee Stone, 208–6741.

Associate Director for—

Administration.—Mary Bradford, 208–6953.

Cultural Resources, Stewardship and Partnership.—Katherine Stevenson, 208–7625.

Natural Resources, Stewardship and Science.—Michael Soukup, 208–3884.

Park Operations and Education.—Maureen Finnerty, 208–5651.

Professional Services.—Charles Clapper (acting), 208–3624.

Assistant Director for External Affairs.—Destry Jarvis, 208–6781.

Legislative and Congressional Affairs.—Kitty L. Roberts, 208–5656.

Congressional Liaison.—[Vacant], 208–5656.

Chief, Office of Public Affairs.—Dave Bama, 208–6843.

Regional Directors:

Alaska Region.—Bob Barbee, 2525 Gambell Street, Anchorage AK 99503, (907) 257–2690, fax (907) 257–2510.

Northeast Region.—Marie Rust, 200 Chestnut Street, Philadelphia PA 19106, (215) 597–7013, fax (215) 597–0815.

Midwest Region.—William Schenk, 1709 Jackson Street, Omaha NE, 68102–2571, (402) 221–3448, fax (402) 341–2039.

National Capital Region.—Terry R. Carlstrom (acting), 1100 Ohio Drive SW, Washington DC 20242, (202) 619–7005, fax (202) 619–7220.

Intermountain Region.—John Cook, PO Box 25287, Denver CO 80225–0287, (303) 969–2500, fax (303) 969–2785.

Southeast Region.—Jerry Belson (acting), 75 Spring Street SW, Atlanta GA 30303, (404) 562–3100, fax (404) 331–3263.

Pacific Western Region.—Stanley T. Albright, 600 Harrison Street, Suite 600, San Francisco CA 94107–1372, (415) 744–3876, fax (415) 744–4050.

ASSISTANT SECRETARY FOR INDIAN AFFAIRS

Interior Building, Room 4160, phone 208–7163

Assistant Secretary.—Ada E. Deer.

Deputy Assistant Secretary.—Michael J. Anderson.

Director, Office of—
Self-Governance.—William Sinclair, (202) 219–0240.
Audit and Evaluation.—Linda Richardson, 208–1916.
American Indian Trust.—Elizabeth Homer, 208–3338.

BUREAU OF INDIAN AFFAIRS

Interior Building, Room 4160, phone 208–5116

Deputy Commissioner.—Hilda Manuel.
Director, Office of—
Management and Administration.—Jim McDivitt (acting), 208–4147.
Trust Responsibilities.—Terry Virden, 208–5831.
Economic Development.—Nancy Jemison, 208–5324.
Tribal Services.—Deborah Maddox, 208–3463.
Director, Office of Indian Education Programs.—Joann Sebastian Morris, 208–3312.
Deputy Director.—William Mehojah, 208–6175.

Area Directors:
Aberdeen.—Delbert Brewer, 115 Fourth Avenue SE, Aberdeen SD 57401, (605) 226–7345, fax (602) 226–7446.
Albuquerque.—Robert Baracker, 615 First Street NW, Box 26567, Albuquerque NM 87125-6567, (505) 766–3171, fax (505) 766–1964.
Anadarko.—Joe Walker (acting), WCD Office Complex, Box 368, Anadarko OK 73005–0368, (405) 247–6673 Ext 314, fax (405) 247–2242.
Billings.—Keith Beartusk, 316 North 26th Street, Billings MT 58101–1397, (406) 247–7943, fax (406) 247–7976.
Eastern.—Franklin Keel, 3701 North Fairfax Drive, Suite 260, Virginia Square, Arlington VA 22203, (703) 235–2571, fax (703) 235–8610.
Juneau.—Niles Cesar, Federal Building, 3rd Floor, PO Box 25520, Juneau AK 99802–5520, (907) 586–7177, fax (907) 586–7169.
Minneapolis.—Larry Morin (acting), 331 Second Avenue South, Minneapolis MN 55401–2241, (612) 373–1000, fax (612) 373–1186.
Muskogee.—James Fields, Fifth and West Okmulgee, Muskogee OK 74401–4898, (918) 687–2296, fax (918) 687–2571.
Navajo.—Wilson Barber, PO Box 1060, Gallup NM 87305–1060, (505) 863–8314, fax (505) 863–8245.
Phoenix.—Theodore Quasula (acting), One North First Street, PO Box 10, Phoenix AZ 85001–0010, (602) 379–6600, fax (602) 379–4413.
Portland.—Stanley Speaks, 911 11th Avenue NE, Portland OR 97232–4169, (503) 231–6702, fax (503) 231–2201.
Sacramento.—Ronald Jaeger, 2800 Cottage Way, Sacramento CA 95835–1884, (916) 979–2600, fax (916) 979–2569.

ASSISTANT SECRETARY FOR LAND AND MINERALS MANAGEMENT

Interior Building, Room 6628, phone 208–5676, fax 208–3144

Assistant Secretary.—Bob Armstrong.
Deputy Assistant Secretary.—Sylvia Baca, 208–6734.

BUREAU OF LAND MANAGEMENT

Interior Building, Room 5660, fax 208–5242

Director.—Sylvia Baca (acting), 208–3801.
Deputy Director.—Mathew Millenbach, 208–6731.
Assistant Director for—
Renewable Resources and Planning.—Maitland Sharpe, 208–4896.
Minerals, Realty and Resource Protection.—W. Hord Tipton, 208–4201.
Information Resources Management.—Gayle Gordon, 208–4587.
Communications.—Gwen Mason, 208–6913.
Human Resources Management.—Carolyn M. Burrell, 501–6724.
Business and Fiscal Services.—Nina Rose Hatfield, 208–4864.

State Directors:
Alaska.—Tom Allen, 222 West Seventh Avenue No. 13, Anchorage AK 99513, (907) 271–5076, fax (907) 271–4596.

Arizona.—Denise Meridith, 222 North Central Avenue, Phoenix AZ 85004–2203, (602) 417–9206, fax (602) 417–9398.
California.—Ed Hastey, 2135 Butano Drive, Sacramento CA 95825–0451, (916) 979–2845, fax (916) 979–2869.
Colorado.—Bob Abbey (acting), 2850 Youngfield Street, Lakewood CO 80215–7076, (303) 239–3700, fax (303) 239–3934.
Eastern States.—Carlson Culp, 7450 Boston Boulevard, Springfield VA 22153, (703) 440–1700, fax (703) 440–1701.
Idaho.—Martha Hahn, 1387 South Vinnell Way, Boise ID 83709, (208) 373–4000, fax (208) 373–3919.
Montana.—Larry Hamilton, Granite Tower, 222 North 32nd Street, Billings MT 59107, (406) 255–2904, fax (406) 255–2995.
Nevada.—Ann Morgan, 850 Harvard Way, Reno NV 89520–0006, (702) 785–6590, fax (702) 785–6601.
New Mexico.—William Calkins, 1474 Rodeo Road, Sante Fe NM 87502, (505) 438–7501, fax (505) 438–7452.
Oregon.—Elaine Zielinski, 1515 Southwest Fifth Avenue, Portland OR 97208–2965, (503) 952–6024, fax (503) 952–6390.
Utah.—Bill Lamb (acting), 324 South State Street, Suite 301, Salt Lake City UT 84145–0155, (801) 539–4010, fax (801) 539–4013.
Wyoming.—Al Pierson, 5353 Yellowstone Road, PO Box 1828, Cheyenne WY 82003, (307) 775–6001, fax (307) 775–6082.

MINERALS MANAGEMENT SERVICE

1849 C Street, MS–4230–MIB, 20240

Director.—Cynthia Quarterman, 208–3500.
Deputy Director.—[Vacant], 208–3500.
Associate Director for—
Offshore Minerals Management.—Carolita Kallaur, 208–3530.
Royalty Management.—Lucy R. Querques, 208–3512.
Administration and Budget.—Robert E. Brown, 208–3220.
Policy and Management Improvement.—Robert E. Brown (acting), 208–3398.
Chief, Office of Communications.—Lyn Herdt, 208–3983, fax 208–3968.

Outer Continental Shelf Regions:
Alaska.—Rance R. Wall (acting), Room 110, 949 East 36th Avenue, Anchorage AK 99508, (907) 271–6010, fax (907) 261–4464.
Gulf of Mexico.—Chris C. Oynes, 1201 Elmwood Park Boulevard, New Orleans LA 70123, (504) 736–2589, fax (504) 736–2589.
Pacific.—J. Lisle Reed, 770 Paseo Camarillo, Camarillo CA 93010, (805) 389–7502, fax (805) 683–7638.

SURFACE MINING RECLAMATION AND ENFORCEMENT

South Interior Building, Room 233, phone 208–4006, fax 219–3106

Director.—Kathrine Henry, (acting).
Deputy Director.—Ed Kay, 208–2807.
Assistant Director for—
Finance and Administration.—Robert Ewing, 208–2560.
Program Support.—Mary Josie Blanchard, 208–2596.
Staff Chiefs:
Equal Opportunity.—James Joiner, 208–5897.
Strategic Planning, Budget and Evaluation.—Victor Christiansen, 208–7837.
Communications.—Nancy Smith, 208–2565.

Regional Director for:
Appalachian Coordinating Center.—Allen Klein, Three Parkway Center, Pittsburgh PA 15220, (412) 937–2828, fax (412) 937–2903.
Mid-Continent Coordinating Center.—Brent Wahlquist, 501 Belle Street, Alton IL 62002, (618) 463–6460, fax (618) 463–6470.
Western Coordinating Center.—Richard Seibel, 1999 Broadway, Suite 3320, Denver CO 80202, (303) 844–1401, fax (303) 844–1522.

Field Office Director for:

Alabama.—Arthur Abbs, 135 Gemini Circle, Suite 215, Homewood AL 35209, (205) 290–7282, fax (205) 290–7280.

Indiana.—Andrew Gilmore, Minton-Capehart Federal Building, 575 North Pennsylvania Street, Room 301, Indianapolis IN 46204, (317) 226–6700, fax (317) 226–6182.

Kentucky.—William Kovacic, 2675 Regency Road, Lexington KY 40503, (606) 233–2894, fax (606) 233–2898.

New Mexico.—Guy Padgett, 505 Marquette Avenue NW, Suite 1200, Albuquerque NM 87102, (505) 248–5070, fax (505) 248–5081.

Oklahoma.—Michael Wolfrom, 5100 East Skelley Drive, Suite 470, Tulsa OK 74135, (918) 581–6430, fax (918) 581–6419.

Pennsylvania.—Robert Biggi, Transportation Center, 415 Market Street, Suite 3C, Harrisburg PA 17101, (717) 782–4036, fax (717) 782–3771.

Tennessee.—George Miller, 530 Gay Street, Suite 500, Knoxville TN 37902, (423) 545–4103, fax (423) 545–4111.

Virginia.—Robert Penn, PO Drawer 1216, Big Stone Gap VA 24219, (540) 523–0001, fax (540) 523–5053.

West Virginia.—Roger Calhoun, 1027 Virginia Street East, Charleston WV 25301, (304) 347–7162, fax (304) 347–7170.

Wyoming.—Guy Padgett, 100 East B Street, Room 2128, Casper WY 82601, (307) 261–6550, fax (307) 261–6552.

ASSISTANT SECRETARY FOR WATER AND SCIENCE

Interior Building, Room 6660, phone 208–4811, fax 371–2815

Assistant Secretary.—Patricia J. Beneke, 208–3186.

Deputy Assistant Secretary.—Mark E. Schaffer, Room 6654, 208–4811.

U.S. GEOLOGICAL SURVEY

12201 Sunrise Valley Drive, Reston VA 20192

phone (703) 648–7415, fax (703) 648–4454

Director.—Dr. Gordon P. Eaton, 648–7411.

Associate Director for—

Programs.—Bonnie A. McGregor, 648–7412.

Operations.—Barbara J. Ryan, 648–7413.

Chief of Staff.—Linda Stanley, 648–7414.

Senior Staff Scientist.—James F. Devine, 648–4423.

Program Planning and Coordination.—Gary L. Hill, 648–4451.

Program Operations.—Martin E. Eckes, 648–4443.

Office of Outreach.—Michael P. McDermott, 648–4460.

Congressional Liaison Officer.—Timothy J. West, 648–4455.

Deputy Bureau Ethics Counselor.—Virginia G. Miles, 648–7474.

Staff Assistant for Special Issues.—Thomas Dolley, 648–7415.

Division Chiefs:

Geologic Division.—P. Patrick Leahy, 648–6600.

National Mapping Division.—Richard E. Witmer (acting) 648–5748.

Water Resources Division.—Robert M. Hirsch, 648–5215.

Biological Resources Division.—Dennis B. Fenn, 648–4050.

Office of Program Support.—William F. Gossman (acting), 648–7200.

BUREAU OF RECLAMATION

18th and C Streets, Room 7654, 20240, phone (202) 208–4157, fax (202) 208–3484

Commissioner.—Eluid L. Martinez, Room 7659, 208–4157.

Director, Policy and External Affairs.—Robert S. (Steve) Richardson, Room 7650, 208–4291.

Chief, Office of—

Congressional and Legislative Affairs.—Lori Sonken, Room 7652, 208–4466.

Public Affairs.—Paul Bledsoe, Room 7642, 208–4662.

Director, Operations.—Stephen V. Magnussen, Room 7645, 208–4081.

RECLAMATION SERVICE CENTER

Federal Center, Denver CO 80225

Director for—

Reclamation Service Center.—James O. Malila, (303) 236–9208.
Program Analysis.—J. Austin Burke, (303) 236–3292.
Organization and Resources Management.—Margaret W. Sibley, (303) 236–7464.
Management Services.—Kathryn E. Gordon, (303) 236–0005.
Technical Service Center.—Felix W. Cook, (303) 236–6985.
Administrative Service Center.—T. Stan Dunn, (303) 969–7200.

Regional Directors:

Pacific Northwest Regional Office.—J.W. Keys III, Boise ID, (208) 378–5012.
Mid-Pacific Regional Office.—Roger K. Patterson, Sacramento CA, (916) 979–2200.
Lower Colorado Regional Office.—Robert W. Johnson, Boulder City NV, (702) 293–8411.
Upper Colorado Regional Office.—Charles A. Calhoun, Salt Lake City UT, (801) 524–3600.
Great Plains Regional Office.—J. Neil Stessman, Billings MT, (406) 247–7600.

DEPARTMENT OF JUSTICE

Main Justice Building

950 Pennsylvania Avenue NW 20530, phone 514–2000, http://www.usdoj.gov

JANET RENO, Attorney General, born and raised in Miami, FL; A.B., chemistry, Cornell University, 1960; LL.B., Harvard Law School, 1963; attorney for the Committee on the Judiciary, Florida House of Representatives; private practice, 1976–78; elected State Attorney for Miami, FL, 1978–93; awarded: Herbert Harley Award, American Judicature Society, 1981; Public Administrator of the Year, American Society for Public Administration, 1983; Medal of Honor Award, Florida Bar Association, 1990; confirmed by the U.S. Senate on March 11, 1993, and entered upon duties March 12, 1993.

OFFICE OF THE ATTORNEY GENERAL

Main Justice Building, Room 5111

950 Pennsylvania Avenue NW 20530, phone 514–2001

Attorney General.—Janet Reno.

Chief of Staff.—John M. Hogan, Room 5111, 514–3892.

Counselor to the Attorney General for Youth Violence.—Kent Markus, Room 5131, 514–3008.

Confidential Assistant to the Attorney General.—Bessie L. Meadows, Room 5111, 514–2001.

Assistants to the Attorney General: Wilfredo Ferrer, Room 5127, 514–2107; David Jones, Room 5121, 514–2291; Cheryl Montgomery, Room 5110, 514–4195; Sidney Espinosa, Room 5116, 514–2148.

Deputy Attorney General.—Seth P. Waxman (acting), Room 4111, phone 514–2101.

Associate Attorney General.—John C. Dwyer (acting), Room 5214, 514–9500.

Assistant Attorney General, Antitrust.—Joel I. Klein (acting), Room 3109, 514–2401.

Assistant Attorney General, Civil Division.—Frank W. Hunger, Room 3143, 514–3301.

Assistant Attorney General Civil Rights Division.—Isabelle Katz Pinzler (acting), Room 5643, 514–2151.

Assistant Attorney General, Criminal Division.—John C. Keeney (acting), Room 2107, 514–2621.

Assistant Attorney General, Environment and Natural Resources Division.—Lois J. Schiffer, Room 2143, 514–2701.

Assistant Attorney General for Administration.—Stephen R. Colgate, Room 1111, 514–3101.

Assistant Attorney General, Office of Justice Programs.—Laurie Robinson.

Assistant Attorney General, Legal Counsel.—Dawn Johnsen (acting), Room 5224, 514–2051.

Assistant Attorney General, Legislative Affairs.—Andrew Fois, phone 514–2141.

Assistant Attorney General, Policy Development.—Eleanor D. Acheson, Room 4234, 514–4601.

Assistant Attorney General, Tax Division.—Loretta C. Argrett, Room 4143, 514–2901.

Co-Directors.—Daniel J. Metcalfe and Richard L. Huff, Flag Building, Suite 570, 514–4251.

Administrator, Drug Enforcement Administration.—Thomas A. Constantine, Room W–12060, 307–8000.

Chair, Foreign Claims Settlement Commission.—Delissa A. Ridgway, Bicentennial Building, 600 E Street NW, Suite 6002, 20579, 616–6985.

Chairman, U.S. Parole Commission.—Michael J. Gaines, Park Place Building, 5550 Friendship Boulevard, Suite 420 Chevy Chase MD 20815, (301) 492–5990.

Chief, Interpol—U.S. National Central Bureau.—John J. Imhoff.

Commissioner, Immigration and Naturalization Service.—Doris Meissner, CAB Room 7100, 514–1900.

Counsel for Intelligence Policy.—James McAdams III, Room 6325, 514–5600.

Counsel.—Michael E. Shaheen, Jr., Room 4304, 514–3365.

Director, Bureau of Prisons.—Kathleen M. Hawk.

Director, Office of Community Orienting Policing Services.—Joseph Brann.
Director, Community Relations Service.—Rose M. Ochi, 600 E Street NW, Suite 2000, 20530, 305–2932.
Director, Executive Office for Immigration Review.—Anthony Moscato.
Director, Executive Office for U.S. Attorneys.—Carol Di Battiste.
Director, Executive Office for U.S. Trustees.—Joseph Patchan, 901 E Street NW, Room 700, 20530, phone 307–1391.
Director, Federal Bureau of Investigation.—Louis J. Freeh, J. Edgar Hoover Building, 935 Pennsylvania Avenue NW, 20535–0001, Room 7176, 324–3444.
Director, Office of Public Affairs.—Bert Brandenburg (acting), Room 1228, 614–2777.
Director, U.S. Marshals Service.—Eduardo Gonzalez.
Inspector General.—Michael R. Bromwich, 1425 New York Avenue NW, Room 4706, Washington DC 20005.
Pardon Attorney.—Margaret C. Love, 1425 New York Avenue NW, Room 4706, Washington DC 20005.
Solicitor General.—Walter E. Dellinger, Room 5143, 514–2201.

OFFICE OF THE DEPUTY ATTORNEY GENERAL

Main Justice Building, Room 4111, phone 514–2101

Deputy Attorney General.—Seth P. Waxman (acting).
Confidential Assistant.—Ginger Trapanotto, Room 4111, 514–2101 or 514–1904.
Principal Associate Deputy Attorney General.—Merrick B. Garland, Room 4206, 514–2105.
Executive Assistant and Counsel.—Dennis M. Corrigan, Room 4113, 616–0419.
Associate Deputy Attorneys General: Paul J. Fishman, Room 4114, 514–3796; David Margolis, Room 4112, 514–4945; David W. Ogden, Room 4208, 514–6909; Catherine Russell, Room 4212, 514–2298; Roslyn A. Mazer, Room 4115, 514–1013.
Special Counsel to the Deputy Attorney General.—Debra Cohn, Room 4119, 514–3052.
Counsels to the Deputy Attorney General: Roger C. Adams, Room 4214, 514–2707; Gerri Lynn Ratliff, Room 4217, 514–3392; Johnathan Schwartz, Room 4116, 514–4375; Charles J. Sgro, Room 4115, 514–3070.

EXECUTIVE OFFICE FOR NATIONAL SECURITY

Director and Associate Deputy Attorney General.—Frederick Baron, Room 4119, 514–6753.
Deputy Director and Associate Deputy Attorney General.—Michael A. Vatis, Room 4129, 307–3667.
Counsel for International Programs.—Regina Hart Nassen, Room 4127, 514–8168.

OFFICE OF THE ASSOCIATE ATTORNEY GENERAL

Main Justice Building, Room 5214, phone 514–9500

Associate Attorney General.—John C. Dwyer (acting), Room 5214, 514–9500.
Confidential Assistant.—Jayne Schreiber, Room 5214, 514–9500.
Deputy Associate Attorneys General: Francis M. Allegra, Room 5132, 514–2987; Reginald Robinson, Room 4315, 616–3535; Lewis Anthony Sutin, Room 5215, 514–8950; Michael Small, Room 4311, 514–0451.

OFFICE OF ALTERNATIVE DISPUTE RESOLUTION

Senior Counsel.—Peter R. Steenland, Jr., Room 5706, 616–9471.

OFFICE OF THE SOLICITOR GENERAL

Main Justice Building, Room 5143, phone 514–2201

Solicitor General.—Walter E. Dellinger.
Deputy Solicitors General: Seth P. Waxman, Room 5141, 514–2206; Lawrence G. Wallace, Room 5609, 514–2211; Edwin S. Kneedler, Room 5139, 514–3261; Michael R. Dreeben, Room 5135, 514–4285.
Tax Assistant.—Kent L. Jones, Room 5623, 514–3948.

Executive Officer.—Carolyn M. Brammer, Room 5140, 514–5507.
Special Assistant.—Cheryl L. Sweitzer, Room 5143, 514–2201.
Legal Administrative Officer, Case Management Section.—Emily C. Spadoni, Room 5614, 514–2218.
Chief, Research and Publications Section.—G. Shirley Anderson, Room 5345, 514–3914.

OFFICE OF THE EXECUTIVE SECRETARIAT
Main Justice Building, Room 4414, phone 514–2063

Director.—Anna-Marie Kilmade Gatons, Room 4414, 514–2149.
Analysis and Quality Control Unit Chief.—Terry R. Samuels, Room 4416, 514–2063.
Operations Unit Chief.—Kathie Harting, Room 4412, 514–2063.
Records Requests/Inquiries, 514–2063.

OFFICE OF THE INSPECTOR GENERAL
Main Justice Building, 1425 New York Avenue NW
Room 4706, Washington DC 20005 (NYAV)

Inspector General.—Michael R. Bromwich.
Counselor to the Inspector General.—Suzanne K. Drouet.
Special Counsel to the Inspector General.—Leonard E. Bailey.
Deputy Inspector General.—Robert L. Ashbaugh.
Assistant Inspectors General:
Audit.—Guy K. Zimmerman, NYAV Room 5007, 616–4633.
Inspections.—Mary W. Demory, NYAV Room 6054, 616–4620.
Investigations.—Thomas J. Bondurant, NYAV Room 7100, 616–4760.
Management and Planning.—Gregory T. Peters, NYAV Room 7000, 616–4550.
General Counsel.—Howard L. Sribnick, Room 4706, 616–0646.

SPECIAL INVESTIGATIONS AND REVIEW UNIT

Director.—Glenn A. Fine, Room 4706, 616–0645

REGIONAL AUDIT OFFICES

Washington: Domenic A. Zazzaro, 1425 New York Avenue NW, Room 6001, Washington DC 20005, (202) 616–4688.
Atlanta: Clark F. Cooper, Suite 2322, 101 Marietta Drive, Atlanta GA 30323–2401, (404) 331–5928.
Chicago: Robert C. Gruensfelder, Suite 3510, Citicorp Center, 500 West Madison, Chicago IL 60661, (312) 353–1203.
Dallas: George W. Stendell, Room 575, Box 4, 207 South Houston Street, Dallas TX 75202, (214) 655–5000.
Denver: David M. Sheeren, Suite 640, 1244 Speer Boulevard, Denver CO 80204, (303) 844–3638.
Philadelphia: Ferris B. Polk, Suite 201, 701 Market Street, Philadelphia PA 19106, (215) 580–2111.
San Francisco: M. Thomas Clark, Suite 201, 1200 Bayhill Drive, San Bruno CA 94066, (415) 876–9220.

REGIONAL INVESTIGATIONS OFFICES

Atlanta: Michael A. Hill, c/o Audit Regional Office, Suite 2322, 101 Marietta Street, Atlanta GA 30323–2401, (404) 331–5037.
Boston: Ellen M. McElroy, Room 1010G, 1003 J.W. McCormack Post Office and Court House, Boston MA 02109, (617) 223–4869.
Chicago: Edward M. Dyner, Suite 3510, 500 West Madison Street, Citicorp Center, Chicago IL 60661, (312) 886–7050.
Colorado Springs: Karen Funk and Paul Sullivan, Suite 312, 111 South Tejon Street, Colorado Springs CO 80903, (719) 635–2366.
Dallas: David A. Mustain, Suite 575, Box 4, 207 South Houston Street, Dallas TX 75202–4724, (214) 655–5000.

El Paso: Stephen P. Beauchamp, Suite 200, 4050 Rio Bravo, El Paso TX 79902, (915) 577–0102.
Los Angeles: Steve F. Turchek, Suite 201, 412 West Broadway, Glendale CA 91204, (818) 637–5080.
McAllen: Wayne D. Beaman, Suite 510, Texas Commerce Center, 1701 West Business Highway 83, McAllen TX 78501, (210) 618–8145.
Miami: Alan J. Hazen, Suite 312, 3800 Inverrary Boulevard, Ft. Lauderdale FL 33319, (954) 356–7142.
New York: Robert H. Goodwin, Building No. 77, North Boundary Road, Pent House 2, Jamaica NY 11430, (718) 553–7520.
San Diego: Ralph F. Paige, Suite 560, 701 B Street, San Diego CA 92101, (619) 557–5970.
San Francisco: Gary N. Overby, Suite 220, 1200 Bayhill Drive, San Bruno CA 94066, (415) 876–9058.
Seattle: Stephen C. Howard, 620 Kirkland Way, Suite 104, Kirkland WA 98033, (206) 828–3998.
Tucson: William L. King, Jr., Suite 105, 10 East Broadway, Tucson AZ 85701 (520) 670–5243.
Washington: David R. Glendinning, 1425 New York Avenue NW, Suite 7100, Washington DC 20005, (202) 616–4766.
Houston: Scott E. Dennis, Bob Casey Federal Courthouse, 515 Rusk Avenue, Room 3037, Suite 3300, Houston TX 77002, (713) 718–4888.

OFFICE OF LEGAL COUNSEL

Main Justice Building, Room 5224, phone 514–2051

Assistant Attorney General.—Dawn Johnsen (acting).
Deputy Assistant Attorneys General: Randolph D. Moss, Room 5228, 514–3745; Beth Nolan, Room 5226, 515–3744; Richard L. Shiffrin, Room 5235, 514–2046.
Special Counsels: Daniel L. Koffsky, Room 5258, 514–2030; Robert J. Delahunty, Room 5239, 514–2054; Paul P. Colborn, Room 5246, 514–2048.
Executive Officer.—Kathleen O. Murphy, Room 5240, 514–2057.

OFFICE OF POLICY DEVELOPMENT

Main Justice Building, Room 4234, phone 514–4601

Assistant Attorney General.—Eleanor D. Acheson.
Special Assistant.—Joe Thesing, Room 4232, 514–2061.
Deputy Assistant Attorneys General: Kevin R. Jones, Room 4245, 514–4604; Harry Litman, Room 4246, 616–2250; Grace L. Mastalli, Room 4237, 514–4606; Sarah L. Wilson, Room 4240, 514–0052; Mark Greenberg, Room 4515, 514–2160.

OFFICE OF PUBLIC AFFAIRS

Main Justice Building, Room 1228, phone 514–2007

Director.—Bert Brandenburg (acting), 614–2777.
Deputy Director.—Myron Marlin. 614–2777.

OFFICE OF INFORMATION AND PRIVACY

Flag Building, Suite 570, phone 514–4251

Co-Directors.—Daniel J. Metcalfe, Richard L. Huff.
Deputy Director.—Margaret A. Irving.

OFFICE OF INTELLIGENCE POLICY AND REVIEW

Main Justice Building, Room 6325, phone 514–5600

Counsel for Intelligence Policy.—James McAdams III.
Deputy Counsel for—
Intelligence Operations.—Allan N. Kornblum, Room 6325, 514–2882.
Intelligence Policy.—Daniel J. Gallington, Room 6325, 514–5604.

OFFICE OF PROFESSIONAL RESPONSIBILITY

Main Justice Building, Room 4304, phone 514–3365

Counsel.—Michael E. Shaheen, Jr.
Deputy Counsel.—Richard M. Rogers.
Associate Counsels: John T. Ezell III; Robert B. Lyon, Jr.; R. Keith Thomas; Judith B. Wish.
Assistant Counsels: Paul L. Colby; George Ellard; Mary Anne Hoopes; Joan L. Goldfrank; Candice M. Will; Alexander S. White; Melanie J. Russell; Mark A. Adler; Marlene M. Wahowiak; James A. Duncan; Phillip A. Talber; Mark G. Fraase.

OFFICE OF LEGISLATIVE AFFAIRS

Main Justice Building, phone 514–2141

Assistant Attorney General.—Andrew Fois.
Deputy Assistant Attorneys General: Ann Harkins, Room 1145, 514–4047; John Trasvina, Room 1605, 514–2111; James Castello, Room 1139, 305–0091.

JUSTICE MANAGEMENT DIVISION

Main Justice Building, Room 1111, 514–3101

Chester Arthur Building, 425 I Street NW, 20536 (CAB)

Ariel Rios Building, 12th and Pennsylvania Avenue NW, 20530 (ARB)

Washington Center, 1001 G Street NW, 20530 (WCTR)

Rockville Building, 1151–D Seven Locks Road, Rockville MD 20854 (ROC)

Bicentennial Building, 600 E Street NW, 20004 (BICN)

National Place Building, 1331 Pennsylvania Avenue NW, 20530 (NPB)

Liberty Place Building, 325 Seventh Street NW, 20530 (LPB)

901 E Street NW, 20530 (901 E)

Assistant Attorney General for Administration.—Stephen R. Colgate, Room 1111, 514–3101.
Deputy Assistant Attorney General for Law and Policy.—Janis A. Sposato, Room 1111, 514–3101.
Senior Policy Advisor.—Warren Oser, Room 1111, 514–0458.
Staff Directors for:
Department Ethics Office.—Mary Braden, Room 6316, 514–8196.
Audit Liaison Office.—Vickie L. Sloan, Room 6316, 514–0469.
Office of General Counsel.—Stuart Frisch, General Counsel, NPB Room 520, 514–3452.
Management and Planning.—Robert F. Diegelman, NPB Room 1400, 307–1800.
Security and Emergency Planning.—D. Jerry Rubino, Room 6525, 514–2094.
Executive Secretariat.—Room 1110, 514–3123.
Procurement Executive.—Janis A. Sposato, NPB Room 1400, 616–3757.
Deputy Assistant Attorney General and Controller.—Michael J. Roper, Room 1114, 514–1843.
Staff Directors for:
Budget.—Adrian A. Curtis, Room 6343, 514–4082.
Finance.—James E. Williams, BIC Room 4070, 616–5800.
Procurement Services.—James W. Johnston, NPB Room 1000, 307–2000.
Office of Small and Disadvantaged Business Utilization.—Joseph (Ken) Bryan, NPB Room 1010, 616–0521.
Asset Forfeiture Management Staff.—Michael Perez, 901 E, Room 832, 616–8000.
Deputy Assistant Attorney General for Debt Collection Management.—Robert N. Ford, LPB Second Floor, 514–5343.
Deputy Assistant Attorney General for Human Resources and Administration.—John C. Vail, Room 1116, 514–5501.
Associate Assistant Attorney General for Federal Law Enforcement Training.—Thomas G.Milburn, Building 70, Glynco GA 31524, (912) 267–2914.
Staff Directors for:
Facilities and Administrative Services.—Benjamin F. Burrell, NPB Room 1050, 616–2995.
Library.—Daphne Sampson, Room 5317, 514–2133.
Personnel.—Henry Romero, NPB Room 1110, 514–6788.
Equal Employment Opportunity.—Ted McBurrows, Room 1246, 616–4800.

Employee Assistance Program.—Ben Elliott, Room 1264, 514–1846.
Office of Attorney Personnel Management.—Linda A. Cinciotta, Room 6150, 514–3396.
Executive Support.—Willistine M. Clark, Room 6257, 514–5537.
Executive Secretariat.—Anna-Marie Kilmade Gatons, Room 4400AA, 514–2063.
Consolidated Administrative Office.—Kathryn F. Harless, Room 1211, 514–2118.

Deputy Assistant Attorney General/Information Resources Management.—Mark A. Boster, Room 1121, 514–0507.

Staff Directors for:

Computer Services.—James E. Price, ROC Room 205, 307–6900.
Telecommunications Services.—David Bittenbender, BICN Room 3064, 514–1600.
Systems Technology.—Andrew J. Boots, Room 1229, 514–3404.
Information Management and Security.—Mary Ellen Condon, WCTR Room 850, 514–4292.

ANTITRUST DIVISION

Main Justice Building, Room 3109, 514–2401

Judiciary Center Building, 555 Fourth Street NW, 20001 (JCB)

City Center Building, 1401 H Street NW, 20530 (CCB)

Bicentennial Building, 600 E Street NW, 20530 (BICN)

Liberty Place Building, 325 Seventh Street NW, 20530 (LPB)

Assistant Attorney General.—Joel I. Klein (acting).

Deputy Assistant Attorneys General: Lawrence R. Fullerton, Room 3114, 514–1157; Andrew S. Joskow, Room 3113, 514–2408; A. Douglas Melamed, Room 3208, 514–2410; Gary R. Spratling, Room 3214, 514–3543; David S. Turetsky, Room 3113, 307–2032.

Director of Operations.—Constance K. Robinson, Room 3214, 514–3544.

Deputy Director of Operations.—Rebecca P. Dick, Room 3208, 514–2562.

Freedom of Information Act Officer.—Ann Lea Harding, LPB Suite 200, 514–2692.

Executive Officer.—Thomas D. King, Room 3242, 514–2421.

Section Chiefs:

Appellate.—Catherine G. O'Sullivan, Room 3224, 514–2413.
Civil Task Force.—Mary Jean Moltenbrey, LPB Suite 300, 616–5935.
Computers and Finance Section.—John F. Greaney, BICN Room 9300, 307–6200.
Competition Policy.—Russell W. Pittman, BICN Suite 10000, 307–6341.
Economic Litigation.—Norman Familant, BICN Suite 10000, 307–6323.
Economic Regulatory.—[Vacant], BICN Suite 10000, 307–6332.
Foreign Commerce.—Charles S. Stark, Room 3264, 514–2464.
Legal Policy.—Robert A. Potter, Room 3121, 514–2512.
Litigation I.—Anthony V. Nanni, CCB Room 3700, 307–6694.
Litigation II.—J. Robert Kramer II, CCB Room 3000, 307–0924.
Merger Task Force.—Craig W. Conrath, CCB Room 4000, 307–0001.
Professions and Intellectual Property (Health Care Task Force).—Gail Kursh, LPB Suite 400, 307–5799.
Telecommunications Task Force.—Donald J. Russell, JCB Room 8104, 514–5621.
Transportation, Energy, and Agriculture.—Roger W. Fones, LPB Suite 500, 307–6351.

FIELD OFFICES

California: Christopher S. Crook (acting), 450 Golden Avenue, Box 36046, San Francisco CA 94102, (415) 436–6660.

Georgia: John T. Orr, Jr., Chief, Richard B. Russell Building, Suite 1176, 75 Spring Street SW, Atlanta GA 30303, (404) 331–7100.

Illinois: James M. Griffin, Chief, Rookery Building, Suite 600, 209 South LaSalle Street, Chicago IL 60604, (312) 353–7530.

New York: Ralph T. Giordano, Chief, Room 3630, 26 Federal Plaza, New York NY 10278–0140, (212) 264–0390.

Ohio: John A. Weedon, Chief, Plaza Nine Building, Seventh Floor, 55 Erieview Plaza, Cleveland OH 44114, (216) 522–4070.

Pennsylvania: Robert E. Connolly, Chief, One Independence Square West, Curtis Center, Suite 650, Seventh and Walnut Streets, Philadelphia PA 19106, (215) 597–7401.

Texas: Alan A. Pason, Chief, Thanksgiving Tower, Suite 4950, 1601 Elm Street, Dallas TX 75201, (214) 880–9401.

CIVIL DIVISION

Main Justice Building, Room 3143, 514–3301
901 E Street NW 20530 (901 E)
1100 L Street NW 20530 (L Street)
National Place Building, 1331 Pennsylvania Avenue NW 20530 (NATP)
1425 New York Avenue NW 20005 (NYAV)

Assistant Attorney General.—Frank W. Hunger, Room 3143, 514–3301.
Counselor.—George J. Phillips, Room 3607, 514–5713.
Special Counsel.—Col. Rick Rosen, Room 3140, 514–3886.
Senior Counsel for Policy.—Donald Remy, Room 3133, 514–3046.

FEDERAL PROGRAMS BRANCH

Deputy Assistant Attorney General.—Gary G. Grindler, Room 3143, 514–1258.
Directors: David J. Anderson, 901E, Room 1064, 514–3354; Dennis G. Linder, 901E, Room 980, 514–3314.
Deputy Directors: Vincent M. Garvey, 901E, Room 1082, 514–3449; Sheila M. Lieber, 901E, Room 974, 514–3786.

COMMERCIAL LITIGATION BRANCH

Deputy Assistant Attorney General.—Stuart E. Schiffer, Room 3611, 514–3306.
Directors: David M. Cohen, L Street, Room 12124, 514–7300; Vito J. DiPietro, L Street, Room 11116, 514–7223; J. Christopher Kohn, L Street, Room 10036, 514–7450; Michael F. Hertz, Room 3647, 7179.
Office of Foreign Litigation.—David Epstein, L Street, Room 11006, 514–7455.
Deputy Directors: Sandra P. Spooner, L Street, Room 10052, 514–7194; Joyce R. Branda, Room 3641, 307–0231; Sharon Y. Eubanks, L Street, Room 12132, 514–7300.
Legal Officer.—James Gresser, American Embassy, London, England, PSC 801, Box 42, FPO AE, New York 09498–4042, 9–011–44–171–629–6794.
Attorney-in-Charge.—Joseph I. Liebman, Suite 339, 26 Federal Plaza, New York NY 10278, (212) 264–9232.

TORTS BRANCH

Deputy Assistant Attorney General.—Eva M. Plaza, Room 3137, 514–3309.
Directors: Gary W. Allen, NYAV Room 10122, 616–4000; Jeffery Axelrad, NATP Room 8098N, 616–4400; Helene M. Goldberg, NYAV Room 8122, 616–4140; J. Patrick Glynn, NATP Room 8028S, 616–4200.
Deputy Directors: JoAnn J. Bordeaux, NATP Room 8024S, 616–4204; John L. Euler, NYAV Room 3122, 616–4088; Paul F. Figley, NATP Room 8096S, 616–4248.
Attorneys-in-Charge: Janis G. Schulmeisters, Suite 320, 26 Federal Plaza, New York NY 10278–0140, (212) 264–0480; Phillip A. Berns, 450 Golden Gate Avenue, 10/6610, Box 36028, San Francisco CA 94102–3463, (415) 556–3146.

APPELLATE STAFF

Deputy Assistant Attorney General.—Stephen W. Preston, Room 3137, 514–4015.
Director.—Robert E. Kopp, Room 3615, 514–3311.
Deputy Director.—William Kanter, Room 7415, 514–4575.

CONSUMER LITIGATION

Director.—Eugene M. Thirolf, NATP Room 9534N, 307–3009.
Deputy Director.—Lawrence G. McDade, NATP Room 9542N, 307–0138.

IMMIGRATION LITIGATION

Deputy Assistant Attorney General.—Philip Bartz, Room 3611, 514–5421.

Director.—Robert L. Bombaugh, NATP Room 7026S, 616–4900.
Deputy Directors: Donald E. Keener, NATP Room 7022S, 616–4878; David J. Kline, NATP Room 7006N, 616–4856; Thomas W. Hussey, NATP Room 7024S, 616–4852.

MANAGEMENT PROGRAMS

Director.—Kenneth L. Zwick, Room 3140, 514–4552.
Directors, Office of:
Administration.—Mary Ann Beck, L Street, Room 9008, 307–0016.
Planning, Budget, and Evaluation.—Linda S. Liner, L Street, Room 9042, 307–0034.
Management Information.—Susan M. Cavanaugh, L Street, Room 9126, 307–0304.
Litigation Support.—Clarisse Abramidis, L Street, Room 8044, 616–5014.
Policy and Management Operations.—Barbara Jean Hong Fong, L Street, Room 8128, 307–0133.

CIVIL RIGHTS DIVISION

Main Justice Building, Room 5643, 514–2151
Home Owners Loan Corporation Building, 320 First Street 20534 (HOLC)
1425 New York Avenue 20005 (NYAV)

Assistant Attorney General.—Isabelle Katz Pinzler (acting), Room 5643, 514–2151.
Counsels to the Assistant Attorney General: Stuart Ishimaru, Room 5541, 514–3845; Elizabeth Savage (acting), Room 5537, 514–4279; Neal Kravitz (acting), Room 5649, 514–2151.
Deputy Assistant Attorneys General: Loretta King, Room 5639, 616–1278; Paul Hancock (acting), Room 5744, 514–1638; William Yeomans (acting), Room 5642, 514–4127.
Special Assistants: Helaine Greenfeld, Room 5649, 514–6860; Policarpio A. Marmolejos, Room 5531, 307–3111; Lisa Winston, Room 5545A, 616–2732; Richard Jerome, Room 5535, 514–8696.
Executive Officer.—DeDe Greene, NYAV Room 5058, 514–4224.
Section Chiefs:
Appellate.—David K. Flynn, Room 5740, 514–2195.
Coordination and Review.—Merrily A. Friedlander, NYAV Room 4012, 307–2222.
Public Access.—John L. Wodatch, NYAV Room 4055, 307–2227.
Criminal.—Richard Roberts, Room 7629, 514–3204.
Educational Opportunities.—Kenneth Mines, Room 7601, 514–4092.
Employment Litigation.—Katherine A. Baldwin, Room 5529, 514–3831.
Housing and Civil Enforcement.—Joan Magagna (acting), Room 7527, 307–2737.
Special Counsel:
Immigration Related Unfair Employment Practices.— Jim Angus (acting), NYAV Room 9030, 616–1950.
Special Litigation.—Steven H. Rosenbaum, Room 1740A, 514–6255.
Voting.—Elizabeth Johnson, HOLC Room 818A, 307–3143.

CRIMINAL DIVISION

Main Justice Building, Room 2107, 514–2601
Bond Building, 1400 New York Avenue NW, 20005 (BB)
Washington Center Building, 1001 G Street NW, (WCTR)
1331 F Street NW, (F Street)

Assistant Attorney General.—John C. Keeney (acting), Room 2107, 514–2621.
Deputy Assistant Attorneys General: John C. Keeney, Room 2107, 514–2621; Mark M Richard, Room 2113, 514–2333; Kevin V. Di Gregory, Room 2112, 514–9725; Robert S. Litt, Room 2112, 514–2636; Mary Lee Warren, Room 2113, 514–3729.
Chief of Staff to the Assistant Attorney General.—Claudia J. Flynn, Room 2106, 305–4758.
Counsel to the Assistant Attorney General.—Mary Frances Harkenrider, Room 2212, 514–2419.
Senior Counsels for National Security Matters: Mary E. Warlow, Room 2117, 514–0008; John B. Bellinger III, Room 2119, 514–8711;
Special Assistants to the Assistant Attorney General: Michael A. Sussmann, Room 2211, 514–5626; L. Jeffrey Ross, Room 2116, 616–1342; John Bentivoglio, Room 2209, 305–4515; Anthony Murry, Room 2213, 305–1283; Jay N. Lerner, Room 2121, 616–2379; Suzanne C. Hayden, Room 2123, 616–6690.

Executive Officer.—Robert K. Bratt, WCTR Suite 800, 514–5749.
Section Chiefs/Office Directors:
Appellate.—Patty M. Stemler, Room 2264, 514–3521.
Fraud.—Mary C. Spearing, BB Room 4100, 514–7023.
Computer Crime and Intellectual Property.—Scott Charney, WCTR Suite 219, 514–1026.
Internal Security.—John L. Martin, BB Room 9100, 514–1187.
Narcotic and Dangerous Drug.—Theresa M.B. VanVliet, BB Room 11100, 514–0917.
Organized Crime and Racketeering.—Paul E. Coffey, WCTR Suite 342, 514–3595.
Public Integrity.—Lee J. Radek, BB Room 12100, 514–1412.
Terrorism and Violent Crime.—James S. Reynolds, Room 2517, 514–0849.
Child Exploitation and Obscenity.—Terry R. Lord (acting), F Street, Room 614 A, 514–5780.
Asset Forfeiture and Money Laundering.—Gerald E. McDowell, BB Room 10100, 514–1263.
Enforcement Operations.—Frederick D. Hess, WCTR Suite 900, 514–3684.
International Affairs.—Frances Fragos Townsend, BB Room 5100, 514–0000.
Policy and Legislation.—Julie E. Samuels, Room 2316, 514–3062; Roger Pauley, Room 2313, 514–3202.
Special Investigations.—Eli M. Rosenbaum, WCTR Suite 1000, 616–2492.
Executive Office for Organized Crime Drug Enforcement Task Forces.—Kenneth Magidson, Room 2229, 514–1860.
International Criminal Investigative Training Assistance Program.—Janice M. Stromsen, F Street, Room 540, 514–1323.

ENVIRONMENT AND NATURAL RESOURCES DIVISION

Main Justice Building, Room 2143, 514–2701
601 Pennsylvania Avenue, (PENN)
801 Pennsylvania Avenue, (MSQ2)
1425 New York Avenue NW, (NYAV)

Assistant Attorney General.—Lois J. Schiffer, Room 2143, 514–2701.
Deputy Assistant Attorneys General: John Cruden, Room 2609, 514–2718, Peter Coppelman, Room 2143, 514–4760; James Simon, Room 2609, 514–3370; Nancy Firestone, Room 2142, 514–0943.
Special Assistant.—Allison Rumseys, Room 2614, 514–0750.
Counsel for State and Environmental Affairs.—Ann Hurley, Room 2612, 514–2744.
Counsel to the Assistant Attorney General.—Ignacia Moreno, Room 2610, 514–5243.
Executive Officer.—Phyllis Gardner, MSQ2 Room 620, 616–3091.
Section Chiefs:
Appellate.—James C. Kilbourne, Room 2339, 514–2748.
Environmental Crimes.—Ron Sarachan, PENN Room 6101, 305–0321.
Environmental Defense.—Letitia J. Grishaw, Room 7110, 514–2219.
Environmental Enforcement.—Joel Gross, NYAV Room 13063, 514–4353.
General Litigation.—William M. Cohen, PENN Room 870, 305–0440.
Indian Resources.—James Clear, PENN Room 6701, 305–0259.
Land Acquisition.—William J. Kollins, PENN Room 6601, 305–0316.
Policy, Legislation, and Special Litigation.—Pauline M. Milius, Room 2133, 514–2586.
Wildlife and Marine Resources.—Eileen Sobeck, PENN Room 5000, 305–0210.

FIELD OFFICES

801 B Street, Suite 504, Anchorage AK 99501–3657

Trial Attorneys: Bruce Landon, (907) 271–5452; Dean Dunsmore, (907) 271–5452; Regina Belt, (907) 271–3456.

999 18th Street, Suite 945, North Tower, Denver CO 80202

Trial Attorneys: Bruce Bernard, (303) 312–7319; Bradley Bridgewater, (303) 312–7318; Dave Carson, (303) 312–7309; Jerilyn DeCotea, (303) 312–7326; James F. DuBois, (303) 312–7341; Jerry Ellington, (303) 312–7331; Robert Foster, (303) 312–7320; Dave Gehlert, (303) 312–7352; Lee Gelman, (303) 312–7302; Mike Gheleta, (303) 312–7303; Alan Greensberg, (303) 312–7234; David Harder, (303) 312–7238; Lynn A. Johnson,

(303) 312–7315; John Lange, (303) 312–7312; Peter Monson, (303) 312–7350; John Moscato, (303) 312–7346; Peter Mounsey, (303) 312–7353; Khaki Schmidt, (303) 312–7327; Andrew Walch, (303) 312–7316.

650 Capital Mall, Fifth Floor, Sacramento CA 95814–4501

Trial Attorneys: Maria Iizuka, (916) 554–2800; Steven MacFarlane, (916) 554–2801.

301 Howard Street, Suite 870, San Francisco CA 94105–2001

Trial Attorneys: Richard Beal, (415) 744–6485; David Glazer, (415) 744–6477; Helen Kang, (415) 744–6482; Robert Klotz, (415) 744–6490.

c/o NOAA/GCNW, 7600 San Point Way NE, BIN C 15700, Seattle WA 98115–0070

Trial Attorneys: James Nicoli, (206) 526–6604; Mike Zevenbergen, (206) 526–6616.

c/o Aspen Systems, Inc., 31 Milk Street, Room 701, Boston MA 02109

Trial Attorney: Catherine Fiske, (617) 695–0341.

TAX DIVISION

Main Justice Building, 514–2901
Judiciary Center Building, 555 Fourth Street NW, 20001 (JCB)
Bicentenial Building, 600 E Street NW, 20004 (BICN)
Max Energy Tower, 7717 North Harwood Street, Suite 400, Dallas TX 75242 (MAX)

Assistant Attorney General.—Loretta C. Argrett, Room 4143, 514–2901.
Deputy Assistant Attorneys General: Mark E. Matthews, Room 4143, 514–2915; Claire Fallon, Room 4137, 514–5109.
Senior Division Counsel.—Stanley F. Krysa, Room 4611, 514–2973.
Chief of Staff and Counsel to the Assistant Attorney General.—Beverly O. Babers, Room 4143, 514–2967.
Counsels to the Assistant Attorney General:
Appellate Matters.—Kevin M. Brown, Room 4140, 514–2553.
Criminal and Budget Matters.—Jill R. Shellow, Room 4610, 616–2844.
Special Assistant.—Noreene C. Stehlik, Room 4608, 514–6489.
Director, Office of Training.—Walter O. Pryor, JCB Room 6102, 514–6722.
Section Chiefs:
Central Region, Civil Trial.—Robert S. Watkins, JCB Room 8921–B, 514–6502.
Eastern Region, Civil Trial.—Edward J. Snyder, JCB Room 6126, 307–6426.
Northern Region, Civil Trial.—Patrick D. Mullarkey, JCB Room 7804–A, 307–6533.
Southern Region, Civil Trial.—Steven Shapiro, JCB Room 6243–A, 514–5905.
Southwestern Region, Civil Trial.—Louise P. Hytken, MET Room 4100, (214) 880–9725.
Western Region, Civil Trial.—Jerome H. Fridkin, JCB Room 7907–B, 307–6413.
Court of Federal Claims.—Mildred L. Seidman, JCB Room 8804–A, 307–6440.
Office of Review.—Milan D. Karlan, JCB Room 6846, 307–6567.
Appellate.—Gary R. Allen, Room 4324, 514–3361.
Criminal Enforcement, Northern Region.—E. Ralph Pierce, Room 4625, 514–0003.
Criminal Enforcement, Southern Region.—J. Randolph Maney, Jr., BICN Room 5154, 514–4334.
Criminal Enforcement, Western Region.—Ronald A. Cimino, BICN Room 5127, 514–5247.
Criminal Appeals and Tax Enforcement Policy.—Robert E. Lindsay, Room 4131, 514–3011.
Executive Officer.—E. Timothy Wagner, BICN Room 5170, 616–2558.
Senior Litigation Counsel.—[Vacant], JCB Room 7201, 307–6398.
Special Litigation Counsels: Ernest J. Brown, Room 4324, 514–3363; Jonathan S. Cohen, Room 4525, 514–2970; Dennis M. Donohue, JCB Room 7104, 307–6492; Donald J. Gavin, JCB Room 7203, 307–6400.

Senior Legislative Counsel.—Stephen J. Csontos, Room 4610, 307–6419.

DRUG ENFORCEMENT ADMINISTRATION

Lincoln Place-1 (East), 600 Army Navy Drive, Arlington VA 22202

Lincoln Place-2 (West), 700 Army Navy Drive, Arlington VA 22202

Administrator.—Thomas A. Constantine, Room W–12060, 307–8000.
Executive Assistant.—David M. Luitweiler, Room W–12060, 307–8003.
Deputy Administrator.—James S. Milford (acting), Room W–12058, 307–7345.
Executive Assistant.—Gilbert Bruce, Room W–12058, 307–8770.
Chief, Office of Congressional and Public Affairs.—Catherine H. Shaw, Room W–12238, 307–7363.
Section Chiefs:
Public Affairs.—James J. McGivney, Room W–12228, 307–7977.
Congressional Affairs.—Gary Wade, Room W–12100, 307–7423.
Demand Reduction.—Robert D. Dey, Room W–4034, 307–7936.
Information Services.—Donald E. Joseph, Room W–12206, 307–7967.
Chief Counsel.—Cynthia R. Ryan, Room W–12051, 307–7322.
Deputy Chief Counsel.—Robert T. Richardson, Room W–10128, 307–8020.
Chief, Office of Administrative Law Judges.—Mary E. Bittner, Room E–2129, 307–8188.

FINANCIAL MANAGEMENT DIVISION

Chief Financial Officer.—Donald P. Quinn, Room W–12142, 307–7330.
Deputy Assistant Administrator, Office of Finance.—Richard Kay, Room E–7397, 307–7002.
Section Chiefs:
Financial Operations.—William Truitt, Room E–7397, 307–7062.
Financial Reports and Systems.—John R. Osterday, Room E–7165, 307–7083.
Deputy Assistant Administrator, Office of Resource Management.—James E. Duke, Room E–7399, 307–7060.
Management Analysis Section.—Peter C. Linn, Room E–7331, 307–7075.
Budget Section.—Jame E. Duke, Room E–7399, 307–7060.
Deputy Assistant Administrator, Office of Acquisition Management.—James M. Whetstone, Room W–5110, 307–7777.
Acquisition Management Section.—Christinia Sisk, Room W–5022, 307–7802.

INSPECTIONS DIVISION

Chief Inspector.—Dennis F. Hoffman, Room W–12042, 307–7358.
Deputy Chief Inspector, Office of Professional Responsibility.—William B. Simpkins, Room W–4176, 307–8232.
Deputy Chief Inspector, Office of Inspections.—Donald V. Stern, Room W–4348, 307–8200.

OPERATIONS DIVISION

Chief of Operations.—Donnie R. Marshall, Room W–12050, 307–7340.
Chief of Domestic Operations.—Gregory K. Williams, Room W–11070, 307–7927.
Section Chiefs:
Financial Operations.—James Borden (acting), Room W–10106, 307–8396.
State and Local.—Michael Pasterchick, Room W–7072, 307–8918.
Domestic East.—[Vacant], Room W–8344, 307–5562.
Domestic West.—Randall Bowman, Room W–8306, 307–4780.
Domestic Liaison.—Calvin McFarland, Room W–7268, 307–8923.
Deputy Chief, Office of Operations Management.—James A. Wooley, Room W–11240, 307–4200.
Section Chief: Operations Budget.—Al Alexander, Room W–11244, 307–4200.
Special Agent-in-Charge, Special Operations Division.—Richard Fiano, Newington VA 703–541–6701.
Deputy Assistant Administrator, Office of Diversion Control.—Jack King, Room E–6295, 307–7165.
Deputy Director.—Terrance W. Woodworth, Room E–6293, 307–7163.

Section Chiefs:
Chemical Operations.—William W. Wolf, Room E–6297, 307–7204.
Drug Operations.—Michael Moy, Room E–6171, 307–7194.
Liaison and Policy.—G. Thomas Gitchel, Room E–6385, 307–7297.
Drug and Chemical.—Frank Sapienza, Room E–6233, 307–7183.
Chief, Office of International Operations.—Michael T. Horn, Room W–11024, 307–4233.
Section Chiefs:
Central America and Caribbean.—Richard D. Barrett, Room W–2116, 307–4266.
Europe and Mid-East.—Mark C. Lloyd, Room W–11104, 307–4252.
Far East.—John E. Driscoll, Room W–11200, 307–4262.
South America.—Sandalio Gonzalez, Room W–2122, 307–4300.

INTELLIGENCE DIVISION

Assistant Administrator.—Craig N. Chretien, Room W–12036, 307–3607.
Special Agent-in-Charge, El Paso Intelligence Center.—John Brown, Building 11339, SSG Sims Street, El Paso TX 79918–5100, (915) 564–2000.
Deputy Assistant Administrator, Office of Investigative Intelligence.—Richard P. Bly, Room W–8264, 307–8050.
Section Chiefs:
Investigative Intelligence.—Michael J. Sapsara, Room W–8072–2, 307–8366.
Special Investigative Support.—Charles L. Updegraph, Jr. Room W–8030, 307–4294.
Deputy Assistant Administrator, Office of Intelligence Liaison and Policy.—Judith E. Bertini, Room W–10190, 307–8748.
Section Chiefs:
Intelligence Policy and Program.—Douglas P. Everett, Room W–7030, 307–8910.
Strategic Intelligence.—Maurice E. Rinfret, Room W–10280, 307–8123.

OPERATIONAL SUPPORT DIVISION

Assistant Administrator.—Anthony R. Bocchichio, Room W–12142, 307–4730.
Chief, Office of Security Programs.—Joseph Parra, W–2340–4, 307–4400.
Deputy Assistant Administrator, Office of Administration.—Bob Richel, Room W–9088, 307–7708.
Section Chiefs:
Facilities and Property Management.—Gregory J. Skorupski, Room W–5242, 307–7792.
Freedom of Information/Records Management.—Tom Wingate (acting), Room W–9174, 307–7709.
Deputy Assistant Administrator, Office of Science and Technology.—Aaron P. Hatcher III, Room W–7342, 307–8866.
Associate Deputy Assistant Administrator, Office of Science and Technology.—Benjamin Perillo, Room W–7344, 307–8868.
Section Chiefs:
Laboratory Operations.— Richard Fox, Room W–7338, 307–8880.
Laboratory Support.—James H. Crockett, Room W–7348, 307–8785.
Investigative Technology.—Edward J. Wisniefski, Newington VA, 703–541–6500.
Deputy Assistant Administrator, Office of Information Systems.—Philip V. Camero, Room E–3105, 307–7454.
Section Chiefs:
Information Resources Management.—Ruth Torres, Room E–3225, 307–5269.
Operations and Support.—Ned Goldberg, Room E–4111, 307–7379.
Systems Applications.—Joseph A. Julian, Room E–3285, 307–7519.
Programs Planning and Control Staff.—Bruce Buchlin, Room E–3153, 307–9875.

HUMAN RESOURCES DIVISION

Assistant Administrator.—Jean D. Mathis, Room W–12010, 307–4680.
Deputy Assistant Administrator, Office of Personnel.—Retha M. Fulmore, Room W–3166, 307–4000.
Section Chiefs:
Personnel Policy and Services.—[Vacant], Room W–3126–2, 307–4004.
Recruitment and Placement.—Kenneth L. Dickinson, Room W–3242, 307–4055.
Equal Employment Opportunity Officer.—Marian E. Moss, Room W–7300, 307–8888.
Career Board Executive Secretary.—John L. Nattinger, Room W–2268, 307–7349.

Chairman, Board of Professional Conduct.—[Vacant], Room W–2170, 307–8980.
Special Agent-in-Charge, Office of Training.—David L. Westrate, DEA/FBI Academy, Building 1, Quantico VA 22135, (703) 640–1105.
Assistant Special Agents-in-Charge:
Domestic Training Section.—Louis A. Pharao, (703) 640–1259.
International Training Section.—James E. Cappola, (703) 640–7419.

FIELD OFFICES

ATLANTA DIVISION:
Special Agent-in-Charge.—John J. Andrejko, Room 740, 75 Spring Street SW, Atlanta GA 30303, (404) 331–4401.
Atlanta Airport Task Force, Suite 302, 3420 Norman Berry Drive, Hapeville GA 30354, (404) 763–7083.
Charleston Resident Office, Suite 300, 5900 Core Avenue, Charleston SC 29406, (803) 308–6660.
Charlotte Resident Office, Suite 200, Nine Woodlawn Green, Charlotte NC 28217, (704) 344–6188.
Chattanooga Post of Duty, Suite 417, East Gate Office Park, Chattanooga TN 37411, (423) 855–6600.
Columbia District Office, Suite 1472, 1835 Assembly Street, Columbia SC 29201, (803) 765–5251.
Columbus Resident Office, PO Box 1565, Columbus GA 31902, (706) 649–7850.
Florence Post of Duty, Room 234, 401 West Evans Street, Florence SC 29501, (803) 661–2171.
Greensboro Resident Office, Suite 201, 1801 Stanley Road, Greensboro NC 27407, (910) 547–4210.
Greenville Post of Duty, PO Box 10195, Federal Station, Greenville SC 29603, (864) 234–0237.
Johnson City Post of Duty, PO Box 4178, Johnson City TN 37602, (423) 854–9100.
Knoxville Resident Office, 3rd Floor, 1721 Midpark Drive, Knoxville TN 37921, (423) 584–9364.
Macon Resident Office, Suite 375, 3920 Arkwright Road, Macon GA 31210, (912) 757–8754.
Memphis Resident Office, Suite 500, Morgan Keegan Tower, 50 North Front Street, Memphis TN 38103–1105, (901) 544–3396.
Nashville District Office, Suite 500, Estes Kefauver Building, FB-USCH, 801 Broadway, Nashville TN 37203, (615) 736–5988.
Raleigh Resident Office, Suite 200, 4505 Falls of Neuse Road, Raleigh NC 27609, (919) 790–3004.
Savannah Resident Office, Suite 401, 300 Drayton Street, Savannah GA 31401, (912) 652–4286.
Wilmington Resident Office, Room 322, Alton Lennon Federal Building, No. 2 Princess Street, Wilmington NC 28401, (910) 815–4513.

BOSTON DIVISION:
Special Agent-in-Charge.—George C. Festa, JFK Federal Building, Room E–400, 15 New Sudsbury Street, Boston MA 02203–0402, (617) 557–2100.
Bridgeport Resident Office, Room 404, 1000 Lafayette Boulevard, Bridgeport CT 06604, (203) 579–5591.
Burlington Resident Office, PO Box 446, 19 Commerce Avenue, Williston VT 05495, (802) 658–4931.
Cape Cod Task Force, PO Box 708, 3010 Main Street, Barnstable MA 02630, (508) 362–2117.
Concord Resident Office, Suite 300, 197 Loudon Road, Concord NH 03301, (603) 225–1574.
Hartford Resident Office, Room 628, 450 Main Street, Hartford CT 06103, (860) 240–3233.
Logan Airport Task Force, Suite 209S, 1 Harbor Side Drive, Boston MA 02128, (617) 561–5764.
Lowell Task Force/C.B.I (Group 1), 900 Chelmsford Street, Tower No. 3, Lowell MA 01851, (508) 452–9191.
New Haven Post of Duty, PO Box 1709, New Haven CT 06507, (203) 773–5288.
Portland Resident Office, Suite D, 1355 Congress Street, Portland ME 04102, (207) 780–3331.
Providence Resident Office, 2 International Way, Warwick RI 02886, (401) 732–2550.
Springfield Resident Office, 10th Floor, 1441 Main Street, Springfield MA 01108, (413) 785–0284.

CARIBBEAN DIVISION:

Special Agent-in-Charge.—Fernando Feliviano, Casa Lee Building, 2432 Loiza Street, San Juan PR 00913, (787) 253–4200.

Bridgetown, Barbados Country Office, DEA/Justice, American Embassy, FPO AA 34055, 9–1–809–437–6337.

Curacao, Netherlands Antilles Country Office, DEA/Justice, Diplomatic Pouch, Washington DC 20537, 9–011–599–9–616985.

Kingston, Jamaica Country Office, DEA/Justice, Diplomatic Pouch, Washington DC 20537, 9–1–876–929–4956.

Ponce Resident Office, PO Box 280, Estacion 6, Ponce PR 00732, (787) 841–3188.

Port-Au-Prince, Haiti Country Office, DEA/Justice, Diplomatic Pouch, Washington DC 20537, 9–011–509–23–8888.

Santo Domingo, Dominican Republic Country Office, DEA/Justice, American Embassy, Unit 5514, APO AA 34041, (809) 687–3754.

St. Croix Post of Duty, PO Box 3240, Christiansted VI 00822, (340) 692–9500.

St. Thomas Resident Office, PO Box 309480, Veterans Drive Station, St. Thomas USVI 00803, (340) 774–2398.

CHICAGO DIVISION:

Special Agent-in-Charge.—Joseph A. Vanacora, Suite 1200, John C. Kluczynski Federal Building, 230 South Dearborn Street, Chicago IL 60604, (312) 353–7875.

Chicago Airport Group, Suite 212, 2350 East Devon, Des Plaines IL 60618, (847) 635–8330.

Fargo Resident Office, Suite 302, Case Plaza Building, One North Second Street, Fargo ND 58102, (701) 239–5331.

Green Bay Post of Duty, 201 West Walnut, Suite 203, Green Bay WI 54301, (414) 448–6241.

Indianapolis District Office, Room 290, 575 North Pennsylvania Avenue, Indianapolis IN 46204, (317) 226–7977.

Indianapolis Airport Task Force, Room 290, 575 North Pennsylvania Avenue, Indianapolis IN 46204, (317) 248–4093.

Madison Post of Duty, Room 307, Federal Plaza, PO Box 92812, 212 East Washington, Madison WI 53701–0981, (608) 264–5111.

Merrillville Resident Office, 1571 East 85th Avenue, Suite 200, Merrillville IN 46410, (219) 681–7000.

Milwaukee Resident Office, Suite 1010, 1000 North Water Street, Milwaukee WI 53202, (414)297–3395.

Minneapolis-St. Paul Resident Office, 402 Federal Building, 110 South Fourth Street, Minneapolis MN 55401, (612) 348–1700.

Rockford Resident Office, 420 West State Street, Rockford IL 61101, (815) 987–4494.

Springfield Resident Office, Suite 302, 400 West Monroe, Springfield IL 62704, (217) 492–4504.

DALLAS DIVISION:

Special Agent-in-Charge.—Julio Mercado, 1880 Regal Row, Dallas TX 75235, (214) 640–0801.

Amarillo Post of Duty, Room 14B, 205 East Fifth Street, PO Box 15307, Amarillo TX 79105–5307, (806) 324–2339.

Dallas-Fort Worth Task Force, PO Box 612645, DFW Airport TX 75261–2645, (214) 574–2111.

Fort Worth Resident Office, Room 13A33, 819 Taylor Street, Fort Worth TX 76102, (817) 978–3455.

Lubbock Resident Office, Suite 401, 5214 68th Street, Lubbock TX 79424, (806) 798–7189.

McAlester Post of Duty, 403 West Carl Albert Parkway, PO Box 3296, McAlester OK 74501, (918) 426–5020.

Midland Post of Duty, Room 225, 1004 North Big Spring Street, Midland TX 79701, (915) 686–0356.

Oklahoma City District Office, Suite 100, 3909 North Classen, Oklahoma City OK 73118, (405) 524–2213.

Tulsa Resident Office, Room 570, 5100 East Skelly Drive, Tulsa OK 74135, (918) 581–6391.

Tyler Resident Office, Suite 280, 909 East SE Loop 323, Tyler TX 75701–9665, (903) 534–0472.

DENVER DIVISION:

Special Agent-in-Charge.—Michael A. Demarte, 115 Inverness Drive East, Englewood CO 80112, (303) 705–7300.

Albuquerque District Office, 301 Martin Luther King, Jr. Avenue NE, Albuquerque NM 87102, (505) 766–8925.

Casper Post of Duty, 100 East B Street, Room 2126, Casper WY 82601, (307) 261–6200.

Cheyenne Resident Office, Room 7010, Federal Center, 2120 Capitol Avenue, Cheyenne WY 82001, (307) 772–2391.

Colorado Springs Resident Office, Suite 306, Plaza of the Rockies, 111 South Tejon, Colorado Springs CO 80901, (719) 471–1749.

Glenwood Springs Resident Office, Suite 300, Valley Professional Building, 401 23rd Street, Glenwood Springs CO 81601, (970) 945–0744.

Las Cruces Resident Office, PO Box 397, Las Cruces NM 88001, (505) 527–6950.

Salt Lake City Resident Office, Suite 401, American Plaza 3, 47 West 200 South, Salt Lake City UT 84101, (801) 524–4156.

DETROIT DIVISION:

Special Agent-in-Charge.—Lawrence Gallina, 431 Howard Street, Detroit MI 48226, (313) 234–4000.

Cincinnati Resident Office, 8504 Federal Building, 550 Main Street, Cincinnati OH 45202, (513) 684–3671.

Cleveland Resident Office, Suite 395, 310 Lakeside NW, Cleveland OH 44113, (216) 522–3705.

Columbus Resident Office, Suite 612, 500 South Front Street, Columbus OH 43215, (614) 469–2595.

Dayton Resident Office, 3464 Successful Way, Dayton OH 45414–4322, (513) 225–2805.

Grand Rapids Resident Office, Room 303, 330 Ionioa Avenue, Grand Rapids MI 49503, (616) 458–0616.

Lexington Resident Office, Room 308, 1500 Leestown Road, Lexington KY 40511, (606) 233–2479.

Louisville Resident Office, 1006 Federal Building, 600 Martin Luther King Place, Louisville KY 40202, (502) 582–5908.

Saginaw Resident Office, Fourth Floor, 301 East Genesee Avenue, Saginaw MI 48607, (517) 758–4133.

Toledo Resident Office, Room 325, 234 North Summit Street, Toledo OH 43604, (419) 259–6490.

HOUSTON DIVISION:

Special Agent-in-Charge.—Ernest L. Howard, 4433 Westloop South, Suite 600, Houston TX 77027, (713) 693–3000.

Alpine Resident Office, 801 North Second Street, Alpine TX 79830, (915)-837–3421.

Austin Resident Office, Suite A–300, 9009 Mountain Ridge Drive, Austin TX 78759, (512) 346–2486.

Beaumont Resident Office, Suite 290, 350 Magnolia, Beaumont TX 77701–2237, (409) 839–2461.

Brownsville Resident Office, Suite 200, 1110 FM 802, Brownsville TX 78521, (210) 504–4100.

Corpus Christi Resident Office, Suite 300, Wilson Plaza, 606 Carancachua, Corpus Christi TX 78476, (512) 888–0150.

Eagle Pass Resident Office, Room 102, 342 Rio Grande, Eagle Pass TX 78852, (210) 773–5378.

El Paso District Office, Suite D–701, 700 East San Antonio Street, El Paso TX 79901, (915) 534–6400.

El Paso Airport Task Force, 700 East San Antonio Street, Suite D–701, El Paso TX 79901,(915) 772–3784.

Galveston Resident Office, Suite 104, 6000 Broadway, Galveston TX 77551–4307, (409) 766–3568.

Houston Airport Task Force, Houston Hobby Airport, Houston TX 77205, (713) 641–1512.

Houston Airport Task Force, Terminal B, Houston Intercontinental Airport, Houston TX 77205, (713) 230–6847.

Laredo Resident Office, PO Drawer 2307, Laredo TX 78041, (210) 722–5201.

McAllen District Office, 1919 Austin Street, McAllen TX 78501–7030, (210) 618–8400.

San Antonio District Office, Suite 200, 10127 Morocco, San Antonio TX 78216, (210) 525–2900.

San Antonio Airport Task Force, 10127 Morocco, San Antonio TX 78216, (210) 829–1007.

Waco Post of Duty, Suite 2000, 6801 Sanger Avenue, Waco TX 76710, (817) 741–1920.

LOS ANGELES DIVISION:

Special Agent-in-Charge.—Robert E. Bender, 255 East Temple Street, 20th Floor, Los Angeles CA 90012, (213) 894–2650.

Los Angeles HIDTA Task Force, 1340 West Sixth Street, Los Angeles CA 90017, (213) 894–3190.

Guam Resident Office, Suite 502C, 238 Archbishop Flores Street, Agana Guam 96910, (200) 472–7384.

Honolulu District Office, 300 Ala Moana Boulevard, Honolulu HI 96850, (808) 541–1930.

Honolulu Airport Task Force, 300 Rogers Boulevard, No. 31, Honolulu HI 96819, (808) 861–8440.

Las Vegas District Office, Suite 640, 600 Las Vegas Boulevard South, Las Vegas NV 89101, (702) 388–6635.
Reno Resident Office, Suite 1320, 300 East Second Street, Reno Nevada 89502, (702) 784–5617.
Riverside District Office, PO Box 2946, Riverside CA 92516–2946, (909) 276–6642.
Santa Ana Resident Office, Suite 720A, 34 Civic Plaza, Santa Ana California 92701, (714) 836–2892.
South Lake/El Dorado Narcotic Enforcement Team, 281 Kingsbury Grade, Stateline NV 89449, (702) 588–8687.
Ventura Resident Office, Suite 300, 770 Paseo Camarillo, Camarillo CA 93010, (805) 383–6454.

MIAMI DIVISION:

Special Agent-in-Charge.—James S. Milford, Phoenix Building, 8400 NW 53rd Street, Miami FL 33166, (305) 590–4870.
Fort Lauderdale District Office, Suite 301, 1475 West Cypress Creek Road, Fort Lauderdale FL 33309, (954) 489–1700.
Fort Myers Resident Office, Suite 501, 12730 New Brittany Boulevard, Fort Myers FL 33907, (941) 275–3662.
Freeport Resident Office, PO Box 9009, Miami FL 33159, (809) 352–5353.
Gainesville Resident Office, Suite 202, 235 South Main Street, Gainesville FL 32601, (352) 371–2077.
Miami HIDTA, Cleveland Building, Suite 200, 8245 NW 53rd Street, Miami FL 33166, (305) 597–2092.
Jacksonville Resident Office, Suite 210, 4077 Woodcock Drive, Jacksonville FL 32207, (904) 232–3566.
Key Largo Resident Office, Suite 6, 95360 Overseas Highway, PO Box 2930, Key Largo FL 33037, (305) 852–7874.
Naples Task Force, 4160 Corporate Square, Naples FL 33941, (941) 643–5550.
Nassau Country Office, American Embassy, PO Box 9009, Miami FL 33159, (242) 322–1700.
Orlando Resident Office, Suite 424, Heathrow Business Center, 300 International Parkway, Heathrow FL 32746, (407) 333–7000.
Panama City Resident Office, Suite 215, Marine Trade Center II, 5323 West Highway 98, Panama City FL 32401, (904) 769–3407.
Pensacola Resident Office, Suite 330, 125 West Romana Street, Pensacola FL 32501, (904) 469–9060.
Tallahassee Resident Office, 3384 Capital Circle, NE, Tallahassee FL 32308, (904) 942–8417.
Tampa District Office, Suite 400, 4950 West Kennedy Boulevard, Tampa FL 33609, (813) 288–1268.
West Palm Beach Resident Office, Commerce Point, Suite 300, 1818 Australian Avenue, West Palm Beach FL 33409–6447, (561) 684–8000.

NEWARK DIVISION:

Special Agent-in-Charge.—John J. Coleman, 80 Mulberry Street, Second Floor, Newark NJ 07102–4206, (201) 645–6060.
Atlantic City Resident Office, 2111 New Road, North Field NJ 08330, (609) 383–3322.
Camden Resident Office, Suite 200, 1000 Crawford Place, Mount Laurel NJ 08054, (609) 757–5407.

NEW ORLEANS DIVISION:

Special Agent-in-Charge.—Ronald J. Caffrey, Suite 1800, Three Lakeway Center, 3838 North Causeway Boulevard, Metairie LA 70002, (504)-840–1100.
Baton Rouge Resident Office, Suite 306, 2237 South Acadian Thruway, Baton Rouge LA 70808, (504) 389–0254.
Birmingham Resident Office, Suite 420W, 234 Goodwin Crest, Birmingham AL 35209, (205) 290–7150.
Fayetteville Resident Office, PO Box 1951, Fayetteville AR 72702, (501) 442–2618.
Gulfport Resident Office, PO Box 1387, Gulfport MS 39502, (601) 863–2992.
Jackson Resident Office, Suite 1213, 100 West Capitol Street, Jackson MS 39269, (601) 965–4400.
Little Rock Resident Office, Suite 317, 10825 Financial Parkway, Little Rock AR 72211, (501) 324–5981.
Mobile Resident Office, Suite 501, 900 Western America Circle, Mobile AL 36609, (334) 441–5831.
Montgomery District Office, 2350 Fairlane Drive, Second Floor, Montgomery AL 36109, (334) 260–1150.
Oxford Resident Office, PO Box 648, Oxford MS 38655–0648, (601) 234–8542.

Shreveport Resident Office, Suite 510, 401 Edwards Street, Shreveport LA 71101–5519, (318) 676–4080.

NEW YORK DIVISION:

Special Agent-in-Charge.—Lewis Rice, 99 10th Avenue New York NY 10011, (212) 337–3900.

Albany Resident Office, Room 746, 930 Leo W. O'Brien Federal Building, Albany NY 12207, (518) 431–4700.

Albany Capital District Task Force, 28 Essex Street, Albany NY 12206, (518) 446–9035.

Buffalo Resident Office, Suite 300, 28 Church Street, Buffalo NY 14202, (716) 551–4421.

JFK Airport Station, D–14, Building 75, Room 232, Halmar Building, Jamaica NY 11430, (718) 553–0195.

Long Island Resident Office, Suite 205, 175 Pinelawn Road, Melville NY 11747, (516) 420–4500.

Rochester Resident Office, PO Box 14120, Rochester NY 14614, (716) 263–3180.

Syracuse Resident Office, 4600 West Genesee Street, Syracuse NY 13219, (315) 468–2772.

Westchester Task Force, Suite 207, 140 Grand Street, White Plains NY 10601, (914) 682–6256.

PHILADELPHIA DIVISION:

Special Agent-in-Charge.—Lawrence P. McElynn, Room 10224, William J. Green Federal Building, 600 Arch Street, Philadelphia PA 19106, (215) 597–9530.

Allentown Resident Office, Suite 2500, U.S. Courthouse and Federal Building, 504 West Hamilton Street, Allentown PA 18101, (610) 770–0940.

Dover Post of Duty, 32 Lockerman Street, Suite 103, Dover DE 19903; Harrisburg Resident Office, PO Box 887, Harrisburg PA 17108–0887, (717) 782–2270.

Pittsburgh Resident Office, Room 1328, Federal Building, 1000 Liberty Avenue, Pittsburgh PA 15222, (412) 644–3390.

Scranton Post of Duty, PO Box 751, Scranton PA 18503, (717) 341–9074.

Wilmington Resident Office, Suite 404, One Rodney Square, 920 King Street, Wilmington DE 19801, (302) 573–6184.

PHOENIX DIVISION:

Special Agent-in-Charge.—Richard E. Gorman, Suite 301, Westmount Place, 3010 North Second Street, Phoenix AZ 85012, (602) 664–5600.

Nogales Resident Office, 1370 West Fairway Drive, Nogales AZ 85621, (520) 281–1727.

Sierra Vista Resident Office, Suite L14, 500 Fry Boulevard, PO Box 2169, Sierra Vista AZ 85636, (520) 458–3691.

Tucson District Office, 3285 East Hemisphere Loop, Tucson AZ 85706, (520) 573–5500.

Yuma Resident Office, 780 East 39th Place, Yuma AZ 85365–4905, (520) 344–9550.

SAN DIEGO DIVISION:

Special Agent-in-Charge.—Errol J. Chavez, 4560 Viewridge Avenue, San Diego CA 92123–1672, (619) 616–4100.

Carlsbad Resident Office, 5810 Newton Drive, Carlsbad CA 92008, (619) 931–2666.

Imperial County Resident Office, PO Box 308, Imperial County CA 92251–0308, (619) 355–0857.

San Ysidro Resident Office, 406 Virginia Avenue, San Ysidro CA 92173, (619) 662–7115.

SAN FRANCISCO DIVISION:

Special Agent-in-Charge.—William J. Mitchell, 450 Golden Gate Avenue, PO Box 36035, San Francisco CA 94102, (415) 436–7900.

Alameda County Drug Enforcement Task Force 333 Hegenberger Road, Room 415, Oakland CA 94621, 510) 568–0411.

San Francisco Airport Task Force, San Francisco International Airport, San Francisco CA 94080, (415) 876–2850.

Fresno Resident Office, Room 200, 1260 M Street, Fresno CA 93721, (209) 487–5410.

Monterey Resident Office, 2560 Garden Road, No. 207, PO Box 3182, Monterey CA 93940, (408) 648–3050.

Sacramento Resident Office, Suite 250, 1860 Howe Avenue, Sacramento CA 95825, (916) 566–7160.

San Jose Resident Office, Suite 405, One North First Street, San Jose CA 95113, (408) 291–7235.

SEATTLE DIVISION:

Special Agent-in-Charge.—George J. Cazenavette, Suite 104, 220 West Mercer, Seattle WA 98119, (206) 553–5443.

Seattle Airport Group, Suite 204, 2800 South 192nd Street, SeaTac WA 98188, (206) 764–3640.

Anchorage Resident Office, Suite 600, 555 Cordova Street, Anchorage AK 99501, (907) 271–5033.

Billings Resident Office, Suite 302, 303 North Broadway, Billings MT 59101, (406) 657–6020.

Blaine Resident Office, 165 Second Street, PO Box 1680, Blaine WA 98231–1680, (360) 332–8692.
Boise Resident Office, Suite 400, 607 North Eighth Street, Boise ID 83702–5518, (208) 334–1620.
Eugene Resident Office, 230 Federal Building, 211 East Seventh Avenue, Eugene OR 97401, (541) 465–6861.
Medford Resident Office, Room B–3, 310 West Sixth Street, Medford OR 97501, (541) 776–4260.
Portland District Office, Room 1525, 1220 SW Third Avenue, Portland OR 97204, (503) 326–3371.
Salem Post of Duty, PO Box 2201, Salem OR 97308–2201, (503) 399–5902.
Spokane Resident Office, Suite L–300, 1124 West Riverside Street, Spokane WA 99201 (509) 353–2964.
Tacoma Post of Duty, PO Box 3109, Federal Way WA 98003, (206) 764–3640.
Tri-Cities Post of Duty, PO Box 6477, Kennewick WA 99336–0627, (509) 545–6010.
Yakima Resident Office, Suite 900, 402 East Yakima Avenue, Yakima WA 98901, (509) 454–4407.

ST. LOUIS DIVISION:

Special Agent-in-Charge.—Joseph Corcoran, Suite 500, 7911 Forsythe Boulevard, St. Louis MO 63105, (314) 425–3241.
Cape Girardeau, Resident Office, Room 158, 339 Broadway, Cape Girardeau MO 63701, (575) 334–1534.
Carbondale Post of Duty, Room 302, 250 West Cherry, Carbondale IL 62901–2678, (618) 457–3605.
Cedar Rapids Post of Duty, Suite 200, 4403 First Avenue SE, Cedar Rapids IA 52402, (319) 393–6075.
Des Moines Resident Office, Room 937, 210 Walnut Street, Des Moines IA 50309, (515) 284–4700.
Fairview Heights Resident Office, 333 Salem Place, Suite 265, Fairview Heights IL 62208, (618) 628–0025.
Garden City Post of Duty, 2225 South Air Service Road, Suite 116, Garden City KS 67846, (316) 275–7798.
Kansas City Resident Office, Suite 200, 8600 Farley Street, Overland Park KS 66212, (913) 236–3257.
Kansas City Airport Task Force, KCI Airport, PO Box 20604, Kansas City MO 64195–0604, (816) 243–6454.
Lambert International Airport Task Force, Box 10009, St. Louis MO 63145, (314) 426–1653.
Omaha Resident Office, Room 1003, 106 South 15th Street, Omaha NE 68102, (402) 221–4222.
Quad Cities Post of Duty, 1830 Second Avenue, Suite 320, PO Box 4088, Rock Island IL 61204–4088, (309) 793–5708.
Rapid City Post of Duty, PO Box 8066, Rapid City SD 57709, (605) 343–4947.
Sioux Falls Resident Office, Suite 407, 230 South Phillips Avenue, Sioux Falls SD 57102, (605) 330–4421.
Sioux City Post of Duty, PO Box 5227, Sioux City IA 51102, (712) 255–9128.
Springfield Resident Office, 901 St. Louis Street, Springfield MO 65806, (417) 831–3948.
Topeka Post of Duty, c/o Special Operations Group, Forbes Field Office, Building 684, Forbes Field, AFB, KS 66619, (913) 862–0812.
Wichita Resident Office, Suite 330, 1919 North Amidon, Wichita KS 67203, (316) 838–2500.

WASHINGTON DC DIVISION:

Special Agent-in-Charge.—Peter F. Gruden, Room 2558, 400 Sixth Street SW, Washington DC 20024, (202) 401–7834.
Baltimore District Office, 200 St. Paul's Place, Room 2222, Baltimore MD 21202, (410) 962–4800.
Charleston Resident Office, Suite 202, Two Monongalia Street, Charleston WV 25302–2349, (304) 347–5209.
Charlottesville Task Force, US Courthouse, Suite 314, 255 West Main Street, Charlottesville VA 22901, (804) 977–9074.
Clarksburg Post of Duty, PO Box 2621, Clarksburg WV 26301–0262, (304) 623–3700.
Hagerstown Post of Duty, PO Box 0949, Hagerstown MD 21741–0949, (301) 733–4111.
HIDTA Task Groups, (DC), 2100 M Street NW, Suite 203, Washington DC 20036, (202) 496–3134.
HIDTA Task Force Groups, (MD), 7500 Greenway Center, Suite 303, Greenbelt MD 20770, (301) 489–1700.
HIDTA Task Force Groups (VA), Suite 303, 6715 Little River Turnpike, Annandale VA 22003, (703) 658–7801.

HIDTA Task Force Groups, (Washington National Airport), East Lab Building, Suite 301, Washington DC 20001, (703) 603–7095.
HIDTA Task Force, (Dulles Airport), Suite 2558, 400 Sixth Street SW, Washington DC 20024, (703) 285–2760.
Norfolk Resident Office, Federal Building, Suite 435, 200 Granby Mall, Norfolk VA 23510, (804) 441–3152.
Richmond Resident Office, 8600 Staples Mill Road, Richmond VA 23228–2719, (804) 771–2871.
Roanoke Resident Office, 105 West Franklin, Roanoke VA 24011, (540) 857–2555.
Salisbury Post of Duty, PO Box 4490, Salisbury MD 21801, (410) 860–4800.

LABORATORIES

Mid-Atlantic Laboratory, 460 New York Avenue NW, Washington DC 20532–0001, (202) 275–6478.
Northeast Laboratory, 99 10th Avenue, Suite 721, New York NY 10011, (212) 620-3684.
North Central Laboratory, Room 800, 536 South Clark Street, Chicago IL 60605, (312) 353–3640.
Southeast Laboratory, 5205 NW 84th Avenue, Miami FL 33166, (305) 590–4830.
South Central Laboratory, 1880 Regal Row, Dallas TX 75235, (214) 640–0964.
Southwest Laboratory, 410 West 35th Street, National City CA 91950, (619) 498–0005.
Special Testing and Research Laboratory, 7704 Old Springhouse Road, McLean VA 22102–3494, (703) 285–2583.
Western Laboratory, 390 Main Street, Room 700, San Francisco CA 94105, (415) 744–7051.

OTHER DEA OFFICES

Special Agent-in-Charge.—John Brown, El Paso Intelligence Center, 11339 SSG Sims Street, El Paso TX 79908–8098, (915) 564–2000.
Special Agent-in-Charge.—Leonard Luke, Aviation Operations Division, 2300 Horizon Drive, Fort Worth TX 76177, (817) 837–2000.
Northeastern Aviation Resident Office, Office D, 401 Industrial Avenue, Teterboro NJ 07608, (201) 645–3370.
Southeastern Aviation Resident Office, Suite 330, 1100 Lee Wagener Boulevard, Houston TX 77032, (954) 359–6449.
South Central Aviation Resident Office, Suite 207, 17555 JFK Boulevard, Houston TX 77032, (713) 821–1054.
Western Aviation Resident Office, PO Box 92799, Long Beach CA 90809–2799, (310) 980–3554.
Office of Professional Responsibility Northeast Field Office, 1 Gateway Center, 100 Mulberry Street, Suite 700, Newark NJ 07102–0842, (201) 645–2000.
Office of Professional Responsibility Southeast Field Office, 499 NW 70th Avenue, Suite 212, Plantation FL 33317, (954) 792–5356.
Office of Professional Responsibility Western Field Office, 350 South Figueroa Street, Suite 725, Los Angeles CA 90071, (213) 894–6395.
Special Agent-in-Charge.—Richard Fiano, (acting) Special Operations Division, 8199 Backlick Road, Lorton VA 22079, (703) 541–6700.
Investigative Technology Section, 8199 Backlick Road, Lorton VA 22079, (703) 541–6500.
Special Agent-in-Charge.—David Westrate, Office of Training, FBI Academy, PO Box 1475, Quantico VA 22134–1475, (703) 640–1631.

FOREIGN OFFICES

Ankara: DEA/Justice, American Embassy, PSC 93, Box 5000, APO AE 09823, 9–011–312–468–6136.
Asuncion: DEA/Justice, American Embassy, Unit 4740, APO AA 34036, 9–1–011–595–21–210–738.
Athens: DEA/Justice, American Embassy, PSC 108, Box 14, APO AE 09842, 9–1–011–30–1–643–4328.
Bangkok: DEA/Justice, American Embassy, Box 49, APO AP 96546, 9–1–011–66–2–205–4622.
Barranquilla: DEA/Justice, American Embassy, Unit 5116, APO AA 34038, 9–1–011–57–53–53024.
Belize: DEA/Justice, American Embassy, Unit 7405, APO AA 34025, 9–011–501–2–33857.
Bern: DEA/Justice, Bern Country Office, Department of State (Bern), Washington DC 20521–5110, 9–011–41–31–357–7367.
Bogota: DEA/Justice, American Embassy, Unit 5116, APO AA 34038, 9–1–011–571–315–2121.

Bombay: DEA/Justice, American Consulate General, Diplomatic Pouch, Washington DC 20521–6240, 9–011–91–22–363–3437.
Bonn: DEA/Justice, American Embassy, PSC 117, Box 290, APO AE 09080–5000, 9–1–011–49–228–339–2307.
Brasilia: DEA/Justice, American Embassy, Unit 3500, APO AA 34030, 9–1–011–55–61–225–7270.
Bridgetown: DEA/Justice, American Embassy, FPO AA 34055, 9–1–246–437–6337.
Brussels: DEA/Justice, American Embassy, PSC 82, Box 002, APO AE 09724, 9–1–011–32–2–508–2420.
Buenos Aires: DEA/Justice, American Embassy, Unit 4309, APO AA 34034–0001, 9–1–011–541–771–4502.
Cairo: DEA/Justice, American Embassy, Unit 64900, Box 24, PO AE 09839–4900, 9–1–011–202–357–2461.
Canberra: DEA/Justice, American Embassy, APO AP 96549–5000, 9–011–61–6–270–5903.
Caracas: DEA/Justice, American Embassy, Unit 4962, APO AA 34037, 9–011–582–977–3852.
Chiang-Mai: DEA/Justice, American Consulate General, Box C, APO AP 96546, 9–011–66–53–217–285.
Cochabamba: DEA/Justice, American Embassy, Unit 3913, APO AA 34032, 9–011–591–4288896.
Copenhagen: DEA/Justice, American Embassy, PSC 73, APO AE 09716, 9–011–45–31–422–680.
Curacao: DEA/Justice, Diplomatic Pouch, Washington DC 20537, 9–011–599–9–6169805.
Frankfurt: DEA/Justice, PSC 115, Frankfurt/DEA, APO AE 09213–7900, 9–011–49–69–75353770.
Freeport: DEA/Justice, 7415 NW 19th Street, Suite Fl, Miami FL 33126, 9–1–809–352–5353.
Guadalajara: DEA/Justice, Guadalajara Resident Office, PO Box 3088, Laredo TX 78044–3088, 9–011–523–825–3064.
Guatemala City: DEA/Justice, American Embassy, Unit 3311, APO AA 34024, 9–011–502–2–314–389.
Guayaquil: DEA/Justice, American Consulate General, Unit 5350, APO AA, 34039, 9–011–593–4–323–715.
The Hague: DEA/Justice, American Embassy, PSC 71, Box 1000, APO AE 09715, 9–011–31–70–310–9327.
Hermosillo: DEA/Justice, Hermosillo Resident Office, PO Box 3087, Laredo TX 78044, 9–011–52–62–17–4715.
Hong Kong: DEA/Justice, American Consulate General, PCS 464, Box 30, FPO AP 96522–0002, 9–011–852–2521–4536.
Islamabad: DEA/Justice, American Embassy, Unit 62215, APO AE 09812–2215, 9–011–92–51–825–258.
Istanbul: DEA/Justice, American Consulate General, PSC 97, Box 0002, APO AE 09827–0002, 9–011–212–251–0160.
Karachi: DEA/Justice, American Consulate, Unit 62041, Box 122, APO AE 09814–2401, 9–011–92–21–5687338..
Kingston: DEA/Justice, Diplomatic Pouch, Kingston Country Office, Washington DC 20521, 9–1–809–929–4956.
Kuala Lumpur: DEA/Justice, American Embassy, APO AP 96535–5000, 9–011–603–248–7951.
Lagos: DEA/Justice, Lagos Country Office, Department of State, Washington DC 20521–8300, 9–011–234–261–9837.
Lahore: DEA/Justice, American Consulate General, Unit 62216, APO AE 09812–2216, 9–011–92–42–636–5530, ext 212.
La Paz: DEA/Justice, American Embassy, Unit 3913, APO AA 34032, 9–011–591–2431481.
Lima: DEA/Justice, American Embassy, Unit 3810, APO AA 34031, 9–011–511–434–3058.
London: DEA/Justice, American Embassy, PSC 801, Box 8, APO AE 09498–4008, 9–011–441–71–408–8026.
Lyon (INTERPOL): DEA/Justice, c/o American Embassy, PSC 116, DEA/Interpol, FPO AE 0948–4008, 9–011–33–7244–7086.
Madrid: DEA/Justice, American Embassy, PSC 61, Box 0014, APO AE 09642, 9–011–341–587–2280.
Manila: DEA/Justice, American Embassy, APO 96440, 9–011–632–521–4899.
Mazatlan: DEA/Justice, Mazatlan Resident Office, PO Box 2708, Laredo TX 78044–3087, 9–011–52–69–821659.
Merida: DEA/Justice, Merida Resident Office, PO Box 3087, Laredo TX 78044–3087, 9–011–52–99–256794.
Mexico City: DEA/Justice, PO Box 3087 Laredo TX 78044–3087, 9–011–525–211–0042.
Milan: DEA/Justice, American Consulate General, PSC 59, Box 60 M, APO AE 09624, 9–011–39–2–655–5766.

Monterrey: DEA/Justice, American Consulate General, PO Box 3098, Laredo TX 78040–3908, 9–011–528–340–1299.

Moscow: DEA/Justice, American Embassy Moscow, PSC 77, APO AE 09721, 9–011–7–095–056–4066.

Nassau: DEA/Justice, American Embassy, PO Box 9009, Miami FL 33159, 9–1–242–322–1700.

New Delhi: DEA/Justice, New Delhi Country Office, Department of State, Washington DC 20521–9000, 9–011–91–11–601–844.

Nicosia: DEA/Justice, American Embassy, PSC 815, Box 1 FPO AE 09836–0001, 9–011–357–2477086.

Ottawa: DEA/Justice, American Embassy Ottawa, Department of State, Washington DC 20521–5480, 9–1–613–238–5633.

Panama City: DEA/Justice, American Embassy, Unit 0945, APO AA 34002, 9–011–507–225–9685.

Paris: DEA/Justice, American Embassy, PSC 116, Box D–401, APO AE 09777, 9–011–33–1–4312–7332.

Peshawar: DEA/Justice, American Consulate General/Peshawar, APO AE 09812, 9–011–92–521–840–424.

Port-Au-Prince: DEA/Justice, Port-Au-Prince, Diplomatic Pouch, Washington DC 20537, 9–011–509–238888.

Quito: DEA/Justice, American Embassy, Unit 5338, APO AA 34039–3420, 9–011–593–2–564–657.

Rangoon: DEA/Justice, American Embassy, Box B, APO AP 96546, 9–011–95–1–282055.

Rome: DEA/Justice, American Embassy, PSC 59, Box 60–M, APO AE 09624, 9–011–39–6–4674–2319.

San Jose: DEA/Justice, American Embassy, Unit 2506, APO AA 34020, 9–011–506–220–2433.

San Salvador: DEA/Justice, American Embassy, Unit 3130, APO AA 34023, 9–011–503–278–6005.

Santa Cruz: DEA/Justice, American Embassy, Unit 3913, APO AA 34032, 9–1–011–591–3–327152.

Santiago: DEA/Justice, American Embassy, Unit 4119, APO AA 34033, 9–011–562–330–3401.

Santo Domingo: DEA/Justice, American Embassy, Unit 5514, APO AA 34031, 9–1–809–687–3754.

Sao Paulo: DEA/Justice, American Embassy, Unit 3502, APO AA 34030, 9–011–55–11–881–6511 ext. 2219.

Seoul: DEA/Justice, American Embassy, Unit 15550, APO AP 96205–0001, 9–011–822–397–4260.

Singapore: DEA/Justice, American Embassy, FPO AP 96534–0001, 9–011–65–338–0251, ext. 286.

Songkhla: DEA/Justice, American Embassy, Box S, APO AP 96546, 9–011–66–74–324–235.

Tegucigalpa: DEA/Justice, American Embassy, Unit 2912, APO AA 34022, 9–011–504–36–6780.

Tokyo: DEA/Justice, American Embassy, Unit 45004, Box 224, APO AP 96337–0001, 9–011–81–33–224–5452.

Udorn: DEA/Justice, American Consulate General, Box UD, APO AP 96546, 9–011–66–42–247–637.

Vienna: DEA/Justice, U.S. Embassy Vienna, U.S. Department of State, Washington DC 20521, 9–011–43–1–514–2251.

FEDERAL BUREAU OF INVESTIGATION

J. Edgar Hoover Building, 935 Pennsylvania Avenue NW
Washington DC 20535–0001, phone (202) 324–3000

Director.—Louis J. Freeh, Room 7176, 324–3444.
Deputy Director.—William J. Esposito, Room 7142, 324–3315.
Chief of Staff.—Robert B. Bucknam, Room 7176, 324–3444.
FBI General Counsel.—[Vacant], Room 7427, 324–6829.
Assistant Directors:
Criminal Justice Information Services Division.—Charles W. Archer, Room 11255, 324–8901. [West Virginia, (304) 625–2700]
Training Division.—Joseph R. Wolfinger, FBI Academy, Quantico VA, (703) 640–1100.
Personnel Division.—Thomas J. Coyle, Room 6012, 324–3515.
Information Resources Division.—Carolyn G. Morris, Room 5829, 324–4840.
National Security Division.—John F. Lewis, Jr., Room 7110, 324–4880.
Criminal Investigative Division.—Robert M. Bryant, Room 7116, 324–4260.
Laboratory Division.—Donald Thompson, Jr. (acting), Room 3090, 324–4410.

Finance Division.—Wade B. Houk, Room 6032, 324–1345.
Inspection Division.—William D. Gore, Room 7825, 324–2901.

Offices:

Public and Congressional Affairs.—Inspector-in-Charge John E. Collingwood, Room 7240, 324–2727.
Equal Employment Opportunity Affairs.—EEO Officer James R. Perez, Room 7901, 324–4128.
General Counsel.—General Counsel [Vacant], Room 7427, 324–6829.

FIELD DIVISIONS

Albany: Fifth Floor, U.S. Post Office and Courthouse, 445 Broadway, Albany NY 12207, (518) 465–7551.
Albuquerque: Suite 300, 415 Silver Avenue SW, Albuquerque NM 87102, (505) 224–2000.
Anchorage: 101 East Sixth Avenue, Anchorage AK 99501–2524, (907) 258–5322.
Atlanta: Suite 400, 2635 Century Parkway NE, Atlanta GA 30345 (404) 679–9000.
Baltimore: 7142 Ambassador Road, Baltimore MD 21244–2754, (410) 265–8080.
Birmingham: 2121 Building, Room 1400, Eighth Avenue North, Birmingham AL 35203–2396, (205) 326–6166.
Boston: John F. Kennedy Federal Office Building, Suite 600, One Center Plaza, Boston MA 02108, (617) 742–5533.
Buffalo: Federal Office Building, Room 1400, One FBI Plaza, Buffalo NY 14202–2698, (716) 856–7800.
Charlotte: Suite 900, 400 South Tryon Street, Charlotte NC 28285–0001, (704) 377–9200.
Chicago: E.M. Dirksen Federal Office Building, Room 905, 219 South Dearborn Street, Chicago IL 60604–1702, (312) 431–1333.
Cincinnati: Room 9023, 550 Main Street, Cincinnati OH 45273–8501, (513) 421–4310.
Cleveland: Federal Office Building, Room 3005, 1240 East Ninth Street, Cleveland OH 44199–9912, (216) 522–1400.
Columbia: Suite 1357, 1835 Assembly Street, Columbia SC 29201–2430, (803) 254–3011.
Dallas: Suite 300, 1801 North Lamar Street, Dallas TX 75202, (214) 720–2200.
Denver: Federal Office Building, Room 1823, 1961 Stout Street, Denver CO 80294–1823, (303) 629–7171.
Detroit: Federal Office Building, 477 Michigan Avenue, Detroit MI 48226, (313) 965–2323.
El Paso: Suite C–600, 700 East San Antonio Avenue, El Paso TX 79901–7020, (915) 533–7451.
Honolulu: Room 4307, 300 Ala Moana Boulevard, Honolulu HI 96850–0053, (808) 521–1411.
Houston: Room 200, 2500 East T.C. Jester Boulevard, Houston TX 77008–1300, (713) 868–2266.
Indianapolis: Federal Building, Room 679, 575 North Pennsylvania Street, Indianapolis IN 46204, (317) 639–3301.
Jackson: Federal Office Building, Suite 1553, 100 West Capitol Street, Jackson MS 39269, (601) 948–5000
Jacksonville: Suite 200, 7820 Arlington Expressway, Jacksonville FL 32211–7499, (904) 721–1211.
Kansas City: United States Courthouse, Room 300, 811 Grand Avenue, Kansas City MO 64106–1926, (816) 221–6100.
Knoxville: Suite 600, 710 Locust Street, Knoxville TN 37092, (423) 544–0751.
Las Vegas: 700 East Charleston Boulevard, Las Vegas NV 89104–1545, (702) 385–1281.
Little Rock: Suite 200, 10825 Financial Centre Parkway, Little Rock AR 72211–3552, (501) 221–9100.
Los Angeles: Federal Office Building, 11000 Wilshire Boulevard, Los Angeles CA 90024, (310) 477–6565.
Louisville: Room 500, 600 Martin Luther King, Jr. Place, Louisville KY 40202, (502) 583–3941.
Memphis: 225 North Humphreys Boulevard, Memphis TN 38120–2107, (901) 747–4300.
Miami: 16320 NW Second Avenue, North Miami Beach FL 33169, (305) 944–9101.
Milwaukee: Suite 600, 330 East Kilbourn Avenue, Milwaukee WI 53202–6627, (414) 276–4684.
Minneapolis: Suite 1100, 111 Washington Avenue South, Minneapolis MN 55401–2176, (612) 376–3200.
Mobile: One St. Louis Centre, One St. Louis Street, Mobile AL 36602, (334) 438–3674.
Newark: One Gateway Center, 22nd Floor, Market Street, Newark NJ 07102–9889, (201) 622–5613.
New Haven: Room 535, Federal Office Building, 150 Court Street, New Haven CT 06510–2020, (203) 777–6311.

New Orleans: Suite 2200, 1250 Poydras Street, New Orleans LA 70113–1829, (504) 522–4671.
New York: 26 Federal Plaza, 23rd Floor, New York NY 10278–0004, (212) 384–1000.
Norfolk: 150 Corporate Boulevard, Norfolk VA 23502–4999, (757) 455–0100.
Oklahoma City: Suite 1600, 50 Penn Place, Oklahoma City OK 73118–1886, (405) 842–7471.
Omaha: Federal Office Building, 10755 Burt Street, Omaha NE 68114–2000, (402) 493–8688.
Philadelphia: William J. Green, Jr., Federal Office Building, Eighth Floor, 600 Arch Street, Philadelphia PA 19106, (215) 829–2700.
Phoenix: Suite 400, 201 East Indianola, Phoenix AZ 85012, (602) 279–5511.
Pittsburgh: Suite 300, USPO, 700 Grant Street, Pittsburgh PA 15219–1906, (412) 471–2000.
Portland: Suite 400, Crown Plaza, 1500 SW First Avenue, Portland OR 97201–5828, (503) 224–4181.
Quantico: FBI Academy, Marine Corps Base, Quantico VA 22135, (703) 640–6131.
Richmond: 111 Greencourt Road, Richmond VA 23228–4948, (804) 261–1044.
Sacramento: 4500 Orange Grove Avenue, Sacramento CA 95841–4205, (916) 481–9110.
St. Louis: Room 2704, 1520 Market Street, St. Louis MO 63103, (314) 241–5357.
Salt Lake City: Suite 1200, 257 East, 200 South, Salt Lake City UT 84111, (801) 579–1400.
San Antonio: Room 200, 615 East Houston Street, San Antonio TX 78205–9998, (210) 225–6741.
San Diego: Federal Office Building, 9797 Aero Drive, San Diego CA 92123–1800, (619) 565–1255.
San Francisco: 450 Golden Gate Avenue, San Francisco CA 94102–9523, (415) 553–7400.
San Juan: Room 526, U.S. Federal Building, 150 Carlos Chardon Avenue, Hato Rey, San Juan PR 00918–1716, (787) 754–6000.
Seattle: Federal Office Building, Room 710, 915 Second Avenue, Seattle WA 98174–1096, (206) 622–0460.
Springfield: Suite 400, 400 West Monroe Street, Springfield IL 62704, (217) 522–9675.
Tampa: Room 610, 500 Zack Street, Tampa FL 33602–3917, (813) 273–4566.
Washington Field Office: 601 Fourth Street NW, Washington DC 20535–0001, (202) 252–7801.

OFFICE OF THE PARDON ATTORNEY

500 First Street NW, Fourth Floor, Washington DC 20530, phone 616–6070

Pardon Attorney.—Margaret C. Love.
Deputy Pardon Attorney.—Raymond P. Theim.
Administrative Officer.—William J. Dziwura.

U.S. PAROLE COMMISSION

Park Place Building, 5550 Friendship Boulevard, Suite 420
Chevy Chase MD 20815, phone (301) 492–5990

Chairman.—Michael J. Gaines.
Commissioners: Edward F. Reilly, Jr., (301) 492–5990; John R. Simpson, (301) 492–5821.
Staff Assistant to Chairman.—Dawn Boozé-Hill, (301) 492–5990.
Staff Director.—Clair D. (Sam) Shoquist (acting), (301) 492–5825.
General Counsel.—Michael Stover, (301) 492–5959.
Executive Officer.—Judy I. Carter, (301) 492–5974.

IMMIGRATION AND NATURALIZATION SERVICE

(CAB) Chester Arthur Building, 425 I Street NW
Washington DC 20536, phone (202) 514–5231
(ULLB) Union Labor Life Building, 111 Massachusetts Avenue NW, Third Floor, 20536
(AFC) 4420 North Fairfax Drive, Arlington VA 22203
Building 64, Federal Law Enforcement Training Center, Glynco GA 31534
Press Information: CAB Room 7021, 514–2648

Commissioner.—Doris Meissner, CAB Room 7100, 514–1900.
Special Assistant.—Alice J. Smith.
Staff Assistant.—Shirley Ballard.
Deputy Commissioner.—Chris Sale.
Chief of Staff.—Peter M. Becraft.
Director of—
Communications.—Julie Anbender, CAB Room 7017, 514–2648.

Congressional Relations.—Alan Erenbaum, CAB Room 7030, 514–5231.
General Counsel.—David Martin, CAB Room 6100, 514–2895.
Director of Internal Audit.—John P. Chase, CAB Room 3260, 514–2373.
Executive Associate Commissioner for Policy and Planning.—Robert L. Bach, CAB Room 6042, 514–3242.
Executive Associate Commissioner for Field Operations.—Brian Perryman (acting), CAB Room 7114, 514–0078.
Regional Directors:
Eastern Region.—Thomas Leupp (acting), 70 Kinball Avenue, South Burlington VT 05403, (802) 660–5000.
Central Region.—Dwayne Peterson (acting), 7701 North Stemmons Freeway, Dallas TX 75247, (214) 767–7020.
Western Region.—Gustavo De La Vina, 24000 Avila Road, PO Box 30080, Laguna Niguel CA 92677–8080, (714) 643–4236.
Director, Office of International Affairs.—Phyllis A. Covan, ULLB Third Floor, 633–1100.
Executive Associate Commissioner for Programs.—Paul Virtue (acting), CAB Room 7309, 514–8223.
Associate Commissioner for Enforcement.—George Rogan (acting), CAB Room 5300, 514–4402.
Assistant Commissioner for—
Border Patrol.—Douglas M. Kruhm, CAB Room 4226, 514–3073.
Detention and Deportation.—Joan C. Higgins, CAB Room 3008, 514–2543.
Intelligence.—Clifford Landsman (acting), CAB Room 5300, 514–4402.
Investigations.—Gregory Bednarz (acting), CAB Room 1000, 514–1189.
Director, Asset Forfeiture.—John F. Shaw, CAB Room 1040, 616–7273.
Associate Commissioner for Examinations.—Louis D. Crocotti, Jr., Room 7252, 514–2982.
Assistant Commissioner for—
Adjudications and Naturalization.—Michael Aytes, CAB Room 3214, 514–3228.
Inspections.—Michael C. Cronin, CAB Room 4064, 514–3019.
Records.—[Vacant], ULLB Third Floor, 514–4258.
Chief, Administrative Appeals.—Terrance M. O'Reilly, ULLB Third Floor.
Executive Associate Commissioner for Management.—George H. Behlinger III, CAB Room 7006, 514–3182.
Director for—
Equal Employment Opportunity.—Diane Weaver (acting), CAB Room 2210, 514–2824.
Office of Security.—Winona Varnon (acting), CAB Room 3038, 514–9615.
Files and Forms Management.—Scott Hastings, ULLB Fourth Floor, 514–2989.
Financial Management.—Joseph O'Leska, CAB Room 6004, 305–1200.
Assistant Commissioner for Budget.—Jeffrey M. Weber, CAB Room 6307, 514–3206.
Assistant Commissioner for Administration.—David Yentzer, Room 2100, 616–2486.
Director for—
Procurement.—Linda Greene, CAB Room 2208, 514–4441.
Facilities.—Richard J. Diefenbeck, CAB Room 2060, 514–3099.
Logistics.—Eugene A. Kupferer, CAB Room 2122, 616–7000.
Assistant Commissioner for Human Resources and Development.—Carol Hall, CAB Room 2006, 514–3636.
Director for—
Human Resources.—Robert Sherman, CAB Room 2006, 514–2520.
Training.—Vance Remillard, Room 2006, 616–2674.
Research and Development.—Magda Colberg, CAB Room 2232, 305–0600.
Assistant Commissioner for Information Resources Management.—Ronald W. Collison, CAB Room 4012, 514–2547.
Assistant Commissioner for—
Data Systems.—Fernanda Young, CAB Room 4114, 514–4518.
Systems Integration.—Alan Shelton, ULLB Second Floor, 514–4477.
Assistant Commissioner for Administrative Centers.—John R. Schroeder, CAB Room 7006, 514–3182.
Washington District Office:
District Director.—William J. Carroll, Fifth Floor, 4420 North Fairfax Drive, Arlington VA 22203, (202) 307–1504.
Deputy District Director.—Nathan Granger, Fifth Floor, (202) 307–1504.
Baltimore District Office:
District Director.—Benedict Ferro, Equitable Tower One, 100 South Charles Street, Baltimore MD 21201, (410) 962–2010.
Deputy District Director.—Warren Lewis, (410) 962–2010.

EXECUTIVE OFFICE FOR UNITED STATES TRUSTEES
901 E Street NW, Washington DC 20530, phone 307–1391

Director.—Joseph Patchan, Room 700, 307–1391.
Deputy Director.—Kevyn D. Orr, Room 700, 307–1391.
Associate Director.—Jeffrey M. Miller, Room 700, 307–1391.
General Counsel.—Martha L. Davis, Room 780, 307–1399.
Deputy General Counsel.—Esther I. Estryn, Room 780, 307–1399.
Assistant Directors Office of—
Administration.—Edward F. Cincinnati, Room 732, 307–2926.
Review and Oversight.—[Vacant], Room 710, 307–2123.
Deputy Assistant Director, Office of Review and Oversight.—Sandra J. Forbes (acting), Room 710, 307–2605.
Office of Research and Planning.—Joseph Gazinski, Room 740, 616–9193.

U.S. TRUSTEES:

Region I:
Room 1184, 10 Causeway Street, Boston MA 02222–1043, (617) 565–6360.
Suite 303, 537 Congress Street, Portland ME 04101, (207) 780–3564.
Suite 440, 44 Front Street, Worcester MA 01608, (508) 793–0555.
Suite 302, 66 Hanover Street, Manchester NH 03101, (603) 666–7908.
Suite 910, 10 Dorrance Street, Providence RI 02903, (401) 528–5551.

Region II:
Third Floor, 80 Broad Street, New York NY 10004, (212) 668–2200.
Room 200, 74 Chapel Street, Albany NY 12207, (518) 434–4553.
Suite 100, 42 Delaware Avenue, Buffalo NY 14202, (716) 551–5541.
Suite 304, 825 East Gate Boulevard, Garden City NY 11530, (516) 228–9220.
Suite 1103, 265 Church Street, New Haven CT 06510, (203) 773–2210.
Room 609, 100 State Street, Rochester NY 14614, (716) 263–5812.
Room 105, 10 Broad Street, Utica NY 13501, (315) 793–8191.

Region III:
Room 950 W, 601 Walnut Street, Philadelphia PA 19106, (215) 597–4411.
Suite 2100, One Newark Center, Newark NJ 07102, (201) 645–3014.
Room 319, 1000 Liberty Avenue, Pittsburgh PA 15222, (412) 644–4756.
Suite 503, 225 Market Street, Harrisburg PA 17101, (717) 782–4907.

Region IV:
Room 2440, 1201 Main Street, Columbia SC 29201, (803) 806–3001.
Room 210, 115 South Union Street, Alexandria VA 22314, (703) 557–7176.
Room 625, 200 Granby Street, Norfolk VA 23510, (757) 441–6012.
Room 590, 500 Virginia Street East, Charleston WV 25301, (304) 347–5310.
Room 806, 280 Franklin Road SW, Roanoke VA 24011, (540) 857–2806.
Room 224, 11 South 12th Street, Richmond VA 23219, (804) 771–8004.
Suite 600, 6305 Ivy Lane, Greenbelt MD 20770, (301) 344–6216.
Suite 350, 300 West Pratt Street, Baltimore MD 21201, (410) 962–3910.

Region V:
Suite 2110, 400 Poydras Street, New Orleans LA 70130, (504) 589–4018.
Suite 3196, 300 Fannin Street, Shreveport LA 71101–3099, (318) 676–3456.
Suite 706, 100 West Capital Street, Jackson MS 39269, (601) 965–5241.

Region VI:
Room 9C60, 1100 Commerce Street, Dallas TX 75242, (214) 767–8967.
Room 300, 110 North College Avenue, Tyler TX 75702, (903) 597–8312.

Region VII:
Suite 3516, 515 Rusk Avenue, Houston TX 77002, (713) 718–4650.
Room 230, 903 San Jacinto, Austin TX 78701, (512) 916–5329.
Suite 533, 615 East Houston Street, San Antonio TX 78205, (210) 472–4647.
Suite 1107, 606 North Carancahua Street, Corpus Christi TX 78476, (512) 888–3270.

Region VIII:
Suite 400, 200 Jefferson Avenue, Memphis TN 38103, (901) 544–3251.
Suite 512, 601 West Broadway, Louisville KY 40202, (502) 582–6091.
Fourth Floor, 31 East 11th Street, Chattanooga TN 37402, (423) 752–5156.
Room 318, 701 Broadway, Nashville TN 37203, (615) 736–2746.
Suite 803, 100 East Vine Street, Lexington KY 40507, (606) 233–2827.

Region IX:
Suite 20–3300, 200 Public Square, Cleveland OH 44114, (216) 522–7800.
Suite 200, 170 North High Street, Columbus OH 43215, (614) 469–7417.

Suite 2030, 36 East Seventh Street, Cincinnati OH 45202, (513) 684–3363.
Room 1760, 477 Michigan Avenue, Detroit MI 48226, (313) 226–7934.
Suite 202, 330 Ionia NW, Grand Rapids MI 49503, (616) 456–2002.

Region X:
Room 1000, 101 West Ohio Street, Indianapolis IN 46204, (317) 226–6101.
Suite 1100, 401 Main Street, Peoria IL 61602, (309) 671–7181.
Suite 555, 100 East Wayne Street, South Bend IN 46601, (219) 236–8105.

Region XI:
Suite 3350, 227 West Monroe Street, Chicago IL 60606, (312) 886–5785.
Room 430, 517 East Wisconsin Avenue, Milwaukee WI 53202, (414) 297–4482.
Suite 304, 780 Regent Street, Madison WI 53715, (608) 264–5522.

Region XII:
Suite 400, 225 Second Street SE, Cedar Rapids IA 52401, (319) 364–2211.
Suite 540, 331 Second Avenue South, Minneapolis MN 55401, (612) 373–1200.
Room 517, 210 Walnut Street, Des Moines IA 50309–2108, (515) 284–4982.
Suite 502, 230 South Philips Avenue, Sioux Falls SD 57104–6321, (605) 330–4450.

Region XIII:
Suite 200, 818 Grand Boulevard, Kansas City MO 64106, (816) 426–7959.
Room 412, 815 Olive Street, St. Louis MO 63101, (314) 539–2976.
Suite 201, 500 South Broadway, Little Rock AR 72201, (501) 324–7357.
Suite 560, 210 South 16th Street, Omaha NE 68102, (402) 221–4300.

Region XIV:
Suite 700, 2929 North Central Avenue, Phoenix AZ 85012, (602) 640–2100.

Region XV:
Suite 600, 402 West Broadway Street, San Diego CA 92101, (619) 557–5013.
Suite 602, 1132 Bishop Street, Honolulu HI 96813–2836, (808) 522–8150.
Room 805, 238 Archbishop Flores, Agana Guam 96910, (671) 472–7736.

Region XVI:
Suite 800, 221 North Figueroa, Los Angeles CA 90012, (213) 894–6811.
Room 501, 600 West Santa Ana Boulevard, Santa Ana CA 92701, (714) 246–8184.
Room 106, 699 North Arrowhead Avenue, San Bernardino CA 92401, (909) 383–5575.

Region XVII:
Suite 1000, 250 Montgomery Street, San Francisco CA 94104–3401, (415) 705–3300.
Suite 6556, 650 Capitol Mall, Sacramento CA 95814, (916) 498–5990.
Suite 1110, 1130 O Street, Fresno CA 93721, (209) 498–7400.
Suite 690N, 1301 Clay Street, Oakland CA 94612–5217, (510) 637–3200.
Suite 430, 600 Las Vegas Boulevard South, Las Vegas NV 89101, (702) 388–6600.
Suite 2129, 300 Booth Street, Reno NV 89509, (702) 784–5335.
Room 268, 280 South First Street, San Jose CA 95113, (408) 535–5525.

Region XVIII:
Room 600, 1200 Sixth Avenue, Seattle WA 98101, (206) 553–2562.
Suite 1300, 851 Southwest Sixth Avenue, Portland OR 97204–1350, (503) 326–4000.
Room 347, 304 North Eighth Street, Boise ID 83702, (208) 334–1300.
Room 593, 920 West Riverside, Spokane WA 99201, (509) 353–2999.
Suite 204, 301 Central Avenue, Great Falls MT 59401, (406) 761–8777.
Suite 258, 605 West Fourth Avenue, Anchorage AK 99501, (907) 271–2600.
Room 285, 211 East Seventh Avenue, Eugene OR 97401, (541) 465–6330.

Region XIX:
Suite 408, 721 19th Street, Denver CO 80202, (303) 844–5188.
Suite 310, 200 West 17th Street, Cheyenne WY 82001, (307) 772–2790.
Suite 100, Nine Exchange Place, Salt Lake City UT 84111, (801) 524–5734.

Region XX:
Room 180, 301 North Main Street, Wichita KS 67202, (316) 269–6637.
Suite 112, 421 Gold Street SW, Albuquerque NM 87102, (505) 248–6544.
Fourth Floor, 201 Northwest Dean A. McGee Avenue, Oklahoma City OK 73102, (405) 231–5950.
Suite 225, 224 South Boulder Avenue, Tulsa OK 74103, (918) 581–6670.

Region XXI:
Room 362, 75 Spring Street SW, Atlanta GA 30303, (404) 331–4437.
Room 638, 150 Chardon Street, Hato Rey PR 00918, (787) 766–5851.
Room 1204, 51 Southwest First Avenue, Miami FL 33130, (305) 536–7285.
Suite 302, 222 West Oglethorpe Avenue, Savannah GA 31401, (912) 652–4112.
Suite 110, 4919 Memorial Highway, Tampa FL 33634, (813) 243–5000.
Suite 510, 433 Cherry Street, Macon GA 31201, (912) 752–3544.
Room 1038, 227 North Bronough Street, Tallahassee FL 32301, (904) 942–8899.
Suite 620, 135 West Central Boulevard, Orlando FL 32801, (407) 648–6301.

COMMUNITY RELATIONS SERVICE

600 E Street NW, Suite 2000, Washington DC 20530, phone 305–2932

Director.—Rose M. Ochi (acting), (202) 305–2932.
General Counsel.—George Henderson (acting), (202) 305–2964.
Media Affairs Officer.—Daryl Borgquist, (202) 305–2966.
Legislative Officer.—Richard Guitierrez, (202) 305–2967.

REGIONAL DIRECTORS

New England.—Martin A. Walsh, 99 Summer Street, Suite 1820, Boston MA 02110–1032, (617) 424–5715.
Northeast Region.—Patricia Glenn, Room 36–118, 26 Federal Plaza, New York NY 10278, (212) 264–0700.
Mid-Atlantic Region.—Jonathan Chace, Customs House, Room 208, Second and Chestnut Streets, Philadelphia PA 19106, (215) 597–2344.
Southeast Region.—Ozell Sutton, Citizens Trust Company Bank Building, Room 900, 75 Piedmont Avenue NE, Atlanta GA 30303, (404) 331–6883.
Midwest Region.—Jesse Taylor, Xerox Center Building, 55 West Monroe Street, Suite 420, Chicago IL 60603, (312) 353–4391.
Southwest Region.—Gilbert J. Chavez, 1420 West Mockingbird Lane, Suite 250, Dallas TX 75247, (214) 655–8175.
Central Region.—Atkins Warren, 1100 Maine Street, Suite 1320, Kansas City MO 64106, (816) 426–7433.
Rocky Mountain Region.—[Vacant], 1244 Speer Boulevard, Room 650, Denver CO 80204–3584, (303) 844–2973.
Northwest Region.—Robert Lamb, Jr., Federal Office Building, 915 Second Avenue, Room 1898, Seattle WA, 98174, (212) 220–6700.
Western Region.—[Vacant], Suite 1840, 33 New Montgomery Street, San Francisco CA 94105, (415) 744–6565.

FOREIGN CLAIMS SETTLEMENT COMMISSION

Bicentennial Building, 600 E Street NW, Suite 6002, 20579, phone 616–6975

Chair.—Delissa A. Ridgway, 616–6985.
Chief Counsel.—David E. Bradley, 616–6975.
Special Assistant.—David C. Blake, 616–6985.
Commissioners: Richard T. White, 616–6975; John R. Lacey, 616–6975.
Administrative Officer.—Judith H. Lock, 616–6986

DEPARTMENT OF LABOR

Frances Perkins Building, Third Street and Constitution Avenue NW 20210
phone (202) 219–5000, http://www.dol.gov

ALEXIS M. HERMAN, of Mobile, AL, Secretary of Labor; graduated form Xavier University, New Orleans, LA in 1969; began her career as a social worker for Catholic Charities, developing training opportunities for unemployed youth, unskilled workers and new entrants to the Mobile labor force at Ingall's Shipbuilding, Inc., in Pascagoula, MS; in the 1980s, founded A.M. Herman and Associates, a human resources consulting firm with corporate and government clients; director of the Women's Bureau, U.S. Department of Labor, during the Carter administration; chief executive officer of the 1992 Democratic National Convention Committee; deputy director of the Presidential Transition Office, 1992; assistant to President Clinton and director of the White House Public Liaison Office; confirmed as the twenty-third Secretary of Labor by the U.S. Senate, May 2, 1997.

OFFICE OF THE SECRETARY

phone 219–8271

Secretary of Labor.—Alexis Herman.
Confidential Assistant.—Ann Delory.
Chief of Staff.—Theodore W. Mastroianni.
Deputy Chief of Staff.—Lee A. Satterfield.
Counselor to the Secretary.—Leslie Loble.
Chief Economist.—Edward B. Montgomery.
Executive Secretary.—T. Michael Kerr.
Director of Scheduling and Advance.—Mark Hunker.

OFFICE OF THE DEPUTY SECRETARY

phone 219–8271

Deputy Secretary.—Cynthia A. Metzler (acting).
Associate Deputy Secretaries: Virginia Apuzzo, William Janvel.
Chief of Staff.—[Vacant].

ADMINISTRATIVE LAW JUDGE

Techworld, 800 K Street NW Suite 4148 20001

Chief Administrative Law Judge.—John N. Vittone (acting), 633–0341.

BENEFITS REVIEW BOARD

200 Constitution Avenue NW Room N5101 20210

Chair.—Betty Jean Hall, 633–7501.

EMPLOYEES COMPENSATION APPEALS BOARD

Reporters Building, 300 Seventh Street SW 20210

Chairman.—Michael J. Walsh, 401–8600.

OFFICE OF SMALL BUSINESS PROGRAMS

Frances Perkins Building, Room C2318

Director.—June M. Robinson, 219–9148.

ADMINISTRATIVE REVIEW BOARD

Frances Perkins Building, Room S4309

Executive Director.—David A. O'Brien (acting), 219–9039.
Deputy Director.—[Vacant], 219–9728.

WAGE APPEALS BOARD AND BOARD OF SERVICE CONTRACT APPEALS

Frances Perkins Building, Room N1651, phone 219–9039

Chair.—David A. O'Brien.
Members: Joyce D. Miller (alternate); Karl J. Sandstrom.
Executive Secretary.—Gerald F. Krizan.
Staff Assistant.—Ernestine Battle.

ASSISTANT SECRETARY FOR CONGRESSIONAL AND INTERGOVERNMENTAL AFFAIRS

Frances Perkins Building, Room S2018, phone 219–4692

Assistant Secretary.—Geri D. Palast.
Special Assistants: Jeffrey Cohen; Todd Flournoy.
Staff Assistant.—[Vacant].
Deputy Assistant Secretaries: Darla J. Letourneau; Mary Ann Richardson, Room S1325, 219–6141.
Legislative Officer: [Vacant].
Legislative Assistant.—[Vacant].
Staff Assistant.—Janice Williams.
Administrative Officer.—Joycelyn J. Daniels, Room S1318, 219–6141.

OFFICE OF INTERGOVERNMENTAL AFFAIRS

Associate Director.—Nancy Kirshner, Room S1325, 219–6141.
Intergovernmental Officers: Dan Chavez; Alina Walker.
Intergovernmental Assistants: Edward M. Flynn; Liz S. Gonchar; Timothy E. Jennings.

EMPLOYMENT STANDARDS

Associate Director.—Ross Eisenbrey, Room S1325, 219–6141.
Legislative Officers: Rich Fiesta; Angela Jackson.

EMPLOYMENT AND TRAINING

Associate Assistant Secretary.—Richard Hobbie, Room S1325, 219–6141.
Associate Director.—Terri G. Bergman.
Legislative Officer.—William Kamela.
Legislative Assistant: Tim Fuller.

WORKER-MANAGEMENT, SAFETY AND HEALTH, AND PENSIONS

Associate Director.—Ross Eisenbrey, Room S1325, 219–6141.
Legislative Officer: Kevin M. Maroney.

HEALTH CARE REFORM

Associate Directors.—Mary Ann Richardson, Kevin Maroney, Room S1325, 219–6141.

REGIONAL OFFICES

Region I.—Connecticut, Maine, Massachusetts, New Hampshire, Rhode Island, Vermont.
Secretary's Representative.—Thomas Davis, One Congress Street, Boston MA 02114–2023, (617) 565–2281.
Deputy Assistant Secretary.—Sean King.

Region II.—New York, New Jersey, Puerto Rico, Virgin Islands.
Secretary's Representative.—Hulbert James, 201 Varick Street, Suite 605, New York NY 10014–4811, (212) 337–2387.

Region III.—Pennsylvania, Delaware, District of Columbia, Maryland, Virginia, West Virginia.
Secretary's Representative.—Patricia Halpin-Murphy, 3535 Market Street, Room 14–120, Philadelphia PA 19104–3309, (215) 596–1116.

Region IV.—Alabama, Georgia, Florida, Kentucky, Mississippi, North Carolina, South Carolina, Tennessee.
Secretary's Representative.—Barbara Kelly, 61 Forsyth SW, Atlanta GA 30303, (404) 562–2000.

Region V.—Illinois, Indiana, Michigan, Minnesota, Ohio, Wisconsin.
Secretary's Representative.—Lois O'Keefe, 230 South Dearborn Street, Suite 3810, Chicago IL 60604, (312) 353–4703.

Region VI.—Texas, Arkansas, Louisiana, New Mexico, Oklahoma.
Secretary's Representative.—[Vacant], Federal Building, Room 735, 525 Griffin Street, Dallas TX 75202, (214) 767–6807.

Region VII.—Iowa, Kansas, Nebraska, Missouri.
Secretary's Representative.—[Vacant], Room 2508, 911 Walnut Street, Kansas City MO 64106, (816) 426–6371.

Region VIII.—Colorado, Montana, North Dakota, South Dakota, Wyoming.
Secretary's Representative.—[Vacant], Federal Building, Room 14561, 1961 Stout Street, Denver CO 80294, (303) 844–4131.

Region IX.—California, Hawaii, Nevada, Arizona, Guam.
Secretary's Representative.—Rick Sawyer, 71 Stevenson Street, Suite 1035, San Francisco CA 94119–3766, (415) 744–6596.

Region X.—Alaska, Idaho, Oregon, Washington.
Secretary's Representative.—Patricia Stell, 1111 Third Avenue, Suite 920, Seattle WA 98101, (206) 553–0574.

ASSISTANT SECRETARY FOR PUBLIC AFFAIRS
Frances Perkins Building, Room S2018, phone 219–5502

Assistant Secretary.—Susan King.
Deputy Assistant Secretaries: Howard Waddell; Nancy Cottey, 219–8211.

REGIONAL OFFICES

Region I.—Connecticut, Maine, Massachusetts, New Hampshire, Rhode Island, Vermont.
Public Affairs Director.—John Chavez, 1 Congress Street, 11th Floor, Boston MA 02114–2023, (617) 565–2072.

Region II.—New York, New Jersey, Puerto Rico, Virgin Islands.
Public Affairs Director.—Chester Fultz, Room 605, 201 Varick Street, New York NY 10014–4811, (212) 337–2319.

Region III.—Delaware, District of Columbia, Maryland, Pennsylvania, Virginia, West Virginia.
Public Affairs Director.—Kate Dugan, Room 14120, 3535 Market Street, Philadelphia PA 19104, (215) 596–1139.

Region IV.—Alabama, Georgia, Florida, Kentucky, Mississippi, North Carolina, South Carolina, Tennessee.
Public Affairs Director.—Dan Fuqua, 61 Forsyth SW, Atlanta GA 30303, (404) 562–2078.

Region V.—Illinois, Indiana, Michigan, Minnesota, Ohio, Wisconsin.
Public Affairs Director.—Brad Mitchell, Room 3192, 230 South Dearborn Street, Chicago IL 60604, (312) 353–6976.

Region VI.—Arkansas, Louisiana, New Mexico, Oklahoma, Texas.
Public Affairs Director.—Sherrie Morna, Room 734, 525 Griffin Street, Dallas TX 75202, (214) 767–4777.

Region VII.—Iowa, Kansas, Nebraska, Missouri.
Public Affairs Director.—Patrick Hand, Room 2509, City Center Square, 11000 Main Street, Kansas City MO 64105, (816) 426–5481.

Region VIII.—Colorado, Montana, North Dakota, South Dakota, Utah, Wyoming.
Public Affairs Director.—Ernest E. Sanchez, Federal Building, Room 1468, 1961 Stout Street, Denver CO 80294, (303) 391–6981.

Region IX.—Arizona, California, Guam, Hawaii, Nevada.
Public Affairs Director.—Joe Kirkbride, Suite 1035, 71 Stevenson Street, San Francisco CA 94119–3766, (415) 744–6675.

Region X.—Alaska, Idaho, Oregon, Washington.
Public Affairs Director.—Mike Shimizu, Building B, Room 805, 1111 Third Avenue, Seattle WA 98101, (206) 553–7620.

BUREAU OF INTERNATIONAL LABOR AFFAIRS

Frances Perkins Building, Room S2235, phone 219–6043

Deputy Under Secretary.—Andrew Samet (acting).
Associate Deputy Under Secretary.—Andrew J. Samet.
Special Assistants: Gabriela Araujo; Todd Howe.
Director, Office of—
Foreign Relations.—John Ferch, 219–7631.
International Economic Affairs.—Jorge Perez-Lopez, 219–7597.
International Organization.—Charles Spring, 219–7682.
Management, Administration and Planning.—Ronald Van Helden (acting), 219–6274.

INSPECTOR GENERAL

Frances Perkins Building, Room S1303, phone 219–6191

Inspector General.—Charles C. Masten, 219–7296.
Deputy Inspector General.—Patricia Dalton.
Assistant Inspector General for—
Audit.—Joseph E. Fisch, Room S5022.
Investigations.—F.M. Broadaway, Room S5512, 357–0492.
Management and Counsel.—Sylvia T. Horowitz, Room S1305, 219–4930.
Freedom of Information and Privacy Act Coordinator.—Pamela Davis, Room S1305, 219–4930.

WOMEN'S BUREAU

Frances Perkins Building, Room S3002, phone 219–6611

Director.—Ida Castro (acting).
Chief, Office of—
Administrative Management.—Wynette Wilson (acting), Room S3305, 219–6606.
Policy Analysis and Information.—Collis N. Phillips, Room S3311, 219–6627.
Programs and Technical Assistance.—Roberta V. McKay, Room S3317, 219–6626.

PENSION AND WELFARE BENEFITS ADMINISTRATION

Frances Perkins Building, Room S2524, phone 219–8233, fax 219–5526

Assistant Secretary.—E. Olena Berg.
Deputy Assistant Secretary for Policy.—Meredith Miller.
Deputy Assistant Secretary.—Alan D. Lebowitz, Room N5677, 219–9048.
Executive Assistant to the Deputy Assistant Secretary.—Sue Ugelow, 219–9048.
Confidential Assistant.—Valerie Washington.
Senior Director for Policy and Legislative Analysis.—Morton Klevan, Room N5677, 219–9044.
Director of—
Program, Planning, Evaluation and Management.—Brian C. McDonnell, Room N–5668, 219–6471.
Chief Accountant.—Ian Dingwall, Room N5508, 219–8818.
Enforcement.—Charles Lerner, Room N5702, 219–8840.
Exemption Determinations.—Ivan L. Strasfeld, Room N5649, 219–8194.
Information Management.—Mervyn A. Schwedt, Room N5459, 219–5514.
Program Services.—Sharon Watson, Room N5625, 219–6999.
Regulations and Interpretations.—Robert Doyle, Room N5669, 219–4504.
Research and Economic Analysis.—Richard Hinz, Room N5718, 219–4505.

EMPLOYMENT STANDARDS ADMINISTRATION

Frances Perkins Building, Room S2321, phone 219–6191

Assistant Secretary.—Bernard E. Anderson.
Deputy Assistant Secretary for Employment Standards.—Gene Karp.
Coordinator, Equal Employment Opportunity Unit.—Carvin Cook, 219–8741.
Wage and Hour Administrator.—John R. Fraser (acting), 219–8305.
Deputy Administrators: [Vacant], John R. Fraser, 219–8305.

Assistant Administrator, Office of—

Policy, Planning and Review.—Charles E. Pugh, 219–5409.

Program Operations.—William W. Gross (acting), 219–8353.

Deputy Assistant Secretary for Federal Contract Compliance Programs.—Shirley J. Wilcher, 219–9475.

Deputy Director.—Joe Kennedy, 219–9476.

Deputy Assistant Secretary for Workers' Compensation Programs.—Shelby Hallmark (acting), 219–7503.

Deputy Director.—Shelby Hallmark, 219–7503.

Director, Division of Planning, Policy and Standards.—Diane B. Svenonius, 219–7491.

Director for—

Coal Mine Worker's Compensation Programs.—James L. DeMarce, 219–6692.

Federal Employees' Compensation Programs.—Thomas M. Markey, 219–7552.

OFFICE OF THE ASSISTANT SECRETARY FOR ADMINISTRATION AND MANAGEMENT

Frances Perkins Building, Room S2514, phone 219–9086

Assistant Secretary.—Patricia W. Lattimore (acting).

Deputy Assistant Secretary.—Patricia W. Lattimore, 219–9088.

Director, Civil Rights Center.—Annabelle T. Lockhart, Room N4123, 219–8927.

Chief, Office of—

Compliance Assistance and Planning.—Lynne Pratico, 219–8927.

Counseling, Mediation and Evaluation.—[Vacant], 219–6362.

Enforcement.—Gregory T. Shaw, 219–7026.

Director, Information Technology Center.—[Vacant], Room N1301, 219–8343.

Director, Office of—

Technical Support.—Greg Storey, 219–6183.

Customized Software Center.—Thomas Byrne, 219–1916.

Electronic Publication and Workgroup Systems Center.—Reggie Moore, 219–7418.

Computer Support and Training Center.—Shirley Malia, 219–9228.

Director, Business Operations Center.—Thomas K. Delaney, 219–7928.

Director, Office of—

Administrative Services Center.—[Vacant], Room S1524, 219–6414.

Finance Center.—George B. Baily, Room S5526, 219–7383.

Financial Advocate.—Adele Paskowski, Room S5526, 219–7801.

Procurement Services.—Daniel Murphy, Room S5220, 219–4631.

Acquisition Advocate.—Melvin Goldberg, Room S1522, 219–9174.

Office of Cost Determination.—Steve Garfinkel, Room S1506, 219–8391.

Office of Business Systems Service.—Michelle Ouellet, Room S1522, 219–8904.

Director, Human Resources Center.—Larry K. Goodwin, Room C5526, 219–6551.

Deputy Director.—Tali Stepp, 219–9191.

Director, Office of—

Work and Family Center.—[Vacant].

Training and Development Center.—Milton Blount, Jr., Room N2305, 219–7401.

Career Management and Assessment Center.—Kim Green, Room N5416, 219–0118.

Labor Management Partnership Center.—Jerry Lelchook, Room N5476, 219–6521.

Personnel Services and Human Resources Analysis and Innovation.—Gary Saturen, C5516, 219–6677.

Director of Office of Safety and Health.—Frederick A. Drayton, Room S2220F, 219–6687.

Safety Services Team.—Helen Li, Room S3217, 219–6188.

Workers' Compensation and Substance Control Team.—Sam DeGenova, Room N1301, 219–6687.

Director, Office of—

Program Coordination and Information Center.—Tali Stepp, 219–6414.

Reinvention Center.—Mark Pelofky, Room N2609, 219–7357.

Executive Services Center.—Kathy Fox, 219–9090.

ASSISTANT SECRETARY FOR POLICY AND BUDGET

Frances Perkins Building, Room S2312, phone 219–6181

Assistant Secretary.—Seth Harris (acting).

Deputy Assistant Secretary.—Roland G. Droitsch, 219–9058.

Associate Deputy Assistant Secretary.—[Vacant], 219–6197.

Director of the Office of Budget.—James E. McMullen, 219–6888.

OFFICE OF THE SOLICITOR

Frances Perkins Building, phone 219–7675

Solicitor.—J. Davitt McAteer (acting).
Confidential Assistant.—Beverly Saunders.
Executive Assistant.—[Vacant], Room S2314, 219–7705.
Special Assistants: Craig W. Hukill, 219–7701; Nancy Rooney, 219–7705.
Deputy Solicitor for—
National Operations.—Oliver B. Quinn, 219–7675.
Regional Operations.—Ronald G. Whiting, 219–7705.
Planning and Coordination.—Judith E. Kramer, 219–7705.

OFFICE OF ADMINISTRATION, MANAGEMENT AND LITIGATION SUPPORT

Director.—Harvey Lewis, Room N2414, 219–6863.
Deputy Director.—Wesley L. Curl.
Financial Managers: Alice Rapport; Cathy Sullivan, Room N2427, 219–5301.
Personnel Officer.—Patricia Friesz, Room N2431, 219–5374.
EEO/Employee Relations.—Rebecca Miller, Room N2431, 219–5276.
Litigation Support.—Raymond Kukulski, Room N2414, 219–6874.
Automation Information Services.—Mary Cline-Buso, Room N2414, 219–6874.

DIVISION OF BLACK LUNG BENEFITS

Associate Solicitor.—Donald S. Shire, Room N2605, 219–4435.
Deputy Associate Solicitor.—Rae Ellen Frank James, 219–4422.
Counsel for—
Administrative Litigation and Legal Advice: Michael J. Rutledge, 219–4419; Richard A. Sied, 219–4402.
Appellate Litigation: Christian Barber; Patricia M. Nece, 219–4417.
Enforcement.—Michael J. Denney, 219–4418.

DIVISION OF CIVIL RIGHTS

Associate Solicitor.—James D. Henry, Room N246, 219–8286.
Deputy Associate Solicitor.—Gary Buff, 219–8293.
Counsel for—
Interpretations and Advice.—Suzan Chastain, 219–8000.
Litigation: William Alexander; Heidi Dalzell-Finger, 219–8000.
Senior Program Attorney.—Penny Dash, 219–8000.
Senior Trial Attorneys: Richard Gilman; Debra A. Millenson, 219–8262.

DIVISION OF EMPLOYEE BENEFITS

Associate Solicitor.—Carol A. DeDeo, Room S4325, 219–4405.
Deputy Associate Solicitor.—[Vacant].
Counsel for—
Claims.—Jeffrey Nesvet, 219–5465.
FECA.—Daniel T. Franklin, 219–4405.
Longshore: Janet Dunlop, 219–4465; Samuel Oshinsky, 219–4405.
Senior Trial Attorney.—Joshua T. Gillelan II, 219–5465.

EMPLOYMENT AND TRAINING LEGAL SERVICES

Associate Solicitor.—Charles D. Raymond, Room N2101, 219–7754.
Deputy Associate Solicitor.—Jonathan H. Waxman, 219–7758.
Counsel for Litigation.—Harry L. Sheinfeld, 219–7836.
Counsel for—
Employment and Immigration Programs.—Bruce W. Alter, 219–7857.
Job Training Program.—A. Robert Pfeffer, 219–7857.
Unemployment Compensation.—Michael Apfelbaum, 219–7874.

FAIR LABOR STANDARDS

Associate Solicitor.—Monica Gallagher, Room N2716, 219–7570.
Deputy Associate Solicitor.—Gail V. Coleman, 219–7577.
Counsel for—
Appellate Litigation.—William J. Stone, 219–7584.
Employment Standards.—Linda Jan S. Pack, 219–7579.
Legal Advice.—Gregory B. Taylor, 219–7626.
Trial Litigation.—Douglas J. Davidson, 219–7620.
Senior Trial Attorney.—Jonathan Kronheim, 219–7550.

DIVISION OF LABOR MANAGEMENT LAWS

Associate Solicitor.—John F. Depenbrock, Room N2475, 219–8607.
Deputy Associate Solicitor.—Barton S. Widom.
Counsel for—
International Affairs/Opinions: Dennis Paquette, 219–8633; Susan M. Webman, 219–8627.
Litigation.—Helene Boetticher, 219–8534.
Attorney Adviser.—Donald D. Carter, 219–8631.

DIVISION OF LEGISLATION AND LEGAL COUNSEL

Associate Solicitor.—Robert A. Shapiro, Room N2428, 219–8201.
Deputy Associate Solicitor.—Bruce Cohen.
Counsel for—
Administrative Law: [Vacant], 219–8065; Miriam Miller, 219–8188.
Ethics.—David Apol, 219–8065.
Labor Relations.—Mark Maxin, 219–8088.
Legislative Reports.—Richard Crone, 219–8065.
Attorney Adviser.—Seth Zinman, 219–8066.

DIVISION OF MINE SAFETY AND HEALTH

Ballston Towers No. 3, 4015 Wilson Boulevard, Arlington VA 22203

Associate Solicitor.—Edward P. Clair, Room 420, (703) 235–1151.
Deputy Associate Solicitor.—Thomas A. Mascolino.
Counsel for—
Appellate Litigation.—W. Christian Schumann, Room 426, (703) 235–1165.
Coal Standards and Advice.—M. Katherine Alejandro, Room 430, (703) 235-1157.
Metal/Non-Metal Standards and Advice.—Deborah K. Green, Room 428, (703) 235–1161.
Trial Litigation.—Douglas White, Room 414, (703) 235–1153.

DIVISION OF OCCUPATIONAL SAFETY AND HEALTH

Associate Solicitor.—Joseph M. Woodward, Room S4004, 219–7723.
Deputy Associate Solicitor.—Donald G. Shalhou, 219–7727.
Counsel for—
Appellate Litigation: Ann Rosenthal, 219–7718; Barbara Werthmann, 219-6823.
General Legal Advice.—Robert Swain, 219–6811.
Health Standards.—Daniel Jacoby, 219–7711.
Safety Standards.—George Henschel, 219–6700.
Trial and OSHRC Litigation.—Daniel Mick, 219–6822.
Senior Trial Attorneys: Kenneth Hellman, 219–6801; Bruce F. Justh, 219–7718.
General Attorneys: Charles P. Gordon; Richard Pfeffer, 219–7711.

DIVISION OF PLAN BENEFITS SECURITY

Associate Solicitor.—Marc I. Machiz, Room N4611, 219–8634.
Deputy Associate Solicitor.—Sherwin Kaplan.
Counsel for—
Decentralized and Special Litigation.—Karen Handorf, 219–7931.
Fiduciary Litigation.—Risa Sandler.

General Litigation.—Leslie Perlmann, 219–6928.
Regulation.—William Taylor, 219–9590.
Senior Trial Attorneys: Daniel McQuire; Timothy Nauser; William Scott; William P. Tedesco, 219–8642; William Zuckerman, 219–8637.

DIVISION OF SPECIAL APPELLATE AND SUPREME COURT LITIGATION

Associate Solicitor.—Allen H. Feldman, Room N2700, 219–8237.
Deputy Associate Solicitor.—Steven J. Mandel, 219–8235.
Counsel for Appellate Litigation.—Nathaniel I. Spiller, 219–8247.
Senior Trial Attorneys: Mark S. Flynn; Edward D. Sieger, 219–8247.

OCCUPATIONAL SAFETY AND HEALTH ADMINISTRATION

Frances Perkins Building, Room S2315, phone 219–6091

Assistant Secretary.—Gregory Watchman (acting).
Deputy Assistant Secretaries: Emily Sheketoff; James W. Stanley; Greg Walchman.
Director, Office of—
Construction and Engineering.—Russell B. Swanson, 219–8644.
Field Programs.—Jimmy Roberts (acting), 219–7725.
Information and Consumer Affairs.—Richard Liblong, 219–8148.
Special Management Programs.—Conchita M. Baylor (acting), 219–8985.
Statistics.—Stephen A. Newell, 219–6463.
Director of—
Administrative Programs.—David C. Zeigler, 219–8576.
Health Standards.—John F. Martonik, 219–7075.
Compliance Programs.—John B. Miles, Jr., 219–9308.
Federal-State Operations.—Paula O. White, 219–7251.
Policy.—Michael A. Silverstein, 219–8021.
Safety Standards Programs.—Thomas Seymore, 219–8063.
Technical Support.—Charles E. Adkins.

EMPLOYMENT AND TRAINING ADMINISTRATION

Frances Perkins Building, Room S2307, phone 219–6050

Assistant Secretary.—Raymond Uhalde (acting).
Deputy Assistant Secretaries: John M. Robinson; Raymond Uhalde.
Chief of Staff.—Stephanie Powers.
Director, Public Affairs.—Bonnie Friedman, Room N4700, 219–6871.
Associate Assistant Secretary for Job Training Programs.—[Vacant], Room N4457, 219–6236.
Director, Office of—
Employment and Training Program.—[Vacant], Room N4666, 219–5580.
Job Corps.—Mary Silva, Room N4508, 219–8550.
Special Targeted Programs.—Paul Mayrand, Room N4641, 219–5585.
Administrator, Office of Financial and Administrative Management.—Bryan T. Keilty, Room N4671, 219–5690.
Director, Office of—
Comptroller.—David T. Duncan, Room S5207, 219–6760.
Grants and Contract Management.—Edward A. Tomchick, Room N4671, 219–5690.
Information Resources Management.—Robert A. Coyer, Room S5207, 219–5741.
Management Support.—Joseph T. Paslawski, Room N4671, 219–5690.
Strategic Planning and Policy Development.—Gerr I. Fiala, Room N5637, 219–8659.
Chief, Division of—
Performance Management and Evaluation.—Karen Greene, Room N5629, 219–8680.
Policy, Legislation and Dissemination.—Gerri Fiala, Room N5637, 219–8659.
Research and Program Demonstration.—Alvin Lafayette Grisby, Room N5637, 219–5677.
Work-Based Learning.—Barbara Farmer, Room N4649, 219–6540.
Director for—
Trade Adjustment Assistance.—Victor Trunzo, Room C4318, 219–5555.
Worker Retraining and Adjustment Programs: Eric Johnson; Shirley Smith, Room N5426, 219–5577.
Regional Management.—Bob Kenyon (acting), Room N5309, 219–5585.

Director for—
Unemployment Insurance.—Grace Kilban, Room S4231, 219–7831.
U.S. Employment Service.—John R. Beverly III, Room N4470, 219–5257.
Bureau of Apprenticeship and Training.—Anthony Swoope, Room N4649, 219–5921.

MINE SAFETY AND HEALTH ADMINISTRATION

4015 Wilson Boulevard, Arlington VA 22203, phone (703) 235–1385, fax 235–1563

Assistant Secretary.—J. Davitt McAteer.
Deputy Assistant Secretaries: Andrea M. Hricko, 235–2625; Edward C. Hugler, 235–2600.
Chief, Office of—
Congressional and Legislative Affairs.—Sylvia Milanese (acting), 235–1392.
Information and Public Affairs.—Wayne E. Veneman, 235–1452.
Standards, Regulations and Variances.—Patricia W. Silvey, 235–1910.
Administrator for—
Coal Mine Safety and Health.—Marvin W. Nichols, Jr., 235–9423.
Metal and Nonmetal Mine Safety and Health.—Vernon R. Gomez, 235–1565.

VETERANS' EMPLOYMENT AND TRAINING SERVICE

Frances Perkins Building, Room S1313, phone 219–9116

Assistant Secretary.—Preston M. Taylor, Jr.
Deputy Assistant Secretary.—Al Borrego.
Executive Assistant.—Charles Lee.
Director, Office of—
Field Operations.—Jeffrey C. Crandell, 219–9105.
Information Management and Budget.—Hary P. Puente-Duany.
Veterans' Employment, Reemployment, and Training.—Jeffrey C. Crandell (acting).

BUREAU OF LABOR STATISTICS

Postal Square Building, Suite 4040, 2 Massachusetts Avenue NE 20212

phone 606–6623, fax 606–6610

Commissioner.—Katherine G. Abraham, Suite 4040, 606–7800.
Deputy Commissioner, Office of Administration and Internal Operations.—William G. Barron, 606–7802.
Quality and Information of Management Staff.—William D. Eisenberg, Suite 4130, 606–6304.
Assistant Commissioner, Office of—
Administration—Daniel J. Lacey, Suite 4060, 606–7777.
Technology and Survey Processing.—Carl J. Lowe, Suite 5025, 606–7600
Director of—
Survey Processing.—John D. Sinks, Suite 5025, 606–7606.
Technology and Computing Services.—Arnold Bresnick, Suite 5015, 606–7603.

ASSOCIATE COMMISSIONER

Compensation and Working Conditions.—Kimberly D. Zieschang, Suite 4130, 606–6302.
Deputy Associate Commissioner.—[Vacant].
Assistant Commissioner, Office of—
Compensation Levels and Trends.—Kathleen M. MacDonald, Suite 4130, 606–6302.
Safety, Health, and Working Conditions.—[Vacant], Suite 4130, 606–6304.
Employment Projection.—Ronald E. Kutscher, Suite 2135, 606–5900.
Employment and Unemployment Statistics.—Thomas J. Plewes, Suite 4925, 606–6400.
Deputy Associate Commissioner.—[Vacant].
Assistant Commissioner, Office of—
Current Employment Analysis.—John E. Bregger, Suite 4675, 606–6388.
Federal/State Programs.—[Vacant], Suite 4840, 606–6500.
Field Operations.—Laura B. King, Suite 935, 606–5800.
Prices and Living Conditions.—Kenneth V. Dalton, Suite 3120, 606–6960.
Deputy Associate Commissioner.—[Vacant].

Assistant Commissioner, Office of—
Consumer Prices and Price Indexes.—Paul Armknecht, Suite 3130, 606–6950.
Industrial Prices and Price Indexes.—John M. Galvin, S3840, 606–7700.
Industrial Price Programs.—Katrian W. Reut, Suite 3955, 606–7100.
Productivity and Technology.—Edwin R. Dean, Suite 2150, 606–5600.
Publications.—Deborah P. Klein, Suite 4915, 606–7398.
Research and Evaluation.—Wesley L. Schaible, Suite 4080, 606–7400.
Assistant Commissioner, Office of—
Economic Research.—Marilyn E. Manser, Suite 4915, 606–7398.
Survey Methods Research.—Cathryn S. Dippo, Suite 4925, 606–7372.

U.S. NATIONAL ADMINISTRATIVE OFFICE

Frances Perkins Building, Room C4327

Secretary of the U.S. National Administrative Office.—Irasema Garza, 501–6653.
Chief Financial Officer.—Edmondo Gonzales, 219–6891.
Deputy Chief Financial Officer.—Ken Breonahon, 219–6891.
Special Assistant.—Harry Echols, 219–6891.
Director, Office of—
Financial Integrity.—William T. Furman, 219–6891.
Accounting and Payment Services.—Norman Perkins (acting), 219–8314.
Financial Systems.—Fred Danzig, 219–4881.
Deputy Assistant Secretary.—Charles Richards, Room S2203, 219–6045.
Special Assistant.—Toni Riley Jones, Room N5402, 219–6098.
Statutory Programs.—Kelley Andrews, Room N5419, 219–4473.
Labor-Management Programs: Ronald Glass, Room N5402, 219–6098; Edward Onanian, Room N5402, 219–6487; Philip Riccobono, Room N5402, 219–6098.
Deputy Assistant Secretary.—John Kotch (acting), Room S2203, 219–7337.
Division of Enforcement.—Lary F. Yud, 219–7353.
Chief, Section of Reports and Disclosure.—Howard Campbell (acting), Room N5616, 219–7353.
Chief, Division of—
Interpretations and Standards.—Kay Oshel, Room N5605, 219–7373.
Liaison, Compliance and Training.—Joseph Fuchs (acting), Room N5605, 219–7320.
Statutory Programs.—Ron Glass, 219–4473.

PRESIDENT'S COMMITTEE ON EMPLOYMENT OF PEOPLE WITH DISABILITIES

331 F Street NW, Washington, DC 20004–1107

phone (202) 376–6200, fax (202) 376–6868, TDD (202) 376–6205

Chairman.—Tony Coelho, Coelho Associates, LLC (Limited Liability Company), 1325 Avenue of the Americas, 26th Floor, New York NY 10019, (212) 424–2610, fax (212) 424–2660.
Vice Chairs:
Ronald W. Drach, National Director of Employment, Disabled American Veterans, 807 Maine Avenue SW, Washington DC 20024, (202) 554–3501, fax 554–3581.
Neil Jacobson, Vice President, Wells Fargo Bank, 201 Third Street, San Francisco CA 94103, (415) 477–7778, fax (415) 477–7721.
Dr. I. King Jordan, President, Gallaudet University, 800 Florida Avenue NE, Washington DC 20002–3695, (202) 651–5005, fax (202) 651–5508.
Karen L. Meyer, President, Karen L. Meyer & Associates, 954 West Montana Street, Chicago IL 60614, (773) 528–8533, TDD (773) 477–8411, fax (773) 477–8422.
Lenore Miller, President, Retail, Wholesale and Department Store Union, 30 East 29th Street, New York NY 10016, (212) 684–5300, fax (212) 779–2809.
Dr. Sylvia Walker, Director, Howard University Research and Training Center, 2900 Van Ness Street NW, Washington DC 20008, (202) 806–8086, TDD (202) 244–7628, fax (202) 806–8148.
Executive Director.—John Lancaster.
Deputy Executive Director.—Paul M. Meyer.

DEPARTMENT OF STATE

2201 C Street NW 20520, phone 647–4000

MADELEINE KORBEL ALBRIGHT, became the 64th Secretary of State on January 23, 1997, the first female Secretary of State and highest ranking woman in the U.S. government; B.A., Wellesley with honors in Political Science; studied at the School of Advanced International Studies at Johns Hopkins University; received Certified from the Russian Institute at Columbia University; Masters and Doctorate from the Department of Public Law and Government, Columbia University; fluent in French and Czech, with good speaking and reading abilities in Russian and Polish; research professor of international affairs and director of Women in Foreign Service Program, Georgetown University School of Foreign Service; taught undergraduate and graduate courses in international affairs, U.S. foreign policy, Russian foreign policy, and central and eastern European polices; United States permanent representative to the United Nations (presenting her credentials at the UN on February 6, 1993); president, Center for National Policy; awarded fellowship, Woodrow Wilson International Center for scholars at the Smithsonian Institute, 1981–82; senior fellow, Soviet and eastern European affairs at the Center for Strategic and International Studies; staff member on the National Security Council and White House staff member, 1978–82; senior fellow, Soviet and eastern European affairs at the Center for Strategic and International Studies; staff member on the National Security Council and White House staff member, 1978–81; chief legislative assistant for Senator Edmund S. Muskie, 1976–78; selected writing: Poland, the Role of the Press in Political Change (New York; Praeger with the Center for Strategic and International Studies, Georgetown University, 1983; The Role of the Press in Political Change: Czechoslovakia 1968 (Ph.D. Dissertation, Columbia University 1976); and The Soviet Diplomatic Service: Profile of an Elite (Master's Thesis, Columbia University 1968); three daughters.

OFFICE OF THE SECRETARY

Secretary of State.—Madeleine K. Albright, 647–5291.
Executive Assistant.—Elaine Shocas, 647–5548.

OFFICE OF THE DEPUTY SECRETARY

Deputy Secretary of State.—Strobe Talbott, Room 7220, 647–8636.
Executive Assistant.—Eric Edelman, 647–8931.

EXECUTIVE SECRETARIAT

Special Assistant and Executive Secretary.—William Burns, Room 7224, 647–5301.
Deputy Executive Secretaries: John Campbell, 647–5302; Alex Wolff, 647–8448; Gretchen Welch, 647–6548.

AMBASSADORS AT LARGE

Ambassador at Large for—
Senior Coordinator for the New Independent States.—James F. Collins, Room 7531, 647–3566.
Burdensharing.—Ray L. Caldwell, Room 7815, 647–2277.
Coordinator, Counter-Terrorism.—Philip C. Wilcox, Jr., Room 2507, 647–9892.

POLICY PLANNING STAFF

Director.—James B. Steinberg, Room 7311, 647–2372.
Deputy Director.—Alan Romberg, Room 7311, 647–2972.

UNDER SECRETARY FOR POLITICAL AFFAIRS

Under Secretary.—Thomas Pickering, Room 7240, 647–2471.
Executive Assistant.—David L. Goldwyn, 647–1598.

UNDER SECRETARY FOR ECONOMIC AND AGRICULTURAL AFFAIRS

Under Secretary.—Joan E. Spero, Room 7256, 647–7575.
Senior Advisor.—John Mallot, Room 7256, 647–7688.

UNDER SECRETARY FOR INTERNATIONAL SECURITY AFFAIRS

Under Secretary.—Lynn E. Davis, Room 7208, 647–1049.
Executive Assistant.—Edward O'Donnell, Room 7210, 647–1749.

UNDER SECRETARY FOR GLOBAL AFFAIRS

Under Secretary.—Timothy E. Wirth, Room 7250, 647–6240.
Executive Assistant.—David Harwood, 647–6240.

UNDER SECRETARY FOR MANAGEMENT

Under Secretary.—Patrick Kennedy (acting), 647–1500.

BUREAUS

AFRICAN AFFAIRS

Assistant Secretary.—George E. Moose, Room 6234–A, 647–4440.
Deputy Assistant Secretaries.—Regina Brown, 647–1818; Judith Johnson, 647–4485; William Twaddell, 647–4493.

EAST ASIAN AND PACIFIC AFFAIRS

Assistant Secretary.—Charles Kartman (acting), Room 6205, 647–9596.
Deputy Assistant Secretaries: Jeffrey Bader, 647–6910; Aurelia Brazeal, 647–6904.

EUROPEAN AND CANADIAN AFFAIRS

Assistant Secretary.—John C. Kornblum, Room 6228, 647–9626.
Deputy Assistant Secretaries: E. Anthony Wayne, 647–6402; Marshall Adair, 647–1126.

INTER-AMERICAN AFFAIRS

Assistant Secretary.—Jeffrey Davidow, Room 6263, 647–5780.
Deputy Assistant Secretaries: Edward Casey, 647–6754; Anne Patterson, 647–8369; John Hamilton, 647–8562; Peter Romero, 647–8387.

NEAR-EASTERN AFFAIRS

Assistant Secretary.—Robert H. Pelletreau, Room 6242, 647–7209.
Deputy Assistant Secretaries.—Art Hughes, 647–7166; Toni Verstandig, 647–7170; David Welch, 647–7207.

SOUTH ASIAN AFFAIRS

Assistant Secretary.—Robin L. Raphael, Room 6254, 736–4325.
Deputy Assistant Secretary.—Gibson Campher, 736–4328.
Senior Advisor.—Stephen A. Rickard, 736–4331.

ADMINISTRATION

Assistant Secretary.—Patrick F. Kennedy, Room 6330, 647–1492.
Procurement Executive.—Lloyd W. Pratsch, Room 603, 1701 North Ft. Meyer Drive Arlington VA 22209, (703) 516–1680.
Deputy Assistant Secretaries: Joseph Lake, Room 4428, 647–2889; Genie Norris, Room 1417, 647–1638; Joseph Sikes, Room 1309, 1701 North Ft. Meyer Drive Arlington VA 22209, (703) 875–6361.

CONSULAR AFFAIRS

Assistant Secretary.—Mary A. Ryan, Room 6811, 647–9576.
Deputy Assistant Secretaries: Donna Hamilton, Ruth Davis 647–9577.

DEMOCRACY, HUMAN RIGHTS AND LABOR

Assistant Secretary.—John H.F. Shattuck, Room 7802, 647–2126.
Deputy Assistant Secretaries: Catharin E. Dalpino, 647–1180; Steven Coffey, 647–2590; Gare Smith, 647–1780.

DIPLOMATIC SECURITY

Assistant Secretary.—Eric Boswell, Room 6316, 647-6290.
Deputy Assistant Secretaries: William D. Clarke, 663–0538; Gregorie Bujac, SA–10, 663–0473.

DIRECTOR GENERAL OF THE FOREIGN SERVICE AND DIRECTOR OF PERSONNEL

Director General.—Anthony Quainton, Room 6218, 647–9898.
Deputy Assistant Secretaries: Jennifer C. Ward, 647–9438; Alex de la Garza, 647–5152, Ralph Frank, 647–5942.

ECONOMIC AND BUSINESS AFFAIRS

Assistant Secretary.—Alan Larson, Room 6828, 647–7971.
Deputy Assistant Secretaries: William Ramsay, 647–1498; Barbara Griffiths, 647–9496; Vonya McCann, 647–5832; Shaun Donnelly, 647–2532; Joel Spiro, 647–4045.

EQUAL EMPLOYMENT OPPORTUNITY AND CIVIL RIGHTS

Deputy Assistant Secretary.—Deidre Davis, Room 4216, 647-9294.
Associate Director.—Thomas Jefferson, Jr., 647-9295.

FINANCE AND MANAGEMENT POLICY

Chief Financial Officer.—Richard L. Greene, 647-8517.
Executive Assistant.—James L. Millette, 647–8514.

FOREIGN MISSIONS

Director.—Eric J. Boswell, Room 6316, 647–6290.
Deputy Director.—Thomas Burns, 647–3416.

FOREIGN SERVICE INSTITUTE

Director.—[Vacant], Room F2102, SA–42, (703) 302–6703.
Deputy Director.—Ruth A. Whiteside, (703) 302–6707.

INTELLIGENCE AND RESEARCH

Assistant Secretary.—Toby L. Gati, Room 6531, 647-9176.
Deputy Assistant Secretaries.—Thomas Finger, 647–633; Daniel C. Kurtzer, 647–7826; Jennifer Sims, 647–7754.

INTERNATIONAL NARCOTICS AND CRIME

Assistant Secretary.—Robert Gelbard, Room 7333, 647-8464.
Deputy Assistant Secretaries.—Jane Becker, 647-6642; Jonathon Winer, 647–6643.

INTERNATIONAL ORGANIZATION AFFAIRS

Assistant Secretary.—Princeton Lyman, Room 6323, 647-9600.
Deputy Assistant Secretaries.—Harold S. Fleming, 647–9431; Melinda L. Kimble, 647–9604; Molly K. Williamson, 647-9602.

LEGISLATIVE AFFAIRS

Assistant Secretary.—Barbara Larkin, Room 7261, 647–4204.
Deputy Assistant Secretaries: Michael Klosson, 647-1050; Meg Donovan, 647–1048.
Deputy Assistant Secretary (Senate).—David Gillette, 647–1048.
Deputy Assistant Secretary (House).—[Vacant], 647–1050.
Senior Policy Adviser.—Peter Yeo, 647–2631.

OCEANS AND INTERNATIONAL ENVIRONMENTAL AND SCIENTIFIC AFFAIRS

Assistant Secretary.—Eileen B. Claussen, Room 7831, 647-1554.
Special Negotiator.—William Milam, 647–1555.
Deputy Assistant Secretaries: Mary Beth West, 647–2396; Rafe Pomerance, 647–2232; Anne K. Solomon, 647–3004.

OFFICE OF THE INSPECTOR GENERAL

Inspector General.—Jacquelyn L. Williams-Bridgers, Room 6817, 647-9450.

LEGAL ADVISER

Senior Adviser.—Michael Matheson (acting), Room 6423, 647–9598.

POLITICO–MILITARY AFFAIRS

Assistant Secretary.—Thomas McNamara, Room 7325, 647–9022.
Deputy Assistant Secretaries: Frances D. Cook, 647–8698; Robert Einhorn, 647–8699; Martha C. Harris, 647–6977; Michael Lemmon, 647–9024; Eric Newsom, 647–9023.

POPULATION, REFUGEES AND MIGRATION

Assistant Secretary.—Phyllis Oakley, Room 8245, 647-7360.
Deputy Assistant Secretaries.—Marguerite Rivera Hooze, 647–5822; Charles L. Sykes, 647–5767.

PROTOCOL

Chief of Protocol.—Molly Raiser, Room 1232, 647–4543.
Deputy Chief.—[Vacant], 647–4120.

PUBLIC AFFAIRS

Assistant Secretary.—Nicholas Bums (acting), Room 6800, 647–5548.
Deputy Assistant Secretaries: Nicholas Burns; Loula Rodriquez, 647–6607.

UNITED STATES DIPLOMATIC OFFICES—FOREIGN SERVICE

(C- Consular Office, N- No Embassy or Consular Office)

AMBASSADORS

ALBANIA (Tirana).—Hon. Marissa Lino.
ALGERIA (Algiers).—Hon. Ronald E. Neumann.
ANGOLA (Luanda).—Hon. Donald K. Steinberg.
ANTIGUA AND BARBUDA (St. John's) (N).—Hon. Jeanette W. Hyde.
ARGENTINA (Buenos Aires).—Hon. James R. Cheek.
ARMENIA (Yerevan).—Hon. Peter Tomsen.
AUSTRALIA (Canberra).—Hon. Genta Hawkins Holmes.
AUSTRIA (Vienna).—Hon. Swanee G. Hunt.
AZERBAIJAN (Baku).—Hon. Richard D. Kauzlarich.
BAHAMAS (Nassau).—Hon. Sidney Williams.
BAHRAIN (Manama).—Hon. David M. Ransom.

BANGLADESH (Dhaka).—
Hon. David N. Merrill.
BARBADOS (Bridgetown).—
Hon. Jeanette W. Hyde.
BELARUS (Minsk).—
Hon. Kenneth S. Yalowitz.
BELGIUM (Brussels).—
Hon. Alan J. Blinken.
BELIZE (Belize City).—
Hon. George C. Bruno.
BENIN (Cotonou).—Hon. John M. Yates.
BERMUDA (Hamilton) (C).—
Hon. Robert A. Farmer.
BOLIVIA (La Paz).—
Hon. Curt W. Kamman.
BOSNIA-HERZEGOVINA (Sarajevo).—
Hon. John K. Menzies.
BOTSWANA (Gaborone).—
Hon. Robert Krueger.
BRAZIL (Brasilia).—Hon. Melvyn Levitsky.
BRUNEI (Bandar Seri Begawan).—
Hon. Glen R. Rase.
BULGARIA (Sofia).—Hon. Avis T. Bohlen.
BURKINA FASO (Ouagadougou).—
Hon. Sharon P. Wilkinson.
BURMA (Rangoon).—
Hon. Kent M. Wiedemann.
BURUNDI (Bujumbura).—
Hon. Morris N. Hughes, Jr.
CAMBODIA (Phnom Penh).—
Hon. Kenneth M. Quinn.
CAMEROON (Yaounde).—
Hon. Charles H. Twining.
CANADA (Ottawa).—[Vacant].
CAPE VERDE (Praia).—
Hon. Lawrence N. Benedict.
CENTRAL AFRICAN REPUBLIC
(Bangui).—Hon. Mosina H. Jordan.
CHAD (N'Djamena).—
Hon. David C. Halsted.
CHILE (Santiago).—
Hon. Gabriel Guerra-Mondragon.
CHINA, PEOPLE'S REPUBLIC OF
(Beijing).—Hon. Jim Sasser.
COLOMBIA (Bogota).—
Hon. Myles R.R. Frechette.
COMOROS (Moroni) (N).—
Hon. Harold W. Geisel.
CONGO (Brazzaville).—
Hon. William C. Ramsay.
CONGO, Democratic Republic of
(Kinshasa).—Hon. Daniel H. Simpson.
COSTA RICA (San Jose).—
Hon. Peter J. De Vos.
COTE D'IVOIRE (Abidjan).—
Hon. Lannon Walker.
CROATIA (Zagreb).—
Hon. Peter W. Galbraith.
CUBA (Havana, U.S. Interests Section).—
Hon. Michael Kozak.
CYPRUS (Nicosia).—Hon. Kenneth C. Brill.
CZECH REPUBLIC (Prague).—
Hon. Jenonne R. Walker.
DENMARK (Copenhagen).—
Hon. Edward E. Elson.
DJIBOUTI, REPUBLIC OF (Djibouti).—
[Vacant].
DOMINICA (Roseau) (N).—
Hon. Jeanette W. Hyde.
DOMINICAN REPUBLIC (Santo
Domingo).—Hon. Donna J. Hrinak.
ECUADOR (Quito).—Hon. Leslie Alexander.
EGYPT (Cairo).—Hon. Edward S. Walker.
EL SALVADOR (San Salvador).—
Hon. Anne W. Patterson.
ERITREA (Asmara).—
Hon. John F. Hicks, Sr.
ESTONIA (Tallinn).—
Hon. Lawrence P. Taylor.
ETHIOPIA (Addis Ababa).—
Hon. David H. Shinn.
FIJI (Suva).—Hon. Don L. Gevirtz.
FINLAND (Helsinki).—Hon. Derek Shearer.
FRANCE (Paris).—[Vacant].
GABON (Libreville).—
Hon. Elizabeth Raspolic.
GAMBIA (Banjul).—Hon. Gerald W. Scott.
GEORGIA (Tbilisi).—
Hon. William H. Courtney.
GERMANY (Bonn).—[Vacant].
GHANA (Accra).—Hon. Edward Brynn.
GREECE (Athens).—
Hon. Thomas M.T. Niles.
GRENADA (St. George) (N).—
Hon. Jeanette W. Hyde.
GUATEMALA (Guatemala City).—
Hon. Donald Planty.
GUINEA (Conakry).—
Hon. Tibor P. Nagy, Jr.
GUINEA-BISSAU (Bissau).—
Hon. Peggy Blackford.
GUYANA (Georgetown).—[Vacant].
HAITI (Port-au-Prince).—
Hon. William L. Swing.
HOLY SEE (Vatican City).—
Hon. Raymond L. Flynn.
HONDURAS (Tegucigalpa).—
Hon. James F. Creagan.
HONG KONG (Hong Kong).—
Hon. Richard Boucher.
HUNGARY (Budapest).—
Hon. Donald M. Blinken.
ICELAND (Reykjavik).—
Hon. Day O. Mount.
INDIA (New Delhi).—Hon. Frank G. Wisner.
INDONESIA (Jakarta).—
Hon. J. Stapleton Roy.
IRELAND (Dublin).—
Hon. Jean K. Smith.
ISRAEL (Tel Aviv).—Hon. Martin S. Indyk.
ITALY (Rome).—
Hon. Reginald Bartholomew.
JAMAICA (Kingston).—
Hon. Jerome G. Cooper.
JAPAN (Tokyo).—[Vacant].
JORDAN (Amman).—Hon. Wesley W. Egan.
KAZAKSTAN (Almaty).—
Hon. A. Elizabeth Jones.
KENYA (Nairobi).—
Hon. Prudence Bushnell.

KIRIBATI (Parawa) (N).—
Hon. Joan M. Plaisted.
KOREA (Seoul).—[Vacant].
KUWAIT (Kuwait).—Hon. Ryan C. Crocker.
KYRGYZ REPUBLIC (Bishkek).—
Hon. Eileen A. Malloy.
LAOS (Vientiane).—
Hon. Wendy J. Chamberlin.
LATVIA (Riga).—Hon. Larry C. Napper.
LEBANON (Beirut).—
Hon. Richard H. Jones.
LESOTHO (Maseru).—
Hon. Bismarck Myrick.
LIBERIA (Monrovia).—
Hon. William B. Milan.
LITHUANIA (Vilnius).—
Hon. James W. Swihart, Jr.
LUXEMBOURG (Luxembourg).—
Hon. Clay Constantinou.
MACEDONIA (Skopje).—
Hon. Christopher R. Hill.
MADAGASCAR (Antananarivo).—
Hon. Vicki J. Huddleston.
MALAWI (Lilongwe).—
Hon. Peter R. Chaveas.
MALAYSIA (Kuala Lampur).—
Hon. John L. Malott.
MALDIVES (Male) (N).—
Hon. A. Peter Burleigh.
MALI (Bamako).—Hon. David P. Rawson.
MALTA (Valletta).—[Vacant].
MARSHALL ISLANDS (Majuro).—
Hon. Joan M. Plaisted.
MAURITANIA (Nouakchott).—
Hon. Dorothy M. Sampas.
MAURITIUS (Port Louis).—
Hon. Harold W. Geisel.
MEXICO (Mexico City).—
Hon. James R. Jones.
MICRONESIA (Kolonia).—[Vacant].
MOLDOVA (Chisinau).—
Hon. John T. Stewart.
MONGOLIA (Ulaanbaatar).—[Vacant].
MOROCCO (Rabat).—
Hon. Marc C. Ginsberg.
MOZAMBIQUE (Maputo).—[Vacant].
NAMIBIA (Windhoek).—
Hon. George Ward, Jr.
NAURU (Yaren) (N).—Hon. Don L. Gevirtz.
NEPAL (Kathmandu).—
Hon. Sandra L. Vogelgesang.
NETHERLANDS (The Hague).—
Hon. K. Terry Dornbush.
NEW ZEALAND (Wellington).—
Hon. Josiah H. Beeman.
NICARAGUA (Managua).—
Hon. John F. Maisto.
NIGER (Niamey).—Hon. Charles O. Cecil.
NIGERIA (Abuja).—
Hon. Walter C. Carrington.
NORWAY (Oslo).—Hon. Thomas A. Loftus.
OMAN (Muscat).—Hon. Frances D. Cook.
PAKISTAN (Islamabad).—
Hon. Thomas W. Simons, Jr.
PALAU (Koror).—Hon. Thomas C. Hubbard.
PANAMA (Panama).—
Hon. William J. Hughes.
PAPUA NEW GUINEA (Port Moresby).—
Hon. Richard W. Teare.
PARAGUAY (Asunción)—
Hon. Robert E. Service.
PERU (Lima).—Hon. Dennis C. Jett.
PHILIPPINES (Manila).—
Hon. Thomas C. Hubbard.
POLAND (Warsaw).—
Hon. Nicholas. A. Rey.
PORTUGAL (Lisbon).—
Hon. Elizabeth F. Bagley.
QATAR (Doha).—Hon. Patrick N. Theros.
ROMANIA (Bucharest).—
Hon. Alfred H. Moses.
RUSSIA (Moscow).—[Vacant].
RWANDA (Kigali).—
Hon. Robert E. Gribbin III.
ST. KITTS AND NEVIS (N).—
Hon. Jeanette W. Hyde.
ST. LUCIA (Castries) (N).—
Hon. Jeanette W. Hyde.
ST. VINCENT AND THE GRENADINES (N).—Hon. Jeanette W. Hyde.
SAO TOME AND PRINCIPE (Sao Tome) (N).—Elizabeth Raspolic.
SAUDI ARABIA (Riyadh).—
Hon. Wyche Fowler, Jr.
SENEGAL (Dakar).—Hon.Mark Johnson.
SERBIA-MONTENEGRO (Belgrade).—
Hon. Richard M. Miles.
SEYCHELLES (Victoria).—[Vacant].
SIERRA LEONE (Freetown).—
Hon. John L. Hirsch.
SINGAPORE (Singapore).—
Hon. Timothy A. Chorba.
SLOVAK REPUBLIC (Bratislava).—
Hon. Ralph R. Johnson.
SLOVENIA (Ljubljana).—
Hon. Victor Jackovich.
SOLOMON ISLANDS (Honiara).—
Hon. Richard W. Teare.
SOUTH AFRICA (Pretoria).—
Hon. James A. Joseph.
SPAIN (Madrid).—Hon. Richard N. Gardner.
SRI LANKA (Colombo).—
Hon. A. Peter Burleigh.
SUDAN (Khartoum).—
Hon. Timothy M. Carney.
SURINAME (Paramaribo).—
Hon. Roger R. Gamble.
SWAZILAND (Mbabane).—
Hon. John T. Sprott.
SWEDEN (Stockholm).—
Hon. Thomas L. Siebert.
SWITZERLAND (Bern).—
Hon. Madeleine M. Kunin.
SYRIAN ARAB REPUBLIC (Damascus).—
Hon. Christopher W.S. Ross.
TAJIKISTAN (Dushanbe).—
Hon. R. Grant Smith.
TANZANIA (Dar es Salaam).—
Hon. J. Brady Anderson.
THAILAND (Bangkok).—
Hon. William H. Itoh.

TOGO (Lome).—Hon. Johnny Young.
TONGA (Nuku'alofa) (N).—
Hon. Don L. Gevirtz.
TRINIDAD AND TOBAGO (Port-of-Spain).—Hon. Brian J. Donnelly.
TUNISIA (Tunis).—Hon. Mary Ann Casey.
TURKEY (Ankara).—Hon. Marc Grossman.
TURKMENISTAN (Ashgabat).—
Hon. Michael W. Cotter.
TUVALU (Funafuti) (N).—
Hon. Don L. Gevirtz.
UGANDA (Kampala).—
Hon. E. Michael Southwick.
UKRAINE (Kiev).—Hon. William G. Miller.
UNITED ARAB EMIRATES (Abu Dhabi).—
Hon. David C. Litt.
UNITED KINGDOM (London).—
Hon. William J. Crowe, Jr.
URUGUAY (Montevideo).—
Hon. Thomas J. Dodd.
UZBEKISTAN (Tashkent).—
Hon. Stanley T. Escudero.
VANUATU (Port Vila) (N).—
Hon. Richard W. Teare.
VENEZUELA (Caracas).—
Hon. Jeffrey Davidow.
VIETNAM (Hanoi).—Hon. Pete Peterson.
WESTERN SAMOA (Apia).—
Hon. Josiah H. Beeman.
YEMEN (Sanaa).—Hon. David G. Newton.
ZAMBIA (Lusaka).—
Hon. Roland K. Kuchel.
ZIMBABWE (Harare).—
Hon. Johnnie Carson.

UNITED STATES PERMANENT DIPLOMATIC MISSIONS TO INTERNATIONAL ORGANIZATIONS

EUROPEAN UNION (Brussels).—
Hon. Stuart E. Eizenstat.
NORTH ATLANTIC TREATY ORGANIZATION (Brussels).—
Hon. Robert E. Hunter.
ORGANIZATION OF AMERICAN STATES (Washington, DC).—
Hon. Harriet C. Babbitt.
ORGANIZATION FOR ECONOMIC COOPERATION AND DEVELOPMENT (Paris).—Hon. David L. Aaron.
UNITED NATIONS (Geneva).—
Hon. Daniel L. Spiegel.
UNITED NATIONS (New York).—
Hon. Bill Richardson.
UNITED NATIONS (Vienna).—
Hon. John B. Ritch III.

DEPARTMENT OF TRANSPORTATION

400 Seventh Street SW 20590
phone 366–4000, http://www.dot.gov

RODNEY E. SLATER, Secretary of Transportation, 13th Secretary in the 30-year history of the department; born February 23, 1955, grew up in Marianna, Arkansas; graduated, Eastern Michigan University; LLB, University of Arkansas; prior to becoming Secretary served four years as Administrator, Federal Highway Administration; Director of Governmental Relations, Arkansas State University; executive assistant, Economic and Community Programs, and special assistant for Community and Minority Affairs for then Arkansas Governor Bill Clinton; Assistant Attorney General-Litigation Division of Arkansas State Attorney General's Office; liaison, Martin Luther King Jr. Federal Holiday Commission; member: Arkansas State Highway Commission, 1987–92, chairman, 1992; married to Cassandra Wilkins; one daughter: Bridgette Josette; named Secretary of Transportation on February 14, 1997.

OFFICE OF THE SECRETARY

Room 10200, phone 366–1111, fax 366–4508

(Created by the act of October 15, 1966; codified under U.S.C. 49)

Secretary of Transportation.—Rodney E. Slater.
Chief of Staff.—[Vacant].
Deputy Chief of Staff.—Jacqueline M. Lowey.
Deputy Secretary.—Mortimer L. Downey, 366–1111.
Associate Deputy Secretary and Director of Intermodalism.—Michael P. Huerta, 366–5781.
Chairman, Board of Contract Appeals (Chief Administrative Judge).—Thaddeus V. Ware, Room 5101, 366–4305.
Director, Office of—
Civil Rights.—[Vacant], Room 10215, 366–4648.
Executive Secretariat.—[Vacant], Room 10205, 366–4277.
Small and Disadvantaged Business Utilization.—Luz A. Hopewell, Room 9414, 366–1930.
Intelligence and Security.—RADM Paul J. Pluta, Room 10401, 366–6535.

GENERAL COUNSEL

General Counsel.—Nancy E. McFadden, Room 10428, 366–4702.
Deputy General Counsel.—Rosalind A. Knapp, 366–4713.
Special Counsel.—Diane R. Liff, Room 6434, 366–0140.
Assistant General Counsel for—
Aviation Enforcement and Proceedings.—Samuel Podberesky, Room 4116, 366–9342.
Environmental, Civil Rights and General Law.—Roberta D. Gabel, Room 10102, 366–4710.
International Law—Donald H. Horn, Room 10105, 366–2972.
Legislation.—Thomas W. Herlihy, Room 10100, 366–4687.
Litigation.—Paul M. Geier, Room 4102, 366–4731.
Regulation and Enforcement.—Neil R. Eisner, Room 10424, 366–4723.
Chairman, Board for Correction of Military Records.—Robert H. Joost, Room 5432, 366–9335.

INSPECTOR GENERAL

Inspector General.—[Vacant], Room 9210, 366–1959.
Deputy Inspector General.—[Vacant], Room 9210, 366–6767.

Senior Counsel to the Inspector General.—Roger Williams, Room 9208, 366–8751.
Associate Deputy Inspector General.—Raymond J. DeCarli, Room 9210, 366–1964.
Assistant Inspector General for Auditing.—Lawrence H. Weintrob, Room 9210, 366–1964.
Deputy Assistant Inspector General for Auditing.—[Vacant], Room 9209, 366–1992.
Director, Office of—
Transporation Program Audits.—Alexis M. Stefani, Room 7128, 366–0500.
Information Technology, Financial and Secretarial Audits.—John L. Meche, Room 7102, 366–1496.
Assistant Inspector General for Investigations and Evaluations.—Wilbur L. Daniels, Room 9210, 366–1454.
Assistant Inspector General for Investigations.—Todd J. Zinser, Room 9208, 366–1967.
Deputy Assistant Inspector General for Investigations.—[Vacant], Room 9200, 366–0681.
Directorate of Administration.—Patricia J. Thompson, Room 9200, 366–0687.
Director, Office of—
Program Planning and Oversight.—Samuel Davis, Room 2440, 366–1968.
Office of Resources.—Glenn C. Griser, Room 7422, 366–1490.
Administrative Services.—Dorothy Bowie, Room 7422, 366–6908.
Financial Services.—Jacquelyn Revetta, Room 7422, 366–1976.
Human Resources.—Patrick Pietrzak, Room 7422, 366–1441.
Information Technology Resources.—James Heminger, Room 7422, 366–1472.

REGIONAL AUDIT OFFICES

Regional Audit Managers:
Region II.—Michael E. Goldstein, Room 200, 1633 Broadway, New York NY 10019, (212) 399–5200.
Region III.—Harry H. Fitzkee, Suite 4500, City Cresent Building, 10 South Howard Street, Baltimore MD 21201, (410) 962–3612.
Region IV.—Dale R. Mills, Suite 376, 1718 Peachtree Road NW, Atlanta GA 30309, (404) 347–7825.
Region V.—Ronald H. Hoogenboom, Room 677, 111 North Canal Street, Chicago IL 60606, (312) 353–0104.
Region VI.—[Vacant], Room 9A27, 819 Taylor Street, Fort Worth TX 76102, (817) 334–3545.
Region IX.—Robin Dorn, 201 Mission Street, Suite 2310, San Francisco CA 94105, (415) 744–3090.
Region X.—Ronald W. Hambrick, Room 644, 915 Second Avenue, Seattle WA 98174, (206) 220–7754.

REGIONAL INSPECTION OFFICES

Regional Inspection Managers:
Region I.—James L. Benson, Room 2440, 400 Seventh Street SW, Washington DC 20590, (202) 366–1302.

REGIONAL INVESTIGATIVE OFFICES

Special Agents-In-Charge:
Region II.—William P. Tompkins, Room 3134, 26 Federal Plaza, New York NY 10278, (212) 264–8701.
Region IV.—Paul D. McGuire, Suite 397, 1718 Peachtree Road NW, Atlanta GA 30309, (404) 347–7836.
Region V.—Dieter H. Harper, Room 677, 111 North Canal Street, Chicago IL 60606, (312) 353–0106.
Region VI.—[Vacant], Room 9A27, 819 Taylor Street, Forth Worth TX 76102, (817) 334–3236.
Region IX.—James Baldwin, Suite 2310, 201 Mission Street, San Francisco CA 94105, (415) 744–3090.

ASSISTANT SECRETARY FOR TRANSPORTATION POLICY

Assistant Secretary.—Frank E. Kruesi, Room 10228, 366–4544.
Deputy Assistant Secretary.—Joseph F. Canny, Room 10228, 366–4540.
Deputy Assistant Secretary.—John N. Lieber, Room 10232, 366–4550.

Director, Office of—
Environment, Energy and Safety.—Donald R. Trilling, Room 9222, 366–4220.
Economics.—[Vacant], Room 10305, 366–4416.

ASSISTANT SECRETARY FOR AVIATION AND INTERNATIONAL AFFAIRS

Assistant Secretary.—Charles A. Hunnicutt, Room 10232, 366–8822.
Deputy Assistant Secretary.—Patrick V. Murphy, Room 10232, 366–4551.
Deputy Assistant Secretary.—Mark Gerchick, Room 10232, 366–8834.
Director, Office of—
International Transportation and Trade.—Bernard Gaillard, Room 10300, 366–4368.
International Aviation.—Paul Gretch, Room 6402, 366–2423.
Aviation Analysis.—John V. Coleman, Room 6401, 366–5903.
Aviation and International Economics.—James Craun, room 6419, 366–1053.

ASSISTANT SECRETARY FOR ADMINISTRATION

Assistant Secretary.—Melissa J. Allen, Room 10314, 366–2332.
Director, Office of—
Personnel.—Glenda M. Tate, Room 9101, 366–4088.
Information Resource Management.—Eugene K. Taylor, Jr., Room 9104, 366–9201.
Hearings, Chief Administrative Law Judge.—Roy A. Maurer, Room 9228, 366–2142.
Acquisition and Grant Management.—David J. Litman, Room 9401, 366–4285.
Security.—[Vacant], Room 7402, 366–4677.

ASSISTANT SECRETARY FOR BUDGET AND PROGRAMS

Assistant Secretary.—Louise F. Stoll, Room 10101, 366–9191.
Deputy Assistant Secretary.—Peter J. Basso, Room 10101, 366–9192.
Deputy Chief Financial Officer.—David K. Kleinberg, Room, 10101, 366–9192.
Director, Office of—
Programs and Evaluation.—George W. McDonald, Room 10118, 366–9603.
Budget.—Beverly Aimaro-Pheto, Room 10117, 366–4594.
Financial Management.—Eileen T. Powell, Room 9130F, 366–1306.

ASSISTANT SECRETARY FOR GOVERNMENTAL AFFAIRS

Assistant Secretary.—Steven O. Palmer, Room 10408, 366–4573.
Deputy Assistant Secretary.—John C. Horsley, Room 10408, 366–4563.
Director, Office of—
Congressional Affairs.—Peter G. Halpin, Room 10406, 366–9714.
Intergovernmental Affairs.—Barbara Leach, Room 10405, 366–1524.

TRANSPORTATION ADMINISTRATIVE SERVICE CENTER

Director.—George C. Fields, Room 10320, 366–9284, fax 366–7211.
Principal of—
Customer Service.—Patricia Parrish, Room 10320, 366–4747.
Business Support.—Edward Hansen (acting), Room 10320, 366–4246.
Worklife Wellness.—Linda Rhoads, Room 9136, 366–9440.
Headquarters Building Management.—Janet Kraus, Room 2303, 366–0815.
Information Services.—Patricia Prosperi, Room 2200C, 366–5135.
Learning and Development.—Frederica Burnett, Room 9103, 366–4168.
Space Management.—Rudy Spruill (acting), Room 2310, 366–2472.
Security Operations.—Jeff Johns, Room 7402, 366–4677.
Systems Development.—Richard Chapman (acting), Room 7404, 366–5636.
Information Technology Operations.—Richard Chapman, Room 9104, 366–9706.
Acquisition Services.—Richard Lieber, Room 9413, 366–4953.

Human Resources Services.—Terry Smith, Room 9113, 366–4140.

OFFICE OF PUBLIC AFFAIRS

Assistant to the Secretary and Director of Public Affairs.—Steve Akey, Room 10414, 366–4570.
Deputy Director.—William Schulz, Room 10414, 366–4531.
Associate Director for—
Speech Writing and Research Division—Ilene Zeldin, Room 9419, 366–5822.
Media Relations and Special Projects Division.—Wendy Jo Burt, Room 10413, 366–5565.

BUREAU OF TRANSPORTATION STATISTICS

400 Seventh Street SW 20590, phone 366–3282

Director.—[Vacant], Room 2104.
Principal Deputy Director.—Tiruvarur Lakshmanan, Room 2104.
Deputy Director.—[Vacant], Room 2104.

U.S. COAST GUARD

2100 Second Street SW 20593, phone 267–2229

Commandant.—Adm. Robert E. Kramek.
Executive Assistant.—Capt. Roy J. Casto.
Special Assistant to the Commandant.—Cmdr. Larry Barrow.
Aide to the Commandant.—Lt. Cmdr. James E. Rendon.
Vice Commandant.—Vice Adm. Richard D. Herr.
Aide to the Vice Commandant.—Lt. James M. Mathieu.
Medical Adviser to the Commandant.—[Vacant].
Chief, Congressional Affairs Staff.—Capt. Jeffrey J. Hathaway. 366–4280.
Chairman, Marine Safety Council.—Rear Adm. Paul M. Blayney
Chief Administrative Law Judge.—Joseph N. Ingolia.
Chief, Office of Civil Rights.—Walter R. Somerville.
Foreign Policy Advisor to the Commandant.—Gerald P. Yoest.
Chief of Staff.—Vice Adm. James M. Loy.
Director of Resources.—Rear Adm. Thad W. Allen.
Director of Finance and Procurement.—William H. Campbell.
Assistant Commandant, for—
Acquisition.—Rear Adm. Paul E. Busick.
Human Resources.—Rear Adm. Gerald F. Woolever.
Marine Safety and Environmental Protection.—Rear Adm. Robert C. North.
Operations.—Rear Adm. Ernest R. Riutta.
Systems.—Rear Adm. John T. Tozzi.
Coast Guard Personnel Command.—Thomas B. Taylor.

MAJOR FIELD COMMANDS

Commanders:
Atlantic Area: Vice Adm. Robert T. Rufe, 431 Crawford Street, Portsmouth VA 23704–5004, (757) 398–6287.
Pacific Area: Vice Adm. James C. Card, Coast Guard Island, Bldg. 51, Room 6, Alameda CA 94501–5100, (510) 437–3196.
Maintenance and Logistics Command—
Atlantic: Rear Adm. Edward J. Barrett, 300 Main Street, Suite 800, Norfolk VA 23510–9104, (757) 628–4275.
Pacific: Rear Adm. Fred L. Ames, 31 Coast Guard Island, Alameda CA 94501–510, (510) 437–3939.
Coast Guard Districts:
First: Rear Adm. Richard M. Larrebee III, 408 Atlantic Avenue, Boston MA 02210–3350, (617) 223–8480.

Fifth: Vice Adm. Roger T. Rufe, 431 Crawford Street, Portsmouth VA 23704–5004, (757) 398–6287.

Seventh: Rear Adm. Norman T. Saunders, Brickell Plaza Federal Building, Room 944, 909 Southeast First Avenue, Miami FL 33130–3050, (305) 536–5654.

Eighth: Rear Adm. Timothy W. Josiah, 501 Magazine Street, Room 1328, New Orleans LA 70130–3396, (504) 589–6298.

Ninth: Rear Adm. John F. McGowan, 1240 East Ninth Street, Cleveland OH 44199–2060, (216) 522–3910.

Eleventh: James C. Card, Coast Guard Island, Alameda CA 94501–5100, 510–437–3196, (510) 437–3196.

Thirteenth: Rear Adm. J. David Spade, 915 Second Avenue, Seattle WA 98174–1067, (206) 220–5078.

Fourteenth: Rear Adm. Thomas H. Collins, 300 Ala Moana Boulevard, Honolulu HI 96850–4982, (808) 541–2051.

Seventeenth: Rear Adm. Terry M. Cross, PO Box 3–5000, Juneau AK 99802–5517, (907) 463–2025.

FEDERAL AVIATION ADMINISTRATION

800 Independence Avenue SW 20591, phone 267–3484

Administrator.—Barry L. Valentine (acting), 267–3111.

Chief of Staff.—Lynne A. Osmus, 267–3111.

Special Assistant To The Administrator.—Peter H. Appel, 267–3111.

Deputy Administrator.—Monte R. Belger (acting), 267–8111.

Executive Assistant To The Deputy Administrator.—Paul Feldman, 267–8111.

Special Assistant To The Deputy Administrator.—Donna Vicars (acting), 267–8111.

Assistant Administrators for System Safety.—Christopher A. Hart, Barry Bermingham, 267–3611.

Chief Counsel.—Nicholas Garaufis, 267–3222.

Assistant Administrator for Civil Rights.—Fanny Rivera, 267–3254; Mary N. Whigham Jones, 267–3264.

Assistant Administrator for Government and Industry Affairs.—A. Bradley Mims, 267–3277; Robert Wrigley, 267–8211.

Assistant Administrator for Public Affairs.—Eliot Brenner, 267–3883; Drucella A. Andersen, 267–3462.

Assistant Administrator for Policy, Planning, and International Aviation.—Louise E. Maillett (acting), 267–3033.

Director of—

Aviation Policy and Plans.—John M. Rodgers, 267–3274

Environment and Energy.—James D. Erickson, 267–3576.

International Aviation.—Joan W. Bauerlein, 267–3213.

Europe, Africa, and Middle East.—Patrick N. Poe, Brussels, (322) 508–2700.

Latin America-Caribbean.—Joaquin Archilla, (305) 526–2551.

Asia-Pacific.—Eugene Ross Hamory, Singapore, 65–543–1466.

Associate Administrator for Commercial Space Transportation.—Patrica Grace Smith (acting), 418–8379.

Associate Administrator for Administration.—Edwin A. Verburg, 267–9105; Ruth A. Leverenz (acting), 267–3751.

Chief Information Officer.—Tim Lawler, 267–7052.

Chief Financial Officer.—Joel C. Taub (acting) and Paulette Lutjens (acting), 267–8928.

Director of Business Information and Consultant.—Larry Covington, 267–7140.

Director of Human Resource Management.—Kay Frances Dolan, 267–3456.

Associate Administrator for Airports.—Susan L. Kurland, 267–9471; Quentin S. Taylor, 267–8738.

Director of Airport Planning and Programming.—Paul L. Galis, 267–8775.

Director of Airport Safety and Standards.—David L. Bennett, 267–3053.

Associate Administrator for Civil Aviation Security (CAS).—Cathal L. Flynn, 267–9863.

Director of CAS Intelligence.—Patrick T. McDonnell, 267–9075.

Director of CAS Operations.—Bruce R. Butterworth, 267–7262.

Director of CAS Policy and Planning.—Anthony Fainberg, 267–7839.

FEDERAL HIGHWAY ADMINISTRATION

Washington Headquarters, Nassif Building, 400 Seventh Street SW 20590

Turner-Fairbank Highway Research Center (TFHRC)

6300 Georgetown Pike, McLean VA 22201

Administrator.—[Vacant], 366–0650.
Deputy Administrator—Jane Garvey, 366–2240.
Executive Director.—Anthony R. Kane, 366–2242.
Chief Counsel.—Jerry L. Malone, Room 4213, 366–0740.
Director of—
Civil Rights.—Edward W. Morris, Jr., Room 4132, 366–0693.
Public Affairs.—[Vacant], Room 4207, 366–0660.
Program Review.—Fred J. Hempel, Room 4210, 366–9393.
Associate Administrator for—
Administration.—George S. Moore, Jr., Room 4316, 366–0604.
Motor Carriers.—George L. Reagle, Room 3103, 366–2519.
Policy.—Gloria J. Jeff, Room 3317, 336–0585.
Program Development.—Thomas Ptak, Room 3212, 366–0371.
Research and Development.—Robert J. Betsold, TFHRC, Room T–306, 285–2051.
Safety and System Applications.—Dennis C. Judycki, Room 3401, 366–2149.

REGIONAL OFFICES

Region 1. *(combines standard Regions 1 and 2).*—Connecticut, Maine, Massachusetts, New Hampshire, New Jersey, New York, Puerto Rico, Rhode Island, Vermont.
Regional Administrator.—Henry P. Rentz, Jr., Leo W. O'Brien, Federal Building, Room 719, Clinton Avenue and North Pearl Street, Albany NY 12207.
Region 3.—Delaware, District of Columbia, Maryland, Pennsylania, Virginia, West Virginia.
Regional Administrator.—David S. Gendell, 10 South Howard Street, Suite 4000, Baltimore MD 21201.
Region 4.—Alabama, Florida, Georgia, Kentucky, Mississippi, North Carolina, South Carolina, Tennessee.
Regional Administrator.—Leon N. Larson, 100 Alabama Street, 17th Floor, Atlanta GA 30303–3104, (404) 562–3570.
Region 5.—Illinois, Indiana, Michigan, Minnesota, Ohio, Wisconsin.
Regional Administrator.—Dale E. Wilkens, 19900 Governors Highway, Suite 301, Olympia Fields IL 60461–1021.
Region 6.—Arkansas, Louisiana, New Mexico, Oklahoma, Texas.
Regional Administrator.—Edward Wueste, 819 Taylor Street, Room 8A00, Fort Worth TX 76102.
Region 7.—Iowa, Kansas, Missouri, Nebraska.
Regional Administrator.—Arthur E. Hamilton, 6301 Rockhill Road, Kansas City MO 64141–6715.
Region 8.—Colorado, Montana, North Dakota, South Dakota, Utah, Wyoming.
Regional Administrator.—Vincent F. Schimmoller, 555 Zang Street, Room 400, Lakewood CO 80228.
Region 9.—Arizona, California, Hawaii, Nevada.
Regional Administrator.—Julie A. Cirillo, 201 Mission Street, Suite 2100, San Francisco CA 94105.
Region 10.—Alaska, Idaho, Oregon, Washington.
Regional Administrator.—Leon J. Wittman, Jr., KOIN Center, Suite 600, 222 SW Columbia Street, Portland OR 97201.

FEDERAL RAILROAD ADMINISTRATION

400 Seventh Street SW 20590

Administrator.—Jolene M. Molitoris, Room 8206, 366–0710.
Deputy Administrator.—Donald M. Itzkoff, 366–0857.
Special Assistant to the Administrator.—Robert C. Land, 366–0154.
Associate Administrator for—
Administration and Finance.—Raymond J. Rogers, Room 8228, 366–0872.
Policy and Program Development.—[Vacant], Room 8302, 366–0173.
Railroad Development.—James T. McQueen, Room 5411, 366–9660.

Safety.—Bruce M. Fine, Room 8320–A, 366–0895.
Chief Counsel.—S. Mark Lindsey, Room 8201, 366–0767.
Civil Rights Director.—Miles S. Washington, Jr., Room 8314, 366–9753.
Public Affairs Director.—David A. Bolger, Room 8204, 366–0881.
Budget Director.—Kathryn B. Murphy, Room 8209, 366–0870.
Resident Engineering Manager, Transportation Test Center.—Gunars Spons, Pueblo CO 81001, (719) 584–0507.

REGIONAL OFFICES (RAILROAD SAFETY)

Region 1.—Northeastern. Connecticut, Maine, Massachusetts, New Hampshire, New Jersey, New York, Rhode Island, Vermont.
Regional Director.—Mark H. McKeon, Room 1077, 55 Broadway, Cambridge MA 02142, (617) 494–2321.
Region 2.—Eastern. Delaware, District of Columbia, Maryland, Pennsylvania, Virginia, West Virginia, Ohio.
Regional Director.—David Myers, International Plaza, Suite 550, Philadelphia PA 19113, (610) 521–8200.
Region 3.—Southern. Kentucky, Tennessee, Mississippi, North Carolina, South Carolina, Georgia, Alabama, Florida.
Regional Director.—Fred Denin, 100 Alabama Street SW, Suite 16T20, Atlanta GA 30303–3104, (404) 562–3800.
Region 4.—Central. Minnesota, Illinois, Indiana, Michigan, Wisconsin.
Regional Director.—[Vacant], Suite 655, 111 North Canal Street, Chicago IL 60606, (312) 353–6203.
Region 5.—Southwestern. Arkansas, Louisiana, New Mexico, Oklahoma, Texas.
Regional Director.—John Megary, 8701 Bedford Euless Road, Suite 425, Hurst TX 76053, (817) 284–8142.
Region 6.—Midwestern. Iowa, Missouri, Kansas, Nebraska, Colorado.
Regional Director.—Darrell J. Tisor, City Center Square, 1100 Maine Street, Suite 1130, Kansas City MO 64105, (816) 426–2497.
Region 7.—Western. Arizona, California, Nevada, Utah.
Regional Director.—James Schultz, 801 I Street, Suite 466, Sacramento, CA 95814 (916) 498–6540.
Region 8.—Northwestern. Idaho, Oregon, Wyoming, Montana, North Dakota, South Dakota, Washington, Alaska.
Regional Director.—Dick Clairmont, 703 Broadway, 650 Murdock Bldg, Vancouver WA 98660, (206) 686–7536.

NATIONAL HIGHWAY TRAFFIC SAFETY ADMINISTRATION

400 Seventh Street SW 20590

Administrator.—Ricardo Martinez, Room 5220, 366–1836.
Deputy Administrator.—Phillip R. Recht, 366–2775.
Executive Director.—Donald C. Bischoff, 366–2111.
Associate Administrator for—
Administration.—Herman Simms, 366–1788.
Safety Assusrance.—Michael Brownlee, 366–9700.
Plans and Policy.—William H. Walsh, Sr., 366–2550.
State and Community Services.—Adele Derby, 366–2121.
Research and Development.—Wiliam A. Boehly, 366–1537.
Safety Performance Standards.—L. Robert Shelton, 366–1810.
Traffic Safety Programs.—James Hedlund, 366–1755.
Director, Office of—
Civil Rights.—George B. Quick, 366–4762.
Public and Consumer Affairs.—[Vacant], 366–9550.
Chief Counsel.—[Vacant], 366–9511.
Director, Executive Correspondence.—Linda Divelbiss, 366–2870.

REGIONAL OFFICES

Region I. Connecticut, Maine, Massachusetts, New Hampshire, Rhode Island, Vermont.
Regional Administrator.—George A. Luciano, Transportation Systems Center, Kendall Square, Code 903, Cambridge MA 02142, (617) 494–3427.

Region II. New York, New Jersey, Puerto Rico, Virgin Islands.
Regional Administrator.—Thomas M. Louizou, Suite 204, 222 Mamaroneck Avenue, White Plains NY 10605, (914) 682–6162.

Region III. Delaware, District of Columbia, Maryland, Pennsylvania, Virginia, West Virginia.
Regional Administrator.—Eugene Peterson, The Cresent Building, 10 South Howard Street, Suite 4000, Baltimore MD 21201, (410) 961–7144.

Region IV. Alabama, Florida, Georgia, Kentucky, Mississippi, North Carolina, South Carolina, Tennessee.
Regional Administrator.—Thomas J. Enright, 100 Alabama Street SW, Suite 17T30, Atlanta GA 30303–3106, (404) 562–3739.

Region V. Illinois, Indiana, Michigan, Minnesota, Ohio, Wisconsin.
Regional Administrator.—Donald J. McNamara, 1990 Governors Drive, Suite 201, Olympia Fields IL 60461, (708) 503–8892.

Region VI. Arkansas, Louisiana, New Mexico, Oklahoma, Texas.
Regional Administrator.—George S. Chakiris, Room 8A38, 819 Taylor Street, Fort Worth TX 76102–6177, (817) 978–3653.

Region VII. Iowa, Kansas, Missouri, Nebraska.
Regional Administrator.—Norman B. McPherson, PO Box 412515, Kansas City MO 64141, (816) 926–7887.

Region VIII. Colorado, Montana, North Dakota, South Dakota. Utah, Wyoming.
Regional Administrator.—Louis R. DeCarolis, Fourth Floor, 555 Zang Street, Denver CO 80228, (303) 969–6917.

Region IX. American Samoa, Arizona, California, Guam, Hawaii, Nevada.
Regional Administrator.—Joseph M. Cindrich, Suite 2230, 201 Mission Street, San Francisco CA 94105, (415) 744–3089.

Region X. Alaska, Idaho, Oregon, Washington.
Regional Administrator.—Curtis Winston, Federal Building, Room 3140, 915 Second Avenue, Seattle WA 98174, (206) 553–5934.

FEDERAL TRANSIT ADMINISTRATION

400 Seventh Street SW 20590, phone 366–4040

Administrator.—Gordon J. Linton, Room 9328.
Deputy Administrator.—[Vacant], 366–4325.
Chief Counsel.—Patrick W. Reilly, Room 9328, 366–4063.
Director, Office of—
Civil Rights.—Arthur Lopez, Room 7412, 366–4018.
Public Affairs.—Bruce C. Frame, Room 9400, 366–4043.
Associate Administrator for—
Administration.—Dorrie Y. Aldrich, Room 7411, 366–4007.
Budget and Policy.—[Vacant], Room 9310, 366–4050.
Programs Management.—Hiram T. Walker, Room 9315, 366–4020.
Research, Demonstration and Innovation.—Edward L. Thomas, Room 6431, 366–4052.

REGIONAL OFFICES

Region 1.—Connecticut, Maine, Massachusetts, New Hampshire, Rhode Island, Vermont.
Regional Administrator.—Richard H. Doyle, Transportation Systems Center, Kendall Square, Suite 920, 55 Broadway, Cambridge MA 02142.

Region 2.—New Jersey, New York, Virgin Islands.
Regional Administrator.—Thomas J. Ryan, Suite 2940, 26 Federal Plaza, New York NY 10278.

Region 3.—Delaware, District of Columbia, Maryland, North Carolina, Pennsylvania, Tennessee, Virginia, West Virginia.
Regional Administrator.—Sheldon A. Kinbar, Suite 500, 1760 Market Street, Philadelphia PA 19103.

Region 4.—Alabama, Florida, Georgia, Kentucky, Mississippi, North Carolina, Puerto Rico, South Carolina, Tennessee.
Regional Administrator.—Susan E. Schruth, 100 Alabama Street NW, Suite T1750, Atlanta GA 30303.

Region 5.—Illinois, Indiana, Michigan, Minnesota, Ohio, Wisconsin.
Regional Administrator.—Joel P. Ettinger, Room 1415, 55 East Monroe Street, Chicago IL 60603.

Region 6.—Arkansas, Louisiana, New Mexico, Oklahoma, Texas.

Regional Administrator.—Wilbur E. Hare, Suite 175, East Lamar Boulevard, Arlington TX 76011.

Region 7.—Iowa, Kansas, Missouri, Nebraska.

Regional Administrator.—Lee O. Waddleton, Suite 303, 6301 Rockhill Road, Kansas City MO 64131.

Region 8.—Colorado, Montana, North Dakota, South Dakota, Utah, Wyoming.

Regional Administrator.—Louis F. Mraz, Columbine Place, 216 16th Street, Denver CO 80202.

Region 9.—Arizona, California, Guam, Hawaii, Nevada, American Samoa.

Regional Administrator.—Leslie T. Rogers, Suite 2210, 201 Mission Street, San Francisco CA 94105.

Region 10.—Alaska, Idaho, Oregon, Washington.

Regional Administrator.—Helen M. Knoll, Suite 3142, 915 Second Avenue, Seattle WA 98174.

SAINT LAWRENCE SEAWAY DEVELOPMENT CORPORATION

400 Seventh Street SW 20590, phone 366–0091, fax 366–7147

Administrator.—Gail C. McDonald.

Director, Office of—

Chief Counsel.—Marc C. Owen.

Development and Logistics.—Robert J. Lewis.

Marketing.—Stephen J. Rybicki.

Staff Directors:

Congressional and Public Affairs Staff.—Ginger W. Vuich.

SEAWAY OPERATIONS

180 Andrews Street, PO Box 520, Massena, NY 13662–0520

phone (315) 764–3200, fax (315) 764–3250

Associate Administrator/Resident Manager.—Erman J. Cocci.

Assistant.—Theodore J. Brue.

Director, Office of—

Operations, Maintenance and Marine Safety.—Stephen C. Hung.

Finance.—Edward Margosian.

Administration.—Mary Ann Hazel.

MARITIME ADMINISTRATION

400 Seventh Street SW 20590, phone 366–5812

Maritime Administrator and Chairman, Maritime Subsidy Board.—A.J. Herberger, Room 7206, 366–5823.

Deputy Administrator and Member, Maritime Subsidy Board.—[Vacant], Room 7206A, 366–1719.

Deputy Administrator for Inland Waterways and Great Lakes.—John E. Graykowski, Room 7206A, 366–1718.

Secretary, Maritime Administration and Maritime Subsidy Board.—Joel Richard, Room 7210, 366–5746.

Chief Counsel and Member, Maritime Subsidy Board.—Joan M. Bondareff, Room 7232, 366–5711.

Director, Office of—

Congressional and Public Affairs.—Cher Brooks, Room 7206, 366–1707.

Maritime Labor, Training and Safety.—Taylor E. Jones, II, Room 7302, 366–5755.

Associate Administrator for—

Administration.—John L. Mann, Jr., Room 7217, 366–5801.

Director, Office of—

Accounting.—John G. Hoban, Room 7322, 366–5852.

Acquisition.—Tim Roark, Room 7310, 366–5757.

Budget.—[Vacant], Room 7307, 366–5778.

Information Resources Management.—Leslie E. Hearn, Room 8311A, 366–4181.

Management Services.—Ralph W. Ferguson, Room 7225, 366–5816.

Personnel.—Sherry D. Gilson, Room 8101, 366–4141.

Policy, International Trade, and Marketing.—Bruce J. Carlton, Room 7216, 366–5772.
Director, Office of—
International Activities.—James A. Treichel, Room 7119, 366–5773.
Policy and Plans.—Bruce J. Carlton, Room 7123, 366–4468.
Statistical and Economic Analysis.—William B. Ebersold, Room 8107, 366–2267.
Ship Financial Assistance and Cargo Preference.—James J. Zok, Room 8126, 366–0364.
Director, Office of—
Cargo Preference.—Thomas W. Harrelson, Room 8118, 366–4610.
Costs and Rates.—Michael P. Ferris, Room 8117, 366–2324.
Financial Approvals.—Richard J. McDonnell, Room 8114, 366–5861.
Ship Financing.—Mitchell D. Lax, Room 8122, 366–5744.
Subsidy and Insurance.—Edmond J. Fitzgerald, Room 8117, 366–2400.
National Security.—James E. Caponti, Room 7300, 366–5400.
Director, Office of—
National Security Plans.—Thomas M. P. Christensen, Room 7300, 366–5900.
Sealift Support.—Raymond R. Barberesi, Room 7300, 366–5900.
Ship Operations.—Michael Delpercio, Jr., Room 2122, 366–1875.
Shipbuilding and Technology Development.—[Vacant], Room 2122, 366–5737.
Director, Office of—
Ship Construction.—Edwin B. Schimler, Room 2126, 366–1880.
Shipyard Revitalization.—Joseph A. Byrne, Room 7326, 366–1931.
Port, Intermodal and Environmental Activities.—Margaret D. Blum, Room 7214, 366–4721.
Director, Office of—
Environmental Activities.—Michael C. Carter, Room 7326, 366–1920.
Intermodal Development.—Richard L. Walker, Room 7201, 366–4357.
Ports and Domestic Shipping.—John M. Pisani, Room 7201, 366–4357.

FIELD ACTIVITIES

North Atlantic Region: *Director.*—Robert F. McKeon, 26 Federal Plaza, Room 3737, New York NY 10278, (212) 264–1300.
Central Region: *Director.*—John W. Carnes, 365 Canal Street, Suite 2590, New Orleans LA 70130–1142, (504) 589–6556.
Great Lakes Region: *Director.*—Alpha H. Ames, Jr., Suite 185, 2860 S. River Road, Des Plaines IL 60018–2413, (708) 298–4535.
Western Region: *Director.*—Francis Johnston III, Suite 2200, 201 Mission Street, San Francisco CA 94105, (415) 744–2580.
South Atlantic Region: *Director.*—Mayank Jain, Building 4D, Room 211, 7737 Hampton Boulevard, Norfolk VA 23505, (804) 441–6393.

U.S. MERCHANT MARINE ACADEMY

Superintendent.—Rear Adm. Thomas T. Matteson, Kings Point, NY 11024–1699, (516) 773–5348.
Assistant Superintendent for—
Academic Affairs (Academic Dean).—Dr. Warren F. Mazek, (516) 773–5357.

RESEARCH AND SPECIAL PROGRAMS ADMINISTRATION

400 Seventh Street SW 20590, phone 366–4433

Administrator.—Dr. D. Sharma, Room 8410, 366–4433.
Deputy Administrator.—Kelley S. Coyner, Room 8410, 366–4461.
Director, Program and Policy Support Staff.—William Vincent, Room 8414, 366–4831.
Chief Counsel.—Judith S. Kaleta, Room 8405, 366–4400.
Director, Office of Civil Rights.—[Vacant], Room 8419, 366–9638.
Associate Administrator for—
Management and Administration.—Garrome Franklin, Room 8321, 366–4347.
Hazardous Materials Safety.—Alan I. Roberts, Room 8420, 366–0656.
Pipeline Safety.—Richard B. Felder, Jr., Room 8417, 366–4995.
Research, Technology and Training.—Edwin F. Felder, Room 8406, 366–4434.
Director, Office of—
Emergency Transportation.—[Vacant], Room 8404, 366–5270.
Research Policy and Technology Transfer.—[Vacant], Room 9402, 366–4208.

TRANSPORTATION SAFETY INSTITUTE

Director.—H. Aldridge Gillespie, 6500 South MacArthur Boulevard, Oklahoma City OK 73125, (405) 954–3521.

VOLPE NATIONAL TRANSPORTATION SYSTEMS CENTER

Director.—Richard R. John, 55 Broadway, Kendall Square, Cambridge MA 02142, (617) 494–2222.

HAZARDOUS MATERIALS SAFETY OFFICES

Eastern Region: *Chief.*—Colleen D. Abbenhaus, 820 Bear Tavern Road, Suite 306, West Trenton NJ 08628, (201) 645–3968.
Central Region: *Chief.*—Kevin Boehne, Suite 136, 2350 East Devon Avenue, Des Plaines IL 60018, (312) 886–0954.
Western Region: *Chief.*—Anthony Smialek, Suite 230, 3200 Inland Empire Boulevard, Ontario CA 91764, (714) 483–5624.
Pipeline Safety Offices:
Eastern Region: *Director.*—William H. Gute, Room 5413, 400 Seventh Street SW, Washington DC 20590, (202) 366–4580.
Southern Region: *Director.*—Frederick A. Joyner, Suite 426 North, 1720 Peachtree Road, Atlanta GA 30309, (404) 347–2632.
Central Region: *Director.*—Ivan A. Huntoon, Room 1811, 911 Walnut Street, Kansas City MO 64106, (816) 426–2654.
Southwest Region: *Director.*—James C. Thomas, Room 2116, 2320 La Branch, Houston TX 77004, (713) 750–1746.
Western Region: *Director.*—Edward J. Ondak, Second Floor, 555 Zang Street, Lakewood CO 80228, (303) 236–3424.

DEPARTMENT OF THE TREASURY

15th and Pennsylvania NW 20220, phone 622–2000, http://www.ustreas.gov

ROBERT E. RUBIN became the 70th Secretary of the Treasury on January 10, 1995; born in New York City on August 29, 1938; A.B., Harvard University *summa cum laude*, 1960; L.L.B., Yale Law School, 1964; attended the London School of Economics; attorney with Cleary, Gottlieb, Steen and Hamilton, 1964–66; associate with Goldman, Sachs and Company in New York City, 1966, and general partner, 1971; joined the management committee in 1980; vice chairman and co-chief operating officer, 1987–90; co-senior partner and co-chairman, 1990–92; memberships include: board of directors of the New York Stock Exchange, Harvard Management Company, New York Futures Exchange, New York City Partnership and the Center for National Policy; served on the board of trustees of the Carnegie Corporation of New York, Mt. Sinai Hospital and Medical School, the President's Advisory Committee for Trade Negotiations, the Securities and Exchange Commission Market Oversight and Financial Services Advisory Committee, the mayor of New York's Council of Economic Advisors and the Governor's Council on Fiscal and Economic Priorities for the State of New York; served in the White House from January 20, 1993, to January 10, 1995, as assistant to the president for economic policy, directing the activities of the National Economic Council; married to Judith Oxenberg Rubin; two adult sons: James and Philip.

OFFICE OF THE SECRETARY

Secretary of the Treasury.—Robert E. Rubin, 622–1100, fax 622–2599.
Executive Assistant.—Annabella Mejia, 622–0425.
Confidential Assistant.—Cheryl Matera, 622–0190.

OFFICE OF THE DEPUTY SECRETARY

Deputy Secretary.—Lawrence H. Summers, 622–1080, fax 622–0081.
Executive Assistant.—Judith Graham, 622–1080.
Confidential Assistant.—Elizabeth Lundquist, 622–1080.
Senior Advisor.—Sheryl Sandberg, 622–1080.

OFFICE OF THE CHIEF OF STAFF

Chief of Staff.—Michael Froman, 622–1906, fax 622–0073.
Review Analyst.—Rosalind Delancy-Mosley, 622–0384.
Deputy Chief of Staff.—Sandy Mancini, 622–0059.
Senior Advisor to the Secretary (Economics and Budget).—Alan Cohen, 622–0056.
Senior Advisor to the Secretary.—Robert Boorstin, 622–0486.
Director of Scheduling.—Esther Watkins, 622–0053.
Special Assistant to the Secretary.—Michael Barr, 622–0016.

OFFICE OF THE EXECUTIVE SECRETARY

Executive Secretary.—J. Benjamin H. Nye, 622–2735, fax 622–0073.
Review Officer.—Linda Johnson, 622–0029.
Deputy Executive Secretary.—Neal Comstock, 622–0064.
Director, Office of Operations.—Alan Keller, 622–1680.
Special Assistant to the Secretary (National Security).—Michael Romey, 622–1841.
Senior National Intelligence Adviser.—John Payne, 622–1843.

OFFICE OF THE GENERAL COUNSEL

General Counsel.—Edward S. Knight, 622–0287, fax 622–2882.
Deputy General Counsel.—Neil S. Wolin, 622–0283.
Associate General Counsel (Legislation, Litigation and Regulation).—Richard S. Carro, 622–1146.
Deputy Associate General Counsel.—Thomas M. McGivern, 622–2317.
Assistant General Counsel (Banking and Finance).—John E. Bowman, 622–1964.
Deputy Assistant General Counsel.—Roberta K. McInerney, 622–1998.
Assistant General Counsel (Enforcement).—Robert M. McNamara, Jr., 622–1913.
Deputy Assistant General Counsel.—Debra Diener, 622–1927.
Assistant General Counsel (General Law and Ethics).—Kenneth R. Schmalzbach, 622–0450.
Deputy Assistant General Counsel.—Rochelle Granat, 622–0450.
Senior Counsel for Ethics.—Henry H. Booth, 622–0450.
Assistant General Counsel (International Affairs).—Russell L. Munk, 622–1899.
Deputy Assistant General Counsel.—Marilyn L. Muench, 622–1986.
Chief Counsel, Foreign Assets Control.—William B. Hoffman, 622–2410.
Tax Legislative Counsel.—Jonathan Talisman, 622–0140.
International Tax Counsel.—Joseph H. Guttentag, 622–0130.
Benefits Tax Counsel.—Mark Iwry, 622–0170.
Counsel to the Inspector General.—Lori Vassar, 622–1090.

OFFICE OF THE INSPECTOR GENERAL

Inspector General.—Valerie Lau, 622–1090, fax 622–2073.
Deputy Inspector General.—Richard Calahan, 622–1090.
Counsel to the Inspector General.—Lori Y. Vassar, 622–1090.
Assistant Inspector General for Investigations and Oversight.—Raisa Otero-Cesario, 927–5260, fax 927–5421.
Deputy Inspector General for Investigations and Oversight.—[Vacant], 927–5260.
Regional Inspector General for Investigations, Eastern Region.—Emily Coleman, 283–1170.
Assistant Inspector General for Resources.—Gary L. Whittington, 927–5200, fax 927–6492.
Deputy Inspector General for Resources.—Clifford H. Jennings, 927–5200.
Assistant Inspector General, Audit.—Dennis S. Schindel, 927–5400, fax 927–5379.
Deputy Assistant Inspector General for Audit (Financial Statements).—William Pugh, 927–5400.

OFFICE OF THE ASSISTANT SECRETARY FOR LEGISLATIVE AFFAIRS AND PUBLIC LIAISON

Assistant Secretary.—Linda L. Robertson, 622–1900, fax 622–0534.
Special Assistant.—Marne Levine, 622–1970.
Scheduling Coordinator.—Janet L. Jones, 622–0581.
Review Analyst.—Linda L. Powell, 622–0535.
Director, Office of Public Affairs.—Gail E. Peterson, 622–1990.
Congressional Inquiries.—Ora Starks, 622–0576.
Deputy Assistant Secretary (International).—Victor Rojas, 622–1980.
Legislative Research Assistant.—Gail Harris-Berry, 622–4401.
Deputy Assistant Secretary (Banking and Finance).—Victoria Rostow, 622–1910.
Legislative Assistant.—Cherry Grayson, 622–0055.
Deputy to the Assistant Secretary (International).—Richard Sinkfield, 622–1960.
Senior Legislative Specialists: Robert Bean, 622–1950; Arthur E. Cameron, 622–1940.
Deputy Assistant Secretary (Public Liaison).—Joyce H. Carrier, 622–2970.
Special Assistant.—Jim Blount, 622–0507.
Director, Office of Business Liaison.—Matthew Gorman, 622–1660.
Staff Assistant.—Verlene Joseph, 622–2970.

OFFICE OF THE ASSISTANT SECRETARY FOR PUBLIC AFFAIRS

Assistant Secretary.—Howard M. Schloss, 622–2910, fax 622–1999.
Special Assistant.—Rebecca Lowenthal, 622–1997.
Review Analyst and Scheduling Cordinator.—Marie F. Strickler, 622–2910.

Deputy Assistant Secretary for Public Affairs.—[Vacant], 622–2910.
Staff Assistant.—Irma Tucker, 622–2920.
Director, Office of Public Affairs.—[Vacant], 622–2960.
Deputy Director.—Michelle Smith, 622–2960.
Public Affairs Specialists: Jon Murchinson, 622–2960; Darren McKinney, 622–2960; Hamilton Dix, 622–2960.
Speech Writer.—David Kurapka, 622–2960.

OFFICE OF THE UNDER SECRETARY FOR INTERNATIONAL AFFAIRS

Under Secretary.—[Vacant], 622–0060, fax 622–0081.
Special Assistant.—Michele Budington, 622–0659.
Senior Advisors: Michael Moynihan, 622–0182; Jenny Sour, 622–7425.

OFFICE OF THE ASSISTANT SECRETARY FOR INTERNATIONAL AFFAIRS

Assistant Secretary.—David Lipton, 622–1270, fax 622–0417.
Special Assistant.—Clay Lowery, 622–0359.
Legislative Coordinator.—[Vacant], 622–2791.
Counselor for Middle East Affairs.—[Vacant], 626–3882.
Director of Program Services.—Daniel A. O'Brien (acting), 622–1211.
Deputy Assistant Secretary for Eurasia and Middle East.—Nancy Lee (acting), 622–0070.
Director, Office of—
Central and Eastern European Nations.—Robert S. Dohner (acting), 622–0121.
Middle Eastern and Central Asian Nations.—Karen Mathiasen (acting), 622–5504.
Deputy Assistant Secretary for International Development, Debt and Environmental Policy.—William Schuerch, 622–0153.
Director, Office of—
Multilateral Development Banks.—Joseph Eichenberger, 622–1231.
International Debt Policy.—Mary E. Chaves, 622–1850.
Deputy Assistant Secretary for Technical Assistance Policy.—James H. Fall III, 622–0667.
Director, Office of Technical Assistance.—Robert Banque (acting), 622–5787.
Director, U.S.-Saudi Arabian Joint Commission Program Office.—Jan Gasserud, 879–4350.
Deputy Assistant Secretary for International Monetary and Financial Policy.—Timothy Geithner, 622–0656.
Director, International Banking and Securities Markets.—William Murden, 622–1255.
Director, Office of—
International Monetary Fund.—James M. Lister, 622–0112.
Industrial Nations and Global Analysis.—Robert Harlow (acting), 622–0138.
Foreign Exchange Operations.—Timothy Dulaney, 622–2052.
Deputy Assistant Secretary for Asia, The Americas and Africa.—Daniel M. Zelikow (acting), 622–7222.
Director, Office of—
East and South Asian Nations.—Todd Crawford, 622–0359.
Latin American Caribbean Nations.—Bruce Juba, 622–1282.
African Affairs.—Edwin L. Barber, 622–1730.
Director, Mexican Task Force.—Wesley McGrew (acting), 622–7392.
Deputy Assistant Secretary for Trade and Investment Policy.—Margrethe Lundsager, 622–4498.
Director Office of—
Trade Finance.—Stephen Tvardek, 622–1739.
International Investment.—Gay S. Hoar, 622–9066.
Financial Services Negotiations.—Matthew Hennesey, 622–0150.
International Trade.—T. Whittier Warthin, 622–1733.

OFFICE OF THE UNDER SECRETARY FOR DOMESTIC FINANCE

Under Secretary.—John D. Hawke, 622–1703, fax 622–0387.
Review Analyst and Scheduling Coordinator.—Gaylen S. Barbour, 622–1703.
Secretary.—Diana Ridway, 622–1703.
Special Assistant.—Sara J. Cavendish, 622–0672.
Staff Assistant.—Jill Grant, 622–0933.

Principal Deputy Assistant Secretary (Government Financial Policy).—Mozelle W. Thompson, 622–2720.
Director, Office of—
Corporate Finance.—[Vacant], 622–2708.
Government Financing.—Charles D. Haworth, 622–2460.
Secretary, Federal Financing Bank.—Charles D. Haworth, 622–2460.
Manager, Federal Financing Bank.—Gary H. Burner, 622–2470.
Director, Office of Synthetic Fuels.—[Vacant], 622–0780.
Deputy Assistant Secretary (Community Development Policy).—Michael Barr, 622–0606.
Director, Community Development Financial Institutions Fund.—Kirsten Moy, 622–8662.
Deputy Director.—Steve Rhode, 622–8662.

OFFICE OF THE FISCAL ASSISTANT SECRETARY

Fiscal Assistant Secretary.—Gerald Murphy, 622–0550, fax 622–0962.
Deputy Fiscal Assistant Secretary.—Donald Hammond, 622–0560.
Assistant Fiscal Assistant Secretary.—John A. Kilcoyne, 622–1805.
Director, Office of Cash and Debt Management.—Donald A. Chiodo, 622–0580.
Senior Advisor for Fiscal Management.—Roger H. Bezdek, 622–1807.

FINANCIAL MANAGEMENT SERVICE

401 14th Street SW 20227, phone 874–6740, fax 874–6743

Commissioner.—Russell D. Morris.
Deputy Commissioner.—Michael T. Smokovich.
Assistant Commissioner for—
Agency Services.—Walter L. Jordan.
Debt Management Services.—Virginia B. Harter.
Federal Finance.—Larry D. Stout.
Financial Information.—Diane E. Clark.
Information Resources.—Constance Craig.
Management (Chief Financial Officer).—Mitchell Levine.
Regional Operations.—Bland T. Brockenborough.
Chief Counsel.—David Ingold.
Director for—
Legislative and Public Affairs.—Jim L. Hagedorn.
Planning.—Michael Merson.
Quality and Diversity.—Sondra Hutchinson.

BUREAU OF THE PUBLIC DEBT

E Street Building, Room 553, 20239–0001, phone 219–3300, fax 219–3391
(Codified under U.S.C. 31, section 306)

Commissioner.—Richard L. Gregg.
Deputy Commissioner.—F. Van Zeck, 219–3303.
Assistant Commissioner for—
Administration.—Thomas W. Harrison, 480–6514, fax 480–6537.
Automated Information Systems.—Noel Keesor, 480–6443, fax 480–6004.
Financing.—Carl M. Locken, Jr., 219–3350, fax 219–3391.
Public Debt Accounting.—Debra Hines, 874–4060, fax 874–3710.
Savings Bond Operations.—Arthur A. Klass, 480–6516, fax 480–6023.
Securities and Accounting Services.—Jane O'Brien, 480–7647, fax 480–6719.
Chief Counsel.—Calvin Ninomiya, 219–3320, fax 219–3391.
Government Securities Regulations Staff.—[Vacant], 219–3632, fax 219–3391.
Executive Director, Savings Bond Marketing Office.—Dino Deconcini, 219–4235, fax 208–1574.

OFFICE OF THE ASSISTANT SECRETARY FOR ECONOMIC POLICY

Assistant Secretary.—Joshua Gotbaum 622–2200, fax 622–2633.
Special Assistant.—David Rubin, 622–2004.
Deputy Assistant Secretary (Economic Policy).—[Vacant], 622–0563.

Director, Office of Financial Analysis.—John Auten, 622–2070.
Deputy Assistant Secretary (Policy Coordination).—Robert F. Gillingham, 622–2220.
Director, Office of—
Economic Analysis.—[Vacant], 622–2020.
Policy Analysis.—John M. Hambor, 622–2350.
Data Management.—Thomas A. McCown, Jr., 622–2250.
Director, Office of Foreign Investment Survey.—William L. Griever, 622–2240.
Deputy Assistant Secretary (Policy Analyst).—Glen Rosselli, 622–0090.

OFFICE OF THE ASSISTANT SECRETARY FOR FINANCIAL INSTITUTIONS

Assistant Secretary.—Richard S. Carnell, 622–2600, fax 622–2027.
Deputy Assistant Secretary (Financial Institutions Policy).—[Vacant], 622–2610.
Director, Office of—
Policy, Planning and Analysis.—Gordon Eastburn, 622–2730.
Financial Institutions Policy.—Joan Affleck-Smith, 622–2740.

OFFICE OF THE ASSISTANT SECRETARY FOR FINANCIAL MARKETS

Assistant Secretary.—[Vacant], 622–2037, fax 622–0265.
Staff Assistants: Jana Carter, 622–2955; Anna Hart, 622–2035.
Senior Advisor, New Currency.—Malcolm Carter, 622–0211.
Deputy Assistant Secretary (Federal Finance).—Roger L. Anderson, 622–2640.
Director, Office of—
Market Finance.—Jill K. Ouseley, 622–2630.
Federal Finance Policy Analysis.—Norman K. Carleton, 622–1855.

OFFICE OF THE ASSISTANT SECRETARY FOR TAX POLICY

Assistant Secretary.—Donald C. Lubick (acting), 622–0050, fax 622–0646.
Scheduling Coordinator.—Rosalind J. Baker, 622–0643.
Senior Advisor.—Jacqueline Wong, 622–0160.
Deputy Assistant Secretary (Tax Policy).—Kenneth Krupsky, 622–0180.
Tax Legislative Counsel.—[Vacant], 622–1334.
Deputy Tax Legislative Counsel.—[Vacant], 622–1334.
Deputy Tax Legislative Counsel for—
Regulatory Affairs.—Robert Miller, 622–1776.
Legislative Affairs.—Michael Thornton, 622–1336.
Associate Tax Legislative Counsels: P. Val Strehlow, 622–0869; John Rooney, 622–1335; John H. Parcell, 622–2578; [Vacant], 622–1129.
International Tax Counsel.—Joseph H. Guttentag, 622–0130.
Deputy International Tax Counsels: Philip West (acting), 622–1762; Daniel Berman, 622–1773.
Associate International Tax Counsels: William W. Crowdus, 622–1779; Joni Walser, 622–1752.
Benefits Tax Counsel.—J. Mark Iwry, 622–0170.
Deputy Benefits Tax Counsel.—Victoria Judson (acting), 622–1357.
Deputy Assistant Secretary (Tax Analysis).—John Karl Scholz, 622–0120.
Director, Office of Tax Analysis.—Lowell Dworin, 622–0269.
Director for—
Economic Modeling and Computer Applications.—Roy A. Wyscarver, 622–0848.
International Taxation.—William Randolph (acting), 622–0455.
Individual Taxation.—James R. Nunns, 622–1328.
Business Taxation.—Geraldine A. Gerardi, 622–1782.
Revenue Estimating.—Joel Platt, 622–0259.

OFFICE OF THE UNDER SECRETARY FOR ENFORCEMENT

Under Secretary.—Raymond Kelley, 622–0240, fax 622–5040.
Scheduling/Review Analyst.—Delores Anderson, 662–0240.
Senior Advisor.—[Vacant], 622–0240.
Director, Office of Finance and Administration.—Anna Fay Dickey, 622–1478.
Director, Office of Policy Development.—David Medina, 622–0300.

OFFICE OF THE ASSISTANT SECRETARY FOR ENFORCEMENT

Assistant Secretary.—James E. Johnson, 622–0200, fax 622–7154.
Deputy Assistant Secretary (Law Enforcement).—Elisabeth A. Bresee, 622–0470.
Director, Project Outreach.—Herbert Jones, 622–0250.
Director, Executive Office for Asset Forfeiture.—Jan Blanton, 622–9600.
Director, Office of Financial Crimes Enforcement Network (FinCEN).—Stanley E. Morris, (703) 905–3591.
Deputy Director.—William Baity, (703) 905–3682.
Deputy Assistant Secretary (Regulatory, Tariff and Trade Enforcement).—John P. Simpson, 622–0230.
Director, Office of Trade and Tariff Affairs.—Dennis M. O'Connell, 622–0220.
Foreign Assets Control.—Richard Newcomb, 622–2510.

BUREAU OF ALCOHOL, TOBACCO AND FIREARMS
650 Massachusetts Avenue NW 20226, phone 927–7777

Director.—John W. Magaw, 927–8700, fax 927–8876.
Deputy Director.—Bradley A. Buckles, 927–8710, fax 927–8876.
Assistant Director for Liaison and Public Information.—Patrick D. Hynes, 927–2617, fax 927–8868.
Executive Assistant for—
Legislative Affairs.—Steve J. Pirotte, 927–8490, fax 927–8863.
Equal Opportunity.—Marjorie R. Kornegay, 927–7760, fax 927–8835.
Chief, Strategic Planning.—Wayne Miller, 927–7720, fax 927–7977.
Ombudsman.—Richard C. Fox, 927–8680, fax 927–8876.
Chief Counsel.—Stephen McHale, 927–7772, fax 927–8673.
Associate Director for Enforcement.—Andrew Vita, 927–7970, fax 927–7756.
Assistant Director for—
Management/CFO.—William T. Earle, 927–8400, fax 927–8786.
Science and Information Technology/SIRMO.—Arthur J. Libertucci, 927–8390, fax 927–3477.
Training and Professional Development.—Gale D. Rossides, 927–9380, fax 927–0752.
Inspection.—Richard J. Hankinson, 927–7800, fax 927–8585.

U.S. CUSTOMS SERVICE
1301 Constitution Avenue NW 20229, phone 927–1000

(Created by act of July 31, 1789; codified under U.S.C. 19, section 2071)

Commissioner of Customs.—George J. Weise, 927–1000, fax 927–1380.
Chief of Staff.—Holm J. Kappler, 927–1000, fax 927–1380.
Special Assistant to the Commissioner for Equal Opportunity.—Linda Lynn Batts, 927–0210, fax 927–1476.
Deputy Commissioner.—Samuel H. Banks, 927–1010, fax 927–1380.
Special Assistant to the Deputy Commissioner.—Robert Mitchell, 927–0210, fax 927–1380.
Trade Ombudsman.—Walter Corley, 927–1440, fax 927–1969.
Assistant Commissioner for—
Congressional and Public Affairs.—Jose Padilla, 927–1760.
Regulations and Rulings.—Stuart Seidel, 482–6900.
Investigations.—Walter Biondi, 927–1600.
International Affairs.—Douglas Browning, 927–0400.
Field Operations.—Robert Trotter, 927–0100.
Chief Financial Officer.—Vincette Goerl, 927–0600.
Information and Technology.—Edward Kwas, 927–0800.
Human Resources Management.—Deborah Spero, 927–1250.

Strategic Trade.—Charles Winwood, 927–1365.
Internal Affairs.—Homer Williams, 927–1800.
Chief Counsel.—Elizabeth Anderson, 927–6900.

U.S. SECRET SERVICE

Suite 800, 1800 G Street 20223, phone 435–5700

(Codified generally under U.S.C. 3 and 18)

Director.—Eljay B. Bowron.
Deputy Director.—Richard Griffin, 435–5705.
Assistant Director for—
Administration.—W. Ralph Basham, Suite 850, 435–5780.
Government Liaison and Public Affairs.—H. Terrence Samway, Suite 805, 435–5708.
Inspection.—K. David Holmes, Suite 848, 435–5766.
Investigations.—Bruce J. Bowen, Suite 820, 435–5716.
Protective Operations.—Richard S. Miller, Suite 810, 435–5721.
Protective Research.—Stephen M. Sergek, Suite 849, 435–5725.
Training.—Lewis C. Merletti, Suite 250, NW, 435–7180.
Chief Counsel.—John J. Kelleher, Suite 842, 435–5771.

FEDERAL LAW ENFORCEMENT TRAINING CENTER

Glynco GA 31524, phone (912) 267–2224, fax (912) 267–2217

Director.—Charles F. Rinkevich, Building 94, (912) 267–2224, fax 230–2495.
Deputy Director.—R.J. Miller, Building 94, (912) 267–2225/2224.
Director, Office of—
Administration.—Kenneth A. Hall, Building 94, (912) 267–2680.
General Training.—Connie Patrick, Building 68, (912) 267–2231.
Special Training.—Ray M. Rice, Building 210, (912) 267–2991.
State, Local and International Training.—Hobart M. Henson, Building 67, (912) 267–2322.
Director.—Jeffrey Hesser, 1300 West Richey Avenue, Artesia NM 88210, phone (505) 748–8000, fax (505) 748–8100.
Associate Director.—John C. Dooher, Room 3100, 650 Massachusetts Avenue NW, Washington DC 20226, phone 927–8940, fax 927–8782.

OFFICE OF THE ASSISTANT SECRETARY FOR MANAGEMENT/CHIEF FINANCIAL OFFICER

Assistant Secretary/Chief Financial Officer.—George Muñoz, 622–0410, fax 622–2337.
Senior Advisor.—Clara Apodaca, 622–5772.
Confidential Assistant.—Susan Ohlenroth, 622–0410.
Review Analyst.—Rochelle Bell, 622–0410.
Deputy Chief Financial Officer.—Steven O. App, 622–0750.
Director, Office of—
Accounting and Internal Control.—James R. Lingebach, 622–1450.
Financial and Budget Execution.—Barry K. Hudson, 622–2207.
Financial Systems and Reports.—Dennis Mitchell, 622–0440.
Security.—Richard P. Riley, 622–1120.
Deputy Assistant Secretary for Departmental Finance and Management.—W. Scott Gould, 622–2400.
Director, Office of—
Small and Disadvantaged Business Utilization.—T.J. Garcia, 622–0530.
Procurement.—Robert Welch, 622–0520.
Management Support Systems.—Robert T. Harper, 622–0500.
Organizational Improvement.—Mary Beth Shaw (acting), 622–1068.
Budget.—Carl L. Moravitz, 622–8614.
Treasury Reinvention.—Anthony M. Fleming, 927–5907.
Strategic Planning.—John Murphy, 622–2228.
Deputy Assistant Secretary for Administration.—Alex Rodriguez, 622–1280.
Director, Office of—
Automated Systems Division.—G. Dale Seward, 622–1000.
Printing and Graphics Division.—Kirk B. Markland, 622–2170.

Director, Facilities Management Division.—James R. Haulsey, 622–1380.
Deputy Director.—Thomas S. Chase, 622–1350.
Director, Office of—
Financial Management Division.—Linda Ripetta (acting), 622–1074.
Procurement Services Division.—Wesley L. Hawley, 622–1300.
Administrative Operations Division.—Ida Hernandez, 622–1500.
Assistant Director—
Disclosure Services.—Alana Johnson, 622–0930.
Library and Information Services.—Susan B. Perella, 622–0980.
Travel and Special Event Services.—Carla Brice, 622–2940.
Director, Management Advisory Services.—William Gillers, 622–0639.
Deputy Assistant Secretary for Information Systems/Chief Information Officer.—James J. Flyzik (acting), 622–1200.
Director, Office of Information Resources Management.—Jane L. Sullivan, 622–1599.
Assistant Director—
Resource Management.—Thomas F. Kingery, 622–1507.
Information Management.—Constance D. Drew, 622–1512.
Policy and Paperwork.—Stephen N. Bryant, 622–1549.
Director, Office of Telecommunications Management.—James J. Flyzik, 622–1592.
Assistant Director—
Network Programs.—Brian P. Carman, 622–1598.
Strategic Planning and Program Administration.—Candace Hardesty, 622–1593.
TCS Executive Agent Program.—[Vacant], 622–4358.
Deputy Assistant Secretary for Human Resources.—David A. Lebryk, 622–0175.
Director, Office of—
Personnel Policy.—Ronald A. Glaser (acting), 622–1890.
Equal Opportunity Program.—Mariam Harvey (acting), 622–1160.
Treasury Integrated Management Information Systems.—Edward B. Powell III, 622–1520.
Treasury Executive Institute.—Suellen Hamby, 622–9311.
Director, Personnel Resources Division.—Debra Tomchek (acting), 622–1410.

OFFICE OF TREASURER OF THE UNITED STATES

Treasurer.—Mary Ellen Withrow, 622–0100, fax 622–2258.
Senior Advisor.—Carol Rowan, 622–0100.
Special Assistant.—Carla Brice, 622–0100.

UNITED STATES MINT

633 Third Street 20220, phone 874–6000, fax 874–6282

Director.—Phillip N. Diehl.
Deputy Director.—John P. Mitchell.
Special Assistant to the Director.—Susan Scates.
Executive Assistant to the Director.—Nancy G. McKenney.
Chief Counsel.—Kenneth B. Gubin.
Associate Director for—
Marketing.—David Pickens.
Policy and Management/CFO.—Jay Weinster.
Associate Director, Chief Operating Officer.—Andrew Cosgarea, Jr.
Deputy Associate Director for Finance/Deputy CFO.—Terry Bowie.
Chief Security/Chief, Mint Police.—William F. Daddio.

BUREAU OF ENGRAVING AND PRINTING

14th and C Streets 20228, phone 874–2000

(Created by act of July 11, 1862; codified under U.S.C. 31, section 303)

Director.—Larry E. Rolufs, 874–2000, fax 874–3879.
Associate Directors:
Chief Financial Officer.—Gregory D. Carper (acting), 874–2020, fax 874–2025.
Chief Operating Officer.—Carla F. Kidwell, 874–2007, fax 874–2009.
Associate Director for—
Management.—Timothy G. Vigotsky, 874–2042, fax 874–2043.
Technology.—Milton J. Seidel, 874–2032, fax 874–2034.

Director, Securities Technology Institute.—Thomas A. Ferguson, 874–2233, fax 874–4087.
Assistant to the Director.—Reese H. Fuller, 874–2769, fax 874–2015.

OFFICE OF THE COMPTROLLER OF THE CURRENCY
250 E Street SW 20219, phone 874–5000

Comptroller.—Eugene A. Ludwig, 874–4900.
Senior Advisor.—Mark P. Jacobsen, 874–4880.
Senior Deputy Comptroller for—
Administration.—Judith A. Walter, 874–5080.
Bank Supervision Operations.—Leann G. Britton, 874–5020.
Bank Supervision Policy.—Samuel P. Golden (acting), 874–5010.
Public Affairs.—Mathew Roberts, 874–4910.
International Affairs.—Susan Krause, 874–5010.
Economic Analysis and Policy Affairs.—James D. Kamihachi, 874–4890.
Chief Counsel.—Julie L. Williams, 874–5200.
Chief National Bank Examiner.—Jimmy F. Barton, 874–5350.
Deputy Chief Counsels: Robert B. Serino, 874–5200; Raymond Natter, 874–5200.
Deputy Comptroller for—
Bank Organization and Structure.—Steven J. Weiss, 874–5060.
Compliance Management.—Stephen M. Cross, 874–5216.
International Banking and Finance.—John M. Abbott, 874–4730.
Multinational Banking.—Ralph E. Sharpe, 874–4620.
Special Supervision.—[Vacant], 874–4450.
Economics.—David Nebhut, 874–5230.
Public Affairs.—Leonora S. Cross, 874–4970.
Resource Management.—Gary W. Norton, 874–4550.
Information Resources Management.—Stephen Cross (acting), 874–4480.
Risk Evaluation.—G. Scott Calhoun, 874–4710.
Senior Advisor for Economic and Policy Analysis.—Emily Marwell, 874–2440.
Senior Technical Advisor.—Allan B. Guerrina, 874–4486.
District Liaison.—Fred D. Finke, 874–5690.
Chief Financial Officer.—Ronald P. Passero, 874–5140.
Director, Congressional Liaison.—Carolyn S. McFarlane, 874–4840.

INTERNAL REVENUE SERVICE
Internal Revenue Building, 1111 Constitution Avenue NW 20224, phone 566–5000
(Created by act of July 1, 1862; codified under U.S.C. 26, section 7802)

Commissioner of Internal Revenue.—Margaret Milner Richardson, Room 3000, 622–4115.
Deputy Commissioner.—Michael P. Dolan, 622–4255.
Assistant to the Deputy Commissioner.—James E. Rogers, Jr., 622–5420.
Special Assistant to the Commissioner.—Helen Bolton, 622–3770.
Assistants to the Commissioner: C. Elizabeth Wagner, 622–5440; Heather Maloy, 622–5280; John Staples, 622–5430.
Special Assistant to the Deputy Commissioner.—Linda Christensen, 622–6600.
Chief, Commissioner's Staff.—James P. Nelson, 622–4091.
Scheduler.—Karen Hunter-Thomas, 622–9511.

OFFICE OF THE TAXPAYER OMBUDSMAN

Taxpayer Advocate.—Lee Monks, 622–6100.
Executive Assistant to the Taxpayer Ombudsman.—Thomas Tiffany, 622–8100.

OFFICE OF THE CHIEF COUNSEL

Chief Counsel.—Stuart Brown, 622–3300.
Deputy Chief Counsel.—Marlene Gross, 622–3310.
Associate Chief Counsel for—
Domestic.—Judy Dunn, 622–4500.
EB/EO.—Sarah Hall Ingram, 622–6000.
Enforcement Litigation.—Eliot Fielding, 622–3400.

Finance and Management.—Richard Mihelcic, 622–3330.
International.—Michael Danilack, 622–3800.
National Director of Appeals.—James Dougherty, 401–6221.

OFFICE OF THE CHIEF COMPLIANCE OFFICER

Chief Compliance Officer.—Jim Donelson, 622–6600.
Executive Assistant.—Dianne Grant, 622–6600.
Fraud Control Executive.—Ted F. Brown, 622–7140.
Assistant Commissioner for—
Collection.—Ronald S. Rhodes, 622–5100.
Criminal Investigation.—Ted F. Brown, 622–3200.
Deputy Assistant Commissioner.—Paul M. Miyahara, 622–6190.
Director of Investigations for—
Central Area of Operations.—Glenda M. Pappillion, (312) 868–5710.
Eastern Area of Operations.—Michael D. Orth, (212) 264–7525.
Southern Area of Operations.—Randall D. Vaughn, (404) 331–6515.
Western Area of Operations.—Robert L. Thomas, (415) 556–0553.
Assistant Commissioner for—
Examination.—Tom Smith, 622–4400.
EP/EO.—Evelyn Petschek, 622–6710.
International.—John Lyons, 874–1900.
Deputy Assistant Commissioner (International).—Deborah Nolan, 874–1910.
National Director, Compliance Research.—Wayne Thomas, 874–0100.
Director, Statistics of Income.—Dan Skally, 874–0700.

OFFICE OF THE CHIEF FINANCIAL OFFICER

Chief Financial Officer.—Tony Musick, 622–6400.
Executive Assistant.—Mike Noble, 622–6410.
Controller/Director, Financial Management Division.—Lisa Fiely, 622–8710.
National Director of—
Office of Budget.—Richard Morgante, 622–8770.
Systems and Accounting Standards.—Patrica Healy, (301) 492–5315.
Financial Analysis Division.—Tom Andretta, 622–8710.

OFFICE OF THE ASSOCIATE COMMISSIONER FOR MODERNIZATION/CHIEF INFORMATION OFFICER

Chief Information Officer.—Arthur A. Gross, 622–8800.
Executive Assistant.—Debbie Pettis, 622–6810.
Deputy Chief Information Officer.—Robert F. Albicker, 622–7100.
Deputy Chief Information Officer (Operations).—[Vacant], 622–6800.
Office of Privacy Advocate.—Rob Veeder, 927–6580
Deputy CIO for—
Resource Management.—Toni Zimmerman, 622–0260.
Government Program Management.—Sarah Witbeck, 622–5380.

OFFICE OF THE CHIEF INSPECTOR

Chief Inspector.—Gary Bell, 622–6500.
Deputy Chief Inspector.—Doug Crouch, 622–6510.
Assistant Chief of—
Internal Audit.—Billy Morrison, 622–8500.
Internal Security.—Sebastian Lorigo, 622–4600.

OFFICE OF THE CHIEF, MANAGEMENT AND ADMINISTRATION

Chief, Management and Administration.—David Mader, 622–4700.
Senior Adviser to the Chief.—Joann Buck, 622–4710.
Assistant Commissioner (Procurement).—Greg Rothwell, 622–8480.
Deputy Assistant Commissioner (Procurement).—Jim Williams, 622–8480.
National Director, EEO and Diversity.—Ed Chavez, 622–5400.
Director, Real Estate Planning and Management.—Lee Keller, 535–4920.

National Director of Education.—Tom Myerchin, (703) 908–6150.
Director of—
Personnel.—Jim A. O'Malley (acting), 874–5840.
Legislative Affairs Division.—Floyd L. Williams III, 622–3720.
Analysis and Studies.—Bill Hannon, 874–6237.
Strategic Planning Division.—Charlotte Perdue, 927–5801.
Chief of—
Office of Planning and Financial Management.—Ted McQuiston, 622–4720.
Office of Executive Support.—Robert Buggs, 622–6320.

OFFICE OF THE CHIEF, TAXPAYER SERVICES

Chief, Taxpayer Services.—Jim Donelson (acting), 622–6880.
Executive Officer for Service Center Operations.—Tom Dega, 622–5700.
National Director, Tax Forms and Publications.—Sheldon Schwartz, 622–5200.
Assistant Commissioner (Taxpayer Service).—Gwen Krauss, 622–0600.

OFFICE OF THE CHIEF, HEADQUARTERS OPERATIONS

Chief, Headquarters Operations.—David Junkins, 622–8600.
Executive Assistant.—Ben Dadd, 622–8600.
Director of—
HQ Human Resources.—Kent Baum, 622–6420.
EEO and Diversity.—Paulette Sewell, 622–4490.
Office of Controller.—Bob Eisenhauer, 622–3490.
Information Technology.—Bill Moss, 927–9370.

OFFICE OF THRIFT SUPERVISION

1700 G Street NW 20552, phone 906–6000, fax 906–7494, 906–7495

(Codified in U.S.C. 12, section 1462a)

Director.—Nicholas P. Retsinas, 906–6590, fax 898–0230.
Executive Director, Supervision.—John F. Downew, 906–6853, fax 906–6518.
Assistant Director for Supervision.—Al Smuzynski, 906–5669, fax 906–6518.
Chief Counsel.—Carolyn J. Buck, 906–6251, fax 906–7606.
Director for—
Executive Research and Analysis.—Kenneth J. Ryder, 906–5727, fax 202–7746.
Minority Affairs.—Nadine Elzy, 906–6579, fax 906–7861.
Executive Administration.—Cora P. Beebe, 906–6547, fax 906–6303.
External Affairs.—John Von Seggern (acting), 906–6288, fax 906–7747.
Public Affairs.—William E. Pulwider (acting), 906–6913, fax 906–7849.
Congressional Affairs.—Kevin Petrasic (acting).
Associate Director for—
Policy.—John C. Price, 906–5762, fax 906–7746.
Information Resources Management.—William J. Durbin, 906–5200, fax 906–6700.
FDIC Operations.—Walter B. Mason, 906–7236, fax 898–0230.
ETC Liaison.—Lee Lassiter, 906–5685, fax 898–0230.

REGIONAL OFFICES

Regional Directors:
Northeast.—Robert C. Albanese, (201) 413–1000, fax (201) 413–7543.
Southeast.—John E. Ryan, (404) 888–0771, fax (404) 892–8128.
Central.—Ronald N. Karr, (312) 917–5000, fax 917–5001.
Midwest.—Frederick R. Casteel, (214) 281–2000, fax (214) 281–2001.
West.—John F. Robinson, (415) 616–1500, fax (415) 616–1752/1753.

DEPARTMENT OF VETERANS AFFAIRS

Many VA offices are located in Techworld Plaza, 801 I Street NW.
Mail should be addressed to 810 Vermont Avenue, Washington DC 20420
phone 535–7023, http://www.va.gov

JESSE BROWN, Secretary of Veterans Affairs; born in Detroit, MI, March 27, 1944; served in U.S. Marine Corps, 1963–65, injured in Vietnam in 1965; A.A., Chicago City College, 1972; national service officer, Disabled American Veterans (DAV), 1967–73; supervisor, national service officer, DAV, 1973–76; supervisor, National Appeals Office, DAV, 1976–81; deputy national service director, 1981–88; executive director, Washington office, DAV, 1988–93; chosen by President-elect Clinton as Secretary of Veterans Affairs-designate on December 17, 1992; nominated by President Clinton on January 20, 1993; confirmed by the U.S. Senate on January 21, 1993; sworn in on January 22, 1993.

OFFICE OF THE SECRETARY

Secretary of Veterans Affairs.—Jesse Brown, 273–4800.
Chief of Staff.—Harold Gracey.
Executive Secretary.—Linda Kaufman.
Special Assistant for Veterans Organization Liaison.—Allen (Gunner) Kent, 273–4835.
General Counsel.—Mary Lou Keener, 273–6660.
Deputy Inspector General.—William T. Merriman, Room 1114, Techworld Building, 565–8620.
Chairman, Board of—
Contract Appeals.—Guy H. McMichael III, Room 545F, 1800 G Street, 273–6743.
Veterans Appeals.—Roger K. Baurer (acting), Room 845 LaFayette Building, 565–5001.

OFFICE OF THE DEPUTY SECRETARY

Deputy Secretary.—Hershel W. Gober, 273–4817.
Director, Office of Small and Disadvantaged Business Utilization (OSDBU).—Scott Denniston, Room 620, Techworld Building, 565–8124.

ASSISTANT SECRETARY FOR CONGRESSIONAL AFFAIRS

Assistant Secretary.—Edward P. Scott, 273–5611.
Deputy Assistant Secretary for Congressional Affairs.—Phil Riggin, Room 504, 273–5615.

ASSISTANT SECRETARY FOR PUBLIC AND INTERGOVERNMENTAL AFFAIRS

Assistant Secretary.—Kathy Jurado, 273–5750.
Deputy Assistant Secretary for—
Public Affairs.—Jim Holley, 273–5710.
Intergovernmental Affairs.—John Hanson, 273–5760.

ASSISTANT SECRETARY FOR POLICY AND PLANNING

Assistant Secretary.—Dennis M. Duffy, 273–5033.
Deputy Assistant Secretary for—
Policy.—Edward Chow, 273–5045.
Planning.—Nora Egan, 273–5068.

ASSISTANT SECRETARY FOR MANAGEMENT

Assistant Secretary.—D. Mark Catlett, 273–5589.
Deputy Assistant Secretary for—
Budget.—Shirley Carozza, 273–5240.
Information Resources Management.—Nada Harris, 273–8855.
Financial Management.—Frank Sullivan, 273–5504.
Acquisition and Materiel Management.—Gary Krump, 273–8029.

ASSISTANT SECRETARY FOR HUMAN RESOURCES MANAGEMENT

Assistant Secretary.—Eugene Brickhouse, 273–4901.
Deputy Assistant Secretary for—
Equal Employment Opportunity.—Gerald K. Hinch, Room 510, Westory Building, 482–6703.
Administration.—Robert W. Schultz, 273–5356.
Human Resources Management.—Ronald Cowles, 273–4920.
Security and Law Enforcement.—John Baffa, 273–5500.

NATIONAL CEMETERY SYSTEM

Director.—Jerry W. Bowen, 273–5145.
Director of—
Field Operations.—Roger R. Rapp, 273–5226.
Operations Support.—Vincent Barile, 273–5153.
Memorial Programs.—Larry DeMeo, Room 819, Techworld Building, 565–4200.

VETERANS BENEFITS ADMINISTRATION

Under Secretary.—Stephen Lemons (acting), Room 520, 1800 G Street, 273–6763.
Deputy Under Secretary.—Stephen Lemons.
Chief Information Officer.—Newell Quinton, Room 436, 1800 G Street, 273–7004.
Chief Financial Officer.—Robert Gardner, Room 623, 1800 G Street, 273–6728.

VETERANS HEALTH ADMINISTRATION

Under Secretary.—Kenneth W. Kizer, M.D., M.P.H., 273–5781.
Deputy Under Secretary.—Thomas L. Garthwaite, M.D., 273–5803.
Chief—
Network Officer.—Jule D. Moravec, Ph.D., 273–5826.
Patient Care Services Officer.—Thomas V. Holohan, M.D., 273–8474.
Research and Development Officer.—John R. Feussner, M.D., 273–8232.
Public Health and Environmental Hazards Officer.—Susan H. Mather, M.D., 273–8456.
Academic Affiliations Officer.—David P. Stevens, M.D., 273–8380.
Administrative Officer.—Lydia B. Mavridis, 273–6309.
Financial Officer.—W. Todd Grams, 273–5662.
Policy, Planning and Performance Officer.—Gregg A. Pane, M.D., 273–8932.

INDEPENDENT AGENCIES, COMMISSIONS, BOARDS

ADVISORY COUNCIL ON HISTORIC PRESERVATION

(Created by Public Law 89–665, amended by Public Laws 94–422, 96–515)

3100 Pennsylvania Avenue NW, Suite 809, 20004
phone 606–8503, http://www.ach.gov

Chairman.—Cathryn Buford Slater, Little Rock, AR.
Vice Chairman.—Stephen B. Hand, New Orleans, LA.
Members:
Margaret Zuehlke Robson, San Francisco, CA.
Arthur Q. Davis, FAIA, New Orleans, LA.
James K. Huhta, Murfreesboro, TN.
Arva Moore Parks McCabe, Miami, FL.
Parker Westbrook, Little Rock, AR.
Bruce D. Judd, FAIA, San Francisco, CA.
Raynard C. Soon, Honolulu, HI.
Governor [Vacant].
Mayor Emmanuel Cleaver II, Kansas City, MO.
Secretary, Department of Agriculture.
Secretary, Department of Housing and Urban Development.
Secretary, Department of Transportation.
Architect of the Capitol.
Administrator, Environmental Protection Agency.
Administrator, General Services Administration.
Nancy Campbell, Chairman, National Trust for Historic Preservation, New York, NY.
Judith Bittner, President, National Conference of State Historic Preservation Officers, Anchorage, AK.
Executive Secretary.—Robert D. Bush, (202) 208–0710.
Acting Executive Director and General Counsel.—John M. Fowler, (202) 606–8503.

AFRICAN DEVELOPMENT FOUNDATION

(Created by Public Law 96–533)

1400 Eye Street NW, Suite 1000, 20005–2248, phone 673–3916, fax 673–3810

BOARD OF DIRECTORS

Chairman.—Ernest G. Green.
Vice Chairman.—Willie Grace Campbell.
Private Members: Cecil J. Banks, Marion Dawson-Carr, Henry E. McKoy.
Public Members: Ambassador George E. Moose, Ambassador John F. Hicks.

STAFF

President.—William R. Ford.
Vice President.—Nathaniel Fields.
Administrative Services Officer.—Genevieve Peterson.
Advisory Committee Management.—Teixeira Nash.
Congressional Liaison Officer.—[Vacant].
General Counsel.—Paul S. Magid.
Budget and Finance Director.—Thomas F. Wilson.
Personnel Director.—Constance Smith-Field.
Acting Director, Program Field Operations.—Rama Bah.
Director, Learning and Dissemination.—Christine Fowles.
Public Affairs Officer.—Teixeira Nash.

AMERICAN BATTLE MONUMENTS COMMISSION

(Created by Public Law 67–534)

Pulaski Building, 20 Massachusetts Avenue NW, Room 5127, 20314–0001
phone (202) 272–0533

Chairman.—Gen. Fred F. Woerner, Jr., U.S. Army (ret).

Commissioners:

Hugh L. Carey
Brig. Gen. Evelyn P. Foote, U.S. Army (ret.)
Rolland E. Kidder
Brig. Gen. Douglas Kinnard, U.S. Army (ret.)
Alfred S. Los Banos
Thomas G. Lyons
Brenda L. Moore
Brig. Gen. Gail M. Reals, U.S. Marine Corps (ret.)
F. Haydn Williams

Secretary.—Maj. Gen. John P. Herrling, U.S. Army (ret.).
Executive Director.—Kenneth S. Pond.
Director for—
Engineering and Maintenance.—Col. Dale F. Means, U.S. Army.
Operations and Finance.—Col. Anthony N. Corea, USAF.
Personnel and Administration.—LtCdr. Theodore Gloukoff, U.S. Army.

AMERICAN NATIONAL RED CROSS

National Headquarters, 430 17th Street NW 20006, phone (202) 737–8300

HONORARY OFFICERS

Honorary Chairman.—William J. Clinton, President of the United States.
General Counsel.—Richard Dashefsky.
Honorary Treasurer.—Robert E. Rubin, Secretary of the Treasury.

OFFICERS

Chairman of the Board of Governors.—Norman R. Augustine.
Vice Chairmen of the Board of Governors:

George McDavid
William R. Usher
Valerie Gwyn

BOARD OF GOVERNORS

C=Elected by the Chartered Units
L=Elected by Board as Member-at-Large
P=Appointed by the President of the United States

D. Inez Andreas (L).
Norman R. Augustine (P).
Hugh J. Baker III (C).
Kenneth D. Brody (P).
Carlton K. Brownell (C).
Deborah D. Carman (L).
Pete E. Chavez (C).
John L. Clendenin (L).
William M. Darr (C).
Mary H. DeKuyper (C).
Frank S. Dickerson III (C).
Robert L. Dilenschneider (C).
F. Joe Falk, Jr. (C).
Russell R. Gifford (C).
Robert N. Grant (C).
Valerie Gwyn (C).
Gray W. Harrison, Jr. (C).
Gwen T. Jackson (C).
Erik E. Joh, (C).
Patricia A. Kennedy (C).
Deborah Karr King (C).
Helen Shores Lee (C).
Michael A. Leven (L).
Jonathan S. Linen (L).
George E. McDavid (C).
D. Richard McFerson (L).
Catherine B. Miller (L).
George A. Nicholson III (C).
Emilio R. Nicolas, Jr. (L).
Miguel A. Nieves (C).
James J. Norton (L).
Donald C. Otto, Jr. (C).
Eddy M. Quijano (C).
Richard W. Riley (P).
Jay Rodriguez (C).
Philip J. Sadler (C).
Donna E. Shalala (P).
John Shalikashvili (P).

Gerald A. Sumida (C).
Lynn R. Swon (C).
Joe A. Taller (C).
William R. Usher (C).
Abigail S. Wexner (C).
James Lee Witt (P).
Thomas G. Yamada (C).

CORPORATE OFFICERS

Chairman.—Norman R. Augustine.
President.—Elizabeth H. Dole.
Treasurer.—[Vacant.]
General Counsel.—Richard L. Dashefsky.
Secretary.—Lois L. Fu.

ADMINISTRATIVE OFFICERS

National Chairman of Volunteers.—Karen K. Goodman.
Chief Operating Officer.—E. Mathew Branam.
Vice President, Finance/Comptroller.—John D. Campbell.
Vice President, Human Resources.—Robert Cherundolo.
Vice President, Information Services.—Thomas H. Woteki.
General Manager, Corporate Planning & Evaluation.—Frederick A. Gervasi.
Senior Vice President, Biomedical Services.—Jimmy D. Ross.
Chief Operating Officer/Responsible Head.—Brian P. McDonough.
Vice President for—
Business Development.—Geoffrey J. Deutsch.
Finance.—Merle Freitag.
Plasma Operations.—Chris Lamb.
Quality Assurance/Regulatory Policy.—Stephen J. Stachelski, Jr.
Research and Development.—Leon W. Hoyer, M.D.
Senior Vice President, Chapter Services.—Susan Morissey Livingstone (acting).
Vice President, Disaster Services.—Donald W. Jones.
Vice President, Armed Forces Emergency Services.—Sue A. Richter.
General Manager, Chapter Organization Administration.—Richard N. Smith.
Senior Vice President, Public Support.—Jennifer L. Dorn.
Vice President, Communications.—Julie Bingham (acting).
Vice President, Development.—Jennifer Dunlap.
Vice President, Marketing.—Suzanne Cox Iglesias.
Vice President, International Services.—Jose Aponte.

APPALACHIAN REGIONAL COMMISSION

1666 Connecticut Avenue NW 20235, phone (202) 884–7660, fax 884–7691

Federal Co-Chairman.—Jesse L. White, Jr.
Alternate Federal Co-Chairman.—[Vacant].
States' Washington Representative.—Michael R. Wenger.
Executive Director.—Thomas M. Hunter.
Congressional Affairs Officer.—Guy Land.

ARMED FORCES RETIREMENT HOME BOARD

PO Box 46362, Washington DC, 20050–6362, phone (703) 892–6815, fax 697–2519

Chair.—Dennis W. Jahnigen, M.D., Gerontologist, Director, Center on Aging, University of Colorado Health Sciences Center.
Vice Chair.—David F. Lacy, Retirement Home Expert, Executive Director, Trinity Terrace.
Members:
Robert B. Armstrong, Retirement Home Expert, Pleasant Hill Health Facility.
Terrie T. Wetle, Ph.D., Gerontologist, Deputy Director, National Institute on Aging.
Laurence G. Branch, PhD, Gerontology, Duke University.
Carolyn H. Becraft, Deputy Assistant Secretary of Defense (Personnel Support, Families and Education).
William E. Coonce, Director, Revolving Fund, Office of the Comptroller, Department of Defense.

Dr. J. F. Mazzuchi, Deputy Assistant Secretary of Defense (Clinical Services).
Cdr. W. D. Newman, U.S. Navy, Office of Associate Deputy General Counsel (Personnel and Health Policy).
LtG. Frederick E. Vollrath, U.S. Army, Deputy Chief of Staff, Personnel.
VADM Daniel T. Oliver, U.S. Navy, Chief of Naval Personnel.
Eric W. Benken, Chief Master Sergeant of the Air Force.
Lewis G. Lee, Sergeant Major of the Marine Corps.
David Morrison, Representative, Office of Management and Budget.
Marsha Goodwin-Beck, Representative, Department of Veterans Affairs.
Rear Adm. Audrey F. Manley, MD, USPHS, Acting Surgeon General.
Gene C. McKinney, Sergeant Major of the Army.
John Hagan, Master Chief Petty Officer of the Navy.
Chief Sergeant Major Robert R. Mix, USA, Military Retiree Counsel Representative.
MG Donald C. Hilbert, U.S. Army (ret.) Director, U.S. Soldiers' and Airmen's Home.
LtG Michael D. McGinty, U.S. Air Force, Chair, U.S. Soldiers' and Airmen's Home Board of Trustees.
F. Michael Fox, Jr., Director, U.S. Naval Home.
Robert J. Walker, Master Chief Petty Officer of the Navy, (ret.) Chair, U.S. Naval Home Board of Trustees.
Martha J. Williams, Chair, Resident Advisory Committee, U.S. Soldiers' and Airmen's Home.
Peter E. Loque, Chair, Resident Advisory Committee, U.S. Naval Home.

U.S. SOLDIERS' AND AIRMEN'S HOME

3700 North Capitol Street 20317, phone (202) 722–3227, fax 722–9087

BOARD OF TRUSTEES

Chair.—LtG. Michael D. McGinty, U.S. Air Force, Deputy Chief of Staff, Personnel.
Vice Chair.—Dr. Richard E. Reichard, Director, National Lutheran Home, Retirement Home Expert.
Members:
LtG. Joe N. Ballard, U.S. Army, CE, Chief of Engineers.
Dr. L. Gregory Pawlson, Chairman, HSC, George Washington University Medical Center, Gerontologist.
MG George T. Stringer, Deputy Assistant Secretary of the Air Force (Budget).
Mr. Sanford M. Garfunkel, Representative, Department of Veterans Affairs.
Martha J. Williams, Chair, Resident Advisory Committee.
William A. Connelly, Sergeant Major of the Army (ret), Retiree Council Representative.
Gene C. McKinney, Sergeant Major of the Army.
Col. (P) Michael Kussman, US Army, Commander, Walter Reed Health Care System.
MG Donald G. Hilbert, U.S. Air Force, The Judge Advocate General.
MG Donald C. Hilbert, U.S. Army, (ret), Director, U.S. Soldiers's and Airmen's Home.
BG Evan Gaddis, Commander, U.S. Army Community and Family Support Center.
Chief Master Sergeant of the Air Force Eric W. Benken.
John Hagan, Master Chief Petty Officer of the Navy.
Sgt. Maj. James L. Lewis, USMC.

OFFICERS OF THE HOME

Director.—MG Donald C. Hilbert, U.S. Army (ret.).
Deputy Director.—Robert J. Grider.
Associate Director, Office of—
Engineering.—[Vacant].
Health Care Services.—BG Paul D. Gleason, M.D., U.S. Air Force (ret.).
Resident Services.—CMSGT Norman T. Parnes, U.S. Air Force (ret.).
Resource Management.—Thomas N. Bellamy.
Support.—Joseph A. Ross, Jr.

U.S. NAVAL HOME

1800 Beach Drive Gulfport MS 39507, phone (601) 897–4003, fax 897–4013

BOARD OF TRUSTEES

Chair.—Robert J. Walker, Master Chief Petty Officer of the Navy (ret.), Representative, Military Retiree Council.

Vice Chair.—RADM Larry R. Marsh, U.S. Navy, Assistant Chief of Naval Personnel.

Members:

J.P. Rathburn, Jr., Headquarters, U.S. Marine Corps MMSR, Senior Chief Service Personnel Representative.

John Hagan, Master Chief Petty Officer of the Navy.

Steven M. Johnson, Retirement Home Expert.

George Rodman, Representative, Department of Veterans Affairs.

Ames Tryon, D.D.S., Ph.D, Gerontologist.

BG Pedro Rivera, U.S. Air Force, Commander, 81st Medical Group, Keesler AFB, MS.

Ty A. Salness, FCCP, M.D., Department of Veterans Affairs.

Ariane L. Whittemore, Financial Management, Office of the Chief of Naval Operations.

CAPT Russell A. Johnson, U.S. Navy Representative, Judge Advocate General Corps.

Peter E. Louque, Chair, Resident Advisory Council.

F. Michael Fox, Jr., Director, U.S. Naval Home.

OFFICERS OF THE HOME

Director.—F. Michael Fox., Jr.

Deputy Director.—Larry R. Weappa.

Office of—

Resource Management Services.—Larry C. Wilson.

Plant Management Services.—James C. Barnett.

Recreation Services.—Donald R. Cross.

Social Services.—Adrenne Dedeaux.

Resident Services.—Robert S. Locke.

Nursing Services.—Helen Donnan.

Clinical Services.—John G. Atwood, M.D.

Pharmacy Services.—Perry Dillard.

BOARD OF GOVERNORS OF THE FEDERAL RESERVE SYSTEM

Constitution Avenue and 20th Street 20551, phone (202) 452–3000

Chairman.—Alan Greenspan.

Vice Chair.—Alice M. Rivlin.

Members:

Edward W. Kelley, Jr.

Susan M. Phillips

Laurence H. Meyer

[Vacant]

[Vacant]

Assistants to the Board:

Public Affairs.—Joseph R. Coyne, 452–3204.

Congressional Liaison.—Donald J. Winn, 452–3456.

Federal Reserve System Affairs.—Theodore E. Allison, 452–2793.

Deputy Congressional Liaison.—Lynn S. Fox.

Special Assistants to the Board: Winthrop P. Hambley, Bob Stahly Moore, Diane Werneke.

Equal Employment Opportunity Programs Adviser.—Portia W. Thompson.

DIVISION OF INTERNATIONAL FINANCE

Staff Director.—Edwin M. Truman.

Senior Associate Directors: Larry J. Promisel, Charles J. Siegman.

Associate Director.—Dale W. Henderson.

Senior Adviser.—David H. Howard.

Assistant Directors: Donald B. Adams, Peter Hooper III, Karen H. Johnson, Ralph W. Smith, Jr., Thomas A. Connors, Catherine L. Mann.

DIVISION OF RESEARCH AND STATISTICS

Director.—Michael J. Prell.
Deputy Directors: Edward C. Ettin, David J. Stockton.
Associate Directors: Martha Bethea, William R. Jones, Myron L. Kwast, Patrick M. Parkinson, Thomas D. Simpson, Lawrence Slifman.
Deputy Associate Directors: Martha S. Scanlon, Peter A. Tinsley.
Assistant Directors: David S. Jones, Stephen A. Rhoades, Charles S. Struckmeyer, Alice Patricia White, Joyce K. Zickler.
Senior Advisers: John J. Mingo, Glenn B. Canner.

DIVISION OF MONETARY AFFAIRS

Director.—Donald L. Kohn.
Deputy Director.—David E. Lindsey.
Associate Director.—Brian F. Madigan.
Deputy Associate Director.—Richard D. Porter.
Assistant Director.—Vincent R. Reinhart.
Special Assistant to the Board.—Normand R.V. Bernard.

DIVISION OF BANKING SUPERVISION AND REGULATION

Director.—Richard Spillenkothen.
Deputy Director.—Stephen C. Schemering.
Associate Director.—William A. Ryback.
Deputy Associate Directors: Herbert A. Biern, Roger T. Cole, James I. Garner.
Assistant Directors: Howard A. Amer, Gerald A. Edwards, Jr., Stephen M. Hoffman, James V. Houpt, Jack P. Jennings, Michael G. Martinson, Rhoger H. Pugh, Sidney M. Sussan, Molly S. Wassom.
Project Director, National Information Center.—William Schneider.

LEGAL DIVISION

General Counsel.—J. Virgil Mattingly, Jr.
Associate General Counsels: Scott G. Alvarez, Richard M. Ashton, Oliver Ireland, Kathleen M. O'Day.
Assistant General Counsels: Robert deV. Frierson, Katherine H. Wheatley.

DIVISION OF CONSUMER AND COMMUNITY AFFAIRS

Director.—Griffith L. Garwood.
Associate Directors: Glenn E. Loney, Dolores S. Smith.
Assistant Directors: Maureen P. English, Irene Shawn McNulty.

DIVISION OF FEDERAL RESERVE BANK OPERATIONS AND PAYMENT SYSTEMS

Director.—Clyde H. Farnsworth, Jr.
Deputy Director (Finance and Control).—David L. Robinson.
Associate Director.—Louise L. Roseman.
Assistant Directors: Charles W. Bennett, Jack Dennis, Jr., Earl G. Hamilton, Jeffrey C. Marquardt, John H. Parrish, Florence M. Young.

OFFICE OF THE SECRETARY

Secretary.—William W. Wiles.
Deputy Secretary of the Board.—Jennifer J. Johnson.
Associate Secretary and Ombudsman.—Barbara R. Lowrey.

STAFF DIRECTOR FOR MANAGEMENT

Staff Director.—S. David Frost.
EEO Programs Director.—Sheila Clark.

DIVISION OF INFORMATION RESOURCES MANAGEMENT

Director.—Stephen R. Malphrus.
Assistant Directors: Marianne M. Emerson, Po Kyung Kim, Raymond H. Massey, Edward T. Mulrenin, Day W. Radebaugh, Jr., Elizabeth B. Riggs, Richard C. Stevens.

DIVISION OF HUMAN RESOURCES MANAGEMENT

Director.—David L. Shannon.
Associate Director.—John R. Weis.
Assistant Directors: Joseph H. Hayes, Jr., Fred Horowitz.

OFFICE OF THE CONTROLLER

Controller.—George E. Livingston.
Assistant Controllers: Stephen J. Clark, Darrell R. Pauley.

DIVISION OF SUPPORT SERVICES

Director.—Robert E. Frazier.
Assistant Directors: George M. Lopez, David L. Williams.

INSPECTOR GENERAL

Inspector General.—Brent L. Bowen.
Assistant Inspectors General: Donald L. Robinson, Barry R. Snyder.

COMMISSION OF FINE ARTS

441 F Street NW, Pension Building 20001, phone (202) 504–2200, fax 504–2195

Commissioners:
J. Carter Brown, Washington, DC.
Carolyn Brody, Washington, DC.
Barbaralee Diamonstein-Spielvogel, New York, NY.
Eden Rafshoon, Washington, DC.
Harry G. Robinson, III, Washington, DC.
Susan Porter Rose, Alexandria, VA.
Secretary and Administrative Officer.—Charles H. Atherton.

BOARD OF ARCHITECTURAL CONSULTANTS FOR THE OLD GEORGETOWN ACT

Stephen Muse
Elliott Carroll
Mary L. Oehrlein

COMMITTEE FOR PURCHASE FROM PEOPLE WHO ARE BLIND OR SEVERELY DISABLED

Crystal Square 3 Room 403, 1735 Jefferson Davis Highway
Arlington VA 22202–3461, phone (703) 603–7740, fax 421–7113

Chairperson.—Gary J. Krump, Department of Veterans' Affairs.
Vice Chairperson.—Evelyne R. Villines, private citizen (knowledgeable about obstacles to employment of persons with other severe disabilities).
Members:
Hugh L. Brennan, Department of Commerce.
Carole A. Dortch, General Services Administration.
W.L. Evey, Department of the Air Force.
Deborah G. Groeber, private citizen (representing nonprofit agency employees with other severe disabilities).
Ira L. Hobbs, Department of Agriculture.
MG Ray E. McCoy, U.S. Army, Department of Defense.
RADM R.M. Mitchell, Jr., USN, Department of the Navy.

Kenneth J. Oscar, Department of the Army.
LeRoy F. Sanders, private citizen (knowledgeable about obstacles to employment of persons who are blind).
Fredic K. Schroeder, Department of Education.
Steven B. Schwalb, Department of Justice.
Suzanne B. Seiden, Department of Labor.
Donald H. Wedewer, private citizen (representing nonprofit agency employees who are blind).

COMMODITY FUTURES TRADING COMMISSION

Three Lafayette Centre, 1155 21st Street NW 20581

phone 418–5000, fax 418–5521, http://www.cfta.gov

Chairperson.—Brooksley Born, 418–5030.
Executive Assistant to the Chairperson.—Susan G. Lee, 418–5030.
Commissioners:
Joseph B. Dial, 418–5050.
John E. Tull, Jr., 418–5060.
Barbara Pedersen Holum, 418–5070.
David D. Spears, 418–5040.
Executive Director.—Donald L. Tendick, 418–5160 (acting).
General Counsel.—Daniel R. Waldman, 418–5120.
Director, Division of—
Economic Analysis.—Blake Imel (acting), 418–5260.
Enforcement.—Geoffrey Aronow, 418–5320.
Trading and Markets.—Andrea Corcoran, 418–5430.
Director, Office of—
Public Affairs.—John C. Phillips, 418–5080.
Legislative and Intergovernmental Affairs.—[Vacant], 418–5075.
Secretary.—Jean A. Webb, 418–5095.
Inspector General.—A. Roy Lavik, 418–5110.

REGIONAL OFFICES

Chicago: 300 South Riverside Plaza, Suite 1600 North, Chicago, IL 60606, (312) 353–5990, fax 353–2993.
Kansas City: 4900 Main Street, Suite 721, Kansas City, MO 64112, (816) 931–7600, fax 931–9643.
Los Angeles: 10900 Wilshire Boulevard, Suite 400, Los Angeles, CA 90024, (310) 235–6783, fax 235–6782.
Minneapolis: 510 Grain Exchange Building, Minneapolis, MN 55415, (612) 370–3255, fax 370–3257.
New York: One World Trade Center, Suite 3747, New York, NY 10048, (212) 466–2061, fax 466–5273.

CONSUMER PRODUCT SAFETY COMMISSION

(Created by Public Law 92–573)

4330 East West Highway, Bethesda MD 20814
phone (301) 504–0990, fax 504–0124, http://www.cpsc.gov

Chairperson.—Ann Brown, 504–0213.
Commissioners:
Mary Sheila Gall, 504–0530
Thomas H. Moore, 504–0290.
Executive Director.—Pamela Gilbert, 504–0550.
Deputy Executive Directors: Clarence T. Bishop, 504–0550; Thomas W. Murr, Jr., 504–0788.
Secretary.—Sadye E. Dunn, 504–0800.
General Counsel.—Jeffery S. Bromme, 504–0980.
Director, Congressional Relations.—Robert J. Wager, 504–0515.

CORPORATION FOR NATIONAL SERVICE

(Executive Order 11603, June 30, 1971; codified in 42 U.S.C., section 4951)

1201 New York Avenue NW 20525
phone (202) 606–5000, http://www.cns.gov

Chief Executive Officer.—Harris Wofford, ext. 167, fax 565–2784.
Chief of Staff.—John Gomperts, ext. 121, fax 565–2784.
Chief Operating Officer.—Frank Beal, (acting), ext. 130, fax 565–2784.
Chief Financial Officer.—Donna H. Cunninghame, ext. 564, fax 565–2784.
Inspector General.—Luise Jordan, ext. 390, fax 565–2795.
Director of AmeriCorps.—Deborah Jospin, (acting), ext. 287, fax 565–2787.
General Counsel.—Barry Stevens (acting), ext. 565, fax 565–2796.
Director, National Senior Service Corps.—Tom Endres, ext 199, fax 565–2789.
Director, Learn and Serve America.—Dr. Marilyn Smith, ext. 138, fax 565–2781.
Director, Office of Congressional and Intergovernmental Relations.—Gene Sofer, ext. 246, fax 565–2784.

DEFENSE NUCLEAR FACILITIES SAFETY BOARD

Indiana Avenue NW, Suite 700, phone 208–6400, fax 208–6518

Chairman.—John T. Conway.
Vice Chairman.—A.J. Eggenberger.
Members:
Joseph J. DiNunno.
Herbert J.C. Kouts.
[Vacant].
General Counsel.—Robert M. Andersen.
General Manager.—Kenneth M. Pusateri.
Technical Director.—George W. Cunningham.

DELAWARE RIVER BASIN COMMISSION

Delaware River Basin Commission, PO Box 7360, West Trenton NJ 08628
phone (609) 883–9500, fax (609) 883–9522

FEDERAL REPRESENTATIVES

Federal Member.—Bruce Babbitt, Secretary of the Interior, Washington, DC 20240, (202) 343–7351.
U.S. Commissioner.—Vincent D'Anna.
Federal Adviser.—Lt. Col. Robert B. Keyser, District Engineer, U.S. Army Corps of Engineers, Second and Chestnut Streets, Philadelphia, PA 19106, (215) 597–4848.

STAFF

Executive Director.—Gerald M. Hansler.
Chief Engineer.—David B. Everett.
Secretary.—Susan M. Weisman.
Chief Administrative Officer.—Richard C. Gore.
General Counsel.—David J. Goldberg, (609) 895–1600.
Public Information Officer.—Christopher M. Roberts.

ENVIRONMENTAL PROTECTION AGENCY

401 M Street SW 20460, (202) 260–4700, http://www.epa.gov

ADMINISTRATOR

Administrator.—Carol M. Browner.
Deputy Administrator.—Fred Hansen, 260–4711.
Environmental Appeals Board Members: Judge Ronald L. McCallum, 501–7060; Judge Edward E. Reich; Judge Kathie A. Stein.
Pollution Prevention Policy Staff Director.—Manik Ratan Roy, 260–8621.
Staff Offices, Director for—
Administrative Law Judge.—Spencer Nissen (acting), 260–0040.
Civil Rights.—Rafael Deleon (acting), 260–9636.
Cooperative Environmental Management.—Clarence Hardy, 260–9741.
Executive Secretariat.—Sandra Hudnall, 260–5044.
Executive Support.—Diane N. Bazzle, 260–4057.
Science Advisory Board.—Donald G. Barnes, 260–4126.
Small and Disadvantaged Business Utilization.—Leon H. Hampton, 305–7777.
Associate Administrator for—
Communication, Education and Public Affairs.—Loretta Ucelli, 260–9828.
Congressional and Legislative Affairs.—Robert W. Hickmott, 260–5200.
Regional Operations and State/Local Relations.—Shelley H. Metzenbaum, 260–4719.

INTERNATIONAL ACTIVITIES

Assistant Administrator.—William A. Nitze, 260–4870.
Principal Deputy Assistant Administrator.—Alan D. Hecht, 260–4870.
Deputy Assistant Administrator.—Alan B. Sielen, 260–4870.

ADMINISTRATION AND RESOURCES MANAGEMENT

Assistant Administrator.—Alvin M. Pesachowitz, 260–4600.
Director, Office of—
Acquisition Management.—Betty L. Bailey, 260–5020.
Administration and Resources Management.—William Henderson, Cincinnati OH (513) 569–7910.
Administration and Resources Management.—William Laxton, Research Triangle Park NC, (919) 541–2258.
Administration.—John C. Chamberlin, 260–8400.
Grants and Debarment.—Harvey G. Pippen, Jr., 260–2523.
Human Resources Management.—Dave O'Connor, 260–4467.
Information Resources Management.—Paul Wohlleben (acting), 260–4465.

CHIEF FINANCIAL OFFICER

Chief Financial Officer.—Sallyanne Harper (acting), 260–4600.
Comptroller.—Kathryn S. Schmoll, 260–9674.

ENFORCEMENT AND COMPLIANCE ASSURANCE

Assistant Administrator.—Steven Alan Herman, 564–2440.
Deputy Assistant Administrator.—Sylvia K. Lowrance, 564–2450.
Deputy Assistant Administrator.—Michael M. Stahl, 564–2445.
Director, Office of—
Compliance.—Elaine G. Stanley, 564–2280.
Criminal Enforcement.—Earl E. Devaney, 564–2480.
Environmental Justice.—Clarice E. Gaylord, 564–2515.
Federal Activities.—Richard E. Sanderson, 564–2400.
Federal Facilities Enforcement.—Craig E. Hooks (acting), 564–2510.
National Enforcement Investigations Center.—Diana Love, (303) 236–5100.
Planning and Analysis.—Eric V. Schaeffer, 564–2530.
Regulatory Enforcement.—Robert Van Heuvelen, 564–2220.
Site Remediation Enforcement.—Barry N. Breen, 564–5110.

GENERAL COUNSEL

General Counsel.—Jonathan Z. Cannon, 260–8040.
Principal Deputy General Counsel.—Scott C. Fulton, 260–8064.
Designated Agency Ethics Official.—Scott C. Fulton, 260–8064.
Associate General Counsel, Division of—
Air and Radiation.—Alan W. Eckert, 260–7606.
Cross-Media Analysis and Review.—James C. Nelson (acting), 260–7622.
Finance and Operations.—Ray E. Spears, 260–5320.
Inspector General.—Marla E. Diamond, 260–5075.
International Activities.—Daniel B. McGraw, Jr., 260–1810.
Pesticides and Toxic Substances.—Patricia A. Roberts (acting) 260–5372.
Solid Waste and Emergency Response.—Patricia A. Roberts (acting), 260–5372.
Water.—Susan G. Lepow, 260–7700.

POLICY, PLANNING AND EVALUATION

Assistant Administrator.—David M. Gardiner, 260–4332.
Deputy Assistant Administrator.—Robert M. Wolcott (acting), 260–4335.
Program Administration and Resources Management Staff.—Mary M. Free, 260–4020.
Director, Office of—
Policy Development.—Maryann B. Froehlich, 260–4034.
Regulatory Management and Evaluation.—Thomas E. Kelly, 260–4001.
Strategic Planning and Environmental Data.—Frederick W. Allen, 260–4028.

INSPECTOR GENERAL

Inspector General.—Nikki L. Tinsley (acting), 260–3137.
Deputy Inspector General.—Nikki L. Tinsley.
Assistant Inspector General for—
Audit.—Kenneth A. Konz, 260–1106.
Investigations.—Allen P. Fallin, 260–1109.
Management.—John C. Jones, 260–4913.

WATER

Assistant Administrator.—Robert Perciasepe, 260–5700.
Deputy Assistant Administrator.—Dana D. Minerva, 260–5700.
Director, Office of—
American Indian Environmental.—Kathy Gorospe, 260–7939.
Ground Water and Drinking Water.—Cynthia C. Dougherty, 260–5543.
Gulf of Mexico Program.—James Giattina, (601) 688–3726.
Policy and Resources Management.—Mark A. Luttner, 260–0643.
Science and Technology.—Tudor T. Davies, 260–5400.
Wastewater Management.—Michael B. Cook, 260–5850.
Wetlands, Oceans and Watersheds.—Robert H. Wayland, III, 260–7166.

SOLID WASTE AND EMERGENCY REPSONSE

Assistant Administrator.—Timothy Fields, Jr. (acting), 260–4610.
Deputy Assistant Administrator.—Timothy Fields, Jr., 260–4610.
Staff Director, Office of Program Management.—Devereaux Barnes, 260–4040.
Director, Office of—
Chemical Emergency Preparedness and Prevention.—James L. Makris, 260–8600.
Emergency and Remedial Response (Superfund).—Stephen D. Luftig, 260–8960.
Solid Waste.—Michael H. Shapiro, (703) 308–8895.
Technology Innovation.—Walter W. Kovalick, Jr., (703) 603–9910.
Underground Storage Tanks.—Joshua Baylson (acting), (703) 603–9900.

AIR AND RADIATION

Assistant Administrator.—Mary D. Nichols, 260–7400.
Deputy Assistant Administrator.—Richard D. Wilson, 260–7400.
Director, Office of—
Air Quality Planning and Standards.—John S. Seitz, Research Triangle Park NC, (919) 541–5616.

Atmospheric Programs.—Paul Stolpman, 233–9689.
Policy Analysis and Review.—Robert D. Brenner, 260–5580.
Program Management Operations.—Jerry A. Kurtzweg, 260–7415.
Mobile Sources.—Margo T. Oge, 260–7645.
Radiation and Indoor Air.—E. Romana Trovato, 233–9320.

PREVENTION, PESTICIDES AND TOXIC SUBSTANCES

Assistant Administrator.—Lynn R. Goldman M.D., 260–2902.
Deputy Assistant Administrators: Susan H. Wayland, 260–2910; James V. Aidala, 260–2897.
Director, Office of—
Pesticide Program.—Daniel Barolo, (703) 305–7090.
Pollution Prevention and Toxics.—William H. Sanders III, 260–3810.
Program Management Operations.—Marylouise M. Uhlig, 260–2906.

RESEARCH AND DEVELOPMENT

Assistant Administrator for Research and Development.—[Vacant], 260–7676.
Deputy Assistant Administrator for—
Management.—Henry L. Longest, II, 260–7676.
Science.—Joseph K. Alexander, 260–7676.
Director, Office of—
Research and Science Integration.—Dorothy E. Patton (acting), 260–7669.
Resources Management and Administration.—Deborah Y. Dietrich, 260–7500.
Science Policy.—Dorothy Patton, 260–6600.
Director, National Exposure Research Laboratory.—Gary J. Foley, Research Triangle Park NC, (919) 541–2106.
Director, National Risk Management Research Laboratory.—Timothy E. Oppelt, Cincinnati OH, (513) 569–7418.
Director, National Health and Environmental Effects Research Laboratory.—Lawrence W. Reiter, Research Triangle Park NC (919) 541–2281.
Director, National Center for Environmental Assessment.—William H. Farland, 260–7315.
Director, National Center for Environmental Research and Quality Assurance.—Peter W. Preuss, 260–5767.

REGIONAL ADMINISTRATION

Region I (Boston): *Regional Administrator.*—John P. Devillars, John F. Kennedy Federal Building, One Congress Street, Boston MA 02203, (617) 565–3400.
Congressional Liaisons: Rudy Brown, Michael Ochs, Al Frezza, (617) 565–3414.
Public Affairs.—Doug Gutro, (617) 565–2905.
Region II (New York): *Regional Administrator.*—Jeanne M. Fox, 290 Broadway, New York NY 10007, (212) 637–3000.
Congressional Liaisons: Jeane Rosiznski, Pat Carr, Barry Shore, (212) 637–3657.
Public Affairs.—Bonnie Bellow, (212) 637–3660.
Region III (Philadelphia): *Regional Administrator.*—W. Michael McCabe, 841 Chestnut Building, Philadelphia PA 19107, (215) 566–2900.
Congressional Liaison.—Micael Burke (215) 566–5120.
Public Out-Reach.—Daniel Ryan, (215) 566–5120.
Region IV (Atlanta): *Regional Administrator.*—John Hankinson, Jr., 100 Alabama Street SW, Atlanta GA 30303, (404) 562–8357.
Congressional Liaisons: Loretta R. Hanks, Marilyn S. Allen, (404) 562–8327.
Public Affairs.—Tom Moore, (404) 562–8327.
Region V (Chicago): *Regional Administrator.*—Valdas V. Adamkus, 77 West Jackson Boulevard, Chicago IL 60604–3507, (312) 886–3000.
Congressional Liaisons: Mary J. Canavan, Tamara Donaldson, (312) 353–3018.
Public Affairs.—Elissa Speizman, (312) 353–2073.
Region VI (Dallas): *Regional Administrator.*—Jane N. Saginaw, First Interstate Bank Tower at Fountain Place, 1445 Ross Avenue, 12th Floor, Suite 1200, Dallas TX 75202–2733, (214) 655–2100.
Congressional Liaison.—David W. Gray, (214) 655–2200.
External Affairs.—David W. Gray, (214) 655–2200.
Region VII (Kansas City): *Regional Administrator.*—Dennis Grams, 726 Minnesota Avenue, Kansas City MO 66101, (913) 551–7006.

Congressional Liaison.—Ronald R. Ritter, (913) 551–7005.
Public Affairs.—Roweena Michaels, (913) 551–7003.

Region VIII (Denver): *Regional Administrator.*—Jack W. McGraw (acting), 999 18th Street, Suite 500, Denver CO 80202–2405, (303) 312–6308.
Congressional Liaison.—Sandy Johnston, (303) 312–6604.
External Affairs.—Nola Cooke, (303) 312–6599.

Region IX (San Francisco): *Regional Administrator.*—Felecia Marcus, 75 Hawthorne Street, San Francisco CA 94105, (415) 744–1001.
Congressional Liaisons: Catherine Roberts, Denise Nelson, (415) 744–1015.
External Affairs.—Enrique Manzanilla, (415) 744–1585.

Region X (Seattle): *Regional Administrator.*—Charles C. Clarke, 1200 Sixth Avenue, Seattle WA 98101, (206) 553–1234.
Congressional Liaison.—Floyd Winsett, (206) 553–1138.
External Affairs.—Melanie Luh, (206) 553–1107.

EQUAL EMPLOYMENT OPPORTUNITY COMMISSION

1801 L Street 20507, phone (202) 663–4900

Chairman.—Gilbert F. Casellas, 663–4001, fax 663–4110.
Executive Director.—Maria Borrero.
Special Assistants: Irene Hill, Brigid Quinn.
Attorney Advisors: Vicky Rovira-Gonzalez, David Lopez.
Vice Chairman.—Paul M. Igasaki, 663–4027, fax 663–7121.

COMMISSIONERS

Paul Steven Miller, 663–4036, fax 663–7101.
Senior Advisor.—R. Paul Richard.
Special Assistants: Lisa S. Cottle, Antionette M. Eates, Andrew J. Imparato.
Reginald E. Jones, 663–4026, fax 663–7086.
Special Assistants: Naomi Levin, Wallace Lew, Cassandra Menoken.
Commissioner.—[Vacant].
Executive Officer.—Frances M. Hart, 663–4070, fax 663–4114.
General Counsel.—C. Gregory Stewart, 663–4705, fax 663–4196.
Attorney Advisor.—Susan Oxford.
Deputy General Counsels: Rosalind Gray, J. Ray Terry.
Legal Counsel.—Ellen J. Vargyas, 663–4637, fax 663–4639.
Inspector General.—Aletha L. Brown, 663–4379, fax 663–7204.
Director, Office of—
Communications and Legislative Affairs.—Claire Gonzales, 663–4900, fax 663–4912.
Program Operations.—Elizabeth M. Thornton, 663–4801, fax 663–4823.
Federal Operations.—Ronnie Blumenthal, 663–4599, fax 663–7022.
Equal Employment Opportunity.—Cynthia C. Matthews, 663–7081, fax 663–7003.

EXPORT-IMPORT BANK OF THE UNITED STATES

811 Vermont Avenue NW 20571, phone (800) 565–EXIM, fax 565–3380

President and Chairman.—Martin A. Kamarck, Room 1215, 565–3510.
First Vice President and Vice Chairman.—[Vacant.]
Directors:
Julie D. Belaga, Room 1257, 565–3540.
Maria L. Haley, Room 1241, 565–3530
Rita M. Rodriguez, Room 1229, 565–3520.
General Counsel.—Kenneth W. Hansen, Room 937, 565–3460.
Chief Financial Officer.—James K. Hess, Room 1055, 565–3240.
Vice President, Claims and Recoveries.—Jeffrey L. Miller, Room 741, 565–3601.
Chief of Staff.—Jackie M. Clegg, Room 1228, 565–3535.
Executive Vice President, Office of the Executive Vice President.—Allan I. Mendelowitz, Room 1115, 565–3220.
Senior Vice President, Business Development.—Richard J. Feeney, Room 919, 565–3901.
Vice President for—
Aircraft.—Julie J. Panaro, Room 933, 565–3402.
Americas.—Charles A. Leik, Room 1157, 565–3401.

Asia and Africa.—Terrence J. Hulihan, Room 1129, 565–3701.
Credit Administration.—Jeffrey Miller (acting), Room 1107, 565–3601.
Engineering and Environment.—James A. Mahoney, Room 1169, 565–3573.
NIS/Central Europe.—Thomas E. Moran, Room 1269, 565–3801.
Insurance.—William W. Redway, Room 719, 565–3633.
Project Finance.—Dianne Rudo, Room 1005, 565–3691
United States.—Sam Z. Zytcer, Room 903, 565–3782.
Information Management and Technology.—Arthur L. Henrichsen, Room 1043, 565–3850.
Communications.—David W. Carter, Room 1027, 565–3203.
Congressional and External Affairs.—Jackie M. Clegg, Room 1228, 565–3535.
Country Risk Analysis.—Daniel L. Bond, Room 9712, 565–3731.
Strategic Planning, Analysis and Program Development.—[Vacant], Room 1243, 565–3763.
Group Vice President, Resource Management.—Dolores Bartning, Room 1017, 565–3561.
Director, Equal Opportunity and Diversity Programs.—Peter Suazo (acting), Room 753, 565–3596
Director, Human Resources.—Joyce E. Savage, Room 771, 565–3329.
Vice President, Administrative Services.—Tamzen C. Reitan, Room 1015, 565–3333.
Director, Employment Development and Training.—Jeanne S. Felix, Room 740, 565–3325.

FARM CREDIT ADMINISTRATION

(Reorganization pursuant to Public Law 99–205, December 23, 1985)

1501 Farm Credit Drive McLean VA 22102–5090
phone (703) 883–4000, fax 734–5784

Chairperson.—Marsha Pyle Martin.
Members:
Doyle L. Cook.
[Vacant].
Secretary.—Floyd J. Fithian, 883–4025.
Chief Operating Officer.—[Vacant], 883–4210.
Director, Office of—
Congressional and Public Affairs.—Eileen M. McMahon, 883–4056, fax 790–3260.
Resources Management.—Donald P. Clark, 883–4200.
Secondary Market Oversight.—Larry W. Edwards, 883–4200.
Policy Development and Risk Control.—Thomas G. McKenzie, 883–4414.
General Counsel.—Jean Noonan, 883–4020.
Inspector General.—Eldon Stoehr, 883–4030.
Chief Examiner and Director, Office of Examination.—Roland E. Smith, 883–4160.
Manager, Equal Employment Opportunity.—Gail Hill, 883–4144.

FEDERAL COMMUNICATIONS COMMISSION

1919 M Street 20554, phone (202) 418–0200, http://www.fcc.gov

Chairman.—Reed E. Hundt, Room 814, 418–1000.
Confidential Assistant.—Ruth Dancey.
Chief of Staff.—Blair Levin.
Senior Legal Advisor.—John Nakahata.
Counsel to the Chairman.—Julius Geneachowsk.
Legal Advisor.—Tom Boasberg.
Commissioner.—James H. Quello, Room 802, 418–2000.
Confidential Assistant.—Ginger Clark.
Senior Legal Advisor.—Rudolfo M. Baca.
Legal Advisor.—Marsha MacBride.
Special Counsel.—James Coltharp.
Commissioner.—Rachelle B. Chong, Room 844, 418–2200.
Confidential Assistant.—Eileen Duff.
Senior Legal Advisor.—Jane Mago.
Legal Advisor.—Daniel Gonzales.

Special Advisor.—Suzanne Toller.
Commissioner.—Susan Ness, Room 832, 418–2100.
Confidential Assistant.—Janice B. Wise.
Senior Legal Advisor.—James L. Casserly.
Legal Advisor.—David R. Siddall, Anita Wallgren.
Commissioner.—[Vacant], 418–2300.

OFFICE OF PLANS AND POLICY

Chief.—Robert M. Pepper, 418–2030.
Deputy Chief.—Elliot Maxwell.
Chief Economist.—Michael H. Riordan.

OFFICE OF PUBLIC AFFAIRS

Director.—Susan Lewis Sallet, 418–0500.
Deputy Director.—Maureen P. Peratino, David Fiske.
Information Technology Manager.—Sheryl A. Segal, 418–0260.
Division Chief for—
Public Service Division.—Martha E. Contee, 418–0260.
Reference Operations Division.—William Cline, 418–0267.

OFFICE OF LEGISLATIVE AND INTERGOVERNMENTAL AFFAIRS

Director.—Karen Kornbluh (acting), 418–1900.
Associate Director.—Stephen Klitzman, 418–1913.
Congressional Correspondence Staff.—418–1910.

OFFICE OF COMMUNICATIONS BUSINESS OPPORTUNITIES

Director.—Catherine Sandoval, 418–0990.
Deputy Director.—Eric L. Jensen.

OFFICE OF ADMINISTRATIVE LAW JUDGES

200 L Street 20554, phone 418–2250

Chief Judge.—Joseph Stirmer.

OFFICE OF GENERAL COUNSEL

General Counsel.—William E. Kennard, 418–1700.
Deputy General Counsels—.Christoper J. Wright, David H. Solomon.
Special Counsels: Peter A. Tenhula, Sheryl Wilkerson, Susan Fox, Ira A. Fishman, James Rubin.
Associate General Counsel for—
Administrative Law.—Sheldon M. Guttmann, 418–1720.
Litigation Division.—Daniel M. Armstrong, 418–1740.
Chief, Competition Division.—John Nakahata, 418–1880.

OFFICE OF INSPECTOR GENERAL

Inspector General.—H. Walker Feaster (acting), 418–0470.
Junior Counsel/Director of Investigations.—Edward W. Hosken.
Director of Audits.—Paul Brachfeld.

OFFICE OF WORKPLACE DIVERSITY

Director.—Jack W. Gravely.
Deputy Director.—Harvey Lee.
EEO Program Manager.—Sandra J. Canery.

OFFICE OF MANAGING DIRECTOR

Managing Director.—Andrew S. Fishel, Room 852, 418–1919.

Deputy Managing Director.—Richard D. Lee, 418–1921.
Assistant Bureau Chief for Management.—Eileen Savell, 418–1927.
The Secretary.—William F. Caton (acting), 418–0300.
Associate Managing Director for—
Human Resources Management.—Michelle A. Oppenheimer, 418–0100.
Information Management.—Ronald Stone, 418–2020.
Operations.—Marilyn J. McDermett, 418–1925.
Program Analysis.—Peter W. Herrick (acting), 2000 M Street, 418–0440.
Division Chief for—
Computer Applications.—John Giuli, 418–0540.
Customer Solutions.—Edward J. McCarthy, 418–1810.
Financial Operations.—Linda King, 418–1970.
Labor Relations and Workforce Effectiveness.—Stephen E. Schumacher.
Operations Management and Services.—Jeffrey R. Ryan, 418–1950.
Personnel Resources.—Michele C. Sutton.
Network Management.—Eric Kanner, 418–1830.

OFFICE OF ENGINEERING AND TECHNOLOGY

2000 M Street 20554, phone 418–2470

Chief.—Richard M. Smith, 418–2470.
Deputy Chief.—Bruce A. Franca.
Associate Chief for—
Networks.—James R. Keegan, 418–2323.
Strategic Communications.—Helena Mitchell.
Technology.—Michael J. Marcus.
Assistant Chief for Management.—Xenia Hajicosti, 418–2471.
Legal Counsel.—Steven S. Kaminer.
Economic Advisor.—R. Alan Stillwell.
Division Chief for—
Allocations and Standards.—Robert M. Bromery, 418–2475.
Equipment Authorization (Columbia, MD).—Julius P. Knapp, (301) 725–1585.
New Technology Development.—Lawrence P. Petak, 418–2478.
Policy and Rules.—Lynn Remly, 418–2472.

CABLE SERVICES BUREAU

2033 M Street 20554, phone 418–7200

Chief.—Meredith Jones.
Deputy Chief (Policy).—William H. Johnson.
Deputy Chief.—John E. Logan.
Associate Chiefs.—Marjorie Greene, Barbara Esbin.
Director of Public Relations.—Morgan Broman.
Special Assistant.—[Vacant].
Legal Advisor.—Meryl S. Icove.
Assistant Chief for Government and Public Outreach.—Margo Domon.
Director of Government Outreach.—Michael S. Perko.
Assistant Chief for Management.—Richard Lee (acting), 418–7079.
Division Chief for—
Consumer Protection and Competition.—Gary Laden, 418–1029.
Engineering and Technical Services.—John Wong, 418–7000.
Financial Analysis and Compliance.—Elizabeth Beaty, 418–2296.
Policy and Rules.—JoAnn Lucanik, 418–7034.

COMMON CARRIER BUREAU

Chief.—Regina Keeney, 418–1500.
Deputy Bureau Chiefs: Kathleen Levitz, A. Richard Metzger, Jr., Mary Beth Richards.
Associate Bureau Chief.—Laurence Atlas.
Assistant Bureau Chief for Management.—Joseph Hall, 2000 M Street, 418–1370.
Chief Economist.—[Vacant].
Counsels to Bureau Chief: Melissa W. Newman, Tim Peterson.
Division Chief for—
Accounting and Audits.—Kenneth P. Moran, 2000 L Street, 418–0800.

Competitive Pricing.—James D. Schlichting, 418–1520.
Enforcement.—John B. Muleta, 2025 M Street, 418–0700.
Industry Analysis.—Peyton L. Wynns, 2033 M Street, 418–0940.
Network Services.—Geraldine Matise, 2000 M Street, 418–2320.
Policy and Program Planning.—Richard Welch, 418–1580.

COMPLIANCE AND INFORMATION BUREAU

FCC National Call Center (Gettysburg, PA), 1–888–Call FCC (1–888–225–5322)

Chief.—Beverly G. Baker, 418–1100.
Deputy Chief.—Arlan K. vanDoorn, 418–1105, Joseph P. Casey.
Assistant Bureau Chief for Law.—Lawrence R. Clance.
Engineering Adviser.—George R. Dillon.
Legal Adviser.—Wayne T. McKee.
Director of—
National Call Center.—Cynthia Jeffries, Gettysburg, PA, (717) 338–2590.
Training Center (Columbia, MD).—Samuel A. Miles, II, (301) 725–3880.
Assistant Bureau Chief for—
Management and Resources.—Robert W. Crisman, 418–1135.
n Resources.—John R. Winston, 418–1100.
Division Chief for—
Compliance.—Magalie Salas (acting), 418–1150.
Technology.—Kenneth R. Nichols, 418–1210.

INTERNATIONAL BUREAU

2000 M Street, phone 418–0420

Chief.—Peter Cowhey.
Deputy Chiefs: Ruth Milkman, Roderick K. Porter.
Associate Chief (Policy).—James L. Ball.
Assistant Chief, Management.—Thomas Sullivan.
Senior Legal Advisors: Bob Calaff, Jonathan Stern.
Senior Counsel for Economics and Competition.—Peter Cowhey.
Division Chief for—
Planning and Negotiations.—Larry Olson (acting), 418–2150.
Satellite and Radiocommunication.—Thomas Tcyz, 418–0719.
Telecommunications.—Diane J. Cornell, 418–1470.

MASS MEDIA BUREAU

Chief.—Roy J. Stewart, 418–2600.
Deputy Chief (Policy).—Renee Licht.
Deputy Chief (Operations).—Mary Ellen Burns.
Senior Legal Assistant.—Robert H. Ratcliffe.
Assistant Chief for—
Engineering.—Keith Larson.
Management and Personnel.—Janet S. Amaya, 418–2610.
Technology Policy.—Saul T. Shapiro.
Chief Economist.—Jerry Duvall.
Special Assistant.—Ray White.
Special Advisor.—Gretchen C. Rubin, 2000 M Street, 418–0425.
Chief Authorization Programming Group.—Thomas Wilchek, 418–2650.
Division Chief for—
Audio Services.—Linda Blair, 418–2780.
Enforcement.—Charles W. Kelley, 2025 M Street, 418–1420.
Policy and Rules.—Douglas W. Webbink, 2000 M Street, 418–2120.
Telecommunications.—Diane J. Cornell, 418–1630.
Video Services.—Barbara A. Kreisman, 418–1600.

WIRELESS TELECOMMUNICATIONS BUREAU

2025 M Street, phone 418–0600

Chief.—Dan Phythyon (acting).

Deputy Bureau Chiefs: Gerald P. Vaughan, Rosalind Allen.
Associate Bureau Chiefs: Karen Brinkmann, Jonathan Cohen.
Associate Bureau Chief for Operations (Gettysburg).—Gary L. Stanford, (717) 338–2501.
Associate Chief for Administration.—Doreen McCarthy.
Assistant Chief.—Karen Gulick.
Chief Engineer.—Thomas Stanley.
Chief Economist.—Walter Strack.
Technical Advisor.—David Wye.
Legal Advisors: Eliabeth Lyle, D'Wanna Speight.
Assistant Chief for Management.—Jennifer Bush, 418–0586.
Division Chief for—
Auctions.—Kathleen O'Brien-Ham, 418–0660.
Commercial Wireless.—David Furth, 418–0620.
Customer Services (Gettysburg).—John Chudovan, (717) 338–2510.
Enforcement.—Howard C. Davenport, 418–0569.
Licensing.—Walter G. Boswell, (717) 338–2601.
Policy.—John Cimko, 418–1310.
Private Wireless.—Robert McNamara, 418–0680.

REGIONAL OFFICES

Northwest Region: Russell D. Monie, Park Ridge Office Center, Room 306, 1550 Northwest Highway, Park Ridge, IL 60068–1460, (847) 298–5412.
Southwest Region: Dennis P. Carlton, Brywood Office Tower, Room 320, 8800 East 63rd Street, Kansas City, MO 64133–4895, (816) 353–9021.
Western Region: Serge Marti-Volkoff, 3777 Depot Road, Room 420, Hayward, CA 94545–1914, (510) 732–6021.

FIELD OFFICES

Anchorage: PO Box 221849, Anchorage, AK 99522–1894, (907) 243–4899.
Atlanta: Koger Center, 3575 Koger Boulevard, Room 320, Duluth, GA 30136–4958, (404) 279–4624.
Boston: One Batterymarch Park, Quincy, MA 02169–7495, (617) 786–9490.
Buffalo: Federal Building, Room 1307, 111 West Huron Street, Buffalo, NY 14202–2398, (716) 846–4536.
Chicago: Park Ridge Office Center, Room 306, 1550 Northwest Highway, Park Ridge, IL 60068–1460, (708) 298–5412.
Columbia: 9200 Farm House Lane, Columbia, MD 21046, (301) 725–1996.
Dallas: 9330 LBJ Freeway, Room 1170, Dallas, TX 75243–3429, (972) 907–0053.
Denver: 165 South Union Boulevard, Room 860, Denver, CO 80228–2213, (303) 969–6496.
Detroit: 24897 Hathaway Street, Farmington Hills, MI 48335–1552, (810) 471–5605.
Honolulu: PO Box 1030, Waipahu, HI 96797–1030, (808) 677–8689.
Houston: 1225 North Loop West, Room 900, Houston, TX 77008–1775, (713) 868–8955.
Kansas City: Brywood Office Tower, Room 320, 8800 East 63rd Street, Kansas City, MO 64133–4895, (816) 353–8934.
Los Angeles: Cerritos Corporate Towers, 18000 Studebaker Road, Room 660, Cerritos, CA 90701–3684, (562) 860–7474.
Miami: 2210 Northwest 82nd Avenue, Miami, FL 33122, (305) 597–4622.
New Orleans: 800 West Commerce Road, Room 505, New Orleans, LA 70123–3333, (504) 589–3684.
New York: 201 Varick Street, Room 305, New York, NY 10014–4870, (212) 620–3389.
Norfolk: 1457 Mount Pleasant Road, Suite 113, Chesapeake, VA 23322, (757) 482–5835.
Philadelphia: One Oxford Valley Office Building, Room 404, 2300 East Lincoln Highway, Langhome, PA 19047–1859, (215) 752–8549.
Portland: 1220 Southwest Third Avenue, Room 1782, Portland, OR 97204–2898, (503) 326–4121.
St. Paul: 2025 Sloan Place, Suite 31, Maplewood, MN 55117–2058, (612) 774–5274.
San Diego: Interstate Office Park, 4542 Ruffner Street, Room 370, San Diego, CA 92111–2216, (619) 557–5698.
San Francisco: 3777 Depot Road, Room 420, Hayward, CA 94545–1914, (510) 732–6021.
San Juan: Federal Building 747, Hato Rey, PR 00918–1731, (787) 766–5439.
Seattle: 11410 Northeast 122nd Way, Room 312, Kirkland, WA 98034–6927, (206) 821–6271.
Tampa: 2203 North Lois Avenue, Room 1215, Tampa, FL 33607–2356, (813) 348–1595.

FEDERAL DEPOSIT INSURANCE CORPORATION

550 17th Street NW 20429

phone (202) 393–8400, http://www.fdic.gov

Chairman.—Ricki Helfer, 898–6974.
Deputy to the Chairman and Chief Operating Officer.—Dennis F. Geer, 898–6948.
Deputy to the Chairman for Policy.—Leslie A. Woolley, 898–7152
Vice Chairman.—Andrew C. Hove, Jr., 898–3888.
Deputy.—Roger A. Hood, 898–3681.
Director.—Joseph H. Neely, 898–8561.
Deputy.—A. David Meadows, 898–3855.
Director.—Eugene Ludwig, 874–4900.
Deputy.—Tom Zemke, 898–6960.
Director.—Nicholas P. Retsinas, 906–6280.
Deputy.—Walter B. Mason, Jr., 898–6965.
Director, Office of Legislative Affairs.—Alice C. Goodman, 898–7055, fax 898–3745/7062.

FEDERAL ELECTION COMMISSION

999 E Street NW 20463

phone (202) 219–3440, Toll Free (800) 424–9530, fax 219–3880, http://www.fec.gov

Chairman.—John Warren McGarry, 219–4104, fax 219–8472.
Vice Chairperson.—Joan D. Aikens, 219–4110, fax 219–8494.
Commissioners:
Lee Ann Elliott, 219–4114, fax 219–8493
Danny L. McDonald,
219–4122, fax 219–8436
Scott E. Thomas, 219–4118, fax 219–8439
[Vacant].
Inspector General.—Lynne A. McFarland, 219–4267.
Staff Director.—John C. Surina, 219–4134, fax 219–2338.
Deputy Staff Director.—James A. Pehrkon, 219–3600.
Assistant Staff Director for—
Audit.—Robert J. Costa, 219–3720.
Disclosure.—[Vacant].
Information Services.—Louise D. Wides, 219–3420.
Reports Analysis.—John D. Gibson, 219–3580.
Director for—
Clearinghouse on Election Administration.—Penelope S. Bonsall, 219–3670.
Data Systems Development Division.—Richard L. Hooper, 219–3730.
Personnel and Labor Management Relations.—David S. Orr, 219–4290.
Planning and Management.—John C. O'Brien, 219–3597.
General Counsel.—Lawrence M. Noble, 219–3690, fax 219–3923.
Associate General Counsel for—
Enforcement.—Lois G. Lerner, 219–3690,
Litigation.—Richard B. Bader, 219–3690.
Policy.—N. Bradley Litchfield, 219–3690.
Public Financing, Ethics and Special Projects.—Kim L. Bright-Coleman, 219–3690.
Administrative Officer.—Larry D. McCoy, 219–3570.
Accounting Officer.—Richard Pullen, 219–3570.
Congressional Affairs Officer.—Christina H. VanBrakle, 219–4136, fax 219–2338.
EEO Director.—Patricia A. Brown, 219–6284.
Library Director (Law).—Leta L. Holley, 219–3312.
Press Officer.—Ronald M. Harris, 219–4155.

FEDERAL EMERGENCY MANAGEMENT AGENCY

500 C Street SW 20472

phone (202) 646–2400, fax 646–2531, http://www.fema.gov

Director.—James Lee Witt, 646–3923.
Executive Deputy Director.—Raymond L. Young, (acting), 646–4211.
Director of Congressional and Governmental Affairs.—Martha S. Braddock, 646–4500.
Associate Director for—
Preparedness, Training and Exercises.—Kay Goss, 642–3651.
Mitigation.—Richard W. Krimm, 646–4622.
Response and Recovery.—Richard W. Krimm, 646–3692.
Executive Administrator for—
Federal Insurance Administration.—Spence Perry, 646–2781.
U.S. Fire Administration.—Carrye B. Brown, 646–4244.
Inspector General.—George Opfer, 646–3298.

FEDERAL HOME LOAN MORTGAGE CORPORATION

8200 Jones Branch Drive McLean, VA 22102, phone (703) 903–2000

Chairman and Chief Executive Officer.—Leland C. Brendsel, (703) 903–3000.
President and Chief Operating Officer.—David Glenn, (703) 903–2700.
Executive Vice President.—John Gibbons, (703) 903–2501.
Vice President for—
Public Relations.—Nancy Stern, (703) 903–2511.
Government and Industry Relations.—Mitchell Delk, (202) 434–8600.
Human Resources.—Ron Majewicz, (703) 905–5050.

FEDERAL HOUSING FINANCE BOARD

(Created by the Financial Institutions Reform, Recovery, and Enforcement Act of August 9, 1989, 103 Stat. 354, 415)

1777 F Street NW 20006, phone 408–2500, fax 408–1435

Chairman.—Bruce A. Morrison, 408–2587.
Board of Directors:
Nicolas P. Retsinas,* 408–2817.
Lawrence U. Costiglio, 408–2828.
J. Timothy O'Neill, 408–2953.
Managing Director.—[Vacant], 408–2544.
Inspector General.—Edward Kelley, 408–2570.
General Counsel.—Deborah Silberman (acting), 408–2570.
Director of Policy.—Karen Crosby (acting), 408–2983
Director Congressional Affairs.—Randall H. McFarlane, 408–2998.
Director of Public Affairs.—Naomi P. Salus, 408–2957.
Director of Resource Management.—Barbara L. Fisher, 408–2586.
Director of Supervision.—Mitchell Berns, 408–2562.

FEDERAL LABOR RELATIONS AUTHORITY

607 14th Street NW 20424–0001, phone (202) 482–6500, fax 482–6659

Chair.—Phyllis N. Segal, Suite 410, 482–6500
Chief Counsel.—Susan D. McCluskey.
Special Assistant for External Affairs.—Kimberly A. Weaver.
Members:
[Vacant].
Chief Counsel.—Steven H. Svartz.
Donald S. Wasserman, Suite 310, 482–6520.

---

*The Secretary of Housing and Urban Development is one of the five Directors of the Federal Housing Finance Board. Secretary Cuomo has designated Nicolas P. Restsinas, the Assistant Secretary for Housing and Commissioner of the Federal Housing Administration, to act for him on the Board of Directors of the Federal Housing Finance Board.

Chief Counsel.—Barbara Franklin.
General Counsel.—Joseph Swerdzewski, Suite 210, 482–6600.
Deputy General Counsel.—David L. Feder.
Director of—
Operations and Resources Management.—Clyde B. Blandford, Jr.
Program Development.—Nancy A. Speight.
Appeals and Special Programs.—Carol W. Pope.
Chief Administrative Law Judge.—Samuel A. Chaitovitz, Suite 440, 482–6630.
Executive Director.—Solly J. Thomas, Suite 420, 482–6560.
Solicitor.—David M. Smith, Suite 330, 482–6620.
Deputy Solicitor.—William R. Tobey.
Inspector General.—Robert Andary, Suite 240, 482–6570.
Chairperson for—
Collaboration and Alternative Dispute Resolution Program.—Thelma C. Colwell, 482–6503.
Federal Service Impasse Disputes Panel.—Betty Bolden, Suite 220, 482–6670.
Executive Director.—H. Joseph Schimansky, Suite 220, 482–6670.
Foreign Service Impasse Disputes Panel.—[Vacant], Suite 220, 482–6670.
Foreign Service Labor Relations Board.—Phyllis N. Segal, Suite 410, 482–6500.

REGIONAL OFFICES

Regional Directors:
Atlanta: Brenda M. Robinson, Marquis Two Tower, Suite 701, 285 Peachtree Center Avenue, Atlanta GA 30303–1270, (404) 331–5212, fax (404) 331–5280.
Boston: Edward S. Davidson, Suite 1500, 99 Summer Street, Boston, MA 02110–1200, (617) 424–5730, fax 424–5743.
Chicago: William E. Washington, Suite 1150, 55 West Monroe, Chicago, IL 60603–9729, (312) 353–6306, fax 886–5977.
Dallas: James E. Petrucci, Suite 926, LB 107, 525 Griffin Street, Dallas, TX 75202–1906, (214) 767–4996, fax 767–0156.
Denver: Marjorie K. Thompson, Suite 100, 1244 Speer Boulevard, Denver, CO 80204–3581, (303) 844–5224, fax 844–2774.
San Francisco: Gerald M. Cole, Suite 220, 901 Market Street, San Francisco, CA 94103–1791, (415) 744–4000, fax 744–4117.
Washington, DC: Michael W. Doheny, 4th Floor, 1255 22nd Street NW, Washington, DC 20037–1206, (202) 653–8500, fax 653–5091.

FEDERAL MARITIME COMMISSION

800 North Capitol Street NW 20573, phone (202) 523–5707, fax 523–3782

OFFICE OF THE CHAIRMAN

Chairman.—Harold J. Creel, Room 1000, 523–5911.
Counsel to the Chairman—Bruce A. Dombrowski.
Confidential Assistant.—Jeannette Cole.
Chief of Staff.—[Vacant].
Commissioner.—[Vacant].
Counsel.—[Vacant].
Commissioner.—Ming C. Hsu, Room 1044, 523–5712.
Counsel.—Francis W. Fraser.
Commissioner.—Joe Scroggins, Room 1032, 523–5715.
Counsel.—Paul Lorenzo-Giguere.
Commissioner.—Delmond J.H. Won, Room 1026, 523–5721.
Counsel.—Raynor T. Tsuneyoshi.

OFFICE OF THE SECRETARY

Secretary.—Joseph C. Polking, Room 1046, 523–5725.
Assistant Secretary.—Ronald D. Murphy.

OFFICE OF INFORMAL INQUIRIES, COMPLAINTS AND INFORMAL DOCKETS

Director.—Joseph T. Farrell, Room 1052, 523–5807.

GENERAL COUNSEL

General Counsel.—Thomas Panebianco, Room 1018, 523–5740.
Deputy General Counsel.—[Vacant].
Librarian.—David J. Vespa, Room 1085, 523–5762.

OFFICE OF ADMINISTRATIVE LAW JUDGES

Chief Judge.—Norman D. Kline, Room 1078, 523–5750.

OFFICE OF EQUAL EMPLOYMENT OPPORTUNITY

Director.—[Vacant].

INSPECTOR GENERAL

Inspector General.—Tony P. Kominoth, Room 1072, 523–5863.

OFFICE OF THE MANAGING DIRECTOR

Managing Director.—Edward P. Walsh, Room 1082, 523–5800.
Deputy Managing Director.—Bruce A. Dombrowski.
Information Resources Management.—George D. Bowers, Room 904, 523–5835.

BUREAU OF ADMINISTRATION

Director.—Sandra L. Kusumoto, Room 900, 523–5866.
Deputy Director.—[Vacant].
Director of—
Administrative Services.—Michael H. Kilby, Room 980, 523–5900.
Budget and Financial Management.—Karon E. Douglass, Room 916, 523–5770.
Personnel.—Harriette H. Charbonneau, Room 924, 523–5773.

BUREAU OF ECONOMICS AND AGREEMENT ANALYSIS

Director.—Austin L. Schmitt, Room 970, 523–5787.
Deputy Director.—Florence A. Carr.
Chief, Office of—
Agreements and Information Management.—Jeremiah D. Hospital, Room 952, 523–5793.
Monitoring (Trade Group I).—Frank J. Schwarz, Room 962, 523–5790.
Monitoring (Trade Group II).—Florence Carr (acting), Room 972, 523–5845.

BUREAU OF TARIFFS, CERTIFICATION AND LICENSING

Director.—Bryant L. VanBrakle, Room 940, 523–5796.
Deputy Director.—[Vacant].
Chief, Office of—
Tariffs.—James G. Cannon, Room 940, 523–5818.
Freight Forwarders.—Betty J. Bennett, Room 940, 523–5843.
Tariff Control Center.—Stanley R. Anderson, Room 940, 523–5828.
Service Contracts and Passenger Vessel Operations.—Theodore A. Zook, Room 940, 523–5856.

BUREAU OF ENFORCEMENT

Director.—Vern W. Hill, Room 1062, 523–5783.
Deputy Director.—Norman W. Littlejohn, Room 928, 523–5860.

AREA REPRESENTATIVES

Los Angeles.—Oliver E. Clark, (310) 514–4905.
Miami.—Andrew Margolis, (305) 536–4316.

New Orleans.—Alvin N. Kellogg, (504) 589–6602.
North Atlantic.—Michael F. Carley, (202) 523–0300.
Seattle.—Michael A. Moneck, (206) 553–0221.

FEDERAL MEDIATION AND CONCILIATION SERVICE

(Codified under 29 U.S.C. 172)

2100 K Street NW 20427, phone (202) 606–8100, fax 606–4251

National Director.—John Calhoun Wells.
Deputy Director for Field Operations.—C. Richard Barnes, 606–8150.
Deputy Director for National Office Operations.—Wilma B. Liebman, 606–8100.
National Representative.—Brian L. Flores, 606–8100.
General Counsel.—Eileen B. Hoffman, 606–5444.
Director for—
Administrative Services.—Dan W. Funkhouser, 606–5477.
ADR/Arbitration Outreach and Training.—John A. Wagner, 606–5445.
Arbitration and Program Services.—Peter L. Regner, 606–8181.
Budget and Finance.—Fran L. Leonard, 606–3660.
Communications.—David L. Helfert, 606–8080.
Human Resources.—William Carlisle, 606–5460.
International Affairs.—James F. Power, 606–9143.
Mediation Information Services.—Lawrence B. Babcock, 606–5499.
Midwestern Region.—Thomas M. O'Brien, (216) 522–4800.
Northeastern Region.—Kenneth C. Kowalski, (212) 399–5038.
Southern Region.—C. Richard Barnes, (404) 331–3995.
Upper Midwestern Region.—Maureen S. Labenski, (612) 370–3300.
Western Region.—Jan Jung-Min Sunoo, (213) 965–3814.

FEDERAL MINE SAFETY AND HEALTH REVIEW COMMISSION

(Created by Public Law 95–164)

Sixth Floor, 1730 K Street, 20006, phone (202) 653–5633, fax 653–5030

Chairperson.—Mary L. Jordan, Room 6009, 653–5660.
Commissioners: Marc L. Marks, Room 6026, 653–5645;
James C. Riley, Room 6010, 653–5653.
Executive Director.—Richard L. Baker, Room 6030, 653–5625.
Chief Administrative Law Judge,—Paul Merlin, Room 6003, 653–5454.
Administrative Officer.—Regina M. Clarke, Room 6053, 653–5615.
General Counsel.—Norman M. Gleichman, Room 6046, 653–5610.

FEDERAL RETIREMENT THRIFT INVESTMENT BOARD

(Authorized by 5 U.S.C. 8472)

1250 H Street 20005, phone (202) 942–1600, fax 942–1676

Executive Director.—Roger W. Mehle, 942–1601.
General Counsel.—John J. O'Meara, 942–1660.
Director, Office of—
Accounting.—David L. Black, 942–1610.
Administration.—Strat D. Valakis, 942–1670.
Automated Systems.—John J. Witters, 942–1440.
Benefits and Program Analysis.—Alisone M. Clarke, 942–1630.
Communications.—Veda R. Charrow, 942–1650.
External Affairs.—Thomas J. Trabucco, 942–1640.
Investments.—Peter B. Mackey, 942–1620.
Chairman.—James H. Atkins, 942–1660.
Board Members:
Scott B. Lukins.
Sheryl R. Marshall.
Jerome A. Stricker.
Thomas A. Fink.

FEDERAL TRADE COMMISSION

Sixth and Pennsylvania Avenue NW 20580

phone 326–2195, http://www.ftc.gov

Chairman.—Robert Pitofsky, Room 440, 326–2100.
Executive Assistant.—James C. Hamill, Room 442, 326–2107.
Commissioners:
Roscoe B. Starek III, Room 540, 326–2150.
Mary L. Azcuenaga, Room 526, 326–2145.
Janet Steiger, Room 338, 325–2159.
Christine Varney, Room 326, 326–2171.
Director, Office of—
Public Affairs.—Victoria A. Streitfeld, Room 423, 326–2718.
Congressional Relations.—Lorraine C. Miller, Room 408, 326–2468.
Deputy Executive Director for Management.—Rosemarie A. Straight, Room 418, 326–2207.
Information and Technology.—Alan Proctor, Room 683, 326–2204.
General Counsel.—Stephen Calkins, Room 570, 326–2481.
Secretary.—Donald S. Clark, Room 172, 326–2514.
Administrative Law Judges.—Lewis F. Parker, Room 112, 326–3632.
Inspector General.—Frederick J. Zirkel, Room 492, 326–2800.
Director, Bureau of—
Competition.—William J. Baer, Room 370, 326–2932.
Consumer Protection.—Jodie Bernstein, Room 470, 326–3430.
Deputy Directors.—Lydia B. Parnes, Room 478, 326–2676; Teresa M. Schwartz, Room 478, 326–2359.
Economics.—Jonathan B. Baker, Room 268, 326–2930.

REGIONAL DIRECTORS

Atlanta: Anthony E. DiResta, 60 Forsyth Street SW., Suite 5M35, Midrise Building, Atlanta GA 30367, (404) 656–1390.
Boston: Phoebe Morse, 101 Merrimac Street, Suite 810, Boston, MA 02222–1073, (617) 424–5960.
Chicago: C. Steve Baker, 55 East Monroe Street, Suite 1860, Chicago, IL 60603–9841, (312) 353–8156.
Cleveland: John M. Mendenhall (acting), 668 Euclid Avenue, Suite 520–A, Cleveland, OH 44114–3006, (216) 522–4210.
Dallas: Thomas B. Carter, 100 N. Central Expressway, Suite 500, Dallas, TX 75201, (214) 979–9350.
Denver: Janice L. Charter (acting), 1961 Stout Street, Suite 1523, Denver, CO 80294–0101, (303) 844–2272.
Los Angeles: Ann I. Jones, 11000 Wilshire Boulevard, Suite 12309, Los Angeles, CA 90024–3679, (310) 235–4040.
New York: Michael J. Bloom, 150 William Street, Suite 1300, New York, NY 10038–2603, (212) 264–8290.
San Francisco: Jeffrey A. Klurfeld, 901 Market Street, Suite 570, San Francisco, CA 94103–1735, (415) 356–5284.
Seattle: Charles A. Harwood, 915 Second Avenue, Suite 2896, Seattle, WA 98174, (206) 220–6366.

FOREIGN–TRADE ZONES BOARD

Herbert C. Hoover Building, 14th and Pennsylvania Avenue NW 20230

phone (202) 482–2862, fax 482–0002

Chairman.—William M. Daley, Secretary of Commerce.
Members:
Robert E. Rubin, Secretary of the Treasury.
Executive Secretary.—John J. Da Ponte, Jr.

GENERAL SERVICES ADMINISTRATION

1800 F Street NW 20405, phone (202) 501–0800, http://www.gsa.gov

OFFICE OF THE ADMINISTRATOR

Administrator.—David J. Barram (acting), 501–0800.
Deputy Administrator.—Thurman M. Davis, Sr., 501–1226.
Chief of Staff.—Martha N. Johnson (acting), 501–1216.
Deputy Chief of Staff.—Eric M. Dodds, 501–1104.

OFFICE OF ENTERPRISE DEVELOPMENT

Associate Administrator.—Dietra L. Ford, 501–1021.
Director, Small and Disadvantaged Business Utilization.—Dietra L. Ford, 501–1021.

OFFICE OF EQUAL EMPLOYMENT OPPORTUNITY

Associate Administrator.—James M. Taylor (acting), 501–0767.

OFFICE OF CONGRESSIONAL AND INTERGOVERNMENTAL AFFAIRS

Associate Administrator.—William R. Ratchford, 501–0563.

OFFICE OF PUBLIC AFFAIRS

Associate Administrator.—Beth W. Newburger, 501–0705.
Deputy Associate Administrator.—Henry (Hap) L. Connors, Jr., 501–0705.

BOARD OF CONTRACT APPEALS

Chairman.—Stephen M. Daniels, 501–0585.
Vice Chairman.—Robert W. Parker, 501–0890.
Chief Counsel.—Anne M. Quigley, 501–1389.
Senior Legal Staff Assistant.—Jean L. Ward, 501–0585.
Board Judges:
Anthony S. Borwick, 501–1852.
Stephen M. Daniels, 501–0585.
Martha H. DeGraff, 208–7922.
Allan H. Goodman, 501–0352.
Catherine B. Hyatt, 501–4594.
Edwin B. Neill, 501–0435.
Robert W. Parker, 501–0890.
Joseph A. Vergilio, 501–1838.
Mary Ellen C. Williams, 501–4668.

OFFICE OF INSPECTOR GENERAL

Inspector General.—William J. Barton, 501–0450.
Executive Assistant.—Gary Day, 501–0450.
Deputy Inspector General.—Joel S. Gallay, 501–1362.
Counsel to the Inspector General.—Kathleen S. Tighe, 501–1932.
Assistant Inspector General for Auditing.—William E. Whyte, 501–0374.
Deputy Assistant Inspector General for Auditing.—Eugene L. Waszily, 501–0374.
Assistant Inspector General for Investigations.—James E. Henderson, 501–1397.
Deputy Assistant Inspector General for Investigations.—Gregory S. Seybold, 501–1397.
Assistant Inspector General for Administration.—James E. Le Gette, 501–2321.

OFFICE OF MANAGEMENT SERVICES AND HUMAN RESOURCES

Associate Administrator.—Martha N. Johnson, 501–0945.
Deputy Associate Administrator.—John J. Landers, 501–0945.
Director of Human Resources.—Gail T. Lovelace, 501–0398.

Director of Management Services.—Gregory L. Knott, 501–0504.
Controller.—Bob Stewart (acting), 501–0625.

OFFICE OF GENERAL COUNSEL

General Counsel.—Emily C. Hewitt, 501–2200.
Associate General Counsel for General Law.—Laurence Harrington, 501–1460.
Associate General Counsel for Personal Property.—Vince L. Crivella, 501–1156.
Special Counsel, Federal Telecomunications Service.—George N. Barclay, 501–1618.
Associate General Counsel for Real Property.—Sharon A. Roach, 501–0430.

OFFICE OF THE CHIEF FINANCIAL OFFICER

Chief Financial Officer.—Dennis J. Fischer, 501–1721.
Director of—
Financial Management Systems.—William J. Topolewski, 501–1057.
Budget.—William B. Early, 501–0719.
Financial Management.—Carole A. Hutchinson, 501–0325.
Finance.—Robert E. Suda, 501–0560.

OFFICE OF THE CHIEF INFORMATION OFFICER

Chief Information Officer.—Joe M. Thompson, 501–1000.
Deputy Chief Information Officer.—Donald Venneberg, 501–1000.
Assistant Chief Information Officer for Planning and Information Architecture.—Shereen G. Remez, 501–3535.
Assistant Chief Information Officer for Information Infrastructure and Support.—Donald P. Heffernan, 208–1534.

OFFICE OF GOVERNMENTWIDE POLICY

Associate Administrator.—G. Martin Wagner, 501–8880.
Chief of Staff.—John G. Sindelar, 501–8880.
Deputy Associate Administrator for Acquisition Policy.—Ida M. Ustad, 501–1043.
Director, Governmentwide Information Systems Division.—Robert Brown, 708–5126.
Deputy Associate Administrator for Real Property.—David Bibb, 501–8880.
Deputy Associate Administrator for Information Technology.—Francis A. McDonough, 501–0291.
Assistant Deputy Associate Administrator for Information Technology.—Lawrence Wolfe (acting), 501–0202.
Deputy Associate Administrator for Transportation and Property Management.—Becky Rhodes, 501–1777.
Director, Regulatory Information Service Center.—Mark G. Schoenberg, 395–6222.
Committee Management Secretariat.—James L. Dean, 273–3563.

PUBLIC BUILDINGS SERVICE

Commissioner.—Robert A. Peck, 501–1100.
Deputy Commissioner.—Paul Chistolini, 501–1100.
Chief of Staff.—Anthony Costa (acting), 501–1100.
Senior Advisor to the Commissioner.—Myron (Mike) Sponder, 501–1459.
Special Assistant to the Commissioner.—Aram H. Kailian, 501–9099.
Controller.—Robin G. Graf, 501–0658.
Chief Information Officer.—James M. Kearns (acting), 501–9171.
Assistant Commissioner for Portfolio Management.—June V. Huber, 501–0638.
Assistant Commissioner for Property Management.—James N. Barnard, Jr. (acting), 501–0971.
Deputy Assistant Commissioner for Property Management.—Jeffrey E. Neely (acting), 501–0971.
Deputy Assistant Commissioner for Special Projects, PBS.—John L. Stanberry, 208–7929.
Assistant Commissioner for Federal Protective Service.—Anthony Artigliere (acting), 501–0907.
Assistant Commissioner for Property Disposal.—Brian K. Polly, 501–0084.

Assistant Commisioner for Property Acquisition and Realty Services.—Hilary W. Peoples, 501–1025.
Assistant Commissioner for Property Development.—John A. Petkewich, 501–0887.
Assistant Commissioner for Business Development.—James A. Williams, 501–0018.
Director of Workplace Initiatives.—Faith A. Wohl, 501–3965.
Director, Cooperative Administrative Support and Telecommuting.—Warren Master, 273–4660.
Acquisition Executive.—Gerald Zaffos (acting), 208–6091.

FEDERAL TELECOMMUNICATIONS SERVICE

Commissioner.—Robert J. Woods, (703) 285–1020.
Deputy Commissioner.—John Okay, (703) 285–1020.
Assistant Commissioner for Information Technology Integration.—Charles Self (acting), (703) 756–4100.
Assistant Commissioner for Service Delivery.—Sandra N. Bates, (703) 760–7444.
Assistant Commissioner for Service Development.—Bruce F. Brignull, (703) 610–2813.
Assistant Commissioner for Strategic Planning and Business Development.—Abby J. Pirnie (acting), (703) 285–1056.
Controller.—Linda F. Vandenberg, (703) 760–7524.
Assistant Commissioner for Acquisition.—C. Allen Olson, (703) 285–1025.
Assistant Commissioner for Regional Services.—Margaret C. Binns, (202) 606–9000.
Assistant Commissioner for Information Security.—Thomas R. Burke, (202) 708–7000.

FEDERAL SUPPLY SERVICE

Commissioner.—Frank P. Pugliese, (703) 305–6667.
Deputy Commissioner.—Donna D. Bennett, (703) 305–6667; Carolyn Alston, (703) 305–7901.
Chief of Staff.—Barbara R. Vogt, (703) 305–6667.
Controller.—Jon A. Jordan, (703) 305–7644.
Assistant Commissioner for—
Acquisition.—William N. Gormley, (703) 305–7901.
Transportation and Property Management.—Janice R. Sandwen (acting), (703) 305–7660.
Business Management and Marketing.—Gary Feit, (703) 305–7970.
Distribution Management.—John R. Roehmer, (703) 305–5202.
FSS Information Systems.—Raymond J. Hanlein, (703) 305–5670.
Quality and Contract Administration.—Patricia M. Mead, (703) 305–7675.

REGIONAL OFFICES

National Capital Region: Seventh and D Streets SW Washington DC 20407, (202) 708–9100
Regional Administrator.—Nelson B. Alcalde,
Deputy.—Wolfgang J. Zoellner (acting), 708–6161.
Assistant for Pubic Buildings Service.—William R. Lawson, 708–5891.
Deputy Assistant for Pubic Buildings Service.—Annie W. Everett, 708–5891.
Assistant for Federal Telecommunications Service.—Craig F. Kennedy (acting), 708–6100.
Deputy Assistant for Federal Supply Service.—James T. Duncan, 619–8900.
New England Region: Thomas P. O'Neill Federal Building, 10 Causeway Street, Boston, MA 02222, (617) 565–5860.
Regional Administrator.—Robert J. Dunfey, Jr.
Assistant for Pubic Buildings Service.—Paul F. Prouty, (617) 565–5694.
Assistant for Federal Telecommunications Service.—William B. Horst, (617) 565–5760.
Northeast and Caribbean Region: 26 Federal Plaza, New York, NY 10278, (212) 264–2600.
Regional Administrator.—Karen R. Adler.
Deputy.—Robert W. Martin.
Assistant for Pubic Buildings Service.—William B. Jenkins, (212) 264–4282.
Assistant for Federal Telecommunications Service.—Stefano (Steve) Ruggiero, (212) 264–1257.
Assistant for Federal Supply Service.—Harold E. Murrell, (212) 264–3590.

Mid-Atlantic Region: 100 Penn Square East, Philadelphia, PA 19107, (215) 656–5501
Regional Administrator.—Ralph Borras (acting).
Deputy.—Larry F. Roush.
Assistant for Pubic Buildings Service.—Jan L. Ziegler, (215) 656–5655.
Assistant for Federal Telecommunications Service.—Paul J. McDermott (acting), (215) 656–6310.
Assistant for Federal Supply Service.—Jack R. Williams, (215) 656–3861.

Southeast Sunbelt Region: 401 West Peachtree Street, Atlanta, GA 30365–2550, (404) 331–3200
Regional Administrator.—Carole A. Dortch.
Assistant for Pubic Buildings Service.—Jimmy H. Bridgeman, (404) 331–5129.
Assistant for Federal Telecommunications Service.—Janice K. Mendenhall, (404) 331–5104.
Assistant for Federal Supply Service.—Ralph M. Wagoner, (404) 331–5114.

Great Lakes Region: 230 South Dearborn Street, Chicago, IL 60604, (312) 353–5395.
Regional Administrator.—William C. Burke.
Deputy.—Kenneth J. Kalscheur.
Assistant for Pubic Buildings Service.—James G. Whitlock, (312) 353–5572.
Assistant for Federal Telecommunications Service.—Ronald Q. Williams, (312) 886–3824.
Assistant for Federal Supply Service.—J. David Hood, (312) 347–1102.

The Heartland Region: 1500 East Bannister Road, Kansas City, MO 64131, (816) 926–7201.
Regional Administrator.—Glen (Woody) W. Overton.
Deputy.—Bond R. Faulwell, (816) 926–7217.
Assistant for Pubic Buildings Service.—Thomas H. Walker, (816) 926–7231.
Assistant for Federal Telecommunications Service.—Ronald G. Decker, (816) 926–5332.
Assistant for Federal Supply Service.—Tyree Varnado, (816) 926–7245.

Greater Southwest Region: 819 Taylor Street, Fort Worth, TX 76102, (817) 978–2321
Regional Administrator.—John C. Pouland.
Deputy.—W. Leighton Waters, (817) 978–4327.
Assistant for Pubic Buildings Service.—Earl W. Eschbacher, Jr., (817) 978–2522.
Assistant for Federal Telecommunications Service.—Marcella F. Banks, (817) 978–2321.
Assistant for Federal Supply Service.—Woody L. Landers, (817) 978–2516.

Rocky Mountain Region: Building 14, Denver Federal Center, Denver, CO 80225–0006, (303) 236–7329
Regional Administrator.—Polly B. Baca.
Deputy.—Marcella F. Banks (acting), (303) 236–7784.
Assistant for Pubic Buildings Service.—Casey Jones (acting), (303) 236–7245.
Assistant for Federal Supply Service.—Kenneth M. Bowen, Jr., (303) 236–7547.

Pacific Rim Region: 450 Golden Gate Avenue, San Francisco, CA 94102–3434, (415) 522–3001.
Regional Administrator.—Kenn N. Kojima.
Deputy.—Aki K. Nakao.
Assistant for Pubic Buildings Service.—Richard B. Welsh, (415) 522–3100.
Assistant for Federal Telecommunications Service.—Bob T. Johnston, (415) 522–4501.
Assistant for Federal Supply Service.—Peter T. Glading, (415) 522–2777.

Northwest/Arctic Region: 400 15th Street, SW, GSA Center, Auburn, WA 98001, (206) 931–7000
Regional Administrator.—L. Jay Pearson.
Executive Director.—William L. DuBray.
Assistant for Pubic Buildings Service.—Robin G. Graf, (206) 931–7200.
Assistant for Federal Telecommunications Service.—John G. Early, (206) 931–7500.
Assistant for Federal Supply Service.—Gary G. Casteel, (206) 931–7146.

HARRY S. TRUMAN SCHOLARSHIP FOUNDATION

(Created by Public Law 93–642)

712 Jackson Place 20006, phone (202) 395–4831, fax 395–6995

BOARD OF TRUSTEES

Chairman.—Elmer B. Staats.
Vice Chairman.—Ike Skelton, Representative from Missouri.

Secretary.—Mrs. Margaret Truman Daniel, New York, NY.
General Counsel.—C. Westbrook Murphy.

Members:
Richard Riley, Secretary of Education.
Christopher S. Bond, Senator from Missouri.
Jo Ann Emerson, Representative from Missouri.
Max Baucus, Senator from Montana.
Joseph E. Stevens, Senior US District Judge from Missouri.
Steven Zinter, Sixth Judicial Circuit from South Dakota.
Susan Bass Levine, Major of Cherry Hill, New Jersey.
Melvin E. Carnahan, Governor of Missouri.
Gordon Gee, President, The Ohio State University.
Norman I. Maldonado, President, University of Puerto Rico.
Luis Rovira, Chief Justice (ret.) from Colorado.
Executive Secretary.—Louis H. Blair.
Administrative Officer.—C. Judy Reed.
Program Support Assistant.—Jonji W. Barrow.
1996–97 Resident Truman Scholar.—Stacey Brandenburg.

INTER-AMERICAN FOUNDATION

901 North Stuart Street, 10th Floor, Arlington VA 22203, phone (703) 841–3800

Chairperson, Board of Director.—María Otero.
Vice Chair, Board of Director.—Neil H. Offen.
President.—George A. Evans.
Senior Vice President and General Counsel.—Adolfo A. Franco.
Vice President for—
Learning and Dissemination.—Anne B. Ternes.
Programs.—David Valenzuela.
Financial Management and Systems.—Winsome Wells.
Congressional Liaison.—Adolfo A. Franco.

INTERNATIONAL BROADCASTING BUREAU

(created by Public Law 103–236)

The International Broadcasting Bureau (IBB) is composed of the Voice of America, WORLDNET Television and Film Service, and Radio and TV Marti. The Broadcasting Board of Governors oversees the operation of the IBB and provides yearly funding grants approved by Congress to two non-profit grantee corporations, Radio Free Europe/Radio Liberty and Radio Free Asia.

Associate Director, International Broadcasting Bureau.—Kevin Close, 619–1009, fax 619–0085.
Director of—
Cube Broadcasting.—Rolando Bonachea (acting), 401–7013, fax 401–3340.
Voice of America.—Evelyn S. Lieberman, 619–2030, fax 401–1327.
Voice of America News Ombudsman.—Mark Hopkins.
WORLDNET Television and Film Service.—John lennon (acting), 501–7806, fax 501–6664.
President, Asia Pacific Network.—Richard Richter.

BROADCASTING BOARD OF GOVERNORS

330 Independence Avenue SW, Suite 3360, 20547, phone 401–3736, fax 401–6605

Chairman.—David Burke.

GOVERNORS

Tom Korologos
Edward Kaufman
Bette Bao Lord
Carl Spielvogel
Cheryl Halpern
Marc Nathanson
Alberto Mora
Joseph Duffey (*ex officio member*)

STAFF

Chief of Staff.—Kathleen Harrington.

Director of Evaluations/Analysis.—Brian Conniff.
Legal Counsel.—John Lindburg.
Program Review Officer.—Bruce Sherman.
Congressional Liaison.—John Beard.
Budget Analyst.—Michael Ringler.
Executive Assistant.—Brenda thomas.
Staff Assistant.—Carolyn Ford.

JOHN F. KENNEDY CENTER FOR THE PERFORMING ARTS

Washington DC 20566, phone 416–8000, fax 416–8205

BOARD OF TRUSTEES

Honorary Chairs:
Mrs. Hillary Rodham Clinton
Mrs. George Bush
Mrs. Ronald Reagan
Mrs. Jimmy Carter
Mrs. Gerald R. Ford
Mrs. Lyndon B. Johnson

Officers:
Chairman.—James A. Johnson
Vice Chairman.—Kenneth M. Duberstein
Vice Chairman.—Alma Johnson Powell
President.—Lawrence J. Wilker
Secretary.—Jean Kennedy Smith
Assistant Secretary.—Charlotte Woolard
Treasurer.—Paul G. Stern
Assistant Treasurer.—Henry Strong
General Counsel.—William Becker

Members Appointed by the President of the United States:
Mrs. Anita Arnold
Mr. Robert B. Barnett
Mr. Stuart A. Bernstein
Mrs. William N. Cafritz
Dr. Ronald I. Dozoretz
Mrs. Phyllis C. Draper
Mr. Kenneth M. Duberstein
Mrs. Max M. Fisher
Mr. Craig L. Fuller
Mrs. Mary Galvin
Mr. Lionel Hampton
Ms. Phyllis Middleton Jackson
Mr. James A. Johnson
Mrs. Ann Jordan
Mr. Donald M. Koll
The Hon. James A. McClure
Mr. Cappy R. McGarr
The Hon. William F. McSweeney
Mr. Frank H. Pearl
Mr. Ronald O. Perelman
Mrs. Alma Johnson Powell
Mrs. Abraham A. Ribicoff
Mr. Miles L. Rubin
Mrs. Joy A. Silverman
The Hon. Jean Kennedy Smith
Mr. Joshua I. Smith
Mr. Jay Stein
Mr. Jerry Weintraub
Mr. Thomas Wheeler
Mr. James D. Wolfensohn

Ex-Officio Members Designated by Act of Congress:
Donna E. Shalala, Secretary of Health and Human Services.
Richard W. Riley, Secretary of Education.
Joseph Duffey, Director, U.S. Information Agency.
Edward M. Kennedy, Senator from Massachusetts.
Max Baucus, Senator from Montana.
John H. Chafee, Senator from Rhode Island.
Trent Lott, Senate Majority Leader from Mississippi.
Ted Stevens, Senator from Alaska.
Joseph M. McDade, Representative from Pennsylvania.
Sidney R. Yates, Representative from Illinois.
James L. Oberstar, Representative from Minnesota.
Bud Shuster, Representative from Pennsylvania.
Newt Gingrich, Speaker of the U.S. House of Representatives from Georgia.
Marion Barry, Mayor, Distirct of Columbia.
I. Michael Heyman, Secretary, Smithsonian Institution.
James H. Billington, Librarian of Congress.
J. Carter Brown, Chairman, Commission of Fine Arts.
Roger G. Kennedy, Director, National Park Service.

Founding Chairman.—Roger Stevens.
Chairman Emeritus.—James D. Wolfensohn.

LEGAL SERVICES CORPORATION

750 First Street NE, 11th Floor 20002–4250

phone (202) 336–8800, fax (202) 336–8952

BOARD OF DIRECTORS

Douglas S. Eakeley, *Chair.*
John N. Erlenborn, *Vice Chair.*
Hulett H. Askew
LaVeeda M. Battle
John T. Broderick, Jr.
F. William McCalpin
Maria Luisa Mercado
Nancy H. Rogers
Thomas F. Smegal, Jr.
Ernestine P. Watlington
Edna Fairbanks-Williams

President.—Martha Bergmark.
General Counsel and Corporate Secretary.—Victor M. Fortuno.
Comptroller/Treasurer.—David Richardson.
Director, Office of—
Program Operations.—John Tull.
Government Relations.—Gail Laster.
Communications.—Robert Echols.
Inspector General.—Edouard Quatrevaux.

NATIONAL AERONAUTICS AND SPACE ADMINISTRATION

300 E Street SW, Room 9F44, 20546

phone 358–1000, http://www.nasa.gov

OFFICE OF THE ADMINISTRATOR

Code A, Room 9F44, phone 358–1010

Administrator.—Daniel S. Goldin.
Executive Assistant.—Jason L. Kessler.
Secretary.—Kelly M. Wilcoxen, 358–1801.
Deputy Administrator.—John R. Dailey (acting), 358–1820.
Associate Deputy Administrator.—John R. Dailey, 358–1820.
Associate Deputy Administrator (Technical).—Michael I. Mott, 358–1807.
Chief Engineer.—Dr. Daniel R. Mulville (acting), Room HQ8W21, 358–1823.
Chief Scientist.—[Vacant].
Chief Information Officer.—Ronald S. West, Room HQ9F44, 358–1824.
Chief Technologist.—Samuel Venneri, Room 4V13, 358–4600.

OFFICE OF THE CHIEF FINANCIAL OFFICER (CFO)/COMPTROLLER

Code B, Room F–8F72, phone 358–2262

Chief Financial Officer (CFO)/Comptroller.—Arnold G. Holz, Room HQ8F72.
Comptroller.—Malcolm L. Peterson.
Deputy Chief Financial Officer.—Kenneth J. Winter.

OFFICE OF HEADQUARTERS OPERATIONS

Code C, Room HQ3Z76, phone 358–2100

Associate Administrator for Headquarters Operations.—Michael D. Christensen, Room HQ3X04.

OFFICE OF EQUAL OPPORTUNITY PROGRAMS

Code E, phone 358–2167

Associate Administrator.—George E. Reese, Room HQ3A11.
Deputy Associate Administrator.—Oceola S. Hall, 358–2163.

OFFICE OF HUMAN RESOURCES AND EDUCATION

Associate Administrator.—Spence M. Armstrong, Room HQ3R11, 358–0520.
Deputy Associate Administrator.—[Vacant], Room HQ3Q13, 358–0520.

GENERAL COUNSEL

Code G, phone 358–2450

General Counsel.—Edward A. Frankle, Room HQ9V31.
Deputy General Counsel.—[Vacant], 358–2053.

OFFICE OF PROCUREMENT

Code H, Room 4L25, phone 358–2090

Associate Administrator.—Deidre A. Lee, Room HQ4L13.
Deputy Associate Administrator.—Thomas S. Luedtke, Room HQ4M11.

OFFICE OF EXTERNAL RELATIONS

Associate Administrator.—John D. Schumacher, Room 7W19, 358–0400.
Deputy Associate Administrator.—John D. Schumacher, Room HQ9U80, 358–0450.
Deputy Associate Administrator (Space Flight).—Michael F. O'Brien, Room HQ7T14, 358–2097.

OFFICE OF MANAGEMENT SYSTEMS AND FACILITIES

Associate Administrator.—Benita A. Cooper, Room HQ3Z29, 358–2800.
Deputy Associate Administrator.—Jeffrey E. Sutton (acting), Room HQ3Y23, 358–1422.

OFFICE OF SMALL AND DISADVANTAGED BUSINESS UTILIZATION

Code K, phone 358–2088

Associate Administrator.—Ralph C. Thomas III, Room HQ9K70.

OFFICE OF LEGISLATIVE AFFAIRS

Code L, Room 9L33, phone 358–1948

Associate Administrator.—Jeff Lawrence, Room HQ9L33.
Deputy Associate Administrator.—Lynn W. Heninger.
Deputy Associate Administrator (Programs).—Mary D. Kerwin.

OFFICE OF SPACE FLIGHT

Code M, phone 358–2015

Associate Administrator.—Wilbur C. Trafton, Room HQ7A11.
Deputy Associate Administrator.—Richard J. Wisniewski, Room HQ7A50, 358–0224.
Deputy Associate Administrator (Space Shuttle).—Stephen S. Oswald, Room HQ7A70, 358–1200.
Director, Space Station Requirements.—Gretchen W. McClain (acting), Room HQ7A40, 358–1854.

OFFICE OF PUBLIC AFFAIRS

Code P

Associate Administrator.—Laurie Boeder, Room HQ9Q39, 358–1898.

Deputy Associate Administrator.—Geoffrey H. Vincent, Room HQ9Q27, 358–1400.

OFFICE OF SAFETY AND MISSION ASSURANCE

Code Q, phone 358–2406

Associate Administrator.—Frederick D. Gregory, Room HQ5W21, 358–2406.
Deputy Associate Administrator.—Dr. Michael A. Greenfield, Room HQ5U11, 358–1930.

OFFICE OF AERONAUTICS AND SPACE TRANSPORTATION TECHNOLOGY

Code R

Associate Administrator.—Dr. Robert E. Whitehead, Room HQ6A70, 358–2693.
Deputy Associate Administrator.—Richard A. Reeves, Room HQ6A51, 358–2695.
Deputy Associate Administrator (Space Transportation Technology).—Gary E. Payton, Room 43Z5, 358–4579.

OFFICE OF SPACE SCIENCE

Code S, Room 5B36, phone 358–1409

Associate Administrator.—Dr. Wesley T. Huntress, Jr., Room HQ5B36, 358–1409.
Deputy Associate Administrator.—Dr. Earle K. Huckins, 358–1413.

OFFICE OF LIFE AND MICROGRAVITY SCIENCES AND APPLICATIONS

Code U

Associate Administrator.—Dr. Arnauld E. Nicogossian (acting), Room HQ8G25, 358–0122.
Deputy Associate Administrator.—Beth M. McCormick (acting), HQ8F32, 358–0215.

OFFICE OF INSPECTOR GENERAL

Code W, phone 358–1220

Inspector General.—Roberta L. Gross, Room HQ8480, 358–1220.

OFFICE OF MISSION TO PLANET EARTH

Code Y, Room 5A20, phone 358–2165

Associate Administrator.—William F. Townsend, (acting), Room HQ5A70, 358–2165.
Deputy Associate Administrator (Technology).—William F. Townsend, Room HQ5A50, 358–0260.
Deputy Associate Administrator (Management).—Michael B. Mann, Room HQ5B72, 358–1132.

OFFICE OF POLICY AND PLANS

Associate Administrator.—Alan M. Ladwig, Room HQ9F44, 358–1617.

NATIONAL OFFICES

Ames Research Center: Moffett Field, CA 94035.
Director.—Dr. Henry McDonald, (415) 604–5000.
Dryden Flight Research Facility: Ames Research Center, PO Box 273, Edwards, CA 93523.
Director.—Kenneth J. Szalai, (805) 258–3311.
Goddard Space Flight Center: Greenbelt Road, Greenbelt, MD 20771.
Director.—John M. Klineberg, (301) 286–2000.
Goddard Institute for Space Studies: Goddard Space Flight Center, 2880 Broadway, New York, NY 10025.
Head.—Dr. James E. Hansen, (212) 678–5500.
Jet Propulsion Laboratory: 4800 Oak Grove Drive, Pasadena, CA 91109.
Director.—Dr. Edward C. Stone, (818) 354–4321.
Lyndon B. Johnson Space Center: Houston, TX 77058.

Director.—George W. S. Abbey, (713) 483–0123.
John F. Kennedy Space Center: Kennedy Space Center, FL 32899.
Director.—Roy D. Bridges, (407) 867–7110.
Resident Office, (Vandenberg AFB): PO Box 425 Lompoc, CA 93438.
Manager.—Ted L. Oglesby, (805) 866–5859.
Langley Research Center: Hampton, VA 23681.
Director.—Jeremiah F. Creedon, (707) 864–1000.
Lewis Research Center: 21000 Brookpark Road, Cleveland, OH 44135.
Director.—Donald J. Campbell, (216) 433–4000.
George C. Marshall Space Flight Center: Marshall Space Flight Center, AL 35812.
Director.—Dr. J. Wayne Lilles, (205) 544–2121.
Michoud Assembly Facility: P.O. Box 29300, New Orleans, LA 70189.
Manager.—John R. Demarest, (504) 257–3311.
NASA Management Office—Jet Propulsion Laboratory: 4800 Oak Grove Drive, Pasadena, CA 91109.
Manager.—Kurt L. Lindstrom, (818) 354–5359.
Slidell Computer Complex: 1010 Gause Boulevard, Slidell, LA 70458.
Manager.—Bobby L. German, (504) 646–7200.
John C. Stennis Space Center: Stennis Space Center, MS 39529.
Director.—Roy S. Estess, (601) 688–2211.
Wallops Flight Facility: Goddard Space Flight Center, Wallops Island, VA 23337, (804) 824–1000.
White Sands Test Facility: Johnson Space Center, PO Drawer MM, Las Cruces, NM 88004.
Manager.—Joseph Freis (acting), (505) 524–5011.

FOREIGN OFFICES

Australian (tracking): APO AP 96549.
NASA Representative.—G. Ted Ankrum.
Spanish (tracking): PSC No. 61, Box 0037, APO AE 09642.
NASA Representative.—Dr. Anthony N. Carro.
European: American Embassy, APO AE 09777–9200.
NASA European Representative.—James V. Zimmerman.
Moscow: U.S Embassy, PSC 77/NASA APO AE 09721.
NASA CIS Representative.—William E. Saxe.

INTERNATIONAL PARTNER COUNTERPARTS TO DEPUTY DIRECTOR, SPACE STATION FREEDOM PROGRAM OFFICE

Space Station Program: Canadian Space Agency, PO Box 7277, 250 Durocher Street, Vanier, Ontario, Canada K1L 8E3.
Director General.—Dr. Karl H. Doetsch.
Columbus Systems and Integration: European Space Agency, ESTEC (MS), Keplerliaan 1–Postbus 299, 2200–AG Noordwijk, The Netherlands.
Manager.—Frank Longhurst.
Space Station Program: Space Station Group, National Space Development Agency of Japan, Shiba Ryoshin Building 6F, 2–5–6 Shiba, Minato-Ku, Tokyo 105, Japan.
Manager.—Kazuhiko Yoneyama.

NASA FOREIGN LIAISON OFFICES

NASA/ESTEC (MO): Keplerlaan 1, 2200–AG Noordwijk, The Netherlands.
Kathleen Laurini, 9–011–31–1719–84866, fax 9–011–31–1719–46278.
C/O U.S. Embassy: PO Box 5000, Ogdensburg, New York 13669–0430.
Dr. Dipak Talapatra, (613) 993–6462, fax (613) 952–9399.
Space Environment Utilization System Department: National Space Development Agency of Japan, Sengen 2–1–1, Rukuba-shi, lbaraki-ken 305, Japan.
Kevin D. Watts, 9–011–81–298–52–1511, fax 9–011–81–298–52–1512.

NATIONAL ARCHIVES AND RECORDS ADMINISTRATION

(Created by Public Law 98–497)

8601 Adelphi Road College Park MD 20740–6001
phone (301) 713–6800, http://www.nara.gov/

Archivist of the United States.—John W. Carlin, (301) 713–6410, fax (301) 713–7141.
Deputy Archivist of the United States and Chief of Staff.—Lewis J. Bellardo, (301) 713–6410, fax (301) 713–7141.
Congressional Affairs.—John A. Constance, (301) 713–7340, fax (301) 713–7344.
General Counsel.—Elizabeth A. Pugh, (301) 713–6937, fax (301) 713–6040
Equal Employment Opportunity and Diversity Programs.—Joyce A. Williams, (301) 713–6935, fax (301) 713–7342.
Policy and Communications Staff Public Affairs.—Lewis J. Bellardo (acting), (301) 713–7360, fax (301) 713–7270.
Information Security Oversight Office.—Steven Garfinkel, (301) 219–5250, fax (301) 219–5385.
National Historical Publications and Records Commission.—Gerald W. George, (202) 501–5600, fax (202) 501–5601.
Director, Office of—
Inspector General.—Kelly A. Sisario, (301) 713–7300, fax (301) 713–7320.
Administrative Services.—Adrienne C. Thomas, (301) 713–6400, fax (301) 713–6497.
Federal Register.—Raymond A. Mosely, (202) 523–4534, fax (202) 523–6866.
Human Resources and Information Services.—L. Reynolds Cahoon, (301) 713–6402, fax (301) 713–7344.
Records Services.—Michael J. Kurtz, (301) 713–7000, fax (301) 713–6915.
Regional Records Services.—Richard L. Claypoole, (301) 713–7200, fax (301) 713–7205.

REGIONAL OFFICES

Northeast Region, Headquarters: Waltham MA. *Regional Director.*—Diane LeBlac, (617) 647–8745
Boston.—380 Trapelo Road, Waltham, MA 02154, (617) 647–8104
Pittsfield.—100 Dan Fox Drive, Pittsfield MA 01201–8230, (413) 445–6885
New York City.—201 Varick St., New York 10014–4811, (213) 337–1301
Bayone.—Building 22, Military Ocean Terminal, Bayonne, NJ 07002–5388, (201) 823–7161
Mid Atlantic Region, Headquarters: Philadelphia, PA. *Regional Director.*—James W. Mouat, (215) 671–9027
Center City Philadelphia.—900 Market Street, Philadelphia, PA, 19107, (215) 597–3000
Northeast Philadelphia.—14700 Townsend Road, Philadelphia, PA 19154, (215) 671–9027
Southeast Region: *Regional Director.*—Gayle P. Peters, (404) 763–7477
Southeast Region.—1557 St. Joseph Avenue, East Point, GA 30344, (404) 763–7474
Great Lakes Region, Headquarters: Chicago, IL, *Regional Director.*—David E. Kuehl, (773) 581–7816
Chicago.—7358 South Pulaski Road, Chicago, IL 60629, (773) 581–9688
Dayton.—3150 Springboro Road, Dayton, OH 45439, (513) 225–2852
Central Plains Region: *Regional Director.*—R. Reed Whitaker, (816) 926–6920
Central Plains Region.—2312 East Bannister Road, Kansas City, MO 64131, (816) 7271
Southwest Region: *Regional Director.*—Kent C. Carter, (817) 334–5515
Southwest Region.—501 W. Felix Street, Ft. Worth, TX 76115, (817) 334–5515
Rocky Mountain Region: *Regional Director.*—Robert Svenningsen, (303) 236–0804
Rocky Mountain Region.—Building 48, Denver Federal Center, Denver, CO 80225, (303) 236–0804
Pacific Region, Headquarters: San Brunco, CA. *Director.*—Sharon L. Roadway, (415) 876–9001
Laguna Niguel.—24000 Avila Road, 1st Floor (East), PO 6719, Laguna Niguel, CA 92607, (714) 360–2626
San Francisco.—1000 Commodore Drive, San Bruno, CA 94066, (415) 876–9001
Pacific Alaska Region, Headquarters: Seattle, WA. *Regional Director.*—Steven M. Edwards, (206) 526–6503
Seattle.—6125 Sand Point Way NE, Seattle, WA 98115, (206) 526–6501
Anchorage.—654 West Third Avenue, Anchorage, AK 99501, (907) 721–2443

National Personnel Records Center: *Director.*—David L. Petree, (314) 538–4201
National Personnel Records Center.—9700 Page Avenue, St. Louis, MO 63132, (314) 538–4201
Presidential Libraries.—David F. Peterson, (202) 501–5700, fax (202) 501–5709.
Director for—
Herbert Hoover Library.—Timothy G. Walch, West Branch, IA 52358–0488, (319) 643–5301.
Franklin D. Roosevelt Library.—Verne W. Newton, Hyde Park, NY 12538–1999, (914) 229–8114.
Harry S. Truman Library.—Larry J. Hackman, Independence, MO 64050–1798, (816) 833–1400.
Dwight D. Eisenhower Library.—Daniel D. Holt, Abilene, KS 67410–2900, (913) 263–4751.
John F. Kennedy Library.—Bradley Gerratt, Boston, MA 02125–3398, (617) 929–4500.
Lyndon Baines Johnson Library.—Harry J. Middleton, Austin, TX 78705, (512) 482–5137.
Gerald R. Ford Library.—Richard Norton Smith, Ann Arbor, MI 48109–2114, (313) 741–2218.
Gerald R. Ford Museum.—Richard Norton Smith, Grand Rapids, MI 49504–5353, (616) 451–9263.
Nixon Presidential Materials Staff.—Karl Weissenbach, Acting, College Park, MD 20740–6001, (301) 713–6950.
Jimmy Carter Library.—Donald B. Schewe, Atlanta, GA 30307–1406, (404) 331–3942.
Ronald Reagan Library.—Mark A. Hunt, Simi Valley, CA 93065–0666, (805) 522–8444.
Bush Presidential Materials Staff.—David E. Alsobrook (acting), College Station, TX 77840–1897, (409) 260–9554.

NATIONAL HISTORICAL PUBLICATIONS AND RECORDS COMMISSION

National Archives Building 20408, phone (301) 713–5600, fax (301) 501–5601

Members:
John W. Carlin, Archivist of the United States, Chairman, National Archives and Records Administration.
Harry A. Blackmun, Associate Justice, U.S. Supreme Court.
Mark O. Hatfield, Senator of Oregon (term expired; serving pending appointment of successor)
William Z. Slany, Director, Historical Office, Department of State.
Alfred Goldberg, Historian, Office of the Secretary, Department of Defense.
Winston Tabb, Director of Public Services and Collections Management I, Library of Congress.
Nicholas C. Burckel, Director of Libraries, Marquette University, Presidential Appointment.
Marvin F. Moss, Presidential Appointment
Constance B. Schulz, University of South Carolina, American Historical Association.
William Chafe, Dean of Faculty, Arts and Sciences, Duke University, Organization of American Historians.
Anne R. Kenney, Associate Director for Preservation and Conservation, Cornell University.
David H. Hoober, Arizona State Archivist, American Association for State and Local History.
Charles T. Cullen, President and Librarian, Newberry Library, Association for Documentary Editing.
Howard P. Lowell, State Archivist and Records Administrator, Delaware Public Archives, National Association of Government Archives and Records Administration.
Executive Directive.—Gerald W. George, 202–501–5600

NATIONAL ARCHIVES TRUST FUND BOARD

phone (301) 713–6405, fax (301) 713–6499

Members:
John W. Carlin, Archivist of the United States, *Chair.*
F. Sheldon Hackney, Chairman, National Endowment for the Humanities.
Gerald Murphy, Fiscal Assistant Secretary, Department of the Treasury.
Secretary.—Sonia R. Rudo, (301) 713–6405.

ADMINISTRATIVE COMMITTEE OF THE FEDERAL REGISTER

800 North Capitol Street, Washington DC, phone (202) 523–4534

Members:
John W. Carlin, Archivist of the United States, *Chair*.
Rosemary Hart, Senior Counsel, Department of Justice.
Michael DiMario, The Public Printer.
Secretary.—Raymond A. Mosley, Director of the Federal Register, National Archives and Records Administration.

NATIONAL CAPITAL PLANNING COMMISSION

801 Pennsylvania Avenue NW, Suite 301, 20576, phone (202) 482–7200, fax 482–7272

APPOINTIVE MEMBERS

Presidential Appointees:
Harvey B. Gantt, *Chairman.*
Robert A. Gaines
Margaret G. Vanderhye
Mayoral Appointees:
Arrington Dixon
Dr. Patricia Elwood, *Vice Chairman*
Ex Officio Members:
Marion Barry, Mayor of the District of Columbia.
First Alternate.—Jill Dennis.
Second Alternate.—[Vacant].
Third Alternate.—David W. Colby.
Linda W. Cropp (acting), Chairman, Council of the District of Columbia.
First Alternate.—Charlene Drew Jarvis.
Second Alternate.—Robert E. Miller.
Third Alternate.—[Vacant].
Bruce Babbitt, Secretary of the Interior.
First Alternate.—Roger Kennedy.
Second Alternate.—Terry R. Carlstrom.
Third Alternate.—John G. Parsons.
William S. Cohen, Secretary of Defense.
First Alternate.—Jerry R. Shiplett.
Second Alternate.—Elbert Humphrey.
Third Alternate.—Michael Brown.
David J. Barram, Administrator of General Services Administration (acting).
First Alternate.—Robert A. Peck.
Second Alternate.—William R. Lawson.
Third Alternate.—Jack Finberg.
Fred Thompson, Chairman, Committee on Governmental Affairs, U.S. Senate.
First Alternate.—Susanne Marshall.
Dan Burton, Chairman, Committee on Government Reform and Oversight, House of Representatives.
First Alternate.—Thomas M. Davis III.
Second Alternate.—Ron Hamm.
Third Alternate.—Roland Gunn.

EXECUTIVE STAFF

Executive Director.—Reginald W. Griffith.
Director, Office of Intergovernmental and Public Affairs.—David S. Julyan.
General Counsel.—Sandra H. Shapiro.
Secretary to the Commission.—Rae N. Allen.
Executive Officer.—Connie M. Harshaw.
Executive Assistant.—Priscilla A. Brown.
Director, Office of—
Planning, Review and Implementation.—George V. Evans (acting).
Technical Planning Services.—Ronald E. Wilson.
Long-Range Planning.—John M. Dugan.
Planning, Information and Technology.—David A. Nystrom.

NATIONAL COMMISSION ON LIBRARIES AND INFORMATION SCIENCE

(Created by Public Law 91–345)

1110 Vermont Avenue NW, Suite 820, 20005, phone 606–9200, fax 606–9203

Chairperson.—Jeanne Hurley Simon.
Vice Chair.—Martha B. Gould, 1690 West Sixth Street, Reno, NV 89503.
Members:
Daniel W. Casey, 202 Scarboro Drive, Syracuse, NY 13209.
Shirley Gray Adamovich, 14 Thompson Lane, Durham, NH 03824.
Dr. James H. Billington, Librarian of Congress, Library of Congress, Washington, DC 20540.
Serves for the Librarian of Congress:
Winston Tabb, Associate Librarian for Collections Services, Library of Congress, Washington, DC 20540.
Carol K. DiPrete, Dean for Academic Services, Roger Williams University, Old Ferry Road, Bristol, RI 02809.
Norman Kelinson, Universal Financial Services, 111 East Third Street, Suite 305, Union Arcade Building, Davenport, IA 52801.
Frank J. Lucchino, Controller, County of Allegheny, 104 Courthouse, Pittsburgh, PA 15219.
Kay W. Riddle, 1900 Grant Street, Suite 850, Denver, CO 80203.
Dr. Bobby L. Roberts, Director, Central Arkansas Library System, 700 Louisiana Street, Little Rock, AR 72201.
Gary N. Sudduth, President and CEO, Minneapolis Urban League, 2000 Plymouth Avenue North, Minneapolis, MN 55411.
Elinor H. Swaim, Member, Executive Committee, 351 Richmond Road, Salisbury, NC 28144.
Barbara J.H. Taylor, 14914 Spring Meadows Drive, Germantown, MD 20874.
Joel D. Valdez, Senior Vice President for Business Affairs, The University of Arizona, 605 Administration Building, Tucson, AZ 85721.
Robert S. Willard, Strategic Customer Relations Director, Mead Data Central, Inc., 9595 Springboro Pike, Miamisburg, OH 45342.
Chairmen Emeritus:
Charles Benton, 5547 North Ravenswood Avenue, Chicago, IL 60640.
Frederick Burkhardt, Box 1067, Bennington, VT 05201.
Elinor M. Hashim, 1320 Old Chain Bridge Road, Suite 350, McLean, VA 22101.
Jerald C. Newman, 63 Captains Road, North Woodmere, NY 11581.
Charles E. Reid, Box 1441, Kennebunkport, ME 04046.
Vice Chairman Emeritus.—Bessie Boehm Moore, 712 Legato Drive, Briarwood, Little Rock, AR 72205.

EXECUTIVE STAFF

Executive Director.—Peter R. Young.
Associate Executive Director.—Mary Alice Hedge.
Secretary to the Staff.—Cherylene W. Rollerson.
Administrative Officer.—Vivian D. Terrell.
Administrative Assistant.—Kim Miller.
Research Associate.—Jane Williams.

LIBRARY STATISTICS STAFF

Coordinator.—John G. Lorenz.
Special Assistant to the Director.—Barbara L. Whiteleather.
Fiscal Officer.—Mimie L. Rutledge.

NATIONAL COUNCIL ON DISABILITY

1331 F Street NW Suite 1050, 20004, phone 272–2004, fax 272–2022

Chairperson.—Marca Bristo, Access Living, Chicago, IL.
Vice Chairperson.—John A. Gannon, Washington, DC.
Acting Executive Director.—Speed Davis.
Members:
Linda W. Allison, New York, NY.
Ellis B. Bodron, Vicksburg, MS.
Larry Brown, Jr., Potomac, MD.
Mary Ann Mobley Collins, Beverly Hills, CA.
Anthony H. Flack, Norwalk, CT.
Robert S. Muller, Grandville, MI.
Bonnie O'Day, Somerville, MA.
Mary M. Raether, McLean, VA.
Shirley W. Ryan, Winnetka, IL.
Anne C. Seggerman, Fairfield, CT.
Michael B. Unhjem, Fargo, ND.
Helen W. Walsh, Greenwich, CT.
Kate Pew Wolters, Grand Rapids, MI.

NATIONAL CREDIT UNION ADMINISTRATION

1775 Duke Street, Alexandria VA 22314–3428, phone (703) 518–6300, fax 518–6300

Chairman.—Norman E. D'Amours.
Vice Chairman.—Shirlee P. Bowné.
Board Member.—Yolanda Townsend Wheat.
Executive Director.—Karl T. Hoyle.
Deputy Executive Director.—Tawana James.
General Counsel.—Robert M. Fenner, 518–6540.
Inspector General.—H. Frank Thomas, 518–6350.
Secretary to the Board.—Becky Baker, 518–6314.
Director, Office of—
Administration.—James L. Baylen, 518–6410.
Community Development Credit Union.—Joyce Jackson, 518–6610.
Chief Financial Officer—Dennis C. Winans, 518–6570.
Corporate Credit Unions.—Robert F. Schafer, 518–6640.
Examination and Insurance.—David M. Marquis, 518–6360.
Human Resources.—Dorothy W. Foster, 518–6510.
Public and Congressional Affairs.—Robert E. Loftus, 518–6330.
Technology and Information Systems.—Doug Verner, 518–6440.

REGIONAL OFFICES

Director, Office of Region I (Albany).—Layne L. Bumgardner, 9 Washington Square, Washington Avenue Extension, Albany, NY 12205, (518) 464–4180, fax 464–4195.

Director, Office of Region II (National Capital Region).—Jane A. Walters, Suite 4206, 1775 Duke Street, Alexandria, VA 22314, (703) 838–0401, fax 838–0571.

Director, Office of Region III (Atlanta).—H. Allen Carver, Suite 1600, 7000 Central Parkway, Atlanta, GA 30328, (404) 396–4042, fax 698–8211.

Director, Office of Region IV (Chicago).—Nicholas Veghts, Suite 125, 4225 Naperville Road, Lisle, IL 60532, (708) 245–1000, fax 245–1015.

Director, Office of Region V (Austin).—Phillip R. Crider, Suite 5200, 4807 Spicewood Springs Road, Austin, TX 78759–8490, (512) 482–4500, fax 482–4511.

Director, Office of Region VI (Concord).—Daniel L. Murphy, Suite 1350, 2300 Clayton Road, Concord, CA 94520, (510) 825–6125, fax 486–3729.

Asset Liquidation Management Center (Austin).—J. Leonard Skiles, President, Suite 5100, 4807 Spicewood Springs Road, Austin, TX 78759–8490, (512) 795–0999, fax 795–8244.

NATIONAL FOUNDATION ON THE ARTS AND THE HUMANITIES

Old Post Office Building, 1100 Pennsylvania Avenue NW 20506, phone (202) 682–5442

NATIONAL ENDOWMENT FOR THE ARTS

Chairman.—Jane Alexander, 682–5414.
Chief of Staff.—Alexander Crary, 682–5652.
Deputy Chairman for—
Management and Budget.—Ana M. Steele, 682–5414.
Grants and Partnership.—Scott Sanders, 682–5441.
Congressional Liaison.—Richard Woodruff, 682–5434.
General Counsel.—Karen Christensen, 682–5418.
Policy, Planning, Research.—Olive Mosier, 682–5424.
Inspector General.—Leon Lilly, 682–5402.
Public Affairs.—Cherie Simon, 682–5570.
Director for Administration.—Laurence M. Baden, 682–5408.

THE NATIONAL COUNCIL ON THE ARTS

Chairman.—Jane Alexander.
Members:
William Bailey
Trisha Brown
Patrick Davidson
Terry Evans
Ronald Feldman
William P. Foster
Barbara W. Grossman
Donald Hall
Hugh Hardy
Marta Istomin
Kenneth M. Jarin
Speight Jenkins
Colleen Jennings-Roggensack
Louise McClure
Wallace D. McRae
Leo J. O'Donovan, S.J.
Jorge Perez
Roberta Peters
Judith O. Rubin
Richard J. Stern
William E. Strickland, Jr.
Luis Valdez
George White
Townsend D. Wolfe III
Rachael Worby

NATIONAL ENDOWMENT FOR THE HUMANITIES

http://ns1.neh.fed.us/

Chairman.—Sheldon Hackney, 606–8310.
Deputy Chairman.—Juan Mestas, 606–8273.
Inspector General.—Sheldon L. Bernstein, 606–8350.
General Counsel.—Michael Shapiro, 606–8322.
Congressional Liaison.—Ann Young Orr, 606–8328.
Public Information Officer.—Joy Evans.
Director, Office of—
Communications Policy.—Gary Krull, 606–8446.
Planning and Budget.—Stephen Cherrington, 606–8428.
Enterprise.—Ann Young Orr, 606–8328.

NATIONAL COUNCIL ON THE HUMANITIES

Members:
Bruce D. Benson
Paul A. Cantor
Bruce Cole
John H. D'Arms
Margaret P. Duckett
David Finn
Billie Davis Gaines
Darryl J. Gless
Ramon A. Gutierrez
Joseph H. Hagan
Theodore S. Hamerow
Mikiso Hane
Charles P. Henry
Henry H. Higuera
Thomas C. Holt
Martha C. Howell
Alicia Juarrero
Nicolas Kanellos
Alan C. Kors
Bev Lindsey
Jon Moline
Robert I. Rotberg
John R. Searle
Harold K. Skramstad, Jr.
Kenny J. Williams

INSTITUTE OF MUSEUM SERVICES

[Transferred to the National Foundation of the Arts and Humanities under the authority of U.S. Code 20, sections 961, 962]

phone (202) 606–8536, fax 202–606–8591

Director.—Diane B. Frankel.
Director of Policy, Planning, and Budget.—Linda Bell.
Program Director.—Rebecca Danvers, 606–8539.
Legislative and Public Affairs.—Mamie Bittner.

NATIONAL MUSEUM SERVICES BOARD

Members:
Robert G. Breunig
John L. Bryant, Jr.
Kinshasha Holman Conwill
Jeanne R. Ferst
Phillip Frost
Alberta Sebolt George
Lisa A. Hembry
Fay S. Howell
Charles Hummell
Ayse Manyas Kenmore
Nancy Marsiglia
Arthur Rosenblatt
Ruth Y. Tamura
David A. Voko
Townsend Wolfe

FEDERAL COUNCIL ON THE ARTS AND HUMANITIES

Federal Council Members:
Jane Alexander, Chairman, National Endowment for the Arts.
Sheldon Hackney, Chairman, National Endowment for the Humanities.
Diane Frankel, Director, Institute of Museum Services.
Richard W. Riley, Secretary, Department of Education.
Earl Powell, Director, National Gallery of Art.
J. Carter Brown, Chairman, Commission of Fine Arts.
James H. Billington, Librarian of Congress, Library of Congress.
John W. Carlin, Archivist of the United States, National Archives and Records Service.
David J. Barram, Acting Administrator, General Services Administration.
Bruce Babbitt, Secretary, Department of the Interior.
Neal Lane, Director, National Science Foundation.
Gary Sisco, Secretary of the Senate.
Michael Heyman, Secretary, Smithsonian Institution.
Joseph Duffey, Director, United States Information Agency.
Fortney Pete Stark, Member, U.S. House of Representatives.
William M. Daley, Secretary, Department of Commerce.
Rodney E. Slater, Secretary, Department of Transportation.
Kinshasha H. Conwill, Chairman, National Museum Services Board.
Andrew M. Cuomo, Secretary, Department of Housing and Urban Development.
Robert A. Peck, Commissioner, Public Buildings Service, Administrator of General Services.
Alexis Herman, Secretary, Department of Labor.
Jesse Brown, Secretary, Department of Veterans' Affairs.
Fernando M. Torres-Gil, Commissioner, Administration on Aging, Department of Health and Human Services.
Staff Contact.—Alice M. Whelihan, Indemnity Administrator, National Endowment for the Arts, 682–5452.

NATIONAL GALLERY OF ART

(Under the direction of the Board of Trustees of the National Gallery of Art)

Constitution Avenue between Third and Seventh Streets 20565
phone (202) 737–4215, fax (202) 289–5446

Board of Trustees:
William H. Rehnquist, Chief Justice of the United States.
Madeleine K. Albright, Secretary of State.
Robert E. Rubin, Secretary of the Treasury.
I. Michael Heyman, Secretary of the Smithsonian Institution.
Paul Mellon, Honorary Trustee.
John R. Stevenson, Trustee Emeritus
Alexander M. Laughlin.
Robert F. Erburu.
Louise W. Mellon.
Chairman.—Ruth Carter Stevenson.
President.—Robert H. Smith.
Director.—Earl A. Powell III.
Deputy Director.—Alan Shestack.
Dean, Center for Advanced Study in the Visual Arts.—Henry A. Millon.
Administrator.—Darrell Willson.
Treasurer.—Ann Leven.
Secretary-General Counsel.—Philip C. Jessup, Jr.
External Affairs Officer.—Joseph J. Krakora.
Directors Emeritus: John Walker; J. Carter Brown.

NATIONAL LABOR RELATIONS BOARD

1099 14th Street NW 20570–0001

Personnel Locator (202) 273–1000, fax 273–4266

Chairman.—William B. Gould IV, 273–1790, fax 273–4270.
Chief Counsel.—Alfred Wolff.
Executive Assistant.—[Vacant].
Special Assistant.—Ralph E. Deeds, Jr.
Members:
Sarah M. Fox, 273–1700.
Chief Counsel.—Elinor H. Stillman.
John C. Truesdale, 273–4270.
Chief Counsel.—Susan Holik.
Margaret A. Browning, 273–1740.
Chief Counsel.—Dennis P. Walsh.
John E. Higgins, 273–1770.
Chief Counsel.—Harold Datz.
Executive Secretary.—John J. Toner, 273–1940, fax 273–4270.
Deputy Executive Secretary.—[Vacant].
Associate Executive Secretaries: [Vacant], Enid W. Weber, Hollace J. Enoch.
Solicitor.—Jeffrey D. Wedekind (acting), 273–2910, fax 273–4270.
Inspector General.—Robert E. Allen (acting), 273–1960, fax 273–4286.
Director, Representation Appeals.—Wayne R. Gold, 273–1980.
Deputy Director.—[Vacant], 273–1980, fax 273–4270.
Director, Division of Information.—David B. Parker.
Associate Director.—Tana M. Adde, 273–1991, fax 273–1789.
Chief Administrative Law Judge.—Robert A. Giannasi, Room 5400, (301) 713–8800, fax (301) 713–8686.
Deputy Chief Administrative Law Judge.—Michael O. Miller.
Associate Chief Administrative Law Judges:
Joel P. Biblowitz, 11th Floor, 120 West 45th Street, New York, NY 10036–5503, (212) 944–2941, fax 944–4904.
William N. Cates, Suite 1708, 401 West Peachtree Street NE, Atlanta, GA 30308–3510, (404) 331–6652, fax 331–2061.
Steven Gross.
Deputy Chief Administrative Law Judge.—William Schmidt, Suite 300, 901 Market Street, San Francisco, CA 94103–1779, (415) 744–6800, fax 744–7905.

GENERAL COUNSEL

phone (202) 273–3700

General Counsel.—Fred L. Feinstein, fax 273–4274.
Deputy General Counsel.—Mary Joyce Carlson, 273–3700.
Assistant General Counsel.—Joseph F. Frankl.
Associate General Counsel, Division of Advice.—Barry J. Kearney, 273–3800, fax 273–4244.
Deputy Associate General Counsel.—Barry J. Kearney.
Assistant General Counsel, Regional Advice Branch.—Jane C. Schnabel, 273–3823.
Assistant General Counsel, Injunction Litigation Branch.—Ellen A. Farrell.
Assistant General Counsel, Legal Research and Policy Planning Branch.—John W. Hornbeck.
Director, Division of Administration.—Gloria J. Joseph, 273–3890, fax 273–4266.
Deputy Director.—Frank V. Battle.
Associate General Counsel, Division of Enforcement Litigation.—Linda R. Sher (acting), 273–2950, fax 273–4244.
Appellate Court Branch:
Deputy Associate General Counsel.—Aileen Armstrong.
Assistant General Counsel.—John Burgoyne.
Supreme Court Branch:
Deputy Associate General Counsel.—Norton J. Come.
Assistant General Counsel.—[Vacant].
Special Litigation Branch:
Assistant General Counsel.—Margery E. Lieber.
Contempt Litigation Branch:
Assistant General Counsel.—Gary Shinners.
Director, Office of Appeals.—Yvonne T. Dixon.
Associate General Counsel, Division of Operations/Management.—Richard Siegel (acting) 273–2900, fax 273–4274.
Deputy Associate General Counsel.—Anne Purcell (acting).
Assistant General Counsels: Shirley A. Bednarz, Celeste Mattina, Eugene L. Rosenfeld, Nicholas E. Karatinos, [vacant].
Executive Assistant.—Carole K. Coleman.
Special Counsel.—Peter A. Eveleth.

NATIONAL MEDIATION BOARD

1301 K Street, Suite 250 East, 20572, phone (202) 523–5920, fax 523–1494

Chairman.—Kenneth B. Hipp, 523–5428.
Board Members:
Ernest W. DuBester, 523–5024
Magdalena Jacobsen, 523–5024.
Chief of Staff.—Stephen E. Crable, 523–5012.
General Counsel.—Ronald M. Etters, 523–5944.
Development and Technical Services.—James E. Armshaw, 523–5623.
Chief Financial Officer.—June King, 523–5950.
Staff Coordinator/Arbitration.—Pirscilla Zeigler, 523–5359.
Information Resources Management.—Donald L. West, 523–5588.

NATIONAL RESEARCH COUNCIL—NATIONAL ACADEMY OF SCIENCES NATIONAL ACADEMY OF ENGINEERING—INSTITUTE OF MEDICINE

2101 Constitution Avenue 20418, phone (202) 334–2000

The National Research Council of the National Academy of Sciences, National Academy of Engineering, and Institute of Medicine, serves as an independent Adviser to the Federal Government on scientific and technical questions of national importance. Although operating under a congressional charter granted the National Academy of Sciences in 1863, the National Research Council and its three parent organizations are private organizations, not agencies of the Federal Government, and receive no appropriation from Congress.

NATIONAL RESEARCH COUNCIL

Chairman.—Bruce M. Alberts, president, National Academy of Sciences, 334–2100.
Vice Chairman.—Robert M. White, president, National Academy of Engineering, 334–3200.
Executive Officer.—E. William Colglazier, 334–3000.
Director, Office of Congressional and Government Affairs.—Stephen A. Merrill (acting), 334–2200.

NATIONAL ACADEMY OF SCIENCES

President.—Bruce M. Alberts, 334–2100.
Vice President.—Jack Halpern, University of Chicago.
Home Secretary.—Peter Raven, Missouri Botanical Garden.
Foreign Secretary.—F. Sherwood Rowland, University of California, Irvine.
Treasurer.—Mildred S. Dresselhaus, Massachusetts Institute of Technology.
Executive Officer.—E. William Colglazier, 334–3000.

NATIONAL ACADEMY OF ENGINEERING

President.—Robert M. White, 334–3200.
Chairman.—Norman R. Augustine, Lockheed Martin Corporation.
Vice President.—Morris Tanenbaum (retired), AT&T.
Home Secretary.—Simon Ostrach, Case Western Reserve University.
Foreign Secretary.—Gerald P. Dinneen (retired), Honeywell, Inc.
Executive Officer.—William Salmon, 334–3677.
(effective July 1, 1995: President-elect.—Dr. Harold Liebowitz).
(effective July 1, 1995: Foreign Secretary-elect.—Dr. Harold K. Forsen).

INSTITUTE OF MEDICINE

President.—Kenneth I. Shine, M.D., 334–3300.
Executive Officer.—Karen Hein, 334–2177.

NATIONAL SCIENCE FOUNDATION

4201 Wilson Boulevard Arlington VA 22230, http://stis.nsf.gov

Director.—Neal F. Lane, Room 1205, (703) 306–1000.
Deputy Director.—Joseph Bordogna, (acting), Room 1205, (703) 306–1000.
Inspector General.—Linda G. Sundro, Room 1135, (703) 306–2100.
Equal Opportunity Coordinator.—Jean W. Riggs, Room 1080, (703) 306–1020.
Director, Office of—
Legislative and Public Affairs.—Julia A. Moore, Room 1245, (703) 306–1070.
Polar Programs.—Cornelius W. Sullivan, Room 755, (703) 306–1030.
Science and Technology Infrastructure.—Nathaniel G. Pitts, Room 1270, (703) 306–1040.
Policy Support.—Susan E. Cozzens, Room 1285, (703) 306–1090.
General Counsel.—Lawrence Rudolph, Room 1265, (703) 306–1060.
Assistant Director for—
Biological Sciences.—Mary E. Clutter, Room 605, (703) 306–1400.
Computer and Information Science and Engineering.—Juris Hartmanis, Room 1105, (703) 306–1900.
Education and Human Resources.—Luther S. Williams, Room 805, (703) 306–1600.
Engineering.—Elbert L. Marsh, (acting), Room 505, (703) 306–1300.
Geosciences.—Robert W. Corell, Room 705, (703) 306–1500.
Mathematical and Physical Sciences.—John B. Hunt, (acting), Room 1005, (703) 306–1801.
Social, Behavorial, and Economic Sciences.—Bennett I. Bertenthal, Room 905, (703) 306–1700.
Director, Office of—
Budget, Finance, and Award Management.—Joseph L. Kull, Room 405, (703) 306–1200.
Information and Resource Management.—Linda P. Massaro, Room 305, (703) 306–1100.

NATIONAL SCIENCE BOARD

Chairman.—Richard N. Zare.

Vice Chairman.—Diana Natalicio.
Executive Officer.—Marta Cehelsky, Room 1225, (703) 306–2000.

MEMBERS

F. Albert Cotton
Sanford D. Greenberg
Charles E. Hess
John Hopcroft
Shirley M. Malcom
Eve L. Menger
Claudia I. Mitchell-Keman
Diana Natalicio
James Powell
Frank H.T. Rhodes
Ian M. Ross
Robert M. Solow
Warren M. Washington
John A. White, Jr.
Richard Neil Zare

NATIONAL TRANSPORTATION SAFETY BOARD

490 L'Enfant Plaza SW 20594, phone (202) 314–6000

Chairman.—Jim Hall, 314–6010, fax 314–6018.
Vice Chairman.—Robert T. Francis, 314–6020, fax 314–6027.
Members:
John A. Hammerschmidt, 314–6030, fax 314–6035.
John J. Goglia, 314–6660, fax 314–6665.
George W. Black, 314–6050, fax 314–6056.
Managing Director.—Kenneth U. Jordan, 314–6060, fax 314–6090.
General Counsel.—Daniel D. Campbell, 314–6080, fax 314–6090.
Director, Office of—
Administration.—B. Michael Levins, 314–6200, fax 314–6203.
Aviation Safety.—Bernard S. Loeb, 314–6300, fax 314–6309.
Government Affairs.—Peter Goelz, 314–6121, fax 314–6122.
Research and Engineering.—Vernon Ellingstad, 314–6500, fax 314–6599.
Safety Recommendations.—Barry M. Sweedler, 314–6170, fax 314–6717.
Surface Transportation Safety.—James A. Arena, 314–6400, fax 314–6406.
Chief Administrative Law Judge.—William W. Fowler, Jr., 314–6150, fax 314–6158.

NEIGHBORHOOD REINVESTMENT CORPORATION

1325 G Street, Room 800, 20005, phone (202) 376–2400, fax 376–2600

BOARD OF DIRECTORS

Chairman.—Gov. Eugene A. Ludwig, Comptroller of the Currency.
Vice Chairman.—Shirlee P. Bowné, Vice Chairman, National Credit Union Administration.
Members:
Laurence H. Meyer, Board of Governors, Federal Reserve System.
Andrew C. Hove, Jr., Vice Chairman, Federal Deposit Insurance Corporation.
Nicolas P. Retsinas, Director, Office of Thrift Supervision.
Andrew D. Cuomo, Secretary, U.S. Department of Housing and Urban Development.
Executive Director.—George Knight, 376–2410.
Deputy Executive Director/Treasurer.—Hubert Guest, 376–2413.
Director for—
Field Operations.—Margo Kelly, (617) 450–0410.
Finance, Program Review and Internal Consulting.—Roy Davis, 376–2623.
Communications and Information Services.—Julia Galdo, 376–3734.
General Counsel/Secretary.—Jeffery Bryson, 376–2441.
Information Technology and Program Review.—Carlos Porrata, 376–2426.
Neighborhood Housing Services of America, Inc.—Mary Lee Widener.
Legislative Representative.—Ali Solis.

NUCLEAR REGULATORY COMMISSION

(Authorized by 42 U.S.C. 5801 and U.S.C. 1201)

Washington DC 20555, phone (301) 415–7000, http//www.nrc.gov

OFFICE OF THE CHAIRMAN

Chairman.—Shirley Ann Jackson, (301) 415–1759.
Executive Assistant and Director, Office of the Chairman.—Martin J. Virgillio, (301) 415–1750.
Deputy Director for Policy Development and Technical Support.—Victor M. McCree, (301) 415–1750.
Deputy Director for Corporate Planning and Management.—Jacqueline E. Silber, (301) 415–1750.
Legal Assistant.—Karla Smith, (301) 415–1750.
Special Assistant for—
Nuclear Material, Waste and Fuel Cycle.—Regis R. Boyle, (301) 415–1750.
Reactors and Research.—James W. Johnson, (301) 415–1750.
Reactors.—Brian E. Holian, (301) 415–1750.
International Affairs.—Janice Dunn Lee, (301) 415–1750.

COMMISSIONERS

Kenneth C. Rogers.—(301) 415–1855.
Technical Assistants: John N. Sorensen, Seth M. Coplan, Morton R. Fleishman.
Legal Assistant.—Myron Karman.
Greta Joy Dicus.—(301) 415–1820.
Executive Assistant.—Bradley W. Jones.
Technical Assistants: Anthony W. Markley, Torre M. Taylor, Terrence L. Chan, Joel O. Lubenau.
Special Assistant.—Donna L. Smith.
Nils J. Diaz.—(301) 415–8420.
Executive Assistant.—Maria E. Lopez-Otin.
Edward McGaffigan, Jr.—(301) 415–1800.
Executive/Legal Assistant.—Joseph R. Gray.
Technical Assistants: Janet R. Schlueter, James E. Beall, Jeffry M. Sharkey.
Special Assistant.—Catherine Grimes.
Administrative Secretary.—Linda D. Lewis.

STAFF OFFICES OF THE COMMISSION

Secretary.—John C. Hoyle, (301) 415–1969.
Commission Appellate Adjudication.—John F. Cordes (acting), (301) 415–1600.
Congressional Affairs.—Dennis K. Rathbun, (301) 415–1776.
General Counsel.—Karen D. Cyr, (301) 415–1743.
International Programs.—Carlton R. Stoiber, (301) 415–1780.
Public Affairs.—William M. Beecher, (301) 415–8200.

ADVISORY COMMITTEE ON NUCLEAR WASTE

Chairman.—Paul W. Pomeroy, (301) 415–7360.

ADVISORY COMMITTEE ON MEDICAL USES OF ISOTOPES

Committee Coordinator.—Torre M. Taylor, (301) 415–7900.

ADVISORY COMMITTEE ON REACTOR SAFEGUARDS

Chairman.—Robert L. Seale, (301) 415–7360,
[Contact John T. Larkins, Director, ACRS/ACNW, (301) 415–7360, fax (301) 415–5589/5422.]

ATOMIC SAFETY AND LICENSING BOARD PANEL

Chief Administrative Judge.—B. Paul Cotter, Jr., (301) 415–7450, fax (301) 415–5599.

INSPECTOR GENERAL

Inspector General.—Hubert Bell, (301) 415–5930, fax (301) 415–5400.
Deputy Inspector General.—David C. Lee, (301) 415–5930.

CHIEF INFORMATION OFFICER

Chief Information Officer.—Anthony J. Galante, (301) 415–8700, fax (301) 415–5079.

CHIEF FINANCIAL OFFICER

Chief Financial Officer.—Jesse L. Funches, (301) 415–7322, fax (301) 415–5388.

OFFICE OF THE EXECUTIVE DIRECTOR FOR OPERATIONS

Executive Director for Operations.—L. Joseph Callan, (301) 415–1700, fax (301) 415–2162.
Deputy Executive Director for—
Regulatory Effectiveness.—Edward L. Jordan, (301) 415–1705, fax (301) 415–2162.
Regulatory Programs.—Hugh L. Thompson, Jr., (301) 415–1713, fax (301) 415–2162.
Management Services.—Patricia G. Norry, (301) 415–7443, fax (301) 415–2162.

STAFF OFFICES OF THE EXECUTIVE DIRECTOR FOR OPERATIONS

Director, Office of—
Administration.—Edward L. Halman, (301) 415–7443, fax (301) 415–5400.
Analysis and Evaluation of Operational Data.—Denwood F. Ross, Jr., (301) 415–7472, fax (301) 415–6382.
Enforcement.—James Lieberman, (301) 415–2741, fax (301) 415–3431.
Investigations.—Guy P. Caputo, (301) 415–2373, fax (301) 415–2370.
Personnel.—Paul E. Bird, (301) 415–7516, fax (301) 415–5106.
Small Business and Civil Rights.—Irene P. Little, (301) 415–7380, fax (301) 415–5953.
State Programs.—Richard L. Bangart, (301) 415–3340, fax (301) 415–3502.

PROGRAM OFFICES

OFFICE OF NUCLEAR MATERIAL SAFETY AND SAFEGUARDS

Director.—Carl J. Paperiello, (301) 415–7800, fax (301) 415–5371.
Deputy Director.—Malcom R. Knapp, (301) 415–7358.
Divisional Directors:
Industrial and Medical Nuclear Safety.—Donald A. Cool, (301) 415–7197.
Fuel Cycle Safety and Safeguards.—Elizabeth Q. Ten Eyck, (301) 415–7212.
Waste Management.—John T. Greeves, (301) 415–7437.

OFFICE OF NUCLEAR REACTOR REGULATION

Director.—Samuel J. Collins, (301) 415–1270, fax (301) 415–1887.
Deputy Director.—Frank J. Miraglia, Jr., (301) 415–1272.
Associate Director for Projects.—Roy P. Zimmerman, (301) 415–1284.
Divisional Directors:
Reactor Projects I, II.—Bruce A. Boger, (301) 415–1403
Reactor Projects III, IV.—Jack W. Roe, (301) 415–1345.
Reactor Program Management.—Brian Grimes, (301) 415–1163.
Associate Director for Technical Assessment.—Thomas T. Martin (acting), (301) 415–1274.
Divisional Directors:
Engineering.—Brian W. Sheron, (301) 415–2722.
Systems Safety and Analysis.—Gary M. Holahan, (301) 415–2884.
Reactor Controls and Human Factors.—Richard L. Spessard, (301) 415–1004.
Project Directorates:
Standardization.—Theodore R. Quay, (301) 415–1118.
License Renewal and Environmental Review.—Christopher I. Grimes, (301) 415–1161.
Non-Power Reactors and Decommissioning.—Seymour H. Weis, (301) 415–2170.

OFFICE OF NUCLEAR REGULATORY RESEARCH

Director.—Ashok C. Phadani (acting), (301) 415–6641, fax (301) 415–5153.
Deputy Director.—Ashok C. Thadani, (301) 415–6641.
Divisional Directors:
Engineering.—Lawrence C. Shao, (301) 415–5678.
Systems Technology.—M. Wayne Hodges, (301) 415–5728.
Regulatory Applications.—Bill M. Morris, (301) 415–6207.

REGIONAL OFFICES

Regional Administrators:
Region I: Hubert J. Miller, 475 Allendale Road, King of Prussia PA 19406–1415, (610) 337–5299, fax 337–5324.
Deputy Regional Administrator.—William L. Axelson, 337–5340.
Divisional Directors:
Radiation Safety and Safeguards.—A. Randolph Blough, 337–5281.
Reactor Projects.—Charles W. Hehl, 337–5229.
Reactor Safety.—James T. Wiggins, 337–5359.
Region II: Luis A. Reyes, 61 Forsyth Street SE, Atlanta, GA 30303 (404) 562–4410.
Divisional Directors:
Radiation Safety and Safeguards.—Bruce S. Mallett, 331–5549.
Reactor Projects.—Jon R. Johnson, 331–5179.
Reactor Safety.—Johns P. Jaudon, 331–5580.
Region III: Arthur B. Beach, 801 Warrensville Road, Lisle, IL 60532–4351, (708) 829–9657, fax 515–1278.
Deputy Regional Administrator.—James L. Caldwell.
Divisional Directors:
Radiation Safety and Safeguards.—Roy J. Caniano (acting), 829–9800.
Reactor Projects.—Geoffrey E. Grant, 829–9600.
Reactor Safety.—Cynthia D. Pederson, 829–9700.
Region IV: Ellis W. Merschoff, Suite 400, 611 Ryan Plaza Drive, Arlington TX 76011–8064, (817) 860–8225, fax 860–8210.
Deputy Regional Administrator.—James E. Dyer, 860–8226.
Divisional Directors:
Radiation Safety and Safeguards.—Ross A. Scarano, 860–8106.
Reactor Projects.—Arthur T. Howell III, 860–8220.
Reactor Safety.—Thomas P. Gwynn, 860–8183.

OCCUPATIONAL SAFETY AND HEALTH REVIEW COMMISSION

(Created by Public Law 91–596)

1120 20th Street NW 20036, phone (202) 606–5100

Chairman.—Stuart E. Weisberg, 606–5374.
Legal Advisor and Special Counsel.—Deborah A. Katz.
Commissioner.—Daniel Guttman.
Counsel to the Commissioner.—Lynn S. McIntosh.
Commissoner.—Velma Montoya, 606–5377.
Counsel to the Commissioner.—William W. Matchneer.
Administrative Law Judges:
James Barkley, 425 Ivanhoe Street, Denver, CO 80220.
Paul L. Brady, 1185 Niskey Lake Road, Atlanta, GA 30331.
Richard DeBenedetto, 11–F Sea Breeze Lane, Nahant, MA 09108.
John H. Frye, III, 1120 20th Street, NW, 9th Floor, Washington, DC 20036–3419.
Sidney Goldstein, 1880 Arapahoe Street, Number 2608, Denver, CO 80202–1858.
Benjamin Loye, 3810 Marshall Street, Wheat Ridge, CO 80033.
Michael H. Schoenfeld, 1120 20th Street, NW, 9th Floor, Washington, DC 20036–3419.
Stanley M. Schwartz, 1244 North Speer Boulevard, Room 250, Denver, CO 80204–3582.
Irving Sommer, 1951 Hopewood Drive, Falls Church, VA 22043.
Nancy L. Spies, 1365 Peachtree Street, NE, Room 240, Atlanta, GA 30309–3119.
Robert A. Yetman, McCormack Post Office and Courthouse, Room 420, Boston, MA 02109–4501.
General Counsel.—Earl R. Ohman, Jr.

Deputy General Counsel.—Patrick E. Moran, 606–5410.
Executive Director.—William J. Gainer, 606–5380.
Director for Management and Administrative Services.—Al Milin.
Executive Secretary.—Ray H. Darling, Jr.
Public Affairs Specialist.—Linda A. Whitsett, 606–5398.

OFFICE OF GOVERNMENT ETHICS

(Created by Act of October 1, 1989; codified in 5 U.S.C, section 401)

1201 New York Avenue NW, Suite 500, 20005, phone (202) 523–5757, fax 523–6325

Director.—Stephen D. Potts.
Executive Secretary.—Janet R. Papinchak.
Deputy Director and General Counsel.—F. Gary Davis.
Deputy Director for Government Relations and Special Projects.—Jane S. Ley.
Special Assistant to the Director.—Stuart C. Gilman.
Deputy General Counsel.—Marilyn L. Glynn.
Associate Director for—
Administration.—Robert E. Lammon.
Agency Programs.—Jack Covaleski.
Education.—Barbara A. Mullen-Roth.
Chief, Information Resources Management.—James V. Parle.

OFFICE OF PERSONNEL MANAGEMENT

Theodore Roosevelt Building, 1900 E Street NW 20415–0001, phone (202) 606–1212

OFFICE OF THE DIRECTOR

Director.—James B. King, 5A09, (202) 606–1000.
Confidential Assistant.—Krysten Wallace, 5A09, (202) 606–1000.
Chief of Staff.—Janice R. Lachance 5305, (202) 606–1000.
Deputy Chief of Staff.—Douglas K. Walker, 5315, (202) 606–1000.
Deputy Chief of Staff/Chief.—Executive Secretariat, Richard B. Lowe, 5319, (202) 606–1100.
Counselor to the Director/Director of Agency Initiatives.—Michael A. Grant, 5305, (202) 606–1000.
Coordinator, Interagency Affairs.—Leigh M. Shein, 5526, (202) 606–1000.
Deputy Director.—[Vacant], 5518, (202) 606–1001.
Executive Assistant.—Evelyn J. Turner, 5518, (202) 606–1001.
Assistant for Field Operations.—Paula L. Bridgham, 5H22, (202) 606–1001.
Extragovernmental Affairs/CFC Operations.—Carol H. Lowe, 5450, (202) 606–2564.

OFFICE OF CONGRESSIONAL RELATIONS

Director.—Cynthia A. Brock-Smith, 5H30, (202) 606–1300.
Deputy Director.—Robert J. Hoke (acting).
Special Assistants: Michael P. Martin, Deborah A. Kendall.
Confidential Assistant.—Thomas Hicks.
Senior Congressional Relations Officers: Robert J. Hoke, David J. Messing.
Congressional Relations Officers.—Janet Chisolm-King.
Chief, Legislative Analysis.—James N. Woodruff, 7520, (202) 606–1424.
Chief, Congressional Liaison Office.—Charlene E. Luskey, B332 Rayburn House Office Building, (202) 632–6296.

OFFICE OF THE INSPECTOR GENERAL

Inspector General.—Patrick E. McFarland, 6400, (202) 606–1200.
Executive Assistant.—M. Fran Seidl.
Deputy Inspector General.—Joseph R. Willever.
Special Counsel.—E. Jeremy Hutton.
Assistant Inspector General for Policy, Resources Management, and Oversight.—J. David Cope.

Assistant Inspector General for Audits.—Harvey D. Thorp.
Deputy Assistant Inspector General for Audits.—Sanders P. Gerson.
Chief, Corporate Audits Division.—Mary L. Detwiler, 2H25.
Chief, Agency Audits Division.—Donna R. Ballard, 6400.
Assistant Inspector General for Investigations.—Gary S. Yauger.
Deputy Assistant Inspector General for Investigations.—Jimmy H. Andrews.
Assistant Inspector General for Evaluation and Inspections.—Kenneth D. Huffman.

FEDERAL PREVAILING RATE ADVISORY COMMITTEE

Chair.—Phyllis G. Foley, (acting), 5559, (202) 606–1500.
Staff Assistant.—Geraldine Coates.

OFFICE OF THE GENERAL COUNSEL

General Counsel.—Lorraine P. Lewis, 7355, (202) 606–1700.
Deputy General Counsel.—Mary Michelson, 7353.
Adminstrative Officer.—Brenda O. Hickey, 7545.
Associate General Counsel (Compensation).—James S. Green, 7554.
Assistant General Counsel (Staffing and Civil Rights).—Rhoda G. Lawrence, 7542.
Assistant General Counsel (Merit Systems).—James F. Hicks, 7536.

OFFICE OF COMMUNICATIONS

Director.—Rosalie A. Cameron, 5F12, (202) 606–1800.
Deputy Director.—Bruce J. Milhans.
Professional Services Center.—Rosa M. Grillo, 5F12, (202) 606–4400.
Interagency Advisory Group Secretariat.—Charles C. Kawecki, 5H22, (202) 606–2166.
External Communications Review.—Vivian L. Mackey, 5H22, (202) 606–1800.

CENTER FOR PARTNERSHIP AND LABOR-MANAGEMENT RELATIONS

Director.—Michael C. Cushing, 7H28, (202) 606–2930.
Labor-Management Relations Staff— Frank L. Milman, Harold E. Fibish, 7H38, (202) 606–2930.
National Partnership Council.—Jean Joines.
National Partnership Clearinghouse Staff.—(202) 606–2040.

OFFICE OF THE CHIEF FINANCIAL OFFICER

Chief Financial Officer.—J. Gilbert Seaux, 5489, (202) 606–1101.
Deputy Chief Financial Officer.—[Vacant].
Office of Financial Management:
Systems, Reports, and Benefits Division.—Robert A. Loring, 5475E.
Employee Services and Accounts Division.—Dory Zamani, 5475C.
Control, Reconciliation, and Accounts Division.—Bradford H. Morrell, 5475.
Office of Budget and Oversight.—Timothy Moriarty, 5447A.
Budget Division.—Elizabeth A. Mautner, 5447C.
Oversight and Reimbursements.—James M. Loiselle, 5439B.

EMPLOYMENT SERVICE

Associate Director.—Mary Lou Lindholm, 6F08, (202) 606–0800.
Deputy Associate Director.—Donna D. Beecher.
Director, Personnel Resources and Developement Center.—Marilyn K. Gowing, 6355, (202) 606–0820.
Assessment Services Division.—[Vacant], 6457.
Workforce Quality Division.—Donna J. Gregory, 6462.
Measurement, Research, and Evaluation Division.—Brian O'Leary, 6457.
Director, Staffing Services Center.—Kenneth P. Mayhew, (912) 744–2072, Macon GA.
Deputy, Director.—C. Lee Willis, Macon GA.
Systems Development Division.—Don A. Peterson, (912) 744–2078, Macon, GA.
Production Division.—[Vacant], Macon GA.
Employment Information Support Division.—Paul Carr, (912) 744–2168, Macon GA.

Director, Performance and Customer Relations Office.—Sandra S. Payne, 6554, (202) 606–0900.
Director, Office of—
Staffing Reinvention.—Patricia H. Paige, 6A12, (202) 606–0830.
Employment Information.—Richard A. Whitford, 2458, (202) 606–2525.
Workforce Restructuring.—Edward P. McHugh, 6504, (202) 600–0960.
Diversity.—Armando E. Rodriquez, 6524, (202) 606–2817.
Washington Service.—Sherry D. Turpenoff, 2525, (202) 606–2525.
Budget and Systems.—Barbara J. Jones, 6355, (202) 606–0900.

EMPLOYMENT SERVICE - FIELD SERVICE CENTERS

Atlanta Service Center: Richard B. Russell Federal Building, 75 Spring Street, SW Suite 940, Atlanta GA 30303–3109.
Director.—Jacqueline Y. Moses, (404) 331–3455
Deputy Director.—Betty McPherson (404) 331–4588
Chicago Service Center: John C. Kluczynski Federal Building, DPN–30–3, 230 Dearborn Street, Chicago IL 60604–1687.
Director.—Karen Johnson, (312) 353–2930.
Dayton Service Center: U.S. Courthouse and Federal Building, 200 West Second Street, Room 507, Dayton OH 45402–0000.
Director.—Michael Pajari, (513) 225–2576.
Denver Service Center: 12345 West Alameda Parkway, PO Box 25167, Denver CO 80225–0000.
Director.—Joseph R. DeLoy, (303) 969–6931.
Detroit Service Center: 477 Michigan Avenue, Room 595, Detroit MI 48226–2574.
Director.—David Nason, (313) 226–7522.
Honolulu Service Center: 300 Ala Moana Boulevard, Box 50028, Honolulu HI 96850–0001.
Director, Paul Miller.—(808) 541–2795.
Huntsville Service Center: 520 Wynn Drive NW, Huntsville AL 35816–3426.
Director.—Carol Y. Toney, (205) 837–1271.
Kansas City Service Center: 601 East 12th Street, Room 131, Kansas City MO 64106–2826.
Director.—James K. Witkop (816) 426–5705.
Norfolk Service Center: Federal Building, 200 Granby Street, Room 500, Norfolk VA 23510–1886.
Director.—Alan Nelson (757) 441–3373.
Philadelphia Service Center: William J. Green, Jr. Federal Building, 600 Arch Street, Room 3256, Philadelphia PA 19106–1596.
Director.—Joe Stix, (215) 597–7670
Deputy Director.—Joyce C. Toppin, (215) 597–7670
Raleigh Service Center: 4407 Bland Road, Suite 2200, Raleigh NC 27609–6296.
Director.—Allan N. Goldberg, (919)790–2817.
San Antonio Service Center: 8610 Broadway, Room 305, San Antonio TX 78217–0001.
Director.—Miguel Hernandez, (210) 805–2423 ext. 201.
San Francisco Service Center: 120 Howard Street, Room 735, San Francisco CA 94105–0001.
Director.—Linda Peterson (415) 281–7094
Deputy Director.—Ira B. Poretsky, (415)281–7095.
San Juan Service Center: Federico Degetau Federal Building, Carlos E. Chardon Street, Hato Rey PR 00918–1710.
Director.—Luis Rodriquez, (787) 765–5259 ext. 22.
Seattle Service Center: 700 Fifth Avenue, Suite 5950, Seattle WA 98104–5012.
Director.—Mary Alice Kline, (206) 553–0870.
Twin Cities Service Center: Federal Building, Room 503, One Federal Drive, Fort Snelling MN 55111–4007.
Director.— Sharon Ellett, (612) 725–3437.

OFFICE OF INFORMATION TECHNOLOGY

Chief Information Technology Officer.—Janet L. Barnes, 5415, (202) 418–3200.
Deputy CITO.—Glenn Sutton.
Plans/Policies.—Robert M. Huley, (acting).
Systems Management and Support.—William A. Farran, Jr.
Investigations Automation Support.—Bernie Springer.

OFFICE OF HUMAN RESOURCES AND EEO

Director.—Rose Gwin, 1447, (202) 606–2440
Personnel Operations Division.—Bonnie C. Maines, (202) 606–2141
Training and Development Division: Barbara J. Garland, Cynthia H. Simpson.
Personnel Programs and Systems Division.—Janet T. Cope.
Equal Employment Opportunity Division.—Alicia O. McPhie, 2441.
Employee and Labor Relations Division.—Suzanne M. Giannetti, 2451.
Boyers Personnel Service Center.—Mark E. Heck, PO Box 9, Boyers PA 16017–0001, (412) 794–5612.

HUMAN RESOURCES SYSTEMS SERVICE

Associate Director.—Steven R. Cohen, (acting), 7508, (202) 606–2800.
Financial Information and Resources Management.—David A. Horne, 7300, (202) 606–2900.
Assistant Director for Employee Relations and Workforce Performance.—Doris Hausser, (acting), 7H12, (202) 606- 2910.
Family Programs and Employee Relations Division.—Marjorie A. Marks, 7425, (202) 606–2920.
Work and Family Program Center.—Anice V. Nelson, 7316, (202) 606–5520.
Performance Management and Incentive Awards Division.—Doris Hausser, 7H12, (202) 606–2720.
Assistant Director for Classification.—Sarah D. Adams, 7H29, (202) 606–2950.
Standards Development Staff.—Del White (acting), 7H29.
Assistant Director for Compensation Policy.—Donald J. Winstead, 6H31, (202) 606–2880.
Wage Systems Division.—Mark Allen, 7H38.
Salary Systems Division.—Ruth M. O'Donnell, 6H31.
Compensation Administration Division.—Jerome D. Mikowicz, 7H24.
Assistant Director for Workforce Information.—Andrew P. Klugh, 7439, (202) 606–2704.
Privacy Act Advisor.—John A. Sanet, 7439, (202) 606–1955.
Statistical Analysis and Services Division.—Andrew P. Klugh (acting), 7439, (202) 606–2704.
Assistant Director Human Resources Development.—Kirke Harper, 7305, (202) 606–2721.
Training Management Assistance Division.—Harold Sega, 1400 Wilson Boulevard, Arlington VA (703) 312–7226.

INVESTIGATIONS SERVICE

Associate Director.—Richard A. Ferris, 5416, (202) 606–1042.
Deputy Associate Director.—[Vacant].
Comptroller.—Charles F. Overend.
Policy and Operations Division.—[Vacant], 5416, (202) 606–1042.
Marketing and Evaluation Division.—John H. Crandell, 5416, (202) 606–1042.
Federal Investigations Processing Center.—Kathy Dillamin, 1137 Branchton Road, Boyers PA 16018–0001, (412) 794–5612.

OFFICE OF MERIT SYSTEMS OVERSIGHT AND EFFECTIVENESS

Associate Director.—Carol J. Okin, 7470, (202) 606–1575.
Administrative Officer.—Jonathan T. McMullen, 7468.
Assistant Director for Merit Systems Oversight.—Steven R. Cohen, 7677, (202) 606–2840.
Classification Appeals/FLSA Programs.—Jeffrey D. Miller, 7679, (202) 606–2990.
Atlanta Oversight Division.—Conrad U. Johnson, (404) 331–3451.
Chicago Oversight Division.—Anna Marie Schuh, (312) 353–2309.
Dallas Oversight Division.—Peter D. Dickson, (214) 767–0561.
Phildelphia Oversight Division.—Albert H. Heumann, (215) 597–4430.
San Francisco Oversight Division.—Theodore G. Shepard, (415) 281–7050.
Washington Oversight Division.—Dana K. Sitnick, 7675, (202) 606–2980.
Assistant Director for Merit Systems Effectiveness.—[Vacant], 7462, (202) 606–2820.
Program Analysis Division.—Craig B. Pettibone, 7659, (202) 606–2820.
Program Development Division.—Mario V. Caviglia, 7456, (202) 606–2820.

OFFICE OF CONTRACTING AND ADMINISTRATIVE SERVICES

Director.—Lynn L. Furman, 1342, (202) 606–2200.
Contracting Division.—Alfred F. Chatterton, III, SB427, (202) 606–2240.
Facilities Services.—Steven Van Rees, 1330, (202) 606–2220.
Health Unit.—Brenda Conaway, 4428, (202) 606–2140.
Security Services.—James S. Conners, 1H17, (202) 606–2007.
Publications Services Division.—Kent Bailey, 5415, (202) 606–2260.
Resources Center.—Leon H. Brody, 5H27, (202) 606–1381.

OFFICE OF EXECUTIVE RESOURCES

Director.—Curtis J. Smith, Charlottesville VA, (804) 980–6221.
Assistant Director for Executive Policy and Services.—K. Joyce Edwards, 6484, (202) 606–1610.
SES Policy and Operations Division.—Ellen Kill Kelley.
SES Services Division.—George J. Sabo.
Director, Eastern Management Development Center.—Thomas C. Dausch, Lancaster PA, (717) 399–0112.
Director, Western Management Development Center.—Rich Liebl, (acting), Aurora CO, (303) 671–1028.
Director, Federal Executive Institute.—Curtis J. Smith, Charlottesville VA, (804) 980–6221.

RETIREMENT AND INSURANCE SERVICE

Associate Director.—William E. Flynn III, 4A10, (202) 606–0600.
Deputy Associate Director.—Frank D. Titus, 4A10, (202) 606–0600.
Agency Services Division.—Mary M. Sugar, 4351.
Retirement Policy Division.—John E. Landers, 4351.
Office of Actuaries.—Nancy H. Kichak, 4307, (202) 606–0722.
Assistant Director of Insurance Programs.—Lucretia F. Myers, 3415, (202) 606–0770.
Insurance Contracts Division I.—Shirley R. Patterson, 3425.
Insurance Contracts Division II.—William J. Washington, 3439.
Insurance Contracts Division III.—Diana M. McKinney, 3415.
Insurance Contracts Division IV.—David A. Lewis, 3415.
Insurance Operations Division.—Ellen E. Tunstall, 3415.
Insurance Policy and Information Division.—Abby L. Block, 3451.
Assistant Director for Financial Control and Management.—Kathleen M. McGettigan 4312, (202) 606–0462.
Budget and Program Information Division.—Arthur G. Linnehan, (acting), 4332.
FERS Design Division.—Larry P. Miller, 3H28
Financial Management Division.—Robert A. Yuran, 4312
Management Services Division.—Arthur G. Linnehan, (acting), 4332.
Quality Assurance Division.—Larry P. Holman, 4316.
Retirement Systems and Operations Division.—George E. Hyder, 2429.
Washington Data Processing Center.—Linwood T. Bonneville, BH03.
Assistant Director for Retirement Programs.—Sidney M. Conley, 3305, (202) 606–0300.
Deputy Assistant Director.—Daniel A. Green.
Retirement Claims Division.—Joseph C. Parker, 4458.
Retirement Services Division.—James K. Freiert, 2H24.
Retirement Information Office.—Gary M. Jacobs, 1323 (202) 606–0500.
Disability and Reconsideration and Appeals Division.—William C. Jackson, 3468.
FERS Division.—John C. Crawford, 4429.
Operations Support Division.—Lorraine E. Dettman, 3349.
Retirement Operations Center.—Donald L. Lacey Boyers PA, (412) 794–2005.
Eligibility Division.—Victor J. Roy, 2336.

OFFICE OF THE SPECIAL COUNSEL

(Authorized by 5 U.S.C. 1101 and 5 U.S.C. 1211)

1730 M Street NW, Suite 300, 20036, phone (202) 653–7188

Special Counsel.—Kathleen Day Koch, Room 300, 653–7122.
Deputy Special Counsel.—James A. Kahl, 653–6000.
Investigations Division.—Ruth Ertel, 653–7193.

Legislative and Public Affairs Division.—Michael Lawrence, 653–9001.
Planning and Advice Division.—Erin McDonnell, 653–8971.
Prosecution Division.—William E. Reukauf, 653–8970.
Management Division.—John Kelly, 653–7144.

PANAMA CANAL COMMISSION

(Created by Public Law 96–70)

1825 I Street NW, Suite 1050, 20006, phone (202) 634–6441, fax 634–6439

Secretary.—John A. Mills.
Assistant to the Secretary for—
Transition Planning.—Michael Bragale.
Board Affairs.—Virginia Allen.
Commission Affairs.—Ruth Huff.
Congressional Affairs.—David R. Ballenger.
Financial Affairs.— Barbara Sanders.
Public Affairs.—Cynthia Riddle.

IN PANAMA

Administrator.—Alberto Aleman.
Deputy Administrator.—Joseph Cornelison.

PEACE CORPS

(Created by Public Law 97–113)

1990 K Street NW, Room 8510, 20526, phone (202) 606–3886, fax (703) 235–9189

Toll-Free Number (800) 424–8580, http://www.peacecorps.gov

OFFICE OF THE DIRECTOR

fax 606–4458

Director.—Mark Gearan.
Senior Advisor to the Director.—Jack Hogan.
Deputy Director.—Charles Baquet III.
Chief of Staff.—Thomas Tighe.
Deputy Chief of Staff.—Kathy Rulon.
Manager for Diversity and EEO.—Mabel Dobarro.
Director of Communications.—André Oliver.
Director of Marketing.—Steve Abbott.
Marketing Manager.—Stephen Maroon.
Director, Press Office.—Brendan Daly.
Editor, Peace Corps Times.—Patricia Cunningham.
Printing Officer.—Rose Green.
Publications Manager.—Annmarie Emmet.
Director, Office of Congressional Relations.—Gloria Johnson.
General Counsel.—Nancy Hendry.
Chief Financial Officer.—Lana Hurdle.
Director, Crisis Corps.—Joan Timoney.
Partnership Program Manager.—Eric Hornberger.
Gifts in Kind Program Manager.—Ann Truxaw.
Director of Planning, Policy and Analysis.—Bill Piatt (acting).
Planning Officer.—Barbara Busch.
Associate Director for:
Private Sector Cooperation and International Volunteerism.—Patricia Garamendi.
Volunteer Support.—Mike Ward (designate).
Management.—Stan Suyat.
Regional Director for:
Africa.—Maureen J. Carroll.
Asia and the Pacific.—Margaret Goodman.
Europe, Central Asia and the Mediterranean.—Donald Movers.
Inter-American.—Kristine Vega (acting).
Director, Office of Domestic Programs.—Sherwood Guernsey.

Assistant Director of:
Domestic Programs for Fellows.—Henry Fernandez.
Domestic Programs for Returned Volunteer Services and Hotline Editor.—Susan Musich.
Domestic Programs for World Wise Schools.—Alyce Hill.
Director, Office of Medical Services.—David Gootnick.

PEACE CORPS REGIONAL OFFICES

Atlanta: 100 Alabama Street, Building 1924, Suite 2R70, Atlanta GA 30303, (404) 562–3456, fax (404) 562–3455 (FL, GA, TN, MS, AL, SC)
Manager.—Maisha Strozler.
Public Affairs Specialist.—Cynthia Glocker.
Boston: Ten Causeway Street, Room 450, Boston MA 02222, (617) 565–5555, fax (617) 565–5539 (MA, VT, NH, RI, ME)
Manager.—Natalie Woodward.
Public Affairs Specialist.—Rae Mims.
Chicago: Xerox Center, 55 West Monroe Street, Suite 450, Chicago IL 60603, (312) 353–4990, fax (312) 353–4192 (IL, IN, MO, MI, OH, KY)
Manager.—Kim Mansaray.
Public Affairs Specialist.—Jennifer Ostermeier.
Dallas: 207 South Houston Street, Room 527, Dallas TX 75202, (214) 767–5435, fax (214) 767–5483 (TX, OK, LA, NM, AR)
Manager.—Morris Baker.
Public Affairs Specialist.—Matthew Seymour.
Denver: 140 East 19th Avenue, Suite 550, Denver CO 80203, (303) 866–1057, fax (303) 866–1068 (CO, KS, NE, UT, WY)
Manager.—Karen Nakandakare.
Public Affairs Specialist.—Jeff Martin.
Los Angeles: 11000 Wilshire Boulevard, Suite 8104, Los Angeles, CA 90024, (310) 235–7444, fax (310) 235–7442 (Southern CA, AZ)
Manager.—John Hartley.
Public Affairs Specialist.—Robin Clark.
Minneapolis: 330 Second Avenue South, Suite 420, Minneapolis, MN 55401, (612) 348–1480, fax (612) 348–1474 (MN, WI, SD, ND, IA)
Manager.—David Belina.
Public Affairs Specialist.—Randy Merideth.
New York: Six World Trade Center, Room 611, New York NY 10048, (212) 466–2477, fax (212) 466–2473 (NY, NJ, CT, PA, PR)
Manager.—John Coyne.
Public Affairs Specialist.—Adrienne Berman.
Rosslyn: 1400 Wilson Boulevard, Suite 400, Arlington VA 22209, (703) 235–9191, fax (703) 235–9189 (DC, MD, NC, WV, DE, VA)
Manager.—Monica Mills.
Public Affairs Specialist.—Felisa Neuringer.
San Francisco: 333 Market Street, Suite 600, San Francisco CA 94105; (415) 977–8800, fax (415) 977–8803 (Northern CA, NV, HI)
Manager.—Maryann Murray.
Public Affairs Specialist.—Heidi Thoren.
Seattle: 2001 Sixth Avenue, Suite 1776, Seattle WA 98121, (206) 553–5490, fax (206) 553–2343 (WA, OR, ID, AK, MT)
Manager.—Dorothy Culjat.
Public Affairs Specialist.—Nancy Chartrand.

PENSION BENEFIT GUARANTY CORPORATION

1200 K Street 20005–4026, (202) 326–4000

BOARD OF DIRECTORS

Chairman.—Secretary of Labor.
Members:
Robert E. Rubin, Secretary of the Treasury.
William Daley, Secretary of Commerce.

OFFICIALS

Executive Director.—John Seal (acting), 326–4010.
Deputy Executive Director and—
Chief Negotiator.—Nell Hennessy, 326–4119.
Chief Operating Officer.—Joseph H. Grant, 326–4010.
Chief Financial Officer.—N. Anthony Calhoun, 326–4170.
Chief Management Officer.—Kathleen Blunt (acting), 326–4180.
Assistant Executive Director for Legislative and Congressional Affairs.—Judy Schub, 326–4010.
Department Director for—
Budget.—Henry R. Thompson, 326–4120.
Communications and Public Affairs.—Judith E. Welles, 326–4040.
Contracts and Controls Review.—Dale Williams, 326–4161.
Corporate Finance and Negotiations.—Abdrew E. Schneider, 326–4070.
Corporate Policy and Research.—Stuart Sirkin, 326–4080.
Facilities and Services.—Janet A. Smith, 326–4150.
Financial Operations Department.—Edward L. Knapp, 326–4060.
Human Resources.—Sharon Barbee-Fletcher, 326–4110.
Information Resources Management.—Cris Birch, 326–4130.
Insurance Operations.—Bennie Hagans, 326–4050.
Participant and Employer Appeals.—Harriet D. Verburg, 326–4090.
Procurement.—Robert W. Herting, 326–4160.
General Counsel.—James J. Keightley, 3267–4020.
Inspector General.—Wayne R. Poll, 326–4030.

POSTAL RATE COMMISSION

1333 H Street NW, Suite 300, 20268–0001, phone (202) 789–6800, fax 789–6861

Chairman.—Edward J. Gleiman, 789–6805.
Vice Chairman.—H. Edward Quick, Jr., 789–6810.
Commissioners:
George W. Haley, 789–6868.
W.H. (Trey) LeBlanc III, 789–6813.
[Vacant].
Chief Administrative Officer and Secretary.—Margaret P. Crenshaw, 789–6840.
Legal Advisor.—Stephen L. Sharfman, 789–6820.
Director, Office of—
Consumer Advocate.—Gail W. Willette, 789–6830.
Rates, Analysis and Planning.—Robert H. Cohen, 789–6850.

SECURITIES AND EXCHANGE COMMISSION

450 Fifth Street NW 20549, phone (202) 942–8088, TTY Relay Service 1–800–877–8339 fax 942–9628, http://www.sec.gov

THE COMMISSION

Chairman.—Arthur Levitt, 942–0100.
Chief of Staff.—Jennifer A. Scardino, 942–0100.
Counselors to the Chairman.—Mark D. Tellini, Gregg W. Corso, Cheryl J. Scarboro, Timothy J. Forde, 942–0120.
Commissioners:
Steven M.H. Wallman, 942–0800.
Counsel to the Commissioner: Andre E. Owen, 942–0907; Luise M. Welby, 942–0806.
Norman S. Johnson, 942–0600.
Counsel to the Commissioner: Paul A. Belvin, 942–0604; Richard D. Capparella, 942–0607; Isaac C. Hunt, Jr., 942–0500.
Counsel to the Commissioner: Michael A. Lainoff, 942–0506; Robert A. Robertson, 942–0507.
Executive Director.—James M. McConnell, 942–4300, fax 942–9588.
Chief Management Analyst.—Diane Campbell, 942–4306.
Chief Administrative Law Judge.—Brenda P. Murray, 942–0399.

OFFICE OF THE SECRETARY

Secretary.—Jonathan G. Katz, 942–7070.
Deputy Secretary.—Margaret H. McFarland, 942–7070.
Library Director.—Jane T. Sessa, 942–7090.

OFFICE OF INVESTOR EDUCATION AND ASSISTANCE

Director.—Nancy M. Smith, 942–7041, fax 942–9634.

OFFICE OF EQUAL EMPLOYMENT OPPORTUNITY

Director.—Victor H. Tynes, Jr, 942–0044, fax 942–9547.

OFFICE OF FREEDOM OF INFORMATION AND PRIVACY ACT OPERATIONS

FOIA/Privacy Act Officer.—Hannah R. Hall, 942–4320.

OFFICE OF THE CHIEF ACCOUNTANT

Chief Accountant.—Michael H. Sutton, 942–4400, fax 942–9656.
Deputy Chief Accountant.—Stephen M. Swad, 942–9440.
Chief Counsel.—Robert E. Burns, 942–4400.

OFFICE OF ECONOMIC ANALYSIS

Chief Economist.—Erik R. Sirri, 942–8020, fax 942–9657.
Deputy Chief Economist.—Robert R. Comment, 942–8020.

OFFICE OF THE GENERAL COUNSEL

General Counsel.—Richard H. Walker, 942–0900, fax 942–9625.
Special Assistant for Management.—Virginia A. Jay, 942–0901.
Solicitor and Deputy General Counsel.—Paul Gonson, 942–0910.
Ethics Counsel.—Barbara Hannigan, 942–0970.
Associate General Counsel for Appellate Litigation and Bankruptcy.—Jacob H. Stillman, 942–0930.

Assistant General Counsels: (Principal Assistant), Eric Summergrad, 942–0911; (Bankruptcy and Appelllate Litigation), Katherine Gresham, 942–0810; (Appellate Litigation), Lucinda McConathy, 942–0904; Susan F. Wyderko, 942–4844.

Associate General Counsel for Litigation and Administranve Practice.—Richard M. Humes, 942–0940.

Assistant General Counsels: (Litigation and Administrative Practice). Susan A. Yashar, 942–0840, James A. Brigagliano, 942–0826; (Litigation and Contracting), George C. Brown, 942–0828.

Associate General Counsel for Legal Policy.—Karen Buck Burgess, 942–0920.

Assistant General Counsels: (Investment Mangement, PUHCA and Administrative Law), Daniel O. Hirsch, 942–0870, (Market Regulation), W. Hardy Callcott, 942–0925, (Corporation Finance and Accounting), Meredith Mitchell, 942–0916, (Legislation and Financial Services), Amy Kroll, 942–0927.

Associate General Counsel for Counseling and Regulatory Policy.—Diane Sanger, 942–0960.

Associate General Counsel for Adjudication.—Anne E. Chafer, 942–0950.

Counselor for Adjudication.—William S. Stern, 942–0949.

Assistant General Counsels: (Principal Assistant), Joan Loizeaux, 942–0990, (Adjudication), Eva Carney, 942–0838; Joan McCarthy, 942–0950.

DIVISION OF INVESTMENT MANAGEMENT

Director.—Barry P. Barbash, 942–0720, fax 942–9659.

Associate Director, Legal and Disclosure.—Heidi Stam, 942–0663.

Assistant Directors: (Disclosure and Review No. 2), Carolyn B. Lewis, 942–0589, (Disclosure and Review No. 1), Barry D. Miller, 942–0587, (Insurance Product), Susan Nash, 942–0670, (Disclosure and Investment Adviser Regulation), Elizabeth R. Krentzman, 942–0721.

Chief Accountant.—(Chief Accountant), Lawrence A. Friend, 942–0590.

Associate Director, Chief Counsel.—Jack W. Murphy, 942–0660.

Assistant Chief Counsels: (International Issues), John V. O'Hanlon, 942–0660, (Financial Institutions), [Vacant], 942–0660.

Associate Director, Regulation.—Robert E. Plaze, 942–0716.

Assistant Directors: (Investment Company Regulation), Elizabeth G. Osterman, 942–0564, (Regulatory Policy), Kenneth J. Berman, 942–0690.

Associate Director, Compliance, Financial Analysis and Public Utility.—Douglas J. Scheidt, 942–0525.

Assistant Directors: (Enforcement Liaison), [Vacant], 942–0535; (Public Utility Regulation), Bonnie Wilkinson, 942–0545.

Chief Financial Analyst (Financial Analysis)—.Paul B. Goldman, 942–0510.

DIVISION OF CORPORATION FINANCE

Director.—Brian J. Lane, 942–2800, fax 942–9525.

Senior Legal Adviser to the Director.—David A. Sirignano, 942–2870.

Deputy Director.—Meredith B. Cross, 942–2810.

Senior Associate Director. (Legal).—William E. Morley, 942–2820.

Senior Associate Director: (Regulatory Policy).—Mauri L. Osheroff, 942–2840.

Associate Directors: (Chief Accountant), Robert A. Bayless, 942–2850; (Operations), Howard F. Morin, 942–2830; (International), David A. Sirignano, 942–2820; (Small Business), Albert S. Dandridge III, 942–2880.

Assistant Directors: Shelly E. Parratt, 942–1840; H. Christopher Owings, 942–1900; James M. Daly, 942–1800; H. Roger Schwall, 942–1870; William L. Tolbert, Jr., 942–1850; Steven C. Duvall, 942–1950; Peggy A. Fisher, 942–1760; Paula Dubberly, 942–1960.

Deputy Chief Accountant.—Wayne Carnall, 942–2960.

Chief Counsel.—Martin Dunn, 942–2900.

Deputy Chief Counsel.—Mark W. Green, 942–2900.

Chief, Office of—

Small Business.—Richard K. Wulff, 942–2950.

International Corporate Finance.—Paul Dudek, 942–2990.

Mergers and Acquisitions.—Catherine T. Dixon, 942–2920.

Information and Analysis.—Herbert D. Scholl, 942–2930.

EDGAR Policy.—Ruben G. Gechter (acting), 942–2940.

DIVISION OF ENFORCEMENT

Director.—William R. McLucas, 942–4500, fax 942–9636.
Deputy Director.—Colleen P. Mahoney, 942–4540.
Assistant Directors: Ellen Ross, 942–4770; Richard Sauer, 942–4777; Antonia Chion, 942–4567.
Associate Director.—Thomas C. Newkirk, 942–4550.
Assistant Directors: James T. Coffman, 942–4574; Jerry A. Isenberg, 942–4652; Erich T. Schwartz, 942–4782.
Associate Director.—Paul V. Gerlach, 942–4560.
Assistant Directors: Gregory S. Bruch, 942–4548; Paul R. Berger, 942–4854; Leonard W. Wang, 942–4828.
Associate Director.—Gary N. Sundick, 942–4570.
Assistant Directors: Paul Huey-Burns, 942–4649; Daniel A. Nathan, 942–4726; William R. Baker, 942–4517;
Director, Regional Office Operations.—James A. Clarkson.
Chief Market Surveillance.—Joseph J. Cella, 942–4559.
Chief Counsel.—Joan E. McKown, 942–4530.
Chief Litigation Counsel.—Christian J. Mixter, 942–4718.
Deputy Chief Litigation Counsel.—Stephen J. Crimmins, 942–4589.
Chief Accountant.—George H. Diacont, 942–4510.
Deputy Chief Accountant.—Edward G. Noakes, 942–4730.
Assistant Chief Accountants: Teresda B. Murrin, 942–4724; Regina M. Barrett, 942–4524.

DIVISION OF MARKET REGULATION

Director.—Richard R. Lindsey, 942–0090, fax 942–9643.
Deputy Director.—Robert L.D. Colby, 942–0080.
Senior Special Counsel.—Herbert Brooks, 942–3076.
Senior Special Counsel.—Belinda Blaine, 942–0167.
Associate Directors: (Risk Management and Control), Larry Bergmann, 942–0770; Michael A. Macchiaroli, 942–0132.
Assistant Directors: Nancy J. Sanow, 942–0772; Jerry Carpenter, 942–4187; Peter Geraghty, 942–0177.
Associate Director, Management Supervision.—Howard Kramer, 942–0180.
Assistant Directors: Katherine England, 942–0154; Sheila Slevin, 942–0796; Ivette Lopez, 942–0765.
Associate Director, Chief Counsel.—Catherine McGuire, 942–0061.
Deputy Chief Counsel.—Paula Jenson, 942–0063.

OFFICE OF INTERNATIONAL AFFAIRS

Director.—Marisa Lago, 942–2770, fax 942–9524.
Deputy Director.—Paul A. Leder, 942–2770.
Assistant Directors: Elizabeth Jacobs, 942–2770; Keith E. Carpenter, 942–2770; Robert D. Strahota, 942–2770; Ester Saverson, Jr., 942–2770.

OFFICE OF LEGISLATIVE AFFAIRS

Director.—Kaye F. Williams, 942–0014.
Legislative Counsel.—Peter S. Kiernan, 942–0015.

OFFICE OF THE INSPECTOR GENERAL

Inspector General.—Walter J. Stachnik, 942–4460, fax 942–9653.
Deputy Inspector General.—Nelson N. Egbert, 942–4462.

OFFICE OF FILINGS AND INFORMATION SERVICES

Associate Executive Director.—Wilson A. Butler, Jr., 942–8938, fax 703–914–1005.
Deputy Director.—Deborah K. Balducchi, 942–8938.
Associate Directors: Ann C. Sykes, 942–8970; Cecilia H. Wilkerson, 942–8925.
Assistant Director.—Shirley A. Slocum, 942–8038.

OFFICE OF PUBLIC AFFAIRS, POLICY EVALUATION AND RESEARCH

Director.—[Vacant], 942–0020, fax 942–9654.
Deputy Directors: John D. Heine, 942–0020; Michael D. Jones, 942–0020.

OFFICE OF THE COMPTROLLER

Comptroller.—James F. Donahue, 942–0340, fax (703) 914–0172.
Assistant Comptroller.—Henry I. Hoffman, 942–0343.

OFFICE OF INFORMATION TECHNOLOGY

Associate Executive Director.—Mike Bartell, 942–8800; fax (703) 914–2621.
Directors: David T. Copenhafer, 942–8805, Richard T. Redfearn, 942–8996; Kenneth A. Drews, 942–8621; Michael Carey, 942–8863.

OFFICE OF ADMINISTRATIVE AND PERSONNEL MANAGEMENT

Associate Executive Director.—Fernando L. Alegria, Jr., 942–4000.
Special Assistant to the Associate Executive Director.—Bonnie M. Westbrook, 942–4003.
Operations Officer.—Richard J. Kanyan, 942–4000.

SEC SPACE RENOVATION PROGRAM

Director.—Kenneth A. Fogash, 942–4100.

REGIONAL OFFICES

Northeast Regional Office: 7 World Trade Center, Suite 1300, New York, NY 10048, (212) 748–8000, fax 748–8032.
Regional Director.—Carmen J. Lawrence, 748–8035.
Deputy Regional Director.—Edwin H. Nordlinger, 748–8038.
Senior Associate Regional Director, Enforcement, Henry Klehm III, 748–8178.
Associate Regional Directors.—Robert B. Blackburn, 748–8185; Andrew J. Geist, 748–8186.
Assistant Regional Directors: Wayne M. Carlin, 748–8292; Eric M. Schmidt, 748–8046; Andrew Wertheim, 748–8242.
Associate Regional Director, Investment Management and Corporate Reorganization.—Douglas Scarff, 748–8300.
Assistant Regional Directors: John J. Costello, 748–8301; Joseph Doyle, 748–8298; Joseph Dimaria, 748–8306.
Associate Regional Director, Broker/Dealer.—Robert A. Sollazzo, 748–8070.
Assistant Regional Directors: Broker/Dealer: Richard D. Lee, 748–8076; John J. Gentile, 948–8073; John M. Nee, 948–8091.
Boston District Office, 73 Tremont Street, Suite 600, Boston, MA 02108–3912, (617) 424–5900, fax 424–5940
District Administrator.—Juan Marcel Marcelino, 424–5934.
Assistant District Administrators: (Enforcement), Grant David Ward, 424–5936; (Regulation), Edward A. Ryan, Jr., 424–5935, Elizabeth Salini, 424–5931.
Philadelphia District Office, The Curtis Center, Suite 1005 East, 601 Walnut Street, Philadelphia, PA 19106–3322, (215) 597–3100, fax 597–5885.
District Administrator.—Ronald C. Long, 597–3106.
Associate District Administrator.—Joy G. Thompson, 597–6135.
Assistant District Administrators: (Enforcement), Merri Jo Gillette, 597–2936; C. Annette Kelton, 597–3107.
Senior Assistant District Administrator (Regulation).—William R. Meck, 597–0789.
Assistant District Administrator (Regulation).— A. Laurence Ehrhart, 597–2983.
Southeast Regional Office: 1401 Brickell Avenue, Suite 200, Miami, FL 33131 (305) 536–4700, fax 982–6333.
Regional Director.—Charles V. Senatore, 982–6332.
Assistant Regional Directors: (Enforcement), Spencer C. Barasch, 982–6338; David P. Nelson, 982–6339.
Associate Regional Director.—John D. Mahoney, 982–6303.
Atlanta District Office, 3475 Lenox Road NE., Suite 1000, Atlanta, GA 30326–1232, (404) 842–7600, fax 842–7666

District Administrator.—Richard P. Wessel, 842–7610.

Associate District Administrator.—Ronald L. Crawford, 842–7630.

Assistant District Administrators: (Enforcement), John E. Birkenheier, 842–7620; (Regulation), Francis P. McGing, 842–7645.

Midwest Regional Office: Citicorp Center, 500 West Madison Street, Suite 1400, Chicago, IL 60661–2511, (312) 353–7390, fax 353–7398.

Regional Director.—Mary Keefe, 353–9338.

Deputy Regional Director.—William M. Hegan, 353–7394.

Associate Regional Directors: (Enforcement), Randall J. Fons, 353–7428; Robert J. Burson, 353–7423; (Regulation), Patricia C. Holland, 353–7402.

Assistant Regional Directors: (Regulation), Michael J. O'Rourke, 353–7436; Lawrence F. Kendra, 886–1496; Thomas N. Kirk, 886–3956; Douglas R. Adams, 886–8513; John R. Lee, 886–8508; Carl E. Hoeck, 353–7219, (Enforcement); Timothy L. Warren, 353–7651; Jeanette L. Lewis, 353–7410; Mark R. Borrelli, 353–5453; John R. Brissman, 353–1679.

Central Regional Office: 1801 California Street, Suite 4800, Denver, CO 80202–2648, (303) 844–1000, fax 844–1010.

Regional Director.—Daniel F. Shea, 844–6889.

Associate Regional Director.—Donald M. Hoerl, 844–1060.

Assistant Regional Directors: (Enforcement), Edward A. Lewkowski, 844–1050; (Regulation), James E. Birchby, 844–1070; Dale E. Coffin, 844–1040.

Fort Worth District Office, 801 Cherry Street, 19th Floor, Fort Worth, TX 76102, (817) 978–3821, fax 978–2700

District Administrator.—T. Harold F. Degenhardt, 978–6469.

Assistant District Administrators: (Enforcement), Hugh M. Wright, 978–6474; (Regulation), Mary Lou Felsman, 978–6425.

Salt Lake District Office, 50 South Main Street, Suite 500, Salt Lake City, UT 84144–0402, (801) 524–5796, fax 524–3558

District Administrator.—Kenneth D. Israel, 524–6745.

Pacific Regional Office, 5670 Wilshire Boulevard, 11th Floor, Los Angeles, CA 90036–3648, (213) 965–3998, fax 965–3816.

Regional Director.—Elaine M. Cacheris, 965–3807.

Associate Regional Director (Enforcement).—Sandra J. Harris, 965–3962.

Assistant Regional Directors: (Enforcement), Ronald E. Wood, 965–3962; Lisa Gok, 965–3835; Kelly Bowers, 965–3924; Diana Tani, 965–3991.

Associate Regional Director (Regulation).—Rosalind R. Tyson, 965–3893.

Assistant Regional Directors: (Regulation), Michael P. Levitt, 525–3634; Stan C. Maekawa, 965–3922; Paul Weiser, 525–3632.

San Francisco District Office, 44 Montgomery Street, Suite 1100, San Francisco, CA 94104, (415) 705–2500, fax 705–2501

District Administrator.—David B. Bayless, 705–2444.

Assistant District Administrators: (Enforcement), Helane L. Morrison, 705–2450; (Regulation), Richard A. Castro, 705–2463.

SELECTIVE SERVICE SYSTEM

1515 Wilson Boulevard, 4th Floor, Arlington, VA 22209–2425

phone (703) 605–4000, fax 605–4133, http://www.sss.gov/

Director.—Gil Coronado, 605–4010

Deputy Director.—[Vacant].

Executive Director.—Willie L. Blanding, Jr., 605–4010.

Chief of Staff.—LtCol. Rogelio Rodriguez, 605–4010.

General Counsel.—Dr. Henry N. Williams, 605–4012.

Inspector General.—Alfred Rascon, 605–4013.

Director for—

Operations.—Col. Justo Gonzalez, 605–4066.

Information Management.—Norman W. Miller, 605–4110.

Registration Information Office, Service System PO Box 94638, Palatine, IL 60094–4638, (847) 688–6888, fax 688–2860.

Resource Management.—[Vacant].

Public and Congressional Affairs.—Lewis C. Brodsky, 605–4100, fax 605–4105.

Planning, Analysis, and Evaluation.—Richard S. Flahavan, 605–4017.

Financial Management.—Joseph S. Tropea, 605–4020.

SMALL BUSINESS ADMINISTRATION

409 Third Street, SW 20416

phone (202) 205–6600, fax (202) 205–7064, http://www.sbaonline.sba.gov/

Administrator.—Aida Alvarez, 205–6605.
Deputy Administrator.—Ginger Lew, 205–6605.
Counselor to the Administrator.—Jeanne Saddler, 205–6606.
Chief of Staff.—Paul Weech, 205–6605.
Director of Executive Secretariat.—Susan Walthall, 205–6608.
General Counsel.—John Spotila, 205–6642.
Chief Counsel for Advocacy.—Jere Glover, 205–6533.
Inspector General.—James F. Hoobler, 205–6580.
Chief Financial Officer.—Larry Wilson, 205–6449.
Director, National Advisory Council.—Michael Novelli, 205–6606.
Associate Administrator for—
Field Operations.—Ken Stram, 205–6808.
Public Communications, Marketing and Customer Service.—Irma Munoz, 205–6740.
Disaster Assistance.—Bernard Kulik, 205–6734.
Assistant Administrator for—
Congressional and Legislative Affairs.—Kris Swedin, 206–6702.
Hearings and Appeals.—Mona Mitnick, 401–8203.
Equal Employment Opportunity and Compliance.—Erline Patrick, 205–6750.
Associate Deputy Administrator for Management and Administration.—Antonella Pianalto, 206–6610.
Assistant Administrator for—
Administration.—Thomas Dumaresq, 205–6630.
Information Resources Management.—Lawrence E. Barrett, 205–6708.
Human Resources.—Carolyn Smith, 205–6782.
Associate Deputy Administrator for Economic Development.—Jean Sclater (acting), 205–6552.
Associate Administrator for—
Business Initiatives.—Monica Harrison, 205–6657.
Small Business Development Centers.—Johnnie Albertson, 205–6766.
Financial Assistance.—Jane Butler (acting), 205–6490.
Investment.—Don Christensen, 205–6510.
Surety Guarantees.—Robert J. Moffitt, 206–6540.
Assistant Administrator for—
International Trade.—Eileen Cassidy, 205–6720.
Veterans' Affairs.—Leon J. Bechet, 205–6773.
Women's Business Ownership.—Sherrye Henry, 205–6673.
Native American Affairs.—Quanah C. Stamps, 205–7364.
Associate Deputy Administrator for Government Contracting and Minority Economic Development.—Ronald Hobson, 205–6459.
Associate Administrator for—
Government Contracting.—Judith A. Roussel, 205–6460.
Minority Enterprise Development.—Calvin Jenkins, 205–6412.
Assistant Administrator for—
Size Standards.—Gary M. Jackson, 205–6618.
Technology.—Daniel O. Hill, 205–6450.

SMITHSONIAN INSTITUTION

Smithsonian Institution Building—The Castle (SIB), 1000 Jefferson Drive SW 20560
phone 357–1300, http://www.si.edu/

The Smithsonian Institution is an independent trust instrumentality created in accordance with the terms of the will of James Smithson of England who in 1826 bequeathed his property to the United States of America "to found at Washington under the name of the Smithsonian Institution an establishment for the increase and diffusion of knowledge among men." Congress pledged the faith of the United States to carry out the trust in 1836 (Act of July 1, 1836, C. 252, 5 Stat. 64), and established the Institution in its present form in 1846 (August 10, 1846, C. 178, 9 Stat. 102), entrusting the management of the institution to its independent Board of Regents.

THE BOARD OF REGENTS

Ex Officio

Chief Justice of the United States.—William H. Rehnquist, Chancellor.
Vice President of the United States.—Albert Gore, Jr.

Appointed by the President of the Senate
Hon. Thad Cochran
Hon. Bill Frist
Hon. Daniel P. Moynihan

Appointed by the Speaker of the House
Hon. Sam Johnson
Hon. Bob Livingston
Hon. Esteban E. Torres

Appointed by Joint Resolution of Congress

Hon. Howard H. Baker, Jr.
Hon. Barber B. Conable, Jr.
Anne d'Harnoncourt
Louis V. Gerstner, Jr.
Dr. Hanna H. Gray
Dr. Manuel L. Ibáñez
Dr. Homer A. Neal
Frank A. Shrontz
Wesley S. Williams, Jr.

NATIONAL BOARD

Jean Bronson, Kilborne, *Chair*

Clives Runnells, *Vice Chair*

Sir Valentine Abdy
Hon. Max N. Berry
Laura Lee Blanton
John M. Bradley
Stephen F. Brauer
Landon T. Clay
Dollie Cole
Peter R. Coneway
Thomas E. Congdon
Allison Stacey Cowles
Frank Arthur Daniels, Jr.
Patricia Frost
Nely Galan
Bert Getz
Marion Edwyn Harrison
Paul Hertelendy
Ruth S. Holmberg
Robert Horchow
Richard Hunt
Robert L. James
Mrs. Donald W. Jeffries
Mrs. James Kinnear
Marie L. Knowles
Hon. Marc Leland
Donald G. Lubin
Elizabeth S. MacMillan
Mrs. John W. Madigan
Frank N. Magid
Mrs. John F. Mars
Michael P. McBride
Nan Tucker McEvoy
Kenneth B. Miller
Hon. Norman Y. Mineta
Thomas D. Mullins
Rupert Murdoch
John N. Nordstrom
Joan Noto
Mrs. Frank Piasecki
Heinz C. Prechter
David S. Purvis
Baron Eric de Rothschild
A. R. Sanchez
Hon. Alan K. Simpson
Kathy Daubert Smith
Kenneth L. Smith
Kelso F. Sutton
Jeffrey N. Watanabe
Hon. Frank A. Weil
Nancy Brown Wellin

Honorary Members

Robert McC. Adams
William S. Anderson
Richard P. Cooley
Joseph F. Cullman, III
Charles D. Dickey, Jr.
Hon. Leonard K. Firestone
Alfred C. Glassell, Jr.
W. L. Hadley Griffin
Hon. William A. Hewitt
Hon. George C. McGhee
Justice Sandra D. O'Connor
S. Dillon Ripley
Francis C. Rooney, Jr.
Wilbur L. Ross, Jr.
Lloyd G. Schermer
Mrs. Gay F. Wray

OFFICE OF THE SECRETARY

Secretary.—I. Michael Heyman.
Executive Assistant to the Secretary.—James M. Hobbins, 357–1869.
Counselor to the Secretary for Biodiversity and Environmental Affairs.—Thomas E. Lovejoy, 786–2263.
Counselor to the Secretary for Community Affairs and Special Projects.—Miguel A. Bretos.
Inspector General.—Thomas D. Blair, 287–3326.
Counselor to the Secretary for Electronic Communications and Special Projects.—Marc J. Pachter, 786–2286.
Office of Planning, Management, and Budget.—L. Carole Wharton, 357–2917.

OFFICE OF THE UNDERSECRETARY

Under Secretary.—Constance Berry Newman, 357–3258.
Executive Director.—Anna B. Martin, 357–4620.
General Counsel.—John E. Huerta, 357–1997.
Director of—

Communications.—David J. Umansky, 357–2627.
Government Relations.—John Berry, 357–2962.

OFFICE OF FINANCE

Chief Financial Officer.—Rick Johnson, 357–4610.
Comptroller.—M. Leslie Casson, 287–3275.
Director, Office of—
Contracting and Property Management.—John W. Cobert, 287–3343.
Risk and Asset Management.—Sudeep Anand, 287–3156.
Sponsored Projects.—Ardelle G. Foss, 287–3796.

OFFICE OF ADMINISTRATION

Office of Equal Employment and Minority Affairs.—Era L. Marshall, 287–3508.
Ombudsman.—Chandra P. Heilman, 357–3261.
Director, Office of—
Human Resources.—Carolyn E. Jones, 287–3646.
Facilities Services.—Richard H. Rice, 357–1872.
Environmental Management and Safety.—F. William Billingsley, 287–3197.
Physical Plant.—Patrick J. Miller, 357–2900.
Protection Services.—David F. Morrell, 357–3062.

OFFICE OF INFORMATION TECHNOLOGY

Senior Information Officer.—A. Lee Denny, 633–9012.
Director, Office of Imaging, Printing, and Photographic Services.—James H. Wallace, Jr., 357–1487.

BUSINESS ADVANCEMENT DIRECTORATE

Smithsonian Magazine.—Ronald C. Walker, 786–2900.
Air and Space/Smithsonian Magazine.—Ronald C. Walker.
The Smithsonian Associates.—Mara Mayor, 357–4800.
Senior Business Officer, Smithonian Businesses/SI Retail.—Roland Banscher (acting), 287–3303.
Smithsonian Press/Productions.—Daniel Goodwin, 287–3738.

INSTITUTIONAL ADVANCEMENT DIRECTORATE

Director, Office of—
Executive Director of Development.—[Vacant].
Executive Associate for the Women's Committee.—Marta H. Doggett, 357–4000.
Membership and Development.—Marie Mattson, 357–4300.
Special Events and Conference Services.—Nicole L. Krakora, 357–2284.

OFFICE OF THE PROVOST

Provost.—J. Dennis O'Connor, 357–2903.
Executive Officer for Administration.—Mary Tanner, 786–2323.
Executive Officers for Programs: Ruth Selig, 786–2296; Barbara Schneider, 357–4837.
Special Assistant/Scheduler.—Sandra Reid, 786–2332.
Director of—
Accessibility Program.—Jan Majewski, 786–2942.
Scientific Diving Program.—Michael Lang, 786–2815.
Institutional Studies Office.—Zahava D. Doering, 786–2232.

SMITHSONIAN MUSEUMS

Anacostia Museum.—Steven Cameron Newsome, Director, 287–3306.
Arthur M. Sackler Gallery.—Milo C. Beach, Director, 357–4880.
Cooper-Hewitt, National Design Museum.—Dianne H. Pilgrim, Director, (212) 860–6868.
Freer Gallery of Art.—Milo C. Beach, Director, 357–4880.

Hirshhorn Museum and Sculpture Garden.—James T. Demetrion, Director, 357–3091.
National Air and Space Museum.—Donald D. Engen, Director, 357–1745.
National Museum of African Art.—Roslyn A. Walker, Director, 357–4600.
National Museum of American Art.—Elizabeth Broun, Director, 357–1959.
National Museum of American History.—Spencer R. Crew, Director, 357–2510.
National Museum of the American Indian.—W. Richard West, Director, 287–2536.
National Museum of Natural History.—Robert W. Fri, Director, 357–2664.
National Portrait Gallery.—Alan Fern, Director, 357–1915.
National Postal Museum.—James H. Bruns, Director, 633–9360.
National Zoological Park.—Michael Robinson, Director, 673–4721.
Renwick Gallery.—Kenneth R. Trapp, Director, 357–2531.

SMITHSONIAN RESEARCH CENTERS

Archives of American Art.—Richard J. Wattenmaker, Director, 357–2782.
Center for Folklife Programs and Cultural Studies.—Richard Kurin, Director, 287–3535.
Conservation Analytical Laboratory.—Lambertus Van Zelst, Director, (301) 238–3700.
Museum Support Center.—U. Vincent Wilcox, Director, (301) 238–3648.
Smithsonian Astrophysical Observatory.—Irwin I. Shapiro, 60 Garden Street, Cambridge MA 02138, Director, (617) 495–7100.
Smithsonian Environmental Research Center.—David L. Correll, PO Box 28, Edgewater MD 21037, Director, (301) 261–4190.
Smithsonian Tropical Research Institute.—Ira Rubinoff, Director, Unit 0948, APO AA 34002–0948, phone 011–507–227–6022.

EDUCATION, MUSEUM AND SCHOLARLY SERVICES

Center for Museum Studies.—Rex M. Ellis, Director, 357–3101.
National Sciences Resources Center.—Douglas M. Lapp, Director, 357–4892.
Office of Exhibits Central.—Michael Headley, Director, 357–1556.
Office of Fellowships and Grants.—Roberta W. Rubinoff, Director, 287–3271.
Office of International Relations.—Francine C. Berkowitz, Director, 357–2519.
Office of the Smithsonian Institution Archives.—Edie Hedlin, Director, 357–3080.
Smithsonian Institution Libraries.—Barbara J. Smith, Museum of Natural History, Director, 357–2240.
Smithsonian Office of Education.—Ann P. Bay, Director, 357–2425.
Smithsonian Early Enrichment Center.—Sharon Shaffer, Director, 786–2531.
Smithsonian Institution Traveling Exhibition Service.—Anna R. Cohn, Director, 357–3168.

SOCIAL SECURITY ADMINISTRATION

International Trade Commission Building, 500 East Street SW 20254, (ITCB)

Altmeyer Building, 6401 Security Boulevard, Baltimore MD 21235, (ALTMB)

Annex Building, 6401 Security Boulevard, Baltimore MD 21235, (ANXB)

National Computer Center, 6201 Security Boulevard, Baltimore MD 21235, (NCC)

West High Rise Building, 6401 Security Boulevard, Baltimore MD 21235, (WHRB)

Gwynn Oak Building, 1710 Gwynn Oak Avenue, Baltimore MD 21207, (GWOB)

Operations Building, 6401 Security Boulevard, Baltimore MD 21235, (OPRB)

Metro West Tower Building, 300 North Greene Street, Baltimore MD 21201, (MWTB)

Security West Tower, 1500 Woodlawn Drive, Baltimore MD 21241, (SWTB)

Van Ness Centre, 4301 Connecticut Avenue NW 20008

One Skyline Tower, 5107 Leesburg Pike, Falls Church VA 22041, (SKY)

http://www.ssa.gov

Commissioner.—John J. Callahan (acting), ITCB, Room 850, (202) 358–6000 or ALTMB, Room 900, (410) 965–3120.
Principal Deputy Commissioner.—John R. Dyer (acting), ALTMB, Room 960, (410) 965–9000.
Chief of Staff.—Brian D. Coyne, ITCB, Room 800, (202) 358–6013.
Senior Executive Officer.—Richard A. Eisinger, ITCB, Room 850, (202) 358–6014.

Director, Executive Secretariat.—Richard A. Eisinger, (acting), ALTMB, Room 900, (410) 965–3620.
Senior Advisor to the Commissioner on Customer Service Integration.—Toni Lenane, ALTMB, Room 960, (410) 965–7767.
Director for Strategic Management.—Carolyn J. Shearin-Jones, ALTMB, Room 946, (410) 965–6210.
Director, Disability Process Redesign Team.—Sue Davis, ALTMB, Room 500, (410) 966–8323.
Deputy Commissioner for Communications.—Joan F. Wainwright, WHRB, Room 4200, (410) 965–1720.
Assistant Deputy Commissioner and Press Officer.—Philip Gambino, WHRB, Room 4200, (410) 965–6448.
Associate Commissioner, Office of—
Communications Policy and Technology.—William H. Hinkle, WHRB, Room 4–J–10, (410) 965–4029.
External Affairs.—Charles Fosler (acting), WHRB, Room 4300, (410) 965–4023.
Public Inquiries.—Charles H. Mullen, ANXB, Room 4100, (410) 965–8187.
Deputy Commissioner for Programs and Policy.—Carolyn W. Colvin, ALTMB, Room 100, (410) 965–4512.
Assistant Deputy Commissioner.—Glennalee K. Donnelly, ALTMB, Room 100, (410) 965–4622.
Associate Commissioner, Office of—
International Policy.—James A. Kissko, ALTMB, Room 142, (410) 965–7389.
Program Benefits Policy.—Marilyn O'Connell (acting), ALTMB, Room 760, (410) 965–6212.
Disability.—Susan M. Daniels, ALTMB, Room 560, (410) 965–3424.
Hearings and Appeals.—Rita Geier, SKY, Room 1600, (703) 305–0200.
Program Support.—Sara A. Hamer, WHRB, Room 440 (410) 965–0500.
Policy and Planning.—Sandy Crank, ALTMB, Room 100, (410) 965–2302.
Research, Evaluation and Statistics.—Peter M. Wheeler, OPRB, Room 4–C–15, (410) 965–2841.
Deputy Commissioner for Operations.—Janice I. Warden, WHRB, Room 1204, (410) 965–3143.
Assistant Deputy Commissioner.—Paul D. Barnes, WHRB, Room 1204, (410) 965–1880.
Associate Commissioner, Office of Public Service and Operations Support.—Marsha Rydstrom, WHRB, Room 1224, (410) 965–3400.
Automation Support.—William Gray (acting), WHRB, Room 1126, (410) 966–8040.
Telephone Services.—Jack McHale, WHRB, Room 1412, (410) 966–7758.
Director, Office of—
Central Records Operations.—W. Burnell Hurt, (acting), SWTB, Room 7200, (410) 966–7000.
Disability and International Operations.—W. Burnell Hurt, SWTB, Room 7200, (410) 966–7000.
Regional Commissioner for—
Boston: Manny Vaz, J.F.K. Federal Building, Government Center, Room 1990, Boston, MA 02203, (617) 565–2870.
New York: Beatrice Disman, 26 Federal Plaza, Room 40–102, New York, NY 12078, (212) 264–3915.
Philadelphia: Larry Massanari, PO Box 8788, 3535 Market Street, Philadelphia, PA 19104, (215) 597–5157.
Atlanta: Gordon Sherman, 101 Marietta Tower, Suite 1902, Atlanta, GA 30323, (404) 331–2475.
Chicago: Myrtle Habersham, Harold Washington Social Security Center, 10th Floor, 600 West Madison Street, Chicago, IL 60661, (312) 353–8277.
Dallas: Horace Dickerson, 1200 Main Tower Building, Suite 1440, Dallas, TX 75202, (214) 767–4210.
Kansas City: Michael Grochowski, Federal Office Building, 601 East 12th Street, Room 436, Kansas City, MO 64106, (816) 426–6548.
Denver: Horace Dickerson, Federal Office Building, 1961 Stout Street, Room 325, Denver, CO 80294, (303) 844–2388.
San Francisco: Linda McMahon, 75 Hawthorne Street, San Francisco, CA 94105, (415) 744–4676.
Seattle: Martin Baer, 2201 Sixth Street, Seattle, WA 98121, (206) 615–2100.
Deputy Commissioner for Finance, Assessment and Management.—Dale W. Sopper (acting), ALTMB, Room 800, (410) 965–2910.
Assistant Deputy Commissioner.—Andria Childs, (acting), ALTMB, Room 800, (410) 965–2914.

Senior Financial Executive.—Norman Goldstein, ALTMB, Room 451, (410) 965–1970.
Associate Commissioner, Office of—
Program and Integrity Review.—Joseph A. Gribbim, ALTMB, Room 860, (410) 965–3894.
Financial Policy and Operations.—Thomas G. Staples, (acting), ANXB, Room 1218, (410) 965–3839.
Budget.—Robert M. Rothenberg, WHRB, Room 2126, (410) 965–3501.
Acquisition and Grants.—James M. Fornataro, GWOB, Room 1–A–7, (410) 965–9459.
Facilities Management.—Barbara S. Sledge, ALTMB, Room 836, (410) 965–4268.
Publications and Logistics Management.—James F. Trickett, ALTMB, Room 826, (410) 965–4262.
Deputy Commissioner for Systems.—D. Dean Mesterharm, ALTMB, Room 400, (410) 965–4721.
Assistant Deputy Commissioner.—Kathleen M. Adams, ALTMB, Room 400, (410) 965–6294.
Associate Commissioner, Office of—
Telecommunications and Systems Operations.—Thomas J. O'Hare, Jr., NCC, Room 535, (410) 965–1500.
Systems Design and Development.—Charles M. Wood, (acting), WHRB, Room 3100, (410) 965–3780.
Systems Requirements.—Richard Gonzalez, WHRB, Room 3224, (410) 965–6018.
Information Management.—Judy Ziolkowski, (acting), WHRB, Room 3420, (410) 965–5311.
Director, Office of Systems Planning and Integration.—B. Carlton Couchoud, ALTMB, Room 322, (410) 965–6290.
Deputy Commissioner for Human Resources.—Ronald E. Brooks (acting), ALTMB, Room 200, (410) 965–1900.
Assistant Deputy Commissioner.—David L. Jenkins, ALTMB, Room 200, (410) 965–3708.
Director, Executive and Special Services Staff.—Evelyn M. Kirby, ALTMB, Room 200, (410) 965–3852.
Associate Commissioner, Office of Personnel.—Maurice O. Brice, WHRB, Room G–314, (410) 965–3318.
Director, Office of—
Labor Management Relations.—Patricia Randle (acting), WHRB, Room G–E–10, (410) 965–4741.
Civil Rights and Equal Opportunity.—Miguel A. Torrado, WHRB, Room 2200, (410) 965–1977.
Training.—Gerald Burton (acting), ANXB, Room 4400, (410) 965–2473.
Workforce Analysis.—G. Kelly Croft, OPRB, Room 4–S–18, (410) 965–3681.
Deputy Commissioner for Legislation and Congressional Affairs.—Judy L. Chesser, ITCB, Room 850, (202) 358–6030.
Assistant Deputy Commissioner.—Diane Garro, ALTMB, Room 152, (410) 965–2386.
Staff Director for—
Disability Insurance Program.—Margy Weiss-LaFond, WHRB, Room 3216, (410) 965–2634.
Congressional Relations.—Edmond DiGiorgio, WHRB, Room 3202, (410) 965–3929.
Supplemental Security Income Program.—David Mattson, WHRB, Room 3227, (410) 965–2615.
Old Age and Survivors Insurance Benefits.—Timothy Kelley, WHRB, Room 3322, (410) 965–3293.
Program Administration and Financing.—Thomas Miller, WHRB, Room 3210, (410) 965–3285.
Chief Actuary.—Harry C. Ballantyne, ALTMB, Room 700, (410) 965–3000.
Deputy Chief Actuary for—
Long Range.—Stephen C. Goss, ALTMB, Room 702, (410) 965–3002.
Short Range.—Eli N. Donkar, OPRB, Room 4–N–29, (410) 965–3004.
General Counsel.—Arthur J. Fried, ALTMB, Room 600, (410) 965–0600.
Principal Deputy General Counsel.—Charlotte Hardnett, ALTMB, Room 600, (410) 965–3114.
Deputy General Counsel.—Randolph Gaines, ALTMB, Room 600, (410) 965–3135.
Associate General Counsel for—
Litigation.—John Sacchetti, (acting), ALTMB, Room 606, (410) 965–3177.
General Law.—Eileen Houghton, ALTMB, Room 654, (410) 965–4816.
Policy and Legislation.—John B. Watson, ALTMB, Room 600, (410) 965–3137.
Regional Chief Counsel for—
Boston: Robert J. Triba, J.F.K. Federal Building, Government Center, Room 2225, Boston, MA 02203, (617) 565–4277.

New York: Barbara I. Spivak, 26 Federal Plaza, Suite 3904, New York, NY 12078, (212) 264–3650, ext. 222

Philadelphia: James A. Winn, PO Box 13716, Philadelphia, PA 19101, (215) 597–4601.

Atlanta: Mary Ann Sloan, 101 Marietta Tower, Suite 221, Atlanta, GA 30323, (404) 331–2238, ext. 155.

Chicago: Thomas W. Crawley, 105 West Adams Street, 19th Floor, Chicago, IL 60603, (312) 353–1640.

Dallas: Frank V. Smith III, (acting), Suite 1310, 1200 Main Tower Building, Dallas, TX 75202, (214) 767–4660, ext. 322

Kansas City: Frank V. Smith III, Federal Office Building, 601 East 12th Street, Room 535, Kansas City, MO 64106, (816) 426–4820.

Denver: Deana R. Ertl-Lombardi, Federal Office Building, 1961 Stout Street, Room 325, Denver, CO 80294, (303) 844–5459.

San Francisco: Dennis Mulshine (acting), United Nations Plaza, Room 420, San Francisco, CA 94102, (415) 437–8053.

Seattle: Lucille Gonzales Meis, 2201 Sixth Avenue M/S–65, Seattle, WA 98121–1833, (206) 615–2662.

Inspector General.—David C. Williams, ALTMB, Room 300, (410) 966–8337.

Counsel to the Inspector General.—Judith Kidwell, OPRB, Room 4–K–1, (410) 965–9750.

Assistant Inspector General for—

Management Services.—Karen Shaffer, ALTMB, Room 306, (410) 966–8808.

Investigations.—James G. Huse, Jr., OPRB, Room 4–S–1, (410) 966–8386.

Audits.—Pamela J. Gardiner, OPRB, Room 4–G–1, (410) 965–9700.

SUSQUEHANNA RIVER BASIN COMMISSION

FEDERAL REPRESENTATIVES

Federal Member.—Bruce Babbitt, Secretary of the Interior.

United States Commissioner.—Kenneth J. Cole.

Federal Adviser.—Colonel Randall R. Inouye, District Engineer, Corps of Engineers, Department of the Army, PO Box 1715, Baltimore, MD 21203.

STAFF

1721 North Front Street, Harrisburg PA 17103, phone (717) 238–0422

Executive Director.—Paul O. Swartz.

Chief Administrative Officer and Treasurer.—Duane A. Friends.

STATE JUSTICE INSTITUTE

1650 King Street, Suite 600, Alexandria VA 22314, phone (703) 684–6100

BOARD OF DIRECTORS

Cochairmen.—David A. Brock, John F. Daffron, Jr.

Secretary.—Sandra A. O'Connor.

Executive Committee Member.—Terrence B. Adamson.

Members:

Joseph F. Baca
Robert N. Baldwin
Carlos R. Garza
Tommy Jewell
Keith McNamara
Florence R. Murray
Janie L. Shores

Officers:

Executive Director.—David I. Tevelin.

Deputy Director.—Richard Van Duizend.

TENNESSEE VALLEY AUTHORITY

One Massachusetts Avenue 20444, phone (202) 898–2999
Knoxville TN 37902, phone (423) 632–2101
Chattanooga TN 37401, phone (423) 751–0011
Muscle Shoals AL 35660, phone (202) 386–2601

BOARD OF DIRECTORS

Chairman.—Craven H. Crowell, Jr., (423) 632–2531 (Knoxville).
Directors: Johnny H. Hayes, (423) 632–3871; William H. Kennoy, (423) 632–2600 (Knoxville).
Chief Administrative Officer.—Norman A. Zigrossi, (423) 632–4144 (Knoxville).
Chief Operating Officer.—Joseph W. Dickey, (423) 632–3108 (Knoxville).
Chief Nuclear Officer.—Oliver D. Kingsley, Jr., (423) 751–4770 (Chattanooga).

CORPORATE VICE PRESIDENTS

Senior Vice President of Communications.—Alan Carmichael, (423) 632–8018 (Knoxville).
Vice President of Quality Improvement.—Camise Paschall, (423) 632–4848 (Knoxville).
Vice President for Government Relations.—Ron Loving, (202) 898–2999 (Washington).
Chief Financial Officer.—David Smith, (423) 632–4049 (Knoxville).
Vice President and General Counsel.—Ed Christenbury, (423) 632–3341, fax 632–4528 (Knoxville).
Inspector General.—George Prosser, (423) 632–4130 (Knoxville).

GENERATING GROUP

Vice President of Fossil Operations.—Joe Bynum, (423) 751–4776 (Chattanooga).
Vice President of Hydro Operations.—Enrique Martinez, (423) 751–2491 (Chattanooga).
Senior Vice President for Nuclear Generation.—Oswald J. (Ike) Zeringue, (423) 751–8682 (Chattanooga).

RESOURCE GROUP

Senior Vice President of Resource Group.—Kathryn J. Jackson (423) 632–3141 (Knoxville).
Senior Vice President of Economic Development.—Betsy L. Child (423) 632–4312 (Knoxville).

CUSTOMER GROUP

Senior Vice President of Customer Group.—Richard L. Tallent (615) 231–7201 (Nashville).
Vice President of Transmission/Power Supply.—William J. Museler (423) 751–4945 (Chattanooga).
Vice President of Service Organization.—Ronald A. Loving (423) 632–3435 (Knoxville).

WASHINGTON OFFICE

(202) 898–2999, fax (202) 898–2998

Vice President of Government Relations.—[Vacant].
Washington Representatives.—Jeannette Pablo, Caroline Nielson, Joe Bailey.

TRADE AND DEVELOPMENT AGENCY

State Annex 16, Room 309, Washington DC 20523–1602, phone (703) 875–4357

Director.—J. Joseph GrandMaison.
Deputy Director.—Nancy D. Frame.
General Counsel.—Kenneth Fries.
Assistant Director for Management Operations.—Deirdre E. Curley.
Special Assistant for Policy/Public Affairs.—Steven Mavigilio.
Congressional Liaison Office.—Edward Cabot.
Export Promotion Director.—[Vacant].

Regional Directors:
Africa and Middle East.—John Richter.
Central, Eastern, and South Europe.—Rod Azama.
New Independent States, South Asia, Mongolia and India.—Daniel D. Stein.
East Asia and Pacific Islands.—Geoff Jackson.
Latin America and Caribbean.—Albert W. Angulo.
Special Projects.—Barbara R. Bradford.
Economist/Evaluation Officer.—David Denny.
Financial Manager.—Noreen St. Louis.
Contracting Officer.—Della Glenn.
Administrative Officer.—Carolyn Hum.

THRIFT DEPOSITOR PROTECTION OVERSIGHT BOARD

(Established August 9, 1989, 12 U.S.C. 1441a)

808 17th Street NW 20232, phone (202) 416–2650

BOARD

Chairman.—Robert E. Rubin, Secretary of Treasury.
Members:
Alan Greenspan
Ricki R. Tigert Helfer
John E. Ryan
Robert C. Larson
Executive Director.—Dietra L. Ford.
Deputy Executive Directors for—
Finance.—Thomas J. Elzey.
Government Affairs and Pubic Liaison.—Kenneth S. Colburn.
Oversight and Evaluation.—Neal D. Peterson.
General Counsel.—Richard H. Farina.
Deputy General Counsel.—Lawrence W. Hayes.

U.S. ADVISORY COMMISSION ON PUBLIC DIPLOMACY

(Created by Executive Order 12048 and Public Law 96–60)

USIA Building, 301 Fourth Street SW, Room 600, 20547
phone (202) 619–4457, fax 619–5489

Chairman.—Lewis Manilow.
Vice Chairman.—William J. Hybl.
Members:
Walter R. Roberts.
Pamela J. Turner.
Harold C. Pachios.
Maria Elena Torano.
Charles H. Dolan.
Staff Director.—Bruce N. Gregory.

U.S. ARMS CONTROL AND DISARMAMENT AGENCY

Department of State Building, 320 21st Street NW 20451, fax 647–6721

Director.—John Holum, 647–9610.
Deputy Director.—Ralph Earle II, 647–8463.
Counselor.—Donald Gross, 647–5553.
Special Assistant.—Carlen Ackerman, 647–9610.
Executive Secretary.—Barbara Starr, 647–8478.
Special Representative.—Thomas Graham Jr., 647–8090.
Special Representative and Chief Science Advisor.—James Sweeney, 647–8090.
Assistant Director, Bureau of—
Multilateral Affairs.—Donald Mahley (acting), 647–8978.
Nonproliferation and Regional Arms Control.—Lawrence Scheinman, 647–3466.
Strategic and Eurasian Affairs.—Michael Nacht, 736–4260.
Intelligence, Verification and Information Management.—O. J. Sheaks (acting), 647–5315.

General Counsel.—Mary Elizabeth Hoinkes, 647–3596.
Director for—
Administration.—Cathleen Lawrence, 647–3442.
Public Affairs.—Mary Dillion, 647–8677.
Congressional Affairs.—Ivo Spalatin, 647–3612.

U.S. COMMISSION ON CIVIL RIGHTS

(Codified in 42 U.S.C., section 1975)

624 Ninth Street 20425, phone (202) 376–7700

Chair.—Mary Francis Berry.
Vice Chairman.—Cruz Reynoso.
Commissioners:
Carl A. Anderson
Arthur A. Fletcher
Robert P. George
Constance Horner
Russell G. Redenbaugh
Charles Pei Wang
Staff Director.—Mary K. Mathews.
Special Assistants: Conner Ball and Jacqueline Johnson.
Executive Assistant to Special Assistants.—Rosalind D. Gray.
Assistant Staff Director for Congressional Affairs.—James S. Cunningham, 376–8317.
Public Affairs Unit Chief.—Charles R. Rivera, 376–8312.
General Counsel.—[Vacant], 376–8351.
Deputy General Counsel.—Stephanie Moore.
Chief, Regional Programs Coordination Unit.—Carol-Lee Hurley.
Assistant Staff Director for Management.—[Vacant].
Office of Civil Rights Evaluation.—Frederick Isler, 376–8582.
Solicitor.—Emma Monroig, 376–8514.

U.S. HOLOCAUST MEMORIAL COUNCIL

The United States Holocaust Memorial Museum, 100 Raoul Wallenberg Place SW 20024

phone 488–0400, fax (202) 488–2690

Appointed by the President:
Chairman.—Miles Lerman, Vineland, NJ.
Vice Chairman.—Ruth B. Mandel, Princeton, NJ.
Members:
Albert Abramson, Bethesda, MD.
Jack Africk, Hollywood, FL.
Gary A. Barron, Miami, FL.
David Berger, Palm Beach, FL.
Allen L. Bildner, Short Hills, NJ.
Bradley A. Blakeman, Valley Stream, NY.
Stanislaus A. Blejwas, Hartford, CT.
Stanley M. Chesly, Cincinnati, OH.
Mimi Weyforth Dawson, Washington, DC.
George Deukmejian, Los Angeles, CA.
Kitty Dukakis, Brookline, MA.
William Anthony Duna, St. Paul, MN.
Dalck Feith, Elkins Park, PA.
Abraham H. Foxman, New York, NY.
Erna I. Gans, Northbrook, IL.
Michael C. Gelman, Chevy Chase, MD.
Barbara George Gold, Chicago, IL.
Steven H. Goldberg, New York, NY.
Louis L. Gonda, Los Angeles, CA.
Sam Halpern, Hillside, NJ.
Robert J. Horn, Washington, DC.
John F. Kordek, Arlington Heights, IL
Cecile B. Kremer, Chase, MD.
Ronald S. Lauder, New York, NY.
Theodore N. Lerner, Chevy Chase, MD.
Deborah E. Lipstadt, Atlanta, GA.
William J. Lowenberg, San Francisco, CA.
Simcha G. Lyons, St. Louis, MO.
Jewell Jackson McCabe, New York, NY.
Benjamin Meed, New York, NY.
Leo Melamed, Chicago, IL.
Harvey M. Meyerhoff, Baltimore, MD.
Ruth R. Miller, Cleveland, OH.
Set C. Momjian, Washington, DC.
Murray Pantirer, Hillside, NJ.
Rev. John T. Pawlikowski, Chicago, IL.
Abe Resnick, Miami Beach, FL.
Sheila Johnson Robbins, New York, NY.
Richard M. Rosenbaum, Rochester, NY.
Menachem Z. Rosensaft, New York, NY.
Dennis B. Ross, Bethesda, MD.
John K. Roth, Claremont, CA.
Samuel Rothberg, Peoria, IL.
Arthur L. Schechter, Houston, TX.
Nathan Shapell, Beverly Hills, CA.
Lawrence M. Small, Washington, DC.
Clifford M. Sobel, Newark, NJ.
Steven E. Some, Princeton, NJ.
Jean Stein, Great Neck, NY.

Arnold Thaler, Chicago, IL.
Sheila Rabb Weidenfeld, Washington, DC.
Abigail S. Wexner, New Albany, OH.
Elie Wiesel, Boston, MA.

Congressional Members:
Appointed by the President Pro Tempore of the Senate:
Charles Grassely, Senator from Iowa.
Orrin G. Hatch, Senator from Utah.
Frank R. Lautenberg, Senator from New Jersey.
Frank H. Murkowski, Senator from Alaska.
Claiborne Pell, Senator from Rhode Island.
Appointed by the Speaker of the House of Representatives:
Benjamin A. Gilman, Representative from New York.
Tom Lantos, Representative from California.
Steven LaTourette, Representative from Ohio.
Ralph Regula, Representative from Ohio.
Sidney R. Yates, Representative from Illinois.
Ex Officio Members:
Department of—
Education.—Madeleine Kunin.
Interior.—Robert G. Stanton.
State.—John Shattuck.
Council Staff:
Founding Museum Director.—Jeshajahu Weinberg.
Executive Director.—Jeffrey LaRiche (acting).
Museum Director.—Jeffrey LaRiche (acting).
Secretary of the Council.—Jeffrey LaRiche.

U.S. INFORMATION AGENCY

(Created by Presidential Reorganization Plan No. 2, 1977)

USIA Building, 301 Fourth Street SW 20547 (USIAB)

Donohoe Building, 400 6th Street SW 20547 (DB)

Health and Human Services North Building

330 Independence Avenue SW 20547 (HHSNB)

Patrick Henry Building, 601 D Street 20547 (PHB)

http://www.usia.gov/

Director.—Joseph Duffey, (USIAB), Room 800, 619–4742, fax 619–6705.
Deputy Director.—Penn Kemble, (USIAB), Room 806, 619–5747, fax 619–6705.
Counselor.—Anne M. Sigmund, (USIAB), Room 820, 619–4618, fax 401–2307.
General Counsel.—Les Jin, (USIAB), Room 700, 619–5078, fax 619–4573.
Associate Director for International Bureau of Broadcasting.—Kevin Klose, (COHEN), Room 3300, 619–1009, fax 619–0085.
Management.—Henry Howard, Jr., (USIAB), Room 816, 619–4626, fax 401–3421.
Information.—Barry Fulton, (USIAB), Room 848, 619–4545, fax 619–6557.
Educational and Cultural Affairs.—John P. Loiello, (USIAB), Room 849, 619–6599, fax 619–5068.
Director for Office of—
Research.—Ann Pincus, (USIAB), Room 352, 619–4965, fax 619–6977.
Congressional and Intergovernmental Affairs.—Carrie Isacco (acting), (USIAB), Room 852, 619–6828, fax 619–6876.
Public Liaison.—Marthena Cowart, (USIAB), Room 602, 619–4355, fax 619–6988.
Voice of America Programs.—Evelyn S. Lieberman, (COHEN), Room 3324, 619–2030, fax 401–1327.
Cuba Broadcasting.—Rolando Bonachea (acting), Room 3350–B, 401–7013, fax 401–3340.
Worldnet Television and Film Services.—John Lennon (acting), (PHB), Room 5000, 501–7806, fax 501–6664.
African Affairs.—Thomas Hull, (USIAB), Room 720, 619–4894, fax 619–5925.
East European and NIS Affairs.—Robert E. McCarthy, (USIAB), Room 868, 619–4563, fax 401–6893.

West European and Canadian Affairs.—C. Miller Croch, (USIAB), Room 868, 619–6565, fax 619–6821.
East Asian and Pacific Affairs.—Frank Scotton, (USIAB), Room 766, 619–4829, fax 619–6684.
American Republics Affairs.—Stephen Chaplin, (USIAB), Room 750, 619–4860, fax 619–5172.
North African, Near Eastern and South Asian Affairs.—Kenton Keith, (USIAB), Room 866, 619–5526, fax 205–0734.

U.S. INSTITUTE OF PEACE

1550 M Street NW 20005–1708

phone (202) 457–1700, fax (202) 429–6063

BOARD OF DIRECTORS

Public Members:
Chairman.—Chester A. Crocker.
Vice Chairman.—Max M. Kampelman.
Members:

Dennis L. Bark
Theodore M. Hesburgh
Seymour Martin Lipset
Christopher Phillips
Mary Louise Smith
W. Scott Thompson
Allen Weinstein
Harriet Zimmerman

Ex Officio:
Deputy Director, U.S. Arms Control and Disarmament Agency.—Ralph Earle II.
Assistant Secretary of State for Intelligence and Research.—Toby Trister Gati.
President, National Defense University.—LG Ervin J. Rokke, USAF.
Principal Deputy Under Secretary of Defense for Policy.—Walter B. Slocome.
Officials:
President.—Richard H. Solomon.
Executive Vice President.—Harriet Hentges.
Vice President.—Charles E. Nelson.
Director of—
Education and Training.—Peter Schoettle.
Research and Studies.—Stanley O. Roth.
Grants Program.—David R. Smock.
Jennings Randolph Fellowship Program for International Peace.—Joseph L. Klaits.
Jeannette Rankin Library Program.—Margarita Studemeister.
Administration.—Bernice J. Carney.
Office of Communications.—Sheryl Brown.
Rule of Law Initiative.—Neil J. Kritz.
Senior Scholar for Religion, Ethics and Human Rights.—David Little.

U.S. INTERNATIONAL DEVELOPMENT COOPERATION AGENCY

New State Department Building, 320 21st Street 20523, phone (202) 647–4000 (NS)

Columbia Plaza Office Building, 2401 E Street 20523

515 22d Street 20523 (SA–1) (SA–2)

Architects Building, 1400 Wilson Boulevard Arlington VA 22209 (SA–8)

1100 Wilson Boulevard Arlington VA 22209 (SA–14)

Rosslyn Plaza Center, 1601 North Kent Street Arlington VA 22209 (SA–18)

http://www.info.usaid.gov/

AGENCY FOR INTERNATIONAL DEVELOPMENT

Administrator.—J. Brian Atwood, Room 5942 (NS), 647–9620, fax 647–1770.
Deputy Administrator.—[Vacant], Room 5894 (NS), 647–8578.
Counselor.—Kelly Kammerer, Room 5644 (NS), 647–4630.

Executive Secretary.—Ryan Conroy, Room 5897 (NS), 647–8000.
Assistant Administrator for Program and Policy Coordination.—Kelly Kammeren, Room 3892 (NS), 647–7028.
Assistant Administrator for—
Africa.—Carol Peasley (acting), Room 6936 (NS), 647–9232.
Asia and the Near East.—Margaret Carpenter, Room 6212 (NS), 647–8298.
Europe and the New Independent States.—Thomas Dine, Room 6724 (NS), 647–9119.
Latin America and the Caribbean.—Mark L. Schneider, Room 4529A (NS), 647–8246.
Humanitarian Response.—Leonard M. Rogers (acting), Room 5314A (NS), 647–0220.
Global Programs, Field Support and Research.—Sally Shelton, Room 4942 (NS), 647–1827.
Management.—Larry E. Byrne, Room 3948 (NS), 647–8646.
Legislative and Public Affairs.—Jill Buckley, Room 4889 (NS), 647–4200.
Chief of Staff.—Richard L. McCall, Jr.
Director, for Equal Opportunity Programs.—Jessalyn L. Pendarvis, Room 1224 (SA–1), 663–1333.
Director of Small and Disadvantaged Business Utilization / Minority Resource Center.—Ivan R. Ashley, Room 1200A (SA–14), (703) 875–1551.
General Counsel.—Singleton McAllister, Room 6895 (NS), 647–8548.
Inspector General.—Jeffrey R. Rush, Jr., Room 5756 (NS), 647–7844.

OVERSEAS PRIVATE INVESTMENT CORPORATION

1100 New York Avenue NW, Washington DC 20527, 336–8400

President and Chief Executive Officer.—Mildred Callear (acting).
Executive Vice President.—[Vacant].
Vice President for Investment Development.—Robert L. Schiffer.
Vice President and General Counsel.—Charles D. Toy.
Vice President and Treasurer.—Mildred O. Callear.
Vice President for—
Finance.—Frank L. Langhammer.
Investment Funds.—Robert D. Stillman.
Insurance.—Daniel W. Riordan.
Management.—William C. Moss.
Director, Legislative Affairs.—Richard Horanburg, 336–8417.

BOARD OF DIRECTORS

Government Directors:
Chairman.—J. Brian Atwood, Administrator, Agency for International Development.
Vice Chairman.—Jeffrey M. Lang, Deputy U.S. Trade Representative.
Ruth Harkin, President and Chief Executive Officer Overseas Private Investment Corporation.
Stuart E. Eizenstat, Under Secretary for International Trade, U.S. Department of Commerce.
Joan E. Spero, Under Secretary for Economic and Agricultural Affairs, U.S. Department of State.
Jeffrey R. Shafer, Under Secretary for International Affairs, U.S. Department of the Treasury.
Bernard E. Anderson, Assistant Secretary for Employment Standards, U.S. Department of Labor.
Private Sector Directors:
John Chrystal, Chairman, Iowa Savings Bank, Coon Rapids, IA.
Simon Ferro, Adorno and Zeder, P.A. Miami, FL.
Gordon D. Giffen, Long, Aldrige and Norman, Atlanta, GA.
George J. Kourpias, President, International Association of Machinists and Aerospace Workers, Upper Marlboro, MD.
Gloria Rose Ott, President, GO Strategies, San Jose, CA.
Lottie Shackleford, Executive Vice President, Global, USA, Little Rock, AR.
Harvey Sigelbaum, President, Amalgamated Life Insurance, New York, NY.

TRADE AND DEVELOPMENT PROGRAM

Room 309, 1621 North Kent Street, Arlington, VA 22209, (703) 875–4357

Director.—J. Joseph Grandmaison.

U.S. INTERNATIONAL TRADE COMMISSION

500 E Street SW 20436

phone (202) 205–1819, fax 205–2798, http://www.usitc.gov

COMMISSIONERS

Chairman.—Marcia E. Miller, Democrat, Indiana; term ending December 16, 2003; entered on duty August 5, 1996; designated Chairman for the term ending June 16, 1998.
Vice Chairman.—Lynn Munroe Bragg, Republican, Maryland; term ending June 16, 2002; entered on duty March 31, 1994; designated Vice Chairman for the term ending June 16, 1998.
Commissioners:
Don E. Newquist, Democrat, Texas; term ending December 16, 1997; entered on duty October 18, 1988.
Carol T. Crawford, Republican, Virginia; term ending June 16, 1999; entered on duty November 22, 1991.
2 vacancies.
Congressional Relations Officer.—Nancy M. Carman, 205–3151.
Secretary.—Donna R. Koehnke.
Director, Office of External Relations.—Daniel F. Leahy, 205–3141.
Administrative Law Judges: Paul J. Luckern, 205–2694; Sidney Harris, 205–2692.
General Counsel.—Lyn M. Schlitt, 205–3061.
Inspector General.—Jane E. Altenhofen, 205–2210.
Director, Office of—
Administration.—Stephen A. McLaughlin, 205–3131.
Economics.—Robert A. Rogowsky (acting), 205–3216.
Equal Employment Opportunity.—Jacqueline A. Waters.
Finance and Budget.—Queen E. Cox, 205–3296.
Industries.—Vern Simpson, 205–3296.
Information Services.—Martin Smith, 205–3258.
Investigations.—William (Lynn) Featherstone, 205–3160.
Management Services.—Dave E. Spencer, 205–2720.
Operations.—Rober A. Rogowsky, 205–2230.
Personnel.—Michael J. Hillier, 205–2651.
Tariff Affairs and Trade Agreements.—Eugene A. Rosengarden, 205–2595.
Unfair Import Investigations.—Lynn I. Levine, 205–2561.

U.S. MERIT SYSTEMS PROTECTION BOARD

(Created by Public Law 95–454)

1120 Vermont Avenue, Room 800, 20419

phone (202) 653–8898, toll-free (800) 209–8960, fax 653–7130

Chairman.—Benjamin L. Erdreich, Room 826, 653–7101.
Vice Chairman.—Beth S. Slavet, 653–7103.
Member.—Antonio C. Amador, 653–7103.
Chief of Staff.—Anita L. Boles, 653–7101.
General Counsel.—Mary L. Jennings, 653–7171.

REGIONAL OFFICES

Regional Directors:
ATLANTA REGIONAL OFFICE: Covering Alabama, Florida, Georgia, Mississippi, South Carolina, Tennessee.—Thomas J. Lamphear, 10th Floor, 401 West Peachtree Street NW, Atlanta, GA 30308, (404) 730–2751, fax 730–2767.
CENTRAL REGIONAL OFFICE: Covering Illinois,Iowa, Kanas City, Kansas, Kentucky, Indiana, Michigan, Minnesota, Missouri, Ohio, Wisconsin.—Martin Baumgaertner, 31st Floor, 230 South Dearborn Street, Chicago, IL 60604–1669, (312) 353–2923, fax 886–4231.
Dallas Field Office: Covering Arkansas, Louisiana, Oklahoma, Texas.—Sharon Jackson, Chief Administrative Judge, Room 6F20, 1100 Commerce Street, Dallas, TX 75242–1001, (214) 767–0555, fax 767–0102.
NORTHEASTERN REGIONAL OFFICE: Covering Delaware, Maryland (except Montgomery and Prince Georges), Pennsylvania, New Jersey (except the counties of Bergen,

Essex, Hudson, and Union), West Virginia.—Lonnie L. Crawford, U.S. Customhouse, Room 501, Second and Chestnut Streets, Philadelphia, PA 19106–2904, (215) 597–9960, fax 597–3456.

Boston Field Office: Covering Connecticut, Maine, Massachusetts, New Hampshire, Rhode Island, Vermont.—William Carroll, Chief Administrative Judge, 99 Summer Street, Suite 1810, Boston, MA 02110, (617) 424–5700, fax 424–5708.

New York Field Office: Covering New York, Puerto Rico, Virgin Islands, the following counties in New Jersey: Bergen, Essex, Hudson, Union.—Arthur Joseph, Chief Administrative Judge, Room 3137, 26 Federal Plaza, New York, NY 10278–0022, (212) 264–9372, fax 264–1417.

WESTERN REGIONAL OFFICE: Covering California and Nevada.—Denis Marachi, Room 2800, 250 Montgomery Street, Suite 400, 4th Floor, San Francisco, CA 94104–3401, (415) 744–3081, fax (415) 705–2945.

Denver Field Office: Covering Arizona, Colorado, Kansas, Montana, Nebraska, Nevada, New Mexico, North Dakota, South Dakota, Utah, Wyoming.—Joseph H. Harman, Chief Administrative Judge, 12567 West Cedar Drive, Suite 100, Lakewood, CO 80228, (303) 969–5101, fax 969–5109.

Seattle Field Office: Covering Alaska, Hawaii, Idaho, Oregon, Washington, Pacific overseas.—Carl Berkenwald, Chief Administrative Judge, Room 1840, 915 Second Avenue, Seattle, WA 98174–1001, (206) 553–0394, fax 553–6484.

WASHINGTON REGIONAL OFFICE: Covering Washington, DC, Maryland (counties of Montgomery and Prince Georges, North Carolina, all overseas areas not otherwise covered), Virginia.—P.J. Winzer, Room 1109, 5203 Leesburg Pike, Falls Church, VA 22041–3473, (703) 756–6250, fax 756–7112.

U.S. PAROLE COMMISSION

5550 Friendship Boulevard, Room 420, Chevy Chase MD 20815, phone (301) 492–5990

Chairman.—Edward F. Reilly, Jr.

Vice Chairman and Chairman of the National Appeals Board.—Jasper R. Clay, Jr.

Commissioners:

Vincent (Vince) J. Fechtel, 492–5917; Michael J. Gaines, 492–5968.

Confidential Assistant to the Chairman.—Dawn M. Booze, 492–5990.

Case Operations Manager.—Tom C. Kowalski, 492–5952.

Deputy Director for Information System.—Sheldon Adelberg, Ph.D., 492–5980.

Executive Officer.—Judy I. Carter, 492–5974.

General Counsel.—Michael Stover, 492–5959.

REGIONAL OFFICES

Kansas City: Carol Pavilack Getty, 10220 North Executive Hills Boulevard, North Pointe Tower, Suite 700, Kansas City, MO 64153, 16) 891–7770.

Eastern Regional Office: John R. Simpson, 5550 Friendship Boulevard, Suite 420, Chevy Chase, MD 20815, (301) 492–5821.

U.S. POSTAL SERVICE

475 L'Enfant Plaza SW 20260–0010, phone (202) 268–2000

BOARD OF GOVERNORS

Chairman.—Tirso del Junco, M.D.

Vice Chairman.—Sam Winters.

Members:

Susan E. Alvarado
Michael S. Coughlin
LeGree S. Daniels
Einar V. Dyhrkopp
S. David Fineman
Bert H. Mackie
Ned R. McWherter
Robert F. Rider
Marvin Runyon

Secretary for the Board of Governors.—Thomas J. Koerber, 268–4800.

OFFICERS OF THE POSTAL SERVICE

Postmaster General.—Marvin Runyon, 268–2500.
Deputy Postmaster General.—Michael S. Coughlin, 268–2525.
Chief Operating Officer and Executive Vice President.—William J. Henderson, 268–4842.
Chief Financial Officer and Senior Vice President.—Michael J. Riley, 268–2454.
Chief Marketing Officer and Senior Vice President.—Allen R. Kane, 268–6990.
General Counsel and Senior Vice President.—Mary S. Elcano, 268–2950.
Vice Presidents:
Chief Postal Inspector.—Kenneth J. Hunter, 268–5615.
Consumer Advocate.—[Vacant]. 268–2281.
Controller.—M. Richard Porras, 268–5272.
Core Business Marketing.—Robert Krause, 268–3595.
Corporate and Legislative Affairs.—Larry M. Speakes, 268–2143.
Customer Relations.—John R. Wargo, 268–2222.
Diversity Development.—Robert F. Harris, 268–6566.
Engineering.—William J. Dowling, (703) 280–7001.
Facilities.—Rudoloph K. Umscheid, (703) 526–2727.
Human Resources.—Yvonne D. Maguire, 268–3783.
Information Systems.—Richard D. Weirich, 268–6900.
International Business.—James F. Grubiak, 268–3153.
Judicial Officer.—James A. Cohen, 268–2128.
Labor Relations.—Joseph J. Mahon, 268–3622.
Legislative Affairs.—[Vacant], 268–3733.
Marketing Systems.—John H. Ward, 268–5839.
Operations Support.—Nicholas F. Barranca, 268–5766.
Purchasing and Materials.—A. Keith Strange, 268–4040.
Quality.—Norman E. Lorentz, 268–6200.
Retail.—Patricia M. Gibert, 268–6965.
Strategic Initiatives.—Darrah Porter, 268–2870.
Tactical Marketing and Sales Development.—Gail G. Sonnenberg, (703) 526–2650.
Workforce Planning and Service Management.—James C. Walton, 268–5381.

U.S. RAILROAD RETIREMENT BOARD

844 North Rush Street, Chicago IL 60611–2092, phone (312) 751–4500, fax 751–4923
Office of Legislative Affairs, 1310 G Street Suite 500, 20005–3001
phone (202) 272–7742, fax 272–7728, http://www.rrb.gov/

Chairman.—Glen L. Bower, (312) 751–4900, fax 751–7193.
Assistants to the Chairman: Eric T. Wooden.
Labor Member.—V.M. Speakerman, Jr., (312) 751–4905, fax 751–7194.
Assistants to the Labor Member: Robert E. Bergeron, James C. Boehner, Geraldine Clark, Lawrence J. LaRocque, David D. Lucci, (202) 272–7742.
Management Member.—Jerome F. Kever, (312) 751–4910, fax 751–7189.
Assistants to the Management Member: Robert M. Perbohner; Joseph Waechter.
Inspector General.—Martin J. Dickman, (312) 751–4690, fax 751–4342.
General Counsel.—Catherine C. Cook, (312) 751–7100, fax 751–7102.
Deputy General Counsel.—Steven A. Bartholow, (312) 751–4935.
Director of Hearings and Appeals.—Dale G. Zimmerman, (312) 751–4793.
Director of Legislative Affairs.—Marian P. Gibson, (202) 272–7742, fax (202) 272–7728.
Librarian.—Kay G. Collins, (312) 751–4927.
Director of—
Programs.—Bobby Ferguson, (312) 751–4980, fax 751–4333.
Office of Operations.—Robert J. Duda, (312) 751–4698.
Policy and Systems.—John L. Thoresdale, (312) 751–4800.
Assessment and Training.—Catherine A. Leyer, (312) 751–4757.
Resource Management Center.—Martha M. Barringer, (312) 751–4812.
Field Service.—Ronald J. Dammon, (312) 751–4950.
Administration.—Kenneth P. Boehne, (312) 751–4930, fax 751–7197.
Chief, Benefit and Employment Analysis.—Marla Huddleston, (312) 751–4779.
Chief Financial Officer.—Peter A. Larson, (312) 751–4590.
Chief Information Officer.—[Vacant], (312) 751–4850.
Director, Bureau of—
Actuary.—Frank Buzzi, (312) 751–4850.

Personnel.—Charlene Kukla, (312) 751–4570.
Quality Assurance.—[Vacant], (312) 751–4760.
Supply and Service.—Henry M. Valiulis, (312) 751–4565.
Director, Office of—
Equal Opportunity.—Leo Franklin, (312) 751–4925.
Public Affairs.—William G. Poulos, (312) 751–4777.

REGIONAL OFFICES

Atlanta: Patricia R. Lawson, Suite 2304, 101 Marietta Street, Atlanta, GA 30323–3001, (404) 331–2691, fax (404) 331–7234.
Denver: Louis E. Austin, Suite 3300, 1999 Broadway, Box 7, Denver, CO 80202–5737, (303) 391–5864, fax (303) 844–0806.
Philadelphia: Richard D. Baird, Suite 670, 1421 Cherry Street, Philadelphia, PA 19102–1413, (215) 656–6947, fax (215) 656–6997.

U.S. SENTENCING COMMISSION

One Columbus Circle NE, Suite 2–500, South Lobby, 20002–8002

phone (202) 273–4500, fax (202) 273–4529

Chairman.—Richard P. Conaboy, (202) 273–4550.
Vice Chairmen:
Michael S. Gelacak, (202) 273–4570; Michael Goldsmith, (202) 273–4560.
Commissioners:
Wayne A. Budd, (202) 273–4560; Deanell R. Tacha, (202) 273–4570.
Commissioners, ex officio: Mary Frances Harkenrider, (202) 273–4560; Michael J. Gaines, (202) 273–4570.
Interim Staff Director.—John H. Kramer, (202) 273–4510.
Deputy Staff Director.—Paul K. Martin, (202) 273–4510.
General Counsel.—John R. Steer, (202) 273–4520.
Director of—
Training and Technical Assistance.—Sharon O. Henegan, (202) 273–4540.
Administration.—[Vacant], (202) 273–4610.
Policy Analysis.—Susan Katzenelson, (202) 273–4530.
Monitoring.—Elizabeth A. McGrath, (202) 273–4620.
Executive Assistant to the Chairman.—Timothy B. McGrath, (202) 273–4550.
Chief Deputy General Counsel.—Donald A. Purdy, Jr., (202) 273–4520.
Legislative Counsel.—Jonathan J. Wroblewski, (202) 273–4520.
Deputy Director of Training and Technical Assistance.—Susan L. Winarsky, (202) 273–4540.
Public Information Specialist.—Michael Courlander, (202) 273–4590.
Public Information (202) 273–4590.
Guideline Application Assistance HelpLine (202) 273–4545.

WASHINGTON METROPOLITAN AREA TRANSIT AUTHORITY

600 Fifth Street 20001, phone (202) 637–1234

General Manager.—Richard A. White.
Deputy General Manager for Operations.—Charles W. Thomas.
General Counsel.—Robert L. Polk.
Secretary.—Harold M. Bartlett.
Assistant General Manager for—
Finance and Comptroller.—Peter Benjamin.
Bus Service.—[Vacant].
Design and Construction.—Nuria I. Fernandez.
Human Resources.—Barbara A. Grier.
Public Service.—Gwendolyn A. Mitchell.
Rail Service.—Nancy Hsu.
Director, Office of—
Government Relations.—Deborah S. Lipman.
Public Affairs.—Leona Agouridas.

WASHINGTON NATIONAL MONUMENT SOCIETY

(Organized 1833; chartered 1859; amended by Acts of August 2, 1876, October, 1888)

740 Jackson Place 20503, phone (202) 842–0806

President Ex Officio.—William J. Clinton, President of the United States.

Vice Presidents Ex Officio.—The Governors of the several states.

First Vice President.—Russell E. Train, Chairman Emeritus, World Wildlife Fund, Suite 500, 1250 24th Street 20037.

Second Vice President.—James W. Symington.

Treasurer.—Henry Ravenel, Jr.,

Secretary.—Roger G. Kennedy, Director for National Park Service, Department of the Interior.

Assistant Secretary.—Edward F. Duffy, Jr., National Park Service.

Members:

Francis Addison, III
Vincent C. Burke, Jr.
Brice Clagett
Robert W. Duemling
Gilbert M. Grosvenor
Mrs. Potter Stewart
Richard P. Williams
C. Boyden Gray
George B. Hartzog, Jr.
John D.H. Kane
Albert James Redway, Jr.
John A. Washington

Members Emeritus:

Harry F. Byrd, Jr.
Samuel Spencer

WOODROW WILSON INTERNATIONAL CENTER FOR SCHOLARS

1000 Jefferson Drive SW 20560 (STB), phone 357–2429, fax 357–4439

(Under the direction of the Board of Trustees of Woodrow Wilson International Center for Scholars)

Director.—Charles Blitzer, 357–2763.

Deputy Director.—Manual F. Wells, Jr., 357–2185.

Deputy Director for Planning and Management.—Dean W. Anderson, 357–2842.

Board of Trustees:

Chairman.—Joseph H. Flom (esq.)

Vice Chairman.—Joseph A. Cari, Jr.

Public Members:

Madeline K. Albright, Secretary of State.
Richard W. Riley, Secretary of Education.
Donna E. Shalala, Secretary of Health and Human Services.
Sheldon Hackney, Chairman of the National Endowment for the Humanities.
I. Michael Heyman, Secretary of the Smithsonian Institution.
James H. Bilington, Librarian of Congress.
John W. Carlin, Archivist of the United States.
Joseph Duffey, Director of the U.S. Information Agency.

Private Members:

James A. Baker III
Steven Alan Bennett
Jean L. Hennessey
Kathryn Walt Hall
Daniel L. Lamaute
Eli Jacobs
Ual Hae Park
S. Dillon Ripley

JUDICIARY

SUPREME COURT OF THE UNITED STATES

One First Street NE 20543, phone 479–3000

WILLIAM HUBBS REHNQUIST, Chief Justice of the United States; born in Milwaukee, WI, October 1, 1924; son of William Benjamin and Margery Peck Rehnquist; married to Natalie Cornell of San Diego, CA; children: James, Janet, and Nancy, member of Faith Lutheran Church, Arlington, VA; served in the U.S. Army Air Corps in this country and overseas from 1943–46; discharged with the rank of sergeant; Stanford University, B.A., M.A., 1948; Harvard University, M.A., 1950; Stanford University, LL.B., 1952, ranking first in class; Order of the Coif; member of the Board of Editors of the Stanford Law Review; law clerk for Justice Robert H. Jackson, Supreme Court of the United States, 1952–53; private practice of law, Phoenix, AZ, 1953–69; engaged in a general practice of law with primary emphasis on civil litigation; appointed Assistant Attorney General, Office of Legal Counsel, by President Nixon in January 1969; nominated Associate Justice of the Supreme Court of the United States by President Nixon on October 21, 1971, confirmed December 10, 1971, sworn in on January 7, 1972; nominated by President Reagan as Chief Justice of the United States on June 17, 1986; sworn in on September 26, 1986.

JOHN PAUL STEVENS, Associate Justice of the Supreme Court of the United States; born in Chicago, IL, April 20, 1920; son of Ernest James and Elizabeth Street Stevens; A.B., University of Chicago, 1941, Phi Beta Kappa, Psi Upsilon; J.D. (magna cum laude), Northwestern University, 1947, Order of the Coif, Phi Delta Phi, co-editor, Illinois Law Review; married to Maryan Mulholland; children: John Joseph, Kathryn Jedlicka, Elizabeth Jane Sesemann, and Susan Roberta Mullen; entered active duty U.S. Navy in 1942, released as Lt. Commander in 1945 after WW II service, Bronz Star; law clerk to U.S. Supreme Court Justice Wiley Rutledge, 1947–48; admitted to Illinois bar, 1949; practiced law in Chicago, Poppenhusen, Johnston, Thompson and Raymond, 1949–52; associate counsel, Subcommittee on the Study of Monopoly Power, Judiciary Committee of the U.S. House of Representatives, 1951–52; partner, Rothschild, Stevens, Barry and Myers, Chicago, 1952–70; member of the Attorney General's National Committee to Study Antitrust Laws, 1953–55; lecturer in Antitrust Law, Northwestern University School of Law, 1950–54, and University of Chicago Law School, 1955–58; chief counsel, Illinois Supreme Court Special Commission to Investigate Integrity of the Judgment of *People* v. *Isaacs*, 1969; appointed U.S. Circuit Judge for the Seventh Circuit, October 14, 1970, entering on duty November 2, 1970, and serving until becoming an Associate Justice of the Supreme Court; nominated to the Supreme Court December 1, 1975, by President Ford; confirmed by the Senate December 17, 1975; sworn in on December 19, 1975.

SANDRA DAY O'CONNOR, Associate Justice of the Supreme Court of the United States; born in El Paso, TX, March 26, 1930; daughter of Harry A. and Ada Mae Wilkey Day; A.B. (with great distinction), Stanford University, 1950; LL.B., Stanford Law School, 1952; Order of the Coif, Board of Editors, Stanford Law Review; married to John Jay O'Connor III, 1952; children: Scott, Brian, and Jay; deputy county attorney, San Mateo County, CA, 1952–53; civilian attorney for Quartermaster Market Center, Frankfurt, Germany, 1954–57; private practice of law in Maryvale, AZ, 1958–60; assistant attorney general, Arizona, 1965–69; elected to the Arizona State senate, 1969–75; senate majority leader, 1974 and 1975; chairman of the State, County, and Municipal Affairs Committee in 1972 and 1973; also served on the Legislative Council, on the Probate Code Commission, and on the Arizona Advisory Council on Intergovernmental Relations; elected judge of the Maricopa County Superior Court, Phoenix, AZ, 1975–79; appointed to the Arizona Court of Appeals by Gov. Bruce Babbitt, 1979–81; nominated by President Reagan as Associate Justice of the U.S. Supreme Court on July 7, 1981; confirmed by the U.S. Senate on September 22, 1981; and sworn in on September 25, 1981; member, National Board of Smithsonian Associates, 1981–present; president, board of trustees, The Heard Museum, 1968–74, 1976–81; member:

Salvation Army Advisory Board, 1975–81, board of trustees, Stanford University, 1976–81, Board of Colonial Williamsburg Foundation, 1988 to present.

ANTONIN SCALIA, Associate Justice of the Supreme Court of the United States; born in Trenton, NJ, March 11, 1936; LL.B., Harvard Law School, 1960; note editor, Harvard Law Review; Sheldon fellow, Harvard University, 1960–61; married to Maureen McCarthy, September 10, 1960; children: Ann Forrest; Eugene, John Francis, Catherine Elisabeth, Mary Clare, Paul David, Matthew, Christopher James, and Margaret Jane; admitted to practice in Ohio (1962) and Virginia (1970); in private practice with Jones, Day, Cockley, and Reavis (Cleveland, OH), 1961–67; professor of law, University of Virginia Law School, 1967–74 (on leave 1971–74); general counsel, Office of Telecommunications Policy, Executive Office of the President, 1971–72; chairman, Administrative Conference of the United States, 1972–74; Assistant Attorney General, Office of Legal Counsel, U.S. Department of Justice, 1974–77; scholar in residence, American Enterprise Institute, 1977; professor of law, University of Chicago, 1977–82; appointed by President Reagan as Circuit Judge of the U.S. Court of Appeals for the District of Columbia Circuit; sworn in on August 17, 1982; appointed by President Reagan as Associate Justice of the U.S. Supreme Court; sworn in on September 26, 1986.

ANTHONY M. KENNEDY, Associate Justice of the Supreme Court of the United States, born in Sacramento, CA, July 23, 1936; son of Anthony James and Gladys McLeod Kennedy; married to Mary Davis, June 29, 1963; children: Justin Anthony, Gregory Davis, and Kristin Marie; Stanford University, 1954–57; London School of Economics, 1957–58; B.A., Stanford University, 1958; LL.B., Harvard Law School, 1961; associate, Thelen, Marrin, Johnson and Bridges, San Francisco, 1961–63; sole practitioner, Sacramento, 1963–67; partner, Evans, Jackson and Kennedy, Sacramento, 1967–75; professor of constitutional law, McGeorge School of Law, University of the Pacific, 1965–88; California Army National Guard, 1961; member: the Judicial Conference of the United States' Advisory Panel on Financial Disclosure Reports and Judicial Activities (subsequently renamed the Advisory Committee of Codes of Conduct), 1979–87; Committee on Pacific Territories, 1979–90 (chairman, 1982–90); board of the Federal Judicial Center, 1987–88; nominated by President Ford to U.S. Court of Appeals for the Ninth Circuit; sworn in on May 30, 1975; nominated by President Reagan as Associate Justice of the U.S. Supreme Court; sworn in on February 18, 1988.

DAVID HACKETT SOUTER, Associate Justice of the Supreme Court of the United States, born in Melrose, MA, September 17, 1939; son of Joseph Alexander and Helen Adams Hackett Souter; Harvard College, A.B., 1961, Phi Beta Kappa, selected Rhodes Scholar; Magdalen College, Oxford, 1963, A.B. in Jurisprudence, 1989, M.A., 1989; Harvard Law School, LL.B., 1966; associate, Orr and Reno, Concord, NH, 1966–68; assistant attorney general of New Hampshire, 1968–71; Deputy Attorney General of New Hampshire, 1971–76; Attorney General of New Hampshire, 1976–78; Associate Justice, New Hampshire Superior Court, 1978–83; Associate Justice, New Hampshire Supreme Court, 1983–90; member: Maine-New Hampshire Interstate Boundary Commission, 1971–75; New Hampshire Police Standards and Training Council, 1976–78; New Hampshire Governor's Commmission on Crime and Delinquency, 1976–78; 1979–83; New Hampshire Judicial Council, 1976–78; Concord Hospital Board of Trustees, 1972–85 (president, 1978–84); New Hampshire Historical Society, 1968–present, (vice-president, 1980–85, trustee, 1976–85); Dartmouth Medical School, Board of Overseers, 1981–87; Merrimack County Bar Association, 1966–present; New Hampshire Bar Association, 1966–present; Honorary Fellow, American Bar Foundation; Honorary Fellow, American College of Trial Lawyers; Honorary Master of the Bench, Gray's Inn, London; Honorary Fellow, Magdalen College, Oxford; Associate, Lowell House, Harvard College; nominated by President Bush to U.S. Court of Appeals for the First Circuit; took oath May 25, 1990; nominated by President Bush as Associate Justice of the U.S. Supreme Court; took oath of office October 9, 1990.

CLARENCE THOMAS, Associate Justice of the Supreme Court of the United States; born in Pin Point, GA (near Savannah), June 23, 1948; son of M.C. and Leola Thomas; raised by his grandparents, Myers and Christine Anderson; married to Virginia Lamp, May 30, 1987; son Jamal Adeen by previous marriage; attended Conception Seminary, 1967–68; A.B. (cum laude), Holy Cross College, 1971; J.D., Yale Law School, 1974; admitted to practice in Missouri, 1974; assistant attorney general of Missouri, 1974–77; attorney in the law department of Monsanto Company, 1977–79; legislative assistant to Senator John Danforth, 1979–81; Assistant Secretary for Civil Rights, U.S. Department of Education, 1981–82; chairman, U.S. Equal Employment Opportunity Commission, 1982–90; nominated by President Bush to U.S. Court of Appeals for the District of Columbia Circuit; took oath March 12, 1990; nominated by President Bush as Associate Justice of the U.S. Supreme Court; took the constitutional oath on October 18, 1991 and the judicial oath on October 23, 1991.

RUTH BADER GINSBURG, Associate Justice of the Supreme Court of the United States; born March 15, 1933, Brooklyn, N.Y., the daughter of Nathan and Celia Amster Bader; married Martin Ginsburg, 1954; two children: Jane C. and James S.; B.A., Phi Beta Kappa, Cornell University, 1954; attended Harvard Law School, 1956–58; LL.B., Columbia Law School, 1959; law clerk to Edmund L. Palmieri, U.S. District Court, Southern District of New York, 1959–61; Columbia Law School Project on International Procedure, 1961–62, associate director, 1962–63; professor, Rutgers University School of Law, 1963–72; professor, Columbia Law School, 1972–80; Fellow, Center for Advanced Study in Behavioral Sciences, 1977–78; American Civil Liberties Union, general counsel, 1973–80; National Board of Directors, 1974–80; Women's Rights Project, founder and Counsel, 1972–80; American Bar Foundation Board of Directors, executive committee, secretary, 1979–89; American Bar Association Board of Editors, 1972–78; ABA Section on Individual Rights and Responsibilities, council member, 1975–81; American Law Institute, council member, 1978–93; American Academy of Arts and Sciences, Fellow, 1982–present; Council on Foreign Relations, 1975–present; nominated by President Carter as a Judge, U.S. Court of Appeals for the District of Columbia Circuit, sworn in on June 30, 1980; nominated Associate Justice by President Clinton, June 14, 1993, confirmed by the Senate, August 3, 1993, and sworn in August 10, 1993.

STEPHEN G. BREYER, Associate Justice of the Supreme Court of the United States; born in San Francisco, CA, August 15, 1938; son of Irving G. and Anne R. Breyer; married Joanna Hare, 1967, three children: Chloe, Nell, and Michael; A.B., Stanford University, 1959; B.A., Oxford University, Magdalen College, Marshall Scholar, 1961; LL.B., Harvard Law School, 1964; law clerk to Associate Justice Arthur J. Goldberg of the Supreme Court of the United States, 1964–65; special assistant to the Assistant Attorney General (Antitrust), Department of Justice, 1965–67; Assistant Special Prosecutor of the Watergate Special Prosecution Force, 1973; Special Counsel of the U.S. Senate Judiciary Committee, Subcommittee on Administrative Practices, 1974–75; Chief Counsel of the U.S. Senate Judiciary Committee, 1979–80; Professor of Law, Harvard Law School, 1970–80; (assistant professor, 1967–70; lecturer, 1980–94); professor, Kennedy School of Government, Harvard University, 1977–80; Nominated by President Carter as a Judge, U.S. Court of Appeals for the First Circuit, sworn in on December 10, 1980; Chief Judge, 1990–94; member, U.S. Sentencing Commission, 1985–89; member, Judicial Conference of the United States, 1990–94; nominated Associate Justice by President Clinton May 13, 1994, confirmed by the Senate July 29, 1994, and sworn in on August 3, 1994.

Retired Members of the Court

WILLIAM J. BRENNAN, JR., Associate Justice of the Supreme Court of the United States (retired); born in Newark, NJ, April 25, 1906; son of William J. and Agnes (McDermott) Brennan; married to Mary Fowler, 1983; previously married to Marjorie Leonard, May 5, 1928 (deceased, 1982); children: William J., Hugh Leonard and Nancy; B.S. (with honors), Wharton School of Business, University of Pennsylvania, 1928; LL.B., Harvard Law School, 1931; associate, Pitney, Hardin and Skinner, Newark, NJ, 1931; member, 1937–42, and again 1945–49, firm name Pitney, Hardin, Ward and Brennan; major, later colonel, U.S. Army, specializing in manpower and personnel work, 1942–45, awarded Legion of Merit; appointed by Governor Driscoll, New Jersey Superior Court, 1949, served as assignment judge, Hudson County, to 1951; appointed to Appellate Division of that court, 1951; appointed by Governor Driscoll, associate justice of New Jersey Supreme Court, 1952; appointed as an Associate Justice of the Supreme Court of the United States by President Eisenhower, a recess appointment on October 15, 1956; sworn in on October 16, 1956; was nominated by President Eisenhower on January 14, 1957; the nomination was confirmed by the Senate on March 19, 1957; was given a new commission on March 21, 1957, and again took the oaths on March 22, 1957; retired on July 20, 1990.

BYRON RAYMOND WHITE, Associate Justice of the Supreme Court of the United States; born in Fort Collins, CO, June 8, 1917; son of Alpha Albert and Maude Burger White; elementary and high school, Wellington, CO; B.A., University of Colorado, 1938; Rhodes scholar, Oxford, England, 1939; officer, USNR, 1942–46; LL.B., Yale Law School, 1946; married to Marion Lloyd Stearns of Denver, CO, June 15, 1946; children: Charles Byron and Nancy Pitkin; law clerk to the Chief Justice of the United States, 1946–47; associate, Lewis, Grant, Newton, Davis and Henry (now Davis, Graham and Stubbs), 1947–50, partner, 1950–60; Deputy Attorney General of the United States, 1961–62; nominated Associate Justice of the Supreme Court of the United States by President Kennedy on April 3, 1962, confirmed by the Senate on April 11, 1962, and sworn in on April 16, 1962; retired June 28, 1993.

HARRY A. BLACKMUN, Associate Justice of the Supreme Court of the United States; born in Nashville, IL, November 12, 1908; son of Corwin M. and Theo (Reuter) Blackmun; A.B. (summa cum laude), Harvard College, 1929; LL.B., Harvard Law School, 1932; married to Dorothy E. Clark, June 21, 1941; children: Nancy Clark (Mrs. John C. Coniaris), Sally Ann (Mrs. Michael V. Elsberry), and Susan Manning (Mrs. William H. Brown); admitted to the Minnesota bar, 1932; law clerk to the Hon. John B. Sanborn, judge of the U.S. Court of Appeals for the Eighth Circuit, 1932–33; associate, junior partner and general partner, Dorsey, Colman, Barker, Scott and Barber and predecessor firms, Minneapolis, MN, 1934–50; occasional member of the faculties of St. Paul College of Law (now William Mitchell College of Law) and University of Minnesota Law School; resident counsel, Mayo Clinic and Mayo Association (now Mayo Foundation), and member of the Section of Administration, Mayo Clinic, Rochester, MN, 1950–59; nominated by President Eisenhower as judge of the U.S. Court of Appeals for the Eighth Circuit, succeeding the Hon. John B. Sanborn, August 18, 1959; confirmed September 14, 1959; sworn in on November 4, 1959; nominated associate justice by President Nixon April 14, 1970, confirmed May 12, 1970; sworn in on June 9, 1970; retired August 3, 1994; numerous honorary degrees; member, Judicial Conference Advisory Committee on Judicial Activities, 1969–79; representative of Judicial Branch, National Historical Publications and Records Commission, 1975–82, 1986–present; chairman of Faculty, Salzburg Seminar on American Studies (Law), July 1977, and member of the faculty, July 1989; participant, Franco-American Colloquium on Human Rights, Paris, France, December 1979; co-moderator, Seminar on Justice and Society, Aspen Institute, 1979–95, inclusive; Brandeis Medal, presented by Brandeis Honor Society, University of Louisville School of Law, 1983; University Citation, presented by Rutgers, The State University of New Jersey–School of Law/Newark, 1985; The Hebrew University Honorary Fellowship, presented at Jerusalem, 1986; Justice Award, presented by Justice Lodge of B'nai B'rith, Philadelphia, 1986; Public Service Award, presented by the Aspen Institute for Humanistic Studies, 1987; Presidents' Award, presented by American Society of Law and Medicine, 1987; UCLA Medal, presented by University of California at Los Angeles, 1989; Distinguished Contributions to Psychology and the Law Award, presented by the American Psychology-Law Society, 1990; Brandeis Medal for Distinguished Legal Service, presented by Brandeis University, 1990; Learned Hand Medal, presented by Federal Bar Council, New York, 1990; Award of Merit, presented by The Decalogue Society of Lawyers, Chicago, 1991; Award, Annual Survey of American Law, New York University School of Law, 1991; Laureate of the Lincoln Academy of Illinois, 1991; American Liberties Medallion, presented by the American Jewish Committee, 1992; Isaac Ray Award, presented by the American Psychiatric Association, 1992; co-moderator, Seminar on Constitutional Justice and Society, Aspen Institute, Italia, Rome, July 1986; visiting instructor on Constitutional Law, Louisiana State University Law School Summer Session at Aix-en-Provence, France, July 1986 and July 1992; visiting instructor on Constitutional Law, Tulane University Law School Summer Session at Berlin, July 1992. Harvard Law School Association Award, 1993; Public Service Award, American College of Obstetricians and Gynecologists, 1994; Madison-Jefferson Award, Americans United for Separation of Church and State, 1994; Association of Trial Lawyers of America, citation, 1994; Kansas City Metropolitan Bar Association Achievement Award, 1994; Blackmun Scholarship Foundation, established by Law Clerks to Justice Blackmun, 1994; Christopher Tietze Humanitarian Award, National Abortion Federation, 1995; Ehrmann Award, Massachusetts Citizen against the Death Penalty, 1995; Joseph Callaway Award for the Defense of Privacy, New York Civil Liberties Union, 1995; National Education Association Award, 1995; Harry A. Blackmun Scholarship of the Harvard-Radcliffe Club of Minnesota, 1995; Carrie Chapman Catt Lifetime Achievement Award presented by the League of Women Voters, 1995; Harry A. Blackmun Reproductive Freedom Award, Family Planning Council of Southeastern Pennsylvania, 1995; National Abortion Rights Action League Lifetime Achievement Award, 1995; Jefferson Award, American Institute for Public Service, 1995; Roger N. Baldwin Civil Liberties Award, New Jersey American Civil Liberties Union, 1995; Reproductive Freedom Award, Voters for Choice, 1995; Blackmun Fellowship, Center for Reproductive Law and Policy, New York City, 1995; William J. Brennan, Jr., Defense of Freedom Award, Libel Defense Resource Center, New York City, 1995; Lifetime Achievement Award, National Family Planning and Reproductive Health Association, 1996.

LEWIS FRANKLIN POWELL, Jr., Associate Justice of the Supreme Court of the United States (retired); born in Suffolk, VA, September 19, 1907; married to Josephine Pierce Rucker, 1936; children: Josephine McRae (Mrs. Richard Stowers Smith), Ann Pendleton (Mrs. Basil Terence Carmody), Mary Lewis Gwathmey (Mrs. Christopher James Sumner), and Lewis Franklin Powell III; B.S., Washington and Lee University, 1929, magna cum laude and Phi Beta Kappa; LL.B., 1931; LL.M., Harvard Law School, 1932; during World War II, served with U.S. Army Air Forces from 1942–46, including service in the European and North African theaters; 319th Bombardment Group, the 12th Air Force, and as Chief of Operational Intelligence for U.S. Strategic Air Forces in Europe; held rank from first lieutenant to full colonel; awarded Legion of Merit, Bronze Star, and France's Croix de Guerre with Palm; attorney, Hunton, Williams, Gay, Powell, and Gibson, Richmond, VA, 1935–71; general counsel, Colonial Williamsburg Foundation, 1957–71; member: National Commission on Law Enforcement and Administration of Justice, appointed by President Johnson, 1965–67; National Advisory Committee on Legal Services to the Poor, established pursuant to the Economic Opportunity Act of 1964; Blue Ribbon Defense Panel, appointed by President Nixon to study the Department of Defense, 1969–70; Virginia State Board of Education, 1961–69 (president, 1968–69); chairman: Richmond Public School Board, 1952–61, and special commission which wrote the charter introducing the manager form of government to the city of Richmond, 1947–48; member, Virginia Constitutional Revision Commission, 1967–68, which proposed the new constitution adopted by the State of Virginia in 1970; trustee emeritus of Washington and Lee University; chairman emeritus of Colonial Williamsburg Foundation; member: American Bar Association (president, 1964–65); American College of Trial Lawyers (president, 1969–70); and American Bar Foundation (president, 1969–71); honorary bencher, Lincoln's Inn, London; nominated by President Nixon as Associate Justice of the U.S. Supreme Court on October 21, 1971, confirmed by the U.S. Senate on December 6, 1971, and sworn in on January 7, 1972; retired on June 26, 1987.

ADMINISTRATIVE ASSISTANT TO THE CHIEF JUSTICE

James C. Duff.

OFFICERS OF THE SUPREME COURT

Clerk.—William K. Suter.
Librarian.—Shelley Dowling.
Marshal.—Dale E. Bosley.
Reporter of Decisions.—Frank D. Wagner.
Counsel.—Mary Ann Willis.
Curator.—Gail A. Galloway.
Budget and Personnel Officer.—Cyril A. Donnelly.
Public Information Officer.—Toni House.
Director of Data Systems.—Donna Clement.

UNITED STATES COURTS OF APPEALS

District of Columbia Judicial Circuit (District of Columbia).—Circuit Justice. *Chief Judge.*—Harry T. Edwards. *Circuit Judges:* Patricia M. Wald; Laurence H. Silberman; Stephen F. Williams; Douglas H. Ginsburg; David B. Sentelle; Karen LeCraft Henderson; A. Raymond Randolph; Judith W. Rogers; David S. Tatel. *Senior Circuit Judges:* Spottswood W. Robinson, III; James L. Buckley. *Circuit Executive.*—Linda Finkelstein Ferren, 273–0340; *Clerk.*—Mark J. Langer, 273–0310, E. Barrett Prettyman United States Courthouse, 333 Constitution Avenue NW, Washington, DC 20001.

First Judicial Circuit (Districts of Maine, Massachusetts, New Hampshire, Puerto Rico, and Rhode Island).—*Chief Judge.*—Juan R. Torruella. *Circuit Judges:* Bruce M. Selya; Michael Boudin; Norman H. Stahl; Sandra L. Lynch. *Senior Circuit Judges:* Bailey Aldrich; Frank M. Coffin; Levin H. Campbell; Hugh H. Bownes; Conrad K. Cyr. *Chief Judge, Bankruptcy Appellate Panel.*—Arthur N. Votolato, Jr. *Judges, Bankruptcy Appellate Panel:* James A. Goodman; James E. Yacos; James F. Queenan, Jr.; Carol J. Kenner; Enrique S. Lamoutte; Sara E. De Jesus; James B. Haines, Jr.; William C. Hillman; Joan N. Feeney; Mark W. Vaughn; Henry J. Boroff; Gerardo A. Carlo-Altieri. *Circuit Executive.*—Vincent Flanagan, (617) 223–9613. *Clerk.*—William H. Ng, 617–223–9057, John W. McCormack Post Office and Courthouse, 90 Devonshire Street, Boston, MA 02109–4590.

Second Judicial Circuit (Districts of Connecticut, New York, and Vermont). *Chief Judge.*—Jon O. Newman. *Circuit Judges:* Amalya Lyle Kearse; Ralph K. Winter, Jr.; John M. Walker, Jr.; Joseph M. McLaughlin; Dennis G. Jacobs; Pierre N. Leval; Guido Calabresi; Jose A. Cabranes; Fred I. Parker. *Senior Circuit Judges:* J. Edward Lumbard; Wilfred Feinberg; James L. Oakes; Ellsworth A. Van Graafeiland; Thomas J. Meskill; Richard J. Cardamone; Roger J. Miner; Frank X. Altimari. *Chief Judge, Bankruptcy Appellate Panel.*—Burton R. Lifland. *Judges, Bankruptcy Appellate Panel:* Robert L. Krechevsky; Alan H.W. Shiff; Tina L. Brozman; Francis G. Conrad; Stephen D. Gerling; Michael J. Kaplan; John Charles Ninfo, II; Jeffry H. Gallet; Carl L. Bucki; Adlai S. Hardin, Jr.; Robert E. Littlefield, Jr. *Circuit Executive.*—Steven Flanders, (212) 857–8700. *Clerk.*—George Lange III, (212) 857–8500, United States Courthouse, 40 Foley Square, New York, NY 10007–1581.

Third Judicial Circuit (Districts of Delaware, New Jersey, Pennsylvania, and Virgin Islands).—*Chief Judge.*—Dolores K. Sloviter. *Circuit Judges:* Edward R. Becker; Walter K. Stapleton; Carol Los Mansmann; Morton I. Greenberg; Anthony J. Scirica; Robert E. Cowen; Richard L. Nygaard; Samuel H. Alito, Jr.; Jane R. Roth; Timothy K. Lewis; Theodore A. McKee. *Senior Circuit Judges:* Collins J. Seitz; Ruggero J. Aldisert; Max Rosenn; Joseph F. Weis, Jr.; Leonard I. Garth. *Circuit Executive.*—Toby D. Slawsky, (215) 597–0718. *Clerk.*—P. Douglas Sisk, (215) 597–2995, United States Courthouse, 601 Market Street, Philadelphia, PA 19106.

Fourth Judicial Circuit (Districts of Maryland, North Carolina, South Carolina, Virginia, and West Virginia). *Chief Judge.*—J. Harrie Wilkinson, III. *Circuit Judges:* Donald Stuart Russell; H. Emory Widener, Jr.; Kenneth K. Hall; Francis D. Murnaghan, Jr.; Sam J. Ervin, III; William W. Wilkins, Jr.; Paul V. Niemeyer; Clyde H. Hamilton; J. Michael Luttig; Karen J. Williams; M. Blane Michael; Diana Gribbon Motz. *Senior Circuit Judges:* John D. Butzner, Jr.; James Dickson Phillips, Jr. *Circuit Executive.*—Samuel W. Phillips, (804) 771–2184. *Clerk.*—Patricia S. Connor, (804) 771–2213, United States Courthouse Annex, 1100 East Main Street, Richmond, VA 23219.

Fifth Judicial Circuit (Districts of Louisiana, Mississippi, and Texas).—*Chief Judge.*—Henry A. Politz. *Circuit Judges:* Carolyn Dineen King; E. Grady Jolly; Patrick E. Higginbotham; W. Eugene Davis; Edith Hollan Jones; Jerry E. Smith; John M. Duhe, Jr.; Jaques L. Weiner, Jr.; Rhesa H. Barksdale; Emilio M. Garza; Harold R. DeMoss, Jr., Fortunato P. Benavides; Carl E. Stewart; Robert M. Parker; James L. Dennis. *Senior Circuit Judges:* John Minor Wisdom; Reynaldo G. Garza; Thomas M. Reavely; Samuel D. Johnson, Jr.; Will L. Garwood. *Circuit Executive.*—Gregory A. Nussel, (504) 589–2730. *Clerk.*—Charles R. Fulbruge, III, (504) 589–6514, John Minor Wisdom United States Court of Appeals Building, 600 Camp Street, New Orleans, LA 70130.

Sixth Judicial Circuit (Districts of Kentucky, Michigan, Ohio, and Tennessee).—*Chief Judge.*—Boyce F. Martin, Jr. *Circuit Judges:* Gilbert S. Merritt; Cornelia G. Kennedy; David M. Nelson; James L. Ryan; Danny J. Boggs; Alan E. Norris; Richard F. Suhrheinrich; Eugene E. Siler, Jr.; Alice M. Batchelder; Martha Craig Daughtrey; Karen Nelson Moore; Ransey Guy Cole, Jr. *Senior Circuit Judges:* Anthony J. Celebrezze; Pierce Lively; Albert J. Engel; Damon J. Keith; Bailey Brown; Nathaniel R. Jones; Leroy J. Contie, Jr., Robert B. Krupansky; Harry W. Wellford; Ralph B. Guy, Jr. *Chief Judge, Bankruptcy Appellate Panel.*—Thomas F. Waldron. *Judges, Bankruptcy Appellate Panel:* Keith M. Lundin; Steven W. Rhodes; Randolph Baxter; David T. Stosberg. *Circuit Executive.*—James A. Higgins, (513) 564–7200. *Clerk.*—Leonard Green, (513) 564–7000, Potter Stewart United States Courthouse, 100 East Fifth Street, Cincinnati, OH 45202–3988.

Seventh Judicial Circuit (Districts of Illinois, Indiana, and Wisconsin).—*Chief Judge.*—Richard A. Posner. *Circuit Judges:* Walter J. Cummings; John L. Coffey; Joel M. Flaum; Frank H. Easterbrook; Kenneth F. Ripple; Daniel A. Manion; Michael S. Kanne; Ilana Diamond Rovner; Diane P. Wood; Terence T. Evans. *Senior Circuit Judges:* Thomas E. Fairchild; Wilbur F. Pell, Jr., William J. Bauer; Harlington Wood, Jr.; Richard D. Cudahy; Jesse E. Eschbach. *Circuit Executive.*—Collins T. Fitzpatrick, (312) 435–5803. *Clerk.*—Thomas F. Strubbe, (312) 435–5850, Everett McKinley Dirksen Building, 219 South Dearborn Street, Chicago, IL 60604.

Eighth Judicial Circuit (Districts of Arkansas, Iowa, Minnesota, Missouri, Nebraska, North Dakota, and South Dakota).—*Chief Judge.*—Richard S. Arnold. *Circuit Judges:* Theodore McMillian; George G. Fagg; Pasco M. Bowman, II; Roger L. Wollman; Frank J. Magill; C. Arlen Beam; James B. Loken; David R. Hansen; Morris S. Arnold; Diana E. Murphy. *Senior Circuit Judges:* Floyd R. Gibson; Donald P. Lay; Gerald W. Heaney; Myron H. Bright; Donald R. Ross; J. Smith Henley; John R. Gibson. *Chief Judge, Bankruptcy Appellate Panel.*—Frank W. Koger. *Judges, Bankruptcy Appellate Panel:* Robert J. Kressel; William A. Hill; Barry S. Schermer; Mary D. Scott; Nancy C. Dreher. *Circuit Executive.*—June L. Boadwine, (612) 290–3311. *Clerk.*—Michael E. Gans, (314) 539–3609, United States Court and Custom House, 1114 Market Street, St. Louis, MO 63101.

Ninth Judicial Circuit (Districts of Alaska, Arizona, California, Guam, Hawaii, Idaho, Montana, Nevada, Northern Mariana Islands, Oregon, and Washington). *Chief Judge.*—Procter Hug, Jr. *Circuit Judges:* James R. Browning; Mary M. Schroeder; Betty B. Fletcher; Harry Pregerson; Stephen Reinhardt; Cynthia H. Hall; Melvin Brunetti; Alex Kozinski; David R. Thompson; Diarmuid F. O'Scannlain; Edward Leavy; Stephen S. Trott; Ferdinand F. Fernandez; Pamela Ann Rymer; Thomas G. Nelson; Andrew J. Kleinfeld; Michael A. Hawkins; A. Wallace Tashima; Sidney R. Thomas. *Senior Circuit Judges:* Eugene A. Wright; Herbert Y.C. Choy; Alfred T. Goodwin; J. Clifford Wallace; Joseph T. Sneed; Otto R. Skopil, Jr.; Jerome Farris; Authur L. Alarcon; Cecil F. Poole; Warren J. Ferguson; Dorothy W. Nelson; William C. Canby, Jr.; Robert Boochever; William A. Norris; Robert R. Beezer; Charles E. Wiggins; John T. Noonan, Jr. *Chief Judge, Bankruptcy Appellate Panel.*—James W. Meyers. *Judges, Bankruptcy Appellate Panel:* Sidney C. Volinn; Robert Clive Jones; Lawrence Ollason; Barry Russell; Alfred C. Hagan; John E. Ryan. *Circuit Executive.*—Gregory B. Walters, (415) 556–6100. *Clerk.*—Cathy Catterson, (415) 556–9800, PO Box 193939, San Francisco, CA 94119–3939.

Tenth Judicial Circuit (Districts of Colorado, Kansas, New Mexico, Oklahoma, Utah, and Wyoming).—*Chief Judge.*—Stephanie K. Seymour. *Circuit Judges:* John C. Porfilio; Stephen H. Anderson; Deanell R. Tacha; Bobby R. Baldock; Wade Brorby; David M. Ebel; Paul J. Kelly, Jr.; Robert H. Henry; Mary Beck Briscoe; Carlos F. Lucero; Michael R. Murphy. *Senior Circuit Judges:* William J. Holloway, Jr.; Robert H. McWilliams; James E. Barrett; Monroe G. McKay; James K. Logan. *Chief Judge, Bankruptcy Appellate Panel.*—Mark B. McFeeley. *Judges, Bankruptcy Appellate Panel:* James A. Pusateri; Stewart Rose; Glen E. Clark; Richard L. Bohanon; John K. Pearson; Judith A. Boulden; Tom R. Cornish; Julie A. Robinson. *Circuit Executive.*—Robert L. Hoecker, (303) 844–2067. *Clerk.*—Patrick J. Fisher, (303) 844–3157, Byron White United States Courthouse, 1823 Stout Street, Denver, CO 80257.

Eleventh Judicial Circuit (Districts of Alabama, Florida, and Georgia). *Chief Judge.*—Joseph W. Hatchett. *Circuit Judges:* Gerald B. Tjoflat; R. Lanier Anderson, III; J.L. Edmondson; Emmett Ripley Cox; Stanley F. Birch, Jr.; Joel F. Dubina; Susan H. Black; Edward E. Carnes; Rosemary Barkett. *Senior Circuit Judges:* David W. Dyer; John C. Godbold; Paul H. Roney; James C. Hill; Peter T. Fay; Phyllis A. Kravitch; Frank M. Johnson, Jr.; Albert J. Henderson; Thomas A. Clark. *Circuit Executive.*—Norman E. Zoller, (404) 331–5724. *Clerk.*—Miguel J. Cortez, Jr., (404) 331–6187, Elbert P. Tuttle Court of Appeals Building, 56 Forsyth Street NW, Atlanta, GA 30303.

Federal Judicial Circuit.—Chief Judge.—Glenn L. Archer, Jr. *Circuit Judges:* Giles S. Rich; Pauline Newman; H. Robert Mayer; Paul R. Michel; S. Jay Plager; Alan D. Lourie; Raymond C. Clevenger, III; Randall R. Rader; Alvin A. Schall; William C. Bryson. *Senior Circuit Judges:* Wilson Cowen; Byron G. Skelton; Marion T. Bennett; Daniel M. Friedman; Edward S. Smith. *Clerk.*—Jan Horbaly, (202) 633–6570, National Courts Building, 717 Madison NW, Washington, DC 20439.

UNITED STATES COURT OF APPEALS

FOR THE DISTRICT OF COLUMBIA CIRCUIT

Room 5423 Courthouse, Third Street and Constitution Avenue 20001, phone 273–0310

HARRY T. EDWARDS, chief judge; born in New York, NY, November 3, 1940; son of George H. Edwards and Arline (Ross) Lyle; B.S., Cornell University, 1962; J.D. (with distinction), University of Michigan Law School, 1965; associate with Seyfarth, Shaw, Fairweather and Geraldson, 1965–70; professor of law, University of Michigan, 1970–75 and 1977–80; professor of law, Harvard University, 1975–77; visiting professor of law, Free University of Brussels, 1974; arbitrator of labor/management disputes, 1970–80; vice president, National Academy of Arbitrators, 1978–80; member (1977–79) and chairman (1979–80), National Railroad Passenger Corporation (Amtrak); Executive Committee of the Association of American Law Schools, 1978–80; public member of the Administrative Conference of the United States, 1977–80; International Women's Year Commission, 1976–77; American Bar Association Commission of Law and the Economy; coauthor of four books: *Labor Relations Law in the Public Sector, The Lawyer as a Negotiator, Higher Education and the Law,* and *Collective Bargaining and Labor Arbitration*; recipient of the Judge William B. Groat Alumni Award, 1978, given by Cornell University; the Society of American Law Teachers Award (for "distinguished contributions to teaching and public service"); the Whitney North Seymour Medal presented by the American Arbitration Association for outstanding contributions to the use of arbitration; and several Honorary Doctor of Laws degrees. Judge Edwards teaches law on a part-time basis; he has recently taught at Duke, Georgetown, Michigan, and Harvard Law Schools, and he is presently teaching a course in Federal Courts at N.Y.U; A.B.A.; married to The Honorable Mildred Matesich Edwards; children: Brent and Michelle; stepchildren: Jessica and Andrew Seidman; appointed to the U.S. Court of Appeals, February 20, 1980; serving as chief judge since September 15, 1994; office: 5400 U.S. Courthouse, Washington, DC 20001.

PATRICIA McGOWAN WALD, circuit judge; born in Torrington, CT, September 16, 1928; daughter of Margaret (O'Keefe) and Joseph McGowan; B.A., Connecticut College, 1948; Phi Beta Kappa; LL.B., Yale Law School, 1951; case editor, Yale Law Journal; Order of the Coif; law clerk, Judge Jerome Frank, U.S. Court of Appeals for the Second Circuit 1951–52: associate, Arnold, Fortas and Porter, Washington, DC, 1952–53; member, President's Commission on Crime in the District of Columbia, 1965–66; attorney, Office of Criminal Justice, Department of Justice, 1967–68; attorney, Neighborhood Legal Services Program, 1968–70; co-director, Ford Foundation Drug Abuse Research Project, 1970; attorney: Center for Law and Social Policy, 1971–72; Mental Health Law Project (litigation director, 1975–77), 1972–77; Assistant Attorney General for Legislative Affairs, Department of Justice, 1977–79; board of trustees, Vera Institute of Justice, 1965–72; American Law Institute (Council, 1978–present; Second Vice President, 1989–93; First Vice President 1993–present); Juvenile Justice Standards Project (IJA–ABA) joint commission member and Executive Commission 1973–77; board of governors, District of Columbia bar (Executive Committee, 1975–76), 1974–77; board of editors, American Bar Association Journal, 1978–84; Institute of Medicine, National Science Foundation, 1978–91; board of trustees, Ford Foundation (Executive Committee, 1975–77), 1972–77; Carnegie Council on Children, 1973–77; Exeter Academy, 1975–77; board of trustees, Connecticut College, 1976–77; Meyer Foundation, 1976–77; married to Robert L. Wald, 1952; children: Sarah, Douglas, Johanna, Frederica, and Thomas. Appointed to the U.S. Court of Appeals for the District of Columbia Circuit by President Jimmy Carter on July 26, 1979, and entered on duty July 31, 1979; served as chief judge July 26, 1986 to January 19, 1991.

LAURENCE HIRSCH SILBERMAN, circuit judge; born in York, PA, October 12, 1935; son of William Silberman and Anna (Hirsch); married to Rosalie G. Gaull, January 5, 1957; children: Robert Stephen, Katherine DeBoer Balaban, and Anne Gaull; B.A., Dartmouth College, 1957; LL.B., Harvard Law School, 1961. Admitted to Hawaii bar, 1962, District of Columbia bar, 1973; associate, Moore, Torkildson and Rice, 1961–64; partner (Moore, Silberman and Schulze), Honolulu, 1964–67; attorney, National Labor Relations Board, Office of General Counsel, Appellate Division, 1967–69; Solicitor, Department of Labor, 1969–70; Under

Secretary of Labor, 1970–73; partner, Steptoe and Johnson, 1973–74; Deputy Attorney General of the United States, 1974–75; Ambassador to Yugoslavia, 1975–77; President's Special Envoy on ILO Affairs, 1976; senior fellow, American Enterprise Institute, 1977–78; visiting fellow, 1978–85; managing partner, Morrison and Foerster, 1978–79 and 1983–85; executive vice president, Crocker National Bank, 1979–83; lecturer, University of Hawaii, 1962–63; board of directors, Commission on Present Danger, 1978–85, Institute for Educational Affairs, New York, NY, 1981–85, member: General Advisory Committee on Arms Control and Disarmament, 1981–85; Defense Policy Board, 1981–85; vice chairman, State Department's Commission on Security and Economic Assistance, 1983–84; American Bar Association (Labor Law Committee, 1965–72, Corporations and Banking Committee, 1973, Law and National Security Advisory Committee, 1981–85); Hawaii Bar Association Ethics Committee, 1965–67; Council on Foreign Relations, 1977–present; Judicial Conference Committee on Court Administration and Case Management, 1994–; Adjunct Professor of Law (Administrative Law) Georgetown Law Center, 1987–94; 1997; Adjunct Professor of Law (Administrative Law) New York University Law School, 1995–96; appointed to the U.S. Court of Appeals for the District of Columbia Circuit by President Ronald W. Reagan on October 28, 1985.

JAMES LANE BUCKLEY, circuit judge, born in New York, NY, March 9, 1923; son of William Frank and Aloise Josephine (Steiner) Buckley; married to Ann Frances Cooley, May 22, 1953; children: Peter, James, Priscilla, William, David, and Andrew; B.A., Yale University, 1943; Lt. (j.g.), U.S. Navy Reserve, 1943–46; LL.B., Yale, 1949; admitted to: Connecticut bar, 1949; District of Columbia bar, 1953; associate: Wiggin and Dana, New Haven, CT, 1949–53; Reasoner and Davis, Washington, DC, 1953–57; vice president, Catawba Corp., New York City, 1957–70; U.S. Senator, 1971–77; director, Executive Committee, Donaldson, Lufkin and Jenrette, New York City, 1977–78; business consultant, 1978–80; Under Secretary for Security Assistance, Science and Technology, U.S. Department of State, 1981–82; president, Radio Free Europe/Radio Liberty, Munich, West Germany, 1982–85; co-chairman, U.S. delegation to the United Nations Conference on the Environment, Nairobi, Kenya, 1982; chairman; U.S. delegation to the United Nations Conference on Population, Mexico City, 1984; appointed to U.S. Court of Appeals (District of Columbia Circuit) in December 1985; retired from active judicial service in September 1996.

STEPHEN F. WILLIAMS, circuit judge; born in New York, NY, September 23, 1936, son of Charles Dickerman Williams and Virginia (Fain); B.A., Yale, 1958, J.D., Harvard Law School, 1961. U.S. Army reserves, 1961–62; associate, Debevoise, Plimpton, Lyons and Gates, 1962–66; Assistant U.S. Attorney, Southern District of New York, 1966–69; associate professor and professor of law, University of Colorado School of Law, 1969–86; visiting professor of law, UCLA, 1975–76; visiting professor of law and fellow in law and economics, University Chicago Law School, 1979–80; visiting George W. Hutchison Professor of Energy Law, SMU, 1983–84; consultant to: Administrative Conference of the United States, 1974–76; Federal Trade Commission on energy-related issues, 1983–85; appointed to the U.S. Court of Appeals for the District of Columbia Circuit by President Ronald Reagan, June 16, 1986; member, American Law Institute; married to Faith Morrow, 1966; children: Susan, Geoffrey, Sarah, Timothy, and Nicholas.

DOUGLAS HOWARD GINSBURG, circuit judge; born in Chicago, IL, May 25, 1946; son of Maurice and Katherine (Goodmont) Ginsburg; married to Claudia DeSecundy, May 31, 1968 (divorced); one child, Jessica J.E. Lubow; married to Hallee Perkins Morgan, May 9, 1981; children, Hallee Katherine Morgan and Hannah Maurice Morgan; education: diploma, Latin School of Chicago, 1963; B.S., Cornell University, 1970 (Phi Kappa Phi, Ives Award); J.D., University of Chicago, 1973 (Mecham Prize Scholarship 1970–73, Casper Platt Award, 1972, Order of Coif, Articles and Book Rev. Ed., 40 U. Chi. L. Rev.); bar admissions: Illinois (1973), Massachusetts (1982), U.S. Supreme Court (1984), U.S. Court of Appeals for the Ninth Circuit (1986). Member: Mont Pelerin Society, American Economic Association, Executive Council of Antitrust Section of the American Bar Association (ex officio, 1985–86); law clerk to: Judge Carl McGowan, U.S. Court of Appeals for the District of Columbia Circuit, 1973–74; Associate Justice Thurgood Marshall, U.S. Supreme Court, 1974–75; previous positions: assistant professor, Harvard University Law School, 1975–81; Professor 1981–83; Deputy Assistant Attorney General for Regulatory Affairs, Antitrust Division, U.S. Department of Justice, 1983–84; administrator for Information and Regulatory Affairs, Executive Office of the President, Office of Management and Budget, 1984–85; Assistant Attorney General, Antitrust Division, U.S. Department of Justice, 1985–86; visiting professor of law, Columbia University, New York City, 1987–88; lecturer in law, Harvard University, Cambridge, MA, 1987–90; foundation professor of law, George Mason University, Arlington, VA, 1988–; Charles J. Merriam visiting scholar, senior lecturer, University of Chicago Law School, 1990, 1992, 1994, and 1996. Appointed to U.S. Court of Appeals for the District of Columbia

Circuit by President Ronald Reagan on October 14, 1986, taking oath of office on November 10, 1986.

DAVID BRYAN SENTELLE, circuit judge, U.S. Court of Appeals (District of Columbia Circuit); 273–0348; born in Canton, NC, February 12, 1943; son of Horace and Maude Sentelle; B.A., University of North Carolina at Chapel Hill, 1965; J.D. with honors, University of North Carolina School of Law, 1968; associate, Uzzell and Dumont, Charlotte, 1968–79; Assistant U.S. Attorney, Charlotte, 1970–74; North Carolina State District Judge, 1974–77; partner, Tucker, Hicks, Sentelle, Moon and Hodge, Charlotte, 1977–85; U.S. District Judge for the Western District of North Carolina, 1985–87; married to Jane LaRue Oldham; daughters: Sharon, Reagan, and Rebecca.

KAREN LECRAFT HENDERSON, circuit judge. [Biographical information not supplied, per Judge Henderson's request.]

A. RAYMOND RANDOLPH, circuit judge; born in Riverside, NJ, November 1, 1943; son of Arthur Raymond Randolph, Sr. and Marile (Kelly); two children: John Trevor and Cynthia Lee Randolph; married to Eileen Janette O'Connor, May 18, 1984. B.S., Drexel University, 1966; J.D., University of Pennsylvania Law School, 1969, summa cum laude; managing editor, University of Pennsylvania Law Review; Order of the Coif. Admitted to Supreme Court of the United States; Supreme Court of California; District of Columbia Court of Appeals; U.S. Courts of Appeals for the First, Second, Fourth, Fifth, Sixth, Seventh, Ninth, Eleventh, and District of Columbia Circuits. Memberships: American Law Institute. Law clerk to Judge Henry J. Friendly, U.S. Court of Appeals for the Second Circuit, 1969–70; Assistant to the Solicitor General, 1970–73; adjunct professor of law, Georgetown University Law Center, 1974–78; George Mason School of Law, 1992; Deputy Solicitor General, 1975–77; Special Counsel, Committee on Standards of Official Conduct, House of Representatives, 1979–80; special assistant attorney general, State of Montana (honorary), 1983–July 1990; special assistant attorney general, State of New Mexico, 1985–July 1990; special assistant attorney general, State of Utah, 1986–July 1990; advisory panel, Federal Courts Study Committee, 1989–July 1990; partner, Pepper, Hamilton and Scheetz, 1987–July 1990; appointed to the U.S. Court of Appeals for the District of Columbia Circuit by President George W. Bush on July 16, 1990, and took oath of office on July 20, 1990; chairman, Committee on Codes of Conduct, U.S. Judicial Conference, 1995.

JUDITH W. ROGERS, circuit judge, born in New York, NY; A.B. (with honors), Radcliffe College, 1961; Phi Beta Kappa honors member; LL.B., Harvard Law School, 1964; LL.M., University of Virginia School of Law, 1988; law clerk, D.C. Juvenile Court, 1964–65; assistant U.S. Attorney for the District of Columbia, 1965–68; trial attorney, San Francisco Neighborhood Legal Assistance Foundation, 1968–69; Attorney, U.S. Department of Justice, Office of the Associate Deputy Attorney General and Criminal Division, 1969–71; general counsel, Congressional Commission on the Organization of the D.C. Government, 1971–72; legislative assistant to D.C. Mayor Walter E. Washington, 1972–79; corporation counsel for the District of Columbia, 1979–83; trustee, Radcliffe College, 1982–90; member of Visiting Committee to Harvard Law School, 1984–90. Appointed by President Ronald W. Reagan to the District of Columbia Court of Appeals as an Associate Judge on September 15, 1983; served as chief judge, November 1, 1988 to March 18, 1994; member of Executive Committee, Conference of Chief Justices, 1993–94. Appointed by President William Jefferson Clinton to the U.S. Court of Appeals for the District of Columbia Circuit on March 11, 1994, and entered on duty March 21, 1994.

DAVID S. TATEL, circuit judge; born in Washington, DC, March 16, 1942; son of Molly and Dr. Howard Tatel; B.A., University of Michigan, 1963; J.D., University of Chicago Law School, 1966; instructor, University of Michigan Law School, 1966–67; associate, Sidley and Austin, Chicago, 1967–69; director, Chicago Lawyers' Committee for Civil Rights Under Law, 1969–70; associate, Sidley and Austin, 1970–72; director, National Lawyers' Committee for Civil Rights Under Law, 1972–74; associate and partner, Hogan and Hartson, 1974–77; director, Office for Civil Rights, U.S. Department of Health, Education and Welfare, 1977–79; partner, Hogan and Hartson, 1979–94; acting general counsel, Legal Services Corporation, 1975–76; lecturer, Stanford University Law School, 1991–92; past activities: board of directors, Spencer Foundation, 1987–97 (chair, 1990–97); Pew Forum on Education Reform; and National Board for Professional Teaching Standards; past memberships: Chicago Council of Lawyers, 1969–70; Mexican American Legal Defense and Educational Fund, 1975–77; Board of Governors, District of Columbia Bar Association, 1980–81; Mental Health Law Project, 1983–90; Refugee Policy Group, 1985–90; Washington Lawyers' Committee for Civil Rights Under Law, co-chair, 1986–87; National Lawyers' Committee for Civil Rights Under Law, co-chair, 1989–91; Disability Rights Council; awards: Stuart Stiller Foundation, Stuart

Stiller Memorial Award, March 1982; Center for Law and Social Policy, Allan Lebow Award, October, 1984; National Association of College and University Attorneys, Distinguished Service Award, June 1993; Lawyers' Committee for Civil Rights Under Law, Segal-Tweed Founders Award, June 1993; National Legal Aid and Defenders Association Award, May 1994; admitted to practice law in Illinois in 1966 and the District Columbia in 1970; married to the former Edith Bassichis, 1965; children: Rebecca, Stephanie, Joshua, and Emily; appointed to the U.S. Court of Appeals for the District of Columbia Circuit by President William Jefferson Clinton on October 7, 1994, and entered on duty October 11, 1994.

Retired Member of the Court

SPOTTSWOOD W. ROBINSON, III, senior circuit judge; born in Richmond, VA, July 26, 1916; son of Spottswood W., Jr., and Inez C. Robinson; B.S. (magna cum laude), Virginia Union University, Richmond, VA, 1937; J.D. (magna cum laude), Howard University, Washington, DC, 1939; LL.D., Virginia Union University, 1955; LL.D., Howard University, 1981; LL.D., Georgetown University, 1983; LL.D., New York Law School, 1986; married to Marian B. Wilkerson; children: Spottswood W., IV, and Nina Cecelia (Mrs. Oswald G.) Govan; admitted to Virginia Bar, 1943; member of faculty, School of Law, Howard University, 1939–48 (on leave 1947–48); practiced law in Richmond, VA, as a member of the firm of Hill and Robinson, later Hill, Martin and Robinson, 1943–55, and as sole practitioner, 1955–60; Dean of School of Law, Howard University, 1960–63; member of U.S. Commission on Civil Rights, 1961–63; vice president and general counsel, Consolidated Bank and Trust Co., Richmond, VA, 1963–64; member of American Bar Association, Virginia State bar (judicial member); Bar Association of the District of Columbia (honorary); Bar Association of the city of Richmond, VA (honorary), fellow, Virginia Law Foundation; nominated by President Kennedy as judge of the U.S. District Court for the District of Columbia on October 1, 1963; following adjournment of the Senate, received recess appointment as judge of said court under commission of President Johnson dated January 6, 1964, and took oath of office on January 7, 1964; nominated by President Johnson as judge of said court on February 3, 1964, confirmed by Senate on July 1, 1964, and took oath of office on July 7, 1964, under commission of President Johnson dated July 2, 1964; nominated by President Johnson as judge of the U.S. Court of Appeals for the District of Columbia Circuit on October 6, 1966, confirmed by Senate on October 20, 1966, and took oath of office on November 9, 1966, under commission of President Johnson dated November 3, 1966 (served as chief judge May 7, 1981 to July 25, 1986).

OFFICERS OF THE UNITED STATES COURT OF APPEALS FOR THE DISTRICT OF COLUMBIA CIRCUIT

Circuit Executive.—Linda J. Ferren.
Clerk.—Ron H. Garvin.
Chief Deputy Clerk.—Marilyn R. Sargent.
Chief Staff Counsel.—Mark J. Langer.

UNITED STATES COURT OF APPEALS

FEDERAL CIRCUIT

717 Madison Place 20439, phone 633–6550

GLENN LEROY ARCHER, JR., chief judge; born March 21, 1929, in Densmore, KS; son of Glenn L. Archer and Ruth Agnes Ford; educated in Kansas public schools; B.A., Yale University, 1951; J.D., with honors, George Washington University Law School, 1954; married to Carole Joan Thomas; children: Susan, Sharon, Glenn III, and Thomas; First Lieutenant, Judge Advocate General's Office, U.S. Air Force, 1954–56; associate (1956–60) and partner (1960–81), Hamel, Park, McCabe and Saunders, Washington, DC; nominated in 1981 by President Ronald Reagan to be Assistant Attorney General for the Tax Division, U.S. Department of Justice, and served in that position from December 1981 to December 1985; nominated in October 1985 by President Ronald Reagan to be circuit judge, U.S. Court of Appeals for the Federal Circuit. Assumed duties of the office on December 23, 1985 and became chief judge on March 19, 1994.

GILES SUTHERLAND RICH, circuit judge; born May 30, 1904, in Rochester, NY; son of Giles Willard and Sarah Sutherland Rich; education: public and private schools in Rochester, Horace Mann School for Boys in New York; S.B., Harvard College, 1926; LL.B., Columbia University School of Law, 1929; admitted to the New York bar and commenced practice in New York City in 1929; formerly married to Gertrude Verity Braun, 1931 (deceased); one daughter, Verity Sutherland (Verity S. Grinnell, M.D.); married, Helen Gill Field of Milton, MA and Washington, DC, 1953; practiced patent and trademark law in New York City as partner in the firms of Williams, Rich and Morse and Churchill; Rich, Weymouth and Engel; lecturer on patent law, Columbia University, 1942–56; adjunct professor of patent law, Georgetown University Law Center, 1963–69; honorary life member: Rochester, NY and Los Angeles Patent Law Associations; LL.D. (honoris causa), John Marshall Law School, Chicago, 1981 and the George Washington University, 1989; add Franklin Pierce Law Center, 1923; Columbia University School of Law's 1994 Medal for Excellence; member: American Bar Association, the Association of the Bar of the city of New York, New York Patent, Trademark and Copyright Law Association (past president), American Intellectual Property Law Association, Phi Delta Phi legal fraternity; appointed judge of the U.S. Court of Customs and Patent Appeals by President Eisenhower on July 19, 1956; assumed duties as judge on July 20, 1956; as of October 1, 1982, continued in office as judge of the U.S. Court of Appeals for the Federal Circuit, pursuant to section 165, Federal Courts Improvement Act of 1982, Public Law 97–164, 96 Stat. 50.

PAULINE NEWMAN, circuit judge; born June 20, 1927, in New York, NY; daughter of Maxwell H. and Rosella G. Newman; B.A. degree from Vassar College in 1947; M.A. in pure science from Columbia University in 1948; Ph.D. degree in chemistry from Yale University in 1952; LL.B. degree from New York University School of Law in 1958; admitted to the New York bar in 1958 and to the Pennsylvania bar in 1979; worked as research scientist for the American Cyanamid Co. from 1951–54; worked for the FMC Corp. from 1954–84 as patent attorney and house counsel and, since 1969, as director of the Patent, Trademark, and Licensing Department; on leave from FMC Corp. worked for the United Nations Educational, Scientific and Cultural Organization as a science policy specialist in the Department of Natural Sciences, 1961–62; offices in scientific and professional organizations include: member of Council of the Patent, Trademark and Copyright Section of the American Bar Association, 1982–84; board of directors of the American Patent Law Association, 1981–84; vice president of the United States Trademark Association, 1978–79, and member of the board of directors, 1975–76, 1977–79; board of governors of the New York Patent Law Association, 1970–74; president of the Pacific Industrial Property Association, 1978–80; executive committee of the International Patent and Trademark Association, 1982–84; board of directors: the American Chemical Society, 1973–75, 1976–78, 1979–81; American Institute of Chemists, 1960–66, 1970–76; member: board of trustees of Philadelphia College of Pharmacy and Science, 1983–84; patent policy board of State University of New York, 1983–84; national board of Medical College of Pennsylvania, 1975–84; board of directors of Research Corp., 1982–84; governmental committees include: State Department Advisory

Committee on International Intellectual Property, 1974–84; advisory committee to the Domestic Policy Review of Industrial Innovation, 1978–79; special advisory committee on Patent Office Procedure and Practice, 1972–74; member of the U.S. Delegation to the Diplomatic Conference on the Revision of the Paris Convention for the Protection of Industrial Property, 1982–84; awarded Wilbur Cross Medal of Yale University Graduate School, 1989, the Jefferson Medal of the New Jersey Patent Law Association, 1988, and the Award for Outstanding Contributions in the Intellectual Property Field of the Pacific Industrial Property Association, 1987; appointed judge of the U.S. Court of Appeals for the Federal Circuit by President Reagan and entered upon duties of that office on May 7, 1984.

H. ROBERT MAYER, circuit judge; born in Buffalo, NY, February 21, 1941; son of Haldane and Myrtle (Gaude) Mayer; educated in the public schools of Lockport, NY; B.S., U.S. Military Academy, West Point, NY, 1963; and J.D., Marshall-Wythe School of Law, The College of William and Mary in Virginia, 1971; editor-in-chief, *William and Mary Law Review,* Omicron Delta Kappa; admitted to practice in Virginia and the District of Columbia; board of directors, William and Mary Law School Association, 1979–85; served in the U.S. Army, 1963–75, in the Infantry and the Judge Advocate General's Corps; awarded the Bronze Star Medal, Meritorious Service Medal, Army Commendation Medal with Oak Leaf Cluster, Combat Infantryman Badge, Parachutist Badge, Ranger Tab, Ranger Combat Badge, Campaign and Service Ribbons; resigned from Regular Army and was commissioned in the U.S. Army Reserve, currently Lieutenant Colonel, retired; law clerk for Judge John D. Butzner, Jr., U.S. Court of Appeals for the Fourth Circuit, 1971–72; private practice with McGuire, Woods and Battle in Charlottesville, VA, 1975–77; adjunct professor, University of Virginia School of Law, 1975–77, 1992–94, George Washington University National Law Center, 1992–present; Special Assistant to the Chief Justice of the United States, Warren E. Burger, 1977–80; private practice with Baker and McKenzie in Washington, DC, 1980–81; Deputy and Acting Special Counsel (by designation of the President), U.S. Merit Systems Protection Board, 1981–82; appointed by President Reagan to the U.S. Claims Court, 1982; appointed by President Reagan to the U.S. Court of Appeals for the Federal Circuit, June 15, 1987; assumed duties of the office, June 19, 1987; Judicial Conference of the U.S. Committee on the International Appellate Judges Conference, 1988–91, Committee on Judicial Resources, 1990–present; married Mary Anne McCurdy, August 13, 1966; two daughters, Anne Christian and Rebecca Paige.

PAUL R. MICHEL, circuit judge; born February 3, 1941, in Philadelphia, PA; son of Lincoln M. Michel and Dorothy Kelley; educated in public schools in Wayne and Radnor, PA; B.A., Williams College, 1963; J.D., University of Virginia Law School, 1966; married Sally Ann Clark, 1965 (divorced, 1987); children, Sarah Elizabeth and Margaret Kelley; married Dr. Elizabeth Morgan, 1989; Second Lieutenant, U.S. Army Reserve (1966–72); admitted to practice: Pennsylvania (1967), U.S. district court (1968), U.S. circuit court (1969), and U.S. Supreme Court (1969); assistant district attorney, Philadelphia, PA (1967–71); Deputy District Attorney for Investigations (1972–74); Assistant Watergate Special Prosecutor (1974–75); assistant counsel, Senate Intelligence Committee (1975–76); deputy chief, Public Integrity Section, Criminal Division, U.S. Department of Justice (1976–78); "Koreagate" prosecutor (1976–78); Associate Deputy Attorney General (1978–81); Acting Deputy Attorney General (Dec. 1979–Feb. 1980); counsel and administrative assistant to Senator Arlen Specter (1981–88); nominated December 19, 1987 by President Ronald Reagan to be circuit judge, U.S. Court of Appeals for the Federal Circuit, confirmed by Senate on February 29, 1988, and assumed duties of the office on March 8, 1988.

S. JAY PLAGER, circuit judge; born May 16, 1931, son of A.L. and Clara (Matross) Plager; educated public schools, Long Branch, NJ; A.B., University of North Carolina, 1952; J.D., University of Florida, with high honors, 1958; LL.M., Columbia University, 1961; Phi Beta Kappa, Phi Kappa Phi, Order of the Coif, Holloway fellow, University of North Carolina; Editor-in-Chief, University of Florida Law Review; Charles Evans Hughes Fellow, Columbia University; married to Ilene H. Nagel; three children; commissioned, Ensign U.S. Navy, 1952; active duty Korean conflict; honorable discharge as Commander, USNR, 1971; professor, Faculty of Law, University of Florida, 1958–64; University of Illinois, 1964–77; Indiana University School of Law, Bloomington, 1977–89; visiting research professor of law, University of Wisconsin, 1967–68; visiting fellow, Trinity College and visiting professor, Cambridge University, 1980; visiting scholar, Stanford University Law School, 1984–85; dean and professor, Indiana University School of Law, Bloomington, 1977–84; counselor to the Under Secretary, U.S. Department of Health and Human Services, 1986–87; Associate Director, Office of Management and Budget, Executive Office of the President of the United States, 1987–88; Administrator, Office of Information and Regulatory Affairs, Office of Management and Budget, Executive Office of the President of the United States, 1988–89; circuit judge, U.S. Court of Appeals for the Federal Circuit, appointed by President George Bush, November

1989; member: Administrative Conference of the United States, vice-chair, National Commission on Judicial Discipline and Removal, Florida bar, Illinois bar; author of numerous articles and books.

ALAN D. LOURIE, circuit judge; born January 13, 1935, in Boston, MA; son of Joseph Lourie and Rose Hurwitz; educated in public schools in Brookline, MA; A.B., Harvard University, (1956); M.S., University of Wisconsin, (1958); Ph.D., University of Pennsylvania, (1965); and J.D., Temple University, (1970); married to the former L. Elizabeth D. Schwartz; children, Deborah L. Rapoport and Linda S. Lourie; employed at Monsanto Company (chemist, 1957–59); Wyeth Laboratories (chemist, literature scientist, patent liaison specialist, 1959–64); SmithKline Beecham Corporation, (Patent Agent, 1964–70; assistant director, Corporate Patents, 1970–76; director, Corporate Patents, 1976–77; vice president, Corporate Patents and Trademarks and Associate General Counsel, 1977–90); vice chairman of the Industry Functional Advisory Committee on Intellectual Property Rights for Trade Policy Matters (IFAC 3) for the Department of Commerce and the Office of the U.S. Trade Representative (1987–90); Treasurer of the Association of Corporate Patent Counsel (1987–89); President of the Philadelphia Patent Law Association (1984–85); member of the board of directors of the American Intellectual Property Law Association (formerly American Patent Law Association) (1982–85); member of the U.S. delegation to the Diplomatic Conference on the Revision of the Paris Convention for the Protection of Industrial Property, October–November 1982, March 1984; chairman of the Patent Committee of the Law Section of the Pharmaceutical Manufacturers Association (1980–85); member of the American Bar Association, the American Chemical Society, the Cosmos Club, and the Harvard Club of Washington; admitted to: Supreme Court of Pennsylvania, U.S. District Court for the Eastern District of Pennsylvania, U.S. Court of Appeals for the Third Circuit, U.S. Court of Appeals for the Federal Circuit, U.S. Supreme Court; nominated January 25, 1990, by President George Bush to be circuit judge, U.S. Court of Appeals for the Federal Circuit, confirmed by Senate on April 5, 1990, and assumed duties of the office on April 11, 1990.

RAYMOND C. CLEVENGER, III, circuit judge, born August 27, 1937, in Topeka, KS; son of R. Charles Clevenger and Mary Margaret Ramsey Clevenger; educated in the public schools in Topeka, Kansas, and at Phillips Academy, Andover, MA; B.A., Yale University, 1959; LL.B., Yale University, 1966; law clerk to Justice White, October term, 1966; practice of law at Wilmer, Cutler and Pickering, Washington, DC, 1967–90. Nominated by President George Bush on January 24, 1990, confirmed on April 27, 1990 and assumed duties on May 3, 1990.

RANDALL R. RADER, circuit judge; born April 21, 1949 in Hastings, NE, son of Raymond A. Rader and Gloria R. Smith; higher education: B.A., Brigham Young University, 1971–74, (magna cum laude), Phi Beta Kappa; J.D., George Washington University Law Center, 1974–78; married the former Sheryl Fluckiger, children: Larke, Samuel, Lisa, and Andrew. 1975–78: legislative assistant to Representative Virginia Smith; 1978–81: legislative director, counsel, House Committee on Ways and Means to Representative Philip M. Crane; 1981–86: General Counsel, Chief Counsel, Subcommittee on the Constitution; 1987–88, Minority Chief Counsel, Staff Director, Subcommittee on Patents, Trademarks and Copyrights, Senate Committee on Judiciary; 1988–90: Judge, U.S. Claims Court; 1990–present, Circuit Judge, U.S. Court of Appeals for the Federal Circuit, nominated by President George Bush on June 12, 1990; confirmed by Senate August 3, 1990, sworn in August 14, 1990, recipient: Outstanding Young Federal Lawyer Award by Federal Bar Association, 1983, bar member: District of Columbia, 1978, Supreme Court of the United States, 1984, U.S. Claims Court, 1988, U.S. Court of Appeals for the Federal Circuit, 1990.

ALVIN A. SCHALL, circuit judge; born April 4, 1944, in New York City, NY; son of the late Gordon W. Schall and the late Helen D. Rogers; preparatory education: St. Paul's School, Concord, NH, 1956–62, graduated *cum laude*; higher education: B.A., Princeton University, 1962–66; J.D., Tulane Law School, 1966–69; married to the former Sharon Frances LeBlanc, children: Amanda and Anthony. 1969–73: associate with the law firm of Shearman and Sterling in New York City; 1973–78: Assistant United States Attorney, Office of the United States Attorney for the Eastern District of New York, chief of the Appeals Division, 1977–78; 1978–87: Trial Attorney, Senior Trial Counsel, Civil Division, United States Department of Justice, Washington, DC; 1987–88: member of the Washington, DC law firm of Perlman and Partners; 1988–92: Assistant to the Attorney General of the United States; 1992–Present: Circuit Judge, United States Court of Appeals for the Federal Circuit, appointed by President George Bush on August 17, 1992, sworn in on August 19, 1992. Author: "Federal Contract Disputes and Forums," Chapter 9 in Construction Litigation: Strategies and Techniques, published by John Wiley and Sons (Wiley Law Publications), 1989. Bar memberships: State of New York (1970), District of Columbia (1980), Supreme Court of the United States (1989), U.S. Court of Appeals for the Second Circuit (1974), U.S. District Courts for the Eastern and Southern Districts of New York (1973), U.S. Court of Appeals for the District of Columbia Circuit (1991), United States District Court for the District of Columbia (1991), U.S. Court of Appeals for the Federal Circuit (1982), and U.S. Court of Federal Claims, formerly the U.S. Claims Court (1978).

WILLIAM CURTIS BRYSON, circuit judge; born August 19, 1945, in Houston, TX; son of William C. Bryson and Jeanne Sherrod; A.B., Harvard University, 1969; J.D., University of Texas School of Law, 1973; married to Julia Penny Clark; children: Alice and Ellen; law clerk to Hon. Henry J. Friendly, circuit judge, U.S. Court of Appeals for the Second Circuit (1973–74), and Hon. Thurgood Marshall, associate justice, U.S. Supreme Court (1974–75); associate, Miller, Cassidy, Larroca and Lewin, Washington, DC (1975–78); Department of Justice, Criminal Division (1979–86), Office of Solicitor General (1978–79, 1986–94), and Office of the Associate Attorney General (1994); nominated in June 1994 by President Clinton to be circuit judge, U.S. Court of Appeals for the Federal Circuit, and assumed duties of the office on October 7, 1994.

WILSON COWEN, senior judge; born near Clifton, TX, December 20, 1905; son of John R. and Florence (McFadden) Cowen; LL.B., University of Texas, 1928; married to Florence Elizabeth Walker, April 18, 1930; children: Wilson Walker and John Elwin; admitted to Texas bar in 1928; private practice in Dalhart, TX, 1928–34; county judge, Dallam County, TX, 1935–38; State director for Texas, 1938–40, and regional director, 1940–42, Farm Security Administration, region XII; commissioner, U.S. Court of Claims, 1942–43; assistant administrator, War Food Administration, 1943–44; returned to the Court of Claims as commissioner in 1945, and was designated chief commissioner in 1959; nominated by President Lyndon B. Johnson as chief judge, U.S. Court of Claims, June 16, 1964, and assumed duties of the office July 14, 1964; retired from active service as chief judge, March 1, 1977, and assumed status as senior judge; as of October 1, 1982, continued in office as senior judge of the U.S. Court of Appeals for the Federal Circuit, pursuant to section 165, Federal Courts Improvement Act of 1982, Public Law 97–164, 96 Stat. 50.

BYRON G. SKELTON, senior judge; born in Florence, Williamson County, TX, September 1, 1905; son of Clarence Edgar and Avis (Bowmer) Skelton; graduated from Clarendon Texas High School in 1923; student at Baylor University, Waco, TX, 1923–24; B.A. (1927), M.A. (1928), and LL.B. (1931), University of Texas, Austin, TX; married to Ruth Alice Thomas, November 28, 1931; children: Sue Helen (Mrs. Jerry Ramsey) and Sandra (Mrs. Robert T. Farrell); admitted to State bar of Texas in 1931; private practice of law in Temple, TX, 1931–42, 1945–66; county attorney of Bell County, TX, 1934–38; special assistant to the U.S. Ambassador to Argentina, 1942–45; city attorney of Temple, TX, 1945–60; admitted to practice before U.S. Circuit Court of Appeals (5th Circuit) (1937), U.S. Supreme Court (1946), Federal Communications Commission (1950), Tax Court of the United States (1952), U.S. Treasury Department (1952), Interstate Commerce Commission (1953); member: Bell-Lampasas-Mills Counties Texas Bar Association (past president), American Bar Association, American Law Institute, American Judicature Society; served on the Grievance Committee, Committee on Administration of Justice and Legislative Committee of the State bar of Texas; Phi Beta Kappa, Pi Sigma Alpha, Delta Theta Phi, and Sigma Delta Pi; appointed judge of the U.S. Court of Claims, August 17, 1966, confirmed by the U.S. Senate, October 20, 1966, and assumed duties of that office on November 9, 1966; retired from active service May 1, 1977, and assumed senior judge status; continued in office as senior judge of the U.S. Court of Appeals for the Federal Circuit, pursuant to section 165, Federal Courts Improvement Act of 1982, Public Law 97–164, 96 Stat. 50; office: W.R. Poage Federal Building, Temple, TX 76504.

MARION T. BENNETT, senior judge; born in Buffalo, MO, June 6, 1914; son of former Congressman Phillip Allen Bennett and Mary Bertha (Tinsley) Bennett; received A.B. degree from Southwest Missouri State University, 1935; J.D. degree, Washington University School of Law; St. Louis, MO (1938); received distinguished awards from both universities; married June Young of Hurley, MO, April 27, 1941; children: Ann and William Philip; admitted to Missouri Bar (1938); private practice of law, Springfield, MO, 1938–43; admitted to bar of the District of Columbia (1956); elected to U.S. House of Representatives (R), 6th District of Missouri, and served in the 78th, 79th, and 80th Congresses, 1943–49; appointed and served as a Commissioner, U.S. Court of Claims, 1949–64, when appointed Chief Commissioner of the Trail Division, serving until July 7, 1972; Colonel (ret.), USAFR, decorated, Legion of Merit; member: Reserve Officers Association, American Bar Association, District of Columbia Bar Association, National Council of the Federal Bar Association (1958–76), United States Association of Former Members of Congress; past president, Bethesda-Chevy Chase chapter of the National Exchange Club; former trustee and chairman (two terms) of the board, Chevy Chase United Methodist Church; nominated by President Richard Nixon as judge of the U.S. Court of Claims on May 22, 1972, confirmed by the Senate on June 28, 1972, and assumed the duties of that office from July 7, 1992 to October 1, 1982; circuit judge, U.S. Court of Appeals for the Federal Circuit, as of October 1, 1982; senior circuit judge as of March 1, 1986.

DANIEL M. FRIEDMAN, senior circuit judge; born New York, NY, February 8, 1916; son of Henry M. and Julia (Freedman) Friedman; attended the Ethical Culture Schools in New York City; A.B., Columbia College, 1937; LL.B., Columbia Law School, 1940; married to Leah L. Lipson (deceased), January 16, 1955; married to Elizabeth M. Ellis, October 18, 1975; admitted to New York bar, 1941; private practice, New York, NY, 1940–42; legal staff, Securities and Exchange Commission, 1942, 1946–51; served in the U.S. Army, 1942–46; Appellate Section, Antitrust Division, U.S. Department of Justice, 1951–59; assistant to the Solicitor General, 1959–62; second assistant to the Solicitor General, 1962–68; First Deputy Solicitor General, 1968–78; Acting Solicitor General, January–March 1977; nominated by President Carter as chief judge of the U.S. Court of Claims, March 22, 1978; confirmed by the Senate, May 17, 1978, and assumed duties of the office on May 24, 1978; as of October 1, 1982, continued in office as judge of the U.S. Court of Appeals for the Federal Circuit, pursuant to section 165, Federal Courts Improvement Act of 1982, Public Law 97–164, 96 Stat. 50.

EDWARD SAMUEL SMITH, senior judge; born in Birmingham, AL, March 27, 1919; son of Joseph Daniel Zadock and Sarah Jane (Tatum) Smith; educated in the public schools of Jefferson County, AL; Alabama Polytechnic Institute (now Auburn University), 1936–38 (mechanical engineering); B.A., University of Virginia, 1941, and LL.B., (now J.D.), University of Virginia Law School, 1947; admitted to the practice of law in Virginia, 1947, the District of Columbia, 1948, and Maryland, 1953; associate and partner, Blair, Korner Doyle and Appel, Washington, 1947–54; partner, Blair, Korner, Doyle and Worth, 1954–61; chief of the Trial Section (1961) and Assistant for Civil Trials (1962–63) Deputy Assistant Attorney General in the Tax Division, U.S. Department of Justice; partner and head of the tax department, Piper and Marbury, Baltimore, 1963–78 (managing partner 1971–74); enlisted USNR, June 1941, active duty September 1941; separated as lieutenant, USNR, February 1946 and retired as commander, USNR, July 1, 1968; member, American Bar Association, Section of Taxation (chairman, Committee on Cooperation With State and Local Bar Associations, 1972–74), Section of Litigation (chairman, Committee on Tax Litigation, 1977–78), Section of Corporation, Banking and Business Law, Section of Economics of Law Practice), Maryland State Bar Association (chairman, Section of Taxation, 1971–72), the Bar Association of the City of Baltimore, Baltimore Association of Tax Counsel, National Tax Association—Tax Institute of America, Federal Bar Association, the Bar Association of the District of Columbia, Virginia State bar, District of Columbia bar, permanent member Judicial Conference of the Fourth Circuit, and chairman, 1979 Court of Claims Judicial Conference; adjunct professor of law, Cumberland School of Law, Samford University, 1992–present; director, Roland Park Civic League, Inc., 1977–78; president, Saint Andrew's Society of Washington, DC, 1956–58; married to Innes Adams Comer, 1942 (deceased 1991); children: Edward S., Jr., and Innes Comer (Mrs. Ronald F. Richards); recommended for appointment to the U.S. Court of Claims by the U.S. Committee on Selection of Federal Judicial Officers and nominated by President Carter to be an associate judge, U.S. Court of Claims on June 30, 1978, confirmed by the U.S. Senate on July 26, 1978, commissioned July 28, 1978, and took the oath of office and assumed duties of the office on August 3, 1978; as of October 1, 1982, continued in office as judge of the U.S. Court of Appeals for the Federal Circuit, pursuant to section 165, Federal Courts Improvement Act of 1982, Public Law 97–164, 96 Stat. 50, assumed senior status June 1, 1989.

OFFICERS OF THE UNITED STATES COURT OF APPEALS FOR THE FEDERAL CIRCUIT

Clerk.—Jan Horbaly, 633–6550.
Chief Deputy Clerk.—[Vacant].
Administrative Services Officer.—Ruth A. Butler, 633–6588.
Senior Technical Assistant.—Melvin L. Halpern, 633–6564.
Librarian.—Patricia McDermott, 633–5871.

UNITED STATES DISTRICT COURT FOR THE DISTRICT OF COLUMBIA

E. Barrett Prettyman U.S. Courthouse, 333 Constitution Avenue 20001
phone (202) 273–0435, FAX 273–0326

JOHN GARRETT PENN, chief judge; born in Pittsfield, MA, March 19, 1932; son of John and Eugenie Heyliger Penn; married to Ann Elizabeth Rollison of Lenox, MA, May 7, 1966; children: John, Karen, and David; MA; A.B., University of Massachusetts (Amherst), 1954; LL.B., Boston University School of Law, 1957; admitted to the bars of Massachusetts, 1957 and District of Columbia, 1970; U.S. Army, first lieutenant, Judge Advocate General Corps, 1958–61; attorney, U.S. Department of Justice, Tax Division, 1961–70; trial attorney, 1961–65, reviewer, 1965–68, assistant chief, 1968–70; National Institute of Public Affairs Fellow, Woodrow Wilson School of Public and International Affairs, Princeton University, 1967–68; Awarded the Charles Hamilton Houston Medallion of Merit by the Washington Bar Association, May 1996; Member of the Judicial Council of the District of Columbia Circuit; Member of the Judicial Conference of the United States; appointed judge, Superior Court of the District of Columbia by President Richard Nixon, October 1970; appointed judge, U.S. District Court for the District of Columbia by President Jimmy Carter, March 23, 1979, and took oath of office, May 15, 1979; Chief Judge March 1, 1992.

NORMA HOLLOWAY JOHNSON, judge; born in Lake Charles, LA; daughter of H. Lee and Beatrice Williams Holloway; married to Julius A. Johnson of St. Louis, MO, June 18, 1964; B.S., University of the District of Columbia, 1955; J.D., Georgetown University Law Center, 1962; admitted to the bar of the District of Columbia, 1962; attorney, civil division, U.S. Department of Justice, 1963–67; Office of Corporation Counsel, District of Columbia, 1967–70; judge, Superior Court of the District of Columbia, 1970–80; appointed judge, U.S. District Court for the District of Columbia by President Jimmy Carter, May 12, 1980, and took oath of office, July 8, 1980.

THOMAS PENFIELD JACKSON, judge; born Washington, DC, January 10, 1937; A.B., Dartmouth College, 1958; LL.B., Harvard Law School, 1964; line officer aboard U.S. Navy destroyer, 1958–61; admitted to bars of District of Columbia (1965), Maryland (1966), and U.S. Supreme Court (1970); private practice of law in the District of Columbia and Maryland, with firm of Jackson and Campbell, P.C., 1965–82; president, bar association of the District of Columbia, 1981–82; fellow, American College of Trial Lawyers; appointed judge of U.S. District Court for the District of Columbia by President Ronald Reagan, June 25, 1982.

THOMAS F. HOGAN, judge; born in Washington, DC, May 31, 1938; son of Adm. Bartholomew W. (MC) (USN) Surgeon Gen., USN, 1956–62, and Grace (Gloninger) Hogan; married to Martha L. Wyrick (M.D.), July 16, 1966; one son, Thomas Garth; Georgetown Preparatory School, 1956; A.B., Georgetown University (classical), 1960; master's program, American and English literature, George Washington University, 1960–62; J.D., Georgetown University, 1966; St. Thomas More Fellow, Georgetown University Law Center, 1965–66; American Jurisprudence Award: Corporation Law; member: bars of the District of Columbia and Maryland; law clerk to Hon. William B. Jones, U.S. District Court for the District of Columbia, 1966–67; counsel, Federal Commission on Reform of Federal Criminal Laws, 1967–68; private practice of law in the District of Columbia and Maryland, 1968–82; adjunct professor of law, Potomac School of Law, 1977–79; adjunct professor of law, Georgetown University Law Center, 1986–88; public member, officer evaluation board, U.S. Foreign Service, 1973; member: American Bar Association, State Chairman, Maryland Drug Abuse Education Program, Young Lawyers Section, 1970–73, District of Columbia Bar Association, Bar Association of the District of Columbia, Maryland State Bar Association, Montgomery County Bar Association, served on many committees, National Institute for Trial Advocacy, Defense Research Institute; chairman, board of directors, Christ Child Institute for Emotionally Ill Children, 1971–74; member, The Barristers, The Lawyers Club, USDC Executive Committee; Conference Committee on Administration of Federal Magistrates System 1988–91; Chairman Inter-Circuit Assignment Committee, 1990–; appointed judge of the U.S. District Court for the District of Columbia by President Ronald Reagan on October 4, 1982.

STANLEY SPORKIN, judge; born in Philadelphia, PA, February 7, 1932; son of Hon. Maurice W. Sporkin (decreased), judge of the Court of Common Pleas, Philadelphia, PA, and Ethel Sporkin (deceased), married to Judith Sally Imber, September 30, 1955; children: Elizabeth Michael, Daniel Paul, and Thomas Abraham; A.B., Pennsylvania State University, 1953; LL.B., Yale University, 1957; member, Pennsylvania and Delaware bars, 1958, and the District of Columbia bar, 1963; admitted to practice before the Pennsylvania Supreme Court, 1958, Delaware Supreme Court, 1958, U.S. district court for the District of Columbia, 1963, U.S. Supreme Court, 1964, U.S. Court of Appeals for the Second Circuit, 1975, and U.S. Court of Appeals for the Fourth Circuit, 1978; law clerk to Hon. Caleb M. Wright, chief judge of the district court for the District of Delaware, 1957–60; law clerk to Hon. Paul Leahy, senior judge for the U.S. district court for the District of Delaware, 1960; practiced law as an associate in the firm of Haley Wollenberg and Bader, 1960–61; Securities and Exchange Commission, 1961–81 (staff attorney, Special Studies of the Securities Markets, 1961–63; Division of Trading and Markets, 1963; chief, Branch of Enforcement, 1963–66; chief enforcement attorney, office of enforcement, 1966–67; assistant director, enforcement, 1966–68; associate director, enforcement, 1968–72; deputy director of enforcement, 1972–74; director of enforcement, 1974–81); general counsel, Central Intelligence Agency, 1981–86; appointed judge of the U.S. District Court for the District of Columbia by President Ronald Reagan on December 17, 1985.

ROYCE C. LAMBERTH, judge; born in San Antonio, TX, July 16, 1943; son of Nell Elizabeth Synder and Larimore S. Lamberth, Sr.; married Janis Kay Jost, June 17, 1979; South San Antonio High School, 1961; B.A., University of Texas at Austin, 1966; LL.B., University of Texas School of Law, 1967; permanent president, class of 1967, University of Texas School of Law; 1967–74, U.S. Army (Captain, Judge Advocate General's Corps, 1968–74; Vietnam Service Medal, Air Medal, Bronze Star with Oak Leaf Cluster, Meritorious Service Medal with Oak Leaf Cluster); 1974–87, assistant U.S. attorney, District of Columbia (chief, civil division, 1978–87); President's Reorganization Project, Federal Legal Representation Study, 1978–79; honorary faculty, Army Judge Advocate General's School, 1976; Attorney General's Special Commendation Award; Attorney General's John Marshall Award, 1982; vice chairman, Armed Services and Veterans Affairs Committee, Section on Administrative Law, American Bar Association, 1979–82, chairman, 1983–84; chairman, Professional Ethics Committee, 1989–91; co-chairman, Committee of Article III Judges, Judiciary Section 1989–present; chairman, Federal Litigation Section, 1986–87; chairman, Federal Rules Committee, 1985–86; deputy chairman, Council of the Federal Lawyer, 1980–83; chairman, Career Service Committee, Federal Bar Association, 1978–80; appointed judge, U.S. District Court for the District of Columbia by President Ronald Reagan, November 16, 1987.

* * *

GLADYS KESSLER, judge, born in New York, NY, January 22, 1938; Education: B.A., Cornell University, 1959; LL.B. Harvard Law School, 1962; member: American Judicature Society (board of directors, 1985–89); National Center for State Courts (board of directors, 1984–87); National Association of Women Judges (president, 1979–81); Women Judges' Fund for Justice, (president, 1980–82); Fellows of the American Bar Foundation; President's Council of Cornell Women; American Law Institute; American Bar Association—committees: Alternative Dispute Resolution, Bioethics and AIDS; private law practice—partner, Roisman, Kessler and Cashdan, 1969–77; associate judge, Superior Court of the District of Columbia, 1977–94; court administrative activites: District of Columbia Courts Joint Committee on Judicial Administration, 1989–94; Domestic Violence Coordinating Council (chairperson, 1993–94); Multi-Door Dispute Resolution Program (supervising judge, 1985–90); family division, D.C. Superior Court (presiding judge, 1981–85); appointed judge, U.S. District Court for the District of Columbia by President Bill Clinton, June 16, 1994, and took oath of office, July 18, 1994.

PAUL L. FRIEDMAN, judge, born in Buffalo, NY, February 20, 1944; son of Cecil A. and Charlotte Wagner Friedman; married to Elizabeth Ann Zicherman, May 25, 1975; education: B.A. (political science), Cornell University, 1965; J.D., *cum laude,* School of Law, State University of New York at Buffalo, 1968; admitted to the bars of the District of Columbia, New York, U.S. Supreme Court, and U.S. Courts of Appeals for the D.C., Federal, Fourth, Fifth, Sixth, Seventh, Ninth and Eleventh Circuits; Law Clerk to Judge Aubrey E. Robinson, Jr., U.S. district court for the District of Columbia, 1968–69; Law Clerk to Judge Roger Robb, U.S. Court of Appeals for the District of Columbia Circuit, 1969–70; Assistant U.S. Attorney for the District of Columbia, 1970–74; assistant to the Solicitor General of the United States, 1974–76; associate independent counsel, Iran-Contra investigation, 1987–88, private law practice, White and Case (partner, 1979–94; associate, 1976–79); member: American Bar Association, District of Columbia bar (president, 1986–

87), American Law Institute, American Academy of Appellate Lawyers, Bar Association of the District of Columbia, Women's Bar Association of the District of Columbia, Washington Bar Association, Hispanic Bar Association, Assistant United States Attorneys Association of the District of Columbia (president, 1976–77), Civil Justice Reform Act Advisory Group (chair, 1991–94), District of Columbia Judicial Nomination Commission (member, 1990–94; chair, 1992–94), Advisory Committee on Procedures, U.S. Court of Appeals for the D.C. Circuit (1982–88), Grievance Committee; U.S. District Court for the District of Columbia (member, 1981–87; chair, 1983–85); fellow, American College of Trial Lawyers; fellow, American Bar Foundation; board of directors: Frederick B. Abramson Memorial Foundation (president, 1991–94), Washington Area Lawyers for the Arts (1988–92), Washington Legal Clinic for the Homeless (member, 1987–92; vice-president 1988–91), Stuart Stiller Memorial Foundation (1980–94), American Judicatur Society (1990–94), District of Columbia Public Defender Service (1989–92); member: Cosmos Club, Lawyers Club of Washington; appointed judge, U.S. District Court for the District of Columbia by President William Clinton, June 16, 1994, and took oath of office August 1, 1994.

RICARDO M. URBINA, judge; 51, sits on the United States District Court for the District of Columbia; born of an Honduran father and Puerto Rican mother in Manhattan, New York; attended Georgetown University and Georgetown Law Center before working as a staff attorney with the D.C. Public Defender Service; after a period of private practice with an emphasis on commerical litigation, joined the faculty of Howard University School of Law, directed the university's criminal justice clinic and taught criminal law, criminal procedure and torts; voted Professor of the Year by the Howard Law School student body, 1978; nominated to the D.C. Superior Court by President Carter, 1980; appointed to the bench as President Reagan's first presidential judicial appointment and the first Hispanic judge in the history of the District of Columbia, 1981; during his thirteen years on the Superior Court, Judge Urbina served as Chief Presiding Judge of the Family Division for three years and chaired the committee that drafted the Child Support Guidelines later adopted as the District of Columbia's child support law; managed a criminal calendar 1989–90 that consisted exclusively of first degree murder, rape and child molestation cases; designated by the Chief Judge to handle a special calendar consisting of complex civil litigation; twice recognized by the United States Department of Health and Human Services for his work with children and families; selected one of the Washingtonians of the Year by *Washington Magazine,* 1986; received Hugh Johnson Memorial Award for his many contributions to "...the creation of harmony among diverse elements of the community and the bar by D.C. Hispanic Bar Association;" received the Hispanic National Bar Association's 1993 award for demonstrated commitment to the "Preservation of Civil and Constitutional Rights of All Americans", and the 1995 NBC-Hispanic Magazine National VIDA Award in recognition of lifetime community service; adjunct professor at the George Washington University Law School since 1993; served as a visting instructor of trial advocacy at the Harvard Law School, 1996–97; appointment by President Clinton to the U.S. District Court for the District of Columbia in 1994 made him the first Latino ever appointed to the federal bench in Washington, D.C. Bar Association, 1994; appointed by Chief Justice Rehnquist to serve on the Federal Judicial Conference Committee on Security, Space and Facilities, 1997.

EMMET G. SULLIVAN, judge; born in Washington, DC, to Emmet A. Sullivan and the late Eileen G. Sullivan; graduated McKinley High School, 1964; B.A., Howard University, 1968; J.D., Howard University Law School, 1971; married to Nan Sullivan; two sons, Emmett and Erik; law clerk to Judge James A. Washington, Jr.; joined the law firm of Houston and Gardner, 1973–80, became a partner; thereafter was a partner with Houston, Sullivan and Gardner; board of directors of the D.C. Law Students in Court Program; D.C. Judicial Conference Voluntary Arbitration Committee; Nominating Committee of the Bar Association of the District of Columbia; U.S. District Court Committee on Grievances; adjunct professor at Howard University School of Law; member: National Bar Association, Washington Bar Association, Lawyer's Club, Bar Association of the District of Columbia, The Fellows of the American Bar Foundation, and the American Bar Association; appointed by President Reagan to the Superior Court of the District of Columbia as an associate judge, 1984; deputy presiding judge and presiding judge of the probate and tax division; chairperson of the rules committees for the probate and tax divisions; member: Court Rules Committee and the Jury Plan Committee; appointed by President George Bush to serve as an associate judge of the District of Columbia Court of Appeals, 1991; chairperson for the nineteenth annual judicial conference of the District of Columbia, 1994; appointed by chief judge Wagner, to chair the "Task Force on Families and Violence for the District of Columbia Courts"; nominated to the U.S. District Court by President William Clinton on March 22, 1994; and confirmed by the U.S. Senate on June 15, 1994.

JAMES ROBERTSON, judge; born in Cleveland, OH; May 18, 1938; son of Frederick Irving and Doris (Byars) Robertson; married to Berit Selma Persson of Ange, Sweden, September 19, 1959; children: Stephen, Catherine, and Peter; educated at Western Reserve Academy, Hudson, OH; A.B., Princeton University, 1959 (Woodrow Wilson School); served as an officer in the U.S. Navy, on destroyers and in the Office of Naval Intelligence, 1959–64; LL.B., George Washington University, 1965 (editor-in-chief, George Washington Law Review); admitted to the bar of the District of Columbia, 1966; associate, Wilmer, Cutler and Pickering, 1965–69; chief counsel, litigation office, Lawyers' Committee for Civil Rights Under Law, Jackson, MS, 1969–70; executive director, Lawyers' Committee for Civil Rights Under Law, Washington, DC, 1971–72; partner, Wilmer, Cutler and Pickering, 1973–94; co-chair, Lawyers' Committee for Civil Rights Under Law, 1985–87, president, Southern Africa Legal Services and Legal Education Project, Inc., 1989–94; president, District of Columbia bar, 1991–92; fellow, American College of trial Lawyers; fellow, American Bar Foundation; appointed U.S. District Judge for the District of Columbia by President Clinton on October 11, 1994 and took oath of office on December 31, 1994.

COLLEEN KOLLAR-KOTELLEY, judge; born in New York City; daughter of Konstantine and Irene Kollar; married to John Kotelly; attended billingual schools in Mexico, Ecuador and Venezualla, and Georgetwon Visitation Preparatory School in Washington, D.C.; received B.A. degree in English at Catholic University (Delta Epsilon Honor Society); received J.D. at Catholic University's Columbus School of Law (Moot Court Board of Governors); law clerk to Hon. Catherine B. Kelly, District of Columbia Court of Appeals, 1968–69; attorney, United States Department of Justice, Criminal Division, Appellate Section (1969–72); chief legal counsel, Saint Elizabeth's Hospital, Department of Health and Human Services, 1972–84; received Saint Elizabeth's Hospital Certificate of Appreciation, 1981; Meritorious Achievement Award from Alcohol, Drug Abuse and Mental Health Administration (ADAMHA), Department of Health and Human Services, 1981, appointed judge, Superior Court of the District of Columbia by President Ronald Reagan, October 3, 1984, took oath of office October 21, 1984; served as Deputy Presiding Judge, Criminial Division, January 1996–April 1997; received Achievement Recognition Award, Hispanic Heritage CORO Awards Celebration, 1996; appointed judge, U.S. District Court for the District of Columbia by President William Jefferson Clinton on March 26, 1997, took oath of office May 12, 1997.

OLIVER GASCH, senior judge; born in Washington, DC, May 4, 1906; son of Herman E. and Marie (Manning) Gasch; married Sylvia Meyer of Washington, DC; one son, Michael Barrett Gasch; A.B., Princeton University, 1928; LL.B., George Washington University Law School, 1932; admitted to the bar of the District of Columbia, 1931; private practice, 1931–37; assistant corporation counsel, District of Columbia 1937–53; principal assistant, U.S. attorney, 1953–56; U.S. attorney for the District of Columbia, 1956–61; partner, Craighill, Aiello, Gasch and Craighill, 1961–65; appointed judge of the U.S. District Court for the District of Columbia by President Johnson and entered upon the duties of that office August 16, 1965; presiding judge, special panel, Regional Rail Reorganization Court; member, general panel, Regional Rail Reorganization Court; president, District of Columbia Bar Association, 1964–65; member, House of Delegates, American Bar Association, 1964–65; fellow, American College of Trial Lawyers; American Law Institute; fellow, American Bar Foundation; chairman, Committee of the General Counsel, Federal Bar Association; the Barristers (past president); the Lawyers Club; the National Lawyers Club; the Counsellors Club; member, Phi Delta Phi Legal Fraternity; Order of the Coif; general counsel, Interstate Commission on Potomac River 1940–60; US Army, 1942–46, (separated as lieutenant colonel).

WILLIAM BENSON BRYANT, senior judge; born Wetumpka, AL, September 18, 1911; son of Benson and Alberta Bryant; married to Astaire A. Gonzalez, August 25, 1934; children: Astaire and William, Jr.; A.B., Howard University, 1932; LL.B., Howard University Law School, 1936; served in U.S. Army, World War II, 1943–47; member of the bar of the District of Columbia and of the Supreme Court of the United States; assistant U.S. attorney for the District of Columbia, 1951–54; private practice of law in District of Columbia as partner in firm of Houston, Bryant and Gardner, 1954–65; member: Committee on Admissions and Grievances of U.S. District Court for District of Columbia, 1959–65; District of Columbia Board of Appeals and Review, District of Columbia Special Police Trial Board, American Bar Association, National Lawyers' Club (honorary); appointed judge of the U.S. District Court for the District of Columbia Circuit by President Lyndon B. Johnson on July 11, 1965, and entered upon the duties of that office on August 16, 1965; served as chief judge, 1977–81; took senior judge status on January 31, 1982.

AUBREY E. ROBINSON, Jr., senior judge; born in Madison, NJ, March 30, 1922; son of Aubrey E. and Mabel J. Robinson; married to Sara E. Payne (deceased), December 31,

1946; children: Paula Elaine Collins and Sheryl Louise; married to Doris A. Washington, March 17, 1973; B.A., Cornell University, 1943; LL.B., Cornell Law School, 1947; served in the U.S. Army, 1943–46; member of the bars of the State of New York and the District of Columbia; private practice of law in the District of Columbia, 1948–65; board of trustees, United Planning Organization, 1963–66; board of directors: Family Service Association of America, 1958–67; Family and Child Services of Washington, DC, 1954–63; Washington Action for Youth, 1962–64; District of Columbia Public Welfare Advisory Council, 1963–65; Eugene and Agnes E. Meyer Foundation, 1969–85; Consortium of Universities of the Washington Metropolitan Area, 1969–74; American Bar Association Advisory Committee on Judges' Function, 1970–72; American Bar Association Committee on Courts and the Community, 1972–78; Judicial Conference Committee on Court Facilities and Design, 1971–78; chairman, National Conference of Federal Trial Judges, 1973–74; Cornell University Council, 1976–78; Judicial Conference Committee on the Administration of Criminal Law, 1976–82; adjunct professor, Washington College of Law, American University, 1975–84; board of directors, Federal Judicial Center, 1978–82; Cornell University Board of Trustees, 1982–91; member, Judicial Conference of the United States, 1982–92; Executive Committee, Judicial Conference of the United States, 1985–90; associate judge of the Juvenile Court of the District of Columbia, 1965–66; appointed judge of the U.S. District Court for the District of Columbia by President Lyndon B. Johnson on November 3, 1966; chief judge of the U.S. District Court for the District of Columbia, September 20, 1982; March 1, 1992, senior status since March 1, 1992.

JUNE LAZENBY GREEN, senior judge; born in Arnold, MD, January 23, 1914; daughter of Eugene H. Lazenby and Jessie (Briggs) Lazenby; married to John Cawley Green, September 5, 1936; J.D., American University (Washington College of Law), 1941; private practice of law in Maryland and District of Columbia for approximately 25 years; bar examiner for the District of Columbia; member: Committee on Admissions and Grievances of U.S. district court for the District of Columbia, 1963–68; president, Women's Bar Association of the District of Columbia, 1955–57; director, Bar Association of the District of Columbia, 1966–68; founder, National Lawyers Club, Washington, DC; member: Kappa Beta Pi legal sorority, American Bar Association; Bar Association of the District of Columbia, and Maryland State Bar Association; appointed judge of U.S. District Court for the District of Columbia by President Johnson, April 11, 1968, and took oath of office June 18, 1968; also appointed judge of the Regional Rail Reorganization Court, April 1987.

THOMAS A. FLANNERY, senior judge; born in Washington, DC, May 10 1918; married to Rita Sullivan; children: Irene and Thomas, Jr.; educated in the parochial schools in Washington; LL.B., Columbus University Law School (now Catholic University), 1940; admitted to the District of Columbia bar, 1940; U.S. Air Force, combat intelligence officer, 1942–45; assistant U.S. attorney for the District of Columbia, 1950–62; partner in law firm of Hamilton and Hamilton, 1962–69; nominated U.S. attorney for the District of Columbia by President Nixon, 1969; served as U.S. attorney, 1969–71; member of the Judicial Conference of the District of Columbia Circuit for many years; served on a number of committees, including Committee on the Administration of Justice of the Judicial Council; active in the District of Columbia Bar Association; member, board of directors of the District of Columbia Bar Association; member of the board of trustees of the Legal Aid Agency of the District of Columbia; special hearing officer for the Department of Justice, 1964–68, in conscientious objector cases; lectured at the Northwestern University School of Law for many years; fellow in the American College of Trial Lawyers; nominated judge, U.S. District Court for the District of Columbia, November 18, 1971, by President Richard M. Nixon, confirmed by the Senate on December 1, 1971.

LOUIS FALK OBERDORFER, senior judge; born in Birmingham, AL, February 21, 1919; son of A. Leo and Stella Falk Oberdorfer; married to Elizabeth Weil of Montgomery, AL, July 31, 1941; children: John, Kathryn, Thomas, and William; A.B., Dartmouth College, 1939; LL.B., Yale Law School, 1946 (editor in chief, Yale Law Journal, 1941); admitted to the bar of Alabama, 1947, District of Columbia, 1949; U.S. Army, rising from private to captain, 1941–45; law clerk to Justice Hugo L. Black, 1946–47; attorney, Paul Weiss, Wharton, Garrison, 1947–51; partner, Wilmer, Cutler and Pickering, and predecessor firms, 1951–61 and 1965–77; Assistant Attorney General, Tax Division, U.S. Department of Justice, 1961–65; president, District of Columbia Bar, 1977; transition chief executive officer, Legal Services Corp., 1975; cochairman, Lawyers' Committee for Civil Rights Under Law, 1967–69; member, Advisory Committee on Federal Rules of Civil Procedure, 1963–84; visiting lecturer, Yale Law School, 1966, 1971; adjunct professor, Georgetown Law Center, 1993–present; appointed judge of the U.S. District Court for the District of Columbia by President Jimmy Carter on October 11, 1977, and took oath of office on November 1, 1977; senior status July 31, 1992.

HAROLD H. GREENE, senior judge; born in Frankfurt, Germany, February 6, 1923; son of Irving and Edith Greene; married to Evelyn Schroer, September 19, 1948; children: Michael David and Stephanie Alison; education: George Washington University, 1949; J.D., George Washington University Law School, 1952; in U.S. Army, 1944–46; admitted to the bars of the District of Columbia, State of Maryland, U.S. Supreme Court, U.S. Court of Appeals for the Fourth, Fifth, and Ninth Circuits, and the U.S. Court of Military Appeals; member: American Bar Association, Bar Association of the District of Columbia, World Trial Judges Association, American Judicature Society, National Lawyers' Club, Order of the Coif, Phi Delta Phi legal fraternity; assistant U.S. attorney for the District of Columbia, 1953–57; Office of Legal Counsel, U.S. Department of Justice, 1957; civil rights division, U.S. Department of Justice, 1958–65; associate judge, District of Columbia Court of General Sessions, 1965–66; chief judge, District of Columbia Court of General Sessions, 1966–71; chief judge, Superior Court of the District of Columbia, 1971–78; appointed judge of the U.S. District Court for the District of Columbia by President Carter, May 17, 1978, and took oath of office June 22, 1978.

JOYCE HENS GREEN, senior judge; born in New York, NY, November 13, 1928; daughter of James S. and Hedy Bucher Hens; married to Samuel Green (deceased), September 25, 1965; children: Michael Timothy, June Heather, and James Harry; education: B.A., University of Maryland, 1949; J.D., George Washington University Law School, 1951; admitted to bars of the District of Columbia, 1951 and Virginia, 1955; member: American Bar Association, District of Columbia bar, Bar Association of the District of Columbia, Virginia State bar, Arlington County, VA, Bar Association, Women's Bar Association of the District of Columbia (president, 1960–62), Federal Judges Association, ABA Judicial Administration Division, Executive Committee, Federal Trial Judges; American Judicature Society, fellow: American Bar Foundation, Kappa Beta Pi, Phi Delta Phi legal fraternity, National Lawyers Club; Lawyers' Club of Washington; board of advisors, George Washington University National Law Center; private law practice, 1951–68; partner, Green and Green, 1966–68; associate judge, District of Columbia Court of General Sessions, 1968–71; associate judge, Superior Court of the District of Columbia, 1971–79; judge, U.S. Foreign Intelligence Surveillance Court, 1988–95, presiding since 1990–95; appointed judge, U.S. District Court for the District of Columbia by President Carter, May 11, 1979, and took oath of office, June 27, 1979.

STANLEY S. HARRIS, senior judge; born in Washington, DC, October 19, 1927; son of Stanley Raymond and Elizabeth Sutherland Harris; married to Rebecca L. Ashley, August 1, 1964; sons: Scott S., Todd A., and Mark A.; U.S. Army (sergeant), 1945–47; attended Virginia Polytechnic Institute, 1945; B.S., University of Virginia, 1951, LL.B., 1953 (articles editor, Virginia Law Review); associate and partner, Hogan and Hartson, Washington, DC, 1953–70; judge, Superior Court of the District of Columbia (appointed by President Nixon), 1971–72; attended National College of State Judiciary, Reno, NV, in 1971; judge, District of Columbia Court of Appeals (appointed by President Nixon), 1972–82; attended senior appellate judges' seminar, N.Y.U., 1973; U.S. attorney for the District of Columbia (appointed by President Reagan), 1982–83; appointed by President Reagan on November 14, 1983, to become U.S. District Judge for the District of Columbia, took oath of office December 2, 1983; member: Committee on Criminal Law of the Judicial Conference of the United States, 1988–94; chairman, Committee on Intercircuit Assignments of the Judicial Conference of the U.S., 1994–present; District of Columbia bar, the Bar Association of the District of Columbia (chairman, Annual Convention Committee, 1969–70; board of directors, 1968–71); the American Bar Association; Federal Communications Bar Association (assistant secretary, 1964–65, secretary, 1965–66, executive committee, 1966–69); board of trustees, Landon School Corporation, 1965–68, 1983–85; member: Chevy Chase Club, The Barristers, Lawyers Club of Washington, Phi Kappa Sigma, The Raven Society, and Pi Delta Epsilon.

OFFICERS OF THE UNITED STATES DISTRICT COURT FOR THE DISTRICT OF COLUMBIA

Clerk.—Nancy Mayer-Whittington.

United States Magistrate Judges.—Patrick J. Attridge; Deborah A. Robinson; Alan Kay.

Bankruptcy Judge.—S. Martin Teel, Jr.

Chief Probation Officer.—Richard A. Houck, Jr.

UNITED STATES COURT OF INTERNATIONAL TRADE

One Federal Plaza, New York NY 10007, phone 212–264–2900

GREGORY W. CARMAN, chief judge; born in Farmingdale, Long Island, NY, January 31, 1937; son of retired District Court Judge Willis B. and Marjorie Sosa Carman; B.A., St. Lawrence University, Canton, NY, 1958; national exchange student, 1956–57, studying at the University of Paris through Sweet Briar College Junior Year in France Program; J.D., St. John's University School of Law, (honors program), 1961; member, St. John's Law Review; University of Virginia Law School, JAG (with honors), 1962; Master in Taxation Program, New York University School of Law; captain, U.S. Army, 1958–64, stationed with the 2d Infantry Division, Fort Benning, GA; received Army Commendation Medal for meritorious service, 1964; admitted to the New York bar, 1961; practiced law with the firm of Carman, Callahan and Sabino, Farmingdale, NY; admitted to practice in U.S. Court of Military Appeals, 1962; certified by Judge Advocate General to practice at general court martial trials, 1962; admitted to practice in the U.S. District Courts, Eastern District of New York and Southern District of New York, 1965; Second Circuit Court of Appeals, 1966; Supreme Court of the United States, 1967; U.S. Court of Appeals, District of Columbia, 1982; Councilman for the town of Oyster Bay, 1972–80; member, U.S. House of Representatives, 97th Congress, appointed to Banking, Finance and Urban Affairs Committee and Select Committee on Aging, 1981–82; member, International Trade, Investment and Monetary Policy Subcommittee of House Banking Committee, 1981–82; U.S. congressional delegate, International I.M.F. Conference, 1982; nominated by President Ronald Reagan, confirmed and appointed to the U.S. Court of International Trade, March 3, 1983; became chief judge, 1996; served as acting chief judge, 1991; bicentennial commission of Nassau County; Rotary International, 1964–present; named a Paul Harris Fellow of the Rotary Foundation of Rotary International; United Way, town of Oyster Bay, chairman, 1973–76; member, Benevolent Protective Order of Elks; past president, savings and loan league committee, New York chapter of the American Bar Association; member: American Bar Association; Fellow American Bar Foundation; member, New York State Bar Association, chairman, NYSBA Committee on Courts and the Community; receipient of 1996 Special Recognition Award from NYSBA's Committee on Courts and the Community; president, Protestant Lawyers Association of Long Island; member, Vestry, St. Thomas's Episcopal Church, Farmingdale, NY, 1992–94; Fellow, American College of Mortgage Attorneys; Phi Delta Phi legal fraternity; district committee, Nassau County Council of Boy Scouts of America, 1964 to present; past vice chairman, Paumanok Boy Scout District; district chairman, United Cerebral Palsy; member: Holland Society; Sigma Chi, social fraternity; married to Judith L. Carman; children: Gregory Wright, Jr., John Frederick, James Matthew, and Mira Catherine.

JANE A. RESTANI, judge; husband, Ira Bloom; born February 27, 1948 in San Francisco, CA; parents, Emilia C. and Roy J. Restani; B.A., University of California at Berkeley, 1969; J.D., University of California at Davis, 1973; law review staff writer, 1971–72; articles editor, 1972–73; member, Order of the Coif; elected to Phi Kappa Phi Honor Society; admitted to the bar of the Supreme Court of the State of California, 1973; joined the civil division of the Department of Justice under the Attorney General's Honor Program, 1973 as a trial attorney; assistant chief commercial litigation section, civil division, 1976–80; director, commercial litigation branch, civil division, 1980–83; assumed the duties of a judge of the U.S. Court of International Trade on November 25, 1983.

THOMAS J. AQUILINO, Jr., judge; born in Mount Kisco, NY, December 7, 1939; son of Thomas J. and Virginia B. (Doughty) Aquilino; attended Cornell University, 1957–59; B.A., Drew University, 1959–60, 1961–62; University of Munich, Germany, 1960–61; Free University of Berlin, Germany, 1965–66; J.D., Rutgers University School of Law, 1966–69; research assistant, Prof. L.F.E. Goldie (Resources for the Future—Ford Foundation) (1967–69); administrator, Northern Region, 1969; Jessup International Law Moot Court Competition; served in the U.S. Army, 1962–65; law clerk, Hon. John M. Cannella, U.S. district court for the Southern District of New York, 1969–71; attorney with Davis Polk and Wardwell, New York, 1971–85; admitted to practice New York, U.S. Supreme Court, U.S. Courts of Appeals for Second and Third Circuits, U.S. Court of International Trade, U.S. Court of Claims, U.S. district courts for Eastern, Southern and Northern Districts of New York,

Interstate Commerce Commission; adjunct professor of law, Benjamin N. Cardozo School of Law, 1984–present; appointed by President Reagan on February 22, 1985; confirmed by U.S. Senate, April 3, 1985; married to Edith Berndt Aquilino; children: Christopher Thomas, Philip Andrew, Alexander Berndt.

R. KENTON MUSGRAVE, judge, U.S. Court of International Trade; born Clearwater, FL, September 7, 1927. Attended Augusta Academy (Virginia); B.A., University of Washington, 1948; editorial staff, Journal of International Law, Emory University; J.D., with distinction, Emory University, 1953; assistant general counsel, Lockheed Aircraft and Lockheed International, 1953–62; vice president and general counsel, Mattel, Inc., 1963–71; director, Ringling Bros. and Barnum and Bailey Combined Shows, Inc., 1968–72; commissioner, BSA (Atlanta), 1952–55; partner, Musgrave, Welbourn and Fertman, 1972–75; assistant general counsel, Pacific Enterprises, 1975–81; vice president, general counsel and secretary, Vivitar Corporation, 1981–85; vice president and director, Santa Barbara Applied Research Corp., 1982–87; trustee, Morris Animal Foundation, 1981—; director Emeritus, Pet Protection Society, 1981—; director, Dolphins of Shark Bay (Australia) Foundation, 1985—; trustee, The Dian Fossey Gorilla Fund, 1987—; vice president and director, South Bay Social Services Group, 1963–70; director, Palos Verdes Community Arts Association, 1973–79; member, Governor of Florida's Council of 100, 1970–73; director, Orlando Bank and Trust, 1970–73; counsel, League of Women Voters, 1964–66; member, State Bar of Georgia, 1953—; State Bar of California, 1962—; Los Angeles County Bar Association, 1962— and chairman, Corporate Law Departments Section, 1965–66; admitted to practice before the U.S. Supreme Court, 1962; Supreme Court of Georgia, 1953; California Supreme Court, 1962; U.S. Customs Court, 1967; U.S. Court of International Trade, 1980. Married May 7, 1949 to former Ruth Shippen Hoppe, of Atlanta, GA. Three children: Laura Marie Musgrave (deceased), Ruth Shippen Musgrave, Esq., and Forest Kenton Musgrave. Nominated by President Ronald Reagan on July 1, 1987; confirmed by the Senate on November 9, and took oath of office on November 13, 1987.

RICHARD W. GOLDBERG, judge; born September 23, 1927 in Fargo, ND; son of Frances and Jacob Goldberg; J.D. from the University of Miami, 1952; served on active duty as an Air Force Judge Advocate, 1953–56; admitted to Washington, DC bar, Florida bar and North Dakota bar; from 1958 to 1983, owned and operated a regional grain processing firm in North Dakota; served as State Senator from North Dakota for two years; was chairman of the Senate Industry, Business and Labor Committee; taught military law for the Army and Air Force ROTC at North Dakota State University; was vice-chairman of the board of Minneapolis Grain Exchange; joined the Reagan administration in 1983 in Washington at the U.S. Department of Agriculture. Served as Deputy Under Secretary for International Affairs and Commodity Programs and later as Acting Under Secretary; in 1990 joined the Washington, DC law firm of Anderson, Hibey and Blair; married Mary Borland, 1964; children: John and Julie.

DONALD C. POGUE, judge; before his appointment to the U.S. Court of International Trade, Judge Pogue served as a Judge in Connecticut's Superior Court; he was appointed to the Connecticut bench in 1994, and presided in criminal court in New Haven; prior to becoming a judge, Mr. Pogue served as chairman of Connecticut's Commission on Hospitals and Health Care, the public agency responsible for regulating Connecticut's health care industry; he was appointed to Commissioner by Governor O'Neill in 1989, and named chairman by Governor Weicker; his responsibilities included leading the agency's adjudication of hospital rate increases and certificates of need for the State's thirty-five acute care hospitals; his accomplishments included initiating the agency's efforts for health care reform, developing legislation and regulations for the agency's regulatory, data collection and budget review processes and initiating and guiding the Commission's efforts to establish a statewide uncompensated care pool; he also was responsible for the Commission's initiative with the General Assembly's Health Care Access Commission to expand outreach for prenatal care to high-risk mothers and to create an insurance program for uninsured children; Mr. Pogue practiced law in Hartford for fifteen years with the firm of Kestell, Pogue, and Gould; Mr. Pogue's practice included service as counsel for pensions and health care benefits for a coalition of eleven unions representing all state employees; he was responsible for developing statewide agreements on pension reform and health care cost containment and his litigation included important cases of employee rights; his law reform efforts included drafting and negotiating the municipal binding arbitration statute; during this period, Mr. Pogue also lectured on labor law, at the University of Connecticut School of Law, and assisted in teaching the Harvard Law School's program on negotiations and dispute resolution for lawyers; he also served as chair of the Connecticut Bar Association's Labor and Employment Law Section, and authored a number of other labor statutes; Mr. Pogue is a magna cum laude, Phi Beta Kappa graduate of Dartmouth College, with highest honors in government, and has done graduate work at the University of Essex, England; he holds a J.D. degree from the

Yale Law School and a master of philosophy from Yale University; he has been listed in Martindale-Hubbell and in the Best Lawyers in America and is a member of the American Leadership Forum; Mr. Pogue has lived in Connecticut with his wife Susan Bucknell, since their marriage in 1971; they now live with their two daughters in Guilford, Connecticut.

JAMES L. WALLACH, judge; born in Superior, AZ, November 11, 1949; son of Albert A. and Sara F. Wallach; married to Katherine Colleen Tobin, 1992; graduate of Acalanes High School, Lafayette, CA, 1967; attended Diablo Valley Junior College, Pleasant Hill, CA, 1967–68; news editor Viking Reporter; member Alfa Gamma Sigma, National Junior College Honor Society, member Junior Varsity Wrestling Team; enlisted United States Army, January, 1969, PVT–SGT, served as Recognizance Sergeant 8th Engineer Bn., 1st Calvary Division (Air Mobile), Republic of Vietnam, 1970–71, Bronze Star Medal, Air Medal, Valorous Unit Citation, Good Conduct Medal; attended University of Arizona, 1971–73, graduated B.A., Journalism (high honors), Phi Beta Kappa, Phi Kappa Phi, Kappa Tau Alfa, Rufenacht French language prize, Douglas Martin Journalism Scholarship; attended University of California, Berkeley, 1973–76, graduated J.D., 1976, research assistant to Prof. Melvin Eisenberg, member of University of California Honor Society; Associate (1976–82) and Partner (1983–95) Lionel Sawyer and Collins, Los Vegas, NV with emphasis on media representation; attended Cambridge University, Cambridge, England, LL.B. (international law) (honors), 1981, member Hughes Hall College Rowing Club, Cambridge University Tennis Club; General Counsel and Public Policy Advisor to U.S. Senator Harry Reid (D) of Nevada, 1987–88; served CAPT–MAJ Nevada Army National Guard, 1989–95; served as Attorney/Advisor, International Affairs Division; Office of the Judge Advocate General of the Army, February–June, 1991–92; Meritorious Service Medal (oak leaf cluster); Nevada Medal of Merit; General Counsel, Nevada Democratic Party, 1978–80, 1982–86; General Counsel, Reid for Congress campaign, 1982, 1984; Reid for Senate campaign, 1986, 1992; General Counsel, Bryan for Senate campaign, 1988; Nevada State Director, Mondale for President campaign, 1984; State Director, Nevada and Arizona Gore for President campaign, 1988; General Counsel Nevada Assembly Democratic Caucus, 1990–95; General Counsel, Society for Professional Journalists, 1988–95; General Counsel, Nevada Press Association, 1989–95; awarded American Bar Association Liberty Bell Award, 1993; Nevada State Press Association President's Award, 1994; Clark County School Librarians Intellectual Freedom Award, 1995; member Nevada Bar, 1977; District of Columbia, 1988; U.S. District Court, District of Nevada, 1977; Ninth Circuit Court of Appeals, 1989; author, Legal Handbook for Nevada Reporters (1994); Comparison of British and American Defense Based Prior Restraint, ICLQ (1984); Treatment of Crude Oil As A War Munition, ICLQ (1992); Three Ways Nevada Unconstitutionally Chills The Media; Nevada Lawyer (1994); Co-Editor, Nevada Civil Practice Handbook (1993).

JAMES L. WATSON, senior judge; born in New York City, NY, May 21, 1922; son of Violet L. and James S. Watson (deceased); first negro jurist elected in New York State; educated in New York City; B.A., New York University, 1947; LL.B., Brooklyn Law School, 1951; wounded in active duty in Italy with the 92d Infantry Division; honorably discharged in 1945; received Battle Star, Purple Heart, Combat Infantry Badge, Good Conduct Medal, European Theater Ribbon, and Army Commendation Ribbon; admitted to the New York State Bar, 1951; admitted to practice in U.S. district court for Southern District, 1951; Board of Immigration Appeals and the Immigration and Naturalization Service, 1952; U.S. district court for Eastern District, 1956; served in New York State Senate as State Senator for the 21st Senatorial District, 1954–63; judge of the Civil Court of the City of New York, 1963–66; nominated by President Lyndon B. Johnson, and confirmed by the U.S. Senate, to the U.S. Customs Court, now U.S. Court of International Trade, March 1966, took senior status February 28, 1991; married D'Jaris Hinton (deceased); children: Karen, and Kris.

HERBERT N. MALETZ, senior judge; born in Boston, MA, October 30, 1913; son of Reuben and Frances Maletz; A.B., cum laude, Harvard College, 1935; LL.B., Harvard Law School, 1939; member, Harvard Legal Aid Bureau, 1938–39; admitted to the practice of law in Massachusetts, 1939, the District of Columbia; 1952; married to Catherine B. Loebach of Montana, 1947; one son, David; review attorney, Marketing Laws Survey, WPA, 1939–41; attorney, Truman Committee of U.S. Senate, 1941–42; served in the U.S. Army, 1942–46, ending as technical sergeant in the Army ground forces; trial attorney, antitrust division, Department of Justice, 1946–51; served in the Office of Price Stabilization as assistant chief counsel and later as chief counsel, 1951–53; private practice of law, District of Columbia, 1953–55; chief counsel, Celler Antitrust Subcommittee, Committee on the Judiciary, U.S. House of Representatives, 1955–61; commissioner, U.S. Court of Claims, 1961–67; lieutenant colonel, U.S. Army Reserve (ret.); member of the bars of Massachusetts, District of Columbia, U.S. Supreme Court, and U.S. Court of Claims; nominated November 6, 1967 by President Lyndon B. Johnson as judge of the U.S. Customs Court (now the U.S. Court of International Trade), confirmed by the Senate, November 16, 1967, and assumed duties of office, December

4, 1967; assumed senior status December 31, 1982; have sat as a visiting judge in the following courts: Court of Customs and Patent Appeals, First and Second Circuits Court of Appeals; United States District Courts for the District of Massachusetts, District of New Hampshire, District of Maine, District of Rhode Island, Eastern District of New York, Eastern District of North Carolina, Central District of California, Southern District of California, District of Maryland continuously from 1987 to the present.

BERNARD NEWMAN, senior judge; born October 28, 1907; son of Isidor J. and Sarah C. Newman; lifelong resident of New York; graduate of New York University College and Law School (B.S., LL.B.); associate editor of Law Review (2 years); president of New York University Law Review Alumni Association (3 years), and currently a governor of the Law Review Alumni Association for upwards of thirty years; admitted to bar of New York and of several U.S. courts; assistant corporation counsel, New York City, assigned to City Chamberlain A.A. Berle, Jr.; secretary to New York State Supreme Court Justice Samuel H. Hofstadter, and official referee for 16 years of appellate division of New York Supreme Court by appointments of presiding justices David W. Peck and Bernard Botein, respectively; lectured at New York University Law School and Practicing Law Institute; counsel to New York County Republican Party; chairman of the New York County Republican Party; chairman of the five county Republican Chairmen comprising New York City; delegate to Republican Judicial and National Nominating Conventions'; referee on special panels of New York State Labor Relations Board and New York State mediation board; government appeals agent, Selective Service; seaman 2d class, Coast Guard Auxiliary Reserve (World War II); active in bar associations; appointed to National Conference of Federal Trial Judges Public Relations Committee of American Bar Association; director, Civic Center Synagogue, Community Synagogue Center, Metropolitan Advisory Board of Anti-Defamation League and LaGuardia Memorial Association; recipient of the Judge Edward Weinfeld Award, and Man of the Year Award, respectively; appointed by Mayor Robert F. Wagner to New York City Family Court; by Governor Nelson A. Rockefeller to New York State Supreme Court; and by President Lyndon B. Johnson to U.S. Customs Court (July 21, 1968), now U.S. Court of International Trade; married to Fritzi W. Rudolph, lifelong friend of the family; previously married to classmate and former law partner Kathryn Bereano (deceased); two daughters: Mrs. Phyllis Cechini and Mrs. Helene Bernstein; five grandsons and five great-grandchildren.

DOMINICK L. DICARLO, senior judge; born March 11, 1928 in Brooklyn, NY; B.A., St. John's College; LL.B., St. John's University School of Law; LL.M., New York University Graduate School of Law; assistant U.S. attorney for the eastern district of New York, 1959–62; counsel to minority leaders of the New York City Council, 1962–65; New York State Assemblyman, 1965–81; chairman, New York State Assembly Standing Committee on Codes; deputy minority leader of the New York State Assembly, 1975–78; Assistant Secretary of State for International Narcotics Matters, 1981–84; representative of the United States on the Commission on Narcotic Drugs of the Economic and Social Council of the United Nations from 1982–84; appointed judge of the U.S. Court of International Trade by President Reagan on June 11, 1984; designated chief judge of the Court by President Bush on December 23, 1991; senior status November 1, 1996; married to Esther Hansen (deceased); children: Vincent, Carl, Robert, and Barbara; married to Susan L. Hauck, 1988.

NICHOLAS TSOUCALAS, senior judge; born August 24, 1926 in New York, NY; one of five children of George M. and Maria (Monogenis) Tsoucalas; received B.S. degree from Kent State University, 1949; received LL.B. from New York Law School, 1951; attended New York University Law School; entered U.S. Navy, 1944–46; reentered Navy, 1951–52 and served on the carrier, *U.S.S. Wasp;* admitted to New York bar, 1953; appointed Assistant U.S. Attorney for the Southern District of New York, 1955–59; appointed in 1959 as supervisor of 1960 census for the 17th and 18th Congressional Districts; appointed chairman, Board of Commissioners of Appraisal; appointed judge of Criminal Court of the City of New York, 1968; designated acting Supreme Court Justice, Kings and Queens Counties, 1975–82; resumed service as judge of the Criminal Court of the City of New York until June 1986; appointed judge of the U.S. Court of International Trade by President Ronald Reagan on September 9, 1985, and confirmed by U.S. Senate on June 6, 1986; assumed senior status on September 30, 1996; former chairman: Committee on Juvenile Delinquency, Federal Bar Association, and the Subcommittee on Public Order and Responsibility of the American Citizenship Committee of the New York County Lawyers' Association; former president: Greek-American Lawyers' Association, and Board of Directors of Greek Orthodox Church of "Evangelismos", St. John's Theologos Society, and Parthenon Foundation; member,

Order of Ahepa, Parthenon Lodge, F.A.M.; married to Catherine Aravantinos; two daughters: Stephanie (Mrs. Daniel Turriago) and Georgia (Mrs. Christopher Argyrople).

OFFICERS OF THE UNITED STATES COURT OF INTERNATIONAL TRADE

Clerk.—Raymond F. Burghardt (212) 264–2814.

UNITED STATES COURT OF FEDERAL CLAIMS

Lafayette Square, 717 Madison Place NW 20005, phone (202) 219–9657

LOREN ALLAN SMITH, chief judge; born December 22, 1944, in Chicago, IL; son of Alvin D. and Selma (Halpern) Smith; B.A., Northwestern University, 1966; J.D., Northwestern University School of Law, 1969; admitted to the Bars of the Illinois Supreme Court; the Court of Military Appeals; the U.S. Court of Appeals, District of Columbia Circuit; the U.S. Court of Appeals for the Federal Circuit; the U.S. Supreme Court; the U.S. Court of Federal Claims; honorary member: The University Club; consultant, Sidley and Austin Chicago, 1972–73; general attorney, Federal Communications Commission, 1973; assistant to the Special Counsel to the President, 1973–74; Special Assistant U.S. Attorney, District of Columbia, 1974–75; chief counsel, Reagan for President campaigns, 1976 and 1980; professor, Delaware Law School, 1976–84; deputy director, Executive Branch Management Office of Presidential Transition, 1980–81; Chairman, Administrative Conference of the Unites States, 1981–85; served as a member of the President's Cabinet Councils on Legal Policy and on Management and Administration; appointed judge of the U.S. Court of Federal Claims on July 11, 1985; entered on duty September 12, 1985; designated Chief Judge on January 14, 1986; married.

JAMES F. MEROW, judge; born in Salamanca, NY, March 16, 1932; son of Walter and Helen (Smith) Merow; A.B. (with distinction), The George Washington University 1953; J.D. (with distinction), The George Washington University Law School, 1956; member: Phi Beta Kappa, Order of the Coif, Omicron Delta Kappa; officer, U.S. Army Judge Advocate General's Corps, 1956–59; trial attorney-branch director, Civil Division, U.S. Department of Justice, 1959–78; trial judge, U.S. Court of Claims, 1978–82; judge, U.S. Court of Federal Claims since October 1, 1982 (reappointed by President Reagan to a 15-year term commencing August 5, 1983); member of Virginia State Bar, District of Columbia Bar, American Bar Association, and Federal Bar Association; married.

JOHN PAUL WIESE, judge; born in Brooklyn, NY, April 19, 1934; son of Gustav and Margaret Wiese; B.A., cum laude, Hobart College, 1962, Phi Beta Kappa; LL.B., University of Virginia School of Law, 1965; married to Alice Mary Donoghue, June 1961; one son, John Patrick; served U.S. Army, 1957–59; law clerk: U.S. Court of Claims, trial division, 1965–66, and Judge Linton M. Collins, U.S. Court of Claims, appellate division, 1966–67; private practice in District of Columbia, 1967–74 (specializing in government contract litigation); trial judge, U.S. Court of Claims, 1974–82; designated in Federal Courts Improvement Act of 1982 as judge, U.S. Court of Federal Claims, reappointed by President Reagan on October 14, 1986, to 15-year term as judge, U.S. Court of Federal Claims; admitted to bar of the District of Columbia, 1966; admitted to practice in the U.S. Supreme Court, the U.S. Court of Appeals for the Federal Circuit, the U.S. Court of Federal Claims; member: District of Columbia Bar Association and American Bar Association.

ROBERT J. YOCK, judge; born in St. James, MN, January 11, 1938; son of Dr. William J. and Erma (Fritz) Yock; B.A. St. Olaf College, 1959; J.D. University of Michigan Law School, 1962; married to Carla M. Moen, June 13, 1964; children: Signe Kara and Torunn Ingrid; admitted to the Minnesota Supreme Court in 1962; Court of Military Appeals, 1964; U.S. Supreme Court, 1965; U.S. District Court for the District of Minnesota, 1966; U.S. District Court for the District of Columbia, 1972; U.S. Court of Claims, 1979; and U.S. Court of Federal Claims, 1982; member: Minnesota State Bar Association, and District of Columbia Bar Association; served in the U.S. Navy, Judge Advocate General's Corps, 1962–66; private practice, St. Paul, MN, 1966–69; entered Government service as chief counsel to the National Archives and Record Services of the General Services Administration, 1969–70; executive assistant and legal advisor to the Administrator of General Services, 1970–72; assistant general counsel at GSA, 1972–77; trial judge, U.S. Court of Claims, 1977–82; designated by Public Law 97–164 as judge, U.S. Court of Federal Claims, 1982–83; renominated by President Reagan as judge, U.S. Court of Federal Claims, June 20, 1983, confirmed by U.S. Senate, August 4, 1983, reappointed to 15-year term, August 5, 1983.

REGINALD W. GIBSON, judge; born in Lynchburg, VA, July 31, 1927; son of McCoy and Julia Gibson; married to Shirley Johnson, 1993; son, Reginald S. Gibson, Jr.; educated in the public schools of Washington, DC; served in the U.S. Army, 1946–47; B.S., Virginia Union University, 1952; Wharton Graduate School of Business Administration, University of Pennsylvania, 1952–53; LL.B., Howard University School of Law, 1956; admitted to the District of Columbia Bar in 1957 and to the Illinois Bar in 1972; Internal Revenue agent, Internal Revenue Service, Washington, DC, 1957–61; trial attorney, tax division, criminal section, Department of Justice, Washington, DC, 1961–71; senior and later general tax attorney, International Harvester Co., Chicago, IL, 1971–82; nominated by President Reagan as judge, U.S. Court of Federal Claims, September 30, 1982; confirmed by the Senate December 10, 1982; entered on duty December 15, 1982.

LAWRENCE S. MARGOLIS, judge; born in Philadelphia, PA, March 13, 1935; son of Reuben and Mollie Margolis; B.A., Central High School, Philadelphia, PA; B.S. in mechanical engineering from the Drexel Institute of Technology (now Drexel University), 1957; J.D., George Washington University Law School, 1961; admitted to the District of Columbia Bar; patent examiner, U.S. Patent Office, 1957–62; patent counsel, Naval Ordnance Laboratory, White Oak, MD, 1962–63; assistant corporation counsel for the District of Columbia, 1963–66; attorney, criminal division, U.S. Department of Justice and special assistant U.S. attorney for District of Columbia, 1966–68; assistant U.S. attorney for the District of Columbia, 1968–71; appointed U.S. magistrate for District of Columbia in 1971; reappointed for a second 8-year term in 1979 and served until December 1982 when appointed a judge, U.S. Court of Federal Claims; chairman, American Bar Association, judicial administration division, 1980–81; chairman, National Conference of Special Court Judges, 1977–78; board of directors, Bar Association of the District of Columbia, 1970–72; editor: DC Bar Journal, 1966–73, Young Lawyers Newspaper editor, 1965–66; executive council, Young Lawyers Section, 1968–69; board of editors, The Judges' Journal and The District Lawyer; president, George Washington University National Law Association, 1983–84; president, George Washington Law Association, District of Columbia Chapter, 1975–76; board of governors, George Washington University General Alumni Association, 1978–85; fellow, Institute of Judicial Administration, 1993–; member, District of Columbia Judicial Conference; former member, board of directors, National Council of U.S. Magistrates; former president, Federal Bar Toastmasters; former technical editor, Federal Bar Journal; faculty, Federal Judicial Center; trustee, Drexel University, 1983–91; member, Rotary Club; president, Washington, D.C. Rotary Club, 1988–89, District governor, 1991–92; American Bar Association Judicial Administration Division Award for distinguished service as chairman for 1980–81; Drexel University and George Washington University Distinguished Alumni Achievement Awards; Drexel University 100 (one of top 100 graduates); Center for Public Resources Alternative Dispute Resolution Achievement Award, 1987; married to Doris May Rosenberg, January 30, 1960; children: Mary Aleta and Paul Oliver; nominated by President Ronald Reagan as a judge on the U.S. Court of Federal Claims on September 27, 1982, confirmed by the Senate and received Commission on December 10, 1982, took oath of office on December 15, 1982.

CHRISTINE ODELL COOK MILLER, judge; born in Oakland, CA, August 26, 1944; married to Dennis F. Miller; B.A., Stanford University, 1966; J.D., University of Utah College of Law, 1969; comment editor, Utah Law Review; member, Utah Chapter Order of the Coif; clerk to chief judge David T. Lewis, U.S. Court of Appeals for the 10th Circuit, 1969–70; trial attorney, civil division, U.S. Department of Justice, 1970–72; trial attorney, Federal Trade Commission, Bureau of Consumer Protection, 1972–74; Hogan and Hartson, litigation section, 1974–76; Pension Benefit Guaranty Corporation, special counsel, 1976–78; U.S. Railway Association, assistant general counsel, 1978–80; Shack and Kimball, P.C., litigation, 1980–83; member of the Bars of the State of California and District of Columbia; Judge Miller was confirmed and appointed on December 10, 1982, as Christine Cook Nettesheim.

MOODY R. TIDWELL III, judge; born in Miami, OK, February 15, 1939; son of Maj. Gen. M.R. Tidwell, Jr., and Dorothy (Thompson) Tidwell; married to Rena C. Tidwell; children: Gregory T. and Jeremy H.; B.A., Ohio Wesleyan University, 1961; J.D., Washington College of Law, American University; LL.M., National Law Center, George Washington University; admitted to the bar of the District of Columbia; admitted to practice in the U.S. Supreme Court, the U.S. Court of Appeals for the Federal Circuit and the U.S. Court of Federal Claims and various other circuit and U.S. district courts; attorney, General Acounting Office, 1965–69; associate solicitor, Divisions of General Law and Energy and Resources, Office of the Solicitor, U.S. Department of the Interior, 1969–77; staff director and vice chairman, Commission on Government Procurement, 1971–73; Associate Solicitor, Mine Safety and Health, Office of the Solicitor, U.S. Department of Labor, 1977–80; corporate secretary and board member, Keco Industries, Inc., 1979–82; deputy solicitor and counsellor to the

Secretary of the Interior, 1980–83; appointed and confirmed by the President as judge in the U.S. Court of Federal Claims, May 17, 1983.

MARIAN BLANK HORN, judge; born in New York, NY, 1943; daughter of Werner P. and Mady R. Blank; married to Robert Jack Horn; daughters: Juli Marie, Carrie Charlotte, and Rebecca Blank; attended Fieldston School, New York, NY, Barnard College, Columbia University and Fordham University School of Law; admitted to practice U.S. Supreme Court, 1973, Federal and State courts in New York, 1970, and Washington, DC, 1973; assistant district attorney, Bronx Couty, NY, 1969–72; attorney, Arent, Fox, Kintner, Plotkin and Kahn, 1972–73; adjunct professor of law, Washington College of Law, American Univeristy 1973–76; litigation attorney, Federal Energy Administration, 1975–76; senior attorney, Office of General Counsel, Strategic Petroleum Reserve Branch, Department of Energy, 1976–79; deputy assistant general counsel for procurement and financial incentives, Department of Energy, 1979–81; deputy associate solicitor, Division of Surface Mining, Department of the Interior, 1981–83; associate solicitor, Division of General Law, Department of the Interior, 1983–85; principal deputy solicitor and acting solicitor, Department of Interior, 1985–86; adjunct professor of law, George Washingotn University National Law Center, 1991–present; Woodrow Wilson Visiting Fellow, 1994; assumed duties of judge, U.S. Court of Federal Claims, April 14, 1986.

ERIC G. BRUGGINK, judge; born in Kalidjati, Indonesia, September 11, 1949; naturalized U.S. citizen, 1961; married to Melinda Harris Bruggink; sons: John and David; B.A., cum laude (sociology), Auburn University, AL, 1971; M.A. (speech), 1972; J.D., University of Alabama, 1975; Hugo Black Scholar and Note and Comments Editor of Alabama Law Review; member, Alabama State Bar and District of Columbia Bar; served as law clerk to chief judge Frank H. McFadden, Northern District of Alabama, 1975–76; associate, Hardwick, Hause and Segrest, Dothan, AL, 1976–77; assistant director, Alabama Law Institute, 1977–79; director, Office of Energy and Environmental Law, 1977–79; associate, Steiner, Crum and Baker, Montgomery, AL, 1979–82; Director, Office of Appeals Counsel, Merit Systems Protection Board, 1982–86; judge, U.S. Court of Federal Claims, April 15, 1986.

WILKES COLEMAN ROBINSON, judge; born September 30, 1925 in Anniston, AL; B.A., University of Alabama, 1948; J.D., University of Virginia, 1951 member: Phi Beta Kappa, Phi Eta Sigma, Phi Alpha Theta, Kappa Alpha fraternity; associate attorney, Bibb and Hemphill, Anniston, AL, 1953–55; city recorder of Anniston, AL, 1953–55; judge, Juvenile and Domestic Relations Court, Calhoun County, AL, 1954–56; attorney: Gulf, Mobile and Ohio Railroad, 1956–58; asst. gen'l. attorney, Seaboard Airline Railroad Company, 1958–66; chief commerce counsel, Monsanto Company, 1966–70; vice president and general counsel, Marion Laboratories, Inc., 1970–80; president and member of board of directors, Gulf and Great Plains Legal Foundation, 1980–85; vice president and general counsel, S.R. Financial Group, Inc., 1986–87; judge, U.S. Court of Federal Claims, assumed duties July 10, 1987; member: Alabama State Bar, Virginia State Bar, Missouri State Bar, Kansas State Bar, U.S. Supreme Court Bar, Tenth Circuit Court of Appeals, Alabama and Missouri U.S. District Courts, U.S. Court of Federal Claims Bar; married to Julia Von P. Rowan; three children: Randolph C., Peyton H. and T. Wilkes C. Robinson.

BOHDAN A. FUTEY, judge; born in Ukraine, June 28, 1939; B.A., Western Reserve University, 1962; M.A., 1964; J.D., Cleveland Marshall Law School, 1968; partner, Futey and Rakowsky, 1968–72; chief assistant police prosecutor, city of Cleveland, 1972–74; executive assistant to the mayor of Cleveland, 1974–75; partner, Bazarko, Futey and Oryshkewych, 1975–84; chairman, U.S. Foreign Claims Settlement Commission, May 1984–87; nominated judge of the U.S. Court of Federal Claims on January 30, 1987, and entered on duty, May 29, 1987; married to the former Myra Fur; three children: Andrew, Lidia, and Daria; member: District of Columbia Bar Association, American Bar Association, the Ukrainian American Bar Association; Judge Futey is actively involved with Democratization and Rule of Law programs organized by the Judicial Conference of the United States, the Department of State, and the American Bar Association in Ukraine and Russia. He has participated in judicial exchange programs, seminars, and workshops and has been a consultant to the working group on Ukraine's Constitution and Ukrainian Parliament; Judge Futey is an advisor to the International Foundation for Election Systems (IFES). He served as an official observer during the parliamentary and presidential elections in 1994 and conducted briefings on Ukraine's election law for international observers; advising the Newly Independent States (NIS) working group on Ukraine which is a CEELI/ABA project.

ROGER B. ANDEWELT, judge; born August 4, 1946, in Brooklyn, NY; son of Samuel F. and Belle (Hockman) Andewelt; B.S., Brooklyn College, 1967; J.D., George Washington University National Law Center, 1971; member: Order of the Coif; married to Maxine

Mitchnick; two children: Alexa Sara and Ian Samuel; patent examiner, U.S. Patent Office, 1968–72; attorney, U.S. Department of Justice, Antitrust Division: trial attorney, 1972–78; assistant chief/chief, Intellectual Property Section, 1978–84; deputy director of operations, 1984–86; deputy assistant attorney general for litigation, 1986–87; adjunct professor of law, George Washington University National Law Center, 1995–present; nominated by President Reagan as judge, U.S. Court of Claims on March 3, 1987, and assumed duties of the office on August 1, 1987.

JAMES T. TURNER, judge; born March 12, 1938, in Clifton Forge, VA; B.A., Wake Forest University, 1960; LL.B., University of Virginia Law School, 1965; private practice of law , Williams, Worrell, Kelly and Greer, 1965–79; U.S. Magistrate for the eastern district of Virginia, 1979–87; president, National Council of U.S. Magistrates, 1984–85; judge, U.S. Court of Federal Claims since July 2, 1987; member of the American Bar Association, Virginia Bar Association, Virginia State Bar, Norfolk and Portsmouth Bar Association.

ROBERT HAYNE HODGES, JR., judge; born in Columbia, SC, September 11, 1944, son of Robert Hayne and Mary (Lawton) Hodges; educated in the public schools of Columbia, SC; attended Wofford College, Spartanburg, SC; B.S., University of South Carolina, 1966; J.D., University of South Carolina Law School, 1969; married to Ruth Nicholson (Lady) Hodges, August 23, 1963; three children; judge, U.S. Court of Federal Claims, April 9, 1990.

DIANE GILBERT WEINSTEIN, judge; born June 14, 1947, in Rochester, NY; daughter of Myron B. and Doris (Robie) Gilbert; married to Dwight D. Sypolt, October, 1995; children: Andrew and David; B.A., Smith College, 1969; visiting student at Stanford University Law School and Georgetown University Law Center, 1977–78; J.D., Boston University Law School, 1979; Boston University Alumnae Association Young Lawyers' Chair, 1989; law clerk, Judge Catherine B. Kelly, District of Columbia Court of Appeals, 1979–80; associate, Peabody, Lambert and Meyers, 1980–83; Assistant General Counsel, Office of Management and Budget, Executive Office of the President, 1983–86; Deputy General Counsel for Departmental Services, U.S. Department of Education, 1986–88; Acting General Counsel, U.S. Department of Education, 1988–89; Counselor to the Vice President of the United States, Counsel to the President's Competitiveness Council, Chair of the Competitiveness Council's Interagency Task Force on Product Liability, 1989–90; nominated by President Bush as judge, U.S. Court of Federal Claims, on July 31, 1990, entered on duty October 22, 1990; admitted to the bars of the Commonwealth of Massachusetts and the District of Columbia; president of the Federal American Inn of Court; member of the Federalist Society, and the University Club.

* * *

KENNETH R. HARKINS, senior judge; born in Cadiz, OH, September 1, 1921; educated in public schools of Zandesville, OH; Ohio State University, B.A. (economics), 1943; LL.B., 1948; J.D., 1967; admitted to practice of law in Ohio, April 1949; married to Helen Mae Dozer, 1942; children: M. Elaine and Richard A.; U.S. Army active duty, July 1943 to June 1946, 500 AFA Battalion, 14th Armored Division, private to 1st lieutenant; attorney, U.S. Housing and Home Finance Agency, 1949–51; trial attorney, Antitrust Division, Department of Justice, 1951–55; cocounsel, Antitrust Subcommittee, Judiciary Committee, House of Representatives, 1955–60; general counsel, Stromberg Carlson Division and Electronics Division, General Dynamics Corp., 1960–64; chief counsel, Antitrust Subcommittee, Judiciary Committee, House of Representatives, 1964–71; commissioner (trial judge), U.S. Court of Claims, 1971–82; judge, U.S. Court of Federal Claims 1982–86, pursuant to Public Law 97–164, section 167(a), October 1, 1982 through November 30, 1986. Recalled to active service in senior status pursuant to 28 U.S.C., section 797, December 1, 1986; senior judge 1986–present.

THOMAS J. LYDON, senior judge; born June 3, 1927 in Portland, ME; educated in the parochial and public schools in Portland; attended University of Maine, 1948–52, B.A.; Georgetown University Law Center, 1952–55, LL.B., 1956–57, LL.M.; trial attorney, Civil Division, Department of Justice, 1955–67; Chief, Court of Claims Section, Civil Division, 1967–72; trial commissioner (trial judge), U.S. Court of Claims, 1972 to September 30, 1982; judge, U.S. Claims Court, October 1, 1982–July 31, 1987; senior judge, August 1, 1987–present.

OFFICERS OF THE UNITED STATES COURT OF FEDERAL CLAIMS

Clerk.—David A. Lampen, (202) 219–9657

Chief Deputy Clerk.—Margaret Earnest.
Financial Officer.—Dale H. DeBuhr.
Building Manager.—[Vacant].

UNITED STATES TAX COURT

400 Second Street 20217, phone (202) 606–8754

MARY ANN COHEN, chief judge—elected Chief Judge, two-year term, June 1, 1996; California; born July 16, 1943, Albuquerque, NM; B.A., University of California at Los Angeles, 1964; J.D., University of Southern California, 1967; admitted to California Bar, 1967; private practice of law, Los Angeles, with firm of Abbott and Cohen, a professional corporation (and predecessors), 1967–82; member: American Bar Association (sections of taxation, litigation, and criminal justice), American Judicature Society, Attorney General's Advisory Committee on Tax Litigation, U.S. Department of Justice (1979–80); appointed to U.S. Tax Court, July 1982 to succeed Cynthia H. Hall; term expires September 24, 1997.

HERBERT L. CHABOT, judge—Maryland; born July 17, 1931, Bronx County, NY; married to Aleen Kerwin, 1951; four children: Elliot C., Donald J., Lewis A., and Nancy Jo; graduated, Stuyvesant High School, 1948; B.A. (cum laude), C.C.N.Y., 1952; LL.B., Columbia University, 1957; LL.M. (taxation), Georgetown University, 1964; enlisted in U.S. Army for 2 years and Army Reserves (civil affairs units), 8 years; served on legal staff, American Jewish Congress, 1957–61; law clerk to tax court Judge Russell E. Train, 1961–65; served on staff of Congressional Joint Committee on Taxation, 1965–78; elected delegate, Maryland Constitutional Convention, 1967–68; adjunct professor, National Law Center, George Washington University, 1974–83; member, American Bar (tax section) and Federal Bar Associations; appointed to the U.S. Tax Court for a 15-year term, beginning April 3, 1978; reappointed for a second 15-year term in 1993.

STEPHEN J. SWIFT, judge—California; born September 7, 1943, Salt Lake City, UT, son of Edward A. Swift and Maurine Jensen; married to Lorraine Burnell Facer, 1972; children: Carter, Stephanie, Spencer, Meredith, and Hunter; graduated, Menlo Atherton High School, Atherton, CA, 1961; B.A., Brigham Young University, political science, 1967; George Washington Law School, J.D. (with honors), 1970; trial attorney (honors program), tax division, U.S. Department of Justice, 1970–74; assistant U.S. attorney, tax division, U.S. attorney's office, San Francisco, CA 1974–77; vice president and senior tax counsel, tax department, BankAmerica N.T. and S.A., San Francisco, CA, 1977–83; adjunct professor, Graduate Tax Program, Golden Gate University, San Francisco, CA 1978–83; member: California Bar, District of Columbia Bar, and American Bar Association (section of taxation); appointed August 16, 1983 to the U.S. Tax Court for a 15-year term expiring August 16, 1998.

JULIAN I. JACOBS, judge—Maryland; born in Baltimore, MD, August 13, 1937; children: Richard and Jennifer; residence: Bethesda, MD; B.A., University of Maryland, 1958; LL.B., University of Maryland Law School, 1960; LL.M. (taxation), Georgetown Law Center, 1965; began legal career with the Internal Revenue Service, first in Washington, DC, drafting tax legislation and regulations from 1961–65, and then in Buffalo, NY, as a trial attorney in the regional counsel's office from 1965–67; entered private practice of law Baltimore City, 1967; partner, Baltimore law firm of Gordon, Feinblatt, Rothman, Hoffberger and Hollander, 1967, and remained until his appointment to the Tax Court on March 30, 1984, for a 15-year term to succeed Senior Judge Theodore Tannenwald, Jr.; chairman, study commission to improve the quality of the Maryland Tax Court, 1978, appointed by Maryland Gov. Blair Lee; member, several study groups to consider changes in the Maryland tax laws and as a commissioner on a commission to reorganize and recodify that article of Maryland law dealing with taxation, 1980, appointed by Maryland Gov. Harry Hughes; lecturer, tax seminars and professional programs; chairman, section of taxation, Maryland State Bar Association.

JOEL GERBER, judge—Virginia; born in Chicago, IL, July 16, 1940; married to Judith Smilgoff, 1963; three sons: Jay Lawrence, Jeffrey Mark, and Jon Victor; B.S., business administration, Roosevelt University, 1962; J.D., DePaul University, 1965; LL.M., taxation, Boston University Law School, 1968; admitted to the Illinois Bar, 1965; Georgia Bar, 1974; Tennessee Bar, 1978; member American Bar Association (section of taxation); served with

U.S. Treasury Department, Internal Revenue Service as: trial attorney, Boston, MA, 1965–72; staff assistant, regional counsel/senior trial attorney, Atlanta, GA, 1972–76; district counsel, Nashville, TN, 1976–80; deputy chief counsel, Internal Revenue Service, Washington, DC, 1980–84; acting chief counsel, Internal Revenue Service, May 1983 to March 1984; recipient of a Presidential Meritorious Rank Award, 1983 and the Secretary of the Treasury's Exceptional Service Award, 1984; lecturer, law, Vanderbilt University, 1976–80; appointed to the Tax Court for a 15-year term, beginning June 18, 1984, to succeed Senior Judge C. Moxley Featherston.

CAROLYN MILLER PARR, judge; born Palatka, FL, daughter of Arthur C. Miller and Audrey Dunklin Miller; married to Jerry S. Parr in 1959; three daughters: Kimberly, Jennifer, and Trish; received B.A. (English) from Stetson University, 1959; M.A. (English), Vanderbilt University, 1960; J.D., Georgetown University Law Center, 1977; served as senior trial attorney, Internal Revenue Service, 1977–82; special counsel to the Assistant Attorney General, and Acting Chief, Office of Special Litigation, Tax Division, Department of Justice, 1982–85; admitted to Maryland and District of Columbia bars, U.S. Supreme Court, and U.S. Tax Court. Member American Bar Association (section of taxation—Court Procedure Committee), Maryland State Bar Association, DC Bar Association, Federal Bar Association, and National Association of Women Judges; chairman, Board of Directors, Heritage Christian Church, 1982; took oath of office on November 25, 1985, for a 15-year term to succeed William M. Fay.

THOMAS B. WELLS, judge; born Akron, OH, July 2, 1945; married Mary Josephine Graham of Vidalia, GA in 1974; children: Kathryn and Graham; received B.S. degree from Miami University, Oxford, OH in 1967; J.D. degree from Emory University School of Law, Atlanta, GA in 1973; LL.M. degree (in Taxation) from New York University Graduate School of Law, New York, NY in 1978; attended Ohio Northern University School of Law, Ada, OH, served as managing editor of the law review until he transferred to Emory University School of Law in 1972; completed active duty in 1970 as a supply corps officer in the U.S. Naval Reserve after tours in Morocco and Vietnam; admitted to the practice of law in the State of Georgia and practiced law in Vidalia, GA with the law firm of Graham and Wells, P.C., served as county attorney for Toombs County, GA and city attorney for the city of Vidalia, GA until 1977, and in Atlanta with the law firm of Hurt, Richardson, Garner, Todd and Cadenhead until 1981 and with the law firm of Shearer and Wells, P.C. until his appointment to the U.S. Tax Court in 1986; member; American Bar Association (section of taxation); State Bar of Georgia, served as a member of its Board of Governors; Board of Editors of the Georgia State Bar Journal; active in the Atlanta Bar Association, served as editor of The Atlanta Lawyer; active in various tax organizations such as the Atlanta Tax Forum; the Atlanta Estate Planning Council, served as a director; and the North Atlanta Tax Council, served as a director; nominated by President Reagan and confirmed by the Senate as a judge of the U.S. Tax Court for a term of 15 years beginning October 12, 1986 to succeed Judge Richard C. Wilbur who retired.

ROBERT PAUL RUWE, judge—Virginia; born July 3, 1941, Cincinnati, Ohio; married to Mary Kay Sayer, Cincinnati, Ohio, 1967; children: Paul, Michael, Christian, and Stephen; graduated Roger Bacon High School, St. Bernard, OH, 1959, Xavier University, Cincinnati, OH, 1963; J.D., Salmon P. Chase College of Law, 1970; admitted to Ohio bar, 1970; joined Office of Chief Counsel, Internal Revenue Service in 1970 and held the following positions, Trial Attorney (Indianapolis), Director, Criminal Tax Division, Deputy Associate Chief Counsel (Litigation), and Director, Tax Litigation Division; member, American Bar Association (Section of taxation); took oath of office as a judge of the U.S. Tax Court, November 20, 1987 for a 15-year term to succeed Judge Charles R. Simpson.

LAURENCE J. WHALEN, judge—Oklahoma; born 1944, Philadelphia, PA; married Nan Shaver Whalen; son: E. Holmes Whalen; A.B., Georgetown University, 1967; J.D., Georgetown University Law Center, 1970; LL.M., 1971; special assistant to the Assistant Attorney General, 1971–72; trial attorney, tax division, 1971–75; private practice in Washington, DC, with Hamel and Park (now Hopkins, Sutter, Hamel and Park), 1977–84; also in Oklahoma City, OK, with Crowe and Dunlevy, 1984–87; member: Oklahoma Bar Association, District of Columbia Bar Association, American Bar Association, and Bar Association of the District of Columbia; appointed to the U.S. Tax Court, November 23, 1987.

JOHN O. COLVIN, judge—Virginia; born November 17, 1946, Canton, OH; married Ava M. Belohlov in 1970; one son: Timothy; graduated from the University of Missouri (A.B., 1968), and Georgetown University Law Center (J.D., Masters of Law in Taxation, 1978). During college and law school, employed by Niedner, Niedner, Nack and Bodeux, St. Charles, MO; Missouri Attorney General John C. Danforth and Missouri State Representative Richard

C. Marshall, Jefferson City, MO; and U.S. Senator Mark O. Hatfield and Congressman Thomas B. Curtis, Washington, DC; admitted to the practice of law in Missouri, 1971 and District of Columbia, 1974. Office of the Chief Counsel, U.S. Coast Guard, Washington, DC, 1971–75; served as tax counsel, Senator Bob Packwood, 1975–84; chief counsel, 1985–87, and chief minority counsel, 1987–88, U.S. Senate Finance Committee; officer of the Tax Section, Federal Bar Association since 1978, and adjunct professor of law, Georgetown University Law Center since 1987. Numerous civic and community activities; Judge Colvin was nominated by President Reagan and confirmed by the Senate as a Judge of the U.S. Tax Court for a term of 15 years beginning September 1, 1988 and expiring August 31, 2003. Judge Colvin filled a vacancy due to the resignation of Judge Samuel B. Sterrett.

JAMES S. HALPERN, judge—District of Columbia; born 1945, New York City; married to Nancy A. Nord; two children: W. Dyer and Hilary Ann; graduated from Hackley School, Terrytown, New York, 1963; Wharton School, University of Pennsylvania, B.S. 1967; Law School, University of Pennsylvania, J.D., 1972; Law School, New York University, LL.M. (in taxation) 1975; associate attorney, Mudge, Rose, Guthrie and Alexander, New York City, 1972–74; assistant professor of law, Law School, Washington and Lee University, 1975–76; assistant professor of law, St. John's University, New York City, 1976–78, visiting professor, Law School, New York University, 1978–79; associate attorney, Roberts and Holland, New York City, 1979–80; Principal Technical Advisor, Assistant Commissioner (Technical) and Associate Chief Counsel (Technical), Internal Revenue Service, Washington, DC, 1980–83; partner, Baker and Hostetler, Washington, DC, 1983–90; adjunct professor, Law School, George Washington University, Washington, DC, 1984–90; Colonel, U.S. Army Reserves; appointed to the U.S. Tax Court on July 3, 1990.

RENATO BEGHE, judge—Illinois; born 1933, Chicago, Illinois; married to Bina House; four children and one grandchild; University of Chicago (A.B. 1951; J.D. 1954); Phi Beta Kappa; Order of the Coif and Law Review co-managing editor; Phi Gamma Delta; admitted New York bar 1955; practiced law with Carter, Ledyard and Milburn, New York City (associate 1954–65; partner 1965–83) and Morgan, Lewis and Bockius, New York City (1983–89); bar associations; Association of the Bar of the City of New York (Chairman, Art Law Committee, 1980–83); New York State Bar Association (tax section chairman 1977–78; Joint Practice Committee of Lawyers and Accountants, co-chairman, 1989–90); American Bar Association (Tax Section); International Bar Association; International Fiscal Association; member American Law Institute and American College of Tax Counsel; member America-Italy Society, Inc. and Honorable Order of Kentucky Counsel; appointed to the Tax Court for 15–year term beginning March 26, 1991, to fill vacancy created by resignation of Judge B. John Williams, Jr.

CAROLYN P. CHIECHI, judge—Maryland; born December 6, 1943, Newark, New Jersey; B.S., Georgetown, University, Washington, DC, magna cum laude, 1965 (Class Rank: 1); J.D., 1969 (Class Rank: 9); LL.M. (Taxation), 1971; admitted to the bar of the District of Columbia, 1969; served as attorney-advisor to Judge Leo H. Irwin, United States Tax Court, 1969–1971; practiced with the law firm of Sutherland, Asbill and Brennan, Washington, D.C. and Atlanta, Georgia (partner, 1976–1992; associate, 1971–1976); member, District of Columbia Bar (served as taxation section Tax Audits and Litigation Committee chairperson, 1987–1988); American Bar Association (Section of Taxation); Federal Bar Association (Section of Taxation); Women's Bar Association of the District of Columbia; elected fellow, American College of Tax Counsel; fellow, American Bar Foundation; member, Board of Regents, Georgetown University; member, National Law Alumni Board, Georgetown University; member, Stuart Stiller Memorial Foundation; appointed by the President to the U.S. Tax Court for a 15–year term beginning October 1, 1992.

DAVID LARO, judge—Michigan; born Flint, MI, March 3, 1942; married to the former Nancy Lynn Wolf on June 18, 1967; two children: Rachel Lynn and Marlene Ellen; graduated from the University of Michigan in 1964 with a B.A.; the University of Illinois Law School in 1967 with a J.D.; and New York University Law School in 1970 with an LL.M. in taxation; admitted to the bar of Michigan in 1968 and the United States District Court (Eastern District) Michigan in 1968, United States Tax Court, 1971; former partner of Winegarden, Booth, Shedd, and Laro, Flint, MI, 1970–75; principal member, Laro and Borgeson, Flint, MI, 1975–86; principal member, David Laro, Attorney at Law, P.C., Flint, MI, 1986–92; of counsel to Dykema Gossett, Ann Arbor, MI, 1989–90; former president and chief executive officer of Durakon Industries, Inc., Lapeer, MI, 1989–91, and former chairman of the board of Durakon Industries, Inc., 1991–92; former chairman of the board of Republic Bank, Ann Arbor, MI, 1986–92, and vice chairman and co-founder of Republic Bancorp, Inc., Ann Arbor, MI, 1986–92. Regent, University of Michigan Board of Regents, Ann Arbor, MI, 1975–81; former member of the Michigan State Board of Education, 1982–

83; former chairman of the Michigan State Tenure Commission, 1972–75; former commissioner, Civil Service Commission, Flint, MI, 1984–1985. Former Commissioner of Police, Flint Township, 1972–74; former member of the Political Leadership Program, the Institute for Public Policy and Social Research, Lansing, MI; frequent speaker and lecturer on tax matters for the Michigan Association of Certified Public Accountants, and the Michigan Institute of Continuing Legal Education and other professional and business groups and organizations; author of numerous articles on taxation; former member of the Ann Arbor Art Association Board of Directors, board member of the Holocaust Foundation (Ann Arbor); appointed to the Tax Court for a 15–year term beginning November 2, 1992, to fill vacancy created by Judge Jules G. Körner III, who assumed senior status.

* * *

MAURICE B. FOLEY, judge—Illinois; born March 28, 1960, Belleville, Illinois; married Cassandra LaNel Green; three children: Malcolm, Corinne, and Nathan; received a Bachelor of Arts degree from Swarthmore College, a Juris Doctor from Boalt Hall School of Law at the University of California at Berkeley, and a Master of Laws in Taxation from Georgetown University Law Center; prior to the appointment to the Court was an attorney for the Legislation and Regulations Division of the Internal Revenue Service, tax counsel for the United States Senate Committee on Finance and Deputy Tax Legislative Counsel in the Treasury's Office of Tax Policy; appointed to the Tax Court for a 15-year term beginning April 10, 1995 to succeed Judge Charles E. Clapp, II.

JUAN F. VASQUEZ, judge—Texas; born in San Antonio, TX on June 24, 1948; married to Mary Theresa (Terry) Schultz in 1970; two children: Juan, Jr. and Jaime; attended Fox Tech High School and San Antonio Junior College, A.D. (Data Processing); received B.B.A (Accounting) from the University of Texas in Austin in 1972; attended State University of New York in Buffalo, 1st year law school in 1975; graduate of University of Houston Law Center in 1977 with a J.D. and New York University Law School in 1978 with an LL.M. in Taxation. Certified in Tax Law by Texas Board of Legal Specialization in 1984; Certified Public Account Certificate from Texas in 1976 and California in 1974; admitted to the bar of Texas in 1977; United States Tax Court in 1978, United States District Court, Southern District of Texas in 1982 and Western District of Texas in 1985, Fifth Circuit Court of Appeals in 1982; private practice of Tax Law, 1987–April 1995; partner, Leighton, Hood and Vasquez, 1982–87, San Antonio, Texas; Trial Attorney, Office of Chief Counsel, Internal Revenue Service, Houston, TX, 1978–82; accountant, Coopers and Lybrand, Los Angeles, California, 1972–74; member American Bar Association (Tax Section); Texas State Bar (Tax and Probate Sections); Fellow of Texas and San Antonio Bar Foundations, Mexican American Bar Association (MABA) of San Antonio (Treasurer); Houston MABA; Texas MABA (Treasurer), National Association of Hispanic CPA's; San Antonio Chapter (founding member), College of State Bar of Texas, National Hispanic Bar Association, Member of Greater Austin Tax Litigation Association; served on Austin Internal Revenue Service District Director's Practitioner Liaison Committee, 1990–91, chairman, 1991; Judge Vasquez was nominated by President Clinton on September 14, 1994, and confirmed by the Senate on March 17, 1995, as a Judge of the United States Tax Court for a term of 15 years beginning on May 1, 1995 to succeed Judge Perry Shields who took senior status.

JOSEPH H. GALE, judge—Virginia; born August 26, 1953, in Smithfield, VA; received A.B., Philosophy, Princeton University, Princeton, New Jersey, 1976; J.D., University of Virginia School of Law, Charlottesville, VA, 1980, where he was a Dillard Fellow; practiced law as an associate attorney at Dewey Ballantine, Washington, DC, and New York, New York, 1980–83, and Dickstein, Shapiro and Morin, Washington, DC, 1983–85; served as Tax Legislative Counsel for Senator Daniel Patrick Moynihan (D–NY), 1985–88; administrative assistant and Tax Legislative Counsel, 1989; chief counsel, 1990–93; chief tax counsel, Committee on Finance, U.S. Senate, 1993–95; minority chief tax counsel, Senate Finance Committee, January 1995-July 1995; minority staff director and chief counsel, Senate Finance Committee, July 1995–January 1996; admitted to the District of Columbia Bar; member: American Bar Association, Section of Taxation; frequent speaker at professional conferences and seminars on various Federal income tax topics; appointed to Tax Court for a 15-year term beginning February 9, 1996, to succeed Judge Edna G. Parker, who assumed senior status.

ARNOLD RAUM, senior judge—Massachusetts; born 1908, Massachusetts; married to Violet Gang Kopp; A.B., Harvard College, (summa cum laude), 1929, and LL.B., Harvard Law School, (magna cum laude), 1932; member of Phi Beta Kappa; member, editorial board of Harvard Law Review, 1930–32; traveling fellowship, Cambridge University, England, 1932; attorney, Reconstruction Finance Corporation, 1932–34; special assistant to Attorney General, Tax Division, Department of Justice, 1934–39; in 1939, entered Solicitor General's office, in charge of Government tax litigation and other types of cases in U.S. Supreme Court; has argued more tax cases in Supreme Court than anyone in history; assistant to Solicitor General (now Deputy Solicitor General), and Acting Solicitor General from time to time; lectured on taxation as a member of faculty at Harvard and Yale; U.S. military service, World War II, lieutenant commander, Coast Guard; oath of office as judge, U.S. Tax Court, September 19, 1950; reappointed for succeeding terms beginning June 2, 1960, and June 2, 1972; retired October 27, 1978; presently serving on senior status.

IRENE FEAGIN SCOTT, senior judge—Alabama; born October 6, 1912, Union Springs, AL; daughter of Arthur H. and Irene Peach Feagin; married to Thomas J. Scott, 1939; children: Thomas J., Jr., and Irene (Mrs. Franklin L. Carroll III); graduated Union Springs High School, 1929; A.B., University of Alabama, 1932; LL.B., University of Alabama, 1936; LL.M., Catholic University of America, 1939; LL.D., University of Alabama, 1978 (honorary); admitted to Alabama bar 1936; attorney, Office of Chief Counsel, Internal Revenue Service, 1937–50; member, Excess Profits Tax Council, Internal Revenue Service, 1950–52; Special Assistant to Head of Appeals Division, Office of Chief Counsel, Internal Revenue Service, 1952–59; staff assistant to the Chief Counsel, Internal Revenue Service, 1959–60; member, Alabama Bar Association; honorary member, The Bar Association of the District of Columbia; member: American Bar Association (section of taxation), Federal Bar Association, Inter-American Bar Association, American Judicature Society, National Association of Women Lawyers, National Association of Women Judges, Kappa Beta Pi; appointed as judge, U.S. Tax Court in May 1960, for term expiring June 1, 1972; reappointed June 1, 1972 for 15-year term; assumed senior status July 1, 1982.

THEODORE TANNENWALD, Jr., senior judge, elected chief judge for a 2-year term beginning July 1, 1981—New York; born 1916, Valatie, NY; married to Selma Peterfreund; two sons: Peter and Robert; graduated Brown University, 1936, A.B., summa cum laude, in political science and mathematics, Phi Beta Kappa, Sigma Xi, Delta Sigma Rho; graduated Harvard Law School, 1939, LL.B., magna cum laude, Fay Diploma for highest 3-year average, note editor, Harvard Law Review; admitted to New York bar, 1939, District of Columbia bar 1946; engaged in practice of law with firm of Weil, Gotshal and Manges, New York, NY, 1939–65, except for absences for service as principal assistant, lend-lease administration, and acting assistant chief, Foreign Funds Control Division, Department of State, 1942–43, special consultant to the Secretary of War, 1943–45, consultant to Secretary of Defense James Forrestal, 1946–49, counsel to Special Assistant to President Truman, W. Averell Harriman, 1950–51, assistant director for Mutual Security, 1951–53, and member of President Kennedy's Task Force on Foreign Assistance and special assistant to Secretary of State, 1961; also served for the State of New York as special counsel to the Moreland Commission for the Investigation of Workmen's Compensation, 1955–58, and New York member, Governors' Tri-State Committee on Taxation of Nonresidents, 1958; member: American Bar Association (tax section), Federal Bar Association, Bar Association of the District of Columbia, and Council on Foreign Relations; honorary chairman and member, board of governors, Hebrew Union College-Jewish Institute of Religion; professional lecturer, George Washington University School of Law 1968–76; University of Miami Law School, 1976 to date; appointed to the U.S. Tax Court for term expiring June 1, 1974, to succeed Judge Clarence V. Opper, deceased; reappointed for a 15-year term expiring June 1, 1989; retired June 30, 1983; presently serving on senior status.

WILLIAM M. FAY, senior judge—Pennsylvania; born Pittston, PA; married to Jean M. Burke, Plainfield, NY, 1945; son, Michael; attended St. John's Academy, Pittston; LL.B., Georgetown and Catholic Universities; 1942; admitted to District of Columbia bar, 1942, and U.S. Supreme Court, 1946; assistant counsel, U.S. Senate Atomic Energy Committee, 1946; executive assistant to Senator McMahon of Connecticut, 1946–48; Office of Chief Counsel, Internal Revenue Service, 1948–57, serving successively as trial attorney, assistant head of civil division, and assistant head of appeals division; assistant regional counsel; military service: 1942–45, serving successively as naval intelligence officer, gunnery officer and legal officer; member of the American Bar (tax section), and the District of Columbia Bar Association; appointed to the U.S. Tax Court on August 3, 1961; retired May 14, 1985; presently serving on senior status.

HOWARD A DAWSON, Jr., senior judge—Arkansas—born October 23, 1922, Okolona, AR, married to Marianne Atherholt; two daughters, Amy and Suzanne; graduated from University of North Carolina, B.S. in business administration, 1946; George Washington University Law School, J.D. with honors, 1949; president, Case Club; secretary-treasurer, Student Bar Association; private practice of law, Washington, DC, 1949–50; served with the U.S. Treasury Department, Internal Revenue Service, as follows: attorney, civil division, Office of Chief Counsel, 1950–53; civil advisory counsel, Atlanta District, 1953–57; regional counsel, Atlanta

Region, 1958; personal assistant to Chief Counsel, December 1, 1958 to June 1, 1959; and assistant chief counsel (administration), June 1, 1959 to August 19, 1962; military service: U.S. Army Finance Corps, 1942–45; served 2 years in European theater; captain, Finance Corps, U.S. Army Reserve; member of District of Columbia Bar, Georgia Bar, American Bar Association (Section of Taxation), Federal Bar Association, National Lawyers Club, Delta Theta Phi Legal Fraternity, George Washington University Law Alumni Association; appointed on August 21, 1962, to the U.S. Tax Court for term expiring June 1, 1970; reappointed on May 21, 1970, to the U.S. Tax Court for a 15-year term expiring June 1, 1985; elected chief judge for a 2-year term beginning July 1, 1973; reelected chief judge for a 2-year term beginning July 1, 1975; again elected chief judge for a 2-year term beginning July 1, 1983. Assumed status as a senior judge on June 2, 1985. David L. Brennan Distinguished Visiting Professor of Law, University of Akron School of Law, spring term, 1986, professor of law and director, Graduate Tax Program, University of Baltimore School of Law, 1986–89; presently serving on senior status.

ARTHUR L. NIMS III, senior judge—New Jersey; elected chief judge for a 2-year term beginning June 1, 1988, re-elected chief judge beginning June 1, 1990; born January 3, 1923, Oklahoma City, OK; married to Nancy Chloe Keyes; two daughters; Deerfield Academy, Deerfield, MA; B.A., Williams College; LL.B., University of Georgia Law School; LL.M. (Tax), New York University Law School; served as an officer, lieutenant (jg.), U.S. Naval Reserve, on active duty in the Pacific theater during World War II; admitted to the bar of Georgia, 1949; and practiced in Macon, GA, 1949–51; served as special attorney, Office of the District Counsel, Internal Revenue Service, New York, NY, 1951–54; attorney, Legislation and Regulations Division, Chief Counsel's Office, Washington, DC, 1954–55; admitted to the bar of New Jersey, 1955; was with the law firm of McCarter and English, Newark, NJ, until 1979, having become a partner in 1961; served as secretary, Section of Taxation, American Bar Association, 1977–79; served as chairman, Section of Taxation, New Jersey State Bar Association, 1969–71; member, American Law Institute; appointed by the President to the U.S. Tax Court, June 21, 1979, to succeed Judge Arnold Raum, who assumed senior status; took office on June 29, 1979; assumed senior status June 1, 1992.

JULES G. KÖRNER III, senior judge—Maryland; born July 27, 1922, Washington, DC; married to Jean McKee in 1943; two children: Jules G. IV and Catherine Anne; graduated from St. Albans School, 1939; University of Virginia (intermediate honors and Dean's List), A.B., 1943; University of Mexico (Mexico, D.F.), Summer school, 1941; University of Virginia Law School, Dean's List, LL.B. (later J.D.), 1947; member of Phi Delta Phi legal fraternity and Kappa Sigma fraternity; commissioned ensign, U.S. Naval Reserve, 1943; served on active duty with U.S. Navy, amphibious forces as commanding officer of amphibious landing ship, 1943–46, in various places, including Pacific theatre and Japan; resigned as lieutenant, USNR, 1960; past commanding officer (1955–56) of Naval Reserve Material Company W-2, under Office of Naval Materiel; member: bars of the District of Columbia, Virginia and Maryland; attorney in the area of federal tax law in the Washington, DC law firm of Blair, Körner, Doyle and Worth (later Körner, Doyle, Worth and Crampton), 1947–70; senior tax partner Pope Ballard and Loos, 1970–81; served as a tax member of a private mission employed by the Government of Ecuador, 1961; served as adjunct professor of law at Georgetown University from 1963–68,appointed to the U.S. Tax Court on November 16, 1981, and took oath of office on January 22, 1982; nominated for a 15-year term to fill one of the three new seats on the court, created by Congress, effective February 1, 1981, term expires January 22, 1997; assumed senior status July 28, 1992.

CHARLES E. CLAPP II, judge—Rhode Island; born Newton, MA, December 25, 1923; married to Elinor L. Jones, 1951; three sons and four daughters; attended Deerfield Academy, Deerfield, MA; B.A., Williams College, 1945; LL.B., Harvard Law School, 1949; served as an officer in the U.S. Navy on active duty during World War II (Pacific theater) and the Korean war, lieutenant (retired), 1953; admitted to Massachusetts bar, 1949, Rhode Island bar, 1956, and Florida bar, 1982; practiced law in the firm of Richardson Wolcott, Tyler and Fassett, Boston, 1949–50; served as law clerk to Judge J. Edgar Murdock of the U.S. Tax Court, 1952–55; joined Edwards and Angell, Providence, RI, 1955, became a member of the firm in 1959, and was senior tax partner at the time of appointment to the Tax Court; member: American Bar Association (tax section); Rhode Island Bar Association (chairman, tax committee, 1966–69 and 1979–82); Florida Bar Association; and executive committee of the Federal Tax Institute of New England; cofounder, Federal Tax Forum, Rhode Island; advisory committee, University of Rhode Island Institute on Federal Taxation; involved in many civic activities including United Way Board and campaign; past president, Narragansett Council, Boy Scouts of America; past president, Barrington (RI) Town Council; appointed to the Tax Court for a term expiring August 15, 1998; retired December 25, 1993; presently serving on senior status.

LAPSLEY WALKER HAMBLEN, Jr., senior judge—Virginia; born December 25, 1926, Chattanooga, TN; married to Claudia Royster Terrell, Lynchburg, VA, 1971; three sons by previous marriage; served in the U.S. Navy, 1945–46, graduated from McCallie School, Chattanooga, TN, 1943; B.A., University of Virginia, 1949; LL.B., 1953; member: Order of the Coif, Raven Society, Omicron Delta Kappa, Phi Alpha Delta, and Phi Delta Theta; admitted to the bar, West Virginia, 1954, Ohio, 1955, and Virginia, 1957; trial attorney, Office of Chief Counsel, Internal Revenue Service (Atlanta, GA), 1955–56, attorney-advisor, Tax Court of the United States (Judge Craig S. Atkins), 1956–57; private practice of law, Lynchburg, VA, as a member of Caskie, Frost, Hobbs and Hamblen and predecessors, 1957–82; Deputy Assistant Attorney General, Tax Division, U.S. Department of Justice, 1982; former chairman, Tax Section Board of Governors, Virginia State Bar; former trustee, Southern Federal Tax Institute, Atlanta, GA; past codirector, Annual Virginia Conference on Federal Taxation, University of Virginia, Charlottesville, VA; fellow, American College of Tax Counsel and American College of Probate Counsel; member: Virginia, Federal and American (tax section) Bar Associations and Virginia State Bar; took oath of office as a judge of the U.S. Tax Court, September 14, 1982, for a 15-year term to succeed Judge Sheldon V. Ekman, deceased; elected chief judge for a 2-year term beginning June 1, 1992.

LAWRENCE A. WRIGHT, senior judge—Vermont; born in Stratton, ME, December 25, 1927; married to Avis Leahy, 1953; five sons: Michael, David, James, Stephen, and Douglas; B.A., government, University of Maine, 1953; J.D., Georgetown University Law School, 1956; LL.M., taxation, Boston University Law School, 1962; practiced law with Gravel, Shea and Wright, Ltd., Vermont; tax commissioner, State of Vermont, 1969–71, senior trial counsel, Chief Counsel's office of the Internal Revenue Service, Boston, 1958–69; admitted to practice in the States of Vermont, Maine, Massachusetts, and the District of Columbia; member, American Bar Association (tax section); chairman, tax committee, Vermont Bar Association; taught the State and Federal tax portion of the Vermont Bar Association bar review course; served on several tax seminars as a panelist on both State and Federal tax matters; served in the U.S. Army 1945–48, second lieutenant; retired, U.S. Army Reserve, 1978, as colonel in the Judge Advocate Branch; appointed to the Tax Court for a 15-year term beginning October 30, 1984.

SPECIAL TRIAL JUDGES OF THE COURT

Robert N. Armen, Jr.; Lewis R. Carluzzo; D. Irvin Couvillion; John F. Dean; Daniel J. Dinan; Stanley J. Goldberg; Larry L. Nameroff; John J. Pajak; Peter J. Panuthos (chief special trial judge); Carleton D. Powell, Norman H. Wolfe.

OFFICERS OF THE COURT

Clerk.—Charles S. Casazza, 606–2754.
Deputy Clerk.—Lynne L. Glasser.
Budget and Accounting Officer.—Washington B. Bowie.
Librarian.—Elsa Silverman.
Reporter.—John T. Fee.

UNITED STATES COURT OF APPEALS FOR THE ARMED FORCES*

450 E Street NW 20442–0001, phone 272–1448, FAX 504–4672

WALTER THOMPSON COX III, chief judge; born August 13, 1942, in Anderson, SC; son of Walter T. Cox and Mary Johnson Cox; married to Vicki Grubbs of Anderson, SC, February 8, 1963; children: Lisa and Walter; B.S., Clemson University, 1964; J.D. (cum laude), University of South Carolina School of Law, 1967; graduated Defense Language Institute (German), 1969; graduated basic course, the Judge Advocate General's School, Charlottesville, VA, 1967; studied procurement law at that same school, 1968. Active duty, U.S. Army judge advocate general's corps, 1964–72 (1964–67, excess leave to U.S.C. Law School). Private law practice, 1973–78. Elected resident judge, 10th Judicial Circuit, South Carolina, 1978–84; also served as acting associate justice of South Carolina supreme court, on the judicial council, on the circuit court advisory committee, and as a hearing officer of the judicial standards commission; member: bar of the Supreme Court of the United States; bar of the U.S. Court of Military Appeals; South Carolina Bar Association; Anderson County Bar Association; the American Bar Association; the South Carolina Trial Lawyers Association; the Federal Bar Association; and the Bar Association of the District of Columbia; has served as a member of the House of Delegates of the South Carolina Bar, and the Board of Commissioners on Grievances and Discipline. Nominated by President Reagan, as judge of U.S. Court of Military Appeals, June 28, 1984, for a term of 15 years; confirmed by the Senate, July 26, 1984; sworn-in and officially assumed his duties on September 6, 1984.

EUGENE R. SULLIVAN, associate judge; born August 2, 1941, in St. Louis, MO; son of Raymond V. and Rosemary K. Sullivan; married to Lis U. Johansen of Ribe, Denmark, June 18, 1966; children: Kim A. and Eugene R. II; B.S., U.S. Military Academy, West Point, 1964; J.D., Georgetown Law Center, Washington, DC, 1971; active duty with the U.S. Army, 1964–69; service included duty with the 3rd Armored Division in Germany, and the 4th Infantry Division in Vietnam; R&D assignments with the Army Aviation Systems Command; one year as an instructor at the Army Ranger School, Ft. Benning, GA; decorations include: Bronze Star, Air Medal, Army Commendation Medal, Ranger and Parachutist Badges, Air Force Exceptional Civilian Service Medal. Following graduation from law school, clerked with U.S. Court of Appeals (8th Circuit), St. Louis, 1971–72; private law practice, Washington, DC, 1972–74; assistant special counsel, White House, 1974; trial attorney, U.S. Department of Justice, 1974–82; deputy general counsel, Department of the Air Force, 1982–84; general counsel of the Department of Air Force, 1984–86; Governor of Wake Island, 1984–86; presently serves on the Board of Governors for the West Point Society of the District of Columbia; the American Cancer Society (Montgomery County Chapter); nominated by President Reagan, as judge, U.S. Court of Military Appeals on February 25, 1986, and confirmed by the Senate on May 20, 1986, and assumed his office on May 27, 1986. President Bush named him the chief judge of the U.S. Court of Military Appeals, effective October 1, 1990.

SUSAN J. CRAWFORD, judge; born April 22, 1947, in Pittsburgh, PA; daughter of William E. and Joan B. Crawford; married to Roger W. Higgins of Geneva, NY, September 8, 1979; one child, Kelley S. Higgins; B.A., Bucknell University, Pennsylvania, 1969; J.D. (cum laude), Dean's Award, Arthur McClean Founder's Award, New England School of Law, Boston, MA, 1977; Career record: history teacher and coach of women's athletics, Radnor High School, Pennsylvania, 1969–74; associate, Burnett and Eiswert, Oakland, MD, 1977–79; Assistant State's Attorney, Garrett County, Maryland, 1978–79; partner, Burnett, Eiswert and Crasford, 1979–81; instructor, Garrett County Community College, 1979–81; deputy general counsel, 1981–83, and general counsel, Department of the Army, 1983–89; special counsel to Secretary of Defense, 1989; inspector general, Department of Defense, 1989–91; member: bar of the Supreme Court of the United States; bar of the U.S. Court of Military Appeals, Maryland Bar Association, District of Columbia Bar Association, American Bar Association, Federal Bar Association, and the Edward Bennett Williams American Inn of Court; member: board of trustees, 1989–present, and Corporation, 1992–present, of New

*Prior to October 5, 1994, United States Court of Military Appeals.

England School of Law; board of trustees, 1988–present, Bucknell University; nominated by President Bush as judge, U.S. Court of Military Appeals, February 19, 1991, for a term of 15 years; confirmed by the Senate on November 14, 1991, sworn in and officially assumed her duties on November 19, 1991.

H.F. ''SPARKY'' GIERKE, judge, born March 13, 1943, in Williston, ND; son of Herman F. Gierke, Jr., and Mary Kelly Gierke; children: Todd, Scott, Craig, and Michelle; B.A., University of North Dakota, 1964; J.D., University of North Dakota, 1966; graduated basic course, the Judge Advocate General's School, Charlottesville, VA, 1967; graduated military judge course, the Judge Advocate General's School, Charlottesville, VA, 1969; active duty, U.S. Army judge advocate general's corps, 1967–71; private practice of law, 1971–83; served as a justice of the North Dakota supreme court from October 1, 1983 until appointment to U.S. Court of Military Appeals. Admitted to the North Dakota Bar, 1966; admitted to practice law before all North Dakota Courts, U.S. District Court for the District of North Dakota, U.S. District Court for the Southern District of Georgia, U.S. Court of Military Appeals, and U.S. Supreme Court; served as president of the State Bar Association of North Dakota in 1982–83; served as president of the North Dakota State's Attorneys Association in 1979–80; served on the board of governors of the North Dakota Trial Lawyers Association from 1977–83; served on the board of governors of the North Dakota State Bar Association from 1977–79 and from 1981–84; served as vice chairman and later chairman of the North Dakota Judicial Conference from June 1989 until November 1991. Fellow of the American Bar Foundation and the American College of Probate Counsel; member of the American Bar Association, American Judicature Society, Association of Trial Lawyers of America, Blue Key National Honor Fraternity, Kappa Sigma Social Fraternity, University of North Dakota President's Club; in 1984, received the Governor's Award from Governor Allen I. Olson for outstanding service to the State of North Dakota; in 1988 and again in 1991, awarded the North Dakota National Leadership Award of Excellence by Governor George A. Sinner; in 1989, selected as the Man of the Year by the Delta Mu Chapter of the Kappa Sigma Fraternity and as Outstanding Greek Alumnus of the University of North Dakota; also awarded the University of North Dakota Sioux Award (UND's alumni association's highest honor); in 1983–84, served as the first Vietnam era state commander of the North Dakota American Legion; in 1988–89, served as the first Vietnam era national commander of the American Legion; nominated by President Bush, October 1, 1991; confirmed by the Senate, November 14, 1991; sworn-in and assumed office on the U.S. Court of Military Appeals, November 20, 1991.

ANDREW S. EFFRON, associate judge; the Court is composed of five civilian judges appointed for 15-year terms by the President with the advice and consent of the Senate; the Court has appellate jurisdiction over cases arising under the Uniform Code of Military Justice; decisions of the Court are subject to review by the United States Supreme Court; Judge Effron joined the Court in 1996; he previously served on the staff of the Senate Armed Services Committee; attorney-adviser, Department of Defense Office of General Counsel and Office of the Staff Judge Advocate, Fort McClellan, Alabama; and legislative aide to the late Representative William A. Steiger; Judge Effron was born in Stamford, Connecticut and raised in Poughkeepsie, New York; he is a graduate of Harvard College, Harvard Law School, and the Judge Advocate General's School, U.S. Army; he and his wife Barbara live in Annandale, Virginia; they have a daughter, Robin, and a son, Michael.

WILLIAM HOLMES COOK, senior judge; born in Carbondale, IL, June 2, 1920; son of Rex H. and Mary Dola (Carter) Cook; prelaw, Southern Illinois University, 1938–40; J.D., Washington University, St. Louis, MO, 1947; active duty in U.S. Army, 1942–46; admitted to bar of Illinois and to practice before the Illinois supreme court, 1947; and before the Supreme Court in 1956; private practice of law in Charleston, IL, 1949–52; joined Federal Trade Commission as an attorney in 1954; became assistant to the chairman in 1957; in 1959, joined the Department of the Navy serving as associate counsel for property and special matters; in 1963, appointed counsel for the Armed Services Committee, House of Representatives; nominated by President Nixon to be an associate judge of U.S. Court of Military Appeals on August 2, 1974, for the remainder of the term expiring May 1, 1976; unanimously confirmed by the Senate on August 16, 1974, and took oath of office on August 21, 1974; commission signed by President Ford on August 20, 1974; reappointed by President Ford on February 10, 1976, and again unanimously confirmed by the Senate for the term expiring May 1, 1991, and took oath of office on April 23, 1976; retired on March 31, 1984 and immediately assumed status of senior judge, returning to full active service until June 30, 1984.

WILLIAM HORACE DARDEN, senior judge; born in Union Point, GA, May 16, 1923; son of William W. and Sara (Newsom) Darden; B.B.A., University of Georgia, 1946; LL.B.,

University of Georgia, 1948; admitted to bar of Georgia and to practice before the Georgia Supreme Court, 1948; active duty in U.S. Navy from July 1, 1943 to July 3, 1946, when released to inactive duty as lieutenant (jg.); married to Mary Parrish Viccellio of Chatham, VA, December 31, 1949; children: Sara Newsom, Martha Hardy, William H., Jr., Daniel Hobson; secretary to U.S. Senator Richard B. Russell, 1948–51; chief clerk of U.S. Senate Committee on Armed Services, 1951–53; professional staff member and later chief of staff, U.S. Senate Committee on Armed Services, February 1953 to November 1968; received recess appointment as judge of the U.S. Court of Military Appeals from President Johnson on November 5, 1968, to succeed the late Judge Paul J. Kilday; took oath of office on November 13, 1968; nominated by President Johnson for the unexpired part of the term of the late Judge Paul J. Kilday ending May 1, 1976; confirmed by Senate on January 14, 1969; designated chief judge by President Nixon on June 23, 1971; resigned December 29, 1973; elected to become senior judge on February 11, 1974.

ROBINSON O. EVERETT, senior judge; born in Durham, NC, March 18, 1928; son of Reuben O. and Kathrine (Robinson) Everett; A.B. (magna cum laude), Harvard College, 1947; J.D. (magna cum laude), Harvard Law School, 1950; LL.M., Duke University, 1959; active duty in U.S. Air Force, 1951–53; thereafter served in U.S. Air Force Reserve and retired as colonel, 1978; married to Linda McGregor of Greensboro, NC, August 27, 1966; children: Robinson O., Jr., McGregor, and Lewis Moore; commissioner, U.S. Court of Military Appeals, 1953–55; private law practice, Durham, NC, 1955–80; assistant professor of law, 1950–51; adjunct professor of law, 1963–66; professor of law, Duke Law School, 1967–present; chairman Durham Urban Redevelopment Commission, 1958–75; counsel, 1961–64; consultant, 1964–66; Subcommittee on Constitutional Rights, Senate Committee on the Judiciary; chairman, Standing Committee on Military Law, American Bar Association, 1977–79; president, Durham County Bar Association, 1976–77; commissioner, National Conference of Commissioners on Uniform State Laws, 1961–73, 1977–present; member, American Law Institute, 1966–present; councillor, North Carolina State Bar, 1978–83; nominated by President Carter as judge of U.S. Court of Military Appeals, February 14, 1980, for the remainder of the term expiring May 1, 1981; unanimously confirmed by the Senate and designated chief judge by President Carter, March 28, 1980; took oath of office, April 16, 1980; term of office extended until April 15, 1990, by Act of December 23, 1980, Public Law 96–579, section 12, 94 Stat. 3369; term of office further extended until Sep. 30, 1990 by Act of November 29, 1989, Public Law 101–189, section 1301, 103 Stat 1575–76. Immediately upon his retirement at the end of his term on September 30, 1990, assumed status of senior judge and returned to full active service pending the appointment of his successor.

OFFICERS OF THE U.S. COURT OF APPEALS FOR THE ARMED FORCES

Clerk of the Court.—Thomas F. Granahan.
Central Legal Staff Director.—William N. Early.
Reporter of Decisions.—John A. Cutts II.
Administrative Officer.—Robert J. Bieber.
Librarian.—Agnes Kiang.

UNITED STATES COURT OF VETERANS APPEALS

625 Indiana Avenue 20004, phone 501–5970

FRANK Q. NEBEKER, chief judge; of Arlington, VA, associate degree, history, Weber College; B.A., political science, University of Utah; law degree, American University; correspondence secretary in the White House; trial attorney, Internal Security Division, Department of Justice, 1956–58; Assistant U.S. Attorney for the District of Columbia, 1958–69; chief, appellate division, Office of the U.S. Attorney for the District of Columbia, 1962–69; associate judge, District of Columbia Court of Appeals, 1969–87; director, Office of Government Ethics; first chief judge, U.S. Court of Veterans Appeals; sworn in July 24, 1989; the court began operating on October 16, 1989; married; father of three adult children.

KENNETH B. KRAMER, judge; born February 19, 1942, in Chicago, IL; B.A., University of Illinois, 1963; J.D., Harvard Law School, 1966; admitted to the bars of the U.S. Supreme Court, the U.S. Court of Military Appeals, the State of Colorado, and the State of Illinois; commissioned in the U.S. Army, captain, Judge Advocate General's Corps, 1967–70; counsel, Army Physical Disability Evaluation Board, which determined ratings and benefits of disabled service personnel at the Fitzsimmons Army Medical Center, Ft. Lewis, WA; trial counsel and defense counsel in numerous general courts-martial cases; chief, administrative law department and legal assistance officer; practiced civil litigation law with the Lord, Bissell and Brook, 1970; prosecutor, Office of the Deputy District Attorney, 4th Judicial District Colorado, 1970–72; practiced law with Holme, Roberts, and Owen, Colorado Springs, CO, 1972–74; practiced law with Floyd, Kramer and Lambrecht in Colorado, 1975–78; elected to the Colorado House of Representatives, 1973–78; serving as the Chairman of the Rules Committee, and member: Judiciary, Business Affairs and Labor, Education Finance and Health Committees; elected to the U.S. House of Representatives, 1979–87; candidate for the U.S. Senate race in Colorado, 1986; vice president, Aries Properties in Colorado Springs, CO, 1987; served as Assistant Secretary of the Army (Financial Management), 1988, until September 1989; confirmed by the U.S. Senate to the Court of Veterans Appeals on September 17, 1989; sworn in October 16, 1989;

JOHN J. FARLEY III, judge, of Bowie, MD; born July 30, 1942 in Hackensack, NJ to John J., Jr. and Patricia F. (Earle) Farley; married June 27, 1970 to Kathleen M. Wells; children: Maura, Brendan, Thomas, and Caitlin; A.B., economics, Holy Cross College, Worcester, MA, 1964; M.B.A., Columbia University Graduate School of Business, 1966 (Samuel Bronfman Fellow, Alpha Kappa Psi); J.D. (cum laude), Hofstra University School of Law, 1973 (first in class, editor-in-chief, Hofstra Law Review); served active duty as private, U.S. Army, 1966; released as Captain in 1970 after service in Vietnam, with Bronze Star with "V" device, three oak leaf clusters, Purple Heart with oak leaf cluster, Army Commendation Medal; career record 1973–78; attorney with the Department of Justice: trial attorney, torts section, 1978–80; assistant director for official immunity, torts branch, 1980–89; director, torts branch, with Civil Division, Department of Justice, 1989–present; admitted to: New York State Bar, 1974; District of Columbia Bar and U.S. Court of Appeals for D.C., 1975; U.S. Supreme Court Bar, 1977; author: "Robin Hood Jurisprudence: The Triumph of Equity in American Tort Law," 65 *St. John's Law Review* 997, 1991; "The New Kid on the Block: The United States Court of Veterans Appeals," *Federal Bar News and Journal*, volume 38, No. 9, Nov./Dec. 1991; "Personal Liability of Federal Investigators and Law Enforcement Officers," *Investigators Journal*, volume 2, Fall 1986; "Senior Executives' Personal Liability," 7, *Action* 4, May 1987; "The Fallout from Westfall," 8 Ibid. 3 March 1988; "From Liability to Immunity: The Roller Coaster Ride of 1988," *The Institute*, 1, February 1989; notable decisions: *Erspamer* v. *Derwinski*, 1990; *Rogozinski* v. *Derwinski*, 1990; *Gilbert* v. *Derwinski*, 1990; *Fegere* v. *Derwinski*, 1990; *Smith* v. *Derwinski*, 1991; *Ashley* v. *Derwinski*, 1992; *Darrow* v. *Derwinski*, 1992; *Zarycki* v. *Brown*, 1993; *Elcyzyn* v. *Brown*, 1994; recipient: Special Achievement Award, Department of Justice, 1979; First Civil Division Special Award for Superior Performance, Department of Justice, 1980; Senior Executive Service Special Achievement Awards, 1984 and 1988; Distinguished Alumni medal, Hofstra University School of Law, 1986; member: Federal Bar Association; Disabled American Veterans; John Carroll Society; Roman Catholic; nominated for appointment on August 29,

1989, by President Bush; confirmed by the Senate September 14, 1989; sworn in September 15, 1989.

RONALD M. HOLDAWAY, judge; born on November 27, 1934, in Afton, WY; parents, O.J. and Fern (Melville) Holdaway; married in December 1958 to Judith K. Janisoski; children: Denise E. Smith and Georgia A. Robinson; higher education: B.A., history, University of Wyoming, 1957; J.D., National Defense University, Washington, DC, 1959; entered active duty, lieutenant, U.S. Army, 1959; retired as Brigadier General in 1989; active duty assignments include: legal staff officer, 4th Infantry Division, Ft. Lewis, WA, 1960–63; legal staff officer, Schofield Barracks, HI, 1963–66; instructor in criminal law, Judge Advocate General's School, VA, 1966–69; staff judge advocate, First Cavalry Division (Airmobile), Vietnam, 1969–70; chief, government appellate division, Office of The Judge Advocate General, 1971–75; chief, of personnel, Judge Advocate General's Corps, Washington, DC, 1975–77; staff judge advocate, U.S. Army VII Corps, Stuttgart, Germany, 1978–80; executive to the Judge Advocate General, 1980–81; Assistant Judge Advocate General, civil law, Headquarters, Department of the Army, Washington, DC, 1981–83; Judge Advocate General (BG), U.S. Army Europe, Heidelberg, Germany, 1983–87; chief judge, U.S. Army Court of Military Review and Commander, U.S. Army Legal Services Agency, Washington, DC, 1987–89; awards and decorations: (2) Distinguished Service Medal, Legion of Merit, Bronze Star Medal, Air Medal, (2) Meritorious Service Medal, Commendation Medal, Republic of Vietnam Campaign Ribbon with four campaign stars, Vietnam Service Medal; admitted to Wyoming bar; U.S. Court of Military Appeals; U.S. Supreme Court Bar; author: "Voire Dire, A Neglected Tool of Advocacy," 43 *Military Law Review,* 1; "Litigating Speedy Trial," *The Army Lawyer*, July 1974; "Litigating Defense Request for Witnesses," *Ibid.*, April 1975; member: Church of Jesus Christ of Latter-day Saints;; nominated for appointment on January 23, 1990, by President Bush; confirmed by the Senate August 3, 1990; sworn in August 7, 1990.

DONALD L. IVERS, judge; A.A., New Mexico Military Institute, 1961; B.A., University of New Mexico, 1963; J.D., American University, 1971; active duty in the U.S. Army, 1963–68, U.S., Europe, and Vietnam; retired from U.S. Army Reserve with the rank of lieutenant colonel; clerk, District of Columbia Superior Court and the District of Columbia Court of Appeals; private practice of law with Brault, Graham, Scott and Brault, Washington, DC, 1972–78; chief counsel, Republican National Committee, 1978–81; chief counsel, Federal Highway Administration, 1981–85; director, Safety Review Task Force, U.S. Department of Transportation, 1984–85; general counsel, Veterans Administration, 1985–89; assistant to the Secretary, United States Department of Veterans Affairs, 1990; resides in Alexandria, VA; married, and the father of two children; nominated by President Bush, confirmed by the U.S. Senate in 1990; sworn in August 7, 1990.

JONATHAN ROBERT STEINBERG, judge; B.A., Cornell University, 1960; L.L.B., cum laude, University of Pennsylvania School of Law. 1963; research and note editor, University of Pennsylvania Law School; Order of the Coif; research assistant, American Law Institute; law clerk for then Judge Warren E.. Burger, U.S. Court of Appeals for the District of Columbia Circuit, 1963–64; attorney advisor, Peace Corps, 1968–69; staff counsel, U.S. Senate Committee on Labor and Public Welfare (Subcommittee on Veterans' Affairs, Subcommittee on Railroad Retirement, and Special Subcommittee on Human Resources) 1969–77; chief counsel/staff director, U.S. Senate Committee on Veterans' Affairs, 1977–81 and 1987–90; minority chief counsel/staff director, Committee on Veterans' Affairs, 1981–87; resides in Potomac, MD with his wife Shellie; two adult children: Andrew and Amy; nominated by President Bush in May 1990, confirmed by the U.S. Senate in August 1990.

OFFICERS OF THE U.S. COURT OF VETERANS APPEALS

Clerk.—Robert F. Comeau, 501–5980.

Chief Deputy Clerk.—James L. Caldwell.

Counsel and Reporter of Decisions.—Jack F. Lane.

Central Legal Staff Director.—Patrick B. O'Brien.

Administrative Officer.—Marlene Davis.

Librarian.—Bernard J. Sussman.

JUDICIAL PANEL ON MULTIDISTRICT LITIGATION

Thurgood Marshall Federal Judiciary Building, Room G–255, North Lobby,
One Columbus Circle NE 20002–8004
phone (202) 273–2800, FAX 273–2810

(National jurisdiction to centralize related cases pending in multiple circuits and districts under 28 U.S.C. §§ 1407 & 2112)

Chairman.—John F. Nangle, U.S. District Judge, Southern District of Georgia.

Judges:

Robert R. Merhige, Jr., Senior U.S. District Judge, Eastern District of Virginia.
William B. Enright, Senior U.S. District Judge, Southern District of California.
Clarence A. Brimmer, U.S. District Judge, District of Wyoming.
John F. Grady, U.S. District Judge, Northern District of Illinois.
Barefoot Sanders, Senior U.S. District Judge, Northern District of Texas.
Louis C. Bechtle, Senior U.S. District Judge, Eastern District of Pennsylvania.

Executive Attorney.—Robert A. Cahn.
Clerk.—Patricia D. Howard.

ADMINISTRATIVE OFFICE OF THE U.S. COURTS

Thurgood Marshall Federal Judiciary Building

One Columbus Circle, NE 20544, phone (202) 273–0107

Director.—Leonidas Ralph Mecham, 273–3000.
Associate Director, Management and Operations.—Clarence A. (Pete) Lee, Jr., 273–3015.
Office of Audit.—David L. Gellman, *Chief,* 273–2080.
Office of Management Coordination.—Cathy A. McCarthy, *Management Coordination Officer,* 273–1150.
Office of Program Assessment.—Duane Rex Lee, *Program Assessment Officer,* 273–1220.
Associate Director and General Counsel.—William R. Burchill, Jr., 273–1100.
Deputy General Counsel.—Robert K. Loesche.
Deputy General Counsel for Contracts and Procurement Law.—Linda Horowitz.
Office of Judicial Conference Executive Secretariat.—Karen K. Siegel, *Assistant Director,* 273–1140.
Deputy Assistant Director.—Wendy Jennis.
Office of Legislative Affairs.—Michael W. Blommer, *Assistant Director,* 273–1120.
Deputy Assistant Director.—Arthur E. White.
Office of Public Affairs.—David A Sellers, *Acting Assistant Director,* 273–0107.
Office of Court Programs.—Noel J. Augustyn, *Assistant Director,* 273–1500.
Deputy for Court Administration.—Robert Lowney.
Court Administration Policy Staff.—Abel J. Mattos, *Chief,* 273–1539.
Appellate Court and Circuit Administration Division.—John P. Hehman, *Chief,* 273–1543.
Bankruptcy Court Administration Division.—Glen K. Palman, *Chief,* 273–1547.
Defender Services Division.—Theodore J. Lidz, *Chief,* 273–1670.
District Court Administration Division.—William M. Moran, Jr., *Acting Chief,* 273–1534.
Federal Corrections and Supervision Division.—Eunice Holt Jones, *Chief,* 273–1610.
Office of Facilities, Security and Administrative Services.—P. Gerald Thacker, *Assistant Director,* 273–1200.
Deputy Assistant Director.—William J. Lehman, 273–1230.
Policy and Resource Management Staff.—Ross Eisenman, *Chief,* 273–1200.
Administrative Office Personnel Office.—Nancy Lee Bradshaw, *Administrative Office Personnel Officer,* 273–2777.
Job Opportunity Recording, 273–2760.
Job Opportunity Request Line, 273–2761.
Administrative Services Office.—Laura C. Minor, *Chief,* 273–4301.
Court Security Office.—Dennis P. Chapas, *Chief,* 273–1517.
Relocation and Travel Management Office.—John R. Breslin, *Chief,* 273–1214.
Contracts Division.—Fred McBride, *Chief,* 273–1430.
Space and Facilities Division.—William J. Lehman, *Chief,* 273–1230.
Office of Finance and Budget.—Joseph J. Bobek, Assistant Director, 273–2000.
Deputy Assistant Director.—George H. Schafer, 273–2000.
Economy Subcommittee Support Office.—Diane V. Margeson, *Chief,* 273–2009.
Financial Liaison Office.—Penny Fleming, *Financial Liaison Officer,* 273–2028.
Accounting and Financial Systems Division.—Philip L. McKinney, *Chief,* 273–2160.
Budget Division.—Gregory D. Cummings, *Chief,* 273–2100.
Office of Human Resources and Statistics.—Myra Howze Shiplett, *Assistant Director,* 273–1277.
Deputy Assistant Director.—R. Townsend Robinson, 501–8090.
Analytical Services Office.—David L. Cook, *Chief,* 273–2159.
Employee Relations and Training Division.—Maurice E. White, *Chief,* 273–1260.
Human Resources Division.—Charlotte G. Peddicord, *Chief,* 273–1270.
Statistics Division.—Steven R. Schlesinger, *Chief,* 273–2240.
Office of Information Technology.—Pamela B. White, *Assistant Director,* 273–2300.
Computer Security and Independent Testing Office.—Frank S. Dozier, *Chief,* 273–2350.
Customer Relations Office.—Dennis E. Morey, *Chief,* 273–2700.
Technology Enhancement Office.—Richard D. Fennell, *Chief,* 273–2730.
Technology Policy, Planning and Acquisitions Office.—Melvin J. Bryson, *Chief,* 273–2305.
Applications Management and Development Division.—Gary L. Bockweg, *Chief,* 273–2500.
Networks and Systems Integration Division.—Charles M. Mayer, *Chief,* 273–2640.

Technology Training and Support Division.—Charles W. Vagner, *Chief,* (210) 530–6200.

Office of Judges Programs.—Peter G. McCabe, *Assistant Director,* 273–1800.

Long Range Planning Office.—Jeffrey A. Hennemuth, *Chief,* 273–1810.

Rules Committee Support Office.—John K. Rabiej, *Chief,* 273–1820.

Article III Judges Division.—John E. Howell, *Chief,* 273–1860.

Bankruptcy Judges Division.—Francis F. Szczebak, *Chief,* 273–1900.

Magistrate Judges Division.—Thomas C. Hnatowski, *Chief,* 273–1830.

FEDERAL JUDICIAL CENTER

One Columbus Circle NE 20002–8003, phone (202) 273–4153

Director.—Judge Rya W. Zobel, 273–4160, fax 273–4019.

Senior Administrative Assistant.—Linda M. Beavers, 273–4160, 273–4164 (fax 273–4019).

Deputy Director.—Russell R. Wheeler, 273–4164, fax 273–4019.

Director of—

Judicial Education.—Robb M. Jones, 273–4059, fax 273–4023.

Court Education.—Emily Z. Huebner, 273–4110, fax 273–4020.

Research.—James B. Eaglin (acting), 273–4071, fax 273–4021.

Planning and Technology.—Gordon Bermant, 273–4200, fax 273–4024.

Publications and Media.—Sylvan A. Sobel, 273–4140, fax 273–4025.

Information Specialist.—Roger Karr, 273–4153, fax 273–4025.

Federal Judicial History Office.—Bruce A. Ragsdale, 273–4181, fax 273–4025.

Interjudicial Affairs Office.—James G. Apple, 273–4161, fax 273–4019.

DISTRICT OF COLUMBIA COURTS

phone 879–1010

Executive Officer.—Ulysses B. Hammond, 879–1700.

Deputy Executive Officer.—[Vacant], 879–4616; fax 879–4829.

Fiscal Officer.—John F. Schultheis, 879–2806; fax 879–2894.

Director, Court Reporting Division.—Shirley Shepard Curley, 879–1016.

DISTRICT OF COLUMBIA COURT OF APPEALS

500 Indiana Avenue 20001

Chief Judge.—Annice M. Wagner, 879–2770.

Associate Judges:

Michael W. Farrell, 879–2790.
John M. Ferren, 879–2750.
Warren King, 879–2740.
Vanessa Ruiz, 879–2761.
John A. Terry, 879–2780.
Frank E. Schwelb, 879–2730.
John M. Steadman, 879–2727.

Retired Judges: Gerard D. Reilly (chief judge), 879–2755; George R. Gallagher, 879–2764; John W. Kern III, 879–2754; William C. Pryor, 879–2745; Julia Cooper Mack, 879–2765; Theodore R. Newman, Jr., 879–2740; James A. Belson, 879–2760.

Clerk.—William H. Ng, 879–2725.

Chief Deputy Clerk.—Joy A. Chapper, 879–2722, fax 626–8847.

Director of Admissions, Committee on Admissions.—Clare M. Root, 879–2714.

SUPERIOR COURT OF THE DISTRICT OF COLUMBIA

phone 879–1010

Chief Judge.—Eugene N. Hamilton, 879–1600, fax 879–7830.

Associate Judges:

Mary Ellen Abrecht, 879–7834.
Geoffrey M. Alprin, 879–1577.
Judith Bartnoff, 879–1988.
John H. Bayly, Jr., 879–7874.
Shellie F. Bowers, 879–1288.
A. Franklin Burgess, Jr., 879–1164.
Arthur L. Burnett, Sr., 879–4883.
Zoe Bush, 879–0023.
Russell F. Canan, 879–1952.
Kaye K. Christian, 879–1668.
Harold L. Cushenberry, Jr., 879–4866.
Rafael Diaz, 879–1125.
Herbert B. Dixon, Jr., 879–4808.
Frederick D. Dorsey, 879–7837.
Stephanie Duncan-Peters, 879–1882.
Mildred M. Edwards, 879–7840.

Stephen F. Eilperin, 879–1566.
Wendell P. Gardner, Jr., 879–1810.
Steffen W. Graae, 879–1244.
Henry F. Greene, 879–1455.
Linda Turner Hamilton, 879–1819.
Brook Hedge, 879–1886.
Ellen Segal Huvelle, 879–1264.
William M. Jackson, 879–1909.
Ann O'Regan Keary, 879–1863.
Henry H. Kennedy, Jr., 879–1202.
Rufus G. King III, 879–1480.
Colleen Kollar-Kotelly, 879–1430.
Noel A. Kramer, 879–1446.
Richard A. Levie, 879–1247.
Cheryl M. Long, 879–1200.
Jose M. Lopez, 879–7877.
Stephen G. Milliken, 879–1823.
George W. Mitchell, 879–1277.
Zinora Mitchell-Rankin, 879–7846.
Gregory E. Mize, 879–1395.
Truman A. Morrison III, 879–1060.
Evelyn E. Queen, 879–4886.
Michael Lee Rankin, 879–1220.
Judith E. Retchin, 879–1866.
Robert I. Richter, 879–1422.
Richard S. Salzman, 879–1717.
Lee F. Satterfield, 879–1918.
Nan R. Shuker, 879–1207.
John H. Suda, 879–4873.
Harriett R. Taylor, 879–1442.
Robert S. Tignor, 879–1252.
Curtis E. von Kann, 879–1210.
Reggie B. Walton, 879–1815.
Paul R. Webber III, 879–1426.
Frederick H. Weisberg, 879–1066.
Susan R. Winfield, 879–1272.
Rhonda Reid Winston, 879–4750.
Patricia A. Wynn, 879–4630.
Joan Zeldon, 879–1590.

Retired Judges:

Bruce D. Beaudin, 879–1575.
Samuel B. Block, 879–1570.
George H. Goodrich, 879–1055.
Margaret A. Haywood, 879–4633.
John R. Hess, 879–1420.
Fred L. McIntyre, 879–1428.
Bruce S. Mencher, 879–1358.
Tim Murphy, 879–1099.
Nicholas S. Nunzio, 879–1440.
Joseph M.F. Ryan, Jr., 879–1448.
Donald S. Smith, 879–1490.
Fred B. Ugast, 879–1890.
Ronald P. Wertheim, 879–1170.
Peter H. Wolf, 879 –1088.

Clerk of the Court.—Duane B. Delaney, 879–1400.
Deputy Clerk of the Court.—Barbara K. Parks, 879–1401; fax: 879–7831.
Auditor-Master.—Anita Isicson, 879–4880; fax: 879–4620.
Directors:
Civil Division.—Deborah Taylor Godwin, 879–1680.
Criminal Division.—William G. Rogers, Sr., 879–1689; fax: 879–1371.
Family Division.—H. Edward Ricks, 879–1633.
Social Services.—Moses McAllister, 508–1800; fax: 508–1603.
Probate, Register of Wills.—Constance G. Evans, 879–4800; fax: 393–5849.
Multi-Door Dispute Resolution Division.—Terrence G. Jones, 879–1334; fax: 879–4619.

OFFICE OF THE REGISTER OF WILLS

500 Indiana Avenue 20001, phone 879–4800

Register of Wills.—Constance G. Evans, 879–4800.
Deputy Register of Wills.—Louis L. Jenkins, 879–7800.

INTERNATIONAL ORGANIZATIONS

EUROPEAN SPACE AGENCY (E.S.A.)

Headquarters: 8–10 Rue Mario Nikis, 75738 Paris, CEDEX 15, France

phone 011–33–1–5369–7654, fax 011–33–1–5369–7651

Chairman Council.—Hugo Parr (Norway).
Director General.—Jean-Marie Luton (France)
Member Countries:

Austria
Belgium
Denmark
Finland
France
Germany
Ireland
Italy
Netherlands
Norway
Spain
Sweden
Switzerland
United Kingdom

Cooperative Agreement.—Canada.
European Space Operations Center (E.S.O.C.), Robert Bosch-Strasse 5, 61, Darmstadt, Germany, phone 011–49–6151–900, telex: 419453, fax 011–49–6151–90495.
European Space Research and Technology Center (E.S.T.E.C.), Keplerlaan 1, 2201, AZ Noordwijk, Zh, Netherlands, phone 011–31–71–565–6565; Telex: 844–39098, fax 011–31–71–565–6040.
Information Retrieval Service (E.S.R.I.N./IRS), Via Galileo Galilei, Casella Postale 64, 00044 Frascati, Italy. Phone, 011–39–6–94–18–01; Telex: 610637, fax 011–39–94–180361.
Washington Office (E.S.A.), Suite 7800, 955 L'Enfant Plaza SW. 20024.
Head of Office.—I.W. Pryke, 488–4158, fax: (202) 488–4930.

GREAT LAKES WATER QUALITY REGIONAL OFFICE

Eighth Floor, 100 Ouellette Avenue, Windsor, Ontario Canada N9A 6T3

phone (519) 257–6700 (Canada), (313) 226–2170 (U.S.)

Director.—Douglas A. McTavish.
Public Affairs Officer.—[Vacant].

CANADIAN SECTION

100 Metcalfe Street 18th Floor, Ottawa, Ontario Canada K1P 5M1, phone (613) 995–2984

Chairman.—Leonard Legault.
Commissioners.—Pierre Béland, Frank Murphy.
Secretary.—Murray Clamen (acting).

INTER-AMERICAN DEFENSE BOARD

2600 16th Street 20441, phone 939–6600, fax 939–6620

Chairman.—MG John C. Thompson, U.S. Army.
Vice Chairman.—Gen. de Brigada Omar A. Vaquernao, El Salvador, Army.
Secretary.—Col. Guillermo Giandoni, U.S. Army.
Vice Secretary.—Col. Sergio Leal da Costa, Brazil, Air Force.
Deputy Secretary for Administration.—[Vacant.]
Conference.—LTC James Branham, U.S. Army, 939–7540.
Finance.—Maj. Hector Colon, U.S. Army, 939–7495.
Protocol.—LTC George Vargas, U.S. Air Force, 939–7490.

CHIEFS OF DELEGATION

Antigua and Barbuda.—LtCol. Trevor Thomas, Army
Argentina.—BG Ricardo Jose Ciaschini, Air Force.
Barbados.—BG Rudyard E.C. Lewis, Army.
Bolivia.—Gen. de Division Freddy Balderrama, Army.
Brazil.—Contra-Almirante Paulo Cesar de Paiva Bastos, Navy
Chile.—BG Carlos Patricio Chacon, Army.
Colombia.—Gen. Ramon Eduardo Niebles Uscategui, Army.
Costa Rica.—Coronel Fernando Herrero, Civilian Guard.
Ecuador.—Coronel Fernando Fiallo, Army.
El Salvador.—Coronel Jose Campos, Army.
Guatemala.—Coronel Cesar A. Ruiz, Army.
Guyana.—[Vacant].
Honduras.—Contralmirante Giordano B. Fontana, Navy.
Mexico.—General Brigadier Jorge A. Cardenas, Army.
Paraguay.—Gen. de Division Santiago Zaracho, Army.
Peru.—Vicealmirante Alfonso Balaguer, Navy.
Trinidad and Tobago.—Col. Hugh Victor Joseph Vidal, Army.
United States.—MG Michael J. Byron, USMC.
Uruguay.—General Oscar Pereira, Army.
Venezuela.—Gen. de Brigada Manuel Delgado, Army.

INTER-AMERICAN DEFENSE COLLEGE

Director.—Same as Chairman Inter-American Defense Board, 646–1337.
Vice Director.—BG Juan Carlos Nielsen, Army, Chile.
Chief of Studies.—General de Brigada Boris Saavedra, Air Force, Venezuela.

INTER-AMERICAN DEVELOPMENT BANK

1300 New York Avenue 20577, phone 623–1000

OFFICERS

President.—Enrique V. Iglesias (Uruguay).
Assistant to the President.—Gabriela G. Sotela.
Chief, Office of the President.—Euric A. Bobb.
Special Advisor.—Jorge Espinosa C.
Advisors: Lionel Y. Nicol, T. Nathaniel Carrera.
Executive Vice President.—Nancy Birdsall (United States).
Chief Advisor.—Joel A. Riley.
Special Advisor.—Robert N. Kaplan.
Senior Advisor.—Roberto Vellutini.
Director, Evaluation Office.—Jean S. Quesnel.
Deputy Director.—Richard D. Fletcher.
Principal Evaluation Officers: Brian A. Thomson, Jean-Michel Houde.
Controller.—Alberto Pico.
Deputy Controller.—Carlos Eduardo Guedes.
Chief Economist.—Ricardo Hausmann.
Senior Advisor.—Frederick Jaspersen.
Auditor General.—William L. Taylor.
External Relations Advisor.—Muni F. de Jiménez.
Associate Deputy Advisor.—David H. Smith.
Ombudsperson.—José Ignacio Estevez.
Manager, Office of—
Multilateral Investment Fund.—Donald F. Terry.
Deputy Managers: Keisuke Nakamura, Abayubá Morey Rolando.
Administration Department.—Richard J. Herring.
Operations Department 1.—Ricardo L. Santiago.
Deputy Manager.—Manuel Rapoport.
Senior Deputy Manager, Regional Support Services.—Frederick W. Schieck.
Deputy Manager, Financial Support Services.—Setsuko Ono.
Regional Operations Department 2—Miguel E. Martínez.

Deputy Manager.—William R. Large, Jr.
Regional Operations Department 3.—Ciro de Falco.
Deputy Manager.—Miguel A. Rivera.
Finance Department.—Charles O. Sethness.
Senior Deputy Manager-Treasurer.—Carlos Santistevan.
Integration and Regional Programs Department.—Nohra Rey de Marulanda.
Private Sector Department.—[Vacant].
Senior Advisor.—Luis A. Rubio O.
Social Programs and Sustainable Development Department.—Waldemar F.W. Wirsig.
Strategic Planning and Operational Policy Department.—Stephen A. Quick.
General Counsel, Legal Department.—John M. Niehuss.
Deputy General Counsel.—J. James Spinner.
Secretary.—Carlos Ferdinand.
Deputy Secretary.—Oscar Rodríguez-Rozic.

BOARD OF EXECUTIVE DIRECTORS

Colombia and Perú.—Julio Angel.
Alternate.—[Vacant].
Bahamas, Barbados, Guyana, Jamaica, Trinidad and Tobago.—Havelock Brewster.
Alternate.—Barry Malcolm.
Dominican Republic and Mexico.—José Cordoba Montoya.
Alternate.—Ruddy E. Perez.
Belize, Costa Rica, El Salvador, Guatemala, Haiti, Honduras, and Nicaragua.—Jorge Ramón Hernandez-Alcerro.
Alternate.—Edgar Ayales.
Panama and Venezuela.—Maritza Izaguirre.
Alternate.—Juan Manuel Castulovich.
Canada.—Guy A. Lavigueur.
Alternate.—William D. Gunn.
Belgium, Denmark, Finland, Germany, Italy, The Netherlands, Norway, Sweden, and United Kingdom.—Gert-Robert Liptau.
Alternate.—Suzanne Rubow.
Argentina and Chile.—A. Humberto Petrei.
Alternate.—Andrés Solimano.
United States.—L. Ronald Scheman.
Alternate.—Larry Harrington.
Brazil, Ecuador, and Suriname.—Antonio Cláudio Sochaczewski.
Alternate.—Jacinto Velez.
Austria, Croatia, France, Israel, Japan, Portugal, Slovenia, Spain, and Switzerland.—Hiroshi Toyoda.
Alternate.—Moshe Gal.
Bolivia, Paraguay, and Uruguay.—Jacques Trigo Loubiere.
Alternate.—Homero Martinez-Lawlor.

INTER-AMERICAN TROPICAL TUNA COMMISSION

Headquarters Office, Scripps Institution of Oceanography, 8604 La Jolla Shores Drive La Jolla CA 92037–1508, phone (619) 546–7100, fax (619) 546–7133

Director—.James Joseph, Ph.D.
Costa Rican Commissioners:
Luis Paris Chaverri, Presidente Ejecutivo.
Jaime Basadre Oreamuno, Commissioner Instituto Costarricense de la Pesca y Acuacultura (INCOPESCA), PO Box 333–5400, Puntarenas, Costa Rica, (506) 661–0846/3269, fax (506) 255–4697/661–0748.
French Commissioners:
Philippė Peronne, Direction des Peches Maritimes, Secretariat d'Etat a la Mer, 3 Place Fontenoy, 75700 Paris, France, (33–1) 4273–505, fax (33–1) 4449–8400.
David Portal, Charge de Mission, Direction des Nations Unies et des Organizations Internationales, Ministere des Affairs Etrangeres, 37 Quai d'Orsay, 75351 Paris, Cedex 07, France. (33–1) 43174666, ext. 460, fax (33–1) 43175558.
Japanese Commissioners:
Minoru Morimoto, Councillor, Oceanic Fisheries Department, Ministry of Agriculture, Forestry and Fisheries, 1–2–1 Kasumigaseki, Chiyoda-Ku, 100 Tokyo, Japan, (81–3) 3502–8111, ext. 5408, fax (81–3) 3504–2649.

Yasuo Takase, Director, Fishery Division, Ministry of Foreign Affairs, 2–2–1 Kasumigaseki, Chiyoda-Ku, 100 Tokyo, Japan. (81–3) 3580–3311, fax (81–3) 3503–3136.
Yamato Ueda, President, Federation of Japanese Tuna Fish Co-op Association, 2–3–22 Kudankita, Chiyoda-Ku, 102 Tokyo, Japan. (81–3) 3264–6167, fax (81–3) 3264–7233.

Nicaraguan Commissioner:

Sergio Martinez Casco, Director, CIRH (Centro de Investigacion de Recursos Hidrobiologicos), Apartado 2020, Managua, Nicaragua. (505–2) 652820, fax (505–2) 653090.

Panamanian Commissioners:

Ricardo Antonio Martans G., Director Gral. de Recursos Marinos
Jose A. Troyano, Viceministro Ministerio de Comercio e Industrias, Apartado 9658, Panama 4, Panama, (507) 274691, fax (507) 273104.
Armando Martinez Valdes, Pradepesca, Apartado 645, Balboa Ancon, Panama, (507) 641909, fax (507) 641864.

United States Commissioners:

Barbara Britten, 801 J Street, Davis, CA 95616. (916) 758–6786, fax (916) 758–8305.
M. Austin Forman, 888 Southeast Third Avenue, Suite 501, Fort Lauderdale FL 33316, (305) 763–8111, fax (305) 522–1969.
James T. McCarthy, 18708 Olmeda Place, San Diego CA 92128, (619) 485–9749, fax (619) 485–0172.
Michael F. Tillman, Southwest Fisheries Science Center, PO Box 271, La Jolla CA 92038, (619) 546–7067, fax (619) 546–7003.

Vanuatuan Commissioner:

Julian Ala, Commissioner of Maritime Affairs, Ministry of Finance, Private Mail Bag 023, Port Vila, Vanuatu. (678) 22247, fax (678) 22242.

Venezuelan Commissioners:

Hugo Alsina Lagos, Director de Asuntos Pesqueros Internacionales, Serv. Autonomo de los Rec. Pesq. y Acuicolas, Ministerio de Agricultura y Cria, Torre Este, Piso 10, Parque Central, Caracas,Venezuela. (58–2) 509–0382, fax (58–2) 81 93 72.
Maria Estela Bermudez, Directora General de Negociaciones Comerciales, Instituto de Comercio Exterior, Centro Comercial Los Cedros, Av. Libertador, Mezz. PH., Caracas, Venezuela. (58–2)531–0026, fax (58–2) 762–3884.

INTERNATIONAL BOUNDARY AND WATER COMMISSION, UNITED STATES AND MEXICO

UNITED STATES SECTION

The Commons, Building C, Suite 310 4171 North Mesa, El Paso TX 79902–1441
phone (915) 534–6700, fax (915) 534–6680

Commissioner.—John M. Bernal, (915) 534–6677.
Secretary.—Manuel R. Ybarra, (915) 534–6698.
Principal Engineers:
Carlo Marin, (915) 534–6703.
Cornelius W. Ruth, (915) 534–6700.
[Vacant], (915) 534–6700.
Director of Personnel.—David D. Skinner, (915) 534–6701.
Administrative Officer.—Robert Ortega, (915) 534–6710.
Staff Counsel.—Randall A. McMains, (915) 534–6696.

MEXICAN SECTION

Avenida Universidad, No. 2180, Ciudad Juarez, Chihuahua, Mexico

PO Box 10525, El Paso TX 79995.

phone 011–52–16–13–7311 or 011–52–16–13–7363 (Mexico)

Commissioner.—Arturo Herrera Solis.
Secretary.—Jose de Jesus Luevano Grano.
Principal Engineers: L. Antonio Rascon Mendoza, Gilberto Elizalde Hernandez.

INTERNATIONAL BOUNDARY COMMISSION, UNITED STATES AND CANADA

UNITED STATES SECTION

1250 23rd Street, Suite 100 20037, phone (202) 736–9100

Commissioner.—Thomas L. Baldini.
Deputy Commissioner.—Clyde R. Moore.
Administrative Officer.—Karen L. McCarthy.

CANADIAN SECTION

Room 130, 615 Booth Street, Ottawa ON, Canada K1A 0E9, phone (613) 995–4960

Commissioner.—Michael J. O'Sullivan.
Engineer to the Commission.—Noel Paquette.

INTERNATIONAL COTTON ADVISORY COMMITTEE

(Permanent Secretariat of the Organization)

Headquarters: 1629 K Street Suite 702, 20006, secretariat@icac.org

phone 463–6660, fax 463–6950, Telex: 701517 ICACOM

MEMBER COUNTRIES

Argentina
Australia
Azerbaijan
Belgium
Brazil
Cameroon
Chad
China (Taiwan)
Colombia
Côte d'Ivoire
Egypt
Finland
France
Germany
Greece
India
Iran
Israel
Italy
Japan
Korea, Republic of
Mali
Netherlands
Pakistan
Paraguay
Philippines
Poland
Russia
South Africa
Spain
Sudan
Switzerland
Syria
Tanzania
Turkey
Uganda
United Kingdom
United States
Uzbekistan
Zimbabwe

Executive Director.—Lawrence H. Shaw.
Statistician.—Terry Townsend.
Economists: Carlos Valderrama; Andre Gultchounts.
Head of Technical Information Section.—M. Rafiq Chaudhry.
Administrative Officer.—Frederico R. Arriola.

INTERNATIONAL JOINT COMMISSION, UNITED STATES AND CANADA

UNITED STATES SECTION

1250 23rd Street 20440, phone (202) 736–9000

Chairman.—Thomas L. Baldini.
Commissioners: Susan Bayh, Alice Chamberlin.
Secretary.—Kathy Prosser.
Legal Adviser.—James G. Chandler.
Engineer Adviser.—Lisa Bourget.
Environmental Adviser.—Joel L. Fisher, Ph.D.
Public Affairs Director.—Frank Bevacqua.
Economic Management Adviser.—Bruce Bandurski.

INTERNATIONAL LABOR ORGANIZATION

Headquarters: Geneva, Switzerland

Washington Branch Office, 1828 L Street 20036, phone 653–7652, fax 653–7687

Liaison Office with the United Nations

220 East 42nd Street, Suite 3101, New York NY 10017–5806

International Labor Office (Permanent Secretariat of the Organization)
Headquarters Geneva:
Director General.—Michel Hansenne.
Deputy Directors General: Mary Chinery-Hesse (Ghana); Katherine Hagen (United States); Kari Tapiola (Finland)
Assistant Directors General:
Jean Francois Tremeaud (France).
Padmanabh Gopinath (India).
Anees Ahmad (Pakistan).
Tadashi Nakamura (Japan).
Shukri Dajani (Jordania).
Victor Tokman (Argentina).
Hans B. Hammar (Sweden).
Elias Mabere (Tanzania).
Mitsuko Horiuchi (Japan).
Ali Taqi (Pakistan).
Heribert Scharrenbroich (Germany).
Washington:
Director.—Anthony G. Freeman.
Assistant Directors.—Jean Decker Mathews, John R. Byrne.
Senior Advisor/Public Affairs.—Mary W. Covington.
Other Branch Offices: Bonn, London, Paris, Rome, Tokyo, Moscow.

INTERNATIONAL MONETARY FUND

700 19th Street 20431, phone (202) 623–7000

MANAGEMENT AND SENIOR OFFICERS

Chairman of the Executive Board.—Michel Camdessus.
Deputy Managing Directors: Stanley Fischer, Alassane D. Ouattara, Shigemetsu Sugisaki.
Economic Counsellor.—Michael Mussa.
Counsellor.—Massimo Russo.
Departmental Directors:
Administration.—Burke Dillon.
African.—Evangelos A. Calamitsis.
Central Asia.—Hubert Neiss.
Monetary and Exchange Affairs.—Manuel Guitian.
European II.—John Odling-Smee.
Policy Development and Review.—John T. Boorman.
External Relations.—Shailendra J. Anjaria.
Fiscal Affairs.—Vito Tanzi.
Legal.—François P. Gianviti.
Middle Eastern.—Paul Chabrier.
Research.—Michael Mussa.
Statistics.—Carol S. Carson.
Western Hemisphere.—Claudio M. Loser.
IMF Institute.—Mohsin S. Khan.
Secretary.—Reinhard Münzberg.
Treasurer.—David Williams.
Bureau Directors:
Computing Services.—Warren N. Minami.
Language Services.—Patrick Delannoy.
Director Office in—
Paris.—Christian Brachet.
Geneva.—[Vacant.]
Asia and Pacific.—Kunio Saito.
Director, Office of—
Budget and Planning.—Lindsay A. Wolfe.
Internal Audit and Review.—Eduard Brau.

EXECUTIVE DIRECTORS AND ALTERNATES

Executive Directors:

Abdulrahman A. Al-Tuwaijri, represents Saudi Arabia.
Alternate.—Sularman M. Al-Turki.
Adviser.—Melhem F. Melhem.

Marc-Antoine Autheman, represents France.
Alternate.—Ambroise Fayolle.
Adviser.—Pierre-Michel Fremann.

Jarle Bergo, represents Denmark, Estonia, Finland, Iceland, Latvia, Lithuania, Norway, Sweden.
Alternate.—Ms. Eva Srejber.
Adviser.—Benny Andersen.

Juan José Torribio, represents Costa Rica, El Salvador, Guatemala, Honduras, Mexico, Nicaragua, Spain, Venezuela.
Alternate.—Javier Guzmán-Calafell.
Advisers: Mario B. Aleman, Tabeila Brizuela.

Thomas A. Bernes, represents Antigua and Barbuda, the Bahamas, Barbados, Belize, Canada, Dominica, Grenada, Ireland, Jamaica, St. Kitts and Nevis, St. Lucia, St. Vincent and the Grenadines.
Alternate.—Charles X. O'Loghlin.
Advisers: Mostafa Askari-Rankouhi, Therese Turner-Huggins.

Dinah Z. Guti, represents Angola, Botswana, Burundi, Eritrea, Ethiopia, Gambia, Kenya, Lesotho, Liberia, Malawi, Mozambique, Namibia, Nigeria, Sierra Leone, Swaziland, Tanzania, Uganda, Zambia, Zimbabwe.
Alternate.—José Pedro de Morais, Jr.
Advisers: Patrick A. Akatu, Lodewyk J. Erasmus.

M. R. Sivaraman, represents Bangladesh, Bhutan, India, Sri Lanka.
Alternate.—H. B. Disanayaka.
Adviser.—Ramalinga Kannan.

Zamani Abdul Ghani, represents Cambodia, Fiji, Indonesia, Lao People's Democratic Republic, Malaysia, Myanmar, Nepal, Singapore, Thailand, Tonga, Viet Nam.
Alternate.—Ommar Sein.

Daniel Kaeser, represents Azerbaijan, Kyrgyz Republic, Poland, Switzerland, Tajikistan, Turkmenistan, Uzbekistan.
Alternate.—Danuta Gotz-Kozierkiewicz.
Adviser.—Roberto F. Cippa.

Alexandre Kafka, represents Brazil, Colombia, Dominican Republic, Ecuador, Guyana, Haiti, Panama, Suriname, Trinidad and Tobago.
Alternate.—Alberto Calderón.
Advisers: Joan John, Helio Mori.

Willy Kiekens, represents Austria, Belarus, Belgium, Czech Republic, Hungary, Kazakhstan, Luxembourg, Slovak Republic, Slovenia, Turkey.
Alternate.—Johann Prader.
Advisers: Ákos Cserés, Jiri Jonas.

Koffi Yao, represents Benin, Burkina Faso, Cameroon, Cape Verde, Central African Republic, Chad, Comoros, Congo, Côte d'Ivoire, Djibouti, Equatorial Guinea, Gabon, Guinea, Guinea-Bissau, Madagascar, Mali, Mauritania, Mauritius, Niger, Rwanda, São Tomé and Principe, Senegal, Togo.
Alternate.—Alexandre Barro Chambrier.
Advisers: Abdel Rehman Ismael, Jean-Christian Obame, Simon N'guiambe, Bernard Konai.

Enzo Grilli, represents Albania, Greece, Italy, Malta, Portugal, San Marino.
Alternate.—Nikolaos Coumbis.
Adviser.—Alessandro Giustinani.

Karin Lissakers, represents United States.
Alternate.—Barry S. Newman.
Adviser.—Mark Sobel.

Hachiro Mesaki, represents Japan.
Alternate.—Hideaki Ono.

Abbas Mirakhor, represents Islamic State of Afghanistan, Algeria, Ghana, Islamic Republic of Iran, Morocco, Pakistan, Tunisia.
Alternate.—Mohammed Daíri.
Advisers: Meekal A. Ahmed, Mohammad-Hadi Mahdavan.

A. Guillermo Zoccali, represents Argentina, Bolivia, Chile, Paraguay, Peru, Uruguay.
Advisers: Jorge Leiva, José Antonio Costa.

Bernd Esdar, represents Germany.
Alternate.—Wolf-Dieter Dunecker.

Adviser.—Andreas Guennewich.

A. Shakour Shaalan, represents Bahrain, Egypt, Iraq, Jordan, Kuwait, Lebanon, Libya, Maldives, Oman, Qatar, Syrian Arab Republic, United Arab Emirates, Yemen.

Alternate.—Yacoob Yousef Mohammed.

Advisers: Toufic K. Gaspard.

Aleksei V. Mohzin, represents Russia.

Alternate.—Andrei Vernikov.

Adviser.—Vitali Verjbitski.

Ewen L. Waterman, represents Australia, Kiribati, Korea, Marshall Islands, Federated States of Micronesia, Mongolia, New Zealand, Papua New Guinea, Philippines, Seychelles, Solomon Islands, Vanuatu, Western Samoa.

Alternate.—Jung-Ho Kang.

Adviser.—Celia M. Gonzalez.

J. de Beaufort Wijnholds, represents Armenia, Bulgaria, Croatia, Cyprus, Georgia, Israel, former Yugoslav Republic of Macedonia, Moldova, Netherlands, Romania, Ukraine.

Alternate.—Yuriy Yakusha.

Advisers: Aziel Levy, Laura van Geest.

Zhang Zhixiang, represents China.

Alternate.—Han Mingzhi.

Adviser.—He Jianxiong.

INTERNATIONAL ORGANIZATION FOR MIGRATION

Headquarters: 17 Route Des Morillons (PO Box 71), CH1211, Geneva 19, Switzerland

Washington Mission: 1750 K Street, NW, Suite 1110, 20006, phone (202) 862–1826

New York Mission: 1123 Broadway, Suite 717, New York NY 10010

phone (212) 463–8422

HEADQUARTERS

Director General.—James N. Purcell, Jr. (United States).

Deputy Director General.—Ambassador Narcisa Escaler (Philippines).

Washington Chief of Mission.—Hans-Petter W. Boe (Norway).

New York Chief of Mission.—Andrew Bruce (New Zealand).

MEMBER STATES

Albania
Angola
Argentina
Armenia
Australia
Austria
Bangladesh
Belgium
Bolivia
Bulgaria
Canada
Chile
Colombia
Costa Rica
Croatia
Cyprus
Czech Republic
Denmark
Dominican Republic
Ecuador
Egypt
El Salvador
Finland
France
Germany
Greece
Guatemala
Haiti
Honduras
Hungary
Israel
Italy
Japan
Kenya
Korea, Republic of
Liberia
Luxembourg
Netherland
Nicaragua
Norway
Pakistan
Panama
Paraguay
Peru
Philippines
Poland
Portugal
Senegal
Slovak Republic
Sri Lanka
Sweden
Switzerland
Tajikistan
Thailand
Uganda
United States of America
Uruguay
Venezuela
Zambia

STATES WITH OBSERVER STATUS

Afghanistan
Belarus
Belize
Bosnia and Herzegovina
Brazil
Cape Verde
Georgia
Ghana
Guinea

Guinea Bissau
Holy See
India
Indonesia
Iran (Islamic Republic of)
Ireland
Jamaica
Jordan
Kyrgyzstan
Latvia
Lithuania
Madagascar
Malta
Mexico
Moldova
Morocco
Mozambique
Namibia
New Zealand
Romania
Russian Federation
Rwanda
San Marino
Sao Tomé and Principe
Slovenia
Somalia
South Africa
Spain
Sudan
Tanzania
Tunisia
Turkey
Ukraine
United Kingdom of Great Britain and Northern Ireland
Vietnam
Yugoslavia
Zaire
Zimbabwe
Soverign Military Order of Malta

IOM OVERSEAS LIAISON AND OPERATIONAL OFFICES

Albania, Tirana
Argentina, Buenos Aires
Australia, Camberra City
Austria, Vienna
Azerbaijan, Nicosia
Belgium/Luxembourg, Brussels
Bolivia, La Paz
Bosnia and Herzegovina, Sarajevo
Chile, Santiago *
Colombia, Bogota
Costa Rica, San Jose *
Croatia, Zagreb
Cyprus, Nicosia
Djibouti
Dominican Republic, Santo Domingo
Ecuador, Quito
Egypt, Cairo
El Salvador, San Salvador
Finland, Helsinki
France, Paris
Georgia, Tbilisi
Germany, Bonn
Ghana, Accra
Greece, Athens
Guatemala, Guatemala City
Haiti, Port Au Prince
Honduras, Tegucigalpa
Hong Kong *
Hungary, Budapest
Indonesia, Tanjung Pinang
Italy, Rome
Japan, Tokyo
Jordan, Jebel Amman
Kenya, Nairobi *
Kuwait, Kuwait City
Liberia, Monrovia
Macau
Malaysia, Kuala Lumpur
Mozambique, Maputo
Netherlands, The Hague
New Zealand, Wellington
Nicaragua, Managua
Pakistan, (Islamabad, Peshawar, Quetta)
Panama, Panama City
Paraguay, Asuncion
Peru, Lima
Philippines, Manila
Portugal, (Lisbon)
Romania, Bucharest
Russia, Moscow *
Singapore
South Africa, Pretoria
Spain, Madrid
Switzerland, Bern
Taiwan, Taipei
Tajikistan, Dushanbe
Thailand, Bangkok *
Turkey, Ankara
Uganda, Kampala
United Kingdom, London
United States of America, Washington, New York, Chicago, Miami
Uruguay, Montevideo
Venezuela, Caracas
Vietnam, Ho Chi Minh City, Hanoi
Yugoslavia, Belgrade
Zambia, Lusaka

INTERNATIONAL PACIFIC HALIBUT COMMISSION
UNITED STATES AND CANADA

Headquarters: University of Washington, Seattle, WA 98105
phone (206) 634–1838, fax (206) 632–2983
Mailing address: PO Box 95009, Seattle WA 98145–2009

American Commissioners:
Ralph G. Hoard, PO Box 79003, Seattle, WA 98119, (206) 282–0988, fax (206) 282–7222.
Ms. Kris Norosz, PO Box 805, Petersburg, AK 99833, (907) 772–9323.
Steven Pennoyer, National Marine Fisheries Service, PO Box 1668, Juneau, AK 99802, (907) 586–7221, fax (907) 586–7131.

Canadian Commissioners:
Dr. Richard J. Beamish, Pacific Biological Station, PO Box 100, Nanaimo, B.C., Canada V9R 5K6, (604) 756–7040, fax (604) 756–7053.
Gregg Best, 1093 Lazo Road, Comox, BC, Canada V9M 3W3, (250) 339–0986, fax (250) 339–6092.
Rodney Pierce, 3044 Kensington Court, Courtenay, BC, Canada V9N 8Z8, (250) 334–0656, fax (250) 897–1238.

* Post includes Regional Coverage.

Director and Secretary (ex officio).—Donald A. McCaughran, PO Box 95009, Seattle, WA 98145–2009.

ORGANIZATION OF AMERICAN STATES

17th Street and Constitution Avenue NW 20006, phone (202) 458–3000, fax 458–3967

PERMANENT MISSIONS TO THE OAS

Antigua and Barbuda.—Ambassador Lionel Alexander Hurst, 3216 New Mexico Avenue NW, Washington DC 20016, phone 362–5122, fax 362–5225.

Argentina.—Ambassador Alicia D. Martinez Rios, 1816 Corcoran Street NW, Washington DC 20009, phone 387–4142, fax 328–1591.

The Bahamas.—Ambassador Arlington Butler, Interim Representative, 2220 Massachusetts Avenue NW, Washington DC 20008, phone 319–2660, fax 319–2668.

Barbados.—Ambassador and Mrs. Courtney Blackman, 2144 Wyoming Avenue NW, Washington DC 20008, phone 939–9200, fax 332–7467.

Belize.—Ambassador and Mrs. Dean Russell Lindo, 2535 Massachusetts Avenue NW, Washington DC 20008–098, phone 332–9636, fax 332–6888.

Bolivia.—Ambassador and Mrs. Carlos Casap Salame, 1735 Eye Street NW, Suite 918/9, Washington DC 20006, phone 785–0218, fax 296–0563.

Brazil.—Ambassador Itamar Franco, Interim Representative, 2600 Virginia Avenue NW, Suite 412, Washington DC 20037, phone 333–4224, fax 333–6610.

Canada.—Ambassador and Mrs. Brian Dickson, 501 Pennsylvania Avenue NW, Washington DC 20001, phone 682–1768, fax 682–7624.

Chile.—Ambassador and Mrs. Edmundo Vargas Carreno, 2000 L Street NW, Suite 720, Washington DC 20036, phone 887–5475, fax 775–0713.

Colombia.—Ambassador Carlos Holmes Trujillo, 1609 22nd Street NW, Washington DC 20008, phone 332–8003, fax 234–9781.

Costa Rica.—Ambassador Fernando Herrero, Interim Representative, 2112 S Street NW, Washington DC 20008, phone 234–9280, fax 986–2274.

Dominica.—3216 New Mexico Avenue, NW 20016, phone 364–6781.

Dominican Republic.—Ambassador Flavio Espinal, Interim Representative, 1715 22nd Street NW, Washington DC 20008, phone 332–9142, fax 265–8057.

Ecuador.—2535 15th Street NW, Washington DC 20009, phone 234–1494, fax 667–3482.

El Salvador.—Ambassador Mauricio Granillo, Interim Representative, 1010 16th Street NW, Fourth Floor, Washington DC 20036, phone 467–0054, fax 467–4261.

Grenada.—Ambassador Denis G. Antoine, 1701 New Hampshire Avenue NW, Washington DC 20009, phone 265–2561, fax 265–2468.

Guatemala.—Ambassador and Mrs. Jose Luis Chea Urruela, 1507 22nd Street NW, Washington DC 20036, phone 833–4015, fax 833–4011.

Guyana.—Ambassador and Mrs. Odeen Ishmael, 2490 Tracy Place NW, Washington DC 20008, phone 265–6900, fax 232–1297.

Haiti.—Ambassador Jean Casimir, 2311 Massachusetts Avenue NW, Washington DC 20008, phone 332–4090, fax 745–7215.

Honduras.—Ambassador Marlene Villela de Talbott and Mr. Jose Jorge Talbott, 5100 Wisconsin Avenue NW, Suite 403, Washington DC 20016, phone 362–9656, fax 537–7170.

Jamaica.—Ambassador and Mrs. Richard Bernal, 1520 New Hampshire Avenue NW, Washington DC 20036, phone 452–0660, fax 452–9395.

Mexico.—Ambassador Carmen Moreno de Del Cueto, 2440 Massachusetts Avenue NW, Washington DC 20008, phone 332–3663, fax 332–9498.

Nicaragua.—Ambassador Felipe Rodriguez, 1627 New Hampshire Avenue NW, Washington DC 20009, phone 332–1643, fax 745–0710.

Panama.—Ambassador and Mrs. Lawrence Chewning Fabrega, 2201 Wisconsin Avenue NW, Suite 240, phone 965–4826, fax 965–4836.

Paraguay.—Ambassador and Mrs. Carlos Victor Montanaro, 1010 16th Street NW, Fourth Floor, Washington DC 20036, phone 244–3003, fax 234–4508.

Peru.—Ambassador Beatriz Ramacciotti, 2201 Wisconsin Avenue NW, Suite 220, Washington DC 20007, phone 232–2881, fax 337–6866.

Saint Kitts and Nevis.—Ambassador Osbert O. Liburd, 3216 New Mexico Avenue NW, Washington DC 20016, phone 686–2636, fax 686–5740.

Saint Lucia.—Ambassador and Mrs. Joseph E. Edmunds, 3216 New Mexico Avenue NW, Washington, DC 20016, phone 364–6792, fax 364–6723.

Saint Vincent and The Grenadines.— Ambassador and Mrs. Kingsley Layne, 1717 Massachusetts Avenue NW, Suite 102, Washington DC 20036, phone 364–6730, fax 364–6736.
Suriname.—Ambassador and Mrs. Willem Udenhout, 4301 Connecticut Avenue NW, Suite 108, Washington, DC 20008, phone 244–7488, fax 244–5878.
Trinidad and Tobago.—Ambassador Corinne McKnight and Mr. David McKnight, 1708 Massachusetts Avenue NW, Washington DC 20036, phone 467–6490, fax 785–3130.
United States of America.—Ambassador Harriet Babbitt and The Honorable Bruce Babbitt, ARA/USOAS Bureau of Inter-American Affairs, Department of State, Room 6494, Washington DC 20520, phone 647–9376, fax 647–0911.
Uruguay.—Ambassador Antonio Mercader, Interim Representative, 2801 New Mexico Avenue NW, Suite 1210, Washington DC 20007, phone 333–0588, fax 337–3758.
Venezuela.—Ambassador Francisco Paparoni, 1099 30th Street NW, Second Floor, Washington DC 20007, phone 342–5837, fax 625–5657.

GENERAL SECRETARIAT

Secretary General.—Cesar Gavirio, 458–3841, fax 458–3624.
Chief of Staff of the Secretary General.—Miguel Silva, 458–3841, fax 458–3624.
Assistant Chief of Staff.—Cesar Negret, 458–3850, fax 458–3624.
Assistant Secretary General.—Christopher R. Thomas, 458–6046, fax 458–3011.
Chief of Staff to the Assistant Secretary General.—Hernan Hurtado Prem, 458–6046, fax 458–3011.
Assistant Secretary for—
Legal Affairs.—Enrique Lagos, 458–3983.
Management.—James R. Harding, 458–3436.
Executive Secretary for Integral Development.—Leonel Zuniga, 458–3325.
Directors:
Department of Public Information.—Jorge Telerman, 458–3754.
Office of Protocol.—Ana C. O'Brien, 458–718, fax 458–6328.
Inter-American Commission of Human Rights (ACHR)
Chairman.—Ambassador John Donaldson, 458–6084.
Executive Secretary.—Ambassador Jorge E. Tallana, 458–6002.
Inter-American Commission of Women (CIM)
Chairperson.—Quezada Martinez, 458–6084, fax 458–6094.
Executive Secretary.—Linda J, poole, 458–6084, fax 458–6094.
Inter-American Drug Abuse Control Commission (CICAD)
Chairman.—[Vacant.]
Executive Secretary.—David Beall, 458–3178.

ORGANIZATION FOR ECONOMIC COOPERATION AND DEVELOPMENT

Headquarters: 2 rue André–ascal, 75775 Paris CEDEX 16, France
phone (331) 4524–8200, fax (331) 4524–8500

Secretary-General.—Donald J. Johnston.
Deputy Secretary-General.—Joanna Shelton.
Member Countries:

Australia	Hungary	Norway
Austria	Iceland	Poland
Belgium	Ireland	Portugal
Canada	Italy	Spain
Czech Republic	Japan	Sweden
Denmark	Korea	Switzerland
Finland	Luxembourg	Turkey
France	Mexico	United Kingdom
Germany	Netherlands	United States
Greece	New Zealand	

OECD PUBLICATIONS AND INFORMATION CENTER, WASHINGTON, DC

2001 L Street 20036, phone (202) 785–6323, fax (202) 785–0350

http://www.oecdwash.org

Washington Representative.—Denis Lamb.
Deputy Head of Center.—Matthew Brosius.

PAN AMERICAN SANITARY BUREAU

REGIONAL OFFICE OF THE WORLD HEALTH ORGANIZATION

525 23rd Street NW Washington DC 20037, phone (202) 974–000, fax (202) 974–3663

PAN AMERICAN SANITARY BUREAU

Director.—Sir George A. O. Alleyne, 974–3408.
Deputy Director.—Dr. David Brandling-Bennett, 974–3178.
Assistant Director.—Dr. Mirta Roses Periago, 974–3404.
Chief of Administration.—Mr. Thomas M. Tracy, 974–3412.
Chief of External Relations.—Dr. Irene Klinger, 974–3194.
Chief of Analysis and Strategic Planning.—Dr. Juan Manuel Sotelo, 974–3187.
Director, Division of—
Communicable Disease Prevention and Control.—Dr. Stephen Corber, 974–3850.
Health and Development.—Dr. Juan Antonio Casas, 974–3210.
Health Promotion and Protection.—Dr. Joao Yunes, 974–3261.
Health Systems and Services.—Dr. Daniel López Acuña, 974–3221.
Health and Environment.—Mr. Horst Otterstetter, 974–3311.
Special Program for Vaccines and Immunization.—Dr. Ciro de Quadros, 974–3247.

FIELD OFFICES

PAHO/WHO Caribbean Program Coordination, PO Box 508, Dayralls and Navy Garden Roads, Christ Church, Bridgetown, Barbados, phone 426–3860, fax 436–9779.
Caribbean Program Coordination.—(Antigua and Barbuda, Barbados, Dominica, Grenada, St. Kitts and Nevis, Saint Lucia, St. Vincent and the Grenadines. Eastern Caribbean: Anguilla, British, Virgin Islands, Montserrat. French Antilles: Guadaloupe, Martinique, St. Martin and St. Bartholomew, French Guiana).
PAHO/WHO Representatives:
Argentina, Oficina Sanitaria Panamericana, Marcelo T. de Alvear 684, 4o. piso, 1058 Buenos Aires, Argentina, phone 312–5301 to 5304, fax 311–9151.
Bahamas (Turks and Caicos), PO Box N 9111, Third Floor Curry House Building, Shirley Street, Royal Victoria Compound, Nassau, Bahamas, phone 326–7390, fax 326–7012.
Belize, PO Box 1834, No. 4 Eyre Street, Belize City, Belize, phone 448–85, fax 309–17.
Bolivia, Casillas Postales 9790 y 2504, Edificio "Foncomin," Av. 20 de octubre No. 2038, 3er Piso, La Paz, Bolivia, phone 362–646, fax 391–296.
Brazil, Caixa Postal 08–29, 70912–70, Setor de Embaixadas Norte, Lote 19, 70800–00, Brasília, D.F., Brasília, phone 312–6565, fax 321–1922.
Chile, Oficina Sanitaria Panamericana, Casilla 9459, Piso 5, Oficina 58, Calle Monjitas 689, Santiago, Chile, phone 6398–209, fax 6393–728.
Colombia, Apartado Aéreo 253367, Carrera 13 No. 32–76, Edificio Urano, 5to Piso, Santafé de Bogotá, DC, Colombia, phone 336–7100, fax 336–7306.
Costa Rica, Apartado 3745, Calle 16, Avenida 6 y 8, Distrito Hospital, San José, Costa Rica, phone 233–8878, fax 233–8061.
Cuba, Oficina Sanitaria Panamericana, Apartado Postal 68, Calle 4 No. 407, entre 17 y 19 Vedado, La Habana, Cuba, phone 323–666, 323–406, fax 333–375.
Dominican Republic, Secretaría de Estado de Salud Pública y Asistencia Social, Apartado 1464, Avenida San Cristóbal, Esquina Ave. Tiradentes, Santo Domingo, República Dominicana, phone 562–1519, fax 544–0322.
Ecuador, Oficina Sanitaria Panamericana, San Javier 295 y Francisco de Orellana, Quito, Ecuador, phone 544–642, fax 502–830.
El Salvador, 73 Avenida Sur No. 135, Colonia Escalón, Apartado 1072, Sucursal Centro, San Salvador, El Salvador, phone 298–3491, fax 298–1168.
Guatemala, Oficina Sanitaria Panamericana, Apartado Postal 383, Edificio Etisa, Plazuela Espana, 7a Avenida 12–23, Zona 9, Guatemala, Guatemala, phone 332–2032, fax 334–3804.
Guyana, PO Box 10969, Lot 8 Brickdam Stabroek, Georgetown, Guyana, phone 751–50, fax 666–54.
Haiti, Boite Postale 1330, No. 295 Avenue John Brown, Port-au-Prince, Haiti, phone 458–666, fax 451–732.
Honduras, Oficina Sanitaria Panamericana, Apartado Postal 728, Colonia Palmira No. 2036, Avenida República de Panamá, frente Embajada China, Tegucigalpa MDC, Honduras, phone 32–3911, fax 32–8942.
Jamaica (Bermuda and Cayman), PO Box 384, Cross Roads, Imperial Life Building, 60 Knutsford Boulevard, Kingston 5, Jamaica, phone 926–1990, fax 929–1182.

México, Oficina Sanitaria Panamericana, Apartado Postal 10–80, Avenida de las Palmas No. 530, Lomas de Chapultepec, C.P. 11000, México, D.F., México, phone 202–8200, fax 520–8868.

Nicaragua, Oficina Sanitaria Panamericana, Apartado Postal 1309, Complejo Nacional de Salud, Camino a la Sabana, Managua, Nicaragua, phone 89–4200, fax 289–4999.

Panamá, Casilla Postal 7260, Zona 5, Ministerio de Salud, Avenida Cuba y Calle 36, Panamá, Panamá, phone 227–0082, fax 227–2270.

Paraguay, Casilla de Correo 839, Edificio ''Faro del Río'' Mcal. López 957 Esq. Estados Unidos, Asunción, Paraguay, phone 450–495, fax 450–498.

Perú, Oficina Sanitaria Panamericana, Los Cedros 269, San Isidro, Lima 27, Perú, Casilla 2117, Lima 100, Perú, phone 421–3030, fax 442–4634.

Suriname, PO Box 1863, Gravenstraat 60 (boven), Paramaribo, Suriname, phone 471–676, fax 471–568.

Trinidad and Tobago, PO Box 898, 49 Jerningham Avenue, Port-of-Spain, Trinidad, phone 624–7524, fax 624–5643.

Uruguay, Casilla de Correo 1821, Avenue Brasil 2697, Apts. 5,6 y 8, Esquina Coronel Alegre, Código Postal 11300, Montevideo, Uruguay, phone 773–590, fax 773–530.

Venezuela (Netherlands Antilles), Oficina Sanitaria Panamericana, Avenida Sexta entre 5a y 6a, Transversal, Altamira, Caracas, Venezuela, Apartado 6722, Carmelitas, Caracas 1010, Venezuela, phone 262–2085, fax 261–6069.

CENTERS

Caribbean Epidemiology Center (CAREC).—Director, PO Box 164, 16–18 Jamaica Boulevard, Federation Park, Port-of Spain, Trinidad, phone 622–4261, fax 622–2792.

Caribbean Food and Nutrition Institute (CFNI).—Director, PO Box 140 - Mona, University of the West Indies, Kingston 7, Jamaica, phone 927–1540, fax 927–2657.

Field Office, United States-Mexico Border (FO/USMB).—Chief, Pan American Sanitary Bureau, 6006 North Mesa, Suite 600, El Paso, Texas 79912, phone (915) 581–6645, fax 833–4768.

Institute of Nutrition of Central America and Panama (INCAP).—Director, Apartado Postal 1188, Carretera Roosevelt, Zona 11, Guatemala, Guatemala, phone 471–5655, fax 473–6529.

Latin American Center and Caribbean Center on Health Sciences Information (BIREME).—Director, Caixa Postal 20381, Rua Botucate 862, Vila Clementino, CEP. 04023–062, Sao Paulo, SP, Brasil, phone 549–2611, fax 571–1919.

Latin American Center for Perinatology and Human Development (CLAP).—Director, Casilla de Correo 627, Hospital de Clínicas, Piso 16, Montevideo, Uruguay, phone 472–929, fax 472–593.

Pan American Institute for Food Protection and Zoonoses (INPPAZ).—Director, Casilla de Correo No. 44, Calle Talcahuano 1660, (CP 1640) Martínez, Provincia de Buenos Aires, Argentina, phone 792–0087, fax 112328.

Pan American Center for Sanitary Engineering and Environmental Sciences (CEPIS).—Director, Calle Los Pinos 259, Urbanización Camacho, Lima 12, Perú, Casilla Postal 4337, Lima 100, Perú, phone 437–7019, fax 437–8289.

Pan American Center for Human Ecology and Health (ECO).—Director, Rancho Guadalupe, Metepec, Estado de México, México, Apartado Postal 37–73, 06696 México, D.F. México, phone 71–10–91, fax 71–10–90.

Pan American Foot-and-Mouth Disease Center (PANAFTOSA).—Director, Avenida Presidente Kennedy 7778, (Antiga Estrada Rio-Petrópolis), 25000 Sao Bento, Duque de Caxias, Rio de Janeiro, Brasil, Caixa Postal 589, 20001 Rio de Janeiro, Brasil, phone 671–3128, fax 671–2387.

PERMANENT JOINT BOARD ON DEFENSE, CANADA-UNITED STATES

CANADIAN SECTION

Ottawa, Ontario, Canada K1A OK2

phone (613) 995–6637

Chairman.—Jesse Flis, (613) 992–2936.
Members:
Air.—BG Cajo Brando, (613) 992–7384.
External Affairs.—Ralph Lysyshyn, (613) 996–2521.
Land.—BG Walt Homes, (613) 945–7242.
Maritime.—Cdr. Bruce MacLean.
Policy.—RADM Jim King, (613) 992–2769.
Secretary.—Charles Court, (613) 992–5457.
Military Secretary.—LtCol. Claude Perras, (613) 995–6637.

UNITED STATES SECTION

**Crystal Gateway North, Room 511, 1111 Jefferson Davis Highway, Arlington VA 22202
phone (703) 604–0488**

Chairman.—Dwight N. Mason, (703) 604–0488.
Members:
Department of State.—Earl A. Wayne, Room 6219, (202) 647–6402.
Joint Staff/Steering and Coordinating.—MG Michael J. Byron, Pentagon, Room 2E996, (703) 697–1887.
Air Force.—MG Terry J. Schwailier, Pentagon, Room 4E–1046, (703) 695–9067.
Navy.—RADM Timothy W. LaFleur, Pentagon, Room 4E–572, (703) 695–2453.
Secretary.—Leonard Kusnitz, Department of State, Room 5227, New State Building, (202) 647–2228.
Military Secretary.—Col(S) Robert W. Tomlinson, CGN, Suite 511, (703) 604–0488.

SOUTH PACIFIC COMMISSION

SECRETARIAT

B.P. D–5, Noumea Cedex, New Caledonia, phone (687) 26.20.00, fax (687) 26.38.18

Secretary General.—Ati George Sokomanu.
Director of Programs.—Vaasatia Poloma Komiti.
Director of Services.—Fusi Caginavanua.

U.S. Contact: Office of Pacific Island Affairs, Bureau of East Asian and Pacific Affairs, Department of State, Washington, DC 20520, phone (202) 647–3546.

American Samoa
Australia
Cook Islands
Federated States of Micronesia
Fiji
France
French Polynesia
Guam
Kiribati
Marshall Islands
Nauru
New Caledonia
New Zealand
Niue
Northern Mariana Islands
Palau
Papua New Guinea
Pitcairn Islands
Solomon Islands
Tokelau
Tonga
Tuvalu
United Kingdom
United States
Vanuatu
Wallis and Futuna
Western Samoa

UNITED NATIONS

GENERAL ASSEMBLY

The General Assembly is composed of all 185 United Nations Member States.

SECURITY COUNCIL

The Security Council has 15 members. The United Nations Charter designates five States as permanent members, and the General Assembly elects 10 other members for two-year terms. The term of office for each non-permanent member of the Council ends on 31 December of the year indicated in parentheses next to its name.

The five permanent members of the Security Council are China, France, Russian Federation, United Kingdom and United States.

The 10 non-permanent members of the Council in 1997 are Chile (1997), Costa Rica (1998), Egypt (1997), Guinea-Bissau (1997), Japan (1998), Kenya (1998), Poland (1997), Portugal (1998), Republic of Korea (1997) and Sweden (1998).

ECONOMIC AND SOCIAL COUNCIL

The Economic and Social Council has 54 members, elected for three-year terms by the General Assembly. The term of office for each member expires on 31 December of the year indicated in parentheses next to its name. In 1997, the Council is composed of the following States:

Argentina (1998)
Australia (1997)
Bangladesh (1998)
Belarus (1997)
Brazil (1997)
Canada (1998)
Cape Verde (1999)
Central African Republic (1998)
Chile (1999)
China (1998)
Colombia (1997)
Congo (1997)
Côte d'Ivoire (1997)
Cuba (1999)
Czech Republic (1998)
Djibouti (1999)
El Salvador (1999)
Finland (1998)
France (1999)
Gabon (1998)
Gambia (1999)
Germany (1999)
Guyana (1998)
Iceland (1999)
India (1997
Jamaica (1997)
Japan (1999)
Jordan (1998)
Latvia (1999)
Lebanon (1998)
Luxembourg (1997)
Malaysia (1997)
Mexico (1999)
Mozambique (1999)
Netherlands (1997)
Nicaragua (1998)
Philippines (1997)
Poland (1997)
Republic of Korea (1999)
Romania (1998)
Russian Federation (1998)
South Africa (1997)
Spain (1999)
Sri Lanka (1999)
Sudan (1997)
Sweden (1998
Thailand (1997)
Togo (1998)
Tunisia (1998)
Turkey (1999)
Uganda (1997)
United Kingdom (1998)
United States (1997)
Zambia (1999)

TRUSTEESHIP COUNCIL

The Trusteeship Council has five members: China, France, Russian Federation, United Kingdom and the United States. With the independence of Palau, the last remaining United Nations trust territory, the Council formerly suspended operation on 1 November 1994. By a resolution adopted on that day, the Council amended its rules of procedure to drop the obligation to meet annually and agreed to meet as occasion required—by its decision or the decision of its President, or at the request of a majority of its members or the General Assembly or the Security Council.

INTERNATIONAL COURT OF JUSTICE

The International Court of Justice has 15 members, elected by both the General Assembly and the Security Council. Judges hold nine-year terms, which end on 5 February of the year indicated in parentheses next to their names.

As of 6 February 1997, the composition of the Court will be: Mohammed Bedjaoui (Algeria) (2006), Carl-August Fleischhauer (Germany) (2003), Gilbert Guillaume (France) (2000), Géza Herczegh (Hungary)(2003), Rosalyn Higgins (United Kingdom) (2000), Shi Jiuyong (China) (2003), Pieter H. Kooijmans (Netherlands) (2006), Abdul G. Koroma (Sierra Leone) (2003), Shigeru Oda (Japan) (2003), Gonzalo Parra-Aranguren (Venezuela) (2000), Raymond Ranjeva (Madagascar) (2000), José Francisco Rezek (Brazil) (2006), Stephen M. Schwebel (United States) (2006), Christopher G. Weeramantry (Sri Lanka) (2000) and Vladlen S. Vereshchetin (Russian Federation) (2006).

UNITED NATIONS SECRETARIAT

One United Nations Plaza, New York NY 10017, (212) 963–1234, http://www.un.org

Secretary General.—Mr. Kofi A. Annan (Ghana).

EXECUTIVE OFFICE OF THE SECRETARY-GENERAL

Chief of Staff.—Mr. Iqbal Riza (Pakistan).
Executive Coordinator for UN Reform.—Mr. Maurice Strong (Canada).
Assistant Secretary-General, External Relations.—Mrs. Gillian Sorensen (USA).
Executive Assistant.—Mrs. Elisabeth Lindenmayer (France).
Executive Assistant.—Mr. Sashi Tharoor (India).

OFFICE OF INTERNAL OVERSIGHT SERVICES

Under-Secretary-General.—Mr. Karl Paschke (Germany).

OFFICE OF LEGAL AFFAIRS

Under-Secretary-General and Legal Counsel.—Mr. Hans Corell (Sweden).

DEPARTMENT OF POLITICAL AFFAIRS

Under-Secretary-General.—Sir Kieran Prendergast (U.K.).
Assistant Secretary-General.—Mr. Alvaro de Soto (Peru).
Assistant Secretary-General.—Mr. Ibrahima Fall (Senegal).

DEPARTMENT OF PEACE-KEEPING OPERATIONS

Under-Secretary-General.—Mr. Bernard Miyet (France).
Assistant Secretary-Genera.—Mr. Hedi Annabi (Tunisia).
Assistant Secretary-General.—Mr. Manfred Eisele (Germany).

DEPARTMENT OF HUMANITARIAN AFFAIRS

Under-Secretary-General.—Mr. Yasushi Akashi (Japan).

DEPARTMENT FOR POLICY COORDINATION AND SUSTAINABLE DEVELOPMENT

Under-Secretary-General.—Mr. Nitin Desai (India).
Special Adviser on Gender Issues and Advancement of Women.—Assistant Secretary-General Ms. Angela King (Jamaica).

DEPARTMENT FOR ECONOMIC AND SOCIAL INFORMATION AND POLICY ANALYSIS

Under-Secretary-General.—[Vacant.]

DEPARTMENT FOR DEVELOPMENT SUPPORT AND MANAGEMENT SERVICES

Under-Secretary-General.—Mr. Yongjian Jin (China).

The Secretary-General announced on 17 March 1997 that the three economic and social departments will be consolidated to one department.

DEPARTMENT OF PUBLIC INFORMATION

Assistant Secretary-General.—Mr. Samir Sanbar (Lebanon).

Spokesman.—Mr. Fred Eckhard (USA).

The Secretary-General announced on 17 March 1997 that the Department of Public Information will be transformed to a new Office of Communications and Media Services.

UNITED NATIONS INFORMATION CENTER

1775 K Street NW, Suite 400, Washington DC 20006, phone (202) 331–8670 fax (202) 331–9191, dpi-washington@un.org

Director.—Mr. Joe Sills (USA).

Deputy Director.—Mrs. Joan L. Hills (USA)

DEPARTMENT OF ADMINISTRATION AND MANAGEMENT

Under-Secretary-General.—Mr. Joseph Connor (USA).

OFFICE OF PROGRAMME PLANNING, BUDGET AND ACCOUNTS

Controller.—Assistant Secretary-General: Mr. Jean-Pierre Halbwachs (Mauritius).

OFFICE OF HUMAN RESOURCES MANAGEMENT

Assistant Secretary-General.—Mr. Denis Halliday (Ireland).

OFFICE OF CONFERENCE AND SUPPORT SERVICES

Assistant Secetary-General.—Mr. Benon Sevan (Cyprus).

UNITED NATIONS AT GENEVA (UNOG)

Palais des Nations, 1211 Geneva 10, Switzerland, phone (41–22) 917–1234.

Director-General of UNOG.—Assistant Secretary-General Mr. Vladimir Petrovsky (Russian Fed.)

UNITED NATIONS AT VIENNA (UNOV)

Vienna International Centre, PO Box 500, A–1400 Vienna, Austria, phone (43–1) 211–31–0.

Director-General of UNOV.—Assistant Secretary-General Giorgio Giacomelli (Italy)

REGIONAL ECONOMIC COMMISSIONS

Economic Commission for Africa (ECA), PO Box 3001, Addis Ababa Ethiopia, phone (251–1) 51–72–00

Under-Secretary-General.—Mr. K.Y. Amoako (Ghana).

Economic Commission for Europe (ECE) Palais des Nations, 1211 Geneva 10, Switzerland, phone (41–22) 917–2893

Under-Secretary-General.—Mr. Yves Berthelot (France).

Economic Commission for Latin American and the Caribebean (ECLAC) Avenida Dag Hammarskjold, Vitacura, Santiago, Chile, phone (56–2) 210–2000, Apartado Postal 6–718, 11570 Mexico, DF, phone (52–5) 2501555

Under-Secretary-General.—Mr. Gert Rosenthal (Guatemala).

Economic and Social Commission for Asia and the Pacific (ESCAP), United Nations Building, Rajdamnern Avenue, Bankok 10200, Thailand, phone (66–2) 288–1234

Under-Secretary-General.—Mr. Adrianus Mooy (Indonesia).

Economic and Social Commission for Western Asia (ESCWA), PO Box 927115, Amman, Jordan, phone (962–6) 694351
Under-Secretary-General.—Mr. Hazem El Beblawi (Egypt).

FUNDS, PROGRAMMES AND BODIES OF THE UN

Advisory Committee on Administrative and Budgetary Questions (ACABQ), One United Nations Plaza, New York NY 10017, phone (212) 963–7456
Chairman.—Mr. C.S.M. Mselle, (UR of Tanzania).

Centre for Human Rights, Palais des Nations, 8–14 Avenue de la Paix, 1211 Geneva 10, Switzerland, phone (41–22) 917–1234
High Commissioner.—Ralph Zacklin (acting).
Officer-in-Charge.—Mr. Ralph Zacklin.
Jose Ayala Lasso resigned as High Commissioner as at 15 March 1997 and Mr. Zacklin will be OIC until his replacement is selected.

International Civil Service Commission (ICSC), One United Nations Plaza, New York NY 10017, phone (212) 963–8464
Chairman.—Mr. Mohsen Bel Hadj Amor (Tunisia).

Joint Inspection Unit (JIU), Palais des Nations, 1211 Geneva 10, Switzerland, phone (41–22) 917–1234
Chairman.—Mr. Fatih Bouyad-Agha (Algeria).

Panel of External Auditors, One United Nations Plaza, New York NY 10017, phone (212) 963–1234
Chairman.—Sir John Bourn, KCB (United Kingdom).

United Nations Centre for Human Settlements (Habitat), UN Office at Nairobi, PO Box 30030, Nairobi Kenya, phone (254–2) 621–234
Assistant Secretary-General: Mr. Wally N'Dow (Gambia).

United Nations Children's Fund (UNICEF), UNICEF House, 3 UN Plaza, New York NY 10017, phone (212) 326–7000
Executive Director.—Ms. Carol Bellamy (USA).

United Nations Conference on Trade and Development (UNCTAD), Palais des Nations, 8–14 Avenue de la Paix, 1211 Geneva 10, Switzerland, phone (41–22) 917–1234
Secretary-General.—Mr. Rubens Ricupero (Brazil).

United Nations Development Fund for Women (UNIFEM), 304 East 45th Street, Sixth Floor, New York NY 10017, phone (212) 906–6400
Director.—Ms. Noeleen Heyzer (Singapore).

United Nations Development Programme (UNDP), 1 United Nations Plaza, New York NY 10017, phone (212) 906–5000
Administrator.—Mr. James Gustave Speth (USA).

United Nations Development Programme (UNDP)1775 K Street NW, Suite 420, Washington DC 20006, phone (202) 331–9130
Director—.Mr. Roy Morey (USA).

United Nations Environment Programme (UNEP), PO Box 30552, Nairobi Kenya, phone (254–2) 621–234
Executive Director.—Under-Secretary-General Elizabeth Dowdeswell (Canada).

United Nations High Commissioner for Refugees (UNHCR), Case Postale 2500, CH–1211 Geneve 2 Depot, Switzerland, phone (41–22) 739–8111
High Commissioner.—Ms. Sadako Ogata (Japan).

United Nations High Commissioner for Refugees (UNHCR), 1775 K Street NW, Third Floor, Washington DC 20006, phone (202) 296–5191
Representative.—Mr. Anne-Willem Bijleveld (Netherlands).

United Nations Institute for Disarmament Research (UNIDIR), Palais des Nations, 1211 Geneva 10, Switzerland, phone (41–22) 917–4292
Director.—Mr. Sverre Lodgaard (Norway).

United Nations Institute for Training and Research (UNITAR), Palais des Nations, 1211 Geneva 10, Switzerland, phone (41–22) 798–5850
Acting Executive Director.—Mr. Marcel A. Boisard (Switzerland).

United Nations International Drug Control Programme (UNDCP), PO Box 500, A–1400 Vienna, Austria, phone (43–1) 21345 ext. 4251
Executive Director.—Mr. Giorgio Giacomelli (Italy).

United Nations International Research and Training, Institute for the Advancement of Women (INSTRAW), PO Box 21747, Santo Domingo, Dominican Republic, phone (1–809) 685–2111
Acting Director.—Ms. Martha Duenas Loza (Ecuador).

United Nations Interregional Crime and Justice Research Institute (UNICRI), Via Giulia 52, 00186 Rome, Italy, phone (39–6) 687–7437
Director.—Mr. Herman Woltring (Australia).

United Nations Office for Project Services (UNOPS), Room 1442, 220 East 42nd Street, New York NY 10017, phone (212) 906–6500
Executive Director.—Mr. Reinhart W.A. Helmke (Germany).

United Nations Population Fund (UNFPA), 220 East 42nd Street, New York NY 10017, phone (212) 297–5000
Executive Director.—Dr. Nafis Sadik (Pakistan).

United Nations Relief and Works Agency for Palestine Refugees in the Near East (UNRWA), Vienna International Centre, PO Box 700, A–1400 Vienna Austria, phone (43–1) 21345 ext. 4531
Commissioner-General.—Mr. Peter Hansen (Denmark).

United Nations Research Institute for Social Development (UNRISD), Palais des Nations, 1211 Geneva 10, Switzerland, phone (41–22) 798–8400
Director.—Mr. Dharam Ghai (Kenya).

United Nations Volunteers Programme (UNV), Postfach 260111, D–53153 Bonn Germany, phone (49–228) 815–2000
Executive Coordinator.—Dr. Brenda Gael McSweeney (USA).

World Food Programme (WFP), 426 Via Cristoforo Colombo, 00145 Rome Italy, phone (39–6) 552–2821
Executive Director.—Ms. Catherine Ann Bertini (USA).

United Nations University (UNU), 53–70, Jingumae 5–Chome, Shibuya-Ku, Tokyo 150, Japan, phone (81–3) 3499–2811
Rector.—Prof. Heitor Gurgulino de Souza (Brazil).

SPECIALIZED AGENCIES

Food and Agricuture Organization (FAO), Washington OfficeVia delle Terme di Caracalla, 00100 Rome, Italy phone (39–6) 52251
Director-General.—Mr. Jacques Diouf (Senegal).

Food and Agriculture Organization, Northern American Regional Office, Suite 300, 1001 22nd Street NW, Washington DC 20437, phone (202) 653–2400
Director.—Mr. Charles Riemenschneider (USA).

International Civil Aviation Organization (ICAO), 1000 Sherbrooke Street West, Montreal, Quebec H3A 2R2 Canada, phone (1–514) 285–8221
Secretary-General.—Dr. Philippe Rochat (Switzerland).

International Fund for Agricultural Development (IFAD), Via del Serafico 107, 00142 Rome, Italy, phone (39–6) 54591
President.—Mr. Fawzi H. Al-Sultan (Kuwait), 1775 K Street NW, Washington DC 20006, phone (202) 331–9099.
Representative.—Mrs. Vera Weill-Halle (USA).

International Labour Organization (ILO), 4, Routes des Morillons, Ch-1211 Geneva 22, Switzerland, phone (41–22) 799–6111
Director-General.—Mr. Michel Hansenne (Belgium).

1828 L Street NW, Suite 801, Washington DC 20036, phone (202) 653–7652
Director.—Mr. Anthony Freeman (USA).

International Maritime Organization (IMO), 4 Albert Embankment, London SE1 7SR, England, phone (44–171) 735–7611
Secretary-General.—Mr. William O'Neil (Canada).

International Monetary Fund (IMF), 700 19th Street NW, Washington, DC 20431, phone (202) 623–7000

Managing Director.—Mr. Michel Camdessus (France).

International Telecommunications Union (ITU), Palais des Nations, 1211 Geneva 20, Switzerland, phone (41–22) 730–5111
Secretary-General.—Mr. Pekka J. Tarjanne (Finland).

United Nations Educational, Scientific and Cultural Organization (UNESCO), 7 Place de Fontenoy, 75732 Paris, 07 SP France, phone (33–1) 4568–1000
Director-General.—Mr. Federico Mayor (Spain).

UNESCO Washington Office: 1775 K Street NW, Washington DC 20006, phone (202) 331–9118
Representative.—Mr. Wadi Haddad (USA).

United Nations Industrial Development Organization (UNIDO), PO Box 300, Vienna International Centre, A–1400 Vienna, Austria, phone (43–1) 21131–0
Director-General.—Mr. Mauricio de Maria Y Campos (Mexico).

Universal Postal Union (UPU), Weltpoststrasse 4, Case Postale, 3000 Berne 15, Switzerland, phone (41–31) 350–3111
Director-General.—Mr. Thomas E. Leavey.

World Bank Group, 1818 H Street NW, Washington DC 20433, phone (202) 477–1234
President.—Mr. James Wolfensohn (USA).

World Health Organization (WHO), 20 Avenue Appia, 1211 Geneva 27, Switzerland, phone (41–22) 791–2111
Director-General.—Dr. Hiroshi Nakajima (Japan).

World Health Organization, 1775 K Street NW, 4th Floor, Washington 2000, phone (202) 331–9081
External Relations Officer.—Ms. Nelle Temple Brown (USA).

World Intellectual Property Organization (WIPO), 34 Chemin des Colombetts, 1211 Geneva 20, Switzerland, phone (41–22) 730–9111
Director General.—Dr. Arpad Bogsch (USA).

World Meteorological Organization (WMO), Case postale No.2300, CH–1211 Geneva 2, Switzerland, phone (41–22) 730–8111
Secretary-Genera.—Mr. G.O.P. Obasi (Nigeria).

RELATED BODY

International Atomic Energy Agency (IAEA), PO Box 100, Vienna International Centre, A–1400 Vienna, Austria, phone (43–1) 2060–0
Director General.—Mr. Hans Blix (Sweden).
The IAEA is an independent intergovernmental organization under the aegis of the UN.

SPECIAL REPRESENTATIVES OR ENVOYS OF THE SECRETARY-GENERAL

Afghanistan: Head of United Nations Special Mission.—Norbert Heinrich Holl (Germany).
Angola: Special Representative.—Alioune Blondin Beye (Mali).
Bosnia and Herzegovina: Special Representative.—Kai Eide (Norway).
Burundi: Special Representative.—Marc Faguy (Canada).
Cambodia: Special Representative.—Benny Widyono (Indonesia).
Croatia: Transitional Administrator for Untaes (United States) (UN Transitional Administration for Eastern Slavonia, Baranja and Western Sirmium).—Jacques Klein.
Cyprus: Special Representative.—Han Sung-Joo (Republic of Korea).
East Timor: Personal Representative.—Jamsheed Marker (Pakistan).
FYROM (former Yugoslav Republic of Macedonia): Special Representative and Chief of Mission for UNPREDEP (UN Preventive Deployment Force in FYROM).—Henryk Sokalski (Poland).
Georgia: Special Envoy.—Edouard Brunner (Switzerland).
Great Lakes: Special Representative.—Mohamed Sahnoun (Algeria).
Greece and The Former Yugoslav Republic of Macedonia: Special Envoy.—Cyrus Vance (USA).
Guatemala: Special Representative.—Jean Arnault (France).
Guyana/Venezuela: Personal Representative.—Sir Alister McIntyre (Grenada).
Haiti: Special Representative.—Enrique Ter Horst (Venezuela).
Liberia: Special Representative.—Anthony B. Nyakyi (Tanzania).
Middle East: Special Representative to the Multilateral Negotiations on the Middle East Peace Talks.—Chinmaya R. Gharekhan (India).

Occupied Territories: Special Coordinator in the Occupied Territories.—Chinmaya R. Gharekhan (India).
Sierra Leone: Special Envo.—Berhanu Dinka (Ethiopia).
Sudan: Special Envoy for Humanitarian Affairs.—Vieri Traxler (Italy).
Tajikistan: Special Representative.—Gerd Merrem (Germany).
Western Sahara: Special Representative.—Sahabzada Yaqub-Khan (Pakistan). Acting Special Representative and Chairman of the Identification Commission.—Erik Jensen (Malaysia)

UN PEACE KEEPING OPERATIONS

The Good Officer Mission in Burundi.—Special Representative to the Mission, Marc Faguy, Canada.
Special Representative of the Secretary-General and Coordinator of United Nations Operations in Bosnia and Herzegovina, Kai Eide, Norway.
UN Angola Verification Mission (UNAVEM III).—Force Commander, Major-General Philip Valenio Sibanda, (Zimbabwe).
UN Disengagement Observer Force (UNDOF).—Force Commander, Major-General Johan Kosters, (Netherlands).
UN Force in Cyprus (UNFICYP).—Force Commander, Major-General Evervisto Arturo de Vergara, (Argentina).
UN Interim Force in Lebanon (UNIFIL).—Force Commander, Major-General Stanislaw Franciszek Wozniak, (Poland).
UN Iraq-Kuwait Observation Mission (UNIKOM).—Force Commander, Major-General Gian Santillo, (Italy).
UN Military Observer Group in India and Pakistan (UNMOGIP).—Chief Military Observer, Major-General Alfonso Pessolano, (Italy).
UN Mission in Bosnia and Herzegovina (UNMIBH).—Commisioner of the International Police Task Force, Mr. Peter Fitzgerald, (Ireland).
UN Mission in Haiti (UNMIH).—Force Commander, Brigadier-General J.R.P. Daigle, (Canada).
UN Mission of Observers in Prevlaka (UNMOP).—Chief Military Observer, Colonel Goran Gunnarsson, (Sweden).
UN Mission for the Referendum in Western Sahara (MINURSO).—Force Commander, Major-General Garcia Leandro, (Portugal).
UN Observer Mission in Georgia (UNOMIG).—Chief Military Observer, Major-General Per Kallstrom, (Sweden).
UN Observer Mission in Liberia (UNOMIL).—Chief Military Observer, Major-General Mahmoud Talha, (Egypt).
UN Mission of Observers in Tajikistan (UNMOT).—Chief Military Observer, Brigadier-General Hasan Abaza, (Jordan).
UN Operation in Somalia (UNOSOM II).—Force Commander, Lieutenant-General Aboo Samah Bin Aboo Bakor, (Malaysia).
UN Peace Keeping Operation In Mozambique (ONUMOZ).—Force Commander, Major-General Mohammed Abdus Salam, (Bangladesh).
UN Preventive Deployment Force (UNPREDEP).—Force Commander, Brigadier-General Bo Lennart Wranker, (Sweden).
UN Transitional Administration in Eastern Slavonia, Baranja and Western Sirmium (UNTAES).—Force Commander, Major-General Jozef Schoups, (Belgium).
UN Transitional Authority in Cambodia (UNTAC).—Force Commander, Lieutenant-General John M. Sanderson, (Australia).
UN Truce Supervision Organization (UNTSO).—Force Commander, Colonel Joseph Bujold, (Canada).
UN Verification Mission in Guatemala (MINUGUA).—Mission Director, Jean Arnault, (France).

WORLD BANK GROUP

The World Bank Group comprises five organizations: the International Bank for Reconstruction and Development (IBRD), the International Development Association (IDA), the International Finance Corporation (IFC), the Multilateral Investment Guarantee Agency (MIGA) and the International Centre for the Settlement of Investment Disputes (ICSID).

Headquarters: 1818 H Street NW 20433, (202) 477–1234

INTERNATIONAL BANK FOR RECONSTRUCTION AND DEVELOPMENT

President.—James D. Wolfensohn.
Managing Director.—Sven Sandstrom.
Managing Director of Finance and Resource Mobilization.—Jessica P. Einhorn.
Managing Director and Chairman of Private Sector Development Group.—Richard H. Frank.
Managing Directors of Operations: Guatam S. Kaji, Caio K. Koch-Weser.
Senior Vice President and Chief Economist.—Joseph Stiglitz.
Senior Vice President and General Counsel.—Ibrahim F. I. Shihata.
Vice President and Controller.—Jules W. Muis.
Secretary.—Zhang Shengman.
Treasurer.—Gary L. Perlin.
Vice President for—
Africa Region: Jean-Louis Sarbib, Callisto Madavo.
East Asia and Pacific Region.—Jean-Michel Severino.
Environmentally Sustainable Development.—M. Ismail Serageldin.
Europe and Central Asia Region.—Johannes Linn.
External Affairs.—Mark Malloch Brown.
Finance and Private Sector Development.—Jean-Francois Rischard.
Financial Policy and Risk Management.—Brian Wilson.
Human Resources.—Dorothy Hamachi Berry.
Latin America and the Caribbean Region.—Shahid Javed Burki.
Middle East and North Africa Region.—Kemal Dervis.
Resource Mobilization and Cofinancing.—Hiroo Fukui.
South Asia Region.—Mieko Nishimizu.
Strategy and Resource Management.—Mark Baird.
Director and Chair, Human Development Department and Network.—David de Ferranti.
Director-General of Operations Evaluations.—Robert Picciotto.

EXECUTIVE DIRECTORS AND ALTERNATES

Bahrain, Arab Republic of Egypt, Jordan, Kuwait, Lebanon, Libya, Maldives, Oman, Qatar, Syrian Arab Republic, United Arab Emirates, Republic of Yemen
Executive Director.—Khalid M. Al-Saad.
Alternate.—Mohamed Wafik Hosny.
Saudi Arabia
Executive Director.—Khalid H. Alyahya.
Alternate.—Ibrahim M. Al-Mofleh.
Brazil, Colombia, Dominican Republic, Ecuador, Haiti, Philippines, Suriname, Trinidad and Tobago
Executive Director.—Juanita D. Amatong.
Alternate.—Murilo Portugal.
France
Executive Director.—Marc-Antoine Autheman.
Alternate.—Olivier Bourges.
Benin, Burkina Faso, Cameroon, Cape Verde, Central African Republic, Chad, Comoros, Congo, Côte d'Ivoire, Djibouti, Equatorial Guinea, Gabon, Guinea, Guinea-Bissau
Madagascar, Mali, Mauritania, Mauritius, Niger, Rwanda, Sao Tome and Principe, Senegal, Togo, Zaire
Executive Director.—Ali Bourhane.
Alternate.—Luc-Abdi Aden.
Afghanistan, Algeria, Ghana, Islamic Republic of Iran, Iraq, Morocco, Pakistan, Tunisia
Executive Director.—Kacim Brachemi.
Alternate.—Abdul Karim Lodhi.
Russian Federation
Executive Director.—Andrei Bugrov.
Alternate.—Eugene Miagkov.
Argentina, Bolivia, Chile, Paraguay, Peru, Uruguay

Executive Director.—Juan Cariaga.
Alternate.—Julio Nogues.
Angola, Botswana, Burundi, Eritrea, Ethiopia, The Gambia, Kenya, Lesotho, Liberia, Malawi, Mozambique, Namibia, Nigeria, Seychelles, Sierra Leone, South Africa, Sudan, Swaziland, Tanzania, Uganda, Zambia, Zimbabwe
Executive Director.—Joaquim R. Carvalho.
Alternate.—Godfrey Gaoseb.
Costa Rica, El Salvador, Guatemala, Honduras, Mexico, Nicaragua, Panama, Spain, Venezuela
Executive Director.—Enzo Del Bufalo.
Alternate.—Roberto Jimenez-Ortiz.
United Kingdom
Executive Director.—Huw Evans.
Alternate.—David Stanton.
Azerbaijan, Kyrgyz Republic, Poland, Switzerland, Tajikistan, Turkmenistan, Uzbekistan
Executive Director.—Jean-Daniel Gerber.
Alternate.—Jan Sulmicki.
Antigua and Barbuda, The Bahamas, Barbados, Belize, Canada, Dominica, Grenada, Guyana, Ireland, Jamaica, St. Kitts and Nevis, St. Lucia, St. Vincent and the Grenadines
Executive Director.—Leonard Good.
Alternate.—Winston Cox.
Austria, Belarus, Belgium, Czech Republic, Hungary, Kazakstan, Luxembourg, Slovak Republic, Slovenia, Turkey
Executive Director.—Luc Hubloue.
Alternate.—Namik Dagalp.
Brunei Darussalam, Fiji, Indonesia, Lao People's Democratic Republic, Malaysia, Myanmar, Nepal, Singapore, Thailand, Tonga, Vietnam
Executive Director.—Jannes Hutagalung.
Alternate.—[Vacant].
Denmark, Estonia, Finland, Iceland, Latvia, Lithuania, Norway, Sweden
Executive Director.—Ruth Jacoby.
Alternate.—Jorgen Varder.
China
Executive Director.—Li Yong.
Alternate.—Zhu Guangyao.
Australia, Cambodia, Kiribati, Republic of Korea, Marshall Islands, Federated States of Micronesia, Mongolia, New Zealand, Papua New Guinea, Solomon Islands, Vanuatu, Western Samoa
Executive Director.—Peter W.E. Nicholl.
Alternate.—Christopher Y. Legg.
Japan
Executive Director.—Atsuo Nishihara.
Alternate.—Rintaro Tamaki.
Albania, Greece, Italy, Malta, Portugal
Executive Director.—Franco Passacantando.
Alternate.—Helena Cordeiro.
Unites States
Executive Director.—Jan Piercy.
Alternate.—Michael Marek.
Germany
Executive Director.—Helmut Schaffer.
Alternate.—Erika Wagenhofer.
Bangladesh, Bhutan, India, Sri Lanka
Executive Director.—Surendra Singh.
Alternate.—Mushfiqur Rahman.
Armenia, Bosnia and Herzegovina, Bulgaria, Croatia, Cyprus, Georgia, Israel, Former Yugoslav Republic of Macedonia, Moldova, Netherlands, Romania, Ukraine
Executive Director.—Pieter Stek.
Alternate.—Sergiy Kulyk.

INTERNATIONAL DEVELOPMENT ASSOCIATION

[The officers, executive directors, and alternates are the same as those of the International Bank for Reconstruction and Development.]

INTERNATIONAL FINANCE CORPORATION

President.—James D. Wolfensohn.
Vice President and Secretary.—Shengman Zhang.
Executive Vice President.—Jannik Lindback.
Director, Operational Evaluation Group.—W.E. Stevenson.
Director, Economics Department.—Guy Pierre Pfefferman.
Vice President, Personnel, Administration and Corporation Business Development.—Christopher Bam.
Manager, Corporation Relations Unit.—Mark Constantine.
Vice President and General Counsel.—Carol Lee.
Deputy General Counsel.—Jennifer Sullivan.
Director, Technical and Environmental Department.—Andreas M. Raczyuski.
Vice President, Investment Operations.—Jernal-ud-din Kassum.
Vice President, Portfolio Management and Advisory Operations.—Assad Jabre.
Director, Financial Sector Issues.—Irving Kuczynski.
Senior Manager, Investment Operations: Robin Glantz; Rashad-Rudolph Kaldany.
Director, Relationship Management.—Peter T. Cook.
Department Director for—
Agribusiness.—Tei Mante.
Asia.—[Vacant].
Central Asia, Middle East and North Africa (CAMENA).—Andre G. Hovaguimian.
Chemicals, Petrochemicals and Fertilizers.—Jean-Phillippe Halphen.
Controller's and Budgeting.—Michael Barth.
Corporate Finance Services.—Robert D. Graffam.
Corporate Planning and Financial Policy.—Nissim Ezekiel.
Europe.—Khosrow Zamani.
Latin America and the Caribbean (LAC).—Karl Voltaire.
Oil, Gas and Mining.—Philippe Lietard.
Power.—Rauf Diwan.
Sub-Saharan Africa.—[Vacant].
Treasury.—Farida Khambata.
Telecommunications, Transportation and Utilities.—Declan Duff.
Manager, Foreign Investment Advisory Service.—Dale R. Weigel.
Manager, Portfolio Analysis and Data Management Unit.—Khalid Mirza.
Manager, Special Operations Unit.—Woonki Sung.
Vice President, Finance and Planning.—Birgitta Kantola.
Principal Financial Adviser.—Vasant H. Karmarker.

MULTILATERAL INVESTMENT GUARANTEE AGENCY

President.—James D. Wolfensohn, 85120, E1227.
Executive Vice President and Secretary.—Akira Ida, 36138, U 12–001.
Vice President and Secretary.—Shengman Zhang, 80242, MC 11–305.

OFFICE OF GUARANTEES

Vice President, Guarantees.—Leigh P. Hollywood, 36168, U 12–141.
Senior Adviser, Guarantees.—Gerald T. West, 32060, U 12–137.
Guarantee Operations.—Christophe Bellinger, 36163, U 12–139.
Regional Management: Europe.—Edward Copoola, 35419, U 12–319.
Regional Management: Asia.—Christina Westholm-Schroder, 36165, U 12–313.
Regional Management: Latin America and Caribbean.—Stine Andersen, 36157, U 12–301.
Regional Management: Africa and Middle East.—Robert Rendall, 35106, U 12–331.

OFFICE OF INVESTMENT MARKETING SERVICES

Administrator.—Martin F. Hartigan, 30687, U 12–401.
Guarantee Operations.—Ken Kwaku, 36142, U 12–357.
Regional Management for—
Africa.—Edward Copoola, 35419, U 12–319.
Asia.—Ghassan Amaoot, 30775, U 12–363.
IPA Services.—Phil Karp, 38710, U 12–407.

OFFICE OF THE VICE PRESIDENT AND GENERAL COUNSEL, LEGAL AFFAIRS AND CLAIMS

Vice President and General Counsel.—Luis Dodero, 35245, U 12–109.
Principal Counsel.—Lorin Weisenfeld, 36141, U 12–101.

OFFICE OF CENTRAL ADMINISTRATION

Manager.—Daniel E. Conway, 32964, U 12–013.
Budget and Accounting.—Esther Lao, 30176, U 12–013.
Information/Document Management.—Manfred Beurgen, 32231, U 12–413.

GOVERNMENT OF THE DISTRICT OF COLUMBIA

COUNCIL OF THE DISTRICT OF COLUMBIA

1350 Pennsylvania Avenue 20004, phone 724–8000

Council Chairman (at Large).—[Vacant], Room 103, 724–8176.
Chairman Pro Tempore (at Large).—Charlene Drew Jarvis (acting).
Council Members:
Frank Smith, Jr., Ward 1, Room 125, 724–8181.
Jack Evans, Ward 2, Room 101, 724–8058.
Kathleen Patterson, Ward 3, Room 111, 724–8062.
Charlene Drew Jarvis, Ward 4, Room 121, 724–8052.
Harry Thomas, Sr., Ward 5, Room 106, 724–8028.
Ward 6, [Vacant], Special Election.
Kevin P. Chavous, Ward 7, Room 108, 724–8068.
Sandy Allen, Ward 8, Room 119, 724–8045.
Council Members (at Large):
Harold Brazil, Room 110, 724–8174.
Hilda H.M. Mason, Room 118, 724–8064.
Carol Schwartz, Room 102, 724–8105.
Linda W. Cropp, Room 116, 724–8032.
Secretary to the Council.—Phyllis Jones, Room 207, 724–8080.
General Counsel.—Charlotte Brookins-Hudson, Room G–24, 724–8026.

EXECUTIVE OFFICE OF THE MAYOR

One Judiciary Square, 441 Fourth Street 20001, phone 727–2980

Mayor of the District of Columbia.—Marion S. Barry.
Chief of Staff.—Barry K. Campbell, Suite 1110, 727–2643, fax 727–2975.
Deputy Chief of Staff.—Jeannette Michael, Suite 1110, 727–2643, fax 727–2975.
Executive Assistant.—Phyllis Anderson, Suite 1100, 727–2980, fax 727–6561.
Director, Mayor's Scheduling Unit.—Laverne Harvey, 727–2980, fax 727–2357.
Secretary of the District of Columbia.—Kathleen E. Arnold, Suite 1130, 727–6306, fax 727–3582.
Special Assistant.—Shiela Harmon Martin.
Inspector General.—[Vacant], 717 14th Street NW, Fifth Floor, 20005, 727–9500, fax 727–9846.
Press Secretary.—Raymone Bain, Suite 1100, 727–5011, fax 727–0505.
General Assistant.—Enid B. Simmons, Suite 930, 727–9218, fax 727–3765.
Special Assistants:
Asian and Pacific Islander Affairs.—Meeja Yu, Suite 1020, 727–3120, fax 727–9291.
Boards and Commissions.—Lucille Knowles, Suite 1050, 727–1372, fax 727–2359.
Labor.—Fran Thomas, Suite 1160, 727–2980, fax 727–0875.
Religious Affairs.—Rev. Dr. William H. Bennett, Suite 1020, 727–6807, fax 727–6526.

OFFICE OF THE CITY ADMINISTRATOR

One Judiciary Square, Suite 1120, 441 Fourth Street 20001

phone 727–6053, fax 727–5445

City Administrator.—Michael C. Rogers.
City Administrator for Finance.—Anthony A. Williams, Suite 1150, 727–2476, fax 737–5258.
Deputy City Administrator for Public Protection.—Thurman Hampton, Suite 1120, 727–6053, fax 727–5445.

Commissions

COMMISSION ON THE ARTS AND HUMANITIES
410 Eighth Street NW, Suite 500, 20004, phone 727–5613, fax 727–4135.
Executive Director.—Anthony Gittens.
COMMISSION ON HEALTH CARE FINANCE
2100 Martin Luther King Jr. Avenue SE, Suite 302, 20020, phone 727–0735, fax 610–3209.
Commissioner.—Paul Offner.
COMMISSION ON MENTAL HEALTH
St. Elizabeth's Campus, 2700 Martin Luther King Jr. Avenue SE 20032, phone 373–7166, fax 373–6484.
Commissioner.—Guido R. Zanni, Ph.D.
COMMISSION ON SOCIAL SERVICES
6098 H Street NE, Fifth Floor 20002, phone 727–5930, fax 727–1687.
Commissioner.—Annie J. Goodson (acting).
TAXICAB COMMISSION
2041 Martin Luther King Jr. Avenue SE, Room 204, 20020, phone 645–6005, fax 889–3604.
Chairperson.—Novell Sullivan (acting).

Departments

DEPARTMENT OF ADMINISTRATIVE SERVICES
441 Fourth Street, Suite 700, 20001, phone 727–1179, fax 727–9878.
Interim Director.—Dallas Evans.
DEPARTMENT OF CONSUMER AND REGULATORY AFFAIRS
615 H Street, Suite 1120, 20001, phone 727–7120, fax 727–8073.
Director.—Hampton Cross.
DEPARTMENT OF CORRECTIONS
1923 Vermont Avenue NW, Room 207, 20001, phone 673–7316, fax 332–1470.
Director.—Margaret A. Moore.
DEPARTMENT OF EMPLOYMENT SERVICES
500 C Street NW, Room 600, 20001, phone 724–7100, fax 724–5683.
Director.—F. Alexis Roberson.
DEPARTMENT OF FIRE AND EMERGENCY MEDICAL SERVICES
1923 Vermont Avenue NW, Suite 201, 20001, phone 673–3320, fax 462–0807.
Fire Chief.—Otis J. Latin, Sr.
DEPARTMENT OF HEALTH
800 Ninth Street SW, Third Floor, 20024, phone 645–5556, fax 645–0526.
Director.—Harvey I. Sloane, M.D. (acting).
DEPARTMENT OF HOUSING AND COMMUNITY DEVELOPMENT
51 N Street NE, Suite 600, 20002, phone 727–6365, fax 727–6703.
Deputy City Administrator for Economic Development.—W. David Watts, 535–1972, fax 535–1584.
DEPARTMENT OF HUMAN RIGHTS AND MINORITY BUSINESS DEVELOPMENT
441 Fourth Street NW, Suite 970, 20001, phone 724–1385, fax 724–3786.
Director.—Gerald Draper.
DEPARTMENT OF HUMAN SERVICES
801 East Building, St. Elizabeth's Campus, 2700 Martin Luther King Jr. Avenue SE 20032, phone 279–6002, fax 279–6014.
Interim Director.—Wayne D. Casey.
DEPARTMENT OF PUBLIC AND ASSISTED HOUSING
1133 North Capitol Street NW, Room 200, 20002 phone 535–1500, fax 535–1740.
Receiver.—David Gilmore.
DEPARTMENT OF PUBLIC WORKS
2000 14th Street NW, Sixth Floor 20009, phone 939–8000, fax 939–8191.
Director.—Cellerino C. Bernardino (acting).
DEPARTMENT OF RECREATION AND PARKS
3149 16th Street 20010, phone 673–7665, fax 673–2087.
Director.—Betty Jo Gaines.

Offices

OFFICE ON AGING
441 Fourth Street NW, Suite 900, 20001, phone 724–5622, fax 724–4979.
Deputy City Administrator for Human Development and Comprehensive Health.—Jearline F. Williams.
OFFICE OF BANKING AND FINANCIAL INSTITUTIONS
717 14th Street NW, Suite 1100, 20005, phone 727–1563, fax 727–1588.
Superintendent.—J. Anthony Romero, III.
OFFICE OF CABLE TELEVISION
2217 14th Street NW 20009, phone 727–0424, fax 332–7020.
Executive Director.—Doreen Thompson.
OFFICE OF COMMUNICATIONS
441 Fourth Street, Suite 1100, 20001, phone 727–6224, fax 727–9561.
Director.—Linda Wharton Boyd (acting).
OFFICE OF THE CORPORATION COUNSEL
441 Fourth Street, Suite 1060, 20001, phone 727–6248, fax 727–9656.
Interim Corporation Counsel.—Jo Anne Robinson, Suite 1060, 727–6248.
OFFICE OF CORRECTIONS
1923 Vermont Avenue, Room 207, 20001, phone 673–7316, fax 332–1470.
Director.—Margaret A. Moore.
OFFICE OF DIVERSITY AND SPECIAL SERVICES
441 Fourth Street, Suite 1160, 20001, phone 727–1620, fax 727–0875.
Director.—Ayo Bryant.
OFFICE OF EMERGENCY PREPAREDNESS
2000 14th Street, Eighth Floor 20009, phone 727–2775, fax 673–2290.
Director.—Samuel H. Jordan.
OFFICE OF FINANCE
One Judiciary Square, 441 Fourth Street 20005, phone 727–2476.
Chief Financial Officer.—Anthony A. Williams.
OFFICE OF INTERGOVERNMENTAL RELATIONS
441 Fourth Street NW, Suite 1010, 20001, phone 727–6265, fax 727–6895.
Director.—Bernard Demczuk.
OFFICE OF INTERNATIONAL AFFAIRS
441 Fourth Street NW, Suite 1140, 20001, phone 727–6365, fax 727–6703.
Director.—Hector Rodriguez (acting).
OFFICE OF LABOR RELATIONS AND COLLECTIVE BARGAINING
441 Fourth Street NW, Suite 200, 20001, phone 724–4953, fax 727–6887.
Deputy Director.—Dean Aqui.
OFFICE OF LATINO AFFAIRS
2000 14th Street NW, Second Floor, 20005, phone 939–8765, fax 673–4557.
Executive Director.—Manuel Uriarte (acting).
OFFICE OF THE OMBUDSMAN
2000 14th Street NW, Room 300, 20009, phone 939–8750, fax 939–8727.
Ombudsman.—Willie Vazquez.
OFFICE OF PERSONNEL
441 Fourth Street NW, Suite 300–S, 20001, phone 727–6406, fax 727–6827.
Deputy City Administrator for Public Management.—Larry A. King.
OFFICE OF POLICY AND EVALUATION
441 Fourth Street NW, Suite 920, 20001, phone 727–6979, fax 727–3765.
Director.— Rodney L. Palmer.
OFFICE OF PLANNING
415 12th Street NW, Suite 500, 20004, phone 727–6492, fax 727–6964.
Director.—Jill Dennis.
OFFICE OF TOURISM AND PROMOTIONS
717 14th Street NW, Suite 1100, 20005 phone 727–4511, fax 727–3784.
Director.—Ann K Pina (acting).

Other

AGENCY FOR HIV/AIDS
717 14th Street NW, Suite 600, 20005, phone 727–2500 ext. 9605, fax 727–8471 and 727–3775.
Administrator.—Melvin H. Wilson.
DISTRICT LOTTERY AND CHARITABLE GAMES
2101 Martin Luther King Jr. Avenue SE 20020, phone 645–8010, fax 645–7914.

Executive Director.—Frederick L. King, Jr.

DISTRICT OF COLUMBIA GENERAL HOSPITAL

1900 Massachusetts Avenue SE, Room 1455A, 20003, phone 675–7654, fax 675–5650.

Executive Director.—John A. Fairman.

DISTRICT OF COLUMBIA PUBLIC LIBRARIES

Martin Luther King Memorial Library (Main Library), 901 G Street, Suite 400, 20001, phone 727–0321.

Director.—Mary E. Raphael (acting), 727–1101, Administrative Office, 727–1101.

DISTRICT OF COLUMBIA PUBLIC SCHOOLS

415 12th Street NW, Suite 1209, 20004, phone 724–4222, fax 724–8855.

Chief Executive Officer.—General Julius Becton.

DISTRICT OF COLUMBIA SPORTS COMMISSION

2400 East Capitol Street SE 20003, phone 547–9077, ext. 729, fax 547–7460.

Executive Director.—James A. Dalrymple.

METROPOLITAN POLICE DEPARTMENT

300 Indiana Avenue NW, Room 5080, 20001, 727–4218, FAX 727–9524.

Police Chief.—Larry Soulsby.

PAROLE BOARD

300 Indiana Avenue NW, Suite 2100, 20001, phone 727–0074, fax 724–6183.

Chairman.—Margaret Quick.

SUPERIOR COURT OF THE DISTRICT OF COLUMBIA

500 Indiana Avenue NW, Suite 3500, 20001, phone 879–1600, fax 879–7830.

Chief Judge.—The Honorable Eugene N. Hamilton.

UNIVERSITY OF THE DISTRICT OF COLUMBIA

4200 Connecticut Avenue NW 20008, phone 274–5100, fax 274–5304.

President.—Dr. Julius I. Nimmons, Jr. (acting).

WASHINGTON CONVENTION CENTER

900 Ninth Street NW 20004, phone 371–3024, fax 789–8365.

General Manager.—Edith Jett-McCloud.

DISTRICT OF COLUMBIA POST OFFICE LOCATIONS

900 Brentwood Road NE 20066–9998, General Information 635–5300

Postmaster.—David A. Clark, 636–1200

Plant Manager.—Ardine Harley, Jr., 636–1334.

Customer Relations.—Gwendolyn Harvey, 636–1205.

CLASSIFIED STATIONS

Station	ZIP Code	Manager	Location/Telephone
Anacostia [1]	20020	S. Osborne	2650 Naylor Rd. SE. 523–2119
Andrews AFB Unit 1	20331	T. Rice	Andrews AFB. (301) 568–2164
B.F. Carriers	20004/5	R. Payne	900 Brentwood Rd. NE. 636–4484
Ben Franklin	20044	B.M. Dennis	1200 Pennsylvania Ave. NW. 523–2387
Benning	20029	I. Tyler	3937–½ Minnesota Ave. NE. 523–2390
Bolling AFB	20332	C. Briggs	Bolling AFB. 767–4419
Brightwood	20011	J. White	6323 Georgia Ave. NW. 523–2392
Brookland [1]	20017	F. Cooper	3401 12th St. NE. 523–2133
Calvert	20007	J. Lintner	2336 Wisconsin Ave. NW. 523–2907
Central	20038	M. Baker	1444 I St. NW. 523–2393
Cleveland Park	20008	C. Lewis	3430 Connecticut Ave. NW. 523–2395
Columbia Heights [1]	20010	E. Cooper	1423 Irving St. NW. 523–2397
Congress Heights [1]	20032	C. Briggs	400 Southern Ave. SE. 523–2107
Customs House [1]	20018	A. Sanford	3178 Bladensburg Rd. NE. 523–2195
Dulles Finance	20041	K. DeVaughn	Dulles International Airport. (703) 471–1868
Farragut	20033	S. Johnson	1145 19th St. NW. 523–2506
Fort Davis	20020	B. Ford	3843 Pennsylvania Ave. SE. 523–2152

CLASSIFIED STATIONS—CONTINUED

Station	ZIP Code	Manager	Location/Telephone
Fort McNair	20319	J. Wilson	300 A. St. SW. 523–2144
Friendship [1]	20016	J. Hotten	4005 Wisconsin Ave. NW. 523–2125
Georgetown	20007	J. Lintner	3050 K St. NW. 523–2405
Headsville	20560	M. Wood	Smithsonian Institute. 357–3029
Kalorama	20009	M. Jones	2300 18th St. NW. 523–2904
Lamond Riggs [1]	20011/12	K. Stevenson	6200 North Capitol St. NW. 523–2041
LeDroit Park	20001	F. Cooper	416 Florida Ave. NW. 483–5617
L'Enfant Plaza	20026	M. Wood	458 L'Enfant Plaza SW. 523–2013
Main Office	20090	K. Melvin	900 Brentwood Rd. NE. 636–1532
Martin L. King	20043	J. Harris	1400 L St. NW. 523–2000
McPherson	20038	M. Baker	1750 Pennsylvania Ave. NW. 523–2393
Mid City	20005	M. Wright	1408 14th St. NW. 523–2567
NASA Conv	20546	B. M. Dennis	300 E St. SW. 358–0235
National Airport [1]	20001	K. DeVaughn	Main Terminal, Room 186. 523–2407
National Capitol	20002	V. English	2 Massachusetts Ave. NE. 523–2628
Naval Research Lab	20390	F. Wilson	Bellevue AFB. 767–3426
Navy Annex	20370	L. Gohlson	Navy Annex, Rm. 1404. (703) 271–6285
Northeast	20002	B. McCoy	1563 Maryland Ave. NE. 523–2565
Northwest	20015	C. Lewis	5632 Connecticut Ave. NW. 523–2569
Palisades	20016	J. Hotten	5136 MacArthur Blvd. NW. 523–2562
Pavilion Postique	20005	M. Wood	1100 Pennsylvania Ave. NW. 523–2571
Pentagon	20050	K. DeVaughn	Pentagon Concourse. (703) 695–6835
Petworth	20011	J. White	4211 9th St. NW. 523–2681
Philatelic Center	20266	M. Wood	475 L'Enfant Plaza SW. 268–4910
Postal Square	20002	J. McRay	2 Massachusetts Ave. NW. 523–2022
Randle	20020	C. Douglas	2306 Prout St. SE. 584–3241
Section 2 [1]	20002	W. Jackson	3300 V St. NE. 523–2108
Southeast	20003	H. Goldring	327 7th St. SE. 523–2173
Southwest [1]	20024/03	C. Dickens	45 L St. SW. 523–2559
State Department	20520	E. Atkins	State Department Bldg. 223–2574
T Street	20056	M. Brown	1915 14th St. NW. 483–9580
Tech World	20091	B. Willis	No. 16, 800 K St. NW. 523–2400
Temple Heights	20009	C. Jones	1921 Florida Ave. NW. 232–7613
Twentieth Street	20036	S. Johnson	2001 M St. NW. 523–2410
Union Station	20002	J. McCray	50 Massachusetts Ave. NE. 523–2057
U.S. Naval	20374	W. Reese	901 M St. SE. 433–2216
Walter Reed	20012	S. Burton	Army Medical Center. 576–3768
Walter Reed No. 1	20012	J. Butler	Forest Glen, Maryland. 523–2679
Ward Place	20006/36 20037	R. Garrett	2121 Ward Pl. NW. 523–2040
Washington Square	20035	V. Roberts	1050 Connecticut Ave. NW 523–2631
Watergate	20037	G. Atkins	2512 Virginia Ave. NW. 965–2730
White House	20500	A. Mendoza	1600 Pennsylvania Ave. NW. 456–2541
Woodridge	20018	A. Sanford	2211 Rhode Island Ave. NE. 523–2414

[1] Carrier Station.

NOTE.—Special Delivery. 636–1549, Government Mails—636–2225; Collections. 636–2221, Wholesale Stamps. 636–1396.

FOREIGN DIPLOMATIC OFFICES IN THE UNITED STATES

AFGHANISTAN
Embassy of the Republic of Afghanistan
2341 Wyoming Avenue NW 20008
phone 234–3770, fax 328–3516
Mr. Yar Mohammad Mohabbat
First Secretary, Chargé d'Affaires ad interim
Consular Office: New York, New York

ALBANIA
Embassy of the Republic of Albania
1511 K Street NW, Suite 1000, 20005
phone 223–4942, fax 628–7342
His Excellency Lublin Dilja
Ambassador E. and P.
Consular Offices:
Massachusetts, Boston
Texas, Houston

ALGERIA
Embassy of the Democratic and Popular Republic of Algeria
2118 Kalorama Road NW 20008
phone 265–2800, fax 667–2174
His Excellency Ramtane Lamamra
Ambassador E. and P.

Iraqi Interests Section
1801 P Street NW 20036
phone 483–7500, fax 462–5066
Dr. Khairi O. T. Alzubaidi
Minister

ANDORRA
Embassy of Andorra
Two United Nations Plaza, 25th Floor
New York NY 10017
phone 212–750–8064, fax 750–6630
His Excellency Juli Minoves Triquell
Ambassador E. and P.

ANGOLA
Embassy of the Republic of Angola
1050 Connecticut Avenue NW, Suite 760, 20036
phone 785–1156, fax 785–1258
His Excellency Antonio dos Santos Franca
Ambassador E. and P.

ANTIGUA AND BARBUDA
Embassy of Antigua and Barbuda
3216 New Mexico Avenue NW 20016
phone 362–5211, fax 362–5225
His Excellency Lionel A. Hurst
Ambassador E. and P.
Consular Office: Florida, Miami

ARGENTINA
Embassy of the Argentine Republic
1600 New Hampshire Avenue NW 20009
phone 939–6400
His Excellency Raul Enrique Granillo Ocampo
Ambassador E. and P.
Consular Offices:
California, Los Angeles
Florida, Miami
Georgia, Atlanta
Illinois, Chicago
New York, New York
Texas, Houston
Tourism Office:
Florida, Coral Gables

ARMENIA
Embassy of the Republic of Armenia
2225 R Street NW 20008
phone 319–1976, fax 319–2982
His Excellency Rouben Robert Shugarian
Ambassador E. and P.
Consular Office: California, Los Angeles

AUSTRALIA
Embassy of Australia
1601 Massachusetts Avenue NW 20036
phone 797–3000, fax 797–3168
His Excellency Andrew Sharp Peacock
Ambassador E. and P.
Consular Offices:
California - Los Angeles, San Francisco
Colorado, Denver
Georgia, Atlanta
Hawaii, Honolulu
Massachusetts, Boston
New York, New York
Texas, Houston
Trust Territories of the Pacific Islands, Pago Pago

AUSTRIA
Embassy of Austria
3524 International Court NW 20008
phone 895–6700, fax 895–6750
His Excellency Helmut Tuerk
Ambassador E. and P.
Consular Offices:

California - Los Angeles, San Francisco
Colorado, Denver
Florida, Miami
Georgia, Atlanta
Hawaii, Honolulu
Illinois, Chicago
Louisiana, New Orleans
Massachusetts, Boston
Michigan, Detroit
Minnesota, Minneapolis
Missouri, Kansas City
New York - Buffalo, New York
Ohio, Columbus
Pennsylvania, Philadelphia
Puerto Rico, San Juan
Texas, Houston
Washington, Seattle

AZERBAIJAN
Embassy of the Republic of Azerbaijan
(Temporary chancery) 927 15th Street NW, Suite 700, 20005
PO Box 27839, 20038–7839
phone 842–0001, fax 842–0004
His Excellency Hafiz Mir Jalal Pashayev
Ambassador E. and P.

BAHAMAS
Embassy of the Commonwealth of The Bahamas
2220 Massachusetts Avenue NW 20008
phone 319–2660, fax 319–2668
His Excellency Sir Arlinton Griffith Butler
Ambassador E. and P.
Consular Offices:
Florida, Miami
New York, New York

BAHRAIN
Embassy of the State of Bahrain
3502 International Drive NW 20008
phone 342–0741, fax 362–2192
His Excellency Muhammad Abdul Ghaffar Abdulla
Ambassador E. and P.
Consular Offices:
California, San Diego
New York, New York

BANGLADESH
Embassy of the People's Republic of Bangladesh
2201 Wisconsin Avenue NW 20007
phone 342–8372
His Excellency K. M. Shehabuddin
Ambassador E. and P.
Consular Offices:
California, Los Angeles
Hawaii, Honolulu
Louisiana, New Orleans
New York, New York

BARBADOS
Embassy of Barbados
2144 Wyoming Avenue NW 20008
phone 939–9200, fax 332–7467
His Excellency Dr. Courtney N. Blackman
Ambassador E. and P.
Consular Offices:
California - Los Angeles, San Francisco
Florida, Miami
Georgia, Atlanta
Illinois, Chicago
Louisiana, New Orleans
Massachusetts, Boston
Michigan, Detroit
New York, New York
Ohio, Cleveland
Oregon, Portland
Texas, Houston

BELARUS
Embassy of the Republic of Belarus
1619 New Hampshire Avenue NW 20009
phone 986–1604, fax 986–1805
His Excellency Valery Tsepkalo
Ambassador E. and P.
Consular Office: New York, New York

BELGIUM
Embassy of Belgium
3330 Garfield Street NW 20008
phone 333–6900, fax 333–3079
His Excellency Andre Adam
Ambassador E. and P.
Consular Offices:
Alaska, Anchorage
Arizona, Phoenix
California - Los Angeles, San Diego, San Francisco
Colorado, Denver
Florida, Miami
Georgia, Atlanta
Hawaii, Honolulu
Illinois, Chicago
Kentucky, Louisville
Maryland, Baltimore
Massachusetts, Boston
Michigan, Detroit
Minnesota, St. Paul
Missouri, St. Louis
New York, New York
Ohio, Cleveland
Oregon, Portland
Pennsylvania - Philadelphia, Pittsburgh
Puerto Rico, San Juan
Texas - Dallas, Houston, San Antonio
Utah, Salt Lake City
Virginia, Norfolk
Washington, Seattle
Wisconsin, Milwaukee

BELIZE
Embassy of Belize
2535 Massachusetts Avenue NW 20008
phone 332–9636, fax 332–6888
His Excellency James S. Murphy
Ambassador E. and P.
Consular Offices:
California - Los Angeles, San Francisco
Florida, Miami
Illinois - Belleville, Chicago
Louisiana, New Orleans
Michigan, Detroit
Puerto Rico, San Juan
Texas - Dallas, Houston

BENIN
Embassy of the Republic of Benin
2737 Cathedral Avenue NW 20008
phone 232–6656, fax 265–1996
His Excellency Lucien Edgar Tonoukouin
Ambassador E. and P.
Consular Office: California - Los Angeles

BHUTAN
Consular Offices:
California, San Francisco
District of Columbia
New York, New York

BOLIVIA
Embassy of the Republic of Bolivia
3014 Massachusetts Avenue NW 20008
phone 483–4410, fax 328–3712
His Excellency Fernando Cossio
Ambassador E. and P.
Consular Offices:
Arizona, Phoenix
California - Los Angeles, San Francisco
Colorado, Aspen
Florida, Miami
Georgia, Atlanta
Illinois, Chicago
Louisiana, New Orleans
Massachusetts, Boston
Missouri, St. Louis
New York, New York
Ohio, Cincinnati
Texas, Houston
Washington, Seattle

BOSNIA AND HERZEGOVINA
Embassy of the Republic of Bosnia and Herzegovina
1707 L Street NW, Suite 760, 20036
phone 833–3612, fax 833–2061
His Excellency Sven Alkalaj
Ambassador E. and P.
Consular Office: New York, New York

BOTSWANA
Embassy of the Republic of Botswana
3400 International Drive, NW, Suite 7M, 20008
phone 244–4990, fax 244–4164
His Excellency Archibald Mooketsa Mogwe
Ambassador E. and P.
Consular Offices:
California, Los Angeles
Texas, Houston

BRAZIL
Brazilian Embassy
3006 Massachusetts Avenue NW 20008
phone 745–2700, fax 745–2827
His Excellency Paulo-Tarso Flecha de Lima
Ambassador E. and P.
Consular Offices:
Alabama, Birmingham
Arizona, Phoenix
California - Los Angeles, San Francisco
Florida, Miami
Georgia, Atlanta
Hawaii, Honolulu
Illinois, Chicago
Massachusetts, Boston
New York, New York
Puerto Rico, San Juan
Texas, Houston
Trust Territories of the Pacific Islands, Hong Kong
Virginia, Norfolk
Washington, Seattle

BRUNEI
Embassy of the State of Brunei Darussalam
Watergate, 2600 Virginia Avenue NW, Suite 300, 20037
phone 342–0159, fax 342–0158
Mr. Shofry Abdul Ghafor
First Secretary, Chargé d'Affaires ad interim

BULGARIA
Embassy of the Republic of Bulgaria
1621 22nd Street NW 20008
phone 387–7969, fax 234–7973
His Excellency Dr. Snejana Damianova Botoucharova
Ambassador E. and P.
Consular Office: New York, New York

BURKINA FASO
Embassy of Burkina Faso
2340 Massachusetts Avenue NW 20008
phone 332–5577
His Excellency Gaetan R. Ouedraogo
Ambassador E. and P.
Consular Offices:
California, Los Angeles
Georgia, Atlanta
Louisiana, New Orleans

BURMA
Embassy of the Union of Burma
2300 S Street NW 20008
phone 332–9044, fax 332–9046
His Excellency Tin Winn
Ambassador E. and P.

BURUNDI
Embassy of the Republic of Burundi
2233 Wisconsin Avenue NW, Suite 212, 20007
phone 342–2574
His Excellency Severin Ntahomvukiye
Ambassador E. and P.
Consular Office: Chicago, Illinois

CAMBODIA
Royal Embassy of Cambodia
4500 16th Street NW 20011
phone 726–7742, fax 726–8381
His Excellency Var Huoth
Ambassador E. and P.

CAMEROON
Embassy of the Republic of Cameroon
2349 Massachusetts Avenue NW 20008
phone 265–8790
His Excellency Jerome Mendouga
Ambassador E. and P.
Consular Offices:
California, San Francisco
Texas, Houston

CANADA
Embassy of Canada
501 Pennsylvania Avenue NW 20001
phone 682–1740, fax 682–7726
His Excellency Raymond A.J. Chretien
Ambassador E. and P.
Consular Offices:
California - Los Angeles, San Diego, San Francisco, San Jose
Florida, Miami
Georgia, Atlanta
Illinois, Chicago
Massachusetts, Boston
Michigan, Detroit
Minnesota, Minneapolis
New Jersey, Princeton
New York - Buffalo, New York
Ohio - Cincinnati, Cleveland
Pennsylvania, Pittsburgh
Texas, Dallas
Washington, Seattle

CAPE VERDE
Embassy of the Republic of Cape Verde
3415 Massachusetts Avenue NW 20007
phone 965–6820, fax 965–1207
His Excellency Corentino Virgilio Santos
Ambassador E. and P.
Consular Offices:
Massachusetts, Boston
Rhode Island, Providence

CENTRAL AFRICAN REPUBLIC
Embassy of Central African Republic
1618 22nd Street NW 20008
phone 483–7800, fax 332–9893
His Excellency Henry Koba
Ambassador E. and P.
Consular Offices:
California, Los Angeles
New York, New York

CHAD
Embassy of the Republic of Chad
2002 R Street NW 20009
phone 462–4009, fax 265–1937
His Excellency Ahmat Mahamat-Saleh
Ambassador E. and P.

CHILE
Embassy of Chile
1732 Massachusetts Avenue NW 20036
phone 785–1746, fax 887–5579
His Excellency John Biehl
Ambassador E. and P.
Consular Offices:
California - Los Angeles, San Diego, San Francisco, Santa Clara
Florida, Miami
Hawaii, Honolulu
Illinois, Chicago
Louisiana, New Orleans
Massachusetts, Boston
New York, New York
Pennsylvania, Philadelphia
Puerto Rico, San Juan
South Carolina, Charleston
Texas - Dallas, Houston
Utah, Salt Lake City

CHINA
Embassy of the People's Republic of China
2300 Connecticut Avenue NW 20008
phone 328–2500
His Excellency Li Daoyu
Ambassador E. and P.
Consular Offices:
California - Los Angeles, San Francisco
Illinois, Chicago
New York, New York
Texas, Houston

COLOMBIA
Embassy of Colombia
2118 Leroy Place NW 20008
phone 387–8338, fax 232–8643

His Excellency Juan Carlos Esguerra
Ambassador E. and P.
Consular Offices:
California - Los Angeles, San Francisco
Florida, Miami
Georgia, Atlanta
Illinois, Chicago
Louisiana, New Orleans
Massachusetts, Boston
New York, New York
Puerto Rico, San Juan
Texas, Houston

COMOROS
Embassy of the Federal and Islamic Republic of the Comoros
(Temporary chancery) care of the Permanent Mission of the Federal and Islamic Republic of the Comoros to the United Nations:
336 East 45th Street, 2nd Floor, New York NY 10017
Consular Office:
New York, New York

CONGO
Embassy of the Democratic Republic of the Congo
1800 New Hampshire Avenue NW 20009
phone 234–7690, fax 686–3631
Consular Office: New York, New York

CONGO
Embassy of the Republic of Congo
4891 Colorado Avenue NW 20011
phone 726–5500, fax 726–1860
His Excellency Dieudonne Antoine Ganga
Ambassador E. and P.

COOK ISLANDS
Consular Offices:
California, Los Angeles
Hawaii, Honolulu

COSTA RICA
Embassy of Costa Rica
2114 S Street NW 20008
phone 234–2945, fax 265–4795
Her Excellency Sonia Picado
Ambassador E. and P.
Consular Offices:
California - Los Angeles, San Diego, San Francisco
Colorado, Denver
Florida, Miami, Tampa
Georgia, Atlanta
Illinois, Chicago
Louisiana, New Orleans
Massachusetts, Springfield
Minnesota, Minneapolis
New Mexico, Albuquerque
New York, New York
North Carolina, Durham
Pennsylvania, Philadelphia
Puerto Rico, San Juan
Texas - Austin, Houston, San Antonio

COTE D'IVOIRE
Embassy of the Republic of Cote d'Ivoire
2424 Massachusetts Avenue NW 20008
phone 797–0300
His Excellency Koffi Moise Koumoue
Ambassador E. and P.
Consular Offices:
California, San Francisco
Michigan, Detroit

CROATIA
Embassy of the Repulic of Croatia
2343 Massachusetts Avenue NW 20008
phone 588–5899, fax 588–8936
His Excellency Miomir Zuzul
Ambassador E. and P.
Consular Offices:
Minnesota, St. Paul
New York, New York
Ohio, Cleveland

CYPRUS
Embassy of the Republic of Cyprus
2211 R Street NW 20008
phone 462–5772, fax 483–6710
His Excellency Andros A. Nicolaides
Ambassador E. and P.
Consular Offices:
Arizona, Phoenix
California - Los Angeles, San Francisco
Georgia, Atlanta
Illinois, Chicago
Indiana, Fort Wayne
Louisiana, Baton Rouge
Massachusetts, Boston
Michigan, Detroit
New York, New York
Ohio, Akron
Oregon, Portland
Pennsylvania, Philadelphia
Texas, Houston
Virginia, Virginia Beach
Washington, Seattle

CZECH
Embassy of the Czech Republic
3900 Spring of Freedom Street NW 20008
phone 274–9101, fax 966–8540
His Excellency Alexandr Vondra
Consular Offices:
California - Los Angeles, San Francisco
Florida, Ft. Lauderdale
Georgia, Atlanta

New York, Buffalo
Oregon, Portland
Pennsylvania, Philadelphia
Texas - Dallas, Houston

DENMARK
Royal Danish Embassy
3200 Whitehaven Street NW 20008
phone 234–4300, fax 328–1470
His Excellency K. Erik Tvgesen
Ambassador E. and P.
Consular Offices:
Alabama, Mobile
Alaska, Anchorage
Arizona, Phoenix
California - Los Angeles, San Diego, San Francisco
Colorado, Denver
Florida - Jacksonville, Miami, Tampa
Georgia - Atlanta, Savannah
Hawaii, Honolulu
Illinois, Chicago
Louisiana, New Orleans
Maryland, Baltimore
Massachusetts, Boston
Michigan, Detroit
Minnesota, Minneapolis
Missouri - St. Louis
Nebraska, Omaha
New York, New York
Ohio, Cleveland
Oklahoma, Oklahoma City
Oregon, Portland
Pennsylvania - Philadelphia, Pittsburgh
Puerto Rico, San Juan
South Carolina, Charleston
Tennessee, Nashville
Texas - Corpus Christi, Dallas, Houston
Utah, Salt Lake City
Virgin Islands, St. Thomas
Virginia, Norfolk
Washington, Seattle
Wisconsin, Milwaukee

DJIBOUTI
Embassy of the Republic of Djibouti
1156 15th Street NW, Suite 515, 20005
phone 331–0270, fax 331–0302
His Excellency Roble Olhaye
Ambassador E. and P.

DOMINICA
Embassy of the Commonwealth of Dominica
3216 New Mexico Avenue NW 20016
phone 364–6781, fax 364–6791
His Excellency Edward I. Watty
Ambassador E. and P.
Consular Office: New York, New York

DOMINICAN REPUBLIC
Embassy of the Dominican Republic
1715 22nd Street NW 20008
phone 332–6280, fax 265–8057
His Excellency Bernardo Vega
Ambassador E. and P.
Consular Offices:
Alabama, Mobile
California - Pasadena, San Francisco
Colorado, Denver
Florida - Jacksonville, Miami, Sarasota
Georgia, Atlanta
Illinois, Chicago
Louisiana - Baton Rouge, Lake Charles, New Orleans
Massachusetts, Boston
Michigan, Detroit
Minnesota, Minneapolis
Missouri, St. Louis
New York, New York
Ohio, Cleveland
Pennsylvania, Philadelphia
Puerto Rico - Humacao, Manati, Mayaguez, Ponce, San Juan
Texas - Dallas, El Paso, Houston
Virgin Islands, St. Thomas

ECUADOR
Embassy of Ecuador
2535 15th Street NW 20009
phone 234–7200
Mr. Fernando Flores
Minister, Chargé d'Affaires ad interim
Consular Offices:
California - Los Angeles, San Francisco
Florida, Miami
Georgia, Atlanta
Illinois, Chicago
Louisiana, New Orleans
Maryland, Baltimore
Massachusetts, Boston
Michigan, Detroit
Nevada, Las Vegas
New Jersey, Newark
New York, New York
Pennsylvania, Philadelphia
Puerto Rico, San Juan
Texas, Houston

EGYPT
Embassy of the Arab Republic of Egypt
3521 International Court NW 20008
phone 895–5400, fax 244–4319
His Excellency Ahmed Maher El Sayed
Ambassador E. and P.
Consular Offices:
California, San Francisco

Illinois, Chicago
New York, New York
Texas, Houston

EL SALVADOR
Embassy of El Salvador
2308 California Street NW 20008
phone 265–9671
Her Excellency Ana Cristina Sol
Ambassador E. and P.
Consular Offices:
Arizona, Phoenix
California - Los Angeles, Oakland, San Francisco
Florida, Miami
Georgia, Atlanta
Illinois, Chicago
Louisiana, New Orleans
Massachusetts, Boston
Missouri, St. Louis
New York, New York
Pennsylvania, Philadelphia
Puerto Rico, Bayamon
Texas - Dallas, Houston

EQUATORIAL GUINEA
Embassy of Equatorial Guinea
1511 K Street NW, Suite 405, 20005
phone 393–0525, fax 393–0348
His Excellency Pastor Micha Ondo Bile
Ambassador E. and P.
Consular Offices: Florida, Miami

ERITREA
Embassy of the State of Eritrea
1708 New Hampshire Avenue NW 20009
phone 319–1991, fax 319–1304
His Excellency Amdemicael Kahsai
Ambassador E. and P.

ESTONIA
Embassy of Estonia
2131 Massachusetts Avenue NW 20008
phone 588–0101, fax 588–0108
His Excellency Grigore-Kalev Stoicescu
Ambassador E. and P.
Consular Offices:
California, Los Angeles
New York, New York
Washington, Seattle

ETHIOPIA
Embassy of Ethiopia
2134 Kalorama Road NW 20008
phone 234–2281, fax 328–7950
His Excellency Berhane Gebre-Christos
Ambassador E. and P.

FIJI
Embassy of the Republic of Fiji
2233 Wisconsin Avenue NW, Suite 240, 20007
phone 337–8320, fax 337–1996
His Excellency Napolioni Masirewa
Ambassador E. and P.
Consular Office: New York, New York

FINLAND
Embassy of Finland
3301 Massachusetts Avenue NW 20008
phone 298–5800, fax 298–6030
His Excellency Jaakko Tapani Laajava
Ambassador E. and P.
Consular Offices:
Alabama, Birmingham
Alaska, Anchorage
Arizona, Phoenix
California - Los Angeles, San Diego, San Francisco
Colorado, Denver
Connecticut, Norwich
Florida, Miami
Georgia, Atlanta
Hawaii, Honolulu
Illinois, Chicago
Louisiana, New Orleans
Maryland, Baltimore
Massachusetts - Boston, Fitchburg
Michigan - Detroit, Marquette
Minnesota, Minneapolis
Montana, Butte
New Mexico, Albuquerque
New York, New York
Oregon - Astoria, Portland
Pennsylvania, Philadelphia
Puerto Rico, San Juan
Texas - Dallas, Houston
Utah, Salt Lake City
Virgin Islands, St. John
Virginia, Norfolk
Washington, Seattle

FRANCE
Embassy of France
4101 Reservoir Road NW 20007
phone 944–6000, fax 944–6166
His Excellency Francois V. Bujon
Ambassador E. and P.
Consular Offices:
Alabama, Birmingham
Alaska, Anchorage
Arizona, Phoenix
Arkansas, Little Rock
California - Los Angeles, Sacramento, San Diego, San Francisco, San Jose
Colorado, Denver
Connecticut, Hartford
Delaware, Wilmington
Florida - Miami, Orlando

Georgia, Atlanta
Guam, Tamuning
Hawaii, Honolulu
Illinois, Chicago
Indiana, Indianapolis
Iowa, Des Moines
Kansas, Kansas City
Kentucky, Louisville
Louisiana - Lafayette, New Orleans
Maine, Portland
Maryland, Baltimore
Massachusetts, Boston
Michigan, Detroit
Minnesota, Minneapolis
Missouri, St. Louis
Montana, Missoula
Nevada, Reno
New Hampshire, Manchester
New Mexico, Santa Fe
New York - Buffalo, New York
North Carolina, Charlotte
Ohio - Cincinnati, Cleveland
Oklahoma, Tulsa
Oregon, Portland
Pennsylvania - Philadelphia, Pittsburgh
Tennessee, Memphis
Texas - Austin, Dallas, Houston, San Antonio
Utah, Salt Lake City
Virgin Islands, St. Thomas
Virginia, Norfolk
Washington, Seattle
Wisconsin, Milwaukee

GABON
Embassy of the Gabonese Republic
2034 20th Street, NW, Suite 200, 20009
phone 797–1000, fax 332–0668
His Excellency Paul Boundoukou-Latha
Ambassador E. and P.
Consular Office: New York, New York

GAMBIA, THE
Embassy of The Gambia
1155 15th Street NW, Suite 1000, 20005
phone 785–1399, fax 785–1430
Mr. Malamin K. Juwara
Minister, Chargé d'Affaires ad interim
Consular Office: California, Los Angeles

GEORGIA
Embassy of the Republic of Georgia
1511 K Street NW, Suite 424, 20005
phone 393–5959, fax 393–4537
His Excellency Dr. Tedo Japaridze
Ambassador E. and P.

GERMANY, FEDERAL REPUBLIC OF
Embassy of the Federal Republic of Germany
4645 Reservoir Road NW 20007
phone 298–4000, fax 298–4249
His Excellency Juergen Chrobog
Ambassador E. and P.
Consular Offices:
Alabama, Mobile
Alaska, Anchorage
American Samoa, Wellington
Arizona, Phoenix
California - Los Angeles, San Diego, San Francisco
Colorado, Denver
Florida - Jacksonville, Miami, St. Petersburg
Georgia - Atlanta, Savannah
Hawaii, Honolulu
Illinois, Chicago
Indiana, Indianapolis
Iowa, Des Moines
Kansas, Kansas City
Kentucky, Louisville
Louisiana, New Orleans
Massachusetts, Boston
Michigan, Detroit
Minnesota, Minneapolis
Mississippi, Jackson
Missouri, St. Louis
Nevada, Las Vegas
New Mexico, Albuquerque
New York - Buffalo, New York
North Carolina, Charlotte
Ohio - Cincinnati, Cleveland, Columbus
Oklahoma, Oklahoma City
Oregon, Portland
Pennsylvania - Philadelphia, Pittsburgh
Puerto Rico, San Juan
South Carolina, Spartanburg
Tennessee, Nashville
Texas - Corpus Christi, Dallas, Houston, San Antonio
Trust Territories of the Pacific Islands, Manila
Utah, Salt Lake City
Washington, Seattle, Spokane

GHANA
Embassy of Ghana
3512 International Drive NW 20008
phone 686–4520, fax 686–4527
His Excellency Ekwow Spio-Garbrah
Ambassador E. and P.
Consular Offices:
Georgia, Atlanta
Illinois, Chicago
New York, New York
Texas, Houston

GREAT BRITAIN
See United Kingdom of Great Britain and Northern Ireland

GREECE
Embassy of Greece
2221 Massachusetts Avenue NW 20008
phone 939–5800, fax 939–5824
His Excellency Loucas Tsilas
Ambassador E. and P.
Consular Offices:
California - Los Angeles, San Francisco
Georgia, Atlanta
Illinois, Chicago
Louisiana, New Orleans
Massachusetts, Boston
New York, New York
Texas, Houston

GRENADA
Embassy of Grenada
1701 New Hampshire Avenue NW 20009
phone 265–2561
His Excellency Denis G. Antoine
Ambassador E. and P.
Consular Offices:
Florida, Miami
Illinois, Chicago
New York, New York

GUATEMALA
Embassy of Guatemala
2220 R Street NW 20008
phone 745–4952, fax 745–1908
His Excellency Pedro Miguel Lamport
Ambassador E. and P.
Consular Offices:
Alabama, Montgomery
California - Los Angeles, San Diego, San Francisco
Florida - Ft. Lauderdale, Miami
Georgia, Atlanta
Illinois, Chicago
Kansas, Leavenworth
Louisiana, New Orleans
New York, New York
Pennsylvania - Philadelphia, Pittsburgh
Puerto Rico, San Juan
Rhode Island, Providence
Tennessee, Memphis
Texas - Houston, San Antonio
Utah, Salt Lake City
Washington, Seattle

GUINEA
Embassy of the Republic of Guinea
2112 Leroy Place NW 20008
phone 483–9420, fax 483–8688
His Excellency Thiam Mohamed Aly
Ambassador E. and P.
Consular Offices:
Florida, Jacksonville
Ohio, Cleveland
Pennsylvania, Philadelphia

GUINEA-BISSAU
Embassy of the Republic of Guinea-Bissau
918 16th Street NW, Mezzanine Suite, 20006
phone 872–4222, fax 872–4226
His Excellency Rufino Jose Mendes
Ambassador E. and P.

GUYANA
Embassy of Guyana
2490 Tracy Place NW 20008
phone 265–6900
His Excellency Mohammed Ali Odeen Ishmael
Ambassador E. and P.
Consular Offices:
California, Los Angeles
Florida, Ft. Lauderdale
New York, New York

HAITI
Embassy of the Republic of Haiti
2311 Massachusetts Avenue NW 20008
phone 332–4090, fax 745–7215
His Excellency Jean Casimir
Ambassador E. and P.
Consular Offices:
California, San Francisco
Colorado, Denver
Florida, Miami
Georgia, Atlanta
Illinois, Chicago
Indiana, Evansville
Louisiana, New Orleans
Massachusetts, Boston
Michigan, Detroit
Missouri, St. Louis
New Jersey, Trenton
New York, New York
Ohio, Cleveland
Pennsylvania - Philadelphia, Pottsville
Puerto Rico, San Juan
Texas, Houston

THE HOLY SEE
Apostolic Nunciature
3339 Massachusetts Avenue NW 20008
phone 333–7121
His Excellency The Most Reverend Agostino Cacciavillan
Apostolic Pro-Nuncio

HONDURAS
Embassy of Honduras
3007 Tilden Street NW 20008
phone 966–7702, fax 966–9751
His Excellency Roberto Flores Bermudez
Ambassador E. and P.

Consular Offices:
California - Los Angeles, San Diego, San Francisco
Florida - Jacksonville, Miami
Georgia, Atlanta
Hawaii, Honolulu
Illinois, Chicago
Louisiana - Baton Rouge, New Orleans
Maryland, Baltimore
Massachusetts, Boston
Michigan, Detroit
Minnesota, Minneapolis
Missouri, St. Louis
New York, New York
Puerto Rico, San Juan
Texas, Houston

HUNGARY
Embassy of the Republic of Hungary
3910 Shoemaker Street NW 20008
phone 362–6730, fax 966–8135
His Excellency Dr. Gyorgy Banlaki
Ambassador E. and P.
Consular Offices:
California - Los Angeles, San Francisco
Colorado, Denver
Florida, Miami
Hawaii, Honolulu
Massachusetts, Boston
New York, New York
Ohio, Cleveland
Texas, Houston
Washington, Seattle

ICELAND
Embassy of Iceland
1156—15th Street, NW, Suite 1200, 20005
phone 265–6653, fax 265–6656
His Excellency Einar Benediktsson
Ambassador E. and P.
Consular Offices:
Alaska, Anchorage
California - Los Angeles, San Francisco
Florida - Hollywood, Tallahassee
Georgia, Atlanta
Illinois, Chicago
Kentucky, Louisville
Louisiana, New Orleans
Massachusetts, Boston
Michigan, Detroit
Minnesota, Minneapolis
Missouri, Grandview
New York, New York
Pennsylvania, Harrisburg
Puerto Rico, San Juan
Texas - Dallas, Houston
Utah, Salt Lake City
Virginia, Norfolk
Washington, Seattle

INDIA
Embassy of India
2107 Massachusetts Avenue NW 20008
phone 939–7000, fax 483–3972
His Excellency Naresh Chandra
Ambassador E. and P.
Consular Offices:
California, San Francisco
Hawaii, Honolulu
Illinois, Chicago
Louisiana, New Orleans
New York, New York
Ohio, Cleveland
Texas, Houston

INDONESIA
Embassy of the Republic of Indonesia
2020 Massachusetts Avenue NW 20036
phone 775–5200, fax 775–5365
His Excellency Arifin Mohamad Siregar
Ambassador E. and P.
Consular Offices:
California - Los Angeles, San Francisco
Hawaii, Honolulu
Illinois, Chicago
New York, New York
Texas, Houston

IRAN
See Pakistan

IRAQ
See Algeria

IRELAND
Embassy of Ireland
2234 Massachusetts Avenue NW 20008
phone 462–3939, fax 232–5993
His Excellency Dermot A. Gallagher
Ambassador E. and P.
Consular Offices:
California, San Francisco
Florida, Ft. Lauderdale
Georgia, Atlanta
Illinois, Chicago
Massachusetts, Boston
Missouri, St. Louis
New York, New York
Texas, Houston

ISRAEL
Embassy of Israel
3514 International Drive NW 20008
phone 364–5500, fax 364–5610
His Excellency Eliahu Ben-Elissar
Ambassador E. and P.
Consular Offices:

California - Los Angeles, San Francisco, Santa Clara (Economic Office)
Florida, Miami
Georgia, Atlanta
Illinois, Chicago
Massachusetts, Boston
New York, New York
Pennsylvania, Philadelphia
Texas, Houston

ITALY
Embassy of Italy
1601 Fuller Street NW 20009
2700—16th Street NW 20009
phone 328–5500, fax 483–2187
His Excellency Ferdinando Salleo
Ambassador E. and P.
Consular Offices:
Alabama, Mobile
Alaska, Anchorage
Arizona, Phoenix
California - Bakersfield, Fresno, Los Angeles, Sacramento, San Diego, San Francisco, San Jose
Colorado, Denver
Connecticut, Hartford
Florida - Jacksonville, Miami, Orlando, Sarasota
Georgia - Atlanta, Savannah
Hawaii, Honolulu
Illinois, Chicago
Indiana, Indianapolis
Kansas, Kansas City
Louisiana, New Orleans
Maryland, Baltimore
Massachusetts - Boston, Springfield, Worcester
Michigan, Detroit
Minnesota, St. Paul
Mississippi, Gulfport
Missouri, St. Louis
Nevada, Las Vegas
New Jersey - Newark, Trenton
New Mexico, Albuquerque
New York - Buffalo, New York, Rochester
Ohio - Cincinnati, Cleveland
Pennsylvania - Philadelphia, Pittsburgh
Puerto Rico, San Juan
Texas - Dallas, Houston
Utah, Salt Lake City
Virginia, Norfolk
Washington, Seattle

JAMAICA
Embassy of Jamaica
1520 New Hampshire Avenue NW 20036
phone 452–0660, fax 452–0081
His Excellency Richard Leighton Bernal
Ambassador E. and P.
Consular Offices:
California - Hayward, Los Angeles
Florida, Miami
Georgia, Atlanta
Illinois, Chicago
Massachusetts, Boston
New York, New York
Texas, Houston
Washington, Seattle

JAPAN
Embassy of Japan
2520 Massachusetts Avenue NW 20008
phone 939–6700, fax 328–2187
His Excellency Kunihiko Saito
Ambassador E. and P.
Consular Offices:
Alabama, Mobile
Alaska, Anchorage
Arizona, Phoenix
California - Los Angeles, San Diego, San Francisco
Colorado, Denver
Florida, Miami
Georgia, Atlanta
Guam, Agana
Hawaii, Honolulu
Illinois, Chicago
Louisiana, New Orleans
Massachusetts, Boston
Michigan, Detroit
Minnesota, Minneapolis
Missouri - Kansas City, St. Louis
New York - Buffalo, New York
Oregon, Portland
Pennsylvania, Philadelphia
Tennessee, Nashville
Texas - Dallas, Houston
Trust Territories of the Pacific Islands - Mariana Islands, Pago Pago
Washington, Seattle

JORDAN
Embassy of the Hashemite Kingdom of Jordan
3504 International Drive NW 20008
phone 966–2664, fax 966–3110
His Excellency Fayez A. Tarawneh
Ambassador E. and P.
Consular Offices:
Illinois, Chicago
Texas, Houston

KAZAKSTAN
Embassy of the Republic of Kazakstan
(Temporary chancery) 3421 Massachusetts Avenue NW 20008
phone 333–4504, fax 333–4509
His Excellency Bolat K. Nurgaliyev
Ambassador E. and P.

KENYA
Embassy of the Republic of Kenya
2249 R Street NW 20008
phone 387–6101, fax 462–3829
His Excellency Benjamin Edgar Kipkorir
Ambassador E. and P.
Consular Offices:
California, Los Angeles
New York, New York

KIRIBATI
Consular Offices: Hawaii, Honolulu

KOREA
Embassy of the Republic of Korea
2450 Massachusetts Avenue NW 20008
phone 939–5600
His Excellency Kun Woo Park
Ambassador E. and P.
Consular Offices:
Alabama, Mobile
Alaska, Anchorage
California - Los Angeles, San Francisco
Colorado, Denver
Florida - Ft. Lauderdale, Miami
Georgia, Atlanta
Guam, Agana
Hawaii, Honolulu
Illinois, Chicago
Louisiana, New Orleans
Massachusetts, Boston
Michigan, Detroit
Minnesota, Minneapolis
New York, New York
Ohio, Cleveland
Oklahoma, Oklahoma City
Oregon, Eagle Point, Portland
Puerto Rico, San Juan
Texas, Dallas, Houston
Washington, Seattle

KUWAIT
Embassy of the State of Kuwait
2940 Tilden Street, NW 20008
phone 966–0702, fax 966–0517
His Excellency Mohammed Sabah Al-Salim Al-Sabah
Ambassador E. and P.

KYRGYZSTAN
Embassy of the Kyrgyz Republic
1732 Wisconsin Avenue NW 20007
phone 338–5141, fax 338–5139
His Excellency Baktybek Abrissaer
Ambassador E. and P.
Consular Office: California, Los Angeles

LAOS
Embassy of the Lao People's Democratic Republic
2222 S Street NW 20008
phone 332–6416, fax 332–4923
His Excellency Hiem Phommachanh
Ambassador E. and P.

LATVIA
Embassy of Latvia
4325 17th Street NW 20011
phone 726–8213, fax 726–6785
His Excellency Ojars Eriks Kalnins
Ambassador E. and P.
Consular Offices:
California, Los Angeles
Illinois, Chicago
Ohio, Cleveland

LEBANON
Embassy of Lebanon
2560 28th Street NW 20008
phone 939–6300, fax 939–6324
Mr. Victor El-Zmeter
Counselor, Chargé d'Affairs ad interim
Consular Offices:
California, Los Angeles
Michigan, Detroit
New York, New York

LESOTHO
Embassy of the Kingdom of Lesotho
2511 Massachusetts Avenue NW 20008
phone 797–5533, fax 234–6815
Her Excellency Dr. Eunice M. Bulane
Ambassador E. and P.
Consular Offices:
Louisiana, New Orleans
Texas, Austin

LIBERIA
Embassy of the Republic of Liberia
5201 16th Street NW 20011
phone 723–0437
T.H. Konah K. Blackett
Minister-Counselor, Chargé d'Affaires ad interim
Consular Offices:
California - Los Angeles, San Francisco
Georgia, Atlanta
Illinois, Chicago
Louisiana, New Orleans
Michigan, Detroit
New York, New York
Pennsylvania, Philadelphia
Texas, Houston

LITHUANIA
Embassy of the Republic of Lithuania
2622 16th Street NW 20009
phone 234–5860, fax 328–0466
His Excellency Alfonsas Eidintas
Ambassador E. and P.

Consular Offices:
- California, Los Angeles
- Illinois, Chicago
- New York, New York
- Ohio, Cleveland

LUXEMBOURG
Embassy of the Grand Duchy of Luxembourg
2200 Massachusetts Avenue NW 20008
phone 265–4171, fax 328–8270
His Excellency Alphonse Berns
Ambassador E. and P.
Consular Offices:
- California - Los Angeles, San Francisco
- Florida, Miami
- Georgia, Atlanta
- Illinois, Chicago
- Indiana, Indianapolis
- Louisiana, New Orleans
- Massachusetts, Boston
- Michigan, Detroit
- Minnesota, St. Paul
- Missouri, Kansas City
- New York, New York
- Ohio - Cleveland, Middletown
- Texas, Dallas
- Washington, Seattle

MACEDONIA
Embassy of the Former Yugoslav Republic of Macedonia
3050 K Street NW, Suite 210, 20007
phone 337–3063
Her Excellency Lubica Z. Acevska
Ambassador E. and P.
Consular Office: New York, New York

MADAGASCAR
Embassy of the Republic of Madagascar
2374 Massachusetts Avenue NW 20008
phone 265–5525
His Excellency Pierrot J. Rajaonarivelo
Ambassador E. and P.
Consular Offices:
- California, Palo Alto
- New York, New York
- Pennsylvania, Philadelphia
- Texas, Houston

MALAWI
Embassy of Malawi
2408 Massachusetts Avenue NW 20008
phone 797–1007
His Excellency Willie Chokani
Ambassador E. and P.
Consular Offices:
- California, Los Angeles
- Washington, Seattle

MALAYSIA
Embassy of Malaysia
2401 Massachusetts Avenue NW 20008
phone 328–2700, fax 483–7661
His Excellency Dato Dali Mahmud Hashim
Ambassador E. and P.
Consular Offices:
- California - Los Angeles, San Francisco
- Hawaii, Honolulu
- New York, New York
- Oregon, Portland

MALI
Embassy of the Republic of Mali
2130 R Street NW 20008
phone 332–2249, fax 332–6603
His Excellency Cheick Oumar Diarrah
Ambassador E. and P.
Consular Offices:
- California, Los Angeles
- Florida, Ft. Lauderdale
- Massachusetts, Boston
- New Mexico, Albuquerque

MALTA
Embassy of Malta
2017 Connecticut Avenue NW 20008
phone 462–3611, fax 387–5470
His Excellency Mark Micallef
Ambassador E. and P.
Consular Offices:
- California, San Francisco
- Florida, Ft. Lauderdale
- Michigan, Detroit
- Minnesota, St. Paul
- Missouri, Independence
- New York, New York
- Texas, Houston

MARSHALL ISLANDS
Embassy of the Republic of the Marshall Islands
2433 Massachusetts Avenue NW 20008
phone 234–5414, fax 232–3236
His Excellency Banny De Brum
Ambassador E. and P.
Consular Offices:
- California, Los Angeles
- Hawaii, Honolulu

MAURITANIA
Embassy of the Islamic Republic of Mauritania
2129 Leroy Place NW 20008
phone 232–5700
His Excellency Bilal Ould Werzeg
Ambassador E. and P.

MAURITIUS
Embassy of Republic of Mauritius
4301 Connecticut Avenue NW, Suite 441, 20008

phone 244–1491, fax 966–0983
His Excellency Chitmansing Jesseramsing
Ambassador E. and P.
Consular Offices:
California, Los Angeles
Georgia, Atlanta

MEXICO
Embassy of Mexico
1911 Pennsylvania Avenue NW 20006
phone 728–1600
His Excellency Jesus Silva Herzog
Ambassador E. and P.
Consular Offices:
Alaska, Anchorage
Arizona - Nogales, Phoenix, Tucson
California - Calexico, Fresno, Los Angeles, San Francisco, San Jose, Santa Ana
Colorado, Denver
Florida - Miami, Orlando, Tampa
Georgia, Atlanta
Hawaii, Honolulu
Illinois, Chicago
Louisiana, New Orleans
Massachusetts, Boston
Michigan, Detroit
Missouri, St. Louis
New Mexico, Albuquerque
New York - Buffalo, New York
North Carolina, Charlotte
Oregon, Portland
Pennsylvania, Philadelphia
Puerto Rico, San Juan
Texas - Austin, Brownsville, Corpus Christi, Dallas, Del Rio, Eagle Pass, El Paso, Fort Worth, Houston, San Antonio
Utah, Salt Lake City
Virginia - Norfolk, Richmond
Washington - Seattle, Spokane
Wisconsin, Madison

Tourism Offices:
California - Oxnard, Sacramento, San Bernardino, San Diego
Texas - Laredo, McAllen, Midland

MICRONESIA
Embassy of the Federated States of Micronesia
1725 N Street NW 20036
phone 223–4383, fax 223–4391
His Excellency Jesse B. Marehalau
Ambassador E. and P.
Consular Offices:
Guam, Tamuning
Hawaii, Honolulu

MOLDOVA
Embassy of the Republic of Moldova
2101 S Street NW 20008
phone 667–1130, fax 667–1204
His Excellency Nicolae Tau
Ambassador E. and P.

MONACO
Consular Offices:
California - Los Angeles, San Francisco
Florida, Palm Beach
Illinois, Chicago
Louisiana, New Orleans
Massachusetts, Boston
New York, New York
Pennsylvania, Philadelphia
Puerto Rico, San Juan
Texas, Dallas

MONGOLIA
Embassy of Mongolia
2833 M Street NW 20007
phone 333–7117, fax 298–9227
His Excellency Jalbuu Choinhor
Ambassador E. and P.
Consular Office: New York, New York

MOROCCO
Embassy of the Kingdom of Morocco
1601 21st Street NW 20009
phone 462–7979, fax 265–0161
His Excellency Mohamed Benaissa
Ambassador E. and P.
Consular Offices:
California, Los Angeles
Kansas, Kansas City
New York, New York
Texas, Houston

MOZAMBIQUE
Embassy of the Republic of Mozambique
1990 M Street NW, Suite 570, 20036
phone 293–7146, fax 835–0245
His Excellency Marcus Geraldo Namashulua
Ambassador E. and P.

MYANMAR
Consular Office: New York, New York

NAURU
Consular Offices:
Guam, Agana
Hawaii, Honolulu
Trust Territories of the Pacific Islands, Pago Pago

NAMIBIA
1605 New Hampshire Avenue NW 20009
phone 986–0540, fax 986–0443
His Excellency Veiccoh Nghiwete
Ambassador E. and P.

NEPAL
Royal Nepalese Embassy
2131 Leroy Place NW 20008
phone 667–4550
His Excellency Bhekh Bahadur Thapa
Ambassador E. and P.
Consular Offices:
California - Los Angeles, San Francisco
Massachusetts, Boston
New York, New York
Ohio, Cleveland

NETHERLANDS
Royal Netherlands Embassy
4200 Linnean Avenue NW 20008
phone 244–5300, fax 362–3430
His Excellency Adriaan Pieter Roetert Jacobovits de Szeged
Ambassador E. and P.
Consular Offices:
Arizona, Phoenix
California - Los Angeles, San Diego, San Francisco
Colorado, Denver
Florida - Jacksonville, Miami, Orlando
Georgia, Atlanta
Hawaii, Honolulu
Illinois, Chicago
Louisiana, New Orleans
Maryland, Baltimore
Massachusetts, Boston
Michigan - Detroit, Grand Rapids
Minnesota, Minneapolis
Missouri - Kansas City, St. Louis
New York, New York
Ohio, Cleveland
Oregon, Portland
Pennsylvania, Philadelphia
Puerto Rico, San Juan
Texas, Houston
Trust Territories of the Pacific Islands, Manila
Utah, Salt Lake City
Virgin Islands, St. Croix
Virginia, Norfolk
Washington, Seattle

NEW ZEALAND
Embassy of New Zealand
37 Observatory Circle NW 20008
phone 328–4800
His Excellency L. John Wood
Ambassador E. and P.
Consular Offices:
California - Los Angeles, San Diego, San Francisco
Georgia, Atlanta
Guam, Tamuning
Illinois, Chicago
New York, New York
Texas, Houston
Trust Territories of the Pacific Islands, Apia
Utah, Salt Lake City
Washington, Seattle

NICARAGUA
Embassy of Nicaragua
1627 New Hampshire Avenue NW 20009
phone 939–6570
His Excellency Francisco Xavier Aguirre Sacasa
Ambassador E. and P.
Consular Offices:
California - Los Angeles, San Francisco
Florida, Miami
Georgia, Atlanta
Louisiana, New Orleans
New York, New York
Pennsylvania, Pittsburgh
Puerto Rico, San Juan
Texas, Houston
Wisconsin, Milwaukee

NIGER
Embassy of the Republic of Niger
2204 R Street NW 20008
phone 483–4224
His Excellency Joseph Diatta
Ambassador E. and P.

NIGERIA
Embassy of the Federal Republic of Nigeria
1333 16th Street NW 20036
phone 986–8400
His Excellency Wakili Hassan Adamu
Ambassador E. and P.
Consular Office: New York, New York

NORWAY
Royal Norwegian Embassy
2720 34th Street NW 20008
phone 333–6000, fax 337–0870
His Excellency Tom Eric Vraalsen
Ambassador E. and P.
Consular Offices:
Alaska, Anchorage
Arizona, Phoenix
California - Los Angeles, San Diego, San Francisco
Colorado, Denver
Florida - Jacksonville, Miami, Pensacola, Tampa
Georgia - Atlanta, Savannah
Hawaii, Honolulu
Illinois, Chicago
Iowa, Des Moines
Louisiana, New Orleans
Maryland, Baltimore
Massachusetts, Boston
Michigan, Detroit

Minnesota, Minneapolis
Missouri, St. Louis
Montana, Billings
Nebraska, Omaha
New York, New York
North Dakota, Fargo
Ohio, Cleveland
Oregon, Portland
Pennsylvania, Philadelphia
Puerto Rico, Ponce
South Carolina, Charleston
South Dakota, Sioux Falls
Texas - Dallas, Houston
Utah, Salt Lake City
Virginia, Norfolk
Washington, Seattle
Wisconsin - Madison, Milwaukee

OMAN
Embassy of the Sultanate of Oman
2535 Belmont Road NW 20008
phone 387--1980, fax 745–4933
His Excellency Abdulla Moh'd Aqueel Al-Dhahab
Ambassador E. and P.
Consular Office: California, Los Angeles

PAKISTAN
Embassy of Pakistan
2315 Massachusetts Avenue NW 20008
phone 939–6200, fax 387–0484
His Excellency Riaz Hussain Khokhar
Ambassador E. and P.
Consular Offices:
California, Los Angeles
Kentucky, Louisville
Massachusetts, Boston
New York, New York

Iranian Interests Section
2209 Wisconsin Avenue NW 20007
phone 965–4990

PALAU
Embassy of the Republic of Palau
2000 L Street NW, Suite 407, 20036
phone 452–6814, fax 452–6281
Mr. David Orrukem
First Secretary, Chargé d'Affaires ad interim

PANAMA
Embassy of the Republic of Panama
2862 McGill Terrace NW 20008
phone 483–1407
His Excellency Eduardo Gonzalez Morgan
Ambassador E. and P.
Consular Offices:
California - Los Angeles, San Diego, San Francisco
Florida - Miami, Tampa (Trade Development)
Georgia, Atlanta
Hawaii, Honolulu
Illinois, Chicago
Louisiana - Baton Rouge, New Orleans
New York, New York
Pennsylvania, Philadelphia
Puerto Rico, San Juan
Texas, Houston

PAPUA NEW GUINEA
Embassy of Papua New Guinea
1615 New Hampshire Avenue NW, 3rd Floor, 20009
phone 745–3680, fax 745–3679
His Excellency Nagora Y. Bogan
Ambassador E. and P.
Consular Office: California, Los Angeles

PARAGUAY
Embassy of Paraguay
2400 Massachusetts Avenue NW 20008
phone 483–6960, fax 234–4508
His Excellency Jorge G. Prieto
Ambassador E. and P.
Consular Offices:
California, Los Angeles
Florida, Miami
Louisiana, New Orleans
Michigan, Detroit
New York, New York
Puerto Rico, San Juan

PERU
Embassy of Peru
1700 Massachusetts Avenue NW 20036
phone 833–9860, fax 659–8124
His Excellency Ricardo V. Luna
Ambassador E. and P.
Consular Offices:
California - Los Angeles, San Francisco
Florida - Miami
Georgia, Atlanta
Hawaii, Honolulu
Illinois, Chicago
Louisiana, New Orleans
Massachusetts, Boston
Missouri, St. Louis
New Jersey, Paterson
New York, New York
Oklahoma, Tulsa
Puerto Rico, San Juan
Texas, Houston
Washington, Seattle

PHILIPPINES
Embassy of the Philippines
1600 Massachusetts Avenue NW 20036
phone 467–9300, fax 328–7614

His Excellency Raul Chaves Rabe
Ambassador E. and P.
Consular Offices:
California - Los Angeles, San Diego, San Francisco
Georgia, Atlanta
Guam, Agana
Hawaii, Honolulu
Illinois, Chicago
Louisiana, New Orleans
Michigan, Detroit
New York, New York
Ohio, Cleveland
Puerto Rico, San Juan
Texas, Houston
Trust Territories of the Pacific Islands, Mariana Islands

POLAND
Embassy of the Republic of Poland
2640 16th Street NW 20009
phone 234–3800, fax 328–6271
His Excellency Jerzy Kozminski
Ambassador E. and P.
Consular Offices:
California, Los Angeles
Illinois, Chicago
Massachusetts, Boston
New York, New York
Puerto Rico, San Juan

PORTUGAL
Embassy of Portugal
2125 Kalorama Road NW 20008
phone 328–8610, fax 462–3726
His Excellency Fernando Andresen Guimaraes
Ambassador E. and P.
Consular Offices:
California - Los Angeles, San Francisco
Connecticut, Waterbury
Florida, Miami
Hawaii, Honolulu
Illinois, Chicago
Massachusetts - Boston, New Bedford
New Jersey, Newark
New York, New York
Pennsylvania, Philadelphia
Puerto Rico, San Juan
Rhode Island, Providence
Texas, Houston

QATAR
Embassy of the State of Qatar
4200 Wisconsin Avenue NW 20016
phone 274–1600
His Excellency Saad Mohamed Al Kobaisi
Ambassador E. and P.

Office of the Cultural Attache:
600 New Hampshire Avenue NW, Suite 950, 20037
phone 338–1700

ROMANIA
Embassy of Romania
1607 23rd Street NW 20008
phone 332–4846, fax 232–4748
His Excellency Mircea Geoana
Ambassador E. and P.
Consular Offices:
California, Los Angeles
New York, New York

RUSSIA
Embassy of the Russian Federation
2650 Wisconsin Avenue NW 20007
phone 298–5700, fax 298–5735
His Excellency Yuli M. Vorontsov
Ambassador E. and P.
Consular Offices:
Alaska, Anchorage
California, San Francisco
New York, New York
Washington, Seattle

RWANDA
Embassy of the Republic of Rwanda
(Temporary chancery) 2141 Wisconsin Avenue NW 20007
phone 232–2882, fax 232–4544
His Excellency Theogene N. Rudasingwa
Ambassador E. and P.
Consular Office: Chicago, Illinois

SAINT KITTS AND NEVIS
Embassy of Street, Kitts and Nevis
3216 New Mexico Avenue NW 20016
phone 686–2636, fax 686–5740
His Excellency Osbert W. Liburd
Ambassador E. and P.
Consular Offices:
Georgia, Atlanta
Texas, Dallas

SAINT LUCIA
Embassy of Saint Lucia
3216 New Mexico Avenue NW 20016
phone 364–6792, fax 364–6728
His Excellency Dr. Joseph Edsel Edmunds
Ambassador E. and P.
Consular Offices:
New York, New York
Texas, Dallas
Virgin Islands, St. Croix

SAINT VINCENT AND THE GRENADINES
Embassy of Saint Vincent and the Grenadines
3216 New Mexico Avenue NW 20016
phone 364–6730, fax 364–6736
His Excellency Kingsley C.A. Layne
Ambassador E. and P.

SAN MARINO
Consular Offices:
District of Columbia
Michigan, Detroit
New York, New York

SAO TOME AND PRINCIPE
Consular Offices:
District of Columbia
Florida, Miami
Illinois, Chicago

SAUDI ARABIA
Embassy of Saudi Arabia
601 New Hampshire Avenue NW 20037
phone 342–3800
His Royal Highness Prince Bandar Bin Sultan
Ambassador E. and P.
Consular Offices:
California, Los Angeles
New York, New York
Texas, Houston

SENEGAL
Embassy of the Republic of Senegal
2112 Wyoming Avenue NW 20008
phone 234–0540
His Excellency Mamadou Mansour Seck
Ambassador E. and P.
Consular Offices:
Florida, Miami
Georgia, Atlanta
Louisiana, New Orleans
Massachusetts, Boston
Texas, Houston

SEYCHELLES
Embassy of the Republic of Seychelles
(Temporary chancery) care of the Permanent Mission of Seychelles to the United Nations
820 Second Avenue, Suite 900F,
New York NY, 10017
phone (212) 972–1785, fax 972–1786
Mr. Claude Morel
Minister-Counselor, Chargé d'Affaires ad interim
Consular Office: Washington, Seattle

SIERRA LEONE
Embassy of Sierra Leone
1701—19th Street NW 20009
phone 939–9261
His Excellency John Ernest Leigh
Ambassador E. and P.

SINGAPORE
Embassy of the Republic of Singapore
3501 International Place NW 20008
phone 537–3100, fax 537–0876
Her Excellency Heng-Chee Chan
Ambassador E. and P.
Consular Offices:
California - Los Angeles, San Francisco
Minnesota, St. Paul

SLOVAK REPUBLIC
Embassy of the Slovak Republic
(Temporary Chancery) 2201 Wisconsin Avenue NW, Suite 250, 20007
phone 965–5161, fax 965–5166
His Excellency Branislav Lichardus
Ambassador E. and P.
Consular Offices:
Colorado, Denver
Illinois, Chicago
Puerto Rico, San Juan

SLOVENIA
Embassy of the Republic of Slovenia
1525 New Hampshire Avenue NW 20036
phone 667–5363, fax 667–4563
His Excellency Dr. Ernest Petric
Ambassador E. and P.
Consular Offices:
California, Los Angeles
New York, New York
Ohio, Cleveland
Texas, Houston

SOLOMON ISLANDS
Embassy of the Solomon Islands
(Temporary chancery) care of Permanent Mission of the Solomon Islands to the United States
820 Second Avenue, Suite 800, New York NY 10017
phone (212) 599–6193

SOMALIA
Embassy of the Somali Democratic Republic
(Embassy ceased operations May 8, 1991)

SOUTH AFRICA
Embassy of the Republic of South Africa
3051 Massachusetts Avenue NW 20008
phone 232–4400, fax 265–1607
His Excellency Franklin Sonn
Ambassador E. and P.
Consular Offices:
Alabama, Mobile
California, Beverly Hills
Illinois, Chicago
New York, New York
Utah, Salt Lake City

SPAIN
Embassy of Spain
2375 Pennsylvania Avenue NW 20037
phone 452–0100, fax 833–5670
His Excellency Antonio Oyarzabal
Ambassador E. and P.
Consular Offices:

Alabama, Mobile
California - Los Angeles, San Francisco
Florida - Miami, Coral Gables, Pensacola
(Spanish Education)
Georgia, Atlanta
Hawaii, Honolulu
Illinois, Chicago
Louisiana, New Orleans
Maryland, Baltimore
Massachusetts, Boston
Michigan, Detroit
Missouri - Kansas City, St. Louis
New Jersey, Newark
New Mexico, Santa Fe
New York, New York
Ohio, Cincinnati
Pennsylvania, Philadelphia
Puerto Rico, San Juan
Texas - Dallas, El Paso, Houston,
San Antonio
Washington, Seattle

SRI LANKA
Embassy of the Democratic Socialist Republic of Sri Lanka
2148 Wyoming Avenue NW 20008
phone 483–4025, fax 232–7181
His Excellency Jayantha Dhanapala
Ambassador E. and P.
Consular Offices:
Hawaii, Honolulu
Louisiana, New Orleans
New York, New York

SUDAN
Embassy of the Republic of the Sudan
2210 Massachusetts Avenue NW 20008
phone 338–8565, fax 667–2406
His Excellency Mahdi Ibrahim Mohamed
Ambassador E. and P.

SURINAME
Embassy of the Republic of Suriname
4301 Connecticut Avenue NW Suite 108, 20008
phone 244–7488, fax 244–5878
Mr. Cicyl G. Alwart
Counselor, Chargé d'Affaires ad interim
Consular Offices:
Florida, Miami
Georgia, Atlanta
Indiana, Indianapolis

SWAZILAND
Embassy of the Kingdom of Swaziland
3400 International Drive NW 20008
phone 362–6683, fax 244–8059
Her Excellency Mary M. Kanya
Ambassador E. and P.

SWEDEN
Embassy of Sweden
1501 M Street NW 20005
phone 467–2600, fax 467–2699
His Excellency Carl Henrik Sihver Liljegren
Ambassador E. and P.
Consular Offices:
Alabama, Mobile
Alaska, Anchorage
Arizona, Phoenix
California - Los Angeles, San Diego,
San Francisco
Colorado, Denver
Florida - Ft. Lauderdale, Jacksonville,
St. Petersburg
Georgia, Atlanta
Hawaii, Honolulu
Illinois, Chicago
Louisiana, New Orleans
Massachusetts, Boston
Michigan, Troy
Minnesota, Minneapolis
Missouri - Kansas City, St. Louis
Nebraska, Omaha
New York - Buffalo, Jamestown,
New York
Ohio, Cleveland
Oregon, Portland
Pennsylvania, Philadelphia
Puerto Rico, San Juan
Texas - Dallas, Houston
Utah, Salt Lake City
Virgin Islands, St. Thomas
Virginia, Norfolk
Washington, Seattle
Wisconsin, Milwaukee

SWITZERLAND
Embassy of Switzerland
2900 Cathedral Avenue NW 20008
phone 745–7900, fax 387–2564
His Excellency Alfred Defago
Ambassador E. and P.
Consular Offices:
Arizona, Phoenix
California - Los Angeles, San Francisco
Colorado, Boulder
Florida, Miami
Georgia, Atlanta
Hawaii, Honolulu
Illinois, Chicago
Indiana, Indianapolis
Louisiana, New Orleans
Massachusetts, Boston
Michigan, Detroit
Minnesota, Minneapolis
Missouri, Kansas City
New York - Buffalo, New York

Ohio, Cleveland
Pennsylvania - Philadelphia, Pittsburgh
Puerto Rico, San Juan
South Carolina, Spartanburg
Texas - Dallas, Houston
Trust Territories of the Pacific Islands, Pago Pago
Utah, Salt Lake City

Cuban Interests Section
2630 16th Street NW 20009
phone 797–8518
Mr. Fernando Remirez de Estenoz
Counselor

SYRIA
Embassy of the Syrian Arab Republic
2215 Wyoming Avenue NW 20008
phone 232–6313, fax 234–9548
His Excellency Walid Al-Moualem
Ambassador E. and P.
Consular Offices:
California, Los Angeles
Texas, Houston

TANZANIA
Embassy of the United Republic of Tanzania
2139 R Street NW 20008
phone 939–6125, fax 797–7408
His Excellency Mustafa Salim Nyang'anyi
Ambassador E. and P.

THAILAND
Royal Thai Embassy
1024 Wisconsin Avenue NW 20007
phone 944–3600, fax 944–3611
His Excellency Nitya Pibulsonggram
Ambassador E. and P.
Consular Offices:
Alabama, Montgomery
California, Los Angeles
Colorado, Denver
Florida, Coral Gables
Georgia, Atlanta
Hawaii, Honolulu
Illinois, Chicago
Louisiana, New Orleans
Massachusetts, Boston
Michigan, Grosse Pointe
Missouri, Kansas City
New York, New York
Oklahoma, Tulsa
Oregon, Portland
Puerto Rico, Hato Rey
Texas - Dallas, El Paso

TOGO
Embassy of the Republic of Togo
2208 Massachusetts Avenue NW 20008
phone 234–4212, fax 232–3190
His Excellency Kossivi Osseyi
Ambassador E. and P.
Consular Office: Miami, Florida

TONGA
Embassy of the Kingdom of Tonga
Consular Offices:
California, San Francisco
Hawaii, Honolulu

TRINIDAD AND TOBAGO
Embassy of the Republic of Trinidad and Tobago
1708 Massachusettes Avenue NW 20036
phone 467–6490, fax 785–3130
Her Excellency Corinne Averille McKnight
Ambassador E. And P.
Consular Office: New York, New York

TUNISIA
Embassy of Tunisia
1515 Massachusetts Avenue NW 20005
phone 862–1850
His Excellency Azouz Ennifar
Ambassador E. and P.
Consular Offices:
California, San Francisco
Florida, Miami
New York, New York

TURKEY
Embassy of the Republic of Turkey
1714 Massachusetts Avenue NW 20036
phone 659–8200
His Excellency Nuzhet Kandemir
Ambassador E. and P.
Consular Offices:
California - Los Angeles, Oakland
Florida, Miami
Georgia, Atlanta
Illinois, Chicago
Kansas, Mission Hills
Maryland, Baltimore
New York, New York
Texas, Houston

TURKMENISTAN
Embassy of Turkmenistan
2207 Massachusetts Avenue NW 20008
phone 588–1500, fax 588–0697
His Excellency Halil Ugur
Ambassador E. and P.

UGANDA
5911 16th Street NW 20011
phone 726–7100, fax 726–1727
Her Excellency Edith Ssempala
Ambassador E. and P.
Consular Office: Chicago, Illinois

UKRAINE
Embassy of Ukraine
3350 M Street NW 20007
phone 333–0606, fax 333–0817
His Excellency Yuriy Mikolayevych Shcherbak
Ambassador E. and P.
Consular Offices:
Illinois, Chicago
New York, New York

UNITED ARAB EMIRATES
Embassy of the United Arab Emirates
3000 K Street NW, Suite 600, 20007
phone 338–6500
His Excellency Mohammad bin Hussein Al-Shaali
Ambassador E. and P.

UNITED KINGDOM OF GREAT BRITAIN AND NORTHERN IRELAND
British Embassy
3100 Massachusetts Avenue NW 20008
phone 588–6500, fax 588–7870
His Excellency Sir John Olav Kerr, KCMG
Ambassador E. and P.
Consular Offices:
Alaska, Anchorage
California - Los Angeles, San Francisco
Colorado, Denver
Florida - Miami, Orlando
Georgia, Atlanta
Illinois, Chicago
Kansas, Kansas City
Louisiana, New Orleans
Massachusetts, Boston
Minnesota, Minneapolis
Missouri, Kansas City
New York, New York
North Carolina, Charlotte
Ohio, Cleveland
Oregon, Portland
Pennsylvania, Philadelphia
Puerto Rico, San Juan
Tennessee, Nashville
Texas - Dallas, Houston
Trust Territories of the Pacific Islands, Nuku'alofa
Utah, Salt Lake City
Washington, Seattle

URUGUAY
Embassy of Uruguay
2715 M Street NW 2000
phone 331–1313, fax 331–8147
His Excellency Dr. Alvaro Diez de Medina
Ambassador E. and P.
Consular Offices:
California - Los Angeles, San Francisco
Florida, Miami
Illinois, Chicago
Louisiana, New Orleans
Massachusetts, Boston
New York, New York
Puerto Rico, San Juan
Washington, Seattle

UZBEKISTAN
Embassy of the Republic of Uzbekistan
1746 Massachusetts Avenue NW 20036
phone 887–5300, fax 293–6804
His Excellency Sadiq Safaev
Ambassador E. and P.
Consular Office: New York, New York

VENEZUELA
Embassy of the Republic of Venezuela
1099 30th Street NW 20007
phone 342–2214, fax 342–6820
His Excellency Pedro Luis Echeverria
Ambassador E. and P.
Consular Offices:
California, San Francisco
Florida, Miami
Illinois, Chicago
Louisiana, New Orleans
Massachusetts, Boston
New York, New York
Puerto Rico, San Juan
Texas, Houston

VIETNAM
Embassy of Vietnam
1233 20th Street NW 20036
phone 861–0737, fax 861–0917
His Excellency Le Van Bang
Ambassador E. and P.

WESTERN SAMOA
Embassy of the Independent State of Western Samoa
820 Second Avenue, Suite 800D, New York, NY 10017
phone 212–599–6196, fax 599–0797
His Excellency Tuiloma Neroni Slade
Ambassador E. and P.
Consular Offices:
California, Los Angeles
Hawaii, Honolulu

YEMEN
Embassy of the Republic of Yemen
2600 Virginia Avenue NW, Suite 705, 20037
phone 965–4760, fax 337–2017
Consular Offices:
California, San Francisco
Michigan, Detroit

YUGOSLAVIA

Embassy of the Former Socialist Federal Republic of Yugoslavia

2410 California Street NW 20008

phone 462–6566

Mr. Nebojsa Vujovic

Counselor, Chargé d'Affaires ad interim

ZAMBIA

Embassy of the Republic of Zambia

2419 Massachusetts Avenue NW 20008

phone 265–9717, fax 332–0826

His Excellency Dunstan Weston Kamana

Ambassador E. and P.

ZIMBABWE

Embassy of the Republic of Zimbabwe

1608 New Hampshire Avenue NW 20009

phone 332–7100, fax 483–9326

His Excellency Amos Bernard Muvengwa Midzi

Ambassador E. and P.

EUROPEAN UNION

Delegation of the European Commission

2300 M Street NW 20037

phone 862–9500, fax 429–1766

His Excellency Hugo Paemen

Ambassador (Head of Delegation)

E. and P.: Extraordinary and Plenipotenitary.

PRESS GALLERIES

SENATE PRESS GALLERY

The Capitol, Room S–316, phone 224–0241

Superintendent.—Robert E. Petersen, Jr.
Deputy Superintendent.—S. Joseph Keenan
Assistant Superintendents:
Merri I. Baker
James D. Saris
Wendy A. Oscarson
Laura E. Lytle

HOUSE PRESS GALLERY

The Capitol, Room H–315, phone 225–3945, 225–6722

Superintendent.—Jerry L. Gallegos
Assistant Superintendents:
Suzanne Seurattan
Frank Lesesne
Charles S. Fuqua
Diana M. Miller

STANDING COMMITTEE OF CORRESPONDENTS

Greg Hitt, Wall Street Journal, *Chairman*
Carroll J. Doherty, Congressional Quarterly, *Secretary*
David Baumann, CongressDaily
Jim Meyers, Tulsa World
Nancy E. Roman, The Washington Times

RULES GOVERNING PRESS GALLERIES

1. Administration of the press galleries shall be vested in a Standing Committee of Correspondents elected by accredited members of the galleries. The Committee shall consist of five persons elected to serve for terms of two years. Provided, however, that at the election in January 1951, the three candidates receiving the highest number of votes shall serve for two years and the remaining two for one year. Thereafter, three members shall be elected in odd-numbered years and two in even-numbered years. Elections shall be held in January. The Committee shall elect its own chairman and secretary. Vacancies on the Committee shall be filled by special election to be called by the Standing Committee.

2. Persons desiring admission to the press galleries of Congress shall make application in accordance with Rule 34 of the House of Representatives, subject to the direction and control of the Speaker and Rule 33 of the Senate, which rules shall be interpreted and administered by the Standing Committee of Correspondents, subject to the review and an approval by the Senate Committee on Rules and Administration.

3. The Standing Committee of Correspondents shall limit membership in the press galleries to bona fide correspondents of repute in their profession, under such rules as the Standing Committee of Correspondents shall prescribe.

4. Provided, however, that the Standing Committee of Correspondents shall admit to the galleries no person who does not establish to the satisfaction of the Standing Committee all of the following:

(a) That his or her principal income is obtained from news correspondence intended for publication in newspapers entitled to second-class mailing privileges.

(b) That he or she is not engaged in paid publicity or promotion work or in prosecuting any claim before Congress or before any department of the government, and will not become so engaged while a member of the galleries.

(c) That he or she is not engaged in any lobbying activity and will not become so engaged while a member of the galleries.

5. Members of the families of correspondents are not entitled to the privileges of the galleries.

6. The Standing Committee of Correspondents shall propose no change or changes in these rules except upon petition in writing signed by not less than 100 accredited members of the galleries.

NEWT GINGRICH,
Speaker of the House of Representatives.

The above rules have been approved by the Committee on Rules and Administration.

JOHN WARNER,
Chairman, Senate Committee on Rules and Administration.

MEMBERS ENTITLED TO ADMISSION

PRESS GALLERIES

Abbott, Charles J.: Reuters
Abrahms, Doug: Washington Times
Abramowitz, Michael: Washington Post
Abrams, James R.: Associated Press
Abramson, David: Oil Daily
Abramson, Jill: Wall Street Journal
Abruzzese, Leo F.: Journal of Commerce
Abse, Nathan: Washington Post
Abu-Nasr, Donna: Associated Press
Achenbach, Joel: Washington Post
Acworth, William: Bridge News
Agres, Theodore J.: Washington Times
Ahearn, David M.: Bloomberg Business News
Akaza, Koichi: Yomiuri Shimbun
Akers, Mary Ann: Washington Times
Akinci, Ugur: Turkish Daily
Al-Sowayel, Naila: Saudi Press Agency
Alderman, Elizabeth J.: Bridge News
Aldinger, Charles: Reuters
Alexander, Andrew: Cox Newspapers
Alexander, Annie: Bridge News
Alfroy, Philippe: Agence France-Presse
Allen, Henry: Washington Post
Allen, Victoria L.: Reuters
Alonso-Zaldivar, Ricardo: Knight-Ridder Newspapers
Alpert, Bruce S.: New Orleans Times-Picayune/Newhouse
Alzaid, Faisal: Kuwait News Agency
Amoako, Ama: Asahi Shimbun
Anason, Dean C.: American Banker
Andenaes, Ulf: Aftenposten
Anderson, Curt L.: Associated Press
Anderson, David E.: Newhouse News Service
Anderson, James P.: German Press Agency - DPA
Anderson, Lucia: Fredericksburg Free Lance-Star
Anderson, Mark: Dow Jones News Services
Anderson, Paul L.: Congressional Quarterly
Anderson, Roger: Scripps Howard News Service
Angle, Martha: Congressional Monitor
Anklam, Jr., Fred: USA Today
Anthan, George P.: Des Moines Register
Anzai, Toshiaki: Kyodo News Service
Apple, R.W., Jr.: New York Times
Archer, Kim: Dow Jones News Services
Archibald, George H.: Washington Times
Arnett, Elisa C.: Knight-Ridder Newspapers
Arnold, Christopher: Jiji Press
Arnold, Dieter E.: Der Bund
Arnold, Holzapfel J.: National Media of South Africa
Arnold, John J.: Associated Press
Arora, C.K.: United News of India
Arshad, Golam: Bangladesh Daily Telegraph
Arthur, William: Bloomberg Business News
Asher, Juiie L.: Catholic News Service
Asher, Robert L.: Washington Post
Aslam, Abid H.: Inter Press Service
Aslan, Ali: Zaman
Asseo, Laurie: Associated Press
Atlas, Terry: Chicago Tribune
Auerbach, Stuart C.: Washington Post
Aukofer, Frank A.: Milwaukee Journal Sentinel
Aulston, Von: New York Times
Austin, Judith B.: Gannett News Service
Averse, Jeannine: Associated Press
Azpiazu, Maria L.: EFE News Service
Babcock, Charles R.: Washington Post
Babington, Charles: Washington Post
Baer, Susan: Baltimore Sun
Bailey, Marilyn: Ottaway News Service
Baker, Donald P.: Washington Post
Baker, Gerard: London Financial Times
Baker, Peter: Washington Post
Baldor, Lolita: Connecticut Post/Thomson Newspapers
Ball, Karen: New York Daily News
Balman, Sid, Jr.: United Press International
Baltimore, Chris: Oil Daily
Balz, Daniel J.: Washington Post
Banales, Jorge A.: United Press International
Banks, Adelle: Newhouse News Service
Barazia, Virginia G.: Thomson Newspapers
Barber, Ben: Washington Times
Barber, Simon: South Africa Times Media
Barker, Jeffrey N.: Arizona Republic
Barnett, James O.: Oregonian
Barr, Gary S.: Washington Post
Barrett, Joyce: Fairchild News Service
Barton, Paul C.: Gannett News Service
Bartz, Diane K.: Agence France-Presse
Basauri, Ignacio: Notimex Mexican News Agency
Bashir, Mustafa A.: Saudi Press Agency
Basken, Paul: United Press International
Bassett, Greg: Thomson Newspapers
Bate, Peter: Reuters
Bater, Jeffrey P.: United Press International
Batog, Jennifer A.: Associated Press
Batt, Tony: Donrey Media Group
Battaile, Janet: New York Times
Bauman, Everett A.: El Universal
Baumann, David: CongressDaily

MEMBERS ENTITLED TO ADMISSION, PRESS GALLERIES—Continued

Bayer, Amy: Copley News Service
Bazinet, Kenneth: United Press International
Beck, Simon L.: South China Morning Post
Beck, Tobin C.: United Press International
Beckett, Paul M.: Dow Jones News Services
Beckner, Steven K.: Market News Service
Bedard, Paul: Washington Times
Beeder, David C.: Omaha World-Herald
Behr, Peter: Washington Post
Belton, Beth M.: USA Today
Beltrame, Julian: Southam News
Benac, Nancy J.: Associated Press
Bender, Bryan D.: Defense Daily
Bender, Penny: Gannett News Service
Benedetto, Richard: USA Today
Benenson, Robert A.: Congressional Quarterly
Benjamin, Matthew K.: Wall Street Journal
Benkelman, Susan: Newsday
Bennet, James: New York Times
Benson, Miles R.: Newhouse News Service
Berke, Richard L.: New York Times
Berry, John, M.: Washington Post
Bettelheim, Adriel: Denver Post
Beyer, Frauke: Springer Foreign News Service
Bian, Chenguang: Science and Technology Daily
Biers, John M.: States News Service
Bilski, Christina: Nikkei
Binder, David: New York Times
Birtel, Marc R.: Congressional Monitor
Biskupic, Joan: Washington Post
Bivins, Larry: Detroit News
Black, Christine M.: Boston Globe
Blaho, Miklos: Magyar Nemzet
Bland, Melissa R.: Reuters
Blecher, Todd: Bloomberg Business News
Blomquist, Brian: New York Post
Blonston, Gary L.: Knight-Ridder Newspapers
Blumenfeld, Laura: Washington Post
Blumenthal, Les: McClatchy Newspapers
Blustein, Paul: Washington Post
Bodipo-Memba, Alejandro: Wall Street Journal
Bohan, Caren: Reuters
Boian, Christopher: Agence France-Presse
Bonabesse, Gaedig: Washington Times
Borchersen-Keto, Sarah: AFX News Service
Borisenko, Igor: Itar-Tass News Agency
Borkowski, Monica C.: New York Times
Bornemeier, James: Los Angeles Times
Bornemeier, Jane B.: New York Times
Boswell, Elizabeth A.: New York Times
Boustany, Nora: Washington Post
Bovard, James: Bovard News Service
Bovee, Timothy K.: Associated Press
Bowers, Paige: Washington Times
Bowman, Curtis Lee: Scripps Howard News Service
Bowman, Rex L.: Washington Times
Boyd, Robert J.: Knight-Ridder Newspapers
Boyer, Dave: Education Daily
Bradford, Allen: Washington Times
Branigin, William: Washington Post
Branson, Amy K.: Legi-Slate News Service
Brasher, Philip: Associated Press
Brazaitis, Thomas J.: Cleveland Plain Dealer
Breaux, Kia: Bridge News
Breem, Thomas: Defense Daily
Brennan, Jeanne K.: New York Times
Brewer, Norm: Gannett News Service
Briand, Xavier: Agence France-Presse
Brinkley, John: Scripps Howard News Service
Briscoe, David: Associated Press
Briscoe, Leonor A.: Minneapolis Star Tribune
Bristol, Nellie O.: Health News Daily
Broder, David S.: Washington Post
Brodie, Ian: London Times
Brodsky, Arthur R.: Communications Daily
Brodzinsky, Sybilla: Agence France-Presse
Brogan, Pamela A.: Gannett News Service
Brogan, Patrick: Glasgow Herald
Brooks, David: La Jornada
Brooks, Jennifer A.: States News Service
Brosnan, James W.: Scripps Howard News Service
Brown, David M.: Washington Post
Brown, Michael H.: Louisville Courier-Journal
Brown, Rene E.: Hartford Courant
Brownstein, Ronald: Los Angeles Times
Brueggemann, Gerd: Die Welt
Brumas, R. Michael: Newhouse News Service
Bruneau, Leon: Agence France-Presse
Bryant, Carleton R.: Washington Times
Bryant, Elizabeth: States News Service
Bunis, Dena: Orange County Register
Bunting, Glenn F.: Los Angeles Times
Burkins, Glenn: Wall Street Journal
Burns, Judith: Dow Jones News Services
Burns, Robert: Associated Press
Burns, Susan: Cox Newspapers
Burrell, Cassandra R.: Associated Press
Byrd, Kenny: Baptist News Service
Cabrera, Denise: Associated Press
Cahir, William J.: Education Daily
Caires, Greg A.: Defense Daily
Calis, Raphael: United Press International
Calmes, Jackie: Wall Street Journal
Calvo-Platero, Mario: Il Sole 24 Ore
Camia, Catalina: Dallas Morning News
Camire, Dennis: Gannett News Service
Campbell, Stephen W.: Portland Press Herald
Canahuate, Alfred T.: Saudi Press Agency
Canas, Rafael: EFE News Service
Cannistraro, Marc, D.: Congressional Information Bureau
Cannon, Carl M.: Baltimore Sun
Cannon, Mary Angela: Knight-Ridder Newspapers
Carelli, Richard: Associated Press
Caretto, Ennio: Corriere Della Sera

MEMBERS ENTITLED TO ADMISSION, PRESS GALLERIES—Continued

Carey, Mary Agnes: Congressional Quarterly
Carlin, John: London Independent
Carlson, Peter: Washington Post
Carmody, John: Washington Post
Carnevale, Mary L.: Wall Street Journal
Carney, Dan: Congressional Quarterly
Carr, Rebecca: Congressional Quarterly
Carreno, Jose: El Universal
Carroll, James R.: Knight-Ridder Newspapers
Carroll, Joe: Irish Times
Carroll, Kathleen: Knight-Ridder Newspapers
Carter, Janelle: Associated Press
Carter, Thomas H.: Washington Times
Carvalho, Orlando Lyra De: ABIM News Agency
Casey, Constance: Newhouse News Service
Cason, James: La Jornada
Cassata, Donna: Congressional Quarterly
Casteel, Chris: Daily Oklahoman
Causey, Mike: Washington Post
Cavelier, Andres: El Tiempo
Cazalas, Robert: Congressional Information Bureau
Chaffee, Kevin: Washington Times
Chambliss, E. Lauren: London Evening Standard
Chandler, Clay: Washington Post
Chandran, Ramesh: Times of India
Chandrasekaran, Rajiv: Washington Post
Chatterjee, Sumana: States News Service
Chavez Lopez, Horacio C.: Notimex Mexican News Agency
Chen, Edwin: Los Angeles Times
Chen, Huang: Central News Agency
Chenglin, Xiao: Xinhua News Agency
Chesser, Larry: Baptist News Service
Chiantaretto, Mariuccia: Il Mattino
Choi, Julia, M.: U.S.-Asian News Service
Christaldi, Mario: Thomson Newspapers
Christensen, Jean: Associated Press
Christensen, Mike: Congressional Quarterly
Christie, Ricky A.: Cox Newspapers
Chung, Sarah, S.: New York Times
Cimons, Marlene: Los Angeles Times
Cindemir, Mehuet K.: Anatolia News Agency
Clark, Bruce: London Financial Times
Clark, Drew: American Banker
Clark, L. Kareema: Bridge News
Clark, Steve: Los Angeles Times
Clavel, Guy: Agence France-Presse
Clayton, William E., Jr.: Houston Chronicle
Cleis, Andreas: Neue Zurcher Zeitung
Clifford, George: Washington Merry-Go-Round
Clifford, Timothy: New York Daily News
Clines, Francis X.: New York Times
Cloud, David: Chicago Tribune
Clymer, Adam: New York Times
Cocco, Marie: Newsday
Cohen, Karen J.: Reuters
Cohen, Patricia: Washington Post
Cohen, Richard: Washington Post
Cohen, Robert: Newhouse News Service
Cohen, Ronald E.: Gannett News Service
Cohn, Laura: Bloomberg Business News
Coker, Margaret E.: United Press International
Colaianni, Deborah M.: Gannett News Service
Collins, Christina W.: Gannett News Service
Collymore, Yvette J.: Inter Press Service
Condon, George E., Jr.: Copley News Service
Conlon, Charles E.: Congressional Quarterly
Connell, Christopher V.: Associated Press
Connolly, Ceci: St. Petersburg Times
Connor, John: Dow Jones News Services
Connors, Thomas J.: Journal of Commerce
Constantine, Gus: Washington Times
Cook, Gretchen: Agence France-Presse
Cook, Rhodes: Congressional Quarterly
Cook, Steven D.: CongressDaily
Coombs, Francis B., Jr.: Washington Times
Cooper, Helene: Wall Street Journal
Cooper, Richard: Los Angeles Times
Copeland, Peter M.: Scripps Howard News Service
Corbett, Jennifer: Dow Jones News Services
Corcoran, Elizabeth: Washington Post
Corcoran, Leila M.: Reuters
Cordray, Ronald: Market News Service
Cornwell, Susan J.: Reuters
Corrigan, Jo Ellen: Cleveland Plain Dealer
Cossette, Lani C.: Yomiuri Shimbun
Costich, Louise R.: Taipei Commercial Times
Cowan, Richard: Bridge News
Cranford, John R.: Bloomberg Business News
Crenshaw, Albert R.: Washington Post
Cromley, Allan W.: Daily Oklahoman
Crutsinger, Martin S.: Associated Press
Cummings, Jeanne M.: Atlanta Journal and Constitution
Curl, Joseph: Washington Times
Curley, Thomas: USA Today
Curta, Francis: Agence France-Presse
Cushman, John H., Jr.: New York Times
Cuthbert, Lori L.: Bridge News
Dahl, David: St. Petersburg Times
Dalgleish, James: Reuters
Dalglish, Arthur R.: Cox Newspapers
Dart, Robert E.: Cox Newspapers
Davidson, Joe: Wall Street Journal
Davidson, Lee: Deseret News
Davies, Hugh: London Daily Telegraph
Davis, Brett: Newhouse News Service
Davis, Robert: Wall Street Journal
Davis, Robert M.: USA Today
Day, John S.: Bangor Daily News
Day, Kathleen: Washington Post
De Carlo, Cesare: La Nazione
De Toledano, Ralph: Creators Syndicate
DeFrank, Thomas M.: New York Daily News
DeParle, Jason: New York Times
DeWitt, Karen E.: New York Times

MEMBERS ENTITLED TO ADMISSION, PRESS GALLERIES—Continued

Dean, Mensah: Washington Times
Deans, Robert E., Jr.: Cox Newspapers
Debenport, Ellen: St. Petersburg Times
Decker, Brett M.: Chicago Sun-Times
Deibel, Mary: Scripps Howard News Service
Del Giudice, Vincent A.: Bloomberg Business News
della Porta, Agostino: German Press Agency-DPA
Del Riccio, Cristiano: ANSA Italian News Agency
Dembicki, Matt: Education Daily
Denniston, Lyle W.: Baltimore Sun
Denver, Cristine: Bridge News
Depledge, Derrick K.: Knight-Ridder Newspapers
Devroy, Ann: Washington Post
Dewar, Heather J.: Knight-Ridder Newspapers
Dewar, Helen: Washington Post
Diamond, John M.: Associated Press
Diemer, Thomas K.: Cleveland Plain Dealer
Dillingham, Susan: Congressional Monitor
Dine, Philip M.: St. Louis Post-Dispatch
di Robilant, Andrea: La Stampa
Dobbin, Muriel: McClatchy Newspapers
Dobbs, Michael S.: Washington Post
Dobbyn, Timothy H.: Reuters
Dodd, Michael P.: USA Today
Dodge, Robert: Dallas Morning News
Doggett, Jr.: Thomas, W.: Dow Jones News Services
Doherty, Carroll: Congressional Quarterly
Dorf, Matthew: Jewish Telegraph Agency
Dorning, Mike: Chicago Tribune
Dorsey, Christine M.: Donrey Media Group
Douglas, William G.: Newsday
Dowd, Maureen: New York Times
Doyle, Michael: McClatchy Newspapers
Drath, Viola H.: Handelsblatt
Drinkard, James P.: Associated Press
Drummond, Bob: Bloomberg Business News
Dryden, Steven J.: Bloomberg Business News
Duff, Christina: Wall Street Journal
Duff, Susanna: States News Service
Duffus, Joseph R.: Thomson Newspapers
Dugas, Martin: Slovak News Agency
Duhanov, Serge P.: Moscow Business World
Duin, Julia: Washington Times
Duncan, Philip D.: Congressional Quarterly
Dunham, Will: Reuters
Dunne, Nancy: London Financial Times
Dunphy, Harry: Associated Press
Dusseau, Brigitte: Agence France-Presse
Dyson, Jessica J.: Bridge News
Eastham, Todd R.: Bloomberg Business News
Easton, Nina J.: Los Angeles Times
Eaton, Sabrina: Cleveland Plain Dealer
Edsall, Thomas B.: Washington Post
Egger, W. Gerald: Bloomberg Business News
Eijsvoogel, Juurd: NRC Handelsblad
Eisler, Peter: USA Today
Eisman, Dale: Virginian-Pilot
El Nasser, Haya: USA Today
El-Ghamry, Atef: Al Ahram International
ElBoghdady, Dina: Orange County Register
Elias, Jorge: La Nacion
Elliott, Polly B.: Ottaway News Service
Elsner, Alan: Reuters
Elving, Ronald: Congressional Quarterly
Emory, Alan S.: Watertown Daily Times
Enda, Jodi A.: Philadelphia Inquirer
Engley, Hollis L.: Gannett News Service
Epstein, Aaron B.: Knight-Ridder Newspapers
Epstein, Keith C.: Cleveland Plain Dealer
Elsasser, Glen R.: Chicago Tribune
Erlanger, Steven: New York Times
Espo, David M.: Associated Press
Esquivel, Jesus P.: Notimex Mexican News Agency
Estevez, Dolia: El Financiero
Estill, Jerry R.: Associated Press
Estill, Robert: Copley News Service
Eurich, Heather J.: Bond Buyer
Evans, Edward: Reuters
Evans, Judith: Washington Post
Evans-Pritchard, Ambrose: London Sunday Telegraph
Fabiani, Christiana: Agence France-Presse
Fagan, Drew: Toronto Globe and Mail
Faiola, Anthony: Washington Post
Faltin, Cornel: Springer Foreign News Service
Fan, Songjiu: Xinhua News Agency
Farhi, Paul: Washington Post
Farragher, Thomas P.: Knight-Ridder Newspapers
Farrell, John A.: Boston Globe
Feeney, Susan: Dallas Morning News
Fehr, Stephen: Washington Post
Feinsilber, Mike: Associated Press
Feldman, Carole: Associated Press
Felker, Edward R.: Small Newspaper Group
Felsenthal, Edward H.: Wall Street Journal
Ferguson, Barbara: Saudi Gazette
Ferguson, Ellyn: Gannett News Service
Ferraro, Thomas M.: Bloomberg Business News
Ferrechio, Susan: Washington Times
Ferris, Craig T.: Bond Buyer
Ferry, Barbara: States News Service
Fialka, John J.: Wall Street Journal
Fields, Gary E.: USA Today
Fields-White Monee: Bloomberg Business News
Fillion, Roger O.: Reuters
Filteau, Jerome F.: Catholic News Service
Fiore, Faye: Los Angeles Times
Fireman, Kenneth: Newsday
Fisher, Marc: Washington Post
Fitzgerald, D'Jamila S.: Los Angeles Times
Fix, Janet, L.: Detroit Free Press
Flanders, Gwen: USA Today
Flanigan, James C.: Kuwait News Agency
Flatin, Paul E.: Kyodo News Service
Flattau, Edward: Global Horizons Syndicate

MEMBERS ENTITLED TO ADMISSION, PRESS GALLERIES—Continued

Fletcher, Martin A.: London Times
Fletcher, Michael: Washington Post
Flynn, Adrianne M.: Arizona Republic
Foerstel, Karen: New York Post
Foote, Sheila: Defense Daily
Forrest, Bonnie L.: Congressional Quarterly
Foskett, Ken: Atlanta Journal and Constitution
Foster, Andrea L.: Congressional Monitor
Foster-Simeon, Ed: USA Today
Fourcade, Marthe: Bloomberg Business News
Fournier, Ronald: Associated Press
Fox, Adrienne: Investor's Business Daily
Fraley, Colette: Congressional Quarterly
Fram, Alan: Associated Press
Frandsen, Jon: Gannett News Service
Frank, Jacqueline: Reuters
Franklin, Mary Beth: Franklin News Features
Fraser, Graham: Toronto Globe and Mail
Fraze, Barbara J.: Catholic News Service
Frederick, Don: Los Angeles Times
Frederick, Robb: Ottaway News Service
Freedberg, Louis: San Francisco Chronicle
Freedman, Allan: Congressional Quarterly
Freedman, Dan: Hearst Newspapers
Freudmann, Aviva: Journal of Commerce
Freyman, Russell A.: Congressional Monitor
Friedman, Robert: Scripps Howard News Service
Friesner, Margery: ANSA Italian News Agency
Frisby, Michael K.: Wall Street Journal
Fritsch, Jane F.: New York Times
Fritz, Sara: Los Angeles Times
Fromson, Brett D.: Washington Post
Fu, Norman: China Times
Fujii, Yasushi: Kyodo News Service
Fujimoto, Naomichi: Yomiuri Shimbun
Fullerton, Jane: Arkansas Democrat-Gazette
Fulwood III, Sam: Los Angeles Times
Funabashi, Yoichi: Asahi Shimbun
Furlow, Robert S.: Associated Press
Gaal, Damien J.: Gas Daily
Gaffney, Lisa L.: Congressional Monitor
Galvin, Kevin: Associated Press
Galvin, Thomas: New York Post
Gamerman, Ellen: Baltimore Sun
Gao, Fengyi: Guangming Daily
Garcia, Richard: Reuters
Garland, William K.: Harte-Hanks Newspapers
Garschagen, Oscar G.: De Volkskrant
Gavin, Jennifer: Denver Post
Gavin, Robert: Newhouse News Service
Gay, Lance C.: Scripps Howard News Service
Gazella, Katherine: St. Petersburg Times
Gedda, George: Associated Press
Gee, Robert W.: Baltimore Sun
Geiger, Robert S.: Knight-Ridder Newspapers
Georges, Chris J.: Wall Street Journal
Geracimos, Ann: Washington Times
Gerdts, Jennifer A.: Tokyo-Chunichi Shimbun
Gerhart, Ann E.: Washington Post
Germond, Jack W.: Baltimore Sun
Gerstenzang, James R.: Los Angeles Times
Gerth, Jeff: New York Times
Gertz, William D.: Washington Times
Gettinger, Steve: Congressional Quarterly
Ghildiyal, Vinod: New Delhi Business & Observer
Giacomo, Carol A.: Reuters
Gibbons, Gene: Reuters
Gigot, Paul: Wall Street Journal
Gimein, Mark: States News Service
Ginsburg, Steven H.: Reuters
Giroux, Gregory L.: Congressional Quarterly
Givhan, Robin: Washington Post
Glachant, Pierre: Agence France-Presse
Glass, Andrew J.: Cox Newspapers
Glass, Joel A.: Lloyd's London Press
Glass, Pamela: Le Mauricien
Glasser, Jeffrey D.: Washington Post
Glover, Keith D.: Congressional Monitor
Goldberg, Benjamin: Asahi Shimbun
Golden, James R.: Gannett News Service
Goldschlag, William: New York Daily News
Goldstein, Amy: Washington Post
Goldstein, David: Kansas City Star
Goldstein, Jacobo: La Tribuna
Goldstein, Joshua F.: Knight-Ridder Newspapers
Goldstein, Steven L.: Philadelphia Inquirer
Golkin, Peter: Reuters
Gonzalez, Maria I.: El Norte & Reforma
Gonzalez, V. Casey: Education Daily
Goodrich, Lawrence J.: Christian Science Monitor
Gordon, Gregory: Minneapolis Star Tribune
Gordon, Marcy G.: Associated Press
Goshko, John M.: Washington Post
Gould, Lee A.: Associated Press
Grady, Ernest S.: Philadelphia Daily News
Graham, Bradley L.: Washington Post
Graham, Brian T.: Bridge News
Graham, Jill: CongressDaily
Granader, Robert: States News Service
Grant, Bill L.: Legi-Slate News Service
Gravely, Robert M.: Congressional Monitor
Gray, Jerry: New York Times
Gray, Kevin M.: New York Times
Green, Charles A.: Knight-Ridder Newspapers
Green, Mark D.: Daily Oklahoman
Green, Stephen J.: Copley News Service
Greenberger, Robert: Wall Street Journal
Greenblatt, Alan: Congressional Quarterly
Greenburg, Jan C.: Chicago Tribune
Greene, Robert T.: Associated Press
Greenfield, Meg: Washington Post
Greenhouse, Linda J.: New York Times
Greve, Frank J.: Knight-Ridder Newspapers
Grier, Peter: Christian Science Monitor

MEMBERS ENTITLED TO ADMISSION, PRESS GALLERIES—Continued

Griffith, Patricia K.: Pittsburgh Post-Gazette/Toledo Blade
Grimaldi, James V.: Seattle Times
Groer, Anne: Washington Post
Grove, Lloyd B.: Washington Post
Gruenwald, Juliana: Congressional Quarterly
Gruley, Bryan: Wall Street Journal
Gugliotta, Guy: Washington Post
Gulino, Denny: Market News Service
Gullo, Karen: Associated Press
Gurdon, Hugo: London Daily Telegraph
Gutfeld, Rose: Congressional Quarterly
Gutman, Roy W.: Newsday
Gvozdas, Susan: USA Today
Haase, David L.: Indianapolis Star-News
Hackett, Laurel E.: Scripps Howard News Service
Hadar, Leon, T.: Singapore Business Times
Hagenbaugh, Barbara: Reuters
Hager, George: Congressional Quarterly
Haggerty, Maryann: Washington Post
Hall, Carol B.: Minneapolis Star Tribune
Hall, John N.: Media General News Service
Hall, Margaret W.: USA Today
Hallinan, Joseph T.: Newhouse News Service
Hallow, Ralph Z.: Washington Times
Hamalainen, Aloysia C.: St. Louis Post-Dispatch
Hamburger, Tom: Minneapolis Star Tribune
Hamilton, Martha A.: Washington Post
Han, Edward N.: Central News Agency
Hanchette, John M.: Gannett News Service
Hand, Mark: Gas Daily
Hanner, Kenneth W.: Washington Times
Hansard, Sara: Bridge News
Hansen, Barbara E.: USA Today
Hanson, Christopher: Hearst Newspapers
Hara, Toshiro: Mainichi Shimbun
Harada, Ryosuke: Nikkei
Harari, Nathaniel: Scripps Howard News Service
Harden, Blaine: Washington Post
Harden, Patrick: Toronto Sun
Hardin, Peter: Richmond Times-Dispatch
Hardy, Michael J.: Newhouse News Service
Hargrove, Thomas K.: Scripps Howard News Service
Harlan, Christi: Austin American-Statesman
Harmon, Bruce: Bridge News
Harper, Jennifer: Washington Times
Harris, John F.: Washington Post
Harris, Katherine E.: Legi-Slate News Service
Harrison, David: Education Daily
Harrison, Katie: Hearst Newspapers
Harrison, Nathaniel: Agence France-Presse
Hartman, Carl: Associated Press
Hartnagel, Nancy J.: Catholic News Service
Hartson, Merrill: Associated Press
Harwood, John J.: Wall Street Journal
Hashim, Salmy M.: Malaysian News Agency
Hasson, Judith B.: USA Today
Hastings, Maribel: La Opinion
Hatty, Michele: Congressional Monitor
Havemann, Joel: Los Angeles Times
Havemann, Judith: Washington Post
Hawkings, David: Congressional Monitor
Hawkins, Charles S.: Bloomberg Business News
Hazar, Hasan M.: Turkiye Daily
Healey, James R.: USA Today
Healy, Melissa: Los Angeles Times
Hebel, Sara: Legi-Slate News Service
Hebert, H. Josef: Associated Press
Hebner, Anna B.: Legi-Slate News Service
Hedges, Michael: Scripps Howard News Service
Heesup, Jun: Yonhap News Agency
Heikes, Drex: Los Angeles Times
Heinicke, Erik: Dow Jones News Services
Heldman, Paul: Bloomberg Business News
Henderson, Jacqueline, M.: USA Today
Hendrickson, Paul J.: Washington Post
Henley, David C.: Lahontan Valley News
Henriksson, Karin: Svenska Dagbladet
Hershey, William L.: Akron Beacon Journal
Hershey, Jr.: Robert D.: New York Times
Hess, David W.: Knight-Ridder Newspapers
Hewett, Jennifer A.: Sidney Morning Herald
Heyniger, Will: Congressional Monitor
Hiatt, Fred: Washington Post
Hicks, Desiree F.: Gannett News Service
Hieronymus, Bill: Bridge News
Hill, Patrice S.: Washington Times
Hillman, G. Robert: Dallas Morning News
Hilzenrath, David: Washington Post
Hines, Cragg: Houston Chronicle
Hinton, Earl: Associated Press
Hitt, Greg A.: Wall Street Journal
Hodges, Sam L.: Newhouse News Service
Hoeffel, John E.: Winston-Salem Journal
Hoffman, Lisa: Scripps Howard News Service
Hohler, Robert T.: Boston Globe
Holland, Judy: Hearst Newspapers
Holmes, Steven: New York Times
Hong, Euntaek: Dong-A Ilbo
Hook, Janet: Los Angeles Times
Hoopes, Cora R.: Roll Call Report Syndicate
Hope, Heather A.: Congressional Quarterly
Horner, Carol J.: Wall Street Journal
Horner, Ferne M.: New York Times
Horowitz, Carl F.: Investor's Business Daily
Horsey, David: Seattle Post-Intelligencer
Hosansky, David: Congressional Quarterly
Hoshi, Hiroshi: Asahi Shimbun
Hoskins, Richard: Reuters
Hosler, Karen A.: Baltimore Sun
House, Julia R.: San Francisco Chronicle
Householder, Michael A.: Associated Press
Hoversten, Paul, M.: USA Today
Howe, Patrick: Small Newspaper Group

MEMBERS ENTITLED TO ADMISSION, PRESS GALLERIES—Continued

Howell, Deborah: Newhouse News Service
Hubler, David, E.: United Press International
Hughes, John: Small Newspapers Group
Hulse, Carl: New York Times Regional Newspapers
Hume, Lynn, S.: Bond Buyer
Hunt, Albert, R.: Wall Street Journal
Hunt, Terence: Associated Press
Hutcheson, Ron, M.: Fort Worth Star-Telegram
Huygen, Maarten: NRC Handelsblad
Hyzy, Ursula: Agence France-Presse
Iiyama, Masashi: Yomiuri Shimbun
Ikemura, Toshiro: Yomiuri Shimbun
Ingersoll, Bruce: Wall Street Journal
Innerst, Carol: Washington Times
Ishiai, Tsutomu: Asahi Shimbun
Ito, Hiroaki: Asahi Shimbun
Ito, Yoshiaki: Mainichi Shimbun
Jackler, Rosalind: Boston Globe
Jackson, David A.: Chicago Tribune
Jackson, David M.: Dallas Morning News
Jackson, Robert L.: Los Angeles Times
Jackson, Sarah: Agence France-Presse
Jacoby, Mary: Chicago Tribune
James Frank E. III: Chicago Tribune
Janofsky, Michael: New York Times
Jaspin, Elliot: Cox Newspapers
Jensen, Kristin: Bloomberg Business News
Jesdanun, Anick: Associated Press
Jingsheng, Zhai: Xinhua News Agency
Johnson, Kevin: USA Today
Johnson, Mark: Media General News Service
Johnson, Sandy K.: Associated Press
Johnson-Settles Mary: McClatchy Newspapers
Johnston, Carl A.: Dow Jones News Services
Johnston, David: New York Times
Jones, David: Washington Times
Jones, Rachel: Knight-Ridder Newspapers
Jones, Wendy, P.: Ottaway News Service
Jordan, Gregory W.: New York Times
Joseph, Ludwina A.: New Delhi Views and News Agency
Jouzaitis, Carol: Chicago Tribune
Joyce, Stacey A.: Reuters
Judson, David: Gannett News Service
Judson, Mark: Mainichi Shimbun
Jukes, Stephen A.: Reuters
Jung, Yun, J.: Han-Kyoreh Shinmun
Kaffsack, Hanns-Jochen: German Press Agency - DPA
Kalabinski, Jacek M.: Gazeta Wyborcza
Kalb, Deborah: Gannett News Service
Kamen, Al: Washington Post
Kanamine, Linda M.: USA Today
Kane, Paul, J.: States News Service
Kang, Stephanie: Travel Management Daily
Kaplan, Lisa F.: Gannett News Service
Kaplan, Peter: Washington Times
Kaplan, Refet: Washington Times
Kaps, Carola: Frankfurter Allgemeine Zeitung
Karey, Gerald: Platt's Oilgram News
Karmin, Monroe W.: Bloomberg Business News
Karp, Aaron: Washington Merry-Go-Round
Karr, Albert R.: Wall Street Journal
Kashiyama, Yukio: Sankei Shimbun
Kasindorf, Martin: Newsday
Kato, Kiyotaka: Jiji Press
Katz, Evan: States News Service
Katz, Jeffrey L.: Congressional Quarterly
Katz, Lee, M.: USA Today
Kaul, Donald W.: Des Moines Register
Kayal, Michele: Journal of Commerce
Kaye, Melissa W.: Congressional Quarterly
Kean, Edward: Bridge News
Keates, Nancy: Dow Jones News Services
Keatley, Robert: Wall Street Journal
Keefe, Stephen R.: Nikkei
Keen, Judith C.: USA Today
Keeton, Jeffrey E.: Scripps Howard News Service
Keil, Richard: Associated Press
Kelley, Jack: USA Today
Kelley, Joanne: Reuters
Kellman, Laurie A.: Washington Times
Kellogg, Sarah M.: Newhouse News Service
Kelly, Brian: Washington Post
Kelly, Erin V.: Gannett News Service
Kelly, Patrick: Bridge News
Kemper, Robert J.: Newport News Daily Press
Kempster, Norman: Los Angeles Times
Kenen, Joanne: Reuters
Kenna, Kathleen: Toronto Star
Kennedy, Barbara F.: Saudi Gazette
Kennedy, Tim: Saudi Gazette
Kessler, Glenn: Newsday
Keto, Laurin A.: Dow Jones News Services
Kiely, Kathy: Arkansas Democrat-Gazette
Kikilo, Vladimir I.: Itar-Tass News Agency
Kil, Jeong-Woo: Joong-Ang Ilbo
Kilian, Michael D.: Chicago Tribune
Kim, Dae-Ho: Maeil Kyungji Daily
Kim, Eun, K.: Associated Press
Kim, Jae-Young: Seoul Shinmun Daily
Kim, James: USA Today
Kim, Jong, H.: Pusan Daily News
King, Colbert: Washington Post
King, John, C.: Associated Press
King, Llewellyn: Energy Daily
King, Peter, H.: Congressional Monitor
Kipling, Bogdan: Kipling News Service
Kirchhoff, Suzanne: Reuters
Kishimoto, Masato: Mainichi Shimbun
Kister, Kurt: Sueddeutsche Zeitung
Kitajima, Shigeji: Asahi Shimbun
Kivlan, Terence J.: Newhouse News Service
Klein, Gilbert F.: Media General News Service
Kliewer, Nancy: Cox Newspapers

MEMBERS ENTITLED TO ADMISSION, PRESS GALLERIES—Continued

Kline, Alan: Washington Times
Klosky, Deborah L.: Dow Jones News Services
Knight, Jerry: Washington Post
Knowlton, Brian B.: International Herald Tribune
Knox, Noelle: Detroit News
Knox, Oliver: Agence France-Presse
Knupfer, Uwe: Westdeutsche Allgemeine
Knutson, Lawrence L.: Associated Press
Koar, Jurgen: Stuttgarter Zeitung
Kocerha, Vladimir: Gestion
Koch, Wendy: Hearst Newspapers
Koike, Hirotsugu: Nikkei
Komarow, Steven: USA Today
Komori, Yoshihisa: Sankei Shimbun
Kong, Huney: Kwangju Ilbo Daily News
Kopecki, Dawn: Washington Times
Korinek, Otakar: Slovak News Agency
Kornelius, Stefan: Sueddeutsche Zeitung
Koszczuk, Jaculine M.: Congressional Quarterly
Kovaleski, Serge F.: Washington Post
Kovski, Alan: Oil Daily
Kozluklu, Fuat: Cumhuriyet Daily
Kramer, Eugene: Associated Press
Kranish, Michael A.: Boston Globe
Kreisher, Otto: Copley News Service
Krishnaswami, Sridhar: The Hindu
Kristiansen, Catherine: Bridge News
Kronholz, June: Wall Street Journal
Kuchiki, Naotumi: Chunichi-Tokyo Shimbun
Kuczynski-Delaney, Sherry K.: Investor's Business Daily
Kuhnhenn, James, L.: Kansas City Star
Kuhon, Albert, P.: Suara Pembaruan
Kunimatsu, Toru: Yomiuri Shimbun
Kuntz, Philip A.: Wall Street Journal
Kurata, Miyuki: Tokyo-Chunichi Shimbun
Kurtzman, Daniel: Jewish Telegraphic Agency
Kuttler, Hillel: Jerusalem Post
LaFraniere, Sharon: Washington Post
LaGesse, David: Dallas Morning News
Labaton, Stephen: New York Times
Labriny, Azeddine: Saudi Press Agency
Lacey, Marc: Los Angeles Times
Lachica, Eduardo: Asian Wall Street Journal
Lamb, David: Los Angeles Times
Lambrecht, William: St. Louis Post-Dispatch
Lambro, Donald: Washington Times
Lan, Dah-Wey: Commons Daily
Landay, Jonathan S.: Christian Science Monitor
Lande, Laurie: Dow Jones News Services
Landers, James M.: Dallas Morning News
Landry, Carole: Agence France-Presse
Lane, Earl: Newsday
Lang, John S.: Scripps Howard News Service
Langan, Michael: Agence France-Presse
Langfitt, Frank D.: Baltimore Sun
Langley, Norma: News Group Publications
Lardner, George: Washington Post
Larsen, Leonard E.: Scripps Howard News Service
Larson, Ruth, I.: Washington Times
Lau, Debra: Yomiuri Shimbun
Lauria, Angela E.: Newspaper Enterprise Association
Lawrence, Christine, C.: Congressional Quarterly
Lawrence, Jill D.: USA Today
Lawrence, Richard: Journal of Commerce
Lawsky, David A.: Reuters
Lawton, Kim A.: Newhouse News Service
Lazarovici, Laureen: Education Daily
Leary, Warren E.: New York Times
Leavitt, Paul W.: USA Today
Lebedev, Ivan: Itar-Tass News Agency
Lee, Jae-Ho: Dong-A Ilbo
Lee, Jessica: USA Today
Lee, Siew Hua: Straits Times
Leffler, Pete: Allentown Morning Call
Lehman, Mary A.: CongressDaily
Leiby, Richard: Washington Post
Lemons, Terry: Arkansas Democrat-Gazette
Leonard, Mary C.: Boston Globe
Leonning, Carol D.: Charlotte Observer
Lesourd, Pierre: Agence France-Presse
Leubsdorf, Carl P.: Dallas Morning News
Lever, Robert: Agence France-Presse
Levy, Douglas A.: USA Today
Lewis, Charles J.: Hearst Newspapers
Lewis, Finlay: Copley News Service
Lewis, Katherine: Dallas Morning News
Lewis, Michael: New York Times
Lewis, Neil A.: New York Times
Lewthwaite, Gilbert A.: Baltimore Sun
Liang, Zhang: Beijing People's Daily
Licitra, Annette: Education Daily
Lieberman, Brett: Newhouse News Service
Liebert, Larry: Congressional Monitor
Lieblich, Julia: Newhouse News Service
Lifshey, Adam: Asahi Shimbun
Lightfoot-Clark, Regina: Education Daily
Lightman, David: Hartford Courant
Lilleston, Thomas R.: Congressional Monitor
Lin, Betty P.: World Journal
Lindberg, Rainer S.: Nachrichten fuer Aussenhandel
Lindberg, Tod M.: Washington Times
Lindsay, John H.: Scripps Howard News Service
Lipman, Laurence M.: Palm Beach Post/Cox Newspapers
Lipold, John: Bridge News
Lippman, Thomas W.: Washington Post
Litvan, Laura M.: Investor's Business Daily
Liu, Marco C.: Taipei Economic Daily
Liu, Ning K.: Youth Daily News
Lobe, James P.: Inter Press Service
Lobsenz, George: Energy Daily
Lochhead, Carolyn: San Francisco Chronicle
Loeb, Vernon F.: Washington Post
Lopez, Jose: Notimex Mexican News Agency

MEMBERS ENTITLED TO ADMISSION, PRESS GALLERIES—Continued

Lorenzetti, Maureen S.: Platt's Oilgram News
Loughlin, Sean M.: New York Times
Love, Alice A.: Associated Press
Lowe, Roger K.: Columbus Dispatch
Lowy, Joan A.: Scripps Howard News Service
Luther, James W.: Associated Press
Lynch, David E.: Lynch News Service
Lyons, Christina: Congressional Monitor
Lytle, Tamara: Orlando Sentinel
Maalouf, Rafic K.: Al Hayat
MacDonald, David M.: McClendon News Service
MacDonald, John A.: Hartford Courant
MacFarland, Margo: Congressional Monitor
MacLeish, Rod: Christian Science Monitor
MacPherson, Karen: Scripps Howard News Service
Macabrey, J.M.: La Tribune Desfosses
Macaluso, Nora G.: Bloomberg Business News
Machacek, John W.: Gannett News Service
Machida, Tetsu: Nikkei
Mackler, Peter: Agence France-Presse
Maddox, Jennifer: Scripps Howard News Service
Magg, Laura A.: States News Service
Maggs, John J.: Journal of Commerce
Magner, Michael J.: Newhouse News Service
Maier, Thomas: German Press Agency - DPA
Majano, Rosendo: EFE News Service
Mak, Matthew: USA Today
Malarstedt, Kurt: Dagens Nyheter
Malone, Julia: Cox Newspapers
Mandel, Susan: Bridge News
Mann, James H.: Los Angeles Times
Mann, William C.: Associated Press
Mannion, James C.: Agence France-Presse
Manthey, Marlene: Zeitungsring
Maraniss, David: Washington Post
Marchak, Elizabeth A.: Cleveland Plain Dealer
Marcus, David, L.: Boston Globe
Marcus, Ruth: Washington Post
Marcy, Steven K.: Bridge News
Marek, Lynne A.: Bloomberg Business News
Margasak, Lawrence N.: Associated Press
Marino, Marie: Gannett News Service
Marlowe, Robert E.: Media General News Service
Marolo, Bruno: ANSA Italian News Agency
Marquis, Christopher: Knight-Ridder Newspapers
Marriott, Anne E.: Washington Times
Marshall, Stephen B.: USA Today
Marshall, Toni L.: Washington Times
Marshall, Tyler: Los Angeles Times
Martin, David K.: Roll Call Report Syndicate
Martin, Fowler W.: Dow Jones News Services
Martin, Gary R.: San Antonio Express-News
Martin, Jurek: London Financial Times
Martin, Kim S.: Dow Jones News Services
Martin, Sean E.: Health News Daily
Martinez, Gebe: Los Angeles Times
Martos, Carlos: EFE News Service
Marwill, Philip: Congressional Monitor
Marx, Claude R.: Investor's Business Daily
Mas, Xavier: La Vanguardia
Masci, David: Congressional Monitor
Mathewson, Judith M.: Ottaway News Service
Mathis, Nancy: Houston Chronicle
Matsuda, Hideaki: Jiji Press
Matsumoto, Hiroshi: Kyodo News Service
Mattheiem, Nathalie: Le Soir
Matthews, Christopher J.: San Francisco Examiner
Matthews, Mark H.: Baltimore Sun
Mauro, Anthony E.: USA Today
Mayer, Caroline F.: Washington Post
Mayer, Luigi: ANSA Italian News Agency
Mays, Andrea L.: USA Today
McAllister, William H.: Washington Post
McBee, Susanna: Hearst Newspapers
McBride, Sarah: Wall Street Journal
McCaney, Kevin P.: Ottaway News Service
McCarthy, Thomas: Los Angeles Times
McCaslin, John L.: Washington Times
McClain, John D.: Associated Press
McClendon, Sarah: McClendon News Service
McClinton, Dennis: Associated Press
McCombs, Philip A.: Washington Post
McConnell, William: American Banker
McCord, Nancy S.: London Financial Times
McCune, Greg A.: Reuters
McCutcheon, Chuck: Congressional Monitor
McDonald, Andrew: New York Times
McDonald, Elizabeth G.: Bloomberg Business News
McDonald, Greg: Houston Chronicle
McDowell, Charles R.: Richmond Times-Dispatch
McFeatters, Ann C.: Scripps Howard News Service
McFeatters, Dale B.: Scripps Howard News Service
McGinley, Laurie: Wall Street Journal
McGray, Kevin: New York Times
McGregor, Deborah: Congressional Quarterly
McGrory, Brian: Boston Globe
McGrory, Mary: Washington Post
McGuinness, Jean E.: Chicago Tribune
McIntyre, David T.: German Press Agency - DPA
McKee, Michael: Bloomberg Business News
McKinney, Joan: Baton Rouge Morning Advocate
McLean, Renwick: El Pais
McLoone, Tracy: CongressDaily
McManus, Doyle: Los Angeles Times
McNulty, Timothy J.: Chicago Tribune
McQuaid, John G.: New Orleans Times-Picayune
McQuillan, Laurence: Reuters
Meadows, Clifton E.: New York Times
Means, Marianne: Hearst Newspapers
Mears, Walter R.: Associated Press
Meckler, Laura: Associated Press
Meinert, Dori: Copley News Service
Meisler, Stanley: Los Angeles Times
Mello, Michael: Ottaway News Service

MEMBERS ENTITLED TO ADMISSION, PRESS GALLERIES—Continued

Melton, Robert H.: Washington Post
Memmott, Mark J.: USA Today
Menon, Nambalat C.: Hindustan Times
Mercer, Marsha D.: Media General News Service
Mercurio, John: Washington Times
Merida, Kevin E.: Washington Post
Merline, John W.: Investor's Business Daily
Merry, Robert: Congressional Quarterly
Meszoly, Robin D.: Bloomberg Business News
Mevel, Jean-Jacques: Le Figaro
Meyer, Harold: Nachrichten fuer Aussenhandel
Miga, Andrew L.: Boston Herald
Minh, Nguyen: Vietnam News Agency
Milius, Peter: Washington Post
Milius, Susan C.: United Press International
Milk, Jeremy L.: Yomiuri Shimbun
Millan, Delia A.: EFE News Service
Miller, Alan C.: Los Angeles Times
Miller, Amy B.: Education Daily
Miller, Jeff: Scripps Howard News Service
Miller, Jill Y.: Fort Lauderdale Sun-Sentinel
Miller, Richard M.: Reuters
Mills, Betty: Griffin-Larrabee News Service
Mills, Mike: Washington Post
Mintz, Elana: Congressional Quarterly
Mintz, John D.: Washington Post
Mironov, Arseny: Itar-Tass News Agency
Mitchell, Alison: New York Times
Miyamoto, Akihiko: Nikkei
Mizuno, Takaaki: Asahi Shimbun
Mkhondo, Rich: Independent Newspapers of S.Africa
Mohammed, Arshad A.: Reuters
Mollison, Andrew R.: Cox Newspapers
Molotsky, Irvin D.: New York Times
Monberg, Helene C.: Monberg News Service
Montet, Virginie: Agence France-Presse
Montgomery, Anne: Health News Daily
Montgomery, Lori A.: Detroit Free Press
Montgomery, Scott: Dayton Daily News/Cox Newspapers
Montoya, Joseph: Reuters
Monyak, Fred: Baltimore Sun
Mooar, Brian: Washington Post
Moon, Julie: U.S.-Asian News Service
Moreno, Elena: EFE News Service
Moreno, Rafael: EFE News Service
Morgan, Dan: Washington Post
Moriarty, JoAnn: Newhouse News Service
Morin, Richard: Washington Post
Morita, Seisaku: Sekai Nippo
Morris, David J.: Associated Press
Morris, Vincent S.: Washington Times
Morrison, Joanne: Bond Buyer
Morrissey, Matthew: CongressDaily
Moser, Patrick: Agence France-Presse
Moyer, Pamela: States News Service
Mulligan, John E.: Providence Journal-Bulletin
Muradian, Vago: Defense Daily
Muramatsu, Masaaki: Nikkei
Muraoka, Shinichiro: Jiji Press
Murayama, Kohei: Kyodo News Service
Murphy, Daniel J.: Investor's Business Daily
Murray, Alan S.: Wall Street Journal
Murray, Frank J.: Washington Times
Murray, Sharon K.: Media General News Service
Murray, William: Dow Jones News Services
Music, Kimberley A.: Oil Daily
Myers, Jim: Tulsa World
Myers, Steven L.: New York Times
Nagai, Toshiharu: Kyodo News Service
Nagoshi, Kenro: Jiji Press
Nakata, Masahiro: Sankei Shimbun
Nakaya, Yuji: Kyodo News Service
Nall, Stephanie: Journal of Commerce
Navarro da Costa, Mario: ABIM News Agency
Neikirk, William R.: Chicago Tribune
Nelson, Jack: Los Angeles Times
Nelson, Lars-Erik: New York Daily News
Nesbitt, Jim: Newhouse News Service
Nesmith, Jeff H.: Cox Newspapers
Neuman, Johanna: USA Today
Neus, Elizabeth: Gannett News Service
Newman, Bud: CongressDaily
Newman-Barnett, Pamela B.: Energy Daily
Nicholson, Jonathan: Munifacts News Wire
Nielsen, David: Scripps Howard News Service
Nishikura, Kazuyoshi: Kyodo News
Nissirio, Patrizio: ANSA Italian News Agency
Nitschke, Lori: Congressional Monitor
Noah, Timothy R.: Wall Street Journal
Nomani, Asra Q.: Wall Street Journal
Nordwall, Eric: United Press International
Norman, Jane M.: Des Moines Register
Norton, Stephen J.: Legi-Slate News Service
Novovitch, Barbara: Reuters
Nozaki, Saiko: Yomiuri Shimbun
Nugroho, Irawan: Jawa Pos Daily
Nutting, Brian W.: Congressional Monitor
Nyhan, Paul: Bloomberg Business News
Nyitray, Joseph P.: Congressional Quarterly
O'Brien, Nancy F.: Catholic News Service
O'Connell, Connie C.: Associated Press
O'Connell, Jim: Scripps Howard News Service
O'Connor, Rory: Knight-Ridder Newspapers
O'Donnell, Jayne: USA Today
O'Donnell, Jr., John B.: Baltimore Sun
O'Driscoll, Mary: Energy Daily
O'Neil, John D.: New York Times
O'Ritter, Hal: USA Today
O'Rourke, Lawrence M.: McClatchy Newspapers
O'Toole, Thomas: Scripps Howard News Service
Ochelli, Victor J.: Reuters
Oden, Henry: Wall Street Journal
Ogrim, Helge: Norwegian News Agency

MEMBERS ENTITLED TO ADMISSION, PRESS GALLERIES—Continued

Okada, Norio: Akahata
Okie, Susan: Washington Post
Oliphant, Cortright W.: Oliphant News Service
Oliphant, John L.: Oliphant News Service
Oliphant, Robert C.: Oliphant News Service
Oliphant, Thomas N.: Boston Globe
Olnhausen, Jeff: Congressional Information Bureau
Omae, Hitoshi: Nikkei
Omicinski, John J.: Gannett News Service
Onishi, Takao: Hokkaido Shimbun
Orantes, Cesar A.: El Grafico
Orin, Deborah: New York Post
Orlov, Arkadiy: RIA Novosti
Orr, J. Scott: Newhouse News Service
Oshima, Hiroshi: Kyodo News Service
Ostroff, Jim: Fairchild News Service
Ostrow, Ronald J.: Los Angeles Times
Ota, Yasuhiko: Nikkei
Otsuka, Ryuichi: Yomiuri Shimbun
Ottaway, David B.: Washington Post
Otten, Alan L.: Wall Street Journal
Otto, Mary C.: Knight-Ridder Newspapers
Overberg, Paul: USA Today
Owens, Jennifer: Fairchild News Service
Pace, David H.: Associated Press
Packer-Tursman, Judy: Pittsburgh Post-Gazette/ Toledo Blade
Page, Susan L.: USA Today
Painter, Kim: USA Today
Pajares, Fernando: EFE News Service
Palmer, Doug: Bridge News
Palmer, Elizabeth: Congressional Monitor
Pan, Herman: Central News Agency
Papandoniou, Lampros: Macedonia News Agency
Paquette, Michael J.: Newhouse News Service
Parasuram, T.V.: Press Trust of India
Parenthoen, Isabelle: Agence France-Presse
Park, Doosik: Chosum Ilbo
Park, In-Kyn: Kyunghyang Shinmun
Parker, Richard: Albuquerque Journal
Parker, Vicki L.: Wall Street Journal
Pasarin, Sorin G.: Evenimentul Zilei
Passarini, Paolo: La Stampa
Patterson, Dean J.: Munifacts News Wire
Pattison, Mark: Catholic News Service
Paul, Sonali J.: Reuters
Payne, Henry: Scripps Howard News Service
Payton, Jack R.: St. Petersburg Times
Pear, Robert L.: New York Times
Pearson, Mark L.: USA Today
Peck, Louis M.: CongressDaily
Pendleton, Keeby: USA Today
Perry, James M.: Wall Street Journal
Pesce, Carolyn: USA Today
Pesek, Jr., William: Dow Jones News Services
Petersen, Rosemary D.: Des Moines Register
Peterson, Denise: Health News Daily
Peterson, Jonathan: Los Angeles Times
Peterson, Margaret: Legi-Slate News Service
Pethel, Blair: Bridge News
Petruska, Anne: Health News Daily
Phillips, Don: Washington Post
Phillips, Michael M.: Wall Street Journal
Philpott, Thomas R.: Military Update
Phinney, David: States News Service
Piacente, Steve: Charleston Post-Courier
Pianin, Eric S.: Washington Post
Pichaske, Peter D.: Phillips News Service
Pierce, Gregory T.: Washington Times
Pierre, Ruetschi: Tribune De Geneve
Pike, David F.: Los Angeles Daily Journal
Pina, Michael: Travel Management Daily
Pincus, Walter: Washington Post
Pine, Art: Los Angeles Times
Pinkerton, James P.: Newsday
Pins, Kenneth W.: Des Moines Register
Pisano, Carl A.: USA Today
Plocek, Joseph E.: Market News Service
Plungis, Jeffrey: Congressional Monitor
Poe, Edgar: New Orleans Times-Picayune
Poling, Bill: Travel Management Daily
Pompa, Frank A.: Gannett News Service
Pomper, Miles A.: Legi-Slate News Service
Poor, Timothy J.: St. Louis Post-Dispatch
Pope, Charles: Columbia State
Popescu, Bianca: Evenimentul Zilei
Porretta, Anthony L.: Congressional Monitor
Pottinger, Matthew, F.: States News Service
Povich, Elaine S.: Newsday
Powell, Stewart M.: Hearst Newspapers
Powelson, Richard: Scripps Howard News Service
Powers, Evelyn T.: USA Today
Powers, Ronald E.: Associated Press
Pressman, Aaron: Reuters
Preston, June R.: United Press International
Prewitt, Bashaan: Gas Daily
Price, David A.: Investor's Business Daily
Price, Deborah J.: Detroit News
Price, Tom: Cox Newspapers
Priddy, Dave: States News Service
Priest, Dana: Washington Post
Pritchard, Justin: Legi-Slate News Service
Pruden, Wesley: Washington Times
Pruitt, Claude Philip: Gannett News Service
Pruzan, Jeffrey S.: Gas Daily
Puente, Maria: USA Today
Puertas, Jose A.: Agence France-Presse
Purdum, Todd S.: New York Times
Purger, Tibor: Magyar Szo
Pyatt, Jr.: Rudolph, A.: Washington Post
Pyun, Jung R.: Kyodo News Service
Quansheng, Fu: Xinhua News Agency
Raasch, Charles: Gannett News Service
Racz, Peter: Hungarian News Agency
Ramadan, Wafik: L'Orient - Le Jour

MEMBERS ENTITLED TO ADMISSION, PRESS GALLERIES—Continued

Ramey, Joanna: Fairchild News Service
Ramjug, Peter A.: Reuters
Ramos, Robert R.: Reuters
Rankin, Robert A.: Knight-Ridder Newspapers
Rauber, Marilyn: New York Post
Raum, Thomas: Associated Press
Reath, Viki: Washington Times
Recer, Paul: Associated Press
Recio, Maria E.: Fort Worth Star-Telegram
Reed, Jennifer E.: Catholic News Service
Reeve, Vicki L.: Saudi Press Agency
Reeves, Pamela: Scripps Howard News Service
Reeves, Tracy A.: Knight-Ridder Newspapers
Rehm, Barbara A.: American Banker
Remez, Michael A.: Hartford Courant
Rennert, Leo: McClatchy Newspapers
Resnick, Amy B.: Bond Buyer
Rhodes, Tom: London Times
Rich, Spencer: Washington Post
Richards, Patrick R.: USA Today
Richey, Warren: Christian Science Monitor
Richter, Paul: Los Angeles Times
Richwine, Lisa: Reuters
Ricks, Thomas E.: Wall Street Journal
Riechmann-Kepler, Deb: Associated Press
Riedler, Monica A.: Die Presse
Rifkin, Ira: Newhouse News Service
Rimscha, Robert von: Der Tagesspeigel
Ringle, Ken: Washington Post
Rios, Delia M.: Newhouse News Service
Ripley, Amanda: Congressional Monitor
Risen, James E.: Los Angeles Times
Riskind, Jonathan: Columbus Dispatch
Ritter, Hal: USA Today
Ritter, John: USA Today
Ritter, Robert: Gannett News Service
Ritter, Scott: Dow Jones News Services
Rizzo, Katherine M.: Associated Press
Roache, Marlo: New York Times Regional Newspapers
Robb, Gregory A.: AFX News Service
Robbins, Carla, A.: Wall Street Journal
Roberson, Peggy: Federal Document Clearinghouse News Service
Roberts, Roxanne: Washington Post
Roberts, Steven: New York Daily News
Roberts, William L. III: Journal of Commerce
Robicheaux, Virginia D.: Deep Dixie News Service
Robinson, James: Los Angeles Times
Robinson, John A.: Defense Daily
Robinson, Loretta E.: Bloomberg Business News
Robinson, Melissa B.: Associated Press
Robinson, Robert G., Jr.: Market News Service
Rodrigo, Alejandro: ANSA Italian News Agency
Rodrigue, George P. III: Dallas Morning News
Rodriguez, Paul M.: Washington Times
Roe, Linda Feldmann: Christian Science Monitor
Rogers, David E.: Wall Street Journal
Rohner, Mark: Bloomberg Business News
Roland, Neil: Bloomberg Business News
Rolnick, Josh: Congressional Monitor
Roman, Nancy E.: Washington Times
Roque, Francisco: EFE News Service
Rosato, Donna: USA Today
Rose, Flemming: Berlingske Tidende
Rosen, James M.: McClatchy Newspapers
Rosenbaum, David E.: New York Times
Rosenberg, Carol: Miami Herald
Rosenberg, Eric M.: Hearst Newspapers
Rosenblatt, Robert: Los Angeles Times
Rosenthal, Harry F.: Associated Press
Ross, Sonya L.: Associated Press
Roth, Bennett: Houston Chronicle
Rothacker, Richard J.: Legi-Slate News Service
Rothberg, Donald M.: Associated Press
Rowold, Manfred: Die Welt
Rozman, Thea D.: Yomiuri Shimbun
Ruane, Michael E.: Knight-Ridder Newspapers
Rubin, Alissa J.: Congressional Quarterly
Rubin, James H.: Associated Press
Ruest, Thomas G.: Tages Anzeiger
Ruffner, Annette R.: Boston Globe
Ruiz, Phillip: Los Angeles Times
Runningen, Roger D.: Bloomberg Business News
Rupprecht, Jody: Congressional Quarterly
Ruzicka, Milan: Journal of Commerce
Ryan, Colleen: Australian Financial Review
Ryan, Richard A.: Detroit News
Ryan, Timothy F.: Reuters
Rzeznitzeck, Peter: Rheinische Post
Saffir, Barbara J.: Washington Post
Safford, David T.: Legi-Slate News Service
Safire, William: New York Times
Sakikawa, Shinichiro: Hokkaido Shimbun
Salisbury, William S.: St. Paul Pioneer Press
Sammon, Richard: Congressional Monitor
Sample, Herbert A.: McClatchy Newspapers
Sanchez, Emilio: EFE News Service
Sanchez, Marcela: El Tiempo
Sanchez, Rene: Washington Post
Sandalow, Marc: San Francisco Chronicle
Sands, David: Washington Times
Sanger, David E.: New York Times
Sansbury, Timothy J.: Journal of Commerce
Santana, Norberto, Jr.: Congressional Monitor
Santini, Jean-Louis: Agence France-Presse
Sanz, Marie: Agence France-Presse
Sase, Moriyoshi: Tokyo-Chunichi Shimbun
Sautter, William H.: Associated Press
Savage, David G.: Los Angeles Times
Sawyer, Jon M.: St. Louis Post-Dispatch
Sawyer, Kathy: Washington Post
Scales, Ann: Boston Globe
Scanlon, Leo F.: Intercontinental Media Service
Scarborough, Rowan: Washington Times

MEMBERS ENTITLED TO ADMISSION, PRESS GALLERIES—Continued

Schatz, Amy J.: Wall Street Journal
Scheibel, Kenneth M.: Washington Bureau News
Scheid, Jon F.: Bridge News
Scherer, Eric: Agence France-Presse
Scherf, Margaret: Associated Press
Schibli, Peter: Basler Zeitung
Schlein, Alan M.: Schlein News Bureau
Schlesinger, Jacob M.: Wall Street Journal
Schmick, William F.: Ottaway News Service
Schmickle, Sharon: Minneapolis Star Tribune
Schmid, Randolph E.: Associated Press
Schmid, Sharon L.: Wall Street Journal
Schmidt, Susan: Washington Post
Schmitt, Eric: New York Times
Schmitt, Richard B.: Wall Street Journal
Schneider, Avinoam: Bridge News
Schouten, Fredreka: Gannett News Service
Schram, Martin: Scripps Howard News Service
Schulte, Brigid: Knight-Ridder Newspapers
Schuster, Larry: United Press International
Schwartz, John: Washington Post
Schwartz, Leland: States News Service
Schwartz, Maralee: Washington Post
Schwed, Craig: Gannett News Service
Schweid, Barry: Associated Press
Schwerzleer, Nancy J.: Legi-Slate News Service
Sciolino, Elaine: New York Times
Scott, Andrew J.: Easton Star Democrat
Scott, Heather: Market News Service
Scully, Sean P.: Washington Times
Seachrist, Lisa: BioWorld Today
Seeley, John P.: Travel Management Daily
Seelye, Katharine Q.: New York Times
Segawa, Shiro: Mainichi Shimbun
Seib, Gerald F.: Wall Street Journal
Seiberg, Jaret: American Banker
Sekles, Maria F.: Jornal Do Brasil
Seper, Jerry: Washington Times
Serrano, Richard A.: Los Angeles Times
Serrin, Judith A.: Knight-Ridder Newspapers
Shafer, Ronald G.: Wall Street Journal
Shakow, Patricia: Washington Post
Shanahan, Eileen: New American News Service
Sharn, Lori: USA Today
Sharpe, Rochelle: Wall Street Journal
Shaw, Cameron: Reuters
Shaw, John T.: Market News Service
Shearer, Cody P.: Shearer and Glen News Enterprise
Shearer, Mary Ellen: Medill News Service
Shenon, Philip: New York Times
Shenoy, Sujatha: New Delhi Business Standard
Shepard, Paul: Associated Press
Shepard, Scott: Cox Newspapers
Shephard, Robert: Shephard News Features
Sherman, Mark J.: Atlanta Journal-Constitution
Sherrell, David M.: Market News Service
Shibuta, Tamio: Nishi-Nippon Shimbun
Shields, Gerard: Scripps Howard News Service
Shields, Mark: Creators Syndicate
Shin, Jae M.: Hankook Ilbo
Shin, Sang I.: Segye Ilbo/Segye Times
Shiner, Josette: Washington Times
Shiver, Jube, Jr.: Los Angeles Times
Shogan, Robert: Los Angeles Times
Shogren, Elizabeth: Los Angeles Times
Shore, Benjamin: Copley News Service
Shorrock, Timothy S.: Journal of Commerce
Shribman, David: Boston Globe
Shrohi, Seema: Calcutta Telegraph
Sia, Richard: Legi-Slate News Service
Sichelman, Lew: United Features Syndicate
Sieff, Martin: Washington Times
Siegel, Stephen J.: Wisconsin State Journal
Silvassy, Kathleen C.: United Press International
Silverman, Elissa C.: States News Service
Simon, Roger: Creators Syndicate
Simpson, Eileen: Congressional Monitor
Simpson, Glenn R.: Wall Street Journal
Singh, Ram A.: Bombay Free Press Journal
Singletary, Michelle: Washington Post
Siniff, John M.: USA Today
Sisk, Richard P.: New York Daily News
Sisnev, Vissarion I.: Trud
Sitov, Andrei K.: Itar-Tass News Agency
Skarzenski, Ronald: New York Times
Skidmore, David W.: Associated Press
Skorneck, Carolyn: Associated Press
Skrzycki, Cindy: Washington Post
Slavin, Barbara: USA Today
Slevin, Peter: Knight-Ridder Newspapers
Sloyan, Patrick J.: Newsday
Smith, Dennis J.: Congressional Monitor
Smith, Donna M.: Reuters
Smith, Hedirck L.: Universal Press Syndicate
Smith, Nichols: Scipps Howard News Service
Smith, R. Jeffery: Washington Post
Smith, Veronica: Agence France-Presse
Sniffen, Michael J.: Associated Press
Snyder, Charles A.: Hong Kong Standard
Sobierai, Sandra J.: Associated Press
Solomon, John F.: Associated Press
Somerville, Glenn F.: Reuters
Sommer, Scott W.: Associated Press
Sotero, Paulo: O Estado De S. Paulo
Sparacino, Micaele: Congressional Quarterly
Specht, Jim: Gannett News Service
Spence, Timothy E.: United Press International
Spitzer, Kirk B.: Gannett News Service
Squeo, Anne Marie: Bloomberg Business News
Squires, Sally: Washington Post
Squitieri, Tom: USA Today
Stamas, Vicky J.: Reuters
Stanton, Michael: Bond Buyer
Starr, Frank: Medill News Service

MEMBERS ENTITLED TO ADMISSION, PRESS GALLERIES—Continued

Stempleman, Neil: Bridge News
Stern, Amy: Congressional Monitor
Stern, Christopher S.: Variety Daily
Stern, Henry: Associated Press
Stern, Marcus, A.: Copley News Service
Stevens, Carol: Detroit News
Stevenson, Richard W.: New York Times
Stewart, B. Scott: Sankei Shimbun
Stewart, Michael R.: Asahi Shimbun
Stewart, Phil: States News Service
Stinson, Jeffrey: Gannett News Service
Stoddard, A.B.: States News Service
Stoffer, Jr., Harry B: Thomson Newspapers
Stohr, Greg: Bloomberg Business News
Stolberg, Sheryl: Los Angeles Times
Stone, Andrea: USA Today
Storey, David: Reuters
Stout, David G.: New York Times
Stout, Hilary: Wall Street Journal
Straub, Bill: Scripps Howard News Service
Strobel, Warren P.: Washington Times
Strong, Thomas J.: Associated Press
Struck, Doug: Washington Post
Stuteville, George: Indianapolis Star-News
Sumikawa, Yuriko: Kyodo News Service
Superville, Darlene E.: Associated Press
Suplec, Curt: Washington Post
Supon, Justin, J.: United Press International
Suzal, Savas: SABAH
Sweet, Lynn: Chicago Sun-Times
Swisher, Lawrence, A.: Northwest Newspapers
Swoboda, Frank: Washington Post
Swope, Christopher: Congressional Quarterly
Szekely, Peter A.: Reuters
Tachimardi, Maria H.: Gazeta Mercantil
Tachio, Ryoji: Tokyo-Chunichi Shimbun
Tackett, Michael: Chicago Tribune
Takahata, Akio: Mainichi Shimbun
Talbott, Basil: Chicago Sun-Times
Tang, Xiao: Xinhua News Agency
Tangonan, Shannon L.: USA Today
Tapscott, Richard: Washington Post
Tarallo, Mark: Bridge News
Tatum, Melanie G.: Saudi Press Agency
Taub, Michael G.: New York Times
Tautfest, Peter: Tageszeitung
Taylor, Andrew B.: Congressional Quarterly
Taylor, April: Detroit News
Taylor, Cynthia A.: Boston Globe
Taylor, Jeff A.: Investor's Business Daily
Taylor, Jeffrey: Wall Street Journal
Temman, Francis: Agence France-Presse
Temple-Raston, Dina S.: Bloomberg Business News
Terashima, Manami: Nikkei
Terzian, Philip: Providence Journal-Bulletin
Tetreault, Stephan, R.: Donrey Media Group
Thomas, Eric: Agence France-Presse
Thomas, Helen: United Press International
Thomas, Jacqueline: Detroit News
Thomas, Jennifer S.: Bloomberg Business News
Thomas, Pierre G.: Washington Post
Thomas, Richard: London Guardian
Thomas, Richard G.: Roll Call Report Syndicate
Thomasson, Dan K.: Scripps Howard News Service
Thomma, Steven R.: Knight-Ridder Newspapers
Thompson, Alan R.: Scripps Howard News Service
Thompson, Jake: Omaha World Herald
Tilman, LeRoy W.: Associated Press
Tilove, Jonathan: Newhouse News Service
Timmons, Suzanne D.: Bridge News
Tisinger, Russ: Congressional Monitor
Tobin, Michael, P.: States News Service
Toedtman, James, S.: Newsday
Tollefson, Chris: Casper Star-Tribune
Tomiyama, Yasushi: Jiji Press
Tomkin, Jennifer: Bloomberg Business News
Tomkins, Richard J.: German Press Agency-DPA
Torry, Jack: Pittsburgh Post-Gazette/Toledo Blade
Torry, Sandra: Washington Post
Toshi, Eiji: Jiji Press
Towell, Pat: Congressional Quarterly
Towle, Michael D.: Fort Worth Star-Telegram
Tranfford, Abigail: Washington Post
Trejos, Nancy: Associated Press
Trescott, Jacqueline: Washington Post
Tsai, Paul: Taipei Liberty Times
Tufty, Harold G.: Tufty News Service
Tumulty, Brian J.: Gannett News Service
Turner, Douglas L.: Buffalo News
Twomey, Stephen M.: Washington Post
Tyson, Rae J.: USA Today
Uchijo, Yoshitaka: Kyodo News Service
Unur, Esen: Hurriyet Daily
Usher, Anne K.: Tokyo-Chunichi Shimbun
Vaida, Bara: AFX News Service
Valenzuela, Francisco-Javier: El Pais
Van der linden, Frank: United States Press
Vartabedian, Ralph: Los Angeles Times
Vedantam, Shankar: Knight-Ridder Newspapers
Velguth, Karen: Mainichi Shimbun
Vicini, James: Reuters
Vieth, Warren: Los Angeles Times
Viollaz, Andre: Agence France-Presse
Vis, Nghi: Vietnam News Agency
Vise, David A.: Washington Post
Vita, Matthew: Cox Newspapers
Vitale, Robert R.: Thomson Newspapers
Vobejda, Barbara: Washington Post
VonDrehle, David J.: Washington Post
Vy, Pham: Vietnam News Agency
Wagman, Robert J.: Newspaper Enterprise Association
Waitz, Nancy H.: Reuters
Wald, Matthew L.: New York Times
Waldmeir, Patti: London Financial Times

MEMBERS ENTITLED TO ADMISSION, PRESS GALLERIES—**Continued**

Walker, Martin: London Guardian
Walker, Penelope: London Daily Telegraph
Wallack, William: Bridge News
Wallison, Ethan S.: States News Service
Walsh, Edmund C.: Oil Daily
Walsh, Sharon: Washington Post
Walte, Juan J.: USA Today
Walters, Nolan: Knight-Ridder Newspapers
Walters, Nolan J.: Columbus Ledger-Enquirer
Walth, Brent: Newhouse News Service
Wamsted, Dennis J.: Energy Daily
Wang, Bill: Central News Agency
Wang, Brice: Taipei Central Daily News
Wang, James C.: Taipei United Daily News
Wang, Yaodong: Shanghai Wen Hui Bao
Ward, David: Bloomberg Business News
Warren, James C.: Chicago Tribune
Warrick, Joby: Washington Post
Wartofsky, Alona: Washington Post
Waters, Donald C.: Associated Press
Watson, Ripley III: Journal of Commerce
Watters, Susan W.: Fairchild News Service
Webb, Ronnie F.: Associated Press
Webb, Thomas J.: Knight-Ridder Newspapers
Weeks, Linton: Washington Post
Wei, Guoqiang: Xinhua News Agency
Weiner, Rebecca: Education Daily
Weinraub, Mark: Reuters
Weintraub, Lisa: Congressional Monitor
Weiser, Carl: Gannett News Service
Weisman, Jonathan: Congressional Quarterly
Weiss, Clyde: Donrey Media Group
Weiss, Rick: Washington Post
Weisskopf, Michael: Washington Post
Welch, William M.: USA Today
Wells, Rob S.: Associated Press
Wells, Robert M.: Congressional Quarterly
Wessel, David: Wall Street Journal
West, Marvin L.: Scripps Howard News Service
West, Paul: Baltimore Sun
Westneat, Daniel: Seattle Times
Westphal, David L.: McClatchy Newspapers
Wetzstein, Cheryl: Washington Times
Wheeler, Lawrence R.: Gannett News Service
Whelan, Charles: Agence France-Presse
White, Dina: New York Daily News
White, Gordon E.: Washington Telecommunications
White, Keith P.: CongressDaily
White, Joseph G., Jr.: Associated Press
Whitmire, Richard: Gannett News Service
Whitney, David L.: McClatchy Newspapers
Whittle, Richard: Dallas Morning News
Whickham, DeWayne: Gannett News Service
Wieland, Leo: Frankfurter Allemeine Zeitung
Wiessler, David A.: Reuters
Wiessler, Judy B.: Houston Chronicle
Wigfield, Mark: Ottaway News Service
Wilke, John R.: Wall Street Journal
Wilkinson, Patrick J.: Congressional Quarterly
Willette, Anne: USA Today
Williams, Betty A.: USA Today
Williams, Larry E.: Knight-Ridder Newspapers
Williams, Vanessa D.: Washington Post
Williams, David: Lost Angeles Times
Wilon, Philip C.: Tampa Tribune
Wilson, John: Associated Press
Wilson, Kinsey S.: Congressional Monitor
Wilson, Peter J.: Australian
Wines, Stephen M.: New York Times
Wing, Jennifer: Associated Press
Winkler, Herbert: German Press Agency-DPA
Winter, Martin E.: Frankfurter Rundschau
Wirz, Benoit V.: Asahi Shimbun
Witcover, Jules: Baltimore Sun
Witham, Larry A.: Washington Times
Witte, Brian: Associated Press
Woellert, Lorraine A.: Washington Times
Wolf, Richard J.: USA Today
Wolman, Jonathan P.: Associated Press
Wood, Daivd B.: Newhouse News Service
Wood, Winston S.: Ottaway News Service
Woodlee, Yolanda M.: Washington Post
Woods, Michael: Pittsburgh Post-Gazette/Toledo Blade
Woodward, Bob: Washington Post
Woodward, Calvin: Associated Press
Woodyard, Christopher B.: Houston Chronicle
Woolworth, Irene C.: Bloomberg Business News
Wright, Gregory L.: Bridge News
Wright, Robin: Los Angeles Times
Wroblewski, Tomaz: Zycie Warszawy
Wyatt, Stephen: Australian Financial Review
Wynn, Randy: Thomson Newspapers
Wysocki, Jr., Bernard: Wall Street Journal
Xiangxin, Su: China News Service
Xingfu, Zhu: Shanghai Wen Hui Bao Daily
Xisheng, Zhou: Xinhua News Agency
Yamahiro, Tsuneo: Kyodo News Service
Yamasaki, Shinji: Akahata
Yancey, Mathhew L.: Associated Press
Yang, John E.: Washington Post
Yaodong, Wang: Shanghai Wen Hui Bao
Yeager, Holly: Hearst Newspapers
Yokoyama, Yuji: Sekai Nippo
Yonan, Alan M.: Wall Street Journal
Yonan, Jr.: Alan: Dow Jones News Services
Yoondho, Ra: Seoul Shinmum Daily
Yoshida, Fumikazu: Koydo News Service
Yoshida, Shigeyuki: Koydo News Service
Yost, Pete: Associated Press
Young, Al: USA Today
Yuan, Bingzhong: Xinhua News Agency
Yuasa, Hiroshi: Sankei Shimbun
Yunfei, Li: Beijng People's Daily
Zaberko, Deborah: Reuters

MEMBERS ENTITLED TO ADMISSION, PRESS GALLERIES—Continued

Zagaroli, Lisa: Detroit News
Zaidi, S.H. Nayyar: Pakistan Daily Jang & News
Zakaria, Tabassum: Reuters
Zakotnik, John M.: Health News Daily
Zalewski, Witold T.: Polish Press Agency
Zapor, Patricia J.: Catholic News Service
Zecchini, Laurent: Le Monde
Zeigler, Kristine: Energy Daily
Zhenhau, Wang: Xinhua News Agency
Zimmerman, Carol: Catholic News Service
Zitner, AAron L.: Boston Globe
Zremaski, Jerry: Buffalo News
Zucconi, Vittorio: La Stampa
Zuckerman, Michael J.: USA Today
Zuckman, Jill: Boston Globe
Zufferey, Sergio S.: Shearer and Glen News Enterprise

NEWSPAPERS REPRESENTED IN PRESS GALLERIES

NEWSPAPERS REPRESENTED IN PRESS GALLERIES—Continued

House Gallery 225–3945, 225–6722 Senate Gallery 224–0241

ABIM NEWS AGENCY—(703) 892–1810; 4107 North 27th Road, Arlington, VA 22207: Orlando Lyra De Carvalho, Jr., Mario Navarro da Costa.

AFX NEWS SERVICE—(202) 347–3237; 835 National Press Building, 20045: Sarah Borchersen-Keto, Gregory A. Robb, Bara Vaida.

ANSA ITALIAN NEWS AGENCY—(202) 628–3317; 1285 National Press Building, 20045: Cristiano Del Riccio, Margery Friesner, Bruno Marolo, Luigi Mayer, Patrizio Nissirio, Alejandro Rodrigo.

AFTENPOSTEN—(202) 785–0658; 2030 M Street, Suite 700, 20036: Ulf Andenaes.

AGENCE FRANCE-PRESSE—(202) 414–0585; 1015 15th Street, Suite 500, 20005: Philippe Alfroy, Diane K. Bartz, Christopher Boian, Xavier Briand, Sybilla Brodzinsky, Leon Bruneau, Guy Clavel, Gretchen Cook, Francis Curta, Brigitte Dusseau, Christiana Fabiani, Pierre Glachant, Nathaniel Harrison, Ursula Hyzy, Sarah Jackson, Oliver Knox, Carole Landry, Michael Langan, Pierre Lesourd, Robert Lever, Peter Mackler, James C. Mannion, Virginie Montet, Patrick Moser, Isabelle Parenthoen, Jose A. Puertas, Jean-Louis Santini, Marie Sanz, Eric Scherer, Veronica Smith, Francis Temman, Eric Thomas, Andre Viollaz, Charles Whelan.

AKAHATA—(202) 393–5238; 978 National Press Building, 20045: Norio Okada, Shinji Yamasaki.

AKRON BEACON JOURNAL—(202) 383–6029; 700 National Press Building, 20045: William L. Hershey.

AL AHRAM INTERNATIONAL—(202) 737–2121; 1112 National Press Building, 20045: Atef El-Ghamry.

AL HAYAT—(202) 783–5544; 1185 National Press Building, 20045: Rafic K. Maalouf.

ALBUQUERQUE JOURNAL—(703) 534–4447, P.O. Box 5627, Arlington, VA 22205: Richard Parker.

ALLENTOWN MORNING CALL—(202) 638–2523; 1333 F Street, Suite 400, 20004: Pete Leffler.

AMERICAN BANKER—(202) 347–5529; 1325 G Street, Suite 900, 20005: Dean C. Anason, Drew Clark, William McConnell, Barbara A. Rehm, Jaret Seiberg Olaf de Senerpont Domis.

ANATOLIA NEWS AGENCY—(301) 718–7966; 4450 South Park Avenue, #1614, Chevy Chase, MD 20815: Mehuet K. Cindemir.

ARIZONA REPUBLIC—(202) 662–7264; 1000 National Press Building, 20045: Jeffrey N. Barker, Adrianne M. Flynn.

ARKANSAS DEMOCRAT-GAZETTE—(202) 662–7690; 1190 National Press Building, 20045: Jane Fullerton, Terry Lemons.

ASAHI SHIMBUN—(202) 783–1000; 1022 National Press Building, 20045: Ama Amoako, Yoichi Funabashi, Benjamin Goldberg, Hiroshi Hoshi, Tsutomu Ishiai, Hiroaki Ito, Shigeji Kitajima, Adam Lifshey, Takaaki Mizuno, Michael R. Stewart, Benoit V. Wirz.

ASIAN WALL STREET JOURNAL—(202) 862–9274; 1025 Connecticut Avenue, 20036: Eduardo Lachica.

ASSOCIATED PRESS—(202) 776–9400; 2021 K Street, 6th Floor, 20006: James R. Abrams, Donna Abu-Nasr, Curt L. Anderson, John J. Arnold, Laurie Asseo, Jeannine Averse, Jennifer A. Batog, Nancy J. Benac, Timothy K. Bovee, Philip Brasher, David Briscoe, Robert Burns, Cassandra R. Burrell, Denise Cabrera, Richard Carelli, Janelle Carter, Jean Christensen, Christopher V. Connell, Martin S. Crutsinger, John M. Diamond, James P. Drinkard, Harry Dunphy, David M. Espo, Jerry R. Estill, Mike Feinsilber, Carole Feldman, Ron Fournier, Alan Fram, Robert S. Furlow, Kevin Galvin, George Gedda, Marcy G. Gordon, Lee A. Gould, Robert T. Greene, Karen Gullo, Carl Hartman, Merrill Hartson, H. Josef Hebert, Earl Hinton, Michael A. Householder, Terence Hunt, Anick Jesdanun, Sandy K. Johnson, Richard Keil, Eun K. Kim, John C. King, Lawrence L. Knutson, Eugene Kramer, Alice A. Love, James W. Luther, William C. Mann, Lawrence N. Margasak, John D. McClain, Dennis McClinton, Walter R. Mears, Laura Meckler, David J. Morris, Connie C. O'Connell, David H. Pace, Ronald E. Powers, Thomas Raum, Paul Recer, Deb Riechmann-Kepler, Katherine M. Rizzo, Melissa B. Robinson, Harry F. Rosenthal, Sonya L. Ross, Donald M. Rothberg, James H. Rubin, William H. Sautter, Margaret Scherf, Randolph E. Schmid, Barry Schweid, Paul Shepard, David W. Skidmore, Carolyn Skorneck, Michael J. Sniffen, Sandra J. Sobieraj, John F. Solomon, Scott W. Sonner, Henry Stern, Thomas J. Strong, Darlene E. Superville, LeRoy W. Tillman, Nancy Trejos, Donald C. Waters, Ronnie F. Webb, Rob S. Wells, Joseph G. White, Jr., John Wilson, Jennifer Wing, Brian Witte, Jonathan P. Wolman, Calvin Woodward, Matthew L. Yancey, Pete Yost.

AUSTIN AMERICAN-STATESMAN—(202) 887–8324; 2000 Pennsylvania Avenue, #10,000, 20006: Christi Harlan.

AUSTRALIAN—(202) 628–7079; 1040 National Press Building, 20045: Peter J. Wilson.

AUSTRALIAN FINANCIAL REVIEW—(202) 639–8084; 1331 Pennsylvania Avenue #904, 20004: Colleen Ryan, Stephen Wyatt.
BALTIMORE SUN—(202) 452–8250; 1627 K Street, Suite 1100, 20006: Susan Baer, Thomas Bowman Carl M. Cannon, Lyle W. Denniston, Ellen Gamerman, Robert W. Gee, Jack W. Germond, Karen A. Hosler, Frank D. Langfitt, Gilbert A. Lewthwaite, Mark H. Matthews, Fred Monyak, John B. O'Donnell, Jr., Paul West, Jules Witcover.
BANGLADESH DAILY TELEGRAPH—(301) 681–6360; 11235 Oakleaf Drive, Apt. H–1020, Silver Spring, MD 20901: Golam Arshad.
BANGOR DAILY NEWS—(202) 397–2566; 1220 Maryland Avenue NE, 20002: John S. Day.
BAPTIST NEWS SERVICE—(202) 544–4226; 200 Maryland Avenue NE, 20002: Kenny Byrd, Larry Chesser.
BASLER ZEITUNG—(301) 530–7903; 5920 Johnson Avenue, Bethesda, 20817 MD: Peter Schibli.
BATON ROUGE MORNING ADVOCATE—(202) 554–0458; 6010 Trailside Drive, Springfield, VA 22150: Joan McKinney.
BEIJING PEOPLE'S DAILY—(202) 966–2285; 3706 Massachusetts Avenue, 20016: Zhang Liang, Li Yunfei.
BERLINGSKE TIDENDE—(202) 347–1744; 1331 Pennsylvania Avenue #506, 20004: Flemming Rose.
BIOWORLD TODAY—(202) 289–4798; 1444 I Street, Suite 1000, 20005: Lisa Seachrist.
BLOOMBERG BUSINESS NEWS—(202) 624–1800; 228 National Press Building, 20045: David M. Ahearn, William Arthur, Todd Blecher, Laura Cohn, John R. Cranford, Vincent A. Del Giudice, Bob Drummond, Steven J. Dryden, Todd R. Eastham, W. Gerald Egger, Thomas M. Ferraro, Monee Fields-White, Marthe Fourcade, Charles S. Hawkins, Paul Heldman, Kristin Jensen, Monroe W. Karmin, Nora G. Macaluso, Lynne A. Marek, Elizabeth G. McDonald, Michael McKee, Robin D. Meszoly, Paul Nyhan, Loretta E. Robinson, Mark Rohner, Neil Roland, Roger D. Runningen, Anne Marie Squeo, Greg Stohr, Dina S. Temple-Raston, Jennifer S. Thomas, Jennifer Tomkins, David Ward, Mark Willen, Irene C. Woolworth.
BOMBAY FREE PRESS JOURNAL—(703) 931–9038; 5597 Seminary Road, Suite 2204–S, Falls Church, VA 22041: Ram A. Singh.
BOND BUYER—(202) 393–1270; 1325 G Street, Suite 900, 20005: Heather J. Eurich, Craig T. Ferris, Lynn S. Hume, Joanne Morrison, Amy B. Resnick, Michael Stanton.
BOSTON GLOBE—(202) 857–5050; 1130 Connecticut Avenue, Suite 520, 20036: Christine M. Black, John A. Farrell, Robert T. Hohler, Rosalind Jackler, Michael A. Kranish, Mary C. Leonard, David L. Marcus, Brian McGrory, Thomas N. Oliphant, Annette R. Ruffner, Ann Scales, David Shribman, Cynthia A. Taylor, AAron L. Zitner, Jill Zuckman.
BOSTON HERALD—(202) 638–1796; 988 National Press Building, 20045: Andrew L. Miga.
BOVARD NEWS SERVICE—(301) 309–6817; 1345 Templeton Place, Rockville, MD 20852: James Bovard.
BRIDGE NEWS—(202) 383–6150; 740 National Press Building, 20045: William Acworth, Elizabeth J. Alderman, Annie Alexander, Kia Breaux, L. Kareema Clark, Richard Cowan, Lori L. Cuthbert, Cristine Denver, Jessica J. Dyson, Brian T. Graham, Bruce Harmon, Bill Hieronymus, Edward Kean, Patrick Kelly, Catherine Kristiansen, John Lipold, Susan Mandel, Steven K. Marcy, Doug Palmer, Blair Pethel, Jon F. Scheid, Avinoam Schneider, Neil Stempleman, Mark Tarallo, Suzanne D. Timmons, William Wallack, Gregory L. Wright.
BUFFALO NEWS—(202) 737–3188; 1141 National Press Building, 20045: Douglas L. Turner, Jerry Zremski.
CALCUTTA TELEGRAPH—(202) 333–0941; 2225 39th Place, 20007: Sirohi.
CASPER STAR-TRIBUNE—(202) 638–4413; 420 7th Street, #305, 20004: Chris Tollefson.
CATHOLIC NEWS SERVICE—(202) 541–3266; 3211 Fourth Street NE, 20017–1100: Julie L. Asher, Jerome F. Filteau, Barbara J. Fraze, Nancy J. Hartnagel, Nancy F. O'Brien, Mark Pattison, Jennifer E. Reed, Patricia J. Zapor, Carol Zimmerman.
CENTRAL NEWS AGENCY—(202) 628–2738; 1173 National Press Building, 20045: Huang Chen, Edward N. Han, Herman Pan, Bill Wang.
CHARLESTON POST-COURIER—(202) 340–8646; 628 Crocus Drive, Rockville, MD 20850: Steve Piacente.
CHARLOTTE OBSERVER—(202) 383–6057; 700 National Press Building, 20045: Carol D. Leonning.
CHICAGO SUN-TIMES—(202) 393–4340; 1750 Pennsylvania Avenue #1312, 20006: Brett M. Decker, Lynn Sweet, Basil Talbott.
CHICAGO TRIBUNE—(202) 637–2030; 1325 G Street, Suite 200, 20005: Terry Atlas, David Cloud, Mike Dorning, Glen R. Elsasser, Jan C. Greenburg, David A. Jackson, Mary Jacoby, Frank E. James III, Carol Jouzaitis, Michael D. Kilian, Jean E. McGuinness, Timothy J. McNulty, William R. Neikirk, Michael Tackett, Vicki Walton, James C. Warren.
CHINA NEWS SERVICE—(703) 920–6223; 1400 S. Joyce Street, Suite 1519, Arlington, VA 22202: Xiangxin Su.
CHINA TIMES—(202) 662–7570; 952 National Press Building, 20045: Norman Fu.
CHOSUN ILBO—(202) 783–4236; 1171 National Press Building, 20045: Chang Kyoon Kim,Doosik Park.
CHRISTIAN SCIENCE MONITOR—(202) 785–4400; 910 16th Street, Suite 200, 20006: Lawrence J. Goodrich, Peter Grier, Jonathan S. Landay, Rod MacLeish, Warren Richey, Linda Feldmann Roe.
CHUNICHI-TOKYO SHIMBUN—(202) 783–9479; 1230 National Press Building, 20045: Naotumi Kuchiki.

CLEVELAND PLAIN DEALER—(202) 638–1366; 930 National Press Building, 20045: Thomas J. Brazaitis, Jo Ellen Corrigan, Thomas K. Diemer, Sabrina Eaton, Keith C. Epstein, Elizabeth A. Marchak.

COLUMBIA STATE—(202) 383–6023; 700 National Press Building, 20045: Charles Pope.

COLUMBUS DISPATCH—(202) 347–3144; 1152 National Press Building, 20045: Roger K. Lowe, Jonathan Riskind.

COLUMBUS LEDGER-ENQUIRER—(202) 383–6045; 700 National Press Building, 20045: Nolan J. Walters.

COMMONS DAILY—(301) 208–6545; 16824 Malibar St, Perwood, MD 20855: Dah-Wey Lan.

COMMUNICATIONS DAILY—(202) 872–9200; 2115 Ward Court, 20037: Arthur R. Brodsky.

CONGRESSDAILY—(202) 739–8400; 1501 M Street, 3rd Floor, 20005: David Baumann, Steven D. Cook, Jill Graham, Mary A. Lehman, Tracy McLoone, Matthew Morrissey, Bud Newman, Louis M. Peck, Keith P. White.

CONGRESSIONAL INFORMATION BUREAU—(703) 516–4801; 3030 Clarendon Boulevard, Suite 202, Arlington, VA 22201: Marc D. Cannistraro, Robert Cazalas, Jeff Olnhausen.

CONGRESSIONAL MONITOR—(202) 887–8500; 1414 22nd Street, 20037: Martha Angle, Marc R. Birtel, Susan Dillingham, Andrea L. Foster, Russell A. Freyman, Lisa L. Gaffney, Keith D. Glover, Robert M. Gravely, Michele Hatty, David Hawkings, Will Heyniger, Peter H. King, Larry Liebert, Thomas R. Lilleston, Christina Lyons, Philip Marwill, Chuck McCutcheon, Lori Nitschke, Brian W. Nutting, Elizabeth Palmer, Jeffrey Plungis, Anthony L. Porretta, Amanda Ripley, Josh Rolnick, Richard Sammon, Norberto Santana, Jr., Eileen Simpson, Dennis J. Smith, Amy Stern, Russ Tisinger, Lisa Weintraub, Kinsey S. Wilson.

CONGRESSIONAL QUARTERLY—(202) 887–8500; 1414 22nd Street, 20037: Paul L. Anderson, F.A. Benenson, Dan Carney, Rebecca Carr, Donna Cassata, Mike Christensen, Charles E. Conlon, Rhodes Cook, Carroll Doherty, Philip D. Duncan, Ronald Elving, Bonnie L. Forrest, Colette Fraley, Allan Freedman, Steve Gettinger, Gregory L. Giroux, Alan Greenblatt, Juliana Gruenwald, Rose Gutfeld, George Hager, Heather A. Hope, David Hosansky, Jeffrey L. Katz, Melissa W. Kaye, Jaculine M. Koszczuk, Christine C. Lawrence, Deborah McGregor, Robert Merry, Elana Mintz, Joseph P. Nyitray, Alissa J. Rubin, Jody Rupprecht, Micaele Sparacino, Christopher Swope, Andrew B. Taylor, Robert Tomkin, Pat Towell, Jonathan Weisman, Robert M. Wells, Patrick J. Wilkinson.

CONNECTICUT POST—(703) 628–2157; 1331 Pennsylvania Avenue #524, 20004: Lolita Baldor.

COPLEY NEWS SERVICE—(202) 737–6960; 1100 National Press Building, 20045: Amy Bayer, George E. Condon, Jr., Robert Estill, Stephen J. Green, Otto Kreisher, Finlay Lewis, Dori Meinert, Benjamin Shore, Marcus A. Stern.

CORRIERE DELLA SERA—(202) 879–6733; 450 National Press Building, 20045: Ennio Caretto.

COX NEWSPAPERS—(202) 887–8334; 2000 Pennsylvania Avenue #10,000, 20006: Andrew Alexander, Susan Burns, Ricky A. Christie, Arthur R. Dalglish, Robert E. Dart, Robert E. Deans, Jr., Andrew J. Glass, Elliot Jaspin, Nancy Kliewer, Julia Malone, Andrew R. Mollison, Jeff H. Nesmith, Tom Price, Scott Shepard, Matthew Vita.

CREATORS SYNDICATE—(202) 223–1196; 500 23rd Street, 20037: Ralph De Toledano; 662–1255; 1009 National Press Building, 20045: Mark Shields; (301) 365–336; 7027 Natelli Woods Lane, Bethesda, MD 20817: Roger Simon.

CUMHURIYET DAILY—(703) 931–6701; 3311 Wyndham Circle, #3200, Alexandria, VA 22302: Fuat Kozluklu.

DAGENS NYHETER—(202) 429–0134; 1726 M Street, 20036: Kurt Malarstedt.

DAILY OKLAHOMAN—(202) 662–7543; 914 National Press Building, 20045: Chris Casteel, Allan W. Cromley, Mark D. Green.

DALLAS MORNING NEWS—(202) 661–8421; 1325 G Street, Suite 250, 20005: Catalina Camia, Robert Dodge, Susan Feeney, G. Robert Hillman, David M. Jackson, David LaGesse, James M. Landers, Carl P. Leubsdorf, Katherine Lewis, George P. Rodrigue, III, Richard Whittle.

DAYTON DAILY NEWS—(202) 887–8328; 2000 Pennsylvania Avenue, #10000, 20006: Scott Montgomery.

DE VOLKSKRANT—(301) 469–6153; 8209 Beech Tree Road, Bethesda, MD 20817: Oscar G. Garschagen.

DEEP DIXIE NEWS SERVICE—(202) 488–5309; 15 3rd Street NE, #4, 20002: Virginia D. Robicheaux.

DEFENSE DAILY—(703) 522–5655; 1111 N. 19th Street, Suite 503, Arlington, VA 22209: Bryan D. Bender, Thomas Breem, Greg A. Caires, Sheila Foote, Vago Muradian, John A. Robinson.

DENVER POST—(202) 662–8990; 1270 National Press Building, 20045: Adriel Bettelheim, Jennifer Gavin.

DER BUND—(301) 229–1570; 7502 Arden Road, Cabin John, MD 20818: Dieter E. Arnold.

DER TAGESSPEIGEL—(202) 234–2168; 1656–B Euclid Street, 20009: Robert von Rimscha.

DES MOINES REGISTER—(703) 907–5002; 1000 Wilson Boulevard, 10th Floor, Arlington, VA 22229: George P. Anthan, Donald W. Kaul, Jane M. Norman, Rosemary D. Petersen, Kenneth W. Pins.

DESERET NEWS—(202) 737–5311; 1061 National Press Building, 20045: Lee Davidson.

DETROIT FREE PRESS—(202) 383–6053; 700 National Press Building, 20045: Janet L. Fix, Lori A. Montgomery.

DETROIT NEWS—(202) 662–7378; 1148 National Press Building, 20045: Larry Bivins, Noelle Knox, Deborah J. Price, Richard A. Ryan, Carol Stevens, April Taylor, Jacqueline Thomas, Lisa Zagaroli.

DIE PRESSE—(202) 986–7032; 1703 Seaton Street,20009: Monica A. Riedler.

DIE WELT—(301) 983–4177; 11148 Powderhorn Drive, Potomac, MD 20854: Gerd Brueggemann, Dr. Manfred Rowold .

DONG-A ILBO—(202) 347–4907; 974 National Press Building, 20045: Euntaek Hong, Jae-Ho Lee.

DONREY MEDIA GROUP—(202) 783–1760; 937 National Press Building, 20045: Tony Batt, Christine M. Dorsey, Stephan R. Tetreault, Clyde Weiss.

DOW JONES NEWS SERVICES—(202) 862–9273; 1025 Connecticut Avenue, Suite 800, 20036: Mark Anderson, Kim Archer, Paul M. Beckett, Judith Burns, John Connor, Jennifer Corbett, Thomas W. Doggett, Jr., Carl A. Johnston, Nancy Keates, Alex A. Keto, Deborah L. Klosky, Laurie Lande, Fowler W. Martin, Kim S. Martin, William Murray, William Pesek, Jr., Scott Ritter, Alan Yonan, Jr.

EFE NEWS SERVICE—(202) 745–7692; 1252 National Press Building, 20045: Maria L. Azpiazu, Rafael Canas, Rosendo Majano, Carlos Martos, Delia A. Millan, Elena Moreno, Rafael Moreno, Fernando Pajares, Francisco Roque, Emilio Sanchez.

EASTON STAR DEMOCRAT—(301) 843–9600; 7 Industrial Park Drive, Waldorf, MD 20602: Andrew J. Scott.

EDUCATION DAILY—(703) 739–6494; 1101 King Street, Suite 444, Alexandria, VA 22313–2053: Dave Boyer, William J. Cahir, Matt Dembicki, V. Casey Gonzalez, David Harrison, Laureen Lazarovici, Annette Licitra, Regina Lightfoot-Clark, Amy B. Miller, Rebecca Weiner.

EL FINANCIERO—(703) 707–0236; 2300 Darius Lane, Reston VA 20191: Dolia Estevez.

EL GRAFICO DAILY NEWS—(703) 360–2997; 8907 Battery Road, Alexandria, VA 22308: Cesar A. Orantes.

EL NORTE & REFORMA—(202) 628–0031; 1265 National Press Building, 20045: Maria I. Gonzalez.

EL PAIS—(202) 638–1533; 1134 National Press Building, 20045: Renwick McLean, Francisco-Javier Valenzuela.

EL TIEMPO—(202) 265–0493; 2828 Connecticut Avenue, #508, 20008: Andres Cavelier, Marcela Sanchez.

EL UNIVERSAL—(202) 966–1024; 4293 Embassy Park Drive, 20016: Everett Bauman, Jose Carreno.

EL UNIVERSAL—(202) 662–7190; 801 National Press Building20045:Jose Carreno-Figueras.

ENERGY DAILY—(202) 638–4260; 627 National Press Building, 20045: Llewellyn King, George Lobsenz, Pamela B. Newman-Barnett, Mary O'Driscoll, Dennis J. Wamsted, Kristine Zeigler.

EVENIMENTUL ZILEI—(202) 965–7732; 2201 Wisconsin Avenue, #520, 20007: Sorin G. Pasarin, Bianca Popescu.

FAIRCHILD NEWS SERVICE—(202) 639–6900; 601 13th Street, Suite 520 South, 20005: Joyce Barrett, Jim Ostroff, Jennifer Owens, Joanna Ramey, Susan W. Watters.

FORT LAUDERDALE SUN-SENTINEL—(202) 824–8256; 1325 G Street, 20005: William Gibson, Jill Y. Miller.

FORT WORTH STAR-TELEGRAM—(202) 466–3121; 1705 DeSales Street, 20036: Ron M. Hutcheson, Maria E. Recio, Michael D. Towle.

FRANKFURTER ALLGEMEINE ZEITUNG—(202) 662–7255; 1093 National Press Building, 20045: Carola Kaps, Leo Wieland.

FRANKFURTER RUNDSCHAU—(202) 265–7240; 1624 19th Street NE, Apt. 301, 20009: Martin E. Winter.

FRANKLIN NEWS FEATURES—(703) 532–1657; 2320 Great Falls Street, Falls Church, VA 22046: Mary Beth Franklin.

FREDERICKSBURG FREE LANCE-STAR—(703) 680–5032; 16007 Laconia Circle, Woodbridge, VA 22191: Lucia Anderson.

GANNETT NEWS SERVICE—(703) 276–5800; 1000 Wilson Boulevard, Arlington, VA 22229: Judith B. Austin, Paul C. Barton, Penny Bender, Norm Brewer, Pamela A. Brogan, Dennis Camire, Ronald E. Cohen, Deborah M. Colaianni, Christina W. Collins, Hollis L. Engley, Ellyn Ferguson, Jon Frandsen, James R. Golden, John M. Hanchette, Desiree F. Hicks, David Judson, Deborah Kalb, Lisa F. Kaplan, Erin V. Kelly, John W. Machacek, Marie Marino, Elizabeth Neus, John J. Omicinski, Frank A. Pompa, Claude Philip Pruitt, Charles Raasch, Robert Ritter, Fredreka Schouten, Craig Schwed, Jim Specht, Kirk B. Spitzer, Jeffrey Stinson, Brian J. Tumulty, Carl Weiser, Lawrence R. Wheeler, Richard Whitmire, DeWayne Wickham.

GAS DAILY—(703) 816–8628; 1616 North Fort Myer Drive, #1000, Arlington, VA 22209: Damien J. Gaul, Mark Hand, Bashaan Prewitt, Jeffrey S. Pruzan.

GAZETA MERCANTIL—(202) 518–3386; 3133 Connecticut Avenue, #1025, 20008: Maria H. Tachinardi.

GAZETA WYBORCZA—(301) 279–9427; 6003 Coral Sea Avenue, Rockville, MD 20851–1722: Jacek M. Kalabinski.

GERMAN PRESS AGENCY-DPA—(202) 783–5097; 969 National Press Building, 20045: James P. Anderson, Hanns-Jochen Kaffsack, Thomas Maier, David T. McIntyre, Richard J. Tomkins, Herbert Winkler, Agostino della Porta.

GESTION—(301) 279–9109; P.O. Box 1887, Rockville, MD 20849–1887: Vladimir Kocerha.

GLASGOW HERALD—(202) 293–4729; 1730 Rhode Island Avenue, 20036: Patrick Brogan.

GLOBAL HORIZONS SYNDICATE—(202) 659–1921; 1330 New Hampshire Avenue, 20036: Edward Flattau.

GRIFFIN-LARRABEE NEWS SERVICE—(202) 554–3579; 2404 Davis Avenue, Alexandria, VA 22302: Betty Mills.

GUANGMING DAILY—(202) 363–0628; 4816 Butterworth Place, 20016: Fengyi Gao.

HAN-KYOREH SHINMUN—(202) 638–2141; 1259 National Press Building, 20045: Yun J. Jung.

HANDELSBLATT—(202) 965–0563; 3206 Q Street, 20007: Viola H. Drath.

HANKOOK ILBO—(202) 783–2674; 961 National Press Building, 20045: Jae M. Shin.

HARTE-HANKS NEWSPAPERS—(202) 628–1585; 958 National Press Building, 20045: William K. Garland.

HARTFORD COURANT—(202) 822–8040; 1730 Rhode Island Avenue, Suite 300, 20036: Rene E. Brown, David Lightman, John A. MacDonald, Michael A. Remez.

HEALTH NEWS DAILY—(301) 657–9830; 5550 Friendship Boulevard, Suite 1, Chevy Chase, MD 20815: Nellie O. Bristol, Sean E. Martin, Anne Montgomery, Denise Peterson, Anne Petruska, John M. Zakotnik.

HEARST NEWSPAPERS—(202) 298–6920; 1701 Pennsylvania Avenue, Suite 610, 20006: Dan Freedman, Christopher Hanson, Katie Harrison, Judy Holland, Wendy Koch, Charles J. Lewis, Susanna McBee, Marianne Means, Stewart M. Powell, Eric M. Rosenberg.

HINDU—(301) 654–9038; 4701 Willard Avenue, Suite 1531, Chevy Chase, MD 20815: Sridhar Krishnaswami.

HINDUSTAN TIMES—(703) 931–9038; 5597 Seminary Road, #2204–S, Falls Church, VA 22041: Nambalat C. Menon.

HOKKAIDO SHIMBUN—(202) 783–6033; 1232 National Press Building, 20045: Takao Onishi, Shinichiro Sakikawa.

HONG KONG STANDARD—(301) 942–2442; P.O. Box 571, Garrett Park, MD 20896: Charles A. Snyder.

HOUSTON CHRONICLE—(202) 393–6880; 1341 G Street, Suite 201, 20005: William E. Clayton, Jr., Cragg Hines, Nancy Mathis, Greg McDonald, Bennett Roth, Judy B. Wiessler, Christopher B. Woodyard.

HUNGARIAN NEWS AGENCY—(301) 565–2221; 8515 Farrell Drive, Chevy Chase, MD 20815: Peter Racz.

HURRIYET DAILY—(703) 526–9829; 1530 N. Key Boulevard, #726, Arlington, VA22209: Esen Unur.

IL MATTINO—(202) 338–4226; 4609 Foxhall Crescent, 20007: Mariuccia Chiantaretto.

IL SOLE 24 ORE—(202) 639–9251; 1285 National Press Building, 20045: Mario Calvo-Platero.

INDEPENDENT NEWSPAPERS OF SOUTH AFRICA—(202) 662–8722; 960–C National Press Building, 20045: Rich Mkhondo.

INDIANAPOLIS STAR-NEWS—(202) 662–7261; 1000 National Press Building, 20045: David L. Haase, George Stuteville.

INTER PRESS SERVICE—(202) 662–7160; 1293 National Press Building, 20045: Abid H. Aslam, Yvette J. Collymore, James P. Lobe.

INTERCONTINENTAL MEDIA SERVICE—(703) 430–1765; 46713 Flicker, Terrace, Sterling, VA 20164: Leo F. Scanlon.

INTERNATIONAL HERALD TRIBUNE—(202) 334–7418; 1150 15th Street, 20071: Brian B. Knowlton.

INVESTOR'S BUSINESS DAILY—(202) 737–2850; 1317 F Street, Suite 930, 20004: Adrienne Fox, Carl F. Horowitz, Sherry K. Kuczynski-Delaney, Laura M. Litvan, Claude R. Marx, John W. Merline, Daniel J. Murphy, David A. Price, Jeff A. Taylor.

IRISH TIMES—(301) 320–2308; 6221 Redwing Road, Bethesda, MD 20817: Joe Carroll.

ITAR–TASS NEWS AGENCY—(202) 662–7080; 1004 National Press Building, 20045: Igor Borisenko, Vladimir I. Kikilo, Ivan Lebedev, Arseny Mironov, Andrei K. Sitov.

JAWA POS DAILY—(703) 528–6530; 307 North George Mason Drive, #4, Arlington, VA 22203: Irawan Nugroho.

JERUSALEM POST—(703) 573–6031; 2813 Lee Oaks Court, #204, Falls Church, VA 22046: Hillel Kuttler.

JEWISH TELEGRAPHIC AGENCY—(202) 737–0935; 1025 Vermont Avenue, Suite 1140, 20005: Matthew Dorf, Daniel Kurtzman.

JIJI PRESS—(202) 783–4330; 550 National Press Building, 20045: Christopher Arnold, Kiyotaka Kato, Hideaki Matsuda, Shinichiro Muraoka, Kenro Nagoshi, Yasushi Tomiyama, Eiji Toshi.

JOONG-ANG ILBO—(202) 347–4006; 416 National Press Building, 20045: Jeong-Woo Kil.

JORNAL DO BRASIL—(301) 320–5296; 5302 Albemarle Street, Bethesda, MD 20816: Maria F. Sekles.

JOURNAL OF COMMERCE—(202) 383–6111; 740 National Press Building, 20045: Leo F. Abruzzese, Thomas J. Connors, Aviva Freudmann, Michele Kayal, Richard Lawrence, John J. Maggs, Stephanie Nall, William L. Roberts, III, Milan Ruzicka, Timothy J. Sansbury, Timothy S. Shorrock, Ripley Watson, III.

KANSAS CITY STAR—(202) 393–2020; 1163 National Press Building, 20045: David Goldstein, James L. Kuhnhenn.

KIPLING NEWS SERVICE—(301) 929–0760; 12611 Farnell Drive, Silver Spring, MD 20906–3873: Bogdan Kipling.

KNIGHT-RIDDER NEWSPAPERS—(202) 383–6030; 700 National Press Building, 20045: Ricardo Alonso-Zaldivar, Elisa C. Arnett, Gary L. Blonston, Robert J. Boyd, Mary Angela Cannon, James R. Carroll, Kathleen Carroll, Derrick K. Depledge, Heather J. Dewar, Aaron B. Epstein, Thomas P. Farragher,

Robert S. Geiger, Joshua F. Goldstein, Charles A. Green, Frank J. Greve, David W. Hess, Rachel Jones, Christopher Marquis, Rory O'Connor, Mary C. Otto, Robert A. Rankin, Tracy A. Reeves, Michael E. Ruane, Brigid Schulte, Judith A. Serrin, Peter Slevin, Steven R. Thomma, Shankar Vedantam, Nolan Walters, Thomas J. Webb, Larry E. Williams.

KUWAIT NEWS AGENCY—(202) 347–5554; 906 National Press Building, 20045: Faisal Alzaid, James C. Flanigan.

KWANGJU ILBO DAILY NEWS—(202) 638–1628; 1115 National Press Building, 20045: Huney Kong.

KYODO NEWS SERVICE—(202) 367–5767; 400 National Press Building, 20045: Toshiaki Anzai, Paul E. Flatin, Yasushi Fujii, Hiroshi Matsumoto, Kohei Murayama, Toshiharu Nagai, Yuji Nakaya, Hiroshi Oshima, Jung R. Pyun, Yuriko Sumikawa, Yoshitaka Uchijo, Tsuneo Yamahiro, Fumikazu Yoshida, Shigeyuki Yoshida.

KYUNGHYANG SHINMUN—(202) 737–3459; 839 National Press Building, 20045: In-Kyu Park.

L'ORIENT - LE JOUR—(202) 342–1213; 1045 31st Street, Apt. 304, 20007: Wafik Ramadan.

LA JORNADA—(202) 547–5852; 132 N. Carolina Avenue, SE, 20003: David Brooks, James Cason.

LA NACION—(202) 628–7907; 901 National Press Building, 20045: Jorge Elias.

LA NAZIONE—(202) 367–0245; 916 National Press Building, 20045: Cesare De Carlo.

LA OPINION—(202) 662–1240; 962 National Press Building, 20045: Maribel Hastings.

LA STAMPA—(202) 347–5233; 916 National Press Building, 20045: Paolo Passarini, Vittorio Zucconi, Andrea di Robilant.

LA TRIBUNA—(202) 737–5349; 960–A National Press Building, 20045: Jacobo Goldstein.

LA TRIBUNE DESFOSSES—(202) 862–6613; 1025 Connecticut Avenue, Suite 800, 20036: J.M. Macabrey.

LA VANGUARDIA—(301) 229–1695; 6812 Algonquin Avenue, Bethesda, MD 20817: Xavier Mas.

LAHONTAN VALLEY NEWS—(301) 951–9590; 5500 Park Street, Chevy Chase, MD 20815: David C. Henley.

LE FIGARO—(202) 342–3199; 1228 30th Street, 20007: Jean-Jacques Mevel.

LE MAURICIEN—(301) 424–3884; 1084 Pipestem Place, Potomac, MD 20854: Pamela Glass.

LE MONDE—(301) 986–8606; 6012 Kenndey Drive, Chevy Chase, MD 20815: Laurent Zecchini.

LE SOIR—(202) 333–4119; 1226 28th Street, 20007: Nathalie Mattheiem.

LEGI-SLATE NEWS SERVICE—(202) 898–3022; 777 North Capitol Street, Suite900, 20002: Amy K. Branson, Bill L. Grant, Katherine E. Harris, Sara Hebel, Anna B. Hebner, Stephen J. Norton, Margaret Peterson, Miles A. Pomper, Justin Pritchard, Richard J. Rothacker, David T. Safford, Nancy J. Schwerzleer.Richard Sia.

LLOYD'S LONDON PRESS—(703) 812–8120; P.O. Box 3696, Arlington, VA 22203: Joel A. Glass.

LONDON DAILY TELEGRAPH—(202) 393–5195; 1331 Pennsylvania Avenue, Suite 904, 20004: Hugh Davies, Hugo Gurdon, Penelope Walker.

LONDON EVENING STANDARD—(301) 270–1022; 8 Jefferson Avenue, Takoma Park, MD 20912: E. Lauren Chambliss.

LONDON FINANCIAL TIMES—(202) 289–5474; 1225 I Street, #810, 20005: Gerard Baker, Bruce Clark, Nancy Dunne, Jurek Martin, Nancy S. McCord, Patti Waldmeir.

LONDON GUARDIAN—(202) 223–2486; 1730 Rhode Island Avenue, #502, 20036: Richard Thomas, Martin Walker.

LONDON INDEPENDENT—(202) 467–4460; 1726 M Street, Suite 700, 20036: John Carlin.

LONDON SUNDAY TELEGRAPH—(202) 393–5195; 1331 Pennsylvania Avenue, #904, 20004: Ivo Dawnay, Ambrose Evans-Pritchard.

LONDON TIMES—(202) 347–7659; 1040 National Press Building, 20045: Ian Brodie, Martin A. Fletcher, Tom Rhodes.

LOS ANGELES DAILY JOURNAL—(202) 484–8255; 1128 National Press Building 20045: David F. Pike, Daniel Shaw.

LOS ANGELES TIMES—(202) 293–4650; 1875 I Street, Suite 1100, 20006: James Bornemeier, Ronald Brownstein, Glenn F. Bunting, Edwin Chen, Marlene Cimons, Steve Clark, Richard Cooper, Nina J. Easton, Faye Fiore, D'Jamila S. Fitzgerald, Don Frederick, Sara Fritz, Sam Fulwood III, James R. Gerstenzang, Joel Havemann, Melissa Healy, Drex Heikes, Janet Hook, Robert L. Jackson, Norman Kempster, Marc Lacey, David Lamb, James H. Mann, Tyler Marshall, Gebe Martinez, Thomas McCarthy, Doyle McManus, Stanley Meisler, Alan C. Miller, Jack Nelson, Ronald J. Ostrow, Jonathan Peterson, Art Pine, Paul Richter, James E. Risen, James Robinson, Robert Rosenblatt, Phillip Ruiz, David G. Savage, Richard A. Serrano, Jube Shiver, Jr., Robert Shogan, Elizabeth Shogren, Sheryl Stolberg, Ralph Vartabedian, Warren Vieth, David Willman, Robin Wright.

LOUISVILLE COURIER-JOURNAL—(703) 276–5423; 1000 Wilson Boulevard, 10th Floor, Arlington, VA 22229: Michael H. Brown.

LYNCH NEWS SERVICE—(202) 488–7943; 7516 Marbury Road, Bethesda, MD 20817: David E. Lynch.

MACEDONIA NEWS AGENCY—(202) 388–0355; 2211 R Street, 20008: Lampros Papandoniou.

MAEIL KYUNGJI DAILY—(202) 637–3258; 909 National Press Building, 20045: Dae-Ho Kim.

MAGYAR NEMZET—(301) 986–5516; 4515 Willard Avenue, Chevy Chase, MD 20815: Miklos Blaho.

MAGYAR SZO—(202) 797–6188; 1775 Massachusetts Avenue, #207, 20036: Tibor Purger.

MAINICHI SHIMBUN—(202) 737–2817; 340 National Press Building, 20045: Toshiro Hara, Yoshiaki Ito, Mark Judson, Masato Kishimoto, Shiro Segawa, Akio Takahata, Karen Velguth.

MALAYSIAN NEWS AGENCY—(703) 356–2087; 7700 Tremayne Place, #307, McLean, VA 22102: Salmy M. Hashim.

MARKET NEWS SERVICE—(202) 371–2121; 552 National Press Building, 20045: Steven K. Beckner, Ronald Cordray, Denny Gulino, Joseph E. Plocek, Robert G. Robinson, Jr., Heather Scott, John T. Shaw, David M. Sherrell.

MCCLATCHY NEWSPAPERS—(202) 393–2228; 624 National Press Building, 20045: Les Blumenthal, Muriel Dobbin, Michael Doyle, Mary Johnson-Settles, Lawrence M. O'Rourke, Leo Rennert, James M. Rosen, Herbert A. Sample, David L. Westphal, David L. Whitney.

MCCLENDON NEWS SERVICE—(202) 483–3791; 3133 Connecticut Avenue, Suite 215, 20008: David M. MacDonald, Sarah McClendon.

MEDIA GENERAL NEWS SERVICE—(202) 662–7664; 1214 National Press Building, 20045: John N. Hall, Mark Johnson, Gilbert F. Klein, Robert E. Marlowe, Marsha D. Mercer, Sharon Murray.

MEDILL NEWS SERVICE—(202) 662–1801; 1325 G Street, Suite 730, 20005: Mary Ellen Shearer, Frank Starr.

MIAMI HERALD—(202) 383–6054; 700 National Press Building, 20045: Carol Rosenberg.

MILITARY UPDATE—(703) 830–6863; P.O. Box 1230, Centreville, VA 20122: Thomas R. Philpott.

MILWAUKEE JOURNAL SENTINEL—(202) 662–7290; 940 National Press Building, 20045: Frank A. Aukofer, Craig Gilbert.

MINNEAPOLIS STAR TRIBUNE—(202) 457–5171; 1627 I Street, Suite 800, 20006: Leonor A. Briscoe, Gregory Gordon, Carol B. Hall, Tom Hamburger, Sharon Schmickle.

MONBERG NEWS SERVICE—(202) 546–1350; 123 6th Street, SE, 20003: Helene C. Monberg.

MOSCOW BUSINESS WORLD—(703) 931–4482; 4500 S. Four Mile Run Drive, #213, Arlington, VA 22204: Serge P. Duhanov.

MUNIFACTS NEWS WIRE—(202) 347–4184; 1325 F Street, Suite 900, 20005: Jonathan Nicholson, Dean J. Patterson.

NRC HANDELSBLAD—(202) 363–6944; 4219 Chesapeake Street, 20016: Juurd Eijsvoogel.

NACHRICHTEN FUER AUSSENHANDEL—(202) 662–7415; 412 National Press Building, 20045: Rainer S. Lindberg, Harald Meyer.

NATIONAL MEDIA OF SOUTH AFRICA—(202) 638–0399; 1263 National Press Building, 20045: Holzapfel J. Arnold.

NEUE ZURCHER ZEITUNG—(202) 298–7906; 3007 P Street, 20007: Andreas Cleis.

NEW AMERICAN NEWS SERVICE—(202) 362–8471; 3608 Van Newss Street, 20008: Eileen Shanahan.

NEW DELHI BUSINESS & OBSERVER—(301) 384–1297; 13106 Collingwood Terrace, Silver Spring, MD 20904: Vinod Ghildiyal.

NEW DELHI BUSINESS STANDARD—(202) 833–4505; 1255 New Hampshire Avenue, #713, 20036: Sujatha Shenoy.

NEW DELHI VIEWS AND NEWS AGENCY—(202) 452–1462; 1255 New Hampshire Avenue, Apt. 630, 20036: Ludwina A. Joseph.

NEW ORLEANS TIMES-PICAYUNE—(202) 383–7861; 1101 Connecticut Avenue, Suite 300, 20036: Bruce S. Alpert, John G. McQuaid, Edgar Poe.

NEW YORK DAILY NEWS—(202) 467–6670; 1615 M Street, Suite 720, 20036: Karen Ball, Thomas M. DeFrank, William Goldschlag, Lars-Erik Nelson, Steven Roberts, Richard P. Sisk, Dina White.

NEW YORK POST—(202) 393–1787; 1114 National Press Building, 20045: Karen Foerstel, Thomas Galvin, Deborah Orin, Marilyn Rauber.

NEW YORK TIMES—(202) 862–0310; 1627 I Street, Suite 700, 20006: R.W. Apple, Jr., Von Aulston, Janet Battaile, James Bennet, Richard L. Berke, David Binder, Monica C. Borkowski, Jane B. Bornemeier, Elizabeth A. Boswell, Jeanne K. Brennan, Sarah S. Chung, Francis X. Clines, Adam Clymer, John H. Cushman, Jr., Jason DeParle, Karen E. DeWitt, Maureen Dowd, Steven Erlanger, Jane F. Fritsch, Jeff Gerth, Jerry Gray, Kevin M. Gray, Linda J. Greenhouse, Robert D. Hershey, Jr., Steven Holmes, Ferne M. Horner, Michael Janofsky, David Johnston, Gregory W. Jordan, Stephen Labaton, Warren E. Leary, Michael Lewis, Neil A. Lewis, Sean M. Loughlin, Andrew McDonald, Clifton E. Meadows, Alison Mitchell, Irvin D. Molotsky, Steven L. Myers, Robert L. Pear, Todd S. Purdum, David E. Rosenbaum, William Safire, David E. Sanger, Eric Schmitt, Elaine Sciolino, Katharine Q. Seelye, Philip Shenon, Ronald Skarzenski, Richard W. Stevenson, David G. Stout, Michael G. Taub, Matthew L. Wald, Michael Wines.

NEW YORK TIMES REGIONAL NEWSPAPERS—(202) 862–0381; 1627 I Street, Suite 700, 20006: Carl Hulse, Marlo Roache.

NEWHOUSE NEWS SERVICE—(202) 463–8777; 1101 Connecticut Avenue, Suite 300, 20036: David E. Anderson, Adelle Banks, Miles R. Benson, R. Michael Brumas, Constance Casey, Robert Cohen, Brett Davis, Robert Gavin, Joseph T. Hallinan, Michael J. Hardy, Sam L. Hodges, Deborah Howell, Sarah M. Kellogg, Terence J. Kivlan, Kim A. Lawton, Brett Lieberman, Julia Lieblich, Michael J. Magner, JoAnn Moriarty, Jim Nesbitt, J. Scott Orr, Michael J. Paquette, Ira Rifkin, Delia M. Rios, Jonathan Tilove, Brent Walth, David B. Wood.

NEWPORT NEWS DAILY PRESS—(202) 824–8224; 1615 L Street, Suite 300, 20036: Robert J. Kemper.

NEWS GROUP PUBLICATIONS—(301) 762–5610; 625 Smallwood Road, Rockville, MD 20850: Norma Langley.

NEWSDAY—(202) 626–8466; 1730 Pennsylvania Avenue, Suite 850, 20006: Susan Benkelman, Marie Cocco, William G. Douglas, Kenneth Fireman, Roy W. Gutman, Martin Kasindorf, Glenn Kessler, Earl Lane, James P. Pinkerton, Elaine S. Povich, Patrick J. Sloyan, James S. Toedtman.

NEWSPAPER ENTERPRISE ASSOCIATION—(301) 365–1999; 1899 L Street, Suite 1200, 20005: Angela E. Lauria, Robert J. Wagman.

NIKKEI—(202) 393–1388; 636 National Press Building, 20045: Christina Bilski, Ryosuke Harada, Stephen R. Keefe, Hirotsugu Koike, Tetsu Machida, Akihiko Miyamoto, Masaaki Muramatsu, Hitoshi Omae, Yasuhiko Ota, Manami Terashima.

NISHI-NIPPON SHIMBUN—(202) 393–5812; 1226 National Press Building, 20045: Tamio Shibuta.

NORTHWEST NEWSPAPERS—(202) 546–2547; 316 3rd Street, NE, 20002: Lawrence A. Swisher.

NORWEGIAN NEWS AGENCY—(301) 229–4500; 5315 Westpath Way, Bethesda, MD 20816: Helge Ogrim.

NOTIMEX MEXICAN NEWS AGENCY—(202) 347–5227; 425 National Press Building, 20045: Ignacio Basauri, Horacio C. Chavez Lopez, Jesus P. Esquivel, Jose Lopez.

O ESTADO DE S. PAULO—(202) 682–3752; 1225 I Street, Suite 810, 20005: Paulo Sotero.

OIL DAILY—(202) 662–0710; 1401 New York Avenue, Suite 500, 20005: David Abramson, Chris Baltimore, Alan Kovski, Kimberley A. Music.

OLIPHANT NEWS SERVICE—(202) 298–7226; P.O. Box 9808, Friendship Station, 20016: Cortright W. Oliphant, John L. Oliphant, Robert C. Oliphant.

OMAHA WORLD-HERALD—(202) 662–7270; 841 National Press Building, 20045: David C. Beeder.

ORANGE COUNTY REGISTER—(202) 628–6381; 1295 National Press Building, 20045: Dena Bunis, Dina ElBoghdady.

OREGONIAN—(202) 383–7800; 1101 Connecticut Avenue, Suite 300, 20036: James O. Barnett.

ORLANDO SENTINEL—(202) 824–8299; 1325 G Street, Suite 200, 20005: Sean M. Holton, Tamara Lytle.

OTTAWAY NEWS SERVICE—(202) 828–3390; 1025 Connecticut Avenue, Suite 310, 20036: Marilyn Bailey, Polly B. Elliott, Robb Frederick, Wendy P. Jones, Judith M. Mathewson, Kevin P. McCaney, Michael Mello, William F. Schmick, Mark Wigfield, Winston S. Wood.

PAKISTAN DAILY JANG & NEWS—(202) 643–1668; 12776 Captains Cove, Woodbridge, VA 22192: S.H.Nayyar Zaidi.

PALM BEACH POST—(202) 887–8340; 2000 Pennsylvania Avenue, 20006: Laurence M. Lipman.

PHILADELPHIA DAILY NEWS—(202) 383–6062; 700 National Press Building, 20045: Ernest S. Grady.

PHILADELPHIA INQUIRER—(202) 383–6051; 700 National Press Building, 20045: Jodi A. Enda, Steven L. Goldstein.

PHILLIPS NEWS SERVICE—(202) 783–2790; 1333 F Street, Suite 400, 20004: Peter D. Pichaske.

PITTSBURGH POST-GAZETTE/TOLEDO BLADE—(202) 662–7070; 955 National Press Building, 20045: Patricia K. Griffith, Judy Packer-Tursman, Jack Torry, Michael Woods.

PLATT'S OILGRAM NEWS—(202) 383–2250; 1200 G Street, Suite 1100, 20005: Gerald Karey, Maureen S. Lorenzetti.

POLISH PRESS AGENCY—(202) 879–6780; 821 National Press Building, 20045: Witold T. Zalewski.

PORTLAND PRESS HERALD—(202) 488–1119; 2716 North Wyoming Street, Arlington, VA 22213: Stephen W. Campbell.

PRESS TRUST OF INDIA—(301) 951–8657; 4450 South Park Avenue, #1719, Chevy Chase, MD 20815: T.V. Parasuram.

PROVIDENCE JOURNAL-BULLETIN—(202) 783–0833; 400 North Capitol Street, Suite 890, 20001: John E. Mulligan, Philip Terzian.

PUSAN DAILY NEWS—(202) 347–8816; 905 National Press Building, 20045: Jong H. Kim.

RIA NOVOSTI—(301) 657–8256; 4701 Willard Avenue, #410, Chevy Chase, MD 20815: Arkadiy Orlov.

REUTERS—(202) 898–8300; 1333 H Street, Suite 410, 20005: Charles J. Abbott, Charles Aldinger, Victoria L. Allen, Peter Bate, Melissa R. Bland, Caren Bohan, Karen J. Cohen, Leila M. Corcoran, Susan J. Cornwell, James Dalgleish, Timothy H. Dobbyn, Will Dunham, Audrey A. Earnhart, Alan Elsner, Edward Evans, Roger O. Fillion, Jacqueline Frank, Richard Garcia, Carol A. Giacomo, Gene Gibbons, Steven H. Ginsburg, Peter Golkin, Barbara Hagenbaugh, Richard Hoskins, Stacey A. Joyce, Stephen A. Jukes, Joanne Kelley, Joanne Kenen, Suzanne Kirchhoff, David A. Lawsky, Greg McCune, Laurence McQuillan, Richard M. Miller, Arshad A. Mohammed, Joseph Montoya, Barbara Novovitch, Sonali J. Paul, Aaron Pressman, Peter A. Ramjug, Robert R. Ramos, Lisa Richwine, Timothy F. Ryan, William F. Scally, Cameron Shaw, Donna M. Smith, Glenn F. Somerville, Vicky J. Stamas, David Storey, Peter A. Szekely, James Vicini, Nancy H. Waitz, Mark Weinraub, David A. Wiessler, Deborah Zabareko, Tabassum Zakaria.

RHEINISCHE POST—(301) 251–2367; 1979 Lancashire Drive, Potomac, MD 20854: Peter Rzeznitzeck.

RICHMOND TIMES-DISPATCH—(202) 662–7669; 1214 National Press Building, 20045: Peter Hardin, Charles R. McDowell.

ROLL CALL REPORT SYNDICATE—(202) 737–1888; 1257–B National Press Building, 20045: Cora R. Hoopes, David K. Martin, Richard G. Thomas.

SABAH—(703) 764–1443; 5432 Midship Court, Burke, VA 22015: Savas Suzal.

SAN ANTONIO EXPRESS-NEWS—(202) 943–9237; 1701 Pennsylvania Avenue, #610, 20006: Gary R. Martin.

SAN FRANCISCO CHRONICLE—(202) 737–7100; 1085 National Press Building, 20045: Louis Freedberg, Julia R. House, Carolyn Lochhead, Marc Sandalow.

SAN FRANCISCO EXAMINER—(202) 298–6920; 1701 Pennsylvania Avenue, Suite 610, 20006: Christopher J. Matthews.

SANKEI SHIMBUN—(202) 347–2015; 330 National Press Building, 20045: Yukio Kashiyama, Yoshihisa Komori, Masahiro Nakata, B. Scott Stewart, Hiroshi Yuasa.

SAUDI GAZETTE—(202) 347–6469; 1145 National Press Building, 20045: Barbara Ferguson, Tim Kennedy.

SAUDI PRESS AGENCY—(202) 861–0324; 1155 15th Street, Suite 1111, 20005: Naila Al-Sowayel, Mustafa A. Bashir, Alfred T. Canahuate, Azeddine Labriny, Vicki L. Reeve, Melanie G. Tatum.

SCHLEIN NEWS BUREAU—(202) 544–5893; 308 East Capitol Street, Apt. 9, 20003: Alan M. Schlein.

SCIENCE AND TECHNOLOGY DAILY—(703) 941–4946; 4507 Highland Green Court, Alexandria, VA 22312: Chenguang Bian.

SCRIPPS HOWARD NEWS SERVICE—(202) 408–1484; 1090 Vermont Avenue, Suite 10,000, 20005: Roger Anderson, Curtis Lee Bowman, John Brinkley, James W. Brosnan, Peter M. Copeland, Mary Deibel, Robert Friedman, Lance C. Gay, Laurel E. Hackett, Nathaniel Harari, Thomas K. Hargrove, Michael Hedges, Lisa Hoffman, Jeffrey E. Keeton, John S. Lang, Leonard E. Larsen, John H. Lindsay, Joan A. Lowy, Karen MacPherson, Jennifer Maddox, Ann C. McFeatters, Dale B. McFeatters, Jeff Miller, David Nielsen, Jim O'Connell, Thomas O'Toole, Henry Payne, Richard Powelson, Pamela Reeves, Martin Schram, Gerard Shields, Nicholas Smith, Bill Straub, Dan K. Thomasson, Alan R. Thompson, Marvin L. West.

SEATTLE POST-INTELLIGENCER—(202) 943–9232; 1701 Pennsylvania Avenue, 20006: Christopher Hanson, David Horsey.

SEATTLE TIMES—(202) 546–4700; 245 2nd Street, NE, 20002–5761: James V. Grimaldi, Daniel Westneat.

SEGYE TIMES—(202) 637–0587; 924 National Press Building, 20045: Sang I. Shin.

SEKAI NIPPO—(202) 879–6786; 924 National Press Building, 20045: Seisaku Morita, Yuji Yokoyama.

SEOUL SHINMUN DAILY—(202) 393–4061; 1126 National Press Building, 20045: Jae-Young Kim, Ra Yoondho.

SHANGHAI WEN HUI BAO—(703) 979–5276; 1600 South Eads Street, #1013N, Arlington, VA 22202: Yaodong Wang, Wang Yaodong, Zhu Xinafu.

SHEARER AND GLEN NEWS ENTERPRISE—(202) 462–6070; P.O. Box 9467, 20016: Cody P. Shearer, Sergio S. Zufferey.

SHEPARD NEWS FEATURES—(703) 941–8946; 4805 Manion Street, Annandale, VA 22003: Robert Shepard.

SIDNEY MORNING HERALD—(202) 737–6360; 1331 Pennsylvania Avenue, #904, 20008: Jennifer A. Hewett.

SINGAPORE BUSINESS TIMES—(301) 654–2389; 4701 Willard Avenue, Suite 1024, 20815: Leon T. Hadar.

SLOVAK NEWS AGENCY—(202) 686–4710; 4501 Connecticut Avenue, #713, 20008: Martin Dugas, Otakar Korinek.

SMALL NEWSPAPER GROUP—(202) 662–7123; 1183 National Press Building, 20045: Edward R. Felker, Patrick Howe.

SOUTH AFRICA TIMES MEDIA—(301) 432–2878; 585 S. Main Street, Keedysville, MD 21756: Simon Barber.

SOUTH CHINA MORNING POST—(202) 332–5731; 1623 Lanier Place, Suite 202, 20009: Simon L. Beck.

SOUTHAM NEWS—(202) 662–7225; 986 National Press Building, 20045–2199: Julian Beltrame.

SPRINGER FOREIGN NEWS SERVICE—(202) 342–3103; 4830 Brandywine Street, 20016: Frauke Beyer, Cornel Faltin.

ST. LOUIS POST-DISPATCH—(202) 298–6880; 1701 Pennsylvania Avenue, 20006: Philip M. Dine, Aloysia C. Hamalainen, William Lambrecht, Timothy J. Poor, Jon M. Sawyer.

ST. PAUL PIONEER PRESS/KR—(202) 383–6042; 700 National Press Building, 20045: William S. Salisbury.

ST. PETERSBURG TIMES—(202) 463–0574; 1100 Connecticut Avenue, Suite 1300, 20045: Ceci Connolly, David Dahl, Ellen Debenport, Katherine Gazella, Jack R. Payton.

STATES NEWS SERVICE—(202) 628–3100; 1333 F Street, Suite 400, 20004: John M. Biers, Jennifer A. Brooks, Elizabeth Bryant, Sumana Chatterjee, Susanna Duff, Barbara Ferry, Mark Gimein, Paul J. Kane, Evan Katz, Laura A. Magg, Pamela Moyer, David Phinney, Matthew F. Pottinger, Dave Priddy, Leland Schwartz, Elissa C. Silverman, Phil Stewart, A. B. Stoddard, Michael P. Tobin, Ethan S. Wallison, Mike Zapler.

STRAITS TIMES—(202) 622–0574; 916 National Press Building, 20045: Siew Hua Lee.

STUTTGARTER ZEITUNG—(301) 983–0735; 11204 Powder Horn Drive, Potomac, MD 20854: Jurgen Koar.

SUARA PEMBARUAN—(301) 881–8173; 4806 Ertter Drive, Rockville, MD 20852–2202: Albert P. Kuhon.

SUEDDEUTSCHE ZEITUNG—(202) 342–3103; 4830 Brandywine Street, NW, 20016: Kurt Kister, Stefan Kornelius.

SVENSKA DAGBLADET—(202) 362–8253; 3601 Connecticut Avenue, #622, 20008: Karin Henriksson.

TAGES ANZEIGER—(202) 833–8290; 3147 Tennyson Place, 20015: Thomas G. Ruest.

TAGESZEITUNG—(202) 986–5042; 1915 Kalorama Road, 20009: Peter Tautfest.

TAIPEI CENTRAL DAILY NEWS—(301) 762–5232; 1 Lawngate Court, Potomac, MD 20854: Brice Wang.

TAIPEI COMMERCIAL TIMES—(703) 573–4376; 3420 Annandale Road, Falls Church, VA 22042: Louise R. Costich.

TAIPEI ECONOMIC DAILY—(202) 737–6426; 1099 National Press Building, 20045: Marco C. Liu.

TAIPEI LIBERTY TIMES—(301) 279–0917; 14431 Pebble Hill Lane, North Potomac, MD 20878: Paul Tsai.

TAIPEI UNITED DAILY NEWS—(202) 737–6426; 1099 National Press Building, 20045: James C. Wang.

TAMPA TRIBUNE—(202) 662–7673; 1214 National Press Building, 20045: Philip L. Willon.

THOMSON NEWSPAPERS—(202) 628–2157; 1331 Pennsylvania Avenue, #524, 20004: Virginia G. Barazia, Greg Bassett, Mario Christaldi, Joseph R. Duffus, Harry B. Stoffer, Jr., Robert R. Vitale, Randy Wynn.

TIMES OF INDIA—(202) 463–1301; 1301 20th Street, #314, 20036: Ramesh Chandran.

TOKYO-CHUNICHI SHIMBUN—(202) 783–9479; 1230 National Press Club, 20045: Jennifer A. Gerdts, Miyuki Kurata, Moriyoshi Sase, Ryoji Tachio, Anne K. Usher.

TORONTO GLOBE AND MAIL—(202) 662–7166; 1331 Pennsylvania Avenue, Suite 524, 20004: Drew Fagan, Graham Fraser.

TORONTO STAR—(202) 662–7390; 982 National Press Building, 20045: Carol Goar, Kathleen Kenna.

TORONTO SUN—(703) 876–0594; 8202 Excalibur Court, Annandale, VA 22003: Patrick Harden.

TRAVEL MANAGEMENT DAILY—(202) 467–8085; 1155 15th Street, Suite 510, 20005: Stephanie Kang, Michael Pina, Bill Poling, John P. Seeley.

TRIBUNE DE GENEVE—(202) 237–5416; 3743 Appleton Street, 20016: Ruetschi Pierre.

TRUD—(301) 656–3744; 4620 North Park Avenue, Suite 501W, Chevy Chase, MD 20815: Vissarion I. Sisnev.

TUFTY NEWS SERVICE—(202) 347–8998; 2107 National Press Building, 20045: Harold G. Tufty.

TULSA WORLD—(703) 484–1424; 1417 North Inglewood Street, Arlington, VA 22205: Jim Myers.

TURKISH DAILY—(301) 571–5204; 4938 Hampden Lane, Suite 238, Bethesda, MD 20814: Ugur Akinci.

TURKIYE DAILY—(202) 737–7800; 495 National Press Building, 20045: Hasan M. Hazar.

U.S.-ASIAN NEWS SERVICE—(202) 638–1117; 1053 National Press Building, 20045: Julia M. Choi, Julie Moon.

USA TODAY—(703) 276–3622; 1000 Wilson Boulevard, Arlington, VA 22229: Fred Anklam, Jr., Beth Belton, Beth M. Belton, Richard Benedetto, Thomas Curley, Robert M. Davis, Michael P. Dodd, Peter Eisler, Haya El Nasser, Gary E. Fields, Gwen Flanders, Ed Foster-Simeon, Susan Gvozdas, Margaret W. Hall, Barbara E. Hansen, Judith B. Hasson, James R. Healey, Jacqueline M. Henderson, Paul M. Hoversten, Kevin Johnson, Linda M. Kanamine, Lee M. Katz, Judith C. Keen, Jack Kelley, James Kim, Steven Komarow, Jill D. Lawrence, Paul W. Leavitt, Jessica Lee, Douglas A. Levy, Matthew Mak, Stephen B. Marshall, Anthony E. Mauro, Andrea L. Mays, Mark J. Memmott, Johanna Neuman, Jayne O'Donnell, Hal O'Ritter, Paul Overberg, Susan L. Page, Mark L. Pearson, Keeby Pendleton, Carolyn Pesce, Carl A. Pisano, Evelyn T. Powers, Maria Puente, Patrick R. Richards, Hal Ritter, John Ritter, Donna Rosato, Lori Sharn, John M. Siniff, Barbara Slavin, Tom Squitieri, Andrea Stone, Shannon L. Tangonan, Rae J. Tyson, Juan J. Walte, William M. Welch, Anne Willette, Betty A. Williams, Richard J. Wolf, Al Young, Michael J. Zuckerman.

UNITED FEATURES SYNDICATE—(301) 262–6699; 12808 Sutters Lane, Bowie, MD 20720: Lew Sichelman.

UNITED NEWS OF INDIA—(703) 486–2696; 1600 South Eads Street, Apt. #1126N, Arlington, VA 22202: C.K. Arora.

UNITED PRESS INTERNATIONAL—(202) 898–8100; 1510 H Street, Suite 800, 20005: Sid Balman, Jr., Jorge A. Banales, Paul Basken, Jeffrey P. Bater, Kenneth Bazinet, Tobin C. Beck, Raphael Calis, Margaret E. Coker, David E. Hubler, Susan C. Milius, Eric Nordwall, June R. Preston, Larry Schuster, Kathleen C. Silvassy, Timothy E. Spence, Justin J. Supon, Helen Thomas.

UNITED STATES PRESS—(301) 229–4063; 5312 Blackistone Road, Bethesda, MD 20816: Frank Van der Linden.

UNIVERSAL PRESS SYNDICATE—(202) 319–1070; 1619 Massachusetts Avenue, 20036: Hedrick L. Smith.

VARIETY DAILY—(703) 448–0510; 1483 Chain Bridge Road, Suite 202, McLean, VA 22101: Christopher S. Stern.

VIETNAM NEWS AGENCY—(202) 530–0854; 2130 P Street, Suite 604, 20037: Nguyen Minh, Nghi Vis, Pham Vy.

VIRGINIAN-PILOT—(703) 913–9872; 7802 Glenister Drive, Springfield, VA 22152: Dale Eisman.

WALL STREET JOURNAL—(202) 862–9200; 1025 Connecticut Avenue, Suite 800, 20036: Jill Abramson, Matthew K. Benjamin, Alejandro Bodipo-Memba, Glenn Burkins, Jackie Calmes, Mary L. Carnevale, Helene Cooper, Joe Davidson, Robert Davis, Christina Duff, Edward H. Felsenthal, John J. Fialka, Michael K. Frisby, Chris J. Georges, Paul Gigot, Robert Greenberger, Bryan Gruley, John J. Harwood, Greg A. Hitt, Carol J. Horner, Albert R. Hunt, Bruce Ingersoll, Albert R. Karr, Robert Keatley, June Kronholz, Philip A. Kuntz, Sarah McBride, Laurie McGinley, Alan S. Murray, Timothy R. Noah, Asra Q. Nomani, Henry Oden, Vicki L. Parker, James M. Perry, Michael M. Phillips, Thomas E. Ricks, Carla A. Robbins, David E. Rogers, Amy J. Schatz, Jacob M. Schlesinger, Sharon L. Schmid, Richard B. Schmitt, Gerald F. Seib, Ronald G. Shafer, Rochelle Sharpe, Glenn R. Simpson, Hilary Stout, Jeffrey Taylor, David Wessel, John R. Wilke, Bernard Wysocki, Jr., Alan M. Yonan.

WASHINGTON BUREAU NEWS—(202) 393–3003; 1325 18th Street, Suite 302, 20036: Kenneth M. Scheibel.

WASHINGTON MERRY-G0–ROUND—(202) 944–3030; 1200 Eton Court, Suite 300, 20007: George Clifford, Aaron Karp.

WASHINGTON POST—(202) 334–6000; 1150 15th Street, 20071: Michael Abramowitz, Nathan Abse, Joel Achenbach, Henry Allen, Robert L. Asher, Stuart C. Auerbach, Charles R. Babcock, Donald P. Baker, Peter Baker, Daniel J. Balz, Charles Barbington, Gary S. Barr, Peter Behr, John M. Berry, Joan Biskupic, Laura Blumenfeld, Paul Blustein, Nora Boustany, William Branigin, David S. Broder, David M. Brown, Peter Carlson, John Carmody, Mike Causey, Clay Chandler, Rajiv Chandrasekaran, Patricia Cohen, Richard Cohen, Elizabeth Corcoran, Albert R. Crenshaw, Kathleen Day, Ann Devroy, Helen Dewar, Michael S. Dobbs, Thomas B. Edsall, Judith Evans, Anthony Faiola, Paul Farhi, Stephen Fehr, Marc Fisher, Michael Fletcher, Brett D. Fromson, Ann E. Gerhart, Robin Givhan, Jeffrey D. Glasser, Amy Goldstein, John M. Goshko, Bradley L. Graham, Meg Greenfield, Anne Groer, Lloyd B. Grove, Guy Gugliotta, Maryann Haggerty, Martha A. Hamilton, Blaine Harden, John F. Harris, Judith Havemann, Paul J. Hendrickson, Fred Hiatt, David Hilzenrath, Robert G. Kaiser, Al Kamen, Brian Kelly, Colbert King, Jerry Knight, Serge F. Kovaleski, Sharon LaFraniere, George Lardner, Richard Leiby, Thomas W. Lippman, Vernon F. Loeb, David Maraniss, Ruth Marcus, Caroline F. Mayer, William H. McAllister, Philip A. McCombs, Mary McGrory, Robert H. Melton, Kevin E. Merida, Peter Milius, Mike Mills, John D. Mintz, Brian Mooar, Dan Morgan, Richard Morin, Susan Okie, David B. Ottaway, Don Phillips, Eric S. Pianin, Walter Pincus, Dana Priest, Rudolph A. Pyatt, Jr., Spencer Rich, Ken Ringle, Roxanne Roberts, Barbara J. Saffir, Rene Sanchez, Kathy Sawyer, Susan Schmidt, John Schwartz, Maralee Schwartz, Patricia Shakow, Michelle Singletary, Cindy Skrzycki, R. Jeffrey Smith, Sally Squires, Doug Struck, Curt Suplee, Frank Swoboda, Richard Tapscott, Pierre G. Thomas, Sandra Torry, Abigail Trafford, Jacqueline Trescott, Stephen M. Twomey, David A. Vise, Barbara Vobejda, David J. VonDrehle, Sharon Walsh, Joby Warrick, Alona Wartofsky, Linton Weeks, Rick Weiss, Michael Weisskopf, Vanessa D. Williams, Yolanda Woodlee, Yolanda M. Woodlee, Bob Woodward, John E. Yang.

WASHINGTON TELECOMMUNICATIONS—(703) 836–2922; P.O. Box 3067, Alexandria, VA 22302: Gordon E. White.

WASHINGTON TIMES—(202) 636–3000; 3600 New York Avenue, NE, 20002: Doug Abrahms, Theodore J. Agres, George H. Archibald, Ben Barber, Paul Bedard, Brian Blomquist, Gaedig Bonabesse, Paige Bowers, Rex L. Bowman, Allen Bradford, Carleton R. Bryant, Thomas H. Carter, Kevin Chaffee, Gus Constantine, Francis B. Coombs, Jr., Joseph Curl, Mensah Dean, Julia Duin, Susan Ferrechio, Ann Geracimos, William D. Gertz, Ralph Z. Hallow, Kenneth W. Hanner, Jennifer Harper, Patrice S. Hill, Carol Innerst, David Jones, Peter Kaplan, Refet Kaplan, Laurie A. Kellman, Alan Kline, Dawn Kopecki, Donald Lambro, Ruth I. Larson, Tod M. Lindberg, Anne E. Marriott, Toni L. Marshall, John L. McCaslin, John Mercurio, Vincent S. Morris, Frank J. Murray, Gregory T. Pierce, Wesley Pruden, Viki Reath, Nancy E. Roman, David Sands, Rowan Scarborough, Sean P. Scully, Jerry Seper, Josette Shiner, Martin Sieff, Warren P. Strobel, Cheryl Wetzstein, Larry A. Witham, Lorraine A. Woellert.

WATERTOWN DAILY TIMES—(202) 662–7085; 1001 National Press Building, 20045: Alan S. Emory.

WESTDEUTSCHE ALLGEMEINE—(301) 469–8933; 8204 Hamilton Spring Court, Bethesda, MD 20817: Uwe Knupfer.

WINSTON-SALEM JOURNAL—(202) 662–7672; 1214 National Press Building, 20045: John E. Hoeffel.

WISCONSIN STATE JOURNAL—(202) 783–2633; 1099 National Press Building, 20045: Stephen J. Siegel.

WORLD JOURNAL—(202) 737–6426; 1121 National Press Building, 20045: Betty P. Lin.

XINHUA NEWS AGENCY—(703) 875–0082; 1740 North 14th Street, #305, Arlington, VA 22209: Xiao Chenglin, Songjiu Fan, Zhai Jingsheng, Fu Quansheng, Xiao Tang, Guoqiang Wei, Zhou Xisheng, Bingzhong Yuan, Wang Zhenhua.

YOMIURI SHIMBUN—(202) 783–0363; 802 National Press Building, 20045: Koichi Akaza, Lani C. Cossette, Naomichi Fujimoto, Masashi Iiyama, Toshiro Ikemura, Toru Kunimatsu, Debra Lau, Jeremy L. Milk, Saiko Nozaki, Ryuichi Otsuka, Thea D. Rozman.

YONHAP NEWS AGENCY—(202) 783–5539; 1299 National Press Building, 20045: Jun Heesup.

YOUTH DAILY NEWS—(301) 983–2368; 8812 Tuckerman Lane, Potomac, MD 20854: Ning Kiang.

ZAMAN—(703) 960–2604; 6036 Richmond Highway, #506, Alexandria, VA 22303: Ali Aslan.

ZEITUNGSRING—(202) 338–6583; 3019 Cambridge Place, 20007: Marlene Manthey.

ZYCIE WARSZAWY—(202) 393–3511; 840 National Press Building, 20045: Tomasz Wroblewski,

PRESS PHOTOGRAPHERS' GALLERY

The Capitol, Room S–317, 224–6548

Superintendent.—Maurie Johnson.
Assistant Superintendent.—Jeff Kent.
Staff Assistant.—Kim M. Magruder.

STANDING COMMITTEE OF PRESS PHOTOGRAPHERS

Tim Dillon, *Chairman*
Dennis Brack, *Secretary-Treasurer*
Steve Crowley
Charles W. Harrity
Joe Marquette
Win McNamee

RULES GOVERNING GALLERY

1. (a) Administration of the Press Photographers' Gallery is vested in a Standing Committee of Press Photographers consisting of six persons elected by accredited members of the Gallery. The Committee shall be composed of one member each from Associated Press Photos, magazine media, and local newspapers and three at-large members. At large members may be, but need not be, selected from a media otherwise represented on the Committee.

(b) The term of office of a member of the Committee elected as the Associated Press Photos member, the local newspapers member and one of the at large members shall expire on the day of the election held in the first odd-numbered year following the year in which the member was elected, and the term of office of a member of the Committee elected as the magazine media member and the remaining two at large members shall expire on the day of the election held in the first even-numbered year following the year in which the member was elected. Whenever two at large seats are up for election the two candidates with the highest number of votes in that category shall be elected. A member elected to fill a vacancy occurring prior to the expiration of a term shall serve for only the unexpired portion of such term.

(c) Elections shall be held as early as practicable in each year, and in no case later than March 31. A vacancy in the membership of the Committee occurring prior to the expiration of a term shall be filled by a special election called for that purpose by the Committee.

(d) The Standing Committee of the Press Photographers' Gallery shall propose no change or changes in these rules except upon petition in writing signed by not less than 25 accredited members of the gallery.

2. Persons desiring admission to the Press Photographers' Gallery of the Senate shall make application in accordance with Rule 33 of the Senate, which rule shall be interpreted and administered by the Standing Committee of Press Photographers subject to the review andapproval of the Senate Committee on Rules and Administration.

3. The Standing Committee of Press photographers shall limit membership in the photographers' gallery to bona fide news photographers of repute in their profession and Headsof Photographic Bureaus under such rules as the Standing Committee of Press Photographers shall prescribe.

4. Provided, however, that the Standing Committee of Press Photographers shall admit to the gallery no person who does not establish to the satisfaction of the Committee all of thefollowing:

(a) That any member is not engaged in paid publicity or promotion work or in prosecuting any claim before Congress or before any department of the Government, and will not become so engaged while a member of the gallery.

(b) That he or she is not engaged in any lobbying activity and will not become so engaged while a member of the gallery.

The above rules have been approved by the Committee on Rules and Administration.

NEWT, GINGRICH,
Speaker, House of Representatives
JOHN WARNER,
Chairman, Senate Committee on Rules and Administration.

MEMBERS ENTITLED FOR ADMISSION

PRESS PHOTOGRAPHERS' GALLERY

Abraham, Mark: Freelance
Ach, Michael: Newsday
Ake, J. David: Reuters News Pictures
Alers, Paul: Freelance
Allen, John: Washington Post
Alpert, Brian: Keystone Press Agency
Andrews, Nancy: Washington Post
Applewhite, J. Scott: Associated Press Photos
Arbogast, Charles: Associated Press Photos
Archambault, Charles: U.S. News & World Report
Arias, Juana: Washington Post
Ashe, James: Time Magazine
Ashley, Douglas: Suburban Communications Corp.
Atlan, Jean-Louis: Freelance
Attlee, Tracey: Freelance
Aubry, Timothy: Reuters News Pictures
Ballard, Karen: Washington Times
Barouh, Stan: Freelance
Barrett, Stephen: Freelance
Beals, Herman: Reuters News Pictures
Beiser, H. Darr: USA/Today
Bentley, PF: Time Magazine
Bereswill, Paul: Newsday
Berg, Lisa: Freelance
Biber, Mehmet: Hurriyet
Biddle, Susan: Washington Post
Binks, Porter: USA/Today
Blass, Eileen: USA/Today
Bloom, Richard: National Journal
Bochatey, Terry: Reuters News Pictures
Borea, Roberto: Associated Press Photos
Borst, Charles: Knight-Ridder Tribune News Service
Boston, Bernard: Freelance
Bouchard, Renee: Freelance
Bowe, Christy: McClendon News Service
Bower, Carl: Freelance
Brack, William: Black Star
Branch-Price, Brian: Wilmington News Journal
Brantley, James: Washington Times
Brown, Robert: Richmond Times Dispatch
Brown, Stephen: Freelance
Burgess, Bob: Associated Press
Burke, William: Impact Visuals
Burnett, David: Contact Press Images
Burns, David: Photo Trends, Inc.
Cameron, Gary: Reuters News Pictures
Cedeno, Ken: Freelance
Clark, Carlton: Legal Times
Clement, Richard: Reuters News Pictures
Cobb, Jodi: National Geographic
Cohen, Marshall: Jennings Publications
Colburn, James: Photoreporters, Inc.
Cook, Dennis: Associated Press Photos
Cooke, Ken: Freelance
Cooper, Karin: Associated Press
Cornell, John: Newsday
Cox, Ernest: Chicago Tribune
Craig, Cameron: Freelance
Crandall, Rob: Freelance
Crowley, Stephen: New York Times
Curtiss, Cathaleen: Washington Times
Cutts, Peter: Freelance
Daugherty, Robert: Associated Press Photos
Davidson, Barbara: Washington Times
Davies, Phillip: Newsday
Davis, Bill: Newsday
DeLort, Jean Guy: Fairchild Publications
Deslich, Steve: Thomson Newspapers
Deutsch, Robert: USA/Today
Devadas, Rajan: Front Line
Diggs, Brian: Associated Press
Dillon, Timothy: USA/Today
Dodge, Thomas: Farm Journal Publishing, Inc.
Dombroski, Joe: Newsday
Dooley, James: Newsday
Downing, Lawrence: Newsweek
Durand, Enrique: Reuters News Pictures
Edmonds, Ronald: Associated Press Photos
Eisele, John: National Journal
Elfers, Steve: Army Times
Ellis, Richard: Sygma
Faram, Mark: Army Times
Ferrell, Scott: Congressional Quarterly
Fetters, Paul: Matrix International
Ficara, John: Newsweek
Fiedler, James: U.S. News & World Report
Florescu, Viorel: Newsday
Fournier, Frank: Contact Press Images
Foy, Mary Lou: Washington Post
Franklin, Ross: Washington Times
Frazza, Luke: Agence France-Presse
Freed, Leonard: Magnum Photos
Freeland, Erik: Freelance
Freeman, Melanie: Christian Science Monitor
Fremson, Ruth: Associated Press Photos
Friar, Jerome: Impact Visuals
Fusco, Paul: Magnum Photos
Gainer, Dennis: USA/Today
Gaines, Julia: Newsday
Garcia, Mannie: Freelance

MEMBERS ENTITLED FOR ADMISSION, PRESS PHOTOGRAPHERS' GALLERY—Continued

Garofalo, John Cleveland: Freelance
Geissinger, Michael A.: Freelance
Gibson, J. Greg: Associated Press Photos
Gilbert, Bruce: Newsday
Gilbert, Kevin: Washington Times
Gilbert, Patrice: Legal Times
Giroux, Robert: Freelance
Glinn, Burton: Magnum Photos
Godfrey, Mark: Freelance
Golon, Maryanne: US News & World Report
Goodrich, Daniel: Newsday
Goulait, Bert: Washington Times
Graham, Douglas: Congressional Quarterly
Grieser, Robert: Los Angeles Times
Griffiths, Philip: Magnum Photos
Guzy, Carol: Washington Post
Halasy, Don: New York Post
Halstead, Dirck: Time Magazine
Hamburg, Harry: New York Daily News
Hanes, Frank: Chicago Tribune
Harari, Nathaniel: Scripps Howard News Service
Harbison, Robert: Christian Science Monitor
Harrington, John: World & I
Harrity, Charles: U.S. News & World Report
Hartmann, Erich: Magnum Photos
Harvey, David: Magnum Photos
Hazen, Pam: Hill, The
Heikes, Darryl: Freelance
Heimsath, Peter: Photo Associate News Service
Heinen, Kenneth: Freelance
Helber, Stephen: Associated Press Photos
Herndon, Craig: Washington Post
Hershorn, Gary: Reuters News Pictures
Holden, Peter: World & I
Horan, Tom: Sygma
Hosefros, Paul: New York Times
Housewerth, Jan: Washington Times
Iuvone, Mary: Asbury Park Press
Jacobsen, Don: Newsday
Jaffe, Stephen: Agence France-Presse
Jenkins, Keith: Washington Post
Jennings, Stan: Jennings Publications
Johns, Christopher: National Geographic
Johnson, Cynthia: Time Magazine
Johnston, Frank: Washington Post
Kanthal, Jack: Newark Star Ledger
Katz, Martin: Chesapeake News Service
Keating, John: Newsday
Keating, Maureen: Roll Call
Keeton, Jeffrey: Scripps Howard News Service
Kelly, James: Freelance
Kennedy, Charles: Freelance
Kennerly, David: Newsweek
Kent, Dazine: Afro-American Newspaper
Kieffer, Gary: Foto Consortium
Kim, Yunghi: Freelance
Kittner, Sam: Freelance
Kleponis, Christopher: Newsweek
Kossoff, Leslie: Freelance
Krafft, Louise: San Juan Star
Kraus, Richard: Newsday
LaVor, Martin: Lavor Group
Laffont, Jean Pierre: Sygma
Lambert, Kenneth: Washington Times
Lee, Wilfredo: Associated Press Photos
Lipski, Richard: Washington Post
Lloyd, Michael: Oregonian
LoScalzo, Jim: U.S. News & World Report
Lopez, Jose: New York Times
Lustig, Raymond: Washington Post
Lynch, M. Patricia: Frontiers News Magazine
MacMillan, Jeffrey: U.S. News & World Report
Madrid, Michael: USA/Today
Mallin, Jay: Impact Visuals
Mallory, Tyler: Freelance
Mark, Leighton: Freelance
Markel, Brad: Capri/ Gamma-Liaison
Maroon, Fred: Freelance
Marquette, Joseph: Associated Press Photos
Martineau, Gerald: Washington Post
Matheny, R. Norman: Christian Science Monitor
Mathieson, Greg: MAI Photo Agency
McCurry, Steven: Magnum Photos
McDonnell, John: Washington Post
McKay, Richard: Cox Newspapers
McNamee, Wallace: Newsweek
McNamee, Win: Reuters News Pictures
Medina, Vidal: Reuters News Pictures
Meiselas, Susan: Magnum Photos
Mendelsohn, Matthew: Freelance
Miller, Ingeborg: Magnum Photos
Mills, Douglas: Associated Press Photos
Mintz, Ari: Newsday
Mohin, Andrea: New York Times
Montgomery, Darrow: City Paper
More, Jose: Chicago Tribune
Morello, Debbi: Freelance
Morris, Larry: Washington Post
Mosley, Leigh: Off Our Backs
Murphy, Timothy: Freelance
Nachtwey, James: Magnum Photos
Naltchayan, Joyce: Agence France-Presse
Naltchayan, Neshan: Freelance
Natoli, Sharon: Washington Times
Norcia, Michael: New York Post
Novovitch, Luc: Freelance
Nozzoli, Akram: Saudi Press Agency
Owen, Clifford: Washington Times
Paganelli, Manuello: Freelance
Panagos, Dimitrios: Greek American News Agency
Pangraze, Jennifer: Freelance
Paraskevas, John: Newsday
Parcell, James: Washington Post
Parsons, Nathan: Scripps Howard News Service

MEMBERS ENTITLED FOR ADMISSION, PRESS PHOTOGRAPHERS' GALLERY—Continued

Patterson, Kathryn: Army Times
Patterson, Laura: Roll Call
Pearman, Reginald: Associated Press
Pearson, Robert: Agence France-Presse
Pensinger, Douglas: Freelance
Peppler, James: Newsday
Peress, Gilles: Magnum Photos
Perkins, Lucien: Washington Post
Perry, William: Gannett News Service
Pokress, David: Newsday
Pokress, Jackson: Observer Newspapers
Poleski, David: Freelance
Powers, Carol: Dallas Morning News
Raia, Alexander: Newsday
Rasmussen, Randy: Oregonian
Reed, Ellis: Magnum Photos
Reeder, Robert: Washington Post
Reinhard, Rick: Impact Visuals
Remsberg, Edwin: Freelance
Rentas, David: New York Post
Ricardel, Vincent: Freelance
Richards, Paul: Agence France-Presse
Richards, Roger: Washington Times
Richardson, Joel: Washington Post
Ries, Barbara: Freelance
Roberts, Joshua: Freelance
Robinson, Scott: Freelance
Ronay, Vivian: Freelance
Rosenbaum, Daniel: Washington Times
Rosenberg, Micheal: Blender Magazine
Roth, Rebecca: Freelance
Rutz, Dean: Seattle Times
Sachs, Arnold: Consolidated News Pictures
Sachs, Howard: Consolidated News Pictures
Sachs, Ronald: Consolidated News Pictures
Salhani, Claude: United Press International
Sargent, Michael: Agence France-Presse
Savoia, Stephan: Associated Press Photos
Sawchuk, Ken: Newsday
Schlein, Lonnie: New York Times
Schroeder, Bjorn: German Newspaper Group
Schumacher, Karl: Freelance
Schwarz, Ira: Freelance
Sell, Blake: Reuters News Pictures
Sherbell, Shepard: Saba Press Photos, Inc.
Sherbow, Robert: People Magazine
Silverman, Joseph: Washington Times
Simon, Martin: Saba Press Photos, Inc.
Sloan, Timothy: Agence France-Presse
Smith, Benjamin: Education Week
Smith, Dayna: Washington Post
Souza, Peter: Freelance
Spencer, Ken: Newsday
Spilotro, Michael: World & I
Stabile, Karen: Newsday
Stanfield, James: National Geographic
Steib, Clint: Washington Blade
Stenzel, Maria: National Geographic
Stephenson, Richard: Freelance
Stubbe, Glen: Washington Times
Sykes, Jack: Professional Pilot Magazine
Takeda, Yasushi: Focus Magazine
Tama, Mario: Prince George's Journal
Tannenbaum, Allan: Sygma
Theiler, Michael: Freelance
Thomas, Margaret: Washington Post
Thresher, James: Washington Post
Tiernan, Audrey: Newsday
Traver, Joseph: Freelance
Trippett, Robert: Sipa Press
Udesen, Betty: Seattle Times
Usher, Chris: Freelance
Van Riper, Frank: Freelance
Varias, Stelios: Reuters News Pictures
Vathis, Paul: Associated Press Photos
Villafuerte, Mario: Army Times
Visser, Robert: Photopress Washington
Walker, Diana: Time Magazine
Walsh, Susan: Associated Press
Ward, Fred: Black Star
Watkins, Jr., Frederick: Johnson Publishing Co.
Watson, Ricardo: United Press International
Wilking, Rick: Reuters News Pictures
Williams, John: Newsday
Williamson, Michael: Washington Post
Wilson, Jym: Gannett News Service
Wilson, Mark: Freelance
Wolfson, Stanley: Newsday
Wood, William: Army Times
Woods, Douglas: Freelance
Woodward, Tracy: Washington Times
Wyman, Ira: Newsweek
Yarwood, Richard: Newsday
Yim, Heesoon: HANA
Young, Bruce: Freelance
Young, Jennifer: Freelance
Yu, Liu: Xinhua News Agency
Ziffer, Steve: Freelance

SERVICES REPRESENTED

PRESS PHOTOGRAPHERS' GALLERY

AFRO-AMERICAN NEWSPAPER—332–0080; 1612 14th St., NW, Washington, DC 20009: Kent, Dazine
AGENCE FRANCE-PRESSE—414–0551; 1015 15th St., NW, 5th floor, Washington, DC 20005: Frazza, Luke;
Jaffe, Stephen; Naltchayan, Joyce; Pearson, Robert; Richards, Paul; Sargent, Michael; Sloan, Timothy
ARMY TIMES—703–750–8170; 6883 Commercial Drive, Springfield, VA 22159–0150: Elfers, Steve; Faram, Mark; Patterson, Kathryn; Villafuerte, Mario; Wood, William
ASSOCIATED PRESS PHOTOS—828–9650; 2021 K Street, NW, Washington, DC 20006: Applewhite, J. Scott; Arbogast, Charles; Borea, Roberto; Burgess, Bob; Cook, Dennis; Cooper, Karin; Daugherty,Robert; Diggs, Brian; Edmonds, Ronald; Fremson, Ruth; Gibson, J. Greg; Helber, Stephen; Lee, Wilfredo; Marquette, Joseph; Mills, Douglas; Pearman, Reginald; Savoia, Stephan; Vathis, Paul; Walsh, Susan
BLACK STAR—547–1176; 7704 Tauxemont Rd., Alexandria, VA 22308: Brack, William; Ward, Fred
BLENDER MAGAZINE—737–7370; 806 15th St., NW Ste. 210, Washington, DC 20005: Rosenberg, Micheal
CHESAPEAKE NEWS SERVICE—338–8550; 1346 Connecticut Ave., Suite 714, Washington, DC 20036: Katz, Martin;
CHICAGO TRIBUNE—824–8221; 1325 G St., NW Ste. 200, Washington, DC 20005: Cox, Ernest; Hanes, Frank; More, Jose;
CHRISTIAN SCIENCE MONITOR—617–262–2300; One Norway Street, Boston, MA 02115–3195: Freeman, Melanie; Harbison, Robert; Matheny, R. Norman
CITY PAPER—347–7534; Suite 202, 724 9th St., Washington, DC 20001: Montgomery, Darrow;
CONGRESSIONAL QUARTERLY—887–8500; 1414 22nd St., Washington, DC 20037: Ferrell, Scott; Graham, Douglas
CONSOLIDATED NEWS PICTURES—543–3203; 10305 Leslie St., Silver Spring, MD 20902: Sachs, Arnold; Sachs, Howard; Sachs, Ronald
CONTACT PRESS IMAGES—212–496–5300; 116 East 27th St. 8th Floor, New York, NY 10016: Burnett, David; Fournier, Frank
COX NEWSPAPERS—887–8348; 2000 Pennsylvannia Ave., Washington, DC 20006: McKay, Richard
DALLAS MORNING NEWS—214–977–8222; PO BOX 655237, Dallas, TX 75265: Powers, Carol
EDUCATION WEEK—364–1039; 4301 Connecticut Ave., Washington, DC 20008: Smith, Benjamin
FAIRCHILD PUBLICATIONS—682–3200; 1333 H St., Washington, DC 20005: DeLort, Jean Guy
FARM JOURNAL PUBLISHING—215–829–4865; 230 W. Square, Philadelphia, PA 19106: Dodge, Thomas
FOCUS MAGAZINE—703–243–1569; 1020 North Quincy St. No. 808, Arlington, VA 22201: Takeda, Yasushi
FOTO CONSORTIUM—703–486–0305; South Oxford St., Arlington, VA 22206–2326: Kieffer, Gary
FRONT LINE—301–340–3338; 214 Hardy Place, Rockville, MD 20852: Devadas, Rajan
FRONTIERS NEWS MAGAZINE—301–229–0635; P.O. Box 634, Glen Echo, MD 20812: Lynch, M. Patricia
GAMMA-LIAISON—212–888–7272; 150 East 58th St., New York, NY 10155: Markel, Brad
GANNETT NEWS SERVICE—703–276–5256; 1000 Wilson Blvd., Arlington, VA 22209: Perry, William; Wilson, Jym;
GERMAN NEWSPAPER GROUP—202–244–6736; 4100 Massachusetts Ave., NW, Washington, DC 20016: Schroeder, Bjorn
GREEK AMERICAN NEWS AGENCY—917–879–0749; 111 Broadway Rt.107, Hicksville, NY 11801: Panagos, Dimitrios
HANA—393–1166; 1111 National Press Building, Washington, DC 20045: Yim, Heesoon
HILL, THE—628–8502; 733 15th St., NW Ste. 1140, Washington, DC 20005: Hazen, Pam
HURRIYET—703–978–8073; 8910 Moreland Lane, Annadale, VA 22033: Biber, Mehmet
IMPACT VISUALS—212–683–9688; Suite 901, 28 West 27th St., New York, NY 10001: Burke, William; Friar, Jerome; Mallin, Jay; Reinhard, Rick
JENNINGS PUBLICATIONS—946–5538; 2600 Pyers Mill Rd., Silver Spring, MD 20902: Cohen, Marshall; Jennings, Stan
JOHNSON PUBLISHING CO.—393–5860; 1750 Pennsylvannia Ave., Washington, DC 20005: Watkins, Jr., Frederick
KEYSTONE PRESS AGENCY—212–924–8123; 202 East 42nd St., 4th Floor, New York, NY 10017: Alpert, Brian

SERVICES REPRESENTED, PRESS PHOTOGRAPHERS' GALLERY—Continued

KNIGHT-RIDDER TRIBUNE NEWS SERVICE—383-6099; Suite 776, 529 14th St., Washington, DC 20045: Borst, Charles;
LAVOR GROUP—703-765-7187; 7710 Lookout Ct., Alexandria, VA 22306: LaVor, Martin LEGAL TIMES—457-0686; 1730 M St., NW, Suite 802, Washington, DC 20036: Clark, Carlton; Gilbert,Patrice;
LOS ANGELES TIMES—293-4650; 1875 I St., Washington, DC 20006: Grieser, Robert
MAGNUM PHOTOS, INC.—212-541-7570; 251 Park Ave., So., New York, NY 10010: Freed, Leonard; Fusco, Paul; Glinn, Burton; Griffiths, Philip; Hartmann, Erich; Harvey, David; McCurry, Steven;Meiselas, Susan; Miller, Ingeborg; Nachtwey, James; Peress, Gilles; Reed, Ellis
MAI PHOTO NEWS AGENCY—703-968-0330; 6601 Ashmere Lane, Centreville, VA 22020: Mathieson, Greg
MATRIX INTERNATIONAL, Inc.—212-362-2393; Suite 2R, 468 West 23rd St., New York, NY 10011: Fetters, Paul
McCLENDON NEWS SERVICE—483-3791; 3133 Connecticut Ave., NW, Washington, DC 20008: Bowe, Christy
NATIONAL GEOGRAPHIC—857-7477; 17th & M Streets, NW, Washington, DC 20036: Cobb, Jodi; Johns, Christopher; Stanfield, James; Stenzel, Maria
NATIONAL JOURNAL—857-1414; 1730 M St., NW, Washington, DC 20036: Bloom, Richard; Eisele, John
NEW YORK DAILY NEWS—212-949-3691; 220 East 42nd St., New York, NY 10017: Hamburg, Harry
NEW YORK POST—212-815-8550; 210 South Street, New York, NY 10002: Halasy, Don; Norcia, Michael; Rentas, David
NEW YORK TIMES—867-0383; 1627 Eye St., NW 9th Floor, Washington, DC 20036: Crowley, Stephen Hosefros, Paul; Lopez, Jose; Mohin, Andrea; Schlein, Lonnie
NEWARK STAR LEDGER—201-877-4141; One Star Ledger Plaza, Newark, NJ 07102: Kanthal,Jack
NEWSDAY—516-454-2832; 235 Pinelawn Dr., Melville, NY 11747: Ach, Michael; Bereswill, Paul; Cornell, John; Davies, Phillip; Davis, Bill; Dombroski, Joe; Dooley, James; Florescu, Viorel; Gaines,Julia; Gilbert, Bruce; Goodrich, Daniel; Jacobsen, Don; Keating, John; Kraus, Richard; Mintz, Ari; Paraskevas, John; Peppler,James; Pokress, David; Raia, Alexander; Sawchuk, Ken; Spencer, Ken; Stabile, Karen; Tiernan, Audrey; Williams, John; Wolfson, Stanley; Yarwood, Richard
NEWSWEEK—626-2060; 1750 Pennsylvania Ave., NW, Washington, DC 20006: Downing, Lawrence; Ficara, John; Kennerly, David; Kleponis, Christopher; McNamee, Wallace; Wyman, Ira
OBSERVER NEWSPAPERS—516-679-9888; 2262 Centre Avenue, Bellmore, NY 11710: Pokress, Jackson;
OFF OUR BACKS—234-8072; 2423 18th St., Washington, DC 20009: Mosley, Leigh
OREGONIAN—503-221-8075; 1320 Southwest Broadway, Portland, OR 97201: Lloyd, Michael; Rasmussen, Randy
PEOPLE MAGAZINE—293-4300; 888 16th St., Washington, DC 20006: Sherbow, Robert
PHOTO ASSOCIATES NEWS SERVICE—965-4428; 3421 M St., NW Ste 1636, Washington, DC 20007: Heimsath, Peter
PHOTO TRENDS, INC.—212-613-3295; Suite 702, 260 West 35th St., New York, NY 10001: Burns, David
PHOTOPRESS WASHINGTON—234-8787; 120 S. Spring St., Falls Church, VA 22046: Visser, Robert
PRINCE GEORGE'S JOURNAL—301-459-3131; 9410 Annapolis Road, Lanham, MD 20706: Tama, Mario
REUTERS NEWS PICTURES—898-8333; 1333 H Street, NW, Washington, DC 20005: Ake, J. David; Aubry, Timothy; Beals, Herman; Bochatey, Terry; Cameron, Gary; Clement, Richard; Durand, Enrique;Hershorn, Gary; McNamee, Win; Medina, Vidal; Sell, Blake; Varias, Stelios; Wilking, Rick
RICHMOND TIMES-DISPATCH—804-649-6486; 333 East Grace St., Ricmond, VA 23229: Brown, Robert
ROLL CALL—289-4900; 900 2nd St., NW, Suite 107, Washington, DC 20002: Keating, Maureen; Patterson, Laura
SABA PRESS PHOTOS—212-679-5454; 159 East 30th St., New York, NY 10116: Sherbell, Shepard; Simon, Martin
SAUDI PRESS AGENCEY—861-0324; 1155 15th St., NW Suite 1111, Washington, DC 20005: Nozzoli, Akram
SCRIPPS HOWARD NEWS SERVICE—480-2723; 1090 Vermont Ave., NW, Washington, DC 20005: Harari, Nathaniel; Keeton, Jeffrey; Parsons, Nathan
SEATTLE TIMES—206-464-2203; 1120 John St., Seattle, WA 98111: Rutz, Dean; Udesen, Betty
SIPA—212-463-0150; 30 West 21st St., New York, NY 10010: Trippett, Robert
SUBURBAN COMMUNICATIONS CORP.—810-645-5164; 805 E. Maple Rd., Birmingham, MI 48009: Ashley, Douglas
SYGMA—212-675-7900; 322 8th Ave., 11th Fl., New York, NY 10001: Ellis, Richard; Horan, Tom; Laffont, Jean Pierre; Tannenbaum, Allan
THOMSON NEWSPAPERS—628-2157; 1331 Pennsylvania Ave., NW #524, Washington, DC 20004: Deslich, Steve
TIME MAGAZINE—861-4062; 1050 Connecticut Ave., NW, Washington, DC 20036: Ashe, James; Bentley, PF; Colburn, James; Halstead, Dirck; Johnson, Cynthia; Walker, Diana

SERVICES REPRESENTED, PRESS PHOTOGRAPHERS' GALLERY—Continued

U.S. NEWS & WORLD REPORT—955–2000; 2400 N Street, NW, Washington, DC 20037: Archambault, Charles; Fiedler, James; Golon, Maryanne; Harrity, Charles; LoScalzo, Jim; MacMillan, Jeffrey

UNITED PRESS INTERNATIONAL—898–8071; 1400 Eye Street, Washington, DC 20005: Salhani, Claude; Watson, Ricardo

USA/TODAY—703–276–3400; 1000 Wilson Boulevard, Arlington, VA 22208: Beiser, H. Darr; Binks, Porter; Blass, Eileen; Deutsch, Robert; Dillon, Timothy; Gainer, Dennis; Madrid, Michael

WASHINGTON BLADE—347–2038; Suite 315, 930 F St., Washington, DC 20017: Steib, Clint

WASHINGTON POST—334–7377; 1150 15th Street, NW, Washington, DC 20071: Allen, John; Andrews, Nancy; Arias, Juana ; Biddle, Susan ; Foy, Mary Lou; Guzy, Carol; Herndon, Craig; Jenkins, Keith; Johnston,Frank; Lipski, Richard; Lustig, Raymond; Martineau, Gerald; McDonnell, John; Morris, Larry;Parcell, James; Perkins, Lucien; Reeder, Robert; Richardson, Joel; Smith, Dayna; Thomas, Margaret; Thresher,James; Williamson, Michael

WASHINGTON TIMES—636–3000; 3600 New York Ave., NE, Washington, DC 20002: Ballard, Karen; Brantley, James; Curtiss, Cathaleen; Davidson, Barbara; Franklin, Ross; Gilbert, Kevin;Goulait, Bert; Housewerth, Jan;Lambert, Kenneth; Natoli, Sharon; Owen, Clifford; Richards, Roger; Rosenbaum, Daniel; Silverman, Joseph; Stubbe, Glen; Woodward, Tracy

WILMINGTON NEWS JOURNAL—302–324–2821; 950 W. Basin Rd., Newcastle, DE 19805: Branch-Price, Brian

WORLD & I—635–4020; 2850 New York Ave., NE, Washington, DC 20002: Harrington, John; Holden, Peter; Spilotro, Michael

XINHUA --703–875–0082; 1740 N. 14 St., Arlington, VA 22209: Yu, Liu

FREELANCE

Abraham, Mark; Alers, Paul; Atlan, Jean-Louis; Attlee, Tracey; Barouh, Stan; Barrett, Stephen; Berg, Lisa; Boston, Bernard; Bouchard, Renee; Bower, Carl; Brown, Stephen; Cedeno, Ken; Cooke, Ken; Craig,Cameron; Crandall, Rob; Cutts, Peter; Freeland, Erik; Garcia, Mannie; Garofalo, John Cleveland; Geissinger, Michael A.; Giroux, Robert; Godfrey, Mark; Heikes, Darryl; Heinen, Kenneth; Kelly, James;Kennedy, Charles; Kim, Yunghi; Kittner, Sam; Kossoff, Leslie; Mallory, Tyler; Mark, Leighton; Maroon, Fred; Mendelsohn, Matthew; Morello, Debbi; Murphy, Timothy; Naltchayan, Neshan; Novovitch, Luc; Paganelli,Manuello; Pangraze, Jennifer; Pensinger, Douglas; Poleski, David; Remsberg, Edwin; Ricardel, Vincent; Ries, Barbara; Roberts, Joshua; Robinson, Scott; Ronay, Vivian; Roth, Rebecca; Schumacher, Karl; Schwarz, Ira; Souza, Peter; Stephenson, Richard; Theiler, Michael; Traver, Joseph; Usher, Chris; Van Riper, Frank; Wilson, Mark; Woods,Douglas; Young, Bruce; Young, Jennifer; Ziffer, Steve

WHITE HOUSE NEWS PHOTOGRAPHERS' ASSOCIATION

7119 Ben Franklin Station 20044–7119, phone 785–5230

OFFICERS

Kevin T. Gilbert, *President*
Steven C. Affens, *Vice President*
Michael Geissinger, *Treasurer*
Donald Watrud, *Secretary*

MEMBERS REPRESENTED

Abercrombie, Thomas: (retired)
Abraham, Mark: Freelance
Aceto, Lorie: Smithsonian Institution
Affens, Steven: WJLA–TV
Alberter, William, Jr.: GOP–TV
Allen, Tom: Washington Post
Allmond, Douglas: ABC
Almanza, Armando: Ventana Productions
Amos, James: Freelance
Andrews, Nancy: Washington Post
Applewhite, J.: Associated Press
Apt Johnson, Roslyn: WJLA–TV
Archambault, Charles: U.S. News & World Report
Arias, Juana: Washington Post
Arneson, Sandra: USA Today
Arrington, Percy: NBC
Ashley, Douglas: Freelance
Atherton, James: (life member)
Attlee, Tracey: Freelance
Aubry, Tim: Reuters
Aufdem-Brinke, Ronald: Freelance
Auth, William: U.S. News & World Report
Bacheler, Peter: Freelance
Bahruth, William: (retired)
Bailey, Joseph: (life member)
Ballard, Karen: Washington Times
Barry, William III: (retired)
Bauer, John H.: ABC
Beals, Herman R.: Reuters
Beene, Richard: AFP Photo
Beiser, H.: USA Today
Bennett, Ronald: Capital Television/Ron
Bethem, Rick: Freelance
Binks, Porter: USA Today
Black, Brad: ABC
Blair, James: Freelance
Blaylock, Kenneth: (life member)
Bochatey, Terry: Reuters
Bodnar, John: CNN
Borst, Charles: Knight Ridder Tribune
Boston, Bernie: Boston Photography: (life member)
Boswell, Victor, Jr.: Freelance
Bowe, Christy: Freelance
Boyer, Robert: NBC
Bozick, Peter: Freelance
Brack, William: Black Star
Brantley, James: Washington Times
Bridgham, Kenneth: (retired)
Brooks, Dudley: Washington Post
Brown, Stephen R.: Freelance
Bryan, Beverly: WJLA–TV
Burnett, David: Contact Press Images
Burroughs, Henry: (life member)
Butler, Francis: Freelance
Cain, Stephen: ABC–TV
Cameron, Gary: Reuters
Carlisle, Stephen: Fuji Film (associate)
Cassetta, Guido: Freelance
Castner, Edward: Freelance
Chase, David: Cox Broadcasting
Cirace, Robert: CNN (life member)
Clarkson, Rich: Rich Clarkson (associate)
Clement, Rich: Reuters
Cobb, Jodi: National Geographic
Cockerham, Richard: Fox News Channel
Cohen, Marshall: Freelance
Colton, William: (retired)
Conger, Dean: (life member)
Cook, Dennis: Associated Press
Coughlan, Gregory: Freelance
Cox, Ernie, Jr.: Chicago Tribune
Craven, Thomas, Jr.: (life member)
Crawford, Walter: WJLA–TV
Crowley, Stephen: New York Times
Cuong, Pham Gia: CBS
Curtiss-Kozak, Cathaleen: Washington Times
Dale, Bruce: Freelance
Darcey, Richard: (life member)
Daugherty, Bob: Associated Press
Davidson, Barbara: Washington Times
Davis, Harry, Jr.: WRC–TV
Desfor, Max: (life member)
DiJoseph, John: (life member)
DiMarco, Salvatore, Jr.: Time Magazine

MEMBERS REPRESENTED—Continued

Disselkamp, Henry: ABC News
Dodson, Richard E.: NBC
Dougherty, Paul: Freelance
Doyle, Ann: Fairfax Hospital Media
duCille, Michel: Washington Post
Dukehart, Thomas: WUSA–TV
Dunmeyer, Earl: WUSA–TV
Dunmire, John: WTTG–TV
Durand, Henry: Reuters
Eaves, James: ABC
Edmonds, Ron: Associated Press
Ehrenberg, Richard, Jr.: ABC News
Elbert, Joseph, II: Washington Post
Elfers, Stephen: The Army Times
Elvington, Glenn: Fisher Broadcasting
Ewing, David: Freelance
Feldman, Randy: Viewpoint
Ficara, John F.: Newsweek
Fiedler, James, Jr.: U.S. News & World Report
Fielman, Sheldon: NBC News
Fine, Holly: CBS
Fine, Paul: CBS
Finnigan, Vincent: Finnigan & Associates
Fletcher, John: (life member)
Folwell, Frank: USA Today
Fookes, Gary: Freelance (associate)
Forcucci, Michael: WJLA–TV
Forrest, James: WRC
Foss, Philip: Eastman Kodak
Fox, Donald: (retired)
Foy, Mary Lou: Washington Post
Frame, John A.: WTTG–TV
Franklin, Ross: Washington Times
Frazza, Luke: AFP
Freeland, Erik: U.S. News & World Report
Freeman, Roland: Freelance
Fremson, Ruth: Associate Press
Fridrich, George: NBC
Fuss, Brian: WJLA–TV
Gainer, Dennis: USA Today
Gaines, Julia: Newsday
Galdabini, Christian: Conus Television
Garcia, Mannie: Freelance
Garofalo, John: Washington Post
Geissinger, Michael: Freelance
Gerlach, George: ABC
Gibson, Craig: Freelance
Gilbert, Kevin: Washington Times
Gilgannon, Pege: WJLA–TV
Gilka, Robert: (life member)
Golon, MaryAnne: U.S. News & World Report
Goodman, Jeffrey: NBC
Goulait, Bert: Washington Times
Goulding, David: Emotion Picture
Grace, Arthur: Freelance
Grieser, Robert, Jr.: Los Angeles Times
Griffiths Belt, Annie: National Geographic
Guzy, Carol: Washington Post
Hackett, Stephen: WJLA–TV
Halstead, Dirck: Time Magazine
Hamburg, Harry: New York News
Harrington, John: Freelance
Harrity, Charles W.: U.S. News & World Report
Harvey, Alan Edward: NBC
Hazen, Pamela: The Hill
Heikes, Darryl L.: U.S. News & World Report
Heilemann, Tami A.: Department of the Interior
Heinen, Ken: Freelance
Herman, Lawrence: WJLA–TV
Hershorn, Gary: Reuters
Hoan, Pham: CBS
Hoiland, Harold: WUSA–TV
Hollenbeck, Paul, Jr.: Cox Broadcasting
Horan, Michael: WTTG–TV
Housewerth, Jan: Washington Times
Hoyt, Michael: Catholic Standard
Irby, Kenneth: Poynter Institute
Iuvone, Mary: Freelance
Jaffe, Stephen: Freelance
Johnson, Fletcher: ABC
Johnson, Kenneth: ABC
Johnston, Frank: Washington Post
Kasmauski, Karen: Freelance
Katz, Marty: Chesapeake News
Kennedy, Charles: Freelance
Kennedy, Thomas: National Geographic
Kennett, Nancy: Eastman Kodak Company
Kieffer, Gary: Photo Press International
Kim, Yunghi: Freelance
Kinney, Barbara: The White House
Kittner, Sam: Freelance
Kleber, David: NBC
Kleponis, Christopher: Freelance
Kobersteen, Kent: National Geographic
Koppelman, A.: Reuters
Kornely, Mike: WFAA–TV
Kos, Martin: Cox Broadcasting
Kossoff, Leslie: LK Photos
Kozak, Rick: (active)
Krebs, Lawrence: (life member)
Kress, G.: (life member)
Krieger, Barbara: NBC/WRC–TV
Lambert, H.M.: (life member)
Lambert, Ken: Washington Times
Langenegger, John: (life member)
Larsen, Gregory: Freelance
Lavies, Bianca: Freelance
LaVor, Marty: Freelance
Lawrence, Jeffrey: Knight-Ridder Tribune
Lee, Wilfredo: Associated Press
Leffler, Warren: (retired)
Levy, John: (life member)
Levy, Sheldon: WUSA–TV
Lion, Harold: Lion Recording Services

MEMBERS REPRESENTED—Continued

Lipski, Richard: Washington Post
Lodovichetti, Arthur: (life member)
Lopez, Jose R.: New York Times
Lorek, Stanley: ABC
LoScalzo, James: U.S. News & World Report
Luce, Robert: Fuji Photo Film USA
Lustig, Ray: Washington Post
Lyons, Paul: NET
MacDonald, Jim: Canadien TV Network
MacMillan, Jeffrey: U.S. News & World Report
Madrid, Michael: USA Today
Maggiolo, Vito: CNN
Manley, Jerold: Freelance
Mark, Leighton: Freelance
Markel, Harry: Fuji Photo Film USA
Maroon, Fred: (retired)
Marquette, Joseph: Associated Press
Martin, Tim: Australian Broadcasting
Martin, James, Jr.: ABC News
Martineau, Gerald: Washington Post
Mason, Thomas: WTTG–TV
Matheny, R.: The Christian Science Monitor
Mathieson, Greg: MAI Photo News Agency
Mazzatenta, O.: National Geographic
McCash, Douglas: ARD German TV
McDermott, Richard: NBC
McDonnell, John: Washington Post
McDougall, Ian: Reuters Television
McKay, Richard: Cox Newspapers
McNamee, Win: Reuters
McNamee, Wallace: Newsweek
McNamee, Bruce II: Reuters
Medina, Vidal: Reuters
Mendelsohn, Matthew: Freelance
Milenic, Alexander: Freelance
Mills, Doug: Associated Press
Mishoe, Philip, Jr.: ABC
Mole, Robert: NBC
Morris, Larry: Washington Post
Moulton, Paul: (retired)
Mummert, John: Associated Press
Murphy, Timothy: Freelance
Murphy, John: Freelance
Naltchayan, Joyce: Agence France Presse
Natoli, Sharon: Washington Times
Nighswander, Marcia: Ohio University
Nighswander, Larry: Ohio University
Nishimura, Jisaburo: (active)
Norling, Richard: Freelance
O'Keefe, Dennis: Freelance (associate)
O'Leary, William: Washington Post
Oates, Walter: (life member)
Ortez, George H.: (retired)
Owen, Cliff: Washington Times
Panzer, Chester: NBC–WRC
Parcell, James: Washington Post
Patterson, Jay: ABC
Patterson, Kathryn B.: Army Times Publishing
Pearson, Robert, Jr.: AFP
Pensinger, Douglas: Allsport Photography
Perkins, Lucian: Washington Post
Peterson, Robert, Jr.: Freelance
Petras, William: NBC
Petros, Bill: National Herald
Pinczuk, Murray: Freelance
Popper, Andrew: Business Week
Potasznik, David: Freelance
Powell, William: NBC
Powell, Dennis: ABC News
Reeder, Robert: Washington Post
Reinstein, Mark: Freelance
Rhodes, James: (retired)
Richards, Roger: Washington Times
Richards, Paul: AFP
Richardson, Joel: Washington Post
Robinson, Clyde, Sr.: NBC
Ronay, Vivian: Freelance
Rosenbaum, Daniel: Washington Times
Roth, Johnie, Jr.: NBC
Rubenstein, Larry: Reuters
Rysak, F.: WTTG–TV
Sargent, Michael: AFP Photo
Scherschel, Joseph: (retired)
Schlegel, Barry: PTSC/CNN
Schmick, Paul A.: Freelance
Schneider, Jack: NBC–TV
Schnitzlein, Bob: Reuters
Schule, James: ITN
Schumacher, Karl: Freelance
Schwarz, Ira: Freelance
Sell, Blake: Reuters
Semiatin, Morris: World News Photos
Serensits, Joseph: ABC
Shannon, Dennis: CBS News
Shaw, Larry: ABC
Sherbell, Shepard: SABA Press Photos, Inc.
Shlemon, Christopher: Independent TV News
Shutt, Charles: Communications
Silverman, Joe: Washington Times
Sisco, Paul: Worldwide TV News
Sisson, Robert: Macro/Nature
Skehan, Michael: Skehan Televideo Service
Smith, James: National Geographic
Smith, Margaret: Washington Post
Smith, Dayna: Washington Post
Sorrell, Maurice: (life member)
Souza, Peter J.: Freelance
Stanfield, James: National Geographic
Stearns, Stan: Freelance
Stein, Norman: Department of Defense
Stein, Arthur III: Freelance
Steinberg, David: Freelance
Stephenson, Al: Freelance
Stoddard, Mark: Freelance

MEMBERS REPRESENTED—Continued

Storey, Alfred: NBC
Stubbe, Glen: Washington Times
Suddeth, Richard: CBN News
Swanson, Richard: Freelance
Sweets, Fred: Associated Press
Swenson, Gordon: ABC
Swiatkowski, Edward: ABC
Sykes, Jack: Professional Pilot
Tasnadi, Charles: (life member)
Taylor, Medford: Freelance
Thalman, Mark: Ventana Productions
Thomas, Ronald: Freelance
Thomas, Margaret: Washington Post
Thresher, James: Washington Post
Thuma, Barry: (retired)
Tinsley, Jeff: Smithsonian Institution
Traver, Joseph: Freelance
Trikosko, Marion: (retired)
Trippett, Robert: Sipa Press
Tuckson, Coleman, D.D.S.: Consolidated News
Valeri, Charlene: National Geographic
Van Riper, Frank: Freelance
Verna, Tressa: NBC–News Dateline
Vicario, Ginny: ABC
Walker, Diana: Time Magazine
Wallace, Jim: Smithsonian Institution
Ward, Fred: Black Star
Warner, Ed: Eastman Kodak Company
Watrud, Donald: WTTG–TV
Webb, David: WJLA–TV
Weik, David: ABC
Weller, George: Freelance
Wells, Jim: Freelance
Wentzel, Volkmar: (retired)
Whyte, Paul: USA Today
Wiegman, Dave, Jr.: (retired)
Wilkes, Douglas: WTTG–TV
Wilking, Rick: Reuters
Williams, Robert: NBC News
Williams, Karen: NBC
Williams, Milton: Freelance
Williamson, Michael: Washington Post
Wilson, Woodrow: (life member)
Wilson, James: New York Times
Wilson, James, II: Gannett News Service
Wingfield, Don: Freelance
Winslow, Donald: CNET: The Computer
Wood, Wayne: NBC–TV
Woodward, Tracy A.: Washington Times
Yates, H. II: Freelance
Yokota, Victoria: Washington Times
Young, Bruce: Freelance
Young, Jennifer: The Evans-McCan Group
Zervos, Stratis: TF–1 French TV
Zimmerman, Catherine: Freelance

RADIO AND TELEVISION CORRESPONDENTS' GALLERIES

SENATE RADIO AND TELEVISION GALLERY
The Capitol, Room S–325, 224–6421

Director.—Lawrence J. Janezich.
Assistant Directors:
Jane Ruyle
Diane Lane
Michael Mastrian
Gloria Halcomb

HOUSE RADIO AND TELEVISION GALLERY
The Capitol, Room H–321, 225–5214

Director.—Tina Tate.
Assistant Directors:
Beverly Braun
Gail Davis
Olga Ramirez
Andrew Elias
Erik LeBlanc

EXECUTIVE COMMITTEE OF THE RADIO AND TELEVISION CORRESPONDENTS' GALLERIES

Victor Ratner, ABC News, *Chairman*
Joe Johns, NBC News
Jim Mills, Fox News Channel
Dave McConnell, WTOP Radio
Brian Naylor, National Public Radio
Keith B. Plummer, Hearst Broadcasting
Evelyn Thomas, CBS News

RULES GOVERNING RADIO AND TELEVISION CORRESPONDENTS' GALLERIES

1. Persons desiring admission to the Radio and Television Galleries of Congress shall make application to the Speaker, as required by Rule 34 of the House of Representatives, as amended, and to the Committee on Rules and Administration of the Senate, as required by Rule 33, as amended, for the regulation of Senate wing of the Capitol. Applicants shall state in writing the names of all radio stations, television stations, systems, or news-gathering organizations by which they are employed and what other occupation or employment they may have, if any. Applicants shall further declare that they are not engaged in the prosecution of claims or the promotion of legislation pending before Congress, the Departments, or the independent agencies, and that they will not become so employed without resigning from the galleries. They shall further declare that they are not employed in any legislative or executive department or independent agency of the Government, or by any foreign government or representative thereof; that they are not engaged in any lobbying activities; that they do not and will not, directly or indirectly, furnish special information to any organization, individual, or group of individuals for the influencing of prices on any commodity or stock exchange; that they will not do so during the time they retain membership in the galleries. Holders of visitors' cards who may be allowed temporary admission to the galleries must conform to all the restrictions of this paragraph.

2. It shall be prerequisite to membership that the radio station, television station, system, or news-gathering agency which the applicant represents shall certify in writing to the Radio and Television Correspondents' Galleries that the applicant conforms to the foregoing regulations.

3. The applications required by the above rule shall be authenticated in a manner that shall be satisfactory to the Executive Committee of the Radio and Television Correspondents' Galleries who shall see that the occupation of the galleries is confined to bona fide news gatherers and/or reporters of reputable standing in their business who represent radio stations, television stations, systems, or news-gathering agencies engaged primarily in serving radio stations, television stations, or systems. It shall be the duty of the Executive Committee of the Radio and Television Correspondents' Galleries to report, at its discretion, violation of the privileges of the galleries to the Speaker or to the Senate Committee on Rules and Administration, and pending action thereon, the offending individual may be suspended.

4. Persons engaged in other occupations, whose chief attention is not given to—or more than one-half of their earned income is not derived from—the gathering or reporting of news for radio stations, television stations, systems, or news-gathering agencies primarily serving radio stations or systems, shall not be entitled to admission to the Radio and Television Galleries. The Radio and Television Correspondents' List in the Congressional Directory shall be a list only of persons whose chief attention is given to or more than one-half of their earned income is derived from the gathering and reporting of news for radio stations, television stations, and systems engaged in the daily dissemination of news, and of representatives of news-gathering agencies engaged in the daily service of news to such radio stations, television stations, or systems.

5. Members of the families of correspondents are not entitled to the privileges of the galleries.

6. The Radio and Television Galleries shall be under the control of the Executive Committee of the Radio and Television Correspondents' Galleries, subject to the approval and supervision of the Speaker of the House of Representatives and the Senate Committee on Rules and Administration.

Approved.

NEWT GINGRICH,
Speaker, House of Representatives.

JOHN WARNER,
Chairman, Senate Committee on Rules and Administration.

MEMBERS ENTITLED TO ADMISSION

RADIO AND TELEVISION CORRESPONDENTS' GALLERIES

Abdul-Jawad, Walid: Middle East Broadcasting
Abernethy, Robert: Freelance
Abid, Rod M.: National Public Radio
Abramson, Larry: National Public Radio
Abshaw, W.H.: Freelance
Acevedo, Victor Ed.: Fox News Channel
Ackerman, Thomas: A.H. Belo Capitol Bureau
Adams, Barbara: Reuters
Adams, Douglas: ABC News
Adams, James M.: NBC4
Adams, Jamile: NBC News
Adelman, Staci: Tribune Broadcasting
Adlerblum, Robin C.: ABC News
Adrine, Lynne: ABC News
Affens, Steven C.: WJLA–TV
Ahlers, Michael M.: CNN
Ahmann, Timothy D.: Freelance
Ahn, Jaehoon: Radio Free Asia
Aiken, Elizabeth: C–SPAN
Aiken, Jonathan F.: CNN
Aizenman, Nurith: CNN
Akinan, Ibrahim: InterStar TV
Alan, Bruce: WTOP Radio
Al Haj, Talal: Min Washington, Inc.
Albano, Thomas: Freelance
Albert, Joel R.: Freelance
Albor, Teresa: APTV–Associated Press
Alexander, Constantin: Radio Free Europe/Radio Liberty
Alexander, Kenny: C–SPAN
Alexander, Leo: NBC4
Alexander, Scott J.: Fox News Channel
Alfredson, Rick: Airwaves, Inc.
Alldredge, Thomas: C–SPAN
Allen, Greg: National Public Radio
Allen, Mark: CNN
Allen, Robert: CBN News
Allen, Victoria: NET–Political NewsTalk Network
Allison, Lynn: WETA–TV
Allmond, Douglas: ABC News
Allyn, Karen: Cable News 21
Almanza, Armando: Ventana Productions
Althage, Robert Y.: WUSA–TV
Altman, Kyoko: CNN
Alvey, Jay: NBC4
Ambrose, Nancy J.: ABC News
Amirault, Theresa L.: C–SPAN
Ammerman, Stuart A.: Freelance
Anastasi, Patrick G.: NBC News
Anderson, Bradley C.: Potomac Television
Anderson, Scott J.: The NewsHour with Jim Lehrer
Anderson, Shawn: WTOP Radio
Andres, Chiara: C–SPAN
Andrews, Wyatt: CBS News
Angle, James L.: Fox News Channel
Anstey, Christopher: TV Asahi
Aoki, Toshiko: TV Tokyo Channel 12, Ltd.
Apokis, Dimitrios: Greek Television-Radio
Ardin, Milagros: WMAL Radio
Arena, Kelli: CNN
Arenstein, Howard: CBS News
Arestad, Anders: Freelance
Aretakis, Nick: C–SPAN
Argueta, Iris J.: NewsChannel 8
Armfield, Robert Ward: PTSC/CNN
Armstrong, Patricia: Freelance
Armstrong, Phyllis: WUSA–TV
Armstrong, Richard: WUSA–TV
Armstrong, Robert: CBS News
Arnold, Elizabeth: National Public Radio
Arobaga, Mary: WINGSPAN
Arraf, Jane: Reuters Television
Arrington, Percy: NBC News
Arteage, Niurka: USIA/TV Marti
Ashe, James F.: Freelance
Asher, Julie: Fox News Channel
Assamann, Karin B.: Spiegel TV/Germany
Atkinson, Rodney Seth: PTSC/CNN
Attkisson, Sharyl: CBS News
Atwell, Laura M.: NET–Political NewsTalk Network
Aubrey, Allison D.: Channel Earth
Aubuchon, John: Freelance
Augenbraum, Marc: APTV–Associated Press
Augenstein, Neal: United Press International
Autry, Jeffery L.: NBC News Channel
Avellino, Jennifer: CNN
Avery, John C.: Black Entertainment Television
Avery-Brown, Verna: Pacifica Radio News
Babarovic, Christina: ABC News
Bacheler, David F.: PTSC/CNN
Badden, David M.: Radio Free Asia
Bae, Jeanie: WTOP Radio
Baer, Jonathan: National Public Radio
Bagnall, Thomas J.: Court TV
Bagnato, Barry: CBS News
Bail, Rachael: Voice of America
Bailey, Becky: Mutual/NBC Radio
Bailey, Douglas: C–SPAN
Bailey, Julia Holmes: National Public Radio
Bailor, Michelle: C–SPAN
Baker, Cissy: Tribune Broadcasting

MEMBERS ENTITLED TO ADMISSION, RADIO AND TELEVISION CORRESPONDENTS' GALLERIES—Continued

Baker, Glenn: America's Defense Monitor
Baker, Les: Cox Broadcasting
Baker, Russell M.: Freelance
Ball, Anne G.: Fox News Channel
Ballou, Jeff: CONUS Communications
Balsamo, Jimmy: Australian Broadcasting Corp.
Baltimore, Dennis: PTSC/CNN
Bamfield, Louise: APTV–Associated Press
Banes, Hildegard: ORF–Austrian Radio and TV
Banker, Stephen: Comm*Tech News
Banks, Mark: ABC News
Banks-Wilson, Katherine: NBC4
Bannigan, Michael: PTSC/CNN
Banville, Lee M.: The NewsHour with Jim Lehrer
Barger, Brian: CNN
Barlett, Cameron C.: Freelance
Barlett, Scott: Freelance
Barnett, Amanda: AP–Broadcast
Baron, Jeffery: AP–Broadcast
Barr, Bruce: CBS News
Barrows, Jessica: Fox News Channel
Barry, Calvin: WETA–TV
Barton, Bruce: Reuters Television
Bascom, Jon: ABC News
Basu, Arin: Radio Free Asia
Batten, Rodney Sims: NBC News
Bauer, John H.: ABC News
Bauley, Patrick: PTSC/CNN
Baumann, Robert: Professional Video Services
Beall, Gary Glenn: NBC News
Beall, Joni: AP–Broadcast
Beard, Robert E.: Washington News Network
Beardsley, Eleanor: TF1–French Television
Beaudin, E. Robert: Worldnet - U.S.I.A TV
Beck, Joanne: NBC4
Becker, Bruce C.: Fox News Channel
Becker, Frank: CBN News
Becker, Michelle: Airwaves, Inc.
Beckford, Edward M.: Washington News Network
Beckman, Patricia N.: APTV–Associated Press
Beery, Nicholas P.: Deutsche Welle German Television
Begleiter, Ralph J.: CNN
Behrens, Thad: Nippon TV Network
Belcher, Christopher: Min Washington, Inc.
Bell, Bradley S.: WJLA–TV
Bell, Karen: Washington News Network
Bellis, Michael: PTSC/CNN
Bellman, Charles: Pyramid National Pressport
Bender, Bob: ABC News
Bender, Sharon: A.H. Belo Capitol Bureau
Benjoar, Maurice: Worldnet-U.S.I.A TV
Bennett, Carol: Washington-Alabama News Report
Bennett, Shepard B.: C–SPAN
Bensen, Jackie: WTTG-Fox Television
Benson, Pamela S.: CNN
Bergen, Peter: CNN
Berger, Catherine A.: ABC News
Berk, Jay: C–SPAN
Berko, Arthur: NBC News
Berman, David Steven: PTSC/CNN
Bernstein, Tracy: Airwaves, Inc.
Berry, Paul L.: WJLA–TV
Betsill, Brett: C–SPAN
Bettag, Thomas: ABC News
Bevis, Mark R.: Pacifica Radio News
Beyer, Kevin: Freelance
Biemann, Barbara: RTL Television Germany
Bierbauer, Charles: CNN
Billmann, Christian: Radio France International
Bilotta, John J.: ABC News
Binder, Robin: Court TV
Bintrim, Tim: PTSC/CNN
Birnholtz, Jeremy: Medill News Service
Bisney, John: CNN
Blackburn, Regina Allen: NBC News
Blackman, Jay Allan: NBC News
Blackman, Keith: NBC News
Blakeslee, Carol: The NewsHour with Jim Lehrer
Blakey, Rea: WJLA–TV
Blanchet, Sharon: British Broadcasting
Blandburg, Victor R.: WJLA–TV
Blaustein, Evan: Image Television
Blaylock, Kenneth L.: ABC News
Blitzer, Wolf: CNN
Block, Kenan S.: NBC News
Blocker, Glay L.: NET–Political NewsTalk Network
Bloom, David Jerome: NBC News
Bloom, Herb: NBC News Stations Division
Blooston, Victoria: NBC News
Blount, Jeffrey: NBC News
Blust, Stephen S.: Televisio De Catalunya
Boag, Keith: Canadian Broadcasting Corporation
Bodenheimer, Carey: CNN
Bodlander, Gerald: AP–Broadcast
Bodnar, John: PTSC/CNN
Boggs, Mae Beth: NBC News Channel
Bohannon, Camille: AP–Broadcast
Bohn, Kevin: CNN
Boilen, Bob: National Public Radio
Bolderson, Claire: British Broadcasting
Bonilla, Angelina: Washington Bureau News Service
Boozer, Diane T.: WJLA–TV
Borniger, Charles F.: German Television/ARD
Borniger, Herta: German Television/ARD
Borzage, Frank E.: F.E.B. Video Productions
Boskent, Amanda: C–SPAN
Bostwich, Stephen: Professional Video Service
Bottorf, Harry: WETA–TV
Boughton, Brian: Fox News Channel
Bowden, John J.: WJLA–TV
Bowen, Timothy: WETA–TV
Bowman, Michael C.: Voice of America
Box, Brenda: CBS News
Boyd, Forrest J.: United News and Information

MEMBERS ENTITLED TO ADMISSION, RADIO AND TELEVISION CORRESPONDENTS' GALLERIES—Continued

Boyd, Janet: Fox News Channel
Boyd, John D.: NBC News
Boyd, Wayne F.: Freelance
Boyer, Robert D.: NBC News
Boyle, Molly A.: Fox News Channel
Boyne, Walter J.: Wingspan Network-Aviation News
Braatz, Matthew: A.H. Belo Capitol Bureau
Bradley, Barbara: National Public Radio
Bradley, Carlotta L.: AP–Broadcast
Brady, Monica: Christian Monitor Radio
Bragale, Charles: NBC4
Branche, Glennwood: ABC News
Bratton, Michael G.: WUSA–TV
Braver, Rita: CBS News
Brawner, Donald: WETA–TV
Braxton, Monique: NewsChannel 8
Brechner, Daniel: Washington-Alabama News Report
Breed, Richard: Freelance
Breiterman, Charles L.: ABC News
Brender, Mark E.: ABC News
Brice, Shirley R.: Tribune Broadcasting
Brislin, Ray: Dutch Television
Brock, Alan Matthew: NewsChannel 8
Brod, Constance D.: C–SPAN
Broder, Jonathan: National Public Radio
Broffman, Craig A.: CNN
Brook, Rovenia M.: Black Entertainment Television
Brooks, Randall: CBN News
Brooks, Sam: ABC News
Brosius, Teddy: Freelance
Brosnan, John E.: The Washington Bureau
Brothers, Lloyd R.: NBC4
Brown, Almadale: NBC News Channel
Brown, Clayton: MSNBC Pro
Brown, Dwight B.: Freelance
Brown, Edgar: Fox News Channel
Brown, Henry Metric: ABC News
Brown, Jeffrey: The NewsHour with Jim Lehrer
Brown, Larry: AP-Broadcast
Brown, Paul: C–SPAN
Brown, Tracey Ann: APTV–Associated Press
Brownstein, Craig: C–SPAN
Brumbaugh, Kathleen M.: Professional Video Services
Bruno, Harold R.: ABC News
Bryan, Beverly: WJLA–TV
Bryn, Ingvilo: Norwegian Broadcasting
Buckhorn, Burke: PTSC/CNN
Buffington, Ann N.: APTV–Associated Press
Buhrow, Tom: German Television/ARD
Bullock, Peter: Reuters
Bundles, A'Lelia: ABC News
Bundock, Susan J.: C–SPAN
Burch, Kevin: C–SPAN
Burdick, Leslie: C–SPAN
Burke, Beverly: WUSA–TV
Burnett, David: WTTG–Fox Television
Bury, Chris: ABC News
Buschschlueter, Nicholas: Deutsche Welle German Television
Buschschluter, Siegfried: Deutschland Radio
Bushyhead, Julia: CONUS Communications
Butler, Allison: Global TV Canada
Butler, Debra Jean: The NewsHour with Jim Lehrer
Butrick, Lesley: The NewsHour with Jim Lehrer
Buzenberg, William E.: National Public Radio
Byrd, David: C–SPAN
Byrne, Matthew: CNN
Cable, Paul: PTSC/CNN
Cagle, Steven: NewsChannel 8
Calhoun, Timothy F.: Tribune Broadcasting
Calo-Christianson, Nancy: C–SPAN
Cameron, Carl: Fox News Channel
Camp, Joseph: WETA–TV
Campbell, Barbara: National Public Radio
Campbell, Cynthia L.: CBS News
Campbell, Jean: Reuters Television
Canizales, Cesar A.: Worldwide Television News
Canter, William M.: Freelance
Caplan, Craig: C–SPAN
Capra, Anthony: NBC News
Caravello, David: CBS News
Carden, Elizabeth: ABC News
Cardwell, Samuel: NBC News
Carey, Julie: NBC4
Carline, Windall: National Public Radio
Carlson, Chris: ABC News
Carlson, Mark: AP–Broadcast
Carlsson, Leif: Swedish Television
Carney, Keith: Federal Network, Inc.
Carpel, Michael: Fox News Channel
Carpenter, Stephen: C–SPAN
Carter, Amanda E.: NET–Political NewsTalk Network
Carter, Hodding: MainStreet Productions
Carter, Kelly M.: Black Entertainment Television
Cassells, Andy: Cox Broadcasting
Cassidy, David Martin: A.H. Belo Capitol Bureau
Castillo, Sharon: USIA/TV Marti
Castner, Edward R.: Finnish Broadcasting
Castrilli, Anthony M.: WUSA–TV
Castro, Margarita: Catholic University of Chile Television
Catrett, David K.: Freelance
Celarier, Karl B.: Pyramid National Pressport
Centanni, Steve: Fox News Channel
Cerletty, Marie: ITN of London
Cha, Eugene: National Public Radio
Chaggaris, Steven: C–SPAN
Chamberlain, Richard: Tribune Broadcasting
Chamberlayne, Pye: United Press International
Champ, Henry S.: Canadian Broadcasting Corp.
Chandonnet, Bridget A.: The NewsHour with Jim Lehrer

MEMBERS ENTITLED TO ADMISSION, RADIO AND TELEVISION CORRESPONDENTS' GALLERIES—Continued

Chang, Hyunju: ABC News
Chapman, Irwin M.: Bloomberg Business News
Charbonneau, Melissa: CBN News
Chase, David: Cox Broadcasting
Chase, Karen: AP–Broadcast
Chatterjee, Sumana: Freelance
Chavez, Miguel A.: Telemundo/WZGS–64
Chen, Huiyi: Radio Free Asia
Chen, Li-Hung: Video News Service
Chernenkoff, Kelly: Fox News Channel
Chester, Allen J.: Zolcer-TV (German TV)
Chi-jou Ku, Jill: Radio Free Asia
Chia-Chi Lu, Annie: Chinese Television Network
Chou, Jennifer: Radio Free Asia
Chrisco, Julie: ESPN
Christian, George: CBS News
Chung, Chen-Fang: Chinese Television System
Chung, Patrice: Fox News Channel
Cinca, Silvia: Radio Free Europe/Radio Liberty
Clancy, Martin: ABC News
Clapman, Leah: The NewsHour with Jim Lehrer
Clark, C. Jaci: Black Entertainment Television
Clark, Jim: C–SPAN
Clark, Robert: ABC News
Clark, Theodore E.: National Public Radio
Clarke, Jim: WJLA–TV
Clarke, John: Reuters Television
Clayton, Cassandra: NBC News
Clemann, William J.: WUSA–TV
Clemente, Michael: CNN
Cloherty, Jack: NBC News
Clough, W.C. (Bill): United Press International
Clugstson, Gregory W.: SRN News/Standard News
Coates, Judith Ann: WJLA–TV
Cochran, Jean: National Public Radio
Cochran, John: ABC News
Cockerham, Richard: Fox News Channel
Cocklin, Anne: Freelance
Cocklin, Stephen: Freelance
Coffman, Mary B.: Medill News Service
Cofske, Harvey: Professional Video Services
Cogan, Amie: C–SPAN
Cohan, Stacey L.: Community Television of Prince George's
Cohen, Aaron Stuart: Freelance
Cohen, Daniel: NBC4
Cohen, Jill: WTOP Radio
Cohen, Jonathan: Metro Teleproductions Inc.
Cohen, Josh: C–SPAN
Cohen, Stuart: British Broadcasting
Colbert, Ron: United Press International
Colby, Alfred: CBS News
Cole, Bryan: Fox News Channel
Cole, Kathryn: C–SPAN
Cole, Thomas C.: National Public Radio
Cole, William: WJLA–TV
Coleman, Korva: National Public Radio
Coleman, Steven E.: AP–Broadcast
Collingwood, Eloise: C–SPAN
Collins, Bruce: C–SPAN
Collins, Pat: NBC4
Collins, Sean: National Public Radio
Collins, Tracey: NET–Political NewsTalk Network
Conan, Neal J.: National Public Radio
Conanan, Ann: Image Television
Conlin, Sheila: NBC News Channel
Connor, James T.: CNN
Connor, William S.D.: Hearst Broadcasting
Conover, William: C–SPAN
Conrad, Jeffrey A.: C–SPAN
Conrad, Monique: Washington News Network
Contreras, Jorge: Univision News
Contreras, Lalnie: AP–Broadcast
Cook, James: PTSC/CNN
Cook, Leslie: National Public Radio
Cooke, Carol Anne: Freelance
Coolidge, Richard: ABC News
Cooper, John M.: Image Television
Cooper, Kyle: WTOP Radio
Cooper, Rebecca: CNN
Corbey, Robert: ABC News
Corcoran, Patricia: WTTG–Fox Television
Corum, Paul H.: CBS News
Cosby, Rita: Fox News Channel
Costantini, Bob: CONUS Communications
Coudoux, Sylvain: Canadian Broadcasting Corporation
Coughlin, Daniel: Pacifica Radio News
Coulter, Pam: CBS Radio
Courson, Paul: Dow Jones Television
Couvillion, Ronald L.: PTSC/CNN
Cowherd, Nayada L.: WTTG–Fox Television
Cox, Lisa Diane: WJLA–TV
Craley, Norman: WETA–TV
Cram, Christopher: NBC News Channel
Cratty, Carol A.: CNN
Craven, William: National Public Radio
Crawford, Robert: ABC News
Crawford, Walter: WJLA–TV
Crawley, Craig: NET–Political NewsTalk Network
Crawley, Plummer: CONUS Communications
Creekmore, Bobby Steve: Freelance
Cremedas, A.E.: ABC News
Crenshaw, Elizabeth: NBC4
Crosariol, Paul M.: Community Television of Prince George's
Crosswhite, Karla: CNN
Crowley, Candy Alt: CNN
Crowley, Dennis: United News and Information
Crowley, Lauren: Fox News Channel
Crutchfield, Curtis A.: Community Television of Prince George's
Cruze, Elizabeth V.: NBC News
Crystal, Lester M.: The NewsHour with Jim Lehrer
Cucinello, Francene: Freelance
Cue, Eduardo: Televisa-Eco Television

MEMBERS ENTITLED TO ADMISSION, RADIO AND TELEVISION CORRESPONDENTS' GALLERIES—Continued

Cullen, Patrick: ABC News
Cummings, Bruce: NBC News
Cunningham, Anthony: Freelance
Cuong Gia, Pham: CBS News
Cupp, Stephen: Freelance
Curley, Ann J.: CNN
Currier, Liam: C–SPAN
Curtis, Mark: Cox Broadcasting
Cutlip, Kerry Arden: WJLA–TV
Cyr, Emily: WUSA–TV
Czechowski, Julie: Radio Free Europe/Radio Liberty
D'Amico, Daniele: APTV–Associated Press
D'Annibale, Thomas J.: ABC News
Dadgar, Maria C.: Native American Television
Dakis, Lynn: NBC News
Dalton, Lynn M.: British Broadcasting
Dames, Sabrina: Black Entertainment Television
Dancy, Christopher: NBC News Channel
Daniel, Roger: PTSC/CNN
Daniels, Brady G.: NBC News
Daouda, Guisset: Washington Bureau News Service
Darya, Folson: WTTG-Fox Television
Daschle, Kelly: APTV–Associated Press
Date, Jack: CNN
Dauchess, Matthew: C–SPAN
Daugherty, Jeffery S.: Worldnet-U.S.I.A TV
Daughtery, Laura Gene: Black Entertainment Television
Davalos, Anna: NBC4
Davenport, Anne Azzi: ABC News
David, Michael M.: PTSC/CNN
Davieaud, Helene: TF1–French Television
Davis, Clinton F.: WTTG–Fox Television
Davis, Harry: NBC4
Davis, James W.: Court TV
Davis, Karla: ABC News
Davis, Pamela: WJLA–TV
Davis, Patricia A.: CNN
Davis, Patrick Alan: CNN
Davis, Phillip: National Public Radio
Davis, Rebecca A.: National Public Radio
Davis, Richard: CNN
Davy, Ernest: ABC News
Day, Richard A.: WTOP Radio
DeFrehn, Raymond C.: Professional Video Services
DeMark, Michael A.: Freelance
DeMoss, Gary S.: Freelance
DePuyt, Bruce: NewsChannel 8
DeVaney, Terri: Professional Video Services
deVogue, Driane: ABC News
DeWitt, Terry: ABC News
Dean, Walter C.: CBS News
Decker, Jonathan P.: Nightly Business Report
Delboni, Chris: Bandeirantes Network-Brazil
Dennis, Derricke M.: WTTG–Fox Television
Derrick, Deborah: C–SPAN
Dessauer, Carin: CNN
Deutsch, David: WETA–TV
Deutschman, Scott: WTTG–Fox Television
Devoney, Steve: C–SPAN
DiBacco, Tom: ABC News
DiBella, Richard B.: Fox News Channel
DiMarco, Joseph: USIA/TV Marti
Dickie, Mary Theresa: NewsChannel 8
Dieguez, Antonio: USIA/TV Marti
Diel, Heike: German Television/ZDF
Dillon, Arlene: CBS News
Dillon, Estel: NBC News Stations Division
Dimassimo, Rick: Native American Television
Dimsdale, John: Marketplace Radio
Disselkamp, Henry: ABC News
Dixson, Charles H.: Freelance
Doane, Martin C.: WJLA–TV
Dodson, Richard E.: NBC News
Doherty, Peter M.: ABC News
Donald, William: Freelance
Donaldson, Jameela: NBC News
Donaldson, Sam: ABC News
Dong, Jun: China Radio International
Dong, Zhenbang: China Radio International
Doniger, Joan: WMAL Radio
Donovan, Kerry: NBC News
Donovan, Mary Ellen: WJLA–TV
Donvan, John: ABC News
Dore, Margaret: NBC News Stations Division
Dore, Robert E.: National Public Radio
Dorman, William G.: CNN
Dorn, Jason M.: Professional Video Services
Dorsee, Karma: Radio Free Asia
Dougherty, Jill M.: CNN
Dougherty, Paul G.: Freelance
Douglass, Linda Diane: ABC News
Douglass, Sheila: Black Entertainment Television
Downey, Sharon: Medill News Service
Downhower, Laura: German Television/ZDF
Doyle, Geoffrey: NBC News
Drake, Bruce: National Public Radio
Drew, Catherine: London News Radio
Drew, Kathleen: ABC News
Driscoll, Barbara: The Blackwell Corporation
Drizin, Julie: Pacifica Radio News
Drum, Jonathan E.: Providence Journal Broadcasting
DuBach, Michele: National Public Radio
Dubinsky, Vladimir: Radio Free Europe/Radio Liberty
Dudley, Don: Wingspan Network-Aviation News
Dukehart, Thomas: WUSA–TV
Dukert, Betty Cole: NBC News
Dunbar, Dennis: Wireless Data Systems
Duncan, Victoria: NBC News
Dunlavey, Thomas J.: CNN
Dunmire, John P.: WTTG–Fox Television
Dupree, Jamie: Cox Broadcasting
Durham, Deborah: Univision News
Durham, Lisa R.: CNN
Durham, Timothy J.: PTSC/CNN

MEMBERS ENTITLED TO ADMISSION, RADIO AND TELEVISION CORRESPONDENTS' GALLERIES—Continued

Duvall, James: Fox News Channel
Dyer, Lois: CBS News
Ebinger, Jonathan: ABC News
Echols, Jerry L.: Fox News Channel
Eck, Christina: Freelance
Eckhardt, Ralph: Voice of America
Edouard, Perrin: TF1–French Television
Edwards, Bob: National Public Radio
Edwards, Bruce: Fox News Channel
Edwards, Catherine: Salem Radio Network
Egy-Rose, Christine: NBC News
Eiras Arlene: WTOP Radio
Eisenbarth, Ronald Ray: Bonneville International Corp.
Eisenhuth, Alfred Scott: Freelance
El-Bardicy, Thabet: Middle East Broadcasting
Eldred, Mary: Reuters Television
Eldridge, James W.: ABC News
Elgart, Joanne L.: Canadian Broadcasting Corporation
Elkins, Brenda: PTSC/CNN
Ellard, Nancy: NBC News Channel
Ellenwood, Gary: C–SPAN
Elliott, John P.: EO Dutch TV and Radio
Ellis, Alyne: National Public Radio
Ellison, Don: WUSA–TV
Elvington, Glenn: Fisher Broadcasting
Encinas, Alvaro: Univision News
Endo, Katsuichi: TV Asahi
Engberg, Eric: CBS News
Engel, Dagmar E.H.: Deutsche Welle German Television
Engel, Seth: C–SPAN
Erbe, Bonnie G.: Mutual/NBC Radio
Erlenborn, Dan: NBC News
Ernst, Charlotte: TV2 Denmark
Esler, Carol: AP–Broadcast
Espinoza, Ana: Univision News
Esposito, Michael J.: NewsChannel 8
Estrada, Peter: NET–Political NewsTalk Network
Etter, Alan: WTOP Radio
Ewing, Samara M.: WUSA–TV
Fabic, Gregory: C–SPAN
Farkas, Daniel: C–SPAN
Farkas, Mark: C–SPAN
Farley, James T.: WTOP Radio
Farnsworth, Amanda Jane: British Broadcasting
Farnsworth, Elizabeth: The NewsHour with Jim Lehrer
Faw, Robert D.: NBC News
Feather, Richard: Professional Video Services
Feig, Christy: CNN
Feinstein, Debra B.: WTOP Radio
Feist, Sam E.: CNN
Felcyn, George: The NewsHour with Jim Lehrer
Feldman, Clifford: Fox News Channel
Feldman, Elizabeth: NBC4
Feldman, Randy: Viewpoint Communications
Felger, Jonathan: Bloomberg Business News
Fendley, Gail: Freelance
Ferder, Bruce: Fox News Channel
Fernandez, Marlene: CNN
Ferrante, Robert: National Public Radio
Fessler, Pam: National Public Radio
Fetzer, Robert: Professional Video Services
Fiddle, Joan: Fox News Channel
Field, Andrew: WABC–ABC NewsOne
Fielman, Sheldon: NBC News
Figueroa, Luis: CBS Telenoticias
Finamore, Charles: ABC News
Findlay, Chad: Gancie Television, Inc.
Finley, Robert: NBC News
Firestone, Richard: Voice of America
Fischer, Elizabeth: NBC News
Fisher, Tobias: CTV Television Network
Flannery, Amy: Freelance
Fleischman, Philip: SRN News/Standard News
Flintoff, Corey: National Public Radio
Flood, Geoffrey: NewsChannel 8
Flores, Cesar: Cox Broadcasting
Flug, Carla: National Narrowcast Network
Fluty, Steve: APTV–Associated Press
Foellmer, Kristin N.: Deutsche Welle German Television
Fogarty, Kevin: NBC News Channel
Fogelson, Marianne: NET–Political NewsTalk Network
Foley, Erin: The Blackwell Corporation
Foley, Kevin Paul: Radio Free Europe/Radio Liberty
Foley, Rita M.: AP–Broadcast
Folson, Darya: WTTG–Fox Television
Font, Silvia: USIA/TV Marti
Forbes, Roy: Potomac Television
Forcey, Diane J.: ABC News
Forcucci, Michael: WJLA–TV
Ford, Michael: Freelance
Forman, David: NBC News
Formica, Salvatore: NBC News
Forner, James E.: WTTG–Fox Television
Forrest, James M.: NBC4
Foster-Dotson, Donna: Black Entertainment Television
Foty, Tom: WTOP Radio
Fouhy, Beth: CNN
Foundas, John David: Tribune Broadcasting
Fowler, Stephanie: Potomac Television
Fox, Peter H.: Reuters Television
Frame, John A.: WTTG–Fox Television
Francis, Betty: Freelance
Francis, Fredrick N.: NBC News
Frank, Patrick: TV Tokyo Channel 12, Ltd.
Frankel, Bruce: TF1–French Television
Franken, Robert: CNN
Fraser, Jr., Wilfred R.: NBC News
Free, Elissa Blake: CNN
Freeman, James B.: The Blackwell Corporation

MEMBERS ENTITLED TO ADMISSION, RADIO AND TELEVISION CORRESPONDENTS' GALLERIES—Continued

Freeman, Jane M.: The Blackwell Corporation
Freeman, Neal: The Blackwell Corporation
Freitas, Rosemary: NBC News
French, F. Patrick: Freelance
Freund, Eugen A.: ORF–Austrian Radio and TV
Fridrich, George: NBC News
Fridrich, George E.: CONUS Communications
Friedenberg, Joan M.: The NewsHour with Jim Lehrer
Friedman, David: Freelance
Frix, Stephanie: Court TV
Froseth, Gary: WTOP Radio
Frost, Nicola: Ventana Productions
Fry, Jim: A.H. Belo Capitol Bureau
Fryer, Alan: CTV Television Network
Fuchs, Joanne: CNN
Fuller, Karen: NBC News Stations Division
Furlong, Timothy: NBC News
Furlow, Tony: CBS News
Furman, Hal E.: CBS News
Fuse, Yuko: Nippon TV Network
Fuss, Brian: WJLA–TV
Fuss, Robert J.: Mutual/NBC Radio
Gabala, Rick: C–SPAN
Gabriel, Oscar Wells: AP–Broadcast
Gaffney, Brian: NBC News
Gaffney, Dennis: Wingspan Network-Aviation News
Gahagan, Kendra: NBC News
Gaito, Vincent: ABC News
Galdabini, Christian: Fox News Channel
Gale, Morgan: National Narrowcast Network
Gallaher, John J.: ABC News
Gallay, Jennifer B.: CONUS Communications
Gamble, William: NBC4
Gancie, Vincent M.: Gancie Television, Inc.
Gangel, Jamie: NBC News
Gao, Jun: China Central Television
Garay, German: Mobile Video Services
Garcia, Edith: USIA/TV Marti
Garcia, Michelle: Pacifica Radio News
Gardner, Cy: Washington News Network
Gardner-Johnson, Regina: C–SPAN
Garofalo, Michael A.: CBN News
Garraty, Timothy C.: PTSC/CNN
Garrett, Julie Kirtz: Hearst Broadcasting
Garske, Jennifer: AP–Broadcast
Gary, Garney: C–SPAN
Gasque, Steve: Cox Broadcasting
Gately, Jim: CONUS Communications
Gates, Gregory S.: Potomac Television
Gato, Pablo: CBS Telenoticias
Gauger, Thomas: United Press International
Gavin, Kristy: British Broadcasting
Gavin, Paul C.: Airwaves, Inc.
Gebhardt, William A.: NBC News
Gelb, Amos: CNN
Gelfman, Andrew: Washington News Network
Genter, Joyce: C–SPAN
Gentilo, Richard S.: APTV–Associated Press
George, Deborah: National Public Radio
George, Maurice: PTSC/CNN
Gerlach, George R.: ABC News
Gerosa, Pietro: Swiss Broadcasting Corp.
Gersh, Darren: Nightly Business Report
Gerstein, Joshua A.: ABC News
Geutzier, Doreen: NBC4
Giacomo, John: Washington News Network
Giammetta, Max: WTTG–Fox Television
Gibbs, Lura Annette: Black Entertainment Television
Gibbs, Richard T.: Black Entertainment Television
Gibson, Jr., Frank L.: NBC News
Giebel, Edward: Freelance
Gildea, Maria: C–SPAN
Gilgannon, Pege: WJLA–TV
Gill, Jacqueline: C–SPAN
Gillan, Jennifer: WTTG–Fox Television
Gillette, David: WETA–TV
Gilley, Robert: PTSC/CNN
Gilliam, Gordon: Freelance
Gilmour, Sandy: NBC News
Ginebra, Nelson: NBC News
Ginsberg, Judah: CNN
Ginsburg, Benson: CBS News
Girshman, Peggy: National Public Radio
Giusto, Thomas: ABC News
Gjelten, Tom: National Public Radio
Glass, R. Pat: Freelance
Glassman, James: The Blackwell Corporation
Glennon, John: Freelance
Glynn, William: NBC News Channel
Goble, Paul: Radio Free Europe/Radio Liberty
Gold, Lawrence: Washington News Network
Gold, Peter: Fuji Television
Gold, Walter L.: Washington News Network
Goldblatt, Jeff: King Broadcasting
Goldfein, Michael: A.H. Belo Capitol Bureau
Goldman, Jeff: CBS News
Goldman, Wendy A.: The Berns Bureau
Goldstein, Stephanie: CNN
Goler, Wendell: Fox News Channel
Gomez, Augusto: Fox News Channel
Gonzalez, Carlos A.: WTTG–Fox Television
Gomez-Boix, Amaro: USIA/TV Marti
Goodknight, Charles: NewsChannel 8
Goodman, Amy: Pacifica Radio News
Goodman, Susan: Marketplace Radio
Gordemer, Barry: National Public Radio
Gordon, Chris: Court TV
Gordon, Patrice: C–SPAN
Gordon, Stuart O.: ABC News
Gorin, Timothy: NBC News
Gorman, James: APTV–Associated Press
Gordon, Herbert J.: Court TV
Gorsky, Edward D.: NBC News
Gorsline Amgjean: The News Hour with Jim Lehrer

MEMBERS ENTITLED TO ADMISSION, RADIO AND TELEVISION CORRESPONDENTS' GALLERIES—Continued

Gottlieb, Brian: The NewsHour with Jim Lehrer
Gottlieb, Carl: WJLA–TV
Goulding, Dave: Freelance
Gourdie, Bryant C.: CONUS Communications
Grabow, Barton: National Public Radio
Grachow, Paul: C–SPAN
Gradison, Robin: ABC News
Grafton, Jennifer: Metro Teleproductions Inc.
Grain, David: Black Entertainment Television
Grassie, John: NBC News
Grasso, Neil J.: CBS News
Graves, Lindsay: PTSC/CNN
Gray, Emma: London News Radio
Gray, Robert: Image Television
Greczyn, Mary Anne: NewsChannel 8
Green, Olivio: NBC News
Green, Sharon: National Public Radio
Greenbaum, Adam: NBC News Channel
Greenberg, Sarah: NBC News
Greenblatt, Larry: Viewpoint Communications
Greene, James M.: PTSC/CNN
Greene, Leslie: PTSC/CNN
Greene, Olin: Potomac Television
Greene, Thomas M.: PTSC/CNN
Greenfield, Heather: AP–Broadcast
Greenhalgh, Jane: National Public Radio
Greenwood, John Kevin: NBC4
Greenwood, William: ABC News
Gregory, Bettina L.: ABC News
Grenda, Jean M.: WTTG–Fox Television
Griffin, Eileen: WETA–TV
Griffin, Gary Keith: Globalvision
Griffin, Kevin: Freelance
Griffith, Gary: Hearst Broadcasting
Griffitts, William J.: Mobile Video Services
Groenhuijsen, Carolus: NOVA Dutch Public Television
Gross, Andrew: ABC News
Gross, Avery: Freelance
Gross, Caitlin: The NewsHour with Jim Lehrer
Gross, David: CBS News
Gross, Eddie S.: PTSC/CNN
Guadalupe, Patricia: Pacifica Radio News
Guarino, Christopher: CNN
Guastadisegni, Richard: WJLA–TV
Gudenkauf, Anne: National Public Radio
Gunn, Ute W.: Fox News Channel
Gursky, Gregg: Fox News Channel
Gutmann, Hanna: Washington Radio And Press Service
Gutzeit, Andreas: Zolcer-TV (German TV)
Guzman, Armando: Univision News
Haberstick, Fred: Fox News Channel
Hackett, Stephen P.: WJLA–TV
Haddad, Tammy: Fox News Channel
Hadler, Elana Beth: National Public Radio
Haederle, Tom: CBS News
Haefeli, Brian: PTSC/CNN
Hagan, Kendall: Fox News Channel
Hagar, Charles: Inside Science
Hager, Jeffery: The Washington Bureau
Hager: Mary K.: CBS News
Hager, Robert M.: NBC News
Hagerty, Michael E.: Fox News Channel
Haggerty, Patrick B.: Channel Earth
Hakel, Peter: WJLA–TV
Hall, David: Canadian Broadcasting Corporation
Hall, David J.: Radio Marti
Hall, Richard: C–SPAN
Hall, Rosemary: Voice of America
Haller, Thomas D.: WUSA–TV
Halsey, Eugenia: CNN
Halton, David: Canadian Broadcasting Corporation
Hamberg, Steven: Freelance
Hamilton, Chris: PTSC/CNN
Hamilton, Holly: WJLA–TV
Hamilton, Jay: Hamilton Productions
Hamilton, John A.: Hamilton Productions
Hamilton Deger, Anne: Hamilton Productions
Hammelburg, David H.: KRO Dutch Radio and Television
Hammer, Michael J.: AP–Broadcast
Hamrick, Mark A.: AP–Broadcast
Han, Myon-taek: Christian Broadcasting System
Hanberry, Steven: Reuters Television
Hanchett, James C.: NBC News Channel
Hand, Catherine: The Hill/UBN
Handelsman, Steve: NBC News Stations Division
Handly, Jim: NBC4
Hanlon, Carl: Global TV Canada
Hanlon, Deirdre: NBC News
Hanoura, Mohamed: C–SPAN
Hansen, Eric: C–SPAN
Hanson, Heidi K.: Image Television
Harding, Christine: Ventana Productions
Harding, Claus: Freelance
Harding, Corrie A.: NBC4
Harding, T. Alejandro: Video News Service
Harding, William: Ventana Productions
Harima, Takushi: Tokyo Broadcasting System
Harmeyer, Nancy: Fox News Channel
Harmon, Catherine: WTOP Radio
Harmon, Elizabeth: National Public Radio
Harrington, Craig J.: WTTG–Fox Television
Harris, Mary: WTTG–Fox Television
Harris, Richard F.: National Public Radio
Harrison, Stella: NET–Political NewsTalk Network
Harter, John Robert: WJLA–TV
Hartge, John: Freelance
Harvey, Alan: NBC News
Hass, Thomas: Freelance
Hassan, Ronnie: Reuters Television
Hassett, Jody: CNN
Hawk, James: Metro Networks, Washington
Hayley, Harold Paul: NBC News
Haynes, Bonnie A.: Airwaves, Inc.

MEMBERS ENTITLED TO ADMISSION, RADIO AND TELEVISION CORRESPONDENTS' GALLERIES—Continued

Haynes, Maurice: C–SPAN
Haywood, Barry: Freelance
Hazard, Colin: C–SPAN
Heacock, Tim: NET–Political Newstalk Network
Headline, William W.: CNN
Hecht, Cynthia: AP–Broadcast
Heffley, William: C–SPAN
Heik, Jens: German Television/ZDF
Heinchon, Tara L.: NewsChannel 8
Heller, James: CNN
Henderson, Susan: European Broadcasting Union
Hendrick, Thomas: WTTG–Fox Television
Henrehan, John: WTTG–Fox Television
Henry, Donald: Voice of America
Herald, Vernon: C–SPAN
Herbst, Christian: Nippon TV Network
Herman, Charlie: ABC News
Herman, Lawrence: WJLA–TV
Herndon, David: ABC News
Herrera, Ken C.: AP–Broadcast
Hertrick, Jeff W.: NewsChannel 8
Hester, Dierdre: CBS News
Hewitt, Candance M.: WJLA–TV
Hewitt, Gavin James: British Broadcasting
Heyman, Douglas: C–SPAN
Hickman, Jutta: German Television/ZDF
Hill, Charles: WETA–TV
Hill, Dana: Fox News Channel
Hill, Wilton: C–SPAN
Hillis, John D.: NewsChannel 8
Hillman, Jeremy: British Broadcasting
Hindes, Walter R.: AP–Broadcast
Hinds, Hugh: WJLA–TV
Hinnewikel, Olivier: European Broadcasting Union
Hirsch, Georg: Freelance
Hirsh, Steve: Fox News Channel
Hirzel, Conrad: PTSC/CNN
Hively, Chester: NBC News
Hoan, Pham Boi: CBS News
Hobbs, Cathy: NBC4
Hoff, George: Canadian Broadcasting Corporation
Hoffman, Sabine: German Television/ARD
Hohn, Natalie: Dow Jones Television
Hoiland, Harald: WUSA–TV
Holland, John: NBC News
Holland, Sarah B.: CNN
Hollenbeck, Paul: Cox Broadcasting
Hollingsworth, Brian: Fox News Channel
Hollis, Jerry: PTSC/CNN
Holly, Dawn: Fox News Channel
Holly, Derrill E.: AP–Broadcast
Holman, Kwame: The NewsHour with Jim Lehrer
Holme, Todd R.: WETA–TV
Holmes, Horace R.: WJLA–TV
Hoose, Monica: The NewsHour with Jim Lehrer
Hoover, Toni: Freelance
Hopkins, Brian C.: CONUS Communications
Hopkins, Moira: Fox News Channel
Hopper, David P.: Freelance
Horan, Michael: WTTG–Fox Television
Horne, Roger: German Television Agency
Hornig Draper, Roberta: NBC News
Houk, Marianne: NewsChannel 8
Houston, Karen Gray: WTTG–Fox Television
Houston, Kermit C.: WUSA–TV
Howard, Stephen G.: WETA–TV
Howell, Richard D.: Fox News Channel
Hsu, Roger: Chinese Television Network
Hubbard, Hal P.: Metro News Network
Hudson, Christian: CNN
Hudson IV, Ira John: NBC4
Huff, Daniel R.: APTV–Associated Press
Hugel, David: PTSC/CNN
Huheey, Thomas Scott: NET–Political NewsTalk Network
Hui, Janice: CNN
Hume, Kim: Fox News Channel
Hunt, Jonathan: Sky News
Hunter, Laura A.: NBC News
Hunter, Regina: C–SPAN
Hunter-Gault, Charlayne: The NewsHour with Jim Lehrer
Hurt, James Allen: NBC News
Huston, Andrew: TV Asahi
Hutchins, Christopher: Tribune Broadcasting
Hutchins, Stacy: King Broadcasting
Hyater, John E.: WETA–TV
Ide, Charles: WETA–TV
Ifill, Gwen: NBC News
Igarashi, Kimitoshi: NHK–Japan Broadcasting
Iiyama, Laura: Pacifica Radio News
Ikehara, Mariko: C–NET
Inches, Andrew: NewsChannel 8
Ingram, Leigh A.: NewsChannel 8
Ingram, Shermaze: The NewsHour with Jim Lehrer
Inskeep, Steve: National Public Radio
Irvin, Paul: NBC4
Irving, John: Metro News Network
Ishaq, Salim: NBC News
Ishihara, Mayumi: Freelance
Itagaki, Nobuyuki: NHK–Japan Broadcasting
Ito, Takanobu: TV Asahi
Iwanciw, Tetiana: Radio Free Europe/Radio Liberty
Izquierdo, Pablo: C–SPAN
Jackson, Brooks: CNN
Jackson, Dimetrius: Worldnet-U.S.I.A TV
Jacobs, Philip: NBC4
Jacobson, Murrey: The NewsHour with Jim Lehrer
Jamison, Dennis: CBS News
Janitschek, Andrew: Radio Free Asia
Janjigian, Janet: NBC News
Jankowski, Judith: Fox News Channel
Jansen, Torsten: Danish Broadcasting
Jarrett, Rick: National Public Radio
Jaskot, Sheila: WTTG–Fox Television

MEMBERS ENTITLED TO ADMISSION, RADIO AND TELEVISION CORRESPONDENTS' GALLERIES—Continued

Jellinek, Sergio A.: NBC News Channel
Jenkins, David A.: PTSC/CNN
Jenkins, Gregory J.: NET–Political NewsTalk Network
Jenkins, Loren: National Public Radio
Jennings, Edward B.: Freelance
Jennings, Mary Ann: WTOP
Jessen, Peder: TV2 Norway
Jia, Wei-ye: The Washington Bureau
Jimenez, Martin: PTSC/CNN
Johannsen, Peggy: AP–Broadcast
Johncox, Douglas P.: WETA–TV
Johnke, Tracy Lyn: CBS Radio
Johns, Joseph E.: NBC News
Johns, Nancy M.: CBS Radio
Johnson, Darryl B.: Professional Video Services
Johnson, David: WTOP Radio
Johnson, Douglas: C–SPAN
Johnson, Fletcher H.: ABC News
Johnson, Gregory D.: Mutual/NBC Radio
Johnson, Julie: ABC News
Johnson, Kathleen: NBC4
Johnson, Kathy Foster: WJLA–TV
Johnson, Kenneth: ABC News
Johnson, Kia: Reuters Television
Johnson, Kyle: WTOP Radio
Johnson, Leroy: NBC News
Johnson, Martha: Hearst Broadcasting
Johnson, Risto: Finnish Broadcasting
Johnson, Rolanda: German Television/ZDF
Johnson, William R.: ABC News
Johnston, Cynthia: National Public Radio
Johnston, Derek: Reuters Television
Johnston, Jeffrey E.: Freelance
Johnston, Lisa: NET–Political NewsTalk Network
Jones, Duane R.: Potomac Television
Jones, Edward M.: National Public Radio
Jones, Hannelore: German Public Radio/ARD
Jones, Morris: WTTG–Fox Television
Jones, Phil: CBS News
Jones, Tony: Australian Broadcasting Corp.
Jordan, Adriene: CBS News
Jordan, Leona: C–SPAN
Joseph, Olga M.: WMAL Radio
Joy, Richard: NET–Political NewsTalk Network
Joya, Steven: ABC News
Joyce, Christopher: National Public Radio
Judd, Jacqueline: ABC News
Judge, Michael C.: Image Television
Juenger, Georg: German Television/ZDF
Just, Sara: ABC News
Justice, Basil A.: WTTG–Fox Television
Kahn, Britt: CNN
Kaiser, Monika: German Television/ARD
Kalbfeld, Brad: AP–Broadcast
Kalfopulos, Joy: ABC News
Kalifa, Bruce E.: PTSC/CNN
Kane, Jim: Christian Monitor Radio
Kane, Lorel: Freelance
Kane, Richard: Freelance
Kane, Ruth: C–SPAN
Kangas, Paul: C–SPAN
Kaplan, Meg: Fox News Channel
Kaplan, Therese: NET–Political NewsTalk Network
Karakashian, Jane: C–SPAN
Karlen, Jane M.: NewsChannel 8
Karmahl, Ingolf: German Broadcasting/ARD
Kambe, Naoto: Nippon TV Network
Karnes, Robert: Potomac Television
Karson, Danielle: Freelance
Kasarda, Amy E.: CNN
Kasell, Carl: National Public Radio
Kast, Sheilah: ABC News
Kaster, Charles G.: Native American Television
Katkov, Mark: CBS News
Katz, Barry: C–SPAN
Kauffman, Michael W.: PTSC/CNN
Kaufmann, Carol: Fox News Channel
Kautz, John: NBC News
Kay, Katty: Freelance
Kaye, Matthew: Berns Bureau
Ke, Sinclair: U.S.I.A. Television
Keator, John C.: National Public Radio
Kelleher, Colleen: APTV–Associated Press
Kelleher, Kristine: APTV–Associated Press
Kellerman, Georg: German Television/ARD
Kellerman, Mike: South African Broadcasting
Kelley, Alice: German Television/ZDF
Kelly, Archie: WJLA–TV
Kelly, Carol Anne: National Public Radio
Kelly, Sarah B.: National Public Radio
Kempf, Deborah: ABC News
Kendall, Bridget: British Broadcasting
Kennedy, Brian: Broadcast News Ltd.
Kennedy, Robert G.: C–SPAN
Kenny, Justin: Freelance
Kent, Lenard: WJLA–TV
Kent, Peter O.: Reuters Television
Kent, Sammy: Washington News Network
Kenyon, Linda: SRN News/Standard News
Kenyon, Peter: National Public Radio
Kerr, Jennifer: AP–Broadcast
Kerr, Roxane: C–SPAN
Kesner, Eric: Freelance
Kessler, Jon: NBC News
Kessler, Lisa Marie: NewsChannel 8
Ketcham, Lew: C–SPAN
Keyes, Charles F.: CNN
Khalid, Sunni M.: National Public Radio
Khananayev, Grigory: Fox News Channel
Kidd, Susan: NBC4
Kikuchi, Madoka: NHK–Japan Broadcasting
Kim, Eugene: AP–Broadcast
Kim, Ho: Radio Free Asia
Kim, Hui Hyon: Radio Free Asia

MEMBERS ENTITLED TO ADMISSION, RADIO AND TELEVISION CORRESPONDENTS' GALLERIES—Continued

Kimura, Eri: NHK–Japan Broadcasting
King, Donna: NET–Political NewsTalk Network
King, Jerry: ABC News
King, Kevin: C–SPAN
King, Kevin G.: WUSA–TV
King, Kristi Sue: WTOP Radio
Kirschner, Natalie Anne: Fox News Channel
Kissal, Bruce: Freelance
Kitasei, Junichi: TV Asahi
Kizer, James S.: NBC4
Klauser, Horst: NDR/WDR German Radio
Kleber, Claus Detlev: German Television/ARD
Klein, Constantin: Deutsche Welle German Television
Klein, Jennifer: PTSC/CNN
Klein, Llissa: Fox News Channel
Klein, Robert: Freelance
Kleine, Kimberly: CNN
Klette, Mary: NBC News
Knapp, Daniel: WETA–TV
Knisely, Thomas: The Blackwell Corporation
Knoll, Jennifer K.: Reuters Television
Knoller, Mark: CBS News
Knott, John W.: ABC News
Knox, Ronald: NBC News
Koch, Kathleen: CNN
Koelsch, Udo: NDR/WDR German Radio
Koenig, Martin: PTSC/CNN
Kohno, Kenji: NHK–Japan Broadcasting
Kohrs, Charlotte: NBC News
Kojovic, Predrag: Reuters Television
Kolodziejczak, Thomas R.: Potomac Television
Komes, Michelle M.: WTOP Radio
Koolhof, Vanessa M.: WUSA–TV
Korich, Kim: Community Television of Prince George's
Kornely, Michael: A.H. Belo Capitol Bureau
Korth, Anja: German Television/ZDF
Kos, Martin: Cox Broadcasting
Koslow, Marc: Freelance
Kotke, Wolfgang: Zolcer-TV (German TV)
Koval, Melissa: Freelance
Kovijanic, Nick: NBC4
Koyama, Orika: TV Asahi
Kozakos, Panayiota: NBC News
Kozel, Sandy: AP–Broadcast
Krakower, Gary: CNN
Krause, Charles A.: The NewsHour with Jim Lehrer
Krebs, Joe: NBC4
Krebs, Larry: WMAL–Radio
Kremer, Stephen: Maryland Public Television
Kretman, Lester A.: NBC News
Kreuz, Greta: WJLA–TV
Kritz, Francesca: MSNBC Pro
Krost, Jack: CNN
Kruse, Peter: German Television/ZDF
Kupperman, Tamara: NBC News
Kur, Bob: NBC News
Kuroiwa, Yuji: Fugi Television
LaComa, Lawrence: Deutsche Welle German Television
LaMonica, John C.: ABC News
LaSalle, Susan Alice: NBC News
Lacey, Donna: C–SPAN
Laflamme, Micheline: Canadian Broadcasting Corporation
Lafrance, Pierre-Leon: Canadian Broadcasting Corporation
Lagan, Christopher: Reuters Television
Lamb, Brian P.: C–SPAN
Lambidakis, Stephanie: CBS News
Landay, Woody: Australian Broadcasting Corp.
Landy, Hope: C–SPAN
Lane, Stanley: Freelance
Lang, Christof: RTL Television Germany
Langmade, Brigette: Potomac Television
Lankes, Elyane C.: Pro Sieben Television (German TV)
Larade, Darren: C–SPAN
Larragoite, Lisa: The NewsHour with Jim Lehrer
Larsen, Gregory: Freelance
Lasker, Phillip: Australian Broadcasting Corp.
Lassoe, Ward: MSNBC Pro
Laughlin, Ara A.: Community Television of Prince George's
Lauterbach, Shannon: Reuters Television
Lavallee, Michael: Tokyo Broadcasting System
Lavon, Neal: Voice of America
Lawn, Connie: Audio-Video News
Lawrence, Michael: National Public Radio
Lawrence, Scot: Providence Journal Broadcasting
Lawson-Muse, Pat: NBC4
LeBrecht, Thelma: AP–Broadcast
LeCroy, Philip L.: APTV–Associated Press
Leake, Myron A.: CONUS Communications
Lee, David: Worldwide TV News
Lee, Donald A.: CBS News
Lee, Edward: WETA–TV
Lee, John W.: NewsChannel 8
Lee, Marietta S.: Court TV
Lee, Nam Sub: Yonhap TV News
Lee, Rich: Salem Radio Network
Lehrer, Jim: The NewsHour with Jim Lehrer
Lehrman, Amy: CBS News
Lehrman, Margaret: NBC News
Leidelmeyer, Ronald H.: Freelance
Lelle, Werner: German Television/ZDF
Lent, David: Freelance
Leonard, Kevin: C–SPAN
Leong, Dexter: Freelance
Leshan, Bruce: WUSA–TV
Levin, Aleksey: Radio Free Europe/Radio Liberty
Levine, Jeffrey B.: CNN
Lewine, Frances L.: CNN
Lewis, Edward: C–SPAN
Lewis, Elizabeth: National Public Radio

MEMBERS ENTITLED TO ADMISSION, RADIO AND TELEVISION CORRESPONDENTS' GALLERIES—Continued

Li, Denise: CBS News
Li, Rong: Chinese Television Network
Liasson, Mara: National Public Radio
Libert, Tara: Swiss Broadcasting Corp.
Lichtenberg, Zita: NHK–Japan Broadcasting
Liffiton, Bruce: Freelance
Lillibridge, Douglas J.: Mutual/NBC Radio
Lilling, David: Metro Teleproductions
Lilly, Judlyne: Fox News Channel
Limbach, Francis J.: AP–Broadcast
Lindauer, Susan: Fox News Channel
Linden, Kim J.: CNN
Linderman, Tamara: Potomac Television
Line, Bill: Fox News Channel
Lisle, John D.: NewsChannel 8
Liss, Liza: CONUS Communications
Little, Craig A.: WTTG–Fox Television
Littlefield, Suzanne: NBC News
Littman, Randy: Hamilton Productions
Liu, Enming: Chinese Television Network
Liu, Ning Rong: Chinese Television Network
Liu, Ping: Broadcasting Corp. of China
Liu, Zhengzhu: China Central Television
Lively, Lydia S.: NBC News
Lockhart, Debbi: NBC4
Lockhart, Kathleen: NBC News
Lodoe, Kalden: Radio Free Asia
Loebach, Joseph W.: NBC News
Loescher, Skip: CNN NewSource
Logan, Laura: ABC News
London, C. Paul: Professional Video Services
Long, Culver: Multinational Media
Long, James V.: NBC News
Longnecker, Emily Marie: The Washington Bureau
Loomans, Kathryn: AP–Broadcast
Loper, Catherine: CTV Television Network
Lopez, Lynda: NBC4
Lormand, John Kenneth: CBN News
Lorson, Laura: National Public Radio
Loucks, Bill: Canadian Broadcasting Corporation
Lougee, Dave: NBC4
Lowe, Matt: CBS News
Lowe, Rachael M.: Mutual/NBC Radio
Lowe, Raimund: ORF – Austrian Radio and TV
Lowman, Wayne: Fox News Channel
Lu, Chiachi: Chinese Television Network
Lucas, Christina L.: Professional Video Services
Lucas, David: NewsChannel 8
Lucas, Diana: SRN News/Standard News
Ludlan, Nick: Zolcer-TV (German TV)
Ludwin, James: AP–Broadcast
Lugato, Giuseppe: RAI–Italian TV News
Luhn, Laura W.: Fox News Channel
Lummis, Sheila: The NewsHour with Jim Lehrer
Lumpkin, Beverley C.: ABC News
Lundberg, Ken: Freelance
Lundh, Lennart: The Swedish News Agency
Lutt, Howard: PTSC/CNN
Lutz, Ellsworth: ABC News
Luzquinos, Julio: Metro Teleproductions Inc.
Lyall, Robert J.: Freelance
Lyle, Robert: Radio Free Europe/Radio Liberty
Lynch, Dotty: CBS News
Lynch, Wayne: NewsChannel 8
Lynker, John: WTOP Radio
Lynn, Gary Earl: PTSC/CNN
Lynn, John V.: CNN
MacCarthy, Dennis: Mutual/NBC Radio
MacDonald, Charles: CTV Television Network
MacDonald, Jim: CTV Television Network
MacHardy, Cybele: Potomac Television
Machado, Carolyn: Freelance
Macias, Shari: NBC4
MacInnis, Jack: PTSC/CNN
Maddux, Catherine V.: National Public Radio
Maer, Peter: Mutual/NBC Radio
Maggi, Yolanda: Fox News Channel
Maggiolo, Vito: CNN
Magnuson, Ron: CBN News
Maguhn, Diana: Pro Sieben Television (German TV)
Mahler, Joerg: German Television/ZDF
Majerus, Marlis: Bonneville International Corporation
Malek, Adel: Contact Middle East
Malesky, Robert: National Public Radio
Malin, Susan: The NewsHour with Jim Lehrer
Mallory, Brenda N.: NBC4
Malone, James: Voice of America
Maltas, Michael L.: CNN
Malveaux, Suzanne: NBC4
Mancuso, Joseph: Mid-Atlantic Media
Mancuso, Michael: Freelance
Mangus, Richard: Talk Radio News Service
Manifold, Geoffrey: WTTG–Fox Television
Manis, Penelope: CNN
Mann, Johnathan A.: WJLA–TV
Mantis, L. Pamela: Radio Marti
Marash, David: ABC News
Marchione, Mark: PTSC/CNN
Marcus, Michael: C–SPAN
Marcus, Ralph: PTSC/CNN
Margolius, Amy: Fuji Television
Marks, Alexandra: NBC News
Marks, Simon: London News Radio
Marques, Autonio: Freelance
Marriott, Mai: Freelance
Marriott, Michael: Freelance
Marshall, Bradley: Washington Bureau News Service
Marshall, Kiersten: C–SPAN
Marshall, Nancy: London News Radio
Martin, Allison A.: The Washington Bureau
Martin, Cheryl: Black Entertainment Television
Martin, Dale Matthew: CBN News

MEMBERS ENTITLED TO ADMISSION, RADIO AND TELEVISION CORRESPONDENTS' GALLERIES—Continued

Martin, David C.: CBS News
Martin, James T.: ABC News
Martin, Jennifer: CNN
Martin, John J.: ABC News
Martin, Mary: CBS News
Martin, Rick: NBC4
Martin, Tim: Ventana Productions
Martinez, Elmy E.: WUNO Notiuno Radio Network
Martinez, Luis E.: ABC News
Martino, Jeff: Freelance
Masciarelli, Anthony: Worldnet-U.S.I.A TV
Mason, Cecelia: West Virginia Public Radio
Mason, Suzanne K: NewsChannel 8
Mason, William Todd: Professional Video Services
Mates, James: ITN of London
Mathews, John Francis: NBC News
Matkosky, Timothy: Potomac Television
Mattesky, Thomas A.: CBS News
Matthews, Barbara Lynn: NewsChannel 8
Matthews, Claude: Freelance
Matthews, Kathleen: WJLA–TV
Matthews, Lisa N.: AP–Broadcast
Matthews, Valerie: C–SPAN
Mattingly, Dave S.: National Public Radio
Maurus, Hans-Jurgen: German Public Radio/ARD
Mawhinnedy, Maxine: Freelance
Maxwell, Darraine: Christian Monitor Radio
McCallister, Doreen: National Public Radio
McCann, Michael: C–SPAN
McCann, Sean: C–SPAN
McCarren, Andrea: NBC News
McCarthy, Lark: WTTG–Fox Television
McCarty, Dennis Page: Swiss Television
McCarty, Donald Jay: Freelance
McCash, Douglas: German Television/ZDF
McCash, Scott: German Television/ZDF
McCaughan, Timothy: CNN
McClam, Kevin J.: C–SPAN
McCleery, Kathleen: The NewsHour with Jim Lehrer
McClure, Tipp K.: German TV Agency
McClurkin, Don: WETA–TV
McConagha, Megan: Fisher Broadcasting
McConnaughey, Brian K.: Wireless Data Systems
McConnell, David F: WTOP Radio
McCoy, Doxie A.: Black Entertainment Television
McDermott, Frank D.: WUSA–TV
McDermott, Richard: NBC News Stations Division
McDougall, Ian: Reuters Television
McDowell, Michael: Canadian Broadcasting Corporation
McGill, Michael: CNN
McGlinchy, James: CBS News
McGoran, Maeve: National Public Radio
McGowan, David: WETA–TV
McGrath, Megan Ann: Freelance
McGrath, Patrick: WTTG–Fox Television
McGraw, Julie: C–SPAN
McGreevy, Allen: Reuters Television
McGuire, Matthew: C–SPAN
McGuire, Michael: CBS News
McHenry, Robert C.: WUSA–TV
McHugh, Mark: CNN
McIntyre, Lynne M.: Canadian Broadcasting Corporation
McKenna, Kate: AP–Broadcast
McKinney, Jerry W.: Voice of America
McManus, Kevin A.: NBC News Channel
McManus, Micheal P.: CNN
McMearty, Michael D: WTOP Radio
McMichael, IV, Sammuel J.: PTSC/CNN
McMurray, Patricia: The NewsHour with Jim Lehrer
McNeil, Tasha Nita: NBC News
McQueen, Michel: ABC News
McWethy, John: ABC News
Mears, Carroll Ann: NBC News
Mears, William C.: CNN
Mederos, Zoila T: Television-Eco Television
Meeks, Brock Nolan: NBC News
Mekour, Dorattasan: NewsChannel 8
Melendy, David R.: AP–Broadcast
Mellen, Roger P.: WJLA–TV
Meluza, Lourdes: Univision News
Melville, Chris: Black Entertainment Television
Meringer, Amy S.: CONUS Communications
Merrill, Robert S.: NBC News
Merritt, Kathleen: WAMU–FM Radio
Meryash, Peter: NBC News
Meserve, Jeanne M.: CNN
Messitte, Zach: CNN
Metil, Adrienne: AP–Broadcast
Meyer, Jill: CBS News
Meyer, Kerry L.: Professional Video Services
Meyer, Richard: CBS News
Michael, Michelle M.: NBC4
Michaels, Peter: National Public Radio
Michaud, Bryant T.: AP–Broadcast
Micheal, Finnigan: Electronic News
Migas, Portia R.: ABC News
Mihalisko, Michael: Radio Free Europe/Radio Liberty
Miklaszewski, James: NBC News
Milenic, Alexander: Freelance
Milford, Robert: Mobile Video Services
Militello, James: AP–Broadcast
Miller, Annette L.: The NewsHour with Jim Lehrer
Miller, Dana: CBS News
Miller, Elizabeth P.: British Broadcasting
Miller, Evan David: NBC News
Miller, Mary: CONUS Communications
Miller, Mitchell: WTOP Radio
Miller, Paul K.: PTSC/CNN
Miller, Scott: CNN
Million, Michael: The NewsHour with Jim Lehrer
Mills, Jim: Fox News Channel
Minner, Richard: NBC News

MEMBERS ENTITLED TO ADMISSION, RADIO AND TELEVISION CORRESPONDENTS' GALLERIES—Continued

Minor, Ronald: NBC4
Mistretta, Brian W.: NewsChannel 8
Mitchell, Andrea: NBC News
Mitchell, Elisabeth: NBC News Channel
Mitchell, Jaqueline N.: NET–Political NewsTalk Network
Mitchell, Russell: CBS News
Mitnick, Steven E.: Freelance
Miville-Dechene, Julie: Canadian Broadcasting Corporation
Miyagi, Yoshinori: NHK–Japan Broadcasting
Mobley, Sarah C.: National Public Radio
Mohen, Peter: PTSC/CNN
Molina-Roman, Adriana: Univision News
Molinares, Ione Indrira: CMI TV News and Radionet
Molineaux, Diana: Radio Marti
Mong, Bryan: Freelance
Montgomery, Jr., Charles: Black Entertainment Television
Moon, Duncan R.: Christian Monitor Radio
Moore, Clifton: WJLA–TV
Moore, Corey B.: Black Entertainment Television
Moore, Dennis E.: Nightly Business Report
Moore, Kristin: NBC News
Moore, Russell T.: NBC News
Moore, Terrence M.: SRN News/Standard News
Mora, Oscar F.: USIA/TV Marti
Moran, James M.: Freelance
Morano, Marc: Mid-Atlantic Media
Moreno, Jaime: USIA/TV Marti
Morgan, John B.: WETA–TV
Morris, Chris: British Broadcasting
Morris, Daniel: ABC News
Morris, Diane: C–SPAN
Morris, Peter: PTSC/CNN
Morrisette, Roland: Bloomberg Business News
Morse, Rick: PTSC/CNN
Morton, Bruce: CNN
Morton, Daniel: C–SPAN
Mortreux, Vincent: Univision News
Mosettig, Michael D.: The NewsHour with Jim Lehrer
Mosher, Brian: Professional Video Services
Mosley, Joseph: PTSC/CNN
Moss, Howard: Mutual/NBC Radio
Moss, Michael: WTOP Radio
Mote, Thomas D.: Freelance
Mottola, Lorraine: European Broadcasting Union
Mueller, John: CBN News
Muhammad, Alverda Ann: National Scene News Bureau
Muhammad, Askia: National Scene News Bureau
Muir, Robert: Reuters Television
Mulera, John H.: NBC News
Muller-Blattau, Beate: Zolcer-TV (German TV)
Mulvey, Julian: C–SPAN
Mun, Jae-Chul: Yonhap TV News
Munoz, Luis: Radio Marti
Munoz, Luis A.: C–SPAN
Munro, Stephen B.: National Public Radio
Muratani, Tateki: Fuji Television
Murney, John M.: Freelance
Murotani, Makiko: Tokyo Broadcasting System
Murphy, Heather: CBS News
Murphy, Kathy: C–SPAN
Murphy, Terence: C–SPAN
Murphy, Thomas P.: PTSC/CNN
Murray, Emily S.: CBN News
Murray, Tim: Ventana Productions
Murrhy, John L.: Freelance
Murtaugh, Peter S.: TF1–French Television
Muta, Akihiro: Nippon TV Network
Myers, Adolyn: NBC News
Myers, Lisa M.: NBC News
Myers, Wayne: WUSA–TV
Myklebust, Gunnar: Norweigan Broadcasting
Nascimento, Aurea: Univision News
Nash, Jim: Freelance
Nash, Jr., John C.: WETA–TV
Navies, Jerome: CBS Radio
Naylor, Brian: National Public Radio
Neary, Lynn: National Public Radio
Neel, Joe R.: National Public Radio
Neely, Prenella: Black Entertainment Television
Neff, Jill: CNN
Nelson, Donna: CBS News
Nelson, Meka: C–SPAN
Nelson, Norman: WETA–TV
Neustadt, James J.: NBC4
Neve, Thomas: C–SPAN
Newman, Patricia A.: Black Entertainment Television
Neyer, Hank: United Press International
Nickles, Ilona: C–SPAN
Nicolaidis, Virginia: CNN
Nielsen, John: National Public Radio
Nielsen, Ulla Pors: TV2 Denmark
Nikkel, Grace Lee: WTTG–Fox Television
Noble, Jeffrey S.: PTSC/CNN
Nolen, John: CBS News
Nonamaker, William T.: Potomac Television
Norins, Jamie F.: Potomac Television
Norland, Dean E.: ABC News
Norling, Richard A.: Freelance
Norling, Richard V.: Freelance
Norman, Dennis: PTSC/CNN
Norton, Charles: WJLA–TV
Norwood, Joelle: Airwaves, Inc.
Nurenberg, Gary: Tribune Broadcasting
Nyirjesy, Christine: APTV–Associated Press
Nyrop, Siri: German Television/ZDF
O'Berry, D. Kerry: Freelance
O'Brien, Tim: ABC News
O'Connor, Herb: ABC News
O'Hara, Victoria L.: National Public Radio

MEMBERS ENTITLED TO ADMISSION, RADIO AND TELEVISION CORRESPONDENTS' GALLERIES—Continued

O'Leary, John M.: CBN News
O'Shea, Daniel J.: Freelance
Oberlander, Sylvie: NBC News
Ochs, David R.: AP–Broadcast
Oesterwinter, Katharina: German Television/ZDF
Ogawa, Jun: Tokyo Broadcasting System
Ogawa, Kazuo: NHK–Japan Broadcasting
Ogoshi, Kumiko: NHK–Japan Broadcasting
Ogulnik, John A.: National Public Radio
Oki, Tom: TV Tokyo Channel 12, Ltd.
Oliva, Jennifer: Fox News Channel
Olsen, Kirsten: Gannett New Media
Olsher, Dean: National Public Radio
Oltarsh, Lauren: CNN
Oo, Thein Htike: Radio Free Asia
Ore, Rolando: Panamericana Television
Orgel, Paul: C–SPAN
Orr, Robert: CBS News
Ortiz, Alberto: CBS News
Ottalini, David: Potomac Television
Overby, Peter: National Public Radio
Owen-Thomas, Gavin: Fox News Channel
Pacheco, Sarah: PTSC/CNN
Pack, Michael: Manifold Productions
Pagano, Jack: Fox News Channel
Palca, Joseph: National Public Radio
Palmer, John S.: NBC News
Panzer, Chester: NBC4
Parenteau, Helene Y.: Canadian Broadcasting Corporation
Park, James I.: Radio Free Asia
Parker, Gill: ABC News
Parker, Robert G.: PTSC/CNN
Parker, Shaun: Black Entertainment Television
Pass, Christine: Reuters Television
Patruznick, Michael: C–SPAN
Patterson, Ferman: NET–Political NewsTalk Network
Patterson, Jay: ABC News
Patterson, Rodney: Freelance
Paxton, Bradford S.: Potomac Television
Peaks, Gershon: Reuters Television
Peleger, Peter: German Television/ZDF
Peltier, Yves: Canadian Broadcasting Corporation
Pena, Maria: United Press International
Pence, Rhonda: Dispatch Broadcast Group
Pendleton, Molette E.: NewsChannel 8
Pennybacker, Jennifer: CONUS Communications
Peppers, Gregory: National Public Radio
Pergram, Chad: C–SPAN
Perkins, Natasha S.: CONUS Communications
Perkins, Richard: Black Entertainment Television
Perry, Craig David: Radio Free Asia
Peters, Mary: AP–Broadcast
Peterson, Gordon W.: WUSA–TV
Peterson, Rebecca S.: CBS News
Peterson, Robert: CBS News
Peterson, Robert: Freelance
Petras, William H.: NBC News
Pettit, Debra: NBC News
Pfeifer, Andreas: ORF–Austrian Radio and TV
Philadelphia, Desa: The NewsHour with Jim Lehrer
Philips, Derek Todd: CNN
Phillips, Steven T.: Reuters Television
Pierce, Maura: C–SPAN
Pillon, Annette: C–SPAN
Pincus, Aileen: Freelance
Pinczuk, Murray: Freelance
Pines, Sarah: NBC News
Pinkas, Boris: Video News Service
Pitcairn, Duncan: Reuters Television
Pitman, John: Voice of America
Pittman, Anthony: Black Entertainment Television
Pitts, Byron A.: CBS News
Pizza, Elizabeth: CNN
Plante, William: CBS News
Plater, Christopher S.: Freelance
Player, Darryl: Black Entertainment Television
Pliszak, Richard K.: ABC News
Plomp, Margaret: N.O.S. National TV The Netherlands
Plotkin, Mark: WAMU–FM Radio
Plummer, Keith B.: Hearst Broadcasting
Polat, Ylmaz F.: Turkish CTV
Polite, Angela: WTOP Radio
Polk, Jackson: Capstone Productions
Poon, Denise L.: NBC News
Popkin, James: NBC4
Porter, Almon L.: CONUS Communications
Pottger, Lisa R.: The NewsHour with Jim Lehrer
Pratt, Carin: CBS News
Preloh, Anne Marie: C–SPAN
Preston, Richard Lee: Mutual/NBC Radio
Presutti, Carolyn: A.H. Belo Capitol Bureau
Pretto, Nancy: WJLA–TV
Price, Lisa: C–SPAN
Prior, James R.: Native American Television
Publicover, Robert: WTOP Radio
Puckett, Richard: Dispatch Broadcast Group
Pugliese, Pat A.: CONUS Communications
Que, Victoria: National Public Radio
Quinn, Diana: CBS News
Quinn, John D.: Worldnet-U.S.I.A TV
Quinnette, John Jay: PTSC/CNN
Quinonez, Omar A.: Freelance
Rabel, Edward: NBC News
Rabin, Carrie: WTOP Radio
Rabin, Mark: Freelance
Rackwitz, Ingolf: German Public Radio/ARD
Rad, Ali: Min Washington, Inc.
Raddatz, Martha: National Public Radio
Rafi, Mary E.: Salem Radio Network
Ragavan, Chitra: National Public Radio
Raker, Lester R.: Capital TV Network
Raker, Patrick L.: Capital TV Network
Raker, Roger A.: Capital TV Network

MEMBERS ENTITLED TO ADMISSION, RADIO AND TELEVISION CORRESPONDENTS' GALLERIES—Continued

Ralston, Paige: NET–Political NewsTalk Network
Ramon, Fausto: MSNBC Pro
Ramsey, Brett: Australian Broadcasting Corp.
Ramshaw, Gregg: The NewsHour with Jim Lehrer
Raphael, Mara: CNN
Rasmussen, Lisa: NBC4
Rasmussen, Torben: Danish Broadcasting
Rathner, Jeff: WETA–TV
Ratliff, Rebecca J.: Tokyo Broadcasting System
Ratner, Ellen F.: Talk Radio News Service
Ratner, Victor: ABC News
Ratns, Timothy: AP–Broadcast
Reals, Gary: WUSA–TV
Reap, Patrick T.: CNN
Redding, Sally: NBC News
Redding, William: ABC News
Reddoor, Charles: Native American Television
Reddy, Deanne: C–SPAN
Redpath, Julia: National Public Radio
Reed, Lloyd A.: Native American Television
Reese, Courtenay K.: NBC News
Reichenau, Maire: Radio Free Europe/Radio Liberty
Reid, Chip: NBC News
Reid, Joseph: AP–Broadcast
Reifenberg, Sabine: NDR/WDR German Radio
Reilly, Paul A.: AP–Broadcast
Reilly, Robert: C–SPAN
Reinsel, Edward M.: Freelance
Reio, Allen Kirk: USIA/TV Marti
Reis, Sean: NBC News Channel
Renaud, Jean R.: Black Entertainment Television
Renfro, Owen: CNN
Resnick, Jonathan: Reuters Television
Revitte, Kathleen N.: ABC News
Reyes, Victor: CBS Telenoticias
Rice, Alan Gregory: NBC News
Rice, Chuck: AP–Broadcast
Rich, Rita: Mutual/NBC Radio
Richard, Sylvain: Canadian Broadcasting Corporation
Richards, Michael W.: Freelance
Richards, Timothy: Canadian Broadcasting
Richerson, Debbie: C–SPAN
Richter, Richard: Radio Free Asia
Rickun, Marcie: NBC News
Rieger, Wendy: NBC4
Rife, Marvin: Washington News Network
Riffle, Luke: Ventana Productions
Riggs, Tyrone W.: PTSC/CNN
Riha, Anne Marie: CONUS Communications
Rinebolt, Roger: Potomac Television
Ringe, Linda: WJLA–TV
Riopedre, Jorge A.: USIA/TV Marti
Rivera, Clara E.: Reuters Television
Rizzolo, Lisa: Fox News Channel
Roach, Emily A.: CBN News
Roberson, David: Freelance
Roberto, Antonini: Swiss Broadcasting Corp.
Roberts, Corinne B.: ABC News
Roberts, Nathan: NewsChannel 8
Robertson, Greg: PTSC/CNN
Robertson, Jo: WTTG–Fox Television
Robertson Stone, Carolyn: PTSC/CNN
Robinson, Charles: Black Entertainment Television
Robinson, Chris: Deutsche Welle German Television
Robinson, Clyde W.: NBC News
Robinson, Douglas M: ORF–Austrian Radio and TV
Robinson, Laura: CNN
Robinson, Margaret L.: The NewsHour with Jim Lehrer
Robinson III, Earle U.: WJLA–TV
Roca, Xavier: Freelance
Rocha, Daniel: American Radio and TV
Rocha, Samuel: American Radio and TV
Roche, John M.: CNN
Rochelle, Carl: CNN
Rockler, Julia: The Washington Bureau
Rodriguez, Eduardo: Telvisa-Eco Television
Rodriguez, Eva M.: Court TV
Rodriguez, Luz: Radio Nacional De Espana
Rodriguez, Martine: The NewsHour with Jim Lehrer
Roeck, Donald: Pacifica Radio News
Rogers, Arthur: CONUS Communications
Rogers, Jeffrey S.: National Public Radio
Rogers, Patrick: CONUS Communications
Rollins, Bonnie: NBC News Stations Division
Romero, Gabe: CBS News
Romilly, George: ABC News
Roof, Peter B.: Freelance
Roper, John: Fox News Channel
Rose, Gail P.: WJLA–TV
Rose, Jeff: WJLA–TV
Rose, Joe: Gancie Television, Inc.
Rose, Joseph: WJLA–TV
Rose, Ray: WJLA–TV
Roselli, H. Michael: CNN
Rosenbaum, Richard: ABC News
Rosenbaum, Thea Luise: German Television/ARD
Rosenberg, Gary: Freelance
Rosenberg, Howard L.: CBS News
Rosenberg, Jeffrey: National Public Radio
Rosenblatt, Steven: Pyramid National Pressport
Rosenfeld, Steven: Freelance
Rosenfelder, Michael J.: Worldwide Television News
Rossetti-Meyer, Misa: Professional Video Services
Roskosh, Joan L.: Freelance
Ross, David Joseph: WTTG–Fox Television
Rosse, Richard Alan: Mutual/NBC Radio
Roth, Johnie F.: NBC News
Roth, Theodore: ABC News
Rovira, Ramon: Televisio De Catalunya
Rowe, Hildrun: German Television/ZDF
Rowe, JoAnn: Rowe News Service

MEMBERS ENTITLED TO ADMISSION, RADIO AND TELEVISION CORRESPONDENTS' GALLERIES—Continued

Rowe, Tom: Reuters Television
Roy, Andrew: British Broadcasting
Royster, William V.: AP–Broadcast
Rubin, Terry: The NewsHour with Jim Lehrer
Rubio, Arturo: Univision
Rudd, Michael: NewsChannel 8
Rudell, Tim Patrick: CONUS Communications
Ruggiero, David S.: PTSC/CNN
Ruggiero, Diane: CNN
Rushlow, Kathleen K.: National Public Radio
Russell, Roxanne: CBS News
Russert, Timothy J.: NBC News
Ruth, Sarah: CNN
Rutherford, John: NBC News
Ruttenberg, Margie: NBC4
Ryan, April: American Urban Radio Networks
Ryan, Karen A.: Freelance
Rysak, F. David: WTTG–Fox Television
Saalwachter, Amy: NBC News
Sabo, Cris: NHK–Japan Broadcasting
Safelle, Jeffrey: Professional Video Services
Sagalyn, Daniel: The NewsHour with Jim Lehrer
Salinas, Eduardo: United Press International
Salinas, Marcos A.: CBN News
Salinas, Mary Alice: NBC4
Saltz, Michael: The NewsHour with Jim Lehrer
Sampaio, Fred: C–SPAN
Sanchez, Claudio: National Public Radio
Sanchez, Pablo: Univision News
Sanders-Smith, Sherry: C–SPAN
Sandler, Lauren O.: National Public Radio
Sandyann, Jeffery R.: National Public Radio
Sanfuentes, Jose A.: NBC News
Santos, Augusto: Televisa-Eco Television
Santos, Jose: WJLA–TV
Sapienza, Stephen: America's Defense Monitor
Sarasohn, Sara Keiko: National Public Radio
Sargeant, Nancy L.: AP–Broadcast
Sargent, Catherine: Fox News Channel
Sargent, Mark E.: WTTG–Fox Television
Sarmiento, Cheryl: NBC News
Sarro, Ron A.: Washington News Network
Sasson, Aaron: Freelance
Saunders, Ernest: C–SPAN
Savage, Craig: Fox News Channel
Savory, Greg: Freelance
Scanlan, Daniel: Mutual/NBC Radio
Scanlon, Jason: C–SPAN
Schaefer, Eugenia F.: NBC News
Schaefer, Frances: NBC News
Schaefer, James: WJLA–TV
Schafer, Alison: Cox Broadcasting
Schaff, Michael L.: CBN News
Schalch, Kathleen N.: National Public Radio
Schantz, Kristine K.: CNN
Schenk, Jenny: German Television/ARD
Scherer, David R.: PTSC/CNN
Scheuer, John: C–SPAN
Schiavone, Louise: CNN
Schick, Carl: CONUS Communications
Schieffer, Robert: CBS News
Schifrin, Debra: National Public Radio
Schindler, Max A.: NBC News
Schlegel, Barry C.: PTSC/CNN
Schloemer, Hans-Peter: German Television/ARD
Schmidt, Robert: Court TV
Schmitz, Michael: German Television/ZDF
Schneider, Rene: The NewsHour with Jim Lehrer
Schoenholtz, Howard: ABC News
Scholl, Christopher: NBC News
Schorr, Daniel: National Public Radio
Schroeder, Bernd Julius, German Radio NDR/WDR
Schroeder: Robert, NHK–Japan Broadcasting
Schuetzeichel: Frank, German Television/ARD
Schule: James, ITN of London
Schultz-Burkel, Gunnar: German Broadcasting/ARD
Schultze, Emily: CBS News
Schwartz, Andy: Fox News Channel
Schweiger, Ellen: C–SPAN
Schweitzer, Murray H.: NBC4
Scicchitano, Carmine: NBC News
Scotchbrook, Ben: ITN of London
Scott, Graham L.: ORF–Austrian Radio and TV
Scott, Ivan: CBS–Radio Stations News Service
Scott, Linda J.: The NewsHour with Jim Lehrer
Scott, Traci Ann: CBS News
Scruggs, Wesley: NBC News
Scully, Steven: C–SPAN
Searle-Grey, Jacquetta J.: ORF–Austrian Television
Sears, Carl: Fox News Channel
Seem, Thomas H.: CBS News
Seium, Michael: Freelance
Selg, Casper: Swiss Broadcasting Corp.
Sell, Dalfa: CONUS Communications
Sellai, Christine: Fox News Channel
Selma, Reginald G.: PTSC/CNN
Selman, Steve: British Broadcasting
Serensits, Joseph S.: ABC News
Sergay, Richard: ABC News
Sesno, Frank: CNN
Sewell, Leslie: NBC News
Sforza, Scott N.: ABC News
Shaffir, Gregory: CBS News
Shalhoup, Joseph F.: NBC4
Shannon, Dennis: CBS News
Sharp, Bridget: NET–Political NewsTalk Network
Sheahan, John: ABC News
Shelton, Steve: Fox News Channel
Shemonsky, Laura: Fox News Channel
Sherrill, Charles L.: Bonneville International Corp.
Sherwood, Tom: NBC4
Shih, Che-Wei: TVBS (Taiwan)
Shine, Thomas: ABC News
Shiraishi, Yoshihiko: Nippon TV Network

MEMBERS ENTITLED TO ADMISSION, RADIO AND TELEVISION CORRESPONDENTS' GALLERIES—Continued

Shlemon, Chris: ITN of London
Shockley, Milton T.: NBC4
Shoffner, Cindy Pena: WJLA–TV
Shoffner, Harry S.: Freelance
Short, Philip: British Broadcasting
Shott, David: Fox News Channel
Shrader, Robert E.: PTSC/CNN
Shuster, David: Fox News Channel
Shwe, Wyein: Radio Free Asia
Siceloff, John: ABC News
Sidel, Adam P.: NewsChannel 8
Siegel, Robert: National Public Radio
Siegloch, Klaus-Peter: German Television/ZDF
Siekkinen, Sinikka: Finnish Broadcasting
Sierra, Joann: CNN
Sierra, Jose Javier: APTV–Associated Press
Sigsgaard, Peter: Danish Broadcasting
Sikka, Madhulika: ABC News
Silberner, Joanne: National Public Radio
Siler, Melanie E.: Black Entertainment Television
Silnicky, Larisa: Radio Free Europe/Radio Liberty
Silva, Ellen: National Public Radio
Silva-Pinto, Lauren: ORF–Austrian Radio and TV
Silver, Amy R.: CNN
Silver, Darwin: WETA–TV
Silver, Janet E.: Australian Broadcasting Corp.
Silver, Quentin: Freelance
Silverberg, Hank: SRN News/Standard News
Silverman, Art: National Public Radio
Silverstein, Mike: ABC News
Simeone, Nicholas: Voice of America
Simon, Julie: Ventana Productions
Simpson, Carole: ABC News
Simpson, Ross W.: Mutual/NBC Radio
Sims, Chinyere: C–SPAN
Sisco, Paul: Worldwide Television News
Sites, Kevin Andrew: NBC News
Skane, William J.: CBS News
Skeans, Ron: Professional Video Services
Sklar, Marc: CNN
Slattery, Andrea: CNN
Slattery, Julie: Bloomberg Business News
Slen, Peter: C–SPAN
Slewka, Stephanie B.: German Television/ARD
Slobogin, Kathy: CNN
Slone, Sean: C–SPAN
Small, William: United Press International
Smee, Bill: CNN
Smith, Cindy: APTV–Associated Press
Smith, Cynthia L.: ABC News
Smith, David: ITN of London
Smith, Gregory: National Public Radio
Smith, Jack P.: ABC News
Smith, Jan: WTTG–Fox Television
Smith, Margaret Low: National Public Radio
Smith, Mark S.: AP–Broadcast
Smith, Mignon C.: Washington-Alabama News Report
Smith, Phillip: A.H. Belo Capitol Bureau
Smith, Raeshawn: C–SPAN
Smith, Renee: Voice of America
Smith, Terence: CBS News
Smith, William B.: Potomac Television
Sneed, Kimberly: NBC News
Snow, Tony: Fox News Channel
Snyder, George: Providence Journal Broadcasting
Sobata, Kenji: NHK–Japan Broadcasting
Soe, Kin Maung: Radio Free Asia
Solomon, Eric: CNN
Solorzano, Gilbert J.: Freelance
Somani, Indira: WJLA–TV
Soneira, Robert: CONUS Communications
Sonne, Werner: German Television/ARD
Sorenson, Randall: PTSC/CNN
Sorimachi, Osamu: Fuji Television
Soucheray, Phil: AP–Broadcast
Soucy, Peggy M.: CNN
Southern, Joel L.: Alaska Public Radio
Sozio, George: ABC News
Spaeth, David: CNN
Spain, Thomas: PTSC/CNN
Speare, Brad: C–SPAN
Speck, Alan: C–SPAN
Speed, Rodney E.: Freelance
Speights, Eric Van: ABC News
Speiser, Matt: ABC News
Spence, Robert: C–SPAN
Spencer, Susan R.: CBS News
Sperrazza, Christine J.: ABC News
Spevak, Joseph: NewsChannel 8
Spillane, Mary: CBS News
Spinrad, Naomi: NBC News
Spoerry, Philip Scott: CNN
Sponder, Myron: Talk Radio News Service
Springham, Lisa Mary: Reuters Television
Sproul, Robin: ABC News
St. John, Jonathan: Potomac Television
Stage, Tina: Bloomberg Business News
Stagneth, Michael: German Television/ZDF
Stalder, Han Peter: Swiss Broadcasting Corp.
Stamberg, Susan L.: National Public Radio
Stanford, David E.: CBS News
Starace, Andrea F.: Standard News Network
Stark, Lisa: ABC News
Statter, Louis David: WUSA–TV
Stauffer, LeeAnn: CNN
Steinhilber, Kathryn E.: CNN
Stenstrom, Oddvar: TV 2 Norway
Steo, Austin: Wingspan Network-Aviation News
Stepney, Eric: C–SPAN
Steuart, Elizabeth: NBC News
Stevens, Pamela: CNN
Stevenson, Louis R.: WTTG–Fox Television
Stewart, Amy: CNN
Stewart, James: CBS News

MEMBERS ENTITLED TO ADMISSION, RADIO AND TELEVISION CORRESPONDENTS' GALLERIES—Continued

Stix, Gabriel: CBS News
Stoddard, Mark: Freelance
Stoll, Karl: NET–Political NewsTalk Network
Storey, Alfred: NBC News
Storey, Rodney: Fox News Channel
Strand, Paul L.: CBN News
Stratton, Frederick: MSNBC Pro
Strei, Jeff: Fox News Channel
Strickland, Kenneth: NBC News
Stringer, Ashley King: CONUS Communications
Stromberg, Sven: Swedish Television
Strong, David: WTTG–Fox Television
Stroud, Andrea Diane: Talk Radio News Service
Stuart, Jessica: NBC News
Stubbs, James: PTSC/CNN
Stultz, Amanda: Reuters Television
Styles, Julian H.: CNN
Suddeth, Rick: Freelance
Suhonen, Alan: A.H. Belo Capitol Bureau
Suissa, Jimmy: PTSC/CNN
Sumler, Jennifer: Cox Broadcasting
Summers, George S.: Freelance
Sundstrom, Bert: Swedish Television
Surbey, Jason: C–SPAN
Suto, Ena: TV Asahi
Sutton, Robert T.: NET–Political NewsTalk Network
Sutton, Todd: NBC News Channel
Suzuki, Jun: Nippon TV Network
Swain, Susan M.: C–SPAN
Swan, David: Voice of America
Swanier, Sherrell: CNN
Swann, Michael D.: NBC4
Sweeney, David: National Public Radio
Swift, Kenneth: CBS News
Swiner, Ricardo: NBC News
Szaroleta, Marjorie: AP–Broadcast
Tamerlani, George: Reuters Television
Tang, Deborah: Black Entertainment Television
Tang, Scott: The NewsHour
Tarrant, Philippa: Reuters Television
Taylor, Allyson Ross: CBS News
Taylor, Ann: National Public Radio
Taylor, Charles W.: ABC News
Taylor, Daniel: PTSC/CNN
Taylor, Kelli: Australian Broadcasting Corp.
Teeples, Joe: C–SPAN
Tenequer: Bob: RainDancer News Bureau
Terrell: Angela: Nightly Business Report
Terry: Janet: WUSA–TV
Tessler, Barton J.: Mutual/NBC Radio
Thalman, Mark: Ventana Productions
Thalman, Mark F.: NewsChannel 8
Thevessen, Elmar: German Television/ZDF
Thiele, Kim Denise: PTSC/CNN
Thinn, Soe: Radio Free Asia
Thomas, Andrew D.: Freelance
Thomas, Arthur: Black Entertainment Television
Thomas, Evelyn: CBS News
Thomas, Hugh: NewsChannel 8
Thompkins, Gwendolyn: National Public Radio
Thompson, Jerry: PTSC/CNN
Thompson, Lea Hopkins: NBC News
Thompson, Ron Talley: WTTG–Fox Television
Thorne, C. Patrick: Washington Bureau News Service
Thornton, Jr., Theodore E.: Black Entertainment Television
Tidler, David: Professional Video Services
Tillery, Richard: The Washington Bureau
Tillman, Thomas E.: CBS News
Tilman, Brandon: C–SPAN
Tin, Annie: C–SPAN
Tobias, Ed: AP–Broadcast
Tollkuhn, Eckhard F.: Deutsche Welle German Television
Tollkuhn, Felicity J.: Deutsche Welle German Television
Tomko, Joe: Video News Service
Tomko, Stephen: Video News Service
Tomko, III, Joseph S.: Worldwide Television News
Toole, Mary Beth: Freelance
Torgerson, Ande: Fox News Channel
Torfey, Robert B.: PTSC/CNN
Totenberg, Nina: National Public Radio
Towne, Charles: CONUS Communications
Tracey, Patrick: Washington Bureau News Service
Trammell, Michael: WUSA–TV
Traynham, Peter C.: CBS News
Trengrove, James Albert: The NewsHour with Jim Lehrer
Troop, William: The World
Troute, Dennis: Image Television
Trull, Armando: Univision News
Tsai, Gary C.: China Television Company
Tschida, Stephen John: NewsChannel 8
Tubbs, Robert V.: Worldnet-U.S.I.A TV
Tubies, Wilma: Wingspan Network-Aviation News
Tucker, Elke: German Television/ZDF
Tuel, Ted Richard: CONUS Communications
Tufeckgian, Denchali: WMAL Radio
Tull, Laura: Court TV
Tune, Melissa D.: Freelance
Tuohey, Ken: Nightly Business Report
Turnbull, Bill: British Broadcasting
Turner, Al Douglas: ABC News
Turnley, William: GVI
Tutman, Dan D.: CBS News
Tyler, Sarah: APTV–Associated Press
Uchima, Charles K.: WTTG–Fox Television
Uchimiya, Ellen: Freelance
Udenans, Vija: ABC News
Uechtritz, Max: Australian Broadcasting Corp.
Ulery, Bradley: Hearst Broadcasting
Uliano, Richard: AP–Broadcast
Umrani, Anthony R.: PTSC/CNN

MEMBERS ENTITLED TO ADMISSION, RADIO AND TELEVISION CORRESPONDENTS' GALLERIES—Continued

Underwood, Colvin: NewsChannel 8
Urman, John F.: PTSC/CNN
Usaeva, Nadia: Radio Free Asia
Uyehara, Otto K.: WETA–TV
Valcarcel, Gus: APTV–Associated Press
Vallese, Julie W.: CNN
Vallete, Robert: Freelance
Van Der Wulp, Gerard: N.O.S. National TV The Netherlands
Van Nguyen, Khanh: Radio Free Asia
Van Susteren, Greta: CNN
Van de Bellen, Erin: NBC News
Vanasse, Robert: Talk Radio News Service
VanderVeen, Lawrence: Mobile Video Services
Vecchione, Allan: WJLA–TV
Veitch, William: Washington Bureau News Service
Velez, Yaromil: NBC News
Vennell, Vicki: ABC News
Verdi, Anthony: NBC News
Verenkotte, Clemens: German Public Radio/ARD
Verna, Terrie: NBC News
Vernon, Wes: CBS Radio
Veron, Ilyse J.: The NewsHour with Jim Lehrer
Ververs, Vaughn: Freelance
Vadilla-Vidaurre, Oscar: Nuevo Mundo Network
Viddy, Laura: CNN
Vineys, Kevin S.: APTV–Associated Press
Vinson, Bryce: Fox News Channel
Viqueria, Michael: NHK–Japan Broadcasting
Voth, Charles: WETA–TV
Vukmer, David: CONUS Communications
Waghorn, Dominic: London News Radio
Wagner, Paul C: WTOP Radio
Wakaizumi, Mitsuhiro: Tokyo Broadcasting System
Wakamatsu, Makoto: Fuji Television
Walker, Brian: Freelance
Walker, James W.: NewsChannel 8
Walker, Kevin C.: AP Broadcast
Walker, Tom: Fisher Broadcasting
Walker, William L.: CBS News
Wallace, James M.: National Public Radio
Wallace, John L.: Fox News Channel
Wallace, Zelda: Cox Broadcasting
Walsh, Joe: Mutual/NBC Radio
Walsh, Mary E.: CBS News
Walsh, Mary F.: ABC News
Walsh Gilmore, Mary Jo: WJLA–TV
Walter, Charles: ITN of London
Walters, Theodore: WJLA–TV
Walworth, A. MacKenzie: CNN
Walz, Mark: PTSC/CNN
Wanzer, John: NBC4
Ward, Derrick: WAMU–FM Radio
Ward, Stacey Y.: Black Entertainment Television
Warehime, Keith: C–SPAN
Warner, Christopher: Image Television
Warner, Craig: Mutual/NBC Radio
Warner, Margaret: The NewsHour with Jim Lehrer
Washburn, Kevin: C–SPAN
Washington, Ervin Steven: Nightly Business Report
Wasser, Fred: National Public Radio
Watkins, Felicia: Black Entertainment Television
Watkins, Richard T.: WJLA–TV
Watson, George H.: ABC News
Watson, James: NewsChannel 8
Watson, Walter Ray: National Public Radio
Watts, Chris: AP–Broadcast
Watts, Michael T.: CNN
Webb, Clifton: NewsChannel 8
Webb, David A.: WJLA–TV
Weinberg, Karin: National Public Radio
Weinfeld, Michael: AP–Broadcast
Weinreub, Lori K.: AP–Broadcast
Weinstein, Lori M.: Hearst Broadcasting
Weisskopf, Arlene: Freelance
Welby, Julianne: WAMU–FM Radio
Weldon, Harry: ABC News
Weller, George: Freelance
Wendy, Carla G.: Fox News Channel
Werner, Dan: The NewsHour with Jim Lehrer
West, Tanzi N.: ABC News
Westaway, Jennifer: Canadian Broadcasting Corporation
Westfall, Richard: NET–Political NewsTalk Network
Westwood, Helen: ABC News
Weyrich, Stephen: NET–Political NewsTalk Network
Wharton, Ned: National Public Radio
Whatley, Mike: NBC4
Wheatley, Marcia: Potomac Television
Wheelock, Robert S.: ABC News
Whelton, Danielle J.: CNN
White, Kenneth: Black Entertainment Television
Whiteman, Doug: AP–Broadcast
Whiteside, John P.: Freelance
Whitley, John: Professional Video Services
Whitney, Michael D.: Washington Bureau News Service
Widmer, Christopher: Freelance
Wiggins, Christopher: NBC News
Wik, Snorre: NewsChannel 8
Wilk, Wendy: WTTG–Fox Television
Wilkes, Douglas H.: WTTG–Fox Television
Wilkinson, Wendla: NBC News
Williams, Danyell T.: National Public Radio
Williams, Debi: National Public Radio
Williams, John A.: Freelance
Williams, Karen: NBC News
Williams, Kenneth E.: CBS News
Williams, LaTanya: C–SPAN
Williams, Louis A.: NBC News
Williams, Robert Toney: NBC News
Williams, Ronald F.: WUSA–TV
Willingham, Dave: NewsChannel 8
Willis, Judith: The NewsHour with Jim Lehrer

MEMBERS ENTITLED TO ADMISSION, RADIO AND TELEVISION CORRESPONDENTS' GALLERIES—Continued

Willman, Dale A.: CNN
Wilmeth, Mary Dorman: NBC News
Wilson, Brenda: National Public Radio
Wilson, Brian G.: WTTG–Fox Television
Wilson, George: American Urban Radio Networks
Wilson, Kristin: Freelance
Wilson, Leigh: Freelance
Wilson, Stephanie S.: WUSA–TV
Windall, Carline: National Public Radio
Windham, R. Craig: National Public Radio
Windham, Ronald: Tribune Broadcasting
Wines, Karen: ABC News
Winkler, Alice: National Public Radio
Winkler, Melissa: Voice of America
Winslow, Linda: The NewsHour with Jim Lehrer
Winter, Sonia: Radio Free Europe/Radio Liberty
Winterhalter, Ruthann: C–SPAN
Wisotzky, Jaimee: C–SPAN
Witt, Holger: German Television/ARD
Witten, Robert: Freelance
Wittlif, Marc R.: Talk Radio News Service
Wolfe, Randy: CBS News
Wolff, Sarah: Canadian Broadcasting Corporation
Wolfson, Charles: CBS News
Wolfson, Paula: Voice of America
Womack, Laura: WAMU–FM Radio
Wood, Geneviere E.: NET–Political NewsTalk Network
Wood, Wayne C.: NBC4
Woods, Madelyne: WJLA–TV
Woods, Stephanie: Nightly Business Report
Wooten, Rodney: Black Entertainment Television
Wordlaw, Gary: WJLA–TV
Wordock, John: Bloomberg Business News
Works, Karol Lyn: Potomac Television
Wotring, Melanie J.: NewsChannel 8
Wright, Brad: CNN
Wright, Crystal S.: ABC News
Wright, Cynthia: WJLA–TV
Wright, Kim: NewsChannel 8
Wright, Linda D.: C–SPAN
Wright, Miriam: WUSA–TV
Wu, Annie: WAMU–FM Radio
Wu, Hsiang-San: Taiwan Television Enterprise
Wurz, Sandra A.: CONUS Communications
Wyatt, Magaly: CBS Telenoticias
Wynn, Audrey: National Public Radio
Wysocki, Jennifer: CNN
Xiao, Yan: Chinese Television Network
Yamada, Junko: Nippon TV Network
Yanaga, Keisuke: Nippon TV Network
Yang, Bettina: Chinese Television Network
Yang, Carter M.: ABC News
Yang, Eun: WUSA–TV
Yates, H. William: Freelance
Ydstie, John: National Public Radio
Yianopoulus, Karen: Fox News Channel
Young, Melissa: ABC News
Young, Nicole: Hearst Broadcasting
Young, Rebekah: CNN
Young, Robert L.: Metro Teleproductions Inc.
Young, Sandra L.: WTTG–Fox Television
Young, Thomas: AP–Broadcast
Young, Tom: WTTG–Fox Television
Yus, Francisca G.: PTSC/CNN
Zabych, Mike: C–SPAN
Zachurski, Tadeusz: Polskie Radio
Zafiropulos, Steve: NewsChannel 8
Zang, GuoHua: Chinese Television Network
Zeidman, Jennifer: CNN
Zelnick, C. Robert: ABC News
Zerros, Stratis J.: Freelance
Zodun, Albert N.: NBC4
Zomorodi, Manoush: British Broadcasting
Zosso, Elizabeth: C–SPAN
Zucker, Joy Allison: NewsChannel 8
Zwadiuk, Oleh: Radio Free Europe/Radio Liberty
Zwerdling, Daniel: National Public Radio

NETWORKS, STATIONS, AND SERVICES REPRESENTED

Senate Gallery 224–6421 House Gallery 225–5214

A.H. BELO CAPITOL BUREAU—(202) 661–8471; 1325 G Street, NW #250 20005: Thomas Ackerman, Sharon Bender, Matthew Braatz, David Martin Cassidy, Jonathan E. Drum, Jim Fry, Jeff Goldblatt, Michael Goldfein, Stacy Hutchins, Michael Kornely, Scot Lawrence, Carolyn Presutti, Phillip Smith, George Snyder, Alan Suhonen.

ABC NEWS—(202) 222–7700; 1717 DeSales Street, NW 20036: Douglas Adams, Robin C. Adlerblum, Lynne Adrine, Douglas Allmond, Nancy J. Ambrose, James F. Ashe, Christina Babarovic, Mark Banks, Jon Bascom, John H. Bauer, Bob Bender, Catherine A. Berger, Thomas Bettag, John J. Bilotta, Kenneth L. Blaylock, Glennwood Branche, Charles L. Breiterman, Mark E. Brender, Sam Brooks, Henry Metric Brown, Hal Bruno, A'Lelia Bundles, Chris Bury, Elizabeth Carden, Chris Carlson, Hyunju Chang, Martin Clancy, Robert E. Clark, John Cochran, Richard Coolidge, Robert Corbey, Pam Coulter, Robert Crawford, Andrew Cremedas, Patrick Cullen, Thomas J. D'Annibale, Anne Davenport, Karla Davis, Ernest Davy, Ariane deVogué, Terry DeWitt, Tom DiBacco, Henry Disselkamp, Peter M. Doherty, Sam Donaldson, John Donvan, Linda Diane Douglass, Kathleen Drew, Jonathan Ebinger, James W. Eldridge, Andrew Field, Charles Finamore, Diane J. Forcey, Andrew R. Field, Vincent Gaito, John J. Gallagher, George R. Gerlach, Joshua A. Gerstein, Thomas Giusto, Stuart O. Gordon, Robin Gradison, Myra P. Green, William Greenwood, Bettina L. Gregory, Andrew Gross, Charles Herman, David Herndon, Fletcher H. Johnson, Julie Johnson, Kenneth Johnson, William R. Johnson, Steven Joya, Jacqueline Judd, Sara Just, Joy Kalfopulos, Sheilah Kast, Deborah Kempf, Jerry King, John W. Knott, John C. LaMonica, Laura Logan, Beverley C. Lumpkin, Ellsworth Lutz, David Marash, James T. Martin, John J. Martin, Luis E. Martinez, Michel McQueen, John McWethy, Portia R. Migas, Daniel Morris, Dean E. Norland, Tim O'Brien, Herb O'Connor, Gillian Parker, Jay Patterson, Victor Ratner, William Redding, Kathleen N. Revitte, Corinne B. Roberts, George Romilly, Richard Rosenbaum, Gary Rosenberg, Howard Schoenholtz, Joseph S. Serensits, Richard Sergay, Scott N. Sforza, John Sheahan, Thomas Shine, John Siceloff, Madhulika Sikka, M.D. Silverstein, Carole Simpson, Cynthia L. Smith, Jack P. Smith, George Sozio, Eric Van Speights, Matthew Speiser, Christine J. Sperrazza, Robin Sproul, Lisa Stark, Charles W. Taylor, Al Douglas Turner, Vija Udenans, Vicki Vennell, Mary F. Walsh, George H. Watson, Harry Weldon, Tanzi N. West, Helen Westwood, Robert S. Wheelock, Karen Wines, Crystal S. Wright, Carter M. Yang, Melissa Young, C. Robert Zelnick.

AP-BROADCAST—(202) 736–9500; 1825 K Street, NW 20006: Amanda Barnett, Jeffery Baron, Joni Beall, Gerald Bodlander, Camille Bohannon, Carlotta L. Bradley, Larry Brown, Mark Carlson, Karen Chase, Steven E. Coleman, Lalnie Contreras, Carol Esler, Rita M. Foley, Oscar Wells Gabriel, Jennifer Garske, Heather Greenfield, Michael J. Hammer, Mark A. Hamrick, Cynthia Hecht, Ken C. Herrera, Walter R. Hindes, Derrill E. Holly, Peggy Johannsen, Brad Kalbfeld, Jennifer Kerr, Eugene Kim, Sandy Kozel, Thelma LeBrecht, Francis J. Limbach, Kathryn Loomans, James Ludwin, Lisa N. Matthews, Kate McKenna, David R. Melendy, Adrienne Metil, Bryant T. Michaud, James Militello, David R. Ochs, Mary Peters, Timothy Ratns, Joseph Reid, Paul A. Reilly, Chuck Rice, William V. Royster, Nancy L. Sargeant, Mark S. Smith, Phil Soucheray, Marjorie Szaroleta, Ed Tobias, Richard Uliano, Kevin Walker, Chris Watts, Michael Weinfeld, Lori K. Weinreub, Doug Whiteman, Thomas Young.

APTV-ASSOCIATED PRESS—(202) 736–9595; 1825 K Street, NW 20006: Teresa Albor, Marc Augenbraum, Louise Bamfield, Patricia N. Beckman, Tracey Ann Brown, Ann N. Buffington, Daniele D'Amico, Kelly Daschle, Steve Fluty, Richard S. Gentilo, James Gorman, Daniel R. Huff, Kristine Kelleher, Philip L. LeCroy, Christine Nyirjesy-Bragale, Jose Javier Sierra, Cindy Smith, Sarah Tyler, Gus Valcarcel, Kevin S. Vineys.

AIRWAVES, INC.—(301) 215–7171; 4300 Montgomery Avenue, #303 Bethesda, MD 20814: Rick Alfredson, Michelle Becker, Tracy Bernstein, Paul C. Gavin, Bonnie A. Haynes, Joelle Norwood.

ALASKA PUBLIC RADIO—(202) 362–1699; 2801 Quebec Street, NW #505 20008: Joel L. Southern.

AMERICA'S DEFENSE MONITOR—(202) 862–0700; 1500 Massachusetts Avenue, NW 20005: Glenn Baker, Stephen Sapienza.

AMERICAN RADIO AND TV, INC.—(202) 822–8774; 1825 K Street, NW #507: Daniel Rocha, Samuel Rocha.

AMERICAN URBAN RADIO NETWORKS—(800) 456–4211; 627 Jefferson Street, NE 20011: April Ryan, George Wilson.

AUDIO-VIDEO NEWS—(703) 354–6795; 3622 Stanford Circle Falls Church, VA 22041: Connie Lawn.

NETWORKS, STATIONS, AND SERVICES REPRESENTED—Continued

AUSTRALIAN BROADCASTING CORPORATION—(202) 626–5170; 529 14th Street, NW #510 20045: Jimmy Balsamo, Tony Jones, Woody Landay, Phillip Lasker, Brett Ramsey, Janet E. Silver, Kelli Taylor, Max Uechtritz.

AUSTRIAN RADIO AND TV/ORF—(202) 822–9570; 1206 Eton Court, NW 20007: Hildegard Banes, Eugen A. Freund, Raimund Loew, Andreas Pfeifer, Douglas M Robinson, Graham L. Scott, Jacquetta J. Searle-Grey, Lauren Silva-Pinto.

BANDEIRANTES NETWORK-BRAZIL—(202) 363–5694; 3101 New Mexico Avenue, NW #815 20016: Chris Delboni.

THE BERNS BUREAU—(202) 628–1430; 400 North Capitol Street, NW #183 20001: Wendy A. Goldman, Matthew Kaye.

BLACK ENTERTAINMENT TELEVISION—(202) 608–2000; 1900 W Street, NE 20018: John C. Avery, Rovenia M. Brook, Kelly M. Carter, C. Jaci Clark, Sabrina Dames, Laura Gene Daughtery, Sheila Douglas, Donna Foster-Dotson, Lura Annette Gibbs, Richard T. Gibbs, David Grain, Helena D. Johnson, Donna Lacey, Cheryl Martin, Doxie A. McCoy, Chris Melville, Charles Montgomery, Jr., Corey B. Moore, Prenella Neely, Patricia A. Newman, Shaun Parker, Richard Perkins, Anthony Pittman, Darryl Player, Jean R. Renaud, Charles Robinson, Melanie E. Siler, Deborah Tang, Arthur Thomas, Theodore E. Thornton, Jr., Stacey Y. Ward, Felicia Watkins, Kenneth White, Rodney Wooten.

BLOOMBERG BUSINESS NEWS—(202) 624–1800; 529 14th Street, NW #228 20045: Irwin M. Chapman, Jonathan Felger, Roland Morrisette, Julie Slattery, Tina Stage, John Wordock.

BONNEVILLE INTERNATIONAL CORPORATION—(202) 737–3100; 400 North Capitol Street, #156 20001: Ronald Ray Eisenbarth, Marlis Majerus, Charles L. Sherrill.

BRITISH BROADCASTING—(202) 223–2050; 2030 M Street, NW #607 20036: Sharon Blanchet, Claire Bolderson, Stuart Cohen, Lynn M. Dalton, Amanda Jane Farnsworth, Kristy Gavin, Gavin James Hewitt, Jeremy Hillman, Katty Kay, Bridget Kendall, Maxine Mawhinney, Elizabeth P. Miller, Chris Morris, Andrew Roy, Steve Selman, Philip Short, Bill Turnbull, Manoush Zomorodi.

BROADCAST NEWS, LTD—(202) 638–3368; 1331 Pennsylvania Avenue, NW 20001: Brian Kennedy.

BROADCASTING CORPORATION OF CHINA—(301) 881–4466; 1641 E. Jefferson Street, #104 Rockville, MD 20852: Ping Liu.

C-NET—(202) 626–7989; 444 North Capitol Street #601D 20009: Mariko Ikehara.

C-SPAN—(202) 737–3220; 400 North Capitol Street, #650 20001: Elizabeth Aiken, Kenny Alexander, Thomas Alldredge, Theresa L. Amirault, Chiara Andres, Nick Aretakis, Douglas Bailey, Michelle Bailor, Shepard B. Bennett, Jay Berk, Brett Betsill, Amanda Boskent, Constance D. Brod, Paul Brown, Craig Brownstein, Susan Bundock, Kevin Burch, Leslie Burdick, David Byrd, Nancy Calo-Christianson, Craig Caplan, Stephen Carpenter, Steven Chaggaris, Jim Clark, Amie Cogan, Josh Cohen, Kathryn Cole, Eloise Collingwood, Bruce Collins, William Conover, Jeffrey Conrad, Liam Currier, Matthew Dauchess, Deborah Derrick, Steve Devoney, Jerry Echols, Gary Ellenwood, Seth Engel, Gregory Fabic, Daniel Farkas, Mark Farkas, Rick Gabala, Regina Gardner-Johnson, Garney Gary, Joyce Genter, Maria Gildea, Jacqueline Gill, Patrice Gordon, Paul Grachow, Richard Hall, Mohamed Hanoura, Eric Hansen, Maurice Haynes, Colin Hazard, William Heffley, Vernon Herald, Douglas Heyman, Wilton Hill, Regina Hunter, Pablo Izquierdo, Douglas Johnson, Leona Jordan, Ruth Kane, Paul Kangas, Jane Karakashian, Barry Katz, Robert G. Kennedy, Roxane Kerr, Lewis Ketcham, Kevin King, Donna Lacey, Brian Lamb, Hope Landy, Darren Larade, Kevin Leonard, Edward Lewis, Michael Marcus, Kiersten Marshall, Valerie Matthews, Michael McCann, Sean McCann, Kevin J. McClam, Julia McGraw, Matthew McGuire, Kate Mills, Diane Morris, Daniel Morton, Julian Mulvey, Luis A. Munoz, Kathy Murphy, Terence Murphy, Meka Nelson, Thomas Neve, Ilona Nickles, Paul Orgel, Michael Patruznick, Ines Perez, Chad Pergram, Maura Pierce, Annette Pillon, Anne Preloh, Lisa Price, Deanne Reddy, Robert Reilly, Deborah Richerson, Fred Sampaio, Sherry Sanders-Smith, Ernest Saunders, Jason Scanlon, John Scheuer, Ellen Schweiger, Steven Scully, Chinyere Sims, Peter Slen, Sean Slone, Raeshawn Smith, Bradley Speare, Alan Speck, Robert Spence, Eric Stepney, Jason Surbey, Susan M. Swain, Joe Teeples, Brandon Tilman, Annie Tin, Keith Warehime, Kevin Washburn, LaTanya Williams, Ruthann Winterhalter, Jaimee Wisotzky, Linda Wright, Michael Zabych, Elizabeth Zosso.

CBN NEWS—(202) 833–2707; 1111 19th Street, NW #950 20036: Robert Allen, Frank Becker, Randall Brooks, Melissa Charbonneau, Michael A. Garofalo, John Kenneth Lormand, Ron Magnuson, D. Matthew Martin, John Mueller, Emily S. Murray, John M. O'Leary, Emily A. Roach, Marcos A. Salinas, Michael L. Schaff, Paul L. Strand.

CBS NEWS—(202) 457–4444; 2020 M Street, NW 20036: Thomas Albano, Wyatt Andrews, Howard Arenstein, Robert Armstrong, Sharyl Attkisson, Barry Bagnato, Bruce Barr, Brenda Box, Rita Braver, David Caravello, George Christian, Barbara Cochran, Alfred Colby, Paul H. Corum, Pham Cuong Gia, Walter C. Dean, Arlene Dillon, Lois Dyer, Eric Engberg, Tony Furlow, Hal E. Furman, Benson Ginsburg, Jeff Goldman, Neil J. Grasso, David Gross, Tom Haederle, Mary K. Hager, Dierdre Hester, Pham Boi Hoan, Dennis Jamison, Tracy Johnke, Nancy Johns, Phil Jones, Adriene Jordan, Mark Katkov, Mark Knoller, Stephanie Lambidakis, Donald A Lee, Amy Lehrman, Denise Li, Matt Lowe, Dotty Lynch, David C. Martin, Mary Martin, Thomas A. Mattesky, James McGlinchy, Michael McGuire, Jill Meyer, Richard Meyer, Dana Miller, Russell Mitchell, Heather Murphy, Donna Nelson, John

NETWORKS, STATIONS, AND SERVICES REPRESENTED—Continued

Nolen, Robert Orr, Alberto Ortiz, Rebecca S. Peterson, Byron A. Pitts, William Plante, Carin Pratt, Diana Quinn, Gabe Romero, Howard L. Rosenberg, Roxanne Russell, Robert Schieffer, Emily Schultze, Traci Ann Scott, Thomas H. Seem, Gregory Shaffir, Kimberlee V. Shaffir, Dennis Shannon, William J. Skane, Terence Smith, Susan R. Spencer, Mary Spillane, David E. Stanford, James Stewart, Gabriel Stix, Kenneth Swift, Allyson Ross Taylor, Evelyn Thomas, Thomas E. Tillman, Peter C. Traynham, Dan D. Tutman, Mary E. Walsh, Kenneth E. Williams, Randy Wolfe, Charles Wolfson.

CBS RADIO—(202) 457–4370; 2020 M Street, NW 20036: Pam Coulter, Tracy Lyn Johnke, Nancy M. Johns, Jerome Navies, Ivan Scott, Wes Vernon.

CBS TELENOTICIAS—(202) 887–9079; 1333 H Street, NW 20005: Luis Figueroa, Pablo Teijeino Gato, Lorestina Montenegro, Victor Reyes, Magaly Wyatt.

CMI TV NEWS AND RADIONET—(202) 822–8774; 1825 K Street, NW #507 20006: Ione Indrira Molinares.

CNN—(202) 898–7900; 820 First Street, NE 20002: Michael M. Ahlers, Jonathan F. Aiken, Nurith Aizenman, Mark Allen, Kyoko Altman, Kelli Arena, Jennifer Avellino, Brian Barger, Ralph J. Begleiter, Pamela S. Benson, Peter Bergen, Charles Bierbauer, John Bisney, Wolf Blitzer, Cary Bodenheimer, Kevin Bohn, Craig A. Broffman, Matthew Byrne, Michael Clemente, James T. Connor, Rebecca Cooper, Carol A. Cratty, Karla Crosswhite, Candy Alt Crowley, Ann J. Curley, Jack Date, Patricia A. Davis, Patrick Alan Davis, Richard Davis, Carin Dessauer, William Dorman, Jill M. Dougherty, Thomas J. Dunlavey, Lisa R. Durham, Christy Feig, Sam E. Feist, Marlene Fernandez, Beth Fouhy, Robert Franken, Elissa Blake Free, Joanne Fuchs, David Futrowsky, Amos Gelb, Judah Ginsberg, Stephanie Goldstein, Christopher Guarino, Eugenia Halsey, Jody Hassett, William W. Headline, James Heller, Natailie Hohn, Sarah B. Holland, Christian Hudson, Janice Hui, Brooks Jackson, Britt Kahn, Amy E. Kasarda, Charles F. Keyes, Kimberly Kleine, Kathleen Koch, Gary Krakower, Jack Krost, Jeffrey B. Levine, Frances L. Lewine, Kim J. Linden, Tamara Linderman, Skip Loescher, John V. Lynn, Vito Maggiolo, Michael L. Maltas, Penelope Manis, Jennifer Martin, Timothy McCaughan, Michael McGill, Mark McHugh, Micheal P. McManus, William C. Mears, Jeanne M. Meserve, Zach Messitte, Scott Miller, Bruce Morton, Jill Neff, Virginia Nicolaidis, Lauren Oltarsh, David Ottalini, D. Todd Philips, Elizabeth Pizza, Mara Raphael, Patrick T. Reap, Owen Renfro, Laura Robinson, John M. Roche, Carl Rochelle, H. Michael Roselli, Diane Ruggiero, Sarah Ruth, Kristine K. Schantz, Louise L. Schiavone, Frank Sesno, Joann Sierra, Amy R. Silver, Marc Sklar, Andrea Slattery, Kathy Slobogin, Bill Smee, Eric Solomon, Peggy M. Soucy, David Spaeth, Philip Scott Spoerry, LeeAnn Stauffer, Kathryn E. Steinhilber, Pamela Stevens, Amy Stewart, Julian H. Styles, Sherrell Swanier, Julie W. Vallese, Greta Van Susteren, Laura Viddy, A. MacKenzie Walworth, Michael T. Watts, Danielle J. Whelton, Dale A. Willman, Brad Wright, Jennifer Wysocki, Rebekah Young, Jennifer Zeidman.

CONUS COMMUNICATIONS—(202) 467–5618; 1825 K Street, NW 9th Floor 20006: Jeff Ballou, Julia Bushyhead, Bob Costantini, Plummer Crawley, George E. Fridrich, Jennifer B. Gallay, Jim Gately, Bryant C. Gourdie, Thomas Hass, Brian Hopkins, Myron A. Leake, Liza Liss, Amy S. Meringer, Mary Miller, Jennifer Pennybacker, Natasha S. Perkins, Almon L. Porter, Pat A. Pugliese, Anne Marie Riha, Patrick Rogers, Tim Patrick Rudell, Carl Schick, Dalfa Sell, Robert Soneira, Ashley King Stringer, Charles Towne, Ted Richard Tuel, David Vukmer, Sandra A. Wurz.

CTV TELEVISION NETWORK—(202) 466–3595; 2030 M Street, NW #602, 20036: Tobias Fisher, Alan Fryer, Catherine Loper, Charles MacDonald, Jim MacDonald.

CABLE NEWS 21—(202) 424–1730; 7548 Standish Place Rockville, MD 20855: Karen Allyn.

CANADIAN BROADCASTING—(202) 383–2905; 529 14th Street, NW #500, 20045: Keith Boag, Henry S. Champ, Sylvain Coudoux, Joanne L. Elgart, David Hall, David Halton, George Hoff, Micheline Laflamme, Pierre-Leon Lafrance, Bill Loucks, Michael McDowell, Lynne M. McIntyre, Julie Miville-Dechene, Helene Y. Parenteau, Yves Peltier, Sylvain Richard, Timothy Richards, Jennifer Westaway, Sarah Wolff.

CAPITAL TV NETWORK—(703) 369–3400; P.O. Box 3150, Manassas, VA 22110: Lester R. Raker, Patrick L. Raker, Roger A. Raker.

CAPSTONE PRODUCTIONS—(301) 948–1468; 12002 Citrus Grove Road, North Potomac, MD 20878: Jackson H. Polk.

CATHOLIC UNIVERSITY OF CHILE TELEVISION—(202) 298–6839; 3435 R Street, NW #22, 20007: Margarita Castro.

CHANNEL EARTH—(301) 942–1996; 9915 Hillridge Drive, Kensington, MD 20895: Allison D. Aubrey, Patrick B. Haggerty.

CHANNEL ONE NEWS—(202) 296–5937; 1825 K Street, NW #915,20006: Sharon McGill.

CHINA RADIO INTERNATIONAL—(703) 892–4572; 2000 South Eads Street, #713 Arlington, VA 22202: Jun Dong, Zhenbang Dong.

CHINA TELEVISION COMPANY—(202) 393–3604; 400 North Capitol Street, #177, 20001: Gary C. Tsai.

CHINA CENTRAL TELEVISION WASHINGTON BUREAU—(202) 362–7382; 4601 Connecticut Avenue, NW #317, 20008: Jun Gao, Zhengzhu Liu.

CHINESE TELEVISION SYSTEM—(202) 662–8950; 529 14th Street, NW #1273, 20045: Chen-fang Chung.

NETWORKS, STATIONS, AND SERVICES REPRESENTED—Continued

CHINESE TELEVISION NETWORK WASHINGTON BUREAU—(202) 331–9110; 1705 DeSales Street, NW, 2nd Floor, 20036; Roger Hsu, Rong Li, Enming Liu, Ning Rong Liu, Chiachi Lu, Yan Xiao, Bettina Yang, GuoHua Zang.

CHRISTIAN BROADCASTING SYSTEM—(202) 737–6031; 529 14th Street, NW #1257A 20045: Myon-taek Han.

CHRISTIAN SCIENCE MONITOR RADIO—(202) 822–0055; 910 16th Street, NW 20006: Monica Brady, Jim Kane, Darraine Maxwell, Duncan R. Moon.

CNBC—(202) 467–5400; 1825 K Street, NW #1003, 20006: Peter Barnes, Matthew P. Cuddy, Stephen Dowling Jr., Louise Ellen Filkins, Robin Gellman, Hampton Pearson, Alen Rochkind, James Vail.

COMM*TECH NEWS—(202) 338–1215; 4410 Lingan Road, NW 20007: Stephen Banker.

COMMUNITY TELEVISION OF PRINCE GEORGE'S—(301) 386–7628; 9475 Lottsford Road, NW #125 Largo, MD 20774: Stacey L. Cohan, Paul M. Crosariol, Curtis A. Crutchfield, Kim Korich, Ara A. Laughlin.

CONTACT MIDDLE EAST—(202) 783–0337; 529 14th Street, NW #1122, 20045: Adel Malek.

COURT TV—(202) 828–0366; 1730 M Street, NW #802, 20036: Thomas J. Bagnall, Robin Binder, James W. Davis, Stephanie Frix, Chris Gordon, Marietta S. Lee, Eva M. Rodriguez, Robert Schmidt, Laura Tull.

COX BROADCASTING—(202) 737–0277; 400 North Capitol Street, #189 20001: Leslie Baker, Andy Cassells, David Chase, Mark Curtis, Jamie Dupree, Cesar Flores, Steve Gasque, Paul Hollenbeck, Martin Kos, Alison Schafer, Jennifer Sumler, Zelda Wallace.

DANISH BROADCASTING—(202) 785–1957; 2030 M Street, NW #700 20036: Torsten Jansen, Torben Rasmussen, Peter Sigsgaard.

DEUTSCHE WELLE GERMAN TELEVISION—(703) 931–6644; 2800 Shirlington Road, #901 Arlington, VA 22206: Nicholas P. Beery, Nicholas Buschschlueter, Dagmar E.H. Engel, Kristin N. Foellmer, Constantin Klein, Lawrence LaComa, Chris Robinson, Eckhard F. Tollkuhn, Felicity J. Tollkuhn.

DEUTSCHLAND RADIO—(703) 821–3792; 6703 Lupine Lane McLean, VA 22101: Siegfried Buschschluter.

DISPATCH BROADCAST GROUP—(202) 737–4630; 529 14th Street, NW #1152, 20045: Rhonda Pence, Richard Puckett.

DOW JONES TELEVISION—(202) 862–6627; 1025 Connecticut Avenue, NW #800 20036: Paul Courson, Natalie Hohn.

DUTCH TELEVISION/NCRV—(703) 276–0558; 3717 North Nelson Street Arlington, VA 22207: Ray Brislin.

DUTCH PUBLIC TELEVISION/NOVA—(202) 775–2960; 2030 M Street, NW #400, 20036: Carolus Groenhuijsen.

DUTCH RADIO AND TELEVISION KRO—(703) 276–0558; 3717 North Nelson Street, Arlington, VA 22207: David Hammelburg.

EO DUTCH TV AND RADIO—(540) 341–0325; 5055 Rock Spring Road Waventon, VA 20187: John P. Elliott.

ESPN—(202) 363–9804; 3309 MaComb Street, NW 20008: Julie Chrisco.

EUROPEAN BROADCASTING UNION—(202) 775–1295; 2030 M Street, NW 20036: Susan Henderson, Olivier Hinnewikel, Lorraine Mottola.

FEDERAL NETWORK, INC.—119 North Henry Street Arlington, VA 22301: Keith Carney.

FINNISH BROADCASTING—(202) 785–2087; 2030 M Street, NW 20036: Edward R. Castner, Risto Johnson, Sinikka Siekkinen.

FISHER BROADCASTING—(202) 783–0322; 444 North Capitol Street, #601, 20001: Glenn Elvington, Megan McConagha, Tom Walker.

FOX NEWS CHANNEL—(202) 824–6369; 400 North Capitol Street, NW #915, 20001: Victor Ed. Acevedo, Scott J. Alexander, James L. Angle, Julie Asher, Anne Ball, Bruce C. Becker, Brian Boughton, Janet Boyd, Molly A. Boyle, Edgar Brown, Carl Cameron, Michael Carpel, Steve Centanni, Kelly Chernenkoff, Patrice Chung, Richard Cockerham, Bryan Cole, Rita Cosby, Lauren Crowley, Richard B. DiBella, James Jed Duvall, Jerry L. Echols, Bruce Edwards, Clifford Feldman, Bruce Ferder, Joan Fiddle, Christian Galdabini, Wendell Goler, Augusto Gomez, Ute W. Gunn, Gregg Gursky, Fred Haberstick, Tammy Haddad, Kendall Hagan, Michael E. Hagerty, Nancy Harmeyer, Dana Hill, Steve Hirsh, Brian Hollingsworth, Dawn Holly, Moira Hopkins, Kim Hume, Judith Jankowski, Meg Kaplan, Carol Kaufmann, Grigory Khananayev, Natalie Anne Kirschner, Llissa Klein, Judlyne Lilly, Susan Lindauer, Bill Line, Wayne Lowman, Laura W. Luhn, Yolanda Maggi, Jim Mills, Jennifer Oliva, Gavin Owen-Thomas, Jack Pagano, Lisa Rizzolo, John Roper, Catherine Sargent, Craig Savage, Andy Schwartz, Carl Sears, Christine Sellai, Steve Shelton, Laura Shemonsky, David Shott, David Shuster, Tony Snow, Rodney Storey, Jeff Strei, Ande Torgerson, Ellen Uchimiya, Bryce Vinson, John L. Wallace, Carla G. Wendy, Karen Yianopoulus.

FUJI TELEVISION—(202) 347–1600; 529 14th Street, NW #330, 20045: Peter Gold, Yuji Kuroiwa, Amy Margolius, Tateki Muratani, Osamu Sorimachi, Makoto Wakamatsu.

GANCIE TELEVISION, INC.—(202) 885–4280; 4001 Nebraska Avenue, NW 20016: Chad Findlay, Vincent M. Gancie, Joe Rose, Joan Roskosh.

NETWORKS, STATIONS, AND SERVICES REPRESENTED—Continued

GANNETT NEWS MEDIA—(703) 276–5967; 1000 Wilson Boulevard 22nd Floor Arlington, VA 22229: Kirsten Olsen.
GERMAN BROADCASTING/ARD—(202) 298–6535; 3132 M Street, NW 20007: Ingolf Karnahl, Gunnar Schultz-Burkel.
GERMAN PUBLIC RADIO/ARD—(202) 625–2503; 1200 Eton Court, NW #200 20007: Hannelore Jones, Hans-Jurgen Maurus, Ingolf Rackwitz, Clemens Verenkotte.
GERMAN RADIO NDR/WDR—(202) 342–1730; 3132 M Street, NW 20007: Horst Duisberg-Klaeuser, Udo Koelsch, Sabine Reifenberg, Bernd Julius Schroeder.
GERMAN TV AGENCY—(202) 393–7571; 529 14th Street, NW #1199, 20045: Roger Horne, Tipp K. McClure.
GERMAN TELEVISION/ARD—(202) 298–6535; 3132 M Street, NW 20007: Charles F. Borniger, Herta Borniger, Tom Buhrow, Sabine Hoffman, Monika Kaiser, Ingolf Karnahl, Georg Kellerman, Claus Detlev Kleber, Thea Luise Rosenbaum, Jenny Schenk, Hans-Peter Schloemer, Gunnar Schltz-Burkel, Frank Schuetzeichel, Stephanie B. Slewka, Werner Sonne, Holger Witt.
GERMAN TELEVISION/ZDF—(202) 333–3909; 1077 31st Street, NW 20007: Heike Diel, Laura Downhower, Jens Heik, Jutta Hickman, Rolanda Johnson, Georg Juenger, Alice Kelley, Anja Korth, Peter Kruse, Werner Lelle, Joerg Mahler, Douglas McCash, Scott McCash, Siri Nyrop, Katharina Oesterwinter, Peter Peleger, Hildrun Rowe, Michael Schmitz, Klaus-Peter Siegloch, Michael Stagneth, Elmar Thevessen, Elke Tucker.
GERMANY TELEVISION/RTL—(202) 530–0829; 1825 K Street, #915 20006: Barbara Biemann, Christof Lang.
GLOBAL TV CANADA—(202) 310–5457; 1333 H Street, NW #505, 20005: Allison Butler, Carl Hanlon.
GLOBALVISION—(202) 546–7760; 617 8th Street, NE 20002: Gary Keith Griffin.
GREEK TELEVISION - RADIO—(202) 253–6336; 4201 Massachusetts Avenue, NW #A249, 20016: Dimitrios Apokis.
HAMILTON PRODUCTIONS—(703) 734–5444; 7732 Georgetown Pike McLean, VA 22102: Jay Hamilton, John A. Hamilton, Anne Hamilton Deger, Randy Littman.
HEARST BROADCASTING—(202) 457–0220; 1825 K Street, NW #720 20006: William S.D. Connor, Julie Kirtz Garrett, Gary Griffith, Martha Johnson, Keith B. Plummer, Bradley Ulery, Lori M. Weinstein, Nicole Young.
INT OF LONDON—(202) 429–9080; 400 North Capitol Street, #899 20001: Marie Cerletty, James Mates, James Schule, Ben Scotchbrook, Chris Shlemon, David Smith, Charles Walter.
IMAGE TELEVISION—(202) 833–3222; 1705 DeSales Street, NW #550 20036: Evan Blaustein, Ann Conanan, John M. Cooper, Robert Gray, Heidi K. Hanson, Michael C. Judge, Dennis Troute, Christopher Warner.
INSIDE SCIENCE—(301) 248–6957; 9614 Pamelia Place Fort Washington, MD 20744: Charles Hagar.
INTERSTAR TV—(703) 931–0586; 5010 7th Road South, #202 Arlington, VA 22204: Ibrahim Serdar Akinan.
KOREAN BROADCASTING SYSTEM— (202) 347–4013; 529 14th & F Streets, NW #414, 20045: Sang Woon Kim.
LONDON NEWS RADIO—(703) 797–2159; 1730 Rhode Island Avenue, NW #205 20036: Catherine Drew, Emma Gray, Simon Marks, Nancy Marshall, Dominic Waghorn.
MSNBC PRO—(202) 639–9448; 400 North Capitol Street, NW #353 20001: Clayton Brown, Ward Lassoe, Fausto Ramon, Frederick Stratton.
MAINSTREET TV—(202) 822–0036; 918 16th Street, NW #400 20006: Hodding Carter.
MANIFOLD PRODUCTIONS—(202) 333–1095; 2804 39th Street, NW 20007: Michael Pack.
MARKETPLACE RADIO—(202) 223–6699; 1333 H Street, NW #1200 West 20005: John Dimsdale, Susan Goodman, Cynthia Ingle.
MARYLAND PUBLIC TELEVISION—(410) 356–5600; 11767 Owings Mills Boulevard, Owings Mills, MD 21117: Stephen Kremer.
MEDILL NEWS SERVICE—(202) 347–8700; 1325 G Street, NW #730 20005: Jeremy Birnholtz, Mary B. Coffman, Sharon Downey.
METRO NETWORKS, WASHINGTON—(301) 718–4949; 5454 Wisconsin Avenue, NW Chevy Chase, MD 20815: James Hawk.
METRO NEWS NETWORK—Hal P. Hubbard, John Irving.
METRO TELEPRODUCTIONS INC.—(301) 608–9077; 8750 Georgia Avenue, #144 Silver Spring, MD 20910: Jennifer Grafton, Dave Lilling, Julio Luzquinos, Robert L. Young.
MID-ATLANTIC MEDIA—(703) 893–8893; 8375 Leesburg Pike, #380 Vienna, VA 22182: Joseph Mancuso, Marc Morano.
MIDDLE EAST BROADCASTING—(202) 637–8889; 1510 H Street, NW 20005: Walid Abdul-Jawad.
MIN WASHINGTON—(703) 524–9300; 1916 Wilson Boulevard, #100 Arlington, VA 22201: Talal Al-Haj, Christopher Belcher, Ali Rad.
MOBILE VIDEO SERVICES—(202) 331–8889; 1620 I Street, NW 20006: Adam D. Bedard, German Garay, William J. Griffitts, Robert Milford, Lawrence VanderVeen.

NETWORKS, STATIONS, AND SERVICES REPRESENTED—Continued

MULTINATIONAL MEDIA—(202) 393–6639; 506 10th Street, NW 20004: Culver Long.

MUTUAL/NBC RADIO—(703) 413–8400; 1755 S. Jefferson Davis Hwy. Arlington, VA 22202: Becky Bailey, Bonnie G. Erbe, Robert J. Fuss, Gregory D. Johnson, Douglas J. Lillibridge, Rachael M. Lowe, Dennis MacCarthy, Peter Maer, Howard Moss, Richard Lee Preston, Rita Rich, Richard Rosse, Daniel Scanlan, Ross Simpson, Barton J. Tessler, Joseph Walsh, Craig Warner.

N.O.S. NATIONAL TV THE NETHERLANDS—Margaret Plomp, Gerard Van Der Wulp.

NBC NEWS—(202) 885–4210; 4001 Nebraska Avenue, NW 20016: Jamile Adams, Robert Abernethy, Joel R. Albert, Patrick Anastasi, Percy Arrington, Rodney Sims Batten, Gary Glenn Beall, Arthur Berko, Regina Allen Blackburn, Jay Allan Blackman, Keith Blackman, Kenan S. Block, David Jerome Bloom, Victoria Blooston, Jeffrey Blount, John D. Boyd, Robert D. Boyer, Anthony Capra, Samuel Cardwell, Cassandra Clayton, Jack Cloherty, Elizabeth V. Cruze, Bruce Cummings, Lynn Dakis, Brady G. Daniels, Robert Decker Faw, Richard E. Dodson, Jameela Donaldson, Kerry Donovan, Geoffrey Doyle, Betty Cole Dukert, Victoria Duncan, Christine Egy-Rose, Daniel Erlenborn, Sheldon Fielman, Robert Finley, Elizabeth Fischer, David Forman, Salvatore Formica, Fredrick N. Francis, Wilfred R. Fraser, Jr., Rosemary Freitas, George Fridrich, Timothy Furlong, Brian Gaffney, Kendra Gahagan, Jamie Gangel, William A. Gebhardt, Frank L. Gibson, Jr., Sandy Gilmour, Nelson Ginebra, Timothy Gorin, Edward D. Gorsky, John Grassie, Olivio Green, Sarah Greenberg, Robert M. Hager, Deirdre Hanlon, Alan Harvey, Harold Paul Hayley, Chester Hively, John Holland, Roberta Hornig Draper, Laura A. Hunter, James A. Hurt, Gwen Ifill, Salim Ibn Ishaq, Janet Janjigian, Joseph E. Johns, Leroy Johnson, John Kautz, Jon Kessler, Mary Klette, Ronald Knox, Charlotte Kohrs, Panayiota Kozakos, Lester A. Kretman, Tamara Kupperman, Robert Kur, Susan Alice LaSalle, Margaret Lehrman, Suzanne Littlefield, Lydia S. Lively, Kathleen Lockhart, Joseph W. Loebach, James V. Long, Alexandra Marks, John Francis Mathews, Claude Matthews, Andrea McCarren, Tasha Nita McNeil, Carroll Ann Mears, Brock Nolan Meeks, Robert S. Merrill, Peter Meryash, James Miklaszewski, Evan David Miller, Richard Minner, Andrea Mitchell, Kristin Moore, Russell T. Moore, John H. Mulera, Adolyn Myers, Lisa M. Myers, Sylvie Oberlander, John S. Palmer, William H. Petras, Debra Pettit, Sarah Pines, Denise L. Poon, Edward Rabel, Sally Redding, Courtenay K. Reese, Charles Reid, Alan Gregory Rice, Marcie Rickun, Clyde W. Robinson, Johnie F. Roth, Timothy J. Russert, John Rutherford, Amy Saalwachter, Jose A. Sanfuentes, Cheryl Sarmiento, Eugenia F. Schaefer, Frances Schaefer, Max A. Schindler, Christopher Scholl, Carmine Scicchitano, Wesley Scruggs, Leslie Sewell, Kevin Andrew Sites, Kimberly Sneed, Naomi Spinrad, Elizabeth Steuart, Alfred Storey, Kenneth James Strickland, Jessica Stuart, Ricardo Swiner, Lea Hopkins Thompson, Erin Van de Bellen, Yaromil Velez, Anthony Verdi, Terrie Verna, Christopher Wiggins, Wendla Wilkinson, Karen Williams, Louis A. Williams, Robert Toney Williams, Mary Dorman Wilmeth.

NBC NEWS CHANNEL—(202) 783–2615; 400 North Capitol Street, #890 20001: Jeffery L. Autry, Mae Beth Boggs, Almadale Brown, Sheila Conlin, Christopher Cram, Christopher Dancy, Nancy Ellard, Kevin Fogarty, William Glynn, Adam Greenbaum, James C. Hanchett, Sergio A. Jellinek, Kevin A. McManus, Elisabeth Mitchell, Sean Reis, Todd Sutton.

NBC NEWS STATIONS DIVISION—(202) 885–4780; 4001 Nebraska Avenue, NW 20016: Herb Bloom, Estel Dillon, Margaret Dore, Karen Fuller, Steve Handelsman, Richard McDermott, Bonnie Rollins.

NBC4—(202) 885–4111; 4001 Nebraska Avenue, NW 20016: James M. Adams, Leo Alexander, Jay Alvey, Katherine Banks-Wilson, Joanne Beck, Charles Bragale, Lloyd R. Brothers, Julie Carey, Daniel Cohen, Pat Collins, Elizabeth Crenshaw, Anna Davalos, Harry Davis, Elizabeth Feldman, Jim M. Forrest, William Gamble, Doreen Geutzier, John Kevin Greenwood, Jim Handly, Corrie A. Harding, Cathy Hobbs, Ira John Hudson, Paul Irvin, Philip Jacobs, Kathleen Johnson, Susan Kidd, James S. Kizer, Nick Kovijanic, Joe Krebs, Pat Lawson-Muse, Debbi Lockhart, Lynda Lopez, Dave Lougee, Shari Macias, Brenda N. Mallory, Suzanne Malveaux, Rick Martin, Michelle M. Michael, Ronald Minor, James J. Neustadt, Chester Panzer, James Popkin, Lisa Rasmussen, Wendy Rieger, Margie Ruttenberg, Mary Alice Salinas, Joseph F. Shalhoup, Murray H. Schweitzer, Tom Sherwood, Milton T. Shockley, Michael D. Swann, John Wanzer, Mike Whatley, Wayne C. Wood, Albert N. Zodun.

NET–POLITICAL NEWSTALK NETWORK—(202) 544–3200; 717 Second Street, NE 20002: Victoria Allen, Laura M. Atwell, Glay L. Blocker, Amanda E. Carter, Tracey Collins, Craig Crawley, Peter Estrada, Marianne Fogelson, Stella Harrison, Tim Heacock, Thomas Scott Huheey, Gregory J. Jenkins, Lisa Johnston, Richard Joy, Therese Kaplan, Donna King, Jaqueline N. Mitchell, Ferman Patterson, Paige Ralston, Bridget Sharp, Karl Stoll, Tamara Stonebarger, Robert T. Sutton, Richard Westfall, Stephen Weyrich, Geneviere E. Wood.

NHK-JAPAN BROADCASTING—(202) 828–5180; 2030 M Street, NW #706 20036: Kimitoshi Igarashi, Nobuyuki Itagaki, Madoka Kikuchi, Eri Kimura, Kenji Kohno, Zita Lichtenberg, Yoshinori Miyagi, Kazuo Ogawa, Kumiko Ogoshi, Koji Okamura, Cris Sabo, Robert Schroeder, Kenji Sobata, Michael Viqueria.

NATIONAL NARROWCAST NETWORK—(202) 966–2211; P.O. Box 9597 20016: Carla Flug, Morgan Gale.

NATIONAL PUBLIC RADIO—(202) 414–2000; 635 Massachusetts Avenue, NW 20001: Rod M. Abid, Larry Abramson, Greg Allen, Elizabeth Arnold, Jonathan Baer, Julia Holmes Bailey, Bob Boilen,

NETWORKS, STATIONS, AND SERVICES REPRESENTED—Continued

Barbara Bradley, Jonathan Broder, William E. Buzenberg, Barbara Campbell, Windall Carline, Eugene Cha, Theodore E. Clark, Jean Cochran, Thomas C. Cole, Korva Coleman, Sean Collins, Neal J. Conan, Leslie Cook, William Craven, Phillip Davis, Rebecca A. Davis, Robert E. Dore, Bruce Drake, Michele DuBach, Bob Edwards, Alyne Ellis, Robert Ferrante, Pam Fessler, Corey Flintoff, Deborah George, Peggy Girshman, Tom Gjelten, Barry Gordemer, Barton Grabow, Sharon Green, Jane Greenhalgh, Anne Gudenkauf, Elana Beth Hadler, Elizabeth Harmon, Richard F. Harris, Steve Inskeep, Rick Jarrett, Loren Jenkins, Cynthia Johnston, Edward M. Jones, Christopher Joyce, Carl Kasell, John C. Keator, Carol Anne Kelly, Sarah B. Kelly, Peter Kenyon, Sunni M. Khalid, Michael Lawrence, Elizabeth Lewis, Mara Liasson, Laura Lorson, Catherine V. Maddux, Robert Malesky, Dave S. Mattingly, Doreen McCallister, Maeve McGoran, Peter Michaels, Sarah C. Mobley, Stephen B. Munro, Brian Naylor, Lynn Neary, Joe R. Neel, John Nielsen, Victoria L. O'Hara, John A. Ogulnik, Dean Olsher, Peter Overby, Joseph Palca, Gregory Peppers, Victoria Que, Martha Raddatz, Chitra Ragavan, Julia Redpath, Jeffrey S. Rogers, Jeffrey Rosenberg, Kathleen K. Rushlow, Claudio Sanchez, Lauren O. Sandler, Jeffery R. Sandyann, Sara Keiko Sarasohn, Kathleen N. Schalch, Debra Schifrin, Daniel Schorr, Robert Siegel, Joanne Silberner, Ellen Silva, Art Silverman, Gregory Smith, Margaret Low Smith, Susan L. Stamberg, David Sweeney, Ann Taylor, Gwendolyn Thompkins, Nina Totenberg, James M. Wallace, Fred Wasser, Walter Ray Watson, Karin Weinberg, Ned Wharton, Danyell T. Williams, Debi Williams, Brenda Wilson, Carline Windall, R. Craig Windham, Alice Winkler, Audrey Wynn, John Ydstie, Daniel Zwerdling.

NATIONAL SCENE NEWS BUREAU—(202) 298–9519; 1422 K Street, NW #691 20005: Alverda Ann Muhammad, Askia Muhammad.

NATIVE AMERICAN TELEVISION—(703) 771–7469; 111–A Fort Evans Road, SE, Leesburg, VA 22075: Maria Dodgar, Rick Dimassimo, Charles G. Kaster, James R. Prior, Charles Bearfighter Reddoor, Lloyd A. Reed.

NEWSCHANNEL 8—(703) 912–5308; 7600 D Boston Boulevard, Springfield, VA 22153: Iris J. Argueta, Monique Braxton, Alan Matthew Brock, Steven Cagle, Bruce DePuyt, Mary Theresa Dickie, Michael J. Esposito, Geoffrey Flood, Charles Goodknight, Mary Anne Greczyn, Tara L. Heinchon, Jeff W. Hertrick, John D. Hillis, Brian C. Hopkins, Marianne Houk, Andrew Inches, Leigh A. Ingram, Jane M. Karlen, Suzanne Mason Kennedy, Lisa Marie Kessler, John W. Lee, John D. Lisle, David Lucas, Wayne Lynch, Barbara Lynn Matthews, Dorattasan Mekour, Brian W. Mistretta, Molette E. Pendleton, Nathan Roberts, Michael Rudd, Adam P. Sidel, Joseph K. Spevak, Mark F. Thalman, Hugh Thomas, Stephen John Tschida, Colvin Underwood, James W. Walker, James T. Watson, Clifton Webb, Snorre Wik, Dave Willingham, Melanie J. Wotring, Kim Wright, Steve Zafiropulos, Joy Allison Zucker.

NIGHTLY BUSINESS REPORT—(202) 682–9029; 1333 H Street, NW #590, 20005: Jonathan P. Decker, Darren Gersh, Dennis E. Moore, Angela Terrell, Ken Tuohey, Ervin Steven Washington, Stephanie Woods.

NIPPON TV NETWORK—(202) 638–0890; 529 14th Street, NW #1036, 20045: Thad Behrens, Yuko Fuse, Naoto Kambe, Christian Herbst, Akihiro Muta, Yoshihiko Shiraishi, Jun Suzuki, Junko Yamada, Keisuke Yanaga.

NORWEGIAN BROADCASTING—(202) 785–1460; 2030 M Street, NW #700, 20036: Ingvilo Bryn, Gunnar Myklebust.

NUEVO MUNDO NETWORK—(301) 365–8224; 7213 Grubby Thicket Way Bethesda, MD 20817: Oscar Padilla-Vidaurre.

PTSC/CNN—(202) 515–2206; 820 First Street, NE 20002: Robert Ward Armfield, Rodney Seth Atkinson, David F. Bacheler, Dennis Baltimore, Michael Bannigan, Patrick Bauley, Michael Bellis, David Steven Berman, Tim R. Bintrim, John Bodnar, Burke Buckhorn, Paul Cable, James Cook, Ronald L. Couvillion, Roger Daniel, Michael M. David, Timothy J. Durham, Brenda Elkins, Timothy C. Garraty, Maurice George, Robert Gilley, Lindsay Graves, James M. Greene, Leslie Greene, Thomas M. Greene, Eddie S. Gross, Brian Haefeli, Chris Hamilton, Conrad W. Hirzel, Jerry Hollis, David Hugel, David A. Jenkins, Martin Jimenez, Bruce E. Kalifa, Michael W. Kauffman, Jennifer Klein, Martin Koenig, Howard Lutt, Gary Earl Lynn, Jack Maclnnis, Mark Marchione, Ralph Marcus, Dwight M. Mayhew, Sammuel J. McMichael, IV, Paul Miller, Peter Mohen, Peter H. Morris, Rick Morse, Joseph Mosley, Thomas P. Murphy, Jeffrey S. Noble, Dennis Norman, Sarah Pacheco, Robert G. Parker, John Jay Quinnette, Tyrone W. Riggs, Greg Robertson, Carolyn Robertson Stone, David S. Ruggiero, David R. Scherer, Barry C. Schlegel, Reginald G. Selma, Robert E. Shrader, Randall Sorenson, Thomas Spain, James Stubbs, Jimmy Suissa, Daniel Taylor, Kim Denise Thiele, Jerry Thompson, Robert B. Torfey, Anthony R. Umrani, John F. Urman, Mark Walz, Francisca G. Yus.

PACIFICA RADIO NEWS—(202) 783–1620; 2390 Champlain Street, NW, 2nd Floor, 20009: Verna Avery-Brown, Mark R. Bevis, Daniel Coughlin, Julie Drizin, Michelle Garcia, Amy Goodman, Patricia Guadalupe, Laura Iiyama, Donald W. Roeck.

PANAMERICANA TELEVISION—(301) 774–7959; 3713 Old Baltimore Drive, Olney, MD 20832: Rolando Ore.

POLSKIE RADIO—(301) 681–5622; 2324 Arthur Avenue Silver Spring, MD 20902: Tadeusz Zachurski.

NETWORKS, STATIONS, AND SERVICES REPRESENTED—Continued

POTOMAC TELEVISION—(202) 783–8000; 500 North Capitol Street, NW 20901: Bradley C. Anderson, Roy Forbes, Stephanie Fowler, Gregory S. Gates, Olin Greene, Duane R. Jones, Robert Karnes, Thomas R. Kolodziejczak, Brigette Langmade, Tamara Linderman, Cybele MacHardy, Timothy Matkosky, William T. Nonamaker, Jamie F. Norins, David Ottalini, Bradford S. Paxton, Roger Rinebolt, William B. Smith, Jonathan St. John, Marcia Wheatley, Karol Lyn Works.

PRO SIEBEN TELEVISION (GERMAN TV)—(202) 965–4404; 3138 P Street, NW 20007: Bridget A. Chandonnet, Elyane C. Lankes, Diana Maguhn.

PROFESSIONAL VIDEO SERVICES—(202) 775–0894; 2030 M Street, NW #400 20036: Robert Baumann, Stephen Bostwich, Kathleen M. Brumbaugh, Harvey Cofske, Raymond C. DeFrehn, Terri DeVaney, Jason M. Dorn, Richard Feather, Robert Fetzer, Darryl B. Johnson, C. Paul London, Christina L. Lucas, William Todd Mason, Kerry L. Meyer, Brian Mosher, Misa Rossetti-Meyer, Jeffrey Saffelle, Ron Skeans, George S. Summers, David Tidler.

PYRAMID NATIONAL PRESSPORT—(202) 783–5030; 480 National Press Building 20045: Charles Bellman, Karl B. Celarier, Steven Rosenblatt.

RAI RADIOTELEVISIONE ITALIANA—(202) 775–1295; c/o EBU 2030 M. Street, NW 20036: Giuseppe Lugato.

RADIO FRANCE INTERNATIONALE—(301) 929–6536; 9519 East Stanhope Road Kensington, MD 20895: Christian Billmann.

RADIO FREE ASIA—(202) 530–4973; 2025 M Street, NW #300 20036: Jaehoon Ahn, David M. Badden, Arin Basu, Huiyi Chen, Jill Chi-jou Ku, Jennifer Chou, Karma Dorsee, Andrew Janitschek, Ho Kim, Hui Hyon Kim, Kalden Lodoe, Thein Htike Oo, James I. Park, Craig David Perry, Richard Richter, Wyein Shwe, Kin Maung Soe, Soe Thinn, Nadia Usaeva, Khanh Van Nguyen.

RADIO FREE EUROPE/RADIO LIBERTY—(202) 457–6959; 1201 Connecticut Avenue, NW 20036: Constantin Alexander, Silvia Cinca, Julie Czechowski, Vladimir Dubinsky, Kevin Paul Foley, Paul Goble, Tetiana Iwanciw, Aleksey Levin, Robert Lyle, Michael Mihalisko, Maire Reichenau, Larisa Silnicky, Sonia Winter, Oleh Zwadiuk.

RADIO MARTI—(703) 641–7961; 400 6th Street, SE 20547: David J. Hall, L. Pamela Mantis, Diana Molineaux, Luis Munoz.

RADIO NACIONAL De ESPANA—(202) 783–0768; 1288 National Press Building, 20045: Luz Rodriguez.

RAINDANCER NEWS BUREAU—(703) 671–2290; 2500 North Van Dorn Street, #625 Alexandria, VA 22302: Bob Tenequer.

REUTERS TELEVISION—(202) 898–0056; 1333 H Street, NW 5th Floor, 20005: Barbara Adams, Jane Arraf, Bruce Barton, Peter Bullock, Jean Campbell, John Clarke, Mary Eldred, Kevin Fogarty, Peter H. Fox, Adam Greenbaum, Steven Hanberg, Ronnie Hassan, Kia Johnson, Derek Johnston, Peter O. Kent, Jennifer K. Knoll, Predrag Kojovic, Culver Jefferson Long, Christopher Lagan, Shannon Lauterbach, Ian McDougall, Allen McGreevy, Robert Muir, Richardo A. Palovecino, Christine Pass, Gershon Peaks, Steven T. Phillips, Duncan Pitcairn, Jonathan Resnick, Clara E. Rivera, Tom Rowe, Lisa Mary Springham, Richard Suddeth, Amanda Stultz, George Tamerlani, Philippa Tarrant.

ROWE NEWS SERVICE—(301) 977–6252; 922 Beacon Square Court, #324, Gaithersburg, MD 20878: JoAnn Rowe.

SRN NEWS/STANDARD NEWS—(703) 528–6213; 1901 North Moore Street, #201, Arlington, VA 20879: Gregory W. Clugstson, Philip Fleischman, Linda Kenyon, Diana Lucas, Terrence M. Moore, Hank Silverberg, Andrea F. Starace.

SALEM RADIO NETWORK—(703) 807–2266; 1901 North Moore Street, #201, Arlington, VA 20879: Catherine Edwards, Rich Lee.

SKY NEWS—(202) 789–8569; 1333 H Street, NW 20005: Jonathan Hunt.

SOUTH AFRICAN BROADCASTING—(202) 686–5885; P.O. Box 954 Rockville, MD 20848: Mike Kellerman.

SPIEGEL TV/GERMANY—(202) 347–1735; 1202 National Press Building, 20045: Karin B. Assamann.

SWEDISH TELEVISION—(202) 785–1727; 2030 M Street, NW #700, 20036: Leif Carlsson, Sven Stromberg, Bert Sundstrom.

SWISS BROADCASTING CORPORATION—(202) 467–6455; 2030 M Street, NW #400, 20036: Pietro Gerosa, Tara Libert, Yves Magat, Dennis Page McCarty, Donald Jay McCarty, Antonini Roberto, Casper Selg, Han Peter Stalder.

TF1–FRENCH TELEVISION—(202) 223–3642; 2100 M Street, NW #302, 20037: Michael G. Stashik, Eleanor Beardsley, Helene Davieaud, Perrin Edouard, Bruce Frankel, Philippe Morand, Peter S. Murtaugh.

TV ASAHI—(202) 347–2933; 670 National Press Building, 20005: Christopher Anstey, Katsuichi Endo, Andrew Huston, Takanobu Ito, Junichi Kitasei, Orika Koyama, Ena Suto.

TV TOKYO CHANNEL 12, LTD—(202) 638–0441; 529 14th, NW #803, 20045: Toshiko Aoki, Patrick Frank, Tom Oki.

TV2 DENMARK—(202) 828–4555; 2030 M Street, NW #511, 20036: Charlotte Ernst, Ulla Pors Nielsen.

TV2 NORWAY—(202) 466–7505; 2030 M Street, NW #510, 20036: Oddvar Stenstrom.

TAIWAN TELEVISION ENTERPRISE—(202) 223–6642; 1705 DeSales Street, NW #302, 20036: Ernie Chuan-yu Ko, Hsiang-San Wu, Che-Wei Shih.

NETWORKS, STATIONS, AND SERVICES REPRESENTED—Continued

TALK RADIO NEWS SERVICE—(202) 337–8715; 2514 Mill Road, NW 20007: Richard Mangus, Ellen F. Ratner, Myron Sponder, Andrea Diane Stroud, Robert Vanasse, Marc R. Wittlif.

TELEMUNDO/WZGS–64—(703) 522–6464; 2000 North 14th Street, #490 Arlington, VA 22201: Miguel A. Chavez.

TELEVISA–ECO TELEVISION—(202) 861–0626; 1705 DeSales Street, NW #306, 20036: Eduardo Cue, Zoila T. Mederos, Eduardo Rodriguez, Augusto Santos.

TELEVISIO DE CATALUNYA—(202) 785–0580; 1620 I Street, NW #150 20006: Stephen S. Blust, Ramon Rovira.

THE BLACKWELL CORPORATION—(703) 524–2300; 1000 Wilson Boulvard, #2702 Arlington, VA 22209: Barbara Driscoll, Erin Foley, James B. Freeman, Jane M. Freeman, Neal Freeman, James Glassman, Thomas Knisely.

THE HILL/UBN—(202) 543–1212, 733 15th Street, NW #1140 20045: Catherine Hand.

THE NEWSHOUR WITH JIM LEHRER—(703) 998–2761; 2117 South Quincy Street, #250 Arlington, VA 22206: Scott J. Anderson, Lee M. Banville, Carol Blakeslee, Jeffrey Brown, Debra Jean Butler, Lesley Butrick, Bridget Chandonnet, Leah Clapman, Lester M. Crystal, Elizabeth Farnsworth, George Felcyn, Joan M. Friedenberg, Amyjean Gorsline, Brian Gottlieb, Caitlin Gross, Kwame Holman, Monica Hoose, Charlayne Hunter-Gault, Shermaze Ingram, Murrey Jacobson, Charles A. Krause, Lisa Larragoite, Jim Lehrer, Sheila Lummis, Susan Malin, Kathleen McCleery, Patricia McMurray, Annette L. Miller, Michael Million, Michael D. Mosettig, Desa Philadelphia, Lisa R. Pottger, Gregg Ramshaw, Margaret L. Robinson, Martine Rodriguez, Terry Rubin, Daniel Sagalyn, Michael Saltz, Rene Scheider, Linda J. Scott, Scott Tang, James Albert Trengrove, Ilyse J. Veron, Margaret Warner, Dan Werner, Judith Willis, Linda Winslow.

THE SWEDISH NEWS AGENCY—(202) 333–5351; 3112 M Street, NW #3rd Floor 20007: Lennart Lundh.

THE WASHINGTON BUREAU—(202) 347–6396; 400 North Capitol Street, NW 20001: John E. Brosnan, Jeffery Hager, Wei-ye Jia, Emily Marie Longnecker, Allison A. Martin, Julia Rockler, Richard Tillery.

THE WORLD—(703) 841–1797; 4414 Carlin Springs, #9 Arlington, VA 22203: William Troop.

TOKYO BROADCASTING SYSTEM—(202) 393–3800; 1088 National Press Building, 20045: Takushi Harima, Michael Lavallee, Makiko Murotani, Jun Ogawa, Rebecca J. Ratliff, Mitsuhiro Wakaizumi.

TRIBUNE BROADCASTING—(202) 824–8444; 1325 G Street, NW #200 20005: Staci Adelman, Cissy Baker, Shirley R. Brice, Timothy F. Calhoun, Richard Chamberlain, John David Foundas, Christopher Hutchins, Gary Nurenberg, Ronald Windham.

TURKISH CTV—(703) 451–5172; 6810 Supreme Court Springfield, VA 22150: Ylmaz F. Polat.

USIA/TV MARTI—(202) 401–7144; 400 Sixth Street, SW 20547: Niurka Arteage, Sharon Castillo, Joseph DiMarco, Antonio Dieguez, Silvia Font, Edith Garcia, Amaro Gomez-Boix, Oscar F. Mora, Jaime Moreno, Allen Kirk Reio, Jorge A. Riopedre.

UNITED NEWS AND INFORMATION—(301) 924–6912; 15602 Cliffs Swallow Way Rockville, MD 20853: Forrest J. Boyd, Dennis Crowley.

UNITED PRESS INTERNATIONAL—(202) 898–8111; 1510 H Street, NW 20005: Neal Augenstein, Pye Chamberlayne, W.C. (Bill) Clough, Ron Colbert, Hank Neyer, Maria Pena, Eduardo Salinas, William Small.

UNIVISION NEWS—(202) 783–7155; 444 North Capitol St., #601G 20001: Perez Arturo Rubio, Jorge Contreras, Deborah Durham, Alvaro Encinas, Ana Espinoza, Armando Guzman, Lourdes Meluza, Adriana Molina-Roman, Vincent Mortreux, Aurea Nascimento, Pablo Sanchez, Armando Trull.

VENTANA PRODUCTIONS—(202) 785–5112; 1825 K Street, NW 5th Floor 20006: Armando Almanza, Nicola Frost, Christine Harding, William Harding, Tim Martin, Tim Murray, Luke Riffle, Julie Simon, Mark Thalman.

VIDEO NEWS SERVICE—(202) 467–4014; 400 North Capitol Street, NW 20001: Li-Hung Chen, Boris Pinkas, Joe Tomko, Stephen Tomko, T. Alejandro Harding S.

VIEWPOINT COMMUNICATIONS—(301) 949–1907; 5000 Euclid Drive, Kensington, MD 20895: Randy Feldman, Larry Greenblatt.

VOICE OF AMERICA—(202) 619–0707; 330 Independence Ave. SW #3500 20547: Michael C. Bowman, Rachael Bail, Ralph Eckhardt, Richard Firestone, Rosemary Hall, Donald Henry, Neal Lavon, James Malone, Jerry W. McKinney, John Pitman, Jim Randle, Nicholas Simeone, Renee Smith, David Swan, Oscar Underwood, Melissa Winkler, Paula Wolfson.

WAMU - FM RADIO—(202) 885–1200; 4000 Brandywine Street, NW 20036: Kathleen Merritt, Mark Plotkin, Derrick Ward, Julianne Welby, Laura Womack, Annie Wu.

WBIS—(202) 862–6645; 1025 Connecticut Avenue, NW #800 Washington, DC 20036: Christine Pass.

WETA-TV—(703) 998–2600; 3620 South 27th Street Arlington, VA 22206: Lynn Allison, Calvin Barry, Harry Bottorf, Timothy Bowen, Donald Brawner, Joseph Camp, Norman Craley, David Deutsch, David Gillette, Eileen Griffin, Charles Hill, Todd R. Holme, Stephen G. Howard, John E. Hyater, Charles Ide, Douglas P. Johncox, Daniel Knapp, Edward Lee, Don McClurkin, David McGowan, John B. Morgan, John C. Nash, Jr., Norman Nelson, Jeff Rathner, Darwin Silver, Otto K. Uyehara, Charles Voth.

NETWORKS, STATIONS, AND SERVICES REPRESENTED—Continued

WGN RADIO—(301) 942–1996; 9915 Hillridge Drive, Kensington, MD 20895: Patrick B. Haggerty.

WINGSPAN NEWS—(202) 293–9464; 1825 K Street, NW 9th Floor 20006: Mary Arobaga, Walter J. Boyne, Don Dudley, Dennis Gaffney, Carolyn Sperry, Austin Steo, Wilma Tubies.

WJLA-TV—(202) 364–7715; 3007 Tilden Street, NW 20008: Steven C. Affens, Bradley S. Bell, Paul L. Berry, Rea Blakey, Victor R. Blandburg, Diane T. Boozer, John J. Bowden, Beverly Bryan, Jim Clarke, Judith Ann Coates, William Cole, Lisa Diane Cox, Walter Crawford, Kerry Arden Cutlip, Pamela Davis, Martin C. Doane, Mary Ellen Donovan, Michael Forcucci, Brian Fuss, Pege Gilgannon, Carl Gottlieb, Richard Guastadisegni, Stephen P. Hackett, Peter Hakel, Holly Hamilton, John Robert Harter, Lawrence Herman, Candance M. Hewitt, Hugh Hinds, Horace R. Holmes, Kathy Foster Johnson, Archie Kelly, Lenard Kent, Greta Kreuz, Johnathan A. Mann, Kathleen Matthews, Roger P. Mellen, Clifton Moore, Charles Norton, Christopher S. Plater, Nancy Pretto, Linda Ringe, Earle U. Robinson III, Gail P. Rose, Jeff Rose, Joseph Rose, Ray Rose, Jose G. Santos, James Schaefer, Cindy Pena Shoffner, Indira Somani, Allan Vecchione, Mary Jo Walsh Gilmore, Theodore Walters, Richard T. Watkins, David A. Webb, Madelyne Woods, Gary Wordlaw, Cynthia Wright.

WMAL RADIO—(202) 686–3020; 4400 Jenifer Street, NW 20015: Milagros Ardin, Joan Doniger, Olga M. Joseph, Larry Krebs, Denchali Tufeckgian.

WTOP RADIO—(202) 362–0504; 3400 Idaho Avenue, NW 20015: Bruce Alan, Shawn Anderson, Jeanie Bae, Jill Cohen, Kyle Cooper, Richard A. Day, Arlene Eiras, Alan Etter, James T. Farley, Debra B. Feinstein, Tom Foty, Gary Froseth, Catherine Harmon, Mary Ann Jennings, David E. Johnson, Kyle Johnson, Colleen Kelleher, Kristi-Sue King, Michelle M. Komes, Judlyne Lilly, John Lynker, David F. McConnell, Michael D. McMearty, Mitchell Miller, Michael Moss, Angela Polite, Robert Publicover, Carrie Rabin, April D. Ryan, Judith Taub Squires, Paul C. Wagner.

WTTG-FOX TELEVISION—(202) 895–3000; 5151 Wisconsin Avenue, NW 20016: Jackie Bensen, David Burnett, Patricia Corcoran, Nayada L. Cowherd, Clinton F. Davis, Derricke M. Dennis, John P. Dunmire, Darya Folson, James E. Forner, John A. Frame, Max Giammetta, Jennifer Gillan, Carlos A. Gonzalez, Jean M. Grenda, Craig J. Harrington, Mary Harris, Thomas Hendrick, John Henrehan, Michael Horan, Karen Gray Houston, Sheila Jaskot, Morris Jones, Basil A. Justice, Craig A. Little, Geoffrey Manifold, Lark McCarthy, Patrick McGrath, Jim Nash, Grace Lee Nikkel, Jo Robertson, David Joseph Ross, F. David Rysak, Mark E. Sargent, Jan Smith, Louis R. Stevenson, Ron Talley Thompson, Charles K. Uchima, Don Watrud, Wendy Wilk, Douglas H. Wilkes, Brian G. Wilson, Sandra L. Young, Tom Young.

WUNO NOTIUNO RADIO NETWORK—(703) 866–4236; P.O. Box 5871 Springfield, VA 22150: Elmy E. Martinez.

WUSA-TV—(202) 895–5700; 4100 Wisconsin Avenue, NW 20016: Robert Y. Althage, Phyllis Armstrong, Richard Armstrong, Michael G. Bratton, Beverly Burke, Anthony M. Castrilli, William J. Clemann, Emily Cyr, Thomas Dukehart, Don Ellison, Samara M. Ewing, Thomas D. Haller, Harald Hoiland, Chris Houston, Keyin G. King, Vanessa M. Koolhof, Bruce Leshan, Frank D. McDermott, Robert C. McHenry, Wayne Myers, Gordon W. Peterson, Gary Reals, Louis David Statter, Janet Terry, Michael Trammell, Ronald F. Williams, Stephanie S. Wilson, Miriam Wright, Eun Yang.

WASHINGTON BUREAU NEWS SERVICE—(202) 544–4800; 236 Massachusetts Avenue, NE #602, 20002: Angelina Bonilla, Daouda Guissrt, Bradley Marshall, C. Patrick Thorne, Patrick Tracey, William Veitch, Michael D. Whitney.

WASHINGTON NEWS NETWORK—(202) 628–4000; 400 North Capitol Street, NW #183, 20001: Robert E. Beard, Edward M. Beckford, Karen Bell, Monique Conrad, Cy Gardner, Andrew Gelfman, John Giacomo, Lawrence Gold, Walter L. Gold, Sammy Kent, Marvin Rife, Ron A. Sarro.

WASHINGTON RADIO AND PRESS SERVICE—(301) 229–2576; 6702 Pawtucket Road Bethesda, MD 20817: Hanna Gutmann.

WASHINGTON-ALABAMA NEWS REPORT—(202) 333–6567; P.O. Box 58058 20037: Carol Bennett, Daniel Brechner, Mignon C. Smith.

WEST VIRGINIA PUBLIC RADIO—Cecelia Mason.

WIRELESS DATA SYSTEMS—(202) 637–3200; 1120 G Street, NW #250 20005: Dennis Dunbar, Brian K. McConnaughey.

WORLDNET–U.S.I.A TV—(202) 401–5454; 330 Independence Avenue, SW 20547: E. Robert Beaudin, Maurice Benjoar, Jeffery S. Daugherty, Dimetrius Jackson, Sinclair Ke, Anthony Masciarelli, John D. Quinn, Robert V. Tubbs.

WORLDWIDE TELEVISION NEWS—(703) 318–9136; 13166 New Parkland Drive Oak Hill, VA 20171: Cesar A. Canizales, Michael J. Rosenfelder, Paul Sisco, Joseph S. Tomko, III.

YONHAP TV NEWS—(202) 289–0773; 1333 H Street, NW #300 20005: Nam Sub Lee, Jae-Chul Mun.

ZOLCER-TV (GERMAN TV)—(202) 333–4842; 38097 W Street, NW 20007: Allen J. Chester, Andreas Gutzeit, Wolfgang Kotke, Nick Ludlan, Beate Muller-Blattau.

FREELANCERS:—Robert G. Abernethy, W.H. Abshaw, Timothy D. Ahmann, Thomas Albano, Joel R. Albert, Stuart A. Ammerman, Anders Alex Arestad, Patricia Armstrong, James F. Ashe, John Aubuchon, Russell M. Baker, Anne G. Ball, Cameron C. Barlett, Scott Barlett, Kevin Beyer, Wayne F. Boyd, Richard Breed, Teddy Brosius, Dwight B. Brown, William M. Canter, David K. Catrett, Sumana

NETWORKS, STATIONS, AND SERVICES REPRESENTED—Continued

Chatterjee, Anne Cocklin, Stephen Cocklin, Aaron Stuart Cohen, Jonathan Cohen, Carol Anne Cooke, Bobby Steve Creekmore, Francene Cucinello, Anthony Cunningham, Stephen Cupp, Michael A. DeMark, Gary S. DeMoss, Charles H. Dixson, William Donald, Paul G. Dougherty, Christina Eck, Alfred Scott Eisenhuth, Gail Fendley, Amy Flannery, Michael Ford, Betty Francis, F. Patrick French, David Friedman, Edward Giebel, Gordon Gilliam, R. Pat Glass, John Glennon, Susan Goodman, Dave Goulding, Kevin Griffin, Avery Gross, Steven Hamberg, Claus Harding, John Hartge, Thomas Hass, Barry Haywood, Georg Hirsch, Toni Hoover, David P. Hopper, Mayumi Ishihara, Edward B. Jennings, Jeffrey E. Johnston, Lorel Kane, Richard Kane, Danielle Karson, Katty Kay, Justin Kenny, Eric Kesner, Bruce Kissal, Robert Klein, Marc Koslow, Melissa Koval, Francesca Kritz, Stanley Lane, Gregory Larsen, David Lee Lee, Ronald H. Leidelmeyer, David Lent, Dexter Leong, Bruce Liffiton, David Lilling, Ken Lundberg, Robert J. Lyall, Carolyn Machado, Michael Mancuso, Autonio Marques, Mai Marriott, Michael Marriott, Jeff Martino, Claude Matthews, Maxine Mawhinnedy, Donald Jay McCarty, Megan Ann McGrath, Finnigan Michael, Alexander Milenic, Rodney Minor, Steven E. Mitnick, Bryan Mong, James M. Moran, Thomas D. Mote, John M. Murney, John L. Murrhy, Jim Nash, Richard A. Norling, Richard V. Norling, D. Kerry O'Berry, Daniel J. O'Shea, Rodney Patterson, Robert Peterson, Aileen Pincus, Murray Pinczuk, Christopher Plater, Mark Rabin, Edward M. Reinsel, Michael W. Richards, David Roberson, Xavier Rocas, Peter B. Roof, Gary Rosenberg, Steven Rosenfeld, Joan L. Roskosh, Karen A. Ryan, Aaron Sasson, Greg Savory, Michael Seium, Harry S. Shoffner, Quentin Silver, Gilbert J. Solorzano, Rodney E. Speed, Mark Stoddard, Rick Suddeth, George S. Summers, Andrew D. Thomas, Mary Beth Toole, Melissa D. Tune, Ellen Uchimiya, Robert Valette, Vaughn Ververs, Brian Walker, William L. Walker, Arlene Weisskopf, George Weller, John P. Whiteside, Christopher Widmer, John A. Williams, Kristin Wilson, Leigh Wilson, Robert Witten, H. William Yates, Stratis J. Zervos.

PERIODICAL PRESS GALLERIES

HOUSE PERIODICAL PRESS GALLERY

The Capitol, H–304, 225–2941

Director.—David Holmes.
Assistant Directors: Anne J. Cobb, Robert L. Stallings.

SENATE PERIODICAL PRESS GALLERY

The Capitol, S–320, 224–0265

Superintendent.—Jim Talbert.
Assistant Superintendents: Louise A. Curran; Edward V. Pesce.

EXECUTIVE COMMITTEE OF CORRESPONDENTS

Craig Winneker, Roll Call, Chairman
Richard Maze, Army Times Publishing Co., Secretary-Treasurer
Richard Dunham, Business Week
Richard Cohen, National Journal
Cheryl Bolen, BNA News
Jay Carney, Time, Inc.
John Godfrey, Tax Notes

RULES GOVERNING PERIODICAL PRESS GALLERIES

1. Persons eligible for admission to the Periodical Press Galleries must be bona fide resident correspondents of reputable standing, giving their chief attention to the gathering and reporting of news. They shall state in writing the names of their employers and their additional sources of earned income; and they shall declare that, while a member of the Galleries, they will not act as an agent in the prosecution of claims, and will not become engaged or assist, directly or indirectly, in any lobbying, promotion, advertising, or publicity activity intended to influence legislation or any other action of the Congress, nor any matter before any independent agency, or any department or other instrumentality of the Executive Branch; and that they will not act as an agent for, or be employed by the Federal, or any State, local or foreign government or representatives thereof; and that they will not, directly or indirectly, furnish special or ''insider'' information intended to influence prices or for the purpose of trading on any commodity or stock exchange; and that they will not become employed, directly or indirectly, by any stock exchange, board of trade or other organization or member thereof, or brokerage house or broker engaged in the buying and selling of any security or commodity. Applications shall be submitted to the Executive Committee of the Periodical Correspondents' Association and shall be authenticated in a manner satisfactory to the Executive Committee.

2. Applicants must be employed by periodicals that regularly publish a substantial volume of news material of either general, economic, industrial, technical, cultural or trade character. The periodical must require such Washington coverage on a continuing basis and must be owned and operated independently of any government, industry, institution, association, or lobbying organization. Applicants must also be employed by a periodical that is published for profit and is supported chiefly by advertising or by subscription, or by a periodical meeting the conditions in this paragraph but published by a nonprofit organization that, first, operates independently of any government, industry, or institution and, second, does not engage, directly or indirectly, in any lobbying or other activity intended to influence any matter before Congress or before any independent agency or any department or other instrumentality of the Executive Branch. House organs are not eligible.

3. Members of the families of correspondents are not entitled to the privileges of the Galleries.

4. The Executive Committee may issue temporary credentials permitting the privileges of the Galleries to individuals who meet the rules of eligibility but who may be on short term assignment or temporarily resident in Washington.

5. Under the authority of Rule 34 of the House of Representatives and of Rule 33 of the Senate, the Periodical Galleries shall be under the control of the Executive Committee, subject to the approval and supervision of the Speaker of the House of Representatives and the Senate Committee on Rules and Administration. It shall be the duty of the Executive Committee, at its discretion, to report violations of the privileges of the Galleries to the Speaker or the Senate Committee on Rules and Administration, and pending action thereon, the offending correspondent may be suspended. The Committee shall be elected at the start of each Congress by members of the Periodical Correspondents' Association, and shall consist of seven members with no more than one member from any one publishing organization. The Committee shall elect its own officers, and a majority of the Committee may fill vacancies on the Committee. The list in the Congressional Directory shall be a list only of members of the Periodical Correspondents' Association.

NEWT GINGRICH,
Speaker, House of Representatives.

JOHN WARNER,
Chairman, Senate Committee on Rules and Administration.

MEMBERS ENTITLED TO ADMISSION

PERIODICAL PRESS GALLERIES

Abadjian, Marguerite: Inside Washington Publishers
Abruscato, Lurdes: Phillips Publishing
Abshire, Michael: Capitol Publications
Aclander, Melanie: Legal Publication Services
Adde, Nicholas L.: Army Times Publishing Co.
Agnew, Bruce A.: Journal of NIH Research
Aguilar, Louis: Hispanic Link News Service
Aihara, Akihiro: Defense Focus
Aikens, Ronald E.: BNA News
Airozo, David: McGraw-Hill
Aker, Janet A.: FDC Reports
Albani, Karin: Capitol Publications
Albergo, Paul F.: BNA News
Albers, Julie Wakefield: Washington City Paper
Albiniak, Paige M.: Broadcasting & Cable
Alden, John R.: Telecommunications Reports
Aldrich, Nancy Lee: Business Publishers
Alger, Elizabeth: Career Pathways Report
Allizon, Marie B.: Internewsletter
Amber, Michelle: BNA News
Amolsch, Arthur L.: FTC Watch
Anand, Vineeta: Crain Communications
Anderson, Burnett: Numismatic News
Anderson, Jon R.: Army Times Publishing Co.
Anderson, Tania: TechNews
Anderson, Wendy Love: Food Chemical News
Anselmo, Joseph C.: Aviation Week
Anthes, Gary H.: IDG Communications
Antonides, David S.: Tax Notes
Archer, Jeffrey Robert: Education Week
Arenstein, Seth: Phillips Publishing
Arian, Michael L.: BNA News
Armbrister, Trevor: Reader's Digest
Armes, Leroy: BNA News
Armstrong, Anne: Federal Computer Week
Arnoult, Sandra: Phillips Publishing
Arthur, Holly E.: McGraw-Hill/Aero
Arthur, Mary Helen: Thompson Publishing Group
Ashton, Jerome C.: BNA News
Ashworth, Jerry: Business Publishers
Ashworth, Susan: IMAS Publishing
Asker, James R.: Aviation Week
Aswad, Nadya: BNA News
Atkins, Pamela S.: BNA News
Atwood, John F.: Washington Service Bureau
Auer, Nathalie: Washington Service Bureau
August, Lissa: Time, Inc.
Aukofer, Matthew: Business Publishers
Auster, Bruce: U. S. News & World Report
Avila, Wanda: Telecommunications Reports
Ayayo, Herman P.: Tax Notes
Ayers, Carl Albert: United Communications Group
Ayoub, Nina Cary: Chronicle of Higher Education
Babbitz, Robert J.: Capitol Publications
Bachman, Kathryn: Radio Business Report
Bader, Aimee: Business Publishers
Baerson, Kevin M.: King Publications
Baez, Jessica L.: BNA News
Bailey, Charles Boileau: BNA News
Bailey, Wendy: Capitol Publications
Baisden, Harry L.: Pasha Publications
Baldassano, Vicki: BNA News
Ballard, Andrew M.: BNA News
Ballard, Peter: FDC Reports
Baldwin, Ian: U.S. News & World Report
Baratta, Lisa J.: Washington Service Bureau
Barber, Jeffrey: McGraw-Hill
Barber, Wayne: Pasha Publications
Barenti, Michael: Business Publishers
Barnard, Richard C.: Army Times Publishing Co.
Barnes, David: Traffic World
Barnes, James A.: National Journal
Barnes, Julian E.: U.S. News & World Report
Barone, Michael Douglas: Reader's Digest
Barras, Jonetta R.: Washington City Paper
Barrett, Amy: Business Week
Barrett, Laurence I.: Time, Inc.
Barrett, R. Morris: Time, Inc.
Barton, Delilah P.: Thompson Publishing Group
Bass, Brad: Federal Computer Week
Bates, Jason: McGraw-Hill/Aero
Baumgarner, James D.: McGraw-Hill/Aero
Beale, LaTaunja: Pasha Publications
Beaven, Lara W.: Inside Washington Publishers
Becker, Bonita: Business Publishers
Beiting, Jan: CD Publications
Bell, John C.: Tax Notes
Beltran-del-rio, Pascal: Proceso
Bendavid, Naftali: Legal Times
Benedetti, Janet: BNA News
Benjamin, Mark: Inside Washington Publishers
Bennefield, Robin: U. S. News & World Report
Bennett, Alison: BNA News
Bennett, Ralph: Reader's Digest
Benton, Nicholas F.: Falls Church News Press
Berenson, Douglas: Inside Washington Publishers
Berger, James R.: Washington Trade Daily
Berger, Mary L.: BNA News
Bergin, Christopher: Tax Notes
Berkman, Harvey: National Law Journal

MEMBERS ENTITLED TO ADMISSION, PERIODICAL PRESS GALLERIES—Continued

Berkowitz, Michael: Business Publishers
Berlau, John: Insight Magazine
Bernard, Roger D.: Futures
Bernhard, Elizabeth: Government Information Services
Bernstein, Aaron: Business Week
Bernstein, Jeremy: Inside Washington Publishers
Bertin, Lou: CMP Media Inc.
Besser, James David: New York Jewish Week
Best, Frank M.: U. S. Medicine
Beswick, Ellen: Natural Gas Intelligence
Biemiller III, Lawrence: Chronicle of Higher Education
Billings, Deborah: BNA News
Billings, Robert: Washington Business Information
Bilson, Don: Inside Washington Publishers
Binker, Mark: CD Publications
Bird, Julie: Army Times Publishing Co.
Birnbaum, Deborah: National Journal
Birnbaum, Jeffrey H.: Time, Inc.
Blackman, Ann: Time, Inc.
Blalock, Cecelia: Periodicals News Service
Blank, Peter L.: Kiplinger Washington Editors
Blanke, Jean Ann: BNA News
Blazar, Ernest: Army Times Publishing Co.
Blum, Debra: Chronicle of Higher Education
Blumel, Robert R.: Reid Publishing Group
Blumenstyk, Goldie: Chronicle of Higher Education
Blumenthal, Sidney: New Yorker
Boatman, John: Jane's Information Group
Bodnar, Janet: Kiplinger Washington Editors
Bodner, Debra G.: BNA News
Boeke, Cynthia: Phillips Publishing
Bolen, Cheryl L.: BNA News
Bond, David: McGraw-Hill/Aero
Booker, Simeon S.: Jet/Ebony
Borger, Gloria: U. S. News & World Report
Borrus, Amy: Business Week
Bosarge, Betty B.: Washington Crime News Services
Botsford, Linda G.: BNA News
Botzum, Jr., John R.: Nautilus Press
Bouvet, Stephen: Capitol Publications
Bowers, Carol L.: Phillips Publishing
Bowie, Karyn S.: BNA News
Boyce, Clayton W.: Traffic World
Boyd, Jr., Ronald D.: Pace Publications
Boyer, Peter: New Yorker
Boyles, William Robert: Health Market Survey
Bradley, Ann: Education Week
Bradley, Eleanor: BNA News
Bradley, Jennifer A.: Roll Call
Brager, Mark E.: FDC Reports
Brandolph, David Barry: BNA News
Brandon, George Everette: Telecommunications Reports
Brandon, Priscilla T.: Kiplinger Washington Editors
Braun, David M.: CMP Media Inc.
Braunberg, Andrew: Phillips Publishing
Brazda, Jerome F.: Crain Communications
Breda, Christina: Capitol Publications
Breeden, II, John: Government Computer News
Breslau, Karen: Newsweek
Bresnahan, John: Inside Washington Publishers
Brevetti, Rossella: BNA News
Brewin, Bob: Federal Computer Week
Breznick, Alan J.: Cable World
Brideau, Alexander W.: Pasha Publications
Brideau, Carol Ann: BNA News
Bridger, Chester T.: Army Times Publishing Co.
Bridges, Jessica H.: Capitol Publications
Briley III, John A.: Food Chemical News
Brindley, David: U. S. News & World Report
Bristow, Melissa Star: Kiplinger Washington Editors
Britt, Angela L.: BNA News
Britt, Julie Anne: Atlantic Information Services
Broderick, Brian J.: BNA News
Bronson, Richard: BNA News
Brooks, Alicia: Time Inc.
Brooks, David: Weekly Standard
Brooks, George A.: Inside Mortgage Finance
Brooks, Susan S.: Research Institute of America Group
Bross, David J.: Phillips Publishing
Brostoff, Steven: National Underwriter
Brousseau, Mark A.: Phillips Publishing
Bruce, Robert C.: BNA News
Brown, Bruce David: Legal Times
Brown, Janice F.: Afro American Newspapers
Brown, Patricia: CMP Media Inc.
Browning, Graeme: National Journal
Brownlee, Shannon: U. S. News & World Report
Bruce, Robert C.: BNA News
Bruninga, Susan: BNA News
Brunori, David E.: Tax Notes
Bryant, Jane: Phillips Publishing
Bryant, Sue: BNA News
Burd, Stephen: Chronicle of Higher Education
Burey, Joseph M.: Inside Washington Publishers
Burger, Timothy J.: Legal Times
Burkhart, Lori: Public Utilities Reports
Burkholder, Randy: FDC Reports
Burlage, John D.: Army Times Publishing Co.
Burleigh, Nina: Time, Inc.
Burnside, Tina: Thompson Publishing Group
Burr, Ronald E.: American Spectator
Burton, Douglas: Insight Magazine
Buskirk, Howard: Natural Gas Week
Butchock, Steve: Medical Devices Report
Byerrum, Ellen: BNA News
Bykowski, Michael S.: International Medical News Group
Byrd, Randy: Pasha Publications
Cage, Mary Crystal: Chronicle of Higher Education
Cahlink, George: Inside Washington Publishers
Caldwell, Christopher: Weekly Standard

MEMBERS ENTITLED TO ADMISSION, PERIODICAL PRESS GALLERIES—Continued

Campbell, Kristina K.: Washington Blade
Campbell, Niles S.: BNA News
Canaday, Henry T.: Phillips Publishing
Canan, Martha M.: BNA News
Cano, Craig S.: McGraw-Hill
Canonica, Rocco: Natural Gas Intelligence
Capaccio, Anthony: King Publications
Carbine, Michael E.: Atlantic Information Services
Carey, John A.: Business Week
Carey, William: Phillips Publishing
Carlozzo, Ann Therese: BNA News
Carlson, Caron: Wireless Week
Carlson, Melissa: FDC Reports
Carlson, Tucker: Weekly Standard
Carnegie, M. D.: American Spectator
Carnevale, Ellen: Thompson Publishing Group
Carney, Eliza Newlin: National Journal
Carney, James: Time, Inc.
Carr, Brian A.: BNA News
Carr, David: Washington City Paper
Carroll, John: Stars & Stripes
Carson, Tom: Village Voice
Cartwright, Linda A.: Green Sheets
Cash, Catherine: McGraw-Hill
Cassell, Barry: Pasha Publications
Cassidy, William B.: Traffic World
Catanzaro, Michael J.: Human Events
Causey, James M.: Capitol Publications
Cauthen, Carey E.: Pace Publications
Cecala, Guy David: Inside Mortgage Finance
Chabel, Bernard S.: BNA News
Chait, Jonathan: New Republic
Chamberlin, Siobhan B.: Thompson Publishing Group
Chapman, Claire: American Banker Newsletters
Chapman, Michael: Human Events
Chappie, Damon: Roll Call
Chase, Jeremy: FDC Reports
Chenoweth, Karin: Black Issues in Higher Education
Cherkasky, Mara: Thompson Publishing Group
Cherry, Sheila R.: CCH Inc.
Chester, David T.: Department of Education Reports
Chetwynd, Josh: U. S. News & World Report
Chibbaro, Jr., Louis M.: Washington Blade
Childs, Nathan D.: International Medical News Group
Chineson, Joel: Legal Times
Chinn, Christopher D.: FDC Reports
Chronister, Gregory M.: Education Week
Chuo, Emily: BNA News
Cislo, Maureen R.: Phillips Publishing
Clapp, Stephen: Food Chemical News
Clark, Charles S.: CQ Researcher
Clark, Colin S.: King Publications
Clark, Shelene: BNA News
Clark, Timothy B.: Government Executive
Clarke, David P.: Inside Washington Publishers
Clarke-Gomez, Irene: BNA News
Clayton, Michelle: American Banker Newsletters
Clemmitt, Marcia: Healthcare Information
Clifford, Garry: Time, Inc.
Clift, Eleanor: Newsweek
Cline, Regina P.: BNA News
Cloud, John A.: Washington City Paper
Cobo, Lucia E.: IMAS Publishing
Coffin, James B.: Public Lands News
Cohen, Amy: Army Times Publishing Co.
Cohen, Daniel: Phillips Publishing
Cohen, Janey: BNA News
Cohen, Joshua T.: Inside Washington Publishers
Cohen, Richard E.: National Journal
Coleman, Janet: FDC Reports
Coles, Adrienne D.: Education Week
Colin, Thomas J.: CQ Researcher
Collett, Camille: Journal of NIH Research
Collins, Brian: National Mortgage News
Collins, Jr., Donald: Time, Inc.
Collogan, David L.: McGraw-Hill/Aero
Combemale, Martine: Milan Presse
Compart, Andrew: Army Times Publishing Co.
Conconi, Charles N.: Washingtonian
Conlan, Michael F.: Drug Topics
Connelly, Joanne M.: Federal Computer Week
Connolly, Paul: Natural Gas Week
Conroy, Declan A.: Food Chemical News
Cook, Barbara C.: Business Travel News
Cook, William James: U. S. News & World Report
Cook, Jr., Charles E.: Cook Political Report
Cooper, Janice: Legal Times
Cooper, Mary H.: CQ Researcher
Cooper, Matthew S.: Newsweek
Cooper, Jr., William P.: Army Times Publishing
Cordes, Colleen: Chronicle of Higher Education
Cordner, Christine: Inside Washington Publishers
Cordwell, Brenda: Capitol Publications
Corley, Matilda Monroe: BNA News
Corn, David: Nation
Corry, John: American Spectator
Cosgrove, Anita Kelly: BNA News
Couteau, Gregory C.: Army Times Publishing Co.
Cowen, Ron: Science News
Cox, Bowman: Pasha Publications
Coyle, Marcia: National Law Journal
Coyne, Martin J.: Inside Washington Publishers
Crabtree, Susan J.: Insight Magazine
Craig, Darlena J.: Army Times Publishing Co.
Craig, David Brian: Army Times Publishing Co.
Craig, Jon: Chronicle of Higher Education
Craig, Theodosia: McGraw-Hill
Craver, Martha L.: Kiplinger Washington Editors
Crawford, Mark H.: King Publications
Cristy, Sam: Washington Business Information
Crock, Stan: Business Week
Cross, Phillip S.: Public Utilities Reports
Crow, Patrick: Oil & Gas Journal

MEMBERS ENTITLED TO ADMISSION, PERIODICAL PRESS GALLERIES—Continued

Crowley, Mary E.: Phillips Publishing
Cruickshank, Paula L.: CCH Inc.
Cuddihy, Kevin: Thompson Publishing Group
Cummins, Ken: Washington City Paper
Cunningham, Robert: Healthcare Information
Cusack, Robert: Inside Washington Publishers
Cushner, Kimberly C.: Thompson Publishing Group
D'Agostino, Joseph A.: Human Events
Dabaie, Michael G.: Business Publishers
Dalecki, Kenneth B.: Kiplinger Washington Editors
Dana, Carol: Government Information Services
Daniel, Lisa: Army Times Publishing Co.
Daniels, Alex: Governing
Danitz, Tiffany: Insight Magazine
Darcey, Sue: Food Chemical News
Davidson, Mark: McGraw-Hill
Davies, Lira Behrens: McGraw-Hill
Davies, Stephen: Endangered Species & Wetlands Report
Davis, Beth: CMP Media Inc.
Davis, Diane: Federal Publications
Davis, Kristin: Kiplinger Washington Editors
Davis, Mary M.: BNA News
Davis, Michael C.: BNA News
Davis, Paris D.: Metro Herald Newspaper
Day, Felicia: Thompson Publishing Group
DeHoff, Michael E.: Tax Notes
DeMott, Kathryn: Capitol Publications
Dean, Eddie: Washington City Paper
Deigh, Gloria: BNA News
Deily, Mary-Ellen P.: Capitol Publications
Del Valle, Christina: Business Week
Della Ratta, J. Raphael: Exchange Monitor Publications
Demko, Paul: Chronicle of Higher Education
Denes, Shary: McGraw-Hill
Denny, Sharon: Army Times Publishing Co.
Dentzer, Susan: U. S. News & World Report
Dern, Adrienne: Food Chemical News
Dervarics, Charles J.: Business Publishers
Desmond, Kathryn J.: BNA News
Desruisseaux, Paul: Chronicle of Higher Education
Dettling, John Charles: Thompson Publishing Group
Dettmer, Jamie: Insight Magazine
DiPasquale, Suzanne: Inside Washington Publishers
Diamond, Phyllis: BNA News
Dickerson, John F.: Time, Inc.
Diegmueller, Karen: Education Week
Dineen, John: Green Sheets
Dizard, Wilson: McGraw-Hill
Doan, Michael F.: Kiplinger Washington Editors
Dobson, Jon: FDC Reports
Doi, Ayako: Japan Digest
Dolan, Michael: Washington Business Information
Donlan, Thomas G.: Barron's
Donmoyer, Ryan J.: Tax Notes
Donnelly, John M.: King Publications
Donnelly, Sally: Time, Inc.
Donoghue, James A.: Penton Publishing
Donohue, Stephen: Phillips Publishing
Doolan, Kelley: McGraw-Hill
Dordbek, Christopher J.: Telecommunications Reports
Doris, Jr., Dennis B.: Press Associates
Dougherty, Carter S.: Inside Washington Publishers
Douglass, David P.: Business Publishers
Dowd, Ann Reilly: Time, Inc.
Downes, Bob: Travel Trade
Doyle, Brian J.: Time, Inc.
Doyle, James S.: Army Times Publishing Co.
Doyle, Kenneth P.: BNA News
Dozier, Damon A.: BNA News
Drew, Elizabeth: New Yorker
Driscoll, Christopher A.: Phillips Publishing
Drolte, Angela: BNA News
Drummond, Steven: Education Week
Duffy, Jennifer: Cook Political Report
Duffy, Michael: Time, Inc.
Duffy, Thomas: Inside Washington Publishers
Duke, Robert M.: CD Publications
Duncan, Leslie A.: Green Sheets
Duncan, Michael J.: Futures
Dundjerski, Marina: Chronicle of Higher Education
Dunham, Richard S.: Business Week
Dunn, William: Research Institute of America Group
Dupont, Daniel G.: Inside Washington Publishers
Durbin, Fran: Travel Weekly
Dwyer, Paula: Business Week
Dykewicz, Paul: Phillips Publishing
Easton, Eric B.: Business Publishers
Easton, Susan: FDC Reports
Eby, William W.: Kiplinger Washington Editors
Eddings, Jerelyn: U. S. News & World Report
Edwards, Charles J.: Government Information Services
Edwards, Tamala: Time, Inc.
Effron, Eric: Legal Times
Ege, Konrad: Blatter
Eggerton, John S.: Broadcasting & Cable
Eilperin, Juliet: Roll Call
Eisele, Albert: The Hill
Eisele, Anne: Army Times Publishing Co.
Eisele, Catherine: The Hill
Eiserer, Elaine R.: Business Publishers
Eiserer, Leonard A. C.: Business Publishers
Eisler, Kim I.: Washingtonian
Elfin, Dana A.: BNA News
Elfin, Mel: U. S. News & World Report
Eliopoulos, Phoebe A.: Atlantic Information Services
Ellingwood, Susan: New Republic
Eng, Warren K.: FDC Reports
Engdahl, Elizabeth: Legal Times
Engel, Diana: United Communications Group
Epstein, Jeffrey H.: Stars & Stripes

MEMBERS ENTITLED TO ADMISSION, PERIODICAL PRESS GALLERIES—Continued

Erlich, Jeff: Army Times Publishing Co.
Esselman, Mary D.: Time, Inc.
Evangelauf, Jean: Chronicle of Higher Education
Evans, David: Phillips Publishing
Evers, Stacey: Jane's Information Group
Ewing, Laurence Lee: Army Times Publishing Co.
Ewy, Bradley J.: FDC Reports
Ezzell, Carol: Journal of NIH Research
Fabian, Thecla: Business Publishers
Fackelmann, Kathy A.: Science News
Fairley, Peter: Chemical Week
Falk, Scott R.: BNA News
Famiglietti, Len: Pasha Publications
Fanning, Odom: Internal Medicine World Report
Farmer, David W.: Roll Call
Favin, Amy: BNA News
Feazel, R. Michael: Warren Publishing
Feder, Jody: Government Information Services
Feldkamp, Robert H.: Washington Crime News Services
Feldman, William H.: LRP Publications
Felsenthal, Mark E.: BNA News
Felsher, Murray: Washington Remote Sensing Letter
Feltman, Peter E.: CCH Inc.
Fenwick, Carla: Washington Service Bureau
Ferguson, Andrew: Weekly Standard
Fernandez III, Robustiano: Phillips Publishing
Ferster, Warren: Army Times Publishing Co.
Festa, Elizabeth D.: American Banker Newsletters
Fickling, Amy L.: Business Research Publications
Field, David: Education Week
Field, Emily: Tax Notes
Fields, Cheryl D.: Black Issues in Higher Education
Fields, Cheryl M.: Chronicle of Higher Education
Fields, Howard: Television Broadcast
Figura, Susannah Z.: Penton Publishing
Fineman, Howard: Newsweek
Finnegan, Philip: Army Times Publishing Co.
Fiore, Catherine: Cancer Letter
Fischer, Craig: Pace Publications
Fischer, David B.: U. S. News & World Report
Fischer, Dean E.: Time, Inc.
Fishbein, Lawrence I.: Kiplinger Washington Editors
Fisher, Mary Jane: National Underwriter
Fitzpatrick, Erika: Government Information Services
Fitzpatrick, James F.: BNA News
Fleming, Heather: Broadcasting & Cable
Fletcher, Jay F.: Food Chemical News
Flint, Perry: Penton Publishing
Flippen, Charles: Phillips Publishing
Flora, Charles Whitt: Business Publishers
Florian, Jeffrey C.: BNA News
Floyd, Bianca P.: Chronicle of Higher Education
Flynn, Joan M.: BNA News
Fodor, Katherine V.: FDC Reports
Fogarty, John R.: Kiplinger Washington Editors
Forror, Mark A.: Professional Pilot Magazine
Forsyth, Gordon: Traffic World
Foster, Lawrence D.: McGraw-Hill
Foster, Michael: Pasha Publications
Fotos, Christopher: McGraw-Hill/Aero
Foullon, Danielle: FDC Reports
Fourney, Susan: Government Executive
Foust, Dean: Business Week
Fowler, Shantelle: BNA News
France, Steve: LRP Publications
Frank, Allan L.: Alfa Publishing
Frank, Richard S.: National Journal
Franklin, Daniel: Economist
Freeman, Edmond B.: Inside Washington Publishers
Freer, Jennifer: Capitol Publications
French, Michael: Warren Publishing
Frick, Robert L.: Kiplinger Washington Editors
Frieden, Joyce: International Medical News Group
Friedly, Jock: The Hill
Friedman, Dorian R.: U. S. News & World Report
Friedman, Roger: Capitol Publications
Friel, Brian: Government Executive
Fries, Laura M.: Satellite Orbit
Fritz, Tina: Research Institute of America Group
Frost, Brendan DuBois: CCH Inc.
Fuentes, Gidget: Army Times Publishing Co.
Fukushima, Craig: Japan Digest
Fulghum, David: Aviation Week
Fulton, April E.: Inside Washington Publishers
Furlong, Vanessa E.: CQ Researcher
Gamber, Glenn: Food Chemical News
Gamble, Jennifer: Green Business Letter
Ganley, Susan: Chronicle of Higher Education
Gardner, Jonathan P.: Crain Communications
Garelik, Glenn: Time, Inc.
Garfield, Bob: Crain Communications
Garland, Susan: Business Week
Garner, W. Lynn: McGraw-Hill
Garvey, Charlotte: Business Publishers
Garwin, Laura J.: Nature
Gasparello, Linda Ann: King Publications
Gatty, Mary Ann: Periodicals News Service
Gatty, Robert C.: Periodicals News Service
Gearey, Robyn: New Republic
Gearon, Christopher: Atlantic Information Services
Geimann, Stephen J.: Warren Publishing
Geisel, Jerome M.: Crain Communications
Geisel, Roseanne W.: Crain Communications
Geraghty, Mary Elizabeth: Chronicle of Higher Education
Gerwig, Kate: CMP Media Inc.
Gest, Ted: U. S. News & World Report
Gibb, Steven K.: Inside Washington Publishers
Gifford, Court: BNA News
Gillooly, Brian: CMP Media Inc.
Gilston, Samuel M.: Gilston Communications Group
Ginburg, Yana: Jane's Information Group
Ginsbach, Pam D.: BNA News
Gizzi, John: Human Events
Glaser, Vera: Washingtonian

MEMBERS ENTITLED TO ADMISSION, PERIODICAL PRESS GALLERIES—Continued

Glass, Michelle A.: BNA News
Glass, Stephen: New Republic
Glasser, Susan B.: Roll Call
Glastris, Paul: U. S. News & World Report
Gleason, Brenda L.: CD Publications
Gleckman, Howard: Business Week
Glenn, Heidi: Tax Notes
Glick, Eric: Cable World
Godfrey, John: Tax Notes
Goebes, Bob: BNA News
Goeller, David: Business Publishers
Gold, Leslie J.: BNA News
Goldberg, Kirsten: Cancer Letter
Goldberg, Paul: Cancer Letter
Goldman, Ted: Legal Times
Goldwasser, Joan: Kiplinger Washington Editors
Golle, Vince: Futures
Golub, Barbra: Research Institute of America Group
Goode, Stephen Ray: Insight Magazine
Goodfellow, Betsy: FDC Reports
Goodgame, Dan: Time, Inc.
Goodman, Jr., Glenn W.: Armed Forces Journal
Goodwin, Anne B.: BNA News
Gordon, Meryl: Elle
Gose, Ben: Chronicle of Higher Education
Gottlick, Jerry: U. S. Medicine
Gough, Bob: Capitol Publications
Goyal, Raghubir: Asia Today
Graham, Oswald G.: Tax Notes
Grandon, Ronald E.: Green Sheets
Grano, John: Inside Washington Publishers
Graves, Desiree Allen: Afro American Newspapers
Gray, Christoher E.: FDC Reports
Gray, Susan: Chronicle of Higher Education
Graziano, Sandra: Education Week
Grebb, Michael B.: Telecommunications Reports
Greczyn, Mary: Crain Communications
Greenberg, Daniel S.: Science & Government Report
Greene, Elizabeth: Chronicle of Higher Education
Gregg, Diana I.: BNA News
Gregory, Erin E.: Satellite Orbit
Griffith, Ellen B.: Washington G-2 Reports
Griffith, Joan H.: BNA News
Grimm, Vanessa Jo: Government Computer News
Grodnitzky, Steven: Tax Notes
Groner, Jonathan: Legal Times
Grossman, Elaine M.: Inside Washington Publishers
Gruber, Peter: Focus
Gruenberg, Mark J.: Press Associates
Grupe, Bob: Business Publishers
Guernsey, Lisa: Chronicle of Higher Education
Haar, Audrey: Pasha Publications
Hadley, Richard D.: United Communications Group
Hagan, Richard: Washington Business Information
Hager, Mary: Newsweek
Haglund, Keith: Journal of NIH Research
Hagstrom, Jerry: National Journal
Hall, Andrea L.: Thompson Publishing Group
Hall, Holly: Chronicle of Higher Education
Halmos, Jr., E.E.: Concrete Products
Halonen, Douglas J.: Crain Communications
Hamelburg, Jamie Kent: Federal Publications
Hamilton, Amy: Tax Notes
Hammond, Brian: Telecommunications Reports
Haniffa, Abdul Aziz: India Abroad
Hannifin, Jerry: Time, Inc.
Hanna, Christina N.: BNA News
Hanson, Christine M.: Federal Publications
Harbrecht, Douglas A.: Business Week
Hardy, Virginia L.: National Journal
Harkness, Peter A.: Governing
Harman, Thomas: Inside Washington Publishers
Harp, Lonnie: Education Week
Harper, Steven R.: Capitol Publications
Harreld, Heather: Federal Computer Week
Harrelson, Robert: Inside Washington Publishers
Harrington, Christine: FDC Reports
Harrington, Timothy P.: FDC Reports
Harris, Christy: Army Times Publishing Co.
Harris, Donna L.: Crain Communications
Harris-Aikens, Donna: BNA News
Harrison, Tom: McGraw-Hill
Hart, Kathleen: McGraw-Hill
Harwood, Margaret C.: Army Times Publishing Co.
Haseley, Donna: Inside Washington Publishers
Hatch, Andrea: Inside Washington Publishers
Hatch, David M.: Crain Communications
Haugerud, Howard E.: Stars & Stripes
Hawkins, Bernadette D.: Army Times Publishing Co.
Haworth, Karla: Chronicle of Higher Education
Hayden, Kathleen J.: Time, Inc.
Hayes, Lisa L.: Government Information Services
Haywood, Richette L.: Jet/Ebony
Hazelwood, Ed: McGraw-Hill/Aero
Healy, Patrick D.: Chronicle of Higher Education
Hearn, Edward T.: Multichannel News
Hedges, Stephen J.: U. S. News & World Report
Heilbrunn, Jacob: New Republic
Heilemann, John: HotWired/Wired
Heinze, Cathy: FDC Reports
Helms, Margaret: Insight Magazine
Henderer, Rhodes: Research Institute of America Group
Henderson, Sheryl: American Spectator
Hendricks, Evan: Privacy Times
Hennig, Jutta: Inside Washington Publishers
Henning, Jonathan: Defense Focus
Henry, Ed: Kiplinger Washington Editors
Henry, Edward M.: Roll Call
Henry, Shannon: TechNews
Herman, Edith: Warren Publishing
Hernandez, Luis: Thompson Publishing Group
Heronema, Jennifer S.: Army Times Publishing Co.
Herzberger, Beth: Pasha Publications

MEMBERS ENTITLED TO ADMISSION, PERIODICAL PRESS GALLERIES—Continued

Hess, Glenn H.: Chemical Marketing Reporter
Hess, Pamela Rae: Inside Washington Publishers
Hetter, Katia: U. S. News & World Report
Hickey, Jennifer: Insight Magazine
Hickman, Enith: Army Times Publishing Co.
Hicks, Darryl R.: National Mortgage News
Higgins, John: McGraw-Hill
Hill, Eleanor S.: Pratt's Letter
Hill, Keith M.: BNA News
Hillebrand, Mary: Satellite Business News
Hillgren, Sonja: Farm Journal
Himali, Ursula: BNA News
Hinkle, Elizabeth T.: Washington Business Information
Hirani, Sindhu G.: BNA News
Hiruo, Elaine: McGraw-Hill
Hitchens, Theresa: Army Times Publishing Co.
Hoar, William: CD Publications
Hobbs, M. Nielsen: FDC Reports
Hobbs, Susan: BNA News
Hoff, David: Education Week
Hoffman, Donald: Government Information Services
Hoffman, Shirlee Gaines: Newsweek
Hofmann, Mark A.: Crain Communications
Hofmeister, Elizabeth W.: BNA News
Hogan, Kevin J.: Thompson Publishing Group
Hogan, Rick: Natural Gas Week
Hoges, Clemens: Der Spiegel
Hogue, Cheryl: BNA News
Holland, Max: Nation
Holloway, Nigel R.: Far Eastern Economic Review
Holly, Christopher P.: McGraw-Hill
Holly, Daniel C.: Army Times Publishing Co.
Holm, Erik W.: King Publications
Holmes, Allan T.: Federal Computer Week
Holmes, Jeremy R.: BNA News
Holmes, Strawn T.: BNA News
Holzer, Robert D.: Army Times Publishing Co.
Hopkin, Karen: Journal of NIH Research
Hopps, Michael: Pasha Publications
Horrock, Nicholas M.: U. S. News & World Report
Horton, Brendan: Nature
Hosenball, Mark: Newsweek
Hotta, Yoshio: Yomiuri America
Howell, Arnesa A.: BNA News
Hubbard, Catherine: Federal Employees News Digest
Hudak, Ronald A.: Phillips Publishing
Hudelson, Dale: Career Pathways Report
Hudson, Neff Karl: Army Times Publishing Co.
Huffer, Karen S.: Phillips Publishing
Huffman, Jason: United Communications Group
Hughes, Janice: Inside Washington Publishers
Hughes, Ken: LRP Publications
Hughes, Siobhan E.: Institutional Investor
Hughes, Jr., John D.: Aviation Week
Hull, Stephen A.: Thompson Publishing Group
Hume, Sandy: The Hill
Hunt, Alicia: Warren Publishing
Hunter, Bridget A.: BNA News
Hutnyan, Joseph D.: McGraw-Hill
Hyneman, Roger T.: Army Times Publishing Co.
Ichniowski, Thomas F.: McGraw-Hill
Idaszak, Jerome: Kiplinger Washington Editors
Idelson, George: Consumer Affairs Letter
Iekel, John F.: Tax Notes
Isikoff, Michael: Newsweek
Ito, Timothy M.: U. S. News & World Report
Ivins, Steven D.: Kiplinger Washington Editors
Iyengar, Sunil: FDC Reports
Jackson, Nicole L.: Phillips Publishing
Jackson, Sara Waldrop: United Communications Group
Jakson, Seth V.: Government Information Services
Jackson, Valarie N.: Business Publishers
Jackson, William K.: Government Computer News
Jacobson, Ken: King Publications
Jacobson, Linda: Education Week
Jacobson, Louis: National Journal
Jaffe, Harry S.: Washingtonian
Jakubowicz, Peter: Business Publishers
Jaschik, Scott: Chronicle of Higher Education
Javers, Eamon: The Hill
Jeffrey, Terence P.: Human Events
Jenkins, Gwendolyn: CCH Inc.
Jenkins, Jr., Kent: U. S. News & World Report
Jennings, Charles: Nature
Jessell, Harry A.: Broadcasting & Cable
Johnson, Carrie: Legal Times
Johnson, Jennifer: Army Times Publishing Co.
Johnson, Wendy: Washington Blade
Johnston, Robert C.: Education Week
Jones, Arthur: National Catholic Reporter
Jones, Christopher P.: Washington Blade
Jones, David: Business Publishers
Jones, David R.: Thompson Publishing Group
Jones, Heather C.: Feedstuffs
Jones, Helen: BNA News
Jones, Ian: Business Research Publications
Jones, James: Inside Washington Publishers
Jones, Joyce: Black Enterprise
Jones, Rochelle: Time, Inc.
Jordan, Anne: Governing
Jordan, Brian D.: McGraw-Hill
Jordan, Melody A.: Army Times Publishing Co.
Jordan, Meredith: Phillips Publishing
Jose, Andy: Phillips Publishing
Jost, Kenneth W.: CQ Researcher
Jowers, Karen Grigg: Army Times Publishing Co.
Judge, Mark: Insight Magazine
Judis, John: New Republic
Kalms, Jennifer L.: BNA News
Kalomiris, Paul: CD Publications
Kaplan, Hugh B.: BNA News
Karam, Samir F.: Al-Kifah Al-Arabi
Karony, Krista L.: Army Times Publishing Co.

MEMBERS ENTITLED TO ADMISSION, PERIODICAL PRESS GALLERIES—Continued

Kasperowicz, Peter I.: Inside Washington Publishers
Kass, Marcia B.: BNA News
Kassabian, Gloria B.: Business Week
Katz, Jennifer L.: CD Publications
Kaufman, Bruce S.: BNA News
Kaut, David P.: BNA News
Kavanagh, Susan: Washington Service Bureau
Kavruck, Angela: Washington Counseletter
Kavruck, Samuel: Washington Counseletter
Kay, Marcia: Washington Jewish Week
Keane, Karol Anne: National Journal
Keen, Lisa Melinda: Washington Blade
Kelleher, Elizabeth: Kiplinger Washington Editors
Keller, Amy M.: Roll Call
Keller, Bess: Education Week
Kelly, Michael: New Republic
Kennedy, Hugh John: Washington Service Bureau
Kennedy, James H.: BNA News
Kennedy, Joan: Food Chemical News
Kent, Christina: Physician's Weekly
Kenyon, Henry S.: Capitol Publications
Kernus, Susan Mary: Washington Crime News Services
Kessler, Elaine: BNA News
Khan, Altaf: BNA News
Kidney, Stephen C.: King Publications
Kiernan, Vincent: New Scientist
Kiesner, Jack: Kiplinger Washington Editors
Kilgore, Christine: International Medical News Group
King, Leslie: BNA News
King, Wendy: Time, Inc.
Kinnander, Ola: Phillips Publishing
Kiplinger, Austin H.: Kiplinger Washington Editors
Kirkland, John Robert: BNA News
Kirschten, Joseph D.: National Journal
Kitfield, James: National Journal
Kittross, David: CD Publications
Klaidman, Daniel: Newsweek
Kleiner, Henry E.: Business Publishers
Kleiner, Kurt: New Scientist
Kline, Jerry Lee: Thompson Publishing Group
Klintberg, Patricia Peak: Farm Journal
Klyce, Juli: Phillips Publishing
Knapik, Michael: McGraw-Hill
Knebl, Charles: Business Publishers
Koenig, David L.: Kiplinger Washington Editors
Koerner, Brendan I.: U. S. News & World Report
Koffler, Keith F.: Inside Washington Publishers
Kondracke, Morton M.: Roll Call
Koppenheffer, Michael: FDC Reports
Kosova, Weston: Newsweek
Kosterlitz, Julie A.: National Journal
Kostreski, Farah: International Medical News Group
Kramer, David F.: McGraw-Hill
Kramer, Linda: Time, Inc.
Kranish, Arthur: Trends Publishing
Krasnow, Jay D.: CD Publications
Krause, Kristin S.: Traffic World
Krehbiel, Gregory A.: Thompson Publishing Group
Kreindler, Anthony L.: Inside Washington Publishers
Kriz, Margaret E.: National Journal
Kubetin, Randy: BNA News
Kuckro, Rod: Business Research Publications
Kuhn, Mark: CD Publications
Kulman, Linda: U. S. News & World Report
Kunz, Clayton: Phillips Publishing
LaBrecque, Louis C.: BNA News
Labash, Matt: Weekly Standard
Lackey, Sue: Thoroughbred Times
Ladov, Mark: FDC Reports
Laing II, Eric: Phillips Publishing
Lake, Eli: Inside Washington Publishers
Lally, Rosemarie: Thompson Publishing Group
Lamoreaux, Denise Anne: Thompson Publishing Group
Landry, Catherine: McGraw-Hill
Lange, Anne M.: BNA News
Lankford, Kimberly: Kiplinger Washington Editors
Lankler, Stephen C.: BNA News
Lardner, Richard: Inside Washington Publishers
Larsen, Kathy Carolin: McGraw-Hill
Lash, Steve: Business Publishers
Late, Michele: U. S. Medicine
Laurent, Anne: Government Executive
Lavelle, Marianne: National Law Journal
Lawson, Chris L.: Army Times Publishing Co.
Lawton, Millicent: Education Week
Lawyer, Gail J.: McGraw-Hill
Leatherman, Courtney: Chronicle of Higher Education
Lebamoff, Craig C.: CCH Inc.
Lederman, Douglas J.: Chronicle of Higher Education
Lee, Bryan: McGraw-Hill
Lee, Christine: FDC Reports
Leeuwenburgh, Todd: Business Publishers
Leiser, Roland: Association Meetings
Lenihan, Mary Anne: Federal Publications
Leopold, George: CMP Media Inc.
Leske, Gisela: Der Spiegel
Lester, Marianne: Army Times Publishing Co.
Levey, Amy: Inside Washington Publishers
Levine, Daniel R.: Reader's Digest
Lewin, David I.: Journal of NIH Research
Lewis, John J.: Inside Mortgage Finance
Lewis, Jr., Arnold: McGraw-Hill/Aero
Liang, John: Inside Washington Publishers
Lief, Louise Joy: U. S. News & World Report
Lightner, Susan: BNA News
Lilly, Stuart: Capitol Publications
Limbacher, Patricia B.: Crain Communications
Limprecht, Jane: BNA News
Lin, Alvin C.: Government Information Services
Linstromberg, Kathryn D.: BNA News

MEMBERS ENTITLED TO ADMISSION, PERIODICAL PRESS GALLERIES—Continued

Lipold, Annmarie Geddes: BNA News
Lipowicz, Alice M.: Crain Communications
Liston, Mary S.: Pasha Publications
Liu, Melinda: Newsweek
Lively, Kit: Chronicle of Higher Education
Lo, Catharine: HotWired/Wired
Lobred, Peter T.: Capitol Publications
Lockett, Brian A.: BNA News
Loeb, Penny: U. S. News & World Report
Logan, Christopher P.: Pasha Publications
Logan, Patricia A.: BNA News
Lopez, Ramon L.: Airline Business
Lord, Mary C.: U. S. News & World Report
Lovece, Joseph: Military Robotics
Loveless, William E.: McGraw-Hill
Lowe, Paul: Aviation International News
Lowry, Rich: National Review
Lowther, William A.: Mail on Sunday
Lucas, Jennifer B.: BNA News
Lucht, Peter: Telecommunications Reports
Lucini, Elena L.: Warren Publishing
Lumb, Jacquelyn: Washington Service Bureau
Lustig, Michael: Pasha Publications
Lynch, Kerry: McGraw-Hill/Aero
Lyons II, Louis M.: Tax Notes
Lytel, Jayne: Institutional Investor
MacKeil, Brian: Army Times Publishing Co.
MacMillan, Robert: Business Research Publications
Mace, Don: Federal Employees News Digest
Macilwain, Colin: Nature
Macko, Carole L.: BNA News
Maggrett, Richard: Stars & Stripes
Magin, Elizabeth: Tax Notes
Magner, Denise K.: Chronicle of Higher Education
Magner, Sarah M.: CQ Researcher
Magnusson, Paul: Business Week
Maguire, Miles: American Banker Newsletters
Mahone, Maria E.: BNA News
Mahoney, Fabia H.: BNA News
Mahtesian, Charles: Governing
Maier, Timothy: Insight Magazine
Makower, Joel: Green Business Letter
Mallaby, Sebastian: Economist
Malloy, Eileen: BNA News
Malone, Bernadette: Phillips Publishing
Maloney, Ann Marie: CCH Inc.
Mann, Paul S.: Aviation Week
Manning, Suzanne Elam: BNA News
Manning, Robert F.: Tax Notes
Mannix, Margaret: U. S. News & World Report
Manzo, Kathleen K.: Education Week
Margolis, Judith E.: BNA News
Mariani, Patricia: Federal Publications
Markley, Theresa Lynn: Research Institute of America Group
Marquardt, Amy: Pasha Publications
Martin, Juliann A.: Tax Notes
Martinez, Luis: BNA News
Marton, Andrew: Time, Inc.
Marvin, Theresa: LRP Publications
Marzec, Colleen: Washington Blade
Mason, Victoria Ann: Telecommunications Reports
Massey, Barton C.: Tax Notes
Masud, Sam: CMP Media Inc.
Mathews, Jim: McGraw-Hill/Aero
Mathur, Vandana: BNA News
Matta, L. Mathew: Investment Dealer's Digest
Matthews, Gary: Kiplinger Washington Editors
Matthews, Martha A.: BNA News
Matthews, Sidney William: Army Times Publishing Co.
Matusow, Barbara: Washingtonian
Maurer, Katherine: International Medical News Group
Mayer, Jane: New Yorker
Mayer, Merry A.: Pasha Publications
Maynard, Nigel F.: Inside Washington Publishers
Maze, Kristina L.: Army Times Publishing Co.
Maze, Richard: Army Times Publishing Co.
McAllister, Jef: Time, Inc.
McAvoy, Kim: Broadcasting & Cable
McBeth, Karen: McGraw-Hill
McCaffery, Richard W.: Army Times Publishing Co.
McCarter, Chris: Phillips Publishing
McCaughan, Michael: FDC Reports
McClain, Jr., Wallis E.: BNA News
McCleary, Hunter: King Publications
McClenahen, John: Penton Publishing
McCollum, Kelly: Chronicle of Higher Education
McConnell, Beth: Pasha Publications
McConnell, Chris: Broadcasting & Cable
McCormack, Richard: Manufacturing News
McCormally, Kevin: Kiplinger Washington Editors
McCracken, Rebecca P.: BNA News
McCullagh, Declan: Time, Inc.
McDaniel, Ann L.: Newsweek
McDermon, Velma Goodwine: Research Institute of America Group
McDonald, Kim A.: Chronicle of Higher Education
McDonell, Brendan: Food Chemical News
McDonough, Edward J.: Atlantic Information Services
McDonough, James: EPIN Publishing
McElroy, Alex: BNA News
McGolrick, Susan J.: BNA News
McGowan, Kevin P.: BNA News
McGuire, David: Capitol Publications
McGuire, Justin: Capitol Publications
McHugh, Jane Claire: Army Times Publishing Co.
McInerney, Susan: BNA News
McIntosh, Toby: BNA News
McIntyre, Kellie M.: Phillips Publishing
McKee, Jane: Roll Call
McKenna III, E. John: FDC Reports
McLane, Paul J.: IMAS Publishing

MEMBERS ENTITLED TO ADMISSION, PERIODICAL PRESS GALLERIES—Continued

McLoone, Sharon A.: Business Research Publications
McMahill, Rosemary J.: Capitol Publications
McMeen, Albert: BNA News
McNamee, Michael D.: Business Week
McShea, Mary G.: Federal Publications
McTague, James: Barron's
McVeigh, Matthew D.: Washington Service Bureau
McVicker, William: Recall
McWilliams, Charlyne: Inside Mortgage Finance
Mead, Holly: FDC Reports
Means, Howard B.: Washingtonian
Mechcatie, Elizabeth: International Medical News Group
Meiselman, Ira: Andrews Communications
Melamed, Dennis: Washington Business Information
Mencimer, Stephanie: Washington City Paper
Mendelsohn, Jennifer: Time Inc.
Mercer, Joye: Chronicle of Higher Education
Mercurio, John: Roll Call
Merrick, Matthew J.: Washington Service Bureau
Merrion, Paul Robert: Crain Communications
Messmer, Ellen: IDG Communications
Messmer, Jack L.: Radio Business Report
Methvin, Eugene H.: Reader's Digest
Meyer, Jennifer S.: BNA News
Meyers, Beth: Washington Information Source
Meyers, David B.: Roll Call
Michels, Jennifer: McGraw-Hill/Aero
Middleton, Amy C.: Research Institute of America Group
Millar, Bruce: McGraw-Hill
Miller, Dorothy G.: HLB Newsletter
Miller, Julie A.: Government Information Services
Miller, Mark Karl: Broadcasting & Cable
Miller, Michael S.: McGraw-Hill/Aero
Miller, Mishelle C.: Thompson Publishing Group
Miller, Reed: Phillips Publishing
Miller, Walter K.: Army Times Publishing Co.
Miller, William H.: Penton Publishing
Minton-Beddoes, Zanny: Economist
Mitchell, Joyce L.: Capitol Publications
Mjoseth, Jeannine: BNA News
Mjoseth, Marcia: BNA News
Mlawsky, David: Atlantic Information Services
Moffett, Anne: Time, Inc.
Mokhiber, Russell: Corporate Crime Reporter
Mollins, Carl W.: Maclean's
Monaco, Monta: Phillips Publishing
Monastersky, Richard: Science News
Moncrief, JoAnne: National Journal
Monroe, Henrietta: Business Publishers
Monroe, John: Federal Computer Week
Montgomery, Heather S.: Phillips Publishing
Montuori, Donald P.: Thompson Publishing Group
Montwieler, Nancy: BNA News
Mooney, Carolyn: Chronicle of Higher Education
Moore, James Gerry: Kiplinger Washington Editors
Moore, Jennifer L.: Chronicle of Higher Education
Moore, John: Federal Computer Week
Moore, Miles David: Crain Communications
Moore, Pamela Susan: Capitol Publications
Moore, Thomas H.: Time, Inc.
Moore, W. John: National Journal
Moorefield, Kesha: Inside Washington Publishers
Moorman, Robert: Penton Publishing
Moorstein, Gail: BNA News
Moragne, Lenora: Black Congressional Monitor
Morgan, Elizabeth Ann: BNA News
Morgan, Joan: Black Issues in Higher Education
Morring, Jr., Frank: McGraw-Hill/Aero
Morris, Jodie: National Journal
Morris, Sheryl: McGraw-Hill
Morris, Walter: FDC Reports
Morrissey, James A.: Textile World
Morton, Peter: Financial Post
Moskowitz, Daniel: Healthcare Information
Mosquera, Mary: BNA News
Moulier, Philippe: U. S. News & World Report
Moulton, Gwen: BNA News
Mower, Bernard H.: BNA News
Mower, Jeff: McGraw-Hill
Mudd, Mary B.: Capitol Publications
Mulholland, David D.: King Publications
Mundy, Alicia: Washingtonian
Munoz, German: News Bites
Munro, Neil P.: TechNews
Muolo, Paul: National Mortgage News
Murphy, Joan: Food Chemical News
Murphy II, Frances L.: Afro American Newspapers
Murray, Bill: Government Computer News
Murray, Joan K.: Bill Communications
Mutcherson-Ridley, Joyce: CCH Inc.
Muth, Katherine P.: Pasha Publications
Mytelka, Andrew C.: Chronicle of Higher Education
Naasz, Kurt D.: BNA News
Nail, Dawson B.: Warren Publishing
Nance, Scott: Phillips Publishing
Nather, David: BNA News
Naughton, James F.: Chronicle of Higher Education
Naylor, Sean D.: Army Times Publishing Co.
Nelan, Bruce W.: Time, Inc.
Nelms, Douglas: Penton Publishing
Nelson, Barbara E.: BNA News
Nelson, Scott Bernard: Kiplinger Washington Editors
Nelson, Susan K.: Countertrade & Offset
Neuben, Stephanie: Warren Publishing
Neumayr, George: American Spectator
Nevin, Tonya M.: United Communications Group
Newkumet, Christopher J.: McGraw-Hill
Newman, Leigh Ann: Capitol Publications
Newman, Richard J.: U. S. News & World Report
Nicholson, Carol: FDC Reports
Nicklin, Julie L.: Chronicle of Higher Education
Nicolaysen, Lisa: Warren Publishing

MEMBERS ENTITLED TO ADMISSION, PERIODICAL PRESS GALLERIES—Continued

Nidecker, Anna: International Medical News Group
Niedowski, Erika: The Hill
Nobel, Carmen: Army Times Publishing Co.
Nobile, Caitlin: Time, Inc.
Nordwall, Bruce D.: Aviation Week
North, David M.: Aviation Week
Novack, Janet: Forbes
Novak, Viveca: Time, Inc.
Novotny, Andrea: Food Chemical News
Nowak, Rachel: New Scientist
Nutting, Rex: CMP Media Inc.
O'Beirne, Kate Walsh: National Review
O'Brien, Sean M.: Tax Notes
O'Connell, Brian R.: Washington Blade
O'Connell, Richard J.: Washington Crime News Services
O'Connell, Jr., Richard J.: Washington Crime News Services
O'Connor, Sheilah: Inside Mortgage Finance
O'Hara, Cindy: McGraw-Hill
O'Hara, Colleen M.: Federal Computer Week
O'Rourke, Kerry: Phillips Publishing
O'Toole, Thomas: BNA News
Oberdorfer, Carol: BNA News
Oberle, Sean: Washington Business Information
Obey, Douglas: Inside Washington Publishers
Ogden, Christopher: Time, Inc.
Ognanovich, Nancy: BNA News
Olson, Catherine: Business Research Publications
Olson, Lynn: Education Week
Omberg, Cynthia S.: BNA News
Onley, Gloria R.: BNA News
Opall, Barbara: Army Times Publishing Co.
Oppenheimer, Mark: New Yorker
Orleans, Anne: Washington New Observer
Orletsky, Heather: Phillips Publishing
Ortman, John: Thompson Publishing Group
Osuna, Juan P.: Federal Publications
Otteman, Scott A.: Inside Washington Publishers
Owens, Anthony: BNA News
Owens, Christopher: Thompson Publishing Group
Page, Paul: Traffic World
Pak, Janne Kum Cha: USA Journal
Pappalardo, Denise: IDG Communications
Parezo, Steve: Natural Gas Week
Parisi, Gretchen: Thompson Publishing Group
Parisien, Lia: Inside Washington Publishers
Park, Scott: American Banker Newsletters
Parker, Liz: Education Week
Parker, Susan T.: Natural Gas Intelligence
Parrish, Molly R.: Pace Publications
Paschal, Mack Arthur: BNA News
Pate, James L.: Soldier of Fortune
Patterson, Kristin: Army Times Publishing Co.
Paulson, William Clifford: FDC Reports
Pearcey, J. Richard: Human Events
Peck, Michael: United Communications Group
Pejman, Payman: Government Computer News
Pekow, Charles: United Communications Group
Pena, Annette: CD Publications
Perlman, Ellen: Governing
Persinos, John: Phillips Publishing
Peters, Katherine M.: Government Executive
Petersen, Tina: McGraw-Hill
Peterson, Donna M.: Army Times Publishing Co.
Peterson, Mark A.: Stars & Stripes
Petrillo, Matthew C.: Telecommunications Reports
Petrush, Liza: McGraw-Hill
Pexton, Patrick B.: Army Times Publishing Co.
Phibbs, Pat: Food Chemical News
Phillips, Andrew: Maclean's
Phillips, Edward H.: Aviation Week
Phillips, Susan: Kiplinger Washington Editors
Piemonte, Philip M.: Capitol Publications
Pierce, Berinthia: Insight Magazine
Pilson, Karen E.: BNA News
Pimley, D. Ward: BNA News
Pleszczynski, Wladyslaw: American Spectator
Podesta, Jane: Time, Inc.
Polen, Danielle M.: Federal Publications
Pollack, Kenan: U. S. News & World Report
Polster, Nathaniel: HLB Newsletter
Pomponio, Angela: Pasha Publications
Pond, Stanley S.: BNA News
Ponessa, Jeanne: Education Week
Ponnuru, Ramesh: National Review
Ponzani, Licia M.: Thompson Publishing Group
Porado, Philip: CD Publications
Porter, Amy: BNA News
Portner, Jessica: Education Week
Postal, Arthur D.: American Banker Newsletters
Porteons, Holly: Inside Washington Publishers
Pound, Edward T.: U. S. News & World Report
Power, Kevin J.: Government Computer News
Power, Maureen J.: Tax Notes
Powers, Martha C.: Mid-Atlantic Research
Powers, William: New Republic
Prah, Pamela M.: BNA News
Price, Elizabeth: Futures
Prothero, P. Mitchell: Inside Washington Publishers
Pryde, Joan A.: BNA News
Pullen, Cynthia: Tax Notes
Pulley, John L.: Army Times Publishing Co.
Quindlen, Terrey: Army Times Publishing Co.
Rabb, Charles: McGraw-Hill/Aero
Radford, Bruce W.: Public Utilities Reports
Rafferty, William: Newsweek
Rainie III, Harrison M.: U. S. News & World Report
Rains, Lon L.: Army Times Publishing Co.
Raloff, Janet Ann: Science News
Ramos, Betty J.: Army Times Publishing Co.
Ramstack, Thomas Phillip: Business Publishers
Rand, Kelly L.: CD Publications
Randolph, Laura Beth: Jet/Ebony
Rankin, Ken: Lebhar-Friedman Publications

MEMBERS ENTITLED TO ADMISSION, PERIODICAL PRESS GALLERIES—Continued

Rash, Jr., Wayne: CMP Media Inc.
Rast, Reynolds R.: Traffic World
Rathbun, Elizabeth: Broadcasting & Cable
Rausch, Howard: Photonics Spectra
Rawson, Kathleen E.: FDC Reports
Razzi, Elizabeth A.: Kiplinger Washington Editors
Reagan, Beth: Thompson Publishing Group
Reagen, Erin: Washington Focus Newsletter
Rebora, Anthony: Research Institute of America Group
Reddy, Tarun: Business Publishers
Rees, John: Mid-Atlantic Research
Rees, Matthew: Weekly Standard
Reeves, M. Sandra: Education Week
Regan, Mary Beth: Business Week
Reichard, John: Healthcare Information
Reid, Kenneth: Washington Information Source
Reinhard, Beth: Education Week
Reinhard, William: Capitol Publications
Reisner, Hiram: Business Research Publications
Reistrup, John V.: JR Publishing
Rendleman, John R.: CMP Media Inc.
Reuter, William P.: FTC Watch
Rhea, Maureen: Army Times Publishing Co.
Rheault, Magali: Kiplinger Washington Editors
Richardson, Martha: FDC Reports
Richman, Sheldon B.: BNA News
Ridgeway, James: Village Voice
Riggs, Manda P.: BNA News
Riley, Michael: Time, Inc.
Ripley, Amanda: Washington City Paper
Rivenbark, Leigh: Army Times Publishing Co.
Rizer, Steven: Alfa Publishing
Robb, David W.: Phillips Publishing
Robelen, Erik W.: Inside Washington Publishers
Roberson, Peter: Institutional Investor
Roberts, Edward S.: Credit Union Journal
Robertson, Jack W.: CMP Media Inc.
Robins, Andrew M.: FDC Reports
Robinson, Paulette J.: Metro Herald Newspaper
Robinson, Thomas S.: Federal News Services
Robinson, Tod: BNA News
Rockelli, Lisa M.: BNA News
Rocker, Jason: CD Publications
Rockwell, Mark: CMP Media Inc.
Rodgers, Lori M.: Public Utilities Reports
Rodriguez, Eva: Legal Times
Rodriguez, Paul M.: Insight Magazine
Roeder, Linda: Business Publishers
Rogers, James O.: Inside Washington Publishers
Rogers, Warren: Associated Features
Roha, Ronaleen: Kiplinger Washington Editors
Rohde, David: IDG Communications
Rollin, Sara Thurin: BNA News
Rombel, Adam J.: Institutional Investor
Ronningen, Judith A.: United Communications Group
Roos, John G.: Armed Forces Journal
Roosa, Dana: Research Institute of America Group
Roosevelt, Ann: Pasha Publications
Rosche, Christopher: Green Sheets
Rose, Lois C.: BNA News
Rosen, Jeffrey: New Republic
Rosen, Stephanie: American Banker Newsletters
Rosin, Hanna: New Republic
Ross, Houkje: Business Publishers
Ross, Patrick C.: Warren Publishing
Ross, Robert S.: Tax Notes
Roth, Siobhan: Legal Times
Roy, Daniel J.: BNA News
Ruark, Jennifer K.: Chronicle of Higher Education
Rubin, Amy Magaro: Chronicle of Higher Education
Rubin, Paul: McGraw-Hill
Ruffins, Paul: Black Issues in Higher Education
Ruscus, Margaret C.: FDC Reports
Rushford, Greg: Rushford Report
Rusnak, Jr., Andrew: Exchange Monitor Publications
Rust, Michael: Insight Magazine
Ryan, Margaret L.: McGraw-Hill
Ryan, Yvonne: Economist
Ryskind, Allan H.: Human Events
Sachs, Adam G.: Atlantic Information Services
Sack, Joetta L.: Education Week
Saenz, Cheryl: BNA News
Sala, Susan J.: BNA News
Salzano, Carlo J.: Waterways Journal
Samuelson, Robert: Newsweek
Sandham, Jessica L.: Education Week
Santa Rita, Michael: Inside Washington Publishers
Sarasohn, Judy: Legal Times
Sarkis, Karen M.: Institutional Investor
Sarkis, Paul A.: BNA News
Satchell, Michael John: U. S. News & World Report
Sayre, David A.: BNA News
Scarbeck, Kathleen M.: International Medical News Group
Scarlett, Thomas: BNA News
Scherman, Bob: Satellite Business News
Schlesinger, Robert E.K.: The Hill
Schlesinger, Jr., James R.: King Publications
Schmidt, Peter G.: Chronicle of Higher Education
Schmidt, Robert: Legal Times
Schnaiberg, Lynn R.: Education Week
Schneider, Alison: Chronicle of Higher Education
Schoenberg, Tom: Legal Times
Schomisch, Jeffrey W.: Pasha Publications
Schorr, Burt: United Communications Group
Schroeder, Michael: Business Week
Schrof, Joannie Marie: U. S. News & World Report
Schuerholz, Katherine: Phillips Publishing
Schuette, Paul A.: Food Chemical News
Schuff, Sally: Agri-Pulse
Schuler, Jr., Joseph F.: Public Utilities Reports
Schulhof, Marc L.: Kiplinger Washington Editors
Schultz, Stacey: FDC Reports

MEMBERS ENTITLED TO ADMISSION, PERIODICAL PRESS GALLERIES—Continued

Schulz, John D.: Traffic World
Schulz, William: Reader's Digest
Schwalm, Steve: Human Events
Schwartz, Christopher A.: Inside Washington Publishers
Schweizer III, Roman G.: Inside Washington Publishers
Scorza, John Forrest: CCH Inc.
Scott, Dean T.: BNA News
Sedgwick, Theodore: Pasha Publications
Seffers, George: Army Times Publishing Co.
Seidenberg, John: Credit Management and Marketplace News
Seitz, Patrick J.: Army Times Publishing Co.
Sellinger, Margery B.: Time, Inc.
Seng, Neang: Time, Inc.
Seng, Vornida: Time, Inc.
Serafini, Marilyn Werber: National Journal
Sergeon, Janet L.: BNA News
Sfiligoj, Mark L.: Kiplinger Washington Editors
Shackelford, Lucy: Newsweek
Shah, Sachin: Phillips Publishing
Shalit, Ruth: New Republic
Shannon, Elaine: Time, Inc.
Shapiro, Elizabeth T.: United Communications Group
Shapiro, Joseph P.: U. S. News & World Report
Shapiro, Michael: Washington Jewish Week
Shay, Lee Ann: Phillips Publishing
Shea, Christopher: Chronicle of Higher Education
Shea, Erich: Business Publishers
Shea, Richard L.: Federal Publications
Shear, Jeffrey: National Journal
Sheffner, Benjamin S.: Roll Call
Shenk, Joshua: U. S. News & World Report
Shepherd, Rachel E.: FDC Reports
Sherfy, Elizabeth Jean: Thompson Publishing Group
Sherman, Jason: Armed Forces Journal
Sherrod, Lawrence: Thompson Publishing Group
Shesgreen, Deirdre: Legal Times
Shifrin, Carole A.: Aviation Week
Shin, Annys: National Journal
Shoop, Thomas J.: Government Executive
Shread, Paul: Food Chemical News
Shute, Nancy: U.S. News & World Report
Sibley, Martin C.: McGraw-Hill/Aero
Sidey, Hugh S.: Time, Inc.
Sietzen, Frank: Pasha Publications
Silva, Jeffrey S.: Crain Communications
Silverberg, David: The Hill
Silverman, Bridget L.: FDC Reports
Silverman, Jennifer: BNA News
Silverstein, Sam: Phillips Publishing
Silverstone, Ken: Business Publishers
Simendinger, Alexis A.: National Journal
Simmon, Christine M.: Thompson Publishing Group
Simmons, Ann: Time, Inc.
Simmons, Lise M.: BNA News
Simmons, Nancy F.: BNA News
Singer, Paul: Inside Washington Publishers
Skilling, Kenneth H.: BNA News
Skolnik, Sam: Legal Times
Skovron, James W.: BNA News
Slaughter, David A.: Thompson Publishing Group
Slee, Kendall Lynn: Export Today
Slevin, Joseph R.: Washington Bond Report
Small, John R.: BNA News
Smith, Darlene W.: Inside Washington Publishers
Smith, Ellen: Legal Publication Services
Smith, John Allen: Thompson Publishing Group
Smith, Leigh: Inside Washington Publishers
Smith, Marc Osgoode: Cablevision
Smith, Marcy L.: Workforce Development Resource
Smith, Paul: McGraw-Hill
Smith, Priscilla: Food Chemical News
Smith, Roger P.: Inside Washington Publishers
Smith, Stephen G.: National Journal
Smith, Van: Baltimore City Paper
Smouse, James S.: Investment Dealer's Digest
Snyder, Anne M.: LRP Publications
Snyder, Jim: Inside Washington Publishers
Sobel, Lindsay: The Hill
Sobie, Brendan: Inside Washington Publishers
Socha, Evamarie: Army Times Publishing Co.
Solomon, Burton R.: National Journal
Solomon, Goody L.: News Bites
Souter, Ericka J.: Time, Inc.
Spangler, Matthew: IMAS Publishing
Speaker, Scott C.: Natural Gas Week
Spears, LaWanza: Afro American Newspapers
Speights, Michael David: Business Publishers
Spence, Charles F.: General Aviation News
Spencer, Patricia S.: BNA News
Spencer, Sarah E.: Business Publishers
Spiegel, Peter: Forbes
Spock, Mary E.: United Communications Group
Spofford, John E.: Phillips Publishing
Sprague, Dean: Budget & Program
Sprague, John: Budget & Program
Srodes, James L.: World Trade
St. John, Eric: Black Issues in Higher Education
Staats, Craig: Time, Inc.
Stabile, Thomas J.: Washington City Paper
Stahl, David: Microbanker
Stahl, Stephanie: CMP Media Inc.
Stainburn, Samantha: Government Executive
Standeford, Dugie: Inside Washington Publishers
Stanfield, Jeffrey E.: Pasha Publications
Stanfield, Rochelle L.: National Journal
Stanglin, Douglas: U. S. News & World Report
Stanley, Scott: Insight Magazine
Stanton, John Roberts: Inside Washington Publishers
Stanton, Lynn E.: Telecommunications Reports
Staples, Edward: Investment Dealers Digest
Starobin, Paul: National Journal

MEMBERS ENTITLED TO ADMISSION, PERIODICAL PRESS GALLERIES—Continued

Starr, Barbara: Jane's Information Group
Starr, Beth: BNA News
Staunton, Jr., John P.: Inside Washington Publishers
Stawick, Susan K.: Futures
Steele, Zaira: Steele Communications
Stehle, Vincent W.: Chronicle of Higher Education
Steinberg, Julie: BNA News
Steinke, Scott A.: FDC Reports
Stellfox, David: McGraw-Hill
Stemler, David McF.: Pratt's Letter
Stencel, Sandra: CQ Researcher
Stevens, Cindy: Phillips Publishing
Stevenson, Jim: Phillips Publishing
Stewart, William H.: Thompson Publishing Group
Stimmel, Katherine M.: BNA News
Stimson, James A.: BNA News
Stimson, Leslie P.: Radio Business Report
Stivers, Rebekah L.: Capitol Publications
Stoddard, A. B.: The Hill
Stoffer, Harry: Crain Communications
Stokeld, Frederick W.: Tax Notes
Stoler, Judith: Time, Inc.
Stoll, Ira E.: Forward
Stone, Peter H.: National Journal
Stover, Stacy: Kiplinger Washington Editors
Stowell, Alan M.: BNA News
Stratton, Sheryl: Tax Notes
Striano, Elizabeth: Public Utilities Reports
Strosnider, Kim: Chronicle of Higher Education
Sturges, Peyton M.: BNA News
Sullivan, Carl: American Banker Newsletters
Sullivan, John H.: BNA News
Sullivan, Mark Eugene: Washington Blade
Sullivan, Martin A.: Tax Notes
Sullivan, Sean D.: Pasha Publications
Sunderland, Kim: Telecommunications Reports
Supervielle, Ana Baron: Editorial Atlantida
Sutton, Eileen C.: BNA News
Swanson, Kathlene C.: National Journal
Sweeney, Terry: CMP Media Inc.
Swit, David: Washington Business Information
Tacconelli, Gail: Newsweek
Taft, Darryl: CMP Media Inc.
Talbot, Jill S.: Thompson Publishing Group
Tallmer, Matthew: Research Institute of America Group
Taube, Herman: Jewish Forward
Taylor, Ihsan K.: Education Week
Taylor, Vincent E.: Pace Publications
Taylor, Jr., Stuart S.: Legal Times
Teinowitz, Ira: Crain Communications
Temin, Thomas R.: Government Computer News
Terry, Shawn M.: Pasha Publications
Teske, Steven: BNA News
Thomas, James C.: Countertrade & Offset
Thompson, Dick: Time, Inc.
Thompson, Mark J.: Time, Inc.
Thornton, Jeannye: U. S. News & World Report
Thyfault, Mary: CMP Media Inc.
Tice, James S.: Army Times Publishing Co.
Tiernan, Tom: McGraw-Hill
Tillett, Scott: Federal Computer Week
Tobias, Susan-Meader: Thompson Publishing Group
Toch, Thomas: U. S. News & World Report
Todaro, Jane: Business Week
Tolchin, Martin: The Hill
Toloken, Lisa: Government Information Services
Toloken, Steve: Crain Communications
Tomich, Nancy: U. S. Medicine
Tosh, Dennis A.: Research Institute of America Group
Travis, John: Science News
Trigoboff, David: Broadcasting & Cable
Trotter, Andrew: Education Week
Tsilas, Vicky: Tax Notes
Tucker, Miriam E.: International Medical News Group
Tumulty, Karen: Time, Inc.
Turner, Margo: CD Publications
Turque, Bill: Newsweek
Tyler, Amanda: McGraw-Hill
Uhlendorf, Karl: FDC Reports
Ullmann, Owen: Business Week
Updyke, Craig A.: Inside Washington Publishers
Usdin, Steve: King Publishing
Viadero, Debra: Education Week
Valmassei, Christine: Warren Publishing
Vample, Gwendolyn C.: Thompson Publishing Group
Van Atta, Dale: Reader's Digest
Van Dongen, Rachel: Roll Call
Van Slooten, Heather: Radio & Records
Van Voorst, L. Bruce: Time, Inc.
VandeHei, James: Inside Washington Publishers
Vandegrift, Beth: Thompson Publishing Group
Varon, Elana: Federal Computer Week
Velez, Elizabeth: Time, Inc.
Venzke, Ben N.: Jane's Information Group
Viadero, Debra: Education Week
Victor, Kirk: National Journal
Vidas, Chris: BNA News
Vise, Albert Avery: McGraw-Hill/Aero
Vistica, Gregory L.: Newsweek
Von Blumencron, Mathias M.: Der Spiegel
Von Ilsemann, Siegesmund: Der Spiegel
Von Zeppelin, Cristina L.: Forbes
Wadman, Meredith: Nature
Wagley, Jr., John R.: The Hill
Wagner, David M.: Insight Magazine
Wahl, Amy E.: CD Publications
Walczak, Lee: Business Week
Walker, Karen S.: BNA News
Walker, Margaret: Army Times Publishing Co.
Walker, Paulette V.: Chronicle of Higher Education
Wall, Robert: McGraw-Hill/Aero
Wallace, Elizabeth: FDC Reports

MEMBERS ENTITLED TO ADMISSION, PERIODICAL PRESS GALLERIES—Continued

Waller, Douglas C.: Time, Inc.
Walsh, Elsa: New Yorker
Walsh, Kenneth T.: U. S. News & World Report
Walsh, Mark: Army Times Publishing Co.
Walsh, Mark A.: King Publications
Walsh, Sheila: Washington Blade
Wanat, Thomas: Chronicle of Higher Education
Wang, Wengong: IMAS Publishing
Ware, Patricia.: BNA News
Warren, Daniel Y.: Warren Publishing
Waterfield, Larry: Vance Publishing
Waters, Angela: Time, Inc.
Watson, Thomas C.: Legal Times
Wayman, Suzanne A.: Inside Washington Publishers
Wayne, Debra: Crain Communications
Weaver, Heather Forsgren: Inside Washington Publishers
Weber, Rick: Inside Washington Publishers
Webster, James C.: Webster Communications
Webster, Susan M.: BNA News
Wechsler, Jill: Pharmaceutical Executive
Weible, Jack: Army Times Publishing Co.
Weil, Jenny: Exchange Monitor Publications
Weiland, Carrie E.: FDC Reports
Weinstein, Gary A.: BNA News
Weiser, Allison: Andrews Publications
Weissenberg, Carrie R.: FDC Reports
Weissenstein, Eric: Crain Communications
Weisskopf, Michael: Time, Inc.
Welch, Jake: National Journal
Welch, Rupert: Furniture Today
Welch, Wayne M.: CD Publications
Wells, Robert J.: Tax Notes
Wells-Lee, Tamera L.: Tax Notes
Wemple, Erik: Washington City Paper
Werble, Cole Palmer: FDC Reports
West, Donald V.: Broadcasting & Cable
Whalen, Jennifer: Phillips Publishing
Whalen, John M.: BNA News
White, Jack E.: Time, Inc.
White, Kerry: Education Week
White, Lisa Putman: FDC Reports
Whitelaw, Kevin: U. S. News & World Report
Whitley, Gigi M.: Inside Washington Publishers
Whitman, David deF.: U. S. News & World Report
Whitten, Daniel: Thompson Publishing Group
Wiener, Leonard: U. S. News & World Report
Wiesemeyer, James: Futures
Wilcox, Melynda D.: Kiplinger Washington Editors
Wildavsky, Ben: National Journal
Wildavsky, Rachel Flick: Reader's Digest
Wildstrom, Stephen H.: Business Week
Wilkins, Francis: Inside Washington Publishers
Willenson, Kim: Japan Digest
Williams, Eric A.: Capitol Publications
Williams, Grant: Chronicle of Higher Education
Williams, Jeanne M.: Government Information Services
Williams, Jeffrey C.: Satellite Business News
Williams, Marjorie C.: Vanity Fair
Williams, Mark A.: BNA News
Williams, Meschelle: Army Times Publishing Co.
Williams, Risa: Tax Notes
Willis, Grant E.: Army Times Publishing Co.
Willner, Jordana M.: Washington Jewish Week
Wilner, Elizabeth: Cook Political Report
Wilson, Benet J.: Phillips Publishing
Wilson, David L.: Chronicle of Higher Education
Wilson, George C.: Army Times Publishing Co.
Wilson, Stanley E.: Institutional Investor
Windish, David F.: Tax Notes
Winebrenner, Jane A.: BNA News
Wingert, Pat: Newsweek
Winneker, Craig A.: Roll Call
Winograd, Jeffrey L.: Yellow Dog Democrat
Winston, Sherie: McGraw-Hill
Winter, Thomas S.: Human Events
Witkin, Gordon: U. S. News & World Report
Witmer, Rachel S.: BNA News
Witt, Elder: Governing
Wittes, Benjamin: Legal Times
Wittrig, Patrice: Radio & Records
Wolffe, James A.: Army Times Publishing Co.
Woodworth, Anne: Thompson Publishing Group
Woolsey, James P.: Penton Publishing
Worsnop, Richard L.: CQ Researcher
Wright, Allison: Food Chemical News
Wright, Carolyn: Tax Notes
Wright, Joseph Michael: National Journal
Wright, Michelle A.: Washington Business Information
Wright, Scott: Black Issues in Higher Education
Wright, Jr., James L.: Afro American Newspapers
Yang, Catherine T.: Business Week
Yaras, Michelle: Federal Publications
Yasin, Rutrell: CMP Media Inc.
Yates, Kerry A.: McGraw-Hill/Aero
Yeager, Eric: BNA News
Yeager, James McCarty: Progressive Populist
Yee, Wendell: BNA News
Yerkey, Gary G.: BNA News
Yochelson, Mindy: BNA News
Yoder, Eric T.: Federal Employees News Digest
Yohannan, Suzanne: Inside Washington Publishers
York, Byron: American Spectator
Yorke, Jeffrey: Radio & Records
Young, Jeffrey R.: Chronicle of Higher Education
Youngstrom, Nina: Atlantic Information Services
Yourish, Karen: Exchange Monitor Publications
Yuill, Barbara: BNA News
Zacaroli, Alec: BNA News
Zagorin, Adam: Time, Inc.
Zastudil, Michael K.: Natural Gas Week
Zavistovich, Alexander: Phillips Publishing
Zirkle, Cynthia: CCH Inc.

MEMBERS ENTITLED TO ADMISSION, PERIODICAL PRESS GALLERIES—Continued

Zuckerman, Edward P.: Political Finance & Lobby Reporter

Zung, Robert Te-Kang: BNA News

Zwillich, Todd: International Medical News Group

PERIODICALS REPRESENTED IN PRESS GALLERIES

House Gallery 225–2941, Senate Gallery 224–0265

Afro American Newspapers—(202) 332–0080; 1612 14th Street NW, Washington DC 20009: Janice F. Brown, Desiree Allen Graves, Frances L. Murphy II, LaWanza Spears, James L. Wright, Jr.

Agri-Pulse—(202) 639–6925; 601 13th Street NW, Suite 520, South, Washington DC 20005: Sally Schuft

Airline Business—(703) 836–7443; 1321 Duke Street, Suite 305, Alexandria VA 22314: Ramon L. Lopez

Al-Kifah Al-Arabi—(703) 471–5125; 3501 Stringfellow Court, Fairfax VA 22033: Samir F. Karam

Alfa Publishing—(301) 565–2532; 9124 Bradford Road, Silver Spring MD 20901: Allan L. Frank, Steven Rizer

American Banker Newsletters—(202) 347–2665, ext. 224; 1325 G Street NW, Suite 900, Washington DC 20005: Claire Chapman, Michelle Clayton, Elizabeth D. Festa, Miles Maguire, Scott Park, Arthur D. Postal, Stephanie Rosen, Carl Sullivan

American Spectator—(703) 243–3733; 2020 North 14th Street, Suite 750, Arlington VA 22201: Ronald E. Burr, M. D. Carnegie, John Corry, Sheryl Henderson, George Neumayr, Wladyslaw Pleszczynski, Byron York

Andrews Communications—(703) 892–2878; 2000 South Eads Street, Arlington VA 22202: Ira Meiselman

Andrews Publications—(202) 462–5569; 2100 Connecticut Avenue NW, Suite 810, Washington, DC 20008: Allison Weiser

Armed Forces Journal—(202) 296–0450; 2000 L Street NW, Suite 520, Washington DC 20036: Glenn W. Goodman, Jr., John G. Roos, Jason Sherman

Army Times Publishing Co.—(703) 750–8670; 6883 Commercial Drive, Springfield VA 22159: Nicholas L. Adde, Jon R. Anderson, Richard C. Barnard, Julie Bird, Ernest Blazar, Chester Bridger, John D. Burlage, Amy Cohen, Andrew Compart, William P. Cooper, Jr., Gregory C. Couteau, Darlena J. Craig, David Brian Craig, Lisa Daniel, Sharon Denny, James S. Doyle, Anne Eisele, Jeff Erlich, Laurence Lee Ewing, Warren Ferster, Philip Finnegan, Gidget Fuentes, Christy Harris, Margaret C. Harwood, Bernadette Hawkins, Jennifer S. Heronema, Enith Hickman, Theresa Hitchens, Daniel C. Holly, Robert D. Holzer, Neff Karl Hudson, Roger T. Hyneman, Jennifer Johnson, Melody A. Jordan, Karen Grigg Jowers, Krista L. Karony, Chris L. Lawson, Marianne Lester, Brian MacKeil, Sidney William Matthews, Kristina L. Maze, Richard Maze, Richard W. McCaffery, Jane Claire McHugh, Walter K. Miller, Sean D. Naylor, Carmen Nobel, Barbara Opall, Kristin Patterson, Donna M. Peterson, Patrick B. Pexton, John L. Pulley, Terrey Quindlen, Lon L. Rains, Betty J. Ramos, Maureen R. Rhea, Leigh Rivenbark, George Seffers, Patrick J. Seitz, Evamarie C. Socha, James S. Tice, Mark Walsh, Margaret Walker, Jack Weible, Meschelle Williams, Grant E. Willis, George C. Wilson, James A. Wolffe

Asia Today—(202) 597–1565; 2020 National Press Building, Washington DC 20045: Raghubir Goyal

Associated Features—(202) 965–0802; 1622 30th Street NW, Washington DC 20007: Warren Rogers

Association Meetings—(301) 589–1692; 2215 Montgomery Street, Silver Spring MD 20910: Roland Leiser

Atlantic Information Services—(202) 775–9008; 1100 17th Street NW, Suite 300, Washington DC 20036: Julie Anne Britt, Michael E. Carbine, Phoebe A. Eliopoulos, Christopher Gearon, Edward J. McDonough, David Mlawsky, Adam G. Sachs, Nina Youngstrom

Aviation International News—(301) 963–9253; 8020 Needwood Road, No. 101, Derwood MD 20855: Paul Lowe

Aviation Week—(202) 383–2300; 1200 G Street NW, Suite 200, Washington DC 20005: Joseph C. Anselmo, James R. Asker, David Fulghum, John D. Hughes, Jr., Paul S. Mann, Bruce D. Nordwall, David M. North, Edward H. Phillips, Carole A. Shifrin

BNA News—(202) 452–4200; 1231 25th Street NW, Washington DC 20037: Ronald E. Aikens, Paul F. Albergo, Michelle Amber, Michael L. Arian, Leroy Armes, Jerome C. Ashton, Nadya Aswad, Pamela S. Atkins, Jessica L. Baez, Charles Boileau Bailey, Vicki Baldassano, Andrew M. Ballard, Janet Benedetti, Alison Bennett, Mary Thomas Berger, Deborah Billings, Jean Ann Blanke, Debra Green, Cheryl L. Bolen, Linda G. Botsford, Karyn S. Bowie, Eleanor Bradley, David Barry Brandolph, Rossella Brevetti, Carol Ann Brideau, Angela L. Britt, Brian J. Broderick, Richard Bronson, Robert C. Bruce, Susan Bruninga, Sue Bryant, Ellen Byerrum, Niles S. Campbell, Martha M. Canan, Ann Therese Carlozzo, Brian A. Carr, Bernard S. Chabel, Emily Chuo, Shelene Clark, Irene Clarke-Gomez, Regina P. Cline, Janey Cohen, Matilda Monroe Corley, Anita Kelly Cosgrove, Mary M. Davis, Michael C. Davis, Gloria Deigh, Kathryn J. Desmond, Phyllis Diamond, Kenneth P. Doyle, Damon A. Dozier, Angela Drolte, Dana A. Elfin, Scott R. Falk, Amy Favin, Mark E. Felsenthal, James F. Fitzpatrick, Jeffrey C. Florian, Joan M. Flynn, Shantelle Fowler, Court Gifford, Pam D. Ginsbach, Michelle Angelique Glass, Bob Goebes, Leslie J. Gold, Anne B. Goodwin, Diana I. Gregg,

PERIODICALS REPRESENTED IN PRESS GALLERIES—Continued

Joan H. Griffith, Christina N. Hanna, Donna M. Harris-Aikens, Keith M. Hill, Ursula Himali, Sindhu G. Hirani, Susan Hobbs, Elizabeth W. Hofmeister, Cheryl Hogue, Jeremy Holmes, Strawn T. Holmes, Arnesa A. Howell, Bridget A. Hunter, Helen Jones, Jennifer L. Kalms, Hugh B. Kaplan, Marcia B. Kass, Bruce S. Kaufman, David P. Kaut, James H. Kennedy, Elaine Kessler, Altaf Khan, Leslie King, John Robert Kirkland, Randy Kubetin, Louis C. LaBrecque, Anne M. Lange, Stephen C. Lankler, Susan Lightner, Jane Limprecht, Kathryn D. Linstromberg, Annmarie G. Lipold, Brian Alexander Lockett, Patricia Anne Logan, Jennifer B. Lucas, Carole L. Macko, Maria E. Mahone, Fabia H. Mahoney, Eileen Malloy, Suzanne Elam Manning, Judith E. Margolis, Luis E. Martinez, Mary Mosquera, Vandana Mathur, Martha A. Matthews, Wallis E. McClain, Jr, Rebecca Pearl McCracken, Alex McElroy, Susan J. McGolrick, Kevin Patrick McGowan, Susan McInerney, Toby McIntosh, Albert McMeen, Jennifer S. Meyer, Jeannine Mjoseth, Marcia Mjoseth, Nancy H. Montwieler, Gail Moorstein, Elizabeth Ann Morgan, Mary Mosquera, Gwen Moulton, Bernard H. Mower, Kurt D. Naasz, David Nather, Barbara E. Nelson, Thomas J. O'Toole, Jr., Carol Oberdorfer, Nancy Ognanovich, Cynthia Omberg, Gloria R. Onley, Anthony Owens, Mack Paschal, Karen E. Pilson, D. Ward Pimley, Stanley S. Pond, Amy L. Porter, Pamela Prah, Joan A. Pryde, Sheldon B. Richman, Manda P. Riggs, Tod Robinson, Lisa M. Rockelli, Sara Thurin Rollin, Lois C. Rose, Daniel J. Roy, Cheryl Saenz, Susan J. Sala, Paul A. Sarkis, David A. Sayre, Thomas Scarlett, Dean Timothy Scott, Janet L. Sergeon, Jennifer Silverman, Lise M. Simmons, Nancy F. Simmons, Kenneth H. Skilling, James W. Skovron, John R. Small, Patricia S. Spencer, Beth L. Starr, Julie A. Steinberg, Katherine M. Stimmel, James A. Stimson, Alan M. Stowell, Peyton Mackay Sturges, John H. Sullivan, Eileen C. Sutton, Steven Teske, Chris Vidas, Karen S. Walker, Patricia Ware, Susan M. Webster, Gary A. Weinstein, John M. Whalen, Mark A. Williams, Jane A. Winebrenner, Rachel S. Witmer, Eric Yeager, Wendell Yee, Gary G. Yerkey, Mindy Yochelson, Barbara Yuill, Alec Zacaroli, Robert Te-Kang Zung

Baltimore City Paper—(410) 523–2300; 812 Park Avenue, Baltimore MD 21201: Van Smith

Barron's—(202) 862–6606; 1025 Connecticut Avenue NW, Suite 800, Washington DC 20036: Thomas G. Donlan, James M. Tague

Bill Communications—(703) 528–4564; 102 North George Mason Road, Arlington VA 22203: Joan K. Murray

Black Congressional Monitor—(202) 488–8879; 607 Fourth Street SW, Washington DC 20013: Lenora Moragne

Black Enterprise—(202) 544–3143; 1507 Massachusetts Avenue SE, Washington DC 20003: Joyce Jones

Black Issues in Higher Education—(703) 385–2981; 10520 Warwick Avenue, Suite B–8, Fairfax VA 22030: Karin Chenoweth, Cheryl D. Fields, Joan Morgan, Paul Ruffins, Eric St. John, Scott Wright

Blatter—(301) 699–3908; 4506 32nd Street, Mt. Rainier MD 20712: Konrad Ege

Broadcasting & Cable—(202) 659–2340; 1705 DeSales Street NW, Washington DC 20036: Paige Albiniak, John S. Eggerton, Heather Fleming, Harry A. Jessell, Kim McAvoy, Chris McConnell, Mark Karl Miller, Elizabeth Rathbun, David Trigoboff, Donald V. West

Budget & Program—(202) 628–3860; P. O. Box 6390, Washington DC 20015: Dean Sprague, John Sprague

Business Publishers—(301) 587–6300; 951 Pershing Drive, Silver Spring MD 20910: Nancy Lee Aldrich, Jerry Ashworth, Matthew Aukofer, Aimee Bader, Michael Barenti, Bonita Becker, Michael Berkowitz, Michael G. Dabaie, Charles J. Dervarics, David P. Douglass, Eric B. Easton, Elaine R. Eiserer, Leonard A. C. Eiserer, Thecla Fabian, Charles Whitt Flora, Charlotte Garvey, David Goeller, Bob Grupe, Valarie N. Jackson, Peter Jakubowicz, David Jones, Henry E. Kleiner, Charles Knebl, Steve Lash, Todd Leeuwenburgh, Henrietta Monroe, Thomas Phillip Ramstack, Tarun Reddy, Linda Roeder, Houkje Ross, Erich Shea, Ken Silverstone, Michael David Speights, Sarah E. Spencer

Business Research Publications—(202) 842–3022; 1333 H Street NW, Suite 200, Washington DC 20045: Amy L. Fickling, Ian Jones, Rod Kuckro, Robert MacMillan, Sharon A. McLoone, Catherine A. Olson, Hiram Reisner

Business Travel News—(703) 642–6422; P. O. Box 11269, Alexandria VA 22312: Barbara C. Cook

CCH Inc.—(202) 508–6751; 655 15th Street NW, Suite 265, Washington DC 20005: Sheila R. Cherry, Paula L. Cruickshank, Peter E. Feltman, Brendan DuBois Frost, Gwendolyn Jenkins, Craig C. Lebamoff, Ann Marie Maloney, Joyce Mutcherson-Ridley, John Forrest Scorza, Cynthia A. Zirkle

CD Publications—(301) 588–6380; 8204 Fenton Street, Silver Spring MD 20910: Jan Beiting, Mark Binker, Bob Duke, Brenda L. Gleason, William P. Hoar, Paul Kalomiris, Jennifer L. Katz, David Kittross, Jay D. Krasnow, Mark Kuhn, Annette Pena, Philip Porado, Kelly L. Rand, Jason Rocker, Margo Turner, Amy E. Wahl, Wayne M. Welch

CMP Media Inc.—(202) 383–4799; 1170 National Press Building, Washington DC 20045: Lou Bertin, David M. Braun, Patricia Brown, Beth Davis, Kate Gerwig, Brian Gillooly, George Leopold, Sam Masud, Rex Nutting, Wayne Rash, Jr., John R. Rendleman, Jack W. Robertson, Mark Rockwell, Stephanie B. Stahl, Terry Sweeney, Darryl K. Taft, Mary Thyfault, Rutrell Yasin

CQ Researcher—(202) 887–8600; 1414 22nd Street NW, Washington DC 20037: Charles S. Clark, Thomas J. Colin, Mary H. Cooper, Vanessa E. Furlong, Kenneth W. Jost, Sarah M. Magner, Sandra Stencel, Richard L. Worsnop

Cable World—(202) 467–8538; 1155 Connecticut Avenue NW, Suite 504, Washington DC 20036: Alan J. Breznick, Eric Glick

PERIODICALS REPRESENTED IN PRESS GALLERIES—Continued

Cablevision—(202) 393–2350; 1511 K Street NW, Suite 1153, Washington DC 20005: Marc Osgoode Smith

Cancer Letter—(202) 362–1809; 3821 Woodley Road NW, Washington DC 20016: Catherine Fiore, Kirsten Goldberg, Paul Goldberg

Capitol Publications—(703) 683–4100; 1101 King Street, Suite 444, Alexandria VA 22314: Michael Abshire, Karin Albani, Robert J. Babbitz, Wendy Bailey, Stephen Bouvet, Christina Breda, Jessica H. Bridges, James M. Causey, Brenda Cordwell, Kathryn DeMott, Mary-Ellen Deily, Jennifer Freer, Roger Friedman, Bob Gough, Steven R. Harper, Henry S. Kenyon, Stuart Lilly, Peter T. Lobred, David McGuire, Justin McGuire, Rosemary J. McMahill, Joyce L. Mitchell, Pamela Susan Moore, Mary B. Mudd, Leigh Ann Newman, Philip M. Piemonte, William Reinhard, Rebekah L. Stivers, Eric A. Williams

Career Pathways Report—(202) 452–8607; 2400 Virginia Avenue NW, Washington DC 20036: Elizabeth Alger, Dale Hudelson

Chemical Marketing Reporter—(202) 393–1444; 1057 C National Press Building, Washington DC 20045: Glenn H. Hess

Chemical Week—(202) 628–3728; 1253 National Press Building, Washington DC 20045: Peter Fairley

Chronicle of Higher Education—(202) 466–1000; 1255 23rd Street NW, Washington DC 20037: Nina Cary Ayoub, Lawrence Biemiller III, Debra E. Blum, Goldie Blumenstyk, Stephen Burd, Mary Crystal Cage, Colleen Cordes, Jon Craig, Paul Demko, Paul Desruisseaux, Marina Dundjerski, Jean Evangelauf, Cheryl M. Fields, Bianca P. Floyd, Susan Ganley, Mary Elizabeth Geraghty, Benjamin P. Gose, Susan Gray, Elizabeth Greene, Lisa Guernsey, Holly Hall, Karla Haworth, Patrick Healy, Scott Jaschik, Courtney Leatherman, Douglas J. Lederman, Kit Lively, Denise Karasiewicz Magner, Kelly McCollum, Kim A. McDonald, Joye Mercer, Carolyn Mooney, Jennifer Lynn Moore, Andrew C. Mytelka, Jim Naughton, Julie L. Nicklin, Jennifer K. Ruark, Amy Magaro Rubin, Peter G. Schmidt, Alison Schneider, Christopher Shea, Vincent W. Stehle, Kim Strosnider, Paulette V. Walker, Thomas Wanat, Grant Williams, David L. Wilson, Jeffrey R. Young

Concrete Products—(301) 972–7440; P. O. Box 132, Poolesville MD 20837: E.E. Halmos, Jr.

Consumer Affairs Letter—(202) 362–4279; 3035 Newark Street NW, Washington DC 20008: George Idelson

Cook Political Report—(202) 789–2434; 900 Second Street NE, Washington DC 20002: Charles E. Cook, Jr., Jennifer Duffy, Elizabeth Wilner

Corporate Crime Reporter—(202) 737–1680; 1209 National Press Building, Washington DC 20045: Russell Mokhiber

Countertrade & Offset—(703) 425–1323; 7703 Woodshade Court, Fairfax Station VA 22039: Susan K. Nelson, James C. Thomas

Crain Communications—(202) 662–7200; 814 National Press Building, Washington DC 20045: Vineeta Anand, Jerome F. Brazda, Jonathan P. Gardner, Bob Garfield, Jerome M. Geisel, Roseanne W. Geisel, Mary Greczyn, Douglas J. Halonen, Donna L. Harris, David M. Hatch, Mark A. Hofmann, Patricia B. Limbacher, Alice M. Lipowicz, Paul Robert Merrion, Miles David Moore, Jeffrey S. Silva, Harry Stoffer, Ira Teinowitz, Steve Toloken, Debra Wayne, Eric Weissenstein

Credit Management and Marketplace News—(703) 256–4748; Post Office Box 1095, Falls Church VA 22041: John Seidenberg

Credit Union Journal—(202) 737–8050; 733 15th Street NW, Suite 1100, Washington DC 20005: Edward S. Roberts

Defense Focus—(703) 528–3770; 1300 North 17th Street, 11th Floor, Arlington VA 22209: Akihiro Aihara, Jonathan Henning

Department of Education Reports—(202) 362–3444; 4401–A Connecticut Avenue NW, #212, Washington DC 20008: David T. Chester

Der Spiegel—(202) 347–5222; 1202 National Press Building, Washington DC 20045: Clemens Hoges, Gisela Leske, Mathias M. Von Blumencron, Siegesmund Von Ilsemann

Drug Topics—(703) 243–8080; 1815 North Fort Myer Drive, Suite 807, Arlington VA 22209: Michael F. Conlan

Economist—(202) 783–5753; 1331 Pennsylvania Avenue NW, Suite 510, Washington DC 20004: Daniel Franklin, Sebastian Mallaby, Zanny Minton-Beddoes, Yvonne Ryan

Editorial Atlantida—(202) 338–5703; 3271 Prospect Street NW, Washington DC 20007: Ana Baron Supervielle

Education Week—(202) 364–4114; 4301 Connecticut Avenue NW, Suite 250, Washington DC 20008: Jeffrey Robert Archer, Ann Bradley, Gregory M. Chronister, Adrienne D. Coles, Karen Diegmueller, Steven Drummond, David Field, Sandra Graziano, Lonnie Harp, David Hoff, Linda Jacobson, Robert Charles Johnston, Bess Keller, Millicent Lawton, Kathleen K. Manzo, Lynn Olson, Liz Parker, Jeanne Ponessa, Jessica Portner, M. Sandra Reeves, Beth Reinhard, Joetta L. Sack, Jessica L. Sandham, Lynn Schnaiberg, Ihsan K. Taylor, Andrew Trotter, Debra Viadero, Kerry White

Elle—(202) 462–2951; 3133 Connecticut Avenue NW, Suite 315, Washington DC 20008: Meryl Gordon

Endangered Species & Wetlands Report—(301) 891–3791; 6717 Poplar Avenue, Takoma Park, MD 20912: Stephen Davies

EPIN Publishing—(301) 365–3621; P. O. Box 21001, Washington DC 20009: James McDonough

Exchange Monitor Publications—(202) 296–2814; 1826 Jefferson Place NW, Suite 100, Washington DC 20036: J. Raphael Della Ratta, Andrew Rusnak, Jr., Jenny Weil, Karen Yourish,

PERIODICALS REPRESENTED IN PRESS GALLERIES—Continued

Export Today—(202) 737–3138; 733 15th Street NW, Suite 1100, Washington DC 20005: Kendall Lynn Slee

FDC Reports—(301) 657–9830; 5550 Friendship Boulevard, Suite One, Chevy Chase MD 20815: Janet A. Aker, Peter Ballard, Mark E. Brager, Randy Burkholder, Melissa Carlson, Jeremy Chase, Christopher D. Chinn, Janet Coleman, Jon Dobson, Susan Easton, Warren K. Eng, Bradley J. Ewy, Katherine V. Fodor, Danielle Foullon, Betsy Goodfellow, Christopher E. Gray, Christine Harrington, Timothy P. Harrington, Cathy Heinze, M. Nielsen Hobbs, Sunil Iyengar, Michael Koppenheffer, Mark Ladov, Christine Lee, Michael McCaughan, E. John McKenna, Holly Mead, Walter Morris, Carol Nicholson, William Clifford Paulson, Kathleen Rawson, Martha Richardson, Andrew M. Robins, Margaret C. Ruscus, Stacey Schultz, Rachel E. Shepherd, Bridget L. Silverman, Scott A. Steinke, Karl Uhlendorf, Elizabeth Wallace, Carrie E. Weiland, Carrie R. Weissenberg, Cole Palmer Werble, Lisa Putman White

FTC Watch—(202) 434–8222; 601 Pennsylvania Avenue NW, Suite 900, Washington DC 20004: Arthur L. Amolsch, William P. Reuter

Falls Church News Press—(703) 532–3267; 929 West Broad Street, Suite 200, Falls Church VA 22046: Nicholas F. Benton

Far Eastern Economic Review—(202) 862–9286; 1025 Connecticut Avenue NW, Suite 800, Washington DC 20036: Nigel R. Holloway

Farm Journal—(202) 824–8250; 1325 G Street NW, Suite 200, Washington DC 20045: Sonja Hillgren, Patricia Peak Klintberg

Federal Computer Week—(703) 876–5100; 3141 Fairview Park Drive, Suite 777, Falls Church VA 22042: Anne Armstrong, Brad Bass, Bob Brewin, Joanne M. Connelly, Heather Harreld, Allan T. Holmes, John Monroe, John Moore, Colleen M. O'Hara, Scott Tillett, Elana Varon

Federal Employees News Digest—(703) 648–0087; 1850 Centennial Park Drive, Suite 520, Reston VA 22091: Catherine Hubbard, Don Mace, Eric T. Yoder

Federal News Services—(703) 548–5177; 1301 East Abingdon Drive, Alexandria VA 22314: Thomas Steven Robinson

Federal Publications—(202) 337–7000; 1120 20th Street NW, Suite 500S, Washington DC 20036: Diane Davis, Jamie Kent Hamelburg, Christine M. Hanson, Mary Anne Lenihan, Patricia Mariani, Mary G. McShea, Juan P. Osuna, Danielle M. Polen, Richard L. Shea, Michelle Yaras

Feedstuffs—(703) 516–9162; 2338 North Taylor, Arlington VA 22207: Heather C. Jones

Financial Post—(202) 842–1190; 1225 Eye Street NW, Suite 810, Washington DC 20005: Peter Morton

Focus—(202) 363–2397; 4527 Windom Place NW, Washington DC 20016: Peter Gruber

Food Chemical News—(202) 544–1980; 1101 Pennsylvania Avenue SE, Washington DC 20003: Wendy Love Anderson, John A. Briley III, Stephen Clapp, Declan A. Conroy, Sue Darcey, Adrienne Dern, Jay F. Fletcher, Glenn Gamber, Joan Kennedy, Brendan McDonell, Joan Murphy, Andrea Novotny, Pat Phibbs, Paul A. Schuette, Paul Shread, Priscilla Smith, Allison Wright

Forbes—(202) 785–1480; 1901 L Street NW, Suite 803, Washington DC 20036: Janet Novack, Peter Spiegel, Cristina L. Von Zeppelin

Forward—(202) 879–6740; 1049 National Press Building, Washington DC 20045: Ira E. Stoll

Furniture Today—(202) 463–8490; 1500 Massachusetts Avenue NW, Suite 748, Washington DC 20005: Rupert Welch

Futures—(202) 842–0800; 1000 Vermont Avenue NW, Suite 810, Washington DC 20005: Roger D. Bernard, Michael J. Duncan, Vince Golle, Elizabeth Price, Susan K. Stawick, James Wiesemeyer

General Aviation News—(301) 330–2715; 1915 Windjammer Way, Gaithersburg MD 20879: Charles F. Spence

Gilston Communications Group—(301) 570–4544; 4816 Sweetbirch Drive, Rockville MD 20853: Samuel M. Gilston

Governing—(202) 862–8802; 2300 N Street NW, Suite 760, Washington DC 20037: Alex Daniels, Peter A. Harkness, Anne Jordan, Charles Mahtesian, Ellen Perlman, Elder Witt

Government Computer News—(301) 650–2000; 8601 Georgia Avenue, Suite 300, Silver Springs MD 20910: John Breeden, Vanessa Jo Grimm, William K. Jackson, Bill Murray, Payman Pejman, Kevin J. Power, Thomas R. Temin

Government Executive—(202) 739–8500; 1501 M Street NW, Suite 300, Washington DC 20005: Timothy B. Clark, Susan Fourney, Brian Friel, Anne Laurent, Katherine M. Peters, Thomas J. Shoop, Samantha Stainburn

Government Information Services—(703) 528–1000; 4301 North Fairfax Drive, Suite 875, Arlington VA 22203: Elizabeth A. Bernhard, Carol Dana, Charles J. Edwards, Jody Feder, Erika Fitzpatrick, Lisa L. Hayes, Donald Hoffman, Seth V. Jackson, Alvin C. Lin, Julie A. Miller, Lisa Toloken, Jeanne M. Williams

Green Business Letter—(202) 332–1700; 1519 Connecticut Avenue NW, Washington DC 20036: Jennifer Gamble, Joel Makower

Green Sheets—(202) 546–2220; 406 E Street SE, Washington DC 20003: Linda A. Cartwright, John Dineen, Leslie A. Duncan, Ronald E. Grandon, Christopher Rosche

PERIODICALS REPRESENTED IN PRESS GALLERIES—Continued

HLB Newsletter—(202) 686–7305; 821 Delaware Avenue SW, Washington DC 20024: Dorothy G. Miller, Nathaniel Polster

Health Market Survey—(202) 362–5408; 4115 Wisconsin Avenue NW, Washington DC 20015: William Robert Boyles

Healthcare Information—(202) 828–4148,251; 1133 15th Street NW, Suite 450, Washington DC 20005: Marcia Clemmitt, Robert Cunningham, Daniel Moskowitz, John Reichard

Hispanic Link News Service—(202) 234–0280; 1420 N Street NW, Washington DC 20005: Louis Aguilar

HotWired/Wired—(202) 872–3830; 888 17th Street NW, Suite 201, Washington DC 20006: John Heilemann, Catharine Lo

Human Events—(202) 546–0966; 422 First Street SE, Suite 400, Washington DC 20003: Michael J. Catanzaro, Michael Chapman, Joseph A. D'Agostino, John Gizzi, Terence P. Jeffrey, J. Richard Pearcey, Allan H. Ryskind, Steve Schwalm, Thomas S. Winter

IDG Communications—(202) 347–0134; 1331 Pennsylvania Avenue NW, Suite 505, Washington DC 20004: Gary H. Anthes, Ellen Messmer, Denise Pappalardo, David Rohde

IMAS Publishing—(703) 998–7600,136; 5827 Columbia Pike, Falls Church VA 22041: Susan Ashworth, Lucia E. Cobo, Paul J. McLane, Matthew Spangler, Wengong Wang

India Abroad—(202) 737–4144; 2046 National Press Building, 529, Washington DC 20045: Abdul Aziz Haniffa

Inside Mortgage Finance—(301) 951–1240; 7910 Woodmont Avenue, Suite 906, Bethesda MD 20814: George A. Brooks, Guy David Cecala, John J. Lewis, Charlyne McWilliams, Sheilah O'Connor

Inside Washington Publishers—(703) 416–8500; 1225 Jefferson Davis Highway, Suite 1400, Arlington VA 22202: Marguerite Abadjian, Lara W. Beaven, Mark Benjamin, Douglas Berenson, Jeremy Bernstein, Don K. Bilson, John Bresnahan, Joseph M. Burey, George Cahlink, David P. Clarke, Joshua T. Cohen, Christine Cordner, Martin J. Coyne, Robert Cusack, Suzanne DiPasquale, Carter S. Dougherty, Thomas Patrick Duffy, Daniel G. Dupont, Edmond B. Freeman, April E. Fulton, Steven K. Gibb, John Grano, Elaine M. Grossman, Thomas Harman, Robert Harrelson, Donna Haseley, Andrea Hatch, Jutta Hennig, Pamela Rae Hess, Janice Hughes, James Jones, Peter I. Kasperowicz, Keith F. Koffler, Anthony L. Kreindler, Eli Lake, Richard Lardner, Amy Levey, John Liang, Nigel F. Maynard, Kesha T. Moorefield, Douglas Obey, Scott A. Otteman, Lia Parisien, Holly Porteons, P. Mitchell Prothero, Erik W. Robelen, James O. Rogers, Michael Santa Rita, Christopher A. Schwartz, Roman G. Schweizer III, Paul B. Singer, Darlene W. Smith, Leigh Smith, Roger P. Smith, Jim Snyder, Brendan Sobie, Dugie Standeford, John Roberts Stanton, John P. Staunton, Jr., Craig A. Updyke, James VandeHei, Suzanne A. Wayman, Heather Forsgren Weaver, Rick W. Weber, Gigi M. Whitley, Francis Wilkins, Suzanne Yohannan

Insight Magazine—(202) 636–8800; 3600 New York Avenue NE, Washington DC 20002: John Berlau, Douglas Burton, Susan J. Crabtree, Tiffany Danitz, Jamie Dettmer, Stephen Ray Goode, Margaret Helms, Jennifer Hickey, Mark Judge,Timothy Maier, Berinthia Pierce, Paul M. Rodriguez, Michael Rust, Scott Stanley, David M. Wagner

Institutional Investor—(202) 393–5555; 1319 F Street NW, Suite 805, Washington DC 20004: Siobhan Hughes, Jayne Levin, Peter Roberson, Adam J. Rombel, Karen M. Sarkis, Stanley Eugene Wilson

Internal Medicine World Report—(301) 530–8430; 9206 Bulls Run Parkway, Bethesda MD 20817: Odom Fanning

International Medical News Group—(301) 816–8700; 12230 Wilkins Avenue, Rockville MD 20852: Michael S. Bykowski, Nathan D. Childs, Joyce Frieden, Christine Kilgore, Farah Kostreski, Katherine Maurer, Elizabeth Mechcatie, Anna Nidecker, Kathleen M. Scarbeck, Miriam E. Tucker, Todd Zwillich

Internewsletter—(202) 347–4575; 1063 National Press Building, Washington DC 20045: Marie B. Allizon

Investment Dealer's Digest—(202) 467–6353; 1130 17th Street NW, Suite 430, Washington DC 20036: L. Mathew Matta, James S. Smouse, Edward Staples

JR Publishing—(703) 532–2235; 6504 Orland Street, Falls Church VA 22043: John V. Reistrup

Jane's Information Group—(703) 683–5367; 1340 Braddock Place, Suite 300, Alexandria VA 22314: John Boatman, Stacey Evers, Yana Ginburg, Barbara Starr, Ben N. Venzke

Japan Digest—(703) 931–2500; 5510 Columbia Pike, Suite 207, Arlington VA 22204: Ayako Doi, Craig Fukushima, Kim Willenson

Jet/Ebony—(202) 393–5860; 1750 Pennsylvania Avenue NW, Suite 1301, Washington DC 20006: Simeon S. Booker, Richette L. Haywood, Laura Randolph

Jewish Forward—(301) 530–8109; 10500 Rockville Pike, Suite 604, Rockville MD 20852: Herman Taube.

Journal of NIH Research—(202) 785–5333,27; 1444 I Street NW, Suite 1000, Washington DC 20005: Bruce A. Agnew, Camille Collett, Carol Ezzell, Keith Alan Haglund, Karen Hopkin, David I. Lewin

King Publications—(202) 638–4260; 627 National Press Building, Washington DC 20045: Kevin M. Baerson, Anthony W. Capaccio, Colin S. Clark, Mark H. Crawford, John M. Donnelly, Linda Ann Gasparello, Erik W. Holm, Ken Jacobson, Stephen C. Kidney, Hunter McCleary, David D. Mulholland, James R. Schlesinger, Jr., Steve Usdin, Mark A. Walsh

Kiplinger Washington Editors—(202) 887–6400; 1729 H Street NW, Washington DC 20006: Peter L. Blank, Janet Bodnar, Priscilla T. Brandon, Melissa Star Bristow, Martha L. Craver, Kenneth B.

PERIODICALS REPRESENTED IN PRESS GALLERIES—Continued

Dalecki, Kristin Davis, Michael F. Doan, William W. Eby, Lawrence I. Fishbein, John R. Fogarty, Robert L. Frick, Joan Goldwasser, Ed Henry, Jerome Idaszak, Steven D. Ivins, Elizabeth Kelleher, Jack Kiesner, Austin H. Kiplinger, David L. Koenig, Kimberly Lankford, Gary L. Matthews, Kevin McCormally, James Gerry Moore, Scott Bernard Nelson, Susan Phillips, Elizabeth A. Razzi, Magali Rheault, Ronaleen Roha, Marc L. Schulhof, Mark Sfiligoj, Stacy Stover, Melynda D. Wilcox

LRP Publications—(703) 684–0510,529; 1555 King Street, Suite 200, Alexandria VA 22314: William H. Feldman, Steve France, Ken Hughes, Theresa Marvin, Anne M. Snyder

Lebhar-Friedman Publications—(301) 924–3033; 17735 Striley Drive, Ashton MD 20861: Ken Rankin

Legal Publication Services—(703) 276–9796; 2008 North Emerson Street, Arlington VA 22207: Melanie Aclander, Ellen E. Smith

Legal Times—(202) 828–0340; 1730 M Street NW, Suite 802, Washington DC 20036: Naftali Bendavid, Bruce David Brown, Timothy J. Burger, Joel Chineson, Janice Cooper, Eric Effron, Elizabeth Engdahl, Ted Goldman, Jonathan Groner, Carrie Johnson, Eva Rodriguez, Siobhan Roth, Judy Sarasohn, Robert Schmidt, Tom Schoenberg, Deirdre Shesgreen, Sam Skolnik, Stuart S. Taylor, Jr., Thomas C. Watson, Benjamin Wittes

Maclean's—(202) 662–7321; 994 National Press Building, Washington DC 20045: Carl W. Mollins, Andrew Phillips

Mail on Sunday—(202) 547–7980; 510 Constitution Avenue NE, Washington DC 20002–5926: William A. Lowther

Manufacturing News—(703) 750–2664; 7713 Newcastle Drive, Falls Church VA 22042: Richard McCormack

McGraw-Hill—(202) 383–2100; 1200 G Street NW, Suite 1100, Washington DC 20005: David Airozo, Jeffrey Barber, Amy Barrett, Aaron Bernstein, Amy Borrus, Craig S. Cano, John A. Carey, Catherine Cash, Theodosia Craig, Stan Crock, Mark Davidson, Lira Behrens Davies, Christina Del Valle, Shary Denes, Wilson Dizard, Kelley Doolan, Richard S. Dunham, Paula Dwyer, Lawrence D. Foster, Dean Foust, Susan Garland, Lynn Garner, Howard Gleckman, Douglas A. Harbrecht, Tom Harrison, Kathleen Hart, John Higgins, Elaine Hiruo, Christopher P. Holly, Joseph D. Hutnyan, Thomas F. Ichniowski, Brian D. Jordan, Gloria B. Kassabian, Michael Knapik, David F. Kramer, Catherine Landry, Kathy Carolin Larsen, Bryan Lee, Gail J. Lawyer, William E. Loveless, Karen McBeth, Paul Magnusson, Michael D. McNamee, Bruce Millar, Sheryl Morris, Jeff Mower, Christopher J. Newkumet, Cindy O'Hara, Tina Petersen, Liza Petrush, Mary Beth Regan, Paul Rubin, Margaret L. Ryan, Michael Schroeder, Paul Smith, David Stellfox, Tom Tiernan, Jane Todaro, Amanda Tyler, Owen Ullmann, Lee Walczak, Stephen H. Wildstrom, Sherie Winston, Catherine T. Yang

McGraw-Hill/Aero—(202) 383–2367; 1200 G Street NW, Suite 200, Washington DC 20005: Holly E. Arthur, Jason Bates, James D. Baumgarner, David Bond, David L. Collogan, Christopher Fotos, Ed Hazelwood, Arnold M. Lewis, Kerry Lynch, James Mathews, Jennifer Lynn Michels, Michael S. Miller, Frank Morring, Jr., Charles Rabb, Martin C. Sibley, Albert Avery Vise, Robert Wall, Kerry A. Yates

Medical Devices Report—(703) 361–6472; 7643 Bland Drive, Manassas VA 22110: Steve Butchock

Metro Herald Newspaper—(703) 548–8891; 901 North Washington Street, Suite 603, Alexandria VA 22314: Paris D. Davis, Paulette J. Robinson

Microbanker—(301) 460–5879; 14119 Pear Tree Lane, Suite 24, Silver Spring MD 20906: David Stahl

Mid-Atlantic Research—800/227–7140; 2805 St. Paul Street, Baltimore MD 21218: Martha C. Powers, John Rees

Milan Presse—(301) 907/7580; 7711 Tilbury Street, Bethesda MD 20814: Martine Combemale

Military Robotics—(202) 723–1600; 19 Rock Creek Church Road NW, Washington DC 20011: Joseph Lovece

Multichannel News—(202) 639–6934; 601 13th Street NW, Suite 520S, Washington DC 20005: Edward T. Hearn

Nation—(202) 546–2239; 110 Maryland Avenue NE, Suite 308, Washington DC 20002: David Corn, Max Holland

National Catholic Reporter—(202) 662–7191; 2060 National Press Building, Washington DC 20045: Arthur Jones

National Journal—(202) 739–8400; 1501 M Street NW, Suite 300, Washington DC 20005: James A. Barnes, Deborah Birnbaum, Graeme Browning, Eliza Newlin Carney, Richard E. Cohen, Richard S. Frank, Jerry Hagstrom, Virginia L. Hardy, Louis Jacobson, Karol Anne Keane, Joseph D. Kirschten, James Kitfield, Julie A. Kosterlitz, Margaret E. Kriz, JoAnne Moncrief, W. John Moore, Jodie Morris, Marilyn W. Serafini, Jeffrey Shear, Annys Shin, Alexis Simendinger, Stephen G. Smith, Burton R. Solomon, Rochelle Stanfield, Paul Starobin, Peter Stone, Kathlene C. Swanson, Kirk Victor, Jake Welch, Ben Wildavsky, Joseph Michael Wright

National Law Journal—(202) 662–8932; 927 National Press Building, Washington DC 20045: Harvey Berkman, Marcia Coyle, Marianne P. Lavelle

National Mortgage News—(202) 822–1261; 1133 15th Street NW, Suite 450, Washington DC 20005: Brian Collins, Darryl R. Hicks, Paul Muolo

National Review—(202) 543–9226; 1126 National Press Building, Washington DC 20045: Rich Lowry, Kate Walsh O'Beirne, Ramesh Ponnuru

PERIODICALS REPRESENTED IN PRESS GALLERIES—Continued

National Underwriter—(202) 783–8443; 1249 National Press Building, Washington DC 20045: Steven Brostoff, Mary Jane Fisher

Natural Gas Intelligence—(703) 318–8848; 22648 Glenn Drive, Suite 305, Sterling VA 20164: Ellen Beswick, Rocco Canonica, Susan T. Parker

Natural Gas Week—(202) 662–0700; 1401 New York Avenue NW, Suite 500, Washington DC 20005: Howard Buskirk, Paul C. Connolly, Rick Hogan, Steve Parezo, Scott C. Speaker, Michael K. Zastudil

Nature—(202) 737–2355; 968 National Press Building, Washington DC 20045: Laura J. Garwin, Brendan Horton, Charles Jennings, Colin Macilwain, Meredith Wadman

Nautilus Press—(202) 347–6643; 1059 National Press Building, Washington DC 20045: John R. Botzum, Jr.

New Republic—(202) 331–7494; 1220 19th Street NW, Suite 600, Washington DC 20036: Jonathan Chait, Susan Ellingwood, Robyn Gearey, Stephen Glass, Jacob Heilbrunn, John B. Judis, Michael Kelly, William Powers, Jeff Rosen, Hanna Rosin, Ruth Shalit

New Scientist—(202) 331–2080; 1150 18th Street NW, Suite 725, Washington DC 20036: Vincent Kiernan, Kurt Kleiner, Rachel Nowak

New York Jewish Week—(703) 978–4724; 8713 Braeburn Drive, Annandale VA 22203: James David Besser

New Yorker—(202) 296–5840; 1156 15th Street NW, Suite 1016, Washington DC 20005: Sidney Blumenthal, Peter Boyer, Elizabeth Drew, Jane Mayer, Mark Oppenheimer, Elsa Walsh

News Bites—(202) 723–2477; 1712 Taylor Street NW, Washington DC 20011: German Munoz, Goody L. Solomon

Newsweek—(202) 626–2000; 1750 Pennsylvania Avenue NW, Suite 1220, Washington DC 20006: Karen Breslau, Eleanor Clift, Matthew S. Cooper, Howard Fineman, Mary Hager, Shirlee Gaines Hoffman, Mark Hosenball, Michael Isikoff, Daniel Klaidman, Weston Kosova, Melinda Liu, Ann L. McDaniel, William Rafferty, Robert Samuelson, Lucy Shackelford, Gail G. Tacconelli, Bill Turque, Gregory L. Vistica, Pat Wingert

Numismatic News—(202) 543–6745; 632 A Street SE, Washington DC 20003: Burnett Anderson

Oil & Gas Journal—(202) 662–7040; 943 National Press Building, Washington DC 20045: Patrick Crow

Pace Publications—(202) 835–0120; 1900 L Street NW, Suite 312, Washington DC 20036: Ronald D. Boyd, Jr., Carey Cauthen, Craig Fischer, Molly R. Parrish, Vincent E. Taylor

Pasha Publications—(703) 528–1244; 1616 North Fort Myer Drive, Suite 1000, Arlington VA 22209: Harry L. Baisden, Wayne Barber, LaTaunja R. Beale, Alexander W. Brideau, Randy Byrd, Barry Cassell, Bowman Cox, Len Famiglietti, Michael Foster, Audrey Haar, Beth Herzberger, Michael Hopps, Mary S. Liston, Christopher P. Logan, Michael Lustig, Amy Marquardt, Merry A. Mayer, Beth McConnell, Katherine P. Muth, Angela Pomponio, Ann Roosevelt, Jeffrey W. Schomisch, Theodore Sedgwick, Frank Sietzen, Jeffrey E. Stanfield, Sean D. Sullivan, Shawn M. Terry

Penton Publishing—(202) 659–8500; 1350 Connecticut Avenue NW, Suite 902, Washington DC 20036: James A. Donoghue, Susannah Z. Figura, Perry Flint, John McClenahen, William H. Miller, Robert Moorman, Douglas Nelms, James P. Woolsey

Periodicals News Service—(301) 854–0660; 5460 Harris farm Lane, Clarksville MD 21029: Cecelia Blalock, Mary Ann Gatty, Robert C. Gatty

Pharmaceutical Executive—(301) 656–4634; 7715 Rocton Avenue, Chevy Chase MD 20815: Jill Wechsler

Phillips Publishing—(301) 340–1520; 1201 Seven Locks Road, Suite 300, Potomac MD 20854: Lurdes DaMaia Ambruscato, Seth Arenstein, Sandra Arnoult, Cynthia Boeke, Carol L. Bowers, Andrew Braunberg, David J. Bross, Mark A. Brousseau, Jane Bryant, Henry T. Canaday, William Carey, Maureen R. Cislo, Daniel Cohen, Mary E. Crowley, Stephen Donohue, Christopher A. Driscoll, Paul Dykewicz, David Evans, Robustiano Fernandez, Charles Flippen, Ronald A. Hudak, Karen S. Huffer, Nicole L. Jackson, Meredith Jordan, Andy Jose, Ola Kinnander, Juli Klyce, Clayton Kunz, Eric Laing II, Bernadette Malone, Chris McCarter, Kellie M. McIntyre, Reed Miller, Monta Monaco, Heather S. Montgomery, Scott Nance, Kerry O'Rourke, Heather Orletsky, John Persinos, David W. Robb, Katherine Schuerholz, Sachin Shah, Lee Ann Shay, Sam Silverstein, John E. Spofford, Cindy Stevens, Jim Stevenson, Jennifer Whalen, Benet J. Wilson, Alexander Zavistovich

Photonics Spectra—(202) 234–3294; 2541 Waterside Drive NW, Washington DC 20007: Howard Rausch

Physician's Weekly—(202) 783–6521; 1129 National Press Building, Washington DC 20045: Christina Kent

Political Finance & Lobby Reporter—(703) 525–7227; 2030 Clarendon Boulevard, Suite 401, Arlington VA 22201: Edward P. Zuckerman,

Pratt's Letter—(703) 528–0145; 1911 Fort Myer Drive, Suite 308, Arlington VA 22209: Eleanor S. Hill, David McF. Stemler

Press Associates—(202) 638–0444; 815 15th Street NW, Suite 1102, Washington DC 20005: Dennis B. Doris, Jr., Mark J. Gruenberg

Privacy Times—(202) 829–3660; 1429 Mantague Street NW, Washington DC 20009: Evan D. Hendricks

Proceso—(202) 393–1966; 986 National Press Building, Washington DC 20045: Pascal Beltran-del-rio

Professional Pilot Magazine—(703) 370–0606; 3014 Colvin Street, Alexandria, VA 22304; Mark A. Forror

PERIODICALS REPRESENTED IN PRESS GALLERIES—Continued

Progressive Populist—(301) 229–0217; 5220 Wapakoneta Road, Bethesda MD 20816–3129: James McCarty Yeager

Public Lands News—(202) 638–7529; 1010 Vermont Avenue NW, Suite 708, Washington DC 20005: James B. Coffin

Public Utilities Reports—(703) 847–7732; 8229 Boone Boulevard, Suite 401, Vienna VA 22182: Lori Burkhart, Phillip S. Cross, Bruce W. Radford, Lori M. Rodgers, Joseph F. Schuler, Jr., Elizabeth Striano

Radio & Records—(202) 783–3822; 975 National Press Building, Washington DC 20045: Heather Van Slooten, Patrice Wittrig, Jeffrey Yorke

Radio Business Report—(703) 719–9500; 6208–B Old Franconia Road, Alexandria VA 22310: Kathryn Bachman, Jack L. Messmer, Leslie P. Stimson

Reader's Digest—(202) 223–9520; 1730 Rhode Island Avenue NW, Washington DC 20036: Trevor Armbrister, Michael Douglas Barone, Ralph Kinney Bennett, Daniel R. Levine, Eugene H. Methvin, William Schulz, Dale Van Atta, Rachel Flick Wildavsky

Recall—(301) 460–8821; 14208 Oakvale Street, Rockville MD 20853: William McVicker

Reid Publishing Group—(703) 527–5653; 655 15th Street NW, Suite 310, Washington DC 20005: Robert R. Blumel

Research Institute of America Group—(202) 393–6449; 1325 G Street NW, Suite 410, Washington DC 20005: Susan S. Brooks, William Dunn, Tina Fritz, Barbra Golub, Rhodes Henderer, Theresa L Markley, Velma D. Goodwine-McDermon, Amy Middleton, Anthony Rebora, Dana Roosa, Matthew Tallmer, Dennis Tosh

Roll Call—(202) 289–4900; 900 Second Street NE, Suite 107, Washington DC 20002: Jennifer A. Bradley, Damon Chappie, Juliet Eilperin, David W. Farmer, Susan B. Glasser, Ed Henry, Amy M. Keller, Morton M. Kondracke, Jane McKee, John Mercurio, David B. Meyers, Benjamin Sheffner, Rachel Van Dongen, Craig A. Winneker

Rushford Report—(703) 938–9420; 1718 M Street NW, Suite 364, Washington DC 20036: Greg Rushford

Satellite Business News—(202) 785–0505; 1730 Rhode Island Avenue NW, Suite 600, Washington DC 20036: Mary Kristine Hillebrand, Bob Scherman, Jeffrey C. Williams

Satellite Orbit—(703) 827–0511,234; 8330 Boone Boulevard, Suite 600, Vienna VA 22182: Laura M. Fries, Erin E. Gregory

Science & Government Report—(202) 244–4135; 3736 Kanawha Street NW, Washington DC 20015: Daniel S. Greenberg

Science News—(202) 785–2255; 1719 N Street NW, Washington DC 20036: Ron Cowen, Kathy A. Fackelmann, Richard Monstersky, Janet Ann Raloff, John Travis

Soldier of Fortune—(301) 293–3577; Post Office Box 401, Myersville, MD 21773: James L. Pate

Stars & Stripes—(301) 486–0839; Post Office Box 624, College Park MD 20740: John Carroll, Jeffrey H. Epstein, Howard E. Haugerud, Richard Maggrett, Mark A. Peterson

Steele Communications—(301) 593–0108; 9922 Tenbrook Drive, Silver Spring MD 20901: Zaira Steele

Tax Notes—(703) 533–4400; 6830 North Fairfax Drive, Arlington VA 22213: David S. Antonides, Herman P. Ayayo, John C. Bell, Christopher E. Bergin, David E. Brunori, Michael E. DeHoff, Ryan J. Donmoyer, Emily Field, Heidi Glenn, John Godfrey, Oswald G. Graham, Steven Grodnitzky, Amy Hamilton, John F. Iekel, Louis M. Lyons II, Elizabeth Magin, Robert F. Manning, Juliann A. Martin, Barton C. Massey, Sean M. O'Brien, Maureen J. Power, Cynthia Pullen, Robert S. Ross, Frederick Stokeld, Sheryl Stratton, Martin A. Sullivan, Vicky Tsilas, Robert J. Wells, Tamera L. Wells-Lee, Risa Williams, David F. Windish, Carolyn Wright

TechNews—(703) 848–2800,133; 8500 Leesburg Pike, Suite 7500, Vienna VA 22182: Tania Anderson, Shannon Henry, Neil P. Munro

Telecommunications Reports—(202) 842–3006; 1333 H Street NW, Suite 100–East Tower, Washington DC 20005: John R. Alden, Wanda Avila, George Everette Brandon, Christopher J. Dordbek, Michael B. Grebb, Brian Hammond, Peter Lucht, Victoria Ann Mason, Matthew C. Petrillo, Lynn E. Stanton, Kim Sunderland

Television Broadcast—(703) 521–4187; 716 South Wayne Street, Arlington VA 22204: Howard Fields

Textile World—(703) 437–4079; 1702 Red Oak Circle, Reston VA 22090: James A. Morrissey

The Hill—(202) 628–8500; 733 15th Street NW, Washington DC 20005: Albert Eisele, Catherine Eisele, Jock Friedly, Sandy Hume, Eamon Javers, Erika Niedowski, Robert E.K. Schlesinger, David Silverberg, Lindsay Sobel, A. B. Stoddard, Martin Tolchin. John R. Wagley, Jr.

Thompson Publishing Group—(202) 872–4000; 1725 K Street NW, Suite 700, Washington DC 20006: Mary Helen Arthur, Delilah P. Barton, Tina Burnside, Ellen Carnevale, Siobhan B. Chamberlin, Mara Cherkasky, Kevin Cuddihy, Kimberly C. Cushner, Felicia Day, John C. Dettling, Andrea L. Hall, Luis Hernandez, Kevin J. Hogan, Stephen A. Hull, Jerry Lee Kline, Gregory A. Krehbiel, Rosemarie Lally, Denise Anne Lamoreaux, Mishelle C. Miller, Donald P. Montuori, John Ortman, Christopher Owens, Gretchen Parisi, Licia M. Ponzani, Beth Reagan, Elizabeth Jean Sherfy, Lawrence Sherrod, Christine M. Simmon, David A. Slaughter, John Allen Smith, William H. Stewart, Jill S. Talbot, Susan-Meader Tobias, Gwendolyn C. Vample, Beth Vandegrift, Daniel Whitten, Anne Woodworth

PERIODICALS REPRESENTED IN PRESS GALLERIES—Continued

Thoroughbred Times—(804) 457–2713; 1208 Ingleside, McLean VA 22101: Sue Lackey

Time Inc.—(202) 463–4000; 1050 Connecticut Avenue NW, Suite 850, Washington DC 20036: Lissa August, Laurence I. Barrett, R. Morris Barrett, Jeffrey H. Birnbaum, Ann Blackman, Alicia Brooks, Nina Burleigh, James Carney, Garry Clifford, Donald Collins, Jr., John F. Dickerson, Sally Donnelly, Ann Reilly Dowd, Brian Doyle, Michael Duffy, Tamala Edwards, Mary D. Esselman, Dean E. Fischer, Glenn Garelik, Dan Goodgame, Jerry Hannifin, Kathleen J. Hayden, Rochelle Jones, Wendy King, Linda Kramer, Andrew Marton, Jef McAllister, Declan McCullagh, Jennifer Mendelsohn, Anne Moffett, Thomas H. Moore, Bruce W. Nelan, Caitlin Nobile, Viveca Novak, Christopher Ogden, Jane Sims Podesta, Michael Riley, Margery B. Sellinger, Neang Seng, Vornida Seng, Elaine Shannon, Hugh S. Sidey, Ann Maria Simmons, Ericka J. Souter, Craig Staats, Judith Stoler, Dick Thompson, Mark J. Thompson, Karen Tumulty, L. Bruce Van Voorst, Elizabeth Velez, Douglas C. Waller, Angela Waters, Michael Weisskopf, Jack E. White, Adam Zagorin

Traffic World—(202) 783–1148; 1230 National Press Building, Washington DC 20045: David Barnes, Clayton W. Boyce, William B. Cassidy, Gordon Forsyth, Kristin S. Krause, Paul Page, Reynolds R. Rast, John D. Schulz

Travel Trade—(703) 451–5130; P. O. Box 2430, Springfield VA 22152: Bob Downes

Travel Weekly—(202) 293–5486; 1156 15th Street NW, Washington DC 20005: Fran Durbin

Trends Publishing—(202) 393–0031; 1079 National Press Building, Washington DC 20045: Arthur Kranish

U. S. Medicine—(202) 463–6000; 1155 21st Street NW, Suite 505, Washington DC 20036: Frank M. Best, Jerry Gottlick, Michele Late, Nancy Tomich

U. S. News & World Report—(202) 955–2439; 2400 N Street NW, Washington DC 20037: Bruce Auster, Ian Baldwin, Julian E. Barnes, Robin Bennefield, Gloria Borger, David Brindley, Shannon Brownlee, Josh Chetwynd, William James Cook, Susan Dentzer, Jerelyn Eddings, Mel Elfin, David B. Fischer, Dorian R. Friedman, Ted Gest, Paul Glastris, Stephen J. Hedges, Katia Hetter, Nicholas M. Horrock, Timothy M. Ito, Kent Jenkins, Jr., Brendan I. Koerner, Linda Kulman, Louise Joy Lief, Penny Loeb, Mary C. Lord, Margaret Mannix, Philippe Moulier, Richard J. Newman, Kenan Pollack, Edward T. Pound, Harrison M. Rainie III, Michael John Satchell, Joannie Marie Schrof, Joseph P. Shapiro, Joshua Shenk, Nancy Shute, Douglas Stanglin, Jeannye Thornton, Thomas Toch, Kenneth T. Walsh, Kevin Whitelaw, David deF. Whitman, Leonard Wiener, Gordon Witkin

USA Journal—(703) 379–2520; 5505 Seminary Road, Suite 1312N, Falls Church VA 22041: Janne Kum Cha Pak

United Communications Group—(301) 287–2700; 11300 Rockville Pike, Suite 1100, Rockville MD 20852: Carl Albert Ayers, Diana Engel, Richard D. Hadley, Jason Huffman, Sara K. Jackson, Tonya M. Nevin, Michael Peck, Charles Pekow, Judith A. Ronningen, Burt Schorr, Elizabeth T. Shapiro, Mary E. Spock

Vance Publishing—(202) 662–7221; 855 National Press Building, Washington DC 20045: Larry Waterfield

Vanity Fair—(202) 882–1157; 616 Whittier Street NW, Washington DC 20012: Marjorie C. Williams

Village Voice—(703) 920–3721; 2818 12th Street, Arlington VA 22204: Tom Carson, James Ridgeway

Warren Publishing—(202) 872–9200; 2115 Ward Court NW, Washington DC 20037: R. Michael Feazel, Michael French, Stephen J. Geimann, Edith Herman, Alicia Hunt, Elena L. Lucini, Dawson B. Nail, Stephanie Neuben, Lisa Nicolaysen, Patrick C. Ross, Christine Valmassei, Daniel Y. Warren

Washington Blade—(202) 797–7000; 1408 U Street NW, 2nd Floor, Washington DC 20009: Kristina K. Campbell, Louis M. Chibbaro, Jr., Wendy Johnson, Christopher P. Jones, Lisa Melinda Keen, Colleen Marzec, Brian R. O'Connell, Mark Eugene Sullivan, Sheila Walsh

Washington Bond Report—(202) 662–7355; 1290 National Press Building, Washington DC 20045: Joseph R. Slevin

Washington Business Information—(703) 247–3424; 1117 North 19th Street, Suite 200, Arlington VA 22209: Robert Billings, Sam Cristy, Michael Dolan, Richard Hagan, Elizabeth T. Hinkle, Dennis Melamed, Sean Oberle, David Swit, Michelle A. Wright

Washington City Paper—(202) 332–2100; 2390 Champlain Street NW, Washington DC 20009: Julie Wakefield Albers, Jonetta R. Barras, David Carr, John A. Cloud, Ken Cummins, Eddie Dean, Stephanie Mencimer, Amanda Ripley, Thomas J. Stabile, Erik Wemple

Washington Counseletter—(202) 244–6709; 5712 26th Street NW, Washington DC 20015: Angela Kavruck, Samuel Kavruck

Washington Crime News Services—(703) 573–1600; 3918 Prosperity Avenue, Suite 318, Fairfax VA 22031: Betty B. Bosarge, Robert H. Feldkamp, Susan Mary Kernus, Richard J. O'Connell, Richard J. O'Connell, Jr.

Washington Focus Newsletter—(202) 234–3689; 1529 18th Street NW, Washington DC 20036: Erin Reagen

Washington G–2 Reports—(202) 789–1034; 1111 14th Street NW, Suite 500, Washington DC 20005: Ellen B. Griffith

Washington Information Source—(301) 770–5553; 6506 Old Stage Road, Suite 100, Rockville MD 20852: Beth Meyers, Kenneth Reid

Washington Jewish Week—(301) 230–2222; 12300 Twinbrook Parkway, Suite 250, Rockville MD 20852: Marcia Kay, Michael Shapiro, Jordana Willner

PERIODICALS REPRESENTED IN PRESS GALLERIES—Continued

Washington New Observer—(301) 657–1966; 5101 River Road, Suite 1204, Potomac MD 20854: Anne Orleans

Washington Remote Sensing Letter—(202) 393–3640; 1057–B National Press Building, Washington DC 20045: Murray Felsher

Washington Service Bureau—(202) 508–0600; 655 15th Street NW, Suite 270, Washington DC 20005: April Anderson, John F. Atwood, Nathalie Auer, Lisa J. Baratta, Carla Fenwick, Susan Kavanagh, Hugh John Kennedy, Jacquelyn Lumb, Matthew D. McVeigh, Matthew J. Merrick

Washington Trade Daily—(301) 946–0817; 2104 National Press Building, Washington DC 20045: James R. Berger

Washingtonian—(202) 296–3600; 1828 L Street NW, Suite 200, Washington DC 20036: Charles N. Conconi, Kim I. Eisler, Vera Glaser, Harry S. Jaffe, Barbara Matusow, Howard B. Means, Alicia Mundy

Waterways Journal—(703) 524–2490; 5220 North Carlin Springs Road, Arlington VA 22203–1307: Carlo J. Salzano

Webster Communications—(703) 525–4512; 1530 North Key Boulevard, PH2, Arlington VA 22209: James C. Webster

Weekly Standard—(202) 293–4900; 1150 17th Street NW, Suite 505, Washington DC 20036: David Brooks, Christopher Caldwell, Tucker Carlson, Andrew Ferguson, Matt Labash, Matthew Rees

Wireless Week—(202) 393–0951; 1511 K Street NW, Suite 1157, Washington DC 20005: Caron Carlson

Workforce Development Resource—(703) 690–6092; 8289 Bark Tree Court, Springfield VA 22153: Marcy L. Smith

World Trade—(202) 393–5130; 1010 Vermont Avenue NW, Suite 721, Washington DC 20005: James L. Srodes

Yellow Dog Democrat—(202) 728–7576; P. O. Box 65538, Washington DC 20035: Jeffrey L. Winograd

Yomiuri America—(703) 525–0576; 2100 Lee Highway, Suite 524, Arlington VA 22201: Yoshio Hotta

CONGRESSIONAL DISTRICT MAPS

ALABAMA—Congressional Districts—(7 Districts)

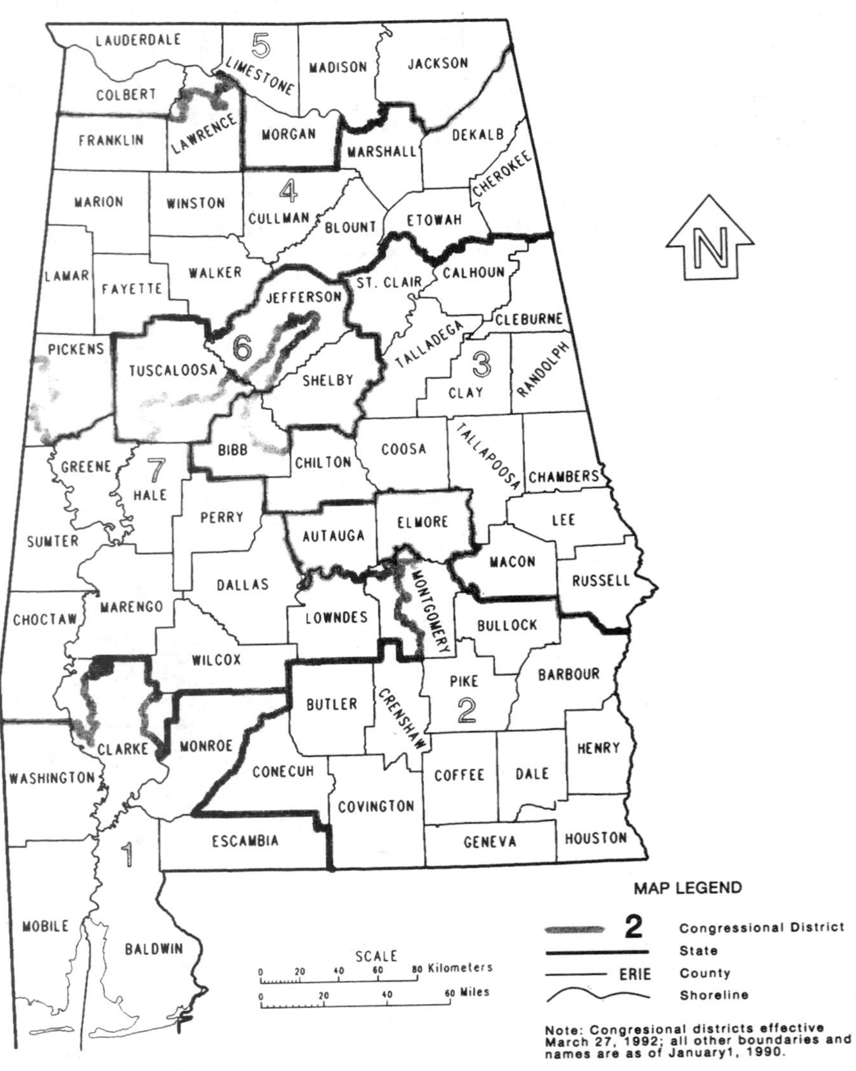

ALASKA—Congressional District—(1 District At Large)

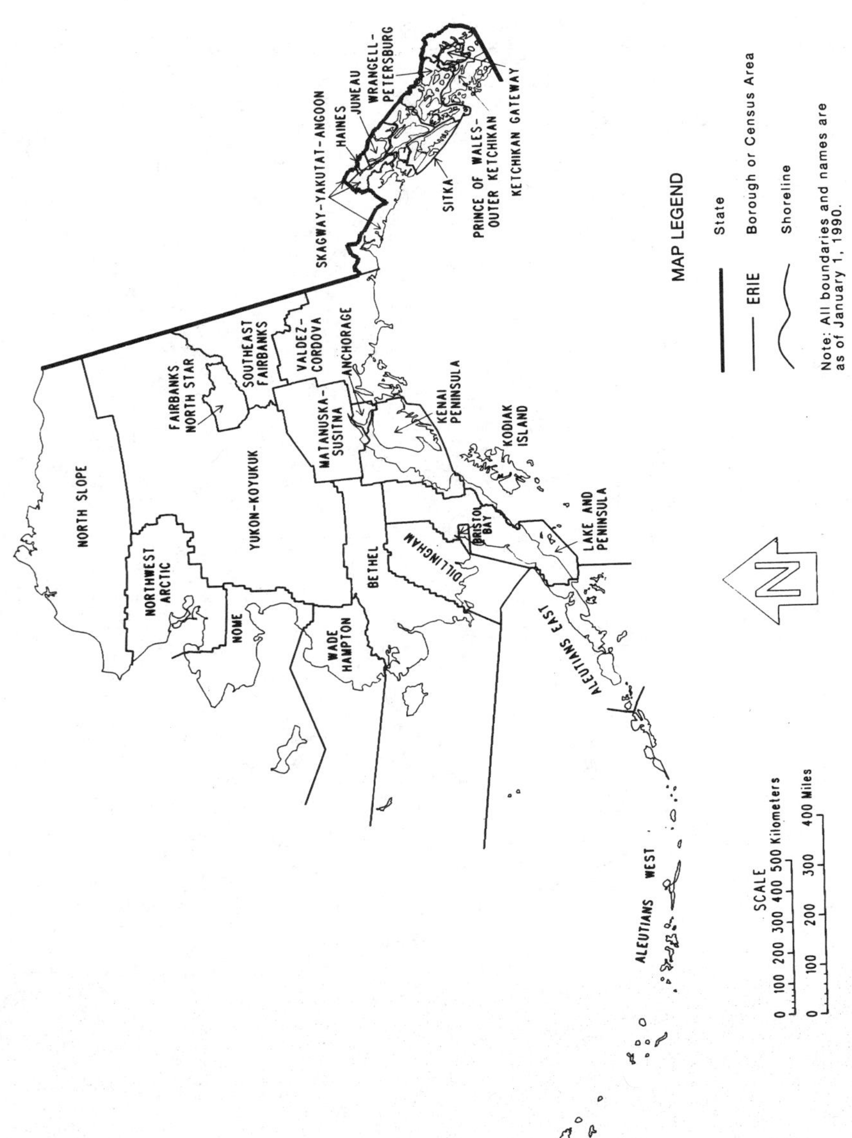

ARIZONA—Congressional Districts—(6 Districts)

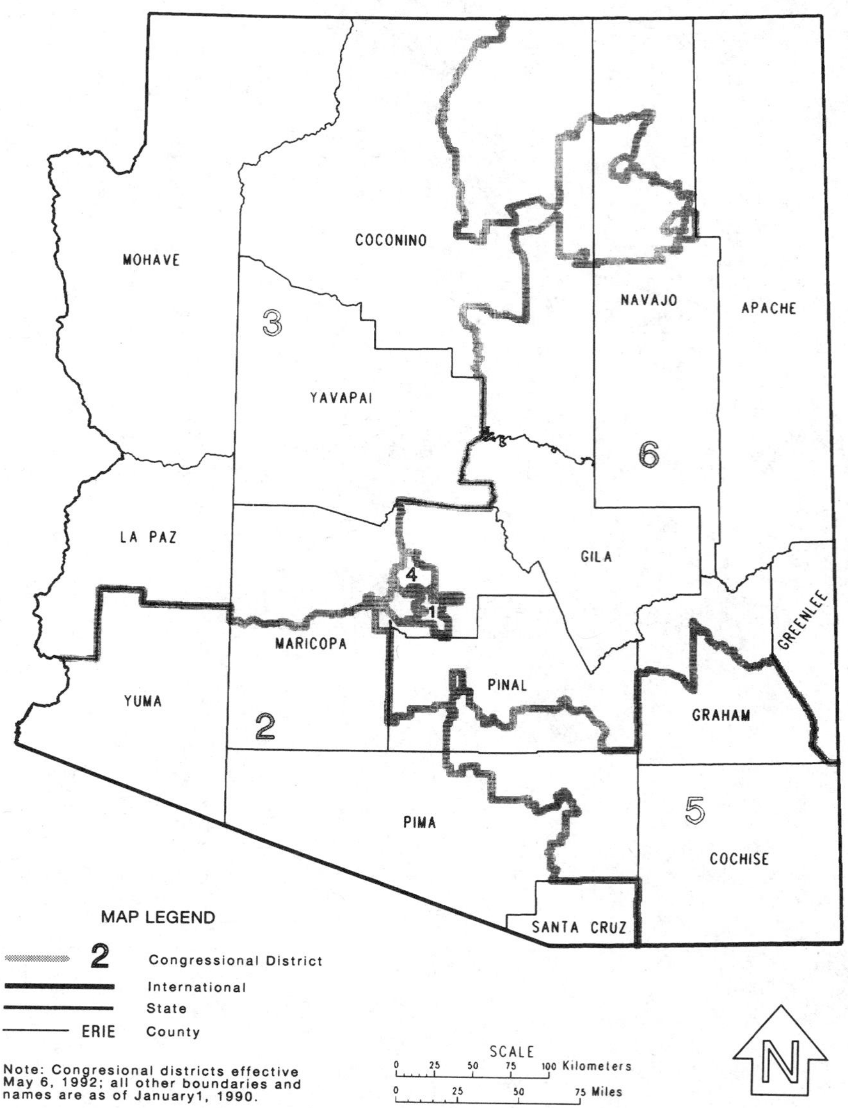

ARKANSAS—Congressional Districts—(4 Districts)

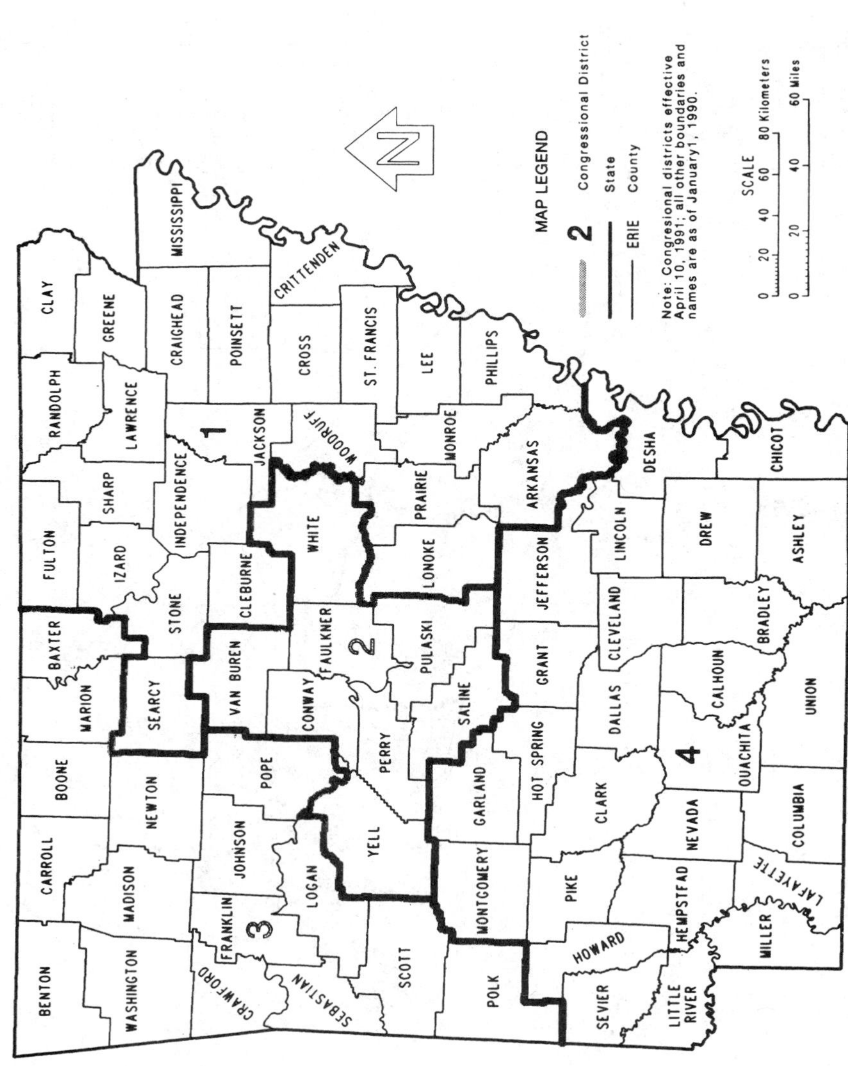

CALIFORNIA—Congressional Districts—(52 Districts)

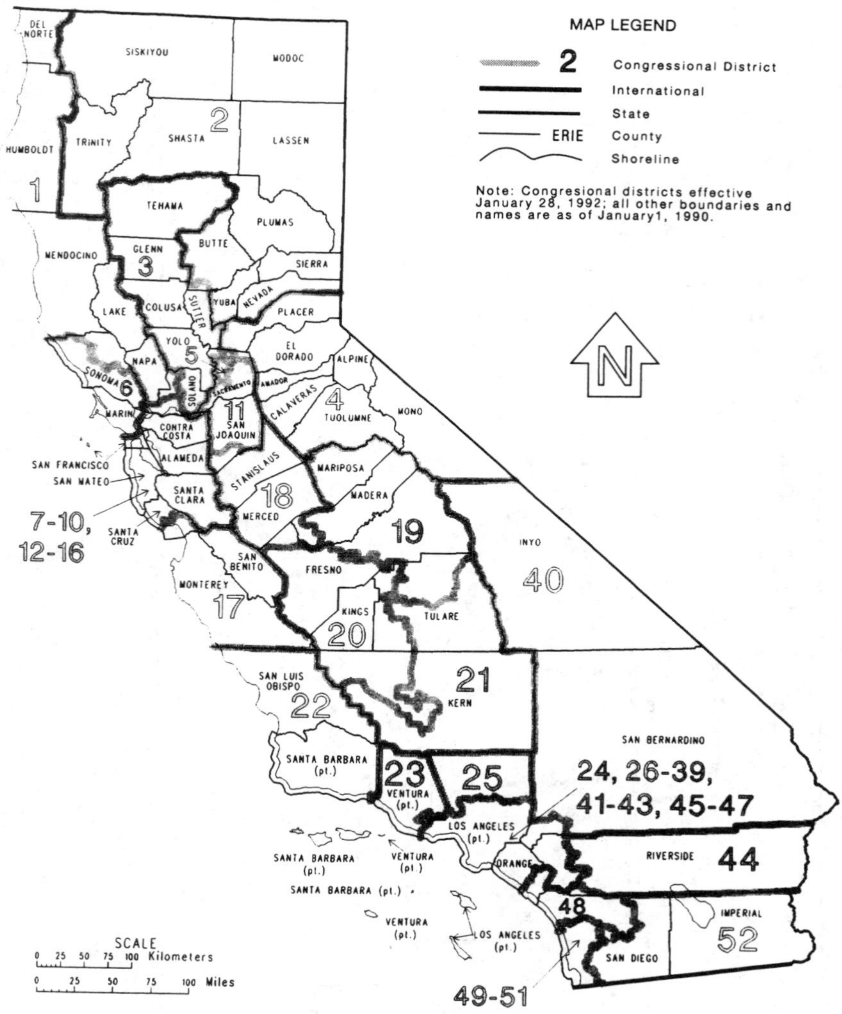

COLORADO —Congressional Districts—(6 Districts)

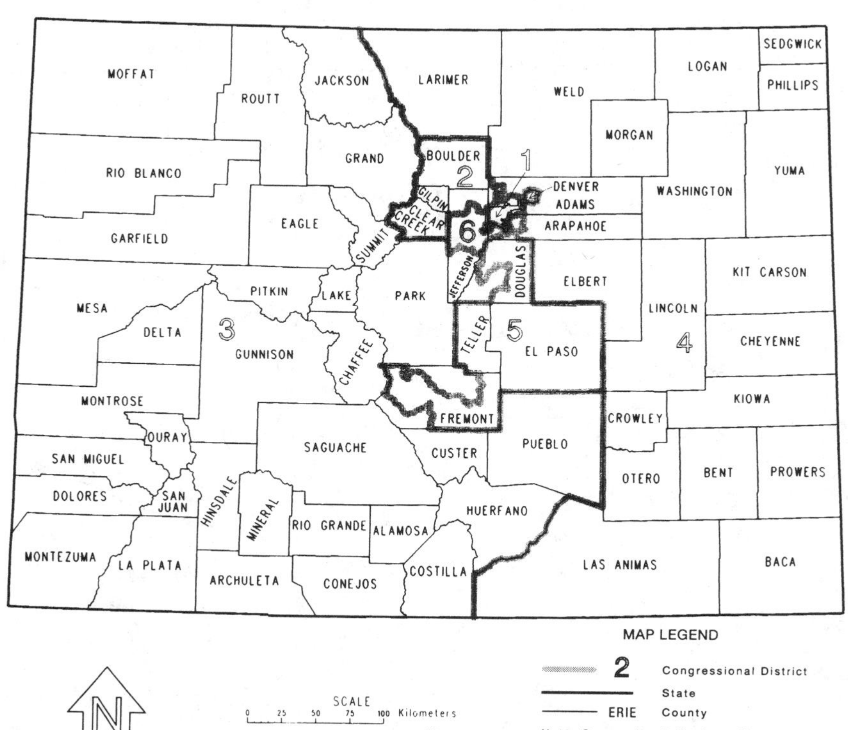

CONNECTICUT—Congressional Districts—(6 Districts)

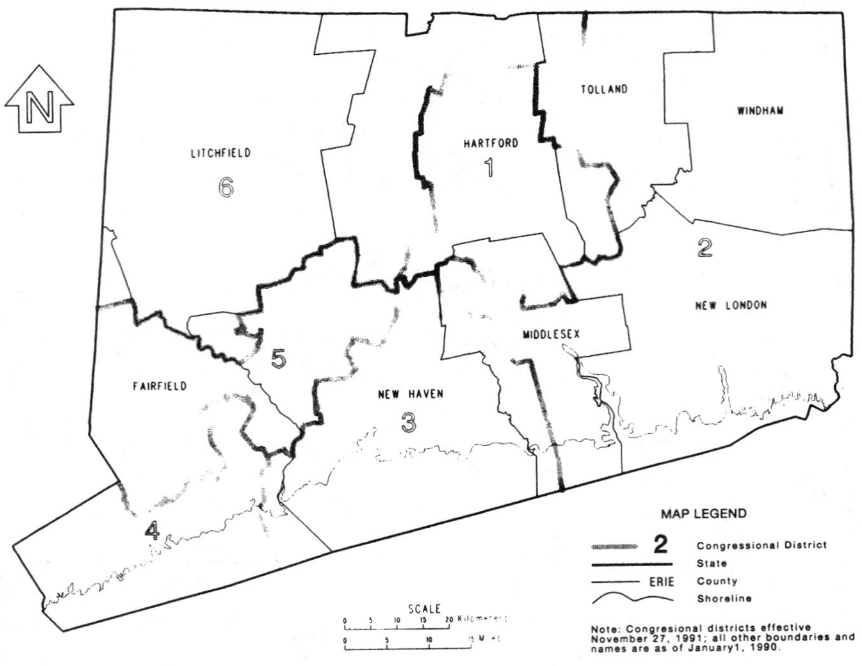

DELAWARE—Congressional District—(1 District At Large)

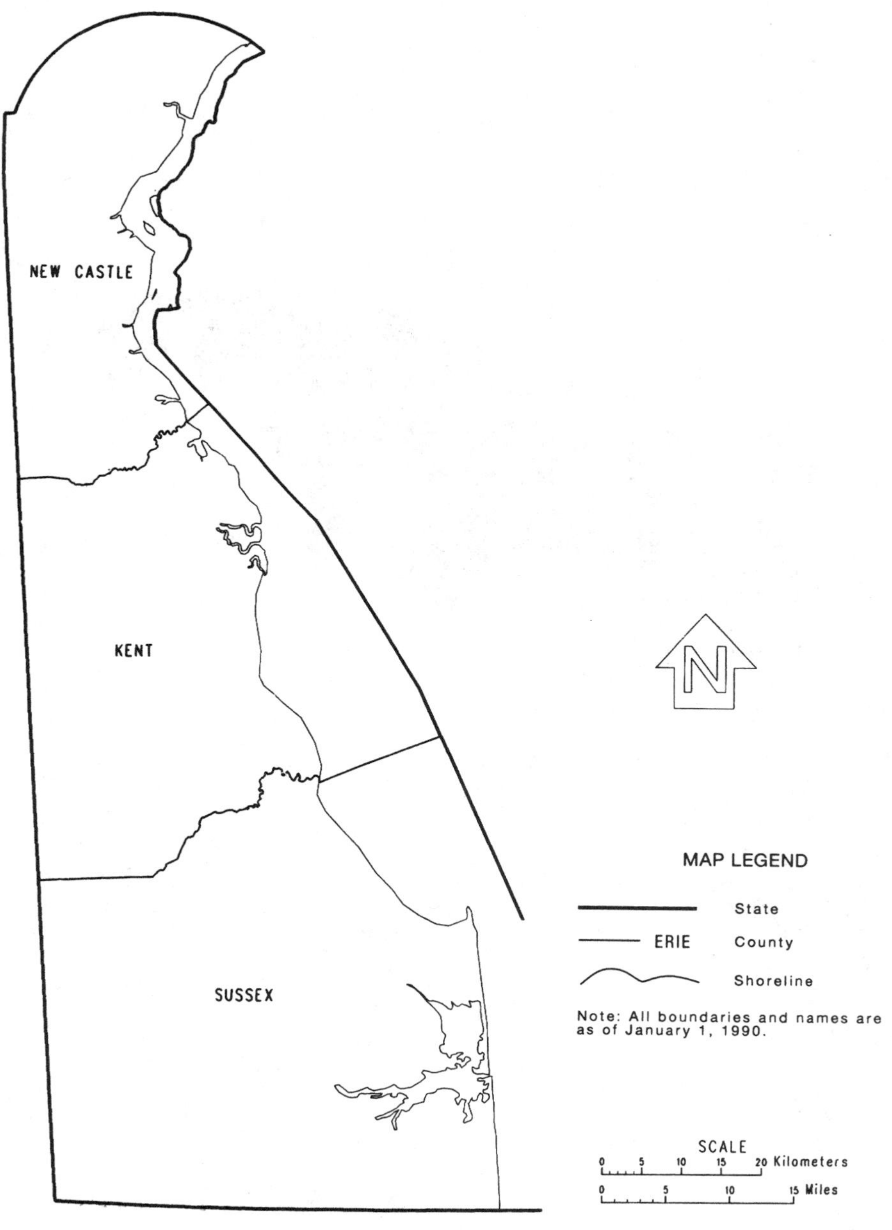

FLORIDA—Congressional Districts—(23 Districts)

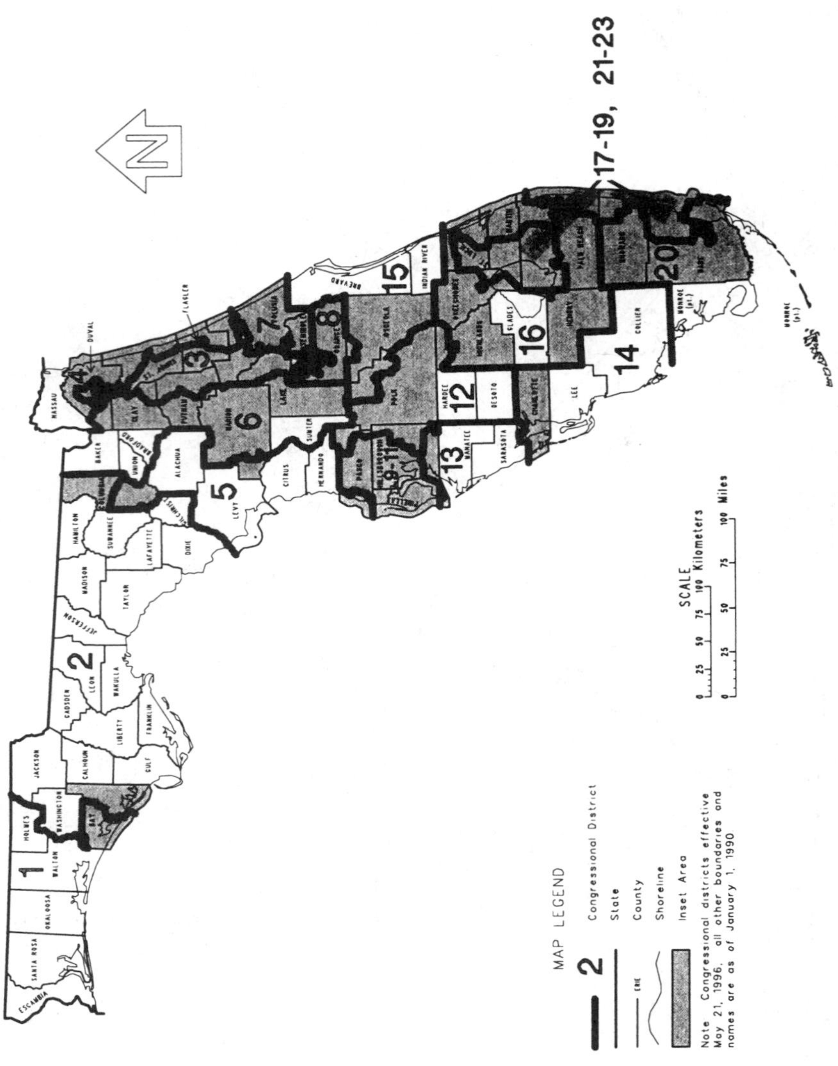

GEORGIA—Congressional Districts—(11 Districts)

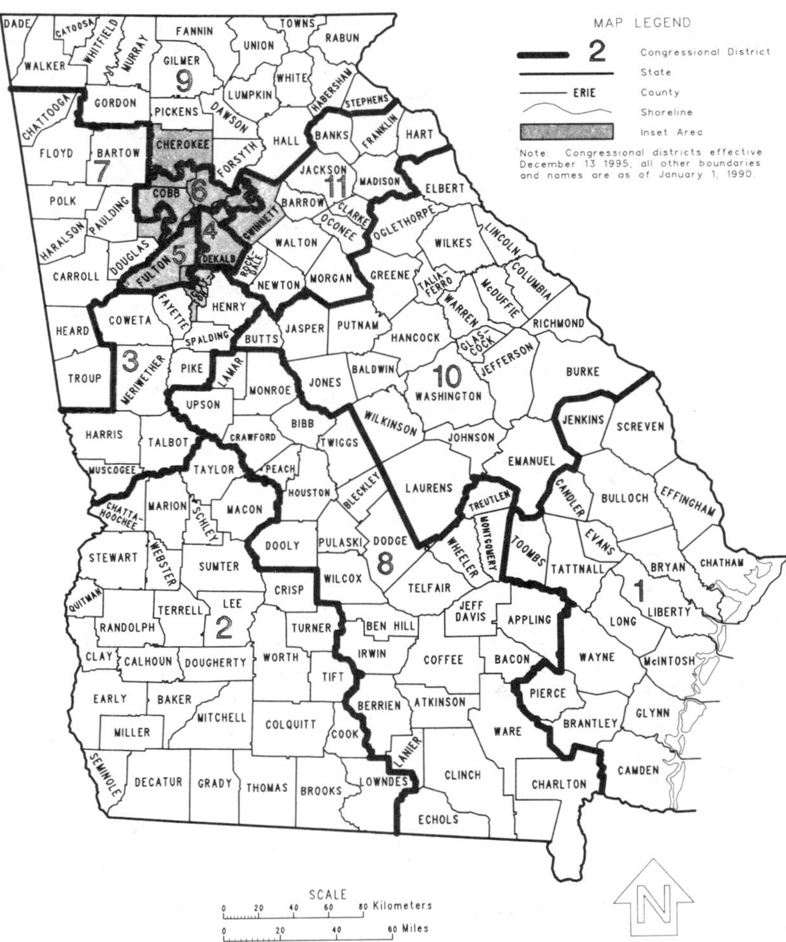

HAWAII—Congressional Districts—(2 Districts)

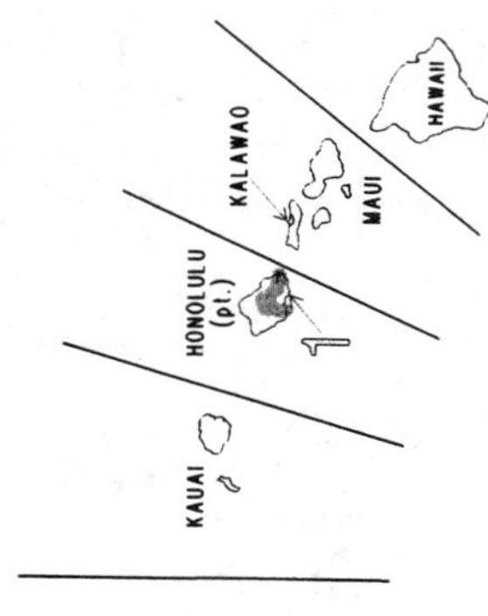

2

HONOLULU
(pt.)

MAP LEGEND

2 Congressional District

ERIE County

Shoreline

Note: Congresional districts effective July 27, 1991; all other bounadries and names are as of January1, 1990.

SCALE

0 100 200 300 Kilometers

0 100 200 Miles

IDAHO—Congressional Districts—(2 Districts)

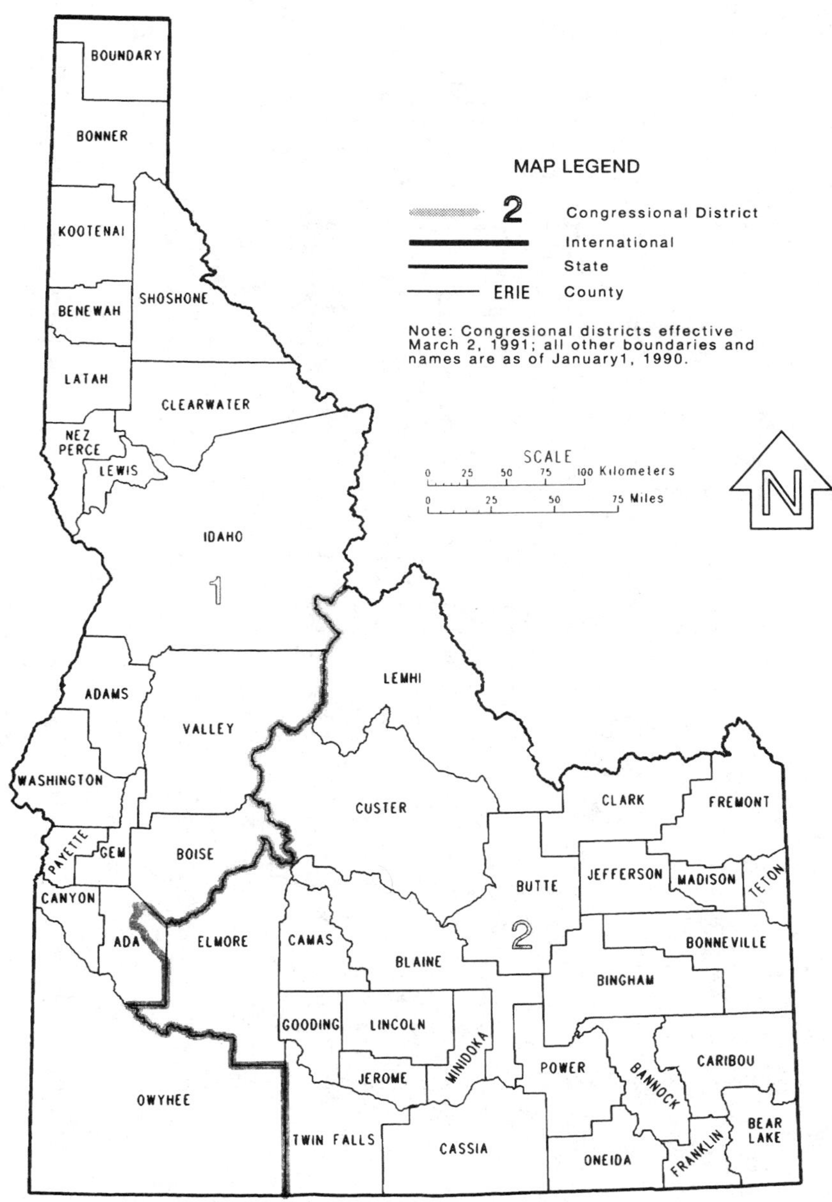

ILLINOIS—Congressional Districts—(20 Districts)

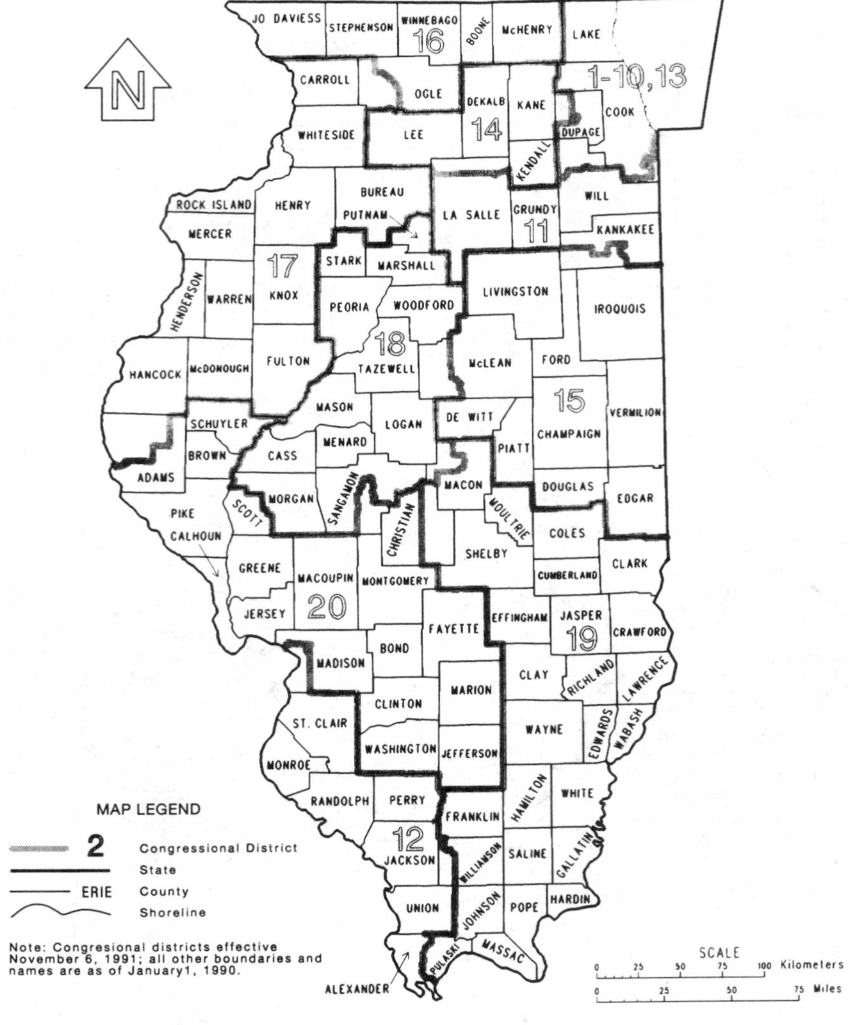

INDIANA—Congressional Districts—(10 Districts)

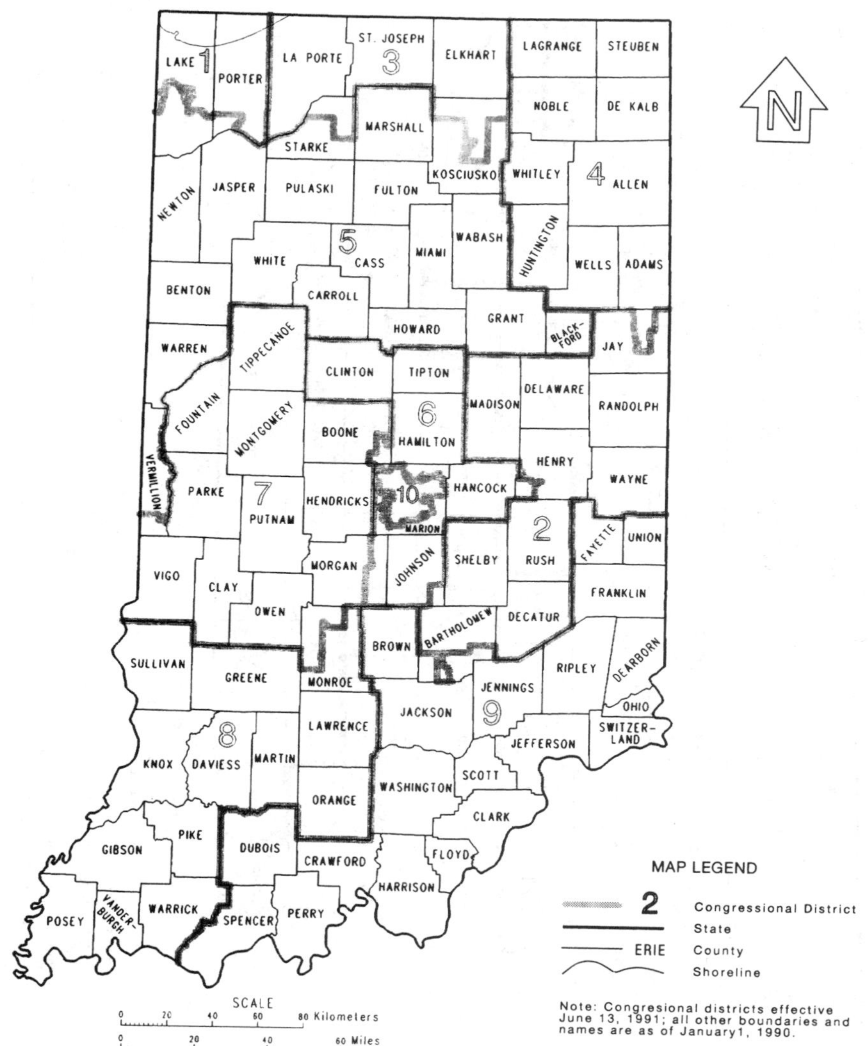

IOWA—Congressional Districts—(5 Districts)

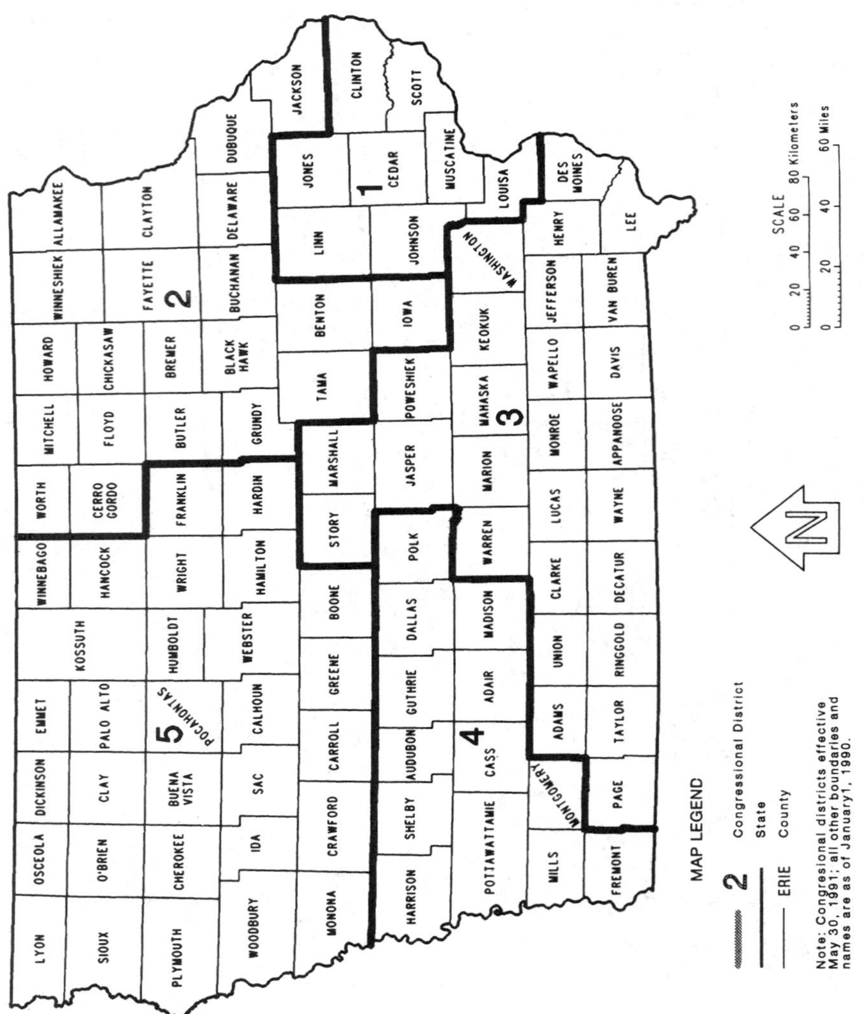

KANSAS—Congressional Districts—(4 Districts)

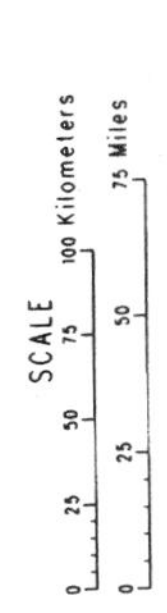

MAP LEGEND

2 Congressional District

State

ERIE County

Note: Congressional districts effective June 3, 1992; all other boundaries and names are as of January1, 1990.

KENTUCKY—Congressional Districts—(6 Districts)

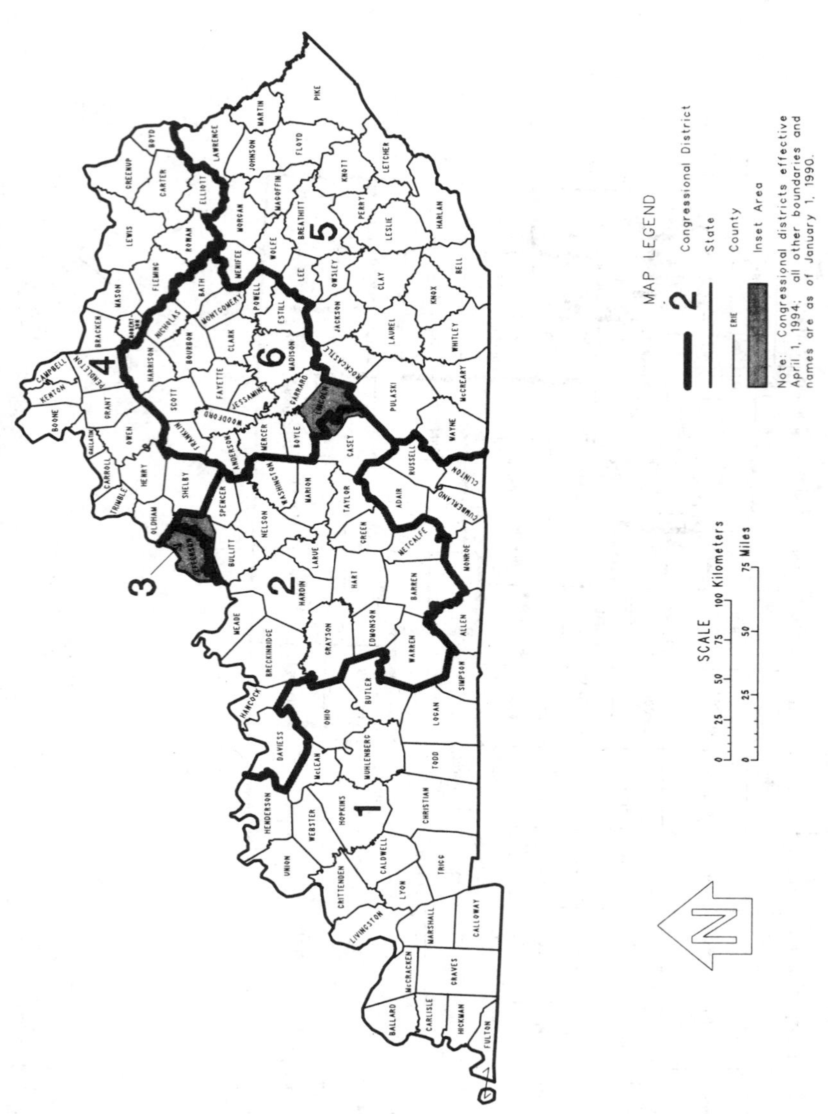

LOUISIANA—Congressional Districts—(7 Districts)

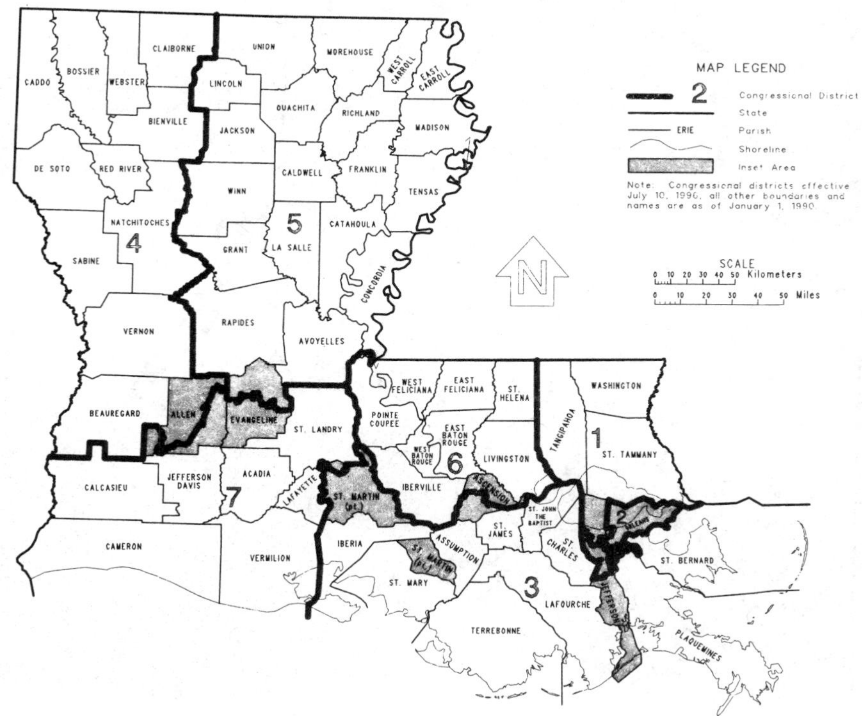

MAINE—Congressional Districts—(2 Districts)

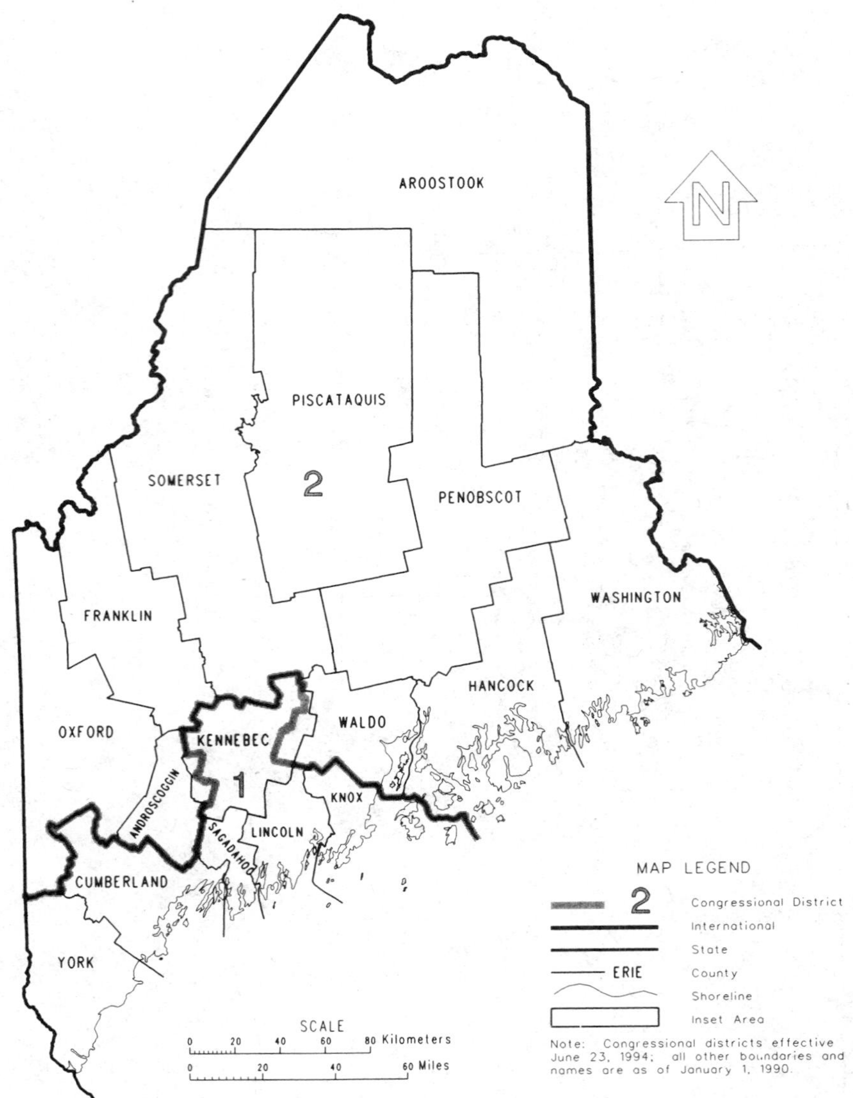

MARYLAND—Congressional Districts—(8 Districts)

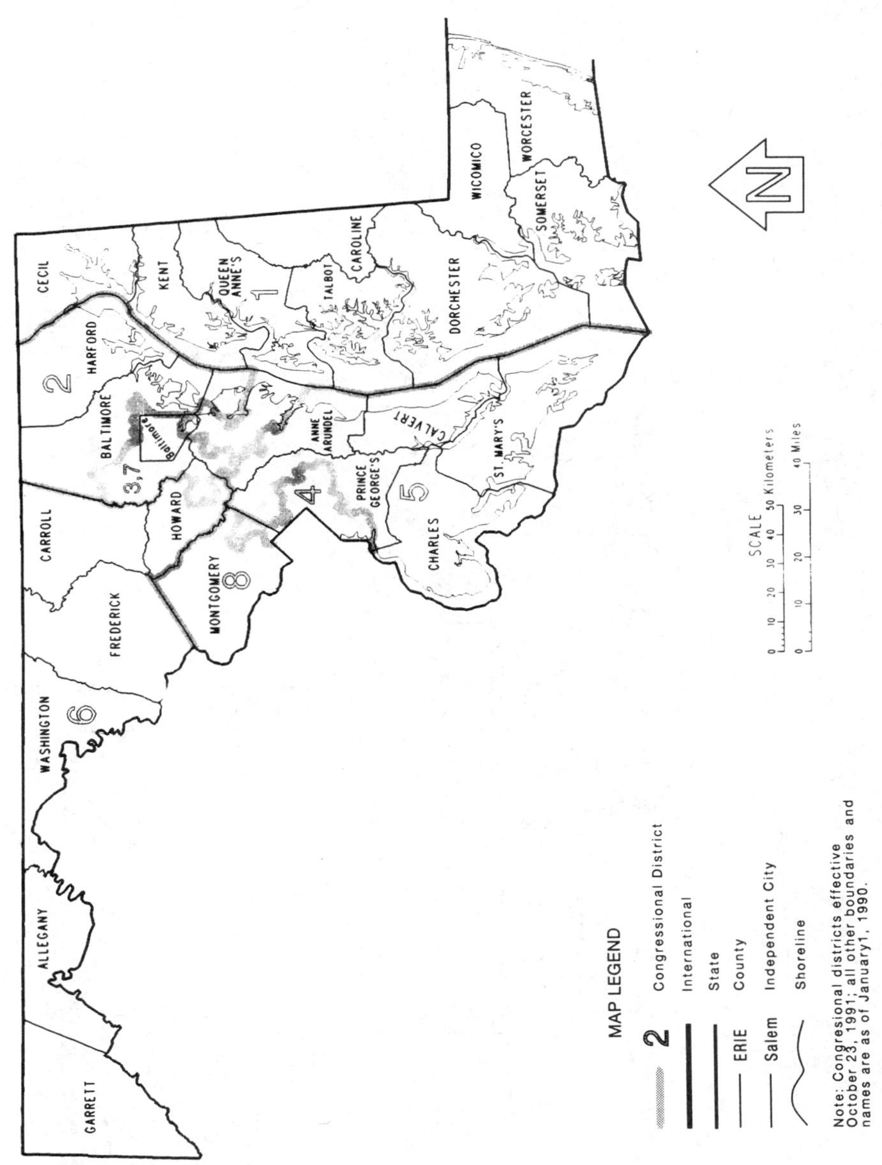

MASSACHUSETTS—Congressional Districts—(10 Districts)

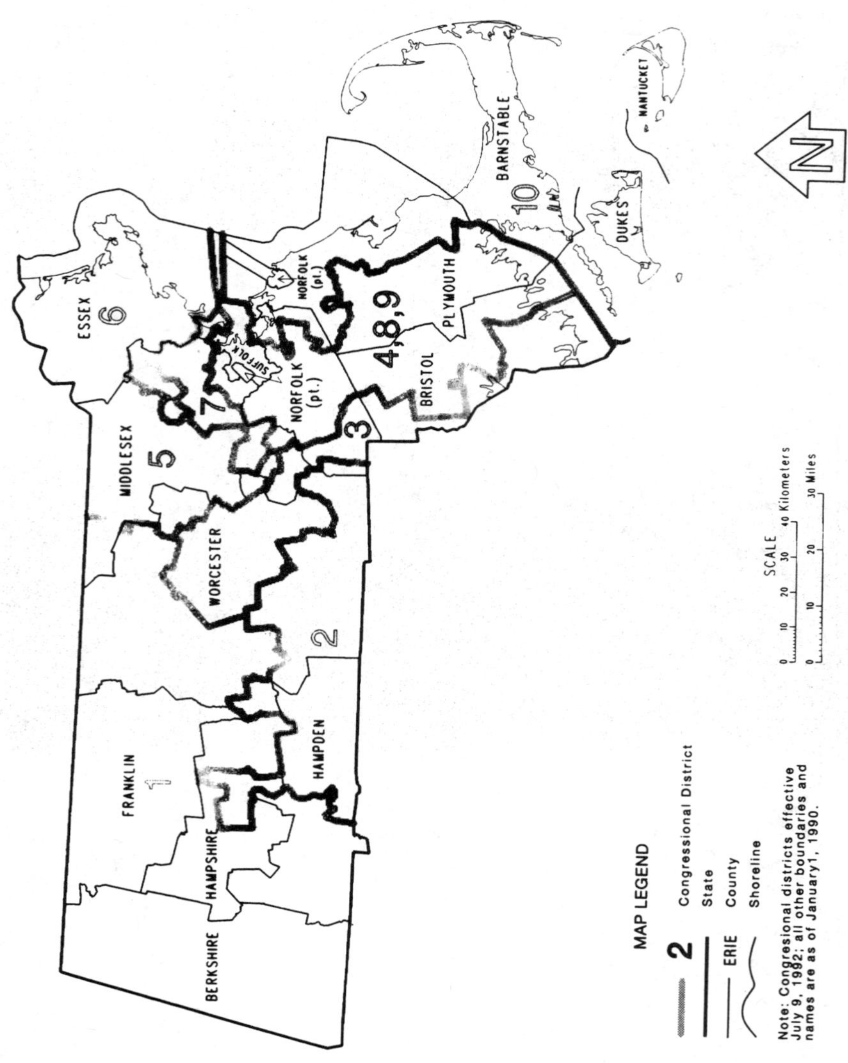

MICHIGAN—Congressional Districts—(16 Districts)

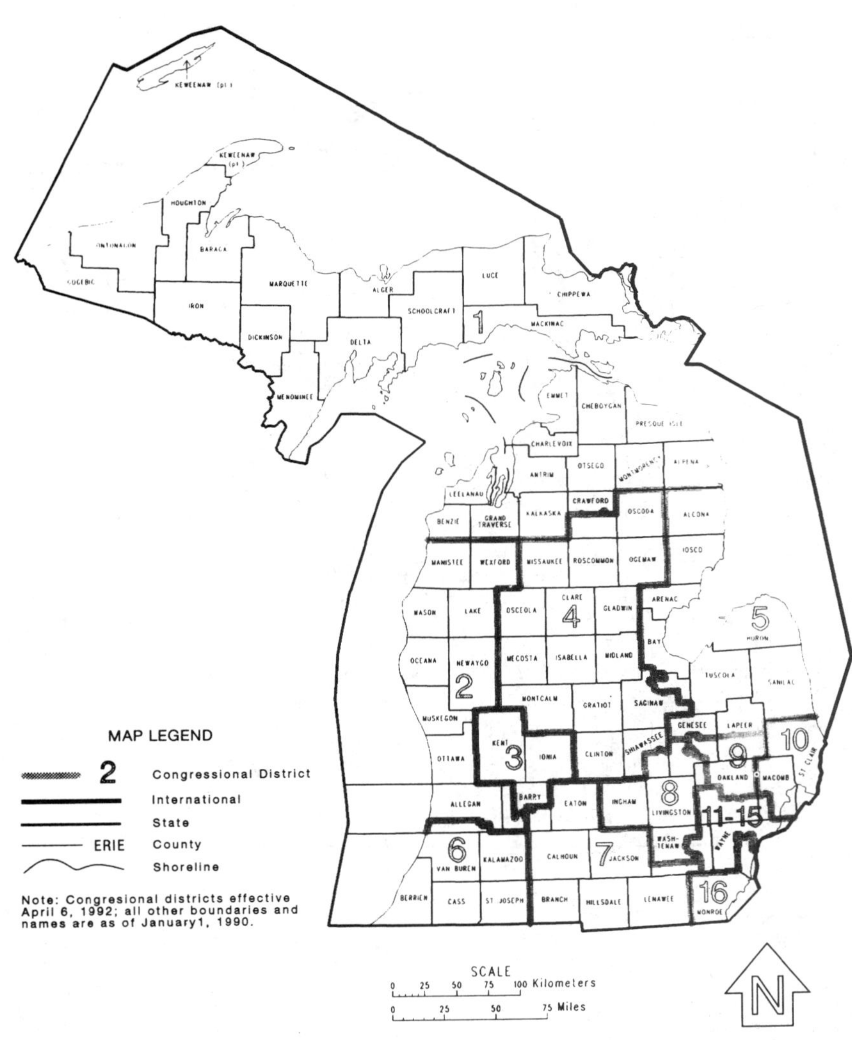

MINNESOTA—Congressional Districts—(8 Districts)

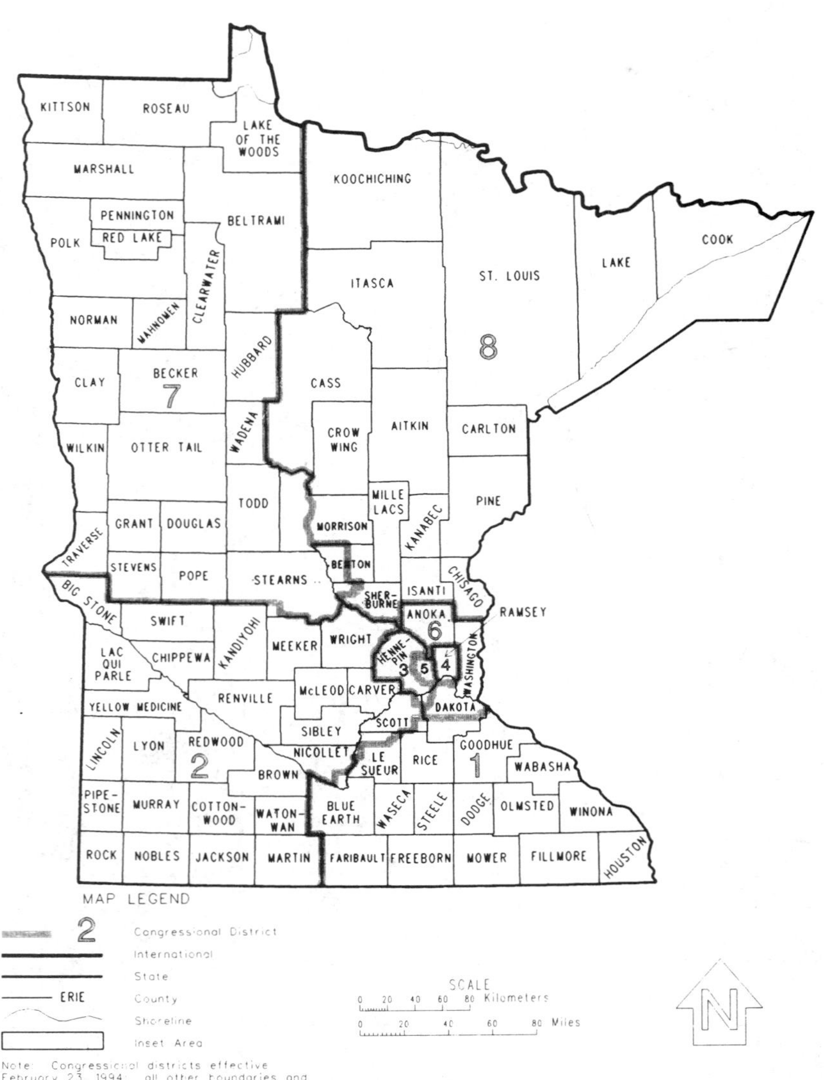

MISSISSIPPI—Congressional Districts—(5 Districts)

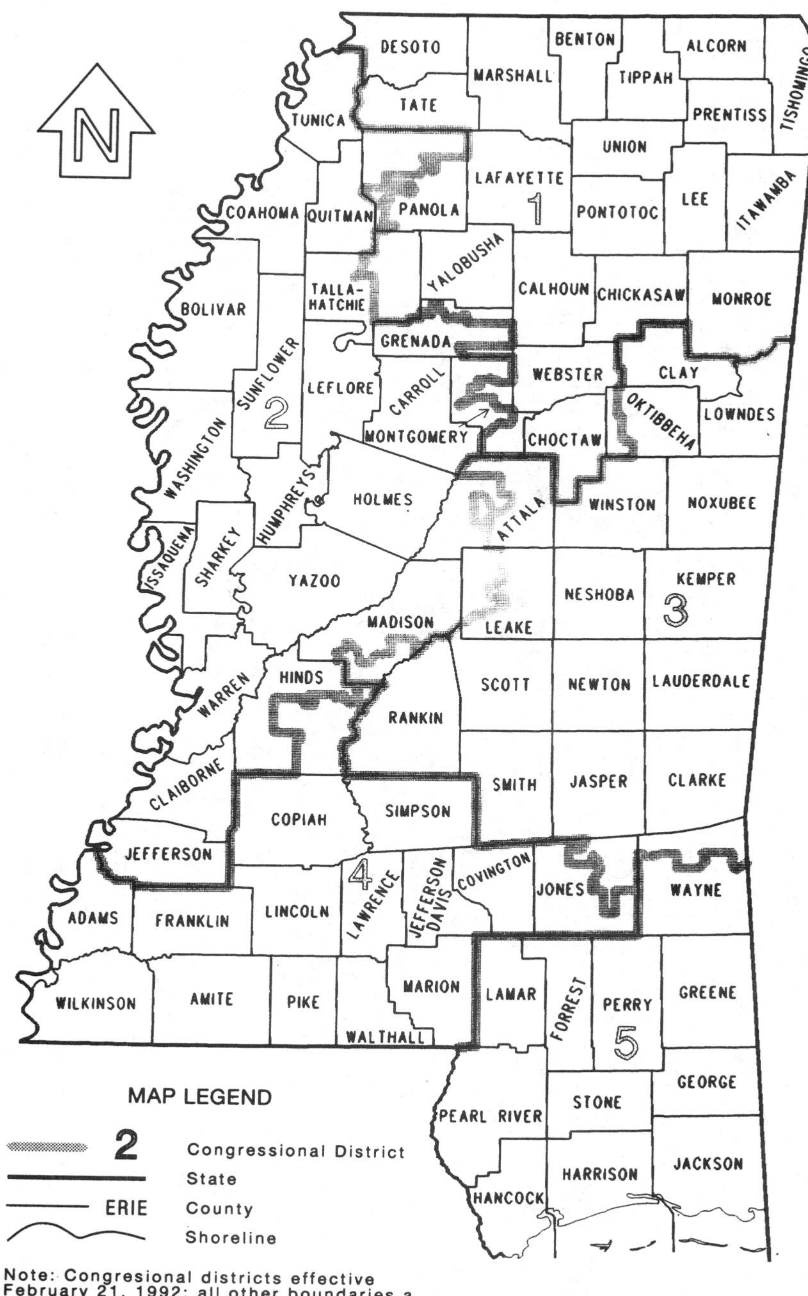

SCALE

0 20 40 60 80 Kilometers

0 20 40 60 Miles

MISSOURI—Congressional Districts—(9 Districts)

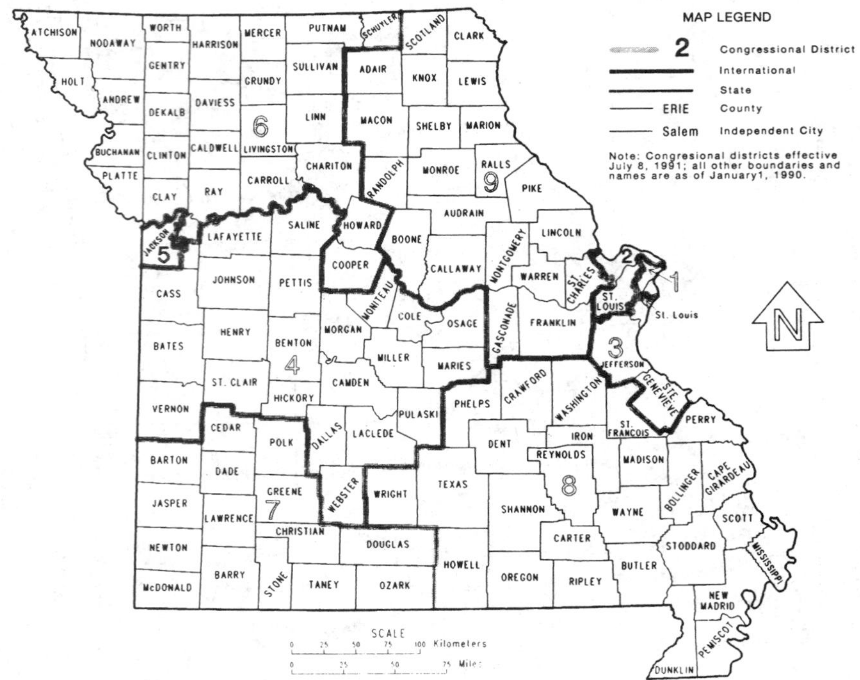

MONTANA—Congressional District—(1 District At Large)

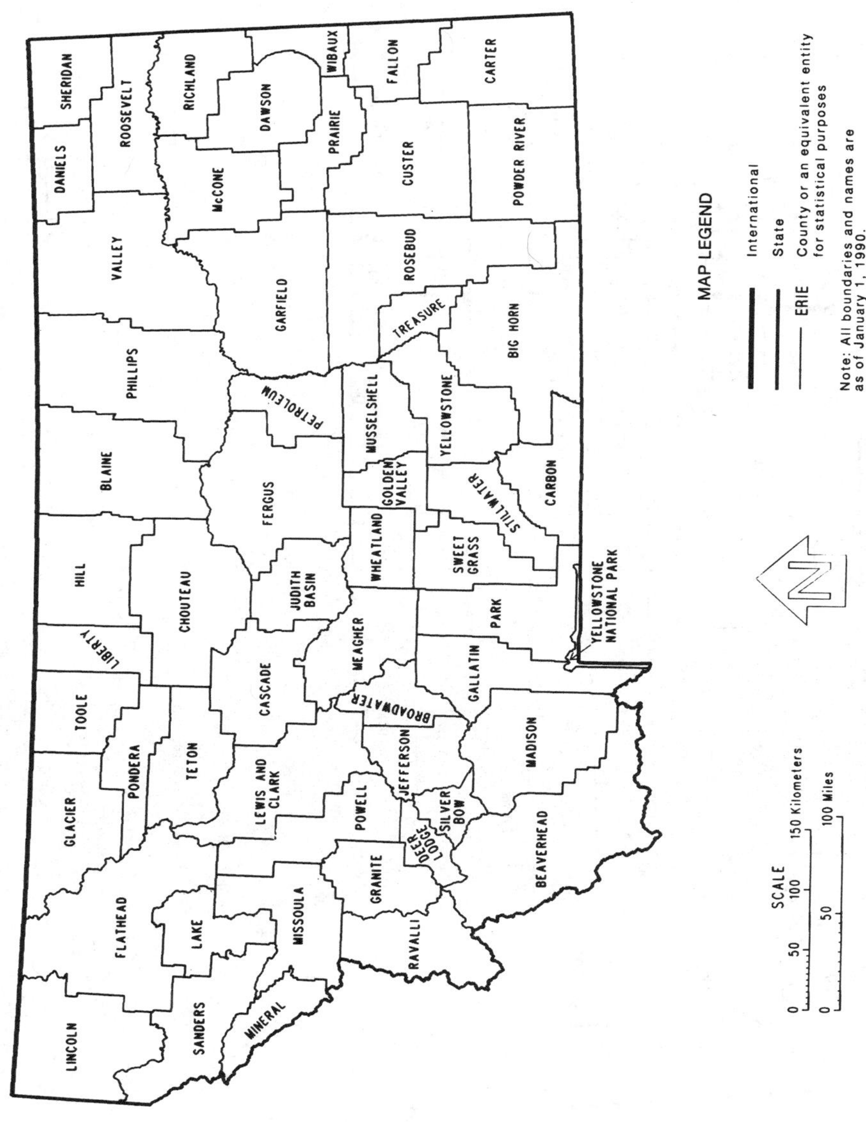

NEBRASKA—Congressional Districts—(3 Districts)

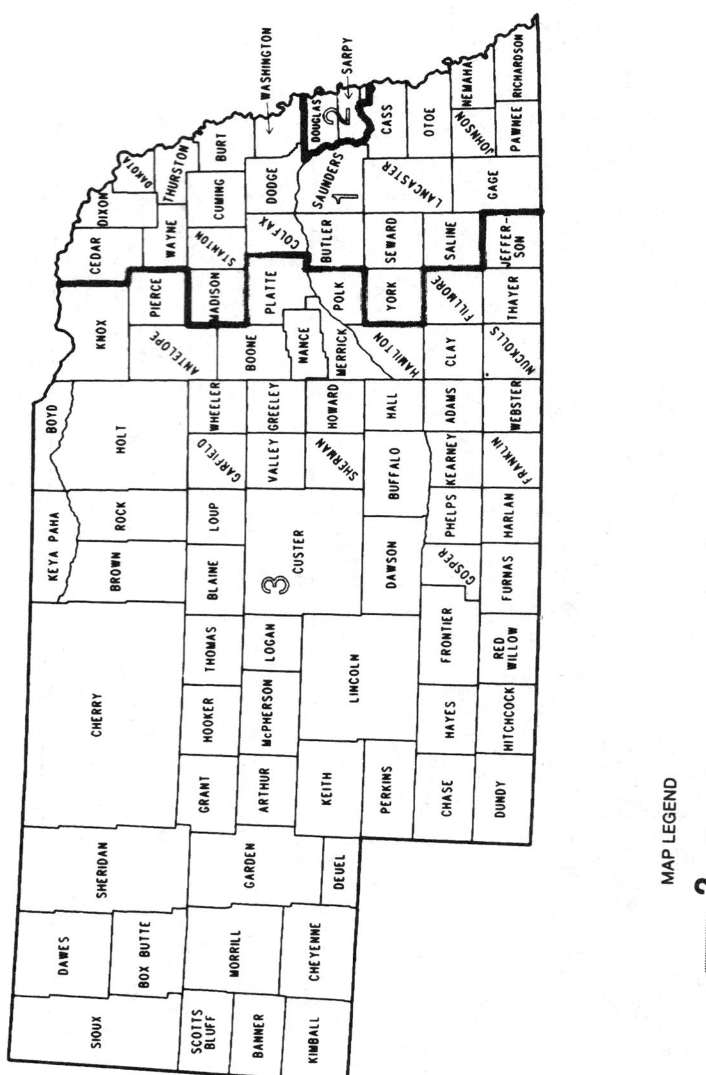

NEVADA—Congressional Districts—(2 Districts)

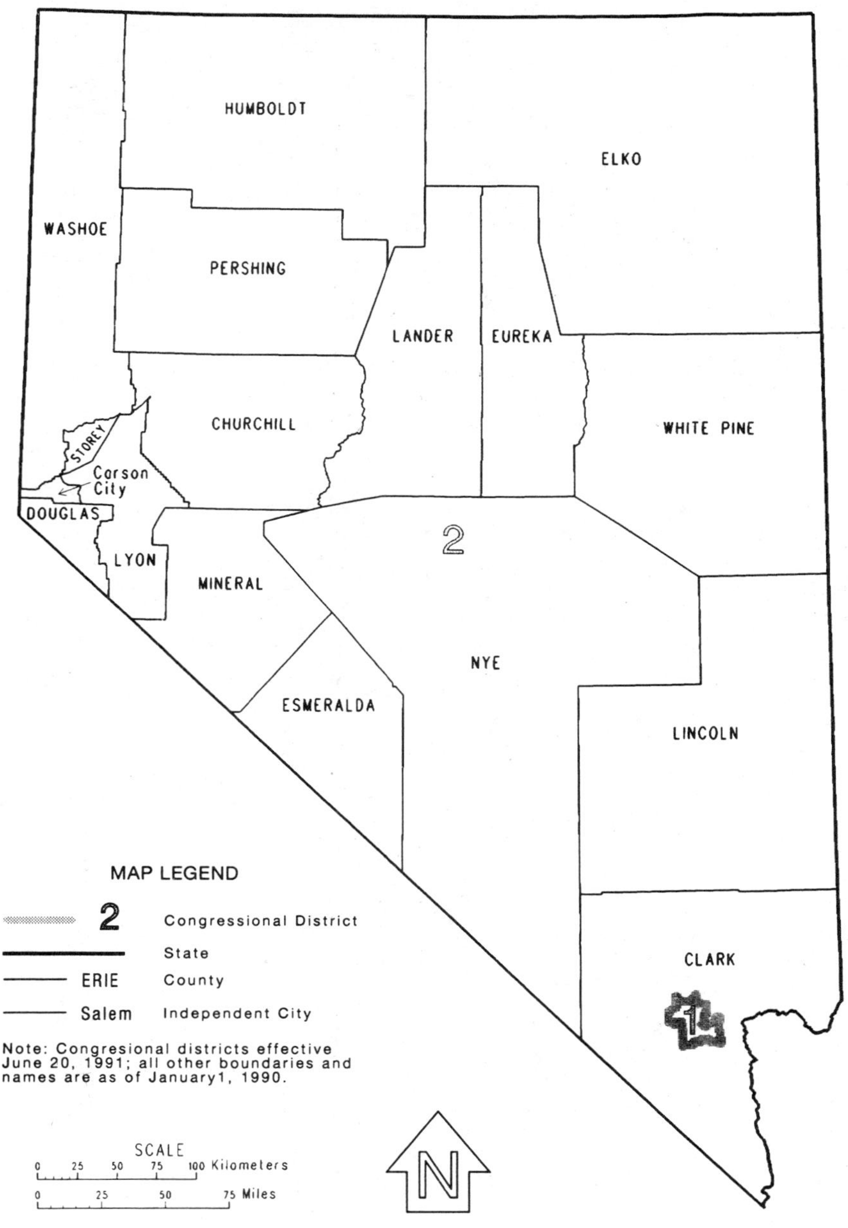

NEW HAMPSHIRE—Congressional Districts—(2 Districts)

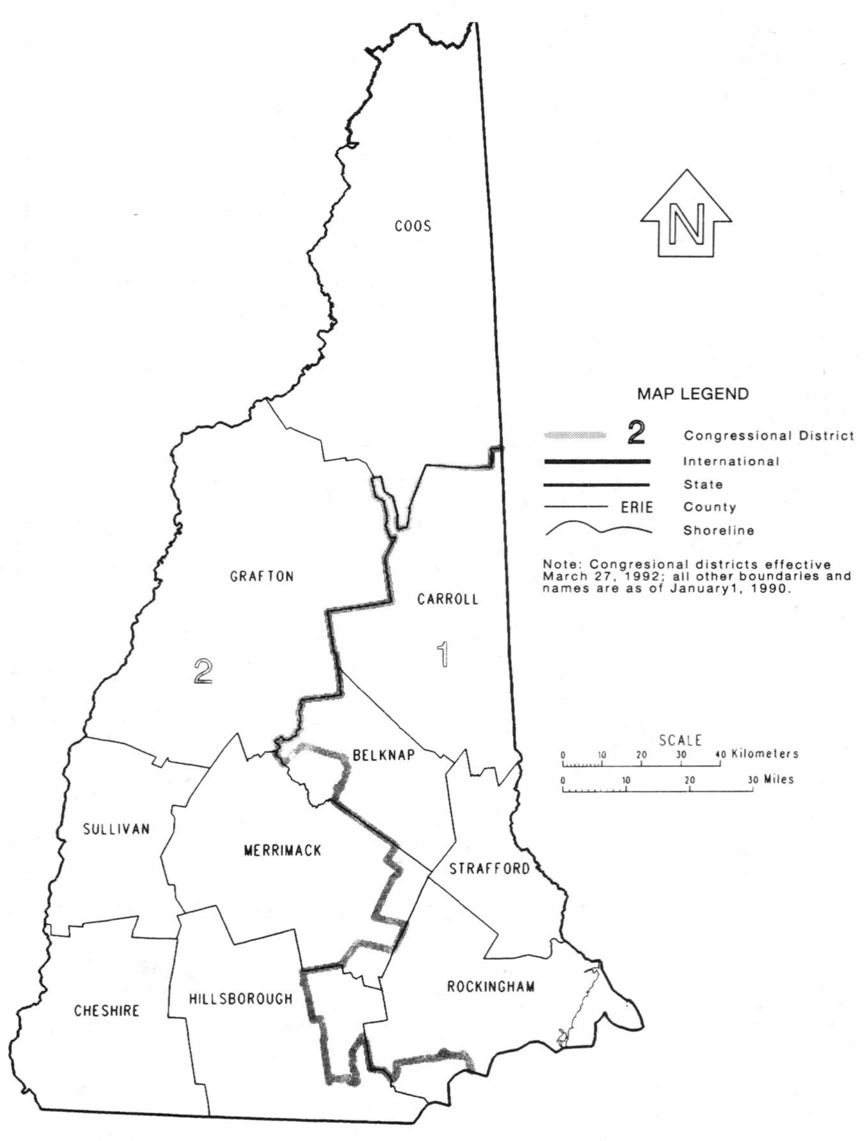

NEW JERSEY—Congressional Districts—(13 Districts)

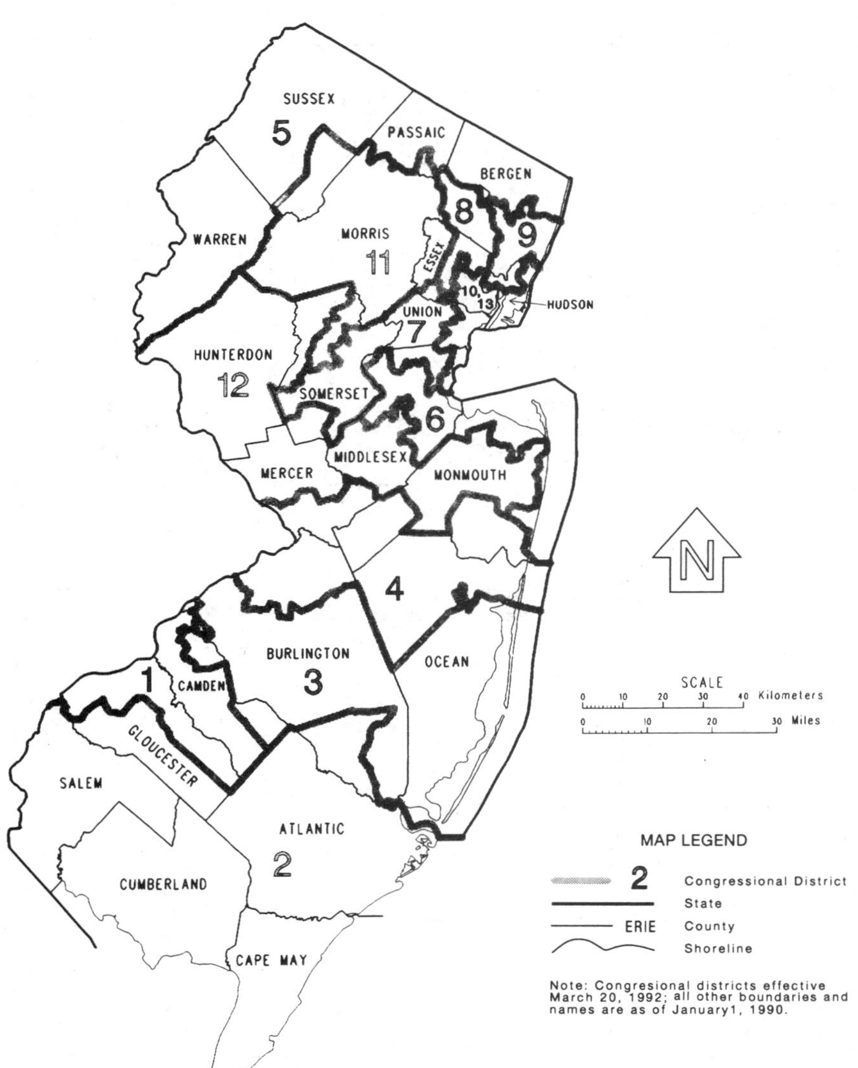

NEW MEXICO—Congressional Districts—(3 Districts)

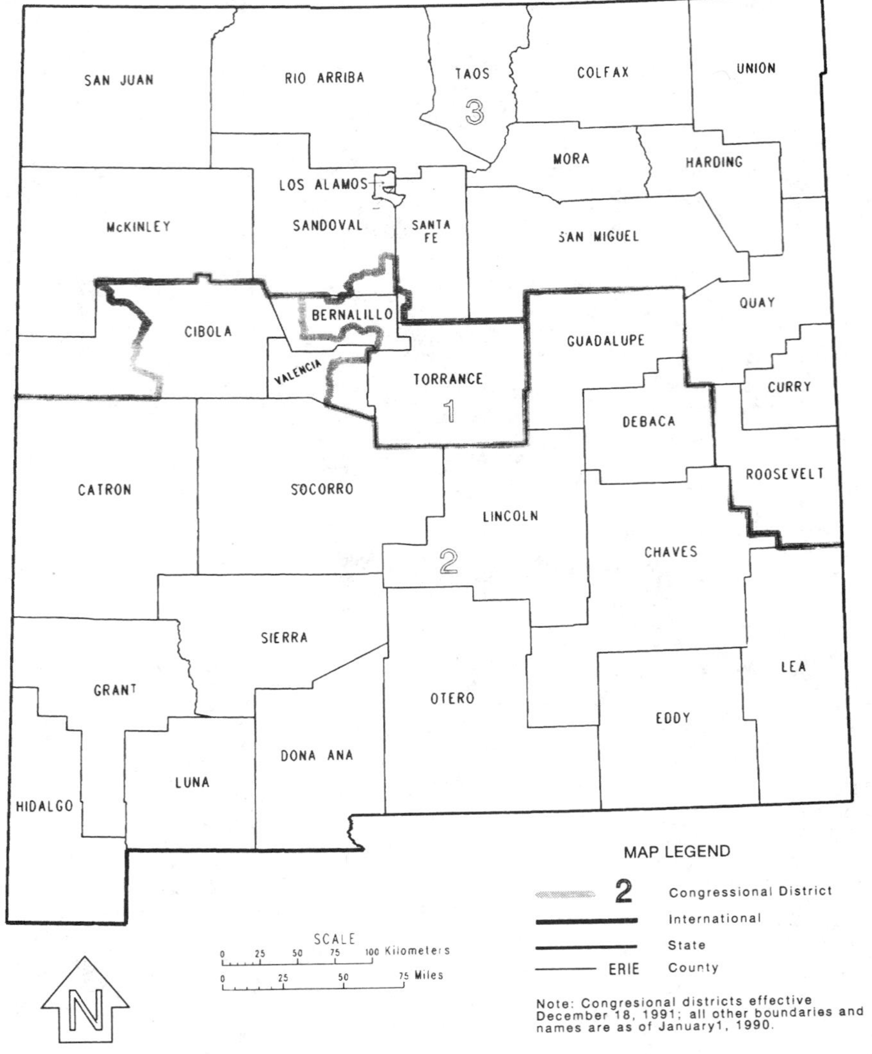

NEW YORK—Congressional Districts—(31 Districts)

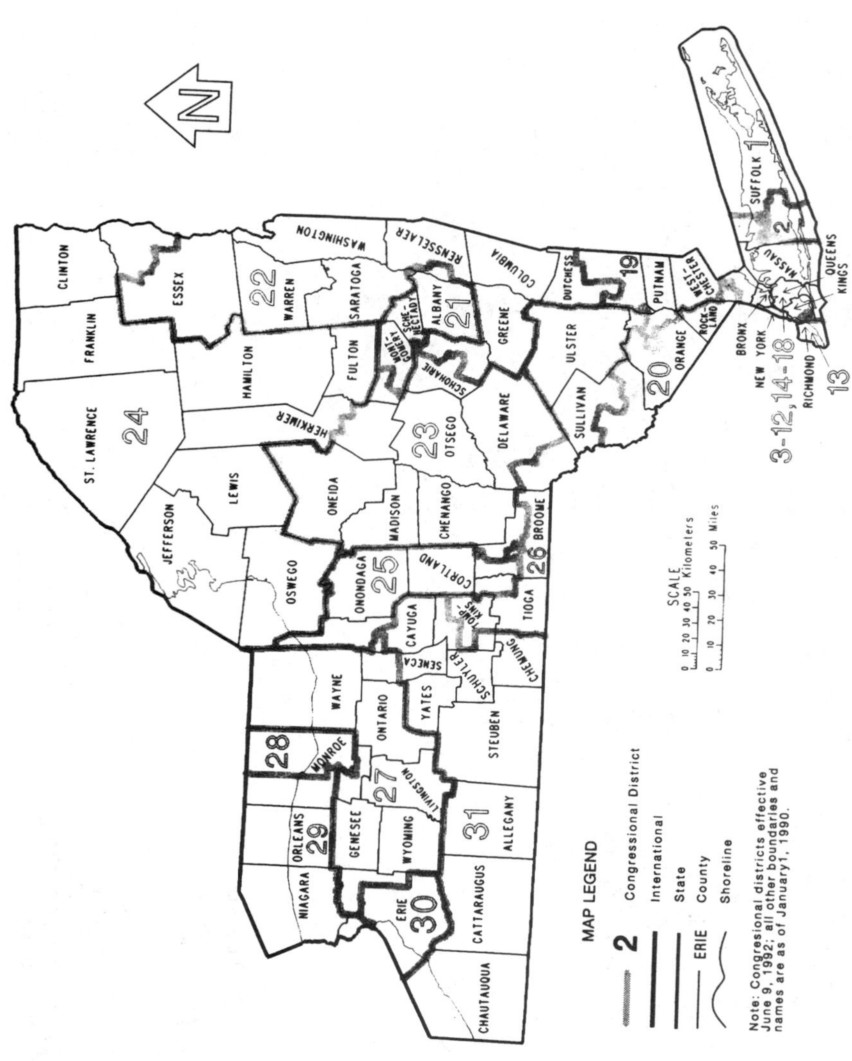

NORTH CAROLINA—Congressional Districts—(12 Districts)

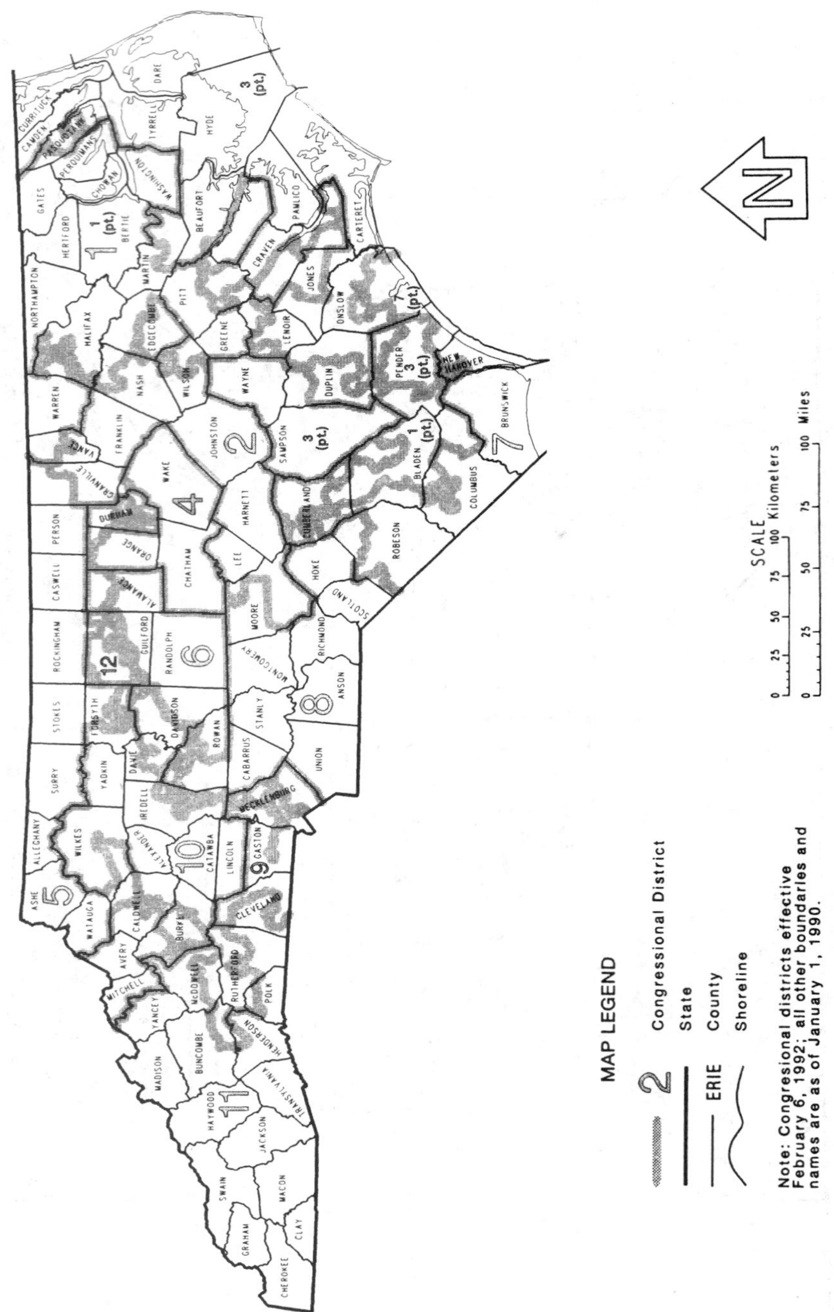

NORTH DAKOTA—Congressional District—(1 District At Large)

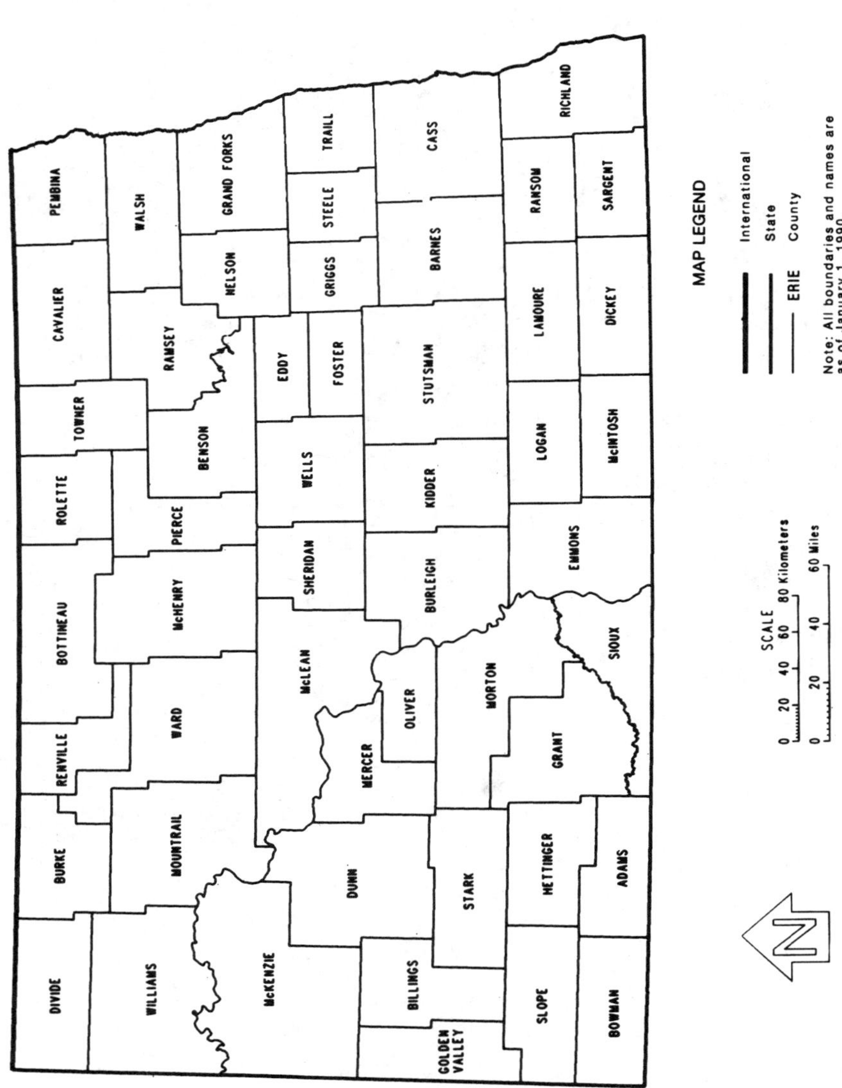

OHIO—Congressional Districts—(19 Districts)

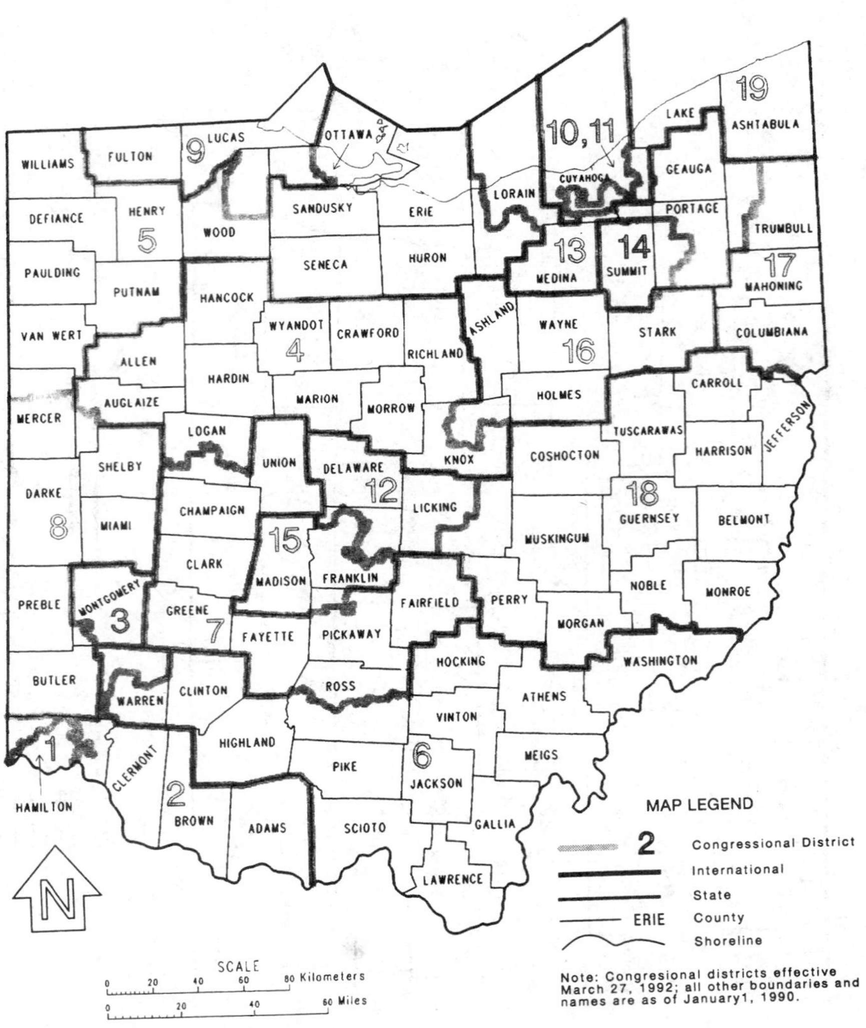

OKLAHOMA—Congressional Districts—(6 Districts)

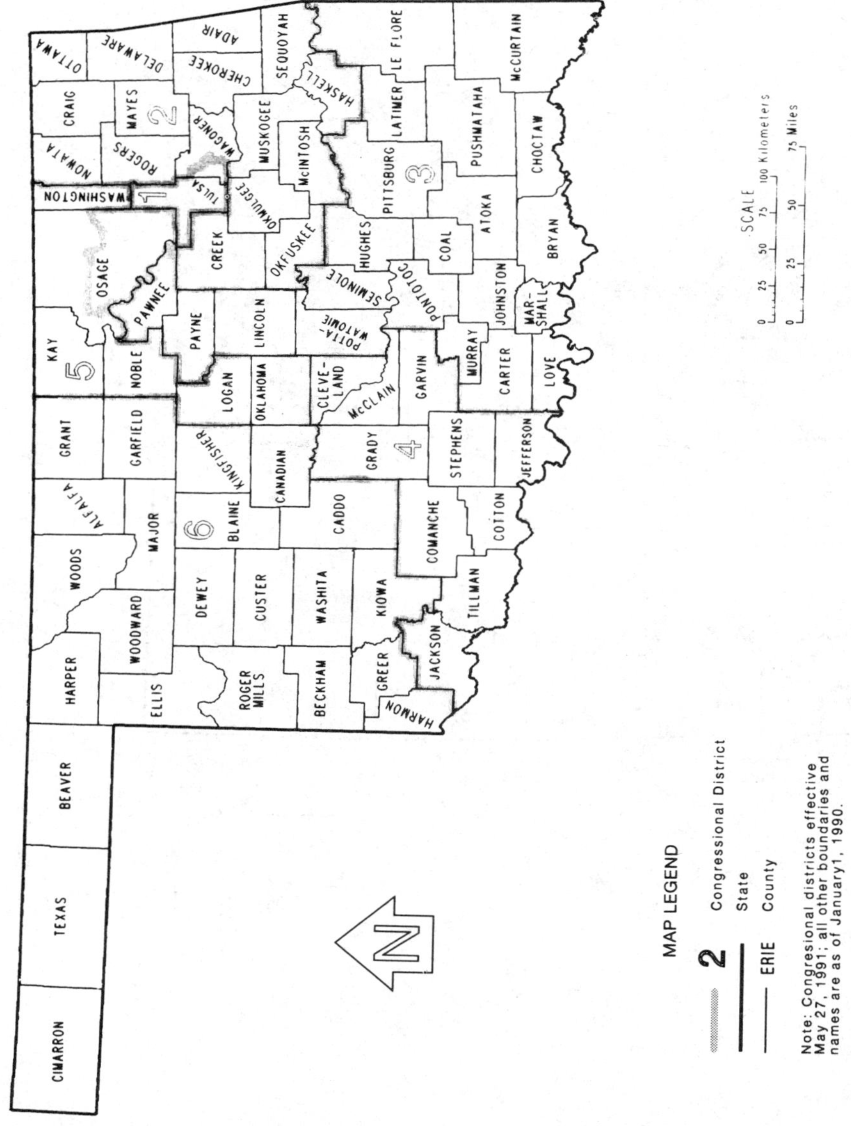

OREGON—Congressional Districts—(5 Districts)

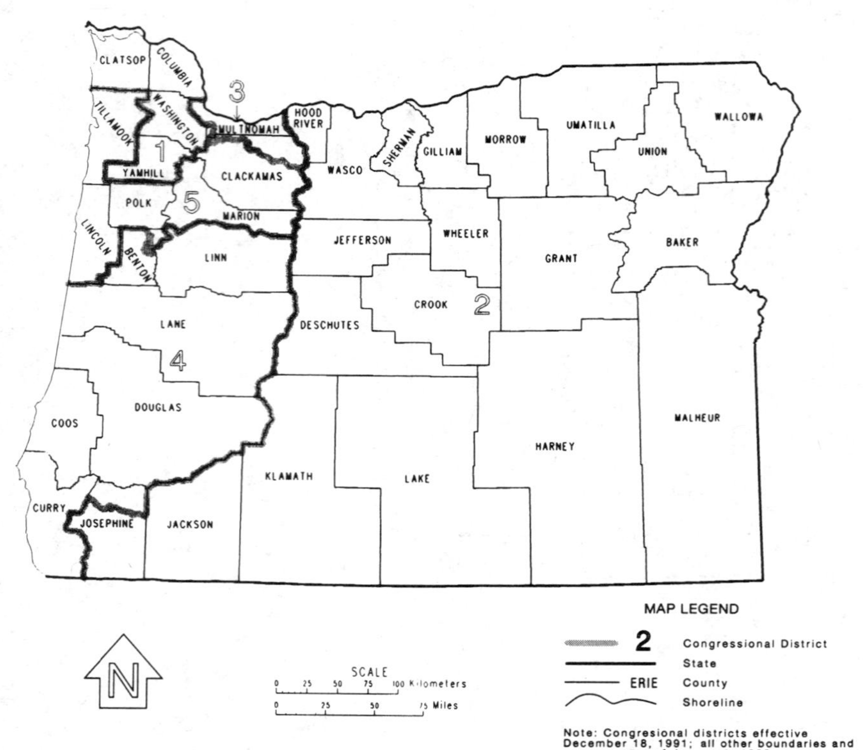

PENNSYLVANIA—Congressional Districts—(21 Districts)

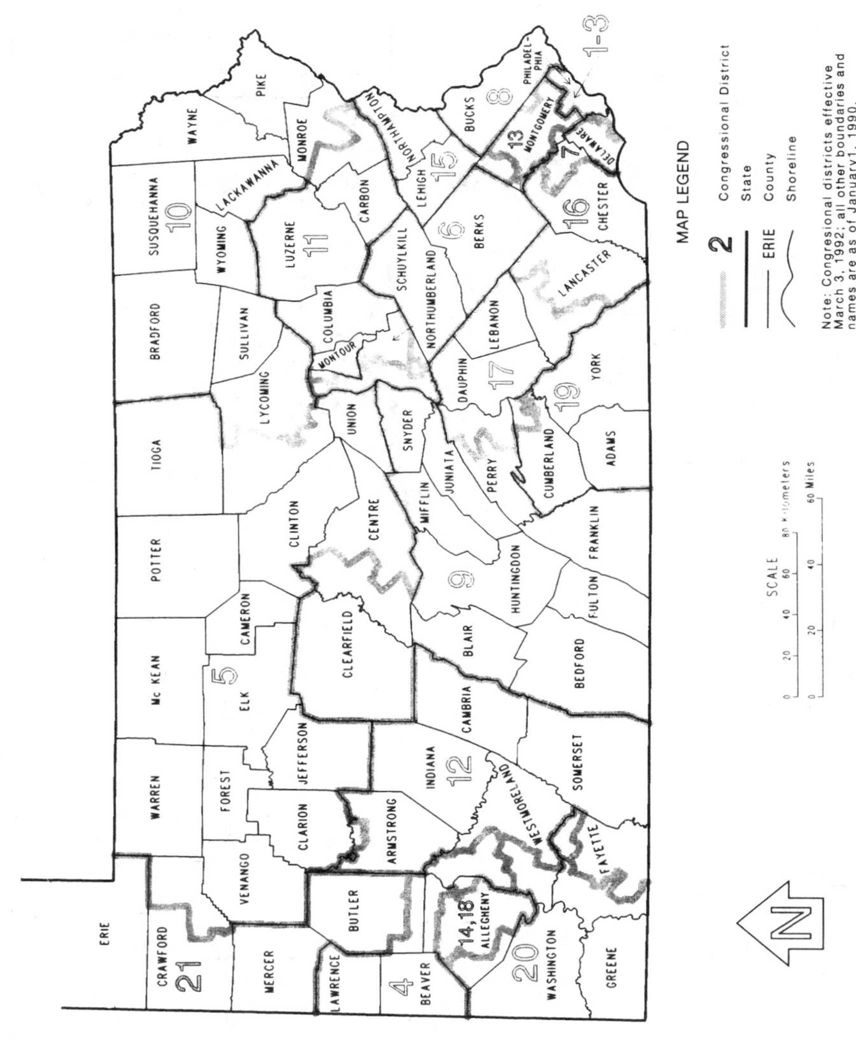

RHODE ISLAND—Congressional Districts—(2 Districts)

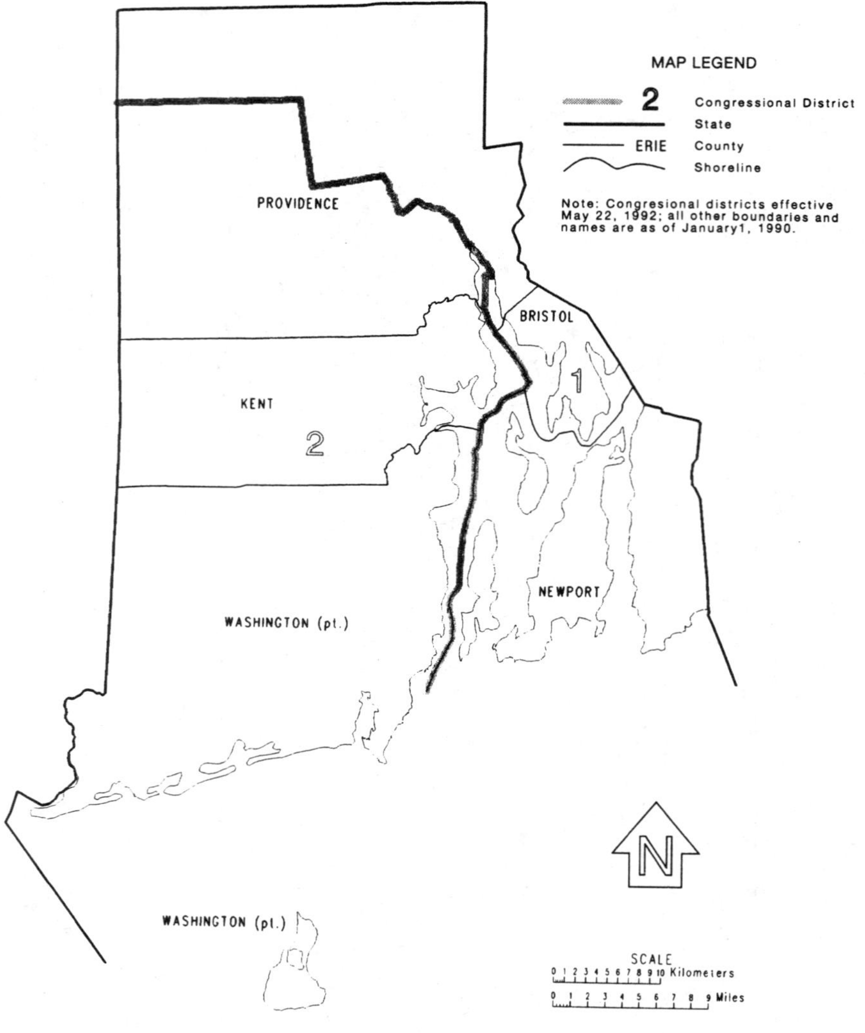

SOUTH CAROLINA—Congressional Districts—(6 Districts)

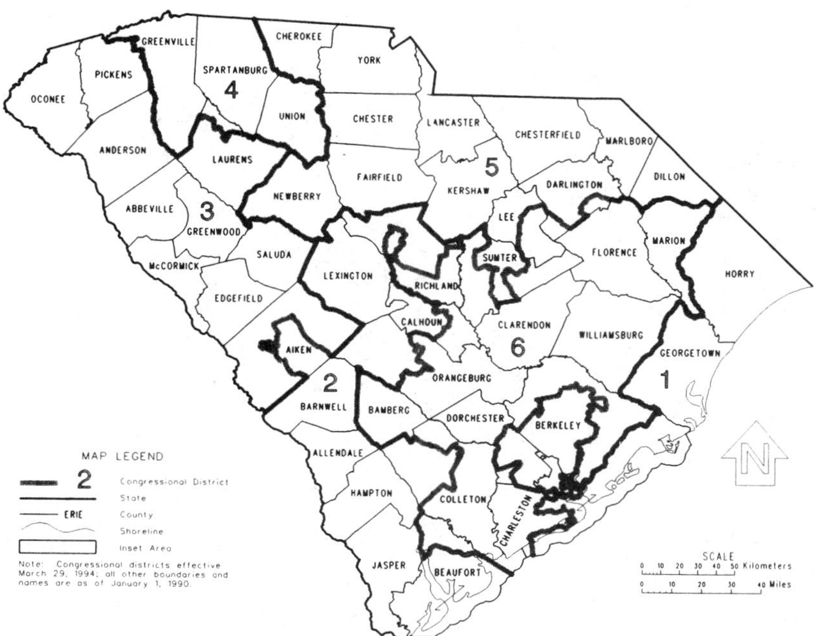

SOUTH DAKOTA—Congressional District—(1 District At Large)

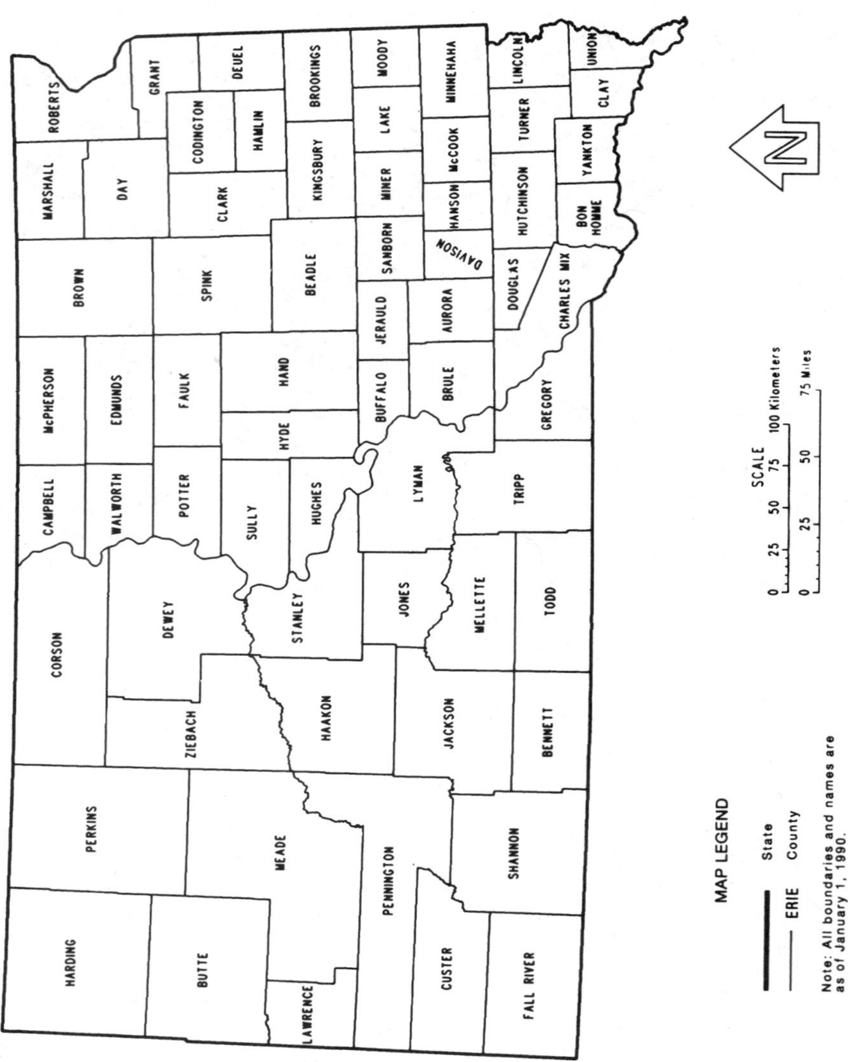

TENNESSEE—Congressional Districts—(9 Districts)

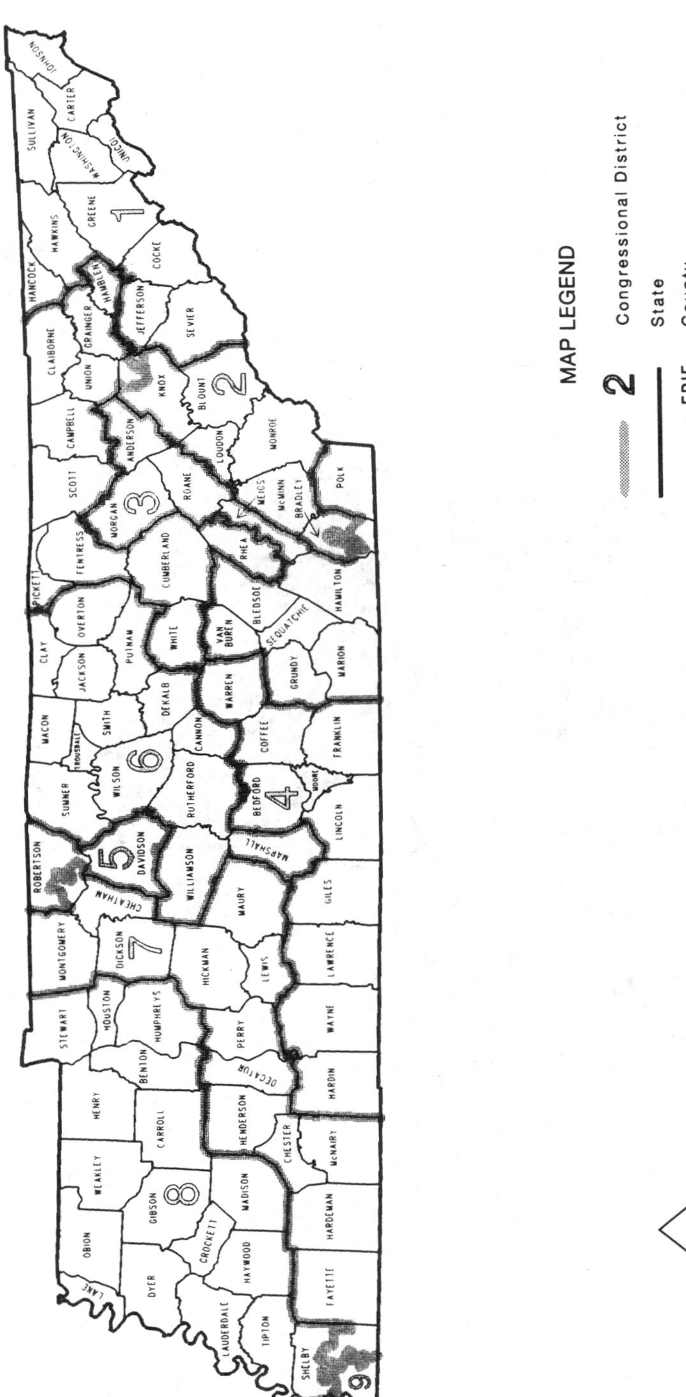

TEXAS—Congressional Districts—(30 Districts)

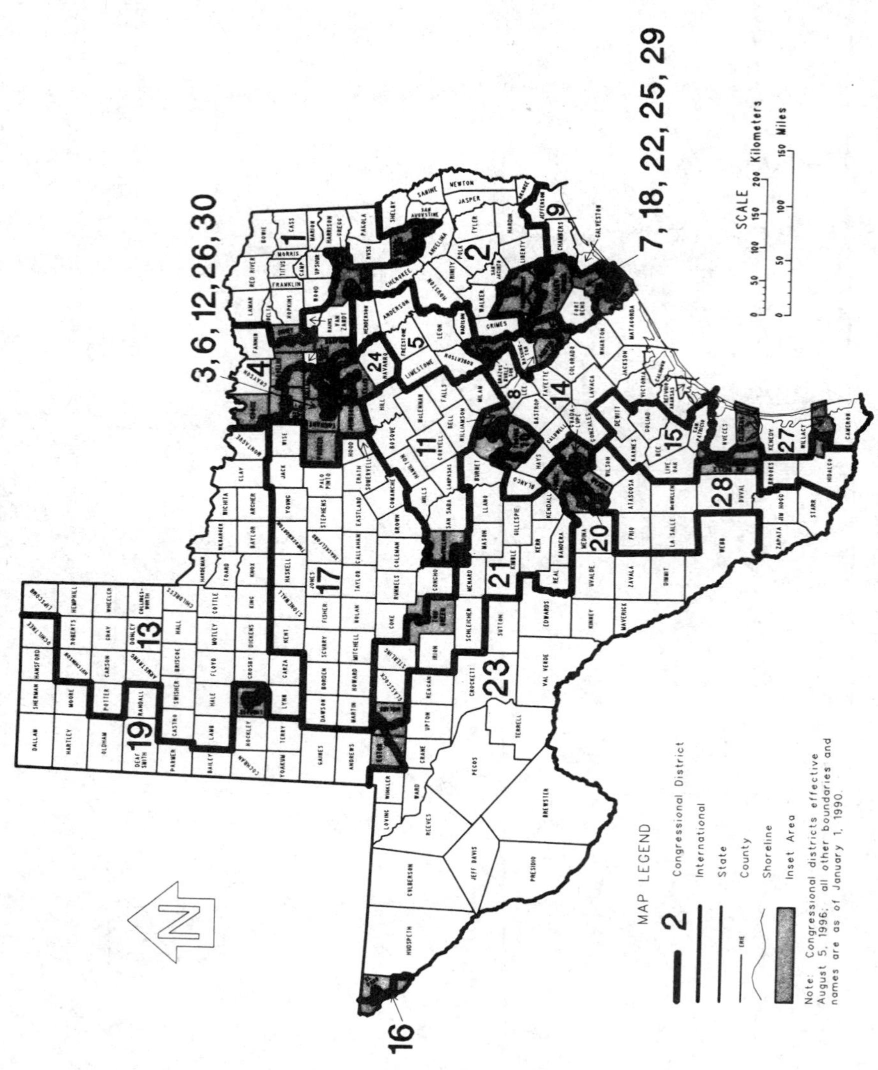

UTAH—Congressional Districts—(3 Districts)

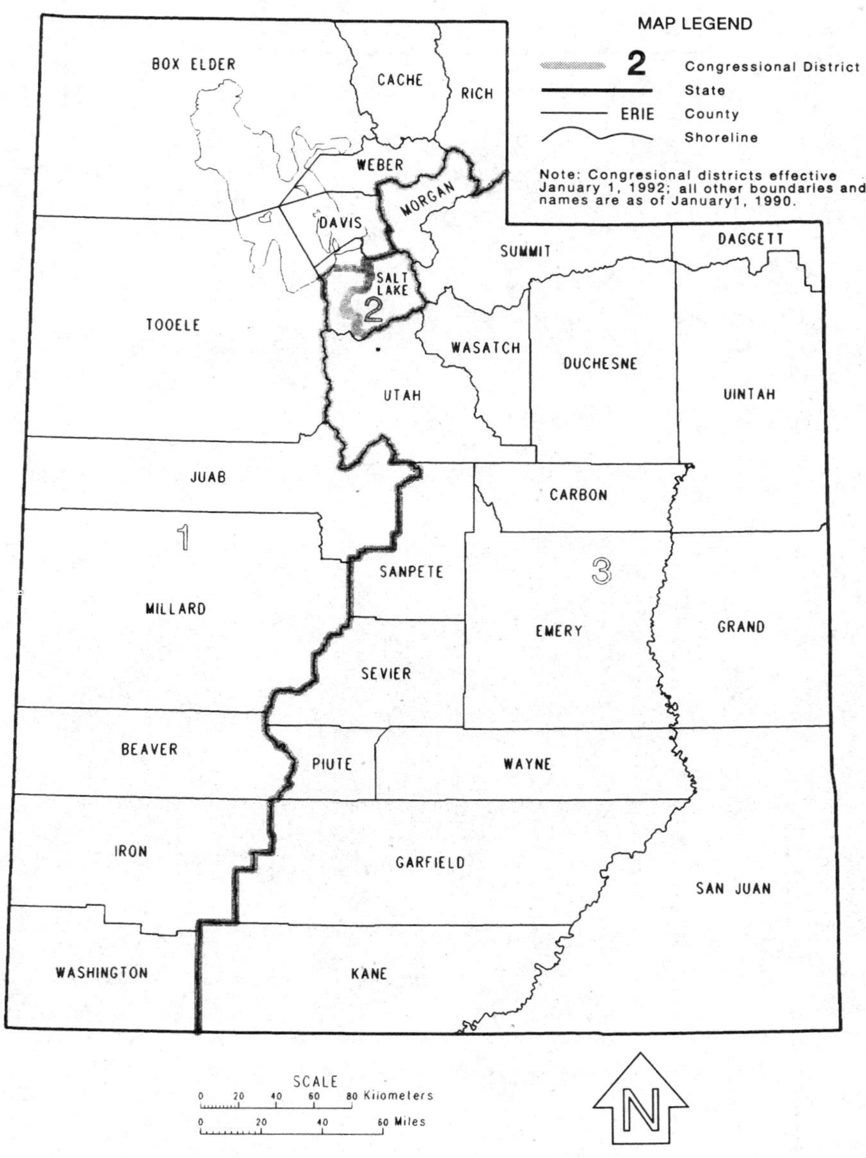

VERMONT—Congressional District—(1 District At Large)

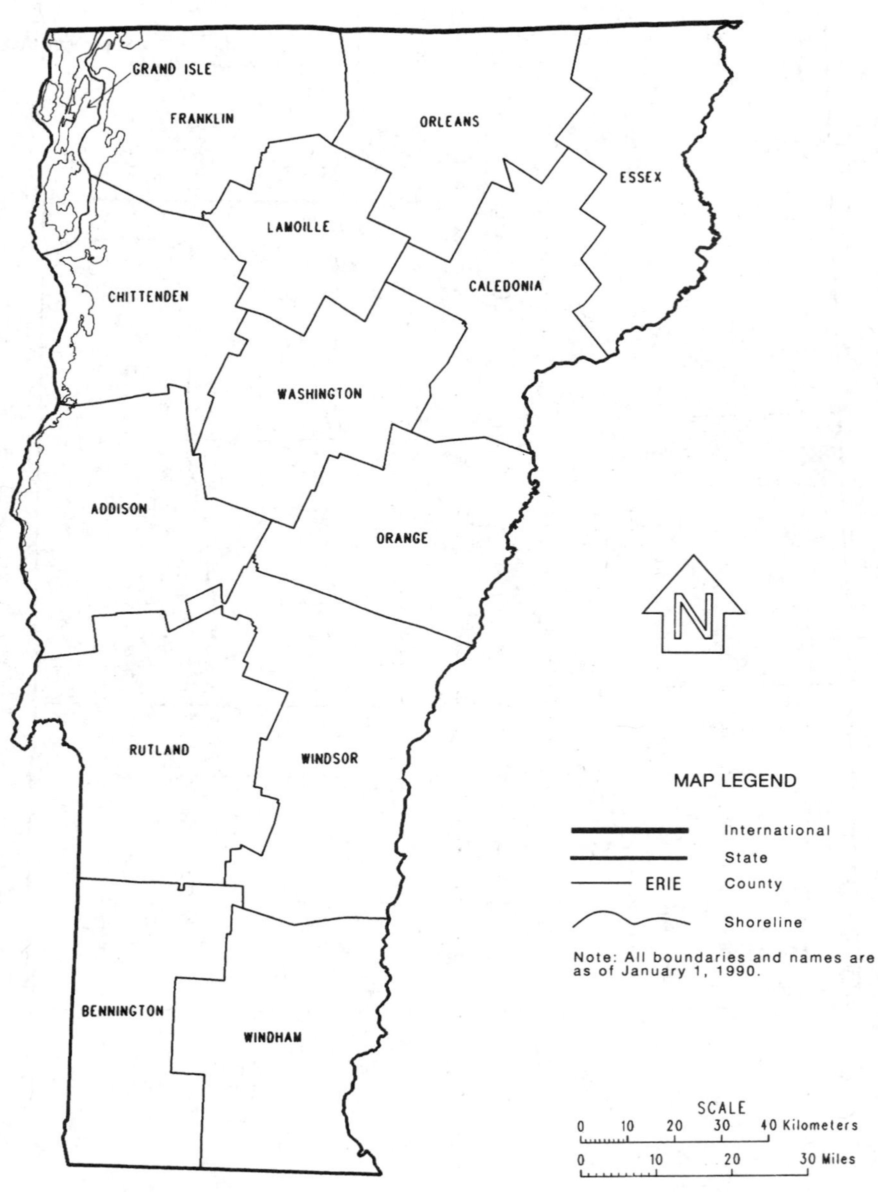

VIRGINIA—Congressional Districts—(11 Districts)

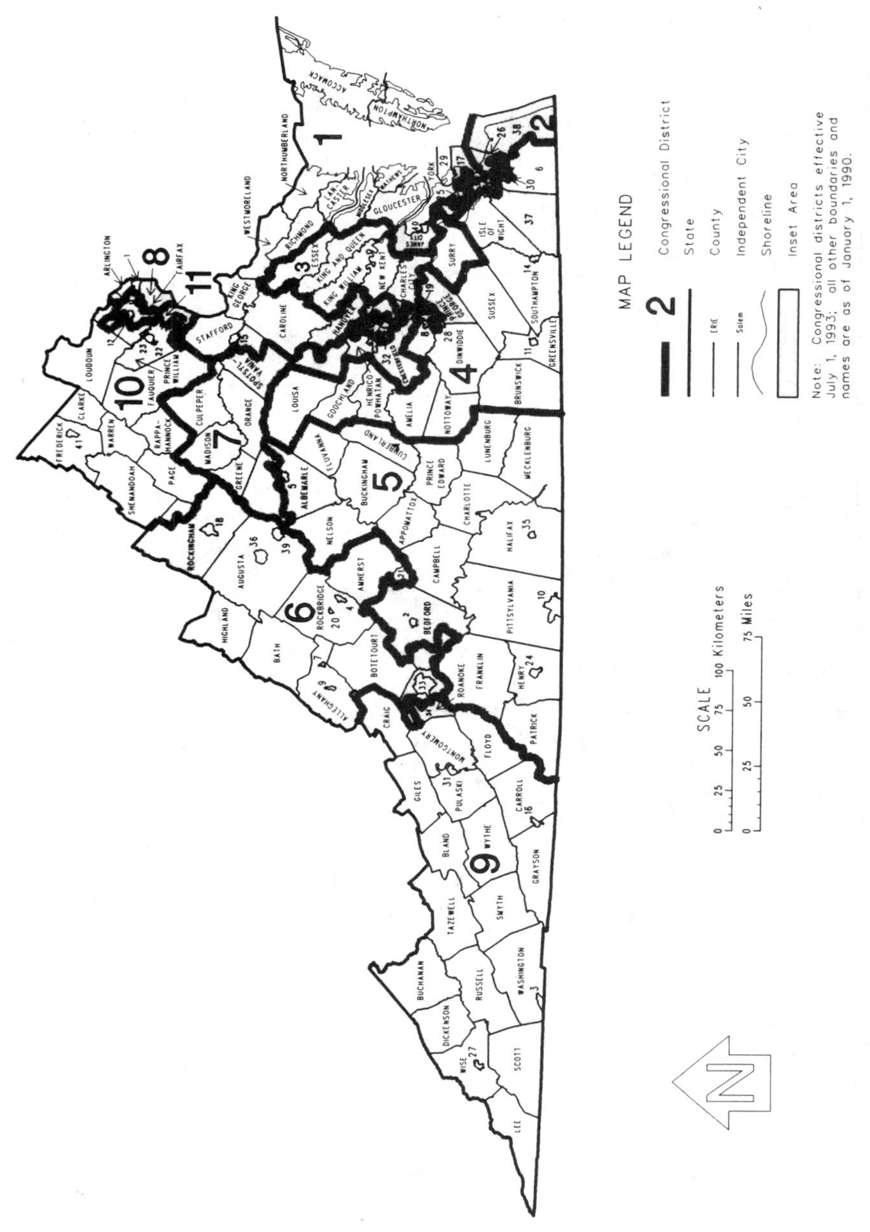

WASHINGTON—Congressional Districts—(9 Districts)

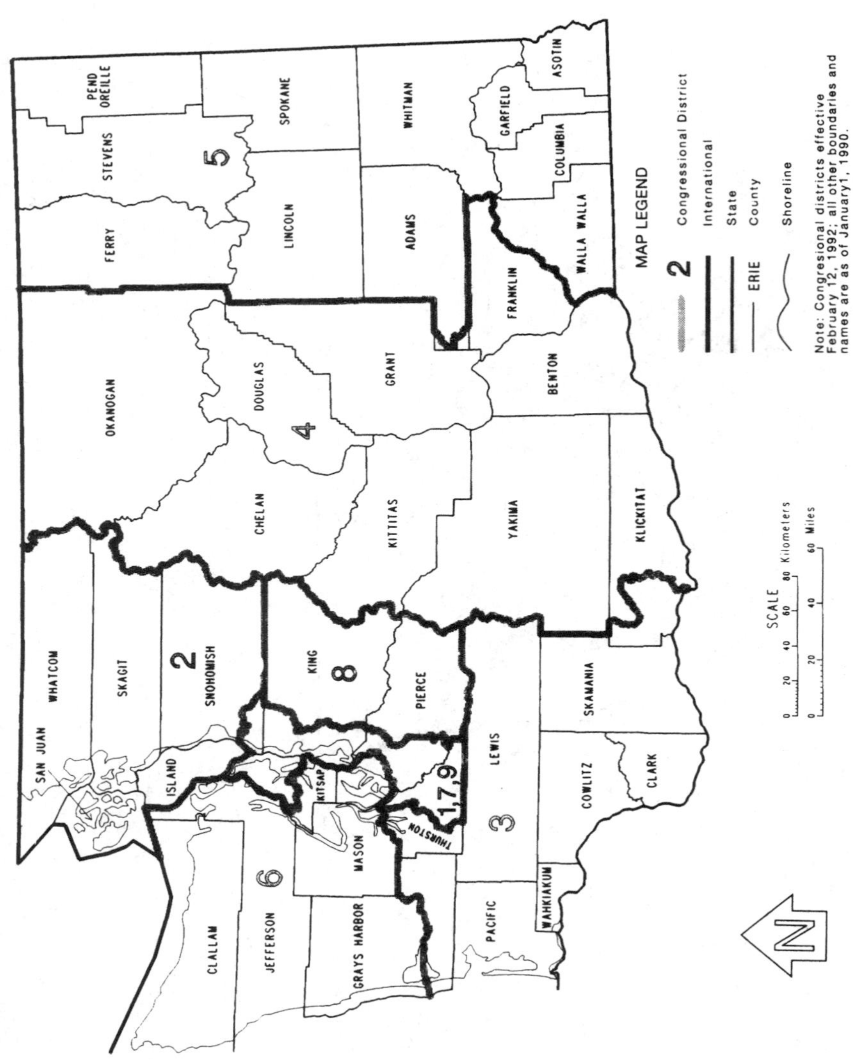

WEST VIRGINIA—Congressional Districts—(3 Districts)

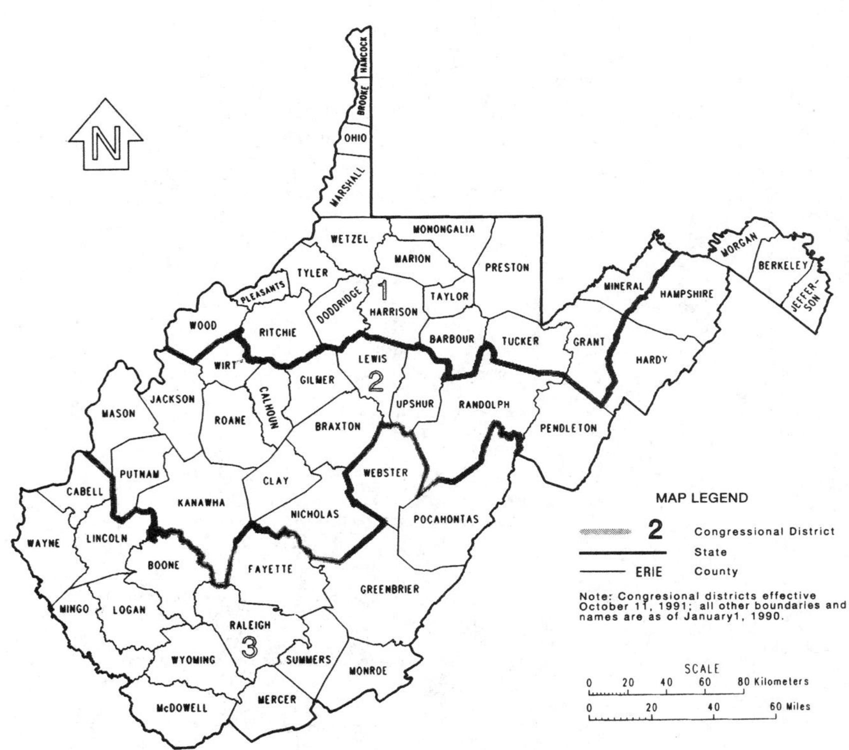

WISCONSIN—Congressional Districts—(9 Districts)

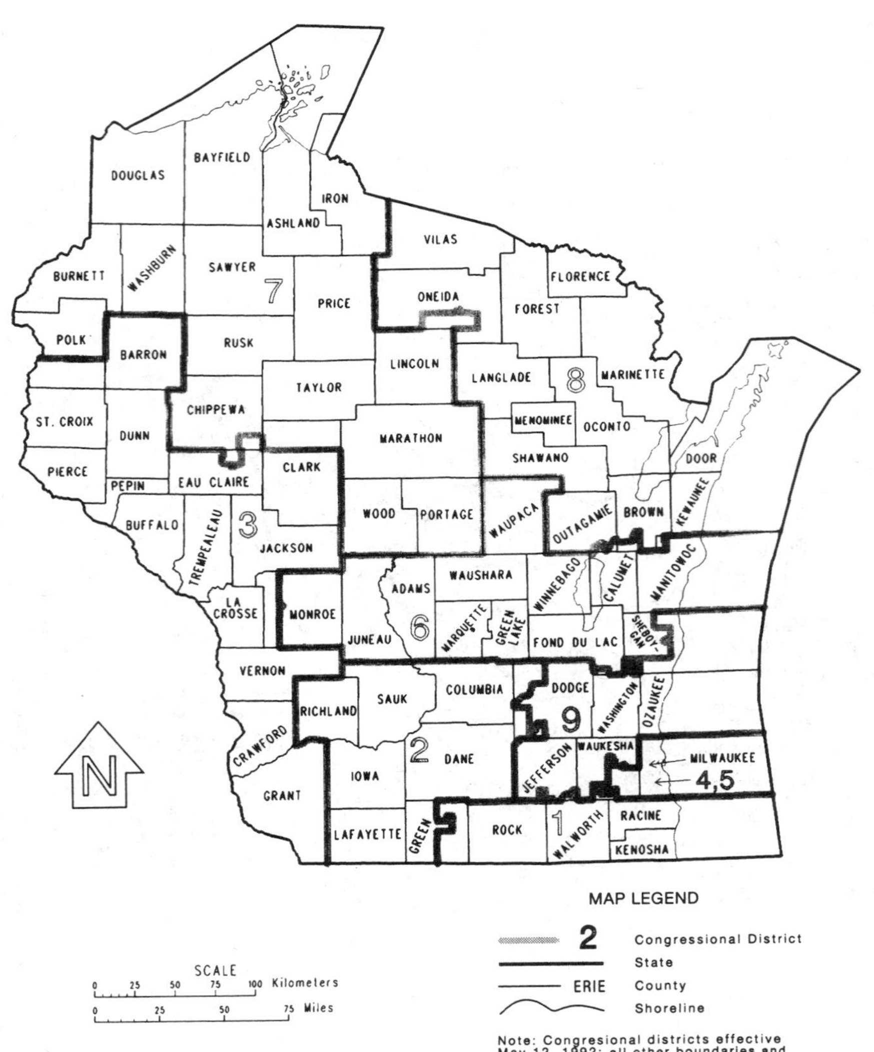

WYOMING—Congressional District—(1 District At Large)

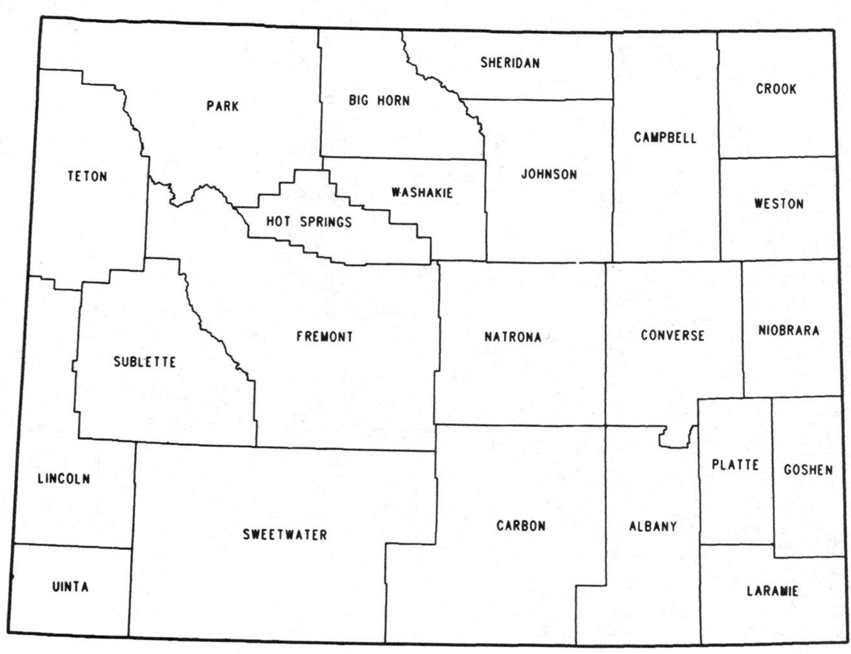

MAP LEGEND

N

SCALE
0 25 50 75 100 Kilometers
0 25 50 75 Miles

State
ERIE County

Note: All boundaries and names are as of January 1, 1990.

AMERICAN SAMOA—(1 Delegate At Large)

ROSE ISLAND

MAP LEGEND

ERIE District or Island

Shoreline

Note: All boundaries and names are as of January 1, 1990.

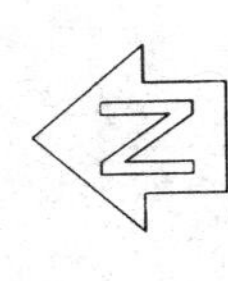

SCALE

0 10 20 30 40 50 Kilometers

0 10 20 30 40 50 Miles

MANU'A

SWAINS ISLAND

DISTRICT OF COLUMBIA—(1 Delegate At Large)

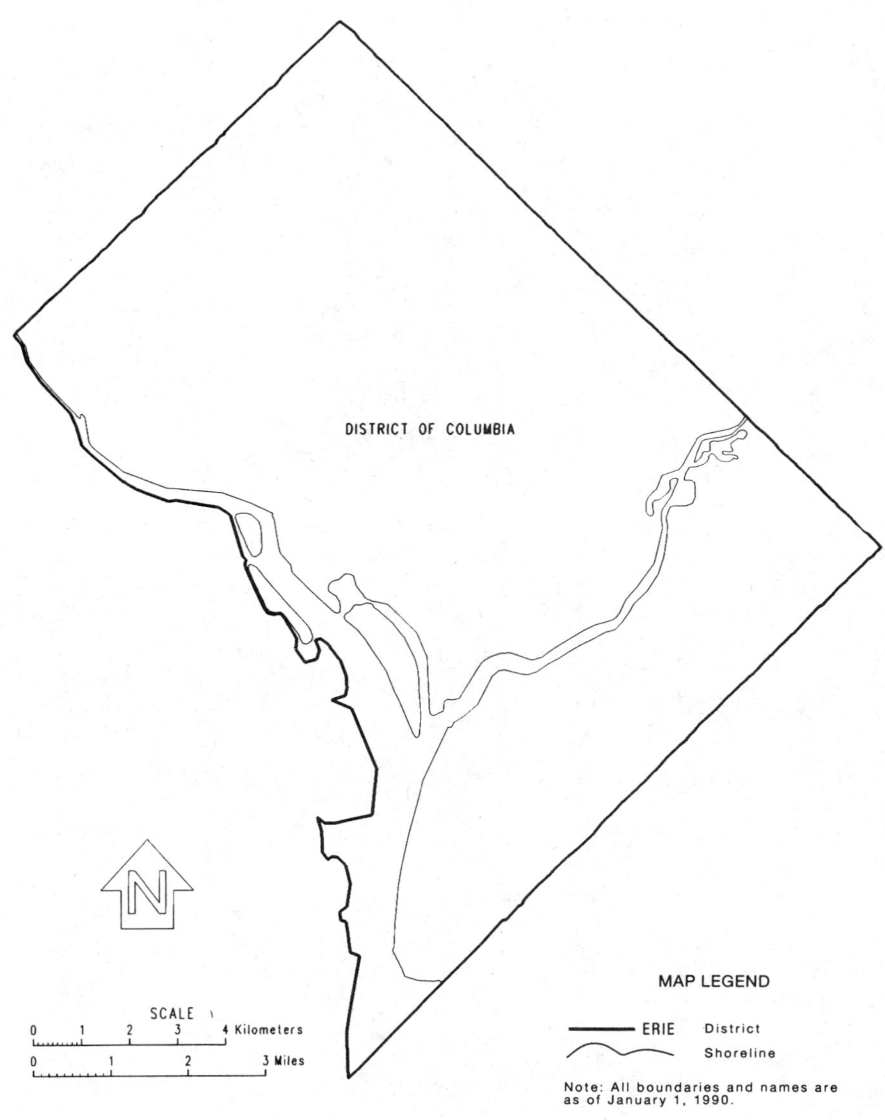

GUAM—(1 Delegate At Large)

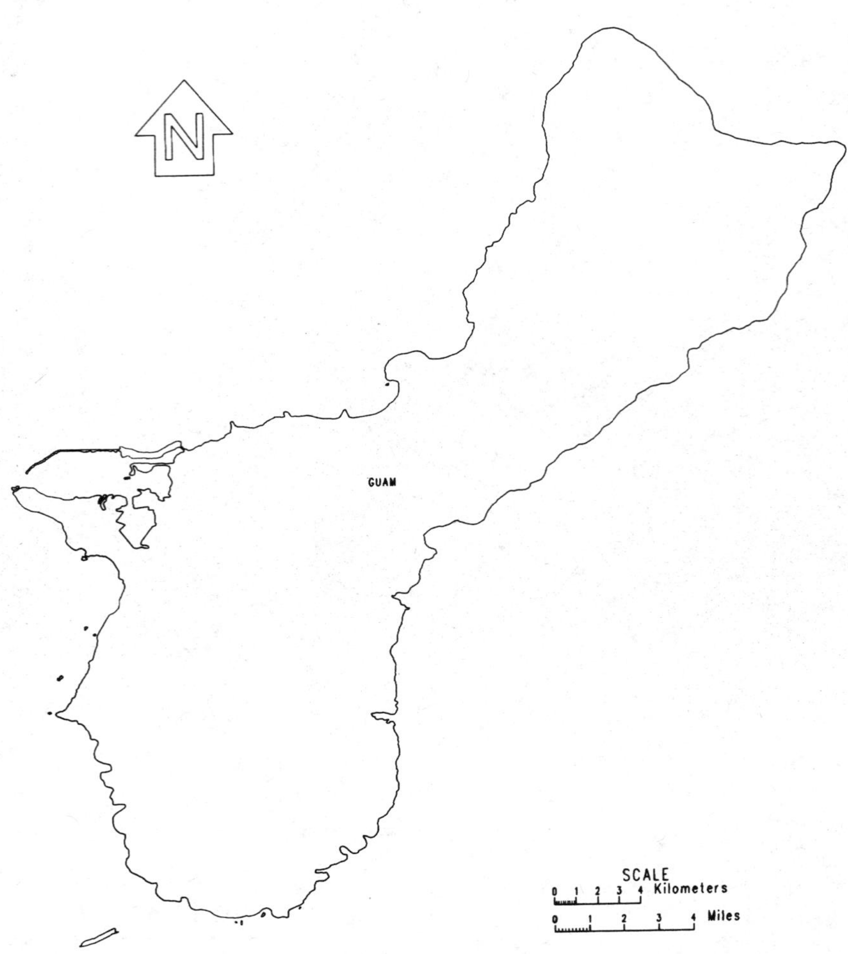

PUERTO RICO—(1 Resident Commissioner At Large)

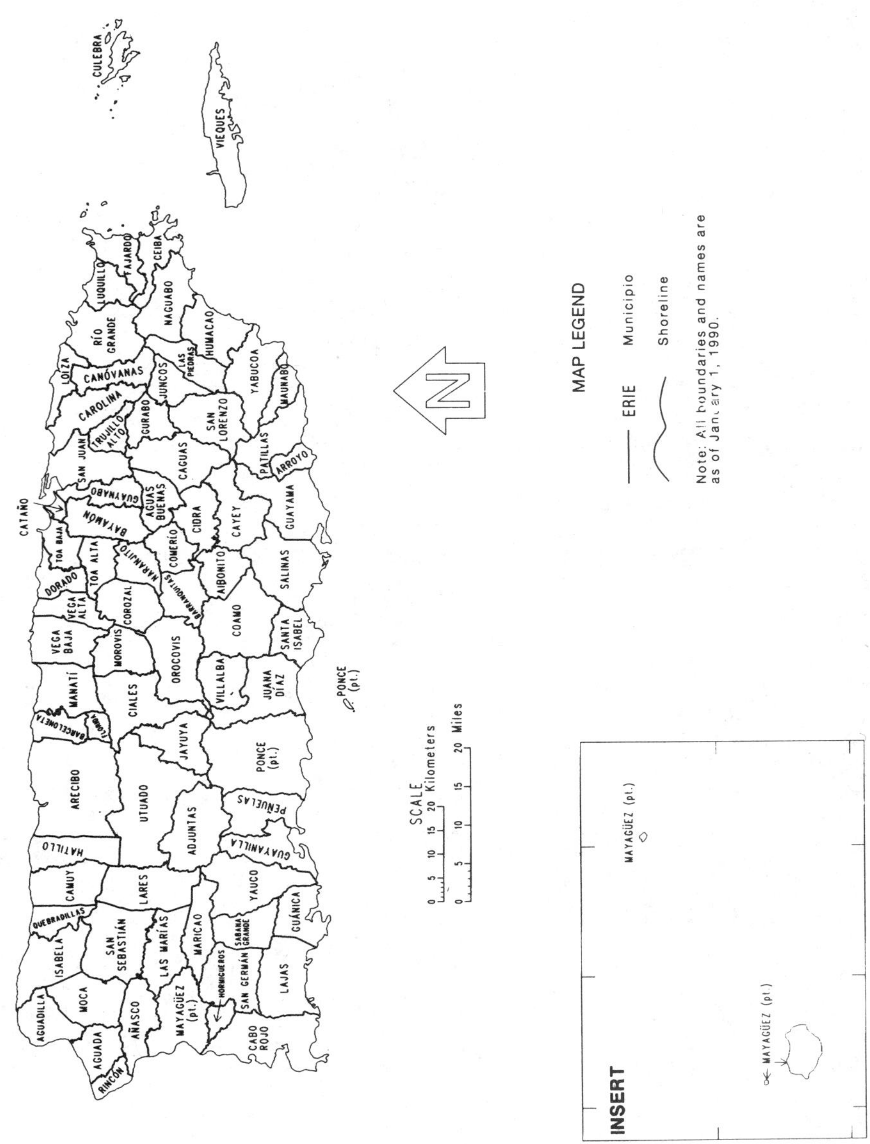

THE VIRGIN ISLANDS OF THE UNITED STATES—(1 Delegate At Large)

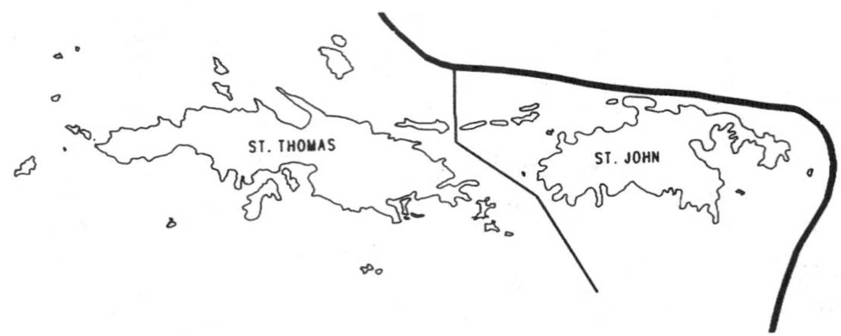

MAP LEGEND

International

ERIE Island

Shoreline

Note: All boundaries and names are as of January 1, 1990.

SCALE

0 1 2 3 4 5 6 7 8 9 10 Kilometers

0 1 2 3 4 5 6 7 8 9 10 Miles

NAME INDEX

C

D

H

P

Q

R

U

○